2013 Standard Catalog of®

FIREARMS

THE COLLECTOR'S PRICE & REFERENCE GUIDE

EDITED BY
JERRY LEE

Published by

Gun Digest® Books, an imprint of F+W Media, Inc.
Krause Publications • 700 East State Street • Iola, WI 54990-0001
715-445-2214 • 888-457-2873
www.krausebooks.com

To order books or other products call toll-free 1-800-258-0929
or visit us online at www.gundigeststore.com

ISBN-13: 978-1-4402-2953-4
ISBN-10: 1-4402-2953-8

Cover & Design by Tom Nelsen & Sandi Carpenter
Edited by Jerry Lee and Jennifer L.S. Pearsall

Printed in the United States of America

CONTENTS

— Manufacturers Directory —

4

8

INTRODUCTION

Welcome to the 23rd edition of *Standard Catalog of Firearms*. It is hard to believe that this publication has now been around for almost a quarter century. The first edition was published in late 1990 and was in bookstores throughout 1991. At the time, gasoline was $1.12 a gallon, George Herbert Walker Bush was in the White House, and you could buy a new Ruger Blackhawk for $300 or a pre-war Model 70 Winchester for under $1,000.

That first edition of *Standard Catalog* had 700 pages—less than half the size of the book in your hand. It has doubled over the years to make room for all the new makes and models that have been introduced, and in this edition you will find information on approximately 18,000 individual guns from almost 1,200 different manufacturers.

We hope you enjoy browsing through what we believe is the most complete source available for gun values, firearms history, and identification. It can also be an "armchair gun show" that provides many hours of reading and learning about guns and reflecting on those that should have been bought, or held on to, long ago.

To get the most from this book, be sure to carefully read the section on our Grading System. Whether you are buying, selling, or simply curious about the value of a gun you already own, be careful and objective when you judge its condition. And remember, the prices shown are *estimated retail* values based upon input from contributing editors and experts in the field.

Thanks for purchasing *Standard Catalog of Firearms* and for your interest and support of the exciting world of guns and the shooting sports.

—Jerry Lee

ACKNOWLEDGMENTS

The editor would like to thank the following individuals for their input, information, advice and support for this 23rd edition of *Standard Catalog of Firearms*.

Jim Supica, Director, and Phil Schreier, Senior Curator of the National Firearms Museum, Tom Turpin, Garry James, Steve Gash, J.B. Wood, Rick Hacker, Holt Bodinson, John Taffin, C. Rodney James, Roy Jinks, David Moore of William Larkin Moore & Co., Alan Heldreth of Cabela's, Mike Clark of Collector's Firearms, and these representatives of some of the top firearms manufacturers: Paul Thompson (Browning), Jason Morton (CZ-USA), Dwight Van Brunt (Kimber), Linda Powell (Mossberg), Jessica Kallam (Remington), Ken Jorgensen (Ruger), Bud Fini (SIG Sauer), Paul Pluff (Smith & Wesson), and Scott Grange (Winchester).

I also want to say thanks to Jennifer L.S.Pearsall, editor of Gun Digest Books, Firearms and Knives Group, graphic designer Tom Nelsen, and data input specialist and proofreader Delores May. Without their help and support, including many long work days, early and late, this book would not exist.

ABOUT THE EDITOR

Jerry Lee has been editor of numerous magazines in the firearms field including *Guns*, *Petersen's Handguns*, *Rifle Shooter*, *Petersen's Shotguns* and many *Guns & Ammo* and *Shooting Times* specialty issues. These include titles like *Book of the 1911*, *Book of the AR-15*, *Book of the Model 70*, *Firearms for Law Enforcement*, *Combat Arms* and many others. He also has been editor of custom magazines for Smith & Wesson, Remington, Ruger, Mossberg, CZ-USA, Hodgdon, Hornady and other companies in the industry. Jerry is also editor of the popular annual book, *Gun Digest*. He is a life-long hunter and shooter, an NRA Life Member, and the author of several articles for the NRA website. Jerry and his wife, Susan, live in West Virginia.

CONTRIBUTING EDITORS

J.B. Barnes
Stevens single-shot rifles and pistols
29 Ridgeview Dr.
Dry Ridge, KY 41035
859-824-5086

Bailey Brower, Jr.
Remington and Savage pistols
P.O. Box 111
Madison, NJ 07940
baileybrower@yahoo.com

Bud Bugni
Winchester Model 42s
P.O. Box 762
Sutter Creek, CA 95685
209-267-5402

Tom Caceci
Blackpowder revolvers
1405 Westover Drive
Blacksburg, VA 24060

Jim Cate
J.P. Sauer Pistols
406 Pine Bluff Dr.
Chattanooga, TN 37412
423-892-6320

Kevin Cherry
Winchester and Colt Commemoratives
3402 West Wendover Ave.
Greensboro, NC 27407
336-854-4182

Joseph Cornell
Browning, Colt, pre-64 Winchesters
2655 West 39th Ave.
Denver, CO 80211
303-455-1717
worthologist@aol.com

Jason Devine
Winchester lever action rifles
250 Commercial Street
Unit 3011
Manchester, NH 03101
Jason@amoskeag.com

Richard Freer
*Belgian Browning and pre-64
Winchester shotguns*
8928 Spring Branch Drive
Houston, TX 77080
713-467-3016

Dr. Daniel Menser
Winchester Model 21 shotguns
320-522-0859
papa_menser@yahoo.com

Gale Morgan
Luger and Mauser pistols
Pre-WWI pistols
P.B. Box 72
Lincoln, CA 95648

Jim Rankin
Walther pistols
3615 Coral Gables, FL 33134
305-446-1792

Bob Rayburn
Colt Woodsman
P.O. Box 97104
Lakewood, WA 98497
rayburn@colt22.com

Dean Rinehart
*Pre-64 Winchester Rifles,
Colt Woodsman*
P.O. Box 5
Gallipolis, OH 45631

AUCTION HOUSES

Among the many resources used by the editors to determine trends in firearms values are the prices realized at recent auctions. These resources include the following auction houses, which are the largest and best in the field of modern and antique firearms.

Amoskeag Auctions, 250 Commercial Street, Suite 3011, Manchester, NH 03101; **www.amoskeag-auction.com**
Bonhams & Butterfields, 220 San Bruno Ave., San Francisco, CA 94103; **www.bonhams.com**
Heritage Auctions, 3500 Maple Ave., 17th Floor, Dallas, TX 75219; **www.ha.com**
James D. Julia, Inc., 203 Skowhegan Rd., Fairfield, ME 04937; **www.juliaauctions.com**
Little John's Auctions, 1740 W. La Veta Ave., Orange, CA 92868; **www.littlejohnsauctions.com**
Rock Island Auction Co., 7819 42nd Street West, Rock Island, IL 61201; **www.rockislanduaction.com**

GRADING SYSTEM

In most cases, the condition of a firearm determines its value. As with all collectible items, a grading system is necessary to give buyers and sellers a measurement that most closely reflects a general consensus on condition. While all grading systems are subjective, the system presented in this publication attempts to describe a firearm in universal terms. It is strongly recommend that the reader be closely acquainted with this grading system before attempting to determine the correct value of a particular firearm.

NIB (NEW IN BOX)

This category can sometimes be misleading. It means that the firearm is in its original factory carton with all of the appropriate papers. It also means the firearm is new, that it has not been fired, and has no wear. This classification brings a substantial premium for both the collector and shooter. It should be noted that NIB values are not the same as MSRP (manufacturer's suggested retail price), but rather are "street prices" that can be considerably lower than the MSRP. A NIB value should closely represent the selling price for a new, unfired gun in the box.

EXCELLENT

Collector quality firearms in this condition are highly desirable. The firearm must be in at least 98 percent condition with respect to blue wear, stock or grip finish, and bore. The firearm must also be in 100 percent original factory condition without refinishing, repair, alterations, or additions of any kind. Sights must be factory original, as well. This grading classification includes both modern and antique (manufactured prior to 1898) firearms.

VERY GOOD

Firearms in this category are also sought after both by the collector and shooter. Modern firearms must be in working order and retain approximately 92 percent original metal and wood finish. It must be 100 percent factory original, but may have some small repairs, alterations, or non-factory additions. No refinishing is permitted in this category. Antique firearms must have 80 percent original finish with no repairs.

GOOD

Modern firearms in this category may not be considered to be as collectible as the previous grades, but antique firearms are considered desirable. Modern firearms must retain at least 80 percent metal and wood finish, but may display evidence of old refinishing. Small repairs, alterations, or non-factory additions are sometimes encountered in this class. Factory replacement parts are permitted. The overall working condition of the firearm must be good, as well as safe. The bore may exhibit wear or some corrosion, especially in antique arms. Antique firearms may be included in this category if the metal and wood finish is at least 50 percent of the factory original.

FAIR

Firearms in this category should be in satisfactory working order and safe to shoot. The overall metal and wood finish on the modern firearm must be at least 30 percent and antique firearms must have at least some original finish or old re-finish remaining. Repairs, alterations, non-factory additions, and recent refinishing would all place a firearm in this classification. However, the modern firearm must be in working condition, while the antique firearm may not function. In either case the firearm must be considered safe to fire if in a working state.

POOR

Neither collectors nor shooters are likely to exhibit much interest in firearms in this condition. Modern firearms are likely to retain little metal or wood finish. Pitting and rust will be seen in firearms in this category. Modern firearms may not be in working order and may not be safe to shoot. Repairs and refinishing would be necessary to restore the firearm to safe working order. Antique firearms in this category will have no finish and will not function. In the case of modern firearms their principal value lies in spare parts. On the other hand, antique firearms in this condition can be used as "wall hangers," or might be an example of an extremely rare variation or have some kind of historical significance.

Example prices are shown for the conditions described above in this format:

NIB	Exc.	V.G.	Good	Fair	Poor
2250	1800	1500	1250	1000	700

PRICING

Prices given in this book are designed as a guide, not as a quote, and the prices given reflect retail values. This is very important to remember. You will seldom realize full retail value if you trade in a gun or sell it to a dealer. In this situation, your gun will be valued at its wholesale price, which is generally substantially below retail value to allow for the seller's profit margin.

It should also be remembered that prices for firearms can vary with the time of the year, geographical location, and the general economy. As might be expected, guns used for hunting are more likely to sell in late summer or early fall as hunting season approaches. Likewise, big-game rifles chambered for powerful magnum cartridges will likely have more appeal in western states than in the Deep South, while semi-automatic rifles or shotguns will not sell well in states where their use for hunting is prohibited, such as is the case in Pennsylvania.

It is not practical to list prices in this book with regard to time of year or location. What is given here is a reasonable price based on sales at gun shows, auction houses, and information obtained from knowledgeable collectors and dealers. In certain cases there will be no price indicated under a particular condition, but rather the notation "N/A" or the symbol "—." This indicates that there is no known price available for that gun in that condition or the sales for that particular model are so few that a reliable price cannot be ascertained. This will usually be encountered only with very rare guns, with newly introduced firearms, or more likely with antique firearms in those conditions most likely to be encountered. Most antique firearms will be seen in the Good, Fair and Poor categories.

Standard Catalog of Firearms can be used as an identification guide and as a source of starting prices for a planned firearms transaction. If you begin by valuing a given firearm according to the values shown in this book, you will not be too far off the mark.

In the final analysis, a firearm is worth only what someone is willing to pay for it. New trends arise quickly, and there are many excellent bargains to be found in today's market. With patience and good judgment—and with this book under your arm—you, too, can find them.

ADDITIONAL CONSIDERATIONS

Firearms have long been admired and coveted not only for their usefulness, but also for their grace and beauty. Since the beginning of the nineteenth century, firearms makers have adorned their guns with engraving, fine woods, or special-order features that set their products apart from the rest. There is no feasible way to give the collector every possible variation of the firearms presented in this book. However, in a general way, certain special factors will significantly influence the price of a firearm.

Perhaps the most recognizable special feature collectors agree that affects the price of a firearm is engraving. The artistry, beauty, and intricate nature of engraving draw all collectors toward it. But firearms engraving is a field unto itself, one that requires years of experience on the part of qualified evaluators to determine proper chronological methods and the ability to identify the engraver in question.

Factory engraving generally brings more of a premium than aftermarket engraving. To be able to determine factory work is a difficult task, one full of pitfalls. In some cases, factories like Colt and Winchester may have records to verify original factory engraving work, whereas other manufacturers such as Parker, Remington, and Savage may not. Whenever a firearm purchase is to be made with respect to an engraved gun, it is in the collector's best interest to secure an expert opinion and/or a factory letter prior to the purchase. Engraved firearms are expensive. A mistake could cost the collector thousands of dollars—proceed with caution.

The nineteenth and twentieth centuries were times when guns were purchased by or given to historically important individuals. Firearms have also been an important part of significant historical events such as the Battle of the Little Bighorn or the Battle of Bull Run. Many of these firearms are in museums where the public can enjoy, see, and appreciate them. Others are in private collections that seldom, if ever, are offered for sale. If the collector should ever encounter one of these historically important firearms, it cannot be stressed strongly enough the necessity of securing an expert determination as to authenticity. Museum curators are perhaps the best source of information for these types of firearms. As with engraved guns, historical firearms are usually expensive, and without documentation their value is questionable.

Special features and variations are also a desirable part of firearms collecting. As with engraving, special-order guns can bring a considerable premium. The Colt factory has excellent records regarding its firearms and will provide the collector with a letter of authenticity. Winchester records are not as comprehensive, but rifles made prior to 1908 may have documentation. Other firearms manufacturers either do not have records or do not provide collectors with documentation. This leaves the collector in a difficult position. Special order sights, stocks, barrel lengths, calibers, and so forth must be judged on their own merits. As with other factors, an expert should be consulted prior to purchase. Experienced collectors, researchers, and museums will generally provide the kind of information a collector needs before purchasing a special order or unique firearm.

Perhaps the best advice is for the collector to take his time. Do not be in a hurry and do not allow yourself to be rushed into making a decision. Learn as much as possible about the firearms you are interested in collecting or shooting. Try to keep current with prices through this publication and the auction houses listed here. Go to gun shows, not just to buy or sell, but to observe and learn. It is also helpful to join a firearms club or association. These groups have experienced collectors who are glad to help the beginner or veteran.

Firearms collecting is a rewarding hobby. Our guns are part of our nation's history and represent an opportunity to learn more about their role in the American experience. If done skillfully, firearms collecting can be a profitable hobby, as well.

GUN VALUES IN TODAY'S ECONOMY

As this edition goes to press, the U.S. economy is still in recovery and the outlook for a turnaround remains uncertain. By the time many of you will be reading this, the latest election cycle will be over and, it is hoped, no longer will distract political leaders from doing what needs to be done. (This may not last very long. Political pundits are already making predictions about the 2014 and 2016 elections.) No matter who is in the White House or in control of Congress, we are probably still a long way from getting over the uncertainties in regard to jobs, the housing market, 401K and IRA values, tax reform (or the lack thereof), and other aspects of the economy. These factors obviously can have a bearing on the values of collectible items such as firearms.

The trends today are sometimes difficult to get a handle on. One common thread in many conversations I have recently had with experts in the field is that prices being paid in the upper end of the market are strong and, in some cases, on the rise. Much of the middle range in gun values could be described as generally flat, while in the lower-priced category, some prices are down as much as 10 to 20 percent. There are many exceptions, but those with money can afford the rare and exceptional, and in auction situations when two or more aficionados of a particular gun are bidding against each other, the sky can be the limit.

Not all "high-end" guns are escalating in value. Collectors of fine guns are not unlike those who like to own fine art, furniture, jewelry, or automobiles. They are subject to the same "what's hot and what's not" syndrome that affects prices of many items. Trends come and go, and the Browning shotgun or Winchester rifle everyone wanted 10 years ago may not be as popular today. Certain items reach their level of value and may stay there.

At the middle and lower price levels, not all values are flat or down. The Winchester Model 67 single-shot .22 rifle, in production from 1934 to 1963, was a $150 to $200 gun for years. Four of five years ago, for some reason, interest in the rifle began to increase. We show a value of $450 in this edition of *Standard Catalog* for one in excellent condition or better.

The soft economy's affect on gun values is complex. As in real estate, location is important, not just due to differences in the popularity of various models, but because the economy is better in some parts of the country, worse in others.

It is important to give some thought as to why we purchase firearms. The answer can be helpful in determining whether or not this is a good time to sell or buy that gun. Some of us are collectors who want to own certain guns because we like them. We enjoy the workmanship, the particular design, the history, and other factors that draw us to certain models and their possession. Others in our ilk are hunters or target shooters who want to use the best in the category. Some want to have a gun or guns primarily for self-protection. And then there are investors or speculators who buy guns like those who buy gold, diamonds or other tangibles. They may not hunt or ever shoot a gun.

My guess is that most buyers of this book tend to be a cross section of these categories and can relate to several if not all of the reasons to buy a gun. And those reasons change from time to time. Perhaps you've always wanted a Model X, but your life has changed, you're older and wiser now, and—wait, what you really should have is a Model Y! All of which makes it more important, and more fun, to spend some time going through the pages of *Standard Catalog of Firearms*.

A

A.A.
Azanza & Arrizabalaga
Eibar, Spain

A.A.

A 6.35mm and 7.65mm caliber semi-automatic pistol with a 6- and 9-shot magazine. Many of these pistols are identifiable by the trademark "AA" on their frames.

Courtesy James Rankin

NIB	Exc.	V.G.	Good	Fair	Poor
—	300	175	150	100	50

Reims

A 6.35mm or 7.65mm caliber semi-automatic pistol with 6- or 8-round magazine capacity. Most of the pistols have their slides marked "1914 Model Automatic Pistol Reims Patent."

Courtesy James Rankin

NIB	Exc.	V.G.	Good	Fair	Poor
—	200	175	150	100	50

A.A.A.
Aldazabal
Eibar, Spain

Modelo 1919

A 7.65mm semi-automatic pistol with 9-round magazine capacity. The trademark of a knight's head over three As is on the side of the slide and the grips.

Courtesy James Rankin

NIB	Exc.	V.G.	Good	Fair	Poor
—	200	175	150	100	50

A. J. ORDNANCE

A delayed blowback action that is unique in that every shot was double-action. This pistol was chambered for the .45 ACP cartridge and had a 3.5" stainless steel barrel with fixed sights and plastic grips. The detachable magazine held 6 shots, and the standard finish was matte blue. Chrome plating was available and would add approximately 15 percent to the values listed.

NIB	Exc.	V.G.	Good	Fair	Poor
1950	1300	800	400	250	175

A-SQUARE
Bedford, Kentucky/Chamberlain, South Dakota

Hannibal Grade

Using the P-17 Enfield action, with a 22" to 26" barrel, this rifle is chambered for 32 calibers from 7mm Rem. Mag. up to and including the .500 A-Square Mag. and .577 Tyrannosaur. Blued with a checkered walnut pistol-grip stock. Introduced in 1986. Weights range from 9 lbs. to 13.25 lbs. depending on caliber. Add 5 percent for Kentucky-built rifles.

NIB	Exc.	V.G.	Good	Fair	Poor
3200	2700	1800	1000	600	350

Caesar Grade

Utilizing a Remington Model 700 action and chambered for the same cartridges as the above, with the exception that A-Square proprietary cartridges are not available. Also made in the left-hand version. Introduced in 1986. Weights are in the 8.5 to 11 lbs. range.

NIB	Exc.	V.G.	Good	Fair	Poor
3200	2700	1800	1000	600	350

Hamilcar Grade

A smaller and lighter version of the Hannibal Grade. It was introduced in 1994. It is designed to be chambered for .30-06 cartridges. Weights are around 8 to 8.5 lbs. Introduced in 1994.

NIB	Exc.	V.G.	Good	Fair	Poor
3200	2700	1800	1000	600	350

Genghis Khan Model

This model is designed for varmint shooting and is fitted with a heavyweight barrel. Offered in .22-250, .243 Win., 6mm Rem., .25-06, .257 Wby., and .264 Win. Barrel length is to customer's specifications, as is length of pull. No iron sights are fitted to this model. Weight is approximately 11 lbs.

NIB	Exc.	V.G.	Good	Fair	Poor
3200	2700	1800	1000	600	350

A & R SALES SOUTH
El Monte, California

A&R Sales South also made frames for custom 1911 builds.

45 Auto

An alloy-frame version of the Colt Model 1911 semi-automatic pistol.

NIB	Exc.	V.G.	Good	Fair	Poor
—	200	175	150	100	50

NIB	Exc.	V.G.	Good	Fair	Poor
475	325	200	150	125	100

Mark IV Sporter

A semi-automatic copy of the M-14 military rifle. Manufactured in .308 cal. (7.65mm NATO) only.

NIB	Exc.	V.G.	Good	Fair	Poor
950	650	500	375	195	100

ABADIE
Liege, Belgium

System Abadie Model 1878

A 9mm double-action revolver with a 6-shot cylinder, octagonal barrel and integral ejector rod.

NIB	Exc.	V.G.	Good	Fair	Poor
—	550	350	175	125	90

System Abadie Model 1886

A heavier version of the above.

NIB	Exc.	V.G.	Good	Fair	Poor
—	575	400	200	125	90

ABBEY, F.J. & CO.
Chicago, Illinois

The Abbey Brothers produced a variety of percussion rifles and shotguns which are all of individual design. The prices listed represent what a plain F.J. Abbey & Company firearm might realize.

Rifle

NIB	Exc.	V.G.	Good	Fair	Poor
—	—	1750	800	450	200

Shotgun

NIB	Exc.	V.G.	Good	Fair	Poor
—	—	2500	1750	575	150

ABBEY, GEORGE T.
Utica, New York, and Chicago, Illinois

George T. Abbey originally worked in Utica, New York, from 1845 to 1852. He moved to Chicago in 1852 and was in business until 1874. He manufactured a wide variety of percussion and cartridge firearms. The values listed represent those of his most common products.

Single-Barrel Shotgun

NIB	Exc.	V.G.	Good	Fair	Poor
—	—	1750	850	550	200

Side-by-Side Shotgun

NIB	Exc.	V.G.	Good	Fair	Poor
—	—	2550	1200	675	250

Over/Under Shotgun

NIB	Exc.	V.G.	Good	Fair	Poor
—	—	2750	1300	975	250

ABESSER & MERKEL
Suhl, Germany

Crown Grade

This model is a single-barrel Trap gun with Greener cross bolt-action with two underbolt locks. Offered in 12 gauge with barrel lengths from 28" to 34". Ventilated rib standard. Skip line checkering. Pistol or straight grip stock. Gun weight is between 7 and 7.5 lbs. Engraved receiver with game scenes.

Courtesy Dan Sheil

NIB	Exc.	V.G.	Good	Fair	Poor
—	6000	4925	3825	1000	—

Diamond Grade

This model is a side-by-side gun offered in 12, 16, 20, and 28 gauge as well as .410 bore. Auto ejectors. Double triggers. Full coverage engraving with artistic stock carving behind the frame. Skip line checkering. Many extras offered on this grade will affect price. Barrel lengths from 25" to 32". Weights are from 6.5 lbs. to 7 lbs. Prices are for standard gun with no extras. **NOTE:** Add 50 percent for 20 gauge guns and 100 percent for 28 gauge or .410 bore guns.

Courtesy Dan Sheil

NIB	Exc.	V.G.	Good	Fair	Poor
—	12000	9200	8050	3000	700

Empire Grade

This shotgun is a side-by-side with an Anson-Deeley action. The receiver is fully engraved with game birds and fine scroll. The stock is carved behind the action. Checkering is a fine skip line-style. Auto ejectors. Pistol or straight grip stock. With or without Monte Carlo and cheekpiece. Prices listed are for pre-war guns with fluid steel barrels. **NOTE:** Add 50 percent for 20 gauge guns and 100 percent for 28 gauge or .410 bore guns.

Courtesy Dan Sheil

NIB	Exc.	V.G.	Good	Fair	Poor
—	13500	11150	9200	2500	700

Excelsior Grade

This side-by-side gun is fitted with engraved side plates. Anson-Deeley action with double triggers. Fine line checkering. Figured walnut stock. All gauges offered from 12 to .410. Barrel lengths from 25" to 32". Many extra cost options available.**NOTE:** Add 50 percent for 20 gauge guns and 100 percent for 28 gauge or .410 bore guns.

Courtesy Dan Sheil

NIB	Exc.	V.G.	Good	Fair	Poor
—	9000	7500	6500	3100	700

Diana Grade

This is an over/under combination gun with Greener cross bolt-action. Safety is located on the side of the pistol grip. Iron sights. Set trigger for rifle barrel. A wide variety of centerfire calibers offered with barrel lengths from 26" to 30".

Courtesy Dan Sheil

NIB	Exc.	V.G.	Good	Fair	Poor
—	9500	8250	6250	3200	700

Vandalia Grade

This is an over/under gun chambered for 2.75" 12 gauge shells. Barrel lengths from 28" to 32". Walnut stock with pistol or straight grip with skip line checkering. Double triggers with extractors. Premium for factory multi-barrel combinations.

Courtesy Dan Sheil

NIB	Exc.	V.G.	Good	Fair	Poor
—	7250	6000	4500	3300	700

Nimrod

This is a drilling with a Greener cross bolt-action and double under bolt. Safety is located on side of grip. Top two barrels may be 12, 16, or 20 gauge. The bottom barrel is offered in a variety of centerfire calibers. Iron sights. Pistol or straight grip stock. Receiver engraved with game scenes. Add 50 percent for 20 gauge.

Courtesy Dan Sheil

NIB	Exc.	V.G.	Good	Fair	Poor
—	13000	9950	6000	4995	700

Magazine Rifle

A bolt-action rifle offered in a wide variety of calibers. Barrel lengths from 24" to 30". Calibers from 6.5mm to .404 Rimless. This model may have a Zeiss scope or other special order features that will affect price. Add $2000 for Magnum actions.

Courtesy Dan Sheil

NIB	Exc.	V.G.	Good	Fair	Poor
—	4900	3950	3350	1100	700

ACCU-MATCH
Mesa, Arizona

Accu-Match Custom Pistol

This is a competition pistol built on the Colt 1911 design. Chambered for the .45 ACP it is fitted with a 5-1/2" match grade stainless steel barrel, stainless steel slide and frame with extended slide release and safety. Fitted with a beavertail grip safety and wraparound finger groove rubber grips, this pistol has a threaded three port compensator and dual action recoil spring system with three dot sight system.

NIB	Exc.	V.G.	Good	Fair	Poor
1050	750	550	400	300	175

ACCU-TEK
Chino, California

AT-380SS

Introduced in 1991 this semi-automatic pistol is chambered for the .380 ACP cartridge. Fitted with a 2.75" barrel with adjustable for windage rear sight. Black composition grips. Stainless steel construction. Furnished with a 5-round magazine. Weight is about 20 oz.

NIB	Exc.	V.G.	Good	Fair	Poor
245	165	100	75	50	25

AT-380 II

Introduced in 2004 this pistol is chambered for the .380 ACP cartridge. It is fitted with a 2.8" barrel. Magazine capacity is 6 rounds. Stainless steel. Magazine release is on bottom of grip. Weight is about 23 oz.

NIB	Exc.	V.G.	Good	Fair	Poor
255	175	125	100	75	35

CP-9SS

This semi-automatic double-action-only stainless steel pistol is chambered for the 9mm cartridge and is fitted with a 3.2" barrel with adjustable for windage rear sight. Magazine capacity is 8 rounds. Grips are black checkered nylon. Weight is about 28 oz. Introduced in 1992.

NIB	Exc.	V.G.	Good	Fair	Poor
295	225	150	100	75	50

CP-45SS

Similar to the Model CP-9SS but chambered for the .45 ACP cartridge. Furnished with a 6-round magazine. Introduced in 1996.

NIB	Exc.	V.G.	Good	Fair	Poor
300	245	195	150	125	75

CP-40SS

Introduced in 1992 and similar to the CP-9SS but chambered for .40 S&W cartridge. Furnished with a 7-round magazine.

NIB	Exc.	V.G.	Good	Fair	Poor
300	245	195	150	125	75

BL-9

This is a semi-automatic double-action-only pistol chambered for 9mm cartridge and furnished with a 5-round magazine. Barrel length is 3". Grips are black composition. Finish is black. Weight is approximately 22 oz. Introduced in 1997.

NIB	Exc.	V.G.	Good	Fair	Poor
295	225	150	100	75	50

BL-380

Similar to the Model BL-9 but chambered for the .380 ACP cartridge. Also introduced in 1997.

NIB	Exc.	V.G.	Good	Fair	Poor
255	175	125	100	75	35

HC-380SS

This .380 ACP semi-automatic pistol has a 2.75" barrel. Stainless steel finish. Weight is about 28 oz. Furnished with a 10-round magazine. Introduced in 1993.

NIB	Exc.	V.G.	Good	Fair	Poor
255	175	125	100	75	35

AT-32SS

Similar to the Model AT-380SS but chambered for the .32 ACP cartridge. Introduced in 1991.

NIB	Exc.	V.G.	Good	Fair	Poor
225	175	110	75	50	40

LT-380

A single-action semi-automatic pistol in .380 ACP with 6-shot magazine, 2.8" barrel. Blued or two-tone stainless slide with aluminum frame. Black, pink, purple or OD green grips. Introduced in 2012.

NIB	Exc.	V.G.	Good	Fair	Poor
250	225	190	150	125	90

ACHA
Domingo Acha
Vizcaya, Spain

Atlas

A 6.35mm semi-automatic pistol manufactured during the 1920s in the style of the Model 1906 Browning. Grips are plain checkered hard rubber. Some grips had the ACHA trademark of the Count's head. The name Atlas appears on the slide. Later models incorporated a grip safety.

Courtesy James Rankin

NIB	Exc.	V.G.	Good	Fair	Poor
—	250	175	100	75	50

Looking Glass (Ruby-Style)

This is a 7.65mm semi-automatic pistol in the Ruby-style. These pistols were furnished with a 7-, 9-, or 12-round magazine.

Courtesy James Rankin

NIB	Exc.	V.G.	Good	Fair	Poor
—	265	195	100	75	50

Looking Glass

A 6.35mm or 7.65mm caliber semi-automatic pistol. Various markings are seen on these pistols and their grips as they were sold in both France and Spain by different distributors. The pistol pictured has two trademarks: "Domingo Acha" on the grips and "Fabrique D'Arms de Guerre De Grande Presision" on the slide.

Courtesy James Rankin

NIB	Exc.	V.G.	Good	Fair	Poor
—	295	175	110	75	50

ACME
See—Davenport Arms Co., Maltby Henley & Co., and Merwin & Hulbert & Co.

ACME ARMS
New York, New York

A trade name found on .22 and .32 caliber revolvers and 12 gauge shotguns marketed by the Cornwall Hardware Company.

.22 Revolver

A 7-shot single-action revolver.

NIB	Exc.	V.G.	Good	Fair	Poor
—	375	275	175	125	75

.32 Revolver

A 5-shot single-action revolver.

NIB	Exc.	V.G.	Good	Fair	Poor
—	400	300	200	150	100

Shotgun

A 12 gauge double-barrel shotgun with external hammers.

NIB	Exc.	V.G.	Good	Fair	Poor
—	400	275	175	125	75

ACME HAMMERLESS
Made by Hopkins & Allen
Norwich, Connecticut

Acme Hammerless

A .32 or .38 caliber 5-shot revolver with either exposed hammer or enclosed hammer. Sometimes known as the "Forehand 1891."

NIB	Exc.	V.G.	Good	Fair	Poor
—	295	225	175	50	25

ACTION ARMS LTD.
Philadelphia, Pennsylvania

AT-84, AT-88

This pistol is the Swiss version of of the CZ-75. It is built at ITM, Solothurn, Switzerland. The AT-84 is chambered for the 9mm cartridge. The AT-88 is chambered for the .41 Action Express. Both have a 4.75" barrel. The 9mm pistol has a magazine capacity of 15 rounds while the .41 AE has a capacity of 10 rounds. Finish is either blue or chrome with walnut grips.

Courtesy James Rankin

NIB	Exc.	V.G.	Good	Fair	Poor
750	550	450	375	300	150

AT-84P, AT-88P

As above, with a 3.7" barrel and smaller frame.

NIB	Exc.	V.G.	Good	Fair	Poor
750	550	450	375	300	150

AT-84H, AT-88H

As above with a 3.4" barrel and smaller frame.

NIB	Exc.	V.G.	Good	Fair	Poor
750	550	450	375	300	150

Timber Wolf Carbine

Introduced in 1989, this slide-action carbine features an 18.5" barrel with adjustable rear sight and blade front sight. Chambered for the .357 Magnum or .38 Special cartridges, it is offered in either blue or hard chrome finish. Weight is approximately 5.5 lbs. Built in Israel by Israel Military Industries.

NIB	Exc.	V.G.	Good	Fair	Poor
850	595	395	300	200	125

Action Arms/IMI Uzi Carbine Models A and B

16" barreled semi-automatic version of the Uzi sub-machine gun chambered in 9mm Parabellum, .41 AE, .45 ACP. Add 10 percent for nylon Uzi case and accessories. Built by IMI (Israeli Military Industries).

NIB	Exc.	V.G.	Good	Fair	Poor
1700	1450	1150	850	600	250

ADAMS/DEANE, ADAMS & DEANE
London, England
London Armoury Co. (After 1856)

Revolvers based upon Robert Adams' patents were manufactured by the firm of Deane, Adams & Deane. Although more technically advanced than the pistols produced by

Samuel Colt, Adams' revolvers were popular primarily in England and the British Empire.

Adams Model 1851 Self-Cocking Revolver

A .44 caliber double-action percussion revolver with a 7.5" octagonal barrel and 5-shot cylinder. The barrel and frame are blued, the cylinder case hardened and the grips are walnut. The top strap is marked "Deane, Adams and Deane 30 King William St. London Bridge." This revolver does not have a hammer spur and functions only as a double-action.

NIB	Exc.	V.G.	Good	Fair	Poor
—	4000	2975	1475	775	400

Adams Pocket Revolver

As above, in .31 caliber with a 4.5" barrel.

NIB	Exc.	V.G.	Good	Fair	Poor
—	3750	2875	1375	750	400

Beaumont-Adams Revolver

As above, fitted with a Tranter Patent loading lever and the hammer made with a spur.

NIB	Exc.	V.G.	Good	Fair	Poor
—	2500	1950	950	695	300

ADAMY GEBRUDER
Suhl, Germany

Over/Under Shotgun

A 12 or 16 gauge double-barrel over/under shotgun with 26" to 30" barrels, double triggers and a walnut stock.

NIB	Exc.	V.G.	Good	Fair	Poor
—	2100	1700	1250	750	400

ADIRONDACK ARMS CO. / A.S. BABBITT CO.
Plattsburgh, New York

Orvil M. Robinson Patent Rifle

The Robinson tube-fed repeating rifle was made in New York between 1870 and 1874. The early models, 1870-1872, are marked "A.S. Babbitt"; the later models, 1872-1874, "Adirondack

Arms Co." The Company was sold to Winchester in 1874, but they never produced the Robinson after that date. The rifle has been found in two styles: The first with small fingers on the hammer to cock and operate the mechanism; the second with buttons on the receiver to retract the bolt and cock the hammer. The rifle was made in .44 caliber with an octagonal barrel usually found in 26" or 28" length. The frames were predominantly brass; but some iron frames have been noted and they will bring a premium of approximately 25 percent. The barrel and magazine tube have a blued finish.

Courtesy Buffalo Bill Historical Center, Cody, Wyoming

First Model

NIB	Exc.	V.G.	Good	Fair	Poor
—	6500	5200	2700	1300	500

Second Model

NIB	Exc.	V.G.	Good	Fair	Poor
—	6500	5200	2700	1300	500

ADLER
Engelbrecht & Wolff
Blasii, Germany

An extremely rare and unusually designed semi-automatic pistol adapted for the 7.25mm Adler cartridge. This is a striker-fired blowback pistol with a 3.4" barrel. Single-column magazine has an 8-round capacity. Weight is approximately 24 oz. Produced in very limited numbers, probably only a few hundred, between 1906 and 1907.

Courtesy James Rankin

NIB	Exc.	V.G.	Good	Fair	Poor
—	—	10000	8750	2750	1250

ADVANCED SMALL ARMS INDUSTRIES
Solothurn, Switzerland

one Pro .45

Introduced in 1997 and built in Switzerland by ASAI, this pistol features a 3" barrel chambered for the .45 ACP cartridge. It is based on a short-recoil operation and is available in double-action or double-action-only. Also available is a kit (purchased separately) to convert the pistol to .400 CorBon caliber. The pistol weighs about 24 oz. empty.

NIB	Exc.	V.G.	Good	Fair	Poor
1000	725	595	425	195	100

ADVANTAGE ARMS U.S.A., INC.
Distributed by Wildfire Sports
St. Paul, Minnesota

Model 422

A .22 or .22 Magnum caliber four-barrel derringer with 2.5" barrels. Entirely made of an aluminum alloy. Finished in either blue or nickel-plate. Manufactured in 1986 and 1987.

NIB	Exc.	V.G.	Good	Fair	Poor
225	125	100	85	65	45

AERO
Manufactura De Armas De Fuego
Guernica, Spain

Model 1914 (Aero)

A 7.65mm caliber semi-automatic pistol with a 3.25" barrel in the Ruby design. The Aero name is on the slide along with an airplane. Magazine capacity is 7 rounds, weight is about 23 oz.

Courtesy James Rankin

NIB	Exc.	V.G.	Good	Fair	Poor
—	350	250	200	125	95

AETNA ARMS CO.
New York

A .22 caliber spur trigger revolver with an octagonal barrel and 7-shot cylinder. The barrel marked "Aetna Arms Co. New York." Manufactured from approximately 1870 to 1880. Copy of the S&W No. 1.

NIB	Exc.	V.G.	Good	Fair	Poor
—	—	550	375	150	100

AFC
Auguste Francotte
Liege, Belgium

This was one of the most prolific makers of revolvers in Liege during the last half of the 19th century. It is estimated that over 150 different revolvers were made and marketed by them before they were forced out of business by the German occupation of 1914. Francotte produced many variations from Tranter copies to pinfires, early Smith & Wesson designs to the 11mm M1871 Swedish troopers revolver. They made break-open revolvers and produced only one semi-auto, a 6.35mm blowback design. A good portion of their pistols were produced for the wholesale market and were sold under other names. These particular revolvers will bear the letters "AF" stamped somewhere on the frame. Because of the vast number and variety of pistols produced by this company, cataloging and pricing is beyond the scope of this or any general reference book. It is suggested that any examples encountered be researched on an individual basis. For more information on Francotte see the information under that listing.

Model 1895

One of the earliest Francotte pistols. Chambered for the 8mm cartridge, it is a lever-operated repeater. Marked "A. Francotte & Co. Makers" on the top of the slide.

Courtesy James Rankin

NIB	Exc.	V.G.	Good	Fair	Poor
—	7000	5500	4150	2300	1500

Trainer

A single-shot target pistol made for competition in .22 caliber short. "AFC" trademark on the left side of the frame. This model was probably not made by Francotte, but sold by that firm and others.

Courtesy James Rankin

NIB	Exc.	V.G.	Good	Fair	Poor
—	3800	3150	2700	2175	1500

Semi-Auto

A 6.35mm, 6-shot detachable magazine pocket pistol with blue finish. This model was marked "A. Francotte A Liege" on the frame.

Courtesy James Rankin

NIB	Exc.	V.G.	Good	Fair	Poor
—	425	300	195	125	90

AFFERBACH, W. A.
Philadelphia, Pennsylvania

This maker is known to have produced copies of Henry Derringer's percussion pocket pistols. Though uncommon, their values would be approximately as listed.

NIB	Exc.	V.G.	Good	Fair	Poor
—	—	2750	2200	995	300

AGNER (SAXHOJ PRODUCTS, INC.)
Copenhagen, Denmark

Model M 80

A .22 caliber single-shot stainless steel target pistol with a 5.9" barrel, adjustable sights and walnut grips. This pistol is fitted with a dry fire mechanism. Also available in a left-hand version. Imported from 1981 to 1986.

Courtesy James Rankin

NIB	Exc.	V.G.	Good	Fair	Poor
—	1250	875	600	450	200

AGUIRRE
Eibar, Spain

A Spanish manufacturer of pistols prior to World War II.

Basculant

A 6.35mm semi-automatic pistol marked on the slide "Cal. 6.35 Automatic Pistol Basculant."

NIB	Exc.	V.G.	Good	Fair	Poor
—	275	150	125	75	50

LeDragon

As above, with the slide marked "Cal. 6.35 Automatic Pistol LeDragon." It is patterned after the Browning Model 1906. A stylized dragon is molded into the grips.

Courtesy James Rankin

NIB	Exc.	V.G.	Good	Fair	Poor
—	275	150	125	75	50

AGUIRRE Y ARANZABAL (AyA)
Eibar, Spain

SIDE-BY-SIDES

Matador

A 12, 16, 20, 28 or .410 bore boxlock double-barrel shotgun with 26", 28" or 30" barrels, single-selective trigger and automatic ejectors. Blued with a walnut stock. Manufactured from 1955 to 1963. **NOTE:** 28 gauge and .410 add 100 percent.

NIB	Exc.	V.G.	Good	Fair	Poor
—	550	415	350	300	200

Matador II

As above, in 12 or 20 gauge with a ventilated rib.

NIB	Exc.	V.G.	Good	Fair	Poor
—	575	425	375	300	200

Matador III

As above, with 3" chambers.

NIB	Exc.	V.G.	Good	Fair	Poor
—	600	450	395	325	200

Bolero

As above, with a non-selective single trigger and extractors. Manufactured until 1984.

NIB	Exc.	V.G.	Good	Fair	Poor
—	500	375	325	295	200

Iberia

A 12 or 20 gauge Magnum boxlock double-barrel shotgun with 26", 28" or 30" barrels, double triggers and extractors. Blued with a walnut stock.

NIB	Exc.	V.G.	Good	Fair	Poor
—	600	450	395	325	200

Iberia II

Similar to the above, in 12 or 16 gauge with 28" barrels and 2.75" chambers.

NIB	Exc.	V.G.	Good	Fair	Poor
—	625	500	425	325	250

Model 106

A 12, 16, or 20 gauge boxlock double-barrel shotgun with 28" barrels, double triggers and extractors. Blued with a walnut stock. Manufactured until 1985.

NIB	Exc.	V.G.	Good	Fair	Poor
—	600	500	400	300	250

Model 107-LI

As above, with the receiver lightly engraved and an English-style stock. In 12 or 16 gauge only.

NIB	Exc.	V.G.	Good	Fair	Poor
—	675	575	495	325	275

Model 116

A 12, 16 or 20 gauge sidelock double-barrel shotgun with 27" to 30" barrels, double triggers and ejectors. Engraved, blued with a walnut stock. Manufactured until 1985.

NIB	Exc.	V.G.	Good	Fair	Poor
—	1095	975	800	500	350

Model 117

As above, with 3" chambers.

NIB	Exc.	V.G.	Good	Fair	Poor
—	1150	1000	850	600	400

Model 117 "Quail Unlimited"

As above in 12 gauge only with 26" barrels and the receiver engraved "Quail Unlimited of North America". Forty-two were manufactured.

NIB	Exc.	V.G.	Good	Fair	Poor
—	1500	1200	875	650	425

Model 210

An exposed hammer, 12 or 16 gauge, boxlock shotgun with 26" to 28" barrels and double triggers. Blued with a walnut stock. Manufactured until 1985.

NIB	Exc.	V.G.	Good	Fair	Poor
—	800	675	550	400	325

Model 711 Boxlock

A 12 gauge boxlock double-barrel shotgun with 28" or 30" barrels having ventilated ribs, single-selective trigger and automatic ejectors. Manufactured until 1984.

NIB	Exc.	V.G.	Good	Fair	Poor
—	900	800	700	500	350

Model 711 Sidelock

As above, with sidelocks. Manufactured in 1985 only.

NIB	Exc.	V.G.	Good	Fair	Poor
—	1200	1000	750	500	400

Senior

A custom order 12 gauge double-barrel sidelock shotgun, gold inlaid and engraved. Made strictly to individual customer's specifications.

NIB	Exc.	V.G.	Good	Fair	Poor
17000	13750	9750	7000	4500	2250

OVER/UNDERS

Model 79 "A"

A 12 gauge boxlock over/under double-barrel shotgun with 26", 28" or 30" barrels, single-selective trigger and automatic ejectors. Blued with a walnut stock. Manufactured until 1985.

NIB	Exc.	V.G.	Good	Fair	Poor
—	1250	1050	925	750	500

Model 79 "B"

As above, with a moderate amount of engraving.

NIB	Exc.	V.G.	Good	Fair	Poor
—	1350	1150	950	800	575

Model 79 "C"

As above, with extensive engraving.

NIB	Exc.	V.G.	Good	Fair	Poor
—	2000	1800	1500	1150	675

Model 77

As above, patterned after the Merkel shotgun.

NIB	Exc.	V.G.	Good	Fair	Poor
—	3000	2700	2000	1500	1000

Coral "A"

A 12 or 16 gauge over/under boxlock double-barrel shotgun with 26" or 28" barrels having ventilated ribs, double triggers and automatic ejectors. Fitted with a Kersten cross bolt. Manufactured until 1985.

NIB	Exc.	V.G.	Good	Fair	Poor
—	1250	900	700	500	300

Coral "B"

As above, with an engraved French case hardened receiver.

NIB	Exc.	V.G.	Good	Fair	Poor
—	1400	1100	750	600	350

RECENTLY IMPORTED SHOTGUNS

SIDELOCK SIDE-BY-SIDES

AyA sidelock shotguns use the Holland & Holland system. They feature double triggers, articulated front trigger, cocking indicators, bushed firing pins, replaceable firing pins, replaceable hinge pins, and chopper lump barrels. Frame and sidelocks are case-colored.

These shotguns weigh between 5 and 7 pounds depending on gauge and barrel length. Barrel lengths are offered in 26", 27", 28", and 29" depending on gauge. All stocks are figured walnut with hand checkering and oil finish. These guns are available with several extra cost options that may affect price. Also influencing price of new guns is the fluctuating dollar in relation to Spanish currency.

Model No. 1

This model is offered in 12 gauge and 20 gauge with special English scroll engraving. Fitted with automatic ejectors and straight grip stock with exhibition quality wood.

NIB	Exc.	V.G.	Good	Fair	Poor
—	10500	8000	4750	2300	700

Model No. 1 Round Body

As above, but with a round body action.

NIB	Exc.	V.G.	Good	Fair	Poor
—	11500	9000	5250	2400	700

Model No. 2

This model is offered in 12, 16, 20, and 28 gauge, and .410 bore. It has automatic ejectors and straight-grip, select walnut stock.

NIB	Exc.	V.G.	Good	Fair	Poor
—	5000	4000	2500	1850	700

Model No. 2 Round Body

As above, but with round body action.

NIB	Exc.	V.G.	Good	Fair	Poor
—	5200	4250	2750	1950	700

Model No. 53

Chambered for 12, 16, and 20 gauge. Features three locking lugs and side clips, automatic ejectors and straight grip stock.

NIB	Exc.	V.G.	Good	Fair	Poor
—	11500	9000	5250	—	—

Model No. 1 Deluxe

A deluxe version of the No. 1 with finer wood and engraving.
NOTE: For round body add $350.

NIB	Exc.	V.G.	Good	Fair	Poor
—	3500	4000	2750	1000	700

Model No. 56

This model is available in 12 gauge only and features three locking lugs, side clips, special wide action body, and raised matted rib. Select walnut, straight-grip stock.

NIB	Exc.	V.G.	Good	Fair	Poor
—	8700	6750	5400	2000	1000

Model XXV

Offered in 12 gauge and 20 gauge only this model is fitted with a Churchill-type rib. Automatic ejectors and select straight grip walnut stock are standard.

NIB	Exc.	V.G.	Good	Fair	Poor
—	5250	4250	3200	1750	1000

BOXLOCK SIDE-BY-SIDES

These AyA guns utilize an Anson & Deeley system with double locking lugs with detachable cross pin and separate trigger plate that gives access to the firing mechanism. Frame is case-colored. The barrels are chopper lump, firing pins are bushed, automatic safety and automatic ejectors are standard. Barrel lengths are offered in 26", 27", and 28" depending on gauge. Weights are between 5 and 7 pounds depending on gauge.

Model XXV

This model is available in 12 and 20 gauge only. The select walnut stock is hand checkered with straight grip stock.

NIB	Exc.	V.G.	Good	Fair	Poor
—	3500	2250	800	600	350

Model No. 4

This model is available in 12, 16, 20, and 28 gauge as well as .410 bore. It is fitted with select hand checkered walnut stock with straight grip. Light scroll engraving on this model. Add 75 percent for 28 and .410.

NIB	Exc.	V.G.	Good	Fair	Poor
—	3000	2650	1250	—	—

Model No. 4 Deluxe

Same as above, but with select walnut stock and slightly more engraving coverage. Add 75 percent for 28 and .410.

NIB	Exc.	V.G.	Good	Fair	Poor
—	5000	3995	1500	1000	550

OVER/UNDERS

These AyA shotguns are similar in design and appearance to the Gebruder Merkel over/under sidelocks with three-part fore-end, Kersten cross bolt, and double under locking lugs.

Model No. 37 Super

This model is available in 12 gauge only with ventilated rib, automatic ejectors, internally gold-plated sidelocks. Offered with three different types of engraving patterns: ducks, scroll, or deep cut engraving. Very few of this model were imported into the U.S.

NIB	Exc.	V.G.	Good	Fair	Poor
—	12000	9500	5000	3500	2000

Model Augusta

This is the top-of-the-line AyA model offered in 12 gauge only. It features presentation wood and deep cut scroll engraving. Very few of this model were imported into the U.S. **NOTE:** For extra cost options add approximately: Pistol grip–$90; Rubber recoil pad–$190; Left-hand gun–$775; Length of pull longer than 15"–$125; Select wood–$235; Deluxe wood–$550; Single non-selective trigger–$400; Single-selective trigger–$600; Chrome-lined barrels–$140; Churchill rib–$375; Raised rib–$180; Extra set of barrels–$1500.

NIB	Exc.	V.G.	Good	Fair	Poor
—	15000	8000	4500	3500	1500

AIR MATCH
Paris, Kentucky

Air Match 500

A .22 caliber single-shot target pistol with a 10.5" barrel, adjustable sights and adjustable front-mounted counterweights. Blued with walnut grips. Imported from 1984 to 1986.

NIB	Exc.	V.G.	Good	Fair	Poor
775	595	425	300	250	125

AJAX ARMY

Single-Action

A spur-trigger, single-action, solid-frame revolver that was chambered for the .44 rimfire cartridge. It had a 7" barrel and was blued with walnut grips. It was manufactured in the 1880s.

NIB	Exc.	V.G.	Good	Fair	Poor
—	750	450	365	275	200

ALAMO RANGER
Spain

A double-action Spanish copy of the Colt SAA, chambered for the .38 Long Colt or .38 Special. The cylinder held 6 shots. The finish was blued; grips were checkered hard rubber. The maker of this pistol is unknown.

NIB	Exc.	V.G.	Good	Fair	Poor
—	350	225	115	75	45

ALASKA
Norwich, Connecticut

See—Hood Firearms Co.

ALDAZABAL
Eibar, Spain
Aldazabal, Leturiondo & CIA

Model 1919

A vest pocket semi-automatic pistol copied from the FN Browning Model 1906. Caliber is 6.35mm.

Courtesy James Rankin

NIB	Exc.	V.G.	Good	Fair	Poor
—	295	175	125	75	50

Military Model

A semi-automatic pistol in the Ruby-style. Caliber is 7.65mm with a 9-round magazine.

Courtesy James Rankin

NIB	Exc.	V.G.	Good	Fair	Poor
—	375	275	195	125	75

Aldazabal

Another typical low-quality, "Eibar"-type semi-automatic. It was a Browning blowback copy, chambered for the 7.65mm cartridge. It had a 7-shot detachable magazine and blued finish with checkered wood grips. This company ceased production before the Spanish Civil War.

NIB	Exc.	V.G.	Good	Fair	Poor
—	295	165	115	65	40

ALERT
Norwich, Connecticut

See—Hood Firearms Co.

ALEXIA
Norwich, Connecticut

See—Hopkins & Allen

ALFA
Eibar, Spain

See—Armero Especialistas Reunides

ALKARTASUNA FABRICA DE ARMAS
Guernica, Spain

This company began production during World War I to help Gabilondo y Urresti supply sidearms to the French. After the hostilities ceased, they continued to produce firearms under their own name. They produced a number of variations in both 6.35mm and 7.65mm marked "Alkar." Collector interest is very thin. The factory burned down in 1920, and by 1922 business had totally ceased.

Alkar

A 6.35mm semi-automatic pistol with a cartridge counter in the grip plates. One variation of many built in either 6.35mm or 7.65mm.

Courtesy James Rankin

NIB	Exc.	V.G.	Good	Fair	Poor
—	295	250	195	125	100

Alkar (Ruby-Style)

A 7.65mm semi-automatic pistol built in the Ruby-style. This pistol was supplied to the French government during World War I.

Courtesy James Rankin

NIB	Exc.	V.G.	Good	Fair	Poor
—	295	225	165	100	90

ALL RIGHT FIREARMS CO.
Lawrence, Massachusetts
Little All Right Palm Pistol

Squeezer-type pocket pistol invented by E. Boardman and A. Peavy in 1876, was made in .22 cal. and had a 5-shot cylinder with a 1-5/8" or 2-3/8" barrel. The barrel is octagonal with a tube on top of it which houses the sliding trigger. The finish is nickel. The black hard rubber grips have "Little All Right" & "All Right Firearms Co., Manufacturers Lawrence, Mass. U.S.A." molded into them. There were several hundred produced in the late 1870s.

Courtesy Milwaukee Public Museum, Milwaukee, Wisconsin

NIB	Exc.	V.G.	Good	Fair	Poor
—	4000	3250	2950	1050	300

ALLEN, ETHAN
Grafton, Massachusetts

The company was founded by Ethan Allen in the early 1800s. It became a prolific gun-making firm that evolved from Ethan Allen to Allen & Thurber, as well as the Allen & Wheelock Company. It was located in Norwich, Connecticut, and Worchester, Massachusetts, as well as Grafton. It eventually became the Forehand & Wadsworth Company in 1871 after the death of Ethan Allen. There were many and varied firearms produced under all of the headings described above. If one desires to collect Ethan Allen firearms, it would be advisable to educate oneself, as there are a number of fine publications available on the subject. The basic models and their values are listed.

First Model Pocket Rifle

Manufactured by Ethan Allen in Grafton, Massachusetts. It was a bootleg-type, under-hammer, single-shot pistol chambered for .31 percussion. Larger-caliber versions have also been noted. It had barrel lengths from 5" to 9" that were part-octagon in configuration. It had iron mountings and was blued with walnut grips. The barrel was marked, "E. Allen/ Grafton/Mass." as well as "Pocket Rifle/Cast Steel/Warranted." There were approximately 2,000 manufactured from 1831 to 1842.

NIB	Exc.	V.G.	Good	Fair	Poor
—	—	—	1650	750	200

Second Model Pocket Rifle

A rounded-frame, round-grip version of the First Model.

NIB	Exc.	V.G.	Good	Fair	Poor
—	—	—	1550	650	200

Bar Hammer Pistol

A double-action pistol with a top-mounted bar hammer. It was chambered for .28 to .36 caliber percussion. The half-octagon barrels were from 2" to 10" in length. They screwed out of the frame so it was possible to breech load them. The finish was blued with rounded walnut grips. They were marked, "Allen & Thurber/ Grafton Mass." There were approximately 2,000 manufactured between the early 1830s and 1860.

NIB	Exc.	V.G.	Good	Fair	Poor
—	—	—	1650	725	200

Tube Hammer Pistol

This version was similar to the Bar Hammer with a curved hammer without a spur. There were only a few hundred manufactured between the early 1830s and the early 1840s.

NIB	Exc.	V.G.	Good	Fair	Poor
—	—	—	2900	1300	400

Side Hammer Pistol

A single-shot, target-type pistol that was chambered for .34, .41, and .45 caliber percussion. It had a part-octagon barrel that was from 6" to 10" in length. There was a wooden ramrod mounted under the barrel. This model had a good quality rear sight that was adjustable. The ornate trigger guard had a graceful spur at its rear. The finish was blued with a rounded walnut grip. The barrel was marked, "Allen & Thurber, Worchester." There were approximately 300 manufactured in the late 1840s and early 1850s.

NIB	Exc.	V.G.	Good	Fair	Poor
—	—	—	1400	650	200

Center Hammer Pistol

A single-action chambered for .34, .36, or .44 percussion. It had a half-octagon barrel from 4" to 12" in length. It had a centrally mounted hammer that was offset to the right side to allow for sighting the pistol. The finish was blued with walnut grips. It was marked, "Allen & Thurber, Allen Thurber & Company." Some specimens are marked, "Allen & Wheelock." There were several thousand manufactured between the late 1840s and 1860.

NIB	Exc.	V.G.	Good	Fair	Poor
—	—	—	1400	650	200

Double-Barrel Pistol

A side-by-side, double-barrel pistol with a single trigger. It was chambered for .36 caliber percussion with 3" to 6" round barrels. The finish was blued with walnut grips. Examples with a ramrod mounted under the barrel have been noted. The flute between the barrels was marked, "Allen & Thurber," "Allen Thurber & Company," or "Allen & Wheelock." There were approximately 1,000 manufactured in the 1850s.

NIB	Exc.	V.G.	Good	Fair	Poor
—	—	—	1250	600	150

Allen & Wheelock Center Hammer Pistol

A single-action pocket pistol chambered for .31 to .38 caliber percussion. It had octagon barrels from 3" to 6" in length. The finish was blued with square butt walnut grips. The barrel was marked, "Allen & Wheelock." There were approximately 500 manufactured between 1858 and 1865.

NIB	Exc.	V.G.	Good	Fair	Poor
—	—	—	1100	550	100

Allen Thurber & Company Target Pistol

A deluxe, single-action target pistol that was chambered for .31 or .36 caliber percussion. It had a heavy, octagon barrel that was from 11" to 16" in length. There was a wooden ramrod mounted underneath the barrel. The mountings were of German silver, and there was a detachable walnut stock with a deluxe, engraved patchbox. This weapon was engraved, and the barrel was marked, "Allen Thurber & Co./Worchester/Cast Steel". This firearm was furnished in a fitted case with the stock, false muzzle, and various accessories. It was considered to be a very high grade target pistol in its era. The values listed are for a complete-cased outfit. There were very few manufactured in the 1850s. **NOTE:** For pistols without attachable stock deduct 75 percent.

NIB	Exc.	V.G.	Good	Fair	Poor
—	—	—	9000	4000	1000

Ethan Allen Pepperboxes

During the period from the early 1830s to the 1860s, this company manufactured over 50 different variations of the revolving, pepperbox-type pistol. They were commercially quite successful and actually competed successfully with the Colt revolving handguns for more than a decade. They were widely used throughout the United States, as well as in Mexico, and during our Civil War. They are widely collectible because of the number of variations that exist. The potential collector should avail himself of the information available on the subject. These pepperboxes can be divided into three categories.

No. 1: Manufactured from the 1830s until 1842, at Grafton, Massachusetts.

No. 2: Manufactured from 1842 to 1847, at Norwich, Connecticut.

No. 3: Manufactured from 1847 to 1865, at Worchester, Massachusetts.

There are a number of subdivisions among these three basic groups that would pertain to trigger type, size, barrel length, etc. It would be impossible to cover all 50 of these variations in a text of this type. We strongly suggest that qualified, individual appraisal be secured if contemplating a transaction. The values of these pepperbox pistols in excellent condition would be between $1,500 and $5,000. Most examples will be seen in the fair to good condition and will bring $1,000 to 2,000 depending on variation.

Large Frame Pocket Revolver

A double-action pocket revolver that was chambered for .34 caliber percussion. It had an octagon barrel from 3" to 5" in length. There were no sights. The 5-shot, unfluted cylinder was game scene engraved. The finish was blued with rounded walnut grips. It had a bar-type hammer. This was the first conventional revolver manufactured by this company, and it was directly influenced by the pepperbox pistol for which Ethan Allen had become famous. It was marked, "Allen & Wheelock" as well as "Patented April 16, 1845." There were approximately 1,500 manufactured between 1857 and 1860.

Courtesy Milwaukee Public Museum, Milwaukee, Wisconsin

NIB	Exc.	V.G.	Good	Fair	Poor
—	—	—	1400	700	350

Small Frame Pocket Revolver

This version was similar to the Large Frame Pocket Revolver except chambered for .31 caliber percussion, with a 2" to 3.5" octagon barrel. It was slightly smaller in size, finished and marked the same. There were approximately 1,000 made between 1858 and 1860.

NIB	Exc.	V.G.	Good	Fair	Poor
—	—	—	1400	700	350

Side Hammer Belt Revolver

A single-action revolver chambered for .34 caliber percussion. It had an octagon barrel from 3" to 7.5" in length. It featured a hammer that was mounted on the right side of the frame and a 5-shot, engraved, unfluted cylinder. The cylinder access pin is inserted from the rear of the weapon. The finish is blued with a case-colored hammer and trigger guard and flared butt walnut grips. It is marked, "Allen & Wheelock." There were two basic types. Values for the early model, of which 100 were manufactured between 1858 and 1861, are listed.

NIB	Exc.	V.G.	Good	Fair	Poor
—	—	—	1500	750	300

Standard Model

The second type was the Standard Model, with a spring-loaded catch on the trigger guard as opposed to a friction catch on the early model. There were approximately 1,000 manufactured between 1858 and 1861.

Courtesy Milwaukee Public Museum, Milwaukee, Wisconsin

NIB	Exc.	V.G.	Good	Fair	Poor
—	—	—	1200	595	200

Side Hammer Pocket Revolver

This version was chambered for .28 caliber percussion and had a 2" to 5" octagon barrel. The frame was slightly smaller than the belt model.

Courtesy Milwaukee Public Museum, Milwaukee, Wisconsin

Early Production

100 manufactured.

NIB	Exc.	V.G.	Good	Fair	Poor
—	—	—	1300	725	250

Standard Production

1,000 manufactured.

NIB	Exc.	V.G.	Good	Fair	Poor
—	—	2100	975	400	225

Side Hammer Navy Revolver

This was a large-frame, military-type revolver that was similar to the Side Hammer Belt Model, chambered for .36 caliber percussion. It features an octagon, 5.5" to 8" barrel with a 6-shot, engraved cylinder. There was an early-production type with a friction catch on the trigger guard. There were approximately 100 manufactured between 1858 and 1861.

Early Production

NIB	Exc.	V.G.	Good	Fair	Poor
—	—	—	4300	1975	575

Standard Model

1,000 manufactured.

NIB	Exc.	V.G.	Good	Fair	Poor
—	—	—	3700	1700	475

Center Hammer Army Revolver

A large, military-type, single-action revolver that was chambered for .44 caliber percussion. It had a 7.5", half-octagon barrel and a 6-shot, unfluted cylinder. The hammer was mounted in the center of the frame. The finish was blued with a case-colored hammer and trigger guard and walnut grips. The barrel was marked, "Allen & Wheelock. Worchester, Mass. U.S./Allen's Pt's. Jan. 13, 1857. Dec. 15, 1857, Sept. 7, 1858". There were approximately 700 manufactured between 1861 and 1862.

Courtesy Milwaukee Public Museum, Milwaukee, Wisconsin

NIB	Exc.	V.G.	Good	Fair	Poor
—	—	7500	4500	1875	500

Center Hammer Navy Revolver

Similar to the Army Revolver except chambered for .36 caliber percussion with a 7.5", full-octagon barrel. Examples have been noted with 5", 6", or 8" barrels. Otherwise, it was similar to the Army model.

NIB	Exc.	V.G.	Good	Fair	Poor
—	—	—	4300	1975	475

Center Hammer Percussion Revolver

A single-action revolver chambered for .36 caliber percussion. It had an octagonal, 3" or 4" barrel with a 6-shot, unfluted cylinder. The finish was blued with walnut grips. This model supposedly was made for the Providence, Rhode Island, Police Department and has become commonly referred to as the "Providence Police Model." There were approximately 700 manufactured between 1858 and 1862.

NIB	Exc.	V.G.	Good	Fair	Poor
—	—	2500	1750	750	200

Lipfire Army Revolver

A large, military-type, single-action revolver that was chambered for the .44 lipfire cartridge. It had a 7.5", half-octagon barrel with a 6-shot, unfluted cylinder that had notches at its rear for the cartridge lips. The finish was blued with a case-colored hammer and trigger guard and square butt walnut grips. The barrel was marked, "Allen & Wheelock, Worchester, Mass." It resembled the Center Hammer Percussion Army Revolver. There were two basic variations, with a total of 250 Lipfire Army Revolvers manufactured in the early 1860s.

Early Model

Top hinged loading gate.

NIB	Exc.	V.G.	Good	Fair	Poor
—	—	—	4500	2200	600

Late Model

Bottom hinged loading gate.

NIB	Exc.	V.G.	Good	Fair	Poor
—	—	—	4000	1700	400

Lipfire Navy Revolver

Similar to the Army model, except chambered for the .36 lipfire cartridge, with an octagonal, 4", 5", 6", 7.5", or 8" barrel. There were approximately 500 manufactured in the 1860s.

NIB	Exc.	V.G.	Good	Fair	Poor
—	—	—	3300	1300	400

Lipfire Pocket Revolver

A smaller version chambered for the .32 lipfire cartridge, with an octagonal, 4", 5", or 6" barrel. There were approximately 200 manufactured in the early 1860s.

NIB	Exc.	V.G.	Good	Fair	Poor
—	—	—	2200	950	250

.32 Side Hammer Rimfire Revolver

A single-action, spur-trigger, pocket revolver chambered for the .32 caliber rimfire cartridge. It had octagonal barrels from 3" to 5" in length. The finish was blued with flared-butt, walnut grips. It was marked "Allen & Wheelock Worchester, Mass." There were three variations with a total of approximately 1,000 manufactured between 1859 and 1862.

First Model

Rounded top strap.

NIB	Exc.	V.G.	Good	Fair	Poor
—	—	1125	800	450	150

Second Model

July 3, 1860 marked on frame.

NIB	Exc.	V.G.	Good	Fair	Poor
—	—	1100	795	425	150

Third Model

1858 and 1861 patent dates.

NIB	Exc.	V.G.	Good	Fair	Poor
—	—	1050	775	400	125

.22 Side Hammer Rimfire Revolver

A smaller version of the .32 revolver, chambered for the .22 rimfire cartridge. It has octagonal barrels from 2.25" to 4" in length. It has a 7-shot, unfluted cylinder. There were approximately 1,500 manufactured between 1858 and 1862. There were many variations.

Early Model First Issue

Access pin enters from rear.

NIB	Exc.	V.G.	Good	Fair	Poor
—	—	1300	850	475	100

Second Issue

Access pin enters from front.

NIB	Exc.	V.G.	Good	Fair	Poor
—	—	1300	850	475	100

Third Issue

Separate rear sight.

NIB	Exc.	V.G.	Good	Fair	Poor
—	—	1425	1250	600	150

Fourth to Eighth Issue

Very similar, values the same.

NIB	Exc.	V.G.	Good	Fair	Poor
—	—	900	750	300	100

Single-Shot Center Hammer

A single-shot derringer-type pistol that was chambered for the .22 caliber rimfire cartridge. It had part-octagon barrels from 2" to 5.5" in length that swung to the right side for loading. Some had automatic ejectors; others did not. The frame was either brass or iron with bird's-head or squared butt walnut grips. It was marked "Allen & Wheelock" or "E. Allen & Co." There were very few manufactured in the early 1860s.

Early Issue

Full-length, octagon barrel and a round, iron frame. It is rarely encountered.

NIB	Exc.	V.G.	Good	Fair	Poor
—	—	1275	1150	400	100

Standard Issue

Squared butt or bird's-head.

NIB	Exc.	V.G.	Good	Fair	Poor
—	—	1175	1050	300	100

.32 Single-Shot Center Hammer

A larger-frame pocket pistol chambered for the .32 rimfire cartridge. It has a part-octagon or full-octagon barrel of 4" or 5" in length. It swung to the right side for loading. Otherwise, this model was similar to the .22-caliber version.

NIB	Exc.	V.G.	Good	Fair	Poor
—	—	1175	1050	300	100

Vest Pocket Derringer

A small pocket pistol chambered for the .22 rimfire cartridge. It had a 2", part-octagon barrel that swung to the right-hand side for loading. The cartridges were manually extracted. It featured a brass frame with a blued or plated barrel and walnut, bird's-head grips. The barrel was marked "Allen & Co. Makers." This was an extremely small firearm, and there were approximately 200 manufactured between 1869 and 1871.

NIB	Exc.	V.G.	Good	Fair	Poor
—	—	1595	975	425	100

.32 Derringer

Similar to the Vest Pocket version, larger in size, and chambered for the .32 rimfire cartridge. It had a part-octagon barrel from 2" to 4" in length that swung to the right for loading. This version featured an automatic extractor. The barrel was marked "E. Allen & Co. Worchester, Mass." This was a very rare firearm, made between 1865 and 1871.

NIB	Exc.	V.G.	Good	Fair	Poor
—	—	1495	875	395	100

.41 Derringer

The same size and configuration as the .32 caliber model except it was chambered for the .41 rimfire cartridge with barrel lengths of 2.5" to 2.75" in length. The markings were the same. There were approximately 100 manufactured between 1865 and 1871.

NIB	Exc.	V.G.	Good	Fair	Poor
—	—	2200	950	350	100

Center Hammer Muzzleloading Rifle

A single-shot rifle chambered for .44 caliber percussion. It had a 36" round barrel with an octagonal breech. It had a center-mounted hammer that was offset to the right for sighting. It had iron mountings. The finish was browned with a case-colored lock. There was a ramrod mounted under the barrel. It had a walnut buttstock with a crescent buttplate and no forearm. There were approximately 100 manufactured in the 1850s.

NIB	Exc.	V.G.	Good	Fair	Poor
—	—	1850	600	250	125

Side Hammer Muzzleloading Rifle

Similar to the Center Hammer model, with the hammer mounted on the right side of the lock. It was chambered for .38 caliber percussion, with an octagon barrel from 28" to 32" in length. It is occasionally found with a patchbox. The barrel is browned with a case-colored lock and a walnut stock with crescent butt-plate. There were several hundred manufactured from the early 1840s to the 1860s.

NIB	Exc.	V.G.	Good	Fair	Poor
—	—	2750	900	350	150

Combination Gun

Either an over/under or side-by-side rifle chambered for 12 gauge and .38 caliber percussion. The barrels were from 28" to 34" in length. It had two hammers and double triggers with a ramrod mounted either beneath or on the right side of the barrels. The finish was browned with a walnut stock. Examples with a patchbox have been noted. Production was very limited, with the over/under versions worth approximately 20 percent more than the side-by-side values given. They were manufactured between the 1840s and the 1860s.

NIB	Exc.	V.G.	Good	Fair	Poor
—	—	6000	4350	1750	600

Side Hammer Breechloading Rifle

A unique rifle chambered for .36 to .50 caliber percussion. It was offered with various-length, part-octagon barrels. It had an unusual breech mechanism that was activated by a rotating lever which resembled a water faucet. The barrel was browned with a case-colored lock and a walnut stock. It was marked "Allen & Wheelock/ Allen's Patent July 3, 1855." There were approximately 500 manufactured between 1855 and 1860.

Courtesy Buffalo Bill Historical Center, Cody, Wyoming

NIB	Exc.	V.G.	Good	Fair	Poor
—	—	3550	1600	500	350

Drop Breech Rifle

This single-shot rifle was chambered for the .22 through the .44 rimfire cartridges. It had a part-octagon barrel from 23" to 28" in length. The breech was activated by the combination trigger guard action lever. Opening the breech automatically ejected the empty cartridge. The external hammer was manually cocked, and it featured an adjustable sight. The barrel was blued with a case-colored frame and a walnut stock. It was marked "Allen & Wheelock/ Allen's Pat. Sept. 18, 1860." There were approximately 2,000 manufactured between 1860 and 1871.

Courtesy Milwaukee Public Museum, Milwaukee, Wisconsin

NIB	Exc.	V.G.	Good	Fair	Poor
—	—	1550	600	200	100

Lipfire Revolving Rifle

A 6-shot, cylinder-type rifle chambered for the .44 caliber lipfire cartridge. It had an unfluted cylinder with slots at its rear to allow for the cartridge lips. The round barrels were 26" to 28" in length with an octagon breech. The finish was blued with a case-colored frame and a walnut buttstock. This model was not marked with the maker's name. There were approximately 100 manufactured between 1861 and 1863.

Courtesy Buffalo Bill Historical Center, Cody, Wyoming

NIB	Exc.	V.G.	Good	Fair	Poor
—	—	18500	7000	2000	775

Double-Barrel Shotgun

A side-by-side gun chambered for 10 or 12 gauge. The barrel length was 28". It was loaded by means of a trapdoor-type breech that had a lever handle. The finish was blued with checkered walnut stock. There were a few hundred manufactured between 1865 and 1871.

NIB	Exc.	V.G.	Good	Fair	Poor
—	—	1800	800	250	125

ALLEN & THURBER
See—Ethan Allen

ALLEN & WHEELOCK
See—Ethan Allen

ALLEN FIREARMS
Santa Fe, New Mexico
See—Aldo Uberti

ALPHA ARMS CO.
Flower Mound, Texas

Alpha Arms Co. produced high-grade bolt-action rifles on a semi-custom basis. It manufactured a number of standard models but offered many options at additional cost. Some of these options were custom sights and finishes and an octagonal barrel. These extra features would add to the value of the models listed. This company operated from 1983 until 1987.

Jaguar Grade I

Built on a Mauser-type action with barrel lengths from 20" to 24". It was chambered for most calibers between .222 Rem. and .338 Win. Mag. The stock was made from a synthetic laminated material that the company called "Alphawood". This model was introduced in 1987 and only produced that year.

NIB	Exc.	V.G.	Good	Fair	Poor
1700	1100	750	500	300	200

Jaguar Grade II

Similar to the Grade I with a Douglas Premium barrel.

NIB	Exc.	V.G.	Good	Fair	Poor
1825	1275	800	500	400	250

Jaguar Grade III

Has the Douglas barrel plus a hand-honed trigger and action and a three-position safety like the Winchester Model 70.

NIB	Exc.	V.G.	Good	Fair	Poor
1950	1500	1050	700	400	200

Jaguar Grade IV

Has all the features of the Grade III with a specially lightened action and sling-swivel studs.

NIB	Exc.	V.G.	Good	Fair	Poor
2000	1750	1200	900	500	250

Alpha Big-Five

Similar to the Jaguar Grade IV chambered for the .300 Win. Mag., .375 H&H Mag. and the .458 Win. Mag. It had a reinforced through-bolt stock to accommodate the recoil of the larger caliber cartridges for which it was chambered. It also had a Decelerator recoil pad. This model was manufactured in 1987 only. Add 20 percent for .458.

NIB	Exc.	V.G.	Good	Fair	Poor
2200	1850	1500	950	600	300

Alpha Grand Slam

Features the same high quality as the Jaguar models and is available in a left-hand model. It has a fluted bolt, laminated stock, and a matte blue finish. Deduct 10 percent for left-hand version.

NIB	Exc.	V.G.	Good	Fair	Poor
1700	1500	1250	700	450	250

Alpha Custom

Similar to the Grand Slam with a select grade stock.

NIB	Exc.	V.G.	Good	Fair	Poor
1700	1500	1250	750	500	250

Alpha Alaskan

Similar to the Grand Slam but chambered for the .308 Win., .350 Rem. Mag., .358 Win. and the .458 Win. Mag. It features all stainless steel construction. Add 20 percent for .458.

NIB	Exc.	V.G.	Good	Fair	Poor
2000	1750	1450	850	500	250

ALSOP, C.R.
Middletown, Connecticut

This firearms manufacturer made revolvers during 1862 and 1863. They made two basic models, the Navy and the Pocket model. Some collectors consider the Alsop to be a secondary U.S. martial handgun, but no verifying government contracts are known to exist.

First Model Navy Revolver

A .36 cal. revolver with a 3.5", 4.5", 5.5", or 6.5" barrel length and a 5-shot cylinder. It has a blued finish, wood grips, and a peculiar hump in its backstrap. The first model has a safety device which blocks the spur trigger. This device is found on serial numbers 1-100. Markings are: "C.R. Alsop Middletown, Conn. 1860 & 1861" on the barrel. The cylinder is marked "C.R. Alsop" & "Nov. 26th, 1861"; the side plate, "Patented Jan. 21st, 1862."

NIB	Exc.	V.G.	Good	Fair	Poor
—	—	3850	1300	500	350

Standard Model Navy Revolver

Exactly the same as the First Model without the safety device. They are serial numbered 101 to 300.

NIB	Exc.	V.G.	Good	Fair	Poor
—	—	3350	900	300	225

Pocket Model Revolver

A .31 cal. 5-shot revolver with spur trigger, 4" round barrel, blued finish, and wood grips. It is very similar in appearance to the Navy model but smaller in size. It is marked "C.R. Alsop Middletown, Conn. 1860 & 1861" on the barrel. The cylinder is marked "C.R. Alsop Nov. 26th, 1861." They are serial numbered 1-300.

Courtesy Milwaukee Public Museum, Milwaukee, Wisconsin

NIB	Exc.	V.G.	Good	Fair	Poor
—	—	1700	700	200	125

AMAC
American Military Arms Corporation
(formerly Iver Johnson)
Jacksonville, Arkansas

The Iver Johnson Arms Co. was founded in 1871 in Fitchburg, Massachusetts. It was one of the oldest and most successful of the old-line arms companies on which our modern era has taken its toll. In 1984 the company moved to Jacksonville, Arkansas; in 1987 it was purchased by the American Military Arms Corporation. This company has released some of the older designs as well as some new models. In 1993 the company went out of business. The original Iver Johnson line is listed under its own heading.

U.S. Carbine .22

This is a semi-automatic, military-style carbine that is patterned after the M1 of WWII fame. It is chambered for the .22 LR cartridge, has an 18.5" barrel and features military-style peep sights and a 15-shot detachable magazine.

NIB	Exc.	V.G.	Good	Fair	Poor
325	250	175	100	75	50

Wagonmaster Lever-Action Rifle

This model is chambered for the .22 rimfire cartridge, has an 18.5" barrel and is styled after the Win. 94. The stock has a straight grip; and the fore-end, a barrel band. There are adjustable sights and a tube magazine that holds 15 LR cartridges.

NIB	Exc.	V.G.	Good	Fair	Poor
295	225	150	100	75	50

Wagonmaster .22 Magnum

This model is the same as the Wagonmaster except that it is chambered for the .22 rimfire magnum.

NIB	Exc.	V.G.	Good	Fair	Poor
325	250	175	125	95	50

Targetmaster Pump-Action Rifle

This model is a slide- or pump-action that is chambered for the .22 rimfire cartridges. It has an 18.5" barrel with adjustable sights and a straight grip stock. It holds 12 LR cartridges.

NIB	Exc.	V.G.	Good	Fair	Poor
325	175	145	115	75	50

Li'L Champ Bolt-Action Rifle

This model is a scaled-down single-shot that is chambered for the .22 rimfire cartridge. It has a 16.25" barrel, adjustable sights, a molded stock, and nickel-plated bolt. This model is 33" overall and is designed to be the ideal first rifle for a young shooter.

NIB	Exc.	V.G.	Good	Fair	Poor
175	125	75	45	35	20

M .30 Cal. Carbine

A military-style carbine styled after the M1 of WWII fame. It is chambered for the .30 Carbine cartridge and has an 18" barrel with military-style sights and hardwood stock. There are detachable 5-, 15-, and 30-round magazines available.

NIB	Exc.	V.G.	Good	Fair	Poor
425	300	225	175	125	90

Paratrooper .30 Carbine

This model is similar to the M1 model with a folding stock.

NIB	Exc.	V.G.	Good	Fair	Poor
495	395	325	250	160	100

Enforcer .30 Carbine

This is a 9.5" pistol version of the M1 Carbine. It has no buttstock.

NIB	Exc.	V.G.	Good	Fair	Poor
625	500	395	300	150	100

Long Range Rifle System/AMAC Model 5100

This is a specialized long-range, bolt-action rifle chambered for the .50 caliber Browning Machine gun cartridge. It has a 33" barrel and a special muzzlebrake system. A custom order version in the .338 or .416 caliber is also available.

NIB	Exc.	V.G.	Good	Fair	Poor
4100	3550	2900	2000	900	450

TP-22 and TP-25

This model is a compact, double-action, pocket automatic that was styled after the Walther TP series. Chambered for either the .22 rimfire or the .25 centerfire cartridges, it has a 2.75" barrel, fixed sights and black plastic grips. The detachable magazine holds 7 shots and the finish is either blue or nickel-plated. The nickel-plated version is worth 10 percent more than the blue.

NIB	Exc.	V.G.	Good	Fair	Poor
265	195	150	100	75	50

AMAC 22 Compact or 25 Compact

This is a compact, single-action, semi-automatic pocket pistol that is chambered for the .22 rimfire or the .25 ACP cartridge. It has a 2" barrel, 5-shot magazine, plastic grips and blue or nickel finish. Add 10 percent for nickel.

NIB	Exc.	V.G.	Good	Fair	Poor
265	195	150	100	75	50

AMERICAN ARMS
Garden Grove, California

Eagle .380

This pistol was a stainless steel copy of the Walther PPKS. It was a semi-auto blowback that was chambered for the .380 ACP. It was double-action and had a 3.25" barrel and a 6-shot detachable magazine. An optional feature was a black Teflon finish that would increase the value by 10 percent. This company ceased production in 1985.

NIB	Exc.	V.G.	Good	Fair	Poor
—	325	250	195	150	100

AMERICAN ARMS CO.
Boston, Massachusetts

The history of American Arms is rather sketchy, but it appears the company was formed in 1853 as the G. H. Fox Co. and then became the American Tool & Machine Co. in 1865. In 1870 they formed a new corporation called American Arms Company with George Fox as the principle stockholder. This corporation was dissolved in 1873; a second American Arms Co. was incorporated in 1877 and a third in 1890. It is unclear if these corporations had essentially the same owners, but George H. Fox appears as a principal owner in two of the three. One could assume that financial problems forced them to bankrupt one corporation and reorganize under another. American Arms manufactured firearms in Boston, Massachusetts, from 1866 until 1893. In 1893 they moved to Bluffton, Alabama and manufactured guns until 1901.

SHOTGUNS

Fox Model "Swing Out" Hammer Double

Manufactured from 1870 to 1884, designed by George H. Fox, not to be confused with A.H. Fox. This model is unusual in that the barrel swings to the right for loading and the barrel release is located on the tang. It comes in 10 and 12 gauge, 26", 28", 30" and 32", with twist, Damascus or laminated barrels. Early production models have conventional soldered together barrels. Later variations after 1878 feature a unique design in that the barrels are dovetailed together. These guns could be ordered with several options and choices of finish; these would add premium value to a particular gun.

NIB	Exc.	V.G.	Good	Fair	Poor
—	—	2000	950	400	150

Semi-Hammerless Double

Manufactured from 1892 to 1901. This model features a cocking lever that cocks an internal firing pin. It comes in 12 gauge with 30" twist barrels.

NIB	Exc.	V.G.	Good	Fair	Poor
—	—	1500	750	350	150

Whitmore Model Hammerless Double

Manufactured from 1890 to 1901. It comes in 10, 12, and 16 gauge with 28", 30" or 32" twist, laminated or Damascus barrels. It is marked "Whitmore's Patent".

Courtesy Nick Niles, Paul Goodwin photo

NIB	Exc.	V.G.	Good	Fair	Poor
—	—	1500	775	375	150

Semi-Hammerless Single-Barrel

Manufactured from 1882 to 1901. It comes in 10, 12, and 16 gauge with 28", 30" or 32" twist or Damascus barrel.

NIB	Exc.	V.G.	Good	Fair	Poor
—	—	1500	750	300	100

TOP-BREAK REVOLVERS

Courtesy Milwaukee Public Museum, Milwaukee, Wisconsin

Spur Trigger Single-Action Five-Shot Revolver

These revolvers were made between 1883 and 1887 in .38 S&W only. They feature an unusual manual ring extractor and double-fluted cylinder. They are nickel plated with hard rubber grips and are marked "American Arms Company Boston Mass."

NIB	Exc.	V.G.	Good	Fair	Poor
—	550	300	100	75	25

Standard Trigger Double-Action Model 1886 Revolver

This model has a standard trigger and trigger guard, comes in .32 short and .38 S&W with a 3.5" barrel, in blue or nickel finish. The early models are equipped with the ring extractor and double fluted cylinder. Later variations have a standard star extractor and single fluted cylinder.

NIB	Exc.	V.G.	Good	Fair	Poor
—	750	300	100	75	25

Hammerless Model 1890 Double-Action

These guns were manufactured from 1890 to 1901. It has an adjustable single- or double-stage trigger pull and several unusual safety devices. It comes in .32 and .38 S&W with a 3.25" ribbed barrel, fluted cylinder, nickel finish, hard rubber grips with logo and ivory or mother of pearl grips. It is marked "American Arms Co. Boston/Pat. May 25, 1886." The top strap is marked "Pat. Pending" on early models and "Pat's May 25'86/Mar 11'89/June 17'90" on later models.

NIB	Exc.	V.G.	Good	Fair	Poor
—	750	300	100	75	25

DERRINGERS

Double-Barrel Derringers

American Arms Co. manufactured a two-barrel derringer-style pocket pistol. The barrels were manually rotated to load and fire the weapon. The pistol had a nickel-plated brass frame, blued barrels, and walnut grips. The markings were: "American Arms Co. Boston, Mass." on one barrel and "Pat. Oct. 31, 1865" on the other barrel. There were approximately 2,000-3,000 produced between 1866 and 1878. Beware of fakes!

Combination .22 caliber R.F. and .32 caliber R.F.

A two-caliber combination with 3" barrel, square butt only. The most common variation.

NIB	Exc.	V.G.	Good	Fair	Poor
—	—	850	350	150	100

.32 caliber R.F., Both Barrels

3" barrel with square butt.

Courtesy Milwaukee Public Museum, Milwaukee, Wisconsin

NIB	Exc.	V.G.	Good	Fair	Poor
—	—	1050	500	195	125

.32 caliber R.F., Both Barrels

2-5/8" barrel with bird's-head grips.

NIB	Exc.	V.G.	Good	Fair	Poor
—	—	1100	550	225	150

.38 caliber R.F., Both Barrels

2-5/8" barrel with bird's-head grips. A rare variation.

NIB	Exc.	V.G.	Good	Fair	Poor
—	—	2500	1075	350	200

.41 caliber R.F., Both Barrels

2-5/8" barrel with square butt only.

NIB	Exc.	V.G.	Good	Fair	Poor
—	—	1850	900	200	100

AMERICAN ARMS, INC.
North Kansas City, Missouri

SIDE-BY-SIDE SHOTGUNS

York/Gentry

These two designations cover the same model. Prior to 1988 this model was called the York. In 1988 the receiver was casecolored and the designation was changed to the Gentry. This model was chambered for 12, 20, 28 gauge and .410. It had chrome-lined barrels from 26" to 30" in length, double triggers, 3" chambers, and automatic ejectors. The boxlock action featured scroll engraving, and the walnut stock was hand checkered. It was introduced in 1986.

NIB	Exc.	V.G.	Good	Fair	Poor
750	625	450	300	200	150

10 Gauge Magnum Shotgun

A 10 gauge with 3.5" chambers and 32" barrels. It featured a scroll-engraved, chromed boxlock action and double triggers. It was imported from Spain in 1986 only.

NIB	Exc.	V.G.	Good	Fair	Poor
850	750	550	350	250	150

12 Gauge Magnum Shotgun

As above but chambered for 12 gauge 3.5" Magnum shell.

NIB	Exc.	V.G.	Good	Fair	Poor
800	700	500	300	200	150

Brittany

Chambered for 12 and 20 gauge with 25" or 27" barrels with screw-in choke tubes. It had a solid matted rib and a case-colored, engraved boxlock action. Automatic ejectors and a single-selective trigger were standard on this model, as was a hand checkered, walnut, straight grip stock with semi-beavertail fore-end. This model was introduced in 1989.

NIB	Exc.	V.G.	Good	Fair	Poor
850	750	600	450	375	200

Turkey Special

A utilitarian model designed to be an effective turkey hunting tool. It is chambered for the magnum 10 and 12 gauges and has 26" barrels. The finish is parkerized, and the stock is also finished in a non-glare matte. Sling-swivel studs and a recoil pad are standard. This model was introduced in 1987.

NIB	Exc.	V.G.	Good	Fair	Poor
800	700	450	350	250	150

Waterfowl Special

Similar to the Turkey Special but chambered for the 10 gauge only. It is furnished with a camouflaged sling. Introduced in 1987.

NIB	Exc.	V.G.	Good	Fair	Poor
950	850	550	350	250	150

Specialty Model

Similar to the Turkey Special and offered in 12 gauge 3.5" Magnum.

NIB	Exc.	V.G.	Good	Fair	Poor
875	750	500	300	200	150

Derby

Chambered for the 12 and 20 gauge. It has 26" or 28" barrels with 3" chambers and automatic ejectors. Either double or single-selective triggers are offered, and the sidelock action is scroll engraved and chromed. The checkered straight grip stock and forearm are oil-finished. This model was introduced in 1986. No longer imported.

NIB	Exc.	V.G.	Good	Fair	Poor
825	700	600	500	350	200

Grulla #2

Top-of-the-line model chambered for 12, 20 and 28 gauge and .410 bore. The barrels are 26" or 28" with a concave rib. The hand-fitted full sidelock action is extensively engraved and case-colored. There are various chokes, double triggers, and automatic ejectors. The select walnut, straight grip stock and splinter fore-

end is hand checkered and has a hand-rubbed oil finish. This model was introduced in 1989. No longer imported.

NIB	Exc.	V.G.	Good	Fair	Poor
2500	1750	1250	900	500	250

OVER/UNDER SHOTGUNS

F.S. 200

A trap or skeet model that was chambered for 12 gauge only. It had 26" Skeet & Skeet barrels or 32" Full choke barrels on the trap model. The barrels were separated and had a vent rib. The boxlock action had a Greener crossbolt and was either black or matte chrome-plated. It featured a single-selective trigger, automatic ejectors, and a checkered walnut pistol grip stock. The F.S. 200 was imported in 1986 and 1987 only.

NIB	Exc.	V.G.	Good	Fair	Poor
—	675	575	465	350	150

F.S. 300

Similar to the F.S. 200 with lightly engraved side plates and a 30" barrel offered in the trap grade. It was imported in 1986 only.

NIB	Exc.	V.G.	Good	Fair	Poor
—	800	675	565	450	250

F.S. 400

Similar to the F.S. 300 with an engraved, matte chrome-plated receiver. It was imported in 1986 only.

NIB	Exc.	V.G.	Good	Fair	Poor
—	1100	950	800	650	350

F.S. 500

Similar to the F.S. 400 with the same general specifications. It was not imported after 1985.

NIB	Exc.	V.G.	Good	Fair	Poor
—	1150	1000	850	700	350

Waterfowl Special

Chambered for the 12 gauge magnum with 3.5" chambers. It has 28" barrels with screw-in choke tubes. There are automatic ejectors and a single-selective trigger. The finish is parkerized with a matte finished stock, sling swivels, and camouflaged sling and a recoil pad. It was introduced in 1987.

NIB	Exc.	V.G.	Good	Fair	Poor
875	700	500	350	300	150

Waterfowl 10 Gauge

The same as the Waterfowl Special but is chambered for the 10 gauge Magnum with double triggers.

NIB	Exc.	V.G.	Good	Fair	Poor
975	850	600	400	300	200

Turkey Special

Similar to the Waterfowl Special 10 gauge with a 26" barrel with screw-in choke tubes.

NIB	Exc.	V.G.	Good	Fair	Poor
975	850	600	350	300	200

Lince

Chambered for the 12 and 20 gauge and has 26" or 28" barrels with 3" chambers and various chokes. The boxlock action has a Greener crossbolt and was either blued or polished and chrome-plated. The barrels were blued with a ventilated rib. It has a single-selective trigger and automatic ejectors. The Lince was imported in 1986 only.

NIB	Exc.	V.G.	Good	Fair	Poor
—	500	425	350	300	200

Silver Model

Similar to the Lince with a plain, unengraved, brushed-chrome-finished receiver. It was imported in 1986 and 1987.

NIB	Exc.	V.G.	Good	Fair	Poor
—	500	425	350	300	200

Silver I

Similar to the Silver but is available in 28 gauge and .410 bore, as well as 12 and 20 gauge. It also has a single-selective trigger, fixed chokes, extractors, and a recoil pad. It was introduced in 1987. **NOTE:** Add $25 for 28 gauge and .410 bore guns.

NIB	Exc.	V.G.	Good	Fair	Poor
650	550	325	275	200	175

Silver II

Similar to the Silver I with screw-in choke tubes, automatic ejectors, and select walnut. It was introduced in 1987. **NOTE:** Add $25 for 28 gauge and .410 bore guns.

NIB	Exc.	V.G.	Good	Fair	Poor
750	650	450	350	300	150

Silver II Lite

Introduced in 1994 this model is designed as an upland game gun. Offered in 12, 20, and 28 gauge with 26" barrels. Chambered for both 2.75" and 3" shells. Frame is made from a lightweight steel alloy. No longer imported.

NIB	Exc.	V.G.	Good	Fair	Poor
875	775	550	400	300	150

Silver Competition/Sporting

Offered in 12 gauge with a choice of 28" or 30" barrels which are made from chrome moly. Barrels have elongated forcing cones, chromed bores and are ported to help reduce recoil. Comes with interchangeable choke tubes. The single-selective trigger is mechanical. Weighs about 7-1/2 pounds. In 1996 a 20 gauge model was added with 28" barrel and 3" chambers.

NIB	Exc.	V.G.	Good	Fair	Poor
950	800	600	400	300	150

Silver Hunter

Introduced in 1999 this model is offered in 12 and 20 gauges with 26" and 28" barrels. Single-selective trigger with extractors.

Choke tubes standard. Weight is about 7 lbs.

NIB	Exc.	V.G.	Good	Fair	Poor
625	500	400	300	200	100

Bristol/Sterling

Chambered for 12 and 20 gauge. It has various barrel lengths with a vent rib and screw-in choke tubes. The chambers are 3", and the chrome-finished action is a boxlock with Greener crossbolt and game scene engraved side plates. There are automatic ejectors and a single-selective trigger. It was introduced in 1986, and in 1989 the designation was changed to the Sterling. No longer imported.

NIB	Exc.	V.G.	Good	Fair	Poor
825	750	675	500	400	200

Sir

Chambered for the 12 and 20 gauge with 3" chambers, various barrel lengths and chokings and a ventilated rib. The chrome-finished sidelock action has a Greener crossbolt and is engraved with a game scene. There are automatic ejectors and a single-selective trigger. This model was imported in 1986. No longer imported.

NIB	Exc.	V.G.	Good	Fair	Poor
—	875	750	625	500	250

Royal

Chambered for the 12 and 20 gauge. It is manufactured in various barrel lengths and chokes with a vent rib and 3" chambers. The chrome-finished sidelock action has a Greener crossbolt and is profusely scroll-engraved. It has automatic ejectors and a single-selective trigger. The select pistol grip walnut stock is hand checkered and oil-finished. This model was imported in 1986 and 1987. No longer imported.

NIB	Exc.	V.G.	Good	Fair	Poor
—	1500	1275	1000	800	400

Excelsior

Similar to the Royal with extensive deep relief engraving and gold inlays. This model was imported in 1986 and 1987. No longer imported.

NIB	Exc.	V.G.	Good	Fair	Poor
—	1750	1500	1200	875	450

SINGLE-BARREL SHOTGUNS

AASB

The standard single-barrel, break-open, hammerless shotgun. It is chambered for 12 and 20 gauge and .410. It has a 26" barrel with various chokes and 3" chambers. It has a pistol grip stock and a matte finish. It was introduced in 1988. No longer imported.

NIB	Exc.	V.G.	Good	Fair	Poor
100	85	75	60	45	25

Campers Special

Similar to the standard model with a 21" barrel and a folding stock. It was introduced in 1988. No longer imported.

NIB	Exc.	V.G.	Good	Fair	Poor
110	95	85	70	50	35

Youth Model

Chambered for the 20 gauge and .410 bore and has a 12.5" stock with a recoil pad. It was introduced in 1989. No longer imported.

NIB	Exc.	V.G.	Good	Fair	Poor
115	100	80	65	50	35

Slugger

This version has a 24" barrel with rifle sights. It is chambered for the 12 and 20 gauge and has a recoil pad. No longer imported.

NIB	Exc.	V.G.	Good	Fair	Poor
115	100	80	65	50	35

10 Gauge Model

Chambered for the 10 gauge 3.5" Magnum. It has a 32" full choke barrel and a recoil pad. This model was introduced in 1988. No longer imported.

NIB	Exc.	V.G.	Good	Fair	Poor
175	145	100	85	60	45

Combo Model

Similar in appearance to the other single-barrel models but is offered in an interchangeable-barreled rifle/shotgun combination—the 28" barreled .22 Hornet and the 12 gauge, or the 26" barreled .22 LR and 20 gauge. This model was furnished with a fitted hard case to hold the interchangeable barrels. It was introduced in 1989. No longer imported.

NIB	Exc.	V.G.	Good	Fair	Poor
250	200	175	145	110	75

SEMI-AUTO SHOTGUNS

Phantom Field

Chambered for 12 gauge and fitted with choice of 24", 26", or 28" barrels. Fitted with 3" chamber. Gas operated action. Choke tubes standard. Five-round magazine. Checkered walnut stock. Weight is about 7 lbs. Introduced in 1999.

NIB	Exc.	V.G.	Good	Fair	Poor
400	350	300	225	125	75

Phantom Synthetic

Same as model above but furnished with checkered synthetic stock. Weight is about 6.75 lbs. Introduced in 1999.

NIB	Exc.	V.G.	Good	Fair	Poor
400	350	300	225	125	75

Phantom HP

This model features a 19" threaded barrel for external choke tubes. Five-round magazine. Weight is about 6.75 lbs. Introduced in 1999.

NIB	Exc.	V.G.	Good	Fair	Poor
400	375	325	300	150	95

RIFLES

ZCY.308

Essentially the same rifle as the ZCY.223, only it is chambered for the .308 cartridge. This model was imported in 1988 only.

NIB	Exc.	V.G.	Good	Fair	Poor
—	500	425	350	300	200

AKY39

The semi-automatic version of the Soviet AK-47 as it is manufactured by Yugoslavia. It is offered with folding tritium night sights and a wooden fixed stock. It was imported in 1988.

NIB	Exc.	V.G.	Good	Fair	Poor
—	600	475	390	300	200

AKF39

The same rifle as the AKY39 with a metal folding stock.

NIB	Exc.	V.G.	Good	Fair	Poor
—	625	550	475	300	200

AKC47

Basically the same rifle as the AKY39 without the tritium night sights.

NIB	Exc.	V.G.	Good	Fair	Poor
—	575	450	375	300	200

AKF47

The same rifle as the AKC47 with a metal folding stock.

NIB	Exc.	V.G.	Good	Fair	Poor
—	625	550	475	300	200

EXP-64 Survival Rifle

A .22 caliber, semi-automatic takedown rifle. It is self-storing in a floating, oversized plastic stock. The rifle has a 21" barrel with open sights and a crossbolt safety. There is a 10-shot detachable magazine. Importation by American Arms began in 1989.

NIB	Exc.	V.G.	Good	Fair	Poor
165	150	125	95	75	50

SM-64 TD Sporter

A .22 LR semi-automatic with a takedown 21" barrel. It has adjustable sights and a checkered hardwood stock and fore-end. Importation began in 1989.

NIB	Exc.	V.G.	Good	Fair	Poor
195	155	110	85	65	45

1860 Henry

Replica of lever action Henry rifle. Brass frame. Steel half-octagon barrel with tube magazine. Chambered for .44-40 or .45 Long Colt. Offered in 24" or 18.5" barrels. Weight with 24" barrel is about 9.25 lbs. Built by Uberti.

NIB	Exc.	V.G.	Good	Fair	Poor
950	800	650	400	300	200

1866 Winchester

Replica of Winchester 1866. Offered in .44-40 or .45 Long Colt. Barrel lengths in 24" or 19". Brass frame. Weight is about 8.25 lbs. for 24" barrel model. Built by Uberti.

NIB	Exc.	V.G.	Good	Fair	Poor
825	700	495	300	200	100

1873 Winchester

Replica of Winchester Model 1873. Offered with choice of 24" or 30" barrels. Chambered for .44-40 or .45 Long Colt. Case hardened steel frame. Weight is about 8.25 lbs. for 24" model. Built by Uberti. **NOTE:** Add $80 for 30" barrel.

NIB	Exc.	V.G.	Good	Fair	Poor
850	725	550	325	225	125

1885 Single-Shot High Wall

Chambered for .45-70 cartridge this Winchester replica is fitted with a 28" round barrel. Weight is about 8.75 lbs. Built by Uberti.

NIB	Exc.	V.G.	Good	Fair	Poor
850	695	550	350	200	100

Sharps Cavalry Carbine

This Sharps replica is fitted with a 22" round barrel and chambered for the .45-70 cartridge. Adjustable rear sight. Weight is about 8 lbs.

NIB	Exc.	V.G.	Good	Fair	Poor
700	600	425	350	200	100

Sharps Frontier Carbine

Similar to the Cavalry carbine but with a 22" octagonal barrel and double set triggers. Weight is about 7.75 lbs.

NIB	Exc.	V.G.	Good	Fair	Poor
775	625	475	375	225	125

Sharps Sporting Rifle

This model features a 28" octagonal barrel chambered for either the .45-70 or .45-120 cartridge. Double set triggers. Adjustable rear sight. Checkered walnut stock. Weight is about 9 lbs.

NIB	Exc.	V.G.	Good	Fair	Poor
775	625	475	375	225	125

Sharps 1874 Deluxe Sporting Rifle

Similar to the above model but with browned barrels.

NIB	Exc.	V.G.	Good	Fair	Poor
800	650	500	395	250	150

HANDGUNS

Model EP-.380

A high-quality, stainless steel pocket pistol that is chambered for the .380 ACP cartridge. It is a double-action semi-automatic that holds 7 shots and has a 3.5" barrel. The grips are checkered walnut. Imported from West Germany beginning in1988.

NIB	Exc.	V.G.	Good	Fair	Poor
425	365	325	275	225	100

Model PK-22

A domestic semi-automatic that is chambered for the .22 LR. It is a double-action with a 3.5" barrel and an 8-shot finger extension magazine. It is made of stainless steel and has black plastic grips. This model is manufactured in the U.S.A. by American Arms.

NIB	Exc.	V.G.	Good	Fair	Poor
245	200	150	125	100	75

Model CX-22

A compact version of the PK-22 with a 2.75" barrel and a 7-shot magazine. Manufacture began in 1989.

NIB	Exc.	V.G.	Good	Fair	Poor
225	200	165	125	100	75

Model TT Tokarev

The Yugoslavian version of the Soviet Tokarev chambered for 9mm Parabellum and with a safety added to make importation legal. It has a 4.5" barrel, 9-shot magazine and a blued finish with checkered plastic grips. Importation began in 1988.

NIB	Exc.	V.G.	Good	Fair	Poor
350	225	175	150	125	100

Model ZC-.380

A scaled-down version of the Tokarev that is chambered for the .380 ACP. It has a 3.5" barrel and holds 8 shots. The finish and grips are the same as on the full-sized version. Importation from Yugoslavia began in 1988.

NIB	Exc.	V.G.	Good	Fair	Poor
295	225	175	150	125	100

Aussie Model

Introduced in 1996, this is an Australian-designed semi-automatic pistol made in Spain. Chambered for the 9mm or .40 S&W cartridge it has a polymer frame with nickeled steel slide. Sold with 10-shot magazine. Barrel length is 4-3/4" and weight is 23 oz.

NIB	Exc.	V.G.	Good	Fair	Poor
400	350	300	250	200	100

Regulator

Built by Uberti this single-action revolver has a case hardened frame, polished brass trigger guard and backstrap. Barrel and cylinder are blued. One piece walnut grips. Choice of chambers in .44-40, .45 LC, or .357 Magnum. Barrel lengths from 4.75", 5.5", to 7.5". Weight is about 34 oz. with 5.75" barrel.

NIB	Exc.	V.G.	Good	Fair	Poor
395	325	275	175	—	—

Regulator Deluxe

Same as above but with steel trigger guard and backstrap. Chambered in .45 Long Colt only.

NIB	Exc.	V.G.	Good	Fair	Poor
375	300	250	150	—	—

AMERICAN BARLOCK WONDER

See—Crescent Arms Co.

AMERICAN CLASSIC

(Eagle Imports)
Wanamassa, NJ

American Classic 1911-A1

Full-size 1911-A1-style semi-auto chambered in .45 ACP. Series 70 lockwork, 8-round magazine with bumper pad, lowered ejection port, throated barrel, checkered wood grips, military-style sights, matte blue or hard chrome finish. Five-inch barrel, weight is 39 ounces. American Classic II has additional features including Novak-style sights, combat trigger and hammer, extended safety and slide stop, front slide serrations, deep blue or hard chrome finish. **NOTE:** Add $35 for Classic II, $50 for hard chrome finish.

NIB	Exc.	V.G.	Good	Fair	Poor
435	400	350	325	250	200

American Classic Commander/Amigo

Same features as American Classic II except 4.25" barrel, weight 35-ounces. Amigo model is Officer's Model style with 3.5" barrel, 7-round magazine. **NOTE:** Add $50 for hard chrome finish, add $35 for Amigo model.

NIB	Exc.	V.G.	Good	Fair	Poor
460	425	360	335	260	200

American Classic Trophy Model

Same features as American Classic II except 5.5-inch barrel, dovetail front fiber optic sight, Novak-style rear, ambidextrous safety, reverse plug recoil system with full-length guide rod, beveled mag well, checkered mainspring housing and hard chrome finish.

NIB	Exc.	V.G.	Good	Fair	Poor
650	600	550	500	400	300

American Classic .22 Model

Full-size, alloy-frame 1911-style pistol chambered for .22 LR. Same dimensions as American Classic with military-type sights, checkered wood grips, matte blue finish, two 10-round magazines.

NIB	Exc.	V.G.	Good	Fair	Poor
300	275	230	200	160	100

AMERICAN DERRINGER CORP.

Waco, Texas

Model 1 Derringer

Fashioned after the Remington over/under derringer this is a high quality, rugged pistol. It is built from high tensile strength stainless steel. There are over 60 different rifle and pistol calibers to choose from on special order. The upper barrel can be chambered different from the lower barrel on request. Available in a high polish finish or a satin finish. Offered with rosewood, bacote, walnut, or blackwood grips. Ivory, bonded ivory, stag, or pearl are available at extra cost. Overall length is 4.8", barrel length is 3", width across the frame is .9", width across the grip is 1.2". Typical weight is 15 oz. in .45 caliber. All guns are furnished with French fitted leatherette case. Prices are determined by caliber. **NOTE:** Premium for rifle cartridges.

Calibers: .22 Long Rifle through .357 Magnum and .45 ACP

NIB	Exc.	V.G.	Good	Fair	Poor
450	375	300	200	100	75

Calibers: .41 Mag., .44-40, .44 Special, .44 Mag., .45 Long Colt, .410 Bore, .22 Hornet, .223 Rem., 30-30, and .45-70 Gov't.

NIB	Exc.	V.G.	Good	Fair	Poor
500	425	350	250	150	100

Model 1 Lady Derringer

Similar to the Model 1 but chambered for the .38 Special, .32 Magnum, .45 Colt, or .357 Magnum. Offered in two grades. **NOTE:** For .45 Colt and .45/.410 add $75. For .357 magnum add $50.

Deluxe

High polished stainless steel with scrimshawed ivory grips with cameo or rose design.

NIB	Exc.	V.G.	Good	Fair	Poor
500	425	350	200	100	75

Deluxe Engraved

Same as above but hand engraved in 1880s style.

NIB	Exc.	V.G.	Good	Fair	Poor
650	550	500	450	250	150

Model 1 NRA 500 Series

Limited edition of 500. Also available in gold and blue finishes over stainless steel.

NIB	Exc.	V.G.	Good	Fair	Poor
425	350	250	125	100	50

Model 1 Texas Commemorative

Built with a solid brass frame and stainless steel barrel. Dimensions are same as Model 1. Grips are stag or rosewood and offered in .45 Colt, .44-40, or .38 Special. Barrels marked "Made in the 150th Year of Texas Freedom". Limited to 500 pistols in each caliber.

Caliber: .38 Special

NIB	Exc.	V.G.	Good	Fair	Poor
425	350	250	150	100	75

Calibers: .45 Colt and .44-40

NIB	Exc.	V.G.	Good	Fair	Poor
450	375	275	200	125	100

Deluxe Engraved

Special serial number engraved on backstrap.

NIB	Exc.	V.G.	Good	Fair	Poor
700	550	395	350	175	125

Model 1 125th Anniversary Commemorative

Built to commemorate the 125th anniversary of the derringer, 1866 to 1991. Similar to the Model 1 but marked with the patent date "December 12, 1865". Brass frame and stainless steel barrel. Chambered for .44-40, .45 Colt, or .38 Special.

NIB	Exc.	V.G.	Good	Fair	Poor
425	350	250	150	100	65

Deluxe Engraved

NIB	Exc.	V.G.	Good	Fair	Poor
650	475	375	250	175	100

Model 2 Pen Pistol

Introduced in 1993 this is a legal pistol that cannot be fired from its pen position but requires that it be pulled apart and bent 80 degrees to fire. Made from stainless steel it is offered in .22 LR, .25 ACP, and .32 ACP. The length in pen form is 5.6" and in pistol form is 4.2". Barrel length is 2". Diameter varies from 1/2" to 5/8". Weight is 5 oz. No longer in production.

NIB	Exc.	V.G.	Good	Fair	Poor
600	395	300	225	100	85

Model 3

This model is a single-barrel derringer. Barrel length is 2.5" and it swings down to load. Frame and barrel are stainless steel. Offered in .38 Special or .32 Magnum. Weighs about 8 oz. Discontinued.

NIB	Exc.	V.G.	Good	Fair	Poor
200	175	115	75	65	50

Model 4

Similar in appearance to the Model 3 but fitted with a 4.1" barrel. Overall length is 6" and weight is about 16.5 oz. Chambered for 3" .410 bore, .45 Long Colt, .44 Magnum, or .357 Magnum. **NOTE:** For .45-70 add $150. For .44 Magnum add $100.

NIB	Exc.	V.G.	Good	Fair	Poor
500	425	350	250	100	75

Engraved

NIB	Exc.	V.G.	Good	Fair	Poor
1000	900	600	400	275	150

Alaskan Survival Model

Similar to the Model 4 but with upper barrel chambered for .45-70 and lower barrel for .45 LC or .410. Both barrels can also be chambered for .44 magnum or .45-70. Comes with oversized rosewood grips.

NIB	Exc.	V.G.	Good	Fair	Poor
700	625	395	250	175	100

Model 6

This double-barrel derringer is fitted with a 6" barrel chambered for the .45 LC or .410 bore. Weighs about 21 oz. Rosewood grips are standard. Optional calibers are .357 magnum or .45 ACP. Oversize grips are optional and add about $35 to value.

NIB	Exc.	V.G.	Good	Fair	Poor
500	450	350	300	150	100

Engraved

NIB	Exc.	V.G.	Good	Fair	Poor
1000	900	700	450	275	150

Double-Action Derringer

High Standard-type double-barrel, double-action derringer is chambered for the .22 LR or .22 Magnum. Its barrel length is 3.5" and overall length is 5.125". Weighs approximately 11 oz. The finish is blue with black grips.

NIB	Exc.	V.G.	Good	Fair	Poor
295	245	175	100	85	75

DA 38 Double-Action Derringer

Similar to above but chambered for .38 Special, .357 Magnum, 9mm Luger, and .40 S&W. Finish is satin stainless. Grip is made from aluminum. Grips are rosewood or walnut. **NOTE:** For .40 S&W add $40.

NIB	Exc.	V.G.	Good	Fair	Poor
400	325	250	200	150	100

Mini Cop 4-Shot

This is a four-barrel derringer chambered for the .22 Magnum Rimfire cartridge.

NIB	Exc.	V.G.	Good	Fair	Poor
600	395	300	225	100	85

Cop 4-Shot

Same as above but chambered for the .357 Magnum cartridge.

NIB	Exc.	V.G.	Good	Fair	Poor
1000	900	500	325	175	100

Model 7 Derringer—Lightweight

Manufactured as a backup gun for police officers. The frame and barrels are made of aircraft aluminum alloy; the other parts are stainless steel. This gun weighs 7.5 oz. Its appearance and function are similar to the Model 1. The finish is a gray matte with thin, matte-finished grips of rosewood or bacote. This model is chambered for and priced as listed.

.32 S&W Long/.32 Magnum

NIB	Exc.	V.G.	Good	Fair	Poor
400	325	250	125	100	75

.38 S&W and .380 ACP

NIB	Exc.	V.G.	Good	Fair	Poor
400	325	250	125	100	75

.22 LR and .38 Special

NIB	Exc.	V.G.	Good	Fair	Poor
400	325	250	125	100	75

.44 Special

NIB	Exc.	V.G.	Good	Fair	Poor
525	450	375	300	250	150

Model 8

This is a single-action two-shot target pistol with a manually operated hammer block safety. Safety automatically disengages when the hammer is cocked. Barrel length is 8". Chambered for the .45 Colt and .410 shotshell. Weight is 24 oz.

NIB	Exc.	V.G.	Good	Fair	Poor
575	500	425	350	175	100

Engraved

NIB	Exc.	V.G.	Good	Fair	Poor
1500	1000	675	450	300	125

Model 10 Derringer

Similar to the Model 1 with a frame of aluminum alloy and all other parts, including the barrels, stainless steel. It has a gray matte finish and thin grips of rosewood or bacote. It weighs 10 oz. and is chambered for the .38 Special, .45 ACP or the .45 Colt. **NOTE:** For .45 Colt add $75.

NIB	Exc.	V.G.	Good	Fair	Poor
400	325	250	125	100	75

Model 11 Derringer

A stainless steel barrel and all other parts aluminum. It weighs 11 oz. and is chambered for the .38 Special, .380 Auto, .32 Mag., .22 LR, and .22 Magnum. The grips and finish are the same as on the Model 10.

NIB	Exc.	V.G.	Good	Fair	Poor
400	325	250	125	100	75

Semmerling LM-4

The LM-4 was designed as the ultimate police backup/defense weapon. It is a manually operated, 5-shot repeater only 5.2" long, 3.7" high, and 1" wide. It is chambered for the .45 ACP and is undoubtedly the smallest 5-shot .45 ever produced. The LM-4 is made of a special tool steel and is either blued or, at extra cost, hard chrome-plated. A stainless steel version is also available. The LM-4 is not a semi-automatic, although it physically resembles one. The slide is flicked forward and back after each double-action squeeze of the trigger. This weapon is virtually hand-built and features high visibility sights and a smooth trigger. **NOTE:** Hard chrome add $200. Stainless steel add 35 percent.

NIB	Exc.	V.G.	Good	Fair	Poor
3000	2500	2000	1500	600	200

LM-5

Built of stainless steel this semi-auto is chambered for the .32 or .25 Auto. The barrel length is 2.25" and the overall length is 4", height is 3". Wooden grips are standard. Offered in limited quantities. Weight is approximately 15 oz. Discontinued.

NIB	Exc.	V.G.	Good	Fair	Poor
425	350	295	150	100	50

Millennium Series 2000

This model chambered for .38 Special, .45 Colt, or .44-40. Single-action. Fitted with scrimshaw grips with a yellow rose of Texas on the left side and the Lone Star flag on the right side. Weight is about 15 oz. Supplied with red velvet box with silver inlay. Introduced in 1999.

NIB	Exc.	V.G.	Good	Fair	Poor
500	325	200	150	100	75

Gambler Millennium 2000

Similar to the Millennium Series above but fitted with rosewood grips with etched Lone Star of Texas. Supplied with brown leatherette box with copper logo inlay.

NIB	Exc.	V.G.	Good	Fair	Poor
500	325	200	150	100	75

Women of Texas Series

This model has the same features as the Millennium Series 2000. Stamped "Women of Texas Series 2000."

NIB	Exc.	V.G.	Good	Fair	Poor
500	325	200	150	100	75

Cowboy Series 2000

This model has the same features as the Gambler Millennium 2000 but with "Cowboy Series 2000" stamped on the barrel.

NIB	Exc.	V.G.	Good	Fair	Poor
500	325	200	150	100	75

AMERICAN FIRE ARMS MFG. CO., INC.
San Antonio, Texas

This company operated between 1972 and 1974, producing a .25 ACP pocket pistol and a stainless steel .38 Special derringer. A .380 auto was produced on an extremely limited basis.

American .38 Special Derringer

A well-made, stainless steel over/under derringer that was similar in appearance and function to the old Remington over/under. It had 3" barrels that pivoted upward for loading. This gun was a single-action that had an automatic selector and a spur trigger. The smooth grips were of walnut. There were approximately 3,500 manufactured between 1972 and 1974.

NIB	Exc.	V.G.	Good	Fair	Poor
—	300	225	150	125	90

American .25 Automatic

A small, blowback, semi-automatic pocket pistol that was chambered for the .25 ACP cartridge. It had a 2" barrel and was made of either stainless steel or blued carbon steel. The grips were of plain uncheckered walnut, and the detachable magazine held 7 shots. It was manufactured until 1974. **NOTE:** For stainless steel add 20 percent.

Courtesy J.B. Wood

NIB	Exc.	V.G.	Good	Fair	Poor
—	275	200	125	100	75

American .380 Automatic

Similar to the .25 except larger. The barrel was 3.5", and the gun was made in stainless steel only. The grips were of smooth walnut, and it held 8 shots. There were only 10 of these .380s manufactured between 1972 and 1974. They are extremely rare, but there is little collector base for this company's products, and the value is difficult to estimate.

NIB	Exc.	V.G.	Good	Fair	Poor
—	600	550	475	375	200

AMERICAN FRONTIER FIREARMS
Aguanga, California

1871, 72 Open Top Standard Model

Offered in .38 or .44 caliber with non-rebated cylinder. Barrel lengths are 7.5" or 8" in round. Blued finish except silver backstrap and trigger guard. Walnut grips.

NIB	Exc.	V.G.	Good	Fair	Poor
795	625	500	400	225	100

Richards & Mason Conversion 1851 Navy Standard Model

Offered in .38 and .44 calibers with Mason ejector assembly and non-rebated cylinder with a choice of octagon barrels in 4.75", 5.5", or 7.5". Blued finish with blued backstrap and trigger guard. Walnut grips.

NIB	Exc.	V.G.	Good	Fair	Poor
795	625	500	400	225	100

1860 Richards Army Model

Chambered for .44 Colt and .38 caliber. Rebated cylinder with or without ejector assembly. Barrel length is 7.5". High polish blue finish with silver trigger guard and case hardened frame. **NOTE:** Guns shipped without ejector assembly will be supplied with a ramrod and plunger typical of the period.

NIB	Exc.	V.G.	Good	Fair	Poor
795	625	500	400	225	100

AMERICAN GUN CO., NEW YORK
Norwich, Connecticut
Maker—Crescent Firearms Co.

Side-by-Side Shotgun

A typical trade gun made around the turn of the century by the Crescent Firearms Co., to be distributed by H. & D. Folsom. These are sometimes known as "Hardware Store Guns," as that is where many were sold. This particular gun was chambered for 12, 16, and 20 gauges and was produced with or without external hammers. The length of the barrels varied, as did the chokes. Some were produced with Damascus barrels; some, with fluid steel. The latter are worth approximately 25 percent more. **NOTE:** For a full listing of most of the variations of the Crescent Arms Co., and shotguns marked with American Gun Co., see "Crescent F.A. Co."

Knickerbocker Pistol—See Knickerbocker

AMERICAN HISTORICAL FOUNDATION
Ashland, Virginia

The American Historical Foundation is a private organization that commissions historical commemoratives. Secondary market sales are infrequent and are difficult to confirm. The American Historical Foundation sells only direct and not through dealers or distributors. For information on past and current issues contact the American Historical Foundation at 10195 Maple Leaf Court, Ashland, VA 23005.

AMERICAN INDUSTRIES
Cleveland, Ohio
aka CALICO LIGHT WEAPONS SYSTEMS
Sparks, Nevada

Calico M-100

A semi-automatic carbine that has a 16.1" barrel with a flash suppressor. It is chambered for the .22 LR and features a folding stock, full shrouding hand guards, a 100-round capacity, helical feed, and detachable magazine. It features an ambidextrous safety, pistol grip storage compartment, and a black finished alloy frame and adjustable sights. This model was introduced in 1986.

NIB	Exc.	V.G.	Good	Fair	Poor
500	400	350	250	200	100

Calico M-100P/M-110

Similar to the M-100 .22 rimfire with a 6" barrel with muzzlebrake and no shoulder stock.

NIB	Exc.	V.G.	Good	Fair	Poor
500	400	350	250	200	75

Calico M-100S Sporter/M-105

Similar to the Model 100 with a futuristically styled walnut buttstock and forearm.

NIB	Exc.	V.G.	Good	Fair	Poor
500	400	350	250	200	75

Calico M-101 Solid Stock Carbine

Introduced in 1994 this rifle features a 100-round magazine and a composite buttstock that is removable.

NIB	Exc.	V.G.	Good	Fair	Poor
550	450	400	300	200	75

Calico M-900

A black polymer-stocked rifle that is similar to the M-100S, chambered for the 9mm Parabellum. It has a delayed blowback action and features a stainless steel bolt and alloy receiver. The cocking handle is non-reciprocating, and the rear sight is fixed with an adjustable front. There is a 50-round magazine standard and a 100-round capacity model optional. This model was introduced in 1989.

NIB	Exc.	V.G.	Good	Fair	Poor
750	575	425	350	275	100

Calico M-950 Pistol

Similar to the Model 900 rifle with a 6" barrel and no shoulder stock.

NIB	Exc.	V.G.	Good	Fair	Poor
750	575	425	350	275	100

Calico M-951

The M-951 is a tactical carbine with a sliding buttstock. The barrel is 16" in length. It weighs about 7 pounds.

NIB	Exc.	V.G.	Good	Fair	Poor
750	575	425	350	275	100

Calico M-951S

Same as above but furnished with more conventional buttstock. Referred to as a light tactical carbine. Weighs about 7-1/4 pounds.

NIB	Exc.	V.G.	Good	Fair	Poor
750	575	425	350	275	100

AMERICAN INTERNATIONAL
Salt Lake City, Utah
aka American Research & Development

180 Carbine (SAM-180)

This firearm, imported from Austria, is a semi-automatic, 16.5" barreled carbine chambered for the .22 LR. The sights are adjustable, and the stock is made of high-impact plastic. The unique drum magazine holds 177 rounds and is affixed to the top of the receiver. There is a select-fire version available for law enforcement agencies only and an optional laser lock sight system. Later manufactured by Feather Industries in Boulder, Colorado. It is now known as the SAM-180.

NIB	Exc.	V.G.	Good	Fair	Poor
1400	1200	650	400	200	100

AMERICAN TACTICAL IMPORTS
Rochester, New York

GSG-522

Semi-auto tactical rifle chambered in .22 LR. Features include 16.25-inch barrel; black finish overall; polymer fore-end and buttstock; backup iron sights; receiver-mounted Picaatinny rail; 10-round magazine. Several other rifle and carbine versions available.

NIB	Exc.	V.G.	Good	Fair	Poor
425	365	325	250	200	100

FX Series

A series of 1911-style .45 ACP pistols imported from the Philippines. Available in single- or double-stack magazines, offered in various barrel lengths with diamond-checkered wood grips, low-profile sights, blue or stainless finishes. FX Thunderbolt model has adjustable sights, Picatinny rail, competition or bull barrel. **NOTE:** Add $200 for Thunderbolt model (shown).

NIB	Exc.	V.G.	Good	Fair	Poor
500	465	425	375	250	150

AMERICAN WESTERN ARMS INC. (AWA)
Delray Beach, Florida

Lightning Rifle LE

A copy of the Colt Lightning slide-action rifle chambered for the .32-20, .38 Special, .38-40, .44-40, or the .45 Colt cartridge. Choice of round barrel lengths in 20" or 24". Engraved AWA logo and stage scene on the receiver. Limited edition to 500 guns.

NIB	Exc.	V.G.	Good	Fair	Poor
1200	950	775	500	300	175

Lightning Rifle

This slide-action rifle is chambered for those cartridges above with a 24" barrel length with the choice of round or octagon barrel. Blued finish. **NOTE:** Add $40 for octagon barrel.

NIB	Exc.	V.G.	Good	Fair	Poor
800	675	500	400	300	175

Lightning Carbine

As above but with 20" barrel in round or octagon. **NOTE:** Add $40 for octagon barrel.

NIB	Exc.	V.G.	Good	Fair	Poor
800	675	500	400	300	175

Lightningbolt

Handgun version of the Lightning rifle with 12-inch barrel and variety of finishes. Chambered in .45 Colt. Values shown are for blued version.

NIB	Exc.	V.G.	Good	Fair	Poor
1000	800	675	500	400	200

AMES, N.P. PISTOLS
Springfield, Massachusetts

Overall length-11-5/8"; barrel length-6"; caliber-.54. Markings: on lockplate, forward of hammer "N.P. AMES/SPRINGFIELD/MASS," on tail, either "USN" or "USR" over date; on barrel, standard U.S. Navy inspection marks. N. P. Ames of Springfield, Massachusetts received a contract from the U.S. Navy in September 1842 for the delivery of 2,000 single-shot muzzleloading percussion pistols. All are distinguished by having a lock mechanism that lies flush with the right side of the stock. On the first 300 Ames pistols, this lock terminates in a point; the balance produced were made with locks with a rounded tail. This "boxlock" had been devised by Henry Nock in England, and was adapted to the U.S. Navy for the percussion pistols they ordered from Ames and Derringer. In addition to the 2,000 pistols for the Navy, the U.S. Revenue

Cutter Service purchased 144 (distinguished by the "U S R" marks) for the forerunner of the U.S. Coast Guard. The latter commands triple the price over the "U S N" marked pistols, while the Navy pistols with pointed tails quadruple the value.

Courtesy Milwaukee Public Museum, Milwaukee, Wisconsin

NIB	Exc.	V.G.	Good	Fair	Poor
—	—	2700	1100	650	400

AMES SWORD CO.
Chicopee Falls, Massachusetts

Turbiaux Le Protector

Ames Sword Co. became one of three U.S. companies that produced this unique, French palm-squeezer pistol. The design consists of a round disk with a protruding barrel on one side and a lever on the other. The disk contains the cylinder that holds either seven 8mm rimfire or ten 6mm rimfire cartridges. The barrel protrudes between the fingers, and the lever trigger is squeezed to fire the weapon. The design was patented in 1883 and sold successfully in France into the 1890s. In 1892 Peter Finnegan bought the patents and brought them to Ames Sword. He contracted with them to produce 25,000 pistols for the Minneapolis Firearms Company. After approximately 1,500 were delivered, Finnegan declared insolvency, and after litigation, Ames secured the full patent rights. The Ames Company produced Protector Revolvers until at least 1917. (See Chicago Firearms Co. and Minneapolis Firearms Co.)

NIB	Exc.	V.G.	Good	Fair	Poor
—	—	3500	1800	900	550

AMT
formerly Arcadia Machine and Tool
Irwindale, California
See also—Galena Industries Inc.

AMT, one of several companies that succeeded Auto Mag Corp., the original manufacturer of Auto Mag pistols, operated from approximately 1984 to 1998. The prices in this section are for these earlier AMT-built guns only. In 1998, Galena Ind., of Sturgis, South Dakota, purchased the rights to produce most of the AMT-developed firearms and manufactured several models from 1999 to 2001. In 2005, the rights to several AMT models were acquired by Crusader Gun Co. of Houston, parent company of High Standard Mfg. Co. Also see listing for Auto Mag.

HANDGUNS

Lightning

A single-action, semi-automatic .22 caliber pistol. Available with barrel lengths of 5" (Bull only), 6.5", 8.5", 10.5" and 12.5" (either Bull or tapered), and adjustable sights, as well as the trigger. The grips are checkered black rubber. Manufactured between 1984 and 1987.

Courtesy John J. Stimson, Jr.

NIB	Exc.	V.G.	Good	Fair	Poor
—	450	350	215	125	85

Bull's Eye Regulation Target

As above, with a 6.5" vent rib bull barrel, wooden target grips, and an extended rear sight. Manufactured in 1986 only.

NIB	Exc.	V.G.	Good	Fair	Poor
—	475	375	250	200	100

Baby Automag

Similar to the above with an 8.5" ventilated rib barrel, and Millett adjustable sights. Approximately 1,000 were manufactured.

Courtesy J.B. Wood

NIB	Exc.	V.G.	Good	Fair	Poor
—	600	450	375	225	150

Automag II

A stainless steel, semi-automatic .22 Magnum pistol. Available with 3-3/8", 4.5", and 6" barrel lengths and Millett adjustable sights, grips of black, grooved, plastic. Was first manufactured in 1987.

NIB	Exc.	V.G.	Good	Fair	Poor
700	600	500	400	225	100

Automag V

Introduced in 1993 this model is similar in appearance to the Automag models but is chambered for the .50 caliber cartridge. A limited production run of 3,000 pistols with special serial number from "1 of 3000" to "3000 of 3000". Barrel length is 6.5" and magazine capacity is 5 rounds. Weighs 46 oz. Production stopped in 1995. Add $300 each for extra conversion barrels in .45 WM or 10mm.

Courtesy J.B. Wood

NIB	Exc.	V.G.	Good	Fair	Poor
700	600	500	400	200	100

Automag III

This semi-automatic pistol is chambered for the .30 Carbine cartridge and the 9mm Winchester Magnum cartridge. Barrel length is 6.37" and overall length is 10.5". The magazine capacity is 8 rounds. Fitted with Millett adjustable rear sight and carbon fiber grips. Stainless steel finish. Pistol weighs 43 oz.

Courtesy J.B. Wood

NIB	Exc.	V.G.	Good	Fair	Poor
800	700	600	500	400	150

Javelina

Produced in 1992 this pistol is chambered for the 10mm cartridge and fitted with a 7" barrel with adjustable sights. Rubber wrap-around grips. Adjustable trigger. Magazine is 8 rounds. Weight is about 47 oz.

Courtesy J.B. Wood

NIB	Exc.	V.G.	Good	Fair	Poor
1000	900	750	600	400	200

Back Up Pistol

This is a small semi-automatic pocket pistol chambered for the .22 LR or the .380 ACP cartridges. This is fitted with a 2.5" barrel and is offered with either black plastic or walnut grips. The pistol weighs 18 oz. Magazine capacity is 5 rounds. Originally manufactured by TDE, then Irwindale Arms Inc., and then by AMT.

NIB	Exc.	V.G.	Good	Fair	Poor
600	500	400	250	100	80

Automag IV

Similar in appearance to the Automag III this pistol is chambered for the .45 Winchester Magnum. Magazine capacity is 7 rounds and weight is 46 oz.

NIB	Exc.	V.G.	Good	Fair	Poor
450	325	175	125	100	85

.45 ACP, .40 S&W, 9mm

Courtesy J.B. Wood

NIB	Exc.	V.G.	Good	Fair	Poor
465	350	200	150	100	85

.38 Super, .357 SIG, .400 CorBon

NOTE: These prices are for current production by High Standard Mfg. Co.

NIB	Exc.	V.G.	Good	Fair	Poor
475	360	250	200	150	100

9mm, .38 Super, .40 S&W, .45 ACP

NIB	Exc.	V.G.	Good	Fair	Poor
475	425	375	325	200	100

.380 Back Up II

Introduced in 1993 this pistol is similar to the Back Up model but with the addition of a double safety, extended finger grip on the magazine, and single-action-only. This was a special order pistol only.

NIB	Exc.	V.G.	Good	Fair	Poor
425	300	250	200	150	100

Hardballer/Government Model

This model is similar to the Colt Gold Cup .45 ACP. It is offered in two versions. The first has fixed sights and rounded slide top, while the second has adjustable Millett sights and matte rib. Magazine capacity is 7 rounds. Wraparound rubber grips are standard. Long grip safety, beveled magazine well, and adjustable trigger are common to both variations. Weight is 38 oz.

Hardballer

Adjustable sights.

Courtesy J.B. Wood

NIB	Exc.	V.G.	Good	Fair	Poor
600	500	350	275	200	125

Government Model

Fixed sights.

NIB	Exc.	V.G.	Good	Fair	Poor
575	475	300	250	150	100

Longslide

Similar to the Hardballer Model but fitted with a 7" barrel. Magazine capacity is 7 rounds. Pistol weighs 46 oz.

NIB	Exc.	V.G.	Good	Fair	Poor
750	550	395	275	200	125

.400 Accelerator

Similar to the models above but chambered for .400 CorBon cartridge and fitted with a 7" barrel. Fully adjustable sights. Introduced in 1997.

NIB	Exc.	V.G.	Good	Fair	Poor
600	500	350	275	200	125

Commando

Built on a Government model-type action and chambered for .40 S&W cartridge. Fitted with a 5" barrel and fully adjustable sights. Introduced in 1997.

NIB	Exc.	V.G.	Good	Fair	Poor
550	425	300	200	125	75

On Duty

This semi-automatic pistol features a double-action-only trigger action or double-action with decocker and is chambered for the 9mm, .40 S&W, or .45 ACP calibers. Barrel length is 4.5" and overall length is 7.75". The finish is a black anodized matte. Carbon fiber grips are standard. Furnished with 3-dot sights. Weighs 32 oz.

NIB	Exc.	V.G.	Good	Fair	Poor
450	350	250	200	150	100

Skipper

Identical to the Hardballer with a 1" shorter barrel and slide. Discontinued in 1984.

NIB	Exc.	V.G.	Good	Fair	Poor
—	450	325	275	200	125

Combat Skipper

Similar to the Colt Commander. Discontinued in 1984.

NIB	Exc.	V.G.	Good	Fair	Poor
—	425	300	250	200	125

RIFLES

Lightning

Patterned after the Ruger 10/22 and said to have been discontinued for that reason, this rifle has a 22" barrel and a 25-round, detachable magazine with a folding stock. Introduced in 1986.

Courtesy J.B. Wood

NIB	Exc.	V.G.	Good	Fair	Poor
375	250	175	125	75	50

Small Game Hunter

As above, with a full stock and 10-round magazine. Introduced in 1986.

NIB	Exc.	V.G.	Good	Fair	Poor
350	225	175	150	125	100

Small Game Hunter II

This semi-automatic rifle is chambered for the .22 LR cartridge. Stock is a checkered black matte nylon and is fitted with a removable recoil pad for ammo, cleaning rod, and knife. Rotary magazine holds 10 rounds. Stainless steel action and barrel. Barrel is a heavyweight target type, 22" long. Weight is 6 lbs.

NIB	Exc.	V.G.	Good	Fair	Poor
350	225	175	150	125	100

Hunter

This semi-automatic rifle is chambered for the .22 Rimfire Magnum cartridge. Stock is checkered black matte nylon. Other features are similar to the Small Game Hunter II including weight.

NIB	Exc.	V.G.	Good	Fair	Poor
375	250	200	150	125	100

Magnum Hunter

Similar to above but chambered for the .22 Rimfire Magnum cartridge and fitted with a 22" accurized barrel. Barrel and action are stainless steel. It comes standard with a 5-round magazine and composite stock but a laminated stock was available at an extra cost as is a 10-round magazine.

NIB	Exc.	V.G.	Good	Fair	Poor
525	400	350	250	200	150

Target Model

A semi-automatic rifle chambered for .22 LR cartridge and fitted with a 20" target barrel. Weight is about 7.5 lbs. Choice of Fajen or Hogue stock. For Hogue stock deduct $50.00.

NIB	Exc.	V.G.	Good	Fair	Poor
600	500	450	300	200	—

Challenge Edition

This is a custom ordered .22 caliber semi-automatic rifle built on a Ruger 10/22-like receiver. Offered in either 18" or 22" barrel lengths with all stainless steel construction, McMillan fiberglass stock, and Weaver-style scope mounts.

NIB	Exc.	V.G.	Good	Fair	Poor
1050	800	550	400	300	175

Single-Shot Standard

Custom-built rifle with choice of barrel length, composite stock, adjustable trigger, post '64 Winchester action, all in stainless and chrome moly steel. Chambered for all standard calibers. First offered in 1996.

NIB	Exc.	V.G.	Good	Fair	Poor
875	675	500	350	200	175

Single-Shot Deluxe

Custom-built rifle on a Mauser-type action with choice of match grade barrel lengths and custom Kevlar stock. Built from stainless and chrome moly steel. Chambered for all standard calibers. First offered in 1996.

NIB	Exc.	V.G.	Good	Fair	Poor
1800	1400	950	650	400	225

Bolt-Action Repeating—Standard

Similar in construction and features to the Standard Single-Shot rifle.

NIB	Exc.	V.G.	Good	Fair	Poor
840	675	500	350	200	175

Bolt-Action Repeating—Deluxe

Similar in construction and features to the Deluxe Single-Shot rifle.

NIB	Exc.	V.G.	Good	Fair	Poor
1800	1400	950	650	400	225

ANCION MARX
Liege, Belgium

This company began production in the 1860s with a variety of cheaply made pinfire revolvers. They later switched to solid-frame, centerfire, "Velo-Dog"-type revolvers chambered for 5.5mm or 6.35mm. They were marketed in various countries under many different trade names. Some of the names that they will be found under are Cobalt, Extracteur, LeNovo, Lincoln, and Milady. The quality of these revolvers is quite poor and collector interest, almost non-existent. Values do not usually vary because of trade names.

NIB	Exc.	V.G.	Good	Fair	Poor
—	—	200	135	75	45

ANDERSON
Anderson, Texas

Under Hammer Pistol

An unmarked, under hammer percussion pistol that was chambered for .45 caliber. It had a 5" half-round/half-octagonal barrel with an all steel, saw handle-shaped frame. It had a flared butt with walnut grips. The finish was blued. There is little information on this pistol.

NIB	Exc.	V.G.	Good	Fair	Poor
—	—	900	400	150	100

ANDRUS & OSBORN
Canton, Connecticut

Under Hammer Pistol

This pistol is of the percussion type and chambered for .25 caliber. The part-round/part-octagonal barrel is 6" long and features small silver star inlays along its length. The barrel is marked "Andrus & Osborn/Canton Conn." with an eagle stamped beside it. It is marked "Cast Steel" near the breech. The grips are of walnut, and the finish is browned. Active 1863 to 1867.

NIB	Exc.	V.G.	Good	Fair	Poor
—	—	1550	625	200	100

ANSCHÜTZ, J.G. GmbH
Ulm, Germany

Originally founded in 1856 by Julius and Lusie Anschutz, the company was originally called J.G. Anschutz and manufactured a wide variety of firearms. In 1950, in Ulm, the new company was founded: J.G. Anschutz GmbH. Values for new guns fluctuate according to currency variations.

Mark 10 Target

A single-shot, bolt-action rifle that is chambered for the .22 LR cartridge. It has a 26" heavy barrel with adjustable target-type sights. The finish was blued, and the walnut target stock had an adjustable palm rest. It was manufactured between 1963 and 1981.

NIB	Exc.	V.G.	Good	Fair	Poor
500	425	350	210	150	100

Model 1403D

A single-shot target rifle chambered for the .22 LR cartridge. It has a 26" barrel and is furnished without sights. It has a fully adjustable trigger and a blued finish with a walnut target-type stock.

NIB	Exc.	V.G.	Good	Fair	Poor
850	775	675	500	375	250

Model 1407

Similar to the Mark 10 but is furnished without sights. It was known as the "I.S.U." model. It was discontinued in 1981.

NIB	Exc.	V.G.	Good	Fair	Poor
525	450	375	235	175	100

Model 1408

A heavier-barreled version of the Model 1407.

NIB	Exc.	V.G.	Good	Fair	Poor
525	450	375	240	180	105

Model 1411

Designed specifically to be fired from the prone position.

NIB	Exc.	V.G.	Good	Fair	Poor
750	650	450	210	150	100

Model 1413 Match

A high-grade, competition version with a heavy target barrel that is furnished without sights; optional sights extra. The walnut stock has an adjustable cheekpiece.

NIB	Exc.	V.G.	Good	Fair	Poor
775	675	550	400	275	150

Model 1416D HB Classic

This model is chambered for the .22 LR cartridge. Magazine capacity is 5 rounds. Fitted with a match grade trigger and target grade barrel. Checkered walnut stock. Built on the 64 action.

NIB	Exc.	V.G.	Good	Fair	Poor
900	725	595	400	225	125

Model 1416D KL Classic

This sporting rifle is chambered for the .22 LR cartridge and is fitted with an American-style stock of European walnut or hardwood. Built on Anschutz Match 64 action. Left-handed model also offered.

NIB	Exc.	V.G.	Good	Fair	Poor
900	725	595	300	200	100

Model 1416D Custom

Chambered for the .22 LR cartridge, this model features a European-style stock with Monte Carlo cheekpiece, and schnabel fore-end.

NIB	Exc.	V.G.	Good	Fair	Poor
875	650	550	300	200	100

Model 1418D KL Mannlicher

A hunting rifle with a full-length, Mannlicher-type stock made with hand-checkered walnut. Chambered for .22 LR with 5-round magazine. Open iron sights. Weight is about 5.5 lbs.

NIB	Exc.	V.G.	Good	Fair	Poor
1200	950	700	450	200	150

Model 1418/19

A lower-priced sporter model that was formerly imported by Savage Arms.

NIB	Exc.	V.G.	Good	Fair	Poor
700	650	425	200	125	85

Model 1433D

This is a centerfire version of the Model 54 target rifle chambered for the .22 Hornet. It is a special-order item and features a set trigger and a 4-round, detachable magazine. The finish was blued with a full length Mannlicher stock. It was discontinued in 1986.

NIB	Exc.	V.G.	Good	Fair	Poor
1500	950	700	400	200	100

Model 1449D Youth

This bolt-action rifle is chambered for the .22 LR cartridge and fitted with a 16" barrel with adjustable rear sight. Stock is European hardwood with 12.25" length of pull. Magazine capacity is 5 rounds. This model is no longer imported.

NIB	Exc.	V.G.	Good	Fair	Poor
450	300	250	100	75	60

Model Woodchucker

Sold by distributor RSR, this bolt-action .22 caliber is similar to the Model 1449D Youth.

NIB	Exc.	V.G.	Good	Fair	Poor
450	300	250	100	75	60

Model 1451E Target

This is a single-shot .22 caliber target rifle fitted with a 22" barrel. Can be fitted with either micrometer iron sights or telescope sights. Checkered pistol grip, adjustable buttplate. Weight is about 6.25 lbs.

NIB	Exc.	V.G.	Good	Fair	Poor
625	500	400	200	125	75

Model 1451R Sporter Target

This is a bolt-action target rifle chambered for the .22 LR cartridge and fitted with a target-style stock and 22" heavy barrel. Furnished with no open sights. Two-stage target trigger is standard. Weight is approximately 6.5 lbs.

NIB	Exc.	V.G.	Good	Fair	Poor
650	525	425	225	175	100

Model 1451D Custom

Similar to the above model but fitted with a checkered walnut sporting stock with Monte Carlo comb and cheekpiece. Barrel length is 22.75" with open sights. Weight is about 5 lbs.

NIB	Exc.	V.G.	Good	Fair	Poor
675	550	450	250	150	100

Model 1451D Classic

Similar to the Model 1451 Custom with the exception of a straight walnut stock. Weight is about 5 lbs.

NIB	Exc.	V.G.	Good	Fair	Poor
700	600	500	300	150	100

Model 1516D KL Classic

Same as above but chambered for .22 Magnum cartridge.

NIB	Exc.	V.G.	Good	Fair	Poor
775	600	500	300	200	100

Model 1516D KL Custom

Same as above but chambered for .22 Magnum cartridge.

NIB	Exc.	V.G.	Good	Fair	Poor
850	650	550	450	250	100

Model 1517D Classic

Based on the 64 action this bolt-action rifle is chambered for the .17 HMR cartridge. Fitted with a 23" barrel. Checkered walnut stock. Magazine capacity is 4 rounds. Weight is about 5.5 lbs. Introduced in 2003.

NIB	Exc.	V.G.	Good	Fair	Poor
850	700	575	395	200	125

Model 1517D HB Classic

Similar to the Model 1516D but fitted with a heavy barrel without sights. Weight is about 6.2 lbs. Introduced in 2003.

NIB	Exc.	V.G.	Good	Fair	Poor
875	725	600	425	200	125

Model 1517D Monte Carlo

Chambered for the .17 HMR cartridge and fitted with a 23" barrel. Checkered walnut stock with schnabel fore-end and Monte Carlo comb. Weight is about 5.5 lbs. Introduced in 2003.

NIB	Exc.	V.G.	Good	Fair	Poor
895	745	625	450	200	125

Model 1517MPR Multi-Purpose Rifle

Introduced in 2003 this model features a 25.5" heavy barrel without sights, a two-stage trigger, a hardwood stock with beavertail fore-end. Chambered for the .17 HMR cartridge. Weight is about 9 lbs. **NOTE:** This model is available with a number of extra cost options.

NIB	Exc.	V.G.	Good	Fair	Poor
925	775	650	475	250	150

Model 1518D Mannlicher

Same as above but chambered for the .22 Magnum.

NIB	Exc.	V.G.	Good	Fair	Poor
1200	950	700	350	225	125

Model 184

A high-grade, bolt-action sporting rifle chambered for the .22 LR cartridge. It has a 21.5" barrel with a folding-leaf sight. The finish is blued with a checkered walnut, Monte Carlo stock with a schnabel fore-end. It was manufactured between 1963 and 1981.

NIB	Exc.	V.G.	Good	Fair	Poor
575	425	315	225	150	100

Model 54 Sporter

A high-grade, bolt-action sporting rifle chambered for the .22 LR cartridge. It has a 24" tapered round barrel and a 5-shot detachable magazine. It features a folding leaf-type rear sight. The finish is blued with a checkered walnut, Monte Carlo stock. It was manufactured between 1963 and 1981.

NIB	Exc.	V.G.	Good	Fair	Poor
750	675	600	350	250	125

Model 54M

This version is chambered for the .22 rimfire Magnum cartridge.

NIB	Exc.	V.G.	Good	Fair	Poor
800	700	625	375	275	125

Model 141

A bolt-action sporter chambered for the .22 LR cartridge. It has a 23" round barrel with a blued finish and walnut Monte Carlo stock. It was manufactured between 1963 and 1981.

NIB	Exc.	V.G.	Good	Fair	Poor
800	650	450	200	150	100

Model 141M

Chambered for the .22 rimfire Magnum cartridge.

NIB	Exc.	V.G.	Good	Fair	Poor
825	675	475	225	175	100

Model 164

This bolt-action rifle is fitted with a 23" round barrel chambered for the .22 LR cartridge. It has a Monte Carlo stock with open sights. Magazine holds 5 rounds.

NIB	Exc.	V.G.	Good	Fair	Poor
700	625	475	325	175	100

Model 164M

Same as model above but chambered for the .22 Win. Magnum cartridge.

NIB	Exc.	V.G.	Good	Fair	Poor
725	650	500	225	175	100

Model 153

A bolt-action sporting rifle chambered for the .222 Remington cartridge. It has a 24" barrel with folding-leaf rear sight. The finish is blued with a checkered French walnut stock featuring a rosewood fore-end tip and pistol grip cap. It was manufactured between 1963 and 1981.

NIB	Exc.	V.G.	Good	Fair	Poor
900	750	575	300	225	150

Model 153-S

This version was offered with double-set triggers.

NIB	Exc.	V.G.	Good	Fair	Poor
950	775	615	350	275	150

Model 64

A single-shot, bolt-action rifle that is chambered for the .22 LR cartridge. It has a 26" round barrel and is furnished without sights. The finish is blued, and the walnut target-type stock featured a beaver-tail forearm and adjustable buttplate. It was manufactured between 1963 and 1981.

NIB	Exc.	V.G.	Good	Fair	Poor
600	450	350	200	150	100

Model 64MS

This version was designed for silhouette shooting and has a 21.25" barrel, blued finish, and a target-type walnut stock with a stippled pistol grip.

NIB	Exc.	V.G.	Good	Fair	Poor
950	850	625	400	300	200

Model 64 MPR

This is a multi-purpose target repeater. Chambered for the .22 LR cartridge and fitted with a 25.5" heavy barrel. Offered with optional sights and choice of stainless steel barrel with beavertail or beavertail with swivel rail. Weight is about 9 lbs.

NIB	Exc.	V.G.	Good	Fair	Poor
975	800	695	400	300	200

Model 64P

Bolt-action pistol with adjustable trigger. The action is grooved for scope mounts, and the stock is synthetic. Barrel length is 10" and is chambered for .22 LR cartridge. Weight is approximately 3 lb. 8 oz. Introduced in 1998.

NIB	Exc.	V.G.	Good	Fair	Poor
595	500	450	250	175	75

Model 64P Mag

Same as model above but chambered for .22 WMR cartridge.

NIB	Exc.	V.G.	Good	Fair	Poor
650	525	475	275	175	75

Model 54.18MS

A high-grade silhouette rifle chambered for the .22 LR cartridge. It has a 22" barrel and a match-grade action with fully adjustable trigger. It is furnished without sights. The finish is blued with a target-type walnut stock.

NIB	Exc.	V.G.	Good	Fair	Poor
2150	1500	995	500	300	200

Model 54.MS REP

A repeating rifle with a five-shot, detachable magazine and a thumbhole stock with vented forearm.

NIB	Exc.	V.G.	Good	Fair	Poor
2100	1600	1050	500	300	200

Model 2000 MK

This single-shot rifle was chambered for the .22 LR cartridge. It has a 26" round barrel with target-type sights. The finish was blued with a walnut stock. It was not imported after 1988.

NIB	Exc.	V.G.	Good	Fair	Poor
650	600	450	200	150	100

Model 2007 Supermatch

Introduced in 1993 this target rifle is chambered for the .22 LR cartridge. It has a 19-3/4" barrel fitted to a Match 54 action. Trigger is a two-stage. The stock is standard ISU configuration with adjustable cheekpiece. Weighs about 10.8 pounds. Offered in left-hand model.

NIB	Exc.	V.G.	Good	Fair	Poor
2350	1850	1350	750	350	200

Model 2013 Supermatch

Similar to the above model but fitted with an International stock with palm rest and buttstock hook. Weighs about 12.5 lbs.

NIB	Exc.	V.G.	Good	Fair	Poor
3200	2600	1850	1250	600	300

Model 1903D

Designed for the advanced junior shooter this target rifle has a 25-1/2" barrel on a Match 64 action with a single stage trigger. The walnut stock is fully adjustable. Weighs about 9.5 pounds and is offered in a left-hand model.

NIB	Exc.	V.G.	Good	Fair	Poor
950	800	700	400	300	200

Model 1803D

A high-grade target rifle chambered for the .22 LR cartridge. It has a 25.5" heavy barrel with adjustable target sights. It features an adjustable trigger. The finish is blued with a light-colored wood stock with dark stippling on the pistol grip and forearm. The stock features an adjustable cheekpiece and buttplate. It was introduced in 1987.

NIB	Exc.	V.G.	Good	Fair	Poor
1200	1000	775	600	450	200

Model 1808D RT Super

A single-shot, running-boar type rifle that is chambered for the .22 LR cartridge. It has a 32.5" barrel furnished without sights. The finish is blued with a heavy target-type walnut stock with thumbhole. It is furnished with barrel weights. Rifle weighs about 9.4 pounds. Also available in a left-hand version.

NIB	Exc.	V.G.	Good	Fair	Poor
1500	1300	1150	750	450	250

Model 1907ISU Standard Match

Chambered for the .22 LR cartridge this rifle is designed for both prone and position shooting. Weight is 11.2 lbs. Built on a Match 54 action and fitted with a 26" barrel this rifle has a two-stage trigger with a removable cheekpiece and adjustable buttstock.

NIB	Exc.	V.G.	Good	Fair	Poor
1600	1350	1000	450	300	200

Model 1910 Super Match II

A high-grade, single-shot target rifle chambered for the .22 LR cartridge. It has a 27.25" barrel and is furnished with diopter-type target sights. The finish is blued with a walnut thumbhole stock with adjustable cheekpiece and buttplate. Hand rest and palm rest are not included.

NIB	Exc.	V.G.	Good	Fair	Poor
2300	1850	1400	900	500	250

Model 1911 Prone Match

This version has a stock designed specifically for firing from the prone position.

NIB	Exc.	V.G.	Good	Fair	Poor
1850	1550	1050	650	400	250

Model 1913 Super Match

A virtually hand-built, match target rifle. It is chambered for the .22 LR cartridge and features a single-shot action. It has adjustable, diopter-type sights on a 27.25" heavy barrel. This is a custom-made gun that features every target option conceivable. The finish is blued with a fully adjustable walnut stock.

NIB	Exc.	V.G.	Good	Fair	Poor
2700	2100	1600	1000	500	250

Model 1827B Biathlon

A repeating, bolt-action target rifle chambered for the .22 LR cartridge. It is specially designed for biathlon competition. Production is quite limited and on a custom basis.

NIB	Exc.	V.G.	Good	Fair	Poor
1850	1500	1150	800	400	250

Model 1827BT Biathlon

Similar to the above model but features a straight-pull Fortner bolt system. Available in left-hand model.

NIB	Exc.	V.G.	Good	Fair	Poor
2900	2350	1750	1000	500	250

Achiever

Introduced in 1993 this target rifle is chambered for the .22 LR cartridge. Designed for the beginning shooter it is furnished with a 5-shot clip but can be converted to a single-shot with an adapter. Barrel length is 19-1/2". Action is Mark 2000 with two-stage trigger. Stock pull is adjustable from 12" to 13". Weighs about 5 lbs.

NIB	Exc.	V.G.	Good	Fair	Poor
525	400	295	150	125	100

Achiever Super Target

Designed for the advanced junior shooter this model has a 22" barrel. Weighs about 6.5 lbs.

NIB	Exc.	V.G.	Good	Fair	Poor
575	450	325	175	125	100

Bavarian 1700

A classic-style sporting rifle chambered for the .22 LR, .22 rimfire Magnum, .22 Hornet, and the .222 Remington cartridges. It features a 24" barrel with adjustable sights. It has a detachable magazine and a blued finish with a checkered walnut, European-style Monte Carlo stock with cheekpiece. It was introduced in 1988. Values shown are for centerfire.

NIB	Exc.	V.G.	Good	Fair	Poor
1300	950	600	400	300	200

Classic 1700

Similar in appearance to the Bavarian but furnished with an American-style stock with fluted comb. Furnished in same calibers as Bavarian but weighs 6.75 lbs. **NOTE:** For "Meister Grade" fancy wood stocks add $175.

NIB	Exc.	V.G.	Good	Fair	Poor
1300	950	600	400	300	200

Custom 1700

Similar to the Bavarian and Classic in caliber offerings but offered with a fancy European walnut stock with roll-over cheekpiece with Monte Carlo. The pistol grip has a palm swell and is fitted with a white lined rosewood grip cap with a white diamond insert. Fore-end is schabel type and stock is checkered in ship line pattern. **NOTE:** For "Meister Grade" fancy wood stocks add $175.

NIB	Exc.	V.G.	Good	Fair	Poor
1650	1275	750	400	300	200

Model 1700 Mannlicher

Similar to the 1700 Classic but fitted with a full-length stock. **NOTE:** For "Meister Grade" fancy wood stocks add $175.

NIB	Exc.	V.G.	Good	Fair	Poor
1550	1200	850	550	350	200

Model 1700 FWT

This model has same specifications as the 1700 Custom but is fitted with a McMillan laminated fiberglass stock. Weighs about 6.25 lbs.

NIB	Exc.	V.G.	Good	Fair	Poor
1225	900	700	500	300	200

Model 1700 FWT Deluxe

Same as above but fitted with a laminated wood grain stock.

NIB	Exc.	V.G.	Good	Fair	Poor
1125	900	800	550	300	200

Model 1710 D Classic

Bolt-action .22 caliber rifle with 23.6" barrel with no sights. Walnut stock is checkered. Magazine capacity is 5 rounds. Weight is about 7.3 lbs.

NIB	Exc.	V.G.	Good	Fair	Poor
1300	1050	800	—	—	—

Model 1710 D HB Classic

Same as above but with heavy barrel. Weight is about 8 lbs.

NIB	Exc.	V.G.	Good	Fair	Poor
1350	1050	750	475	300	150

Model 1710 D KL Monte Carlo

Same as the Classic but with Monte Carlo stock and folding leaf rear sight with hooded front sight. Weight is about 7.5 lbs.

NIB	Exc.	V.G.	Good	Fair	Poor
1300	1000	775	425	325	175

Model 1710 D HB Classic 150 Years Anniversary Version

Similar to Model 1710 D HB Classic but with heavy stainless barrel and stock laser-engraved with 150th anniversary and 1901 "Germania" logos. Introduced in 2007. Only 150 units were produced.

NIB	Exc.	V.G.	Good	Fair	Poor
2100	1700	1200	700	400	200

Model 1712 Silhouette Sporter

Chambered in .22 LR. Features include two-stage trigger, deluxe walnut stock, 21.6" blued sightless barrel, 5-shot magazine.

NIB	Exc.	V.G.	Good	Fair	Poor
1150	925	675	425	200	100

Model 1702 D HB Classic

Chambered in .17 Mach 2. Features include finely-tuned double-stage trigger, walnut stock, 23" blued heavy sightless barrel, 5-shot magazine.

NIB	Exc.	V.G.	Good	Fair	Poor
1300	1150	700	450	250	125

Model 1502 D HB Classic

Similar to Model 1702 D HB but with single-stage trigger, fewer refinements. Add 10 percent for beavertail fore-end.

NIB	Exc.	V.G.	Good	Fair	Poor
600	400	300	200	100	50

Model 1907 Club

Single-shot economy target rifle chambered in .22 LR. Features include target trigger, short lock time, 26" blued barrel, micrometer rear peep and hood front sights, ambidextrous removable cheekpiece and walnut buttstock with rubber buttplate and stock spacers. Weighs 9.7 lbs.

NIB	Exc.	V.G.	Good	Fair	Poor
1800	1500	1200	900	—	—

Model 1717 D Classic

This bolt-action model is chambered for the .17 HMR cartridge. Fitted with a 23.6" barrel with no sights. Checkered walnut stock. Weight is about 7.3 lbs.

NIB	Exc.	V.G.	Good	Fair	Poor
1375	1000	675	475	300	150

Model 1717 D HB Classic

Same as above but with heavy barrel. Weight is about 8 lbs.

NIB	Exc.	V.G.	Good	Fair	Poor
1475	1200	700	495	325	175

Model 1730 D Classic

This bolt-action rifle is chambered for the .22 Hornet cartridge and fitted with a 23.6" barrel. Magazine capacity is 5 rounds. Checkered walnut stock. No sights. Weight is about 7.3 lbs.

NIB	Exc.	V.G.	Good	Fair	Poor
1625	1325	750	525	350	225

Model 1730 D HB Classic

Same as above but fitted with a heavy barrel. Weight is about 8 lbs.

NIB	Exc.	V.G.	Good	Fair	Poor
1550	1250	700	495	325	175

Model 1730 D KL Monte Carlo

This model has a Monte Carlo stock and folding leaf rear sight with hooded front sight. Weight is about 7.5 lbs.

NIB	Exc.	V.G.	Good	Fair	Poor
1625	1325	750	525	350	225

Model 1733D KL Mannlicher

Introduced in 1993 this model features a Mannlicher stock built on a Match 54 action. The stock has a rosewood schnabel tip and checkering is done in a skip-line pattern. Chambered for .22 Hornet. Weighs about 6.25 lbs.

NIB	Exc.	V.G.	Good	Fair	Poor
1450	1150	675	475	300	175

Model 1740 D Classic

This bolt-action model is chambered for the .222 Remington cartridge. Checkered walnut stock with no sights. Magazine capacity is 3 rounds. Weight is about 7.3 lbs.

NIB	Exc.	V.G.	Good	Fair	Poor
1625	1325	750	525	350	225

Model 1740 D HB Classic

Same as above but fitted with a heavy barrel. Weight is about 7.3 lbs.

NIB	Exc.	V.G.	Good	Fair	Poor
1550	1250	700	495	325	175

Model 1740 D KL Monte Carlo

This model is fitted with a Monte Carlo stock and folding leaf rear sight and hooded front sight. Weight is about 7.3 lbs.

NIB	Exc.	V.G.	Good	Fair	Poor
1625	1325	750	525	350	225

Model 520/61

A blowback-operated, semi-automatic rifle that is chambered for the .22 LR cartridge. It has a 24" barrel and a 10-round, detachable magazine. The finish is blued with a checkered walnut stock. This rifle was discontinued in 1983.

NIB	Exc.	V.G.	Good	Fair	Poor
675	550	300	200	100	85

Model 525 Sporter

This semi-automatic rifle is chambered for the .22 LR cartridge. It has a 24" barrel with adjustable sights and a 10-round, detachable magazine. The finish is blued with a checkered Monte Carlo-type stock. It was introduced in 1984. A carbine version with a 20" barrel was originally offered but was discontinued in 1986.

NIB	Exc.	V.G.	Good	Fair	Poor
725	600	450	250	175	100

Exemplar

A bolt-action pistol that is built on the Model 64 Match Action. It is chambered for the .22 LR cartridge and has a 10" barrel with adjustable sights and a 5-shot, detachable magazine. It features an adjustable two-stage trigger with the receiver grooved for attaching a scope. The walnut stock and fore-end are stippled. It was introduced in 1987. Discontinued 1997.

NIB	Exc.	V.G.	Good	Fair	Poor
500	400	300	225	175	100

Exemplar XIV

Similar to the standard Exemplar with a 14" barrel. It was introduced in 1988.

NIB	Exc.	V.G.	Good	Fair	Poor
600	500	400	250	200	100

Exemplar Hornet

Chambered for the .22 Hornet cartridge. It was introduced in 1988.

NIB	Exc.	V.G.	Good	Fair	Poor
800	650	575	300	200	100

ANTI GARROTTER
England

Percussion belt pistol, marked "Balls Pat. Steel." Oval is 7" long and the barrel protrudes 1-1/2"; approximately .45 caliber. A cord runs from the lock up and through the sleeve and is fired by pulling the cord. Beware of modern fakes.

NIB	Exc.	V.G.	Good	Fair	Poor
—	—	7500	3000	800	400

APACHE
Eibar, Spain

See—Ojanguren Y Vidosa

APALOZO HERMANOS
Zumorraga, Spain

Spanish manufacturer from approximately 1920 to 1936. The trademark, a dove-like bird, is normally found impressed into the grips.

Apaloza

Copy of a Colt Police Positive revolver.

NIB	Exc.	V.G.	Good	Fair	Poor
—	275	150	100	65	45

Paramount

Copy of the Model 1906 Browning chambered for 6.35mm. "Paramount" is stamped on the slide and at the top of each grip plate.

Courtesy James Rankin

NIB	Exc.	V.G.	Good	Fair	Poor
—	275	175	100	50	30

Triomphe

A copy of the Browning Model 1906 in caliber 6.35mm. The slide is inscribed "Pistolet Automatique Triomphe Acier Comprime." "Cal. 6.35mm" is stamped on each grip plate along with the dove logo.

Courtesy James Rankin

NIB	Exc.	V.G.	Good	Fair	Poor
—	275	175	100	50	30

AR-7 INDUSTRIES
Meriden, Connecticut

AR-7 Explorer

Semi-automatic .22 caliber takedown rifle fitted with a 16" barrel and 8-round magazine. Adjustable rear peep sight. Weight is 2.5 lbs.

NIB	Exc.	V.G.	Good	Fair	Poor
200	150	90	65	50	25

AR-7C Explorer

Same as above but with camo stock.

NIB	Exc.	V.G.	Good	Fair	Poor
225	175	100	65	50	25

AR-7 Sporter

Similar to the standard AR-7, but with a metal skeleton stock and aluminum ventilated shrouded barrel. Weight is about 3.8 lbs.

NIB	Exc.	V.G.	Good	Fair	Poor
250	150	120	75	65	35

AR-7 Target

This model features a tubular stock with cantilever 3-9x40mm scope. Fitted with 16" bull barrel. Weight is about 5.7 lbs.

NIB	Exc.	V.G.	Good	Fair	Poor
300	200	150	75	65	35

AR-7 Bolt-Action

This model is similar in all respects to the standard semi-automatic AR-7, but with a bolt action.

NIB	Exc.	V.G.	Good	Fair	Poor
225	120	90	65	50	25

ARCUS
Bulgaria

Arcus-94

Introduced in 1998 this is a semi-automatic pistol chambered for the 9mm cartridge. Fitted with an ambidextrous safety and 10-round magazine. Imported from Bulgaria.

NIB	Exc.	V.G.	Good	Fair	Poor
425	325	275	200	150	100

ARIZAGA, G.
Eibar, Spain

Spanish manufacturer prior to World War II.

Arizaga (Model 1915)

A 7.65mm semi-automatic pistol. Patterned after the Ruby-style military pistols. Magazine capacity is 9 or 12 rounds. Wood grips.

NIB	Exc.	V.G.	Good	Fair	Poor
—	275	195	100	75	45

Mondial

Similar design to the Astra pistol in the 100 series. Chambered for the 6.35mm cartridge. It has the Owl and Mondial on each grip plate.

NIB	Exc.	V.G.	Good	Fair	Poor
—	300	190	145	75	45

Pinkerton

Arizaga's standard model known to exist with a cartridge counter. Slide is marked "Pinkerton Automatic 6.35."

NIB	Exc.	V.G.	Good	Fair	Poor
—	295	175	100	75	45

Warwick

Same design as the Mondial but in caliber 7.65mm. "Warwick" appears on each grip plate.

NIB	Exc.	V.G.	Good	Fair	Poor
—	300	190	145	75	45

ARIZMENDI, ZULAICA
Eibar, Spain

Cebra Pistol

A semi-automatic 7.65mm pistol patterned after the Ruby-style of Spanish automatics. The slide is marked "Pistolet Automatique Cebra Zulaica Eibar", together with the letters "AZ" in an oval. Generally found with checkered wood grips.

Courtesy James Rankin

NIB	Exc.	V.G.	Good	Fair	Poor
—	250	150	100	50	35

Cebra Revolver

Copy of a Colt Police Positive revolver marked "Made in Spain" with the word "Cebra" cast in the grips.

NIB	Exc.	V.G.	Good	Fair	Poor
—	250	150	125	75	50

ARIZMENDI, FRANCISCO
Eibar, Spain

Originally founded in the 1890s, the company was reformed in 1914 and manufactured semi-automatic pistols.

Singer

The Singer was manufactured in a number of different variations and in calibers 6.35mm and 7.65mm. It was earlier called the Victor. The 6.35mm models resembled the Browning 1906. The 7.65mm model resembled the Browning Model 1910.

6.35mm

Courtesy James Rankin

NIB	Exc.	V.G.	Good	Fair	Poor
—	225	195	100	50	35

7.65mm

Courtesy James Rankin

NIB	Exc.	V.G.	Good	Fair	Poor
—	175	125	75	50	35

Teuf Teuf

The Teuf Teuf was chambered in calibers 6.35mm and 7.65mm. The 7.65mm was only slightly larger than the 6.35mm model. The pistol copied its name from the Browning Model 1906 and from the Belgium Teuf Teuf. The pistol shown is a cartridge indicator model.

Courtesy James Rankin

6.35mm

NIB	Exc.	V.G.	Good	Fair	Poor
—	225	195	100	50	35

7.65mm

NIB	Exc.	V.G.	Good	Fair	Poor
—	225	195	100	50	35

Walman

The Walman was manufactured in a number of variations, and in calibers 6.35mm, 7.65mm, and .380. Earliest semi-automatic production was in 1908 through 1926. Certain variations were called the American Model. The model in .380 caliber had a squeeze grip safety.

6.35mm

Courtesy James Rankin

NIB	Exc.	V.G.	Good	Fair	Poor
—	225	195	100	50	35

7.65mm

Courtesy James Rankin

NIB	Exc.	V.G.	Good	Fair	Poor
—	250	200	125	60	35

.380

Courtesy James Rankin

NIB	Exc.	V.G.	Good	Fair	Poor
—	260	225	145	60	35

Arizmendi

Solid-frame, folding-trigger revolver chambered for 7.65mm or .32 caliber. Normal markings are the trademark "FA" and a circled five-pointed star.

NIB	Exc.	V.G.	Good	Fair	Poor
—	200	150	80	50	25

Boltun—1st Variation

The Bolton semi-automatic pistol was made in both calibers 6.35mm and 7.65mm. It was almost an exact copy of the Belgian Pieper. The 7.65mm model was only slightly larger than the 6.35mm model.

6.35mm

NIB	Exc.	V.G.	Good	Fair	Poor
—	250	195	125	60	35

7.65mm

NIB	Exc.	V.G.	Good	Fair	Poor
—	250	195	125	60	35

Boltun—2nd Variation

The Boltun 2nd variation is chambered for the 7.65mm cartridge and is almost an exact copy of the Browning Model 1910. It was made into the 1930s.

NIB	Exc.	V.G.	Good	Fair	Poor
—	250	195	125	60	35

Roland

Chambered for 6.35 and 7.65mm cartridges, this model was manufactured during the 1920s. The 7.65mm was only slightly larger than the 6.35mm model.

Courtesy James Rankin

6.35mm

NIB	Exc.	V.G.	Good	Fair	Poor
—	250	150	90	60	35

7.65mm

NIB	Exc.	V.G.	Good	Fair	Poor
—	250	150	90	60	35

Puppy

A variation of the "Velo-Dog" revolver with the barrel stamped "Puppy" and the frame bearing the "FA" trademark.

NIB	Exc.	V.G.	Good	Fair	Poor
—	250	195	125	60	35

Pistolet Automatique

Normal markings include the "FA" trademark.

NIB	Exc.	V.G.	Good	Fair	Poor
—	250	195	125	60	35

Kaba Spezial

A 6.35mm semi-automatic pistol patterned after the Browning Model 1906. The Kaba Spezial was originally made by August Menz of Suhl, Germany and sold by Karl Bauer of Berlin, Germany. The name "Kaba" was derived from the first two initials of Karl Bauer. These two pistols do not look alike.

Courtesy James Rankin

NIB	Exc.	V.G.	Good	Fair	Poor
—	275	150	100	50	35

Ydeal

The Ydeal was manufactured in four variations and in calibers 6.35mm, 7.65mm, and .380. All four variations resemble the Browning Model 1906, with the 7.65mm and .380 caliber being slightly larger.

Courtesy James Rankin

6.35mm

NIB	Exc.	V.G.	Good	Fair	Poor
—	225	175	100	60	35

7.65mm

NIB	Exc.	V.G.	Good	Fair	Poor
—	225	175	100	60	35

.380

NIB	Exc.	V.G.	Good	Fair	Poor
—	225	175	100	60	35

ARMALITE, INC.
Costa Mesa, California
Geneseo, Illinois (current production)

In 1995 Eagle Arms purchased the Armalite trademark and certain other assets. The new companies are organized under the Armalite name. The original company, formed in the mid 1950s, developed the AR-10, which in turn led to the development of the M-16 series of service rifles still in use today. All current models are produced at the Geneseo, Illinois, facility.

AR-24 Pistol

15-shot 9mm double-action semi-auto. Steel frame, fixed or adjustable sights. Compact version available. Introduced 2006. Pricing is for full-size pistol with adjustable sights. Deduct 15 percent for fixed sight versions.

NIB	Exc.	V.G.	Good	Fair	Poor
595	450	325	275	200	125

AR-24 Tactical Custom

Similar to above with tactical refinements including stippled front and back straps, 3-dot luminous sights, etc. Also available in compact version (shown).

NIB	Exc.	V.G.	Good	Fair	Poor
630	475	350	300	225	150

AR-17 Shotgun

A gas-operated semi-automatic 12 gauge shotgun, with a 24" barrel and interchangeable choke tubes. The receiver and the barrel are made of an aluminum alloy, with an anodized black or gold finish. The stock and forearm are of plastic. Approximately 2,000 were manufactured during 1964 and 1965. Add 10 percent for gold finish.

NIB	Exc.	V.G.	Good	Fair	Poor
750	625	400	300	225	100

AR-7 Explorer Rifle

A .22 LR semi-automatic carbine with a 16" barrel. The receiver and barrel are partially made of an alloy. The most noteworthy feature of this model is that it can be disassembled and the component parts stored in the plastic stock. Manufactured between 1959 and 1973. Reintroduced in 1999.

NIB	Exc.	V.G.	Good	Fair	Poor
375	300	200	150	100	85

AR-7 Custom

As above with a walnut cheekpiece stock, manufactured between 1964 and 1970.

NIB	Exc.	V.G.	Good	Fair	Poor
475	400	300	250	200	185

AR-180

A gas-operated semi-automatic rifle chambered for the .223 or 5.56mm cartridge. The AR-180 is the civilian version of the AR18, which is fully automatic. It is a simple and efficient rifle that was tested by various governments and found to have potential. This rifle was also manufactured by Howa Machinery Ltd. and Sterling Armament Co. of England. The most common version is manufactured by Sterling. Those built by Armalite and Howa bring a small premium.

Howa

NIB	Exc.	V.G.	Good	Fair	Poor
1500	1250	900	700	450	200

Sterling

NIB	Exc.	V.G.	Good	Fair	Poor
1150	900	700	500	350	175

AR-180B

Similar to the original AR-180. Chambered for the .223 cartridge and fitted with a 19.8" barrel with integral muzzlebrake. Lower receiver is polymer while the upper receiver is sheet steel. Trigger group is standard M15. Accepts standard M15 magazines. Weight is about 6 lbs.

NIB	Exc.	V.G.	Good	Fair	Poor
750	625	500	400	300	125

AR-10A4 Rifle

Introduced in 1995 this model features a 20" stainless steel heavy barrel chambered for the .308 Win. or .243 Win. cartridge. Has a flattop receiver, optional two-stage trigger, detachable carry handle, scope mount. Equipped with two 10-round magazines. Weight is about 9.6 lbs. **NOTE:** For stainless steel barrel add $100.

NIB	Exc.	V.G.	Good	Fair	Poor
1500	1250	900	700	500	200

AR-10A4 Carbine

Similar to above model but chambered for .308 Win. cartridge and fitted with a 16" barrel. Flattop receiver. Sold with two 10-round magazines. Weight is approximately 9 lbs. **NOTE:** For stainless steel barrel add $100.

NIB	Exc.	V.G.	Good	Fair	Poor
1500	1250	900	700	500	200

AR-10A2 Rifle

This model has a 20" heavy barrel chambered for the .308 cartridge but without the removable carry handle. Weight is about 9.8 lbs. **NOTE:** For stainless steel barrel add $100.

NIB	Exc.	V.G.	Good	Fair	Poor
1500	1250	900	700	500	200

AR-10A2 Carbine

Similar to model above but fitted with a 16" barrel. Weight is approximately 9 lbs. **NOTE:** For stainless steel barrel add $100.

NIB	Exc.	V.G.	Good	Fair	Poor
1500	1250	900	700	500	200

AR-10B

Chambered for the .308 cartridge and fitted with a 20" barrel. The trigger is a single-stage or optional two-stage match type. This model has several of the early M16 features such as a tapered handguard, pistol grips, and short buttstock in original brown color. Fitted with early charging handle. Limited production. Weight is about 9.5 lbs. Introduced in 1999.

NIB	Exc.	V.G.	Good	Fair	Poor
1600	1250	900	700	500	200

AR-10(T) Rifle

This model features a 24" heavy barrel with a two-stage trigger. The front sight and carry handle are removable. The handguard is fiberglass. Weight is approximately 10.4 lbs.

NIB	Exc.	V.G.	Good	Fair	Poor
1850	1400	875	600	450	225

AR-10(T) Carbine

Similar to the AR-10T but fitted with a 16.25" target weight barrel. Weight is approximately 8.5 lbs.

NIB	Exc.	V.G.	Good	Fair	Poor
1850	1400	875	600	450	225

AR-10(T) Ultra

Chambered for the .300 Remington Ultra Short Action Magnum cartridge. Barrel length is 24". Two-stage National Match trigger. Offered in choice of green or black stock. Sold with a 5-round magazine.

NIB	Exc.	V.G.	Good	Fair	Poor
1850	1400	875	600	450	225

AR-10 SOF

Introduced in 2003 this model features an M4-style fixed stock. Flattop receiver. Chambered for the .308 cartridge. Offered in both A2 and A4 configurations.

NIB	Exc.	V.G.	Good	Fair	Poor
1850	1400	875	600	450	225

AR-10 .338 Federal

Similar to AR-10 but chambered in .338 Federal. Suggested retail price: Approximately $1500.

NIB	Exc.	V.G.	Good	Fair	Poor
1500	1250	900	700	500	200

M15 SOF

This model is chambered for the .223 cartridge and is fitted with a flattop receiver and M4-style fixed stock. Introduced in 2003. Offered in both A2 and A4 configurations.

NIB	Exc.	V.G.	Good	Fair	Poor
1150	925	675	475	300	150

M15A2 HBAR

This model was introduced in 1995 and features a 20" heavy barrel chambered for .223 cartridge. A2-style forward assist, recoil check brake. Formerly sold with a 10-round magazine. Weight is approximately 8.2 lbs.

NIB	Exc.	V.G.	Good	Fair	Poor
1100	850	600	500	375	125

M15A2 National Match

Chambered for the .223 cartridge this variation features a 20" stainless steel match barrel with two-stage trigger, A2-style forward assist and hard coated anodized receiver. Equipped with a 10-round magazine. Weight is about 9 lbs.

NIB	Exc.	V.G.	Good	Fair	Poor
1475	1200	850	600	375	200

M15A2-M4A1C Carbine

Similar to the M15A2 heavy barrel but with a 16" heavy barrel. Flattop receiver with detachable carry handle. Introduced in 1995. **NOTE:** Add $100 for Match trigger.

NIB	Exc.	V.G.	Good	Fair	Poor
1100	900	700	500	300	125

M15A2-M4C Carbine

Similar to the M4A1C Carbine but with the flattop receiver and detachable carry handle.

NIB	Exc.	V.G.	Good	Fair	Poor
1000	850	600	500	300	125

M15A4(T) Eagle Eye

Chambered for the .223 cartridge and fitted with a 24" stainless steel heavy weight barrel this rifle has a National Match two-stage trigger, Picatinny rail, NM fiberglass handguard tube. Sold with a 7-round magazine and 4-section cleaning rod with brass tip, sling, owner's manual, and lifetime warranty.

NIB	Exc.	V.G.	Good	Fair	Poor
1500	1100	800	600	350	150

M15A4 Special Purpose Rifle (SPR)

This model is fitted with a 20" heavy barrel with detachable front sight, detachable carry handle with NM sights, Picatinny rail. Weight is about 7.8 lbs.

NIB	Exc.	V.G.	Good	Fair	Poor
1200	900	750	600	375	175

M15A4 Action Master

This variation features a 20" stainless steel heavy barrel with two-stage trigger, Picatinny rail, and fiberglass handguard tube. Weight is approximately 9 lbs.

NIB	Exc.	V.G.	Good	Fair	Poor
1450	1000	850	600	375	175

M15A4 Eagle Spirit

This version is similar to the Action Master above but fitted with a 16" stainless steel barrel. Weight is about 7.6 lbs.

NIB	Exc.	V.G.	Good	Fair	Poor
1450	1000	850	600	375	175

Armalite M15 A4 Carbine 6.8 & 7.62x39

Shorty, carbine version of AR-15 chambered in 6.8 Remington and 7.62x39. 16" chrome-lined barrel with flash suppressor, front and rear picatinny rails for mounting optics, two-stage tactical trigger. Ten-round magazine. Anodized aluminum/phosphate finish. Overall length 36.6". Weight: 7 lbs. Suggested retail price: $1107.

AR-30M

Chambered for the .338 Lapua, .300 Winchester Magnum, or the .308 Winchester cartridges. Barrel length is 26" with muzzlebrake. Adjustable butt stock. Weight is about 12 lbs. This model is a reduced version of the AR-50. **NOTE:** Add $150 for .338 Lapua.

NIB	Exc.	V.G.	Good	Fair	Poor
1600	1400	1250	1000	500	195

AR-50

Introduced in 2000 this rifle is chambered for the .50 BMG cartridge. Fitted with a 31" tapered barrel threaded for recoil check (muzzlebrake). Trigger is single-stage. Stock is a 3-section type with extruded fore-end. Pachmayr buttplate. Picatinny rail. Buttplate is adjustable. Finish is magnesium phosphated steel and hard anodized aluminum. Bipod. Weight is about 33 lbs.

NIB	Exc.	V.G.	Good	Fair	Poor
3400	2650	2000	1500	750	300

PRE-BAN MODELS

Golden Eagle

Fitted with a 20" stainless extra-heavy barrel with NM two-stage trigger and NM sights. Sold with a 30-round magazine. Weight is about 9.4 lbs.

NIB	Exc.	V.G.	Good	Fair	Poor
1500	1200	950	800	400	200

HBAR

This pre-ban rifle has a 20" heavy barrel, a 30-round magazine, and sling. Weight is approximately 8 lbs.

NIB	Exc.	V.G.	Good	Fair	Poor
1300	1000	850	700	350	175

M4C Carbine

This pre-ban variation is fitted with a 16" heavy barrel, collapsible stock, and fixed flash suppressor. Weight is about 6.2 lbs.

NIB	Exc.	V.G.	Good	Fair	Poor
1300	1000	850	700	350	175

ARMAS DE FUEGO
Guernica, Spain

See—Alkartasuna Fabrica de Armas

ARMERO ESPECIALISTAS
Eibar, Spain

Alfa

"Alfa" was a trademark given a number of revolvers based upon both Colt and Smith & Wesson designs in calibers ranging from .22 to .44. Add 50 percent for S&W N-frame copies.

NIB	Exc.	V.G.	Good	Fair	Poor
—	250	200	100	75	50

Omega

A semi-automatic 6.35 or 7.65mm pistol marked "Omega" on the slide and grips.

NIB	Exc.	V.G.	Good	Fair	Poor
—	225	175	100	75	50

ARMES DE CHASSE
Chadds Ford, Pennsylvania

Importer of firearms manufactured by Franchi, P. Beretta, and other arms manufactured in Germany.

Model EJ

An over/under Anson & Deeley action 12 gauge shotgun with double triggers as well as automatic ejectors. Blued barrels, silver finished receiver and checkered walnut stock. Manufactured in Germany and introduced in 1989.

NIB	Exc.	V.G.	Good	Fair	Poor
1500	1250	900	650	500	250

Model EU

As above with a ventilated rib barrel and a nonselective single trigger. Introduced in 1989.

NIB	Exc.	V.G.	Good	Fair	Poor
1600	1300	850	650	500	250

Highlander

A side-by-side double-barrel 20 gauge shotgun with a boxlock action. Available in various barrel lengths and choke combinations, with double triggers and manual extractors. Blued with a checkered walnut stock. Manufactured in Italy and introduced in 1989.

NIB	Exc.	V.G.	Good	Fair	Poor
1350	800	650	350	250	125

Chesapeake

As above but chambered for the 3.5" 12 gauge shell. The bores are chrome-lined and suitable for steel shot. Fitted with automatic ejectors and double triggers. Manufactured in Italy, it was introduced in 1989.

NIB	Exc.	V.G.	Good	Fair	Poor
1450	995	700	475	400	200

Balmoral

English-style straight grip 12, 16, or 20 gauge boxlock shotgun, fitted with false side plates. Receiver and side plates case hardened, the barrels blued. Fitted with a single trigger and automatic ejectors. Manufactured in Italy and introduced in 1989.

NIB	Exc.	V.G.	Good	Fair	Poor
1200	925	725	500	400	200

Model 70E

A 12, 16, or 20 gauge side-by-side shotgun fitted with 27" or 28" barrels. The action based upon the Anson & Deeley design with a Greener crossbolt. The receiver is case hardened, barrels are blued and the walnut stock checkered. Manufactured in Germany and introduced in 1989.

NIB	Exc.	V.G.	Good	Fair	Poor
1225	925	725	500	400	200

Model 74E

As above with game scene engraving and more fully figured walnut stock. Introduced in 1989.

NIB	Exc.	V.G.	Good	Fair	Poor
1475	1050	900	650	500	250

Model 76E

As above with engraved false side plates and fully figured walnut stock. Introduced in 1989.

NIB	Exc.	V.G.	Good	Fair	Poor
2000	1500	1100	750	600	300

ARMINEX LTD.
Scottsdale, Arizona

Tri-Fire

A semi-automatic pistol chambered for 9mm, .38 Super or .45 ACP cartridges. Available with conversion units that add approximately $130 if in excellent condition. Fitted with 5", 6", or 7" stainless steel barrels. Presentation cases were available at an extra cost of $48. Approximately 250 were manufactured from 1981 to 1985.

Courtesy James Rankin

NIB	Exc.	V.G.	Good	Fair	Poor
950	800	600	300	175	100

Target Model

As above with a 6" or 7" barrel.

Courtesy James Rankin

NIB	Exc.	V.G.	Good	Fair	Poor
1000	850	650	350	225	100

ARMINUS
See—Freidrich Pickert
See—Hermann Weirauch
See—F. I. E.

ARMITAGE INTERNATIONAL, LTD.
Seneca, South Carolina

Scarab Skorpion

A blowback-operated, semi-automatic pistol, patterned after the Czechoslovakian Scorpion submachine gun. Chambered for the 9mm cartridge with a 4.6" barrel having military-type sights. Fitted with a 32-round, detachable box magazine. The standard finish is matte black and the grips are plastic.

NIB	Exc.	V.G.	Good	Fair	Poor
650	550	400	300	175	100

ARMSCO FIREARMS CORP.
Ankara, Turkey
U.S.A.—Des Plaines, Illinois

Built by Huglu Hunting Firearms Corporation in Turkey, which was established in 1927. Armsco is the U.S. representive. First year of business in the U.S. was 2002.

SINGLE-SHOT

Model 301A

This single-shot model is offered in 12, 16, 20, 28 gauge as well as .410 bore. Barrel lengths from 22" to 32" depending on gauge. Checkered walnut stock. Weight varies from 5 lbs. to 5.5 lbs. depending on gauge.

NIB	Exc.	V.G.	Good	Fair	Poor
200	150	75	50	35	25

SIDE-BY-SIDES

Model 202B

Boxlock gun offered in 12, 16, 20, and 28 gauge as well as .410 bore with barrel lengths from 22" to 32" depending on gauge. Double triggers. Hand engraved about 50 percent coverage. Fixed chokes or choke tubes. Checkered walnut stock with cheekpiece. Weight is about 6.4 lbs. to 7.3 lbs. depending on gauge.

NIB	Exc.	V.G.	Good	Fair	Poor
550	425	325	200	125	50

Model 202A

Same as above but offered with standard buttstock.

NIB	Exc.	V.G.	Good	Fair	Poor
775	625	450	300	175	75

Model 201A

Offered in gauges from 12 to .410 with sideplates with 50 percent hand engraving. Choice of single or double triggers.

NIB	Exc.	V.G.	Good	Fair	Poor
695	525	450	300	175	75

Model 200A

Boxlock in gauges 12 to .410 with single trigger. Hand engraved 50 percent coverage.

NIB	Exc.	V.G.	Good	Fair	Poor
750	575	450	300	175	75

Model 205A

Offered in gauges 12 to .410 with barrel lengths 22" to 32" depending on gauge. Boxlock frame with 60 percent hand engraving coverage. Single trigger. Checkered walnut stock. Weights are 6.1 lbs. to 6.8 lbs. depending on gauge.

NIB	Exc.	V.G.	Good	Fair	Poor
990	750	600	425	200	100

Model 210AE

Offered in 12, 16, and 20 gauge with single trigger and automatic ejectors. Boxlock frame is 60 percent hand engraved. Optional fixed or choke tubes.

NIB	Exc.	V.G.	Good	Fair	Poor
1250	950	700	450	300	200

Model 210BE

Same as above but with double triggers.

NIB	Exc.	V.G.	Good	Fair	Poor
1150	850	675	450	300	200

OVER/UNDERS

Model 104A

Chambered for the 12 through .410 bores with double triggers and barrel lengths from 22" to 32" depending on gauge. Ventilated rib. Checkered walnut stock. Fixed or choke tubes. Weight is from 6.6 lbs. to 7.3 lbs. depending on gauge. Receiver is 15 percent hand engraved.

NIB	Exc.	V.G.	Good	Fair	Poor
425	300	250	200	125	75

Model 103D

Same as model above but with single trigger and schnabel forearm.

NIB	Exc.	V.G.	Good	Fair	Poor
595	475	375	325	175	75

Model 103DE

Same as above but with automatic ejectors.

NIB	Exc.	V.G.	Good	Fair	Poor
750	575	525	425	200	75

Model 103C

Similar to the Model 103D but with blued receiver with gold inlaid birds with 40 percent engraving coverage.

NIB	Exc.	V.G.	Good	Fair	Poor
720	550	525	425	200	75

Model 103CE

Same as above but with automatic ejectors.

NIB	Exc.	V.G.	Good	Fair	Poor
870	650	575	475	225	100

Model 103F

Similar to the Model 103D but with 80 to 100 percent hand engraved side plates.

NIB	Exc.	V.G.	Good	Fair	Poor
850	625	550	450	225	100

Model 103FE

Same as above but with automatic ejectors.

NIB	Exc.	V.G.	Good	Fair	Poor
970	750	600	475	250	125

Model 101SE

Offered in 12 gauge only with 28", 30", or 32" barrels with ventilated rib. Single trigger and automatic ejectors. Hand engraved receiver. Checkered walnut stock. Weight is from 6.6 lbs. to 7.3 lbs. depending on barrel length.

NIB	Exc.	V.G.	Good	Fair	Poor
1325	975	750	450	275	125

Model 101BE

Same as above but with adjustable comb.

NIB	Exc.	V.G.	Good	Fair	Poor
1325	975	750	450	275	125

SEMI-AUTOS

Model 401A

This semi-automatic shotgun uses a short-recoil inertia-operated system. Chambered for the 12 gauge shell up to 3". Barrel lengths from 22" to 32". Ventilated rib. Plastic or walnut stock. Fixed or choke tubes. Fully engraved receiver. Weight is from 6.9 lbs. to 7.2 lbs. depending on barrel length. Magazine capacity is 6 rounds.

NIB	Exc.	V.G.	Good	Fair	Poor
425	350	275	225	125	75

Model 401B

Same as model above but with 4-round magazine capacity.

NIB	Exc.	V.G.	Good	Fair	Poor
425	350	275	225	125	75

Model 501GA

This is a gas-operated shotgun chambered for the 3" 12 gauge shell. Barrel lengths are from 22" to 32". Black receiver with 15 percent hand engraving coverage. Magazine capacity is 7 rounds. Walnut or plastic stock. Weight is from 6.8 lbs. to 7.3 lbs. depending on barrel length.

NIB	Exc.	V.G.	Good	Fair	Poor
425	350	275	225	125	75

Model 501GB

Same as above but with 4-round magazine.

NIB	Exc.	V.G.	Good	Fair	Poor
425	350	275	225	125	75

Model 601GB

Same as the Model 501GB but with a full engraving coverage silver receiver.

NIB	Exc.	V.G.	Good	Fair	Poor
450	375	300	250	125	75

Model 601GA

Same as Model 501GA with 7-round magazine capacity.

NIB	Exc.	V.G.	Good	Fair	Poor
450	375	300	250	125	75

Model 701GA

This model is chambered for the 20 gauge 3" shell and fitted with barrel lengths from 22" to 32". Ventilated rib. Walnut stock. Fixed or choke tubes. Magazine capacity is 7 rounds. Weight is 6 lbs. to 6.4 lbs. depending on barrel length.

NIB	Exc.	V.G.	Good	Fair	Poor
450	375	300	225	125	75

Model 701GB

Same as above but with 4-round magazine.

NIB	Exc.	V.G.	Good	Fair	Poor
450	375	300	225	125	75

PUMP-ACTIONS

Model 801A

This is a slide-action 12 gauge shotgun with plastic stock. Barrel length is from 22" to 32". Fixed or choke tubes. Magazine capacity is 7 rounds. Weight is about 7 lbs.

NIB	Exc.	V.G.	Good	Fair	Poor
300	275	250	175	100	50

Model 801B

Same as above but with 4-round magazine.

NIB	Exc.	V.G.	Good	Fair	Poor
300	275	250	175	100	50

ARMSCOR PRECISION INTERNATIONAL
Pahrump, Nevada

Armscor Precision International, imports firearms made by Arms Corporation of the Philippines.

RIFLES

M14R

A civilian version of the U.S. M14 rifle manufactured from new and surplus parts. Introduced in 1986.

NIB	Exc.	V.G.	Good	Fair	Poor
1350	900	500	300	200	100

M14 National Match

As above but built to A.M.T.U. MIL specifications. Introduced in 1987.

NIB	Exc.	V.G.	Good	Fair	Poor
1650	1250	800	500	400	200

FAL

A civilian version of the FN FAL rifle assembled from new and Argentine surplus parts. Introduced in 1987.

NIB	Exc.	V.G.	Good	Fair	Poor
1600	1250	800	400	300	150

M36 Israeli Sniper Rifle

A specialized weapon built upon the Armscorp M14 receiver in the Bullpup style. Barrel length 22" and of free floating design for accuracy, chambered for the .308 cartridge. There is an integral flash suppressor and a bipod. It is furnished with a 20-shot detachable magazine. This civilian version was first offered for sale in 1989.

NIB	Exc.	V.G.	Good	Fair	Poor
3200	2650	2000	1500	850	400

Expert Model

A .22 caliber semi-automatic rifle with a 21" barrel, open sights, and 10-shot magazine. Introduced in 1989.

NIB	Exc.	V.G.	Good	Fair	Poor
225	200	175	145	100	80

Model M14P

A .22 caliber bolt-action rifle fitted with a 23" barrel, open sights, and a 5-shot detachable magazine. Mahogany stock.

NIB	Exc.	V.G.	Good	Fair	Poor
150	90	75	50	35	25

Model M14D

As above with an adjustable rear sight and checkered stock. Manufactured in 1987 only.

NIB	Exc.	V.G.	Good	Fair	Poor
165	100	85	60	40	25

Model 14Y

This bolt-action rifle is chambered for .22 LR cartridge. It is fitted with an 18" barrel and 10-round magazine. Weight is approximately 5.2 lbs.

NIB	Exc.	V.G.	Good	Fair	Poor
150	125	100	75	50	25

Model 12Y

This bolt-action rifle is a single-shot and chambered for the .22 LR. It is fitted with an 18" barrel. Weight is about 5 lbs.

NIB	Exc.	V.G.	Good	Fair	Poor
125	100	75	50	35	25

Model 1400

This is a bolt-action rifle chambered for the .22 LR cartridge. Fitted with a 22.5" barrel and a 10-round magazine. Weight is about 6.5 lbs.

NIB	Exc.	V.G.	Good	Fair	Poor
225	200	150	125	100	75

Model M1500

A .22 Magnum bolt-action rifle fitted with a 22.5" barrel, open sights, 5-shot magazine and checkered mahogany stock. Weight is approximately 6.5 lbs.

NIB	Exc.	V.G.	Good	Fair	Poor
250	200	150	125	100	75

Model M1600

A .22 caliber copy of the U.S. M16 rifle with an 18" barrel and detachable 15-round magazine. Weight is about 6.2 lbs.

NIB	Exc.	V.G.	Good	Fair	Poor
300	200	125	100	75	50

Model M1600R

As above with a stainless steel collapsible stock and shrouded barrel. No longer in production.

NIB	Exc.	V.G.	Good	Fair	Poor
325	225	150	125	100	75

Model M1600C

As above with a 20" barrel and fiberglass stock. No longer in production.

NIB	Exc.	V.G.	Good	Fair	Poor
300	200	125	100	75	50

Model M1600W

As above with a mahogany stock. No longer in production.

NIB	Exc.	V.G.	Good	Fair	Poor
300	200	125	100	75	50

Model M1800

A .22 Hornet bolt-action rifle fitted with a 22.5" barrel, 5-shot magazine and a mahogany Monte Carlo-style stock. Weight is approximately 6.6 lbs.

NIB	Exc.	V.G.	Good	Fair	Poor
250	200	150	75	50	35

Model 20C

Chambered for .22 LR with a 15-round magazine and fitted with an 18.25" barrel. Weight is about 6.2 lbs.

NIB	Exc.	V.G.	Good	Fair	Poor
175	150	90	70	50	40

Model M20P

A .22 caliber 15-shot semi-automatic rifle fitted with a 20.75" barrel, open sights and plain mahogany stock. Weight is about 6.3 lbs.

NIB	Exc.	V.G.	Good	Fair	Poor
175	150	90	70	50	40

Model M2000

As above with adjustable sights and a checkered stock. Weight is approximately 6.4 lbs.

NIB	Exc.	V.G.	Good	Fair	Poor
175	150	90	70	50	40

Model AK22S

A .22 caliber semi-automatic rifle resembling the Russian AKA47. Barrel length of 18.5", 15-round magazine and mahogany stock. Weight is about 7.5 lbs.

NIB	Exc.	V.G.	Good	Fair	Poor
275	225	195	125	75	50

Model AK22F

As above with a folding stock. No longer in production.

NIB	Exc.	V.G.	Good	Fair	Poor
275	225	195	125	75	50

HANDGUNS

Hi-Power

An Argentine-made version of the Browning semi-automatic pistol chambered for 9mm with a 4.75" barrel. Matte finish with checkered synthetic grips. Introduced in 1989.

NIB	Exc.	V.G.	Good	Fair	Poor
450	350	300	250	200	100

Detective HP—Compact

As above with a 3.5" barrel.

NIB	Exc.	V.G.	Good	Fair	Poor
475	375	350	275	200	100

P22

A copy of the Colt Woodsman .22 caliber semi-automatic pistol available with either 4" or 6" barrels and a 10-shot magazine. Finish blued, grips of checkered hardwood. Introduced in 1989.

NIB	Exc.	V.G.	Good	Fair	Poor
250	150	125	100	75	50

SD9

An Israeli-made 9mm double-action semi-automatic pistol with a 3" barrel. Assembled extensively from sheet metal stampings. Loaded chamber indicator and 6-round magazine. This model is also known as the Sirkus SD9 manufactured by Sirkus Industries in Israel. Introduced in 1989.

Courtesy Jim Rankin

NIB	Exc.	V.G.	Good	Fair	Poor
300	250	200	150	100	75

Armscor 1911A1-45 FS GI

1911-style semi-automatic pistol chambered in .45 ACP (8 rounds) , 9mm Parabellum, .38 Super (9 rounds). Features include checkered plastic or hardwood grips, 5" barrel, parkerized steel frame and slide, drift adjustable sights. **NOTE:** Add $50 for Commander or Officer's model.

NIB	Exc.	V.G.	Good	Fair	Poor
400	350	300	250	200	100

Model M100

A double-action, swing-out cylinder revolver chambered for .22, .22 Magnum, and the .38 Special cartridges. Has a 4" ventilated rib barrel. Six-shot cylinder and adjustable sights. Blued with checkered mahogany grips. No longer in production.

NIB	Exc.	V.G.	Good	Fair	Poor
200	175	150	110	80	50

Model 200P

Introduced in 1990 this 6-shot revolver is chambered for the .38 Special cartridge. It is fitted with a 4" barrel, fixed sights and wood or rubber grips. Weighs about 26 ozs.

NIB	Exc.	V.G.	Good	Fair	Poor
180	150	125	100	85	60

Model 200TC

Introduced in 1990 this model is similar to above but is fitted with adjustable sights and checkered wood grips. Weight is about 28 oz.

NIB	Exc.	V.G.	Good	Fair	Poor
200	175	150	125	100	75

Model 200DC

Similar to the Model 200P but fitted with a 2.5" barrel. Weight is about 22 oz.

NIB	Exc.	V.G.	Good	Fair	Poor
175	150	125	100	85	60

Model 201S

Similar to the Model 200P but in stainless steel.

NIB	Exc.	V.G.	Good	Fair	Poor
200	175	150	125	100	75

Model 202

Chambered for the 38 Special cartridge this 6-shot revolver is fitted with a 4" barrel and fixed sights. Blued finish. Weight is about 27 oz.

NIB	Exc.	V.G.	Good	Fair	Poor
150	120	95	75	50	25

Model 206

Similar to the Model 202 but with a 2.88" barrel. Weight is about 25 oz.

NIB	Exc.	V.G.	Good	Fair	Poor
180	140	110	75	50	25

Model 210

Same as the Model 202 but with adjustable sights. Weight is about 27 oz.

NIB	Exc.	V.G.	Good	Fair	Poor
200	150	125	75	50	25

MAP1 FS

Single/double-action 9mm semi-automatic with 16+1 capacity. Fixed sights, 4.45" barrel, 40.5 oz. nickel alloy steel frame and slide. (Shorter, lighter MS model has 3.66" barrel.) Introduced 2006.

NIB	Exc.	V.G.	Good	Fair	Poor
—	350	300	200	125	75

MAPP1 FS

Single/double-action 9mm semi-automatyic with 16+1 capacity. Fixed sights, 4.45" barrel, 40.5 oz. polymer frame with integrated accessory rail, and nickel alloy steel slide. (Shorter, lighter MS model has 3.66" barrel.) Introduced 2006.

NIB	Exc.	V.G.	Good	Fair	Poor
—	350	300	200	175	75

Model 1911-A1

A semi-automatic pistol similar in design to the Colt Model 1911 pistol. Chambered for the .45 ACP cartridge and fitted with a 5" barrel. Blued finish. Magazine capacity is 8 rounds. Weight is about 39 oz. Also sold under the Charles Daly name.

NIB	Exc.	V.G.	Good	Fair	Poor
500	400	300	200	150	75

Model 1911-A2

Same as above but fitted with a double column magazine with a 13-round capacity. Weight is approximately 43 oz. **NOTE:** For two-tone finish add $100. For chrome finish add $130.

NIB	Exc.	V.G.	Good	Fair	Poor
600	500	375	250	195	110

SHOTGUNS

Model 30D

A slide-action 12 gauge shotgun fitted with either 28" or 30" barrels with various chokes. The magazine holds 6 cartridges. Weight is about 7.6 lbs.

NIB	Exc.	V.G.	Good	Fair	Poor
200	175	150	125	100	75

Model 30DG

As above with a 20" barrel, fitted with rifle sights and a 7-shot magazine. Weight is about 7.2 lbs.

NIB	Exc.	V.G.	Good	Fair	Poor
175	150	125	100	80	70

Model 30R

As above with shotgun bead sights, 20" or 18.5" barrel. Weight is between 7 and 7.2 lbs. depending on barrel length.

NIB	Exc.	V.G.	Good	Fair	Poor
175	150	125	100	80	70

Model 30RP

As above with an auxiliary black composition pistol grip and an 18.5" barrel.

NIB	Exc.	V.G.	Good	Fair	Poor
175	150	125	100	80	70

Model 30 SAS1

Slide-action 12 gauge with 20" barrel with heat shield. Chambered for the 3" shell. Open cylinder choke. Parkerized finish finish. Weight is about 8 lbs.

NIB	Exc.	V.G.	Good	Fair	Poor
200	150	100	75	50	25

ARNOLD ARMS
Arlington, Washington

This company offered a wide range of rifles and calibers including its own proprietary cartridges, from the 6mm Arnold to the .458 Arnold. Rifles were built on a choice of actions including the Apollo, Remington, Sako, and Winchester. These action choices affect the base price of the rifle. Out of business in 2002. Values vary with geography. **NOTE:** Add $1100 for Apollo actions to all applicable models, unless otherwise noted.

Varminter I

This model features a heavy match grade barrel with straight taper. Lengths are from 24" to 26". Calibers are from .222 Rem. to .257 Arnold Magnum. Choice of McMillian Varmint stock in various finishes and Pacific Research Varmint stock in flat black. Rifles weigh from 9 to 11 lbs. depending on caliber and configuration.

NIB	Exc.	V.G.	Good	Fair	Poor
2600	2000	1450	1050	700	200

Varminter II

This variation features a 24" to 26" medium weight match barrel with choice of McMillan or Pacific Research sporter stocks. Choice of triggers. Weight is 7.5 to 9 lbs. depending on configuration. Calibers from .223 Rem. to .257 Arnold Magnum.

NIB	Exc.	V.G.	Good	Fair	Poor
2600	2000	1450	1050	700	200

Alaskan

This is a bolt-action rifle chambered for calibers from .223 to .338 Win. Mag. Barrel lengths are from 22" to 26" depending on caliber. Stocks are synthetic in black woodland or arctic camo. Sights are optional. Rifle is drilled and tapped for scope mounts. Trigger is fully adjustable. Choice of chrome moly steel or stainless steel. Introduced in 1996.

NIB	Exc.	V.G.	Good	Fair	Poor
2600	2000	1450	1050	700	200

Alaskan Trophy

Similar to the Alaskan Rifle except chambered for .300 Magnums to .458 Win. Mag. Barrel lengths are 24" to 26" depending on caliber. Choice of walnut, synthetic, or fibergrain stock. Fitted with iron sights. Choice of stainless or chrome moly steel. Introduced in 1996.

NIB	Exc.	V.G.	Good	Fair	Poor
3100	2500	1450	1050	700	200

Alaskan Guide

This model is offered in choice of calibers from .257 to .338 Magnum. Barrel lengths are 22" to 26" depending on caliber. Buyer has a choice of "A" English walnut stock or deluxe synthetic stock. No open sights.

Synthetic Stock

NIB	Exc.	V.G.	Good	Fair	Poor
3700	2900	2200	1400	650	300

Walnut Stock

NIB	Exc.	V.G.	Good	Fair	Poor
4300	3400	2500	1475	700	325

Grand Alaskan

This version is fitted with AAA fancy select or exhibition wood. Built in calibers from .300 Magnum to .458 Win. Magnum.

"AAA" English Walnut

NIB	Exc.	V.G.	Good	Fair	Poor
6000	5000	3750	2500	1500	450

"Exhibition" Grade Walnut

NIB	Exc.	V.G.	Good	Fair	Poor
7400	6000	5000	3900	1650	325

Safari

Introduced in 1996 this model features calibers from .223 to .458 Win. Mag. Barrel lengths are from 22" to 26" depending on caliber. The Apollo is a controlled or push feed type with one-piece, cone-head bolt. Fully adjustable trigger with chrome moly or stainless steel construction. Sights are optional but the rifle is drilled and tapped for scope mounts. Choice of A fancy English or AA fancy English walnut.

"A" Fancy English Walnut

NIB	Exc.	V.G.	Good	Fair	Poor
4300	3500	2700	1650	800	300

"AA" Fancy English Walnut

NIB	Exc.	V.G.	Good	Fair	Poor
4400	3500	2700	1650	800	300

African Trophy

Similar to the Safari Rifle except stocked in AAA fancy walnut with wraparound checkering.

NIB	Exc.	V.G.	Good	Fair	Poor
6300	5000	3250	2500	1750	300

Grand African

Similar to the Safari rifle with the addition of Exhibition Grade wood. Calibers are from .338 to .458.

NIB	Exc.	V.G.	Good	Fair	Poor
7600	6100	5000	3900	1650	325

Serengeti Synthetic

Similar to the Safari rifle with a fibergrain stock in classic or Monte Carlo style. Checkering or stipple finish. Calibers are .243 to .300 Magnum. Introduced in 1996.

NIB	Exc.	V.G.	Good	Fair	Poor
2600	2100	1600	1150	700	225

African Synthetic

Similar to the Safari rifle with fibergrain stock, checkering or stipple finish. Calibers are .338 Mag. to .458 Mag.

NIB	Exc.	V.G.	Good	Fair	Poor
3300	2600	1800	1400	750	250

Neutralizer Mark I

Built on a Remington 700 or Winchester action this bolt-action rifle is chambered in a choice of calibers from .223 to .300 Win. Mag. Barrel lengths are from 24" to 26" depending on caliber with Magnum barrels up to 28". A fiberglass tactical stock with adjustable cheekpiece and buttplate is standard in various finishes. Winchester action is $400 less.

NIB	Exc.	V.G.	Good	Fair	Poor
2900	2300	1700	1300	700	275

Neutralizer Mark II

Same as above but with Apollo action.

NIB	Exc.	V.G.	Good	Fair	Poor
4000	3200	2250	1700	900	325

Benchrest Rifles

Custom built. Unable to price individual rifles.

Prone Rifles

Custom built. Unable to price individual rifles.

X-Course Rifles

Custom built. Unable to price individual rifles.

1,000 Yard Match Rifles

Custom built. Unable to price individual rifles.

Fully Accurized Production Rifles

These rifles are offered in standard blue or stainless steel with walnut or synthetic stock. Chambered from .223 to .338 Win. mag. and built on Remington, Ruger, or Winchester actions.

NIB	Exc.	V.G.	Good	Fair	Poor
1250	1100	750	600	400	200

AROSTEGUI, EULOGIO
Eibar, Spain

Azul Royal (Model 31)

A semi-automatic or full automatic pistol in calibers 7.63 Mauser, 9mm Bergmann, or .38 ACP. Manufactured between 1935 and 1940. Fitted with a 10-round integral magazine. **NOTE:** Add 300 percent for fully automatic machine pistol version. NFA/BATFE regulations apply.

Courtesy James Rankin

NIB	Exc.	V.G.	Good	Fair	Poor
—	3000	2500	1000	500	300

Super Azul (M-34)

A semi-automatic or full automatic pistol in 7.63mm Mauser, 9mm Bergmann, and .38 ACP. Manufactured between 1935 and 1940. It has a removable box magazine with capacity of 10, 20, or 30 rounds. Also known as the War Model or the Standard Model. **NOTE:** Add 300 percent for fully automatic machine pistol version. NFA/BATFE regulations apply.

Courtesy James Rankin

NIB	Exc.	V.G.	Good	Fair	Poor
—	3000	2500	1000	500	300

Azul 6.35mm

A 6.35mm semi-automatic pistol copied after the Model 1906 Browning. The frame is marked with the letters "EA" in a circle and a retriever is molded in the grips. Magazine capacity is 6 or 9 rounds.

NIB	Exc.	V.G.	Good	Fair	Poor
—	250	200	150	100	75

Azul 7.65mm

A 7.65mm semi-automatic pistol copied after the Model 1910 FN. Magazine capacity is 7 or 9 rounds.

NIB	Exc.	V.G.	Good	Fair	Poor
—	250	200	150	100	75

Velo-Dog

A folding trigger 5.5mm or 6.35mm revolver bearing the trademark "EA" on the grips.

NIB	Exc.	V.G.	Good	Fair	Poor
—	175	100	75	50	30

ARRIETA S.L.
Elgoibar, Spain

This company produces a wide variety of double-barrel shotguns in a price range from $450 to more than $30,000. It is recommended that highly engraved examples, as well as small bore arms, be individually appraised. **NOTE:** For 20 or 28 gauge and .410 bore add 10 percent to the values shown.

490 Eder

A double-barrel boxlock shotgun with double triggers and extractors. Discontinued in 1986.

NIB	Exc.	V.G.	Good	Fair	Poor
—	550	425	325	250	100

500 Titan

A Holland & Holland-style sidelock double-barrel shotgun with French case hardened and engraved locks. Double triggers on extractors. No longer imported after 1986.

NIB	Exc.	V.G.	Good	Fair	Poor
—	675	500	400	300	150

501 Palomara

As above, but more finely finished. Discontinued in 1986.

NIB	Exc.	V.G.	Good	Fair	Poor
—	800	600	500	400	200

505 Alaska

As above, but more intricately engraved. Discontinued in 1986.

NIB	Exc.	V.G.	Good	Fair	Poor
—	900	750	600	500	250

510 Montana

A Holland & Holland-style sidelock double-barrel shotgun with the internal parts gold-plated.

NIB	Exc.	V.G.	Good	Fair	Poor
3200	2750	1250	850	500	250

550 Field

As above, without the internal parts gold-plated.

NIB	Exc.	V.G.	Good	Fair	Poor
3200	2750	1250	850	500	250

557 Standard

As above, but more finely finished.

NIB	Exc.	V.G.	Good	Fair	Poor
3750	3000	1750	1250	800	400

558 Patria

As above, but more finely finished.

NIB	Exc.	V.G.	Good	Fair	Poor
3650	3150	1750	1250	800	400

560 Cumbre

As above, but featuring intricate engraving.

NIB	Exc.	V.G.	Good	Fair	Poor
3800	3200	1800	1200	800	400

570 Lieja

NIB	Exc.	V.G.	Good	Fair	Poor
4400	3500	2000	1500	750	500

575 Sport

NIB	Exc.	V.G.	Good	Fair	Poor
4750	3750	2250	1700	1200	750

578 Victoria

This model is engraved in the English manner with floral bouquets.

NIB	Exc.	V.G.	Good	Fair	Poor
6000	5000	3750	2250	1000	750

585 Liria

As above, but more finely finished.

NIB	Exc.	V.G.	Good	Fair	Poor
6500	5500	4250	3000	2000	1000

588 Cima

NIB	Exc.	V.G.	Good	Fair	Poor
4800	4000	2250	1500	900	400

590 Regina

NIB	Exc.	V.G.	Good	Fair	Poor
4250	3500	2700	1750	1000	500

595 Principe

As above, but engraved with relief-cut hunting scenes.

NIB	Exc.	V.G.	Good	Fair	Poor
7500	6000	4000	3000	2000	1000

600 Imperial

This double-barrel shotgun has a self-opening action.

NIB	Exc.	V.G.	Good	Fair	Poor
8500	7000	6000	4500	3000	2000

601 Imperial Tiro

As above, but nickel-plated. Fitted with a self-opening action.

NIB	Exc.	V.G.	Good	Fair	Poor
9000	7500	6500	4000	2500	1500

801

A detachable sidelock, self-opening action, double-barrel shotgun engraved in the manner of Churchill.

NIB	Exc.	V.G.	Good	Fair	Poor
10000	8500	7500	5000	3000	2000

802

As above, with Holland & Holland-style engraving.

NIB	Exc.	V.G.	Good	Fair	Poor
11000	9000	8000	6000	4000	2000

803

As above, with Purdey-style engraving.

NIB	Exc.	V.G.	Good	Fair	Poor
9500	7500	6000	4000	3000	2000

871

This model features hand detachable sidelocks with Holland ejectors. Scroll engraving.

NIB	Exc.	V.G.	Good	Fair	Poor
5300	4400	2500	1500	1000	750

872

This model has same features as the Model 871 with the addition of more engraving coverage using a tighter scroll.

NIB	Exc.	V.G.	Good	Fair	Poor
12500	10500	9000	7000	5000	2000

873

This model features hand detachable sidelocks and game scene engraving.

NIB	Exc.	V.G.	Good	Fair	Poor
13000	11000	9000	7000	5000	2000

874

Same features as above model but with the addition of a blued frame with gold line outlines.

NIB	Exc.	V.G.	Good	Fair	Poor
11000	9000	8000	6000	4000	2000

875

A custom manufactured sidelock, double-barrel shotgun built solely to the customer's specifications.

NIB	Exc.	V.G.	Good	Fair	Poor
15000	11500	9000	7000	5000	2000

R-1 Double Rifle

NIB	Exc.	V.G.	Good	Fair	Poor
15000	12500	10500	6000	3000	1000

R-2 Double Rifle

NIB	Exc.	V.G.	Good	Fair	Poor
18000	16000	14000	11000	5000	2000

ARRIZABALAGA, HIJOS de C.
Eibar, Spain

Arrizabalaga

A 7.65mm semi-automatic pistol with a 9-shot magazine and a lanyard ring fitted to the butt. Checkered wood grips. "ARRIZABALAGA" on the slide.

Courtesy James Rankin

NIB	Exc.	V.G.	Good	Fair	Poor
—	275	175	125	75	50

Campeon

The Model 1919 6.35mm, 7.65mm, or 9mm Kurtz semi-automatic pistol with the slide marked "Campeon Patent 1919" and the plastic grips "Campeon". Supplied with 6- or 8-round magazines. "CAMPEON" appears on the slide. **NOTE:** Add 25 percent for 9mm Kurtz.

Courtesy James Rankin

NIB	Exc.	V.G.	Good	Fair	Poor
—	325	275	195	75	50

Jo Lo Ar

The Model 1924 semi-automatic pistol with a tip-up barrel, cocking lever, and no trigger guard. The Jo Lo Ar was built in six calibers: 6.35mm, 7.65mm, 9mm Kurtz, 9mm Largo, and .45 ACP. "Jo-Lo-Ar" appears on the slide and the grips. Premium for larger calibers. **NOTE:** Add 400 percent for .45.

Courtesy James Rankin

NIB	Exc.	V.G.	Good	Fair	Poor
—	1100	925	800	450	200

Sharpshooter

A 6.35mm, 7.65mm or 9mm Corto (short) semi-automatic pistol fitted with a cocking lever. The barrel tips up for cleaning or when using the pistol as a single-shot. "SHARPSHOOTER" appears on the slide.

Courtesy James Rankin

NIB	Exc.	V.G.	Good	Fair	Poor
—	400	300	225	150	100

ARSENAL, INC.
Las Vegas, Nevada

SA M-7

Semi-automatic rifles manufactured in U.S. similar to the AK-47 in appearance. Chambered for the 7.62x39 cartridge and fitted with a 16" barrel. Black polymer stock.

NIB	Exc.	V.G.	Good	Fair	Poor
1000	800	550	325	200	125

SA M-7 Classic

As above but with blonde wood stock.

NIB	Exc.	V.G.	Good	Fair	Poor
1050	850	600	325	200	125

SA M-7S

Similar to the SA M-7 but with scope rail added.

NIB	Exc.	V.G.	Good	Fair	Poor
1025	875	575	325	200	125

SA RPK-7

Chambered for the 7.62x39 cartridge this rifle is similar to the RPK. Fitted with a 23" barrel with bipod. Solid blonde wood stock with trap in stock for cleaning kit.

NIB	Exc.	V.G.	Good	Fair	Poor
975	800	595	325	200	125

ASCASO
Cataluna, Spain

Spanish Rebublican Government

A copy of the Astra Model 400 chambered for the 9mm Largo cartridge. The barrel marked "F. Ascaso Tarrassa" in an oval. Built by the Spanish government during the Spanish Civil War. Very few were made.

Courtesy James Rankin

NIB	Exc.	V.G.	Good	Fair	Poor
—	850	750	550	300	200

ASHEVILLE ARMORY
Asheville, North Carolina

Enfield-Type Rifle

A .58 caliber percussion rifle with a 32.5" barrel and full stock secured by two iron barrel bands. Finished in the white brass trigger guard and buttplate with a walnut stock. The lockplate is marked "Asheville, N.C." Approximately 300 were made in 1862 and 1863.

Courtesy Milwaukee Public Museum, Milwaukee, Wisconsin

NIB	Exc.	V.G.	Good	Fair	Poor
—	—	42000	19200	5000	3250

ASHTON, PETER & WILLIAM
Middletown, Connecticut

Under Hammer Pistol

A .28 to .38 caliber single-shot percussion revolver with 4" or 5" half-octagonal barrels marked "P.H. Ashton" or "W. Ashton". Blued or browned with walnut grips. Active 1850s.

NIB	Exc.	V.G.	Good	Fair	Poor
—	—	1100	500	200	100

ASTON, H./H. ASTON & CO. PISTOLS
Middleton, Connecticut

Overall length 14"; barrel length 8-1/2"; caliber .54. Markings: on lockplate, forward of hammer "U S/H. ASTON" or "U S/H. ASTON & CO.," on tail "MIDDTN/CONN/(date)"; on barrel, standard government inspection marks. Henry Aston of Middleton, Connecticut received a contract from the U.S. War Department in February 1845 for 30,000 single-shot percussion pistols. These were delivered between 1846 and 1852, after which Ira N. Johnston continued production under a separate contract. Three thousand of these pistols were purchased for Navy usage and many of these were subsequently marked with a small anchor on the barrel near the breech. These Navy purchases will command a slight premium.

Courtesy Milwaukee Public Museum, Milwaukee, Wisconsin

NIB	Exc.	V.G.	Good	Fair	Poor
—	—	4700	4500	1750	500

ASTRA-UNCETA SA
Guernica, Spain

Astra is a brand name placed on guns built by Esperanza y Unceta and then Unceta y Cia. This Spanish company has now incorporated its trade name into its corporate name and is now know as Astra-Unceta SA. The firm under the direction of Don Pedron Unceta and Don Juan Esperanza began business in Eibar on July 17, 1908 and moved to Guernica in 1913. The Astra trademark was adopted on November 25, 1914. Esperanza began production of the Spanish Army's Campo Giro pistol in 1913. The Model 1921 was marketed commercially as the Astra 400. After the Spanish Civil War Unceta was one of only four handgun companies permitted to resume manufacturing operations. An interesting and informative side note is that pistols with 1000 to 5000 model numbers were made after 1945. Astra merged with Star before going out of business in 2006.

Victoria

A 6.35mm semi-automatic pistol with a 2.5" barrel. Blued with black plastic grips. Manufactured prior to 1913.

NIB	Exc.	V.G.	Good	Fair	Poor
—	300	250	200	150	100

Astra 1911

A 6.35mm and 7.65mm semi-automatic pistol. External hammer and checkered hard rubber grips. The 7.65mm model was manufactured before the 6.35mm model.

Courtesy James Rankin

NIB	Exc.	V.G.	Good	Fair	Poor
—	375	275	175	100	75

Astra 1924

A 6.35mm semi-automatic pistol with a 2.5" barrel. The slide marked "Esperanza y Unceta Guernica Spain Astra Cal 6.35 .25." Blued with black plastic grips.

NIB	Exc.	V.G.	Good	Fair	Poor
—	300	200	125	100	75

Astra 100 (Old Model)

A semi-automatic pistol in caliber 7.65mm. Checkered hard rubber grips. Magazine capacity is 12 rounds. Introduced after WWII.

Courtesy James Rankin

NIB	Exc.	V.G.	Good	Fair	Poor
—	550	400	300	200	100

Astra 200

A 6.35mm semi-automatic pistol with a 2.5" barrel and 6-shot magazine fitted with a grip safety. Also known as the "Firecat" in the United States. Manufactured from 1920 to 1966. Add 25 percent for factory engraving.

Courtesy James Rankin

NIB	Exc.	V.G.	Good	Fair	Poor
—	300	200	125	100	75

Astra 400 or Model 1921

A 9x23 Bergman (9mm Largo) caliber semi-automatic pistol with a 6" barrel. Blued with black plastic grips. This model was adopted for use by the Spanish Army. Approximately 106,000 were made prior to 1946. Recent importation has depressed the price of these guns. Any with Nazi proofs marks are worth a 100 percent premium, but caution is advised.

NIB	Exc.	V.G.	Good	Fair	Poor
—	475	400	250	75	40

Astra 300

As above, in 7.65mm or 9mm short. Those used during World War II by German forces bear Waffenamt marks. Approximately 171,000 were manufactured prior to 1947. **NOTE:** Nazi-proofed add 25 percent.

Courtesy Orvel Reichert

NIB	Exc.	V.G.	Good	Fair	Poor
—	650	475	250	150	100

Astra 600

Similar to the Model 400, but in 9mm Parabellum. In 1943 and 1944 approximately 10,500 were manufactured. Some of these World War II guns will have Nazi proof stamp and bring a premium. A further 49,000 were made in 1946 and commercially sold.

NIB	Exc.	V.G.	Good	Fair	Poor
—	575	375	275	175	100

Astra 700

A single-action semi-automatic pistol in caliber 7.65mm. Magazine capacity is 9 rounds. Introduced in 1926.

Courtesy James Rankin

NIB	Exc.	V.G.	Good	Fair	Poor
—	500	400	300	150	100

Astra 800

Similar to the Model 600 with an external hammer and loaded chamber indicator. Blued with plastic grips having the tradename "Condor" cast in them. Approximately 11,400 were made from 1958 to 1969.

NIB	Exc.	V.G.	Good	Fair	Poor
—	1500	1200	850	500	300

Astra 900

A modified copy of the Mauser Model C96 semi-automatic pistol. Blued with walnut grips. **NOTE:** Early examples with a small Bolo grip marked "Hope" on the chamber will bring a 20 percent premium. Serial numbers 32,788 through 33,774 were used by the German Army in WWII and bring a 50 percent premium. Add 50 percent for matching Astra-made stock.

NIB	Exc.	V.G.	Good	Fair	Poor
—	3000	2250	1500	600	300

Astra 1000

A single-action semi-automatic pistol in caliber 7.65mm. Magazine capacity is 12 rounds. Introduced after WWII.

Courtesy James Rankin

NIB	Exc.	V.G.	Good	Fair	Poor
—	750	600	450	200	100

Astra 2000

In a single-action semi-automatic pistol in .22 or 6.35mm caliber without a grip safety and with an external hammer. Blued with plastic grips.

NIB	Exc.	V.G.	Good	Fair	Poor
—	225	200	175	150	90

Astra 3000

The Model 300 in 7.65mm or 9mm short with a 6- or 7-shot magazine and loaded chamber indicator. Manufactured from 1948 to 1956.

Paul Goodwin photo

NIB	Exc.	V.G.	Good	Fair	Poor
—	600	500	325	200	100

Astra 4000 Falcon

A semi-automatic pistol that was known later as the Falcon. Calibers were .22 LR, 7.65mm, and 9mmK with magazine capacity of 10, 8, and 7 rounds. Manufactured beginning 1955.

Courtesy James Rankin

NIB	Exc.	V.G.	Good	Fair	Poor
—	575	475	325	200	100

Astra 5000 Constable

A .22, 7.65mm or 9mm short semi-automatic pistol (resembling a Walther PP pistol) with a 3.5" barrel. Blued, chrome-plated or stainless steel with plastic grips. Also available with a 6" barrel as a sport model. Introduced in 1965. **NOTE:** Add 15 percent for Constable Sport version with 6" barrel and adjustable sight.

NIB	Exc.	V.G.	Good	Fair	Poor
—	395	300	250	200	100

Astra 7000

An enlarged version of the Model 2000 in .22 caliber.

NIB	Exc.	V.G.	Good	Fair	Poor
—	575	475	325	200	100

Astra A-80

A .38 Super, 9mm or .45 caliber double-action semi-automatic pistol with a 3.75" barrel and either a 9- or 15-shot magazine depending upon the caliber. Blued or chrome-plated with plastic grips. Introduced in 1982.

Courtesy James Rankin

NIB	Exc.	V.G.	Good	Fair	Poor
450	350	300	250	200	100

Astra A-90

As above, in 9mm or .45 caliber only. Introduced in 1986.

NIB	Exc.	V.G.	Good	Fair	Poor
400	350	300	250	200	100

Constable A-60

A .380 caliber double-action semi-automatic pistol with a 3.5" barrel, adjustable sights and 13-shot magazine. Blued with plastic grips. Introduced in 1986.

NIB	Exc.	V.G.	Good	Fair	Poor
400	300	200	150	100	75

Astra Cadix

A .22 or .38 Special double-action swing-out cylinder revolver with a 4" or 6" barrel and either 9- or 5-shot cylinder. Blued with plastic grips. Manufactured from 1960 to 1968.

NIB	Exc.	V.G.	Good	Fair	Poor
—	225	175	125	90	70

.357 Double-Action Revolver

Similar to Cadix but in .357 Magnum caliber with a 3", 4", 6", or 8.5" barrel, adjustable sights and 6-shot cylinder. Blued or stainless steel with walnut grips. Manufactured from 1972 to 1988. **NOTE:** Stainless steel add 10 percent.

NIB	Exc.	V.G.	Good	Fair	Poor
295	250	175	125	100	75

.44/.45 Double-Action Revolver

As above, in .41 Magnum, .44 Magnum or .45 ACP caliber with 6" or 8.5" barrels and a 6-shot cylinder. Blued or stainless steel with walnut grips. Manufactured from 1980 to 1987. **NOTE:** Stainless steel add 25 percent.

NIB	Exc.	V.G.	Good	Fair	Poor
—	375	325	250	200	100

Terminator

As above, in .44 Special or .44 Magnum with a 2.75" barrel, adjustable sights and 6-shot cylinder. Blued or stainless steel with rubber grips. **NOTE:** Stainless steel add 10 percent.

NIB	Exc.	V.G.	Good	Fair	Poor
—	380	330	255	200	100

Convertible Revolver

Similar to the .357 D/A revolver but accompanied by a cylinder chambered for 9mm Parabellum. Barrel length 3". Blued with walnut grips. Introduced in 1986.

NIB	Exc.	V.G.	Good	Fair	Poor
—	395	325	275	150	100

RECENTLY IMPORTED PISTOLS

Model A-70

This is a lightweight semi-automatic pistol chambered for the 9mm cartridge or .40 S&W cartridge. It is fitted with 3-dot combat sights. The barrel is 3.5" long and the magazine capacity is 8 rounds for 9mm and 7 rounds for the .40 S&W. Black plastic grips and blue finish are standard. Weight is 29 oz. **NOTE:** Add $35 for nickel finish.

NIB	Exc.	V.G.	Good	Fair	Poor
350	275	225	175	150	100

Model A-75

Introduced in 1993 this model features all of the standard features of the Model 70 plus selective double or single trigger action and decocking lever. Chambered for 9mm, .40 S&W, or .45 ACP. Offered in blue or nickel finish and steel or alloy frame in 9mm only. Weight for steel frame in 9mm and .40 S&W is 31 oz., for .45 ACP weight is 34.4 oz. Featherweight 9mm weight is 23.5 oz. **NOTE:** Add $35 for nickel finish.

NIB	Exc.	V.G.	Good	Fair	Poor
375	325	250	200	150	100

Model A-100

This semi-automatic service pistol is chambered for the 9mm Parabellum, .40 S&W, or .45 ACP cartridges. The trigger action is double-action for the first shot, single-action for follow-up shots. Equipped with a decocking lever. The barrel is 3.8" long and the overall length is 7.5". Magazine capacity for the 9mm is 17 rounds, .40 S&W is 13 rounds, while the .45 holds 9 rounds. A blue or nickel finish is standard. Weight is approximately 34 oz. Also available in a featherweight model 9mm at only 26.5 oz. **NOTE:** Add $35 for nickel finish.

NIB	Exc.	V.G.	Good	Fair	Poor
400	350	300	250	200	100

Model A-100 Carry Comp

Similar to the Model A-100 but fitted with a 4.25" barrel and 1" compensator. Blue finish only. Weight is approximately 38 oz. Magazine capacity for 9mm is 17 rounds and for the .40 S&W and .45 ACP 10 rounds.

NIB	Exc.	V.G.	Good	Fair	Poor
475	375	300	250	200	100

ATCSA
Armas de Tiro y Casa
Eibar, Spain

Colt Police Positive Copy

A .38 caliber 6-shot revolver resembling a Colt Police Positive.

NIB	Exc.	V.G.	Good	Fair	Poor
—	250	125	100	60	40

Target Pistol

A .22 caliber single-shot target pistol utilizing a revolver frame.

NIB	Exc.	V.G.	Good	Fair	Poor
—	300	175	125	100	55

AUBREY, A.J.
Meriden, Connecticut

Double-Barrel Shotguns

Good quality doubles made for Sears. Value depends on condition, grade, and model. Prices range between $100 and $1,500.

AUER, B.
Louisville, Kentucky

Pocket Pistol

A .60 caliber percussion pocket pistol with a 4" octagonal barrel and a long tang extending well back along the grip. Browned, silver furniture and a checkered walnut stock. The lock is marked "B. Auer." Produced during the 1850s.

NIB	Exc.	V.G.	Good	Fair	Poor
—	—	1700	700	250	100

AUGUSTA MACHINE WORKS
Augusta, Georgia
1851 Colt Navy Copy

A .36 caliber percussion revolver with an 8" barrel and 6-shot cylinder. Unmarked except for serial numbers with either 6 or 12 stop cylinder slots. Blued with walnut grips. This is a very rare revolver.

NIB	Exc.	V.G.	Good	Fair	Poor
—	—	62500	40000	17500	5000

AUSTIN & HALLECK, INC.
Weston, Missouri; later Provo, Utah
Model 320 LR BLU

An in-line percussion, bolt-action rifle fitted with a 26" half octagon-half round barrel in .50 caliber. Receiver and barrel are blue. Adjustable trigger and receiver drilled and tapped for scope mount. Stock is black synthetic with checkering. Weight is about 7.87 lbs.

NIB	Exc.	V.G.	Good	Fair	Poor
450	375	300	250	200	100

Model 320 S/S

Similar to the above model but fitted with stainless steel barrel and action.

NIB	Exc.	V.G.	Good	Fair	Poor
500	400	300	250	200	100

Model 420 LR Classic

Similar to the Model 320 series but fitted with a standard lightly figured Maple stock in classic configuration. Available in blue or stainless steel. Premium for fancy wood.

NIB	Exc.	V.G.	Good	Fair	Poor
500	425	300	250	200	100

Model 420 LR Monte Carlo

Same as classic series but with Monte Carlo stock and cheekpiece. Premium for fancy wood.

NIB	Exc.	V.G.	Good	Fair	Poor
500	425	300	250	200	100

Mountain Rifle

This is a .50 caliber percussion or flintlock rifle with double-set triggers, 32" octagonal barrel, buckhorn sights, curly Maple stock

and crescent steel buttplate. Weight is approximately 7.5 lbs. Premium for fancy wood.

NIB	Exc.	V.G.	Good	Fair	Poor
500	400	300	250	200	100

AUSTRALIAN AUTOMATIC ARMS LTD.
Tasmania, Australia
SAR

A 5.56mm semi-automatic rifle with a 16.25" or 20" barrel, 5-shot or 20-shot magazine, black plastic stock and fore-end. Imported from 1986 to 1989.

NIB	Exc.	V.G.	Good	Fair	Poor
1200	950	650	350	250	125

SAP

A 10.5" barreled pistol version of the above. Imported from 1986 to 1989.

NIB	Exc.	V.G.	Good	Fair	Poor
1150	900	600	325	250	125

SP

A sporting rifle version of the SAR, fitted with a wood stock and 5-shot magazine. Introduced in 1989.

NIB	Exc.	V.G.	Good	Fair	Poor
975	850	575	300	250	125

AUTAUGA ARMS INC.
Prattville, Alabama
MK II

This is a .32 ACP semi-automatic blowback pistol with a double-action trigger. Barrel length is 2.25". Fixed sights. Overall length 4.25". Weight is about 13.5 oz. Magazine capacity is 6 rounds. Introduced in 1999.

NIB	Exc.	V.G.	Good	Fair	Poor
325	275	225	195	150	100

AUTO MAG
Various Manufacturers

This popular stainless steel semi-automatic pistol was developed by the Sanford Arms Company of Pasadena, California, in the 1960s and was chambered for a special cartridge known as the .44 AMP which had a 240-grain .44 caliber bullet. Production of this arm has been carried out by a number of companies over the past 40 years. It is believed that fewer than 10,000 have been produced by the eight manufacturers involved.

AMT "C" SERIES

There were 100 guns produced in this series. The first 50 were serial numbered with a "C" prefix. The second 50 were serial numbered "LAST 1" through "LAST 50". They were available with a 6.5" vent rib or 10" tapered barrel.

AUTO MAG, INC.
Irwindale, California

In 1998 this company was formed to produce 1,000 Harry Sanford Commemorative pistols. Chambered for .44 AMP cartridge. Each pistol comes in a walnut display case, a special serial number, Harry Sanford's signature and the name Auto Mag on the receiver. The last retail price for the Auto Mag is $2,750.

AUTO MAG CORP.
Pasadena, California

Serial number range A0000 through A3300, made with a 6.5" vent rib barrel, chambered in .44 AMP only.

.44 AMP

NIB	Exc.	V.G.	Good	Fair	Poor
2700	1850	1475	995	600	300

HIGH STANDARD (2)
Hamden, Connecticut

High Standard was the national distributor for Auto Mag in 1974 and 1975. These guns were chambered for the .44 AMP and .357 AMP. HS Cat. #9346 for .44 AMP, #9347 for .357 AMP.

High Standard sold 134 Auto Mags with the "H" prefix. Serial numbers are between H1 and H198, one at H1566 and three between H17219 and H17222. Of these 108 were .44 AMP and 26 were .357 AMP.

High Standard also sold 911 Auto Mags between serial numbers A05278 and A07637. Of these, 777 were .44 AMP and 108 were .357 AMP.

NIB	Exc.	V.G.	Good	Fair	Poor
2200	1900	1350	900	600	300

KENT LOMONT

As pistols made by this maker are essentially prototypes, it is advised that potential purchasers secure a qualified appraisal.

L. E. JURRAS CUSTOM

This custom maker produced a limited number of Auto Mag pistols in 1977. These arms are worth approximately 35-50 percent more than standard production models.

TDE CORP.
El Monte, California

Serial number range A05016 through A08300, 6.5" vent rib barrel standard. Also available in 8" and 10" barrel lengths, chambered for .44 AMP and .357 AMP.

.357 AMP

NIB	Exc.	V.G.	Good	Fair	Poor
1750	1300	900	700	500	300

.44 AMP

NIB	Exc.	V.G.	Good	Fair	Poor
1950	1550	1000	800	600	300

TDE CORP.
North Hollywood, California

Serial number range A3400 through A05015, made with a 6.5" vent rib barrel, chambered in .44 AMP and .357 AMP.

.357 AMP

NIB	Exc.	V.G.	Good	Fair	Poor
2300	1850	1325	900	600	300

.44 AMP

NIB	Exc.	V.G.	Good	Fair	Poor
2150	1700	1250	850	600	300

TDE-OMC

This is known as the solid-bolt or "B" series. The serial number range is B00001 through B00370. Either 6.5" vent rib or 10" tapered barrels are available.

NIB	Exc.	V.G.	Good	Fair	Poor
2550	2100	1600	1000	600	300

AUTO ORDNANCE CORP.

Auto Ordnance makes reproductions of the 1911 Government Model pistol, the Thompson sub-machine gun (semi-auto only) and the M-1 Carbine. Variations of the 1911 are marketed under both the Auto Ordnance and Thompson brand names. In 1999 the company was bought by Kahr Arms and moved from West Hurley, New York to Worcester, Massachusetts.

Auto Ordnance 1911A1

Standard model in .45 ACP with 5-inch barrel, Parkerized finish, fixed sights, plastic or checkered walnut grips. Also offered in 9mm, .38 Super, 10 mm (all discontinued in 1996), and .40 S&W (disc. 1993). Blue, satin nickel and two-tone finish were optional until 2005. In 2011 a 100th Anniversary Model was introduced with appropriate rollmarks. **NOTE:** Add $35 for nickel or two-tone finish, or for 100th Anniversary Model.

NIB	Exc.	V.G.	Good	Fair	Poor
565	525	475	400	300	200

Thompson Model 1911TC

.45 ACP semi-auto with fixed sights and 7+1 capacity. Stainless frame and slide. 5" barrel, 39 oz. Laminate grips.

NIB	Exc.	V.G.	Good	Fair	Poor
650	525	395	300	200	100

Thompson Model 1911CAF

.45 ACP semi-auto with fixed sights and 7+1 capacity. Aluminum frame and stainless slide. 5" barrel, 31.5 oz. Laminate grips.

NIB	Exc.	V.G.	Good	Fair	Poor
650	525	395	300	200	100

Thompson 1911 A1—Standard

A 9mm, .38 Super or .45 caliber copy of the Colt Model 1911 A1. Pistol weighs 39 oz. **NOTE:** For 9mm and .38 Super add $20. The 9mm and .38 Super models were discontinued in 1997.

NIB	Exc.	V.G.	Good	Fair	Poor
475	325	275	200	150	100

Thompson 1911 A1—Parkerized

NIB	Exc.	V.G.	Good	Fair	Poor
475	325	275	200	150	100

Thompson 1911 A1—Deluxe

Same as above but Hi-profile 3 white dot sight system. Black textured, rubber wraparound grips.

NIB	Exc.	V.G.	Good	Fair	Poor
800	650	500	300	150	100

Thompson 1911 A1 Custom High Polish

Introduced in 1997 this model features a special high polish blued finish with numerous special options. Stocks are rosewood with medallion. Fitted with 5" barrel and chambered for .45 ACP. Weight is about 39 oz.

NIB	Exc.	V.G.	Good	Fair	Poor
575	475	—	—	—	—

Thompson 1911 A1—10mm

Same as above but chambered for the 10mm cartridge. Magazine capacity is 8 rounds. Discontinued in 1997.

NIB	Exc.	V.G.	Good	Fair	Poor
700	550	400	250	175	100

Thompson 1911 A1—Duo Tone

Chambered for the .45 ACP, the slide is blued and the frame is satin nickel. Discontinued in 1997.

NIB	Exc.	V.G.	Good	Fair	Poor
500	425	350	225	150	100

Thompson 1911 A1—Satin Nickel

Chambered for .45 ACP or .38 Super the finish is a satin nickel on both frame and slide. Blade front sight and black checkered plastic grips. Discontinued in 1997.

NIB	Exc.	V.G.	Good	Fair	Poor
500	425	350	225	150	100

Thompson 1911 A1—Competition

Chambered for .45 ACP or .38 Super the pistol is fitted with a 5" barrel with compensator and other competition features such as custom Commander hammer, flat mainspring housing, beavertail grip safety, full-length recoil guide rod, extended ejector, slide stop and thumb safety. Pistol weighs 42 oz. and is 10" overall. Discontinued in 1997. **NOTE:** For .38 Super add $10.

NIB	Exc.	V.G.	Good	Fair	Poor
700	625	500	350	300	150

Thompson 1911 A1—Pit Bull

Chambered for .45 ACP and fitted with a 3-1/2" barrel this model has high profile sights and black textured rubber wraparound grips. Magazine capacity is 7 rounds and weight is 36 oz.

NIB	Exc.	V.G.	Good	Fair	Poor
500	425	350	225	150	100

Thompson 1911 A1—General

This is a Commander-size pistol with 4-1/2" barrel, high profile sights. Chambered for .45 ACP or .38 Super. Weighs 37 oz. Discontinued in 1997.

NIB	Exc.	V.G.	Good	Fair	Poor
500	425	350	225	150	100

ZG-51 "Pit Bull"

Same as above, with a 3.5" barrel in .45 caliber. Introduced in 1988 and renamed "PIT BULL" in 1994. Discontinued.

NIB	Exc.	V.G.	Good	Fair	Poor
500	425	350	225	150	100

Thompson 1927 A1 Standard (New York Production)

A semi-automatic version of the Thompson submachine gun, chambered for the .45 ACP cartridge with a 16-1/2" barrel that is 18" with compensator. Blued with walnut stock. Weight is 13 lbs.

NIB	Exc.	V.G.	Good	Fair	Poor
1250	850	650	400	300	150

1927 A1 Deluxe/Model T1

As above, with a finned barrel, adjustable sights, pistol grip forearm, and a 50-round drum magazine costing an additional $250. The violin-shaped carrying case adds approximately $150 to the values listed.

NIB	Exc.	V.G.	Good	Fair	Poor
1350	950	695	400	300	150

1927 A1C/Model T5

As above, with an aluminum alloy receiver. Introduced in 1984.

NIB	Exc.	V.G.	Good	Fair	Poor
1175	825	625	400	300	150

1927 A1 Commando/Model T1-C

Introduced in 1998 this version features a 16.5" finned barrel with compensator. The finish is parkerized with black wood finish. Furnished with 30-round magazine and black nylon sling. Weight is about 13 lbs.

NIB	Exc.	V.G.	Good	Fair	Poor
1250	850	650	400	300	150

1927 A5 Pistol/TA5

A pistol version of the Model 1927 A1 with a 13" finned barrel, aluminum alloy receiver and no shoulder stock. Reintroduced in 2008 with 10-inch barrel as Model TA5. Value of the original model is debatable, with advertised prices higher than those shown here, but few apparent sales. The TA5 version is expected to depress value of original 1927 A5s.

NIB	Exc.	V.G.	Good	Fair	Poor
2200	1300	1000	800	500	150

1927 A3

A .22 caliber variation of the Model 1927 A1 with a 16" barrel and aluminum alloy receiver. No longer in production. Add $500 for drum magazine.

NIB	Exc.	V.G.	Good	Fair	Poor
1350	900	675	550	425	150

T1SB

Short-barreled (10.5" finned and compensated) variant of semi-auto M1. Accepts drum magazines. Requires Form 3. Introduced 2005.

NIB	Exc.	V.G.	Good	Fair	Poor
1500	1150	695	400	300	150

M1SB

Short-barreled (10.5" finned and compensated) variant of semi-auto M1. Does not accept drum magazines. Requires Form 3.

NIB	Exc.	V.G.	Good	Fair	Poor
1500	1150	695	400	300	150

M1 Carbine

Newly manufactured replica of the military M1 carbine chambered in .30 Carbine. Introduced 2005. Birch stock, parkerized finish. **NOTE:** Add 5 percent for walnut stock.

NIB	Exc.	V.G.	Good	Fair	Poor
950	800	650	500	300	125

AUTO POINTER
Yamamoto Co.
Tokyo, Japan

Auto Pointer Shotgun

A 12 or 20 gauge semi-automatic shotgun with 26", 28" or 30" barrels and an aluminum alloy frame. Blued with a checkered walnut stock. Originally imported by Sloan's but no longer available. Clone of Browning A-5.

NIB	Exc.	V.G.	Good	Fair	Poor
—	475	350	250	175	100

AXTELL RIFLE CO.
Riflesmith, Inc.
Sheridan, Montana

#1 Long Range Creedmore

This single-shot rifle is chambered for the .40-50BN, .40-70SS, .40-70BN, .40-90, .45-70, .45-90, and .45-100. Weight is about 10 lbs. Numerous options will affect price.

NIB	Exc.	V.G.	Good	Fair	Poor
4700	3750	3000	2200	1400	300

New Model Sharps 1877

Chambered for the .45-90, .45-100, and the .45-70 cartridges and fitted with a choice of 30" to 34" half round-half octagon barrel with double-set triggers.

NIB	Exc.	V.G.	Good	Fair	Poor
5200	4000	3250	2500	1500	250

#2 Long Range

The Long Range #2 rifle is chambered for all the same calibers as the #1 Long Range Creedmore. Weight is about 10 lbs.

NIB	Exc.	V.G.	Good	Fair	Poor
3900	3000	1900	900	550	300

Lower Sporting Rifle

Chambered for same calibers as above. Weight is between 9 and 12 lbs. depending on barrel options.

NIB	Exc.	V.G.	Good	Fair	Poor
2600	2000	1375	700	400	200

Business Rifle

Same calibers as above. Weight is about 8.5 lbs.

NIB	Exc.	V.G.	Good	Fair	Poor
2400	1800	1275	700	400	200

Overbaugh Schuetzen

Chambered for the .40-50BN and the .40-50 straight. Weight is 11 to 14 lbs. depending on barrel options.

NIB	Exc.	V.G.	Good	Fair	Poor
4400	3500	3000	2200	1400	300

AZPIRI
Eibar, Spain

A Spanish manufacturer of pistols prior to World War II.

Avion

A 6.35mm semi-automatic pistol copied after the Model 1906 Browning. Marked "Pistolet Automatique Avion Brevete" on the slide as well as on each side of the grip plate along with an airplane logo. Manufactured from 1914 to 1918.

Courtesy James Rankin

NIB	Exc.	V.G.	Good	Fair	Poor
—	250	175	100	75	45

Colon

As above, in 6.35mm caliber, marked "Automatic Pistol Colon."

NIB	Exc.	V.G.	Good	Fair	Poor
—	250	175	100	75	45

B

B.R.F.
South Africa

B.R.F.

This is a .25 caliber semi-automatic pistol similar to the P.A.F. with a 2" barrel and 6-shot magazine. "U-SA" means Union of South Africa. Little is known about the manufacturer of this pistol, its origin, or dates of manufacture.

NIB	Exc.	V.G.	Good	Fair	Poor
—	295	195	125	100	70

BABBIT, A. S.
Plattsburgh, New York
See—Adirondack Arms

BABCOCK, MOSES
Charlestown, Massachusetts

Babcock Under Hammer Cane Gun

A .52 caliber percussion cane gun with a 27" barrel and overall length of approximately 33". Folding trigger, under hammer with a wood handle. The hammer is marked "Moses Babcock/Charlestown." Active 1850s and 1860s.

NIB	Exc.	V.G.	Good	Fair	Poor
—	—	2950	950	350	200

BACON ARMS CO.
Norwich, Connecticut

Bacon Arms operated from 1862 until 1891. They have become known primarily for the production of cheaply made, solid-frame, rimfire revolvers known as "Suicide Specials." Bacon manufactured and sold under a number of different trademarks. They were: Bacon, Bonanza, Conqueror, Express, Gem, Governor, Guardian, and Little Giant. Collector interest is low, and values for all trademarks are quite similar.

Courtesy Milwaukee Public Museum, Milwaukee, Wisconsin

NIB	Exc.	V.G.	Good	Fair	Poor
—	295	225	100	75	50

BAER CUSTOM, LES
Hillsdale, Illinois

This long-standing 1911 pistolsmith is now producing custom quality 1911 pistols on a semi-production basis. Each pistol features a large number of custom characteristics such as forged steel frame and full slide recoil rod, double-serrated slide, beveled magazine well, checkered front strap, beavertail safety, extended magazine release button, Bo-Mar sights, and many others depending on the specific model. A representative sampling of these fine Baer pistols appears below.

COMPETITION PISTOLS

Baer 1911 Ultimate Master Combat Pistol-Compensated

Chambered for the .45 ACP and fitted with a triple-port, tapered cone compensator.

NIB	Exc.	V.G.	Good	Fair	Poor
2660	1850	1000	750	600	300

Baer 1911 Ultimate Master Steel Special

Designed for steel targets and Bianchi-style competition this model is similar to above but designed for light loads. Chambered for .38 Super. Hard chrome finish.

NIB	Exc.	V.G.	Good	Fair	Poor
2900	2250	1500	950	750	350

Baer 1911 Ultimate Master Combat Pistol

Similar to the other Baer Master series pistols this model is offered in .45 ACP, .400 Cor-Bon, and .38 Super. It is fitted with a large number of special features. Offered in a 5" or 6" version. The 5" version is also offered in 9x23 caliber.

6" Model

NIB	Exc.	V.G.	Good	Fair	Poor
2600	1950	1350	850	650	350

5" Model

NIB	Exc.	V.G.	Good	Fair	Poor
2670	1920	1425	800	600	350

Baer 1911 Ultimate Master Para

Designed for IPSC competition and offered either in Unlimited version with compensator and scope or Limited version with iron sights and no compensator.

Unlimited Model

.45 ACP, .38 Super, 9x23.

NIB	Exc.	V.G.	Good	Fair	Poor
3400	2700	1750	1200	850	400

Limited Model

NIB	Exc.	V.G.	Good	Fair	Poor
2900	2000	1500	900	650	300

Baer 1911 Bullseye Wadcutter Pistol

Designed for use with wadcutter loads only. Chambered for .45 ACP. **NOTE:** This version is also offered with a Baer Optical mount. Add $125 for this option. For a 6" slide with LoMount BoMar sight add $200.

NIB	Exc.	V.G.	Good	Fair	Poor
1650	1250	800	600	500	250

Baer 1911 National Match Hardball Pistol

Designed for DCM matches. Chambered for .45 ACP.

NIB	Exc.	V.G.	Good	Fair	Poor
1425	1050	700	500	400	200

Baer 1911 Target Master

Designed for NRA centerfire matches. Chambered for .45 ACP.

NIB	Exc.	V.G.	Good	Fair	Poor
1450	1150	750	550	450	250

Baer 1911 IPSC Action Pistol

Chambered for .45 ACP with blued slide and frame.

NIB	Exc.	V.G.	Good	Fair	Poor
1700	1350	850	600	450	300

Baer 1911 P.P.C. Distinguished Match

Introduced in 1999 this pistol features a 5" barrel with an adjustable Aristrocrat rear sight. Many, many special features such as double serrated slide, lowered and flared ejection port, extended ambi safety, checkered front strap, etc. Offered in .45 ACP, and 9mm with supported chamber. Blued finish and one magazine. **NOTE:** Add approximately $400 for 9mm model.

NIB	Exc.	V.G.	Good	Fair	Poor
1950	1450	900	650	475	300

Baer 1911 P.P.C. Open Class

Similar to the model above but fitted with a 6" barrel and slide. Chambered for .45 ACP, and 9mm with supported chamber. Blued finish. Introduced in 1999. **NOTE:** Add approximately $400 for 9mm model.

NIB	Exc.	V.G.	Good	Fair	Poor
2150	1550	950	700	500	350

DUTY & DEFENSE PISTOLS

Baer 1911 Premier II

Designed as a duty or defense pistol this model is chambered for the .45 ACP, .400 CorBon, and 9x23 cartridges. Fitted with a 5" slide. **NOTE:** For stainless steel version add $150 to above prices. Add $100 for .400 CorBon and $250 for 9x23.

NIB	Exc.	V.G.	Good	Fair	Poor
1790	1350	900	600	450	250

Baer 1911 Premier II—6" barrel

Same as above but fitted with a 6" match grade barrel. **NOTE:** Add $100 for .400 CorBon and $300 for .38 Super. 9x23 not offered with 6" slide.

NIB	Exc.	V.G.	Good	Fair	Poor
1990	1600	1100	900	700	350

Baer 1911 Premier II—Light Weight (LW1)

Has the same features as the standard Premier II but with reduced weight aluminum frame. Furnished with low mount LCB adjustable rear sight. Offered in .45 ACP only.

NIB	Exc.	V.G.	Good	Fair	Poor
1900	1550	1100	900	700	350

Baer 1911 Premier II—Light Weight (LW2)

Same as above but with fixed combat-style rear sight.

NIB	Exc.	V.G.	Good	Fair	Poor
1900	1550	1100	900	700	350

Baer 1911 Premier II Super-Tac

Similar to the standard Premier II models but with low mount adjustable rear night sight and front sight. Special BEAR COAT finish. Offered in .45 ACP, .40 S&W, .400 CorBon. **NOTE:** Dual caliber .45 ACP/.400 CorBon combo add $200.

NIB	Exc.	V.G.	Good	Fair	Poor
2280	1700	1200	900	700	350

Baer 1911 Prowler III

Similar to the Premier II but with a tapered cone stub weight, a full-length guide rod, and a reverse plug. Special order only.

NIB	Exc.	V.G.	Good	Fair	Poor
2580	1700	1200	950	700	350

Baer 1911 Prowler IV

Chambered for .45 ACP or .38 Super this model is built on a Para-Ordnance oversize frame. Fitted with a 5" slide. Special order only. **NOTE:** For optional 6" barrel and slide add $300.

NIB	Exc.	V.G.	Good	Fair	Poor
2580	1900	1250	900	650	300

Baer 1911 Custom Carry—Commanche Length

Chambered for .45 ACP this model has several options including 4.5" barrel, stainless steel slide and frame, lightweight aluminum frame with blued steel slide. As of 2000 this model is furnished with night sights. **NOTE:** For stainless steel add $40. For lightweight frame add $130.

NIB	Exc.	V.G.	Good	Fair	Poor
1850	1400	950	600	450	250

Baer 1911 Custom Carry—5"

Same as above but offered with 5" slide. Not offered in aluminum frame. **NOTE:** Add $40 for stainless steel.

NIB	Exc.	V.G.	Good	Fair	Poor
2120	1700	950	600	450	250

Baer 1911 Thunder Ranch Special

This model features a steel frame and slide with front and rear serrations. Deluxe fixed rear sight with tritium insert. Checkered front strap. Numerous special features. Slim line grips with Thunder Ranch logo. Seven-round magazine standard. Special serial numbers with "TR" prefix. Offered in .45 ACP. **NOTE:** Add 10 percent for Comanche length; add 5 percent for home defense model.

NIB	Exc.	V.G.	Good	Fair	Poor
1990	1500	950	600	450	250

Baer 1911 Thunder Ranch Special Engraved Model

As above but with engraved frame and slide.

NIB	Exc.	V.G.	Good	Fair	Poor
6600	4750	2500	1500	1150	650

Baer S.R.P. (Swift Response Pistol)

Chambered for .45 ACP and built on a Para-Ordnance frame this unit is similar to the one supplied to the FBI. Supplied with wooden presentation box. **NOTE:** For S.R.P. models built on a Baer frame or shorter 4.5" frame subtract $300 from NIB through Fair prices.

NIB	Exc.	V.G.	Good	Fair	Poor
2590	2250	1750	1200	850	400

Baer 1911 Monolith

Introduced in 1999 this model features a 5" barrel and slide with extra long dust cover. Chambered in .45 ACP, .400 CorBon, .40 S&W, 9x23, 9mm, or .38 Super all with supported chamber. Many special features such as BoMar sights, Commander-style hammer, speed trigger, etc. Blued finish with one magazine. Weight is approximately 37 oz. **NOTE:** For all other supported calibers add $250.

NIB	Exc.	V.G.	Good	Fair	Poor
1850	1500	950	675	500	325

Baer 1911 Monolith Heavyweight

Introduced in 1999 this model is similar to the Monolith but with the addition of a heavier frame that adds 3.5 oz. Same calibers as available on the Monolith. Weight is approximately 40 oz. **NOTE:** For all other supported calibers add $200.

NIB	Exc.	V.G.	Good	Fair	Poor
1930	1700	1100	775	425	250

Baer 1911 Monolith Tactical Illuminator

This model, introduced in 1999, has the same features as the Monolith Heavyweight above but with the addition of light mounted under the dust cover. Offered in .45 ACP and .40 S&W with supported chamber. Weight with light is approximately 44 oz. **NOTE:** For all other supported calibers add $275.

NIB	Exc.	V.G.	Good	Fair	Poor
1850	1500	1050	795	425	250

Baer 1911 Monolith Commanche

Fitted with a 4.25" slide and a dust cover that covers the length of the slide. Has all the features of the standard Monolith. Comes with night sights and a deluxe fixed rear sight. Edges rounded for tactical carry. Chambered in .45 ACP only. Introduced in 2001.

NIB	Exc.	V.G.	Good	Fair	Poor
1990	1750	1100	650	400	225

Baer 1911 Monolith Commanche Heavyweight

Exactly as above but with thicker dust cover to add an additional 2 oz. of weight. Introduced in 2001.

NIB	Exc.	V.G.	Good	Fair	Poor
2150	1800	1000	600	375	200

Baer 1911 Stinger

This model features a shorter Officer's grip frame and Commanche slide and barrel. Many special features. Offered in .45 ACP. Choice of aluminum frame with blued slide, aluminum frame with stainless steel slide and stainless steel frame and slide. Weight in aluminum is about 28 oz., with stainless steel about 34 oz. Introduced in 1999. **NOTE:** For aluminum frame and blued slide with supported calibers add $300. For aluminum frame with stainless slide and supported chamber add $340. For stainless frame and slide with supported chamber add $140.

NIB	Exc.	V.G.	Good	Fair	Poor
1890	1600	1050	750	400	225

Baer 1911 Stinger Stainless

Same as above but with stainless steel frame and slide. Introduced in 2001.

NIB	Exc.	V.G.	Good	Fair	Poor
1970	1670	1100	775	425	250

NEW CONCEPT PISTOLS

This line of 1911 pistols offers custom features at a slightly lower cost. Each succeeding grade offers a few more features.

Baer 1911 Concept I

Chambered for .45 ACP and fitted with BoMar sights.

NIB	Exc.	V.G.	Good	Fair	Poor
1690	1450	975	750	550	300

Baer 1911 Concept II

Same as above but fitted with Baer adjustable sights.

NIB	Exc.	V.G.	Good	Fair	Poor
1690	1450	975	750	550	300

Baer 1911 Concept III

Same as above but with stainless steel frame with blued steel slide with BoMar sights.

NIB	Exc.	V.G.	Good	Fair	Poor
1950	1890	975	800	550	300

Baer 1911 Concept V 6"

This model is identical to the Concept V with the addition of a 6" barrel and slide. Introduced in 1999.

NIB	Exc.	V.G.	Good	Fair	Poor
1840	1550	975	800	550	300

Baer 1911 Concept IV

Same as above but with Baer adjustable sights.

NIB	Exc.	V.G.	Good	Fair	Poor
2050	1990	1075	900	650	350

Baer 1911 Concept VI

Same as above but fitted with Baer adjustable sights.

NIB	Exc.	V.G.	Good	Fair	Poor
1840	1550	975	800	550	300

Baer 1911 Concept V

This model has both stainless steel slide and frame with BoMar sights.

NIB	Exc.	V.G.	Good	Fair	Poor
2050	1990	1075	900	650	350

Baer 1911 Concept VI L.W.

Same as above but built on aluminum frame with supported chamber and National Match barrel.

NIB	Exc.	V.G.	Good	Fair	Poor
2050	1990	1075	900	650	350

Baer 1911 Concept VII

Features all blued 4.5" steel frame and slide with Baer fixed night sights.

NIB	Exc.	V.G.	Good	Fair	Poor
2050	1990	1075	900	650	350

Baer 1911 Concept VIII

Same as above but with stainless steel slide and frame. Fixed combat night sights standard.

NIB	Exc.	V.G.	Good	Fair	Poor
2100	1850	1500	1250	700	300

Baer 1911 Concept IX

This version has a lightweight aluminum frame with 4.5" steel slide.

NIB	Exc.	V.G.	Good	Fair	Poor
2100	1850	1500	1250	700	300

Baer 1911 Concept X

This model features a 4.5" stainless steel slide with a lightweight aluminum frame.

NIB	Exc.	V.G.	Good	Fair	Poor
2100	1850	1500	1250	700	300

Baer Lightweight .22 caliber 1911 Models
4.5" Model with fixed sights

NIB	Exc.	V.G.	Good	Fair	Poor
1525	1400	950	800	550	300

5" Model with fixed sights

NIB	Exc.	V.G.	Good	Fair	Poor
1625	1400	950	800	550	300

5" Model with Bo-Mar sights

NIB	Exc.	V.G.	Good	Fair	Poor
1700	1475	1000	850	600	300

Baer Limited Edition Presentation Grade 1911

A fully hand engraved Baer 1911 with special bluing in presentation wooden box.

NIB	Exc.	V.G.	Good	Fair	Poor
6590	3995	2500	1750	1150	500

Model 1911 Twenty-Fifth Anniversary

Custom-engraved limited collector edition .45 ACP semi-automatic. Built on fully functional, fully equipped Baer Premier II. Hand engraved, both sides of slide and frame. Les Baer signature. Inlaid with white gold. Ivory grips. Deep blue finish. Presentation box. Introduced 2006.

NIB	Exc.	V.G.	Good	Fair	Poor
6590	3995	2500	1750	1150	500

Ultimate Recon

Semi-automatic with integral Picatinny rail, 5" barrel, .45 ACP. Blue or chrome. Comes with SureFire X-200 light. Fixed sights. 4-pound trigger. Two 8-round magazines. Cocobolo grips. Add $500 for hard chrome.

NIB	Exc.	V.G.	Good	Fair	Poor
3070	2590	1650	1100	775	450

RIFLES

AR .223 Ultimate Super Varmint

Fitted with a choice of 18", 20", or 24" heavy barrels with 1-in-12 twist. Flat top rail. Choice of single or two-stage trigger. Aluminum free-floating handguard. Bear Coat finish. Introduced in 2000.

NIB	Exc.	V.G.	Good	Fair	Poor
1975	1600	1300	900	600	300

AR .223 Ultimate Super Match

Introduced in 2002 this model features a wide number of custom features with barrel lengths from 18" to 24". Special match carrier with integral rail system.

NIB	Exc.	V.G.	Good	Fair	Poor
2125	1700	1400	1000	750	500

AR .223 M4-A2 Flattop

This model features a flat top rail and match bolt and carrier. The 16" barrel has a integral compensator. Single-stage trigger. Knights Armament Systems rail adapter. Bear Coat finish. Introduced in 2000.

NIB	Exc.	V.G.	Good	Fair	Poor
2175	1725	1425	1025	675	400

AR .223 IPSC Action Model

Similar to the model above but with 18" Super Match heavy barrel with integral compensator. Introduced in 2000.

NIB	Exc.	V.G.	Good	Fair	Poor
2300	1875	1550	1100	700	450

AR .223 Ultimate NRA Match

This model features numerous custom features and is fitted with a 30" barrel, special front and rear sights. **NOTE:** Add $750 for special sight package.

NIB	Exc.	V.G.	Good	Fair	Poor
2500	2000	1350	900	600	375

Bullpup Muzzleloader

This .50 caliber muzzleloader is fitted with a 28" stainless steel barrel with a Williams front sight and M16 National Match rear sight. Maple or synthetic stock. Internal ignition system. Discontinued. **NOTE:** Add $30 for maple stock and stainless steel.

NIB	Exc.	V.G.	Good	Fair	Poor
750	575	395	300	225	165

Thunder Ranch Rifle

This .223 model is fitted with a bench-rest 16" barrel. Upper receiver has a carry handle and a top rail. Free-floating handguard, jewel two-stage trigger, floating front sight, and many other custom features. "Thunder Ranch" logo stamped on lower receiver. Weight is about 7.5 lbs. Introduced in 2004.

NIB	Exc.	V.G.	Good	Fair	Poor
2500	2000	1350	900	600	375

Monolith .308 S.W.A.T.

Military type match sniper rifle chambered in .308 Winchester. Solid full-length Picatinny rail for scope mounting. DuPont-S coating on barrel, two-stage trigger group with choice of 18, 20 (standard) or 24" barrel. Two magazines and soft case included. Introduced in 2011.

NIB	Exc.	V.G.	Good	Fair	Poor
3500	3000	2600	2000	1000	500

BAFORD ARMS, INC.
Bristol, Tennessee

Thunder Derringer

A .410 bore or .44 Special single-shot pistol with 3" interchangeable barrels and a spur trigger. Additional interchangeable barrels are chambered in calibers from .22 to 9mm. Also available with a scope. Blued with a walnut grip. Introduced in 1988. **NOTE:** Add $50 for interchangeable barrel.

NIB	Exc.	V.G.	Good	Fair	Poor
175	110	85	70	55	35

Fire Power Model 35

A 9mm semi-automatic pistol with a 4.75" barrel, Millett adjustable sights and 14-shot magazine. Fitted with a combat safety and hammer, and Pachmayr grips. Stainless steel. Introduced in 1988.

NIB	Exc.	V.G.	Good	Fair	Poor
550	450	365	300	250	125

BAIKAL
Izhevsk, Russia

Baikal is a Russian firearms manufacturer with a history that goes back to World War II when it made military weapons like the Tokarev pistols for the old Soviet Union. After the war, the company expanded into sporting firearms, mainly shotguns.

Baikal IJ-27E1C

A 12 or 20 gauge Magnum over/under shotgun with 26" Skeet-Skeet or 28" Modified-Full ventilated rib barrels, single-selective trigger and extractors. Blued with a walnut stock.

NIB	Exc.	V.G.	Good	Fair	Poor
375	275	200	150	100	75

Baikal TOZ - 34

A 12 or 28 gauge double-barrel shotgun with 26" or 28" barrels, double triggers, cocking indicators and extractors. Blued with a checkered walnut stock. This model was also available with a silver-plated receiver.

NIB	Exc.	V.G.	Good	Fair	Poor
400	300	250	200	100	75

Model MC-8-0

A 12 gauge double-barrel shotgun with 26" Skeet-Skeet or 28 Full-Modified barrels, hand fitted action and engraved receiver.

NIB	Exc.	V.G.	Good	Fair	Poor
2000	1250	950	700	500	250

Model MC-5-105

The Model TOZ-34 with an engraved receiver.

NIB	Exc.	V.G.	Good	Fair	Poor
1200	850	700	500	300	150

Model MC-7

As above, with a relief engraved receiver.

NIB	Exc.	V.G.	Good	Fair	Poor
2250	1750	1200	800	550	250

IZH18/MP18

This is a single-barrel shotgun chambered for 12, 20, or .410 bore. Choice of 26.5" or 29.5" barrels. Hardwood stock. Ejectors. Introduced in 1999.

NIB	Exc.	V.G.	Good	Fair	Poor
95	75	50	35	25	10

IZK18MAX

Similar to the above model but with polished nickel receiver, vent rib, walnut stock, screw-in chokes, and ejectors. Offered in 12 and 20 gauge as well as .410 bore.

NIB	Exc.	V.G.	Good	Fair	Poor
170	125	100	75	50	25

IZH43

This side-by-side gun is available in 12, 16, 20, 28, and .410 bore. In barrel lengths for 20" to 28" depending on gauge. Internal hammers. Single-selective trigger, ejectors. Walnut stock. **NOTE:** Add $80 for 28 gauge and .410 bore guns.

NIB	Exc.	V.G.	Good	Fair	Poor
350	275	200	150	100	75

IZH43K

Introduced in 1999 this is a 12 or 20 gauge 3" side-by-side external hammer gun with choice of barrel lengths of 18.5", 20", 24", 26", and 28". Single-selective trigger or double trigger. Engraved side plates. Walnut stock with pistol grip. Weight is about 7.3 lbs. **NOTE:** Deduct $40 for double triggers.

NIB	Exc.	V.G.	Good	Fair	Poor
375	300	250	175	125	100

MP213 Coach Gun

Similar to the above model but with internal hammers. Single or double triggers. Weight is about 7 lbs. Barrel inserts for .45-70 were offered. **NOTE:** Add 25 percent for .45-70 inserts.

NIB	Exc.	V.G.	Good	Fair	Poor
650	500	400	350	100	75

IZH27

This is an over/under gun chambered for 12, 20, 28, and .410 bore. Choice of 26.5" or 28.5" barrels. Walnut stock. Single trigger with ejectors. Fixed chokes. **NOTE:** Add $35 for screw-in chokes. Add $85 for 28 gauge and .410 bore guns.

NIB	Exc.	V.G.	Good	Fair	Poor
350	275	200	150	100	75

MP233

This over/under gun is chambered for the 12 gauge 3" shell with a choice of 26", 28", or 30" barrels. Walnut checkered stock. Single or double triggers. Screw-in chokes. Removable trigger assembly. Weight is about 7.3 lbs. Introduced in 1999.

NIB	Exc.	V.G.	Good	Fair	Poor
700	600	500	400	175	100

IZH94/MP94

This is an over/under combination gun with a 12 gauge upper barrel and centerfire rifle barrel on the under barrel. Barrel length is 24" or 26". This model is offered as an over/under rifle in calibers .222, .223, 6.5x55, .308, .30-06, or 7.62x39. A .410/.22LR or .410/.22 WMR model is available. Walnut stock single or double trigger. Weight is about 8 - 10 lbs. Open sights. **NOTE:** Deduct 40 percent for .410.

NIB	Exc.	V.G.	Good	Fair	Poor
525	475	425	350	300	175

IZH81

This is a pump-action shotgun chambered for 12 gauge 3" shells. Barrel lengths are a choice of 20", 26", or 28". Five-round detachable magazine. Walnut stock. **NOTE:** Add $60 for vent rib.

NIB	Exc.	V.G.	Good	Fair	Poor
300	225	165	125	97	50

MP131K

This is a pump-action shotgun with a choice of two different feeding sources: a tubular magazine or a detachable 3-round or 5-round box magazine.

NIB	Exc.	V.G.	Good	Fair	Poor
300	225	165	125	97	50

MP133

This is a slide-action shotgun chambered for the 12 gauge 3.5" shell. Available with barrel lengths of 20", 24", 26", or 28". Vent rib or all barrel lengths except 20". Walnut stock. Choke tubes for all barrel lengths except 20" (Cylinder choke). Introduced in 2001.

NIB	Exc.	V.G.	Good	Fair	Poor
300	225	165	125	95	50

MP153

This is a semi-automatic shotgun chambered for 12 gauge 3" shell. Choice of 26" or 28" barrels. Choice of walnut or black synthetic stock. Weight is about 7.8 lbs. Screw-in chokes. Introduced in 1999.

NIB	Exc.	V.G.	Good	Fair	Poor
400	325	250	200	100	65

IZH35

This is a semi-automatic pistol chambered for the .22 LR cartridge. Fully adjustable target grip, adjustable trigger assembly, cocking indicator, detachable scope. Fitted with a 6" barrel. Introduced in 2000.

NIB	Exc.	V.G.	Good	Fair	Poor
500	400	350	200	165	95

MP310

Originally imported as the Model IZH2, this over/under is now marketed as the MP310. Offered in 12 gauge, 20 gauge or .410 bore with 26" or 28" barrels. Hammer forged barrels, machined steel receiver and monoblock, checkered walnut two-piece stock. Hard chrome-lined barrels, ventilated rib, ejectors, auto safety and single selective trigger.

NIB	Exc.	V.G.	Good	Fair	Poor
475	425	350	300	250	200

MP220

This side-by-side field gun has single selective trigger, ejectors, machined steel boxlock receiver, checkered walnut stock with recoil pad, splinter fore-end, automatic tang safety and screw-in chokes. In 12, 16, 20, 28 gauge and .410 bore. Weight is 8 to 10 lbs.

NIB	Exc.	V.G.	Good	Fair	Poor
300	250	200	175	150	100

CURRENTLY IMPORTED BAIKAL SHOTGUNS

Importer—European American Armory

A custom-made O/U shotgun with detachable sidelocks. Produced in limited quantities and most often to the purchaser's specifications.

BAILONS GUNMAKERS, LTD.
Birmingham, England

Most of the products of this company are produced strictly on custom order.

Hunting Rifle

A bolt-action sporting rifle produced in a variety of calibers with a 24" barrel, open sights, double-set triggers and a 3- or 4-shot magazine. Blued with a well-figured walnut stock. The values listed are for a standard grade rifle.

NIB	Exc.	V.G.	Good	Fair	Poor
3500	2950	2450	1900	675	325

BAKER GAS SEAL
London, England

A .577 caliber percussion revolver with a 6.5" octagonal barrel and 6-shot cylinder. When the hammer is cocked, the cylinder is forced forward tightly against the barrel breech, thus creating a gas seal. Blued, case hardened with walnut grips.

NIB	Exc.	V.G.	Good	Fair	Poor
—	2500	1900	1500	875	350

BAKER GUN & FORGING CO.
Batavia, New York

The Baker Gun & Forging Company was founded in early 1890, by Elias Baker, brother of William Baker. Made from drop forged parts, Baker single and double barrel shotguns quickly gained a reputation for strength and reliability among shooters of the period. Offered in a wide variety of grades, from plain utilitarian to heavily embellished models, Baker shotguns have in recent years become highly collectible. The company was sold on December 24, 1919, to H. & D. Folsom Arms Company of Norwich, Connecticut. The Folsom Company had for almost 20 years been the Baker Company's sole New York City agent and had marketed at least one Baker model that was only made for them. From 1919 to approximately 1923, Folsom continued to assemble and make Baker shotguns. Late model Bakers were made by the Crescent Firearms Company and have serial numbers with an "F" suffix.

The Baker Gun & Forging Company was the first American arms manufacturer to:
1. Make a single barrel trap shotgun.
2. Make a single barrel trap shotgun with a ventilated rib.
3. Make arms with an intercepting firing pin block safety.
4. Make a double barrel shotgun with hammers directly behind the firing pins.
5. Use a long swinging sear that once adjusted gave consistent trigger pull throughout the working life of an arm.

Those Baker shotguns manufactured between 1913 and 1923 that were engraved by Rudolph J. Kornbrath command substantial price premiums over the values listed.

Baker Trap Gun

A 12 gauge single barrel boxlock shotgun with either a 30" or 32" barrel. Blued, case hardened with a walnut stock.

NIB	Exc.	V.G.	Good	Fair	Poor
—	1800	1450	1050	500	250

Elite Grade

Standard scrollwork and simple game scenes engraved on receiver.

NIB	Exc.	V.G.	Good	Fair	Poor
—	2800	2400	1500	1000	600

Superba

Heavily engraved on receiver and sides of barrel breech.

NIB	Exc.	V.G.	Good	Fair	Poor
—	4500	3300	1800	1200	1000

Expert Grade Double Shotgun

The highest grade shotgun manufactured by the Baker Gun & Forging Company. General specifications as above. The stock of imported English or French walnut. The engraving of full coverage type and partially chiselled. Automatic ejectors and single trigger if requested. Built on special order only.

NIB	Exc.	V.G.	Good	Fair	Poor
—	7000	5500	4000	1800	750

Deluxe Grade Double Shotgun

The designation given those Expert Grade shotguns produced by H. & D. Folsom from 1919 to 1923. Characteristics identical to those listed for the Baker Expert Grade Double Shotgun. Add 80 percent for this model. Very rare.

Black Beauty Double Shotgun

Made solely for H. & D. Folsom Arms Company. A 12 or 16 gauge double barrel shotgun with sidelocks and 26", 28", 30", or 32" barrels in 12 gauge and 26", 28", or 30" barrels in 16 gauge. The barrels are blued, the receiver is case hardened, the sideplates are finished with black oxide and the stock is walnut. Automatic ejectors and single trigger are extra cost options.

NIB	Exc.	V.G.	Good	Fair	Poor
—	1150	1000	850	700	250

Grade S Double Shotgun

As above, with simple engraving.

NIB	Exc.	V.G.	Good	Fair	Poor
—	1550	1250	950	500	250

Grade R Double Shotgun

As above, with case hardened sideplates and engraved with simple scrollwork and game scenes.

NIB	Exc.	V.G.	Good	Fair	Poor
—	1950	1500	1100	600	300

Paragon Grade Shotgun

As above, with finely cut scrollwork and detailed game scenes engraved on the sideplates. The stock of finely figured walnut.

NIB	Exc.	V.G.	Good	Fair	Poor
—	4000	3000	2200	1000	500

Paragon Grade—Model NN

As above, but more finely engraved. Built on special order only. Automatic ejectors.

NIB	Exc.	V.G.	Good	Fair	Poor
—	4500	3500	2700	2000	800

Batavia Special

A 12 or 16 gauge double barrel shotgun with sidelocks and 28", 30", or 32" barrels in 12 gauge and 28" or 30" barrels in 16 gauge. Blued, case hardened with a walnut stock and double triggers.

NIB	Exc.	V.G.	Good	Fair	Poor
—	850	550	450	225	175

Batavia Brush Gun

A 12 or 16 gauge double barrel shotgun with sidelocks and 26" barrels. Blued, case hardened with walnut stock. Sling rings and swivels optional.

NIB	Exc.	V.G.	Good	Fair	Poor
—	750	600	550	225	175

Batavia Leader

A 12 or 16 gauge double barrel shotgun with sidelocks and 26", 28", 30", or 32" barrels in 12 gauge and 26", 28", or 30" barrels in 16 gauge. Blued, case hardened with a walnut stock and double triggers.

NIB	Exc.	V.G.	Good	Fair	Poor
—	1500	1000	600	400	200

Batavia Damascus

As above with Damascus barrels.

NIB	Exc.	V.G.	Good	Fair	Poor
—	1750	1200	600	225	175

Baker Hammer Gun

A 10, 12, or 16 gauge double barrel shotgun with sidehammers and 30" and 32" barrels in 10 gauge, 26" to 32" barrels in 12 gauge and 26" to 30" barrels in 16 gauge. Browned, case hardened with walnut stock and double triggers.

NIB	Exc.	V.G.	Good	Fair	Poor
—	450	350	275	195	100

Batavia Automatic Rifle

A .22 caliber semi-automatic rifle with a 24" round barrel and a detachable 7-shot magazine. Blued with a walnut stock.

NIB	Exc.	V.G.	Good	Fair	Poor
—	625	550	300	160	70

BAKER, M.A.
Fayetteville, North Carolina

In business from 1857 through 1862, Baker produced sporting arms prior to the Civil War. During the Civil War Baker altered muskets and "common rifles". In addition, it is thought that Baker made rifles for the State of North Carolina with lockplates stamped "M.A. Baker/Fayetteville/N.C.". These rifles resembled the U.S. Model 1841 Rifle and had these characteristics: Overall length 51.5"; Barrel length 35-1/8; Caliber .50.

NIB	Exc.	V.G.	Good	Fair	Poor
—	—	26000	13500	3200	1500

BAKER, THOMAS

Baker shotguns and rifles were extensively imported into the United States during the nineteenth and early twentieth centuries. His premises were as follows:

1 Stonecutter Street	1838-1844
Bury Street, St. James	1844-1850
34 St. James Street	1850
88 Fleet Street	1851-1881
88 Fleet Street & 21 Cockspur Street	1882-1898
88 Fleet Street & 29 Glasshouse Street	1899-1905
29 Glasshouse Street	1905-1915
64 Haymarket	1915

BAKER, WILLIAM
Marathon, Syracuse and Ithaca, New York

William Baker designed and built double barrel shotguns from approximately 1869 until his death in 1889. His hammerless designs were used by the Baker Gun & Forging Company of Batavia, New York, which was established by his brother Elias in early 1890.

BALL REPEATING CARBINE
Lamson & Co.
Windsor, Vermont

Ball Repeating Carbine

A .50 caliber lever-action repeating carbine with a 20.5" round barrel and 7-shot magazine. The receiver is marked "E.G. Lamson & Co./Windsor, Vt./U.S./Ball's Patent/June 23, 1863/Mar. 15, 1864". Blued, case hardened with a walnut stock. Late production examples of this carbine have been noted with browned or bright barrels. In excess of 1,500 were made between 1864 and 1867.

Courtesy Milwaukee Public Museum, Milwaukee, Wisconsin

NIB	Exc.	V.G.	Good	Fair	Poor
—	—	5500	3000	1100	500

BALLARD PATENT ARMS
(until 1873; after 1875, see MARLIN)

On Nov. 5, 1861, C.H. Ballard of Worcester, Massachusetts, received a patent for a breechloading mechanism that would remain in production for nearly thirty years. Ballard patented a breechblock that tilted down at its front to expose the breech by activating the lever/triggerguard. During the twelve years that followed, Ballard rifles, carbines, and shotguns were produced by five interrelated companies. Four of these were successive: Ball & Williams, R. Ball & Co. (both of Worcester,

Massachusetts), Merrimack Arms & Manufacturing Co. and Brown Manufacturing Company (both of Newburyport, Massachusetts). These four companies produced Ballard arms in a successive serial range (1 through approximately 22,000), all marked upon the top of the frame and the top of the barrel where it joins the frame. In 1863, another company, Dwight, Chapin & Company of Bridgeport, Connecticut, also produced Ballard rifles and carbines in a larger frame size, but in a different serial range (1 through about 1,900), usually marked on the left side of the frame below the agents' mark. The large frame carbines and rifles were produced to fulfill a U.S. War Department contract initially for 10,000 of each, subsequently reduced to 1,000 of each, issued to Merwin & Bray, the sole agents for the Ballard patent arms between 1862 and 1866. Most of the production during this period concentrated on military contracts, either for the U.S. War Department or the state of Kentucky, although the state of New York also purchased 500 for its state militia.

Ballard (Ball & Williams) Sporting Rifles, First Type (Serial numbers 1-100)

Barrel length 24"; caliber .38 rimfire. Markings: "BALL & WILLIAMS/ Worcester, Mass.", and BALLARD'S PATENT/Nov. 5, 1861" on octagonal barrel. The distinctive feature of the earliest production of the Ballard rifles is the presence of an internal extractor conforming to the patent specifications. After approximately 100 rifles, this feature was dropped in favor of a manual extractor located under the barrel.

Courtesy Milwaukee Public Museum, Milwaukee, Wisconsin

NIB	Exc.	V.G.	Good	Fair	Poor
—	—	5000	3000	1250	500

Ballard (Ball & Williams) Sporting Rifles, Second Type (Serial numbers 200-1600, and 1600-14,000, interspersed with martial production)

Barrel length 24", 28", or 30", usually octagonal, but part round/ part octagonal as well; calibers .32, .38, and .44 rimfire. Markings: "BALL & WILLIAMS/Worcester, Mass.", "BALLARD'S PATENT/ Nov. 5, 1861", and "MERWIN & BRAY, AGT'S/ NEW YORK", on facets of barrel until about serial no. 9000, thereafter the patent name and date on the right side of the frame and the manufacturer and agents on the left side of the frame. On early production (200 to 1500), the extractor knob is smaller and crescent shaped. Early production (prior to about serial no. 10,000) have solid breechblocks; after that number breechblocks are made in two halves. A few of these arms were made with bronze frames to facilitate engraving and plating. These should command a higher premium.

NIB	Exc.	V.G.	Good	Fair	Poor
—	—	2000	1650	730	280

Ballard (Ball & Williams) Sporting Rifles, Third Type (Serial numbers 14,000-15,000)

These arms are essentially the same as the second type in characteristics but have Merwin & Bray's alternate percussion mechanism built into the breechblock. The hammer is accordingly marked on the left side "PATENTED JAN. 5, 1864".

NIB	Exc.	V.G.	Good	Fair	Poor
—	—	1400	1100	550	225

Ballard (Ball & Williams) Military Carbines (Serial numbers 1500-7500, and 8500-10500)

Overall length 37.25"; barrel (bore) length 22"; caliber .44 rimfire. Markings: same as Ballard/Ball & Williams sporting rifles, second type. Additional marks on U.S. War Department purchases include inspector's initials "MM" or "GH" on left side of frame, and "MM" on barrel, breechblock, buttplate, and on left side of buttstock in script within an oval cartouche. Three thousand of the earlier production (serial numbers 1700 through about 5000) of these carbines were sold to the state of Kentucky under an August 1862 contract, extended in April 1863. In November 1863, Kentucky contracted for an additional 1,000 carbines. In the interim, the state of New York purchased 500 for distribution to its militia. The U.S. War Department ordered 5,000 under a contract signed in January of 1864, but Ball & Williams delivered only 1,500 (serial numbers noted in range of 9800 through 10600) while concentrating production on their more lucrative Kentucky contract. Another 600 of the federal contract were partially inspected (serial numbers about 6500 to 7100-MM in cartouche in stock only) but were rejected because the barrels had been rifled prior to proofing; these were sold to Kentucky in September 1864 on an open market purchase. The carbines marked with federal inspection marks usually bring a premium.

Courtesy Milwaukee Public Museum, Milwaukee, Wisconsin

NIB	Exc.	V.G.	Good	Fair	Poor
—	—	5775	4150	1750	675

Ballard (Ball & Williams) "Kentucky" Half-Stock Rifles

Overall length 45-3/8"; barrel (bore) length 30"; caliber .44 rimfire. These half-stock rifles bear the standard Ball & Williams markings upon their barrels and in addition have the state ownership mark "KENTUCKY" on the barrel forward of the rear sights. A total of 1,000 (serial numbers about 7100 through 8550) were contracted for by Kentucky in November 1863 and delivered between January and April 1864.

Courtesy Milwaukee Public Museum, Milwaukee, Wisconsin

NIB	Exc.	V.G.	Good	Fair	Poor
—	—	2300	1900	800	350

Ballard (Ball & Williams) "Kentucky" Full-Stock Rifles

Overall length 45.25"; barrel (bore) length 30"; caliber .46 rimfire. Marked on the frame with standard Ball & Williams manufacturer (left), agent (left), and patent (right) markings, these rifles are additionally distinguished by the state ownership mark "KENTUCKY" stamped into the top of the frame near the breech. Kentucky contracted for 3,000 of these arms in November 1863, initially in .56 caliber. However, by mutual consent of the state and the contractors, in February 1864 the caliber of the arms was changed to .46. All deliveries were made in this caliber, beginning in July 1864 and continuing until March 1865 (serial numbers 10,400 to 14,500).

Courtesy Milwaukee Public Museum, Milwaukee, Wisconsin

NIB	Exc.	V.G.	Good	Fair	Poor
—	—	2100	1750	620	295

Ballard (Dwight, Chapin & Co.) Carbines

Overall length 37.75"; barrel (bore) length 22"; caliber .56 rimfire. Markings: On left side of round-topped frame "BALLARD'S PATENT/NOV. 5 1861"; on right side of frame "DWIGHT, CHAPIN & CO./BRIDGEPORT CONN." (through serial no. about 125, deleted after that number) over "MERWIN & BRAY/AGT'S

N.Y." over serial no. Inspection letters "D" frequently appear on carbines with the Dwight, Chapin, & Co. markings, indicative of preliminary inspection by E. M. Dustin, of the U.S. Ordnance Department. Often mistaken as early Ballard production from a fictitious Fall River, Massachusetts, factory, these carbines and their complementing rifles were in fact not placed into production until 1863, as evident by the split, two-piece breechblocks. Both carbines and rifles originated from a contract entered into between the U.S. War Department and Merwin & Bray in October 1862 for 10,000 of each arm, subsequently reduced to 1,000 of each by the Commission on Ordnance and Ordnance Stores. Because Ball & Williams facilities were tied up with Kentucky contracts, Merwin & Bray turned to the small parts maker of Dwight, Chapin & Co. in Bridgeport, Connecticut. Although they tooled for production, they fell short of scheduled delivery dates, and although about 100 carbines had been inspected, no deliveries were accepted (due to caliber problems) by the U.S. government, effectively bankrupting Dwight, Chapin & Co. The completed carbines and unfinished parts were sent to Worcester and assembled by Ball & Williams, and Merwin & Bray sold all 1,000 carbines in Kentucky in April 1864 on an open market purchase.

Courtesy Milwaukee Public Museum, Milwaukee, Wisconsin

NIB	Exc.	V.G.	Good	Fair	Poor
—	—	2450	2000	825	350

Ballard (Dwight, Chapin & Co.) Full-Stock Rifles

Overall length 53"; barrel (bore) length 30"; caliber .56 rimfire. Markings: same as Dwight, Chapin & Co. carbines, but none found with "DWIGHT, CHAPIN & CO./BRIDGEPORT, CONN." stamping above agents marks. The history of these rifles is the same as the .56 caliber carbines, with serial numbers interspersed in the production of the carbines (1 through 1850). Evidently only about 650 of the rifles were completed of the 1,000 set up. Of these, 35 were sold to a U.S. agent in Florida in February 1864 and 600 to Kentucky in April 1864 with the 1,000 carbines.

NIB	Exc.	V.G.	Good	Fair	Poor
—	—	2450	2000	825	350

Ballard (R. Ball & Co.) Sporting Rifles

Overall length varies according to barrel length; barrel (bore) length usually 24", 28", and 30"; calibers .32, .38, .44, and .46 rimfire. Markings: The frame markings of R. Ball & Co. rifles are similar to Ball & Williams production, only eliminating the Ball & Williams marking on the left side. Cartridge size, e.g. "No. 44", usually also stamped upon the top of the barrel or frame. Merwin & Bray's patented alternate ignition device usually present with left side of hammer usually marked "PATENTED JAN. 5, 1864". Serial numbers (which follow in sequence with Ball & Williams production. i.e. after no. about 15,800) appear on top of barrel and top of frame. After William Williams withdrew from the Ball & Williams partnership in mid-1865, the business continued under the name of R. Ball & Co., with Richard Ball's son-in-law, E.J. Halstead, in charge after the former's paralytic stroke in the fall of 1865.

Courtesy Rock Island Auction Company

NIB	Exc.	V.G.	Good	Fair	Poor
—	—	2650	2200	975	400

Ballard (R. Ball & Co.) Carbines

Overall length 37.25"; barrel (bore) length 22" caliber .44 rimfire. Markings: same as R. Ball & Co. sporting rifles; "No. 44" on top of frame near breech. Although firm evidence is elusive, approximately 1,000 of these carbines were manufactured in anticipation of a Canadian contract, which never came to fruition. Serial numbers are interspersed with sporting rifles, in the 16,400 through 17,700 range. All are equipped with the Merwin & Bray dual ignition block.

NIB	Exc.	V.G.	Good	Fair	Poor
—	—	1825	1500	580	225

Ballard (Merrimack Arms & Manufacturing Co.) Sporting Rifles

Overall length varies with barrel length; usual barrel lengths 24", 28", 30"; calibers .22, .32, .44, .46, .50 rimfire. Markings: Left side of frame marked with both manufacturing and patent marks, "MERRIMACK ARMS & MFG. CO./NEWBURYPORT, MASS." over "BALLARD'S PATENT/ NOV. 5, 1861". Caliber usually marked on top of barrel or frame, e.g. "No. 38" together with serial no. Left side of hammer marked "PATENTED JAN. 5, 1864" if breech fitted with Merwin & Bray's alternate ignition device. In the spring of 1866, Edward Bray of Brooklyn, New York, and former partner of Joseph Merwin purchased the Ballard machinery from R. Ball & Co. and set up a new plant in Newburyport, Massachusetts, primarily for the production of sporting rifles. The glut of surplus arms on the market following the American Civil War, however, forced him into bankruptcy in early 1869, after producing only about 2,000 Ballard rifles, carbines and a limited number of 20 gauge shotguns. Serial numbers continue in the sequence of the Ball & Williams/R. Ball & Co. production (serial numbers about 18,000 through 20,300). Prices of these rifles will vary considerably depending on the degree of finish or engraving.

NIB	Exc.	V.G.	Good	Fair	Poor
—	—	2200	1900	775	350

Ballard (Merrimack Arms & Manufacturing Co.) Carbines

Overall length 37.25"; barrel (bore) length 22"; caliber .44 rimfire. Markings: same as Merrimack Arms & Mfg. Co. sporting rifles. In March 1866, the state of New York purchased 100 Ballard carbines (serial numbers about 18,500 to 18,600) for use by its prison guards. In January 1870, an additional 70 (serial numbers 19,400 to 19,500) were purchased from New York City arms merchants Merwin, Hulbert & Co. to arm guards at Sing Sing Prison. Between these two purchases Merrimack Arms & Mfg. Co. had shortened its new "tangless" frames by 1/8", the prime distinction between the two purchases. Despite the rarity of both types of carbines, they do not command high prices.

NIB	Exc.	V.G.	Good	Fair	Poor
—	—	1750	1400	550	300

Ballard (Brown Mfg. Co.) Sporting Rifles

Dimensions: same as Merrimack Arms & Mfg. Co. sporting rifles. Markings: left side of frame marked with manufacturer, "BROWN MFG. CO. NEWBURYPORT, MASS." Over patent, "BALLARD'S PATENT/ NOV. 5, 1861". Serial no. on top of barrel and frame. Upon the failure of Merrimack Arms & Manufacturing Company in early 1869, the plant was purchased by John Hamilton Brown, who continued producing Ballard patent rifles until 1873 in a serial range consecutive with that of its three predecessors (Ball & Williams, R. Ball & Co., and Merrimack Arms & Mfg. Co.). Approximately 2,000 Ballard arms were produced during the period of Brown's manufacture of the Ballard (serial numbers about 20,325 through 22,100). Brown-made Ballards tend to exhibit finer finishing than earlier produced rifles, accounting for their average higher value. Special features, such as breakdown facility and side extractors (on .22 cal. rifles) will also positively affect the prices.

Courtesy Rock Island Auction Company

NIB	Exc.	V.G.	Good	Fair	Poor
—	—	2200	1825	675	350

Ballard (Brown Mfg. Co.) Full-Stock Military Rifles

Overall length 52.5" barrel (bore) length 30"; caliber .46 rimfire. Markings: The same as Brown Mfg. Co. sporting rifles, with the addition of the caliber marking, "No. 46", on the top of the barrel forward of the rear sight. The cause for the production of the Ballard/Brown military rifle has yet to be determined, but it has been speculated that they were possibly manufactured in anticipation of a sale to France during the Franco-Prussian War. In any event, the sale was not culminated, and many, if not most, of the estimated 1,000 produced were "sporterized" by shortening the forestock and sold by commercial dealers in the United States. Serial numbers concentrate in the 20,500 through 21,600 range, with sporting rifles interspersed in the sequence. Rifles that have not been sporterized command a premium.

NIB	Exc.	V.G.	Good	Fair	Poor
—	—	2350	1950	800	350

BALLARD RIFLE AND CARTRIDGE CO.
Onsted, Michigan

All models feature American black walnut stocks, case hardening, and rust blued barrels. There are a number of special order features that are available with these rifles.

No. 1½ Hunter's Rifle

This model features a 30" round barrel, single trigger, S lever, plain forend, and rifle buttstock. Blade front sight and Rocky Mountain rear sight are standard. Calibers from .32-40 to .50-70. Weight is about 10.5 lbs.

NIB	Exc.	V.G.	Good	Fair	Poor
3000	2350	1950	1200	700	300

No. 1¾ Far West Rifle

Offered with 30" round barrel in standard or heavy weight. Single or double-set triggers, S lever, ring-style lever, blade front sight, and Rocky Mountain rear sight. Offered in calibers from .32-40 to .50-90. Weight with standard 30" barrel is approximately 10.5 lbs., with heavyweight barrel 11.75 lbs.

NIB	Exc.	V.G.	Good	Fair	Poor
2900	2400	1900	1200	700	300

No. 2 Sporting Model

Stocked in plain walnut with crescent butt and offered in 24", 26", 28", or 30" octagon barrel with blade front and Rocky Mountain rear sights. A straight-grip action with S lever, in calibers .38-40, .44-40, and .45 Colt. Discontinued.

NIB	Exc.	V.G.	Good	Fair	Poor
2050	1650	1300	1225	700	300

No. 3 Gallery Rifle

Chambered for the .22 caliber rimfire cartridge this model features a choice of 24", 26", or 30" lightweight octagon barrel with rifle-style buttstock with steel crescent buttplate, S lever, blade and Rocky Mountain sights. Weight with standard 26" barrel is about 7.5 lbs.

NIB	Exc.	V.G.	Good	Fair	Poor
3000	2650	2300	1200	700	300

No. 3F Fine Gallery Rifle

Same as above model but with fancy checkered walnut stock, pistol grip, single or double-set triggers, full-loop lever, light Schuetzen buttstock, globe front sight and gallery tang sight. Weight with standard 26" barrel is approximately 7.75 lbs.

NIB	Exc.	V.G.	Good	Fair	Poor
3500	3000	2400	1500	750	300

No. 4 Perfection Model

This model features a plain walnut stock with rifle or shotgun butt. Offered in 28", 30" or 32" octagon barrel with blade front sight and Rocky Mountain rear sight. Straight-grip action with single or double-set triggers with S lever or ring lever in calibers from .32-40 to .50-90.

NIB	Exc.	V.G.	Good	Fair	Poor
3400	2900	2300	1200	700	300

No. 4½ Mid-Range Model

This model features checkered fancy walnut stock, standard or heavy weight half octagon barrel 30" or 32" with single or double-set triggers, pistol grip, hard rubber or steel shotgun butt, horn fore-end cap, full-loop lever, and globe front sight. Offered in calibers from .32-40 to .40-70. Weight with standard barrel 10.75 lbs. and with heavy barrel 11.5 lbs.

NIB	Exc.	V.G.	Good	Fair	Poor
3200	2650	2100	1100	600	250

No. 5 Pacific Model

This model features a 30" or 32" octagon barrel in either standard or heavy weight, stocks in rifle or shotgun configuration, double-set triggers, ring lever, blade front sight, and Rocky Mountain rear sight. Calibers from .38-55 to .50-90. Weight with standard 30" barrel is 10.75 lbs., with heavyweight barrel 12 lbs.

NIB	Exc.	V.G.	Good	Fair	Poor
3350	2600	2250	1200	700	300

No. 5½ Montana Model

This model has a fancy walnut stock, double-set triggers, and ring lever. Shotgun steel butt. Barrels are either 28", 30" or 32", extra heavy octagon, in calibers .45-70, .45-110, and .50-90. Under barrel wiping rod. Weight is approximately 14.5 lbs.

NIB	Exc.	V.G.	Good	Fair	Poor
3300	2600	2000	110	600	225

No. 6 Off-Hand Rifle Model (Schuetzen)

This rifle features a fancy walnut checkered stock with hand rubbed finish, heavy Schuetzen buttplate, and horn insert on fore-end. Choice of 30", 32", or 34" half-octagon barrel with globe front sight. Straight-grip action with double-set triggers, Schuetzen ball, spur lever and deluxe rust blueing. Offered in .22 LR, .32-40, .38-55, .40-65, and .40-70 calibers.

NIB	Exc.	V.G.	Good	Fair	Poor
3300	2700	2100	1100	600	250

No. 7 Long Range Model

This model features a fancy walnut checkered stock with 32" or 34" standard or heavy weight half octagon barrel. Pistol-grip stock with rubber or steel shotgun butt, single or double-set triggers, full-loop lever, horn fore-end cap, and globe front sight. Calibers from .32-40 to .45-110. Weight with standard 32" barrel 11.75 lbs., with heavyweight barrel 12.25 lbs.

NIB	Exc.	V.G.	Good	Fair	Poor
3100	2550	2200	1100	600	250

No. 8 Union Hill Model

This model features a 30" or 32" half-octagon standard or heavy barrel, single or double-set triggers, pistol-grip stock with cheekpiece, full-loop lever, hook Schuetzen buttplate and fancy walnut checkered stock. Offered in calibers from .22 LR to .40-70. Weight with standard barrel in .32 caliber 10.5 lbs, with heavyweight barrel in .40 caliber 11.5 lbs. This model is not furnished with sights.

NIB	Exc.	V.G.	Good	Fair	Poor
3600	2000	1700	900	450	200

Model 1885 High Wall

This single-shot rifle is chambered for a wide variety of calibers from .18 Bee to .577 Express. Barrel lengths to 34". American walnut stock. Many options to choose from that will affect price. Introduced in 2000.

NIB	Exc.	V.G.	Good	Fair	Poor
3050	2500	2000	1175	650	275

BALLESTER—MOLINA

See—Hafdasa

BALLARD, C. H.

Worcester, Massachusetts

Single-Shot Derringer

A .41 caliber rimfire spur trigger single-shot pistol with a 2.75" barrel marked "Ballard's". Blued with silver-plated frame and walnut grips. Manufactured during the 1870s. **NOTE:** Iron frame model add 20 percent.

NIB	Exc.	V.G.	Good	Fair	Poor
—	—	1775	1450	550	225

BARRETT, F.A. MFG. CO.

Murfreesboro, Tennessee

Barrett MRAD

Chambered in the .338 Lapua Magnum with user-changeable barrel system. Match-grade trigger. Thumb-operated safety can be configured to right or left. Folding stock has adjustable cheekpiece and length of pull. Finished in Barrett's Multi-Role Brown. Introduced in 2011.

NIB	Exc.	V.G.	Good	Fair	Poor
5500	4675	3950	2500	1000	500

Model 82 Rifle

A .50 caliber BMG semi-automatic rifle with a 37" barrel and 11-shot magazine. The barrel fitted with a muzzlebrake, and the

receiver with a telescope. Approximate weight 35 lbs. Parkerized. Manufactured from 1985 to 1987.

NIB	Exc.	V.G.	Good	Fair	Poor
6000	5500	4750	2250	1500	400

Model 82A1

As above, with a 29" barrel without sights, and a 10-round magazine. A 10X telescope and iron sights are optional. Comes with hard carrying case. Weight is 28.5 lbs.

NIB	Exc.	V.G.	Good	Fair	Poor
8000	7000	4000	2750	1600	400

Model 95M

Introduced in 1995 this .50 caliber BMG bolt-action model features a 29" barrel and 5-round magazine. Scope optional. Weight is 22 lbs.

NIB	Exc.	V.G.	Good	Fair	Poor
6000	4000	3200	2000	1400	300

Model 99

This model is a single-shot bolt-action rifle chambered for the .50 BMG or .416 Barrett. Standard barrel length is 32". Optional barrel lengths of 29" or 25". Rifle weight is about 25 lbs. with 32" barrel. **NOTE:** Add $200 for fluted barrel.

NIB	Exc.	V.G.	Good	Fair	Poor
4300	3450	1700	1200	600	175

Model 107

Chambered for the .50 caliber cartridge this model is a semi-automatic rifle fitted with a 29" barrel with muzzlebrake. Bipod is detachable and adjustable. M1913 accessory rail. Supplied with two 10-round magazines. Weight is about 32 lbs.

NIB	Exc.	V.G.	Good	Fair	Poor
9650	8000	7000	6000	4000	1000

Model 468

Built on a semi-automatic AR-15-style lower receiver, this rifle features a 16" barrel with muzzlebrake chambered for the 6.8 SPC cartridge. Folding front sight and integrated Rail system. Folding rear sight. Weight is about 7.3 lbs.

NIB	Exc.	V.G.	Good	Fair	Poor
2800	2100	1450	975	650	225

BARRETT, J. B. and A.B. & CO.
Wytheville, Virginia
Barrett Muskets and Rifled Muskets

Overall length 57.75"; barrel length 41.5" to 42"; caliber .69. Markings: Although the Barretts placed no marks of their own on their alterations, most were effected on Virginia Manufactory muskets, whose lockplates are marked "VIRGINIA/Manufactory" forward of the hammer and "RICHMOND/(date)" on the tail. For many years collectors considered the adaptations of Hall rifles and carbines from breechloaders to muzzleloaders to be the product of J.B. Barrett & Co. of Wytheville. Recent evidence, however, confirms that those adaptations were actually effected in Danville, Virginia, by another firm (see READ & WATSON). Nevertheless, the Barretts of Wytheville did adapt arms during the early years of the American Civil War. The adaptation, effected almost exclusively upon Virginia Manufactory flintlock muskets, consisted of percussioning by means of the cone-in-barrel and rifling of the barrels with seven narrow grooves. In 1861 and 1862, the Barretts percussioned a total of 1250 muskets, of which 744 were rifled.

Courtesy Milwaukee Public Museum, Milwaukee, Wisconsin

NIB	Exc.	V.G.	Good	Fair	Poor
—	—	—	16500	6750	2200

BAR-STO PRECISION MACHINE
Burbank, California
Bar-Sto 25

A .25 caliber semi-automatic pistol with a brushed stainless steel receiver and slide. Walnut grips. Produced in 1974.

NIB	Exc.	V.G.	Good	Fair	Poor
—	325	275	175	125	100

BASCARAN, MARTIN A.
Eibar, Spain

A Spanish manufacturer of pistols prior to World War II.

Martian 6.35mm

A 6.35mm semi-automatic pistol. The slide is marked "Automatic Pistol Martian". Blued with black plastic grips having the monogram "MAB" cast in them.

NIB	Exc.	V.G.	Good	Fair	Poor
—	275	195	135	100	75

Martian 7.65mm

A semi-automatic pistol patterned after the Ruby military pistols. "Martian" is stamped on the slide with wood grips and a lanyard loop.

Courtesy James Rankin

NIB	Exc.	V.G.	Good	Fair	Poor
—	275	195	135	100	75

Thunder

A semi-automatic pistol in caliber 6.35mm. Almost a duplicate of the Martian above except for the sight placement. "Thunder" is stamped on the slide and each grip plate.

Courtesy James Rankin

NIB	Exc.	V.G.	Good	Fair	Poor
—	275	195	135	100	75

BAUER, F. A. CORP.
Fraser, Michigan

The Rabbit

A .22 caliber-by-.410 bore combination rifle/shotgun, with a tubular metal stock. Manufactured between 1982 and 1984. Similar to Garcia Bronco.

NIB	Exc.	V.G.	Good	Fair	Poor
—	325	300	225	125	75

Bauer 25 Automatic

A .25 caliber semi-automatic pistol made of stainless steel with a 2.5" barrel and 6-shot magazine. Walnut or imitation pearl grips. Manufactured from 1972 to 1984. After 1984 this pistol was produced under the name of Fraser for a few years. Add 15 percent for NIB.

Courtesy James Rankin

NIB	Exc.	V.G.	Good	Fair	Poor
250	200	165	125	80	

BAYARD
Herstal, Belgium
See—Pieper, H. & N. and Bergmann

BAYONNE, MANUFACTURE D'ARMES
aka MAB
Bayonne, France

Model A

Manufactured in 1921 and chambered for the 6.35mm cartridge. Patterned after the Browning Model 1906. Squeeze grip safety with a 6-round magazine.

Courtesy James Rankin

NIB	Exc.	V.G.	Good	Fair	Poor
—	295	175	115	75	50

Model B

Manufactured in 1932. Chambered for 6.35mm cartridge and has an exposed hammer, no grip safety, and a 6-round magazine.

Courtesy James Rankin

NIB	Exc.	V.G.	Good	Fair	Poor
—	275	165	90	75	50

Model C

Manufactured in 1933 and chambered for the 7.65mm and .380 cartridge. Patterned after the Browning Model 1910. Seven-round magazine.

Courtesy James Rankin

NIB	Exc.	V.G.	Good	Fair	Poor
—	325	225	200	125	90

Model D

Manufactured in 1933. Chambered for 7.65mm and .380 cartridge. Basically a Model C with a longer barrel and a 9-round magazine. **NOTE:** Add 100 percent for Nazi-marked pistols.

Courtesy James Rankin

NIB	Exc.	V.G.	Good	Fair	Poor
—	400	300	250	125	100

Model E

Manufactured in 1949 and chambered for the 6.35mm cartridge. Patterned after the Model D with streamlined grips and a 10-round magazine.

NIB	Exc.	V.G.	Good	Fair	Poor
—	425	325	300	150	125

Model F

Manufactured in 1950 and chambered for the .22 LR cartridge. Interchangeable barrel lengths, target grips, and a 10-round magazine.

Courtesy James Rankin

NIB	Exc.	V.G.	Good	Fair	Poor
—	425	325	200	150	125

Model G

Manufactured in 1951, chambered for the .22 LR cartridge and 7.65mm cartridge. Some with Dural frames. Magazine capacity is 10 rounds for .22 LR and 8 rounds for the 7.65mm.

Courtesy James Rankin

NIB	Exc.	V.G.	Good	Fair	Poor
—	450	350	225	150	125

Model GZ

Manufactured in calibers .22 LR, 6.35mm, 7.65mm, and .380. Almost identical to the Model G. Dural frames and two-tone finishes on some variations.

NIB	Exc.	V.G.	Good	Fair	Poor
—	450	350	275	150	125

Model P-8 & P-15

In 1966 MAB manufactured the Model P-8 and Model P-15 in 9mm Parabellum with 8- and 15-round magazine capacity. Basically it is the same gun with different magazine capacities. The Model P-15 went to the French military as well as some commercial sales.

Courtesy James Rankin

NIB	Exc.	V.G.	Good	Fair	Poor
—	475	350	300	250	175

Model P-15 M1 Target

The MAB Model P-15 was manufactured for target shooting using the 9mm Parabellum cartridge. Most M1 Target MABs were purchased by the French military for their target teams.

Courtesy James Rankin

NIB	Exc.	V.G.	Good	Fair	Poor
—	875	750	500	350	175

Model R

Manufactured in caliber 7.65mm Long in 1951 the Model R was similar to the Model D. Model Rs were later produced in several calibers. The .22 LR was furnished with a 10-round magazine and two different barrel lengths. The 7.65mm had a 9-round magazine while the .380 and 9mm Parabellum were fitted with 8-round magazines. **NOTE:** Deduct 15 percent for 7.65 Long.

.22 Long Rifle

NIB	Exc.	V.G.	Good	Fair	Poor
—	350	250	225	150	125

7.65mm & 7.65mm Long & .380

NIB	Exc.	V.G.	Good	Fair	Poor
—	350	250	225	150	125

9mm Parabellum

NIB	Exc.	V.G.	Good	Fair	Poor
—	400	300	250	150	125

Model R PARA Experimental

In the late 1950s MAB began experimenting with the Model R in caliber 9mm Parabellum. There were many of these experimental-type pistols and the 8-round, rotating barrel Model R shown led directly to the Model P-15 series.

Courtesy James Rankin

NIB	Exc.	V.G.	Good	Fair	Poor
—	1500	1250	1000	500	250

Model "Le Chasseur"

Manufactured in 1953 the Le Chasseur was a target model in .22 LR and had a 9-round magazine. It had an external hammer, target sights, and target grips. **NOTE:** MAB pistols that were sold in the U.S.A. were retailed by the Winfield Arms Company of Los Angeles, California, and are marked "Made in France for WAC". This does not affect value.

Courtesy James Rankin

NIB	Exc.	V.G.	Good	Fair	Poor
—	500	350	225	175	100

NIB	Exc.	V.G.	Good	Fair	Poor
—	300	200	150	125	90

BEATTIE, J.
London, England

Beattie produced a variety of revolvers during the percussion period, some of which were imported into the United States. During the period this firm was in business, it was located at these London addresses:

Beattie Gas Seal Revolver

A .42 caliber single-action percussion revolver with a 6.25" octagonal barrel. When the hammer is cocked, the cylinder is forced forward against the barrel breech, thus effecting a gas seal. Blued, case hardened with walnut grips.

NIB	Exc.	V.G.	Good	Fair	Poor
—	—	5100	3500	2200	1100

BEAUMONT
Maastrict, Netherlands
1873 Dutch Service Revolver, Old Model

A 9.4mm double-action 6-shot revolver weighing 2 lbs. 12 oz.

NIB	Exc.	V.G.	Good	Fair	Poor
—	—	695	400	200	100

1873 Dutch Service Revolver, New Model

As above, with a 6-shot cylinder.

NIB	Exc.	V.G.	Good	Fair	Poor
—	—	695	400	200	100

1873 KIM, Small Model

As above, with an octagonal barrel and 5-shot cylinder.

NIB	Exc.	V.G.	Good	Fair	Poor
—	—	775	500	250	125

BEAUMONT, ADAMS
See—Adams

BECKER AND HOLLANDER
Suhl, Germany

Beholla

A semi-automatic pistol in caliber 7.65mm. Introduced in 1908 in Germany. It was manufactured by Becker & Hollander until 1920. After that date three different companies produced the Beholla under the names Stenda, Menta, and Leonhardt.

BEEMAN PRECISION ARMS, INC.
Santa Rosa, California

Although primarily known as an importer and retailer of airguns, Beeman Precision Arms, Inc., has marketed several firearms.

MP-08

A .380 caliber semi-automatic pistol, with a 3.5" barrel and 6-shot magazine, resembling the German Luger. Blued. Introduced in 1968.

NIB	Exc.	V.G.	Good	Fair	Poor
475	375	275	225	200	125

P-08

As above, in .22 caliber with an 8-shot magazine and walnut grips. Introduced in 1969.

NIB	Exc.	V.G.	Good	Fair	Poor
475	375	275	225	200	125

SP Standard

A .22 caliber single-shot target pistol with 8" to 15" barrels. Fitted with adjustable sights and walnut grips. Imported in 1985 and 1986.

NIB	Exc.	V.G.	Good	Fair	Poor
325	225	200	175	150	100

SP Deluxe

As above, with a walnut fore-end.

NIB	Exc.	V.G.	Good	Fair	Poor
350	250	225	200	150	100

BEERSTECHER, FREDERICK
Philadelphia, Pennsylvania (1846-1856)
Lewisburg, Pennsylvania (1857-1868)
Superposed Load Pocket Pistol

A .41 caliber superposed load percussion pistol with an average barrel length of 3", German silver mounts and walnut stock. The hammer is fitted with a movable twin striker head so that the first charge in the barrel can be fired and then the second fired. The lock is normally marked "F. Beerstecher's/Patent 1855". Prospective purchasers are advised to secure a qualified appraisal prior to acquisition.

NIB	Exc.	V.G.	Good	Fair	Poor
—	—	6400	4800	3500	1050

BEHOLLA
See—Becker and Hollander

BEISTEGUI, HERMANOS
Eibar, Spain
See—Grand Precision

BENELLI
Italy

SHOTGUNS

SL SERIES

Model SL-121 V

This is a semi-automatic 12 gauge with 3" chambers and various barrel lengths and chokes. It has a black anodized alloy receiver and was discontinued in 1985.

NIB	Exc.	V.G.	Good	Fair	Poor
500	450	400	350	300	150

Model SL-121 Slug

This model is similar to the SL-121 V with a 21" cylinder-bore barrel and rifle sights. It, too, was discontinued in 1985.

NIB	Exc.	V.G.	Good	Fair	Poor
500	450	400	350	300	150

Model SL-123 V

This model has the improved, fast, third-generation action. Otherwise it resembles the earlier SL-121.

NIB	Exc.	V.G.	Good	Fair	Poor
550	475	425	350	300	150

Model SL-201

This is a 20 gauge with a 26", Improved Cylinder barrel. It is similar in appearance to the SL-123.

NIB	Exc.	V.G.	Good	Fair	Poor
500	475	425	350	300	150

M SERIES

M3 Super 90

This is an improved version of the Benelli pump-action and semi-automatic inertia recoil system. The shotgun can be converted from pump to semi-automatic by turning a spring-loaded ring located at the end of the forearm. It has a rotating bolt system and is chambered for 12 gauge, with a 3" chamber. This model has a 19.75" barrel with cylinder bore and rifle sights with a 7-round tubular magazine. It has a matte black finish and a black fiberglass pistol-grip stock and forearm. This model was introduced in 1986. **NOTE:** Add $50 for open rifle sights.

NIB	Exc.	V.G.	Good	Fair	Poor
1300	1100	900	700	450	300

M3 Super 90 Folding Stock

Same as above but furnished with a folding tubular steel stock.

NIB	Exc.	V.G.	Good	Fair	Poor
1600	1350	1150	850	600	300

M4

Adopted by the U.S. Marine Corps this 12 gauge shotgun features a choice of three modular buttstock and two barrel configurations. Top-mounted Picatinny rail. Barrel length is 18.5". Magazine capacity is 6 rounds. Ghost ring sights. Weight is about 8.4 lbs. Matte black finish. Introduced in 2003. The civilian version does not have a collapsible buttstock.

M4 with skeleton stock with cheekpiece

M4 with standard stock

M4 with pistol-grip stock

NIB	Exc.	V.G.	Good	Fair	Poor
1550	1150	875	725	500	200

M1014 Limited Edition

Introduced in 2003 this version of the M4 is fitted with a skeleton buttstock and a special U.S. flag engraving on the receiver. Fitted with an 18.5" barrel and Picatinny rail with ghost ring sights. Limited to 2,500 shotguns.

NIB	Exc.	V.G.	Good	Fair	Poor
1600	1200	900	750	550	250

M1 Practical

This model was designed for IPSC events and features an oversized safety, speed loader, larger bolt handle, muzzlebrake, and adjustable ghost ring sight and optics rail. Offered with 26" barrel with extended magazine tube. Weighs about 7.6 lbs.

NIB	Exc.	V.G.	Good	Fair	Poor
1150	900	750	500	275	125

M1 Super 90 Tactical

This is a semi-automatic 12 gauge shotgun with an inertia recoil system. It features an 18.5" plain barrel with three screw-in choke tubes. Available in either standard polymer stock or pistol-grip stock. Ghost ring sights are standard. Gun weighs 6.5 lbs. First introduced in 1993.

NIB	Exc.	V.G.	Good	Fair	Poor
900	700	600	500	450	250

M1 Super 90 Slug Gun

Equipped with a standard black polymer stock with 19.75" plain barrel. Fitted with a 7-shot magazine. Ghost ring sights are an option. Weighs 6.7 lbs. Camo model introduced in 2000. **NOTE:** Add $100 for Camo model.

NIB	Exc.	V.G.	Good	Fair	Poor
1000	750	550	450	350	250

M1 Super 90 Entry Gun

This model is fitted with a black polymer pistol-grip stock with 14" plain barrel. Magazine holds 5 shells. Plain or ghost ring sights

available. **CAUTION:** NFA Weapon, Restricted sale, Class III Transfer required.

M1 Super 90 Defense Gun

Comes standard with polymer pistol-grip stock, 19.75" barrel, plain sights, or ghost ring sights. Offered in 12 gauge only. Weighs 7.1 lbs.

NIB	Exc.	V.G.	Good	Fair	Poor
900	700	600	500	450	250

M1 Super 90 Field

This model is similar to other Super 90 series guns with a 21", 24", 26", or 28" vent rib barrel with screw-in choke tubes. In 1998 this model was available with 24" rifled bore with matte rib. Add $80 for this barrel. Left-hand model added in 2000. In 2001 this model was offered in 20 gauge as well.

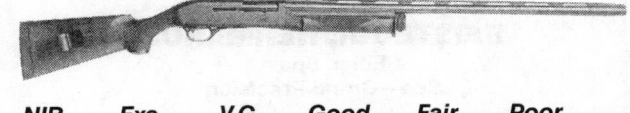

NIB	Exc.	V.G.	Good	Fair	Poor
900	650	600	550	450	200

M1 Super 90 Camo Field

Same as above but with camouflage receiver, barrel, buttstock and forearm. Offered in 24", 26", and 28" vent rib barrels. Introduced in 1997. In 1998 this model was also offered with a 21" vent rib barrel. Left-hand model added in 2000. In 2001 this model was offered in 20 gauge as well.

M1 20 gauge

M1 Field Steady Grip

Introduced in 2003 this model features a vertical pistol grip, drilled and tapped receiver and extra Full choke tube. Barrel length is 24". Weight is about 7.3 lbs.

NIB	Exc.	V.G.	Good	Fair	Poor
1175	900	600	325	175	100

M1 Super 90 Sporting Special

Introduced in 1993 this 12 gauge shotgun is similar to the Super 90 with the addition of non-reflective surfaces, 18.5" plain barrel with 3 choke tubes (IC, Mod, Full). The gun is fitted with ghost ring sights.

NIB	Exc.	V.G.	Good	Fair	Poor
725	600	500	400	350	200

M2 Practical with ComforTech

Introduced in 2005 this model is chambered for the 12 gauge 3" shell and fitted with a 25" plain barrel with compensator and ghost-ring rear sight. Receiver is fitted with a Picatinny rail. Magazine capacity is 8 rounds. Weight is about 7.6 lbs.

NIB	Exc.	V.G.	Good	Fair	Poor
1335	1000	750	595	400	275

M2 Tactical

This 12 gauge 3" gun is fitted with a 18.5" barrel with choke tubes and choice of rifle or ghost-ring sights. Pistol grip or extended pistol grip. Black synthetic stock. Magazine capacity is 5 rounds. Weight is about 7 lbs. **NOTE:** Add $70 for ComforTech version and $65 for ghost ring sights.

NIB	Exc.	V.G.	Good	Fair	Poor
1100	850	600	525	300	200

M2 Field with ComforTech

In 12 gauge, this model is offered with a 21", 24", 26" or 28" barrel with a black matte synthetic finish or Max-4, Timber or APG camo. The 20 gauge has a 24" or 26" barrel in black, Timber or APG. Average 12 gauge weight is 7 lbs.; average 20 gauge weight is 5.8 lbs. Add $75 for camo.

NIB	Exc.	V.G.	Good	Fair	Poor
1000	750	500	525	300	200

M2 Field without ComforTech

Same features as above without ComforTech features. Available only in satin walnut with 26" or 28" barrel.

NIB	Exc.	V.G.	Good	Fair	Poor
1075	825	550	525	300	200

MONTEFELTRO SERIES

Montefeltro Super 90

Introduced in 1987, this model is similar to the Super 90 Field with a checkered walnut stock and forearm with gloss finish. Offered with 21", 24", 26", or 28" vent rib barrel. Available in 12 gauge only with 3" chambers. This shotgun offered in left-hand model also.

NIB	Exc.	V.G.	Good	Fair	Poor
900	700	600	500	450	350

Montefeltro 20 Gauge

Introduced in 1993, this model features a walnut checkered stock with 26" vent rib barrel. In 1995 a 24" vent rib barrel was offered as well. Gun weighs 5.75 lbs. **NOTE:** Add $75 for short stock model.

NIB	Exc.	V.G.	Good	Fair	Poor
900	700	600	500	450	350

Montefeltro 20 Gauge Camo

Same as above with Realtree Camo finish and offered with 26" vent rib barrel. Introduced in 1998.

NIB	Exc.	V.G.	Good	Fair	Poor
950	750	700	600	500	400

Montefeltro 20 Gauge Limited

Introduced in 1995 this version features a finely etched nickel plate receiver with scroll and game scenes highlighted in gold. The stock is a select grade walnut and is fitted with a 26" vent rib barrel.

NIB	Exc.	V.G.	Good	Fair	Poor
1750	1250	800	500	400	350

Montefeltro (2005)

This is an updated version of the Montefeltro series of guns with a slight change in the receiver, a different trigger, upgraded wood, and the name "Montefeltro" in gold on the receiver. Offered in 12 or 20 gauge with 3" chambers. Checkered select walnut stock with pistol grip. Choice of 24", 26", or 28" vent rib barrel with choke tubes and red bar front sight. Weight for 12 gauge is about 6.9 lbs. and the 20 gauge is about 5.6 lbs.

NIB	Exc.	V.G.	Good	Fair	Poor
1300	1000	950	700	500	350

BLACK EAGLE SERIES

Black Eagle Competition Gun

Offered in 12 gauge only this model is fitted with an etched receiver, mid rib bead, competition stock, and 5 screw-in choke tubes. Available in either 26" or 28" vent rib barrel. The upper receiver is steel while the lower receiver is lightweight alloy. Weighs 7.3 lbs.

NIB	Exc.	V.G.	Good	Fair	Poor
1300	800	750	700	400	275

Black Eagle

Similar to the Black Eagle Competition Model but with standard grade wood and matte black finish on the receiver. Introduced in 1997.

NIB	Exc.	V.G.	Good	Fair	Poor
900	600	475	325	225	150

Black Eagle Executive Series

Offered in 12 gauge only this is a special order only shotgun. It is offered with a choice of 21", 24", 26", 28" vent rib barrels. Each grade or level of gun is engraved with increasing levels of coverage. The stock is fancy walnut.

Grade I

NIB	Exc.	V.G.	Good	Fair	Poor
5000	4000	2500	1200	700	300

Grade II

NIB	Exc.	V.G.	Good	Fair	Poor
5700	4500	3000	1500	950	400

Grade III

NIB	Exc.	V.G.	Good	Fair	Poor
6600	5000	3250	1700	1050	550

SUPER BLACK EAGLE SERIES

Super Black Eagle

This model is similar to the Montefeltro Super 90 Hunter with a polymer or walnut stock and forearm. It is offered with a 24", 26", or 28" vent rib barrel with 5 screw-in choke tubes. Chambered for 12 gauge from 2.75" to 3.5". It was introduced in 1989. The 24" barrel was introduced in 1993.

NIB	Exc.	V.G.	Good	Fair	Poor
1200	950	650	500	300	200

Super Black Eagle Left-Hand

Introduced in 1999 this model is the same as the Black Eagle but in a left-hand version. A Camo version is available.

NIB	Exc.	V.G.	Good	Fair	Poor
1200	950	650	500	300	200

Super Black Eagle Custom Slug Gun

This 12 gauge model has a 24" rifled barrel with 3" chamber. It comes standard with matte metal finish. Gun weighs 7.6 lbs.

NIB	Exc.	V.G.	Good	Fair	Poor
1100	800	750	600	500	350

Super Black Eagle Camo Gun

Introduced in 1997 this model features 24", 26", or 28' vent rib barrels chambered for 12 gauge shells. Has a Realtree Xtra Brown Camo finish. Stock is camo polymer as is forearm.

NIB	Exc.	V.G.	Good	Fair	Poor
1300	1000	750	600	500	400

Super Black Eagle Steady Grip

Similar to the model above but equipped with a vertical pistol grip. Drilled and tapped receiver. Extra Full choke tube. Barrel length is 24". Weight is about 7.3 lbs. Introduced in 2003.

NIB	Exc.	V.G.	Good	Fair	Poor
1465	1100	650	575	325	225

Super Black Eagle Limited Edition

Introduced in 1997 this shotgun features a 26" vent rib barrel, matte metal finish, and satin select grade wood stock. The nickel plated receiver is finely etched with scroll and game scenes. Limited to 1,000 guns.

NIB	Exc.	V.G.	Good	Fair	Poor
2000	1500	1050	750	525	375

SUPER BLACK EAGLE II SERIES

This series of guns was introduced in 2005. Major features are a new butt pad, grip, and cryogenically treated barrels for which specially designed longer choke tubes are required. Benelli offers this series with or without "ComforTech" features. This system reduces recoil up to 48 percent and muzzle climb by 15 percent.

Super Black Eagle II with ComforTech

Offered in 12 gauge with 3.5" chambers. Barrel lengths are 24", 26", or 28" with choke tubes and red bar front sight. Available in synthetic or various camo finishes. Magazine capacity is 3 rounds. Weight is about 7.2 lbs. with 26" barrel.

NIB	Exc.	V.G.	Good	Fair	Poor
1465	1100	700	600	365	250

Super Black Eagle II without ComforTech

This model, without ComforTech, has the same options as the one above with the addition of a walnut stock. **NOTE:** Add $60 for walnut stock. Add $110 for camo models.

NIB	Exc.	V.G.	Good	Fair	Poor
1355	1000	650	575	325	225

Super Black Eagle II Rifled Slug with ComforTech

This is a 12 gauge 3" chamber gun with 24" rifled barrel with adjustable sights. Available with synthetic stock or Timber HD camo stock. Weight is about 7.4 lbs. **NOTE:** Add $120 for Camo version.

NIB	Exc.	V.G.	Good	Fair	Poor
1535	1150	650	575	325	225

Super Black Eagle II Turkey Gun

This 12 gauge 3" chamber shotgun (3.5" chambers on non-ComforTech guns) is fitted with 24" smooth bore barrels with choke tubes. Red bar front sight. Weight is about 7.1 lbs. Available with Timber HD camo stock with or without ComforTech. **NOTE:** Add $130 for ComforTech version.

NIB	Exc.	V.G.	Good	Fair	Poor
1455	1050	700	600	365	250

Super Black Eagle II Steady Grip

This 12 gauge 3.5" chamber gun is fitted with a 24" barrel with red bar front sight. Choke tubes. Stock is camo with steady grip pistol grip. Weight is about 7.3 lbs. This model comes without ComforTech.

NIB	Exc.	V.G.	Good	Fair	Poor
1200	950	650	500	300	200

LEGACY SERIES

Legacy

This model features a coin finished alloy receiver and was introduced in 1998. Chambered for the 12 gauge 2.75" or 3" shell. It is fitted with a choice of 26" or 28" vent rib barrel with mid and front sights. Weight is about 7.5 lbs. Buttstock and forearm are select walnut. A 20 gauge was added in 1990 with 24" or 26" vent rib barrels. Weight 6 lbs.

NIB	Exc.	V.G.	Good	Fair	Poor
1300	800	750	700	400	275

Legacy Limited Edition

Offered in both 12 and 20 gauge this model features select walnut stock and etched game scenes with gold filled accents. The 12 gauge features waterfowl scenes while the 20 gauge has upland game scenes. The 12 gauge is fitted with a 28" barrel while the 20 gauge has a 26" barrel. This model was introduced in 2000 and is limited to 250 guns in each gauge.

NIB	Exc.	V.G.	Good	Fair	Poor
1600	1200	900	550	375	295

Legacy (2005)

This is a updated version of the Legacy model with changes in the engraving pattern, upgraded wood, improved trigger, and a slightly different receiver style. Offered in 12 and 20 gauge with 3" chambers and choice of 26" or 28" vent rib barrel with choke tubes. Red bar front sight. Checkered select walnut stock with pistol grip. Magazine capacity is 4 rounds. Weight for 12 gauge is about 7.4 lbs. and the 20 gauge is about 5.8 lbs. **NOTE:** Add $30 for 20 gauge.

NIB	Exc.	V.G.	Good	Fair	Poor
1435	1050	900	575	325	225

NOVA SERIES
Nova

Introduced in 1999 this model features polymer molded frame with steel cage chambered for 3.5" shells. Choice of 24", 26", or 28" vent rib barrels. A 18.5" slug barrel is also offered. Two- or four-shot magazine extensions are offered as well. Weight with 28" barrel is 8 lbs. Choice of camo or black synthetic pistol-grip stock. In 2001 this model was offered in 20 gauge as well.

Nova Pump with vent rib barrel

Nova Camo Model

NIB	Exc.	V.G.	Good	Fair	Poor
350	275	225	175	150	75

Nova Slug

This 12 gauge shotgun has a 18.5" cylinder bored barrel with open rifle or ghost ring sights. Black synthetic stock. Chambered for 2.75" or 3" shells. Magazine capacity is 4 rounds. Weight is about 7.2 lbs. Introduced in 2000. **NOTE:** Add $40 for ghost ring sights.

NIB	Exc.	V.G.	Good	Fair	Poor
350	275	225	200	150	95

Nova Rifled Slug

Introduced in 2000 this 12 gauge model features a 24" rifled barrel with open rifle sights. Black synthetic stock or Timber HD camo stock. Chambered for 2.75" or 3" shells. Magazine capacity is 4 rounds. Weight is about 8 lbs. **NOTE:** Add $75 for Camo version.

NIB	Exc.	V.G.	Good	Fair	Poor
525	425	350	250	175	125

Nova Field Slug Combo

This 12 gauge 3" gun is equipped with a 26" and 24" barrel. The 26" barrel is fitted with a vent rib and choke tube while the 24" barrel is rifled and fitted with a cantilever scope mount. Black synthetic stock.

NIB	Exc.	V.G.	Good	Fair	Poor
545	425	325	250	175	125

Nova H2O Pump

Introduced in 2003 this model features a largely polymer exterior with corrosion-resistant finish. Barrel, magazine tube, magazine cap, trigger group and other internal parts are nickel plated. Chambered for 12 gauge. Fitted with an 18.5" barrel. Black synthetic stock. Magazine capacity is 4 rounds. Open rifle sights. Weight is about 7.2 lbs.

NIB	Exc.	V.G.	Good	Fair	Poor
465	375	295	225	150	95

Supernova

Introduced in 2006, the Supernova incorporates Benelli's ComforTech stock system into the Nova pump shotgun. Available in 24", 26" and 28" barrel lengths in matte black synthetic, 24" and 26" barrel lengths in Advantage Timber camo, and 26" and 28" barrel lengths in Max-4 camo. Weight is about 8 lbs. with 28" barrel. All versions are chambered for 3.5" shells. Three choke tubes. Add 15 percent for camo versions.

NIB	Exc.	V.G.	Good	Fair	Poor
475	375	250	175	150	75

Supernova SteadyGrip

As above but with extended pistol grip in 24" barrel only. Matte black synthetic or Advantage Timber stock. Add 15 percent for camo model.

NIB	Exc.	V.G.	Good	Fair	Poor
455	375	250	175	150	75

Supernova Tactical

Matte black synthetic stock with 18" barrel. Available with ComforTech or pistol grip stock. Fixed cylinder bore. Open rifle sights. Ghost ring sights optional.

NIB	Exc.	V.G.	Good	Fair	Poor
400	325	225	150	125	75

SPORT SERIES
Sport Model

This model was introduced in 1997 and is the first shotgun with removable, interchangeable carbon fiber vent ribs. This model is offered in 12 gauge only with choice of 26" or 28" barrels or 20 gauge with 28" barrel. Buttpad is adjustable. Weight is 7 lbs. for 26" models and 7.3 lbs. for 28" models.

NIB	Exc.	V.G.	Good	Fair	Poor
1300	1000	650	400	250	100

SuperSport with ComforTech

Introduced in 2005 this model is offered in 12 gauge with 3" chamber or 20 gauge with 28" barrel. Choice of 28" or 30" carbon fiber barrel with choke tubes and red bar front sight. Weight is about 7.25 lbs.

NIB	Exc.	V.G.	Good	Fair	Poor
1670	1250	800	575	395	200

Sport II Model

Introduced in 2003 this model features cryogenically treated barrels and extra-long choke tubes. Chambered for the 12 gauge shell in either 2.75" or 3" with 28" or 30" barrel or 20 gauge with 28" barrel. Vent rib and choke tubes. Magazine capacity is 4 rounds. Red bar front sight. Weight is approximately 7.9 lbs.

NIB	Exc.	V.G.	Good	Fair	Poor
1470	1100	700	475	325	150

Cordoba

This model, introduced in 2005, is chambered for the 12 gauge 3" shell and fitted with cryogencially treated ported barrels in 28" or 30" lengths with extended choke tubes. Vent rib is 10mm width. Synthetic stock with adjustable length butt pads. Red bar front sight. Weight is about 7.25 lbs.

NIB	Exc.	V.G.	Good	Fair	Poor
1800	1530	1200	850	375	295

Benelli Vinci

Gas-operated semi-automatic shotgun chambered for 2.75" and 3" 12 gauge. Features include modular disassembly; interchangeable choke tubes; 24" to 28" ribbed barrel; black, MAX-4HD or APG HD finish; synthetic contoured stocks; optional Steady-Grip model. Weight 6.7 to 6.9 lbs.

NIB	Exc.	V.G.	Good	Fair	Poor
1200	1000	850	600	400	300

Benelli Super Vinci

Unlike the Vinci, the Super Vinci fires 12 gauge 2.75", 3" and 3.5" magnum ammunition interchangeably. Barrel lengths: 26" or 28". Features Crio chokes, red bar front sight, metal bead mid sight. Receiver drilled and tapped for scope mounting. Weight is approx. 7 lbs. Available in black synthetic, Realtree MAX-4 or Realtree APG camo finish. New in 2011. **NOTE:** Add $100 for camo finish.

NIB	Exc.	V.G.	Good	Fair	Poor
1400	1150	900	650	450	350

Ultra Light

Inertia-driven 12 gauge semi-automatic features an alloy receiver, carbon fiber rib and small proportions to bring weight down to about 6 lbs. Walnut stock with Weathercoat finish. Chambered for 3" shells. Offered in 24" or 26" barrel only with 5 Crio chokes. Introduced 2006.

NIB	Exc.	V.G.	Good	Fair	Poor
1435	1050	900	575	325	225

RIFLES

Model R1 Rifle

Introduced in 2003 this rifle is chambered for the .30-06 or .300 Win. Magnum cartridge. Barrels are cryogenically treated. Action is gas operated. Interchangeable barrel offered in 20" and 22" in .30-06 and 20" and 24" in .300 Win. Magnum. Walnut stock.

Detachable magazine has a 4-round capacity. Weight is about 7 to 7.2 lbs. depending on caliber and barrel length. In 2005 the .270 WSM and .300 WSM calibers were added to the R1 rifle.

NIB	Exc.	V.G.	Good	Fair	Poor
1080	850	675	500	350	225

Model R1 Carbine

As above but with 20" barrel chambered for the .30-06 or .300 Win. Magnum calibers. Weight is about 7 lbs.

NIB	Exc.	V.G.	Good	Fair	Poor
1080	850	675	500	350	225

R1 ComforTech Rifle

Similar to Model R1 but with ComforTech recoil-absorbing stock. Additional chamberings .270 and .300 WSM. Introduced 2006. Add 10 percent for RealTree camo and adjustable comb.

NIB	Exc.	V.G.	Good	Fair	Poor
1350	1100	700	475	325	150

Benelli MR1 Rifle

Gas-operated semi-automatic rifle chambered in 5.56 NATO. Features include 16" 1:9 hard chrome-lined barrel, synthetic stock with pistol grip, rotating bolt, military-style aperture sights with picatinny rail. Comes equipped with 5-round detachable magazine but accepts M16 magazines.

NIB	Exc.	V.G.	Good	Fair	Poor
1135	965	800	550	350	250

HANDGUNS

Model B-76

This is an all-steel, double-action semi-automatic chambered for the 9mm Parabellum. It has a 4.25" barrel, fixed sights, and an 8-round detachable magazine.

NIB	Exc.	V.G.	Good	Fair	Poor
525	400	350	300	200	100

Model B-76S

This is the target version of the B-76. It has a 5.5" barrel, adjustable sights, and target grips.

NIB	Exc.	V.G.	Good	Fair	Poor
625	500	400	300	200	100

Model B-77

This model is similar to the B-76 except that it is chambered for the .32 ACP.

NIB	Exc.	V.G.	Good	Fair	Poor
425	300	250	200	150	100

Model B-80

This is another model similar to the B-76 except that it is chambered for the .30 Luger cartridge.

NIB	Exc.	V.G.	Good	Fair	Poor
525	395	300	200	150	100

Model B-80S

This is the target version of the B-80 with a 5.5" barrel and adjustable sights. It also features target grips.

NIB	Exc.	V.G.	Good	Fair	Poor
575	475	400	300	200	100

Model MP90S Match (World Cup)

This is a semi-automatic single-action pistol chambered for the .22 Short, .22 LR, or .32 S&W wadcutter. It is fitted with a 4-3/8" barrel with walnut match style fully adjustable grips, blade front sight and fully adjustable rear sight. Barrel has adjustable weights below. Magazine capacity is 5 rounds. Weight is about 39 oz. Previously imported by European American Armory, now imported by Benelli USA. **NOTE:** Add 10 percent for .32 S&W.

NIB	Exc.	V.G.	Good	Fair	Poor
1200	950	700	500	300	150

Model MP95E Match (Atlanta)

Similar to the above model but with anatomically shaped grips. Choice of blue or chrome finish. Previously imported by European American Armory, now imported by Benelli U.S.A. **NOTE:** Add $60 for chrome finish.

NIB	Exc.	V.G.	Good	Fair	Poor
750	600	450	350	225	125

BENTLEY, DAVID
Birmingham, England

Bentley was a prolific maker of both percussion and cartridge arms between 1845 and 1883. Those arms in cases can be dated by the addresses listed.

New Church Street	1845-1849
55 Hockley Street	1849-1854
5 Lower Loveday Street	1855-1860
61 & 62 Lower Loveday Street	1860-1863
44 Shadwell Street	1863-1871
Tower Works, Aston	1871-1883

BENTLEY, JOSEPH
Birmingham and Liverpool, England

Best known for his transitional and later patented percussion revolvers, Bentley worked at these addresses:

Birmingham11 Steelhouse Lane	1829-1837
14 St. Mary's Row	1840-1864
Liverpool143 Dale Street	1840-1842
12 South Castle Street	1842-1851
40 Lime Street & 65 Castle	1852-1857
65 Castle & 37 Russell Street	1857-1862

Bentley Revolver

A .44 caliber double-action percussion revolver with a 7" barrel and 5-shot cylinder. Blued, case hardened with walnut grips.

NIB	Exc.	V.G.	Good	Fair	Poor
—	—	4500	2750	2000	750

BERETTA, DR. FRANCO
Brescia, Italy

This series of shotguns was made by the Beretta company in Brescia, Italy and imported under the Dr. Franco Beretta name in the 1980s.

Black Diamond Field Model

Over/under series offered in all standard gauges. Walnut stock, coin-finished receiver, fixed chokes, SST and auto ejectors. **NOTE:** Four embellished grades were offered, Grades One through Four, with increasing levels of scrollwork, engraving and higher grades of French walnut stocks.

NIB	Exc.	V.G.	Good	Fair	Poor
800	650	500	400	300	200

Grade One

NIB	Exc.	V.G.	Good	Fair	Poor
1400	1200	1000	850	400	200

Grade Two

NIB	Exc.	V.G.	Good	Fair	Poor
1600	1400	1200	1000	500	300

Grade Three

NIB	Exc.	V.G.	Good	Fair	Poor
2200	1900	1650	1400	600	300

Grade Four

NIB	Exc.	V.G.	Good	Fair	Poor
3500	2800	2250	1750	700	350

Gamma Standard

A 12, 16, or 20 gauge boxlock over/under shotgun with 26" or 28" barrels, single trigger and automatic ejectors. Blued, French case hardened with a walnut stock. Imported from 1984 to 1988.

NIB	Exc.	V.G.	Good	Fair	Poor
900	775	600	425	250	100

Gamma Deluxe

As above, but more finely finished.

NIB	Exc.	V.G.	Good	Fair	Poor
1200	975	800	600	350	125

Gamma Target

As above, in a trap or skeet version. Imported from 1986 to 1988.

NIB	Exc.	V.G.	Good	Fair	Poor
1200	975	800	600	350	125

America Standard

A .410 bore boxlock over/under shotgun with 26" or 28" barrels. Blued, French case hardened with a walnut stock. Imported from 1984 to 1988.

NIB	Exc.	V.G.	Good	Fair	Poor
650	475	325	275	200	100

America Deluxe

As above, but more finely finished.

NIB	Exc.	V.G.	Good	Fair	Poor
695	525	375	300	225	100

Europa

As above, with a 26" barrel and engraved action. Imported from 1984 to 1988.

NIB	Exc.	V.G.	Good	Fair	Poor
800	725	575	425	275	100

Europa Deluxe

As above, but more finely finished.

NIB	Exc.	V.G.	Good	Fair	Poor
850	775	625	475	300	1005

Francia Standard

A .410 bore boxlock double-barrel shotgun with varying barrel lengths, double triggers and manual extractors. Blued with a walnut stock. Imported from 1986 to 1988.

NIB	Exc.	V.G.	Good	Fair	Poor
600	500	375	250	125	100

Alpha Three

A 12, 16, or 20 gauge boxlock double-barrel shotgun with 26" or 28" barrels, single triggers and automatic ejectors. Blued, French case hardened with a walnut stock. Imported from 1984 to 1988.

NIB	Exc.	V.G.	Good	Fair	Poor
750	650	500	325	150	100

Beta Three

A single-barrel, break-open, field-grade gun chambered for all gauges and offered with a ventilated rib barrel from 24" to 32" in length. The receiver chrome-plated, and the stock of walnut. Imported from 1985 to 1988.

NIB	Exc.	V.G.	Good	Fair	Poor
325	225	200	175	125	40

BERETTA, PIETRO
Brescia, Italy

PISTOLS

Model 1915

A 7.65mm and 9mm Glisenti caliber semi-automatic pistol with 3.5" barrel, fixed sights and 8-shot magazine. Blued with walnut grips. The 7.65mm pistol has a single-line inscription while the 9mm Glisenti has a double line. There are various styles of wood grips on this model. Manufactured between 1915 and 1922. Replaced by the Model 1915/19.

Model 1915 in 7.65mm

Courtesy James Rankin

Model 1915 in 9mm Glisenti

Courtesy James Rankin

NIB	Exc.	V.G.	Good	Fair	Poor
—	1000	800	600	400	250

Model 1915/1919

This model is an improved version of the above pistol but chambered for the 7.65mm cartridge. It also incorporates a new barrel-mounting method and a longer cutout in the top of the slide.

Courtesy Orvel Reichert

NIB	Exc.	V.G.	Good	Fair	Poor
—	500	350	275	200	100

Model 1919

Similar to Model 1915, in 6.35mm caliber. Manufactured with minor variations and different names between 1919 and the 1940s.

Courtesy James Rankin

NIB	Exc.	V.G.	Good	Fair	Poor
—	550	450	350	300	150

Model 1923

A 9mm Glisenti caliber semi-automatic pistol with 4" barrel and 8-shot magazine. Blued with steel grips. The slide is marked, "Brev 1915-1919 Mlo 1923". Manufactured from 1923 to 1935.

NIB	Exc.	V.G.	Good	Fair	Poor
—	1600	1200	600	265	175

Model 1931

A 7.65mm caliber semi-automatic pistol with 3.5" barrel and open-top slide. Blued with walnut grips and marked, "RM" separated by an anchor.

NIB	Exc.	V.G.	Good	Fair	Poor
—	495	425	325	250	180

Model 1934

As above, with 9mm short (.380 ACP) caliber. The slide is marked, "P. Beretta Cal. 9 Corto-Mo 1934 Brevet Gardone VT." This inscription is followed by the date of manufacture that was given numerically, followed by a Roman numeral that denoted the year of manufacture on the Fascist calendar which began in 1922. Examples are marked, "RM" (Navy), "RE" (Army), "RA" (Air Force), and "PS" (Police). Manufactured between 1934 and 1959.

Courtesy Orvel Reichert

NIB	Exc.	V.G.	Good	Fair	Poor
—	400	365	250	175	100

Air Force "RA" marked

NIB	Exc.	V.G.	Good	Fair	Poor
—	575	500	375	250	175

Navy "RM" marked

NIB	Exc.	V.G.	Good	Fair	Poor
—	650	575	400	275	200

Model 1934 Rumanian Contract

This model is identical to the Model 1934 except the slide is marked "9mm Scurt" instead of 9mm Corto.

NIB	Exc.	V.G.	Good	Fair	Poor
—	500	450	375	275	175

Model 1935

As above, in 7.65mm caliber. Post-war versions are known. Manufactured from 1935 to 1959.

Courtesy Orvel Reichert

NIB	Exc.	V.G.	Good	Fair	Poor
—	400	375	250	175	125

Model 318

An improved version of the old Model 1919 with the butt reshaped to afford a better grip. Chambered for the .25 ACP cartridge and has a 2.5" barrel. Variety of finishes with plastic grips. In the United States it is known as the "Panthe". Manufactured between 1935 and 1946.

NIB	Exc.	V.G.	Good	Fair	Poor
—	350	275	250	175	125

Model 418

As above, with a rounded grip and a cocking indicator. It is known as the "Bantam" in the U.S. Introduced in 1947.

NIB	Exc.	V.G.	Good	Fair	Poor
—	275	225	175	125	90

Model 420

An engraved and chrome-plated Model 418.

NIB	Exc.	V.G.	Good	Fair	Poor
—	350	300	275	200	150

Model 421

An engraved, gold-plated Model 418 with tortoise-shell grips.

NIB	Exc.	V.G.	Good	Fair	Poor
—	475	425	325	250	150

Model 948

A .22 LR version of the Model 1934. It has either a 3.5" or 6" barrel.

NIB	Exc.	V.G.	Good	Fair	Poor
—	350	300	200	125	90

Model 949 Olympic Target

A .22 caliber semi-automatic pistol with 8.75" barrel, adjustable sights and muzzlebrake. Blued with checkered, walnut grips. Manufactured from 1959 to 1964.

NIB	Exc.	V.G.	Good	Fair	Poor
—	750	600	500	400	200

U22 Neos 4.5/6.0

This semi-automatic .22 caliber pistol was first introduced in 2002. It is chambered for the .22 LR cartridge and fitted with a choice of 4.5" or 6" barrel with integral scope rail. Magazine capacity is 10 rounds. Weight is about 32 oz. to 36 oz. depending on barrel length.

NIB	Exc.	V.G.	Good	Fair	Poor
250	200	165	125	100	75

U22 Neos 4.5 Inox/6.0 Inox

Same as above but with special two-tone finish.

NIB	Exc.	V.G.	Good	Fair	Poor
300	250	195	150	100	75

U22 Neos 6.0/7.5 DLX

Introduced in 2003 this model features a 6" or 7.5" barrel with target sights and polymer grips with inlays. Adjustable trigger and interchangeable sights. Laser-engraved slide. Weight is about 36 oz.

NIB	Exc.	V.G.	Good	Fair	Poor
335	275	200	150	100	75

U22 Neos 6.0/7.5 Inox DLX

As above but with Inox finish.

NIB	Exc.	V.G.	Good	Fair	Poor
385	300	215	165	115	90

BERETTA 70 SERIES

These pistols began production in 1958 replacing Models 1934, 1935, 948, and 949. During the late 1960s several of these models briefly utilized a 100 series designation for the U.S. market. During the latter part of the 1970s a magazine safety was added to the 70 series and the pistols became known as the Model 70S. The 70S designation replaced model designations 70 through 75 making these older model numbers obsolete. Only the Model 76 designation continued.

The 70 Series design included a cross bolt safety, sear block safety, a slide hold-open device, and a push-button magazine release. Shorty after its introduction the cross bolt safety pushbutton was replaced with a lever-type sear block safety located in the same place.

NOTE: The above information was supplied by contributing editor John Stimson, Jr.

Model 70 (Model 100)

The Model 948 with cross bolt safety, hold-open device, and a push-button magazine release. Fixed sights. There are a number of sub-variations available chambered for the .22 LR, .32 ACP, and the .380 ACP cartridges. Available with a 3.5" or 5.9" barrel and has a detachable magazine. Also known as the "Puma" when marketed in the U.S. by J.L. Galef & Sons. It was introduced in 1958 and discontinued in 1985.

NIB	Exc.	V.G.	Good	Fair	Poor
525	450	350	275	125	85

Model 70S

This is an improved Model 70. Chambered for the 7.65 (.32 ACP), 9mm Corto (.380 ACP), and the .22 LR cartridge. Magazine capacity is 7, 8, and 9 rounds respectively.

NIB	Exc.	V.G.	Good	Fair	Poor
550	475	375	295	125	85

Model 71/Jaguar (Model 101)

Similar to above model and chambered for .22 LR cartridge. Magazine capacity is 10 rounds. Frame is alloy and is fitted with a 5.9" barrel. Models imported into the U.S. prior to 1968 were fitted with 3.5" barrels.

NIB	Exc.	V.G.	Good	Fair	Poor
425	375	300	225	125	85

Model 72

This is essentially a Model 71 but sold with two sets of barrels; a 3.5" and 5.9". Fixed sights.

NIB	Exc.	V.G.	Good	Fair	Poor
450	400	325	250	150	125

Model 76 (102)

This is a .22 LR target pistol. The barrel is shrouded with an aluminum sleeve, with the rear part of the sleeve extended above the slide to hold an adjustable rear sight. Marketed in the U.S. as the "Sable". Magazine capacity is 10 rounds. Briefly after 1968 imported into the U.S. as the Model 102, the "New Sable".

Courtesy John J. Stimson, Jr.

NIB	Exc.	V.G.	Good	Fair	Poor
450	400	300	200	125	75

Model 950/Minx

A .22 caliber semi-automatic pistol with 2.25" barrel hinged at the front that could be pivoted forward for cleaning or loading, making this either a semi-automatic or single-shot pistol. Blued with plastic grips. Introduced in 1955. A 4" barrel version also available. This model was known as the "Minx" in the U.S.

NIB	Exc.	V.G.	Good	Fair	Poor
325	250	215	145	95	50

Model 950B/Jetfire

As above, in .25 caliber, known as the "Jetfire" in the U.S.

NIB	Exc.	V.G.	Good	Fair	Poor
325	250	215	145	95	50

Model 950 Jetfire Inox

Same as the Model 950 Jetfire but with stainless steel finish. Introduced in 2000.

NIB	Exc.	V.G.	Good	Fair	Poor
335	250	175	135	85	50

Model 3032 Tomcat

This is a double-action semi-automatic pistol similar in appearance to the Model 950 but chambered for the .32 ACP cartridge. Barrel length is 2.45" and overall length is 5". Fixed blade front sight and drift adjustable rear sight. Plastic grips. Seven-round magazine. Blued or matte black finish. Weight is 14.5 oz. **NOTE:** For blued finish add $30.

NIB	Exc.	V.G.	Good	Fair	Poor
375	325	250	200	1350	75

Model 3032 Tomcat Inox

Same as above but with stainless steel finish. Introduced in 2000.

NIB	Exc.	V.G.	Good	Fair	Poor
400	325	250	195	125	75

Model 3032 Tomcat Titanium

Same as above but with titanium finish and plastic grips. Weight is about 16 oz. Introduced in 2001.

NIB	Exc.	V.G.	Good	Fair	Poor
575	450	350	290	210	150

Alley Cat

Introduced in 2001 as a special limited run promotion pistol. Chambered for the .32 ACP cartridge this model is a Tomcat with special features such as AO Big Dot night sights. Supplied with an Alcantara inside-the-pants holster.

Alley Cat AO Big Dot night sights

NIB	Exc.	V.G.	Good	Fair	Poor
575	450	350	290	210	150

Model 951

A 9mm caliber semi-automatic pistol with 4.5" barrel and fixed sights. Blued with plastic grips. It was also known as the "Brigadier" at one time. Introduced 1952.

NIB	Exc.	V.G.	Good	Fair	Poor
—	450	375	275	150	100

Model 20

A .25 ACP double-action pistol with 2.5" barrel and 9-shot magazine. Blued with either walnut or plastic grips. Discontinued in 1985.

NIB	Exc.	V.G.	Good	Fair	Poor
300	250	195	150	90	75

Model 21 Bobcat

This small frame semi-automatic pistol, chambered for the .22 LR or .25 ACP cartridge, features a 2.4" tip-up barrel with fixed sights and a magazine capacity of 8 rounds (.25 ACP) or 7 rounds (.22 LR). Comes with either plastic or walnut grips and a deluxe version with gold line engraving. Pistol weighs about 11 to 11.8 oz. depending on caliber.

Standard Model

NIB	Exc.	V.G.	Good	Fair	Poor
325	275	250	225	175	95

Model 21EL

Gold engraved model.

NIB	Exc.	V.G.	Good	Fair	Poor
395	350	325	280	195	110

Model 21 Inox

Stainless steel.

NIB	Exc.	V.G.	Good	Fair	Poor
325	250	200	140	95	75

Model 90

A double-action, semi-automatic .32 auto pocket pistol with a 3.5" barrel and 8-round magazine. Manufactured from 1969 to 1983.

NIB	Exc.	V.G.	Good	Fair	Poor
—	395	350	295	200	125

Model 92

A 9mm caliber double-action, semi-automatic pistol with a 5" barrel, fixed sights and a 16-round, double-stack magazine. Blued with plastic grips. Introduced in 1976 and is now discontinued.

NIB	Exc.	V.G.	Good	Fair	Poor
800	600	500	400	250	200

Model 92SB-P

As above, but with a polished finish. Manufactured from 1980 to 1985.

NIB	Exc.	V.G.	Good	Fair	Poor
625	475	400	325	250	200

Model 92SB Compact

As above, with a 4.3" barrel and a shortened grip frame that holds a 14-shot magazine. Either blued or nickel-plated with wood or plastic grips. The nickel version would be worth an additional 15 percent. The wood grips would add $20 to the value. Introduced in 1980 and discontinued in 1985.

NIB	Exc.	V.G.	Good	Fair	Poor
500	425	375	325	250	200

Model 92FS

The current production Model 92 chambered for the 9mm Parabellum cartridge. Barrel length is 4.9" and rear sight is a 3-dot combat drift adjustable. The magazine capacity is 15 rounds. This semi-automatic pistol features a double- or single-action operation. The safety is manual type. The frame is a light alloy

sandblasted and anodized black. The barrel slide is steel. Grips are plastic checkered with black matte finish. Equipped with spare magazine cleaning rod, and hard carrying case. Pistol weighs 34.4 oz. empty.

NIB	Exc.	V.G.	Good	Fair	Poor
550	450	350	300	200	150

Model 92FS Inox

Introduced in 2001 this pistol is chambered for the 9mm cartridge and fitted with a 4.9" barrel. The slide is black stainless steel with lightweight frame and combat-style trigger guard, reversible magazine release, and ambidextrous safety. Gray wrap-around grips. Weight is about 34 oz.

NIB	Exc.	V.G.	Good	Fair	Poor
695	575	425	350	225	175

Model 96

Identical to Model 92FS but fitted with a 10-round magazine and chambered for the .40 S&W. Introduced in 1992.

NIB	Exc.	V.G.	Good	Fair	Poor
550	450	350	300	200	150

Model 96 Combat

Introduced in 1997 this model is single-action-only with a competition tuned trigger. Developed for practical shooting competition. The barrel length is 5.9" and is supplied with a weight as standard. Rear sight is adjustable target type. Tool kit included as standard. Weight is 40 oz.

NIB	Exc.	V.G.	Good	Fair	Poor
1700	1300	950	575	350	175

Model 96 Stock

Similar to the Model 96 but in double-/single-action with a half-cock notch for cocked and locked carry. Fitted with a 4.9" barrel with fixed sights. Three interchangeable front sights are supplied as standard. Weight is 35 oz. Introduced in 1997. No longer in the U.S. product line.

NIB	Exc.	V.G.	Good	Fair	Poor
1350	950	775	500	325	150

Model 92/96FS Inox

Same as above except the barrel, slide, trigger, extractor, and other components are made of stainless steel. The frame is made of lightweight anodized aluminum alloy. The Model 96FS was discontinued in 1993.

NIB	Exc.	V.G.	Good	Fair	Poor
650	550	450	350	300	200

Model 92/96FS Centurion

Chambered for either the 9mm or .40 S&W (Model 96) this model features a 4.3" barrel, but retains a full grip to accommodate a 15-round magazine (9mm) or 10 rounds (.40 S&W). Pistol weighs approximately 33.2 oz. Introduced in 1993. Black sandblasted finish.

NIB	Exc.	V.G.	Good	Fair	Poor
550	450	400	300	200	150

Model 92FS/96 Brigadier

Same as the 92FS and 96 but with a heavier slide to reduce felt recoil. Removable front sight. Weight is about 35 oz.

NIB	Exc.	V.G.	Good	Fair	Poor
700	550	400	300	150	75

Model 92FS/96 Brigadier Inox

Same as above but with stainless steel finish. Introduced in 2000.

NIB	Exc.	V.G.	Good	Fair	Poor
750	600	475	325	175	100

Model 92G-SD/96G-SD

Introduced in 2003 this model features a decock mechanism built around a single-action/double-action trigger system. In addition, the pistol has an integral accessory rail on the frame. Fitted with a 9mm or .40 S&W 4.9" barrel with heavy slide and 3-dot tritium sights. Weight is about 35 oz.

NIB	Exc.	V.G.	Good	Fair	Poor
1000	750	500	350	195	125

Model 92F

A 9mm Parabellum caliber double-action semi-automatic pistol with a 4.9" barrel, fixed sights and a 15-shot double-stack magazine with an extended base. Matte blued finish with walnut or plastic grips. Introduced in 1984. No longer in production.

NIB	Exc.	V.G.	Good	Fair	Poor
500	400	350	300	200	150

Model 92F Compact

As above, with a 4.3" barrel and a 13-shot magazine. No longer in production.

NIB	Exc.	V.G.	Good	Fair	Poor
500	400	350	300	200	150

Model 92/96 Compact "Type M"

Essentially the same as the Model 92FS Compact but with the exception of a single column magazine that holds 8 rounds and reduces the grip thickness of the pistol. Pistol weighs 30.9 oz. Discontinued in 1993 and reintroduced in 1998. The Model 96 version (.40 S&W) was introduced in 2000. **NOTE:** Add $90 for Tritium night sights.

NIB	Exc.	V.G.	Good	Fair	Poor
700	550	350	300	200	150

Model 92/96M Compact Inox

Same as above but with stainless steel slide and frame. Introduced in 2000.

NIB	Exc.	V.G.	Good	Fair	Poor
700	550	450	350	300	200

Model 92D Compact Type M

Same as above but with double-action-only trigger function. **NOTE:** Add $90 for Tritium night sights.

NIB	Exc.	V.G.	Good	Fair	Poor
550	450	350	300	200	150

Model 92FS Deluxe

Identical dimensions to the full size Model 92FS with the addition of gold-plated engraved frame with gold-plated extra magazine in fitted leather presentation hard case. Grips are walnut briar with gold initial plate. Introduced in 1993.

NIB	Exc.	V.G.	Good	Fair	Poor
5500	4500	3000	2000	1500	1000

Model 92FS "470th Anniversary" Limited Edition

This model is limited to only 470 pistols worldwide. Features high polish finish with stainless steel, gold-filled engravings, walnut grips, Anniversary logo on top of slide and on the back of the chrome plated magazine. Supplied with walnut case.

NIB	Exc.	V.G.	Good	Fair	Poor
2075	1300	800	600	375	200

Model 92/96D

Same specifications as the standard Model 92 and Model 96 except that this variation has no visible hammer and is double-action-only. This model has no manual safety. Pistol weighs 33.8 oz.

NIB	Exc.	V.G.	Good	Fair	Poor
425	375	325	275	200	150

Model 92/96DS

Same as above but with the same manual safety as found on the 92FS pistol. Introduced in 1994.

NIB	Exc.	V.G.	Good	Fair	Poor
425	375	325	275	200	150

Model 92G/96G

Designed for the French Gendarmerie, this model has now been adopted for the French Air Force as well as other government agencies. This model features a hammer drop lever that does not function as a safety when the lever is released but lowers the hammer and returns to the ready to fire position automatically. Offered to law enforcement agencies only.

NIB	Exc.	V.G.	Good	Fair	Poor
650	550	475	400	250	100

Model 92/96 Vertec

Introduced in 2002 this pistol is chambered for the 9mm or .40 S&W cartridges. Fitted with a 4.7" barrel. Double and single-action trigger. Features a new vertical grip design with a shorter trigger reach and thin grip panels. Removable front sight and integral accessory rail on frame. Magazine capacity is 10 rounds. Weight is about 32 oz.

NIB	Exc.	V.G.	Good	Fair	Poor
700	575	425	300	225	165

Model 92 Competition Conversion Kit

The kit includes a 7.3" barrel with counterweight and elevated front sight, semi-automatic, walnut grips, and fully adjustable rear sight. Comes in special carrying case with the basic pistol. **NOTE:** Kit Price Only.

NIB	Exc.	V.G.	Good	Fair	Poor
500	350	300	200	150	100

Model 92/96 Combo

This model features a specially designed Model 96 pistol with an extra 92FS slide and barrel assembly. Barrel lengths are 4.66". Sold with one 10-round magazine in both 9mm and .40 S&W.

NIB	Exc.	V.G.	Good	Fair	Poor
850	725	600	425	275	200

Model M9 Limited Edition

Introduced in 1995 to commemorate the 10th anniversary of the U.S. military's official sidearm this 9mm pistol is limited to 10,000 units. Special engraving on the slide with special serial numbers. Slide stamped "U.S. 9mm M9-BERETTA U.S.A.-65490".

Standard Model

NIB	Exc.	V.G.	Good	Fair	Poor
825	700	450	300	200	100

Deluxe Model

Walnut grips with gold plated hammer and grip screws.

NIB	Exc.	V.G.	Good	Fair	Poor
875	750	500	350	200	100

Model 92 Billennium

Introduced in 2001 this is a limited production pistol of 2,000 units world wide. Chambered for the 9mm cartridge. Steel frame with checkered front and backstrap. Nickel alloy finish with unique engraving. Carbon fiber grips. Interchangeable sights with adjustable rear sight. Carry case standard. Single action.

NIB	Exc.	V.G.	Good	Fair	Poor
1200	1000	800	600	475	325

92 Steel-I

Steel-frame semi-automatic in 9mm or .40 S&W. Single- or single/double-action. 15+1 capacity, 4.7" barrel, 42.3 oz. IDPA certified. Fixed, 3-dot sights. Introduced 2006.

NIB	Exc.	V.G.	Good	Fair	Poor
1075	850	600	475	300	150

M9A1

Semi-automatic, single-/double-action in 9mm developed for U.S. Marine Corps. Capacity 10+1 or 15+1. Fixed sights. Introduced 2006.

NIB	Exc.	V.G.	Good	Fair	Poor
825	650	450	300	195	125

ELITE TEAM SERIES

In 1999 Beretta introduced a new series of pistols based on the company's M92/96 pistol. Each of these pistols has specific features for specific shooting requirements.

Model 92/96 Custom Carry

This model is fitted with a 4.3" barrel, shortened grip, and low profile control levers. Safety lever is left side only. Magazine capacity is 10 rounds. "CUSTOM CARRY" engraved on the slide. Chambered for either 9mm or .40 S&W calibers.

NIB	Exc.	V.G.	Good	Fair	Poor
625	500	400	300	200	100

Model 92/96 Border Marshall

This is the commercial version of the pistol built for the Immigration and Naturalization Service. It is fitted with a heavy-duty steel slide and short 4.7" I.N.S. style barrel. Rubber grips and night sights are standard. "BORDER MARSHALL" engraved on the slide. Offered in either 9mm or .40 S&W calibers.

NIB	Exc.	V.G.	Good	Fair	Poor
750	600	475	350	225	150

Model 92G/96G Elite

Chambered for 9mm or .40 S&W calibers this pistol is fitted with a 4.7" stainless steel barrel and heavy-duty Brigadier-style slide. The action is decock only. Slide has both front and rear serrations. Hammer is skeletonized. Beveled magazine well. Special "ELITE" engraving on the slide. Weight is about 35 oz.

NIB	Exc.	V.G.	Good	Fair	Poor
825	650	450	375	250	165

Model 92G Elite II

This version of the Elite was developed for the competition shooter. Fitted with a 4.7" barrel fitted with a heavy slide, it also has a skeletonized hammer. Beveled magazine well. Extended magazine release. Checkered front and backstrap grip. Weight is about 35 oz.

NIB	Exc.	V.G.	Good	Fair	Poor
925	725	550	395	275	150

Model 92FS Inox Tactical

This model has a satin matte finish on its stainless steel slide. The frame is anodized aluminum. Black rubber grips and night sights are standard. Offered in 9mm only.

NIB	Exc.	V.G.	Good	Fair	Poor
775	625	500	350	225	100

COUGAR SERIES

Model 8000/8040/8045 Cougar

This is a compact size pistol using a short recoil rotating barrel. It features a firing pin lock, chrome lined barrel, anodized aluminum alloy frame with Bruniton finish. Overall length is 7", barrel length is 3.6", overall height 5.5", and unloaded weight is 33.5 oz. Offered in double-/single-action as well as double-action-only. Magazine holds 10 rounds. Available in 9mm or .40 S&W. In 1998 Beretta added the .45 ACP caliber to this model. **NOTE:** Add $50 for .45 ACP models

NIB	Exc.	V.G.	Good	Fair	Poor
625	525	400	350	250	150

Model 8000/8040/8045 Mini Cougar

This pistol was introduced in 1997 and is similar in design to the full size model. Offered in 9mm or .40 S&W or .45 ACP. The pistol is fitted with a 3.6" barrel (3.7" on .45 ACP). Empty weight is 27 oz. Offered in double-/single-action or double-action-only. Magazine capacity is 10 rounds for 9mm and 8 rounds for .40 S&W model. Weight is between 27 oz. and 30 oz. depending on caliber. **NOTE:** Add $50 for .45 ACP models

NIB	Exc.	V.G.	Good	Fair	Poor
500	450	350	225	125	75

Model 8000F—Cougar L

Similar to the model above but fitted with a shortened grip frame. Chambered for the 9mm cartridge and fitted with a 3.6" barrel. Overall height as been reduced by .4". Weight is about 28 oz. Introduced in 2003.

NIB	Exc.	V.G.	Good	Fair	Poor
600	500	400	300	175	95

Model 9000F

Introduced in 2000 this pistol is chambered for the 9mm or .40 S&W cartridge. It is fitted with a 3.4" barrel and has a polymer frame. The "F" type has a single-/double-action trigger. Fixed sights. Magazine capacity is 10 rounds. Weight is about 27 oz. Overall length is 6.6" and overall height is 4.8". External hammer and black finish.

NIB	Exc.	V.G.	Good	Fair	Poor
550	450	350	200	125	75

Model 9000D

Same as above but with double-action-only trigger.

NIB	Exc.	V.G.	Good	Fair	Poor
550	450	350	275	150	100

Model 9000S

This model is chambered for the 9mm or .40 S&W cartridges. Magazine capacity is 10 rounds. With optional spacer Model 92/96 magazines can also be used. Three-dot sight system. An accessory magazine bottom that extends when griped but retracts when holstered is standard. Steel alloy frame and slide. Weight is about 27 oz. Introduced in 2001.

NIB	Exc.	V.G.	Good	Fair	Poor
550	450	350	200	125	75

CHEETAH SERIES

Model 84/Cheetah

This is a small semi-automatic pistol chambered for the .380 cartridge. It has a double-column magazine that holds 13 rounds. Offered in blue or nickel finish. Grips are checkered black plastic or checkered wood.

NIB	Exc.	V.G.	Good	Fair	Poor
450	375	325	275	200	150

Model 84BB

Similar to the Model 84 but incorporates different features such as a firing pin blocking device and loaded chamber indicator. Single-column magazine holds 8 rounds of .380 shells. Discontinued in 1993.

NIB	Exc.	V.G.	Good	Fair	Poor
425	375	325	275	200	150

Model 85/Cheetah

Similar in appearance to the Model 84, but features a single-column magazine with a capacity of 8 rounds. Available in blue or nickel finish. Grips are checkered black plastic. Pistol weighs 22 oz.

NIB	Exc.	V.G.	Good	Fair	Poor
600	475	325	275	200	150

Model 86/Cheetah

This .380 ACP semi-automatic pistol has a 4.4" tip-up barrel. Magazine capacity is 8 rounds. Furnished with checkered wood grips. Pistol weighs 23 oz.

NIB	Exc.	V.G.	Good	Fair	Poor
675	500	300	250	200	150

Model 87/Cheetah

A .22 caliber double-action, semi-automatic target pistol with a 3.8" or 6" barrel, adjustable sights with a 7-shot magazine. Blued with checkered walnut grips. Introduced in 1986.

NIB	Exc.	V.G.	Good	Fair	Poor
650	525	375	250	200	150

Model 87 Target

This is a .22 caliber single-action target pistol. It features an adjustable rear sight, integral scope base, and external hammer. Anodized aluminum frame. Weight is about 41 oz. Introduced in 2000.

NIB	Exc.	V.G.	Good	Fair	Poor
700	600	395	250	200	150

Model 89/Gold Standard

A .22 caliber, semi-automatic target pistol with adjustable sights, and 10-shot, detachable magazine. Matte finish with hand-fitting walnut grips. Introduced in 1988.

NIB	Exc.	V.G.	Good	Fair	Poor
900	725	550	400	300	150

Px4 Storm Pistol

Introduced in 2005 this pistol features a single/double action trigger with decocker and is chambered for the 9mm, .45 ACP or .40 S&W cartridges. Fitted with a 4" barrel. Interchangeable grip backstraps. Reversible magazine release button. Picatinny rail. Fixed sights. Magazine capacity is 14 rounds for the .40 S&W and 17 rounds for the 9mm. Weight is about 27.5 lbs. Compact model has 3.2" barrel and smaller grip frame with magazine capacity reduced by two rounds.

NIB	Exc.	V.G.	Good	Fair	Poor
500	450	375	250	195	125

Model PX4 Storm Subcompact

Similar to above but with smaller dimensions and chambered in 9mm and .40 S&W only, 10- (.40) or 13- (9mm) round capacity. Overall length 6.2". Weight: 26.1 oz.

NIB	Exc.	V.G.	Good	Fair	Poor
500	450	375	250	195	125

Model PX4 Storm SD (Special Duty)

Similar to PX4 Storm but in .45 ACP only and with matte black slide and OD polymer frame, 9- or 10-round magazine. Overall length 8.2". Weight 28.6 oz.

NIB	Exc.	V.G.	Good	Fair	Poor
900	750	575	450	300	150

90-Two

Wrap-around polymer grip, standard or slim. Single/double-action semi-automatic in 9mm (10+1, 15+1 or 17+1 capacity) or .40 S&W (10+1 or 12+1 capacity). Types D, F or G. Fixed sights. 4.9" barrel, 32.5 oz. Introduced 2006. **NOTE:** Add 10 percent for luminous sights.

NIB	Exc.	V.G.	Good	Fair	Poor
600	475	350	290	210	150

BU9 Nano

Micro-compact DA-only 9mm with 6+1 round capacity, 3" barrel, polymer frame, adjustable sights. Weight: 17 oz. Introduced 2011.

NIB	Exc.	V.G.	Good	Fair	Poor
425	375	300	225	150	100

Stampede Blue

Introduced in 2003, this single-action revolver is chambered for the choice of .45 Colt, .44-40, or .357 Magnum cartridge. Choice of 4.75", 5.5", or 7.5" barrel. Blued with Beretta case color and black polymer grips. Weight is about 2.3 lbs. depending on barrel length.

NIB	Exc.	V.G.	Good	Fair	Poor
525	400	275	195	125	75

Stampede Nickel

As above but with brushed nickel finish and walnut grips.

NIB	Exc.	V.G.	Good	Fair	Poor
500	400	295	195	125	75

Stampede Deluxe

As above but with charcoal blue finish and Beretta case color with select walnut grips.

NIB	Exc.	V.G.	Good	Fair	Poor
620	500	375	250	195	125

Stampede Bisley

Single action 6-shot Bisley replica revolver in .45 Colt or .357 Magnum. Blued with 4.75", 5.5" or 7.5" barrel. Introduced 2006. **NOTE:** Add 10 percent for nickel.

NIB	Exc.	V.G.	Good	Fair	Poor
620	500	375	250	195	125

Laramie

Break-open single-action revolver reminiscent of S&W #3 chambered for .45 LC or .38 Special. Six-shot cylinder. Adjustable rear sight. 5" or 6.5" barrels. Introduced 2006. Made by Beretta subsidiary Uberti. **NOTE:** Add 10 percent for nickel finish.

NIB	Exc.	V.G.	Good	Fair	Poor
1000	875	595	375	225	145

RIFLES

1873 Renegade Short Lever-Action Rifle

Lever-action rifle chambered in .45 Colt, .357 Magnum. Patterned after 1873 Winchester. Features include 20" round barrel, blued finish, checkered walnut buttstock and fore-end, adjustable rear sight and fixed blade front. Ten-round tubular magazine.

NIB	Exc.	V.G.	Good	Fair	Poor
1400	1050	875	595	375	225

Gold Rush Slide-Action Rifle and Carbine

External replica of old Colt Lightning Magazine Rifle chambered in .357 Magnum and .45 Colt. Features include a 20" round or 24.5" octagonal barrel, case-hardened receiver, walnut buttstock and fore-end, crescent buttplate, 13-round (rifle) or 10-round (carbine) magazine. Available as Standard Carbine, Standard Rifle, or Deluxe Rifle.

NIB	Exc.	V.G.	Good	Fair	Poor
1400	1050	875	595	375	225

Cx4 Storm

Introduced in 2003, this semi-automatic carbine has a 16.6" barrel. Chambered for the 9mm, .40 S&W, or .45 ACP cartridge. Synthetic stock with rubber recoil pad has adjustable stock spacers. Ghost ring rear sight with adjustable post front sight. Forward accessory rail. Magazine capacity is 10 rounds for 9mm or .40 S&W and 8 rounds for the .45 ACP model. Weight is about 5.75 lbs.

NIB	Exc.	V.G.	Good	Fair	Poor
650	785	495	350	195	100

AR-70

A .223 caliber, semi-automatic rifle with a 17.7" barrel, adjustable diopter sights, and an 8- or 30-shot magazine. Black epoxy finish with a synthetic stock. Weight is approximately 8.3 lbs. No longer imported into the U.S.

NIB	Exc.	V.G.	Good	Fair	Poor
2100	1900	1500	1000	750	400

BM-59 Standard Grade

A gas-operated semi-automatic rifle with detachable box magazine. Chambered for .308 cartridge. Walnut stock. Barrel length is 19.3" with muzzlebrake. Magazine capacity is 5,10, or 20 rounds. Weight is about 9.5 lbs.

NIB	Exc.	V.G.	Good	Fair	Poor
3000	2700	2100	1500	400	200

Model 500 Custom

A bolt-action rifle in three action lengths, 24" barrel, open sights. Chambered in .222 Rem., .223 Rem., .243 Win., .270 Win., .308 Win., .30-06. Blued finish and checkered walnut stock. This model was offered in several grades.

NIB	Exc.	V.G.	Good	Fair	Poor
—	600	525	400	325	275

Model 500S

NIB	Exc.	V.G.	Good	Fair	Poor
—	625	550	425	350	300

Model 500DL

NIB	Exc.	V.G.	Good	Fair	Poor
—	1400	1250	1000	775	650

Model 500DEELL

NIB	Exc.	V.G.	Good	Fair	Poor
—	1600	1450	1200	975	800

Model 500DEELLS

NIB	Exc.	V.G.	Good	Fair	Poor
—	1625	1475	1225	1000	825

Model 501

A .243 or .308 caliber bolt-action rifle with a 23" barrel, furnished without sights and a 6-shot magazine. Blued with a checkered walnut stock. It was discontinued in 1986. It was offered in the same variations as the Model 500 series-501S, 501DL, 501DLS, 501EELL, and 501EELLS. The values for this series are the same as for the 500 series rifles.

Model 502

A .270, 7mm Remington Magnum, and .30-06 caliber bolt-action rifle with a 24" barrel (without sights) and a 5-shot magazine. Blued with a checkered walnut stock. Discontinued in 1986. It is also available in the same variations as the Model 500 and the Model 501 but is valued at approximately 10 percent higher in each variation.

Mato Standard

Bolt-action rifles built on Mauser 98 type action with controlled-round feed, three-position safety, adjustable trigger. Chambered in .270 Win., .280 Rem., .30-06, .300 Win. Magnum, .338 Win. Magnum. Composite stock.

NIB	Exc.	V.G.	Good	Fair	Poor
1200	1000	800	600	300	175

Mato Deluxe

This bolt-action rifle was introduced into the Beretta product line in 1997. The stock is XXX Claro walnut with a hand-rubbed oil finish and black fore-end tip. Chambered for .270 Win., .280, .30-06, 7mm Magnum, .300 Magnum, .338 Magnum, and .375 H&H. Weight is about 8 lbs.

NIB	Exc.	V.G.	Good	Fair	Poor
2000	1500	1000	750	350	200

PREMIUM RIFLES

Model S689 Sable

A 9.3x74R or the .30-06 caliber over/under rifle with a boxlock action, 23" ribbed barrels and express-type sights. Blued, case hardened or nickel-plated with checkered walnut stock. Double triggers and automatic ejectors. Offered in three grades. **NOTE**: Extra 20 gauge barrel with forearm add $1,200. Scope with claw mounts add $2,000.

Silver Sable

NIB	Exc.	V.G.	Good	Fair	Poor
3850	3000	2500	1750	1200	300

Gold Sable

NIB	Exc.	V.G.	Good	Fair	Poor
6500	5500	4500	3000	1500	350

Diamond Sable

NIB	Exc.	V.G.	Good	Fair	Poor
12750	10000	7500	5500	2000	1000

SSO Express

A .375 Holland & Holland and .458 Winchester Magnum caliber over/under, double barrel rifle with 23" barrels, folding express sights, double triggers, and automatic ejectors. Furnished with a fitted case. This firearm is available on a custom order basis and should be individually appraised.

NIB	Exc.	V.G.	Good	Fair	Poor
18000	13000	9500	6000	3500	2500

SSO5 Express

A more finely finished version of the above.

NIB	Exc.	V.G.	Good	Fair	Poor
20000	15000	11000	8000	5000	3000

SSO6

This is a premium grade sidelock over/under express rifle. Equipped with double triggers. It is offered in 9.3x74R, .375 H&H Magnum, and .458 Win. Magnum. It is fitted with a 24" barrel with express sights. Claw mounts for Zeiss scopes are available from the factory. The receiver is case-colored with light scroll engraving. Special select walnut is used in the stock and forearm with fine line checkering. Stock comes with cheekpiece and rubber recoil pad. Furnished with leather case. Rifle weighs about 11 lbs.

NIB	Exc.	V.G.	Good	Fair	Poor
55000	45000	34000	24000	15000	10000

SSO6 EELL

Offered in the same calibers as above but furnished with hand engraved game scenes with gold inlays. Walnut stock is special select briar with fine diamond line checkering.

NIB	Exc.	V.G.	Good	Fair	Poor
95000	70000	50000	30000	18000	10000

Model 455

This is a premium grade side-by-side express rifle with slide locks. Available in these calibers: .375 H&H Magnum, .458 Win. Magnum, .470 Nitro Express, .500 Nitro Express, and .416 Rigby. The receiver is case-colored without engraving and the walnut stock is highly figured with fine line checkering. Comes supplied with express sights. Claw mounts and Zeiss scope offered at customer's request only on .375, .458, and .416. Weighs about 11 lbs.

NIB	Exc.	V.G.	Good	Fair	Poor
53000	40000	30000	15000	6750	2000

Model 455 EELL

Same as above model but furnished with case-colored game scene engraving with gold inlays. Walnut briar stock with fine diamond line checkering. Supplied with leather case and accessories.

NIB	Exc.	V.G.	Good	Fair	Poor
95000	70000	50000	30000	18000	10000

SHOTGUNS

Beretta shotguns are marked with a symbol or "0" stamping to indicate the type of fixed choke in the barrel or barrels. Usually this stamping is on the side of the barrel in the rear, near the receiver on semi-automatics and near the ejectors on double barrel shotguns. Beretta shotguns with screw-in Mobilchoke tubes will have notches cut in them to indicate the amount of choke placed in the tube.

BL SERIES

The BL series of over/under shotguns were manufactured between 1968 and 1973. They are chambered for 12 or 20 gauge and were offered with 26", 28", or 30" vent ribbed barrels with various choke combinations. They feature boxlock actions and were offered with either single or double triggers, and manual extractors or automatic ejectors. The finishes are blued with checkered walnut stocks. The configurations differ basically in the quality of materials and workmanship and the degree of ornamentation.

BL-1

NIB	Exc.	V.G.	Good	Fair	Poor
—	500	450	350	225	150

BL-2

NIB	Exc.	V.G.	Good	Fair	Poor
—	425	375	300	250	200

BL-2/S (Speed Trigger)

NIB	Exc.	V.G.	Good	Fair	Poor
—	450	400	325	275	225

BL-2 Stakeout

18" barrel.

NIB	Exc.	V.G.	Good	Fair	Poor
—	400	350	275	225	175

BL-3

NIB	Exc.	V.G.	Good	Fair	Poor
—	600	550	475	425	350

BL-3 Competition

NIB	Exc.	V.G.	Good	Fair	Poor
—	650	600	525	475	400

BL-4

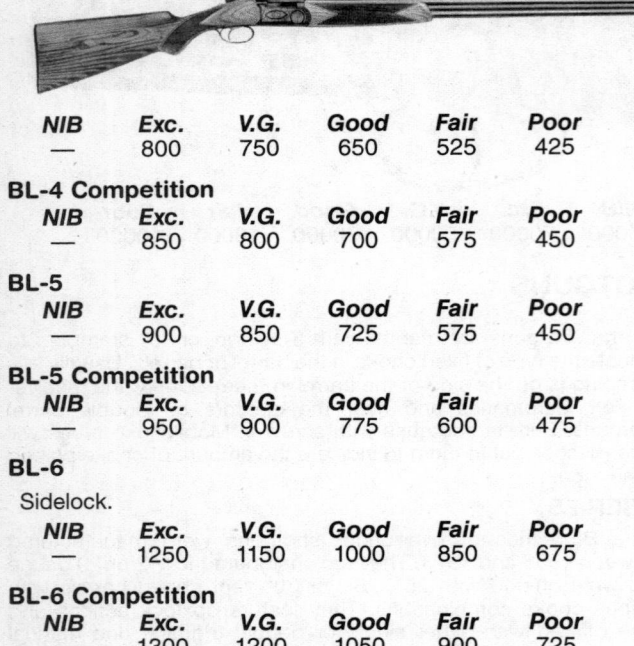

NIB	Exc.	V.G.	Good	Fair	Poor
—	800	750	650	525	425

BL-4 Competition

NIB	Exc.	V.G.	Good	Fair	Poor
—	850	800	700	575	450

BL-5

NIB	Exc.	V.G.	Good	Fair	Poor
—	900	850	725	575	450

BL-5 Competition

NIB	Exc.	V.G.	Good	Fair	Poor
—	950	900	775	600	475

BL-6

Sidelock.

NIB	Exc.	V.G.	Good	Fair	Poor
—	1250	1150	1000	850	675

BL-6 Competition

NIB	Exc.	V.G.	Good	Fair	Poor
—	1300	1200	1050	900	725

Model S55 B

A 12 or 20 gauge over/under shotgun with 26", 28", or 30" ventilated rib barrels, various choke combinations and boxlock action with a single-selective trigger and extractors. Blued with a checkered walnut stock.

NIB	Exc.	V.G.	Good	Fair	Poor
—	550	500	400	325	275

Model S56 E

As above, but more finely finished.

NIB	Exc.	V.G.	Good	Fair	Poor
—	600	550	450	375	325

Model S58 Competition

As above, with either 26" or 30" barrels, wide vent ribs and competition-type stocks.

NIB	Exc.	V.G.	Good	Fair	Poor
—	700	650	550	475	400

Silver Snipe

A 12 or 20 gauge over/under shotgun with 26", 28", or 30" barrels, boxlock action with a double trigger and extractors. Blued with a checkered walnut stock. Manufactured from 1955 through 1967.

A single-selective trigger version with ventilated rib and automatic ejectors would be worth approximately 50 percent additional.

NIB	Exc.	V.G.	Good	Fair	Poor
—	600	475	325	275	200

Golden Snipe

As above with a ventilated rib and automatic ejectors. If it has a single-selective trigger, add 10 percent.

NIB	Exc.	V.G.	Good	Fair	Poor
—	800	675	500	350	200

Model 57 E

As above, but more finely finished. Manufactured between 1955 and 1967.

NIB	Exc.	V.G.	Good	Fair	Poor
—	825	775	600	475	250

ASEL Model

A 12 or 20 gauge over/under shotgun with 26", 28", or 30" ventilated rib barrel with various choke combinations. Single-selective trigger and automatic ejectors. Blued with a checkered pistol-grip stock. Manufactured between 1947 and 1964. Prices listed are for 20 gauge guns. **NOTE:** For 12 gauge guns deduct $1000 from Exc. condition price. For EELL grade add 30 percent.

NIB	Exc.	V.G.	Good	Fair	Poor
—	4250	2500	1200	750	400

Model 409 PB

A 12, 16, 20, and 28 gauge boxlock, double-barrel shotgun with 27", 28", or 30" barrels with double triggers and extractors and various choke combinations. Blued with a checkered walnut stock. Manufactured between 1934 and 1964. **NOTE:** Add 50 percent for 20 gauge, 100 percent for 28 gauge.

NIB	Exc.	V.G.	Good	Fair	Poor
—	775	700	625	500	250

Model 410

As above, with a 32" Full-choke barrel. Blued with a checkered walnut stock. Introduced in 1934 in 10 gauge only.

NIB	Exc.	V.G.	Good	Fair	Poor
—	1000	925	750	600	300

Model 410 E

More finely finished version of 409PB.

NIB	Exc.	V.G.	Good	Fair	Poor
—	900	825	650	500	275

Model 411 E

The Model 410 with false sideplates and more heavily engraved. Manufactured between 1934 and 1964.

NIB	Exc.	V.G.	Good	Fair	Poor
—	1800	1400	950	800	425

Model 424

A 12 and 20 gauge boxlock shotgun with 26" or 28" barrels, double triggers, various choke combinations, and extractors. Blued with a checkered walnut stock. In 20 gauge it is designated the Model 426 and would be worth an additional 50 percent.

NIB	Exc.	V.G.	Good	Fair	Poor
—	950	875	675	500	225

Model 426 E

As above, with silver inlays and heavier engraving, single-selective trigger and automatic ejectors. Not imported after 1983.

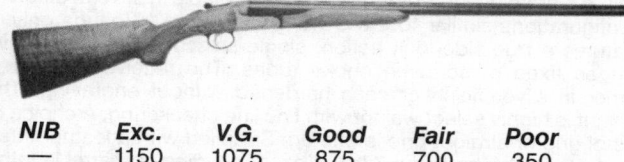

NIB	Exc.	V.G.	Good	Fair	Poor
—	1150	1075	875	700	350

Model 625

A 12 or 20 gauge boxlock, double-barrel shotgun with 26", 28", or 30" barrels, various choke combinations, double triggers and extractors. Moderately engraved and blued with a checkered walnut grip. Imported between 1984 and 1986. **NOTE:** Add 50 percent for 20 gauge.

NIB	Exc.	V.G.	Good	Fair	Poor
—	800	750	600	500	250

GR Series

Moderately priced series of side-by-side boxlock double shotguns imported from 1968 to about 1976. Offered in 12 or 20 gauge with fixed chokes. GR-2 has double triggers with folding front trigger, extractors. GR-3 has single selective trigger, better wood. GR-4 has automatic ejectors, higher grade wood. Prices shown are for 12 gauge models. **NOTE:** Add 50 percent for 20 gauge.

GR-1

NIB	Exc.	V.G.	Good	Fair	Poor
1000	850	700	600	500	350

GR-2

NIB	Exc.	V.G.	Good	Fair	Poor
1150	950	800	700	600	400

GR-3

NIB	Exc.	V.G.	Good	Fair	Poor
1250	1050	900	800	700	500

Silver Hawk

A 10 or 12 gauge boxlock, double-barrel shotgun with 30" barrels, double triggers and extractors. Blued with a silver-finished receiver and a checkered walnut stock. The 10 gauge version would be worth an additional 20 percent. Discontinued in 1967.

NIB	Exc.	V.G.	Good	Fair	Poor
—	700	500	375	250	150

Model 470 Silver Hawk

Introduced in 1997 to commemorate Beretta's 470 years in the gunmaking business, this shotgun is offered in either 12 or 20 gauge configurations. The receiver is silver chrome with engraving. The top lever is checkered with a gold inlaid hawk's head. The gun is fitted with a straight grip stock with splinter forearm of select walnut with oil finish. Choice of 26" or 28" barrels with auto ejection or manual extraction. Weight of 12 gauge about 6.5 lbs. The 20 gauge weighs approximately 6 lbs.

NIB	Exc.	V.G.	Good	Fair	Poor
2400	2000	1500	—	—	—

Model 470 Silver Hawk EL

Introduced in 2002 this model features color case hardened frame with side plates with gold filled game scene engraving. Offered in 12 or 20 gauge with choice of 26" or 28" barrels. Weight is 5.9 lbs. for 20 gauge and 6.5 lbs. for 12 gauge.

NIB	Exc.	V.G.	Good	Fair	Poor
4800	4000	3000	—	—	—

471 Silver Hawk

Introduced in 2003, this side-by-side shotgun has a boxlock receiver and is offered in 12 and 20 gauge with a choice of 26" or 28" barrels. This model is also offered with a choice of pistol grip with beavertail fore-end or straight grip stock with splinter fore-end. A straight grip stock with case color receiver is also available at a premium. Select walnut stock with oil finish. Single-selective trigger. Weight is about 6.5 lbs. in 12 gauge and 5.9 lbs. in 20 gauge. **NOTE:** Add $350 for straight grip stock with case color receiver.

NIB	Exc.	V.G.	Good	Fair	Poor
2875	2250	1300	800	450	300

"SO" SERIES & OTHER PREMIUM SHOTGUNS

These over/under shotguns were fitted with side-locks, automatic ejectors, single or double triggers. Barrel ranges in length from 26" to 30" with a wide variety of choke combinations. These guns were introduced in 1948 in 12 gauge only and no longer imported as a production gun in 1986. Many of these SO guns were sold through the firm of Garcia, a sporting goods firm and distributor. The various grades are priced according to quality of wood, finish engraving coverage, and the like. Do not confuse these earlier Beretta shotguns with the present line of premium grade Berettas now being imported into the U.S.

SO-1

NIB	Exc.	V.G.	Good	Fair	Poor
—	3000	2400	1500	800	400

Model SO-2

NIB	Exc.	V.G.	Good	Fair	Poor
—	4000	2700	2000	900	500

SO-3

NIB	Exc.	V.G.	Good	Fair	Poor
—	5000	4400	3500	1500	1000

SO-4 (Garcia SO3EL)

NOTE: For fully engraved Garcia Model SO3-EL add 80 percent.

NIB	Exc.	V.G.	Good	Fair	Poor
—	7900	6900	3500	2000	1500

SO-5 (Garcia SO-3 EELL)

NIB	Exc.	V.G.	Good	Fair	Poor
—	—	7900	5900	3500	2500

SO-6 (450 or 451 EL) Side-by-Side

This model is fitted with Holland & Holland-style sidelocks and third fastener.

NIB	Exc.	V.G.	Good	Fair	Poor
—	7500	6500	5500	3500	2500

SO-7 (451 EELL) Side-by-Side

NIB	Exc.	V.G.	Good	Fair	Poor
—	8900	7900	5900	4000	3000

SO-5 Trap

A premium grade Beretta over/under shotgun built for competition trap shooting. Available in 12 gauge with 30" vent rib barrels standard. Barrels in 28" and 32" may be special ordered. Receiver is silver with light scroll engraving. The stock is select highly figured walnut with pistol grip and offered in International or Monte Carlo dimensions. Special trap rubber recoil pad is furnished. Weighs 8 lbs. 2 oz. Furnished with leather case and tools.

NIB	Exc.	V.G.	Good	Fair	Poor
20500	16000	12000	6500	3000	600

SO-5 Trap 2 Barrel Set

NIB	Exc.	V.G.	Good	Fair	Poor
23500	18500	13000	6500	3000	600

SO-5 Sporting Clays

Offered in 12 gauge only with choice of 28", 30", or 32" barrels; 26" on special order. Sporting clay dimension walnut stock with pistol grip and rubber recoil pad. Weighs 7 lbs. 8 oz.

SO-5 sidelocks

NIB	Exc.	V.G.	Good	Fair	Poor
20500	10000	7500	5000	2750	500

SO-5 Skeet

Same general specifications as SO-5 Trap but furnished to skeet dimensions. Offered in 12 gauge only with 26" or 28" vent rib barrels choked skeet. Weighs 7 lbs. 8 oz.

NIB	Exc.	V.G.	Good	Fair	Poor
20500	16000	7500	5000	2750	500

SO-6 EL

This is a premium grade Beretta that is available in several different configurations similar to the SO-5. Available in 12 gauge only. It features a true side-lock action, single-selective or nonselective trigger, fixed or screw-in choke tubes. The receiver is offered either in silver finish or case hardened without engraving. The walnut is highly select walnut with fine line checkering. A choice of pistol grip or straight grip is offered. Supplied with a leather fitted hard case. Weighs about 7 lbs. 4 oz. depending on barrel length.

SO-6 receiver

SO-6 Trap

NIB	Exc.	V.G.	Good	Fair	Poor
26500	13000	8500	5000	1700	500

SO-6 Skeet

NIB	Exc.	V.G.	Good	Fair	Poor
26500	13000	8500	5000	1700	500

SO-6 Sporting Clays

NIB	Exc.	V.G.	Good	Fair	Poor
26500	13000	8500	5000	1700	500

SO-6 EELL

A higher grade in the SO-6 series that features a silver receiver with custom engraving with scroll or game scenes. Gold inlays are available on request. Choice of barrel lengths from 26" to 30". Choice of pistol grip or straight grip. All of the same features of the SO-6, but with higher fit and finish. Offered in 12 gauge only.

NIB	Exc.	V.G.	Good	Fair	Poor
43750	33500	27000	20000	12000	600

SO-6 EESS

Same specifications as the SO-6 EELL grade but with ruby, sapphire, or emerald side plates with diamond brilliants.

NIB	Exc.	V.G.	Good	Fair	Poor
88850	75000	50000	2250	1750	600

SO-7

One of Beretta's best-grade, sidelock, double-barrel shotgun. It is elaborately engraved and has the highest grade walnut in the stock. No longer in production.

SO-9 with close-ups of engraving patterns

NIB	Exc.	V.G.	Good	Fair	Poor
—	10500	8850	7250	5500	4500

SO-9

This model over/under is Beretta's highest grade. Offered in 12, 20, and 28 gauge, and .410 bore. The true side lock (removable) receiver is highly engraved with scroll or game scenes by Italy's finest craftsmen. Barrel lengths are offered from 26" to 30" with solid hand filed rib. The walnut stock is the finest available with either pistol grip or straight grip. Stock dimensions to customers request. A custom fitted leather case with accessories is supplied with gun. A custom order gun. An independent appraisal is strongly suggested prior to a sale. Suggested Retail Price: From $44,500 to $98,000.

Jubilee Field Grade (Giubileo)

This model was introduced in 1998 and is Beretta's finest boxlock over/under shotgun. The model is fitted with sideplates without screws. Offered in 12, 20, 28, and .410 bore with 26" to 30" barrel depending on gauge. Each gun is richly engraved with fine scroll and signed by master engravers. Highly figured walnut with pistol or straight grip. Weights range from about 7 lbs. in 12 gauge to 5.5 lbs. in .410 bore.

Single Gun

NIB	Exc.	V.G.	Good	Fair	Poor
14750	12000	825	4500	2200	600

Matched Pair

NIB	Exc.	V.G.	Good	Fair	Poor
32650	—	—	—	—	—

Jubilee Sporting Grade

Similar to the above model in terms of finish but offered in 12 gauge only with choice of 30" or 32" barrels. Pistol grip standard. **NOTE:** For two barrel combination with 20 gauge barrel and extended chokes add $1,500.

NIB	Exc.	V.G.	Good	Fair	Poor
14750	12000	8250	4500	2200	600

Jubilee II (Giublio)

This is a side-by-side model offered in 12 or 20 gauge only with straight grip stocks. Choice of 26" or 28" barrels. Full coverage scroll engraving and highly figured walnut. Double triggers are by special order only. The 12 gauge weighs about 6.5 lbs. while the 20 gauge weighs about 6 lbs.

Single Gun

NIB	Exc.	V.G.	Good	Fair	Poor
14750	12000	8250	4500	2200	600

Matched Pair

NIB	Exc.	V.G.	Good	Fair	Poor
32650	2600	17000	9200	4000	900

ASE Deluxe Sporting

This boxlock over/under gun is offered in 12 gauge only with choice of 28" or 30" barrels. Classic European scroll engraving. Offered in both field and competition configuration. Weights are about 7.5 lbs. for the 12 gauge.

NIB	Exc.	V.G.	Good	Fair	Poor
25000	18500	12000	900	700	400

Model 687 EELL Gallery Special

A special version of this model. These are especially engraved guns with upgraded wood that are only made for the Beretta Galleries. Offered in 12, 20, 28, and .410 bore.

Single Gun

NIB	Exc.	V.G.	Good	Fair	Poor
8500	7300	5900	4500	3300	500

Special Combo—20/28 Gauge

NIB	Exc.	V.G.	Good	Fair	Poor
9500	8600	6700	5800	4000	600

Matched Pair

NIB	Exc.	V.G.	Good	Fair	Poor
17100	15500	11500	8000	4750	700

Imperiale Montecarlo

This is a side-by-side gun chambered for the 12, 20, or 28 gauge shell. True sidelock action. Choice of 26", 27", or 28" barrels with fixed chokes. Other lengths by special request. Weight is about 7.3 lbs. for 12 gauge, 6.5 lbs. for 20 gauge, and 6.2 lbs. for 28 gauge. Master engraved and signed.

Diana

This side-by-side gun is chambered for the 12 or 20 gauge with choice of barrel lengths. Action is true sidelock with exposed hammers. Weight for 12 gauge is about 7.2 lbs. and for the 20 gauge about 6.4 lbs. Master engraved and signed. **NOTE:** To scarce to value. Seek qualified appraisal.

Model 451 Series

A custom order sidelock shotgun. The lowest priced version would be worth approximately $8,000 in excellent condition; and the top-of-the-line model, approximately $25,000. Prospective purchasers are advised to secure a qualified appraisal prior to acquisition.

Model 450 Series

This model is the same as the 451 series with the exception of being a Holland & Holland sidelock design. Prospective purchasers are advised to secure a qualified appraisal prior to acquisition.

Model 452

This is a premium grade side-by-side shotgun fitted with sidelocks (removable). Offered in 12 gauge only with 26", 28", or 30" solid rib barrels. The receiver is a highly polished silver finish without engraving. Triggers may be double, single-selective, or single non-selective. The stock and forearm are special select walnut with fine line checkering with a choice of pistol or straight grip. Comes with leather hard case. Weighs about 6 lbs. 13 oz.

NIB	Exc.	V.G.	Good	Fair	Poor
24000	19000	14500	8500	4500	2500

Model 452 EELL

Same as above but furnished with fine scroll or game scene engraving. The highest grade of walnut is furnished for the stock and forearm. Leather case with accessories furnished.

NIB	Exc.	V.G.	Good	Fair	Poor
31000	27500	19500	11000	7000	600

ONYX SERIES

This series designation was first used in 2003 to simplify the product line. Instead of using numeric model references the company now refers to these guns and others by series name.

Onyx

This over/under gun is offered in 12, 20, and for 2003, 28 gauge. With a choice of 26" or 28" barrels. It features a boxlock action with select checkered walnut stock, single-selective trigger, schnabel fore-end and auto safety. Black rubber recoil pad. Blued barrels and action. Weight is about 6.8 lbs. for 12 gauge.

NIB	Exc.	V.G.	Good	Fair	Poor
1675	1350	950	650	475	200

Onyx Waterfowler 3.5

As above but in 12 gauge with 3.5" chamber and matte black finish.

NIB	Exc.	V.G.	Good	Fair	Poor
1750	1400	1050	700	500	250

White Onyx

Introduced in 2003 this model features a receiver machined in a jeweled pattern with satin nickel alloy. Offered in 12, 20, and 28 gauge with choice of 26" or 28" barrels. Select checkered walnut stock with schnabel fore-end. Weight is about 6.8 lbs. for 12 gauge.

NIB	Exc.	V.G.	Good	Fair	Poor
1775	1425	1250	700	500	250

Onyx Pro

Introduced in 2003 this over/under shotgun is offered in 12, 20 and 28 gauge with a choice of 26" or 28" vent rib barrels with choke tubes. Single-selective trigger. Checkered X-Tra wood stock. Gel-Tek recoil pad. Supplied with plastic carry case. Weight is about 6.8 lbs.

NIB	Exc.	V.G.	Good	Fair	Poor
1700	1300	1000	600	400	200

Onyx Pro 3.5

As above in 12 gauge with 3.5" chamber. Weight is approximately 6.9 lbs. Introduced in 2003.

NIB	Exc.	V.G.	Good	Fair	Poor
1700	1300	1000	600	400	200

682 SERIES
682/682 Gold

This is a high-grade, quality-built over/under shotgun. Offered in 12 and 20 gauge, it is also available in some configurations in 28 gauge and .410 bore with barrel lengths from 26" to 34" depending on the type of shooting required. It is fitted with single-selective trigger and automatic ejectors. Barrels are fitted with ventilated rib and various fixed or screw-in choke combinations are available. The stock is a high-grade walnut with fine checkering in stock dimensions to fit the function of the gun. The frame is silver with light scroll borders on most models. This model covers a wide variety of applications and these are listed by grade and/or function:

NOTE: The Beretta Competition Series shotguns have been renamed as of 1994. These shotguns are also referred to as the 682 Gold Competition Series guns, such as Model 682 Gold Trap or Model 682 Gold X Trap Combo and so forth.

682 Super Skeet

This model is offered in 12 gauge only with 28" vent rib barrels choked skeet and skeet. Single-selective trigger and auto ejectors are standard. This Super Skeet features ported barrels and adjustable length of pull and drop. A fitted hard case is standard. Gun weighs 7 lbs. 8 oz.

NIB	Exc.	V.G.	Good	Fair	Poor
2400	1850	1500	1250	750	450

682 Skeet

This is the standard 12 gauge skeet model that features a choice of 26" or 28" vent rib barrels choked skeet and skeet. Walnut stock is of International dimensions with special skeet rubber recoil pad. Gun is supplied with hard case. Weighs 7 lbs. 8 oz.

NIB	Exc.	V.G.	Good	Fair	Poor
2000	1750	1500	1250	750	450

682 4 Barrel Set

This skeet gun is fitted with 4 barrels in 12, 20, 28 gauge, and .410 bore. Each barrel is 28", choked skeet and skeet, and fitted with a vent rib.

NIB	Exc.	V.G.	Good	Fair	Poor
4000	3500	3000	2500	2000	650

682 Super Sporting/682 Gold Sporting Ported

Built for sporting clays this 12 gauge or 20 gauge model features ported barrel and adjustable length of pull and drop. Fitted with 28" or 30" vent barrel with screw-in chokes; fixed chokes on special order. Checkered walnut stock with pistol grip and recoil pad. Supplied with case. Introduced in 1993. Weight of 12 gauge is 7 lbs. 8 oz. and 20 gauge weighs 6 lbs. 3 oz.

NIB	Exc.	V.G.	Good	Fair	Poor
2400	2000	1600	1100	700	350

682 Gold Sporting

The standard version of the 12 gauge or 20 gauge Super Sporting model with a choice of 28" or 30" vent rib barrel with screw-in chokes. Checkered walnut stock with recoil pad. Introduced in 1993.

NIB	Exc.	V.G.	Good	Fair	Poor
2000	1650	1400	1250	950	350

682 Sporting Combo

Similar to the 682 Sporting with the addition of two 12 gauge 28" and 30" barrels fitted with screw-in chokes. Supplied with hard case.

NIB	Exc.	V.G.	Good	Fair	Poor
3200	2700	2250	1750	1250	650

682 Super Trap

This 12 gauge trap model (a 20 gauge set of barrels is available on special order) features ported 30" or 32" ventilated rib barrels with either fixed or screw-in chokes. Automatic ejectors are standard as is a single non-selective trigger. The checkered walnut stock can be adjusted for length of pull and drop of comb and is offered in either Monte Carlo or International dimensions. Weight is approximately 8 lbs. 6 oz.

NIB	Exc.	V.G.	Good	Fair	Poor
2300	2000	1700	1250	950	500

682 Top Single Super Trap

Same as the Super Trap but available in a single barrel configuration of either 32" or 34".

NIB	Exc.	V.G.	Good	Fair	Poor
2600	2150	1700	1350	950	500

682 Top Combo Super Trap

This configuration features a single barrel and an over/under barrel, both interchangeable. The combinations are: 30", 32", and 30", 34".

NIB	Exc.	V.G.	Good	Fair	Poor
3300	2975	2350	1750	1250	650

682 Trap

This model is the standard variation Beretta trap gun. This 12 gauge comes standard with 30" vent rib barrels. However, 28" and 32" barrels can be special ordered. Fixed or screw-in chokes are available. The three-position sliding trigger allows for adjustable length of pull. A checkered walnut stock with recoil pad is standard. Stock is available in either Monte Carlo or International dimensions. Customer has choice of either silver or black receiver. Comes cased.

NIB	Exc.	V.G.	Good	Fair	Poor
2300	1950	1700	1250	900	450

682 Top Single Trap

This 12 gauge single barrel trap gun is available in 32" or 34" vent rib barrel.

NIB	Exc.	V.G.	Good	Fair	Poor
2000	1600	1200	1000	600	450

682 Mono Combo Trap

A special configuration that features a single barrel with vent rib set to place single barrel in bottom position of what would normally be an over/under setup. A second barrel that is an over/under is also provided as part of the set. Single barrel is 34" and the over/under set is 32" in length.

NIB	Exc.	V.G.	Good	Fair	Poor
2500	2100	1500	1200	750	500

682 Top Combo

This trap combination features a standard placement single barrel with an interchangeable over/under barrel. Barrel sets available in 30"/32", 30"/34", and 32"/34". Barrels are fitted with ventilated rib.

NIB	Exc.	V.G.	Good	Fair	Poor
2500	2000	1500	1000	950	500

682 Gold Trap with Adjustable Stock

Introduced in 1998 this over/under features a choice of 30" or 32" barrels with Monte Carlo stock and adjustable drop, cast, and comb. Trigger is adjustable for length of pull. Selected walnut stock with oil finish. Black rubber recoil pad standard. Weight is approximately 8.8 lbs. **NOTE:** Add $800 for Top Combo set.

NIB	Exc.	V.G.	Good	Fair	Poor
2200	1800	1500	—	—	—

682 Gold Skeet with Adjustable Stock

Introduced in 1999 this 12 gauge model features a skeet stock with adjustable comb. Stock drop and cast may also be adjusted. Graystone receiver. Comes with case. Offered in choice of 28" or 30" barrels. Single-selective trigger adjustable for length of pull. Black rubber recoil pad standard. Weight is about 7.5 lbs.

NIB	Exc.	V.G.	Good	Fair	Poor
2000	1700	1500	1200	900	600

682 Gold "Live Bird"

Introduced in 1995 this model has a gray receiver with select walnut stock. Single-selective trigger is adjustable for length of pull. Offered in 12 gauge only with 30" barrels. Average weight is 8.8 lbs.

NIB	Exc.	V.G.	Good	Fair	Poor
2550	1950	1595	1150	850	400

S682 Gold E Trap

Chambered for 12 gauge 3" chambers with choice of 30" or 32" barrels overbored and choke tubes. Highly select walnut stock with black rubber pad. Single-selective trigger with adjustable length of pull. Beavertail fore-end. Adjustable Monte Carlo stock. Front white bead with mid bead sight. Carry case standard. Weight is about 8.8 lbs. Introduced in 2001.

NIB	Exc.	V.G.	Good	Fair	Poor
3900	3300	2750	1800	900	450

S682 Gold E Trap Combo

Offers the same features as the Trap model but with interchangeable over/under barrels and top single barrel with under rib. Introduced in 2001.

NIB	Exc.	V.G.	Good	Fair	Poor
5600	4400	3100	1700	800	350

S682 Gold E Skeet

This 12 gauge skeet gun features a special skeet-style stock with beavertail fore-end. Adjustable stock. Barrel lengths are 28" or 30". Single-selective trigger. Weight is about 7.5 lbs. Introduced in 2001.

NIB	Exc.	V.G.	Good	Fair	Poor
4000	3600	2750	1500	625	350

S682 Gold E Sporting

This 12 gauge model has a choice of 28", 30", or 32" barrels with extended choke tubes and tapered top rib with white front sight and mid bead. Sporting clay-style stock of select walnut. Weight is about 7.6 lbs. Introduced in 2001.

NIB	Exc.	V.G.	Good	Fair	Poor
4150	3200	2350	1200	475	300

Model 685

A lower priced over/under chambered for 12 or 20 gauge with 3" chambers, a satin-chromed boxlock action with a single trigger and extractors. Not imported after 1986.

NIB	Exc.	V.G.	Good	Fair	Poor
—	750	675	550	375	200

686 SERIES

686/686 Silver Perdiz Sporting

This Beretta over/under shotgun is available in a number of different configurations. This basic model features ventilated rib barrels from 24" to 30"; 30" is a special order. Screw-in chokes or fixed chokes are available. All configurations are offered in 12 gauge and 20 gauge with 28 gauge and .410 bore available in special order only. The gun is fitted with checkered American walnut stock with black rubber recoil pad and special grip cap. Some models have silver receiver with scroll engraving and others have black receivers with gold-filled contours. This 686 series was renamed in 1994.

686 Essential/Silver Essential

Introduced in 1994 this 686 model is designed to be an entry level 686. It offers all of the mechanical features of the 686 series without any of the frills. Offered in 12 gauge only with 26" or 28" barrels with open-side rib. Plain walnut stock with checkering and plain blue receiver. Weighs about 6.7 lbs. Renamed the Silver Essential in 1997.

Beretta 686 Silver Essential w/close-up view of engraving

NIB	Exc.	V.G.	Good	Fair	Poor
900	750	600	450	350	200

686 Ultra Light Onyx

This model features a black anodized light alloy receiver accented with an engraved gold-filled "P. Beretta" signature. Available in 12 gauge only with 26" or 28" vent rib barrels. Chokes are either fixed or screw-in type. Weighs 5 lbs. 1 oz.

NIB	Exc.	V.G.	Good	Fair	Poor
1050	850	750	600	500	400

686 Onyx

Similar in appearance to the Ultra Light Onyx, but available in either 12 gauge or 20 gauge with vent rib barrel lengths from 26" to 28". Chambers are either 3" or 3.5". Checkered walnut stock offered in pistol grip or straight grip. Choice of choke types. Weight of 12 gauge 6 lbs.13 oz.; 20 gauge 6 lbs. 3 oz. A 12 gauge version with 3.5" chambers and 28" barrel is offered (new in 1999) with matte wood finish, matte black receiver, beavertail fore-end with fingerwells, and silver finish trigger.

NIB	Exc.	V.G.	Good	Fair	Poor
1800	1350	950	650	500	400

686 Onyx 2 Barrel Set

Same as above but supplied with a 20 gauge 28" vent rib barrel and a 28 gauge 26" vent rib barrel.

NIB	Exc.	V.G.	Good	Fair	Poor
2100	1650	1500	800	650	500

686 Silver Receiver

This model is the basic 686. It features a plain semi-matte silver receiver and is available in either 12 or 20 gauge; 28 gauge available on special order. Vent rib barrels are offered in lengths from 24" to 30" with fixed chokes or choke tubes.

NIB	Exc.	V.G.	Good	Fair	Poor
1200	895	775	650	500	400

686 L/686 Silver Perdiz

Same as above but furnished with a scroll engraved silver receiver. Offered in 28 gauge with 26" or 28" vent rib barrels. Gun weighs 5 lbs. 5 oz.

NIB	Exc.	V.G.	Good	Fair	Poor
1200	950	750	650	500	400

686 Silver Pigeon

Introduced in 1996 this model replaces the Silver Perdiz. It has an electroless nickel finish on a scroll engraved receiver. Offered in 12, 20, and 28 gauge with 26" or 28" barrels. Average weight is 6.8 lbs. A new variation, introduced in 1999, features a 20 gauge gun with 28" barrels, straight grip stock, and matte nickel receiver.

NIB	Exc.	V.G.	Good	Fair	Poor
1800	1450	950	600	400	200

Sporting

NIB	Exc.	V.G.	Good	Fair	Poor
1500	1050	750	600	400	200

Trap (30")

NIB	Exc.	V.G.	Good	Fair	Poor
1400	1000	700	500	400	300

Trap Top Mono (32" or 34")

NIB	Exc.	V.G.	Good	Fair	Poor
1300	900	600	500	400	300

686 Silver Pigeon S

Essentially the same as the Silver Pigeon models but packaged with a carrying case that includes five choke tubes, accessory recoil pad, and sling swivels. A .410-bore offering on a proportionally smaller receiver was added in 2006. **NOTE:** Add $700 for two barrel 20/28 gauge set.

NIB	Exc.	V.G.	Good	Fair	Poor
2000	1600	1275	825	575	350

686E Sporting

Offered in 12 or 20 gauge with choice of 28" or 30" barrels. Five Beretta screw-in chokes. Modern ellipsis receiver engraving. Special carrying case. Introduced with new styling in 2001.

NIB	Exc.	V.G.	Good	Fair	Poor
2100	1700	1350	825	575	350

686 EL/Gold Perdiz

This model is available in 12 gauge or 20 gauge with 26" or 28" vent rib barrels. The receiver is silver with scroll engraving and fitted with side plates. A fitted hard case comes with the gun.

NIB	Exc.	V.G.	Good	Fair	Poor
1900	1350	1100	800	700	350

686 Hunter Sport

A sporting clay 12 gauge or 20 gauge shotgun that features a silver receiver with scroll engraving. Wide 12.5mm target rib. Radius recoil pad. Offered in 26" or 28" vent rib barrels with screw-in chokes. Offered for the first time in 1993.

NIB	Exc.	V.G.	Good	Fair	Poor
1200	950	750	600	500	250

686 Onyx Hunter Sport

Same as above but offered in 12 gauge only with matte black finish on receiver and barrels. Weighs 6 lbs.13 oz. Introduced in 1993.

NIB	Exc.	V.G.	Good	Fair	Poor
1100	850	650	600	500	250

WING SERIES
686 Whitewing

Introduced in the fall of 1998, this over/under shotgun is chambered for the 12 gauge shell and fitted with 26" or 28" barrels with Beretta's choke system. The receiver is polished nickel with engraved game scenes, and gold-plated trigger. Walnut pistol-grip stock with gloss finish.

NIB	Exc.	V.G.	Good	Fair	Poor
1350	1025	800	550	375	250

686 Blackwing

This model, introduced in 2002, is similar to the Whitewing model with the exception of a blued receiver and schnabel fore-end.

NIB	Exc.	V.G.	Good	Fair	Poor
1450	1100	900	600	425	300

686 Sporting Combo

Same specifications as the Hunter Sport with the addition of an interchangeable 30" 12 gauge barrel.

NIB	Exc.	V.G.	Good	Fair	Poor
1900	1600	1250	1000	700	325

686 Collection Trap

Introduced in 1996 this model features a special multi-colored stock and fore-end. Offered in 12 gauge only with 30" barrels. Factory recoil pad standard. Average weight is 7.7 lbs.

NIB	Exc.	V.G.	Good	Fair	Poor
1500	1000	750	500	400	300

686 Collection Sport

Similar to above but offered with 28" barrels.

NIB	Exc.	V.G.	Good	Fair	Poor
1500	975	750	500	400	300

686 Quail Unlimited 2002 Covey Limited Edition

Offered in 20 or 28 gauge with 26" or 28" vent rib barrels. Choke tubes. Engraved receiver with gold quail inlays. Weight is about 6.8 lbs.

NIB	Exc.	V.G.	Good	Fair	Poor
1950	1550	1250	1000	700	325

686 Ringneck Pheasants Forever

Introduced in 2003 this model is chambered for 12 or 20 gauge and fitted with 26" or 28" vent rib barrels. Checkered walnut stock with pistol grip. Single-selective trigger. Gel-Tek recoil pad. Schnabel fore-end. Weight is about 6.8 lbs. on 12 gauge.

NIB	Exc.	V.G.	Good	Fair	Poor
2025	1550	1100	750	450	275

ULTRALIGHT SERIES
Ultralight

This over/under model is chambered for 12 gauge 2.75" shells and fitted with a choice of 26" or 28" barrels. The receiver is light aluminum alloy with nickel finish with game scene engraving. Black rubber recoil pad is standard. Single-selective trigger, pistol grip, and schnabel forearm. Weight is approximately 5.75 lbs.

Ultralight receiver

NIB	Exc.	V.G.	Good	Fair	Poor
1900	1500	900	600	375	175

Ultralight Deluxe

Similar to the above model but offered only with 28" barrels. Nickel receiver is gold game scene engraved. First offered in 1998.

NIB	Exc.	V.G.	Good	Fair	Poor
2400	2000	1600	1100	700	350

687/PIGEON SERIES

687/687 Silver Pigeon Sporting

This model is similar to the Model 686 but in a slightly more ornate version. This series was renamed in 1994.

687 L/Silver Pigeon

This model is offered in 12 gauge or 20 gauge with 26" or 28" vent rib barrels. The boxlock receiver is scroll engraved with game scenes. Auto ejectors and double or single triggers are offered.

NIB	Exc.	V.G.	Good	Fair	Poor
1800	1100	950	800	650	300

687 Silver Pigeon II

Introduced in 1999, this model features a deep relief game scene engraving on a silver receiver. Select walnut stock with oil finish. Available in 12 gauge only with choice of 26" or 28" vent rib barrels. Single-selective trigger. Weight is about 6.8 lbs.

NIB	Exc.	V.G.	Good	Fair	Poor
2500	1900	1250	700	425	300

687 Silver Pigeon Sporting

A sporting clays version available in 12 or 20 gauge with 28" or 30" barrels.

NIB	Exc.	V.G.	Good	Fair	Poor
1900	1400	1000	700	425	300

687 Silver Pigeon II Sporting

Introduced in 1999, this model features a deep relief engraving with oil finished select walnut stock with schnabel fore-end. Single-selective trigger. Offered in 12 gauge only with choice of 28" or 30" barrels. Black rubber recoil pad. Weight is about 7.7 lbs.

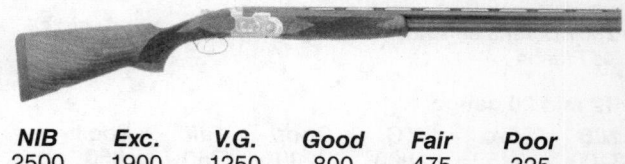

NIB	Exc.	V.G.	Good	Fair	Poor
2500	1900	1250	800	475	325

Silver Pigeon S

New in 2007, the Silver Pigeon S Series features scroll and floral engraving on a satin nickel-alloy finished receiver. It is available in 12, 20 and 28 gauge with 26" or 28" barrels, and .410 bore with 28" barrels. All come with five chokes. Weight is about 6.8 lbs.

NIB	Exc.	V.G.	Good	Fair	Poor
1800	1475	900	600	375	275

Silver Pigeon S Combo

Combo model comes with 26" 20 gauge barrels and 28" 28 gauge barrels.

NIB	Exc.	V.G.	Good	Fair	Poor
2200	1875	100	900	600	300

687 Sporting Combo

Offered in 12 gauge only with two sets of 12 gauge interchangeable vent rib barrels in 28" and 30".

NIB	Exc.	V.G.	Good	Fair	Poor
2500	2100	1850	1500	750	400

687 Silver Pigeon IV

Introduced in 2003 for the U.S. market this shotgun features a black finish receiver with full scroll engraving with gold-filled game birds. Select oil-finished walnut stock with Gel-Tek recoil pad. Offered in 12, 20, or 28 gauge with 26" or 28" barrels. Single-selective trigger with fluted beavertail fore-end. Weight is about 6.8 lbs. in 12 gauge.

NIB	Exc.	V.G.	Good	Fair	Poor
2665	1950	1850	1500	750	400

687 Silver Pigeon V

This is the top-of-the-line model in the Silver Pigeon Series. Available in 12, 20 and 28 gauges with 26" and 28" barrels and .410 bore (added in 2006). Pistol-grip stock of richly figured walnut with oil finish. Color case-hardened receiver with gold-filled game bird inlays. English stocked versions of the 20 and 28 gauges and .410 bore were added in 2006.

NIB	Exc.	V.G.	Good	Fair	Poor
3595	2400	1700	1250	750	375

687 EL/687 Gold Pigeon

This model is offered with scroll engraved gold inlaid game animals. Fitted with side plates. The stock is highly figured walnut with fine line checkering. Available in 12, 20, 28 gauge or .410 bore in 26" or 28" vent rib barrels with screw-in chokes. Comes with fitted hard case. Weights for 12 gauge: 6 lbs. 13 oz.; 20 gauge: 6 lbs. 3 oz.; 28/.410: 5 lbs. 5 oz. Series was renamed in 1994.

In 2001 Beretta enhanced the engraving on the Model 687EL Gold Pigeon

12 and 20 gauge

NIB	Exc.	V.G.	Good	Fair	Poor
3400	2450	1800	1200	750	350

28 gauge and .410 bore

NIB	Exc.	V.G.	Good	Fair	Poor
3450	2500	1850	1250	800	400

687 EL Gold Pigeon Sporting

A sporting clays model chambered for 12 gauge and fitted with 28" or 30" vent rib barrels. Offered new in 1993. Comes with fitted hard case.

NIB	Exc.	V.G.	Good	Fair	Poor
3400	2450	1750	1250	900	450

687 EELL/Diamond Pigeon

Same as above, including gauge and barrel offerings, but furnished with more fully figured walnut and finer checkering. Fitted with side plates that are scroll engraved with fine cut game scenes. This grade is also available in a straight grip English stock version in 20 gauge as well as a combo set of 20 gauge and 28 gauge interchangeable 26" barrels. All 687 EELL Models are fitted with hard case. Series was renamed in 1994.

12 and 20 gauge

NIB	Exc.	V.G.	Good	Fair	Poor
6500	5200	4500	3000	1500	700

28 gauge and .410 bore

NIB	Exc.	V.G.	Good	Fair	Poor
7000	5500	4500	3000	1500	700

Combo

NIB	Exc.	V.G.	Good	Fair	Poor
8000	6800	5000	3500	1300	500

687 EELL Diamond Pigeon Skeet

Same as above with the addition of a skeet configuration. A 12 gauge version is offered with 28" vent rib barrels choked skeet and skeet. Weighs about 7 lbs. 8 oz. A 4 barrel set is also offered with interchangeable 12, 20, 28 gauge, and .410 bore barrels choked Skeet and Skeet.

12 gauge

NIB	Exc.	V.G.	Good	Fair	Poor
3500	3000	2500	1750	1450	475

4 Barrel Set

NIB	Exc.	V.G.	Good	Fair	Poor
6400	5000	4500	3750	2500	1500

with Adjustable Stock

Same as the Skeet version above but with adjustable comb, drop and cast. Introduced in 1999.

NIB	Exc.	V.G.	Good	Fair	Poor
5000	4000	3200	2500	1500	500

687 EELL Diamond Pigeon Sporting

A sporting clays version of the 687 EELL in 12 gauge only with 28" vent rib barrels fitted with screw-in chokes.

NIB	Exc.	V.G.	Good	Fair	Poor
6000	4750	3500	2500	1750	1200

687 EELL Trap

This model is fitted with either International or Monte Carlo trap stock dimensions. Offered in 12 gauge with 30" vent rib barrels fixed or screw-in choke tubes. Weighs about 8 lbs. 6 oz.

NIB	Exc.	V.G.	Good	Fair	Poor
4000	3000	2500	2000	1500	1000

687 EELL Top Combo

A single barrel trap gun with choice of one single barrel set and one over/under steel rod barrel in either 30" and 32" or 32" and 34".

NIB	Exc.	V.G.	Good	Fair	Poor
4700	3500	3000	2250	2000	1000

Model 687 EELL King Ranch

Similar to Silver Pigeon Grade IV with special cowboy and western engraving. In 20 or 28 gauge only. Introduced 2006, discontinued in 2009.

NIB	Exc.	V.G.	Good	Fair	Poor
3300	2750	2200	1700	1250	800

Model 626 Field Grade

A 12 or 20 gauge boxlock double barrel shotgun with a 26" or 28" barrel, various choke combinations, single trigger and automatic ejectors. Engraved, blued with a checkered walnut stock. Imported between 1984 and 1988.

NIB	Exc.	V.G.	Good	Fair	Poor
—	1000	825	700	575	475

626 Onyx

This model is a boxlock side-by-side shotgun offered in 12 gauge and 20 gauge. With choice of 26" or 28" solid rib barrels with screw-in chokes. Double triggers are standard but single trigger is available on request. Receiver is anti-glare black matte finish. Stock is walnut with hand checkering and pistol grip. The 12 gauge weighs 6 lbs. 13 oz. and the 20 gauge weighs 6 lbs. 13 oz.

NIB	Exc.	V.G.	Good	Fair	Poor
1350	950	850	750	500	400

627 EL

This model is offered in 12 gauge only with choice of 26" or 28" solid rib barrels. The walnut is highly figured and fine cut checkered. The receiver is silver with side plates engraved with scroll. Comes with hard case.

NIB	Exc.	V.G.	Good	Fair	Poor
2600	2000	1750	1500	1250	650

627 EELL

Same as above but fitted with scroll engraved side plates with game scenes. Walnut is highly figured with fine line checkering. A straight-grip stock is also offered in this model. Comes with hard case.

NIB	Exc.	V.G.	Good	Fair	Poor
3850	3500	3000	2500	1500	1000

FS-1

A single-barrel boxlock shotgun in all gauges and a 26" or 28" full choke barrel. Blued with a checkered walnut stock. This model was also known as the "Companion."

NIB	Exc.	V.G.	Good	Fair	Poor
—	300	225	175	125	90

TR-1 Trap

A 12 gauge, single-barrel boxlock trap gun, 32" ventilated rib full choke barrel. Blued with a checkered, Monte Carlo stock. Manufactured between 1968 and 1971.

NIB	Exc.	V.G.	Good	Fair	Poor
—	375	250	200	150	100

TR-2 Trap

As above, with a high, competition-type vent rib. It was manufactured between 1969 and 1973.

NIB	Exc.	V.G.	Good	Fair	Poor
—	400	275	225	175	125

Mark II Trap

A 12 gauge, boxlock single-barrel trap shotgun with a 32" or 34", full-choke barrel, competition-type rib and automatic ejector. Blued with a checkered, Monte Carlo type, walnut stock. Manufactured between 1972 and 1976.

NIB	Exc.	V.G.	Good	Fair	Poor
—	800	625	525	450	275

ASE 90/Gold Series

This is a competition trap model over/under shotgun. It features a trigger lock assembly that is removable in the field so a spare can be used in the event of failure. The single non-selective trigger has a three-way adjustment. The ventilated rib is wide and the side ribs are also ventilated. Walnut stock and forearms are interchangeable. Special trap recoil pad is standard. Receiver is silver with gold inlays or blued on special order. The ASE 90 weighs about 8 lbs. 6 oz.

ASE 90 Pigeon

Equipped with 28" barrels choked Improved-Modified and Full.

NIB	Exc.	V.G.	Good	Fair	Poor
6750	5250	3750	2750	1200	500

ASE 90 Trap

Comes standard with 30" vent rib barrels.

NIB	Exc.	V.G.	Good	Fair	Poor
5950	5250	3750	2750	1200	500

ASE 90 Gold X Trap Combo

Introduced in 1993 this set features a single barrel and interchangeable over/under barrels in 30", 32" and 30", 34" combinations.

NIB	Exc.	V.G.	Good	Fair	Poor
6950	2500	1750	1200	700	350

ASE 90 Skeet

This model is a skeet version of the ASE 90 series. Features the same basic specifications as the trap model but configured for competition skeet. Offered in 12 gauge only with 28" Skeet and Skeet chokes. Weighs about 7 lbs. 11 oz.

NIB	Exc.	V.G.	Good	Fair	Poor
5950	2500	1750	1200	700	350

ASE 90 Sporting Clay

Configured for sporting clays competition. Offered in 12 gauge only with 28" or 30" vent rib barrels.

NIB	Exc.	V.G.	Good	Fair	Poor
6950	5200	4000	3000	1500	1000

SL-2

A 12 gauge slide-action shotgun, 26", 28", or 30", ventilated rib barrels with various chokes. Blued with a checkered walnut stock. Manufactured between 1968 and 1971.

NIB	Exc.	V.G.	Good	Fair	Poor
—	350	300	250	200	150

Pigeon Series

As above, in three grades.

Silver Pigeon

NIB	Exc.	V.G.	Good	Fair	Poor
—	300	250	200	150	110

Gold Pigeon

NIB	Exc.	V.G.	Good	Fair	Poor
—	450	400	300	250	200

Ruby Pigeon

NIB	Exc.	V.G.	Good	Fair	Poor
—	600	550	450	375	275

DT 10 TRIDENT SERIES

These shotguns feature removable trigger mechanism, overbored barrels, and special choke tubes.

DT 10 Trident Trap

This is a 12 gauge over/under gun with a number of options. The barrel is 30" or 32" and the highly select walnut stock is fitted with a Monte Carlo comb. Stock is also adjustable. Rib type is 3/8" with progressive step. Full black rubber recoil pad. Weight is about 8.8 lbs. A top single model is also offered with 34" barrel. Introduced in 2000.

NIB	Exc.	V.G.	Good	Fair	Poor
8000	6000	5000	2750	1600	500

DT 10 Trident Trap Combo Top

Same as above with both over/under barrels and single barrel combo.

NIB	Exc.	V.G.	Good	Fair	Poor
10000	8000	6500	4700	3000	500

DT 10 Trident Trap Bottom Single

Introduced in 2001 this model features a choice of 30"/34" barrel combo or 32"/34" barrel combo. Select walnut stock. Fitted with an adjustable point-of-impact rib. Weight is about 8.8 lbs.

NIB	Exc.	V.G.	Good	Fair	Poor
13250	10500	7500	4700	3000	500

DT 10 Trident Skeet

This 12 gauge skeet model is fitted with either 28" or 30" barrel. Walnut stock is adjustable. Weight is about 8 lbs. Introduced in 2000.

NIB	Exc.	V.G.	Good	Fair	Poor
8000	7000	5000	2850	1875	400

DT 10 Trident Sporting

This 12 gauge over/under gun is fitted with a choice of 28", 30", or 32" barrels. Highly figured walnut stock with schnabel fore-end. Weight is about 8 lbs. Introduced in 2000.

NIB	Exc.	V.G.	Good	Fair	Poor
12000	10000	6000	2850	1875	400

SV10 Perennia

New in 2008, the Perennia over/under is a 3" 12 gauge featuring an oil-finished, select walnut stock and a laser-engraved, nickel high-phosphorous-based finish on the receiver. The barrels are 26" or 28" and feature the Optimachoke HP system introduced in 2008. User-selectable automatic or mechanical shell extraction. Beretta's Kick-Off recoil reduction system is available on the 28" Perennia. Includes five choke tubes and plastic carrying case. Add $400 for Kick-Off version.

NIB	Exc.	V.G.	Good	Fair	Poor
3250	2000	1450	800	600	300

SEMI-AUTOMATIC SHOTGUNS

AL SERIES

A 12 or 20 gauge semi-automatic shotgun with 26", 28", or 30" barrels and various choke combinations. Blued with a checkered walnut stock. Manufactured between 1969 and 1976.

AL-1

NIB	Exc.	V.G.	Good	Fair	Poor
—	400	375	300	225	150

AL-2

NIB	Exc.	V.G.	Good	Fair	Poor
—	350	300	250	175	125

AL-2 Competition

NIB	Exc.	V.G.	Good	Fair	Poor
—	400	350	300	225	175

AL-2 Magnum

NIB	Exc.	V.G.	Good	Fair	Poor
—	425	375	325	250	200

AL-3

NIB	Exc.	V.G.	Good	Fair	Poor
—	400	350	300	225	175

AL-3 Deluxe Trap

NIB	Exc.	V.G.	Good	Fair	Poor
—	775	700	600	500	425

301

Improved version of the AL Series manufactured between 1977 and 1982. It is also available as a slug gun with a 22" barrel with rifle sights.

NIB	Exc.	V.G.	Good	Fair	Poor
—	400	350	300	225	175

1200 Field Grade

A 12 gauge semi-automatic shotgun, 28" ventilated rib barrel, screw-in choke tubes and a 4-round, tubular magazine. Matte blued with either a checkered walnut or black synthetic stock. Introduced in 1984.

NIB	Exc.	V.G.	Good	Fair	Poor
585	525	425	325	250	200

1200 Magnum

3" chamber.

NIB	Exc.	V.G.	Good	Fair	Poor
585	525	425	325	250	200

1200 Riot

20" cyl. bore barrel.

NIB	Exc.	V.G.	Good	Fair	Poor
585	525	425	325	250	200

1201

This 12 gauge semi-automatic shotgun has a short recoil system and features a synthetic stock with matte black finish and lightweight alloy receiver. Available in two basic configurations: the Field Grade with choice of 24", 26", and 28" vent rib barrel with screw-in chokes and Riot Models with 18" plain Cylinder choked barrel with either full stock or pistol-grip-only stock (introduced in 1993). Field Grade weighs about 6 lbs. 12 oz. and the Riot Model about 6 lbs. 5 oz. **NOTE:** For Riot Models with pistol grip add $40. For Riot Models with Tritium sights add $75. For ghost ring sights add $100.

Field Grade

NIB	Exc.	V.G.	Good	Fair	Poor
450	400	350	300	200	150

Riot Model

NIB	Exc.	V.G.	Good	Fair	Poor
650	500	400	350	250	175

302

A 12 or 20 gauge semi-automatic shotgun using 2.75" or 3" shells interchangeably, various barrel lengths and screw-in choke tubes. Blued with a checkered walnut stock. Manufactured between 1982 and 1987.

NIB	Exc.	V.G.	Good	Fair	Poor
—	400	350	275	200	150

302 Super Lusso

As above, with a heavily engraved receiver and gold-plated, contrasting parts. Presentation grade walnut was used for the hand checkered stock. Discontinued in 1986.

NIB	Exc.	V.G.	Good	Fair	Poor
—	2150	2000	1600	1050	850

Vittoria/Pintail

This semi-automatic 12 gauge shotgun was introduced to the Beretta product line in 1993. It has a short recoil operation and is offered with a 24" or 26" vent rib barrel with screw-in chokes. A 24" rifled choke tube version for slugs is also available. A non-reflective matte finish is put on all wood and metal surfaces. Equipped with sling swivels and walnut stock. Weighs about 7 lbs. Renamed in 1994.

NIB	Exc.	V.G.	Good	Fair	Poor
600	500	420	350	250	200

ES100 Pintail Synthetic

Introduced in 1999, this model is essentially the same as the Pintail model above with the addition of a black synthetic stock. Offered with a choice of 24", 26", or 28" vent rib barrels with screw-in chokes. Weight is about 7 lbs.

NIB	Exc.	V.G.	Good	Fair	Poor
550	450	385	325	250	200

ES100 Pintail Rifled Slug

Introduced in 1997 this model features a 24" fully rifled barrel with adjustable rear sight and removable blade front sight. The receiver is drilled and tapped for scope mount. Hardwood stock with matte finish. Anodized aluminum alloy receiver. Weight is approximately 7 lbs. Fitted with 3" chambers.

NIB	Exc.	V.G.	Good	Fair	Poor
650	550	450	400	250	200

ES100 Rifled Slug

This variation is the same as the Pintail Rifled Slug model above with the addition of a black synthetic stock. Introduced in 1999.

NIB	Exc.	V.G.	Good	Fair	Poor
600	500	425	350	250	200

ES100 Rifled Slug Combo

Same as above but with the addition of a 28" smooth bored barrel.

NIB	Exc.	V.G.	Good	Fair	Poor
700	600	525	450	350	250

ES100 NWTF Special Camo

This 12 gauge model is fitted with a 24" barrel with 3" chambers. Stock is Mossy Oak camo. Metal is black matte finish. Weight is about 7.3 lbs. Introduced in 1999.

NIB	Exc.	V.G.	Good	Fair	Poor
975	750	550	375	210	150

A-303 SERIES

A 12 or 20 gauge semi-automatic shotgun, 26", 28", 30", or 32" ventilated rib barrels with screw-in choke tubes. Blued with a checkered walnut stock. Introduced in 1987. The various models offered differ slightly in configuration and/or quality of materials.

A-303

NIB	Exc.	V.G.	Good	Fair	Poor
650	600	475	375	300	250

A-303 Upland

24" barrel.

NIB	Exc.	V.G.	Good	Fair	Poor
680	650	525	425	350	300

A-303 Sporting Clay

NIB	Exc.	V.G.	Good	Fair	Poor
735	700	575	475	400	350

A-303 Competition (Trap or Skeet)

NIB	Exc.	V.G.	Good	Fair	Poor
675	650	530	425	350	300

A-303 Slug Gun

22" barrel with sights.

NIB	Exc.	V.G.	Good	Fair	Poor
680	650	525	425	350	300

A-303 Youth Gun

This version of the Model 303 is available in 20 gauge with a shorter length of pull, 13.5", than standard. It is fitted with a rubber recoil pad, screw-in choke tubes, and checkered walnut stock.

NIB	Exc.	V.G.	Good	Fair	Poor
500	450	400	300	250	200

A-303 Ducks Unlimited

A commemorative version of the Model 303. It is chambered for 12 or 20 gauge. There were 5,500 manufactured in 12 gauge in 1986 and 1987. There were 3,500 manufactured in 20 gauge in 1987 and 1988. These commemorative firearms are collectible when NIB with all furnished materials.

12 Gauge

NIB	Exc.	V.G.	Good	Fair	Poor
575	500	425	325	275	225

20 Gauge

NIB	Exc.	V.G.	Good	Fair	Poor
675	600	525	425	375	325

MODEL AL390/MALLARD SERIES

This series of 12 gauge semi-automatic shotguns features a self-compensating, gas-operating recoil system. All loads from target to 3" Magnums can be used in the same gun. The Field Model features an anodized light alloy receiver with scroll engraving and matte black receiver top. Magazine capacity is 3 rounds. Checkered walnut stock with recoil pad. Available in vent rib barrel lengths from 24" to 30" with 32" on special request. A 22" or 24" slug plain barrel is also available. Chokes are fixed or screw-in at customer's option. Shotgun weighs about 7 lbs. Beginning in 1996 Beretta offered the Silver Mallard shotguns chambered for the 20 gauge shell and available with 24", 26, or 28" barrels. Average weight for these 20 gauge guns is 6.4 lbs.

AL390 Field Grade

NIB	Exc.	V.G.	Good	Fair	Poor
800	600	450	350	300	200

AL390 Slug Gun

NIB	Exc.	V.G.	Good	Fair	Poor
800	600	450	350	300	200

AL390 Synthetic Stock

NIB	Exc.	V.G.	Good	Fair	Poor
800	600	450	350	300	200

AL390 Camouflage

NIB	Exc.	V.G.	Good	Fair	Poor
800	600	450	350	300	200

AL390 Deluxe Grade/Gold Mallard

Gold-filled game animals and select walnut stock.

NIB	Exc.	V.G.	Good	Fair	Poor
700	650	500	350	300	200

AL390 Trap

NIB	Exc.	V.G.	Good	Fair	Poor
675	600	500	400	300	200

AL390 Super Trap

Features ported barrels in 30" or 32", adjustable length of pull, adjustable comb.

NIB	Exc.	V.G.	Good	Fair	Poor
800	700	600	500	300	200

AL390 Skeet

NIB	Exc.	V.G.	Good	Fair	Poor
625	550	450	350	250	200

AL390 Super Skeet

Features ported barrel, adjustable cast and length of pull, and adjustable drop. 12 gauge only.

NIB	Exc.	V.G.	Good	Fair	Poor
1000	800	600	500	300	200

AL390 Sporting

NIB	Exc.	V.G.	Good	Fair	Poor
700	550	450	350	250	200

20 gauge

Same as above but in 20 gauge. Introduced in 1997. Weight about 6.8 lbs.

NIB	Exc.	V.G.	Good	Fair	Poor
800	600	450	350	250	200

Ported

NIB	Exc.	V.G.	Good	Fair	Poor
725	650	550	400	300	200

AL390 Sport Gold Sporting

Introduced in 1997 this model is similar to above models but with silver sided receiver with gold engraving. Select walnut stock. 12 gauge only with choice of 28" or 30" vent rib barrels. Weight about 7.6 lbs.

NIB	Exc.	V.G.	Good	Fair	Poor
1100	900	700	450	300	175

AL390 Sport Sporting Youth

This semi-automatic shotgun is offered in 20 gauge only with 26" vent rib barrel. Length of pull is 13.5" with adjustable drop and cast on the buttstock. Introduced in 1997. Weight is approximately 6.7 lbs.

NIB	Exc.	V.G.	Good	Fair	Poor
825	675	500	350	200	175

AL390 NWTF Special Youth

Introduced in 1999, this model features a shortened walnut stock with 24" 20 gauge vent rib barrel. Black matte finish. Weight is about 6.4 lbs.

NIB	Exc.	V.G.	Good	Fair	Poor
900	700	525	375	225	175

AL390 Sport Sporting Youth Collection

Same as above but with multi-colored stock and forearm. Introduced in 1997.

NIB	Exc.	V.G.	Good	Fair	Poor
900	750	525	375	225	175

AL390 Sport Diamond Sporting

Introduced in 1998 this model features a silver sided receiver with gold engraving. Select walnut stock with oil finish and adjustable for drop and cast. Available in 12 gauge with 28" or 30" barrels.

Sold with spare trigger group and orange front sight beads. Weight is approximately 7.6 lbs.

NIB	Exc.	V.G.	Good	Fair	Poor
3000	2600	1950	1300	600	300

AL390 Camo

This 12 gauge shotgun is offered with either a 24" or 28" vent rib barrel. Barrel, receiver, stock and forearm have woodland camo finish. Weight is about 7.5 lbs. Offered for first time in 1997.

NIB	Exc.	V.G.	Good	Fair	Poor
995	775	595	450	300	150

AL390 Waterfowl/Turkey Model

Matte finish.

NIB	Exc.	V.G.	Good	Fair	Poor
550	500	450	350	300	250

AL390 NWTF Special Camo

NIB	Exc.	V.G.	Good	Fair	Poor
1100	875	625	500	325	150

AL390 NWTF Special Synthetic

NIB	Exc.	V.G.	Good	Fair	Poor
925	750	595	450	300	150

AL390 Super Trap

Ported barrels, adjustable comb and length of pull.

NIB	Exc.	V.G.	Good	Fair	Poor
975	800	650	500	325	175

AL390 Super Skeet

Ported barrels, adjustable comb and length of pull.

NIB	Exc.	V.G.	Good	Fair	Poor
950	800	650	500	325	175

3901 SERIES

This series was introduced in 2005 and is built around the A390 shotgun. The 3901 guns feature a gas operating system, choke tubes, and a removable trigger group.

3901

Introduced in 2003, this semi-automatic shotgun is offered in 12 gauge with choice of 26" or 28" barrel. Charcoal gray synthetic stock. Black rubber recoil pad. Non-reflective black finish. Weight is about 7.5 lbs.

NIB	Exc.	V.G.	Good	Fair	Poor
730	575	450	300	225	175

3901 RL

As above, but in 20 gauge with reduced-length buttstock. Introduced in 2003.

NIB	Exc.	V.G.	Good	Fair	Poor
730	575	450	300	225	175

3901 Camo

This 12 gauge model is offered in Mossy Oak Shadowgrass camo stock. Choice of 24" or 26" barrel. Introduced in 2003.

NIB	Exc.	V.G.	Good	Fair	Poor
840	650	475	350	250	175

3901 Citizen

Offered in 12 or 20 gauge with choice of 26" or 28" vent rib barrels with choke tubes. Black synthetic stock. Rubber recoil pad. Weight is about 7.6 lbs. for 12 gauge and 7 lbs. for 20 gauge.

NIB	Exc.	V.G.	Good	Fair	Poor
750	600	450	300	225	175

3901 Statesman

As above but with checkered walnut stock.

NIB	Exc.	V.G.	Good	Fair	Poor
850	675	475	325	250	175

3901 Ambassador

This model has all the features of the Statesman but is fitted with a select checkered X-tra wood stock with Gel-Tek recoil pad. Weight for 12 gauge is about 7.2 lbs. and 6.6 lbs. for 20 gauge.

NIB	Exc.	V.G.	Good	Fair	Poor
950	750	525	450	350	200

3901 Target RL

Gas-operated semi-automaticchambered in 3" 12-gauge. Specifically designed for smaller-stature shooters with adjustable length of pull from 12" to 13". Stock is adjustable for cast on or cast off. Adjustable comb and Sporting style flat rib. Available in 12 gauge only with 26" or 28" barrel.

NIB	Exc.	V.G.	Good	Fair	Poor
895	700	550	400	295	175

AL 391 URIKA SERIES

Urika

Introduced in 2000 this semi-automatic shotgun is offered in both 12 and 20 gauge. Choice of barrels from 24" to 30" depending on gauge. Stock is walnut with checkered grip and fore-end. Rubber recoil pad. Gold trigger. Choke tubes. Weight for 12 gauge is about 7.3 lbs. while the 20 gauge is about 6 lbs.

NIB	Exc.	V.G.	Good	Fair	Poor
850	750	600	450	300	175

Urika Synthetic

Same as above but fitted with a black synthetic stock with gripping inserts. Offered in 12 gauge only. Introduced in 2000.

NIB	Exc.	V.G.	Good	Fair	Poor
950	750	625	525	325	200

Urika Camo

This 12 gauge model is offered with either Realtree Hardwoods camo or Advantage Wetlands camo. In 24" or 26" barrels. Weight is about 7.3 lbs. First introduced in 2000.

NIB	Exc.	V.G.	Good	Fair	Poor
1050	800	650	550	300	175

Urika Gold

This model features a 26" or 28" barrels with choke tubes. The black receiver model is offered in both 12 and 20 gauge with a weight of about 7.3 lbs. The silver receiver model (lightweight) is available in 12 gauge only and weighs about 6.6 lbs. Both configurations are fitted with highly figured walnut stock. Gold trigger. Introduced in 2000.

NIB	Exc.	V.G.	Good	Fair	Poor
900	825	750	675	325	200

Urika Youth

This 20 gauge model features a walnut stock with a shorter length of pull than standard and a 24" barrel. Weight is about 6 lbs. Introduced in 2000.

NIB	Exc.	V.G.	Good	Fair	Poor
900	800	600	450	275	195

Urika Sporting

This model is offered in both 12 and 20 gauge. Fitted 28" or 30" barrels. Select walnut checkered stock. Gold trigger. Chambered for 3" shells. Weight of 12 gauge is about 7.3 lbs. and the 20 gauge is about 6 lbs. Introduced in 2000.

NIB	Exc.	V.G.	Good	Fair	Poor
1100	750	600	500	350	175

Urika Gold Sporting

This model is offered in 12 gauge with a choice of black or silver receiver. The 20 gauge models are offered with black receiver only. Fitted with 28" or 30" barrels. Highly select checkered walnut stock. Chambered for 3" shells. Introduced in 2000. **NOTE:** Add $30 for 12 gauge silver receiver.

NIB	Exc.	V.G.	Good	Fair	Poor
1295	950	700	600	450	175

Urika Trap

This 12 gauge model is fitted with a choice of 30" or 32" barrels. Select checkered walnut stock with Monte Carlo comb. Chambered for 3" shells. Weight is about 7.2 lbs. Introduced in 2000.

NIB	Exc.	V.G.	Good	Fair	Poor
1000	750	600	500	350	175

Urika Gold Trap

This model is similar to the standard Urika Trap but with highly selected checkered walnut stock and black receiver.

NIB	Exc.	V.G.	Good	Fair	Poor
1295	950	700	600	450	175

Urika Parallel Target RL/SL

This 12 gauge competition model is fitted with 28" or 30" barrels and select walnut Monte Carlo stock. The "RL" has standard stock configurations while the "SL" has a shorter length of pull.

NIB	Exc.	V.G.	Good	Fair	Poor
1100	750	600	500	350	200

URIKA OPTIMA MODELS

First offered in 2003 this shotguns are similar to the standard Urika model but feature Beretta's Optima-Bore overbored barrels with flush Optima-Choke Plus tubes.

Urika Optima

Offered in 12 gauge with 26" or 28" vent rib barrel. Checkered select walnut stock. Gold trigger. Chamber is 3". Weight is about 7.3 lbs.

NIB	Exc.	V.G.	Good	Fair	Poor
1500	1175	825	650	450	300

Urika Synthetic Optima

As above but with synthetic stock with rubber inserts. Weight is about 7.4 lbs.

NIB	Exc.	V.G.	Good	Fair	Poor
1300	1105	750	575	400	325

Urika Optima Camo

As above but with camo stock.

NIB	Exc.	V.G.	Good	Fair	Poor
1350	1195	950	625	450	250

URIKA 2 SERIES

Introduced in 2007, the Urika 2 is an enhanced version of the original AL391 Urika. Improvements include the addition of a spinning, self-cleaning action for faster cycling and longer functioning periods between cleanings.

Urika 2 X-Tra Grain

This series features Beretta's wood-enhancement treatment to highlight the color contrast of the wood. Offered in 3" 12 and 20 gauge with 26" and 28" barrels. A 20 gauge youth model with shorter stock and 24" barrel is also offered.

NIB	Exc.	V.G.	Good	Fair	Poor
1000	900	725	575	400	250

Urika 2 Gold

Select oil-finished wood stock and fore-end with gold-filled game bird inlays on the receiver. The 12 gauge has a 28" barrel and the 20 gauge has a 26" barrel.

NIB	Exc.	V.G.	Good	Fair	Poor
1350	1075	725	500	375	250

Urika 2 Kick-Off

These waterfowl models feature Beretta's Kick-Off recoil reduction system. Matte black synthetic, Max-4 or Realtree AP finish with 26" or 28" barrel. Deduct 30 percent for models without Kick-Off. Add 10 percent for camo finish.

NIB	Exc.	V.G.	Good	Fair	Poor
1200	950	700	475	350	225

Urika 2 Sporting X-Tra Grain

Sporting clays models in 12 and 20 gauge with 28" or 30" barrel.

NIB	Exc.	V.G.	Good	Fair	Poor
1200	950	700	475	350	225

Urika 2 Gold Sporting

Enhanced wood with gold inlays and floral motif engraving on receiver in 12 gauge with 28" or 30" barrel.

NIB	Exc.	V.G.	Good	Fair	Poor
1300	1025	775	525	375	275

Urika 2 Parallel Target X-Tra Grain

Target model in 12 gauge with 28", 30" or 32" barrel.

NIB	Exc.	V.G.	Good	Fair	Poor
1250	975	750	525	375	295

Urika 2 Gold Parallel Target

Enhanced wood with gold inlays and floral motif engraving on receiver in 12 gauge with 30" or 32" barrel.

NIB	Exc.	V.G.	Good	Fair	Poor
1400	1075	750	525	395	265

Covey

Introduced in 2003 this model is offered in 20 gauge with a 26" or 28" vent rib barrel. Select walnut stock. Gold-filled game scenes. Weight is about 5.9 lbs. Limited to 1,000 guns.

NIB	Exc.	V.G.	Good	Fair	Poor
1350	1075	725	500	375	250

Ringneck

As above but with gold-filled pheasants. In 12 gauge only. Weight is about 7.3 lbs. Limited to 1,000 guns. Introduced in 2003.

NIB	Exc.	V.G.	Good	Fair	Poor
1360	1075	800	550	400	300

Teknys

This model features a nickel receiver with polished sides and anti-glare top. Offered in 12 or 20 gauge with 26" or 28" vent rib barrel. Xtra-wood stock with Gel-Tek recoil. Weight is about 7.2 lbs. for 12 gauge and 5.9 lbs. for the 20 gauge. Introduced in 2003.

NIB	Exc.	V.G.	Good	Fair	Poor
1150	900	750	500	350	250

Teknys Gold

As above, but with engraved hunting scene on the receiver, gold plated trigger, jeweled breech bolt and carrier. Select walnut checkered stock with oil finish. Introduced in 2003.

NIB	Exc.	V.G.	Good	Fair	Poor
1465	1100	850	575	425	325

Teknys Gold Target

Similar to AL391 Teknys Gold but with adjustable comb, 8.5 oz. recoil reducer and additional stepped rib for trap shooting. 30" barrel.

NIB	Exc.	V.G.	Good	Fair	Poor
1665	1300	975	600	450	350

Teknys King Ranch

Introduced in 2005.

NIB	Exc.	V.G.	Good	Fair	Poor
1650	1300	1000	725	625	375

XTREMA SERIES

Xtrema 3.5

Introduced in 2002 this model is a Urika overbuilt to handle 12 gauge 3.5" super magnum loads. Offered with a choice of 24", 26", or 28" vent rib barrels with black synthetic stock or choice of various camo stocks. Weight is about 7.8 lbs. **NOTE:** Add $100 for camo finish.

NIB	Exc.	V.G.	Good	Fair	Poor
1150	900	750	500	350	250

Xtrema2

An upgraded version of the Xtrema with additional recoil-reducing features was introduced in 2005. Available with 24", 26" or 28" barrels with black, Max-4 HD or Hardwoods HD synthetic stock. Optima-Bore five choke system. Optional Kick Off recoil reduction feature available. Add 10 percent for camo finish. Add 30 percent for Kick Off option.

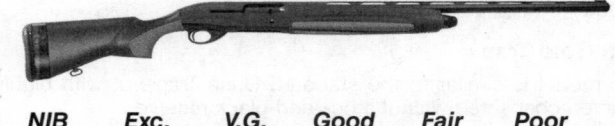

NIB	Exc.	V.G.	Good	Fair	Poor
1300	950	800	650	400	300

Xtrema2 Slug Gun

24" rifled barrel version of Xtrema2. Introduced in 2006. Black synthetic only. Add 10 percent for Kick Off option.

NIB	Exc.	V.G.	Good	Fair	Poor
1200	925	800	650	400	300

UGB25 XCEL

Introduced in 2005 this is a semi-automatic break-open competition trap gun chambered for the 12 gauge 2.75" shell. The gun is fed from the side with bottom ejection. Choice of 30" or 32" barrel with high trap-style interchangeable rib. Choke tubes. The checkered walnut has an adjustable comb and length of pull. Weight is about 7.7 to 9 lbs. depending on barrel length and rib.

NIB	Exc.	V.G.	Good	Fair	Poor
3595	2800	2150	1675	850	450

A400 Xplor Unico

Self-regulation gas-operated shotgun chambered to shoot all 12-gauge loads from 2.75" to 3.5". Features include Kick-Off hydraulic damper; 26" or 28" "Steelium" barrel with interchangeable choke tubes; anodized aluminum receiver; sculpted, checkered walnut buttstock and fore-end. **NOTE:** Add $100 for Kick-Off Recoil reduction system.

NIB	Exc.	V.G.	Good	Fair	Poor
1500	1250	1050	800	550	300

A400 Xcel Sporting

Similar to Xplor Unico except designed to Sporting Clays competition. 12 gauge, 3" chambers, with 28" 30" and 32" barrels. Blue aluminum receiver, optional Kick-Off recoil reduction system. Gun Pod optional system available with digital readout of temperature, ammo pressure and other information. **NOTE:** Add $100 for Kick-Off Recoil reduction system or for Gun Pod.

NIB	Exc.	V.G.	Good	Fair	Poor
1600	1300	1050	800	550	300

TX4 Storm

Gas-operated semi-automatic shotgun chambered for 3" 12 gauge shells. Features include 18" barrel with interchangeable choke tubes; adjustable ghost ring rear sight with military-style front sight; adjustable length of pull; integral picatinny rail on receiver; 5+1 capacity; soft rubber grip inlays in buttstock and fore-end.

NIB	Exc.	V.G.	Good	Fair	Poor
1200	1000	750	500	350	250

BERGER, JEAN MARIUS
St. Etienne, France

Berger

The Berger was a magazine-fed repeating pistol in 7.65mm. It was a self loader and self cocker. It had all the characteristics of a semi-automatic except for the recoil operating system.

Courtesy James Rankin

NIB	Exc.	V.G.	Good	Fair	Poor
—	5900	4750	3750	3000	2000

BERGMANN, THEODOR
Gaggenau, Germany

Theodor Bergmann was a successful industrialist, designer and sometimes inventor with a deep interest in firearms based in Gaggenau, Germany. His first automatic pistol patent dates from 1892, and by 1894 he had prototype pistols, refined with the help of Louis Schmeisser, being evaluated by various governments. When his designs went into commercial production in 1896, however, they were actually manufactured by the firm of V. Charles Schilling in Suhl, the heart of German arms manufacture. Later he licensed manufacture of his "Mars" pistol to Anciens Establishment Pieper ("Bayard"), and after WWI affiliated with the Lignose firm, producing a line of .25 caliber pocket pistols, first under the Bergmann name but later marketed as Lignose. Still later several pistol designs from the August Menz firm were marketed under the "Bergmann Erben" trademark, though it's doubtful if the Bergmann firm actually had much part in their production or sale.

Model 1894 Bergmann Schmeisser

The Model 1894 was made in prototype form only, with only a few examples surviving and known serial numbers no higher than the mid teens. Most are large framed and chambered for the 8mm Bergmann-Schmeisser cartridge, though at least one was made in 7.5mm Swiss revolver for Swiss army testing and a few very compact versions, with a unique folding trigger, for 5mm Bergmann. Early Bergmann pistols had no extractor, counting on gas pressure to blow the fired (rimless-grooveless) cartridge from the chamber. Too rare to price.

Model 1896 Number 2

The 1896 Number 2 pistols were quite compact and chambered for the 5mm Bergmann cartridge. Early Number 2s also featured a folding trigger and no extractor, but after serial 500 or so reverted to a more conventional in-the-frame trigger and an extractor was added. About 2000 of the later model were produced. Cased sets are known, and add about 50 percent to the value.

Folding Trigger

Courtesy James Rankin

NIB	Exc.	V.G.	Good	Fair	Poor
—	4700	3700	2800	1500	800

Conventional

Courtesy James Rankin

NIB	Exc.	V.G.	Good	Fair	Poor
—	3700	3200	2250	1375	800

Model 1896 Number 3

The Number 3 was a larger version of the Number 2, chambered for the 6.5mm Bergmann cartridge. Early examples had a slim gripframe and, up to about serial 800, were made without extractor like the early Number 2s. These bring about a 20 percent premium over the later examples. Number 3 serials range to a little over 4000. Add about 20 percent for dealer markings (usually English), and 50 percent for cased sets. A few target models, with long barrel, adjustable sights and set triggers are known and will bring about three times the price of a standard Number 3.

First Variation

Courtesy James Rankin

NIB	Exc.	V.G.	Good	Fair	Poor
—	4050	3500	2750	1650	800

Second Variation

Courtesy James Rankin

NIB	Exc.	V.G.	Good	Fair	Poor
—	3500	3200	2500	1650	800

Third Variation

Courtesy James Rankin

NIB	Exc.	V.G.	Good	Fair	Poor
—	3700	3200	2500	1650	800

Holster and Stock Model

Courtesy James Rankin

NIB	Exc.	V.G.	Good	Fair	Poor
—	6300	5700	4950	3250	2750

Model 1896 Number 4

The Number 4 is identical to the Number 3 but chambered for a unique 8mm Bergmann cartridge and serialed in the same series with the Number 3. Both the Number 4 and its cartridge are rare; probably fewer than 200 were ever made.

NIB	Exc.	V.G.	Good	Fair	Poor
—	8000	6500	5000	3700	2900

Model 1897 Number 5

This was Bergmann's first attempt at a more powerful arm for the military market, with a unique side-moving locking system and a 10-shot removable box magazine. The 7.8mm cartridge resembled the 7.63mm Mauser, but with a longer neck. Add 60 percent for original metal framed leather holster-stock.

NIB	Exc.	V.G.	Good	Fair	Poor
—	8550	6900	4950	3000	2250

Model 1897 Number 5 Carbine

A limited number of the approximately 1000 Bergmann Model 5s were made with a 12-inch barrel and solid wood detachable buttstock and marked "Karabiner Bergmann" on the action cover. A very few were made with a full-length Mannlicher-type stock and sold as the Bergmann Model 1897/07 Sporting Carbine; these are worth about 50 percent more than the long barreled pistol with detachable stock.

Courtesy Joe Schroeder

NIB	Exc.	V.G.	Good	Fair	Poor
—	12500	10000	6000	3000	2000

Bergmann Simplex

The Simplex combined some features of the 1896 pistols with improvements developed from the "Mars," resulting in a reasonable compact pocket pistol that came on the market in the early 1900s. It was chambered for the unique Bergmann-Simplex 8mm cartridge, however, and that and competition from better Browning and other designs doomed it to a short production life. Very early examples had checkered wood grips and bring a premium, as do very late examples (above serial 3000) that have the magazine release behind the magazine instead of on the front of the frame.

NIB	Exc.	V.G.	Good	Fair	Poor
—	3450	2950	2000	900	600

Bergmann Mars

The Mars was Bergmann's first really successful pistol aimed at the military market. Early examples, about 100 of the total 1000 or so Mars pistols made, were chambered for the 7.63mm Mauser cartridge but later Mars pistols, identified by a large "9mm" on the chamber, were chambered for the special 9mm cartridge that later became known as the 9mm Bergmann-Bayard. The Mars was adopted by the Spanish government in 1905 as their first military automatic pistol, but none were ever delivered by Bergmann. At least two Mars pistols were also made in .45 caliber for U.S. Army trials in 1906, but did not perform well and were dropped from the trials; these are too rare to price. **NOTE:** Add 25 percent for low serial number guns chambered for 7.63mm Mauser; add 50 percent for original Bergmann Mars holster stock.

NIB	Exc.	V.G.	Good	Fair	Poor
—	7000	5300	3850	2500	1650

Bergmann Bayard Model 1908

Shortly after receiving the Spanish contract for the Mars pistol, Bergmann's arrangement with Schilling to produce Bergmann pistols ended. However, he negotiated an arrangement with Anciens Establishment Pieper (Bayard) to produce the Mars and, after some minor modifications, AEP filled the Spanish contract. They also marketed the gun commercially, and later secured a production contract from the Danish army as the Model 1910. Spanish contract (proofed with a small circle divided into three segments) and very early commercial pistols have hard rubber grips that proved very fragile in service; these bring a premium as do original unmodified Danish contract guns (with a contract number and Danish letter D proof). A few Model 1908 Bergmann Bayards were equipped with leather and wood holster stocks; a complete rig is worth at least twice the price of an unslotted pistol.

Courtesy James Rankin

NIB	Exc.	V.G.	Good	Fair	Poor
—	1950	1600	1000	775	550

Bergmann Post War Pistols

Shortly after WWI ended Bergmann came on the market with a line of .25 caliber pocket pistols; the 2 and 3 were conventional vest pocket designs with a short and long gripframe respectively; the 2a and 3a were identical except for an "Einhand" (one-hand) feature that enabled the user to cycle the slide by pulling the front of the trigger guard with his trigger finger. Soon into production (at about serial 8000) Bergmann affiliated with the Lignose firm and later Model 2 and 3 pistols were marketed under the Lignose name.

Model 2 and 3

Courtesy Joe Schroeder

NIB	Exc.	V.G.	Good	Fair	Poor
—	325	275	200	150	100

Model 2a and 3a

Courtesy Joe Schroeder

NIB	Exc.	V.G.	Good	Fair	Poor
—	400	375	325	275	150

BERGMANN ERBEN PISTOLS

The Bergmann Erben pistols appear to be an attempt by the Bergmann family to keep the Bergmann name associated with firearms without actually investing any design or production effort. The Bergmann Erben pistols were all August Menz designs, and were undoubtedly made by Menz as well. Most noteworthy was the "Spezial" model, a very sophisticated double-action .32 pocket pistol that could be cocked for single-action fire by pulling and then releasing the trigger. Also noteworthy were several compact vest pocket .25s that also bore the Bergmann Erben name.

Bergmann Erben Spezial

NIB	Exc.	V.G.	Good	Fair	Poor
—	1650	1350	900	650	400

Bergmann Erben Model II Pistol

Courtesy James Rankin

NIB	Exc.	V.G.	Good	Fair	Poor
—	550	495	330	225	125

BERGMANN, EINHAND
See—Lignose

BERNARDELLI, VINCENZO
Brescia, Italy

Established in the 1721, this company originally manufactured military arms and only entered the commercial sporting arms market in 1928.

HANDGUNS

Vest Pocket Model

Similar to the Walther Model 9, in a 6.35mm caliber semi-automatic pistol with a 2.25" barrel, and 5-shot magazine. An extended 8-shot version was also available. Blued with plastic grips. Manufactured between 1945 and 1948.

NIB	Exc.	V.G.	Good	Fair	Poor
—	350	250	180	125	100

Pocket Model

As above, in 7.65mm caliber. This model was also offered with extended barrels that protruded beyond the end of the slide. Introduced in 1947.

NIB	Exc.	V.G.	Good	Fair	Poor
—	300	225	200	150	100

Baby Model

As above, in .22 short or LR. Manufactured between 1949 and 1968.

NIB	Exc.	V.G.	Good	Fair	Poor
—	300	225	175	125	95

Sporter Model

A .22 caliber semi-automatic pistol with 6", 8", or 10" barrels and adjustable sights. Blued with walnut grips. Manufactured between 1949 and 1968.

NIB	Exc.	V.G.	Good	Fair	Poor
—	325	250	200	150	125

Revolvers

A .22 rimfire and .32 caliber double-action revolver with 1.5", 2", or 5" barrels. A .22 caliber, 7" barrel version with adjustable sights also available. Manufactured between 1950 and 1962.

NIB	Exc.	V.G.	Good	Fair	Poor
—	250	175	150	125	100

Model 60

A .22, .32 ACP or .380 ACP caliber semi-automatic pistol with 3.5" barrel and fixed sights. Blued with plastic grips. Manufactured since 1959.

NIB	Exc.	V.G.	Good	Fair	Poor
—	275	200	175	150	115

Model 68

A .22 rimfire caliber or .25 ACP semi-automatic pistol with a 2" barrel and 5-shot magazine. Blued with plastic grips. No longer imported into the U.S.

NIB	Exc.	V.G.	Good	Fair	Poor
—	200	175	150	100	75

Model 80

A .22 or .380 ACP caliber semi-automatic pistol with a 3.5" barrel and adjustable sights. Blued with plastic grips. Imported between 1968 and 1988.

NIB	Exc.	V.G.	Good	Fair	Poor
—	250	200	150	125	95

Model AMR

As above, with a 6" barrel.

NIB	Exc.	V.G.	Good	Fair	Poor
450	350	200	150	100	90

Model 69

A .22 caliber semi-automatic target pistol with a 6" heavy barrel, and a 10-shot magazine. Blued with checkered walnut grips.

NIB	Exc.	V.G.	Good	Fair	Poor
450	375	300	225	150	100

Model PO10

A .22 caliber, single-action, semi-automatic target pistol with a 6" barrel, adjustable target sights, barrel weights, and an adjustable trigger. Matte-black finish with stippled walnut grips. Introduced in 1989. Weight 40 oz. Sold with special hard case.

NIB	Exc.	V.G.	Good	Fair	Poor
800	700	500	300	200	100

Model PO18

A 7.65mm or 9mm Parabellum caliber, double-action, semi-automatic pistol with a 4.75" barrel and a 16-shot, double stack, detachable magazine. All-steel construction. Blued with plastic grips. Walnut grips are available for an additional $40. Introduced in 1985.

NIB	Exc.	V.G.	Good	Fair	Poor
550	450	300	275	200	100

Model PO18 Compact

As above, with a 4" barrel and a shorter grip frame with a 14-shot, double-column magazine. Introduced in 1989.

NIB	Exc.	V.G.	Good	Fair	Poor
550	450	300	275	200	100

Model P. One

A full-size semi-automatic pistol chambered for the 9mm or .40 S&W calibers. Fitted with a 4.8" barrel. Can be fired double-action or single-action. Ten-shot magazine. Weight is 2.14 lbs. Available in black or chrome finish. Add $50 for chrome finish.

NIB	Exc.	V.G.	Good	Fair	Poor
625	525	400	275	200	100

Model P. One-Compact

Same as above but with 4" barrel and offered in .380 caliber as well as 9mm and .40 S&W. Weight is 1.96 lbs.

NIB	Exc.	V.G.	Good	Fair	Poor
650	550	400	275	200	100

Practical VB Target

Designed for Practical shooting this 9mm pistol has a 6" barrel with choice of 2 or 4 port compensator. It is fitted with numerous extra features. Weights is 2.2 lbs.

NIB	Exc.	V.G.	Good	Fair	Poor
1500	1200	850	600	400	200

Practical VB Custom

As above but designed for IPSC rules.

NIB	Exc.	V.G.	Good	Fair	Poor
2250	1900	1400	900	600	300

Model USA

A .22, .32 ACP or .380 ACP caliber semi-automatic pistol with a 3.5" barrel, adjustable sights, steel frame and a loaded chamber indicator. Blued with plastic grips.

NIB	Exc.	V.G.	Good	Fair	Poor
450	350	200	150	100	90

SHOTGUNS

MODEL 115 SERIES

A 12 gauge over/under, boxlock, double-barrel shotgun with various barrel lengths and choke combinations, single triggers and automatic ejectors.

Model 115

NIB	Exc.	V.G.	Good	Fair	Poor
1525	1250	900	700	550	300

Model 115S

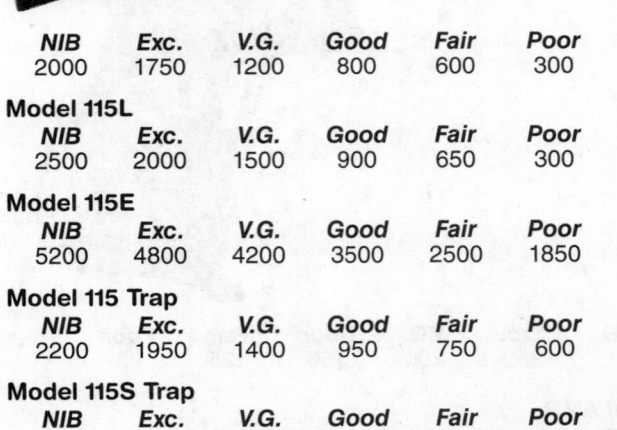

NIB	Exc.	V.G.	Good	Fair	Poor
2000	1750	1200	800	600	300

Model 115L

NIB	Exc.	V.G.	Good	Fair	Poor
2500	2000	1500	900	650	300

Model 115E

NIB	Exc.	V.G.	Good	Fair	Poor
5200	4800	4200	3500	2500	1850

Model 115 Trap

NIB	Exc.	V.G.	Good	Fair	Poor
2200	1950	1400	950	750	600

Model 115S Trap

NIB	Exc.	V.G.	Good	Fair	Poor
2700	2450	1900	1450	1150	900

Model 115E Trap

NIB	Exc.	V.G.	Good	Fair	Poor
5250	4800	4200	3500	2500	1850

MODEL 190 SERIES

A 12 gauge, over/under shotgun with various barrel lengths and choke combinations, a single-selective trigger and automatic ejectors. Engraved and silver-finished with a checkered walnut stock. Introduced in 1986. The various versions differ in the degree of ornamentation and quality of materials utilized in construction.

Model 190

NIB	Exc.	V.G.	Good	Fair	Poor
1050	950	750	600	475	400

Model 190MC

NIB	Exc.	V.G.	Good	Fair	Poor
1150	1050	850	700	575	500

Model 190 Special

NIB	Exc.	V.G.	Good	Fair	Poor
1350	1150	950	800	675	600

Model 190 Combo Gun

A .243, .308 or .30-06 caliber and 12, 16, or 20 gauge combination over/under rifle shotgun with a boxlock action, double triggers and automatic ejectors. Blued with a checkered walnut stock. Introduced in 1989.

NIB	Exc.	V.G.	Good	Fair	Poor
1625	1425	925	775	650	575

ORIONE SERIES

A 12 gauge boxlock over/under shotgun with various barrel lengths and choke combinations. Finishes and triggers were optional, as were extractors or automatic ejectors.

Orione

NIB	Exc.	V.G.	Good	Fair	Poor
1150	900	700	500	400	200

Orione S

NIB	Exc.	V.G.	Good	Fair	Poor
1150	900	700	500	400	200

Orione L

NIB	Exc.	V.G.	Good	Fair	Poor
1250	1000	800	600	500	250

Orione E

NIB	Exc.	V.G.	Good	Fair	Poor
1350	1150	850	600	500	250

S. Uberto I Gamecock

A 12, 16, 20, or 28 gauge boxlock side-by-side shotgun with either 25.75" or 27.5" barrels, various chokes, double triggers and extractors. Automatic ejectors were available and would be worth a 20 percent premium. Blued with a checkered stock.

NIB	Exc.	V.G.	Good	Fair	Poor
—	950	700	500	350	250

Brescia

A 12, 16, or 20 gauge sidelock double-barrel shotgun with exposed hammers, various barrel lengths, choke combinations, a sidelock action, double triggers, and manual extractors. Blued with an English-style, checkered walnut stock.

NIB	Exc.	V.G.	Good	Fair	Poor
1850	900	700	450	350	225

Italia

This is a higher grade version of the Brescia.

NIB	Exc.	V.G.	Good	Fair	Poor
2250	1250	750	600	400	250

Italia Extra

This is the highest grade hammer gun that Bernardelli produces.

NIB	Exc.	V.G.	Good	Fair	Poor
5900	2750	1500	1000	750	300

UBERTO SERIES

A 12, 16, 20 or 28 gauge Anson & Deeley boxlock double barrel shotgun with various barrel lengths and choke combinations. The increased value of the various models depends on the degree of engraving, options, and quality of materials and workmanship utilized in their construction.

S. Uberto 1

NIB	Exc.	V.G.	Good	Fair	Poor
1000	800	650	475	350	250

S. Uberto 1E

NIB	Exc.	V.G.	Good	Fair	Poor
1100	900	700	500	350	250

S. Uberto 2

NIB	Exc.	V.G.	Good	Fair	Poor
1500	1100	800	500	350	250

S. Uberto 2E

NIB	Exc.	V.G.	Good	Fair	Poor
1750	1350	950	600	400	250

S. Uberto F.S.

NIB	Exc.	V.G.	Good	Fair	Poor
2000	1500	1100	800	400	250

S. Uberto F.S.E.

NIB	Exc.	V.G.	Good	Fair	Poor
2250	1750	1200	800	400	250

ROMA SERIES

Similar to the S. Uberto Series with false sideplates. The values of the respective variations result from the degree of ornamentation and quality of materials and workmanship utilized in the construction.

Roma 3

NIB	Exc.	V.G.	Good	Fair	Poor
1550	1200	800	600	300	200

Roma 3E

NIB	Exc.	V.G.	Good	Fair	Poor
1750	1300	900	650	300	200

Roma 4

NIB	Exc.	V.G.	Good	Fair	Poor
1950	1400	1100	750	400	250

Roma 4E

NIB	Exc.	V.G.	Good	Fair	Poor
2000	1500	1200	750	400	250

Roma 6

NIB	Exc.	V.G.	Good	Fair	Poor
2100	1750	1400	850	500	250

Roma 6E

NIB	Exc.	V.G.	Good	Fair	Poor
2200	1800	1400	850	500	250

Roma 7

NIB	Exc.	V.G.	Good	Fair	Poor
2900	2500	1800	1200	700	350

Roma 8

NIB	Exc.	V.G.	Good	Fair	Poor
3500	3000	2250	1550	850	400

Roma 9

NIB	Exc.	V.G.	Good	Fair	Poor
4000	3500	2750	1700	950	450

Elio

A 12 gauge boxlock double-barrel shotgun with various barrel lengths and choke combinations, lightweight frame, double triggers and extractors. Scroll-engraved, silver-finished receiver, blued barrels and a select, checkered walnut stock.

NIB	Exc.	V.G.	Good	Fair	Poor
1000	800	600	500	350	250

Elio E

As above, with automatic ejectors.

NIB	Exc.	V.G.	Good	Fair	Poor
1100	900	700	550	350	250

Hemingway

As above, with coin finished receiver, engraved with hunting scenes, 23.5" barrels, double triggers or single trigger and a select, checkered walnut stock. Available in 12, 20 and 28 gauge.

NIB	Exc.	V.G.	Good	Fair	Poor
1750	1350	900	700	400	250

Hemingway Deluxe

Same as above but fitted with full side plates.

NIB	Exc.	V.G.	Good	Fair	Poor
2250	1750	1200	800	400	250

Las Palomas Pigeon Model

A live pigeon gun in 12 gauge with single trigger.

NIB	Exc.	V.G.	Good	Fair	Poor
3800	3250	2500	2000	1500	750

HOLLAND V.B. SERIES

A 12 or 20 gauge sidelock shotgun with various barrel lengths, detachable Holland & Holland-type locks, single triggers, and automatic ejectors. The models listed vary in the amount of engraving and the quality of their wood. Prospective purchasers are advised to secure a qualified appraisal prior to acquisition.

Holland V.B. Liscio

NIB	Exc.	V.G.	Good	Fair	Poor
8000	5500	4000	3000	2000	1000

Holland V.B. Inciso

NIB	Exc.	V.G.	Good	Fair	Poor
10250	7500	5250	4000	2500	1250

Holland V.B. Lusso

NIB	Exc.	V.G.	Good	Fair	Poor
11000	8000	6000	4500	2500	1250

Holland V.B. Extra
NIB	Exc.	V.G.	Good	Fair	Poor
13000	10000	7500	5500	3000	1500

Holland V.B. Gold
NIB	Exc.	V.G.	Good	Fair	Poor
45000	30000	22500	15000	7500	3000

Luck

An over/under shotgun with single-selective trigger or double triggers, automatic ejectors with choice of fixed chokes or choke tubes. Available in 12 gauge. Blued or coin finish receiver.

NIB	Exc.	V.G.	Good	Fair	Poor
1400	1100	850	600	400	200

Giardino/Garden Gun (9mm Rimfire)

This is a semi-automatic shotgun chambered for the 9mm shot cartridge. Fitted with a 4-round magazine. Weight is 5 lbs.

NIB	Exc.	V.G.	Good	Fair	Poor
850	595	425	300	250	100

RIFLES

Carbina VB Target

A semi-automatic carbine chambered for the .22 LR cartridge. Barrel is 20.8" and magazine capacity is 10 rounds.

NIB	Exc.	V.G.	Good	Fair	Poor
650	550	400	300	200	100

Comb 2000

A rifle-shotgun combination in 12 or 16 gauge with a variety of centerfire calibers to choose from. Barrels are 23.5" long. Set trigger, special rib for scope mount and cheekpiece stock with pistol grip. Weight is 6.75 lbs.

NIB	Exc.	V.G.	Good	Fair	Poor
2900	2100	1200	800	400	250

Express 2000

An over/under double rifle chambered for a variety of European calibers. Fitted with automatic ejectors, double-set triggers or single trigger, muzzle adjustment device. Barrel length is 23.5".

NIB	Exc.	V.G.	Good	Fair	Poor
3350	2550	1700	1200	600	300

Express VB

A side-by-side double rifle chambered for a variety of European calibers up to .375 H&H. Double or single trigger, auto ejectors, and finely engraved receiver with beavertail forearm. Cheekpiece stock with pistol grip.

NIB	Exc.	V.G.	Good	Fair	Poor
5900	4900	3750	2000	1000	750

Express VB Deluxe

Same as above but with side plates and select walnut stock finely checkered.

NIB	Exc.	V.G.	Good	Fair	Poor
6300	5200	4000	2000	1000	750

Minerva

A side-by-side double rifle with exposed hammers chambered for the 9.3x74R cartridge. Fitted with fancy walnut stock, double triggers, hand-cut rib, and other high-quality features.

NIB	Exc.	V.G.	Good	Fair	Poor
6700	5900	4550	2500	1200	750

BERNARDON MARTIN
St. Etienne, France

This small firm was active between 1906 and 1912. The gun designer was Martin and the money man was Bernadon.

1907/8 Model

A 7.65mm caliber semi-automatic pistol. The left side of the slide is marked "Cal. 7.65mm St. Etienne". The trademark "BM" is molded into the grips. Sometimes found with a 32-round horseshoe magazine. Occasionally the Bernardon Martin pistol will be noted with the word "Hermetic" stamped on the slide in letters that do not match the other markings on the weapon. This was but another name for the Model 1907/8. Guns with this stamping were most likely assembled after the company ceased operations. **NOTE:** Add 50 percent for horseshoe magazine.

Courtesy James Rankin

NIB	Exc.	V.G.	Good	Fair	Poor
—	1100	875	700	450	275

1908/9 Model

Introduced late in 1908 this model is similar to the Model 1907/8 with the addition of a grip safety.

NIB	Exc.	V.G.	Good	Fair	Poor
—	925	775	600	375	225

BERNEDO, VINCENZO
Eibar, Spain

B C

The B C is in caliber 6.35mm and most of the barrel is exposed. The recoil spring is housed in the rear of the receiver. The B C closely resembles the Tanque pistol.

Courtesy James Rankin

NIB	Exc.	V.G.	Good	Fair	Poor
—	325	225	200	175	150

Bernado

This model 7.65mm is in the Spanish style of the Ruby automatic pistols.

Courtesy James Rankin

NIB	Exc.	V.G.	Good	Fair	Poor
—	225	150	125	75	50

BERSA
Ramos Mejia, Argentina

Model 644

This model is a blowback pocket pistol chambered for the .22 LR. The trigger system is single-action. Barrel length is 3.5", overall length is 6.57", and empty weight is approximately 28 oz. This is the basic Bersa model from which its other models derive their design and function.

NIB	Exc.	V.G.	Good	Fair	Poor
275	175	150	125	100	75

Model 622

Similar to the Model 644 but with a slightly longer barrel.

NIB	Exc.	V.G.	Good	Fair	Poor
275	175	150	125	100	75

Model 97

This model is a slightly larger version of the Model 644 chambered for the 9mm Short.

NIB	Exc.	V.G.	Good	Fair	Poor
275	175	150	125	100	75

Model 23

A .22 rimfire caliber, double-action, semi-automatic pistol with a 3.5" barrel and 10-shot detachable magazine. Either blued or satin nickel-plated with checkered walnut grips.

NIB	Exc.	V.G.	Good	Fair	Poor
300	200	150	125	100	75

Model 223

As above, with a squared trigger guard and nylon grips. Imported after 1988.

NIB	Exc.	V.G.	Good	Fair	Poor
—	275	175	125	100	75

Model 224

As above, with a 4" barrel. Imported after 1988.

NIB	Exc.	V.G.	Good	Fair	Poor
—	275	175	125	100	75

Model 225

As above, with a 5" barrel. Discontinued in 1986.

NIB	Exc.	V.G.	Good	Fair	Poor
—	275	175	125	100	75

Model 226

As above, with a 6" barrel. Discontinued in 1988.

Courtesy John J. Stimson, Jr.

NIB	Exc.	V.G.	Good	Fair	Poor
—	275	175	125	100	75

Model 323

A .32 ACP caliber single-action semi-automatic pistol, with a 3.5" barrel, fixed sights and a 7-shot detachable magazine. Blued with molded plastic grips. Not imported after 1986.

NIB	Exc.	V.G.	Good	Fair	Poor
—	225	125	100	75	50

Model 383

As above, in .380 caliber. Discontinued in 1988.

NIB	Exc.	V.G.	Good	Fair	Poor
—	250	150	125	90	75

Model 383A

A .380 ACP caliber double-action semi-automatic pistol with a 3.5" barrel with fixed sights and 7-shot magazine. Blued with checkered walnut grips. Overall length is 6.6" and weight is about 24 oz. Available in blue or nickel finish.

NIB	Exc.	V.G.	Good	Fair	Poor
300	200	150	125	100	75

Model 83

Similar to the above model but with double-action operating system. Weighs about 26 oz. Introduced in 1988.

NIB	Exc.	V.G.	Good	Fair	Poor
300	200	150	125	100	75

Model 85

As above, with a double-column magazine. Introduced in 1988.

NIB	Exc.	V.G.	Good	Fair	Poor
350	250	200	150	100	75

Model 86

Similar to the Model 85 .380 caliber, but features a matte blue or satin nickel finish, wrap around rubber grips, and three-dot sight. Magazine capacity is 13 rounds.

NIB	Exc.	V.G.	Good	Fair	Poor
350	250	225	200	150	100

Thunder 9

Introduced in 1993 this model is a double-action 9mm pistol that features ambidextrous safety, reversible extended magazine release, ambidextrous slide release, adjustable trigger stop, combat-style hammer, three-dot sights, and matte blue finish. Magazine capacity is 15 rounds.

NIB	Exc.	V.G.	Good	Fair	Poor
350	275	250	200	150	100

Series 95/Thunder 380

This is a semi-automatic double-action pistol chambered for the .380 cartridge. Choice of matte blue or nickel finish. Barrel length is 3.5". Fixed sights. Magazine capacity is 7 rounds. Weight is about 23 oz. Add $50 for nickel.

NIB	Exc.	V.G.	Good	Fair	Poor
260	200	150	100	75	50

Thunder 380 Matte Plus

Semi-automatic double-action blued pistol in .380 with 15-round magazine. Fixed sights and polymer grips. Introduced 2006.

NIB	Exc.	V.G.	Good	Fair	Poor
350	275	250	200	150	100

Thunder 9 Ultra Compact

Available blued or stainless with 10- or 13-round capacity. Double-action chambered for 9mm. 3.5" barrel, 25 oz., fixed sights and polymer grips. Introduced 2006. **NOTE:** Add $50 for stainless.

NIB	Exc.	V.G.	Good	Fair	Poor
395	300	250	200	150	100

Thunder 9/40 High Capacity Series

Double-action semi-automatic available chambered for 9mm or .40 S&W and in matte blued or satin nickel-plate. Fixed sights and polymer grips. LOA 7-1/2", 4-1/4" barrel, 26 oz. Introduced 2006.

NIB	Exc.	V.G.	Good	Fair	Poor
395	300	250	200	150	100

Thunder Deluxe

This semi-automatic double-action pistol is chambered for the .380 cartridge. Blued finish. Fixed sights. Barrel length is 3.5". Weight is about 23 oz. Magazine capacity is 9 rounds.

NIB	Exc.	V.G.	Good	Fair	Poor
325	225	175	100	75	50

BERTRAND, JULES
Liege, Belgium

Le Novo

A 6.35mm caliber double-action revolver. Manufactured in the 1890s. The only identifying markings are the "JB" trademark on the grips.

NIB	Exc.	V.G.	Good	Fair	Poor
—	300	225	175	100	50

Lincoln

As above, in 7.65mm caliber.

NIB	Exc.	V.G.	Good	Fair	Poor
—	300	225	175	100	50

Le Rapide

A 6.35mm caliber, semi-automatic pistol. The Jules Bertrand logo is on the slide, as well as Le Rapide. Both are on each side of the grip plates.

NIB	Exc.	V.G.	Good	Fair	Poor
—	350	275	200	125	50

BERTUZZI
Brescia, Italy

OVER/UNDER SHOTGUNS

Zeus

A 12, 16, 20, or 28 gauge sidelock shotgun with automatic ejectors, single-selective trigger, and deluxe checkered walnut stock. Custom order in various barrel lengths and chokes. Engraved. Rarely seen on the used gun market.

NIB	Exc.	V.G.	Good	Fair	Poor
18000 - 39000					

Zeus Extra Lusso

As above, but with best wood and engraving. Cased.

NIB	Exc.	V.G.	Good	Fair	Poor
35000 - 79000					

Zeus Boss System

This gun is chambered for the 12, 16, 20, or 28 gauge and is fitted with the Boss locking system with ejectors. One-of-a-kind gun with best quality wood and engraving.

NIB	Exc.	V.G.	Good	Fair	Poor
65000 - 134000					

Gull Wing

This is Burtuzzi's best gun with a unique sidelock design mounted on a center plate with a release located on top of the safety to allow sidelock access. These shotguns usually take about three years to build. Consult the distributor about options and availability.

NIB	Exc.	V.G.	Good	Fair	Poor
125000 +					

Ariete Extra Lusso

This is a best quality hammer gun in all gauges from 12 to 28. Limited quantities.

NIB	Exc.	V.G.	Good	Fair	Poor
65000 +					

SIDE-BY-SIDE SHOTGUNS

Orione

A 12, 16, 20 or 28 gauge boxlock shotgun with Anson & Deeley through bolt, in various barrel lengths and chokes, single-selective trigger and automatic ejectors. Hand checkered, walnut stock with a semi-beavertail forearm. Engraving.

NIB	Exc.	V.G.	Good	Fair	Poor
25500 - 39950					

Venere

This is a best quality sidelock gun with either a traditional or round frame. Special order to customer specifications. Engraved guns bring a premium.

NIB	Exc.	V.G.	Good	Fair	Poor
29000 - 69000					

Ariete

Best quality hammer gun with or without self cocking hammers and ejectors. Offered in 12 bore through .410. Many options.

NIB	Exc.	V.G.	Good	Fair	Poor
25000 - 55000					

Gull Wing

This is a one-of-a-kind custom built gun with quick release sidelocks. Delivery time about three years. Contact distributor for more information.

NIB	Exc.	V.G.	Good	Fair	Poor
85000 +					

BIG HORN ARMORY
Cody, Wyoming

Big Horn Armory Model 89 Rifle and Carbine

Lever-action rifle or carbine chambered for .500 S&W Magnum. Features include 22" or 18" barrel; walnut or maple stocks with pistol grip; aperture rear and blade front sights; recoil pad; sling swivels; enlarged lever loop; magazine capacity 5 (rifle) or 7 (carbine) rounds. Price: $1889.

BIGHORN ARMS CO.
Watertown, South Dakota

Target Pistol

A .22 caliber single-shot pistol resembling a semi-automatic. Ventilated rib barrel 6" in length. Stock of molded plastic.

NIB	Exc.	V.G.	Good	Fair	Poor
—	275	175	100	85	65

Shotgun

A single-shot 12 gauge shotgun with a 26" barrel. Blued with a plastic stock.

NIB	Exc.	V.G.	Good	Fair	Poor
—	195	115	65	50	30

BIGHORN RIFLE CO.
Orem, Utah

Bighorn Rifle

Custom order in any caliber, double-barrel, bolt-action rifle with optional barrel lengths and finishes. Double triggers and walnut stock.

NIB	Exc.	V.G.	Good	Fair	Poor
2500	1750	1500	1000	750	400

BILHARZ, HALL & CO.
Location Unknown

CONFEDERATE CARBINES

Bilharz, Hall & Co. Breechloading ("Rising Breech") Carbine

Overall length 40"; barrel length 21"; caliber 54. Markings: either "P" or "P/CS" on upper left side of barrel and top of rising breech. The peculiar feature of this carbine is the manner in which the breechblock exposes the chamber. A box-like chamber at the rear of the barrel rises vertically to expose the chamber for a paper cartridge by activating the lever/triggerguard mechanism. Only 100 of this type were delivered to the Confederacy in September 1862. Two types of front sight blades are known, but neither affects the value.

Courtesy Milwaukee Public Museum, Milwaukee, Wisconsin

NIB	Exc.	V.G.	Good	Fair	Poor
—	—	50000	22500	5000	2100

Bilharz, Hall & Co. Muzzleloading Carbine

Overall length 37.5"; barrel length 22"; caliber .58. Markings: "P/CS" on upper left of barrel near breech; "CSA" on top near breech. Modeled after the Springfield U.S. M1855 rifle carbine, the Bilharz, Hall & Co. muzzleloading carbine has often been mistakenly identified as a product of D.C. Hodgkins & Sons of Macon, Georgia. Serial numbers (found internally) belie that identification. Instead these arms are part of deliveries made to Richmond from the middle of 1863 until March 1864. Serial numbers, noted in excess of 700, suggest that about 1,000 were produced. Two basic types, the earlier (through serial number 300) were made with brass nosecaps; the later type (about serial number 310 through at least 710) have pewter nosecaps on the short forestock; neither type affects value.

NIB	Exc.	V.G.	Good	Fair	Poor
—	—	25000	10000	3000	1650

BILLINGHURST, WILLIAM
Rochester, New York

Billinghurst originally worked for James and John Miller of Rochester. After James Miller's death in 1837, Billinghurst established his own shop where he produced revolving rifles based upon Miller's 1829 patent. While these arms were originally made with percussion ignition systems (either pill or percussion cap), later examples using self-contained metallic cartridges are sometimes encountered. Billinghurst also established a well-deserved reputation for making extremely accurate percussion target pistols and rifles.

Under Hammer Pistol

This pistol is somewhat different than most of the under hammers encountered. The barrels are 12" to 18" in length and of a heavy octagonal construction. They are chambered from .30 to .38 caliber and utilize the percussion ignition system. Higher grade versions feature a part-round barrel, and it is important to note that no two pistols are alike. These pistols were furnished with detachable shoulder stocks, and a good many were cased with telescopic sights and false muzzles. This is a high quality weapon; and if encountered with the optional accessories, it would definitely warrant an individual appraisal. This firearm was manufactured in the 1850s and 1860s. **NOTE:** Shoulder stock add 50 percent.

NIB	Exc.	V.G.	Good	Fair	Poor
—	—	4750	2150	800	400

Revolving Rifle

Calibers vary from .40 to .50 with barrels from 24" to 29"; walnut stocks. The barrels marked: "W. Billinghurst, Rochester, N.Y.", or "W. Billinghurst".

NIB	Exc.	V.G.	Good	Fair	Poor
—	—	7900	3700	950	400

BILLINGS
Location Unknown

Pocket Pistol

A .32 rimfire caliber single-shot spur trigger pistol with a 2.5" round barrel and an unusually large grip. The barrel is stamped "Billings Vest Pocket Pistol Pat. April 24, 1866". Blued with walnut grips. Manufactured between 1865 and 1868.

NIB	Exc.	V.G.	Good	Fair	Poor
—	—	3500	1500	550	195

BINGHAM LTD.
Norcross, Georgia

PPS 50

A .22 rimfire caliber semi-automatic rifle patterned after the Soviet PPSH submachine gun with 16" barrel and a 50-round drum magazine. Blued, walnut or beech stock with a vented handguard. Manufactured between 1976 and 1985.

NIB	Exc.	V.G.	Good	Fair	Poor
—	575	400	275	225	100

AK-22

A .22 rimfire caliber semi-automatic rifle patterned after the Soviet AK-47 with either a 15- or 29-shot magazine. Walnut or beech stock. Manufactured between 1976 and 1985.

NIB	Exc.	V.G.	Good	Fair	Poor
—	365	225	150	100	75

Bantam

A .22 rimfire or .22 rimfire magnum caliber bolt-action rifle with an 18.5" barrel. Manufactured between 1976 and 1985.

NIB	Exc.	V.G.	Good	Fair	Poor
—	200	85	70	50	35

BISMARCK
Location Unknown

Pocket Revolver

A .22 caliber spur trigger revolver with a 3" round ribbed barrel and a 7-shot, unfluted cylinder. Brass frame and the remainder was plated with rosewood grips. The barrel is marked "Bismarck." Manufactured in the 1870s.

NIB	Exc.	V.G.	Good	Fair	Poor
—	—	550	225	90	50

BITTERLICH, FRANK J.
Nashville, Tennessee

A .41 caliber single-shot percussion pistol in a variety of octagonal barrel lengths, German silver mounts, walnut stock. The barrel and locks are marked "Fr.J. Bitterlich/Nashville, Tenn." Produced between 1861 and 1867.

NIB	Exc.	V.G.	Good	Fair	Poor
—	—	5500	4900	1900	850

BITTNER, GUSTAV
Wieport, Bohemia

Bittner

A 7.7mm Bittner caliber repeating pistol with a 4.5" barrel. The bolt containing the firing pin rotates to lock the breech and is operated by the finger lever that encloses the trigger. Manufactured in mid-1890s. Fewer than 500 were made.

NIB	Exc.	V.G.	Good	Fair	Poor
—	15000	10500	8000	4000	2000

BLAKE, J. H.
New York, New York

Blake Bolt-Action Rifle

A .30-40 Krag caliber bolt-action rifle with a 30" barrel, and a 7-shot magazine. The stock is secured by three barrel bands. Blued with a walnut stock. Manufactured between 1892 and 1910.

Courtesy Milwaukee Public Museum, Milwaukee, Wisconsin

NIB	Exc.	V.G.	Good	Fair	Poor
—	—	3500	1700	675	200

BLANCH, JOHN
London, England

Blanch Percussion Pistol

A .69 caliber single-shot, percussion pistol with a 5" Damascus barrel. Engraved frame and hammer with a walnut grip. Manufactured in the 1830s.

NIB	Exc.	V.G.	Good	Fair	Poor
—	—	6750	2950	1450	875

BLAND, THOMAS & SONS
London, England

Established in 1840, this firm has produced or marketed a wide variety of percussion and cartridge arms. Over the years, the firm has occupied a variety of premises in London, some of them concurrently.

41 Whittall Street	1840-1867
41, 42, 43 Whittall Street	1867-1886
106 Strand	1872-1900
430 Strand	1886-1900
2 William IV Street	1900-1919
4-5 William IV Street	1919-1973
New Row, St. Martin's Lane	1973-

BLASER JAGDWAFFEN
Germany

RIFLES

Model K77

A single-shot rifle chambered in a variety of calibers with a 24" barrel and silver-plated as well as engraved receiver. Walnut stock. Introduced in 1988. **NOTE:** Extra barrels add $750 per barrel.

NIB	Exc.	V.G.	Good	Fair	Poor
3900	3050	2200	1500	900	450

Model R-84

A bolt-action sporting rifle chambered in a variety of calibers with either a 23" or 24" barrel. Interchangeable barrels are available for this model. Walnut stock. Imported beginning in 1988.

NIB	Exc.	V.G.	Good	Fair	Poor
2700	2300	2000	1800	1100	450

Model R-93 LX

This is a straight-pull-back bolt-action rifle with interchangeable barrels in calibers from .22-250 to .416 Rem. Magnum. Barrel length for standard calibers is 22" and for Magnum calibers 26". Magazine capacity is 3 rounds. Receiver is drilled and tapped for Blaser scope mounts. Weight is approximately 7 lbs. Two-piece walnut stock. Introduced by SIGARMS into the U.S. in 1998. **NOTE:** Add $200 for left-hand rifles, add $800 for .416 Remington Magnum.

NIB	Exc.	V.G.	Good	Fair	Poor
2000	1400	1100	800	600	300

Model R-93 Prestige

An updated and upgraded standard model with all the features of the R-93 LX. Light scroll engraving on receiver.

NIB	Exc.	V.G.	Good	Fair	Poor
3275	2750	1800	1300	700	350

Model R-93 Classic

Similar to the model above in choice of calibers and barrel lengths but with the addition of highly figured walnut stock and game scene engraved receiver. **NOTE:** Add $200 for left-hand rifles, add $800 for .416 Remington Magnum.

NIB	Exc.	V.G.	Good	Fair	Poor
3500	3000	2400	1750	800	400

Model R-93 Luxus

This is an updated and upgraded model of the R-93 Classic. It features a high grade Turkish walnut stock with ebony fore-end. Side plates are engraved with game scenes.

NIB	Exc.	V.G.	Good	Fair	Poor
5000	4000	3000	2000	1000	500

Model R-93 Synthetic

Also available in the same wide range of interchangeable barrels and calibers. This model features a one-piece black synthetic stock. **NOTE:** Add $200 for left-hand rifles, add $800 for .416 Remington Magnum.

NIB	Exc.	V.G.	Good	Fair	Poor
3000	2400	2000	1500	1000	400

Model R-93 Attache

This model features a custom made stock of highly figured walnut with cheekpiece, leather covered buttplate, silver pistol-grip cap, ebony fore-end tip, and custom checkering. Sold with a leather carrying case. **NOTE:** Add $200 for left-hand rifles.

NIB	Exc.	V.G.	Good	Fair	Poor
5100	4000	3000	2000	900	400

Model R-93 Safari Synthetic

This model is chambered for the .416 Remington Magnum cartridge and fitted with a 24" heavy barrel with open sights. Weight is 9.5 lbs. Black synthetic stock. Other Blaser barrels will interchange on this model.

NIB	Exc.	V.G.	Good	Fair	Poor
2100	1700	1250	875	500	275

Model R-93 Safari LX

Same as the R-93 Safari Synthetic with the exception of a two-piece walnut stock.

NIB	Exc.	V.G.	Good	Fair	Poor
2500	2000	1550	1000	750	350

Model R-93 Safari Classic

This model features an engraved receiver and fancy walnut stock.

NIB	Exc.	V.G.	Good	Fair	Poor
2500	2000	1550	1000	750	350

Model R-93 Safari Attache

This is a top-of-the-line version of the R-93 series. It features engraved receiver, fancy walnut stock and other custom options found on the R-93 Attache model.

NIB	Exc.	V.G.	Good	Fair	Poor
6000	5000	3950	2900	1500	400

Model R-93 Grand Luxe

Offered in the same wide range of calibers as other Blaser models with the addition of a high grade walnut stock, fully hand engraved

receiver, and matching scroll sideplates. Introduced in 1999.
NOTE: Add $200 for left-hand rifles.

NIB	Exc.	V.G.	Good	Fair	Poor
6000	5000	4000	2000	1000	395

Model R-8 Professional

Improved variation of R-93 action with detachable magazine. Offered in many calibers from .222 Rem. to 10.3x60R. Offered in several high grade models similar to those in R-93 series. Prices shown are for basic model with synthetic stock. **NOTE:** Add 15 to 300 percent for high grade versions.

NIB	Exc.	V.G.	Good	Fair	Poor
3000	2300	1700	1200	750	300

Model K-95 Standard

This is a single-shot model with break-open action. The receiver is aluminum with engraving on the side plates. Barrel length is 23.6" for standard calibers and 25.6" for magnum calibers. Oil finish Turkish walnut stock. Interchangeable barrels in calibers from .243 to .300 Wby. Magnum. Weight is about 5.5 lbs. Introduced in 2001.

NIB	Exc.	V.G.	Good	Fair	Poor
3500	2500	1500	1150	700	325

Model K-95 Luxus

Same as above but with fancy Turkish walnut stock and hand engraving on receiver and side plates.

NIB	Exc.	V.G.	Good	Fair	Poor
4300	3750	2500	1900	900	400

Model K-95 Stutzen

Introduced in 2003 this break-action single-shot rifle is offered in 23 calibers. Fancy walnut Mannlicher-style, two-piece stock. Interchangeable barrels.

NIB	Exc.	V.G.	Good	Fair	Poor
5400	4650	3200	2250	1000	450

Ultimate Bolt-Action

Unique bolt-action design imported into the U.S. in the 1980s. Chambered in most popular calibers from .22-250 to .375 H&H. Features include interchangeable barrels and bolt heads, single set trigger, exposed hammer and left-hand models at no additional cost. Available in several high-grade models. Prices shown are for standard model. **NOTE:** Add premium of 15 to 200 percent for higher grade engraving and wood.

NIB	Exc.	V.G.	Good	Fair	Poor
1500	1200	1000	800	550	300

Model R-93 Long Range Sporter

Introduced in 1998, this bolt-action rifle is chambered for the .308 Win. cartridge. The barrel length is 24" without muzzlebrake. Removable box magazine holds 10 rounds. The stock is aluminum and fully adjustable. Weight is approximately 10.4 lbs. No longer in production.

NIB	Exc.	V.G.	Good	Fair	Poor
2200	1775	1250	875	500	275

Model R-93 (LRS2)

This model, introduced in 2000, is a second generation version of the Long Range Sporter model above. It is chambered for the .300 Win. Magnum and the .308 both of which are interchangeable. It is also chambered for the .338 Lapua cartridge which does not interchange with the other calibers. The cheekpiece is improved and a new front rail has been added to this model. Barrel length is 24" without muzzlebrake. Weight is about 10.4 lbs. **NOTE:** For .338 Lapua add $350.

NIB	Exc.	V.G.	Good	Fair	Poor
3475	2700	1900	1275	800	375

Blaser S2 Double Rifle

A series of side-by-side double rifles offered in two different models, Standard and Safari. Standard calibers range from .22 Hornet to 9.3x74R, including several European rimmed cartridges. The Safari model chamberings are for .375 H&H, .470 NE, .500/416 NE and 500 NE. Both series are available in standard or five higher grades offering increasing levels of wood and engraving. Higher grade models are, in order, Luxus, Super Luxus, Exclusive, Super Exclusive and Imperial. Prices shown are for basic standard models. Extra sets of barrels in different calibers offered, including shotgun barrels. Barrel sets are not interchangeable between Standard and Safari models. **NOTE:** Add 15 to 200 percent or more for higher grades.

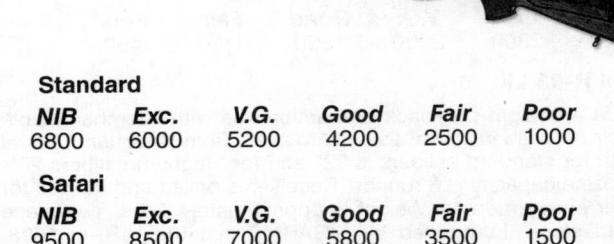

Standard

NIB	Exc.	V.G.	Good	Fair	Poor
6800	6000	5200	4200	2500	1000

Safari

NIB	Exc.	V.G.	Good	Fair	Poor
9500	8500	7000	5800	3500	1500

SHOTGUNS

F3 Series

Over/under series of shotguns offered in standard, sporting, skeet and trap models in 12 or 20 gauge. Available with various barrel lengths and options, including extra barrel sets. Add 40 percent for additional set of barrels. Offered in several higher grades, each with increasing levels of engraving and wood upgrades. For higher grades, add the following to prices shown below: Luxus Grade: 20 percent, Grand Lux Grade: 60 percent, Super Lux Grade: 80 percent, Baroness Grade: 100 percent, Exclusive Grade: 115 percent, Super Exclusive Grade: 200 percent, Imperial Grade: 300 percent.

NIB	Exc.	V.G.	Good	Fair	Poor
—					

Game Standard

NIB	Exc.	V.G.	Good	Fair	Poor
5500	4700	3900	3000	2000	1000

Sporting Standard and Skeet

NIB	Exc.	V.G.	Good	Fair	Poor
6500	5500	4600	3750	2500	1000

Super Trap and Super Sport

NIB	Exc.	V.G.	Good	Fair	Poor
7500	6750	5900	4500	3000	1000

HANDGUNS

Blaser HHS

This single-shot pistol has an R93 receiver and is fitted with a 14" barrel and pistol-grip fancy Turkish walnut stock. All R93 calibers are offered. Offered in both right- and left-hand models. Introduced in 2003. **NOTE:** Add $100 for left-hand models.

NIB	Exc.	V.G.	Good	Fair	Poor
4250	3250	2000	1300	70	400

BLISS, F. D.
New Haven, Connecticut

Bliss Pocket Revolver

A .25 caliber spur trigger revolver with a 3.25" octagon barrel, 6-shot magazine, and a square butt. Blued with either hard rubber or walnut grips. The barrel is stamped "F.D. Bliss New Haven, Ct." There was an all-brass framed version made early in the production, and this model would be worth approximately 50 percent more than the values listed here for the standard model. Approximately 3,000 manufactured circa 1860 to 1863.

NIB	Exc.	V.G.	Good	Fair	Poor
—	—	975	525	125	75

BLISS & GOODYEAR
New Haven, Connecticut

Pocket Model Revolver

A .28 caliber percussion revolver with a 3" octagonal barrel, 6-shot magazine, unfluted cylinder and a solid frame with a removable side plate. Blued with a brass frame and walnut grips. Approximately 3,000 manufactured in 1860.

NIB	Exc.	V.G.	Good	Fair	Poor
—	—	1800	550	225	150

BLUNT & SYMS
New York, New York

Under Hammer Pepperbox

Pepperboxes produced by Blunt & Syms are noteworthy for the fact that they incorporate a ring trigger cocking/revolving mechanism and a concealed under hammer. They were produced in a variety of calibers and the standard finish was blued. Normally these pistols are found marked simply "A-C" on the face of the barrel group. Some examples though are marked "Blunt & Syms New York". This firm was in business from approximately 1837 to 1855.

Small Frame Round Handle .25-.28 Caliber

NIB	Exc.	V.G.	Good	Fair	Poor
—	—	1800	1300	675	175

Medium Frame Round Handle .31 Caliber

NIB	Exc.	V.G.	Good	Fair	Poor
—	—	1850	1450	725	195

Round Handle Dragoon .36 Caliber

NIB	Exc.	V.G.	Good	Fair	Poor
—	—	2900	1050	900	295

Medium Frame Saw Handle .31 Caliber

NIB	Exc.	V.G.	Good	Fair	Poor
—	—	2000	750	375	175

Saw Handle Dragoon .36 Caliber

NIB	Exc.	V.G.	Good	Fair	Poor
—	—	2800	1350	750	225

Dueling Pistol

A .52 caliber percussion single-shot pistol with an octagonal barrel normally of 9" length. Steel furniture with a walnut stock. Barrel marked "B&S New York/Cast Steel".

NIB	Exc.	V.G.	Good	Fair	Poor
—	—	1750	725	325	

Single-Shot Bar Hammer

A .36 caliber single-shot percussion pistol with a 6" half-octagonal barrel and a bar hammer. Blued or browned with walnut grips. Marked as above.

NIB	Exc.	V.G.	Good	Fair	Poor
—	—	1200	700	450	200

Side Hammer Pocket Pistol

A .31 or .35 caliber single-shot percussion pistol with a 2.5" to 6" octagonal barrel. Blued with walnut grips.

NIB	Exc.	V.G.	Good	Fair	Poor
—	—	1250	650	425	195

Side Hammer Belt Pistol

As above, in calibers ranging from .36 to .44 with barrel lengths of 4" or 6".

NIB	Exc.	V.G.	Good	Fair	Poor
—	—	1400	750	375	150

Ring Trigger Pistol

A .36 caliber percussion single-shot pistol with a 3" to 5" half-octagonal barrel and a ring trigger. Blued with walnut grips.

NIB	Exc.	V.G.	Good	Fair	Poor
—	—	1025	650	375	150

Double Barrel Pistol

A .36 to .44 caliber percussion double barrel pistol with 7.5" barrels and walnut grips. A ring trigger variation of this model is known.

NIB	Exc.	V.G.	Good	Fair	Poor
—	—	1350	650	275	125

Double Barrel Under Hammer Pistol

As above, with two under hammers and in .34 caliber with 4" barrels.

NIB	Exc.	V.G.	Good	Fair	Poor
—	—	1750	875	425	200

Derringer Style Pistol

A .50 caliber single-shot percussion pistol with a 3" barrel, German silver mounts and a walnut stock. The lock is marked "Blunt & Syms/New York".

NIB	Exc.	V.G.	Good	Fair	Poor
—	—	1800	675	395	200

BODEO
Location Unknown

Italian Service Revolver

System Bodeo Modello 1889 (Enlisted Model)

NIB	Exc.	V.G.	Good	Fair	Poor
—	750	550	400	250	100

Modello 1889 (Officer's Model)

NIB	Exc.	V.G.	Good	Fair	Poor
—	750	550	400	250	100

BOLUMBURO, G.
Eibar, Spain

Bristol

A semi-automatic pistol in caliber 7.65mm made in the style of the Ruby military pistols. "Bristol" is stamped on the slide. Wood grips.

Courtesy James Rankin

NIB	Exc.	V.G.	Good	Fair	Poor
—	295	185	150	90	40

Marina 6.35mm

A semi-automatic pistol in caliber 6.35mm. "Marina" is stamped on each grip's plate.

Courtesy James Rankin

NIB	Exc.	V.G.	Good	Fair	Poor
—	295	195	150	90	40

Marina 7.65mm

As above but in 7.65mm with "Marina" stamped on the slide. Wood grips and a lanyard loop.

Courtesy James Rankin

NIB	Exc.	V.G.	Good	Fair	Poor
—	275	195	150	90	40

Rex

A semi-automatic pistol in caliber 7.65mm. "Rex" is stamped on the slide with wood grips and a lanyard loop.

Courtesy James Rankin

NIB	Exc.	V.G.	Good	Fair	Poor
—	275	195	150	90	40

BOND ARMS INC.
Grandbury, Texas

Texas Defender

This is a stainless steel over/under derringer chambered for a variety of calibers such as .45 Colt/.410, .357 Magnum, 9mm, .45 ACP, and .44 Magnum. Removable triggerguard. Barrels are interchangeable. Grips are laminated black ash or rosewood. Barrel length is 3" with blade front sight and fixed rear sight. Weight is approximately 21 oz. Introduced in 1997. Add 300 percent for fully factory engraved model.

NIB	Exc.	V.G.	Good	Fair	Poor
—	400	300	200	150	100

Snake Slayer IV

Modern variation of the Remington over/under derringer. Interchangeable 4.5" barrel assemblies, rosewood grip panels, stainless finish, fixed sights. Chambered for .410-bore shotshell/.45 LC, 9mm, 10mm, .40 S&W, .45 ACP.

NIB	Exc.	V.G.	Good	Fair	Poor
—	400	300	200	150	100

Snake Slayer

3.5" barrels; weighs 22 oz. Interchangeable barrel assemblies, rosewood grip panels, stainless, fixed sights. Chambered for .410-bore shotshell/.45 LC, 9mm, 10mm, .40 S&W, .45 ACP).

NIB	Exc.	V.G.	Good	Fair	Poor
—	400	300	200	150	100

Cowboy Defender

Derringer with 3" barrels. Weighs 19 oz. Interchangeable barrels, rosewood grip panels, stainless, fixed sights. Variety of chambering options such as .410-bore, .45 LC, .357 Magnum, .38 Special, .45 ACP, .44 Special, .44-40 Win, .40 S&W, 10mm, etc. No trigger guard. Automatic extractor (except for 9mm, 10mm, .40 S&W, .45 ACP).

NIB	Exc.	V.G.	Good	Fair	Poor
395	350	300	225	150	75

Century 2000

Similar to Cowboy Defender but with 3.5" barrels to allow use of .410 Magnum, shotshells..357/.38 Special, .45 ACP, .44 Special, .44-40 Win, .40 S&W, 10mm, etc. Automatic extractor (except for 9mm, 10mm, .40 S&W, .45 ACP).

NIB	Exc.	V.G.	Good	Fair	Poor
425	375	300	225	150	75

BOOM
Hatfield, Massachusetts
See—Shattuck, C.S.

BORCHARDT
Berlin, Germany
Waffenfabrik Lowe

Borchardt

A forerunner of the German Luger. The Borchardt was a semi-automatic pistol chambered for the 7.65mm Borchardt cartridge. It was fitted with a 6.5" barrel and the magazine held 8 rounds. The pistol was designed by Hugo Borchardt and manufactured by Ludwig Lowe of Berlin. Later models were manufactured by DWM, Deutsch Waffen Und Munitionsfabriken, Berlin. Many Borchardts come with a case which holds shoulder stock, holster, extra magazines, and numerous other accessories.

Courtesy James Rankin

Pistol Only

NIB	Exc.	V.G.	Good	Fair	Poor
—	23000	15000	8000	4000	2000

Pistol with Case and Accessories

NIB	Exc.	V.G.	Good	Fair	Poor
—	35000	20000	12000	7500	4000

BORSIG
East Germany

The Borsig is the East German version of the Soviet Makarov pistol. It is a double-action, chambered for the Soviet 9x18mm cartridge. Its appearance is nearly identical to the Makarov.

NIB	Exc.	V.G.	Good	Fair	Poor
—	300	225	150	100	75

BOSIS, LUCIANO
Brescia, Italy

Bosis is a maker of high-grade sidelock over/under and side-by-side guns in gauges 12, 20, 28, and .410. These guns are made on a custom-order basis.

Over/Under

Values for used guns in excellent condition begin at $30,000. Secure an expert appraisal prior to sale.

Side-by-Side

Values for used guns in excellent condition begin at $20,000. Secure an expert appraisal prior to sale. **NOTE:** Small gauge guns will bring a premium of 20 percent.

BOSS & CO.
London, England

Thomas Boss worked for the great British gunmaker Joseph Manton before becoming a pieceworker to the London trade. In 1891 John Robertson was taken in as a partner and under his control the firm was established as one of London's best gunmakers, rivaled only by James Purdey. Current Boss shotgun prices begin at around £60,000 ($96,000 U.S.) and double rifles about £85,000 ($136,000 U.S.). Many of the older models are encountered on the used gun market. A professional appraisal is strongly advised before establishing a buying or selling price.

A cased pair of Boss & Co. sidelock shotguns

BOSWELL, CHARLES
London, England

One of England's more established makers of best-quality rifles and shotguns. In 1988 the company was purchased by an American consortium and the Cape Horn Outfitters of Charlotte, North Carolina, was appointed their sole agent.

Double Rifle, Boxlock

A .300 Holland & Holland, .375 Holland & Holland or .458 Winchester Magnum double-barrel boxlock rifle with double triggers and a walnut stock. Other features were made to the customer's specifications. A .600 Nitro Express version was also available. **NOTE:** .600 Nitro Express add 25 percent.

NIB	Exc.	V.G.	Good	Fair	Poor
—	47000	39500	29500	19950	600

Double Rifle, Sidelock

As above, with Holland & Holland-style sidelocks. **NOTE:** .600 Nitro Express add 25 percent.

NIB	Exc.	V.G.	Good	Fair	Poor
—	63000	47500	35000	22000	600

BOSWORTH, B. M.
Warren, Pennsylvania

Under Hammer Pistol

A .38 caliber single-shot percussion pistol with an under hammer and a 6" half-octagonal barrel. The frame is marked "BM Bosworth." Browned with brass grips forming part of the frame. Made circa 1850 to 1860.

NIB	Exc.	V.G.	Good	Fair	Poor
—	—	1850	800	295	125

BRAENDLIN ARMOURY
London, England

A .450 caliber 8-barrel pistol with hinged barrels, rotating firing pin and double-action lock. Manufactured during the 1880s.

NIB	Exc.	V.G.	Good	Fair	Poor
—	—	8550	5500	3500	1850

BRAND
New York
Maker—E. Robinson

Breech Loading Carbine

A .50 rimfire caliber carbine with a 22" barrel secured by one barrel band. The frame is marked "Brand's Patent July 29,1862/E. Robinson Manfr/New York". This carbine was produced in limited numbers, primarily for trial purposes.

NIB	Exc.	V.G.	Good	Fair	Poor
—	—	6800	2950	1250	550

BREDA, ERNESTO
Milan, Italy

Andromeda Special

A 12 gauge boxlock shotgun with various barrel lengths and chokes, single-selective triggers and automatic ejectors. Engraved, satin-finished with checkered walnut stock.

NIB	Exc.	V.G.	Good	Fair	Poor
—	1150	775	595	425	300

Vega Special

A 12 gauge boxlock over/under shotgun with 26" or 28" barrels, various choke combinations, single-selective trigger and automatic ejectors. Engraved and blued with a checkered walnut stock.

NIB	Exc.	V.G.	Good	Fair	Poor
—	850	700	600	375	275

Vega Special Trap

As above with a competition-styled stock and 30" or 32" barrels with full chokes.

NIB	Exc.	V.G.	Good	Fair	Poor
—	1350	1050	850	500	350

Sirio Standard

Similar to the Vega with extensive engraving and a higher degree of finishing. There is a 28" barreled skeet version available in this model.

NIB	Exc.	V.G.	Good	Fair	Poor
—	2750	2000	1950	1350	650

Standard Semi-Automatic

A 12 gauge semi-automatic shotgun with 25" or 27" ventilated rib barrels, screw-in choke tubes, an engraved receiver, and checkered walnut stock.

NIB	Exc.	V.G.	Good	Fair	Poor
—	375	275	225	175	125

Grade I

As above, with more engraving and finer wood.

NIB	Exc.	V.G.	Good	Fair	Poor
—	650	475	325	225	175

Grade II

A more elaborately engraved version of the Grade I.

NIB	Exc.	V.G.	Good	Fair	Poor
—	850	600	450	375	250

Grade III

The most deluxe version in this line with select walnut and extensive engraving.

NIB	Exc.	V.G.	Good	Fair	Poor
—	1050	800	650	575	250

Magnum Model

Same as the standard but in 12 gauge Magnum.

NIB	Exc.	V.G.	Good	Fair	Poor
—	435	325	250	175	75

Gold Series Antares Standard

A 12 gauge semi-automatic shotgun with a 25" or 27" ventilated rib barrel and screw-in choke tubes. Blued with a checkered walnut stock.

NIB	Exc.	V.G.	Good	Fair	Poor
—	650	425	350	275	225

Gold Series Argus

As above, with alloy frame.

NIB	Exc.	V.G.	Good	Fair	Poor
—	650	475	375	300	250

Gold Series Aries

As above, except in 12 gauge Magnum.

NIB	Exc.	V.G.	Good	Fair	Poor
—	700	495	400	325	275

M1 Garand

Virtual duplicate of the US M1 Garand chambered in .30-06. Made in the mid-1950s by Breda under contract for Denmark. Values shown are for correct, non-import marked specimens. Deduct up to 50 percent for built-up parts guns or non-matching guns.

NIB	Exc.	V.G.	Good	Fair	Poor
—	2200	1595	800	400	250

BREN 10
Huntington Beach, California
See—Dornaus & Dixon Inc.

Manufactured from 1983 until 1986. Deduct 15 percent for aftermarket magazines.

Standard Bren 10

A 10mm caliber double-action semi-automatic pistol with a 5" barrel and 10-shot magazine. Stainless frame and satin-blued slide. Manufactured between 1983 and 1986. Value includes original factory magazine.

NIB	Exc.	V.G.	Good	Fair	Poor
2625	1925	1400	850	550	325

M & P Model

As above, with a matte black finish.

NIB	Exc.	V.G.	Good	Fair	Poor
2700	2100	1550	925	595	385

Special Forces Model

Chambered for 10mm cartridge and is similar to the M&P model. Offered in two models: Model D has a dark finish while Model L has a light finish. Prices listed are for Model D, add 25 percent for Model L.

NIB	Exc.	V.G.	Good	Fair	Poor
2800	2200	1750	1000	800	500

Dual-Master Presentation Model

As above, with a .45 caliber, extra barrel and slide and a fitted walnut case.

NIB	Exc.	V.G.	Good	Fair	Poor
6125	4375	2190	1225	875	500

Marksman Model

Similar to the Standard Model but in .45 caliber. There were 250 manufactured for the "Marksman Shop" in Chicago, Illinois.

NIB	Exc.	V.G.	Good	Fair	Poor
2450	1750	1325	700	300	275

Jeff Cooper Commemorative

There were supposed to be 2,000 of these manufactured in 1986, but no one knows how many were actually produced. Some estimates are less than 10. They are chambered for the 10mm and have a high-gloss blue finish with 22 kt. gold-plated details. The grips are laser engraved, and the whole affair is furnished in a walnut display case.

NIB	Exc.	V.G.	Good	Fair	Poor
6125	4375	—	—	—	—

Bren 10 (2010 Series)

Several Bren 10 models were manufactured by Vltor in Tucson, Arizona from 2010 to 2011. Limited production of approximately 2000 guns. Specifications similar to original Standard and Marksman models with choice of 4" or 5" barrels, 10mm or .45 ACP chambering, stainless or two-tone finish.

NIB	Exc.	V.G.	Good	Fair	Poor
1100	1000	850	700	500	300

BRETTON
Ste. Etienne, France

Baby Standard

A 12 or 20 gauge over/under shotgun with various barrel lengths and choke combinations and double triggers. Blued, checkered walnut stock.

NIB	Exc.	V.G.	Good	Fair	Poor
1350	975	725	550	400	325

Deluxe Grade

A 12, 16, and 20 gauge over/under shotgun. Engraved, coin-finished receiver with walnut stock.

NIB	Exc.	V.G.	Good	Fair	Poor
2150	1875	1400	800	500	325

BRIGGS, H. A.
Norwich, Connecticut

Single-Shot Pistol

A .22 caliber single-shot spur trigger pistol with a 4" part-round/part-octagonal barrel with a downward rotating breechblock. Blued with walnut grips. Frame is marked "H.A. Briggs/Norwich, Ct." Manufactured in the 1850s and 1860s.

NIB	Exc.	V.G.	Good	Fair	Poor
—	—	2950	1250	450	200

BRILEY MANUFACTURING INC.
Houston, Texas

El Presidente Model—Unlimited

This 1911-style pistol can be built on a Caspian Arms, STI, or SVI frame. Includes scope mount, compensator, match barrel, cocking sight, lowered and flared ejection port, front and rear serrations, aluminum guide rod, and numerous other custom features. Offered in most calibers. Blued finish.

NIB	Exc.	V.G.	Good	Fair	Poor
2400	2000	1450	1000	700	350

Versatility Plus Model—Limited

Built on a 1911 frame with BoMar sight, checkered mainspring housing and checkered front strap. Many other custom features. Available in .45 ACP, .40 S&W, and 9mm.

NIB	Exc.	V.G.	Good	Fair	Poor
1950	1650	1200	800	400	225

Versatility Model—Limited

Similar to the above model but without several features such as the checkered front strap. Available in .45 ACP, .40 S&W, 9mm.

NIB	Exc.	V.G.	Good	Fair	Poor
1475	1150	800	575	265	195

Lightning Model—Action Pistol

Built on a 1911 frame this pistol features many custom components including a titanium compensator. Weight no more than 40 oz. Available in 9mm and .38 Super only.

NIB	Exc.	V.G.	Good	Fair	Poor
2450	1950	1300	850	425	200

Carry Comp Model—Defense

Built on a 1911 frame this model features a dual port cone compensator with many custom features. Barrel length is about 5". Offered in .45 ACP only.

NIB	Exc.	V.G.	Good	Fair	Poor
2450	2000	1550	1000	500	250

BRIXIA
Brescia, Italy

Model 12

A commercial version of the Model 1910 Glisenti in 9mm Glisenti caliber. The Brixia was a simplified Glisenti and was made to replace the Glisenti for the military market. The Italian military did not accept them and only a few were made for the commercial market. The only markings are the monogram eagle holding a shield cast in the grips.

Courtesy James Rankin

NIB	Exc.	V.G.	Good	Fair	Poor
—	1300	950	7850	450	325

BRNO ARMS
Uhersky Brod, Czech Republic

Brno firearms have been manufactured since 1918 in what was once known as Czechosolvakia, now the Czech Republic. Various Brno rifles, pistols, shotguns and combination guns have been brought into the U.S. since the late 1940s by several importers including Continental Arms, Magnum Research, Bohemia Arms, EAA and others. There has been a close association between Brno and CZ (Ceska Zbrojovka) for many years. CZ-USA of Kansas City, Kansas, is the current importer of both brands. The only Brno models currently being imported are single-shot and over/under rifles and over/under combination rifle/shotguns.

ZG-47

A bolt-action rifle based on the Mauser system. Chambered for .270, 7x57, 7x64, .30-06, 8x57, 8x60, 8x64S, 9.3x62, and on special order 10.75x68. Barrel length is 23.6". Adjustable trigger. Hinged floorplate. Weight is about 7.7 lbs.

Standard

NIB	Exc.	V.G.	Good	Fair	Poor
—	1000	900	800	650	400

Deluxe

NIB	Exc.	V.G.	Good	Fair	Poor
—	1100	950	850	600	450

ZH-SERIES

A double barrel over/under boxlock series of shotguns with interchangeable barrels in shotgun and rifle configurations, of various lengths, double triggers and automatic ejectors. The models listed represent the different gauges and/or calibers offered. **NOTE:** For ZH models with set triggers and cheekpiece add $75. For interchangeable barrels add between $300 and $400 depending on gauge and caliber.

ZH-300

NIB	Exc.	V.G.	Good	Fair	Poor
—	675	575	400	325	250

ZH-301

12gauge/12gauge.

NIB	Exc.	V.G.	Good	Fair	Poor
	600	500	400	350	200

ZH-302

12gauge/12gauge Skeet.

NIB	Exc.	V.G.	Good	Fair	Poor
—	600	550	450	400	250

ZH-303 12

12gauge/12gauge Trap.

NIB	Exc.	V.G.	Good	Fair	Poor
—	600	550	450	400	250

ZH-304

12gauge/7x57R.

NIB	Exc.	V.G.	Good	Fair	Poor
—	1000	800	500	400	250

ZH-305

12gauge/6x52R.

NIB	Exc.	V.G.	Good	Fair	Poor
—	900	700	500	400	225

ZH-306

12gauge/6x50R Magnum.

NIB	Exc.	V.G.	Good	Fair	Poor
—	850	650	450	350	200

ZH-308

12gauge/7x65R.

NIB	Exc.	V.G.	Good	Fair	Poor
	850	700	500	400	225

ZH-309

12gauge/8x57 JRS.

NIB	Exc.	V.G.	Good	Fair	Poor
—	850	700	500	400	225

ZH-321

16gauge/16gauge.

NIB	Exc.	V.G.	Good	Fair	Poor
—	750	625	450	400	225

ZH-324

16gauge/7x57R.

NIB	Exc.	V.G.	Good	Fair	Poor
—	875	700	500	400	225

ZH-328

16gauge/7x65R.

NIB	Exc.	V.G.	Good	Fair	Poor
—	850	700	500	400	225

Model 300 Combo

The model ZH-300 with 8 interchangeable barrels in a fitted case. Introduced in 1986.

NIB	Exc.	V.G.	Good	Fair	Poor
5000	4000	3000	2750	2000	1500

Model 500

The model ZH-300 with acid-etched decoration, automatic ejectors and in 12 gauge.

NIB	Exc.	V.G.	Good	Fair	Poor
—	800	600	425	350	275

ZP-49

A 12 gauge sidelock double-barrel shotgun with double triggers and automatic ejectors. Blued with a walnut stock. Imported in 1986 only.

NIB	Exc.	V.G.	Good	Fair	Poor
—	1050	800	650	450	325

ZP-149

As above, without engraving.

NIB	Exc.	V.G.	Good	Fair	Poor
—	600	500	400	300	200

ZP-349

As above, with the buttstock having a cheekpiece and a beavertail forearm.

NIB	Exc.	V.G.	Good	Fair	Poor
—	800	650	500	350	250

ZBK-100

A single barrel shotgun in 12 or 20 gauge with 27" barrel and walnut stock. Weight is approximately 5.5 lbs.

NIB	Exc.	V.G.	Good	Fair	Poor
250	200	150	125	100	75

RIFLES

ZKW-465 (Hornet Sporter)

A .22 Hornet caliber bolt-action rifle with a 23" barrel, express sights and double-set triggers. Blued with a walnut stock.

NIB	Exc.	V.G.	Good	Fair	Poor
—	1500	1100	950	800	550

Model 21H

A 6.5x57mm, 7x57mm or 8x57mm caliber bolt-action sporting rifle with a 23-5/8" barrel, express sights and double-set triggers. Blued with a walnut stock.

NIB	Exc.	V.G.	Good	Fair	Poor
—	1250	1050	900	750	600

Model 22F

As above, with a Mannlicher-style stock. Barrel length is 20.5".

NIB	Exc.	V.G.	Good	Fair	Poor
—	1295	1100	900	650	500

Model I

A .22 caliber bolt-action rifle with a 22.75" barrel having folding leaf rear sights. Blued with a walnut stock.

NIB	Exc.	V.G.	Good	Fair	Poor
—	550	400	300	250	200

Model II

As above, with a more finely figured walnut stock.

NIB	Exc.	V.G.	Good	Fair	Poor
—	595	450	350	300	225

ZKM 611

This is a semi-automatic rifle chambered for the .17 HMR or .22 WRM cartridge. It is fitted with a 20" barrel and has a magazine capacity of 6 rounds. Weight is approximately 6.2 lbs.

NIB	Exc.	V.G.	Good	Fair	Poor
700	625	525	300	175	125

ZKM 451

This is a semi-automatic rifle chambered for the .22 LR cartridge and fitted with a 22" barrel. Magazine capacity is 7 rounds. Weight is about 5.25 lbs.

NIB	Exc.	V.G.	Good	Fair	Poor
450	300	250	125	100	75

ZKM 451 LUX

Same as above but with select walnut stock.

NIB	Exc.	V.G.	Good	Fair	Poor
500	350	250	150	125	100

ZBK 680

A .22 Hornet or .222 caliber bolt-action rifle with a 23.5" barrel, double set triggers and 5-shot magazine. Blued with a walnut stock.

NIB	Exc.	V.G.	Good	Fair	Poor
925	750	550	400	325	225

Super Express Rifle

An over/under sidelock double-barrel rifle, with 23.5" barrels, double triggers and automatic ejectors. Engraved, blued with a walnut stock. Available in 6 grades:

Standard Model

NIB	Exc.	V.G.	Good	Fair	Poor
5500	4150	3000	2500	1750	1250

Grade I

NIB	Exc.	V.G.	Good	Fair	Poor
7500	5900	4750	4500	3600	3250

Grade II

NIB	Exc.	V.G.	Good	Fair	Poor
6500	5150	4000	3500	2750	2250

Grade III

NIB	Exc.	V.G.	Good	Fair	Poor
6250	4900	3950	3250	2750	2250

Grade IV

NIB	Exc.	V.G.	Good	Fair	Poor
6000	4700	3500	3000	2500	2250

Grade V

NIB	Exc.	V.G.	Good	Fair	Poor
5750	3950	3250	2750	2250	1750

Grade VI

NIB	Exc.	V.G.	Good	Fair	Poor
4900	4250	3100	2600	1950	1500

ZH-344/348/349

An over/under rifle chambered for 7x57R, 7x65R, or 8x57JRS.

NIB	Exc.	V.G.	Good	Fair	Poor
1500	975	700	550	400	275

Model 98 Standard

This bolt-action rifle is chambered for a variety of calibers from the 7x64 to the 9.3x62. It is fitted with a 23" barrel and figured walnut stock with buttplate and open sights. Weight is approximately 7.25 lbs. **NOTE:** For set trigger add $100.

NIB	Exc.	V.G.	Good	Fair	Poor
800	650	400	300	200	150

Model 98 Full Stock

Same as above but with full one-piece stock and set trigger.

NIB	Exc.	V.G.	Good	Fair	Poor
1000	700	500	400	350	200

ZK 99

This is a tip-up centerfire rifle chambered for a wide variety of calibers from 6.5x57R to .30-06. Barrel length is 23" and weight is about 5.75 lbs.

NIB	Exc.	V.G.	Good	Fair	Poor
995	750	550	395	200	150

ZBK 110

This is a single-shot tip-open rifle chambered for the .22 Hornet, .222 Rem., the 5.6x50R Magnum, and the 5.6x52R. Barrel length is 23.5". Open sights. Walnut stock without checkering. Weight is about 6 lbs.

NIB	Exc.	V.G.	Good	Fair	Poor
450	350	250	200	150	75

ZBK 110 LUX

Same as above but with select walnut stock with checkering. Open sights.

NIB	Exc.	V.G.	Good	Fair	Poor
440	350	250	200	150	75

ZBK 110 Super Lux

Same as above but with fancy walnut stock with checkering. Open sights.

NIB	Exc.	V.G.	Good	Fair	Poor
650	525	400	300	150	75

HANDGUNS

ZKR 551

This is a double- or single-action revolver with a 6-round cylinder. Adjustable rear sight. Walnut grips. Fitted with 6" barrel. Chambered for .38, .32 S&W Long, and .22 LR. Weight is about 35 oz.

NIB	Exc.	V.G.	Good	Fair	Poor
1800	1350	900	700	500	275

BROLIN ARMS
La Verne, California

Brolin Arms was in business from approximately 1995 to 2000 and imported handguns from Hungary, Mauser military rifles from Europe and shotguns from China. The company also manufactured a series of 1911-pattern pistols

LEGEND SERIES—1911 AUTO PISTOL
L45—Standard Auto Pistol

This is the standard model with 5" barrel chambered for the .45 ACP. Fitted with throated match barrel, polished feed ramp, lowered ejection port, beveled magazine well and fixed sights. Other custom features as well. Finish is matte blue with 7-round magazine. Weight is about 36 oz.

NIB	Exc.	V.G.	Good	Fair	Poor
550	400	295	200	125	75

L45C—Compact Auto Pistol

Similar to the above standard model but with a 4.5" barrel. Weight is about 32 oz.

NIB	Exc.	V.G.	Good	Fair	Poor
595	550	325	225	150	100

L45T

This version of the L45 series was introduced in 1997 and is fitted with a compact slide on a full-size frame. Weight is 36 oz. **NOTE:** For Novak sights add $50.

NIB	Exc.	V.G.	Good	Fair	Poor
595	550	325	200	125	75

PATRIOT SERIES—DPC CARRY-COMP PISTOLS
P45 Comp—Standard Carry Comp

This model features a 4" barrel with integral compensator cut into the slide. Other features are a custom beavertail grip safety, adjustable aluminum trigger, flat-top slide, and checkered wood grips. Weight is about 37 oz.

NIB	Exc.	V.G.	Good	Fair	Poor
600	550	375	225	110	95

P45C Comp—Compact Carry Comp

Similar to the above model but fitted with a 3.25" barrel. Weight is about 33 oz. **NOTE:** For two-tone finish add $20.

NIB	Exc.	V.G.	Good	Fair	Poor
600	550	375	225	110	95

P45T

This addition to the Patriot Series was introduced in 1997 and has all of the features of the Patriot pistols but is fitted with a compact slide and full size frame. Weight is about 35 oz. Also available in two-tone finish for an additional $20. **NOTE:** For Novak sights add $50.

NIB	Exc.	V.G.	Good	Fair	Poor
600	550	375	225	110	95

TAC SERIES—TACTICAL 1911 PISTOLS
TAC-11

This series and model were introduced in 1997 and have all of the features of the L45 series with the additions of a special 5" conical match barrel, Novak Low Profile sights, black rubber contour grips, "iron claw" extractor, and optional night sights. Chambered for the .45 ACP the pistol is supplied with an 8-round magazine. Weight is approximately 37 oz. **NOTE:** For Tritium night sights add $90.

NIB	Exc.	V.G.	Good	Fair	Poor
650	575	395	250	150	100

TAC SERIES—DOUBLE-ACTION PISTOLS
MS45

This is a full-size double-action pistol chambered for the .45 ACP cartridge. It is fitted with an 8-round magazine and low-profile 3-dot sights. Standard finish is matte blue. **NOTE:** Add $20 for royal blue finish.

NIB	Exc.	V.G.	Good	Fair	Poor
650	575	395	250	150	100

M45

Similar to the model above but with a longer barrel. Chambered for .45 ACP and 8-round magazine. **NOTE:** Add $20 for royal blue finish.

NIB	Exc.	V.G.	Good	Fair	Poor
550	475	300	250	150	100

M40

Same as M45 but chambered for .40 S&W cartridge. Magazine capacity is 10 rounds. **NOTE:** For Novak sights add $50.

NIB	Exc.	V.G.	Good	Fair	Poor
500	400	275	250	150	100

M90

Same as M45 model but chambered for 9mm cartridge. Magazine capacity is 10 rounds. **NOTE:** Add $20 for royal blue finish.

NIB	Exc.	V.G.	Good	Fair	Poor
500	400	300	250	150	100

MC40

This is compact version of the full-size double-action models. It is fitted with a full-size frame but shorter slide. Chambered for .40 S&W cartridge. Magazine capacity is 10 rounds. **NOTE:** Add $20 for royal blue finish.

NIB	Exc.	V.G.	Good	Fair	Poor
600	500	300	250	150	100

MC90

Same as above but chambered for 9mm cartridge.

NIB	Exc.	V.G.	Good	Fair	Poor
500	400	275	250	150	100

MB40

This is super-compact double-action pistol. Features a concealed hammer. Chambered for .40 S&W cartridge. Magazine capacity is 6 rounds. **NOTE:** Add $20 for royal blue finish.

NIB	Exc.	V.G.	Good	Fair	Poor
550	450	300	250	150	100

MB90

Same as above but chambered for 9mm cartridge.

NIB	Exc.	V.G.	Good	Fair	Poor
550	450	300	250	150	100

PRO SERIES—COMPETITION PISTOL
Pro-Stock—Competition Pistol

Chambered for the .45 ACP, this pistol is designed for the competition shooter. Many special features are standard such as full-length recoil guide, front strap high relief cut, serrated flat mainspring housing, ambidextrous thumb safety and fully adjustable rear sight. Barrel length is 5" and weight is about 37 oz. **NOTE:** For two-tone finish add $20.

NIB	Exc.	V.G.	Good	Fair	Poor
700	600	500	350	175	100

Pro-Comp—Competition Pistol

Similar to the competition model above but fitted with an integral compensator and 4" barrel. Weight is about 37 oz. **NOTE:** For two-tone finish add $20.

NIB	Exc.	V.G.	Good	Fair	Poor
750	650	500	375	200	100

PUMP-ACTION SHOTGUNS

LAWMAN SERIES—PERSONAL SECURITY SHOTGUN
HL18SB

This is a pump-action 12 gauge shotgun with an 18.5" barrel, black synthetic stock and bead sights. Weight is about 7 lbs. Introduced in 1997. A copy of the Remington Model 870.

NIB	Exc.	V.G.	Good	Fair	Poor
295	250	195	150	95	50

HL18SR

Same as above but fitted with rifle sights.

NIB	Exc.	V.G.	Good	Fair	Poor
325	275	225	175	125	65

HL18SBN

Same as above but with nickel finish.

NIB	Exc.	V.G.	Good	Fair	Poor
270	200	150	100	75	50

HL18WB

This version has a wood stock and bead sights.

NIB	Exc.	V.G.	Good	Fair	Poor
295	250	195	150	95	50

HL18WR

Same as above but fitted with rifle sights.

NIB	Exc.	V.G.	Good	Fair	Poor
270	200	150	100	75	50

FIELD SERIES—PUMP-ACTION FIELD GUN
HF24SB

This is a 12 gauge pump-action shotgun with a 24" barrel, matte finish, and black synthetic stock with bead sights. Weight is about 7.3 lbs. Introduced in 1997.

NIB	Exc.	V.G.	Good	Fair	Poor
270	200	150	100	75	50

HF28SB

Same as above but fitted with a 28" barrel. Weight is 7.4 lbs.

NIB	Exc.	V.G.	Good	Fair	Poor
270	200	150	100	75	50

HF24WB

This model features a 24" barrel with wood stock.

NIB	Exc.	V.G.	Good	Fair	Poor
270	200	150	100	75	50

HF28WB

Same as above but with 24" barrel.

NIB	Exc.	V.G.	Good	Fair	Poor
270	200	150	100	75	50

Slug Special

This slide-action shotgun is chambered for 3" 12 gauge shells and is available with choice of 18.5" or 22" barrels with rifle or ghost ring sights. Available with fixed improved cylinder choke, 4" extended rifled choke, or fully rifled barrel. Choice of wood or synthetic stocks.

NIB	Exc.	V.G.	Good	Fair	Poor
270	200	150	100	75	50

Turkey Special

This 12 gauge 3" model is fitted with a 22" extra full choke vent rib barrel with a choice of wood or synthetic stock.

NIB	Exc.	V.G.	Good	Fair	Poor
270	200	150	100	75	50

FIELD COMBO—TWO BARREL COMBO SET

HC28SB

This set consists of an 18.5" barrel and 28" barrel with synthetic stock pistol grip, and bead sights.

NIB	Exc.	V.G.	Good	Fair	Poor
300	250	200	125	75	50

HC28SR

Same as above but with rifle and bead sights.

NIB	Exc.	V.G.	Good	Fair	Poor
320	250	200	125	75	50

HC28WB

This model features a wood stock, pistol grip, and bead sights.

NIB	Exc.	V.G.	Good	Fair	Poor
300	250	200	125	75	50

HC28WR

Same as above but with wood stock with rifle and bead sights.

NIB	Exc.	V.G.	Good	Fair	Poor
320	250	200	125	75	50

SEMI-AUTOMATIC SHOTGUNS

BL-12 Security

This 12 gauge shotgun has a 3" chamber and 5 round magazine. It is fitted with a 18.5" vent rib barrel. Synthetic stock is standard.

NIB	Exc.	V.G.	Good	Fair	Poor
350	325	295	200	150	75

BL-12 Field

Similar to the above model but with a 28" vent rib barrel and choice of wood or synthetic stock.

NIB	Exc.	V.G.	Good	Fair	Poor
350	325	295	200	150	75

SAS-12 Security

This 12 gauge shotgun is chambered for 2.75" 12 gauge shells and fitted with 24" vent rib barrel or rifle sight barrel. Detachable box magazine; 3 round standard, 5 round optional. Synthetic stock.

NIB	Exc.	V.G.	Good	Fair	Poor
350	325	295	200	150	75

RIFLES

Legacy

This is a .50 caliber muzzleloader with in-line ignition system. It has a walnut stain hardwood stock with recoil pad. Finish is blue or chrome. **NOTE:** Add $20 for chrome finish.

NIB	Exc.	V.G.	Good	Fair	Poor
180	150	100	75	50	15

Mitchell PPS-50

This is a semi-automatic rifle chambered for the .22 LR cartridge. It has a detachable 10-round magazine. It is a copy of the Russian PPSh machine gun used in WWII.

NIB	Exc.	V.G.	Good	Fair	Poor
400	325	275	225	175	100

MAUSER RIFLES

All of these Mauser rifles were introduced in 1998 to the Brolin product line.

Lightning Model

This model features a sliding bolt that locks directly into the barrel. Chambered for 7.62x39mm cartridge as well as the .308 Win. Blue finish with choice of colored synthetic stocks. Open sights are standard.

NIB	Exc.	V.G.	Good	Fair	Poor
550	450	350	325	200	100

Lightning Hunter Model

This model features a detachable magazine, recoil pad, blued finish, checkered wood stock, and choice of open sights or no sights with scope mounts included. Calibers from .243 to .300 Win. Magnum. **NOTE:** Add $50 for open sights, $50 for stainless steel.

NIB	Exc.	V.G.	Good	Fair	Poor
650	500	350	325	200	100

Lightning Hunter All Weather Model

Same as above but with black synthetic stock.

NIB	Exc.	V.G.	Good	Fair	Poor
700	550	350	325	200	100

Lightning Varmint Model

The features of this model are the same as the Lightning Hunter Model with the addition of a heavy fluted barrel with special varmint wood or synthetic stock. Chambered for .22-250 and .243 cartridges.

NIB	Exc.	V.G.	Good	Fair	Poor
900	700	550	450	300	125

Lightning Sniper

This model features a heavy fluted barrel with detachable magazine and a choice of special wood or synthetic stock with built-in bi-pod rail. Offered in .308 or 300 Win. Magnum calibers.

NIB	Exc.	V.G.	Good	Fair	Poor
1000	800	600	450	300	125

Lightning Professional

This model has a heavy fluted barrel, no sights, and recoil compensator. A tuned trigger system is standard. All-weather adjustable stock with pistol grip. Available in .308 or .300 Win. Magnum calibers.

NIB	Exc.	V.G.	Good	Fair	Poor
900	700	550	395	300	125

2000 Classic

The 2000 Classic features an interchangeable caliber system for cartridges in the same action length. Detachable magazine. High-grade walnut stock with cut checkering and rosewood fore-end. Single set trigger is standard. Offered in .270, .308, .30-06, 7mm Rem. Magnum, and .300 Win. Magnum.

NIB	Exc.	V.G.	Good	Fair	Poor
1500	1250	800	495	300	125

2000 Varmint

This model features a heavy fluted barrel with special varmint wood stock with accessory rail. Offered in .22-250, and .243 calibers. Standard without sights.

NIB	Exc.	V.G.	Good	Fair	Poor
2200	1700	1200	800	400	200

2000 Sniper

This model features an interchangeable caliber system, heavy fluted barrel, no sights, single set trigger, all-weather stock with built-in bi-pod rail. Offered in .308 and .300 Win. Magnum calibers.

NIB	Exc.	V.G.	Good	Fair	Poor
2200	1750	1250	800	400	200

2000 Professional

This model has all of the features of the Sniper rifle with the addition of a recoil compensator and special all-weather pistol-grip stock. Each rifle is custom built.

NIB	Exc.	V.G.	Good	Fair	Poor
3500	2750	1700	90	550	250

20/22

This is a high-quality .22 bolt-action rifle chambered for the .22 LR or .22 Magnum cartridge. Available in both a standard and deluxe configuration. Add $100 for deluxe version.

NIB	Exc.	V.G.	Good	Fair	Poor
750	575	475	395	300	125

1898 Commemorative

This model celebrates the 100 year anniversary of the '98 Mauser. Chambered for the 8mm Mauser cartridge. This is a limited edition rifle.

NIB	Exc.	V.G.	Good	Fair	Poor
2300	1750	1400	1000	675	300

98

This is the original Mauser action built to Safari calibers. Chambered for .375 H&H or .416 Rigby.

NIB	Exc.	V.G.	Good	Fair	Poor
10000	8000	6250	5000	1500	400

CUSTOM SHOP

Formula One RZ

This is a high-performance competition race gun with many special features such as supported barrel chamber, 6-port compensator, tuned trigger, extended magazine release, and many other options as standard. Chambered for .38 Super, .40 S&W cartridges. Blue finish. Add $400 for double-action.

NIB	Exc.	V.G.	Good	Fair	Poor
2500	2000	1400	1050	700	350

Formula One RS

Designed as a Limited Class competition gun with 5" barrel and chambered for .38 Super, .40 S&W, or .45 ACP calibers. Features adjustable rear sight, tuned trigger, checkered front strap and mainspring housing and other special features. Add $300 for double-action.

NIB	Exc.	V.G.	Good	Fair	Poor
2000	1600	1250	875	500	350

Formula Z

This model is a custom-built combat pistol chambered for .40 S&W, .400 CorBon, or .45 ACP calibers. Fitted with a 5" or 4" barrel. Features many extra-cost features as standard.

NIB	Exc.	V.G.	Good	Fair	Poor
1300	1000	650	425	300	150

MITCHELL SINGLE-ACTION REVOLVERS

Single-Action Army Model

Offered in 4.75", 5.5", or 7.5" barrel lengths and chambered for the .45 Long Colt, .357 Magnum, or .44-40 calibers. Offered in blue finish with case hardened frame or nickel finish. Also available with dual cylinders, i.e. .45 LC/.45 ACP. Add $50 for nickel finish, and $150 for dual cylinder models.

NIB	Exc.	V.G.	Good	Fair	Poor
395	350	275	175	125	75

BRONCO
Eibar, Spain

See— Echave & Arizmendi
(Firearms International & Garcia)

BROOKLYN F. A. CO.
Brooklyn, New York

Slocum Pocket Revolver

A .32 caliber spur-trigger revolver with a 3" round barrel. The frame is silver-plated brass and scroll engraved; the remainder is either blued or plated with walnut grips. The barrel is marked "B.A. Co. Patented April 14, 1863". Approximately 10,000 were manufactured in 1863 and 1864. The cylinder has five individual tubes that slide forward to open for loading and then for ejecting the spent cartridges.

NIB	Exc.	V.G.	Good	Fair	Poor
—	975	325	120	75	

Slocum Unfluted Cylinder Pocket Revolver

As above, but in .22 or .32 caliber with 5- or 7-shot cylinder. Approximately 250 were manufactured in .32 rimfire and 100 in .22 rimfire. **NOTE:** .22 caliber add 25 percent.

NIB	Exc.	V.G.	Good	Fair	Poor
—	—	1300	450	225	125

BROWN, ED PRODUCTS
Perry, Missouri

There are a number of extra options available on Ed Brown handguns and rifles that may affect values. In August of 2010, Ed Brown announced that he would no longer be accepting orders for new rifles and, for an indefinite period of time, would be focusing on his core business of handguns. Rifle parts and limited services remain available.

HANDGUNS

Commander Bobtail

This model features a 4.25" barrel chambered for the .45 ACP, .400 CorBon, .40 S&W, .38 Super, 9x23, or 9mm Luger cartridge. Modified Hogue grips from exotic wood are standard. This pistol is completely handmade and is built to the customer's specifications. Many available options.

NIB	Exc.	V.G.	Good	Fair	Poor
2200	1700	1200	700	500	300

Classic Custom

Chambered for the .45 ACP cartridge. This is a custom built pistol with many extra features such as Videki trigger, Ed Brown wide thumb safety, stainless steel thumb safety, and extended safety, adjustable rear sight, etc. All hand-fitted parts.

NIB	Exc.	V.G.	Good	Fair	Poor
3100	2400	1700	950	450	300

Class A Limited

This is a custom-built pistol offered in a number of different calibers from .45 ACP to 9mm Luger. Fitted with a 4.25" Commander length slide. Many special features. Price listed is for the basic pistol.

NIB	Exc.	V.G.	Good	Fair	Poor
2450	1750	1300	800	500	325

Kobra Custom .45

Introduced in 2002 this pistol features a snakeskin treatment on forestrap, mainspring housing, and slide. Novak night sights and Hogue checkered wood grips standard. Many other custom features.

NIB	Exc.	V.G.	Good	Fair	Poor
1995	1400	1150	675	400	250

Kobra Carry .45

Same as above but with shorter grip frame and barrel.

NIB	Exc.	V.G.	Good	Fair	Poor
2195	1500	1200	700	425	275

Executive Target

1911 Executive Elite modified for target/range with adjustable BoMar rear sight, ambidextrous safety. 38 oz. 5" barrel chambered for .45 ACP. 7-round magazine.

NIB	Exc.	V.G.	Good	Fair	Poor
2550	2000	1500	950	450	300

Executive Elite

Government model 5" barrel, 38 oz., chambered for .45 ACP. 7-round magazine. Fixed sights. Blue/blue, stainless/blue or all-stainless.

NIB	Exc.	V.G.	Good	Fair	Poor
2300	1800	1350	900	400	275

Executive Carry

A 4.25" commander model .45 ACP with Ed Brown Bobtail. 38 oz. 7-round magazine, fixed sights. Blue/blue, stainless/blue or all-stainless.

NIB	Exc.	V.G.	Good	Fair	Poor
2400	1900	1500	950	450	300

Special Forces

Blue/blue 1911 semi-automatic with 5" barrel and fixed 3-dot night sights. Chambered for .45 ACP. 38 oz.; 7-round magazine. Cocobolo grips.

NIB	Exc.	V.G.	Good	Fair	Poor
2195	1600	1150	800	550	275

RIFLES

Savanna

Fitted with a long action and chambered for calibers from .257 Ackley to .338 Win. Magnum. Barrel is a lightweight 24" for standard calibers and a 24" medium weight for magnum calibers. Talley scope mounts included. Fiberglass stock, recoil pad, steel trigger guard and floorplate are standard.

NIB	Exc.	V.G.	Good	Fair	Poor
3800	3000	1995	1500	900	400

Damara

Similar to Savanna but in a lightweight configuration with natural-finish stainless barrel.

NIB	Exc.	V.G.	Good	Fair	Poor
3200	2650	2000	1300	650	400

Varmint

This is a custom-made rifle with a short single-shot action, 26" medium weight barrel or 24" heavyweight barrel. H-S Precision stock. Available in calibers from .222 to 6.5/.284.

NIB	Exc.	V.G.	Good	Fair	Poor
3500	2800	2000	1300	750	400

Bushveld

This model is based on a Dakota controlled feed action. Fitted with a 24" medium or heavyweight barrel. Calibers from .330 Dakota to .458 Win. Magnum. Detachable box magazine. Monte Carlo fiberglass stock, recoil pad, steel trigger and floorplate are standard as is Talley scope mounts. Weight is approx. 8.5 lbs.

NIB	Exc.	V.G.	Good	Fair	Poor
4400	3250	2000	1500	900	400

Express

Centerfire bolt-action rifle chambered for a wide variety of large Africa-class calibers. Dropped box magazine, fully controlled feed, fluted bolt, McMillan stock, iron sights.

NIB	Exc.	V.G.	Good	Fair	Poor
3600	2900	2350	1600	800	400

Marine Sniper

Duplicate of Vietnam-era McMillan sniper rifle, controlled feed, fluted bolt, hinged floorplate, woodland camo stock, blackened stainless steel barrel and receiver. Offered in .308 and .300 Win. Magnum calibers. Weight is about 9.25 lbs.

NIB	Exc.	V.G.	Good	Fair	Poor
3700	2950	2350	1600	900	400

Light Tactical

This is a short-action rifle with light weight floorplate and trigger guard. Fitted with a 21" medium-weight barrel. Black fiberglass stock with aluminum bedding block. Available in calibers from .22-250 to .308.

NIB	Exc.	V.G.	Good	Fair	Poor
4100	2950	2000	1500	900	400

Tactical

This is similar to the above model but built on a long action with heavy weight 26" blued barrel. McMillan A-3 black tactical stock. Available in .308 and .300 Win. Magnum.

NIB	Exc.	V.G.	Good	Fair	Poor
3900	3350	2500	1600	950	400

Ozark

This rifle is built on a short action with a blind magazine. A 21" lightweight barrel is fitted for standard calibers and a medium weight 21" barrel for magnum calibers. Chambered for calibers from .22-250 to .308. Talley scope mounts are included as is a fiberglass stock, recoil pad, steel trigger guard and floorplate.

NIB	Exc.	V.G.	Good	Fair	Poor
3800	3000	1995	1500	900	400

Denali

This is a lighter-weight version of the Ozark with a 22" super light weight barrel. Chambered for calibers .25-06 to .300 WSM. Weight is about 6.75 lbs.

NIB	Exc.	V.G.	Good	Fair	Poor
3800	3000	1995	1500	900	400

Peacekeeper

This is a single-shot long-action rifle chambered for .30-378 Wby., .338-378 Wby., or the .338 Lapua caliber. Fitted with a heavy 26" barrel with muzzlebrake. Fiberglass tactical stock with recoil pad. Leupold Mark 4 scope mounts standard. Weight is approx. 13 lbs.

NIB	Exc.	V.G.	Good	Fair	Poor
4500	3250	2100	1300	800	400

BROWN MANUFACTURING CO.
Newburyport, Massachusetts
Also See—Ballard Patent Arms

Southerner Derringer

A .41 caliber spur-trigger single-shot pocket pistol with a pivoted 2.5" or 4" octagonal barrel marked "Southerner." Silver-plated or blued with walnut grips. This pistol was manufactured by the Merrimack Arms Co. from 1867 to 1869 and by the Brown Manufacturing Co. from 1869 to 1873.

Courtesy W. P. Hallstein III and son Chip

Brass Framed
2.5" barrel.

NIB	Exc.	V.G.	Good	Fair	Poor
—	—	875	600	325	125

Iron Frame
2.5" barrel (Brown Mfg. only).

NIB	Exc.	V.G.	Good	Fair	Poor
—	—	1025	800	500	200

Brass Frame 4" Barrel

NIB	Exc.	V.G.	Good	Fair	Poor
—	—	3700	2000	1500	500

Brown Mfg. Co./Merrill Patent Breechloading Rifles

Overall length 54.75"; barrel (bore) length 35"; caliber .577. Markings: On breechblock-bolt mechanism, "BROWN MFG. CO. NEWBURYPORT, MASS./PATANTED OCT. 17, 1871". The patent issued to George Merrill in 1871, permitted the Brown Manufacturing Co. to alter probably up to 1,000 English P1853 rifle-muskets to a single-shot breechloading system. The large bolt handle projecting upward at the end of the breech readily distinguishes these arms.

Courtesy Milwaukee Public Museum, Milwaukee, Wisconsin

NIB	Exc.	V.G.	Good	Fair	Poor
—	—	2500	1250	800	300

BROWN PRECISION, INC.
Los Molinos, California

Although known as a manufacturer of stocks, this company also produced custom-order rifles.

High Country Standard

A .243 to .30-06 bolt-action rifle with a 22" barrel and Kevlar stock. **NOTE:** Gray camo stock, stainless barrel and Leupold 2.5 x 10 scope add $650.

NIB	Exc.	V.G.	Good	Fair	Poor
985	775	600	500	400	200

Open Country Varmint Rifle

Similar to the above, with a heavy barrel. Introduced in 1989.

NIB	Exc.	V.G.	Good	Fair	Poor
1100	800	650	550	400	200

Law Enforcement Model

A .308 caliber Remington Varmint action rifle with a 20" barrel, Zeiss telescope and Kevlar stock.

NIB	Exc.	V.G.	Good	Fair	Poor
1050	800	650	550	400	200

Pro-Hunter

A .375 Holland & Holland or .458 Winchester Magnum bolt-action rifle. Blued, electroless nickel-plated or Teflon coated.

NIB	Exc.	V.G.	Good	Fair	Poor
1800	1400	950	700	500	250

Brown Precision Rifle

A .270 or .30-06 bolt-action rifle with a 22" featherweight barrel and Kevlar stock.

NIB	Exc.	V.G.	Good	Fair	Poor
600	475	350	250	150	100

Blaser Rifle

Built on the Camex-Blaser action with a Brown Precision stock.

NIB	Exc.	V.G.	Good	Fair	Poor
1600	1300	850	550	400	200

BROWN, E.A. MANUFACTURING CO.
Alexandria, Minnesota

Brown Classic Single-Shot Pistol

This is a falling block single-shot pistol with 15" match grade barrel. Chambered for calibers from .17 Ackley to .45-70 Government. Walnut thumbrest grips. Handfitted. Introduced in 1998.

NIB	Exc.	V.G.	Good	Fair	Poor
1200	1000	750	600	400	200

Brown Model 97D Single-Shot Rifle

This is a single-shot falling block rifle chambered for calibers from .17 Ackley to .45-70 Government. Barrel lengths up to 26". Sporter-style stock with pistol grip, cheekpiece, and schnabel fore-end. Blue/black finish. Weight is about 6 lbs. No sights.

NIB	Exc.	V.G.	Good	Fair	Poor
1200	1000	750	600	400	200

BROWNING ARMS CO.
Morgan, Utah

Early Semi-Automatic Pistols

In the period between 1900 and the development of the Model 1935 Hi-Power Pistol, Browning had a number of semi-automatic pistols manufactured by Fabrique Nationale of Herstal, Belgium. They were the Models 1900, 1903, 1905, 1910, 1922, the Baby, and the 1935 Model Hi-Power. These firearms will be listed in more detail with their respective values in the Fabrique Nationale section of this text.

Hi-Power Modern Production

This version of the FN Model 1935 is quite similar in appearance to the original described in the FN section. It is chambered for the 9mm Parabellum cartridge and has a 4.75" barrel. Models built before the passage of the crime bill have a double column, 13-round, detachable box magazine and is blued with checkered walnut grips. It has fixed sights and has been produced in its present configuration since 1954. Add a 10 percent premium for adjustable sights. A matte-nickel version, offered between 1980 and 1984, was also available and would be worth approximately 15 percent additional. From 1994 to 2010, available in .40 S&W.

NOTE: Add $60 for adjustable sights. Add 35 percent for internal extractor.

Hi-Power with spur hammer and adjustable sights

Spur Hammer Version

NIB	Exc.	V.G.	Good	Fair	Poor
875	750	600	500	300	150

Round Hammer Version

NIB	Exc.	V.G.	Good	Fair	Poor
1050	900	725	600	450	200

Hi-Power—.30 Luger

This version is similar to the standard Hi-Power except that it is chambered for the .30 Luger cartridge. There were approximately 1,500 imported between 1986 and 1989. The slide is marked "FN". The Browning-marked versions are quite rare and worth approximately 30 percent additional.

NIB	Exc.	V.G.	Good	Fair	Poor
1000	900	725	450	300	200

Tangent Sight Model

This version is similar to the standard Hi-Power with the addition of an adjustable rear sight calibrated to 500 meters. There were approximately 7,000 imported between 1965 and 1978. **NOTE:** If the grip frame is slotted to accept a detachable shoulder stock, add approximately 20 percent to the value; but be wary of fakes. Add an additional 10 percent for "T" series serial numbers.

NIB	Exc.	V.G.	Good	Fair	Poor
1200	1050	900	650	450	200

Renaissance Hi-Power

This is a heavily engraved version with a matte-silver finish. It features synthetic-pearl grips and a gold-plated trigger. Import on this model ended in 1979.

Spur Hammer Model

NIB	Exc.	V.G.	Good	Fair	Poor
2950	2600	2100	1750	1000	600

Ring Hammer Model

NIB	Exc.	V.G.	Good	Fair	Poor
3100	2850	2400	2000	1500	900

Adjustable Sight Spur Hammer Model

NIB	Exc.	V.G.	Good	Fair	Poor
3000	2650	2100	1750	1000	600

Renaissance .25 Caliber

NIB	Exc.	V.G.	Good	Fair	Poor
2400	2100	1700	1500	1000	600

Renaissance .380 Caliber

With pearl grips.

NIB	Exc.	V.G.	Good	Fair	Poor
2700	2400	2000	1600	1000	600

Renaissance .380 Caliber (Model 1971)

With wood grips and adjustable sights.

NIB	Exc.	V.G.	Good	Fair	Poor
2300	2000	1700	1500	900	500

Cased Renaissance Set

This features one example of a fully engraved and silver-finished .25 ACP "Baby", one .380 ACP pistol, and one Hi-Power. The set is furnished in a fitted walnut case or black leatherette and was imported between 1955 and 1969. **NOTE:** For early coin finish sets add 30 percent.

Courtesy Rock Island Auction Company

NIB	Exc.	V.G.	Good	Fair	Poor
8400	6000	4000	2000	—	—

Louis XVI Model

This is a heavily engraved Hi-Power pistol that features a leaf-and-scroll pattern. It is satin-finished and features checkered walnut grips. It is furnished in a fitted walnut case. To realize its true potential, this pistol must be NIB. It was imported between 1980 and 1984.

Diamond Grip Model

NIB	Exc.	V.G.	Good	Fair	Poor
3150	2500	2000	800	400	300

Medallion Grip Model

NIB	Exc.	V.G.	Good	Fair	Poor
1950	1750	1600	800	400	300

Hi-Power Centennial Model

This version is similar to the standard fixed-sight Hi-Power but is chrome-plated with the inscription, "Browning Centennial/1878-1978" engraved on the slide. It is furnished with a fitted case. There were 3,500 manufactured in 1978. As with all commemorative pistols, in order to realize its collector potential, this model should be NIB with all supplied material. Prices are for pistols built in Belgium

NIB	Exc.	V.G.	Good	Fair	Poor
1075	875	700	450	300	200

Hi-Power Capitan

This is a new version of the Hi-Power model fitted with tangent sights. Introduced in 1993. Furnished with walnut grips. Weighs about 32 oz. Assembled in Portugal.

NIB	Exc.	V.G.	Good	Fair	Poor
750	575	450	400	250	200

Hi-Power Practical

First introduced in 1993 this version is furnished with a blued slide and chrome frame. Has Pachmayr wraparound rubber grips, round-style serrated hammer, and removable front sight. Available with adjustable sights. Weighs 36 oz. Assembled in Portugal.

NIB	Exc.	V.G.	Good	Fair	Poor
845	625	500	300	200	175

Hi-Power Silver Chrome Model

Furnished in hard chrome and fitted with wraparound Pachmayr rubber grips. Weighs 36 oz. Assembled in Portugal. Add 10 percent for models with all Belgian markings. This pistol was introduced in 1981 and dropped from the Browning product line in 1984. It was reintroduced in 1991.

NIB	Exc.	V.G.	Good	Fair	Poor
750	575	500	425	225	200

Hi-Power .40 S&W

Introduced in 1994, this new version of the Hi-Power is furnished with adjustable sights, molded grips, 5" barrel and a 10-round magazine. Weighs about 35 oz. Discontinued 2010.

NIB	Exc.	V.G.	Good	Fair	Poor
800	600	450	300	200	150

Hi-Power Mark III

The pistol, introduced in 1991, has a matte blued or green finish, low-profile fixed sights, and two-piece molded grips with thumb rest. Weighs 32 oz.

NIB	Exc.	V.G.	Good	Fair	Poor
900	700	500	300	200	175

Baby Browning

This .25 caliber semi-automatic is the same as the FN Baby model made by Fabrique Nationale in Belgium from 1931 until 1983. Many were imported into the U.S. with the Browning rollmark from 1954 to 1968. See Baby Model under the Fabrique Nationale section for more details. Prices shown are for the Browning-marked model.

NIB	Exc.	V.G.	Good	Fair	Poor
650	550	500	450	350	200

Browning Model 1955

This semi-automatic pistol is the same as the FN Model 1910, from 1912 to 1983 in .32 ACP and .380 ACP. See the Fabrique Nationale section for more information. The pistol was imported into the U.S. by Browning from 1954 to 1968. Prices shown are for Browning-marked pistols. **NOTE:** Add $200 for .32 ACP

NIB	Exc.	V.G.	Good	Fair	Poor
750	650	550	450	350	200

Pro-9/Pro-40

This 9mm or .40 S&W double-action pistol is fitted with a 4" barrel. Stainless steel slide. Grips are composite with interchangeable backstrap inserts. Magazine capacity is 16 rounds for 9mm and 14 rounds for the .40 S&W. Weight is about 30 oz.

NIB	Exc.	V.G.	Good	Fair	Poor
725	500	375	—	—	—

BDA-380

This is a double-action, semi-automatic pistol chambered for the .380 ACP cartridge. It features a 3.75" barrel with a 14-round, double-stack, detachable magazine. The finish is either blued or nickel-plated with smooth walnut grips. This pistol was manufactured in Italy by Beretta and introduced in 1977. **NOTE:** Add 10 percent for nickel finish.

NIB	Exc.	V.G.	Good	Fair	Poor
625	400	325	275	200	150

Model BDA

This is a double-action, semi-automatic pistol manufactured between 1977 and 1980 for Browning by SIG-Sauer of Germany. It is identical to the SIG-Sauer Model 220. It is chambered for 9mm Parabellum, .38 Super, and the .45 ACP cartridges. The .38 Super would be worth approximately 30 percent additional.

NIB	Exc.	V.G.	Good	Fair	Poor
—	525	425	375	300	235

BDM Pistol

This is a double-action, semi-automatic pistol chambered for the 9mm cartridge. The pistol is fitted with a selector switch that allows the shooter to choose between single-action model or double-action model. It features a 4.75" barrel with adjustable rear sight. The magazine capacity is 15 rounds. Weighs 31 oz. First introduced in 1991.

NIB	Exc.	V.G.	Good	Fair	Poor
560	450	350	250	200	150

Model BDM Silver Chrome

This variation of the BDM was introduced in 1997 and features a silver chrome finish on the slide and frame. The balance of the pistol is in a contrasting matte blue finish.

NIB	Exc.	V.G.	Good	Fair	Poor
560	450	350	250	200	150

Model BDM Practical

This model, also introduced in 1997, is the same as above but with the silver chrome on the frame only.

NIB	Exc.	V.G.	Good	Fair	Poor
560	450	350	250	200	150

Model BPM-D

Introduced in 1997 this new version of the BDM (Browning Pistol Model Decocker) features a double-action pistol with the first shot fired double-action and subsequent shots fired single-action. There is no manual safety. A decock lever also releases the slide.

NIB	Exc.	V.G.	Good	Fair	Poor
525	400	300	250	200	150

Model BRM-DAO

This 9mm pistol is a redesigned version of the Model BDM but the initials stand for "Browning Revolver Model Double-Action-Only." This pistol also has a finger support trigger guard for two-handed control. All other features are the same as the BPM-D pistol. Weight is approximately 31 oz.

NIB	Exc.	V.G.	Good	Fair	Poor
525	400	300	250	200	150

Nomad

This is a blowback-operated, semi-automatic pistol chambered for the .22 LR cartridge. It was offered with a 4.5" or 6.75" barrel. It has a 10-round, detachable magazine with adjustable sights and all-steel construction. The finish is blued with black plastic grips. It was manufactured between 1962 and 1974 by FN.

NIB	Exc.	V.G.	Good	Fair	Poor
500	360	275	150	75	50

Challenger

This is a more deluxe target pistol chambered for the .22 LR cartridge. It was offered with a 4.5" or 6.75" barrel and has a 10-round magazine. It is constructed entirely of steel and has adjustable sights. The finish is blued with a gold-plated trigger and checkered, wraparound, walnut grips. It was manufactured between 1962 and 1974 by FN.

Courtesy John J. Stimson, Jr.

NIB	Exc.	V.G.	Good	Fair	Poor
600	475	300	250	200	140

Renaissance Challenger

This version is fully engraved with a satin-nickel finish and furnished with a fleece-lined pouch.

NIB	Exc.	V.G.	Good	Fair	Poor
2600	2300	1600	750	500	350

Gold Line Challenger

This version is blued and has a gold-inlaid line around the outer edges of the pistol. It was cased in a fleece-lined pouch. Built in Belgium.

NIB	Exc.	V.G.	Good	Fair	Poor
2600	2300	1600	750	500	350

Challenger II

This is a blowback-operated, semi-automatic pistol chambered for the .22 LR cartridge. It has a 6.75" barrel with an alloy frame. The finish is blued with phenolic impregnated hardwood grips. This pistol was manufactured between 1976 and 1982 in Salt Lake City, Utah.

NIB	Exc.	V.G.	Good	Fair	Poor
—	450	325	175	140	100

Challenger III

This version features a 5.5" bull barrel with adjustable sights. It was manufactured between 1982 and 1984 in Salt Lake City, Utah. A 6.75", tapered-barrel version was also available and known as the Sporter.

NIB	Exc.	V.G.	Good	Fair	Poor
—	400	300	150	125	90

Browning Collector's Association Edition

Fully engraved, 100 manufactured. This model was fitted with a two-piece grip.

NIB	Exc.	V.G.	Good	Fair	Poor
2950	2250	1650	1200	800	400

Medalist

This is a high-grade, semi-automatic target pistol chambered for the .22 LR cartridge. It has a 6.75", vent rib barrel with adjustable target sights. It was supplied with three barrel weights and a dry-fire-practice mechanism. The finish is blued with target type, thumbrest, walnut grips. It was manufactured between 1962 and 1974 by FN. There were four additional high-grade versions of this pistol that differed in the degree of ornamentation.

NIB	Exc.	V.G.	Good	Fair	Poor
1350	1000	800	675	375	250

International Medalist

About 700 were sold in the U.S. from 1977 to 1980. Barrels were 5-7/8" long. Built in Belgium.

Courtesy John J. Stimson, Jr.

NIB	Exc.	V.G.	Good	Fair	Poor
1200	900	600	450	300	150

Second Model International Medalist

Same as above but with flat-sided barrel, dull finish, and adjustable palm rest. Built in Belgium.

Courtesy John J. Stimson, Jr.

NIB	Exc.	V.G.	Good	Fair	Poor
875	725	450	300	200	150

Gold Line Medalist

Introduced in 1962 and discontinued in 1974 with only an estimated 400 guns produced.

NIB	Exc.	V.G.	Good	Fair	Poor
3350	2750	2250	1000	750	500

Renaissance Medalist

This model was built entirely in Belgium from 1970 to 1974. Built with a one-piece grip.

NIB	Exc.	V.G.	Good	Fair	Poor
3750	3000	2500	1200	900	700

BUCK MARK SERIES
Buck Mark

This is a blowback-operated, semi-automatic pistol chambered for the .22 LR cartridge. It has a 5.5" bull barrel with adjustable sights. It has an 11-round, detachable magazine and is matte blued with skip-line checkered synthetic grips. It was introduced in 1985. Produced in the U.S. NOTE: Add $25 for stainless steel version introduced in 2005.

NIB	Exc.	V.G.	Good	Fair	Poor
350	250	175	135	110	85

Buck Mark Plus

This version is similar to the standard, with plain wood grips. It was introduced in 1987. Produced in the U.S.

NIB	Exc.	V.G.	Good	Fair	Poor
395	300	200	150	100	75

Nickel

Introduced in 1991. **NOTE:** Add $35 to above prices.

Buck Mark Varmint

This version has a 9.75" bull barrel with a full-length ramp to allow scope mounting. It has no sights. It was introduced in 1987 and produced in the U.S.

NIB	Exc.	V.G.	Good	Fair	Poor
395	300	250	200	175	125

Buck Mark Silhouette

This version features a 9.75" bull barrel with adjustable sights. Introduced in 1987.

NIB	Exc.	V.G.	Good	Fair	Poor
450	350	285	220	185	140

Buck Mark 22 Micro

This version of the Buck Mark 22 is fitted with a 4" bull barrel. Available in blue, matte blue, or nickel finish. Also available in Micro Plus variation with walnut grips. Weighs 32 oz. Introduced in 1992. **NOTE:** Add $25 for stainless steel version introduced in 2005.

NIB	Exc.	V.G.	Good	Fair	Poor
350	275	175	135	110	85

Plus

NIB	Exc.	V.G.	Good	Fair	Poor
350	275	175	150	125	90

Plus Nickel

Introduced in 1996. **NOTE:** Add $75 to above prices.

Buck Mark 5.5

This .22 caliber pistol has a 5.5" heavy bull barrel fitted with target sights. It is offered in three separate models:

Blued Target

This version has a blued finish, contoured walnut grips, target sights. Weighs 35.5 oz. Introduced in 1990.

NIB	Exc.	V.G.	Good	Fair	Poor
475	395	250	150	100	100

Blued Target (2005)

Introduced in 2005 this model features a new target-style Cocabolo grips, a full length scope mount, and hooded target sights. Weight is 35 oz.

NIB	Exc.	V.G.	Good	Fair	Poor
525	425	300	200	150	100

Gold Target

Same as above but has a gold anodized frame and top rib. Slide is blue. Walnut grips. Introduced in 1991.

NIB	Exc.	V.G.	Good	Fair	Poor
550	425	300	200	150	125

Field

Same action and barrel as the Target Model but with adjustable field sights. Sights are hoodless. Slide and barrel are blued while the rib and frame are anodized blue. Grips are walnut. Introduced in 1991.

NIB	Exc.	V.G.	Good	Fair	Poor
450	345	225	150	100	100

Field (2005)

This model features new target style grips and full-length scope rail. Weight is about 35 oz.

NIB	Exc.	V.G.	Good	Fair	Poor
525	425	295	225	165	100

Buck Field Plus

This .22 caliber pistol has a 5.5" barrel with Truglo/Marbles' front sight. Grips are laminated rosewood. Barrel is polished blue. Weight is about 24 oz.

NIB	Exc.	V.G.	Good	Fair	Poor
425	325	225	200	150	75

Buck Mark Bullseye

Introduced in 1996 this pistol is designed for metallic silhouette competition. The fluted barrel is 7.25" long. Adjustable trigger pull, adjustable rear sight, removable barrel are some of the features. Weight is about 36 oz. Choice of laminated wood grips or rubber grips. Add $150 for stainless. **NOTE:** For rosewood target grips add $90.

NIB	Exc.	V.G.	Good	Fair	Poor
550	425	275	175	125	75

Buck Mark Unlimited Match

This pistol is fitted with a 14" barrel with top rib. The front sight hood is slightly rearward of the muzzle for a maximum sight radius of 15". All other features are the same as the Silhouette model. Weighs 64 oz.

NIB	Exc.	V.G.	Good	Fair	Poor
700	525	375	225	175	125

Buck Mark Challenge

Introduced in 1999 this model features a lightweight 5.5" barrel with adjustable rear sight. Smaller grip diameter. Matte blue finish and 10-round magazine capacity. Weight is about 25 oz.

NIB	Exc.	V.G.	Good	Fair	Poor
350	250	200	175	125	100

Buck Mark Camper

This model is fitted with a heavy 5.5" barrel and has a matte blue finish. Ten-round magazine capacity. Weight is about 34 oz. Introduced in 1999. **NOTE:** Add $60 for stainless steel version.

NIB	Exc.	V.G.	Good	Fair	Poor
300	225	150	125	100	75

Buck Mark Camper Cocobola UDX

Similar to above but with cocobolo Ultra DX grips and TruGlo front sight. Introduced 2008.

NIB	Exc.	V.G.	Good	Fair	Poor
375	295	245	150	100	75

Buck Mark Practical URX Fiber Optic

Matte grey finish, 5.5" tapered bull barrel, Ultragrip RX ambi-grips, adjustable ProTarget rear sight with TruGlo fiber optic front sight. Introduced 2008.

NIB	Exc.	V.G.	Good	Fair	Poor
350	300	20	150	100	75

Buck Mark Hunter

This .22 pistol features a 7.25" heavy round barrel with Tru-glo/Marbles front sights, adjustable rear sight and integrated scope base. Grips are Cocabolo target-style. Weight is about 38 oz. Introduced in 2005.

NIB	Exc.	V.G.	Good	Fair	Poor
375	275	225	175	125	100

Buck Mark Limited Edition 25th Anniversary

This model is limited to 1,000 pistols and features a 6.75" barrel with matte blued finish and scrimshaw etched ivory grips. Pistol rug furnished as standard equipment.

NIB	Exc.	V.G.	Good	Fair	Poor
495	350	300	225	150	125

Buck Mark Bullseye Target

Blowback, single action .22 LR semi-automatic. Matte blued, heavy 7.25" round and fluted stainless bull barrel. Laminated rosewood grip, adjustable sights. Introduced 2006.

NIB	Exc.	V.G.	Good	Fair	Poor
695	450	300	225	150	175

Buck Mark Bullseye Target URX

Blowback, single-action semi-automatic in .22 LR. Matte blued, heavy 7.25" round and fluted bull barrel. Grooved, rubberized grip, 39 oz., adjustable sights. Introduced 2006.

NIB	Exc.	V.G.	Good	Fair	Poor
475	400	325	225	150	175

Buck Mark Contour 5.5 URX

Blowback, single-action .222 semi-automatic. Matte blued, contoured 5.5" barrel. Full-length scope base, 36 oz., adjustable sights. Multiple barrel lengths and options. Introduced 2006.

NIB	Exc.	V.G.	Good	Fair	Poor
425	365	300	250	200	100

Buck Mark Contour Lite 5.5 URX

.22 LR blowback, single-action semi-automatic. Matte blued, contoured 5.5" barrel. Full-length scope base, 28 oz. Adjustable sights. Multiple barrel lengths and options. Introduced 2006.

NIB	Exc.	V.G.	Good	Fair	Poor
475	395	325	275	225	150

Buck Mark FLD Plus Rosewood UDX

22 LR blowback single-action semi-automatic. "FLD" sculpted grip with rosewood panels. Blued, contoured 5.5" barrel, 34 oz., adjustable rear sight, fiber optic front sight. Multiple barrel lengths and options. Introduced 2006.

NIB	Exc.	V.G.	Good	Fair	Poor
475	395	325	275	225	150

Buck Mark Lite Splash 5.5 URX

Blowback single-action semi-automatic. Matte blued finish, gold splash anodizing. Chambered for .22 LR, 5.5" barrel. Rubberized ambidextrous grip. Adjustable sights; fiber optic front sight. 28 oz. Also available with 7.5" barrel. Introduced 2006.

NIB	Exc.	V.G.	Good	Fair	Poor
450	375	325	275	225	150

Buck Mark Micro Standard Stainless URX

With a 4" stainless barrel, this .22 LR weighs 32 oz. Ambidextrous rubberized grip and adjustable sights. Also available in alloy steel. Introduced 2006.

NIB	Exc.	V.G.	Good	Fair	Poor
395	350	325	275	225	150

Buck Mark Micro Bull

4" stainless bull barrel; .22 LR; weight 33 oz. Plastic grip panels and adjustable sights. Introduced 2006.

NIB	Exc.	V.G.	Good	Fair	Poor
350	275	225	175	125	100

Buck Mark Plus Stainless Black Laminated UDX

Similar to Buck Mark Standard. Stainless UDX but with ambidextrous grips. Introduced 2007.

NIB	Exc.	V.G.	Good	Fair	Poor
495	375	300	225	150	125

Buck Mark Plus UDX

Similar to Buck Mark FLD Plus but with ambidextrous walnut grips. Introduced 2007.

NIB	Exc.	V.G.	Good	Fair	Poor
425	350	300	225	150	125

Full Line Dealer Buck Mark Plus Rosewood UDX

Similar to Buck Mark Plus UDX but with ambidextrous rosewood grips. Available only to full-line and Medallion-level Browning dealers. Introduced 2007.

NIB	Exc.	V.G.	Good	Fair	Poor
425	350	300	225	150	125

Buck Mark Plus Stainless UDX

.22 LR semi-automatic with finger-grooved wood grips. 5.5" barrel, 34 oz. Adjustable sights, fiber optic front sight. Also available blued alloy steel. Introduced 2006.

NIB	Exc.	V.G.	Good	Fair	Poor
450	350	300	225	150	125

Buck Mark Standard Stainless URX

.22 LR semi-automatic. 5.5" stainless bull barrel; 34 oz. ambidextrous rubberized grip and adjustable sights. Also available in alloy steel. Introduced 2006.

NIB	Exc.	V.G.	Good	Fair	Poor
400	325	275	200	125	100

Browning 1911-22

A scaled-down version of the 1911A1 chambered in .22 LR. Aluminum slide, alloy frame, blowback operated with a single-action trigger. Controls are standard 1911 including thumb and grip safeties. Other features include 10-round magazine, brown composite grips, matte blue finish. Weight is 16 ounces, barrel length is 4.25". Compact model has 3-5/8" barrel. Introduced in 2011. **NOTE:** Add $400 for Anniversary Edition.

NIB	Exc.	V.G.	Good	Fair	Poor
500	450	400	350	300	200

SHOTGUNS

SUPERPOSED SHOTGUNS

This series of over/under, double-barrel shotguns is chambered for 12, 20, and 28 gauges, as well as the .410 bore and is offered with vent rib barrels from 26.5" to 32" in length. It features various choke combinations. This shotgun is built on a boxlock action and features either double or single-selective triggers and automatic ejectors. There were a number of versions offered that differ in the amount of ornamentation and the quality of the materials and workmanship utilized in manufacture. Values for small-bore models are generally higher. This series was introduced in 1930 and is manufactured by Fabrique Nationale in Belgium. For factory restored guns or very fine non-factory restorations Superposed guns will bring close to factory original prices.

For extra factory installed barrels add $1000 to $2500 depending on the grade of the gun.

PRE-WAR SUPERPOSED, 1930-1940

Browning Superposed shotgun prices are divided into three different categories. The first category is for pre-war guns built from 1930 to 1940. These pre-war Superposed guns were manufactured in 12 gauge only from serial number 1 to around 17,000. These shotguns were offered in four different grades: Grade I, Pigeon, Diana, and Midas. **NOTE:** For twin-single triggers add 15 percent. For vent rib add 10 percent. For recoil pads or shorter than standard stocks deduct 25 percent.

Grade I

Rock Island Auction Company, August, 2004

NIB	Exc.	V.G.	Good	Fair	Poor
—	2500	1950	1200	450	300

Pigeon

NIB	Exc.	V.G.	Good	Fair	Poor
—	4900	3800	2800	1500	800

Diana

NIB	Exc.	V.G.	Good	Fair	Poor
—	7500	6000	4700	2000	900

Midas

NIB	Exc.	V.G.	Good	Fair	Poor
—	12500	9500	5000	2500	1000

SUPERPOSED FROM 1947-1959

The second category of Superposed was produced and sold from 1947 to 1959. These were built in 12 and 20 gauge as well as the 28 gauge and .410 bore which were introduced in 1959. These shotguns were graded using a Roman numeral system instead of names. They are: Grade I, Grade II, Grade III, Grade IV, Grade V, and Grade VI. The values listed are for 12 gauge. Add the premium or deductions as listed. The number of 28 gauge and .410 bore guns sold in late 1959 number less than 100. The number of Grade VIs sold in North America is unknown, but it was most likely very small. This is a very rare grade. Proceed with caution. **NOTE:** 20 gauge add 60 percent; 28 gauge add 100 percent (1959 only); .410 add 100 percent (1959 only). Trap deduct 40 percent. Standard weight 12 gauge Grade I deduct 10 percent.

Grade I

NIB	Exc.	V.G.	Good	Fair	Poor
3700	2500	1400	900	300	250

Grade II

NIB	Exc.	V.G.	Good	Fair	Poor
6500	4500	2500	1200	600	375

Grade III

NIB	Exc.	V.G.	Good	Fair	Poor
7000	6000	3900	2200	750	450

Grade IV

NIB	Exc.	V.G.	Good	Fair	Poor
10000	8500	4500	2400	1200	550

Grade V

NIB	Exc.	V.G.	Good	Fair	Poor
10000	7500	4000	2400	1200	650

Grade VI

NIB	Exc.	V.G.	Good	Fair	Poor
17000	15000	8500	4000	2200	850

SUPERPOSED FROM 1960-1976

Browning Superposed shotguns built from 1960 to 1976 revert back to the older grade names. They are Grade I, Pigeon, Pointer, Diana, and Midas. These shotguns were available in 12, 20, and 28 gauge as well as .410 bore. This last production period is a little more complicated due to manufacturing changes that some collectors consider important such as round knobs and long tangs.

Prices listed reflect Superposed field guns produced from 1960 to 1965 in round pistol grip knob with long trigger guard tang in 12 gauge. For all other variations during this period one should consider:

For salt wood damage deduct a minimum of 60 percent. For round knob short tang (circa 1966-1969) deduct 50 percent. For flat knob short tang (circa 1969-1971) deduct 50 percent. For flat knob long tang (circa 1971-1976) deduct 25 percent. For New Style Skeet and Lightning Trap (recoil pad, flat knob, full beavertail forearm) with long trigger guard tang (1971-1976) deduct 35 percent; with short trigger guard tang deduct 40 percent; if Broadway rib deduct an additional 10 percent. For skeet chokes on field guns deduct 5 percent. For recoil pads on 2.75" chambered field guns deduct 20 percent. For Master engraver signed guns (Funken, Watrin, Vrancken) add 10 percent. For shorter than standard stock length deduct 25 percent. For barrel lengths of 32" add 10 percent. For 20 gauge add 50 percent. For 28 gauge add 100 percent. For .410 bore add 60 percent.

Grade I Standard Weight

NIB	Exc.	V.G.	Good	Fair	Poor
3000	2000	1500	700	500	250

SUPERPOSED FROM 1960-1976

Grade I Lightweight

NIB	Exc.	V.G.	Good	Fair	Poor
3200	2200	1600	800	600	300

SUPERPOSED FROM 1960-1976

Pigeon Grade

NIB	Exc.	V.G.	Good	Fair	Poor
6500	5500	3800	2000	1000	600

Pointer Grade—(Rare)

NIB	Exc.	V.G.	Good	Fair	Poor
10500	8050	5600	3000	2000	1000

Diana Grade

NIB	Exc.	V.G.	Good	Fair	Poor
11000	8250	5700	3000	2000	1000

Midas Grade

FN also built Exhibition Grades that were sold in this country under the Browning name. Collectors consider a true Exhibition Grade as one not having a "C" prefix in the serial number. These particular guns are considered quite desirable and should be appraised on an individual basis. Superposed in this category can range in price from $10,000 to $20,000 depending on gauge, engraving coverage, and options.

The second type of Exhibition Grade is know as the "C" type that was first sold in the United States from about 1973 to 1977 and is so called because of the "C" prefix in the serial number. There were about 225 of these guns sold in the United States. They came in quite a few grades and some were specially ordered. Although the lower grades are not considered by some to be true exhibitions (pre-C series) the highest "C" series grades are a match to the best of the older exhibitions. In 2000, an all option Superlight 2 barrel set with sideplates engraved by Vranken sold for $22,000. Generally, depending on the gun, prices will range between $6,000 and $25,000. These "C" grade guns should also be appraised individually.

NIB	Exc.	V.G.	Good	Fair	Poor
15000	12000	9000	7000	5000	4000

Superposed Superlight

This model was first introduced in 1967 in 12 gauge and in 1969 in 20 gauge. Special order 28 gauge as well as .410 bore are also seen. It was offered in 26.5" barrel lengths with 27.5" barrels in 12 gauge and 28" barrels in smaller bores available on special order. It features a rounded frame and straight grip stock with tapered solid or vent rib barrels. Regular production on the Superlight ended in 1976 for the grades listed. Production did continue for the Superlight in the P series beginning in 1977. **NOTE:** For 20 gauge guns add a 50 percent premium. For 28 gauge guns add a 100 percent premium. For .410 bore guns add 30 percent premium.

Grade I

NIB	Exc.	V.G.	Good	Fair	Poor
4500	3750	1800	700	500	250

Pigeon Grade

NIB	Exc.	V.G.	Good	Fair	Poor
7000	5900	4000	2500	1000	800

Pointer Grade—(Rare)

NIB	Exc.	V.G.	Good	Fair	Poor
11000	9000	6000	3500	2000	1000

Diana Grade

NIB	Exc.	V.G.	Good	Fair	Poor
11000	8500	6500	3500	2000	1000

Midas Grade

NIB	Exc.	V.G.	Good	Fair	Poor
15500	12000	9000	7000	5000	4000

SUPERPOSED PRESENTATION GRADE SERIES

The superposed shotguns listed were manufactured between 1977 and 1984 by FN in Belgium. The models listed differ in the amount of ornamentation and the quality of materials and workmanship utilized in construction. This series was also available in a superlight configuration.

NOTE: Due to the tremendous variation of P-Series guns, prices here reflect the Superlight configuration. An all option superlight with a checkered butt, oil finish, and three-piece fore-end will bring 25-30 percent more. For all other variations one should consider:

For trap guns deduct 35 percent. For new style skeet deduct 30 percent. For skeet choked field guns deduct 5 percent. For recoil pads on field guns deduct 30 percent. For flat knob long tang hunting guns with no options deduct 35 percent. For flat knob long tang hunting guns with all options add 25 percent. For guns signed by J. Baerten add 5 percent. For P-4V guns with no gold deduct 20 percent. For hand filed vent rib add 5 percent.

For Presentation Grade guns with extra sets of barrels add approximately $1,500 to $2,500 depending on gauge and combination.

For P1, P2, and P3 grades add the premium listed:

For 20 gauge guns—55 percent.

For 28 gauge guns—100 percent.

For .410 bore—30 percent.

For the P4 grade add the premium listed:

For 20 gauge guns—55 percent.

For 28 gauge guns—100 percent.

For .410 bore—40 percent.

Presentation 1 (without gold inlays)

NIB	Exc.	V.G.	Good	Fair	Poor
4500	3700	1900	1000	600	500

Presentation 1 Gold-inlaid

NIB	Exc.	V.G.	Good	Fair	Poor
7500	6000	3250	1400	700	500

Presentation 2 (without gold inlays)

NIB	Exc.	V.G.	Good	Fair	Poor
6250	5250	3700	1800	1000	600

Presentation 2 Gold-inlaid

NIB	Exc.	V.G.	Good	Fair	Poor
10000	8500	4950	2500	1500	1000

Presentation 3 Gold-inlaid

NOTE: For early hand-engraved P3 models (approximately 25 produced) add 40 percent. These early guns are rare, proceed with caution.

NIB	Exc.	V.G.	Good	Fair	Poor
12000	9500	5500	4000	2000	1300

Presentation 4 Gold-inlaid

NIB	Exc.	V.G.	Good	Fair	Poor
17500	15000	9800	6750	5000	3500

NOTE: For P4 Grade guns with no gold, deduct approximately 20 percent.

SUPERPOSED WATERFOWL LIMITED EDITION SERIES

This model was issued in three different versions: Mallard, Pintail, and Black Duck. Each edition was limited to 500 guns, all in 12 gauge.

1981 Mallard Issue

NIB	Exc.	V.G.	Good	Fair	Poor
9500	7000	4900	3300	1900	1100

1982 Pintail Issue

NIB	Exc.	V.G.	Good	Fair	Poor
9500	7000	4900	3300	1900	1100

1983 Black Duck Issue

NIB	Exc.	V.G.	Good	Fair	Poor
10000	7000	4900	3300	1900	1100

Bicentennial Model

Produced in 1976 to commemorate the 200 year anniversary of America. A total of 53 guns were built in this special edition. All of these Superposed were 12 gauge with 28" barrels and each was numbered for one of the fifty states plus the District of Columbia. Two additional guns were built for the Smithsonian Institution and the Liege Firearms Museum. All were fitted with side plates with gold inlays. To reflect the true value, guns must be in unfired condition, in their original case and with all the papers.

NIB	Exc.	V.G.	Good	Fair	Poor
15000	9000	5950	2750	1500	1000

FN/BROWNING SUPERPOSED

A number of FN Browning Superposed B-25 shotguns were imported into this country by Browning in various grades. These Superposed were intended originally for FN's European market. There are a large number of variations and grades. It is strongly suggested that an expert appraisal be sought prior to the sale. These guns are marked with both the Browning and FN barrel address.

Classic

Produced in 1986, this model was offered in 20 gauge with 26" barrels. About 2,500 guns were produced. Silver gray receiver with engraving.

NIB	Exc.	V.G.	Good	Fair	Poor
4000	3200	2650	2000	800	300

Gold Classic

This shotgun was similar to the above model but more finely finished and engraved with gold inlays. About 350 of these guns were built in 1986.

NIB	Exc.	V.G.	Good	Fair	Poor
12500	8500	5000	2450	1750	400

Custom Shop B25 & B125 Superposed

These special order Superposed are currently available with a delivery time of 6 to 8 months. A number of options are offered that affect price. B125 guns are assembled in Belgium with components made in other countries to hold down costs. The B25 is made entirely in Belgium and is the more expensive version of the Superposed. Prices listed are retail only. **NOTE:** Retail prices for current production guns change often. Contact Browning for the present prices.

B-125

Trap Retail Price—$8,125

12 Gauge Sporting

A Style	Retail Price—$4,475
B Style	Retail Price—$4,800
C Style	Retail Price—$5,275

12 & 20 Gauge Hunting and Superlight

A Style	Retail price—$4,475
B Style	Retail price—$4,800
C Style	Retail price—$5,275

B-25

Grade I	Retail price—$19,500
Pigeon Grade	Retail price—$21,000
Pointer Grade	Retail price—$23,000
Diana Grade	Retail price—$24,000
Midas Grade	Retail price—$30,000

Custom Shop BSL

This side-by-side shotgun is equipped with Browning sidelock barrel, Holland & Holland-type locks with double trigger and auto ejectors. The gun is assembled and finished by Labeau-Courally. It is offered in both 12 and 20 gauge. Engraved grayed receiver or case colored receiver. Introduced into the Browning product line in 2001.

Case Colored Receiver (BSL Grade LC1)

NIB	Exc.	V.G.	Good	Fair	Poor
13000	11000	9000	—	—	—

Engraved Gray Receiver (BSL Grade LC2)

NIB	Exc.	V.G.	Good	Fair	Poor
18000	15000	12500	—	—	—

Liege

This is an over/under shotgun chambered for 12 gauge. It was offered with 26.5", 28", or 30" vent rib barrels with various choke combinations. It features a boxlock action with a nonselective single trigger and automatic ejectors. The finish is blued with a checkered walnut stock. There were approximately 10,000 manufactured between 1973 and 1975. U.S. versions were marked Browning Arms Company on the barrel.

NIB	Exc.	V.G.	Good	Fair	Poor
1500	850	650	450	300	200

B27

This improved version of the Liege was imported into the U.S., some without the Browning Arms Company markings and only the FN barrel address. Others may have both barrel addresses. It was offered in a number of variations that differed in the amount of ornamentation and quality of materials and workmanship utilized. It features the same action as the Liege over/under gun.

Standard

NIB	Exc.	V.G.	Good	Fair	Poor
1200	950	650	350	250	200

Deluxe

NIB	Exc.	V.G.	Good	Fair	Poor
1600	1200	850	500	350	250

Deluxe Trap

NIB	Exc.	V.G.	Good	Fair	Poor
1600	1200	850	450	300	250

Deluxe Skeet

NIB	Exc.	V.G.	Good	Fair	Poor
1600	1200	850	450	300	250

Grand Deluxe

NIB	Exc.	V.G.	Good	Fair	Poor
2000	1500	1000	650	500	400

City of Liege Commemorative

250 manufactured.

NIB	Exc.	V.G.	Good	Fair	Poor
2500	1650	1000	600	450	300

ST-100

This is an over/under trap gun that features separated barrels with an adjustable point of impact. It is chambered for 12 gauge and has a 30" or 32" barrel with full choke and a floating ventilated rib. It features a single trigger and automatic ejectors. The finish is blued with a checkered walnut stock. It was manufactured by FN between 1979 and 1981.

NIB	Exc.	V.G.	Good	Fair	Poor
3750	2700	1800	1000	700	400

CITORI SERIES

This is an over/under, double-barrel shotgun chambered for all gauges and offered with vent rib barrels of 26" through 30" in length. It has a boxlock action with a single-selective trigger and automatic ejectors. The various grades differ in the amount of ornamentation and the quality of materials and workmanship utilized in construction. This series is manufactured in Japan by B.C. Miroku and was introduced in 1973. **NOTE:** For all Citori models, add a 15-20 percent premium for 28 gauge and .410. Add premium of 30 percent for 16 gauge guns. Add 10 percent for small gauges.

NIB	Exc.	V.G.	Good	Fair	Poor
2750	1700	1400	1000	700	400

Grade I

NIB	Exc.	V.G.	Good	Fair	Poor
1200	900	725	550	425	300

Upland Special—Grade I

Offered with straight-grip stock and 24" rib barrels. Available in 12- or 20 gauge. Weighs 6 lbs. 11 oz. in 12 gauge and 6 lbs. in 20 gauge. Introduced in 1984.

NIB	Exc.	V.G.	Good	Fair	Poor
1350	950	700	600	400	300

Grade II—1978 to 1983

NIB	Exc.	V.G.	Good	Fair	Poor
—	1500	1300	1000	650	400

Grade II—Choke Tubes

NIB	Exc.	V.G.	Good	Fair	Poor
1600	1400	1000	775	650	400

Grade V—1978 to 1984

NIB	Exc.	V.G.	Good	Fair	Poor
2900	2300	1600	950	750	400

Grade V with sideplates—1981 to 1984

NIB	Exc.	V.G.	Good	Fair	Poor
2950	2500	2100	1500	800	400

Grade VI—Choke Tubes

NIB	Exc.	V.G.	Good	Fair	Poor
1950	1650	1200	1000	750	500

Citori Hunter

This model features a full pistol-grip stock with beavertail forearm with high-gloss walnut. Chambered for 12 with 2.75", 3", or 3.5" chambers and choice of 26", 28" or 30" barrels in 12 gauge. The 20 gauge models have a choice of 26" or 28" barrels. Twelve gauge guns weigh from 7 lbs. 13 oz. to 8 lbs. 9 oz. depending on barrel length. Twenty gauge guns weigh about 6.75 lbs. **NOTE:** Add $75 for 3.5" models.

NIB	Exc.	V.G.	Good	Fair	Poor
1500	1100	850	650	550	450

Citori Sporting Hunter

This model has the same features as the Hunting model with the exception of the stock configuration. The Sporting Hunter has a Sporting model buttstock and a Superposed-style forearm. Fitted with a contoured sporting recoil pad. Introduced in 1998. **NOTE:** Add $75 for 3.5" models.

NIB	Exc.	V.G.	Good	Fair	Poor
1550	1400	1050	750	550	450

Citori Satin Hunter

This model is chambered for 12 gauge shells, has a hunting-style stock, choice of 26" or 28" barrels, and a special satin wood finish with matte black receiver and barrels. Offered in Grade I only. Weight is about 8 lbs. Introduced in 1999. **NOTE:** Add $100 for 3.5" chamber.

NIB	Exc.	V.G.	Good	Fair	Poor
1250	1000	825	700	500	375

Citori Satin Hunter Micro Midas

A budget-priced Citori with the same features and handling qualities that have made other Citoris so popular. Available in 12 or 20 gauge with 24" or 26" barrels. Satin-finished walnut stock with 13" length of pull. Vector-Pro lengthened forcing cones. Weight: 6 lbs. 3 oz. to 6 lbs. 10 oz. New in 2011.

NIB	Exc.	V.G.	Good	Fair	Poor
1300	1050	900	800	500	300

Citori Lightning

This is a lightweight version that features a slimmer profile and has a checkered, round-knob, pistol-grip stock. It is offered in all gauges and in the same barrel lengths as the standard Citori. It features screw-in choke tubes known as Invectors. It was introduced in 1988. Offered in 12, 20 and 28 gauge and .410 bore. Weights are 6.5 lbs. to 8 lbs. depending on gauge and barrel length. The models differ in the amount of ornamentation and quality of materials and workmanship utilized. **NOTE:** Add $300 for 28 and .410 models.

Grade I

NIB	Exc.	V.G.	Good	Fair	Poor
1650	1200	900	600	450	375

Grade III

NIB	Exc.	V.G.	Good	Fair	Poor
2450	1900	1400	975	600	450

Grade IV

12 Gauge

20 & 28 Ga., .410

NIB	Exc.	V.G.	Good	Fair	Poor
2610	1950	1450	1025	650	500

Grade VI

NIB	Exc.	V.G.	Good	Fair	Poor
3800	3000	2250	1500	700	550

Grade VII

12 Gauge

20 & 28 Ga., .410

NIB	Exc.	V.G.	Good	Fair	Poor
4145	3100	2500	1750	775	575

Citori Lightning Feather

Introduced in 1999 this model features a lightweight alloy receiver. Offered in 12 gauge Grade I only with choice of 26" or 28" barrels.

Weight with 28" barrels is about 7 lbs. 11 oz. In 2000 this model was offered in 20 gauge as well with 26" or 28" barrels with 3" chambers. Weight of 20 gauge is about 6.5 lbs.

NIB	Exc.	V.G.	Good	Fair	Poor
1870	1400	975	595	400	300

Citori Lightning Feather Combo

This model features a 20 gauge and 28 gauge barrel, both 27" long. The 20 gauge with 3" chambers the 28 gauge with 2.75" chambers. Pistol grip stock. Weight is about 6.25 lbs. Supplied with Browning luggage case. Introduced in 2000.

NIB	Exc.	V.G.	Good	Fair	Poor
3035	2250	1700	1250	700	550

Citori Feather XS

This model is offered in 12, 20, 28, and .410 bore. It has a lightweight alloy receiver. Fitted with a walnut stock with pistol grip, black recoil pad and schnabel forearm. Triple trigger system and Hi-Viz Comp sight system standard. Weight is about 7 lbs. for 12 gauge; 6.5 lbs. for 20 gauge; 6 lbs. for 28 gauge; and 6 lbs. for .410 bore. Introduced in 2000.

NIB	Exc.	V.G.	Good	Fair	Poor
2000	1500	1200	900	600	400

Citori Superlight Feather

Chambered for the 12 or 20 gauge with straight grip stock and schnabel forearm. This model has an alloy receiver. Checkered walnut stock. Offered with 26" barrels. Weight is about 6 lbs. Introduced in 2002.

NIB	Exc.	V.G.	Good	Fair	Poor
1940	1450	1100	800	550	350

Citori Super Lightning Grade I

Introduced in 2005 this 12 or 20 gauge model features a blued receiver with gold line border. Checkered satin finished select walnut stock with pistol grip and schnabel forearm. Barrels are 26" or 28" with choke tubes. Recoil pad on 12 gauge. Weight is about 8 lbs. for the 12 gauge and 6.75 lbs. for the 20 gauge.

NIB	Exc.	V.G.	Good	Fair	Poor
1865	1400	1050	750	500	300

Citori Classic Lightning Grade I

Offered in 12 or 20 gauge with choice of 26" or 28" vent rib barrels with choke tubes. Receiver is scroll engraved on a silver nitride finish. Checkered select walnut stock with oil finish. Forearm is

Lightning style. Recoil pad on 12 gauge. Weight is about 8 lbs. for 12 gauge and about 6.75 lbs. for the 20 gauge. Introduced in 2005.

NIB	Exc.	V.G.	Good	Fair	Poor
1890	1425	1075	775	525	325

Citori Classic Lightning Feather Grade I

This model, introduced in 2005, features a high relief engraved alloy receiver. Chambered for the 12 or 20 gauge and fitted with 26" or 28" vent rib barrels with choke tubes. Checkered select stock with schnabel forearm. Recoil pad on 12 gauge. Weight is about 7 lbs. for 12 gauge and about 6.25 lbs. for 20 gauge.

NIB	Exc.	V.G.	Good	Fair	Poor
1950	1450	1100	775	525	325

Citori 525 Sporting

Introduced in 2002 this model is chambered for the 12 or 20 gauge and fitted with a choice of 28" or 30" vent rib ported barrels. The stock is redesigned with a Euro checkering pattern and more pronounced palm swell. Weight is about 8 lbs. for the 12 gauge and 7 lbs. for the 20. In 2003 this model was offered in both 28 gauge and .410 bore. **NOTE:** Add $275 for adjustable comb.

NIB	Exc.	V.G.	Good	Fair	Poor
2320	1750	1250	800	550	350

Citori 525 Field

As above but with a choice of 26" or 28" barrels. Barrels are unported. Ventilated recoil pad. Introduced in 2002. In 2003 this model was offered in both 28 gauge and .410 bore.

NIB	Exc.	V.G.	Good	Fair	Poor
1980	1475	950	700	500	325

Citori 525 Golden Clays Sporting

This model has the same features as the 525 Sporting but with an oil-finished high stock and engraved receiver with gold inlays. In 2003 this model was offered in both 28 gauge and .410 bore.

NIB	Exc.	V.G.	Good	Fair	Poor
4450	3250	2600	1950	1200	550

Citori 525 Feather

This lightweight Citori features an alloy receiver with a steel breech face and high-relief engraving. The stock and schnabel fore-end are Grade II/III oil finished walnut. Available in 12, 20 and 28 gauges and .410 bore with 26" or 28" barrels. All but 28 gauge have 3" chambers. Weight is about 6.9 lbs. in 12 gauge and 5.5 to 5.7 lbs. in others. Three choke tubes.

NIB	Exc.	V.G.	Good	Fair	Poor
2300	1750	1250	800	550	350

Citori 625 Sporting

Introduced in 2008, this 2.75" 12 gauge has 28", 30" or 32" ported barrels with Browning's Vector Pro lengthened forcing cones system. The stock and schnabel fore-end are Grade III/IV walnut. The steel receiver has a silver nitride finish with high-relief engraving and gold embellishment. Five choke tubes included. Weight is 7.9 to 8.2 lbs. Add 5 percent for adjustable comb stock.

NIB	Exc.	V.G.	Good	Fair	Poor
3500	2700	1975	1200	850	550

Citori 625 Sporting Left-Hand

As above but configured for left-hand shooters.

NIB	Exc.	V.G.	Good	Fair	Poor
3500	2700	1975	1200	850	550

Citori 625 Field

26" or 28" barrels and a gloss oil finish Grade II/III walnut stock and schnabel fore-end. Steel receiver with silver nitride finish and high-relief engraving. Three choke tubes. Chambered for 12, 20, 28 gauge and .410. Weight: 7 lbs., 14 oz. to 6 lbs., 12 oz.

NIB	Exc.	V.G.	Good	Fair	Poor
2400	1900	1400	975	600	450

Citori Esprit

Introduced in 2002 this model features removable decorative sideplates, schnabel forearm, and high-grade walnut stock. Offered in 12 gauge only with 28" vent rib barrels. Weight is about 8.25 lbs.

NIB	Exc.	V.G.	Good	Fair	Poor
2450	1975	1400	975	600	450

Citori Sporting Clays

Specifically designed for sporting clays shooting. Offered in 12 gauge only, each model is back-bored, ported and fitted with Invector-Plus choke tubes. Barrels are chrome-plated. Receiver is blued with gold inscription. Pigeon Grade has gold detailing and high grade gloss walnut stock. Signature Grade features a red and black print on the stock with gold decals. Trigger is adjustable to three length of pull positions. Comes with three interchangeable trigger shoes. Each model is fitted with rubber recoil pad.

NIB	Exc.	V.G.	Good	Fair	Poor
2450	1975	1400	975	600	450

Citori Lightning Sporting

This model features a rounded pistol grip and Lightning forearm with choice of high or low vent rib. Chambered for 3" shells. Offered in 28" or 30" barrels. Weighs about 8.5 lbs. Introduced in 1989.

NIB	Exc.	V.G.	Good	Fair	Poor
1400	1000	800	600	450	300

Pigeon Grade

NIB	Exc.	V.G.	Good	Fair	Poor
1450	1100	900	650	450	300

Golden Clays

First introduced in 1994.

NIB	Exc.	V.G.	Good	Fair	Poor
2800	2250	1650	900	450	300

Citori Privilege

This high-grade model features game scene engraved sideplates, unique checkering pattern, oil finish high-grade walnut stock with pistol grip. Offered in 12 gauge only with choice of 26" or 28" barrels. Weight is about 8 lbs. Introduced in 2000. In 2001 a 20 gauge version with 26" or 28" barrels was introduced.

Citori Privilege left side.

NIB	Exc.	V.G.	Good	Fair	Poor
5475	4250	3500	2800	1300	550

Citori XS Sporting Clays

Introduced in 1999, this model features silver nitride receiver with gold accents and European-style stock with schnabel fore-end. Available in 12 or 20. Choice of 28", 30" or 32" barrels. Weight varies from 8 lbs. in 12 gauge to 7 lbs. for the 20 gauge.

NIB	Exc.	V.G.	Good	Fair	Poor
2600	2050	1450	1000	625	475

Citori Ultra XS Skeet

This model is offered in 12 gauge only with choice of 28" or 30" ported barrels chambered for 2.75" shells. Semi-beavertail forearm. Triple trigger system standard. Adjustable comb optional. Walnut stock with pistol grip and black recoil pad. Weight is about 7.75 lbs. Introduced in 2000. In 2001 a 20 gauge version was introduced with a choice of 28" or 30" barrels. **NOTE:** Add $275 for adjustable comb.

NIB	Exc.	V.G.	Good	Fair	Poor
2535	1900	1375	950	600	450

Citori XS Special

This is a 12 gauge 2.75" chamber gun with choice of 30" or 32" vent rib barrels with porting and extended choke tubes. Checkered walnut stock with adjustable comb and pistol grip. Semi-beavertail forearm. Silver engraved receiver. Weight is about 8.7 lbs.

NIB	Exc.	V.G.	Good	Fair	Poor
2825	2100	1550	1100	675	475

Citori Plus

This model features an adjustable point of impact from 3" to 12" above point of aim. Receiver on Grade I is blued with scroll engraving. Walnut stock is adjustable and forearm is a modified beavertail style. Available in 30" or 32" barrels that are backbored and ported. Non-ported barrels are optional. Weighs about 9 lbs. 6 oz. Introduced in 1989.

Grade I

NIB	Exc.	V.G.	Good	Fair	Poor
1300	1075	750	500	400	300

Pigeon Grade

NIB	Exc.	V.G.	Good	Fair	Poor
1850	1500	950	700	500	300

Signature Grade

NIB	Exc.	V.G.	Good	Fair	Poor
1750	1450	950	700	500	300

Golden Clays

NIB	Exc.	V.G.	Good	Fair	Poor
2850	2295	1500	900	450	300

Citori Trap Combination Set

This version is offered in Grade I only and features a 34" single barrel and a 32" set of over/under barrels. It is furnished in a fitted case and has been discontinued.

NIB	Exc.	V.G.	Good	Fair	Poor
—	1950	1350	950	800	700

GTI Model

This model features a 13mm wide rib, ventilated side ribs, pistol-grip stock, semi-beavertail forearm. Offered in 28" or 30" barrel. Weighs about 8 lbs. This model not offered in Pigeon Grade. Introduced in 1989.

Grade I

NIB	Exc.	V.G.	Good	Fair	Poor
1200	975	750	600	450	300

Signature Grade

NIB	Exc.	V.G.	Good	Fair	Poor
1200	975	750	600	450	300

Golden Clays

NIB	Exc.	V.G.	Good	Fair	Poor
2575	1975	1250	900	450	300

Ultra Sporter - (Sporting Clays)

This model was introduced in 1995 and replaces the GTI model. It features a 10mm to 13mm tapered rib and is offered with either a blued or gray receiver with walnut stock with pistol grip and semi-beavertail forearm. Fitted with adjustable comb. Adjustable length of pull. Offered in 12 gauge only with 28" or 30" barrels. Average weight is 8 lbs. **NOTE:** For Ultra Sporters with adjustable comb add $200 to NIB price.

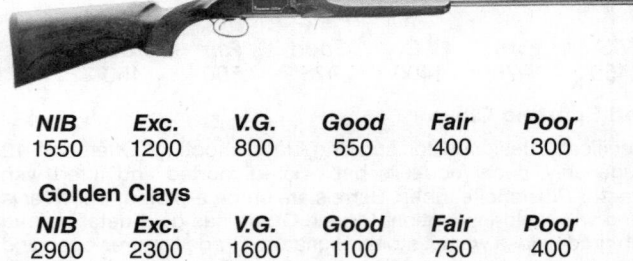

NIB	Exc.	V.G.	Good	Fair	Poor
1550	1200	800	550	400	300

Golden Clays

NIB	Exc.	V.G.	Good	Fair	Poor
2900	2300	1600	1100	750	400

NOTE: For Ultra Sporters with adjustable comb add $200 to NIB price.

Citori Superlight

This is a lighter-weight version of the Citori chambered for all gauges and offered with the same features as the Lightning Series. The grades differ in the amount of ornamentation and quality of materials and workmanship utilized. This series was introduced in 1983.

Citori Superlight Feather

Introduced in 1999 this model features a straight grip stock with schnabel fore-end. Lightweight alloy receiver. Offered in 12 gauge Grade I only with choice of 26" or 28" barrels. Weight with 28" barrels is about 6 lbs. 6 oz.

NIB	Exc.	V.G.	Good	Fair	Poor
1700	1250	895	600	475	350

Micro Lightning

Offered in 20 gauge only and has reduced dimensions for smaller shooters. Available with 24" vent rib barrels. Weighs 6 lbs. 3 oz. Introduced in 1991.

NIB	Exc.	V.G.	Good	Fair	Poor
1100	895	700	600	400	300

Gran Lightning

This is essentially a Grade I Lightning with a high grade select walnut stock with satin finish. Receiver and barrels are blued. Offered in 12 gauge and 20 gauge with choice of 26" or 28" vent rib barrels. Choke tubes standard. Weighs about 8 lbs. in 12 gauge and 6 lbs. 11 oz. in 20 gauge. Introduced in 1990. In 2004 the 28 gauge and .410 bore were added.

NIB	Exc.	V.G.	Good	Fair	Poor
2550	1900	1300	975	650	350

Grade I

NIB	Exc.	V.G.	Good	Fair	Poor
1300	975	750	500	425	350

Grade III

NIB	Exc.	V.G.	Good	Fair	Poor
1625	1375	1050	750	550	450

Grade V

Discontinued 1984.

NIB	Exc.	V.G.	Good	Fair	Poor
—	1800	1350	950	750	500

Grade VI

NIB	Exc.	V.G.	Good	Fair	Poor
2000	1750	1300	1000	800	500

Citori White Lightning

Introduced in 1998 this model features a silver nitride scroll engraved receiver. Offered in 3" 12 and 3" 20 gauge with choice of 26" or 28" barrels. In 2004 this model is also available in 28 gauge as well as .410 bore. Weight is approximately 8 lbs. for 12 gauge models and 6.8 lbs. for 20 gauge models. Invector-Plus chokes standard. Lightning-style stock. **NOTE:** Add $75 for 28 and .410 models.

NIB	Exc.	V.G.	Good	Fair	Poor
1500	1200	950	700	600	375

Citori White Upland Special

Introduced in 2000 this model features a shortened straight-grip stock, schnabel forearm, and 24" barrel. Fitted with 2.75" chambered for 12 gauge and 20 gauge only. Weight is about 6.75 lbs.

NIB	Exc.	V.G.	Good	Fair	Poor
1650	1200	975	725	625	395

Citori Skeet

This series of guns was chambered for all gauges and was designed for competition skeet shooting. It is similar to the standard Citori with a high-post target rib and 26" or 28" barrels. The versions differ in the amount of engraving and the quality of materials and workmanship utilized.

Grade I

NIB	Exc.	V.G.	Good	Fair	Poor
1000	925	750	550	425	350

Grade II

Discontinued 1983.

NIB	Exc.	V.G.	Good	Fair	Poor
—	1000	900	750	450	300

Grade III

NIB	Exc.	V.G.	Good	Fair	Poor
1500	1200	900	750	450	300

Grade V

Discontinued 1984.

NIB	Exc.	V.G.	Good	Fair	Poor
1600	1200	900	750	450	300

Grade VI

NIB	Exc.	V.G.	Good	Fair	Poor
2000	1750	1200	900	450	300

Golden Clays

First introduced in 1994.

NIB	Exc.	V.G.	Good	Fair	Poor
2400	2000	1500	900	450	300

3 Gauge Sets

Consists of 20 gauge, 28 gauge, and .410 bore interchangeable 28" vent rib barrels. Introduced in 1987.

Grade I

NIB	Exc.	V.G.	Good	Fair	Poor
2200	1950	1700	1250	900	700

Grade III

NIB	Exc.	V.G.	Good	Fair	Poor
2600	2250	1900	1400	1100	800

Grade VI

NIB	Exc.	V.G.	Good	Fair	Poor
3000	2500	2000	1500	1200	900

4 Gauge Sets

This set has a 12 gauge, 20 gauge, 28 gauge, and .410 bore interchangeable vent rib barrels in either 26" or 28" lengths. Introduced in 1981.

Grade I

NIB	Exc.	V.G.	Good	Fair	Poor
3400	2750	2250	1700	1250	900

Grade III

NIB	Exc.	V.G.	Good	Fair	Poor
3500	2900	2500	1900	1350	900

Grade VI

NIB	Exc.	V.G.	Good	Fair	Poor
3900	3300	2900	2250	1400	950

Citori Trap

This version is similar to the standard Citori, offered in 12 gauge only with 30" or 32" barrels. It features a high rib and a Monte Carlo-type stock with recoil pad. The versions differ as to the amount of ornamentation and the quality of materials and workmanship utilized.

Grade I

NIB	Exc.	V.G.	Good	Fair	Poor
1200	975	750	550	425	350

Plus Trap

Adjustable rib and stock. Introduced in 1989.

NIB	Exc.	V.G.	Good	Fair	Poor
1700	1450	1000	750	600	500

Grade II

Discontinued 1983.

NIB	Exc.	V.G.	Good	Fair	Poor
—	1200	1000	675	450	350

Grade III

NIB	Exc.	V.G.	Good	Fair	Poor
1600	1450	1000	750	600	500

Grade V

Discontinued 1984.

NIB	Exc.	V.G.	Good	Fair	Poor
—	1500	1350	900	650	450

Grade VI

NIB	Exc.	V.G.	Good	Fair	Poor
2200	1900	1550	1250	1000	800

Citori XT Trap

Introduced in 1999, this trap model is fitted with contoured beavertail with Monte Carlo stock with or without adjustable comb. The grayed receiver is highlighted in gold with light scroll work. Choice of 32" or 30" barrels. Weight is approximately 8 lbs. 11 oz. **NOTE:** Add $275 for adjustable comb.

NIB	Exc.	V.G.	Good	Fair	Poor
2500	1700	1200	900	650	395

Golden Clays

First introduced in 1994.

NIB	Exc.	V.G.	Good	Fair	Poor
2950	2250	1500	900	450	300

Signature Grade

NIB	Exc.	V.G.	Good	Fair	Poor
2150	1750	900	600	450	300

Citori XT Trap Gold

Introduced in 2005 this model features a gold game scene engraving pattern on a silver receiver. Choice of 30" or 32" vent rib ported barrels with choke tubes. Checkered select walnut stock with adjustable comb and semi-beavertail forearm. Stock also has adjustable length of pull and recoil reduction system. Weight is about 9 lbs.

NIB	Exc.	V.G.	Good	Fair	Poor
4520	3300	2900	2250	1400	650

Model 325 Sporting Clays

Introduced in 1993 this model has a European design that features a scroll-engraved, grayed receiver schnabel forearm, 10mm wide vent rib, three interchangeable and adjustable trigger shoes, and back-bore barrels that are ported and fitted with choke tubes. Available in 12 gauge and 20 gauge. The 12 gauge is offered with 28", 30", or 32" barrels while the 20 gauge is offered with 28" or 30" barrel fitted with conventional chokes. The 12 gauge weighs about 7 lbs. 14 oz., while the 20 gauge weighs about 6 lbs. 12 oz.

NIB	Exc.	V.G.	Good	Fair	Poor
1550	1200	900	700	450	300

Special Sporting

Similar to the Sporting model but fitted with a 2.75" chamber and choice of 28", 30", or 32" barrels. Barrels are ported. Barrels are also fitted with a high post rib. Stock has a full pistol grip and optional adjustable comb. Depending on barrel length weighs about 8.3 lbs.

Grade I

NIB	Exc.	V.G.	Good	Fair	Poor
1350	975	750	600	450	300

Signature Grade

NIB	Exc.	V.G.	Good	Fair	Poor
1350	1000	750	600	450	300

Pigeon Grade

NIB	Exc.	V.G.	Good	Fair	Poor
1500	1300	850	600	450	300

Golden Clays

NIB	Exc.	V.G.	Good	Fair	Poor
2600	1975	1250	900	450	300

Model 425 Sporting Clays

This Citori over/under gun is offered in both 12 and 20 gauge with a choice of 28" and 30" barrel with 32" barrels available on the 12 gauge as well. Barrels are fitted with a 10mm wide rib. Invector chokes are standard. Average weight is 7 lbs. 14 oz. Introduced in 1995.

NIB	Exc.	V.G.	Good	Fair	Poor
1650	1200	850	600	450	300

Model 425 Golden Clays

Same as above but with high-grade wood and engraved receiver. **NOTE:** For Model 425 with adjustable comb add $200 to NIB price.

NIB	Exc.	V.G.	Good	Fair	Poor
3000	2450	1650	1100	600	300

Light Sporting 802ES (Extended Swing)

Introduced in 1996 this model features a 28" vent rib barrel with 2" stainless steel extension tubes for an extended swing of 30". An additional 4" extension is also included. Thus the barrel can be 28", 30" or 32" according to needs. Chambered for 12 gauge with adjustable length of pull. Walnut stock with pistol grip and schnabel forearm. Weight is about 7.5 lbs.

NIB	Exc.	V.G.	Good	Fair	Poor
—	1500	900	700	500	250

Citori Plus Combo

This model features a single-barrel trap and an interchangeable over/under set of barrels. Other features are similar to Citori Plus Grade 1. Barrel combinations are 32" over/under with 34" single barrel or 30" over/under barrel with 32" or 34" single barrel. Introduced in 1989.

NIB	Exc.	V.G.	Good	Fair	Poor
2500	2100	1750	1100	700	450

Citori Ultra XS Prestige

New in 2008, this 12 gauge sporting clays model features an adjustable comb and Grade III/IV walnut stock with right hand palm swell. Ported barrels are 28", 30" or 32". Gold accented, high relief Ultra XS Special engraving on the steel/silver nitride finish receiver. Weight is about 8 lbs.

NIB	Exc.	V.G.	Good	Fair	Poor
4500	3300	2900	2250	1400	600

BT-99 SERIES

BT-99

This is a break-open, single-barrel trap gun chambered for 12 gauge only. It is offered with a 32" or 34" vent rib barrel with screw-in choke tubes. It features a boxlock action with automatic ejectors. The finish is blued with a checkered walnut stock and beavertail forearm. It was introduced in 1968 by B.C. Miroku.

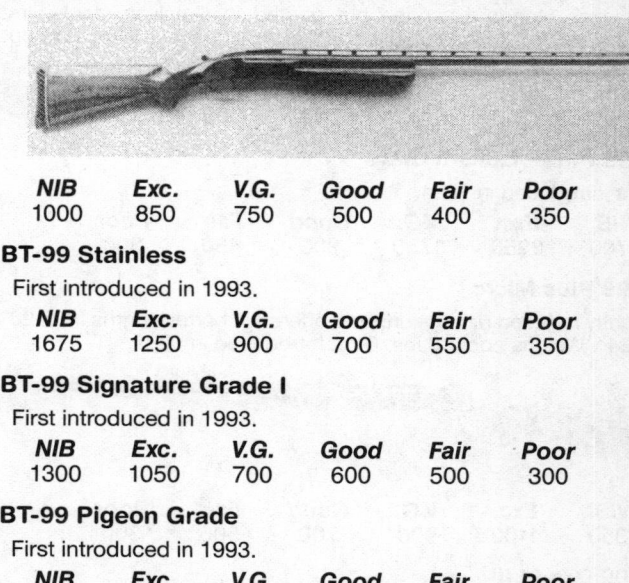

NIB	Exc.	V.G.	Good	Fair	Poor
1000	850	750	500	400	350

BT-99 Stainless

First introduced in 1993.

NIB	Exc.	V.G.	Good	Fair	Poor
1675	1250	900	700	550	350

BT-99 Signature Grade I

First introduced in 1993.

NIB	Exc.	V.G.	Good	Fair	Poor
1300	1050	700	600	500	300

BT-99 Pigeon Grade

First introduced in 1993.

NIB	Exc.	V.G.	Good	Fair	Poor
1600	1250	800	650	500	300

BT-99 Golden Clays

First introduced in 1994. In 2003 this model was offered with an adjustable comb. Weight is about 9 lbs. Available with either a 32" or 34" barrel.

NIB	Exc.	V.G.	Good	Fair	Poor
3700	2500	1750	1100	500	300

BT-99 Plus

This version features an adjustable vent rib and a recoil reduction system. It has an adjustable stock and recoil pad, as well as a back-bored barrel. It was introduced in 1989.

NIB	Exc.	V.G.	Good	Fair	Poor
1350	1200	900	700	500	300

BT-99 Plus—Pigeon Grade

NIB	Exc.	V.G.	Good	Fair	Poor
1700	1300	900	800	550	350

BT-99 Plus—Signature Grade

NIB	Exc.	V.G.	Good	Fair	Poor
1600	1200	850	700	500	300

BT-99 Plus Stainless—Grade I

Same as standard version but offered in stainless steel. First introduced in 1993. Available in 32" and 34" barrels. Weighs about 8 lbs. 11 oz.

NIB	Exc.	V.G.	Good	Fair	Poor
1700	1350	900	700	500	350

BT-99 Plus—Golden Clays

First introduced in 1994.

NIB	Exc.	V.G.	Good	Fair	Poor
2700	2250	1750	900	450	300

BT-99 Plus Micro

Slightly reduced dimensions and offered in barrel lengths from 28" to 34". Weighs about 8 lbs. 6 oz. Introduced in 1991.

NIB	Exc.	V.G.	Good	Fair	Poor
1350	1100	900	700	500	300

BT-99 Grade III

New in 2008, this BT-99 features a gloss finish Monte Carlo Grade III/IV walnut stock and gold accented high relief engraving on the receiver. Add 10 percent for adjustable comb stock.

NIB	Exc.	V.G.	Good	Fair	Poor
2400	1950	1250	750	550	350

BT-100 SERIES
Model BT-100

First introduced in 1995 this single-barrel trap features an adjustable trigger pull and length of pull. The stock is either a Monte Carlo version or an adjustable comb version. Barrel is either 32" or 34". Choice of blue or stainless finish. Weight is about 8.9 lbs.

NIB	Exc.	V.G.	Good	Fair	Poor
2500	1900	1200	700	500	300

Model BT-100 Satin

Introduced in 1999, this model features a matte black receiver and barrels without ejector selector. Available in 32" or 34" barrels. Available in Grade I only.

NIB	Exc.	V.G.	Good	Fair	Poor
1950	1300	1050	600	400	200

Model BT-100 Thumbhole

This model is the same as the standard BT-100, but with the additional feature of a thumbhole stock. Offered in both blue and stainless.

NIB	Exc.	V.G.	Good	Fair	Poor
2575	2000	1350	1000	600	400

Recoilless Trap

First introduced in 1993 this model features an advanced design that eliminates recoil up to 72 percent. The receiver is a special bolt-action single-shot. Receiver is black anodized. It is fitted with an adjustable ventilated rib so the point of impact can be moved. Adjustable length of pull. The Standard Model is a 12 gauge with 30" barrel while the Micro Model is fitted with 27" barrels. Choke tubes are supplied. Standard Model weighs 9 lbs. 1 oz., while the Micro Model weighs 8 lbs. 10 oz.

NIB	Exc.	V.G.	Good	Fair	Poor
1250	1100	900	700	500	350

BSS SERIES
BSS

This is a side-by-side, double-barrel shotgun chambered for 12 or 20 gauge. It was offered with a 26", 28", or 30" barrel with various choke combinations. It features a boxlock action and automatic ejectors. Early guns had a nonselective single trigger; late production, a selective trigger. The finish is blued with a checkered walnut stock and beavertail forearm. It was manufactured between 1978 and 1987 by B.C. Miroku. **NOTE:** Single-selective trigger add 20 percent. 20 gauge add 50 percent.

NIB	Exc.	V.G.	Good	Fair	Poor
1500	1300	1000	800	650	400

BSS Grade II

This version features game scene engraving and a satin, coin finished receiver. It was discontinued in 1984. **NOTE:** Add 50 percent for 20 gauge.

NIB	Exc.	V.G.	Good	Fair	Poor
1700	1500	1100	850	600	500

BSS Sporter

This version features an English-style, straight-grip stock and a splinter forearm. The stock was oil-finished. It was offered with a 26" or 28" barrel. **NOTE:** For 20 gauge add 25 percent.

NIB	Exc.	V.G.	Good	Fair	Poor
2400	2000	1550	975	650	400

BSS Sidelock

This version features an engraved sidelock action and was offered in 12 or 20 gauge. It was offered with a 26" or 28" barrel and has a straight-grip stock and splintered forearm. It was manufactured in Korea between 1983 and 1987. The last few dozen 12 gauge sidelocks produced were an uncatalogued version of earlier guns. These guns had very finely engraved game scenes with English scroll. Add a 30 percent premium for this variation. **NOTE:** Add 30 percent to these prices for 20 gauge guns.

NIB	Exc.	V.G.	Good	Fair	Poor
4000	3500	2200	1750	800	500

CYNERGY SERIES

This series was introduced in 2004. Browning calls it the third generation over/under gun. The Cynergy has a number of new design features such as a monolock hinge system for a lower profile, an inflex recoil pad, a new mechanical trigger system, an adjustable comb, back-bored barrels, and impact ejectors.

Cynergy Field

This 12 gauge 3" model features a checkered walnut stock and forearm. Silver nitrate receiver with engraving. Choice of 26" or 28" vent rib barrels with choke tubes. Weight is about 7.75 lbs. A synthetic stock with adjustable comb is also offered. **NOTE:** Deduct $40 for synthetic stock.

NIB	Exc.	V.G.	Good	Fair	Poor
2050	1800	1400	1000	575	325

Cynergy Classic Field

This more traditionally styled 12 gauge was added to the Cynergy line in 2006. It features a steel receiver with silver nitride finish and game bird scenes on each side. Satin finish walnut stock and schnabel style fore-end. Three choke tubes. Available in barrel lengths of 26" and 28" with an average weight of 7.75 lbs.

NIB	Exc.	V.G.	Good	Fair	Poor
2150	1850	1400	1000	575	325

Cynergy Field Small Gauge

Introduced in 2005 this model is chambered for the 20 or 28 gauge or .410 bore. Choice of 26" or 28" vent rib barrels. Weight is about 6.25 lbs.

NIB	Exc.	V.G.	Good	Fair	Poor
2100	1850	1450	1050	575	325

Cynergy Sporting

As above but with higher grade walnut stock and choice of 28", 30", or 32" vent rib barrels with choke tubes. Ported barrels. Hi-Viz front sight. Weight is about 8 lbs. A synthetic stock with adjustable comb is also offered. **NOTE:** For synthetic stock deduct $40.

NIB	Exc.	V.G.	Good	Fair	Poor
2000	1600	1200	900	500	300

Cynergy Classic Sporting

New for 2006, this traditionally styled version of the Cynergy Sporting is available in 12 gauge with 28", 30" or 32" ported barrels. Oil finish walnut stock with schnabel fore-end and Browning logo on steel receiver with silver nitride finish. Three Invector-Plus Midas Grade choke tubes. Average weight 7.75 lbs.

NIB	Exc.	V.G.	Good	Fair	Poor
2750	2200	1800	900	500	300

Cynergy Classic Field Grade III

Similar to Classic Cynergy Field but with full coverage high-relief engraving on receiver and top lever, gloss finish Grade III/IV walnut.

NIB	Exc.	V.G.	Good	Fair	Poor
3400	2600	2000	1650	950	550

Cynergy Classic Field Grade VI

Similar to Cynergy Classic Field Grade III but with more extensive, gold-highlighted engraving.

20 GA.

12 GA.

NIB	Exc.	V.G.	Good	Fair	Poor
5100	4200	3450	2300	1400	600

Cynergy Sporting Adjustable Comb

Similar to Cynergy Sporting but with a comb adjustable for cast and drop. Average weight 8.2 lbs. Introduced 2006.

NIB	Exc.	V.G.	Good	Fair	Poor
2900	2000	1475	1050	750	450

Cynergy Sporting Small Gauge

As above but in 20" or 28" gauge. Choice of 28", 30", or 32" ported barrels in 20 gauge and 28" or 30" ported barrels in 28 gauge. Weight is about 6.25 to 6.5 lbs. depending on barrel length. Introduced in 2005.

NIB	Exc.	V.G.	Good	Fair	Poor
2300	1750	1200	850	625	400

Cynergy Feather

This lightweight Cynergy 12 gauge was introduced in 2006, followed by 20 and 28 gauge and .410 bore versions in 2008. Satin finish walnut stock. Weight is about 6.5 lbs. in 12 gauge and about 5 lbs. in others.

NIB	Exc.	V.G.	Good	Fair	Poor
2400	1800	1300	950	675	450

Cynergy Feather Composite

As above but with synthetic stock and fore-end in 12 gauge only.

NIB	Exc.	V.G.	Good	Fair	Poor
2300	1700	1200	950	675	450

Cynergy Euro Sporting

Sporting clays and skeet version comes in 2.75" 12 and 20 gauge with 28", 30" or 32" barrels. Stock is oil finish Grade III/IV walnut. Three choke tubes. Weight is about 8 lbs. in 12 gauge and 6.5 lbs. in 20 gauge.

NIB	Exc.	V.G.	Good	Fair	Poor
3500	2800	2200	1650	950	550

Cynergy Euro Field

Similar to Cynergy Euro Sporting but has Invenctor Plus tubes in 12 and 20 gauge, standard Invector tubes on 28 gauge and .410.

NIB	Exc.	V.G.	Good	Fair	Poor
2500	1900	1200	700	500	300

Cynergy Euro Sporting Composite with Adjustable Comb

Similar to Euro Sporting Composite but with adjustable comb.

NIB	Exc.	V.G.	Good	Fair	Poor
3800	3000	2000	1650	950	550

Cynergy Classic Trap Unsingle Combo

Trap shotgun in 12 gauge comes with a double barrel set in 32/34", 32/32", 30/34" or 30/32". Gloss finish Monte Carlo Grade III/IV walnut stock with right hand palm swell and adjustable comb. Weight is about 8.9 lbs. Four choke tubes. Aluminum fitted carrying case.

NIB	Exc.	V.G.	Good	Fair	Poor
4800	3800	2900	2250	1400	600

EARLY PRODUCTION AUTO-5

This series of recoil-operated, semi-automatic shotguns was designed by John M. Browning and was offered in 12 or 16 gauge. The barrel lengths were 26", 28", 30", or 32" with various chokes and ribs. It has a unique, square-back action that has become instantly recognizable. The finish is blued with a checkered, walnut, round-knob stock. The various versions differ in the amount of ornamentation, type of rib, and quality of materials and workmanship utilized in construction. This series was manufactured in Belgium by FN between 1903 and 1939. The first example appeared in the United States in 1923. Pre-WWI 16 gauge guns, introduced in 1936, had 2-9/16" chambers; early models should be inspected by a qualified gunsmith before firing.

NOTE: For 16 gauge not converted to 2.75" chamber deduct 30 percent. Grade III or Grade IV prices are not nearly as affected by chamber length because of their rarity. Original pre-war barrels were serial numbered to the gun. For extra barrels serial numbered to the gun add $100 for plain barrels, $200 for matte rib barrels, $275 for vent rib barrels. For extra barrels on Grade IV guns add an additional 30 percent to these barrel prices. Prices given are for guns with original barrels serial numbered to the gun. Remember the safety is located in front of the trigger guard. Deduct 10 to 25 percent for "suicide safety" in trigger guard.

Grade I—Plain Barrel

NIB	Exc.	V.G.	Good	Fair	Poor
—	500	400	300	250	150

Grade I—Matte Rib

NIB	Exc.	V.G.	Good	Fair	Poor
—	750	600	400	300	175

Grade I—Vent Rib

NIB	Exc.	V.G.	Good	Fair	Poor
—	950	650	475	375	200

Grade II—Plain Barrel

NIB	Exc.	V.G.	Good	Fair	Poor
—	950	800	700	250	150

Grade II—Matte Rib

NIB	Exc.	V.G.	Good	Fair	Poor
—	1150	850	750	350	175

Grade II—Vent Rib

NIB	Exc.	V.G.	Good	Fair	Poor
—	1400	1000	800	400	200

Grade III—Plain Barrel

NIB	Exc.	V.G.	Good	Fair	Poor
—	1900	1500	850	500	250

Grade III—Matte Rib

NIB	Exc.	V.G.	Good	Fair	Poor
—	3000	2500	1350	600	250

Grade III—Vent Rib

NIB	Exc.	V.G.	Good	Fair	Poor
—	3500	3000	1350	600	300

Grade IV—Plain Barrel

NIB	Exc.	V.G.	Good	Fair	Poor
—	4000	3250	2250	850	350

Grade IV—Matte Rib

NIB	Exc.	V.G.	Good	Fair	Poor
—	4850	4150	3000	1000	400

Grade IV—Vent Rib

Courtesy Amoskeag Auction Company

Browning Grade IV

NIB	Exc.	V.G.	Good	Fair	Poor
—	5500	4750	3500	1500	500

American Browning Auto-5

This recoil-operated, semi-automatic shotgun was another variation of the early-production Auto-5. It was chambered for 12, 16, or 20 gauge and was manufactured by the Remington Company for Browning. It is quite similar to Remington's Model 11 shotgun but features the Browning logo and a different type of engraving. There were approximately 45,000 manufactured between 1940 and 1942. **NOTE:** Vent rib add 20 percent. 20 gauge add 10 percent.

NIB	Exc.	V.G.	Good	Fair	Poor
—	675	575	450	375	200

MID-PRODUCTION AUTO-5—FN MANUFACTURE STANDARD WEIGHT

This version of the recoil-operated, semi-automatic Auto-5 shotgun was manufactured by FN in Belgium between 1952 and 1976. It was offered in 12 or 16 gauge with 26" through 32" barrels with various chokes. The finish is blued with a checkered walnut stock and a black buttplate that was marked "Browning Automatic" with "FN" in center oval. Guns made prior to 1967 will be found with round knob pistol grips. The flatbottom variation was introduced in 1967. **NOTE:** Add 25 percent for guns with round-knob pistol grip and 35 percent for straight-grip stock. Add 20 percent for 20 gauge guns. Add 40 percent for 16 and 20 gauge guns NIB.

Plain Barrel

NIB	Exc.	V.G.	Good	Fair	Poor
800	600	475	400	250	175

Matte Rib

NIB	Exc.	V.G.	Good	Fair	Poor
900	725	500	400	275	200

Vent Rib

NIB	Exc.	V.G.	Good	Fair	Poor
1150	800	600	450	300	250

Auto-5 Lightweight

This version was chambered for 12 or 20 gauge and featured a lighter-weight, scroll-engraved receiver. It was manufactured between 1952 and 1976 by FN. The 20 gauge was not introduced until 1958. **NOTE:** Vent rib add 15 percent. For 20 gauge add 35 percent.

NIB	Exc.	V.G.	Good	Fair	Poor
1000	800	600	450	275	200

Auto-5 Magnum

This version featured 3" chambers and was offered with 26" through 32", full-choke barrels. It was manufactured between 1958 and 1976 by FN. The 12 gauge was introduced in 1958 and the 20 gauge brought out in 1967. **NOTE:** Vent rib add 20 percent. Add 10 to 15 percent for 20 ga.

NIB	Exc.	V.G.	Good	Fair	Poor
—	950	750	550	375	200

Auto-5 Skeet

This version is similar to the Lightweight Model, chambered for 12 or 20 gauge with a 26" or 28", vent rib, skeet-choked barrel.

NIB	Exc.	V.G.	Good	Fair	Poor
—	850	575	525	425	250

Auto-5 Trap Model

This version is similar to the standard-weight model except chambered for 12 gauge only, with a 30", vent rib, full-choke barrel. It was manufactured by FN until 1971.

NIB	Exc.	V.G.	Good	Fair	Poor
—	675	550	475	300	225

Sweet Sixteen

This version is similar to the standard-weight and is chambered for 16 gauge only. It has a gold-plated trigger and was manufactured by FN between 1936 and 1976. **NOTE:** Not all A-5 16-gauges are Sweet Sixteens. Look for the gold-plated trigger, "Sweet Sixteen" script, and the lack of a suicide safety. **NOTE:** Matte rib add 25 percent. Vent rib add 50 percent.

NIB	Exc.	V.G.	Good	Fair	Poor
1500	950	700	400	300	200

Buck Special

This version features a 24", cylinder-bore barrel with adjustable rifle sights. It was produced in 12 and 20 gauge 2.75" and 3" Magnum, and in 16 gauge with 2.75" chambers. It was manufactured by FN between 1963 and 1976. Prices are for 12 gauge guns.

NIB	Exc.	V.G.	Good	Fair	Poor
—	750	650	525	400	275

Two Millionth Commemorative

This version commemorated the two millionth Auto-5 shotgun produced by FN. It was engraved with a special high-polish blue finish and high-grade, checkered walnut in the stock. It was furnished in a black fitted case along with a book on the Browning Company. There were 2,500 manufactured between 1971 and 1974. As with all commemoratives, it must be NIB to realize its top potential.

NIB	Exc.	V.G.	Good	Fair	Poor
3200	1850	950	625	475	300

LATE PRODUCTION AUTO-5—B.C. MIROKU MANUFACTURE

In 1976 production of the Auto-5 shotgun was begun by B.C. Miroku in Japan. This move was accomplished after approximately 2,750,000 Auto-5 shotguns were manufactured by FN in Belgium between 1903 and 1976. The Japanese-manufactured guns, in the opinion of many knowledgeable people, show no less quality or functionality but are simply not as desirable from a collector's standpoint. In 1999 Browning discontinued production of the Auto-5 shotgun.

NOTE: Since the discontinuance of the Auto-5, values for Japanese examples have risen, approaching those of Belgian guns.

Auto-5 Light 12

This version is chambered for 12 gauge 2.75" chamber only and is offered with a lightweight receiver. The barrel has a vent rib and choke tubes. It was introduced in 1975.

NIB	Exc.	V.G.	Good	Fair	Poor
750	650	500	400	350	250

Auto-5 Light 20

This version is similar to the Light 12 except chambered for 20 gauge only.

NIB	Exc.	V.G.	Good	Fair	Poor
800	650	550	425	350	250

Auto-5 Magnum

This version features 3" chambers and is offered with 26", 28", 30", or 32" barrels. It was introduced in 1976 by Miroku and discontinued in 1996.

NIB	Exc.	V.G.	Good	Fair	Poor
900	775	575	450	325	250

Auto-5 Buck Special

This version has a 24" barrel cylinder-bored with adjustable sights. It was introduced by Miroku in 1976.

NIB	Exc.	V.G.	Good	Fair	Poor
725	625	500	425	300	200

Auto-5 Skeet

This is a competition model that features 26" or 28" skeet-bored barrels with a vent rib. It was manufactured between 1976 and 1983 by Miroku.

NIB	Exc.	V.G.	Good	Fair	Poor
825	550	450	350	—	200

Sweet Sixteen

This version is similar to the Belgian-produced Sweet Sixteen, but is offered standard with a vent rib and screw-in Invector choke tubes. It was introduced in 1988 by Miroku and discontinued in 1992.

NIB	Exc.	V.G.	Good	Fair	Poor
1350	1100	750	550	375	225

A-5 DU 50th Anniversary

This was a high-grade version of the Auto-5 produced to commemorate the 50th anniversary of Ducks Unlimited. It is highly engraved and features high-gloss bluing and a fancy checkered walnut stock. There were approximately 5,500 manufactured by Miroku in 1987. They were auctioned by the Ducks Unlimited chapters to raise money for the organization, and because of this fact, it is difficult to furnish an accurate value. This is a commemorative firearm and, as such, must be NIB with all furnished materials to command premium collector value. We furnish what we feel is a general value.

NIB	Exc.	V.G.	Good	Fair	Poor
3000	2000	800	600	450	300

A-5 DU Sweet Sixteen

This was a special version of the Miroku-manufactured Sweet Sixteen that was auctioned by the Ducks Unlimited chapters in 1988. There were 5,500 produced. All specifications and cautions that were furnished for the 50th Anniversary gun also apply here.

NIB	Exc.	V.G.	Good	Fair	Poor
2500	1500	850	600	400	300

Auto-5 Classic

This is a special limited edition series of A-5 shotguns built in 12 gauge only. The Classic is photo-etched with game scenes on a silver gray receiver. 5,000 of these guns were manufactured in 1984. The Gold Classic is similar in appearance but features gold inlays and is limited to 500 guns.

Classic

NIB	Exc.	V.G.	Good	Fair	Poor
2000	1675	1200	750	525	300

Gold Classic

Produced by FN.

NIB	Exc.	V.G.	Good	Fair	Poor
8500	7000	5000	3000	—	—

Auto-5 Light Buck Special

This model is a lightweight version of the Buck Special. Chambered for the 2.75" shell and fitted with a 24" vent rib barrel. Conventional choked for slug or buckshot. Barrel has adjustable rear sight and ramp front sight. Weighs 8 lbs.

NIB	Exc.	V.G.	Good	Fair	Poor
850	650	550	450	375	225

Auto-5 Stalker

New for 1992, this model is available in either a lightweight version or a magnum version. The Light Stalker is available in 12 gauge with either 26" or 28" barrel with choke tubes. The Magnum Stalker is offered in 12 gauge (3" chamber) with 28" or 30" barrel and choke tubes. The Light Stalker weighs 8 lbs. 4 oz. and the Magnum Stalker weighs 8 lbs. 11 oz.

Light Stalker

NIB	Exc.	V.G.	Good	Fair	Poor
775	600	550	400	300	225

Magnum Stalker

NIB	Exc.	V.G.	Good	Fair	Poor
800	650	600	375	275	250

Auto-5 Final Tribute Limited Edition

Introduced in 1999, this commemorative A-5 is limited to 1,000 shotguns. It represents the final production of this model. Chambered for the 12 gauge shell and fitted with a 28" vent rib barrel this shotgun has a special engraved receiver.

NIB	Exc.	V.G.	Good	Fair	Poor
5000	3750	2500	2000	1300	500

Browning A5

With a squared "hump-back" receiver, the A5 is similar in appearance to the classic Auto-5 but is a totally different semi-automatic shotgun. It operates with Browning's new short-recoil Kinematic action. In 12 gauge only with a 3" chamber, the A5 is designed to function with a wide range of 2.75" and 3" loads. Barrel length is 26", 28" or 30" with ventilated rib, brass bead front and ivory bead middle sights, three Invector DS choke tubes. A5 Hunter model has checkered walnut stock. Also offered with black composite stock (A5 Stalker) or Mossy Oak Duck Blind or Break-Up Infinity camo finish or with black composite stock. All are shim adjustable for cast and drop. Introduced in 2012. **NOTE:** Subtract $100 for Stalker model.

NIB	Exc.	V.G.	Good	Fair	Poor
1400	1200	950	700	—	—

Double Automatic Shotgun

This is a short recoil-operated, semi-automatic shotgun chambered for 12 gauge only. It was offered with a 26", 28", or 30" barrel that was either plain or vent ribbed. It has various chokes. The receiver is steel, and the finish is blued or silver with a checkered walnut stock. The tubular magazine holds only two shots—hence its name. It was manufactured between 1954 and 1972. **NOTE:** Vent rib add 25 percent.

NIB	Exc.	V.G.	Good	Fair	Poor
—	625	500	350	275	225

Twelvette Double Auto

This version is similar to the Double Automatic except that it has an aircraft aluminum alloy frame color-anodized in either blue, silver, green, brown, or black. Red-, gold-, or royal blue-colored receivers were the rarest colors and would command approximately a 50 to 75 percent premium. It was offered with either a plain or vent rib barrel. There were approximately 65,000 produced between 1954 and 1972. **NOTE:** Vent rib add 25 percent.

NIB	Exc.	V.G.	Good	Fair	Poor
—	875	595	350	275	225

Twentyweight Double Auto

This version is similar in all respects to the Twelvette except that it is three-quarters of a pound lighter and was offered with a 26.5" barrel. It was manufactured between 1952 and 1971. **NOTE:** Vent rib add 25 percent.

NIB	Exc.	V.G.	Good	Fair	Poor
—	850	595	375	300	250

2000 SERIES
B-2000

This is a gas-operated, semi-automatic shotgun chambered for 12 or 20 gauge and offered with a 26", 28", or 30", vent rib barrel with various chokes. The finish is blued with a checkered walnut stock. This shotgun was assembled in Portugal from parts that were manufactured by FN in Belgium. There were approximately 115,000 imported between 1974 and 1981.

NIB	Exc.	V.G.	Good	Fair	Poor
625	550	475	300	225	175

B-2000 Magnum

This version features a barrel with 3" chambers and was offered standard with a recoil pad.

NIB	Exc.	V.G.	Good	Fair	Poor
775	575	500	300	225	175

B-2000 Buck Special

This version has a 24", cylinder-bored barrel with rifle sights.

NIB	Exc.	V.G.	Good	Fair	Poor
625	475	425	275	225	175

B-2000 Trap

This version has a 30", full-choke barrel with a floating rib and a Monte Carlo-type trap stock.

NIB	Exc.	V.G.	Good	Fair	Poor
600	475	425	275	225	175

B-2000 Skeet

This version features a 26", skeet-bored barrel with a floating vent rib and a skeet-type stock. **NOTE:** Add 20 percent for 20 gauge guns.

NIB	Exc.	V.G.	Good	Fair	Poor
—	595	450	375	275	200

80 SERIES
B-80

This is a gas-operated, semi-automatic shotgun chambered for 12 or 20 gauge. It features 3" magnum potential by simply exchanging the barrel. It features various-length barrels and was offered with screw-in Invector chokes as of 1985. The receiver is either steel or lightweight aluminum alloy. The finish is blued with a checkered walnut stock. This gun was assembled in Portugal from parts manufactured by Beretta in Italy. It was manufactured between 1981 and 1988. **NOTE:** Add 20 percent for 20 gauge guns.

NIB	Exc.	V.G.	Good	Fair	Poor
—	550	450	375	325	225

B-80 Buck Special

This version features a 24", cylinder-bored barrel with rifle sights. It was discontinued in 1984.

NIB	Exc.	V.G.	Good	Fair	Poor
—	495	400	350	300	200

B-80 DU Commemorative

This version was produced to be auctioned by American Ducks Unlimited chapters. In order to realize the collector potential, it must be NIB with all supplied materials. Values supplied are general.

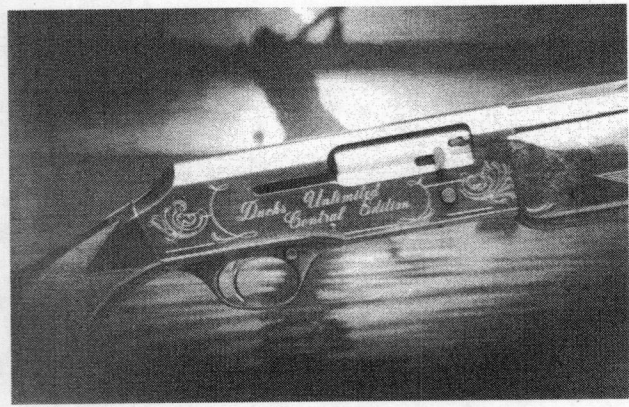

NIB	Exc.	V.G.	Good	Fair	Poor
950	650	550	425	325	275

GOLD SERIES
Gold 10

Introduced for the first time in 1993 this is a gas-operated 5-shot semi-automatic shotgun chambered for the 10 gauge shell. Offered with 26", 28", or 30" vent rib barrel. The standard model has a walnut stock, blued receiver and barrel while the Stalker Model is fitted with a graphite composite stock with non-glare finish on receiver and barrel. Both models are fitted with choke tubes. Weighs about 10 lbs. 10 oz.

NIB	Exc.	V.G.	Good	Fair	Poor
950	700	550	450	300	150

Gold Evolve

Introduced in 2004 this model is an updated version of the original Gold gun. It features newly designed receiver, magazine cap, ventilated rib design, checkering pattern and Hi-Viz sights. Offered in 12 gauge 3" with choice of 26", 28", or 30" barrel with choke tubes. Weight is about 7 lbs. for the 28" model.

NIB	Exc.	V.G.	Good	Fair	Poor
1195	875	700	525	400	225

Gold Light 10 Gauge Camo

This 10 gauge model is offered with 26" or 28" barrels with Mossy Oak or Shadow Grass camo. Lightweight alloy receiver reduces weight to 9 lb. 10 oz. Introduced in 2001.

NIB	Exc.	V.G.	Good	Fair	Poor
1275	975	775	595	450	250

Gold 10 Gauge Combo

This 10 gauge model has a choice of two vent rib barrels in lengths of 24" and 26", or 24" and 28". Walnut stock with black ventilated recoil pad. Weight with 28" barrels is about 10 lbs. 10 oz.

NIB	Exc.	V.G.	Good	Fair	Poor
1150	800	675	500	375	250

Gold Stalker

NIB	Exc.	V.G.	Good	Fair	Poor
1025	725	550	450	300	150

Gold Classic Stalker

Introduced in 1999 this model features a classic Browning squared receiver and shim-adjustable stock. This model is chambered for 12 gauge shells with choice 26" or 28" vent rib barrels. Gun has 3" chambers. Black synthetic stock. Weight is about 7 lbs. 3 oz.

NIB	Exc.	V.G.	Good	Fair	Poor
850	675	550	400	275	125

Gold 3½" 12 Gauge

Introduced in 1997 this model features a 3.5" chamber. It can operate 2.75", or 3" shells as well. Choice of barrel lengths from 26" to 30". Invector-Plus chokes. Magazine capacity is four 2.75" shells or three 3" shells or three 3.5" shells. The weight is approximately 7 lbs. 10 oz.

NIB	Exc.	V.G.	Good	Fair	Poor
1000	795	595	450	200	150

Gold 12 Gauge Hunter

Introduced in 1994 this semi-automatic shotgun is built on the same gas operating system as the Gold 10. Offered with 26", 28", or 30" barrel it has a magazine capacity of four 3" shells. Walnut stock has full checkered pistol grip with black rubber recoil pad. Invector-Plus choke tubes supplied. Weighs about 7.5 lbs. Also available (1998) in Stalker version with non-glare matte metal parts and stocks.

NIB	Exc.	V.G.	Good	Fair	Poor
750	525	400	300	200	150

Gold Classic Hunter

Introduced in 1999, this model features a squared receiver, fully adjustable stock, selected walnut stock, and deep blued barrels. Choice of 26", 28", or 30" vent rib barrel. Offered with 3" chamber 12 gauge only.

NIB	Exc.	V.G.	Good	Fair	Poor
850	600	500	400	275	225

Gold Classic 20 Gauge

Offered with choice of 26" or 28" vent rib barrels with select walnut stock. Shim-adjustable. Squared receiver. Weight is about 6 lbs. 12 oz. Introduced in 1999.

NIB	Exc.	V.G.	Good	Fair	Poor
795	600	500	400	275	225

Gold Classic High Grade

Introduced in 1999, this model features a traditional square receiver with engraved silver gray finish. Offered in 12 gauge only with 3" chambers and 28" vent rib barrel. Select walnut stock. Weight is about 7 lbs. 6 oz.

NIB	Exc.	V.G.	Good	Fair	Poor
1500	1200	775	500	225	165

Gold Deer Hunter

Introduced in 1997, this model features a choice of a fully rifled barrel or a smooth bore barrel with Invector choke system. Both versions come with a cantilever scope mount. Stock and forearm are of select walnut. Receiver has non-glare black finish. Barrel is satin finish. Barrel length is 22" on both barrels. Weight is about 7 lbs. 12 oz. Price listed are for smoothbore barrel. **NOTE:** For fully rifled version add $40.

NIB	Exc.	V.G.	Good	Fair	Poor
875	650	500	400	200	150

Gold Deer Hunter 20 Gauge

Same as above but chambered for 20 gauge 3" shell. Furnished with fully rifled 22" barrel. Cantilever scope mount. Introduced in 2001.

NIB	Exc.	V.G.	Good	Fair	Poor
1025	900	625	495	300	200

Gold Deer Stalker

This model, introduced in 1999, is the same as the model above but fitted with a black synthetic stock.

NIB	Exc.	V.G.	Good	Fair	Poor
950	700	600	500	300	150

Gold Deer Mossy Oak

Introduced in 1999 with camo finish.

NIB	Exc.	V.G.	Good	Fair	Poor
825	675	575	450	200	125

Gold Waterfowl Mossy Oak Shadow Grass

Introduced in 1999 with camo finish.

NIB	Exc.	V.G.	Good	Fair	Poor
950	700	600	500	200	125

Gold Waterfowl Mossy Oak Breakup

Introduced in 2000 with camo finish.

NIB	Exc.	V.G.	Good	Fair	Poor
950	700	575	450	200	125

Gold Turkey/Waterfowl Mossy Oak

Introduced in 1999 with camo finish.

NIB	Exc.	V.G.	Good	Fair	Poor
950	700	575	450	200	125

Gold Turkey/Waterfowl Stalker

Introduced in 1999, this model features a black synthetic stock, 24" barrel, Hi-Viz sight, and 3" or 3.5" chambers. Weight is approximately 7 lbs. 4 oz.

NIB	Exc.	V.G.	Good	Fair	Poor
900	650	575	450	200	125

Gold Turkey/Waterfowl Hunter

This 12 gauge 3" or 3.5" chambered gun is offered with 24" vent rib barrel. Select walnut stock with black ventilated recoil pad. Weight is about 7 lbs. Introduced in 1999.

NIB	Exc.	V.G.	Good	Fair	Poor
875	625	550	450	200	125

Gold NWTF Series

This model is finished in a Mossy Oak Breakup pattern and bears the "NWTF" logo on the buttstock. Fitted with a 24" barrel, Hi-Viz front sight, X-full extended Turkey choke. Offered in the configurations listed.

Gold Light 10 Gauge

NIB	Exc.	V.G.	Good	Fair	Poor
1350	950	775	600	425	175

Gold 12 Gauge

3.5" Chamber, Shadow Grass

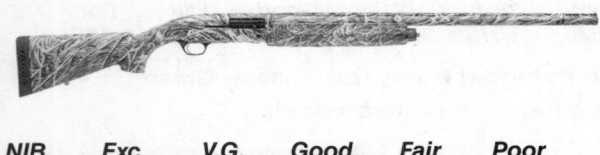

NIB	Exc.	V.G.	Good	Fair	Poor
1275	900	725	550	375	150

3" Chamber

NIB	Exc.	V.G.	Good	Fair	Poor
1100	775	650	575	375	150

3.5" Chamber Ultimate Turkey Gun

NIB	Exc.	V.G.	Good	Fair	Poor
1280	1000	900	725	375	200

Gold Hunter

Chambered for 12 and 20 gauge and offered in 26" or 28" barrel lengths. Weighs about 6.8 lbs.

NIB	Exc.	V.G.	Good	Fair	Poor
750	625	400	300	200	150

Gold Sporting Clays

Introduced in 1996, this model features a ported barrel in 28" or 30" lengths. Recoil pad is standard. Weight is about 7.5 lbs.

NIB	Exc.	V.G.	Good	Fair	Poor
800	675	475	375	200	150

Gold Ladies/Youth Sporting Clays

Offered in 12 gauge only with 2.75" chambers this model features a 28" vent rib barrel. Overall dimensions have been adjusted to fit women. Black solid recoil pad. Weight is about 7 lbs. 6 oz. Introduced in 1999.

NIB	Exc.	V.G.	Good	Fair	Poor
1200	895	625	450	300	125

Gold "Golden Clays" Ladies Sporting Clays

Introduced in 2005 this 12 gauge 2.75" chambered gun is fitted with a 28" vent rib ported barrel with 4 choke tubes. Silver receiver is engraved with gold enhancements. Weight is about 7.75 lbs.

NIB	Exc.	V.G.	Good	Fair	Poor
1900	1375	1050	800	575	300

Gold "Golden Clays" Sporting Clays

As above but with standard stock dimensions and choice of 28" or 30" barrels. Introduced in 2005.

NIB	Exc.	V.G.	Good	Fair	Poor
1800	1300	1050	800	575	300

Gold Micro

Introduced in 2001 this model features a 20 gauge gun with 26" barrel, smaller pistol grip, shorter length of pull, and back-bored barrel with choke tubes. Weight is about 6 lb. 10 oz.

NIB	Exc.	V.G.	Good	Fair	Poor
925	650	575	475	300	125

Gold Upland

Offered in 12 or 20 gauge. The 12 gauge offered with 24" barrel and the 20 gauge with 26" barrel. Straight grip stock with 3" chamber. Weight is 7 lbs. for 12 gauge and 6.75 lbs. for 20 gauge. Introduced in 2001.

NIB	Exc.	V.G.	Good	Fair	Poor
950	700	600	475	300	125

Gold Fusion

This model features a new style vent rib, adjustable comb pro-comp sight, and five choke tubes. Offered in 12 gauge with 3" chambers with 26" or 28" barrels. Introduced in 2001. In 2002 this model was offered in 20 gauge as well as 12 with choice of 26" or 28" vent rib barrel. Weight for 12 gauge is about 7 lbs. and for 20 gauge about 6.5 lbs.

NIB	Exc.	V.G.	Good	Fair	Poor
900	725	650	495	300	125

Gold Fusion High Grade

Similar to the Gold Fusion with the addition of a high grade Turkish walnut stock, silver nitride receiver with game scene in gold. Five choke tubes and a hard case are standard. Introduced in 2005.

NIB	Exc.	V.G.	Good	Fair	Poor
1600	1250	900	625	450	300

Golden Clays

Introduced in 1999, this model features chambered for the 12 gauge shell with 2.74" chambers. Choice of 28" or 30" vent rib ported barrels. Engraved silver gray receiver. Select walnut stock. Weight is about 7 lbs. 3 oz.

NIB	Exc.	V.G.	Good	Fair	Poor
1250	1000	825	675	425	300

Gold Superlite Hunter

Introduced in 2006, this gun uses an aluminum alloy receiver and alloy magazine tube to reduce weight to about 7 lbs. in 12 gauge. Gloss finish walnut stock. Available with 3" or 3.5" chamber and 26" or 28" barrel. Magazine cut-off feature on 3.5" model. A 6.5 lb. 20 gauge with 3" chamber and 26" or 28" barrel is also offered. Three choke tubes. Add 15 percent for 3.5" chamber.

NIB	Exc.	V.G.	Good	Fair	Poor
900	650	575	475	300	125

Gold Superlite FLD Hunter

Similar to Gold Superlite Hunter but with semi-humpback style receiver and satin finish walnut stock and 3" chamber only.

Magazine cut-off on 12 gauge models. Adjustable shim system and three choke tubes.

NIB	Exc.	V.G.	Good	Fair	Poor
925	650	575	475	300	125

Gold Superlite Micro

Similar to Gold Superlite Hunter but with compact dimensions for smaller shooters. Only in 20 gauge with 26" barrel. Weighs about 6.25 pounds. Three choke tubes.

NIB	Exc.	V.G.	Good	Fair	Poor
925	650	575	475	300	125

A-500 SERIES

A-500G/A-500R

This is a self-adjusting, gas-operated, semi-automatic shotgun chambered for 12 gauge only. It is offered with 26", 28", or 30" barrels with a vent rib and screw-in Invector choke tubes. It has 3" chambers and can fire any load interchangeably. The finish is blued with a checkered walnut stock and recoil pad. It features light engraving. It was introduced in 1987. The 2008 recoil version (A-500R) has a slightly better reputation for functioning than the gas-operated A-500G, but values are roughly similar.

NIB	Exc.	V.G.	Good	Fair	Poor
575	490	425	350	275	225

A-500G Sporting Clays

This gas-operated version is designed for sporting clays and features a choice of 28" or 30" vent rib barrel with semi-gloss finish with gold lettering "Sporting Clays." Ventilated recoil pad standard. Weighs about 8 lbs.

NIB	Exc.	V.G.	Good	Fair	Poor
550	425	350	300	200	150

A-500R Hunting Model

Similar in appearance to the A-500G with the exception that this model operates on a short recoil design. The buttstock features a full pistol grip. Available with 26", 28", or 30" vent rib barrels. Choke tubes standard. Weighs about 7 lbs. 13 oz.

NIB	Exc.	V.G.	Good	Fair	Poor
475	385	300	250	200	150

A-500R Buck Special

Same as Hunting Model with the addition of adjustable rear sight and contoured front ramp sight with gold bead. Choke tubes standard, as is 24" barrel. Weighs 7 lbs. 11 oz.

NIB	Exc.	V.G.	Good	Fair	Poor
500	425	350	300	225	150

SILVER SERIES

This value-priced series of gas-operated autoloaders was introduced in 2006. All models feature a semi-humpback design and aluminum alloy receiver. Weights vary from 7.25 to 7.5 lbs. depending on barrel length and stock material. Three choke tubes provided with all models.

Silver Hunter

This version features a satin finish walnut stock and fore-end. It is available with a 3" chamber in 26", 28" and 30" barrel lengths or with a 3.5" chamber in 26" or 28" barrel length. Add 15 percent for

3.5" chamber. A 20 gauge version with 26" or 28" barrel became available in 2008.

NIB	Exc.	V.G.	Good	Fair	Poor
850	700	575	400	295	200

Silver Stalker

Similar to Silver Hunter but with matte black composite stock and fore-end. Sling swivel studs. 3.5" chamber only.

NIB	Exc.	V.G.	Good	Fair	Poor
825	675	550	375	275	175

Silver Micro

This is a 20 gauge with a 26" barrel and shorter stock dimensions for smaller shooters.

NIB	Exc.	V.G.	Good	Fair	Poor
825	695	550	375	275	175

Silver Sporting Micro

This 2.75" 12 gauge includes adjustment spacers for changing stock length. Barrel is 28". Three choke tubes included. Weight is about 7 lbs.

NIB	Exc.	V.G.	Good	Fair	Poor
1150	900	725	600	375	250

Silver NWTF

New in 2008, this 3" 12 gauge turkey gun is fully camouflaged with Mossy Oak's New Break-Up pattern. The 24" barrel is outfitted with fiber-optic rifle sights. Weight is about 7 lbs. Add 10 percent for 3.5" chamber.

NIB	Exc.	V.G.	Good	Fair	Poor
1100	900	725	600	375	250

Silver Rifled Deer

New in 2008, this 3" 12 gauge slug gun features a rifled barrel with cantilever scope mount. Finishes include satin walnut, black composite and Mossy Oak New Break-Up camo. Add 10 percent for camo finish.

NIB	Exc.	V.G.	Good	Fair	Poor
1100	900	725	600	375	250

Silver–Mossy Oak

Similar to Silver Stalker but in choice of Mossy Oak New Break-Up with 26" barrel or Mossy Oak New Shadow Grass with 26" or 28" barrel.

NIB	Exc.	V.G.	Good	Fair	Poor
925	650	575	475	300	125

MAXUS SERIES

Introduced in 2009 as a replacement for the Gold line.

Maxus

Autoloading shotgun chambered for 3" or 3.5" shells. Aluminum receiver, lightweight profile 26" or 28" barrel with vent rib, composite stock, Vector Pro lengthened forcing cone, DuraTouch Armor Coating overall. Weight: 6-7/8 lbs.

Maxus Stalker

Matte black finish overall. Add $150 for 3.5".

NIB	Exc.	V.G.	Good	Fair	Poor
1200	975	800	625	475	300

Maxus Mossy Oak Duck Blind

Mossy Oak Duck Blind finish overall. Add $150 for 3.5".

NIB	Exc.	V.G.	Good	Fair	Poor
1300	975	800	625	475	300

Maxus Hunter

Gas-operated auto-loader available with 3" or 3.5" magnum chambers. Barrel lengths: 26", 28", 30" (22" for rifled version). Lengthened forcing cone. Stock is shim-adjustable for length of pull, cast and drop. Glossy-finished walnut stock with 22 lpi checkering. Also offered in Mossy Oak Break-Up Infinity camo, and as Rifled Deer version with Mossy Oak Break-up Infinity camo. Weight: approx. 7 pounds. Introduced in 2011.

NIB	Exc.	V.G.	Good	Fair	Poor
1200	1000	850	650	400	300

Maxus Sporting Carbon

Gas-operated 12-gauge auto-loader with 3" chamber. Aluminum alloy receiver has satin nickel finish, laser engraving. Barrel length: 28" or 30". Gloss-finished high-grade walnut stock. Also available with carbon fiber stock and as Rifled Deer Stalker version with cantilevered scope base and 22" barrel. New 2011. **NOTE:** Deduct 15 percent for Deer Stalker/Carbon

NIB	Exc.	V.G.	Good	Fair	Poor
1390	1200	950	700	450	350

BPS SERIES

This is a slide-action shotgun chambered for 10, 12, or 20 gauge. It is offered with various length vent rib barrels with screw-in Invector chokes. It features 3" magnum chambers and a bottom-ejection system that effectively makes it ambidextrous. It has double slide bars and a 5-shot tubular magazine. It is constructed of all steel. It was introduced by B.C. Miroku in 1977.

BPS Field Grade

NIB	Exc.	V.G.	Good	Fair	Poor
350	300	275	200	200	150

28 Gauge

Introduced in 1994. Weight approximately 7 lbs.

NIB	Exc.	V.G.	Good	Fair	Poor
425	325	295	225	210	150

BPS Magnum

10 or 12 gauge, 3.5" chambers.

NIB	Exc.	V.G.	Good	Fair	Poor
510	400	350	300	250	150

BPS Waterfowl 12 Gauge Camo

Introduced in 1999.

NIB	Exc.	V.G.	Good	Fair	Poor
525	425	350	300	250	150

BPS Waterfowl 12 Gauge Mossy Oak Break-Up

NIB	Exc.	V.G.	Good	Fair	Poor
575	475	375	325	250	150

BPS Mossy Oak New Break-up

Similar to BPS Hunter but with Mossy Oak New Break-up camo finish overall; 3" and 3.5" 12-gauge only.

NIB	Exc.	V.G.	Good	Fair	Poor
750	625	400	300	200	150

BPS Mossy Oak Duck Blind

Similar to above but with Mossy Oak Duck Blind finish overall.

NIB	Exc.	V.G.	Good	Fair	Poor
750	625	400	300	200	150

BPS Rifled Deer Mossy Oak New Break-up

Similar to BPS Rifled Deer Hunter but with Mossy Oak New Break-up camo finish overall.

NIB	Exc.	V.G.	Good	Fair	Poor
750	625	400	300	200	150

BPS NWTF Series

This model is finished in a Mossy Oak Breakup pattern and bears the NWTF logo on the buttstock. Fitted with a 24" barrel, Hi-Viz front sight, Extra Full extended turkey choke. Introduced in 2001. Offered in the configurations listed.

10 Gauge

NIB	Exc.	V.G.	Good	Fair	Poor
625	475	400	325	200	125

12 Gauge 3.5" Chamber

NIB	Exc.	V.G.	Good	Fair	Poor
625	475	400	325	200	125

12 Gauge 3" Chamber

NIB	Exc.	V.G.	Good	Fair	Poor
550	450	375	325	200	125

BPS Stalker

Matte finish, black stock.

NIB	Exc.	V.G.	Good	Fair	Poor
435	390	325	275	200	150

BPS Stalker—Combo

A combination of a 28" vent rib barrel and a choice of 22" fully rifles barrel or 20.5" Invector barrel with Extra Full turkey choke. Introduced in 2000.

NIB	Exc.	V.G.	Good	Fair	Poor
650	525	475	325	200	125

BPS Game Gun

These models are designed for turkey and deer with 20.5" barrels with Invector chokes or rifled barrels. Deer model has 5" rifled choke tube while the turkey model has Extra Full choke tube. The Cantilever model has a fully rifled barrel. Weight is approximately 7.7 lbs. Introduced in 1998. Add $30 for deer model and $60 for Cantilever model.

NIB	Exc.	V.G.	Good	Fair	Poor
450	350	300	250	200	125

BPS 10 Gauge Mossy Oak Shadow Grass Camo

Introduced in 1999.

NIB	Exc.	V.G.	Good	Fair	Poor
575	475	375	325	175	125

BPS 10 Gauge Turkey

Fitted with a 24" vent rib barrel and black synthetic stock with black solid recoil pad, this model was introduced in 1999. Weight is about 9 lbs. 2 oz.

NIB	Exc.	V.G.	Good	Fair	Poor
525	425	375	325	200	125

BPS Micro 20 Gauge

This model features a 22" vent rib barrel with shorter pistol grip stock and lighter weight. Weight is about 6.75 lbs. Introduced in 2001.

NIB	Exc.	V.G.	Good	Fair	Poor
450	350	300	250	200	125

BPS Upland Special

This model is chambered for the 20 gauge shell and fitted with a 22" vent rib barrel. The walnut stock is a straight grip. Weight is about 6.5 lbs. This model comes in 12 or 20 gauge with a 22" barrel and straight grip stock. A 16 gauge version with a 24" or 26" barrel was introduced in 2008. A very beautiful little pump.

NIB	Exc.	V.G.	Good	Fair	Poor
550	375	300	275	200	125

BPS Small Gauge

Introduced in 2000 this model is chambered for the 28 gauge and the .410 bore. The 28 gauge is offered with a choice of 26" or 28" vent rib barrel with Invector chokes. The .410 is available with 26" vent rib barrel with Invector chokes. Both the 28 gauge and .410 bore weigh about 6.75 lbs.

NIB	Exc.	V.G.	Good	Fair	Poor
525	450	325	275	200	125

BPS Pigeon Grade

Furnished in 12 gauge only with high grade walnut stock and gold trimmed receiver.

NIB	Exc.	V.G.	Good	Fair	Poor
500	400	300	225	175	125

BPS Game Gun

Offered in 12 gauge only this model is available in either a Turkey Special or a Deer Special. Both have 20.5" plain barrel and drilled and tapped receivers. The stock is walnut. The turkey gun is fitted with an Extra Full choke. The deer gun has a special rifled choke tube for slugs. Both weigh about 7 lbs. 7 oz.

NIB	Exc.	V.G.	Good	Fair	Poor
300	250	175	125	100	50

BPS Buck Special

24" barrel with sights.

NIB	Exc.	V.G.	Good	Fair	Poor
450	400	350	300	225	175

BPS Trap Model

NIB	Exc.	V.G.	Good	Fair	Poor
—	375	325	275	200	150

BPS Micro Trap

Similar to BPS Trap Model but with compact dimensions (13.75" length of pull, 48.25" overall length). 12 gauge only. **CAUTION:** Do not interchange Invector choke tubes with Invector-Plus choke tubes. May cause personal injury.

NIB	Exc.	V.G.	Good	Fair	Poor
700	—	—	—	—	—

BPS Youth Model

Short stock, 22" barrel.

NIB	Exc.	V.G.	Good	Fair	Poor
435	390	325	275	200	150

BPS Waterfowl Deluxe

This version is chambered for 12 gauge with a 3" chamber and features an etched receiver with a gold-plated trigger. Otherwise, it is similar to the standard BPS.

NIB	Exc.	V.G.	Good	Fair	Poor
—	600	525	425	325	250

BPS Ducks Unlimited Versions

These were limited-edition guns produced to be auctioned by Ducks Unlimited. They were furnished with a case and must be NIB with furnished materials to realize their collector potential.

NIB	Exc.	V.G.	Good	Fair	Poor
650	525	425	325	250	175

MODEL 12

Grade I

This is a slide-action shotgun chambered for 20 and 28 gauge with a 26", modified choke, vent rib barrel. It is a reproduction of the Winchester Model 12 shotgun. It has a 5-round, tubular magazine with a floating, high-post rib. It has a takedown feature and is blued with a walnut stock. Introduced in 1991, total production was limited to 7,000 guns.

NIB	Exc.	V.G.	Good	Fair	Poor
825	625	425	300	250	200

Grade V

This is an extensively engraved version of the Grade I Model 12. It features a select walnut stock with deluxe checkering and a high-gloss finish. There are gold inlays. It was introduced in 1991, and production was limited to 5,000 guns. Discontinued 1992. **NOTE:** For 28 gauge add 30 percent.

NIB	Exc.	V.G.	Good	Fair	Poor
1300	950	700	450	—	—

LIMITED EDITION MODEL 42

A new version of the .410 bore pump shotgun that was last produced by Winchester in 1963. Available in two grades both fitted with 26" vent rib barrels. The Grade I features a plain blued receiver with walnut stock. The Grade V features a blued receiver with scroll engraving and gold inlays. Both models are choked Full and weigh 6 lbs. 4 oz.

Grade I

NIB	Exc.	V.G.	Good	Fair	Poor
900	600	500	400	—	—

Grade V

NIB	Exc.	V.G.	Good	Fair	Poor
1450	1000	700	500	—	—

A-BOLT SHOTGUN

Introduced in 1995 this bolt-action shotgun was offered in 12 gauge with 3" chamber. Rifled barrel version is 22" long while the Invector barrel version is 23" long with a 5" rifle tube installed. Has a 2-shot detachable magazine. Average weight is about 7 lbs. This is considered the "Rolls Royce" of bolt shotguns and is becoming quite desirable. Manufacture ceased in 1998. **NOTE:** For Invector rifled choke tube model deduct $50.

Hunter Version

NIB	Exc.	V.G.	Good	Fair	Poor
1000	850	750	500	300	100

Stalker Version

NIB	Exc.	V.G.	Good	Fair	Poor
900	750	650	400	200	100

RIFLES

High-Power Bolt-Action Rifle

This was a high-grade, bolt-action sporting rifle manufactured by FN in Belgium (from 1959 to 1975) or Sako of Finland (from 1961 to 1975). It was built on either a Mauser or a Sako action and chambered for a number of popular calibers from the .222 Remington up to the .458 Winchester Magnum. There were three basic grades that differed in the amount of ornamentation and the quality of materials and workmanship utilized. Certain calibers are considered to be rare and will bring a premium from collectors of this firearm. We recommend securing a qualified appraisal on these rifles if a transaction is contemplated. We furnish general values only.

NOTE: From 1959 through 1966 FN Mauser actions with long extractors were featured. These Mauser actions will bring a premium depending on caliber. From 1967 on, FN Supreme actions with short extractors were used. Only .30-06 and .270 calibers continued with long extractor Mauser actions.

CAUTION: For buyer and seller alike some rare calibers may be worth as much as 100 percent or more over prices listed for rare calibers such as .284 Win., .257 Roberts, 300 H&H, and .308 Norma Magnum. The High-Power bolt-action rifles seemed to be particularly hard hit by salt wood. That is why short extractor rifles bring less than long extractor guns. No factory replacement stocks are known to still be available. Deduct 20-25 percent for short extractor rifles. Proceed with caution.

Safari Grade

Standard model and calibers.

NIB	Exc.	V.G.	Good	Fair	Poor
1600	1350	1100	850	400	300

Medallion Grade

Scroll engraved, standard calibers.

NIB	Exc.	V.G.	Good	Fair	Poor
3200	2500	1900	1400	750	400

Olympian Grade

Extensive game scene engraving, standard calibers.

NIB	Exc.	V.G.	Good	Fair	Poor
8500	6300	5250	4250	2500	1500

Model BBR

This is a bolt-action sporting rifle chambered for various popular calibers. It has a 24" barrel with an adjustable trigger and fluted bolt. It features a detachable magazine under the floorplate and was furnished without sights. The finish is blued with a checkered, walnut, Monte Carlo stock. It was manufactured between 1978 and 1984 by Miroku.

NIB	Exc.	V.G.	Good	Fair	Poor
675	575	400	350	275	200

BOSS™ SYSTEM

Introduced by Browning in 1994 this new accuracy system allows the shooter to fine-tune his Browning rifle to the particular load he is using. Consists of a tube on the end of the rifle muzzle that allows the shooter to select the best setting for the ammunition type. The system also reduces recoil. BOSS stands for "Ballistic Optimizing Shooting System". This option will add approximately $80 to the value of the particular Browning rifle on which it is fitted.

X-BOLT SERIES

Introduced in 2008, the X-Bolt series of rifles features an adjustable three-position Feather Trigger system, a newly-designed bolt release, an improved scope mounting system, tang safety, and a generally slimmer, sleeker profile.

X-Bolt Composite Stalker

Features include steel receiver with matte blue finish, free-floating crowned barrel, matte black composite stock with palm swell, Inflex recoil pad. Various barrel lengths depending on chambering, which include both medium and long cartridges ranging from .243 Winchester to .338 Winchester Magnum. Introduced in 2008.

NIB	Exc.	V.G.	Good	Fair	Poor
850	700	600	500	350	200

X-Bolt Stainless Stalker

Similar to above but with stainless steel receiver and barrel. Various barrel lengths depending on chambering, which include both medium and long cartridges ranging from .243 Winchester to .375 H&H Magnum. Introduced in 2008.

NIB	Exc.	V.G.	Good	Fair	Poor
850	700	600	500	350	200

X-Bolt Hunter

Similar to above but with sculpted, satin-finished walnut stock with cut checkering and low-luster blued barrel and receiver. Various barrel lengths depending on chambering, which include both medium and long cartridges ranging from .243 Winchester to .338 Winchester Magnum. Left-hand model available.

NIB	Exc.	V.G.	Good	Fair	Poor
850	700	600	500	350	200

X-Bolt Medallion

Similar to above but with high-gloss finish and engraved, blued barrel and receiver. Various barrel lengths depending on chambering, which include both medium and long cartridges ranging from .243 Winchester to .375 H&H Magnum. Introduced in 2008. Available in left-hand version.

NIB	Exc.	V.G.	Good	Fair	Poor
1000	850	700	600	500	350

X-Bolt Micro Hunter

Similar to Browning X-Bolt Hunter but with compact dimensions (13-5/16" length of pull, 41.25" overall length). Left-hand available.

NIB	Exc.	V.G.	Good	Fair	Poor
800	700	600	500	350	200

X-Bolt Varmint Stalker

Similar to X-Bolt Stalker but with medium-heavy free-floated barrel, target crown, composite stock. .223, .22-250, .243 Winchester and .308 Winchester only.

NIB	Exc.	V.G.	Good	Fair	Poor
1000	850	700	600	500	350

X-Bolt RMEF White Gold

Similar to X-Bolt Medallion but with gold-engraved matte stainless finish and Rocky Mountain Elk Foundation grip cap. Chambered in .325 WSM only.

NIB	Exc.	V.G.	Good	Fair	Poor
1300	1000	850	650	550	375

X-Bolt RMEF Special Hunter

Similar to above but with matte blued finish without gold highlights.

NIB	Exc.	V.G.	Good	Fair	Poor
900	700	600	500	350	200

A-BOLT SERIES

NOTE: In 2004 new calibers were offered for the A-Bolt series depending on model. They are the .25 WSSM and the .223 Rem. All A-Bolt II Descriptions: "II" designation dropped from A-Bolt name in 2006.

A-Bolt Hunter

This is the current bolt-action rifle manufactured by B.C. Miroku. It is chambered for various popular calibers and offered with a 22", 24", or 26" barrel. It has either a short or long action, an adjustable trigger, and a detachable box magazine that is mounted under the floorplate. It is furnished without sights and is blued with a checkered walnut stock. It was introduced in 1985.

NIB	Exc.	V.G.	Good	Fair	Poor
575	400	350	300	250	200

A-Bolt II Hunter

Introduced in 1994 this new model features a newly designed anti-bind bolt and improved trigger system. In 2001 the .300

Winchester Short Magnum cartridge was offered for this model. In 2003 a left-hand model was introduced.

NIB	Exc.	V.G.	Good	Fair	Poor
795	575	400	300	250	200

A-Bolt II Hunter WSSM

Similar to the A-Bolt Hunter but chambered for the .223 WSSM and .243 WSSM cartridges. The stock design is also different from the A-Bolt Hunter with the addition of a longer pistol grip and thicker forearm. Weight is about 6.25 lbs. Introduced in 2003.

NIB	Exc.	V.G.	Good	Fair	Poor
795	575	400	300	250	200

A-Bolt II Micro Hunter

Introduced in 1999, this model features a shorter length of pull and a shorter barrel length than the Hunter model. Offered in .22 Hornet, .22-250, 7mm-08, .308, .243, and .260 calibers. Weight is about 6 lbs. In 2003 the .270 WSM, 7mm WSM, and .300 WSM calibers were added for this model as well as a left-hand version. **NOTE:** Add $30 for left-hand model and $30 for WSM calibers.

NIB	Exc.	V.G.	Good	Fair	Poor
650	525	350	250	200	150

A-Bolt II Classic Hunter

This model features a Monte Carlo stock, low luster bluing, select walnut, and double bordered checkering. Offered in .30-06, .270, 7mm Rem. Magnum, and .300 Win. Magnum. No sights. Weight is about 7 lbs. Introduced in 1999.

NIB	Exc.	V.G.	Good	Fair	Poor
675	500	395	250	200	150

A-Bolt Stainless Hunter

This model features a black composite stock, stainless steel receiver and barrel, no sights. Chamberings range from .243 Winchester to .300 WSM. Weight is about 6.5 lbs. Introduced in 2008.

NIB	Exc.	V.G.	Good	Fair	Poor
800	650	450	300	250	200

A-Bolt Classic Hunter WSSM

As above but chambered for the .223 WSSM and .243 WSSM cartridges. Weight is about 6.25 lbs. Introduced in 2003.

NIB	Exc.	V.G.	Good	Fair	Poor
800	650	450	300	250	200

A-Bolt Mountain Ti

This model features a lightweight stainless steel 23" barrel, titanium receiver, and lightweight fiberglass stock. Chambered for the .270 WSM, 7mm WSM, and the .300 WSM cartridges. Weight is about 5.5 lbs. Calibers: .243, 7mm-08, .308, .325 WSM. Introduced in 2004.

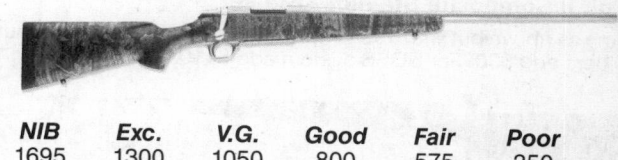

NIB	Exc.	V.G.	Good	Fair	Poor
1695	1300	1050	800	575	350

A-Bolt Composite Stalker

Supplied with composite stock and matte finish bluing. Offered in .338 Win. Magnum, .300 Win. Magnum, 7mm Rem. Magnum, .25-06, .270, .280, .30-06. Introduced in 1988. In 2001 the .300 Winchester Short Magnum cartridge was offered for this model. Calibers: .223 WSSM, .243 WSSM, .25 WSSM, .223, .243, .7mm-08, .270 WSM, 7mm WSM, .300 WSM, .325 WSM, .25-06, .270, .280, .30-06, 7mm RM, .300 WM, .338 WM. Add 10 percent for BOSS or left-hand version.

NIB	Exc.	V.G.	Good	Fair	Poor
550	350	300	250	200	150

A-Bolt II Composite Stalker

Same as above but with 1994 improvements. **NOTE:** Add $80 for BOSS system.

NIB	Exc.	V.G.	Good	Fair	Poor
670	525	400	300	250	200

A-Bolt Composite Stalker WSSM

As above but chambered for the .223 WSSM or the .243 WSSM cartridge. Weight is about 6 lbs. Introduced in 2003.

NIB	Exc.	V.G.	Good	Fair	Poor
700	550	400	300	250	200

A-Bolt Stainless Stalker

Bolt-action rifle. Calibers: .223 WSSM, .243 WSSM, .25 WSSM, .223, .243, .7mm-08, .270 WSM, 7mm WSM, .300 WSM, .325 WSM, .25-06, .270, .280, .30-06, 7mm RM, .300 WM, .338 WM, .375 H&H. Barrel: 22", 23", 24", 26" stainless steel, sightless (except for .375 H&H). Magazine: Detachable box. Stock: Black composite. Add 10 percent for BOSS system and left-hand version. **NOTE:** For .300 and .338 calibers add $30.

NIB	Exc.	V.G.	Good	Fair	Poor
600	450	400	350	300	250

A-Bolt II Composite Stainless Stalker

Same as above but with 1994 improvements. **NOTE:** For magnum calibers add $30. For BOSS system add $110.

NIB	Exc.	V.G.	Good	Fair	Poor
850	650	550	400	300	250

A-Bolt Stainless Stalker WSSM

As above but chambered for the .223 WSSM and .243 WSSM calibers. Stock design is slightly different from standard A-Bolt Stalker. Weight is about 6 lbs. Introduced in 2003.

NIB	Exc.	V.G.	Good	Fair	Poor
880	675	550	400	300	250

A-Bolt Carbon Fiber Stainless Stalker

This model features a Christensen Arms patent carbon barrel. Chambered for .22-250 or .300 Win. Magnum. Weight is about 6.25 lbs. for short action and 7 lbs. for long action. Introduced in 2000. In 2001 the .300 Winchester Short Magnum cartridge was offered for this model.

NIB	Exc.	V.G.	Good	Fair	Poor
1400	1200	1000	900	700	350

A-Bolt II Heavy Barrel Varmint

Introduced in 1994 this model features all of the A-Bolt II improvements in a heavy barrel varmint rifle. Offered in .22-250 and .223 Rem. calibers with 22" barrel. Equipped with black laminated wood stock.

NIB	Exc.	V.G.	Good	Fair	Poor
685	600	525	425	325	250

A-Bolt Varmint Stalker

Introduced in 2002 this model features a new armor coated synthetic stock. Matte blue metal finish. Chambered for the .223 Rem. and .22-250 Rem. cartridges. Fitted with a 24" barrel on the .223 and a 26" barrel on the .22-250. Weight is about 8 lbs.

NIB	Exc.	V.G.	Good	Fair	Poor
790	650	525	425	325	250

A-Bolt Varmint Stalker WSSM

As above but chambered for the .223 WSSM and .243 WSSM cartridges. Weight is about 7.75 lbs. Introduced in 2003.

NIB	Exc.	V.G.	Good	Fair	Poor
815	650	525	425	325	250

A-Bolt Eclipse M-1000

Thumbhole stock. Calibers: .270, .30-06, 7mm RM, .22-250, .308, .270 WSM, .7mm WSM, .300 WSM. Add 10 percent for BOSS. The rifle is fitted with a 26" barrel with BOSS system. The stock is a laminated hardwood with gray/black finish. The forearm is a benchrest style. Weight is approximately 9 lbs. 13 oz.

NIB	Exc.	V.G.	Good	Fair	Poor
1135	700	625	450	350	250

A-Bolt Eclipse M-1000 WSM & Stainless

Introduced in 2004 this model is offered in all of the WSM calibers. The M-1000 is blued with a heavy barrel, while the stainless is fitted with a heavy bull barrel. Barrel length is 26". Weight is 9.85 lbs. No sights. **NOTE:** Add $200 for the stainless model.

A-Bolt Eclipse M-1000 Stainless

NIB	Exc.	V.G.	Good	Fair	Poor
1050	825	675	500	350	200

A-Bolt Eclipse Varmint

Introduced in 1996 this model features a thumbhole stock made from gray/black laminated hardwood. Offered in two version: a short-action, heavy-barrel version, and a long and short action with standard-weight barrel. Eclipse Varmint weighs about 9 lbs. and the standard-barrel version weighs about 7.5 lbs. depending on caliber.

NIB	Exc.	V.G.	Good	Fair	Poor
950	800	600	500	400	250

Euro-Bolt

First introduced in 1993 this A-Bolt variation features a rounded bolt shroud, Mannlicher-style bolt handle, continental-style stock with cheekpiece, schnabel-style forearm. The finish is a low-luster blue. Offered in .270, .30-06, and 7mm Rem. Magnum calibers. Weighs about 7 lbs.

NIB	Exc.	V.G.	Good	Fair	Poor
650	500	450	350	250	150

A-Bolt II Euro Bolt

Same as above but with 1994 improvements.

NIB	Exc.	V.G.	Good	Fair	Poor
850	500	450	350	250	150

NRA A-Bolt Wildlife Conservation Collection

Commemorates NRA's Environment Conservation and Hunting Outreach Program. Caliber: .243 Win. Barrel: 22" blued sightless. Stock is satin-finish walnut with NRA Heritage logo lasered on buttstock. MSRP: $797.

A-Bolt Medallion Model

Calibers: .223 WSSM, .243 WSSM, .25 WSSM, .223, .243, .7mm-08, .270 WSM, 7mm WSM, .300 WSM, .325 WSM, .25-06, .270, .280, .30-06, 7mm RM, .300 WM, .338 WM. Add 10 percent for BOSS or left-hand version. **NOTE:** Add $35 for .300 and .338 calibers.

NIB	Exc.	V.G.	Good	Fair	Poor
800	600	500	400	300	250

A-Bolt II Medallion

Same as above but with 1994 improvements. In 2003 this model was offered in a left-hand version.

NIB	Exc.	V.G.	Good	Fair	Poor
765	600	450	350	300	250

A-Bolt II Medallion WSSM

As above but chambered for the .223 WSSM or the .243 WSSM cartridge. Weight is about 6.25 lbs. Introduced in 2003.

NIB	Exc.	V.G.	Good	Fair	Poor
795	650	525	450	400	325

A-Bolt Gold Medallion

This version has a fancy grade walnut stock with a cheekpiece. It is lightly engraved and has gold-inlaid letters. It was introduced in 1988.

NIB	Exc.	V.G.	Good	Fair	Poor
690	625	550	450	400	325

A-Bolt II Gold Medallion

Same as above but with 1994 improvements.

NIB	Exc.	V.G.	Good	Fair	Poor
690	625	550	450	400	325

A-Bolt II White Gold Medallion

This model features a gold engraved stainless receiver and barrel, select walnut stock with brass spacers and rosewood caps. European-style cheekpiece. No sights. Introduced in 1999. Offered in .30-06, .270, 7mm Rem. Magnum, and .300 Win. Magnum. Weight is about 7 lbs. 8 ozs.

NIB	Exc.	V.G.	Good	Fair	Poor
1100	800	650	500	425	350

A-Bolt White Gold Medallion RMEF

Introduced in 2003 this model is a special edition for the Rocky Mountain Elk Foundation. Chambered for the 7mm Rem. Magnum and fitted with a 26" barrel. Both action and barrel are stainless steel. Special RMEF logo on the grip cap. Weight is about 7.75 lbs. Add 5 percent for WSM calibers.

NIB	Exc.	V.G.	Good	Fair	Poor
1200	950	750	600	450	325

A-Bolt Custom Trophy

Introduced in 1998 this model features gold highlights on the barrel and receiver, select walnut stock, with shadowline cheekpiece and skeleton pistol grip. The barrel is octagonal. Chambered for .270 and .30-06 with 24" barrel and 7mm Rem. Magnum and .300 Win. Magnum with 26" barrel. Weight varies from 7 lbs. 11 oz. to 7 lbs. 3 oz. depending on caliber.

NIB	Exc.	V.G.	Good	Fair	Poor
1300	1000	800	650	425	300

A-Bolt Big Horn Sheep Issue

This is a high-grade version of the A-Bolt chambered for the .270 cartridge. It features a deluxe skipline checkered walnut stock with a heavily engraved receiver and floorplate. It has two gold sheep inlays. There were 600 manufactured in 1986 and 1987.

NIB	Exc.	V.G.	Good	Fair	Poor
1050	800	600	450	400	325

A-Bolt Micro-Medallion

This is a smaller version of the A-Bolt Hunter chambered for popular cartridges that fit a short action. It has a 20" barrel without sights and a 3-round magazine. It was introduced in 1988.

NIB	Exc.	V.G.	Good	Fair	Poor
525	475	400	350	300	250

A-Bolt II Micro-Medallion

Same as above but with 1994 improvements.

NIB	Exc.	V.G.	Good	Fair	Poor
525	475	400	350	300	250

A-Bolt Pronghorn Issue

This is a deluxe version of the A-Bolt chambered for the .243 cartridge. It is heavily engraved and gold inlaid and features a presentation-grade walnut stock with skipline checkering and pearl-inlaid borders. There were 500 manufactured in 1987.

NIB	Exc.	V.G.	Good	Fair	Poor
1300	1000	750	500	400	325

A-Bolt Special Hunter RMEF

Similar to A-Bolt Hunter but honors Rocky Mountain Elk Foundation. Chambered in .325 WSM. Satin finish. Introduced 2007.

NIB	Exc.	V.G.	Good	Fair	Poor
800	600	500	400	300	250

A-Bolt White Gold RMEF

Similar to A-Bolt Special Hunter RMEF but with stainless barrel and receiver and glossy finish. Introduced 2007.

NIB	Exc.	V.G.	Good	Fair	Poor
1100	775	600	475	325	200

A-Bolt Target

Similar to A-Bolt but with 28" heavy bull blued barrel, blued receiver, satin finish gray laminated stock with adjustable comb and semi-beavertail fore-end. Chambered in .223, .308 Winchester and .300 WSM.

NIB	Exc.	V.G.	Good	Fair	Poor
1275	1000	800	650	425	300

A-Bolt Target Stainless

Similar to above but with stainless receiver and barrel.

NIB	Exc.	V.G.	Good	Fair	Poor
1500	1275	1000	800	650	425

A-Bolt .22 Grade I

This is a bolt-action sporting rifle chambered for the .22 LR or .22 Magnum cartridges. It features a 60-degree bolt and a 22" barrel available either with or without open sights. It has a 5-round, detachable magazine and an adjustable trigger. The finish is blued with a checkered walnut stock. It was introduced in 1986. **NOTE:** .22 Magnum add 15 percent.

NIB	Exc.	V.G.	Good	Fair	Poor
340	275	210	150	125	100

A-Bolt .22 Gold Medallion

This deluxe, high-grade version features a select stock with rosewood pistol-grip cap and fore-end tip. It is lightly engraved and has gold-filled letters. It was introduced in 1988.

NIB	Exc.	V.G.	Good	Fair	Poor
450	400	350	300	225	175

T-BOLT SERIES

T-Bolt Model T-1

This is a unique, straight-pull, bolt-action sporting rifle chambered for .22 caliber cartridges. It has a 22" barrel with open sights and a 5-round magazine. The finish is blued with a plain walnut stock. It was manufactured between 1965 and 1974 by FN. Many T-Bolt rifles were affected by salt wood. Proceed with caution. Reintroduced 2006 with rotary magazine.

NIB	Exc.	V.G.	Good	Fair	Poor
—	550	395	350	150	100

T-Bolt Model T-2

This version is similar to the T-1 with a select, checkered walnut stock and a 24" barrel.

NIB	Exc.	V.G.	Good	Fair	Poor
800	600	450	375	250	200

T-Bolt (2006)

Reintroduction of classic and collectible T-bolt straight-pull .22 rifle. Introduced in 2006. Chambered for .17 HMR, .22 WMR or .22 LR.

NIB	Exc.	V.G.	Good	Fair	Poor
600	475	450	375	250	200

T-Bolt Target/Varmint

Similar to reintroduced T-Bolt but with floating heavy target barrel and other accurizing refinements. Introduced 2007.

NIB	Exc.	V.G.	Good	Fair	Poor
650	525	500	425	300	250

T-Bolt Target/Varmint Stainless

Similar to above but with stainless steel receiver and barrel. Introduced 2008.

NIB	Exc.	V.G.	Good	Fair	Poor
850	725	650	525	350	325

T-Bolt Composite Hunter

Sporter version of the new T-Bolt with black composite Monte Carlo stock and glossy blue barrel and receiver. Chambered in .17 HMR, .22 WMR or .22 LR. Scope not included. Introduced 2008.

NIB	Exc.	V.G.	Good	Fair	Poor
675	525	500	425	300	250

T-Bolt Composite Target/Varmint

Sporter version of the new T-Bolt Target/Varmint with black composite Monte Carlo stock and glossy blue barrel and receiver. Chambered in .17 HMR, .22 WMR or .22 LR. Scope not included. Introduced 2008.

NIB	Exc.	V.G.	Good	Fair	Poor
700	550	525	450	325	275

T-Bolt Composite Target/Varmint Left-Hand

Similar to T-Bolt Composite Target/Varmint but in left-hand version.

NIB	Exc.	V.G.	Good	Fair	Poor
725	550	525	450	325	275

T-Bolt Sporter

Sporter version of the new T-Bolt with satin walnut stock and bright blue barrel and receiver. Scope not included. Introduced 2008.

NIB	Exc.	V.G.	Good	Fair	Poor
700	550	525	450	325	275

T-Bolt Sporter Left-Hand

Similar to Browning T-Bolt Sporter but in left-hand version.

NIB	Exc.	V.G.	Good	Fair	Poor
700	550	525	450	325	275

T-Bolt Composite Sporter Left-Hand

Similar to Browning T-Bolt Sporter Left-Hand but with composite stock.

NIB	Exc.	V.G.	Good	Fair	Poor
700	550	525	450	325	275

Acera Straight Pull Rifle

Introduced in 1999, this model features a straight-action bolt system. It is chambered for the .30-06 with a 22" barrel and the .300 Win. Magnum with 24" barrel. Open sights are optional as is the BOSS system. Detachable box magazine. Checkered walnut stock. Prices listed are for .30-06 with no sights and no BOSS. **NOTE:** Add $100 for .300 Win. Magnum with no sights and no BOSS.

NIB	Exc.	V.G.	Good	Fair	Poor
1100	775	600	475	325	200

Model 52 Limited Edition

This model is based on the design of the original Winchester Model 52 .22 caliber bolt-action rifle. Fitted with a 24" barrel and walnut stock with oil finish. Metal pistol-grip cap and rosewood fore-end tip. Drilled and tapped for scope. Five-round detachable magazine. Blued finish. Weight is about 7 lbs. From 1991 to 1992 5,000 Model 52s were built.

NIB	Exc.	V.G.	Good	Fair	Poor
850	750	650	550	—	—

BPR-22

This is a short-stroke, slide action rifle chambered for the .22 LR and Magnum cartridges. It has a 20.25" barrel with open sights and an 11-round, tubular magazine. The finish is blued with a checkered walnut stock. It was manufactured between 1977 and 1982. **NOTE:** Add $100 for models chambered for .22 Magnum.

NIB	Exc.	V.G.	Good	Fair	Poor
—	500	350	215	125	95

BPR-22 Grade II

This version is engraved and has a select walnut stock. **NOTE:** Add 20 percent for models chambered for .22 Magnum.

NIB	Exc.	V.G.	Good	Fair	Poor
—	600	400	275	225	150

Trombone Model

This is a slide-action rifle chambered for the .22 LR cartridge. It has a 24" barrel with open sights and a takedown design. It has a tubular magazine and a hammerless action. There were approximately 150,000 manufactured by FN between 1922 and 1974. Approximately 3,200 were imported by Browning in the 1960s. They are marked with either the FN barrel address or the Browning Arms address. The Browning-marked guns are worth approximately 20 percent additional. The values given are for FN-marked guns.

NIB	Exc.	V.G.	Good	Fair	Poor
1000	750	600	450	375	275

.22 Caliber Semi-Auto

This is a blowback-operated, semi-automatic rifle chambered for the .22 Long Rifle or Short cartridge. It features a take-down barrel design with a 19.25" barrel and an 11-round, tubular magazine inside the buttstock. It is loaded through a hole in the middle of the buttstock. The finish is blued with a checkered walnut stock and beavertail forearm. This lightweight, compact firearm was manufactured by FN between 1956 and 1974 for U.S. marked guns. There are a number of versions that differ in the amount of ornamentation and the quality of materials and workmanship.

Grade I

NOTE: For Grade I short add 50 percent. Early Wheel Sight manufactured 1956-1960 add 10 percent.

NIB	Exc.	V.G.	Good	Fair	Poor
750	525	400	325	220	125

Grade II

French grayed receiver. **NOTE:** For Grade II short add 300 percent.

NIB	Exc.	V.G.	Good	Fair	Poor
1600	1200	900	700	300	200

Grade III

French grayed receiver. **NOTE:** For premium engravers add 40 percent to Grade III. For Grade III short add 800 percent. For unsigned Grade III, 1956-1960 deduct 20 percent.

NIB	Exc.	V.G.	Good	Fair	Poor
3250	2700	1900	1200	700	400

.22 Semi-Auto/Model SA-22 (Miroku Mfg.)

This model is similar to the Belgian FN except that it was produced as of 1976 by B.C. Miroku in Japan. Collector interest is not as high as in the FN version.

Grade I

NIB	Exc.	V.G.	Good	Fair	Poor
700	575	400	275	125	100

Grade II

Discontinued 1984.

NIB	Exc.	V.G.	Good	Fair	Poor
900	700	525	375	225	150

Grade III

Discontinued 1983.

NIB	Exc.	V.G.	Good	Fair	Poor
1300	1000	750	500	300	200

Grade VI

Gold plated animals.

NIB	Exc.	V.G.	Good	Fair	Poor
1200	950	750	525	325	275

BAR-22

This is a blowback-operated, semi-automatic rifle chambered for the .22 LR cartridge. It has a 20.25" barrel with open sights and a 15-round, tubular magazine. It features a polished, lightweight alloy receiver. It was finished in blue with a checkered walnut stock. It is manufactured between 1977 and 1985 by Miroku.

NIB	Exc.	V.G.	Good	Fair	Poor
—	600	525	290	160	125

BAR-22 Grade II

This is a deluxe version with an engraved, silver-finished receiver. It has a select walnut stock. It was discontinued in 1985.

NIB	Exc.	V.G.	Good	Fair	Poor
—	695	575	375	175	150

Buck Mark Rifle

This model uses the same design as the Buck Mark pistol. It is fitted with an 18" barrel (heavy on the target model) and thumbhole pistol grip. Magazine capacity is 10 rounds. Integral rail scope mount. Introduced in 2001. Weight is about 4.25 lbs. for Sporter and 5.5 lbs. for the Target model.

Target Model

NIB	Exc.	V.G.	Good	Fair	Poor
595	460	325	250	195	125

Sporter Model

NIB	Exc.	V.G.	Good	Fair	Poor
590	450	325	250	195	125

Buck Mark Field Target Gray Laminate

Introduced in 2003 this model features a lightweight carbon composite barrel, gray laminate stock and integral scope rail. Chambered for the .22 cartridge and fitted with an 18" barrel. Weight: 5.5 lbs. for standard; 3.75 lbs. for Lite model.

NIB	Exc.	V.G.	Good	Fair	Poor
650	525	400	325	250	175

Patent 1900 High Power

This is a semi-automatic sporting rifle chambered for the .35 Remington cartridge. It is similar in configuration to the Remington Model 8 rifle. It has a 22" barrel with open sights and a 5-round, integral magazine. The finish is blued with a plain walnut stock. There were approximately 5,000 manufactured between 1910 and 1931. A deluxe model with a ribbed barrel and checkered walnut stock was also available and would be worth approximately 15 percent additional. Very rare in the USA.

NIB	Exc.	V.G.	Good	Fair	Poor
—	1500	1000	700	475	300

BAR SERIES

Bar High Power Rifle

This is a gas-operated, semi-automatic sporting rifle chambered for various popular calibers from the .243 up to the .338 Magnum cartridges. It was offered with either a 22" or 24" barrel with folding leaf sight until 1980. The finish is blued with a checkered walnut stock. The various grades offered differed in the amount of ornamentation and the quality of materials and workmanship utilized. Earlier models were manufactured in Belgium by FN; these guns would be worth approximately 15 percent additional over guns assembled in Portugal from parts manufactured by FN. The early .338 Magnum model is rarely encountered and would be worth approximately 25 percent additional. The Grade I values furnished are for Portuguese-assembled guns from 1977 until the introduction of the BAR Mark II in 1993. This model was introduced in 1967 and discontinued in 1977.

Grade I

NIB	Exc.	V.G.	Good	Fair	Poor
1000	725	650	475	225	100

Grade I Magnum

NIB	Exc.	V.G.	Good	Fair	Poor
1150	750	675	400	250	125

Grade II Deluxe

1967-1974.

NIB	Exc.	V.G.	Good	Fair	Poor
1200	900	825	475	300	175

Grade II Deluxe Magnum

1968-1974.

NIB	Exc.	V.G.	Good	Fair	Poor
1275	950	850	500	325	200

Grade III

Discontinued 1984. **NOTE:** The Grade III was offered in two variations. The first was hand-engraved and produced in Belgium. The second was photo-etched and built in Belgium and assembled in Portugal. This second variation will not be as valuable as the first.

NIB	Exc.	V.G.	Good	Fair	Poor
1450	1200	900	600	375	250

Grade III Magnum

Discontinued 1984. **NOTE:** Prices indicated above are for 1970 through 1974 production. For guns assembled in Portugal deduct 30 percent. .338 Win. Magnum caliber is rare in Grade III; add 75 percent premium.

NIB	Exc.	V.G.	Good	Fair	Poor
1500	1300	950	650	400	275

Grade IV

Game scene engraved. This grade was hand-engraved from 1970 through 1976 then was etched thereafter. Grade IV rifles were discontinued in 1984. **NOTE:** Pre-1977 rifles add 40 percent. Premium engraving add 10 percent.

NIB	Exc.	V.G.	Good	Fair	Poor
1900	1500	1050	800	650	400

Grade IV Magnum

NIB	Exc.	V.G.	Good	Fair	Poor
2000	1600	1075	850	650	425

Grade V

Gold Inlaid. 1971-1974.

NIB	Exc.	V.G.	Good	Fair	Poor
5500	4800	3500	2800	1200	600

Grade V Magnum

1971-1974. **NOTE:** For special order variations on Grade V rifles add up to 100 percent.

NIB	Exc.	V.G.	Good	Fair	Poor
5600	4900	3600	2900	1250	600

North American Deer Rifle Issue

This is a deluxe version of the BAR chambered for .30-06 only. It features a photo etched, silver-finished receiver and a deluxe, checkered walnut stock. There were 600 produced and furnished with a walnut case and accessories. This model was discontinued in 1983. As with all commemoratives, it must be NIB to command premium values.

NIB	Exc.	V.G.	Good	Fair	Poor
4000	3600	2400	1800	450	250

BAR Mark II Safari Rifle

This is an improved version of the BAR first introduced by Browning in 1967. Announced in 1993 this Mark II design uses a new gas system with a newly designed buffering system to improve reliability. This model also has a new bolt release lever, a new easily removable trigger assembly. Available with or without sights. Walnut stock with full pistol grip and recoil pad on magnum gun are standard. The receiver is blued with scroll engraving. Rifles with magnum calibers have a 24" barrel while standard calibers are fitted with a 22" barrel. Available in .243, .308, .270, .30-06, 7mm Rem. Magnum, .300 Win. Magnum, .338 Win. Magnum. Standard calibers weigh about 7 lbs. 9 oz. and magnum calibers weigh about 8 lbs. 6 oz. **NOTE:** Add 30 percent for .270 Wby. Magnum, which was made for one year only.

NIB	Exc.	V.G.	Good	Fair	Poor
825	750	600	450	250	150

BAR Mark II Lightweight

This version of the Mark II was introduced in 1997 and features a lightweight alloy receiver and shortened 20" barrel. It is offered in .30-06, .270 Win., .308 Win., and .243 Win. calibers. It is not offered with the BOSS system. Weight is approximately 7 lbs. 2 oz.

NIB	Exc.	V.G.	Good	Fair	Poor
900	725	550	425	175	125

BAR Composite Stalker

Introduced in 2001 this model features a composite buttstock and fore-end with removable magazine. It is offered in short action (.243 and .308) with sights, and in standard action (.270 and .30-06) with no sights. In magnum calibers (7mm, .330 Win., and .338) it is offered with no sights and with the BOSS system as well. **NOTE:** For magnum calibers add $75, and for BOSS add $140.

NIB	Exc.	V.G.	Good	Fair	Poor
900	725	550	425	175	125

BAR High Grade Models

These models will feature high grade walnut stock with highly polished blued barrel. Receivers will be grayed with game animals: mule deer and whitetail on the standard calibers (.270 and .30-06) and elk and moose on magnum calibers (7mm magnum and .300 Win. Magnum).

NIB	Exc.	V.G.	Good	Fair	Poor
1825	1450	1100	800	550	400

BAR ShortTrac

Introduced in 2004 this model features the ability to chamber magnum cartridges. Offered in .270 WSM, 7mm WSM, .325 WSM and .300 WSM as well as .243 and .308. Fitted with a 23" barrel in magnum calibers and 22" barrel in non-magnum. Receiver is alloy steel. Redesigned stock adjustable for length of pull. Weight is about 7.25 lbs. for magnum calibers and 6 75 lbs. for others. Add 10 percent for camo finish.

NIB	Exc.	V.G.	Good	Fair	Poor
950	650	450	350	250	200

BAR ShortTrac Stalker

Similar to BAR ShortTrac but with matte blue barrel and composite stock. Introduced 2006.

NIB	Exc.	V.G.	Good	Fair	Poor
850	670	550	450	350	250

BAR ShortTrac Left-Hand

Similar to BAR ShortTrac but in left-hand. Introduced 2007.

NIB	Exc.	V.G.	Good	Fair	Poor
950	650	450	350	250	200

BAR ShortTrac Mossy Oak New Break-up

Similar to BAR ShortTrac but with Mossy Oak Break-up finish overall.

NIB	Exc.	V.G.	Good	Fair	Poor
1275	1000	750	600	475	350

BAR ShortTrac Digital Green

Similar to above but with Digital Green camo finish overall.

NIB	Exc.	V.G.	Good	Fair	Poor
1275	1000	750	600	475	350

BAR LongTrac

Similar to the above model but made for long action calibers such as .270, .30-06, 7mm Rem. Magnum and .300 Win. Magnum. Barrel length is 22" for the .270 and .30-06 and 24" for the other two calibers. Weight is about 7 lbs. for .270 and .30-06 and 7.5 lbs. for 7mm and .300. Introduced in 2004. Add 10 percent for camo finish. **NOTE:** Add $75 for magnum calibers.

NIB	Exc.	V.G.	Good	Fair	Poor
950	650	450	350	250	200

BAR LongTrac Stalker

Long-action version of the BAR ShortTrac Stalker.

NIB	Exc.	V.G.	Good	Fair	Poor
850	670	550	450	350	250

BAR LongTrac Left-Hand

Similar to BAR Long-Trac but in left hand. Introduced 2007.

NIB	Exc.	V.G.	Good	Fair	Poor
950	1000	750	600	475	350

BAR LongTrac Mossy Oak New Break-up

Similar to BAR LongTrac but with Mossy Oak Break-up finish overall.

NIB	Exc.	V.G.	Good	Fair	Poor
1275	1000	750	600	475	350

Model BPR

The initials "BPR" stands for Browning Pump Rifle. It was introduced in 1997 and is similar in appearance to the BAR. Offered in both long action and short action calibers with barrel lengths from 22" to 24". Short action calibers are: .243 Win., and .308 Win. Long Action calibers are: .270 Win., .30-06, 7mm Rem. Magnum, and .300 Win. Magnum. Weight is about 7 lbs. 3 oz. Discontinued 2003.

NIB	Exc.	V.G.	Good	Fair	Poor
800	675	525	400	300	200

BL SERIES

BL-22 Grade I

This is a lever-action rifle chambered for the .22 rimfire cartridge. It has an 18" barrel with a tubular magazine and a folding leaf rear sight. It is a Western-style firearm that features an exposed hammer. The finish is blued with a walnut stock. It was introduced in 1970 by Miroku.

NIB	Exc.	V.G.	Good	Fair	Poor
450	350	200	150	125	100

BL-22 Grade II

This version is similar with a scroll-engraved receiver and a checkered, select walnut stock.

NIB	Exc.	V.G.	Good	Fair	Poor
475	350	225	175	150	125

BL-22 Field Series Grade I

Introduced in 2005 this rifle features a satin nickel receiver. Walnut stock with no checkering. Blued trigger. Magazine capacity is 16 rounds. Weight is about 5 lbs.

NIB	Exc.	V.G.	Good	Fair	Poor
495	375	350	200	150	100

BL-17 Field Series Grade I

As above but chambered for the .17 Mach 2 cartridge. Weight is about 5.2 lbs.

NIB	Exc.	V.G.	Good	Fair	Poor
650	575	400	200	150	100

BL-22 Field Series Grade II

As above but with checkered stock, gold trigger, and scroll engraving on the receiver.

NIB	Exc.	V.G.	Good	Fair	Poor
555	425	350	200	150	125

BL-17 Field Series Grade II

As above but chambered for the .17 Mach 2 cartridge.

NIB	Exc.	V.G.	Good	Fair	Poor
700	600	450	250	150	125

BL-22 Grade II Octagon

Introduced in 2005 this model has a 24" octagon barrel chambered for the .22 Long and Long Rifle cartridges. Receiver is silver nitride with scroll engraving and gold trigger. Magazine capacity is 16 rounds. Gold bead front sight. Weight is about 5.25 lbs.

NIB	Exc.	V.G.	Good	Fair	Poor
725	550	375	275	200	150

BL-17 Grade II Octagon

As above but chambered for the .17 Mach 2 cartridge. Magazine capacity is 16 rounds. Weight is about 5.35 lbs. Introduced in 2005.

NIB	Exc.	V.G.	Good	Fair	Poor
750	575	375	275	200	150

BL-22 Classic

This model was introduced in 1999 and has the same features as the BL-22 Grade I.

NIB	Exc.	V.G.	Good	Fair	Poor
425	375	275	200	175	125

BL-22 NRA Grade 1

Similar to BL-22 Grade 1 but with "NRA" logo lasered on buttstock.

NIB	Exc.	V.G.	Good	Fair	Poor
500	450	350	300	—	—

BL-22 Gray Laminate Stainless

Similar to BL-22 but with gray laminated stock, nickeled receiver and stainless steel barrel. Introduced 2006.

NIB	Exc.	V.G.	Good	Fair	Poor
725	550	375	275	200	150

BL-22 Micro Midas

Chambered for the .22 LR. Designed for younger shooters with 12" length of pull. Lever action with short 33-degree throw. Full-length tubular magazine, American walnut stock, gloss finish, straight grip. Receiver is steel with blued finish and grooved for scope mounts. New 2011.

NIB	Exc.	V.G.	Good	Fair	Poor
400	350	300	250	200	150

Model 81 BLR

This is a contemporarily designed, lever-action sporting rifle chambered for various popular calibers from .22-250 up to .358 Winchester. It has a 20" barrel with adjustable sights. It features a 4-round, detachable magazine and a rotary locking bolt. The finish is blued with a checkered walnut stock and recoil pad. It was introduced in 1971 and manufactured that year in Belgium. In 1972 manufacture moved to Miroku in Japan. In 2003 a straight-grip stock was introduced and WSM calibers were added from .270 to .300. Weight is about 6.5 lbs. **NOTE:** Belgian-manufactured version add 20 percent.

NIB	Exc.	V.G.	Good	Fair	Poor
895	675	500	300	200	150

BLR Lightning (Lightweight)

Introduced in 1996 this model features a lightweight aluminum receiver with walnut stock and checkered pistol grip. Offered in both long and short action calibers from .223 Rem. to 7mm Rem. Magnum. Barrel length is 20" for short action calibers and 22" to 24" for long action calibers. Open sights are standard. Weight is about 7 lbs. depending on caliber. In 2003 a straight- grip stock was introduced.

NIB	Exc.	V.G.	Good	Fair	Poor
740	600	450	300	200	150

BLR Lightweight '81

This model features a straight grip checkered walnut stock. Fitted with a 20" or 22" barrel depending on caliber. Magazine capacity is 4 or 5 rounds depending on caliber. Chambered for calibers .22-25-, .243, 7mm-08, .308, .358, .450 Marlin, .270 WSM, .300 WSM, and .325 WSM. Also offered in a long action version chambered for the .270, .30-06, 7mm Rem. Magnum, and the .300 Win. Magnum. Weight is from 6.5 lbs. to 7.75 lbs. depending on caliber. **NOTE:** Add 20 percent for long action rifles and $70 for WSM calibers.

NIB	Exc.	V.G.	Good	Fair	Poor
730	550	425	325	225	125

BLR Lightweight Takedown

Similar to BLR Lightweight but with takedown feature. Introduced 2007.

NIB	Exc.	V.G.	Good	Fair	Poor
775	650	575	375	200	150

BLR Lightweight '81 Stainless Takedown

Similar to above but with stainless steel barrel and receiver. Introduced 2008.

NIB	Exc.	V.G.	Good	Fair	Poor
975	850	695	475	350	225

Model B-78

Introduced in 1973 this single-shot, lever-action falling block was offered in several calibers from .22-250 to .45-70. Barrel lengths from 24" to 26" in either round or octagonal shape with no sights except .45-70. Checkered walnut stock. First built in 1973 and discontinued in 1983. **NOTE:** Add 15 percent for .45-70 caliber.

NIB	Exc.	V.G.	Good	Fair	Poor
1400	1100	850	600	350	250

Model 53

Offered in 1990 this model is a reproduction of the Winchester Model 53 and like the original is chambered for the .32-20 cartridge. This is a limited edition offering confined to 5,000 rifles. It features hand-cut checkering, high-grade walnut stock with full pistol grip and semi-beavertail fore-end. Pistol grip is fitted with a metal grip cap. Barrel length is 22" and the finish is blue.

NIB	Exc.	V.G.	Good	Fair	Poor
900	800	650	500	325	200

Model 65 Grade I

This was a limited-edition, lever-action rifle chambered for the .218 Bee cartridge. It has a tapered, round, 24" barrel with open sights. It was patterned after the Winchester Model 65 rifle. It has a 7-round, tubular magazine. The finish is blued with a plain walnut stock and metal buttplate. There were 3,500 manufactured in 1989.

NIB	Exc.	V.G.	Good	Fair	Poor
850	675	500	300	—	150

Model 65 High Grade

This is a deluxe version that features a silver-finished, scroll engraved receiver with gold animal inlays and a gold-plated trigger. It features a select, checkered walnut stock. There were 1,500 manufactured in 1989.

NIB	Exc.	V.G.	Good	Fair	Poor
1650	1200	825	500	—	—

Model 71 Grade I

This was a reproduction of the Winchester Model 71, chambered for the .348 cartridge. It has either a 20" or 24" barrel with open sights and a 4-round, tubular magazine. The finish is blued with a plain walnut stock. There were 4,000 20" carbines and 3,000 24" rifles manufactured in 1986 and 1987.

NIB	Exc.	V.G.	Good	Fair	Poor
—	950	750	595	400	250

Model 71 High Grade

This version was similar to the Grade I except that it had a scroll engraved, grayed receiver with a gold-plated trigger and gold inlays. There were 3,000 rifles and 3,000 carbines manufactured in 1986 and 1987.

NIB	Exc.	V.G.	Good	Fair	Poor
—	1400	950	750	500	325

Jonathan Browning Centennial Mountain Rifle

This is a limited edition blackpowder rifle chambered for the .50 ball. It is fitted with a 30" octagon barrel with single set trigger. Figured walnut stock and engraved lock plate. Cased with powder horn. Limited to 1,000 rifles in 1978.

NIB	Exc.	V.G.	Good	Fair	Poor
1250	750	600	450	—	250

Jonathan Browning Mountain Rifle

Same as above but without fancy wood, case, or engraving. Also chambered for .45 or .54 caliber.

NIB	Exc.	V.G.	Good	Fair	Poor
800	500	400	300	—	175

Model 1878 (Original)

Based on John M. Browning's first patent this single-shot rifle was the only firearm manufactured by the Browning brothers. Offered in several calibers, only a few hundred probably exist with the Ogden, Utah, barrel address. This design was later sold to Winchester and sold under that company's name as the Model 1885 High Wall.

NIB	Exc.	V.G.	Good	Fair	Poor
—	20000	12500	8500	3500	1000

Model 1885 High Wall

This is a single-shot rifle with falling block action and octagonal free-floating barrel similar to the Model 78. Introduced in 1985. The stock is a high grade walnut with straight grip and recoil pad. Furnished with 28" barrel it is offered in these calibers: .223, .22-250, .270, .30-06, 7mm Rem. Magnum, .45-70 Gov't. Weighs about 8 lbs. 12 oz.

NIB	Exc.	V.G.	Good	Fair	Poor
1275	950	650	500	200	100

Model 1885 Low Wall

Introduced in 1995 this rifle is similar to the above but in a more accurate version of the original Low Wall. The thin octagon barrel is 24" in length. Trigger pull is adjustable. The walnut stock is fitted with a pistol grip and schnabel forearm. Offered in .22 Hornet, .223 Rem. and the .243 Win. calibers. Weight is about 6.4 lbs.

NIB	Exc.	V.G.	Good	Fair	Poor
1150	850	550	400	300	150

Model 1885 Low Wall Traditional Hunter

Introduced in 1998 this model is similar to the Low Wall but with a half-octagon half-round 24" barrel chambered for the .357 Magnum, .44 Magnum, and .45 Colt cartridges. Case colored receiver and crescent butt with tang sight are also features. Weight is approximately 6.5 lbs.

NIB	Exc.	V.G.	Good	Fair	Poor
1150	850	550	400	300	150

Model 1885 BPCR (Black Powder Cartridge Rifle)

This model was introduced in 1996 for BPCR metallic silhouette shoots. Chambered for the .45-70 or .40-60 caliber the receiver is case colored and the 28" round barrel is fitted with vernier sight with level. The walnut stock has a checkered pistol grip and is fitted with a tang sight. Weight is approximately 11 lbs.

NIB	Exc.	V.G.	Good	Fair	Poor
1600	1300	800	400	300	150

Model 1885 BPCR Creedmore Type

Introduced in 1998 this model is chambered for the 45-90 cartridge and features a 34" heavy half-round barrel with long range tang sight and wind gauge front sight. Weight is approximately 11 lbs. 13 oz.

NIB	Exc.	V.G.	Good	Fair	Poor
1500	1250	875	750	525	300

Model 1885 High Wall Traditional Hunter

This variation of the Model 1885 series was introduced in 1997. It is fitted with an oil finish walnut stock with crescent buttplate. The barrel is octagonal and 28" in length. The rear sight is buckhorn and the rifle is fitted with a tang-mounted peep sight. The front sight is gold bead classic style. The rifle is chambered for the .30-30, .38-55, and .45-70 cartridges. Weight is approximately 9 lbs. In 1998 the .454 Casull caliber was added to this rifle.

NIB	Exc.	V.G.	Good	Fair	Poor
1200	950	700	575	400	275

Model 1886 Grade I

This was a lever action sporting rifle patterned after the Model 1886 Winchester rifle. It was chambered for the .45-70 cartridge and has a 26", octagonal barrel with a full-length, tubular magazine. The finish is blued with a walnut stock and crescent buttplate. There were 7,000 manufactured in 1986.

NIB	Exc.	V.G.	Good	Fair	Poor
1350	950	725	600	450	300

Carbine

NIB	Exc.	V.G.	Good	Fair	Poor
950	650	550	400	325	250

Model 1886 High Grade

This deluxe version of the Model 1886 features game scene engraving with gold accents and a checkered, select walnut stock. "1 of 3,000" is engraved on the top of the barrel. There were 3,000 manufactured in 1986.

NIB	Exc.	V.G.	Good	Fair	Poor
1900	1600	1000	700	—	—

Carbine

NIB	Exc.	V.G.	Good	Fair	Poor
1600	1100	900	600		

Model 1886 Montana Centennial

This version is similar to the High Grade with a different engraving pattern designed to commemorate the centennial of the State of Montana. There were 2,000 manufactured in 1986. As with all commemoratives, it must be NIB with all supplied materials to command collector interest.

NIB	Exc.	V.G.	Good	Fair	Poor
2000	1600	1200	—	—	—

B-92 Carbine

This is a lever-action sporting rifle patterned after the Winchester Model 92. It was chambered for the .357 Magnum and the .44 Magnum cartridges. It has a 20" barrel with an 11-round, tubular magazine. The finish is blued with a walnut stock. It was discontinued in 1986. **NOTE:** Add 10 percent for Centennial Model. For .357 Magnum add 30 percent.

NIB	Exc.	V.G.	Good	Fair	Poor
—	700	625	400	250	120

Model 1895 Grade I

This is a lever-action sporting rifle chambered in .30-40 Krag and the .30-06 cartridge. It was patterned after the Model 1895 Winchester rifle. It has a 24" barrel and a 4-round, integral box magazine. It has a buckhorn rear sight and a blade front. The finish is blued with a walnut stock. There were 6,000 manufactured in .30-06 and 2,000 chambered for the .30-40 Krag. It was manufactured in 1984.

NIB	Exc.	V.G.	Good	Fair	Poor
—	950	675	475	375	275

Model 1895 High Grade

This is the deluxe engraved version of the Model 1895. It has gold-inlaid game scenes and a gold-plated trigger and features a checkered select walnut stock. There were 2,000 produced in 1984—1,000 in each caliber.

NIB	Exc.	V.G.	Good	Fair	Poor
—	1500	1250	900	700	400

Express Rifle

This is an over/under, superposed rifle chambered for the .270 Winchester or the .30-06 cartridges. It has 24" barrels with folding express sights and automatic ejectors. It features a single trigger. The receiver is engraved and is finished in blue with a deluxe checkered walnut stock. Introduced in 1980 and discontinued in 1986.

NIB	Exc.	V.G.	Good	Fair	Poor
—	6500	3950	2000	1100	800

Custom Shop Express Rifles

Produced in two different models, the Herstall and the CCS 375. Both are custom-built with choice of engraving patterns.

Herstal Express Rifle

NIB	Exc.	V.G.	Good	Fair	Poor
N/A	23000	17500	12000	5500	700

Continental Set

This consists of an Express Rifle chambered for the .30-06 cartridge and furnished with an extra set of 20 gauge, over/under barrels. The shotgun barrels are 26.5" in length. There is a single trigger, automatic ejectors, and a heavily engraved receiver. The select walnut stock is hand checkered and oil-finished. It was furnished with a fitted case. There were 500 manufactured between 1978 and 1986.

NIB	Exc.	V.G.	Good	Fair	Poor
10000	9250	8000	4500	2000	1000

BRUCE & DAVIS
Webster, Massachusetts

Double-Barreled Pistol

A .36 caliber double-barrel percussion pistol with 3" to 6" round barrels. The barrel rib marked "Bruce & Davis." Blued with walnut grips. Manufactured during the 1840s.

NIB	Exc.	V.G.	Good	Fair	Poor
—	—	925	400	175	100

BRUCHET
Ste. Etienne, France

Model A Shotgun

A 12 or .410 bore side-by-side shotgun with double triggers, and automatic ejectors. The barrel lengths and chokes are to customer specifications. Produced on a limited basis (50 per year) since 1982. Base price is listed.

NIB	Exc.	V.G.	Good	Fair	Poor
3600	2750	1900	1450	1000	500

Model B

As above, with a finer finish and a spring-assisted action opener. Imported since 1982.

NIB	Exc.	V.G.	Good	Fair	Poor
6950	5250	4000	3000	2250	1250

BRUFF, R.P.
New York, New York

Pocket Pistol

A .41 caliber single-shot percussion pistol with 2.5" to 3" barrels The pistol is marked "R.P. Bruff NY" in an arch and "Cast Steel." German silver with a checkered walnut stock. Manufactured between 1861 and 1870.

NIB	Exc.	V.G.	Good	Fair	Poor
—	—	1900	825	225	100

BRYCO ARMS
Carson City, Nevada
See—Jennings

BSA GUNS LTD.
Birmingham, England

Established in 1861, this firm has produced a wide variety of firearms over the years. The more common of these arms that are currently available in the United States are listed.

SINGLE-SHOT RIFLES

No. 12 Cadet Martini

A .310 caliber single-shot Martini action rifle with a 29" barrel, adjustable sights and straight-gripped walnut stock. Approximately 80,000 were manufactured from 1911 to 1913. Many of those imported into the United States were altered to .22 caliber.

NIB	Exc.	V.G.	Good	Fair	Poor
—	750	500	300	150	100

Centurian Match Rifle

As above, in .22 caliber with a 24" barrel, adjustable sights and a pistol-grip walnut stock.

NIB	Exc.	V.G.	Good	Fair	Poor
—	600	450	300	200	100

Model 13 Sporter

As above, in .22 Hornet with hunting sights.

NIB	Exc.	V.G.	Good	Fair	Poor
—	650	425	300	225	100

Martini International Match

As above, with a heavy match barrel, ISU-style sights and a match stock. Manufactured from 1950 to 1953.

NIB	Exc.	V.G.	Good	Fair	Poor
—	750	575	325	250	125

Martini International Light

As above, with a 26" barrel of lighter weight.

NIB	Exc.	V.G.	Good	Fair	Poor
—	750	575	325	250	125

Martini International ISU

As above, meeting ISU specifications with a 28" barrel. Manufactured from 1968 to 1976.

NIB	Exc.	V.G.	Good	Fair	Poor
—	850	675	400	325	200

BOLT-ACTION RIFLES

Royal

A bolt-action sporting rifle manufactured in a variety of calibers and a 24" barrel, with a checkered French walnut stock.

NIB	Exc.	V.G.	Good	Fair	Poor
—	550	500	250	200	100

Majestic Deluxe

A .22 Hornet, .222, .243, 7x57mm, .308 or .30-06 bolt-action sporting rifle with a 22" barrel, having a folding rear sight and a checkered walnut stock with a schnabel fore-end tip. Imported from 1959 to 1965. **NOTE:** Add 60 percent for .22 Hornet.

NIB	Exc.	V.G.	Good	Fair	Poor
—	550	350	250	200	100

Majestic Deluxe Featherweight

As above, in .270 or .458 Magnum with a thinner barrel. Add 25 percent for .458. Add 75 percent for .458.

NIB	Exc.	V.G.	Good	Fair	Poor
—	550	350	250	200	100

Monarch Deluxe

As above, drilled and tapped for telescopic sight and also available in a heavy barreled varmint version in .222 or .243 caliber. Imported from 1966 to 1974.

NIB	Exc.	V.G.	Good	Fair	Poor
—	550	375	275	225	100

HERTERS U9

The firm of Herters, Inc. of Waseca, Minnesota, imported BSA rifle actions beginning in 1965 that were used for custom-made rifles. Commencing in 1986, BSA began production of a new line of bolt-action sporting rifles on the Model CF-2 action. The standard production models are listed.

Sporter/Classic

A hunting rifle available in a variety of calibers with a checkered walnut stock. Introduced in 1986.

NIB	Exc.	V.G.	Good	Fair	Poor
—	450	325	275	200	100

Varminter

As above, with a matte-finished heavy barrel in .222, .22-250 or .243 caliber. Introduced in 1986.

NIB	Exc.	V.G.	Good	Fair	Poor
—	350	275	225	175	100

Stutzen Rifle

As above, with a 20.5" barrel and a Mannlicher-style stock.

NIB	Exc.	V.G.	Good	Fair	Poor
—	475	350	275	225	100

Regal Custom

As above, with an engraved receiver, checkered walnut stock and an ebony fore-end. Imported only in 1986.

NIB	Exc.	V.G.	Good	Fair	Poor
—	925	750	600	500	250

CFT Target Rifle

A .308 caliber single-shot version of the above with a 26.5" barrel and adjustable sights. Imported only in 1987.

NIB	Exc.	V.G.	Good	Fair	Poor
—	750	600	550	400	200

SHOTGUNS

Royal

This side-by-side is chambered for either 12 or 20 gauge 3" shells. Choice of 26" or 28" barrels with multi-chokes. Checkered select walnut stock with straight grip. Splinter forearm. Case colored receiver with side plates. Single selective trigger. Recoil pad standard. Weight is about 7.25 lbs. for 12 gauge and about 6.75 lbs. for the 20 gauge.

NIB	Exc.	V.G.	Good	Fair	Poor
1500	1150	900	675	—	—

Classic

This side-by-side gun is offered in 12, 16, 20, 28 gauge as well as .410 bore. Choice of 26" or 28" barrels except for 28 and .410 where 26" barrels are the only length offered. Checkered walnut stock with pistol grip. Case colored box lock receiver with scroll engraving. Semi-beavertail forearm. Recoil pad standard. Choke tubes standard. Weight is about 7.25 lbs. for 12 gauge, 6.75 lbs. for 16 gauge, 6.6 lbs. for 20 gauge, 6.25 lbs. for 28 gauge. .410 bore weighs about 6.5 lbs.

NIB	Exc.	V.G.	Good	Fair	Poor
1300	975	800	600	400	200

Falcon

This is an over/under gun in either 12 or 20 gauge 3" chambers. Choice of 26" or 28" barrels with ventilated rib and choke tubes. Checkered walnut stock with pistol grip. Case colored scroll engraved receiver. Single selective trigger. Automatic ejectors. Recoil pad is standard. Weight is about 7.25 lbs. for the 12 gauge and 7 lbs. for the 20 gauge.

NIB	Exc.	V.G.	Good	Fair	Poor
1200	900	875	500	300	150

Falcon Sporting

Similar to the Falcon but offered only in 12 gauge with 2.75" chambers. Choice of 2" or 30" ventilated rib barrels with 5 chokes tubes. Barrels are ported. Checkered walnut stock with schnabel forearm. Weight is about 7.7 lbs.

NIB	Exc.	V.G.	Good	Fair	Poor
1250	950	775	475	275	125

Silver Eagle

This over/under gun is chambered for either the 12 or 20 gauge 3" shell. Fitted with 26" or 28" vent rib barrels with choke tubes. Checkered walnut stock with pistol grip. Single selective trigger. Blued box lock receiver. Recoil is standard. Weight for 12 gauge is about 7.2 lbs. and 6.75 lbs. for the 20 gauge.

NIB	Exc.	V.G.	Good	Fair	Poor
490	375	300	250	200	125

Silver Eagle II

Similar to the Silver Eagle above with the addition of automatic ejectors.

NIB	Exc.	V.G.	Good	Fair	Poor
590	425	275	225	175	100

200 Series

This is a series of semi-automatic shotgun chambered for 12, 16, 20, 28 gauge as well as the .410 bore. The 12, 16, and 20 gauge guns are offered with choice of 26" or 28" vent rib barrels with choke tubes. The 28 and .410 are available in 26" barrels only. All gauges are offered with a choice of walnut or synthetic stocks. The 20 gauge gun is offered in a youth model with shortened stock. All gauges have 3" chambers except for the 28 gauge with 2.75" chambers. Weights range from 7.4 lbs. to 6.5 lbs. **NOTE:** Add $70 for walnut stock.

NIB	Exc.	V.G.	Good	Fair	Poor
390	290	225	200	100	75

300 SM Series

This semi-automatic series is offered in 12 gauge only with 3.5" chambers. Choice of 24", 26", or 28" vent rib barrels with choke tubes. Synthetic stock. Weights are about 7.3 lbs.

NIB	Exc.	V.G.	Good	Fair	Poor
420	315	250	225	175	100

BUCO
Germany
Gas Pistol

This odd firearm looks more like a telescope than a pistol. It is chambered for a 10.55mm gas cartridge and is a single-shot. Overall it is approximately 5.5" long in its open or cocked position. The barrel is smooth bore and 3.75" in length. This pistol has no sights and no safety—one simply pulls the inner tube back much like extending a telescope, unscrews the end cap, inserts the round, and screws the cap back into place. When it is needed, a thumbnail is used to depress the sear and fire the pistol. They are marked on the end cap "Buco DRGM". No more information is available as to quantity or year of manufacture.

NIB	Exc.	V.G.	Good	Fair	Poor
—	—	650	500	350	150

BUDISCHOWSKY
Norton Armament Corp.
Mt. Clemens, Michigan
TP-70

A .22 or .25 ACP caliber semi-automatic pistol with a 2.5" barrel, fixed sights and 6-shot magazine. Stainless steel with plastic grips. Manufactured between 1973 and 1977.

NOTE: The German-designed Budischowsky was originally made in Michigan by Norton Armament Corp. Michigan-made Budischowsky's are considered better quality than later examples made in Florida and Utah. Deduct 15% for non-Michigan manufacture.

.22 Rimfire Caliber

NIB	Exc.	V.G.	Good	Fair	Poor
550	425	350	300	225	150

.25 ACP Caliber

NIB	Exc.	V.G.	Good	Fair	Poor
525	400	325	275	175	125

BUL TRANSMARK LTD.
Tel-Aviv, Israel
Model M5

Introduced for the first time in the U.S. in 1996 this semi-automatic pistol bears a resemblance to the Model 1911. The frame is polymer and the slide is stainless steel. Available in 9mm, .38 Super, .40 S&W, and .45 ACP. Magazine limited to 10 rounds.

NIB	Exc.	V.G.	Good	Fair	Poor
750	600	450	350	200	100

BULLARD REPEATING ARMS CO.
Springfield, Massachusetts

Designed by James H. Bullard, the rifles listed were manufactured in competition with those produced by the Whitney Arms Company and the Winchester Repeating Arms Company. Approximately 12,000 were made between 1886 and 1890.

Small Frame

A .32-40 and .38-45 caliber lever action rifle with a 26" octagonal barrel and either a half or full length magazine tube. Blued or case hardened with a walnut stock. The receiver is stamped "Bullard Repeating Arms Company/Springfield, Mass., U.S.A. Pat. Aug. 16, 1881". The caliber is marked on top of the frame.

Courtesy Milwaukee Public Museum, Milwaukee, Wisconsin

NIB	Exc.	V.G.	Good	Fair	Poor
—	—	4000	2050	675	300

Large Frame

A .40-75 through .45-85 caliber lever action rifle with 28" octagonal barrel. Other features and markings as above. Can be custom ordered in .50-95 and .50-115.

NIB	Exc.	V.G.	Good	Fair	Poor
—	—	5150	2500	875	400

Carbine

A .45-70 caliber lever action rifle with a 22" round barrel and a sliding dust cover on the receiver. Marking and finish as above.

NIB	Exc.	V.G.	Good	Fair	Poor
—	—	7950	3800	1500	500

Musket

A .45-70 caliber lever action rifle with a 30" round barrel with a full-length stock secured by two barrel bands. There is a rod under the barrel, military sights, and the same sliding cover on the receiver as found on the Carbine. There have been examples noted without the manufacturer's markings.

NIB	Exc.	V.G.	Good	Fair	Poor
—	—	7500	3500	1500	500

BULLDOG
SINGLE-SHOT PISTOL
Connecticut Arms & Manufacturing Co.
Naubuc, Connecticut
Bulldog

A .44 or .50 caliber single-shot spur trigger pistol with 4" or 6" barrels, and a pivoting breechblock that moves to the left for loading. Blued, case hardened and stamped "Connecticut Arms & Manf. Co. Naubuc Conn. Patented Oct. 25, 1864". There were only a few hundred manufactured, and the .50 caliber, 6" barreled versions would be worth an additional 40 percent. Produced between 1866 and 1868.

NIB	Exc.	V.G.	Good	Fair	Poor
—	—	1650	675	275	150

BURGESS GUN CO.
Buffalo, New York
Also See—Colt and Whitney

One of the most prolific 19th century designers was Andrew Burgess who established his own company in 1892. The Burgess Gun Company manufactured slide action shotguns and rifles operated by a unique pistol grip prior to their being purchased by the Winchester Repeating Arms Company in 1899. Arms based on Burgess' patents were manufactured by a variety of American gun makers. Serial numbers for all Burgess shotguns begin at 1000.

12 Gauge Slide Action Shotgun

A 12 gauge slide-action shotgun with a 28" or 30" barrel. Blued with a walnut stock. This model was available with 6 grades of engraving. The values listed are for the standard, plain model.

Burgess engraving grades (1-4)

NIB	Exc.	V.G.	Good	Fair	Poor
—	—	1700	700	250	125

Folding Shotgun

As above, with a 19.5" barrel that is hinged so that it may be folded back against the buttstock.

NIB	Exc.	V.G.	Good	Fair	Poor
—	—	4550	1750	650	300

Slide Action Rifle

An extremely rare rifle based upon the shotgun design described above. Manufactured in at least three calibers with varying barrel lengths. Blued with a walnut stock.

NIB	Exc.	V.G.	Good	Fair	Poor
—	—	3950	1500	500	250

BURGSMULLER, K.
Krelensen, Germany

Burgo

The Rohm RG10 under another name. It is a poor quality, inexpensive .38 caliber revolver. The examples marketed by Burgsmuller are so marked. **Virtually worthless.**

Regent

The Regent is a .22 caliber revolver that resembles the Colt Police Positive in appearance. It is of a higher quality than the Burgo. The manufacturer is not known.

NIB	Exc.	V.G.	Good	Fair	Poor
—	165	125	75	50	5

BURNSIDE RIFLE CO.
Bristol Firearms Co.
Providence, Rhode Island

Bristol, Rhode Island

This is a historically desirable firearm for Civil War collectors as the designer, Ambrose E. Burnside, was to become a well- known Union general. The rifle, of which there were four distinct models, was used quite extensively in the Civil War.This carbine was manufactured first by the Bristol Firearms Co., which made the entire production of the first model and also some of the second model. In 1862 the Burnside Firearms Co. was formed, and they produced the remainder of the second models and all of the third and fourth models. Production ceased entirely in 1865.

Burnside Carbine 1st Model

This model was produced by Bristol and was chambered for the .54 caliber. It is a breechloader that uses the percussion ignition

system but features a cartridge of sorts made of copper, and a tape priming device that was located inside the frame. It has a 22" round barrel with no fore-end and a walnut stock with inspector's cartouche. The finish is blued and case-colored, and the frame is stamped "Burnside's /Patent/March 25th/1856". There were approximately 250 1st Models manufactured.

NIB	Exc.	V.G.	Good	Fair	Poor
—	—	15000	6000	1500	500

2nd Model

The 2nd Model features an improved breechblock opening mechanism located inside the trigger guard. The barrel is 21" long, and the other features are similar to the 1st Model. They are marked either "Bristol Firearm Co." or "Burnside Rifle Co./ Providence-R.I.". The barrel is marked "Cast Steel 1861" and some of the breechblock devices are marked "G.P. Foster Pat./ April 10th 1860". There were approximately 1,500 2nd Models manufactured in 1861 and 1862.

Courtesy Milwaukee Public Museum, Milwaukee, Wisconsin

NIB	Exc.	V.G.	Good	Fair	Poor
—	—	5500	2500	750	300

3rd Model

This model differs from the 2nd Model in that it has a fore-end with a barrel band and a slightly modified hammer. The markings are the same as the Burnside-manufactured 2nd Models. There were approximately 2,000 produced in 1862.

NIB	Exc.	V.G.	Good	Fair	Poor
—	—	3500	1250	500	250

4th Model

This model differs from the others in that it features a hinged breech that permits simpler loading of the odd-shaped Burnside percussion cartridge. The frame is marked "Burnside's Patent/ Model of 1864". The other features are similar to the 3rd Model. There were approximately 50,000 manufactured between 1862 and 1865.

Courtesy Milwaukee Public Museum, Milwaukee, Wisconsin

NIB	Exc.	V.G.	Good	Fair	Poor
—	—	4000	2000	800	400

BUSHMASTER FIREARMS INTERNATIONAL
Ilion, New York

In 2006, Bushmaster was purchased by the Freedom Group, the parent company of Remington, Marlin/H&R, DPMS, Para USA and Dakota Arms. In 2011, the Bushmaster plant in Maine was closed and production moved to the Remington facility in Ilion, New York.

XM15-E2S Target Model

Furnished with a 20" heavy barrel and A-2 stock. Weight is 8.35 lbs. **NOTE:** Add $10 for 24" barrel and $20 for 26" barrel. Add $75 for A3 carry handle.

NIB	Exc.	V.G.	Good	Fair	Poor
800	675	550	400	300	200

XM15-E2S V-Match Competition Rifle

This model is a specially designed competition rifle with 20", 24", or 26" barrel lengths. Fitted with a black anodized aluminum handguard. Weight is about 8.1 lbs. **NOTE:** Add $75 for A3 carry handle.

NIB	Exc.	V.G.	Good	Fair	Poor
950	800	700	450	350	250

XM15-E2S V-Match Carbine

As above but with 16" barrel. Weight is about 6.9 lbs. **NOTE:** Add $75 for A3 carry handle.

NIB	Exc.	V.G.	Good	Fair	Poor
900	700	575	450	350	250

XM15-E2S Shorty Carbine

This "post-ban" model of the M16 is a gas-operated semi-automatic rifle chambered for the .223 Remington cartridge. It is fitted with a heavy 16" barrel and a 30-round magazine. Overall length is 35" and empty weight is 6.72 lbs. **NOTE:** Add $50 for fluted barrel. Add $75 for A3-type carry handle.

NIB	Exc.	V.G.	Good	Fair	Poor
—	675	550	450	300	200

XM15-E2S Dissipator

Similar to the above model with a 16" barrel but fitted with a longer plastic handguard to give a longer sight radius. Weight is 7.2 lbs. **NOTE:** Add $75 for A3 carry handle.

NIB	Exc.	V.G.	Good	Fair	Poor
950	775	600	450	300	200

M4 Post-Ban Carbine

Introduced in 2001 this rifle features a 14.5" barrel with permanently attached Mini Y Comp muzzlebrake (total length 16") and pinned, fixed-length Tele-style stock. Chambered for .223 caliber. M16A2 rear sight. Supplied with 10-round magazine. Weight is about 6.6 lbs.

NIB	Exc.	V.G.	Good	Fair	Poor
1050	900	750	450	300	200

M4A3 Post-Ban Carbine

Same as above but with removable carry handle. Introduced in 2001.199

NIB	Exc.	V.G.	Good	Fair	Poor
1125	975	825	500	400	300

DCM Competition Rifle

This model features a 20" extra heavy barrel with free floating fore-end. Competition sights and trigger. Supplied with buttstock weight and hard carrying case. 10-round magazine.

NIB	Exc.	V.G.	Good	Fair	Poor
1350	1075	800	600	500	350

11.5" Barrel Carbine

AR-style carbine chambered in 5.56/.223. Features include an 11.5" chrome-lined barrel with permanently attached BATF-approved 5.5" flash suppressor, fixed or removable carry handle, optional optics rail, 30-round magazine. Overall length 31.625". Weight: 6.46 or 6.81 lbs.

NIB	Exc.	V.G.	Good	Fair	Poor
900	775	600	450	300	200

Heavy-Barreled Carbine

AR-style semi-automatic carbine chambered in 5.56/.223. Features include a chrome-lined, heavy profile 16" vanadium steel barrel, fixed or removable carry handle, six-position telestock. Overall length 32.5". Weight: 6.93 lbs. to 7.28 lbs.

NIB	Exc.	V.G.	Good	Fair	Poor
1000	850	700	550	300	200

Modular Carbine

AR-style carbine chambered in 5.56/.223. Features include 16" chrome-lined chrome-moly vanadium steel barrel, skeleton stock or six-position telestock, clamp-on front sight and detachable flip-up dual aperture rear, 30-round magazine. Overall length 36.25". Weight: 7.3 lbs.

NIB	Exc.	V.G.	Good	Fair	Poor
1450	1200	1000	750	400	250

M17S Bullpup

This model is a gas-operated semi-automatic rifle in the bull-pup design. Chambered for the .223 cartridge and fitted with a 21.5" barrel. Weight is 8.2 lbs.

NIB	Exc.	V.G.	Good	Fair	Poor
800	675	500	400	300	200

Gas Piston Rifle

Semi-automatic AR-style rifle chambered in .223. Features include a 16" barrel, telescoping stock, carry handle, 30-round magazine, and piston assembly rather than direct gas impingement. Overall length 32.5". Weight: 7.46 lbs.

NIB	Exc.	V.G.	Good	Fair	Poor
1750	1375	1050	800	650	300

6.8 SPC Carbine

AR-style semi-automatic rifle chambered in 6.8 SPC. Features include 16" M4 profile barrel with Izzy muzzle brake, 26-round magazine, six-position telestock. Available in A2 (fixed carry handle) or A3 (removable carry handle) configuration. Overall length 32.75". Weight: 6.57 lbs. Also chambered in 7.62x39mm.

NIB	Exc.	V.G.	Good	Fair	Poor
1200	1150	950	800	650	300

Carbon 15 9mm Carbine

Semi-automatic carbine chambered in 9mm Parabellum. Carbon fiber frame, 16" steel barrel, six-position telescoping stock, 30-round detachable magazine. Introduced 2006.

NIB	Exc.	V.G.	Good	Fair	Poor
1000	850	700	550	475	300

Carbon 15 Top Loading Rifle

Semi-automatic rifle chambered in .223. Carbon fiber frame, 16" steel barrel, retractable stock, Picatinny rail, 10-round fixed magazine. Based on AR-15. Introduced 2006.

NIB	Exc.	V.G.	Good	Fair	Poor
1000	850	700	550	475	300

Predator

Semi-automatic rifle chambered in .223. 20" DCM-type barrel, fixed composite buttstock, 2-stage competition trigger, Picatinny rail, 1/2" scope risers. Based on AR-15. Introduced 2006.

NIB	Exc.	V.G.	Good	Fair	Poor
1100	900	750	600	525	325

Carbon 15 .22 Rimfire Rifle

Similar to Shorty carbine but chambered in .22 LR. Blowback; 10-round magazine. MSRP: $790.

NIB	Exc.	V.G.	Good	Fair	Poor
625	495	350	275	200	150

.308 Hunter

Designed for the hunter, chambered in .308 Winchester with a 20" heavy-fluted barrel with chrome lined bore and chamber. Features include 5-round magazine, mid-length gas system, two .75" mini risers for optics mounting, Hogue rubberized pistol grip, standard A2 stock. Vista Hunter has A2 grip. Approx. weight 8.5 pounds. **NOTE:** Add $100 for Vista Hunter if NIB.

NIB	Exc.	V.G.	Good	Fair	Poor
1400	1100	925	775	500	300

ORC Series

The Optics Ready Carbine series is for shooters who wish to add various optical holograph, red dot or scope sights. Chambered in .223/5.56 with magazine capacity of 30 rounds or .308 with 20-round magazine. The gas piston system taps gas from the barrel much like AK and FAL designs. Provides a cleaner operation with less recoil. Detented plug in the gas block allows for easy cleaning. Barrel length is 16", weight is 6.6 pounds (.223) to 7.75 pounds (.308). **NOTE:** Add $60 for .308 chambering.

NIB	Exc.	V.G.	Good	Fair	Poor
1125	965	825	700	500	300

.450 Carbine

Chambered for the .450 Bushmaster cartridge, providing big-bore power in the AR platform. Developed with Hornady Mfg. the cartridge propels a 250-grain bullet at 2200 fps, ideal for most North American big game. Barrel length of 16 or 20", A3 flattop receiver with Picatinny rail, weight is approx. 8.5 pounds.

NIB	Exc.	V.G.	Good	Fair	Poor
1200	1025	900	750	550	350

Bushmaster AK Carbine

AR-type rifle with AK-type muzzle brake and permanently pinned suppressor. 5.56 Nato caliber.

NIB	Exc.	V.G.	Good	Fair	Poor
1100	950	800	650	300	200

Bushmaster .300 AAC Blackout

AR-type rifle chambered for .300 AAC cartridge, developed by Advanced Armament Corporation, which is now part of the Freedom Group that owns Bushmaster. The round's ballistics are similar to the 7.62x39 and the .300 Whisper wildcat. The .300 AAC is factory loaded by Remington, including a sub-sonic load. It is compatible with AR-15 magazines.

NIB	Exc.	V.G.	Good	Fair	Poor
1300	1050	875	700	300	200

BA50 .50 BMG Rifle and Carbine

A bolt-action, 10-round repeater intended for long-range target shooting. 30" barrel, muzzle brake. Carbine has 20" barrel.

NIB	Exc.	V.G.	Good	Fair	Poor
5000	4200	3700	3000	—	—

Carbon 15 .223 Pistol

AR-style semi-automatic pistol chambered in 5.56/.223. Features include a 7.5" stainless steel barrel, carbon composite receiver, shortened handguard, full-length optics rail, A2-type front sight with dual-aperture flip-up rear. 30-round magazine. Overall length 20". Weight: 2.88 lbs.

NIB	Exc.	V.G.	Good	Fair	Poor
800	700	550	400	300	200

Carbon-15 9mm Pistol

Operating controls similar to AR-type rifles, 30 round capacity. Weight with loaded magazine 5.5 lbs. Carbon fiber receiver, fore-end and grip with Chrome Moly steel barrel. Full length Picatinny rail.

NIB	Exc.	V.G.	Good	Fair	Poor
800	700	550	400	300	200

Type 97 Pistol

Similar to above but without handguard.

NIB	Exc.	V.G.	Good	Fair	Poor
750	650	500	400	300	200

BUTLER, WM. S.
Rocky Hill, Connecticut

Single-Shot Pistol

A .36 caliber single-shot percussion pocket pistol with a 2.5" barrel and the frame and grip made in one piece. The frame marked "Wm. S. Butler's Patent/Patented Feb.3, 1857".

NIB	Exc.	V.G.	Good	Fair	Poor
—	—	975	385	150	50

BUTTERFIELD, JESSE
Philadelphia, Pennsylvania

Butterfield Army Revolver

A .41 caliber revolver with a 7" octagonal barrel, an unfluted 5-shot cylinder and features a special priming device, a disk that was loaded in front of the trigger guard. A brass frame, blued with walnut grips. The frame is stamped "Butterfield's Patent Dec. 11, 1855/Phila.". Approximately 650 manufactured in 1861 and 1862.

Courtesy Milwaukee Public Museum, Milwaukee, Wisconsin

NIB	Exc.	V.G.	Good	Fair	Poor
—	—	6000	2250	875	450

Butterfield Pocket Pistol

A .41 caliber single-shot percussion pistol with a 2" to 3.5" barrel. German silver with walnut stocks. The lock is marked "Butterfield's/Patent Dec 11, 1855". Extremely rare. Manufactured in the 1850s.

NIB	Exc.	V.G.	Good	Fair	Poor
—	—	9000	4250	1650	1000

C

CABANAS INDUSTRIAS S.A.
Aguilas, Mexico

This company manufactures a variety of bolt-action single-shot rifles that utilize .22 caliber blanks to propel a .177 caliber pellet. Scarce, but not especially valuable.

Mini-82 Youth

NIB	Exc.	V.G.	Good	Fair	Poor
75	65	50	40	30	20

R-83 Larger Youth

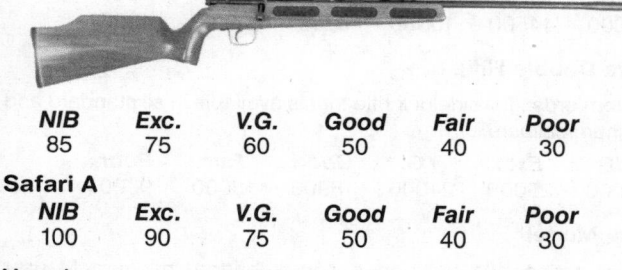

NIB	Exc.	V.G.	Good	Fair	Poor
85	75	60	50	40	30

Safari A

NIB	Exc.	V.G.	Good	Fair	Poor
100	90	75	50	40	30

Varmint

NIB	Exc.	V.G.	Good	Fair	Poor
125	110	90	75	—	35

Espronceda IV

NIB	Exc.	V.G.	Good	Fair	Poor
125	110	90	75	50	35

Leyre

NIB	Exc.	V.G.	Good	Fair	Poor
140	125	100	85	65	50

Master

NIB	Exc.	V.G.	Good	Fair	Poor
150	130	110	100	75	60

CALICO
Cleveland, Ohio
See—American Industries, Inc.

CAMEX-BLASER USA, INC.
Ft. Worth, Texas
See—Blaser Jagdwaffen

CAMPO GIRO
Eibar, Spain

Esperanza y Unceta Model 1904

Designed by Lt. Col. Venancio Aguirre. This pistol was produced in limited numbers.

NIB	Exc.	V.G.	Good	Fair	Poor
—	3000	2000	1500	1000	800

Model 1910

Similar to the above, in 9mm Largo. Tested, but not adopted, by the Spanish army.

NIB	Exc.	V.G.	Good	Fair	Poor
—	2000	1500	1000	800	600

Model 1913

An improved version of the above, about 1,300 made.

Courtesy James Rankin

NIB	Exc.	V.G.	Good	Fair	Poor
—	1500	1250	850	600	500

Model 1913/16

An improved version of the above, about 13,000 built.

Courtesy James Rankin

NIB	Exc.	V.G.	Good	Fair	Poor
—	2000	1550	1000	600	350

CARACAL

Caracal-F

Chambered for the 9mm Parabellum, the Caracal has a DAO trigger and is striker-fired. Features include a polymer frame, steel slide, ambidextrous magazine releases and an 18-round magazine. Weight is 26.5 ounces, barrel length is 4.1", finish is matte blue. Caracal-C is compact variation with 3.5" barrel, weighs 24.7 oz. Made in the United Arab Emirates. Introduced in 2011.

CARACAL "F"

NIB	Exc.	V.G.	Good	Fair	Poor
535	465	400	300	200	100

CARD, S. W.
Location Unknown

Under Hammer Pistol

A .34 caliber single-shot percussion pocket pistol with a 7.75" half octagonal barrel marked "S.W. Card" and "Cast Steel". Blued with walnut grips.

NIB	Exc.	V.G.	Good	Fair	Poor
—	—	1500	450	150	50

CARLTON, M.
Haverhill, New Hampshire

Under Hammer Pistol

A .34 caliber percussion under hammer single-shot pistol with a 3.5" to 7.75" half-octagonal barrel marked "M. Carleton & Co." Browned with walnut grips. Active 1830s and 1840s.

NIB	Exc.	V.G.	Good	Fair	Poor
—	—	1800	600	200	100

CASARTELLI, CARLO
Brescia, Italy

Sidelock Shotgun

Custom order sidelock shotgun that is available in any gauge, barrel length, choke, automatic ejectors and single-selective trigger and choice of engraving style.

NIB	Exc.	V.G.	Good	Fair	Poor
16000	14500	10500	8250	6000	4000

Kenya Double Rifle

Custom order, full sidelock rifle that is available in all standard and magnum calibers.

NIB	Exc.	V.G.	Good	Fair	Poor
33000	29000	24000	18900	13000	9000

Africa Model

A bolt-action rifle built on a square-bridge magnum Mauser action. It is chambered for the heavy magnum calibers and can be taken down for transport. The other features are on a custom order basis.

NIB	Exc.	V.G.	Good	Fair	Poor
9750	8800	7500	5750	4750	3750

Safari Model

Built on a standard Mauser bolt-action and is chambered for the non-magnum calibers.

NIB	Exc.	V.G.	Good	Fair	Poor
8000	7200	5800	4500	3250	2500

CASE WILLARD & CO.
New Hartford, Connecticut

Under Hammer Pistol

A .31 caliber single-shot percussion pistol with a 3" half-octagonal barrel marked "Case Willard & Co./New Hartford Conn." Blued, brass frame with walnut grips.

NIB	Exc.	V.G.	Good	Fair	Poor
—	—	1400	550	200	100

CASPIAN ARMS, LTD.
Hardwick, Vermont

This company is primarily a 1911 component manufacturer.

Vietnam Commemorative

Government Model engraved by J.J. Adams and nickel-plated. The walnut grips have a branch service medallion inlaid, and gold plating was available for an additional $350. There were 1,000 manufactured in 1986.

NIB	Exc.	V.G.	Good	Fair	Poor
1800	1350	950	650	475	300

CASULL ARMS, INC.
Afton, Wyoming

CA 2000

Chambered for the .22 LR cartridge this stainless steel revolver has a 5-round cylinder with fold-up trigger. Double-action-only. Palm sized. The most recently produced "Velo-Dog". Discontinued.

NIB	Exc.	V.G.	Good	Fair	Poor
550	425	350	250	200	175

CA 3800

Chambered for the .38 Casull cartridge (124 gr. 1800+fps) this pistol is fitted with a 6" match barrel and has a magazine capacity of 8 rounds. Full-length two-piece guide rod. Checkering on front strap and mainspring housing is 20 lpi. Match trigger and numerous other special features. Weight is about 40 oz. Introduced in 2000. Discontinued. **NOTE:** Add $300 for extra .45 ACP barrel.

NIB	Exc.	V.G.	Good	Fair	Poor
2600	2050	1700	1200	650	300

CENTURY GUN COMPANY
Evansville, Knightstown & Greenfield, Indiana

Former manufacturer of large-caliber revolvers made in Evansville or Knightstown, Indiana between 1973 and 2001, or Greenfield, Indiana between 2002 and 2004.

Model 100

Single-action revolver with six-round capacity, chambered originally for .45-70 Government and later for .30-30 Win., .375 Win., .444 Marlin, .50-70 and .50-110. Barrel lengths from 6.5" to 12", wight from 5.5- to 6 lbs. Adjustable sights, crossbolt safety. Prices shown are for .45-70 caliber. **NOTE:** Add 100 percent for .50-110 caliber, 20 percent for others. For early production .45-70 guns marked Evansville, Indiana, add 100 to 200 percent, if in excellent condition.

NIB	Exc.	V.G.	Good	Fair	Poor
1200	1100	900	750	400	200

CENTURY INTERNATIONAL ARMS CO.
Delray Beach, Florida

Century International Arms is a leading importer of military firearms. It was founded in 1961 in Albans, Vermont, moved to Boca Raton, Florida in 1997 and to Delray Beach in 2004. Many models are original military surplus, others have been re-stocked or re-barreled to make satisfactory hunting rifles. Inventory changes frequently and some models are imported in limited quantities. The company also imports new handguns, rifles and shotguns from various manufacturers and countries. The listed firearms represent only a few of the many models imported recently or in the past.

Centurion Over/Under Shotgun

This is a new shotgun in 12, 20, and 28 gauge as well as .410 bore with 2.75" chambers. The walnut stock is checkered. The receiver is blue. Offered in 28" vent-rib barrels in full and modified chokes. Weight is about 7.35 lbs. for the 12 gauge and 5.3 lbs. for the .410 bore.

NIB	Exc.	V.G.	Good	Fair	Poor
—	375	325	225	175	125

Centurion 98 Sporter

This is refinished and rebuilt on a surplus German Mauser 98 action with new commercial 22" barrel. No sights. A synthetic stock with recoil pad is standard. Chambered for .270 or .30-06. Weighs about 7 lbs. 13 oz.

NIB	Exc.	V.G.	Good	Fair	Poor
—	300	250	175	150	100

Century Centurion 14

This bolt-action rifle uses an Enfield Pattern 14 action drilled and tapped for scope mount. Barrel is 24" and chambered for 7mm Rem. Magnum. Walnut stock is checkered with pistol grip and Monte Carlo comb. No sights.

NIB	Exc.	V.G.	Good	Fair	Poor
350	300	250	175	150	100

Enfield Sporter No. I Mark III

This refinished rifle has a cut down Sporter-style stock. Action and sights are original. Caliber is .303.

NIB	Exc.	V.G.	Good	Fair	Poor
—	250	200	150	100	50

Enfield Sporter No. 4 Mark I

With new walnut stock.

LEE ENFIELD
No 4 Mark I Sporter
R1682 / 10LE41S
Nov 11, 1992

NIB	Exc.	V.G.	Good	Fair	Poor
—	260	210	150	100	50

TOZ-17

An original Russian rifle chambered for the .22 LR. Has a 21" barrel and 5-round magazine. Checkered stock and iron sights. Weighs about 5.4 lbs.

NIB	Exc.	V.G.	Good	Fair	Poor
—	175	135	110	50	40

TOZ-17-1

Same as above with hooded front sight and tangent rear sight. Receiver is grooved for scope mount.

NIB	Exc.	V.G.	Good	Fair	Poor
—	185	145	120	60	50

Mexican Mauser Model 1910 Sporter

This rifle has been converted from a military rifle to a sporter by cutting down the stock. The metal is refinished and the barrel has been rebored and rechambered for the .30-06 cartridge. The box magazine holds 5 rounds. Barrel is 23" and rifle weighs about 8 lbs.

NIB	Exc.	V.G.	Good	Fair	Poor
—	185	145	120	60	50

FAL Sporter

This is a refinished FAL receiver and barrel installed in a synthetic thumbhole stock. The flash suppressor and bayonet lug have been removed. Barrel is 20.75" and weight is approximately 10 lbs.

NIB	Exc.	V.G.	Good	Fair	Poor
1000	850	650	450	350	150

M-14 Rifle

Imported from China by Century International this rifle features a 22" barrel chambered for the .308 Win. cartridge. Stock is walnut with rubber pad. Parkerized finish. Weight is approximately 8.25 lbs.

NIB	Exc.	V.G.	Good	Fair	Poor
750	650	550	300	150	100

Tiger Dragunov Rifle

This is a shortened version of the Russian SVD sniper rifle. Fitted with a 20.8" barrel and chambered for the 7.62x54R cartridge the rifle is sold with a 5-round magazine and a 4x range finding scope. Imported from Russia. Weight is about 8.5 lbs.

NIB	Exc.	V.G.	Good	Fair	Poor
1000	850	700	500	350	150

GP WASR 10 Rifle

AK-47 design in 7.62x39mm caliber. Comes with two double-stack, 30-round magazines. Also available with 5- or 10-round fixed magazine. New. Made by Romarm in Romania.

NIB	Exc.	V.G.	Good	Fair	Poor
500	400	325	275	200	100

Shooter's Arms 1911 Pistol

Standard 1911-A .45 ACP design in full-size version with 5" barrel or Commodore model with 4.25" barrel. Magazine capacity if 8 shots. New. Manufactured in the Philippines.

NIB	Exc.	V.G.	Good	Fair	Poor
450	375	325	275	200	100

Saiga Semi-auto Shotgun

A 12 gauge shotgun based on AK-47 design. Five-round capacity. Weight 7.9 lbs. Has a 19" barrel, black synthetic stock, sight rail. Made in Russia.

NIB	Exc.	V.G.	Good	Fair	Poor
600	500	425	375	200	100

S.A.R. Series

AK-47 style semi-automatic rifle with wood stock and forearm. Capacity, 10 or 30 rounds. Chambered for 7.62x39mm, 5.45x39mm, or .223. Made in Romania by Romarm.

NIB	Exc.	V.G.	Good	Fair	Poor
800	650	500	350	200	100

CETME
Madrid, Spain

Cetme Autoloading Rifle

A .308 caliber semi-automatic rifle with a fluted chamber, a 17.74" barrel, an aperture rear sight and a 20-round detachable magazine. Black with a military-style wood stock. It is identical in appearance to the H&K 91 assault rifle.

NIB	Exc.	V.G.	Good	Fair	Poor
1500	1100	800	600	350	200

CHAMPLIN FIREARMS
Enid, Oklahoma

Champlin Firearms Company manufactures custom order rifles built to the customer's specifications. Prospective purchasers are advised to secure a qualified appraisal prior to purchase.

Bolt-Action Rifle

These arms featured round or octagonal barrels, set triggers, a variety of sights and well figured walnut stocks.

NIB	Exc.	V.G.	Good	Fair	Poor
5500	4500	3500	2900	2200	1500

CHAPMAN, CHARLES
Chattanooga, Tennessee

Chapman produced a limited number of percussion carbines and rifles during the Civil War. Carbines had an overall length of 39.5" and .54 caliber barrels 24" in length. Their furniture was of brass. Chapman rifles resembled the U.S. Model 1841 rifle, but did not have patchboxes. Overall length 48.5", barrel length 33", caliber .58. Chapman rifles and carbines are marked "C. CHAPMAN" on the lockplates. Prospective purchasers are strongly advised to secure an expert appraisal prior to acquisition.

Courtesy Milwaukee Public Museum, Milwaukee, Wisconsin

NIB	Exc.	V.G.	Good	Fair	Poor
—	—	38000	17500	3000	1000

CHAPMAN, G. & J.
Philadelphia, Pennsylvania
Chapman Pocket Revolver

A .32 caliber revolver with a 4" round barrel and 7-shot cylinder. The frame is made of brass while the barrel and cylinder are of steel. The barrel is marked "G.& J. Chapman/Philada/Patent Applied For/1861". Manufactured during the1860s.

NIB	Exc.	V.G.	Good	Fair	Poor
—	—	2550	1050	550	275

CHAPUIS ARMES
France
RGP Shotgun

A 16, or 20 gauge boxlock shotgun. Most options are available on order.

NIB	Exc.	V.G.	Good	Fair	Poor
3000	2500	2000	1800	1250	900

RG Express Model 89 Rifle

A 7x65R, 8x57 JRS, 9.3x74R, and .375 Holland & Holland caliber sidelock, double-barreled rifle. The other features are at the customer's order.

NIB	Exc.	V.G.	Good	Fair	Poor
6500	5750	4800	4000	3000	1500

Utility Grade Express Model Rifle

A side-by-side boxlock-action double rifle with case colored or coin finish receiver. Offered in a variety of calibers: 9.3x74R, 8x57JRS, 7x65R, 8x75RS, and .30-06. Checkered walnut stock with pistol grip.

NIB	Exc.	V.G.	Good	Fair	Poor
6000	4800	4000	3000	1500	750

St. Bonnet Model Shotgun

This model is a side-by-side shotgun with sideplates on a boxlock-action. Scroll engraved case colored receiver. Straight grip stock and double triggers. Offered in 12, 16, or 20 gauge.

NIB	Exc.	V.G.	Good	Fair	Poor
4000	3250	2000	1250	800	500

Super Orion Rifle Series

This series of over/under rifles was offered in a wide range of European calibers plus, .30-06 and .300 Win. Magnum. Several grades were available. Prices shown are for C-15 model which was imported in the 1990s. These rifles also were offered with a set of shotgun barrels. Currently imported by William Larkin Moore in Scottsdale, Arizona.

NIB	Exc.	V.G.	Good	Fair	Poor
8000	7000	5200	4000	2000	1000

African PH Model Grade I Rifle

A boxlock-action double rifle offered in a wide variety of calibers. Caliber determines retail price. Hand engraved case colored receiver. Pistol grip stock with European-style cheekpiece.

.470 Nitro & .416 Rigby

NIB	Exc.	V.G.	Good	Fair	Poor
12500	9500	8500	6000	3750	700

.375 H&H

NIB	Exc.	V.G.	Good	Fair	Poor
9500	7500	6250	4000	2500	600

.300 Win. Magnum

NIB	Exc.	V.G.	Good	Fair	Poor
8500	6500	5250	3000	1750	500

.30-06, 9.3x74R

NIB	Exc.	V.G.	Good	Fair	Poor
8000	6000	5000	3000	1750	500

African PH Model Grade II

Same as above but with master engraving with game scenes. Add 20 percent to 25 percent to above NIB prices.

CHARTER ARMS
Shelton, Connecticut

Founded in 1962, Charter Arms has had several name and location changes. Original production was in Stratford, Connecticut until 1991 and in Ansonia, Connecticut from 1992 to 1996. From 1998 to 2005 the company name was Charter 2000. It was located in Shelton, Connecticut, where the current company, again known as Charter Arms is headquartered.

Bulldog

Chambered for the .44 Special cartridge and fitted with a 2.5" barrel. Stainless steel or blued frame with 5-round cylinder. Round butt and fixed sights. Weight is 21 oz. **NOTE:** For stainless steel add $20.

NIB	Exc.	V.G.	Good	Fair	Poor
320	250	175	125	75	50

Police Bulldog

This model is chambered for the .38 Special cartridge and fitted with a 4" bull or tapered barrel. Full rubber grips. Blued finish. Weight is about 24 oz. Introduced in 2002.

NIB	Exc.	V.G.	Good	Fair	Poor
320	250	175	125	75	50

Undercover

Chambered for the .38 Special cartridge and fitted with a 2" barrel. Stainless steel or blued frame with 5-round cylinder. Round butt. Weight is about 20 oz. **NOTE:** For stainless steel add $20.

NIB	Exc.	V.G.	Good	Fair	Poor
280	225	175	150	100	75

Off Duty

This .38 Special revolver has an aluminum frame and 2" barrel. Combat grips. Double-action-only. Weight is about 12 oz. Introduced in 2002.

NIB	Exc.	V.G.	Good	Fair	Poor
350	250	200	150	100	75

Pathfinder

This is a stainless steel revolver chambered for the .22 caliber cartridge. Fitted with a 2" barrel and wood grips. Weight is about 17 oz. Introduced in 2002.

NIB	Exc.	V.G.	Good	Fair	Poor
265	200	165	125	75	50

Mag Pug

Chambered for the .357 Magnum cartridge and fitted with a 2.2" ported barrel. Stainless steel or blued frame. Weight is about 24 oz.

NIB	Exc.	V.G.	Good	Fair	Poor
320	250	175	125	75	50

Dixie Derringer

Stainless steel with 1.125" barrels. Chambered for the .22 LR or .22 Magnum cartridges. Weight is about 8 oz. Introduced in 2002. **NOTE:** For .22 Magnum model add $10.

NIB	Exc.	V.G.	Good	Fair	Poor
190	150	125	100	50	25

Field King Rifle

Available with blue or stainless steel finish and chambered for .25-06, .270, .30-06, or .308 with 22" barrel. Magazine capacity is 4 rounds. Checkered fiberglass stock with cheekpiece. Weight is about 8 lbs.

NIB	Exc.	V.G.	Good	Fair	Poor
300	225	175	125	75	50

Field King Carbine

Same as above but with 18" barrel with compensator (20" total) and chambered for .308.

NIB	Exc.	V.G.	Good	Fair	Poor
350	250	200	150	75	50

CHARTER ARMS CORP.
Ansonia, Connecticut/Shelton, Connecticut

Police Undercover

This model is chambered for the .38 Special or the .32 Magnum. It is fitted with a 2" barrel in blue or stainless steel finish. Offered with walnut or rubber grips. The overall length is 6.25" and weight is between 16 oz. and 19 oz. depending on grips and finish.

NIB	Exc.	V.G.	Good	Fair	Poor
350	300	175	150	100	75

Undercover Stainless Steel

As above, in stainless steel.

NIB	Exc.	V.G.	Good	Fair	Poor
390	325	225	175	125	100

Undercover Lite

Similar to Undercover but with lightweight aluminum alloy frame. Frame finishes: black/stainless, red/stainless, and red/black.

NIB	Exc.	V.G.	Good	Fair	Poor
390	325	225	175	125	100

Undercoverette

As above, with a thinner grip and in .32 S&W.

NIB	Exc.	V.G.	Good	Fair	Poor
350	300	250	125	100	75

Bulldog

Similar to the Undercover model, but in .44 Special caliber with a 2.5" or 3" barrel and 5-shot cylinder. Discontinued; replaced by Target and Pug models.

NIB	Exc.	V.G.	Good	Fair	Poor
325	275	225	175	125	100

Stainless Steel Bulldog

As above, in stainless steel.

NIB	Exc.	V.G.	Good	Fair	Poor
350	300	250	200	150	125

Target Bulldog

As above, in .357 Magnum or .44 Special with a 4" barrel fitted with adjustable rear sights. Blued with walnut grips. Manufactured from 1986 to 1988, later reintroduced.

NIB	Exc.	V.G.	Good	Fair	Poor
350	300	250	200	150	125

Pathfinder

Similar to the above, but in .22 LR or .22 Magnum caliber with a 2", 3", or 6" barrel with adjustable sights.

NIB	Exc.	V.G.	Good	Fair	Poor
350	300	250	200	150	125

Pathfinder Stainless Steel

As above, in stainless steel.

NIB	Exc.	V.G.	Good	Fair	Poor
360	310	260	210	160	135

Bulldog Pug

Chambered for the .44 Special cartridge it is fitted with a 2.5" barrel. Available with walnut or neoprene grips in blue or stainless steel finish with choice of spur or pocket hammer. The cylinder holds 5 rounds. Overall length is 7" and weight is between 20 oz. and 25 oz. depending on grip and finish.

NIB	Exc.	V.G.	Good	Fair	Poor
350	300	250	200	150	125

Stainless Steel Bulldog

As above, in stainless steel.

NIB	Exc.	V.G.	Good	Fair	Poor
375	325	275	225	175	125

Bulldog Tracker

As above, with a 2.5", 4", or 6" barrel in .357 Magnum only.

NIB	Exc.	V.G.	Good	Fair	Poor
375	325	275	225	175	125

Police Bulldog

As above, in .32 H&R Magnum, .38 Special or .44 Special with 3.5" or 4" barrel.

NIB	Exc.	V.G.	Good	Fair	Poor
350	300	250	200	150	125

Stainless Steel Police Bulldog

As above, in stainless steel and available also in .357 Magnum.

NIB	Exc.	V.G.	Good	Fair	Poor
350	300	250	200	150	125

Off Duty

Chambered for the .38 Special or .22 LR this revolver is fitted with a 2" barrel. Offered with either walnut or rubber grips in blue or stainless finish with choice of spur or pocket hammer.

Weight of the .38 special version is between 17 oz. and 23 oz., depending on grip and finish. The .22 LR version weighs between 19 oz. and 22 oz. The overall length is 4.75". A nickel finish with rubber grips is also offered.

NIB	Exc.	V.G.	Good	Fair	Poor
325	275	225	175	125	100

Pit Bull

A 9mm Federal, .38 Special or .357 Magnum caliber double-action revolver with a 2.5", 3.5", or 4" barrel. Blued with rubber grips.

NIB	Exc.	V.G.	Good	Fair	Poor
400	350	250	175	125	90

The Mag Pug

A 5-shot revolver chambered for .357 Magnum. Stainless or blue. Ported 2.2" barrel. 23 oz. Fixed sights, rubber grips.

NIB	Exc.	V.G.	Good	Fair	Poor
350	300	250	200	150	125

Charter Arms Southpaw

Five-shot snubnose revolver chambered in .38 Special +P. Five-shot cylinder, 2" barrel, matte black aluminum alloy frame with stainless steel cylinder. Cylinder latch and crane assembly are on right side of frame for convenience of left-hand shooters. Rubber Pachmayr-style grips. Weight: 12 oz.

NIB	Exc.	V.G.	Good	Fair	Poor
400	350	250	175	125	90

Pink Lady

Similar to Undercover Lite but with pink anodized frame. .38 Special only.

NIB	Exc.	V.G.	Good	Fair	Poor
375	325	275	225	175	125

Goldfinger

Similar to Undercover Lite but with gold anodized frame. .38 Special only.

NIB	Exc.	V.G.	Good	Fair	Poor
375	325	275	225	175	125

Patriot

Built on Bulldog frame but chambered in .327 Federal Magnum (six-shot). Rubber grips, 2.2" or 4" barrel. Comes with Kershaw "327" knife.

NIB	Exc.	V.G.	Good	Fair	Poor
425	300	225	175	150	100

Dixie Derringer

Stainless mini-revolver chambered for .22 LR (5 oz.) or .22 Magnum (6 oz.). 5-shot, 1.175" barrel.

NIB	Exc.	V.G.	Good	Fair	Poor
175	140	100	75	50	25

Explorer II Pistol

A .22 caliber semi-automatic pistol with 6", 8", or 10" barrels. Available with a camo, black, silver, or gold finish and plastic grips. Discontinued in 1986.

NIB	Exc.	V.G.	Good	Fair	Poor
225	175	125	65	45	25

Model 40

A .22 caliber double-action semi-automatic pistol with a 3.5" barrel and 8-shot magazine. Stainless steel with plastic grips. Manufactured from 1984 to 1986.

NIB	Exc.	V.G.	Good	Fair	Poor
—	275	225	200	150	100

Model 79K

A .32 or .380 caliber double-action semi-automatic pistol with a 3.5" barrel and 7-shot magazine. Stainless steel with plastic grips. Manufactured from 1986 to 1988.

NIB	Exc.	V.G.	Good	Fair	Poor
—	350	300	250	180	125

Model 42T

A .22 caliber semi-automatic pistol with a 6" barrel and adjustable sights. Blued with walnut grips. Manufactured in 1984 and 1985.

NIB	Exc.	V.G.	Good	Fair	Poor
500	450	400	325	265	200

AR-7 Explorer Rifle

A .22 caliber semi-automatic rifle with a 16" barrel, 8-shot magazine and hollow plastic stock which can house the barrel when detached.

NIB	Exc.	V.G.	Good	Fair	Poor
175	125	80	60	40	25

CHEYTAC
Arco, Idaho

M-200

This bolt-action rifle is chambered for the .408 CheyTac cartridge. Detachable barrel length is 30" with muzzlebrake. Magazine capacity is 7 rounds. Integral bipod. No sights, but receiver has attachable Picatinny rail. Weight is about 27 lbs.

NIB	Exc.	V.G.	Good	Fair	Poor
10995	8250	6900	5400	3000	700

M-310

This is a single-shot bolt-action rifle chambered for the .408 CheyTac cartridge. Fitted with a 25" barrel with muzzlebrake. McMillian A-5 stock with adjustable cheekpiece. Match grade trigger. Picatinny rail. Weight is about 16.5 lbs.

NIB	Exc.	V.G.	Good	Fair	Poor
4395	3250	2750	1875	1300	500

CHIAPPA ARMS
Dayton, Ohio

1911-22

1911-style semi-automatic pistol chambered in .22 LR. Features include alloy frame; steel barrel; matte blue-black or bright nickel finish, walnut-like grips, two 10-round magazines, fixed sights. Straight blowback action. **NOTE:** Add $25 for target model with adjustable sights, $25 for OD or tan finish.

NIB	Exc.	V.G.	Good	Fair	Poor
260	225	200	150	100	75

Rhino 14

Unique revolver chambered in .357 Magnum. Features include 2", 4", 5" or 6" barrel; fixed or adjustable sights; visible hammer or hammerless design. Weight 24 to 33 oz. Walnut or synthetic grips with black frame; hexagonal-shaped cylinder. Unique design fires from bottom chamber of cylinder. **NOTE:** Add $75 for wood grips, $50 for brushed nickel finish.

NIB	Exc.	V.G.	Good	Fair	Poor
650	600	525	475	300	200

Model 1886 Kodiak Rifle

Lever-action rifle chambered for .45-70 Government cartridge. Replica of Winchester 1886 with 18.5" half-octagon barrel, express sights, black synthetic stock and hard-chrome matte gray finish. Standard model has four-round, half-length tubular magazine. Trapper model has 6-shot magazine, blue finish and walnut stock. **NOTE:** Deduct $150 for Trapper model.

NIB	Exc.	V.G.	Good	Fair	Poor
1200	1050	900	700	500	400

Model 1887 Shotgun

Lever-action limited edition replica of Model 1887 Winchester 12 gauge with 5-shot magazine, 22" or 28" barrel with choke tubes.

NIB	Exc.	V.G.	Good	Fair	Poor
1000	900	750	600	400	250

CHICAGO, F. A. CO.
Chicago, Illinois
Protector Palm Pistol — Standard Model Nickel-Plated/Black Grips

A .32 caliber radial cylinder revolver designed to fit in the palm of the hand and to be operated by a hinged lever mounted to the rear of the circular frame. The sideplates are marked "Chicago Firearms Co., Chicago, Ill." and "The Protector". Blued with hard rubber grip panels or nickel-plated with pearl grip panels. Manufactured by the Ames Manufacturing Company. **NOTE:** Add 25 percent for pearl grip panels without cracks or chips. Add 50 percent for blued finish.

NIB	Exc.	V.G.	Good	Fair	Poor
—	—	3000	2000	1000	750

CHIPMUNK RIFLES/ROGUE RIFLE CO.
Lewiston, Idaho
Chipmunk Single-Shot Standard Rifle

A .22 or the .22 rimfire Magnum caliber bolt-action rifle with 16.25" barrel, and open sights. Weight is approximately 3.5 lbs.

NIB	Exc.	V.G.	Good	Fair	Poor
185	150	125	100	80	60

Deluxe Chipmunk

As above, with a hand-checkered walnut stock.

NIB	Exc.	V.G.	Good	Fair	Poor
230	180	135	100	80	60

Chipmunk .17 HMR

Similar to the Standard Model but chambered for the .17 HMR cartridge. Introduced in 2002.

NIB	Exc.	V.G.	Good	Fair	Poor
200	160	125	100	75	45

Chipmunk TM

Introduced in 2002 this model features a micrometer rear sight. Stock has accessory rail installed and is adjustable for length of pull. Barrel is an 18" heavy type. Weight is about 5 lbs.

NIB	Exc.	V.G.	Good	Fair	Poor
325	250	150	125	100	75

Silhouette Pistol

A .22 caliber bolt-action pistol with a 14.5" barrel, open sights and pistol-grip walnut stock.

NIB	Exc.	V.G.	Good	Fair	Poor
150	125	100	80	60	40

CHRISTENSEN ARMS
Gunnison, Utah

There are a number of custom options offered by this company for its rifles. Many of these options may affect price. Prices listed are for standard models with standard features.

Carbon One

This is a bolt-action rifle with Remington 700 action chambered for .17 through .243 caliber. It is fitted with a custom trigger, match-grade stainless steel barrel and black synthetic stock. Weight is about 6 lbs.

NIB	Exc.	V.G.	Good	Fair	Poor
3900	2750	1900	1200	700	500

Carbon Lite

This model is similar to above but weighs about 5 lbs.

NIB	Exc.	V.G.	Good	Fair	Poor
3900	2750	1900	1200	700	500

Carbon King

This model utilizes a Remington 700 BDL long action and is chambered for .25 caliber through .30-06. Stainless steel barrel, custom trigger, and black synthetic stock are standard. Weight is approximately 6.5 lbs.

NIB	Exc.	V.G.	Good	Fair	Poor
3900	2750	1900	1200	700	500

Carbon Cannon

Similar to above model and chambered for belted magnum calibers. Weight is about 7 lbs.

NIB	Exc.	V.G.	Good	Fair	Poor
3900	2750	1900	1200	700	500

Carbon Challenge I

This rifle is built on a Ruger 10/22 action. It is fitted with a Volquartsen trigger, stainless steel bull barrel and black synthetic stock. Weight is approximately 3.5 lbs. Add 20 percent for .17 caliber.

NIB	Exc.	V.G.	Good	Fair	Poor
1800	1300	875	600	400	175

Carbon Challenge II

Similar to above model but fitted with an AMT action and trigger. Weight is about 4.5 lbs. Discontinued.

NIB	Exc.	V.G.	Good	Fair	Poor
1295	995	700	550	325	125

Carbon Tactical

This bolt-action model uses a Remington 700 BDL action and is available in most any caliber. It is fitted with a custom trigger, match-grade stainless steel barrel and black synthetic stock. Weight is about 7 lbs.

NIB	Exc.	V.G.	Good	Fair	Poor
3900	2750	1900	1200	700	500

Carbon Conquest

Chambered for the .50 caliber BMG cartridge this rifle is built on a McMillan stainless steel bolt action with magazine capacity of 5 rounds. Barrel length is 32" with muzzlebrake. Composite stock. Weight is about 20 lbs. **NOTE:** For single-shot model deduct $1,000.

NIB	Exc.	V.G.	Good	Fair	Poor
6250	4000	3250	1700	875	400

Carbon One Hunter

Semi-custom bolt-action rifle built around choice of receivers; steel barrel encased in carbon alloy shroud; synthetic stock. All popular calibers. Weight: 6.5-7 lbs.

NIB	Exc.	V.G.	Good	Fair	Poor
1500	1300	875	550	375	125

Carbon Ranger Repeater

Semi-custom bolt-action rifle chambered in .50 BMG. Five-shot magazine; steel Pac-Nor barrel encased in carbon alloy. Muzzle brake. Weight: 20 lbs.

NIB	Exc.	V.G.	Good	Fair	Poor
8000	7000	5500	4000	2000	1000

Carbon Ranger Single Shot

Similar to Repeater but single shot.

NIB	Exc.	V.G.	Good	Fair	Poor
6500	5000	3000	2000	1100	500

CHURCHILL
Various European Manufacturers and Importers

SIDE-BY-SIDE SHOTGUNS

Windsor I

A 10, 12, 16, 20, 28, and .410 bore Anson & Deeley double-barrel boxlock shotgun with barrel lengths from 23" through 32", various choke combinations, double triggers and extractors. Scroll-engraved, silver-finished, with checkered walnut pistol grip and fore-end.

NIB	Exc.	V.G.	Good	Fair	Poor
800	600	500	400	300	200

Windsor II

As above, in 10, 12, and 20 gauge only with automatic ejectors. Not imported after 1987.

NIB	Exc.	V.G.	Good	Fair	Poor
800	600	550	450	350	250

Windsor VI

As above with sidelocks. Chambered for 12 and 20 gauge only with automatic ejectors. Not imported after 1987.

NIB	Exc.	V.G.	Good	Fair	Poor
1100	800	750	650	500	350

Royal

A 12, 20, 28 and .410 bore boxlock double-barrel shotgun with various barrel lengths and chokes, double triggers and extractors. Case hardened with checkered walnut stock. Introduced in 1988.

NIB	Exc.	V.G.	Good	Fair	Poor
650	500	425	350	275	125

OVER/UNDER SHOTGUNS

Monarch

A 12, 20, 28, or .410 bore over/under shotgun with a boxlock-action, 25", 26", or 28" ventilated-rib barrels, either double- or a single-selective trigger, extractors, and a checkered walnut stock.

NIB	Exc.	V.G.	Good	Fair	Poor
600	475	425	375	300	150

Windsor III

A 12 and 20 and .410 bore boxlock double-barrel shotgun with 27" or 30" ventilated-rib barrels, extractors, a single-selective trigger, scroll-engraved, silver finished and a checkered walnut stock.

NIB	Exc.	V.G.	Good	Fair	Poor
700	575	525	475	400	200

Windsor IV

As above, with screw-in choke tubes standard. Introduced in 1989.

NIB	Exc.	V.G.	Good	Fair	Poor
975	775	650	500	425	200

Regent

As above, in 12 and 20 gauge with 27" ventilated-rib barrels, screw-in choke tubes, scroll-engraved false sideplates, automatic ejectors, a single-selective trigger, and a checkered walnut stock. Not imported after 1986.

NIB	Exc.	V.G.	Good	Fair	Poor
950	750	650	550	450	250

Regent II

As above with finer overall finishing.

NIB	Exc.	V.G.	Good	Fair	Poor
1250	1000	850	750	500	250

OTHER SHOTGUNS

Regent Shotgun/Rifle Combination

A .222, .223, .243, .270, .308, or .30-06 caliber/12 gauge over/under rifle/shotgun with a 25" ventilated rib, automatic ejectors and single-selective trigger. Silver finished, scroll engraved with a checkered walnut stock.

NIB	Exc.	V.G.	Good	Fair	Poor
1050	825	725	600	450	250

Windsor Grade Semi-Automatic

A 12 gauge semi-automatic shotgun with 26", 28", or 30" ventilated-rib barrels and screw-in choke tubes. An etched and anodized alloy receiver with a checkered walnut stock.

NIB	Exc.	V.G.	Good	Fair	Poor
500	375	325	275	225	175

Regent Grade Semi-Automatic

Chambered for 12 gauge with choice of 26", 28", or 30" barrels. Standard chokes or choke tubes. Walnut stock with pistol grip. Introduced in 1984 and discontinued in 1986. Weight is about 7.5 lbs.

NIB	Exc.	V.G.	Good	Fair	Poor
500	375	325	275	225	175

Windsor Grade Slide-Action

A 12 gauge slide-action shotgun with a 26" through 30" ventilated-rib barrel, various chokes, double slide rails, and an anodized alloy receiver. Checkered walnut stock. Discontinued in 1986.

NIB	Exc.	V.G.	Good	Fair	Poor
—	500	375	300	250	175

RIFLES

Highlander

A .25-06 through .300 Winchester Magnum caliber bolt-action rifle with a 22" barrel, with or without sights, a 3-shot magazine, and a checkered walnut stock.

NIB	Exc.	V.G.	Good	Fair	Poor
575	425	375	300	250	200

Regent

As above, with a Monte Carlo-style comb and cheekpiece. Discontinued in 1988.

NIB	Exc.	V.G.	Good	Fair	Poor
—	650	500	425	350	275

CHURCHILL, E. J. LTD.
London, England

One of One Thousand Rifle

A .270 to .458 Magnum caliber bolt-action rifle with 24" barrel and a select French walnut stock with a trap pistol-grip cap and recoil pad. Only 100 actually produced for the 20th anniversary of Interarms in 1973.

NIB	Exc.	V.G.	Good	Fair	Poor
—	1750	1050	850	700	550

Premier Over/Under

This is a sidelock ejector gun available in 12, 20 or 28 gauge. Single- or double-trigger with choice of finish. Barrel lengths built to order. Deluxe Turkish walnut with choice of grip. Fine scroll engraving. Weight for 12 gauge gun about 7 lbs., for 20 gauge guns about 6.75 lbs. Many extra cost options available. **NOTE:** Add $3,000 for 28 gauge guns.

NIB	Exc.	V.G.	Good	Fair	Poor
47000	36500	26000	20000	10000	800

Premier Side-by-Side

Similar to the over/under gun but with side-by-side barrels. Also offered in 16 gauge as well as 12, 20, and 28 gauge. Weights are about 6.5 lbs. for 12 gauge; 6 lbs. for 16 gauge; and 5.8 lbs. for 20 gauge. Many extra options are available. **NOTE:** Add $3,000 for 28 gauge guns.

NIB	Exc.	V.G.	Good	Fair	Poor
38000	30000	20000	16500	7000	600

Premier Double Rifle

Similar in construction to the side-by-side shotgun, this rifle is chambered for the .300 H&H, .375 H&H, or .500 Nitro Express. Weight is 9.5 lbs. for the .300, 9.75 lbs. for the 375, and 12.5 lbs. for the .500. Many extra-cost options. **NOTE:** Add $3,000 for .500 N.E. guns.

NIB	Exc.	V.G.	Good	Fair	Poor
55000	45000	35000	20000	13000	800

Baronet Magazine Rifle

This rifle uses the standard Mauser 98 action with fully adjustable trigger, 3 position safety, and box release floor plate. Barrel length is custom to order. Border engraving. Chambered for the .30-06 or .375 H&H. Weight for .30-06 is about 8.5 lbs., for the .375 about 9 lbs. Many extra-cost options offered. Seek an expert opinion prior to a sale.

NIB	Exc.	V.G.	Good	Fair	Poor
13000	9750	7000	45000	2750	575

CHYLEWSKI, WITOLD
Switzerland

A 6.35mm caliber semi-automatic pistol with a 6-round magazine, marked "Brevete Chylewski" and bears the name "Neuhausen" on the left side of the pistol. Approximately 1,000 were made between 1910 and 1918. This pistol was designed to be cocked with one hand.

NIB	Exc.	V.G.	Good	Fair	Poor
—	—	1250	850	550	275

CIMARRON, F. A. CO.
Fredericksburg, Texas

In business since 1984 this company imports quality firearms from Uberti, Armi San Marco, Pedersoli and others. Cimarron also sells Uberti-manufactured blackpowder Colt reproductions, from the Patterson to the Model 1862 Pocket. For prices and specifications on these models see the Uberti section.

Model No. 3 Schofield

This version of the Schofield is manufactured for Cimarron by Armi San Marco in Italy. Its parts are interchangeable with the original. It is offered in several variations and calibers. Discontinued. Beware of latch locking problems. **NOTE:** For standard nickel finish add $100 and for custom nickel finish add $150.

Civilian Model

Fitted with 7" barrel and offered in .38 Special, .44 Russian/.44 Special, .44 WCF, .45 Schofield, .45 Long Colt.

NIB	Exc.	V.G.	Good	Fair	Poor
875	600	525	425	300	125

Military Model

Essentially the same as the Civilian Model except for its markings.

NIB	Exc.	V.G.	Good	Fair	Poor
875	600	525	425	300	125

Wells Fargo

Similar to the Military and Civilian Model but fitted with a 5" barrel. Calibers are the same.

NIB	Exc.	V.G.	Good	Fair	Poor
875	600	525	425	300	125

Model 1872 Open Top

This revolver is offered in a number of different calibers and configurations. It is chambered for the .44 SP, .44 Colt, .44 Russian, .45 Schofield, .38 Colt, .38 Special. It can be fitted with Army or Navy grips. Barrel lengths are 4.75", 5.5", or 7.5". Offered in regular blued finish, charcoal blue finish, or original finish. **NOTE:** Add $40 for charcoal finish and $50 for original finish. Add $25 for silver-plated back strap and trigger guard.

NIB	Exc.	V.G.	Good	Fair	Poor
575	425	350	300	200	100

COLT SINGLE-ACTION ARMY CONFIGURATIONS

Cimarron Arms reproduction of the 1873 Colt Single-Action Army revolver comes in two basic configurations. First is the "Old Model" with the black powder frame screw-in cylinder pin retainer and circular bull's eye ejector head. Second is the "pre-war Model" style frame with spring loaded cross-pin cylinder retainer and half moon ejector head. Old Model revolvers are available in authentic old style charcoal blue finish at an extra charge. Unless otherwise stated all of these Colt reproductions are produced by Uberti of Italy. Plain walnut grips are standard unless noted. **NOTE:** Relic finish offered by Cimarron as an extra cost item on its revolvers. This finish duplicates the old worn antique finish seen on many used historical Colts. Add $40 to the NIB price for any Cimarron revolver with this finish.

General Custer 7th Cavalry Model

Has U.S. military markings and is fitted with 7.5" barrel on an Old Model frame. Offered in .45 LC only.

NIB	Exc.	V.G.	Good	Fair	Poor
650	450	350	300	200	100

Rough Rider U.S. Artillery Model

This version of the Old Model is fitted with a 5.5" barrel and chambered for .45 LC.

NIB	Exc.	V.G.	Good	Fair	Poor
650	450	350	300	200	100

Frontier Six Shooter

This revolver is offered with a choice of 4.75", 5.5", or 7.5" barrel. It is chambered for .38 WCF, .357 Magnum, .44 WCF, .45 LC, or

.45 LC with extra .45 ACP cylinder. **NOTE:** For charcoal blue finish add $40 to NIB price. For extra .45 ACP cylinder add $30. For stainless steel add $50.

NIB	Exc.	V.G.	Good	Fair	Poor
575	350	300	275	175	75

Sheriff's Model no ejector

Fitted with a 3" barrel and chambered in .44 WCF or .45 LC. Built on an Old Model frame.

NIB	Exc.	V.G.	Good	Fair	Poor
550	350	300	275	175	75

New Sheriff's Model w/ejector

This variation is fitted with a 3.5" barrel with ejector and is available in .357 Magnum, .44 WCF, .44 Special, and .45 LC. For checkered walnut grips add $35.

NIB	Exc.	V.G.	Good	Fair	Poor
575	400	325	275	175	75

Wyatt Earp Buntline

This is a limited edition model fitted with a 10" barrel chambered for the .45 LC cartridge. Model P frame. Silver shield inlaid in grip.

NIB	Exc.	V.G.	Good	Fair	Poor
775	600	500	425	300	125

New Thunderer

The frame is based on the Old Model fitted with a bird's-head grip with a choice of plain or checkered walnut grips. Originally offered in 3.5" or 4.75" barrel lengths; in 1997 5.5" barrels were offered. Chambered for .357 Magnum, .44 WCF, .44 Special, or .45 LC/.45 ACP. Add $35 for checkered grips.

NIB	Exc.	V.G.	Good	Fair	Poor
575	450	325	275	175	75

Thunderer Long Tom

Same as the New Thunderer except for a barrel length of 7.5".

NIB	Exc.	V.G.	Good	Fair	Poor
550	425	350	275	175	75

Lightning

Similar to the Thunderer but with a smaller grip frame. Chambered for the .38 Special cartridge or .22 LR and fitted with 3.5", 4.75", or 5.5" barrel. Finish is blue with case hardened frame.

NIB	Exc.	V.G.	Good	Fair	Poor
475	375	315	250	150	65

Lightning .32s

This model features two cylinders chambered for the .32-20 and the .32 H&R cartridges. Choice of 3.5", 4.75", or 5.5" barrel. Introduced in 2004.

NIB	Exc.	V.G.	Good	Fair	Poor
550	400	350	275	175	75

New Model P

Offered in either Old Model or Pre-War styles in a choice of 4.75", 5.5", or 7.5" barrel. Chambered for .32 WCF, .38 WCF, .44 WCF, .44 Special, or .45 LC.

NIB	Exc.	V.G.	Good	Fair	Poor
475	400	325	275	175	75

Stainless Frontier Model P

This model is a Model P in stainless steel. Chambered for the .357 Magnum or .45 LC cartridge. Barrels are 4.75", 5.5", or 7.5". Introduced in 2004.

NIB	Exc.	V.G.	Good	Fair	Poor
550	450	400	300	200	100

A.P. Casey Model P U.S. Cavalry

Fitted with a 7.5" barrel and chambered for .45 LC this revolver has U.S. markings (APC) on an Old Model frame.

NIB	Exc.	V.G.	Good	Fair	Poor
550	375	325	250	150	75

Rinaldo A. Carr Model P U.S. Artillery

This is a Model P built on an Old Model frame and chambered for .45 LC and fitted with a 5.5" barrel. U.S. markings (RAC).

NIB	Exc.	V.G.	Good	Fair	Poor
550	425	375	275	175	100

Evil Roy Model

This model features a Model P frame with wide square-notch rear sight and wide-width front sight. Slim grips checkered or smooth. Tuned action with lightened trigger. Chambered for the .357 Magnum, .45 LC, or .44-40 cartridge. Barrel lengths are 4.75" or 5.5". Introduced in 2004.

NIB	Exc.	V.G.	Good	Fair	Poor
625	550	475	375	250	125

Model P Jr.

Similar to the Model P but sized 20 percent smaller. Chambered for the .38 Special cartridge and fitted with 3.5" or 4.75" barrels. Blue with case hardened frame.

NIB	Exc.	V.G.	Good	Fair	Poor
475	400	325	250	150	75

Model P Jr. .32s

This model, introduced in 2004, features two cylinders chambered for the .32-20 and the .32 H&R cartridges. Choice of 3.5", 4.75", or 5.5" barrel.

NIB	Exc.	V.G.	Good	Fair	Poor
550	400	350	250	150	75

Cimarron 1880 Frontier Flat Top

Introduced in 1998 this model is a target version of the Colt Single-Action Army. Rear sight is adjustable for windage and front adjustable for elevation. Offered with choice of 4.75", 5.5", or 7.5" barrels and chambered for .45 LC, .45 Schofield, .44 WCF, and .357 Magnum. Choice of Model P frame or Pre-War frame.

NIB	Exc.	V.G.	Good	Fair	Poor
550	450	325	225	150	100

Cimarron Bisley

Exact copy of the Colt Bisley with case hardened frame. Choice of 4.75", 5.5", or 7.5" barrels and calibers from .45 LC, .45 Schofield, .44 WCF, to .357 Magnum. Introduced in 1998.

NIB	Exc.	V.G.	Good	Fair	Poor
550	450	325	225	150	100

Cimarron Bisley Flat Top

Offered in the same barrel lengths and caliber as the standard Bisley with the addition of a windage adjustable rear sight and elevation adjustable front sight. Introduced in 1998.

NIB	Exc.	V.G.	Good	Fair	Poor
550	450	325	225	150	100

El Pistolero

This budget-priced revolver was introduced in 1997 and features a brass backstrap and trigger guard with plain walnut grips. Offered in 4.75", 5.5", and 7.5" barrel lengths. Chambered for .45 LC or .357 Magnum.

NIB	Exc.	V.G.	Good	Fair	Poor
350	250	200	125	75	50

Doc Holliday Thunderer

This nickel-plated SAA in .45 LC has a 3.5" barrel, Cimarron Tru Ivory grips, and comes with a matching numbered dagger and a shoulder holster designed to carry both items.

NIB	Exc.	V.G.	Good	Fair	Poor
1150	1000	800	650	450	300

Rooster Shooter SAA

Replica of SAA used by John Wayne in many movies. Chambered in .357 Magnum, .44-40 or .45 LC with antique grey finish, artificial ivory grips. Introduced in 2010.

NIB	Exc.	V.G.	Good	Fair	Poor
700	625	525	400	300	250

Man With No Name SAA

Replica of gun used by Clint Eastwood in several "spaghetti westerns" in .45 LC with 4.75" or 5.5" barrel, cased-colored finish, wood grips with rattlesnake inlay. Introduced in 2010.

NIB	Exc.	V.G.	Good	Fair	Poor
750	650	550	425	300	250

RICHARDS CONVERSIONS

NOTE: Relic finish offered by Cimarron as an extra cost item on its revolvers. This finish duplicates the old worn antique finish seen on many used historical Colts. Add $40 to the NIB price for any Cimarron revolver with this finish.

Model 1851

Chambered for .38 Special, .38 Colt, and .44 Colt. Fitted with 5" or 7" barrels.

NIB	Exc.	V.G.	Good	Fair	Poor
550	450	325	225	150	100

Model 1861

Chambered for .38 Special, .38 Colt, and .44 Colt. Fitted with 5" or 7" barrels.

NIB	Exc.	V.G.	Good	Fair	Poor
550	450	325	225	150	100

Model 1860

Chambered for .38 Special, .38 Colt, and .44 Colt. Fitted with 5" or 7.5" barrels.

NIB	Exc.	V.G.	Good	Fair	Poor
550	450	325	225	150	100

Model 1911A1

Manufactured by Chiappa, standard full-size replica of Colt .45 ACP Government Model in blue, polished blue or nickel finish. **NOTE:** For nickel finish add 40 percent, for polished blue finish add 30 percent.

NIB	Exc.	V.G.	Good	Fair	Poor
525	450	400	325	250	200

RIFLES

Model 1865 Spencer

Chambered for the .56-50 centerfire cartridge.

NIB	Exc.	V.G.	Good	Fair	Poor
1350	975	775	650	375	250

Henry Civil War Model

Offered in .44 WCF or .45 LC with 24.25" barrel. **NOTE:** For charcoal blue or white finish add $80.

NIB	Exc.	V.G.	Good	Fair	Poor
1400	1200	1000	625	350	200

Henry Civilian Model

Same as above but without military markings.

NIB	Exc.	V.G.	Good	Fair	Poor
1200	925	750	625	350	200

Model 1866 Yellowboy Carbine

Reproduction of the Winchester model 1866. Fitted with a 19" barrel and chambered for .38 Special, .44 WCF, or .45 LC. **NOTE:** For charcoal blue add $40.

NIB	Exc.	V.G.	Good	Fair	Poor
1000	850	600	525	300	150

Model 1866 Yellowboy Rifle

Same as above but fitted with a 24.25" barrel. **NOTE:** For charcoal blue add $40.

NIB	Exc.	V.G.	Good	Fair	Poor
1100	900	600	525	300	150

Model 1866 Yellowboy Trapper

As above but with a 16" barrel.

NIB	Exc.	V.G.	Good	Fair	Poor
950	725	600	525	300	150

Model 1873 Winchester Rifle

This lever-action rifle is offered in .357 Magnum, .44 WCF, or .45 LC. Fitted with a 24.25" barrel. **NOTE:** For charcoal blue add $40. For pistol grip option add $140.

NIB	Exc.	V.G.	Good	Fair	Poor
1150	925	750	675	400	200

Model 1873 Long Range Rifle

Similar to the Model 1873 but fitted with a 30" barrel. **NOTE:** For pistol grip option add $140. For 1 of 1000 engraving option add $1,250.

NIB	Exc.	V.G.	Good	Fair	Poor
1175	950	775	675	400	200

Model 1873 Carbine

Same as the standard Model 1873 but fitted with a 19" barrel. **NOTE:** For charcoal blue add $40.

NIB	Exc.	V.G.	Good	Fair	Poor
1150	925	750	675	400	200

Model 1873 Short Rifle

This model is fitted with a 20" barrel. Production ceased in 1998. **NOTE:** For charcoal blue add $40.

NIB	Exc.	V.G.	Good	Fair	Poor
1150	925	750	675	400	200

Model 1873 Trapper

As above but with 16" barrel.

NIB	Exc.	V.G.	Good	Fair	Poor
1150	925	750	675	400	200

Model 1873 Deluxe Sporting Rifle

This model is fitted with a 24" barrel, checkered walnut stock with pistol grip.

NIB	Exc.	V.G.	Good	Fair	Poor
1220	925	850	725	400	200

Model 1873 Evil Roy Rifle

This model is chambered for the .357 or .45 Colt cartridge and fitted with a 20" barrel.

NIB	Exc.	V.G.	Good	Fair	Poor
1450	1200	950	700	400	200

Model 1873 Larry Crow Signature Series Rifle

Chambered for the .357 Magnum or .45 Colt cartridge and fitted with a 20" barrel.

NIB	Exc.	V.G.	Good	Fair	Poor
1550	1300	1050	800	400	200

Model 1892 Solid Frame Rifle

Offered with either 20" or 24" octagon barrels and chambered for the .357 Magnum, .44WCF, or .45 Colt cartridges.

NIB	Exc.	V.G.	Good	Fair	Poor
850	675	575	450	300	150

Model 1892 Takedown Rifle

As above but with takedown feature.

NIB	Exc.	V.G.	Good	Fair	Poor
975	775	675	525	375	200

Model 1886

Replica of Winchester 1886. Caliber .45-70 Government.

NIB	Exc.	V.G.	Good	Fair	Poor
1400	1250	900	750	400	250

Billy Dixon Model 1874 Sharps

A reproduction of the Model 1874 Sharps rifle chambered for the .45-70 cartridge. Fitted with a 32" tapered octagon barrel. Stock is hand checkered with oil finish walnut. Double set triggers standard.

NIB	Exc.	V.G.	Good	Fair	Poor
1650	1225	1100	700	500	250

Remington Rolling Block

This Remington reproduction was introduced to Cimarron in 1997 and represents the Rolling Block Sporting rifle with 30" tapered octagon barrel and chambered for .45-70 cartridge. Hand-checkered, satin-finished walnut stock.

NIB	Exc.	V.G.	Good	Fair	Poor
1300	1000	900	550	300	175

Adobe Walls Rolling Block

This model is chambered for the .45-70 cartridge and is fitted with a 30" octagon barrel. Hand-checkered walnut stock with hand finishing. Case colored receiver and German silver nose cap. Weight is about 10.13 lbs. Introduced in 2004.

NIB	Exc.	V.G.	Good	Fair	Poor
1425	1050	950	600	350	225

Model 1885 High Wall

Reproduction of the Winchester Model 1885 chambered for .45-70, .45-90, .45-120, .40-65, .348 Win., .30-40 Krag, or .38-55 cartridges. Fitted with a 30" barrel. Walnut stock and case colored receiver.

NIB	Exc.	V.G.	Good	Fair	Poor
995	800	650	500	300	125

Model 1885 Deluxe High Wall

As above but with checkered walnut stock with pistol grip.

NIB	Exc.	V.G.	Good	Fair	Poor
1175	875	700	550	300	125

Model 1885 Low Wall

Introduced in 2004 this model is chambered for the .22 LR, .22 Hornet, .30-30, .32-20, .38-40, .357 Magnum, .44-40, and .44 Magnum cartridges. Hand checkered walnut stock with pistol grip. Octagon barrel is 30" long. Single or double-set trigger.

NIB	Exc.	V.G.	Good	Fair	Poor
1175	850	700	550	300	125

Texas Ranger Carbine

This model is a copy of the Sharps Model 1859 Military Carbine. Round barrel is 22" long. Receiver is case colored. Stock is American black walnut. Chambered for the .45-70 cartridge. Marked "T*S" on the barrel. Introduced in 2004.

NIB	Exc.	V.G.	Good	Fair	Poor
1200	900	725	600	350	150

Sharps Silhouette

Offered in .45-70 or .40-65 calibers with 32" octagon barrel. Introduced in 1998.

NIB	Exc.	V.G.	Good	Fair	Poor
1095	850	700	600	350	150

Quigley Sharps Sporting Rifle

This rifle is chambered for the .45-70 or .45-120 caliber and fitted with a heavy 34" octagon barrel. Introduced in 1998.

NIB	Exc.	V.G.	Good	Fair	Poor
1725	1350	1175	700	450	275

Sharp's No. 1 Sporting Rifle

Plain walnut stock with pistol grip. Fitted with a 32" barrel. Chambered for the .45-70 cartridge.

NIB	Exc.	V.G.	Good	Fair	Poor
1350	1050	900	500	300	150

Pride of the Plains Model

Based on the Sharps Model 1874 Sporting Rifle, this model, chambered for the .45-70 cartridge, features a 32" octagon barrel, hand-checkered walnut stock with pistol grip, coin nickel receiver, Creedmore tang sight, and target front sight with inserts. Introduced in 2004.

NIB	Exc.	V.G.	Good	Fair	Poor
1620	1200	925	500	300	150

Professional Hunter Model

This model is the basic Sharps Model 1874 chambered for the .45-70 cartridge. Fitted with a 32" barrel, case colored receiver, walnut stock with shotgun butt and double-set triggers. Introduced in 2004.

NIB	Exc.	V.G.	Good	Fair	Poor
1160	850	725	500	300	150

Big Fifty Model

Chambered for the .50-90 cartridge and fitted with a 34" half-octagon barrel. Fancy walnut stock with hand checkering and pistol grip. Case colored receiver, German silver nose cap, and Hartford-style Soule Creedmore sights with spirit level and globe front sight. Weight is about 11 lbs. Introduced in 2004.

NIB	Exc.	V.G.	Good	Fair	Poor
1890	1400	1150	700	450	275

Springfield Trapdoor Carbine

Based on the famous Springfield design. Chambered for the .45-70.

NIB	Exc.	V.G.	Good	Fair	Poor
995	800	625	425	250	125

Springfield Trapdoor Officer's Model

This is the Officer's version of the Springfield Trapdoor model. Chambered for .45-70.

NIB	Exc.	V.G.	Good	Fair	Poor
1150	900	775	500	275	150

SHOTGUNS

1878 Coach Gun

Side-by-side double-barrel 12 gauge with hammers, double triggers, 22" or 26" barrels. Standard or polished blue "U.S.A." finish. **NOTE:** Add $100 for U.S.A. finish.

NIB	Exc.	V.G.	Good	Fair	Poor
500	425	375	300	250	200

1881 Coach Gun

Side-by-side double barrel in 12 or 20 gauge with 22", 26", 28" or 30" barrels. Hammerless design. Interchangeable choke tubes. Walnut stock with straight or pistol grip.

NIB	Exc.	V.G.	Good	Fair	Poor
600	500	400	325	275	225

Model 1887 Shotgun

Lever-action limited edition replica of Model 1887 Winchester 12 gauge with 5-shot magazine, 20", 22", 24" or 28" barrel. Color case-hardened frame.

NIB	Exc.	V.G.	Good	Fair	Poor
1150	975	750	600	400	250

Model 1897 Shotgun

Replica of Winchester 12 gauge pump-action model. Exposed hammer, semi-pistol grip walnut stock, choke tubes.

NIB	Exc.	V.G.	Good	Fair	Poor
500	400	350	300	200	150

CLAPP, HOFFMAN & CO. / CLAPP, GATES & CO. RIFLES
Alamance, North Carolina

Maker of Confederate Civil War rifles, 1862 - 1864. Overall length: Types I, II, & III 51.25" to 52", Type IV varies between 46.5" and 51"; barrel length: Types I, II, & III 35.25" to 36", Type IV varies between 31.25" and 35-7/8"; caliber: Types I, II, & III .50, Type IV .577; markings: none. Despite the absence of makers marks, the Clapp, Gates & Co. products are readily distinguished by their part-round, part-octagonal (octagonal section on Types I to III, about 4" long, 4.75" to 5.5" on Type IV rifles) barrels having only a slightly raised bolster projecting from the upper right quarter. This small bolster accommodates the boxlock that distinguished the first 100 rifles produced. This gave way to a standard percussion lock on subsequent production, which required that the hammer bend sharply to the left to strike the cone. Type I and Type II rifles were adapted to a "footprint" saber bayonet lug on the right side of the barrel; Types III and IV also had a saber bayonet lug on the right side of the barrel but of the standard pattern. Types III and IV are distinguished by their caliber, the former being .50, the latter .577. Prices reflect Type II through IV production; Type I (while extant) has never been offered for sale and would presumably bring a significantly higher premium.

NIB	Exc.	V.G.	Good	Fair	Poor
—	—	39500	19500	3900	1200

CLARK, F. H.
Memphis, Tennessee

Pocket Pistol

A .41 caliber single-shot percussion pistol with a 3.5" to 5" barrel, German silver mounts and end cap, and the barrel is stamped "F.H. Clark & Co./Memphis". Manufactured in the 1850s and 1860s.

NIB	Exc.	V.G.	Good	Fair	Poor
—	—	5350	1900	550	200

CLASSIC DOUBLES
Tochigi City, Japan

Importer of Japanese shotguns formerly imported by Winchester as the Model 101 and Model 23. These models were discontinued by Winchester in 1987 and imported by Classic Doubles until 1990.

Model 201 Classic

A 12 or 20 gauge boxlock side-by-side double-barrel shotgun with 26" ventilated-rib barrels, screw-in choke tubes single-selective trigger and automatic ejectors. Blued with checkered walnut stock and beavertail forearm.

NIB	Exc.	V.G.	Good	Fair	Poor
2400	1950	1700	1500	1250	900

Model 201 Small Bore Set

As above, with a smaller receiver and two sets of barrels chambered for 28 gauge and .410. The barrels are 28" in length.

NIB	Exc.	V.G.	Good	Fair	Poor
4100	3500	2950	2250	1750	1250

Model 101 Classic Field Grade I

A 12 or 20 gauge over/under shotgun with 25.5" or 28" ventilated-rib barrels, screw-in choke tubes, automatic ejectors and a single-selective trigger. Engraved, blued with checkered walnut stock.

NIB	Exc.	V.G.	Good	Fair	Poor
2000	1750	1500	1250	1000	700

Classic Field Grade II

As above, in 28 gauge and .410, highly engraved with a coin-finished receiver and a deluxe walnut stock with a round knob pistol grip and fleur-de-lis checkering.

NIB	Exc.	V.G.	Good	Fair	Poor
2500	2000	1750	1500	1250	900

Classic Sporter

As above, in 12 gauge only with 28" or 30" barrels, ventilated rib and screw-in choke tubes. The frame is coin-finished with light engraving and a matted upper surface to reduce glare. The stock is select walnut. This model was designed for sporting clays.

NIB	Exc.	V.G.	Good	Fair	Poor
2250	1800	1500	1250	1000	700

Waterfowl Model

As above with 30" barrels, 3" chambers, vent-rib, and screw-in choke tubes. The overall finish is a subdued matte with light engraving.

NIB	Exc.	V.G.	Good	Fair	Poor
1650	1350	1000	850	650	500

Classic Trap Over/Under

Designed for competition trap shooting with 30" or 32" barrels, a ventilated center and top rib, automatic ejectors, screw-in choke tubes, and a single trigger. Blued with light engraving and a walnut stock in straight or Monte Carlo style.

NIB	Exc.	V.G.	Good	Fair	Poor
2250	1750	1500	1250	1000	700

Classic Trap Single

As above, with a single 32" or 34" barrel.

NIB	Exc.	V.G.	Good	Fair	Poor
2250	1800	1500	1250	1000	700

Classic Trap Combo

As above, with a single barrel and a set of over/under barrels.

NIB	Exc.	V.G.	Good	Fair	Poor
3000	2500	2000	1750	1250	1000

Classic Skeet

As above, with 27.5" barrels.

NIB	Exc.	V.G.	Good	Fair	Poor
2250	1750	1500	1250	1000	700

Classic Skeet 4 Gauge Set

As above, furnished with four sets of barrels chambered for 12, 20, 28 gauge, and .410.

NIB	Exc.	V.G.	Good	Fair	Poor
4150	3750	3000	2500	1850	1500

CLEMENT, CHAS.
Liege, Belgium

Model 1903

A 5.5mm Glisenti caliber semi-automatic pistol. Barrel raises at the muzzle to begin the loading procedure.

Courtesy James Rankin

NIB	Exc.	V.G.	Good	Fair	Poor
—	575	475	350	220	110

Model 1907

As above, but in 6.35mm and 7.65mm caliber.

Courtesy Orvel Reichert

NIB	Exc.	V.G.	Good	Fair	Poor
—	475	395	325	200	100

Model 1908

Similar to the Model 1907 but with the magazine release at the bottom of the frame. Fitted with a larger grip.

Courtesy J.B. Wood

NIB	Exc.	V.G.	Good	Fair	Poor
—	575	450	295	200	125

Model 1909

A semi-automatic pistol in 6.35mm and 7.65mm calibers. Similar to the Model 1908 but with barrel and chamber housing in one piece.

Courtesy James Rankin

NIB	Exc.	V.G.	Good	Fair	Poor
—	575	450	300	225	100

Model 1910

Redesigned version of the above with the barrel and housing all one piece. This unit is held in position by the trigger guard.

Courtesy Orvel Reichert

NIB	Exc.	V.G.	Good	Fair	Poor
—	575	475	395	350	275

Model 1912

A 6.35mm caliber semi-automatic pistol marked "Clement's Patent" ; others, "Model 1912 Brevet 243839". This model is quite different from earlier Clement models.

Courtesy James Rankin

NIB	Exc.	V.G.	Good	Fair	Poor
—	425	295	250	195	100

American Model

Revolver copy of the Colt Police Positive. It was chambered for .38 caliber.

NIB	Exc.	V.G.	Good	Fair	Poor
—	425	295	250	150	90

CLERKE PRODUCTS
Santa Monica, California

Hi-Wall

A copy of the Winchester Model 1885 High Wall rifle with the action activated by a lever, and the receiver is case colored. This rifle is chambered for almost all of the modern calibers and features a 26" barrel and a walnut stock with a pistol grip and a schnabel fore-end. It was manufactured between 1972 and 1974.

NIB	Exc.	V.G.	Good	Fair	Poor
975	850	650	425	300	200

Deluxe Hi-Wall

As above, with a half-round/half-octagonal barrel, select walnut stock, and a recoil pad. It was manufactured between 1972 and 1974.

NIB	Exc.	V.G.	Good	Fair	Poor
1100	975	750	525	400	250

COBRA ENTERPRISES, INC.
Salt Lake City, Utah

DERRINGERS

Standard Series

Offered chambered in .22 LR, .22 WMR, .25 ACP, and .32 ACP. Over/under barrels are 2.4". Pearl or laminate wood grips. Weight is about 9.5 oz. grips. Introduced in 2002.

NIB	Exc.	V.G.	Good	Fair	Poor
250	200	160	125	100	75

Long Bore Series

This series is chambered for the .22 WMR, .38 Special, or the 9mm cartridge. Fitted with a 3.5" barrel. Black synthetic, laminate oak, or laminate rosewood grips. Chrome or black finish. Weight is about 16 oz.

NIB	Exc.	V.G.	Good	Fair	Poor
250	200	160	125	100	75

Big Bore Series

Chambered for the .22 WMR, .32 H&R Mag., and the .38 Special. Barrel length is 2.75". Choice of black synthetic, laminate oak, or laminate rosewood grips. Chrome or black finish. Weight is about 14 oz.

NIB	Exc.	V.G.	Good	Fair	Poor
250	200	160	125	100	75

SEMI-AUTOMATIC PISTOLS

C-32/C-380

Chambered for the .32 ACP or .380 cartridges. Fitted with a 2.8" barrel. Chrome or black finish. Magazine capacity is 5 rounds for the .380 and 6 rounds for the .32 ACP. Weight is about 22 oz.

NIB	Exc.	V.G.	Good	Fair	Poor
175	125	80	60	40	25

C-9mm

This is a double-action-only pistol chambered for the 9mm cartridge. Fitted with a 3.3" barrel. Magazine capacity is 10 rounds. Load indicator. Polymer grips. Weight is about 21 oz.

NIB	Exc.	V.G.	Good	Fair	Poor
275	215	150	115	75	45

Patriot .45

This is double-action-only pistol chambered for the .45 ACP cartridge. Barrel length is 3". Frame is black polymer. Slide is stainless steel. Magazine capacity is 6 rounds. Weight is about 20 oz.

NIB	Exc.	V.G.	Good	Fair	Poor
350	225	150	115	75	45

COBRAY INDUSTRIES
S.W.D., Inc.
Atlanta, Georgia

M-11 Pistol

A 9mm caliber semi-automatic pistol. It fires from the closed bolt and is made of steel stampings with a parkerized finish. It is patterned after, though a good deal smaller than, the Ingram Mac 10. **NOTE:** Add $70 for stainless steel. Add $150 for pre-ban models.

NIB	Exc.	V.G.	Good	Fair	Poor
—	375	295	150	100	75

M-12

Same as above but chambered for the .380 ACP cartridge. **NOTE:** Add $150 for pre-ban models.

NIB	Exc.	V.G.	Good	Fair	Poor
—	375	295	150	100	75

TM-11 Carbine

As above in 9mm caliber, with a 16.25" shrouded barrel and a telescoping metal shoulder stock.

NIB	Exc.	V.G.	Good	Fair	Poor
—	450	350	225	150	100

TM-12 Carbine

As above but chambered for the .380 ACP cartridge.

NIB	Exc.	V.G.	Good	Fair	Poor
—	450	350	225	150	100

Terminator Shotgun

A single-shot 12 or 20 gauge shotgun that fires from an open bolt position. The cocked bolt is released to slam home on the shell when the trigger is pulled. The 18" barrel is cylinder bored. There is a telescoping wire stock and the finish is Parkerized. We have seen many of these advertised at sky-high prices, but junk is junk.

NIB	Exc.	V.G.	Good	Fair	Poor
—	175	125	80	60	40

COCHRAN TURRET
C. B. Allen
Springfield, Massachusetts

Under Hammer Turret Rifle

A .36 or .40 caliber percussion radial cylinder rifle with 31" or 32" octagonal barrels and walnut stocks. The barrel marked "Cochrans/Many/Chambered/&/Non Recoil/Rifle" and the top strap "C.B. Allen / Springfield". These rifles were produced in the variations listed. Manufactured during the late 1830s and 1840s.

1st Type

Fitted with a circular top strap secured by two screws. Serial numbered from 1 to approximately 30.

NIB	Exc.	V.G.	Good	Fair	Poor
—	—	—	18000	6500	2150

2nd Type

Fitted with a rectangular hinged top strap, the locking catch of which serves as the rear sight. Serial numbered from approximately 31 to 155.

NIB	Exc.	V.G.	Good	Fair	Poor
—	—	29500	15000	5100	1800

3rd Type

As above, with a smaller hammer and a plain trigger guard.

NIB	Exc.	V.G.	Good	Fair	Poor
—	—	18000	15000	5100	1800

Pistol

Action similar to above with 4" to 7" barrels.

NIB	Exc.	V.G.	Good	Fair	Poor
—	—	26500	21000	9700	3000

CODY, MICHAEL & SONS
Nashville, Tennessee

Received a contract with the State of Tennessee for "Mississippi" rifles with brass patchboxes in late 1861. Barrel length 36"; caliber .54. Cody often used reworked Model 1817 rifle barrels and sporting pattern single screw lockplates. Rifles are unmarked except for large engraved serial number on top of breech plug tang.

NIB	Exc.	V.G.	Good	Fair	Poor
—	—	29500	13000	2150	775

COFER, T. W.
Portsmouth, Virginia

Cofer Navy Revolver

A .36 caliber spur trigger percussion revolver with a 7.5" octagonal barrel and 6-shot cylinder. The top strap is marked "T.W. Cofer's/ Patent" and the barrel "Portsmouth, Va." This revolver was manufactured in limited quantities during the Civil War.

NIB	Exc.	V.G.	Good	Fair	Poor
—	—	120000	43500	6500	1500

COGSWELL
London, England

Cogswell Pepperbox Pistol

A .47 caliber 6-shot percussion pepperbox with case hardened barrels, German silver frame and walnut grips. Normally marked "B. Cogswell, 224 Strand, London" and "Improved Revolving Pistol".

NIB	Exc.	V.G.	Good	Fair	Poor
—	—	4400	1950	975	550

COLTON MANUFACTURING CO.
Toledo, Ohio

The Colton Manufacturing Co. provided Sears with its first American-made hammerless house brand double. Sears advertised their sidelock hammerless gun as "the equal of any gun made, regardless of price" in their 1900 Fall catalog No. 110. There were four models: three sideplated boxlock-types and a unique unitized coil spring driven striker assembly version. All these, especially the latter, were designed to be mass produced. Many of the distinctive sidelock-within-a-sideplated model were produced but they are seldom seen today either because they were used-up or did not hold up well and were scrapped. Sears replaced Colton with the more traditional design Fryberg gun in 1902. Values depend on grade. There appear to be at least two levels of quality and condition ranging from $300 to $1,500. Colton-marked guns are scarce.

Courtesy Nick Niles, Paul Goodwin photo

COLT'S PATENT FIRE ARMS MANUFACTURING COMPANY
Hartford, Connecticut

COLT PATERSON MODELS

Pocket or Baby Paterson Model No. 1

The Paterson was the first production revolver manufactured by Colt. It was first made in 1837. The Model 1 or Pocket Model is the most diminutive of the Paterson line. The revolver is serial numbered in its own range, #1 through #500. The numbers are not visible without dismantling the revolver. The barrel lengths run from 1.75" to 4.75". The standard model has no attached loading lever. The chambering is .28 caliber percussion and it holds five shots. The finish is all blued, and the grips are varnished walnut. It has a roll-engraved cylinder scene, and the barrel is stamped "Patent Arms Mfg. Co. Paterson N.J. Colt's Pt." Cased examples in Very Good or better condition can bring upwards of $200,000.

NIB	Exc.	V.G.	Good	Fair	Poor
—	—	125000	50000	19500	5000

Belt Model Paterson No. 2

The Belt Model Paterson is a larger revolver with a straight-grip and an octagonal barrel that is 2.5" to 5.5" in length. It is chambered for .31 caliber percussion and holds five shots. The finish is all blued, with varnished walnut grips and no attached loading lever. It has a roll-engraved cylinder scene, and the barrel is stamped "Patent Arms Mfg. Co. Paterson N.J. Colt's Pt." The serial number range is #1-#850 and is shared with the #3 Belt Model. It was made from 1837-1840. An excellent cased example was auctioned by Rock Island Auction in 2007 for $414,000.

Courtesy Buffalo Bill Historical Center, Cody, Wyoming

NIB	Exc.	V.G.	Good	Fair	Poor
—	400000	225000	75000	28500	7500

Belt Model Paterson No. 3

This revolver is quite similar to the Model #2 except that the grips are curved outward at the bottom to form a more handfilling configuration. They are serial numbered in the same #1-#850 range. Some attached loading levers have been noted on this model, but they are extremely rare and would add approximately 35 percent to the value.

NIB	Exc.	V.G.	Good	Fair	Poor
—	—	250000	95000	40000	10000

Ehlers Model Pocket Paterson

John Ehlers was a major stockholder and treasurer of the Patent Arms Mfg. Co. when it went bankrupt. He seized the assets and inventory. These revolvers were Pocket Model Patersons that were not finished at the time. Ehlers had them finished and marketed them. They had an attached loading lever, and the abbreviation "Mfg Co." was deleted from the barrel stamping. There were 500 revolvers involved in the Ehlers variation totally, and they were produced from 1840-1843.

NIB	Exc.	V.G.	Good	Fair	Poor
—	—	—	75000	30000	8000

Ehlers Belt Model Paterson

The same specifications apply to this larger revolver as they do to the Ehlers Pocket Model. It falls within the same 500 revolver involvement and is rare.

NIB	Exc.	V.G.	Good	Fair	Poor
—	—	—	75000	30000	8000

Texas Paterson Model No. 5

This is the largest and most sought after of the Paterson models. It is also known as the Holster Model. It has been verified as actually seeing use by both the military and civilians on the American frontier. It is chambered for .36 caliber percussion, holds five shots, and has an octagonal barrel that ranges from 4" to 12" in length. It has been observed with and without the attached loading lever, but those with it are rare. The finish is blued, with a case-colored hammer. The grips are varnished walnut. The cylinder is roll-engraved; and the barrel is stamped "Patent Arms Mfg. Co. Paterson, N.J. Colts Pt." Most Texas Patersons are well used and have a worn appearance. One in excellent or V.G. condition would be highly prized. A verified military model would be worth a great deal more than standard, so qualified appraisal would be essential. The serial number range is #1-#1000, and they were manufactured from 1838-1840. The attached loading lever brings approximately a 25 percent premium. An 1836 Colt Paterson Revolver sold in September, 2011, for $977,500 at a Heritage Auction in Dallas, Texas. (The price includes a 15% buyer's premium.) This is believed to be a world record for the sale of a single American firearm. The very rare No. 5 Holster Model with a 9" barrel, ivory grips, attached loading lever and accessories in a box, is the finest known surviving example of Samuel Colt's first revolver. Two other Colt percussion revolvers were sold at the same auction for more than $800,000. (See Third Model Dragoon and Model 1861 Navy listings.) Such prices are extreme exceptions to the values of typical models.

NIB	Exc.	V.G.	Good	Fair	Poor
—	—	300000	150000	60000	17500

COLT REVOLVING LONG GUNS 1837-1847

First Model Ring Lever Rifle

This was actually the first firearm manufactured by Colt; the first revolver appeared a short time later. There were 200 of the First Models made in 1837 and 1838. The octagonal barrel of the First Model is 32" long and browned, while the rest of the finish is blued. The stock is varnished walnut with a cheekpiece inlaid with Colt's trademark. The ring lever located in front of the frame is pulled to rotate the 8-shot cylinder and cock the hammer. The rifle is chambered for .34, .36, .38, .40, and .44 caliber percussion. The cylinder is roll-engraved, and the barrel is stamped "Colt's Patent/ Patent Arms Mfg. Co., Paterson, N. Jersey". This model has a top strap over the cylinder. They were made both with and without an attached loading lever. The latter is worth approximately 10 percent more.

Courtesy Bonhams & Butterfields, San Francisco, California

NIB	Exc.	V.G.	Good	Fair	Poor
—	—	—	90000	40000	9750

Second Model Ring Lever Rifle

This model is quite similar in appearance to the First Model. Its function is identical. The major difference is the absence of the top strap over the cylinder. It had no trademark stamped on the cheekpiece. The Second Model is offered with a 28" and a 32" octagonal barrel and is chambered for .44 caliber percussion, holding 8 shots. There were approximately 500 produced from 1838-1841. The presence of an attached cheekpiece would add approximately 10 percent to the value.

Courtesy Bonhams & Butterfields, San Francisco, California

NIB	Exc.	V.G.	Good	Fair	Poor
—	—	—	80000	19500	8000

Model 1839 Shotgun

This model is quite similar in appearance to the 1839 Carbine. It is chambered for 16 gauge and holds six shots. It has a Damascus pattern barrel, and the most notable difference is a 3.5" (instead of a 2.5") long cylinder. There were only 225 of these made from 1839-1841. The markings are the same as on the Carbine.

Courtesy Bonhams & Butterfields, San Francisco, California

NIB	Exc.	V.G.	Good	Fair	Poor
—	—	37500	29500	11000	6000

Model 1839 Carbine

This model has no ring but features an exposed hammer for cocking and rotating the 6-shot cylinder. It is chambered for .525 smoothbore and comes standard with a 24" round barrel. Other barrel lengths have been noted. The finish is blued, with a browned barrel and a varnished walnut stock. The cylinder is roll-engraved, and the barrel is stamped "Patent Arms Mfg. Co. Paterson, N.J.-Colt's Pt." There were 950 manufactured from 1838-1841. Later variations of this model are found with the attached loading lever standard, and earlier models without one would bring approximately 25 percent additional. There were 360 purchased by the military and stamped "WAT" on the stock. These would be worth twice what a standard model would bring.

Courtesy Bonhams & Butterfields, San Francisco, California

NIB	Exc.	V.G.	Good	Fair	Poor
—	—	6300	45000	13500	7900

Model 1839/1850 Carbine

In 1848 Colt acquired a number of Model 1839 Carbines (approximately 40) from the state of Rhode Island. In an effort to make them marketable they were refinished and the majority fitted with plain cylinders (brightly polished) having integral ratchets around the arbor hole. Barrel length 24"; caliber .525; barrel browned; cylinder polished; frame blued; furniture case hardened; walnut stock varnished.

NIB	Exc.	V.G.	Good	Fair	Poor
—	—	70000	55000	18500	6500

Model 1854 Russian Contract Musket

In 1854 Colt purchased a large number of U.S. Model 1822 flintlock muskets that the company altered to percussion cap ignition and rifled. The reworked muskets are dated 1854 on the barrel tang and at the rear of the lockplate. In most instances the original manufactory marks, such as Springfield or Harpers Ferry at the rear of the lockplate, have been removed, while the U.S. and eagle between the hammer and bolster remain. The percussion nipple bolster is marked COLT'S PATENT. Some examples have been noted with the date 1858. Barrel length 42"; caliber .69; lock and furniture burnished bright; walnut stock oil finished.

NIB	Exc.	V.G.	Good	Fair	Poor
—	15000	10000	5000	1500	750

COLT WALKER-DRAGOON MODELS

Walker Model Revolver

The Walker is a massive revolver. It weighs 4 lbs., 9 oz. and has a 9" part-round/part-octagonal barrel. The cylinder holds six shots and is chambered for .44 caliber percussion. There were 1,000 Walker Colts manufactured in 1847, and nearly all of them saw extremely hard use. Originally this model had a roll-engraved cylinder, military inspection marks, and barrel stamping that read "Address Saml. Colt-New York City". Practically all examples noted have had these markings worn or rusted beyond recognition. Because the Walker is perhaps the most desirable and sought-after Colt from a collector's standpoint and because of the extremely high value of a Walker in any condition, qualified appraisal is definitely recommended. These revolvers were serial numbered A, B, C, and D Company 1-220, and E Company 1-120. An Excellent example was auctioned by James D. Julia in 2008 for $920,000.

Courtesy Buffalo Bill Historical Center, Cody, Wyoming

NIB	Exc.	V.G.	Good	Fair	Poor
—	900000	675000	400000	200000	59500

Civilian Walker Revolver

This model is identical to the military model but has no martial markings. They are found serial numbered 1001 through 1100.

NIB	Exc.	V.G.	Good	Fair	Poor
—	500000	395000	195000	58000	

Whitneyville Hartford Dragoon

This is a large, 6-shot, .44 caliber percussion revolver. It has a 7.5" part-round/part-octagonal barrel. The frame, hammer, and loading lever are case colored. The remainder is blued, with a brass trigger guard and varnished walnut grips. There were only 240 made in late 1847. The serial numbers run from 1100-1340.

This model is often referred to as a Transitional Walker. Some of the parts used in its manufacture were left over from the Walker production run. This model has a roll-engraved cylinder scene, and the barrel is stamped "Address Saml. Colt New York-City". This is an extremely rare model.

NIB	Exc.	V.G.	Good	Fair	Poor
—	—	140000	100000	55000	28500

Walker Replacement Dragoon

This extremely rare Colt (300 produced) is sometimes referred to as the "Fluck" in memory of the gentleman who first identified it as a distinct and separate model. They were produced by Colt as replacements to the military for Walkers that were no longer fit for service due to mechanical failures. They were large, 6-shot, .44 caliber percussion revolvers with 7.5" part-round/part-octagonal barrels. Serial numbers ran from 2216 to 2515. The frame, hammer, and loading lever are case-colored; the remainder, blued. The grips, which are longer than other Dragoons and similar to the Walkers, are of varnished walnut and bear the inspectors mark "WAT" inside an oval cartouche on one side and the letters "JH" on the other. The frame is stamped "Colt's/ Patent/U.S." The letter "P" appears on various parts of the gun.

NIB	Exc.	V.G.	Good	Fair	Poor
—	—	75000	55000	25000	6000

First Model Dragoon

Another large, 6-shot, .44 caliber percussion revolver. It has a 7.5" part-round/part-octagonal barrel. The frame, hammer, and loading lever are case colored; the remainder, blued with a brass grip frame and square backed trigger guard. The trigger guard is silver-plated on the Civilian Model only. Another distinguishing feature on the First Model is the oval cylinder stop notches. The serial number range is 1341-8000. There were approximately 5,000 made. The cylinder is roll-engraved; and the barrel stampings read "Address Saml. Colt, New York City." "Colt's Patent" appears on the frame. On Military Models the letters "U.S." also appear on the frame.

Military Model

NIB	Exc.	V.G.	Good	Fair	Poor
—	110000	75000	40000	20000	3500

Civilian Model

NIB	Exc.	V.G.	Good	Fair	Poor
—	90000	55000	35000	18000	3000

Second Model Dragoon

Most of the improvements that distinguish this model from the First Model are internal and not readily apparent. The most obvious external change is the rectangular cylinder-stop notches. This model is serial numbered from 8000-10700, for a total production of approximately 2,700 revolvers manufactured in 1850 and 1851. There is a Civilian Model, a Military Model, and an extremely rare variation that was issued to the militias of New Hampshire and Massachusetts (marked "MS.").

Civilian Model

NIB	Exc.	V.G.	Good	Fair	Poor
—	75000	55000	35000	25000	3500

Military Model

NIB	Exc.	V.G.	Good	Fair	Poor
—	85000	62500	40000	30000	3000

Militia Model

NIB	Exc.	V.G.	Good	Fair	Poor
—	90000	75000	45000	30000	3000

Third Model Dragoon

This is the most common of all the large Colt percussion revolvers. Approximately 10,500 were manufactured from 1851 through 1861. It is quite similar in appearance to the Second Model, and the most obvious external difference is the round trigger guard. The Third Model Dragoon was the first Colt revolver available with a detachable shoulder stock. There are three basic types of stocks, and all are quite rare as only 1,250 were produced. There are two other major variations we will note—the "C.L." Dragoon, which was a militia-issued model and is rare, and the late-issue model with an 8" barrel. These are found over serial number 18000, and only 50 were produced.

An historic, cased, Gustave Young-engraved, ivory-gripped Colt Third Model Dragoon was sold for $805,000 at a Texas auction in 2011. The revolver was inscribed "Colonel P.M. Milliken". Milliken was an officer of the 1st Ohio volunteer calvary and was killed leading a charge against the Confederate Army at Stone River, Tennessee in 1862. Two other Colt percussion revolvers were sold at the same auction for more than $800,000. (See Texas Paterson No. 5 and Model 1861 Navy listings.) Such prices are extreme exceptions to the values of typical models.

Courtesy Buffalo Bill Historical Center, Cody, Wyoming

Courtesy Buffalo Bill Historical Center, Cody, Wyoming

Civilian Model

NIB	Exc.	V.G.	Good	Fair	Poor
—	50000	35000	15000	2500	1000

Military Model

NIB	Exc.	V.G.	Good	Fair	Poor
—	65000	47000	30000	17500	3000

Shoulder Stock Cut Revolvers

NIB	Exc.	V.G.	Good	Fair	Poor
—	70000	51000	35000	20000	3000

Shoulder Stocks

NIB	Exc.	V.G.	Good	Fair	Poor
—	—	15000	8000	4000	2000

C.L. Dragoon

Hand engraved, not stamped.

NIB	Exc.	V.G.	Good	Fair	Poor
—	80000	60000	57500	17500	3000

8" Barrel Late Issue

NIB	Exc.	V.G.	Good	Fair	Poor
—	67000	55000	42500	25000	3000

Hartford English Dragoon

This is a variation of the Third Model Dragoon. The only notable differences are the British proofmarks and the distinct #1-#700 serial number range. Other than these two features, the description given for the Third Model would apply. These revolvers were manufactured in Hartford but were finished at Colt's London factory from 1853-1857. Some bear the hand-engraved barrel marking "Col. Colt London". Many of the English Dragoons were elaborately engraved, and individual appraisal would be a must. Two hundred revolvers came back to America in 1861 to be used in the Civil War.

NIB	Exc.	V.G.	Good	Fair	Poor
—	50000	35000	25000	12000	3000

Model 1848 Baby Dragoon

This is a small, 5-shot, .31 caliber percussion revolver. It has an octagonal barrel in lengths of 3", 4", 5", and 6". Most were made without an attached loading lever, although some with loading levers have been noted. The frame, hammer, and loading lever (when present) are case colored; the barrel and cylinder, blued. The grip frame and trigger guard are silver-plated brass. There were approximately 15,500 manufactured between 1847 and 1850. The serial range is between 1-5500. The barrels are stamped "Address Saml. Colt/New York City". Some have been noted with the barrel address inside brackets. The frame is marked "Colt's/Patent". The first 10,000 revolvers have the Texas Ranger/Indian roll-engraved cylinder scene; the later guns the stagecoach holdup scene. This is a popular model, and many fakes have been noted. **NOTE:** Attached loading lever add 15 percent.

Texas Ranger/Indian Scene

Courtesy Bonhams & Butterfields, San Francisco, California

Courtesy Bonhams & Butterfields, San Francisco, California

NIB	Exc.	V.G.	Good	Fair	Poor
—	—	19500	12000	6500	2000

Stagecoach Holdup Scene

NIB	Exc.	V.G.	Good	Fair	Poor
—	—	20500	13000	7000	2000

Model 1849 Pocket Revolver

This is a small, either 5- or 6-shot, .31 caliber percussion revolver. It has an octagonal barrel 3", 4", 5", or 6" in length. Most had loading gates, but some did not. The frame, hammer, and loading lever are case colored; the cylinder and barrel are blued. The grip frame and round trigger guard are made of brass and are silver plated. There are both large and small trigger guard variations noted. This is the most plentiful of all the Colt percussion revolvers, with approximately 325,000 manufactured over a 23-year period, 1850-1873. There are over 200 variations of this model, and one should consult an expert for individual appraisals. There are many fine publications specializing in the field of Colt percussion revolvers that would be helpful in the identification of the variations. The values represented here are for the standard model.

Courtesy Rock Island Auction Company

NIB	Exc.	V.G.	Good	Fair	Poor
—	4000	3400	2950	1200	300

London Model 1849 Pocket Revolver

Identical in configuration to the standard 1849 Pocket Revolver, the London-made models have a higher quality finish and their own serial number range, 1-11000. They were manufactured from 1853 through 1857. They feature a roll-engraved cylinder scene, and the barrels are stamped "Address Col. Colt/London". The first 265 revolvers, known as early models, have brass grip frames and small round trigger guards. They are quite rare and worth approximately 50 percent more than the standard model that has a steel grip frame and large oval trigger guard.

NIB	Exc.	V.G.	Good	Fair	Poor
—	6000	5000	3500	1200	300

Model 1851 Navy Revolver

This is undoubtedly the most popular revolver Colt produced in the medium size and power range. It is a 6-shot, .36-caliber percussion revolver with a 7.5" octagonal barrel. It has an attached loading lever. The basic model has a case colored frame hammer, and loading lever, with silver-plated brass grip frame and trigger guard. The grips are varnished walnut. Colt manufactured approximately 215,000 of these fine revolvers between 1850 and 1873. The basic Navy features a roll-engraved cylinder scene of a battle between the navies of Texas and Mexico. There are three distinct barrel stampings—serial number 1-74000, "Address Saml. Colt New York City"; serial number 74001-101000 "Address Saml. Colt. Hartford, Ct."; and serial number 101001-215000 "Address Saml. Colt New York U.S. America". The left side of the frame is stamped "Colt's/Patent" on all variations. This model is also available with a detached shoulder stock, and values for the stocks today are nearly as high as for the revolver itself. Careful appraisal should be secured before purchase. The number of variations within the 1851 Navy model designation makes it necessary to read specialized text available on the subject.

Square Back Trigger Guard, 1st Model, Serial #1-1000

Courtesy Rock Island Auction Company

NIB	Exc.	V.G.	Good	Fair	Poor
—	—	50000	42500	27000	5500

Square Back Trigger Guard, 2nd Model, Serial #1001-4200

NIB	Exc.	V.G.	Good	Fair	Poor
—	—	37500	30000	10000	2500

Small Round Trigger Guard, Serial #4201-85000

Courtesy Milwaukee Public Museum, Milwaukee, Wisconsin

NIB	Exc.	V.G.	Good	Fair	Poor
—	—	9500	8000	2500	500

Large Round Trigger Guard, Serial #85001-215000

NIB	Exc.	V.G.	Good	Fair	Poor
—	—	9500	8000	2500	500

Martial Model

"U.S." stamped on the left side of frame; inspector's marks and cartouche on the grips.

NIB	Exc.	V.G.	Good	Fair	Poor
—	—	42000	20000	7000	1000

Shoulder Stock Variations

1st and 2nd Model Revolver cut for stock only. An expert appraisal is recommended prior to a purchase of these very rare variations.

Stock Only

NIB	Exc.	V.G.	Good	Fair	Poor
—	—	22000	17000	7000	1250

3rd Model Cut For Stock

Revolver only.

NIB	Exc.	V.G.	Good	Fair	Poor
—	—	17500	11500	4000	1250

Stock Only for 3rd Model

NIB	Exc.	V.G.	Good	Fair	Poor
—	—	12500	9000	3750	1000

London Model 1851 Navy Revolver

These revolvers are physically similar to the U.S.-made model with the exception of the barrel address, which reads "Address Col. Colt. London". There are also British proofmarks stamped on the barrel and cylinder. There were 42,000 made between 1853 and 1857. They have their own serial number range, #1-#42,000. There are two major variations of the London Navy, and again a serious purchaser would be well advised to seek qualified appraisal as fakes have been noted.

1st Model

Serial #1-#2,000 with a small round brass trigger guard and grip frame. Squareback guard worth a 40 percent premium.

NIB	Exc.	V.G.	Good	Fair	Poor
—	—	16500	8000	2150	700

2nd Model

Serial #2,001-#42,000, steel grip frame, and large round trigger guard.

NIB	Exc.	V.G.	Good	Fair	Poor
—	—	15000	7500	1800	600

Hartford Manufactured Variation

Serial numbers in the 42,000 range.

NIB	Exc.	V.G.	Good	Fair	Poor
—	—	15000	7500	1800	600

COLT SIDE HAMMER MODELS

Model 1855 Side Hammer "Root" Pocket Revolver

The "Root," as it is popularly known, was the only solid-frame revolver Colt ever made. It has a spur trigger and walnut grips, and the hammer is mounted on the right side of the frame. The standard finish is a case colored frame, hammer, and loading lever, with the barrel and cylinder blued. It is chambered for both .28 caliber and .31 caliber percussion. Each caliber has its own serial number range—1-30000 for the .28 caliber and 1-14000 for the .31 caliber. The model consists of seven basic variations, and the serious student should avail himself of the fine publications dealing with this model in depth. Colt produced the Side Hammer Root from 1855-1870.

Models 1 and 1A Serial #1-384

3.5" octagonal barrel, .28 caliber, roll-engraved cylinder, Hartford barrel address without pointing hand.

Courtesy Milwaukee Public Museum, Milwaukee, Wisconsin

NIB	Exc.	V.G.	Good	Fair	Poor
—	—	12000	6000	3500	1200

Model 2 Serial #476-25000

Same as Model 1 with pointing hand barrel address.

NIB	Exc.	V.G.	Good	Fair	Poor
—	—	7500	3500	1900	500

Model 3 Serial #25001-30000

Same as the Model 2 with a full fluted cylinder.

NIB	Exc.	V.G.	Good	Fair	Poor
—		7500	3500	1900	500

Model 3A and 4 Serial #1-2400

.31 caliber, 3.5" barrel, Hartford address, full fluted cylinder.

NIB	Exc.	V.G.	Good	Fair	Poor
—		7250	3250	1800	500

Model 5 Serial #2401-8000

.31 caliber, 3.5" round barrel, address "Col. Colt New York".

NIB	Exc.	V.G.	Good	Fair	Poor
—	—	6500	2900	1300	300

Model 5A Serial #2401-8000

Same as Model 5 with a 4.5" barrel.

Courtesy Milwaukee Public Museum, Milwaukee, Wisconsin

NIB	Exc.	V.G.	Good	Fair	Poor
—		6500	2900	1300	300

Models 6 and 6A Serial #8001-11074

Same as Model 5 and 5A with roll-engraved cylinder scene.

NIB	Exc.	V.G.	Good	Fair	Poor
—		6750	2995	1350	300

Models 7 and 7A Serial #11075-14000

Same as Models 6 and 6A with a screw holding in the cylinder pin.

NIB	Exc.	V.G.	Good	Fair	Poor
—		6750	2995	1350	300

COLT SIDE HAMMER LONG GUNS

Model 1855 Sporting Rifle, 1st Model

This is a 6-shot revolving rifle chambered for .36 caliber percussion. It comes with a 21", 24", 27", or 30" round barrel that is part octagonal where it joins the frame. The stock is walnut with either an oil or a varnish finish. The frame, hammer, and loading lever are case colored; the rest of the metal, blued. The hammer is on the right side of the frame. The 1st Model has no fore-end, and an oiling device is attached to the barrel underlug. The trigger guard has two spur-like projections in front and in back of the bow. The roll-engraved cylinder scene depicts a hunter shooting at five deer and is found only on this model. The standard stampings are " Colt's Pt./1856" and "Address S. Colt Hartford, Ct. U.S.A."

Early Model

Low serial numbers with a hand-engraved barrel marking "Address S. Colt Hartford, U.S.A."

NIB	Exc.	V.G.	Good	Fair	Poor
—	—	16500	15000	5500	1500

Production Model

NIB	Exc.	V.G.	Good	Fair	Poor
—		15000	12000	3000	1000

Model 1855 1st Model Carbine

Identical to the 1st Model Rifle but offered with a 15" and 18" barrel.

Courtesy Milwaukee Public Museum, Milwaukee, Wisconsin

NIB	Exc.	V.G.	Good	Fair	Poor
—	—	12500	9500	3000	1000

Model 1855 Half Stock Sporting Rifle

Although this rifle is quite similar in appearance and finish to the 1st Model, there are some notable differences. It features a walnut fore-end that protrudes halfway down the barrel. There are two types of trigger guards—a short projectionless one or a long model with a graceful scroll. There is a 6-shot model chambered for .36 or .44 caliber or a 5-shot model chambered for .56 caliber. The cylinder is fully fluted. The markings are "Colt's Pt/1856" and "Address Col. Colt/Hartford Ct. U.S.A." There were approximately 1,500 manufactured between 1857 and 1864.

Courtesy Milwaukee Public Museum, Milwaukee, Wisconsin

NIB	Exc.	V.G.	Good	Fair	Poor
—		12500	9500	3500	1000

Model 1855 Full Stock Military Rifle

This model holds 6 shots in its .44 caliber chambering and 5 shots when chambered for .56 caliber. It is another side hammer revolving rifle that resembles the Half Stock model. The barrels are round and part-octagonal where they join the frame. They come in lengths of 21", 24", 27", 31", and 37". The hammer and loading lever are case colored; the rest of the metal parts, blued. The walnut buttstock and full length fore-end are oil finished, and this model has sling swivels. The cylinder is fully fluted. Military models have provisions for affixing a bayonet and military-style sights and bear the "U.S." martial mark on examples that were actually issued to the military. The standard stampings found on this model are "Colt's Pt/1856" and "Address Col. Colt Hartford, Ct. U.S.A." There were an estimated 9,300 manufactured between 1856 and 1864.

Courtesy Milwaukee Public Museum, Milwaukee, Wisconsin

Martially Marked Models

NIB	Exc.	V.G.	Good	Fair	Poor
—	—	42500	25000	9500	2000

Without Martial Markings

NIB	Exc.	V.G.	Good	Fair	Poor
—		13500	9750	3500	1000

Model 1855 Full Stock Sporting Rifle

This model is similar in appearance to the Military model, with these notable exceptions. There is no provision for attaching a bayonet, there are no sling swivels, and it has sporting-style sights. The buttplate is crescent shaped. This model has been noted chambered for .56 caliber in a 5-shot version and chambered for .36, .40, .44, and .50 caliber in the 6-shot variation. They are quite scarce in .40 and .50 caliber and will bring a 10 percent premium. The standard markings are "Colt's Pt/1856" and "Address Col. Colt/Hartford Ct. U.S.A." Production on this model was quite limited (several hundred at most) between the years 1856 and 1864.

NIB	Exc.	V.G.	Good	Fair	Poor
—	—	20000	13500	4000	1000

Model 1855 Revolving Carbine

This model is similar in appearance to the 1855 Military Rifle. The barrel lengths of 15", 18", and 21" plus the absence of a fore-end make the standard Carbine Model readily identifiable. The markings are the same. Approximately 4,400 were manufactured between 1856 and 1864.

NIB	Exc.	V.G.	Good	Fair	Poor
—	—	13500	9500	4000	1000

Model 1855 Artillery Carbine

Identical to the standard carbine but chambered for .56 caliber only, it has a 24" barrel, full-length walnut fore-end, and a bayonet lug.

NIB	Exc.	V.G.	Good	Fair	Poor
—	—	23500	17000	5500	1500

Model 1855 British Carbine

This is a British-proofed version with barrel lengths of up to 30". It has a brass trigger guard and buttplate and is chambered for .56 caliber only. This variation is usually found in the 10000-12000 serial number range.

NIB	Exc.	V.G.	Good	Fair	Poor
—	—	18500	13000	3750	1000

Model 1855 Revolving Shotgun

This model very much resembles the Half Stock Sporting Rifle but was made with a 27", 30", 33", and 36" smoothbore barrel. It has a 5-shot cylinder chambered for .60 or .75 caliber (20 or 10 gauge). This model has a case-colored hammer and loading lever; the rest of the metal is blued, with an occasional browned barrel noted. The buttstock and fore-end are of walnut, either oil or varnish-finished. This model has no rear sight and a small trigger guard with the caliber stamped on it. Some have been noted with the large scroll trigger guard; these would add 10 percent to the value. The rarest shotgun variation would be a full stocked version in either gauge, and qualified appraisal would be highly recommended. This model is serial numbered in its own range, #1-#1100. They were manufactured from 1860-1863.

Courtesy Amoskeag Auction Company

.60 Caliber (20 gauge)

NIB	Exc.	V.G.	Good	Fair	Poor
—	—	22500	10000	3500	1000

.75 Caliber (10 gauge)

NIB	Exc.	V.G.	Good	Fair	Poor
—	—	22500	10000	3500	1000

Model 1861 Single-Shot Rifled Musket Production Model

With the advent of the Civil War, the army of the Union seriously needed military arms. Colt was given a contract to supply 112,500 1861-pattern percussion single-shot muskets. Between 1861 and 1865, 75,000 were delivered. They have 40" rifled barrels chambered for .58 caliber. The musket is equipped with military sights, sling swivels, and a bayonet lug. The metal finish is bright steel, and the stock is oil-finished walnut. Military inspector's marks are found on all major parts. "VP" over an eagle is stamped on the breech along with a date. The Colt address and a date are stamped on the lockplate. A large number of these rifles were altered to the Snyder breech loading system for the Bey of Egypt.

Courtesy Milwaukee Public Museum, Milwaukee, Wisconsin

NIB	Exc.	V.G.	Good	Fair	Poor
—	—	5500	2000	750	450

COLT PERCUSSION REVOLVERS

Model 1860 Army Revolver

This model was the third most produced of the Colt percussion handguns. It was the primary revolver used by the Union Army during the Civil War. Colt delivered 127,156 of these revolvers to be used during those hostilities. This is a 6-shot .44 caliber percussion revolver. It has either a 7.5" or 8" round barrel with an attached loading lever. The frame, hammer, and loading lever are case colored; the barrel and cylinder are blued. The trigger guard and front strap are brass, and the backstrap is blued steel. The grips are one-piece walnut. The early models have the barrels stamped "Address Saml. Colt Hartford Ct." Later models are stamped "Address Col. Saml. Colt New-York U.S. America". "Colt's/Patent" is stamped on the left side of the frame; ".44 Cal.", on the trigger guard. The cylinder is roll engraved with the naval battle scene. There were a total of 200,500 1860 Army Revolvers manufactured between 1860 and 1873.

Martial Marked Model

NIB	Exc.	V.G.	Good	Fair	Poor
—	—	8500	7500	3500	900

Civilian Model

This model is found in either 3- or 4 screw variations and it may or may not be cut for a shoulder stock. Civilian models are usually better finished.

Courtesy Milwaukee Public Museum, Milwaukee, Wisconsin

NIB	Exc.	V.G.	Good	Fair	Poor
—	—	7500	6000	3000	800

Full Fluted Cylinder Model

Approximately 4,000 Army's were made with full fluted cylinders. They appear in the first 8,000 serial numbers.

Courtesy Milwaukee Public Museum, Milwaukee, Wisconsin

Shoulder Stock 2nd Type

NIB	Exc.	V.G.	Good	Fair	Poor
—	—	16500	15000	7000	2000

Model 1861 Navy Revolver

This model is a 6-shot, 7.5" round-barreled, .36 caliber percussion revolver. The frame, hammer, and attached loading lever are case colored. The barrel and cylinder are blued. The grip frame and trigger guard are silver-plated brass. The grips are of one-piece walnut. The cylinder has the roll-engraved naval battle scene, and the barrel stamping is "Address Col. Saml. Colt New-York U.S. America". The frame is stamped "Colts/Patent" with "36 Cal." on the trigger guard. There are not many variations within the 1861 Navy model designation, as less than 39,000 were made between 1861 and 1873.

A very exceptional cased and engraved presentation-grade Model 1861 Navy was sold at auction in 2011 for $805,000. Three Colt percussion revolvers sold for over $800,000 at the auction. (See Texas Paterson No. 5 and Third Model Dragoon listings.) Such prices are extreme exceptions to the values of typical models.

Courtesy Rock Island Auction Company

Fluted Cylinder Model

Approximately the first 100 were made with full fluted cylinders.

NIB	Exc.	V.G.	Good	Fair	Poor
—	35000	25000	15000	6000	3000

Military Model

Marked "U.S." on frame, inspector's cartouche on grip. 650 were marked "U.S.N." on the butt.

NIB	Exc.	V.G.	Good	Fair	Poor
—	30000	22000	14000	5500	2500

Shoulder Stock Model

Only 100 3rd-type stocks were made. They appear between serial #11000-#14000. These are very rare revolvers.

Revolver

|-----|------|------|------|------|------|
Revolver

NIB	Exc.	V.G.	Good	Fair	Poor
—	—	—	—	5000	1500

Stock

NIB	Exc.	V.G.	Good	Fair	Poor
—	—	—	10000	4250	1000

Civilian Model

NIB	Exc.	V.G.	Good	Fair	Poor
—	18000	9000	6000	4000	2000

Model 1862 Pocket Navy Revolver

This is a smaller, 5-shot, .36 caliber percussion revolver that resembles the configuration of the 1851 Navy. It has a 4.5", 5.5", or 6.5" octagonal barrel with an attached loading lever. The frame, hammer, and loading lever are case colored; the barrel and cylinder, blued. The grip frame and trigger guard are silver-plated brass; and the one-piece grips, of varnished walnut. The stagecoach holdup scene is roll-engraved on the cylinder. The frame is stamped "Colt's/Patent"; and the barrel, "Address Col. Saml. Colt New-York U.S. America". There were approximately 19,000 manufactured between 1861 and 1873. They are serial numbered in the same range as the Model 1862 Police. Because a great many were used for metallic cartridge conversions, they are quite scarce today.

The London Address Model with blued steel grip frame would be worth more than the standard model. Add 50 percent. **NOTE:** Longer barrels will bring a premium over the 4.5" length.

Standard Production Model

NIB	Exc.	V.G.	Good	Fair	Poor
—	—	6000	3750	1200	500

Model 1862 Police Revolver - Standard Production Model

This is a slim, attractively designed revolver that some consider to be the most aesthetically pleasing of all the Colt percussion designs. It has a 5-shot, half-fluted cylinder chambered for .36 caliber. It is offered with a 3.5", 4.5", 5.5", or 6.5" round barrel. The frame, hammer, and loading lever are case colored; the barrel and cylinder, blued. The grip frame is silver-plated brass; and the one-piece grips, varnished walnut. The barrel is stamped "Address Col. Saml Colt New-York U.S. America"; the frame has "Colt's/Patent" on the left side. One of the cylinder flutes is marked "Pat Sept. 10th 1850". There were approximately 28,000 of these manufactured between 1861 and 1873. Many were converted to metallic cartridge use, so they are quite scarce on today's market. **NOTE:** The London Address Model would be worth approximately twice the value of the standard model. Longer barrels will bring a premium over the 3.5" or 4.5" length.

Courtesy Milwaukee Public Museum, Milwaukee, Wisconsin

NIB	Exc.	V.G.	Good	Fair	Poor
—	—	6000	2950	1000	400

COLT METALLIC CARTRIDGE CONVERSIONS

Thuer Conversion Revolver

Although quite simplistic and not commercially successful, the Thuer Conversion was the first attempt by Colt to convert the percussion revolvers to the new metallic cartridge system. This conversion was designed around the tapered Thuer cartridge and consists of a ring that replaced the back part of the cylinder, which had been milled off. This ring is stamped "Pat. Sep./15, 1868". The ejection position is marked with the letter "E". These conversions have rebounding firing pins and are milled to allow loading from the front of the revolver. This conversion was undertaken on the six different models listed; and all other specifications, finishes, markings, etc., not directly affected by the conversion would be the same as previously described. From a collectible and investment standpoint, the Thuer Conversion is very desirable. Competent appraisal should be secured if acquisition is contemplated. **NOTE:** Blued models will bring higher prices than nickel models in the same condition.

Model 1849 Pocket

NIB	Exc.	V.G.	Good	Fair	Poor
—	60000	35000	15500	4000	2000

Model 1851

Courtesy Milwaukee Public Museum, Milwaukee, Wisconsin

NIB	Exc.	V.G.	Good	Fair	Poor
—	—	28000	18000	5000	2000

Model 1860 Army

NIB	Exc.	V.G.	Good	Fair	Poor
—	—	30000	19500	6000	2000

Model 1861 Navy

NIB	Exc.	V.G.	Good	Fair	Poor
—	—	30000	19500	6000	2000

Model 1862 Police

NIB	Exc.	V.G.	Good	Fair	Poor
—	—	20000	13500	3500	1500

Model 1862 Pocket Navy

NIB	Exc.	V.G.	Good	Fair	Poor
—	—	25000	16000	3500	1500

Richards Conversion, 1860 Army Revolver

This was Colt's second attempt at metallic cartridge conversion, and it met with quite a bit more success than the first. The Richards Conversion was designed for the .44 Colt cartridge and has a 6-shot cylinder and an integral ejector rod to replace the loading lever that had been removed. The other specifications pertaining to the 1860 Army Revolver remain as previously described if they are not directly altered by the conversion. The Richards Conversion adds a breechplate with a firing pin and its own rear sight. There were approximately 9,000 of these Conversions manufactured between 1873 and 1878. **NOTE:** Blued models will bring higher prices than nickel models in the same condition.

NIB	Exc.	V.G.	Good	Fair	Poor
—	—	10000	3950	2000	600

Martially Marked

This variation is found with mixed serial numbers and a second set of conversion serial numbers. The "U.S." is stamped on the left side of the barrel lug, and inspector's cartouche appears on the grip. This is a very rare Colt revolver.

Courtesy Little John's Auction Service, Inc., Paul Goodwin photo

NIB	Exc.	V.G.	Good	Fair	Poor
—	—	18000	15000	8000	2000

Transition Richards Model

This variation is marked by the presence of a firing pin hammer.

Courtesy Bonhams & Butterfields, San Francisco, California

NIB	Exc.	V.G.	Good	Fair	Poor
—	—	9500	7000	3000	1200

Richards-Mason Conversion, 1860 Army Revolver

This conversion is different from the Richards Conversion in a number of readily apparent aspects. The barrel was manufactured with a small lug much different in appearance than seen on the standard 1860 Army. The breechplate does not have its own rear sight, and there is a milled area to allow the hammer to contact the base of the cartridge. These Conversions were also chambered for the .44 Colt cartridge, and the cylinder holds 6 shots. There is an integral ejector rod in place of the loading lever. The barrels on some are stamped either "Address Col. Saml. Colt New-York U.S. America" or "Colt's Pt. F.A. Mfg. Co. Hartford, Ct." The patent dates 1871 and 1872 are stamped on the left side of the frame. The finish of these revolvers, as well as the grips, were for the most part the same as on the unconverted Armies; but for the first time, nickel-plated guns are found. There were approximately 2,100 of these Conversions produced in 1877 and 1878. **NOTE:** Blued models will bring higher prices than nickel models in the same condition.

NIB	Exc.	V.G.	Good	Fair	Poor
—	—	13500	7000	2500	800

Richards-Mason Conversions 1851 Navy Revolver

These revolvers were converted in the same way as the 1860 Army previously described, the major difference being the caliber .38, either rimfire or centerfire. Finishes are mostly the same as on unconverted revolvers, but nickel-plated guns are not rare. **NOTE:** Blued models will bring higher prices than nickel models in the same condition.

Production Model Serial #1-3800

Courtesy Bonhams & Butterfields, San Francisco, California

NIB	Exc.	V.G.	Good	Fair	Poor
—	—	11000	5500	2000	800

U.S. Navy Model Serial #41000-91000

"USN" stamped on butt; steel grip frame.

NIB	Exc.	V.G.	Good	Fair	Poor
—	—	16000	9500	3000	1000

Richards-Mason Conversion 1861 Navy Revolver

The specifications for this model are the same as for the 1851 Navy Conversion described above, with the base revolver being different. There were 2,200 manufactured in the 1870s. **NOTE:** Blued models will bring higher prices than nickel models in the same condition.

Courtesy Wallis & Wallis, Lewes, Sussex, England

Standard Production Model Serial #100-3300

NIB	Exc.	V.G.	Good	Fair	Poor
—	—	11500	6250	1500	500

U.S. Navy Model Serial #1000-9999

NIB	Exc.	V.G.	Good	Fair	Poor
—	—	15000	7500	3500	1000

Model 1862 Police and Pocket Navy Conversions

The conversion of these two revolver models is the most difficult to catalog of all the Colt variations. There were approximately 24,000 of these produced between 1873 and 1880. There are five basic variations with a number of sub-variations. The confusion is usually caused by the different ways in which these were marked. Depending upon what parts were utilized, caliber markings could be particularly confusing. One must also consider the fact that many of these conversion revolvers found their way into secondary markets, such as Mexico and Central and South America, where they were either destroyed or received sufficient abuse to obliterate most identifying markings. The five basic variations are all chambered for either the .38 rimfire or the .38 centerfire cartridge. All held 5 shots, and most were found with the round roll-engraved stagecoach holdup scene. The half-fluted cylinder from the 1862 Police is quite rare on the conversion revolver and not found at all on some of the variations. The finishes on these guns were pretty much the same as they were before conversion, but it is not unusual to find nickel-plated specimens. **NOTE:** Blued models will bring a premium over nickel in the same condition. Half-fluted cylinder add 20 percent.

Round Barrel Pocket Navy with Ejector

NIB	Exc.	V.G.	Good	Fair	Poor
—	—	7500	3500	1600	800

3.5" Round Barrel Without Ejector

NIB	Exc.	V.G.	Good	Fair	Poor
—	—	5500	2500	1000	300

4.5" Octagonal Barrel Without Ejector

NIB	Exc.	V.G.	Good	Fair	Poor
—	—	6500	3500	1200	400

Model 1862 Pocket Navy Octagon Barrel with Ejector

NIB	Exc.	V.G.	Good	Fair	Poor
—	—	7500	3850	1500	600

Model 1862 Police Round Barrel with Ejector

NIB	Exc.	V.G.	Good	Fair	Poor
—	—	7500	3850	1500	600

Model 1871-1872 Open Top Revolver

This model was the first revolver Colt manufactured especially for a metallic cartridge. It was not a conversion. The frame, 7.5" or 8" round barrel, and the 6-shot cylinder were produced for the .44 rimfire metallic cartridge. The grip frame and some internal parts were taken from the 1860 Army and the 1851 Navy. Although this model was not commercially successful and was not accepted by the U.S. Ordinance Department, it did pave the way for the Single-Action Army that came out shortly thereafter and was an immediate success. This model is all blued, with a case colored hammer. There are some with silver-plated brass grip frames, but most are blued steel. The one-piece grips are of varnished walnut. The cylinder is roll-engraved with the naval battle scene. The barrel is stamped "Address Col. Saml. Colt New-York U.S. America". The later production revolvers are barrel stamped "Colt's Pt. F.A. Mfg. Co. Hartford, Ct. U.S.A." The first 1,000 revolvers were stamped "Colt's/Patent". After that, 1871 and 1872 patent dates appeared on the frame. There were 7,000 of these revolvers manufactured in 1872 and 1873. **NOTE:** Blued models will bring higher prices than nickel models in the same condition.

1860 Army Grip Frame

NIB	Exc.	V.G.	Good	Fair	Poor
—	—	27500	15000	4500	800

1851 Navy Grip Frame

NIB	Exc.	V.G.	Good	Fair	Poor
—	—	29000	17500	4000	1200

COLT DERRINGERS AND POCKET REVOLVER

First Model Derringer

This is a small all-metal single-shot. It is chambered for the .41 rimfire cartridge. The 2.5" barrel pivots to the left and downward for loading. This model is engraved with a scroll pattern and has been noted blued, silver, or nickel-plated. The barrel is stamped "Colt's Pt. F.A. Mfg. Co./Hartford Ct. U.S.A/ No.1." ".41 Cal." is stamped on the frame under the release catch. There were approximately 6,500 of this model manufactured from 1870-1890. It was the first single-shot pistol Colt produced.

Courtesy Rock Island Auction Company

NIB	Exc.	V.G.	Good	Fair	Poor
—	—	3750	2500	1200	400

Second Model Derringer

Although this model has the same odd shape as the First Model, it is readily identifiable by the checkered varnished walnut grips and the "No 2" on the barrel after the address. It is also .41 rimfire and has a 2.5" barrel that pivots in the same manner as the First Model. There were approximately 9,000 of these manufactured between 1870 and 1890.

Courtesy Wallis & Wallis, Lewes, Sussex, England

NIB	Exc.	V.G.	Good	Fair	Poor
—	—	3200	2000	900	400

Third Model Derringer

This model was designed by Alexander Thuer who was also responsible for Colt's first metallic cartridge conversion. It is often referred to as the "Thuer Model" for this reason. It is also chambered for the .41 rimfire cartridge and has a 2.5" barrel that pivots to the right (but not down) for loading. The Third Model has a more balanced appearance than its predecessors, and its commercial success (45,000 produced between 1875 and 1910) reflects this. The barrel on this model is stamped "Colt" in small block letters on the first 2,000 guns. The remainder of the production features the "COLT" in large italicized print. The ".41 Cal." is stamped on the left side of the frame. This model will be found with the barrel blued or plated in either silver or nickel and the bronze frame plated. The grips are varnished walnut. **NOTE:** Blued models will bring a premium over nickel in the same condition.

First Variation, Early Production

This has a raised area ("pregnant frame") on the underside of the frame through which the barrel screw passes, and the spur is not angled. Small block "Colt" lettering on barrel.

NIB	Exc.	V.G.	Good	Fair	Poor
—	—	4000	3000	2200	1000

First Variation, Late Production

This is similar to early production but has large italicized "COLT" on barrel.

NIB	Exc.	V.G.	Good	Fair	Poor
—	—	3400	2200	1500	600

Production Model

NIB	Exc.	V.G.	Good	Fair	Poor
—	—	1800	800	400	200

House Model Revolver

There are two basic versions of this model. They are both chambered for the .41 rimfire cartridge. The 4-shot version is known as the "Cloverleaf" due to the shape of the cylinder when viewed from the front. Approximately 7,500 of the nearly 10,000 House revolvers were of this 4-shot configuration. They are offered with a 1.5" or 3" barrel. The 1.5" length is quite rare, and some octagonal barrels in this length have been noted. The 5-shot round-cylinder version accounts for the rest of the production. It is found with serial numbers over 6100 and is offered with a 2-7/8" length barrel only. This model is stamped on the top strap "Pat. Sept. 19, 1871". This model has brass frames that were sometimes nickel-plated. The barrels are found either blued or plated. The grips are varnished walnut or rosewood. There were slightly fewer than 10,000 of both variations manufactured from 1871-1876.

Cloverleaf with 1.5" Round Barrel

NIB	Exc.	V.G.	Good	Fair	Poor
—	3750	3000	2000	1250	400

Cloverleaf with 3" Barrel

Courtesy Buffalo Bill Historical Center, Cody, Wyoming

NIB	Exc.	V.G.	Good	Fair	Poor
—	—	1750	1500	500	200

House Pistol with 5-Shot Round Cylinder

NIB	Exc.	V.G.	Good	Fair	Poor
—	—	1550	1300	500	200

Open Top Pocket Revolver

This is a .22-caliber rimfire, 7-shot revolver that was offered with either a 2-3/8" or a 2-7/8" barrel. The model was a commercial success, with over 114,000 manufactured between 1871 and 1877. There would undoubtedly have been a great deal more sold had not the cheap copies begun to flood the market at that time, forcing Colt to drop this model from the line. This revolver has a silver or nickel-plated brass frame and a nickel-plated or blued barrel and cylinder. The grips are varnished walnut. The cylinder bolt slots are found toward the front on this model. "Colt's Pt. F.A. Mfg. Co./Hartford, Ct. U.S.A." is stamped on the barrel and ".22 Cal." on the left side of the frame.

Early Model with Ejector Rod

Courtesy Bonhams & Butterfields

NIB	Exc.	V.G.	Good	Fair	Poor
—	—	2000	1750	800	400

Production Model without Ejector Rod

NIB	Exc.	V.G.	Good	Fair	Poor
—	—	1250	600	300	150

New Line Revolver .22

This was the smallest framed version of the five distinct New Line Revolvers. It has a 7-shot cylinder and a 2.25" octagonal barrel. The frame is nickel-plated, and the balance of the revolver is either nickel-plated or blued. The grips are of rosewood. There were approximately 55,000 of these made from 1873-1877. Colt also stopped production of the New Lines rather than try to compete with the "Suicide Specials". "Colt New .22" is found on the barrel; and ".22 Cal.", on the frame. The barrel is also stamped "Colt's Pt. F.A. Mfg.Co./Hartford, Ct. U.S.A." **NOTE:** Blued models will bring higher prices than nickel models in the same condition.

1st Model

Short cylinder flutes.

NIB	Exc.	V.G.	Good	Fair	Poor
—	—	1300	600	300	150

2nd Model

Long cylinder flutes.

Courtesy Bonhams & Butterfields, San Francisco, California

NIB	Exc.	V.G.	Good	Fair	Poor
—	—	750	500	250	125

New Line Revolver .30

This is a larger version of the .22 New Line. The basic difference is the size, caliber, caliber markings, and the offering of a blued version with case colored frame. There were approximately 11,000 manufactured from 1874-1876.

Courtesy Wallis & Wallis, Lewes, Sussex, England

NIB	Exc.	V.G.	Good	Fair	Poor
—	—	1000	750	300	150

New Line Revolver .32

This is the same basic revolver as the .30 caliber except that it is chambered for the .32-caliber rimfire and .32-caliber centerfire and is so marked. There were 22,000 of this model manufactured from 1873-1884. **NOTE:** This model was offered with the rare 4" barrel, and this variation would be worth nearly twice the value of a standard model. Prices listed are for nickel finish. Blued models will bring a premium of 100 percent.

Courtesy Bonhams & Butterfields, San Francisco, California

NIB	Exc.	V.G.	Good	Fair	Poor
—	—	1550	850	300	150

New Line Revolver .38

There were approximately 5,500 of this model manufactured between 1874 and 1880. It is chambered for either the .38 rimfire or .38 centerfire caliber and is so marked. This model in a 4" barrel would also bring twice the value. **NOTE:** Prices are for nickel finish. Blued models will bring a premium of 100 percent.

Courtesy Rock Island Auction Company

NIB	Exc.	V.G.	Good	Fair	Poor
—	—	1500	800	400	200

New Line Revolver .41

This is the "Big Colt, as it was sometimes known in advertising of its era. It is chambered for the .41 rimfire and the .41 centerfire and is so marked. The large caliber of this variation makes this the most desirable of the New Lines to collectors. There were approximately 7,000 of this model manufactured from 1874-1879. **NOTE:** A 4"-barreled version would again be worth a 100 percent premium.

NIB	Exc.	V.G.	Good	Fair	Poor
—	—	2000	1375	650	300

New House Model Revolver

This revolver is similar to the other New Lines except that it features a square-butt instead of the bird's-head configuration, a 2.25" round barrel without ejector rod, and a thin loading gate. It is chambered for the .32 (rare), .38, and the .41 centerfire cartridges. The finish was either full nickel-plated or blued, with a case colored frame. The grips are walnut, rosewood or (for the first time on a Colt revolver) checkered hard rubber, with an oval around the word "Colt". The barrel address is the same as on the other New Lines. The frame is marked "New House", with the caliber. There were approximately 4,000 manufactured between 1880-1886. .32 caliber model would bring a 10 percent premium.

Courtesy Milwaukee Public Museum, Milwaukee, Wisconsin

NIB	Exc.	V.G.	Good	Fair	Poor
—	—	1495	1000	450	250

New Police Revolver

This was the final revolver in the New Line series. It is chambered for .32, .38, and .41 centerfire caliber. The .32 and .41 are quite rare. It is offered in barrel lengths of 2.25", 4.5", 5.5", and 6.5". An ejector rod is found on all but the 2.5" barrel. The finish is either nickel or blued and case colored. The grips are hard rubber with a scene of a policeman arresting a criminal embossed on them; thusly the model became known to collectors as the "Cop and Thug" model. The barrel stamping is as the other New Lines, and the frame is stamped "New Police .38". There were approximately 4,000 of these manufactured between 1882-1886. **NOTE:** The .32 and .41 caliber versions of this model will bring a 40-50 percent premium. Blued models and models with 5.5" or 6.5" barrels will bring a premium. Short barrel model will bring about 50 percent of the listed prices.

Courtesy Milwaukee Public Museum, Milwaukee, Wisconsin

Long Barrel Model with Ejector

NIB	Exc.	V.G.	Good	Fair	Poor
—	—	—	3250	1400	700

COLT'S SINGLE-ACTION ARMY REVOLVER

The Colt Single-Action Army, or Peacemaker as it is sometimes referred to, is one of the most widely collected and recognized firearms in the world. With few interruptions or changes in design, it has been manufactured from 1873 until the present. It is still available on a limited production basis from the Colt Custom Shop. The variations in this model are myriad. It has been produced in 30 different calibers and barrel lengths from 2.5" to 16", with 4.75", 5.5", and 7.5" standard. The standard finish is blued, with a case colored frame. Many are nickel-plated. Examples have been found silver- and gold-plated, with combinations thereof. The finest engravers in the world have used the SAA as a canvas to display their artistry. The standard grips from 1873-1883 were walnut, either oil-stained or varnished. From 1883 to approximately 1897, the standard grips were hard rubber with eagle and shield. After this date, at serial number 165000, the hard rubber grips featured the Rampant Colt. Many special-order grips were available, notably pearl and ivory, which were often checkered or carved in ornate fashion. The variables involved in establishing values on this model are extreme. Added to this, one must also consider historical significance, since the SAA played a big part in the formative years of the American West. Fortunately for those among us interested in the SAA, there are a number of fine publications available dealing exclusively with this model. It is my strongest recommendation that they be acquired and studied thoroughly to prevent extremely expensive mistakes. The Colt factory records are nearly complete for this model, and research should be done before acquisition of rare or valuable specimens. For our purposes we will break down the Single-Action Army production as follows: Antique or Black Powder, 1873-1898, serial number 1-175000. The cylinder axis pin is retained by a screw in the front of the frame. Pre-war, 1899-1940, serial number 175001-357859. The cylinder axis pin is retained by a spring-loaded button through the side of the frame. This method is utilized on the following models, as well. Post-war 2nd Generation, 1956-1978, serial number 0001SA-99999SA. 3rd Generation, 1978-Present, serial #SA1001. A breakdown of production by caliber will follow the chapter. It is important to note that the rarer calibers and the larger calibers bring higher values in this variation.

NOTE: As a rule of thumb, nickel guns will bring a deduction of 20-30 percent. For revolvers with 4.75" barrels add 10-15 percent. For checkered grips add 20 percent.

COLT ANTIQUE SINGLE ACTION ARMY REVOLVER

1st Year Production "Pinched Frame" 1873 Only

It is necessary to categorize this variation on its own. This is one of the rarest and most interesting of all the SAAs—not to mention that it is the first. On this model the top strap is pinched or constricted approximately one-half inch up from the hammer to form the rear sight. The highest surviving serial number having this feature is #156, the lowest #1. From these numbers, it is safe to assume that the first run of SAAs were all pinched-frame models; but there is no way to tell how many there were, since Colt did not serial number the frames in the order that they were manufactured. An educated guess would be that there were between 50 and 150 pinched frame guns in all and that they were all made before mid-July 1873. The reason for the change came about on the recommendation of Capt. J.R. Edie, a government inspector who thought that the full fluted top strap would be a big improvement in the sighting capabilities of the weapon. The barrel length of the first model is 7.5"; the standard caliber, .45 Colt; and the proper grips were of walnut. The front sight blade is German silver. Needless to say, this model will rarely be encountered; and if it is, it should never be purchased without competent appraisal.

NIB	Exc.	V.G.	Good	Fair	Poor
—	—	275000	250000	125000	90000

Early Military Model 1873-1877

The serial number range on this first run of military contract revolvers extends to #24000. The barrel address is in the early script style with the # symbol preceding and following. The frame bears the martial marking "US", and the walnut grips have the inspector's cartouche stamped on them. The front sight is steel as on all military models; the barrel length, 7.5". The caliber is .45 Colt, and the ejector rod head is the bull's-eye or donut style with a hole in the center of it. The finish features the military polish and case colored frame, with the remainder blued. Authenticate any potential purchase; many spurious examples have been noted.

NIB	Exc.	V.G.	Good	Fair	Poor
—	115000	75000	40000	30000	15000

Early Civilian Model 1873-1877

This model is identical to the Early Military Model but has no military acceptance markings or cartouches. Some could have the German silver front sight blade. The early bull's-eye ejector rod head is used on this model. The Civilian Model has a higher degree of polish than is found on the military models, and the finish on these early models could be plated or blued with a case colored frame. This model also has a script barrel address. The grips are standard one-piece walnut. Ivory-grip models are worth a premium.

NIB	Exc.	V.G.	Good	Fair	Poor
—	65000	50000	35000	20000	10000

.44 Rimfire Model 1875-1880

This model was made to fire the .44 Henry Rimfire cartridge. It was to be used as a compatible companion sidearm to the Henry and Winchester 1866 rifles that were used extensively during this era. However, this was not the case; and the .44 Rimfire was doomed to economic failure as soon as it appeared on the market. By that time, it had already been established that large-caliber centerfire cartridges were a good deal more efficient than their rimfire counterparts. The large-caliber rimfires were deemed obsolete before this Colt ever hit the market. The result of this was that Colt's sales representatives sold most of the production to obscure banana republics in South and Central America, where this model received much abuse. Most had the original 7.5" barrels cut down; and nearly all were denied even the most basic maintenance, making the survival rate of this model quite low. All this adds to its desirability as a collector's item and makes the risk of acquiring a fake that much greater. This model is unique in that it was the only SAA variation to have its own serial number range, starting with #1 and continuing to #1892, the latest known surviving specimen. The block style barrel markings were introduced during this production run. At least 90 of these revolvers were converted by the factory to .22 rimfire, and one was shipped chambered for .32 rimfire.

NIB	Exc.	V.G.	Good	Fair	Poor
—	80000	60000	47000	20000	10000

Late Military Model 1878-1891

The later Military Models are serial numbered to approximately #136000. They bear the block-style barrel address without the # prefix and suffix. The frames are marked "US," and the grips have the inspector's cartouche. The finish is the military-style polish, case colored frame; and the remainder, blued. Grips are oil-stained walnut. On the military marked Colts, it is imperative that potential purchases be authenticated as many fakes have been noted. **NOTE:** Revolvers produced from 1878 to 1885 will command a premium. Seek an expert appraisal prior to sale.

NIB	Exc.	V.G.	Good	Fair	Poor
—	68000	39500	14000	10000	6000

Artillery Model 1895-1903

A number of "US" marked SAAs were returned either to the Colt factory or to the Springfield Armory, where they were altered and refinished. These revolvers have 5.5" barrels and any combination of mixed serial numbers. They were remarked by the inspectors of the era and have a case colored frame and a blued cylinder and barrel. Some have been noted all blued within this variation. This model, as with the other military marked Colts, should definitely be authenticated before purchase. Some of these revolvers fall outside the 1898 antique cutoff date that has been established by the government and, in our experience, are not quite as desirable to investors. They are generally worth approximately 20 percent less.

NIB	Exc.	V.G.	Good	Fair	Poor
—	18000	12500	8000	4000	3000

London Model

These SAAs were manufactured to be sold through Colt's London Agency. The barrel is stamped "Colt's Pt. F.A. Mfg. Co. Hartford, Ct. U.S.A. Depot 14 Pall Mall London". This model is available in various barrel lengths. They are generally chambered for .45 Colt, .450 Boxer, .450 Eley, .455 Eley, and rarely .476 Eley, the largest of the SAA chamberings. A good many of these London Models were cased and embellished, and they should be individually appraised. This model should be authenticated as many spurious examples have been noted.

NIB	Exc.	V.G.	Good	Fair	Poor
—	22000	15000	10000	4500	2000

Frontier Six-Shooter 1878-1882

Several thousand SAAs were made with the legend "Colt's Frontier Six Shooter" acid-etched into the left side of the barrel instead of being stamped. This etching is not deep, and today collectors will become ecstatic if they discover a specimen with mere vestiges of the etched panel remaining. These acid-etched SAAs are serial numbered #45000-#65000. They have various barrel lengths and finishes, but all are chambered for the .44-40 caliber.

Courtesy Little John's Auction Service, Inc., Paul Goodwin photo

NIB	Exc.	V.G.	Good	Fair	Poor
—	40000	20000	14000	7000	5000

Sheriff's or Storekeeper's Model 1882-1898

This model was made in several barrel lengths: 2.5", 3", 3.5", 4", 4.75" and 7.5". The 2.5" and 7.5" guns are very rare and can bring premiums of 25 to 50 percent, depending on condition. Most have 4" barrels. It features no ejector rod or housing, and the frame is made without the hole in the right forward section to accommodate the ejector assembly. The Sheriff's or Storekeeper's Model is numbered above serial #73000. It was manufactured with various finishes and chambered for numerous calibers. This model continued after 1898 into the smokeless or modern era. Examples manufactured in the pre-war years are worth approximately 20 percent less. Although faking this model is quite difficult, it has been successfully attempted. **NOTE:** Nickel models will command a premium.

Courtesy Little John's Auction Service, Inc., Paul Goodwin photo

NIB	Exc.	V.G.	Good	Fair	Poor
—	65000	50000	40000	25000	10000

Flattop Target Model 1888-1896

This model is highly regarded and sought after by collectors. It is not only rare (only 925 manufactured) but is an extremely attractive and well-finished variation. It is chambered for 22 different calibers from .22 rimfire to .476 Eley. The .22 rimfire, .38 Colt, .41, and .45 Colt are the most predominant chamberings. The 7.5" barrel length is the most commonly encountered. The serial number range is between #127000-#162000. Some have been noted in higher ranges. The finish is all blued, with a case colored hammer. The checkered grips are either hard rubber or walnut. The most readily identifying feature of the flattop is the lack of a groove in the top strap and the sight blade dovetailed into the flattop. The front sight has a removable blade insert. The values given are for a standard production model chambered for the calibers previously mentioned as being the most common. It is important to have other calibers individually appraised as variance in values can be quite extreme. **NOTE:** Nickel models will command a premium.

NIB	Exc.	V.G.	Good	Fair	Poor
—	35000	25000	15000	8000	4000

Bisley Model 1894-1915

This model was named for the target range in Great Britain, where their National Target Matches were held since the nineteenth century. The model was designed as a target revolver with an odd humped-back grip that was supposed to better fill the hand while target shooting. It is also easily identified by the wide low profile hammer spur, wide trigger, and the name "Bisley" stamped on the barrel. The Bisley production fell within the serial number range #165000-#331916. There were 44,350 made. It was offered in 16 different chamberings from .32 Colt to .455 Eley. The most common calibers were .32-20, .38-40, .41, .44-40, and .45 Colt. The barrel lengths are 4.75", 5.5", and 7.5". The frame and hammer are case-colored; the remainder, blued. Smokeless powder models produced after 1899 utilized the push-button cylinder pin retainer. The grips are checkered hard rubber. This model was actually designed with English sales in mind; and though it did sell well over there, American sales accounted for most of the Bisley production. The values we provide here cover the standard calibers and barrel lengths. Rare calibers and/or other notable variations can bring greatly fluctuating values.

NIB	Exc.	V.G.	Good	Fair	Poor
—	9000	6500	4500	2500	1200

Bisley Model Flattop Target 1894-1913

This model is quite similar to the Standard Bisley Model, with the flattop frame and dovetailed rear sight feature. It also has the removable front sight insert. It has an all-blued finish with case-colored hammer only and is available with a 7.5" barrel. Smokeless powder models produced after 1899 utilized the push-button cylinder pin retainer. The calibers are the same as the standard Bisley. Colt manufactured 976 of these revolvers. The advice regarding appraisal would also apply. **NOTE:** Nickel models will command a premium.

NIB	Exc.	V.G.	Good	Fair	Poor
—	25000	16000	9500	3500	1800

Standard Civilian Production Models 1876-1898

This final designated category for the black powder or antique SAAs includes all the revolvers not previously categorized. They have barrel lengths from 4.75", 5.5", and 7.5" and are chambered for any one of 30 different calibers. The finishes could be blued, blued and case colored, or plated in nickel, silver, gold, or combinations thereof. Grips could be walnut, hard rubber, ivory, pearl, stag, or bone. The possibilities are endless. The values given here are for the basic model, and we again strongly advise securing qualified appraisal when not completely sure of any model variation. **NOTE:** Add a 20 percent premium for serial numbers between 54000 and 130000, 40 percent for serial numbers between 22000 and 54000. Add 20 to 30 percent for original box, depending on condition. Add 10 percent for 4.75" barrel.

NIB	Exc.	V.G.	Good	Fair	Poor
—	30000	18000	12000	8000	3000

COLT PRE-WAR SINGLE-ACTION ARMY REVOLVER 1899-1940

Standard Production Pre-war Models (1899-1940)

The 1899 cutoff has been thoroughly discussed, but it is interesting to note that the actual beginning production date for smokeless models was 1900. The pre-war Colts are, all in all, quite similar to the antiques—the finishes, barrel lengths, grips, etc. Calibers are also similar, with the exception of the obsolete ones being dropped and new discoveries added. The most apparent physical difference between the smokeless powder and black powder models is the previously discussed method of retaining the cylinder axis pin. The pre-war Colts utilized the spring-loaded button through the side of the frame. The black powder models utilized a screw in the front of the frame. The values we furnish for this model designation are for these standard models only. The serial number range on the pre-war SAAs is 175001-357859. Any variation can have marked effects on value fluctuations, and qualified appraisal should be secured. **NOTE:** Scarce chamberings command 30 percent to 100 percent premium.

NIB	Exc.	V.G.	Good	Fair	Poor
—	15000	10000	6000	4000	2000

Long Fluted Cylinder Model (1913-1915)

Strange as it may seem, the Colt Company has an apparent credo they followed to never throw anything away. That credo was never more evident than with this model. These Long Flute Cylinders were actually left over from the model 1878 Double-Action Army Revolvers. Someone in the hierarchy at Colt had an inspiration that drove the gunsmiths on the payroll slightly mad: to make these cylinders fit the SAA frames. There were 1,478 of these Long Flutes manufactured. They are chambered for the .45 Colt, .38-40, .32-20, .41 Colt, and the .44 Smith & Wesson Special. They were offered in the three standard barrel lengths and were especially well-polished, having what has been described as Colt's "Fire Blue" on the barrel and cylinder. The frame and hammer are case colored. They are fitted with checkered hard rubber grips and are particularly fine examples of Colt's craft. Rare.

NIB	Exc.	V.G.	Good	Fair	Poor
—	17500	1000	6000	3250	2000

COLT POST-WAR SINGLE-ACTION ARMY REVOLVER (AKA SECOND GENERATION)

Standard Post-war Model (1956-1975)

In 1956 the shooting and gun-collecting fraternity succeeded in convincing Colt that there was a market for a re-introduced SAA. The revolver was brought back in the same external configuration. The only changes were internal. The basic specifications as to barrel length and finish availability were the same. The calibers available were .38 Special, .357 Magnum, .44 Special, and .45 Colt. The serial number range of the re-introduced 2nd Generation Colt is #000ISA-73000SA. Values are established by four basic factors: caliber (popularity and scarcity), barrel length, finish, and condition. Shorter barrel lengths are more desirable than the 7.5". The .38 Special is the rarest caliber, but the .45 Colt and .44 Special are more sought after than the .357 Magnum. Special feature revolvers, such as the 350 factory-engraved guns produced during this period, must be individually appraised. The

ivory situation in the world today has become quite a factor, as ivory grips are found on many SAAs. Remember as always, when in doubt secure a qualified appraisal. **NOTE:** 4.75" barrel add 25 percent. 5.5" barrel add 15 percent. Nickel finish add 25 percent. Ivory grips add $250.

7.5" Barrel Model .38 Special

NIB	Exc.	V.G.	Good	Fair	Poor
3500	2750	1700	1100	800	600

.357 Magnum

NIB	Exc.	V.G.	Good	Fair	Poor
3000	2000	1200	900	700	600

.44 Special

NIB	Exc.	V.G.	Good	Fair	Poor
3750	3000	1800	1100	1000	750

.45 Colt

NIB	Exc.	V.G.	Good	Fair	Poor
4000	3500	2000	1500	1000	750

Sheriff's Model (1960-1975)

Between 1960 and 1975, there were approximately 500 Sheriff's Models manufactured. The first of these were marketed by Centennial Arms. They have 3" barrels and no ejector rod assemblies. The frames were made without the hole for the ejector rod to pass through. They were blued, with case colored frames; 25 revolvers were nickel-plated and would bring a sizable premium if authenticated. The barrels are marked "Colt Sheriff's Model". The serial number has an "SM" suffix. They are chambered for the .45 Colt cartridge. **NOTE:** Nickel finish add 100 percent.

NIB	Exc.	V.G.	Good	Fair	Poor
3000	2200	1800	1200	850	600

Buntline Special (1957-1975)

The "Buntline Special" was named after a dime novelist named Ned Buntline, who supposedly gave this special long barrel revolver to Wyatt Earp. The story is suspected to be purely legend as no Colt records exist to lend it credence. Be that as it may, the Colt factory decided to take advantage of the market and produced the 12" barreled SAA from 1957-1974. There were approximately 3,900 manufactured. They are chambered for the .45 Colt cartridge and are offered in the blued and case colored finish. Only 65 Buntlines are nickel-plated, making this an extremely rare variation that definitely should be authenticated before purchase. Walnut grips are the most commonly noted, but they are also offered with the checkered hard rubber grips. The barrels are marked on the left side "Colt Buntline Special .45". **NOTE:** Nickel finish add 100 percent.

NIB	Exc.	V.G.	Good	Fair	Poor
2400	1600	1250	850	600	500

New Frontier (1961-1975)

The New Frontier is readily identified by its flattop frame and adjustable sight. It also has a high front sight. Colt manufactured approximately 4,200 of them. They are chambered for the .357 Magnum, .45 Colt, .44 Special (255 produced), and rarely (only 49 produced) in .38 Special. A few were chambered for the .44-40 cartridge. The 7.5" barrel length is by far the most common, but the 4.75" and 5.5" barrels are also offered. The standard finish is case colored and blued. Nickel-plating and full blue are offered but are rarely encountered. Standard grips are walnut. The barrel is stamped on the left side "Colt New Frontier

Colt Single-Action Army Production Breakdown by Caliber Antique and Pre-war

NOTE: Rare calibers can increase values 300-500 percent in extreme cases.

CALIBER	SAA	FLATTOP SAA	BISLEY	FLATTOP BISLEY
.22 R.F.	107	93	0	0
.32 R.F.	1	0	0	0
.32 Colt	192	24	160	44
.32 S&W	32	30	18	17
.32-44	2	9	14	17
.32-20	29,812	30	13,291	131
.38 Colt (1914)	1,011	122	412	96
.38 Colt (1922)	1,365	0	0	0
.38 S&W	9	39	10	5
.38 Colt Sp.	82	7	0	0
.38 S&W Sp.	25	0	2	0
.38-44	2	11	6	47
.357 Mag.	525	0	0	0
.380 Eley	1	3	0	0
.38-40	38,240	19	12,163	98
.41	16,402	91	3,159	24
.44 SmBr.	15	0	1	0
.44 R. F.	1,863	0	0	0
.44 Germ.	59	0	0	0
.44 Russ.	154	51	90	62
.44 S&W	24	51	29	64
.44 S&W Sp.	506	1	0	0
.44-40	64,489	21	6,803	78
.45 Colt	150,683	100	8,005	97
.45 SmBr.	4	0	2	0
.45 ACP	44	0	0	0
.450 Boxer	729	89	0	0
.450 Eley	2,697	84	5	0
.455 Eley	1,150	37	180	196
.476 Eley	161	2	0	0
Total	**310,386**	**914**	**44,350**	**976**

The above chart covers the production by caliber of the Single-Action Army Revolvers manufactured between 1873 and 1940. These are the antique and the pre-war firearms. This chart readily informs us as to which are the rare calibers.

S.A.A." The serial has the "NF" suffix. **NOTE:** 4.75" barrel add 25 percent. 5.5" barrel add 20 percent. Full Blue add 50 percent. .38 Special add 50 percent. .44 Special add 30 percent. 44-40 add 30 percent.

NIB	Exc.	V.G.	Good	Fair	Poor
2500	1850	1200	800	600	500

New Frontier Buntline Special (1962-1967)

This model is rare, as Colt only manufactured 70 during this five-year period. They are similar to the standard Buntline, with a 12" barrel. They are chambered for .45 Colt only.

NIB	Exc.	V.G.	Good	Fair	Poor
5500	3750	2000	1500	1000	700

COLT THIRD GENERATION SINGLE-ACTION ARMY 1976-1981

In 1976 Colt made some internal changes in the SAA. The external configuration was not altered. The serial number range began in 1976 with #80000SA, and in 1978 #99999SA was reached. At this time the suffix became a prefix, and the new serial range began with #SA01001. This model's value is determined in much the same manner as was described in the section on the 2nd Generation SAAs. Caliber, barrel length, finish, and condition are once again the four main determining factors. The prevalence of special-order guns was greater during this period, and many more factory-engraved SAAs were produced. Colt's Custom Shop was quite active during this period. Custom guns are valued according to the prevailing market. **NOTE:** 4.75" barrel add 25 percent. 5.5" barrel add 10 percent. Nickel plated add 10 percent. Ivory grips add $250.

7.5" Barrel .357 Magnum

NIB	Exc.	V.G.	Good	Fair	Poor
1500	1100	895	750	600	500

.44-40

NIB	Exc.	V.G.	Good	Fair	Poor
1950	1550	900	750	600	500

.44-40 Black Powder Frame
(Screw Retaining Cylinder Pin)

NIB	Exc.	V.G.	Good	Fair	Poor
1900	1400	1150	1000	800	600

.44 Special

NIB	Exc.	V.G.	Good	Fair	Poor
2000	1200	900	700	550	500

.45 Colt

NIB	Exc.	V.G.	Good	Fair	Poor
1750	1300	900	750	600	500

Sheriff's Model 3rd Generation

This model is similar to the 2nd Generation Sheriff's Model. The serial number and the fact that this model is also chambered for the .44-40 are the only external differences. Colt offered this model with interchangeable cylinders—.45 Colt/.45 ACP or .44-40/.44 Special—available in 3" barrel, blued and case colored finish standard. **NOTE:** Interchangeable cylinders add 30 percent. Nickel finish add 10 percent. Ivory grips add $250.

NIB	Exc.	V.G.	Good	Fair	Poor
1500	1275	950	600	450	400

Buntline Special 3rd Generation

This is the same basic configuration as the 2nd Generation with the 12" barrel. Standard finish blued and case-colored, it is chambered for .45 Colt and has checkered hard rubber grips. **NOTE:** Nickel finish add 20 percent.

NIB	Exc.	V.G.	Good	Fair	Poor
1500	1275	950	600	450	400

New Frontier 3rd Generation

This model is similar in appearance to the 2nd Generation guns. The 3rd Generation New Frontiers have five-digit serial numbers; the 2nd Generation guns, four-digit numbers. That and the calibers offered are basically the only differences. The 3rd Generations are chambered for the .44 Special and .45 Colt and are rarely found in .44-40. Barrel lengths are 7.5" standard, with the 4.75" and 5.5" rarely encountered. **NOTE:** .44-40 add 20 percent. 4.75" barrel add 35 percent. 5.5" barrel add 25 percent.

NIB	Exc.	V.G.	Good	Fair	Poor
1650	1225	750	550	500	400

COLT RECENT PRODUCTION SINGLE-ACTION ARMY 1982-PRESENT

Standard Single-Action Army Optional Features:

Nickel finish add $125. Royal blue finish add $200. Mirror brite finish add $225. Gold plate add $365. Silver plate add $365. Class A engraving add $875. Class B engraving add $1,200. Class C engraving add $1,500. Class D engraving add $1,750. Buntline engraving add 15 percent.

NIB	Exc.	V.G.	Good	Fair	Poor
1050	950	850	650	500	300

Colt Cowboy (CB1850)

Introduced in 1998 this model is a replica of the Single-Action Army that features a modern transfer bar safety system. Made in USA using some Canadian-built parts. Offered with 5.5" barrel and chambered for .45 Colt. Sights are fixed with walnut grips. Blued barrel with case colored frame. Discontinued in 2003.

NIB	Exc.	V.G.	Good	Fair	Poor
850	650	500	400	300	200

Colt Single-Action Army "Legend Rodeo"

A limited-edition revolver built to commemorate Colt's official PRCA sponsorship. Limited to 1,000. Chambered for .45 LC fitted with a 5.5" barrel. Nickel finish Buffalo horn grips with gold medallions. Machine engraved and washed in gold. Discontinued 1998.

NIB	Exc.	V.G.	Good	Fair	Poor
2750	2250	—	—	—	—

Frontier Six Shooter (2008)

New reintroduction of classic .44-40 Peacemaker. Black powder-style frame and 4.75", 5.5" and 7.5" barrel lengths. Blued finish with color casehardened frame or nickel. Discontinued 2010.

NIB	Exc.	V.G.	Good	Fair	Poor
1550	1100	750	600	400	200

Sheriff's and Storekeeper's Model (2008)

New reintroduction of classic Sheriff's (4" barrel) and Storekeeper's Model (3" barrel) without ejector assembly. Black powder-style frame. Blued finish with color casehardened frame or nickel. .45 Colt or .44-40. Discontinued 2010.

NIB	Exc.	V.G.	Good	Fair	Poor
1550	1100	750	600	400	200

175th Anniversary SAA Limited Edition

From the Colt Custom Shop to celebrate the 175th anniversary of the Colt Company, this model was introduced in 2011 with production limited to 175 units in each of the three standard barrel lengths of 4.75", 5.5" and 7.5". In .45 Colt only, features include a black powder frame, Royal Blue finish, 24 karat Gold plated scroll on the frame, cylinder and barrel depicting the Rampant Colt icon, Colt Dome, Serpentine Colt, Sam Colt signature and a banner with the text "1836 — 175th Anniversary — 2011".

NIB	Exc.	V.G.	Good	Fair	Poor
1425	1350	1000	—	—	—

New Frontier Third Generation

Reintroduction of the adjustable-sighted, flattop-frame version of the Single Action Army that was last made in 1975. Chambered in .357 Magnum, .44 Special or .45 Colt and in all three standard barrel lengths. The rear sight is adjustable for windage and elevation, and there is a ramp style front sight. Finish is Colt's Royal Blue on both the barrel and cylinder with a color case hardened frame. Two-piece walnut grips are decorated with a gold medallion. Introduced in 2011.

NIB	Exc.	V.G.	Good	Fair	Poor
1300	1225	900	700	600	500

COLT SCOUT MODEL

A surprising number of Colt pistols are still found in their original boxes, even older models. This can add 100 percent to the value of the pistol. My thanks to Bruce Buckner, Jr., for his suggestions for and corrections to this section. Anyone wishing to procure a factory letter authenticating a Single-Action Army should do so by writing to: COLT HISTORIAN, P.O. BOX 1868, HARTFORD, CT 06101. There is a charge of $50 per serial number for this service. If Colt cannot provide the desired information, $10 will be refunded. Enclose the Colt model name, serial number, and your name and address, along with the check.

Frontier Scout (1957-1971)

This is a scaled-down version of the SAA that is chambered for the .22 LR with an interchangeable .22 Magnum cylinder. It is offered with a 4.75", or a 9.5" barrel. The frame is alloy. First year production frame were duotone with frame left in the white and the balance of the revolver blued. All blue models and wood grips became available in 1958. In 1961 the duotone model was dropped from production. All the Q series guns were offered in duotone finish; F series guns were made in duotone and full blue. A .22 Magnum model was first offered in 1959. In 1964 dual cylinders were introduced. These revolvers have "Q" or "F" serial number suffixes. In 1960 the "K" series Scout was introduced and featured a heavier frame, nickel plating, and wood grips. The majority of commemorative revolvers are of this type. This series was discontinued in 1970. Prices are about 15 percent higher than for the "Q" and "F" series guns. **NOTE:** 9.5" Buntline add 50 percent. Extra cylinder add 10 percent.

NIB	Exc.	V.G.	Good	Fair	Poor
450	325	200	175	125	90

Peacemaker & New Frontier .22

This model is similar to the Frontier Scout, with a steel case-colored or blued frame. Fitted with old style black plastic eagle grips. Peacemaker .22 and New Frontier .22 revolvers were initially offered with 4.75", 6" and 7.5" barrels (Buntline). After about one year of production the 4.75" barrel was discontinued and a 4.4" barrel was offered in each model. It also has an interchangeable .22 Magnum cylinder.

The Peacemaker .22 was only available with a steel receiver with a color-casehardened finish. The grip frames were alloy. The same is true of the New Frontier .22 revolvers except that (as noted in the book), the New Frontier .22 GS series was available with color-casehardened or blue receivers. Both Peacemaker .22 and New Frontier .22 revolvers were available in the single caliber (.22 LR only) and dual caliber (.22 LR and .22 Magnum) models. The factory had separate model numbers for these variations. Also, the factory offered "P" series or "62" model Frontier Scouts and Buntline Scouts. This was a significant model variation. Most of these revolvers had a "G" suffix although some built in 1974 had a

"L" suffix. In 1982 through 1986 a New Frontier model with cross-bolt safety was offered. This model is often referred to as the "GS" series. This revolver was offered with adjustable sights only. No Peacemakers were offered in this series.

NIB	Exc.	V.G.	Good	Fair	Poor
550	475	300	200	150	100

Scout Model SAA (1962-1971)

This is basically a scaled-down version of the SAA chambered for the .22 LR cartridge. This model is offered with a 4.75", 6", or 7" barrel. The earlier production has case-colored frames with the remainder blued; later production is all blued. Grips are checkered hard rubber. This model was discontinued in 1986.

NIB	Exc.	V.G.	Good	Fair	Poor
400	275	200	150	100	75

COLT ANTIQUE LONG ARMS

Berdan Single-Shot Rifle

This is a scarce rifle on today's market. There were approximately 30,200 manufactured, but nearly 30,000 of them were sent to Russia. This rifle was produced from 1866-1870. It is a trapdoor-type action chambered for .42 centerfire. The standard model has a 32.5" barrel; the carbine, 18.25". The finish is blued, with a walnut stock. This rifle was designed and the patent held by Hiram Berdan, Commander of the Civil War "Sharpshooters" Regiment. This was actually Colt's first cartridge arm. The 30,000 rifles and 25 half-stocked carbines that were sent to Russia were in Russian Cyrillic letters. The few examples made for American sales have Colt's name and Hartford address on the barrel.

Courtesy Milwaukee Public Museum, Milwaukee, Wisconsin

Russian Order

30,000 manufactured.

NIB	Exc.	V.G.	Good	Fair	Poor
—	15000	10000	5000	1500	750

Carbine Russian Order

25 manufactured.

NIB	Exc.	V.G.	Good	Fair	Poor
—	18000	12500	6500	1800	750

U.S. Sales

100 manufactured.

NIB	Exc.	V.G.	Good	Fair	Poor
—	15000	10000	5000	1500	750

Carbine U.S. Sales

25 manufactured.

NIB	Exc.	V.G.	Good	Fair	Poor
—	18000	12500	6500	1800	750

Colt-Franklin Military Rifle

This is a rifle that was not a successful venture for Colt. The patents were held by William B. Franklin, a vice-president of the company.

This was a bolt-action rifle with a primitive, gravity-fed box magazine. It is chambered for the .45-70 government cartridge, has a 32.5" barrel, and is blued, with a walnut stock. The rifle has the Colt Hartford barrel address and is stamped with an eagle's head and U.S. inspectors marks. There were only 50 of these rifles produced, and it is believed that they were prototypes intended for government sales. This was not to be, and production ceased after approximately 50 were manufactured in 1887 and 1888.

NIB	Exc.	V.G.	Good	Fair	Poor
—		9500	5000	2000	1100

Colt-Burgess Lever-Action Rifle

This represented Colt's only attempt to compete with Winchester for the lever-action rifle market. It is said that when Winchester started to produce revolving handguns for prospective marketing, Colt dropped the Burgess from its line. This rifle is chambered for .44-40. It has a 25.5" barrel and a 15-shot tubular magazine. The Carbine version has a 20.5" barrel and 12-shot magazine. The finish is blued, with a case-colored hammer and lever. The stock is walnut with an oil finish. The Colt Hartford address is on the barrel, and "Burgess Patents" is stamped on the bottom of the lever. There were 3,775 rifles manufactured—1,219 with round barrels and 2,556 with octagonal barrels. There were also 2,593 Carbines. The Burgess was produced from 1883-1885.

Courtesy Buffalo Bill Historical Center, Cody, Wyoming

Rifle - Octagonal Barrel

NIB	Exc.	V.G.	Good	Fair	Poor
—	—	6000	4000	2000	1000

Rifle - Round Barrel

NIB	Exc.	V.G.	Good	Fair	Poor
—	—	5800	3800	1800	800

Carbine

NIB	Exc.	V.G.	Good	Fair	Poor
—	—	10000	7500	3000	1500

Baby Carbine

Lighter frame and barrel (RARE).

NIB	Exc.	V.G.	Good	Fair	Poor
—	—	12500	9000	4000	1500

Lightning Slide-Action, Medium-Frame

This was the first slide-action rifle Colt produced. It is chambered for .32-20, .38-40, and .44-40 and was intended to be a companion piece to the SAAs in the same calibers. The rifle has a 26" barrel with 15-shot tube magazine; the carbine, a 20" barrel with 12-shot magazine. The finish is blued, with case-colored hammer; the walnut stock is oil-finished; and the fore-end, usually checkered. The Colt name and Hartford address are stamped on the barrel along with the patent dates. There were approximately 89,777 manufactured between 1884 and 1902.

Courtesy Bonhams & Butterfields, San Francisco, California

Rifle

NIB	Exc.	V.G.	Good	Fair	Poor
—	—	4750	3500	2000	1000

Carbine

NIB	Exc.	V.G.	Good	Fair	Poor
—	—	5500	4000	2500	1500

Military Rifle or Carbine

.44-40 caliber, short magazine tube, bayonet lug, and sling swivels.

NIB	Exc.	V.G.	Good	Fair	Poor
—	7000	4000	2000	1500	

Baby Carbine

1 lb. lighter version of standard carbine.

Courtesy Richard M. Kumor Sr.

NIB	Exc.	V.G.	Good	Fair	Poor
—	8750	5500	3000	2000	

San Francisco Police Rifle

.44-40 caliber, #SFP 1-SFP401 on bottom tang.

NIB	Exc.	V.G.	Good	Fair	Poor
—	—	9000	6000	3000	2000

Lightning Slide-Action Small-Frame

This is a well-made rifle and the first of its type that Colt manufactured. It is chambered for the .22 Short and Long. The standard barrel length is 24"; the finish, blued with a case-colored hammer. The stock is walnut; some were checkered; some, not. The barrel is stamped with the Colt name and Hartford address and the patent dates. There were 89,912 manufactured between 1887 and 1904.

Courtesy Bonhams & Butterfields, San Francisco, California

NIB	Exc.	V.G.	Good	Fair	Poor
—	4000	2500	2000	1500	1000

Lightning Slide-Action, Large-Frame (Express)

This rifle is similar in appearance to the medium-frame Lightning, though larger in size. It is chambered in larger rifle calibers of the era, from .38-56 up to .50-95 Express. The larger calibers are more desirable from a collector's standpoint. The rifle has a 28" barrel; the carbine, a 22" barrel. The finish is blued, with a case-colored hammer. The stock is oiled walnut; the fore-end, checkered. The Colt name and Hartford address are stamped on the barrel along with the patent dates. This rifle is quite large and has come to be known as the "Express model". Colt manufactured 6,496 between 1887 and 1894.

Rifle - Octagonal Barrel 28"

NIB	Exc.	V.G.	Good	Fair	Poor
—	—	7500	3750	750	500

Rifle - Round Barrel 28"

NIB	Exc.	V.G.	Good	Fair	Poor
—	—	7500	3750	750	500

Carbine

22" barrel.

NIB	Exc.	V.G.	Good	Fair	Poor
—	—	9000	5500	2500	750

Baby Carbine

22" barrel 1 lb. lighter.

NIB	Exc.	V.G.	Good	Fair	Poor
—	—	12500	6500	2500	950

Model 1878 Double-Barrel Shotgun

This model is chambered in 10 or 12 gauge and has 28", 30", or 32" barrels. It is a sidelock double-trigger hammer gun with case-colored locks and breech. The barrels are browned Damacus-patterned. The checkered walnut stock is varnished or oil-finished. The Colt's Hartford address is stamped on the barrel rib; and Colt's name, on the lock. This has been regarded as one of the finest shotguns made in America, although Colt had difficulty competing with the less expensive European imports of the day. They ceased production after only 22,690 were manufactured between 1878 and 1889. **NOTE:** Fully engraved model add 300 percent.

NIB	Exc.	V.G.	Good	Fair	Poor
—	—	4500	2250	750	300

Model 1883 Double-Barrel Shotgun

This model is a hammerless boxlock, chambered for 8, 10 or 12 gauge. The barrels are 28", 30", or 32"; and it features double triggers. The frame and furniture are case-colored; the barrels, browned with Damascus pattern. The checkered walnut stock is varnished or oil-finished. Colt's Hartford address is stamped on the barrel rib. "Colt" is stamped on each side of the frame. Again, as in the Model 1878, this is rated as one of the finest of all American-made shotguns. There were many special orders, and they require individual appraisal. Colt manufactured 7,366 of these guns between 1883 and 1895. **NOTE:** Fully engraved model add 300 percent. For 8 gauge add 200 percent.

NIB	Exc.	V.G.	Good	Fair	Poor
—	3000	2000	1400	775	400

Double-Barrel Rifle

This is one of the rarest of all Colt firearms and is a prize for the Colt collector. There were only 35 of these guns manufactured. They were said to be the special interest of Caldwell Hart Colt, Samuel Colt's son, who was an avid arms collector. It is said that most of the 35 guns produced wound up in his collection or those of his friends. This gun is chambered for .45-70 or one of the larger variations thereof. It is an exposed hammer sidelock with double triggers. The locks, breech, and furniture are case-colored; the barrels, browned or blued. The barrels are 28" in length, and the checkered stock was oil-finished or varnished walnut. The barrel rib is stamped with the Colt name and Hartford address. The locks are also stamped "Colt". One must exercise extreme caution in dealing with this model as there have been Model 1878 shotguns converted into double rifles. Colt manufactured the 35 guns over the period 1879-1885.

Courtesy Bonhams & Butterfields, San Francisco, California

NIB	Exc.	V.G.	Good	Fair	Poor
—	95000	75000	35500	—	—

COLT DOUBLE-ACTION REVOLVERS

Model 1877 "Lightning" and "Thunderer"

The Model 1877 was Colt's first attempt at manufacturing a double-action revolver. It shows a striking resemblance to the Single-Action Army. Sales on this model were brisk, with over 166,000 produced between 1877 and 1909. Chambered for two different cartridges, the .38 Colt, known as the "Lightning," and .41 Colt, as the "Thunder." The standard finishes are blued, with case-colored frame and nickel plate. The bird's-head grips are of checkered rosewood on the early guns and hard rubber on the majority of the production run. The barrel lengths most often encountered are 2.5" and 3.5" without an ejector rod, and 4.5" and 6" with the rod. Other barrel lengths from 1.5" through 10" were offered. The Model 1877 holds 6 shots in either caliber. There were quite a few different variations found within this model designation. Values furnished are for the standard variations. Antiques made before 1898 would be more desirable from an investment standpoint. Note that these revolvers have a reputation as "watchmaker's nightmares" and non-functioning examples command substantially reduced prices. **NOTE:** Premium for blued guns add 25 percent. Premium for shorter than 2.5" add 50 percent. .41 Caliber "Thunderer" add 10 percent. Over 6" barrel add 50 percent. London barrel address add 20 percent. .32 caliber add 50 percent. Rosewood grips add 10 percent.

Without Ejector, 2.5" and 3.5" Barrel

NIB	Exc.	V.G.	Good	Fair	Poor
—	3000	2000	800	500	350

With Ejector, 4.5" and 6" Barrel

NIB	Exc.	V.G.	Good	Fair	Poor
—	3000	1800	800	750	450

Model 1878 "Frontier"

This model is a large and somewhat ungainly looking revolver. It has a solid frame with a removable trigger guard. The cylinder does not swing out, and there is a thin loading gate. It has bird's-head grips made of checkered hard rubber; walnut would be found on the early models. The finish is either blued and case-colored or nickel-plated. The Model 1878 holds 6 shots, and the standard barrel lengths are 4.75", 5.5", and 7.5" with an ejector assembly and 3", 3.5", and 4" without. The standard chamberings for the Model 1878 are .32-20, .38-40, .41 Colt, .44-40, and .45 Colt. This model was fairly well received because it is chambered for the large calibers that were popular in that era. Colt manufactured 51,210 between 1878 and 1905. Antique models made before 1898 would be more desirable from an investment standpoint. **NOTE:** Add a 15 percent premium for blued revolvers. Add 10-50 percent premium for calibers other than .44-40 or .45.

Standard

Courtesy Bonhams & Butterfields, San Francisco, California

NIB	Exc.	V.G.	Good	Fair	Poor
—	5000	3200	1600	800	400

Omnipotent

This is a special order version of the model above with the name "Omnipotent" stamped on the barrel.

NIB	Exc.	V.G.	Good	Fair	Poor
—	8000	7000	6000	3000	1000

Sheriff's Model

Chambered for .44-40 or .45 Colt with barrels lengths of 3.5" or 4".

NIB	Exc.	V.G.	Good	Fair	Poor
—	6000	4000	2000	1000	800

Model 1902 (Philippine or Alaskan Model)

This is a U.S. Ordnance contract Model 1878. It has a 6" barrel and is chambered for .45 Colt. The finish is blued, and there is a lanyard swivel on the butt. This model bears the U.S. inspector's marks. It is sometimes referred to as the Philippine or the Alaskan model. The trigger guard is quite a bit larger than standard.

Courtesy Bonhams & Butterfields

NIB	Exc.	V.G.	Good	Fair	Poor
—	5500	3500	1800	1000	600

Model 1889 Navy—Civilian Model

The 1889 Navy is an important model from a historical standpoint as it was the first double-action revolver Colt manufactured with a swing-out cylinder. They produced 31,000 of them between 1889 and 1894. The Model 1889 is chambered for the .38 Colt and the .41 Colt cartridges. The cylinder holds 6 shots. It is offered with a 3", 4.5", or 6" barrel; and the finish was either blued or nickel-plated. The grips are checkered hard rubber with the "Rampant Colt" in an oval molded into them. The patent dates 1884 and 1888 appear in the barrel marking, and the serial numbers are

stamped on the butt. **NOTE:** Add premium for blued models. For 3" barrel add 20 percent.

NIB	Exc.	V.G.	Good	Fair	Poor
—	2250	1500	1000	600	300

Model 1889 U.S. Navy—Martial Model

This variation has a 6" barrel, is chambered for .38 Colt, and is offered in blued finish only. "U.S.N." is stamped on the butt. Most of the Navy models were altered at the Colt factory to add the Model 1895 improvements. An original unaltered specimen would be worth as much as 50 percent premium over the altered values listed.

Courtesy Bonhams & Butterfields, San Francisco, California

NIB	Exc.	V.G.	Good	Fair	Poor
—	6000	5000	2500	1000	500

Model 1892 "New Army and Navy" —Civilian Model

This model is similar in appearance to the 1889 Navy. The main differences are improvements to the lockwork function. It has double bolt stop notches, a double cylinder locking bolt, and shorter flutes on the cylinder. The .38 Smith & Wesson and the .32-20 were added to the .38 Colt and .41 Colt chamberings. The checkered hard rubber grips are standard, with plain walnut grips found on some contract series guns. Barrel lengths and finishes are the same as described for the Model 1889. The patent dates 1895 and 1901 appear stamped on later models. Colt manufactured 291,000 of these revolvers between 1892 and 1907. Antiques before 1898 are more desirable from an investment standpoint. **NOTE:** For 3" barrel add 20 percent.

NIB	Exc.	V.G.	Good	Fair	Poor
—	1500	800	500	200	100

Model 1892 U.S. Navy—Martial Model

Courtesy Bonhams & Butterfields, San Francisco, California

NIB	Exc.	V.G.	Good	Fair	Poor
—	2500	2000	800	600	400

Model 1892 U.S. Army—Martial Model

NIB	Exc.	V.G.	Good	Fair	Poor
—	2500	2000	800	600	400

Model 1896/1896 Army

NIB	Exc.	V.G.	Good	Fair	Poor
—	2200	2000	800	600	400

Model 1905 Marine Corps

This model is a variation of the New Army and Navy Model. It was derived from the late production with its own serial range #10001-10926. With only 926 produced between 1905 and 1909, it is quite rare on today's market and is eagerly sought after by Colt Double-Action collectors. This model is chambered for the .38 Colt and the .38 Smith & Wesson Special cartridges. It holds 6 shots, has a 6" barrel, and is offered in a blued finish only. The grips are checkered walnut and are quite different than those found on previous models. "U.S.M.C." is stamped on the butt; patent dates of 1884, 1888, and 1895 are stamped on the barrel. One hundred twenty-five of these revolvers were earmarked for civilian sales and do not have the Marine Corps markings; these will generally be found in better condition. Values are similar.

Courtesy Faintich Auction Services, Inc., Paul Goodwin photo

NIB	Exc.	V.G.	Good	Fair	Poor
—	3000	2500	2000	1500	750

New Service Model

This model was in continual production from 1898 through 1944. It is chambered for 11 different calibers: .38 Special, .357 Magnum, .38-40, .44 Russian, .44 Special, .44-40, .45 ACP, .45 Colt, .450 Eley, .455 Eley, and .476 Eley. It is offered in barrel lengths from 2" to 7.5", either blued or nickel-plated. Checkered hard rubber grips were standard until 1928, and then checkered walnut grips were used with an inletted Colt medallion. This was the largest swing-out cylinder double-action revolver that Colt ever produced, and approximately 356,000 were manufactured over the 46 years they were made. There are many different variations of this revolver, and one should consult a book dealing strictly with Colt for a thorough breakdown and description. **NOTE:** Add 30 percent for nickel finish, 40 percent for factory ivory or pearl grips.

Courtesy Cherry's Collector Firearms Auction, Paul Goodwin photo

Early Model, #1-21000

NIB	Exc.	V.G.	Good	Fair	Poor
—	1700	1000	600	200	125

Early Model Target, #6000-15000

Checkered walnut grips, flattop frame, 7.5" barrel.

Courtesy Faintich Auction Services, Inc., Paul Goodwin photo

NIB	Exc.	V.G.	Good	Fair	Poor
—	3000	1500	550	300	200

Improved Model, #21000-325000

Has internal locking improvements.

Courtesy Faintich Auction Services, Inc., Paul Goodwin photo

NIB	Exc.	V.G.	Good	Fair	Poor
—	1150	850	450	175	150

Improved Target Model, #21000-325000

Courtesy Faintich Auction Services, Inc., Paul Goodwin photo

NIB	Exc.	V.G.	Good	Fair	Poor
	2250	1500	550	300	200

U.S. Army Model 1909, #30000-50000

5.5" barrel, .45 Colt, walnut grips, "U.S. Army Model 1909" on butt.

NIB	Exc.	V.G.	Good	Fair	Poor
—	1750	900	550	300	200

U.S. Navy Model 1909, #50000-52000

Same as above with "U.S.N." on butt.

NIB	Exc.	V.G.	Good	Fair	Poor
—	2600	1800	1000	350	250

U.S. Marine Corps Model 1909, #21000-23000

Checkered walnut grips, "U.S.M.C." on butt.

NIB	Exc.	V.G.	Good	Fair	Poor
—	3000	2000	1200	650	450

U.S. Army Model 1917, #150000-301000

Smooth walnut grips, 5.5" barrel, .45 ACP. Model designation stamped on butt.

Courtesy Faintich Auction Services, Inc., Paul Goodwin photo

NIB	Exc.	V.G.	Good	Fair	Poor
—	1300	900	600	300	225

Model 1917 Civilian, #335000-336000

Approximately 1,000 made in .45 ACP only from Army parts overrun. No military markings.

NIB	Exc.	V.G.	Good	Fair	Poor
—	1500	950	600	250	200

Late Model New Service, #325000-356000

Checkered walnut grips and internal improvements.

NIB	Exc.	V.G.	Good	Fair	Poor
—	1550	975	650	300	225

Shooting Master, #333000-350000

Round-butt, checkered walnut grips with Colt medallion, 6" barrel, "Colt Shooting Master" on barrel, flattop frame with target sights.

Chambered for the .38 Special cartridge. **NOTE:** Add 100 percent premium for .44 Special, .45 ACP, and .45 Colt.

Courtesy Faintich Auction Services, Inc., Paul Goodwin photo

NIB	Exc.	V.G.	Good	Fair	Poor
—	1950	1200	850	400	300

Magnum Model New Service, Over #340000

Chambered for .357 Magnum, .38 Special.

NIB	Exc.	V.G.	Good	Fair	Poor
—	2400	2000	1000	500	200

New Pocket Model

This was the first swing-out cylinder, double-action pocket revolver made by Colt. It is chambered for .32 Colt and .32 Smith & Wesson. It holds 6 shots and is offered with barrel lengths of 2.5", 3.5", 5", and 6". The finish is blued or nickel-plated, and the grips are checkered hard rubber with the oval Colt molded into them. "Colt's New Pocket" is stamped on the frame. 1884 and 1888 patent dates are stamped on the barrel of later-production guns. There were approximately 30,000 of these manufactured between 1893 and 1905. Antiques made before 1898 are more desirable. **NOTE:** Early production without patent dates add 25 percent. 5" barrel add 10 percent.

NIB	Exc.	V.G.	Good	Fair	Poor
—	750	450	300	250	150

Pocket Positive

Externally this is the same revolver as the New Pocket, but it has the positive lock feature. It was manufactured between 1905 and 1940.

NIB	Exc.	V.G.	Good	Fair	Poor
—	700	475	325	225	125

Army Special Model

This is a heavier-framed improved version of the New Army and Navy revolver. It is chambered for the .32-20, .38 Colt, .38 Smith & Wesson, and .41 Colt. It is offered with a 4", 4.5", 5", and 6" barrel. The finish is blued or nickel-plated, and the grips are checkered hard rubber. The serial number range is #291000-#540000, and they were manufactured between 1908-1927.

NIB	Exc.	V.G.	Good	Fair	Poor
—	650	475	250	200	150

New Police Model

This model appears similar to the New Pocket Model. The frame is stamped "New Police." It is chambered for the .32 Colt, .32 Colt New Police, and .32 Smith & Wesson cartridges. The barrel lengths are 2.5", 4", and 6". The finishes are blued or nickel-plated. Colt manufactured 49,500 of this model from 1896-1907. The New York City Police Department purchased 4,500 of these revolvers, and the backstraps are so marked. There was also a target model of this revolver, which features a 6" barrel with a flattop frame and target sights, of which 5,000 were produced. **NOTE:** New York Police marked add 30 percent. Target model add 20 percent.

NIB	Exc.	V.G.	Good	Fair	Poor
—	600	350	225	150	100

Police Positive

This is externally the same as the New Police with the addition of the positive lock feature and two new chamberings—the .38 New Police and the .38 Smith & Wesson. They were manufactured from 1905-1947.

NIB	Exc.	V.G.	Good	Fair	Poor
—	700	475	250	200	150

Police Positive Target

This is basically the same as the New Police Target with the positive lock feature. It is chambered in .22 LR, the .22 WRF, as well as the other cartridges offered in the earlier model. Deduct 20 percent for WRF. **NOTE:** A .22 caliber Police Positive chambered for the .22 Short and Long cartridge may be seen with British

proofs. Several such revolvers were sold to London Armory in this configuration during the late 1920s. A NIB example recently sold for $1,200.

NIB	Exc.	V.G.	Good	Fair	Poor
—	800	600	300	175	100

Police Positive Special

This model is similar to the Police Positive but has a slightly larger frame to accept the longer cylinder needed to chamber more powerful cartridges such as the .38 Special, in addition to the original chamberings. They were manufactured from 1907-1973.

NIB	Exc.	V.G.	Good	Fair	Poor
—	600	450	250	150	100

Police Positive Special Mark V

Introduced in 1994 this is an updated version of the Police Positive Special. This model features an underlug 4" barrel with rubber grips and fixed sights. The butt is rounded. The revolver is rated to fire .38 caliber +P rounds. Overall length is 9" and weighs approximately 30 oz.

NIB	Exc.	V.G.	Good	Fair	Poor
550	400	300	150	100	85

Officer's Model Target 1st Issue

This revolver is chambered for the .38 Special cartridge. It has a 6" barrel and is blued. It has a flattop frame with adjustable target sights. Colt manufactured this model from 1904-1908.

NIB	Exc.	V.G.	Good	Fair	Poor
—	1000	750	350	300	200

Officer's Model Target 2nd Issue

This model is similar to the 1st Issue but is offered in .22 LR and .32 Police Positive caliber, as well as in .38 Special. It also is furnished with a 4", 4.5", 5", 6", and 7.5" barrel in .38 Special only. It has checkered walnut grips. Colt manufactured this model between 1908 and 1940.

Courtesy Faintich Auction Services, Inc., Paul Goodwin photo

NIB	Exc.	V.G.	Good	Fair	Poor
—	700	550	300	250	150

Camp Perry Single-Shot

This model was created by modifying an Officer's Model frame to accept a special flat single-shot "cylinder." This flat chamber pivots to the left side and downward for loading. The pistol is chambered for .22 LR and is offered with an 8" (early production) or 10" (late production) barrel. The finish is blued, with checkered walnut grips. The name "Camp Perry Model" is stamped on the left side of the chamber; the caliber is on the barrel. Colt named this model after the site of the U.S. Target Competition held annually at Camp Perry, Ohio. They manufactured 2,525 of these between 1920 and 1941. **NOTE:** This gun serial numbered 101-2525 with 2488 produced from 1926-1941. In 1934 standard barrel length was reduced from 10" to 8" at approximately serial number 2150. **NOTE:** Add 100 percent premium for 10" barrel. Add 50 percent premium for original box.

NIB	Exc.	V.G.	Good	Fair	Poor
—	2500	1750	950	600	400

Officer's Model Match

Introduced in 1953 this model is similar to the Officer's Model Target and chambered for either the .22 caliber cartridge or the .38 Special with 6" barrel. The revolver is fitted with a heavy tapered barrel and wide hammer spur with adjustable rear sight and ramp front sight. It was sold with checkered walnut target grips. Blued finish is standard. Discontinued in 1970. The standard of long action could be fired both double- or single-action. **NOTE:** The .22 caliber version prices are listed. Officer's Model Match in .38 caliber will bring approximately 20 percent less. This model was also produced in .22 Magnum. This is rather a rare gun in this caliber with approximately 800 produced.

NIB	Exc.	V.G.	Good	Fair	Poor
—	750	600	450	350	250

.22 Caliber in Short Action—Single-Action-Only

NIB	Exc.	V.G.	Good	Fair	Poor
—	1000	750	600	500	350

Official Police

This was a popular revolver in the Colt line for many years. It was manufactured from 1927 to 1969. It is chambered for .32-20 and .41 Colt. These calibers were discontinued in 1942 and 1930, respectively. The .38 Special was chambered throughout the entire production run, and .22 LR was added in 1930. This model holds 6 shots, has a square-butt, and is offered with 2", 4", 5", and 6" barrel lengths. The grips are checkered walnut. The finish is either blued or nickel-plated. **NOTE:** Nickel-plated add 10 percent. .22 LR add 20 percent.

NIB	Exc.	V.G.	Good	Fair	Poor
—	600	425	350	200	150

Commando Model

This model, for all intents and purposes, is an Official Police chambered for .38 Special, with a 2", 4", or 6" barrel. This model is Parkerized and stamped "Colt Commando" on the barrel. There were approximately 50,000 manufactured between 1942-1945 for use in World War II. **NOTE:** Add 30 percent for 2" barrel.

Courtesy Richard M. Kumor, Sr.

NIB	Exc.	V.G.	Good	Fair	Poor
—	950	750	375	150	100

Marshall Model

This is an Official Police that is marked "Colt Marshall" on the barrel and has an "M" suffix in the serial number. It has a 2" or 4" barrel and a round butt. The finish is blued. There were approximately 2,500 manufactured between 1954 and 1956.

NIB	Exc.	V.G.	Good	Fair	Poor
—	1000	700	500	250	150

Colt .38 SF-VI

Introduced in 1995 this model is essentially a Detective Special in stainless steel with a new internal mechanism. Has a transfer bar safety mechanism. Fitted with a 2" barrel and cylinder holds 6 rounds of .38 Special. A 4" barrel in bright stainless steel is also available. Weight is 21 oz. and overall length is 7".

NIB	Exc.	V.G.	Good	Fair	Poor
650	475	350	225	150	100

Colt .38 SF-VI Special Lady

Introduced in 1996 this 2" barrel version is similar to the above model with the addition of a bright finish and bobbed hammer. Weight is 21 oz.

NIB	Exc.	V.G.	Good	Fair	Poor
650	450	300	200	150	100

Detective Special 1st Issue / 2nd Issue

This model is actually a Police Positive Special with a 2" barrel. It was originally chambered for .32 New Police, .38 New Police, (which were discontinued) and .38 Special, which continued until the end of the production run. The finish is blued or nickel and it is offered with wood or plastic grips. There were over 400,000 manufactured between 1926 and 1972. A few 2nd issue (post WWII) units came with 3" barrels. **NOTE:** For pre-war 1st issue (serial number 331000 - 490000) add 50 percent. For nickel finish add 25 percent. For 3" barrel add 30 percent.

NIB	Exc.	V.G.	Good	Fair	Poor
—	850	650	525	200	100

Detective Special 3rd Issue

This is basically a modernized, streamlined version with a 2" or 3" barrel with a shrouded ejector rod, wraparound checkered walnut grips and is chambered for .38 Special. It was finished in blue or nickel plate. Made from 1973 to 1986 and 1993 to 1995. **NOTE:** Add $50 for nickel finish.

NIB	Exc.	V.G.	Good	Fair	Poor
750	600	500	350	200	100

Detective Special II (DS-II)

Introduced in 1997 this version of the Detective special features new internal lock work and a transfer bar safety mechanism. It is fitted with a 2" barrel, has a capacity of six rounds, and is chambered for the .38 Special. In 1998 this model was offered chambered for .357 Magnum cartridge as well. Rubber combat style grips are standard. Weight is approximately 21 oz. Stainless steel finish.

NIB	Exc.	V.G.	Good	Fair	Poor
650	475	300	225	—	—

Colt Magnum Carry

Introduced in 1999, this model is essentially a renamed Detective Special II. Stainless steel finish. Weight is 21 oz.

NIB	Exc.	V.G.	Good	Fair	Poor
650	475	300	250	—	—

Banker's Special

The Bankers Special is a 2" barreled, easily concealed revolver. It was designed with bank employees in mind. It is chambered for .38 Special and was offered in blued finish. The revolver was also offered in .22 caliber. The grips are rounded but full-sized, and Colt utilized this feature in advertising this model. The U.S. Postal Service equipped its railway mail clerks with this model. There were approximately 35,000 manufactured between 1926 and 1943. **NOTE:** Nickel models will command a premium. A Banker's Special in .22 caliber will command a premium.

NIB	Exc.	V.G.	Good	Fair	Poor
—	1500	975	500	250	150

Cobra 1st Issue

The Cobra is simply an alloy-framed lightweight version of the Detective Special. It weighs only 15 oz. The Cobra is chambered for .32, .38 Special, and .22 LR. This model is available in either a round-butt or square-butt version with a 4" barrel only. They were manufactured between 1950 and 1973.

NIB	Exc.	V.G.	Good	Fair	Poor
—	850	650	525	200	100

Cobra 2nd Issue

The same as the 1st Issue in .38 Special only, this is streamlined with wraparound walnut grips and shrouded ejector rod. **NOTE:** For nickel add 30 percent.

NIB	Exc.	V.G.	Good	Fair	Poor
—	525	375	250	150	100

Agent 1st Issue

This revolver is basically the same as the 1st Issue Cobra with a shortened grip frame. This was done to make the Agent more concealable. Colt manufactured the Agent 1st Issue from 1955-1973.

NIB	Exc.	V.G.	Good	Fair	Poor
—	650	400	225	150	100

Border Patrol

This model is quite rare, as Colt manufactured only 400 of them in 1952. It is basically a Police Special with a heavy 4" barrel. It is chambered for the .38 Special and was built to be strong. The finish is blued and serial numbered in the 610000 range.

NIB	Exc.	V.G.	Good	Fair	Poor
—	5000	3000	2000	1000	500

Agent L.W. 2nd Issue

This is a streamlined version with the shrouded ejector rod. In the last four years of its production, it was matte finished. Colt manufactured this model between 1973 and 1986.

NIB	Exc.	V.G.	Good	Fair	Poor
—	550	400	275	175	150

Aircrewman Special

This model was especially fabricated for the Air Force to be carried by their pilots for protection. It is extremely lightweight at 11 oz. The frame and the cylinder are made of aluminum alloy. It has a 2" barrel and is chambered for the .38 Special. The finish was blued, with checkered walnut grips. There were approximately 1,200 manufactured in 1951, and they are marked "U.S." or "A.F."

NIB	Exc.	V.G.	Good	Fair	Poor
—	4500	2500	1500	800	250

Courier

This is another version of the Cobra. It features a shorter grip frame and a 3" barrel. This model is chambered for .32 and .22 rimfire. There were approximately 3,000 manufactured in 1955 and 1956. **NOTE:** .22 Rimfire add 20 percent.

NIB	Exc.	V.G.	Good	Fair	Poor
1300	750	600	500	350	150

Trooper

This model was designed specifically by Colt to fill the need for a large, heavy-duty, powerful revolver that was accurate. The Trooper filled that need. It was offered with a 4" or 6" barrel and blued or nickel finishes with checkered walnut grips. The Trooper is chambered for the .38 Special, .357 Magnum, and there is a .22 rimfire version for the target shooters. This model was manufactured between 1953 and 1969. Add 10 percent for .357 or .22.

NIB	Exc.	V.G.	Good	Fair	Poor
—	600	475	300	150	100

Colt .357 Magnum

This is a deluxe version of the Trooper. It is offered with a special target wide hammer and large target-type grips. The sights are the same as Accro target model. It features a 4" or 6" barrel and a blued finish and was manufactured between 1953 and 1961. There were fewer than 15,000 produced.

NIB	Exc.	V.G.	Good	Fair	Poor
—	675	495	300	200	150

Diamondback

This model is a medium-frame, duty-type weapon suitable for target work. It has the short frame of the Detective Special with the ventilated rib 2.5", 4", or 6" barrel. It is chambered for .38 Special and .22 rimfire for the target shooters. The finish is blued or nickel-plated, with checkered walnut grips. The Diamondback features adjustable target sights, wide target hammer, and a steel frame. It was manufactured between 1966 and 1986. **NOTE:** Premium of 100 percent for 2.5" barrel or nickel finish.

NIB	Exc.	V.G.	Good	Fair	Poor
1500	1200	900	500	250	150

Viper

This is an alloy-framed revolver chambered for the .38 Special. It has a 4" barrel and was manufactured between 1977 and 1984. The Viper is essentially a lightweight version of the Police Positive.

NIB	Exc.	V.G.	Good	Fair	Poor
1000	750	500	200	125	100

Python

The Python was often described as the Cadillac of the Colt double-action revolve line. It was originally designed to be a large-frame .38 Special target revolver but shortly before the Python was introduced in 1955, Colt management decided to chamber it for the .357 Magnum. (A .38 Special 8" barrel variation was made in the early 1980s. See separate listing.) The Python was offered in barrel lengths of 2.5", 3" (very rare), 4", 6" and 8". Features included a ventilated rib, full lug barrel and an adjustable rear sight. Finish choices were Royal Blue, nickel plated, matte stainless and high polished "Ultimate" stainless. The Python remained in the catalog as a regular production item until 1996. The following year the Colt Custom Shop started making the Python on a special-order-only basis. Known as the Python Elite, it was produced by the Custom Shop until 2006. **NOTE:** The early (pre-1970) production guns in very good to excellent condition can command premiums from 10 to 25 percent and those with 3-inch barrels up to 50 percent. Nickel-plated, 3" barreled Pythons should be confirmed with a Colt factory letter and can command premiums of 400 to 500 percent.

NIB	Exc.	V.G.	Good	Fair	Poor
1700	1200	900	500	400	225

Matte Stainless Steel

NIB	Exc.	V.G.	Good	Fair	Poor
1550	1100	775	600	500	275

"The Ultimate" Bright Stainless

NIB	Exc.	V.G.	Good	Fair	Poor
1600	1150	850	600	500	300

Python Elite

This Custom Shop model features a stainless steel satin finish or blued finish. Adjustable red ramp front sight. Custom wood grips and choice of 4" or 6" barrel.

NIB	Exc.	V.G.	Good	Fair	Poor
1600	1300	900	675	400	300

Python .38 Special

This is an 8" barreled Python chambered for the .38 Special only. It was a limited-production venture that was not a success. It was offered in blue only.

NIB	Exc.	V.G.	Good	Fair	Poor
—	950	700	475	300	225

Python Hunter

The Hunter was a special 8" .357 Magnum Python with an extended eye relief Leupold 2X scope. The grips are neoprene with gold Colt medallions. The revolver, with mounted scope and accessories, was fitted into a Haliburton extruded aluminum case. The Hunter was manufactured in 1981 only.

NIB	Exc.	V.G.	Good	Fair	Poor
2000	1650	1000	500	400	300

Metropolitan MK III

This revolver is basically a heavier-duty version of the Official Police. It is chambered for .38 Special and fitted with a 4" heavy barrel. It is finished in blue only and was manufactured from 1969-1972.

NIB	Exc.	V.G.	Good	Fair	Poor
750	525	350	250	100	75

Lawman MK III

This model is offered chambered for the .357 Magnum with a 2" or 4" barrel. It has checkered walnut grips and is either blued or nickel-plated. Colt manufactured the Lawman between 1969 and 1983.

NIB	Exc.	V.G.	Good	Fair	Poor
—	550	400	300	200	100

Lawman MK V

This is an improved version of the MK III. It entailed a redesigned grip, a shorter lock time, and an improved double-action. It was manufactured 1982-1985.

NIB	Exc.	V.G.	Good	Fair	Poor
525	375	300	200	150	100

Trooper MK III

This revolver was intended to be the target-grade version of the MK III series. It is offered with a 4", 6", or 8" vent-rib barrel with a shrouded ejector rod similar in appearance to the Python. It is chambered for the .22 LR and the .22 Magnum, as well as .357 Magnum. It features adjustable target sights, checkered walnut target grips, and is either blued or nickel-plated. This model was manufactured between 1969 and 1983.

NIB	Exc.	V.G.	Good	Fair	Poor
750	400	325	200	150	100

Trooper MK V

This improved version of the MK III was manufactured between 1982 and 1985.

NIB	Exc.	V.G.	Good	Fair	Poor
825	550	375	200	150	100

Boa

This is basically a deluxe version of the Trooper MK V. It has all the same features plus the high polished blue found on the Python. Colt manufactured 1,200 of these revolvers in 1985, and the entire production was purchased and marketed by Lew Horton Distributing Company in Southboro, Massachusetts.

NIB	Exc.	V.G.	Good	Fair	Poor
1200	850	475	325	250	150

Peacekeeper

This model was designed as a duty-type weapon with target capabilities. It is offered with a 4" or 6" barrel chambered for .357 Magnum. It features adjustable sights and neoprene combat-style grips and has a matte blued finish. This model was manufactured between 1985 and 1987.

NIB	Exc.	V.G.	Good	Fair	Poor
650	475	375	200	150	100

King Cobra

The King Cobra has a forged steel frame and barrel and a full length ejector rod housing. The barrel is fitted with a solid rib. This model is equipped with an adjustable, white outline rear sight and a red insert front sight. Colt black neoprene combat style grips are standard. In 1998 all King Cobras were drilled and tapped for scope mounts. Discontinued.

Blued

NIB	Exc.	V.G.	Good	Fair	Poor
875	650	375	250	200	100

Stainless Steel

Offered in 4" or 6" barrel lengths. In 1997 this model was introduced with optional barrel porting. No longer in production.

NIB	Exc.	V.G.	Good	Fair	Poor
975	725	400	275	200	125

High Polish Stainless Steel

NIB	Exc.	V.G.	Good	Fair	Poor
975	725	400	275	200	125

Anaconda

This double-action .44 Magnum revolver was introduced in 1990. It is offered with 4", 6", or 8" barrel lengths. The 4" model weighs 47 oz., the 6" model weighs 63 oz., and the 8" model weighs 59 oz. The Anaconda holds 6 rounds and is available with a matte stainless steel finish. For 1993 a new chambering in .45 Colt was offered for the Anaconda. This model was offered with a 6" or 8" barrel in a matte stainless steel finish revolver chambered for the .44 Remington Magnum cartridge. It is currently offered with a 6" or 8" barrel and adjustable red-insert front and white-outline rear sights. It is constructed of matte-finished stainless steel and has black neoprene fingergroove grips with gold Colt medallions. In 1996 the Realtree model was offered with 8" barrel. Chambered for the .44 Magnum cartridge. Furnished with either adjustable rear sight and ramp front sights or special scope mount. No longer in production. Reintroduced in 2001 In .44 Magnum with 4", 6", or 8" barrel. In 1998 the Anaconda was drilled and tapped for scope mounts and buyers had the option of barrel porting. Once again, discontinued.

.44 Magnum

NIB	Exc.	V.G.	Good	Fair	Poor
1300	950	650	495	300	200

.45 Colt

NIB	Exc.	V.G.	Good	Fair	Poor
1200	850	600	450	300	200

Realtree Camo Model—Adjustable Sights

NIB	Exc.	V.G.	Good	Fair	Poor
1600	1100	750	575	350	250

Realtree Camo Model—Scope Mounts

NIB	Exc.	V.G.	Good	Fair	Poor
1600	1100	750	575	350	250

COLT SEMI-AUTOMATIC PISTOLS

The Colt Firearms Co. was the first of the American gun manufacturers to take the advent of the semi-automatic pistol seriously. This pistol design was becoming popular among European gun makers in the late 1880s and early 1900s. In the United States, however, the revolver was firmly ensconced as the accepted design. Colt realized that if the semi-auto could be made to function reliably, it would soon catch on. The powers that be at Colt were able to negotiate with some of the noted inventors of the day, including Browning, and to secure or lease the rights to manufacture their designs. Colt also encouraged the creativity of their employees with bonuses and incentives and, through this innovative thinking, soon became the leader in semi-auto pistol sales—a position that they have never really relinquished to any other American gun maker. The Colt semi-automatic pistols represent an interesting field for the collector of Colt handguns. There were many variations with high enough production to make it worthwhile to seek them out. There are a number of fine books on the Colt semi-automatics, and anyone wishing to do so will be able to learn a great deal about them. Collector interest is high in this field, and values are definitely on the rise.

Model 1900

This was the first of the Colt automatic pistols. It was actually a developmental model with only 3,500 being produced. The Model 1900 was not really a successful design. It was quite clumsy and out of balance in the hand; however it was reliable in function during Army trials. This model is chambered for the .38 Rimless smokeless cartridge. It has a detachable magazine that holds seven cartridges. The barrel is 6" in length. The finish is blued, with a case-colored hammer and safety/sight combination. The grips are either plain walnut, checkered walnut, or hard rubber. This pistol is a Browning design, and the left side of the slide is stamped "Browning's Patent" with the 1897 patent date. Colt sold 200 pistols to the Navy and 200 to the Army for field trials and evaluation. The remaining 3,300 were sold on the civilian market. This model was manufactured from 1900-1903. **NOTE:** Many of the original 1900 pistols had the original sight/safety converted to Model 1902 configuration. These are worth about 50 percent less than unconverted pistols.

Standard Civilian Production

NIB	Exc.	V.G.	Good	Fair	Poor
—	10000	7500	3500	1250	750

U.S. Navy Military Model

NIB	Exc.	V.G.	Good	Fair	Poor
—	17500	12000	7500	2500	1000

U.S. Army Military Model—1st Contract

NIB	Exc.	V.G.	Good	Fair	Poor
—	20000	15000	10000	4000	2000

U.S. Army Military Model—2nd Contract

NIB	Exc.	V.G.	Good	Fair	Poor
—	16000	10000	6300	2000	1500

Model 1902 Sporting Pistol

This model is chambered for the .38 ACP cartridge. It has a 7-round detachable magazine and a 6" barrel and is blued, with checkered hard rubber grips featuring the "Rampant Colt" molded into them. The most notable features of the 1902 Sporting Model are the rounded butt, rounded hammer spur, dovetailed rear sight, and the 1897-1902 patent dates. Colt manufactured approximately 7,500 of these pistols between 1903 and 1908.

Paul Goodwin photo

NIB	Exc.	V.G.	Good	Fair	Poor
—	4000	3000	2000	750	450

Model 1902 Military Pistol

Early Model with Front of Slide Serrated

NIB	Exc.	V.G.	Good	Fair	Poor
—	6000	5000	4000	1500	750

Standard Model with Rear of Slide Serrated

NIB	Exc.	V.G.	Good	Fair	Poor
—	5000	4000	3000	1000	400

U.S. Army Marked, #15001-15200 with Front Serrations

NIB	Exc.	V.G.	Good	Fair	Poor
—	12000	10000	7500	2000	1000

Model 1903 Pocket Hammer Pistol

This was the first automatic pocket pistol Colt produced. It is essentially identical to the 1902 Sporting Model with a shorter slide. The barrel length is 4.5", and it is chambered for the .38 ACP cartridge. It is blued, with a case-colored hammer, with checkered hard rubber grips that have the "Rampant Colt" molded into them. The detachable magazine holds 7 rounds. There were approximately 26,000 manufactured between 1903 and 1929.

Paul Goodwin photo

NIB	Exc.	V.G.	Good	Fair	Poor
—	4000	3000	1200	800	400

Model 1903 Hammerless, .32 Pocket Pistol (Model M)

This was the second pocket automatic Colt manufactured. It was another of John Browning's designs, and it developed into one of Colt's most successful pistols. This pistol is chambered for the .32 ACP cartridge. Initially the barrel length was 4"; this was shortened to 3.75". The detachable magazine holds 8 rounds. The standard finish is blue, with quite a few nickel plated. The early model grips are checkered hard rubber with the "Rampant Colt" molded into them. Many of the nickel plated pistols had pearl grips. In 1924 the grips were changed to checkered walnut with the Colt medallions. The name of this model can be misleading as it is not a true hammerless but a concealed hammer design. It features a slide stop and a grip safety. Colt manufactured 572,215 civilian versions of this pistol and approximately 200,000 more for military contracts. This model was manufactured between 1903 and 1945. **NOTE:** Early Model 1897 patent date add 40 percent. Nickel-plated with pearl grips add $100. 4" barrel to #72,000 add 20 percent.

Courtesy Richard M. Kumor, Sr.

NIB	Exc.	V.G.	Good	Fair	Poor
1200	1000	500	450	300	200

U.S. Military Model

Serial prefix M, marked "U.S. Property" on frame, Parkerized finish. **NOTE:** Pistols issued to General Officers will command a premium of 50 percent.

NIB	Exc.	V.G.	Good	Fair	Poor
2000	1500	1000	800	600	500

Model 1908 Hammerless .380 Pocket Pistol

This model is essentially the same as the .32 Pocket Pistol, chambered for the more potent .380 ACP, also known as the 9mm Browning short. Other specifications are the same. Colt manufactured approximately 138,000 in this caliber for civilian sales. An unknown number were sold to the military. **NOTE:** Nickel with pearl grips add $100.

Standard Civilian Model

NIB	Exc.	V.G.	Good	Fair	Poor
1600	1300	1000	700	500	350

Military Model

Serial prefix M, marked "U.S. Property" on frame, blue finish. General Officer's pistol add 50 percent.

NIB	Exc.	V.G.	Good	Fair	Poor
—	2800	2000	1300	800	500

Model 1908 Hammerless .25 Vest Pocket Model

This was the smallest automatic Colt made. It is chambered for the .25 ACP cartridge, has a 2" barrel, and is 4.5" long overall. It weighs a mere 13 oz. This is a true pocket pistol. The detachable magazine holds 6 shots. This model was offered in blue or nickel-plate, with grips of checkered hard rubber and checkered walnut on later versions. This model has a grip safety, slide lock, and a magazine disconnector safety. This was another Browning design, and Fabrique Nationale manufactured this pistol in Belgium before Colt picked up the rights to make it in the U.S. This was a commercial success by Colt's standards, with approximately 409,000 manufactured between 1908 and 1941. **NOTE:** Add 30 percent for nickel finish, 50 percent for factory pearl grips.

Courtesy Orvel Reichert

Civilian Model

NIB	Exc.	V.G.	Good	Fair	Poor
—	750	500	300	200	100

Military Model

"U.S. Property" marked on right frame. Very rare.

NIB	Exc.	V.G.	Good	Fair	Poor
—	3500	2500	1350	450	300

Model 1905 .45 Automatic Pistol

The Spanish American War and the experiences with the Moros in the Philippine campaign taught a lesson about stopping power or the lack of it. The United States Army was convinced that they needed a more powerful handgun cartridge. This led Colt to the development of a .45 caliber cartridge suitable for the semi-automatic pistol. The Model 1905 and the .45 Rimless round were the result. In actuality, this cartridge was not nearly powerful enough to satisfy the need, but it led to the development of the .45 ACP. Colt believed that this pistol/cartridge combination would be a success and was geared up for mass production. The Army actually bought only 200 of them, and the total production was approximately 6,300 from 1905 to 1911. The pistol has a 5" barrel and detachable 7-shot magazine and is blued, with a case-colored hammer. The grips are checkered walnut. The hammer was rounded on the first 3,600 pistols and was changed to a spur hammer on the later models. The right side of the slide is stamped "Automatic Colt / Caliber 45 Rimless Smokeless". This model was not a commercial success for Colt—possibly because it has no safety whatsoever except for the floating inertia firing pin. The 200 military models have grip safeties only. A small number (believed to be less than 500) of these pistols were grooved to accept a shoulder stock. The stocks were made of leather and steel and made to double as a holster. These pistols have been classified "Curios and Relics" under the provisions of the Gun Control Act of 1968.

Civilian Model

NIB	Exc.	V.G.	Good	Fair	Poor
—	7000	5000	3000	1500	800

Military Model, Serial #1-201

NIB	Exc.	V.G.	Good	Fair	Poor
—	15000	12000	8000	4000	1000

COLT 1911/1911A1

Verified proof

Courtesy Karl Karash

Early Colt "1911 Commercial Government Model"

Serial numbers through about C4500, high polish on all parts and fire-blue finish on the trigger, slide stop, thumb safety, hammer pins, ejector, and stock screws. Pistols in the latter part of the serial range did not have fire blued stock screws. Pistols through about serial C350 had the dimpled magazine catch. The main spring housing pin was rounded on both ends in the pistols through about serial C2000. Keyhole (punch and sawcut) magazines were shipped on pistols through serial C3500. **NOTE:** Three-digit serial number add 20 percent. Two-digit serial number add 40 percent. For finish 99-100 percent add 30-50 percent.

Courtesy Karl Karash

NIB	Exc.	V.G.	Good	Fair	Poor
—	10000	6500	3000	1400	900

Standard Colt "1911 Commercial Model" with Un-numbered Slide

Above about serial # C4500 with un-numbered slide to about serial #C127300. No fire blue. Polished finished but not mirror finish. Loop magazine until about C90000. A number of variations exist within this wide serial range such as slide nomenclature and position of the "Rampant Colt", but none currently receives any particular premium. **NOTE:** Finish 99-100 percent add 20-50 percent.

NIB	Exc.	V.G.	Good	Fair	Poor
—	3750	2400	1600	1000	800

Standard Colt "1911 Commercial Government Model" with Numbered Slide

Colt started to number the slide with the receiver's serial number at about serial #C127300. This practice continued for commercial production through WWII, and all 1911 commercial pistols after about serial C127300 to about serial C136000

(when 1911A1 production had taken over). The first numbered slide pistols (in the C127xxx range) had the slide numbered on the bottom of the slide rail. This only lasted a short time and the numbering was moved to behind the firing pin stop plate by serial C128000. Subtract 20 percent for a mismatched slide number. The changes between the 1911 Commercial Government Model and the 1911A1 Commercial Government were phased in during this period. **NOTE:** Finish 99-100 percent add 20-50 percent.

NIB	Exc.	V.G.	Good	Fair	Poor
—	3500	2100	1400	900	650

FOREIGN CONTRACTS

Colt "1911 Commercial Government Model" Argentine Contracts

Multiple contracts were awarded by Argentina between 1914 and 1948 to supply .45 caliber pistols to their armed forces, police, and government agencies. these contracts totaled 21,616 pistols of which 2,151 were the 1911 model. Pistols differ from the Standard Government Model in that they are usually marked with an Argentine crest as well as the normal Colt commercial markings including the C prefix serial number. Colt also supplied Argentina the 1911A1 model "modelo 1927" that had its own serial number range of #1 to #10000 with no C prefix. Most of these pistols are well used, reblued, had mixed parts, and have import markings. Prices listed are for completely original pistols. Reblue=Fair/Poor. **NOTE:** Finish 99-100 percent add 20-100 percent.

Courtesy Karl Karash

An example of one style of Argentine crest

NIB	Exc.	V.G.	Good	Fair	Poor
—	1500	1100	750	500	400

Colt "1911 Commercial Government Model" Russian Order

This variation is chambered for .45 ACP and has the Russian version of "Anglo Zakazivat" stamped on the frame. There were about 51,000 of these blued pistols manufactured in 1915-1916. They are found between serial numbers C21000 and C89000. This variation is rarely encountered today, but a few have recently been imported and advertised. One should be extremely cautious and verify the authenticity if contemplating a purchase, as fakes have been noted. Despite market uncertainties demand for original pistols is high. Reblue=Fair/Poor

Courtesy Karl Karash

Russian frame stamping

NIB	Exc.	V.G.	Good	Fair	Poor
10000	5500	3900	2350	1600	1000

Colt "1911 Commercial Government Model" Canadian Contract

This group of 5099 pistols serial numbered between about C3077 and C13500 were purchased by the Canadian Government in 1914. Most observed pistols appear to be unmarked and can be identified only by a Colt factory letter. Others have been observed with the Canadian Broad Arrow property mark as well as unit markings. Often these unit markings are applied in a very rudimentary manner that detracts considerably from the appearance. (Any applied markings done crudely, deduct 10-50 percent.) Due to the nature of these markings, a Colt factory letter is probably a requirement to authenticate these pistols. Refinish=Fair/Poor. **NOTE:** Finish. 99-100 percent add 20-50 percent.

NIB	Exc.	V.G.	Good	Fair	Poor
—	3100	2200	1450	950	650

Colt "1911 Commercial Government Model" British Contract

This series is chambered for the British .455 cartridge and is so marked on the right side of the slide. The British "Broad Arrow" proofmark will often be found. These pistols were made in 1915-1919 and follow the same numeric serial number sequence as the normal Government models, except that the "C" prefix was replaced with a "W". They are commercial series pistols. The magazine well of these .455 pistols is slightly larger than a standard Cal. .45 Auto pistol and will accept a Cal.45 magazine, but a standard Cal. 45 will not accept a Cal. .455 magazine. All pistols in the W19001 to W19200 range as well as some in the W29000 range are believed to be JJ marked above the left trigger guard bow. Add 25 percent for JJ marked. Some pistols in the C101000 to about C109000 range have RAF marks as well as a welded ring in the lanyard loop. Most RAF pistols have been refinished and many have been converted to .45 cal. by changing the barrels. Refinish=Fair/Poor. **NOTE:** Finish 99-100 percent add 20-50 percent. Add 25 percent for RAF. Wrong barrel less 35 percent.

Broad Arrow

Courtesy Karl Karash

NIB	Exc.	V.G.	Good	Fair	Poor
—	3200	2000	1250	850	650

Norwegian Kongsberg Vapenfabrikk Pistol Model 1912 (Extremely Rare)

Serial number 1-96. **NOTE:** These pistols are so rare that almost any price would not be out of order for an original pistol. Finish 99-100 percent add 20-30 percent.

NIB	Exc.	V.G.	Good	Fair	Poor
—	5000	3200	2200	1600	1200

Norwegian Kongsberg Vapenfabrikk Pistol Model 1914

Serial number 97-32854. **NOTE:** Finish 99-100 percent add 20-50 percent.

NIB	Exc.	V.G.	Good	Fair	Poor
—	1350	1050	900	770	600

Norwegian Kongsberg Vapenfabrikk Model 1914 (Copy)

Serial number 29615 to 30535. Waffenamt marked on slide and barrel. **CAUTION:** Fakes have been reported. Any Waffenamt-marked pistol outside this serial range is probably counterfeit. **NOTE:** Finish 99-100 percent add 20-30 percent.

NIB	Exc.	V.G.	Good	Fair	Poor
—	4500	2700	2000	1200	900

MODEL 1911 U.S. MILITARY SERIES

For a complete look at the many variations of the Colt Model 1911 that were made for U.S. Military forces, see Standard Catalog of Military Firearms, 6th Edition. This publication covers history, technical data, photos and values of the world's military arms and accessories. The following is a brief summary of estimated values for Model 1911 pistols manufactured for U.S. forces between 1912 and 1919.

Colt 1912

Serial number range 1-17250.

NIB	Exc.	V.G.	Good	Fair	Poor
—	10000	7000	5000	2500	800

Colt 1913-1915

Serial number ranges 17251-72570, 83856-102596, 107597-113496, 120567-125566, 133187-137400.

NIB	Exc.	V.G.	Good	Fair	Poor
—	5800	4500	3000	1500	500

Colt 1917-1918

Serial number range 137401-594000.

NIB	Exc.	V.G.	Good	Fair	Poor
—	4500	3000	2000	1000	500

Springfield Armory 1914-1916

Serial number ranges 72751-83855, 102597-107596, 113497-120566, 125567-133186.

NIB	Exc.	V.G.	Good	Fair	Poor
—	6000	4750	3500	2000	800

Remington-UMC 1918-1919

Serial number range 1-21676.

NIB	Exc.	V.G.	Good	Fair	Poor
—	6000	4750	3500	2000	800

North American Arms 1918

Less than 100 manufactured in Canada but none delivered to the U.S. government. One of the most rare 1911 models, so beware of fakes. Get an expert appraisal before buying or selling.

NIB	Exc.	V.G.	Good	Fair	Poor
—	—	30000	20000	10000	—

MODEL 1911 AUTOMATIC PISTOL, MILITARY SERIES

For a complete listing of Colt 1911 military pistols with photos, technical data, and prices see the *Standard Catalog of Military Firearms*.

The commercial "Government Models" made by Colt between the wars may be the best pistols that Colt ever produced. The civilian configurations of the 1911 and 1911A1 were known as "Government Models". They were identical to the military models, with the exception of the fit, finish, and markings. However, commercial production of the 1911A1 pistols was stopped when WWII started. Therefore, production changes of the 1911A1 pistols were not carried over to the contemporary commercial pistols because there was no contemporary commercial production. The "C" serial number prefix designated the commercial series until 1950, when it was changed to a "C" suffix. The "Government Model" pistols were polished and blued until about serial number C230,000, when the top, bottom, and rear were matte finished. The words "Government Model" as well as the usual "Verified Proof" mark were stamped on all but about the first 500 pistols when post-war production commenced at C220,000. Some of these first 500 also lacked the verified proof mark. These first post-war pistols used some leftover military parts such as triggers and stocks. Pre-war pistols all had checkered walnut grips. Post-war pistols generally had plastic grips until the "midrange" serial when the wood grips returned. There were a number of different commercial models manufactured. They are individually listed.

PRE-WWII COLT "1911A1 COMMERCIAL GOVERNMENT MODEL"

Manufactured by Colt from 1925-1942 from about serial number C136000 to about serial number C215000. Only a few pistols from serial #C202000 to C215000 were shipped domestically, as most were shipped to Brazil or renumbered into military models. See Model 1911A1 commercial to military conversions.

Standard Colt "1911A1 Commercial Government Model" Domestic Sales

These pistols have numbered slides, no foreign markings, no Swartz safeties and no additions whatsoever. **NOTE:** Finish 99-100 percent add 30-60 percent.

NIB	Exc.	V.G.	Good	Fair	Poor
—	4500	3500	2500	1000	500

Standard Colt "1911A1 Commercial Government Model" Export Sales

Usually with foreign crest or foreign inscription of a county such as Argentina or Brazil. This pistol has a numbered slide. Some variations with the foreign markings are more rare than the standard domestic pistols and have a developed local followings who have raised their prices considerably. The Argentine pistols do not have the collector interest that the others or the "Standard" domestic pistols have. Four factors have reduced collector interest in the Argentine Colt pistols compared to the rest:

1. Most of the Argentine-marked pistols have been recently imported and have the legally required important markings.
2. Many of the Argentine-marked pistols have been advertised and sold in the wholesale trade publications at utility prices.
3. Most of the recent import pistols from Argentina have been refinished or are in "well used" condition.
4. Most of the recent import pistols from Argentina have had some parts changed or swapped with other pistols and are not in original condition. The few Argentine pistols that remain in original and excellent or better condition usually sell for less than their "plain Jane" counterparts, and they sell for much less than the rarer Brazilian and Mexican pistols.

Argentine Colt-made 1911A1 model pistols without Swartz safeties

NOTE: Finish 99-100 percent add 20-30 percent.

NIB	Exc.	V.G.	Good	Fair	Poor
—	1500	1000	650	550	450

Brazilian, Mexican, and other South American (except Argentina)

Colt-made "1911A1 Commercial Government Model" pistols.
NOTE: Finish 99-100 percent add 20-100 percent.

NIB	Exc.	V.G.	Good	Fair	Poor
—	6500	4500	2800	1700	1000

Colt National Match Caliber .45, Pre-WWII, .45 (without Swartz safeties)

The National Match Commercial pistol was introduced by Colt at the 1930 National Matches at Camp Perry. Production began in 1932. The right side of the slide was marked "NATIONAL MATCH" and the mainspring housing had no lanyard loop. The National Match modifications to the standard pistol, as described in Colt literature included: "A tighter barrel, better sights, and a hand polished action." The "tighter barrel" probably amounted to a tighter fit between the barrel bushing and barrel. The hand polishing of the action probably produced a greatly improved trigger pull, but overall, the barrel slide lockup was probably only superficially improved. Colt also advertised a "Selected Match Grade" barrel. Colt advertising indicated that scores using the National Match pistols improved greatly and they probably did to a degree, but most of the improvement was probably due to the improved (wider) sights and improved trigger pull. The very first pistols had fixed sights, but by about SN C177,000 the "Stevens Adjustable Rear Target Sight" was available. Both fixed and adjustable sights were available thereafter throughout production. The total number of National Match pistols with each type of sight is not known, but one author (Kevin Williams, Collecting Colt's National Match Pistols) estimates that the percentage of adjustable sight equipped National Match pistols may have been only 20 percent. Note that the Colt National Match pistol is not referred to here as a "1911A1" because this pistol lacks the military lanyard loop that is present in all Standard Government Models. This is simply a matter of personal preference. Also note that "Colt National Match" Pre-war pistols are also "Government models" as the receiver was marked as such throughout production.
NOTE: Finish 99-100 percent add 30-60 percent.

With Adjustable Sights

Stevens adjustable sight   Courtesy Karl Karash

NIB	Exc.	V.G.	Good	Fair	Poor
—	9000	6500	4500	2500	900

Fixed Sights

NIB	Exc.	V.G.	Good	Fair	Poor
—	7500	5000	3000	1750	750

Swartz Safeties, Pre-WWII, Firing Pin and Hammer/Sear

The "Swartz Safeties" are a pair of devices that Colt installed in 1911A1 Commercial Government Models" and 1911A1 Commercial National Match pistols in the late 1930s and early 1940s. The first device, a firing pin block that was actuated by the grip safety, prevented the firing pin from moving forward unless the grip safety was squeezed. The second Swartz safety device, the Hammer/Sear safety prevented a possible unsafe half cock position. The Swartz firing pin block safety can be observed by pulling the slide back all the way and looking at the top of the frame. A Swartz-safety-equipped 1911A1 pistol will have a second pin protruding up, next to the conventional disconnector pin. This second pin pushes a spring loaded piston in the rear part of the slide that is visible when the slide is pulled back and the slide is viewed from underneath. This piston, in turn, blocks the firing pin when relaxed. A second Swartz safety (the Swartz Sear Safety), is usually built into pistols equipped with the Swartz firing pin block safety. The sear safety can sometimes be detected by the drag marks of the notched sear on the round portion of the hammer that the sear rides on. Pulling the hammer all the way back will expose these drag marks if they are visible. Presence of the drag marks, however, does not ensure that the Swartz-modified sear safety parts are all present. Disassembly may be required to verify the correct parts are all present. The Swartz Safeties are referred to in Colt Factory letters as the "NSD" (New Safety Device).(From SN C162,000 to C215,000 about 3,000 total National Match pistols were made with and without Swartz safeties.) The number of National Match pistols having the Swartz safeties is unknown. However only a few pistols below serial C190000 had the safeties installed and of the pistols made after C190000, most were Standard Models shipped to Brazil and Argentina. The Brazilian pistols were without the safeties or the cutouts. The Argentine pistols were shipped in two batches of 250 pistols each. Both of these Argentine batches appear to have had the safeties installed as a number of them have recently been imported into the U.S.A.

Probably much less than half of the total Colt made National Match pistols had the Swartz safeties. The total number of pistols (both Standard Government Model and National Match) shipped with Swartz safeties is probably much less than 3,000. And probably much less than half of the total Colt made National Match pistols had the Swartz safeties. Swartz safeties were also installed in late Super .38 and Super Match .38 pistols.

Standard Colt 1911A1 Commercial "GOVERNMENT MODEL" Marked Pistol with Numbered Slide

"Swartz safeties", no foreign markings. Fixed sights only, no additions whatsoever. Rare, seldom seen. **NOTE:** Finish 99-100 percent add 20-50 percent.

NIB	Exc.	V.G.	Good	Fair	Poor
—	5500	4200	3000	1500	850

Colt National Match Caliber Pre-WWII, .45. Pre-WWII (with "Swartz Safeties")

Serial number C186,000-C215,000 probably less than 1,500 pistols. Colt would rework fixed sights equipped pistols on a repair order with Stevens adjustable sight. Therefore, a Colt letter showing that the pistol was originally shipped with adjustable sights is in order for any adjustable sight-equipped pistol. **NOTE:** Finish 99-100 percent add 30-60 percent.

Stevens Adjustable Sights

NIB	Exc.	V.G.	Good	Fair	Poor
—	10000	7500	5000	3000	1500

Fixed Sights

NIB	Exc.	V.G.	Good	Fair	Poor
—	8500	6000	4000	2500	1200

Standard 1911A1 Pre-WWII, "GOVERNMENT MODEL" Export Sales

With "Swartz Safeties" and usually a foreign crest or foreign inscription mainly from Argentina. The vast majority of Swartz equipped foreign contract pistols were shipped to Argentina, but Argentine pistols do not have the collector interest that the others or the plain domestic pistols have. Four factors reduce collector interest in the Colt made Argentine pistols compared to the rest:

Colt 1911/1911A1 Pistols

Photos courtesy of Karl Karash

Arched mainspring   *Flat mainspring*

Long grip safety   *Short grip safety*

No finger groove   *Finger groove*

1. Most of the Argentine-marked pistols have been recently imported and have the legally required Import Markings. 2. Many of the Argentine-marked pistols have been advertised and sold in the wholesale trade publications at utility prices. 3. Most of the recent import Argentine pistols have been refinished or are in "well used" condition. 4. Most of the recent import pistols from Argentina have had some parts changed or swapped with other pistols and are not in original condition.

The few of these Argentine Swartz equipped pistols that remain in original and excellent or better condition usually sell for less than their "plain Jane" domestic counterparts, and they sell for much less than the much rarer Brazilian and Mexican pistols. Perhaps these depressed prices represent a bargin for collectors with an eye to the future when the supply of these extremely rare pistols dries up. 100 percent reblue = Fair/Poor. **NOTE:** Finish 99-100 percent add 20-30 percent.

NIB	Exc.	V.G.	Good	Fair	Poor
—	1400	1050	900	650	550

Normal Brazilian and Mexican Pistols (with Swartz Safeties)

These pistols do not normally have Swartz safeties, but if any were found, they would be expected to sell for at least the amount listed. **NOTE:** Finish 99-100 percent add 20-30 percent.

NIB	Exc.	V.G.	Good	Fair	Poor
—	9500	7000	4000	2500	1200

Argentine Contract Pistols "Modelo Argentino 1927, Calibre .45"

These pistols were delivered to Argentina in 1927. The right side of the slide is marked with the two-line inscription "Ejercito Argentino Colt Cal .45 Mod. 1927". There is also the Argentine National Seal and the "Rampant Colt". SN 1-10,000. Verified proof, Assembler's mark, and Final inspectors mark under left stock by upper bushing. None had Swartz Safeties. Most of these pistols were reblued. Reblued = Fair/Poor. **NOTE:** The abundance of these and other refinished Argentine pistols has depressed the prices of all original finish Argentine pistols. Finish 99-100 percent add 20-50 percent

NIB	Exc.	V.G.	Good	Fair	Poor
—	1400	1050	850	600	400

"Military to Commercial Conversions"

Some 1911 Military pistols that were brought home by GIs were subsequently returned to the Colt factory by their owners, for repair or refinishing. If the repair included a new barrel, the pistol would have been proof fired and a normal Verified proof mark affixed to the trigger guard bow in the normal commercial practice. If the pistol was refinished between about 1920 and 1942, the slide would probably be numbered to the frame again in the normal commercial practice. These pistols are really remanufactured Colt pistols of limited production and should be valued at least that of a contemporary 1911A1 commercial pistol. Only pistols marked with identifiable Colt markings should be included in this category. Very seldom seen. Since Colt rework records are lost, reworked and refinished pistols without identifiable Colt applied markings are probably not verifiable as Colt reworks, and should be considered refinished pistols of unknown pedigree. **NOTE:** Finish 99-100 percent add 30 percent.

NIB	Exc.	V.G.	Good	Fair	Poor
—	1900	1300	975	550	425

Super .38 1929 Model, Pre-WWII

This pistol is identical in outward physical configuration to the .45 ACP Colt Commercial. It is chambered for the .38 Super cartridge and has a magazine that holds 9 rounds. The right side of the slide is marked "Colt Super .38 Automatic" in two lines, followed by the "Rampant Colt." The last few thousand pre-war Super .38 pistols made had the Swartz Safety parts installed, but some pistols were assembled post-war with leftover parts. These post-war-assembled pistols did not have the Swartz safeties installed but most (possibly all) had the cutouts. In 1945, 400 pistols were purchased by the U.S. Government. These 400 pistols bear

the G.H.D. acceptance mark as well as the Ordnance crossed cannons. (G.H.D. and Ordnance marked add 30-50 percent. A factory letter is probably necessary here.) Some collectors feel that post-war assembly and post-war chemical tank bluing adds a premium, others feel that it requires a deduction. Post-war assembly may add 15 percent or it may deduct 15 percent. **NOTE:** Finish 99-100 percent add 33 percent. Swartz Safeties add 20 percent. For nickel finish add 50 percent.

NIB	Exc.	V.G.	Good	Fair	Poor
—	5000	4000	3000	2000	1000

Super Match .38 1935 Model, Pre-WWII

Only 5,000 of these specially fit and finished target-grade pistols were manufactured. They have fixed sights or the Stevens adjustable sights, and the top surfaces are matte-finished to reduce glare. Twelve hundred of these pistols were purchased and sent to Britain in 1939, at the then-costly rate of $50 per unit. The last few thousand pre-war Super .38 pistols made had the Swartz safety parts installed, but some pistols were assembled post-war with leftover parts. These post-war-assembled pistols did not have the Swartz safeties installed but most (possibly all) had the cutouts. In 1945, 400 pistols were purchased by the U.S. Government. These 400 pistols bear the G.H.D. acceptance mark as well as the Ordnance crossed cannons. G.H.D. and Ordnance marked add 30-50 percent. A factory letter is probably necessary here. Swartz Safeties add 20 percent. Some collectors feel that post-war assembly and post-war chemical tank bluing adds a premium, others feel that it requires a deduction. Post-war assembly may add 15 percent or it may deduct 15 percent. **NOTE:** Finish 99-100 percent add 20-75 percent for both models.

Adjustable Sights

NIB	Exc.	V.G.	Good	Fair	Poor
—	11500	8000	5000	3000	2000

Fixed Sights

NIB	Exc.	V.G.	Good	Fair	Poor
—	10000	6500	4000	2000	1250

PRE-WWII COLT "1911A1 COMMERCIAL GOVERNMENT MODEL"

MODEL 1911A1 U.S. MILITARY SERIES

For a complete look at the many variations of the Colt Model 1911A1 that were made for U.S. Military forces, see Standard Catalog of Military Firearms, 6th Edition. This publication covers history, technical data, photos and values of the world's military arms and accessories. The following is a summary of estimated values for Model 1911A1 pistols manufactured for U.S. forces between 1924 and the end of WWII in 1945.

Colt

NOTE: For Army or Navy variations with blue finish made between 1937 and 1939 add 100 to 200 percent. Serial number range 710000-717281.

NIB	Exc.	V.G.	Good	Fair	Poor
—	3500	3200	2500	1000	500

Ithaca

NIB	Exc.	V.G.	Good	Fair	Poor
—	2000	1650	1200	900	600

Remington Rand

NIB	Exc.	V.G.	Good	Fair	Poor
—	2000	1650	1200	900	600

Union Switch & Signal

NIB	Exc.	V.G.	Good	Fair	Poor
—	5000	4200	3200	2400	1200

Singer Mfg. Co.

NOTE: This is a highly collectible model and fakes are known to exist. Five hundred of these guns were made with serial numbers from S800001 to S800500. An appraisal from a recognized Colt expert is strongly suggested, whether buying or selling.

NIB	Exc.	V.G.	Good	Fair	Poor
—	48000	40000	28000	18000	6000

COLT 1911A1 POST WWII COMMERCIAL PRODUCED, DOMESTIC SALES, 1946-1969

SN C220,000 to about C220,500

No "GOVERNMENT MODEL" marking, a few have no verified proof. Many parts are leftover military. **NOTE:** Finish 99-100 percent add 20-50 percent.

NIB	Exc.	V.G.	Good	Fair	Poor
—	2300	1650	1150	950	750

SN C220,500 to about C249,000 verified proof and "GOVERNMENT MODEL" marking

Many parts are leftover military in the first few thousand pistols. No foreign markings. **NOTE:** Finish 99-100 percent add 20-30 percent. Less 30 percent for foreign markings.

NIB	Exc.	V.G.	Good	Fair	Poor
—	1600	1100	750	500	400

SN 255,000-C to about 258,000-C Slide Factory Roll Marked "PROPERTY OF THE STATE OF NEW YORK," verified proof, and "GOVERNMENT MODEL" marking (250 pistols total)

A few leftover military parts are still used. A few pairs of pistols remain as consecutive pairs. **NOTE:** Finish 99-100 percent add 20-50 percent. Add 10 percent for consecutive pairs.

Courtesy Karl Karash

NIB	Exc.	V.G.	Good	Fair	Poor
—	1700	1200	800	550	450

SN 249,500-C to about 335,000-C, verified proof and "GOVERNMENT MODEL" marking

No foreign markings. **NOTE:** Finish 99-100 percent add 20-30 percent. Less 30 percent for foreign markings.

NIB	Exc.	V.G.	Good	Fair	Poor
—	1600	1100	750	500	400

SN 334,500-C to about 336,169-C, BB (Barrel Bushing) marked

About 1000 pistols. Verified proof and "GOVERNMENT MODEL" marking. **NOTE:** Finish 99-100 percent add 20-50 percent.

NIB	Exc.	V.G.	Good	Fair	Poor
—	1500	1000	700	575	450

ACE and SERVICE MODEL ACE

Rebuilt from service pistols at Springfield Armory between 1955 and about 1967 and at Rock Island in 1968. These pistols were built and rebuilt each year with a portion being sold to competitors by the NRA. Each year improvements were added to the rebuild program. Four articles in the "National Rifleman" document these pistols well: August 1959, April 1963, June 1966, and July 1966. Many parts for these pistols have been available and many "Look Alike" pistols have been built by basement armorers. Pistols generally came with a numbered box and shipping papers. Prices listed are for pistols with numbered box or papers. Less box and papers deduct 30 percent. When well-worn, these pistols will offer little over a standard pistol. Early pistols are much less commonly seen, but seem to be less sought after since they look largely like normal issue pistols.

Ace Model .22 Pistol

Starting on June 21, 1913, the U.S. Military along with "Springfield Armory" and "Colt Patented Firearms Manufacturing Co." attempted to develop a .22 cal rimfire pistol that could be used for training purposes. By 1927, the military became convinced that a pistol identical to the standard "Service Pistol" but in .22 cal rimfire was impractical and dropped the idea. In 1930 Colt purchased advertising that, in effect, requested the shooting public to let the company know if they would be interested in a .22 rimfire pistol built similar to the Government Model. The response must have been positive because in 1931 the Colt Ace appeared on the market. The Ace uses the same frame as the Government Model with a highly modified slide and a heavy barrel. It is chambered for .22 LR cartridge only. The size is the same as the larger-caliber version, and the weight is 36 oz. The operation is straight blowback. The Ace has a 10-round detachable magazine and features the "Improved Ace Adjustable Target Sight." The markings on the left side of the slide are the same as on the Government Model; the right side reads "Colt Ace 22 Long Rifle." At first the Army purchased a few pistols (totaling 206) through 1936. The Army concluded that the function of the Ace was less than perfect, as they concluded the .22 rimfire lacked the power to consistently and reliably operate the slide. Approximately 11,000 Ace pistols were manufactured, and in 1941 they were discontinued. Many owners today find that although the ACE is somewhat selective to ammunition, with full power loads, it is a highly reliable pistol when properly cleaned and maintained. **NOTE:** Finish 99-100 percent add 33 percent.

NIB	Exc.	V.G.	Good	Fair	Poor
—	4500	3000	1800	950	700

Pre-1945 Service Model Ace .22 R. F. Pistol

In 1937 Colt introduced this improved version of the Ace Pistol. It utilizes a floating chamber invented by David "Carbine" Williams, the firearm's designer who invented the "Short Stroke Gas Piston" that is the basis of the MI carbine while serving time on a Southern chain gang. Colt's advertised that this pistol with its floating chamber would give the Service Model Ace the reliability and "feel" of a .45 Auto. Today, owners of the Service Model ACE pistols find that they require regular maintenance and cleaning in order to keep the close-fitting floating chamber from binding. Furthermore, fouling appears to be much worse with some brands and types of ammunition. Most owners feel that although the perceived recoil of the Service Model ACE is noticeably greater than that of the ACE, it falls far short of a .45 Auto's recoil. The serial number is prefixed by the letters "SM." The external configuration is the same as the Ace, and the slide is marked "Colt Service Model Ace .22 Long Rifle." Most were sold to the Army and some on a commercial basis. There were a total of 13,803 manufactured before production ceased in 1945. **NOTE:** Finish 99-100 percent add 20-30 percent for both models. Add 20 percent for "US Property" marking.

Blued pistols (before about SN SM 3840)

NIB	Exc.	V.G.	Good	Fair	Poor
—	7000	5000	3000	1150	1000

Parkerized pistols (after about SN SM 3840)

NIB	Exc.	V.G.	Good	Fair	Poor
—	5000	3000	1800	950	700

Service Model Ace-Post-War

Introduced in 1978 this model is similar to the pre-war model. Production ceased in 1982. **NOTE:** Finish 99-100 percent add 20-30 percent.

NIB	Exc.	V.G.	Good	Fair	Poor
—	1100	950	875	800	600

Conversion Units .22-.45, .45-.22

In 1938 Colt released a .22-caliber conversion unit. With this kit, one who already owned a Government Model could simply switch the top half and fire inexpensive .22 rimfire ammunition. The unit consists of a slide marked "Service Model Ace," barrel with floating chamber, ejector, slide lock, bushing, recoil spring, 10-shot magazine, and box. The Conversion Units feature the Stevens adjustable rear sight. Later that same year, a kit to convert the Service Model Ace to .45 ACP was offered. In 1942 production of these units ceased. The .22 kit was reintroduced in 1947; the .45 kit was not brought back. (Finish 99-100 percent add 20-30 percent.) Subtract 20 percent if box is missing. Be alert, as sometimes a conversion unit is found on a Service Model ACE receiver and a Service model Ace upper is sold as a "Conversion Unit." Conversion Units are ALWAYS marked "Conversion Unit." Service Model ACE" pistols lack the "Conversion Unit" marking. **NOTE:** Finish 99-100 percent add 20-30 percent.

Pre-war and Post-war "U" numbered Service Model Ace Conversion Unit, .22-.45 (to convert .45 cal. to .22 cal.)

The pre-war conversion units were serial numbered U1-U2000.

Courtesy Karl Karash

NIB	Exc.	V.G.	Good	Fair	Poor
—	1200	950	550	500	450

Post-war Conversion Units

These were serial numbered U2001-U2670.

NIB	Exc.	V.G.	Good	Fair	Poor
—	650	550	500	450	425

Pre-war Service Model Ace (Re-)Conversion Unit, .45-22

To convert Convert SMA .22 Cal. to .45 Cal. SN 1-SN 112. Watch out for fakes.

NIB	Exc.	V.G.	Good	Fair	Poor
5000	3500	2500	1500	750	550

Post-war .22 Conversion Unit Unnumbered

30 percent premium for Stevens adjustable sights, 1946 only.

NIB	Exc.	V.G.	Good	Fair	Poor
600	400	350	250	225	175

Military National Match .45 Pistols

Rebuilt from service pistols at Springfield Armory between 1955 and about 1967 and at Rock Island in 1968. These pistols were built and rebuilt each year with a portion being sold to competitors by the NRA. Each year improvements were added to the rebuild program. Four articles in the "National Rifleman" document these pistols well: August 1959, April 1963, June 1966 and July 1966. Many parts for these pistols have been available and many "Look Alike" pistols have been built by basement armorers. Pistols generally came with a numbered box and shipping papers. Prices listed are for pistols with numbered box or papers. Less box and papers deduct 30 percent. When well-worn, these pistols will offer little over a standard pistol. Early pistols are much less commonly seen, but seem to be less sought after since they look largely like normal issue pistols. **NOTE:** Finish 99-100 percent add 20-30 percent.

Paul Goodwin photo

NIB	Exc.	V.G.	Good	Fair	Poor
—	1500	1075	775	600	475

Military National Match Pistols (Drake Slide)

In 1964, Springfield Armory used some of these specially machined and hardened slides to build the Military National Match pistols that year. This year's pistol is perhaps the most identifiable NM pistol due to the unique slide marking. However, Drake was only the supplier of the slides that year. Colt supplied the slides in the following year (1965). **NOTE:** Finish 99-100 percent add 20-30 percent.

Courtesy Karl Karash

NIB	Exc.	V.G.	Good	Fair	Poor
—	1550	1100	790	610	485

Gold Cup National Match (pre-Series 70)

This model is chambered for the .45 ACP, features the flat mainspring housing of the 1911, and has a match-grade barrel and bushing. The parts were hand fitted, and the slide has an enlarged ejection port. The trigger is the long version with an adjustable trigger stop, and the sights are adjustable target type. The finish is blued, with checkered walnut grips and gold medallions. The slide is marked "Gold Cup National Match," and the serial number is prefixed by the letters "NM." This pistol was manufactured from 1957 to 1970. **NOTE:** Finish 99-100 percent add 20-30 percent.

NIB	Exc.	V.G.	Good	Fair	Poor
—	1100	850	625	500	400

Gold Cup MKIII National Match

This pistol is identical to the Gold Cup .45 except that it is chambered for the .38 Mid-Range Wad Cutter round. It was manufactured from 1961 until 1974. **NOTE:** Finish 99-100 percent add 20-30 percent.

Courtesy John J. Stimpson

NIB	Exc.	V.G.	Good	Fair	Poor
1800	1500	1000	600	450	350

Colt 1911A1 AMU (Army Marksmanship Unit)

NOTE: For Army modified pistols deduct 70 percent.

NIB	Exc.	V.G.	Good	Fair	Poor
—	2700	2250	1450	900	400

COLT LICENSED AND UNLICENSED FOREIGN-MADE 1911A1 AND VARIATIONS

Argentine D.G.F.M.

Direccion General de Fabricaciones Militares made at the F.M.A.P. (Fabrica Militar de Arms Portatiles [Military Factory of Small Arms]). Licensed copies SN 24,000 to 112,494. Parts are generally interchangeable with Colt-made 1911A1 type pistols. Most pistols were marked "D.G.F.M. - (F.M.A.P.)." Late pistols were marked FM within a cartouche on the right side of the slide. These pistols are found both with and without import markings, often in excellent condition, currently more often in refinished condition, and with a seemingly endless variety of slide markings. None of these variations have yet achieved any particular collector status or distinction, unless new in box. In fact many of these fine pistols have and continue to be used as the platforms for the highly customized competition and target pistols that are currently popular. Refinished=Fair/Poor. **NOTE:** Finish 99-100 percent-NIB add 10-30 percent)

Courtesy Karl Karash

NIB	Exc.	V.G.	Good	Fair	Poor
1500	1000	700	400	350	300

Argentine-Made Ballester Molina

Un-licensed, Argentine redesigned versions. (Parts are NOT interchangeable with Colt except for the barrel and magazine.) These pistols are found both with and without import markings. Pistols without import markings usually have a B prefix number stamped on the left rear part of the mainspring housing and are often in excellent to new original condition. The vast majority of currently available pistols are found in excellent but refinished condition. Only the pistols with no import markings that are in excellent-to-new original condition have achieved any particular collector status. Most of these pistols that are being sold today are being carried and shot rather than being collected. Refinished = Fair/Poor. **NOTE:** Finish 99-100 percent-NIB add 10-30 percent.

Courtesy Karl Karash

NIB	Exc.	V.G.	Good	Fair	Poor
—	600	375	300	215	190

Brazilian Models 1911A1

Made by "Fabrica de Itajuba" in Itajuba, Brazil, and the Imbel Model 973, made by "Industriade Material Belico do Brazil" in Sao Paulo, Brazil. The Itajuba is a true copy of the Colt 1911A1, and the Imbel is also believed to be a true copy. However, an Imbel has yet to be examined by the author. Too rarely seen in the U.S.A. to establish a meaningful price.

COLT MODEL 1911A1 1970 - CURRENT

The Model 1911A1 was manufactured by Colt until 1971 when the Series 70 Government Model superseded it. The modifications in the new model were a slightly heavier slide and a slotted collet barrel bushing. In 1983 Colt introduced the Series 80 models which had an additional passive firing pin safety lock. The half-cock notch was also redesigned. At the beginning of 1992 another change was made to the Model 1911A1 model in the form of an enhanced pistol. Included were the Government models, the Commander, the Officer's model, the Gold Cup, and the Combat Elite. These modifications are the result of Colt's

desire to meet the shooters demand for a more "customized" pistol. Colt chose some of the most popular modifications to perform on their new enhanced models. They include beavertail safety grip, a slotted Commander-style hammer, a relief cut under the trigger guard, a beveled magazine well, a slightly longer trigger, a flat top rib, and angled slide serrations. The Model 1911A1 may be the most modified handgun in the world.

MKIV Series 70 Government Model

This model is essentially a newer version of the 1911A1. It has the prefix "70G" from 1970-1976, "G70" from 1976-1980, and "70B" from 1980-1983, when production ceased. This model is offered in blue or nickel plate and has checkered walnut grips with the Colt medallion. It is chambered for .45 ACP, .38 Super, 9mm, and 9mm Steyr (foreign export only). **NOTE:** Add 25 percent for nickel finish, 15 percent for .38 Super.

NIB	Exc.	V.G.	Good	Fair	Poor
950	775	600	400	250	200

MKIV Series 70 Gold Cup National Match

This is the newer version of the 1957 National Match. It features a slightly heavier slide and Colt Elliason sights. The chambering is .45 ACP only. The Accurizer barrel and bushing was introduced on this model. It was manufactured from 1970-1983.

NIB	Exc.	V.G.	Good	Fair	Poor
1500	1200	1000	650	500	400

Series 70 Gunsite Pistol

This model features a 5" barrel, thin rosewood grips, Gold Cup serrations, Heinie front sight and Novak rear sight, and several other special features. Available in blue of stainless steel. Introduced in 2004.

NIB	Exc.	V.G.	Good	Fair	Poor
1200	1050	825	600	400	200

Series 70 Gunsite Pistol Commander

As above but with 4.25" barrel.

NIB	Exc.	V.G.	Good	Fair	Poor
1200	1050	825	600	400	200

COLT ENHANCED GOVERNMENT MODELS

In 1992 Colt introduced a new set of features for its Model 1911A1 series pistols. These new features include: a flattop slide, angled rear slide serrations, scalloped ejection port, combat style hammer, beavertail grip safety, relief cut-under trigger guard and long trigger. The models that are affected by this new upgrade are the: Delta Elite, Combat Elite, Government Model, Combat Commander, Lightweight Commander, Officer's ACP, Officer's ACP Lightweight.

COMMANDER SERIES

This is a shortened version of the Government model. It has a 4.25" barrel, a lightweight alloy frame, and a rounded spur hammer. The total weight of the Commander is 27.5 oz. The serial number has the suffix "LW." The Commander is chambered for the .45 ACP, 9mm, and .38 Super. Some were chambered for 7.65 Parabellum for export only. The Commander was introduced in 1949.

Pre-70 Series (1949-1969)

NOTE: Deduct 20 percent for 9mm.

NIB	Exc.	V.G.	Good	Fair	Poor
1500	1250	1000	800	600	400

Series 70 (1970-1983)

NIB	Exc.	V.G.	Good	Fair	Poor
1200	1000	850	700	600	300

Series 80 (1983-1996)

NIB	Exc.	V.G.	Good	Fair	Poor
900	750	600	500	400	300

Combat Commander

The Combat Commander was produced in response to complaints from some quarters about the excessive recoil and rapid wear of the alloy-framed Commander. This model is simply a Commander with a steel frame. The Combat Commander weighs 32 oz. and is offered in blue or satin nickel with walnut grips. No longer in production. **NOTE:** Add 40 percent for Series 70 model

NIB	Exc.	V.G.	Good	Fair	Poor
850	550	475	375	300	200

MK IV Series 80 Government Model

This model was introduced in 1983. It is, for all purposes, the same externally as the Series 70. The basic difference is the addition of the new firing pin safety on this model. No longer in production.

Blued

NIB	Exc.	V.G.	Good	Fair	Poor
850	725	600	500	400	250

Nickel Plated

NIB	Exc.	V.G.	Good	Fair	Poor
1000	800	650	500	400	250

Stainless Steel

NIB	Exc.	V.G.	Good	Fair	Poor
950	800	650	500	400	250

Polished Stainless Steel

NIB	Exc.	V.G.	Good	Fair	Poor
1000	800	700	500	400	250

Colt 1991A1

Introduced in 1992 this Colt Government Model is designed to resemble the original GI service issue Government Model. Offered in .45 ACP, a 5" barrel, 7-round magazine, black composition grips, and a special parkerized finish. In 1996 this model was also chambered for the 9x23 cartridge. No longer in production. **NOTE:** This pistol was offered in stainless steel in 1996. Add $50 to the these prices.

NIB	Exc.	V.G.	Good	Fair	Poor
800	550	400	300	225	125

M1991A1 Compact

Chambered for the .45 ACP this model has a 3.25" barrel. It is 1.5" shorter than the standard M1991A1 model and .375" shorter in height. Its magazine holds 6 rounds. No longer in production. **NOTE:** In 1997 Colt offered this model in stainless steel with fixed white dot sights. Add $50 to NIB price.

NIB	Exc.	V.G.	Good	Fair	Poor
850	750	500	350	150	125

M1991A1 Commander

Chambered for the .45 ACP this model has all of the same features as the standard M1991A1 with a slightly shorter 4.25" barrel. Reintroduced in 2004. **NOTE:** In 1997 Colt offered this model in stainless steel with fixed white dot sights. Add $100 to NIB price.

NIB	Exc.	V.G.	Good	Fair	Poor
850	600	425	300	150	125

MK IV Series 80 Gold Cup National Match

Externally the same as the Series 70 Gold Cup with the new firing pin safety. No longer in production.

Blued

NIB	Exc.	V.G.	Good	Fair	Poor
1200	900	675	500	350	250

Stainless Steel

NIB	Exc.	V.G.	Good	Fair	Poor
1200	900	675	500	350	250

Polished Stainless Steel

NIB	Exc.	V.G.	Good	Fair	Poor
1200	900	675	500	350	250

Officer's ACP

This is a shortened version of the Government Model. It has a 3.5" barrel and weighs 37 oz. It is chambered for the .45 ACP only and has checkered walnut grips. The Officer's ACP was introduced in 1985. No longer in production.

Blued

NIB	Exc.	V.G.	Good	Fair	Poor
1000	700	525	325	250	200

Matte Blued

NIB	Exc.	V.G.	Good	Fair	Poor
1000	700	525	325	250	200

Satin Nickel

Discontinued 1985.

NIB	Exc.	V.G.	Good	Fair	Poor
1050	750	575	375	295	200

Stainless Steel

NIB	Exc.	V.G.	Good	Fair	Poor
1100	800	625	425	345	200

Lightweight Officer's ACP

This is an alloy-framed version that weighs 24 oz. It was introduced in 1986. No longer in production.

NIB	Exc.	V.G.	Good	Fair	Poor
1000	700	525	325	250	200

Concealed Carry Officer's Model

This model features a lightweight aluminum frame with stainless steel Commander slide. Barrel length is 4.25" and it is chambered for .45 ACP cartridge. Fitted with lightweight trigger, combat style hammer, and Hogue grips. Weight is approximately 34 oz. Introduced in 1998. No longer in production.

NIB	Exc.	V.G.	Good	Fair	Poor
1000	700	525	325	250	200

Delta Gold Cup

Introduced in 1992 the Delta Gold Cup is chambered for the 10mm, features a 5" barrel, stainless steel finish, adjustable Accro sights, special trigger, and black rubber wraparound grips. Features all of the new "Enhanced" model features. No longer in production.

NIB	Exc.	V.G.	Good	Fair	Poor
1050	875	700	600	400	200

Delta Elite

This model is chambered for the 10mm Norma cartridge. It is offered in blue or stainless steel. The grips are black neoprene with the Delta medallion. It features a high-profile three-dot combat sight system. The Delta Elite was introduced in 1987. No longer in production.

Blued

NIB	Exc.	V.G.	Good	Fair	Poor
1200	925	650	425	300	250

Stainless Steel

NIB	Exc.	V.G.	Good	Fair	Poor
1250	950	675	400	300	250

Polished Stainless Steel

NIB	Exc.	V.G.	Good	Fair	Poor
1250	950	675	400	300	250

Combat Elite

This is a specialized Government model that has a 5" barrel and adjustable Accro sights. It is chambered either in .45 ACP or .38 Super. It weighs 38 oz. and has an 8-round magazine for the .45 ACP and a 9-round magazine for the .38 Super. Finish can be either blue or matte stainless steel. No longer in production. Colt issued a recall notice for the safety on this model in June 2009. Pistols with serial numbers from CG10000E to CG11293E should be sent to the factory for parts replacement.

NIB	Exc.	V.G.	Good	Fair	Poor
1050	875	700	600	400	200

Combat Target Model

Introduced in 1996 this 5" barrel 1911 model features a fitted barrel, Gold Cup-style trigger, tuned action, flat top slide, relieved ejection port, skeletonized hammer, wide grip safety, high cut trigger guard, beveled magazine well, and adjustable sights. Weight is 39 oz. Offered in both blue and stainless steel. In 1996 this model was also chambered for the new 9x23 cartridge as well as the .45 ACP and the .38 Super. No longer in production. In 1997 Colt expanded this Target Model to include a number of different variations. They are listed. **NOTE:** Add $50 for stainless steel version.

NIB	Exc.	V.G.	Good	Fair	Poor
1050	875	700	600	400	200

Combat Target Combat Commander

Barrel length is 4.25". Chambered for .45 ACP. Stainless steel finish. Weight is 36 oz. Has all other Combat Target features. No longer in production.

NIB	Exc.	V.G.	Good	Fair	Poor
1050	875	700	600	400	200

Combat Target Officer's ACP

Fitted with a 3.5" barrel and chambered for .45 ACP. Stainless steel finish. Weight is about 34 oz. Has all other Combat Target features. No longer in production.

NIB	Exc.	V.G.	Good	Fair	Poor
1050	875	700	600	400	200

Special Combat Government

This pistol features a 5" barrel, double diamond rosewood grips, extended ambidextrous thumb safety, and steel checkered mainspring housing with extended magazine well. Chambered for the .45 ACP or .38 Super cartridges. Adjustable Bomar rear sight. Magazine capacity is 8 rounds. Choice of hard chrome or blue/satin nickel finish.

NIB	Exc.	V.G.	Good	Fair	Poor
2000	1500	—	—	—	—

Colt Special Combat Government Carry Model

1911-style semi-automatic pistol chambered in .45 ACP (8+1) or .38 Super (9+1). Semi-custom features include Novak front and rear night sights, skeletonized three-hole trigger, slotted hammer, black/silver synthetic grips, Smith & Alexander upswept beavertail grip palm swell safety and extended magazine well, Wilson tactical ambidextrous safety. Five-inch barrel. Available in blued, hard chrome, or blue/satin nickel finish, depending on chambering.

NIB	Exc.	V.G.	Good	Fair	Poor
1450	1100	—	—	—	—

XSE SERIES MODEL O PISTOLS

Introduced in 1999, these models are an enhanced version of the Colt 1911 and features front slide serrations, checkered, double diamond rosewood grips, adjustable McCormick trigger, three-dot dovetail rear sights, ambidextrous safety, enhanced tolerances, aluminum frame, and stainless steel slide. Chambered for .45 ACP cartridge.

Colt O-Model Government (01070XS)

Fitted with a 5" barrel and 8-round magazine.

NIB	Exc.	V.G.	Good	Fair	Poor
1200	775	595	475	350	200

Colt O-Model Concealed Carry Officer's (09850XS)

Fitted with a 4.25" barrel and 7-round magazine.

NIB	Exc.	V.G.	Good	Fair	Poor
1250	800	625	475	350	200

Colt O-Model Commander (04012XS)

Fitted with a 4.25" barrel and 8-round magazine.

NIB	Exc.	V.G.	Good	Fair	Poor
1200	775	595	475	350	200

Colt O-Model Lightweight Commander (04860XS)

Fitted with a 4.25" barrel and 8-round magazine. Weight is about 26 oz.

NIB	Exc.	V.G.	Good	Fair	Poor
1200	775	595	475	350	200

1991 SERIES MODEL O PISTOLS

This series of pistol was introduced in 1991 and is to replace the standard Colt 1911 series pistols. These pistols feature checkered rubber composite grips, smooth trigger, fixed sights, beveled magazine well and standard thumb safety and service style grip safety. Chambered for .45 ACP cartridge and 7-round magazines.

Colt O-Model Government Matte (01991)

Fitted with a 5" barrel, black matte finish, carbon steel frame and slide.

NIB	Exc.	V.G.	Good	Fair	Poor
800	650	495	350	295	200

Colt O-Model Government Stainless (01091)

Fitted with a 5" barrel, mattel stainless finish on stainless steel frame and slide.

NIB	Exc.	V.G.	Good	Fair	Poor
920	700	550	400	300	200

Colt O-Model Commander Stainless (04091U)

Fitted with a 4.25" barrel and matte stainless finish with stainless steel frame and slide.

NIB	Exc.	V.G.	Good	Fair	Poor
920	700	550	400	300	200

Colt O-Model Commander (04691)

Fitted with a 4.25" barrel and black matte finish with carbon steel frame and slide.

NIB	Exc.	V.G.	Good	Fair	Poor
870	650	—	—	—	—

Colt O-Model Gold Cup

This model has the same features as the O-Model Commander with the addition of a 5" barrel with a stainless steel frame and slide. Slide top is rounded. Magazine capacity is 8 rounds. Weight is about 39 oz. Introduced in 1999.

NIB	Exc.	V.G.	Good	Fair	Poor
1400	1050	800	575	300	200

Colt Defender

This single-action pistol was introduced in 1998. This model features a lightweight aluminum alloy frame and stainless steel slide. It is chambered for the .45 ACP or .40 S&W cartridge and is fitted with a 3" barrel. Magazine capacity is 7 rounds. Rubber wraparound grips. Weight is approximately 23 oz. and overall length is 6.75".

NIB	Exc.	V.G.	Good	Fair	Poor
850	650	475	300	250	200

Colt Defender Model O (07000D)

This model takes the place of Defender and was introduced in 2000. It has a brushed stainless finish with a 3" barrel. Skeletonized composite trigger, beveled magazine well, extended thumb safety and upswept beavertail with palm swell. Chambered for .45 ACP only. Colt issued a recall notice for the guide pad on this model in June 2009. Pistols with serial numbers from DR33036 o DR35948 should be sent to the factory for parts replacement.

NIB	Exc.	V.G.	Good	Fair	Poor
950	700	525	350	200	145

1911 – WWI Replica

Single-action semi-auto chambered in .45 ACP. Faithful external reproduction of the WWI-era service pistol with original-style rollmarks, grips, sights, carbonia blue finish, etc. Series 70 lockwork. Made from 2003 - 2009.

NIB	Exc.	V.G.	Good	Fair	Poor
1025	850	625	575	400	200

1911 - WWI 1918 Replica

Based on the military model made in 1918. Black finish and World War I rollmarks. This model was also offered in a Presentation Grade with blue or nickel finish and Colt Custom Shop "A" engraving. In excellent or new condition, this could add a premium of 100 percent. Made in 2008 and 2009. Colt issued a recall notice for the safety on this model in June of 2009. Pistols with serial numbers from 1001WWI to 3431WWI should be sent to the factory for parts replacement.

NIB	Exc.	V.G.	Good	Fair	Poor
900	800	600	500	400	200

1911A1 - WWII Replica

Replica of U.S. Military sidearm of World War II. Parkerized finish, WWII-ear rollmarks, lanyard loop, original style composite grips and packaging. Made in .45 ACP only by the Colt Custom Shop from 2001 to 2004. Series 70 lockwork. Colt issued a recall notice for the safety on this model in June 2009. Pistols with serial numbers from 4597WMK to 5414WMK should be sent to the factory for parts replacement.

NIB	Exc.	V.G.	Good	Fair	Poor
1075	950	700	575	400	200

Colt New Agent Double Action Only

Similar to New Agent single action except has double-action-only operating system. Spur-less hammer design with second-strike capability and no manual safety. Double-diamond slim fit grips, snag free trench sighting system, 7-shot magazine. In .45 ACP only. Colt issued a recall notice for the safety and guide pad on this model in June of 2009. Pistols with serial numbers from GT01001 to GT04505 should be sent to the factory for parts replacement.

NIB	Exc.	V.G.	Good	Fair	Poor
850	750	600	500	400	200

Colt Model 1991 DAO

Double-action-only version of the Lightweight Government Model. Spur-less hammer design with second-strike capability and no manual safety. Double-diamond slim fit grips, 7-shot magazine. In .45 ACP only. Introduced in 2011.

NIB	Exc.	V.G.	Good	Fair	Poor
950	800	700	550	400	250

Colt Model 1911 100th Anniversary Series

These two limited edition Model 1911s were introduced in 2011 to commemorate the 100th anniversary of the legendary pistol. Model 1911ANVIII is based on the 1918 configuration with custom rollmarks on the receiver relating to the 100th anniversary. The higher grade version, Model 1911ANVII, features scroll engraving and historic Colt symbols highlighted in 24 karat gold, and comes in a glass-topped walnut display case. Production for this model was to be limited to 750 units. Higher grade variants limited to 100 units with A, B, C or D levels of engraving were also scheduled at prices ranging from $2640 to $6528.

1911ANVII

NIB	Exc.	V.G.	Good	Fair	Poor
2150	1800	1500	—	—	—

1911ANVIII

NIB	Exc.	V.G.	Good	Fair	Poor
1075	900	750	—	—	—

Colt Government Model 1911 .22 LR Series

A licensed reproduction of the 1911A1 in .22 Long Rifle manufactured by Umarex USA. Blow-back action with 12-shot magazine and other standard 1911 specifications including 5-inch barrel, thumb and grip safeties, diamond checkered wood grips, blue finish and drift-adjustable rear sight. (Gold Cup has fully adjustable sight.) Weight is approximately 33 ounces. Offered in three variants: standard model, Rail Gun, and Gold Cup. Introduced in 2011. Prices below are for standard model.

NIB	Exc.	V.G.	Good	Fair	Poor
350	300	275	225	175	100

Colt Concealed Carry

Chopped, lightweight 1911-style semi-automatic chambered in .45 ACP. Weighs 25 oz. unloaded; overall length 6.75"; 7+1 capacity; Series 80 lockwork; black anodized aluminum frame with double-diamond wood grips. Introduced 2007.

NIB	Exc.	V.G.	Good	Fair	Poor
950	700	525	350	200	150

New Agent

7+1 .45 ACP semi-automatic with aluminum frame, fized sights, Series 80 action, slim-fit grips and 6.75" overall length. Introduced 2007.

NIB	Exc.	V.G.	Good	Fair	Poor
950	700	525	350	200	150

Colt Rail Gun

1911-style semi-automatic pistol chambered in .45 ACP. Stainless steel frame and slide, front and rear slide serrations, skeletonized trigger, integral; accessory rail, Smith & Alexander upswept beavertail grip palm swell safety, white dot front sight and Novak rear. Rosewood double diamond grips, tactical thumb safety, National Match barrel. Capacity 8+1.

NIB	Exc.	V.G.	Good	Fair	Poor
950	700	525	350	200	150

Double Eagle

This is a double-action semi-automatic pistol chambered for the 10mm Auto and the .45 ACP cartridges. It has a 5" barrel and an 8-round detachable box magazine. It is constructed of stainless steel and has checkered black synthetic grips. The sights are fixed and utilize the three-dot system. No longer in production.

NIB	Exc.	V.G.	Good	Fair	Poor
1200	775	595	475	350	200

Double Eagle Officer's Model

This is a compact version of the double-action Double Eagle pistol chambered for .45 ACP only. No longer in production.

NIB	Exc.	V.G.	Good	Fair	Poor
1025	850	625	575	400	200

Double Eagle Combat Commander

Based on the standard Double Eagle design but with a slightly shorter 4.25" barrel, the Double Eagle Combat Commander fits

between the standard model and the smaller Officer's Model. Available in .45 ACP and .40 S&W (1993) this model weighs about 36 oz., holds 8 rounds, has white dot sights, and checkered Xenoy grips. The finish is matte stainless steel. No longer in production.

NIB	Exc.	V.G.	Good	Fair	Poor
1025	850	625	575	350	200

Double Eagle First Edition

This version of the double-action Double Eagle pistol is chambered for the 10mm Auto and is furnished with a Cordura holster, double-magazine pouch, and three magazines, as well as a zippered black Cordura case.

NIB	Exc.	V.G.	Good	Fair	Poor
1100	875	650	500	375	300

.38 Super (2006)

1911-style single-action semi-auto chambered in .38 Super. Nine-shot magazine, double-diamond walnut or checkered hard rubber stocks, fixed 3-dot sights, 5" barrel. Stainless, bright stainless or blued finish.

NIB	Exc.	V.G.	Good	Fair	Poor
1100	875	650	500	375	300

Pocket Nine

This double-action semi-automatic pistol is chambered for the 9mm cartridge. The frame is aluminum alloy and the slide is stainless steel. Barrel length is 2.75". Magazine capacity is 6 rounds. Wraparound rubber grips standard. Overall length is 5.5". Weight is approximately 17 oz. No longer in production.

NIB	Exc.	V.G.	Good	Fair	Poor
950	700	525	350	250	175

Tac Nine

Introduced in 1999, this double-action-only semi-automatic pistol is chambered for the 9mm cartridge. It has a 2.75" barrel with an aluminum alloy frame and stainless steel slide. Tritium night sights. Wraparound rubber grips are standard. The finish is black oxide. Enhanced tolerances. Weight is about 17 oz. No longer in production.

NIB	Exc.	V.G.	Good	Fair	Poor
975	725	550	375	250	175

Mustang

This is a more compact version of the .380 Government Model. It has a 2.75" barrel and a 5-round detachable magazine. No longer in production. **NOTE:** Nickel finish add 10 percent. Stainless steel add 10 percent.

NIB	Exc.	V.G.	Good	Fair	Poor
850	650	475	300	250	200

Mustang PocketLite

A lightweight version of the Mustang that features an aluminum alloy receiver. The finish is blued only, and it has synthetic grips. It was introduced in 1987. Discontinued 1999. Reintroduced 2012. **NOTE:** Deduct 20 percent for 2012 model.

NIB	Exc.	V.G.	Good	Fair	Poor
800	600	475	300	250	200

Government Pocketlite LW

Similar to the Mustang but fitted with a 3.25" barrel and a 7-round magazine. This model has an aluminum frame and stainless steel slide. Fixed sights. Black composition grips. Weight is approximately 15 oz. No longer in production.

NIB	Exc.	V.G.	Good	Fair	Poor
850	650	475	300	250	200

Mustang Plus II

This version of the Mustang pistol features the 2.75" barrel with the longer grip frame that accommodates a 7-round magazine. It was introduced in 1988 and is offered in blue, as well as stainless steel. No longer in production. **NOTE:** Stainless steel add 10 percent.

NIB	Exc.	V.G.	Good	Fair	Poor
850	650	475	300	250	200

Colt Pony

Introduced in 1997 this semi-automatic pistol is chambered for the .380 ACP. It is fitted with a 2.75" barrel and a bobbed hammer. It is double-action-only. The grips are black composition. Sights are a ramp front with fixed rear. Finish is Teflon and stainless steel. Magazine capacity is 6 rounds. Overall length is 5.5". Weight is 19 oz. No longer in production.

NIB	Exc.	V.G.	Good	Fair	Poor
850	650	475	300	250	200

Colt Pony PocketLite

Same as above but with aluminum and stainless steel frame. Weight is approximately 13 oz. No longer in production.

NIB	Exc.	V.G.	Good	Fair	Poor
850	650	475	300	250	200

.380 Series 80 Government Model

This is a single-action, blowback-operated semi-automatic pistol chambered for the .380 ACP cartridge. It has a 3.25" barrel and a 7-round magazine. The sights are fixed. It is available either blued, nickel plated, or stainless steel. It has synthetic grips and was introduced in 1985. No longer in production. **NOTE:** Nickel finish add 10 percent. Stainless steel add 10 percent.

NIB	Exc.	V.G.	Good	Fair	Poor
875	675	500	325	275	200

Colt CZ40

Introduced in 1998 this double-action .40 S&W pistol was built for Colt by CZ in the Czech Republic. It is fitted with a 4" barrel and has black polymer grips. The frame is alloy with a carbon steel slide with blue finish. Magazine capacity is 10 rounds. Weight is approximately 34 oz. No longer in production.

NIB	Exc.	V.G.	Good	Fair	Poor
900	750	600	500	400	225

Colt Model 2000

Introduced in 1992, the Model 2000 was a new departure for Colt from its traditional service style semi-automatic pistols. Chambered for the 9mm, the Model 2000 is a double-action-only pistol with a 4.5" barrel and a choice between a polymer frame or an aluminum alloy frame. The polymer frame model weighs 29 oz. while the aluminum alloy frame weighs 33 oz. Grips are black composition and sights are white dot. Pistol was dropped from the Colt line in 1994.

NIB	Exc.	V.G.	Good	Fair	Poor
700	595	400	300	250	200

COLT .22 RIMFIRE SEMI-AUTOMATIC PISTOLS

For the Colt Ace see the Model 1911 section.

COLT WOODSMAN

The original Colt .22 Target Model was designed by John Moses Browning and improved by engineers at Colt Firearms prior to the start of production in 1915, and major design updates were made in 1947 and again in 1955. Those three designs constitute what collectors call the three series of Woodsman pistols. First Series refers to all those built on the frame used prior to and during World War II. Second Series includes all versions built on the second frame design from 1947 until 1955, and Third Series means the third frame design as used from 1955 to the end of production in 1977.

Each series had a Target Model, a Sport Model, and a Match Target Model. All models are very similar: the Sport Model, for example, is merely the Target Model with a short barrel, and in some cases different sights or grips. The Match Target is nearly the same as the Sport or Target Model, but with a heavier, slab-sided barrel, a squared-off frame at the front of the receiver to mate with the heavy barrel, and improved sights. In the post-war years only there were also three very similar economy models: First the Challenger, then the Huntsman, and finally the Targetsman. The actions of the economy models are identical to the higher-end models of the same period internally; they lack only some of the refinements.

These guns were not assembled in strict numerical sequence. Furthermore, even when changes were made, old parts were used up at the same time new parts were being introduced. As a result, there is no hard and fast serial number dividing line for any particular feature, and serial number overlaps of several thousand are common.

All models of the Woodsman line, in all three series, are discussed here, but there are numerous variations in details that are primarily of interest to specialized collectors. For more details see Bob Rayburn's Colt Woodsman Pocket Guide, a 96-page pocket-sized guide to the Colt Woodsman line, available for $10 (including shipping) from:

Bob Rayburn
PO Box 97104
Lakewood, WA 98497Or online at www.colt22.com or www.coltwoodsman.com

Values listed here are for the pistol only, without extras, for guns in the middle of each condition range. These are guidelines to the prevailing retail values for the collector or shooter who is buying it as the end user, not what one might expect to receive from a gun dealer who is buying it to resell. Furthermore, within the Excellent and Very Good condition categories, there is a considerable spread in value, especially for the older and more collectible versions. Excellent, for example, means 98 percent or more original blue, but a very nice pre-Woodsman with 100 percent of the original blue would likely be worth twice as much to a serious collector as one with only 98 percent. At the other end of the condition scale, in the Fair and Poor categories, the individual values of component parts become significant, and effectively set a floor value. A poor condition, rusty, pitted pre-Woodsman or First Series Match Target would still have good value if it included the original magazine and grips in nice condition, for example. In addition, there are sometimes rare variations within the broad categories that can significantly enhance the value. Include the original crisp condition box, instructions, and tools, and the value goes up more, especially for high condition early guns. On the other hand, rust, pitting (even very minor), rebluing, or other non-factory modifications will significantly reduce the values from those listed in the Very Good category or better.

FIRST SERIES

In 1915 the intended market was the target shooter, and there was only one model: the Colt .22 LR Automatic Target Pistol. That model, however, proved to be very popular not only with target shooters, but also with hunters, trappers, campers, and other outdoorsmen. Management at Colt noticed this, of course, and decided to give the pistol a new name that more closely reflected its widespread use. THE WOODSMAN was the name chosen, and that roll mark was added to the side of the receiver in 1927, at approximately serial number 54000. To further satisfy the broader market, Colt introduced the Sport Model in 1933, and the Match Target Model in 1938. The compact and beautifully balanced Sport Model was a near perfect "kit gun" for the outdoorsman, and the Match Target was designed for the special needs of the serious target shooters. Approximately 54,000 pre-Woodsmans (all with 6-5/8 inch barrels) and a combined total of approximately 110,000 Woodsman marked Sport and Target Models were produced in the first series. The Sport Model and Target Model were serial numbered together after the Sport Model was added to the line in 1933, so it is not possible to easily determine how many of each were manufactured. It is safe to say that the Target Model far outnumbered the Sport Model. During the war years of 1942-45 the Match Target was the only Woodsman model built, and virtually the entire production was for the US military.

Pre-Woodsman

This model was made from 1915-1927. It has a 10-round magazine capacity, blue finish, checkered walnut grips, and 6-5/8" barrel. It was designed for .22 LR standard velocity ammunition. The rear sight is adjustable for windage, the front sight for elevation. Up until approximately serial number 31000 the barrel was a very thin, so-called "pencil barrel". The barrel weight and diameter were increased slightly in 1922 to what collectors now call the "medium weight barrel". There were also numerous small changes in the grips, magazines, and markings over the years. Approximately 54,000 were made in all variations.

An early pre-Woodsman

A checkered pattern in an oval on the mainspring housing (left) indicates a pre-Woodsman or First Series Woodsman Target model that was designed for standard velocity .22 Long Rifle ammunition only. A series of horizontal parallel lines in a rectangular pattern (right) indicates one that was designed for high-velocity .22 Long Rifle ammunition. All guns in the series

made after 1932 were designed for high-velocity ammunition, and that includes all Sport, Match Target, Challenger, Huntsman, and Targetsman models. The post-WWII guns have no pattern on the mainspring housing but they were all made for high-velocity ammunition.

The three barrel profiles used with the Colt pre-Woodsman and First Series Target Model: from left to right, in order used, the pencil barrel, medium weight barrel and straight taper barrel.

NIB	Exc.	V.G.	Good	Fair	Poor
2400	1600	1000	500	250	200

Woodsman Target

Initially this was exactly the same as the late pre-Woodsman, with the exception of THE WOODSMAN marking on the side of the receiver. Later there were small changes in the sights, trigger, and markings. In 1934 the barrel profile was again modified to a larger diameter, heavier barrel. This third and final pre-WWII barrel profile lacked the fillet, or step-down, as was present on the earlier pencil barrel and medium barrel, and is therefore commonly called the "straight taper" barrel. A significant modification occurred in 1932 when a new heat-treated mainspring housing and stiffer recoil spring were phased in to allow the use of the increasingly popular high velocity .22 LR ammunition. While this change has been widely reported to have taken place at serial number 83790, it was actually phased in over a period of time and a range of serial numbers, spanning at least 81000-86000, within which range both standard and high speed versions can be found. Fortunately Colt changed the marking on the back of the mainspring housing (see photo) to allow visual differentiation. Colt also sold a conversion kit to modify the older guns for use with high velocity ammunition. The kit consisted of a new style mainspring housing, a stiffer recoil spring, and a coil type magazine spring for use in the very early guns that had a Z type magazine spring.

First Series Target Model

NIB	Exc.	V.G.	Good	Fair	Poor
1800	1600	1000	500	250	200

Woodsman Sport

With the Woodsman proving to be increasingly popular with outdoorsmen of all types, Colt decided to market a Woodsman better suited for a "take along" gun for hiking, camping, etc. This was accomplished in 1933 by merely shortening the barrel from 6-5/8 inches to 4.5", and announcing the new Sport Model. Other than barrel length, the only difference between the Target Model and the Sport Model was an adjustable front sight on the Target Model and a fixed front sight on the Sport Model. Later a front sight adjustable for elevation would be an available option for the

Sport Model. Colt called this arrangement "Target Sights," and indeed it was the same front sight used on the Target Model. A First Series Sport Model with an adjustable front sight will command a premium of approximately 25 percent over the values listed.

First Series Sport Model

NIB	Exc.	V.G.	Good	Fair	Poor
2000	1700	1200	600	250	200

Woodsman Match Target

Colt introduced the Match Target Woodsman in 1938, with its own serial number series beginning at MT1, and continuing until 1944 with serial number MT16611. The new features included larger grips, a heavier barrel (6-5/8"), and a rear sight fully adjustable for both windage and elevation. To signify its intended market a Bullseye Target pattern was placed on the side of the barrel. That led to its nickname of "Bullseye Match Target." The elongated, one-piece wraparound walnut grips also picked up a nickname, due to their unusual shape. Unfortunately, the so-called "Elephant Ear" grips are somewhat fragile and are often broken. In addition, many of the serious target shooters of the day replaced them with custom grips with thumb rest and palm swell, and the original grips were set aside and eventually lost or discarded. For those reasons the original grips are often missing, and that severely affects the value. Values listed assume original one-piece walnut wraparound Elephant Ear grips with no cracks, repairs, or modifications, and a correct Match Target marked magazine. The values listed for Fair and Poor condition are primarily salvage value, and reflect the high value of original "Elephant Ear" grips and Match Target marked magazines for spare parts. Approximately 11,000 were produced for the civilian market from 1938-1942.

First Series Match Target

NIB	Exc.	V.G.	Good	Fair	Poor
3600	3400	1900	1000	700	600

Military Woodsman Match Target

After the United States entered World War II at the end of 1941, civilian production at Colt was stopped and the total effort was devoted to the U.S. military. Slightly more than 4000 First Series Match Target Woodsmans were delivered on U.S. Government contract from 1942-1944. Most of them, but not all, had serial numbers above MT12000. With possible rare exceptions they all had U.S. Property or U.S. military markings, standard blue finish, 6-5/8" barrel, and extended length plastic stocks. The plastic stocks are sometimes erroneously called elephant ear stocks. The military plastic stocks are still relatively easy to find and inexpensive

and, since they will fit any First Series Colt Woodsman, they are often used as replacement grips on non-military guns. Since the military guns had plastic grips, rather than the costly and desirable "Elephant Ear" grips, the salvage value in the Fair and Poor condition range is less than that for the civilian model.

NIB	Exc.	V.G.	Good	Fair	Poor
—	3400	1900	950	550	350

SECOND SERIES

After World War II Colt entered a lengthy period of clearing up government contracts and retooling for the civilian market. The Woodsman line was extensively revised and modernized. The second series guns began appearing near the end of 1947, although no appreciable numbers were shipped until 1948. The Second Series Woodsman had essentially the same action and many of the same internals as the first series guns, but were larger and heavier, with a longer grip frame. New features included a magazine safety, automatic slide stop when the magazine was emptied, fully adjustable rear sight, heavier barrels, and a 6" barrel length on the Target and Match Target Models, rather than 6-5/8 inches, as on the first series. Other new features included a push button magazine release just aft of the trigger guard, like that on the large frame Government Model semi-automatics, a lanyard ring concealed in the butt, and a provision for attaching a plastic grip adapter to the backstrap, thereby accommodating different sized hands. Elevation adjustment was incorporated into the rear sight of all Woodsman models, and the adjustable front sight was replaced with a fixed blade. Serial numbers were restarted at 1-S, and are intermixed for all three models. Approximately 146,000 of the three models were produced.

In 1950 Colt added the Challenger to the line of second series pistols, the first of the economy models. Internally the Challenger is nearly identical to the Woodsman pistols of the same era, but externally it lacks most of the refinements introduced with the Second Series Woodsman. It has no magazine safety, automatic slide stop, adjustable sights, push button magazine release, lanyard ring, or grip adapters. It was available with either a 6-inch or 4.5" barrel, and had its own serial number series beginning with 1-C. Approximately 77,000 were produced.

Woodsman Target 6" barrel

Second Series Target Model

NIB	Exc.	V.G.	Good	Fair	Poor
1400	1000	750	500	250	150

Woodsman Sport 4.5" barrel

Second Series Sport Model

NIB	Exc.	V.G.	Good	Fair	Poor
—	1200	900	600	350	150

Woodsman Match Target 6" barrel

Second Series Match Target Model with 6" barrel.

NIB	Exc.	V.G.	Good	Fair	Poor
1800	1400	1200	800	450	250

Woodsman Match Target 4.5" barrel

Introduced in 1950.

Second Series Match Target Model with 4.5" barrel.

Second Series Woodsman magazine catch

NIB	Exc.	V.G.	Good	Fair	Poor
2000	1700	1300	900	600	300

Challenger 4.5" barrel

Colt Challenger (Second Series only) with 4.5" barrel.

NIB	Exc.	V.G.	Good	Fair	Poor
950	850	550	400	200	150

Challenger 6" barrel

Colt Challenger (Second Series only) with 6" barrel.

NIB	Exc.	V.G.	Good	Fair	Poor
750	650	425	350	200	150

THIRD SERIES

In 1955 Colt again redesigned the Woodsman line. The most obvious change was in the location of the magazine release, which was again placed at the heel of the butt, just as on the first series guns. Other changes were made over time in the markings, grips, sights, and trigger. The Sport, Target, and Match Target models continued. The Challenger was replaced by the very similar Huntsman, with either a 4.5" or 6" barrel. In 1959 the Targetsman was added to the line. The Targetsman differs from the Huntsman only in having an adjustable rear sight and a thumbrest on the left grip panel, and was available with a 6" barrel only. All Third Series models had black plastic grips until 1960, and checkered walnut grips thereafter. The Huntsman has no thumbrest on the grips. All other Third Series models have a thumbrest on the left grip panel.

It is difficult to impossible to determine how many of each model were produced in the third series, due to a very complex serial numbering scheme. Approximately 1000 Third Series Sport, Target, and Match Target Models were numbered at the end of the second series serial number range, from 146138-S to 147138-S. Numbers were then restarted at 160001-S, so there are no post-WWII Woodsmans with numbers in the 148xxx-S to 159xxx-S range. The Challenger serial numbers, meantime, had reached approximately 77143-C prior to the Challenger being replaced by the Huntsman (note the C suffix, for Challenger). The Huntsman initially continued in the Challenger serial number series, although numbers skipped forward to 90000-C before restarting. The Targetsman, when added to the line early in 1959, joined the Huntsman in using the -C suffix serial numbers, which were by then up to 129300-C. Then in 1969, when Woodsman serial numbers had reached 241811-S and the -C numbers had reached 194040-C, Colt decided to integrate the serial numbers for all versions of the Woodsman, Huntsman, and Targetsman and restart numbering again. This time they started with 001001S. That worked fine until numbers reached 099999S, and rolled over to 100000S. Numbers used in 1951-52 were then being inadvertently duplicated, with one small exception: the earlier guns had a -S suffix while the later ones had only an S (no hyphen before the S). Apparently that was not enough of a distinction to satisfy federal regulations, so when Colt discovered the error after approximately 1,330 had already been numbered, the existing "double headers" were hand stamped with an S prefix, in addition to the S suffix, in order to salvage them. Serial numbers were then restarted yet again, this time at 300000S, and continued to 317736S, when production ended.

Woodsman Target 6" barrel

NIB	Exc.	V.G.	Good	Fair	Poor
950	850	550	400	250	150

Woodsman Sport 4.5" barrel

NIB	Exc.	V.G.	Good	Fair	Poor
1000	900	600	400	250	150

Woodsman Match Target 6" barrel

NIB	Exc.	V.G.	Good	Fair	Poor
1100	1000	750	525	350	150

Woodsman Match Target 4.5" barrel

Added to the line in 1950.

With the introduction of the Third Series guns, Colt moved the magazine catch back to the heel of the butt, where it had been on the first series.

NIB	Exc.	V.G.	Good	Fair	Poor
1400	1200	850	600	350	150

Huntsman 6.5" barrel

NIB	Exc.	V.G.	Good	Fair	Poor
750	650	450	325	200	150

Targetsman 6" barrel, 4.5" (rare)

NIB	Exc.	V.G.	Good	Fair	Poor
775	675	475	350	200	150

Colt Junior Pocket Model

This diminutive unit is only 4.5" long overall and weighs 12 oz. Colt did not manufacture this pistol, but rather had it made for them by Astra in Spain. The pistol was introduced in 1958 chambered for .25 ACP. One year later a .22 Short version appeared. Both had external hammers and detachable 6-round magazines. The passage of the 1968 Gun Control Act made import of a weapon of this size illegal, so Colt discontinued its relationship with Astra. The pistol was re-introduced in 1970 as an American-made product and was produced for two more years. Production ceased in 1972. Astra also made this pistol and called it the Cub. **NOTE:** .22 Short add 25 percent.

NIB	Exc.	V.G.	Good	Fair	Poor
525	375	250	175	125	75

Cadet / Colt .22

Introduced in 1994 this .22 caliber semi-automatic pistol is offered with a 4.5" barrel and stainless steel finish. The model was renamed Colt .22 in 1995. The sights are fixed and magazine capacity is 11 rounds. Overall length is 8-5/8" and weight is approximately 33 oz.

NIB	Exc.	V.G.	Good	Fair	Poor
350	300	265	225	125	50

Colt .22 Target

Introduced in 1995 this model features a 6" bull barrel with removable front sight and adjustable rear sight. Black composite monogrip stock. Stainless steel finish. Weight is 40.5 oz.

NIB	Exc.	V.G.	Good	Fair	Poor
475	325	300	250	150	75

COLT MODERN LONG ARMS

Colteer I-22

This is a single-shot bolt-action rifle chambered for .22 LR or .22 Magnum. It has a plain uncheckered walnut stock, 20" barrel, and adjustable sights. There were approximately 50,000 manufactured between 1957 and 1966.

NIB	Exc.	V.G.	Good	Fair	Poor
350	300	175	125	90	25

Stagecoach

This is a semi-automatic, saddle ring carbine. It is chambered for .22 LR and has a 16.5" barrel and a 13-shot tubular magazine. The stock is fancy walnut, and the receiver has the stagecoach holdup scene roll-engraved on it. There were approximately 25,000 manufactured between 1965 and 1975.

NIB	Exc.	V.G.	Good	Fair	Poor
450	400	350	200	150	100

Courier

This model is similar to the Stagecoach, with a pistol-grip stock and beavertail forearm. It was manufactured between 1970 and 1975.

NIB	Exc.	V.G.	Good	Fair	Poor
425	400	300	200	125	90

Colteer

This is a less-expensive version of the Stagecoach. It features a 19.5" barrel, has a 15-shot tubular magazine, and is stocked in a plainer grade walnut. There is no roll engraving. Approximately 25,000 were manufactured between 1965 and 1975. Add 50 percent for .22 rimfire magnum.

NIB	Exc.	V.G.	Good	Fair	Poor
425	400	300	175	100	90

Colt "57" Bolt-Action Rifle

This rifle was manufactured for Colt by the Jefferson Mfg. Co of New Haven, Connecticut. It utilizes a Fabrique Nationale Mauser action and has a checkered American walnut stock with a Monte Carlo comb. The rifle is offered with adjustable sights. It is chambered for .243 or .30-06. There is also a deluxe version that features higher-grade wood. There were approximately 5,000 manufactured in 1957. **NOTE:** Deluxe version add 20 percent.

NIB	Exc.	V.G.	Good	Fair	Poor
675	550	450	350	300	225

Coltsman Bolt-Action Rifle

The Coltsman was manufactured for Colt by Kodiak Arms. It utilizes either a Mauser or Sako action. The rifle is offered in .243, .308, .30-06, and .300 Winchester Magnum. It has a barrel length of 22", 24" in the Magnum chambering. The stock is checkered

American walnut. There were approximately 10,000 manufactured between 1958 and 1966. There is a deluxe version that features a higher-grade, skipline-checkered walnut stock and rosewood fore-end tip; this is called "The Coltsman Custom". **NOTE:** Coltsman Custom add 50 percent.

NIB	Exc.	V.G.	Good	Fair	Poor
700	650	550	450	350	250

Coltsman Pump Shotgun

This model was manufactured by Jefferson Arms, utilizing an aluminum alloy frame made by Franchi. It is chambered for 12, 16, and 20 gauge and has a 26" or 28" plain barrel. There were approximately 2,000 manufactured between 1961 and 1965.

NIB	Exc.	V.G.	Good	Fair	Poor
375	350	300	275	200	150

Semi-Automatic Shotgun

This shotgun was manufactured for Colt by the firm of Luigi Franchi in Italy. It features an aluminum alloy receiver and is chambered for 12 or 20 gauge. The barrel length is 26", 28", 30", or 32"—either vent-rib or plain. A deluxe version, "The Custom Auto", features a fancy walnut stock and a hand engraved receiver. There were approximately 5,300 manufactured between 1962 and 1966. **NOTE:** Custom Auto add 25 percent.

NIB	Exc.	V.G.	Good	Fair	Poor
400	375	325	300	225	175

Double-Barrel Shotgun

During 1961 and 1962, Colt had approximately 50 side-by-side shotguns made for them by a French gun manufacturer. They have the Colt name on the breech area of the barrels and are in the 467000-469000 serial range. There is little information available on this gun, and Colt never went past the test-market stage.

NIB	Exc.	V.G.	Good	Fair	Poor
—	1200	950	650	500	400

Colt Light Rifle

Introduced in 1999, this bolt-action rifle is offered in both long and short action calibers from .243 to .300 Win. Magnum. Fitted with a 24" barrel and adjustable trigger. Stock is black synthetic. Action and barrel are matte black. Long action calibers. Weight about 6 lbs., with short action rifle about 5.4 lbs. Adjustable trigger. No sights.

NIB	Exc.	V.G.	Good	Fair	Poor
—	700	600	500	400	200

Colt Sauer Bolt-Action Rifle

This is a high quality and unique rifle manufactured for Colt by the firm of J.P. Sauer & Son of Germany. The rifle features a non-rotating bolt that makes the Colt Sauer action smoother functioning than most. It has a 24" barrel, skipline-checkered walnut stock with rosewood fore-end tip, pistol grip cap, and recoil pad. There are five basic configurations: the Standard Action, chambered for .25-06, .270 Winchester, and .30-06; the Short Action, chambered for .22-250, .243 Winchester, and .308 Winchester; the Magnum Action, chambered for .7mm Remington Magnum, .300 Winchester Magnum, and .300 Weatherby Magnum; also the "Grand Alaskan" and the "Grand African", heavier versions chambered for .375 Holland & Holland Magnum

and .458 Winchester Magnum, respectively. These rifles were all discontinued by Colt in 1985.

Colt Sauer Short Action

NOTE: Standard Action add $50. Magnum Action add 20 percent. "Grand Alaskan" add 50 percent. "Grand African" add 75 percent.

NIB	Exc.	V.G.	Good	Fair	Poor
2000	1950	1850	1500	800	500

Colt Sauer Drilling

This is a rather unique firearm and one with which many American enthusiasts are not familiar—a 3-barreled gun. It features a side-by-side shotgun in 12 gauge over a .30-06 or .243 rifle barrel. The name was based on the German word for three, as this is where the concept was developed. They are quite popular in Europe where the game preserve style of hunting is prevalent but have little use in America where our hunting seasons don't often overlap. This drilling has 25" barrels and pop-up sights for the rifle barrel and is nicely engraved. It was discontinued by Colt in 1985.

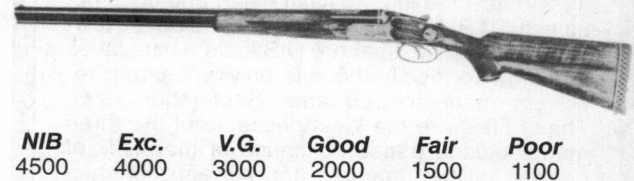

NIB	Exc.	V.G.	Good	Fair	Poor
4500	4000	3000	2000	1500	1100

Colt-Sharps Rifle

Introduced in 1970 as the last word in sporting rifles, the Colt-Sharps is a falling-block action that was advertised as a modern Sharps-Borchardt. This undertaking was first-class all the way. The finish is high polish blue with a deluxe-grade hand-checkered walnut stock and fore-end. This rifle is chambered for .17 Remington, .22-250, .243, .25-06, 7mm Remington Magnum, .30-06, and .375 Holland & Holland Magnum; and it was offered cased with accessories. This model was manufactured between 1970 and 1977. Add 25 percent for .375.

NIB	Exc.	V.G.	Good	Fair	Poor
6000	4900	3200	1550	800	500

COLT AR-15 & SPORTER RIFLES

NOTE: It is estimated that the value of pre-ban AR-15s declined 10-15 percent since the 1994-2004 Assault Weapons ban has lapsed but the market has once again spiked due to demand. The pricing status of the AR-15 is still volatile.

AR-15 Sporter (Model #6000)

A semi-automatic rifle firing from a closed bolt was introduced into the Colt product line in 1964. Similar in appearance and function to the military version, the M-16. Chambered for the .223 cartridge. It is fitted with a standard 20" barrel with no forward assist, no case deflector, but with a bayonet lug. Weighs about 7.5 lbs. Dropped from production in 1985.

NIB	Exc.	V.G.	Good	Fair	Poor
2150	1800	1600	1500	600	400

COLT AR-15 AND COLT SPORTER TERMINOLOGY

There are three different and distinct manufacturing cycles that not only affect the value of these rifles but also the legal consequences of their modifications.

Pre-Ban Colt AR-15 rifles (Pre-1989): Fitted with bayonet lug, flash hider, and stamped AR-15 on lower receiver. Rifles that are NIB have a green label. It is legal to modify this rifle with any AR-15 upper receiver. These are the most desirable models because of their pre-ban features.

Colt Sporters (Post-1989-pre-September 1994): This transition model has no bayonet lug, but it does have a flash hider. There is no AR-15 designation stamped on the lower receiver. Rifles that are NIB have a blue label. It is legal to modify this rifle with upper receivers made after 1989, i.e. no bayonet lug. These rifles are less desirable than pre-ban AR-15s.

Colt Sporters (Post-September 1994): This rifle has no bayonet lug, no flash hider, and does not have the AR-15 designation stamped on the lower receiver. Rifles that are NIB have a blue label. It is legal to modify this rifle only with upper receivers manufactured after September 1994. These rifles are the least desirable of the three manufacturing periods because of their lack of pre-ban military features and current manufacture status.

AR-15 Sporter w/Collapsible Stock (Model #6001)

Same as above but fitted with a 16" barrel and folding stock. Weighs approximately 5.8 lbs. Introduced in 1978 and discontinued in 1985.

NIB	Exc.	V.G.	Good	Fair	Poor
2750	2450	2100	1800	600	400

AR-15 Carbine (Model #6420)

Introduced in 1985 this model has a 16" standard weight barrel. All other features are the same as the previous discontinued AR-15 models. This version was dropped from the Colt product line in 1987.

NIB	Exc.	V.G.	Good	Fair	Poor
2200	1900	1700	1600	600	400

AR-15 9mm Carbine (Model #6450)

Same as above, chambered for 9mm cartridge. Weighs 6.3 lbs.

NIB	Exc.	V.G.	Good	Fair	Poor
2250	1950	1750	1650	700	400

AR-15A2 Sporter II (Model #6500)

Introduced in 1984 this was an updated version with a heavier barrel and forward assist. The AR sight was still utilized. Weighs approximately 7.8 lbs.

NIB	Exc.	V.G.	Good	Fair	Poor
1850	1500	1300	1050	550	400

AR-15A2 Government Model Carbine (Model #6520)

Added to the Colt line in 1988 this 16" standard barrel carbine featured for the first time a case deflector and the improved A2 rear sight. This model is fitted with a 4-position telescoping buttstock. Weighs about 5.8 lbs.

NIB	Exc.	V.G.	Good	Fair	Poor
2300	2000	1750	1650	700	400

AR-15A2 Government Model (Model #6550)

This model was introduced in 1988 is the rifle equivalent to the Carbine. It features a 20" A2 barrel, forward assist, case deflector, but still retains the bayonet lug. Weighs about 7.5 lbs. Discontinued in 1990. USMC model.

NIB	Exc.	V.G.	Good	Fair	Poor
2300	2000	1750	1650	700	400

AR-15A2 H-Bar (Model #6600)

Introduced in 1986 this version features a special 20" heavy barrel. All other features are the same as the A2 series of AR15s. Discontinued in 1991. Weighs about 8 lbs.

NIB	Exc.	V.G.	Good	Fair	Poor
1950	1750	1500	950	700	500

AR-15A2 Delta H-Bar (Model #6600DH)

Same as above but fitted with a 3x9 scope and detachable cheekpiece. Dropped from the Colt line in 1990. Weighs about 10 lbs.

NIB	Exc.	V.G.	Good	Fair	Poor
2350	2100	1800	1650	850	600

Sporter Lightweight Rifle

This lightweight model has a 16" barrel and is finished in a matte black. It is available in either a .223 Rem. caliber (Model #6530) that weighs 6.7 lbs., a (Model #6430) 9mm caliber weighing 7.1 lbs., or a (Model #6830) 7.65x39mm that weighs 7.3 lbs. The .223 is furnished with two five-round box magazines as is the 9mm and 7.65x39mm. A cleaning kit and sling are also supplied with each new rifle. The buttstock and pistol grip are made of durable nylon and the handguard is reinforced fiberglass and aluminum lined. The rear sight is adjustable for windage and elevation. These newer models are referred to simply as Sporters and are not fitted with a bayonet lug and receiver block has different size pins. **NOTE:** The Model 6830 will bring about $25 less than these prices.

NIB	Exc.	V.G.	Good	Fair	Poor
1500	1300	1000	600	400	300

Sporter Target Model Rifle (Model #6551)

This 1991 model is a full size version of the Lightweight Rifle. The Target Rifle weighs 7.5 lbs. and has a 20" barrel. Offered in .223 Rem. caliber only with target sights adjustable to 800 meters. New rifles are furnished with two 5-round box magazines, sling, and cleaning kit. **NOTE:** For post-9/94 guns deduct 30 percent.

NIB	Exc.	V.G.	Good	Fair	Poor
1700	1400	1100	650	400	300

Sporter Match H-Bar (Model #6601)

This 1991 variation of the AR-15 is similar to the Target Model but has a 20" heavy barrel chambered for the .223 caliber. This model weighs 8 lbs. and has target type sights adjustable out to 800 meters. Supplied with two 5-round box magazines, sling, and cleaning kit.

NIB	Exc.	V.G.	Good	Fair	Poor
11700	1400	1100	650	400	300

AR-15 (XM16E1)

This rifle was made upon request for foreign contracts. Very rare. Proceed with caution. This variation will command a premium price over the standard AR-15 rifle. Secure an appraisal before a purchase.

Courtesy Richard M. Kumor, Sr.

Sporter Match Delta H-Bar (Model #6601 DH)

Same as above but supplied with a 3x9 scope. Weighs about 10 lbs. Discontinued in 1992.

NIB	Exc.	V.G.	Good	Fair	Poor
2300	1900	1600	1300	600	400

Match Target H-BAR Compensated (Model #6601C)

Same as the regular Sporter H-BAR with the addition of a compensator.

NIB	Exc.	V.G.	Good	Fair	Poor
2200	1900	1600	1300	600	400

Colt Match Target M4

Similar to above but with carbine-length barrel.

NIB	Exc.	V.G.	Good	Fair	Poor
2200	1900	1600	1300	600	400

Sporter Competition H-Bar (Model #6700)

Introduced in 1992, the Competition H-Bar is available in .223 caliber with a 20" heavy barrel counterbored for accuracy. The carry handle is detachable with target sights. With the carry handle removed the upper receiver is dovetailed and grooved for Weaver-style scope rings. This model weighs approximately 8.5 lbs. New rifles are furnished with two 5-round box magazines, sling, and cleaning kit. **NOTE:** For post-9/94 guns deduct 35 percent.

NIB	Exc.	V.G.	Good	Fair	Poor
1800	1500	1300	1000	500	350

Sporter Competition H-Bar Select w/scope (Model #6700CH)

This variation is identical to the Sporter Competition with the addition of a factory mounted scope. The rifle has also been selected for accuracy and comes complete with a 3-9X rubber armored variable scope, scope mount, carry handle with iron sights, and nylon carrying case.

NIB	Exc.	V.G.	Good	Fair	Poor
2000	1800	1400	1000	600	400

Match Target Competition H-BAR Compensated (Model #6700C)

Same as the Match Target with a compensator.

NIB	Exc.	V.G.	Good	Fair	Poor
2000	1800	1400	1000	600	400

AR-15 Carbine Flat-top Heavyweight/Match Target Competition (Model #6731)

This variation in the Sporter series features a heavyweight 16" barrel with flat-top receiver chambered for the .223 cartridge. It is equipped with a fixed buttstock. Weight is about 7.1 lbs.

NIB	Exc.	V.G.	Good	Fair	Poor
1200	1000	800	600	400	300

AR-15 Tactical Carbine (Model #6721)

This version is similar to the above model with the exception of the buttstock which is telescoping and adjusts to 4 positions. Chambered for the .223 cartridge with a weight of about 7 lbs. A majority of these guns were for law enforcement only. Only 134 rifles are pre-ban. **NOTE:** 100 percent premium if serial number is below BD000135.

NIB	Exc.	V.G.	Good	Fair	Poor
1400	1200	1000	800	600	400

Sporter H-Bar Elite/Accurized Rifle (Model #6724)

This variation was introduced in 1996 and features a free floating 24" stainless steel match barrel with an 11 degree target crown and special Teflon coated trigger group. The handguard is all-aluminum with twin swivel studs. Weight is approximately 9.26 lbs.

NIB	Exc.	V.G.	Good	Fair	Poor
1500	1250	900	550	400	300

Colt SP901

New hunting type modular rifle chambered in .308 Winchester with interchangeable upper receiver in .223 Remington. Fully floating 16" chrome lined barrel. One-piece monolithic receiver ready for optical sights. Adjustable front and rear sights. Ambidextrous magazine release, bolt catch and safety. Scheduled to be introduced in late 2012.

NIB	Exc.	V.G.	Good	Fair	Poor
1700	1600	—	—	—	—

Colt SP6920

Sporter version of the classic Colt M4 carbine. Chambered for .223 Remington with chrome-lined bore with 6 grooves, 1" to 7" right hand twist. Four-position collapsible stock. Flattop receiver with removable carry handle. Matte black finish. Introduced in 2011.

NIB	Exc.	V.G.	Good	Fair	Poor
975	850	725	600	400	200

Colt SP6940

Same gun as SP6920 but with one-piece upper receiver, fully floated barrel which allows easier mounting of optical, laser or light accessories. No carry handle. Matte black finish. Introduced in 2011.

NIB	Exc.	V.G.	Good	Fair	Poor
1275	1075	900	700	500	300

COLT CUSTOM SHOP

The Colt Custom Shop has developed several models over the years that are available to the public. The basis of these offerings are standard Colt Models upgraded to perform special functions.

Special Combat Government Model (Competition)

This is a competition ready model. Chambered for the .45 ACP it comes fitted with a skeletonized trigger, upswept grip safety, custom tuned action, polished feed ramp, throated barrel, flared ejection port, cutout commander hammer, two 8-round magazines, hard chromed slide and receiver, extended thumb safety, Bomar rear sight, Clark dovetail front sight, and flared magazine funnel. The pistol has been accurized and is shipped with a certified target.

NIB	Exc.	V.G.	Good	Fair	Poor
1750	1200	800	500	300	200

Special Combat Government Model (Carry)

This model has all of the same features as the competition model except that it has a royal blue finish, special bar-dot night sights, ambidextrous safety. It has also been accurized and shipped with a certified target.

NIB	Exc.	V.G.	Good	Fair	Poor
1550	1000	700	400	300	200

Gold Cup Commander

Chambered for the .45 ACP and has these features: heavy-duty adjustable target sights, beveled magazine well, serrated front strap, checkered mainspring housing, wide grip safety, Palo Alto wood grips, and stainless steel or royal blue finish.

NIB	Exc.	V.G.	Good	Fair	Poor
1400	875	650	600	500	375

U.S. Shooting Team Gold Cup

This is a limited edition Gold Cup .45 ACP with special blue, sights, grips. The U.S. Shooting Team logo is rolled on the slide. Limited to 500 pistols and built for Lew Horton..

NIB	Exc.	V.G.	Good	Fair	Poor
1400	875	650	600	500	375

Gold Cup Trophy

Introduced in 1997 this model features .45 ACP 5" barrel 1911 with a choice of stainless steel or blue finish. Several custom features such as skeletonized hammer and trigger. Adjustable rear sight and wraparound rubber grips are standard. The pistol has been accurized and is shipped with a target. Magazine capacity is 7 or 8 rounds. Weight is approximately 39 oz.

NIB	Exc.	V.G.	Good	Fair	Poor
1000	900	675	625	525	400

McCormick Commander

This is a limited edition pistol made for Lew Horton in 1995 and limited to 100 pistols. It has many special features. The slide is engraved and there is a gold rampant colt on the slide.

NIB	Exc.	V.G.	Good	Fair	Poor
1600	1000	750	600	500	375

McCormick Officer

This Lew Horton exclusive pistol has factory installed McCormick parts and a hard chrome finish. A total of 500 guns were built in 1995.

NIB	Exc.	V.G.	Good	Fair	Poor
1500	875	650	600	500	375

McCormick Factory Racer

This is a limited edition pistol from Lew Horton. It is a full size government model with hard chrome finish, special barrel, trigger safety, and other custom features. Each gun is rollmarked "McCormick Factory Racer" on the slide. Special serial numbers from MFR001 to MFR500.

NIB	Exc.	V.G.	Good	Fair	Poor
1300	775	650	600	500	375

Colt Classic .45 Special Edition

This Lew Horton model is limited to 400 pistols and features a royal blue polish with special "Classic .45" gold etched on the slide. Pearlite grips.

NIB	Exc.	V.G.	Good	Fair	Poor
1300	775	650	600	500	375

125th Anniversary Edition Peacemaker

Introduced in 1998 this model features a V-shaped rear sight with two-line patent date. Barrel is 4.75" and is chambered for .45 Colt cartridge. The cylinder is the second generation type and the hammer is knurled. Frame and hammer are case colored with blue barrel. Grips are two piece walnut with oil finish. Special serial number range SA74000 to SA75999.

NIB	Exc.	V.G.	Good	Fair	Poor
1950	1350	950	600	500	375

Custom Anaconda

Custom-tuned action, Magnaported barrel, with Elliason rear sight. The contoured trigger is polished smooth. Comes with Pachmayr grips and brushed stainless steel finish.

NIB	Exc.	V.G.	Good	Fair	Poor
1950	1275	800	600	300	200

Ultimate Python

Custom tuned action with both Elliason and Accro sighting systems. Both rubber and walnut grips are included. Bright stainless steel or royal blue finish. Available only with 6" barrel.

NIB	Exc.	V.G.	Good	Fair	Poor
1800	1275	800	600	300	200

Anaconda Hunter

Comes with a Leupold 2X scope, heavy-duty mounts, cleaning accessories, both walnut and rubber grips, in a hard case. Furnished only with an 8" barrel.

NIB	Exc.	V.G.	Good	Fair	Poor
1800	1275	800	600	300	200

Bobbed Detective Special

First offered in 1994 this model features a bobbed hammer, a front sight with night sight, and honed action. Available in either chrome or blue finish.

NIB	Exc.	V.G.	Good	Fair	Poor
775	600	450	300	150	100

Limited Class .45 ACP

1911 auto. Designed for tactical competition. Supplied with a parkerized matte finish, lightweight composite trigger, extended ambidextrous safety, upswept grip safety, beveled magazine well, accurized, and shipped with a signed target. Introduced in 1993.

NIB	Exc.	V.G.	Good	Fair	Poor
1450	1050	650	450	300	200

Compensated Model .45 ACP

This competition pistol has a hard chrome receiver, bumper on magazine, extended ambidextrous safety, blue slide with full profile BAT compensator, Bomar rear sight, and flared funnel magazine well. Introduced in 1993.

NIB	Exc.	V.G.	Good	Fair	Poor
1450	1050	650	450	300	200

Compensated .45 ACP Commander

Introduced in 1998 and limited to 500 pistols. This model is fitted with a full-length guide rod, extended beavertail safety, skeletonized hammer, Novak-style sights, and checkered walnut double-diamond grips.

NIB	Exc.	V.G.	Good	Fair	Poor
1350	975	575	400	300	200

Nite Lite .380

Supplied with a bar-dot night sight, special foil mark on barrel slide, Teflon-coated alloy receiver, stainless slide, high-capacity grip-extension magazine, and a standard magazine. Shipped with a soft carrying case. Introduced in 1993.

NIB	Exc.	V.G.	Good	Fair	Poor
1350	975	575	400	300	200

Standard Tactical Model

Built for 20th Anniversary of IPSC competition shooting in 1996. Built on the Colt Government model with round top slide and chamber for .45 ACP. Many special features special serial numbers. Limited to 1,500 pistols.

NIB	Exc.	V.G.	Good	Fair	Poor
1450	875	600	450	300	200

Superior Tactical Model

Same as above but built on an enhanced frame with many custom features. Special serial numbers limited to 500 pistols.

NIB	Exc.	V.G.	Good	Fair	Poor
1550	975	700	550	400	200

COLT COMMEMORATIVES

The field of commemoratives can be fascinating and frustrating, depending on one's point of view. For someone who collects things from purely an aesthetic sense, commemoratives are quite desirable. Most are embellished and have had great care put into their fit and finish. They are attractively cased, and the proliferation of them makes acquisition relatively simple except from a financial standpoint. On the other hand, the collector who has an eye for the investment potential of his collections has found that the commemorative market has been soft and as investments they historically have not done well. The reason for this is twofold. The limited production appeal is not always what it seems. Many times the amounts produced are greater than one would consider limited. It is also a fact that if one fires a commemorative, its collectibility is gone. Even excessive handling can cause this problem. This means that since the majority of these firearms are kept new in the original boxes, the supply will usually outstrip the demand. Because of the limited numbers built, it is difficult to furnish accurate prices for the secondary market. Today's collectors are attracted to those Commemoratives with low production numbers and are willing to pay modest premiums for those where production was 2,500 or less. Few commemoratives are ever lost or worn out. Collectors who seek firearms for their historic significance are usually not interested in the commemoratives, as even though they may have been issued to commemorate a specific historic person or event, they are not a part of the era and are regarded as "instant" collectibles. In some areas one will find that the Colt Commemoratives are not as desirable, saleable, or expensive as the plain out-of-the-box versions. This is especially true in the Single-Action Army Models. We list the commemoratives made by Colt in chronological order. Remember that the prices reflect new-in-the-box as it came from the factory—all papers, books, etc., intact and included. We also include the issue price for comparison. If the model with which you are concerned has been fired or is not in its original casing or box, deduct as much as 50 percent from these prices. It is interesting to note that in some areas shooters are taking advantage of the soft commemorative market and are buying SAAs at lower prices than the plain 3rd Generation guns—then shooting them. This can perhaps have a positive effect on appreciation. One final note. There are a number of Colt Commemoratives that were produced by Colt but offered for sale by private companies to commemorate an event of their choosing. This publication does not cover most of these private commemoratives because it is difficult, if not impossible, to determine a secondary market value. It is also difficult to construct any meaningful comprehensive list of these private offerings. While the market for Colt factory remains soft the market for private commemoratives is usually very soft. the few that come on the market sometimes sell for less than half of their initial offering price. For those who enjoy collecting these firearms without investment goals these private commemoratives offer an additional outlet.

1961	Issue Price	NIB	Amount Mfg.
Geneseo, IL. 125th Anniv. Derringer	$ 28	$ 650	104
Sheriff's Model (Blue & Case)	130	2250	478
Sheriff's Model (Nickel)	140	6000	25
Kansas Statehood Scout	75	450	6,197
125th Anniv. Model SAA .45	150	1495	7,390
Pony Express Cent. Scout	80	600	1,007
Civil War Cent. Pistol	75	300	24,114
1962			
Rock Island Arsenal Cent. Scout	$ 39	$ 250	550
Columbus, OH. Sesquicent. Scout	100	550	200
Ft. Findlay, OH. Sesquicent. Scout	90	650	110
Ft. Findlay Cased Pair	185	2500	20
New Mex. Golden Anniv. Scout	80	550	1,000
Ft. McPherson, Nebraska Cent. Derringer	29	500	300
West Virginia Statehood Cent. Scout	75	550	3,452
1963			
West Virginia Statehood Cent. SAA .45	$ 150	$1495	600
Ariz. Terr. Cent. Scout	75	550	5,355
Ariz. Terr. Cent. SAA .45	$150	1495	1,280
Carolina Charter Tercent Scout	75	550	300

1963 *(cont.)*	Issue Price	NIB	Amount Mfg.
Carolina Charter Tercent .22/.45 Comb.	$ 240	$ 2200	251
H. Cook 1 To 100 .22/.45 Comb.	275	2500	100
Ft. Stephenson, Oh. Sesquicent. Scout	75	550	200
Battle of Gettysburg Cent. Scout	90	650	1,019
Idaho Terr. Cent. Scout	75	550	902
Gen. J.H. Morgan Indiana Raid Scout	75	650	100
1964			
Cherry's 35th Anniv. .22/.45 Comb.	$ 275	$ 2500	100
Nevada Statehood Cent. Scout	75	450	3,984
Nevada Statehood Cent. SAA .45	150	1600	1,688
Nevada Statehood Cent. .22/.45 Comb.	240	2100	189
Nevada Statehood Cent. .22/.45 W/extra Cyls.	350	2200	577
Nevada Battle Born Scout	85	550	981
Nevada Battle Born SAA .45	175	1900	80
Nevada Battle Born .22/.45 Comb.	265	2595	20
Montana Terr. Cent. Scout	75	550	2,300
Montana Terr. Cent. SAA .45	150	1600	851
Wyoming Diamond Jubilee Scout	75	550	2,357
General Hood Cent. Scout	75	550	1,503
New Jersey Tercent Scout	75	450	1,001
New Jersey Tercent SAA .45	150	1600	250
St. Louis Bicent. Scout	75	450	802
St. Louis Bicent. SAA .45	150	1600	200
St. Louis Bicent .22/.45 Comb.	240	2100	250
California Gold Rush Scout	80	575	500
Pony Express Pres. SAA .45	250	1750	1,004
Chamizal Treaty Scout	85	550	450
Chamizal Treaty SAA .45	170	1700	50
Chamizal Treaty .22/.45 Comb	280	2400	50
Col. Sam Colt Sesquicent. SAA .45	225	1600	4,750
Col. Sam Colt Deluxe SAA .45	500	3500	200
Col. Sam Colt Special Deluxe SAA .45	1000	5000	50
Wyatt Earp Buntline SAA .45	250	2750	150
1965			
Oregon Trail Scout	$ 75	$ 550	1,995
Joaquin Murietta .22/.45 Comb.	350	2100	100
Forty-Niner Miner Scout	85	550	500
Old Ft. Des Moines Reconst. Scout	90	600	700
Old Ft. Des Moines Reconst. SAA .45	170	1600	100
Old Ft. Des Moines Reconst. .22/.45 Comb.	290	2100	100
Appomattox Cent. Scout	75	600	1,001
Appomattox Cent. SAA .45	150	1600	250
Appomattox Cent. .22/.45 Comb.	240	2200	250
General Meade Campaign Scout	75	550	1,197
St. Augustine Quadracent. Scout	85	550	500
Kansas Cowtown Series Wichita Scout	85	500	500
1966			
Kansas Cowtown Series Dodge City Scout	$ 85	$ 550	500
Colorado Gold Rush Scout	85	600	1,350
Oklahoma Territory Scout	85	550	1,343
Dakota Territory Scout	85	600	1,000
General Meade SAA .45	165	1600	200
Abercrombie & Fitch Trailblazer N.Y.	275	1400	200
Abercrombie & Fitch Trailblazer Chic.	275	1400	100
Abercrombie & Fitch Trailblazer S.F.	275	1400	100
Kansas Cowtown Series Abilene Scout	95	550	500
Indiana Sesquicent. Scout	85	600	1,500
Pony Express 4-Square Set .45 4 Guns	1,400	7000	N/A
California Gold Rush SAA .45	175	1700	130
1967			
Lawman Series Bat Masterson Scout	$ 90	$ 600	3,000
Lawman Series Bat Masterson SAA .45	180	1700	500
Alamo Scout	85	500	4,250

1967 *(cont.)*	Issue Price	NIB	Amount Mfg.
Alamo SAA .45	$165	$ 1650	750
Alamo .22/.45 Comb.	265	2100	250
Kansas Cowtown Series Coffeyville Scout	95	450	500
Kansas Trail Series Chisolm Trail Scout	100	450	500
WWI Series Chateau Thierry .45 Auto	200	1000	7,400
WWI Series Chateau Thierry Deluxe	500	1350	75
WWI Series Chateau Thierry Sp. Deluxe	1000	2950	25
1968			
Nebraska Cent. Scout	$ 100	$ 450	7,001
Kansas Trail Series Chisolm Trail Scout	100	450	500
WWI Series Belleau Wood .45 Auto	200	1000	7,400
WWI Series Belleau Wood Deluxe	500	1350	75
WWI Series Belleau Wood Sp. Deluxe	1000	2950	25
Lawman Series Pat Garrett Scout	110	600	3,000
Lawman Series Pat Garrett SAA .45	220	1700	500
1969			
Nathan B. Forrest Scout	$ 110	$ 450	3,000
Kansas Trail Series Santa Fe Trail Sct.	120	450	501
WWI Ser. 2nd Battle of Marne .45 Auto	220	1000	7,400
WWI Ser. 2nd Battle of Marne Deluxe	500	1350	75
WWI Ser. 2nd Battle of Marne Sp. Del.	1000	2950	25
Alabama Sesquicent. Scout	110	450	3,001
Alabama Sesquicent. SAA .45	N/A	15000	1
Golden Spike Scout	135	550	11,000
Kansas Trail Ser. Shawnee Tr. Scout	120	450	501
WWI Ser. Meuse-Argonne .45 Auto	220	1000	7,400
WWI Ser. Meuse-Argonne Deluxe	500	1350	75
WWI Ser. Meuse-Argonne Sp. Deluxe	1000	2950	25
Arkansas Terr. Sesquicent. Scout	110	450	3,500
Lawman Ser. Wild Bill Hickok Scout	117	600	3,000
Lawman Ser. Wild Bill Hickok SAA .45	220	1650	500
California Bicent. Scout	135	550	5,000
1970			
Kansas Ft. Ser. Ft. Larned Scout	$ 120	$ 450	500
WWII Ser. European Theatre	250	1000	11,500
WWII Ser. Pacific Theatre	250	1000	11,500
Texas Ranger SAA .45	650	2250	1,000
Kansas Ft. Ser. Ft. Hays Scout	130	450	500
Marine Sesquicent. Scout	120	450	3,000
Missouri Sesquicent. Scout	125	450	3,000
Missouri Sesquicent. SAA .45	220	1600	900
Kansas Ft. Ser. Ft. Riley Scout	130	450	500
Lawman Ser. Wyatt Earp Scout	125	600	3,000
Lawman Ser. Wyatt Earp SAA .45	395	2750	500
1971			
NRA Centennial SAA .45	$ 250	$ 1600	5,000
NRA Centennial SAA .357 Mag.	250	1600	5,000
NRA Centennial Gold Cup .45 Auto	250	1295	2,500
U.S. Grant 1851 Navy	250	750	4,750
Robt. E. Lee 1851 Navy	250	750	4,750
Lee - Grant Set 1851 Navies	500	1500	250
Kansas Ft. Ser. Ft. Scott Scout	130	450	500
1972			
Centennial Cased Set Florida Terr. Sesquicent. Scout	$ 125	$ 550	2,001
Arizona Ranger Scout	135	550	3,001
1975			
Peacemaker Centennial SAA .45	$ 300	$ 1700	1,500
Peacemaker Centennial SAA .44-40	300	1700	1,500
Peacemaker	625	3600	500

1976	**Issue Price**	**NIB**	**Amount Mfg.**
U.S. Bicentennial Set	$ 1695	$ 2995	1,776
1977			
2nd Amendment .22	$ 195	$ 450	3,020
U.S. Cavalry 200th Anniversary Set	995	1450	3,000
1978			
Statehood 3rd Model Dragoon	$ 12500	$ 7500	52
1979			
Ned Buntline SAA N.F. .45	$ 895	$ 1295	3,000
Ohio President's Spec. Edit. .45 Auto	N/A	995	250
Tombstone Cent. .45 SAA	550	1500	300
1980			
Drug Enforcement Agency .45 Auto	$ 550	$ 1100	910
Olympics Ace Spec. Edition .22	1000	1295	200
Heritage Walker .44 Percussion	1495	950	1,847
1981			
John M. Browning .45 Auto	$ 1100	$ 995	3,000
Ace Signature Series .22	1000	1200	1,000
1982			
John Wayne SAA	$ 2995	$ 2250	3,100
John Wayne SAA Deluxe	10000	7500	500
John Wayne SAA Presentation	20000	13500	100
1983			
Buffalo Bill Wild West Show Cent. SAA	$ 1350	$ 1595	500
1984			
1st Edition Govt. Model .380 ACP	$ 425	$ 750	1,000
Duke Frontier .22	475	850	1,000
Winchester/Colt SAA .44-40	N/A	2500	4,000
USA Edition SAA .44-40	4995	3500	100
Kit Carson New Frontier .22	550	550	1,000
2nd Edition Govt. Model .380 ACP	525	750	1,000
Officer's ACP Commencement Issue	700	1000	1,000
Theodore Roosevelt SAA .44-40	1695	1995	500
No Amer. Oilmen Buntline SAA .45	3900	3500	200
1985			
Mustang 1st Edition .380 ACP	$ 475	$ 750	1,000
Officer's ACP Heirloom Edition	1575	1550	N/A
Klay-Colt 1851 Navy	1850	1850	150
Klay-Colt 1851 Navy Engraved Edit.	3150	3150	50
Double Diamond Set .357 & .45 Auto	1575	3000	1,000
1986			
150th Anniversary SAA .45	$ 1595	$ 1995	1,000
150th Anniv. Engraving Sampler	1613	3500	N/A
150th Anniv. Engraving Sampler .45 Auto	1155	2000	N/A
Texas 150th Sesquicent. Sheriff's .45	836	1695	N/A
1987			
Combat Elite Custom Edition .45 Auto	$ 900	$ 1100	500
12th Man Spirit of Aggieland .45 Auto	950	995	999
1989			
Snake Eyes Ltd. Edit. 2-2.5" Pythons	$ 2950	$ 3200	500

Deluxe Tactical Model

Same as above but with added features. Limited to 250 pistols.

NIB	Exc.	V.G.	Good	Fair	Poor
1650	1075	800	650	500	300

COLT REPRODUCTION PERCUSSION REVOLVERS

The revolvers listed were manufactured in a variety of styles (cylinder form, stainless steel, etc.) that affect prices. Factory engraved examples command a considerable premium over the prices listed. Imported from Italy.

Walker

Made from 1979 to 1981; serial numbers 1200-4120 and 32256 to 32500.

NIB	Exc.	V.G.	Good	Fair	Poor
950	750	500	—	—	—

Walker Heritage Model

NIB	Exc.	V.G.	Good	Fair	Poor
1000	—	—	—	—	—

First Model Dragoon

Made from 1980 to 1982; serial numbers 24100-34500.

NIB	Exc.	V.G.	Good	Fair	Poor
595	400	300	—	—	—

Second Model Dragoon

Made from 1980 to 1982; serial numbers as above.

NIB	Exc.	V.G.	Good	Fair	Poor
595	400	300	—	—	—

Third Model Dragoon

Made from 1980 to 1982; serial numbers as above.

NIB	Exc.	V.G.	Good	Fair	Poor
595	400	300	—	—	—

Model 1848 Pocket Pistol

Made in 1981; serial numbers 16000-17851.

NIB	Exc.	V.G.	Good	Fair	Poor
600	425	325	—	—	—

Model 1851 Navy Revolver

Made from 1971 to 1978; serial numbers 4201-25100 and 24900-29150.

NIB	Exc.	V.G.	Good	Fair	Poor
595	400	300	—	—	—

Model 1860 Army Revolver

Made from 1978 to 1982; serial numbers 201000-212835.

NIB	Exc.	V.G.	Good	Fair	Poor
595	400	300	—	—	—

Model 1861 Navy Revolver

Made during 1980 and 1981; serial numbers 40000-43165.

NIB	Exc.	V.G.	Good	Fair	Poor
595	400	300	—	—	—

Model 1862 Pocket Pistol

Made from 1979 to 1984; serial numbers 8000-58850.

NIB	Exc.	V.G.	Good	Fair	Poor
595	400	300	—	—	—

Model 1862 Police Revolver

Made from 1979 to 1984; serial numbers in above range.

NIB	Exc.	V.G.	Good	Fair	Poor
595	400	300	—	—	—

COLT BLACKPOWDER ARMS
Brooklyn, New York

These blackpowder revolvers and rifles were made under license from Colt. Imported from Italy. No longer in business.

Special order Paterson Colt No. 5 Holster Model

1842 Paterson Colt No. 5 Holster Model

This model is a copy of the No. 5 Holster model and is chambered for the .36 caliber ball. Fitted with a 7.5" octagon barrel. Hand engraved. This is a special order revolver.

Special order Paterson Colt No. 5 Holster Model

NIB	Exc.	V.G.	Good	Fair	Poor
1900	1200	900	600	450	200

Walker

This .44 caliber large-frame revolver is fitted with a 9" barrel.

NIB	Exc.	V.G.	Good	Fair	Poor
975	600	350	300	200	150

Walker 150th Anniversary Model

Marked "A Company No. 1" in gold. Introduced 1997.

NIB	Exc.	V.G.	Good	Fair	Poor
975	600	350	300	200	150

Whitneyville Hartford Dragoon

Similar in appearance to the Walker colt this revolver is fitted with a 7.5" barrel and a silver plated iron backstrap and trigger guard. This is a limited edition with a total of 2,400 guns built with serial numbers between 1100 through 1340.

NIB	Exc.	V.G.	Good	Fair	Poor
1075	700	450	32	225	200

Marine Dragoon

Special limited edition presentation grade in honor of U.S. Marine Corps.

NIB	Exc.	V.G.	Good	Fair	Poor
1100	725	450	32	225	200

3rd Model Dragoon

Another large-frame revolver with 7.5" barrel with a brass backstrap, 3-screw frame, and unfluted cylinder.

NIB	Exc.	V.G.	Good	Fair	Poor
675	500	350	300	200	150

Steel Backstrap

NIB	Exc.	V.G.	Good	Fair	Poor
600	425	375	325	200	150

Fluted Cylinder

NIB	Exc.	V.G.	Good	Fair	Poor
610	435	375	325	200	150

Cochise Dragoon

This is a commemorative issue Third Model with gold inlay frame and barrel with special grips.

NIB	Exc.	V.G.	Good	Fair	Poor
975	600	350	300	200	150

Colt 1849 Model Pocket

A small-frame revolver chambered in .31 caliber with a 4" barrel. Fitted with one-piece walnut grips.

NIB	Exc.	V.G.	Good	Fair	Poor
575	475	325	275	200	150

Colt 1851 Model Navy

This is medium-frame revolver chambered in .36 caliber with 7.5" barrel. Walnut grips and case color frame.

NIB	Exc.	V.G.	Good	Fair	Poor
635	575	400	300	200	125

Dual Cylinder

NIB	Exc.	V.G.	Good	Fair	Poor
675	595	400	300	200	125

Colt Model 1860 Army

This model is chamber in .44 caliber with roll engraved cylinder and one piece walnut grips. Barrel length is 8".

NIB	Exc.	V.G.	Good	Fair	Poor
675	575	400	300	200	125

Dual Cylinder

NIB	Exc.	V.G.	Good	Fair	Poor
700	600	450	350	225	150

Fluted Cylinder

NIB	Exc.	V.G.	Good	Fair	Poor
675	575	400	300	200	125

Colt 1860 Officer's Model

This is a deluxe version of the standard 1860 with a special blued finish and gold crossed sabres. This is a 4-screw frame with 8" barrel and 6-shot rebated cylinder.

NIB	Exc.	V.G.	Good	Fair	Poor
675	575	450	375	250	150

Colt Model 1860 Army Gold U.S. Cavalry

Features a gold engraved cylinder and gold barrel bands.

NIB	Exc.	V.G.	Good	Fair	Poor
650	575	450	375	250	150

Stainless Steel

NIB	Exc.	V.G.	Good	Fair	Poor
575	400	350	300	200	150

Colt 1860 Heirloom Edition

This is an elaborately engraved revolver done in the Tiffany-style and fitted with Tiffany-style grips.

NIB	Exc.	V.G.	Good	Fair	Poor
4100	3000	2175	1400	850	450

Colt Model 1861 Navy

This .36 caliber revolver features a 7.5" barrel with engraved cylinder, case colored frame and one piece walnut grips.

NIB	Exc.	V.G.	Good	Fair	Poor
700	550	350	300	200	150

General Custer

Same as above but with engraved frame and cylinder.

NIB	Exc.	V.G.	Good	Fair	Poor
975	850	700	500	300	200

Colt Model 1862 Pocket Navy

This small-frame revolver is fitted with a round engraved cylinder with a 5" octagon barrel with hinged loading lever. Chambered for .36 caliber.

NIB	Exc.	V.G.	Good	Fair	Poor
550	475	325	275	200	150

Colt Model 1862 Trapper-Pocket Police

This small-frame revolver is fitted with a 3.5" barrel, silver backstrap, and trigger guard. The cylinder is semi-fluted and chambered in .36 caliber.

NIB	Exc.	V.G.	Good	Fair	Poor
600	475	325	275	200	150

Colt 1861 Musket

This Civil War musket is chambered in the .58 caliber. Lockplate, hammer, buttplate, and three barrel bands, and 40" barrel are finished bright. The stock is a one-piece oil-finish affair. Bayonet and accessories are extra.

NIB	Exc.	V.G.	Good	Fair	Poor
800	650	500	325	275	150

Colt 1861 Musket—Artillery Model

Same as above but fitted with a 31.5" barrel.

NIB	Exc.	V.G.	Good	Fair	Poor
800	650	500	325	275	150

Colt 1861 Musket Presentation 1 of 1000

Limited to 1,000 guns these are special finished with a high polish and Colt's signature in gold on the trigger guard. Sold with special custom wooden case.

NIB	Exc.	V.G.	Good	Fair	Poor
1650	1300	750	600	450	300

Colt 1861 Musket Presentation 1 of 1000 —Artillery Model

Same as above but 31.5" barrel.

NIB	Exc.	V.G.	Good	Fair	Poor
1650	1300	750	600	450	300

Colt Gamemaster .50

Introduced in 1997 this rifle issimilar to the above in general outline and is in .50 caliber. It is fitted with a 31.5" barrel and weighs about 13 lbs.

NIB	Exc.	V.G.	Good	Fair	Poor
800	650	475	300	225	125

COLUMBIA ARMORY
Columbia, Tennessee

A trade name applied to a variety of solid frame cartridge revolvers made by John T. Smith Company of Rock Falls, Connecticut. They were marked "SAFETY HAMMERLESS REVOLVER". This model was made under several trade names.

NIB	Exc.	V.G.	Good	Fair	Poor
—	—	225	110	75	50

COLUMBUS F. A. MFG. CO.
Columbus, Georgia
Columbus Revolver

A .36-caliber double-action percussion revolver with a 6-shot, unfluted cylinder and a 7.5" octagonal barrel. Similar in appearance to the 1851 Colt Navy. The pistol is browned steel, with brass gripstraps and walnut grips. The barrel is marked "Columbus Fire Arms Manuf. Co/Columbus Ga." 100 revolvers were manufactured in 1863 and 1864.

NIB	Exc.	V.G.	Good	Fair	Poor
—	—	115000	55000	35000	12500

COMANCHE
Buenos Aires, Argentina
See—Firestorm
Comanche I

Single-/double-action revolver chambered in .22 LR. Nine-shot cylinder, 6" barrel, adjustable sights, blued or stainless steel construction with rubber grips.

NIB	Exc.	V.G.	Good	Fair	Poor
225	150	100	65	35	15

Comanche II

Similar to above but in .38 Special with 2", 3" or 4" barrel.

NIB	Exc.	V.G.	Good	Fair	Poor
225	150	100	65	35	15

Comanche III

Similar to above but in .357 Magnum and additional 6" barrel option.

NIB	Exc.	V.G.	Good	Fair	Poor
250	150	100	65	35	15

Super Comanche

Single-shot break-action pistol chambered in .410/.45 Colt. Matte black finish, rubber grips.

NIB	Exc.	V.G.	Good	Fair	Poor
195	150	125	85	50	25

COMMANDO ARMS
Knoxville, Tennessee

Formerly known as Volunteer Enterprises. The name change took place in 1978.

Mark III Carbine

A .45 ACP caliber semi-automatic rifle with a 16.5" barrel, a peep rear sight and a vertical foregrip. Manufactured between 1969 and 1976.

NIB	Exc.	V.G.	Good	Fair	Poor
675	550	375	300	225	150

Mark 9 Carbine

As above, in 9mm caliber.

NIB	Exc.	V.G.	Good	Fair	Poor
675	550	375	300	225	150

Mark .45

The new designation for the Mark III after the company changed its name.

NIB	Exc.	V.G.	Good	Fair	Poor
675	550	375	300	225	150

COMPETITOR CORP.
New Ipswich, New Hampshire

Competitor Single-Shot

This single-shot pistol is chambered for calibers from .22 LR to .50 Action Express. Choice of barrels lengths from 10.5", 14", and 16". Ramp front sight. Adjustable single stage trigger. Interchangeable barrels. Matte blue finish. Weight is approximately 59 oz. depending on barrel length. Introduced in 1988.

NIB	Exc.	V.G.	Good	Fair	Poor
465	325	275	225	175	125

CONNECTICUT ARMS CO.
Norfolk, Connecticut

Pocket Revolver

A .28 caliber spur trigger revolver with 3" octagonal barrel, 6-shot unfluted cylinder, using a cup-primed cartridge and loads from the front of the cylinder. There is a hinged hook on the side of the frame under the cylinder that acts as the extractor. Silver-plated brass, blued with walnut grips. The barrel is marked "Conn. Arms Co. Norfolk, Conn." Approximately 2,700 manufactured in the 1860s.

NIB	Exc.	V.G.	Good	Fair	Poor
—	—	950	750	300	100

CONNECTICUT SHOTGUN MANUFACTURING COMPANY
New Britain, Connecticut

RBL Side-By-Side Shotgun

Round-action SXS shotguns made in the USA. Chambered in 12, 16, 20 and 28 gauge with scaled frames. Barrel lengths 26", 28", 30" and 32" with five TruLock choke tubes. Deluxe fancy-grade walnut buttstock and fore-end, Quick Change recoil pad in two lengths. Various dimensions and options available depending on gauge. Values shown are for 12 gauge. **NOTE:** For 16 gauge add 10 percent, for 20 or 28 gauge add 20 percent.

NIB	Exc.	V.G.	Good	Fair	Poor
4000	2950	2000	1275	800	400

A-10 American

Sidelock design in 12, 20 or 28 gauge with XX grade walnut stock and light scroll engraving. Offered in standard barrel lengths from 26 to 32 inches. Options include higher-grade wood and engraving. Prices shown are for standard mode. Introduced in 2010

NIB	Exc.	V.G.	Good	Fair	Poor
7500	6000	4500	3500	—	—

Model 21

This is a faithful rendition of the famous Winchester side-by-side shotgun that was in production from 1931 to 1959 and on custom-order from 1960 to 1993. Made in all gauges and standard barrel lengths with many options. Each gun is custom made to order. Introduced in 2002. Prices are for standard 12, 16 and 20-gauge models. **NOTE:** Add $3000 for 28 or .410, plus $10,000 if made on optional small frame.

NIB	Exc.	V.G.	Good	Fair	Poor
15000	12000	9500	7000	3500	—

Model 21 Grand American

As above with high-grade, gold-inlayed engraving, AAA-grade walnut stock with elaborate checkering and carving patterns. Comes with two sets of barrels. **NOTE:** Add $3000 for 28 or .410, plus $10,000 if made on optional small frame.

NIB	Exc.	V.G.	Good	Fair	Poor
25000	20000	17500	15000	8000	—

CONNECTICUT VALLEY ARMS CO.
Norcross, Georgia

RIFLES

Express Rifle

A .50 caliber double-barrel percussion rifle with 28" barrels. Blued with a walnut stock. **NOTE:** Deluxe version add 25 percent.

NIB	Exc.	V.G.	Good	Fair	Poor
625	475	425	375	325	200

Over/Under Rifle

A .50 caliber double-barrel over/under rifle with 26" barrels. Blued with a walnut stock.

NIB	Exc.	V.G.	Good	Fair	Poor
600	475	425	375	325	200

Hawken Rifle

A .50 caliber with a 28" octagonal barrel, double set triggers and a walnut stock.

NIB	Exc.	V.G.	Good	Fair	Poor
450	325	275	225	150	100

Presentation Grade Hawken

As above, with an engraved lock, patchbox, and finely figured stock.

NIB	Exc.	V.G.	Good	Fair	Poor
550	425	375	325	275	200

Pennsylvania Long Rifle

A .50 caliber flintlock rifle with a 40" octagonal barrel, double set triggers and a walnut stock.

NIB	Exc.	V.G.	Good	Fair	Poor
475	400	350	300	250	175

Kentucky Rifle

A .45 caliber percussion rifle with a 33.5" octagonal barrel and walnut stock.

NIB	Exc.	V.G.	Good	Fair	Poor
275	225	175	150	100	75

Mountain Rifle

A .50 or .54 caliber percussion half-stock rifle.

NIB	Exc.	V.G.	Good	Fair	Poor
300	225	175	125	100	75

Blazer Rifle

A .50 caliber percussion rifle with a 28" octagonal barrel and walnut stock.

NIB	Exc.	V.G.	Good	Fair	Poor
150	125	100	85	65	45

Apollo Shadow SS

Introduced in 1993 this rifle features an in-line stainless steel bolt spring-action, a 24" blued round barrel with octagonal one piece receiver, drilled and tapped. Stock is black hardwood-textured with Dura Grip with pistol grip and recoil pad. Offered in either .50 or .54 caliber. Weighs about 9 lbs.

NIB	Exc.	V.G.	Good	Fair	Poor
175	150	125	100	75	50

Apollo Classic

Similar to the above Apollo Model but with dark brown stained laminated hardwood stock with pistol grip, raised comb, and recoil pad. Weighs about 8.5 lbs.

NIB	Exc.	V.G.	Good	Fair	Poor
215	175	150	125	100	75

Apollo Carbelite

Offered in .50 caliber with percussion bolt and 27" blued round taper barrel with octagonal receiver, drilled and tapped. Fitted with Carbelite composite stock with Monte Carlo and cheekpiece with pistol grip. Weighs approximately 7.5 lbs.

NIB	Exc.	V.G.	Good	Fair	Poor
280	225	175	150	100	75

Apollo Starfire

Chambered for the .50 caliber bullet this rifle is an in-line type with 24" stainless steel barrel with synthetic stock with checkered pistol grip, raised comb, and cheekpiece. Weight is about 6.5 lbs.

NIB	Exc.	V.G.	Good	Fair	Poor
225	175	150	125	100	75

Apollo Eclipse Rifle

Offered in either .50 or .54 caliber with 24" round barrel with blued steel receiver. Synthetic stock with checkered pistol, raised comb, and cheekpiece. Approximate weight is 6.5 lbs.

NIB	Exc.	V.G.	Good	Fair	Poor
175	150	125	100	85	65

Apollo Dominator

Fitted with a synthetic thumbhole stock and a 24" round barrel this rifle is chambered for the .50 caliber bullet. Introduced in 1996. Weight is approximately 8.5 lbs.

NIB	Exc.	V.G.	Good	Fair	Poor
300	225	175	150	100	75

Apollo Brown Bear

This .50 caliber rifle is fitted with a hardwood stock with pistol grip with raised comb and cheekpiece. The barrel is round and 24". Introduced in 1996. Weight is about 6.5 lbs.

NIB	Exc.	V.G.	Good	Fair	Poor
200	175	150	125	100	75

Frontier Carbine

Fitted with a 24" blued barrel this rifle is offered in .50 caliber percussion or flintlock. Case hardened lock with hardwood stock. Weighs about 6.75 lbs.

NIB	Exc.	V.G.	Good	Fair	Poor
150	125	100	85	75	50

Plainsman Rifle

This .50 caliber percussion rifle has a 26" octagonal barrel with case hardened lock and hardwood stock. Weight is about 6.5 lbs.

NIB	Exc.	V.G.	Good	Fair	Poor
130	115	100	85	75	50

Panther Carbine

This percussion rifle is available in either .50 or .54 caliber. It is fitted with a 24" blued octagonal barrel with Hawken-style case hardened lock. Stock is textured black Dura Grip over hardwood with Monte Carlo comb, cheekpiece, and pistol grip. Weight approximately 7.5 lbs.

NIB	Exc.	V.G.	Good	Fair	Poor
150	125	100	85	75	50

Bushwacker Rifle

This .50 caliber percussion rifle is fitted with a 26" octagonal barrel with case hardened engraved lock and brown stained hardwood stock with rounded nose. Weight is about 7.5 lbs.

NIB	Exc.	V.G.	Good	Fair	Poor
135	115	100	85	75	50

Trophy Carbine

This carbine is fitted with a 24" half-round half-octagon barrel with Hawken-style lock. The stock is walnut with Monte Carlo comb, cheekpiece, and pistol grip. Offered in .50 or .54 caliber percussion and weighs about 6.75 lbs.

NIB	Exc.	V.G.	Good	Fair	Poor
215	175	150	125	100	75

Varmint Rifle

This is a lightweight percussion rifle in .32 caliber with 24" octagon barrel and case-colored lock. The stock is hardwood. Weighs about 6.75 lbs.

NIB	Exc.	V.G.	Good	Fair	Poor
175	150	125	100	85	75

Woodsman Rifle LS

Introduced in 1994 this rifle features a 26" blued octagon barrel with dark brown stained laminated hardwood stock. Offered in .50 or .54 caliber percussion. Weighs about 6.5 lbs.

NIB	Exc.	V.G.	Good	Fair	Poor
135	115	100	85	75	50

Frontier Hunter Carbine

Offered in either .50 or .54 caliber this percussion rifle is fitted with a 24" blued octagon barrel and case hardened 45° offset hammer. The stock is dark stained laminated hardwood. Weighs about 7.5 lbs.

NIB	Exc.	V.G.	Good	Fair	Poor
170	150	125	100	75	50

Grey Wolf Rifle

Offered in either .50 or .54 caliber percussion this rifle is fitted with a 26" matte blue octagon barrel with a case hardened engraved lock. The stock is matte gray composite with raised comb, checkered pistol grip, and buttplate. Weighs about 6.5 lbs.

NIB	Exc.	V.G.	Good	Fair	Poor
160	125	100	85	75	50

Lone Grey Wolf Rifle

Introduced in 1994 this .50 caliber percussion rifle features a 26" matte blued octagon barrel. The trigger guard is oversized. The composite stock is black and has a raised comb, checkered pistol grip, and recoil pad. Weighs about 6.5 lbs.

NIB	Exc.	V.G.	Good	Fair	Poor
185	150	125	100	75	50

Timber Wolf Rifle

Introduced in 1994 this model is similar to the above model but is furnished with Realtree composite stock with raised comb, checkered pistol grip, and buttplate. Weighs about 6.5 lbs.

NIB	Exc.	V.G.	Good	Fair	Poor
185	165	140	100	75	50

Tracker Carbine LS

Introduced in 1994 this carbine is fitted with a 21" blued, half-round, half-octagon barrel with a Hawken-style lock. The stock is laminated dark brown with matte finish, and straight grip. Chambered for .50 caliber percussion. Weighs about 6.5 lbs.

NIB	Exc.	V.G.	Good	Fair	Poor
185	165	140	100	75	50

Stag Horn

Introduced in 1996 this in-line rifle is chambered for the .50 or .54 caliber bullet. The round barrel is 24" with blued finish. The stock is synthetic with checkered pistol grip, raised comb, and cheekpiece. Weight is about 6.5 lbs.

NIB	Exc.	V.G.	Good	Fair	Poor
175	150	125	100	85	65

Electra

A .50-caliber inline muzzleloader that uses electronic-arc ignition rather than caps or primers. Powered by common 9v battery. Finishes include stainless/camo, stainless/black composite, and blued/black composite. Introduced in 2007. Price given is for stainless/camo version.

NIB	Exc.	V.G.	Good	Fair	Poor
600	500	400	300	200	100

SHOTGUNS

Brittany 11 Shotgun

A .410 bore double-barrel percussion shotgun with 24" barrels, double triggers and a walnut stock.

NIB	Exc.	V.G.	Good	Fair	Poor
425	350	250	150	125	75

Trapper Shotgun

A 12 gauge percussion single barrel shotgun with a 28" barrel threaded for choke tubes, and a walnut stock.

NIB	Exc.	V.G.	Good	Fair	Poor
275	250	225	175	150	100

Classic Turkey Double-Barrel Shotgun

This is a 12 gauge percussion breech-loading shotgun with 28" barrel. The checkered stock is European walnut with straight grip. Weighs about 9 lbs.

NIB	Exc.	V.G.	Good	Fair	Poor
495	375	275	200	175	100

Trapper Shotgun

This is a single barrel 12 gauge shotgun with a 28" barrel. The stock is a straight grip hardwood with checkering. Supplied with three interchangeable chokes. Weighs about 6 lbs.

NIB	Exc.	V.G.	Good	Fair	Poor
295	250	200	150	100	75

PISTOLS

Made by Pedersoli, Uberti and other Italian makers.

Siber

A .45 caliber percussion pistol patterned after the Swiss Siber.

NIB	Exc.	V.G.	Good	Fair	Poor
450	325	275	225	150	100

Kentucky

A .45 caliber single-shot percussion pistol with a 10" barrel and walnut stock.

NIB	Exc.	V.G.	Good	Fair	Poor
140	125	100	80	60	40

Philadelphia Derringer

A .45 caliber single-shot percussion pistol with a 3.25" barrel and walnut stock.

NIB	Exc.	V.G.	Good	Fair	Poor
125	95	50	40	30	20

Sheriff's Model

A .36 caliber percussion revolver, nickel-plated with walnut grips.

NIB	Exc.	V.G.	Good	Fair	Poor
225	200	175	150	125	100

3rd Model Dragoon

NIB	Exc.	V.G.	Good	Fair	Poor
225	200	175	150	125	100

Colt Walker Replica

NIB	Exc.	V.G.	Good	Fair	Poor
425	295	225	200	175	150

Remington Bison

NIB	Exc.	V.G.	Good	Fair	Poor
250	225	200	175	150	125

Pocket Police

NIB	Exc.	V.G.	Good	Fair	Poor
135	110	100	85	65	45

Pocket Revolver

Chambered for .31 caliber. Fitted with 4" octagon barrel. Cylinder holds five bullets. Solid brass frame. Weighs about 15 oz.

NIB	Exc.	V.G.	Good	Fair	Poor
225	150	85	75	60	50

Wells Fargo

NIB	Exc.	V.G.	Good	Fair	Poor
225	150	85	75	60	50

1851 Navy

NIB	Exc.	V.G.	Good	Fair	Poor
250	225	200	175	150	125

1861 Navy

NIB	Exc.	V.G.	Good	Fair	Poor
250	225	200	175	150	125

1860 Army

NIB	Exc.	V.G.	Good	Fair	Poor
250	225	200	175	150	125

1858 Remington

NIB	Exc.	V.G.	Good	Fair	Poor
275	225	125	100	75	50

1858 Remington Target

As above, but fitted with adjustable sights.

NIB	Exc.	V.G.	Good	Fair	Poor
275	225	125	100	75	50

Bison

A 6-shot .44 caliber revolver with 10.25" octagonal barrel. Solid brass frame. Weighs about 48 oz.

NIB	Exc.	V.G.	Good	Fair	Poor
275	225	125	100	75	50

Hawken Pistol

This is a .50 caliber percussion pistol with 9.75" octagon barrel. The stock is hardwood. Weighs about 50 oz.

NIB	Exc.	V.G.	Good	Fair	Poor
250	180	115	75	65	50

CONSTABLE, R.
Philadelphia, Pennsylvania

Pocket Pistol

A single-shot percussion pistol with a 3" round or octagonal barrel. German-silver mounts and walnut stock. These pistols are marked "R. Constable Philadelphia" and were manufactured during the late 1840s and 1850s.

NIB	Exc.	V.G.	Good	Fair	Poor
—	—	2200	1100	550	200

CONTENTO/VENTUR
SIDE-BY-SIDES

Model 51

A 12, 16, 20, 28, and .410 bore boxlock double-barrel shotgun with 26", 28", 30", and 32" barrels, various chokes, extractors and double triggers. Checkered walnut stock. Introduced in 1980 and discontinued in 1985.

NIB	Exc.	V.G.	Good	Fair	Poor
—	500	350	300	225	150

Model 52

As above in 10 gauge.

NIB	Exc.	V.G.	Good	Fair	Poor
—	500	350	300	225	150

Model 53

As above, with scalloped receiver, automatic ejectors and available with a single-selective trigger. Discontinued in 1985.
NOTE: Single-selective trigger add 25 percent.

NIB	Exc.	V.G.	Good	Fair	Poor
—	550	400	350	250	200

Model 62

A 12, 20, or 28 gauge Holland & Holland sidelock shotgun with various barrel lengths and chokes, automatic ejectors, cocking indicators, a floral engraved receiver, a checkered, walnut stock. Discontinued in 1982.

NIB	Exc.	V.G.	Good	Fair	Poor
—	1150	800	750	600	450

Model 64

As above, but more finely finished. No longer in production.

NIB	Exc.	V.G.	Good	Fair	Poor
—	1250	900	850	700	550

OVER/UNDERS

Over/Under

A 12 gauge Over/Under shotgun with 32" barrels, screw-in choke tubes, a high ventilated rib, automatic ejectors, and a standard single-selective trigger. Checkered, with Monte Carlo walnut stock.

NIB	Exc.	V.G.	Good	Fair	Poor
—	1250	900	750	600	500

Mark 2

As above, with an extra single barrel and fitted in a leather case.

NIB	Exc.	V.G.	Good	Fair	Poor
—	1500	1200	1050	900	800

Mark 3

As above, but engraved with a finely figured walnut stock.

NIB	Exc.	V.G.	Good	Fair	Poor
—	1850	1500	1250	1100	950

Mark 3 Combo

As above, with an extra single barrel and fitted in a leather case.

NIB	Exc.	V.G.	Good	Fair	Poor
—	3200	2600	2250	1750	1300

CONTINENTAL
RWM
Cologne, Germany

Continental Pocket Pistol (6.35mm)

A 6.35mm caliber semi-automatic pistol with a 2" barrel, internal hammer, and a 7-shot detachable magazine. Blued with plastic grips, and the slide is marked "Continental Kal. 6.35". Produced during the 1920s.
NOTE: This pistol may have been manufactured in Spain and carried German proof marks, because it was sold by RWM in Germany.

NIB	Exc.	V.G.	Good	Fair	Poor
—	300	150	125	100	75

Continental Pocket Pistol (7.65mm)

This is a German-made pistol chambered for the 7.65mm cartridge. It is fitted with a 3.9" barrel. Rear sight is a U-notch in the slide. Magazine capacity is 8 rounds. Weight is about 20 oz. Made prior to 1914.

NIB	Exc.	V.G.	Good	Fair	Poor
—	500	300	225	150	100

CONTINENTAL ARMS CO.
Norwich, Connecticut

Pepperbox

A .22 caliber 5-barrel pepperbox with a spur trigger and 2.5" barrels marked "Continental Arms Co. Norwich Ct. Patented Aug. 28, 1866". Some examples of this pistol are to be found marked "Ladies Companion".

Courtesy Milwaukee Public Museum, Milwaukee, Wisconsin

NIB	Exc.	V.G.	Good	Fair	Poor
—	—	2250	1000	350	250

CONTINENTAL ARMS CO.
Leige, Belgium

Double Rifle

A .270, .303, .30-40, .30-06, .348, 375 H&H, .400 Jeffreys, .465, .475, .500, and .600 Nitro Express caliber Anson & Deeley boxlock double-barreled rifle with 24" or 26" barrels, and double triggers. Checkered walnut stock.

NIB	Exc.	V.G.	Good	Fair	Poor
—	6500	4500	3750	3000	2250

COOK & BROTHER RIFLES AND CARBINES
New Orleans, Louisiana

In early 1861, Ferdinand W.C. Cook and his brother, Francis L. Cook, both English emigres, joined to form Cook & Brother in New Orleans to manufacture rifles and carbines following the English P1853 series for the newly seceded state of Louisiana and its neighbors. Between June 1861 and the federal occupation of New Orleans in April 1862, this firm produced about 200 cavalry and artillery carbines and about 1000 rifles. Having successfully moved the armory's machinery before federal occupation, the firm continued manufacture of rifles in Selma, Alabama, during 1862, probably completing another 1,000 rifles with the New Orleans lock markings from the parts brought with them. Re-established in Athens, Georgia, in early 1863, the firm continued to build both carbines and rifles, manufacturing more than 5,500 above the New Orleans production through 1864. The firm's products were clearly among the best small arms made within the Confederacy.

Cook & Brother Rifles (New Orleans & Selma production)

Overall length 48.75"; barrel length 33"; caliber .58. Markings: representation of a Confederate flag ("Stars & Bars") and "COOK & BROTHER/N.O./1861 (or) 1862" on lock; same usually on barrel, together with serial number and "PROVED" near breech. Rifles in the early production have long range rear sights and unusual two piece block and blade front sights as well as an integral bayonet lug with guide on right side of barrel. Later production utilizes a brass clamping ring for the bayonet, a block open rear sight and a simple block and blade front sight. Earlier production will claim a premium if in good condition.

Courtesy Milwaukee Public Museum, Milwaukee, Wisconsin

NIB	Exc.	V.G.	Good	Fair	Poor
—	—	35000	15500	3000	1650

Cook & Brother Carbines (New Orleans production)

Overall length 40" (artillery), 37" (cavalry); barrel length 24" (artillery), 21" to 21.5" (cavalry); caliber .58. Markings: As on Cook & Brother rifles (New Orleans production) artillery and cavalry carbines were produced in New Orleans in a separate serial range from the rifles. Total production is thought not to have exceeded 225, divided evenly between 1861 and 1862 dates. In addition to the overall and barrel lengths, the main difference between the artillery and cavalry carbines is the manner in which they were carried. The former bears standard sling rings on the upper band and the trigger guard strap, the latter has a bar with a ring on the left side of the stock. Both are exceedingly rare.

NIB	Exc.	V.G.	Good	Fair	Poor
—	—	20000	8500	5000	1500

Cook & Brother Rifles (Athens production)

Overall length 49"; barrel length 33"; caliber .58. Markings: representation of a Confederate flag ("Stars & Bars") and "COOK & BROTHER/ATHENS GA./date (1863 or 1864), and serial number on lock; "PROVED" on barrel near breech; serial number on various metal parts. After re-establishing their plant at Athens, Georgia, in the spring of 1863, Cook & Brother continued to manufacture rifles in a consecutive serial range after their New Orleans/Selma production (beginning about serial number 2000) and continued to make arms well into 1864 (through at least serial number 7650) until Sherman's army threatened the plant and necessitated the employment of its workforce in a military capacity as the 23rd Battalion Georgia State Guard.

Courtesy Milwaukee Public Museum, Milwaukee, Wisconsin

NIB	Exc.	V.G.	Good	Fair	Poor
—	—	21000	9300	3000	900

Cook & Brother Carbines (Athens production)

Overall length 40" (artillery) or 37" (cavalry); barrel lengths 24" (artillery) or 21" to 21-1/2" (cavalry); caliber .58. Markings: same as on Athens production rifles. Artillery and cavalry carbines were manufactured in the same serial range as the Athens production rifles (about 2000 through 7650). As in New Orleans production, the artillery and cavalry carbines are distinguished from one another by their respective lengths. Unlike New Orleans/Selma production, however, some of the cavalry carbines are mounted with sling swivels of the artillery style, while others bear the sling ring on the left side and additionally have a swivel ring to secure the ramrod.

Courtesy Milwaukee Public Museum, Milwaukee, Wisconsin

NIB	Exc.	V.G.	Good	Fair	Poor
—	—	27500	9800	3900	1250

COONAN ARMS/COONAN INC.
Blaine, Minnesota

The original Coonan Arms was based in St. Paul, Minnesota from 1983 to 1994 and in Maplewood, Minnesota from 1994 to 1998. That company ceased operations in 1998. The current manufacturer was established as Coonan Inc. in 2009 and is located in Blaine, Minnesota. **NOTE:** For 6" barrel add $40; Bomar adjustable sights add $130; .38 Special conversion add $40; checkered walnut grips add $40; with Teflon slide add $100; with Teflon frame add $100.

Model A

A .357 Magnum semi-automatic pistol with a 5" barrel, a 7-shot, detachable magazine, and fixed sights. Stainless steel with walnut grips. Introduced in 1981 and discontinued in 1984.

NIB	Exc.	V.G.	Good	Fair	Poor
1200	1000	875	500	350	275

Model B

An improved version of the above with a linkless barrel system, extended grip safety, enclosed trigger bar, and a more contoured grip. A 6" barrel is available, as are adjustable sights, as extra cost options. A .38 Special conversion is also available. Introduced in 1985. A number of other options are also available that will affect value.

NIB	Exc.	V.G.	Good	Fair	Poor
1300	1175	925	675	500	300

Comp I

As above, with 6" barrel and attached compensator and a stippled front grip strap. Introduced in 1989.

NIB	Exc.	V.G.	Good	Fair	Poor
1600	1250	1000	700	550	350

Comp I Deluxe

As above, with a blued stainless steel slide, checkered grip straps, and a finer finishing.

NIB	Exc.	V.G.	Good	Fair	Poor
1650	1300	1050	750	600	400

Classic (Current Production)

This model features an integrated compensator with 5" barrel. Pistol is supplied with checkered walnut grips, Millett adjustable rear sight, and two-tone Teflon finish. Magazine capacity is 7 rounds, weight is 42 oz., and overall length is 8.3".

NIB	Exc.	V.G.	Good	Fair	Poor
1000	900	700	600	—	—

Cadet

Chambered for the .357 magnum cartridge this model has a 3.9" barrel with smooth walnut grips, and fixed rear sight. Magazine capacity is 6 rounds; weight is about 39 oz., and overall length is 7.8". Height of the pistol is 5.3". Coonan Arms refers to this model as the "Short Grip".

NIB	Exc.	V.G.	Good	Fair	Poor
1150	875	675	500	400	400

Cadet II

Same as above but with a standard grip. Magazine capacity of this model is 7 rounds.

NIB	Exc.	V.G.	Good	Fair	Poor
1150	875	675	500	400	200

.41 Magnum Model

Introduced in 1997 this model is chambered for the .41 Magnum cartridge and fitted with a 5" barrel with smooth walnut grips and fixed sights.

NIB	Exc.	V.G.	Good	Fair	Poor
1700	1250	975	800	550	350

COOPER, J. M. & CO.
Philadelphia, Pennsylvania

Pocket Revolver

A .31 caliber percussion double-action revolver with 4", 5", or 6" octagonal barrel, and a 6-shot unfluted cylinder. Blued with walnut grips. During the first two years of production they were made in Pittsburgh, Pennsylvania, and were so marked. Approximately 15,000 were manufactured between 1864 and 1869. **NOTE:** Pittsburgh-marked models add 20 percent.

Courtesy Milwaukee Public Museum, Milwaukee, Wisconsin

NIB	Exc.	V.G.	Good	Fair	Poor
—	—	1850	775	200	100

COOPER ARMS
Stevensville, Montana

Model 36 Marksman

This is a premium bolt-action rifle chambered for the .22 LR cartridge and in centerfire calibers of .17 CCM and .22 Hornet. The 23" Shilen barrel is mated to a solid bar stock receiver. High grade walnut is used in stocks that are fine-lined checkered.

Standard

NIB	Exc.	V.G.	Good	Fair	Poor
1600	900	700	500	300	2000

Classic

NIB	Exc.	V.G.	Good	Fair	Poor
1800	1200	800	600	400	200

Custom Classic

NIB	Exc.	V.G.	Good	Fair	Poor
2000	1650	1150	850	600	300

Western Classic

Octagon barrel and case color metal.

NIB	Exc.	V.G.	Good	Fair	Poor
2400	1900	1350	900	700	300

BR-50 w/Jewell Trigger

NIB	Exc.	V.G.	Good	Fair	Poor
1800	1450	1100	800	600	300

IR-50-50 w/Jewell Trigger

NIB	Exc.	V.G.	Good	Fair	Poor
1800	1450	1100	800	600	300

Featherweight w/Jewell Trigger

NIB	Exc.	V.G.	Good	Fair	Poor
1800	1450	1100	800	600	300

Model 38/40

This bolt-action rifle is chambered for the .17 AK Hornet, .22 K Hornet, or the .22 Hornet.

Classic

NIB	Exc.	V.G.	Good	Fair	Poor
1800	1500	1100	800	600	300

Custom Classic

NIB	Exc.	V.G.	Good	Fair	Poor
2000	1750	1250	850	600	300

Western Classic

NIB	Exc.	V.G.	Good	Fair	Poor
2200	1800	1250	850	600	300

Model 21

This bolt-action rifle is chambered for these cartridges: .221 Fireball, .222, .223, 6x45, 6x47, .17 Mach IV, and the .17 Rem. A 24" stainless steel Shilen match grade barrel is fitted. AAA claro walnut is used. Oval forearm, ambidextrous palm swell, 22 lpi checkering, oil finish, and Pachmayr buttpad are all standard features. Weighs approximately 8 lbs.

Varmint Extreme

NIB	Exc.	V.G.	Good	Fair	Poor
1600	1250	900	700	500	250

Classic

NIB	Exc.	V.G.	Good	Fair	Poor
1600	1250	900	700	500	250

Custom Classic

NIB	Exc.	V.G.	Good	Fair	Poor
1900	1700	1300	850	600	300

Western Classic

NIB	Exc.	V.G.	Good	Fair	Poor
2200	1800	1250	850	600	300

Benchrest w/Jewell Trigger

NIB	Exc.	V.G.	Good	Fair	Poor
2100	1800	1250	850	600	300

Model 22

This is a bolt-action single rifle chambered for a variety of calibers: 6mm PPC, .22-250, .220 Swift, .243, .25-06, .308, .22 BR, 7.62x39, 6.5x55. A Pachmayr decelerator pad is standard. Weight is approximately 8.5 lbs.

Pro Varmint Extreme

NIB	Exc.	V.G.	Good	Fair	Poor
1750	1500	1200	800	600	300

Benchrest w/Jewell Trigger

NIB	Exc.	V.G.	Good	Fair	Poor
2100	1800	1300	900	650	300

Model 22 Repeater

Same as above but with magazine and chambered for .22-25, .308, 7mm-08, and .243.

Classic

NIB	Exc.	V.G.	Good	Fair	Poor
2400	2000	1750	1250	800	325

Custom Classic

NIB	Exc.	V.G.	Good	Fair	Poor
2650	2200	1850	1400	900	400

Western Classic

NIB	Exc.	V.G.	Good	Fair	Poor
2200	1800	1250	850	600	300

Model 52 Classic

Long-action repeater offered virtually any centerfire caliber from .22-250 to .340 Weatherby. Model 52 Classic has oil-finished AA Claro walnut stock, hand checkering, matte finish. Also offered with synthetic stock as Excalibur. Custom Classic has more extensive checkering, ebony fore-end cap. Western Classic available in any caliber, has octagon barrel, case-hardened action, engraving. Introduced in 2007. **NOTE:** Add $150 for Excalibur, $1200 for Custom Classic, $2000 for Western Classic.

NIB	Exc.	V.G.	Good	Fair	Poor
1500	1300	1000	800	500	300

Model 54

Similar to above except with short action and in these calibers: .22-250, .243 Win., .250 Savage, .260 Rem., 7mm-08 Rem., .308 Win. Optional models same as Model 52 plus three varmint variants. **NOTE:** Add $150 for Excalibur, $400 for Varmint Extreme, $1200 for Custom Classic, $2000 for Western Classic.

NIB	Exc.	V.G.	Good	Fair	Poor
1500	1300	1000	800	500	300

Model 57

Bolt-action repeater chambered for the following rimfire calibers: .17 Mach II, .17 HMR, .22 LR, or .22 Win. Magnum. Offered in several versions including standard model with checkered walnut stock, matte finish, steel grip cap. **NOTE:** Add $500 for Custom Classic, $1200 for Western Classic

NIB	Exc.	V.G.	Good	Fair	Poor
1400	1200	950	750	500	300

COOPERATIVA OBRERA
Eibar, Spain

Longines

A 7.65mm caliber semi-automatic pistol. The slide is marked "Cal. 7.65 Automatic Pistol Longines".

NIB	Exc.	V.G.	Good	Fair	Poor
—	275	175	150	110	85

COPELAND, FRANK
Worcester, Massachusetts

Copeland Pocket Revolver .22

A .22 cartridge spur trigger revolver with a 2.5" barrel, 7-shot magazine, an unfluted cylinder and lock notches on the front. Frame is brass, blued walnut, or rosewood grips. The barrel marked "F. Copeland, Worcester, Mass." Manufactured in the 1860s.

NIB	Exc.	V.G.	Good	Fair	Poor
—	—	700	300	125	100

Copeland .32 Revolver

A .32 caliber spur trigger revolver with a 5-shot fluted cylinder and an iron frame. Nickel-plated. The barrel marked "F. Copeland, Sterling, Mass." Manufactured in the 1860s.

NIB	Exc.	V.G.	Good	Fair	Poor
—	—	700	300	150	75

COSMI, A. & F.
Torrette, Italy

Semi-Automatic

A 12 and 20 gauge top-break semi-automatic shotgun with various barrel lengths and chokes, an 8-shot magazine, and a ventilated rib. This is basically a custom-built, made-to-order gun. There is a standard and a deluxe model, with differences in the degree of embellishment.

Standard Model

NIB	Exc.	V.G.	Good	Fair	Poor
14000	8500	4750	3250	2200	1500

Deluxe Model

NIB	Exc.	V.G.	Good	Fair	Poor
15500	9500	6000	4250	3250	1750

COSMOPOLITAN ARMS CO.
Hamilton, Ohio

Breechloading Rifle

A .52 single-shot percussion rifle with a 31" round barrel. The frame marked "Cosmopolitan Arms Co. Hamilton 0. U.S./Gross Patent". Blued with a walnut buttstock. Approximately 100 were made between 1859 and 1862.

NIB	Exc.	V.G.	Good	Fair	Poor
—	—	7000	2750	775	450

COWLES & SON
Chicopee, Massachusetts

Single-Shot Pistol

A .22 or .30 caliber single-shot spur trigger pistol with a 3.25" round barrel. Silver-plated brass frame, blued with walnut grip. Approximately 200 manufactured in 1865.

Courtesy Richard M. Kumor Sr.

NIB	Exc.	V.G.	Good	Fair	Poor
—	—	1500	775	250	100

CPA RIFLES
Dingman's Ferry, Pennsylvania

This company builds rifles based on the Stevens Model 44-1/2. Several different configurations are offered, which are listed. **NOTE:** There are a number of special order options and custom features available at extra charge that will affect value.

Schuetzen Rifle

This model is usually built to order as to stock style, caliber, and barrel size, shape and length. Many calibers are available from .22 Short to .40-65 Winchester. Sights are extra.

NIB	Exc.	V.G.	Good	Fair	Poor
2900	2250	1600	975	600	300

Silhouette Rifle

This model as produced is approved for BPCR competition by the NRA. This model has either a sporting-style stock with low comb or the Model 52 style with more drop. Calibers are from .38-55 to .45-110 with other calibers available. Standard barrel is #4 part octagon 30" in length. Sights are extra.

NIB	Exc.	V.G.	Good	Fair	Poor
2550	1900	1350	700	550	250

Sporting Rifle

This model uses a sporting-style stock with standard forearm with schnabel tip. Rifles are offered in rimmed calibers including .222,

.225, .22 Hornet and others. Standard barrels are round or part octagon with weights from #1 to #5 and up to 28" in length. Sights are extra.

NIB	Exc.	V.G.	Good	Fair	Poor
2475	1900	1350	700	550	250

Varmint Rifle

As above but with a semi-beavertail forearm.

NIB	Exc.	V.G.	Good	Fair	Poor
2475	1900	1350	700	550	250

CRAUSE, CARL PHILLIP MUSKETS AND RIFLES
Herzberg, Germany

Carl Phillip Crause (who signed his products only with his last name) operated a gun manufactory in Herzberg on the Harz in the northwestern German kingdom of Hannover from the close of the Napoleonic Wars until 1857. The main production of his factory was devoted to military arms for Hannover and the surrounding principalities. Weapons of his manufacture included the Brunswick M1835 and M1848 rifles, the Hannovarian M1850 and M1854 rifle-muskets and yager rifles, and the M1840 and M1849 rifle-muskets of the Hanseatic League (a coalition of the north German states of Oldenberg, Hamburg, Bremen, and Lubeck). The latter two arms were subsequently altered to accept the elongated projectiles popular during the 1850s, and a few thousand evidently were imported into the United States and saw service during the American Civil War.

Hanseatic League M1840 Rifled Musket

Overall length 55.5"; barrel length 40.25"; caliber .70. Markings: on lockplate forward of hammer, "Crause in Herzberg" in script, the "s" in the archaic form, appearing as an "f". Of the 6,000 muskets of this type made, approximately half were sent to the United States in 1861 during the arms crisis that accompanied the outbreak of the American Civil War. A total of 2,680 of these were issued to Ohio and at least one regiment (the 56th Ohio) was armed with these rifled muskets. These arms were mistakenly identified during the period as being Saxon due to the similarity of the large squared off foresection of the lockplate.

Courtesy Milwaukee Public Museum, Milwaukee, Wisconsin

NIB	Exc.	V.G.	Good	Fair	Poor
—	—	1700	800	375	200

Oldenberg M1849 Rifled Musket

Overall lengths 55.5" to 56-5/8" (long version), 49.5" (short version); barrel lengths 39" to 39-1/8" (long version), 33" (short version); caliber .69-.72 (rifled). Markings: "Crause in Herzberg" inscribed in script on the backstrap of the hammer housing, the "s" in archaic form, appearing as an "f". Nicknamed the "Cyclops" because its large, center-hung hammer is pierced with a large window that served as its rear sight, a few hundred of these clumsy rifled muskets may have been intermixed with the shipments of "Saxon" muskets imported in 1861 or 1862 into the United States during the American Civil War.

Courtesy Milwaukee Public Museum, Milwaukee, Wisconsin

NIB	Exc.	V.G.	Good	Fair	Poor
—	—	1975	850	400	250

CRESCENT F. A. CO.
Norwich, Connecticut

The company made good quality inexpensive single and double-barrel shotguns at its Norwich works, beginning about 1892. It was bought by H&D Folsom of New York City, large importers and distributors of firearms and sporting goods, so they could add an American-made sidelock hammer, side-by-side to their extensive range of imported guns. The Crescent guns were offered in 12, 16, 20, and 28 gauges and later, 44XL shot caliber with Damascus twist laminated or Armory steel barrels depending on the shooter's wants. In 1898 VL&D said these were the best American hammer guns in the market for the money.

Huge quantities of these "Hardware Guns" were produced in a profusion of private brands as well as in Folsom's house brand "American Gun Co. of NY." In 1922 the Crescent brand replaced the "American Gun Co. of NY" and can be found on many thousands of doubles. In 1905 Crescent's first hammerless sidelock was introduced as the American Gun Co. "Knickerbocker" Model No. 6. This very popular model became the Crescent "Peerless" No. 6 in 1922. In 1928 it became the Crescent "Empire" No. 60 and in 1931 the Crescent-Davis "New Empire" No. 88, "New Empire" No. 9, and "Empire" No. 9.

Crescent was bought by J. Stevens Arms Co., Division of Savage Arms Corp. about 1930. It was merged with Davis-Warner Arms Corp. successors to N.R. Davis & Sons Co. and became Crescent-Davis Arms Corp. In 1932 the operation was moved to the Stevens plant at Springfield, Mass. where some sidelock doubles were assembled. Crescent-Davis brand guns remained in Steven's full line catalog until 1941 but from 1937 to 1941 the doubles sold in the C-D brand were on either Stevens or Davis boxlock frames.

DOUBLES

Triumph—Hammerless Boxlock

NIB	Exc.	V.G.	Good	Fair	Poor
—	800	650	425	300	200

Model 2655—Laminated Barrels Hammer Sidelock

NIB	Exc.	V.G.	Good	Fair	Poor
—	575	450	325	200	150

Model 2665—Damascus Barrels Hammer Sidelock

NIB	Exc.	V.G.	Good	Fair	Poor
—	575	450	325	200	150

Crescent American Hammer Gun No. 0—Hammer Sidelock

NIB	Exc.	V.G.	Good	Fair	Poor
—	400	325	250	200	100

American Machine Made 2641—Hammer Sidelock

NIB	Exc.	V.G.	Good	Fair	Poor
—	450	350	300	250	200

American Machine Made 2650—Hammer Sidelock

NIB	Exc.	V.G.	Good	Fair	Poor
—	575	450	325	200	150

American Machine Made 2660—Damascus Barrels Hammer Sidelock

NIB	Exc.	V.G.	Good	Fair	Poor
—	700	550	400	275	175

American Gun Co. NY No. 1 Armory—Hammerless Sidelock

NIB	Exc.	V.G.	Good	Fair	Poor
—	450	325	250	200	100

American Gun Co. NY No. 2—Hammerless Sidelock

NIB	Exc.	V.G.	Good	Fair	Poor
—	575	450	300	250	200

American Gun Co. No. 3—Damascus Barrels Hammer Sidelock

NIB	Exc.	V.G.	Good	Fair	Poor
—	700	550	425	300	250

American Gun Co. No. 4—Hammer Sidelock

NIB	Exc.	V.G.	Good	Fair	Poor
—	800	650	525	400	300

American Gun Co. No. 5—Damascus Barrels Hammer Sidelock

NIB	Exc.	V.G.	Good	Fair	Poor
—	925	800	650	450	350

Folsom Arms Co. No. 0 Armory—Hammer Sidelock

NIB	Exc.	V.G.	Good	Fair	Poor
—	450	325	250	200	100

Folsom Arms Co. No. 2—Hammer Sidelock

NIB	Exc.	V.G.	Good	Fair	Poor
—	575	450	300	200	150

Folsom Arms Co. No. 3—Damascus Barrel

NIB	Exc.	V.G.	Good	Fair	Poor
—	700	550	425	300	200

Knickerbocker No. 6 Armory—Hammerless Sidelock

Courtesy Nick Niles, Paul Goodwin photo

NIB	Exc.	V.G.	Good	Fair	Poor
—	450	325	250	200	100

Knickerbocker No. 7—Hammerless Sidelock

NIB	Exc.	V.G.	Good	Fair	Poor
—	450	325	250	200	100

Knickerbocker No. 8—Damascus Barrels Hammerless Sidelock

NIB	Exc.	V.G.	Good	Fair	Poor
—	575	450	300	250	200

New Knickerbocker Armory—Hammerless Sidelock

NIB	Exc.	V.G.	Good	Fair	Poor
—	450	325	250	200	100

New Knickerbocker WT—Hammerless Sidelock

Courtesy Nick Niles, Paul Goodwin photo

NIB	Exc.	V.G.	Good	Fair	Poor
—	500	375	250	200	150

New Knickerbocker Damascus Barrels—Hammerless Sidelock

NIB	Exc.	V.G.	Good	Fair	Poor
—	575	450	300	250	200

American Gun Co. Small Bore No. 28—Straight Stock Hammer Sidelock

NIB	Exc.	V.G.	Good	Fair	Poor
—	925	775	650	400	300

American Gun Co. Small Bore No. 44—Straight Stock Hammer Sidelock

NIB	Exc.	V.G.	Good	Fair	Poor
—	1025	825	700	475	350

American Gun Co. No. 0—Armory Straight Stock—Hammer Sidelock

Courtesy Nick Niles, Paul Goodwin photo

NIB	Exc.	V.G.	Good	Fair	Poor
—	400	300	250	200	100

American Gun Co. No. 28—Nitro Straight Stock—Hammer Sidelock

NIB	Exc.	V.G.	Good	Fair	Poor
—	925	775	650	400	300

American Gun Co. No. 44—Nitro Straight Stock—Hammer Sidelock

NIB	Exc.	V.G.	Good	Fair	Poor
—	1025	825	700	475	350

American Gun Co. Midget Field No. 28—Hammer Sidelock

NIB	Exc.	V.G.	Good	Fair	Poor
—	925	775	650	400	300

American Gun Co. Midget Field No. 44—Hammer Sidelock

Courtesy Nick Niles, Paul Goodwin photo

NIB	Exc.	V.G.	Good	Fair	Poor
—	1025	825	700	500	350

Crescent 1922 Model No. 66—Quail—Hammerless Sidelock

NIB	Exc.	V.G.	Good	Fair	Poor
—	700	550	400	275	175

Crescent Fire Arms Co. No. 0—Hammer Sidelock

NIB	Exc.	V.G.	Good	Fair	Poor
—	450	350	250	200	150

Crescent Fire Arms Co. No. 0—Nickel—Hammer Sidelock

NIB	Exc.	V.G.	Good	Fair	Poor
—	600	450	350	250	200

Crescent Fire Arms Co. No. 6—Peerless—Hammerless Sidelock

NIB	Exc.	V.G.	Good	Fair	Poor
—	450	350	250	200	150

Crescent Fire Arms Co. No. 6E—Peerless Engraved—Hammerless Sidelock

NIB	Exc.	V.G.	Good	Fair	Poor
—	700	550	400	275	175

Crescent Fire Arms Co. No. 66—Quail—Hammerless Sidelock

NIB	Exc.	V.G.	Good	Fair	Poor
—	750	550	425	300	200

Crescent Fire Arms Co. No. 60—Empire—Hammerless Sidelock

Courtesy Nick Niles, Paul Goodwin photo

NIB	Exc.	V.G.	Good	Fair	Poor
—	500	400	350	300	200

Crescent Fire Arms Co. No. 6—Peerless—Hammerless Sidelock

NIB	Exc.	V.G.	Good	Fair	Poor
—	450	350	300	200	150

Crescent Fire Arms Co. No. 44—Improved—Hammer Sidelock

NIB	Exc.	V.G.	Good	Fair	Poor
—	800	600	500	400	300

Crescent Empire No. 60—Hammerless Sidelock

NIB	Exc.	V.G.	Good	Fair	Poor
—	400	300	250	200	100

New Crescent Empire Red Butt—Hammerless Sidelock

NIB	Exc.	V.G.	Good	Fair	Poor
—	450	350	250	200	150

Crescent New Empire No. 88—Hammerless Sidelock

NIB	Exc.	V.G.	Good	Fair	Poor
—	450	350	250	200	150

Crescent New Empire No. 9—Hammerless Sidelock

Courtesy Nick Niles, Paul Goodwin photo

NIB	Exc.	V.G.	Good	Fair	Poor
—	400	300	250	200	100

Crescent Certified Empire No. 60—Hammerless Sidelock

NIB	Exc.	V.G.	Good	Fair	Poor
—	450	300	250	200	150

Crescent Certified Empire No. 9—Hammerless Sidelock

NIB	Exc.	V.G.	Good	Fair	Poor
—	500	375	300	250	200

Crescent Certified Empire No. 88—Hammerless Sidelock

Courtesy Nick Niles, Paul Goodwin photo

NIB	Exc.	V.G.	Good	Fair	Poor
—	575	450	400	350	300

Crescent Davis No. 600—Hammerless Boxlock

Courtesy Nick Niles, Paul Goodwin photo

NIB	Exc.	V.G.	Good	Fair	Poor
—	450	350	300	250	200

Crescent Davis No. 900—Hammerless Boxlock

NIB	Exc.	V.G.	Good	Fair	Poor
—	575	450	400	350	300

Single-Shot

Made in 12, 16, 20, and 28 gauge and .410. Barrel lengths were 26", 28", 30", and 32", with various chokes. It had an exposed hammer, fluid steel barrel, and walnut pistol grip stock.

NIB	Exc.	V.G.	Good	Fair	Poor
—	200	125	100	75	50

Revolver

A typical S&W copy made by Crescent in Norwich, Connecticut. It was a top-break double-action- that was found either blued or nickel-plated with checkered, black hard rubber grips. The cylinder held 5 shots and was chambered for the .32 S&W cartridge.

NIB	Exc.	V.G.	Good	Fair	Poor
—	250	150	125	85	40

Crescent Certified Shotgun NFA, Curio or Relic

The Crescent Certified Shotgun is a .410 smooth bore pistol with a 12.25" barrel, manufactured from approximately 1930 to 1932 by the Crescent-Davis Arms Corp., Norwich, Connecticut, and possibly thereafter until 1934 by the J. Stevens Arms Co., which purchased the company. In various distributor catalogs, it is termed the "Ever-Ready" Model 200, and advertised with a blued frame. Specimens have been observed with "tiger-stripe" (like an H&R Handy-Gun) or Colt SAA or Winchester-type case hardening. Total production is unknown but serial numbers ranging from 1305 to 3262 have been observed, suggesting it may have been fewer than 4,000. The Treasury Department ruled the .410 Crescent to be a "firearm" in the "any other weapon" category under the NFA in 1934, when its retail price was about $11.

The barrel is marked proof tested 410 gauge on top and 2-1/2 IN SHELLS on the middle left side. The receiver's left side is stamped crescent certified shotgun/crescent-davis arms corporation/ norwich, conn., u.s.a. The earliest guns also have .410 stamped at the top of the left side of the receiver near the breech, but this marking does not appear on later guns. It is a rather heavy (57 oz. unloaded) handgun. **NOTE:** Add $100 to $300 for original cardboard box.

NIB	Exc.	V.G.	Good	Fair	Poor
—	975	725	550	350	250

Brand Names Used by Crescent Arms

American Bar Lock Wonder made for Sears, Roebuck & Co.
American Boy made for Townley Metal & Hardware Co.
American Gun Co. (H & D Folsom house brand)
American Gun Company of New York
American Nitro
Armory Gun Co.Baker Gun Co. (if no foreign proof marks)
T. Barker New York-if a sidelock hammerless double without proofs.
Bellmore Gun Co.Berkshire No. 3000 made for Shapleigh Hardware Co. of St. Louis, MO
Black Beauty-hammerless doubles
Bluefield Clipper
Bluegrass Arms Co. made for Belknap Hardware Co. of Louisville, KY
Blue Whistler
Bridge Black PrinceBridge Gun Co.
Bridge Gun Works
Bridgeport Arms Co. (if no foreign proof marks)
Bright Arms Co.
Canadian Belle
Carolina Arms Co. made for Smith Wadsworth Hardware Co. of Charlotte, NC
Caroline Arms
Central Arm Co. made for Shapleigh Hardware Co. of St. Louis, MO
Chatham Arms Co.
Cherokee Arms Co. made for C. M. McClung Co. of Knoxville, TN
Chesapeake Gun Co.
Chicago Long Range Wonder 1908-1918 made for Sears, Roebuck & Co. of Chicago, IL
Colonial
Columbian New York Arms Co.
Compeer made for Van Camp Hardware & Iron Co. of Indianapolis, IN
Connecticut Arms Co.
Cumberland Arms Co.
Crescent Fire Arms Co.
Creve Cour (if no foreign proof marks) made for Isaac Walker Hardware Co. of Peoria, IL
CrusoDaniel Boone Gun Co. made for Belknap Hardware Co. of Louisville, KY
Delphian Arms Co. (some models without foreign proof marks) made for Supplee-Biddle Hardware Co. of Philadelphia, PA
Delphian Manufacturing Co. (some models)
Diamond Arms Co. (some models) made for Shapleigh Hardware Co. of St. Louis, MO
Dunlap Special made for Dunlap Hardware Co. of Macon, GAE.C. Mac made for E.C. Meacham Arms Co. of St. Louis, MO
Elgin Arms Co. made for Strauss & Schram and Fred Biffar & Co. both of Chicago, IL

Elmira Arms Co.
Empire Arms Co. made for Sears, Roebuck & Co. of Chicago, IL
Empire State Arms Co.
Enders Oakleaf made for Shapleigh Hardware Co. of St. Louis, MO
Enders Special Service made for Shapleigh Hardware Co.
Enders Royal Service made for Shapleigh Hardware Co.
Essex made for Belknap Hardware Co. of Louisville, KY
Excel made for Montgomery Ward & Co. of Chicago, IL
Farwell Arms Co. made for Farwell, Ozmun & Kirk of St. Paul, MN
Faultless made for John M. Smythe Co. of Chicago, IL
Faultless Goose Gun made for John M. Smyth Co. of Chicago, IL
The Field after 1894
Folsom Arms Co. (also used by H & D Folsom on Belgian imports)
F.F. Forbes (H & D Folsom house brand)
Fort Pitt Arms Co.
Fremont Arms Co. (also used on Belgian imports)
Gold Medal Wonder
Greenfield (some models) made for Hibbard, Spencer, Bartlett & Co. of Chicago, ILH.B.C. (some models) made for Hudson's Bay Co. of Canada
H.S.B. & Co. (some models) made for Hibbard, Spencer,Bartlett & Co. of Chicago, IL
Hanover Arms Co. (if no foreign proof marks)
S.H. Harrington (if no foreign proof marks)
Hartford Arms Co. made for both Simmons Hardware and Shapleigh Hardware Co. of St. Louis, MO
Harvard (H & D Folsom house brand)
Hermitage (some models) made for Grey-Dusley Hardware Co. of Nashville, TN
Hip Spe Bar (some models) made for Hibbard, Spencer, Bartlett & Co. of Chicago, IL
Hibbard (some models) made for Hibbard, Spencer, Bartlett & Co. of Chicago, IL
Howard Arms Co. made for Fred Biffar & Co. of Chicago, IL
Hudson (some models) made for Hibbard, Spencer, Bartlett & Co. of Chicago, IL
Hunter made for Belknap Hardware Co. Louisville, KY
Interstate Arms Co. made for Townley Metal & Hardware Co. of Kansas City, MO
Jackson Arms Co. made for C.M. McClung & Co. of Knoxville, TN
Joseph Arms Co. Norwich, Conn.
K K and Keen Kufter (some models) made for Shapleigh Hardware Co. of St. Louis, MO
Kingsland Special and Kingsland 10 Star made for Geller, Ward & Hasner of St. Louis, MO
Kirk Gun Co. made for Farwell, Ozmun & Kirk of St. Paul, MN
Knickerbocker (up to 1915, H & D Folsom house brand)
Knockabout (before 1925) made for Montgomery Ward & Co. of Chicago, IL
Knoxall (only hammerless doubles)
Laclede Gun Co.
Lakeside made for Montgomery Ward & Co. of Chicago, IL
Leader Gun Co. made for Charles Williams Stores of New York, NY
Lee's Special and Lee's Munner Special made for Lee Hardware Co. of Salina, KS
Long Range Marvel, Long Range Winner, and Long Range Wonder made between 1893 to 1909 for Sears, Roebuck & Co. of Chicago, IL
F.A. LoomisMarshwoodMassachusetts Arms Co. made before 1920 for Blish, Mizet and Silliman Hardware Co. of Atchison, KS
Mears (if no foreign proof marks)
Metropolitan made for Siegal-Cooper Co. of New York, NY
Minnesota Arms Co. made for Farwell, Ozmun, Kirk & Co. of St. Paul, MN
Mississippi Arms Co. St. Louis (some models) made for Shepleigh Hardware Co. of St. Louis, MO
Mississippi Valley Arms Co. (some models) made for Shapleigh Hardware Co. of St. Louis, MO
Mohawk made for Glish, Mizet and Lilliman Hardware Co. of Atchison, KS

Monitor

R. Murdock, National Firearms Co. (some models)

National Arms Co. hammer doubles (without foreign proof marks) and hammerless doubles made for May Hardware Co. of Washington, D.C. and Moskowitz and Herbach Co. of Philadelphia, PA

New Britain Arms Co.'s Monarch

New Elgin Arms Co.

New EmpireNew England (some models after 1914) made for Sears, Roebuck & Co.

New England Arms Co. (some models)

Newport Model CN made for Hibbard, Spencer, Bartlett and Co. of Chicago

Newport Model WN (some models) made for Hibbard, Spencer, Bartlett and Co. of Chicago

New Rival made for Van Camp Hardware and Iron Co. of Indianapolis, IN

New York Arms Co. made for Garnet Carter Co. of Chattanooga, TN

New York Machine Made (some models)

New York Match Gun (some models)

New York Nitro Hammerless

Nitro Bird made for Conover Hardware Co. of Kansas City, MO

Nitro Hunter made for Belknap Hardware Co. of Louisville, KY

Nitro King 1908 to 1917 made for Sears, Roebuck & Co. of Chicago, IL

Norwich Arms Co.

Not-Noc Manufacturing Co. made for Belknap Hardware Co. of Louisville, KY and Canton Hardware Co. of Canton, OH

Osprey made for Lou J. Eppinger, Detroit, MI

Oxford made for Belknap Hardware Co. of Louisville, KY

Peerless (H & D Folsom house brand)

Perfection made for H. G. Lipscomb & Co. of Nashville, TN

Piedmont made for Piedmont Hardware Co. of Danville, PA

Piedmont Arms Co.

Pioneer Arms (if no foreign proof marks) made for Kruse and Baklmann Hardware Co. of Cincinnati, OH

Quail (H & D Folsom house brand)

Queen City made for Elmira Arms Co. of Elmira, NY

Red Chieftan (model 60) made for Supplee Biddle Hardware Co. of Philadelphia, PARev-O-Noc (some models) made for Hibbard, Spencer, Bartlett & Co. of Chicago, IL

Rich-Con made for Richardson & Conover Hardware Co.Charles Richter (some models) made for New York Sporting Goods Co. of New York, NY

Rickard Arms Co. made for J. A. Rickard Co. of Schenectady, NYRival (some models) made for Van Camp Hardware and Iron Co. of Indianapolis, IN

Rocket SpecialRoyal Service made for Shapleigh Hardware Co. of St. Louis, MO

Rummel Arms Co. made for A. J. Rummel Arms Co. of Toledo, OH

Ruso (if no foreign proof marks)St. Louis Arms Co. (sidelock hammerless doubles) made for Shapleigh Hardware Co. of St. Louis, MO

Seminole (hammerless) unknown

Shue's Special made for Ira M. Shue of Hanover, PA

Smithsonian (some models)

John M. Smythe & Co. made for John M. Smythe Hardware Co. of Chicago, IL

Southern Arms Co. (some models)

Special Service made for Shapleigh Hardware Co. of St. Louis, MO

Spencer Gun Co. made for Hibbard, Spencer, Bartlett & Co. of Chicago, IL

Sportsman (some models) made for W. Bingham & Co. of Cleveland, OH

Springfield Arms Co. used until 1930. (H & D Folsom house brand). This brand was also used by Stevens and James Warner guns.Square Deal made for Stratton, Warren Hardware Co. of Memphis, TN

Star Leader (some models)

State Arms Co. made for J.H. Lau & Co. of New York, NY

Sterling Arms Co.

Sullivan Arms Co. made for Sullivan Hardware Co. of Anderson, SC

Superior (some models) made for Paxton & Gallagher Co. of Omaha, NE

Syco (some models) made for Wyeth Hardware Co. of St. Joseph, MO

Ten Star & Ten Star Heavy Duty (if no foreign proof marks) made for Geller, Ward & Hasner Co. of St. Louis, MO

Tiger (if no foreign proof marks) made for J.H. Hall & Co. of Nashville, TN

Townley's Pal and Townley's American Boy made for Townley Metal & Hardware Co. of Kansas City, MO

Trap's Best made for Watkins, Cottrell Co. of Richmond, VA

Triumph (some models) made for Sears, Roebuck & Co. of Chicago, IL

Tryon Special (some models) made for Edward K. Tryon Co. of Philadelphia, PA

U.S. Arms Co. (if no foreign proof marks) made for Supplee-Biddle Hardware Co. of Philadelphia, PA

U.S. FieldUtica Firearms Co. (some models) made for Simmons Hardware Co. of St. Louis, MO

Victor & Victor Special made for Hibbard, Spencer, Bartlett & Co. of Chicago, IL

Virginia Arms Co. made for Virginia-Carolina Co. of Richmond, VA

Volunteer (some models) made for Belknap Hardware Co. of Louisville, KY

Vulcan Arms Co. made for Edward K. Tryon Co. of Philadelphia, PA

Warren Arms Co. (if no foreign proof marks)

Washington Arms Co. (some models)

Wauregan (some models)

Wautauga (some models) made for Wallace Hardware Co. Morristown, TN

Wildwood made for Sears, Roebuck & Co. of Chicago, IL

Wilkinson Arms Co. (if no foreign proof marks) made for Richmond Hardware Co. of Richmond, VA

Wilshire Arms Co. made for Stauffer, Eshleman & Co. of New Orleans, LA

Winfield Arms Co. (H & D Folsom house brand)

Winoca Arms Co. made for Jacobi Hardware Co. of Philadelphia, PA

Witte Hardware Co. (some models) made for Witte Hardware Co. of St. Louis, MO

Wolverine Arms Co. made for Fletcher Hardware Co. of Wilmington, NC

Worthington Arms Co. made for George Worthington Co. of Cleveland, OH

CRISPIN, SILAS
New York, New York

Crispin Revolver

A .32 Crispin caliber 5- or 6-shot revolver produced in limited quantities. Some are marked "Smith Arms Co., New York City. Crispin's Pat. Oct. 3, 1865". The most noteworthy feature of these revolvers is that the cylinder is constructed in two pieces so that the belted Crispin cartridge can be used. It is believed that these revolvers were only made on an experimental basis, between 1865 and 1867.

NIB	Exc.	V.G.	Good	Fair	Poor
—	—	19000	7500	2500	1000

CROSSFIRE
LaGrange, Georgia

This combination rifle/shotgun is manufactured by Saco Defense, Inc. for Crossfire. It is the first production firearm to combine the shotgun and rifle into a pump action, multi-shot weapon.

MK-1

This model is designed to fire both a .223 Rem. cartridge and a 12 gauge 3" shotgun shell from two different barrels. It is a dual action long gun operated with a pump action. Overall length of the gun is 38". The shotgun has a 4-round detachable magazine while the rifle has an AR-15 type 5-round magazine. Shotgun barrel is furnished with choke tubes. Offered in black oxide finish or camo finish. Weight is approximately 8.6 lbs. Introduced in 1999. **NOTE:** Add $100 for camo finish.

NIB	Exc.	V.G.	Good	Fair	Poor
2200	1700	1350	775	500	250

CRUCELEGUI, HERMANOS
Eibar, Spain

A 5mm, 6.35mm, 7.65mm, and 8mm caliber double-action revolver. The trade names used were; Puppy, Velo-Mith, Le-Brong, Bron-Sport, C.H., and Brong-Petit.

NIB	Exc.	V.G.	Good	Fair	Poor
—	250	150	80	60	35

CUMMINGS, O. S.
Lowell, Massachusetts
Cummings Pocket Revolver

A .22 caliber spur trigger revolver with a 3.5" ribbed round barrel, and a 7-shot fluted cylinder. Nickel-plated with rosewood grip. The barrel is stamped "O.S. Cummings Lowell, Mass." Approximately 1,000 manufactured in the 1870s.

NIB	Exc.	V.G.	Good	Fair	Poor
—	—	675	300	150	100

CUMMINGS & WHEELER
Lowell, Massachusetts
Pocket Revolver

Similar to the Cummings Pocket Revolver with subtle differences such as the length of the flutes on the cylinder and the size and shape of the grip. The barrel is slightly longer and is marked "Cummings & Wheeler, Lowell, Mass."

NIB	Exc.	V.G.	Good	Fair	Poor
—	—	750	350	150	100

CUSTOM GUN GUILD
Doraville, Georgia
Wood Model IV

A falling block single-shot rifle produced in a number of popular calibers with barrel lengths from 22" to 28". The stock of select checkered walnut. This is a lightweight rifle, at approximately 5.5 lbs. It was manufactured for one year only, 1984, and is not often encountered on today's market.

NIB	Exc.	V.G.	Good	Fair	Poor
—	3750	2750	2500	1750	1000

CZ/CZ-USA
(Ceska Zbrojovka)
Uhersky Brod, Czech Republic

Established by Karel Bubla and Alois Tomiska in 1919. This company later merged with Hubertus Engineering Company. In 1949 the company was nationalized. CZ regularly exports 90 percent of its production to over 80 countries. As of 1998, CZ firearms have been imported exclusively by CZ-USA, a wholly-owned distribution subsidiary of Ceska Zbrojovka a.s. Uhersky Brod, (CZUB) of the Czech Republic.

Fox

A 6.35mm caliber semi-automatic pistol with a 2-1/8" barrel, tubular slide, a folding trigger and no trigger guard. Fox and CZ are inscribed on the slide. The CZ logo is on each grip plate. Blued with plastic grips. Manufactured between 1919 and 1936.

Courtesy James Rankin

NIB	Exc.	V.G.	Good	Fair	Poor
—	900	750	600	400	200

CZ 1921 Praga

A semi-automatic pistol in 7.65mm caliber. The first service pistol manufactured in Czechoslovakia. Production began in 1920. Praga is stamped on the slide and on each grip plate for commercial models. The service models were fitted with wood grips.

Courtesy James Rankin

NIB	Exc.	V.G.	Good	Fair	Poor
—	650	550	475	350	200

Army Pistol 1922 (Nickl-Pistole)

Designed by Josef Nickl of Mauser. First approved by the Army in 1921, this pistol was chambered for the .380 ACP (9mmKurtz/9x17mm) cartridge. Plagued by design problems, it was produced only in 1922 and 1923. Fewer than 22,000 were built.

NIB	Exc.	V.G.	Good	Fair	Poor
—	650	500	350	200	150

CZ 1922

A semi-automatic pistol in caliber 6.35mm. Very similar to the Fox above. It has no sights but is fitted with a conventional trigger guard. CZ is stamped on the slide and the CZ logo on each grip plate. Grips are plastic or wood. Manufactured between 1922 and 1936.

NIB	Exc.	V.G.	Good	Fair	Poor
—	550	450	350	300	200

CZ 1924

The first large-production military pistol produced by CZ. Chambered for the 9mmK cartridge. It is the first of the CZ models with wraparound grips of both wood and plastic. CZ logo is seen on plastic grips. A lanyard loop is attached to the base of the butt. Manufactured from 1925 to 1932.

Courtesy James Rankin

NIB	Exc.	V.G.	Good	Fair	Poor
—	650	500	400	300	200

CZ 1927

A semi-automatic pistol chambered for the 7.65mm cartridge, marked the same as the CZ 1924, but the cocking grooves on the slide are cut vertically instead of sloped as on the earlier model. This model was blued with checkered, wrap-around, plastic grips. These early guns were beautifully made and marked, "Ceska Zbrojovka AS v Praze". After the war, these pistols continued in production until 1951. There were more than 500,000 manufactured.

NOTE: Some of these pistols were made with an extended barrel for the use of a silencer. This variation brings a large premium. Fewer than 10 CZ27s were made in .22 caliber. An expert opinion is suggested if a sale is contemplated. Nazi-proofed add 50 percent.

Commercial markings

Courtesy Orvel Reichert

NIB	Exc.	V.G.	Good	Fair	Poor
—	650	475	300	200	165

CZ 1936

A 6.35mm caliber semi-automatic pistol with 2.5" barrel, and double-action-only lockwork. It has plastic wraparound grips with the CZ logo on each side. It replaced the Model 1922 in 1936. Discontinued in 1940 because of wartime production.

Courtesy James Rankin

NIB	Exc.	V.G.	Good	Fair	Poor
—	450	350	300	200	100

CZ 1938

A semi-automatic double-action pistol in caliber 9mmK. Manufactured for the Czechoslovakian military from 1938 to 1940. Barrel length is 4.7". Weight is about 32 oz. Magazine capacity is 8 rounds. Wraparound plastic grips with the CZ logo on each side.

Courtesy James Rankin

NIB	Exc.	V.G.	Good	Fair	Poor
—	550	500	400	300	200

CZ 1945

This model is a small .25 caliber (6.35mm) pocket pistol that is double-action-only. It was produced and sold after World War II. It is a modified version of the CZ 1936. Approximately 60,000 were built between 1945 and 1949.

Courtesy James Rankin

NIB	Exc.	V.G.	Good	Fair	Poor
—	350	300	250	175	125

CZ 1950

This is a blowback-operated, semi-automatic, double-action pistol chambered for the 7.65mm cartridge. It is patterned after the Walther Model PP with a few differences. The safety catch is located on the frame instead of the slide; and the trigger guard is not hinged, as on the Walther. It is dismantled by means of a catch on the side of the frame. Although intended to be a military pistol designed by the Kratochvil brothers, it proved to be underpowered and was adopted by the police. There were few released on the commercial market.

Courtesy James Rankin

NIB	Exc.	V.G.	Good	Fair	Poor
—	250	150	125	100	50

CZ 1952

This Czech army sidearm is a semi-automatic pistol chambered for the 7.62mm cartridge and fitted with a 4.7" barrel. It has a very complex locking system using two rollers inside the frame. Magazine capacity is 8 rounds. Weight is about 34 oz. Production ended in 1956.

NIB	Exc.	V.G.	Good	Fair	Poor
—	300	275	225	125	75

Model 1970

This model was an attempt to correct dependability problems with the Model 50. There is little difference to see externally between the two except for markings and the grip pattern. Production began during the 1960s and ended in 1983.

Courtesy Rock Island Auction Company

NIB	Exc.	V.G.	Good	Fair	Poor
—	250	200	150	100	75

RIFLES

Model 52 (7.62x45) Carbine

NIB	Exc.	V.G.	Good	Fair	Poor
—	450	300	250	200	125

Model 52/57 (7.62 x 39)

NIB	Exc.	V.G.	Good	Fair	Poor
—	525	325	275	225	150

CURRENTLY IMPORTED CZ GUNS—CZ-USA, Kansas City, Kansas

CZ first entered the U.S. market in 1990 through various distributors. In January 1998 CZ-USA opened its office in Kansas City, Kansas. This office includes full sales and warranty service as well as an on-site gunsmith.

RIFLES

CZ Model 3

This bolt-action rifle, introduced in 2004, is produced in the U.S.A. Offered in both right- and left-hand configurations. Chambered for the Winchester Short Magnums: .270, 7mm, and .300. Walnut stock with choice of stainless steel or blue finish. Fitted with a 24" barrel. No sights. Magazine is 3 rounds. Weight is about 7.5 lbs. **NOTE:** Add $30 for stainless steel.

NIB	Exc.	V.G.	Good	Fair	Poor
970	675	575	400	200	100

CZ 452-2E LUX

This bolt-action rifle is chambered for the .22 LR or .22 Win. Magnum cartridge. It is fitted with a 24.8" barrel with hooded front and adjustable rear sight. Trigger is adjustable for pull. The pistol grip stock is a European-style Turkish walnut. Supplied with a 5-round magazine. Blued finish. Weight is approximately 6.6 lbs. **NOTE:** Add $40 for .22 WMR.

NIB	Exc.	V.G.	Good	Fair	Poor
490	350	225	150	125	100

CZ ZKM-452D

As above, with a walnut, Monte Carlo-style stock.

NIB	Exc.	V.G.	Good	Fair	Poor
—	425	300	225	150	100

CZ 452-2E ZKM Style

Similar to the above model but chambered for .22 LR only and fitted with a black synthetic stock and matte nickel finish. Fitted with a 22.5" barrel. Weight is about 6 lbs.

NIB	Exc.	V.G.	Good	Fair	Poor
475	325	225	175	125	100

CZ 452 Training Rifle

Chambered for the .22 LR cartridge and fitted with a 24.8" barrel. Detachable magazine has a 5-round capacity. Beechwood stock. Adjustable sights. Weight is about 5.4 lbs.

NIB	Exc.	V.G.	Good	Fair	Poor
375	275	175	150	125	100

CZ 452 American Classic

This model is chambered for the .22 LR and .22 Win. Magnum cartridge and features an American-style Circassian walnut stock with 18 lpi checkering. Fitted with a 21" barrel with recessed target crown. Supplied with a 5-round magazine. Blued finish. Weight is about 6.5 lbs. Introduced in 1999. In 2005 the .17 Mach 2 caliber was offered. **NOTE:** Add $40 for .22 WMR. or .17 HMR.

NIB	Exc.	V.G.	Good	Fair	Poor
465	350	250	150	12	100

CZ 452 Varmint

This bolt-action rifle is chambered for the .22 LR cartridge and is fitted with a 20" barrel. American-style Turkish walnut stock. Blued finish. Weight is about 7.5 lbs. In 2005 the .17 Mach 2 was offered. **NOTE:** Add $20 for .17 Mach 2 caliber.

NIB	Exc.	V.G.	Good	Fair	Poor
420	300	250	200	150	125

CZ 452 Scout

This model is designed for the younger shooter and features a shortened buttstock, 16.2" barrel, and reduced weight receiver. Chambered for the .22 LR cartridge. Open adjustable sights. Weight is 3.9 lbs. Introduced in 2000.

NIB	Exc.	V.G.	Good	Fair	Poor
275	200	150	125	100	75

CZ 452 Style

Chambered for the .22 LR cartridge and fitted with a 22.5" barrel, this model features a synthetic stock with matte nickel finish. Magazine capacity is 5 or 10 rounds. Weight is about 5.3 lbs.

NIB	Exc.	V.G.	Good	Fair	Poor
400	300	250	225	125	75

CZ 452 Silhouette

Designed for small silhouette competition shooting, this .22 caliber rifle has a synthetic stock and blued finish. Barrel length is 22.5". Weight is about 5.3 lbs.

NIB	Exc.	V.G.	Good	Fair	Poor
400	300	250	225	125	75

CZ 452 FS

This model, introduced in 2004, is chambered for the .22 LR or .22 WMR cartridge and fitted with a full-length Turkish walnut stock. Barrel length is 20.5". Adjustable sights. Weight is about 6.5 lbs.

NIB	Exc.	V.G.	Good	Fair	Poor
475	350	265	200	150	100

CZ 513 Basic

This model is a simplified version of the CZ 452. It features a plain beechwood stock with no checkering. Iron sights. Chambered for the .22 LR cartridge. Barrel length is 21". Weight is about 5.4 lbs. Introduced in 2004.

NIB	Exc.	V.G.	Good	Fair	Poor
275	200	170	125	100	75

CZ 511

This is a semi-automatic rifle chambered for the .22 LR cartridge. Fitted with a 22" barrel. Two-position rear sight. Supplied with an 8-round magazine. Cross bolt safety. Turkish walnut stock. Blued finish. Weight is approximately 5.4 lbs.

NIB	Exc.	V.G.	Good	Fair	Poor
400	335	250	175	125	75

CZ Model 527

This bolt-action model is chambered for the .22 Hornet, .222 Rem., and the .223 Rem. The rear sight is adjustable and the checkered stock is walnut. Barrel length is 23.6" and magazine capacity is 5 rounds. Weight is approximately 6.2 lbs.

NIB	Exc.	V.G.	Good	Fair	Poor
600	500	400	300	225	125

CZ 527 American Classic

Introduced in 1999, this model features a 20.5" barrel with American-style Turkish walnut stock. Weight is approximately 7.6 lbs. Blued finish. In 2005 this model was chambered for the .204 Ruger cartridge with 22" barrel. **NOTE:** Add $170 for English walnut stock, $200 for fancy American walnut, $30 for maple, and $30 for laminate stock.

NIB	Exc.	V.G.	Good	Fair	Poor
600	500	400	300	200	100

CZ 527 Lux

This is a bolt-action center fire rifle chambered for the .22 Hornet, .222 Rem., or the .223 Rem. cartridge. Fitted with a 23.6" barrel with a hooded front sight and fixed rear sight. The trigger is an adjustable single-set type. The Turkish walnut stock is in the Bavarian style. Blued finish. Supplied with a 5-round magazine. Weight is approximately 6.6 lbs.

NIB	Exc.	V.G.	Good	Fair	Poor
600	475	350	250	150	100

CZ 527 Premium (Lux)

Introduced in 2000 this model features hand fitted actions, fancy walnut stock, 18 lpi checkering, and satin finish. Offered in .22 Hornet and .223 Rem. Barrel length is 22". Magazine capacity is 5 rounds. Weight is about 6.2 lbs.

NIB	Exc.	V.G.	Good	Fair	Poor
650	525	400	300	175	125

CZ 527 FS

Similar to the above model but fitted with a 20.5" barrel with Mannlicher-style stock. Blued finish. Weight is about 6 lbs.

NIB	Exc.	V.G.	Good	Fair	Poor
690	525	400	300	175	125

CZ 527 Varmint

Chambered for the .17 Remington or .204 Ruger cartridge and fitted with a 24" heavy barrel. Checkered Turkish walnut stock. No sights. Detachable magazine. Weight is about 7.2 lbs.

NIB	Exc.	V.G.	Good	Fair	Poor
600	475	350	175	125	100

CZ 527 Varmint Laminate

Chambered for the .223 Rem. cartridge and fitted with a 24" heavy barrel. Gray laminate stock. Magazine capacity is 5 rounds. Weight is about 8 lbs. Introduced in 2002.

NIB	Exc.	V.G.	Good	Fair	Poor
695	525	400	300	200	100

CZ 527 Varmint

As above but with an H-S Kevlar stock. Weight is about 7.5 lbs. Introduced in 2002. In 2004 this model was also offered with a Turkish walnut stock.

NIB	Exc.	V.G.	Good	Fair	Poor
800	625	400	300	200	100

CZ 527 Carbine

This model, introduced in 2000, is chambered for the 7.62x39 cartridge and fitted with a 18.5" barrel. Detachable magazine capacity is 5 rounds. Open sights. Weight is about 6 lbs.

NIB	Exc.	V.G.	Good	Fair	Poor
600	475	350	225	175	100

CZ 527 Prestige

An upgraded CZ 527 American with jeweled bolt and semi-fancy Turkish walnut with hand rubbed finish. Chambered for the .22 Hornet or .223 Remington cartridges. Barrel length is 21.9". Weight is about 6.2 lbs. Introduced in 2001.

NIB	Exc.	V.G.	Good	Fair	Poor
880	675	600	475	275	150

CZ Model 537

This bolt-action rifle is chambered for the .270, .308, and .30-06 cartridges. The rear sight is adjustable and the stock is checkered walnut. Barrel length is 23.6". Magazine capacity is 5 rounds. Weight is approximately 7.9 lbs. Discontinued.

NIB	Exc.	V.G.	Good	Fair	Poor
600	475	375	250	200	100

CZ 550 American Classic

Similar to the Model CZ 550 this rifle is chambered for the .243, .308, .270, and .30-06 cartridges. It is fitted with a 20.5" barrel and American-style Turkish walnut stock. No sights. Supplied with 5-round internal magazine. Blued finish. Weight is about 7.6 lbs. Introduced in 1999.

NIB	Exc.	V.G.	Good	Fair	Poor
620	500	400	300	200	100

CZ Model 550

Chambered for the .243, .270, .308, and .30-06 cartridges, this bolt-action rifle features a 24" barrel and high comb walnut stock. No open sights. Weight is about 7.25 lbs.

NIB	Exc.	V.G.	Good	Fair	Poor
700	525	400	300	200	100

CZ Model 550 Battue Lux

Chambered for the .30-06 cartridge. Ramp rear sight. Barrel length is 20.25". Weight is approximately 7.25 lbs. Checkered walnut stock.

NIB	Exc.	V.G.	Good	Fair	Poor
700	525	400	300	200	100

CZ Model 550 FS Battue

Same as above but with full-length stock.

NIB	Exc.	V.G.	Good	Fair	Poor
750	600	500	375	200	100

CZ Model 550 Minnesota

This model is chambered for the .270 Win. and .30-06 calibers. Barrel length is 23.5". Weight is approximately 7.25 lbs. No sights. Supplied with recoil pad.

NIB	Exc.	V.G.	Good	Fair	Poor
650	550	450	325	225	125

CZ Model 550 Minnesota DM

Same as above but with detachable magazine. Calibers are .270 Win. and .308.

NIB	Exc.	V.G.	Good	Fair	Poor
725	575	475	350	225	125

CZ 550 Prestige

This model is similar to the CZ 550 American with the added features of jeweled bolt, semi-fancy walnut and hand rubbed finish. Chambered for the .270 or .30-06 cartridges with 23.6" barrel. Weight is approximately 7.3 lbs. Introduced in 2001.

NIB	Exc.	V.G.	Good	Fair	Poor
700	625	550	425	300	175

CZ 550 Lux

This rifle is chambered for the 7x57, 6.5x55 SE, and the 9.3x62 cartridges. Barrel length is 23.6". Fixed magazine capacity is 5 rounds. Bavarian-style stock with Turkish walnut. Open sights. Weight is about 7.3 lbs.

NIB	Exc.	V.G.	Good	Fair	Poor
575	450	375	200	150	75

CZ 550 Varmint

This model is chambered for the .308 Win. cartridge and is fitted with a 25.6" heavy barrel. No sights. Checkered walnut varmint-style stock. Ventilated recoil pad. Single set trigger. Detachable magazine holds 4 rounds. Weight is about 9.3 lbs. In 2004 an HS Precision Kevlar stock was also offered on this model. **NOTE:** Add $200 for Kevlar stock.

NIB	Exc.	V.G.	Good	Fair	Poor
650	500	400	300	200	100

CZ 550 Varmint Laminate

As above but with a gray laminate stock and offered in .22-250. Introduced in 2002.

NIB	Exc.	V.G.	Good	Fair	Poor
750	600	450	350	200	125

CZ 550 Safari Magnum

Chambered for the .300 Win. Magnum, .375 H&H, .458 Win. Magnum, and the .416 Rigby cartridges, this bolt-action rifle is fitted with a 25" barrel and 5-round internal magazine. Sights are one standing and two folding express rear with a hooded front sight. Blued finish. Bavarian-style Turkish walnut stock. Weight is about 9.2 lbs.

NIB	Exc.	V.G.	Good	Fair	Poor
925	750	500	400	300	200

CZ 550 American Safari Magnum

Introduced in 2004 this model is similar to the Safari Magnum above but with an American pattern stock. Offered with American walnut, brown laminate, or camo laminate stock. This model is also offered with fancy American walnut stock. **NOTE:** For laminate stock add $200, for fancy wood stock add $600.

NIB	Exc.	V.G.	Good	Fair	Poor
925	750	500	400	300	200

CZ 550 Ultimate Hunting Rifle

Similar to CZ550 Safari Magnum but chambered for .300 Win. Magnum only and with custom select wood. 23.6" barrel. Accuracy guaranteed at one MOA to 1000 yards. Introduced 2006.

NIB	Exc.	V.G.	Good	Fair	Poor
3600	3000	2450	1500	675	300

CZ 550 Premium

Introduced in 2000 this model features a hand fitted action with fancy walnut stock and 18 lpi checkering. Chambered for .30-06 and .270 Win. cartridges. Barrel length is 23.6". Weight is about 7.3 lbs.

NIB	Exc.	V.G.	Good	Fair	Poor
925	750	500	400	300	200

CZ 550 Medium Magnum

This model is designed around a mid-sized magnum action. Fitted with a 23.6" barrel and has a fixed magazine capacity of 5 rounds. Chambered for the .300 Win. Magnum or the 7mm Rem. Magnum. Single set trigger and adjustable rear sight. Weight is about 7.3 lbs. Introduced in 2001.

NIB	Exc.	V.G.	Good	Fair	Poor
700	575	425	300	200	100

CZ 550 Safari Classic Custom

Chambered for the .404 Jeffery, .450 Rigby, or the .505 Gibbs. Fancy grade checkered walnut stock. Single set trigger. Express sights. **NOTE:** Add $100 for .505 Gibbs.

NIB	Exc.	V.G.	Good	Fair	Poor
2400	2000	1400	750	400	300

CZ 584

A combination 12 gauge/7x57Rmm, .222 or .308 caliber over/under combination rifle/shotgun with 24.5" ventilated rib barrels, single triggers and automatic ejectors. Blued with a walnut stock.

NIB	Exc.	V.G.	Good	Fair	Poor
1000	775	600	500	400	200

CZ ZKK 600

Offered in 7x57mm, 7x64mm, .270, or .30-06. Features a Mauser-type bolt-action with controlled feed, non-rotating extractor, and dovetailed receiver in three action lengths. **NOTE:** Add $100 to prices for pop-up receiver sight that was discontinued in 1977.

NIB	Exc.	V.G.	Good	Fair	Poor
750	625	500	425	325	175

CZ ZKK 601

As above, in .243 or .308 caliber.

NIB	Exc.	V.G.	Good	Fair	Poor
700	600	500	425	325	175

CZ ZKK 602

As above, in .300 Holland & Holland, .375 Holland & Holland or .458 Winchester Magnum.

NIB	Exc.	V.G.	Good	Fair	Poor
800	700	600	500	400	200

CZ 700 Sniper M1

Introduced in 2001 this rifle is chambered for the .308 Winchester cartridge and fitted with a 25.6" heavy barrel. Receiver has permanently attached Weaver rail. Laminated stock has adjustable cheekpiece and buttplate with adjustable trigger. Magazine capacity is 10 rounds. Weigh is approximately 12 lbs.

NIB	Exc.	V.G.	Good	Fair	Poor
2350	1800	1300	700	400	200

CZ 750 Sniper

Bolt-action rifle; .308 Win. 10-shot detachable magazine, 26" blued barrel, two scope mount systems, polymer stock, weighs 12 lbs. Introduced 2006.

NIB	Exc.	V.G.	Good	Fair	Poor
2000	1750	1550	1050	600	325

CZ 455

Updated version of the popular CZ 452. Action forged from steel billets. Walnut stock, cut checkering, oil finish. No sights furnished, 20.5" barrel. Trigger adjustable for weight and pull. Detachable magazine. Available with CZ Switch Barrel Set in .22 LR and .17 HMR. Single barrel guns chambered for the .22LR, .22 WMR or .17 HMR.

NIB	Exc.	V.G.	Good	Fair	Poor
350	300	250	220	170	100

CZ 512

Rimfire, semi-automatic rifle. Dual guide rods for smooth operation. Hammer forged barrel, adjustable sights. Receiver is machined for 11mm dovetail mounts. Field stripping via a coin, modular design for simple takedown. Aluminum upper receiver with polymer lower. Beechwood stock. Chambered for the .22LR and .22 WMR.

NIB	Exc.	V.G.	Good	Fair	Poor
400	350	295	220	185	125

CZ 550 Urban Sniper

Compact profile in a modern sniper rifle. Free floating 16" barrel with target crown. Surefire muzzle brake with suppressor compatibility. Bell & Carlson fiberglass stock, aluminum bedding block, oversized bolt handle and single stage trigger. Available with a 5- or 10-round magazine. Chambered for the .308 Winchester with other calibers on request.

NIB	Exc.	V.G.	Good	Fair	Poor
2000	1725	1400	950	500	300

SHOTGUNS

CZ 581

A 12 gauge over/under double-barrel boxlock shotgun with 28" ventilated rib barrels, single trigger, and automatic ejectors. Blued with a walnut stock.

NIB	Exc.	V.G.	Good	Fair	Poor
875	700	600	450	400	200

CZ 712

This is a gas-operated semi-automatic 12 gauge 3" chamber shotgun built on a lightweight alloy receiver. Offered with a choice of 26" or 28" vent rib barrels. Magazine is 4 rounds. Checkered walnut stock with blued finish. Weight is about 7 lbs. Introduced in 2004.

NIB	Exc.	V.G.	Good	Fair	Poor
425	325	275	200	150	100

CZ 720

This model is similar to the above but chambered for the 20 gauge 3" shell. Offered with a choice of 26" or 28" vent rib barrels. Walnut stock. Weight is about 6 lbs. Introduced in 2004.

NIB	Exc.	V.G.	Good	Fair	Poor
425	325	275	200	150	100

Redhead

This over/under is available in 12, 20, or 28 gauge with choke tubes, and .410 bore with fixed chokes. Barrel lengths are 26" or 28". Single-selective trigger with extractors on 28 and .410 models. Checkered walnut stock with pistol grip. Receiver finish is silver. Weight from 8 lbs. to 6 lbs. depending on gauge.

NIB	Exc.	V.G.	Good	Fair	Poor
795	625	500	350	200	150

Canvasback

This over/under gun is offered in 12 or 20 gauge fitted with 26" or 28" barrels with choke tubes. Single-selective trigger with extractors. Black receiver finish. Weight is about 7.5 lbs.

NIB	Exc.	V.G.	Good	Fair	Poor
695	550	450	350	200	150

Woodcock

Available in 12, 20, 28 and .410 bore with 26" or 28" barrel with chokes tubes except for fixed chokes on the .410. Single-selective trigger with ejectors except for the 12 and 20 gauge. Receiver is case colored with sideplate. Checkered walnut stock with pistol grip. **NOTE:** Add $75 for 28 and .410 models.

NIB	Exc.	V.G.	Good	Fair	Poor
1055	825	625	450	300	225

Woodcock Custom Grade

Similar to the Woodcock model, but stocked with Grade IV walnut and offered only in 20 gauge with 28" barrels.

NIB	Exc.	V.G.	Good	Fair	Poor
1500	1250	975	600	400	200

Mallard

This 12 or 20 gauge over and under gun is fitted with double triggers and extractors. Barrel length is 28". Checkered walnut stock with pistol grip. Coin finish receiver.

NIB	Exc.	V.G.	Good	Fair	Poor
695	550	450	350	200	150

Durango

This side-by-side gun is offered in 12 or 20 gauge with 20" barrels with choke tubes. Extractors. Case colored receiver. Single trigger. Checkered walnut with pistol grip.

NIB	Exc.	V.G.	Good	Fair	Poor
795	625	550	400	300	200

Amarillo

As above but with double triggers.

NIB	Exc.	V.G.	Good	Fair	Poor
700	550	425	350	250	150

Ringneck

This side-by-side gun is chambered for the 12, 16, 20, 28, or .410 bore with 26" or 28" barrels with choke tubes. Case colored receiver with side plates. Single-selective trigger with extractors. Checkered walnut stock with pistol grip. **NOTE:** Add $100 for 16 gauge; add $175 for 28 and .410 models.

NIB	Exc.	V.G.	Good	Fair	Poor
870	675	575	400	300	200

Ringneck Custom Grade

Select Grade IV walnut is used in the manufacture of this 20 gauge with 28" barrels.

NIB	Exc.	V.G.	Good	Fair	Poor
1200	1000	700	450	300	200

Bobwhite

As above but with straight grip stock and double triggers.

NIB	Exc.	V.G.	Good	Fair	Poor
795	625	550	400	300	200

Partridge

New in 2008, this side-by-side is available in 12, 20 and 28 gauge and .410 bore with 3" chambers (2.75" in 28 gauge), each with a frame scaled to its bore size. White chrome-plated receiver with scroll engraving. Boxlock action and double triggers. Straight grip stock and splinter fore-end. Barrels are 28" in 12 and 20 gauge and 26" in 28 and .410. Includes five choke tubes (.410 is choked IC/MOD). Add 20 percent for 28 gauge and .410 bore.

NIB	Exc.	V.G.	Good	Fair	Poor
795	625	550	400	300	200

Grouse

New in 2008, the Grouse is a single trigger side-by-side in 12, 20 and 28 gauge and .410 bore with 3" chambers (2.75" in 28 gauge). White chrome-plated receiver with scroll engraving. Prince of Wales grip and semi-beavertail schnabel fore-end. Barrels are 28" in 12 and 20 gauge and 26" in 28 and .410. Includes five choke tubes (.410 is choked IC/MOD). Add 20 percent for 28 gauge and .410 bore.

NIB	Exc.	V.G.	Good	Fair	Poor
995	800	700	550	450	300

CZ Sporting

This dedicated sporting clays over/under is a 12 gauge with an adjustable comb stock and fore-end of #3 Circassian walnut. It features chrome-lined barrels back-bored to .736 and automatic ejectors. Barrels are 30" or 32". Five choke tubes included. Weight is about 9 lbs.

NIB	Exc.	V.G.	Good	Fair	Poor
2400	1800	1300	700	400	200

Hammer Coach

12-gauge cowboy gun with double triggers, color case hardened receiver, external hammers and Turkish walnut pistol grip stock and fore-end. Fixed IC and Modified chokes. Introduced 2006.

NIB	Exc.	V.G.	Good	Fair	Poor
795	625	550	400	300	200

PISTOLS

All currently imported CZ pistols can be ordered with tritium night sights with the exception of models CZ 97B and CZ 100. Add $80 for this option. **NOTE:** Substantial premium for factory-engraved examples.

CZ 75

Designed by the Koucky brothers in 1975, this model bears little resemblance to previous CZ pistols. Considered by many, including the late Jeff Cooper, to be the best pistol ever to come from the Czech Republic and one of the finest semi-automatics in the world. Chambered for the 9mm Parabellum cartridge it is copied in many countries. This pistol has a breechlock system utilizing a Browning-style cam. The slide rides on the inside of the slide rails. Magazine capacity is 15 rounds, barrel length is 4.72", overall length is 8", and the empty pistol weighs 34.5 oz. Offered in black paint, matte or polished blue finish.

NIB	Exc.	V.G.	Good	Fair	Poor
500	450	425	400	325	250

CZ 75 B

Introduced in 1994 this CZ model is an updated version of the original CZ 75. It features a pinned front sight, a commander hammer, non-glare ribbed barrel, and a squared trigger guard. Also offered in .40 S&W chamber. **NOTE:** For .40 S&W add $30. For glossy blue add $20, for dual tone finish $25, and for nickel add $25. For tritium night sights add $80.

NIB	Exc.	V.G.	Good	Fair	Poor
510	400	300	250	175	125

CZ 75 30th Anniversary

Introduced in 2005 this model features special 30th anniversary engraving, gold inlays, gold plated controls, high gloss blue finish, engraved blonde finished birch grips. Magazine capacity is 15 rounds. Limited to 1,000 pistols.

NIB	Exc.	V.G.	Good	Fair	Poor
850	675	500	400	300	200

CZ 75 Compact

Introduced in 1992, this is a compact version of the CZ 75. The barrel length is 3.9", the overall length is 7.3", and the weight is about 32 oz. Offered in black paint, matte or polished blue finish. Traditional single-action double-action. **NOTE:** In 2005 this model was offered with accessory rail and ambidextrous manual safety. Add $50 to prices. For .40 S&W add $30. For glossy blue add $20, for dual tone finish $25, and for nickel add $25. For tritium night sights add $80.

NIB	Exc.	V.G.	Good	Fair	Poor
475	425	300	250	175	125

CZ 75 D Compact

Essentially the same as the CZ 75 Compact but with a decocking double-action system and lightweight alloy frame. Weight approximately 25 oz. **NOTE:** Only 20 of these pistols were imported into the U.S. No longer in production. Expert appraisal suggested prior to sale.

NIB	Exc.	V.G.	Good	Fair	Poor
555	450	300	225	150	100

CZ 75 B Tactical

Chambered for the 9mm Luger cartridge and fitted with a 4.7" barrel. This pistol has a single-action/double-action trigger. Fixed sights. Rubber grips. Slide is black polycoat and the frame is a military green finish. Weight is about 35 oz. Add 10 percent for night sights.

NIB	Exc.	V.G.	Good	Fair	Poor
475	400	325	250	175	125

CZ 75 BD

Has all the same features as the Model 75 B but with the addition of a decocking double-action. Black polycoat finish.

NIB	Exc.	V.G.	Good	Fair	Poor
450	400	300	225	150	100

CZ BD Compact

Introduced in 2001 this model features a 3.9" barrel with decocking lever. Chambered for the .40 S&W cartridge. Blued finish. Magazine capacity is 10 rounds. Weight is about 32 oz. All other features same as CZ 75 B Compact.

NIB	Exc.	V.G.	Good	Fair	Poor
400	350	300	225	150	100

CZ BD Compact Carry

Same as the model above but with rounded edges including trigger guard.

NIB	Exc.	V.G.	Good	Fair	Poor
425	375	300	225	150	100

CZ 75 SA

This model was introduced in 2000 and features a single-action trigger designed for competitive shooting that can be carried in condition one. Fitted with a straight trigger, manual safety, and chambered for the 9mm cartridge. Weight is about 35 oz.

NIB	Exc.	V.G.	Good	Fair	Poor
520	400	325	225	150	100

CZ 75 Semi-Compact

This model was introduced in 1994 and has the same barrel length as the Compact (3.9") but has the same full-size grip as the CZ 75. Magazine capacity is 15 rounds of 9mm. Overall length is 7.3".

NIB	Exc.	V.G.	Good	Fair	Poor
495	350	300	250	175	100

CZ 75 D PCR Compact

Introduced in 2000 this pistol is chambered for the 9mm cartridge and features a light alloy frame and 3.9" barrel. Trigger is both single and double-action with decocking lever. Low profile sights. Serrated front and rear backstrap. Designed for the Czech national police force. Magazine capacity is 10 rounds. Weight is about 27 oz.

NIB	Exc.	V.G.	Good	Fair	Poor
525	425	350	225	150	100

CZ 75 Champion

This model is chambered for the .40 S&W, 9mm, and 9x21 cartridges. Single-action-only trigger with straight trigger. Fitted with a 4.5" barrel with low profile adjustable sights and three port compensator. Furnished with blue slide and nickel frame. Hand fitted. Weight is about 36 oz.

NIB	Exc.	V.G.	Good	Fair	Poor
1475	1150	975	675	500	300

CZ 75 DAO

This model is similar to the CZ 75 but with a double-action-only trigger, no safety lever and a spurless hammer. Offered in 9mm and .40 S&W. Barrel length is 4.7". Weight is about 35 oz. Introduced in 2000.

NIB	Exc.	V.G.	Good	Fair	Poor
695	525	450	350	250	175

CZ P-01

Introduced in 2002 this pistol replaced the CZ 75 with the Czech National Police. It features a forged aluminum alloy frame and 3.8" barrel. Decocker single-action/double-action. Fixed sights. Fitted with M3 accessory rail. Rubber grips. Ten-round magazine. Black polycoat finish. Weight is about 29 oz.

NIB	Exc.	V.G.	Good	Fair	Poor
600	525	450	350	250	175

CZ 75 Standard IPSC (ST)

Designed and built for IPSC competition. Chambered for .40 S&W and fitted with a 5.4" barrel. Single-action-only trigger. Special high-profile sights. Weight is about 45 oz.

NIB	Exc.	V.G.	Good	Fair	Poor
1000	850	775	625	500	300

CZ 75 M IPSC

Similar to the CZ 75 Standard IPSC with the addition of a two-port compensator with blast shield to protect frame-mounted optics. Slide racker standard. Red Dot optics. Barrel length is 3.9". Weight is about 45 oz. Introduced in 2001.

NIB	Exc.	V.G.	Good	Fair	Poor
1350	1200	1050	675	550	325

CZ 75 Silver Anniversary Model

This model commemorates the 25th anniversary of the CZ Model 75 pistol. It features a high polish nickel finish with walnut grips. The number "25" is inlaid in the grips. A total of 1000 pistols will be produced with about 500 allocated for the U.S. market.

NIB	Exc.	V.G.	Good	Fair	Poor
850	700	600	500	400	225

CZ 75 B Stainless

All steel construction, double-stack magazines, 3-dot fixed sights and chambered for 9mm. 16+1 or 10+1 capacity with 4.72" barrel. The first stainless from CZ. Introduced 2006.

NIB	Exc.	V.G.	Good	Fair	Poor
675	550	425	350	275	150

CZ 75 SP-01 Shadow

Chambered 9mm for IPSC "Production" Division competition. 19+1 capacity, 4.72" barrel. 41 oz., wood grip. Introduced 2006.

NIB	Exc.	V.G.	Good	Fair	Poor
650	600	500	400	300	175

CZ 75 SP-01 Shadow Custom

Chambered in 9mm Parabellum. Steel slide and frame, CZ Custom Shop trigger job. Cold hammer-forged barrel, fiber-optic front sight, aluminum grips and 19-round magazine. Weight 36 ounces, 4.7" barrel and dual-tone finish. Customized for IPSC Production division. Introduced in 2011.

NIB	Exc.	V.G.	Good	Fair	Poor
1000	900	750	650	450	300

CZ 75 TS Czechmate

Comes with all parts necessary to compete in IPSC Open or Limited divisions. Chambered in 9mm Parabellum. Steel slide and frame, single-action grips, comes with compensator and C-More red dot sight installed and ambidextrous slide racker. Includes front-sight adapter that replaces compensator, rear sight, ambidextrous safeties, aluminum grips, magazine well, one 26- and three 20-round magazines. Weight 48 ounces, 5.4" barrel, matte blue finish. Introduced in 2011.

NIB	Exc.	V.G.	Good	Fair	Poor
2900	2500	2000	1500	800	350

CZ 75 Tactical Sport

Single-action for IPSC competition. Chambered in 9mm and .40 S&W. Dual tone (nickel/blued). Capacity 20+1 (9mm) or 16+1 (.40 S&W). 5.4" barrel; 45 oz. Introduced 2006.

NIB	Exc.	V.G.	Good	Fair	Poor
1100	900	675	500	400	200

CZ 85 B

This model is similar in appearance to the CZ 75 but offers some new features such as ambidextrous safety and slide stop levers, squared trigger guard, adjustable sight, and ribbed slide. Caliber, magazine capacity, and weight are same as CZ 75. **NOTE:** For .40 S&W add $30. For glossy blue add $20, for dual tone finish $25, and for nickel add $25.

NIB	Exc.	V.G.	Good	Fair	Poor
525	475	425	300	250	175

CZ 85 Combat

Similar to the CZ 85 but with the addition of adjustable sights, walnut grips, round hammer, and free dropping magazine. **NOTE:** For .40 S&W add $30. For glossy blue add $20, for dual tone finish $25, and for nickel add $25.

NIB	Exc.	V.G.	Good	Fair	Poor
500	450	325	250	175	125

CZ 40B

Introduced in 2002 this model is similar to the CZ 75 but features an alloy frame similar in shape to the Colt Model 1911. It is a single-action/double-action design. Barrel length is 4.7". Magazine capacity is 10 rounds. Chambered for the .40 S&W cartridge. Weight is about 35 oz.

NIB	Exc.	V.G.	Good	Fair	Poor
625	500	400	300	200	125

CZ Kadet

Chambered for the .22 LR cartridge and fitted with a 4.7" barrel. This model is a fixed barrel blowback semi-automatic pistol. Adjustable sights and blue finish. Weight is about 36 oz.

NIB	Exc.	V.G.	Good	Fair	Poor
510	400	300	225	175	100

CZ 75 Kadet Conversion

This is a separate conversion kit for the CZ 75/85 series. It converts these pistols to .22 LR. Adjustable rear sight. Supplied with 10-round magazine.

NIB	Exc.	V.G.	Good	Fair	Poor
300	225	200	150	100	50

CZ 2075 RAMI

Introduced in 2004 this 9mm or .40 S&W pistol is fitted with a 3" barrel. It has a single-action/double-action trigger. The design is based on the CZ Model 75. Magazine capacity is 10 rounds for the 9mm and 8 rounds for the .40 S&W. Weight is about 25 oz.

NIB	Exc.	V.G.	Good	Fair	Poor
450	400	350	300	250	175

CZ 83

This is a fixed-barrel .380 caliber pistol. It features an ambidextrous safety and magazine catch behind the trigger guard. The pistol is stripped by means of a hinged trigger guard. Barrel length is 3.8", overall length is 6.8", and weight is about 23 oz. **NOTE:** For nickel finish add $5. In 1993 Special Editions of this pistol were introduced. These Special Editions consist of special finishes for the then-currently imported CZ pistols. They are high polish blue, nickel, chrome, gold, and a combination of these finishes. These Special Edition finishes may affect price;

they add between $100 and $250 to the cost of the pistol when new.

NIB	Exc.	V.G.	Good	Fair	Poor
475	325	200	175	150	125

CZ 97 B

This pistol was planned for production in the summer of 1997. It is chambered for the .45 ACP cartridge. It is fitted with a 4.8" barrel and has a single-/double-action mode. Magazine capacity is 10 rounds. Wood grips with blue finish. Weight is approximately 40 oz.

NIB	Exc.	V.G.	Good	Fair	Poor
665	525	400	300	175	100

CZ 100

This is a semi-automatic pistol, introduced in 1996, chambered for the 9mm or .40 S&W cartridge. It has a plastic frame and steel slide. Barrel length is 3.75". Weight is approximately 24 oz. U.S. magazine capacity is 10 rounds.

NIB	Exc.	V.G.	Good	Fair	Poor
525	450	325	2000	150	100

CZ
Strakonice, Czech Republic

This firm is a separate company from the one located in Uhershy Brod. Prior to the collapse of the Soviet Union both companies were owned and operated by the state.

Model TT 40/45/9

This is semi-automatic pistol chambered for the .40 S&W, .45 ACP, or 9mm cartridges. Fitted with a 3.8" barrel. Trigger is single-/double-action or double-action-only. Magazine capacity is 10 rounds. Weight is about 26 oz.

NIB	Exc.	V.G.	Good	Fair	Poor
575	425	300	200	125	100

D

D. W. M.
Berlin, Germany
See—Luger & Borchardt

Model 22

A 7.65mm caliber semi-automatic pistol with 3.5" barrel. Blued with walnut grips; later changed to plastic grips. Approximately 40,000 manufactured between 1921 and 1931.

NIB	Exc.	V.G.	Good	Fair	Poor
—	950	775	500	400	250

DAEWOO
Pusan, Korea

DH-40

This semi-automatic pistol is chambered for the .40 S&W cartridge. It has a 4.13" barrel and a magazine capacity of 11 rounds. Weight is approximately 32 oz.

NIB	Exc.	V.G.	Good	Fair	Poor
495	375	300	250	175	100

DP-51B

This semi-automatic pistol is chambered for the 9mm cartridge and is fitted with a 4.13" barrel. Magazine capacity is 13 rounds. Overall length is 7.5" and weight is approximately 28 oz.

NIB	Exc.	V.G.	Good	Fair	Poor
400	325	275	225	175	100

DP-51SB

This is a more compact design with 3.6" barrel and 10-round magazine. Weight is 27 oz. Stainless steel finish.

NIB	Exc.	V.G.	Good	Fair	Poor
450	395	275	225	175	100

DP-51CB

Same as above but fitted with a 3.6" barrel. Magazine capacity is 10 rounds. Weight is about 26 oz.

NIB	Exc.	V.G.	Good	Fair	Poor
450	375	300	250	175	100

DP-52

This semi-automatic pistol is chambered for the .22 LR cartridge. It has a 3.82" barrel length and a magazine capacity of 10 rounds. It operates in double-action and single-action modes. Overall length is 6.7" and weight is approximately 23 oz.

NIB	Exc.	V.G.	Good	Fair	Poor
395	325	250	200	150	100

DH380

Introduced in 1996 this semi-automatic pistol is chambered for the .380 ACP cartridge. It is fitted with a 3.8" barrel and has a magazine capacity of 8 rounds. The firing model is double- or single-action. Weight is approximately 24 oz.

NIB	Exc.	V.G.	Good	Fair	Poor
425	375	275	225	150	100

DR200

Introduced in 1996 this post-ban semi-automatic rifle is chambered for the .223 Rem. cartridge. It features a black matte finish with a synthetic thumbhole stock. Barrel length is 18.3". Uses AR-15 magazines, not included with the rifle. Weight is about 9 lbs.

NIB	Exc.	V.G.	Good	Fair	Poor
975	875	500	400	300	150

K-2/AR-100 (Max I)

A 5.56mm caliber pre-ban semi-automatic rifle with an 18" barrel, gas-operated rotary bolt-action, magazines interchangeable with those from the M-16. Black. Introduced in 1985, but is no longer imported.

NIB	Exc.	V.G.	Good	Fair	Poor
1450	1200	950	700	500	400

K1A1 (Max II)

This rifle is quite similar to the K-2/AR-100 but with a folding composite stock.

NIB	Exc.	V.G.	Good	Fair	Poor
1450	1200	950	700	500	400

DAISY
Rogers, Arkansas

VL Rifle

A .22 combustible cartridge single-shot rifle with an 18" barrel and plastic stock. Cartridge is ignited by compressed air. Manufactured during 1968 and 1969. It is believed that fewer than 20,000 were made. Add considerable premium if large quantity of VL ammunition is present.

NIB	Exc.	V.G.	Good	Fair	Poor
275	100	85	75	50	25

VL Presentation Model

As above, with a walnut stock. Approximately 4,000 were made in 1968 and 1969.

NIB	Exc.	V.G.	Good	Fair	Poor
275	150	125	100	75	50

VL Cased Presentation Model

As above, with a gold plaque inlaid in the stock and with a fitted case containing 300 VL cartridges.

NIB	Exc.	V.G.	Good	Fair	Poor
325	200	175	125	100	75

Model 2201/2211

A bolt-action single-shot rifle chambered for .22 LR cartridge. Fitted with a 19" barrel with octagon shroud. Ramp blade front sight with adjustable notch rear sight. Synthetic stock on Model 2211 and walnut stock on Model 2201. Trigger is adjustable. Weight is about 6.5 lbs.

NIB	Exc.	V.G.	Good	Fair	Poor
200	150	100	60	50	25

Model 2202/2212

Similar to the above model in appearance but fitted with a 10-round rotary magazine. The synthetic stock is Model 2212 and the walnut stock is Model 2202. Weight is about 6.5 lbs.

NIB	Exc.	V.G.	Good	Fair	Poor
200	150	100	60	50	25

Model 2203/2213

This is a semi-automatic rifle chambered for .22 long rifle cartridge. Has a 7-round magazine and a 19" barrel. The synthetic stock is Model 2213 and the walnut stock is Model 2203. Weight is approximately 6.5 lbs.

NIB	Exc.	V.G.	Good	Fair	Poor
225	175	125	75	75	50

DAKIN GUN CO.
San Francisco, California

Model 100

A 12 and 20 gauge boxlock double-barrel shotgun with 26" or 28" barrels, various chokes, extractors and double triggers. Engraved, blued, with a checkered walnut stock. Manufactured in the 1960s.

NIB	Exc.	V.G.	Good	Fair	Poor
—	475	325	275	200	100

Model 147

As above, with ventilated rib barrels.

NIB	Exc.	V.G.	Good	Fair	Poor
—	450	375	250	200	100

Model 160

As above with a single-selective trigger.

NIB	Exc.	V.G.	Good	Fair	Poor
—	700	600	450	250	150

Model 215

As above, but more finely finished.

NIB	Exc.	V.G.	Good	Fair	Poor
—	1800	1600	1100	500	250

Model 170

A 12, 16, and 20 gauge over/under shotgun with 26" or 28" ventilated rib barrels, various chokes, and double triggers. Blued and lightly engraved. Discontinued in the 1960s.

NIB	Exc.	V.G.	Good	Fair	Poor
—	500	425	350	275	150

DAKOTA ARMS, INC.
Sturgis, South Dakota

This company was formed by Don Allen. He was a fine craftsmen in the field of custom rifles. The company offers four basic models with a number of options to fit the customers' needs or wants. The workmanship and materials are of the highest quality. In business since 1987, the company was purchased by Remington Arms Co. in 2009. **NOTE:** All prices are base prices. Dakota offers a number of extra cost options that can greatly affect the value of its rifles and shotguns.

RIFLES

Dakota 76 Classic

A .257 Roberts, .270 Winchester, .280 Remington, .3006, 7mm Remington Magnum, .338, .300 Winchester Magnum, and the .458 Winchester Magnum bolt-action rifle with a 23" barrel, and Mauser-type extractor. Checkered walnut stock. Manufactured in 1987.

NIB	Exc.	V.G.	Good	Fair	Poor
5000	4250	3000	1650	800	400

Dakota 76 Varmint Grade

Introduced in 1996 this rifle is chambered for a variety of cartridges from the .17 Rem. to the 6mm PPC. This is a single-shot bolt-action design available in right- or left-hand versions. Barrel length is 24". The Varmint-style stock is semi-fancy walnut with oil finish and no checkering. Many extra cost options are offered for this model.

NIB	Exc.	V.G.	Good	Fair	Poor
2500	2000	1500	1100	800	400

Varmint Hunter

This model is built on a Model 97 action. Standard features are fiberglass stock, round-action single-shot, adjustable trigger, and black recoil pad. Barrel length is 24". Offered in calibers from .220 Swift to .308 Winchester. Weight is about 8 lbs. Introduced in 1999.

NIB	Exc.	V.G.	Good	Fair	Poor
2195	1750	1000	750	600	300

Safari Grade

Chambered in .375 Holland & Holland, .458 Winchester Magnum, and other short Magnum calibers. Features an ebony fore-end tip, one-piece magazine assembly and open sights. Weighs approximately 8-1/2 lbs.

NIB	Exc.	V.G.	Good	Fair	Poor
6500	5250	2000	1350	700	350

Alpine Grade

As above, but lighter in weight and chambered for .22-250, .243, 6mm, 250-3000, 7mm/08, .308, and .358. Introduced in 1989.

NIB	Exc.	V.G.	Good	Fair	Poor
5400	3950	3000	2000	700	350

African Grade

As above in .416 Rigby, .416 Dakota, .404 Jeffery, and .450 Dakota with walnut especially selected for strength, with crossbolts through the stock. Weighs between 9 and 10 lbs.

NIB	Exc.	V.G.	Good	Fair	Poor
7300	5750	4500	2200	1075	400

Model 10 Single-Shot

Built on a single-shot falling action this rifle features a 23" barrel and choice of XX grade wood with oil finish. Fine line checkering, steel gripcap, and 1/2" recoil pad are also standard. Weighs about 5.5 lbs.

NIB	Exc.	V.G.	Good	Fair	Poor
4500	4000	2750	1550	900	400

Model 10 Single-Shot Magnum

Same as above but in calibers .338 Win. Mag to .416 Dakota. Weight about 6.5 lbs.

NIB	Exc.	V.G.	Good	Fair	Poor
5895	4600	3200	1900	1000	450

Dakota .22 Long Rifle Sporter

Fitted with a 22" barrel and X grade oil finish walnut with fine line checkering and steel gripcap. A 1/2" black recoil pad is standard. Weighs about 6.5 lbs. This model ceased production in 1998.

NIB	Exc.	V.G.	Good	Fair	Poor
1750	1300	800	650	500	275

Dakota .22 Long Rifle Sporter (New Model)

This is a reintroduction (2003) of the Dakota .22 rifle.

NIB	Exc.	V.G.	Good	Fair	Poor
2800	2500	2000	1350	700	350

Model 97 Long Range Hunter

Introduced in 1997 this bolt-action rifle is offered in 13 calibers: .250-6, .257 Roberts, .270 Win., .280 Rem., 7mm Rem. Mag., 7mm Dakota Mag., .30-06, .300 Win. Mag., .300 Dakota Mag., .338 Win. Mag., .330 Dakota Mag., .375 H&H, .375 Dakota Mag. Barrel lengths depend on caliber but are either 24" or 26". The trigger is fully adjustable. Many other special features. Stock is black synthetic with one-piece bedding. Black recoil pad is standard. Weight is approximately 7.7 lbs.

NIB	Exc.	V.G.	Good	Fair	Poor
2800	2400	2200	1500	800	375

Model 97 Lightweight Hunter

Introduced in 1998 this rifle features barrel lengths from 22" to 24" in both short- and long-actions. A special lightweight composite stock is used. Calibers offered range from .22-250 to .330 Dakota Magnum. Weights are between 6.15 to 6.5 lbs. depending on caliber and barrel length. **NOTE:** Add 50 to 70 percent for Deluxe with AAA grade wood.

NIB	Exc.	V.G.	Good	Fair	Poor
2000	1500	1100	800	500	375

Model T-76 Longbow Tactical Rifle

This long range tactical bolt-action rifle is available in 3 calibers: .338 Lapua, .300 Dakota Mag., and .330 Dakota Mag. The fiberglass stock is an A-2 McMillan in black or olive green. Adjustable length of pull with bipod spike in forearm. The 28" stainless steel is .950 diameter at the muzzle with muzzlebrake. The rifle is sold with a number of accessories such as a case with bipod, tool kit and tool box. Weight is about 13.7 lbs.

NIB	Exc.	V.G.	Good	Fair	Poor
4600	4250	3000	1650	800	400

Model 76 Traveler

This model was introduced in 1999 and is built on a modified Model 76 design and stocked in wood. Disassembly is threadless. It is offered in standard length action, short magnum-action, and long-actions in both left and right hand. Offered in three grades.

Classic

NIB	Exc.	V.G.	Good	Fair	Poor
6200	5500	4000	2700	1800	900

Safari

NIB	Exc.	V.G.	Good	Fair	Poor
6900	5900	4200	3000	2000	1200

African

NIB	Exc.	V.G.	Good	Fair	Poor
7600	6500	5000	3200	2000	1200

Classic Predator

This bolt-action rifle is chambered for the .17 VarTarg, .17 Rem., .17 Tactical, .20 VarTarg, .20 Tactical, .20 PPC, .204 Ruger, .221 Rem. Fireball, .222 Rem., .222 Rem. Mag., .223 Rem., .22 BR, 6 PPC, and the 6 BR. Fitted with a 22" stainless steel barrel, Checkered special select Claro walnut stock with cheekpiece.

NIB	Exc.	V.G.	Good	Fair	Poor
3800	3000	2200	1700	800	375

Serious Predator

As above but with AAA Claro walnut stock.

NIB	Exc.	V.G.	Good	Fair	Poor
3000	2250	2000	1650	800	400

All-Weather Predator

As above but with varmint style composite stock.

NIB	Exc.	V.G.	Good	Fair	Poor
2500	2000	1600	1000	500	300

Double Rifle

Available in most common calibers. Fitted with exhibition walnut with pistol grip. Barrel is 25". Round-action with selective ejectors, recoil, pad and hard case. Prices listed are for guns without engraving.

NIB	Exc.	V.G.	Good	Fair	Poor
30000	24000	18000	10000	3500	800

Little Sharps Rifle

Introduced in 2003 this is a smaller version (20 percent) of the full size Sharps rifle. Standard rifle has a 26" octagon barrel, straight grips stock with XX walnut, steel buttplate and blade front sight. Offered in calibers from .17 HMR to .30-40 Krag. Weight is around 8 lbs.

NIB	Exc.	V.G.	Good	Fair	Poor
5500	3950	2750	2000	1500	400

Limited Edition .30-06 Model 76

Ultra-decked-out version of Model 76; commemorates 100th anniversary of .30-06 cartridge; production limited to 101 units. Introduced 2006.

NIB	Exc.	V.G.	Good	Fair	Poor
8000	5500	4000	2650	1700	500

Limited Edition .30-06 Model 10

Ultra-decked-out version of Model 10; commemorates 100th anniversary of .30-06 cartridge; production limited to 101 units. Introduced 2006.

NIB	Exc.	V.G.	Good	Fair	Poor
8000	5500	4000	2650	1700	500

SHOTGUNS

Classic Grade

This grade features a case colored round-action with straight grip and fancy walnut oil finish stock. Forearm is splinter type. Double trigger standard with choice of chokes. This model is no longer in production.

NIB	Exc.	V.G.	Good	Fair	Poor
7950	5200	4400	3000	2000	600

Premier Grade

This grade features a case colored round-action with 50 percent engraving coverage. Exhibition grade English walnut stock with straight grip and splinter forearm. Oil rubbed finish. Double triggers are standard with choice of chokes. NOTE: Add 10 percent for 28 gauge and .410 bore.

NIB	Exc.	V.G.	Good	Fair	Poor
13950	9500	7000	4750	2900	500

Dakota American Legend

Introduced in 1996, this side-by-side shotgun is offered in 12, 20 and 28 gauge, and .410 bore with 27" barrels, concave rib, splinter forearm, double triggers, straight grips stock, and full scroll engraving on the frame. Many additional extra cost options are offered that can greatly affect the price. The base price is listed.

NIB	Exc.	V.G.	Good	Fair	Poor
18000	14000	11500	7900	5000	600

Dakota Shotgun

Similar to the American Legend but offered in two grades of finish. These new grades were first offered in 1997.

DAKOTA ARMS INC.—FERLIB SHOTGUNS

In 2000 Dakota Arms Inc. became the exclusive importer of Ferlib shotgun in the U.S. The models listed are imported and sold by Dakota Arms Inc.

Model 7

NIB	Exc.	V.G.	Good	Fair	Poor
10950	8000	6500	5000	4000	700

Prince Model

NIB	Exc.	V.G.	Good	Fair	Poor
11950	9000	7500	6000	4500	700

Prince Model Side-Lever

NIB	Exc.	V.G.	Good	Fair	Poor
14500	10500	8500	7000	5500	700

Rex

NIB	Exc.	V.G.	Good	Fair	Poor
14950	11000	8500	7000	5500	700

Premier

NIB	Exc.	V.G.	Good	Fair	Poor
16950	12500	10000	7200	5500	600

Sideplate Model

NIB	Exc.	V.G.	Good	Fair	Poor
14400	10500	8500	7000	5500	700

Sideplate Model with Gold

NIB	Exc.	V.G.	Good	Fair	Poor
15100	11250	10000	7200	5500	600

Sideplate with Scroll

NIB	Exc.	V.G.	Good	Fair	Poor
14000	10500	8500	7000	5500	700

Hammer Gun

NIB	Exc.	V.G.	Good	Fair	Poor
19000	14000	12000	10000	5000	700

H.H. Model—no engraving

NIB	Exc.	V.G.	Good	Fair	Poor
20000	15000	13000	11000	570	675

Esposizione

NIB	Exc.	V.G.	Good	Fair	Poor
25500	18000	13000	10000	7000	700

L'Inglesina

NIB	Exc.	V.G.	Good	Fair	Poor
25500	18000	13000	10000	7000	700

Model E "Fantasy"

NIB	Exc.	V.G.	Good	Fair	Poor
39500	27500	22000	15500	11000	700

Boss—no engraving

NIB	Exc.	V.G.	Good	Fair	Poor
29500	20000	15000	10000	7000	750

DAKOTA ARMS INC.—SIACE SHOTGUNS

Imported from Italy in 2004 and called the Dakota SuperLight. These shotguns are side-by-sides with boxlock actions.

Field

Available in 12, 20, 24, and 28 gauge as a well as 16, 32 and .410. Case colored receiver with select Turkish walnut. Checkereing is 24 lpi. Double triggers. Border engraving. Weight is about 5.5 lbs. for the 20 gauge. **NOTE:** Add $600 for 16, 32, and .410 bores.

NIB	Exc.	V.G.	Good	Fair	Poor
4500	3500	2400	1775	1100	500

Grade II

As above but with 65 percent coverage of English scroll. **NOTE:** Add $700 for 16, 32, and .410 bores.

NIB	Exc.	V.G.	Good	Fair	Poor
5500	4250	3200	1600	800	400

Grade III

As above but with deeply cut vine and leaf scroll with deluxe Turkish walnut and 65 percent coverage of English scroll. **NOTE:** Add $800 for 16, 32, and .410 bores.

NIB	Exc.	V.G.	Good	Fair	Poor
6500	5000	4000	3000	1650	400

DALY, CHARLES

Charles Daly was co-founder of the Schoverling & Daly sporting goods company in New York City in 1865. The company imported some of the better-made shotguns from Europe and Charles Daly was used as the brand name. The Daly trademark was sold several times over the years with the various owners importing guns from Belgium, Germany, Japan, Italy and other countries.

EARLY PRUSSIAN GUNS

Commander Over/Under Model 100

A boxlock over/under Anson & Deeley action shotgun chambered all gauges, choice of barrel length and chokes, double triggers (standard) or single-selective trigger. Blued with a checkered walnut stock. Manufactured in Belgium in the late 1930s.

NIB	Exc.	V.G.	Good	Fair	Poor
—	1000	750	475	275	200

Commander Over/Under Model 200

As above, with a better-grade walnut stock.

NIB	Exc.	V.G.	Good	Fair	Poor
—	1100	850	550	300	200

Superior Side-by-Side

As above, with an Anson & Deeley boxlock action and double triggers. Blued with a walnut stock. Not manufactured after 1933. **NOTE:** Add $600 for 20 gauge, $1000 for 10 gauge.

NIB	Exc.	V.G.	Good	Fair	Poor
—	1400	950	650	450	250

Empire Side-by-Side

As above, but engraved with a better grade of walnut. **NOTE:** Prices shown for Empire and Diamond grade models are for those manufactured by Sauer. Add 20 to 30 percent for Linder manufacture.

NIB	Exc.	V.G.	Good	Fair	Poor
—	3750	3000	2250	1250	600

Diamond Grade Side-by-Side

A deluxe version of the above. **NOTE:** Prices shown for Empire and Diamond grade models are for those manufactured by Sauer. Add 20 to 30 percent for Linder manufacture.

NIB	Exc.	V.G.	Good	Fair	Poor
—	5750	4500	3750	3000	1200

Regent Diamond Grade Side-by-Side

A custom order version of the above.

NIB	Exc.	V.G.	Good	Fair	Poor
—	11500	8500	7000	5500	2500

Empire Over/Under

A 12, 16, and 20 gauge Anson & Deeley boxlock shotgun with choice of barrel length and choke, double triggers and automatic ejectors. Engraved with fine quality scrollwork and walnut stock. Discontinued in 1933.

NIB	Exc.	V.G.	Good	Fair	Poor
—	3500	2750	2000	1150	500

Diamond Grade Over/Under

As above, but more finely finished.

NIB	Exc.	V.G.	Good	Fair	Poor
—	5500	3750	3250	2500	1250

SEXTUPLE SINGLE-BARREL TRAP

Empire Grade

A 12 gauge boxlock single-barrel shotgun with 30"-34" Full choke barrels, ventilated rib and automatic ejectors. The strong action features six locking lugs. Engraved with a walnut stock. Manufactured after 1933.

NIB	Exc.	V.G.	Good	Fair	Poor
—	2950	2450	1850	1500	750

Regent Diamond Grade

As above, with more engraving and a better grade walnut stock.

NIB	Exc.	V.G.	Good	Fair	Poor
—	7500	6300	5500	4500	2000

DRILLINGS

Superior Grade

A 12, 16, and 20 gauge over/under rifle/shotgun with a rifle barrel in .25-20, .25-35, or .30-30. Engraved with a walnut stock. Not manufactured after 1933.

NIB	Exc.	V.G.	Good	Fair	Poor
—	3700	2450	1800	1450	800

Diamond Grade

As above, with more engraving and a better grade of walnut in the stock.

NIB	Exc.	V.G.	Good	Fair	Poor
—	5250	4500	3750	3000	1500

Regent Diamond Grade

As above, with elaborate engraving and the highest quality walnut stock.

NIB	Exc.	V.G.	Good	Fair	Poor
—	12500	9500	7200	5800	3000

B.C. MIROKU GUNS

Empire Grade Side-by-Side

A 12, 16, and 20 gauge Anson and Deeley boxlock shotgun with 26", 28", and 30" barrels, various chokes, extractors, and a single trigger. Blued with a checkered walnut stock. Manufactured between 1968 and 1971. **NOTE:** Add 10 percent for ventilated rib barrels and/or 20 gauge.

NIB	Exc.	V.G.	Good	Fair	Poor
—	750	550	375	200	100

Superior Grade Single Barrel Trap

A 12 gauge boxlock shotgun with 32" or 34" ventilated rib barrels, Full choke, and automatic ejector. Blued with Monte Carlo walnut stock. Manufactured between 1968 and 1976.

NIB	Exc.	V.G.	Good	Fair	Poor
—	675	525	450	350	200

Over/Unders

A 12, 20, and 28 gauge and .410 bore boxlock shotgun with 26", 28", and 30" barrels with ventilated ribs. Various choke combinations were offered with single-selective triggers and automatic ejectors. Blued with checkered walnut stocks. The differences between the grades are the degree and quality of the engraving and the grade of walnut used for the stock. The smaller-bore guns bring a premium as listed. Manufactured between 1963 and 1976 by B.C. Miroku. **NOTE:** 20 gauge add 10 percent. 28 gauge add 20 percent. .410 add 30 percent.

Venture Grade

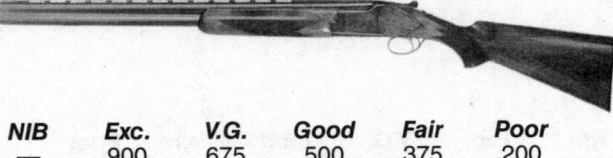

NIB	Exc.	V.G.	Good	Fair	Poor
—	900	675	500	375	200

Venture Grade Skeet or Trap

Offered with either 26" Skeet & Skeet or 30" Full choke.

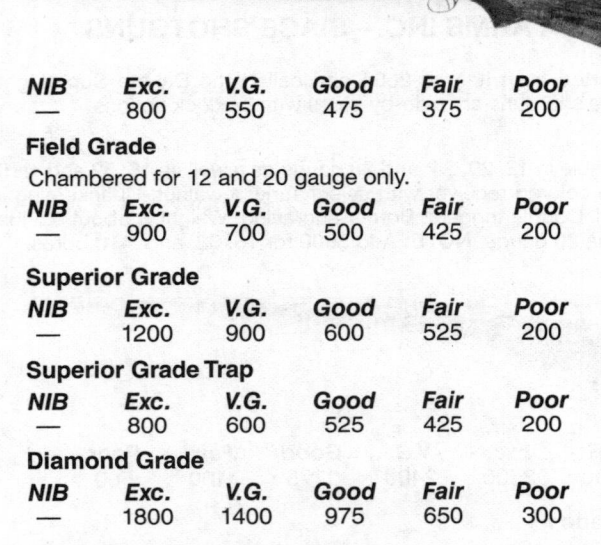

NIB	Exc.	V.G.	Good	Fair	Poor
—	800	550	475	375	200

Field Grade

Chambered for 12 and 20 gauge only.

NIB	Exc.	V.G.	Good	Fair	Poor
—	900	700	500	425	200

Superior Grade

NIB	Exc.	V.G.	Good	Fair	Poor
—	1200	900	600	525	200

Superior Grade Trap

NIB	Exc.	V.G.	Good	Fair	Poor
—	800	600	525	425	200

Diamond Grade

NIB	Exc.	V.G.	Good	Fair	Poor
—	1800	1400	975	650	300

Diamond Grade Trap or Skeet

With either 26" Skeet & Skeet or 30" Full choke barrels and Monte Carlo stocks. **NOTE:** Wide rib add 5 percent.

NIB	Exc.	V.G.	Good	Fair	Poor
—	1500	1100	800	650	350

ITALIAN MANUFACTURE
SEMI-AUTOMATIC SHOTGUNS

Manufactured by the firm of Breda in Milan, Italy. The semi-automatic "Novamatic" was produced in 1968. All other models began Italian production in 1976. Imported by KBI, Inc. until 2010.

Novamatic Lightweight

A 12 gauge semi-automatic shotgun with a 26" or 28" ventilated-rib barrel and screw-in choke tubes. The receiver is alloy, with checkered walnut stock. Imported under the Daly name in 1968 only.

NIB	Exc.	V.G.	Good	Fair	Poor
—	400	325	275	175	125

Novamatic Trap

As above, with a Monte Carlo stock and a 30" full choke barrel.

NIB	Exc.	V.G.	Good	Fair	Poor
—	415	340	290	200	150

Charles Daly Automatic

A 12 gauge Magnum semi-automatic shotgun with 26" or 28" ventilated rib barrels, screw-in choke tubes and a 5-shot magazine. There is a slug gun available with rifle sights. Checkered walnut grip in two versions—a pistol grip and an English-style straight grip. **NOTE**: The choke-tube model would be worth a 10 percent premium.

NIB	Exc.	V.G.	Good	Fair	Poor
—	475	395	300	225	150

Field Grade

Introduced in 1999, this model has several variations all in 12 gauge. The standard gun has a choice of 24", 26", 28", or 30" barrels with screw-in chokes and synthetic stocks. A slug gun is offered with 22" barrel in blue or nickel finish. A full coverage camo model is offered in the same configurations as the field grade. **NOTE**: Add $30 for nickel slug gun, add $100 for camo gun.

NIB	Exc.	V.G.	Good	Fair	Poor
425	365	255	200	150	100

Superior Grade Hunter

Offered in 12 gauge with choice of 26", 28", or 30" vent-rib barrels. Walnut stock with hand checkering. Gold trigger and gold highlights. Introduced in 1999.

NIB	Exc.	V.G.	Good	Fair	Poor
550	425	365	245	160	100

Superior Grade Sporting

Same as above but with a 28" or 30" ported barrel and select walnut stock.

NIB	Exc.	V.G.	Good	Fair	Poor
570	450	365	245	160	100

Superior Grade Trap

This 12 gauge model is offered with a choice of 30" or 32" vent-rib barrel. Walnut stock with hand checkering. Introduced in 1999.

NIB	Exc.	V.G.	Good	Fair	Poor
625	475	390	270	185	100

Field Hunter VR-MC

This series of 3" semi-automatic 12 gauges is finished in one of four Realtree/Advantage camo patterns or matte black. Barrels are 24", 26" or 28". Advantage Timber model is available in 20 gauge and black matte is available in 20 and 28 gauge. Add 15 percent for camo.

NIB	Exc.	V.G.	Good	Fair	Poor
425	365	255	200	150	100

Field Hunter VR-MC Youth

As above but with a 1.6-inch shorter stock and 22" barrel. In 20 gauge only.

NIB	Exc.	V.G.	Good	Fair	Poor
400	345	230	165	125	100

Superior II

New in 2007, the Superior II line of semi-autos features oil-finished Turkish walnut stocks and three chokes.

NIB	Exc.	V.G.	Good	Fair	Poor
600	525	395	275	200	100

Hunter

Available in 12 and 20 gauge with 26" or 28" barrel and 28 gauge with 26" barrel.

NIB	Exc.	V.G.	Good	Fair	Poor
600	525	395	275	200	100

Sport

In 12 gauge only with 28" or 30" ported barrel and wide rib.

NIB	Exc.	V.G.	Good	Fair	Poor
600	525	395	275	200	100

Trap

In 12 gauge, 30" ported barrel only with Monte Carlo comb and wide rib.

NIB	Exc.	V.G.	Good	Fair	Poor
650	550	425	275	200	100

Field Hunter Maxi-Mag VR-MC Semi-Auto

This 3.5" 12 gauge comes in one of three Realtree/Advantage camos and matte black with 24", 26" or 28" ported barrel. Add 15 percent for camo.

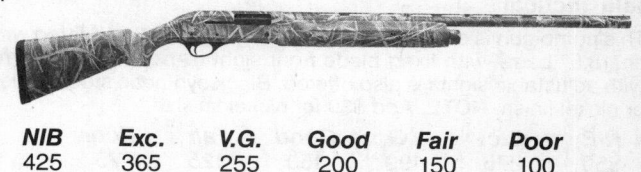

NIB	Exc.	V.G.	Good	Fair	Poor
425	365	255	200	150	100

TURKISH SHOTGUNS

Model 105

This 3" 12 gauge over/under features an engraved nickel-plated steel receiver, double triggers and extractors. Chokes are fixed Modified and Full with 28" barrels or Modified and Improved Cylinder with 26" barrels.

NIB	Exc.	V.G.	Good	Fair	Poor
600	450	395	300	175	100

Model 106/206

Similar to Model 105 but in 12, 20 and 28 gauge and .410 bore. The Model 106 has a blued receiver with raised gold ducks and a rounded pistol grip. All but the .410 include three screw-in chokes. Barrels are 26" or 28" in 12 and 20 gauge and 26" in 28 gauge and .410. Frames are scaled to gauge. **NOTE:** Add $50 for 28 and .410. Add $50 for model 206 with SST, ejectors.

NIB	Exc.	V.G.	Good	Fair	Poor
650	495	395	300	175	100

Model 306

This 3" side-by-side is offered in 12 and 20 gauge with 26" or 28" barrels. Turkish walnut stock, gold-plated single selective trigger and extractors. Three choke tubes.

NIB	Exc.	V.G.	Good	Fair	Poor
400	350	295	175	115	75

PUMP SHOTGUNS

Field Grade

This 12 gauge pump gun is offered with 24", 26", 28", or 30" barrels. With fixed chokes. A slug gun is offered with 18.5" barrels with blue or nickel finish. A camo version is also offered. First introduced in 1999. This model is also offered in 20 gauge in both full size and youth. **NOTE:** Add $10 for nickel gun, add $80 for full camo gun.

NIB	Exc.	V.G.	Good	Fair	Poor
300	225	165	125	100	65

Field Tactical

This pump gun is chambered for the 12 gauge shell and fitted with an 18.5" barrel with fixed blade front sight . An 18.5" slug barrel with adjustable sights is also offered. Black synthetic stock. Blued or nickel finish. **NOTE:** Add $30 for nickel finish.

NIB	Exc.	V.G.	Good	Fair	Poor
350	275	190	150	125	75

Field Hunter MM (Maxi-Mag)

This is a 12 gauge pump gun chambered for the 3.5" Magnum shell. Offered with choice of 24", 26", or 28" vent-rib ported barrels. Black synthetic stock with camo stock also available. Weight is about 6.75 lbs. **NOTE:** Add $50 for camo finish.

NIB	Exc.	V.G.	Good	Fair	Poor
275	225	150	125	100	65

Field Hunter Maxi-Mag VR-MC Pump

Newer versions of the Maxi-Mag are recognized by an updated fore-end and availability in Timber or Hardwoods camo or matte black. All are 3.5" 12 gauges with a 24", 26" or 28" ported barrel. **NOTE:** Add 15 percent for camo.

NIB	Exc.	V.G.	Good	Fair	Poor
350	300	255	200	150	100

OVER/UNDER GUNS

Country Squire Over/Under Folding

This model features a folding stock with over/under vent-rib barrels 25.5" in length, gold double triggers and walnut stock. Chokes are Full and Full.

NIB	Exc.	V.G.	Good	Fair	Poor
550	450	325	250	175	125

Field II Hunter

A 12, 20, 28, and .410 gauge over/under shotgun with 26" or 28" chrome-lined ventilated rib barrels with a crossbolt boxlock-action, single-selective trigger, and extractors. Blued with a stamped checkered walnut stock. Introduced in 1989. Weight for 12 gauge guns about 7 lbs. Weight for 28 and .410 guns about 6.75 lbs. **NOTE:** Add $150 for ejectors.

NIB	Exc.	V.G.	Good	Fair	Poor
900	775	575	400	250	200

Field Ultra Light

Introduced in 1999, this model is offered in either 12 or 20 gauge with 26" barrel choked Improved Cylinder/Modified. The receiver is aluminum alloy. Walnut stock with pistol grip and slim fore-end. Weight is approximately 5.5 lbs.

NIB	Exc.	V.G.	Good	Fair	Poor
950	850	650	450	—	—

Field III

This is an economy level model in 12 or 20 gauge, imported from Turkey in the 1980s.

NIB	Exc.	V.G.	Good	Fair	Poor
400	350	300	250	200	150

Empire

Similar to Field II Hunter with automatic ejectors, screw-in choke tubes, and a silver-finished receiver. The walnut stock is hand-checkered. Introduced in 1989.

NIB	Exc.	V.G.	Good	Fair	Poor
1150	1000	750	500	400	200

Empire II EDL Hunter

Offered in 12, 20, 28, and .410 bores this gun features 26" or 28" vent rib barrels (26" only on 28 or .410), choke tubes on the 12 and 20 gauge guns and fixed chokes on the 28 and .410 guns. Receiver has game scene engraving with nine gold enlays. Weight is 6.25 to 7.25 lbs. depending on gauge.

NIB	Exc.	V.G.	Good	Fair	Poor
2000	1500	1100	700	375	200

Empire Sporting

This model is offered in 12 gauge with a choice of 28" or 30" barrels. Fitted with a Monte Carlo stock and automatic ejectors.

NIB	Exc.	V.G.	Good	Fair	Poor
1850	1425	1000	600	375	200

Empire Grade Combination

This is an over/under with a 12 gauge top barrel and a rifle lower barrel. Rifle calibers are .22 Hornet, .223 Rem., .22-250, .243, .270, .308 and .30-06. Barrel length is 23.5". Weight is about 7.25 lbs.

NIB	Exc.	V.G.	Good	Fair	Poor
2190	1600	1150	800	375	200

Empire Trap

This 12 gauge model features a Monte Carlo stock with 30" barrels.

NIB	Exc.	V.G.	Good	Fair	Poor
2250	1650	1200	750	325	150

Empire Grade Trap Combo

This model features a 30" over/under barrel with an additional 32" single barrel. Buttstock has fully adjustable comb. Introduced in 1999. **NOTE:** Deduct $600 for non-adjustable stock.

NIB	Exc.	V.G.	Good	Fair	Poor
4000	3000	2000	1450	675	375

Diamond GTX DL Hunter

As above in 12 and 20 gauge Magnum with various barrel lengths and screw-in choke tubes, single trigger, automatic ejectors, and select walnut stock. Extra fancy walnut stock and hand engraved frame.

NIB	Exc.	V.G.	Good	Fair	Poor
9000	8000	6000	5000	2000	1000

Diamond GTX Sporting

This 12 gauge model features a choice of 28" or 30" barrels with automatic ejectors and Monte Carlo stock.

NIB	Exc.	V.G.	Good	Fair	Poor
5900	4500	2750	1250	900	450

Diamond GTX Trap or Skeet

As above, with 26" or 30" barrels. Available in 1989. **NOTE:** Wide rib add 5 percent.

NIB	Exc.	V.G.	Good	Fair	Poor
5900	4500	2750	1250	900	400

Diamond GTX Trap Combo

This model has a fully adjustable stock. Choice of 30" over/under barrels and 32" single barrel.

NIB	Exc.	V.G.	Good	Fair	Poor
7500	5700	4250	2650	1000	450

Presentation Grade

As above, with a Purdey-type boxlock action and engraved false sideplates. The stock is of deluxe French walnut. Discontinued in 1986.

NIB	Exc.	V.G.	Good	Fair	Poor
—	5500	3750	1650	900	450

Superior II

A 12, 20, 28, and .410 gauge over/under shotgun with 26" or 28" ventilated rib barrels, various chokes, single trigger, and automatic ejectors. Engraved, blued with a walnut stock. Weight for 12 and 20 gauge guns about 7 lbs. For 28 and .410 guns weight is about 6.75 lbs.

NIB	Exc.	V.G.	Good	Fair	Poor
625	550	350	300	200	150

Superior II Sporting

This 12 gauge model is fitted with a choice of 28" or 30" barrels. Monte Carlo stock and automatic ejectors.

NIB	Exc.	V.G.	Good	Fair	Poor
650	575	375	325	225	165

Superior Grade Trap

This 12 gauge gun is fitted with 30" barrels, Monte Carlo stock and automatic ejectors.

NIB	Exc.	V.G.	Good	Fair	Poor
1700	1250	900	625	425	200

Superior Grade Combination

This is an over/under with a 12 gauge top barrel and a rifle lower barrel. Rifle calibers are .22 Hornet, .223 Rem., and .30-06. Barrel length is 23.5". Weight is about 7.25 lbs.

NIB	Exc.	V.G.	Good	Fair	Poor
1480	1100	800	550	350	175

SINGLE-BARREL SHOTGUNS

Empire Trap Mono

This is a single barrel trap gun with choice of 30" or 32" barrels. Automatic ejectors and Monte Carlo fully adjustable stock. **NOTE:** Deduct $600 for non-adjustable stock.

NIB	Exc.	V.G.	Good	Fair	Poor
2450	1800	1250	900	375	175

Diamond GTX Mono

This model has a fully adjustable stock. Barrel choice is 30". Automatic ejectors are standard.

NIB	Exc.	V.G.	Good	Fair	Poor
6500	5250	3750	1750	900	400

SIDE-BY-SIDE GUNS

Field Hunter

A side-by-side boxlock gun chambered for 10, 12, 20, 28 and .410. Barrel length from 26" to 32" depending on gauge. Extractors are standard. Add $100 for ejectors. Weight from 8.75 lbs. to 6.75 lbs. depending on gauge. Nickel receiver with game scene engraving. **NOTE:** Add $40 for 28 and .410 guns, add $100 for automatic ejectors.

NIB	Exc.	V.G.	Good	Fair	Poor
1190	850	600	400	250	100

Superior Hunter

A 12, 20, and 28 gauge as well as .410 bore boxlock double-barrel shotgun with 26" or 28" barrels, various chokes, a boxlock action and single trigger. Blued with a walnut stock. In 2002 this model was offered in 10 gauge with 28" barrels. **NOTE:** Add $50 for 28 and .410 gauge guns.

NIB	Exc.	V.G.	Good	Fair	Poor
1660	1200	850	600	350	150

Empire Hunter

Offered in 12 and 20 gauge with 26" or 28" barrels. Chokes are fixed. Weight is about 7 lbs. Silver receiver with game scene engraving, straight stock, splinter forearm, automatic ejectors.

NIB	Exc.	V.G.	Good	Fair	Poor
2120	1500	1100	700	400	200

Diamond DL

Offered in 12, 20, 28, and .410 with 26" or 28" barrels and fixed chokes. Fancy walnut straight grip stock, hand detachable sidelocks, 100 percent hand engraving coverage. Hand fit and finished. Weight for 12 and 20 gauge guns is about 6.75 lbs., while the 28 and .410 guns weigh about 5.75 lbs. This model is generally made on special order only. **NOTE:** Add $450 for 28 and .410 bores.

NIB	Exc.	V.G.	Good	Fair	Poor
6700	5000	3500	1500	750	350

Diamond Regent DL

High grade model of above, with best quality engraving, hand-checkered AAA-grade walnut stock, fixed chokes. Limited importation in 1997.

NIB	Exc.	V.G.	Good	Fair	Poor
18000	16000	12500	—	—	—

Country Squire Side-by-Side Folding

This model features a folding stock with 25.5" barrels, gold double triggers and walnut stock. Chokes are Full and Full.

NIB	Exc.	V.G.	Good	Fair	Poor
475	375	275	200	145	100

Model 306

In 12 or 20 gauge with 26" or 28" barrels, choke tubes, single trigger and extractors. Imported from Turkey from 2006 to 2008.

NIB	Exc.	V.G.	Good	Fair	Poor
600	525	450	300	200	150

Classic Coach

Same features as Model 306 above, except with 20" barrels and in 12 gauge only.

NIB	Exc.	V.G.	Good	Fair	Poor
650	575	500	350	200	150

RIFLES

Field Grade Mauser 98

This bolt-action rifle is offered in a wide variety of calibers from .243 Win. to .458 Win. Mag. Barrel length is 23" for all calibers. Stock is black synthetic. Open sights. Add $175 for .375 H&H and .458 Win. Mag. **NOTE:** Add $50 for stainless steel.

NIB	Exc.	V.G.	Good	Fair	Poor
460	350	300	225	150	100

Field Grade Mini-Mauser 98

This version is chambered for short cartridges such as the .22 Hornet, .223, .22-250, and 7.62x39mm. Barrel length is 19.25". Magazine capacity is 5 rounds.

NIB	Exc.	V.G.	Good	Fair	Poor
600	475	350	250	175	125

Superior Grade Mauser 98

This model is similar to the Field Grade Mauser with the addition of a hand-checkered walnut stock.

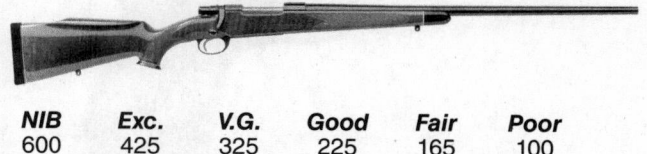

NIB	Exc.	V.G.	Good	Fair	Poor
600	425	325	225	165	100

Superior Grade Mini-Mauser 98

Same as the Field Grade Mini-Mauser with the addition of a hand-checkered walnut stock.

NIB	Exc.	V.G.	Good	Fair	Poor
600	450	325	250	150	100

Field Grade Rimfires

Chambered for .22 LR cartridge and fitted with a 22" barrel in the bolt-action version, 20" barrel in semi-auto version or 17.5" barrel in bolt-action. Youth model, or 16.25" barrel in bolt-action single-shot True Youth model. **NOTE**: Add $25 for True Youth model.

NIB	Exc.	V.G.	Good	Fair	Poor
120	100	75	50	25	10

Superior Grade Rimfires

Chambered for .22 LR or .22 Magnum or .22 Hornet in bolt-action or .22 LR semi-automatic. Walnut stock with checkering. Open sights. **NOTE**: Add $20 for .22 Magnum model and $170 for .22 Hornet model.

NIB	Exc.	V.G.	Good	Fair	Poor
175	125	100	75	50	25

This version was introduced in 2005 and is chambered for the .22 Long Rifle, .22 WMR, or the .17 HMR cartridges. Fitted with a 22" barrel with open sights on the .22 LR and drilled and tapped for scope mounts on the .22 WMR and .17 HMR models. Oiled walnut stocks with checkering. **NOTE**: Add $40 for .22 Mag. model and $75 for .17 HMR.

NIB	Exc.	V.G.	Good	Fair	Poor
260	200	175	150	125	100

Empire Grade Rimfires

Empire Grade has select walnut stock with 24 lpi hand-cut checkering. Grip and forearm caps highly polished and blued metal finish. Same configurations as Superior Grade rifles. **NOTE**: Add $20 For .22 Mag. model and $100 for .22 Hornet model.

NIB	Exc.	V.G.	Good	Fair	Poor
335	275	225	175	125	100

Superior Grade Express

Chambered for the .30-06 cartridge and fitted with 23.5" barrel. Open sights with dovetail receiver for scope mounting. Silver receiver with game scene engraving. Checkered walnut stock with sling swivels. Weight is about 7.75 lbs.

NIB	Exc.	V.G.	Good	Fair	Poor
3250	2700	1800	1475	1000	500

Empire Express

Chambered for the .30-06, .375H&H, or .416 Rigby cartridge with open sights and dovetail receiver for scope mounting. Barrel length is 23.5". Checkered walnut stock with Bavarian-style cheekpiece. Silver game scene engraved receiver. Weight is about 8 lbs. **NOTE**: Add $700 for .375 H&H and .416 Rigby models.

NIB	Exc.	V.G.	Good	Fair	Poor
3600	3000	2300	1775	1250	600

DM-4 Series

This series of rifles and carbines was manufactured in 2008 and 2009 with forged aluminum alloy receivers, manganese phosphate or stainless barrels, forward assist and other features typically found on quality made AR-type models. All were chambered in 5.56 NATO. Many of the popular AR configurations were offered with 16" or 20" barrels, sighting and grip options, mounting rails, finishes and other regular features found in the AR family. Prices shown are for standard DM-4 Carbine. The many available options can double these values.

NIB	Exc.	V.G.	Good	Fair	Poor
950	825	700	500	—	—

HANDGUNS

Daly ZDA

Introduced in 2005 this pistol is chambered for the 9mm or .40 S&W cartridge. Fitted with a 4.5" ramped barrel. Ambidextrous slide release/dececker/lock as well as magazine release. Loaded chamber indicator. Magazine capacity is 15 rounds for 9mm and 12 rounds for the .40 S&W.

NIB	Exc.	V.G.	Good	Fair	Poor
590	450	375	300	175	100

Field 1911-A1 FS/MS/CS

Chambered for .45 ACP with a choice of 5" (FS), 4" (MS), or 3.5" (CS) barrel and various special features such as front and rear slide serrations, extended beavertail safety, and lightweight trigger. Magazine capacity is 8 rounds. Overall length is 8.75".

NIB	Exc.	V.G.	Good	Fair	Poor
575	400	300	200	175	115

Superior 1911-A1 EFS/EMS/ECS

Same as the Field Grade described above but with a blued frame and stainless steel slide. Introduced in 1999.

NIB	Exc.	V.G.	Good	Fair	Poor
550	450	350	200	175	115

Empire 1911-A1 EFS

Same as the Field Grade but in full stainless with both stainless steel slide and frame. Introduced in 1999.

NIB	Exc.	V.G.	Good	Fair	Poor
630	475	350	225	195	125

Field 1911-A2P

Same as above but with 10-round magazine.

NIB	Exc.	V.G.	Good	Fair	Poor
570	450	350	225	195	125

.22 Caliber Conversion Kit

Offered with adjustable sights for models with 5" barrel only. First offered in 1999.

NIB	Exc.	V.G.	Good	Fair	Poor
200	150	100	65	45	25

Field 1911-A1 PC

This model is fitted with a 4" barrel and slide. It also has a polymer frame. Produced under license from STI. Introduced in 1999.

NIB	Exc.	V.G.	Good	Fair	Poor
575	400	300	200	175	115

Superior 1911-A1 PC

Same as the model above but with stainless steel slide and black polymer frame. Introduced in 1999.

NIB	Exc.	V.G.	Good	Fair	Poor
595	425	325	225	195	125

Field 1911 Target EFST

Fitted with a 5" barrel and chambered for the .45 ACP cartridge. Eight-round magazine. Blued finish. Fully adjustable rear sight with dovetail front sight. Weight is about 40 oz.

NIB	Exc.	V.G.	Good	Fair	Poor
620	475	350	240	195	125

Empire 1911 Target EFST

As above but with stainless steel finish.

NIB	Exc.	V.G.	Good	Fair	Poor
790	600	475	350	240	125

Empire Custom Match Target

Same as Empire target but with hand polished stainless steel finish with 20 lpi checkered front strap.

NIB	Exc.	V.G.	Good	Fair	Poor
800	600	500	375	255	135

Daly HP

Introduced in 2003 this U.S.-made 9mm pistol is similar to the famous Browning Hi-Power. Fitted with a 5" barrel. XS sighting system. Weight is about 35 oz.

NIB	Exc.	V.G.	Good	Fair	Poor
550	400	350	225	195	125

Daly M-5 Government

This is a polymer frame pistol chambered for the 9mm, .40 S&W, or the .45 ACP cartridge. Fitted with a 5" barrel, high rise beavertail and ambidextrous safety. Low profile sights. Weight is around 34 oz. Made in Israel by BUL. Introduced in 2003.

NIB	Exc.	V.G.	Good	Fair	Poor
720	575	400	275	225	100

Daly M-5 Commander

Same as above but fitted with a 4.375" barrel. Weight is about 30 oz.

NIB	Exc.	V.G.	Good	Fair	Poor
720	575	400	275	225	100

Daly M-5 Ultra-X

This is an ultra compact model.

NIB	Exc.	V.G.	Good	Fair	Poor
720	575	400	275	225	100

Daly M-5 IPSC

This model has a 5" barrel and is fitted with a stainless steel slide with adjustable sights. Flared and lowered ejection port and extended mag release. Weight is about 34 oz.

NIB	Exc.	V.G.	Good	Fair	Poor
1500	1150	725	600	325	125

Daly Classic 1873 Single-Action Revolver

Chambered for the .45 Colt or the .357 Mag., this revolver is offered with 4.75", 5.5", or 7.5" barrel. Choice of walnut or simulated Ivory grips. Stainless steel, blue or case colored finish. Introduced in 2005. Imported from Italy. **NOTE:** Add $30 for steel backstrap and trigger guard. Add $200 for stainless steel.

NIB	Exc.	V.G.	Good	Fair	Poor
450	350	285	250	195	150

DAN ARMS OF AMERICA
Allentown, Pennsylvania

These are Italian-made shotguns manufactured by Silmer and imported by Dan Arms of America. Production ceased in 1988.

SIDE-BY-SIDES

Field Grade

A boxlock shotgun chambered for all gauges with 26" or 28" barrels, various choke combinations, double triggers and extractors. Blued with a walnut stock.

NIB	Exc.	V.G.	Good	Fair	Poor
—	325	265	225	150	125

Deluxe Field Grade

As above, with a single trigger and automatic ejectors.

NIB	Exc.	V.G.	Good	Fair	Poor
—	465	400	325	250	200

OVER/UNDERS

Lux Grade I

A 12 and 20 gauge over/under shotgun with a 26", 28" or 30" ventilated rib barrels, double triggers and extractors. Blued finish with a walnut stock.

NIB	Exc.	V.G.	Good	Fair	Poor
—	325	265	200	150	100

Lux Grade II

As above, in 12 gauge only with a single trigger.

NIB	Exc.	V.G.	Good	Fair	Poor
—	350	300	250	200	150

Lux Grade III

As above, in 20 gauge only with automatic ejectors.

NIB	Exc.	V.G.	Good	Fair	Poor
—	400	325	275	225	175

Lux Grade IV

As above in 12 gauge only with screw-in choke tubes.

NIB	Exc.	V.G.	Good	Fair	Poor
—	450	375	325	275	200

Silver Snipe

A 12 or 20 gauge shotgun manufactured to custom order with engraved false sideplates and a select walnut stock.

NIB	Exc.	V.G.	Good	Fair	Poor
—	1250	1000	800	600	350

DANCE & BROTHERS CONFEDERATE REVOLVERS
Columbia, Texas

J.H., G.P., and D.E. Dance began production of percussion revolvers for the Confederate States of America in Columbia, Texas, in mid-1862, moving to Anderson, Texas, in early 1864. Based on surviving serial numbers, the combined output at both places did not exceed 350 pistols. Most of these were in the "Army" (.44 caliber) size but a limited number of "Navy" (.36 caliber) were also manufactured. Nearly all are distinguished by the absence of a "recoil shield" on the frame behind the cylinders. As Colt M1851 "Navy" revolvers closely resemble the Dance Navy revolvers, great care must be exercised in examining revolvers purported to be Dance Navies.

.36 Caliber

Courtesy Milwaukee Public Museum, Milwaukee, Wisconsin

NIB	Exc.	V.G.	Good	Fair	Poor
—	—	85000	67500	20000	7000

.44 Caliber

NIB	Exc.	V.G.	Good	Fair	Poor
—	—	90000	68000	20000	5500

DANSK REKYLRIFFEL SYNDIKAT
Copenhagen, Denmark

This firm was founded in 1896. In 1936 it became known as Madsen, makers of the famous Madsen light machine gun. The Schouboe pistols were designed by Jens Schouboe, the chief engineer for Dansk. They were developed in 1900-1902. The first year of manufacture was in 1902.

Schouboe Model 1902

A 7.65mm caliber semi-automatic pistol with a conventional blowback design. Production began in 1903 and ended in 1908, with fewer than 1,000 manufactured.

Courtesy James Rankin

NIB	Exc.	V.G.	Good	Fair	Poor
—	15500	12000	8200	5000	3000

Schouboe Model 1904

A semi-automatic pistol in caliber 11.35mm. The Model 1904 was an enlarged Model 1902. The name Dansk Rekylriffel is stamped on the slide.

Courtesy James Rankin

NIB	Exc.	V.G.	Good	Fair	Poor
—	24500	20500	16500	11000	5000

Schouboe Model 1907

An 11.35mm caliber semi-automatic pistol designed to fire a 55-grain, copper-aluminum-and-wood projectile at a velocity of 1625 fps. The pistol has the name Dansk Rekylriffel and Schouboe stamped on the slide. Some of these pistols had grip frames slotted for stocks. Five hundred were manufactured before production stopped in 1917. **NOTE:** Combination holster/shoulder stocks were made for this model, but are extremely rare. If present with a pistol, they would add approximately $5,000 to the value.

Courtesy James Rankin

NIB	Exc.	V.G.	Good	Fair	Poor
—	24000	20000	16000	10500	5000

Schouboe Model 1907 9mm

As above but chambered for the 9mm cartridge. Very few of these pistols were built.

Courtesy James Rankin

NIB	Exc.	V.G.	Good	Fair	Poor
—	14000	11000	8250	5500	3000

Schouboe Model 1910/12

This model is chambered for the 11.35mm cartridge and was involved in U.S. military tests in 1912.

Courtesy James Rankin

NIB	Exc.	V.G.	Good	Fair	Poor
—	24500	21500	16500	11000	5000

Schouboe Model 1916

This model is also chambered for the 11.35mm cartridge. It is fitted with a very large slide release and safety lever on the left side of the pistol. The name of the manufacturer is stamped on the slide.

Courtesy James Rankin

NIB	Exc.	V.G.	Good	Fair	Poor
—	24000	21050	16500	11000	5000

DARDICK CORP.
Hamden, Connecticut

Perhaps one of the most unusual firearms to have been designed and marketed in the United States during the 20th century. It utilizes a "tround," which is a triangular plastic case enclosing a cartridge. The action of these arms consists of a revolving carrier that brings the trounds from the magazine into line with the barrel. Discontinued in 1962. **NOTE:** Values below are for boxed examples with supply of tround ammunition. Deduct 50 to 75 percent for unboxed, loose examples without ammunition.

Series 110

3" barrel. Chambered in .38 Dardick only.

NIB	Exc.	V.G.	Good	Fair	Poor
—	2500	1650	1500	1100	500

Series 1500

6" barrel. Chambered for the .22, .30, and the .38 Dardick. **NOTE:** A carbine conversion kit consisting of a long barrel and shoulder stock was available and would bring a premium of $750 to $1400 depending on the condition.

NIB	Exc.	V.G.	Good	Fair	Poor
—	5000	3000	1750	1500	900

DARLING, B. & B. M.
Belingham, Massachusetts

Pepperbox Pistol

A .30 caliber percussion 6-shot pepperbox with 3.25" length barrels. Blued with walnut grips. This is one of the rarest American pepperboxes and copies are known to have been made. Consequently, prospective purchasers are advised to secure a qualified appraisal prior to acquisition. Manufactured during the late 1830s.

NIB	Exc.	V.G.	Good	Fair	Poor
—	—	4950	1950	600	600

DARNE, S. A.
St. Etienne, France

SIDE-BY-SIDE SHOTGUNS

A 12, 16, 20, or 28 gauge sliding breech double-barrel shotgun manufactured in a variety of barrel lengths and with numerous optional features. Manufactured from 1881 to 1979. **NOTE:** Darnes have been undergoing a surge in popularity in the last few years because of their unique design. Depending on the circumstances, and the amount of factory engraving and ornamentation present, individual examples may bring considerably in excess of the values listed below. Deduct 25 percent for 2.5-inch chambers.

Model R11

NIB	Exc.	V.G.	Good	Fair	Poor
—	2500	2000	1200	800	550

Model R13

NIB	Exc.	V.G.	Good	Fair	Poor
—	3000	2600	2250	1100	750

Model R15

NIB	Exc.	V.G.	Good	Fair	Poor
—	4000	3000	2450	1500	750

Model V19

NIB	Exc.	V.G.	Good	Fair	Poor
—	4500	3600	2950	2050	1250

Model V22

NIB	Exc.	V.G.	Good	Fair	Poor
—	5000	4100	3500	2500	1700

Model V Hors Series No. I

NIB	Exc.	V.G.	Good	Fair	Poor
—	7500	5500	4050	3250	1500

DAVENPORT FIREARMS CO.
Providence, Rhode Island
Norwich, Connecticut

Text and prices by Nick Niles. William Hastings Davenport's company also made and marked double-barrel, visible hammer guns in Providence, R.I. on Orange St., 1880-1882 and in Norwich, Conn. ca. 1890-1909. All are monobloc designs of which there were four models. The 1st model made at Providence, ca. 1881, had hammers rising out of the boxlock frame. The 2nd model, made in Norwich, Conn. about 1898, is a typical boxlock. The 3rd model made in Norwich, Conn., ca. 1909, has small sidelocks set in larger boxlock frames. Its barrels have unnotched extensions and notched underlugs. The 4th model, also from Norwich, possibly made after the 1901 takeover by Hopkins & Allen, also has sidelocks set in boxlock frames but the barrels have half moon lugs and notched barrel extensions. Few Davenport doubles are seen although single barrel guns are often found.

1st Model

NIB	Exc.	V.G.	Good	Fair	Poor
—	1200	875	500	400	300

2nd Model

Courtesy Nick Niles

NIB	Exc.	V.G.	Good	Fair	Poor
—	700	450	300	200	150

3rd Model

NIB	Exc.	V.G.	Good	Fair	Poor
—	1200	875	500	400	300

4th Model

NIB	Exc.	V.G.	Good	Fair	Poor
—	900	450	300	250	200

Single-Barrel Shotgun

A 10, 12, 16, or 20 gauge side-hammer single-barrel shotgun with 26" to 36" barrels and extractors. Blued, case hardened with a walnut stock. Manufactured from approximately 1880 to 1915.

NIB	Exc.	V.G.	Good	Fair	Poor
—	—	450	300	150	75

8 Gauge Goose Gun

As above, in 8 gauge.

NIB	Exc.	V.G.	Good	Fair	Poor
—	—	550	250	175	100

Falling Block Single-Shot Rifle

A .22, .25, or .32 rimfire single-shot rifle with a 24" round barrel and exposed hammer. Blued with a walnut stock. The barrel marked "The W.H. Davenport Fire Arms Co. Norwich, Conn. U.S.A. Patented Dec. 15, 1891." Manufactured between 1891 and 1910.

NIB	Exc.	V.G.	Good	Fair	Poor
—	—	675	425	325	200

DAVIDSON, F.A.
Eibar, Spain

Arms bearing this name were manufactured in Spain by Fabrica De Armas.

Model 63B

A 12, 16, 20, 28, or .410 bore double-barrel boxlock shotgun with 25" to 30" barrels. Engraved, nickel-plated with a walnut stock. Made from 1963 to 1976.

NIB	Exc.	V.G.	Good	Fair	Poor
—	350	225	200	150	100

Model 69 SL

A 12 or 20 gauge sidelock double-barrel shotgun with 26" or 28" barrels and finished as above.

NIB	Exc.	V.G.	Good	Fair	Poor
—	425	350	300	225	125

Stagecoach Model 73

A 12 or 20 gauge Magnum sidelock double-barrel shotgun with 20" barrels and exposed hammers.

NIB	Exc.	V.G.	Good	Fair	Poor
—	300	250	175	150	100

DAVIS, A. JR.
Stafford, Connecticut

Under Hammer Pistol

A .31 caliber single-shot under hammer percussion pistol with a 7.5" half octagonal barrel and brass frame. The grips are of maple and formed with a bottom tip. The top strap marked "A. Davis Jr./ Stafford Conn."

NIB	Exc.	V.G.	Good	Fair	Poor
—	—	1250	775	350	100

DAVIS, N.R. & CO./DAVIS, N.R. & SONS
(See also Davis-Warner Arms Corporation)

Manufacturer of percussion, and later, cartridge shotguns from 1853 to 1919. The cartridge shotguns embodied Nathan R. Davis' patented improvements of 1879, 1884, and 1886. Though only made in plain, serviceable grades, Davis shotguns were extremely well made and lived up to the company's motto "As Good as the Best."

Grade A and B Hammerless Shotguns

Made in 12 or 16 gauge with 28", 30", or 32" barrels.

NIB	Exc.	V.G.	Good	Fair	Poor
—	900	675	400	200	100

Grade C Hammerless Shotgun

Made in 10 gauge with 30" or 32" barrels.

NIB	Exc.	V.G.	Good	Fair	Poor
—	900	675	400	200	100

Grade D and DS Hammer Shotguns
Made in 12 or 16 gauge with 28", 30", or 32" barrels.

NIB	Exc.	V.G.	Good	Fair	Poor
—	875	675	425	200	100

Grade E and F Single-Barrel Shotguns
Made in 12 or 16 gauge with 30" or 32" barrels.

NIB	Exc.	V.G.	Good	Fair	Poor
—	350	250	125	75	50

N.R. DAVIS BRAND

1st Button Opener—Hammer Boxlock
NIB	Exc.	V.G.	Good	Fair	Poor
—	475	325	250	150	100

1st Sidelever—Hammer Boxlock
NIB	Exc.	V.G.	Good	Fair	Poor
—	475	325	250	150	100

2nd Sidelever—Hammer Boxlock

Courtesy Nick Niles, Paul Goodwin photo

NIB	Exc.	V.G.	Good	Fair	Poor
—	475	325	250	150	100

1st Toplever—Hammer Boxlock

Courtesy Nick Niles, Paul Goodwin photo

NIB	Exc.	V.G.	Good	Fair	Poor
—	475	325	250	150	100

2nd Toplever—Hammer Boxlock
NIB	Exc.	V.G.	Good	Fair	Poor
—	475	325	250	150	100

3rd Toplever—Hammer Boxlock
NIB	Exc.	V.G.	Good	Fair	Poor
—	475	325	250	150	100

1879 1st Model—Hammer Boxlock
NIB	Exc.	V.G.	Good	Fair	Poor
—	475	325	250	150	100

1879 2nd Model—Damascus Barrel—Hammer Boxlock
NIB	Exc.	V.G.	Good	Fair	Poor
—	475	325	250	150	100

1885—Hammerless Boxlock
NIB	Exc.	V.G.	Good	Fair	Poor
—	475	325	250	150	100

1886 Rival—Hammerless Boxlock
NIB	Exc.	V.G.	Good	Fair	Poor
—	350	275	200	150	100

1886 Rival Improved—Hammerless Boxlock
NIB	Exc.	V.G.	Good	Fair	Poor
—	350	275	200	150	100

1897 "G" —Hammer Sidelock
NIB	Exc.	V.G.	Good	Fair	Poor
—	350	275	200	150	100

N.R. DAVIS & SONS BRAND

Hammerless 1900—Boxlock
NIB	Exc.	V.G.	Good	Fair	Poor
—	350	275	200	150	100

Hammerless A—Damascus Barrel—Boxlock
NIB	Exc.	V.G.	Good	Fair	Poor
—	350	275	200	150	100

Hammerless B—Boxlock
NIB	Exc.	V.G.	Good	Fair	Poor
—	350	275	200	150	100

Hammerless C—Engraved Damascus Barrel—Boxlock
NIB	Exc.	V.G.	Good	Fair	Poor
—	400	325	250	150	100

Hammerless D—Engraved—Boxlock
NIB	Exc.	V.G.	Good	Fair	Poor
—	475	375	300	250	200

New Model—Hammerless Boxlock
NIB	Exc.	V.G.	Good	Fair	Poor
—	350	275	200	150	100

"D.S." Straight Stock—Engraved—Hammerless Boxlock
NIB	Exc.	V.G.	Good	Fair	Poor
—	350	275	200	150	100

Davis Special—Hammerless Boxlock
NIB	Exc.	V.G.	Good	Fair	Poor
—	925	650	500	400	250

Davis "B" Manga Steel—Hammerless Boxlock
NIB	Exc.	V.G.	Good	Fair	Poor
—	925	650	500	400	250

CRESCENT-DAVIS BRAND

Model No. 600—Hammerless Boxlock
NIB	Exc.	V.G.	Good	Fair	Poor
—	700	550	300	200	100

Model No. 900—Hammerless Boxlock

NIB	Exc.	V.G.	Good	Fair	Poor
—	700	550	300	200	100

DAVIS & BOZEMAN
Central, Alabama

Pattern 1841 Rifle

A .58 caliber single-shot percussion rifle with a 33" round barrel, full walnut stock, two barrel bands, brass furniture and an iron ramrod. The lock marked "D. & B. Ala." as well as the serial number and date of manufacture.

NIB	Exc.	V.G.	Good	Fair	Poor
—	—	40000	16500	3500	1750

DAVIS INDUSTRIES
Mira Loma, California

This company was founded in 1987 by Jim Davis in Chino, California. The company ceased operations in 2001. Remaining stocks and production machinery purchased by Cobra Enterprises, 1960 S. Milestone Drive, Suite F, Salt Lake City, UT 84104.

D-Series Deringer

A .22 LR, .22 WMR, .25 ACP and .32 ACP caliber double-barrel over/under derringer with 2.4" barrels. Black Teflon or chrome-plated finish with laminated wood grips. Weighs approximately 9.5 oz.

NIB	Exc.	V.G.	Good	Fair	Poor
150	75	40	30	25	20

Big Bore D-Series

Similar to the above model but chambered for the .38 Special and .32 H&R Magnum. Barrel length is 2.75". Weighs about 11.5 oz.

NIB	Exc.	V.G.	Good	Fair	Poor
150	75	40	30	25	20

Long Bore D-Series

Introduced in 1994 this two-shot pistol is chambered for the .22 LR , .22 WMR, .32 ACP, .32 H&R Mag., .380 ACP, 9mm, and .38 Special cartridges. Barrel length is 3.75", overall length is 5.65" and weight is approximately 13 oz.

NIB	Exc.	V.G.	Good	Fair	Poor
150	75	40	30	25	20

P-32

A .32-caliber semi-automatic pistol with a 2.8" barrel and 6-shot magazine. Black Teflon or chrome-plated finish with laminated wood grips. Overall length is 5.4". Weighs approximately 22 oz.

NIB	Exc.	V.G.	Good	Fair	Poor
150	75	40	30	25	20

P-380

As above, in .380 caliber.

NIB	Exc.	V.G.	Good	Fair	Poor
175	85	65	50	40	30

DAVIS-WARNER ARMS CORPORATION
Norwich, Connecticut

Established in 1917, when N.R. Davis & Sons purchased the Warner Arms Company. Manufactured shotguns, as well as revolvers and semi-automatic pistols. Ceased operations in 1930. The Crescent Arms Company purchased the proprietary rights to the name and briefly assembled shotguns under the name (probably from parts acquired in the purchase) until Crescent was in turn purchased by J.C. Stevens. Initially, the Davis-Warner shotguns were identical to those made by Davis, but they subsequently made a Davis Grade B.S. Hammerless, Davis-Warner Expert and Davis Grade D.S. The pistols made by the company included .32 caliber revolvers and two Browning Patent semi-automatics made in Belgium for the company.

Davis Grade B.S. Hammerless Shotgun

Made in 12, 16, or 20 gauge with 28", 30", or 32" barrels.

Courtesy William Hammond

NIB	Exc.	V.G.	Good	Fair	Poor
—	875	650	400	200	100

Davis-Warner Expert Hammerless

Made in 12, 16, or 20 gauge with 26", 28", 30", or 32" barrels.

Courtesy Nick Niles, Paul Goodwin photo

NIB	Exc.	V.G.	Good	Fair	Poor
—	875	650	400	200	100

"BS"—Hammerless Boxlock

NIB	Exc.	V.G.	Good	Fair	Poor
—	350	275	200	150	100

"Maximin"—Hammerless Boxlock

Courtesy Nick Niles, Paul Goodwin photo

NIB	Exc.	V.G.	Good	Fair	Poor
—	475	325	250	200	150

"DS"—Hammerless Boxlock

NIB	Exc.	V.G.	Good	Fair	Poor
—	350	275	200	150	100

Deluxe—Hammerless Boxlock

NIB	Exc.	V.G.	Good	Fair	Poor
—	350	275	200	150	100

Premier—Hammerless Boxlock

NIB	Exc.	V.G.	Good	Fair	Poor
—	350	275	200	150	100

Peerless Ejector—Hammerless Boxlock

Courtesy Nick Niles, Paul Goodwin photo

NIB	Exc.	V.G.	Good	Fair	Poor
—	475	325	250	200	150

Hypower—Hammerless Boxlock

NIB	Exc.	V.G.	Good	Fair	Poor
—	475	325	250	200	150

Ajax (Model 800)

Courtesy Nick Niles, Paul Goodwin photo

NIB	Exc.	V.G.	Good	Fair	Poor
—	475	325	250	150	100

Ajax—Hammerless Boxlock

Courtesy Nick Niles, Paul Goodwin photo

NIB	Exc.	V.G.	Good	Fair	Poor
—	350	275	200	150	100

Certified (Savage)

Courtesy Nick Niles, Paul Goodwin photo

NIB	Exc.	V.G.	Good	Fair	Poor
—	475	325	250	150	100

Deluxe Special (Model 805)

Automatic ejectors.

NIB	Exc.	V.G.	Good	Fair	Poor
—	575	450	300	200	150

Premier Special (Model 802)

NIB	Exc.	V.G.	Good	Fair	Poor
—	575	450	300	200	150

Premier (Model 801)

NIB	Exc.	V.G.	Good	Fair	Poor
—	475	325	250	150	100

Warner Infallible Semi-Automatic Pistol

Fyrberg Patent .32 ACP. Not a particularly robust design.

NIB	Exc.	V.G.	Good	Fair	Poor
—	350	275	175	125	75

Davis-Warner Swing-Out Revolver

Double-action .32 caliber revolver with a 5" or 6" barrel.

NIB	Exc.	V.G.	Good	Fair	Poor
—	200	150	120	75	50

Davis-Warner Semi-Automatic Pistols

Browning Patent .25 ACP, .32 ACP or .380 caliber pistols.

NIB	Exc.	V.G.	Good	Fair	Poor
—	350	275	175	125	75

DAW, G. H.
London, England

Revolver

A .38 caliber double-action percussion revolver with a 5.5" barrel marked "George H. Daw, 57 Threadneedle St. London, Patent No. 112." Blued, with walnut grips. Manufactured in the 1860s.

NIB	Exc.	V.G.	Good	Fair	Poor
—	—	5750	3500	1975	1000

DEANE-HARDING
London, England

Revolver

A .44 caliber percussion revolver with a 5.25" barrel and 5-shot cylinder. Blued, case hardened with walnut grips. Manufactured during the late 1850s.

Courtesy Bonhams & Butterfields, San Francisco, California

NIB	Exc.	V.G.	Good	Fair	Poor
—	—	8500	2750	1475	850

DECKER, WILHELM
Zella St. Blasii, Germany

A 6.35mm double-action revolver with a 6-shot cylinder and concealed hammer. Unusual bar-type trigger design. Blued with plastic grips. Manufactured prior to 1914. Very few of these revolvers were produced.

Revolver

NIB	Exc.	V.G.	Good	Fair	Poor
—	2100	1500	750	325	100

DEMIRETT, J.
Montpelier, Vermont

Under-Hammer Pistol

A .27 caliber single-shot percussion pistol with 3" to 8" barrels and an under hammer. The barrel marked "J. Demerrit / Montpelier / Vermont." Blued with maple, walnut or stag horn grips. Active from 1866 to the mid-1880s.

NIB	Exc.	V.G.	Good	Fair	Poor
—	—	2700	825	350	200

DEMRO
Manchester, Connecticut

XF-7 Wasp Carbine

A 9mm or .45-caliber semi-automatic carbine with a 16.5" barrel and folding stock. Fires from open bolt.

NIB	Exc.	V.G.	Good	Fair	Poor
—	750	600	450	300	150

T.A.C. Model 1

As above, with a fixed stock.

NIB	Exc.	V.G.	Good	Fair	Poor
—	750	600	450	300	150

DERINGER REVOLVER AND PISTOL CO.
Philadelphia, Pennsylvania

After Henry Deringer's death, his name was used by I.J. Clark who manufactured rimfire revolvers on Charles Foehl's patents between 1870 and 1879.

Deringer Model I

A .22 caliber spur trigger revolver with a hinged octagonal barrel and 7-shot cylinder. Manufactured circa 1873.

NIB	Exc.	V.G.	Good	Fair	Poor
—	—	—	650	275	150

Deringer Model II

As above, with a round barrel and also available in .32 caliber.

NIB	Exc.	V.G.	Good	Fair	Poor
—	—	—	425	200	100

Centennial 1876

A .22, .32, or .38 caliber solid frame revolver.

NIB	Exc.	V.G.	Good	Fair	Poor
—	—	—	900	450	200

DERINGER RIFLES AND PISTOLS, HENRY
Philadelphia, Pennsylvania

Henry Deringer Sr. and his son, Henry Jr., were well established in Philadelphia by the close of the War of 1812, having made both sporting and military rifles at that place since the turn of the century. Henry Jr. continued in the gun trade until the outbreak of the American Civil War, primarily producing flintlock and percussion military rifles, at least 2,500 "Northwest guns" and 1,200 rifles for the Indian trade, a few percussion martial pistols, but most importantly the percussion pocket pistols that became so popular that they took on his misspelled name as a generic term, the "derringers."

Deringer U.S. M1814 Military Rifle

Overall length 48-1/2"; barrel length 32-3/4"; caliber .54. Markings: on lockplate, "US/H. DERINGER/PHILADA," on top flat of barrel, "H. DERINGER/PHILADA" and standard U.S. proofmarks. The U.S. M1814 rifle is distinguished by its part octagonal barrel, whose bands were secured by wedge-shaped spring bands, and the distinctive finger ridges on the triggerguard strap. Henry Deringer Sr. received a contract for 2,000 of these rifles in 1814, but delivered only 50 that year, devoting his resources instead to a more lucrative Pennsylvania state contract for rifles.

NIB	Exc.	V.G.	Good	Fair	Poor
—	—	9000	2950	1500	850

Deringer U.S. M1817 Military Rifle (Types I & II)

Overall length 51-1/4"; barrel length 36"; caliber .54. Markings: on lockplate, "US/H. DERINGER/PHILADA" forward of cock, date on tail; standard U.S. proofmarks on barrel. The U.S. M1817 "common" rifle followed much of the same design elements as its predecessor, the U.S. M1814 rifle; however, the barrel is fully round with its bands secured by full band springs, and on the earlier production, the finger ridges on the triggerguard strap were

eliminated in favor of a plain strap formed into a handgrip. On the 6,000 rifles manufactured under his 1840 contract, Deringer eliminated the "pistol grip" in favor of a plain strap, distinguishing Type 11 production from Type 1. As one of the four major contractors for the U.S. M1817 rifle, Deringer produced a total of 111,000 rifles for the U.S. War Department. Many of the rifles from first two contracts (2,000 in 1821, 3,000 in 1823) were distributed to Southern states under the 1808 Militia Act. Accordingly, Deringer M1817 rifles altered to percussion by traditional Southern methods may generate a premium.

In Flintlock

NIB	Exc.	V.G.	Good	Fair	Poor
—	—	8000	3500	1750	800

Altered to Percussion

NIB	Exc.	V.G.	Good	Fair	Poor
—	—	4000	1250	600	400

Deringer Original Percussion Martial Rifles (Types I & II)

Overall length 51-1/4"; barrel length 36"; caliber .54. Markings: Type I-on lockplate forward of hammer "DERINGER/PHILA"; also known to exist with standard U.S. M1817 lock markings and barrel marks; Type II-on lockplate forward of hammer "US/DERINGER/PHILADELA" or "DERINGER/PHILADELA" and same on top of barrel. Although the Type I rifle of this series appears at first glance to be a late contract rifle altered to percussion by means of the cone-in barrel method, in fact it is an original percussion rifle made by Deringer from modified spare parts that remained after the completion of his 1840 contract. The Type 11 rifle also evidences having been made from modified parts; however, its cone is set in an elongated bolster brazed to the right side of the barrel. Speculation concerning these rifles is rampant; however, the available evidence indicates that Deringer produced about 600 of these most likely produced at the beginning of the American Civil War.

Courtesy Milwaukee Public Museum, Milwaukee, Wisconsin

NIB	Exc.	V.G.	Good	Fair	Poor
—	—	4750	1550	800	450

Deringer Original Percussion Rifle-Muskets

Overall length 57-3/4"; barrel length 42"; caliber .69. Markings: on lock forward of hammer, "US/DERINGER/PHILADELA." Just as the original percussion rifle appears to be an altered arm, the rare Deringer rifle muskets at first appear to have been flintlocks. However, these arms are original percussion, having been made from spare or rejected parts from the U.S. M1816 muskets. The brazed bolsters are identical in style to that of the Type 11 original percussion rifles made by Deringer. Barrels are rifled with seven grooves, and the barrels accordingly bear a rear sight. Deringer probably assembled a hundred of these rifles in 1861 to arm some company of Pennsylvania's early war regiments.

Courtesy Milwaukee Public Museum, Milwaukee, Wisconsin

NIB	Exc.	V.G.	Good	Fair	Poor
—	—	4000	1300	725	450

Deringer U.S. Navy Contract "Boxlock" Pistols

Overall length 11-5/8"; barrel length 6"; caliber .54. Markings: on lockplate, "US/DERINGER/ PHILADELIA" or merely "DERINGER/ PHILADEL\" in center, the tail either plain or marked "U.S.N./ (date)"; barrels sometimes marked with U.S. Navy inspection marks.Deringer was granted a contract with the U.S. Navy in 1845 for 1,200 of the new "boxlock" percussion pistols also made by Ames. All of these appear to have been delivered. From the extra parts, Deringer is thought to have assembled several hundred extra pistols, some of which he rifled. The latter bring a premium, even though quantities remain enigmatic.

NIB	Exc.	V.G.	Good	Fair	Poor
—	—	4050	1550	1225	750

Deringer Percussion Pocket Pistols

The most famous of Henry Deringer's products, an estimated 15,000 were produced between the Mexican War through the Civil War, usually in pairs. The popularity of the pistol is attested in the large number of imitations and the nickname "Derringer" applied to them, even when clearly not Deringer's products. Prices can fluctuate widely based on agent marks occasionally found on barrel. Care is advised in purchasing purported "true" derringers. Beware of fakes!

Courtesy Milwaukee Public Museum, Milwaukee, Wisconsin

NIB	Exc.	V.G.	Good	Fair	Poor
—	—	7000	2250	1600	800

Principal Makers of Deringer-Style Pocket Pistols

William AFFLERBACH, Philadelphia, PA
Balthaser AUER, Louisville, KY
Frederick BEERSTECHER, Philadelphia and Lewisburg, PA
Franz J. BITTERLICH, Nashville, TN
BLUNT & SYMS, New York, NY
Richard P. BRUFF, New York, NY
Jesse S. BUTTERFIELD, Philadelphia, PA
Daniel CLARK, Philadelphia, PA
Richard CONSTABLE, Philadelphia, PA
DELONG & SON, Chattanooga, TN
MOSES DICKSON, Louisville, KY
Horace E. DIMICK, St. Louis, MO
Gustau ERICHSON, Houston, TX
B.J. EUSTACE & Company, St. Louis, MO
James E. EVANS, Philadelphia, PA
W.S. EVANS, Philadelphia, PA
FIELD, LANGSTROTH & Company, Philadelphia, PA
Daniel FISH, New York, NY
FOLSOM BROTHERS & Company, New Orleans, LA
August G. GENEZ, New York, NY
George D. H. GILLESPIE, New York, NY
Frederick G. GLASSICK, Memphis, TN
James GOLCHER, Philadelphia, PA
Joseph GRUBB & Company, Philadelphia, PA
John H. HAPPOLDT, Charlestown, SC
John M. HAPPOLDT, Columbus, GA & Charlestown, SC
HAWS & WAGGONER, Columbia, SC
HODGKINS & SONS, Macon, GA
Louis HOFFMAN, Vicksburg, MS

HYDE & GOODRICH, New Orleans, LA
Joseph JACOB, Philadelphia, PA
William W. KAYE, Philadelphia, PA
Benjamin KITTERIDGE, Cincinnati, OH
Peter W. KRAFT, Columbia, SC
John KRIDER, Philadelphia, PA
Jacob KUNTZ, Philadelphia, PA
Martille La FITTE, Natchitoches, LA
A. Frederich LINS, Philadelphia, PA
C. LOHNER, Philadelphia, PA
John P. LOWER, Denver, CO
A.R. MENDENHALL, Des Arc, AK
John MEUNIER, Milwaukee, WI
William D. MILLER, New York, NY
MURPHY & O'CONNELL, New York, NY
—— NEWCOMB, Natchez, MS
Charles A. OBERTEUFFER, Philadelphia, PA
Stephen O'DELL, Natchez, MS
Henry C. PALMER, St. Louis, MO
R. PATRICK, New York, NY
REID & TRACY, New York, NY
William ROBERTSON, Philadelphia, PA
ROBINSON & KRIDER, Philadelphia, PA
Ernst SCHMIDT & Company, Houston, TX
SCHNEIDER & GLASSICK, Memphis, TN
W.A. SEAVER, New York, NY
Paul J. SIMPSON, New York, NY
SLOTTER & Company, Philadelphia, PA
Patrick SMITH, Buffalo, NY
SPRANG & WALLACE, Philadelphia, PA
Adam W. SPIES, New York, NY
Casper SUTER, Selma, AL
Jacob F. TRUMPLER, Little Rock, AK
Edward TRYON, Jr., Philadelphia, PA
George K. TRYON, Philadelphia, PA
TUFTS & COLLEY, New York, NY
WOLF, DASH & FISHER, New York, NY
Alfred WOODHAM, New York, NY
Andrew WURFFLEIN, Philadelphia, PA
John WURFFLEIN, Philadelphia, PA

Agent Names Found on Deringer Pocket Pistols

W.C. ALLEN, San Francisco, CA
W.H. CALHOUN, Nashville, TN
CANFIELD & BROTHERS, Baltimore, MD
F. H. CLARK & CO., Memphis, TN
COLEMAN & DUKE, Cahaba, AL
M.W. GALT & BROTHER, Washington, DC
J.B. GILMORE, Shreveport, LA
A.B. GRISWOLD & CO., New Orleans, LA
HYDE & GOODRICH, New Orleans, LA
LULLMAN & VIENNA, Memphis, TN
A.J. MILLSPAUGH, Shreveport, LA
H.G. NEWCOMB, Natchez, MS
A.J. PLATE, San Francisco, CA
J.A. SCHAFER, Vicksburg, MS
S.L. SWETT, Vicksburg, MS
A.J. TAYLOR, San Francisco, CA
WOLF & DURRINGER, Louisville, KY

DESENZANI, LABORATORIES ARMI
Brescia, Italy

Over/Under

These custom made guns are all unique. Used guns in excellent condition will bring $35,000. Values increase depending on the small gauges and amount and coverage of engraving.

Side-By-Side

These custom made guns are all unique. Used guns in excellent condition will bring $25,000. Values increase depending on the small gauges and amount and coverage of engraving.

DESERT EAGLE

The Desert Eagle is a semi-automatic gas-operated pistol chambered for the .357 Magnum, .41 Magnum, .44 Magnum, and

.50 Action Express. It was produced by Israel Military Industries until 2009 and are now made in the U.S. The pistols are furnished with a standard 6" barrel but 10" and 14" interchangeable barrels are offered as options. Also available are these interchangeable barrels that are Mag-Na-Ported. The standard material used for frame is steel, but stainless and aluminum are also available. The standard finish for these pistols is black oxide but custom finishes are available on special order. These special finishes are: gold, stainless steel, satin nickel, bright nickel, polished blue, camo, matte chrome, polished chrome, brushed chrome, and matte chrome with gold. All of these special order finishes as well as the optional barrels will affect the prices of the pistols. Prices listed here will reflect standard pistols only.

Desert Eagle .357 Magnum

Standard with 6" barrel and black oxide finish. Magazine capacity is 9 rounds. Standard weight is 58 oz.

NIB	Exc.	V.G.	Good	Fair	Poor
1250	900	700	500	400	250

Desert Eagle .41 Magnum/.44 Magnum

Standard barrel length is 6" with black oxide finish. Magazine capacity is 8 rounds. Weight for standard pistol is 63 oz. Add 10 percent for .41.

NIB	Exc.	V.G.	Good	Fair	Poor
1350	900	700	500	400	250

Desert Eagle .50 Action Express

Standard barrel length is 10" with black oxide finish. Magazine capacity is 7 rounds. Standard weight is 72 oz.

Interchangeable barrels make the Desert Eagle a truly versatile handgun. The .50 AE shown here will handle the biggest game in North America.

NIB	Exc.	V.G.	Good	Fair	Poor
1450	900	700	500	400	250

Desert Eagle Mark XIX

Introduced in 1996 this new design is manufactured in the U.S. and allows the interchangeability of barrels to switch calibers between the same receiver. A single receiver can be turned into six different pistols in three Magnum calibers. Available are the

.50 A.E., .44 Mag., and .357 Mag. in barrel lengths of 6" or 10". Separate magazines are also required. Eight different finishes are offered as well. A separate bolt assembly is necessary to convert the .44/.50 calibers to the .357. There are so many different possibilities with this design that only the basic pistol prices are given. Extra barrel assemblies are an additional cost. Prices range from $280 to $160 depending on caliber and length. NOTE: These custom shop finishes for Desert Eagle pistols are available: Satin nickel, bright nickel, polished and deep blued, matte hard chrome, polished hard chrome, brushed hard chrome, 24K gold. All finishes except gold add $195 to price of pistol. For gold finish add $500. For gold appointments add $195.

.50 A.E. w/6" Barrel

NIB	Exc.	V.G.	Good	Fair	Poor
1450	900	700	500	300	200

.50 A.E. w/10" Barrel

NIB	Exc.	V.G.	Good	Fair	Poor
1350	1000	750	500	300	200

.44 Mag. w/6" Barrel

NIB	Exc.	V.G.	Good	Fair	Poor
1250	900	700	450	300	200

.44 Mag. w/10" Barrel

NIB	Exc.	V.G.	Good	Fair	Poor
1350	1000	750	500	300	200

.357 Mag. w/6" Barrel

NIB	Exc.	V.G.	Good	Fair	Poor
1250	900	700	450	300	200

.357 Mag. w/10" Barrel

NIB	Exc.	V.G.	Good	Fair	Poor
1350	1000	750	500	300	200

.440 CorBon w/6" Barrel (1999)

NIB	Exc.	V.G.	Good	Fair	Poor
1200	950	700	600	500	300

.440 CorBon w/10" Barrel (1999)

NIB	Exc.	V.G.	Good	Fair	Poor
1300	1000	750	650	550	325

Bolt Assembly—.44/.50 or .357

NIB	Exc.	V.G.	Good	Fair	Poor
220	175	150	100	75	50

Mark XIX Component System

Introduced in 2000 this system features a Mark XIX frame with a .44 magnum 6" and 10" barrels; .50AE with 6" and 10" barrel; and .357 magnum with 6" and 10" barrel. Supplied with ICC aluminum case. Also offered with 6" only barrel components or 10" only barrel components.

6" & 10" Component System

NIB	Exc.	V.G.	Good	Fair	Poor
3990	2990	2500	1875	1150	500

6" Component System

NIB	Exc.	V.G.	Good	Fair	Poor
2575	1900	1500	1200	700	350

10" Component System

NIB	Exc.	V.G.	Good	Fair	Poor
2815	2100	1600	1325	725	400

Baby Eagle

The Baby Eagle is a smaller version of the Desert Eagle. It is an all-steel construction, extra long slide rail, nylon grips, combat style trigger guard, ambidextrous thumb safety, decocking safety. It is a double-action design and available in 9mm, .40 S&W, .41 Action

Express. Standard finish is black oxide but matte chrome and brushed are offered as optional finishes. Fixed sights are standard. Fixed night sights and adjustable night sights are options.

.40 S&W (Standard)

Supplied with 4.5" barrel and black oxide finish, it has a magazine capacity of 10 rounds. Empty weight is 38 oz.

NIB	Exc.	V.G.	Good	Fair	Poor
500	400	350	300	250	200

9mm (Standard)

Fitted with a 4.5" barrel and black oxide finish, this model has a magazine capacity of 16 rounds. Empty weight is 38 oz.

NIB	Exc.	V.G.	Good	Fair	Poor
500	400	350	300	250	200

.41 Action Express

This model has a 4.7" barrel and black oxide finish. Magazine capacity is 11 rounds. Empty weight is 38 oz.

NIB	Exc.	V.G.	Good	Fair	Poor
500	400	350	300	250	200

Short Barrel (Semi-Compact)

This 9mm, 40 S&W, or .45 ACP model features a 3.6" barrel with frame-mounted safety. Weight is about 36 oz. Magazine holds 10 rounds.

NIB	Exc.	V.G.	Good	Fair	Poor
500	400	350	300	250	200

Short Barrel/Short Grip (Compact)

This 9mm or .40 S&W version has a 3.6" barrel and shorter grip (3.25") than standard. Magazine capacity is still 10 rounds. Weight is about 38 oz. Frame-mounted safety.

NIB	Exc.	V.G.	Good	Fair	Poor
500	400	350	300	250	200

Semi-Compact Polymer

This pistol has a polymer frame and a 3.9" barrel chambered for the 9mm or .40 S&W cartridge. Weight is about 29 oz.

NIB	Exc.	V.G.	Good	Fair	Poor
500	400	325	285	225	175

Compact Polymer

As above but with 3.6" barrel and short grip. Weight is about 27 oz. **NOTE:** These custom shop finishes for Desert Eagle pistols are available: Satin nickel, bright nickel, polished and deep blued, matte hard chrome, polished hard chrome, brushed hard chrome, 24K gold. All finishes except gold add $195 to price of pistol. For gold finish add $500. For gold appointments add $195.

NIB	Exc.	V.G.	Good	Fair	Poor
500	400	325	285	225	175

Mountain Eagle

This semi-automatic pistol is chambered for the .22 LR cartridge. It features a 6.5" barrel with adjustable rear sight. The grip is a one-piece molded plastic, checkered with raised side panels. The magazine capacity is 15 rounds with 20-round magazine available as an option. A black oxide finish is standard. The pistol weighs 21 oz.

NIB	Exc.	V.G.	Good	Fair	Poor
275	175	150	125	100	75

Mountain Eagle Target Edition

Similar to the standard Mountain Eagle but fitted with an 8" accurized barrel, two-stage target trigger, jeweled bolt, adjustable sights with three interchangeable blades, and range case.

NIB	Exc.	V.G.	Good	Fair	Poor
295	225	195	150	125	85

Mountain Eagle Compact Edition

Similar to above but fitted with a 4.5" barrel and short grip.

NIB	Exc.	V.G.	Good	Fair	Poor
295	225	195	150	125	85

Lone Eagle

This is a single-shot rotating breech pistol designed to fire centerfire cartridges. The standard finish is a black oxide blue luster. The barrel is drilled and tapped for scope mounts. Standard barrel length is 14". Fixed, adjustable, or silhouette sights are offered as options. Stock assembly is made from Lexan. The handgun is offered in these calibers: .22-250, .223, .22 Hornet, .243, .30-30, .30-06, .308, .357 Mag., .358 Win., .35 Rem., .44 Mag., .444 Marlin, 7mm-08, 7mm Bench Rest. Weighs between 4 lbs. 3 oz. to 4 lbs. 7 oz. depending on caliber.

NIB	Exc.	V.G.	Good	Fair	Poor
400	300	275	250	200	125

Lone Eagle (New Model)

Introduced in 1996 this new Lone Eagle model features 15 interchangeable barreled actions from .22 Hornet to .444 Marlin. Available in both black and chrome actions with or without muzzlebrake. The 7.62x39 action was introduced in 1996 also. Sights can be fixed, adjustable or silhouette type. Weight is from 4 lbs. 3 oz. to 4 lbs. 7 oz. depending on caliber. Prices listed reflect black action and fixed sights. **NOTE**: Add $100 for muzzlebrake; $30 for chrome action; $35 for adjustable sights; $130 for silhouette sights.

NIB	Exc.	V.G.	Good	Fair	Poor
425	325	175	150	125	100

Micro Desert Eagle Pistol

Small-frame DAO pocket pistol chambered in .380 ACP. Features include a 2.22" barrel, fixed low-profile sights, steel slide, aluminum alloy frame, nickel-teflon finish, six-round capacity. Overall length 4.52". Weight: 14 oz.

NIB	Exc.	V.G.	Good	Fair	Poor
450	350	250	200	150	100

Mountain Eagle Rifle

A limited edition rifle (1,000) with a Sako action and composite stock. Chambered for the .270, .280, .30-06, .300 Win., .338 Win, 7mm Mag. Introduced in 1994. Additional calibers are .300 Weatherby, .375 H&H, .416 Rem., and 7mm STW. Barrel length is 24". Average weight is about 7.74 lbs. **NOTE**: For muzzlebrake add $150. For .375 H&H and .416 Rem. add $300. For left-hand actions add $100.

NIB	Exc.	V.G.	Good	Fair	Poor
2295	1700	1150	800	400	175

Mountain Eagle Varmint Edition

Chambered for the .222 Rem. and the .223 Rem. cartridges and fitted with a 26" stainless Krieger barrel. Kevlar-graphite stock. Weight is approximately 9 lbs. 13 oz.

NIB	Exc.	V.G.	Good	Fair	Poor
2295	1750	1150	800	400	175

Magnum Lite Rimfire Rifles

These rifles are built with Ruger 10/22 actions and graphite barrels. There are several variations depending on stock configuration. **NOTE:** For Clark Custom Upgrades add $130 to price of each Magnum Lite rifle.

Hogue and Fajen Scope-Hi Stock

NIB	Exc.	V.G.	Good	Fair	Poor
650	495	400	300	200	125

Fajen Thumbhole Sporter

NIB	Exc.	V.G.	Good	Fair	Poor
700	550	450	300	200	125

Fajen Thumbhole Silhouette

NIB	Exc.	V.G.	Good	Fair	Poor
800	650	500	300	200	125

Turner Barracuda

NIB	Exc.	V.G.	Good	Fair	Poor
800	650	500	300	200	125

Magnum Lite Centerfire Rifles

These rifles are built on Sako actions and are fitted with graphite barrels. Introduced in 1999. Offered in two configurations, both with synthetic stock.

Heavy Barrel

Fitted with a 26", 1.2" diameter barrel with a 1-in-14 twist. Chambered for .223 cartridge. Weight is approximately 7.8 lbs.

NIB	Exc.	V.G.	Good	Fair	Poor
2295	1700	1150	800	400	295

Sport Taper Barrel

Fitted with a 24" tapered barrel and chambered for the .280 Rem., 7mm Mag, .30-06, .300 Win. Mag. Weight is about 6.4 lbs.

NIB	Exc.	V.G.	Good	Fair	Poor
2295	1700	1150	800	400	295

Tactical Rifle

Introduced in 2000 this rifle features a 26" match grade barrel chambered for the .223, .22-250, .308, or .300 Win. Mag. cartridges. The barrel is made from carbon fiber. The action is a Remington Model 700. H-S Precision tactical stock with adjustable comb. Adjustable trigger. Weight is approximately 8.3 lbs.

NIB	Exc.	V.G.	Good	Fair	Poor
2400	1800	1250	850	400	295

DESERT INDUSTRIES
Las Vegas, Nevada
SEE—Steel City Arms

DESTROYER CARBINE
Spain

Destroyer Carbine

A 9mm Bayard/Large caliber bolt-action rifle with a 20" barrel and 7-shot magazine. Full length stock with two barrel bands.

NIB	Exc.	V.G.	Good	Fair	Poor
—	500	395	200	100	35

DETONICS FIREARMS INDUSTRIES / NEW DETONICS / DECTONICS USA LLC
Bellevue, Washington / Phoenix, Arizona / Pendergrass, Georgia

This series of compact 1911-type pistols was first manufactured by Detonics Firearms Industries in Bellvue, WA from 1976 to 1988. That firm was sold to New Detonics Mfg. Corp. of Phoenix, AZ, which operated from 1989 to 1992. In 2004 the brand was resurrected and returned to production by Detonics USA in Pendergrass, GA. Then in 2007 Detonics USA and all if its predecessors was sold to a group of investors who established the current company, known only as Detonics, in Middlestadt, IL.

Mark I

A .45 caliber semi-automatic pistol with a 3.25" barrel and 6-shot magazine. Matte blued with walnut grips. Discontinued in 1981.

NIB	Exc.	V.G.	Good	Fair	Poor
—	550	450	400	300	200

Mark II

As above, with satin nickel-plated finish. Discontinued in 1979.

NIB	Exc.	V.G.	Good	Fair	Poor
—	550	450	400	300	200

Mark III

As above, with hard chrome plating. Discontinued in 1979.

NIB	Exc.	V.G.	Good	Fair	Poor
—	600	500	450	350	250

Mark IV

As above, with polished blue finish. Discontinued in 1981.

NIB	Exc.	V.G.	Good	Fair	Poor
—	550	450	400	300	200

Combat Master

The Mark I in 9mm, .38 Super, or .45 caliber.

NIB	Exc.	V.G.	Good	Fair	Poor
975	800	600	500	400	250

Combat Master Mark V

As above, in stainless steel with a matte finish. Discontinued in 1985.

NIB	Exc.	V.G.	Good	Fair	Poor
975	800	600	500	400	250

Combat Master Mark VI

As above, with adjustable sights and the sides of the slide polished. 1,000 were made in .451 Detonics Magnum caliber. **NOTE**: .451 Detonics Magnum add 40 percent.

NIB	Exc.	V.G.	Good	Fair	Poor
900	750	600	500	400	250

Combat Master Mark VII

As above, without sights. **NOTE**: .451 Detonics Magnum add 40 percent.

NIB	Exc.	V.G.	Good	Fair	Poor
900	750	600	500	400	250

Military Combat MC2

As above, in 9mm, .38 Super or .45 caliber with fixed sights, dull finish and Pachmayr grips. Discontinued in 1984.

NIB	Exc.	V.G.	Good	Fair	Poor
675	600	500	425	300	200

Scoremaster

As above, in .45 or .451 Detonics Magnum with a 5" or 6" barrel, Millet sights and a grip safety.

NIB	Exc.	V.G.	Good	Fair	Poor
1250	1000	800	600	400	250

Janus Competition Scoremaster

As above, in .45 caliber with a compensated barrel. Introduced in 1988.

NIB	Exc.	V.G.	Good	Fair	Poor
1750	1450	1250	850	650	300

Servicemaster

As above, with a 4.25" barrel, interchangeable sights and matte finish. Discontinued in 1986.

NIB	Exc.	V.G.	Good	Fair	Poor
—	1000	800	600	400	200

Pocket 9

A 9mm double-action semi-automatic pistol with a 3" barrel and 6-shot magazine. Matte finish stainless steel. Discontinued in 1986.

NIB	Exc.	V.G.	Good	Fair	Poor
—	400	350	275	225	175

Combat Master

Fitted with a 3.5-inch barrel chambered for the .45 ACP, .40 S&W, .357 SIG, .38 Super, or the 9mm Para cartridges. Checkered rosewood grips. Low profile fixed sights. Magazine capacity is 6-rounds. Height of pistol is 4.75-inches. Overall length is 7-inches. Weight is about 34 oz. All stainless steel including springs. Introduced in 2005, by Detonics USA.

NIB	Exc.	V.G.	Good	Fair	Poor
1300	1050	650	425	300	175

Street Master

Chambered for the .45 ACP cartridge and fitted with a 5-inch barrel. Checkered rosewood grips. All stainless steel including springs. Height is 4.75-inches. Overall length is 8.5-inches. Weight is about 39 oz. Magazine capacity is 6-rounds. Fixed sights. Introduced in 2005, by Detonics USA.

NIB	Exc.	V.G.	Good	Fair	Poor
1200	950	675	450	325	195

Model 9-11-01

This model, introduced in 2005 by Detonics USA, is chambered for the .45 ACP cartridge and fitted with a 5-inch barrel. All stainless steel construction. Checkered rosewood grips. Height is about 5.5-inches. Overall length is 8.625-inches. Weight is about 43 oz. Magazine capacity is 7-rounds. Fixed sights.

NIB	Exc.	V.G.	Good	Fair	Poor
1200	950	675	450	325	195

DETONICS
Middlestadt, Illinois

Current manufacturer of Detonics 1911-style pistols.

Combat Master

The latest version of the very first compact 1911 developed in the 1970s by the original Detonics company. In .45 ACP with a 3.5-inch octagonal barrel, two-tone finish, aluminum/Dymondwood grips, 6+1 capacity, stainless steel frame and slide, weight 30 oz. Introduced in 2010.

NIB	Exc.	V.G.	Good	Fair	Poor
850	775	700	550	—	—

Nemesis HT

Full-size with 5-inch barrel, chambered in .40 S&W, weight 38 oz., capacity 9+1. Other features same as above. Introduced in 2011.

NIB	Exc.	V.G.	Good	Fair	Poor
1950	1800	1500	1100	—	—

DTX

A polymer-frame, double-action-only pistol chambered in 9mm or .40 S&W, Barrel is 4.25-inches, weight 25 oz., capacity 16+1 (9mm), 14+1 (.40). Introduced in 2011.

NIB	Exc.	V.G.	Good	Fair	Poor
975	900	775	625	450	250

DEUTSCHE WERKE
Erfurt, Germany

Ortgies

A semi-automatic pistol in 6.35mm and 7.65mm. The 6.35mm pistol was manufactured in 1921 and the 7.65mm model in 1922 by the Ortgies Company. The pistols had the "HO" logo for Heinrich Ortgies on each grip. Later the Ortgies Company was bought by Deutsche Werke. The grip logo was "D." Over the period the Ortgies were manufactured with four different slide legends.

Courtesy James Rankin

NIB	Exc.	V.G.	Good	Fair	Poor
—	450	325	275	200	100

Ortgies 9mm

As above but with the addition of a hold-open button on the left side of the slide. Caliber is 9mmk, aka .380 ACP.

Courtesy James Rankin

NIB	Exc.	V.G.	Good	Fair	Poor
—	450	375	250	175	100

DEVISME, F. P.
Paris, France

One of the more popular French gunsmiths of the mid-19th century, F.P. Devisme manufactured a wide variety of firearms including single-shot percussion pistols, double-barrel percussion rifles and shotguns, percussion revolvers and cane guns. After 1858 this maker manufactured cartridge weapons of the same style as his percussion arms. The quality of all of his products is uniformly high and it is impossible to provide a generalized price guide.

DIAMOND
Turkey

Gold Series Semi-Auto Shotgun

Chambered for the 12 gauge shell with 3" chamber. Barrel length is 28". Turkish walnut stock or synthetic stock. Black receiver with gold-filled engraving. Also available with 24" slug barrel with sights. **NOTE**: Add $50 for walnut stock.

NIB	Exc.	V.G.	Good	Fair	Poor
350	300	200	150	100	75

Gold Series Pump-Action Shotgun

Offered with the same features as the semi-auto Gold gun but with a slide-action. **NOTE**: Add $25 for walnut stock.

NIB	Exc.	V.G.	Good	Fair	Poor
300	250	175	125	100	75

Silver Series Mariner Semi-Auto Shotgun

This is a 12 gauge stainless steel and anodized alloy semi-auto gun with 3" chambers and fitted with 22" vent-rib barrel and synthetic stock.

NIB	Exc.	V.G.	Good	Fair	Poor
425	350	275	200	150	100

Silver Series Mariner Pump-Action Shotgun

A 12 gauge pump gun with 20" slug barrel and symthetic stock. Stainless steel and alloy.

NIB	Exc.	V.G.	Good	Fair	Poor
350	275	200	150	100	75

Diamond Elite Semi-Auto Shotgun

This 12 gauge 3" chamber shotgun is offered with 22" to 28" barrels with 3 choke tubes. Engraved receiver.

NIB	Exc.	V.G.	Good	Fair	Poor
325	275	200	150	100	75

Diamond Panther Pump-Action Shotgun

As above but in a slide-action configuration.

NIB	Exc.	V.G.	Good	Fair	Poor
250	200	200	150	100	75

Diamond Panther Semi-Auto Shotgun

A 12 gauge gun with 3" chambers with 20" or 28" vent-rib barrel. Furnished with three choke tubes. Synthetic stock.

NIB	Exc.	V.G.	Good	Fair	Poor
325	275	200	150	100	75

Diamond Elite Pump-Action Shotgun

As above but with slide-action. Also offered with 18.5" slug barrel.

NIB	Exc.	V.G.	Good	Fair	Poor
300	250	175	125	100	75

Diamondback DB9 Semi-Auto Pistol

A polymer-frame, striker-fired, mimi-compact 9mm with 6+1 capacity and weight of 11 oz. Very compact design with a 3" barrel, overall length of 5.6", height of 4" and width of .80". Available in several finishes including black, stainless, pink, orange and teal. Introduced in 2011. Add $200 for Crimson Trace laser grip.

NIB	Exc.	V.G.	Good	Fair	Poor
435	385	325	300	—	—

Diamondback DB380 Semi-Auto Pistol

Small variation of DB9. Chambered for .380. Barrel length is 2.8" and weight is 8.8 oz. Introduced in 2011. Add $200 for Crimson Trace laser grip.

NIB	Exc.	V.G.	Good	Fair	Poor
385	325	285	250	—	—

DICKINSON, E. L. & J.
Springfield, Massachusetts
Ranger Revolver

A .32 caliber spur trigger revolver with a 6-shot cylinder.

NIB	Exc.	V.G.	Good	Fair	Poor
—	—	525	450	200	100

Single-Shot Pistol

A .32 caliber single-shot pistol with a 3.75" hinged barrel, silver plated brass frame, blued barrel and walnut grips.

NIB	Exc.	V.G.	Good	Fair	Poor
—	—	775	650	250	100

DICKSON, NELSON & CO.
Dawson, Georgia
Rifle

A .58 caliber single-shot percussion rifle with a 34" barrel, full stock secured by two barrel bands, brass furniture and iron loading rod. The lock marked "Dickson/Nelson & Co./C.S." as well as "Ala." and the date of manufacture. Prospective purchasers are advised to secure a qualified appraisal prior to acquisition. A carbine version of this arm is known and has a 24" barrel.

NIB	Exc.	V.G.	Good	Fair	Poor
—	—	39500	14000	3000	2000

DIMICK, H.E.
St. Louis, Missouri
Percussion Pistol

While this maker is primarily known for half stock Plains Rifles, he also manufactured a limited number of percussion pistols. These vary in length, caliber, stock form and type of furniture. The values listed should only be used as a rough guide. Prospective purchasers should secure a qualified appraisal prior to acquisition. Active 1849 to 1873.

NIB	Exc.	V.G.	Good	Fair	Poor
—	—	—	7500	2750	900

DOMINGO ACHA
See—Acha

DOMINO
Brescia, Italy
Model OP 601 Match Pistol

A .22-caliber short semi-automatic pistol with a 5.6" vented barrel, target sights, adjustable and removable trigger. Blued with adjustable walnut grips.

NIB	Exc.	V.G.	Good	Fair	Poor
1700	1200	800	550	300	175

Model SP 602 Match Pistol

As above, in .22 LR caliber.

Courtesy John J. Stimsom, Jr.

NIB	Exc.	V.G.	Good	Fair	Poor
1700	1200	800	550	300	175

DORNAUS & DIXON ENTERPRISES, INC.
Huntington Beach, California
See—Bren 10

DORNHEIM, G.C.
Suhl, Germany

Gecado Model 11

A 6.35mm semi-automatic pistol bearing the name "Gecado" on the slide. Fitted with a 2.2" barrel. Magazine capacity is 6 rounds. Weight is about 15 oz. Marketed by G.C. Dornheim. Copy of the FN Browning Model 1906.

Courtesy James Rankin

NIB	Exc.	V.G.	Good	Fair	Poor
—	300	225	125	75	50

Gecado 7.65mm

A 7.65mm semi-automatic pistol bearing the name "Gecado" on the slide. Fitted with a 2.6" barrel. Magazine capacity is 7 rounds. Weight is about 21 oz. Marketed by G.C. Dornheim.

NIB	Exc.	V.G.	Good	Fair	Poor
—	275	150	125	75	50

DOUBLESTAR CORP.
Winchester, Kentucky

Star EM-4

Chambered for the .223 cartridge and fitted with a 16" barrel. Rifle is supplied with A-2 or flat top upper and Colt M-4 handguard.

NIB	Exc.	V.G.	Good	Fair	Poor
915	750	600	500	275	125

Star-15

This model has a 20" barrel, A-2 buttstock, and A-2 handguard. Supplied with A-2 or flat top upper. In .223 or 7.62x39 calibers.

NIB	Exc.	V.G.	Good	Fair	Poor
775	625	575	450	225	100

Star Lightweight Tactical Rifle

Fitted with a 15" fluted barrel with permanently attached muzzlebrake. Fitted with a short tactical buttstock. Supplied with an A-2 or flat top upper.

NIB	Exc.	V.G.	Good	Fair	Poor
880	700	575	450	225	100

Star Carbine

This model has a 16" match grade barrel. Supplied with either an A-2 buttstock or non-collapsing CAR buttstock. Upper receiver is A-2 style or flat top. In .223 or 7.62x39 calibers.

NIB	Exc.	V.G.	Good	Fair	Poor
775	625	575	450	225	100

Star DS-4 Carbine

This model features a 16" M-4 barrel with 6 position buttstock, oval handguard, and A2 flash hider. Weight is about 6.75 lbs. Choice of A2 or flattop upper receiver.

NIB	Exc.	V.G.	Good	Fair	Poor
875	700	575	450	225	100

Star Super Match Rifle

Choice of match grade barrel lengths of 16", 20", 22", or 24". Rifle supplied with flat top upper or tactical Hi-Rise upper. **NOTE:** Add $50 for .204 Ruger or 6.8 SPC; $100 for 6.5 Grendel, all discontinued.

NIB	Exc.	V.G.	Good	Fair	Poor
950	800	675	450	225	100

Star Critterslayer

This model is fitted with a 24" fluted super match barrel with a flat top upper and free floating handguard. Match 2 stage trigger. Fitted with a Harris LMS swivel bipod and Ergo grip with palm swell.

NIB	Exc.	V.G.	Good	Fair	Poor
1300	1000	750	600	395	175

DSC Expedition Rifle

Offered with a 16" or 20" lightweight barrel with integral muzzlebrake. Stock, sights, and receiver are A2 configuration.

NIB	Exc.	V.G.	Good	Fair	Poor
825	650	575	450	225	100

DSC Star-15 CMP Service Rifle

Fitted with a 20" chrome lined heavy match barrel. National Match front and rear sights. CMP free float handguard. National Match trigger. A2 upper receiver.

NIB	Exc.	V.G.	Good	Fair	Poor
1000	750	650	575	450	225

DSC Star CMP Improved Service Rifle

Similar to the above model but with 20" Wilson Arms premium grade heavy match barrel. McCormick single- or two-stage Match trigger and Tippie Competition rear sight.

NIB	Exc.	V.G.	Good	Fair	Poor
1299	975	825	650	575	300

DSC Star 15 Lightweight Tactical

This model is fitted with a 16" fluted heavy barrel with tactical "shorty" A-2 buttstock.

NIB	Exc.	V.G.	Good	Fair	Poor
880	700	575	450	225	100

DSC Star Dissipator

This model features a 16" barrel with full length handguard. Available with A2 or flattop upper receiver.

NIB	Exc.	V.G.	Good	Fair	Poor
875	700	575	450	225	100

DSC Star 15 9mm Carbine

Chambered for the 9mm cartridge and fitted with a 16" heavy barrel. A2 or flattop upper receiver. Available with A2 or CAR buttstock.

NIB	Exc.	V.G.	Good	Fair	Poor
995	750	650	575	450	225

1911 Combat Pistol

Full-size Government Model .45 ACP with 5-inch barrel, stainless slide, forged frame, black finish. Novak white-dot LoMount sights, Picatinny rail, 8-shot magazine, checkered wood grips. Introduced 2010.

NIB	Exc.	V.G.	Good	Fair	Poor
1150	1000	875	700	400	300

DOUG TURNBULL MANUFACTURING CO.
Bloomfield, New York

This company began operation in 1983 as a one-man shop. Today the company numbers 14 people and does finish work for most major firearms manufacturers. The company also installs Miller single triggers. The models listed are a series of special run firearms produced by Turnbull.

DT Colt

This model is a current Colt SAA reworked to look like the pre-1920 SAA. Assigned serial numbers beginning with 001DT these revolvers are offered in .45 Colt, .44-40, and .38-40 calibers. Barrel lengths are 4.75", 5.5", and 7.5". The standard DT has color case hardened frame and the rest of the gun charcoal blue. Cylinder flutes are enlarged and the front of the cylinder is beveled. Many special options offered which will affect cost. Prices listed are for standard revolvers. Valuues for these very special guns is strictly what the market will bear.

Year Offered—1998

NIB	Exc.	V.G.	Good	Fair	Poor
1795	—	—	—	—	—

Year Offered—1999

NIB	Exc.	V.G.	Good	Fair	Poor
2250	—	—	—	—	—

Year Offered—2000

NIB	Exc.	V.G.	Good	Fair	Poor
2500	—	—	—	—	—

EHBM Colt

This is a Colt SAA current production revolver limited to 50 guns chambered of the .45 Colt and fitted with a 5.5" barrel. Special features. Serial numbers EHBM01 to EHBM50. First offered in 2000.

NIB	Exc.	V.G.	Good	Fair	Poor
2650	2300	1600	1250	700	500

Smith & Wesson No. 3 Schofield

Introduced in 2002 this is a special new production S&W Schofield with special serial numbers with a "DTR" prefix starting with serial number 0001. The frame, barrel, and cylinder are charcoal blued while the trigger, trigger guard, and barrel latch are bone color case hardened. Factory wood grips are standard. Engraving is optional.

NIB	Exc.	V.G.	Good	Fair	Poor
2300	2450	1900	1550	875	500

Colt/Winchester Cased Set

A cased set with a Colt Model 1873 engraved revolver and a Winchester Model 1894. Colt is chambered for the .45 Colt cartridge and fitted with a 7.5" barrel. Engraving is "B" coverage. Model 1894 is chambered for the .45 Colt cartridge and is in the saddle ring configuration. Engraving pattern is #9 with deer. Checkered walnut stock. Limited to five sets total. Serial numbers 160DT to 164DT.

NIB	Exc.	V.G.	Good	Fair	Poor
5750	4300	3750	2500	1500	600

General Patton Colt

This limited run of engraved Colt Model 1873 Single Action Army revolvers is fitted with ivory grips and full-coverage engraving. Chambered for the .45 Colt cartridge and fitted with a 4.75" barrel. Helfricht-style engraving. Silver-plated finish. Limited to 10 revolvers total. Serial numbers GP01 to GP10.

NIB	Exc.	V.G.	Good	Fair	Poor
5250	4000	3250	2000	1000	400

Theodore Roosevelt Colt

This Colt SAA revolver features carved ivory grips, full coverage engraving with gold cylinder, hammer and ejector rod. Chambered for the .44-40 cartridge and fitted with a 7.5" barrel. Nimschke-style engraving. Balance of gun is silver plated. Supplied with fitted case. Limited to 25 revolvers total. Serial numbers TR01 to TR25.

NIB	Exc.	V.G.	Good	Fair	Poor
7750	6000	5000	4000	3000	600

Theodore Roosevelt Winchester Model 1876

This custom rifle is limited to 25 pieces and will be serial numbered from TR01 to TR-25. Each rifle is engraved and checkered in the style of the original and chambered for the .45-70 cartridge. It is fitted with a 28" half round barrel. Gold inlaid stock oval. A portion of the proceeds of each rifle goes to benefit the Doug Turnbull Conservation Laboratory at the National Firearms Museum.

NIB	Exc.	V.G.	Good	Fair	Poor
29000	—	—	—	—	—

Cowboy Classic

Custom-tuned and authentically finished USFA 1873-style single-action revolver. Chambered in virtually all historically-correct centerfire cartridges. Barrel: 4.75, 5.5 and 7.5 inches. Black hard rubber grips standard. Bone charcoal case-hardened and charcoal blue finish. Introduced 2006.

NIB	Exc.	V.G.	Good	Fair	Poor
1650	1300	950	675	400	300

DOWNSIZER CORPORATION
Santee, California

Model WSP

Introduced in 1998, this is billed as the world's smallest pistol by the manufacturer. It is a single-shot, double-action-only pistol with tip-up barrel. It is chambered for .22 Mag., .32 Mag, .357 Mag., 9mm, .40 S&W, and .45 ACP cartridges. Barrel length is 2.1". Overall length is 3.25". Height is 2.25", thickness is .9". Weight is approximately 11 oz. Built from stainless steel.

NIB	Exc.	V.G.	Good	Fair	Poor
400	325	275	225	175	125

DPMS
St. Cloud, Minnesota

Panther Bull A-15

This A-15 type rifle is chambered for the .223 cartridge and fitted with a 20" stainless steel bull barrel. A2-style buttstock. No sights. Barrel has 1:9 twist. Flat top receiver. Handguard is aluminum free float tube. Upper and lower receivers are hard coated black. Weight is about 9.5 lbs. Each rifle comes standard with two 7-round magazines, sling, and cleaning kit.

NIB	Exc.	V.G.	Good	Fair	Poor
900	700	550	400	275	125

Panther Bull 24

Similar to the model above but fitted with a 24" bull barrel. Flat top receiver. Weight is about 10 lbs.

NIB	Exc.	V.G.	Good	Fair	Poor
950	750	600	400	275	125

Panther Deluxe Bull 24 Special

This model is fitted with a 24" stainless steel fluted bull barrel. Adjustable A2 style buttstock. Flat top receiver. Adjustable sniper pistol grip. Weight is about 10 lbs.

NIB	Exc.	V.G.	Good	Fair	Poor
1150	900	750	400	275	125

Panther Extreme Super Bull 24

This model is fitted with a 24" stainless steel extra heavy bull barrel (1.150" dia.). Skeletonized stock. Flat top receiver. Weight is about 11.75 lbs.

NIB	Exc.	V.G.	Good	Fair	Poor
1200	800	650	400	275	125

Panther Bulldog

Fitted with a 20" stainless steel fluted bull barrel with black synthetic A2-style buttstock. Flat top receiver. Adjustable trigger. Weight is about 10 lbs.

NIB	Exc.	V.G.	Good	Fair	Poor
1200	975	800	400	275	125

Panther Bull Sweet 16

This model is fitted with a 16" stainless steel bull barrel with flat top receiver. Weight is about 7.75 lbs.

NIB	Exc.	V.G.	Good	Fair	Poor
1100	900	550	400	275	125

Panther Bull SST 16

Similar to the model above but with stainless steel lower receiver. Weight is about 9 lbs.

NIB	Exc.	V.G.	Good	Fair	Poor
1300	975	650	400	275	125

Panther Bull Classic

This model is fitted with a 20" 4150 steel bull barrel. Square front post sight, adjustable A2 rear sight. Weight is about 9.75 lbs.

NIB	Exc.	V.G.	Good	Fair	Poor
1200	800	650	400	275	125

Panther Arctic

This model is similar to the model above but with 20" fluted bull barrel and flat top receiver. Black A2-style buttstock with white coat finish on receiver and handguard. Black Teflon finish on barrel. Weight is about 8.25 lbs.

NIB	Exc.	V.G.	Good	Fair	Poor
1075	850	700	400	275	125

Panther Classic

Fitted with a 20" 4150 steel heavy barrel with square front post sight and A2 rear sight. A2 round handguard. Weight is about 9.5 lbs.

NIB	Exc.	V.G.	Good	Fair	Poor
800	600	500	400	275	125

Panther DCM

This model is similar to the model above but with 20" stainless steel heavy barrel and NM rear sight. DCM free-float handguard. Adjustable trigger. Weight is about 9.5 lbs.

NIB	Exc.	V.G.	Good	Fair	Poor
950	750	600	400	275	125

Panther Classic 16 Post Ban

This model is fitted with a 1" 4150 steel heavy barrel. A2-style sights. Round handguard. Weight is about 7.25 lbs.

NIB	Exc.	V.G.	Good	Fair	Poor
775	600	500	400	275	125

Panther Free Float 16 Post Ban

Similar to the model above with 16" barrel but fitted with a vented free-floated barrel and vented free-float tube handguard. Weight is approximately 7.25 lbs.

NIB	Exc.	V.G.	Good	Fair	Poor
825	650	550	400	275	125

Panther Southpaw Post Ban

This model is fitted with a 20" 4150 steel heavy barrel with A2-style sights. Upper receiver has been modified for left-hand ejection. Weight is about 9.5 lbs.

NIB	Exc.	V.G.	Good	Fair	Poor
875	700	600	400	275	125

Panther Race Gun

Similar to Panther Bull but with 24-inch fluted bull barrel. Sights: JP Micro adjustable rear, JP front sight adjustable for height. Includes Lyman globe and Shaver inserts.

NIB	Exc.	V.G.	Good	Fair	Poor
1875	1500	800	500	275	125

Panther Tuber

Similar to Panther Bull 24 but with 16-inch barrel with cylindrical aluminum shroud.

NIB	Exc.	V.G.	Good	Fair	Poor
700	600	500	400	275	125

Single Shot Rifle

AR-15-style single-shot rifle with manually-operated bolt, no magazine.

NIB	Exc.	V.G.	Good	Fair	Poor
775	500	400	275	125	100

Panther Pardus

Similar to Panther Post Ban but with 16-inch bull barrel, telescoping buttstock and tan Teflon finish. Introduced 2006.

NIB	Exc.	V.G.	Good	Fair	Poor
1200	850	700	400	275	200

Panther 20th Anniversary Rifle

Similar to Panther Post-ban but with 20-inch bull barrel and engraved, chrome-plated lower receiver. Introduced 2006.

NIB	Exc.	V.G.	Good	Fair	Poor
2500	2000	1550	800	500	300

Panther 6.8 Rifle

Similar to Panther DCM but with 20-inch chrome-moly barrel and chambered for 6.8x43 Remington SPC. Introduced 2006.

NIB	Exc.	V.G.	Good	Fair	Poor
1000	850	700	400	275	125

Panther Mark 12

Similar to other Panthers but with flash hider and other refinements. Introduced 2007.

NIB	Exc.	V.G.	Good	Fair	Poor
1300	850	700	400	275	125

Panther SDM-R

Similar to other Panthers but with stainless steel barrel and Harris bipod. Introduced 2007.

NIB	Exc.	V.G.	Good	Fair	Poor
1200	850	700	400	275	125

LRT-SASS

Semi-automatic rifle based on AR-15 design. Chambered in .308 Win. With 18-inch stainless steel barrel with flash hider, collapsible Vitor Clubfoot carbine stock and 19-rd. detachable magazine. Introduced 2006.

NIB	Exc.	V.G.	Good	Fair	Poor
1900	1600	1475	1000	600	350

LR-260

Similar to LRT-SASS but with 24" stainless steel barrel and chambered in .260 Remington. Also available with 20" chrome-moly barrel as LR-260H. Introduced 2006.

NIB	Exc.	V.G.	Good	Fair	Poor
1300	1000	900	800	500	300

LR-243

Similar to LR-260 but with 20" chrome-moly barrel and chambered in .243 Win. Introduced 2006.

NIB	Exc.	V.G.	Good	Fair	Poor
1150	950	800	650	500	300

LR-204

Similar to LRT-260 but chambered in .204 Ruger. Introduced 2006.

NIB	Exc.	V.G.	Good	Fair	Poor
1000	800	650	500	400	300

Panther Arms 5.56 Oracle

Semi-auto AR-style rifle chambered in 5.56 NATO. Features include 16-inch 4140 chrome-moly 1:9 barrel; phosphated steel bolt; oval Glacier Guard hand guard; flattop upper with Picatinny rail; aluminum lower; two 30-round magazines; Pardus 6-position telescoping stock. Also available on larger platform in .308 Winchester/7.62 NATO.

NIB	Exc.	V.G.	Good	Fair	Poor
700	575	500	400	300	200

Panther 3G1

Semi-auto AR-style rifle chambered in 5.56 NATO. Features include 18-inch 416 stainless 1:9 barrel; phosphated steel bolt; VTAC modular hand guard; flattop upper with Picatinny rail; aluminum lower; two 30-round magazines; Magpul CTR adjustable stock.

NIB	Exc.	V.G.	Good	Fair	Poor
1000	850	700	600	400	300

Prairie Panther

Semi-auto AR-style rifle chambered in 5.56 NATO. Features include 20" 416 stainless fluted heavy 1:8 barrel; phosphated steel bolt; free-floated carbon fiber hand guard; flattop upper with Picatinny rail; aluminum lower; two 30-round magazines; skeletonized Zytel stock; finished in King Desert Shadow camo overall.

NIB	Exc.	V.G.	Good	Fair	Poor
1150	1000	850	700	450	300

Panther RAPTR

Semi-auto AR-style rifle chambered in 5.56 NATO. Features include 16-inch 4140 chrome-moly 1:9 barrel; phosphated steel bolt; ERGO Z-Rail 4-rail hand guard; front vertical grip; standard A2 sights; aluminum lower; four 30-round magazines. Price: $1649.

NIB	Exc.	V.G.	Good	Fair	Poor
1350	1025	800	625	350	250

Panther REPR

Semi-auto AR-style rifle chambered in .308 Win./7.62 NATO. Features include 18-inch 416 stainless steel 1:10 barrel; phosphated steel bolt; 4-rail free-floated hand guard; no sights; aluminum lower; two 19-round magazines; Coyote Brown camo finish overall.

NIB	Exc.	V.G.	Good	Fair	Poor
2100	1850	1400	1000	650	350

Panther 308 Mk12

Semi-auto AR-style rifle chambered in .308 Win./7.62 NATO. Features include 16" 4140 chrome-moly heavy 1:10 barrel; phosphated steel bolt; 4-rail free-floated hand guard; flip-up front and rear sights; aluminum lower; two 19-round magazines; matte black finish overall; Magpul CTR adjustable stock.

NIB	Exc.	V.G.	Good	Fair	Poor
1500	1100	850	700	450	300

Panther A-15 Pump Rifle

This model has a 20" 4150 steel heavy barrel with A2-style sights. Fitted with an A2 compensator and modified to slide-action. Weight is about 8.5 lbs.

NIB	Exc.	V.G.	Good	Fair	Poor
1400	1050	700	600	500	300

Panther A-15 Pump Pistol

Same as above but fitted with a 10.5" barrel. Weight is about 5 lbs.

NIB	Exc.	V.G.	Good	Fair	Poor
1450	1100	750	575	450	300

Panther DCM .22 LR

Rimfire version of Panther series with 20" fluted stainless H-Bar barrel, A2 upper receiver, National Match sights. Also available with 16" barrel (Panther AP4) with flat-top receiver. **NOTE:** Deduct $75 for AP4 model

NIB	Exc.	V.G.	Good	Fair	Poor
850	750	600	450	300	150

Panther Lite 308/338

Chambered for .308 Win. or .338 Federal. A3 Flattop design with 20" free-floated barrel and handguard. Various options offered.

NIB	Exc.	V.G.	Good	Fair	Poor
1350	1200	900	650	400	200

Panther 6.5

Basic Panther model chambered for 6.5 Creedmoor. Stainless steel free-floated 24" barrel, A3 Flattop upper, mil-spec stock.

NIB	Exc.	V.G.	Good	Fair	Poor
1100	975	750	550	350	200

6.8 SPCII Hunter

Chambered for Remington 6.8 SPC cartridge with 18" barrel and Miculek compensator. A3 Flattop design with forward assist, skeletonized stock.

NIB	Exc.	V.G.	Good	Fair	Poor
1150	1025	800	600	400	250

300 AAC Blackout

Chambered for .300 AAC cartridge. Chrome-lined 16" heavy barrel comes with Blackout suppressor adapter. AP4 stock, free-float handguard.

NIB	Exc.	V.G.	Good	Fair	Poor
1100	975	750	550	350	200

308 Recon

Similar to 300 AAC Blackout model except chambered for .308 Winchester. Standard weight, 16" barrel with Blackout suppressor adapter. A3 Flattop upper receiver, Magpul MOE stock with 4-Rail handguard.

NIB	Exc.	V.G.	Good	Fair	Poor
1350	1200	1000	750	500	250

DREYSE

See—Rheinmetall

DRISCOLL, J.B.

Springfield, Massachusetts

Single-Shot Pocket Pistol

A small pistol chambered for .22 rimfire. It has a 3.5" octagonal barrel that pivots downward for loading after a trigger-like hook under the breech is pulled. It has a spur trigger, silver-plated brass frame, and a blued barrel. The square butt is flared at the bottom, and the grips are walnut. There were approximately 200 manufactured in the late 1860s.

NIB	Exc.	V.G.	Good	Fair	Poor
—	—	1000	375	100	50

DRULOV

Czech Republic

This company was part of the national co-operative under communist rule when the Czech Republic was part of Czechoslovakia. The company was formed in 1948. The company specialized in low-cost but well made rimfire target pistols.

Model 70 Standard

This model is a bolt-action single-shot pistol chambered for the .22 Long Rifle. A knob at the rear of the frame opened the bolt. When the bolt is closed the firing pin is cocked. The barrel is 9.75" long with an adjustable front sight for windage. The rear sight is adjustable for elevation. Wooden wraparound grips with thumb rest are standard. Weighs about 44 oz.

NIB	Exc.	V.G.	Good	Fair	Poor
—	300	200	175	100	75

Model 70 Special

Same as above but with the addition of a set trigger.

NIB	Exc.	V.G.	Good	Fair	Poor
—	350	250	200	150	100

Model 75

This model features a set trigger, better sights, and grip. The rear sight is fully adjustable.

NIB	Exc.	V.G.	Good	Fair	Poor
—	400	300	250	200	150

Pav

This target pistol was introduced between World War I and World War II. It is an inexpensive pistol with a fixed front sight and a notch for the rear sight. Like the other models above it is also a single-shot chambered for the .22 Long Rifle cartridge. The barrel is 10.25" and weighs about 35 oz.

Courtesy Orvel Reichert

NIB	Exc.	V.G.	Good	Fair	Poor
—	175	150	100	75	50

DSA, INC.

Barrington, Illinois

DSA, Inc. began selling its rifles to the public in 1996. Based on actual blueprints of the famous FN/FAL rifle, SA58 rifles are made in the US. All SA58 rifles are fitted with fully adjustable gas system, Type I, II, or III forged receiver, hand-lapped barrel, muzzlebrake, elevation adjustable post front sight, windage adjustable rear peep sight with 5 settings from 200 to 600 meters, detachable metric magazine, adjustable sling and hard case. DSA also manufactures a series of AR-15 type rifles and carbines. Virtually all parts are made by DSA.

SA58

SA58 24" Bull

Fitted with a 24" stainless steel barrel with .308 match chamber. Overall length is 44.5". Weight is approximately 11.5 lbs.

NIB	Exc.	V.G.	Good	Fair	Poor
1750	1500	1150	800	500	300

SA58 21" Bull

Same as the above but fitted with a 21" stainless steel barrel. Weight is about 11.1 lbs.

NIB	Exc.	V.G.	Good	Fair	Poor
1750	1500	1150	800	500	300

SA58 Medium Contour

This model is offered with a 21" barrel in either stainless steel or blued steel. Weight is about 10.5 lbs. **NOTE:** Add $250 for stainless steel.

NIB	Exc.	V.G.	Good	Fair	Poor
1550	1300	1150	800	500	300

SA58 Carbine

This model is fitted with a 16.25" barrel. Barrel is cut for factory light bipod. Blued finish. A stainless steel version is also available. Overall length is 37.5". Weight is about 8.35 lbs. **NOTE:** Add $250 for stainless steel.

NIB	Exc.	V.G.	Good	Fair	Poor
1600	1400	1150	800	500	300

SA58 Standard

This model has a 21" barrel cut for factory light bipod. Weight is about 8.75 lbs. Blued finish.

NIB	Exc.	V.G.	Good	Fair	Poor
1600	1400	1150	800	500	300

SA58 Tactical

Fitted with a 16.25" fluted barrel, black synthetic stock, Type I receiver, adjustable sights, and detachable magazine. Blued finish. Weight is about 8.25 lbs.

NIB	Exc.	V.G.	Good	Fair	Poor
1600	1400	1150	800	500	300

SA58 Congo

This .308 model features a 18" bipod-cut barrel with short Belgian-style flash hider. Type I receiver with carry handle. Synthetic buttstock and pistol grip. Aluminum lower. Detachable magazine. Adjustable sights. Weight is about 8.6 lbs.

NIB	Exc.	V.G.	Good	Fair	Poor
1800	1550	1250	800	500	300

SA58 Para Congo

This model is fitted with a Type II receiver with carry handle and a 18" bipod-cut barrel with short Belgian-style flash hider. Steel lower. Folding steel Para stock. Adjustable sights. Weight is about 9.85 lbs.

NIB	Exc.	V.G.	Good	Fair	Poor
1800	1550	1250	800	500	300

SA58 Predator

Offered in .308, .260 Rem., or .243. This rifle has a Type I receiver, a 16" medium carbine barrel with target crown or 19" medium barrel with target crown. Green furniture. Aluminum lower. Picatinny rail. Weight is about 9 lbs. with 16" barrel.

NIB	Exc.	V.G.	Good	Fair	Poor
1600	1450	1100	800	475	200

SA58 Graywolf

This .308 model is fitted with a 21" match grade barrel with target crown. Type I receiver. Aluminum lower. Extended safety. Picatinny rail. Target pistol grip with standard or X-series buttstock. Versa-pod bipod. Weight is about 13 lbs.

NIB	Exc.	V.G.	Good	Fair	Poor
2100	1600	1250	800	500	300

SA58 T48 Replica

Chambered for the .308 cartridge and fitted with a 21" barrel with replica Browning flash hider. Supplied with 10- or 20-round fixed magazine with stripper clip top cover. Wooden stock. Weight is about 9.7 lbs.

NIB	Exc.	V.G.	Good	Fair	Poor
1600	1400	1250	800	475	200

DS-AR

S1 Rifle

Introduced in 2004 this 5.56 caliber rifle features a 20" or 24" bull barrel with Picatinny gas black sight base. Flattop receiver. Free floating aluminum handguard. A2 stock. Ten-round magazine. Discontinued.

NIB	Exc.	V.G.	Good	Fair	Poor
950	750	600	425	225	150

CVI Carbine

Similar to the model above but with a 16" barrel with forged front sight base and integral muzzlebrake. D-4 handguard. Fixed CAR buttstock. Ten-round magazine. Discontinued.

NIB	Exc.	V.G.	Good	Fair	Poor
900	700	600	425	225	150

LE4 Carbine

As above but with pre-ban features. For law enforcement only. Discontinued.

NIB	Exc.	V.G.	Good	Fair	Poor
1150	850	600	425	225	150

DS-AR S Series Rifle

Introduced in 2005 this rifle is chambered for the .223 cartridge and fitted with a choice of 16", 20", or 24" stainless steel match grade bull barrel. A2 stock with free floating handguard. Flattop receiver, National Match 2 stage trigger. Magazine capacity is 10, 20, or 30 rounds.

NIB	Exc.	V.G.	Good	Fair	Poor
1350	1050	800	525	225	150

DS-AR Carbine

Chambered for the .223 cartridge and fitted with a 16" D4 barrel with flash hider. Choice of fixed or collapsible stock. Choice of forged flattop or A2 upper receiver. Magazine capacity is 10, 20, or 30 rounds. Introduced in 2005.

NIB	Exc.	V.G.	Good	Fair	Poor
1350	1050	800	525	225	150

DS-AR Rifle

As above but with 20" heavy barrel with flash hider and fixed stock. Introduced in 2005.

NIB	Exc.	V.G.	Good	Fair	Poor
1350	1050	800	525	225	150

DS-AR DCM Rifle

Chambered for the .223 cartridge with Wylde chamber. Fitted with a 20" match grade Badger barrel. DCM free float handguard system. National Match two-stage trigger. National Match rear sight. A2 upper receiver. Introduced in 2005.

NIB	Exc.	V.G.	Good	Fair	Poor
1595	1250	950	625	425	225

DS-AR CQB MRP

Introduced in 2005 this model features a 16" chrome lined barrel with A2 flash hider. Collapsible stock with MRP quad rail. Monolithic rail platform upper. Flattop or A2 upper receiver. Supplied with 30-round magazine.

NIB	Exc.	V.G.	Good	Fair	Poor
2595	1850	1400	1025	600	300

DSA Z4 Gas Trap Carbine (GTC)

This model, introduced in 2005, is fitted with a 16" chrome lined barrel with M4 profile fluted with Vortec flash hider. Collapsible 6-position stock with free float tactical rail. Gas trap system. Flattop upper receiver. Magazine capacity is 10, 20, or 30 rounds.

NIB	Exc.	V.G.	Good	Fair	Poor
1675	1250	950	625	425	225

ZM-4 Series

This series of AR-15 type models features forged upper and lower receivers, flattop upper, fixed or collapsible stocks, 16" or 20" barrels, black finish or OD Green. **NOTE:** Add $200 for Spartan model with Robar bolt, Magpul trigger guard, Phantom Flashider, 30-round magazine.

NIB	Exc.	V.G.	Good	Fair	Poor
750	650	600	500	300	150

BOLT-ACTION RIFLES

DS-MP1

This is a bolt-action rifle chambered for the .308 cartridge. It is built on a custom Remington 700 action and fitted with a 21" Badger barrel with target crown. Black McMillan A5 stock. Matte black finish. Introduced in 2004.

NIB	Exc.	V.G.	Good	Fair	Poor
2800	2100	1675	1050	650	425

HANDGUNS

B&T TP9 Tactical Pistol

Swiss made recoil-operated, rotating-bolt semi-automatic chambered in 9mm Parabellum. Semi-automatic, civilian-legal version of B&T TP9SF select-fire sub-machine gun. Planned to be imported in 2007.

NIB	Exc.	V.G.	Good	Fair	Poor
1100	950	775	600	475	350

DUBIEL ARMS CO.
Sherman, Texas

Dubiel Arms was a manufacturer of custom bolt-action rifles in Sherman, Texas from 1975 to about 1987. Joseph Dubiel and Dr. John Tyson were the founders and co-owners of the company. Dubiel's father was John Dubiel, a well-known gunsmith in Oklahoma in the 1920s and '30s. It is believed that the Texas rifles were based on his original designs. The actions featured a bolt with five locking lugs and a short 36-degree bolt rotation. These rifles were available with many options, stock designs and custom features and were made in most popular centerfire calibers. Several Dubiel rifles are on display at the Buffalo Bill Historical Center in Cody, Wyoming. In May of 2012, co-founder Dr. John Tyson made a presentation of nine rifles to the NRA National Firearms Museum in Fairfax, Virginia. Prices shown are estimated values of basic models. Various options would increase these values significantly.

NIB	Exc.	V.G.	Good	Fair	Poor
5000	3500	2800	2000	—	—

DUMOULIN
Herstal, Belgium

The guns produced by Ernest Dumoulin are essentially handmade to the customer's order. They are of the highest quality, both in materials and workmanship. There are many options available that have a tremendous impact on value fluctuations. The models and values listed here are base prices.

SHOTGUNS

Europa Model

A side-by-side double-barrel chambered for 12, 20, and 28 gauge and .410 bore. It is available in any length barrel and choke combination, with an Anson & Deeley boxlock action and automatic ejectors. One has the option of double- or single-selective triggers and a choice of six different moderate engraving patterns. The select walnut stock is oil-finished. This model was introduced in 1989. Basic values are listed.

NIB	Exc.	V.G.	Good	Fair	Poor
3500	2750	1950	1250	800	400

Leige Model

A side-by-side double chambered for 12, 16, 20, and 28 gauge. It is similar to the Europa, with a greater degree of finish and more engraving. The walnut is of a higher grade. This model was introduced in 1986.

NIB	Exc.	V.G.	Good	Fair	Poor
5750	4200	2750	1500	950	425

Continental Model

A side-by-side chambered for 12, 20, and 28 gauge and .410. Barrel lengths and chokes are on a custom-order basis. This is a true sidelock action with automatic ejectors and choice of triggers. There are six different engraving patterns, and the stock is made of high grade, hand-checkered, oil-finished walnut. This model was introduced in 1989.

NIB	Exc.	V.G.	Good	Fair	Poor
7500	6000	4500	3000	1500	400

Etendart Model

A side-by-side chambered for 12, 20, and 28 gauge. This best grade side-by-side is built on a purely made-to-order basis. It is profusely engraved and uses exhibition grade walnut in its stock. There are 12 different engraving patterns from which to choose, and the cost is according to embellishments chosen. Values given here are for the basic model.

NIB	Exc.	V.G.	Good	Fair	Poor
14500	11000	8500	4000	3000	700

Superposed Express International

An over/under chambered for 20 gauge and is furnished with a set of rifle barrels in the customer's choice of seven calibers. The walnut is of a deluxe grade, and engraving is available at extra cost. This is a made-to-order gun, and the value here is for the most basic model. This gun was discontinued in 1985.

NIB	Exc.	V.G.	Good	Fair	Poor
—	2500	2000	1250	750	400

Boss Royal Model

The best grade over/under, chambered for 12, 20, and 28 gauge. It is a full sidelock gun that is made to the customer's specification using the finest materials and workmanship available. This model was introduced in 1987.

NIB	Exc.	V.G.	Good	Fair	Poor
18500	15000	12000	8000	4500	700

Eagle Model Combination Gun

This model has a rifle barrel or the shotgun barrel that is chambered for 12 or 20 gauge. The rifle calibers available are .22 Hornet, .222 Remington, .222 Remington Magnum, 6mm, .243, .25-06, .30-06, 6.5 x 57R, 7 x 57R, 8 x 57JRS, and 9.3 x 74R. The action is a boxlock with automatic ejectors, and the other specifications are on a custom-order basis. This model was introduced in 1989.

NIB	Exc.	V.G.	Good	Fair	Poor
2750	2250	1500	950	750	400

DOUBLE RIFLES

Europa I

A made-to-order, over/under, double-barreled rifle available in the same calibers as the Eagle Combination gun. It has an Anson & Deeley boxlock and all other options to the customer's specifications.

NIB	Exc.	V.G.	Good	Fair	Poor
6000	4700	3500	4000	1250	500

Continental I Model

A more deluxe over/under rifle with a true sidelock-action. The calibers are the same as the Europa. The specifications are to the customer's order with 12 engraving patterns to choose from at extra cost. This model was introduced in 1989.

NIB	Exc.	V.G.	Good	Fair	Poor
9000	7150	5500	4000	2000	600

Pionier Express Rifle

A side-by-side double rifle chambered for the .22 Hornet through the .600 Nitro Express. It has the Anson & Deeley boxlock-action and is quite deluxe throughout. The specifications are to the customer's order, and there are basically 12 models available (P-1 through P-XII). The differences among these models are in the degree of ornamentation and quality of the walnut used for the stock. Values range from approximately $10,000 to $15,000 for the basic models.

Aristocrat Model

A low-profile single-shot chambered for all calibers up to .375 Holland & Holland. This is a deluxe, made-to-order rifle with exhibition-grade walnut and 12 engraving patterns available.

NIB	Exc.	V.G.	Good	Fair	Poor
—	9500	7500	5800	3000	700

BOLT-ACTION RIFLES

Centurion Model

A custom-order rifle built on a Mauser or Sako action and chambered for all calibers from .270 to .458 Winchester Magnum. The barrel lengths available were 21.5", 24", and 25.5"; and there were many engraving options from which to choose. The stock is of deluxe French walnut, with rosewood fore-end tip and pistol gripcap. This rifle was discontinued in 1986.

NIB	Exc.	V.G.	Good	Fair	Poor
7500	6000	5000	4000	—	—

Centurion Classic

Similar to the Mauser-actioned Centurion chambered for the non-Magnum calibers only. The walnut used for the stock is a better grade.

NIB	Exc.	V.G.	Good	Fair	Poor
1275	950	750	600	500	400

Diane

A more deluxe version of the Centurion Classic.

NIB	Exc.	V.G.	Good	Fair	Poor
1800	1550	1250	900	650	500

Amazone

A 20" barreled, full-length stocked, upgraded version of the Diane.

NIB	Exc.	V.G.	Good	Fair	Poor
2100	1750	1400	950	700	500

Bavaria Deluxe

Similar to the Centurion, with the same barrel lengths and calibers available. The engraving styles available are more deluxe. This model was discontinued in 1985.

NIB	Exc.	V.G.	Good	Fair	Poor
2350	1800	1400	950	700	500

Safari Model

Similar to the Bavaria Deluxe, but it is chambered for the heavy Magnum calibers only.

NIB	Exc.	V.G.	Good	Fair	Poor
3275	2700	1900	1450	900	500

Safari Sportsman

Built on a Magnum Mauser action and is chambered for the .375 Holland & Holland, .404 Jeffreys, .416 Rigby, and the .505 Gibbs. This is a true big game rifle that was made available in 1986.

NIB	Exc.	V.G.	Good	Fair	Poor
4500	3650	2400	1550	1100	—

African Pro

A more deluxe version of the Safari Sportsman, with a folding leaf rear sight, hooded front sight, and an ebony or buffalo horn fore-end tip.

NIB	Exc.	V.G.	Good	Fair	Poor
5200	3950	2700	1700	1300	750

DUSEK, F.
Opocno, Czech Republic

Dusek commenced business in the mid-1920s and continued to make firearms through WWII. They manufactured pistols for Nazi Germany under the contract code "aek." After the war the communists took over, and Dusek's designs were relegated to the CZ factory.

Perla

This 6.35mm pistol has a fixed barrel and open-topped slide. It resembles a Walther design and is striker-fired. The slide is marked "Automat Pistole Perla 6.35mm" ; the grips, "Perla 6.35." Dusek made this model from the early 1930s until WWII.

NIB	Exc.	V.G.	Good	Fair	Poor
—	335	225	165	100	80

Duo

DAK-5Replace with DAK-6-7. **NOTE:** Nazi-marked examples will bring a 25 percent premium.

Courtesy J.B. Wood

NIB	Exc.	V.G.	Good	Fair	Poor
—	375	250	195	100	80

E

E.M.F. CO., INC.
Santa Ana, California
See—Uberti, Aldo

An importer and a distributor of quality Italian-made reproduction firearms. Most of its offerings are listed in the section dealing with Aldo Uberti firearms. E.M.F. also markets a line of 1911 pistols made in the Philippines.

Hartford Bisley

This single-action revolver is fitted with a Colt Bisley grip. Chambered for .45 Long Colt as well as .32-20, .357 Magnum, .38-40, and .44-40 calibers. Barrel lengths are 4-3/4", 5-1/2", and 7-1/2". Plain walnut grips.

NIB	Exc.	V.G.	Good	Fair	Poor
525	425	300	225	145	105

Hartford Express

A single-action Colt SAA frame and barrel with a Colt Lightning-style grip. Chambered for .45 Long Colt in 4-3/4", 5-1/2", or 7-1/2" barrel lengths.

NIB	Exc.	V.G.	Good	Fair	Poor
525	425	300	225	145	105

Hartford Pinkerton

This model features a 4" barrel with ejector and a bird's-head grip. Chambered for 45 Long Colt, .32-20, .357 Magnum, .38-40, .44-40, and .44 Special.

NIB	Exc.	V.G.	Good	Fair	Poor
525	425	300	225	145	105

Citadel 1911

Full-size 1911A1-type pistol in .45 ACP with skeletonized trigger and hammer. Extended ambidextrous thumb safety and slide stop, front and rear slide grooves and flared ejection port. Built by Armscor in the Philippines.

NIB	Exc.	V.G.	Good	Fair	Poor
500	425	350	300	250	200

EAGLE ARMS, DIVISION OF ARMALITE
Geneseo, Illinois

Previous manufacturer of AR-15 type rifles from 1990 to 2005. From 1995 to 2002, a division of ArmaLite, Inc.

PRE-BAN MODELS

Golden Eagle

This model is identical in design to the AR-15. Fitted with a 20" stainless steel extra-heavy barrel with National Match sights and two-stage trigger. Weight is about 9.4 lbs.

NIB	Exc.	V.G.	Good	Fair	Poor
1050	950	750	575	400	225

HBAR

Similar to the above model but with a heavy 20" barrel. Weight is approximately 8 lbs.

NIB	Exc.	V.G.	Good	Fair	Poor
1250	950	750	575	400	225

SPR

This is similar to the above model with the exception of a detachable carry handle. Weight is about 7.6 lbs.

NIB	Exc.	V.G.	Good	Fair	Poor
1250	950	750	575	400	225

M4C Carbine

This model features a 16" barrel with a 4.33" flash suppressor. Retractable stock. Weight is approximately 6.2 lbs.

NIB	Exc.	V.G.	Good	Fair	Poor
1250	950	750	575	400	225

M4A1C Carbine

Similar to the above model but with detachable carry handle. Weight is about 6 lbs.

NIB	Exc.	V.G.	Good	Fair	Poor
1250	950	750	575	400	225

POST-BAN MODELS

Golden Eagle

Reintroduction of earlier model. Limited production in 2002.

NIB	Exc.	V.G.	Good	Fair	Poor
1050	850	750	575	400	225

AR-10 Match Rifle

Chambered for .308 Win. with 20" or 24" chrome-moly barrel. Features include flattop upper receiver, black stock and forearm, 10-round magazine.

NIB	Exc.	V.G.	Good	Fair	Poor
1000	900	750	500	400	200

Model M15 Series

Chambered for .223 or .308 in various AR-15 type configurations. Manufactured from 2002 to 2005. **NOTE:** For .308 caliber add $200 and Eagle Spirit model with National Match accessories, add $150.

ECHAVE & ARIZMENDI
Eibar, Spain

Basque, Echasa, Dickson, or Dickson Special Agent

These four pistols are the same semi-automatic pistols but chambered in .22 LR, 6.35mm, 7.65mm, and 9mmK respectively. Their magazine capacities are 10, 9, 7, and 6 rounds. They are manufactured with alloy frames and various finish combinations. The specific model names are stamped on the slides and grip plates.

Courtesy James Rankin

NIB	Exc.	V.G.	Good	Fair	Poor
—	295	185	125	90	50

Bronco Model 1913

A semi-automatic pistol in caliber 6.35mm. Patterned after the Browning Model 1906 with a squeeze grip safety. Bronco is stamped on the slide and on each side of the grip plate.

Courtesy James Rankin

NIB	Exc.	V.G.	Good	Fair	Poor
—	295	185	125	90	50

Bronco Model 1918

A semi-automatic pistol chambered for both 6.35mm or 7.65mm. Both are patterned after the Browning Model 1906 with a squeeze grip safety. The 7.65mm pistol is approximately 1/2" longer and higher than the 6.35mm. It has a magazine capacity of 7 rounds. The 6.35mm pistol has a magazine capacity of 6 rounds.

Courtesy James Rankin

NIB	Exc.	V.G.	Good	Fair	Poor
—	295	185	125	90	50

Echasa

Similar to the 6.35mm Bronco, without a grip safety. It is marked "Model 1916."

NIB	Exc.	V.G.	Good	Fair	Poor
—	295	185	125	90	50

Lightning

A renamed version of the Bronco in 6.35mm.

NIB	Exc.	V.G.	Good	Fair	Poor
—	295	185	125	90	50

Lur Panzer

A copy of the Luger toggle-lock-action, chambered for .22 rimfire. This is an almost exact copy except for a different trigger assembly and a less robust mainspring. It is marked "Lur Cal.22 LR Made in Spain." The plastic grips have "Panzer" molded into them.

NIB	Exc.	V.G.	Good	Fair	Poor
—	265	225	150	125	100

Pathfinder

A semi-automatic pistol similar to the Bronco above but in caliber 6.35mm and 7.65mm. Sold in the U.S. by Stoeger. The 7.65mm Pathfinder holds 12 rounds. The values listed are for both pistol models.

NIB	Exc.	V.G.	Good	Fair	Poor
—	295	185	125	90	50

Protector Model 1915 and 1918

A semi-automatic pistol in caliber 6.35mm. Similar to the Echasa model. "Protector" is stamped on the slide while the grip plates have various logos of the firms that marketed the pistol.

Courtesy James Rankin

NIB	Exc.	V.G.	Good	Fair	Poor
—	275	185	100	70	40

Selecta Model 1918

A semi-automatic pistol chambered for 7.65mm cartridge. Patterned after the Protector but chambered for the 7.65mm. "Selecta" is stamped on the slide and Echave Arizmendi logo is on each of the grip plates.

Courtesy James Rankin

NIB	Exc.	V.G.	Good	Fair	Poor
—	295	185	125	90	50

ECHEVERRIA, STAR-BONIFACIO SA (STAR)
Eibar, Spain

An old-line Spanish company that survived the Spanish civil war. It was founded in 1908 by Jean Echeverria, but the early records of the company were lost during the civil war. The early pistols the company produced were patterned after the Mannlicher designs, and the trade name Star was the closest thing to Steyr that could be used. After the close of WWI, the company began production of the open-topped slide Star for which they have become known. They also produced a large 1911-type pistol that was successful. During the civil war, the plant was damaged and the company records destroyed; but after the cessation of hostilities, they were one of only three gun companies that were allowed to remain in business. The company is now defunct.

Star Model 1908

The first pistol produced under the Star banner. It is a Mannlicher copy that is chambered for 6.35mm. It has a 3" fixed barrel and an open-topped slide. The detachable magazine holds 8 shots. The finish is blued, and the grips are checkered plastic. The slide is marked "Automatic Pistol Star Patent."

Courtesy James Rankin

NIB	Exc.	V.G.	Good	Fair	Poor
—	350	275	200	150	100

Star Model 1914

Similar to the Model 1908, with a 5" barrel and larger grips that have the Star name molded into them. This model was the first to have the six-pointed star surrounded by rays of light (that became the Star trademark) stamped on its slide.

Courtesy James Rankin

NIB	Exc.	V.G.	Good	Fair	Poor
—	350	275	200	150	100

Star Model 1919

Also a copy of a Mannlicher design and differs from its predecessors chiefly in the way the pistol is disassembled. This model has a spring catch at the top of the trigger guard. This model also has a small spur on the hammer, and the magazine release was relocated to a button behind the trigger guard instead of a catch at the bottom of the butt. This model was chambered for 6.35mm, 7.65mm and 9mm short, with various barrel lengths offered. The maker's name, as well as the Star trademark, is stamped into the slide. This model was produced until 1929.

Courtesy James Rankin

NIB	Exc.	V.G.	Good	Fair	Poor
—	350	275	200	150	100

Star Model 1919 New Variation

Same as above but with full spur hammer.

Courtesy James Rankin

NIB	Exc.	V.G.	Good	Fair	Poor
—	350	275	200	150	100

Modelo Militar

Represents the first pistol Star produced that was not a Mannlicher design copy. This model was copied from the Colt 1911. It was chambered initially for the 9mm Largo in hopes of securing a military contract. When this contract was awarded to Astra, Star chambered the Model 1919 for the .38 Super and the .45 ACP and put it on the commercial market. This model is like the Colt 1911—it has a Browning-type swinging link and the same type of lock up. However there is no grip safety, and the thumb safety functions differently. **NOTE:** Add 30 percent for guns marked .38 Super.

NIB	Exc.	V.G.	Good	Fair	Poor
—	425	325	245	175	125

Star Model A

A modification of the Model 1919, chambered for the 7.65mm, 7.63mm Mauser, 9mm Largo, and the .45 ACP cartridge. The slide is similar in appearance to the 1911 Colt, and the spur hammer has a small hole in it. Early models had no grip safety, but later production added this feature. Some models are slotted for addition of a shoulder stock.

NIB	Exc.	V.G.	Good	Fair	Poor
—	425	325	245	175	125

Star Model B

Similar to the Model A except that it is almost an exact copy of the Colt 1911. It is chambered for 9mm Parabellum and has a spur hammer with no hole. This model was introduced in 1928.

Courtesy Orvel Reichert

NIB	Exc.	V.G.	Good	Fair	Poor
—	425	325	245	175	125

Star Model C

The Model B chambered for the 9mm Browning Long cartridge. It was manufactured in the 1920s.

NIB	Exc.	V.G.	Good	Fair	Poor
—	350	265	175	125	90

Star Model CO

A pocket pistol similar to the early open-topped Star pistols. It is chambered for the 6.35mm cartridge, and the finish is blued with checkered plastic grips that bear the Star name and logo. This model was manufactured between 1930 and 1957.

Courtesy James Rankin

NIB	Exc.	V.G.	Good	Fair	Poor
—	275	195	125	100	75

Star Model D

A medium-sized pistol that is similar in appearance to a smaller Model A. It is chambered for the 9mm Short cartridge and was called the "Police and Pocket Model" after it was adopted by the Spanish police. It was manufactured between 1930 and 1941.

NIB	Exc.	V.G.	Good	Fair	Poor
—	500	400	300	200	100

Star Model DK Starfire

Single-action .380 with 3-1/8" barrel, fixed sights, brown plastic grips. Imported from 1957 until 1968. Alloy frame was available in blue finish or in various colors. Add $100 for colored frame.

Courtesy James Rankin

NIB	Exc.	V.G.	Good	Fair	Poor
550	425	400	350	300	150

Star Model E

A pocket pistol chambered for the 6.35mm cartridge. It has a 2.5" barrel and an external hammer. The detachable magazine holds 5 rounds, and the finish is blued with checkered plastic grips. This model was manufactured between 1932 and 1941.

NIB	Exc.	V.G.	Good	Fair	Poor
—	250	195	165	110	80

Star Model F

The first of the .22-caliber Star pistols. It has a 4" barrel, a 10-shot magazine, and fixed sights. The finish is blued, and the plastic grips are checkered. This model was manufactured between 1942 and 1967.

NIB	Exc.	V.G.	Good	Fair	Poor
—	300	265	200	110	75

Star Model F Target

Similar to the Model F, with a 6" barrel.

NIB	Exc.	V.G.	Good	Fair	Poor
—	325	275	210	125	100

Star Model F Sport

Has a 5" barrel. Manufactured between 1962 and 1967.

NIB	Exc.	V.G.	Good	Fair	Poor
—	325	275	210	125	100

Star Model F Olympic

Has a 6" barrel and adjustable sights. It is furnished with a muzzlebrake and barrel weights. It was manufactured between 1942 and 1967.

Courtesy James Rankin

NIB	Exc.	V.G.	Good	Fair	Poor
—	350	265	175	125	90

Star Model F Olympic Rapid Fire

Similar to the Olympic but is chambered for .22 Short only.

NIB	Exc.	V.G.	Good	Fair	Poor
—	375	295	185	150	125

Star Model FR

Has an adjustable sight and a slide stop. The 4" barrel is heavier, with flattened sides. It was manufactured between 1967 and 1972.

NIB	Exc.	V.G.	Good	Fair	Poor
—	325	275	210	125	100

Star Model FRS

Similar to the Model FR, with a 6" barrel. It is also available chrome-plated with white checkered plastic grips. It was introduced in 1967.

NIB	Exc.	V.G.	Good	Fair	Poor
—	295	225	175	125	100

Star Model FM

A heavier-framed version of the Model FRS. It has a 4.5" barrel and is available in blue or chrome-plated. It was introduced in 1972.

NIB	Exc.	V.G.	Good	Fair	Poor
—	325	275	210	125	100

Star Model H

Similar to the old Model CO—only larger in size. It is chambered for the 7.65mm cartridge and was manufactured between 1932 and 1941.

NIB	Exc.	V.G.	Good	Fair	Poor
—	250	195	150	125	100

Star Model HK

A pocket-sized version of the Model F chambered for .22 Short. It has a 2.5" barrel and is quite scarce on today's market.

NIB	Exc.	V.G.	Good	Fair	Poor
—	325	275	210	125	100

Star Model HN

Simply the Model H chambered for the 9mm Short cartridge. It was manufactured and discontinued at the same time as the Model H was.

NIB	Exc.	V.G.	Good	Fair	Poor
—	275	202	165	125	100

Star Model I

An improved version of the Model H with a 4" barrel and a recontoured grip. It was chambered for 7.65mm and was produced until 1941. After the war it was resumed and survived until the mid-1950s, when it was replaced by the modernized Model IR that would be valued approximately the same.

NIB	Exc.	V.G.	Good	Fair	Poor
—	250	195	150	125	100

Star Model M

Similar to the Model B, chambered for the .38 Auto (NOT .38 Super) cartridge.

NIB	Exc.	V.G.	Good	Fair	Poor
—	375	295	185	150	125

Star Model P

The post-war version of the Model B, fitted with a 5" barrel and chambered for the .45 ACP cartridge. Checkered walnut grips and blued finish.

NIB	Exc.	V.G.	Good	Fair	Poor
—	400	350	265	195	125

Star Model CU "Starlet"

Similar to the Model CO, with an alloy frame that was anodized in black, blue, gray, green, or gold. It has a steel slide that is blued or chrome-plated. It has checkered, white plastic grips and is chambered for the .25 ACP cartridge. It has a 2.5" barrel, fixed sights, and a 5-shot magazine. This model was introduced in 1975 and was not imported after 1986.

NIB	Exc.	V.G.	Good	Fair	Poor
—	250	175	145	100	75

Star Model 1941 S

Add 100 percent to prices listed for pistols issued to Spanish Air Force with box, cleaning rod, instruction sheet, and two numbered magazines.

Courtesy Richard M. Kumor Sr.

NIB	Exc.	V.G.	Good	Fair	Poor
—	250	210	175	125	75

Star Model BKS "Starlight"

The smallest locked-breech automatic chambered for the 9mm cartridge at the time. It has an alloy frame and a 4.25" barrel. It is similar in appearance to a scaled-down Colt 1911 without a grip safety. It has an 8-shot magazine and is either blued or chrome-plated, with checkered plastic grips. This model was manufactured between 1970 and 1981.

NIB	Exc.	V.G.	Good	Fair	Poor
—	325	275	210	125	100

Star Model PD

Chambered for the .45 ACP cartridge and has a 4" barrel. It has an alloy frame and a 6-shot magazine and adjustable sights and is blued with checkered walnut grips. It was introduced in 1975.

NIB	Exc.	V.G.	Good	Fair	Poor
400	325	275	225	175	125

Star Model BM

A steel-framed 9mm that is styled after the Colt 1911. It has an 8-shot magazine and a 4" barrel. It is available either blued or chrome-plated.

NIB	Exc.	V.G.	Good	Fair	Poor
350	300	250	200	150	125

Star Model BKM

Similar to the Model BM, with an alloy frame.

NIB	Exc.	V.G.	Good	Fair	Poor
450	350	300	250	200	125

Star Model 30/PK

Similar to the Models 28 and 30M, with a lightweight alloy frame.

NIB	Exc.	V.G.	Good	Fair	Poor
450	350	300	250	200	125

Megastar

This is a double-action semi-automatic pistol chambered for the 10mm or .45 ACP cartridge. It features a three-position ambidextrous selective decocking lever, rubber grips, combat-style trigger guard, slotted hammer, and checkered mainspring housing. Barrel length is 4.6" and the magazine capacity is 12 rounds. Available in either blue or Starvel (brushed chrome). The pistol weighs 47.6 oz.

NIB	Exc.	V.G.	Good	Fair	Poor
375	325	275	225	175	125

Star Model 28

The first of Star's Super 9s. It is a double-action semi-automatic chambered for the 9mm Parabellum cartridge. It has a 4.25" barrel and a steel frame. The magazine holds 15 shots. The construction of this pistol was totally modular, and it has no screws in its design. It is blued with checkered synthetic grips and was manufactured in 1983 and 1984.

NIB	Exc.	V.G.	Good	Fair	Poor
500	450	350	250	200	100

Firestar M43, M40, and M45

This is a compact large caliber semi-automatic pistol offered in 9mm, the M43, .40 S&W, the M40, and the .45 ACP, the M45. It features an ambidextrous safety, steel frame and slide, checkered rubber grips. The barrel is 3.4" on the M43 and M40 and 3.6" on the M45. Choice of finish is blue or Starvel (brushed chrome). A finger rest magazine is optional. Weight for the M43 and M40 is 30 oz. while the M56 weighs 35 oz. Introduced in 1990.

NIB	Exc.	V.G.	Good	Fair	Poor
425	365	295	200	150	100

Star Model 30M

An improved version of the Model 28, that is quite similar in appearance. It was introduced in 1985.

NIB	Exc.	V.G.	Good	Fair	Poor
400	300	250	200	150	100

Starfire Model 31P

This model evolved from the Models 28 and 30. It is chambered for either the 9mm Parabellum or .40 S&W. The trigger action is double-action/single-action. Barrel length is 3.9". It is fitted with a two-position safety/decocking lever. The magazine capacity for the 9mm is 15 rounds, while the .40 S&W holds 11 rounds. The pistol weighs 39 oz.

NIB	Exc.	V.G.	Good	Fair	Poor
425	350	300	250	200	100

Starfire Model 31PK

Similar to the Model 31P but built on an alloy frame. Chambered for 9mm only with a 15-round magazine capacity. Weight is 30 oz.

NIB	Exc.	V.G.	Good	Fair	Poor
400	325	275	225	200	100

Ultrastar

Introduced in 1994, this compact 9mm or .40 S&W semi-automatic pistol with a polymer frame features a 3.57" barrel, a 9-round magazine, a blued finish and an overall length of 7". It weighs about 26 oz. It has a double-action operating system, a windage adjustable rear sight, and an ambidextrous two-position safety.

NIB	Exc.	V.G.	Good	Fair	Poor
400	365	305	275	200	100

ECLIPSE
Enterprise Gun Works
Pittsburgh, Pennsylvania

Single-Shot Derringer

This pocket pistol was made by the firm of James Bown & Son, doing business as the Enterprise Gun Works. It is chambered for .22 or .32-caliber rimfire cartridges. A few in .25 rimfire have been noted and would add approximately 25 percent to the values listed. The barrel is 2.5" in length and is part-round/part-octagonal. It pivots sideways for loading. It has a spur trigger and a bird's-head grip. The barrel is stamped "Eclipse." It is made of nickel-plated iron, with walnut grips. There were approximately 10,000 manufactured between 1870 and 1890.

NIB	Exc.	V.G.	Good	Fair	Poor
—	—	650	250	100	75

84 GUN CO.
Eighty Four, Pennsylvania

In business for a brief time in the early 1970s, this company produced three basic bolt-action rifles—each in four grades that differ in amounts of embellishment and grades of wood. There is little known about this company and its products. The basic models are listed, and values are approximate.

Classic Rifle

Grade 1 - Grade 4 available. $650—$1800

Lobo Rifle

Grade 1 - Grade 4 available. $625—$2700

Pennsylvania Rifle

Grade 1 - Grade 4 available. $625—$2800

EL DORADO ARMS
See—United Sporting Arms, Inc.

ELGIN CUTLASS
(C.B. Allen / Merrill, Mossman & Blair)
Springfield and Amherst, Massachusetts

Manufactured by two companies—C.B. Allen of Springfield, Massachusetts, and Morrill, Mossman and Blair of Amherst, Massachusetts. It is a unique pistol that has an integral knife attachment affixed to the gun barrel. It was designed and patented by George Elgin and simultaneously produced by the two companies. The inspiration for this weapon was supposedly Jim Bowie, who at that time had made a name as a knife fighter with his large "Bowie" knife. The blades for these pistols were supplied by N.P. Ames of the famed Ames Sword Co. These pistols are much sought after, and one must exercise caution as fraudulent examples have been noted.

C.B. ALLEN-MADE PISTOLS

U.S. Navy Elgin Cutlass Pistol

Chambered for .54-caliber percussion and has a 5" octagonal smooth-bore barrel. The Bowie-style blade is 11" long by 2" wide and is forged together with the trigger guard and the knuckle guard that protects the grip. The handle is walnut. This pistol was issued to the U.S. Navy's Wilkes-South Sea Exploration Expedition, and the markings are "C.B. Allen / Springfield / Mass." "Elgin's Patent" and the letters "CB" , "CBA" along with the date 1837. If the sheath that was issued with this knife pistol is included and in sound condition, it would add approximately $700 to the value. There were 150 manufactured for the U.S. Navy in 1838.

NIB	Exc.	V.G.	Good	Fair	Poor
—	—	35500	14000	7500	4750

Civilian Model

Chambered for .35- or .41-caliber percussion and has a 4" octagonal barrel with a 7.5"-10" knife blade. It has a round trigger guard but does not have the knuckle bow across the grip, as found on the military model. They are marked "C.B. Allen Springfield, Mass." Blades marked "N.P. Ames" have been noted. There were approximately 100 manufactured in 1837.

NIB	Exc.	V.G.	Good	Fair	Poor
—	—	33500	13000	6250	3250

MORRILL, MOSSMAN & BLAIR-MADE PISTOLS

Small Model

The main difference in the pistols of the two makers is that this model has a round barrel and a square-back trigger guard that comes to a point at the rear. This version is chambered for .32-caliber percussion and has a 2.75" barrel. The knife blade is 7.5" in length and is screwed to the frame. This model is unmarked except for a serial number. The number produced is unknown, and they were manufactured in 1837.

NIB	Exc.	V.G.	Good	Fair	Poor
—	—	33500	13000	6250	3250

Large Model

Chambered for .36-caliber percussion and has a 4" round barrel and a 9" knife blade. The pistol is usually marked "Cast Steel" and serial numbered. The blade is etched with an American eagle, stars, and an urn with flowers. "Elgin Patent" is etched in the center. This model was also manufactured in 1837.

Courtesy Milwaukee Public Museum, Milwaukee, Wisconsin

NIB	Exc.	V.G.	Good	Fair	Poor
—	—	37000	14500	7000	3900

ELLS, JOSIAH
Pittsburgh, Pennsylvania
POCKET REVOLVER

Three distinct variations of this percussion revolver. They are chambered for .28- and .31-caliber and have 6-shot unfluted cylinders. They have been noted with 2.5", 3", and 3.75" octagonal barrels.

Model 1

The first model has an open-topped frame and is chambered for .28 caliber. The cylinder holds 5 or 6 shots, and the hammer is of the bar type. It was offered with a 2.5" or 3" barrel. The markings are "J. Ells; Patent; 1854." There were approximately 625 manufactured between 1857 and 1859.

Courtesy Milwaukee Public Museum, Milwaukee, Wisconsin

NIB	Exc.	V.G.	Good	Fair	Poor
—	—	1700	875	375	200

Model 2

The second model is similar to the first, with a solid-topped frame. They have 5-shot cylinders and 3.75" long barrels. There were approximately 550 manufactured.

Courtesy Milwaukee Public Museum, Milwaukee, Wisconsin

NIB	Exc.	V.G.	Good	Fair	Poor
—	—	1750	750	365	200

Model 3

The third model is radically different from its forerunners. It has a closed-top frame and a conventional spur-type hammer that strikes from the right side. It functions either as a double- or single-action. It is chambered for .28 caliber and has a 5-shot cylinder

and a 3.75" barrel. There were only about 200 manufactured between 1857 and 1859.

NIB	Exc.	V.G.	Good	Fair	Poor
—	—	1850	995	425	200

ENDERS, CARL
Suhl, Germany
Side-by-Side Shotgun

Percussion damascus double-barrel side-by-side in 12 gauge. Ornate checkering with cheekpiece and engraved metal work. This firm made high-quality firearms, mostly side-by-side guns. The gun pictured was made circa 1850-1860. The firm was in business from about 1835 to approximately 1890.

Courtesy Jim Cate

NIB	Exc.	V.G.	Good	Fair	Poor
—	—	1250	550	300	150

ENFIELD AMERICAN, INC.
Atlanta, Georgia
MP-45

A blowback-operated, semi-automatic assault pistol chambered for the .45 ACP cartridge. It was offered with a barrel length of 4.5" through 18.5". The long barrel features a shroud. The finish is Parkerized, and there were four different magazines available in 10, 20, 30, and 50-round capacities. This firearm was manufactured in 1985 only.

NIB	Exc.	V.G.	Good	Fair	Poor
—	575	475	295	175	125

ENTERPRISE ARMS, INC.
Irwindale, California
ELITE SERIES

This is the basic model with stainless steel barrels, fixed sights, squared trigger guard, adjustable match trigger, checkered slide release, high ride grip safety, flat mainspring housing, and a number of other special features. Magazine capacity is 10 rounds.

Elite P500

Chambered for .45 ACP and fitted with a 5" barrel. Weight is about 40 oz.

NIB	Exc.	V.G.	Good	Fair	Poor
600	500	400	350	200	100

Elite P425

This model has a 4.25" barrel. Weight is approximately 38 oz.

NIB	Exc.	V.G.	Good	Fair	Poor
600	500	400	350	200	100

Elite P325

This model has a 3.25" barrel with a weight of 36 oz.

NIB	Exc.	V.G.	Good	Fair	Poor
600	500	400	350	200	100

TACTICAL SERIES

This model has an ambidextrous thumb lock with lightweight match hammer with matching sear. National match barrel with match extractor, full length one-piece guide rod, Novak sights, dovetail front sight, matte black finish, and a host of other features. Magazine capacity is 10 rounds.

Tactical P500

This model is chambered for the .45 ACP cartridge and has a 5" barrel and a weight of approximately 40 oz.

NIB	Exc.	V.G.	Good	Fair	Poor
900	795	600	495	350	100

Tactical P425

This model is fitted with a 4.25" barrel and weighs about 38 oz.

NIB	Exc.	V.G.	Good	Fair	Poor
900	795	600	495	350	100

Tactical P325

This model is fitted with a 3.25" barrel and has a weight of 36 oz.

NIB	Exc.	V.G.	Good	Fair	Poor
900	795	600	495	350	100

Tactical P325 Plus

This model features a 3.25" barrel and is fitted to a full size Government model frame. Weight is about 37 oz.

NIB	Exc.	V.G.	Good	Fair	Poor
950	800	615	500	365	105

TITLEIST NATIONAL MATCH SERIES

This model is chambered for either the .45 ACP or .40 S&W cartridge. It has all the features of the Elite Series with an adjustable rear sight and dovetail Patridge front sight. Many other special features.

Titleist P500

This model is fitted with a 5" barrel. Weight is about 40 oz. **NOTE:** Add $20 for .40 S&W chambering.

NIB	Exc.	V.G.	Good	Fair	Poor
900	795	600	495	350	100

Boxer Model

Chambered for the .45 ACP cartridge and fitted with a 5" barrel this model features a ramped bull barrel, wide ambi safety and high-mass chiseled slide. Weight is approximately 44 oz.

NIB	Exc.	V.G.	Good	Fair	Poor
1200	975	750	600	375	125

TOURNAMENT SERIES

These are the top-of-the-line models that feature all of the Elite Series features plus oversized magazine release button, checkered front strap, and flared extended magazine well.

TSM I

This is a limited class competition pistol. All these model are hand crafted. Fitted with a 5" barrel and choice of calibers. Weight is about 40 oz.

NIB	Exc.	V.G.	Good	Fair	Poor
1900	1750	1375	900	675	300

TSM II

This is a long slide model with cocking serrations on front and rear of slide. Barrel is 6". Weight is about 44 oz.

NIB	Exc.	V.G.	Good	Fair	Poor
2300	1750	1375	900	675	300

TSM III

This is an open class pistol designed for scope mount. Barrel is 5.5" long. Fitted with 7 port compensator. Many other custom features. Weight is about 44 oz.

NIB	Exc.	V.G.	Good	Fair	Poor
2500	2000	1525	1050	700	310

ERA
Brazil

ERA Side-by-Side Shotgun

An inexpensive shotgun chambered for 12 and 20 gauge, as well as .410. It was offered with 26", 28", or 30" barrels with various choke combinations. It has double triggers and extractors, with a checkered hardwood pistol-grip stock. This gun is also available as a Quail model with a 20" barrel and as a Riot model with an 18" barrel. These two models are not offered in .410 bore.

NIB	Exc.	V.G.	Good	Fair	Poor
—	200	150	125	100	75

ERA Over/Under Shotgun

Chambered for 12 or 20 gauge, with 28" ventilated rib barrels that were choked full and modified. It is a boxlock with double triggers, extractors, and a hardwood stock. It was also offered in a trap model and a skeet model chambered for 12 gauge only and appropriately choked. These latter two models would be worth a 10 percent premium over the values listed.

NIB	Exc.	V.G.	Good	Fair	Poor
—	325	275	250	200	150

ERICHSON, G.
Houston, Texas

Pocket Pistol

A close copy of the Philadelphia-style Henry Deringer. It is chambered for .45-caliber percussion and has a 3.25" barrel. The mountings are German silver and not engraved; the stock is walnut. The hammer is deeply fluted, and the fore-end carved. The barrel is marked "G. Erichson / Houston, Texas." The number produced is unknown, but examples are scarce. They were manufactured in the 1850s and 1860s.

NIB	Exc.	V.G.	Good	Fair	Poor
—	—	6500	3000	1000	400

ERMA WERKE WAFFENFABRIK
Erfurt, Germany
Post-war Dachau, Germany

Known primarily as a manufacturer of submachine guns, but they are also in the handgun and rifle business. In 1933 they answered the German army's need for an inexpensive practice weapon by producing a .22 rimfire conversion unit for the Luger pistol. This was marketed commercially and was available for many years. The success of this unit led the company to produce other inexpensive target and plinking pistols. After the war they were reorganized in the western sector and resumed submachine gun production. In 1964 they returned to the sporting firearms business with the introduction of their .22 rimfire Luger-lookalike pistol. Since then, they have produced many like-quality firearms. They were imported by Excam of Hialeah, Florida. This association is now terminated, and they are currently imported by Beeman Precision in Santa Rosa, California, and Mandell Shooting Supplies in Scottsdale, Arizona.

PISTOLS

Erma .22 Luger Conversion Unit

Produced for the German army in 1933 and then became a successful commercial item. It would turn a standard 9mm or 7.65mm Luger into an inexpensive-to-shoot .22 rimfire. The unit consists of a barrel insert, a breech block, and toggle unit with its own lightened recoil spring, and a .22 magazine. This unit was furnished with a wooden box. There were many different sized units to fit various caliber and barrel-length Lugers, but all used the same parts and concept. These units have become desirable to Luger collectors.

NIB	Exc.	V.G.	Good	Fair	Poor
—	500	425	350	275	200

.22 Target Pistol (Old Model)

A semi-automatic target pistol in caliber .22 LR. This model was offered with 4", 6", or 8" barrels. The frame is made from a cast zinc alloy, and there is an external hammer. There are adjustable sights, and balance weights were available. Magazine capacity is 10 rounds. Weight is about 35 oz. This pistol was manufactured in 1936 and 1937.

Courtesy James Rankin

NIB	Exc.	V.G.	Good	Fair	Poor
—	800	725	500	350	100

.22 Target Pistol (New Model)
Master Model

An improved version of the old model that features a new grip angle and a magazine and takedown device like that of the Luger. There were interchangeable barrels and three basic models — the "Sport," "Hunter," and the "Master." The difference was the length of the barrels — 4", 8", and 12", respectively. Magazine capacity is 10 rounds. Weight is about 39 oz. These pistols were manufactured between 1937 and 1940, when they were discontinued due to Erma's involvement in the war effort.

Courtesy James Rankin

NIB	Exc.	V.G.	Good	Fair	Poor
—	850	700	500	400	125

KGP SERIES

Made to resemble the Luger quite closely. They utilized the mechanical features of the .22 conversion unit and developed a pistol around it. There are many different versions of this pistol chambered for .22 rimfire, .32 ACP, and .380 ACP. The original designation was the KGP-68; but the Gun Control Act of 1968 required that a magazine safety be added, and the model was redesignated the KGP-68A. The last designations for the three calibers are KGP-22, KGP-32, and KGP-38. These pistols were manufactured between 1964 and 1986, and their values are listed.

KGP-68

A 4" barrel and is chambered for the .32 ACP and the .380 ACP cartridges. It has a 6-shot magazine and an anodized alloy receiver. Weight is about 23 oz. This model is also known as the Beeman MP-08.

Courtesy James Rankin

NIB	Exc.	V.G.	Good	Fair	Poor
—	450	400	300	200	100

KGP-69

A .22 rimfire version of this series, with an 8-shot magazine capacity. Weight is about 30 oz. It is also known as the Beeman P-08.

NIB	Exc.	V.G.	Good	Fair	Poor
	300	200	150	100	75

KGP-22

The later version of the KGP-69 chambered for .22 rimfire.

NIB	Exc.	V.G.	Good	Fair	Poor
—	350	300	250	200	125

KGP-32 & KGP-38

These two designations are the later versions of the KGP-68 and 68A.

NIB	Exc.	V.G.	Good	Fair	Poor
	350	300	250	200	125

ET-22 "Navy Luger" Long-Barreled Pistol

A rare firearm. According to some estimates only 375 were produced. It features an 11.75" barrel and is chambered for the .22 rimfire cartridge. It has an artillery Luger-type rear sight and checkered walnut grips, with a smooth walnut fore-end. The pistol was furnished with a red-felt-lined, black leatherette case.

NIB	Exc.	V.G.	Good	Fair	Poor
—	900	675	400	250	150

ESP 85A

A high-quality target pistol imported by Mandall Shooting Supply. It features an interchangeable barrel system that converts the chambering from .22 rimfire to .32 S&W long wad cutter. The barrels are both 6" in length, and there are adjustable and interchangeable sights and a 5- or 8-shot detachable magazine. Weight is about 41 oz. The finish is blued, and the grips are stippled target types. The gun is furnished in a padded hard case with two extra magazines and takedown tools. This unit was introduced in 1989.

NIB	Exc.	V.G.	Good	Fair	Poor
1100	1000	850	700	550	450

EP-25

A semi-automatic pistol in caliber 6.35mm. Fitted with 2.75" barrel. Weight is about 18 oz. Mostly marketed outside of Germany. It has a polished blue finish and wood grips. Erma is stamped on the slide and on each of the grip's plates.

Courtesy James Rankin

NIB	Exc.	V.G.	Good	Fair	Poor
—	275	195	150	100	75

RX-22 and PX-22

A semi-automatic .22 rimfire copy of the Walther PPK. It has a 7-round magazine. Assembled in the U.S. with parts from Germany by various companies that marketed the pistol in the U.S. It has a black plastic wraparound grips with the Erma logo on each side.

Courtesy James Rankin

NIB	Exc.	V.G.	Good	Fair	Poor
—	240	175	150	100	75

REVOLVERS

ER-772 Match

A target revolver chambered for the .22 rimfire and has a 6" shrouded barrel with a solid rib. The swing-out cylinder holds

6 shots, and the sights are adjustable. The finish is blued, with stippled target grips. This model was introduced in 1989.

NIB	Exc.	V.G.	Good	Fair	Poor
1000	800	600	350	250	200

ER-773 Match

Similar to the ER-772 except that it is chambered for the .32 S&W long cartridge.

NIB	Exc.	V.G.	Good	Fair	Poor
900	750	500	375	250	200

ER-777

Basically a similar revolver to the ER-773 except that it has a 4.5" or 5" barrel and is chambered for the .357 Magnum cartridge. The revolver is larger and has standard sport grips. This model was introduced in 1989.

NIB	Exc.	V.G.	Good	Fair	Poor
800	600	450	350	250	200

RIFLES

EM1.22

A semi-automatic .22 rimfire version of the M1 Carbine. It has an 18" barrel and a 15-round magazine. It was manufactured between 1966 and 1976.

NIB	Exc.	V.G.	Good	Fair	Poor
—	350	225	150	125	100

EG-72, EG-722

A 15-shot slide-action carbine chambered for .22 rimfire, with a 18.5" barrel and open sights. The finish is blued, and it was manufactured between 1970 and 1985.

NIB	Exc.	V.G.	Good	Fair	Poor
—	250	165	100	75	50

EG-712, EG-73

A lever copy of the Winchester 94 Carbine chambered for the .22 rimfire or the .22 rimfire Magnum (EG-73). It has an 18.5" barrel and holds 15 shots in a tubular magazine. It was manufactured between 1973 and 1985.

NIB	Exc.	V.G.	Good	Fair	Poor
—	250	175	150	125	100

SR-100

This is long-range precision bolt-action rifle chambered for .308 Win., .300 Win. Mag., or .338 Lapua calibers. Barrel length on the .308 Win. caliber is 25.25", other calibers are 29.25". All barrels are fitted with a muzzlebrake. Trigger is adjustable. Stock is laminated with thumbhole and adjustable recoil pad and cheekpiece. Weight is approximately 15 lbs.

NIB	Exc.	V.G.	Good	Fair	Poor
8800	7000	5000	2750	1300	600

ERQUIAGA
Eibar, Spain

Another Spanish company that commenced business during WWI as a subcontractor on the French "Ruby" contract. They manufactured the usual poor quality, 7.65mm Eibar-type pistol.

Fiel

The trade name found on the Ruby subcontract pistol described above. It is marked "Erquiaga y Cia Eibar Cal. 7.65 Fiel."

Courtesy James Rankin

NIB	Exc.	V.G.	Good	Fair	Poor
—	200	150	125	100	75

Fiel 6.35

After the end of WWI, a 1906 Browning copy was made. It is chambered for the 6.35mm cartridge. The markings are "Automatic Pistol 6.35 Fiel No. 1." Later models had "EMC" molded into the grip.

NIB	Exc.	V.G.	Good	Fair	Poor
—	195	135	100	75	50

Marte

Another poor-quality "Eibar" -type pistol that is chambered for the 6.35mm and that was made in the early 1920s.

NIB	Exc.	V.G.	Good	Fair	Poor
—	195	135	100	75	50

ERRASTI, A.
Eibar, Spain

Errasti manufactured a variety of inexpensive yet serviceable pistols from the early 1900s until the Spanish Civil War.

Velo Dog

Usual cheap, solid-frame, folding-trigger revolvers one associates with the model designation. They were chambered in 5.5mm and 6.35mm and were made in the early 1900s.

NIB	Exc.	V.G.	Good	Fair	Poor
—	195	135	100	75	50

M1889

In 1915-1916 Errasti produced the 10.4mm Italian army service revolver. The quality was reasonably good. They were marked "Errasti Eiber" on the right side of the frame.

NIB	Exc.	V.G.	Good	Fair	Poor
—	400	295	200	125	75

Errasti

Two "Eibar"-type Browning copies were made under this trade name. One was chambered for the 6.35mm, the other the 7.65mm. They were both marked "Automatic Pistol Errasti."

Courtesy James Rankin

NIB	Exc.	V.G.	Good	Fair	Poor
—	195	135	110	75	50

Errasti Oscillante

Manufactured in the 1920s, these revolvers were copied from the Smith & Wesson Military & Police design. They were chambered for the .32, .38, and .44 calibers with the .38 being the most frequently encountered. **NOTE:** Add 30 percent for .44.

NIB	Exc.	V.G.	Good	Fair	Poor
—	250	195	125	95	50

Dreadnaught, Goliath and Smith Americano

These three trade names were found on a group of poor quality nickel-plated revolvers. They were made from 1905 through 1920 and were obvious copies of the Iver Johnson design. They had break-open actions, ribbed barrel, and were chambered for .32, .38, and .44 calibers. They are scarce today, as most have long since fallen apart. **NOTE:** Add 30 percent for .44.

NIB	Exc.	V.G.	Good	Fair	Poor
—	225	175	100	75	50

ESCODIN, M.
Eibar, Spain

This company made a Smith & Wesson revolver copy from 1924 through 1931. It is chambered for the .32 and the .38 Special. The only marking is a coat of arms stamped on the left side of the frame.

NIB	Exc.	V.G.	Good	Fair	Poor
—	175	125	100	75	50

ESPIRIN, HERMANOS
Eibar, Spain

Euskaro

This poor-quality, often unsafe revolver was manufactured from 1906 until WWI. They are copies of the Iver Johnson design break-open actions, chambered for .32. .38, and .44. This product epitomizes the worst Eibar had to offer during the pre-Civil War era. **NOTE:** Add 30 percent for .44.

NIB	Exc.	V.G.	Good	Fair	Poor
—	200	125	75	50	25

ESCORT
Turkey

SEMI-AUTOMATIC SHOTGUNS

Model AS

This 12 gauge 3" model is fitted with a 28" vent rib barrel with choke tubes. Walnut stock. Black finish. Magazine capacity is 4 rounds. Weight is about 7 lbs.

NIB	Exc.	V.G.	Good	Fair	Poor
450	365	245	200	150	100

Model PS

This 12 gauge 3" model is similar to the above but with a black polymer stock and black finish. Also offered in Shadow Grass camo or Mossy Oak Break-Up camo. Choice of Spark or TriViz front sights. Barrel length is 28" except for TriViz variation with 24" barrel. Weight is about 7 lbs. **NOTE:** Add $100 for camo coverage; add $45 for TriViz model.

NIB	Exc.	V.G.	Good	Fair	Poor
500	400	300	200	150	100

Model PS AimGuard

This 12 gauge 3" model is fitted with a 20" fixed choke barrel in Cylinder bore. Black polymer stock with black finish. Magazine capacity is 5 rounds. Weight is about 6.4 lbs.

NIB	Exc.	V.G.	Good	Fair	Poor
400	295	200	125	100	75

Combo Model

This 12 gauge 3" model is offered with two sets of barrels: one 28" with Full choke tube and the other 24" with Turkey choke tube. Polymer stock with Mossy Oak Break-Up. Receiver is fitted with a dovetail mount. Weight is about 7 lbs.

NIB	Exc.	V.G.	Good	Fair	Poor
575	425	365	295	200	100

Escort Semi-Auto Slug Gun

This slug gun is available in 12 or 20 gauge. Rifled barrel is 22 inches long with 1:26 twist. Self-regulating gas piston. It has Hi-Viz sights and is equipped with a cantilevered scope base. Black synthetic stock. Overall length, 42 inches. Weight: 6.3 lbs. (20 ga.), 7 lbs. (12 ga.).

NIB	Exc.	V.G.	Good	Fair	Poor
530	475	375	300	250	200

Escort Extreme Series

Available for either the 12 gauge 3" or 3.5" Magnum with 28" barrel, Hi-Viz sights, choke tubes and several camo patterns for turkey or waterfowl hunting. Extreme Waterfowl Youth model available in 20 gauge with 22" barrel.

Extreme 3.5"

NIB	Exc.	V.G.	Good	Fair	Poor
800	675	500	400	300	200

Extreme 3"

NIB	Exc.	V.G.	Good	Fair	Poor
700	600	450	400	300	150

Extreme Waterfowl Youth

NIB	Exc.	V.G.	Good	Fair	Poor
600	525	400	350	300	150

PUMP-ACTION SHOTGUNS

Field Hunter

This 12 gauge 3" model is fitted with a 28" vent rib barrel with choke tubes. Offered with a black polymer stock of Mossy Oak Break-Up or Shadow Grass camo pattern. A 24" barrel with TriViz is also offered. Magazine capacity is 4 rounds. Weight is about 7 lbs. **NOTE:** For camo finish add $50. For TriViz sights add $100.

NIB	Exc.	V.G.	Good	Fair	Poor
325	225	165	135	100	75

AimGuard

This 12 gauge 3" model is fitted with a 20" barrel with fixed Cylinder bore choke. Black polymer stock. Magazine capacity is 5 rounds. Weight is about 6.4 lbs. Add 10 percent for 18" barrel and nickel finish.

NIB	Exc.	V.G.	Good	Fair	Poor
325	225	165	135	100	75

Escort Pump Slug Gun

Same specifications as semi-automatic except slide-action. Weight: 6 lbs. (20 gauge), 6.7 lbs. (12 gauge).

NIB	Exc.	V.G.	Good	Fair	Poor
430	385	290	250	200	150

EUROARMS OF AMERICA
Winchester, Virginia

An importer of blackpowder muzzleloading firearms, primarily replicas of early American weapons.

REVOLVERS

1851 Navy

A replica of the Colt revolver chambered for .36 or .44 caliber percussion. It has a squareback, silver-plated trigger guard and a 7.5" barrel.

NIB	Exc.	V.G.	Good	Fair	Poor
275	225	170	110	75	45

1851 Navy Police Model

Chambered for .36 caliber with a 5-shot, fluted cylinder and a 5.5" barrel.

NIB	Exc.	V.G.	Good	Fair	Poor
275	225	170	110	75	45

1851 Navy Sheriff's Model

A 5" barreled version of the Navy Model.

NIB	Exc.	V.G.	Good	Fair	Poor
275	225	170	110	75	45

1851 "Schneider & Glassick" Navy

A replica of the Confederate revolver chambered for .36 or .44 caliber percussion.

NIB	Exc.	V.G.	Good	Fair	Poor
150	100	80	60	50	35

1851 "Griswold & Gunnison" Navy

A replica of this Confederate revolver chambered for .36 or .44 caliber percussion.

NIB	Exc.	V.G.	Good	Fair	Poor
285	235	170	110	75	45

1862 Police

A replica of the Colt Model 1862 chambered for .36 caliber percussion, with a 7.5" barrel and a steel frame.

NIB	Exc.	V.G.	Good	Fair	Poor
275	225	170	110	75	45

1860 Army

A replica of the Colt revolver chambered for .44 caliber percussion. It was offered with a 5" or 8" barrel.

NIB	Exc.	V.G.	Good	Fair	Poor
275	225	170	110	75	45

1861 Navy

A replica of the Colt revolver chambered for .36 caliber percussion.

NIB	Exc.	V.G.	Good	Fair	Poor
275	225	170	110	75	45

1858 Remington Army or Navy

Replicas of the Remington percussion revolvers chambered for .36 or .44 caliber.

NIB	Exc.	V.G.	Good	Fair	Poor
275	225	170	110	75	45

RIFLES

The rifles listed are modern replicas of early American and British firearms. They are of good quality and are quite serviceable.

Cook & Brother Carbine

NIB	Exc.	V.G.	Good	Fair	Poor
595	500	375	250	195	100

1863 J.P. Murray

NIB	Exc.	V.G.	Good	Fair	Poor
595	500	375	250	195	100

1853 Enfield Rifled Musket

NIB	Exc.	V.G.	Good	Fair	Poor
610	525	375	250	195	100

1858 Enfield Rifled Musket

NIB	Exc.	V.G.	Good	Fair	Poor
610	525	375	250	195	100

1861 Enfield Musketoon

NIB	Exc.	V.G.	Good	Fair	Poor
500	375	250	195	100	65

1803 Harper's Ferry

NIB	Exc.	V.G.	Good	Fair	Poor
595	500	375	250	195	100

1841 Mississippi Rifle

NIB	Exc.	V.G.	Good	Fair	Poor
595	500	375	250	195	100

Pennsylvania Rifle

NIB	Exc.	V.G.	Good	Fair	Poor
400	350	275	225	150	100

Hawken Rifle

NIB	Exc.	V.G.	Good	Fair	Poor
400	350	275	225	150	100

Cape Gun

NIB	Exc.	V.G.	Good	Fair	Poor
450	395	325	275	200	150

Buffalo Carbine

NIB	Exc.	V.G.	Good	Fair	Poor
450	395	325	275	200	150

1862 Remington Rifle

NIB	Exc.	V.G.	Good	Fair	Poor
450	395	325	275	200	150

Zouave Rifle

NIB	Exc.	V.G.	Good	Fair	Poor
450	395	325	275	200	150

SHOTGUNS

Duck Gun

A single-barreled percussion fowling piece chambered for 8, 10, or 12 gauge. It has a 33" smoothbore barrel and a case-colored hammer and lock. The stock is walnut with brass mountings. This model was introduced in 1989. Add 20 percent for 8 gauge.

NIB	Exc.	V.G.	Good	Fair	Poor
450	395	325	275	200	150

Standard Side-by-Side

A side-by-side chambered for 12 gauge percussion. It has 28" barrels with engraved locks and a walnut stock.

NIB	Exc.	V.G.	Good	Fair	Poor
475	400	350	295	200	125

EUROPEAN AMERICAN ARMORY CORP./U.S. SPORTING GOODS, INC.

Rockledge, Florida

EAA WITNESS PISTOLS

EAA Witness P-Series Full Size

Introduced in 1998 this is a full size polymer frame pistol chambered for 9mm, .40 S&W, .45 ACP, .38 Super, and 10mm cartridges. Barrel length is 4.55". Overall length is 8.5" with an empty weight of 31 oz. Rear sight is adjustable for windage. Magazine capacity for 9mm is 28 rounds and .40 S&W is 15 rounds while the .45 ACP model holds 10 rounds. For the 10mm model magazine capacity is 15 rounds. **NOTE:** Add $30 for ported barrel.

NIB	Exc.	V.G.	Good	Fair	Poor
525	425	325	225	180	100

EAA Witness P-Series Carry-Comp

This model is fitted with a 4.25" ported barrel. Chambered for .45 ACP.

NIB	Exc.	V.G.	Good	Fair	Poor
470	375	275	200	150	100

EAA Witness P-Series Compact

Similar to the above model but with a barrel length of 3.55". Weight is about 26 oz. **NOTE:** Add $30 for ported barrel.

NIB	Exc.	V.G.	Good	Fair	Poor
450	350	250	200	150	100

EAA Witness P-S Series

Built on a different frame size from the P-Series pistols. This model is chambered for the .22 LR, 9mm, or .40 S&W cartridges. Barrel length is 4.55". Weight is about 31 oz.

NIB	Exc.	V.G.	Good	Fair	Poor
400	325	275	200	150	100

EAA Witness Carry Comp

This model is offered in 9mm, .41 AE, .40 S&W, and .45 ACP. It features a 1" steel compensator. The barrel is 4.1" long. Overall length is the same as the standard model as is magazine capacity. Offered in blue or blue chrome finish. Weighs 34 oz. **NOTE:** For .45 ACP add 15 percent.

Old Configuration

NIB	Exc.	V.G.	Good	Fair	Poor
425	350	300	250	200	175

New Configuration

NIB	Exc.	V.G.	Good	Fair	Poor
500	450	375	325	250	175

EAA Witness Standard

Available in 9mm, .41 AE, .40 S&W, and .45 ACP with 4.5" barrel. Magazine capacity: 9mm-16 rounds, .41 AE-11 rounds, .40 S&W-12 rounds, .45 ACP-10 rounds. Offered in blue, chrome, two-tone, and stainless steel. Weighs approximately 33 oz. **NOTE:** For chrome, two-tone, and stainless steel add 5 percent.

Old Configuration

NIB	Exc.	V.G.	Good	Fair	Poor
385	325	275	225	175	125

New Configuration

NIB	Exc.	V.G.	Good	Fair	Poor
500	375	295	225	175	125

EAA Witness Subcompact

Offered in the same calibers as the standard model but fitted with a 3.66" barrel and shorter grip. Magazine capacity: 9mm-13 rounds, .41 AE-9 rounds, .40 S&W 9 rounds, .45 ACP-8 rounds. Weighs about 30 oz. Offered in blue, chrome, two-tone, and stainless steel. **NOTE:** For chrome, two-tone, and stainless steel add 5 percent.

Old Configuration

NIB	Exc.	V.G.	Good	Fair	Poor
425	350	295	235	175	125

New Configuration

NIB	Exc.	V.G.	Good	Fair	Poor
460	350	275	225	175	125

EAA Witness Sport L/S

This model features a longer slide for its 4.75" barrel. Offered in 9mm, .41 AE, .40 S&W, and .45 ACP. Magazine capacity: 9mm-19 rounds, .41 AE-13 rounds, .40 S&W 14 rounds, and .45 ACP-11 rounds. This model is also fitted with adjustable rear sight and extended safety. Available in two-tone finish. Weighs about 34.5 oz. A ported barrel is offered as an option. **NOTE:** For .45 ACP add 10 percent to prices.

Old Configuration

NIB	Exc.	V.G.	Good	Fair	Poor
625	550	500	400	300	200

New Configuration

NIB	Exc.	V.G.	Good	Fair	Poor
625	550	500	400	300	200

EAA Witness Combo 9/40

This model offers a 9mm conversion kit, and a .40 S&W conversion kit. These kits consist of a slide, barrel, recoil spring and guide, and magazine. Available in standard or subcompact size in blue, chrome, or two-tone finish. **NOTE:** For chrome or two-tone finish add 5 percent.

NIB	Exc.	V.G.	Good	Fair	Poor
595	495	425	350	275	175

EAA Witness Silver Team Match

This is designed as a competition pistol. It is fitted with a 5.25" barrel. It has these features: dual chamber compensator, single-action trigger, extended safety, competition hammer, paddle

magazine release, checkered walnut grips, and adjustable rear sight or drilled and tapped for scope mount. Offered in 9mm-19 rounds, .40 S&W 14 rounds, .41 AE-13 rounds, .45 ACP-11 rounds, and 9 x 21. Finish is blue and weight is approximately 34 oz.

NIB	Exc.	V.G.	Good	Fair	Poor
900	800	700	600	450	300

EAA Witness Sport

This model is built on the standard Witness frame with the addition of an adjustable rear sight and extended safety. Offered in 9mm, .41 AE, .40 S&W, .45 ACP in standard model magazine capacity. Weighs 33 oz. Available in two-tone finish. **NOTE:** For .45 ACP add 10 percent.

Old Configuration

NIB	Exc.	V.G.	Good	Fair	Poor
550	475	400	300	200	150

New Configuration

NIB	Exc.	V.G.	Good	Fair	Poor
550	475	400	300	200	150

EAA Witness Hunter

This model features a camo finish with a 6" barrel. Chambered for the .45 ACP or 10mm cartridge. Drilled and tapped for scope mount and adjustable sights. Magazine capacity is 10 rounds. Weight is about 41 oz. Also available with blued finish.

NIB	Exc.	V.G.	Good	Fair	Poor
975	800	575	395	250	150

EAA Witness Gold Team Match

This is a full race competition pistol with triple chamber compensator, beaver tail grip safety, beveled magazine well, adjustable rear sight or drilled and tapped for scope mount, extended safety and magazine release, competition hammer, square trigger guard, checkered front and backstrap, competition grips, and hard chrome finish. Same barrel length, magazine capacity, and calibers as the Silver Team Match. Weighs 38 oz.

NIB	Exc.	V.G.	Good	Fair	Poor
1700	1250	900	750	600	400

EAA Witness Limited Class Pistol

This model is built on the Witness Match frame with competition grips, high-capacity magazine, extended safety and magazine release, single-action trigger, long slide with adjustable rear sight, and match grade barrel. Offered in 9mm, .40 S&W, .38 Super, and .45 ACP with blue finish.

NIB	Exc.	V.G.	Good	Fair	Poor
1200	975	725	550	400	300

EAA Witness Stock

Introduced in 2005 this pistol features a 4.5" tapered cone barrel chambered for the 9mm, .40S&W, .45ACP, or .10mm cartridge.

Hard chrome finish, extended safety, wood checkered grips, and fully adjustable sights. Weight is about 33 oz.

NIB	Exc.	V.G.	Good	Fair	Poor
825	695	595	400	200	100

EAA Witness Multi Class Pistol Package

This package consists of one Witness Limited Class pistol with a complete unlimited class top half. The top half is made up of a standard length slide with super sight, recoil guide and spring, match grade competition barrel (threaded for compensator), and a dual chamber compensator. Available in 9mm, .40 S&W, 9 x 21, .45 ACP, 9 x 23, and .38 Super. Finish is blue.

NIB	Exc.	V.G.	Good	Fair	Poor
1700	1350	850	600	300	200

EAA Witness Elite Match

Single action semi-auto featuring 4.5" polygonal rifled steel barrel, adjustable rear sights, rubber grips. Two-tone finish. Chambered for 9 mm (18+1), 10 mm (15+1), 38 Super (15+1), .40 S&W (15+1) and .45 ACP (10+1). 33 oz. Introduced 2006.

NIB	Exc.	V.G.	Good	Fair	Poor
725	600	450	300	200	100

Zastava EZ Pistol

CZ75 clone. Single-/double-action pistol with 4" (Full Size) or 3.5" (Compact) barrel, polymer frame. Chambered in 9mm, .40 S&W or .45 ACP. Magazine capacity varies from 7 rounds (.45 ACP) to 15 (9mm).

NIB	Exc.	V.G.	Good	Fair	Poor
375	300	265	225	165	100

Thor

This is a single-shot pistol chambered for the .223 Rem., .270 Win., .30-06, .300 Win., .308, .375 Win., .44 Magnum, .45-70, .50 S&W, .7mm-08, or the .7mm Rem. Magnum. Fitted with a 14" barrel, the receiver has an integral top rail for scope mount. Weight is about 5 lbs.

NIB	Exc.	V.G.	Good	Fair	Poor
1150	850	675	500	355	145

OTHER EAA IMPORTED FIREARMS

BUL 1911 SERIES
BUL Government

Chambered for the .45 ACP cartridge and fitted with 4.8" barrel. Polymer frame. Tactical rear sight with dovetail front sight. Fully checkered grip. Black or stainless steel slide. Weight is about 24 oz. Magazine capacity is 10 rounds. Introduced in 2002. **NOTE**: Add $50 for stainless steel slide.

NIB	Exc.	V.G.	Good	Fair	Poor
550	450	300	200	125	75

Commander

Same as above but fitted with 3.8" barrel.

NIB	Exc.	V.G.	Good	Fair	Poor
550	450	300	200	125	75

Stinger

This model has a 3" barrel.

NIB	Exc.	V.G.	Good	Fair	Poor
550	450	300	200	125	75

EAA Big Bore Bounty Hunter

This model is a single-action revolver made in Germany. It features three-position hammer, forged barrel, and walnut grips. Offered in .357 Mag., .45 Long Colt, and .44 Mag. in 4.5", 5.5", or 7.5" barrel lengths. Choice of finish includes blue or case-colored frame, chrome, gold, or blue and gold. **NOTE**: For chrome, gold, or blue and gold finish add 20 percent.

NIB	Exc.	V.G.	Good	Fair	Poor
400	300	225	175	150	125

EAA Small Bore Bounty Hunter

This is a single-action .22-caliber revolver. It has wood grips and is available in blue or blue and brass finish. Barrel lengths are 4.75", 6", and 9". It is chambered for .22 LR or .22 Winchester Rimfire Magnum.

NIB	Exc.	V.G.	Good	Fair	Poor
275	200	145	125	75	60

EAA Bounty Hunter Shotgun—External Hammers

This is a side-by-side shotgun with external hammers chambered for 10, 12, 16, 20, 28, and .410 bores. It is offered in barrel lengths of 20", 24", and 26".

NIB	Exc.	V.G.	Good	Fair	Poor
375	300	250	175	150	125

EAA Bounty Hunter Shotgun—Traditional

Same as above but with internal hammers. Offered in 12 or 20 gauge.

NIB	Exc.	V.G.	Good	Fair	Poor
300	250	200	150	100	75

EAA F.A.B. 92 Pistol

This model is a semi-automatic pistol similar to the Witness, but fitted with a hammer drop safety and slide mounted safety, that is both a double-action or single-action. It is available in either a full size (33 oz.) or compact size (30 oz.). The full size version has a 4.5" barrel while the compact is fitted with a 3.66" barrel. Offered in 9mm or .40 S&W in blue, two-tone, or chrome finish.

NIB	Exc.	V.G.	Good	Fair	Poor
395	300	225	175	125	100

EAA European Standard Pistol

This is a single-action semi-automatic pistol with external hammer, slide grip serrations, wood grips, and single column magazine. The barrels length is 3.2" and overall length is 6.5". Chambered for .22 LR, 380 ACP, and .32 ACP. The magazine capacity is 10 rounds for the .22 LR, 7 rounds for .380, and 7 rounds for .32. Offered in blue, blue/chrome, chrome, blue/gold. Weighs 26 oz.

NIB	Exc.	V.G.	Good	Fair	Poor
195	155	110	95	75	50

EAA European Target Pistol

This model features adjustable rear sight, external hammer, single-action trigger, walnut target grips, and adjustable weight system. Chambered for .22 LR. Offered in blue finish and weighs 40 oz.

NIB	Exc.	V.G.	Good	Fair	Poor
355	295	225	175	150	100

EAA Windicator Standard Grade

This German-built model is a double-action revolver chambered for the .22 LR, .22 Winchester Rimfire Magnum, .32 H&R, and .38 Special. It is offered in 2", 4", and 6" barrel lengths. The cylinder capacity for the .22 LR/.22 WRM is 8 rounds, .32 H&R is 7 rounds, and the .38 Special is 6 rounds. The cylinder is unfluted. Finish is blue.

NIB	Exc.	V.G.	Good	Fair	Poor
275	165	135	110	75	60

EAA Windicator Basic Grade

This model is chambered for the .38 Special or the .357 Magnum with 2" barrel. The fluted cylinder holds 6 rounds. Finish is blue.

NIB	Exc.	V.G.	Good	Fair	Poor
275	165	135	110	75	60

EAA Windicator Tactical Grade

This model is similar in appearance to the standard grade but is chambered for the .38 Special with 2" or 4" barrel. The 4" barrel has an integral compensator. Finish is blue.

2" Barrel

NIB	Exc.	V.G.	Good	Fair	Poor
190	150	125	100	80	60

4" Barrel

NIB	Exc.	V.G.	Good	Fair	Poor
250	200	150	125	100	75

EAA Windicator Target Grade

This model has these special features: adjustable trigger pull, walnut grips, adjustable rear sight, drilled and tapped for scope mount, target hammer, adjustable trigger stop. Fitted with 6" target barrel. Chambered for .22 LR, .38 Special, .357 Mag. Blue finish.

NIB	Exc.	V.G.	Good	Fair	Poor
350	275	225	200	150	100

EAA PM2 Shotgun

This is a pump-action 12 gauge shotgun with 6-round box magazine. Barrel length is 20" and finish is either blue or chrome. Stock is black composite. Weight is 6.8 lbs. This model was discontinued in 1993. **NOTE:** Add $100 for optional night sights.

NIB	Exc.	V.G.	Good	Fair	Poor
450	350	300	250	200	150

EAA HW 60 Rifle

This German-made target rifle is chambered for the .22 LR. It features an adjustable trigger and other target and match grade components. The barrel length is 26.8", the stock is stippled walnut, and the finish is blue. Weighs approximately 10.8 lbs.

Target Grade

NIB	Exc.	V.G.	Good	Fair	Poor
700	595	500	400	300	200

Match Grade

NIB	Exc.	V.G.	Good	Fair	Poor
795	675	550	450	350	250

EAA SABATTI

These firearms are made by the Sabatti firm in Gardone, Italy. It is a old line company, having been in the firearms business since 1674. The company also produces and supplies component parts to many of Italy's premier gun makers. These shotguns and rifles are manufactured for the cost-conscious buyer.

EAA Sabatti Falcon

This is a field grade over/under shotgun with checkered walnut stock with pistol grip, boxlock action, double triggers, and extractors. Offered in 12 or 20 gauge with 3" chambers. Also available in 28 gauge and .410 bore with 26" or 28" barrels. Barrel lengths are available in 26", 28", or 30". Chokes are fixed.

12/20 Gauge

NIB	Exc.	V.G.	Good	Fair	Poor
575	425	400	350	300	250

28/.410

NIB	Exc.	V.G.	Good	Fair	Poor
625	480	425	375	325	275

EAA SP 1822

This Sabatti rifle is chambered for the .22 LR. It is a semi-automatic carbine with a two-piece adjustable stock.

NIB	Exc.	V.G.	Good	Fair	Poor
225	175	125	100	85	60

EAA SP 1822H

This a heavy barrel version of the above model without sights. The receiver is fitted with scope mount base.

NIB	Exc.	V.G.	Good	Fair	Poor
225	175	125	100	85	60

EAA SP 1822TH

This variation also has a heavy barrel without sights but with base mounts. A one-piece Bell and Carlson thumb hole stock is the feature of this model.

NIB	Exc.	V.G.	Good	Fair	Poor
350	260	225	175	125	90

EAA Sporting Clay Basic

This model features a single-selective trigger, extractors, checkered walnut stock with pistol grip, extra wide rib, and blued receiver with scroll engraving. Offered in 12 gauge only with 28" fixed choke barrel.

NIB	Exc.	V.G.	Good	Fair	Poor
350	275	250	200	150	100

EAA Sporting Clay Pro

This model is similar to the basic sporting clay model with the addition of a select walnut stock, screw-in choke tubes, automatic ejectors, recoil pad. Comes with hard shell case.

NIB	Exc.	V.G.	Good	Fair	Poor
950	720	650	550	450	300

EAA Sporting Clay Pro Gold

Same as above but with gold inlay receiver.

NIB	Exc.	V.G.	Good	Fair	Poor
1000	750	650	550	450	300

EAA Saba

This model is a side-by-side shotgun that features an engraved silver boxlock receiver, double or single triggers, selective ejectors, solid raised matted rib, and select European walnut checkered stock. Offered in 12, 20, and 28 gauge as well as .410 bore. Barrel length are 26" or 28" with fixed chokes.

NIB	Exc.	V.G.	Good	Fair	Poor
775	600	500	400	300	250

EAA/Saiga Shotgun

A semi-automatic shotgun based on the AK-47 design. Chambered for the 12, 20 and .410 bore. Barrel length are 20", 24", 26", or 28". Blued finish with optional camo finish. Detachable 5-round box magazine. Introduced in 1999. **NOTE:** Deduct $175 for .410 variation.

NIB	Exc.	V.G.	Good	Fair	Poor
600	525	450	350	200	125

EAA/Saiga Rifle

Same as above but chambered for 7.62x39 or .308 cartridge. Fitted with a 20" barrel. Choice of wood or synthetic stock. Introduced in 1999. **NOTE:** Add $100 for .308 caliber.

NIB	Exc.	V.G.	Good	Fair	Poor
550	450	300	200	125	75

EAA Rover 870

This is a high-quality bolt-action rifle. The walnut stock is checkered with rubber recoil pad. Adjustable rear sight and receiver is drilled and tapped for scope mount. Barrel length is 22". Chambered for these cartridges: .22-250, .243, .25-06, .270, .308, .30-06, 7mm Rem. Magnum, .300 and .338 Win. Magnum.

NIB	Exc.	V.G.	Good	Fair	Poor
585	445	375	300	200	125

EAA Benelli Silhouette Pistol

This is a specialized competition pistol with a semi-automatic action. The stocks are match type walnut with stippling. The palm shelf is adjustable. The barrel is 4.3" long. Fully adjustable sights. It is chambered for the .22 LR, .22 Short, and the .32 WC. Supplied with loading tool and cleaning rod. The .22 Caliber version weighs 38.5 oz. Overall length is 11.7".

NIB	Exc.	V.G.	Good	Fair	Poor
2000	1350	995	750	600	400

EVANS REPEATING RIFLE CO.
Mechanic Falls, Maine

Incorporated in 1873, this firm produced repeating rifles based upon patents issued to Warren R. Evans (1868-1871) and later George F. Evans (1877, 1878 and 1879). The most distinctive feature of these arms is that they used a butt magazine operating on the principle of an Archimedean screw. Distributed by Merwin, Hulbert & Company, as well as Schuyler, Hartley & Graham, Evans rifles met with some success. One of their earliest advocates was William F. Cody (Buffalo Bill). The company ceased operations in 1879, after approximately 15,000 arms had been made.

LEVER-ACTION RIFLES

This rifle is totally unique for a number of reasons. It holds the most rounds of any repeating rifle that did not have a detachable magazine, with capacities up to 38 rounds on some models. This rifle was chambered for its own cartridge—the .44 Evans of which there were two versions: a 1" cartridge in the "Old Model" and the "Transition Model" and a 1.5" cartridge in the "New Model." The finish on these rifles is blued, with nickel-plated levers and buttplates noted on some examples. The stocks are walnut. There were approximately 12,250 of all models manufactured between 1873 and 1879.

Old Model

This variation is chambered for the 1" .44 Evans cartridge and has a butt stock that covers only the top half of the revolving 34-shot magazine located in the butt of the rifle. The buttplate appears as if it is reversed, and the markings on the "Old Model" are "Evans Repeating Rifle/Pat. Dec. 8, 1868 & Sept. 16, 1871". There are three versions of the Old Model listed. They were manufactured between 1874 and 1876 and serial numbered 1-500.

Military Musket

This version has a 30" barrel, with two barrel bands and provisions for a bayonet. There were only 50 estimated manufactured.

NIB	Exc.	V.G.	Good	Fair	Poor
—	—	3750	1700	500	200

Sporting Rifle

Approximately 300 of this model produced with a 26", 28", or 30" octagonal barrel.

NIB	Exc.	V.G.	Good	Fair	Poor
—	—	1950	900	500	200

Carbine

This variation has a 22" barrel, with one barrel band and a sling swivel. There were 150 produced.

NIB	Exc.	V.G.	Good	Fair	Poor
—	—	3500	1450	500	200

Transitional Model

Has a buttstock that covers both the top and bottom of the rotary magazine, with an exposed portion in the middle of the butt. The buttplate does not have the backward appearance, and the barrel is marked "Evans Repeating Rifle Mechanic Falls Me./Pat Dec. 8, 1868 & Sept. 16, 1871". This version was manufactured in 1876 and 1877 and was serial numbered between 500-2185, for a total of approximately 1,650 manufactured.

Military Musket

Has a 30" barrel and two barrel bands. 150 were produced.

NIB	Exc.	V.G.	Good	Fair	Poor
—	—	3000	1750	650	200

Carbine

Four hundred-fifty of these were produced, with a 22" barrel and one barrel band.

NIB	Exc.	V.G.	Good	Fair	Poor
—	—	2950	1700	600	200

Sporting Rifle

Has a 26", 28", or 30" barrel. There were 1,050 produced.

NIB	Exc.	V.G.	Good	Fair	Poor
—	—	2250	1000	300	150

"Montreal Carbine"

A special issue marked "Montreal", sold by R.H. Kilby, Evans' Canadian sales agent. There were between 50 and 100 produced.

NIB	Exc.	V.G.	Good	Fair	Poor
—	—	3250	1150	450	250

New Model

Approximately 10,000 of the New Model were produced, chambered for the 1.5" .44 Evans cartridge with a magazine capacity reduced to 28. The frame was redesigned and rounded at the top, and the fore-end fit flush to the receiver. The lever and hammer are streamlined, and there is a dust cover over the loading gate. The markings are the same as on the Transitional Model with "U.S.A." added to the last line. This version was not serial numbered, and any numbers found are assembly numbers only.

Military Musket

3,000 produced, with a 30" barrel and two barrel bands.

Courtesy Bonhams & Butterfields, San Francisco, California

NIB	Exc.	V.G.	Good	Fair	Poor
—	—	3950	1750	450	275

Carbine

4,000 produced with a 22" barrel, one barrel band, and a sling swivel.

Courtesy Buffalo Bill Historical Center, Cody, Wyoming

NIB	Exc.	V.G.	Good	Fair	Poor
—	—	2150	950	500	250

Sporting Rifle

3,000 produced with 26", 28", or 30" octagonal barrels.

NIB	Exc.	V.G.	Good	Fair	Poor
—	—	2500	2000	800	300

EVANS, J. E.
Philadelphia, Pennsylvania

Pocket Pistol

A copy of the Philadelphia-made Henry Deringer pistol and is chambered for .41 caliber. It utilizes the percussion ignition system and has barrels from 2.5" to 3" in length. The stock is of walnut with a checkered grip, and the mountings are scroll engraved German silver. The barrel is marked "J.E. Evans Philada." These pistols were manufactured in the 1850s.

NIB	Exc.	V.G.	Good	Fair	Poor
—	—	1250	1850	775	350

EXCAM
Hialeah, Florida

An importer of firearms, not a manufacturer. The Erma and Uberti products imported by this company are under their own heading in this book. The other products that they imported are listed here. They are no longer in business.

TA 76

Patterned after the Colt Single Action Army and is chambered for the .22 rimfire cartridge. It has a 4.75", 6", or 9" barrel and blue finish with wood grips. It is offered with brass trigger guard and backstrap and also offered chrome-plated. A combo model with an extra .22 Magnum cylinder is available and would add 10 percent to the listed values.

NIB	Exc.	V.G.	Good	Fair	Poor
—	100	75	65	40	25

TA 38 Over/Under Derringer

A two-shot derringer patterned after the Remington derringer. It is chambered for the .38 Special cartridge, has 3" barrels that pivot upward for loading, and is blued with checkered nylon grips. This model was discontinued in 1985.

NIB	Exc.	V.G.	Good	Fair	Poor
—	100	75	65	40	25

TA 90

A double-action, semi-automatic copy of the CZ-75 that some experts rate as the finest combat handgun in the world. It is chambered for the 9mm Parabellum and has a 4.75" barrel. It is constructed of steel and is finished with a matte blue or chrome with checkered wood or rubber grips. The detachable magazine holds 15 rounds.

NIB	Exc.	V.G.	Good	Fair	Poor
425	375	325	275	200	150

BTA-90B

A compact version of the TA 90, that has a 3.5" barrel and a 12-round detachable magazine. It is similar in all other respects to the standard model, with rubber grips only.

NIB	Exc.	V.G.	Good	Fair	Poor
425	375	325	275	200	150

TA 90 SS

A competition version of the TA 90, that is similar to the standard model except that it is compensated and features adjustable sights. It is offered either blued or chrome-plated and was introduced in 1989.

NIB	Exc.	V.G.	Good	Fair	Poor
650	575	500	400	325	225

TA 41, 41C, and 41 SS

This series of pistols is identical to the TA 90 series except that they are chambered for the .41 Action Express cartridge. Their values are about 10 percent higher than the 9mm versions. They were introduced in 1989.

Warrior Model W 722

A double-action revolver chambered for the .22 rimfire and the .22 rimfire Magnum with an interchangeable cylinder. It has a 6" barrel, adjustable sights, and an 8-shot cylinder capacity. It is blued, with checkered plastic grips. This model was not imported after 1986.

NIB	Exc.	V.G.	Good	Fair	Poor
—	100	75	50	35	20

Model W384

A double-action revolver chambered for the .38 Special cartridge, with a 4" or 6" vent rib barrel, blued finish, and plastic grips. It was discontinued in 1986.

NIB	Exc.	V.G.	Good	Fair	Poor
—	175	125	100	75	50

Model W357

Similar to the W384 except that it is chambered for the .357 Magnum cartridge. It was discontinued in 1986.

NIB	Exc.	V.G.	Good	Fair	Poor
—	200	150	125	100	75

Targa GT 26

A blowback-operated, semi-automatic pistol chambered for the .25 ACP cartridge. It has a 2.5" barrel and a 6-shot detachable magazine. It is finished in blue or matte chrome, with a choice of alloy or steel frame. The grips are wood.

Steel Frame Version

NIB	Exc.	V.G.	Good	Fair	Poor
125	90	75	50	40	30

Alloy Frame Version

NIB	Exc.	V.G.	Good	Fair	Poor
100	75	50	35	30	25

GT 22

A semi-automatic pistol chambered for the .22 LR cartridge. It has a 4" barrel, fixed sights, and a 10-round magazine. Available either blued or matte chrome-plated and has wooden grips.

NIB	Exc.	V.G.	Good	Fair	Poor
200	175	150	125	90	70

GT 22T

Similar to the GT 22, with a 6" barrel and adjustable target-type sights.

NIB	Exc.	V.G.	Good	Fair	Poor
225	200	175	150	100	75

GT 32

A blowback-operated semi-automatic pistol chambered for the .32 ACP cartridge. It has a 7-round magazine and is either blued or matte chrome-plated with wood grips.

NIB	Exc.	V.G.	Good	Fair	Poor
200	175	150	125	90	75

GT 380

Similar to the GT 32 except that it is chambered for the .380 ACP cartridge.

NIB	Exc.	V.G.	Good	Fair	Poor
225	175	150	125	100	75

GT 380XE

Similar to the GT 380, with an 11-shot, high-capacity, detachable magazine.

NIB	Exc.	V.G.	Good	Fair	Poor
225	200	175	150	125	100

EXCEL INDUSTRIES
Chino, California

Accelerator Pistol

This is a semi-automatic pistol available in .22 WMR or .17 HMR. Barrel length is 8.5" with a .875" diameter. Stainless steel with polymer grip. The barrel is fitted with an aluminum rib with target sights and a Weaver base. Magazine capacity is 9 rounds. Weight is about 54 oz. Introduced in 2004.

NIB	Exc.	V.G.	Good	Fair	Poor
425	320	250	165	125	75

Accelerator Rifle

As above but with an 18" fluted stainless steel barrel and black polymer pistol-grip stock. Fully adjustable removable sights on a Weaver rail. Weight is about 8 lbs. Introduced in 2004.

NIB	Exc.	V.G.	Good	Fair	Poor
465	350	275	195	150	100

F

F.A.S.
Italy

Model 601

A high-grade, competition target pistol chambered for the .22 Short cartridge. It is a semi-automatic, with a 5.5" barrel and adjustable target sights. The detachable magazine holds 5 rounds, and the finish is blued with wraparound target grips. This model was discontinued in 1988.

NIB	Exc.	V.G.	Good	Fair	Poor
—	1450	1150	775	550	300

Model 602

Similar to the Model 601 except that it is chambered for the .22 LR. It was discontinued in 1987.

NIB	Exc.	V.G.	Good	Fair	Poor
—	1250	10500	725	500	250

Model 603

Chambered for the .32 S&W wadcutter cartridge and features adjustable grips. It was discontinued in 1987.

NIB	Exc.	V.G.	Good	Fair	Poor
—	1350	1075	775	500	250

F.I.E.
Hialeah, Florida

Firearms Import and Export was engaged in the business of importing the Franchi shotgun (which is listed under its own heading) and the Arminius revolver (which is made in Germany). They were also distributors for the Titan semi-automatic pistols, which are manufactured in the U.S.A. They were also importing a series of 9mm pistols from Italy that are produced by Tanfoglio and known as the TZ series. F.I.E. was no longer in business as of 1990.

HANDGUNS

TZ 75

A copy of the CZ 75 Czechoslovakian combat pistol produced by Tanfoglio in Italy. It is a 9mm, double-action semi-automatic with a 4.75" barrel, all-steel construction, fixed sights, and a 15-shot magazine. It is offered either blued or matte chrome plated, with wood or rubber grips.

NIB	Exc.	V.G.	Good	Fair	Poor
450	350	300	250	200	150

TZ 75 Series 88

An improved version that is also chambered for the .41 Action Express cartridge. It has a firing pin safety and can be carried cocked and locked. There are a few other minor changes. It was introduced in 1988.

NIB	Exc.	V.G.	Good	Fair	Poor
500	375	325	250	200	150

KG-99

A blowback-operated, semi-automatic assault pistol chambered for the 9mm Parabellum cartridge. It has a 36-round magazine. It was discontinued in 1984.

NIB	Exc.	V.G.	Good	Fair	Poor
550	450	350	250	200	150

Spectre Assault Pistol

An assault-type semi-automatic pistol chambered for the 9mm Parabellum. It has a 30- or 50-round magazine available. It was introduced in 1989.

NIB	Exc.	V.G.	Good	Fair	Poor
800	675	575	400	300	200

Titan II .22

A semi-automatic pistol chambered for the .22 LR. It has a 10-shot magazine and a blued finish with walnut grips. It is made in the U.S.A.

NIB	Exc.	V.G.	Good	Fair	Poor
275	150	100	75	50	25

Titan E32

A single-action, blowback-operated, semi-automatic pistol that was chambered for the .32 ACP and is now chambered for the .380 ACP cartridge. The finish is blue or chrome-plated, and the grips are walnut.

NIB	Exc.	V.G.	Good	Fair	Poor
300	175	150	125	100	75

Super Titan 11

Similar to the Titan except that it has a 12-round, high-capacity magazine.

NIB	Exc.	V.G.	Good	Fair	Poor
325	200	175	150	100	75

Titan 25

A smaller version of the Titan Series chambered for the .25 ACP cartridge. It is blued or chrome-plated.

NIB	Exc.	V.G.	Good	Fair	Poor
200	75	50	40	30	20

Titan Tigress

Similar to the Titan 25 except that it is gold-plated and cased.

NIB	Exc.	V.G.	Good	Fair	Poor
225	115	90	75	50	30

D38 Derringer

A two-shot, over/under, Remington-style derringer chambered for the .38 Special cartridge. It is chrome-plated and was dropped from the line in 1985.

NIB	Exc.	V.G.	Good	Fair	Poor
145	75	45	35	25	20

D86 Derringer

A single-shot derringer with a 3" barrel. It is chambered for the .38 Special cartridge and is chrome-plated. There is an ammunition storage compartment in the butt and a transfer bar safety that makes it safer to carry. This model was introduced in 1986.

NIB	Exc.	V.G.	Good	Fair	Poor
150	80	65	50	35	20

SINGLE ACTION ARMY REPLICA REVOLVERS

There is a series of single-action, .22-caliber revolvers that were patterned after the Colt Single Action Army. They were manufactured in the U.S.A. or Brescia, Italy. They are inexpensive and of fair quality. The differences between these models are basically barrel lengths, type of sights, and finish. They all are chambered for the .22 LR and have interchangeable .22 Magnum cylinders. We list them for reference purposes.

Cowboy

NIB	Exc.	V.G.	Good	Fair	Poor
250	125	100	80	75	50

Gold Rush

NIB	Exc.	V.G.	Good	Fair	Poor
250	125	100	80	75	50

Texas Ranger

NIB	Exc.	V.G.	Good	Fair	Poor
200	85	75	50	35	20

Buffalo Scout

NOTE: Add 50 percent for faux "gold"-plated Yellow Rose of Texas variant.

NIB	Exc.	V.G.	Good	Fair	Poor
175	80	70	50	35	20

Legend S.A.A.

NIB	Exc.	V.G.	Good	Fair	Poor
250	125	100	80	75	50

ARMINIUS REVOLVERS
Hombre

A single-action made in Germany by Arminius. It is patterned after the Colt Single Action Army revolver. The Hombre is chambered for the .357 Magnum, .44 Magnum, and .45 Colt cartridges. It is offered with a 5.5", 6", or 7.5" barrel, case-colored frame, and blued barrel and cylinder, with smooth walnut grips. The backstrap and trigger guard are offered in brass and will bring a 10 percent premium.

NIB	Exc.	V.G.	Good	Fair	Poor
325	225	175	125	100	75

Model 522TB

A swing-out cylinder, double-action revolver chambered for the .22 rimfire cartridge. It has a 4" barrel and is blued with wood grips.

NIB	Exc.	V.G.	Good	Fair	Poor
250	125	100	75	50	30

722

Similar to the 522, with an 8-shot cylinder and a 6" barrel. It is available with a chrome finish.

NIB	Exc.	V.G.	Good	Fair	Poor
250	125	100	75	50	30

532TB

A 7-shot, double-action revolver chambered for the .32 S&W cartridge. It has a 4" barrel and adjustable sights and is finished in either blue or chrome.

NIB	Exc.	V.G.	Good	Fair	Poor
250	130	110	80	60	40

732B

Similar to the 532TB, with a 6" barrel and fixed sights. It was discontinued in 1988.

NIB	Exc.	V.G.	Good	Fair	Poor
225	100	80	65	50	35

Standard Revolver

A double-action, swing-out cylinder revolver chambered for .32 Magnum or .38 Special. It has a 4" or 6" barrel and fixed sights and is blued with wood grips. This model is made in the U.S.A. and was introduced in 1989.

NIB	Exc.	V.G.	Good	Fair	Poor
225	100	75	50	35	20

Models 384TB and 386TB

These two models are double-action chambered for the .38 Special cartridge. The 384 has a 4" barrel; and the 386, a 6" barrel. They are available in blue or chrome plate and were discontinued in 1985.

NIB	Exc.	V.G.	Good	Fair	Poor
250	125	100	85	65	50

Model 357TB

Similar to the 384TB except that it is chambered for the .357 Magnum cartridge and is offered with a 3", 4", or 6" barrel.

NIB	Exc.	V.G.	Good	Fair	Poor
250	125	100	85	65	50

222, 232, and 382TB

These models are double-action swing-out cylinder revolvers chambered for .22 rimfire, .32 S&W, and .38 Special. They are 2"-barreled snub-nosed revolvers, with either blued or chrome-plated finishes. They were discontinued in 1985.

NIB	Exc.	V.G.	Good	Fair	Poor
200	100	75	50	40	25

Model 3572

A similar revolver to the 382TB except that it is chambered for the .357 Magnum cartridge. It was discontinued in 1984.

NIB	Exc.	V.G.	Good	Fair	Poor
250	125	100	85	65	50

SHOTGUNS AND RIFLES

Model 122

A bolt-action rifle chambered for .22 rimfire, with a 21" barrel and adjustable sights. It has a 10-shot magazine and a walnut Monte Carlo stock. It was introduced in 1986.

NIB	Exc.	V.G.	Good	Fair	Poor
200	100	75	50	35	25

Single-Shot

Brazilian made and chambered for 12 or 20 gauge and .410. It is a single-barreled break-open, with 25" through 30" barrel and various chokes. It is blued with a wood stock and was introduced in 1985.

NIB	Exc.	V.G.	Good	Fair	Poor
150	100	60	45	35	25

S.O.B.

Similar to the single-shot, with an 18.5" barrel and a pistol grip instead of a standard stock. This model was discontinued in 1984.

NIB	Exc.	V.G.	Good	Fair	Poor
165	110	60	45	35	25

Sturdy Over/Under

Chambered for 12 and 20 gauge and has 3" chambers and 28" vent-rib barrels with various chokes. This is an over/under with double triggers and extractors. The frame is engraved and silver finished. It was manufactured in Italy by Maroccini and imported between 1985 and 1988.

NIB	Exc.	V.G.	Good	Fair	Poor
400	300	225	175	150	100

Brute

A side-by-side chambered for 12 and 20 gauge and .410. It has 19" barrels, double triggers, and extractors. It has a wood stock and was dropped from the line in 1984.

NIB	Exc.	V.G.	Good	Fair	Poor
300	200	125	100	75	50

SPAS-12

A unique shotgun in that it can function as a pump or an automatic with the touch of a button. It is a paramilitary-type shotgun chambered for 12 gauge, with a 21.5" barrel and a 9-shot tube magazine. It has an alloy receiver and an optional folding stock. The finish is all black. This model is manufactured by Franchi in Italy. **NOTE:** Some early models had detachable wood stocks. These are rarely encountered. Seek a qualified appraiser for evaluations.

NIB	Exc.	V.G.	Good	Fair	Poor
1500	1100	900	700	400	300

LAW-12

A paramilitary-type, 12-gauge, semi-automatic shotgun that is gas-operated and has a 9-shot tube magazine. The barrel is 21.5" in length and choked cylinder bore. It has a military special black finish and a black synthetic stock.

NIB	Exc.	V.G.	Good	Fair	Poor
850	650	400	300	200	100

SAS-12

A paramilitary-type, slide-action shotgun chambered for 12 gauge. It has a 21.5" barrel, choked cylinder bore. The finish is similar to the LAW-12, and it is manufactured by Franchi in Italy.

NIB	Exc.	V.G.	Good	Fair	Poor
850	650	500	400	300	200

FABARM
Brescia, Italy

In 1998 H&K took over the importation of the Fabarm shotgun line in the U.S. Imported by Tristar and Sig Arms from 2005 - 2009. Currently imported by Fabarm USA.

SEMI-AUTOMATIC SHOTGUNS

Ellegi Standard

A gas-operated, semi-automatic shotgun chambered for 12 gauge. It has a 28" vent-rib barrel with choice of choke. The receiver is blue anodized alloy with a photo-etched game scene, and the stock and forearm are checkered walnut. This model was introduced in 1989. The Ellegi Model is available in six other configurations. The differences are in the barrel length and choke, type of choke tubes, and finish. Basically the guns are quite similar to the standard model. These variations are listed.

NIB	Exc.	V.G.	Good	Fair	Poor
700	625	525	450	350	250

Ellegi Multichoke

NIB	Exc.	V.G.	Good	Fair	Poor
700	625	525	450	350	250

Ellegi Innerchoke

NIB	Exc.	V.G.	Good	Fair	Poor
725	650	550	475	375	275

Ellegi Magnum

NIB	Exc.	V.G.	Good	Fair	Poor
725	650	550	475	375	275

Ellegi Super Goose

NIB	Exc.	V.G.	Good	Fair	Poor
800	725	625	550	450	350

Ellegi Slug

NIB	Exc.	V.G.	Good	Fair	Poor
775	700	600	525	425	325

Ellegi Police

NIB	Exc.	V.G.	Good	Fair	Poor
575	500	450	400	300	225

SLIDE-ACTION SHOTGUNS

Model S.D.A.S.S.

Chambered for 12 gauge with a 3" chamber. It is offered with a 20" or 24.5" barrel threaded for external choke tubes. This model has an 8-shot tube magazine, twin action bars, an alloy receiver and a matte black finish. It is a defensive-type shotgun and has been imported since 1989. The Special Police and the Martial Model are variations of the basic slide-action and differ in barrel length and choke. The Police Model has a shrouded barrel.

NIB	Exc.	V.G.	Good	Fair	Poor
350	275	200	150	100	75

Special Police

NIB	Exc.	V.G.	Good	Fair	Poor
525	475	425	350	275	200

Martial Model

NIB	Exc.	V.G.	Good	Fair	Poor
475	425	375	300	225	175

SINGLE-SHOT SHOTGUNS

Omega Standard

Has an alloy receiver and is chambered for 12 and 20 gauge, as well as .410. It has 26" or 28" barrels with various chokes. The finish is black with a beech stock. It was introduced in 1989.

NIB	Exc.	V.G.	Good	Fair	Poor
150	125	100	75	50	40

Omega Goose Gun

Chambered for 12 gauge only, with a 35.5" full-choke barrel.

NIB	Exc.	V.G.	Good	Fair	Poor
195	140	125	100	75	50

SIDE-BY-SIDE SHOTGUNS

Beta Model

This double-barrel is chambered for 12 gauge only, with choice of barrel length and choke. It has a boxlock action with false side plates. It has a single trigger and automatic ejectors, and the finish is blued with a checkered, select walnut stock. This model was introduced in 1989.

NIB	Exc.	V.G.	Good	Fair	Poor
925	850	750	600	450	300

Beta Europe

A deluxe version that features single-selective triggers and a game scene engraved, coin-finished receiver. The stock is the straight English style with a splinter forend. This model was introduced in 1989.

NIB	Exc.	V.G.	Good	Fair	Poor
1750	1500	1250	1000	750	500

OVER/UNDER SHOTGUNS

Field Model

Chambered for 12 gauge and has 29" vent-rib barrels with various chokes. The receiver is coin-finished, and the stock is checkered walnut. This Model was discontinued in 1985.

NIB	Exc.	V.G.	Good	Fair	Poor
900	700	600	500	400	300

Gamma Field

Chambered for 12 or 20 gauge and is offered with 26", 28", or 29" vent-rib barrels and various choke combinations. Screw-in choke tubes are available and would be worth a 10 percent premium. This model has a boxlock, coin-finished receiver that is moderately engraved and a checkered walnut stock.

NIB	Exc.	V.G.	Good	Fair	Poor
925	850	775	650	500	350

Gamma Paradox Gun

Chambered for 12 gauge only, and the top barrel is rifled for accurate placement of slugs. The barrels are 25" long with vent-rib, and the bottom barrel has three screw-in choke tubes. This model has a single-selective trigger and automatic ejectors. The finish is similar to the Field Model. It was introduced in 1989.

NIB	Exc.	V.G.	Good	Fair	Poor
1000	900	825	750	600	450

Gamma Trap or Skeet

Competition-grade guns with either a 27.5" barrel with five screw-in choke tubes on the skeet model or a 29" barrel with screw-in trap chokes. Both models feature single-selective triggers and automatic ejectors; and the trap model has a Monte Carlo stock. They have moderately engraved, coin-finished boxlock actions and were introduced in 1989.

NIB	Exc.	V.G.	Good	Fair	Poor
1000	900	825	750	600	450

Gamma Sporting Competition Model

Designed for Sporting Clays and is chambered for 12 gauge only. The 29" barrel has a wide rib and is furnished with five screw-in choke tubes. It has a single-selective trigger, automatic ejectors, and a checkered walnut stock with a competition recoil pad. It is finished like the skeet and trap models and was introduced in 1989.

NIB	Exc.	V.G.	Good	Fair	Poor
1000	900	825	750	600	450

H&K POST-1997 IMPORTED SHOTGUNS

Camo Lion

Introduced in 1999, this 12 gauge model features a ported barrel system in 24", 26", or 28" lengths. Wetlands camo finish. Five chokes tubes and hard plastic case included. Weight is about 7 lbs.

NIB	Exc.	V.G.	Good	Fair	Poor
800	650	450	300	175	100

Red Lion

This is a 12 gauge semi-auto with 3" chambers, three-shot magazine, matte finish, walnut stock, rubber vented recoil pad with leather cover, and set of five choke tubes. Available with 24", 26", or 28" vent-rib barrel. Weight is about 7 lbs.

NIB	Exc.	V.G.	Good	Fair	Poor
800	650	450	300	175	100

Red Lion Ducks Unlimited 2001

This model is offered only through the Ducks Unlimited banquet program only. This is a 12 gauge 28" barrel with select walnut stock. Oil finish. Unique serial numbers from 0001DU2001 to 3600DU2001. Receiver is engraved with waterfowl scene and DU logo. Comes with lockable case. Limited to 3,600 shotguns.

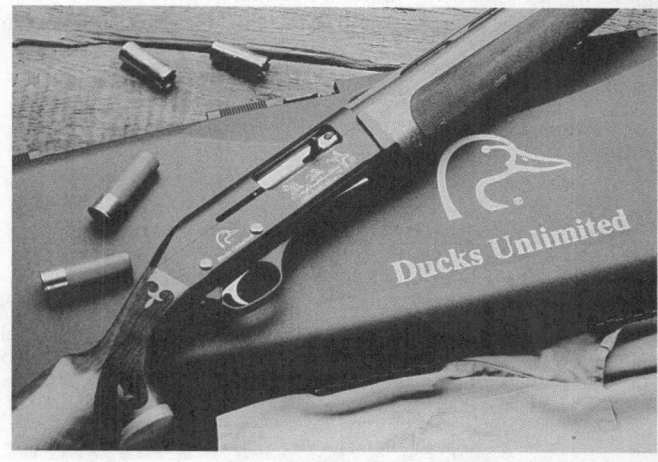

NIB	Exc.	V.G.	Good	Fair	Poor
975	775	625	500	325	200

Gold Lion

Has many of the features of the Red Lion model with the addition of a high-grade oil-finished walnut stock with Olive wood pistol grip cap. Trigger is gold plated.

NIB	Exc.	V.G.	Good	Fair	Poor
800	650	450	300	175	100

Gold Lion Mark III

This semi-automatic model is an improved version of the Gold Lion with the addition of an enhanced walnut stock, lightweight receiver with scroll and engraving and gold enlays. Fitted with a 28" TriBore barrel and chambered for the 3" 12 gauge shell. Supplied with five choke tubes. Weight is about 7.2 lbs.

NIB	Exc.	V.G.	Good	Fair	Poor
975	775	625	500	325	200

Sporting Clays Lion

This model, introduced in 1999, features a ported barrel and special "TriBore" system. Offered in 12 gauge with 28" barrel. Walnut stock with rubber recoil pad, gold-plated trigger, matte blue finish, red front sight bar, 10mm channeled rib, two extra front sights (green and white), and a set of five choke tubes. Weight is about 7.2 lbs.

NIB	Exc.	V.G.	Good	Fair	Poor
975	775	625	500	325	200

Rex Lion

Introduced in 2002 this model features a 12 gauge gun with 3" chambers with 26" or 28" vent-rib barrel. Choke tubes. High-grade walnut stock with Olive wood grip cap. Silver and black frame with scroll engraving with gold inlay. Weight is about 7 lbs. A limited edition.

NIB	Exc.	V.G.	Good	Fair	Poor
1050	800	650	450	300	175

Sporting Clays Extra

Introduced in 2000 this model features a 28" or 30" vent-rib barrel with carbon fiber finish on both barrel and receiver. This model also supplied with eight competition choke tubes. Stock is adjustable. Supplied with fitted luggage case. Weight is about 7.3 lbs.

NIB	Exc.	V.G.	Good	Fair	Poor
850	675	450	300	175	100

Tactical Semi-Auto

This is a 12 gauge semi-automatic shotgun fitted with a 20" barrel threaded for chokes. Receiver-mounted Picatinny rail. Flip-up front sight. Optional magazine extension has 7-round capacity. Also optional pistol grip. Weight is about 6.6 lbs. Introduced in 2001.

NIB	Exc.	V.G.	Good	Fair	Poor
650	550	400	265	150	100

Home Security HD

This semi-automatic shotgun is chambered for the 12 gauge 3" shell. Fitted with a 20" plain barrel with cylinder screw-in choke. Matte black finish. Black polymer stock. Magazine capacity is 5 rounds. Weight is about 7.5 lbs.

NIB	Exc.	V.G.	Good	Fair	Poor
600	475	300	225	150	100

H368

This 12 gauge 3" model features a 28" tri-bore vent rib barrel, matte black synthetic stock or Realtree camo stock. Lightweight

alloy matte black receiver. Magazine capacity is 2 rounds. Weight is about 7.2 lbs. Introduced in 2003. Also available in a left-hand model. **NOTE:** Add $60 for camo stock and $90 for left-hand model.

NIB	Exc.	V.G.	Good	Fair	Poor
650	550	400	265	150	100

FP6 Field Pump

Introduced in 2001 this model features a black alloy receiver with screw-in chokes. Chambered for 12 gauge with 28" barrel. Black synthetic stock. Optional 24" rifles barrel. Weight is about 7 lbs. Also available in Mossy Oak Break-up Camo.

NIB	Exc.	V.G.	Good	Fair	Poor
375	350	275	225	175	100

FP6

This model is a 12 gauge slide-action shotgun with 3" chamber, 20" barrel with heat shield, black polymer stock, threaded barrel for exterior chokes. Weight is about 6.6 lbs. This model is also available with a carbon fiber finish.

NIB	Exc.	V.G.	Good	Fair	Poor
500	400	300	200	125	100

FP6 with Rail

Introduced in 1999, this model is similar to the standard FP6 with the addition of a Picatinny rail mounted on the top of the receiver. Also fitted with a flip-up front sight. In 2003 this model was offered with a 20" tri-bore barrel with barrel threaded choke, new style front sight, and ghost ring rear sight. **NOTE:** This model is also available with 14" barrel. This requires a BATF tax and all NFA rules apply to purchase and sale of this restricted shotgun. An accessory wire stock and pistol grip are available for an additional $150.

NIB	Exc.	V.G.	Good	Fair	Poor
510	410	300	200	125	100

Max Lion

This over/under gun is chambered for the 12 or 20 gauge, 3" shell and fitted with single-selective trigger, auto ejectors, high grade walnut stock, leather covered recoil pad, set of five choke tubes and a fitted luggage-style case. Choice of 26", 28", or 30" barrels on 12 gauge guns and 26" or 28" on 20 gauge guns. Weight is about 7.5 lbs. for 12 gauge and 7 lbs. for 20 gauge. **NOTE:** In 1999 the Max Lion was offered with the TriBore barrel system. For models with this system add $70 to NIB price.

NIB	Exc.	V.G.	Good	Fair	Poor
1200	900	700	550	300	175

Max Lion Light

Introduced in 2000 this model features 24" barrels in both 12 and 20 gauge. Receiver has gold game bird inlay. Single trigger, automatic ejectors and select walnut stock. Weight is about 7 lbs.

NIB	Exc.	V.G.	Good	Fair	Poor
1200	900	700	550	300	175

Max Lion Paradox

Introduced in 2002 this model features a 12 gauge 3" gun with 24" barrels. The bottom barrel is rifled. Case hardened receiver with checkered walnut stock. Weight is about 7.6 lbs.

NIB	Exc.	V.G.	Good	Fair	Poor
1425	1175	900	700	550	300

Sporting Clays Competition Lion

This model is available in 12 or 20 gauge with 28" 10mm channeled rib barrels. Single-selective trigger and automatic ejectors. Recoil reducer installed in buttstock. Ported barrels. Set of 5 choke tubes standard. Leather covered recoil pad. High grade walnut stock. Introduced in 1999.

NIB	Exc.	V.G.	Good	Fair	Poor
925	825	600	500	300	150

Sporting Clays Max Lion

Chambered for the 12 gauge 3" shell and fitted with a 32" tri-bore vent rib barrel. Select walnut stock with hand checkering, adjustable trigger, and leather covered recoil pad. Engraved gold inlay receiver is case colored. Supplied with eight choke tubes. Weight is approximately 7.9 lbs. Introduced in 2003.

NIB	Exc.	V.G.	Good	Fair	Poor
925	825	600	500	300	150

Sporting Clays Competition Extra

This 12 gauge model features a a choice of 28" or 30" barrels. Walnut stock is adjustable. Finish is carbon fiber. Gun is supplied with set of eight choke tubes. Introduced in 2000. Weight is about 7.8 lbs.

NIB	Exc.	V.G.	Good	Fair	Poor
1000	775	625	500	400	150

Black Lion Competition

Similar to the Max Lion in choice of gauges and barrel lengths and features but with less figured walnut stock and black receiver finish.

NIB	Exc.	V.G.	Good	Fair	Poor
1050	795	650	525	425	175

Monotrap

This is a single barrel trap gun with 30" vent-rib barrel. Forearm has built-in recoil reduction system. Single-selective trigger and automatic ejectors. Adjustable comb. This shotgun is a 12 gauge built on a 20 gauge receiver. Weight is about 6 lbs. Introduced in 2000.

NIB	Exc.	V.G.	Good	Fair	Poor
1800	1350	1100	750	600	500

Silver Lion

This model is available in both 12 and 20 gauge and with 26", 28" barrel and 30" barrels in 12 gauge. The silver finish receiver is etched and stock is high quality walnut with leather covered pad. Scalable forearm is standard and is single-selective trigger and auto ejectors. Five chokes tubes are included. Weight is about 7.5 lbs. for 12 gauge guns and 7 lbs. for 20 gauge.

NIB	Exc.	V.G.	Good	Fair	Poor
925	825	600	500	300	150

Silver Lion Youth

This 20 gauge over/under features a shortened buttstock and 24" ported barrels. Single-selective trigger and automatic ejectors standard. Walnut stock. Rubber recoil pad. Silver steel receiver. Weight is approximately 6 lbs. Introduced in 1999.

NIB	Exc.	V.G.	Good	Fair	Poor
800	775	675	500	325	150

Super Light Lion Youth

Similar to the Silver Lion Youth model but chambered for 12 gauge shells. Aluminum receiver and 24" ported barrels. Introduced in 1999. Weight is about 6.5 lbs.

NIB	Exc.	V.G.	Good	Fair	Poor
800	775	675	500	325	150

Ultra Mag Lion

This model is a 12 gauge gun with 3.5" chambers, black receiver, single-selective trigger, auto ejectors, blackened walnut stock, leather covered recoil pad, and set of five choke tubes. Barrel length is 28". Weight is 7.9 lbs.

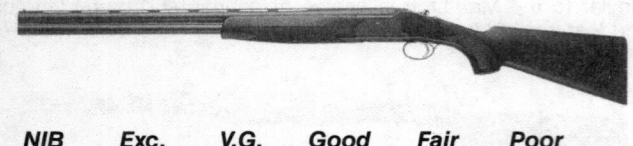

NIB	Exc.	V.G.	Good	Fair	Poor
800	775	675	500	325	150

Super Light Lion

This model features a lightweight alloy receiver with 12 gauge 24" barrels, single-selective trigger, non-auto ejectors, walnut stock, five choke tubes, and leather covered recoil pad. Weight is about 6.5 lbs. **NOTE:** For TriBore system add $125.

NIB	Exc.	V.G.	Good	Fair	Poor
800	775	675	500	325	150

Camo Turkey Mag

Introduced in 1999, this model features an unported TriBore 20" barrel. Receiver has Picatinny rail on top. Full extra brown camo finish. Chambered for 12 gauge with 3.5" chambers. Weight is about 7.5 lbs.

NIB	Exc.	V.G.	Good	Fair	Poor
925	825	600	500	300	150

Ultra Camo Mag Lion

This 12 gauge 3.5" model is fitted with 28" barrels. Wetlands camo pattern finish. Non-automatic ejectors. Weight is about 8 lbs. Introduced in 1999. Standard with steel screw-in chokes and regular screw-in chokes.

NIB	Exc.	V.G.	Good	Fair	Poor
925	825	600	500	300	150

Classic Lion Grade I

Offered in 12 gauge with 3" chambers, single-selective trigger, auto-ejectors, walnut stock, buttplate, and fitted with 26" barrels. Weight is about 7 lbs.

NIB	Exc.	V.G.	Good	Fair	Poor
1200	925	825	600	500	300

Classic Lion Grade II

Similar to the Grade I but with the addition of oil finished stock and removable sideplates with game scene engraving. Weight is 7.2 lbs.

NIB	Exc.	V.G.	Good	Fair	Poor
1200	925	825	600	500	300

Classic Lion Elite

Introduced in 2002, this 12 gauge model features 26" or 28" barrels with case colored receiver and straight grip stock. Fixed chokes. Weight is about 7 lbs.

NIB	Exc.	V.G.	Good	Fair	Poor
1300	1025	850	650	525	315

Famarb USA XLR5 Velocity

Semi-automatic 12 gauge shotgun design for clay target shooting with 2.75" chamber, Turkish walnut stock, adjustable comb and rib, 30" or 32" barrel and five choke tubes. Also available in left-hand configuration. Velocity Silver model has titanium receiver. As of 2012, the only Fabarm model imported into the U.S. **NOTE:** Add $150 for left-hand model, $300 for Velocity Silver.

NIB	Exc.	V.G.	Good	Fair	Poor
2300	2000	1650	1350	—	—

FABBRI ARMI
Gardone V.T., Italy

Fabbri Armi currently manufactures one of the best shotguns in the world. They are available as a custom made-to-order item, and they are not often seen in the used gun market. The values for guns of this nature and quality are impossible to accurately establish in a book of this nature as there are so many options and conditions that make the prices fluctuate greatly. We give an estimated figure as a base starting point. See Karl Lippard's book *Fabbri Shotguns,* Colorado Springs, Colorado, VM Publications, 1998, for more value details.

Side-by-Side Shotgun

Chambered for 12 or 20 gauge with all other features on a custom-order basis. This model is no longer in production. **NOTE:** Deduct $10,000 for Type One Model.

NIB	Exc.	V.G.	Good	Fair	Poor
39500	27000	18500	15000	10000	8000

Over/Under Shotgun

Chambered for 12 or 20 gauge with all other features on a custom-order basis. Prices listed are for Boehler barrels. **NOTE:** Add 50 percent for vacuum arc remelted steel barrels. Deduct 50 percent for Phoenix barrels.

NIB	Exc.	V.G.	Good	Fair	Poor
41500	26000	18500	15000	10000	8000

FABRIQUE NATIONALE
Herstal, Belgium

In 1889 Fabrique Nationale (or FN) was founded by a group of Belgian investors for the purpose of manufacturing Mauser rifles for the Belgian army. This was to be accomplished under license from Mauser, with the technical assistance of Ludwig Loewe of Berlin. A few years later, in the late 1890s, John Browning arrived in Europe seeking a manufacturer for his semi-automatic shotgun. He had severed his ties with Winchester after a disagreement. This led to a long association that worked out extremely well for both parties. Later Browning became associated with Colt, and the world market was divided—with the Eastern Hemisphere going to FN and the Western Hemisphere to Colt. In this section, we list arms that bear the FN banner. The FN-manufactured firearms produced under the Browning banner are listed in the Browning section of this book.

PISTOLS

Model 1900

A blowback-operated semi-automatic pistol chambered for the 7.65mm cartridge. It has a 4" barrel and fixed sights and is blued with molded plastic grips. It was manufactured between 1899 and 1910. This model is referred to as the "Old Model."

NIB	Exc.	V.G.	Good	Fair	Poor
—	750	525	350	200	150

Model 1903

A considerable improvement over the Model 1900. It is also a blowback-operated semi-automatic; but the recoil spring is located under the barrel, and the firing pin travels through the slide after being struck by a hidden hammer. The barrel is held in place by five locking lugs that fit into five grooves in the frame. This pistol is chambered for the 9mm Browning long cartridge and has a 5" barrel. The finish is blued with molded plastic grips, and the detachable magazine holds 7 rounds. There is a detachable shoulder stock/holster along with a 10-round magazine that was available for this model. These accessories are extremely rare and if present would make the package worth approximately five

times that of the pistol alone. There were approximately 58,000 manufactured between 1903 and 1939.

NIB	Exc.	V.G.	Good	Fair	Poor
—	1000	750	500	275	175

Model 1905/1906

A smaller version of the Model 1903, designed to be a pocket pistol and chambered for the 6.35mm cartridge. It became known as the "Vest Pocket" model and was also the basis for many Eibar copies. It has a 2.5" barrel and was produced in two distinct variations. The first variation had no safety lever or slide lock and relied on the grip safety. The second variation, that occurred at approximately serial number 100000, added this safety lever and slide lock, which helped simplify dismantling of the pistol. This model was available either blued or nickel-plated. The plated models would bring a 10 percent premium. There were approximately 1,086,100 manufactured between 1906 and 1959. It is known in the U.S. as the Model 1905 and in Europe as the Model 1906.

1st Variation, Under Serial Number 100000

NIB	Exc.	V.G.	Good	Fair	Poor
—	500	395	275	200	125

2nd Variation, Over Serial Number 100000

NIB	Exc.	V.G.	Good	Fair	Poor
—	475	350	250	175	100

Model 1910 "New Model"

Chambered for 7.65mm and 9mm short. It has a 3.5" barrel, is blued, and has molded plastic grips. The principal difference between this model and its predecessors is that the recoil spring on the Model 1910 is wrapped around the barrel. This gives the slide a more graceful tubular appearance instead of the old slab-sided look. This model has the triple safety features of the 1906 Model 2nd variation. This model was adopted by police forces around the world. It was manufactured between 1912 and 1954.

Courtesy Orvel Reichert

NIB	Exc.	V.G.	Good	Fair	Poor
—	600	500	400	175	125

Model 1922

A variation of the Model 1910 made for military and police use in several European countries between 1922 and 1944. **NOTE:** Add 75 percent if Nazi marked with original magazine; add 100 percent for "WaA613" marking.

NIB	Exc.	V.G.	Good	Fair	Poor
—	350	225	175	125	100

"Baby" Model

A smaller and lighter version of the Model 1906. It is chambered for the 6.35mm cartridge and has a 2" barrel. There is no grip safety or slide lock on this model, and it appears to be more square in shape than the Model 1906. This model was offered in blue, with molded plastic grips. Early models have the word "Baby" molded into the grips; post-1945 versions do not. There is also a nickel-plated version with pearl grips. There were over 500,000 of these manufactured between 1931 and 1983. Late-production specimens command a slight premium.

NIB	Exc.	V.G.	Good	Fair	Poor
800	650	500	300	225	150

The last design from John Browning and was developed between 1925 and 1935. This pistol is known as the Model 1935, the P-35, Hi-Power or HP, and also as the GP (which stood for "Grand Puissance") and was referred to by all those names at one time or another. The HP is essentially an improved version of the Colt 1911 design. The swinging link was replaced with a fixed cam, which was less prone to wear. It is chambered for the 9mm Parabellum and has a 13-round detachable magazine. The only drawback to the design is that the trigger pull is not as fine as that of the 1911, as there is a transfer bar instead of a stirrup arrangement. This is necessary due to the increased magazine capacity resulting in a thicker grip. The barrel is 4.75" in length. It has an external hammer with a manual and a magazine safety and was available with various finishes and sight options and was furnished with a shoulder stock. The Model 1935 was used by many countries as their service pistol as such there are many variations. We list these versions and their approximate values.

MODEL 1935/HI-POWER/GP

Pre-War Commercial Model

Found with a sliding tangent rear sight and is slotted for a detachable shoulder stock. It was manufactured from 1935 until 1940. **NOTE:** Wood holster stock add 50 percent.

NIB	Exc.	V.G.	Good	Fair	Poor
—	2000	1800	1500	1000	400

Pre-War Military Contract

The Model 1935 was adopted by many countries as a service pistol, and they are listed.

Belgium

NIB	Exc.	V.G.	Good	Fair	Poor
—	3000	2600	2000	600	375

Canada and China

NIB	Exc.	V.G.	Good	Fair	Poor
—	2500	2000	950	650	400

Great Britain

NIB	Exc.	V.G.	Good	Fair	Poor
—	2500	1700	1000	550	325

Estonia

NIB	Exc.	V.G.	Good	Fair	Poor
—	3000	2600	2000	600	375

Holland

NIB	Exc.	V.G.	Good	Fair	Poor
—	3000	2600	2000	650	400

Latvia

NIB	Exc.	V.G.	Good	Fair	Poor
—	3000	2600	2000	775	500

Lithuania

NIB	Exc.	V.G.	Good	Fair	Poor
—	2800	2000	1200	650	400

Romania

NIB	Exc.	V.G.	Good	Fair	Poor
—	3000	2600	2000	775	500

German Military Pistole Model 640(b)

In 1940 Germany occupied Belgium and took over the FN plant. The production of the Model 1935 continued, with Germany taking the output. The FN plant was assigned the production code "ch," and many thousands were produced. The finish on these Nazi guns runs from as fine as the Pre-war Commercial series to downright crude, and it is possible to see how the war was progressing for Germany by the finish on their weapons. One must be cautious with some of these guns as there have been fakes noted with their backstraps cut for shoulder stocks, producing what would appear to be a more expensive variation. Individual appraisal should be secured if any doubt exists.

Fixed Sight Model

NIB	Exc.	V.G.	Good	Fair	Poor
—	1000	750	400	300	250

Tangent Sight Model

50,000 manufactured.

Courtesy Orvel Reichert

NIB	Exc.	V.G.	Good	Fair	Poor
—	1500	1000	700	550	400

Captured Pre-war Commercial Model

These pistols were taken over when the plant was occupied. They are slotted for stocks and have tangent sights. There were few produced between serial number 48,000 and 52,000. All noted have the WA613 Nazi proof mark. Beware of fakes!

NIB	Exc.	V.G.	Good	Fair	Poor
—	1700	1400	1150	750	500

Post-War Military Contract

Manufactured from 1946, and they embody some design changes—such as improved heat treating and barrel locking. Pistols produced after 1950 do not have barrels that can interchange with the earlier model pistols. The earliest models have an "A" prefix on the serial number and do not have the magazine safety. These pistols were produced for many countries, and there were many thousands manufactured.

Fixed Sight

NIB	Exc.	V.G.	Good	Fair	Poor
—	750	425	375	300	250

Tangent Sight

NIB	Exc.	V.G.	Good	Fair	Poor
—	1000	675	575	400	300

Slotted and Tangent Sight

NIB	Exc.	V.G.	Good	Fair	Poor
—	1500	1050	750	500	400

Post-War Commercial Model

Introduced in 1950 and in 1954. Those imported into the U.S.A. are marked Browning Arms Co. These pistols have the commercial polished finish.

Fixed Sight

NIB	Exc.	V.G.	Good	Fair	Poor
—	850	500	350	300	250

Tangent Sight

NIB	Exc.	V.G.	Good	Fair	Poor
—	1000	650	500	400	350

Slotted and Tangent Sight

NIB	Exc.	V.G.	Good	Fair	Poor
—	1500	1100	800	550	450

RIFLES

Model 1889

NIB	Exc.	V.G.	Good	Fair	Poor
—	350	250	200	125	100

Model 1949 or SAFN 49

NIB	Exc.	V.G.	Good	Fair	Poor
—	600	500	300	225	150

Model 30-11 Sniper Rifle

NIB	Exc.	V.G.	Good	Fair	Poor
—	5000	4500	3500	2750	2000

FN-FAL

50.00—21" Rifle Model

NIB	Exc.	V.G.	Good	Fair	Poor
3000	2750	2250	2000	1850	1000

50.63—18" Paratrooper Model

NIB	Exc.	V.G.	Good	Fair	Poor
3800	3350	2950	2750	2450	1100

50.64—21" Paratrooper Model

NIB	Exc.	V.G.	Good	Fair	Poor
3300	3000	2700	2200	1900	1000

50.41—Synthetic Butt H-Bar

NIB	Exc.	V.G.	Good	Fair	Poor
2800	2400	2000	1800	1200	1000

50.42—Wood Butt H-Bar

NIB	Exc.	V.G.	Good	Fair	Poor
2800	2400	2000	1800	1200	1000

FN-FAL "G" Series (Type I Receiver)

Standard

NIB	Exc.	V.G.	Good	Fair	Poor
6500	5000	4000	3000	2000	1000

Lightweight

NIB	Exc.	V.G.	Good	Fair	Poor
6500	5000	4000	3000	2000	1000

FN CAL

NIB	Exc.	V.G.	Good	Fair	Poor
7000	6500	5000	3000	1500	1000

FNC

NOTE: These above prices are for Belgian-made guns only.

Standard

Fixed stock, 16" or 18" barrel.

NIB	Exc.	V.G.	Good	Fair	Poor
3000	2800	2500	2000	1500	1000

Paratrooper Model

Folding stock, 16" or 18" barrel.

NIB	Exc.	V.G.	Good	Fair	Poor
3000	2800	2500	2000	1500	1000

Musketeer Sporting Rifles

A bolt-action rifle built on the Mauser-action chambered for various popular cartridges. It has a 24" barrel and is blued, with a checkered walnut stock. It was manufactured between 1947 and 1963.

NIB	Exc.	V.G.	Good	Fair	Poor
—	450	350	300	250	200

Deluxe Sporter

A higher-grade version of the Musketeer with the same general specifications. It was also manufactured between 1947 and 1963.

NIB	Exc.	V.G.	Good	Fair	Poor
—	550	450	400	275	200

FN Supreme

Chambered for the popular standard calibers and has a 24" barrel with an aperture sight and a checkered walnut stock. It was manufactured between 1957 and 1975.

NIB	Exc.	V.G.	Good	Fair	Poor
—	800	650	500	400	400

Supreme Magnum Model

Similar to the standard Supreme except that it is chambered for .264 Win. Mag., 7mm Rem. Mag., and .300 Win. Mag. It is furnished with a recoil pad and was manufactured between the same years as the standard model.

NIB	Exc.	V.G.	Good	Fair	Poor
—	800	650	500	400	400

FAIRBANKS, A. B.
Boston, Massachusetts

Fairbanks All Metal Pistol

This odd pistol was produced of all metal, with a one-piece cast brass frame and handle and an iron barrel and lock system. It is chambered for .33 caliber and utilizes the percussion ignition system. The barrel lengths noted are of 3" to 10". The barrels are marked "Fairbanks Boston. Cast Steel." They were manufactured between 1838 and 1841.

NIB	Exc.	V.G.	Good	Fair	Poor
—	—	1050	350	150	75

FALCON FIREARMS
Northridge, California

Portsider

A copy of the Colt 1911 built for a left-handed individual. It is constructed of stainless steel and is similar in all other respects to the Colt. It was introduced in 1986. A scarce 1911.

NIB	Exc.	V.G.	Good	Fair	Poor
700	575	450	375	300	225

Portsider Set

A matching serial numbered pair consisting of a left-handed and a right-handed version of this model. It was cased, and there were only 100 manufactured in 1986 and 1987.

NIB	Exc.	V.G.	Good	Fair	Poor
1400	1250	1000	750	600	475

Gold Falcon

The frame was machined from solid 17-karat gold. The slide is stainless steel, and the sights have diamond inlays. It was engraved to the customer's order, and there were only 50 manufactured.

NIB	Exc.	V.G.	Good	Fair	Poor
50000	30000	25000	15000	7500	700

FAMARS, A. & S.
Brescia, Italy

The Famars shotgun is one of the world's finest and is available on a custom-order basis. This makes it quite difficult to accurately establish values in a book of this nature. We list them and give an estimated value in their basic form only.

Engraving Pattern Descriptions
(Older Discontinued Patterns)

S2—Traditional fully engraved fine English scroll with coverage highlighting selected areas of the receiver and fore-end metal. Wood grade is AA.

S3—Traditional hand-engraved scroll with some open areas around the scroll coverage on the receiver and fore-end metal. Wood grade is AAA.

S4—Traditional full coverage, intricate and high in detail. Patterns may be English, German, or game scene. Wood grade is AAAA.

S5—Grade S4 patterns with animals inlaid in 24k gold. Wood grade is AAAA.

S4E—Extremely high detail scenes and elaborate ornamental work where the subject matter is selected by the customer. Wood grade is AAAAA.

S5E—Similar to the S4E level but with raised or flush gold inlay work. Wood grade is AAAAA.

SXO—The best work by the world's best engravers. Museum quality. Wood grade is AAAAAA.

Zeus

An engraved side-by-side boxlock in 12, 20, 28, and .410 bore. **NOTE:** Add 10 percent for smaller gauges.

In the white

NIB	Exc.	V.G.	Good	Fair	Poor
19000	12000	9000	6500	4750	750

D2 pattern

NIB	Exc.	V.G.	Good	Fair	Poor
20000	12000	9000	6500	4750	750

S3 pattern

NIB	Exc.	V.G.	Good	Fair	Poor
22000	20000	12000	9000	6500	900

Tribute

An engraved side-by-side droplock offered in 12 or 20 gauge.

In the white

NIB	Exc.	V.G.	Good	Fair	Poor
21400	20800	12000	9000	6500	900

D2 pattern

NIB	Exc.	V.G.	Good	Fair	Poor
22600	20500	12000	9000	6500	900

S3 pattern

NIB	Exc.	V.G.	Good	Fair	Poor
24300	22000	12000	9000	6500	900

Venus

A side-by-side sidelock shotgun with choice of engraving patterns and coverage. Offered in 12, 20, 28, or .410 bore.

In the white

NIB	Exc.	V.G.	Good	Fair	Poor
32700	30500	20000	12000	9000	900

D2 pattern

NIB	Exc.	V.G.	Good	Fair	Poor
33900	31500	—	—	—	—

D3 pattern

NIB	Exc.	V.G.	Good	Fair	Poor
37000	10500	—	—	—	—

D4 pattern

NIB	Exc.	V.G.	Good	Fair	Poor
42800	39000	—	—	—	—

D5 pattern

NIB	Exc.	V.G.	Good	Fair	Poor
48200	42000	—	—	—	—

D4E pattern

NIB	Exc.	V.G.	Good	Fair	Poor
53500	47500	—	—	—	—

D5E pattern

NIB	Exc.	V.G.	Good	Fair	Poor
58500	51500	—	—	—	—

DXO pattern

NIB	Exc.	V.G.	Good	Fair	Poor
85000	55000	—	—	—	—

Veneri

A side-by-side sidelock shotgun.

NIB	Exc.	V.G.	Good	Fair	Poor
32000	30000	—	—	—	—

D2 pattern

NIB	Exc.	V.G.	Good	Fair	Poor
32700	30500	—	—	—	—

Jorema Royal

An over/under shotgun with sidelocks. Offered in 12, 20, 28, and .410 bore. **NOTE:** Add 15 percent for smaller gauges.

In the white

NIB	Exc.	V.G.	Good	Fair	Poor
32700	26000	—	—	—	—

S2 pattern

NIB	Exc.	V.G.	Good	Fair	Poor
33900	20000	—	—	—	—

S3 pattern

NIB	Exc.	V.G.	Good	Fair	Poor
37300	29500	—	—	—	—

S4 pattern

NIB	Exc.	V.G.	Good	Fair	Poor
42900	33500	—	—	—	—

S5 pattern

NIB	Exc.	V.G.	Good	Fair	Poor
48200	29500	—	—	—	—

S4E pattern

NIB	Exc.	V.G.	Good	Fair	Poor
53500	42500	—	—	—	—

S5E pattern

NIB	Exc.	V.G.	Good	Fair	Poor
53500	42500	—	—	—	—

SXO pattern

NIB	Exc.	V.G.	Good	Fair	Poor
85000	66500	—	—	—	—

Excaliber BL

An over/under shotgun with removable trigger group. Offered in 12, 20, 28, and .410 bore with single trigger.

NIB	Exc.	V.G.	Good	Fair	Poor
11800	6500	—	—	—	—

Excalibur BL Extra

Finer engraving than standard.

NIB	Exc.	V.G.	Good	Fair	Poor
15455	8900	—	—	—	—

Excalibur BL Prestige

Finer engraving than BL Extra.

NIB	Exc.	V.G.	Good	Fair	Poor
17820	10750	—	—	—	—

Excalibur BLX

Over/under shotgun with sideplates.

NIB	Exc.	V.G.	Good	Fair	Poor
11150	9000	—	—	—	—

Excalibur BLX Extra

Same as above but with finer engraving.

NIB	Exc.	V.G.	Good	Fair	Poor
16759	14000	—	—	—	—

Excalibur BLX Prestige

Finer engraving than the BLX Extra.

NIB	Exc.	V.G.	Good	Fair	Poor
16900	13750	—	—	—	—

Excalibur SL

Over/under shotgun with sidelocks.

NIB	Exc.	V.G.	Good	Fair	Poor
26125	14800	—	—	—	—

Excalibur SL Extra

Same as above with finer engraving.

NIB	Exc.	V.G.	Good	Fair	Poor
30000	16000	—	—	—	—

Excalibur SL Prestige

Finer engraving than the SL Extra.

NIB	Exc.	V.G.	Good	Fair	Poor
33000	18000	—	—	—	—

Excalibur Express

An over/under double rifle in calibers from 7x65R to .375 H&H.

NIB	Exc.	V.G.	Good	Fair	Poor
20196	11500	—	—	—	—

Excalibur Express Extra

Same as above but with finer engraving.

NIB	Exc.	V.G.	Good	Fair	Poor
27060	12000	—	—	—	—

Excalibur Express Prestige

Finer engraving than the Express Extra.

NIB	Exc.	V.G.	Good	Fair	Poor
32065	15250	—	—	—	—

African Express

A side-by-side boxlock double rifle. Calibers from .22 Long Rifle to .600 NE.

NIB	Exc.	V.G.	Good	Fair	Poor
34000	17500	—	—	—	—

Venus Express Professional

A side-by-side double rifle with sidelocks.

NIB	Exc.	V.G.	Good	Fair	Poor
45000	34500	—	—	—	—

Venus Express Extra

A side-by-side double rifle with sidelocks. Calibers from .375 H&H to .500 NE.

NIB	Exc.	V.G.	Good	Fair	Poor
95750	50000	—	—	—	—

FARROW ARMS CO.
Holyoke, Massachusetts
Mason, Tennessee

Farrow Falling Block Rifle

Designed by W.M. Farrow, a target shooter who had worked on the Ballard rifles for the Marlin company. The Farrow rifles are chambered for various calibers and have barrel lengths from 28"- 36" of octagonal configuration. They feature tang sights and are either all blued or have a nickel-plated receiver. The stocks are walnut. There were two grades offered that varied according to the grade of wood used. These rifles are quite scarce on today's market, and the number manufactured between 1885 and 1900 is unknown.

No. 1 Model

Fancy walnut with checkering and a Schutzen buttplate.

NIB	Exc.	V.G.	Good	Fair	Poor
—	—	13500	4500	1950	750

No. 2 Model

Plainer wood and no checkering.

NIB	Exc.	V.G.	Good	Fair	Poor
—	—	11000	3300	1600	500

FAUSTI, STEFANO
Italy

Fausti has been manufacturing quality over/under and side-by-side shotguns in Italy for the European market since 1948. In 2009, the company established an office in Fredericksburg, Virginia and now imports a wide range of models

OVER/UNDER SHOTGUNS

Low-profile boxlock design scaled to various gauges. All standard barrel lengths with five choke tubes (.410 has fixed M/F). Offered in 12, 16, 20, 28 gauges and .410 bore in four grades: Caledon (shown), Caledon SL, Class and Class SL, each with increased level of walnut, laser engraving and inlays. Features include automatic ejectors, single selective trigger, rounded pistol grip. SL models have false side plates. Prices shown are for 12 and 20 gauge models. **NOTE:** Add $500 for 16, 28, or .410.

Caledon

NIB	Exc.	V.G.	Good	Fair	Poor
1800	1450	1200	950	600	400

Caledon SL
NIB	Exc.	V.G.	Good	Fair	Poor
2500	2000	1600	1350	900	500

Class
NIB	Exc.	V.G.	Good	Fair	Poor
2200	1750	1400	1100	750	500

Class SL
NIB	Exc.	V.G.	Good	Fair	Poor
2900	2250	1700	1450	1000	500

Round Body

Similar to other over/under models except built on Fausti-designed rounded receiver. AAA grade oil finished walnut stock. Not available in 12 gauge. Prices shown are for 20 gauge. **NOTE:** Add $500 for 16, 28 or .410.

NIB	Exc.	V.G.	Good	Fair	Poor
3750	3200	2600	2000	1200	500

MAGNIFICENT SERIES

Higher grade series with AAA+ walnut stock and deep-sculpted engraving. Offered in a field version and a sporting clays model (shown). Prices shown are for 12 or 20 gauge. **NOTE:** Add $500 for 16, 28 gauge or .410.

Magnificent Field
NIB	Exc.	V.G.	Good	Fair	Poor
4500	3600	3000	2400	1600	700

Magnificent Sporting

NIB	Exc.	V.G.	Good	Fair	Poor
5400	4500	3750	3000	2000	900

SIDE-BY-SIDE SHOTGUNS

Model DEA

Built on a low boxlock action with modified Anson & Deeley mechanism. Straight-grip AAA-grade oil-finished walnut stock. Automatic ejectors, non-selective single trigger. Made in 12, 16, 20 and 28 gauges and .410 bore. Also offered as Duetto model with interchangeable 28 and .410 barrel sets. Prices shown are for 12 or 20 gauge. **NOTE:** Add $500 for other gauges; add $1800 for Duetto model.

NIB	Exc.	V.G.	Good	Fair	Poor
3000	2500	2000	1600	1000	500

RIFLES

Classic Express Rifle

Over/under design with oil finished walnut stock, automatic ejectors and choice of double or single trigger. Calibers are .30-06, .444 Marlin, .45-70, 30R Blaser, 8x57 JRS and 9.3x74R. Barrels are 24" with adjustable fiber optic sight.

NIB	Exc.	V.G.	Good	Fair	Poor
4500	3600	3000	2400	1600	700

FAYETTEVILLE ARMORY PISTOLS AND RIFLES
Fayetteville, North Carolina

In 1861, the U.S. Arsenal at Fayetteville, North Carolina, was seized by the officials of that state and later turned over to the government of the Confederate States of America. While still controlled by the state of North Carolina, a number of inferior flintlock arms were altered at the arsenal from flint to percussion, including a number of U.S. M1836 pistols and U.S. M1819 Hall rifles (the latter also shortened and remodeled into cavalry carbines). In accordance with an agreement between the governors of Virginia and North Carolina, the rifle machinery seized at the former U.S. Armory at Harpers Ferry, Virginia, was also sent to Fayetteville, where in 1862 the Confederacy began the construction of rifles modeled after the U.S. M1855 rifle. Production continued until 1865 when the advance of Sherman's armies necessitated the evacuation of the armory.

Fayetteville Armory Percussion Pistols
(U.S. M1836 Pistols, Altered)

Overall length 13.25"; barrel length 8.5"; caliber .54. Markings: same as U.S. M1836 contact pistols, i.e. the locks either marked with eagle head over "A. WATERS/MILBURY MS./(date)" or "US/R. JOHNSON/MIDDN CONN./(date)" and various barrel proofmarks; also occasionally marked "N. CAROLINA".

The Fayetteville Armory altered approximately 900 U.S. M1836 pistols from flintlock to percussion. These arms were altered by enlarging the flint touchhole and screwing in a cylindrical drum in place of the pan and frizzen. The distinguishing feature of the Fayetteville alteration is the clean-out screw at the face of the cylinder and the "S" shaped hammer, not unlike that used on post-1862 dated rifles.

Courtesy Milwaukee Public Museum, Milwaukee, Wisconsin

NIB	Exc.	V.G.	Good	Fair	Poor
—	—	3250	1350	950	400

Fayetteville Armory Rifles (Types I through IV)

Overall length 49-1/8"; barrel length 33"; caliber .58. Markings: on barrel, an eagle over "C.S.A./FAYETTEVILLE" forward of the hammer and the date on the rounded tail. "CSA" also found on buttplates; date on top of barrel; proofmarks (eagle head, "V" and "P") on left quarter of barrel near breech.

From 1862 to early 1865, the Fayetteville Armory produced four variants of the old U.S. M1855 rifle on the machinery that had been lent to North Carolina by Virginia after its capture in April 1861. The earliest 1862 production (Type I) utilized unmilled lockplates captured at Harpers Ferry and are distinguished by having a "hump" (where the Maynard primer would have been milled) that extends to the arc of the hammer. Type II production utilized the newly made locks received from Richmond during the balance of 1862; they had a relatively low "hump" whose upper surface matched the contour of the stock. By the end of 1862, Fayetteville was producing its own lock, the plate of which resembled the U.S. M1861 rifle musket, but with a distinctive "S" shaped hammer. This lock distinguishes both type III and type IV production. All rifles made through 1863 continued to bear a saber bayonet lug on the right side of the barrel. In 1864, however, this was eliminated in favor of a triangular socket bayonet. The absence of the saber bayonet lug and remodeled front sight distinguishes type IV production. Because the barrel machinery went to Richmond, production at Fayetteville was continually hindered, seldom reaching more than 300 per month in the three years that the Fayetteville rifle was manufactured. (Note: The rarity of Type I production will usually generate a premium for that variant.)

Courtesy Milwaukee Public Museum, Milwaukee, Wisconsin

NIB	Exc.	V.G.	Good	Fair	Poor
—	—	27500	10500	4000	800

FEATHER INDUSTRIES, INC.
Trinidad, Colorado

AT-22

A blowback-operated semi-automatic chambered for the .22 LR cartridge. It has a removable, shrouded 17" barrel and a folding metal stock. There are adjustable sights, and the finish is black. There is a detachable 20-round magazine. This model was introduced in 1986.

NIB	Exc.	V.G.	Good	Fair	Poor
450	200	175	150	110	75

AT-9

Similar to the AT-22 except that it is chambered for the 9mm Parabellum cartridge and has a 16" barrel and 32-round magazine. It was introduced in 1988.

NIB	Exc.	V.G.	Good	Fair	Poor
800	675	300	250	175	125

KG-9

A 9mm, semi-automatic assault rifle that was introduced in 1989.

NIB	Exc.	V.G.	Good	Fair	Poor
725	500	425	375	300	250

KG-22

Similar in appearance to the KG-9 except that it is chambered for .22 LR and has a 20-round detachable magazine. It was introduced in 1989.

NIB	Exc.	V.G.	Good	Fair	Poor
400	275	225	175	125	100

SAR-180

The current incarnation of the old American 180, which was manufactured in Austria a number of years ago. It is chambered for .22 LR and has a 17.5" barrel. It is a blowback-operated semi-automatic that has a 165-round drum magazine that sits on top of the action on the flat side. The rear sight is adjustable, and the finish is blued with a walnut stock, pistol grip, and fore-end. This model was revived by Feather Industries in 1989.

NIB	Exc.	V.G.	Good	Fair	Poor
750	675	600	475	300	200

Mini-AT

A blowback-operated semi-automatic pistol chambered for the .22 LR cartridge. It is a 5.5"-barreled version of the AT-22 rifle and has a 20-round magazine. This model was manufactured between 1986 and 1989.

NIB	Exc.	V.G.	Good	Fair	Poor
375	250	175	150	125	100

Guardian Angel

A two-shot, over/under, derringer-style pistol. It is chambered for the 9mm Parabellum and can be converted to fire the .38 Super cartridge. It is constructed of stainless steel and has an internal hammer and fully enclosed trigger. It was introduced in 1988.

NIB	Exc.	V.G.	Good	Fair	Poor
225	125	100	75	50	40

FEDERAL ENGINEERING CORP.
Chicago, Illinois

XC-220

A blowback-operated, semi-automatic rifle chambered for the .22 LR cartridge. It has a 16.5" barrel and a steel receiver that is blued. The stock is black synthetic. This model was introduced in 1984.

NIB	Exc.	V.G.	Good	Fair	Poor
650	450	375	225	175	125

XC-450

Similar in appearance to the XC-220 except that it is chambered for the .45 ACP cartridge. It has a 30-round detachable magazine.

NIB	Exc.	V.G.	Good	Fair	Poor
750	525	450	400	300	250

XC-900

A 9mm Parabellum version of the same basic firearm. It has a 32-round magazine and was introduced in 1984.

NIB	Exc.	V.G.	Good	Fair	Poor
750	525	450	400	300	250

FEDERAL ORDNANCE, INC.
South El Monte, California

An importer as well as a manufacturer that basically fabricates new and custom firearms out of existing older military parts. The firearms they import are military surplus weapons. The firearms covered here are of Federal Ordnance manufacture.

M-14 Semi-Automatic

A semi-automatic version of the M-14 service rifle. It is constructed of a newly manufactured receiver that has no selector and select surplus G.I. parts. The rifle is refinished to original specifications and furnished with a 20-round magazine and either a wood or fiberglass stock. This model was introduced in 1986. Although this model is a battle rifle and falls into the category affected by the wild price fluctuations we have been experiencing, prices for this gun have stayed fairly stable due to a fairly constant supply. This model has been manufactured since 1986.

NIB	Exc.	V.G.	Good	Fair	Poor
—	750	600	550	450	375

Model 714 Broomhandle Mauser

A remanufactured C96-type pistol chambered for 7.63mm or 9mm Parabellum. It utilizes a new manufactured frame and surplus parts. It features a 10-round detachable magazine, adjustable sights, and walnut grips. Manufactured 1986 to 1991. A Bolo Model with a smaller grip was produced in 1988 only.

NIB	Exc.	V.G.	Good	Fair	Poor
650	500	400	300	250	100

Model 713 Mauser Carbine

A 16"-barreled version of the Mauser with a fixed walnut stock. It has a standard magazine and is chambered for 7.63mm or 9mm Parabellum. It is refinished and was introduced in 1987.

NIB	Exc.	V.G.	Good	Fair	Poor
—	1250	1000	900	700	575

Model 713 Deluxe

Chambered for 7.63mm and has a 16" barrel with a detachable shoulder stock made of deluxe walnut. It has been modified to accept detachable magazines and is furnished with two 20-shot units. It has a 1000-meter adjustable sight and is furnished in a fitted leather case. There were only 1,500 manufactured in 1986.

NIB	Exc.	V.G.	Good	Fair	Poor
2000	1750	1500	1250	1000	800

Standard Broomhandle

A refurbished surplus C-96 Mauser pistol with a new 7.63mm or 9mm barrel. All springs are replaced, and the entire gun is refinished. It is furnished with a shoulder stock/holster of Chinese manufacture.

NIB	Exc.	V.G.	Good	Fair	Poor
800	650	525	450	350	275

Ranger 1911A1

Federal Ordnance's version of the 1911A1 Colt service pistol. It is made of all steel, is chambered for .45 ACP, and has checkered walnut grips and phiosphate-style finish. It was introduced in 1988.

NIB	Exc.	V.G.	Good	Fair	Poor
500	375	325	275	225	150

FEG (FEGYVER ES GAZKESZULEKGYAR)
Budapest, Hungary

Rudolf Frommer was a first-class engineer who became associated with Fegyvergyar in 1896. In 1900 he became the manager and held that position until his retirement in 1935. He died one year later in 1936. His designs were successful and prolific. They were used militarily and sold on the commercial market as well.

PISTOLS

Model 1901

An odd pistol that was not successful at all. It was chambered for an 8mm cartridge that was the forerunner of the 8mm Roth Steyr. It has a long, slender barrel, which was actually a collar with the barrel within. It has a rotary bolt and external hammer and is recoil-operated. There is a 10-round integral magazine, and it is loaded from the top via a stripper clip. This pistol was manufactured from 1903 to 1905.

Courtesy James Rankin

NIB	Exc.	V.G.	Good	Fair	Poor
—	2450	1795	1000	700	350

Model 1906

An improved version of the 1901, chambered for the 7.65mm Roth-Sauer cartridge. It is, for all intents and purposes, the same action; but on later models a detachable 10-round magazine was adopted. It was manufactured between 1906 and 1910 in small quantity.

NIB	Exc.	V.G.	Good	Fair	Poor
—	2300	1750	1000	700	350

Model 1910

The final version in this series of pistols and is similar with the addition of a grip safety. Chambered for 7.65mm Browning.

NIB	Exc.	V.G.	Good	Fair	Poor
—	2600	1950	1100	700	350

Frommer Stop Model 1912

A semi-automatic pistol in caliber 7.65mm or 9mmK. It is unusual in that it operates on a long recoil system. Frommer is stamped on the slide as well as the Frommer Stop logo on each side of the wood or plastic grip plates.

Courtesy James Rankin

NIB	Exc.	V.G.	Good	Fair	Poor
—	450	300	225	150	50

Frommer Baby Model

A smaller version of the Stop that was designed as a pocket pistol with a 2" barrel and chambered for the same calibers. It was manufactured at the same time as the Stop Model.

Courtesy James Rankin

NIB	Exc.	V.G.	Good	Fair	Poor
—	375	250	200	125	75

Frommer Lilliput

This pocket pistol is chambered for 6.35mm and outwardly resembles the Baby. It is actually a simple, blowback-operated, semi-automatic pistol and was a good deal less complex to produce. This model was introduced in 1921.

Courtesy James Rankin

NIB	Exc.	V.G.	Good	Fair	Poor
—	350	225	175	125	75

Model 1929

A semi-automatic pistol in 9mmK. It is based on the Browning designed blowback-action. This pistol replaced the earlier models. A few of these pistols were made in .22 Long Rifle.

Courtesy James Rankin

NIB	Exc.	V.G.	Good	Fair	Poor
—	450	350	225	175	100

.22 Caliber

NIB	Exc.	V.G.	Good	Fair	Poor
—	975	825	725	450	250

Model 1937

A semi-automatic pistol in caliber 7.65mm or 9mmK. This pistol was designed by Frommer and manufactured by Femaru. It is also known as the Model 1937.

Courtesy James Rankin

Nazi Proofed 7.65mm Version

NIB	Exc.	V.G.	Good	Fair	Poor
—	450	350	225	175	100

9mm Short Hungarian Military Version

NIB	Exc.	V.G.	Good	Fair	Poor
—	425	325	200	175	100

Model R-9

A copy of the Browning Hi-Power semi-automatic pistol. It is chambered for 9mm Parabellum and has a 4.75" barrel. The frame is steel, and the finish is blued with checkered wood grips. The detachable magazine holds 13 shots, and the sights are fixed. This model was imported in 1986 and 1987 only.

NIB	Exc.	V.G.	Good	Fair	Poor
—	375	250	225	175	100

Model AP-9

This pistol has been manufactured in Hungary under a number of different names. It is known as the AP-9, Walam 48, AP-66, and the Attila. It is a semi-automatic pistol in calibers 7.65mm and 9mmK. It is similar to the Walther Model PP. It has a 7-round magazine and alloy frame. There are various styles of grip plates.

Courtesy James Rankin

NIB	Exc.	V.G.	Good	Fair	Poor
—	325	200	150	100	50

Model PPH

A copy of the Walther PP, chambered for the .380 ACP cartridge. It is a double-action semi-automatic with a 3" barrel, alloy frame, and a blued finish, with thumb rest checkered plastic grips. It was imported in 1986 and 1987 only.

NIB	Exc.	V.G.	Good	Fair	Poor
—	350	200	175	100	75

Model B9R

This semi-automatic pistol is chambered for the .380 ACP cartridge and fitted with a 4" barrel, it features double or single-action trigger operation. The frame is alloy and weighs about 25 oz. Magazine capacity is 15 rounds.

NIB	Exc.	V.G.	Good	Fair	Poor
375	225	200	175	125	75

Model PA-63

Same as above but chambered for the 9mm Makarov (9x18mm) cartridge.

NIB	Exc.	V.G.	Good	Fair	Poor
—	275	175	125	100	50

Model FP-9

This model is a copy of the Browning Hi-Power pistol. Chambered for the 9mm Luger cartridge. It features a walnut checkered grip with blue finish. Barrel is 5" and overall length is 8". The top of the slide features a full-length ventilated rib with fixed sights. Weighs 35 oz. Magazine capacity is 14 rounds.

NIB	Exc.	V.G.	Good	Fair	Poor
300	175	150	125	90	70

Model P9R

This is similar to the model above and follows the Browning Hi-Power lines with the exception of the ventilated rib. Barrel length is 4.66" and the pistol is offered in blue or chrome finish. Magazine capacity is 15 rounds.

Blue

NIB	Exc.	V.G.	Good	Fair	Poor
325	200	150	125	90	70

Chrome

NIB	Exc.	V.G.	Good	Fair	Poor
350	225	175	150	120	80

Model P9RK

Similar to model above but fitted with 4.12" barrel and 7.5" overall length. Finger grooves on front strap and backstrap is serrated. Weighs about 34 oz.

NIB	Exc.	V.G.	Good	Fair	Poor
300	200	150	125	90	70

RIFLES

SA-2000-M

Introduced in 1999, this model is a semi-automatic rifle chambered for the 7.62x39mm cartridge or the .223 cartridge. Fitted with a detachable 10-round magazine, synthetic stock and muzzlebrake.

NIB	Exc.	V.G.	Good	Fair	Poor
575	450	350	250	150	95

AMD-65 AK47

Hungarian AK-47 clone chambered in 7.62xc39. Fixed or folding-stock versions are available.

NIB	Exc.	V.G.	Good	Fair	Poor
650	495	375	275	175	125

FEINWERKBAU
Oberndorf, Germany

Known predominately for the production of high quality, extremely accurate air rifles and pistols. They also produce some of the most accurate target .22 caliber firearms in the world today. These firearms are listed:

Model 2000 Universal

A single-shot, bolt-action target rifle chambered for the .22 rimfire cartridge. It has a 26.5" barrel with adjustable aperture sights and a fully adjustable trigger. There were four different stock configurations offered with stippled pistol grips and forearms. An electronic trigger was available as a $450 option. This model was discontinued in 1988.

NIB	Exc.	V.G.	Good	Fair	Poor
—	1800	1250	950	650	550

Mini 2000

Has a 22" barrel, and the electronic trigger was available at the additional cost.

NIB	Exc.	V.G.	Good	Fair	Poor
—	1550	1050	850	550	450

Running Boar Rifle

Has a thumbhole stock with an adjustable cheekpiece and is furnished without sights. It was specially designed for the offhand Running Boar Competitions.

NIB	Exc.	V.G.	Good	Fair	Poor
—	1800	1250	950	650	550

Match Rifle

Has a 26.75" barrel and an adjustable cheekpiece stock.

NIB	Exc.	V.G.	Good	Fair	Poor
—	1650	1095	850	550	450

Model 2600 Ultra Match Free Rifle

Similar to the Model 2000, with a laminated thumbhole stock and a heavy 26" barrel, fully adjustable sights, and trigger. It is offered with an electronic trigger for an additional $400. This model was introduced in 1986.

NIB	Exc.	V.G.	Good	Fair	Poor
1950	1400	1150	850	650	550

FEMARU
Budapest, Hungary

Hungary became a communist satellite in the mid-1950s. At this time the Femaru company was designated to replace the firm of Fegyvergyar as the official Hungarian arms manufacturer. The products are of good quality.

Model 37

This semi-automatic pistol was built in both 7.65mm and 9mm Short calibers. It is well designed pistol of quality construction. It is fitted with a grip safety and exposed hammer. The Hungarian military adopted the pistol in 1937. It was produced until the late 1940s. Early guns were marked "Femaru Fegyver es Gepgyar RT Budapest" but during the war the Nazi code for these guns was "jhv." The 9mm models have a 7-round magazine while the 7.65mm models have an 8-round magazine. During World War II the Germans designed this pistol the "Pistol Mod 37 Kal 7.65 (Ung)." Add 75 percent for Nazi proofed examples.

Courtesy Richard M. Kumor, Sr.

NIB	Exc.	V.G.	Good	Fair	Poor
—	350	275	225	150	100

Hege

A complete copy of the Walther PP. It is chambered for the 7.65mm and manufactured to be sold by Hegewaffen of Germany. The slide is so marked, along with a Pegasus in a circle. The designation "AP 66 Cal.7.65" also appears. The pistol was intended for export sales in the U.S. and other western countries.

NIB	Exc.	V.G.	Good	Fair	Poor
—	350	225	175	125	100

Tokagypt

15,000 of these pistols were built in 1958, under contract for the Egyptian army. It is a modified version of the Soviet TT-33 Tokarev chambered for the 9mm Parabellum with a safety added. The balance were sold commercially, some under the trademark "Firebird."

NIB	Exc.	V.G.	Good	Fair	Poor
—	475	350	275	200	125

Walam

Another Walther PP copy of excellent quality chambered for the 9mm short or .380 ACP. The pistols were sold on the commercial market—some designated Model 48.

NIB	Exc.	V.G.	Good	Fair	Poor
—	350	225	175	125	100

FERLIB
Gardone V.T., Italy

Model F.VI

A high-grade, side-by-side shotgun chambered for all gauges and is essentially custom-ordered. It is available in various barrel lengths and chokes and has an Anson and Deeley boxlock-action, double triggers, and automatic ejectors. The action is case-colored, and the stock is hand-checkered select walnut. Single-selective triggers are available for an additional $375. **NOTE:** 28 gauge and .410 add 10 percent.

NIB	Exc.	V.G.	Good	Fair	Poor
4750	3600	—	—	—	—

Model F.VII

Has a scroll-engraved, coin-finished frame but otherwise is similar to the Model F.VI. Single trigger option and small gauge premium are the same.

NIB	Exc.	V.G.	Good	Fair	Poor
12000	8500	—	—	—	—

Model F.VII/SC

A more deluxe version with gold inlays and a game scene-engraved receiver. Options and premium are the same.

NIB	Exc.	V.G.	Good	Fair	Poor
13000	9500	—	—	—	—

Model F.VII Sideplate

Features false sideplates that are completely covered with game scene engraving. This model is standard with a single-selective trigger, but the small gauge premium is applicable.

NIB	Exc.	V.G.	Good	Fair	Poor
15000	10500	—	—	—	—

Model F.VII/SC Sideplate

The false sideplate model with gold inlays accenting the full coverage engraving. **NOTE:** 28 gauge and .410 add 10 percent.

NIB	Exc.	V.G.	Good	Fair	Poor
16000	11500	—	—	—	—

Hammer Gun

Features a boxlock action with external hammers. Its other features are custom ordered to the purchaser's specifications.

NIB	Exc.	V.G.	Good	Fair	Poor
20000	14500	—	—	—	—

FERRY, ANDREWS & CO.
Stafford, Connecticut

Under Hammer Pistol

This boot pistol is chambered for .36 caliber percussion and has a 3" part-round, part-octagonal barrel. They are similar to the other under hammer pistols that were produced in Connecticut and Massachusetts. The top strap was marked "Andrews Ferry & Co." The number manufactured is unknown. They were produced in the 1850s.

NIB	Exc.	V.G.	Good	Fair	Poor
—	—	1550	700	395	125

FIALA ARMS COMPANY
New Haven, Connecticut

Fiala Repeating Target Pistol

A different type of pistol than what is commonly encountered. Outwardly it resembles a semi-automatic Colt Woodsman; in actuality it is a manually operated firearm that must be cycled by hand after every shot. It was chambered for the .22 rimfire and was offered with interchangeable barrels in lengths of 3", 7.5", and 20". Also offered was a detachable buttstock. The finish is blued, and the grips are found in both smooth and ribbed walnut. The rear sight is a square-notched blade that tips up into an elevation-adjustable peep sight. They are marked "Fiala Arms and Equipment Co. Inc. / New Haven Conn. / Patents Pending" on the right side of the frame behind the grip and Model 1920/Made in U.S.A. on the right side of the frame above the trigger guard. The left side of the frame was marked "FIALA ARMS" above the image of the polar bear with the "TRADE MARK" below the polar bear in the area above the trigger guard. This pistol was also furnished in one of three variations of cases that were optionally available: a canvas case, a black leatherette case, velvet-lined and fitted with a lock and key, and a tan leather version of the leatherette case. A fixed 7.5" barrel variation was also produced. A 7.5" smoothbore barrel was catalogued as a silencer. Some 20" smoothbore barrels were produced. Some pistols bear the names "Columbia Arms Company," and "Botwinik Brothers." The government has classified this pistol with its stock as a "Curio or Relic" and in its complete state is a very desirable collectible. See also Schall & Co.

Courtesy Butterfield & Butterfield, San Francisco, California

Complete, Three Barrels, Stock, Tools, and Case

NIB	Exc.	V.G.	Good	Fair	Poor
—	2500	2100	1250	675	550

Gun Only

Courtesy Dr. Jon Miller

NIB	Exc.	V.G.	Good	Fair	Poor
—	800	700	450	275	175

FINNISH LION
Valmet, Sweden

ISU Target Rifle

A single-shot, bolt-action rifle chambered for the .22 rimfire cartridge. It has a 27" heavy barrel and a target stock with accessories. It features target adjustable sights and was manufactured between 1966 and 1977.

NIB	Exc.	V.G.	Good	Fair	Poor
—	475	325	275	200	125

Champion Free Rifle

Has a 29" heavy barrel and double-set triggers. Otherwise it is similar to the ISU model. It was manufactured between 1965 and 1972.

NIB	Exc.	V.G.	Good	Fair	Poor
—	900	750	600	375	275

Match Rifle

Similar to the Champion rifle, with a thumbhole stock and an adjustable buttplate. It was manufactured between 1937 and 1972.

NIB	Exc.	V.G.	Good	Fair	Poor
—	900	750	600	375	275

FIOCCHI OF AMERICA, INC.
Ozark, Missouri

See—Pardini and A. Zoli

Imports the above firearms, and they are listed in their own respective sections.

FIREARMS INTERNATIONAL
Washington, D.C.

See—Star and Garcia

Was once the importer of the Star Model D as it was sold in the U.S.A. They also imported various other .25 caliber Colt copies that are not considered collectible and would be valued in the $150-and-under range. For the .22/.410 Bronco, see "Garcia."

FIRESTORM
Argentina

Firestorm .22 LR

A semi-automatic pistol chambered for the .22 Long Rifle cartridge. Ten-round magazine capacity. Matte blue finish or duotone.

NIB	Exc.	V.G.	Good	Fair	Poor
250	185	135	100	75	45

Firestorm .32

Double-action semi-auto chambered for .32 with 10+1 capacity. Blued, 3.5" barrel, 23 oz. Fixed sights and rubber grips. Introduced 2006.

NIB	Exc.	V.G.	Good	Fair	Poor
275	215	155	125	95	50

Firestorm .380

This semi-auto double-action pistol is chambered for the .380 ACP cartridge and fitted with a 3.5" barrel. Fixed three-dot combat sights. Matte blue or duotone finish. Magazine capacity is 7 rounds. Weight is about 23 oz.

NIB	Exc.	V.G.	Good	Fair	Poor
295	225	195	150	95	50

Mini Firestorm 9mm

This 9mm semi-auto double-action pistol is fitted with a 3.5" barrel. White outline drift adjustable target sights. Matte blue finish. Polymer grips. Magazine capacity is 10 rounds. Weight is about 25 oz.

NIB	Exc.	V.G.	Good	Fair	Poor
350	275	215	165	115	75

Mini Firestorm .40 S&W

As above but chambered for the .40 S&W cartridge.

NIB	Exc.	V.G.	Good	Fair	Poor
350	275	215	165	115	75

Firestorm .45 Government

This is a single-action semi-automatic pistol chambered for the .45 ACP cartridge. Fitted with a 5.125" barrel and 3 dot fixed combat sights. Magazine capacity is 7 rounds. Black rubber grips. Matte blue, nickel, or duotone finish. Weight is about 36 oz.

NIB	Exc.	V.G.	Good	Fair	Poor
350	275	215	165	115	75

Compact Firestorm .45 Government

As above but with 4.25" barrel. Weight is about 34 oz.

NIB	Exc.	V.G.	Good	Fair	Poor
350	275	215	165	115	75

Mini Firestorm .45 Government

As above but with 3.14" barrel. Black polymer grips and magazine capacity of 10 rounds. Weight is about 31 oz.

NIB	Exc.	V.G.	Good	Fair	Poor
350	275	215	165	115	75

1911 Mil-Spec Standard Government

1911A1-style single-action semi-auto chambered in .45 ACP; 5.125" barrel, steel frame, 7- or 8-round magazine, steel frame, plastic or wood grips, matte blue or deluxe polished blue finish.

NIB	Exc.	V.G.	Good	Fair	Poor
350	275	215	165	115	75

FLETCHER BIDWELL, LLC
Viroqua, Wisconsin

Spencer 1860 Military Carbine

Introduced in 2001 this is a faithful reproduction of the original Spencer Carbine. It is chambered for the .56-50 black powder cartridge but in centerfire. Fitted with a blued 22" round barrel. Magazine capacity is 7 rounds in butt tube. Bone charcoal case hardened receiver. Walnut stock. Blade front sight with ladder rear sight adjustable to 800 yards. Weight is about 9 lbs. Built in U.S.

NIB	Exc.	V.G.	Good	Fair	Poor
2750	1950	1500	900	625	400

FLORENCE ARMORY

Florence, Guilford Counry, North Carolina

Founded in 1862 as a repair facility to alter sporting arms for military use. Majority of work done by H.C. Lamb & Company. In 1862, Captain Z. Coffin ordered stocks, barrels and locks to assemble newly made rifles. Furniture of these arms varied, either being supplied by Glaze & Company or being the remainders from Searcy & Moore's production. Number made estimated to be in excess of 300 rifles in both .50 and .54 calibers. These arms (particularly the barrels) exhibit characteristics of North Carolina contract pieces.

NIB	Exc.	V.G.	Good	Fair	Poor
—	—	29500	12500	4000	1450

FNH USA, INC.

McLean, Virginia

This company is a subsidiary of FN Herstal in Belgium. It is essentially the sales and marketing arm for FN in the U.S. market.

PISTOLS

Model Forty-Nine

This pistol is built by FN Manufacturing, Inc. in Columbia, S.C. It has a polymer frame and stainless steel slide. Chambered for 9mm or .40 S&W cartridge. Barrel length is 4.25". Magazine capacity is 16 rounds for law enforcement and 10 rounds for commercial sales. It features a repeatable secure striker trigger system. Offered in stainless steel slide or black coated slide. Weight is about 26 oz. Offered primarily for sale to law enforcement agencies. Introduced in 2000.

NIB	Exc.	V.G.	Good	Fair	Poor
470	375	300	250	225	135

Model FNP-9/FNP-40

Introduced in 2003, this pistol is chambered for the 9mm or .40 S&W cartridge. Fitted with a 4" barrel and featuring a polymer frame. The action is a double-action/single-action design with an ambidextrous manual decocking lever. Fixed sights. Ten-round magazine capacity. Weight is about 33 oz.

NIB	Exc.	V.G.	Good	Fair	Poor
550	425	375	300	250	125

FNP-45

A longer-frame version of the FNP-9 chambered for .45 ACP. Barrel length is 4.5 inches and weight is 33.3 ounces. Ambidextrous mag release and decocker/safety, forward slide serrations. Magazine capacity: 10 or 15 rounds. Black or Flat Dark Earth finish. Interchangeable backstrap inserts.

NIB	Exc.	V.G.	Good	Fair	Poor
700	625	500	375	250	150

FNP-45 Tactical

Developed for the U.S. Joint Combat Pistol Program, this .45 ACP tactical model has a 5.3-inch threaded barrel for a suppressor or other accessories, high-profile combat sights, two mounting bases for optional red dot sights, MIL-STD 1913 rail. Black or Flat Dark Earth finish. Weight: 33.6 oz.

NIB	Exc.	V.G.	Good	Fair	Poor
1250	1050	850	625	350	250

FNP-45 Competition

Designed as a major caliber competition pistol. Same overall features as FNP-45 plus fiber optic front sight and Picatinny rail. Introduced in 2011.

NIB	Exc.	V.G.	Good	Fair	Poor
1050	850	700	500	300	250

FNX-9, FNX-40

Chambered in 9mm or .40 S&W. Magazine capacity: 17 (9mm), 14 (.40). Weight 22 to 24 ounces. Stainless steel slide has front and rear cocking serrations. Other features include ambidextrous operating controls. Four interchangeable back-strap inserts.

NIB	Exc.	V.G.	Good	Fair	Poor
600	535	450	325	250	150

FNH Five-seveN

Single-action design chambered for 5.7x28mm round. Magazine capacity: 10 or 20 rounds. Matte black, olive drab green or Flat

Dark Earth finish. Ambidextrous safety and accessory mounting rail. Barrel length, four inches, weight 21 ounces. Three-dot combat sights, adjustable rear.

NIB	Exc.	V.G.	Good	Fair	Poor
1100	975	800	575	250	150

Model HP-SA

This is the famous John Browning design Hi-Power pistol. Chambered for the 9mm or .40 S&W cartridge. Barrel length is 4.6". Magazine capacity is 10 rounds. Weight is around 32 oz. Blued finish.

NIB	Exc.	V.G.	Good	Fair	Poor
900	750	595	400	200	125

Model HP-SA-SFS

Introduced in 2003 this variant of the Hi-Power pistol features a single-action double-action mechanism that allows cocked-and-locked carry with the hammer and slide locked. When the safety is pushed off the hammer is set in the cocked position and is fired single action.

NIB	Exc.	V.G.	Good	Fair	Poor
900	750	595	400	200	125

Model HP-DA/HP-DAO

This model is offered in two different configurations. The first is with double-action/single-action trigger while the second is double-action-only. Chambered for the 9mm cartridge, the pistol is fitted with fixed sights. Magazine capacity is 15 rounds for law enforcement and 10 rounds for commerical sales. Weight is about 31 oz. Intended primarily for law enforcement sales. Introduced in 2000.

NIB	Exc.	V.G.	Good	Fair	Poor
900	750	595	400	200	125

Model HP-DA/HP-DAO Compact

As above but in a smaller and lighter package.

NIB	Exc.	V.G.	Good	Fair	Poor
900	750	595	400	200	125

Model BDA/BDAO Compact

This is a short recoil compact pistol chambered for the 9mm Parabellum cartridge. Fitted with a double-action/single-action trigger or double-action-only trigger. Each configuration has a 10-round magazine capacity. Weight is about 28 oz. Corrosion-resistant finish. Fixed sights.

NIB	Exc.	V.G.	Good	Fair	Poor
800	650	500	395	200	125

RIFLES

These rifles are produced at FN manufacturing in the U.S.

SPECIAL POLICE RIFLES (FN SPR)
FNAR

Semi-auto chambered in .308 Winchester. Cold hammer-forged 16-inch standard or 20-inch heavy barrel. Magazine capacity: 5 or 10 rounds. Weight: 8.5 to 10 lbs. Receiver-mounted optical rail with additional rails on fore-end. Matte black synthetic stock with fully adjustable comb and length of pull via interchangeable inserts. Match-grade model available.

NIB	Exc.	V.G.	Good	Fair	Poor
1600	1350	1050	800	450	300

FN A1 SPR

Chambered for the .308 7.62x51mm cartridge. Bolt-action. Fitted with a 24" heavy barrel with no sights. Choice of hinged floorplate or detachable box magazine. Stock is McMillan A3 tactical. Weight is about 10.75 lbs.

NIB	Exc.	V.G.	Good	Fair	Poor
1600	1350	1175	900	725	375

FN A1a SPR

Similar to the above model but fitted with a 20" heavy fluted barrel. McMillan A3 tactical stock. Weight is about 9.75 lbs.

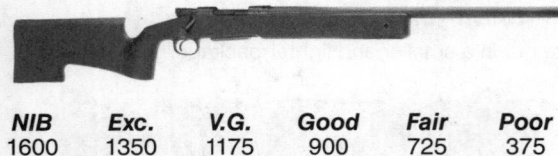

NIB	Exc.	V.G.	Good	Fair	Poor
1600	1350	1175	900	725	375

FN A2 SPR

Fitted with a 24" heavy barrel with McMillan A4 tactical stock and Badger Ordinance scope base. Weight is about 10.75 lbs.

NIB	Exc.	V.G.	Good	Fair	Poor
2190	1750	1550	1275	900	400

FN A3 SPR

This model has a 24" heavy barrel with McMillan A4 adjustable stock, Badger Ordinance scope base and Badger Ordinance or FN scope rings. Supplied with FNH Parker-Hale type or Harris bipod. Weight is about 10.75 lbs.

NIB	Exc.	V.G.	Good	Fair	Poor
2450	1950	1650	1375	950	450

FN A4 SPR

Fitted with a 24" heavy barrel with McMillan A4 adjustable tactical stock. Scope base and rings standard. Choice of several tactical scopes. Bipod. Sling. Drag bag. Kill flash. Tool kit. Cleaning kit. Hard case. Weight is about 10.75 lbs.

NIB	Exc.	V.G.	Good	Fair	Poor
5725	4350	3000	2350	1200	700

FN A5 SPR

This model has a 20" heavy fluted barrel threaded for a suppressor. Special McMillan tactical stock. The rest of the features are the same as the FN A4 model.

NIB	Exc.	V.G.	Good	Fair	Poor
7600	5750	4000	2400	1600	700

FN A5a SPR

This model has a 20" heavy fluted barrel threaded for a suppressor. Special SPR McMillan adjustable tactical stock. Weight is about 9.75 lbs.

NIB	Exc.	V.G.	Good	Fair	Poor
2460	1975	1650	1375	950	450

FN PBR (Patrol Bolt Rifle)

Introduced in 2004 this rifle is chambered for the .308 or .300 WSM. Offered with four different barrel lengths: 18", 20", 22", or 24". Fitted with a two-piece MIL spec M1913 rail. Black Hogue stock. Magazine capacity is 4 rounds. Weight is about 9 lbs.

NIB	Exc.	V.G.	Good	Fair	Poor
1000	950	900	800	700	400

PGM PRECISION RIFLES

These rifles are made by PGM Precision, a subsidary of FN, in Poisy Cedex, France.

Ultima Ratio Intervention

This bolt-action rifle is chambered for the .308 7.62x51mm cartridge and fitted with a 23.6" ribbed barrel with integral muzzle-brake. Folding bipod. Stock, trigger group, and action are fixed to a rigid metal girder. Stock is adjustable. No sights. Magazine capacity is 5 or 10 rounds. Weight is about 13.25 lbs. depending on configuration.

NIB	Exc.	V.G.	Good	Fair	Poor
9000	7995	6000	3250	1795	700

Ultima Ratio Commando I

Similar to the above model but with 18.5" fluted barrel with muzzlebrake. Weight is about 12 lbs.

NIB	Exc.	V.G.	Good	Fair	Poor
9100	8050	6100	3250	1795	700

Ultima Ratio Commando II

Similar to the Commando I but with folding stock.

NIB	Exc.	V.G.	Good	Fair	Poor
8320	—	—	—	—	—

FN-Mini-Hecate

Chambered for the .308 cartridge this bolt-action rifle features a free-loading interchangeable 18.5", 19.7", 21.7", or 23.6" match-grade barrel. Collapsible buttstock. Magazine capacity is 10 rounds. Weight is about 14 lbs. Introduced in 2001.

NIB	Exc.	V.G.	Good	Fair	Poor
9100	8050	6100	3250	1795	700

.338 Lapua

Similar to the Mini-Hecate but chambered for the .33 Lapua cartridge and fitted with a 27.2" barrel with integral muzzlebrake. Collapsible buttstock. Weight is about 15 lbs. Magazine capacity is 10 rounds.

NIB	Exc.	V.G.	Good	Fair	Poor
10500	9000	7750	6000	3750	1475

Hecate II

Chambered for the .50 BMG cartridge. Fitted with a 27.6" heavy barrel with integral muzzlebrake. Bipod. Adjustable stock. Magazine capacity is 7 rounds. Weight is about 36 lbs.

NIB	Exc.	V.G.	Good	Fair	Poor
N/A	—	—	—	—	—

OM .50 Nemesis

Chambered for the .50 caliber Browning cartridge (12.7x99mm) this bolt-action rifle features an adjustable buttstock, bipod, and other characteristics that make it a long range material rifle. Weight is approximately 28 lbs.

NIB	Exc.	V.G.	Good	Fair	Poor
N/A	—	—	—	—	—

SHOTGUNS

FN Police Shotgun

This is a slide-action 12 gauge shotgun chambered for the 3" 12 gauge shell. Barrel length is 18". Magazine capacity is 7 rounds. Black synthetic stock. Corrosion-resistant finish. Weight is about 6.5 lbs.

NIB	Exc.	V.G.	Good	Fair	Poor
350	275	200	150	125	100

FN Tactical Police

Similar to the standard model but with ported barrel and collapsible stock with pistol grip. Weight is about 6.5 lbs.

NIB	Exc.	V.G.	Good	Fair	Poor
550	475	400	300	200	100

FN Self-Loading Police

This shotgun is a gas-operated semi-automatic shotgun fitted with a picatinny rail and short stock. Chambered for the 12 gauge shell. Magazine capacity is 6 rounds. Weight is about 7.75 lbs.

NIB	Exc.	V.G.	Good	Fair	Poor
1000	800	600	400	300	200

FOEHL & WEEKS
Philadelphia, Pennsylvania

Columbian

A .32 or .38 caliber revolver marked with the patent date "20 January 1891."

NIB	Exc.	V.G.	Good	Fair	Poor
—	—	350	150	75	50

Columbian Automatic

A .38 caliber revolver with a hinged barrel and cylinder assembly.

NIB	Exc.	V.G.	Good	Fair	Poor
—	—	400	200	100	75

Perfect

As above, with a concealed hammer and also in .32 caliber.

NIB	Exc.	V.G.	Good	Fair	Poor
—	—	400	200	100	75

FOEHL, C.
Philadelphia, Pennsylvania

Derringer

A .41 caliber percussion single-shot pistol with a 2" barrel, German silver mounts and a walnut stock. The lock marked "C. Foehl."

NIB	Exc.	V.G.	Good	Fair	Poor
—	—	1950	750	300	110

FOGARTY
American Repeating Rifle Co.
Boston, Massachusetts

Fogarty Repeating Rifle and Carbine

A limited number of repeating rifles and carbines based upon Valentine Fogarty's patents were produced between 1866 and 1867. The calibers of these arms varies and the normal barrel lengths are 20" and 28". Blued, casehardened with walnut stocks. The American Repeating Rifle Company was purchased by the Winchester Repeating Arms Company in 1869.

Rifle

Courtesy Buffalo Bill Historical Center, Cody, Wyoming

NIB	Exc.	V.G.	Good	Fair	Poor
—	—	9500	4050	1250	450

Carbine

Courtesy Buffalo Bill Historical Center, Cody, Wyoming

NIB	Exc.	V.G.	Good	Fair	Poor
—	—	9500	4050	1250	450

FOLSOM, H.
St. Louis, Missouri

Derringer

A .41 caliber single-shot percussion pocket pistol with a 2.5" barrel, German silver mounts and a walnut stock. The barrel marked "H. Folsom."

NIB	Exc.	V.G.	Good	Fair	Poor
—	—	1150	800	350	275

FOLSOM, H&D ARMS CO.

Large distributor of double and single barrel shotguns produced by Crescent Firearms Co., Norwich, Connecticut. Folsom owned and later sold to Savage Arms Co. the Crescent Firearms Co., Davis Warner Co., and Baker Gun Co. around 1930. For more information see also Crescent Firearms Co.

FOREHAND & WADSWORTH
Worcester, Massachusetts

Established in 1871 and operated under the above name until 1890 when it became the Forehand Arms Company. Hopkins & Allen purchased the company in 1902.

Single-Shot Derringer

A .22 caliber single-shot pocket pistol with a 2" half-octagonal pivoted barrel, spur trigger and nickel- or silver-plated frame. Walnut grips. The barrel marked "Forehand & Wadsworth Worcester."

NIB	Exc.	V.G.	Good	Fair	Poor
—	1450	600	250	100	

Single-Shot .41 Derringer

As above in .41 caliber with a 2.5" round barrel.

Courtesy Milwaukee Public Museum, Milwaukee, Wisconsin

NIB	Exc.	V.G.	Good	Fair	Poor
—	—	1000	850	450	200

Side-Hammer .22

A .22 caliber spur trigger revolver with a 2.25" to 4" octagonal barrel and 7-shot cylinder. Blued or nickel-plated with walnut grips.

NIB	Exc.	V.G.	Good	Fair	Poor
—	—	675	475	200	100

Center Hammer

A .32 caliber spur trigger revolver with a 3.5" octagonal barrel and 6-shot cylinder. Blued or nickel-plated with rosewood or walnut grips. The top strap commonly found marked "Terror."

Courtesy Milwaukee Public Museum, Milwaukee, Wisconsin

NIB	Exc.	V.G.	Good	Fair	Poor
—	—	400	300	200	100

Old Model Army Single-Action Revolver

A .44 Russian caliber revolver with a 7.5" round barrel and 6-shot cylinder. The barrel marked "Forehand & Wadsworth, Worchester, Mass. U.S. Patd. Oct. 22, '61, June 27, '71 Oct. 28, '73." Blued with walnut grips. Approximately 250 were manufactured between 1872 and 1878.

NIB	Exc.	V.G.	Good	Fair	Poor
—	—	4000	3250	2000	500

New Model Army Single-Action Revolver

Similar to the above, with a 6.5" barrel and half-cock notch on the hammer. Approximately 250 were made between 1878 and 1882. Intersting note: In 2008, United States Fire Arms announced plans to remanufacture this model.

NIB	Exc.	V.G.	Good	Fair	Poor
—	—	3750	3000	2250	500

Double-Action Revolver

A .32 or .38 centerfire or rimfire caliber double-action revolver with a 3.5" barrel and 6- or 7-shot cylinder. The .32 caliber version marked "Forehand & Wadsworth Double-Action," and the .38 caliber "American Bulldog." Manufactured from 1871 to 1890.

NIB	Exc.	V.G.	Good	Fair	Poor
—	400	300	200	100	35

British Bulldog

A .32 or .38 centerfire solid frame double-action revolver resembling the Webley Bulldog.

NIB	Exc.	V.G.	Good	Fair	Poor
—	—	395	300	150	75

British Bulldog .44

As above in .44 Webley caliber with a 5" barrel and 5-shot cylinder.

NIB	Exc.	V.G.	Good	Fair	Poor
—	—	450	325	175	100

Swamp Angel

A .41 caliber single-action revolver with a 3" barrel and 5-shot cylinder. The top strap marked "Swamp Angel."

NIB	Exc.	V.G.	Good	Fair	Poor
—	—	425	275	100	50

FOREHAND ARMS CO. 1898-1902
Perfection Automatic

A .32 or .38 caliber double-action revolver with a hinged barrel and cylinder assembly. Varying barrel lengths. Blued or nickel-plated with hard rubber grips.

NIB	Exc.	V.G.	Good	Fair	Poor
—	275	250	100	75	50

Double-Barrel Shotguns

Good quality hammer and hammerless doubles but few produced until taken over by Hopkins and Allen Firearms Co. Values from $100 to $1,000 depending on grade and condition.

FOWLER, B. JR.
Hartford, Connecticut

Percussion Pistol

A .38 caliber single-shot percussion pistol with a 4" half octagonal barrel, iron frame and maple grips. The barrel marked "B. Fowler, Jr." Manufactured between 1835 and 1838.

NIB	Exc.	V.G.	Good	Fair	Poor
—	—	995	550	325	150

FOX, A. H.
Philadelphia, Pennsylvania

Ansley H. Fox established the Fox Gun Company in Baltimore, Maryland, in 1896. Subsequently, he made arms under the name Philadelphia Gun Company. As of 1905, he operated under the name A.H. Fox. In 1930, this company was purchased by the Savage Arms Company who continued manufacturing all grades of Fox shotguns. As of 1942, the Savage Company only made the plainer grades. For Fox Model B double shotguns see Savage Arms Co.

Sterlingworth

A 12, 16, or 20 gauge boxlock double-barrel shotgun with 26", 28", or 30" barrels, double triggers and extractors. Automatic ejectors were also available and would add approximately 30 percent to the values listed. Blued, casehardened with a walnut stock. Manufactured from 1911 to 1946. **NOTE:** 20 gauge add 50 percent. Add 25 percent for 16 gauge.

Courtesy Nick Niles, Paul Goodwin photo

NIB	Exc.	V.G.	Good	Fair	Poor
—	2000	1600	1000	500	275

Sterlingworth Deluxe

As above, with an ivory bead, recoil pad and optional 32" barrel. **NOTE:** 20 gauge add 50 percent. Add 25 percent for 16 gauge.

NIB	Exc.	V.G.	Good	Fair	Poor
—	2500	1900	1250	700	400

SP Grade

A 12, 16, or 20 gauge boxlock double-barrel shotgun with varying length barrels, double triggers and extractors. **NOTE:** 20 gauge add 35 percent. Automatic ejectors add 15 percent. Add 25 percent for 16 gauge.

NIB	Exc.	V.G.	Good	Fair	Poor
—	1600	1325	1050	450	225

HE Grade

Similar to the early A Grade and offered in 12 and 20 gauge. Chambers were 2-1/4" standard with 3" chambers available on request. This model is marked on the barrel "Not Warranted." this referred to pattern density, not barrel quality. Only sixty 20 gauge HE Grades appear in factory records. Manufactured from 1923 to 1942. **NOTE:** Single-selective trigger add 20 percent. Add 30 percent premium for 20 gauge.

NIB	Exc.	V.G.	Good	Fair	Poor
—	3250	2800	2225	1000	650

High Grade Guns A-FE

The Fox Company as well as the Savage Arms Company produced a variety of shotguns decorated in varying grades. They were available in 12, 16, and 20 gauge. As the value for these arms depends on the particular features of these arms, prospective purchasers are advised to secure a qualified appraisal prior to acquisition. NOTE: A 25 percent premium should be added to the grades below for small gauge guns and guns with single selective trigger.

A Grade

Built from 1905 to 1942.

NIB	Exc.	V.G.	Good	Fair	Poor
—	2100	1700	1225	600	400

AE Grade (Automatic Ejectors)

Built from 1905 to 1946.

NIB	Exc.	V.G.	Good	Fair	Poor
—	2400	2000	1600	900	700

B Grade

Built from 1905 to 1918.

NIB	Exc.	V.G.	Good	Fair	Poor
—	3100	2700	1950	1100	500

BE Grade

Built from 1905 to 1918.

NIB	Exc.	V.G.	Good	Fair	Poor
—	3500	3050	2500	1500	900

C Grade

Built from 1905 to 1913.

NIB	Exc.	V.G.	Good	Fair	Poor
—	3300	2700	2150	1100	550

CE Grade

Built from 1905 to 1946.

NIB	Exc.	V.G.	Good	Fair	Poor
—	3800	3350	2550	1700	950

XE Grade

Built from 1914 to 1945.

Courtesy William Hammond

NIB	Exc.	V.G.	Good	Fair	Poor
—	6500	5900	4150	2250	1100

D Grade

Built from 1906 to 1913.

NIB	Exc.	V.G.	Good	Fair	Poor
—	9300	8000	5150	2750	1000

DE Grade

Built from 1906 to 1945.

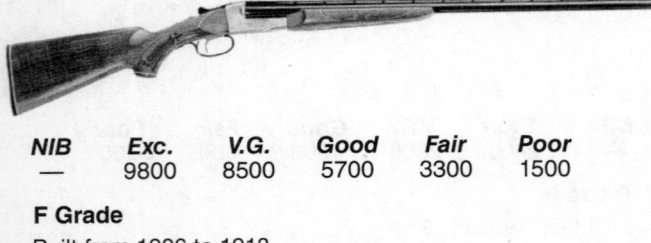

NIB	Exc.	V.G.	Good	Fair	Poor
—	9800	8500	5700	3300	1500

F Grade

Built from 1906 to 1913.

NIB	Exc.	V.G.	Good	Fair	Poor
—	25000	16800	9000	5700	3000

FE Grade

Built from 1906 to 1940.

NIB	Exc.	V.G.	Good	Fair	Poor
—	28000	21000	11500	7700	5000

Single Barrel Trap Guns

A 12 gauge single barrel boxlock shotgun with 30" or 32" ventilated rib barrels and automatic ejector. There were approximately 571 single-barrel trap guns manufactured. Produced in four grades as listed:

J Grade

Built from 1919 to 1936.

NIB	Exc.	V.G.	Good	Fair	Poor
—	3100	2400	1750	1050	600

K Grade

Built from 1919 to 1931. Approximately 75 built.

NIB	Exc.	V.G.	Good	Fair	Poor
—	4350	3300	2450	1650	950

L Grade

Built from 1919 to 1931. Approximately 25 built.

NIB	Exc.	V.G.	Good	Fair	Poor
—	5750	3900	3150	2150	1200

M Grade

Built from 1919 to 1932. A total of 9 guns built.

NIB	Exc.	V.G.	Good	Fair	Poor
—	15000	10000	6500	4700	2500

RECENTLY MANUFACTURED A.H. FOX SHOTGUNS

In 1993 the Connecticut Shotgun Manufacturing Company of New Britain, Connecticut, announced the production of the A.H. Fox shotgun in 20 gauge exclusively. The gun is hand-built and constructed to the same dimensions and standards as the original Fox. The gun is offered in five grades with many standard features and several optional ones as well. Each shotgun is built to order. Because these guns are newly built and have no pricing history, only manufacturer's retail price for the base gun will be given. Extra sets of barrels, single triggers, and other extra costs options will greatly affect price.

CE Grade

Retail price: $15,500

XE Grade

Retail price: $17,000

DE Grade

Retail price: $20,500

FE Grade

Retail price: $25,500

Exhibition Grade

This is the company's highest grade and features any optional detail the customer desires including custom engraving and exhibition quality wood.

Retail price: On request from CSMC.

FRANCHI, L.
Brescia, Italy

BOXLOCK SIDE-BY-SIDE-SHOTGUNS

Astore

A 12 gauge boxlock shotgun manufactured in a variety of barrel lengths with double triggers and automatic ejectors. Blued with a straight walnut stock. Manufactured from 1937 to 1960.

NIB	Exc.	V.G.	Good	Fair	Poor
2900	1600	750	500	350	200

Astore II

As above, but more finely finished.

NIB	Exc.	V.G.	Good	Fair	Poor
3150	1850	900	700	450	250

Astore 5

As above, but more finely finished.

NIB	Exc.	V.G.	Good	Fair	Poor
3350	2150	1250	950	600	300

Airone

Similar to the Astore. Manufactured during the 1940s.

NIB	Exc.	V.G.	Good	Fair	Poor
2900	1600	750	500	350	200

SIDELOCK SIDE-BY-SIDE SHOTGUNS

A 12, 16, or 20 gauge sidelock double-barrel shotgun manufactured in a variety of barrel lengths with a single-selective trigger and automatic ejectors. Produced in the following grades they differ as to engraving coverage and quality of wood:

Condor

NIB	Exc.	V.G.	Good	Fair	Poor
7500	6500	4500	3500	2500	1250

Imperial

NIB	Exc.	V.G.	Good	Fair	Poor
10000	8500	6000	4500	3250	1500

Imperiales

NIB	Exc.	V.G.	Good	Fair	Poor
10500	9000	6500	5000	3500	1500

No. 5 Imperial Monte Carlo

NIB	Exc.	V.G.	Good	Fair	Poor
15000	12500	9000	7500	5000	2000

No. 11 Imperial Monte Carlo

NIB	Exc.	V.G.	Good	Fair	Poor
16000	13500	10000	8000	5500	2000

Imperial Monte Carlo Extra

NIB	Exc.	V.G.	Good	Fair	Poor
20000	17500	12500	9500	7500	3500

Highlander

Introduced in 2003 this model features either a 12, 20, or 28 gauge gun fitted with 26" barrels and fixed chokes. Select walnut straight grip stock with splinter fore-end. Coin finished steel receiver. Single trigger. Weight is 6.4 lbs. for 12 gauge; 5.8 lbs. for 20 gauge, and 5.7 lbs. for 28 gauge. **NOTE:** Add $150 for 28 gauge.

NIB	Exc.	V.G.	Good	Fair	Poor
1800	1600	1200	850	475	300

OVER/UNDER SHOTGUNS

Priti Deluxe Model

A 12 or 20 gauge over/under boxlock double-barrel shotgun with 26" or 28" ventilated rib barrels, single trigger and automatic ejectors. Introduced in 1988.

NIB	Exc.	V.G.	Good	Fair	Poor
400	350	300	250	200	150

Falconet

A 12, 16, 20, and 28 gauge as well as .410 bore boxlock double-barrel shotgun with single-selective trigger and automatic ejectors. The receiver was anodized in tan, ebony, or silver finishes. Manufactured from 1968 to 1975. **NOTE:** Silver receiver add 10 percent. 28 gauge and .410 add 25 percent.

NIB	Exc.	V.G.	Good	Fair	Poor
650	550	425	350	250	200

Falconet Skeet

As above, with a 26" skeet barrel with a wide rib and the receiver casehardened. Manufactured from 1970 to 1974.

NIB	Exc.	V.G.	Good	Fair	Poor
950	850	700	550	450	250

Falconet International Skeet

As above, but more finely finished.

NIB	Exc.	V.G.	Good	Fair	Poor
1050	950	750	600	475	250

Falconet Trap

As above, with a 30" modified and full choke barrel, and trap stock. Manufactured from 1970 to 1974.

NIB	Exc.	V.G.	Good	Fair	Poor
1000	900	700	550	450	250

Falconet International Trap

As above, but more finely finished.

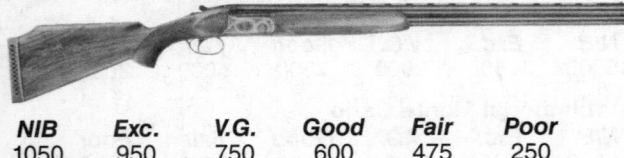

NIB	Exc.	V.G.	Good	Fair	Poor
1050	950	750	600	475	250

Peregrine Model 451

A 12 gauge boxlock double-barrel shotgun with 26" or 28" ventilated rib barrels, alloy receiver, single-selective trigger and automatic ejectors. Manufactured in 1975.

NIB	Exc.	V.G.	Good	Fair	Poor
800	675	495	375	275	200

Peregrine Model 400

As above, with a steel frame.

NIB	Exc.	V.G.	Good	Fair	Poor
850	775	600	400	300	200

Aristocrat

Similar to the above, with 26", 28", or 30" ventilated rib barrels. Manufactured from 1960 to 1969.

NIB	Exc.	V.G.	Good	Fair	Poor
850	725	600	400	300	200

Aristocrat Magnum

As above, with 3" chambers and 32" full choke barrels.

NIB	Exc.	V.G.	Good	Fair	Poor
895	775	675	450	300	200

Aristocrat Silver King

As above, with a French case hardened receiver, and available in four grades of decoration.

NIB	Exc.	V.G.	Good	Fair	Poor
950	875	775	475	350	200

Aristocrat Deluxe

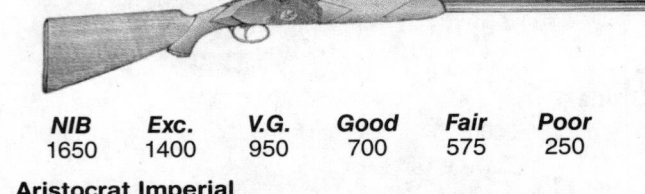

NIB	Exc.	V.G.	Good	Fair	Poor
1250	1000	875	575	400	200

Aristocrat Supreme

NIB	Exc.	V.G.	Good	Fair	Poor
1650	1400	950	700	575	250

Aristocrat Imperial

NIB	Exc.	V.G.	Good	Fair	Poor
2950	2450	1950	1250	950	450

Aristocrat Monte Carlo

NIB	Exc.	V.G.	Good	Fair	Poor
3750	3200	2950	2000	1500	750

Model 2003 Trap

A 12 gauge boxlock double-barrel shotgun with 30" or 32" ventilated rib barrels, single-selective trigger and automatic ejectors. Manufactured in 1976.

NIB	Exc.	V.G.	Good	Fair	Poor
1450	1300	900	650	500	250

Model 2004 Trap

A single-barreled version of the Model 2003.

NIB	Exc.	V.G.	Good	Fair	Poor
1450	1300	900	650	500	250

Model 2005 Combination Trap

The Model 2003 with both a single and set of over/under barrels.

NIB	Exc.	V.G.	Good	Fair	Poor
2800	2400	1950	1200	950	450

Model 3000 "Undergun"

As above, with a single barrel fitted with a high ventilated rib so that it fires from the lower barrel position.

NIB	Exc.	V.G.	Good	Fair	Poor
3050	2850	2200	1500	1200	600

Alcione Classic

Introduced in 2004 this 12 gauge 3" model features 26" or 28" ventilated rib barrels. Side rib is ventilated. Walnut stock with schnabel fore-end. Optional 20 gauge barrels. Weight is about 7.5 lbs.

NIB	Exc.	V.G.	Good	Fair	Poor
1300	975	800	600	500	250

Alcione T (Titanium)

Introduced in 2002 this model is similar to the Alcione Field but has an aluminum alloy frame with titanium inserts. Available in 12 and 20 gauge with 3" chambers. Choice of 26" or 28" vent rib barrels with choke tubes. Weight is about 6.8 lbs. for 12 and 20 gauge.

NIB	Exc.	V.G.	Good	Fair	Poor
1400	1150	950	700	600	300

Alcione T Two-Barrel Set

As above but with a two-barrel set: One 12 gauge 28" and the other is a 20 gauge 26". Introduced in 2004.

NIB	Exc.	V.G.	Good	Fair	Poor
1600	1275	1100	800	650	350

Alcione Field Model

A 12 gauge boxlock double-barrel shotgun with 26" or 28" ventilated rib barrels, single-selective trigger and automatic ejectors. Engraved silver receiver. Weight is about 7.5 lbs.

NIB	Exc.	V.G.	Good	Fair	Poor
1200	995	800	525	300	150

Alcione Sporting

This over/under gun is designed for sporting clays competition. Fitted with mechanical triggers and ported barrels. Offered in 12 gauge only with 30" barrels. Select walnut stock. Removable sideplates. Weight about 7.5 lbs.

NIB	Exc.	V.G.	Good	Fair	Poor
1550	1250	995	775	400	00

Alcione LF

This 12 or 20 gauge model features barrels of 26" and 28" in 12 gauge and 26" in 20 gauge. Both gauges are chambered for 3" shells. Walnut stock. Receiver is aluminum alloy with etched games scenes with gold fill. Weight is about 6.8 lbs.

Alcione LF receiver—Right side view

NIB	Exc.	V.G.	Good	Fair	Poor
1300	1050	700	450	300	200

Alcione SL Sport

As above, but more finely finished and with a French casehardened receiver.

NIB	Exc.	V.G.	Good	Fair	Poor
1375	1125	775	525	375	275

Alcione SP

Chambered for the 12 gauge shell and fitted with 28" vent rib barrels with choke tubes. Full slide lock-style side plates with engraving and gold pheasants and mallards. Weight is about 7.5 lbs. Introduced in 2003.

NIB	Exc.	V.G.	Good	Fair	Poor
1700	1450	975	700	575	345

ALCIONE SIDEPLATES

Alcione Classic SX

This 12 gauge 3" model is similar to the Alcione Field SX above but with blued receiver. Available with choice of 26" or 28" vent rib barrels. An extra 12 gauge 30" ported barrel and 20 gauge barrels are also optional. Weight is about 7.5 lbs. Introduced in 2004.

NIB	Exc.	V.G.	Good	Fair	Poor
1400	1150	950	700	600	300

Alcione Field SX

This model is fitted with a high grade walnut stock, fine checkering, and engraved receivers with gold filled etched side plates. Offered with 28" or 26" barrels. Weight is about 7.3 lbs.

NIB	Exc.	V.G.	Good	Fair	Poor
1600	1250	995	775	400	00

Veloce

Introduced in 2001 this model is chambered for the 20 or 28 gauge only with 26" or 28" barrels for 20 gauge guns and 26" barrels for 28 gauge guns. Aluminum alloy receiver. Engraved side plates with gold filled game scenes. Mechanical trigger. Select walnut stock. Weight of 20 gauge guns is about 5.8 lbs. and 28 gauge guns about 5.5 lbs.

NIB	Exc.	V.G.	Good	Fair	Poor
1375	1125	775	525	375	275

Veloce English Stock

Introduced in 2002 this model is similar ot the Veloce but with a straight-grip stock. Offered in 20 and 28 gauge with 26" vent-rib barrels. Choke tubes. Weight is about 5.7 lbs. in 20 gauge and 5.5 lbs. in 28 gauge.

NIB	Exc.	V.G.	Good	Fair	Poor
1400	1150	950	700	600	300

Veloce Grade II

This 20 or 28 gauge model features an extra-select-grade walnut stock with gold-filled birds and scroll engraving. The 20 gauge is offered with either a 26" or 28" vent-rib barrel, while the 28 gauge is fitted with a 26" vent-rib barrel. The 20 gauge gun weighs about 5.75 lbs., while the 28 gauge gun weighs about 5.5 lbs.

NIB	Exc.	V.G.	Good	Fair	Poor
1600	1275	1100	800	650	350

Veloce Squire Set

This model features a two-barrel set in 20 and 28 gauge. Each barrel set is fitted with 26" vent-rib barrels. Select walnut stock, gold-embellished game scenes, jeweled monoblocs, and filigreed top lever. Weight is about 5.5 lbs. Introduced in 2003.

NIB	Exc.	V.G.	Good	Fair	Poor
2100	1775	1600	1200	800	400

Renaissance

The Renaissance Series was introduced in 2006. These over/unders feature ultra-light alloy receivers, oil-finished walnut stocks, Prince of Wales pistol grips, cut checkering and Twin Shock Absorber recoil pads with gel insert. The 3" 12 and 20 gauges have 26" or 28" barrels; the 28 gauge has a 26" barrel. Weights average 6.2 lbs. in 12 gauge, 5.8 lbs. in 20 gauge and 5.5 lbs. in 28 gauge. Add 5 percent to values shown for 28 gauge.

Field

Walnut stock with engraved receiver.

NIB	Exc.	V.G.	Good	Fair	Poor
1600	1250	995	775	400	00

Classic

A-Grade walnut with gold inlaid receiver.

NIB	Exc.	V.G.	Good	Fair	Poor
1650	1300	1050	825	450	250

Elite

AA-Grade Walnut with gold inlaid receiver.

NIB	Exc.	V.G.	Good	Fair	Poor
1900	1550	1295	1050	650	275

Sporting

This 3" 12 gauge model was introduced in 2007. It features a 30" barrel, A-Grade walnut stock, engraved receiver with gold inlay and adjustable comb. Weight is about 7.9 lbs.

NIB	Exc.	V.G.	Good	Fair	Poor
1975	1625	1350	1300	825	325

SEMI-AUTOMATIC SHOTGUNS

AL48

A 12 or 20 gauge semi-auto shotgun with 24" to 30" ventilated-rib barrels (those made after 1989, threaded for choke tubes) and an alloy receiver. Walnut stock. Manufactured since 1950. Values shown are for current production. **NOTE:** Magnum Model add 10 percent. Add $75 for 28 gauge model.

NIB	Exc.	V.G.	Good	Fair	Poor
725	550	300	250	150	100

AL 48 Short Stock (Modern)

Same as above but in 20 gauge with shorter length of pull. First imported in 2000.

NIB	Exc.	V.G.	Good	Fair	Poor
700	525	275	250	150	100

AL 48 Deluxe English Stock (Modern)

Similar to the standard AL 48 but with straight grip stock. Offered in 20 and 28 gauge with 26" vent-rib barrel with choke tubes. Weight is about 5.5 lbs. Introduced in 2002.

NIB	Exc.	V.G.	Good	Fair	Poor
800	625	375	275	175	100

Hunter Model AL48 (1950-1970)

As above with an etched receiver and more finely figured wood. **NOTE:** Magnum Model add 10 percent.

NIB	Exc.	V.G.	Good	Fair	Poor
550	350	300	250	200	150

Eldorado AL48 (1954-1975)

As above, but more finely finished. Manufactured from 1954 to 1975.

NIB	Exc.	V.G.	Good	Fair	Poor
600	425	325	250	200	150

Crown Grade

As above, with hand-done engraving and finely figured walnut stocks.

NIB	Exc.	V.G.	Good	Fair	Poor
1800	1450	1200	800	475	250

Diamond Grade

As above, with hand-done engraving and finely figured walnut stocks.

NIB	Exc.	V.G.	Good	Fair	Poor
2300	1850	1375	900	575	300

Imperial Grade

As above, with hand-done engraving and finely figured walnut stocks.

NIB	Exc.	V.G.	Good	Fair	Poor
2800	2450	1850	1250	950	450

Model 500

A 12 gauge semi-automatic shotgun with a 28" ventilated-rib barrel and walnut stock. Introduced in 1976. **NOTE:** Deluxe version add 10 percent.

NIB	Exc.	V.G.	Good	Fair	Poor
500	425	375	295	150	100

Model 520 "Eldorado Gold"

An engraved and gold-inlaid version of the above.

NIB	Exc.	V.G.	Good	Fair	Poor
1250	1050	850	550	300	150

Model 530 Trap

The Model 500 with a 30" or 32" ventilated-rib barrel and trap stock.

NIB	Exc.	V.G.	Good	Fair	Poor
675	600	500	400	300	150

Prestige Model

A 12 gauge semi-automatic shotgun manufactured in a variety of barrel lengths. After 1989 the barrels threaded for choke tubes. Alloy receiver and walnut stock.

NIB	Exc.	V.G.	Good	Fair	Poor
675	550	475	350	250	150

Elite Model

As above, with an etched receiver and more finely figured stock.

NIB	Exc.	V.G.	Good	Fair	Poor
700	600	525	350	250	150

SPAS12

A 12 gauge slide-action/semi-automatic shotgun with a 21.5" barrel and 9-shot magazine. Anodized, black finish with a composition folding or fixed stock.

NIB	Exc.	V.G.	Good	Fair	Poor
1450	1000	800	600	475	300

Black Magic Game Model

A 12 gauge Magnum semi-automatic shotgun with 24" to 28" ventilated rib barrels threaded for choke tubes, gold anodized alloy receiver, blackened barrel and walnut stock. Also available in trap or skeet configuration. **NOTE:** Skeet Model add 10 percent. Trap Model add 15 percent.

NIB	Exc.	V.G.	Good	Fair	Poor
750	600	525	300	250	100

Black Magic Hunter

A 12 or 20 gauge Magnum double-barrel shotgun with 28" ventilated-rib barrels threaded for choke tubes, single-selective triggers and automatic ejectors. Blued with a walnut stock. Introduced in 1989.

NIB	Exc.	V.G.	Good	Fair	Poor
700	550	475	300	250	100

Black Magic Lightweight Hunter

As above, with 26" barrels and 2.75" chambers.

NIB	Exc.	V.G.	Good	Fair	Poor
975	850	650	400	300	150

Variomax 912

Introduced in 2001 this model is chambered for the 12 gauge 3.5" shell. It is offered with a choice of 24", 26", 28", or 30" barrels with vent-rib. Black synthetic stock. Weight is about 7.6 lbs. Choke tubes. In 2002 a walnut stock was added as an option. **NOTE:** Add $50 for walnut stock.

NIB	Exc.	V.G.	Good	Fair	Poor
700	550	475	300	250	100

Variomax 912 Camo

Same as above but with Advantage Timber camo finish.

NIB	Exc.	V.G.	Good	Fair	Poor
750	600	525	300	250	10

Variomax 912 SteadyGrip

Introduced in 2005 this model features a extended pistol grip and Advantage H-D camo stock with 24" vent rib barrel and choke tubes. Weight is about 8 lbs.

NIB	Exc.	V.G.	Good	Fair	Poor
775	625	550	325	265	10

Variopress 612 Sporting

This is a 12 gauge semi-automatic gas-operated shotgun with 30" ported barrel. Extended choke tubes. Select walnut stock with stock drop kit. Magazine capacity is 5 rounds. Weight is about 7 lbs. First imported in 2000.

NIB	Exc.	V.G.	Good	Fair	Poor
700	550	475	300	250	100

Variopress 612 Field

This 12 gauge model is offered with barrel lengths from 24" to 28". Stock configurations are walnut, synthetic, or camo. Magazine capacity is 5 rounds. Weight is about 7 lbs. depending on barrel length.

NIB	Exc.	V.G.	Good	Fair	Poor
700	550	475	300	250	100

Variopress 612 Defense

This 12 gauge gun is fitted with an 18.5" barrel and black synthetic stock. Matte black finish. Choke is cylinder. Weight is about 6.5 lbs. Magazine capacity is 5 rounds. First imported in 2000.

NIB	Exc.	V.G.	Good	Fair	Poor
600	500	425	350	250	150

Variopress 620 Field

This model is offered in 20 gauge with a choice of walnut or camo stock. Barrel lengths from 24" to 28". Magazine capacity is 5 rounds. Weight is about 6 lbs. **NOTE:** Add $50 for camo stock.

NIB	Exc.	V.G.	Good	Fair	Poor
700	550	475	300	250	100

Variopress 620 Short Stock

Same as above but with 12.5" length of pull and walnut stock. First imported in 2000.

NIB	Exc.	V.G.	Good	Fair	Poor
700	550	475	300	250	100

Model 712

This is semi-automatic shotgun chambered for the 12 gauge 3" shell. Available with choice of 24", 26", or 28" vent rib barrels with choke tubes. Also offered in several different finishes: Weathercoat (synthetic wood), Max-4 camo and Timber HD. Choice of synthetic wood, black synthetic, or camo stock. Weight is about 6.8 lbs. to 7 lbs., depending on stock and barrel length. Introduced in 2004.

Weathercoat

NIB	Exc.	V.G.	Good	Fair	Poor
700	600	500	375	200	100

Camo

NIB	Exc.	V.G.	Good	Fair	Poor
725	625	525	400	225	125

Synthetic

NIB	Exc.	V.G.	Good	Fair	Poor
775	650	550	425	250	150

Model 720

Similar to the Model 712 but chambered for the 20 gauge 3" shell. Offered with 24", 26", or 28" vent rib barrels. Choice of Max-4, Timber HD finish or walnut stock with 12.5" lop. Introduced in 2004.

Camo

NIB	Exc.	V.G.	Good	Fair	Poor
750	650	550	425	250	150

Walnut Short Stock

NIB	Exc.	V.G.	Good	Fair	Poor
725	625	525	400	225	125

Weathercoat

Introduced in 2005 with 28" vent rib barrel. Weight is about 6.2 lbs.

NIB	Exc.	V.G.	Good	Fair	Poor
775	650	550	425	250	150

I-12

Introduced in 2005 this 12 gauge model is offered with 3" chambers and choice of 24", 26", or 28" vent rib barrels. Available with synthetic, walnut, Max-4, or Timber H-D stock. Choke tubes. Weight is about 7.5 lbs. depending on barrel length.

NIB	Exc.	V.G.	Good	Fair	Poor
1200	900	600	500	350	200

I-12 White Gold

Similar to Inertia I-12 but with highly figured walnut stock and white gold game bird scene on a satin nickel receiver. Introduced in 2006. Available only with 28" barrel. Weight is about 7.7 lbs.

NIB	Exc.	V.G.	Good	Fair	Poor
1400	1050	750	600	425	250

RIFLES

Centennial Semi-Automatic

A .22 caliber semi-automatic rifle with a 21" barrel, adjustable sights, Alloy receiver and walnut stock. Manufactured in 1968 only. **NOTE:** Deluxe Engraved Model add 20 percent.

NIB	Exc.	V.G.	Good	Fair	Poor
550	375	325	250	175	125

FRANCOTTE, A.
Liege, Belgium

For pistols and revolvers See—AFC.

Jubilee

A 12, 16, 20, and 28 gauge Anson & Deeley boxlock double-barrel shotgun with various barrel lengths and chokes, automatic ejectors, double triggers and walnut stock.

NIB	Exc.	V.G.	Good	Fair	Poor
—	2000	1350	1100	850	450

No. 14

Courtesy William Hammond

NIB	Exc.	V.G.	Good	Fair	Poor
—	3000	2050	1700	1300	650

No. 18

NIB	Exc.	V.G.	Good	Fair	Poor
—	3500	3000	2200	1500	750

No. 20

NIB	Exc.	V.G.	Good	Fair	Poor
—	4000	3600	2250	1750	900

No. 25

NIB	Exc.	V.G.	Good	Fair	Poor
—	5000	3900	2750	2000	1000

No. 30

Courtesy William Hammond

NIB	Exc.	V.G.	Good	Fair	Poor
—	6000	4200	3500	3000	1500

Eagle Grade No. 45

NIB	Exc.	V.G.	Good	Fair	Poor
—	9000	7000	3500	2000	1000

Knockabout

A plain version of the Jubilee Model in 12, 16, 20, and 28 gauge and .410 bore. **NOTE:** 20 gauge add 20 percent; 28 gauge add 30 percent; .410 add 40 percent.

NIB	Exc.	V.G.	Good	Fair	Poor
—	2700	2000	1000	650	500

Sidelock Side-by-Side

A 12, 16, 20, and 28 gauge and .410 bore sidelock shotgun ordered per customer's specifications. Extensive scroll engraving, deluxe walnut stock and finely checkered. **NOTE:** The .410 will bring a premium of from $1,200-$1,500.

NIB	Exc.	V.G.	Good	Fair	Poor
25000	20000	12000	6500	5000	3500

Deluxe Sidelock Side-by-Side

As above, with gold-inlaid hunting scenes.

NIB	Exc.	V.G.	Good	Fair	Poor
30000	24000	16000	8000	5750	4800

CUSTOM MADE SHOTGUNS & RIFLES

These shotguns and rifles were all custom built to the customer's specifications. Gauge (including 24 and 32 gauge), caliber, barrel length, engraving, wood type and style are all individually produced. No two are alike. These shotguns and rifles should be individually appraised before the sale. Prices listed are subject to fluctuations in international currency.

Custom Side-by-Side Shotguns

Available in 12, 16, 20, 28 gauge and .410 bore in either boxlock or sidelock actions. Barrel length, engraving, wood type and style are at the customer's discretion. Retail prices range from: Basic Boxlock with 27.5" barrels and walnut stock with double triggers in 12, 16, and 20 gauge without engraving—$18,000 Basic Boxlock in 28 gauge or .410 bore without engraving—$14,000 Basic Boxlock with 26.5" or 28" barrels and deluxe walnut stock with scroll engraving, and double triggers in 12, 16, and 20 gauge—$23,000 Basic Boxlock in 28 gauge or .410 bore—$28,000 Prices for 24 and 32 gauge are extra. These prices do not include engraving.

Custom Double Rifles

These custom built double rifles were offered in calibers from 9.3x74R to .470 Nitro Express in boxlock or sidelock actions. Barrel length, engraving, wood type and style are at the customer's discretion. Retail prices range from: Prices for 24 and 32 gauge are extra. These prices do not include engraving. Boxlock in 9.3x74R, 8x57JRS and other European calibers-$14,000 Boxlock in.375 H&H and.470 NE—$19,000 Sidelock in 9.3x74R, etc.—$23,700. Sidelock in large calibers—$32,000

Custom Single-Shot Mountain Rifles

These single-shot rifles were offered in rimmed cartridges but rimless cartridge rifles can be built on special request. Barrel length, engraving, wood type and style are at the customer's discretion. Retail prices range from: Boxlock in rimmed calibers—Prices start at $13,000. Sidelock in 7x65R and 7mm Rem. Mag.—Prices start at $24,000

Custom Bolt-Action Rifles

These bolt-action rifles utilize a Mauser 98 type action with adjustable trigger. They were offered in calibers from .17 Bee to .505 Gibbs. Barrel lengths are 21" to 24.5", engraving wood type and style are at the customers' discretion. Retail prices range from: Standard bolt-action calibers: .270, .30-06, 7x64, 8x60S and 9.3x62—Prices start at $7,650 Short-action calibers: .222, .223—Prices start at $9,100 Magnum-action calibers: 7mm Rem. Mag., .300 Win. Mag., .338 Win. Mag., .375 H&H and .458 Win. Mag.—Prices start at $8,400 African calibers: .416 Rigby, .460 Wby., .505 Gibbs—Prices start at $12,250. Please note that the prices listed are for the basic models. They do not reflect the extensive list of options available on these custom firearms.

FRANKLIN, C. W.
Liege, Belgium

Manufacturer of utilitarian shotguns with either exposed or enclosed hammers. Circa 1900.

Single-Barrel

NIB	Exc.	V.G.	Good	Fair	Poor
—	150	75	50	35	20

Damascus Barrel Double

NIB	Exc.	V.G.	Good	Fair	Poor
—	250	150	125	100	65

Steel Barrel Double

NIB	Exc.	V.G.	Good	Fair	Poor
—	300	175	150	125	90

FRANKONIA JAGD
Favorit, Germany

Seldom seen in USA. Values extremely variable, based on local market, chambering, and other factors.

Favorit Standard

Chambered for various European calibers, this bolt-action rifle has a 24" barrel and set triggers. Blued, with a checkered walnut stock.

NIB	Exc.	V.G.	Good	Fair	Poor
—	450	295	260	175	125

Favorit Deluxe

As above, with a more finely figured stock.

NIB	Exc.	V.G.	Good	Fair	Poor
—	475	325	275	200	150

Safari Model

As above, in Magnum calibers.

NIB	Exc.	V.G.	Good	Fair	Poor
—	1400	950	675	275	200

Heeren Rifle

A best quality single-shot rifle with a 26" octagonal barrel, double-set triggers, and adjustable sights. Engraved with hand checkered, high-grade walnut. Blued. Produced in a variety of calibers.

NIB	Exc.	V.G.	Good	Fair	Poor
—	5000	3050	2500	1700	1250

FRASER F. A. CORP.
Fraser, Michigan

Fraser .25 cal.

A .25 ACP caliber semi-automatic pistol with a 2.25" barrel and 6-round magazine. Stainless steel with black nylon grips. There is a 24 kt. gold-plated model that is worth approximately $100 additional. Later made under Fraser name by different company in 1990.

NIB	Exc.	V.G.	Good	Fair	Poor
250	175	125	100	50	35

FREEDOM ARMS
Freedom, Wyoming

"Percussion" Mini-Revolver

A .22 caliber spur trigger revolver with 1", 1.75", or 3" barrel lengths, 5-shot cylinder and a bird's-head grip. Stainless steel. A belt buckle is available that houses the pistol for an additional $40.

NIB	Exc.	V.G.	Good	Fair	Poor
300	250	195	125	100	75

Bostonian (aka Boot Gun)

As above, with a 3" barrel, in .22 Magnum. Discontinued 1992.

NIB	Exc.	V.G.	Good	Fair	Poor
375	300	225	150	80	60

Patriot (aka Boot Gun)

As above, in .22 LR caliber. Discontinued 1992.

NIB	Exc.	V.G.	Good	Fair	Poor
375	300	225	150	80	60

Minuteman

As above, with a 3" barrel. Discontinued in 1988.

NIB	Exc.	V.G.	Good	Fair	Poor
375	300	225	150	80	60

Ironsides

As above, in .22 Magnum with a 1" or a 1.75" barrel.

NIB	Exc.	V.G.	Good	Fair	Poor
375	300	225	150	80	60

Celebrity

As above, with the belt buckle mount for either .22 or .22 Magnum revolvers. **NOTE:** .22 Magnum Model add $25.

NIB	Exc.	V.G.	Good	Fair	Poor
400	325	275	225	150	100

PREMIER AND FIELD GRADE REVOLVERS

Both grades use the same materials and machining tolerances. The difference is in the finish, standard components, and warranty. The PREMIER GRADE has a bright brushed finish, screw adjustable rear sight, laminated hardwood grips, and a limited lifetime warranty. The FIELD GRADE has a matte finish, adjustable rear sight for elevation only, Pachmayr rubber grips, and a one year warranty.

Casull Field Grade Model 83

A .454 Casull Magnum revolver with a 4.75", 6", 7.5", and a 10" barrel and standard fixed sights. Fires a 225-grain bullet. Also offered in .50 AE, .475 Linebaugh, .44 Rem. Mag, .41 Magnum, and .357 Magnum. Adjustable sights available as a $75 option. Matte stainless steel with black rubber Pachmayr grips. Introduced in 1988. **NOTE:** Add $75 for .454 Casull, .475 Linebaugh, or .50

AE calibers.

NIB	Exc.	V.G.	Good	Fair	Poor
1825	1400	800	550	—	—

Casull Premier Grade Model 83

A .454 Mag., .44 Rem. Mag., .45 Win. Mag., .475 Linebaugh, and .50 AE, with replaceable forcing and walnut grips. The finish is a brush stainless steel. The adjustable sights are an extra cost option on this model as well. Offered in barrel lengths of 4.75", 6", 7.5", and 10" except for .475 Casull. .55 Wyoming Express added 2006. **NOTE:** Extra cylinders are available for these models in .45 Colt, .45 Win. Mag., and .45 ACP. Add $250 to the price of the gun for each cylinder. Add $75 for .454 Casull, .475 Linebaugh, or .50 AE calibers.

NIB	Exc.	V.G.	Good	Fair	Poor
2150	1800	1250	850	500	350

Model 97

This revolver is chambered for either the .357 Magnum, .45 Colt, .44 Special, and .22 Long Rifle cartridges. Available in Field or Premier grades. Available with a choice of 4.25", 5.5" or 7.5" barrel. Optional .45 ACP cylinder of .45 Colt and optional .38 Special cylinder for .357 Magnum model. In 2004 this model was also offered in .17 HMR and .32 H&R Magnum calibers. **NOTE:** There are a number of extra-cost options that will affect the price. Some of these options are sights, grips, Mag-Na-Port barrels, slings and trigger overtravel screws. Add $265 for extra .38 Special, .45 ACP or .22 WMR cylinder. Add $475 for extra fitted .22 Long Rifle match grade cylinder. Add $215 for match grade chambered instead of .22 Long Rifle sport chamber.

NIB	Exc.	V.G.	Good	Fair	Poor
1800	1350	1000	600	400	300

Model 353

Chambered for .357 Magnum cartridge with choice of 4.75", 6", 7.5", or 9" barrel length. Adjustable sights. This model designation no longer used; see Model 97.

Field Grade

NIB	Exc.	V.G.	Good	Fair	Poor
1650	1300	950	550	350	250

Premier Grade

NIB	Exc.	V.G.	Good	Fair	Poor
2150	1800	1250	700	500	300

Signature Edition

As above, with a highly polished finish, rosewood grips, 7.5" barrel only and a fitted case. The serial numbers are DC1-DC2000. (The DC represents Dick Casull, the designer of the firearm.) A total of 2,000 were made.

NIB	Exc.	V.G.	Good	Fair	Poor
2500	1950	1300	750	550	350

Model 252

This is a stainless steel version of the large frame revolver chambered for the .22 Long Rifle cartridge. Available in 5.12", 7.5", or 10" barrel lengths. Matte finish. This designation no longer used, see Model 97. **NOTE:** Optional .22 magnum cylinder available for $250.

Silhouette Class

10" barrel.

NIB	Exc.	V.G.	Good	Fair	Poor
1700	1150	850	600	450	250

Varmint Class

5.12" or 7.5" barrel.

NIB	Exc.	V.G.	Good	Fair	Poor
1700	1150	850	600	450	250

Model 757

Introduced in 1999, this five-shot revolver is chambered for the .475 Linebaugh cartridge. Fitted with adjustable sights and offered in both Field and Premier grades. Choice of 4.75", 6", or 7.5" barrel. This designation no longer used; see Model 83.

Field Grade

NIB	Exc.	V.G.	Good	Fair	Poor
1400	1100	750	500	400	300

Premier Grade

NIB	Exc.	V.G.	Good	Fair	Poor
1800	1450	1100	750	500	400

Model 654

This five-shot revolver is chambered for the .41 Magnum cartridge. Adjustable sights. Introduced in 1999. This designation no longer used; see Model 97.

Field Grade

NIB	Exc.	V.G.	Good	Fair	Poor
1325	1050	750	500	400	300

Premier Grade

NIB	Exc.	V.G.	Good	Fair	Poor
1750	1400	1100	750	500	400

Model 83 .500 Wyoming Express

Similar to Model 83 but chambered in .500 Wyoming Express. Introduced 2007.

NIB	Exc.	V.G.	Good	Fair	Poor
2150	1800	1250	700	500	300

FREEMAN, AUSTIN T.
Hoard's Armory
Watertown, New York

Freeman Army Model Revolver

A .44 caliber percussion revolver with a 7.5" round barrel and a 6-shot unfluted cylinder with recessed nipples. Blued, casehardened rammer and hammer, and walnut grips. The frame is marked "Freeman's Pat. Dec. 9, 1862/Hoard's Armory, Watertown, N.Y." Several thousand were manufactured in 1863 and 1864.

NIB	Exc.	V.G.	Good	Fair	Poor
—	—	5800	2200	550	200

FRIGON
Clay Center, Kansas

An importer of guns manufactured by Marocchi of Italy.

FT I

A 12 gauge boxlock single-barrel shotgun with a 32" or 34" ventilated rib barrel, full choke, automatic ejector and interchanged stock. Blued. Introduced in 1986.

NIB	Exc.	V.G.	Good	Fair	Poor
950	750	650	550	450	300

FTC

As above, with two sets of barrels (a single ventilated rib trap barrel and a set of over/under ventilated rib barrels). In a fitted case. Introduced in 1986.

NIB	Exc.	V.G.	Good	Fair	Poor
1750	1400	1150	800	650	500

FS-4

A four gauge set (12, 20, and 28 gauge and .410 bore). Introduced in 1986.

NIB	Exc.	V.G.	Good	Fair	Poor
2500	2100	1750	1500	1100	750

FROMMER
See—FEG (Fegyver Es Gazkeszulekgyar)

FRUHWIRTH
Austria

M1872 Fruhwirth System Rifle

An 11mm bolt-action rifle with a 25" barrel and 6-shot magazine. Blued with a full-length walnut stock.

NIB	Exc.	V.G.	Good	Fair	Poor
—	650	425	300	195	100

FUNK, CHRISTOPH
Suhl, Germany

Christoph Funk began his gun business before 1900. The vast majority of long guns were best quality. Some collectors believe that J.P. Sauer built receivers for Funk but this is not known for certain. Funk produced shotguns, shotgun-rifle combinations, and double rifles. Some were exported to England and the U.S. Most of the U.S. imports are in the more common North American calibers such as .300 Savage, 30-30, 32-20 Winchester, and 12 or 16 gauge. Most are found with only a right-hand extension arm which locks into the receiver, but some higher grades have both extension arms. The quality of these guns is extremely high. Guns were probably not made after 1940. Quality of engraving and caliber determines value. American calibers will command a higher price. Prices listed are for American calibers.

Double Rifles

Courtesy Jim Cate

NIB	Exc.	V.G.	Good	Fair	Poor
—	2950	2250	1450	600	400

Prewar Drilling in 16 or 12 gauge

NIB	Exc.	V.G.	Good	Fair	Poor
—	4500	3750	2500	1200	—

FURR ARMS
J. & G. Sale, Inc.
Prescott, Arizona

In addition to producing reproductions of various cannon, this company also manufactured one-tenth to three-quarter scale reproductions of Gatling guns. Furr products are highly desirable in some circles, with the Gatling .22 reproductions typically commanding prices in excess of $18,000 in mint, unfired condition.

FYRBERG, ANDREW
Worcester and Hopkinton, Massachusetts

Double-Barrel Shotguns

Fyrberg did work for Iver Johnson and C.S. Shattuck Co. of Hatfield, Mass. He began producing a hammerless double about 1902, a well designed boxlock with coil mainsprings. An estimated 2,000 were produced at Hopkinton and Worcester, Mass. Some have been made at Meriden, Conn. Sears cataloged the Fyrberg guns in 1902 to about 1908.

NIB	Exc.	V.G.	Good	Fair	Poor
—	525	425	300	200	150

Revolvers

A 3"-barreled .32 caliber and a 3.5" .38 caliber revolver with round ribbed barrels and round butts. The grips bear the trademark, "AFCo." This model was most likely made by Iver Johnson for Andrew Fyrberg.

NIB	Exc.	V.G.	Good	Fair	Poor
—	250	145	100	75	50

G

GABBET-FAIRFAX, H.
Birmingham, England

Mars

Designed by Hugh Gabbet-Fairfax, this semi-automatic pistol was first produced on an experimental basis by Webley & Scott Revolvers in the 1890s. After Webley gave up on the idea an extremely limited number were built by the Mars Automatic Pistol Syndicate, Ltd., 1897 to 1905. The pistol was produced in four calibers; the 8.5mm Mars, 9mm Mars, .45 Mars Short Case, and .45 Mars Long Case. This was the most powerful handgun cartridge of its time and remained so until well after World War II. It is estimated that only about 80 of these pistols were ever produced. **NOTE:** Webley examples are worth a premium.

Courtesy James Rankin

NIB	Exc.	V.G.	Good	Fair	Poor
—	45000	30500	19500	9200	6000

GABILONDO Y CIA
See—Llama

GABILONDO Y URRESTI
Guernica, Spain
Elgoibar, Spain

See—Llama

This Spanish firm was founded in 1904 to produce inexpensive revolvers of the Velo-Dog type. Sometime around 1909 the firm began to manufacture the Radium revolver. In 1914 the company produced a semi-automatic pistol distributed as the Ruby. This pistol soon became the mainstay of the company with orders of 30,000 pistols a month for the French army. With the end of WWI Gabilondo Y Urresti moved to Elgoeibar, Spain. The company produced a Browning 1910 replica pistol until the early 1930s. It was at this point that Gabilondo began to manufacture a Colt Model 1911 copy that became known as the Llama. For information of specific Llama models see the Llama section. The pistols listed reflect the pre-Llama period and are so marked with the trade name of that particular model. The monogram "GC" frequently appears on the grips but not on the slide.

Velo-Dog Revolver

A 6.35mm double-action revolver with a 1.5" barrel, folding trigger and concealed hammer. Blued with walnut grips. Manufactured from 1904 to 1914.

NIB	Exc.	V.G.	Good	Fair	Poor
—	295	195	125	75	50

Radium

A semi-automatic pistol in caliber 7.65mm. Produced both for the commercial and military market in the Ruby style. "Radium" is stamped on the slide as well as the top of each grip plate.

Courtesy James Rankin

NIB	Exc.	V.G.	Good	Fair	Poor
—	295	195	125	100	70

Ruby

A 7.65mm caliber semi-automatic pistol. Discontinued in 1930.

NIB	Exc.	V.G.	Good	Fair	Poor
—	250	175	150	100	75

Bufalo 6.35mm

A semi-automatic pistol in caliber 6.35mm. A copy of the Browning Model 1906 with a squeeze grip safety. Has "Bufalo" stamped on the slide and the Gabilondo logo along with a buffalo's head on each side of the grip plates. Manufactured between 1918 and 1925. NOTE: The spelling of "Bufalo" is as it appears on the pistol.

Courtesy James Rankin

NIB	Exc.	V.G.	Good	Fair	Poor
—	275	175	150	100	75

Bufalo 7.65mm

A semi-automatic pistol in caliber 7.65mm. Patterned after the Browning Model 1910 with a squeeze grip safety. There were two models, with either a 7-round or a 9-round magazine. The model with the 9-round magazine usually is fitted with wood grips and a lanyard ring. A buffalo's head is inset in each grip plate. Manufactured between 1918 and 1925.

Courtesy James Rankin

NIB	Exc.	V.G.	Good	Fair	Poor
—	275	175	125	100	75

Bufalo 9mmK

A semi-automatic pistol in caliber 9mmK. Nearly the same pistol as the 7.65mm model but fitted with a grip safety. "Bufalo" is stamped on the slide and the Gabilondo logo and buffalo's head are on each grip plate. Manufactured between 1918 and 1925.

Courtesy James Rankin

NIB	Exc.	V.G.	Good	Fair	Poor
—	295	205	145	105	70

Danton 6.35mm

A semi-automatic pistol in caliber 6.35mm. Patterned after the Browning Model 1906 with a grip safety. "Danton" appears on the slide as well as the grips. The Gabilondo logo is on each grip plate. Manufactured between 1925 and 1931.

Courtesy James Rankin

NIB	Exc.	V.G.	Good	Fair	Poor
—	275	175	125	100	75

Danton War Model

A semi-automatic pistol in caliber 7.65mm. Similar to the Bufalo above and it was made with and without a grip safety. It came in two models with 9- and 20-round magazines. Fitted with a lanyard ring. "Danton" stamped on the slide and the grips. The Gabilondo log is on each side of the grip plates. Manufactured between 1925 and 1931.

Courtesy James Rankin

With Nine-Round Magazine

NIB	Exc.	V.G.	Good	Fair	Poor
—	275	175	125	100	75

With Twenty-Round Magazine

NIB	Exc.	V.G.	Good	Fair	Poor
—	550	325	250	200	100

Perfect

This semi-automatic pistol was chambered for the 6.35mm and 7.65mm cartridges. It was a cheap, low-priced pistol marketed by Mugica. These pistols usually have the word "Perfect" on the grips. The slide may be stamped with the name MUGICA but many are not.

NIB	Exc.	V.G.	Good	Fair	Poor
—	275	175	125	100	75

Plus Ultra

This pistol is chambered for the 7.65mm cartridge and was built from 1925 to 1933. It had a 20-round magazine that gave the pistol an unusual appearance. "Plus Ultra" appears on the slide and the grips. A Gabilondo logo is on each grip plate. Equipped with a lanyard ring.

Courtesy James Rankin

NIB	Exc.	V.G.	Good	Fair	Poor
—	1200	875	650	425	250

GALAND, C.F.
Liege, Belgium

Galand, Galand & Sommerville, Galand Perrin (Galand M1872)

A 7mm, 9mm, and 12mm caliber double-action revolver with a 6-shot cylinder, open frame, a unique ejection system that, by means of rotating a lever downward from the trigger guard, causes the barrel and cylinder to slide forward, leaving the ejector and the spent cases behind. Circa 1872.

Courtesy Bonhams & Butterfields

NIB	Exc.	V.G.	Good	Fair	Poor
—	—	1350	875	550	150

Velo-Dog

A 5.5mm Velo-Dog caliber fixed trigger and guard double-action revolver with open-top design. Later models (.22 and 6.35mm caliber) feature folding triggers and no trigger guards.

NIB	Exc.	V.G.	Good	Fair	Poor
—	250	165	125	75	50

Le Novo

As above, with a concealed hammer and in 6.35mm caliber.

NIB	Exc.	V.G.	Good	Fair	Poor
—	250	165	125	75	50

Tue-Tue

A .22 short, 5.5mm Velo-Dog, and 6.35mm caliber double-action revolver with a concealed hammer, folding trigger, and a swing-out cylinder with central extractor. Introduced in 1894.

NIB	Exc.	V.G.	Good	Fair	Poor
—	250	165	125	75	50

GALAND & SOMMERVILLE
Liege, Belgium

See—Galand

GALEF (ZABALA)
Zabala Hermanos & Antonio Zoli
Spain

Zabala Double

A 10, 12, 16, and 20 caliber boxlock shotgun with a 22" to 30" barrel and various chokes. Hardwood stock. Add 50 percent for 10 gauge.

NIB	Exc.	V.G.	Good	Fair	Poor
—	450	300	175	100	75

Companion

A folding 12 to .410 bore single-shot underlever shotgun with a 28" or 30" barrel.

NIB	Exc.	V.G.	Good	Fair	Poor
—	200	145	105	50	25

Monte Carlo Trap

A 12 gauge underlever single-shot shotgun with a 32" ventilated rib barrel.

NIB	Exc.	V.G.	Good	Fair	Poor
—	325	275	150	100	75

Silver Snipe, Golden Snipe, and Silver Hawk

See—Antonio Zoli

GALENA INDUSTRIES INC.
Sturgis, South Dakota

In 1998 Galena Industries purchased the rights to use the AMT trademark and manufacturing rights to many, but not all, AMT designs. For AMT models made by AMT see that section. This company's designs have been acquired by Crusader/High Standard of Houston, Texas.

AMT Backup

This model features a double-action-only trigger system and is offered in both stainless steel and matte black finish. The small frame .380 Backup weighs 18 oz. with its 2.5" barrel. The large frame Backups are fitted with a 3" barrel and are offered in 9mm, .38 Super, .357 Sig., .40 S&W, .400 CorBon, and .45 ACP. Weights are approximately 23 oz. and magazine capacity is 5 to 6 rounds, depending on caliber. **NOTE:** Add $50 for .38 Super, .357 SIG, and .400 CorBon.

Galena .380 DAO Backup

NIB	Exc.	V.G.	Good	Fair	Poor
525	375	275	200	125	100

Automag II

This semi-automatic pistol is chambered for the .22 WMR cartridge. Offered in 3.38", 4.5", or 6" barrel lengths. Magazine capacity is 9 rounds except for the 3.38" model where capacity is 7 rounds. Weight is about 32 oz.

NIB	Exc.	V.G.	Good	Fair	Poor
695	550	325	225	125	100

Automag III

This pistol is chambered for the .30 Carbine cartridge. Barrel length is 6.38" and weight is about 43 oz. Stainless steel finish.

NIB	Exc.	V.G.	Good	Fair	Poor
800	675	375	250	150	100

Automag IV

This model is chambered for the .45 Winchester Magnum cartridge. It is fitted with a 6.5" barrel and has a magazine capacity of 7 rounds. Weight is approximately 46 oz.

NIB	Exc.	V.G.	Good	Fair	Poor
800	675	375	250	150	100

Automag .440 CorBon

This semi-automatic pistol is chambered for the .440 CorBon cartridge and fitted with a 7.5" barrel. Magazine capacity is 5 rounds. Finish is matte black. Weight is about 46 oz. Checkered walnut grips. Introduced in 2000. Special order only.

NIB	Exc.	V.G.	Good	Fair	Poor
1000	900	750	575	400	175

Galena Accelerator

This model has a 7" barrel built on a 1911 frame and is chambered for the .400 CorBon. Magazine capacity is 7 rounds. Weight is about 46 oz. Finish is stainless steel.

NIB	Exc.	V.G.	Good	Fair	Poor
850	725	550	400	300	100

Galena Hardballer

This pistol is based on the Colt Model 1911 design and is chambered for the .45 ACP cartridge. It is fitted with a 5" barrel and has a magazine capacity of 7 rounds. Finish is stainless steel. Adjustable trigger and beveled magazine well. Also offered chambered for the .40 S&W and .400 CorBon cartridges. Weight is about 38 oz.

NIB	Exc.	V.G.	Good	Fair	Poor
1000	900	750	575	400	175

Galena Longslide

This model is chambered for the .45 ACP cartridge and fitted with a 7" barrel. Magazine capacity is 7 rounds with weight about 46 oz. Finish is stainless steel.

NIB	Exc.	V.G.	Good	Fair	Poor
850	725	550	400	300	10

Galena Commando

The Commando is chambered for the .40 S&W cartridge and fitted with a 4" barrel. Magazine capacity is 8 rounds. Weight is about 38 oz. Finish is stainless steel.

NIB	Exc.	V.G.	Good	Fair	Poor
550	400	295	225	175	100

GALESI, INDUSTRIA ARMI
Brescia, Italy

Rino Galesi Armi, Collebeato, Italy, manufactured shotguns, revolvers, and automatic pistols. The firm's name changed from Rino Galesi Armi to Industria Armi Galesi, to Rigarmi di Rino Galesi. Their semi-automatic pistols were designated by model year, model number, and a 500 Series. Most models named in the 500 Series came after the firm changed its name to Industria Armi Galesi.

Model 1923

A 6.35mm and 7.65mm caliber semi-automatic pistol. Has a squeeze grip safety and wood grip plates with crest. Model 1923 is stamped on the slide.

Courtesy James Rankin

NIB	Exc.	V.G.	Good	Fair	Poor
—	275	195	145	75	50

Model 1930

A 6.35mm and 7.65mm caliber semi-automatic pistol. A very few were made in 1946 in 9mm Parabellum. Based on the 1910 Browning design. Blued with plastic grips. The slide marked "Brevetto Mod. 1930".

Courtesy James Rankin

NIB	Exc.	V.G.	Good	Fair	Poor
—	275	195	145	75	50

9mm Parabellum

NIB	Exc.	V.G.	Good	Fair	Poor
—	600	500	400	300	100

Model 6

Updated Model 1930. Manufactured approximately 1938 to 1948 in calibers; 22 Short, .22 Long, .22 LR, 6.35mm, 7.65mm, and 9mm Short.

Courtesy James Rankin

NIB	Exc.	V.G.	Good	Fair	Poor
—	350	175	100	75	50

Model 9

Manufactured from approximately 1947 to 1956 in calibers .22 Short, .22 Long, .22 LR, 6.35mm, 7.65mm, and 9mm Short. Also, listed under the 500 Series. The .22 versions were marketed as "the smallest .22 pistols ever built".

Courtesy James Rankin

NIB	Exc.	V.G.	Good	Fair	Poor
—	295	175	100	75	50

GALIL
Israel Military Industries
Israel

Model AR (.223)
NOTE: Add $600 for .308 caliber.

NIB	Exc.	V.G.	Good	Fair	Poor
3000	2400	2000	1500	900	700

Model ARM

NIB	Exc.	V.G.	Good	Fair	Poor
3400	2700	2000	1500	900	700

Sniper Rifle

NIB	Exc.	V.G.	Good	Fair	Poor
8500	7500	6000	4000	3000	2000

Hadar II

NIB	Exc.	V.G.	Good	Fair	Poor
1300	1100	800	650	500	400

GALLAGER
Richardson & Overman
Philadelphia, Pennsylvania

Gallager Carbine

A .50 caliber single-shot percussion carbine with a 22.25" barrel, saddle ring and walnut stock. Blued and case hardened. Approximately 23,000 were made during the Civil War.

Percussion Model

As above, in .56-62 rimfire caliber. Approximately 5,000 of this model were made.

Courtesy Milwaukee Public Museum, Milwaukee, Wisconsin

NIB	Exc.	V.G.	Good	Fair	Poor
—	—	3900	2450	1500	500

Spencer Cartridge Model

NIB	Exc.	V.G.	Good	Fair	Poor
—	—	3425	1950	1350	400

GAMBA, RENATO
Gardone V. T., Italy

SIDE-BY-SIDE SHOTGUNS

Hunter Super

A 12 gauge Anson & Deeley boxlock double-barrel shotgun with a variety of barrel lengths and chokes, double triggers and extractors. Engraved and silver-plated.

NIB	Exc.	V.G.	Good	Fair	Poor
1250	900	700	550	450	250

Principessa

A 12, 20 or 28 gauge boxlock shotgun. Engraved, checkered stock.

NIB	Exc.	V.G.	Good	Fair	Poor
1850	1250	900	700	500	250

Oxford 90

A 12 or 20 gauge sidelock shotgun with various barrel lengths and chokes, the Purdey locking system, double triggers, and automatic ejectors. Walnut stock.

NIB	Exc.	V.G.	Good	Fair	Poor
4250	3250	1700	900	600	300

Oxford Extra

Same as above but with fine engraving.

NIB	Exc.	V.G.	Good	Fair	Poor
5200	4000	2250	1500	900	450

Gamba 624 Prince

Fitted with a Wesley Richards-type frame, select walnut stock, and fine hand engraving. Offered in 12 gauge with 28" barrels.

NIB	Exc.	V.G.	Good	Fair	Poor
4800	3900	2500	1500	850	400

Gamba 624 Extra

Same as above but with deep floral engraving.

NIB	Exc.	V.G.	Good	Fair	Poor
8000	5000	4500	2500	1250	600

London

A 12 or 20 gauge Holland & Holland sidelock shotgun with various barrel lengths and chokes, double- or single-selective trigger, automatic ejectors. Walnut stock.

NIB	Exc.	V.G.	Good	Fair	Poor
7000	5500	4500	2500	1250	700

London Royal

As above with engraved hunting scenes.

NIB	Exc.	V.G.	Good	Fair	Poor
8000	6500	5000	3750	2000	950

Ambassador Gold and Black

A 12 and 20 gauge Holland & Holland sidelock shotgun with various barrel lengths and choke combinations, single-selective trigger, automatic ejectors, and a single gold line engraved on the barrels and the frame. Walnut stocks.

NIB	Exc.	V.G.	Good	Fair	Poor
25000	19000	13500	9500	5000	2500

Ambassador Executive

Gamba's best quality shotgun produced in 12 or 20 gauge to the customer's specifications.

NIB	Exc.	V.G.	Good	Fair	Poor
28000	20000	15000	10000	5000	2500

OVER/UNDER SHOTGUNS

Country Model

A 12 and 20 gauge over/under shotgun with 28" or 30" barrels with ventilated rib, double triggers, extractors, and walnut stock.

NIB	Exc.	V.G.	Good	Fair	Poor
650	550	400	300	275	200

Grifone Model

A 12 and 20 gauge over/under shotgun with 26", 28", or 30" ventilated-rib barrels, a single-selective trigger, and automatic ejectors. The boxlock action is silver-plated, with walnut stock. Available with screw-in chokes, and this would add 10 percent to the values.

NIB	Exc.	V.G.	Good	Fair	Poor
800	650	550	350	250	200

Europa 2000

A 12 gauge over/under shotgun in various barrel lengths and choke combinations, single-selective trigger, and automatic ejectors. Engraved, silver-plated, boxlock action with false sideplates and walnut stock.

NIB	Exc.	V.G.	Good	Fair	Poor
1250	900	700	550	350	250

Grinta Trap and Skeet

A 12 gauge over/under shotgun with 26" Skeet or 30" Full choke barrels, a single-selective trigger, automatic ejectors, and some engraving. Walnut stock.

NIB	Exc.	V.G.	Good	Fair	Poor
1350	900	700	550	350	250

Victory Trap and Skeet

As above, but more finely finished.

NIB	Exc.	V.G.	Good	Fair	Poor
1650	1150	850	600	400	250

Edinburg Match

As above, with slightly different engraving patterns.

NIB	Exc.	V.G.	Good	Fair	Poor
1250	1000	800	600	400	250

Boyern 88 Combination Gun

A 12 gauge combination over/under rifle/shotgun with double triggers, and extractors. Engraved game scenes and coin-finished with walnut stock.

NIB	Exc.	V.G.	Good	Fair	Poor
1250	900	700	500	400	250

DAYTONA SERIES

This is a competition shotgun, first introduced into the US in 1986 as the Type I. The Type I was available in different configurations with the base model selling for about $4,000 until 1991. In 1994 Gamba introduced the Daytona in a wide variety of configurations and grades under a new designation called the Type II. The primary difference was in the location of the stock bolt. Only about 80 Daytona Type II shotguns are allocated to the US per year. They are a high quality shotgun with an excellent reputation. Prices are listed for 12 gauge guns. 20 gauge guns are available on special request.

Daytona Trap

Offered in 12 gauge with 30" or 32" barrels. Select walnut stock with hand checkering. Removable trigger group, improved Boss lock-up and boxlock receiver.

NIB	Exc.	V.G.	Good	Fair	Poor
5900	4750	3000	2250	1200	600

Daytona Sporting

Available in 12 gauge with 30" barrel with screw-in chokes and single-selective trigger.

NIB	Exc.	V.G.	Good	Fair	Poor
4000	3250	2500	1900	1200	700

Daytona Skeet

Offered in 12 gauge with 29" barrels and single-selective trigger.

NIB	Exc.	V.G.	Good	Fair	Poor
4000	3250	2500	1900	1200	700

Daytona America Trap

Offered in 12 gauge with 30" or 32" barrels, high adjustable rib, adjustable stock, and single trigger.

NIB	Exc.	V.G.	Good	Fair	Poor
4000	3250	2500	1900	1200	700

Daytona Game

Offered in 12 gauge with 28" barrels and single trigger. **NOTE:** Add $300 for black frame with gold inlaid names and logo.

NIB	Exc.	V.G.	Good	Fair	Poor
3900	3500	3000	2250	1200	700

Daytona Grade 6 Engraving

Fine English scroll hand engraving edged with gold line work.

Trap and Skeet Models

NIB	Exc.	V.G.	Good	Fair	Poor
13000	5000	4000	3000	1500	700

Sporting Model

NIB	Exc.	V.G.	Good	Fair	Poor
13500	5000	4000	3000	1500	700

Daytona Grade 5 Engraving

Deep relief floral engraving with gold inlaid griffons.

Trap and Skeet Models

NIB	Exc.	V.G.	Good	Fair	Poor
14000	9000	6500	5000	2500	1200

Sporting Model

NIB	Exc.	V.G.	Good	Fair	Poor
14500	9000	6500	5000	2500	1200

Daytona Grade 4 Engraving

A flying eagle in a landscape and very fine English scroll by master engravers.

Trap and Skeet Models

NIB	Exc.	V.G.	Good	Fair	Poor
16250	10000	7500	5500	3000	1500

Sporting Model

NIB	Exc.	V.G.	Good	Fair	Poor
16750	10000	7500	5500	3000	1500

Daytona SL Grade 3 Engraving

Fitted with sideplates with engraved game scenes and fine English scroll by master engravers.

Trap and Skeet Models

NIB	Exc.	V.G.	Good	Fair	Poor
18750	15000	11000	7500	3500	1750

Sporting Model

NIB	Exc.	V.G.	Good	Fair	Poor
19250	11000	9000	6500	3500	1750

Game Model

NIB	Exc.	V.G.	Good	Fair	Poor
18750	11000	9000	6500	3500	1750

Daytona SLHH Grade 2 Engraving

Fitted with sideplates and Boss lock-up system, automatic ejectors, figured walnut stock, and fine game scene engraving signed by a master. Offered in 12 gauge with 28" barrels.

NIB	Exc.	V.G.	Good	Fair	Poor
36250	16000	12500	9500	6000	3000

Daytona SLHH Grade 1 Gold Engraving

Same as above but with gold inlaid game scenes and floral-style engraving signed by master engraver. Offered in 12 gauge with 28" barrels.

NIB	Exc.	V.G.	Good	Fair	Poor
43500	17000	13000	9500	5500	2500

Daytona SLHH "One of Thousand"

Same as above but game scene is executed at customers direction and is a totally custom ordered gun. Available in all configurations.

NIB	Exc.	V.G.	Good	Fair	Poor
125000	70000	35000	15500	7500	600

CONCORDE GAME SHOTGUNS

This over/under model is offered as a slightly less expensive alternative to the Daytona Series guns. The base gun is available with a blued or chromed action. Extra barrel are interchangeable in both 12 and 20 gauges with 28" barrels and single triggers.

NIB	Exc.	V.G.	Good	Fair	Poor
6000	4250	3000	1500	750	450

Concorde Trap

Available in 12 gauge with 30" or 32" barrels with single trigger.

NIB	Exc.	V.G.	Good	Fair	Poor
—	2000	1500	1000	600	450

Concorde Skeet

Available in 12 gauge with 29" barrels and single trigger.

NIB	Exc.	V.G.	Good	Fair	Poor
6000	4250	3000	1500	750	450

Concorde Sporting

Offered in 12 gauge with 30" barrels, screw-in chokes, and single-selective trigger.

NIB	Exc.	V.G.	Good	Fair	Poor
6100	2900	2000	1500	900	500

Concorde Game Grade 7 Engraving

Game scene engraving with fine English scroll.

NIB	Exc.	V.G.	Good	Fair	Poor
8700	4000	3250	2250	1200	600

Concorde Game Grade 8 Engraving

English scroll engraving.

NIB	Exc.	V.G.	Good	Fair	Poor
6250	3000	2500	1750	1000	500

Concorde 2nd Generation

Similar to the Concorde series but with fixed trigger group. Black or chrome frame. Automatic ejectors. Select walnut stock. Choice of 12 or 20 gauge with 28" or 30" barrels and single trigger. Introduced in 2002.

NIB	Exc.	V.G.	Good	Fair	Poor
6100	4850	3200	1950	750	300

Le Mans

This model is chambered for the 12 gauge shell and fitted with a choice of 28" or 30" barrels. Automatic ejectors. Single-selective trigger. Five choke tubes. Introduced in 2002.

NIB	Exc.	V.G.	Good	Fair	Poor
1750	1200	850	625	475	200

Hunter II

This 12 gauge model has an alloy frame with reinforced barrel with automatic ejectors. Five choke tubes. Single-selective trigger. Barrel lengths of 26" to 27.5". Introduced in 2002.

NIB	Exc.	V.G.	Good	Fair	Poor
1600	1100	750	525	375	150

RIFLES

Safari Express

A 7x65R, 9.3x74R, or .375 H&H caliber boxlock double barrel rifle with 25" barrels, open sights, double triggers, automatic ejectors, and a coin-finished scroll engraved receiver. Walnut stock.

NIB	Exc.	V.G.	Good	Fair	Poor
8500	6500	4500	1750	750	350

Mustang

A 5.6x50, 6.5x57R, 7x65R, .222 Rem., .270 Win., or .30-06 caliber sidelock single barrel rifle with double set triggers, engraved sidelock action and walnut stock.

NIB	Exc.	V.G.	Good	Fair	Poor
8500	6500	4500	1750	750	350

RGZ 1000

7x64, .270 Win., 7mm Rem. Magnum, and .300 Win. Magnum caliber Mauser 98 bolt-action with a 20.5" barrel. Walnut pistol grip stock with a cheekpiece.

NIB	Exc.	V.G.	Good	Fair	Poor
1100	900	750	550	400	200

RGX 1000 Express

As above, with double set triggers and a 23.75" barrel.

NIB	Exc.	V.G.	Good	Fair	Poor
1250	950	750	550	400	200

PISTOLS

SAB G90

A 7.65 Parabellum or 9mm caliber double-action semi-automatic pistol with a 4.75" barrel, and 15-shot magazine. Blued or chrome-plated with walnut grips.

NIB	Exc.	V.G.	Good	Fair	Poor
575	450	350	300	250	175

SAB G91 Compact

As above, with a 3.5" barrel and a 12-shot magazine.

NIB	Exc.	V.G.	Good	Fair	Poor
550	400	325	275	225	150

Trident Fast Action

A .32 S&W or .38 Special caliber double-action revolver with a 2.5" or 3" barrel and 6-shot cylinder. Blued, with walnut grips.

NIB	Exc.	V.G.	Good	Fair	Poor
500	400	300	250	200	150

Trident Super

As above, with a 4" ventilated-rib barrel.

NIB	Exc.	V.G.	Good	Fair	Poor
550	400	325	275	225	150

Trident Match 900

As above, with 6" heavy barrel, adjustable sights and target type, walnut grips.

NIB	Exc.	V.G.	Good	Fair	Poor
850	700	550	400	350	200

GARAND
(U.S. M-1 Rifle)

This was the standard issue rifle for U.S. military services from 1936 to 1957. In .30-06 caliber, it is a gas-operated semi-automatic, fed by an 8-round clip that is inserted in the open action from above. The Garand series was made in several variants and was manufactured by many different companies over its 20 years of service. For a complete history of John Garand's great rifle, see *Standard Catalog of Military Firearms*, published by Gun Digest Books/Krause Publications. **NOTE:** Prices shown below are for rifles in original, unaltered condition. Many of the rifles seen on today's market have been restored or refinished and values should be reduced from 30 to 50 percent.

Rebuilt Rifle, any manufacture

NIB	Exc.	V.G.	Good	Fair	Poor
1200	1000	800	600	—	—

DCM Rifles

NIB	Exc.	V.G.	Good	Fair	Poor
—	850	575	450	—	—

Navy Trophy Rifles U.S.N. Crane Depot Rebuild

NIB	Exc.	V.G.	Good	Fair	Poor
—	1800	1000	900	—	—

AMF Rebuild

NIB	Exc.	V.G.	Good	Fair	Poor
—	1000	900	750	—	—

H&R Rebuild

NIB	Exc.	V.G.	Good	Fair	Poor
—	900	800	700	—	—

NOTE: These rifles MUST be original and validated by experts.

SPRINGFIELD ARMORY PRODUCTION

Gas trap sn: ca 81-52,000

NIB	Exc.	V.G.	Good	Fair	Poor
—	40000	35000	25000	—	—

Gas trap/modified to gas port

NIB	Exc.	V.G.	Good	Fair	Poor
—	5000	3500	2500	—	—

Pre-Dec. 7, 1941 gas port production sn: ca 410,000

NIB	Exc.	V.G.	Good	Fair	Poor
—	4000	2200	1300	900	400

WWII Production sn: ca 410,000-3,880,000

NIB	Exc.	V.G.	Good	Fair	Poor
—	1400	1100	900	750	500

Post-WWII Production sn: ca 4,200,000-6,099,361

NIB	Exc.	V.G.	Good	Fair	Poor
—	1100	850	650	500	450

Winchester Educational Contract sn: 100,000-100,500

NIB	Exc.	V.G.	Good	Fair	Poor
—	10000	6000	4500	2000	700

Winchester sn: 100,501-165,000

NIB	Exc.	V.G.	Good	Fair	Poor
—	6500	4500	3000	1100	550

Winchester sn: 1,200,00-1,380,000

NIB	Exc.	V.G.	Good	Fair	Poor
—	5500	4500	2500	750	400

Winchester sn: 2,305,850-2,536,493

NIB	Exc.	V.G.	Good	Fair	Poor
—	3500	2800	1500	500	300

Winchester sn: 1,601,150-1,640,000 "win-13"

NIB	Exc.	V.G.	Good	Fair	Poor
—	3500	2200	1800	1500	850

Harrington & Richardson Production

NIB	Exc.	V.G.	Good	Fair	Poor
—	1800	1200	900	600	300

International Harvester Production

NIB	Exc.	V.G.	Good	Fair	Poor
—	2200	1500	800	500	250

International Harvester/with Springfield Receiver (postage stamp)

NIB	Exc.	V.G.	Good	Fair	Poor
—	2800	1500	1000	—	—

International Harvester/with Springfield Receiver (arrow head)

NIB	Exc.	V.G.	Good	Fair	Poor
—	2800	1500	1000	—	—

International Harvester/with Springfield Receiver (Gap letter)

NIB	Exc.	V.G.	Good	Fair	Poor
—	2800	1500	1000	—	—

International Harvester/with Harrington & Richardson Receiver

NIB	Exc.	V.G.	Good	Fair	Poor
—	1900	1200	900	—	—

British Garands (Lend Lease)

NIB	Exc.	V.G.	Good	Fair	Poor
—	1300	1200	875	500	275

M1 Garand Cutaway

NIB	Exc.	V.G.	Good	Fair	Poor
—	3000	2500	1000	600	500

NOTE: For examples with documentation add 300 percent.

SCOPED VARIANTS (SNIPER RIFLES)

NOTE: Sniper rifles must have sales or verification papers.

M1C

NIB	Exc.	V.G.	Good	Fair	Poor
—	10000	8000	5000	—	—

M1D (USMC Issue) MC 1952

NIB	Exc.	V.G.	Good	Fair	Poor
—	3800	3000	2000	—	—

National Match

Type I

NIB	Exc.	V.G.	Good	Fair	Poor
—	4500	2500	1800	—	—

Type II

NIB	Exc.	V.G.	Good	Fair	Poor
—	3200	2200	1500	—	—

GARATE, ANITUA/G.A.C.
Eibar, Spain

Charola

A 5.5mm Clement semi-automatic pistol with the magazine located in front of the trigger and with an exposed hammer.

Courtesy James Rankin

NIB	Exc.	V.G.	Good	Fair	Poor
—	1500	1200	750	500	400

Cosmopolite

A .38 caliber copy of the Colt Police Positive. Manufactured from 1920 to 1930.

NIB	Exc.	V.G.	Good	Fair	Poor
—	275	165	125	100	75

El Lunar

Resembling the Colt Police Positive in 8mm Lebel caliber, this revolver was made for the French government in 1915 and 1916.

NIB	Exc.	V.G.	Good	Fair	Poor
—	300	175	150	125	100

G.A.C.

A copy of the Smith & Wesson Military & Police revolver, manufactured between 1930 and 1936, in .32-20 caliber. Marked "G.A.C. Firearms Mfg. Co."

NIB	Exc.	V.G.	Good	Fair	Poor
—	250	150	125	100	75

"Modelo Militar"

A close copy of the Smith & Wesson Triple Lock/New Century N-frame revolver chambered in .44 Special. Marked "G.A.C."

NIB	Exc.	V.G.	Good	Fair	Poor
—	325	250	200	175	75

Express or Danton

A 7.65mm caliber "Eibar" semi-automatic pistol with 9-shot magazine.

NIB	Exc.	V.G.	Good	Fair	Poor
—	275	150	100	75	50

British Service Old Pattern No.2 Mk. I Trocaola Aranzabal Military Revolver

A .455 caliber double-action break-open revolver with a 5" barrel, adopted by the Royal Army in November of 1915 and known as "Pistol OP No. 1 Mark 1".

NIB	Exc.	V.G.	Good	Fair	Poor
—	450	250	200	150	100

L'Eclair

A 5.5mm Velo-Dog caliber folding-trigger double-action revolver with 6-shot cylinder. Manufactured from 1900 to 1914. Not to be confused with the chocolate confectionary.

NIB	Exc.	V.G.	Good	Fair	Poor
—	250	145	100	75	50

Sprinter

A 6.35mm caliber semi-automatic pistol marked "The Best Automatique Pistol Sprinter Patent 6.35mm Cartridge.". Manufactured before WWI.

NIB	Exc.	V.G.	Good	Fair	Poor
—	250	145	125	75	50

La Lira

A copy of the Mannlicher Model 1901 in .32 ACP caliber with removable magazine marked "System La Lira" on the breech; "Para Cartoucho Browning 7.65mm", on the barrel; and "G.A.C.", on the grips. Produced prior to WWI.

Courtesy James Rankin

NIB	Exc.	V.G.	Good	Fair	Poor
—	1200	1000	700	400	300

Triumph

Identical to the La Lira model but marked "Triumph Automatic Pistol".

NIB	Exc.	V.G.	Good	Fair	Poor
—	1200	1000	700	400	300

GARATE, HERMANOS
Ermua, Spain

Cantabria

A 6.35mm caliber folding-trigger double-action revolver with a concealed hammer, cocking spur and a short barrel resembling the slide on a semi-automatic. The name "Cantabria" is stamped on the left side.

NIB	Exc.	V.G.	Good	Fair	Poor
—	300	175	125	100	75

Velo-Stark

A double-action folding-trigger revolver with concealed hammer.

NIB	Exc.	V.G.	Good	Fair	Poor
—	250	150	100	75	50

GARBI
Eibar, Spain

Model 51-B

A 12 gauge boxlock shotgun, also available in 16 and 20 gauge, with double triggers, automatic ejectors, case hardened or coin-finished receiver and walnut stock.

NIB	Exc.	V.G.	Good	Fair	Poor
1750	1200	850	600	—	—

Model 62-B

A 12 gauge sidelock shotgun, also chambered for 16 and 20 gauge with double triggers, extractors and cocking indicators. Engraved, case hardened or coin-finished receiver and walnut stock.

NIB	Exc.	V.G.	Good	Fair	Poor
1500	1050	850	650	325	175

Model 71

A 12, 16, or 20 gauge Holland & Holland sidelock shotgun with various barrel lengths and choke combinations, automatic ejectors and a single-selective trigger. Engraved with fine English-style scrollwork and walnut stock. Discontinued in 1988.

NIB	Exc.	V.G.	Good	Fair	Poor
2500	2000	1800	1500	700	225

Model 100

A 12, 16, or 20 gauge Holland & Holland sidelock shotgun with chopper-lump barrels, automatic ejectors, and a single trigger. Engraved in the Purdey style, with walnut stock.

NIB	Exc.	V.G.	Good	Fair	Poor
3500	3000	2500	2000	900	250

Model 101

As above, with floral engraving. Discontinued in 1988 in this form, then furnished with hand-engraved Continental scroll with round body action.

NIB	Exc.	V.G.	Good	Fair	Poor
6100	5250	3250	2500	1000	350

Model 102

As above, with Holland & Holland style, engraving and also in 28 gauge. Discontinued in 1988.

NIB	Exc.	V.G.	Good	Fair	Poor
4500	3750	3200	1600	600	250

Model 103A

This model has Purdey-style engraving with high grade wood and checkering.

NIB	Exc.	V.G.	Good	Fair	Poor
14100	10000	7500	5500	2750	1000

Model 103A Royal

Same as above but with special high quality engraving, very fancy wood, hand matted rib.

NIB	Exc.	V.G.	Good	Fair	Poor
16000	12500	8500	6500	3750	1200

Model 103B

In 12, 16, 20, or 28 gauge, Holland & Holland sidelock shotgun with various barrel lengths and choke combinations, chopper-lump barrels, Holland & Holland easy-opening mechanism, automatic ejectors, single-selective trigger, and Purdey-type scroll engraving.

NIB	Exc.	V.G.	Good	Fair	Poor
21600	16750	10500	7750	6000	1500

Model 103B Royal

Same as above but with high quality engraving, very fancy wood, hand matted rib.

NIB	Exc.	V.G.	Good	Fair	Poor
22500	18000	13000	8500	4200	1600

Model 120

As above, with engraved hunting scenes. Discontinued in 1988.

NIB	Exc.	V.G.	Good	Fair	Poor
21600	16750	10500	7750	6000	1500

Model 200

As above, Magnum proofed, double locking screws and 100 percent floral scroll engraving.

NIB	Exc.	V.G.	Good	Fair	Poor
17100	13500	9500	6500	300	1250

Model Special

A special order gun. Too rare to price.

Express Rifle

This is a best-quality sidelock side-by-side double rifle. Stock has pistol grip and cheekpiece. Choice of English scroll or floral engraving. Calibers are 7x65R, 9.3x74R, or .375 H&H.

NIB	Exc.	V.G.	Good	Fair	Poor
21000	15000	12000	7750	6000	1500

GARCIA
(formerly Firearms International of Wash., D.C.)

Garcia Bronco

A single-shot .410 shotgun or .22 LR or .22 Magnum rifle with swing out action, modeled somewhat after the old Hamilton No. 7. Barrel length is 18.5". Stock is a one-piece metal skeletonized affair. Weight is approximately 3.5 lbs. Introduced in 1968 and discontinued in 1978. Built in U.S.A.

NIB	Exc.	V.G.	Good	Fair	Poor
350	250	225	125	90	50

Garcia Bronco .22/.410

This is an over/under shotgun/rifle combination. The over barrel is .22 LR and the under barrel is chambered for .410 bore. Barrel length is 18.5". One-piece metal skeletonized stock. Introduced in 1976 and discontinued in 1978. Weight is about 4 lbs.

NIB	Exc.	V.G.	Good	Fair	Poor
500	375	295	200	115	75

Garcia Musketeer

This model is a bolt-action rifle chambered for the .243, .264, .270, .30-06, .307 Win. Magnum, .308 Norma, 7mm Rem. Magnum, and .300 Win. Magnum. Fitted with a checkered walnut stock, open sights, pistol grip, hinged floorplate, and adjustable trigger. Introduced in 1970 and discontinued in 1972.

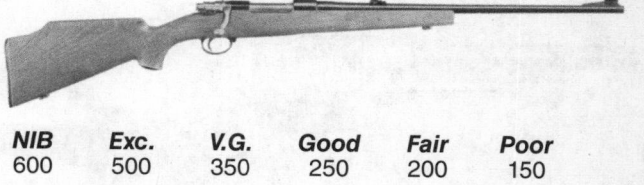

NIB	Exc.	V.G.	Good	Fair	Poor
600	500	350	250	200	150

GARRET, J. & F. CO.
Greensboro, North Carolina

Garrett Single-Shot Pistol

A .54 caliber single-shot percussion pistol with an 8.5" round barrel, swivel ramrod, walnut stock and brass mounts. Marked on the barrel breech "G.W." or "S.R." Approximately 500 were made in 1862 and 1863.

Courtesy Bonhams & Butterfields

NIB	Exc.	V.G.	Good	Fair	Poor
—	—	4550	165	1000	500

GASSER, LEOPOLD
Ottakring, Austria

M1870

An 11mm caliber double-action revolver with a 14.75" or 9.3" barrel, and 6-shot cylinder. Marked "Gasser Patent, Guss Stahl". It also bears an Austrian eagle and an apple pierced by an arrow, with the words "Schutz Mark".

NIB	Exc.	V.G.	Good	Fair	Poor
—	650	425	230	175	125

M1870/74

As above, with a steel frame.

NIB	Exc.	V.G.	Good	Fair	Poor
—	650	425	350	175	125

Gasser-Kropatschek M1876

An M1870/74 weighing 1 lb., 11 oz. and 9mm caliber.

NIB	Exc.	V.G.	Good	Fair	Poor
—	600	400	300	150	100

Montenegrin Gasser

A 10.7mm caliber double-action revolver with 5" or 6" barrels, and 5-shot cylinder. Engraved, silver and gold inlay, and ivory or bone grips. Values given are for the plain, unadorned model. Embellished models will need individual appraisal.

NIB	Exc.	V.G.	Good	Fair	Poor
—	650	425	350	200	150

Rast & Gasser M1898

A 8mm caliber double-action revolver with 4.75" barrel, 8-shot cylinder, solid-frame revolver with loading gate and an integral ejector rod.

NIB	Exc.	V.G.	Good	Fair	Poor
—	650	425	350	175	125

GATLING ARMS CO.
Birmingham, England

Established in 1888, this company remained in operation until approximately 1890. Although primarily involved with the marketing of Gatling Guns, it did market the one revolver listed.

Kynoch-Dimancea

A .38 or .45 caliber double-action hammerless revolver with a 6-shot cylinder. The loading system is rather unusual—a spur that resembles a hammer is pulled down, allowing the barrel and cylinder to pivot and to be pulled forward. During this motion the empty cases are ejected and new ones could be inserted. Marked "The Gatling Arms and Ammunition Co. Birmingham"; some are also marked "Dimancea Patent".

NIB	Exc.	V.G.	Good	Fair	Poor
—	—	2400	1275	750	350

GAUCHER
France

GN 1

This is a single-shot, bolt-action pistol chambered for the .22 LR. It is fitted with a 10" barrel with blade front sight and adjustable rear sight. Adjustable trigger. Hardwood target grips. Weight is approximately 38 oz. Introduced in 1990.

NIB	Exc.	V.G.	Good	Fair	Poor
525	425	350	225	145	100

GAULOIS
St. Etienne, France

See—Le Francais

GAVAGE, A.
Liege, Belgium

A 7.65mm caliber semi-automatic pistol with a fixed barrel and a concealed hammer. Similar in appearance to the Clement. Markings with "AG" molded into the grips. Some have been found bearing German Waffenamts. Manufactured from 1930s to 1940s.

NIB	Exc.	V.G.	Good	Fair	Poor
—	450	325	250	150	100

GAZANAGA, ISIDRO
Eibar, Spain

Destroyer M1913

A 6.35mm or 7.65mm caliber semi-automatic pistol. The 6.35mm model is copied after the 1906 Browning. "Destroyer" is stamped on the slide with the Isidro logo on each side of the grip plate. Produced through WWI.

NIB	Exc.	V.G.	Good	Fair	Poor
—	295	195	145	75	50

Destroyer M1916

A 7.65mm caliber semi-automatic pistol with a 7- or 9-shot magazine. A Ruby style pistol manufactured by the Spanish during World War I. "Destroyer" stamped on the slide. Wood grips.

NIB	Exc.	V.G.	Good	Fair	Poor
—	325	225	125	75	50

Destroyer Revolver

A good quality .38 caliber copy of the Colt Police Positive.

NIB	Exc.	V.G.	Good	Fair	Poor
—	295	165	155	100	75

Super Destroyer

A 7.65mm caliber copy of the Walther PP. The slide is stamped "Pistola Automatica 7.65 Super Destroyer".

NIB	Exc.	V.G.	Good	Fair	Poor
—	325	195	175	100	75

Surete

As above in 7.65mm caliber. Marked "Cal. 7.65 Pistolet Automatique Surete" with "IG" stamped on the frame.

NIB	Exc.	V.G.	Good	Fair	Poor
—	295	165	155	100	75

GECO
See—Genschow, G.

GEHA
Germany

An altered Mauser 98 rifle re-barreled for use with 12 gauge shotgun shells. Barrel length 26.5", military stock shortened to half length and the butt inlaid with a brass medallion marked "Geha". Manufactured from approximately 1919 to 1929.

NIB	Exc.	V.G.	Good	Fair	Poor
—	375	225	150	100	75

GEM
Bacon Arms Company
Norwich, Connecticut

See—Bacon Arms Company

Gem Pocket Revolver

A .22 caliber spur trigger revolver with a 1.25" octagonal barrel. The frame is iron, engraved, nickel-plated, with walnut or ivory grips. The barrel marked "Gem". Manufactured between 1878 and 1883.

NIB	Exc.	V.G.	Good	Fair	Poor
—	—	1950	700	300	145

GENEZ, A. G.
New York, New York

Located at 9 Chambers Street, Genez made a wide variety of firearms during his working life (ca. 1850 to 1875). The most commonly encountered of his arms today are single-shot percussion pistols and percussion double-barrel shotguns. More rarely seen are single-shot percussion target rifles. A number of the arms he made were decorated by Louis D. Nimschke. Genez products signed by Nimschke command considerable premiums over the values for the standard firearms listed.

Double-Barrel Shotgun

Most often encountered in 12 gauge with varying barrel lengths; blued steel furniture, and walnut stock.

NIB	Exc.	V.G.	Good	Fair	Poor
—	—	2800	1950	500	250

Pocket Pistol

A .41 caliber single-shot percussion pistol with a 3" barrel, German silver mountings and a walnut stock. Manufactured in the 1850s and 1860s.

NIB	Exc.	V.G.	Good	Fair	Poor
—	—	3950	1850	500	175

GENSCHOW, G.
Hamburg, Germany

Geco

A 6.35mm, 7.65mm, .32 Long, and 8mm Lebel caliber folding trigger double-action revolver.

NIB	Exc.	V.G.	Good	Fair	Poor
—	275	175	100	75	50

German Bulldog

A .32, .38, and .45 caliber folding trigger double-action revolver with solid frames, integral ejector rods, and loading gates. The proofmarks indicate Belgian manufacture.

NIB	Exc.	V.G.	Good	Fair	Poor
—	275	175	110	75	50

GEORGIA ARMORY
Milledgeville, George

Established in 1862, this concern produced a rifle based upon the U.S. Model 1855 Harper's Ferry Rifle. Nearly identical in all respects to the Harpers Ferry, the Georgia Armory rifle had a lockplate patterned after the U.S. Model 1841 Rifle. Lock marked "G.A. ARMORY" over the date (1862 or 1863). Buttplate tangs marked with serial numbers. The highest known serial number is 309. These rifles were fitted with saber bayonets.

NIB	Exc.	V.G.	Good	Fair	Poor
—	—	65000	22000	10500	3000

GERING, H. M. & CO.
Arnstadt, Germany

Leonhardt

A semi-automatic pistol in caliber 7.65mm. Almost identical to the Beholla pistol made by Becker. Leonhardt is stamped on the slide along with the Gering logo on each of the grip plates.

Courtesy James Rankin

NIB	Exc.	V.G.	Good	Fair	Poor
—	425	325	250	200	100

GERSTENBERGER & EBERWEIN
Gussenstadt, Germany

Em-Ge, G.& E., Omega & Pic

A series of poor-quality revolvers sold in the U.S.A. before 1968. .22 and .32 calibers with 2.25" barrels, and 6-shot cylinder. The editor does not consider these safe to shoot, even if new in the box.

NIB	Exc.	V.G.	Good	Fair	Poor
—	Worthless.	—	—	—	—

GEVARM
St. Etienne, France

Model A-6

This .22 caliber semi-automatic rifle fires from an open bolt. It is fitted with a one-piece stock. Furnished with a 8-round magazine. The E-1 20 magazine will not fit the A-6 without hand fitting. Add 15 percent for higher-end A7 model. These rifles are increasingly popular on the secondary market because of their open-bolt design.

NIB	Exc.	V.G.	Good	Fair	Poor
—	800	695	475	275	165

E-1 Autoloading Rifle

A .22 caliber semi-automatic rifle with a 19" barrel, 8-shot magazine, blued with walnut grips. Two-piece stock. A 20-round magazine is an option.

NIB	Exc.	V.G.	Good	Fair	Poor
—	550	450	295	200	150

GIB
Eibar, Spain

10 Gauge Shotgun

A 10 gauge Magnum boxlock double-barrel shotgun with 32" matte-ribbed barrels. Case hardened, blued with walnut grips.

NIB	Exc.	V.G.	Good	Fair	Poor
—	700	495	275	150	100

GIBBS
New York, New York

Gibbs Carbine

A .52 caliber single-shot percussion carbine with a sliding 22" round barrel. Blued, case hardened with a walnut stock. The lock marked with an American eagle and "Wm. F. Brooks/Manf New York/1863". The breech marked "L.H. Gibbs/Patd/Jany 8, 1856". There were only 1,050 produced.

Courtesy Milwaukee Public Museum, Milwaukee, Wisconsin

NIB	Exc.	V.G.	Good	Fair	Poor
—	—	5950	2200	900	350

Gibbs Pistol

A caliber percussion pistol made by Hull & Thomas of Ilion, New York, in 1855 or 1856.

Courtesy Milwaukee Public Museum, Milwaukee, Wisconsin

NIB	Exc.	V.G.	Good	Fair	Poor
—	—	3600	2750	1250	400

GIBBS, J. & G. / LATER GIBBS, GEORGE
Bristol, England

Established in 1835, this concern continues in business to this day.

J. & G. Gibbs	4 Redcliffe Street	1835-1842
George Gibbs	142 Thomas Street	
	Clare Street	
	39 Corn Street	

While initially known for exceptionally accurate single-shot rifles, the firm subsequently established a reputation for first quality bolt-action magazine rifles in a variety of large bore calibers. Bolt rifles by Gibbs, Rigby and others havebecome extremely desirable, especially in the African chamberings.

GIBBS GUNS, INC.
Greenback, Tennessee

Mark 45 Carbine

A .45 ACP caliber semi-automatic rifle with a 16.5" barrel, a 5-, 15-, 30-, or 90-shot magazine. Blued, with a walnut buttstock and forend. **NOTE:** A nickel-plated model was available as an option and would bring approximately $25 additional. Discontinued in 1988.

NIB	Exc.	V.G.	Good	Fair	Poor
650	475	275	200	125	100

GIBBS RIFLE COMPANY
Martinsburg, West Virginia

This company imports Parker Hale black powder replicas and WW II surplus military firearms such as the Mauser Model 1888, Model 71/84, and the Israeli K98. The company also produced historical remakes and specialty rifles.

Enfield No. 5 Jungle Carbine

This is a remake of the original British rifle. Chambered for the .303 cartridge and fitted with a 20" barrel with flash hider. Magazine capacity is 10 rounds. Weight about 7.75 lbs. New stock.

NIB	Exc.	V.G.	Good	Fair	Poor
350	295	200	150	100	50

Enfield No. 7 Jungle Carbine

This model is chambered for the .308 Winchester cartridge. Fitted with a 20" barrel with flash hider. Magazine capacity is 12 rounds. Adjustable rear sight. Original wood. Weight is about 8 lbs.

NIB	Exc.	V.G.	Good	Fair	Poor
650	575	475	350	250	200

Quest Extreme Carbine

An updated design of the No. 5 Jungle Carbine. Chambered for .303 cartridge with 20" barrel. Nickel finish and new hardwood stock. Brass butt trap. Weight is about 7.75 lbs.

NIB	Exc.	V.G.	Good	Fair	Poor
350	295	200	150	100	50

Quest II Extreme Carbine

Updated version of the No. 7 Jungle Carbine with nickel finish, see through scope mount and hardwood stock. Chambered for the .308 cartridge. Magazine capacity is 12 rounds. Barrel length is 20" and weight is about 8 lbs.

NIB	Exc.	V.G.	Good	Fair	Poor
350	295	200	150	100	50

Quest III Extreme Carbine

Similar to Quest II but with synthetic stock.

NIB	Exc.	V.G.	Good	Fair	Poor
400	325	200	150	100	50

Summit 45-70 Carbine

This bolt-action is built on the Enfield No. 4 action and rebarreled to .45-70 caliber. Fitted to a 21" barrel. MIL SPEC peep sight and checkered walnut stock. Weight is about 8.5 lbs.

NIB	Exc.	V.G.	Good	Fair	Poor
400	325	225	175	125	75

Mauser M71/84

Chambered for the 11mm Mauser cartridge and fitted with a 31.5" barrel. This model has been arsenal reconditioned but is otherwise original.Weight is about 10 lbs.

NIB	Exc.	V.G.	Good	Fair	Poor
300	250	175	150	100	50

Mauser M88 Commission Rifle

Fitted with a 30" barrel and chambered for the 8mm cartridge. This model has been arsenal reconditioned but is otherwise original. Weight is about 10 lbs.

NIB	Exc.	V.G.	Good	Fair	Poor
200	175	120	100	65	50

M98K Israeli Mauser

Re-barreled to .308 Win. by the Israeli Arsenal. Made in three grades; Standard, Grade 2 and Grade 1 (best grade). **NOTE:** Add $50 for Grade 2, $100 for Grade 1.

NIB	Exc.	V.G.	Good	Fair	Poor
350	300	250	200	150	100

M1903-A4 Springfield Sniper Model

Replica of 1903-A3 with original Remington action, new barrels in .30-06, C model stock, new copy of M73B1 scope with Redfield-type rings and mounts, Parkerized finish.

NIB	Exc.	V.G.	Good	Fair	Poor
900	800	650	500	300	150

GIBBS TIFFANY & CO.
Sturbridge, Massachusetts

Under Hammer Pistol

A .28 caliber single-shot percussion pistol with 3" to 8" barrels. A browned iron frame, walnut or maple pointed handle trimmed with brass. The top strap is marked "Gibbs Tiffany & Co." Active 1820 to 1838.

NIB	Exc.	V.G.	Good	Fair	Poor
—	—	1250	650	250	100

GILLESPIE
New York, New York
Derringer Type Pocket Pistol

A .41 caliber single-shot percussion pistol with a 2.5" barrel and a walnut stock. Manufactured from 1848 to 1870.

NIB	Exc.	V.G.	Good	Fair	Poor
—	—	2950	1350	500	200

GLAZE, W. & CO.
Columbia, South Carolina
See—B. & B. M. Darling

GLOCK
Deutsch-Wagram, Austria
Smyrna, Georgia

First imported into the U.S.A. in 1985. Completely manufactured in Austria until 2004 when Glock opened its plant in Georgia to produce the polymer frames. Offered in many models but main differences are caliber, sighting systems, barrel and slide length and grip length/magazine capacity. In 2010 the Gen4 (fourth generation) of Glock pistols was introduced. Gen4 features include three interchangeable back-straps, reversible magazine release button, improved recoil spring assembly and rough-textured frame (RTF) to enhance grip traction. As of 2012, all new-production units of the following models had the Gen4 features: M17, M19, M20, M21, M22, M23, M26, M27, M29, M30, M31, M35, M37. **NOTE:** Add $70 if equipped with Meprolight night sights. Add $90 if equipped with Trijicon night sights. Add $30 if equipped with adjustable sights. Add 10 percent for Gen4 if NIB.

Glock 17

This model is chambered for the 9mm Parabellum cartridge. It is a double-action-only semi-automatic that has a 4.49" barrel and a 17-shot detachable magazine. The empty weight of this pistol is 21.91 oz.

NIB	Exc.	V.G.	Good	Fair	Poor
520	425	325	300	275	175

Glock 17C

Similar to the Model 17 but with the additional feature of an integral ported barrel. Specifications are the same except for weight: 17C weighs 21.9 oz. Also available with OD green frame.

NIB	Exc.	V.G.	Good	Fair	Poor
525	475	350	300	275	175

Glock 17CC

Introduced in 1998 this is a compensated competition version of the C variation. It is fitted with an extended slide stop lever, extended magazine release, adjustable sights and a target trigger pull. This is special order item only.

NIB	Exc.	V.G.	Good	Fair	Poor
650	600	500	400	300	200

Glock 17L Competition Model

This version features a 6" compensated barrel and adjustable sights. The trigger is fine-tuned to provide between 5 to 8 lbs. trigger pull. This model was introduced in 1988. In 1990 this pistol won the I.P.S.C. World Stock Gun Championship. This pistol has limited availability in the U.S. Also available with OD green frame.

NIB	Exc.	V.G.	Good	Fair	Poor
700	600	475	350	300	225

Glock 19

This is similar in appearance to the Model 17 but is a compact version with a 4" barrel and a smaller grip that will accept either a 15-round or the standard 17-round magazine that protrudes a bit. Weight for this model is 20.99 oz. empty. The grip straps on this model are serrated as they are on the other Glock models. It was introduced in 1988 and is currently in production. Also available with OD green frame.

NIB	Exc.	V.G.	Good	Fair	Poor
525	475	350	300	275	175

Glock 19C

Same as above but with integral ported barrel. Weight is 20.7 oz. Also available with OD green frame.

NIB	Exc.	V.G.	Good	Fair	Poor
550	475	350	300	275	175

Glock 19CC

Introduced in 1998 this is a compensated competition version of the C variation. It is fitted with an extended slide stop lever, extended magazine release, adjustable sights and a target trigger pull. This is special order item only.

NIB	Exc.	V.G.	Good	Fair	Poor
700	600	500	350	300	275

Glock 22

Almost identical in appearance to the Model 17, the Model 22 is chambered for the .40 S&W cartridge. It comes standard with a

15-round clip. It has a slightly larger and heavier slide. Weight is 22.36 oz. Also available with OD green frame.

NIB	Exc.	V.G.	Good	Fair	Poor
525	475	350	300	275	175

Glock 22C

Same as the Glock 22 model but with the addition of an integral ported barrel. Weight is 22.5 oz. Also available with OD green frame.

NIB	Exc.	V.G.	Good	Fair	Poor
550	475	350	300	275	175

Glock 22CC

Introduced in 1998 this is a compensated competition version of the C variation. It is fitted with an extended slide stop lever, extended magazine release, adjustable sights and a target trigger pull. This is special order item only.

NIB	Exc.	V.G.	Good	Fair	Poor
700	600	500	350	300	275

Glock 23

Model 23 is chambered for the .40 S&W cartridge. Its slide is slightly heavier and larger than the Model 19. Weight is 21.67 oz. The Glock 23 magazine holds 13 rounds. Also available with OD green frame.

NIB	Exc.	V.G.	Good	Fair	Poor
525	475	350	300	275	175

Glock 23C

Same as above but with integral ported barrel. Weight is 20.9 oz. Also available with OD green frame.

NIB	Exc.	V.G.	Good	Fair	Poor
550	475	350	300	275	175

Glock 23CC

Introduced in 1998 this is a compensated competition version of the C variation. It is fitted with an extended slide stop lever, extended magazine release, adjustable sights and a target trigger pull. This is special order item only.

NIB	Exc.	V.G.	Good	Fair	Poor
700	600	500	350	300	275

Glock 24

Chambered for the .40 S&W cartridge, it is fitted with a 6" barrel. Weight is 26.5 oz.

NIB	Exc.	V.G.	Good	Fair	Poor
675	550	400	350	300	175

Glock 24C

Same as above but with a ported barrel.

NIB	Exc.	V.G.	Good	Fair	Poor
700	525	400	300	250	200

Glock 24CC

Introduced in 1998 this is a compensated competition version of the C variation. It is fitted with an extended slide stop lever, extended magazine release, adjustable sights and a target trigger pull. This is special order item only.

NIB	Exc.	V.G.	Good	Fair	Poor
700	600	500	350	300	275

Glock 20 and Glock 21

Both of these models are identical in physical appearance except for the caliber: the Model 20 is chambered for the 10mm cartridge while the Model 21 is chambered for the .45 ACP. Both have a barrel length of 4.60". The Model 20 has a 15-round clip and weighs 26.35 oz. while the Model 21 has a 13-round magazine and weighs 25.22 oz. Also available with OD green frame.

NIB	Exc.	V.G.	Good	Fair	Poor
550	425	350	300	250	200

Glock 20 SF Short Frame Pistol

DAO semi-auto similar to Glock Model 20 but with short-frame design. Chambered in 10mm Auto. Features include 4.61" barrel with hexagonal rifling, fixed sights, extended sight radius. Overall length 8.07" . Weight: 27.51 oz.

NIB	Exc.	V.G.	Good	Fair	Poor
550	475	350	300	275	175

Glock 21 SF

Slenderized version of Model 21 with slimmer frame and ambidextrous magazine catch. Introduced 2007.

Courtesy Ken Lunde

NIB	Exc.	V.G.	Good	Fair	Poor
550	475	350	300	275	175

Glock 20C and 21C

Same as Models 20 and 21 but with integral ported barrel. Also available with OD green frame.

NIB	Exc.	V.G.	Good	Fair	Poor
600	475	400	325	250	200

Glock 20CC/21CC

Introduced in 1998 this is a compensated competition version of the C variation. It is fitted with an extended slide stop lever, extended magazine release, adjustable sights and a target trigger pull. This is special order item only.

NIB	Exc.	V.G.	Good	Fair	Poor
700	600	500	350	300	275

Glock 26 and Model 27

Both of these models are identical except for caliber. Introduced in 1995 these are subcompact versions of the full-size Glocks. The Model 26 is chambered for the 9mm cartridge, while the Model 27 is chambered for the .40 S&W cartridge. The 9mm version magazine capacity is 10 rounds and the 40 caliber version holds 9 rounds. The overall length is 6.25" with a barrel length of 3.5". The height is 4-3/16" and the width is 1.25". Weight for both models is about 20 oz. Standard are a dot front sight and white outline rear adjustable sight. Also available with OD green frame.

NIB	Exc.	V.G.	Good	Fair	Poor
550	475	350	300	275	175

Glock 29 and Glock 30

These two pistols were introduced in 1997. The Model 29 is chambered for the 10mm cartridge while the Model 30 is chambered for the .45 ACP cartridge. Barrel length is 3.78". Weight is about 24 oz. Overall length is 6.77". The Model 29 has a magazine capacity of 10 rounds while the Model 30 has a standard capacity of 10 rounds with a optional capacity of 9 rounds. With the 10-round magazine in place the Model 30 magazine protrudes slightly below the grip. With the 9-round magazine in place the magazine fits flush with the bottom of the grip. Also available with OD green frame.

Model 30 with 10-round magazine

NIB	Exc.	V.G.	Good	Fair	Poor
550	475	350	300	275	175

Glock Model 29 SF Short Frame Pistol

DAO semi-auto similar to Glock Model 29 but with short-frame design. Chambered in 10mm Auto. Features include 3.78" barrel with hexagonal rifling, fixed sights, extended sight radius. Overall length 6.97" . Weight: 24.52 oz.

NIB	Exc.	V.G.	Good	Fair	Poor
575	495	350	300	275	175.

Glock 31

Chambered for the .357 SIG cartridge this pistol is fitted with a 4.5" barrel and a magazine capacity of 10 rounds (15 rounds law enforcement). Overall length is 7.3" and the height is 5.4". Weight is about 23.3 oz. Introduced in 1998. Also available with OD green frame.

NIB	Exc.	V.G.	Good	Fair	Poor
550	475	350	300	275	175

Glock 31C

Same as the Model 31 but with an integral compensator. Also available with OD green frame.

NIB	Exc.	V.G.	Good	Fair	Poor
575	495	350	300	275	175

Glock 31CC

Introduced in 1998 this is a compensated competition version of the C variation. It is fitted with an extended slide stop lever, extended magazine release, adjustable sights and a target trigger pull. This is special order item only.

NIB	Exc.	V.G.	Good	Fair	Poor
700	600	500	350	300	275

Glock 32

Similar to the Glock 31 except fitted with a 4" barrel. Overall length is 6.85" and height is 5". Magazine capacity is 10 rounds (13 rounds law enforcement). Weight is approximately 21.5 oz. Introduced in 1998. Also available with OD green frame.

NIB	Exc.	V.G.	Good	Fair	Poor
575	495	350	300	275	175

Glock 32C

Same as above but fitted with integral ported barrel and slide. Also available with OD green frame.

NIB	Exc.	V.G.	Good	Fair	Poor
700	600	500	350	300	275

Glock 32CC

Introduced in 1998 this is a compensated competition version of the C variation. It is fitted with an extended slide stop lever, extended magazine release, adjustable sights and a target trigger pull. This is special order item only.

NIB	Exc.	V.G.	Good	Fair	Poor
700	600	500	350	300	275

Glock 33

This .357 SIG model has a 3.5" barrel and an overall length of 6.3". Height is 4.2" and weight is about 17.7 oz. Introduced in 1998. Also available with OD green frame.

NIB	Exc.	V.G.	Good	Fair	Poor
575	495	350	300	275	175.

Glock 34

This model is chambered for the 9x19 cartridge and has a 5.3" barrel, overall length of 8.2", and a magazine capacity of 10 rounds. Empty weight is approximately 23 oz. Also available with OD green frame.

NIB	Exc.	V.G.	Good	Fair	Poor
575	495	350	300	275	175.

Glock 35

The Glock 35 is chambered for the .40 S&W cartridge. It has the same dimensions as the Glock 34 except for weight, which is 24.5 oz. Also available with OD green frame.

NIB	Exc.	V.G.	Good	Fair	Poor
700	600	500	350	300	275

Glock 36

Introduced in 1999, this model is similar to the Model 30 but fitted with a single-column magazine with a capacity of 6 rounds. The width of the pistol is .14" less than the Model 30. Barrel length is 3.78". Weight is 20 oz. Also available with OD green frame.

NIB	Exc.	V.G.	Good	Fair	Poor
575	495	350	300	275	175.

Glock 37

This semi-automatic pistol is chambered for the .45 G.A.P. cartridge, which is slightly shorter than the .45 ACP cartridge. This cartridge has a muzzle speed of 951 fps and muzzle energy of 405 ft. lbs. Fitted with a 4.49" barrel. Height is 5.5". Overall length is 7.3". Weight is about 26 oz. Also available with OD green frame.

NIB	Exc.	V.G.	Good	Fair	Poor
575	495	350	300	275	175

Glock 38

This .45 G.A.P. pistol is fitted with a 4" barrel. Height is 5" and overall length is 6.85". Magazine capacity is 8 rounds. Weight is about 24 oz. Introduced in 2005. Also available with OD green frame.

NIB	Exc.	V.G.	Good	Fair	Poor
575	495	350	300	275	175

Glock 39

Introduced in 2005 this sub-compact .45 G.A.P. pistol has a 3.46" barrel. Height is 4.17" and overall length is 6.3". Magazine capacity is 8 rounds. Weight is about 19.3 oz. Also available with OD green frame.

NIB	Exc.	V.G.	Good	Fair	Poor
575	495	350	300	275	175

GODDARD

See—B. & B. M. Darling

GOLDEN EAGLE

Nikko Limited
Tochigi, Japan

SHOTGUNS

Golden Eagle Model 5000 Grade I

A 12 or 20 gauge over/under shotgun with of 26", 28", and 30" barrels with ventilated ribs and various choke combinations, a single-selective trigger and automatic ejectors. Blued, with a walnut stock that has an eagle's head inlaid into the pistol grip cap. Manufactured between 1976 and the early 1980s.

NIB	Exc.	V.G.	Good	Fair	Poor
1000	900	750	600	475	250

Grade I Skeet

As above, with a 26" or 28" barrel having a wide competition rib.

NIB	Exc.	V.G.	Good	Fair	Poor
1100	900	750	600	475	250

Grade I Trap

Similar to the skeet model, with a 30" or 32" barrel.

NIB	Exc.	V.G.	Good	Fair	Poor
1200	900	750	600	475	250

Model 5000 Grade II

As above, but more finely finished with an eagle's head inlaid in the receiver in gold.

NIB	Exc.	V.G.	Good	Fair	Poor
1100	1000	800	600	475	250

Grandee Grade III

As above, but more elaborately engraved.

NIB	Exc.	V.G.	Good	Fair	Poor
2500	2000	1750	1400	850	500

RIFLES

Model 7000 Grade I

A Mauser bolt-action rifle chambered for all popular American calibers with a 24" or 26" barrel, walnut stock and a rosewood pistol-grip cap and fore-end tip.

NIB	Exc.	V.G.	Good	Fair	Poor
700	600	500	375	300	200

Model 7000 African

As above in .375 H&H and .458 Win. Magnum caliber with open sights.

NIB	Exc.	V.G.	Good	Fair	Poor
800	650	550	400	325	250

Model 7000 Grade II

As above, but engraved.

NIB	Exc.	V.G.	Good	Fair	Poor
900	750	625	450	350	275

GONCZ CO.
Hollywood, California

GC Carbine

A 7.63mm Mauser, 9mm Parabellum, .38 Super, and .45 ACP caliber semi-automatic rifle with a 16.1" barrel. Black with a walnut stock. Later production models were stainless steel.

NIB	Exc.	V.G.	Good	Fair	Poor
650	500	395	275	200	125

GC Stainless

As above, in stainless steel. Introduced in 1987.

NIB	Exc.	V.G.	Good	Fair	Poor
800	550	425	325	250	175

GC Collector's Edition

A limited edition with hand-polished finish.

NIB	Exc.	V.G.	Good	Fair	Poor
875	600	500	425	350	225

Halogen Carbine

The GC Carbine with a powerful light source mounted under the barrel. Chambered for 9mm and .45 ACP only.

NIB	Exc.	V.G.	Good	Fair	Poor
750	500	395	275	200	125

Laser Carbine

As above, with a laser sighting system effective to 400 yards.

NIB	Exc.	V.G.	Good	Fair	Poor
1500	1250	1000	750	650	500

GA Pistol

The GC Carbine with a 9.5" shrouded barrel and a 16- or 18-shot magazine. Black with a one-piece grip. Manufactured between 1985 and 1987.

NIB	Exc.	V.G.	Good	Fair	Poor
525	400	295	200	150	100

GAT-9 Pistol

As above, in a 9mm caliber with an adjustable trigger and hand-honed action.

NIB	Exc.	V.G.	Good	Fair	Poor
600	475	375	300	225	150

GA Collector's Edition

A hand-polished stainless steel limited production of the above.

NIB	Exc.	V.G.	Good	Fair	Poor
825	675	600	500	400	300

GS Pistol

The Model GA with a plain 5" barrel. In 1987 pistols were made in stainless steel.

NIB	Exc.	V.G.	Good	Fair	Poor
350	275	225	175	125	75

GS Collector's Edition

A hand-polished, limited-production, stainless steel version of the GS.

NIB	Exc.	V.G.	Good	Fair	Poor
775	625	550	475	350	250

GOUDRY, J.F.
Paris, France

Double-action 10-shot turret pistol. Marked on barrel rib "J.F. Goudry Paris and Systeme A. Norl." By raising the gate on the left side the turret can be removed and reloaded or another preloaded turret inserted.

NIB	Exc.	V.G.	Good	Fair	Poor
—	—	6500	2000	1000	500

GOVERNOR
Norwich, Connecticut

Governor Pocket Revolver

A .22 caliber spur trigger revolver with a 3" barrel and 7-shot cylinder. These revolvers were made from modified Bacon pepperboxes. The top strap marked "Governor." Manufactured from approximately 1868 to 1874.

NIB	Exc.	V.G.	Good	Fair	Poor
—	—	725	650	250	100

GRABNER G.
Kolibri Rehberg, Austria

See—Kolibri

GRAND PRECISION, FABRIQUE D'ARMES DE
Eibar, Spain

Bulwark Model 1913

This model is chambered for the 6.35mm cartridge and is an exact copy of the Browning Model 1906 complete with squeeze grip safety. Marketed by Beistegui Hermanos. "Bulwark" is stamped on the slide and "B.H." stamped on the grip plate.

Courtesy James Rankin

NIB	Exc.	V.G.	Good	Fair	Poor
—	295	195	150	75	40

Bulwark Model 1914

Chambered for the 7.65mm cartridge and in the style of the Ruby military pistols of WWI. Magazine capacity is 9 rounds.

Courtesy James Rankin

NIB	Exc.	V.G.	Good	Fair	Poor
—	275	225	150	75	40

Bulwark 6.35mm

A semi-automatic pistol in caliber 6.35mm patterned after the Browning Model 1906, and marketed by Beistegue Hermanos.

Courtesy James Rankin

NIB	Exc.	V.G.	Good	Fair	Poor
—	250	175	115	75	40

Libia 6.35mm

This model is also patterned after the Browning Model 1906 with squeeze safety. "Libia" is stamped on the slide and each grip plate. Marketed by Beistegui Hermanos.

Courtesy James Rankin

NIB	Exc.	V.G.	Good	Fair	Poor
—	275	225	150	750	40

Libia 7.65mm

Similar to the model above but chambered for the 7.65mm cartridge.

Courtesy James Rankin

NIB	Exc.	V.G.	Good	Fair	Poor
—	275	225	150	75	40

GRANGER, G.
St. Etienne, France

Side-by-Side Shotgun

A custom-order 12, 16, and 20 gauge boxlock double-barrel shotgun. Manufactured since 1902. Because the gun is imported the value of the dollar frequently determines price movement.

NIB	Exc.	V.G.	Good	Fair	Poor
—	16500	13000	8500	4250	1500

GRAS
France

Model 1874

An 11mm caliber bolt-action rifle with a 32" barrel with a walnut stock, a barrel band and a metal tip. The bayonet is a spike blade with a wood handle and a brass butt cap.

NIB	Exc.	V.G.	Good	Fair	Poor
—	500	375	225	150	75

GREAT WESTERN ARMS COMPANY
Los Angeles, California

During the 10 years that Great Western was in business the quality of its firearms was inconsistent due to uncertain management and finances. This left the company's reputation damaged and allowed Colt and Ruger to dominate the single-action market. By 1961 Great Western Arms Company was no longer able to compete. Despite, or perhaps because of, the company's unstable history there is considerable collector interest in these firearms. Approximately 22,000 single-action revolvers were built and fewer than 3,500 derringers were manufactured from 1953 to 1961. Standard barrel lengths were: 4.75", 5.5" and 7.5". Standard calibers were: .38 Special, .357 Magnum, .357 Atomic, .44 Special, .44-40, .44 Magnum, .45 Colt, and .22 LR. Standard finishes were: Case hardened frame, blued barrel and cylinder, or all blue finish. **NOTE:** For guns to be in NIB condition they must have original boxes and paper work. Factory engraved guns must be supported by some type of invoice, letter, or other provenance to realize full value. Great Westerns were also available in kit form. Assembled kit guns are not as valuable as factory-built guns. Deduct 25-40 percent for kit guns unless in disassembled form.

Centerfire Single-Action

Courtesy John C. Dougan

NIB	Exc.	V.G.	Good	Fair	Poor
900	750	500	350	250	200

.22 Long Rifle Single-Action
NIB	Exc.	V.G.	Good	Fair	Poor
450	335	295	250	200	150

Fast Draw Model
Brass backstrap and trigger guard.
NIB	Exc.	V.G.	Good	Fair	Poor
700	550	475	400	300	225

Deputy Model
4-inch barrel with full length sight rib. **NOTE:** For calibers other than standard such as .22 Hornet, .32-20, .45 ACP, .22 Magnum, .30 Carbine or .357 Atomic add 10 percent premium. For factory plated pistols add 10 percent. For factory cased pistols add 20 percent. For Sheriff's Model or Buntline Special add 15 percent. For factory ivory grips add $175; for stag grips add $95, and for pearl grips add $150. Factory-engraved guns will add $750 to $3,500 to above prices depending on coverage.
NIB	Exc.	V.G.	Good	Fair	Poor
1000	850	600	425	250	—

Derringer Models
These two-shot over/unders were based on the Remington Derringer of the late 19th Century. Chambered for either .38 S&W or .38 Special. Some models were factory engraved and presented to Hollywood celebrities.

Engraved Model

Courtesy John C. Dougan

NIB	Exc.	V.G.	Good	Fair	Poor
—	1100	900	700	400	150

Standard Model

Courtesy John C. Dougan

NIB	Exc.	V.G.	Good	Fair	Poor
—	625	475	275	175	100

GREEN, E.
Cheltenham, England
Green
A .450 and .455 caliber double-action revolver, popular with its military users in the late 1800s.
NIB	Exc.	V.G.	Good	Fair	Poor
—	—	2000	875	550	300

GREENE
Milbury, Massachusetts
Greene Breechloading Rifle
A .53 caliber single-shot bolt-action percussion rifle with a 35" barrel, under hammer and full length walnut stock secured by three barrel bands. Marked "Greene's Patent/Nov. 17, 1857". Approximately 4,000 were made by the A.H. Waters Armory between 1859 and 1862.

Courtesy Milwaukee Public Museum, Milwaukee, Wisconsin

NIB	Exc.	V.G.	Good	Fair	Poor
—	—	3250	1050	400	200

GREENER, W. W. LTD.
Birmingham, England
Perhaps the best known manufacturer of double-barrel shotguns in England during the 19th Century. Greener was also a prolific

author. His name will forever be associated with the "Greener Crossbolt". Greener hammer-model shotguns were quite popular in the United States during the last half of the 19th century. The company is still in business in Birmingham and makes a limited number of custom guns. Current prices on the used gun market range for basic boxlock, non-ejector models in the $1,500 to $2,000 range. Top of the line models from the first half of the 20th century can bring $100,000 or more. Because of the wide range of models and grades, a professional appraisal would be necessary before any transaction.

GREIFELT & CO.
Suhl, Germany

OVER/UNDER SHOTGUNS

Grade No. 1

NOTE: 28 gauge and .410 add 25 percent.

NIB	Exc.	V.G.	Good	Fair	Poor
—	3750	3250	2950	1750	1000

Grade No. 3

Similar to the No. 1, with less engraving. Manufactured prior to WWII. **NOTE:** 28 gauge and .410 add 25 percent.

NIB	Exc.	V.G.	Good	Fair	Poor
—	3250	2700	1850	1250	750

Model 143E

The post-war version of the No. 1. Not made in 28 gauge or .410 bore.

NIB	Exc.	V.G.	Good	Fair	Poor
—	2750	2300	1650	1200	750

Combination Gun

A combination over/under rifle/shotgun manufactured in all bores and a variety of rifle calibers with 24" or 26" barrels. Made prior to 1939. **NOTE:** Deduct 40 percent if rifle caliber is obsolete. 28 gauge and .410 add 25 percent. Automatic ejectors add 10 percent.

NIB	Exc.	V.G.	Good	Fair	Poor
—	5800	4750	3950	2500	1250

SIDE-BY-SIDE SHOTGUNS

Model 22

A 12 or 20 gauge boxlock double-barrel shotgun with 28" or 30" barrels, sideplates, double triggers and extractors. Blued, case hardened with a walnut stock. Manufactured after 1945.

NIB	Exc.	V.G.	Good	Fair	Poor
—	2500	1950	1500	500	200

Model 22E

As above, with automatic ejectors.

NIB	Exc.	V.G.	Good	Fair	Poor
—	2750	2300	1650	550	225

Model 103

A 12 and 16 gauge boxlock shotgun with a 28" or a 30" barrel, double triggers and extractors. Walnut stock with a pistol or straight English-style grip. Post-war model.

NIB	Exc.	V.G.	Good	Fair	Poor
—	2250	1800	1350	400	175

Model 103E

As above, with automatic ejectors.

NIB	Exc.	V.G.	Good	Fair	Poor
—	2500	1950	1500	500	200

Drilling

A 12, 16, or 20 gauge double-barrel shotgun fitted with a rifle barrel, chambered for a variety of cartridges. Barrel length 26", boxlock-action, double triggers, extractors and folding rear sight. Manufactured prior to 1939. **NOTE:** Deduct 40 percent if rifle caliber is obsolete. 20 gauge add 10 percent.

NIB	Exc.	V.G.	Good	Fair	Poor
—	3750	3200	2950	900	300

GRENDEL, INC.
Rockledge, Florida

P-10 Pistol

A .380 caliber semi-automatic pistol with a 3" barrel, 11-shot magazine, matte black finish with black plastic grips. The pistol has a plastic frame with plastic magazine. It is offered in electroless nickel-plate, as well as a green Teflon finish for a slightly higher price. **NOTE:** Green finish add $5. Electroless nickel add $15.

NIB	Exc.	V.G.	Good	Fair	Poor
295	250	195	150	125	75

P-12

This semi-automatic double-action pistol is chambered for the .380 ACP cartridge. Fitted with a 3" barrel, checkered polymer grips, and blued finish. Magazine capacity is 10 rounds. Weight is about 13 oz. Introduced in 1992.

NIB	Exc.	V.G.	Good	Fair	Poor
295	250	195	150	125	75

P-30

Introduced in 1990 this is a double-action semi-automatic pistol chambered for the .22 WMR cartridge. Fitted with a 5" barrel or 8" barrel. Fixed sights. Magazine capacity is 30 rounds. Weight is about 21 oz. Discontinued in 1994.

NIB	Exc.	V.G.	Good	Fair	Poor
450	350	275	125	85	75

P-30L

Same as above model but in 8" barrel only. Also discontinued in 1994.

NIB	Exc.	V.G.	Good	Fair	Poor
450	350	275	125	85	75

P-30M

Similar to the P-30 but fitted with a removable muzzlebrake.

NIB	Exc.	V.G.	Good	Fair	Poor
450	350	275	125	85	75

P-31

This is a semi-automatic pistol chambered for .22 WMR cartridge. Fitted with an 11" barrel, muzzlebrake. Black matte finish. Weight is approximately 48 oz. Introduced in 1991 but no longer in production.

NIB	Exc.	V.G.	Good	Fair	Poor
450	350	275	125	85	75

RIFLES

SRT-20F Compact Rifle

A .308 caliber bolt-action rifle with 20" finned match grade barrel, 9-shot magazine, a folding synthetic stock, integral bipod and no sights.

Courtesy Jim Supica, Old Town Station

NIB	Exc.	V.G.	Good	Fair	Poor
575	500	425	325	250	100

SRT-24

As above, with a 24" barrel. Discontinued in 1988.

NIB	Exc.	V.G.	Good	Fair	Poor
600	525	450	350	275	100

R-31 Carbine

This semi-automatic carbine was introduced in 1991 and is chambered for the .22 WMR cartridge. Fitted with a 16" barrel with muzzlebrake and a telescoping tubular stock. Magazine capacity is 30 rounds. Weight is about 4 lbs. Discontinued in 1994.

NIB	Exc.	V.G.	Good	Fair	Poor
300	250	200	150	125	100

GRIFFIN & HOWE
Bernardsville, New Jersey

Established in 1923, this firm manufactures, on custom order, a variety of bolt-action sporting rifles. These rifles have an excellent reputation and are quite desirable. Starting prices for currently manufactured rifles is around $15,000. Values of older models in excellent condition range from $4,000 to $10,000 and much higher for engraved rifles. Griffin & Howe also are agents for various European shotgun makers.

GRIFFON
South Africa

Griffon 1911 A1 Combat

This semi-automatic single-action pistol is chambered for the .45 ACP cartridge and fitted with a 4" ported barrel. Aluminum trigger and high-profile sights are standard. Frame is chrome and slide is blued. Magazine capacity is 7 rounds.

NIB	Exc.	V.G.	Good	Fair	Poor
600	500	400	295	200	125

GRISWOLD & GRIER
See—Griswold & Gunnison

GRISWOLD & GUNNISON
Griswoldville, Georgia

1851 Navy Type

A .36 caliber percussion revolver with a 7.5" barrel and 6-shot cylinder. The frame and grip straps made of brass and the barrel as well as cylinder made of iron. Approximately 3,700 were made between 1862 and 1864, for the Confederate government. **NOTE:** This revolver is sometimes referred to as the Griswold and Grier.

Courtesy Milwaukee Public Museum, Milwaukee, Wisconsin

NIB	Exc.	V.G.	Good	Fair	Poor
—	—	38500	14000	2750	1350

GROSS ARMS CO.
Tiffin, Ohio

Pocket Revolver

A .25 and .30 caliber spur trigger revolver with a 6" octagonal barrel, a 7-shot cylinder and marked "Gross Arms Co., Tiffin, Ohio". Blued, with walnut grips. Only a few hundred were manufactured between 1864 and 1866.

NIB	Exc.	V.G.	Good	Fair	Poor
—	—	1700	600	300	150

GRUBB, J. C. & CO.
Philadelphia, Pennsylvania

Pocket Pistol

A .41 caliber single-shot percussion pistol with various barrel lengths. German silver, walnut stock and engraved lock and trigger guard. The lock is marked "J.C. Grubb". Several hundred were manufactured between 1860 and 1870.

NIB	Exc.	V.G.	Good	Fair	Poor
—	—	1550	800	650	170

GRULLA
Eibar, Spain

Model 216RL

This side-by-side shotgun is offered in 12, 16, 20, and 28 gauge, as well as .410 bore. Barrel length is 28". Articulated double triggers. Action body is H&H side locks. Select walnut with straight grip and splinter fore-end. Fixed chokes. Choice of different styles of engraving. Weight range from 7.1 lbs. for 12 gauge to 6 lbs. for .410 bore. **NOTE:** Add $300 for 28 gauge and .410 bore.

NIB	Exc.	V.G.	Good	Fair	Poor
9000	5750	3500	2000	1350	500

Royal

As above but fitted with a 7-pin H&H-style lock.

NIB	Exc.	V.G.	Good	Fair	Poor
9500	6250	3800	2500	1750	750

GUERINI, CAESAR
Italy

This line of Italian over/under guns was introduced into the U.S.A. in 2004.

Flyway

This over/under 12 gauge 3" gun is offered with either 28" or 30" vent-rib barrels with choke tubes. Checkered walnut stock with pistol grip. Trap-style forearm with finger grooves. Single-selective trigger and ejectors. Weight is about 8 lbs. depending on barrel length.

NIB	Exc.	V.G.	Good	Fair	Poor
2795	2300	1750	1300	900	500

Woodlander

This model is offered in 12, 20 and 28 gauge with choice of 26" or 28" vent-rib barrels and choke tubes. Frame is case hardened with gold ruffed grouse on bottom of receiver. The checkered Circassian walnut stock with straight grip is oil finished. Single-

selective trigger and ejectors. Weight is about 6.25 lbs. for the 20 gauge and 6.15 lbs. for the 28 gauge.

NIB	Exc.	V.G.	Good	Fair	Poor
2795	2300	1750	1300	900	500

Magnus Light

This model is offered in 12, 20, or 28 gauge with choice of 26" or 28" vent-rib barrels with choke tubes. Alloy frame with Tinaloy finish with side plates. Scroll engraved with gold game birds. Checkered walnut stock with Prince of Wales-style pistol grip. Weight of 12 gauge is about 6 lbs.; 20 gauge is 5.4 lbs. and the 28 gauge is about 5.25 lbs.

NIB	Exc.	V.G.	Good	Fair	Poor
3500	2995	2000	1500	1000	500

Magnus

Similar to the Magnus Light but with case hardened steel receiver. Weight is about 6.75 lbs. for the 12 gauge, 6.5 lbs. for the 20 gauge, and 6.25 lbs. for the 28 gauge.

NIB	Exc.	V.G.	Good	Fair	Poor
3500	2995	2000	1500	1000	500

Tempio

This over/under gun is offered in 12, 20, and 28 gauge with choice of 26" or 28" barrels with choke tubes. Checkered Circassian walnut stock with Prince of Wales-style pistol grip. Alloy receiver is a gray finish of Tinaloy. Engraved with scroll and gold game birds. Single-selective trigger with ejectors. Weight is about 6.8 lbs. for 12 gauge, 6.4 lbs. for 20 gauge, and 6.25 lbs. for the 28 gauge.

NIB	Exc.	V.G.	Good	Fair	Poor
2450	2000	1500	1050	600	250

Forum/Forum Sporting

This model is offered in 12, 20 and 28 gauge, with choice of 26" or 28" barrels on the Forum and 30", 32", or 34" on the Forum Sporting. Gun has silver receiver with scroll and game scene engraving with side plates. **NOTE:** Add $300 for Forum Sporting.

NIB	Exc.	V.G.	Good	Fair	Poor
7250	6000	4750	3250	1600	700

Summit Sporting/Summit Limited

Offered in 12, 20, or 28 gauge with choice of 30" or 32" vent-rib barrels with extended choke tubes. Alloy receiver with engraving. Single-selective trigger is adjustable for length of pull. Ejectors. Checkered walnut stock with pistol grip. Weight of 12 gauge is about 8 lbs., the 20 gauge about 7.5 lbs., and the 28 gauge about 7.45 lbs. **NOTE:** For Summit Limited add $300.

NIB	Exc.	V.G.	Good	Fair	Poor
2950	2300	1650	1200	750	300

Magnus Sporting

This model is similar to the Summit but with upgraded wood and sidelock-style receiver with scroll engraving and gold game birds.

NIB	Exc.	V.G.	Good	Fair	Poor
3500	2900	2300	1650	1000	500

Essex

New in 2006, this over/under with oil-finished stock and coin finished receiver with scroll engraving is available in 12, 20 and 28 gauges and .410 bore, all with 3" chambers.

NIB	Exc.	V.G.	Good	Fair	Poor
4250	3500	2300	1650	1000	500

Ellipse Evo

Rounded action in 12, 20 or 28 gauge with coin-finished receiver, hand-rubbed oil-finished stock with rounded grip, choke tubes and 28" barrels. Choice of selective or non-selective trigger, manual or automatic safety. Also offered in 12 gauge sporting (Evolution) and Limited versions. **NOTE:** Add $1800 for Evolution model, deduct $1500 for Limited.

NIB	Exc.	V.G.	Good	Fair	Poor
5000	4000	2800	2000	1500	700

GUION, T. F.
New Orleans, Louisiana

Pocket Pistol

A .41 caliber single-shot percussion pistol with a 2.5" barrel, German silver mountings, and a walnut stock. Manufactured in the 1850s.

NIB	Exc.	V.G.	Good	Fair	Poor
—	—	2150	1850	550	275

GUNWORKS LTD.
Buffalo, New York

Model 9 Derringer

An over/under derringer chambered in 9mm, .38 Special, .38 Super, and .357 Magnum caliber with 2.5" barrels, with a spur trigger and Millet sights. Nickel-plate, with walnut grips. Manufacturing ceased in 1986.

NIB	Exc.	V.G.	Good	Fair	Poor
—	175	125	90	75	50

GUSTAF, CARL
Eskilstuna, Sweden

Bolt-Action Rifle

A 6.5x55, 7x64, .270, 7mm Magnum, .308, .30-06, and 9.3x62 caliber bolt-action rifle with a 24" barrel. Blued with a walnut stock in either the classic style or with a Monte Carlo cheekpiece. Manufactured between 1970 and 1977.

NIB	Exc.	V.G.	Good	Fair	Poor
—	700	600	450	325	150

Grade II

As above, with better walnut and a rosewood pistol grip cap and fore-end tip.

NIB	Exc.	V.G.	Good	Fair	Poor
—	850	650	475	375	175

Grade III

As above, with a high-gloss finish and a finely figured walnut stock.

NIB	Exc.	V.G.	Good	Fair	Poor
—	950	700	550	475	275

Deluxe Bolt-Action

As above, with an engraved floorplate and trigger guard, a Damascened bolt, and a high-grade French walnut stock. Manufactured between 1970 and 1977.

NIB	Exc.	V.G.	Good	Fair	Poor
—	1250	900	650	450	300

Varmint Model

A .222, .22-250, .243, and 6.5x55 caliber bolt-action rifle with 27" barrel and a large bolt knob made of Bakelite. Furnished without open sights and has a heavy target-type stock. Manufactured in 1970 only.

NIB	Exc.	V.G.	Good	Fair	Poor
—	700	600	450	325	150

Grand Prix Target

A .22 caliber single-shot, bolt-action rifle with a 27" barrel and adjustable weights. Furnished without sights and with an adjustable butt target stock. Only manufactured in 1970.

NIB	Exc.	V.G.	Good	Fair	Poor
—	700	600	450	325	150

Model 2000

A 6.5x55, .243, .270, .308, and .30-06 caliber bolt-action rifle with a 60 percent bolt lift and a cold swagged barrel and action. Furnished with open sights. Blued, walnut stock with a Monte Carlo cheekpiece. Manufactured until 1985.

NIB	Exc.	V.G.	Good	Fair	Poor
—	675	575	400	300	150

GWYN & CAMPBELL
Hamilton, Ohio

Union Carbine

A .52 caliber single-shot breech loading percussion carbine with a round/octagonal 20" barrel marked "Gwyn & Campbell/Patent/1862/ Hamilton,O". Blued, case hardened with a walnut stock. Approximately 8,500 were made between 1862 and 1865.

Courtesy Milwaukee Public Museum, Milwaukee, Wisconsin

NIB	Exc.	V.G.	Good	Fair	Poor
—	—	4000	1975	500	300

H.J.S. INDUSTRIES, INC.
Brownsville, Texas

Frontier Four Derringer

A .22 caliber four-barreled pocket pistol with 2.5" sliding barrels, stainless steel frame and barrel grip and walnut grips. Recalled due to risk of unintentional discharge.

NIB	Exc.	V.G.	Good	Fair	Poor
—	450	400	275	150	50

Lone Star Derringer

A .38 Special caliber single-shot spur trigger pistol with a 2.5" barrel. Stainless steel with wood grips.

NIB	Exc.	V.G.	Good	Fair	Poor
—	300	250	175	125	50

H-S PRECISION, INC.
Rapid City, South Dakota

SPR Sporter Rifle

This bolt-action rifle is offered in both long and short actions with any standard SAAMI caliber. Match grade stainless steel barrel lengths are 22", 24", or 26" with optional muzzlebrake available. Synthetic stock is offered in various colors. Weight is between 7.5 and 7.75 lbs. depending on barrel length. Magazine capacity is 4 rounds for standard calibers and 3 rounds for magnum calibers.

NIB	Exc.	V.G.	Good	Fair	Poor
2375	1800	1400	900	500	250

SPL Lightweight Sporter

Introduced in 2005 this model features a 22", 24", or 26" fluted barrel with choice of short or long action calibers. Detachable magazine. No sights. Pro-series synthetic stock. Weight is under 7 lbs.

NIB	Exc.	V.G.	Good	Fair	Poor
2400	1825	1425	925	525	275

PHR Professional Hunter Rifle

This bolt-action rifle is chambered for magnum calibers only and is fitted with 24" or 26" stainless steel match grade fluted barrel (except .416 Rigby). Built in recoil reduced in synthetic stock with choice of colors. Matte black finish. Weight is between 7.75 lbs. and 8.25 depending on barrel length and caliber. Offered in any standard SAAMI caliber. Magazine capacity is 3 rounds.

NIB	Exc.	V.G.	Good	Fair	Poor
3000	2400	1650	1050	575	300

BHR Big Game Professional Hunter Rifle

Introduced in 2005 this model has the same features as the PHR series with the addition of adjustable iron sights and specially designed stock. Weight is about 7.75 to 8.25 lbs. depending on caliber and barrel length.

NIB	Exc.	V.G.	Good	Fair	Poor
3100	2500	1850	1175	625	350

PHL Professional Hunter Lightweight Rifle

This model features a weight of 5.75 lbs. Fitted with a Pro-Series stock and choice of 20" or 22" contoured fluted stock. Matte

black teflon finish. Detachable magazine. Chambered for short action calibers. Introduced in 2005.

NIB	Exc.	V.G.	Good	Fair	Poor
3100	2500	1850	1175	625	350

VAR Varmint Rifle

Offered in long or short action with .17 Rem., 6mm PPC, and .223 Rem. in single-shot. Fitted with match grade stainless steel fluted barrel in 24" or 26" lengths. Also available is a lightweight 20" barrel. Synthetic stock in choice of colors with 20" barrel guns offered with thumbhole stocks. Black matte finish. Weight is between 8 and 8.25 lbs. for standard rifles and 7.5 and 7.75 lbs. for 20" barrel guns. Available in any standard SAAMI caliber.

NIB	Exc.	V.G.	Good	Fair	Poor
2600	2050	1650	1050	575	300

Varmint Take-Down Rifle

This take-down bolt-action rifle is offered in a stainless steel long or short action with 24" stainless steel match grade fluted barrel. Matte black finish. Weight is between 8.5 and 9 lbs. **NOTE:** Add $1,000 for extra barrel with same head size caliber and $1,200 for extra barrel with different head size caliber.

NIB	Exc.	V.G.	Good	Fair	Poor
3700	2900	2050	1450	600	400

Professional Hunter Take-Down Rifle

This take-down rifle is offered in magnum and super magnum calibers with 24" fluted stainless steel barrel. Built in recoil reducer. Matte black finish. Weight is between 8.25 and 8.75 lbs.

NIB	Exc.	V.G.	Good	Fair	Poor
4500	3200	2400	1650	750	450

Varmint Pistol

Bolt-action single-shot pistol chambered for a wide variety of calibers from .17 Rem. to 7mm BR. Fitted with a heavy contour fluted stainless steel match barrel. Synthetic stock with center grip. Matte black finish. Weight is about 5.25 to 5.5 lbs.

NIB	Exc.	V.G.	Good	Fair	Poor
2200	1500	950	600	400	225

Silhouette Pistol

Same as above but with sporter contoured barrel. Weight is about 4.5 lbs.

NIB	Exc.	V.G.	Good	Fair	Poor
2100	1400	950	600	400	225

HTR Heavy Tactical Rifle

This bolt-action model features a stainless steel long or short action with fluted stainless steel 24" heavy barrel. Stock is synthetic with adjustable cheekpiece and length of pull. Any standard SAAMI caliber is available. Weight is about 10.75 to 11.25 lbs. Matte black finish.

NIB	Exc.	V.G.	Good	Fair	Poor
2750	2250	1850	1175	625	350

Short Tactical

Chambered for the .308 cartridge and fitted with a 20" fluted barrel with matte teflon finish. Pro-Series tactical stock.

NIB	Exc.	V.G.	Good	Fair	Poor
2750	2250	1850	1175	625	350

RDR Rapid Deployment Rifle

This is similar to the model above but with 20" stainless steel fluted barrel and smaller stock. Thumbhole stock on request. Magazine is 4 rounds. Matte black finish. Offered in any short action SAAMI calibers. Weight is between 7.5 and 7.75 lbs.

NIB	Exc.	V.G.	Good	Fair	Poor
2750	2250	1850	1175	625	350

TTD Tactical Take-Down System

This take-down rifle is chambered for any standard SAAMI caliber and fitted with a 24" fluted heavy stainless steel barrel. Magazine capacity is 4 rounds for standard calibers and 3 rounds for magnum calibers. Synthetic stock that is adjustable for length of pull and cheekpiece. Matte black finish. Weight is between 11.25 and 11.75 lbs.

NIB	Exc.	V.G.	Good	Fair	Poor
4600	3800	2400	1650	750	450

HAENEL, C. G.
Suhl, Germany

Established in 1840, this company began to manufacture semi-automatic pistols after Hugo Schmeisser joined the firm in 1921 as its chief engineer.

Model 1

A 6.35mm caliber semi-automatic pistol with a 2.48" barrel, striker-fired, a 6-shot magazine. Weight is approximately 13.5 oz. The left side of the slide is stamped "C.G. Haenel Suhl-Schmeisser Patent". Each grip panel is marked "HS" in an oval.

NIB	Exc.	V.G.	Good	Fair	Poor
—	500	400	295	200	125

Model 2

As above, but shorter (2" barrel) and lighter in weight (12 oz.). "Schmeisser" is molded into the grips.

Courtesy Orvel Reichert

NIB	Exc.	V.G.	Good	Fair	Poor
—	550	425	350	225	150

HAFDASA
Buenos Aires, Argentina
Ballester-Molina

A copy of the Colt Model 1911 semi-automatic pistol differing only in the absence of a grip safety, smaller grip and the finger grooves on the slide. The slide stamped "Pistola Automatica Cal. .45 Fabricado por HAFDASA Patentes Internacional Ballester Molina Industria Argentina" on the slide. Introduced in 1941.

Courtesy James Rankin

NIB	Exc.	V.G.	Good	Fair	Poor
—	475	400	300	225	100

Criolla

A .22 caliber automatic pistol, similar to the Ballester-Molina. Some were sold commercially under the trademark "La Criolla".

NIB	Exc.	V.G.	Good	Fair	Poor
—	1000	800	650	500	250

Hafdasa

A .22 caliber semi-automatic pistol with a tubular receiver. A true hammerless, striker-fired, with an angled grip. Markings are "HA" on the butt.

NIB	Exc.	V.G.	Good	Fair	Poor
—	400	325	275	200	100

Zonda

As above, but marked "Zonda".

NIB	Exc.	V.G.	Good	Fair	Poor
—	400	325	275	200	100

Rigaud

A semi-automatic copy of the Colt Model 1911 with no grip safety. Caliber is .45 ACP and later .22 LR. Barrel length is 5". Magazine capacity is 7 rounds. The .22 caliber was introduced in 1940.

Courtesy James Rankin

NIB	Exc.	V.G.	Good	Fair	Poor
—	475	400	300	225	100

Campeon

The same as the Ballester-Molina but with a floating chamber to accommodate the .22 LR cartridge. There were three variations of the target model: Sights, trigger, and barrel lengths. The pistol was first introduced in 1941 and produced until 1953.

Courtesy James Rankin

NIB	Exc.	V.G.	Good	Fair	Poor
—	750	550	400	300	200

HAHN, WILLIAM
New York, New York

Pocket Pistol

A .41 caliber single-shot percussion pistol with a 2.5" round barrel, German silver mountings, and a walnut stock. Manufactured in the 1860s and 1870s.

NIB	Exc.	V.G.	Good	Fair	Poor
—	—	1950	1050	475	250

HALE, H. J.
Bristol, Connecticut

Under Hammer Pistol

A .31 caliber single-shot, under hammer percussion pistol with a 5" or 6" part-round, part-octagonal barrel and an iron frame with either a pointed or a round walnut butt. Markings read "H.J.Hale/Warranted/Cast Steel". Manufactured during the 1850s.

NIB	Exc.	V.G.	Good	Fair	Poor
—	—	995	375	245	125

HALE & TULLER
Hartford, Connecticut

Under Hammer Pistol

A .44 caliber single-shot under hammer percussion pistol with a 6" tapered round barrel and a pointed walnut grip. Manufactured at the Connecticut State Prison between 1837 and 1840.

NIB	Exc.	V.G.	Good	Fair	Poor
—	—	975	450	200	125

HALL, ALEXANDER
New York, New York

Revolving Rifle

A .58 caliber percussion revolving rifle with a 15-shot open centered cylinder. The frame was made of brass, the barrel and cylinder of iron and the stock of walnut. Manufactured during the 1850s in limited quantities. This is a very rare firearm.

NIB	Exc.	V.G.	Good	Fair	Poor
—	—	27500	12500	3750	1300

HALL-NORTH
Middletown, Connecticut

MODEL 1840 CARBINE

This carbine was manufactured by Simeon North and was chambered for .52 caliber percussion. It is a single-shot, breech-loading, smoothbore with a 21" round barrel. It has a full-length stock held on by two barrel bands. There is a ramrod mounted under the barrel, and the mountings are of iron. The lock is case hardened, and the barrel is brown. The stock is walnut. The markings are "US/S. North/Midltn/ Conn." There are two distinct variations, both produced under military contract.

Type 1 Carbine

This model has a squared, right-angled breech lever mounted on the trigger plate. There were 500 of these manufactured in 1840.

NIB	Exc.	V.G.	Good	Fair	Poor
—	—	9000	4000	1750	1000

Type 2 Carbine

This variation features a curved, breech-operating lever that is known as a fishtail. There were approximately 6,000 of these manufactured from 1840 to 1843. Some have an 8" bar and ring.

NIB	Exc.	V.G.	Good	Fair	Poor
—	—	7500	2500	1100	550

HAMBUSH, JOSEPH
Ferlach, Austria

Boxlock Side-by-Side Shotgun

A custom-order boxlock double-barrel shotgun chambered for all gauges, single-selective or double trigger and automatic ejectors. It features workmanship of a high order, and all specifications could vary with the customer's wishes. Engraved with hunting scenes. This is a rare gun and is not often encountered on today's market. **NOTE:** Pricing is only estimated as not enough are traded to provide accurate values.

NIB	Exc.	V.G.	Good	Fair	Poor
—	1950	1100	950	575	375

Sidelock Side-by-Side Shotgun

Similar to the above, but features a full sidelock-action.

NIB	Exc.	V.G.	Good	Fair	Poor
—	3800	2500	1750	1600	1350

HAMILTON RIFLE COMPANY
Plymouth, Michigan

Manufacturer of inexpensive .22 caliber rifles established by Clarence J. Hamilton and his son Coello. The company was established in 1898 in Plymouth, Michigan. The company ceased production in 1945. Over 1 million rifles were produced between 1900 and 1911.

NOTE: Despite the fact that there were many Hamilton rifles sold, most of these little guns were used hard and many did not survive. Hamilton rifles in excellent condition are hardly ever encountered. No prices are quoted for rifles in this condition as few exist. Further information about these rifles is gratefully accepted by the editor.

Model 7

The first rifle produced by the company, it was made entirely of castings and stampings. It was nickel plated. Chambered for the .22 Short cartridge with an 8" brass-lined barrel that pivots for loading. The stock was a metal skeleton. Production ceased in 1901 with a total of 44,000 rifles produced.

Hamilton Model 7

Courtesy William F. Krause

NIB	Exc.	V.G.	Good	Fair	Poor
—	750	500	450	300	195

Model 11

Similar to the Model 7 but fitted with a board-like walnut stock. There are markings stamped into the buttstock: "Hamilton Rifles Co., Plymouth, Mich., Pat. Pending No. 11".. The Model 11 was produced from 1900 to 1902 and approximately 22,000 were sold.

NIB	Exc.	V.G.	Good	Fair	Poor
—	700	475	300	200	150

Model 15

Produced from 1901 to 1910 the Model 15 was chambered for the .22 Short with an 8" brass lined barrel. Walnut stock. The design was an under lever single-shot with the loading port under the barrel. The cocking knob is located at the rear of the frame. Blued finish. Approximately 234,000 of these rifles were sold.

NIB	Exc.	V.G.	Good	Fair	Poor
—	675	400	200	150	100

Model 19

This is similar to the Model 15 with a modified loading port and a 12" barrel. A few Model 19s have been seen with 13" barrels. These will bring a premium. Produced from 1903 to 1910 there were about 59,000 of these models sold.

NIB	Exc.	V.G.	Good	Fair	Poor
—	700	475	300	200	150

Model 23

This was the first bolt-action rifle made by the company. The receiver is a steel tube with a loading port in the top where the barrel joins the receiver. The bolt handle is located at the extreme rear of the bolt. The cocking knob must be operated manually. Walnut stock either rounded or flat. Chamber for the .22 Short and .22

Long cartridges. 15" brass lined barrel. Blued finish. Weighs about 3 lbs. Produced from 1905 to 1909. About 25,000 guns were sold.

NIB	Exc.	V.G.	Good	Fair	Poor
—	700	475	300	200	150

Model 27

Single-shot tip-up .22 caliber rifle with stamped steel receiver. Barrel length 16" brass lined or 14-7/8"; overall length 30". First produced in 1906.

NIB	Exc.	V.G.	Good	Fair	Poor
	475	300	200	150	100

Model 027

As above with a walnut stock. First produced in 1908.

NIB	Exc.	V.G.	Good	Fair	Poor
—	495	300	200	150	100

Model 31

Introduced in 1910 this single-shot rifle is chambered for the .22 Short and Long cartridge. Fitted with a 15.75" barrel with brass liner. It is a tip-up design. Blued finish. Weighs about 2.25 lbs.

NIB	Exc.	V.G.	Good	Fair	Poor
—	725	575	400	250	200

Model 35 or Boys' Military Rifle

Single-shot .22 caliber rifle with a full-length oval walnut straight-grip stock and 15.75" brass lined barrel. Produced from 1915 to 1918. Sold with a stamped steel bayonet. Few bayonets survive. **NOTE:** Add $150 for bayonet to prices.

NIB	Exc.	V.G.	Good	Fair	Poor
—	950	700	450	250	125

Model 39

This was the only repeating rifle built by the company. It is a hammerless slide-action design with a tubular magazine. Magazine capacity is 15 rounds of .22 Short. Barrel length is 16" with brass liner. Walnut stock with blade front sight. Produced from 1922 to 1930. Weighs about 4 lbs.

NIB	Exc.	V.G.	Good	Fair	Poor
—	575	300	200	150	100

Model 43

This is a bolt-action design with the loading port on the top of the barrel. There is no external cocking knob but the bolt is pulled to the rear when in the locked position. Chambered for the .22 Short and .22 Long cartridges. 15.75" brass lined barrel. Fitted with an oval walnut stock with blade front sight and open non-adjustable rear sight. Weighs about 3 lbs. Built from 1924 to 1932.

NIB	Exc.	V.G.	Good	Fair	Poor
—	575	300	200	150	100

Model 47

This is a bolt-action single-shot rifle with the loading port located on top of the barrel. It was chambered for the .22 Short and Long cartridges. The cocking knob is located at the rear of the bolt handle. Early Model 47 were built with 16" brass lined barrels. Later examples were fitted with 18.25" steel lined barrels. Early guns had an oval buttstock while later guns had a pistol grip stock. Very late guns had an all-steel barrel. Produced from 1927 to 1932.

NIB	Exc.	V.G.	Good	Fair	Poor
—	575	475	300	200	150

Model 51

This was a conventional type bolt-action rifle with the cocking knob located at the rear of the bolt. Two styles of buttstocks were used: a flat style or later an oval shape. This was the first Hamilton rifle chambered for the .22 LR cartridge. Barrel was 20" steel. Finish was blue. Weight was approximately 3.5 lbs. Produced from 1935 to 1941.

NIB	Exc.	V.G.	Good	Fair	Poor
—	550	400	250	200	150

Model 55

This bolt-action rifle was chambered for the .22 Short, Long, and LR cartridges. Fitted with a 20" steel barrel with bead front sight and open adjustable rear sight. Walnut stock. This is the rarest Hamilton rifle. Only one example is known. Produced from late 1941 to early 1942.

NIB	Exc.	V.G.	Good	Fair	Poor
—	1000	—	—	—	—

HAMMERLI, SA
Lenzburg, Switzerland

RIFLES

Model 45 Smallbore Rifle

A .22 caliber bolt-action single-shot, with a 27.5" heavy barrel, an aperture rear and globe target front sight and a match rifle-type thumbhole stock. Manufactured between 1945 and 1957.

NIB	Exc.	V.G.	Good	Fair	Poor
—	825	700	595	450	250

Model 54 Smallbore Rifle

As above, with an adjustable buttplate. Manufactured between 1954 and 1957.

NIB	Exc.	V.G.	Good	Fair	Poor
—	850	725	625	475	275

Model 503 Smallbore Free Rifle

Similar to the Model 54, with a free rifle-style stock.

NIB	Exc.	V.G.	Good	Fair	Poor
—	800	675	575	450	225

Model 506 Smallbore Match Rifle

The later version of the Smallbore target series. Manufactured between 1963 and 1966.

NIB	Exc.	V.G.	Good	Fair	Poor
—	850	725	625	475	275

Olympic 300 Meter

A 7x57, .30-06, or .300 H&H Magnum caliber bolt-action, single-shot, rifle with a 20.5" heavy barrel, an aperture rear, globe target front sight, double-set triggers and a free rifle-type, adjustable thumbhole stock with a wide beavertail forearm and schuetzen-style buttplate. Manufactured between 1945 and 1959.

NIB	Exc.	V.G.	Good	Fair	Poor
—	1050	900	725	550	325

Sporting Rifle

A bolt-action, single-shot rifle chambered for many popular calibers (American and European), double-set triggers and a classic-style stock.

NIB	Exc.	V.G.	Good	Fair	Poor
—	800	675	575	450	225

PISTOLS

Model 100 Free Pistol

A .22 caliber single-shot Martini-action target pistol with an 11.5" octagonal barrel, adjustable sights, single set trigger and walnut stocks. Manufactured from 1933 to 1949.

NIB	Exc.	V.G.	Good	Fair	Poor
—	1000	825	700	550	325

Model 101

As above, with a heavy round barrel and more sophisticated target sights. A matte-blued finish and was manufactured between 1956 and 1960.

NIB	Exc.	V.G.	Good	Fair	Poor
—	1000	825	700	550	325

Model 102

As above, with highly polished blue finish. Manufactured between 1956 and 1960.

NIB	Exc.	V.G.	Good	Fair	Poor
—	1000	825	700	550	325

Model 103

Similar to the Model 101, with a lighter-weight octagonal barrel, high-polished blued finish. Manufactured between 1956 and 1960.

NIB	Exc.	V.G.	Good	Fair	Poor
—	1100	925	825	650	425

Model 104

As above, with a lightweight round barrel. Manufactured between 1961 and 1965.

NIB	Exc.	V.G.	Good	Fair	Poor
—	950	625	550	450	300

Model 105

As above, with a redesigned stock and an improved action. Manufactured between 1962 and 1965.

NIB	Exc.	V.G.	Good	Fair	Poor
—	950	625	550	450	300

Model 106

As above, with an improved trigger.

NIB	Exc.	V.G.	Good	Fair	Poor
—	950	625	550	450	300

Model 107

This variation is fitted with a five-level set trigger. Introduced in 1965 and discontinued in 1971.

NIB	Exc.	V.G.	Good	Fair	Poor
—	950	625	550	450	300

Model 107 Deluxe

As above, but engraved and with a carved stock.

NIB	Exc.	V.G.	Good	Fair	Poor
—	1500	1250	900	800	500

Model 120-1 Free Pistol

A bolt-action, single-shot pistol in .22 LR caliber with a a 9.9" barrel, adjustable target sights, activated for loading and cocking by an alloy lever on the side of the bolt. Blued, with checkered walnut grips

NIB	Exc.	V.G.	Good	Fair	Poor
—	1200	975	600	425	250

Model 120-2

As above with contoured grips.

NIB	Exc.	V.G.	Good	Fair	Poor
—	1200	975	600	425	250

Model 120 Heavy Barrel

As above, with a 5.7" heavy barrel.

NIB	Exc.	V.G.	Good	Fair	Poor
—	1200	975	600	425	250

Model 150

A single-shot, Martini-action .22 caliber pistol with an 11.25" barrel, adjustable sights, contoured grips and a single-set trigger. Blued with walnut stocks.

NIB	Exc.	V.G.	Good	Fair	Poor
—	1500	1100	775	500	350

Model 152

As above, with an 11.25" barrel, and an electronic release trigger.

NIB	Exc.	V.G.	Good	Fair	Poor
—	1800	1300	1050	600	450

International Model 206

A .22 caliber semi-automatic pistol with a 7.5" barrel, an integral muzzlebrake, adjustable sights, and walnut grips. Manufactured between 1962 and 1969.

NIB	Exc.	V.G.	Good	Fair	Poor
—	825	700	575	425	300

International Model 207

As above, with adjustable grips.

NIB	Exc.	V.G.	Good	Fair	Poor
—	850	725	600	450	325

International Model 208

A .22 caliber semi-automatic pistol with a 6" barrel, adjustable sights and an 8-shot magazine, adjustable trigger, and target grips. The barrel is drilled and tapped for the addition of barrel weights. Manufactured between 1966 and 1988.

NIB	Exc.	V.G.	Good	Fair	Poor
—	1850	1550	1250	1000	750

International Model 208 Deluxe

As above, with an engraved receiver, and carved grips. Discontinued in 1988.

NIB	Exc.	V.G.	Good	Fair	Poor
—	3250	2750	2500	2000	1500

International Model 209

A .22 Short caliber semi-automatic pistol with a 4.75" barrel, a muzzlebrake, adjustable target sights, and 5-shot magazine. Blued, with walnut grips. Manufactured between 1966 and 1970.

NIB	Exc.	V.G.	Good	Fair	Poor
—	1200	975	600	425	250

International Model 210

As above, with adjustable grips.

NIB	Exc.	V.G.	Good	Fair	Poor
—	1225	1000	625	450	275

International Model 211

As above, with non-adjustable thumb rest grips.

NIB	Exc.	V.G.	Good	Fair	Poor
—	1300	1075	700	475	300

Model 212

A .22 caliber semi-automatic pistol with a 5" barrel, and adjustable sights. Blued with walnut grips.

NIB	Exc.	V.G.	Good	Fair	Poor
—	1300	1075	700	475	300

Model 230

A .22 Short caliber semi-automatic pistol with a 6.3" barrel, a 5-shot magazine, adjustable sights and walnut grip. Manufactured between 1970 and 1983.

NIB	Exc.	V.G.	Good	Fair	Poor
—	1350	1125	750	525	325

Model 232

A .22 short caliber semi-automatic pistol with a 5" barrel, adjustable sights, and a 6-shot magazine. Contoured walnut grips. Introduced in 1984.

NIB	Exc.	V.G.	Good	Fair	Poor
—	1300	1075	700	475	300

Model 280

This is the new state-of-the-art target pistol from Hammerli. It features a modular design and has a frame of carbon fiber material. It has a 4.6" barrel with adjustable sights, trigger, and grips. It is chambered for .22 LR or .32 wadcutter. The magazine holds 5 rounds, and the pistol was introduced in 1988.

NIB	Exc.	V.G.	Good	Fair	Poor
—	1800	1500	1350	1000	600

Model SP 20

Introduced in 1998, this pistol has a very low sight line and features a wide variety of special items such as adjustable buffer system, anatomically shaped trigger in various sizes, various receiver colors, change over caliber system from .22 LR to .32 S&W.

NIB	Exc.	V.G.	Good	Fair	Poor
1750	1325	900	800	500	—

HAMMERLI-WALTHER
Lenzburg, Switzerland

These target pistols were produced by Hammerli under license from Walther after WWII. This project continued until approximately 1963, when production was ceased.

Olympia Model 200 Type 1952

A .22 caliber semi-automatic pistol with a 7.5" barrel, a 10-shot magazine, adjustable target sights, and a blued with walnut grips. Manufactured between 1952 and 1958.

NIB	Exc.	V.G.	Good	Fair	Poor
—	900	775	575	475	350

Model 200 Type 1958

As above with an integral muzzlebrake. Manufactured between 1958 and 1963.

NIB	Exc.	V.G.	Good	Fair	Poor
—	950	725	625	495	350

Model 201

A Model 200 Type 1952 with a 9.5" barrel. Manufactured between 1955 and 1957.

NIB	Exc.	V.G.	Good	Fair	Poor
—	950	725	625	495	350

Model 202

Similar to the Model 201, with adjustable walnut grips. Manufactured between 1955 and 1957.

NIB	Exc.	V.G.	Good	Fair	Poor
—	950	725	625	495	350

Model 203

Similar to the Model 200, with the adjustable grips, available with or without a muzzlebrake.

NIB	Exc.	V.G.	Good	Fair	Poor
—	950	725	625	495	350

Model 204

A .22 caliber semi-automatic pistol with a 7.5" barrel, a muzzlebrake, and barrel weights. Manufactured between 1956 and 1963.

NIB	Exc.	V.G.	Good	Fair	Poor
—	975	750	650	525	375

Model 205

As above, with adjustable target grips. Manufactured between 1956 and 1963.

NIB	Exc.	V.G.	Good	Fair	Poor
—	1000	775	675	575	450

HAMMOND BULLDOG
Connecticut Arms & Mfg. Co.
Naubuc, Connecticut

Hammond Bulldog

A .44 rimfire single-shot spur trigger pistol with a 4" octagonal barrel that pivots to open. Blued with checkered walnut grips. Manufactured from 1864 to approximately 1867.

NIB	Exc.	V.G.	Good	Fair	Poor
—	775	550	375	250	100

HAMMOND MFG. CO., GRANT
New Haven, Connecticut
Military Automatic Pistol

A .45 ACP caliber semi-automatic pistol with a 6.75" barrel and an 8-shot magazine. Blued, with checkered walnut grips. Marked on the right of the slide "Grant Hammond Mfg. Corp. New Haven, Conn." The left side shows the patent dates. Manufactured in 1917. As all the known specimens of this pistol exhibit differences, it is believed that they were only made as prototypes. The highest serial number known is under 20. **TOO RARE TO PRICE.**

Courtesy Horst Held

Grant Hammond 7.65mm Pistol

A semi-automatic pistol in 7.65mm caliber. Has a blow-forward action and a spur hammer. **TOO RARE TO PRICE.**

Courtesy James Rankin

H&R 1871, LLC
Gardner, Massachusetts
See—Harrington & Richardson

HANKINS, WILLIAM
Philadelphia, Pennsylvania

Pocket Revolver

A .26 caliber spur trigger percussion revolver with a 3" octagonal barrel, and a 5-shot unfluted cylinder. Blued with walnut grips. Approximately 650 were manufactured in 1860 and 1861.

Courtesy Milwaukee Public Museum, Milwaukee, Wisconsin

NIB	Exc.	V.G.	Good	Fair	Poor
—	—	3250	1700	600	200

HANUS, BILL
Newport, Oregon

Bill Hanus Classic

Bill Hanus is a dealer and importer of various European shotguns. In the 1980s and 1990s he imported his own private brand of side-by-side doubles, from Ignacio Ugartechea in Italy, in 16, 20, 28 gauges and .410 bore. These guns had double triggers, ejectors and English-style stocks.

NIB	Exc.	V.G.	Good	Fair	Poor
2500	2000	1350	900	625	350

HARRINGTON & RICHARDSON, INC.
Madison, North Carolina

Established in 1877 by G.H. Harrington and W.A. Richardson. The arms originally produced by this company were marketed under the trade name Aetna. In November 2000 the Marlin Firearms Company purchased the assets of Harrington & Richardson. In 2008 it was announced that H&R/NEF/Marlin had been acquired by Remington Arms, and that H&R's Gardner, Mass., plant would be closed and absorbed into Remington's existing production facilities.

Model No. 1

A .32 or .38 caliber spur-trigger single-action revolver with a 3" octagonal barrel, solid frame, a 7-shot or a 5-shot cylinder, depending on the caliber. Nickel-plated with checkered rubber bird's-head grips. Barrel marked "Harrington & Richardson Worcester, Mass." Approximately 3,000 were manufactured in 1877 and 1878.

NIB	Exc.	V.G.	Good	Fair	Poor
—	300	250	200	125	75

Model No. 1-1/2

A .32 caliber spur-trigger, single-action revolver with a 2.5" octagonal barrel and a 5-shot cylinder. Nickel-plated, round-butt rubber grips with an "H&R" emblem molded in. Approximately 10,000 were manufactured between 1878 and 1883.

NIB	Exc.	V.G.	Good	Fair	Poor
—	300	150	125	75	50

Model No. 2-1/2

As above, with a 3.25" barrel and a 7-shot cylinder. Approximately 5,000 were manufactured between 1878 and 1883.

NIB	Exc.	V.G.	Good	Fair	Poor
—	300	150	125	75	50

Model No. 3-1/2

Similar to the Model 2-1/2 except in .38 rimfire caliber with a 3.5" barrel and a 5-shot cylinder. Approximately 2,500 were manufactured.

NIB	Exc.	V.G.	Good	Fair	Poor
—	300	175	150	100	75

Model No. 4-1/2

A .41 rimfire caliber spur trigger revolver with a 2.5" barrel and 5-shot cylinder. Approximately 1,000 were manufactured.

NIB	Exc.	V.G.	Good	Fair	Poor
—	600	400	200	125	90

Model 1880

A .32 or .38 S&W centerfire caliber double-action revolver with a 3" round barrel, a solid frame, and a 5- or 6-shot cylinder, depending on the caliber. Nickel-plated with hard rubber grips. Marked "Harrington & Richardson Worchester, Mass." Approximately 4,000 were manufactured between 1880 and 1883.

NIB	Exc.	V.G.	Good	Fair	Poor
—	250	200	175	125	90

The American Double-Action

A .32, .28, or .44 centerfire caliber double-action revolver with a 2.5", 4.5", or 6" round or octagonal barrel, a 5- or 6-shot fluted cylinder, depending on the caliber, and solid frame, nickel-plated, with some blue models noted. The grips are hard rubber. Marked "The American Double Action." Some noted are marked "H&R Bulldog." Approximately 850,000 were manufactured between 1883 and 1940. Add 150 percent for .44.

NIB	Exc.	V.G.	Good	Fair	Poor
—	250	125	100	85	65

The Young America Double-Action

A .22 rimfire or .32 S&W centerfire caliber, double-action revolver, with 2", 4.5", or 6" round or octagonal barrels, solid frame, and a 5- or 7-shot cylinder, depending on the caliber. Blued or nickel-plated, with hard rubber grips. Marked "Young America Double Action" or "Young America Bulldog." Approximately 1,500,000 were manufactured between 1884 and 1941.

NIB	Exc.	V.G.	Good	Fair	Poor
—	200	125	100	85	65

Hunter

A .22 caliber double-action revolver with a 10" octagonal barrel and a 9-shot fluted cylinder. Blued, with checkered walnut grips.

NIB	Exc.	V.G.	Good	Fair	Poor
—	400	300	200	150	100

Trapper

As above, with a 6" octagonal barrel and a 7-shot cylinder. Otherwise it is similar to the Hunter.

NIB	Exc.	V.G.	Good	Fair	Poor
—	300	200	125	100	75

Self-Loader

A 6.35mm or 7.65mm semi-automatic pistol with a 2" or 3.5" barrel, a 6- or 8-shot magazine. Similar in outline to the Webley. The larger 7.65 model has a grip safety. Blued or nickel-plated with checkered, hard rubber grips that bear the H&R monogram. The slide is marked, "H&R Self-Loading" with 1907 or 1909 patent dates. Approximately 16,500 were manufactured in 6.35mm between 1912 and 1916 and 34,500 in 7.65mm manufactured between 1916 and 1924. Add 10 percent for .32.

NIB	Exc.	V.G.	Good	Fair	Poor
—	500	400	275	200	125

First Model Hand Ejector

A .32 or .38 centerfire caliber double-action revolver with a 3.25" ribbed round barrel. This version does not feature the automatic ejection found on later models. Nickel-plated, with hard rubber grips. The company name is marked on the barrel. Approximately 6,000 were manufactured between 1886 and 1888.

NIB	Exc.	V.G.	Good	Fair	Poor
—	200	150	125	90	65

Model 1 Double-Action Revolver

A .32, .32 Long, and the .38 S&W caliber double-action revolver with a 3.25" ribbed round barrel, and a 5- or 6-shot cylinder, depending on the caliber. Nickel-plated, with hard rubber grips. Approximately 5,000 were manufactured between 1887 and 1889.

NIB	Exc.	V.G.	Good	Fair	Poor
—	175	145	110	80	50

Model 2

Similar to the Model 1, with 2.5", 3.25", 4", 5", or 6" barrels. The grips feature the H&R target logo. There were approximately 1,300,000 manufactured between 1889 and 1940.

NIB	Exc.	V.G.	Good	Fair	Poor
—	125	100	80	65	40

Knife Model

The Model 2 with a 4" ribbed round barrel having a folding 2.25" double-edged knife mounted under the barrel. Blued or nickel-plated. Approximately 2,000 were manufactured between 1901 and 1917.

NIB	Exc.	V.G.	Good	Fair	Poor
—	1500	1000	700	500	150

Model 922 First Issue

A .22 caliber double-action revolver with a 2.5", 4", or 6" barrel. Blued, with checkered walnut grips.

NIB	Exc.	V.G.	Good	Fair	Poor
—	150	125	100	75	50

Target Model

A .22 LR or .22 WRF caliber double-action revolver with 7-shot cylinder, a break-open frame and a 6" barrel with fixed sights. Blued, with checkered walnut grips.

NIB	Exc.	V.G.	Good	Fair	Poor
—	150	125	100	75	50

.22 Special

A .22 LR or the .22 WRF double-action, break-open revolver with a 6" barrel and a 7-shot cylinder. Blued, with checkered walnut grips.

NIB	Exc.	V.G.	Good	Fair	Poor
—	300	200	125	90	65

Expert

As above, with a 10" barrel.

NIB	Exc.	V.G.	Good	Fair	Poor
—	400	300	200	100	50

No. 199 Sportsman

A .22 caliber single-action, break-open revolver with a 6" barrel, adjustable target sights and a 9-shot cylinder. Blued, with checkered walnut grips.

NIB	Exc.	V.G.	Good	Fair	Poor
—	275	200	150	100	75

Ultra Sportsman

As above, but more finely finished with a special, wide target hammer and an improved action.

NIB	Exc.	V.G.	Good	Fair	Poor
—	325	215	175	125	90

Defender

A .38 S&W caliber double-action, break-open revolver with a 4" or 6" barrel and fixed sights. Blued, with plastic grips.

NIB	Exc.	V.G.	Good	Fair	Poor
—	275	200	145	75	50

New Defender

A .22 caliber double-action, break-open revolver with a 2" barrel and a 9-shot cylinder. Blued with checkered, walnut round-butt grips.

NIB	Exc.	V.G.	Good	Fair	Poor
—	225	200	175	125	90

.22 U.S.R.A./Model 195 Single-Shot Match Target Pistol

Also called the Model 195, this pistol underwent nearly constant modifications from its inception in 1928 until production ceased in 1941. Its development was greatly influenced by the United States Revolver Association (USRA), which established certain rules for target pistol shooting. The lack of any H&R-published model chronology for the estimated 3,500 guns manufactured makes model determination by examination complicated; a further difficulty is that H&R supplied newly designed parts to owners of older variations, who would then retrofit their pistols with newer triggers, hammers, sights, and trigger guards. Extracted from the available literature, the parts represent approximately: 14 different stocks and virtually endless custom variations by Walter F. Roper; 5 different trigger guards; 3 different triggers; 2 different hammers; 2 different extractors; 3 barrel lengths (7", 8", 10"); and 3 barrel rib styles. From this array of potential characteristics, at least four distinct variations can be identified.

.22 U.S.R.A./Model 195 Pistol, Variations 1 to 3

NIB	Exc.	V.G.	Good	Fair	Poor
—	2500	1800	1000	600	200

.22 U.S.R.A./Model 195 Pistol, Variation 4

NIB	Exc.	V.G.	Good	Fair	Poor
—	2200	1500	800	325	250

Variation 1, pre-U.S.R.A., 1928-30: Not marked **U.S.R.A.**, and known as the "H&R Single-Shot Pistol." There is no finger rest between the trigger guard and front grip strap; it was advertised with "sawhandle" shape grip copied from the Model 1 or 2 smooth bore H&R Handy-Gun, manufactured with a 10" "hourglass" barrel with a deeply undercut rib. These are the first 500 pistols.

Variation 2, U.S.R.A. Keyhole Barrel, 1930-31: This is the standard "early" model marked **U.S.R.A.**, has a finger rest, and non-sawhandle grips; however, several grip shapes were offered as options. The grip screw goes from rear of grip into threaded hold in back grip strap.

Variation 3, Modified Keyhole Barrel, 1931: Modification of Variation 2 to improve rear sight, barrel catch changed, reduced spent cartridge force by replacing cylindrical extractor with less powerful hinged type, and the hammer cocking spur and finger rest were made wider. The 8" barrel was offered as an option to standard 10" length, and the number of different grip shapes was increased. This is a transition model between "early" Variation 2 and "final" Variation 4 designs.

Variation 4, Tapered Slabside Barrel, 1931-41: New "truncated teardrop" barrel cross section shape; new standard barrel length of 7", with 10" optional; adjustable trigger; new sear; grip screw location was changed to front of grip; and front sight was adjustable for elevation. The trigger design was changed from curved to straight beveled type with relocated cocking surfaces, and the number of grip shapes increased further to 13 types. A front sight protector was supplied as standard equipment, and luggage style case offered as an option. It appears that Variation 4 was introduced around 1931; the 1932 advertisements describe the fully redesigned gun, but picture Variation 2, indicating H&R probably did not re-photograph the new design. The final variation has a special, tight bore .217" in diameter, with bullet seating .03125" (1/32") into rifling, and is among the most accurate of single-shot .22 caliber pistols. The Model 195/U.S.R.A. was relatively expensive, costing approximately $30 in 1932, and increased to slightly more than $36 by the time production ended in 1941, yet was the least expensive of all single-shot .22 target pistols of quality.

Model 504

A .32 H&R Magnum caliber double-action, swing-out cylinder revolver with a 4" or 6" heavy barrel, adjustable sights, and 5-shot cylinder. Blued, with either black plastic or walnut grips. Smaller version manufactured with a 3" or 4" barrel and a round butt.

NIB	Exc.	V.G.	Good	Fair	Poor
—	350	275	150	90	65

Model 532

As above, but with a cylinder that has to be removed for loading. Manufactured in 1984 and 1985.

NIB	Exc.	V.G.	Good	Fair	Poor
—	275	175	125	75	50

Model 586

A .32 H&R Magnum caliber double-action revolver with a 4.5", 5.5", 7.5", or 10" barrel, adjustable sights and a 5-shot cylinder. Blued, with either black plastic or walnut grips.

NIB	Exc.	V.G.	Good	Fair	Poor
—	325	275	175	150	100

Model 603

A .22 rimfire Magnum caliber double-action revolver with a 6" flat-sided barrel and swing-out 6-shot cylinder. Blued, with smooth walnut grips.

NIB	Exc.	V.G.	Good	Fair	Poor
—	225	165	140	110	85

Model 604

As above, with a 6", ribbed, heavy barrel.

NIB	Exc.	V.G.	Good	Fair	Poor
—	295	215	175	125	100

Model 622

A .22 caliber solid-frame double-action revolver with a 2.5" or 4" barrel. Blued, with round-butt plastic grips.

NIB	Exc.	V.G.	Good	Fair	Poor
—	150	100	65	50	25

Model 623

As above, but nickel-plated.

NIB	Exc.	V.G.	Good	Fair	Poor
—	165	110	80	60	40

Model 632

As above in .32 centerfire.

NIB	Exc.	V.G.	Good	Fair	Poor
—	150	90	75	60	30

Model 642

As above, in .22 rimfire Magnum.

NIB	Exc.	V.G.	Good	Fair	Poor
—	150	80	65	50	25

Model 649

The Model 622, with a 5.5" or 7.5" barrel.

NIB	Exc.	V.G.	Good	Fair	Poor
—	150	125	100	75	50

Model 650

As above, but nickel-plated.

NIB	Exc.	V.G.	Good	Fair	Poor
—	175	150	125	75	50

Model 660

A .22 caliber solid-frame, Western-style revolver with a 5.5" barrel and is a double-action. Blued, with walnut grips. It is also known as the "Gunfighter".

NIB	Exc.	V.G.	Good	Fair	Poor
—	150	125	100	50	25

Model 666

A .22 or .22 rimfire Magnum caliber double-action revolver with a 6" barrel and a 6-shot cylinder. Blued, with plastic grips. Manufactured between 1976 and 1982.

NIB	Exc.	V.G.	Good	Fair	Poor
—	150	125	100	50	25

Model 676

Similar to the Model 660. Blued, with a case colored frame. It has walnut grips. Manufactured between 1976 and 1982.

NIB	Exc.	V.G.	Good	Fair	Poor
—	175	150	100	75	50

Model 686

Similar to the Model 660 "Gunfighter" with a 4.5", 5.5", 7.5", 10", or 12" barrel.

NIB	Exc.	V.G.	Good	Fair	Poor
—	175	150	125	100	75

Model 732

A .32 caliber double-action, solid-frame revolver with a swingout cylinder, a 2.5" or 4" barrel and a 6-shot cylinder. Blued, with black plastic grips. Also known as the "Guardsman."

NIB	Exc.	V.G.	Good	Fair	Poor
—	150	125	90	65	45

Model 733

As above, but nickel-plated and a 2.5" barrel.

NIB	Exc.	V.G.	Good	Fair	Poor
—	175	150	100	75	50

Model 900

A .22 caliber solid-frame revolver with a removable cylinder, a 2.5", 4", or 6" barrel and a 9-shot cylinder. Blued, with black plastic grips. Manufactured between 1962 and 1973.

NIB	Exc.	V.G.	Good	Fair	Poor
—	150	125	90	60	40

Model 901

As above, but chrome-plated with white plastic grips. Manufactured in 1962 and 1963 only.

NIB	Exc.	V.G.	Good	Fair	Poor
—	150	125	90	60	40

Model 903

As above, with a swing-out cylinder, a flat-sided, 6" barrel, and a 9-shot cylinder. Blued, with walnut grips.

NIB	Exc.	V.G.	Good	Fair	Poor
—	150	125	90	75	50

Model 904

As above, with a ribbed heavy barrel.

NIB	Exc.	V.G.	Good	Fair	Poor
—	175	150	125	100	50

Model 905

As above, but nickel-plated.

NIB	Exc.	V.G.	Good	Fair	Poor
—	200	175	150	80	65

Model 922 Second Issue

A .22 rimfire caliber solid-frame revolver with a 2.5", 4", or 6" barrel. Blued, with black plastic grips. Manufactured between 1950 and 1982.

NIB	Exc.	V.G.	Good	Fair	Poor
—	150	90	80	60	40

Model 923

As above, but nickel-plated.

NIB	Exc.	V.G.	Good	Fair	Poor
—	160	90	80	60	40

Model 925

A .38 S&W caliber double-action, break-open, hand ejector revolver with a 2.5" barrel, adjustable sights and a 5-shot cylinder. Blued, with a one-piece wraparound grip. Manufactured between 1964 and 1984.

NIB	Exc.	V.G.	Good	Fair	Poor
—	250	175	125	75	50

Model 935

As above, but nickel-plated.

NIB	Exc.	V.G.	Good	Fair	Poor
—	260	200	150	100	50

Model 929

A .22 rimfire solid-frame, swing-out revolver with a 2.5", 4", or 6" barrel and a 9-shot cylinder. Blued, with plastic grips. It is also known as the "Sidekick." Manufactured between 1956 and 1985.

NIB	Exc.	V.G.	Good	Fair	Poor
—	225	150	125	65	45

Model 929 Sidekick—New Model

Reintroduced in 1996 this single- and double-action revolver chambered for the .22 short, long, or LR cartridges. Cylinder holds 9 rounds. Sold with a lockable storage case, nylon holster, and gun oil and gun grease samples. Weighs about 30 oz. Discontinued. Made from 1996 - 1999.

NIB	Exc.	V.G.	Good	Fair	Poor
250	175	150	100	75	50

Model 929 Sidekick Trapper Edition

Same as above but with grey laminate grips and special "NTA" Trapper Edition roll stamp on barrel. Made in 1996.

NIB	Exc.	V.G.	Good	Fair	Poor
275	175	150	100	75	50

Model 930

As above, but nickel-plated and not available with a 6" barrel.

NIB	Exc.	V.G.	Good	Fair	Poor
—	250	150	125	65	45

Model 939 Ultra Sidekick

As above, with a ventilated rib, flat sided 6" barrel, adjustable sights, thumb rest grips and features a safety device whereby the pistol could not be fired unless it was unlocked by a furnished key. Manufactured between 1958 and 1982.

NIB	Exc.	V.G.	Good	Fair	Poor
—	225	200	150	75	50

Model 939 Premier

Similar to the above models but fitted with a 6" barrel with sighting rib, adjustable rear sight, hard wood grips, high polished blued finish. Weighs about 36 oz. Made from 1995 - 1999.

NIB	Exc.	V.G.	Good	Fair	Poor
250	225	200	125	75	50

Model 940

A round-barreled version of the above.

NIB	Exc.	V.G.	Good	Fair	Poor
—	225	200	125	75	50

Model 949

A .22 caliber double-action, Western-type revolver with a 5.5" barrel with an ejector rod, 9-shot, gate-loaded cylinder and adjustable sights. Blued, with walnut grips. Manufactured between 1960 and 1985.

NIB	Exc.	V.G.	Good	Fair	Poor
—	200	175	150	75	50

Model 949 Western

Similar to the above model this revolver is offered with a choice of 5.5" or 7.5" barrel. Adjustable rear sight, walnut grips, and case colored frame and backstrap with blued cylinder and barrel. Weight is about 36 oz.

NIB	Exc.	V.G.	Good	Fair	Poor
250	200	150	100	75	50

Model 950

As above, but nickel-plated.

NIB	Exc.	V.G.	Good	Fair	Poor
—	250	175	125	75	50

Model 976

As above, with a case-hardened frame.

NIB	Exc.	V.G.	Good	Fair	Poor
—	200	150	100	75	50

Model 999 Sportsman

A .22 rimfire caliber double-action, break-open, self ejecting revolver with a 6" or 4" barrel ventilated rib barrel and windage

adjustable sights. Blued, with walnut grips. Weighs about 30 oz. with 4" barrel and 34 oz. with 6" barrel.

NIB	Exc.	V.G.	Good	Fair	Poor
500	425	350	295	175	100

Model 999 Engraved

As above, but engraved.

NIB	Exc.	V.G.	Good	Fair	Poor
550	450	375	300	200	125

Amtec 2000

This is a German-designed (Erma) and American-built double-action revolver introduced in 1996. Offered in 2" or 3" barrel and chambered for .38 Special cartridge. Pachmayr composition grips. Cylinder holds 5 rounds. Weight is approximately 25 oz. Discontinued.

NIB	Exc.	V.G.	Good	Fair	Poor
250	200	200	150	75	50

SHOTGUNS

Hammerless Double

A 10 or 12 gauge Anson & Deeley hammerless boxlock double-barrel shotgun with 28", 30", or 32" Damascus barrels in various choke combinations, double triggers and extractors. Engraved, case hardened and walnut stock. Four grades were available. They differ in the amount of engraving and the quality of materials and workmanship utilized. Approximately 3,500 were manufactured between 1882 and 1885.

D Grade

NIB	Exc.	V.G.	Good	Fair	Poor
—	650	550	425	300	175

C Grade

NIB	Exc.	V.G.	Good	Fair	Poor
—	750	650	500	400	275

B Grade

NIB	Exc.	V.G.	Good	Fair	Poor
—	900	750	600	500	350

A Grade

NIB	Exc.	V.G.	Good	Fair	Poor
—	2000	1750	1500	1000	550

Harrich No. 1

A 12 gauge boxlock single barrel shotgun with a 32" or 34", ventilated rib, full-choke barrel and automatic ejector. Engraved, blued with a checkered, walnut stock. Imported between 1971 and 1975.

NIB	Exc.	V.G.	Good	Fair	Poor
—	1750	1500	1150	850	650

Single-Barrel Shotguns

Harrington & Richardson manufactured a series of single-barrel, break-open shotguns between 1908 and 1942. They were chambered for various gauges and had various barrel lengths and chokes. The finishes were blued with walnut stocks. There is little collector interest in these guns and, if in sound condition, are desirable as shooters only. They are the Models 3, 5, 6, 7, 8, and 9, as well as a hinged-frame, folding design.

NIB	Exc.	V.G.	Good	Fair	Poor
—	125	100	85	65	40

Turkey Mag

A single-shot break-open side release gun chambered for the 12 gauge 3.5" shell with screw-in Full choke. The hardwood stock has a Mossy Oak finish. Barrel length is 24" with a bead front sight. Weight is about 6 lbs.

NIB	Exc.	V.G.	Good	Fair	Poor
175	150	125	100	75	50

Youth Turkey Gun

Similar in appearance to the Turkey Mag but on a smaller scale. Chambered for the 20 gauge 3" shell with 22" barrel. Weighs about 5.5 lbs.

NIB	Exc.	V.G.	Good	Fair	Poor
165	140	115	90	60	40

Topper (New Production)

This is a break-open side release single-shot available in 12 and 20 gauge as well as .410 bore. The 12 gauge is offered with a 28" barrel while the others are fitted with 26" barrel. Blued finish with hardwood stock in black finish with semi-pistol grip. Weight is approximately 6 lbs.

NIB	Exc.	V.G.	Good	Fair	Poor
150	100	80	60	45	30

Topper Deluxe

NIB	Exc.	V.G.	Good	Fair	Poor
170	125	90	70	50	40

Topper Jr. in 20 Gauge and .410 Bore Only

NIB	Exc.	V.G.	Good	Fair	Poor
150	100	80	60	45	30

Topper Jr. Classic

Similar to the Topper Jr. Features a black walnut stock with butt checkering, white line spacer and black recoil pad. Weighs about 7.5 lbs.

NIB	Exc.	V.G.	Good	Fair	Poor
150	100	80	60	45	30

Topper Deluxe Slug

This 12 gauge single-shot has a 24" fully rifled barrel with built-in compensator.

NIB	Exc.	V.G.	Good	Fair	Poor
150	115	90	70	50	40

Topper Deluxe Classic

Introduced in 2004, this 12 gauge 3" single shot gun is fitted with a 28" vent rib barrel with screw-in modified choke. American black walnut stock with pistol grip and ventilated recoil pad. Barrel has black finish while the receiver has a nickel finish. Weight is about 5.5 lbs. In 2005 this model was offered in 20 gauge.

NIB	Exc.	V.G.	Good	Fair	Poor
245	200	150	100	75	50

Topper Trap Gun

Similar to above but with select checkered walnut stock and fore-end with fluted comb and full pistol grip; 30" barrel with two white beads and screw-in chokes (Improved Modified Extended included); deluxe Pachmayr trap recoil pad. Suggested retail price $360.

NIB	Exc.	V.G.	Good	Fair	Poor
350	275	200	165	145	75

Tamer

This single-shot gun is chambered for the .410 shell with 3" chamber. It is fitted with a 19.5" barrel and had a matte nickel finish. The stock is matte black polymer. Weighs about 6 lbs.

NIB	Exc.	V.G.	Good	Fair	Poor
160	125	90	60	45	30

Ultra Slug Hunter

Introduced in 1995 this model uses a heavy 10 gauge action fitted with a 24" 12 gauge barrel. Weight is about 8 lbs.

NIB	Exc.	V.G.	Good	Fair	Poor
150	115	90	70	50	40

Ultra Slug Hunter Deluxe 20 Gauge

Introduced in 1997 this model is chambered for 20 gauge shells and features a hand checkered camo laminated wood stock. Fitted with a fully rifled heavy slug barrel 24" long.

NIB	Exc.	V.G.	Good	Fair	Poor
315	250	200	150	100	75

Ultra Slug Hunter Deluxe 12 Gauge

Same as above but in 12 gauge with 3" chamber.

NIB	Exc.	V.G.	Good	Fair	Poor
315	250	200	150	100	75

Ultra Slug Youth Model

As above but chambered for 20 gauge shell. Weight is approximately 7 lbs.

NIB	Exc.	V.G.	Good	Fair	Poor
260	200	150	100	60	45

Ultra Slug Hunter Bull Barrel

Same as above but chambered for 20 gauge.

NIB	Exc.	V.G.	Good	Fair	Poor
150	100	80	60	45	30

Ultra Slug Hunter Thumbhole Stock

Similar to above but with laminated thumbhole stock and blued or stainless steel finish. Weight: 8.5 lbs. Add 10 percent for stainless.

NIB	Exc.	V.G.	Good	Fair	Poor
350	275	—	—	—	—

Ultra Slug Youth Bull Barrel

Same as above but with 22" barrel.

NIB	Exc.	V.G.	Good	Fair	Poor
150	100	80	60	45	30

Ultra Lite Slug Hunter

Single-shot break-open shotgun. 12- or 20-gauge with 3" chamber; fully rifled 24" barrel; hardwood stock with walnut finish, full pistol grip, recoil pad and sling swivels. No iron sights; scope base included. Overall length 40", weight 5.25 lbs. 20-ga. Youth Model has 20" rifled barrel. Deluxe Model has checkered laminated stock and fore-end.

NIB	Exc.	V.G.	Good	Fair	Poor
275	225	150	100	75	50

Camo Laminate Turkey NWTF Edition

Introduced in 1999 this single barrel model features a 12 gauge, 3.5" chamber, 22" barrel choked Turkey full. Polished receiver has laser engraved NWTF logo. Stock is hand checkered and is hardwood laminate with a green, brown, and black pattern. Ventilated recoil pad and sling swivels and camo sling are standard.

NIB	Exc.	V.G.	Good	Fair	Poor
250	200	150	100	75	50

Camo Laminate Turkey Youth NWTF Edition

Similar to the Camo Turkey above but chambered for 20 gauge with 3" chambers. Stock is laminated hardwood but with special shorter dimensions.

NIB	Exc.	V.G.	Good	Fair	Poor
250	200	150	100	75	50

H&R Handy-Gun (rifled barrel) Curio or Relic

Rifled-barrel H&R Handy-Guns were manufactured about 1930-34, but details of their production are not well documented. In H&R catalog #19 (copyright 1931) and #20, the .22 and .32-20 are listed as available with blued frame only, 12.25" barrel, with an optional ($1.50) detachable shoulder stock. Whether the .22 W.R.F. version listed on page 83 of the 1932 *Stoeger's Bible* was manufactured is unknown. Guns that were originally factory fitted for the shoulder stock (all are extremely rare) have *H.&R. ARMS COMPANY/WORCESTER, MASS.U.S.A./PAT.PENDING* stamped on the bottom of the grip in .125" letters. Production of the rifled-barrel H&R Handy-Gun was halted in 1934 when the Treasury Department classified it as a "firearm" under the NFA, because it was available with a shoulder stock. Any rifled-barrel H&R Handy-Gun is (and always was) exempt from the NFA, if not accompanied by a shoulder stock.

.32-20 W.C.F. serial range mostly from 43851 (?) to 43937 (?)

NIB	Exc.	V.G.	Good	Fair	Poor
—	1600	1100	950	700	600

.22 rimfire serial range from 1 (?) to 223 (?)

NIB	Exc.	V.G.	Good	Fair	Poor
—	1400	1000	750	650	500

H&R Handy-Gun (smooth bore) NFA, Curio or Relic

The .410 bore or 28 gauge H&R Handy-Gun is a single-shot pistol with an 8" or 12.25" smooth bore barrel, made from 1921 to 1934 by the Harrington & Richardson Arms Co., Worcester, Massachusetts. It shares internal parts with H&R Model 1915 (No. 5) shotgun, but the Handy-Gun's shorter receiver is designed for a pistol grip, its barrels won't fit the No. 5, and these firearms are serial numbered separately. About 54,000 H&R Handy-Guns were manufactured, nearly all for 2.5" shells. Production was halted after the government ruled the H&R Handy-Gun to be a "firearm" in the "any other weapon" category under the NFA, when its retail price was about $16. An H&R Handy-Gun with an 18" smooth bore barrel is subject to the NFA, but exempt if accompanied by an original (detachable) wire shoulder stock. **NOTE:** Rare variations command premiums: 8" barrel, 25 to 50 percent; 18" barrel (rarest), 200 to 300 percent; unchoked .410, 20 to 30 percent; 28 gauge or Model 3 (only) with factory-equipped original detachable shoulder stock, 150 percent or more; holster, $75 to $200; serial matching box, $100 to $200 or more (i.e., a box for an 8" barrel 28 gauge could be quite expensive).

.410 bore, Model 2, Types II and III

NIB	Exc.	V.G.	Good	Fair	Poor
—	2000	1200	500	250	175

28 gauge, Model 2, Type I

NIB	Exc.	V.G.	Good	Fair	Poor
—	1500	1100	850	695	525

H&R manufactured "private-branded" or "trade-branded" H&R Handy-Guns for other distributors. One variation has *ESSEX GUN WORKS* on the left side of the receiver. Another has *HIBBARD* stamped on the left side, and *MODEL W.H.* stamped on the right; a holster with identical stampings was also available. Most have nickel-plated receivers and are serial numbered within the same ranges as, and have other characteristics identical to, regular-production H&R Handy-Guns, by variation. None of those inspected during this research had any markings identifying H&R as the original manufacturer. Anecdotal evidence suggests H&R manufactured a Handy-Gun for an independent telephone company in Colorado; none were located during this research. These materials are copyright 1998 by Eric M. Larson.

Topper (Old Production)

A single-shot, break-open shotgun chambered for various gauges with various barrel lengths, chokes. Blued, with a hardwood stock. Introduced in 1946.

NIB	Exc.	V.G.	Good	Fair	Poor
—	145	95	75	60	40

Model 088

An external hammer single-shot, break-open shotgun chambered for all gauges with various barrel lengths, chokes and an automatic ejector. Blued, with a case colored frame and hardwood stock.

NIB	Exc.	V.G.	Good	Fair	Poor
—	80	65	50	40	30

Model 099

As above, but matte, electroless, nickel-plated.

NIB	Exc.	V.G.	Good	Fair	Poor
—	110	95	75	60	40

Model 162

A 12 or 20 gauge boxlock single-shotgun with a 24" barrel with rifle sights.

NIB	Exc.	V.G.	Good	Fair	Poor
—	125	100	80	65	45

Model 176

A 10-gauge, 3.5" Magnum caliber boxlock single barrel shotgun with a heavyweight 36" barrel and a Full choke. Manufactured between 1977 and 1985.

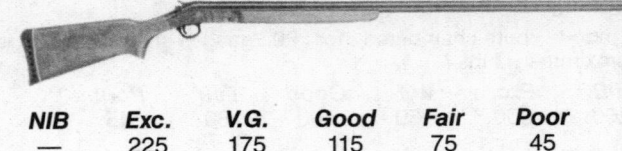

NIB	Exc.	V.G.	Good	Fair	Poor
—	225	175	115	75	45

Model 400

A 12, 16, or 20 gauge slide-action shotgun with a 28" Full choke barrel. Blued, with a hardwood stock. Manufactured between 1955 and 1967.

NIB	Exc.	V.G.	Good	Fair	Poor
—	150	125	100	75	50

Model 401

As above, with a variable choke device. Manufactured between 1956 and 1963.

NIB	Exc.	V.G.	Good	Fair	Poor
—	175	150	125	90	65

Model 402

As above, in a .410 bore. Manufactured between 1959 and 1967.

NIB	Exc.	V.G.	Good	Fair	Poor
—	175	150	125	90	65

Model 440

A 12, 16, or 20 gauge slide-action shotgun with a 26", 28", or 30" barrel in various chokes. Blued, with a hardwood stock. Manufactured between 1968 and 1973.

NIB	Exc.	V.G.	Good	Fair	Poor
—	150	125	100	75	50

Model 442

As above with a ventilated rib barrel and a checkered stock. Manufactured between 1969 and 1973.

NIB	Exc.	V.G.	Good	Fair	Poor
—	175	150	125	90	65

Model 403

A .410 bore semi-automatic shotgun with a 26", Full choke barrel. Blued, with a hardwood stock. Manufactured in 1964.

NIB	Exc.	V.G.	Good	Fair	Poor
—	300	250	175	100	75

Model 404

A 12, 20, or .410 bore boxlock double-barrel shotgun with 26" or 28" barrels, double triggers and extractors. Blued with a walnut stock. Manufactured by Rossi in Brazil and imported between 1969 and 1972.

NIB	Exc.	V.G.	Good	Fair	Poor
—	175	150	125	90	65

Pardner Pump Field Gun Full-Dip Camo

Pump-action shotgun with steel receiver, double action bars, cross-bolt safety, easy take-down. 28" barrel with 3" chamber and ventilated rib, screw-in Modified choke tube. Synthetic stock with ventilated recoil pad and grooved fore-end with Realtree APG-HDTM full camo dip finish. Overall length 48-1/8", weight 7.5 lbs. Also available in several variations with hardwood stock or black synthetic stock. Suggested retail for full camo version $278.

Excell

Introduced in 2005 this semi-automatic shotgun is chambered for the 12 gauge 3" shell and fitted with a 28" vent rib barrel with choke tubes. Checkered black synthetic stock. Magazine capacity is 5 rounds. Weight is about 7 lbs.

NIB	Exc.	V.G.	Good	Fair	Poor
400	365	295	200	150	100

Excell Waterfowl

As above but with Real Tree Advantage Wetlands camo finish. Introduced in 2005.

NIB	Exc.	V.G.	Good	Fair	Poor
425	375	325	225	175	125

Excell Turkey

This model is fitted with a 22" barrel with choke tubes and fiber optic front sight. Real Tree Advantage Hardwoods camo finish. Weight is 7 lbs. Introduced in 2005.

NIB	Exc.	V.G.	Good	Fair	Poor
425	375	325	225	175	125

Excell Combo

This model has a black synthetic stock and two barrels: 28" vent rib with choke tubes, and 24" rifled barrel. Weight is about 7 lbs. depending on barrel length. Introduced in 2005.

NIB	Exc.	V.G.	Good	Fair	Poor
450	395	350	250	195	145

Pinnacle

This is an over/under gun chambered for the 12 or 20 gauge with 3" chambers. Barrel length for the 12 gauge is 28" and for the 20 gauge 26"; both with vent ribs. Choke tubes. Checkered walnut stock with recoil pad and pistol grip. Weight is about 6.75 lbs. for the 12 gauge and 6.25 lbs. for the 20 gauge. Introduced in 2005.

NIB	Exc.	V.G.	Good	Fair	Poor
700	600	500	325	175	125

Model 1212

A 12 gauge over/under boxlock shotgun with 28" ventilated rib barrels. Blued with a walnut stock. Also available with 30" barrels having 3" chambers. Manufactured by Lanber Arms of Spain and imported after 1976.

NIB	Exc.	V.G.	Good	Fair	Poor
—	450	375	325	200	125

Long Tom Classic

Introduced in 1996 this limited edition single-barrel shotgun features a case hardened frame with 32" Full choked barrel. Stock is hand-checkered black walnut with crescent buttplate. Chambered for 12 gauge. Weight is about 7.5 lbs.

NIB	Exc.	V.G.	Good	Fair	Poor
425	395	325	250	175	125

Harrington & Richardson/New England Firearms Handi-Rifle/Slug Gun Combos

Single-shot break-open rifle/shotgun combos (one rifle barrel, one shotgun barrel per combo) chambered in .44 Magnum/12 gauge rifled slug and .357 Magnum/20 gauge rifled slug. Rifle barrels are not interchangeable; shotgun barrels are interchangeable. Stock is black matte high-density polymer with sling swivel studs, molded checkering and recoil pad. Rifle barrel 22" for both calibers; shotgun barrels 28" (12 gauge) and 24" (20 gauge) fully rifled. No iron sights; scope rail included. Overall length 38" (both rifle chamberings); 42" (12 gauge) and 40" (20 gauge). Weight 7 - 8 lbs.

NIB	Exc.	V.G.	Good	Fair	Poor
—	300	250	175	100	75

RIFLES

Model 058

A 20-gauge, .22 Hornet, .30-30, .357 Magnum, or .44 Magnum caliber rifle/shotgun outfit with interchangeable barrels. Blued with a hardwood stock.

NIB	Exc.	V.G.	Good	Fair	Poor
—	200	150	100	75	50

Model 258

As above, but with a matte, electroless nickel-plate finish.

NIB	Exc.	V.G.	Good	Fair	Poor
—	225	175	125	100	75

Reising Model 60

A .45 ACP caliber semi-automatic rifle with an 18.25" barrel and a 12- or 20-round detachable magazine. Blued, with a walnut stock. It operates on a retarded blowback system and was developed to be used as a police weapon. Manufactured between 1944 and 1946.

Courtesy Richard M. Kumor, Sr.

NIB	Exc.	V.G.	Good	Fair	Poor
—	2000	1600	1000	450	250

Model 65 Military (Model 58C)

A .22 LR caliber semi-automatic rifle with a 23" barrel and Redfield peep sights. Blued, with a walnut stock. Manufactured between 1944 and 1956. **NOTE:** Add 100 percent if USMC marked.

Courtesy Richard M. Kumor, Sr.

NIB	Exc.	V.G.	Good	Fair	Poor
—	500	300	200	125	90

Model 150

A .22 LR caliber semi-automatic rifle with a 20" barrel and a 5-shot magazine. Blued, with a walnut stock. Manufactured between 1949 and 1953.

NIB	Exc.	V.G.	Good	Fair	Poor
—	100	80	60	45	30

Model 155 (Shikari)

This is a single-shot, break-open rifle chambered for the .44 Magnum or the .45-70 cartridge. It has a 20" barrel with fixed sights. The finish is blued, with a full-length walnut stock. It was introduced in 1972.

NIB	Exc.	V.G.	Good	Fair	Poor
—	375	300	225	150	100

Model 157

As above in .22 Magnum, .22 Hornet, and .30-30 caliber.

NIB	Exc.	V.G.	Good	Fair	Poor
—	350	275	200	125	75

Model 158

A .357 or .44 Magnum single-shot side lever rifle with a 22" barrel. Blued, case hardened with a walnut stock. Available with an interchangeable 26" 20 gauge barrel. Manufactured prior to 1986.

NIB	Exc.	V.G.	Good	Fair	Poor
—	350	275	200	125	75

Model 300 Ultra

A .22-250 up to the .300 Winchester Magnum caliber, bolt-action rifle with a 22" or 24" barrel and without sights. High polished blue, and checkered walnut stock. Manufactured between 1965 and 1978.

NIB	Exc.	V.G.	Good	Fair	Poor
—	450	400	350	275	175

Model 301 Carbine

As above with an 18" barrel and a full-length, Mannlicher-style stock.

NIB	Exc.	V.G.	Good	Fair	Poor
—	450	400	350	275	175

Model 317 Ultra Wildcat

A .17 Rem., .17-223, .222 Rem., and the .223 Rem. caliber short Sako bolt-action rifle with a 20" barrel furnished without sights. Blued, with a checkered walnut stock. Manufactured between 1968 and 1976.

NIB	Exc.	V.G.	Good	Fair	Poor
—	550	400	350	275	175

HANDI-RIFLE

Break-action single-shot rifle that's been around in one form or another since God invented dirt. Side lever release, automatic ejection, hardwood stock, transfer bar passive safety. Available in nearly every conceivable rimfire and centerfire chambering (except the biggest centerfires) and now made under the auspices of Marlin, this rifle is as good a bargain today as it ever was. Some newer models feature factory scopes, bull barrels, thumbhole stocks and other niceties, but they are still Handi-Rifles. Value is generally under $300 even in New or Excellent condition, sometimes remarkably under. **NOTE:** The latest iteration of the Handi-Rifle (2008) is available in a wide variety of chamberings, from .223 to .500 S&W Magnum.

Synthetic

Basic Handi-Rifle design but with synthetic buttstock and fore-end (either grooved or beavertail). Available with iron sights or picatinny rail for mounting optics.

NIB	Exc.	V.G.	Good	Fair	Poor
275	200	175	150	100	50

Stainless

Similar to above but with stainless barrel. Chambered in .223, .270 or .30-06.

NIB	Exc.	V.G.	Good	Fair	Poor
295	225	200	175	115	75

Synthetic Handi-Rifle/Slug Gun Combo

Similar to above but with extra slug barrel. Available in .44 Magnum/12 gauge and .357 Magnum/20 gauge. Introduced in 2008.

NIB	Exc.	V.G.	Good	Fair	Poor
—	325	300	225	175	100

Superlite Compact

Similar to Synthetic Handi-Rifle but weighs only 5.5 lbs. Chambered in .223 and .243. Also available with optional scope.

NIB	Exc.	V.G.	Good	Fair	Poor
295	225	200	175	115	75

Ultra Varmint Rifle

This single-shot rifle is chambered for the .223 Rem. or the .22-250 cartridge. It is fitted with a 22" heavy barrel. The stock is hand checkered curly maple (older models) or laminated (newer models) with Monte Carlo cheekpiece. Comes with picatinny rail for mounting optics. Weighs about 7.5 lbs.

NIB	Exc.	V.G.	Good	Fair	Poor
350	295	175	125	75	50

Ultra Varmint Thumbhole

Similar to above but with laminated thumbhole stock.

NIB	Exc.	V.G.	Good	Fair	Poor
375	325	200	150	100	75

Stainless Steel Ultra Varmint Thumbhole

Similar to above but with stainless steel barrel and matte nickel receiver.

NIB	Exc.	V.G.	Good	Fair	Poor
375	325	200	150	100	75

Ultra Varmint Fluted

Introduced in 2005 this model is chambered for the .204 Ruger, .22-250, or the .223 Rem. cartridge. Fitted with a 24" fluted barrel

with no sights. Stock is black synthetic with vertical adjustable adjustment knob, recoil pad, and adjustable bipod mount. Weight is about 7 lbs.

NIB	Exc.	V.G.	Good	Fair	Poor
350	295	175	125	75	50

Model 317P

As above, but more finely finished. Manufactured between 1968 and 1976.

NIB	Exc.	V.G.	Good	Fair	Poor
—	500	475	425	375	250

Ultra Rifle—Hunting

Single-shot rifle chambered for .25-06, .308 Win., and .357 Rem. Max. The .25-06 has a 26" barrel, the other two are fitted with 22" barrels. A Cinnamon laminated stock is standard. Weight is about 7 lbs. In 2001 the .450 Marlin cartridge was added.

NIB	Exc.	V.G.	Good	Fair	Poor
275	200	175	150	100	50

Harrington & Richardson/New England Firearms Stainless Ultra Hunter with Thumbhole Stock

Single-shot break-open rifle chambered in .45-70 Government. 24" stainless steel barrel and receiver with scope mount rail; hammer extension; cinnamon laminate thumbhole stock. Overall length 40"; weight 8 lbs.

NIB	Exc.	V.G.	Good	Fair	Poor
375	325	200	150	100	75

Ultra Rifle—Varmint

Same as above but chambered for .223 Rem. with 22" barrel. Laminated stock with checkered pistol grip.

NIB	Exc.	V.G.	Good	Fair	Poor
375	325	200	150	100	75

Ultra .22 Magnum Rifle

Same as above but chambered for the .22 Winchester Magnum. Introduced in 2001.

NIB	Exc.	V.G.	Good	Fair	Poor
295	225	200	175	115	75

Ultra Rifle—Comp

Introduced in 1997 this single-shot rifle features an integral muzzlebrake on the end of the barrel. Available in .270 Win. and .30-06 calibers with 24" barrels. Camo laminated stock.

NIB	Exc.	V.G.	Good	Fair	Poor
295	225	200	175	115	75

Ultra Rifle Rocky Mountain Elk Foundation Commemorative

A limited edition single rifle chambered for the .35 Whelen cartridge. Selected laminated stock with Monte Carlo. Barrel length is 26".

NIB	Exc.	V.G.	Good	Fair	Poor
—	450	400	350	275	175

Sportster .17 HMR

A .17 HMR version of the Handi-Rifle with black polymer Monte Carlo stock and picatinny rail for moutning optics. Overall length 38.25".

NIB	Exc.	V.G.	Good	Fair	Poor
—	250	200	150	100	50

Sportster

A .22 LR or .22 WMR version of the Handi-Rifle with black polymer stock, fluted fore-end and iron sights. Overall length 36.25".

NIB	Exc.	V.G.	Good	Fair	Poor
—	175	150	100	75	50

Sportster Compact

Similar to above but in .22 LR only and 2" shorter length of pull.

NIB	Exc.	V.G.	Good	Fair	Poor
—	150	125	100	75	50

Buffalo Classic

This rifle was first produced in 1995. It is chambered for the .45-70 and .38-55 cartridges. Barrel length is 32" with no sights but dovetail front and drilled and tapped rear. Hand checkered walnut stock with case colored crescent steel buttplate. Weight is approximately 8 lbs. Since its introduction in 1995 there have been about 2,000 guns produced. The factory anticipates about 1,000 of these rifles being built each year.

NIB	Exc.	V.G.	Good	Fair	Poor
375	315	225	175	125	50

Wesson & Harrington Brand 125th Anniversary Rifle

Introduced in 1996 this rifle commemorates the 125th anniversary of the partnership. This special rifle is chambered for the .45-70 Government cartridge. The receiver is hand engraved. The barrel length is 32". The stock is American black walnut with crescent steel butt.

NIB	Exc.	V.G.	Good	Fair	Poor
395	325	250	200	150	75

Ultra Rifle Whitetails Unlimited 1997 Commemorative Edition

Introduced in 1997 and chambered for the .45-70 Govt. cartridge, this model features a hand checkered black walnut stock. Special laser engraving on the action and pewter finished medallion inletted into stock. Barrel length is 22".

NIB	Exc.	V.G.	Good	Fair	Poor
325	275	225	175	125	75

CR Carbine

Single-shot rifle based on the Handi-Rifle design. Two-piece checkered walnut stock with schnabel fore-end. Marble front and rear sights, Crescent steel buttplate. Chambered in .45 Colt. Introduced in 2007.

NIB	Exc.	V.G.	Good	Fair	Poor
375	315	225	150	100	50

Model 333

The Model 300 in 7mm Magnum caliber. Manufactured in 1974.

NIB	Exc.	V.G.	Good	Fair	Poor
—	250	200	175	125	100

Model 340

A .243 to .308 Winchester caliber bolt-action rifle with a 22" barrel and a 5-shot magazine. Blued, with a checkered walnut stock.

NIB	Exc.	V.G.	Good	Fair	Poor
—	400	350	300	225	150

Model 360 Ultra Automatic

A .243 Win. and the .308 Win. caliber semi-automatic rifle with a 22" barrel, adjustable sights and a 3-shot detachable magazine. Blued, with a checkered walnut stock. Manufactured between 1965 and 1978.

NIB	Exc.	V.G.	Good	Fair	Poor
—	425	375	275	195	100

Model 451 Medalist

A .22 LR caliber bolt-action rifle with a 26" barrel, open sights and a 5-shot detachable magazine. Blued, with a walnut stock. Manufactured between 1948 and 1961.

NIB	Exc.	V.G.	Good	Fair	Poor
—	175	150	125	100	75

Model 700

A .22 rimfire Magnum caliber, semi-automatic rifle with a 22" barrel, adjustable sights and a 5-round, detachable magazine. Blued, with a checkered walnut stock. Manufactured between 1977 and 1985.

NIB	Exc.	V.G.	Good	Fair	Poor
—	225	200	150	125	85

Model 700 DL

As above, with a checkered walnut stock with a 4X scope. Manufactured until 1985.

NIB	Exc.	V.G.	Good	Fair	Poor
—	300	250	200	150	100

Model 750

A .22 LR bolt-action single-shot rifle with a 22" barrel with sights and a short stock. Blued, and the stock is hardwood.

NIB	Exc.	V.G.	Good	Fair	Poor
—	100	80	60	45	25

Model 865

A .22 LR caliber bolt-action rifle with a 22" barrel, open sights and a 5-shot magazine. Blued, with a hardwood stock.

NIB	Exc.	V.G.	Good	Fair	Poor
—	100	80	60	45	25

Model 5200

A .22 LR caliber bolt-action, single-shot rifle with a 28" heavy barrel without sights, and an adjustable trigger. Blued, with a target-type walnut stock.

NIB	Exc.	V.G.	Good	Fair	Poor
—	400	350	300	225	125

Model 5200 Sporter

A .22 LR caliber bolt-action rifle with a 24" barrel, adjustable sights and a 5-shot magazine. Blued with a walnut stock. Not manufactured after 1983.

NIB	Exc.	V.G.	Good	Fair	Poor
—	400	350	300	225	125

100th Anniversary Officer's Model

A commemorative replica of the Officer's Model 1873 Trapdoor Springfield Rifle, with a 26" barrel. Engraved, and an anniversary plaque mounted on the stock. Blued, with a case colored receiver and a pewter fore-end tip. There were 10,000 manufactured in 1971. As with all commemorative's, this model is most desirable when NIB with all supplied material.

NIB	Exc.	V.G.	Good	Fair	Poor
850	695	500	375	250	175

Custer Memorial Issue

A limited production issue commemorating George Armstrong Custer's Battle of the Little Bighorn. Heavily engraved and gold inlaid with a high-grade checkered walnut stock. Furnished in a mahogany display case that included two books dealing with the subject. There were two versions produced—an Officer's Model, of which 25 were issued commemorating the 25 officers that fell with Custer, and another version commemorating the 243 enlisted men who lost their lives at the Little Bighorn. As with all commemorative's, to be collectible they must be NIB with all furnished material.

Officer's Model

25 manufactured.

NIB	Exc.	V.G.	Good	Fair	Poor
3000	2000	1600	1200	500	200

Enlisted Men's Model

243 manufactured.

NIB	Exc.	V.G.	Good	Fair	Poor
1500	1000	600	400	250	150

Model 171

A reproduction of the Model 1873 Trapdoor Springfield Carbine with a 22" barrel. Blued, with a case colored receiver and a walnut stock.

NIB	Exc.	V.G.	Good	Fair	Poor
—	500	450	300	200	125

Model 171-DL

As above, but more finely finished.

NIB	Exc.	V.G.	Good	Fair	Poor
—	550	500	325	250	175

Model 174

A plain copy of the Springfield Model 1873 Carbine in .45-70 caliber with a 22" barrel. Manufactured in 1972.

NIB	Exc.	V.G.	Good	Fair	Poor
—	525	400	325	250	175

Model 178

A copy of the Springfield Model 1873 rifle with a 32" barrel. Manufactured from 1973 to 1984.

NIB	Exc.	V.G.	Good	Fair	Poor
—	525	400	325	250	175

HARRIS GUNWORKS
Phoenix, Arizona

There are a wide range of extra costs options for all Harris Gunworks models that in many cases will dramatically affect price.

National Match Rifle

Introduced in 1989 this model features a bolt-action rifle chambered for the 7mm-08 or .308 with 5-round magazine. It is fitted with a 24" stainless steel match grade barrel with Canjar trigger. The stock is fiberglass with adjustable buttplate. Weight is about 11 lbs.

NIB	Exc.	V.G.	Good	Fair	Poor
3500	2750	1750	950	600	300

Model 86 Sniper Rifle

Chambered for .308, .30-06, .300 Win. Magnum with 24" heavy match grade barrel. The stock is a special design McHale fiberglass with textured grip and forearm. Fitted with a recoil pad. Supplied with a bipod. Weight is about 11.25 lbs. **NOTE:** Add $100 for take-down model.

NIB	Exc.	V.G.	Good	Fair	Poor
2700	2100	1600	1000	600	350

Model 87 Series

These are single-shot rifles chambered for .50 BMG. Fitted with a 29" barrel with muzzlebrake. Fiberglass stock. Introduced in 1987. Weight is approximately 21.5 lbs. **NOTE:** For Model 87R 5-shot repeater add $600. For Model 87 5-shot repeater add $400. For Model 92 Bullpup add $300.

NIB	Exc.	V.G.	Good	Fair	Poor
6000	4750	3000	2000	1000	500

Model 88

These bolt-action .50 BMG rifles are offered in two different configurations. One is fitted with a 20" carbon graphite barrel with add-on recoil arrestor with black teflon finish. The second variation is fitted with a 16.5" stainless steel barrel with integral recoil arrestor. Both rifles weigh about 14 lbs. Titanium action is available for further weight reduction.

NIB	Exc.	V.G.	Good	Fair	Poor
6000	4750	3000	2000	1000	500

Model 89 Sniper Rifle

This bolt-action rifle is chambered for .308 cartridge. Fitted with a 28" barrel. Supplied with a bipod. Stock is fiberglass with adjustable length of pull and fitted with a recoil pad. Weight is about 15.25 lbs.

NIB	Exc.	V.G.	Good	Fair	Poor
2700	2100	1600	1000	600	350

Model 93

Bolt-action .50 BMG rifle with folding hinge stock assembly. Furnished with a 10- or 20-round magazine. Barrel length is 29". Weight is approximately 21 lbs.

Model 93 folding model

NIB	Exc.	V.G.	Good	Fair	Poor
6000	4750	3000	2000	1000	500

Model 95

This is a lightweight variation of the .50 BMG models featuring Titanium and graphite. Supplied with bipod. Barrel length is 29". Weight is approximately 18 lbs.

NIB	Exc.	V.G.	Good	Fair	Poor
6000	4750	3000	2000	1000	500

Model 96

This is a gas-operated semi-automatic .50 BMG sniper rifle. Barrel length is 29". Detachable 5-round magazine. Weight is approximately 25 lbs.

NIB	Exc.	V.G.	Good	Fair	Poor
7500	6500	4000	2500	1500	750

Long Range Rifle

Chambered for a variety of cartridges such as the .300 Win. Magnum, 7mm Rem. Magnum, .300 Phoenix, .338 Lapua. This is a single-shot rifle fitted with a 26" match grade stainless steel barrel. Fiberglass stock with adjustable buttplate and cheekpiece. Weight is about 14 lbs.

Target/Benchrest Rifle on top and Long Range Rifle on bottom

NIB	Exc.	V.G.	Good	Fair	Poor
3900	2850	1500	1000	700	350

Target/Benchrest Rifle

Offered in .243, .308, 6mm BR, 6mm PPC, and 6mm Rem. This model is custom built for the customer. Available in both left- and right-hand. Weight is about 11 lbs.

NIB	Exc.	V.G.	Good	Fair	Poor
3500	2750	1750	950	600	300

Antietam Sharps Rifle

This is a replica of the Sharps Model 1874 sidehammer introduced in 1994. Chambered for the .40-65 or the .45-70. Choice of 30" or 32" octagon or round barrel. Stock is fancy walnut with either straight, pistol grip, or Creedmoor with schnabel forearm. Many optional sights offered. Weight is about 11.25 lbs.

NIB	Exc.	V.G.	Good	Fair	Poor
2600	1950	1200	800	450	200

Signature Classic Sporter

This is a left- or right-handed bolt-action model introduced in 1987 with a choice of calibers from .22-250 to .375 H&H. Barrel lengths are 22", 24", or 26" depending on caliber. Choice of fiberglass stocks in green, beige, brown, or black. A wood stock is optional. Weight is about 7 lbs. for short action calibers.

NIB	Exc.	V.G.	Good	Fair	Poor
3150	2550	1500	1150	500	250

Signature Classic Stainless Sporter

Same as above but with barrel and action made from stainless steel. A .416 Rem. Magnum is available in this variation also. This model is also available with interchangeable barrels. **NOTE:** Add $600 for interchangeable barrels.

NIB	Exc.	V.G.	Good	Fair	Poor
3200	2650	1600	1250	600	300

Signature Super Varminter

Similar to the Classic Sporter except fitted with a heavy contoured barrel, adjustable trigger, and special hand-bedded fiberglass stock. Chambered for .223, .22-250, .220 Swift, .243, 6mm Rem., .25-06, 7mm-08, 7mm BR, .308, .350 Rem. Introduced in 1989.

NIB	Exc.	V.G.	Good	Fair	Poor
2900	2250	1600	1050	700	350

Signature Alaskan

Similar to the Classic Sporter except fitted with a match grade barrel with single leaf rear sight. Nickel finish. Walnut Monte Carlo stock with cheekpiece and palm swell grip. Chambered for .270 to .375 H&H. Introduced in 1989.

NIB	Exc.	V.G.	Good	Fair	Poor
3950	3200	2200	1500	700	350

Signature Titanium Mountain Rifle

Similar to the Classic Sporter except action is made of titanium alloy and barrel of chrome-moly steel. Stock is graphite reinforced fiberglass. Chambered for .270 to .300 Win. Magnum. Weight is about 5.5 lbs. Introduced in 1989. **NOTE:** Add $400 for graphite steel barrel.

NIB	Exc.	V.G.	Good	Fair	Poor
3500	2750	1750	950	600	300

Sportsman 97

This bolt-action rifle is chambered for a variety of calibers from .270 Win. to .338 Win. The stock is fancy grade walnut, Bastogne, or English. A Talon action is fitted.

NIB	Exc.	V.G.	Good	Fair	Poor
2900	2250	1600	1050	700	350

Talon Safari Rifle

This bolt-action rifle is chambered for 16 different calibers from .300 Win. Magnum to .460 Weatherby Magnum. The finish is a matte black with fiberglass Safari stock. Weight is between 9 and 10 lbs. depending on caliber.

NIB	Exc.	V.G.	Good	Fair	Poor
4200	3350	2200	1600	1200	600

Talon Sporter Rifle

This bolt-action rifle, introduced in 1991, uses a pre-64 Model 70 type action with cone breech. Barrel and action are stainless steel. Chambered for a wide variety of calibers from .22-250 to .416 Rem. Magnum. Choice of walnut or fiberglass stock. Most barrel lengths are 24". Weight is about 7.5 lbs. depending on caliber.

NIB	Exc.	V.G.	Good	Fair	Poor
3150	2550	1500	1150	500	250

Double Rifle/Shotgun

This side-by-side gun is offered in .470 NE or .500 NE as well as 12 and 20 gauge guns. Engraved receiver, AAA fancy walnut stocks and 3-leaf express sights are standard. Offered in boxlock and side lock models.

Boxlock

NIB	Exc.	V.G.	Good	Fair	Poor
15000	12500	9000	5000	2750	1500

Side Lock

NIB	Exc.	V.G.	Good	Fair	Poor
21000	16500	12000	7500	3100	1750

HARTFORD ARMS & EQUIPMENT CO.
Hartford, Connecticut

Established in 1925, this firm was purchased by the High Standard Company in 1932.

Single-Shot Target

A .22 caliber single-shot pistol with a 6.75" round barrel, fixed sights and either walnut or composition grips. The frame marked "Manfd. by the/ Hartford Arms and Equip. Co./ Hartford, Conn./ Patented .22 cal./ l.r." on the left side in front of their breach. Although this pistol resembles a semi-automatic, it is in fact a single-shot manually operated pistol. **NOTE:** Add $150 premium for guns in original Hartford Arms box numbered to the gun. Add $250 premium for guns in original High Standard box numbered to the gun.

Courtesy John J. Stimson, Jr.

NIB	Exc.	V.G.	Good	Fair	Poor
—	595	450	325	250	150

Model 1925

Semi-automatic pistol chambered for .22 caliber with 6.75" round barrel, checkered hard black rubber grips or ribbed walnut grips. Magazine capacity is 10 rounds. The frame is marked, "manfd. by/ the hartford arms and equip. co./ hartford, conn./ patented/ .22 cal/ long rifle" on the left side in front of the breach. Approximately 5,000 were produced from 1925 to 1932. **NOTE:** Add $150 premium for guns in original Hartford Arms box numbered to the gun.

Courtesy John J. Stimson, Jr.

NIB	Exc.	V.G.	Good	Fair	Poor
—	600	475	365	225	175

HATFIELD RIFLE COMPANY
St. Joseph, Missouri

Squirrel Rifle

A flintlock or percussion rifle in .32 to .50 caliber with a 39" barrel, double set triggers, adjustable sights, brass mounts and maple stocks. Available in a wide variety of forms, which affect the values. The values listed are for plain, standard models.

NIB	Exc.	V.G.	Good	Fair	Poor
550	400	350	300	225	150

SHOTGUNS

Uplander Grade I

A 20 gauge boxlock double-barrel shotgun with a 26" improved cylinder and modified barrel with a matte raised rib, single-selective trigger and automatic ejectors. Case hardened, blued with a deluxe-grade, hand-checkered walnut stock. Introduced in 1987.

NIB	Exc.	V.G.	Good	Fair	Poor
1250	1050	750	600	475	200

Uplander Pigeon Grade II

As above, with scroll engraving with a fitted leather case.

NIB	Exc.	V.G.	Good	Fair	Poor
2250	1750	1275	900	650	500

Uplander Super Pigeon Grade III

As above, with deep-relief cut engraving and a leather case.

NIB	Exc.	V.G.	Good	Fair	Poor
2500	2200	1700	1400	1000	700

Uplander Golden Quail Grade IV

A gold-inlaid version of the above.

NIB	Exc.	V.G.	Good	Fair	Poor
4000	3500	2750	2000	1700	1300

Uplander Woodcock Grade V

As above, with seven 24 kt. gold inlays and best quality engraving. Furnished with a leather case.

NIB	Exc.	V.G.	Good	Fair	Poor
5600	5000	4250	3500	2750	2000

HAVILAND & GUNN
Ilion, New York

Gallery Pistol

A .17 caliber rimfire single-shot pistol with a 5" barrel. The barrel and frame made of one piece of iron and nickel plated. There are no markings on these pistols whatsoever. Believed to have been made during the 1870s.

NIB	Exc.	V.G.	Good	Fair	Poor
—	—	1150	550	175	100

HAWES
Los Angeles, California

An importer of handguns primarily made in Europe.

Courier

A .25 caliber, blowback, semi-automatic pocket pistol manufactured by Galesi.

NIB	Exc.	V.G.	Good	Fair	Poor
—	125	100	75	50	25

Diplomat

A .380 ACP pistol with an external hammer.

NIB	Exc.	V.G.	Good	Fair	Poor
—	150	125	100	75	50

Trophy

A J.P. Sauer & Sohn, manufactured revolver with a swing-out cylinder and a 6" barrel. Chambered for the .22 LR and the .38 Special. Has adjustable sights.

NIB	Exc.	V.G.	Good	Fair	Poor
—	250	200	175	125	90

Medalion

As above, with a 3", 4", or 6" barrel and fixed sights.

NIB	Exc.	V.G.	Good	Fair	Poor
—	200	175	125	100	75

Tip-Up Target Pistol

Replica of the Stevens Model 35 .22 LR single-shot. Globe front sight, adjustable rear.

NIB	Exc.	V.G.	Good	Fair	Poor
—	275	200	135	75	35

MARSHAL SINGLE-ACTION ARMY REVOLVERS

J. P. Sauer made a Western-styled series for Hawes based in appearance on the Colt Single-Action Army.

Silver City

A .22 LR or .22 rimfire Magnum caliber single-action revolver with a 5.5" barrel, 6-shot cylinder, and fixed sights.

NIB	Exc.	V.G.	Good	Fair	Poor
—	150	125	95	50	25

Western

A .357 Magnum, .44 Magnum, .45 Colt, .45 ACP, .44-40, 9mm, .22 LR, and .22 rimfire Magnum single-action revolver with fixed sights. Blued.

NIB	Exc.	V.G.	Good	Fair	Poor
—	350	275	195	100	75

Texas

As above, but nickel-plated.

NIB	Exc.	V.G.	Good	Fair	Poor
—	350	275	195	100	75

Montana

The Western Marshal with a brass backstrap and trigger guard.

NIB	Exc.	V.G.	Good	Fair	Poor
—	350	275	195	100	75

Deputy

A .22 LR and .22 rimfire Magnum single-action revolver with a 5.5" barrel, and 6-shot cylinder.

NIB	Exc.	V.G.	Good	Fair	Poor
—	150	125	95	50	25

Chief

A .357 Magnum, .44 Magnum, and the .45 Colt caliber revolver with a 6.5" barrel, and 6-shot cylinder and adjustable sights. Blued.

NIB	Exc.	V.G.	Good	Fair	Poor
—	350	275	195	100	75

Federal

A 6-shot single-action revolver in .357 Magnum, .44 Magnum, and the .45 Colt caliber.

NIB	Exc.	V.G.	Good	Fair	Poor
—	350	275	195	100	75

HAWES & WAGGONER
Philadelphia, Pennsylvania

Pocket Pistol

A .41 caliber single-shot percussion pistol with a 3" barrel, German silver mountings, and a walnut stock. Manufactured in the 1850s.

NIB	Exc.	V.G.	Good	Fair	Poor
—	—	2250	925	475	275

HAWKEN
St. Louis, Missouri

During the early part of the 19th century, Jacob and Samuel Hawken manufactured a variety of flintlock, percussion and cartridge rifles, shotguns and pistols. They are best known, however, for half stock Plains Rifles. Though of a plain nature, these arms were recognized for their accuracy and dependability. Early Hawken rifles will be worth a substantial premium over later examples. Some examples in very good condition may be worth as much as $50,000. Proceed with caution.

HDH, SA.
Henrion, Dassy & Heuschen
Liege, Belgium

Cobold

A 9.4mm Dutch, 10.6mm German, .38, and .45 caliber double-action five-shot revolver with solid frame, octagonal barrel, and an odd safety catch that locks the cylinder.

NIB	Exc.	V.G.	Good	Fair	Poor
—	500	325	275	150	100

Puppy

A 5.5mm to 7.65mm caliber folding trigger, double-action revolver. Most are "Velo-Dogs".

NIB	Exc.	V.G.	Good	Fair	Poor
—	200	150	100	75	50

Lincoln

A .22 caliber folding trigger, double-action revolver with a solid frame, imitation pearl or ivory grips, and engraving.

NIB	Exc.	V.G.	Good	Fair	Poor
—	200	150	100	75	50

Lincoln-Bossu

A 5.5mm or 6.35mm caliber folding trigger double-action revolver ("Velo-Dog" type) with solid-frame and hammerless.

NIB	Exc.	V.G.	Good	Fair	Poor
—	200	150	100	75	50

Left Wheeler

A Colt Police Positive copy in .32 or .38 caliber. The last revolver HDH manufactured.

NIB	Exc.	V.G.	Good	Fair	Poor
—	200	150	125	100	75

HEAVY EXPRESS INC.
Colorado Springs, Colorado

This company built, custom-built, rifles using its proprietary nonbelted cartridges from .260 Heavy Express Magnum to the .416 Heavy Express Magnum. The company's rifles were built on Ruger Model 77 Mark II and Winchester Model 70 Classic actions. Barrels are 4140 chrome-moly blue and 416R stainless steel. Stocks include factory walnut, laminated, or composite designs. The prices listed are for the basic guns. Options are not included and will affect price.

Heavy Express Premier—Ruger M77 Mk II

This rifle is chambered for the .260 HE Magnum, .284 HE Magnum, or .300 HE Magnum. Choice of walnut, laminated, or composite stocks. **NOTE:** Add $200 for stainless steel.

NIB	Exc.	V.G.	Good	Fair	Poor
1500	1150	800	600	350	175

Heavy Express Monarch—Winchester M70 Classic

Same as above but built on a Winchester M70 Classic action. Choice of stocks. **NOTE:** Add $200 for stainless steel.

Close-up of Model 70 Classic stainless steel action.

NIB	Exc.	V.G.	Good	Fair	Poor
1775	1400	1000	750	500	250

Heavy Express Monarch—Ruger 77 MK II

This rifle is built on a Ruger M77 action and is chambered for the .338, .350, .375, .416, and .460 HE Magnum cartridges. Choice of stocks. **NOTE:** Add $200 for stainless steel.

NIB	Exc.	V.G.	Good	Fair	Poor
1775	1400	1000	750	500	250

Heavy Express Single-Shot—Ruger #1

This rifle is chambered in .300, .338, .350, and .416 HE Magnum cartridges. Choice of stocks. **NOTE:** Add $200 for stainless steel.

NIB	Exc.	V.G.	Good	Fair	Poor
1775	1400	1000	750	500	250

Heavy Express Premier—Ruger M77 Mk II

This rifle is built on a Ruger M77 Mk II action in .260 HE Magnum, .284 HE Magnum, or .300 HE Magnum. Choice of stocks. **NOTE:** Add $200 for stainless steel.

NIB	Exc.	V.G.	Good	Fair	Poor
1500	1150	800	500	400	200

HECKLER & KOCH
Oberndorf/Neckar, Germany

At the end of WWII, the French dismantled the Mauser factory as part of their reparations; and the buildings remained idle until 1949, when firearms production was again allowed in Germany. Heckler & Koch was formed as a machine tool enterprise and occupied the vacant Mauser plant. In the early 1950s Edmund Heckler and Theodor Koch began to produce the G3 automatic rifle based on the Spanish CETME design and progressed to machine guns and sub-machine guns and eventually to the production of commercial civilian rifles and pistols. In 1990 the company got into financial difficulties because of a failed contract bid. In December 1990 the French state consortium GIAT announced the purchase of Heckler and Koch, but a little more than a year later the contract was canceled. Later in 1991 the company was purchased by Royal Ordnance of Britain. In 2002 the company was sold to a combined group of European investors and long-time company managers.

Model 91 A2

This rifle is recoil-operated, with a delayed-roller lock bolt. It is chambered for the .308 Winchester cartridge and has a 17.7" barrel with military style aperture sights. It is furnished with a 20-round detachable magazine and is finished in matte black with a black plastic stock. Some areas of the country have made its ownership illegal.

NIB	Exc.	V.G.	Good	Fair	Poor
2800	2400	2000	1500	1150	800

Model 91 A3

This model is simply the Model 91 with a retractable metal stock.

NIB	Exc.	V.G.	Good	Fair	Poor
3100	2700	2250	1700	1350	900

Model 93 A2

This model is similar to the Model 91 except that it is chambered for the .223 cartridge and has a 16.4" barrel. The magazine holds 25 rounds, and the specification are the same as for the Model 91.

NIB	Exc.	V.G.	Good	Fair	Poor
3000	2500	2000	1500	1150	800

Model 93 A3

This is the Model 93 with the retractable metal stock.

NIB	Exc.	V.G.	Good	Fair	Poor
3250	2650	2250	1700	1350	900

Model 94 A2

This is a carbine version chambered for the 9mm Parabellum cartridge, with a 16.5" barrel. It is a smaller-scaled weapon that has a 15-shot magazine.

NIB	Exc.	V.G.	Good	Fair	Poor
4000	3750	3500	3100	2500	1250

Model 94 A3

This model is a variation of the Model 94 with the addition of a retractable metal stock.

NIB	Exc.	V.G.	Good	Fair	Poor
4200	3950	3750	3300	2700	1000

Model 270

This model is chambered for the .22 LR cartridge. It is a sporting-styled rifle with a 16.5" barrel. It is furnished with either a 5- or a 20-round magazine and is blued, with a checkered walnut stock. This rifle was discontinued in 1985.

NIB	Exc.	V.G.	Good	Fair	Poor
800	675	500	350	250	150

Model 300

This model is similar to the Model 270 except that it is chambered for the .22 rimfire Magnum cartridge. It was not imported after 1988.

NIB	Exc.	V.G.	Good	Fair	Poor
1000	800	500	350	250	150

Model 630

This model is chambered for the .223 and features the same roller-delayed semi-automatic action as found on the paramilitary-type weapons. This is a sporting-style rifle that has a polished blue finish and a checkered walnut stock. The barrel is 17.7" long, and the magazines offered holds either 4 or 10 rounds. Importation was discontinued in 1986.

NIB	Exc.	V.G.	Good	Fair	Poor
1795	1350	900	650	450	300

Model 770

This model is similar to the Model 630 except that it is chambered for the .308 Winchester cartridge and has 19.7" barrel. It was not imported after 1986.

NIB	Exc.	V.G.	Good	Fair	Poor
1795	1350	900	650	450	300

Model 940

This model is essentially the same as the Model 770 except that it is chambered for the .30-06 cartridge. It has a 21" barrel and was not imported after 1986.

NIB	Exc.	V.G.	Good	Fair	Poor
2000	1600	1000	600	400	300

Model SL6

This is Heckler & Koch's current sporting rifle chambered for the .223 cartridge. It has a 17.7" barrel and features the same basic action as the military versions. It has a matte black finish and a walnut stock with a vented walnut hand guard. The magazine holds 4 rounds.

NIB	Exc.	V.G.	Good	Fair	Poor
1600	1300	950	650	350	300

Model SL7

This model is similar to the SL6 except that it is chambered for the .308 Winchester cartridge and has a 3-round magazine.

NIB	Exc.	V.G.	Good	Fair	Poor
1600	1300	950	650	350	300

Model SR9

This model was introduced into the U.S. market after the federal government prohibited the importation of H&K's other semi-automatic rifles. The SR9 is similar to the HK91 but has been certified by the BATFE as a sporting rifle. This model features a special thumb hole stock made of Kevlar reinforced fiberglass. The action is a delayed-roller locked bolt semi-automatic design chambered for the .308 Winchester cartridge. The barrel is 19.7" in length and features adjustable rear sight with hooded front sight. The rifle weighs 10.9 lbs.

NIB	Exc.	V.G.	Good	Fair	Poor
2900	2400	2000	1400	700	500

Model SR9 (T) Target

Similar to the standard model SR9 but with the addition of a special MSG90 adjustable buttstock, PSG-1 trigger group, and a PSG-1 contoured hand grip. Rifle weighs 10.6 lbs.

NIB	Exc.	V.G.	Good	Fair	Poor
3000	2500	2200	1650	950	600

Model SR9 (TC) Target Competition

Similar to the Model SR9 (T) but with the addition of the PSG-1 adjustable buttstock. Rifle weighs 10.9 lbs.

NIB	Exc.	V.G.	Good	Fair	Poor
3300	3000	2300	1950	1100	700

BASR Model

This is a bolt-action rifle chambered for various popular calibers. It has a stainless steel barrel and was essentially custom built to the customer's specifications. The stock is of Kevlar. This model is quite rare because only 100 were manufactured in 1968.

NIB	Exc.	V.G.	Good	Fair	Poor
—	4000	3600	2750	1300	800

PSG-1

This rifle is a high precision sniping rifle that features the delayed-roller semi-automatic action. It is chambered for the .308 Winchester cartridge and has a 5-shot magazine. Barrel length is 25.6". It is furnished with a complete array of accessories including a 6x42-power illuminated Hensoldt scope. Rifle weighs 17.8 lbs.

NIB	Exc.	V.G.	Good	Fair	Poor
14500	12500	9000	7500	6000	4000

Model SL8-1

This is a new generation .223 rifle modeled after the military Model G36 and introduced in 2000. It is built of carbon fiber polymer and is gas operated. Thumbhole stock with cheekpiece. Barrel length is 20.8". Magazine capacity is 10 rounds. Adjustable sights. Weight is approximately 8.6 lbs.

NIB	Exc.	V.G.	Good	Fair	Poor
1800	1625	1050	700	500	325

SLB 2000

Introduced in 2001 this gas-operated semi-automatic rifle is chambered for the .30-06 cartridge. The receiver is built of lightweight alloy. The barrel is 16.7" in length and will accept interchangeable barrels at some future date. Oil finished walnut stock. Open sights with both barrel and receiver drilled and tapped for scope mounts. Magazine capacity is 2, 5, or 10 rounds. Weight is about 7.25 lbs.

NIB	Exc.	V.G.	Good	Fair	Poor
1200	1000	800	600	400	225

Model USC

Introduced in 2000 this semi-automatic blowback carbine is derived from H&K's UMP submachine gun. Chambered for the

.45 ACP cartridge and fitted with a 16" barrel. Skeletonized stock. Accessory rail on top of receiver. Adjustable sights. Magazine capacity is 10 rounds. Weight is approximately 6 lbs.

NIB	Exc.	V.G.	Good	Fair	Poor
1700	1275	1000	750	400	200

Model MR556A1

Direct descendant of the HK416, Semi-automatic, gas-piston operating system. Free floating rail hand-guard system with four Picatinny rails for mounting of optical or lighting accessories. Two-stage trigger. Retractable butt-stock can be locked in any position to suit individual requirements. Chambered for the 5.56x45mm NATO round. Magazine capacities: 10, 20 or 30 rounds.

NIB	Exc.	V.G.	Good	Fair	Poor
2900	2475	2100	1300	650	300

PISTOLS

HK4

This is a blowback-operated semi-automatic pistol based on the Mauser HSc design. It is chambered for .22 LR, .25 ACP, .32 ACP, and .380. These calibers were easily converted by switching the barrels, recoil springs and magazines. The rimfire model could be changed by rotating the breechface. The conversion kits were available for all calibers. The barrel is 3" long; and the finish is blued, with molded plastic thumb rest grips. This pistol was sold from 1968-1973 as the Harrington & Richardson HK4 and is so marked. It was discontinued in 1984.

.22 Caliber or .380 Caliber

NIB	Exc.	V.G.	Good	Fair	Poor
—	475	350	250	200	100

.25 Caliber or .32 Caliber

NIB	Exc.	V.G.	Good	Fair	Poor
—	350	300	250	200	100

Conversion Units

NIB	Exc.	V.G.	Good	Fair	Poor
—	150	125	90	60	30

P9

This is a single-action, delayed-blowback semi-automatic pistol chambered for 9mm or 7.65mm Parabellum. The action is based on the G-3 rifle mechanism. The barrel is 4" in length, and the pistol has an internal hammer and a thumb-operated hammer drop and decocking lever. There is also a manual safety and a loaded-chamber indicator. The finish is Parkerized, and the grips are molded plastic and well contoured. It has fixed sights. This model was manufactured between 1977 and 1984. This model is rarer than the P9S model.

NIB	Exc.	V.G.	Good	Fair	Poor
800	650	500	400	300	200

P9S

This model is similar to the Model P9 except that the action features a double-action capability and it is chambered for the .45 ACP and the 9mm Parabellum with a 5.5" barrel. This model was also manufactured between 1977 and 1984.

NIB	Exc.	V.G.	Good	Fair	Poor
800	650	500	400	300	200

P9S Target Model

This version is similar to the Model P9S chambered for the 9mm or .45 ACP cartridges, with adjustable sights, and an adjustable trigger. It was discontinued in 1984.

NIB	Exc.	V.G.	Good	Fair	Poor
1400	1100	900	600	500	300

P9S Competition

Similar to the P9S target but with the addition of barrel weights and special competition grips.

NIB	Exc.	V.G.	Good	Fair	Poor
3000	2000	1200	750	500	275

VP 70Z

This is a blowback-operated semi-automatic chambered for the 9mm Parabellum cartridge. It is striker-fired and double-action-only. The barrel is 4.5" long, and the double-column magazine holds 18 rounds. The finish is blued, and the receiver and grip are molded from plastic. This model was discontinued in 1984.

NIB	Exc.	V.G.	Good	Fair	Poor
700	500	350	300	250	200

P7 PSP

This was the first of the squeeze-cocked H&K pistols. It is a single-action semi-automatic that is placed in the firing position by pressure on the front of the grip strap. This moves the striker into battery; and firing is then accomplished by a single action pressure on the trigger, releasing the grip strap cocking device and decocking the mechanism. This particular model does not have the extended finger guard on the trigger and also does not have an ambidextrous safety. It was discontinued in 1984.

NIB	Exc.	V.G.	Good	Fair	Poor
1100	900	700	600	500	400

P7 K3

This is the "Squeeze Cocker" chambered for either the .380 or .22 LR caliber. It has a recoil buffer that is oil-filled and a 3.8" barrel. The magazine holds 8 rounds. This model was introduced in 1988.

NIB	Exc.	V.G.	Good	Fair	Poor
1800	1600	1350	900	500	300

.22 Caliber Conversion Kit

This unit will convert the P7 K3 to fire the .22 LR cartridge.

NIB	Exc.	V.G.	Good	Fair	Poor
1500	1200	650	300	150	75

.32 ACP Caliber Conversion Kit

NIB	Exc.	V.G.	Good	Fair	Poor
1000	900	400	100	75	50

P7 M8

This is the 8-shot newer version of the "squeeze cocker". It has the heat-shield finger guard and the ambidextrous safety. It has a 4" barrel and a 3-dot sight system. The finish is matte blue or nickel with stippled black plastic grips. This model is no longer in production. **NOTE:** For night sights, introduced in 1993, add $100.

NIB	Exc.	V.G.	Good	Fair	Poor
1500	1200	900	700	500	300

P7 M10

A new addition to the P7 series in 1993, this variation is chambered for the .40 S&W cartridge. Magazine holds 10 rounds and the finish is available in either blue or nickel. Pistol weighs 2.69 lbs. **NOTE:** For night sights add $100.

NIB	Exc.	V.G.	Good	Fair	Poor
2000	1600	1000	650	500	300

P7 M13

This version is similar to the P7 M8 except that it has a double column 13-shot magazine. **NOTE:** For night sights add $100.

NIB	Exc.	V.G.	Good	Fair	Poor
2200	1750	1200	650	500	300

SP89

Introduced in the early 1990s, this is a large frame semi-automatic pistol chambered for the 9mm cartridge. It features a 15-round magazine and a square notch rear sight with a hooded front sight. The pistol has a 4.5" barrel and is 13" overall. It weighs 4.4 lbs. In August 1993 this model was no longer imported due to a ban on assault pistols.

NIB	Exc.	V.G.	Good	Fair	Poor
4000	3600	3200	2500	1800	1000

USP SERIES

Late in 1999 H&K began shipping its USPs and Mark 23s with an internal locking system. This lock-out is installed in the grip and blocks the movement of the hammer, trigger, and slide. It is operated with a two pronged key, supplied with the pistol. This system is in addition to the traditional trigger lock that is sold with each H&K firearm. In 2001 the stainless steel version of these pistols was discontinued.

In 2005 H&K offered a limited edition run of color frame variations for the USP line. These colors are Desert tan, green and gray.

Gray: USP 45 and USP 40 Compact
Green: USP 45, USP 40, USP 40 Compact, and USP 45
Tactical Desert Tan: USP 45, USP 40, USP 40 Compact, and USP 45 Tactical and Mark 23

Retail prices are the same for these color variations as the standard black frame pistols

USP 40

Introduced in 1993 this new semi-automatic H&K pistol features a new design that incorporates a short recoil modified Browning action. Chambered for the .40 S&W cartridge this model has a 4.13" barrel and a magazine capacity of 13 rounds. Stainless steel model introduced in 1996. It weighs 1.74 lbs. Available in seven different variations from traditional double-action to double-action-only and various safety locations and styles. These variants numbered by H&K are listed.

1.DA/SA with safe position and control lever on left side of frame. 2.DA/SA with safe position and control lever on right side of frame. 3.DA/SA without safe position and decocking lever on left side of frame. 4.DA/SA without safe position and decocking lever on left side of frame. 5.DA only with safe position and safety lever on left side of frame. 6.DA only with safe position and safety lever on right side of frame. 7.DA only without control lever. 9.DA/SA with safe position and safety lever on left side of frame. 10.DA/SA with safety lever on the right side of frame. **NOTE:** For stainless steel model add $45.

NIB	Exc.	V.G.	Good	Fair	Poor
900	800	650	300	250	125

USP 9

Same as the USP 40 but chambered for the 9mm cartridge. Magazine holds 16 rounds and pistol weighs 1.66 lbs. This model also has the choice of seven variations as listed above for the USP 40. New for 1993. **NOTE:** For stainless steel model add $45.

NIB	Exc.	V.G.	Good	Fair	Poor
900	800	650	300	250	125

USP 9SD

This variation of the USP 9 is fitted with target sights to see over an optional sound suppressor. The barrel is threaded left-hand and does not have an O-ring and does not require a thread cap. Introduced in 2004.

NIB	Exc.	V.G.	Good	Fair	Poor
975	825	675	325	275	150

USP 40 Compact

Same as 9mm Compact model but chambered for .40 S&W cartridge. Weight is about 27 oz. All other dimensions are the same.

NIB	Exc.	V.G.	Good	Fair	Poor
900	800	650	300	250	125

USP 45

Introduced in 1995 this version is slightly larger than the 9mm and .40 S&W models. Barrel length is 4.41" and overall length is 7.87". Weight is 1.9 lbs. The USP 45 is available in the same variants as the other USP models. Magazine capacity is 12 rounds. **NOTE:** For stainless steel model add $45.

H&K Stainless Steel Model

NIB	Exc.	V.G.	Good	Fair	Poor
1100	950	775	500	350	200

USP 9 Compact

Introduced in 1997 this 9mm model is a smaller version of the full size USP 9. There are some internal differences due to size. Barrel length is 3.58". Overall length is 6.81". Magazine capacity is 10 rounds. Weight is approximately 26 oz. **NOTE:** Also available with stainless steel slide. Add $45 to NIB price.

NIB	Exc.	V.G.	Good	Fair	Poor
800	600	450	300	200	150

USP Compact LEM (Law Enforcement Modification)

This model, introduced in 2002, is identical to the USP Compact .40 S&W Variant 7, but with a double-action-only trigger with a special trigger mechanism. The mechanism improves the double-action trigger performance and reduces the weight of pull to between 7.5 and 8.5 lbs. Offered in blued finish.

NIB	Exc.	V.G.	Good	Fair	Poor
1150	1000	750	500	300	150

USP 45 Match

Introduced in 1997 this model is a match grade variation of the USP. It is chambered for the .45 ACP cartridge. Fitted with a 6.02" barrel with barrel weight assembly. Adjustable rear sight and target front sight. Adjustable trigger stop. Blued finish. Weight is approximately 38 oz. Also available in a stainless steel version. **NOTE:** Add $60 for stainless steel.

NIB	Exc.	V.G.	Good	Fair	Poor
1500	1300	1050	800	475	275

USP 45 Compact

Introduced in 1997 this pistol is chambered for the .45 ACP cartridge. It has a 3.8" barrel and an overall length of 7.1". It weighs approximately 28 oz. Magazine capacity is 8 rounds.

NIB	Exc.	V.G.	Good	Fair	Poor
1100	950	775	500	350	200

USP 45 Compact Tactical

Blued semi-automatic .45 ACP. Double-action with 4.46" barrel, 8 round capacity. 27.5 oz. Polymer grip.

NIB	Exc.	V.G.	Good	Fair	Poor
1100	950	775	500	350	200

USP .357 Compact

Introduced in mid-1998 this pistol is built on the same frame as the .40 S&W Compact but chambered for the .357 SIG cartridge. Magazine capacity is 10 rounds. Weight is about 28 oz.

NIB	Exc.	V.G.	Good	Fair	Poor
1000	850	4675	375	250	150

USP 45 Expert

Introduced in the fall of 1998, this .45 ACP pistol is fitted with a 5.2" barrel and slide and 10-round magazine. Overall length is 8.7" and height is 1.87". Weight is approximately 30 oz. Adjustable low-profile sights. Limited availability of between 1,000 and 2,500 pistols. In 2003 this model was also offered chambered for the 9mm and the .40 S&W cartridge. **NOTE:** H&K price reduction in 2005.

NIB	Exc.	V.G.	Good	Fair	Poor
1355	1200	900	600	300	150

USP 45 Tactical

This pistol was introduced in 1998. It is an enhanced version of the USP 45. It is fitted with a 4.9" threaded barrel with adjustable high profile target sights. Overall length is 8.6" and weight is approximately 36 oz. Magazine capacity is 10 rounds. Availability limited to between 1,000 and 2,500 pistols.

NIB	Exc.	V.G.	Good	Fair	Poor
875	700	500	350	250	125

NIB	Exc.	V.G.	Good	Fair	Poor
1100	850	625	425	300	175

USP Elite

Introduced in 2003 this model features a 6.2" barrel chambered for the 9mm or .45 ACP cartridge. Fitted with a match trigger, adjustable trigger stop, adjustable micrometer rear target sights, extended floorplate and loaded chamber indicator. Weight is about 30 oz. empty. Magazine capacity is 10 rounds. **NOTE:** H&K price reduction in 2005.

P2000 SK

This semi-automatic double-action pistol is a subcompact version of the P2000. It is chambered for the 9mm or .40 S&W cartridge as well as the .357 SIG .It has a 2.5" barrel with an overall length of 6.4". Magazine capacity is 10 rounds for 9mm, 12 rounds for the .357 SIG, and 9 rounds for the .40 S&W. Weight is about 21 oz. Introduced in 2004.

NIB	Exc.	V.G.	Good	Fair	Poor
1400	1150	800	575	250	135

NIB	Exc.	V.G.	Good	Fair	Poor
1100	850	625	425	300	175

USP 45 50th Anniversary Commemorative

Limited to 1,000 pistols this pistol features a high polish blue with 50th anniversary logo engraved in gold and silver. Supplied with custom-made wooden box with commemorative coin. Introduced in 2000.

NIB	Exc.	V.G.	Good	Fair	Poor
1100	850	625	425	300	175

P2000 GPM

Introduced in 2003 this model is similar to the USP compact LEM pistol but with several modular features, such as interchangeable back straps, ambidextrous slide release, and short trigger reset distance. Chambered for the 9mm or .40 S&W cartridge and fitted with a 3.62" barrel. Fixed sights. Magazine capacity is 12 rounds for the .40S&W and .357 SIG, and 13 rounds for the 9mm. Weight is about 22 oz. **NOTE:** Add $30 for magazine disconnect.

Mark 23

Very similar to the H&K's US government contract pistol developed for special Operation Units. Chambered for the .45 ACP and fitted with a 5.87" barrel, this pistol has a polymer frame with steel slide. Magazine capacity is 10 rounds on civilian models and 12 rounds on law enforcement models. Barrel is threaded for noise suppressor. Weight is about 42 oz.

NIB	Exc.	V.G.	Good	Fair	Poor
2200	1850	1200	875	500	250

HK45

Full-size autoloader chambered in .45 ACP. Features include polygonal bore, front and rear slide serrations, integrated picatinny rail, ambi mag release levers, interchangeable backstrap panels, polymer frame, modular action design allowing for double- single action or double action-only operation. Measures 7.52" overall length. 10+1 capacity.

NIB	Exc.	V.G.	Good	Fair	Poor
1100	850	625	425	300	175

HK45 Compact

Similar to above but with 8 round capacity; overall length 7.2".

NIB	Exc.	V.G.	Good	Fair	Poor
1100	850	625	425	300	175

P30

Polymer-frame 9mm autoloader. Features include loaded chamber indicator, integral picatinny rail, oversized trigger guard, double or single action firing mode with decocker, "Hostile Environment" black finish, ambidextrous, oversized controls. **NOTE:** Add 10 percent for longslide variant.

NIB	Exc.	V.G.	Good	Fair	Poor
850	675	575	450	250	150

HEINZELMANN, C.E.
Plochipnam Neckar, Germany

Heim

A 6.35mm semi-automatic pistol with a 2" barrel. Detachable magazine holds 6 rounds. Weight is approximately 11 oz. Manufactured during the 1930s and marked on the frame "C.E. Heinzelmann Plochingen A.N. Patent Heim-6.35".

NIB	Exc.	V.G.	Good	Fair	Poor
—	800	675	550	400	200

HELFRICHT
Zella-Mehlis, Germany

Model 3 Pocket Pistol

A 6.35mm semi-automatic pistol with a 2" barrel and 6-shot magazine. Weight is about 11 oz. Blued with checkererd black plastic grips having the monogram "KH" cast in them. These pistols have no external sights.

Courtesy James Rankin

NIB	Exc.	V.G.	Good	Fair	Poor
—	500	400	300	200	100

Model 4 Pocket Pistol

A semi-automatic pistol in caliber 6.35mm. It has checkered black plastic grips with the "KH" logo on each grip.

Courtesy James Rankin

NIB	Exc.	V.G.	Good	Fair	Poor
—	400	300	200	150	100

HENRION & DASSY
Liege, Belgium

Semi-Automatic

A 6.35mm semi-automatic pistol with a 2.5" barrel and 5-shot magazine. Blued with black plastic grips. Marked "H&D."

NIB	Exc.	V.G.	Good	Fair	Poor
—	600	500	450	375	275

HENRY
See—Winchester

HENRY, ALEXANDER
Edinburgh, Scotland

Noted for both the rifling system he developed and the falling block single-shot rifles he made, Alexander Henry conducted business at these locations:

12 South Street, Andrew Street	1853-1858
8 South Street, Andrew Street	1858-1862
12 South Street, Andrew Street	1862-1871
12 and 14 South Street, Andrew Street	1871-1875
12 South Street, Andrew Street	1875-1895
18 Frederick Street	1895-1911
22 Frederick Street	1911-

Single-Shot Rifle

A high-grade single-shot that features a true falling-block action that is activated by a side lever on the action. It was available in the popular European cartridges of the era, and the barrel length varies from 22" to 28" in length. This rifle exhibits fine quality materials and workmanship. The select-grade walnut stock and schnabel fore-end are hand checkered. The finish of the rifle is scroll-engraved and blued. This company manufactured firearms from 1869 until 1895.

NIB	Exc.	V.G.	Good	Fair	Poor
—	—	3800	1500	700	400

Double Rifle

A side-by-side, double-barreled Express Rifle chambered for the .500/450 Black Powder Express cartridge. It has Damascus barrels and double triggers. This gun is hammerless and features ornate scroll engraving as well as a high-grade hand checkered walnut stock and fore-end. It was furnished with a fitted leather case and accessories. This rifle was manufactured in the 1890s.

NIB	Exc.	V.G.	Good	Fair	Poor
—	—	9000	5000	1750	800

HENRY REPEATING ARMS COMPANY
Brooklyn, New York

Lever-Action

Chambered for the .22 LR, Long, and Short cartridges It is fitted with a 18.25" barrel and weighs 5.5 lbs. Magazine capacity is 15 rounds for the .22 LR cartridge. Rear sight is adjustable and the front sight is hooded.

NIB	Exc.	V.G.	Good	Fair	Poor
280	200	155	125	75	50

Carbine

Similar to the above model but with an overall length of 34". It features a large loop lever.

NIB	Exc.	V.G.	Good	Fair	Poor
280	200	155	125	75	50

Youth Model

Similar to the carbine model above but with an overall length of 33".

NIB	Exc.	V.G.	Good	Fair	Poor
280	200	155	125	75	50

Lever-Action .22 Magnum

Fitted with a 19.5" barrel with a tubular magazine capacity of 11 rounds. Checkered deluxe walnut stock. Weight is about 5.5 lbs.

NIB	Exc.	V.G.	Good	Fair	Poor
350	300	250	195	125	75

Lever-Action Frontier Model

Similar to Lever Action but with 20" octagon barrel. Chambered in .22 WMR and .17HMR. Introduced 2006.

NIB	Exc.	V.G.	Good	Fair	Poor
375	300	250	175	115	85

Golden Boy

This lever-action rifle is chambered for the .22 LR, Short, or Long cartridges as well as the .22 WRM cartridge in a separate model. Fitted with a brass receiver and 20" octagon barrel. Walnut stock. Weight is about 6.75 lbs. **NOTE:** Add $70 for .22 WRM model or .17 HMR. Add $20 for large loop lever. Add $600 for hand-engraved model.

NIB	Exc.	V.G.	Good	Fair	Poor
550	400	295	200	125	85

Golden Boy Deluxe

Chambered for the .22 Long Rifle cartridge and fitted with a 20" octagon barrel. Fancy walnut stock. Deeply engraved receiver.

NIB	Exc.	V.G.	Good	Fair	Poor
1250	995	650	400	200	125

Deluxe Engraved Golden Boy Magnum

Similar to Golden Boy Deluxe but chambered in .22 WMR. Features deluxe deep-cut German-style engraving on receiver. Introduced 2006.

NIB	Exc.	V.G.	Good	Fair	Poor
1275	1000	675	425	225	150

Varmint Express

This lever-action rifle is chambered for the .17 HMR cartridge and fitted with a 20" round barrel. Checkered American walnut stock. Scope mount included. Magazine capacity is 11 rounds. Weight is about 5.75 lbs.

NIB	Exc.	V.G.	Good	Fair	Poor
45	350	225	175	100	75

Big Boy

This lever-action model is chambered for the .44 Magnum or .45 Colt cartridge. Octagonal barrel is 20". Magazine capacity is 10 rounds. American walnut stock with straight grip. Weight is about 8.7 lbs. .357 Magnum added 2006.

NIB	Exc.	V.G.	Good	Fair	Poor
725	595	400	300	200	150

Big Boy Deluxe Engraved .44 Magnum

Similar to Big Boy but with deluxe deep-cut German-style engraving on receiver. Introduced 2006.

NIB	Exc.	V.G.	Good	Fair	Poor
1350	1100	850	550	275	175

Big Boy .44 Magnum "Wildlife Edition"

Similar to Big Boy .44 Magnum but with fore-end and buttstock laser-engraved with whitetail deer scenes. Introduced in 2007.

NIB	Exc.	V.G.	Good	Fair	Poor
875	750	625	500	250	125

Big Boy .45 Colt "Cowboy Edition"

Similar to Big Boy .45 Colt but with fore-end and buttstock laser-engraved with Old West scenes. Introduced in 2007.

NIB	Exc.	V.G.	Good	Fair	Poor
1350	1100	850	550	275	175

.30-30

.30-30 caliber Winchester. Features a 20" barrel, straight-grip American walnut stock with rubber butt-pad, XS ghost ring sights, blue finish, weight of 7 lbs. Also available with brass receiver, octagon barrel and adjustable Marble's buck-horn rear sight, bead front. **NOTE:** Add 30 percent for brass receiver/octagon barrel.

NIB	Exc.	V.G.	Good	Fair	Poor
650	575	500	400	300	200

Mare's Leg

Caliber: .45 Colt or .22 S/L/LR. Has large-loop lever based on rifle seen in classic Steve McQueen western TV series "Wanted: Dead or Alive". Barrel length is 12.9", overall length 25". Weight: 5.8 lbs. (.45 Colt), 4.5 lbs. (.22). Lanyard ring, blue finish, straight-grip walnut stock. Sights are Marble's adjustable semi-buckhorn rear and brass bead front (.45 Colt): adjustable rear and hooded front (.22).

.45 Colt

NIB	Exc.	V.G.	Good	Fair	Poor
800	675	500	400	300	200

.22

NIB	Exc.	V.G.	Good	Fair	Poor
315	275	220	175	110	85

Pump-Action Rifle

Introduced in 1999 this .22 caliber is fitted with a 18.25" barrel and chambered for the .22 LR cartridge. Walnut stock and adjustable rear sight. Weight is approximately 5.5 lbs.

NIB	Exc.	V.G.	Good	Fair	Poor
350	250	185	135	100	75

U.S. Survival Rifle

This model is an improved version of the AR-7 .22 caliber survival rifle issued to the Air Force. It is a breakdown design and features a waterproof stock, a steel-lined barrel and adjustable sights. Furnished with two 8-round magazines. Overall length when broken down is 16.5".

NIB	Exc.	V.G.	Good	Fair	Poor
250	175	115	85	65	40

Pump-Action .22 Octagon Rifle

Similar to Pump-Action Rifle but with 20" octagon barrel. Introduced 2006. Add 10 percent for .22 WMR.

NIB	Exc.	V.G.	Good	Fair	Poor
495	350	225	150	125	75

Mini Bolt

This single-shot bolt-action .22 caliber rifle is designed for young shooters. Barrel length is 16.25". Overall length is 30.25" Stainless steel barrel and receiver. Colored stocks available. Adjustable sights. Weight is about 3.25 lbs.

NIB	Exc.	V.G.	Good	Fair	Poor
210	165	100	75	50	25

Acu-Bolt

Chambered for the .22 LR, .22 WMR, or the .17 HMR cartridges and fitted with a 20" barrel. Fiberglass stock. Scope mounts. Weight is about 4.25 lbs. Add 10 percent for factory scope.

NIB	Exc.	V.G.	Good	Fair	Poor
315	275	200	150	100	75

HERITAGE MANUFACTURING, INC.
Opa Locka, Florida

Stealth

This is a 9mm semi-automatic pistol. It has a black polymer frame with stainless steel slide. Barrel length is 3.9" with overall length at 6.3". Magazine capacity is 10 rounds. Weight is approximately 20 oz. A .40 S&W version was scheduled to be introduced in the summer of 1996. Offered with a black finish, two-tone black chrome with stainless steel side panels, or black chrome.

NIB	Exc.	V.G.	Good	Fair	Poor
275	225	175	150	125	100

Model H25S

A semi-automatic pistol chambered for the .25 ACP cartridge. Barrel length is 2.25" and overall length is 4.58". Weight is about 13.5 oz. Frame mounted safety. Single-action-only. Available in blue or nickel.

NIB	Exc.	V.G.	Good	Fair	Poor
150	125	100	85	65	50

Sentry

This is a double-action revolver chambered for the .38 Special. Cylinder holds 6 rounds. Barrel length is 2". Weight is about 23 oz. Blue or nickel finish.

NIB	Exc.	V.G.	Good	Fair	Poor
130	100	85	65	50	30

Rough Rider

Single-action revolver chambered for the .22 caliber cartridges. Barrel lengths are 4.75", 6.5", and 9". Cylinder holds 6 rounds. Weight is about 34 oz. Available in blue or nickel finish.

NIB	Exc.	V.G.	Good	Fair	Poor
165	125	100	75	50	30

With Combination Cylinder—.22 Magnum

NIB	Exc.	V.G.	Good	Fair	Poor
190	150	120	75	50	30

With Bird's-Head Grip & Combo Cylinder

NIB	Exc.	V.G.	Good	Fair	Poor
190	150	120	75	50	30

Rough Rider .17 HMR

Introduced in 2004.

NIB	Exc.	V.G.	Good	Fair	Poor
190	150	120	75	50	30

Rough Rider .32

Six-shot revolver chambered for .32 H&R Magnum centerfire (interchangeably .32 S&W, .32 S&W Long). Black satin finish. Offered with 3.5", 4.75" or 6.5" barrels. 35 oz. (6.5" bbl.). 11.785" LOA.) Fixed sights. Bird's head grip available.

NIB	Exc.	V.G.	Good	Fair	Poor
240	190	140	95	75	50

Rough Rider Big-Bore Series

Six-shot, steel-frame revolver chambered for .357, .44-40 or .45 Long Colt. Barrel lengths 4.75", 5.5" or 7.5". 36 oz. Fixed sights.
NOTE: Add 10 percent for chrome finish.

NIB	Exc.	V.G.	Good	Fair	Poor
350	275	200	150	100	50

HEROLD
Franz Jaeger
Suhl, Germany

Bolt-Action Rifle

A .22 Hornet bolt-action sporting rifle with a 24" ribbed barrel, adjustable sights, double set triggers and walnut stock. Imported by Charles Daly and Stoeger Arms prior to WWII.

NIB	Exc.	V.G.	Good	Fair	Poor
—	1500	850	600	400	250

HERTER'S
Waseca, Minnesota

An importer and retailer of European-made firearms. Active until approximately 1980.

REVOLVERS

Guide

A .22 caliber double-action swing-out cylinder revolver with a 6" barrel and 6-shot cylinder. Blued with walnut grips.

NIB	Exc.	V.G.	Good	Fair	Poor
—	125	95	70	45	30

Power-Mag Revolver

A .357 Magnum, .401 Herter Power Magnum, and .44 Magnum caliber single-action revolver with a 4" or 6" barrel and 6-shot cylinder. Blued, with walnut grips. Add 10 percent for .401.

NIB	Exc.	V.G.	Good	Fair	Poor
—	400	325	200	125	75

Western

As above, in .22 caliber.

NIB	Exc.	V.G.	Good	Fair	Poor
—	200	150	125	75	50

RIFLES

J-9 or U-9 Hunter

Mauser-action sporting rifles manufactured in England (J-9) and Yugoslavia (U-9), with 24" barrels and Monte Carlo-style walnut stocks.

NIB	Exc.	V.G.	Good	Fair	Poor
—	475	200	155	100	75

J-9 or U-9 Presentation or Supreme

As above, with checkering and sling swivels.

NIB	Exc.	V.G.	Good	Fair	Poor
—	550	325	200	150	100

HESSE ARMS
Inver Grove Heights, Minnesota

FAL-H RIFLES

All FAL-H rifles include these features: military spec internal parts, new or as new barrel, military finish, post ban legal muzzlebrake, one magazine, new metric pattern Type 3 receiver, adjustable gas system, refinished or new pistol grip, hard case, carry handle, sling, and manual. All rifles chambered for .308 Winchester cartridge. Additional calibers in .22-250 and .243 are also available. Weights are from 8.5 to 14 lbs. depending on model. **NOTE:** Value on Hesse Arms products can fluctuate widely.

FALO Tactical Rifle

This model features a free floating handguard assembly.

NIB	Exc.	V.G.	Good	Fair	Poor
1150	900	700	400	200	100

FALO Heavy Barrel

This model features a heavy barrel and is based on the Israeli FALO rifle.

NIB	Exc.	V.G.	Good	Fair	Poor
950	750	600	400	200	100

FAL-H High Grade

This model is available in any configuration and features a new walnut stock, pistol grip, and handguard. Trigger is gold plated.

NIB	Exc.	V.G.	Good	Fair	Poor
1350	1050	850	500	300	150

FAL-H Standard Grade

This is standard model that is similar in appearance to the original FAL.

NIB	Exc.	V.G.	Good	Fair	Poor
950	750	600	400	200	100

FAL-H Congo Rifle

This model features a 16" barrel.

NIB	Exc.	V.G.	Good	Fair	Poor
1000	800	650	400	200	100

FALO Congo Rifle

Similar to the model above but fitted with a 16" heavy barrel.

NIB	Exc.	V.G.	Good	Fair	Poor
1000	800	650	400	200	100

HAR-15 RIFLES

All of the HAR-15 rifles have these features: military spec internal parts, heavy match grade barrels, post ban legal muzzle-brake, A2 upper receiver, A2 round handguards with heat shields, A2 stock, A2 lower receiver. Each rifle comes with hard case, manual, and sling. Rifles are chambered for .223 Remington but can be chambered in other calibers as well. These are: .17 Rem. add $145, 9mm NATO add $85, 6mm PPC add $145, 6mmx45 add $95, .300 Fireball add $195, 7.62x39 add $45.

Omega Match

Fitted with a 1" diameter stainless steel barrel, adjustable match trigger, E2 stock, flat top receiver, free floating handguard.

NIB	Exc.	V.G.	Good	Fair	Poor
1000	800	650	400	200	100

HAR-15A2 Standard Rifle

This model has all of the standard features offered for HAR-15 rifles.

NIB	Exc.	V.G.	Good	Fair	Poor
725	575	475	325	150	75

HAR-15A2 National Match

This model is fitted with special bolt carrier, adjustable match trigger. Designed as Match grade rifle.

NIB	Exc.	V.G.	Good	Fair	Poor
1000	800	650	400	200	100

HAR-15A2 Bull Gun

This model is fitted with a 1" stainless steel barrel with special front sight base.

NIB	Exc.	V.G.	Good	Fair	Poor
775	600	475	225	150	75

HAR-15A2 Dispatcher

Fitted with a 16" barrel with full length handguard.

NIB	Exc.	V.G.	Good	Fair	Poor
725	575	450	225	150	75

HAR-15A2 Carbine

Fitted with a 16" heavy barrel and a non-collapsing stock with short handguard.

NIB	Exc.	V.G.	Good	Fair	Poor
725	575	475	225	150	75

H-22 RIFLES

All H-22 rifles include these features: new internal parts interchangeable with Ruger 10/22 rifle, heavy stainless steel barrel with match chamber, stainless steel receiver, laminated stock, hard case, magazine, and manual. All rifle are chambered for .22 LR. For an additional $250 any H-22 rifle can be converted to .22 Magnum. Weight of these rifles is approximately 7 lbs.

H-22 Tigershark

Special forearm and skeleton stock with heavy fluted barrel. Special trigger pack with over travel screw and glass bedded stock.

NIB	Exc.	V.G.	Good	Fair	Poor
800	650	525	375	195	125

H-22 Competition Rifle

This model features a gloss finished laminated competition thumbhole stock.

NIB	Exc.	V.G.	Good	Fair	Poor
550	450	350	225	150	75

H-22 Wildcat

This model has a screwed-in heavy barrel and a special laminated stock.

NIB	Exc.	V.G.	Good	Fair	Poor
550	450	350	225	150	75

H-22 Standard Rifle

Has all the standard features of the H-22 rifle including a buttstock with cheekpiece.

NIB	Exc.	V.G.	Good	Fair	Poor
475	375	300	200	125	50

OTHER RIFLES

M14-H Standard Rifle

This is a semi-automatic version of the M14 rifle chambered for the .308 cartridge. It is fitted with a new receiver, walnut stock or synthetic stock. Each rifle is sold with a sling, annual, and 10-round magazine and an extra original M145 stock.

NIB	Exc.	V.G.	Good	Fair	Poor
1000	800	650	400	200	100

M14-H Brush Rifle

This model has the same features as the standard rifle but with an 18" barrel.

NIB	Exc.	V.G.	Good	Fair	Poor
1050	800	650	450	225	125

Hesse Model 47 Rifle

This is a copy of the AK-47 and it is chambered for the 7.63x39 cartridge. It is also available in .223 caliber.

NIB	Exc.	V.G.	Good	Fair	Poor
600	475	375	275	150	75

HEYM, F. W.
Suhl, Germany

Established in 1865 in Suhl, Germany, this company was re-established after WWII in Munnerstadt. The company remained there until 1996 when it moved back to a suburb of Suhl. Post-war arms were originally imported by Paul Jaeger of Grand Junction, Tennessee.

SINGLE-SHOT RIFLES

Model HR-30

Built on the Ruger No. 1 falling-block-action and chambered for most calibers with a 24" round barrel or a 26" barrel in the magnum calibers. There is a quarter rib with express sights, and the single-set trigger is made by Canjar. The rifle is engraved with a game scene motif, and the stock is deluxe, hand checkered French walnut with a classic European-style cheekpiece. French case hardened and blued.

NIB	Exc.	V.G.	Good	Fair	Poor
—	5000	3900	3250	1750	1250

Model HR-38

As above, with an octagonal barrel.

NIB	Exc.	V.G.	Good	Fair	Poor
—	5200	4250	3500	2000	1500

DOUBLE RIFLES

Model 22 Safety

An over/under combination rifle/shotgun chambered for 16 or 20 gauge over .22 Hornet, .22 WMR, .222 Remington, .222 Remington Magnum, .223, 5.6x50Rmm, 6.5x57Rmm, and 7x57Rmm with 24" barrels. Boxlock action with a single trigger, automatic ejectors, and automatic decocking mechanism. French case hardening, blued with a walnut stock.

NIB	Exc.	V.G.	Good	Fair	Poor
—	3500	3000	2750	1200	900

Model 77B/55B Over/Under Rifle

An over/under rifle manufactured in a variety of calibers with 25" barrels having open sights and a boxlock-action with Kersten double cross bolts. The action is heavily engraved with a game scene motif and is silver plated. This model has double triggers, cocking indicators, automatic ejectors, and select walnut stock. The barrels machined to accept a Zeiss scope with claw mounts.

NIB	Exc.	V.G.	Good	Fair	Poor
—	6000	5500	4000	3250	2500

Model 55BSS

As above with sidelocks.

NIB	Exc.	V.G.	Good	Fair	Poor
—	10500	9500	8500	5000	3500

Model 55BF/77BF

Similar to the Model 55B, except one barrel is rifled and the other smooth in 12, 16, or 20 gauge.

NIB	Exc.	V.G.	Good	Fair	Poor
—	6000	5500	5000	3250	2500

Model 55BFSS

As above, with sidelocks.

NIB	Exc.	V.G.	Good	Fair	Poor
—	10500	9500	8500	5000	3500

Model 88 B

A large bore double-barrel boxlock rifle with 24" barrels, automatic ejectors, double triggers, and select walnut stock.

NIB	Exc.	V.G.	Good	Fair	Poor
—	12500	9750	8750	5500	4000

Model 88 BSS

As above with sidelocks.

NIB	Exc.	V.G.	Good	Fair	Poor
20000	18000	15000	10500	6500	5250

Model 88 Safari

As above, but chambered for .375 Holland & Holland, .458 Winchester Magnum, .470, or .500 Nitro Express calibers with 25" barrels.

NIB	Exc.	V.G.	Good	Fair	Poor
20000	18000	15000	10000	7000	4750

DRILLINGS

Model 33

A boxlock drilling manufactured in a variety of American and European calibers and gauges with 25" barrels, double triggers and extractors. Case hardened, blued with a walnut stock.

NIB	Exc.	V.G.	Good	Fair	Poor
—	7000	6000	5250	3750	2000

Model 33 Deluxe

Same as above but with game scene engraving.

NIB	Exc.	V.G.	Good	Fair	Poor
—	8500	7000	5750	4500	2500

Model 37

Similar to the Model 33 Standard but with full sidelocks.

NIB	Exc.	V.G.	Good	Fair	Poor
—	17500	13000	9500	6000	2500

Model 37 Deluxe

Similar to the above Model 37 but with hand engraved scroll work and fancy walnut stock.

NIB	Exc.	V.G.	Good	Fair	Poor
—	20000	16500	12000	6000	3000

BOLT-ACTION RIFLES

Model SR-20

A Mauser-action sporting rifle manufactured in a variety of calibers with 21", 24", or 26" barrels, open sights, adjustable trigger or set trigger. Blued with a walnut stock.

NIB	Exc.	V.G.	Good	Fair	Poor
2450	2250	1650	750	600	450

Model SR-20 Alpine

As above with a 20" barrel and Mannlicher stock. Introduced in 1989.

NIB	Exc.	V.G.	Good	Fair	Poor
—	2500	2000	1250	850	600

SR-20 Classic Safari

As above, but chambered for .404 Jeffries, .425 Express, and the .458 Winchester Magnum with a 24" barrel having express sights. Introduced in 1989.

NIB	Exc.	V.G.	Good	Fair	Poor
—	3000	2500	2000	1250	750

SR-20 Classic Sportsman

This model features a round barrel without sights. Chambered for many calibers from .243 to .375 H&H. Introduced in 1988. Add $100 for Magnum calibers.

NIB	Exc.	V.G.	Good	Fair	Poor
2650	2250	1900	900	500	300

SR-20 Trophy

Similar to the above Classic Sportsman model but with German bead ramp sight and open quarter rib rear sight. Select walnut stock with oil finish. Octagonal barrel and rosewood grip cap.

NIB	Exc.	V.G.	Good	Fair	Poor
3000	2500	2250	1800	900	300

Heym Magnum Express

This bolt-action rifle is chambered for .338 Lapua, .375 H&H, .416 Rigby, .500 Nitro Express, .500 A-Square, and a few were built in .600 Nitro Express. Fitted with a 24" barrel. Adjustable front sight, three leaf rear express sight. Select hand checkered European walnut stock, and many other special features. Introduced in 1989. **NOTE:** Add $4,000 for .600 N.E.

NIB	Exc.	V.G.	Good	Fair	Poor
10000	8000	5000	2500	1750	500

HI-POINT FIREARMS
MKS Supply
Dayton, Ohio

Model C

This is a 9mm single-action compact semi-automatic pistol with a 3.5" barrel. Magazine capacity is 8 rounds. Black or chrome finish. Weight is 32 oz.

NIB	Exc.	V.G.	Good	Fair	Poor
125	100	85	75	65	50

Model C Polymer

Same as above but with polymer frame. Weight is 28 oz.

NIB	Exc.	V.G.	Good	Fair	Poor
140	110	85	75	65	50

Model C Comp

Introduced in 1998 this 9mm model features a 4" barrel with compensator, adjustable sights and 10-round magazine.

NIB	Exc.	V.G.	Good	Fair	Poor
170	130	100	90	75	50

Model JH

All steel construction chambered for .45 ACP with 4.5" barrel. Magazine capacity is 7 rounds. Weight is 39 oz.

NIB	Exc.	V.G.	Good	Fair	Poor
180	135	100	85	75	50

Model 40SW

Same as above but chambered for the .40 S&W cartridge. Eight-round magazine capacity. Weight is 39 oz.

NIB	Exc.	V.G.	Good	Fair	Poor
180	135	100	85	75	50

Model .45 Polymer

This model has a polymer frame and 4.5" barrel chambered for the .45 ACP cartridge. Magazine capacity is 9 rounds. Weight is about 32 oz.

NIB	Exc.	V.G.	Good	Fair	Poor
180	135	100	85	75	50

Model .40 Polymer

As above but chambered for the .40 S&W cartridge with a magazine capacity of 10 rounds. Weight is about 32 oz.

NIB	Exc.	V.G.	Good	Fair	Poor
180	135	100	85	75	50

Model CF

This pistol is chambered for the .380 ACP cartridge and is fitted with a polymer frame. Magazine capacity is 8 rounds. Barrel length is 3.5". Weight is 29 oz. **NOTE:** Add $25 for compensator model.

NIB	Exc.	V.G.	Good	Fair	Poor
120	95	65	40	30	25

.380 ACP Compensated

Semi-automatic with fully-adjustable 3-dot sights, muzzle compensator, 4" barrel, 31 oz, polymer frame. Two magazines: one 10-round, one 8-round. **NOTE:** Add 50 percent for laser sight.

NIB	Exc.	V.G.	Good	Fair	Poor
150	125	100	85	75	50

.40 S&W Carbine

.40 S&W semi-automatic carbine. Features include all-weather, black, polymer stock, 10 shot magazine, 17.5" barrel, sling swivels, grip mounted clip release, quick on & off thumb safety, rear peep sight, 32.5" OAL and a scope mount. Add $85 for red dot sight.

NIB	Exc.	V.G.	Good	Fair	Poor
275	200	150	100	75	50

Model 995 Carbine

Similar to .40 S&W Carbine but chambered for 9mm Parabellum.

NIB	Exc.	V.G.	Good	Fair	Poor
285	210	160	110	75	50

HIGGINS, J. C.
Chicago, Illinois

The Sears, Roebuck & Company of Chicago used the trade name J.C. Higgins on the firearms and other sporting goods it sold between 1946 and 1962. Arms bearing this tradename were manufactured by a variety of American gunmakers. See High Standard, Mossberg, etc.

HIGH STANDARD
New Haven, Connecticut 1932-1945
Hamden, Connecticut 1946-1977
East Hartford, Connecticut 1977-1984

See High Standard Manufacturing Co., Houston, TX at the end of this semi-automatic pistol section.

LETTER MODELS
Model B

A .22 LR caliber semi-automatic pistol with either a 4.5" or a 6.75" round barrel and a 10-shot magazine. Blued; came with checkered hard rubber grips (later production versions have checkered grips impressed with the High Standard monogram). Introduced 1932, with serial numbers beginning at 5000. Early production utilized Hartford parts. Approximately 65,000 made. Add $75 premium for Type-I-B takedown. Add a $75 premium for early models with Hartford Arms front sight, safety, and takedown levers. Box with papers add premium of 15 percent. C&R eligible. Most guns are found in serial number ranges from 5,000 to about 95,894 and 148198 to about 151021.

NIB	Exc.	V.G.	Good	Fair	Poor
—	600	475	215	125	90

Model B-US

A version of the Model B with slight contour modifications to the back of the frame. Approximately 14,000 were made for the U.S. government in 1942-1943. Most are marked "PROPERTY OF U.S." on the top of the barrel and on the right side of the frame. Monogrammed hard rubber grips. Most guns are found in serial number range 92344 to about 111631. **NOTE:** Box with papers add premium of 20 percent.

NIB	Exc.	V.G.	Good	Fair	Poor
—	800	520	375	175	125

Model C

Like the Model B except in .22 Short. Introduced 1936; approximately 4,700 made. Both plain and monogrammed hard rubber grips. Available with either a 4.5" or a 6.75" round barrel. **NOTE:** Add $75 premium for I-A takedown. Add $175 premium for I-B takedown. Box with papers add premium of 15 percent.

NIB	Exc.	V.G.	Good	Fair	Poor
—	725	450	300	225	150

Model A

Similar to the Model B but with checkered walnut grips over an extended grip and an adjustable sight. Introduced 1938; approximately 7,300 made. Available with either a 4.5" or a 6.75" round barrel. The same light barrel as the Model B. **NOTE:** Add

$175 premium for I-B takedown. Box with papers add premium of 15 percent.

NIB	Exc.	V.G.	Good	Fair	Poor
—	750	500	400	175	125

Model D

Similar to a Model A but with a heavier weight barrel. (The middle weight barrel.) Available with either a 4.5" or a 6.75" barrel and optional checkered walnut grips. Introduced 1938; approximately 2,500 made. **NOTE:** Add $175 premium for I-B takedown. Box with papers add premium of 15 percent.

NIB	Exc.	V.G.	Good	Fair	Poor
—	835	490	310	200	130

Model E

Like the Model D but with a still heavier weight barrel (the heavy weight barrel). Available with either a 4.5" or a 6.75" barrel. Checkered walnut grips with thumb rest. Introduced 1938; approximately 2,600 made. **NOTE:** Add $175 for I-B takedown. Box with papers add premium of 18 percent.

NIB	Exc.	V.G.	Good	Fair	Poor
—	1300	925	650	250	140

Model S

Not a production model. Like the model B but with a smooth bore. Nine registered as Model S. Additional five with Model C slides

are registered, Model C/S. Note ivory bead front sight. Others may exist but only 14 are registered with BATF. Manufactured in 1939 and 1940. Values for both variations are equal. 6.75" barrels. **NOTE:** Serial numbers for registered samples. Model S: 48142; 48143; 48144; 48145; 48146; 59458; 59459; 59474 Model C/S: 59279; 59460; 59469; 59473; 59478

NIB	Exc.	V.G.	Good	Fair	Poor
—	5250	3950	3000	—	—

HAMMER LETTER MODELS

Second models made. Like the letter models but with external hammers.

Model H-B, Type 1 Pre-War

Like the Model B but with exposed hammer. Introduced 1940; approximately 2,100 made. **NOTE:** Box with papers add premium of 15 percent.

NIB	Exc.	V.G.	Good	Fair	Poor
—	725	425	275	175	125

Model H-B, Type 2 Post-War

Post-war variation has an external safety. Approximately 25,000 made. **NOTE:** Box with papers add premium of 15 percent.

NIB	Exc.	V.G.	Good	Fair	Poor
—	550	375	225	150	100

Model H-A

Like the Model A but with exposed hammer. Introduced 1940; approximately 1,040 made. **NOTE:** Box with papers add premium of 15 percent.

NIB	Exc.	V.G.	Good	Fair	Poor
—	1600	1100	750	500	300

Model H-D

Like the Model D but with exposed hammer. Introduced 1940; approximately 6,900 made. **NOTE:** Box with papers add premium of 15 percent.

Model H-D with 6.75" barrel

NIB	Exc.	V.G.	Good	Fair	Poor
—	1500	1000	650	400	250

Model H-E

Like the Model E but with exposed hammer. Introduced 1940; approximately 2,100 made. **NOTE:** Box with papers add premium of 15 percent.

NIB	Exc.	V.G.	Good	Fair	Poor
—	1800	950	700	275	150

Model USA—Model HD

Similar to the Model HD but 4.5" barrel only. Had fixed sights, checkered black hard rubber grips and an external safety. Early models blued; later model Parkerized. Introduced 1943; approximately 44,000 produced for the U.S. government. **NOTE:** Box with papers add premium of 20 percent.

NIB	Exc.	V.G.	Good	Fair	Poor
—	800	625	450	225	125

Model USA—Model HD-MS

A silenced variation of the USA Model HD. Approximately 2,000 produced for the OSS during 1944 and 1945. 6.75" shrouded barrel. Early models blued; later model Parkerized. Only a few are registered with BATFE for civilian ownership.

NIB	Exc.	V.G.	Good	Fair	Poor
—	6600	5500	—	—	—

Model H-D Military

Similar to the HD but with external safety. Early production had checkered plastic grips; later production changed to checkered walnut. Introduced 1945; approximately 150,000 produced. **NOTE:** Box with papers add premium of 15 percent.

NIB	Exc.	V.G.	Good	Fair	Poor
—	600	450	275	200	125

LEVER LETTER MODELS

Third design models incorporate interchangeable barrels with a lever takedown.

G-.380

A .380 caliber semi-automatic pistol with a 5" barrel and 6-shot magazine. Blues with checkered plastic grips. Fixed sights. Introduced 1947, discontinued 1950; approximately 7,400 made. High Standard's only production centerfire pistol. **NOTE:** Box with papers add premium of 10 percent.

NIB	Exc.	V.G.	Good	Fair	Poor
—	750	550	375	150	115

G-B

Similar characteristics with the Model B but with interchangeable 4.5" or 6.75" barrels. Sold with either barrel or as a combination with both barrels. Fixed sights. Blued with monogrammed plastic grips. Last short frame model produced. Introduced 1949, discontinued 1950; approximately 4,900 produced. **NOTE:** Box with papers add premium of 15 percent. Add $225 premium for factory combination.

NIB	Exc.	V.G.	Good	Fair	Poor
—	575	350	250	135	100

G-D

Similar characteristics with the Model D but with interchangeable 4.5" or 6.75" barrels. Sold with either barrel or as a combination with both barrels. Adjustable sights. Blued with checkered walnut grips. Optional checkered thumb rest walnut grips. Introduced 1949, discontinued 1950; approximately 3,300 produced. **NOTE:** Add $325 premium for factory combination, $50 premium for factory target grips. Box with papers add premium of 15 percent.

NIB	Exc.	V.G.	Good	Fair	Poor
—	975	750	450	195	125

G-E

Similar characteristics with the Model E but with interchangeable 4.5" or 6.75" barrels. Sold with either barrel or as a combination with both barrels. Adjustable sights. Blued with checkered thumb rest walnut grips. Introduced 1949, discontinued 1950; approximately 2,900 produced. **NOTE:** Add $375 premium for factory combination. Box with papers add premium of 15 percent.

NIB	Exc.	V.G.	Good	Fair	Poor
—	1275	800	450	225	135

Olympic (commonly called "G-O")

New gun design for competitive shooting in .22 Short caliber. 4.5" or 6.75" barrels. Sold with either barrel or as a combination with both barrels. Grooved front and back straps on frame. Adjustable sights. Blued with checkered thumb rest walnut grips. Introduced 1949, discontinued 1950; approximately 1,200 produced. This model uses a special curved magazine. A few guns will utilize a straight-back magazine. The majority of these Olympics use the curved magazine with a humped back. **NOTE:** Add $375 premium for factory combination. Box with papers add premium of 15 percent. Add $300 for the straight magazine variation.

NIB	Exc.	V.G.	Good	Fair	Poor
—	1500	875	550	225	125

LEVER NAME MODELS

Fourth design models evolving from the lever letter series designs with slight changes.

Supermatic

.22 LR caliber pistol with 10-shot magazine. Heavy round barrel, blued finish; adjustable sights and brown plastic thumb rest grips. Grooved front and back straps on frame. Available with 4.5" or 6.75" barrels or combination with both barrels. Ribbed barrels and provisions for weights. A 2 oz. and a 3 oz. weight were provided with this model, as was a filler strip for when the weights were not used. **NOTE:** Add $250 for factory combination. Box with papers add premium of 15 percent.

NIB	Exc.	V.G.	Good	Fair	Poor
—	750	550	400	275	135

Olympic

.22 Short caliber pistol with 10-shot magazine. Heavy round barrel, blued finish, adjustable sights and brown plastic thumb rest grips. Grooved front and back straps on frame. Available with 4.5" or 6.75" barrels or combination with both barrels. Ribbed barrels and provisions for weights. Weights of 2 oz. and 3 oz. were provided with this model, as was a filler strip for when the weights were not used. **NOTE:** Add $250 for factory combination. Box with papers add premium of 15 percent.

NIB	Exc.	V.G.	Good	Fair	Poor
—	1000	750	575	275	150

Field King

.22 LR caliber pistol with 10-shot magazine. Heavy round barrel, blued finish, adjustable sights and brown plastic thumb rest grips. Available with 4.5" or 6.75" barrels or combination with both barrels. No rib on barrels or provisions for weights. **NOTE:** Add $225 premium for factory combination. Box with papers add premium of 15 percent.

NIB	Exc.	V.G.	Good	Fair	Poor
—	575	380	250	150	125

Sport King

.22 caliber pistol with 10-shot magazine. Lightweight round barrel, blued finish, fixed sights and brown plastic thumb rest grips. Available with 4.5" or 6.75" barrels or combination with both barrels. Early models did not have a slide holdback when the magazine was empty. Early variation without holdback was produced in about twice the quantity as the later models incorporating this feature. **NOTE:** Add $200 premium for factory combination. Box with papers add premium of 15 percent. Add a $25 premium for guns with holdback feature.

NIB	Exc.	V.G.	Good	Fair	Poor
—	425	300	225	155	110

100 SERIES MODELS

Fifth design models evolving from the lever name series designs. This series introduced the small pushbutton barrel release takedown and deletes the shrouded breach.

Supermatic S-100

Like the lever takedown Supermatic but with new takedown. Available with 4.5", 6.75", or a combination with both barrel lengths. Grooved front and back straps on frame. This model produced briefly in 1954. Weights of 2 oz. and 3 oz. were provided with this model, as was a filler strip for when the weights were not used. **NOTE:** Add $250 for factory combination. Box with papers add premium of 15 percent.

NIB	Exc.	V.G.	Good	Fair	Poor
—	825	600	400	175	125

Olympic O-100

Like the lever takedown Olympic but with new takedown. Available with 4.5", 6.75", or a combination with both barrel lengths. Grooved front and back straps on frame. This model produced briefly in 1954. Weights of 2 oz. and 3 oz. were provided with this model, as was a filler strip for when the weights were not used. **NOTE:** Add $250 for factory combination. Box with papers add premium of 15 percent.

NIB	Exc.	V.G.	Good	Fair	Poor
—	1250	700	475	250	135

Field King FK-100

Like the lever takedown Field King but with new takedown. Available with 4.5", 6.75", or a combination with both barrel lengths. This model produced briefly in 1954. **NOTE:** Add $225 premium for factory combination. Box with papers add premium of 15 percent.

NIB	Exc.	V.G.	Good	Fair	Poor
—	750	495	385	175	125

Sport King SK-100

Like the lever takedown Sport King but with new takedown. Available with 4.5", 6.75", or a combination with both barrel lengths. This model produced 1954 to 1957. In late 1958 Col. Rex Applegate imported about 300 of these pistols into Mexico. These guns are marked with his company's name "ARMAMEX." Marked "ARMAMEX, MEXICO" on the right side of the barrel and "SPORT KING/CAL .22 L.R." on the left side of the barrel. Serial numbers around 870,084-870,383. Note that the Applegate guns were made after the 102 series was in production. Armamex catalog number 1910. **NOTE:** Add $200 premium for factory combination. Add $250 premium for Armamex version. Box with papers add premium of 10 percent.

NIB	Exc.	V.G.	Good	Fair	Poor
—	425	250	200	135	100

Sport King Lightweight SK-100

Aluminum frame like Flite King LW-100 but in .22 LR caliber. Produced 1956 to 1964. Also available nickel plated 1957 to 1960. **NOTE:** Add $150 premium for nickel finish, $200 premium for factory combination. Box with papers add premium of 12 percent.

NIB	Exc.	V.G.	Good	Fair	Poor
—	525	325	200	140	100

Flite King LW-100

.22 Short caliber semi-automatic pistol with 10-shot magazine. Blued finish with black anodized aluminum frame and slide. Brown plastic checkered thumb rest grips. Fixed sights. Available with 4.5", 6.75", or a combination with both barrel lengths. This model produced 1954 to 1957. **NOTE:** Add $200 for factory combination. Box with papers add premium of 12 percent.

NIB	Exc.	V.G.	Good	Fair	Poor
—	550	400	285	145	100

Dura-Matic M-100

.22 LR caliber semi-automatic pistol with 10-shot magazine. Striker-fired, fixed sights, blued finish, brown checkered plastic one-piece grip. Takedown by thumb nut. Available with 4.5", 6.5", or a combination with both barrel lengths. This model produced briefly in 1954. **NOTE:** Add $150 premium for factory combination. Box with papers add premium of 12 percent.

NIB	Exc.	V.G.	Good	Fair	Poor
—	350	225	165	150	95

101 SERIES MODELS

Sixth design models evolving from the 100 series. This series continued the small pushbutton barrel release takedown.

Olympic O-101

A .22 Short caliber semi-automatic pistol with a 10-shot magazine. Heavy round barrel, blued finish, adjustable sights and brown plastic thumb rest grips. Grooved front and back straps on frame. Available with 4.5", 6.75", or a combination with both barrel lengths. The 6.75" barrel incorporates a muzzlebrake with one slot on either side of the front sight. **NOTE:** Add $250 premium for factory combination. Box with papers add premium of 13 percent.

NIB	Exc.	V.G.	Good	Fair	Poor
—	950	600	450	200	175

Supermatic S-101

A .22 LR caliber semi-automatic pistol with a 10-shot magazine. Heavy round barrel, blued finish, adjustable sights and brown plastic thumb rest grips. Grooved front and back straps on frame. Available with 4.5", 6.75", or a combination with both barrel lengths. The 6.75" barrel incorporates a muzzlebrake with one slot on either side of the front sight. Also produced with U.S. marking for the military. **NOTE:** Add $250 premium for factory combination. Box with papers add premium of 13 percent.

NIB	Exc.	V.G.	Good	Fair	Poor
—	775	475	360	190	130

Field King FK-101

A .22 LR caliber semi-automatic pistol with a 10-shot magazine. Heavy round barrel, blued finish, adjustable sights and brown plastic thumb rest grips. Available with 4.5", 6.75", or a combination with both barrel lengths. **NOTE:** Add $225 premium for factory combination. Box with papers add premium of 15 percent.

NIB	Exc.	V.G.	Good	Fair	Poor
—	625	475	360	175	125

Dura-Matic M-101

Like the Dura-matic M-100 with slightly different locking method for thumb nut takedown. Produced 1954 to 1970. Later appeared renamed "Plinker" M-101 in 1971 to 1973. Plinker not available with both barrel combinations. A slightly modified version was sold by Sears Roebuck & Co. as the J. C. Higgins M-80. **NOTE:** Add $150 premium for factory combination. Box with papers add premium of 10 percent.

NIB	Exc.	V.G.	Good	Fair	Poor
—	350	225	140	110	80

Conversion Kits

These kits convert .22 LR to .22 Short and include a barrel, an aluminum slide, and magazine for .22 Short to .22 LR in which case the slide is steel. Prices are for the kit in original factory boxes. **NOTE:** First advertised for 101 Series guns. Later versions were produced for lever takedown guns. Catalog numbers are unknown for conversion kits for lever takedown guns.

NIB	Exc.	V.G.	Good	Fair	Poor
—	600	475	—	—	—

102 & 103 SERIES MODELS

The 102 Series was a major design change incorporating a new frame with a large pushbutton takedown release. Also new was a superb adjustable sight. There is little difference between the two series.

Supermatic Trophy

A .22 LR caliber semi-automatic pistol with a 10-shot magazine. A tapered barrel with an enlarged register at the muzzle end to hold a removable muzzlebrake. Super polished blue finish; adjustable sights; 2 and 3 oz. adjustable weights and checkered walnut thumb rest grips. Grooved front and back straps on frame. Available with 6.75", 8" or 10" barrels. Occasionally sold as a combination including two barrels. Premiums for 10" barrels and combinations in original boxes. 5.5" bull barrel available in 103s after April 1962, 7.25" fluted barrels available in 103s after April 1963. **NOTE:** Add $125 premium for 8" barrel and $225 premium for 10" barrel. Box with papers add premium of 12 percent. Occasionally found with the optional light oak case, which will command a premium of about 14 percent.

NIB	Exc.	V.G.	Good	Fair	Poor
—	1100	775	525	200	120

Supermatic Citation

Like the Supermatic Trophy with checkered plastic grips. Blued finish without the trophy's super polished finish. Grooved front and back straps on frame. 5.5" bull barrel available in 103s after April 1962. Also produced with U.S. marking for the military. **NOTE:** Add $100 premium for 8" barrel and $200 premium for 10" barrel. Box with papers add premium of 12 percent. Occasionally found with optional light oak case, which will command a premium of about 18 percent.

NIB	Exc.	V.G.	Good	Fair	Poor
—	725	495	375	165	120

Supermatic Tournament

A .22 LR caliber semi-automatic pistol with a 10-shot magazine. Barrels are round and tapered. Blued finish, adjustable sights and checkered plastic grips. Available with 4.5", 6.75", or a combination with both barrels. Combinations available in 102 Series only. 5.5" bull barrel replaced the 4.5" barrel in early 1962. Also produced with U.S. marking for the military. **NOTE:** Add $200 premium for factory combination. Box with papers add premium of 12 percent.

NIB	Exc.	V.G.	Good	Fair	Poor
—	640	475	275	155	110

Olympic

A .22 Short caliber version of the Supermatic Citation. Early models marked "Olympic Citation," changed to "Olympic" only in 1960. Grooved front and back straps on frame. 6.75", 8" and 10" barrels produced. 5.5" bull barrel available on later 103 production. **NOTE:** Add $125 premium for 8" barrel and $225 premium for 10" barrel and $150 premium for "Olympic Citation" marked guns. Box with papers add premium of 12 percent.

NIB	Exc.	V.G.	Good	Fair	Poor
—	1150	600	375	175	120

Olympic ISU

Like an Olympic but only available with a 6.75" barrel with integral muzzlebrake. Grooved front and back straps on frame. **NOTE:** Box with papers add premium of 12 percent.

NIB	Exc.	V.G.	Good	Fair	Poor
—	1150	675	360	165	120

Olympic Trophy ISU

An Olympic ISU with a Supermatic Trophy finish. Grooved front and back straps on frame. Produced in the 103 Series only. Fewer than 500 produced. **NOTE:** Box with papers add premium of 10 percent.

NIB	Exc.	V.G.	Good	Fair	Poor
—	2400	775	375	165	135

Sport King

A .22 LR caliber semi-automatic pistol with a 10-shot magazine. Barrels are lightweight, round, and tapered. Blued finish; fixed sights and checkered plastic grips. Available with 4.5", 6.75", or a combination with both barrel lengths. Produced 1957 to 1970 and 1974 to 1977. Also available 1974 to 1977 with nickel finish. $100 premium for nickel finish and $200 premium for factory combination. **NOTE:** Box with papers add premium of 20 percent.

NIB	Exc.	V.G.	Good	Fair	Poor
—	350	300	250	150	100

Flite King

A .22 Short caliber version of the Sport King Models 102 and 103. These models have steel frames. **NOTE:** Add $200 premium for factory combination. Box with papers add premium of 12 percent.

NIB	Exc.	V.G.	Good	Fair	Poor
—	475	360	265	150	100

Sharpshooter

A .22 LR caliber semi-automatic pistol with a 10-shot magazine. 5.5" bull barrel, blued finish, adjustable sights, checkered plastic grips. Some produced with Model 103-marked slides. Although the 103-marked guns have 1969 and later serial numbers they were shipped after the introduction of the Sharpshooter in 1971 and were probably converted from unsold Sport Kings. No premium for 103-marked. Variation without series marked on slide is the most plentiful. Produced 1971 to 1977. **NOTE:** Box with papers add premium of 15 percent.

NIB	Exc.	V.G.	Good	Fair	Poor
—	500	325	265	154	110

Conversion Kits

These kits convert .22 LR to .22 Short and include a barrel, an aluminum slide, and magazine. Prices are for kits in original boxes.

NIB	Exc.	V.G.	Good	Fair	Poor
900	700	575	—	—	—

104 SERIES MODELS

The last of the slant grip gun designs. The early production marked "Model 104". Later production is unmarked.

Supermatic Trophy

A .22 LR caliber semi-automatic pistol with a 10-shot magazine. Super polished blue finish; adjustable sights; 2 and 3 oz. adjustable weights, checkered walnut thumb rest grips. Grooved front and back straps on frame. Available with 5.5" bull or 7.25" fluted barrels. Both barrels accept the removable muzzlebrake. **NOTE:** Add $150 premium for high polish blue finish. Box with papers add premium of 12 percent.

NIB	Exc.	V.G.	Good	Fair	Poor
—	1050	625	425	175	110

Supermatic Citation

A .22 LR caliber semi-automatic pistol with a 10-shot magazine. Blue finish; adjustable sights; 2 and 3 oz. adjustable weights, checkered walnut thumb rest grips. Grooved front and back straps on frame. **NOTE:** Box with papers add premium of 12 percent.

NIB	Exc.	V.G.	Good	Fair	Poor
—	725	500	325	125	110

Olympic

Like the 103 Series 8" barrel models. **NOTE:** Box with papers add premium of 12 percent.

NIB	Exc.	V.G.	Good	Fair	Poor
—	1200	650	375	175	110

Olympic ISU

Like the 103 model. 6.75" barrel with integral brake. 5.5" version introduced in 1964. Catalogs and price list refer to the 9295 as both Olympic and Olympic ISU. It met the ISU regulations and included a removable muzzlebrake and weights. **NOTE:** Box with papers add premium of 12 percent.

NIB	Exc.	V.G.	Good	Fair	Poor
—	1100	625	360	175	110

Victor

A .22 LR caliber semi-automatic pistol with a 10-shot magazine. 4.5" and 5.5" slab-sided barrels with either ventilated or solid ribs. The adjustable sights are integral with the rib. Blue finish, barrel tapped for weight, checkered walnut thumb rest grips. Grooved front and back straps on frame. Probably fewer than 600 of these slant grip Victors in all configurations. Probably fewer than 40 each of the 4.5" guns. Trigger is adjustable for both pull and over-travel. Most guns in serial number range above 2401xxx with a few in the ML serial number series. Note the early vent rib barrels were steel and later ones aluminum without a change in catalog numbers. BEWARE—fakes exist. **NOTE:** Add $75 premium for steel rib, $200 premium for solid rib, and $200 premium for 4.5" barrel. Box with papers add premium of 15 percent.

Victor with 4.5" solid-rib barrel

Victor with 5.5" vent rib barrel

NIB	Exc.	V.G.	Good	Fair	Poor
—	2750	1500	600	425	250

106 SERIES MODELS

Referred to as military models, this series was designed to provide the same grip angles and feel of the Colt military model 1911. This design was introduced in 1965 and continued through most of 1968.

Supermatic Trophy

Like the 104 Series Supermatic Trophy with the new military frame. Stippled front and back straps on frame. **NOTE:** Add $100 premium for high polish blue finish, $200 premium for guns with boxes and accessories if factory records verify model numbers. Box with papers add premium of 12 percent.

NIB	Exc.	V.G.	Good	Fair	Poor
—	1000	600	425	190	120

Supermatic Citation

Like the 104 Series Supermatic Citation with the new military frame. Stippled front and back straps on frame. **NOTE:** Add $150 premium for guns with boxes and accessories if factory records verify model numbers. Box with papers add premium of 12 percent.

NIB	Exc.	V.G.	Good	Fair	Poor
—	675	475	300	200	120

Supermatic Tournament

Like the 104 Series Supermatic Tournament with the new military frame. Stippled front and back straps on frame. **NOTE:** Add $125 premium for guns with boxes and accessories if factory records verify model numbers. Box with papers add premium of 12 percent.

NIB	Exc.	V.G.	Good	Fair	Poor
—	600	375	250	165	120

Olympic

Listed in catalog but not in shipping records. Catalog number 9235 for 5.5" barrel. **WARNING:** There is no evidence that this model was actually produced.

Olympic ISU

Like the 104 Series Olympic ISU with the new military frame. Stippled front and back straps on frame. **NOTE:** Add $200 premium for guns with boxes and accessories if factory records verify model numbers. Box with papers add premium of 12 percent.

NIB	Exc.	V.G.	Good	Fair	Poor
—	1050	650	385	200	120

107 SERIES MODELS

The evolutionary successor to the 106 Series. This series had the frame redesigned to eliminate the plugging of the spring hole produced with the old tooling. During the time of this series production, the MILITARY marking on the frame was removed and then later reappeared near the end of the end of the traditional serial number series. The MILITARY marking is absent from the guns with the ML prefixed serial numbers. There is no premium associated with these variations.

Olympic ISU

Like the 106 Series Olympic ISU. **NOTE:** Box with papers add premium of 12 percent.

NIB	Exc.	V.G.	Good	Fair	Poor
—	1100	675	525	225	110

Olympic ISU 1980 Commemorative

A limited edition of the 107 Olympic ISU with 1,000 produced. "USA" prefix on serial numbers from 0001 to 1000. Engraved, right side of slide has the five gold ring Olympic logo. Offered with lined presentation case. **NOTE:** Prices are for guns with box, papers, and presentation case; otherwise deduct $250 for guns in excellent condition.

NIB	Exc.	V.G.	Good	Fair	Poor
—	1500	850	525	300	175

Supermatic Trophy

Like the 106 Series Supermatic Trophy. **NOTE:** Box with papers add premium of 12 percent.

NIB	Exc.	V.G.	Good	Fair	Poor
—	925	550	360	200	120

Supermatic Trophy 1972 Commemorative

A limited edition of the 107 Supermatic Trophy with 1000 planned. "T" prefix on serial numbers from 0000 to 999. Engraved, right side of slide has the five gold ring Olympic logo. Offered with lined presentation case. Only 107 guns listed in the shipping records, plus one frame. A couple of prototypes believed to exist in the regular serial number series. Prices are for guns in original presentation cases. **NOTE:** One fully engraved gun is known.

NIB	Exc.	V.G.	Good	Fair	Poor
6250	4500	—	—	—	—

Supermatic Citation

Like the 106 Series Supermatic Citation. **NOTE:** Box with papers add premium of 12 percent.

NIB	Exc.	V.G.	Good	Fair	Poor
—	625	425	300	225	110

Supermatic Tournament

Like the 106 Series Supermatic Tournament. Smooth front and back straps on frame. **NOTE:** Box with papers add premium of 12 percent.

NIB	Exc.	V.G.	Good	Fair	Poor
—	550	360	300	175	110

Sport King

Like the 103 Series Sport King with the military frame. **NOTE:** Box with papers add premium of 12 percent.

NIB	Exc.	V.G.	Good	Fair	Poor
—	345	225	195	155	100

Sharpshooter

Like the 103 Series Sharpshooter with the military frame. **NOTE:** Box with papers add premium of 12 percent.

NIB	Exc.	V.G.	Good	Fair	Poor
—	450	300	225	175	110

Survival Kit

An electroless nickel Sharpshooter with 5.5" barrel in a canvas carrying case with an extra electroless nickel magazine. **NOTE:** Deduct $100 for guns without the case and $65 for guns without the extra magazine for guns in excellent condition.

NIB	Exc.	V.G.	Good	Fair	Poor
—	750	500	300	175	110

Victor

A .22 LR caliber semi-automatic pistol with a 10-shot magazine. 4.5" and 5.5" slab-sided barrels with either ventilated or solid ribs. The adjustable sights are integral with the rib. Blue finish, barrel tapped for weight, checkered walnut thumb rest grips. Stippled front and back straps on frame. Early ventilated ribs were steel; aluminum replaced the steel on later ventilated ribs. Still later a clearance groove was added for spent shell ejection behind the barrel. Early models marked THE VICTOR on the left side of the barrel; later guns marked simply VICTOR on the left side of the frame. A few transition guns marked in both locations. **NOTE:** Add $125 premium for steel ribs, $125 premium for solid rib guns, premium for 4.5" barreled guns, $140 premium for Hamden guns (7-digit serial numbers and ML prefix serial numbers below ML 25,000). Box with papers add premium of 12 percent.

NIB	Exc.	V.G.	Good	Fair	Poor
—	775	500	350	200	120

10-X

A .22 LR caliber semi-automatic pistol with a 10-shot magazine. Matte blue finish, adjustable sights, checkered walnut thumb rest grips painted black. Stippled front and back straps on frame.

Available with 5.5" bull barrel. Assembled by a master gunsmith. Gunsmith's initials stamped in frame under left grip panel. Produced in 1981. **NOTE:** Prices are for guns with box and papers including test target. Otherwise deduct $175.

NIB	Exc.	V.G.	Good	Fair	Poor
—	2750	1550	900	350	125

SH SERIES MODELS

The final design produced by High Standard. A change in takedown from the large pushbutton introduced with the 102 Series and continuing through the 107 Series, to a hex socket head cap screw takedown.

Supermatic Trophy

Like the 107 Supermatic Trophy with a new takedown. **NOTE:** Box with papers add premium of 10 percent.

NIB	Exc.	V.G.	Good	Fair	Poor
—	600	375	275	165	120

Supermatic Citation

Like the 107 Supermatic Citation with a new takedown. **NOTE:** Box with papers add premium of 10 percent.

NIB	Exc.	V.G.	Good	Fair	Poor
—	525	350	250	175	120

Citation II

A new gun like the Supermatic Citation but with the barrel slabbed on the sides like the Victor and smooth front and back straps on frame. 5.5" and 7.25" barrels available. Blued finish, adjustable sights. Electroless nickel version utilized in some survival kits. **NOTE:** Box with papers add premium of 10 percent.

NIB	Exc.	V.G.	Good	Fair	Poor
—	475	350	250	155	110

Sport King

Like the 107 Sport King with a new takedown. Electroless nickel finish also available. **NOTE:** Box with papers add premium of 10 percent.

NIB	Exc.	V.G.	Good	Fair	Poor
—	300	225	165	140	90

Victor

Like the 107 Victor with a new takedown. Only available with 5.5" barrel. **NOTE:** Box with papers add premium of 10 percent.

NIB	Exc.	V.G.	Good	Fair	Poor
—	550	330	250	175	110

Sharpshooter

Like the 107 Sharpshooter with a new takedown. Electroless nickel version utilized in some survival kits. **NOTE:** Box with papers add premium of 10 percent.

NIB	Exc.	V.G.	Good	Fair	Poor
—	375	250	200	155	110

10-X

Like the 107 10-X with a new takedown. Also available with 7.25" fluted barrel and a 5.5" ribbed barrel like a Victor. **NOTE:** Prices are for guns with box and papers including test target. Otherwise deduct $150. Add $500 premium for 7.25" barrel, $1,000 for ribbed barrel like Victor.

NIB	Exc.	V.G.	Good	Fair	Poor
—	2350	1450	825	350	125

Survival Kit

Either an electroless nickel Sharpshooter or electroless nickel Citation II with 5.5" barrel in a canvas carrying case with an extra electroless nickel magazine. Two different fabrics utilized during production. **NOTE:** Deduct $100 for guns without the case and $65 for guns without the extra magazine for guns in excellent condition.

NIB	Exc.	V.G.	Good	Fair	Poor
—	700	475	275	200	110

Conversion Kits for Military Frame Guns

These kits convert .22 LR to .22 Short and include a barrel, an aluminum slide, and 2 magazines. **NOTE:** Prices are for kits in original boxes.

NIB	Exc.	V.G.	Good	Fair	Poor
—	625	390	—	—	—

HIGH STANDARD MANUFACTURING CO.
Houston, Texas

This company was established in 1993. Among its employees are several who worked for the High Standard Company that closed its doors in Connecticut in 1984. The remaining semi-automatic pistols in this section were made in Houston. This firm expanded in 2004 by purchasing the assets of AMT-Auto Mag and Interarms.

Supermatic Citation

Chambered for the .22 LR and fitted with a 5.5" barrel. Matte blue or Parkerized finish. Weight is about 44 oz. Discontinued.

NIB	Exc.	V.G.	Good	Fair	Poor
425	325	275	225	175	100

Supermatic Citation MS

Designed for metallic silhouette shooting and introduced in 1996. Fitted with a 10" barrel. Weight is approximately 49 oz. Discontinued.

NIB	Exc.	V.G.	Good	Fair	Poor
675	575	425	350	250	125

Supermatic Tournament

Chambered for .22 LR and fitted with a 5.5" barrel. Matte blue finish. Weight is approximately 44 oz.

NIB	Exc.	V.G.	Good	Fair	Poor
600	450	350	250	175	100

Supermatic Trophy

Offered with 5.5" or 7.25" barrels and chambered for .22 LR. Adjustable trigger, barrel weights, gold-plated trigger, safety, slide stop and magazine catch. Matte blue or Parkerized finish. Weight is about 45 oz. Add 10 percent for 7.25" barrel.

NIB	Exc.	V.G.	Good	Fair	Poor
600	450	350	250	150	100

Olympic Model

Chambered for .22 Short and fitted with a 5.5" bull barrel. Blued finish. Weight is approximately 44 oz.

NIB	Exc.	V.G.	Good	Fair	Poor
625	425	300	250	200	100

Olympic ISU

Similar to the previous model but fitted with a 6.75" barrel with internal stabilizer. Magazine capacity is 5 rounds. Checkered walnut grips. Weight is approximately 45 oz. This model was discontinued in 1995.

NIB	Exc.	V.G.	Good	Fair	Poor
600	500	350	300	200	150

Olympic Rapid Fire

Introduced in 1996. Chambered for the .22 Short cartridge with a 4" barrel, integral muzzlebrake and forward mounted compensator. Special grips. Weight is about 46 oz. Discontinued.

NIB	Exc.	V.G.	Good	Fair	Poor
1995	1550	1200	900	600	—

Sport King

Chambered for .22 LR and fitted with a 4.5" or 6.75" barrel. Adjustable rear sight. Weight is about 44 oz. Limited edition.

NIB	Exc.	V.G.	Good	Fair	Poor
650	400	225	150	100	80

Victor

With 4.5" barrel and blue or Parkerized finish.

NIB	Exc.	V.G.	Good	Fair	Poor
625	525	350	300	200	125

10-X

Fitted with 5.5" barrel. Weight is about 44 oz. From HS Custom Shop.

NIB	Exc.	V.G.	Good	Fair	Poor
850	700	550	450	350	200

10-X—Shea Model

Fitted with a 4.5" or 5.5" barrel. Limited to 150 pistols per year. Add 10 percent for 5.5 barrel.

NIB	Exc.	V.G.	Good	Fair	Poor
1100	850	700	500	350	200

Olympic Trophy Space Gun

Semi-automatic pistol chambered in .22 LR. Recreation of famed competition "Space Gun" from 1960s. Features include 8- or 10" barrel; 10-round magazine; adjustable sights; barrel weight; adjustable muzzle brake; blue-black finish with gold highlights.

NIB	Exc.	V.G.	Good	Fair	Poor
950	850	725	550	400	200

DERRINGERS

A .22 caliber or .22 Magnum caliber over/under double-action-only derringer with 3.50" barrels. They are found with three different types of markings.

Type 1 Markings

Type 1 Markings are found on early models which are marked "HI-STANDARD" / "DERRINGER" and have the EAGLE logo on the left side of the barrel. These models were marked "D-100" for the .22 caliber and "DM-101" for the .22 Magnum on the left side of the barrel. Date range 1962 to about 1967.

Type 2 Markings

Type 2 Markings are found on later models were marked "HI-STANDARD" / "DERRINGER" and had the TRIGGER logo. The early .22 caliber models were marked "D-100" and the later .22 caliber models beginning about 1969 were marked "D-101" on the left side of the barrel. The .22 Magnum models were marked "DM-101" on the left side of the barrel. Date range 1967 to about 1970.

Type 3 Markings

Type 3 Markings are found on the latest models were marked simply "DERRINGER" without HI STANDARD, or either logo. These models were also marked "D-101" for the .22 caliber and "DM-101" for the .22 Magnum on the left side of the barrel.

Blued finish, white or black grips, 1962-1984

NIB	Exc.	V.G.	Good	Fair	Poor
—	250	185	140	80	65

Nickel Finish black grips, introduced 1970

NIB	Exc.	V.G.	Good	Fair	Poor
—	250	185	140	80	65

Electroless Nickel Finish with checkered walnut grips

NIB	Exc.	V.G.	Good	Fair	Poor
—	275	190	145	80	65

Silver-Plated Derringer

A .22 Magnum derringer with a presentation case. Faux black mother of pearl grips. 501 made. Serial numbers SP 0 through SP 500. Produced in 1981.

NIB	Exc.	V.G.	Good	Fair	Poor
—	500	275	175	90	75

Gold-Plated Derringers

NIB	Exc.	V.G.	Good	Fair	Poor
—	450	300	200	100	80

NOTE: Prices are for GP serial number guns with presentation case. $100 premium for DM prefix guns in Exc. condition with presentation case. $150 premium for 1960s gold guns in Exc. condition with presentation cases.

REVOLVERS

POLICE-STYLE REVOLVERS

The revolvers begin with the R-100 design series and continue through the R-109 design series. Later steel-framed Sentinels carry no design series markings. The changes of design series designations indicate design changes to the guns. The only R-105 known to date is a private label gun made for Sears. The design series designations and the associated catalog numbers listed are the best estimates at the time of publication.

Earliest Sentinels in 1955 were in a seperate serial number series from 1 through approximately 45000. Then they were included in serial number series common to all handguns. In 1974 they were again put in a separate serial number series with an S prefix: S101 through S79946. Many of the later guns had a V suffix which indicated the gun was visually imperfect but guaranteed to work properly.

Sentinel Aluminum Frames

A 9-shot single-action or double-action revolver with swing-out cylinder for .22 Short, Long, or LR cartridges. Fixed sights. The Sentinel snub 2.375" barrel model had a bobbed hammer from its introduction until 1960. Beginning in 1961 this changed to a standard spur hammer with no change in the catalog number. Beginning with R-102 series the ejector had a spring return. Available in configurations listed.

High Standard private-labeled the aluminum-framed Sentinels for both Sears and Western Auto. From 1957 through 1962 High Standard offered the 2.375" snub-barreled Sentinel in three different color anodized frames. These guns had nickel-plated cylinders, triggers, and hammers. The grips were round-butt ivory-colored plastic. **NOTE:** Add $20 premium for nickel. Deduct $15 for early models without spring return ejector. Add $20 for R-102 marked guns.

NIB	Exc.	V.G.	Good	Fair	Poor
—	300	200	125	95	

Gold

NIB	Exc.	V.G.	Good	Fair	Poor
—	500	275	185	80	55

Turquoise

NIB	Exc.	V.G.	Good	Fair	Poor
—	575	300	185	80	55

Pink

NIB	Exc.	V.G.	Good	Fair	Poor
—	575	270	185	80	55

Sentinel Imperial

Has two-piece walnut square-butt grips, ramp front and adjustable rear sights. **NOTE:** Add $15 premium for nickel.

NIB	Exc.	V.G.	Good	Fair	Poor
—	300	200	125	95	70

Sentinel Deluxe

Has two-piece walnut square-butt grips and fixed sights. **NOTE:** Add $20 premium for nickel.

NIB	Exc.	V.G.	Good	Fair	Poor
—	300	200	125	95	70

Sentinel Snub

Has a 2.375" barrel with round-butt grips. **NOTE:** Add $20 premium for nickel.

NIB	Exc.	V.G.	Good	Fair	Poor
—	300	200	125	95	70

Sentinel Steel Frames

This model is like the Mark I sentinels without the Mark I markings. Offered as a combination with cylinders for .22 LR and .22 Win. Magnum. Prices are for guns with both cylinders. **NOTE:** Add $25 premium for adjustable sights. Deduct $50 for guns with only one cylinder.

NIB	Exc.	V.G.	Good	Fair	Poor
—	350	295	250	115	55

Kit Gun

A 9-shot single- or double-action revolver with swing-out cylinder for .22 Short, Long, or LR cartridges. Blue finish, aluminum frame, 4.0" barrel, and adjustable sights. Wood round-butt grips.

NIB	Exc.	V.G.	Good	Fair	Poor
—	275	195	125	80	55

Camp Gun

A nine-shot single- or double-action revolver with swing-out cylinder for .22 Short, Long, or LR cartridges or for .22 magnum. Also available as a combination with both cylinders. Blue finished steel frame, adjustable sights. **NOTE:** Add $50 premium for combination with both cylinders.

NIB	Exc.	V.G.	Good	Fair	Poor
—	275	195	120	80	55

Sentinel Mark I

A 9-shot single- or double-action revolver with swing-out cylinder for .22 Short, Long, or LR cartridges. Steel frame, and fixed sights. Available with blue and nickel finishes in 2", 3", and 4" barrels. Adjustable sights available on 3" and 4" barreled guns only. Wood square-butt grips. **NOTE:** Add $25 premium for adjustable sights. Add $25 for nickel.

NIB	Exc.	V.G.	Good	Fair	Poor
—	255	180	135	80	55

Sentinel Mark IV

Like the Mark I above except in .22 Magnum. **NOTE:** Add $25 premium for nickel. $25 premium for adjustable sights.

NIB	Exc.	V.G.	Good	Fair	Poor
—	275	200	145	80	55

Sentinel Mark II

A .357 Magnum single- or double-action 6-shot revolver with swing-out cylinder. Blue finish, steel frame, fixed sights. Produced by Dan Wesson for High Standard. Sold 1974 through 1975.

NIB	Exc.	V.G.	Good	Fair	Poor
—	325	265	175	90	60

Sentinel Mark III

Like the Mark II above except with adjustable sights. Sold 1974 through 1975.

NIB	Exc.	V.G.	Good	Fair	Poor
—	350	290	200	90	60

Power Plus

A five-shot single- or double-action revolver with swing-out cylinder for .38 Special cartridges. Blue finished steel frame. Only 177 guns produced. Serial numbers between PG 1010 and PG 1273.

NIB	Exc.	V.G.	Good	Fair	Poor
—	575	400	275	110	70

Crusader

A .44 Magnum or .45 Colt caliber double-action swing-out cylinder revolver with a unique geared action. Adjustable sights. 6-shot cylinder. The first 51 guns had the long barrels, special engraving, a gold crusader figure on the side plate, and an anniversary rollmark to commemorate High Standard's 50th anniversary.

.45 Colt

NOTE: Prices for serial numbers 0 through 50 with the 8.375" barrels.

NIB	Exc.	V.G.	Good	Fair	Poor
—	1000	750	500	350	200

.44 Magnum

NOTE: Prices for serial numbers 51 through 500 with the 6.5" barrels.

NIB	Exc.	V.G.	Good	Fair	Poor
—	1200	800	550	375	225

WESTERN-STYLE REVOLVERS

The Western-style revolvers begin with the W-100 design series and continue through the W-106 design series. Later steel-framed Sentinels carry no design series markings. The changes of design series designations indicate design changes to the guns. The design series designations and the associated catalog numbers which are listed are the best estimates at the time of publication.

High Standard private labeled the aluminum-framed Western-style revolvers for both Sears and Western Auto.

Double Nine with Aluminum Frame

A 9-shot single-action or double-action revolver for .22 Short, Long, or LR cartridges for all aluminum frame guns. One model has grip straps and trigger guard with gold plating contrasting with the blue frame. **NOTE:** Add $25 premium for nickel.

NIB	Exc.	V.G.	Good	Fair	Poor
—	325	250	195	100	55

Double Nine with Steel Frame

Available as .22 Short/Long/LR, .22 magnum, or a combination with both cylinders. **NOTE:** Add $45 premium for combination models, $20 premium for nickel.

NIB	Exc.	V.G.	Good	Fair	Poor
—	325	250	195	100	55

Longhorn

A 9-shot single- or double-action revolver for .22 Short, Long, or LR cartridges for all aluminum frame guns. Blue finish, fixed sights, and square-butt grips. One model has grip straps and trigger guard with gold plating contrasting with the blue frame. A Sears version exists.

NIB	Exc.	V.G.	Good	Fair	Poor
—	375	300	250	200	100

Longhorns with Steel Frame

Guns available as .22 Short/Long/LR, .22 magnum, or a combination with both cylinders. **NOTE:** Add $45 premium for combination models and $25 premium for adjustable sights.

NIB	Exc.	V.G.	Good	Fair	Poor
—	375	300	250	200	100

Marshall

A nine-shot single- or double-action revolver for .22 Short, Long, or LR cartridges. Blue finish. Aluminum frame, 5.5" barrel, fixed sights and square-butt stag style plastic grips. Offered in a special promotion package with a holster, trigger lock and spray can of G-96 gun scrubber. Price is for gun only. Add $40 premium if box, papers and accessories are present and in excellent condition.

NIB	Exc.	V.G.	Good	Fair	Poor
—	350	250	125	80	55

Posse

A nine-shot single- or double-action revolver for .22 Short, Long, or LR cartridges. Blue finish with brass colored grip straps and trigger guard. Aluminum frame, 3.5" barrel, fixed sights and square-butt walnut grips.

NIB	Exc.	V.G.	Good	Fair	Poor
—	400	275	135	90	55

Natchez

A 9-shot single- or double-action revolver for .22 Short, Long, or LR cartridges. Aluminum frame, 4.5" barrel, fixed sights and bird's-head-style ivory-colored plastic grips.

NIB	Exc.	V.G.	Good	Fair	Poor
—	450	325	225	125	60

Hombre

A 9-shot single- or double-action revolver for .22 Short/Long/LR cartridges. Blue or nickel finish. Aluminum frame, 4" barrel, fixed sights and square-butt walnut grips. **NOTE:** Add $20 premium for nickel.

NIB	Exc.	V.G.	Good	Fair	Poor
—	375	300	250	200	100

Durango

A 9-shot single- or double-action revolver for .22 Short/Long/LR cartridges. Blue or nickel finish. Aluminum or steel frame, 4.5" or 5.5" barrel, fixed or adjustable sights and square-butt walnut grips. Two models have their grip straps and trigger guard with contrasting plating to the blue frame. **NOTE:** Add $20 premium for nickel. Add $25 premium for steel frame and $25 premium for adjustable sights.

NIB	Exc.	V.G.	Good	Fair	Poor
—	375	300	250	200	100

The Gun/High Sierra

A 9-shot single- or double-action revolver for .22 Short, Long, or LR cartridges. Also available as a combination model with a second cylinder in .22 Magnum. Blued finish with gold plated grip straps and trigger guard. Steel frame, 7" octagonal barrel, fixed or adjustable sights and square-butt walnut grips. This revolver was introduced as "The Gun" in the February 1973 price list and the name was changed to "High Sierra" by November 1973 price list. Note that early "The Gun" had neither "High Sierra" markings nor any other name. **NOTE:** Add $60 premium for presentation case, $55 premium for combination models, $25 for adjustable sights.

NIB	Exc.	V.G.	Good	Fair	Poor
—	375	300	250	200	100

BLACKPOWDER REVOLVERS

These guns were a series of .36 caliber cap-and-ball revolvers that began production in 1974 and ran through 1976. These are reproductions of the Confederate copies of the Colt Model 1851 Navy. **NOTE:** Most Confederate copies of the Colt had round barrels, not octagonal as found on Colts. The frames were made by High Standard and the balance of the parts by Uberti. The guns were assembled and finished by High Standard.

Griswold & Gunnison

Blued finish with a brass frame. Six-shot single-action. Commemorative gun came with a pine presentation case and a brass belt plate depicting the Georgia state seal. **NOTE:** Price is for gun in case with accessories. Deduct $100 for gun only in Exc. condition.

NIB	Exc.	V.G.	Good	Fair	Poor
—	325	—	175	—	—

Leech & Rigdon

Blued finish with a steel frame. Six-shot single-action. Commemorative gun came with a presentation case and a reproduction of a Civil War belt buckle. **NOTE:** Price is for gun in case with accessories. Deduct $100 for gun only in Exc. condition.

NIB	Exc.	V.G.	Good	Fair	Poor
—	325	235	175	—	—

Schneider & Glassick

Blued finish with a steel frame. Six-shot single-action. Commemorative gun came with a presentation case and a modern version of a Confederate "D" guard Bowie knife.

NIB	Exc.	V.G.	Good	Fair	Poor
—	450	235	175	—	—

Bicentennial 1776-1976

Blued finish with a steel frame. Six-shot single-action. Guns came with two versions of presentation case. One case is pine, marked "High Standard" and the trigger logo is on the lid with a powder flask and silver dollar-sized medallion inside. The other is a brown leatherette covered case with "American Bicentennial 1776-1976" and contains a pewter Bicentennial belt buckle.

NIB	Exc.	V.G.	Good	Fair	Poor
—	450	235	175	—	—

Special Presentation Bicentennial

100 guns were available in presentation cases with "US" serial number prefixes. Serial numbers US 11 through US 50 are in walnut presentation cases with purple fitted lining and a pewter Bicentennial belt buckle. The top of the case is marked "Limited Edition / American Bicentennial / 1776 – 1976". The guns are engraved on the frame, cylinder barrel, loading lever, and hammer. Catalog number 9339 has a steel frame with a round barrel and catalog number 9340 has a brass frame with an octagonal barrel.

NIB	Exc.	V.G.	Good	Fair	Poor
—	675	500	350	—	—

SHOTGUNS

SEMI-AUTOMATIC SHOTGUNS

Supermatic Field

Gas-operated semi-automatic shotgun. Blued finish, plain pistol-grip walnut stock and forearm, 4-round magazine capacity. Supermatic Field models were superseded by models in the Supermatic Deluxe group beginning in 1966. The 12 gauge guns have 2.75" chambers while the 20 gauge guns have 3" chambers. **NOTE:** Slight premium for 20 gauge.

NIB	Exc.	V.G.	Good	Fair	Poor
—	300	250	195	100	75

Supermatic Special

Like the Supermatic Field except with 27" barrel with 6-position click-stop adjustable choke. Supermatic Special models were superseded by models in the Supermatic Deluxe group beginning in 1966. The 12 gauge guns have 2.75" chambers.

NIB	Exc.	V.G.	Good	Fair	Poor
	300	250	195	100	75

Supermatic Deluxe

Gas-operated semi-automatic shotgun. Blued finish, Checkered pistol grip walnut stock and forearm. Four-round magazine capacity. The adjustable choke had 6 click-stop positions. Recoil pad beginning 1966. The 12 gauge guns have 2.75" chambers while the 20 gauge guns have 3" chambers. **NOTE:** Add $20 premium for vent rib versions.

NIB	Exc.	V.G.	Good	Fair	Poor
—	325	275	210	125	95

Supermatic Citation

Same as Trophy except without ventilated rib. Six click-stop adjustable choke. Catalog number 8220 has a compensator integral with the adjustable choke. The 12 gauge guns have 2.75" chambers.

NIB	Exc.	V.G.	Good	Fair	Poor
—	300	250	195	100	75

Supermatic Trophy

Gas-operated semi-automatic shotgun. Blued finish, checkered walnut stock and fore-end. 4-round magazine capacity. Six click-stop adjustable choke. Catalog number 8230 has a compensator integral with the adjustable choke. The 12 gauge guns have 2.75" chambers while the 20 gauge guns have 3" chambers.

NIB	Exc.	V.G.	Good	Fair	Poor
—	300	250	195	100	75

Supermatic Duck

Gas-operated semi-automatic shotgun chambered for 3" magnum and suitable for all 2.75" shells. Blued finish. Checkered pistol-grip walnut stock and forearm. Magazine capacity: five 2.75" shells, four 3" shells. Recoil pad. **NOTE:** Add $20 premium for vent rib versions.

NIB	Exc.	V.G.	Good	Fair	Poor
—	325	275	210	125	95

Supermatic Deer Gun

Like Supermatic Deluxe with rifle sight. Recoil pad. Receiver tapped for peep sight on catalog number 8246. The 12 gauge guns have 2.75" chambers.

NIB	Exc.	V.G.	Good	Fair	Poor
—	300	250	195	100	75

Supermatic Skeet

Same features as Supermatic Deluxe except select American walnut stock and forearm and no recoil pad. The 12 gauge guns have 2.75" chambers while the 20 gauge guns have 3" chambers.

NIB	Exc.	V.G.	Good	Fair	Poor
—	325	275	210	125	95

Supermatic Trap

Same features as Supermatic Deluxe except select American walnut stock and forearm. Recoil pad. Catalog number 8266 is the Executive Trap model with Fajen Monte Carlo stock. The 12 gauge guns have 2.75" chambers.

NIB	Exc.	V.G.	Good	Fair	Poor
—	325	275	210	125	95

PUMP SHOTGUNS

Model 200

An economy 12 gauge pump shotgun sold as part of a promotional package beginning in 1971. The package included the Model 200, a zippered gun case, a plastic trigger lock, and G-96 gun lubricant. Prices are for gun alone. Add $30 for gun with complete promotional package.

NIB	Exc.	V.G.	Good	Fair	Poor
—	175	130	105	90	65

Flite King Field

Slide-action shotgun. Blued finish, plain pistol grip walnut stock and forearm. Catalog number 8450, magazine capacity: five 2.5" shells, four 3" shells. The 12 gauge guns have 2.75" chambers while the 20 gauge guns have 3" chambers. **NOTE:** Add 50 percent for .410 bore.

NIB	Exc.	V.G.	Good	Fair	Poor
—	250	195	150	100	65

Flite King Brush

Like the Flite King Field except has adjustable rifle sights. Receiver is tapped for the Williams sight and provision exist for sling swivels. Deluxe models have Williams receiver sight, a leather sling with swivels, and a recoil pad. The 12 gauge guns have 2.75" chambers. **NOTE:** Add $10 premium for deluxe model.

Flite King Brush Deluxe

NIB	Exc.	V.G.	Good	Fair	Poor
—	265	205	160	100	75

Flite King Special

Like the Flite King Field except for a 27" barrel with 6-click-stop adjustable choke. The 12 gauge guns have 2.75" chambers while the 20 gauge guns have 3" chambers.

NIB	Exc.	V.G.	Good	Fair	Poor
—	250	195	150	100	65

Flite King Deluxe

Slide-action shotgun. Blued finish, checkered pistol grip walnut stock and forearm. Five-round magazine capacity. Available with and without a vent rib. 8411 and 6411 were the boys "Converta Pump" sold with two stocks: one youth size and one full size. The adjustable choke had six click-stop positions. Recoil pad beginning 1966 except .410 models.The 12 gauge guns have 2.75" chambers, the 16 gauge has 2.75" chambers, the 20 gauge guns have 3" chambers, the 28 gauge has 2.75" chambers, and the .410 bore has 3" chambers. **NOTE:** Add $20 for vent rib.

NIB	Exc.	V.G.	Good	Fair	Poor
—	265	205	160	100	75

Flite King Citation

Like the Flite King Trophy without the vent rib. Catalog number 8130 has a compensator integral with the 6 position click-stop adjustable choke. The 12 gauge guns have 2.75" chambers while the 16 gauge guns have 2.75" chambers as well.

NIB	Exc.	V.G.	Good	Fair	Poor
—	250	195	150	100	65

Flite King Trophy

Slide-action shotgun. Blued finish, checkered pistol grip walnut stock and forearm. Five-round magazine capacity. Ventilated rib. Catalog number 8140 has a compensator integral with the adjustable choke. The 12 gauge guns have 2.75" chambers while the 20 gauge guns have 3" chambers.

NIB	Exc.	V.G.	Good	Fair	Poor
—	250	195	150	100	65

Flite King Skeet

Same features as Flite King Deluxe except select American walnut stock and forearm and no recoil pad. The 12 gauge guns have 2.75" chambers, the 20 gauge guns have 3" chambers, the 28 gauge has 2.75" chambers, and the .410 bore has 3" chambers.

NIB	Exc.	V.G.	Good	Fair	Poor
—	290	200	150	100	75

Flite King Trap

Same features as Flite King Deluxe except select American walnut stock and forearm. Recoil pad. 8166 is the Executive Trap model with Fajen Monte Carlo stock. Catalog number 6165 is a model with provisions for interchangeable barrels. The 12 gauge guns have 2.75" chambers. **NOTE:** Add $25 for Fajen Monte Carlo stock.

NIB	Exc.	V.G.	Good	Fair	Poor
—	275	185	150	100	75

BOLT-ACTION SHOTGUNS

Model 514

The Sears version of this shotgun was recalled for safety considerations in the late 1990s. The catalog numbers listed are from a parts book which does not provide production dates.

NIB	Exc.	V.G.	Good	Fair	Poor
—	135	85	60	45	25

POLICE SHOTGUNS

Semi-Automatic

A gas-operated semi-automatic 12 gauge shotgun. Plain oiled pistol grip walnut stock and forearm. Magazine capacity is four. Recoil pad.

NIB	Exc.	V.G.	Good	Fair	Poor
—	265	205	160	100	75

Model 10-A

A gas-operated semi-automatic 12 gauge shotgun in bullpup configuration with pistol grip. Integral carrying handle and integral flashlight on top of gun. Magazine capacity is four.

NIB	Exc.	V.G.	Good	Fair	Poor
—	900	725	575	325	225

Model 10-B

A gas-operated semi-automatic 12 gauge shotgun in bullpup configuration with pistol grip. Fitted with a integral folding carrying handle and mounting provisions for a flashlight. Magazine capacity is four. Carrying case catalog number 50284 and attachable flashlight catalog number 50285 sold optionally. **NOTE:** Values are for gun with flashlight.

NIB	Exc.	V.G.	Good	Fair	Poor
—	900	725	575	325	225

Pump

A slide-action 12 gauge shotgun. Plain pistol-grip oiled walnut stock and forearm—changed from walnut to stained and lacquered birch in the mid 1970s. 8111/8113 magazine capacity six. 8104/8129 magazine capacity five. A 1963 flyer mentions the #8105 Flite King Brush 20" and the #8107 Flite King Deluxe 20" as riot guns. The data on the #8105 and #8107 is listed under Flite King Brush.

NIB	Exc.	V.G.	Good	Fair	Poor
—	230	160	125	100	75

IMPORTED SHOTGUNS

Supermatic Shadow Automatic

A gas-operated semi-automatic shotgun in 12 and 20 gauge, interchangeable barrels. Checkered walnut stock and forearm. Special "airflow" rib. Imported from Nikko in Japan.

NIB	Exc.	V.G.	Good	Fair	Poor
—	395	280	200	130	100

Supermatic Shadow Indy Over/Under

A boxlock over/under 12 gauge shotgun with selective auto ejectors and single trigger. Receiver is fully engraved. Skipline checkered walnut stock with pistol grip. Ventilated forearm. Recoil pad. Special "airflow" rib. Imported from Nikko in Japan.

NIB	Exc.	V.G.	Good	Fair	Poor
—	860	730	625	475	350

Supermatic Shadow Seven Over/Under

Like the Shadow Indy but with a standard size vent rib, conventional forearm, no recoil pad, standard checkering, and less engraving. Imported from Nikko in Japan.

NIB	Exc.	V.G.	Good	Fair	Poor
—	695	585	480	350	300

RIFLES

Sport King/Flite King

A .22 caliber slide-action rifle capable of using Short/Long/LR ammunition interchangeably. 24" barrel, open sights, and a tubular magazine. Magazine capacity 21 Short, 17 Long or 15 LR.

NIB	Exc.	V.G.	Good	Fair	Poor
—	175	110	80	65	45

Sport King Field

A .22 caliber semi-automatic rifle capable of using Short/Long/LR ammunition interchangeably. 22.25" barrel, open sights, and a tubular magazine. Magazine capacity 21 Short, 17 Long, or 15 LR. Walnut stock.

NIB	Exc.	V.G.	Good	Fair	Poor
—	165	95	70	60	40

Sport King Special

Like the Sport King Field except Monte Carlo walnut stock with pistol grip.

NIB	Exc.	V.G.	Good	Fair	Poor
—	185	130	100	60	40

Sport King Deluxe/Sport King

The Sport King Special with a new name. Catalog number 6005 is also the same gun but called just Sport King. A promotional package was offered that included the Sport King rifle, a zippered gun case, a plastic trigger lock, and G-96 gun lubricant. This package was catalog number 8007. **NOTE:** Add a 10 percent premium for complete 8007 package in original box.

NIB	Exc.	V.G.	Good	Fair	Poor
—	215	145	110	80	50

Sport King Carbine

A .22 carbine semi-automatic rifle capable of using Short/Long/LR ammunition interchangeably. 18.25" barrel, open sights, and a tubular magazine. Magazine capacity 17 Short, 14 Long, or 12 LR. Straight grip walnut stock with barrel band and sling.

NIB	Exc.	V.G.	Good	Fair	Poor
—	195	145	110	80	50

Hi-Power Field Grade

A .270 or .30-06 caliber bolt-action rifle with a 22" barrel, open sights and a 4-shot magazine. Blued with a walnut stock.

NIB	Exc.	V.G.	Good	Fair	Poor
—	350	265	225	150	100

Hi-Power Deluxe

Like the Field Grade except has a Monte Carlo-style stock.

NIB	Exc.	V.G.	Good	Fair	Poor
—	400	330	275	175	130

HILL, W.J.
Birmingham, England

Hill's Self-Extracting Revolver

A .32 caliber double-action folding trigger revolver with a 3.75" barrel and 6-shot cylinder. Marked "Hill's Patent Self Extractor." Blued with walnut grips.

NIB	Exc.	V.G.	Good	Fair	Poor
		1025	495	295	150

HILLIARD, D. H.
Cornish, New Hampshire

Under Hammer Pistol

A .34 caliber under hammer percussion pistol with varying barrel lengths. Blued with walnut grips. Active 1842 to 1877.

NIB	Exc.	V.G.	Good	Fair	Poor
—	—	950	475	200	100

HINO-KOMURA
Tokyo, Japan

A 7.65mm or 8mm Nambu semi-automatic pistol manufactured in limited quantities between 1905 and 1912. The operation of this pistol involves pulling the muzzle forward until the slide engages a catch on the trigger assembly. Pulling the trigger at this point allows the barrel to move back and engage the cartridge nose into the chamber. Squeezing the grip safety then allows the barrel to slam back into the fixed firing pin on the breechblock. Prospective purchasers are advised to secure a qualified appraisal prior to acquisition.

NIB	Exc.	V.G.	Good	Fair	Poor
—	3850	3600	3000	2250	1000

HODGKINS, D. C. & SONS
Macon, Georgia
See—Bilharz, Hall & Co.

HOFER, P.
Feriach, Austria

A gunmaker specializing in double-barrel rifles made strictly to custom order. Value depends on local demand, chamberings, and other factors.

HOFFMAN, LOUIS
Vicksburg, Mississippi

Pocket Pistol

A .41 caliber percussion pocket pistol with a 3" barrel, German silver mounts and walnut stock. Active 1857 to 1886.

NIB	Exc.	V.G.	Good	Fair	Poor
—	—	900	525	200	100

HOLDEN, C. B.
Worcester, Massachusetts

Open Frame Rifle

A .44 rimfire single-shot rifle with a 28" barrel, open sights, silver plated bronze frame and walnut stock. The barrel marked "C.B. Holden Worcester-Mass.". Produced in limited quantities during the mid-1860s.

NIB	Exc.	V.G.	Good	Fair	Poor
—	—	2600	1850	675	300

HOLECK, EMANUEL
Czechoslovakia

Holeck Rifle

Chambered for the .276 cartridge this semi-automatic rifle was submitted for testing for U.S. military trials in the 1920s. Barrel length is 21.5" with upper portion slotted for operating handle. Rotating dial at barrel band. Rarely encountered. **NOTE:** Thanks to Jim Supica for the research found in his Old Town Station Dispatch, in which one of these rifles was offered for sale.

NIB	Exc.	V.G.	Good	Fair	Poor
—	4250	—	—	—	—

HOLLAND & HOLLAND, LTD.
London, England

Established in 1835, Holland & Holland has manufactured a wide variety of shotguns and rifles during its existence. The greater part of these arms are made to custom order.

DOUBLE RIFLES

No. 2 Grade Double Rifle

A sidelock double-barrel rifle produced in a variety of calibers with 24" barrels, double triggers, automatic ejectors and express sights. Obsolete cartridges could be worth less.

NIB	Exc.	V.G.	Good	Fair	Poor
—	19500	15500	10200	7700	4000

Royal Side-by-Side Rifle

Price depends on caliber.

H&H .700 Bore Side-by-Side Rifle

A .700 Holland & Holland double-barrel rifle with a weight of approximately 18 lbs. Currently manufactured. Because of the uniqueness of the piece, buyers should seek qualified appraisal.

BOLT-ACTION RIFLES

Best Quality Rifle

Price depends on caliber and extra cost options. Retail prices for magazine rifles begin around $30,000, depending on the value of the dollar. Due to the uniqueness of each rifle an independent appraisal is a must prior to a sale.

HOLLOWAY ARMS CO.
Ft. Worth, Texas

HAC Model 7

A 7.62x54mm semi-automatic rifle with a 20" barrel, adjustable sights, integral telescope mount and 20-shot magazine. Black anodized finish with folding stock. No longer in production.

NIB	Exc.	V.G.	Good	Fair	Poor
2500	2000	1750	1200	600	500

HAC Model 7C

As above, with a 16" barrel.

NIB	Exc.	V.G.	Good	Fair	Poor
2750	2500	2000	1400	700	500

HAC Model 7S

As above, with a heavy barrel.

NIB	Exc.	V.G.	Good	Fair	Poor
2850	2650	2100	1500	700	500

HOLMES FIREARMS
Wheeler, Arkansas

MP-22

A .22 caliber semi-automatic pistol with a 6" barrel and alloy receiver. Anodized black finish with a walnut grip. Manufactured in 1985.

NIB	Exc.	V.G.	Good	Fair	Poor
425	325	250	200	150	100

MP-83

Similar to the above, but in 9mm or .45 caliber. Manufactured in 1985. **NOTE:** Several of the Holmes pistols have been declared machine guns by the BATFE because of their easy conversion to full automatic. Make sure before purchase that a Class III license is not required.

NIB	Exc.	V.G.	Good	Fair	Poor
550	425	325	250	200	125

HOOD F. A. CO.
Norwich, Connecticut

A manufacturer of spur trigger .22 or .32 caliber revolvers with varying length barrels and finishes. Many of these revolvers are found stamped only with trade names. This type of handgun is often referred to as a suicide special to denote its poor quality and lack of reliability.

NIB	Exc.	V.G.	Good	Fair	Poor
—	—	250	145	75	50

HOPKINS & ALLEN
Norwich, Connecticut
See—Bacon Arms Co. & Merwin Hulbert & Co.

Established in 1868, this company produced a variety of spur trigger revolvers in .22, .32, .38, or .41 caliber often marked with trade names such as: Acme, Blue Jacket, Captain Jack, Chichester, Defender, Dictator, Hopkins & Allen, Imperial Arms Co., Monarch, Mountain Eagle, Ranger, Tower's Police Safety, Universal and XL.

Some of these revolvers are hinged-frame, double-action break-opens with round-ribbed barrels of various lengths. Blued or nickel-plated, with checkered plastic grips.

Courtesy Milwaukee Public Museum, Milwaukee, Wisconsin

NIB	Exc.	V.G.	Good	Fair	Poor
—	—	550	275	125	75

Dictator

A .36 caliber percussion or .38 rimfire single-action revolver with a 4" barrel and 5-shot cylinder. Blued with walnut grips. The barrel marked "Dictator". Approximately 6,000 percussion revolvers were made and 5,000 rimfire.

NIB	Exc.	V.G.	Good	Fair	Poor
—	—	1000	725	400	125

Falling Block Rifle

A .22 to .38-55 caliber single-shot rifle with a 24", 26", or 28" octagonal barrel. Blued with a walnut stock. Manufactured between 1888 and 1892.

NIB	Exc.	V.G.	Good	Fair	Poor
—	—	1250	650	325	175

Schuetzen Rifle

A .22 or .25-20 caliber single-shot rifle with a 26" octagonal barrel, double-set trigger and a Schuetzen-type buttplate. Blued with a walnut stock.

NIB	Exc.	V.G.	Good	Fair	Poor
—	—	2750	1025	550	200

Navy Revolver

A .38 caliber rimfire single-action revolver with a 6.5" barrel marked, "Hopkins & Allen Mfg. Co., Pat. Mar. 28, 71, Apr. 27, 75" and a 6-shot cylinder. The top strap marked "XL Navy." Blued or nickel-plated with walnut grips. Several hundred were made between 1878 and 1882.

NIB	Exc.	V.G.	Good	Fair	Poor
—	—	1950	1650	675	175

Army Revolver

As above, in .44 rimfire with a 4.5", 6", or 7.5" barrel. The top strap marked "XL No. 8." Several hundred were manufactured between 1878 and 1882.

NIB	Exc.	V.G.	Good	Fair	Poor
—	—	2800	2500	925	350

Derringer

A .22 caliber single-shot pistol with a hinged 1.75" barrel that pivots downwards for loading. Blued or nickel-plated with walnut, ivory, or pearl grips. The frame marked, "Hopkins & Allen Arms Co., Norwich, Conn. U.S.A." Several hundred were manufactured in the 1880s and 1890s.

NIB	Exc.	V.G.	Good	Fair	Poor
—	—	2750	950	330	150

Double-Barrel Shotguns

Hopkins & Allen also made good quality single and double-barrel shotguns in large numbers. Many were sold under private brand names such as Seminole and King Nitro. Both hammer and hammerless versions were offered. Values vary from $100 to $1,000 depending on model and condition.

HOWA MACHINE COMPANY
Japan

This company manufactured bolt-action rifles for Smith & Wesson until 1985 and then for Mossberg in 1986 and 1987. From 1988 to 2000 Howa firearms were imported by Interarms of Alexandria, Virginia. These rifles are now imported by Legacy Sports of Alexandria, Virginia.

Model 1500 Hunter

A .22-250, .223, .243, .270, 7mm Remington Magnum .308, .30-06, .300 Win. Magnum, and .338 Winchester Magnum caliber bolt-action sporting rifle with a 22" or 24" barrel and 3- or 5-shot magazine. Blued or stainless steel with a checkered walnut stock. In 2002 this rifle was offered with black polymer stock. Weight is approximately 7.6 lbs. **NOTE:** Add $70 for stainless steel.

NIB	Exc.	V.G.	Good	Fair	Poor
600	500	450	325	225	175

Model 1500 JRS Classic

Offered in blue or stainless steel with laminated stock, these rifles are chambered for the .223 through .338 Win. Magnum calibers. Barrel length is 22" or 24", depending on caliber. Weight is about 8 lbs. **NOTE:** Add $70 for stainless steel.

NIB	Exc.	V.G.	Good	Fair	Poor
650	575	500	375	250	195

Model 1500 Mountain

Introduced in 2004 this bolt-action model is chambered for the .243, .308, or 7mm-08 cartridges. Fitted with a 20" contoured barrel with no sights. Blued finish with black hardwood stock. Stainless steel offered in .308 only. Magazine capacity is 5 rounds. Weight is about 6.4 lbs. **NOTE:** Add $115 for stainless steel.

NIB	Exc.	V.G.	Good	Fair	Poor
600	500	450	325	225	175

Model 1500 Trophy

As above, but with more finely figured walnut stocks and checkering. Introduced in 1988. No longer imported.

NIB	Exc.	V.G.	Good	Fair	Poor
650	525	450	375	250	195

Model 1500 Varmint

As above, in .22-250 or .223 caliber with a 24" heavy barrel. Choice of walnut or synthetic stock, in blue or stainless. Weight is about 9.3 lbs. Introduced in 1988. **NOTE:** Add $70 for stainless steel and $20 for walnut stock.

NIB	Exc.	V.G.	Good	Fair	Poor
650	600	500	375	250	195

Model 1500 Varmint Supreme

This model features a stainless steel barrel chambered for the .223, .22-250, .308, and .243 with no sights. Choice of black synthetic, or laminated stock with Monte Carlo comb. **NOTE:** Add $110 for thumbhole stock.

NIB	Exc.	V.G.	Good	Fair	Poor
650	525	450	375	250	195

Model 1500 Lightning Rifle

Introduced in 1993, this model has a black composite checkered stock with schnabel fore-end. The buttstock is Monte Carlo. Choice of blue or stainless steel. Offered in .223, .22-250, .243, .270, .308, .30-06, 7mm Rem. Magnum, .300 and .338 Win. Magnum/ Weighs about 7.5 lbs. **NOTE:** Add $70 for stainless steel.

NIB	Exc.	V.G.	Good	Fair	Poor
600	525	450	325	225	175

Model 1500 Youth

This model is chambered for the .243, .308, or 7mm-08 cartridge. Barrel length is 20". Black hardwood stock with 1" shorter length of pull than standard. Weight is about 6.3 lbs. Introduced in 2004. **NOTE:** Add $115 for stainless steel .308 version.

NIB	Exc.	V.G.	Good	Fair	Poor
600	500	400	275	175	125

Model 1500 Thumbhole Sporter

As above but with thumbhole stock. Weight is about 8.25 lbs. **NOTE:** Add $70 for stainless steel.

NIB	Exc.	V.G.	Good	Fair	Poor
750	625	500	400	275	150

Model 1500 Custom

Chambered for the .300 WSM or .300 Win. Magnum cartridge this rifle is fitted with a 22" or 24" barrel, depending on caliber. Polymer or laminated stock. Weight is around 8 lbs. Blued or stainless steel. **NOTE:** Add $70 for stainless steel.

NIB	Exc.	V.G.	Good	Fair	Poor
950	800	700	495	325	175

Realtree Camo Rifle

Introduced in 1993, this bolt-action model features a composite stock and a 22" barrel. Both the metal and stock finish are a brown leaf pattern. The receiver is a mono-block system. The floorplate is hinged and the magazine holds 5 rounds. The receiver is drilled and tapped for scope mounts. Fitted with a sling swivel and recoil pad. Offered in .30-06 and .270 calibers. Weighs 8 lbs.

NIB	Exc.	V.G.	Good	Fair	Poor
650	525	400	275	175	125

Texas Safari Rifle

Chambered for the .270 Win. or .300 Win. Magnum cartridge, this rifle is modified by gunsmith Bill Wiseman. Blue Teflon finish and

---

22" or 24" barrel depending on caliber. Laminated stock. Weight is about 7.8 lbs.

NIB	Exc.	V.G.	Good	Fair	Poor
1200	800	650	525	400	150

Model 1500 PCS (Police Counter Sniper)

This bolt-action is offered in .308 Winchester and fitted with a 24" heavy barrel. Magazine capacity is 5 rounds. Available in blue or stainless steel and walnut or synthetic stock. Weight is approximately 9.3 lbs.

NIB	Exc.	V.G.	Good	Fair	Poor
1200	800	650	525	400	150

HOWARD-WHITNEY
New Haven, Connecticut
See—Whitney Arms Co.

HUGLU
Turkey

SIDE-BY-SIDES

Bobwhite

Offered in 12, 20, 28 gauge as well as .410 bore with 26" or 28" barrel with choke tubes. The .410 bore has fixed chokes. Double triggers with no auto ejectors. Manual safety. Box lock receiver with silver finish. Walnut stock with round knob pistol grip and splinter schnabel fore-end. **NOTE:** Add $200 for 28 gauge or .410 models.

NIB	Exc.	V.G.	Good	Fair	Poor
700	550	400	275	175	125

Ringneck

Similar to the Bobwhite but with single trigger and case colored frame with side plates. Choice of round knob pistol grip or straight grip. Fore-end is beavertail schnabel. **NOTE:** Add $200 for 28 gauge or .410 models.

NIB	Exc.	V.G.	Good	Fair	Poor
1000	750	600	495	300	150

OVER/UNDERS

Woodcock

This gun is available in 12, 20, or 28 gauge as well as .410 bore. Choice of 26" or 28" vent rib barrels with choke tubes, except for fixed chokes on the .410. Single trigger. No auto ejectors. Manual safety. Receiver finish is case colored. Checkered walnut stock with round knob pistol grip and schnabel fore-end. **NOTE:** Add $150 for 28 gauge or .410 models.

NIB	Exc.	V.G.	Good	Fair	Poor
1050	825	600	495	300	150

Woodcock Deluxe

As above but in 12 gauge with auto ejectors and side plates.

NIB	Exc.	V.G.	Good	Fair	Poor
1200	900	750	550	350	185

Redhead

Available in 12, 20, 28, and .410. Choice of 26" or 28" vent rib barrels with choke tubes, except for .410 with fixed chokes. The 20 gauge is also offered with 24" barrels. Single trigger, no auto ejectors, and manual safety. Boxlock receiver with silver finish.

Checkered walnut stock with round knob pistol grip and schnabel forearm. **NOTE:** Add $150 for 28 gauge or .410 models.

NIB	Exc.	V.G.	Good	Fair	Poor
800	625	500	400	275	150

Redhead Deluxe

As above but in 12 and 20 gauge only with 26" or 28" barrels. Auto ejectors.

NIB	Exc.	V.G.	Good	Fair	Poor
900	750	675	395	200	100

Mallard

This 12 or 20 gauge gun is fitted with 28" vent rib barrels with choke tubes. Double triggers and no auto ejectors. Silver receiver. Checkered walnut stock with round knob pistol grip and schnabel fore-end.

NIB	Exc.	V.G.	Good	Fair	Poor
550	425	300	200	150	75

Canvasback

This gun is available in 12, 20, 28, and .410 bore. Choice of 26" or 28" vent rib barrels with choke tubes, except for the .410 with fixed chokes. Single trigger with no auto ejectors and manual safety. Black boxlock receiver. Checkered walnut stock with round knob pistol grip and schnabel fore-end. **NOTE:** Add $150 for 28 gauge or .410 models.

NIB	Exc.	V.G.	Good	Fair	Poor
800	625	500	400	275	150

Canvasback Deluxe

As above but in 12 and 20 gauge only with auto ejectors.

NIB	Exc.	V.G.	Good	Fair	Poor
900	750	675	395	200	100

COWBOY & SINGLE-SHOT

Cottontail

This is a single-barrel shotgun in 12 or 20 gauge as well as .410 bore with choice of 24" or 28" barrels. Modified choke. No auto ejectors. Silver receiver with blued barrel. Checkered walnut stock with pistol grip.

NIB	Exc.	V.G.	Good	Fair	Poor
200	150	100	75	50	25

Durango

This side-by-side shotgun is chambered for the 12 or 20 gauge with single trigger and choke tubes. Barrel lengths are 20". No auto ejectors. The boxlock receiver is case colored. Checkered walnut grips with round knob pistol grip and schnabel fore-end.

NIB	Exc.	V.G.	Good	Fair	Poor
850	650	500	400	275	150

Amarillo

Similar to the Durango but with a flat-side receiver.

NIB	Exc.	V.G.	Good	Fair	Poor
700	525	400	300	195	125

SEMI-AUTOMATIC

Sharptail

This 12 gauge 3" gun is fitted with a choice of 26" or 28" vent rib barrels with choke tubes. Black receiver. Checkered walnut stock with pistol grip. Weight is about 7.3 lbs.

NIB	Exc.	V.G.	Good	Fair	Poor
550	425	300	200	150	95

Canadian

As above but with an alloy frame and matte black finish. Weight is about 7 lbs.

NIB	Exc.	V.G.	Good	Fair	Poor
650	525	400	275	165	115

Teal

This model is a 20 gauge with 3" chambers and a choice of 26" or 28" vent rib barrels with choke tubes. Black alloy receiver. Checkered walnut stock with pistol grip.

NIB	Exc.	V.G.	Good	Fair	Poor
550	425	300	200	150	95

COMPETITION GUNS

Vandalia Trap

This 12 gauge trap gun is offered with either a single- double-barrel combo; single barrel only, or double barrel only. Five choke tubes. Engraved silver receiver. Checkered walnut stock with pistol grip and adjustable comb. **NOTE:** For Combo model add $300.

NIB	Exc.	V.G.	Good	Fair	Poor
1900	1400	995	650	395	200

English Sporter

This is a sporting clays model chambered for the 12 gauge shell and fitted with a 30" barrel with ten choke tubes. Black receiver. Adjustable comb with checkered walnut stock with pistol grip.

NIB	Exc.	V.G.	Good	Fair	Poor
1900	1400	995	650	395	200

CUSTOM GRADES

Custom Grade II

This is a custom-built side-by-side gun in the customer's choice of gauge. Engraved case colored receiver with side plates. Choice of barrel lengths. Select walnut stock with hand checkering and round knob pistol grip.

NIB	Exc.	V.G.	Good	Fair	Poor
2200	1600	1200	950	500	300

Custom Grade IV

This custom-built side-by-side features a silver scroll engraved receiver with side plates. Straight grip stock. Choice of bore and barrel lengths.

NIB	Exc.	V.G.	Good	Fair	Poor
2800	1900	1400	650	600	350

Custom Grade IV with Upgrade

This is an over/under gun with extra fancy walnut stock and elaborately engraved silver receiver. Choice of gauge and barrel lengths.

NIB	Exc.	V.G.	Good	Fair	Poor
3150	2200	1600	750	650	350

Custom Grade VI

This is the highest grade offered with the finest walnut stock and engraving.

NIB	Exc.	V.G.	Good	Fair	Poor
3500	26500	1900	950	775	475

HUNGARY

SA-85M

This is pre-ban semi-automatic copy of the AKM rifle. Chambered for the 7.62x39mm cartridge. Fixed or folding stock.

NIB	Exc.	V.G.	Good	Fair	Poor
1800	1600	1200	850	600	500

HUNT
New Haven, Connecticut
See—Winchester Repeating Arms Co.

HUNTER ARMS CO.
Fulton, New York
See—L. C. Smith

HUSQVARNA
Husqvarna, Sweden

PISTOLS

Model 1907

This pistol is a copy of the FN Browning Model 1903 made for the Swedish Army. It is identical in every way to the FN model. Many were converted to the .380 caliber and imported into the U.S.
NOTE: If converted to .380 caliber reduce values by 50 percent.

Courtesy Orvel Reichert

NIB	Exc.	V.G.	Good	Fair	Poor
—	400	325	225	150	100

Lahti

A 9mm caliber semi-automatic pistol with a 5.5" barrel and 8-shot magazine. Designed by Aino Lahti and adopted as the standard Swedish sidearm in 1940. Add 75 percent for complete military rig with holsters and magazines.

NIB	Exc.	V.G.	Good	Fair	Poor
—	800	675	475	225	150

BOLT-ACTION RIFLES

Hi-Power

A bolt-action sporting rifle manufactured in a variety of calibers with a 24" barrel, open sights and beechwood stock. Manufactured between 1946 and 1951.

NIB	Exc.	V.G.	Good	Fair	Poor
—	500	375	275	200	150

Model 1100 Deluxe

As above, with a walnut stock. Manufactured between 1952 and 1956.

NIB	Exc.	V.G.	Good	Fair	Poor
—	550	400	325	250	200

Model 1000 Super Grade

As above, with a Monte Carlo-style stock. Manufactured between 1952 and 1956.

NIB	Exc.	V.G.	Good	Fair	Poor
—	575	475	350	250	200

Model 3100 Crown Grade

A bolt-action sporting rifle manufactured in a variety of calibers with a 24" barrel, walnut stock with a black composition fore-end tip and pistol grip cap. Manufactured between 1954 and 1972.

NIB	Exc.	V.G.	Good	Fair	Poor
—	575	475	350	300	200

Model 4100 Lightweight

As above, with a schnabel fore-end tip. Manufactured between 1954 and 1972.

NIB	Exc.	V.G.	Good	Fair	Poor
—	575	475	350	300	200

Model 456

As above, with a full length Mannlicher-style stock. Manufactured between 1959 and 1970.

NIB	Exc.	V.G.	Good	Fair	Poor
—	600	500	375	325	200

Model 6000

The Model 4100 with express folding sights and a finely figured walnut stock. Manufactured between 1968 and 1970.

NIB	Exc.	V.G.	Good	Fair	Poor
—	600	500	400	300	200

Model 9000 Crown Grade

A bolt-action sporting rifle manufactured in a variety of calibers with a 23.5" barrel, open sights, adjustable trigger and walnut stock. Manufactured in 1971 and 1972.

NIB	Exc.	V.G.	Good	Fair	Poor
—	500	425	350	300	250

Model 8000 Imperial Grade

As above, with an engraved magazine floor plate, machine jeweled bolt and finely figured walnut stock. Manufactured in 1971 and 1972.

NIB	Exc.	V.G.	Good	Fair	Poor
—	675	550	475	400	300

DOUBLE SHOTGUNS

A number of pre-war Husqvarna side-by-side shotguns have been imported over the years. While sturdy, excellent shotguns, their collector value is rather limited. Those following values apply only to modern, fluid-steel (nitro proofed) guns.

NIB	Exc.	V.G.	Good	Fair	Poor
—	500	425	350	300	250

HY-HUNTER, INC.
Burbank, California

Chicago Cub

A .22 caliber folding trigger double-action revolver with a 2" barrel and 6-shot cylinder.

NIB	Exc.	V.G.	Good	Fair	Poor
—	50	40	30	25	20

Detective

A .22 or .22 WMR caliber double-action revolver with a 2.5" barrel and 6-shot cylinder. Blued with plastic grips.

NIB	Exc.	V.G.	Good	Fair	Poor
—	65	50	40	30	25

Frontier Six Shooter (rimfire)

A .22 or .22 WMR caliber single-action revolver with a 6-shot cylinder.

NIB	Exc.	V.G.	Good	Fair	Poor
—	125	95	50	40	30

Frontier Six Shooter(centerfire)

As above, in .357 Magnum, .44 Magnum or .45 Colt.

NIB	Exc.	V.G.	Good	Fair	Poor
—	225	195	175	100	50

Maxim

A .25 caliber semi-automatic pistol with a 2" barrel and 5-shot magazine.

NIB	Exc.	V.G.	Good	Fair	Poor
—	75	65	50	40	30

Military

A .22, .32 or .380 caliber double-action semi-automatic pistol with a 4" barrel and 6-shot magazine.

NIB	Exc.	V.G.	Good	Fair	Poor
—	100	80	60	50	40

Stingray

A .25 caliber semi-automatic pistol with a 2.5" barrel and 5-shot magazine.

NIB	Exc.	V.G.	Good	Fair	Poor
—	75	65	50	40	30

Panzer

A .22 caliber semi-automatic pistol with a 4" barrel and 7-shot magazine.

NIB	Exc.	V.G.	Good	Fair	Poor
—	75	65	50	40	30

Stuka

Similar to the above.

NIB	Exc.	V.G.	Good	Fair	Poor
—	75	65	50	40	30

Automatic Derringer

A .22 caliber over/under pocket pistol patterned after the Remington Double Derringer.

NIB	Exc.	V.G.	Good	Fair	Poor
—	50	40	30	25	20

Accurate Ace

A .22 caliber Flobert-action pistol.

NIB	Exc.	V.G.	Good	Fair	Poor
—	50	40	30	25	20

Favorite

A .22 or .22 WMR caliber copy of the Steven's single-shot pistol with a 6" barrel and nickel-plated frame.

NIB	Exc.	V.G.	Good	Fair	Poor
—	100	80	70	50	25

Gold Rush Derringer

A .22 caliber spur trigger single-shot pistol with a 2.5" barrel.

NIB	Exc.	V.G.	Good	Fair	Poor
—	100	80	70	50	25

Target Model

A .22 or .22 WMR bolt-action single-shot pistol with a 10" barrel, adjustable sights and walnut grip.

NIB	Exc.	V.G.	Good	Fair	Poor
—	50	40	30	25	20

HYDE & SHATTUCK
Hatfield, Massachusetts

Queen Derringer

A .22 caliber spur trigger single-shot pistol with a 2.5" half octagonal barrel. Blued or nickel-plated with walnut grips. The barrel normally marked "Queen", but sometimes "Hyde & Shattuck". Manufactured between 1876 and 1879.

NIB	Exc.	V.G.	Good	Fair	Poor
—	—	650	400	300	150

HYPER
Jenks, Oklahoma

Single-Shot Rifle

A custom made falling block-action single-shot rifle manufactured in a variety of calibers, barrel lengths, barrel types, and stock styles. Manufactured until 1984.

NIB	Exc.	V.G.	Good	Fair	Poor
—	2750	2000	1750	1450	80

I

I.G.I.
Itaiguns International
Zingone de Tressano, Italy

Domino SP602

A .22 caliber semi-automatic target pistol with a 6" barrel and 5-shot magazine (that is inserted into the action from the top), adjustable trigger and customized grips.

NIB	Exc.	V.G.	Good	Fair	Poor
—	950	725	625	450	250

Domino OP601

As above, but in .22 short caliber.

NIB	Exc.	V.G.	Good	Fair	Poor
—	950	725	625	450	250

IAB
Industria Armi Bresciane
Brescia, Italy

S-300

A 12 gauge boxlock single-barrel trap gun with 30" or 32" barrels having a wide ventilated rib and walnut trap-style stock.

NIB	Exc.	V.G.	Good	Fair	Poor
—	1600	1325	1050	850	450

C-300 Combo

A 12 gauge over/under boxlock double-barrel shotgun with 30" or 32" barrels, single-selective trigger, automatic ejectors, trap-style walnut stock, accompanied by two extra single barrels.

NIB	Exc.	V.G.	Good	Fair	Poor
—	2850	2300	1875	1500	800

C-300 Super Combo

As above, but more finely finished.

NIB	Exc.	V.G.	Good	Fair	Poor
—	3600	2800	2275	1750	900

IAI-AMERICAN LEGENDS
Houston, Texas

RIFLES

M-888 M1 Carbine

A re-creation of the U.S. M1 Carbine in .30 caliber. Barrel length is 18". Weight is about 5.5 lbs. Uses surplus magazines of 15 to 30 rounds. Comes with 10-round magazine. Options of wooden or metal handguard and walnut or birchwood stock.

NIB	Exc.	V.G.	Good	Fair	Poor
675	575	400	325	200	100

M-333 M1 Garand

Re-manufactured to GI specifications. Fitted with 24" barrel and GI wood stock. Eight-round capacity. Parkerized finish. Weight is about 9.5 lbs.

NIB	Exc.	V.G.	Good	Fair	Poor
900	800	625	495	350	150

PISTOLS

M-2000

This is a Government model .45 ACP pistol fitted with a 5" barrel and 7-round magazine. Fixed sights. Wood grips. Parkerized finish. Weight is about 38 oz.

NIB	Exc.	V.G.	Good	Fair	Poor
475	375	325	250	175	100

M-999

Similar to the above model but with rubber-style combat grips, extended slide stop, safety, and magazine release. Fixed sights. Offered with stainless steel slide and blued frame or all stainless steel. Supplied with 7-round magazine. Weight is about 38 oz. **NOTE:** Add $25 for stainless steel frame.

NIB	Exc.	V.G.	Good	Fair	Poor
475	350	275	200	125	75

M-777

Same as M-999 but fitted with 4.25" barrel. Weight is about 36 oz. **NOTE:** Add $25 for stainless steel frame.

NIB	Exc.	V.G.	Good	Fair	Poor
475	350	275	200	125	75

M-6000

This .45 ACP pistol is fitted with a 5" barrel, plastic grips, extended slide stop, safety, and magazine release. Safety is ambidextrous. Magazine capacity is 8 rounds. Fixed sights. Weight is about 38 oz.

NIB	Exc.	V.G.	Good	Fair	Poor
475	375	325	250	175	100

M-5000

This model is similar to the M-6000 but fitted with a 4.25" barrel. Weight is about 36 oz.

NIB	Exc.	V.G.	Good	Fair	Poor
475	375	325	250	175	100

IGA
Veranopolis, Brazil

Single-Barrel Shotgun

A 12 or 20 gauge or .410 bore single barrel shotgun with an exposed hammer, 28" barrel and hardwood stock.

NIB	Exc.	V.G.	Good	Fair	Poor
150	90	75	50	40	30

Single-Barrel Shotgun Youth Model

Offered in 20 gauge and .410 bore this model features a 22" barrel and shorter than standard buttstock. Weighs 5 lbs.

NIB	Exc.	V.G.	Good	Fair	Poor
150	100	80	60	50	35

Coach Gun

A 12 and 20 gauge as well as .410 bore boxlock double-barrel shotgun with 20" barrels, double triggers and extractors. Blued with a hardwood stock. **NOTE:** Add $50 for nickel finish. Add $60 for engraved butt stock.

NIB	Exc.	V.G.	Good	Fair	Poor
425	325	250	150	100	75

Standard Side-by-Side Uplander

Offered in 12, 20, 28 gauge, and .410 bore with 26" and 28" barrels. Checkered hardwood stock with pistol grip or straight grip in 20 gauge only. Weighs 6.75 lbs. **NOTE:** Add $40 for choke tubes.

NIB	Exc.	V.G.	Good	Fair	Poor
425	325	250	150	100	75

Uplander Youth

Same as above but offered in .410 bore with 24" barrel or 20 gauge with 24" barrels. Shorter length of pull. Recoil pad standard.

NIB	Exc.	V.G.	Good	Fair	Poor
450	325	250	150	100	75

Uplander Supreme

Introduced in 2000 this model features a high grade walnut stock with checkering, single-selective trigger, choke tubes, and automatic ejectors. Offered in 12 and 20 gauge with 26" or 28" barrels. Chambered for 3" shells. Soft rubber recoil pad standard.

NIB	Exc.	V.G.	Good	Fair	Poor
600	450	375	300	200	100

Standard Over/Under Condor I

This model is offered in 12 or 20 gauge with 26" or 28" barrels. Fitted with extractors and single trigger. Choke tubes are standard. Checkered hardwood stock with pistol grip and recoil pad. Weighs 8 lbs.

NIB	Exc.	V.G.	Good	Fair	Poor
425	300	225	200	150	100

Condor II

Same as above but with double triggers and plastic buttplate.

NIB	Exc.	V.G.	Good	Fair	Poor
400	250	200	150	100	75

Condor Supreme Deluxe

This model is similar to the standard Condor model but has a high grade walnut stock, hand checkering, recoil pad, single-selective trigger, and automatic ejectors. Offered in 12 and 20 gauge with 26" or 28" vent rib barrels. Chambered for 3" shells. Choke tubes standard. First offered in 2000.

NIB	Exc.	V.G.	Good	Fair	Poor
550	400	325	200	150	100

Deluxe Over/Under ERA 2000

Offered in 12 gauge only with 26" or 28" barrels. Fitted with single trigger and extractors. Choke tubes are standard. Barrels are chrome lined and stock is hand checkered.

NIB	Exc.	V.G.	Good	Fair	Poor
450	325	250	150	100	75

INDIAN ARMS CORP.
Detroit, Michigan

Indian Arms .380

A .380 caliber semi-automatic pistol with a 3.25" barrel and 6-shot magazine. Made of stainless steel and finished either in the white or blued with walnut grips. Manufactured from 1975 to 1977.

NIB	Exc.	V.G.	Good	Fair	Poor
—	350	250	200	150	100

INDUSTRIA ARMI GALESI
Brescia, Italy
See—Galesi

INGRAM
Military Armament Corp.
Atlanta, Georgia

MAC 10

A 9mm or .45 caliber open-bolt semi-automatic pistol with a 5.75" barrel and 32-shot magazine. Anodized with plastic grips. Discontinued. **NOTE:** Accessory kit (barrel extension and extra magazine) add 20 percent.

NIB	Exc.	V.G.	Good	Fair	Poor
750	500	375	250	175	100

MAC 10AI

As above, but firing from a closed bolt. Add 300 percent for earlier open-bolt model. **NOTE:** Accessory kit add 20 percent.

NIB	Exc.	V.G.	Good	Fair	Poor
750	600	250	200	150	100

MAC 11

As above in a smaller version and chambered for the 9mm cartridge. Add 300 percent for earlier open-bolt model. **NOTE:** Accessory kit add 20 percent.

NIB	Exc.	V.G.	Good	Fair	Poor
800	650	350	150	100	50

INTERARMS
Alexandria, Virginia

An importer of arms made by Howa Machine, Star and Walther. This firm is no longer in business.

RIFLES

Mark X Viscount

Bolt-action sporting rifle made in a variety of calibers with a 24" barrel, open sights, adjustable trigger and magazine holding either 3 or 5 cartridges. Manufactured in Yugoslavia. Blued with a walnut stock.

NIB	Exc.	V.G.	Good	Fair	Poor
450	300	250	200	175	125

Mark X Lightweight

As above, with a 20" barrel and composition stock. Introduced in 1988.

NIB	Exc.	V.G.	Good	Fair	Poor
450	300	250	200	175	125

Mini Mark X

As above, with a short action in .223 caliber only with a 20" barrel, open sights, adjustable trigger and 5-shot magazine. Introduced in 1987.

NIB	Exc.	V.G.	Good	Fair	Poor
450	300	250	200	175	125

Mark X American Field

As above, with a finely figured walnut stock, ebony fore-end tip, pistol grip cap, sling swivels and recoil pad. Introduced in 1984.

NIB	Exc.	V.G.	Good	Fair	Poor
525	400	350	300	250	175

Whitworth Express Rifle

A .375 Holland & Holland or .458 Winchester Magnum bolt-action sporting rifle with a 24" barrel, express sights and 3-shot magazine. Blued with a walnut stock. Introduced in 1974.

NIB	Exc.	V.G.	Good	Fair	Poor
950	750	550	350	250	200

Whitworth Mannlicher Carbine

A .243, .270, 7x57mm, .308, and the .30-06 caliber bolt-action rifle with a 20" barrel, open sights, sling swivels and a full length stock. Manufactured between 1984 and 1987.

NIB	Exc.	V.G.	Good	Fair	Poor
—	725	550	375	250	200

Cavalier

A bolt-action sporting rifle made in a variety of calibers with a modern styled stock having a rollover cheekpiece. Discontinued.

NIB	Exc.	V.G.	Good	Fair	Poor
—	500	400	350	200	150

Mannlicher Carbine

As above, with a 20" barrel and full length stock. Discontinued.

NIB	Exc.	V.G.	Good	Fair	Poor
—	600	500	425	275	195

Continental Carbine

As above, with double set triggers. Discontinued.

NIB	Exc.	V.G.	Good	Fair	Poor
—	625	525	450	300	225

Alaskan Model

Similar to the Mark X, in .375 Holland & Holland or .458 Winchester Magnum with a 24" barrel. Discontinued in 1985.

NIB	Exc.	V.G.	Good	Fair	Poor
—	950	750	550	350	200

22-ATD

A .22 caliber semi-automatic rifle with a 19.4" barrel, open sights, and 11-shot magazine. Blued with a hardwood stock. Manufactured by Norinco. Introduced in 1987.

NIB	Exc.	V.G.	Good	Fair	Poor
195	125	95	65	50	40

HANDGUNS

Helwan Brigadier

A 9mm semi-automatic pistol with a 4.5" barrel, fixed sights, and 8-shot magazine. Blued with plastic grips. Introduced in 1988.

NIB	Exc.	V.G.	Good	Fair	Poor
375	275	200	175	125	100

FEG R-9

A 9mm semi-automatic pistol patterned after the Browning 35 with a 13-shot magazine. Blued with walnut grips. Manufactured in 1986 and 1987.

NIB	Exc.	V.G.	Good	Fair	Poor
—	350	250	185	145	100

FEG PPH

A .380 caliber double-action semi-automatic pistol with a 3.5" barrel and 6-shot magazine. Blued with plastic grips.

NIB	Exc.	V.G.	Good	Fair	Poor
—	300	175	150	125	100

Mark II AP

A copy of the Walther PP. Chambered for the .380 ACP or .22 LR cartridge.

NIB	Exc.	V.G.	Good	Fair	Poor
300	175	125	100	75	50

Mark II APK

A copy of the Walther PPK. Chambered for the .380 ACP cartridge only.

NIB	Exc.	V.G.	Good	Fair	Poor
300	175	125	100	75	50

Mauser Parabellum Karabiner

A 9mm caliber semi-automatic carbine with an 11.75" barrel and detachable shoulder stock. Fitted in a leather case. **NOTE:** Only 100 were imported into the United States and this arm is subject to BATE registration.

NIB	Exc.	V.G.	Good	Fair	Poor
6500	5750	5000	4000	3000	2250

Mauser Parabellum Cartridge Counter

A reproduction of the cartridge counter Luger. Fitted in a leather case with only 100 units imported into the United States.

NIB	Exc.	V.G.	Good	Fair	Poor
4000	3000	2500	2000	1500	1000

Virginian Dragoon

A .44 Magnum single-action revolver with a 6", 7.5", 8.75", or 12" barrel, adjustable sights and 6-shot cylinder. Originally made in Switzerland and then in the U.S.A. Discontinued in 1984. Add 20 percent for Swiss manufacture.

NIB	Exc.	V.G.	Good	Fair	Poor
—	325	275	200	150	100

Stainless Dragoon

As above, in stainless steel.

NIB	Exc.	V.G.	Good	Fair	Poor
—	375	300	245	175	105

Virginian .22 Convertible

As above, in .22 caliber with a 5.5" barrel.

NIB	Exc.	V.G.	Good	Fair	Poor
—	275	200	125	100	75

Virginian Stainless .22 Convertible

As above, in stainless steel.

NIB	Exc.	V.G.	Good	Fair	Poor
—	295	225	165	100	80

INTERDYNAMICS OF AMERICA
Miami, Florida

KG-9

A 9mm caliber semi-automatic pistol with a 3" barrel and 36-shot magazine. Manufactured from 1981 and 1983. Note that earliest models fire from open bolt and are valued at approximately 150 percent of the values shown here.

NIB	Exc.	V.G.	Good	Fair	Poor
—	800	650	575	500	300

KG-99

As above, with a barrel shroud. Manufactured from 1981 and 1984.

NIB	Exc.	V.G.	Good	Fair	Poor
—	800	650	575	500	300

KG-99 Stainless

As above, in stainless steel. Manufactured in 1984.

NIB	Exc.	V.G.	Good	Fair	Poor
—	800	650	575	500	300

KG-99M

A more compact version of the above. Manufactured in 1984.

NIB	Exc.	V.G.	Good	Fair	Poor
—	800	650	575	500	300

INTRATEC USA, INC.
Miami, Florida

TEC-9

A 9mm caliber semi-automatic pistol with a 5" shrouded barrel and 36-shot magazine. Introduced in 1985.

NIB	Exc.	V.G.	Good	Fair	Poor
450	350	295	200	15	100

TEC-9C

As above, with a 16" barrel and a folding stock. Manufactured in 1987.

NIB	Exc.	V.G.	Good	Fair	Poor
—	450	350	295	200	100

TEC-9M

As above, with a 3" barrel and 20-shot magazine. Also made in stainless steel.

NIB	Exc.	V.G.	Good	Fair	Poor
450	350	295	200	15	100

TEC-22 "Scorpion"

Similar to the above, but in .22 caliber with a 4" barrel and 30-shot magazine.

NIB	Exc.	V.G.	Good	Fair	Poor
325	225	175	100	75	50

TEC-38

A .38 caliber over/under double-action derringer with 3" barrels. Manufactured between 1986 and 1988.

NIB	Exc.	V.G.	Good	Fair	Poor
—	195	125	90	65	45

IRVING, W.
New York, New York

Single-Shot Derringer

A .22 caliber spur trigger single-shot pistol with a 2.75" half octagonal barrel. Silver plated brass frame, blued barrel and rosewood grips. The barrel marked "W. Irving". Manufactured in the 1860s. The .32 caliber variation has a 3" barrel and is worth approximately 40 percent more than the values listed.

NIB	Exc.	V.G.	Good	Fair	Poor
—	—	1050	475	195	125

Pocket Revolver 1st Model

A .31 caliber spur trigger percussion revolver with a 3" octagonal barrel, 6-shot cylinder and brass frame. The barrel marked "W. Irving". Approximately 50 were made between 1858 and 1862.

NIB	Exc.	V.G.	Good	Fair	Poor
—	—	2500	925	275	175

Pocket Revolver 2nd Model

A .31 caliber percussion revolver with a 4.5" round barrel, loading lever and either brass or iron frame. The barrel marked "Address W. Irving. 20 Cliff St. N.Y.". Approximately 600 manufactured with a brass frame and 1,500 with a frame of iron. The brass-frame version will bring a premium of about 35 percent.

NIB	Exc.	V.G.	Good	Fair	Poor
—	—	1450	495	200	100

IRWINDALE ARMS, INC.
Irwindale, California
See—AMT

ISRAELI MILITARY INDUSTRIES
Israel

Civilian firearms manufactured by this firm have been and are being retailed by Action Arms Limited, Magnum Research, and Mossberg.

ITHACA GUN CO.
Ithaca, New York

This material was supplied by Walter C. Snyder and is copyrighted in his name. Used with the author's permission.

The Ithaca Gun Company was founded by William Henry Baker, John VanNatta, and Dwight McIntyre. Gun production started during the latter half of 1883 at an industrial site located on Fall Creek, Ithaca, New York. Leroy Smith joined the company by 1885 and George Livermore joined the firm in 1887. By 1894 the company was under the exclusive control of Leroy Smith and George Livermore. Many of the company's assets were purchased by the Ithaca Acquisition Corporation in 1987 and moved to King Ferry, New York, where it operated until May, 1996. Now dba Ithaca Gun Company of Upper Sandusky, Ohio.

HAMMER MODELS

Ithaca Baker Model

The first model produced by the company was designed by W.H. Baker and was manufactured from 1883 through 1887. It was offered in six grades; Quality A ($35) through Quality F ($200) in either 10 or 12 gauge. All Ithaca-produced Baker models had exposed hammers. **NOTE:** Grades above Quality B are seldom encountered and an expert appraisal is recommended.

Quality A

Courtesy Walter C. Snyder

NIB	Exc.	V.G.	Good	Fair	Poor
—	900	500	300	200	100

Quality B

NIB	Exc.	V.G.	Good	Fair	Poor
—	1850	1350	750	300	100

New Ithaca Gun

The New Ithaca Gun was introduced in 1888 and discontinued during 1915. Like its predecessor, it was introduced in the same seven grades, Quality A through Quality F. Later, the Quality F was discontinued. By 1900, a "condensed steel" barreled model, named Quality X, was introduced. The New Ithaca Gun was produced in gauges 10, 12, and 16, and very rarely, 20. Lower grade models carried the logo, "New Ithaca Gun", usually within a banner, on each side of the frame.**NOTE:** Like its predecessor, grades above Quality B are seldom encountered, and an expert appraisal is recommended. Sixteen gauge guns command a 30 percent price premium. The extremely rare 20 gauge model requires an expert appraisal.

Quality A

Courtesy Walter C. Snyder

NIB	Exc.	V.G.	Good	Fair	Poor
—	1100	775	295	175	100

Quality AA

NIB	Exc.	V.G.	Good	Fair	Poor
—	1100	775	295	175	100

Quality B

NIB	Exc.	V.G.	Good	Fair	Poor
—	1300	875	450	225	100

Quality X

NIB	Exc.	V.G.	Good	Fair	Poor
—	1300	875	450	225	100

The "New Double Bolted Hammer Gun"

During 1915, the Ithaca Gun Company replaced the New Ithaca Gun with a model it referred to as "our new model two bolt hammer gun". The new hammer gun had coil springs powering the external hammers. The "two bolt" lock up was accomplished by a bottom bolt and by the top lever engagement with the rear nub of the rib extension. Lower grade models were marked on both sides of the frame with a setter dog and the logo, "Ithaca Gun Co.". The 1915 catalog is the last year hammer guns were advertised but the old records indicate a few were sold as late as 1919.

Grades offered were X, A, AA, B, C, D, and E. The 1915 catalog advertised a price of $29 for an A Quality model and $150 for the elaborately engraved Quality E. All grades were available in 10, 12, and 16 gauges. **NOTE:** Like the New Ithaca Gun, grades above Quality B are seldom encountered, and an expert appraisal is recommended. Sixteen gauge guns command a 30 percent price premium. The extremely rare 20 gauge model requires an expert appraisal.

Quality A

NIB	Exc.	V.G.	Good	Fair	Poor
—	1300	875	350	225	100

Quality AA

NIB	Exc.	V.G.	Good	Fair	Poor
—	1600	1075	450	250	100

Quality B

NIB	Exc.	V.G.	Good	Fair	Poor
—	1600	1075	450	250	100

Quality X

NIB	Exc.	V.G.	Good	Fair	Poor
—	1600	1075	450	250	100

HAMMERLESS MODELS

The first hammerless Ithaca gun was introduced in 1888. All Ithaca double guns were discontinued in 1948. The gauge and grade can usually be found on the left front corner of the water table of the frame, the serial number is usually found on the right side of the same water table, on the barrel flats, and the fore-end iron.

Crass Model

The Crass Model, named after Ithaca's Frederick Crass who designed it, was introduced in 1888. It was offered in Quality 1 through Quality 7. The Quality 1P, a model with no engraving, was introduced in 1898. The Crass Model underwent three major frame redesigns before it was discontinued during 1901. The gun was available in 10, 12, and 16 gauge. Automatic ejectors were introduced in 1893 and were available in any quality gun at extra cost. **NOTE:** Sixteen gauge guns will command a 20 percent price premium. Guns above Quality 4 are seldom encountered, and an expert appraisal is necessary. For automatic ejectors add $250. The serial number range for the Crass Model is approximately 7000 to 50000.

Quality 1

NIB	Exc.	V.G.	Good	Fair	Poor
—	900	575	400	225	100

Quality 1-1/2

NIB	Exc.	V.G.	Good	Fair	Poor
—	900	575	400	225	100

Quality 1P

NIB	Exc.	V.G.	Good	Fair	Poor
—	900	575	400	225	100

Quality 2

Courtesy Walter C. Snyder

NIB	Exc.	V.G.	Good	Fair	Poor
—	1300	875	600	250	100

Quality 3

NIB	Exc.	V.G.	Good	Fair	Poor
—	1800	1300	775	325	100

Quality 4

NIB	Exc.	V.G.	Good	Fair	Poor
—	2250	1850	1075	325	100

Lewis Model

Chester Lewis, an Ithaca Gun employee, was credited with the design of the gun that now bears his name. The gun was bolted through the rib extension in addition to the traditional under bolt. The model was available from 1901 through 1906, and was offered in Qualities 1 through 7. It was made in 10, 12, and 16 gauge, and after 1906, 20 gauge. Automatic ejectors were offered at added cost. **NOTE:** Automatic ejectors add about $250 to grades below Quality 4. The serial number range for the Lewis Model is approximately 55000 to 123600.

Quality 1

NIB	Exc.	V.G.	Good	Fair	Poor
—	900	575	325	175	100

Quality 1 Special

NIB	Exc.	V.G.	Good	Fair	Poor
—	900	575	325	175	100

Quality 1-1/2

NIB	Exc.	V.G.	Good	Fair	Poor
—	950	600	350	200	100

Quality 2

NIB	Exc.	V.G.	Good	Fair	Poor
—	1150	725	500	225	100

Quality 3

NIB	Exc.	V.G.	Good	Fair	Poor
—	1850	1500	850	425	100

Quality 4

NIB	Exc.	V.G.	Good	Fair	Poor
—	2700	2350	1900	475	100

Quality 5

NIB	Exc.	V.G.	Good	Fair	Poor
—	3700	3150	2100	725	300

Quality 6

NIB	Exc.	V.G.	Good	Fair	Poor
—	6300	4750	3200	775	300

Quality 7

NIB	Exc.	V.G.	Good	Fair	Poor
—	6300	4750	3200	775	300

Minier Model

The Minier Model, named after Ithaca's David Minier, was introduced in 1906 and was available through 1908. It was offered in Qualities Field through 7 and any grade could be ordered with ejectors. The Minier Model was the first Ithaca gun to use coil springs to power the internal hammers. This model was triple bolted, e.g., two fastenings at the rib extension and the under bolt. Gauges 10, 12, 16, and 20 were offered. **NOTE:** Automatic ejectors add $250 to guns below Quality 4. The serial number range for the Minier Model is approximately 130000 to 151000.

Field Grade

NIB	Exc.	V.G.	Good	Fair	Poor
—	1150	725	500	225	100

Quality 1

NIB	Exc.	V.G.	Good	Fair	Poor
—	1150	725	500	225	100

Quality 1 Special

NIB	Exc.	V.G.	Good	Fair	Poor
—	1150	725	500	225	100

Quality 1-1/2

NIB	Exc.	V.G.	Good	Fair	Poor
—	1150	725	500	225	100

Quality 2

NIB	Exc.	V.G.	Good	Fair	Poor
—	1350	700	475	225	100

Quality 3

Courtesy Walter C. Snyder

NIB	Exc.	V.G.	Good	Fair	Poor
—	2250	1200	575	450	100

Quality 4

Courtesy Amoskeag Auction Company

NIB	Exc.	V.G.	Good	Fair	Poor
—	2700	1325	875	450	100

Quality 5

NIB	Exc.	V.G.	Good	Fair	Poor
—	3700	3150	2100	725	300

Quality 6

NIB	Exc.	V.G.	Good	Fair	Poor
—	5250	4100	1550	725	300

Quality 7

NIB	Exc.	V.G.	Good	Fair	Poor
—	6800	4300	1700	800	300

Flues Model

The Flues Model Ithaca gun was built on a three-piece lock mechanism invented and patented by Emil Flues. Introduced in 1908, it remained in production through 1926 when it was replaced by the Ithaca New Double. It was offered in gauges 10, 12, 16, 20, and 28, and enjoyed the longest production life of any Ithaca double gun. Several grades were offered beginning with the Field grade and ending with the Sousa Special. The Flues Model had the same bolting system as used on the Minier Model. Any grade could have been ordered with automatic ejectors at extra cost. A single-selective trigger made by the Infallible Trigger company was offered after 1914 and was the first single trigger offered from the company. **NOTE:** Add $200 for factory-ordered single trigger,

add $200 for automatic ejectors on grades lower than Grade 4. Small gauges command a price premium. A 20 gauge gun may command up to a 50 percent price premium; a 28 gauge field grade perhaps as much as 200 percent. The serial number range for the Flues is approximately 175000 to 399000. Expert appraisals are recommended on higher-grade, small-gauge models as they are seldom encountered.

Field Grade

Courtesy Walter C. Snyder

NIB	Exc.	V.G.	Good	Fair	Poor
—	1100	700	375	250	100

Grade 1

NIB	Exc.	V.G.	Good	Fair	Poor
—	1100	700	375	250	100

Grade 1 Special

NIB	Exc.	V.G.	Good	Fair	Poor
—	1100	700	375	250	100

Grade 1-1/2

NIB	Exc.	V.G.	Good	Fair	Poor
—	1250	850	500	350	100

Grade 2

NIB	Exc.	V.G.	Good	Fair	Poor
—	1350	900	575	400	100

Grade 3

NIB	Exc.	V.G.	Good	Fair	Poor
—	2300	1600	800	500	100

Grade 4

NIB	Exc.	V.G.	Good	Fair	Poor
—	2300	1600	800	500	100

Grade 5

NIB	Exc.	V.G.	Good	Fair	Poor
—	2800	2200	1650	600	200

Grade 6

Courtesy Walter C. Snyder

NIB	Exc.	V.G.	Good	Fair	Poor
—	11000	6000	2750	1100	300

Grade 7

NIB	Exc.	V.G.	Good	Fair	Poor
—	11500	7000	3000	1250	300

Sousa

NIB	Exc.	V.G.	Good	Fair	Poor
—	17000	12000	7500	3750	N/A

The New Ithaca Double

The New Ithaca Double, commonly referred to as the NID, was manufactured from 1926 to 1948. It has the distinction of being the last double gun manufactured by the factory. The NID was bolted by a single rotary top bolt. External cocking indicators were standard on all NID models until about 1934, when they were eliminated from the design. Selective and non-selective single triggers and automatic ejectors were optional at additional costs. A special variation of the NID was introduced in 1932 to accommodate 10 gauge 3.5" magnum ammunition and was named, appropriately, the Magnum 10. All NID were available in grades Field, 1, 2, 3, 4, 5, 7, and Sousa (renamed the $1,000 grade after 1936). Gauges Magnum 10, standard 10, 12, 16, 20, 28, and .410 bore were offered.

NOTE: Like most collectible double guns, the smaller gauges command a price premium over the 12 gauge model. A 16 gauge field grade may command a 25 percent price premium, a 20 gauge field grade may command up to a 50 percent price premium, and the 28 gauge, and .410 caliber field-grade models perhaps as much as 250-300 percent. It is recommended that an expert opinion be sought for the valuation of high-grade, small-gauge models. Of late, the Magnum 10 gauge model also commands a price premium. Few of these guns trade, and the advice of an expert appraiser is suggested.

Non-selective single trigger add $150. Single-selective trigger add $250. Ventilated rib add $300. Automatic ejectors for grades below Grade 4 add $300. Beavertail forearm add $200. Monte Carlo buttstock add $300.

Field Grade

NIB	Exc.	V.G.	Good	Fair	Poor
—	1100	700	375	250	100

Grade 1

NIB	Exc.	V.G.	Good	Fair	Poor
—	1350	850	475	250	100

Grade 2

Courtesy Walter C. Snyder

NIB	Exc.	V.G.	Good	Fair	Poor
—	1650	900	725	350	100

Grade 3

NIB	Exc.	V.G.	Good	Fair	Poor
—	2600	1600	1075	425	100

Grade 4

NIB	Exc.	V.G.	Good	Fair	Poor
—	3250	2700	1600	475	100

Grade 5

Courtesy Walter C. Snyder

NIB	Exc.	V.G.	Good	Fair	Poor
—	4300	3400	2200	775	200

Grade 7

NIB	Exc.	V.G.	Good	Fair	Poor
—	12000	7500	4250	1100	300

Sousa Grade

NIB	Exc.	V.G.	Good	Fair	Poor
—	28000	15000	8000	4000	800

THE NEW ITHACA DOUBLE (MODERN-1999)

Special Field Grade

This side-by-side double is offered in 16, 20, 28, and .410 bore with a choice of matted rib barrel lengths of 26", 28", or 30". Ivory bead front sight. The action is case colored with light line border engraving. The stock is feather crotch black walnut with 22 lpi checkering. Choice of pistol or straight grip. Double trigger is standard. Weight in 20 gauge is about 5 lbs. 14 oz. 28 gauge is about 5 lbs. 8 oz., and .410 bore weighs about 5 lbs. 5 oz.

NIB	Exc.	V.G.	Good	Fair	Poor
6200	4750	4000	1700	800	300

Grade 4E

This model is also available in 16, 20, 28, and .410 with 26", 28", and 30" barrels. This model has gold plated triggers jeweled barrel flats and hand tuned locks. Black walnut stock has 28 lpi checkering with a fleur-de-lis pattern. Pistol or straight grip stock. Action is hand engraved with three game scenes and bank note scroll. Case colored frame.

NIB	Exc.	V.G.	Good	Fair	Poor
8000	6000	3000	1750	775	300

Grade 7E

This model has all of the gauges and barrel lengths of the above gun. Action is hand engraved with gold two tone inlays. Exhibition grade, black walnut stock with elaborate patterns. Custom built dimensions.

NIB	Exc.	V.G.	Good	Fair	Poor
11000	8750	7500	4250	1100	300

Sousa Grade

This model, available in the same gauges and barrel lengths as the above guns is stocked with presentation grade black walnut, hand carved with 32 lpi checkering. The action is hand engraved with bank note scroll and gold inlays. The entire gun is hand fitted and polished. Extremely limited availability. Special order only.

NIB	Exc.	V.G.	Good	Fair	Poor
35000	28000	15000	—	—	—

LEFEVER ARMS COMPANY, INC.

During 1921, Ithaca Gun, under the name "The Lefever Arms Company, Inc." introduced a line of lower-cost, boxlock guns. See the Lefever Arms Company section of this book for prices concerning those guns.

WESTERN ARMS CORPORATION

During 1929 the Ithaca Gun Company created the Western Arms Corporation, which introduced a new, low-cost double gun. That new double gun was named The Long Range Double and it was produced in 12, 16, and 20 gauges, and .410 caliber. Twenty gauge guns often command a 20 percent premium, a .410 caliber can command up to a 250 percent premium. This model was last made at the start of World War II.

The Long Range Double

The Long Range Double had walnut stocks that were not checkered. **NOTE:** Single trigger guns will add $100 and automatic ejectors will add $200.

NIB	Exc.	V.G.	Good	Fair	Poor
—	550	450	200	150	N/A

The Long Range Double Deluxe

Usually made exclusively for the Montgomery Ward Company and sold by them under the name, Western Field Deluxe. This model had a line checkering pattern at the grip and on the splinter fore-end. Many of the Ithaca produced Western Field Deluxe guns had automatic ejectors and that fact was stamped into the right barrel. **NOTE:** Single triggers add $100. Automatic ejectors add $200.

NIB	Exc.	V.G.	Good	Fair	Poor
—	575	475	300	150	N/A

ITHACA SINGLE-BARREL TRAP GUNS

The Ithaca Gun Company introduced a single-barrel trap gun in 1914. This gun was based upon the Emil Flues three piece lock design used for the double gun and has become known as the Flues Model Single-Barrel Trap. The Flues Model was discontinued during 1922 and was replaced that year by a model designed by Ithaca's Frank Knickerbocker, commonly referred to as the "Knick". The Knick Model was discontinued in 1988, shortly after the Ithaca Acquisition Corp. purchased the assets of the Ithaca Gun Company. For many years, The Ithaca Single-Barrel Trap Gun was the gun of choice for many champion shooters.

Flues Model Single-Barrel Trap Gun (1914 to 1922)

The Flues Model trap gun was introduced in 1914 and offered in Grades 4, 5, 6, and 7. A lower cost Victory grade was introduced in 1919 and the highest cost variety, the Sousa Special was introduced in 1918. All Flues model trap guns were made within the same serial number sequence as the double guns but do have the letter "T" for Trap following the serial number. All Flues Models with the exception of the Victory Grade were produced with an automatic ejector. A rubber anti-recoil pad was an option. Guns having a pre-1916 engraving pattern will command the highest prices.

Courtesy Walter C. Snyder

Victory Grade

NIB	Exc.	V.G.	Good	Fair	Poor
—	1300	900	700	300	N/A

Grade 4E

NIB	Exc.	V.G.	Good	Fair	Poor
—	2350	1900	1300	400	N/A

Grade 5E

Courtesy Walter C. Snyder

NIB	Exc.	V.G.	Good	Fair	Poor
—	4200	3100	2550	600	N/A

Grade 6E

NIB	Exc.	V.G.	Good	Fair	Poor
—	6300	5250	3200	900	N/A

Grade 7E

NIB	Exc.	V.G.	Good	Fair	Poor
—	8350	6200	4100	1050	N/A

Sousa Grade

NIB	Exc.	V.G.	Good	Fair	Poor
—	16500	11000	9000	2500	N/A

Knick Model Single-Barrel Trap

The Knick Model trap gun was introduced during 1922 and was based on a design credited to Frank Knickerbocker. The design was simple and very serviceable, had been in continues production until 1988 when it was discontinued. The model was available in Victory, 4, 5, 7, and Sousa Special Grades. The Sousa was replaced by the $1,000 Grade in about 1936, which was replaced by the $2,000 Grade by 1952, the $2,500 Grade by 1960, the $3,000 Grade by 1965, the $5,000 Grade by 1974, and finally the Dollar Grade in the early 1980s as the cost of production increased. All Knick models were produced with an automatic ejector and a rubber anti-recoil pad.

Victory Grade

Courtesy William Hammond

NIB	Exc.	V.G.	Good	Fair	Poor
2500	1350	900	700	300	N/A

Grade 4E

Courtesy C. Hadley Smith

NIB	Exc.	V.G.	Good	Fair	Poor
3300	2450	1950	1100	500	N/A

Grade 5E

NIB	Exc.	V.G.	Good	Fair	Poor
5500	4400	3300	2750	875	N/A

Grade 7E

Courtesy Walter C. Snyder

NIB	Exc.	V.G.	Good	Fair	Poor
8800	5500	4450	3300	1100	N/A

Sousa Grade

NIB	Exc.	V.G.	Good	Fair	Poor
19000	11000	6600	4400	N/A	N/A

$1,000 to $2,500 Grades

Courtesy Walter C. Snyder

NIB	Exc.	V.G.	Good	Fair	Poor
16500	13500	8800	6500	2200	N/A

$3,000 through the Dollar Grade

NIB	Exc.	V.G.	Good	Fair	Poor
13500	11000	6500	5500	2200	N/A

Century Grade Trap (SKB)

A 12 gauge boxlock single-barrel shotgun with a 32" or 34" ventilated rib barrel and automatic ejector. Blued with a walnut stock. Manufactured by SKB during the 1970s.

NIB	Exc.	V.G.	Good	Fair	Poor
—	900	700	550	350	300

Century II (SKB)

An improved version of the above model.

NIB	Exc.	V.G.	Good	Fair	Poor
—	950	700	600	450	350

ITHACA MODEL 66

Model 66 Supersingle—1963-1978

A 12, 20 or .410 bore lever action single-shot shotgun with a 24" barrel. Blued with a walnut stock. The 20 gauge and .410 bore command a 50 percent premium.

Courtesy C. Hadley Smith

NIB	Exc.	V.G.	Good	Fair	Poor
300	180	150	125	100	50

Model 66 Youth Grade

A special gun offered for the youth market in 20 gauge and .410 bore.

NIB	Exc.	V.G.	Good	Fair	Poor
300	180	150	125	100	50

Model 66 Buck Buster (RS Barrel)

As above, in 20 gauge with a Deerslayer 22" barrel fitted with rifle sights.

NIB	Exc.	V.G.	Good	Fair	Poor
325	250	200	150	125	75

Model 66 Vent Rib

NIB	Exc.	V.G.	Good	Fair	Poor
325	250	200	150	125	75

ITHACA AUTO & BURGLAR GUN
NFA, CURIO OR RELIC

The Ithaca Auto & Burglar Gun is a double-barreled 20 gauge smooth bore pistol manufactured by Ithaca Gun Company, Ithaca, New York, from 1922 to 1934. Total production was approximately 4,500. They were made by modifying Ithaca's standard field grade double-barrel shotgun by shortening the barrels and fitting the receiver with a pistol grip. Standard factory guns had blued 10" barrels, case hardened receivers with the legend "Auto & Burglar Gun/ Ithaca Gun Co./Ithaca, New York", and the figure of a pointing dog stamped on each side. The barrel length on 21 guns inspected varied to 10.25" (typically in increments divisible by .125"), apparently from inexact factory quality control. Ithaca set a $37.50 retail price when the gun was in production, but some dealers sold it for $40 or more. Production was halted when the government ruled the Ithaca Auto & Burglar Gun to be a "firearm" in the "any other weapon" category under the National Firearms Act (NFA) of 1934.

There are two variations, termed Model A and Model B. Model A utilizes the so-called Flues frame (named after Emil Flues, who designed it in 1908), and its distinctive grip has a curving butt and a large spur. Model A is designed for 2.5" shells, and is not considered safe to fire using modern ammunition. Approximately 2,500 Model A Auto & Burglar Guns were manufactured from 1922 to 1925, when the Flues model was discontinued.

Model B utilizes the so-called NID frame (short for New Ithaca Double), introduced in 1926 and discontinued in 1948. The NID is designed for modern ammunition and 2.75" shells, has cocking indicators, and a different pistol grip that is perpendicular to the barrel and which lacks the distinctive spur. Some Model Bs have been observed with rosettes or "stars" engraved in each side of the receiver; their significance is unknown at this time, but they probably are decorations. Approximately 2,000 Model B Auto & Burglar Guns were manufactured from 1926 to 1934.

Model A
Serial numbered from 343336 to 398365

NIB	Exc.	V.G.	Good	Fair	Poor
—	2500	2000	1750	900	500

Model B
Serial numbered from 425000 to 464699

NIB	Exc.	V.G.	Good	Fair	Poor
—	2750	2200	2000	950	550

NOTE: Nonstandard or special order guns command premiums of 100 percent or more. Original holsters (marked Auto and Burglar Gun/made by/ITHACA GUN CO./ithaca, n.y.) are extremely rare and worth $300 to $500 or more.

ITHACA MODEL 37 REPEATER

The Ithaca Model 37 Repeater was introduced in 1937 in 12 gauge, 1938 in 16 gauge, and in 1939 in 20 gauge. It underwent very few design changes throughout its long life which ended in 1987 when the Ithaca Acquisition Corp. acquired the assets of the Ithaca Gun Company during 1987 and renamed the gun Model 87. The name has recently been changed again to the M37 after the assets of the Ithaca Acquisition Corp. were purchased in May of 1996 by the Ithaca Gun Company, LLC. All Model 37 guns were chambered only for 2.75 ammunition until 1983, when the Magnum with 3" chamber was introduced to some configurations. Most Model 37 guns had blued metal and walnut stocks with the exception of the Model 37 Field Grade series which had matte finished metal and Birch stocks. The 16 gauge guns were discontinued in 1973. Ithaca Gun closed in April, 2005, but reopened in 2006 as Ithaca Guns USA of Upper Sandusky, Ohio. **NOTE:** The 20 gauge guns made before 1968 will generally command a price premium.

Model 37/Standard Grade—1937-1983

Guns made before 1968 will enjoy a 15 percent price premium; those made before World War II, a 30 percent price premium.

Courtesy C. Hadley Smith

NIB	Exc.	V.G.	Good	Fair	Poor
—	350	200	175	125	75

Model 37S/Skeet Grade—1937-1953

Guns made before World War II will enjoy a 50 percent price premium.

NIB	Exc.	V.G.	Good	Fair	Poor
—	600	400	350	250	100

Model 37T/Trap—1937-1953

Guns made before World War II will enjoy a 50 percent price premium.

NIB	Exc.	V.G.	Good	Fair	Poor
—	600	400	350	250	100

Model 37T/Target—1954-1961

NIB	Exc.	V.G.	Good	Fair	Poor
—	600	400	350	250	100

Model 37R/Solid Rib—1940-1967

Guns made before World War II will enjoy a 50 percent price premium.

Courtesy Walter C. Snyder

NIB	Exc.	V.G.	Good	Fair	Poor
—	400	275	225	200	75

Model 37 Military Marked (WWII)

This is one of the scarcest military shotguns. It was built in three different configurations; 30" barrel, 20" barrel, and 20" barrel with handguard and bayonet lug (Trench Gun). A rare shotgun, proceed with caution. **NOTE:** Add $200 for government release papers and 150 percent for Trench Gun configuration.

Courtesy Richard M. Kumor, Sr.

Model 37 with 20" barrel and release papers

NIB	Exc.	V.G.	Good	Fair	Poor
—	2000	1800	1500	—	—

Model 37RD/Deluxe Solid Rib—1954-1962

Courtesy C. Hadley Smith

NIB	Exc.	V.G.	Good	Fair	Poor
—	500	375	300	200	100

Model 37 Deerslayer—1959-1987

All Deerslayer models made before 1968 will enjoy a 10 percent to 20 percent price premium.

Courtesy C. Hadley Smith

NIB	Exc.	V.G.	Good	Fair	Poor
—	300	250	200	125	75

Model 37 Deluxe Deerslayer—1959-1971

NIB	Exc.	V.G.	Good	Fair	Poor
—	300	250	225	125	75

Model 37 Super Deluxe Deerslayer—1959-1987

Courtesy C. Hadley Smith

NIB	Exc.	V.G.	Good	Fair	Poor
—	450	325	275	200	100

Model 37 Supreme Grade—1967-1987

NIB	Exc.	V.G.	Good	Fair	Poor
—	700	450	350	200	100

Model 37 Field Grade Standard—1983-1985

NIB	Exc.	V.G.	Good	Fair	Poor
—	350	200	150	125	75

Model 37 Field Grade Vent Rib—1983-1986

NIB	Exc.	V.G.	Good	Fair	Poor
—	350	250	200	125	75

Model 37 Basic Featherlight—1979-1983

Manufactured in 12 gauge only.

Courtesy Walter C. Snyder

NIB	Exc.	V.G.	Good	Fair	Poor
—	300	250	200	125	75

Model 37V/Vent Rib—1961-1983

Guns made before 1968 will enjoy a 10 percent to 20 percent price premium.

NIB	Exc.	V.G.	Good	Fair	Poor
—	350	300	175	150	75

Model 37RV/Deluxe Vent Rib—1961-1966

Courtesy Walter C. Snyder

NIB	Exc.	V.G.	Good	Fair	Poor
—	750	500	300	200	75

Model 37D/Deluxe—1955-1977

Guns made before 1968 will enjoy a 10 percent to 20 percent price premium.

Courtesy C. Hadley Smith

NIB	Exc.	V.G.	Good	Fair	Poor
—	400	250	175	125	75

Model 37DV/Deluxe Vent Rib—1961-1987

Guns made before 1968 will enjoy a 10 percent to 20 percent price premium.

NIB	Exc.	V.G.	Good	Fair	Poor
—	450	300	200	150	100

Model 37 Magnum 3" Chamber—1978-1987

NIB	Exc.	V.G.	Good	Fair	Poor
—	400	300	225	125	75

Model 37 Field Grade Magnum—1984-1987

NIB	Exc.	V.G.	Good	Fair	Poor
—	300	225	175	125	75

Model 37 UltraLight—1978 to 1987

The UltraLight had an aluminum alloy frame and trigger plate. The barrels are marked Ultra Featherlight and the serial number is prefaced with the mark, "ULT". Both the 12 and 20 gauges were offered.

NIB	Exc.	V.G.	Good	Fair	Poor
—	475	400	300	150	100

Model 37 English UltraLight—1982-1987

This gun is the same as the Model 37 UltraLight, but has an English-style straight grip stock.

NIB	Exc.	V.G.	Good	Fair	Poor
—	500	450	350	150	100

Model 37 Camo

Introduced in 1985, this model is available with either a green or brown camouflage finish and was offered only in 12 gauge.

NIB	Exc.	V.G.	Good	Fair	Poor
—	350	300	200	150	100

Model 37 Bicentennial

A special model produced during 1976 to commemorate the 200 year anniversary of the United States. The gun came with a full-length trunk-style hard case and a pewter belt buckle number to the gun. The serial number was prefaced with "U.S.A." **NOTE:** Subtract 35 percent if the original case and belt buckle are missing.

NIB	Exc.	V.G.	Good	Fair	Poor
650	500	300	200	125	75

Model 37 Ducks Unlimited Commemorative, Auction Grade

Special edition made during 1977. Serial number sequence was 40-DU0001 to 40-DU1125.

NIB	Exc.	V.G.	Good	Fair	Poor
650	400	300	150	100	75

Model 37 Ducks Unlimited Commemorative, Trade Grade

Special edition made during 1977. Lower grade version of the Auction Grade. Serial number preceded with the mark, DU37040.

NIB	Exc.	V.G.	Good	Fair	Poor
450	400	350	200	N/A	N/A

Model 37 2500 Series Centennial

A commemorative Model 37 12 gauge shotgun with silver-plated receiver and press checkered stocks. Manufactured in 1984.

NIB	Exc.	V.G.	Good	Fair	Poor
800	500	300	150	100	75

Model 37 Presentation Series Centennial

A commemorative Model 37 12 gauge with a gold-plated receiver and high grade hand checkered stocks. It was manufactured during 1980, but is still available as of August 1997.

NIB	Exc.	V.G.	Good	Fair	Poor
1500	800	500	150	100	—

Hi-Grade Ithaca Model 37 Guns

The Ithaca Gun company offered custom engraving services either from its in-house engraver, one of which was retained until about 1972, or through an outside contract engraver who was usually William Mains. Many customers requested some degree of custom work and guns with various patterns turn up from time to time. There were four standard engraving patterns offered to customers, Grade 1, Grade 2, Grade 3, and the very elaborate $1,000 Grade pattern. Increasing production costs forced the $1,000 Grade to become the $2,000 Grade, the $2,500, and finally the $3,000 Grade over the years. **NOTE:** All factory engraved Model 37 guns are rare and require an expert appraiser to determine an accurate value.

$1,000 Grade

The Model 37 with an engraved receiver, gold inlays, and a well-figured walnut stock. Manufactured between 1940 and 1942.

NIB	Exc.	V.G.	Good	Fair	Poor
10000	5000	3000	2000	N/A	N/A

$2,000 Grade

Manufactured from 1946 to 1957.

NIB	Exc.	V.G.	Good	Fair	Poor
10000	5000	3000	2000	N/A	N/A

$3,000 Grade

As above. Manufactured from 1958 to 1967.

NIB	Exc.	V.G.	Good	Fair	Poor
8000	4000	2500	1500	N/A	N/A

Model 37 Law Enforcement Weapons

The Ithaca Gun Company entered the law enforcement market in 1962 when it introduced the Model 37 Military and Police (M&P) and the Model 37DS Police special (DSPS). The M&P Model was styled after the riot guns made for various military contracts. The DSPS was styled after the Ithaca Deerslayer. Both models were offered with 8-shot capacity after 1968. A chrome finish was an available option after 1976. Both models usually had ring turned slide handles. Only those models available to the general public, i.e. barrel lengths of 18" or longer, are listed. Add 25 percent if marked with police department. **NOTE:** Add 20 percent for an 8-shot model in NIB or EXC. condition, and add an additional 15 percent for chrome plated models in similar condition.

Military and Police (M&P)—1962-1986

NIB	Exc.	V.G.	Good	Fair	Poor
550	450	250	200	125	75

DS Police Special—1962-1986

NIB	Exc.	V.G.	Good	Fair	Poor
575	450	250	200	125	75

ITHACA MODEL 87 REPEATER

During 1987 many of the assets of the bankrupt Ithaca Gun Company were purchased by the Ithaca Acquisition Corporation. Manufacture of the Model 37 was resumed that summer after the gun was renamed the Model 87. Many of the Models offered by the old company were continued. All Model 87 field guns were produced with ventilated ribs. All Deerslayer models continued the rifle sights used on the Model 37 guns.

Model 87 Basic—1989-1994

Early models had birch stocks, later production had walnut stocks. All had ring turned slide handles.

NIB	Exc.	V.G.	Good	Fair	Poor
350	300	250	175	125	75

Model 87 Magnum

A 12 or 20 gauge magnum slide action shotgun with a 25" barrel fitted with screw-in choke tubes and a ventilated rib that is similar to the Model 37. Blued with a walnut stock.

NIB	Exc.	V.G.	Good	Fair	Poor
400	350	300	225	150	100

Model 87 Field Grade—1987-1990

Stocks were walnut with pressed checkering.

NIB	Exc.	V.G.	Good	Fair	Poor
325	250	200	175	125	75

Model 87 Camo—1987-1994

NIB	Exc.	V.G.	Good	Fair	Poor
300	250	200	175	125	75

Model 87 Turkey Gun—1987-1996

Courtesy C. Hadley Smith

NIB	Exc.	V.G.	Good	Fair	Poor
325	250	200	175	125	75

Model 87 Deluxe—1987-1996

The buttstocks and slide handle were walnut with a machine cut checkered pattern.

Courtesy C. Hadley Smith

NIB	Exc.	V.G.	Good	Fair	Poor
375	300	250	200	125	75

Model 87 Ultralite—1987-1990

All IAC manufactured Ultralite guns carry the old Model 37 serial number.

NIB	Exc.	V.G.	Good	Fair	Poor
500	350	250	175	125	75

Model 87 English—1993-1996

Courtesy C. Hadley Smith

Hand-checkered walnut stocks. The slide handle was styled after the pre-war Model 37 slide handle.

NIB	Exc.	V.G.	Good	Fair	Poor
400	350	250	175	125	75

Model 87 Ultralite Deluxe

NIB	Exc.	V.G.	Good	Fair	Poor
400	350	300	250	125	75

Model 87 Supreme Grade—1987-1996

High grade walnut stocks with hand checkering. Metal had extra fine polish and finish.

Courtesy C. Hadley Smith

NIB	Exc.	V.G.	Good	Fair	Poor
1000	700	500	300	250	100

Model 87 Deerslayer Basic—1989-1996

Walnut, oil finish butt and slide handle stocks. Slide handle was classic ring turned style.

NIB	Exc.	V.G.	Good	Fair	Poor
300	275	250	200	125	75

Model 87 Deerslayer—1989-1996

It was sometimes advertised as the Model 87 Deerslayer Field. Buttstock and slide handle were walnut and usually had a pressed checkered pattern. The slide handle was the beavertail style.

Courtesy C. Hadley Smith

NIB	Exc.	V.G.	Good	Fair	Poor
350	300	250	200	125	75

Model 87 Deluxe Deerslayer—1989-1996

Butt stock and slide handle were walnut with a machine-cut checkering pattern. The slide handle was beavertail.

NIB	Exc.	V.G.	Good	Fair	Poor
400	350	250	200	125	75

Model 87 Deerslayer II—1988-1996

This model had a fixed rifle barrel and a Monte Carlo buttstock. A small number of guns were specially made with a fast twist barrel to handle Brenneke ammunition and are marked "BRENNEKE" on the receiver. **NOTE:** Brenneke-marked guns will command a 30 percent price premium.

Courtesy C. Hadley Smith

NIB	Exc.	V.G.	Good	Fair	Poor
550	450	350	200	125	75

Model 87 Home Protection and Law Enforcement

The Ithaca Acquisition Corporation continued production of many of the law enforcement firearms produced by the Ithaca Gun Company. Only those models available to the general public are listed.

Military & Police—1987-1996

Generally produced with a non-checkered walnut buttstock and a ring turned slide handle, both of which were oil finished. Add 20 percent for an 8-shot model in NIB or excellent condition. **NOTE:** Add an additional 15 percent for chrome plated models in similar condition.

NIB	Exc.	V.G.	Good	Fair	Poor
450	395	275	200	125	75

DS Police Special—1987-1996

Produced with either a pressed checkered or a non-checkered walnut buttstock, and a ring-turned slide handle, both lacquer finished. The metal was usually finished with a commercial polished blue but a chrome-plated finish was also available. **NOTE:** Add 20 percent for an 8-shot model in NIB or excellent condition, and add an additional 15 percent for a chrome plated models in similar condition.

NIB	Exc.	V.G.	Good	Fair	Poor
450	395	275	200	125	75

NEW MODEL 37

During 1996, the assets of the bankrupt Ithaca Acquisition Corporation were purchased by a new company named the Ithaca Gun Company, LLC. One of the first public actions of the new firm was to rename the Model 87 the Model 37, before resuming production later that year, the serial number of the new Model 37 is prefaced with the letter "M". A used market for the new Model 37 has not been established at this time. Suggested retail prices for each model currently produced are listed. In 2001 a Legacy Edition upgrade featuring a laser carved handwritten message in the stock was available for an additional $125.

Model 37 Deerslayer II

This model is offered in both 12 and 20 gauge. Fitted with either 20" or 25" barrels with rifled bores. These barrels are fixed to the receiver. Magazine capacity is 5 rounds. Walnut stock. Weight is approximately 7 lbs. In 2001 a 16 gauge version with fixed rifled barrel was offered.

NIB	Exc.	V.G.	Good	Fair	Poor
640	500	375	275	200	100

Smooth Bore Deluxe

Offered in 12, 16, or 20 gauge with interchangeable barrels in 20" or 25" with smoothbore for deer. Walnut stock. Magazine capacity is 5 rounds. Weight is approximately 6.75 lbs.

NIB	Exc.	V.G.	Good	Fair	Poor
675	400	350	275	200	100

Rifled Deluxe

Same as above but in 12 and 20 gauge only with rifled barrels.

NIB	Exc.	V.G.	Good	Fair	Poor
675	400	350	275	200	100

Deerslayer III Slug Shotgun

Updated, slug-only version of the classic Model 37 pump-action shotgun. 12 or 20 gauge. Fully rifled, heavy fluted 26" barrel with 1:28 twist. Bottom ejection. Fancy black walnut stock and fore-end, blued barrel and receiver.

NIB	Exc.	V.G.	Good	Fair	Poor
1350	1000	750	500	300	150

Model 37 28 Gauge

28 gauge pump action shotgun. Scaled down receiver with traditional Model 37 bottom ejection and easy takedown. 26" or 28" barrel. Available in Fancy "A", Fancy "AA", and Fancy "AAA" grades with increasingly elaborate receiver engraving and decoration. Special order only. Values shown are for "Fancy A" grade.

NIB	Exc.	V.G.	Good	Fair	Poor
1000	750	575	400	300	200

Model 37 Deluxe Field

This model is offered in 12, 16, and 20 gauge with interchangeable vent rib barrels of 26", 28", or 30" (12 gauge only). Walnut stock. Magazine capacity is 5 rounds. Weight is about 7 lbs.

NIB	Exc.	V.G.	Good	Fair	Poor
625	475	375	250	150	100

Model 37 Deluxe Field English Style

This model is offered in 20 gauge only with 24", 26", or 28" vent rib barrels. Walnut stock. Weight is about 7 lbs. Magazine capacity is 5 rounds.

NIB	Exc.	V.G.	Good	Fair	Poor
650	475	375	250	150	100

Model 37 Ultra Featherlight Grouse Special

Based on the Classic Model 37 with bottom ejection this model features an aluminum receiver and 24" vent rib barrel with choke tubes. Straight grip stock of American black walnut.

NIB	Exc.	V.G.	Good	Fair	Poor
650	525	395	275	150	100

Model 37 Ultra Featherlight Youth

Similar to the above model but with a 22" barrel and 12.75" length of pull buttstock with ventilated recoil pad.

NIB	Exc.	V.G.	Good	Fair	Poor
600	475	375	250	150	100

Model 37 Sporting Clays

This model features a choice of 24", 26", or 28" wide vent rib barrels with Briley choke tubes. Receiver has an antiqued finish with scroll engraving and high grade American black walnut.

NIB	Exc.	V.G.	Good	Fair	Poor
1350	1000	750	575	300	150

Model 37 Trap

This model has similar features as the sporting clays but with 30" wide vent rib barrel.

NIB	Exc.	V.G.	Good	Fair	Poor
1350	1000	750	500	300	150

Model 37 Women's Endowment Shotgun

Offered in 16 or 20 gauge with straight grip stock and a length of pull designed for the woman's height of 5'5". American walnut stock with cut checkering.

NIB	Exc.	V.G.	Good	Fair	Poor
635	500	375	250	150	100

Model 37 Waterfowler

Available in 12 gauge only with 28" steel shot barrel. Camo pattern stock. Weight is about 7 lbs. Magazine capacity is 5 rounds.

NIB	Exc.	V.G.	Good	Fair	Poor
595	475	375	250	150	10

Model 37 New Classic

Available in 12, 20, or 16 gauge with hand checkered walnut stock with choice of pistol grip or straight grip and high polish bolt and other component parts. Sunburst recoil pad. Interchangeable vent rib barrels in either 26" or 28". Weight is about 7 lbs.

NIB	Exc.	V.G.	Good	Fair	Poor
810	625	475	375	250	150

Model 37 Turkeyslayer

The first version of this model was made from 1996 to 2004 with a 22" barrel and camo stock. It was offered in 12 or 20 gauge. A later model, introduced in 2010, is in 12 gauge only with a 24" fixed barrel and synthetic stock with a matte black or camo finish. Also available with laminated thumb-hole stock. Other features include a Briley extended and ported extra-full turkey choke, lengthened forcing cone, Pachmayr Decelerator recoil pad, Tru-Glo fiber optic front sight. Weight: 7.6 pounds with standard stock, 8.2 pounds with thumb-hole.

NIB	Exc.	V.G.	Good	Fair	Poor
575	500	450	400	300	200

Model 37 Home Defense

In 12 or 20 gauge with 18.5" or 20" barrel, rifle sights, matte blue finish. Black synthetic or wood stock, 20" fixed barrel, rifle sights. Magazine holds 8 rounds (12 gauge only) or 5 rounds (12 or 20 gauge).

NIB	Exc.	V.G.	Good	Fair	Poor
425	385	340	295	250	200

Model 37 Hogslayer

In 12 gauge with 20" rifled barrel with rifle sights, matte blued finish. Tubular magazine holds 8 rounds. Matte blued barrel and action. Synthetic stock.

NIB	Exc.	V.G.	Good	Fair	Poor
450	400	355	300	250	200

MODEL 51

A 12 or 20 gauge semi-automatic shotgun with 26", 28", or 30" ventilated rib barrels. Blued with a walnut stock. Manufactured from 1970 to 1985 as listed.

Model 51A Standard

Plain barrel. **NOTE:** Vent rib add $100.

Courtesy C. Hadley Smith

NIB	Exc.	V.G.	Good	Fair	Poor
—	400	325	250	150	75

Model 51A Magnum

3" chamber. **NOTE:** Vent rib add $100.

NIB	Exc.	V.G.	Good	Fair	Poor
—	425	350	275	175	75

Model 51A Waterfowler

Matte finished.

NIB	Exc.	V.G.	Good	Fair	Poor
—	425	350	275	175	75

Model 51A Deerslayer

Courtesy C. Hadley Smith

NIB	Exc.	V.G.	Good	Fair	Poor
—	325	275	225	150	75

Model 51A Turkey Gun

Courtesy C. Hadley Smith

NIB	Exc.	V.G.	Good	Fair	Poor
—	425	350	275	175	75

Model 51 Supreme Trap

NIB	Exc.	V.G.	Good	Fair	Poor
—	425	375	325	250	75

Model 51 Supreme Skeet

NIB	Exc.	V.G.	Good	Fair	Poor
—	450	400	350	275	200

Model 51 Ducks Unlimited Commemorative

NIB	Exc.	V.G.	Good	Fair	Poor
600	500	375	325	275	200

Model 51 Presentation

Engraved receiver.

NIB	Exc.	V.G.	Good	Fair	Poor
1500	1250	1000	750	500	300

MAG-10

A 10 gauge magnum semi-automatic shotgun manufactured in a variety of barrel lengths, styles and finishes. Manufactured from 1975 to 1986 as listed. **NOTE:** The market for Ithaca Mag-10s has declined somewhat with the success of the 3.5" 12 gauge load. This is apparently because most owners consider their Mag-10s as hunting weapons, not collectors' pieces. Nevertheless, NIB or Excellent+ examples still command fairly high prices, if the right buyer can be found.

Standard Grade

NIB	Exc.	V.G.	Good	Fair	Poor
—	750	600	650	300	250

Standard Vent Rib Grade

NIB	Exc.	V.G.	Good	Fair	Poor
—	850	675	700	550	250

Deluxe Vent Rib Grade

NIB	Exc.	V.G.	Good	Fair	Poor
—	1000	750	775	600	250

Supreme Grade

NIB	Exc.	V.G.	Good	Fair	Poor
—	1100	850	850	700	250

Roadblocker—Military and Police Model

NIB	Exc.	V.G.	Good	Fair	Poor
—	750	600	650	300	250

Presentation Grade

Engraved, gold-inlaid, 200 made.

NIB	Exc.	V.G.	Good	Fair	Poor
1875	1500	1100	900	750	300

National Wild Turkey Federation

1985 manufacture.

NIB	Exc.	V.G.	Good	Fair	Poor
850	700	600	550	450	350

RIFLES

Model X5-C

A .22 caliber semi-automatic rifle with a 7-shot magazine. A 10-shot magazine was available as an extra cost option. Blued with a walnut stock. Manufactured between 1958 and 1964.

NIB	Exc.	V.G.	Good	Fair	Poor
400	200	150	100	75	50

Model X5T Lightning

A .22 caliber tubular feed auto-loading rifle produced between 1959 and 1963. Some models were stocked with curly maple stocks. These guns will command a 25 percent price premium.

NIB	Exc.	V.G.	Good	Fair	Poor
450	175	150	100	75	50

Model X-15 Lightning

Similar to the above, but manufactured between 1964 and 1966.

NIB	Exc.	V.G.	Good	Fair	Poor
450	175	150	100	75	50

Model 49 Saddlegun—1961-1979

A .22 caliber lever action single-shot rifle with an 18.5" barrel, fixed sights, alloy receiver and hardwood stock. It was offered chambered for the .22 Magnum in 1962. Deduct 20 percent for .22 LR.

Courtesy C. Hadley Smith

NIB	Exc.	V.G.	Good	Fair	Poor
350	220	175	100	50	25

Model 49 Saddlegun

Deluxe Grade

Fitted with gold plated trigger, hammer, and equipped with sling and sling swivels.

NIB	Exc.	V.G.	Good	Fair	Poor
400	250	200	125	50	25

Presentation Grade

High grade wood and engraved frame.

NIB	Exc.	V.G.	Good	Fair	Poor
425	300	250	200	50	25

Model 49R—1968-1971

A lever action .22 caliber tubular feed repeater. Magazine capacity is 15 LR cartridges.

NIB	Exc.	V.G.	Good	Fair	Poor
350	250	200	150	50	25

Model 72 Saddlegun—1973-1979

A .22 or .22 Magnum caliber lever action rifle with an 18.5" barrel, tubular magazine, open sights and walnut stock. Made by Erma in Germany.

NIB	Exc.	V.G.	Good	Fair	Poor
300	250	225	200	100	25

LSA-55 OR 65

A bolt-action sporting rifle manufactured in a variety of calibers and barrel lengths by Tikka of Finland. Imported between 1969 and 1977 in the models listed.

LSA-55 Standard

NIB	Exc.	V.G.	Good	Fair	Poor
—	500	350	300	250	175

LSA-55 Deluxe

NIB	Exc.	V.G.	Good	Fair	Poor
—	600	375	325	275	200

LSA-55 Varmint Heavy Barrel

NIB	Exc.	V.G.	Good	Fair	Poor
—	600	400	350	300	225

LSA-55 Turkey Gun

A 12 gauge by .222 Remington caliber over/under combination rifle/shotgun with 24.5" barrels, single trigger, exposed hammer and walnut stock. Manufactured in Finland by Tikka between 1970 and 1981.

NIB	Exc.	V.G.	Good	Fair	Poor
—	900	700	450	350	275

LSA-65 Long Action

NIB	Exc.	V.G.	Good	Fair	Poor
—	500	350	300	250	175

LSA-65 Deluxe

NIB	Exc.	V.G.	Good	Fair	Poor
—	600	375	325	275	200

HANDGUNS

Model 1911

The first 1911 made by Ithaca since WWII. Chambered in .45 ACP with hand-lapped carbon steel frame and slide, checkered front strap, skeletonized hammer and trigger, checkered cocobolo grips, and choice of adjustable Novak Combat or Bomar Target sights. Other features include a stainless steel Match grade barrel and bushing, and a full-length, two-piece guide rod. Optional lockable canvas case. Introduced in 2011. **NOTE:** Add $100 for case.

NIB	Exc.	V.G.	Good	Fair	Poor
1440	1225	1000	750	—	—

X-Caliber

A .22 to .44 Magnum caliber single-shot pistol with 10" or 15" barrels featuring a dual firing pin system so that interchangeable barrels could be used. The Model 20 is blued; the Model 30 is Teflon coated. Introduced in 1988. Made by Sterling Arms. Add 20 percent premium for .44.

NIB	Exc.	V.G.	Good	Fair	Poor
600	475	300	225	175	125

IVER JOHNSON ARMS, INC.
Middlesex, New Jersey
See—AMAC

Established in 1883 in Fitchburg, Massachusetts, this company has produced a wide variety of firearms during its existence.

HANDGUNS

Trade Name Revolvers

A series of spur trigger revolvers were made by Iver Johnson bearing only the trade names such as Encore, Eclipse, Favorite, Tycoon, and Eagle. In general, the value for these revolvers are listed.

NIB	Exc.	V.G.	Good	Fair	Poor
—	250	170	120	95	65

Safety Automatic Double-Action

A .22, .32 CF, or .38 CF caliber double-action revolver produced in a variety of barrel lengths with or without exposed hammers. Manufactured between 1893 and 1950.

NIB	Exc.	V.G.	Good	Fair	Poor
—	250	170	120	95	65

Model 1900

A .22 to .38 caliber double-action revolver with a 2.5", 4.5", or 6" barrel. Blued or nickel-plated with rubber grips and no cartridge ejecting system. Manufactured between 1900 and 1947.

NIB	Exc.	V.G.	Good	Fair	Poor
—	250	170	120	95	65

Safety Cycle Automatic

Similar to the Safety Automatic with a 2" barrel.

NIB	Exc.	V.G.	Good	Fair	Poor
—	250	170	120	95	65

Petite

A .22 Short caliber double-action folding trigger revolver with a 1" barrel and 7-shot cylinder. Nickel-plated with rubber grips. Introduced in 1909.

NIB	Exc.	V.G.	Good	Fair	Poor
—	350	250	200	150	100

Supershot Sealed 8

A .22 caliber double-action revolver with a 6" barrel and counterbored 8-shot cylinder. Blued with rubber grips. Manufactured from 1919 to 1957.

NIB	Exc.	V.G.	Good	Fair	Poor
—	250	170	120	95	65

Protector Sealed 8

As above, with a 2.5" barrel.

NIB	Exc.	V.G.	Good	Fair	Poor
—	250	170	120	95	65

Supershot 9

Similar to the Supershot Sealed 8 with a 9-shot uncounterbored cylinder. Manufactured between 1929 and 1949.

NIB	Exc.	V.G.	Good	Fair	Poor
—	250	170	120	95	65

Trigger Cocker Single-Action

A .22 caliber single-action revolver with a 6" barrel and 8-shot counterbored cylinder. Blued with walnut grips. Manufactured between 1940 and 1947.

NIB	Exc.	V.G.	Good	Fair	Poor
—	200	125	100	50	25

.22 Target Single-Action

As above, with adjustable sights and adjustable grips. Manufactured between 1938 and 1948.

NIB	Exc.	V.G.	Good	Fair	Poor
—	250	190	150	125	65

Model 844

A .22 caliber double-action revolver with a 4.5" or 6" barrel, adjustable sights, and an 8-shot cylinder. Manufactured in the 1950s.

NIB	Exc.	V.G.	Good	Fair	Poor
—	225	140	100	80	40

Model 855

As above, but single-action with a 6" barrel. Manufactured in the 1950s.

NIB	Exc.	V.G.	Good	Fair	Poor
—	225	140	100	80	40

Model 55A Sportsmen Target

A .22 caliber single-action revolver with a 4.75" or 6" barrel, fixed sights and 8-shot cylinder. Blued with walnut grips.

NIB	Exc.	V.G.	Good	Fair	Poor
—	200	125	100	75	35

Model 55S-A Cadet

A .22 to .38 caliber single-action revolver with a 2.5" barrel and fixed sights. Blued with plastic grips. Introduced in 1955.

NIB	Exc.	V.G.	Good	Fair	Poor
—	250	170	120	95	65

Model 57A Target

As above, with a 4.5" or 6" barrel and adjustable sights. Manufactured between 1955 and 1975.

NIB	Exc.	V.G.	Good	Fair	Poor
—	175	110	85	60	35

Model 66 Trailsman

A .22 caliber double-action revolver with a 6" barrel, adjustable sights, and 8-shot cylinder. Blued with walnut grips. Manufactured between 1958 and 1975.

NIB	Exc.	V.G.	Good	Fair	Poor
—	125	75	65	50	25

Model 67 Viking

As above, with a safety hammer.

NIB	Exc.	V.G.	Good	Fair	Poor
—	125	75	65	50	25

Model 67S Viking Snub

Same as above but fitted with 2" barrel.

NIB	Exc.	V.G.	Good	Fair	Poor
—	125	75	65	50	25

Model 50

A .22 or .22 Magnum single-action revolver with a 4.75" or 6" barrel, 8-shot cylinder and either fixed or adjustable sights. Also known as the Sidewinder. Manufactured between 1961 and 1975.

NIB	Exc.	V.G.	Good	Fair	Poor
—	125	75	65	50	25

American Bulldog

A .22 to .38 caliber double-action revolver with a 2.5" or 4" barrel and adjustable sights. Blued or nickel-plated with plastic grips. Manufactured between 1974 and 1976.

NIB	Exc.	V.G.	Good	Fair	Poor
—	175	100	75	50	25

Rookie

A .38 caliber revolver with a 4" barrel and 5-shot cylinder. Blued or nickel-plated with plastic grips.

NIB	Exc.	V.G.	Good	Fair	Poor
—	175	100	75	50	25

Cattleman Series

Manufactured by Aldo Uberti and listed under that name in this book.

Model X300 Pony

A .380 semi-automatic pistol with a 3" barrel and 6-shot magazine. Blued with plastic grips. Introduced in 1975.

NIB	Exc.	V.G.	Good	Fair	Poor
—	275	195	165	135	85

Trailsman

A .22 caliber semi-automatic pistol with a 4.5" or 6" barrel and 10-shot magazine. Blued with plastic or walnut grips.

NIB	Exc.	V.G.	Good	Fair	Poor
—	275	195	165	135	85

TP22/TP25 Pistol

A .22 or .25 ACP caliber double-action semi-automatic pistol with a 2.8" barrel and 7-shot magazine. Blued or nickel-plated with plastic grips.

NIB	Exc.	V.G.	Good	Fair	Poor
—	275	195	165	135	85

THE "NEW" IVER-JOHNSON BRAND (2006)

The Iver Johnson name resurfaced in 2006 in connection with a line of firearms based in Rockledge, Florida.

Frontier Four Derringer

Four-barrel, stainless .22 LR single-action derringer with unique rotating firing pin. Based on old Sharps derringer. 5.5 oz. Introduced 2006.

NIB	Exc.	V.G.	Good	Fair	Poor
195	150	100	75	50	—

Eagle Target Series 1911 .45

All-steel 7+1 capacity 1911 .45 ACP with 5" Government or 4.5" Commander barrel. Adjustable white outline rear sight. Adjustable trigger. Polished blue. Introduced 2006.

NIB	Exc.	V.G.	Good	Fair	Poor
650	550	425	315	250	150

Eagle Target Series 1911 .22 LR

Aluminum slide and frame, 15+1 capacity 1911 .22 LR with 5" Government or 4.5" Commander barrel. 19 oz. Adjustable white outline rear sight. Adjustable trigger. Blued or stainless. Introduced 2006.

NIB	Exc.	V.G.	Good	Fair	Poor
600	500	400	300	200	100

Raven Series 1911 .45

All-steel 7+1 capacity 1911 .45 ACP with 5" Government or 4.5" Commander barrel. Fixed sights. Matte blue, Parkerized or two-tone. Introduced 2006.

NIB	Exc.	V.G.	Good	Fair	Poor
550	425	315	250	150	100

Raven Series 1911 .22 LR

Aluminum slide and frame, 15+1 capacity 1911 in .22 LR with 5" Government or 4.5" Commander barrel. 19 oz. Fixed sights. Matte blued or stainless two-tone finish. Introduced 2006.

NIB	Exc.	V.G.	Good	Fair	Poor
550	425	315	250	150	100

RIFLES

Model X

Bolt action .22 caliber single-shot rifle fitted with 22" barrel with open sights, pistol grip. Manufactured between 1927 and 1932.

NIB	Exc.	V.G.	Good	Fair	Poor
—	175	110	90	70	40

Model XA

As above but with Lyman receiver sight, swivels, leather strap, and ivory bead. Manufactured between 1927 and 1932.

NIB	Exc.	V.G.	Good	Fair	Poor
—	325	225	175	130	80

Model 2X

Fitted with a 24" heavy barrel and adjustable sights. Manufactured between 1932 and 1955.

NIB	Exc.	V.G.	Good	Fair	Poor
—	400	300	250	150	100

Li'L Champ

Chambered for the .22 LR cartridge this is a bolt-action single-shot rifle that weighs about 3 lbs.

NIB	Exc.	V.G.	Good	Fair	Poor
—	125	85	70	50	30

Long Range Rifle

This is a single-shot bolt-action rifle chambered for the .50 caliber Browning cartridge. Fitted with a 29" fluted barrel and adjustable trigger. Bipod. Comes supplied with a 20 power Leupold scope.

Limited production. Weight is about 36 lbs. Manufactured between 1988 and 1993.

NIB	Exc.	V.G.	Good	Fair	Poor
—	4600	4000	3000	2500	1000

JJ 9mm Carbine

This is a copy of the U.S. military M1. Blued finish and hardwood stock. Magazine is 20 rounds. Chambered for the 9mm cartridge. Built between 1985 and 1986. **NOTE:** Add 10 percent for folding stock. Deduct 5 percent for plastic stock.

NIB	Exc.	V.G.	Good	Fair	Poor
—	500	400	250	175	100

Delta-786 Carbine

Similar to the M1 carbine but in 9mm only. Matte finish. Manufactured in 1989.

NIB	Exc.	V.G.	Good	Fair	Poor
—	500	400	250	175	100

Carbine .30 Caliber

Similar to the M1 carbine and chambered for the .30 carbine cartridge. Offered in various stock configurations. Built from 1985 to 1986 and again in 1988 to 1993. **NOTE:** For paratrooper model add $50, for Johnson 5.7mm caliber deduct $75, no premium for stainless steel.

NIB	Exc.	V.G.	Good	Fair	Poor
—	600	485	315	250	150

U.S. Carbine .22 Caliber

Same as above but chambered for the .22 LR or .22 Magnum cartridge. Built in 1985 and 1986 and again in 1988. Fitted with 15-round magazine.

NIB	Exc.	V.G.	Good	Fair	Poor
—	350	295	225	150	75

Slide Action Targetmaster

Chambered for the .22 LR or .22 Magnum cartridge this rifle has a 15-round tubular magazine. Manufactured between 1985 and 1988 and again in 1990.

NIB	Exc.	V.G.	Good	Fair	Poor
—	250	170	125	100	50

Wagonmaster Model EW .22 HBL Lever Action

Chambered for the .22 LR or .22 Magnum cartridge and fitted with a hardwood stock. Blued finish. Grooved scope mounts. Built in 1985 and 1986 and again between 1988 and 1990.

NIB	Exc.	V.G.	Good	Fair	Poor
—	250	175	130	100	50

Model IJ .22 HB Semi-Automatic (Trail Blazer)

Chambered for .22 LR only with 10-round magazine. Manufactured in 1985 only.

NIB	Exc.	V.G.	Good	Fair	Poor
—	225	130	100	60	40

SHOTGUNS

Champion

A single barrel shotgun manufactured in a variety of gauges as well as .44 or .45 caliber with 26" to 32" barrels, external hammers, and automatic ejectors. Blued with a walnut stock. Manufactured between 1909 and 1956.

NIB	Exc.	V.G.	Good	Fair	Poor
—	250	200	150	75	25

Matted Rib Grade

As above, in 12, 16, or 20 gauge with a matte rib barrel. Manufactured between 1909 and 1948.

NIB	Exc.	V.G.	Good	Fair	Poor
—	275	225	175	95	50

Trap Grade

As above, in 12 gauge with a 32" ventilated rib barrel. Manufactured between 1909 and 1942.

NIB	Exc.	V.G.	Good	Fair	Poor
—	525	350	275	175	100

Hercules Grade

A boxlock double-barrel shotgun manufactured in a variety of gauges with 26" to 32" barrels, double triggers and extractors. Blued with a walnut stock.

NIB	Exc.	V.G.	Good	Fair	Poor
—	1350	1050	775	550	350

NOTE: Add premium for these features:
Single trigger—25 percent   Ejectors—25 percent
28 gauge—100 percent   .410 bore—100 percent
20 gauge—50 percent   16 gauge—20 percent
Engraving—100 percent   Vent rib—25 percent

Skeeter Model

As above, but more finely finished. Discontinued in 1946.

NIB	Exc.	V.G.	Good	Fair	Poor
—	2250	1600	1050	750	300

NOTE: Add premium for these features:
Single trigger—25 percent   Ejectors—25 percent
28 gauge—100 percent   .410 bore—100 percent
20 gauge—50 percent   16 gauge—20 percent
Engraving—100 percent   Vent rib—25 percent

Super Trap

A 12 gauge boxlock double barrel shotgun with a 32" full choked barrels, and extractors. Discontinued in 1942. **NOTE:** Add 50 percent for Miller single selective trigger and 35 percent for non-selective single trigger.

NIB	Exc.	V.G.	Good	Fair	Poor
—	2650	2000	1350	850	350

Silver Shadow

A 12 gauge boxlock over/under shotgun with a 26" or 28" ventilated rib barrels, double triggers and extractors. Blued with a walnut stock. Manufactured in Italy and imported by Iver Johnson. **NOTE:** Also available with a single trigger, which would increase the values listed by approximately 25 percent.

NIB	Exc.	V.G.	Good	Fair	Poor
—	550	400	350	300	200

IXL
New York, New York

Pocket Revolver

A .31 caliber double-action percussion revolver with a 4" octagonal barrel and 6-shot cylinder. Blued with walnut grips. The barrel marked "IXL N.York." Approximately 750 were made without hammer spurs and 150 with side mounted hammers during the 1850s.

NIB	Exc.	V.G.	Good	Fair	Poor
—	—	—	1250	600	300

Navy Revolver

As above in .36 caliber. Approximately 100 were made with both center and side mounted hammers during the 1850s.

NIB	Exc.	V.G.	Good	Fair	Poor
—	—	—	3250	1400	500

J

JACQUESMART, JULES
Liege, Belgium

Le Monobloc

A 6.35mm semi-automatic pistol with a 2" barrel and 6-shot magazine. The slide marked "Le Monobloc/Pistolet Automatique/ Brevefte." Blued with composition grips. Production ceased in 1914.

Courtesy James Rankin

NIB	Exc.	V.G.	Good	Fair	Poor
—	550	450	350	200	100

JACQUITH, ELIJAH
Brattleboro, Vermont

Revolving Under Hammer Rifle

An extremely rare .40 caliber percussion revolving rifle with a 34" round-octagonal barrel and 8-shot cylinder. It is believed that approximately 25 of these rifles were made in 1838 and 1839. The barrel marked "E. Jaquith Brattleboro. Vt." Prospective purchasers should secure a qualified appraisal prior to acquisition.

NIB	Exc.	V.G.	Good	Fair	Poor
—	—	18000	7250	2200	2200

JAGER WAFFENFABIK
Suhl, Germany

Jager Semi-Automatic Pistol

A 7.65mm caliber semi-automatic pistol with a 3" barrel and 7-shot magazine. Largely made from steel stampings. Weight is approximately 23 oz. Blued with plastic grips. The slide marked "Jager-Pistole DRP Angem". Approximately 5,500 were made prior to 1914. **NOTE:** Add 50 percent for Imperial proofed examples.

Courtesy Richard M. Kumor, Sr.

NIB	Exc.	V.G.	Good	Fair	Poor
—	500	375	325	175	100

JEFFERY, W. J. & CO. LTD.
London, England

This company produced high quality shotguns and rifles. Their products have been used by wealthy sportsmen for many years. They produced guns under their own banner and also as contractors for other distributors. They made the guns sold by the Army & Navy Department Store in London. Guns of this type were basically custom-ordered and as such are extremely hard to evaluate on a general basis. We supply estimated values for standard rifle models.

Single-Shot

Built on the Farquharson Falling Block action and was chambered for many calibers up to the .600 Nitro Express. This was also a custom-order gun, and the barrel length was optional. There are usually folding express sights, and the finish is usually blued with a select, hand-checkered walnut stock. These were high quality firearms, and the values would be determined, for the most part, by the options and embellishments on the particular specimen. Individual appraisal is definitely advised. The caliber in which a rifle is chambered will also have an effect on the value. Obsolete calibers bring less, and the larger express calibers bring more.

NIB	Exc.	V.G.	Good	Fair	Poor
—	9000	6750	3750	21700	900

Boxlock Double Rifle

A boxlock chambered for many different calibers. It can be found with either a top or underlever action and has folding express sights. The stock and forearm are select, hand-checkered walnut, and the finish is usually blue. This was a custom-order proposition, and values can be affected by many variables such as caliber, options, and embellishment. Damascus barreled hammerguns are worth approximately 50 percent less.

NIB	Exc.	V.G.	Good	Fair	Poor
—	22000	15250	10950	3850	2500

Sidelock Double Rifle

Has detachable sidelocks and otherwise is comparable to the boxlock version.

NIB	Exc.	V.G.	Good	Fair	Poor
—	35000	22500	12250	7000	4000

JENISON, J. & CO.
Southbridge, Connecticut

Under Hammer Pistol

A .28 caliber single-shot under hammer percussion pistol with a 4" half-octagonal barrel marked "J.Jenison & Co./Southbridge, Mass.". Blued with a maple or oak grip. Manufactured during the 1850s.

NIB	Exc.	V.G.	Good	Fair	Poor
—	—	1550	850	400	200

JENKS CARBINE
Springfield, Massachusetts
Manufacturer—N. P. Ames

Jenks "Mule Ear Carbine"

A .54 caliber percussion side hammer carbine with a 24.5" round barrel and full length stock secured by two barrel bands.

The lock case hardened, the barrel browned and the furniture of brass. The lock marked "N.P.Ames/Springfield/Mass.". The barrel stamped "Wm.Jenks/USN" followed by the inspector's initials. The buttstock carries an inspector's cartouche. Approximately 4,250 were made between 1841 and 1846. Some were marked "USR" for the "U.S. Revenue Cutter Service", and these would bring approximately an 80 percent premium over the values listed. However, prospective purchasers should secure a qualified appraisal prior to acquisition.

Courtesy Milwaukee Public Museum, Milwaukee, Wisconsin

NIB	Exc.	V.G.	Good	Fair	Poor
—	—	4500	3750	1500	600

Jenks Navy Rifle

As above, with a 30" round barrel and full-length stock secured by three barrel bands. Approximately 1,000 were made for the U.S. Navy in 1841.

Courtesy Milwaukee Public Museum, Milwaukee, Wisconsin

NIB	Exc.	V.G.	Good	Fair	Poor
—	—	5000	4250	1750	750

JENKS-HERKIMER
New York
Manufacturer—E. Remington & Son

Jenks Carbine

Identical to the Jenks "Mule Ear Carbine" listed in the previous entry except that the barrel length is 24.25" and the lock is fitted with a Maynard tape primer. The lock marked "Remington's/Herkimer/N.Y." The barrel is marked "W. Jenks/USN/RC/P/Cast Steel". Approximately 1,000 of these carbines manufactured circa 1846.

NIB	Exc.	V.G.	Good	Fair	Poor
—	—	5000	4250	1750	750

JENKS-MERRILL
Baltimore, Maryland

An alteration of the Jenks Carbine listed previously to a breech loading system developed by J.H. Merrill. The conventional sidelock marked "J. H. Merrill Balto./Pat. July 1858". The breech retains the mark "Wm.Jenks/USN". Approximately 300 were altered between 1858 and 1860.

NIB	Exc.	V.G.	Good	Fair	Poor
—	—	9750	8500	3500	950

JENNINGS
Windsor, Vermont
Manufacturer—Robbins & Lawrence
See—Winchester Repeating Arms

JENNINGS F. A., INC.
Carson City, Nevada

Distributors of arms manufactured by Calwestco in Chino, California, and Bryco Firearms in Carson City, Nevada.

J-22

A .22 caliber semi-automatic pistol with a 2.5" barrel and 6-shot magazine. Aluminum, finished in bright chrome, Teflon, or satin nickel with plastic or wood grips.

NIB	Exc.	V.G.	Good	Fair	Poor
150	90	75	65	50	35

Bryco Model 25

A .25 caliber semi-automatic pistol with a 2.5" barrel and 6-shot magazine. Constructed and finished as above.

NIB	Exc.	V.G.	Good	Fair	Poor
150	90	75	65	50	35

Bryco Model 38

A .22, .32, or .380 semi-automatic pistol with a 2.8" barrel and 6-shot magazine. Constructed and finished as above.

NIB	Exc.	V.G.	Good	Fair	Poor
150	90	75	65	50	35

Bryco Model 48

Similar to the above, with a redesigned trigger guard with a squared forward section. Introduced in 1988.

NIB	Exc.	V.G.	Good	Fair	Poor
150	90	75	65	50	35

JERICHO
Israeli Military Industries, Israel

Jericho

A 9mm or .41 Action Express double-action semi-automatic pistol with a 4.72" barrel, polygonal rifling, ambidextrous safety and fixed sights. Blued with plastic grips.

NIB	Exc.	V.G.	Good	Fair	Poor
575	500	400	350	300	200

JIEFFCO
Liege, Belgium
See—Robar et Cie

JOHNSON, STAN, BYE & CO.
Worcester, Massachusetts

Established in 1871 by Martin Bye and Iver Johnson. This company primarily manufactured inexpensive pistols. In 1883 Johnson assumed full control of the company and renamed it the Iver Johnson Arms Company.

Defender, Eagle, Encore, Eureka, Favorite, Lion, Smoker, and Tycoon

A .22, .32, .38, or .44 caliber spur trigger revolver manufactured with various barrel lengths and normally nickel-plated. The barrel marked with one of the above trade names.

NIB	Exc.	V.G.	Good	Fair	Poor
—	—	500	200	75	25

Eclipse

A .22 caliber spur trigger single-shot pistol with a 1.5" barrel. Blued with walnut grips.

NIB	Exc.	V.G.	Good	Fair	Poor
—	—	250	100	50	25

American Bulldog

A .22, .32, or .38 caliber double-action revolver with a 3" barrel. Blued or nickel-plated with walnut or composition grips.

NIB	Exc.	V.G.	Good	Fair	Poor
—	—	250	100	50	25

JOSLYN
Milbury, Massachusetts
Manufacturer—A. H. Waters

Model 1855 Carbine

A .54 caliber breech loading single-shot percussion carbine with a 22.5" barrel secured to the fore-end by one barrel band. Blued, case hardened with brass mounts. The lock marked "A.H.Waters & Co./Milbury, Mass.", and the patent dates stamped on the breech lever. Approximately 1,000 manufactured in 1855 and 1856.

NIB	Exc.	V.G.	Good	Fair	Poor
—	—	2750	2000	950	300

Model 1855 Rifle

Similar to the above, in .58 caliber with a 38" barrel secured by three barrel bands. Several hundred were made in 1856.

NIB	Exc.	V.G.	Good	Fair	Poor
—	—	4500	3250	1100	400

JOSLYN
Springfield, Massachusetts
Manufacturer—Springfield Armory

Joslyn Breechloading Rifle

The first mass-produced, true breechloading cartridge firearm manufactured in a national armory. The actions were supplied by the Joslyn Firearms Company, and the rifles were chambered for the .56-50 rimfire cartridge. This rifle has a 35.5" round barrel and a full-length stock that is held on by three barrel bands. The lock is marked "U.S./Springfield" with "1864" at the back. The barrel is marked "B. F. Joslyn's Patent/ Oct. 8th, 1861 / June 24th, 1862". There were approximately 3,000 of these manufactured circa 1865. They were probably issued to Union forces, but it is unknown if they saw action before the end of the Civil War.

NIB	Exc.	V.G.	Good	Fair	Poor
—	—	5500	3495	1950	500

.50-70 Alteration

Approximately 1,600 Joslyn rifles were rechambered to fire the .50-70 centerfire cartridge. The conversion consisted of rechambering and drilling a new firing pin hole after the rimfire pin was sealed. There was no specific serial number range in which these conversions were done. Most of these weapons were eventually converted to smoothbores and sold in Africa. The original military specimens are extremely scarce.

NIB	Exc.	V.G.	Good	Fair	Poor
—	—	6000	4200	2500	750

JOSLYN FIREARMS COMPANY
Stonington, Connecticut

Model 1862 Carbine

A .52 rimfire breechloading single-shot carbine with a 22" round barrel secured by one barrel band. Blued, case hardened with brass mounts. The lock marked "Joslyn Firearms Co./Stonington/Conn.", and the patent date marked on the barrel. The trigger plate is 8" long, and the upper tang measures 4.5". Approximately 4,000 manufactured in 1862.

Courtesy Milwaukee Public Museum, Milwaukee, Wisconsin

NIB	Exc.	V.G.	Good	Fair	Poor
—	—	4500	3700	1500	400

Model 1864 Carbine

As above, with case hardened iron mounts, a 7" trigger plate and 2" upper tang. Approximately 12,000 were made in 1864 and 1865.

Courtesy Milwaukee Public Museum, Milwaukee, Wisconsin

NIB	Exc.	V.G.	Good	Fair	Poor
—	—	4200	3300	1100	400

Army Model Revolver

A .44 caliber side hammer percussion revolver with an 8" octagonal barrel and 5-shot cylinder. Blued, case hardened with walnut grips. The barrel marked "B. F. Joslyn/Patd. May 4, 1858". Martially marked examples are worth a premium of approximately 25 percent over the values listed.

First Model

With a brass trigger guard and iron butt cap. Approximately 500 made in 1861.

NIB	Exc.	V.G.	Good	Fair	Poor
—	—	6000	4750	2000	650

Second Model

Fitted with an iron trigger guard and without a butt cap. Approximately 2,500 were made in 1861 and 1862.

NIB	Exc.	V.G.	Good	Fair	Poor
—	—	5500	4250	1600	500

JURRAS, LEE
Prescott, Arizona
See—Auto Mag

While Jurras is best known for manufacturing the last model of the Auto Mag, he also produced the pistol listed sold by J. & G. Sales in Prescott, Arizona.

Howdah Pistol

A .375, .416, .460, .475, .500, and .577 caliber single-shot pistol with a 12" barrel, adjustable sights and Nitex finish, built on a Thompson/Center Contender frame. Supposedly approximately 100 produced.

NIB	Exc.	V.G.	Good	Fair	Poor
—	1750	1100	800	650	500

JUSTICE, P. S.
Philadelphia, Pennsylvania

Percussion Rifle

A .58 caliber percussion rifle with a 35" round barrel secured by two barrel bands, browned barrel, polished lock and brass furniture. The lock marked "P.S. Justice/Philada.". Approximately 2,500 were manufactured in 1861.

Courtesy Milwaukee Public Museum, Milwaukee, Wisconsin

NIB	Exc.	V.G.	Good	Fair	Poor
—	—	2300	1900	875	450

K

K.F.C. (KAWAGUCHIYA FIREARMS CO.)
Japan

E-1 Trap or Skeet Over/Under

A 12 gauge boxlock double-barrel shotgun with 26" or 30" barrels, competition rib, single-selective trigger, and automatic ejectors. Engraved, blued with a walnut stock. Manufactured until 1986.

NIB	Exc.	V.G.	Good	Fair	Poor
—	950	800	700	500	300

E-2 Trap or Skeet Over/Under

As above, but more finely finished.

NIB	Exc.	V.G.	Good	Fair	Poor
—	1400	1250	1000	750	350

Field Grade Over/Under

As above, with a narrow rib and 26" or 28" barrels. Discontinued in 1986.

NIB	Exc.	V.G.	Good	Fair	Poor
—	650	575	500	400	275

Model 250

A 12 gauge semi-automatic shotgun with 26", 28", or 30" barrels fitted for choke tubes. Matte blued with a walnut stock. Manufactured from 1980 to 1986.

NIB	Exc.	V.G.	Good	Fair	Poor
—	350	300	275	200	100

KAHR ARMS
Blauvelt, New York

K9

This is a semi-automatic pistol chambered for the 9mm cartridge. It is a ultra-compact size. The barrel length is 3.5" and the overall length is 6". The width at the slide is .9". The magazine capacity is 7 rounds. Available in blue or electroless nickel finish. Weight is 25 oz. **NOTE:** Add $30 for blackened stainless steel slide; $130 for night sights.

NIB	Exc.	V.G.	Good	Fair	Poor
550	425	325	250	150	75

Lady K9

Same as above but with lightened recoil spring.

NIB	Exc.	V.G.	Good	Fair	Poor
500	375	300	225	125	50

K9 Elite

Introduced in 2003 this 9mm model features a 3.5" barrel and polished stainless steel slide. Magazine capacity is 7 rounds. Weight is about 25 oz. **NOTE:** Add $110 for night sights.

NIB	Exc.	V.G.	Good	Fair	Poor
575	425	350	275	150	100

MK9 Elite

Introduced in 2003 this 9mm model features a 3" barrel and polished stainless steel slide. Magazine capacity is 7 rounds. Weight is about 24 oz. **NOTE:** Add 15 percent for laser grips or night sights.

NIB	Exc.	V.G.	Good	Fair	Poor
725	595	450	300	175	100

P9 Compact Polymer

Introduced in 1999 this 9mm model features a 3.5" barrel with double-action-only trigger. Black polymer frame with stainless steel slide. Overall length is 6", height is 4.5". Weight is about 18 oz. Magazine capacity is 7 rounds.

NIB	Exc.	V.G.	Good	Fair	Poor
625	550	475	325	250	100

K9 Compact Polymer Covert

Same as the model above but with 1/2" shorter grip frame. Weight is about 17 oz. Magazine capacity is 6 rounds. Introduced in 1999.

NIB	Exc.	V.G.	Good	Fair	Poor
625	550	475	325	250	100

TP9

Introduced in 2004 this 9mm model features a black polymer frame with matte stainless steel slide. Fitted with a 4" barrel. Weight is about 20 oz. **NOTE:** Add 15 percent for Novak night sights.

NIB	Exc.	V.G.	Good	Fair	Poor
700	600	475	325	250	100

PM9 Micro

Fitted with a 3" barrel and chambered for the 9mm cartridge this pistol weighs about 16 oz. Polymer frame and stainless steel slide. Introduced in 2002.

NIB	Exc.	V.G.	Good	Fair	Poor
625	550	475	325	250	100

TP40

Double-action-only semi-automatic pistol chambered in .40 S&W. Black polymer frame, matte stainless slide, 4" barrel, textured polymer grips, 6- or 7-round capacity depending on magazine. Drift-adjustable white bar-dot sights or Novak two-dot tritium sights. Introduced 2006.

NIB	Exc.	V.G.	Good	Fair	Poor
625	550	475	325	250	100

PM9

This 9mm model is fitted with a 3" barrel with blackened stainless steel slide and black polymer frame. Magazine capacity is 6 rounds. Weight is about 16 oz. Introduced in 2004. **NOTE:** Add 15 percent for night sights.

NIB	Exc.	V.G.	Good	Fair	Poor
700	600	400	300	200	100

K40

This model is similar to the K9 but is chambered for the .40 S&W cartridge. Magazine capacity is 6 rounds. Weight is 26 oz. **NOTE:** Add 15 percent for night sights.

NIB	Exc.	V.G.	Good	Fair	Poor
750	650	450	350	250	150

K40 Elite

Introduced in 2003 this .40 S&W model features a 3.5" barrel and polished stainless steel slide. Magazine capacity is 6 rounds, beveled magazine well. Weight is about 26 oz. **NOTE:** For night sights add 15 percent. For nickel finish add 10 percent. For black titanium finish add $15 percent. For the K40 stainless steel version add 5 percent.

NIB	Exc.	V.G.	Good	Fair	Poor
800	700	575	400	300	175

K40 Covert

Similar to the K40 with a 1/2" shorter grip frame and flush fitting 5-round magazine. Barrel length is 3.5". Weight is about 25 oz. Finish is matte stainless steel.

NIB	Exc.	V.G.	Good	Fair	Poor
575	425	350	275	150	100

MK40

This .40 S&W model is fitted with a 3" barrel. Its overall length is 5.4" and height is 4". Finish is matte stainless steel. Magazine capacity is 5 rounds. Uses same magazines as K40 Covert. Introduced in 1999.

NIB	Exc.	V.G.	Good	Fair	Poor
700	600	400	300	200	100

MK40 Elite

Introduced in 2003 this .40 S&W model features a 3" barrel and polished stainless steel slide. Magazine capacity is 5 rounds, beveled magazine well. Weight is about 25 oz. **NOTE:** Add 10 percent for night sights.

NIB	Exc.	V.G.	Good	Fair	Poor
750	625	525	425	225	150

P40

Similar to the P9 but chambered for the .40 S&W cartridge. Fitted with a 3.5" match grade barrel and matte stainless steel slide and black polymer frame. Supplied with two 6-round stainless steel magazines. Weight is approximately 19 oz. Introduced in 2001. **NOTE:** Add $30 for blackened stainless steel slide; $130 for night sights.

NIB	Exc.	V.G.	Good	Fair	Poor
550	425	325	250	150	75

P45

Introduced in 2005 this polymer frame stainless steel slide model is chambered for the .45 ACP cartridge. Barrel length is 3.5". Fixed sights. Magazine capacity is 6 rounds. Height of pistol is 4.8". Overall length is 6.3". Slide width is 1". Weight is about 18.5 oz. **NOTE:** Add 15 percent for night sights.

NIB	Exc.	V.G.	Good	Fair	Poor
675	550	375	275	170	125

MK9

This is a 9mm model with double-action-only trigger. Barrel length is 3". Overall length is 5.5" and height is 4". Weight is approximately 22 oz. One 6-round magazine and one 7-round magazine with grip extension standard. This model is fitted with a specially designed trigger for shorter trigger stroke. **NOTE:** Add 15 percent for night sights or laser grips.

NIB	Exc.	V.G.	Good	Fair	Poor
700	600	400	300	200	100

CW9

This 9mm model, introduced in 2005, features a 3.5" barrel, polymer frame, and stainless steel slide. Magazine capacity is 7 rounds. Height of pistol is 4.5". Overall length is 6". Slide width is .9".

NIB	Exc.	V.G.	Good	Fair	Poor
475	375	250	200	150	100

CW40

Semi-automatic with textured polymer grip chambered for .40 S&W and 6+1 capacity. Double-action with 3.6" barrel, 16.8 oz. Adjustable rear sights. Introduced 2006.

NIB	Exc.	V.G.	Good	Fair	Poor
500	375	300	225	125	50

Wilson Combat Kahr Pistols

Offered in both the K9 and K40 models this is a customized pistol by Wilson's Gun Shop. It features hard chrome frame, black slide, 30 lpi checkering on front strap, beveled magazine well and several other special features. Initial production for the K40 is 50 pistols and for the K9 25 pistols.

NIB	Exc.	V.G.	Good	Fair	Poor
1300	1050	800	550	325	200

Model 1911PKZ

This model uses the Auto-Ordnance 1911 pistols re-engineered by Kahr Arms. This model includes a Parkerized finish, lanyard loop and U.S. Army roll mark of the slide. Seven-round magazine standard. Introduced in 2001.

NIB	Exc.	V.G.	Good	Fair	Poor
475	375	250	—	—	—

Model 1911 Standard

This model features a blued finish, plastic grips with Thompson medallion and bullet logo on the slide. Seven-round magazine. Introduced in 2001.

NIB	Exc.	V.G.	Good	Fair	Poor
450	325	250	200	150	100

Model 1911C

Similar to the Standard Model but with a 4.25" barrel.

NIB	Exc.	V.G.	Good	Fair	Poor
500	400	250	200	150	100

Model 1911WGS Deluxe

This model has a blued finish, rubber wrap-around grips with Thompson medallion, high profile white dot sights, and Thompson bullet logo on the slide. Seven-round magazine. Introduced in 2001.

NIB	Exc.	V.G.	Good	Fair	Poor
575	475	425	300	225	125

P380 .380 ACP Pistol

DAO semi-automatic pocket pistol chambered in .380 ACP. Features include a 2.5" Lothar Walther barrel, black polymer frame and grips, stainless steel slide, 6+1 capacity. Overall length 4.9". Weight: 11.3 oz. **NOTE:** Add 15 percent for night sights.

NIB	Exc.	V.G.	Good	Fair	Poor
625	500	400	295	175	75

KASSNAR IMPORTS, INC.
Harrisburg, Pennsylvania

Standard Over/Under

A 12, 20, 28 or .410 bore boxlock double-barrel shotgun with 26"
or 28" barrels, ventilated ribs, single trigger and extractors. Blued
with a walnut stock.

NIB	Exc.	V.G.	Good	Fair	Poor
350	275	225	200	150	100

Deluxe Over/Under

As above, with a more finely figured stock.

NIB	Exc.	V.G.	Good	Fair	Poor
400	325	250	225	175	100

Standard Side-by-Side

A 20, 28 or .410 bore boxlock folding double-barrel shotgun with
26" barrels, double triggers and extractors. Blued with a walnut
stock.

NIB	Exc.	V.G.	Good	Fair	Poor
250	200	175	150	100	75

Deluxe Side-by-Side

As above, in .410 bore only and with more finely figured wood.

NIB	Exc.	V.G.	Good	Fair	Poor
300	250	200	175	125	75

KBI, INC.
Harrisburg, Pennsylvania

This company previously imported firearms from several
manufacturers. These brands included Charles Daly handguns,
shotguns and rifles, which are listed in the "D" section under
Daly, Charles.

Kassnar PSP-25

A .25 caliber semi-automatic pistol with a 2" barrel manufactured
in Charlottesville, Virginia, under license from Fabrique Nationale.
Introduced in 1989.

NIB	Exc.	V.G.	Good	Fair	Poor
275	200	175	150	100	—

KEBERST INTERNATIONAL
Kendall International
Paris, Kentucky

Model 1A

A .338 Lapua Magnum, .338-416 Rigby, or .338-06 caliber bolt-
action rifle with a 24" barrel having an integral muzzle-brake, and
fitted with a 3-9 power Leupold telescope. Matte blued with a
camouflaged composition stock. Manufactured in 1987 and 1988.

NIB	Exc.	V.G.	Good	Fair	Poor
—	3750	3000	2500	1800	900

KEL-TEC CNC INDUSTRIES
Cocoa, Florida

Kel-Tec PMR-30

Caliber: .22 WMR, steel barrel and slide, glass reinforced Zytel grip
frame and slide cover, 30-round magazine, single-action trigger,
ambidextrous manual safety, fiber optic sights and accessory rail.
Weight: 13.6 ounces, 4.3" fluted barrel with matte black finish.
New 2011.

NIB	Exc.	V.G.	Good	Fair	Poor
360	310	250	200	150	75

P-11

This is a semi-automatic pistol chambered for the 9mm cartridge.
It is double-action-only with a barrel length of 3.1". Overall length
is 5.6". Weight is 14 oz. Magazine capacity is 10 rounds. Standard

model has blued slide with black grip. Stainless steel and Parkerized finish are offered as well. **NOTE:** Add $100 for stainless steel and $40 for Parkerized finish. Add $60 for hard chrome.

NIB	Exc.	V.G.	Good	Fair	Poor
320	225	175	125	100	100

P-32

This .32 caliber semi-automatic pistol is fitted with a 2.68" barrel. The action is double-action-only. Overall length is 5", overall height is 3.5". Magazine capacity is 7 rounds. Weight is about 6.6 oz. Blued slide and frame. **NOTE:** Add $40 for Parkerized finish. Add $60 for hard chrome.

NIB	Exc.	V.G.	Good	Fair	Poor
305	225	175	125	100	100

P-3AT

This model is chambered for the .380 cartridge and fitted with a 2.75" barrel. Blued finish. Magazine capacity is 6 rounds. Weight is about 7.3 oz. **NOTE:** Add $40 for Parkerized finish and $60 for hard chrome.

NIB	Exc.	V.G.	Good	Fair	Poor
310	225	175	125	100	100

P-40

This model is similar to the P-11 but chambered for the .40 S&W cartridge. Barrel length is 3.3". Magazine capacity is 9 rounds. Weight is approximately 16 oz. Blued finish. NOTE: Add $40 for Parkerized finish. Add $60 for hard chrome.

NIB	Exc.	V.G.	Good	Fair	Poor
320	225	175	125	100	100

SUB-2000 Rifle

Introduced in 1996 this is a semi-automatic rifle chambered for the 9mm or .40 S&W cartridge. The barrel length is 16.1". The rifle can be folded closed with an overall length of 16". Weight is approximately 4.6 lbs. Different grip assembly can be fitted to this rifle allowing for the use of different magazines.

NIB	Exc.	V.G.	Good	Fair	Poor
375	295	175	125	75	50

SU-16

This semi-automatic gas operated rifle is chambered for the .223 cartridge. It is fitted with an 18" barrel. This rifle has several unique features: the fore-end folds down to form a bipod, the stock can store spare magazines and the rifle folds into two parts for carry. Weight is about 5 lbs. SU-16A, 18.5" barrel; SU-16B, 16" lightweight barrel; SU-16C, 16" barrel, folding stock; SU-16CA, 16" standard barrel and standard stock.

NIB	Exc.	V.G.	Good	Fair	Poor
625	525	400	295	200	125

PLR-16

A 5.56mm NATO gas-operated, semi-automatic AR-15-style long-range pistol. Windage-adjustable rear sight. Picatinny rail. Muzzle threaded for muzzle-brake. 9.2" barrel, 51 oz. 10-round or M-16 magazine. Blued finish, polymer construction. Introduced 2006.

NIB	Exc.	V.G.	Good	Fair	Poor
650	550	425	325	200	100

RFB Rifle

Bullpup semi-automatic rifle with 32", 24" or 18" barrel, black laminated stock, third swivel for bipod. Forward ejection; takes FAL-type magazines. Chambered in .308 Winchester. Announced in 2007. Price shown is for sporter.

NIB	Exc.	V.G.	Good	Fair	Poor
1850	1600	—	—	—	—

KEMPER, SHRIVER & COMPANY
Nashville, Tennessee

Delivered rifles made from sporting arm parts to the Ordnance Department at Nashville from December 1861 to March 1862. In all 150 arms were assembled. Overall length 48.5"; octagonal barrels shortened 33" and bored to .48 caliber; some fitted with saber bayonet lugs; stocks of military with brass furniture.

NIB	Exc.	V.G.	Good	Fair	Poor
—	—	4750	2000	1500	700

KENDALL, INTERNATIONAL
Paris, Kentucky
See—Keberst International

KENDALL, NICANOR
Windsor, Vermont

Under Hammer Pistol

A .31 to .41 caliber under hammer percussion pistol with 4" to 10" octagonal/round barrels marked "N.Kendall/Windsor,Vt." Browned or blued with brass mounts and maple grips. Manufactured in the 1850s.

NIB	Exc.	V.G.	Good	Fair	Poor
—		1950	600	200	125

KENO
Unknown

Derringer

A .22 caliber single-shot spur trigger pistol with a 2.5" barrel, brass frame, and walnut grips. The barrel blued or nickel-plated and marked "Keno."

NIB	Exc.	V.G.	Good	Fair	Poor
—		750	500	175	100

KERR
London, England

Kerr Revolver

A .44 caliber double-action percussion revolver with a 5.5" barrel and 6-shot cylinder. Blued with walnut grips. The frame marked "Kerr's Patent 648" and "London Armoury Bermondsey".

Courtesy Bonhams & Butterfields, San Francisco, California

NIB	Exc.	V.G.	Good	Fair	Poor
—	—	4250	2000	800	300

KESSLER ARMS CORPORATION
Silver Creek, New York

Bolt-Action Shotgun

A 12, 16, or 20 gauge shotgun with 26" or 28" barrels. Blued with a walnut stock. Manufactured between 1951 and 1953.

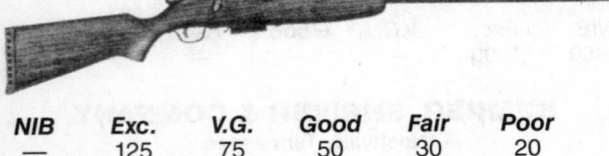

NIB	Exc.	V.G.	Good	Fair	Poor
—	125	75	50	30	20

Levermatic Shotgun

A 12, 16, or 20 gauge lever-action shotgun with a 26" or 28" barrel. Blued with a walnut stock. Manufactured between 1951 and 1953. A nice low-end collectible.

NIB	Exc.	V.G.	Good	Fair	Poor
—	300	275	200	150	75

KETTNER, EDWARD
Suhl, Germany

Drilling

This is a high-quality three-barreled firearm chambered for 12x12 gauge or 16x16 gauge over various metric rifle cartridges. The barrels are 25" in length and feature ejectors, selective triggers, and pop-up rifle sights that appear when the rifle barrel is selected. This gun is deep-relief engraved in the German style and has a high-grade checkered walnut stock. It was manufactured between 1922 and 1939.

NIB	Exc.	V.G.	Good	Fair	Poor
—	—	3200	1700	900	500

KIMBALL ARMS COMPANY
Detroit, Michigan

Semi-Automatic Pistol

A .30 carbine caliber semi-automatic pistol with a 3.5" or 5" barrel. Blued with plastic grips. Also believed to have been made in .22 Hornet and .357 Magnum, though few legitimate examples have been seen. Manufactured from 1955 to 1958. Approximately 238 were made.

NIB	Exc.	V.G.	Good	Fair	Poor
—	3000	2000	1500	1000	450

KIMBER MFG., INC.
Yonkers, New York

Kimber of Oregon was established in April 1979 by Greg and Jack Warne. The company produced high quality rimfire and centerfire rifles until going out of business in early 1991. Kimber produced approximately 60,000 rifles during its operation. In April 1993, Greg Warne opened Kimber of America in Clackamas, Oregon. This new company presently manufactures the same high-quality rifles built on an improved Model 82 Sporter action and stock, but in rimfire only. In 1995 the company expanded its product line to include centerfire rifles as well as a 1911 .45 ACP semi-automatic pistol line. In 1997 manufacturing operations were consolidated in the New York pistol factory and the two factories in Oregon were closed. Guns may be found stamped "Kimber of America", "Kimber, Yonkers, NY", or "Kimber, Clackamas, Oregon".

DISCONTINUED MODELS

Model 82 Classic

A .22, .22 Magnum, or .22 Hornet bolt-action rifle with a 22" barrel furnished without sights and 4- or 5-shot magazine. Blued with a walnut stock. Discontinued in 1988. **NOTE:** For Model 82 Series rifles in .22 Magnum caliber add 10 percent. For rifles chambered for .22 Hornet add 15 percent.

NIB	Exc.	V.G.	Good	Fair	Poor
—	700	600	550	450	350

Cascade

As above, with a Monte Carlo-style stock.

NIB	Exc.	V.G.	Good	Fair	Poor
—	750	650	600	500	400

Custom Classic

As above, in .218 Bee or .25-20.

NIB	Exc.	V.G.	Good	Fair	Poor
—	800	725	650	400	300

Mini Classic

The Model 82 with an 18" barrel. Manufactured in 1988.

NIB	Exc.	V.G.	Good	Fair	Poor
—	600	550	475	400	300

Deluxe Grade

Similar to the Custom Classic. Introduced in 1989.

NIB	Exc.	V.G.	Good	Fair	Poor
1000	850	650	550	450	350

Model 82A Government

A .22 caliber bolt-action rifle with a 25" heavy barrel fitted with telescope mounts. Matte blued with a walnut stock. Introduced in 1987.

NIB	Exc.	V.G.	Good	Fair	Poor
675	550	450	375	300	200

Continental

Similar to the Custom Classic with a 20" barrel, open sights, and full length Mannlicher-style stock. Introduced in 1987.

NIB	Exc.	V.G.	Good	Fair	Poor
1200	1000	750	500	400	300

Super Continental

As above, but more finely finished. Discontinued in 1988.

NIB	Exc.	V.G.	Good	Fair	Poor
1600	1300	1000	750	600	300

Super America

The Model 82 but more finely finished. Discontinued in 1988.

NIB	Exc.	V.G.	Good	Fair	Poor
1600	1300	950	850	650	500

Super Grade

As above, introduced in 1989.

NIB	Exc.	V.G.	Good	Fair	Poor
11600	1300	900	750	600	475

Centennial

A commemorative rifle moderately engraved including a special match barrel, skeleton buttplate, hand-selected walnut stock, and light engraving. Issued to commemorate the 100th anniversary of the .22 LR cartridge. One hundred were manufactured in 1987.

NIB	Exc.	V.G.	Good	Fair	Poor
2500	2250	2000	1750	1500	1150

Brownell

In 1986, 500 commemorative rifles were produced in honor of Leonard Brownell, featuring a high-grade, Mannlicher-style, full-length walnut stock.

NIB	Exc.	V.G.	Good	Fair	Poor
2000	1500	1000	800	600	500

MODEL 84 SERIES—DISCONTINUED MODELS

A bolt-action rifle manufactured in a variety of smallbore centerfire calibers with a 22" or 24" barrel and 5-shot magazine. Blued with a walnut stock. Variations are listed.

Classic

NIB	Exc.	V.G.	Good	Fair	Poor
1000	900	600	400	250	200

Custom Classic

NIB	Exc.	V.G.	Good	Fair	Poor
1300	1000	700	500	350	200

Deluxe Grade Sporter

NIB	Exc.	V.G.	Good	Fair	Poor
1200	1000	850	750	500	250

Continental

NIB	Exc.	V.G.	Good	Fair	Poor
1800	1300	900	700	500	250

Super Continental

NIB	Exc.	V.G.	Good	Fair	Poor
2000	1700	1100	700	575	250

Super America

NIB	Exc.	V.G.	Good	Fair	Poor
2000	1700	1100	825	600	300

Super Grade

NIB	Exc.	V.G.	Good	Fair	Poor
2100	1800	1200	850	650	300

Ultra Varmint

As above, with a 24" stainless steel barrel and laminated birch wood stock. Introduced in 1989.

NIB	Exc.	V.G.	Good	Fair	Poor
1500	1100	900	750	550	250

Super Varmint

As above with a walnut stock. Introduced in 1989.

NIB	Exc.	V.G.	Good	Fair	Poor
1750	1250	1000	850	650	300

Predator

A .221 Fireball, .223 Rem., 6mm TCU, 7mm TCU, or the 6x45mm caliber single-shot bolt-action pistol based upon the Model 84 action with a 14.75" barrel adopted for a telescope. Blued with a walnut stock and available in two grades as listed. Manufactured in 1987 and 1988 only.

Hunter Grade

NIB	Exc.	V.G.	Good	Fair	Poor
1800	1350	950	600	400	300

Super Grade

NIB	Exc.	V.G.	Good	Fair	Poor
2500	2000	1500	1000	500	400

MODEL 89 SERIES/BGR (BIG GAME RIFLES)

A bolt-action sporting rifle produced in .270 Winchester to .505 Gibbs caliber with a 22" or 24" barrel. Blued with a walnut stock. The variations of this model are listed.

Classic

NIB	Exc.	V.G.	Good	Fair	Poor
800	650	550	400	300	200

Custom Classic

NIB	Exc.	V.G.	Good	Fair	Poor
1000	850	650	450	350	250

Deluxe Grade

NIB	Exc.	V.G.	Good	Fair	Poor
1400	1150	900	650	450	250

Super America

NIB	Exc.	V.G.	Good	Fair	Poor
1800	1250	900	700	500	250

Super Grade

NIB	Exc.	V.G.	Good	Fair	Poor
1800	1250	900	700	500	250

NOTE: Add 10 percent for .375 H&H or .505 Gibbs.

NIB	Exc.	V.G.	Good	Fair	Poor
5500	4250	3200	2400	1200	500

MODEL 82C SERIES

In 1998 the Model 82C series rifles went out of production.

Classic

Bolt-action rifle chambered for the .22 LR cartridge. Receiver drilled and tapped for sights. Fitted with a 22" barrel. Detachable magazine holds 4 rounds. Stock is plain with standard grade Claro Walnut. Checkering is 18 lpi with 4 point side panel pattern. Red rubber butt pad and polished steel pistol grip cap are standard. Weight is approximately 6.5 lbs. Reintroduced in 1989.

NIB	Exc.	V.G.	Good	Fair	Poor
900	650	500	400	—	—

Super America

Same as above but fitted with AAA fancy grade Claro Walnut with ebony tip and beaded cheekpiece. Hand checkering is 22 lpi in a full-coverage pattern. Steel buttplate and steel pistol grip cap are standard.

NIB	Exc.	V.G.	Good	Fair	Poor
2200	1500	1100	750	300	300

Custom Match

This bolt-action .22 caliber has a 22" barrel. The stock is AA French walnut with full coverage checkering. Finish is rust blued. Weight is about 6.75 lbs.

NIB	Exc.	V.G.	Good	Fair	Poor
2000	1600	950	700	400	200

Custom Shop Super America (Basic)

Same as above but furnished with a number of special order options that greatly affect the value. Seek an independent appraisal before the sale.

Stainless Classic Limited Edition

Introduced in 1996 this limited edition Model 82C is chambered for the .22 long rifle cartridge The stainless steel barrel is 22" long. A 4-shot magazine is included. Production limited to about 600 rifles.

NIB	Exc.	V.G.	Good	Fair	Poor
1900	1750	1100	800	500	300

SVT (Short Varmint/Target)

First introduced in 1996 this .22 caliber rifle is a single-shot. It is fitted with an 18" stainless steel fluted barrel. The walnut stock is a target style with no checkering. Weight is about 7.5 lbs.

NIB	Exc.	V.G.	Good	Fair	Poor
1350	1050	700	500	400	175

HS (Hunter Silhouette)

Introduced in 1997 this model features a 24" half-fluted barrel. Chambered for .22 Long Rifle cartridge. Stock is American walnut with high comb. Trigger is fully adjustable. Four-round magazine is standard. Weight is about 7 lbs.

NIB	Exc.	V.G.	Good	Fair	Poor
1350	1050	700	500	400	175

Single-Shot Varmint

Chambered for the .17 Rem. or .223 Rem. cartridge this rifle is fitted with a 25" stainless steel fluted barrel. Claro walnut stock with varmint-style forearm. Weight is approximately 7.5 lbs. In 1998 the Model 84C series rifle went out of production.

NIB	Exc.	V.G.	Good	Fair	Poor
1500	1175	900	600	400	200

Sporterized Model 98 Swedish Mausers

These are reconditioned and reworked Mausers that are fitted with new match grade stainless steel fluted barrels in 24" or 26" depending on caliber. The stock is new synthetic checkered. Chambered in .257 Roberts, .270 Win., .280 Rem., .30-06, 7mm Rem. Magnum, .300 Win. Magnum, .338 Win. Magnum, and the .220 Swift with a 25" barrel. **NOTE:** Suggested retail price is $535 for standard calibers and $560 for Magnums.

MODEL 84C SERIES

Sporterized Model 96 Swedish Mausers

Similar to the above in terms of reworking and reconditioning. Chambered for these calibers:

.22-250 w/stainless steel heavy barrel fluted—Retail $500.
.243 Win.—$400 to $465 depending on finish.
6.5x55mm—$340 to $370 depending on finish.
7mm-08 Rem.—$415 to $465 depending on finish.
.308 Win.—$415 to $520 depending on finish and barrel configuration.

RECENT PRODUCTION MODELS

17 SERIES

This series of .17 Mach 2 rifles was introduced in 2005. Features are similar to the 22 Series.

Hunter

Fitted with a 22" light sporter barrel with no sights. Checkered walnut stock with black pad and clear stock finish. Magazine capacity is 5 rounds. Weight is about 6.5 lbs.

NIB	Exc.	V.G.	Good	Fair	Poor
900	700	500	375	250	125

SVT (Short Varmint/Target) (Centerfire)

This model is fitted with a 18.25" stainless steel bull fluted barrel with no sights. Checkered walnut stock with black pad and oil finish. Magazine capacity is 5 rounds. Weight is about 7.9 lbs.

NIB	Exc.	V.G.	Good	Fair	Poor
1200	950	775	575	350	150

Pro Varmint

This model features a 20" stainless steel heavy sporter fluted barrel with no sights. Stock is gray laminate with oil finish and no checkering. Magazine capacity is 5 rounds. Weight is about 6.75 lbs.

NIB	Exc.	V.G.	Good	Fair	Poor
1150	875	675	500	325	150

Classic Varmint

Fitted with a 20" heavy sporter fluted barrel with no sights. Checkered walnut stock with oil finish. Magazine capacity is 5 rounds. Weight is about 6.5 lbs.

NIB	Exc.	V.G.	Good	Fair	Poor
1200	950	775	575	350	150

22 SERIES

In 1999 Kimber introduced a new line of bolt-action .22 caliber rimfire rifles. First deliveries were made early in 2000. This series is built on a totally new design from bolt, to magazine, to barrel. All rifles in this series have a 5-round magazine capacity. This line replaces the Model 82-C series of rifles.

Classic

This .22 caliber rifle is fitted with a 22" barrel with fully adjustable trigger. Stock is A grade Claro walnut with 18 lpi checkering. Fitted with a Model 70 style safety. Blued finish. Weight is about 6.5 lbs.

NIB	Exc.	V.G.	Good	Fair	Poor
1200	950	775	575	350	150

Custom Classic

Fitted with a 22" barrel, ebony fore-end tip, hand-rubbed oil finish, and 24 lpi checkering, This rifle was introduced in 2003. Weight is about 6.5 lbs.

NIB	Exc.	V.G.	Good	Fair	Poor
1425	1100	850	675	450	150

Super America

This model features a 22" barrel with fully adjustable trigger. Stock is AAA grade Claro walnut with 22 lpi wrap-around checkering and ebony fore-end tip. Black recoil pad. Weight is about 6.5 lbs.

NIB	Exc.	V.G.	Good	Fair	Poor
1900	1400	1075	775	500	200

SVT (Short Varmint/Target)

Fitted with an 18" fluted stainless steel barrel and gray laminated wood stock with high target comb. This model weighs about 7.5 lbs. In 2004 this model was also offered in the .17 Mach 2 caliber.

NIB	Exc.	V.G.	Good	Fair	Poor
1150	875	675	500	325	150

Classic Varmint

Introduced in 2003, this model features a 20" barrel with hand-rubbed oil finish and 20 lpi checkering. Weight is about 6.5 lbs. In 2004 this model is also available in the .17 Mach 2 caliber.

NIB	Exc.	V.G.	Good	Fair	Poor
1150	875	675	500	325	150

Pro Varmint

This model features a heavy fluted 20" stainless steel barrel and a gray laminated stock. No sights. Magazine capacity is 5 rounds. Weight is about 6.75 lbs. Introduced in 2004. This model is also available in .17 Mach 2 caliber.

NIB	Exc.	V.G.	Good	Fair	Poor
1200	950	775	575	350	150

HS (Hunter Silhouette)

This model is fitted with a 24" medium sporter match grade barrel with match chambered and half fluting. Walnut stock with 18 lpi checkering and Monte Carlo comb. Weight is about 7 lbs.

NIB	Exc.	V.G.	Good	Fair	Poor
900	700	500	375	250	125

Youth

Introduced in 2002 this .22 caliber rifle is fitted with a 18.5" barrel. Checkered Claro walnut stock with 12.25" length of pull. Weight is about 5.25 lbs.

NIB	Exc.	V.G.	Good	Fair	Poor
850	675	495	300	200	100

Hunter

This is a lower-priced version of the Classic.

NIB	Exc.	V.G.	Good	Fair	Poor
800	650	550	400	300	200

Custom Match Limited Edition

Introduced in 2004 this is a limited edition of 300 rifles. This rifle features a checkered French walnut stock of AAA wood and several custom features. Serial numbered from KAN25001-KAN25300.

NIB	Exc.	V.G.	Good	Fair	Poor
2850	2300	—	—	—	—

MODEL 84M SERIES

Classic

Introduced in 2001 this centerfire bolt-action rifle is chambered for the .243 Win., .260 Rem., 7mm-08 Rem., and the .308 Win. In 2005 this model was offered chambered for the .22-250 cartridge. Fitted with a 22" light sporter match grade barrel Claro walnut stock with 20 lpi checkering and satin wood finish. Matted blue finish. Fitted with a 1" Pachmayr Decelerator recoil pad. Weight is about 5.75 lbs.

NIB	Exc.	V.G.	Good	Fair	Poor
1100	895	700	475	300	150

Montana

This model is essentially a stainless steel version of the Model 84M Classic with a black synthetic stock. Weight is about 5.25 lbs. Introduced in 2003.

NIB	Exc.	V.G.	Good	Fair	Poor
1200	950	775	575	350	150

Super America

This model was first offered in 2003 and is available in .243, .260 Rem., 7mm-08 Rem., and .308 Win. Fitted with a 22" barrel. In 2005 this model was offered chambered for the .223 cartridge. Stock is select walnut with 24 lpi checkering and fitted with an ebony fore-end tip, cheekpiece, and hand-rubbed oil finish. Weight is approximately 5.75 lbs. depending on caliber. Magazine capacity is 5 rounds.

NIB	Exc.	V.G.	Good	Fair	Poor
1800	1350	1000	650	325	175

Pro Varmint

This rifle is chambered for the .22-250 Win. cartridge and fitted with a 24" stainless steel fluted barrel with no sights. In 2005 offered in 204 Ruger and .223 calibers. Gray laminated stock. Magazine capacity is 5 rounds. Weight is 7.25 lbs. Introduced in 2004.

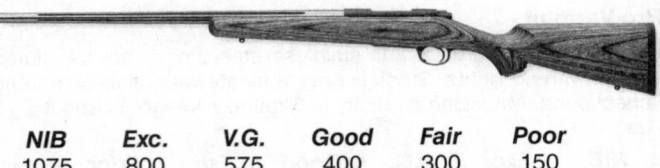

NIB	Exc.	V.G.	Good	Fair	Poor
1075	800	575	400	300	150

Varmint

Similar to the Classic but fitted with a stainless steel 26" match grade barrel. Chambered for the .22-250 Rem. cartridge. In 2005 offered in the .204 Ruger caliber. Fitted with a .5" solid recoil pad. Weight is approximately 7.4 lbs.

NIB	Exc.	V.G.	Good	Fair	Poor
1000	750	500	375	300	150

SVT

Stocked in gray laminate with Monte Carlo comb. Barrel length is 18.25" in stainless steel and fluted. Chambered for the .223 cartridge. Magazine capacity is 5 rounds. Weight is about 8.3 lbs.

NIB	Exc.	V.G.	Good	Fair	Poor
1200	950	775	575	350	150

LongMaster VT

This bolt-action rifle is chambered for the .22-250 cartridge and is fitted with a 26" fluted stainless steel match grade barrel. Special laminated target stock. Weight is about 10 lbs. No sights. Introduced in 2002.

NIB	Exc.	V.G.	Good	Fair	Poor
1200	950	775	575	350	150

LongMaster Classic

Same features as the Model 84M Classic but with 24" fluted stainless steel barrel chambered for the .308 Win. cartridge. In 2005 offered in .223 caliber. Checkered walnut stock. Weight is about 7.25 lbs. Introduced in 2002.

NIB	Exc.	V.G.	Good	Fair	Poor
1200	950	775	575	350	150

LongMaster Pro

This model, introduced in 2003, is a single-shot bolt-action rifle fitted with a 24" fluted heavy barrel chambered for the .308 Win. or .22-250 cartridge. Fitted with a synthetic benchrest stock. Weight is about 7.25 lbs.

NIB	Exc.	V.G.	Good	Fair	Poor
1350	1050	700	500	400	175

Tactical

Based on Model 84 action but with 24" medium weight fluted match barrel, black laminated stock, third swivel for bipod. Chambered in .308 Winchester. Introduced in 2007.

NIB	Exc.	V.G.	Good	Fair	Poor
1075	800	575	400	300	150

Model 84L Classic Rifle

Bolt-action rifle chambered in .270 Win. and .30-06. Features include 24" sightless matte blue sporter barrel; hand-rubbed A-grade walnut stock with 20 lpi panel checkering; pillar and glass bedding; Mauser claw extractor; 3-position M70-style safety; 5-round magazine; adjustable trigger.

NIB	Exc.	V.G.	Good	Fair	Poor
1000	850	720	400	300	200

Model 84L Montana

Long-action variation of Model 84 action. Chambered in .25-06 Remington, .270 Winchester, .280 Ackley Improved and .30-06 Springfield. Capacity is 4-rounds in blind magazine. Kevlar-reinforced carbon fiber stock. Match-grade barrel, chamber and trigger. Free-floating 24" barrel is both pillar and glass bedded. Model 70-type 3-position safety. Weight is under 6 pounds. Introduced in 2011.

NIB	Exc.	V.G.	Good	Fair	Poor
1150	1000	850	600	300	200

MODEL 8400 SERIES

This series was introduced in 2003 and features the smallest action size compatible with the WSM family of cartridges.

Classic

This model is fitted with a select walnut stock with 20 lpi checkering. Chambered for the WSM calibers: .270, 7mm, .300, and .325. Barrel length is 24" with no sights. Magazine capacity is 3 rounds. Weight is about 6.6 lbs. **NOTE:** Add $140 for French walnut.

NIB	Exc.	V.G.	Good	Fair	Poor
1000	795	600	475	300	150

Montana

This model features a 24" stainless steel barrel with no sights. Stock is black synthetic with no checkering. Same calibers as the Classic. Weight is about 6.25 lbs.

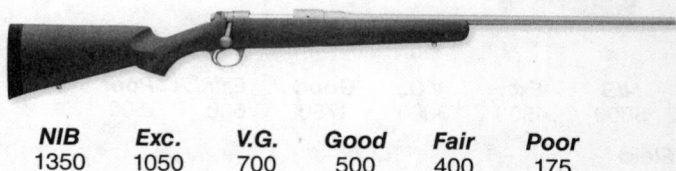

NIB	Exc.	V.G.	Good	Fair	Poor
1350	1050	700	500	400	175

SuperAmerica

This model is fitted with a AAA walnut stock with 24 lpi checkering. Cheekpiece and ebony fore-end tip are standard. Barrel length is 24" with no sights and chambered for the same calibers as the Classic. Weight is about 6.6 lbs.

NIB	Exc.	V.G.	Good	Fair	Poor
1875	1350	1000	650	325	175

Classic Select Grade

Similar to 8400 Classic but with hand-rubbed, oil-finished select stock of Claro or French walnut. Introduced 2006.

NIB	Exc.	V.G.	Good	Fair	Poor
1100	895	700	475	300	150

Tactical

24" heavyweight match barrel, stippled black McMillan stock, third swivel for bipod. Chambered in .308 Winchester. Introduced in 2007.

NIB	Exc.	V.G.	Good	Fair	Poor
1650	1200	800	550	300	150

Advanced Tactical

Similar to Model 8400 Tactical but with KimPro II Dark Earth finish, fully-adjustable stock and hard case. Introduced in 2007.

NIB	Exc.	V.G.	Good	Fair	Poor
1800	1350	1000	650	325	175

Patrol Rifle

Bolt action tactical rifle chambered in .308 Win. Features include 20" 1:12 fluted sightless matte blue heavy barrel; black epoxy-coated laminated wood stock with 20 lpi panel checkering; pillar and glass bedding; Mauser claw extractor; 3-position M70-style safety; 5-round magazine; adjustable trigger.

NIB	Exc.	V.G.	Good	Fair	Poor
1300	1100	850	500	350	200

AUGUSTA SHOTGUNS

These shotguns are made in Italy for Kimber. Based on a Boss-type action, each model is fitted with H-Viz sights and Pachmayr Decelerator recoil pads. Back bored. Single-selective trigger and automatic ejectors. Introduced in 2002.

Sporting

Chambered for the 12 gauge shell and fitted with a choice of barrel lengths from 28.5" to 32". Checkered walnut stock with pistol grip and schnabel forearm. Blued finish with silver frame. Weight is about 7.75 lbs.

NIB	Exc.	V.G.	Good	Fair	Poor
5000	4500	3000	1750	600	300

Field

Also chambered for the 12 gauge shell and choice of barrel lengths from 26" to 27.5". Checkered with pistol grip and beavertail forearm. Weight is about 7 lbs.

NIB	Exc.	V.G.	Good	Fair	Poor
4750	3900	2650	1500	475	225

Trap

This 12-gauge model is offered in barrel lengths from 30" to 34". Beavertail forearm. Wide ramped ventilated rib. Weight is about 7.75 lbs.

NIB	Exc.	V.G.	Good	Fair	Poor
5200	4700	3000	1750	600	300

Skeet

This 12-gauge gun has a choice of 26" or 27.5" barrels. Barrels are fitted with an 11mm flat rib. Checkered walnut stock with beavertail forearm. Weight is about 7.5 lbs.

NIB	Exc.	V.G.	Good	Fair	Poor
5200	4700	3000	1750	600	300

VALIER SHOTGUNS

These side-by-side guns were introduced into the Kimber line in 2005.

Grade I

A lightweight, properly-scaled side-by-side in 16- and 20-gauge. Double triggers and extractors. Choked IC and Mod. Color case-hardened receiver, straight stock and splinter fore-end. Hand checkered wood at 24 lpi. Chambered for 2.75" shells in 16 gauge and 3" shells in 20 gauge.

NIB	Exc.	V.G.	Good	Fair	Poor
3300	2900	2300	1250	600	300

Grade II

Similar to Valier Grade I but with higher grade wood and choice of color case, blued or bone charcoal receiver in 20 gauge; bone charcoal only in 16 gauge. Automatic ejectors.

NIB	Exc.	V.G.	Good	Fair	Poor
4900	3500	2700	1500	700	300

MARIAS SHOTGUNS

Grade I

This single-trigger sidelock over/under features scroll hand engraving and bone charcoal case colors with 24 lpi checkered wood. Grade I is available with 28" barrels and Prince of Wales stock in 12 and 20 gauge. Chambered for 3" shells. Automatic ejectors. Comes with 5 choke tubes.

NIB	Exc.	V.G.	Good	Fair	Poor
4600	3300	2300	1200	600	300

Grade II

Similar to Marias Grade I but with higher grade wood. Available in 12 gauge with PW stock or 20 gauge with PW or straight stock in 26", 28" or 30" barrels.

NIB	Exc.	V.G.	Good	Fair	Poor
4900	3500	2700	1500	700	300

CLASSIC .45 PISTOLS

CUSTOM SERIES

First introduced in 1996 this is a quality built American-made 1911 designed by Chip McCormick for Kimber. **NOTE:** In 2001 Kimber phased in a new safety system on its pistols: the Kimber firing pin safety. Models with this new firing pin safety will bear the designation "II" as part of their model name.

Custom

Barrel length is 5" with black oxide finish fixed sights. Black synthetic grips. Magazine capacity is 8 rounds. Weight is about 38 oz. **NOTE:** For night sights add $100.

NIB	Exc.	V.G.	Good	Fair	Poor
850	750	650	475	300	150

Custom II

NIB	Exc.	V.G.	Good	Fair	Poor
825	675	500	375	250	125

NOTE: For Walnut grips add $10.00. For night sights add $100.

Custom Heritage Edition

Chambered for .45 ACP cartridge and fitted with a 5" barrel. Magazine capacity is 7 rounds. Checkered front strap, ambidextrous thumb safety, aluminum trigger, hand checkered rosewood grips, special edition markings on slide. Sights are low-profile fixed. Weight is about 38 oz. Introduced in 2000.

NIB	Exc.	V.G.	Good	Fair	Poor
1150	950	700	495	300	150

Custom Stainless

Similar to Custom but in stainless steel. **NOTE:** For night sights add $100.

NIB	Exc.	V.G.	Good	Fair	Poor
1000	800	650	475	300	150

Stainless Limited Edition

Similar to the Custom Stainless except for black thumb release, black grip safety, black magazine release button, and black barrel bushing. Limited to approximately 1,200 pistols.

NIB	Exc.	V.G.	Good	Fair	Poor
1200	950	775	575	350	150

Custom Target

The Custom Target has the same features as the Custom with the addition of an adjustable rear sight.

NIB	Exc.	V.G.	Good	Fair	Poor
825	675	500	375	250	125

Custom TLE II (Tactical Law Enforcement)

Introduced in 2003 this model features Meprolight three-dot night sights and 30 lpi checkering on the front strap. Magazine capacity is 7 rounds. Weight is about 38 oz. **NOTE:** In 2004 a stainless steel version was offered. Add $135 for this model.

NIB	Exc.	V.G.	Good	Fair	Poor
900	700	500	375	250	125

Custom TLE/RL II

This model is similar ot the TLE with the addition of an integral tactical rail. Weight is about 39 oz. Introduced in 2004.

NIB	Exc.	V.G.	Good	Fair	Poor
1050	825	675	450	295	150

Stainless II

Chambered for the .45 ACP or .40 S&W cartridge and fitted with a 5" barrel with fixed low profile sights. Both frame and slide are satin stainless steel. Magazine capacity for the .45 ACP is 7 rounds and 8 rounds for the .40 S&W. Weight is about 38 oz.

NIB	Exc.	V.G.	Good	Fair	Poor
865	650	450	275	150	100

Stainless II (polished)

As above but chambered for the .38 Super cartridge. Frame and slide are polished stainless steel. Magazine capacity is 9 rounds. Weight is about 38 oz. Introduced in 2005.

NIB	Exc.	V.G.	Good	Fair	Poor
1150	950	700	495	300	150

Stainless Ultra TLE II

1911-style semi-automatic pistol chambered in .45 ACP. Features include 7-round magazine; full length guide rod; aluminum frame with stainless slide; satin silver finish; checkered frontstrap; 3" barrel; tactical gray double diamond grips; tritium 3-dot night sights.

NIB	Exc.	V.G.	Good	Fair	Poor
1000	900	750	650	500	400

Stainless Target II

Chambered for the .45 ACP or .38 Super cartridge with a slide and frame machined from stainless steel. Weight is 38 oz.

NIB	Exc.	V.G.	Good	Fair	Poor
980	750	600	400	250	125

Stainless Target II 9mm/10mm

As above but chambered for the 9mm or 10mm cartridge. The 9mm pistol has a magazine capacity of 9 rounds and the 10mm has a magazine capacity of 8 rounds. Both of these pistols are produced on a one-run basis only with production in the low hundreds. Introduced in 2003.

NIB	Exc.	V.G.	Good	Fair	Poor
1150	950	700	495	300	150

Stainless Target II (polished)

As above but chambered for the .38 Super cartridge. Frame and slide are polished stainless steel. Magazine capacity is 9 rounds. Weight is about 38 oz. Introduced in 2005.

NIB	Exc.	V.G.	Good	Fair	Poor
1200	950	775	575	350	150

Stainless Target Limited Edition

Similar to the Stainless Target but with black thumb safety, black grip safety, black slide release, and black barrel bushing. This model is limited to approximately 700 pistols. Introduced in 1998.

NIB	Exc.	V.G.	Good	Fair	Poor
900	700	500	375	250	125

Custom Royal

This has all the features of the Custom plus a high polish blue finish, hand checkered walnut grips, and long guide rod.

NIB	Exc.	V.G.	Good	Fair	Poor
900	700	500	375	250	125

Custom Royal II

NIB	Exc.	V.G.	Good	Fair	Poor
1500	1100	750	400	250	125

Custom TLE/RL II Special Edition

This .45 ACP pistol is fitted with a 5" barrel with fixed night sights. Steel frame and slide with tactical accessory rail on frame. Black rubber grips. Black matte finish. Magazine capacity is 7 rounds. Weight is about 38 oz. Introduced in 2003.

NIB	Exc.	V.G.	Good	Fair	Poor
1150	950	700	495	300	150

Warrior

This model, introduced in 2005, is chambered for the .45 ACP cartridge and fitted with a 5" barrel with night sights. Grips are Kimber G-10 Tactical with lanyard loop. Accessory rail on frame. KimPro finish. Magazine capacity is 7 rounds. Weight is about 39 oz.

NIB	Exc.	V.G.	Good	Fair	Poor
1200	950	775	575	350	150

Desert Warrior

This model is similar to the Warrior but with a desert tan finish and lighter tan G10 tactical grips.

NIB	Exc.	V.G.	Good	Fair	Poor
1200	950	775	575	350	150

25th ANNIVERSARY LIMITED EDITIONS

Anniversary Custom

Introduced in 2004 this is a limited edition of 1,911 pistol. Chambered for the .45 ACP cartridge. Select walnut grips. Serial numbered: KAPC0001-KAPC1911.

NIB	Exc.	V.G.	Good	Fair	Poor
850	650	450	275	150	100

Anniversary Gold Match

This .45 ACP pistol is limited to 500 pistols. Serial numbered KAPG0001-KAPG0500.

NIB	Exc.	V.G.	Good	Fair	Poor
1200	950	775	575	350	150

Anniversary Match Pair Custom

This is a matched pair of Custom pistols in .45 ACP. Matching serial numbers and presentation case. Limited to 250 pairs.

NIB	Exc.	V.G.	Good	Fair	Poor
2500	2100	—	—	—	—

GOLD MATCH SERIES

Gold Match

All of the features of the Custom Royal plus BoMar adjustable sights, fancy checkered diamond grips.

NIB	Exc.	V.G.	Good	Fair	Poor
1200	950	775	575	350	150

Gold Match II

NIB	Exc.	V.G.	Good	Fair	Poor
1200	950	775	575	400	150

Stainless Gold Match

Similar to the Gold Match except slide and frame are stainless steel. Introduced in 1998.

NIB	Exc.	V.G.	Good	Fair	Poor
1200	950	775	575	350	150

Gold Team Match II

Introduced in 2003 this .45 ACP 5" barrel model features a stainless steel slide and frame along with a Kimber Tactical Extractor with loaded chamber indicator. Front strap is checkered 30 lpi and the grips are red, white, and blue USA Shooting Team logo. Weight is about 38 oz.

NIB	Exc.	V.G.	Good	Fair	Poor
1350	1225	950	575	400	150

Team Match II .38 Super

As above but without external extractor. Limited production run. Introduced in 2003.

NIB	Exc.	V.G.	Good	Fair	Poor
1600	1300	1000	575	400	150

TEN II SERIES

In 2002 the Polymer series pistols were upgraded to the Ten II series with the addition of a firing pin block safety, a Kimber-made frame of improved dimensions, and an external extractor. The original Polymer pistol magazines of 10 and 14 rounds will interchange with the newer Ten II Series pistols.

Polymer

This model features a polymer frame with a matte black oxide slide. Sights are McCormick low profile. Barrel length is 5" and overall length is 8.75". Weight is about 34 oz. Magazine is 14 rounds. One 14-round magazine is supplied with gun when new.

NIB	Exc.	V.G.	Good	Fair	Poor
700	600	550	395	200	100

Polymer Stainless

Similar to the Polymer model but with a stainless steel slide. Weight is the same as the Polymer model; 34 oz.

NIB	Exc.	V.G.	Good	Fair	Poor
750	650	550	425	225	125

Polymer Target

Introduced in 1998 this pistol has a matte black oxide slide with adjustable sights. Magazine is 14 rounds. Weight is about 34 oz.

NIB	Exc.	V.G.	Good	Fair	Poor
950	775	625	450	245	150

Polymer Stainless Target

Same as above but with stainless steel slide. Introduced in 1998.

NIB	Exc.	V.G.	Good	Fair	Poor
950	775	625	450	245	150

Polymer Pro Carry Stainless

Chambered for the .45 ACP cartridge with a 4" barrel. McCormick Low Profile sights. Stainless steel slide with black polymer frame. Weight is about 32 oz. Magazine capacity is 14 rounds. Introduced in 1999.

NIB	Exc.	V.G.	Good	Fair	Poor
750	675	550	395	200	100

Polymer Stainless Gold Match

This model is similar to the Polymer Gold Match with the addition of a stainless steel slide. This model is also chambered for several calibers: .45 ACP, .40 S&W, 9mm, and .38 Super. Weight is about 34 oz.

NIB	Exc.	V.G.	Good	Fair	Poor
1000	850	775	575	350	150

Pro Carry Ten II

This .45 ACP model features a 4" bull barrel with no barrel bushing. Stainless steel slide. Weight is about 28 oz.

NIB	Exc.	V.G.	Good	Fair	Poor
850	675	550	395	200	100

Ultra Ten CDP II

Introduced in 2003 this model features night sights and rounded edges. Fitted with a 3" bull barrel. Chambered for the .45 ACP. Weight is about 24 oz.

NIB	Exc.	V.G.	Good	Fair	Poor
900	800	700	575	350	150

Gold Match Ten II

This .45 ACP 5" barrel model has all of the standard features of the Gold Match with a black Polymer frame and blued steel slide. Magazine capacity is 14 rounds. Weight is approximately 34 oz.

NIB	Exc.	V.G.	Good	Fair	Poor
1200	950	775	575	350	150

BP Ten II

This .45 ACP pistol has a 5" barrel and a 10-round magazine capacity. Steel slide with polymer frame. Fixed sights. Black matte finish. Weight is about 30 oz. Introduced in 2003.

NIB	Exc.	V.G.	Good	Fair	Poor
750	675	550	395	200	100

Pro BP Ten II

As above but with 4" barrel. Weight is about 31 oz. Introduced in 2003.

NIB	Exc.	V.G.	Good	Fair	Poor
750	675	550	395	200	100

COMPACT SERIES

Compact

These steel frame and slide pistols are fitted with a 4" bull barrel and shortened grip (.4" shorter than full size). Offered in .45 ACP. Finish is matte black oxide. Grips are black synthetic. Overall length is 7.7". Weight is about 43 oz. Introduced in 1998.

NIB	Exc.	V.G.	Good	Fair	Poor
675	550	400	300	200	100

Compact Aluminum

This model has the same appearance as the Compact but with an aluminum frame. Matte black finish. Weight is approximately 28 oz. Introduced in 1998.

NIB	Exc.	V.G.	Good	Fair	Poor
675	550	400	300	200	100

Compact Stainless

Same as the Compact model but with a stainless steel slide and frame. Offered in both .45 ACP and .40 S&W. Introduced in 1998.

NIB	Exc.	V.G.	Good	Fair	Poor
850	700	550	395	200	100

Pro Carry Stainless Night Sights

As above but fitted with night sights.

NIB	Exc.	V.G.	Good	Fair	Poor
950	750	625	450	275	175

NIB	Exc.	V.G.	Good	Fair	Poor
850	675	550	395	200	100

Compact Stainless II

NIB	Exc.	V.G.	Good	Fair	Poor
900	675	500	375	250	125

Compact Stainless Aluminum

Offered in both .45 ACP and .40 S&W this model features a 4" barrel with stainless steel slide and aluminum frame. Weight is about 28 oz. **NOTE:** Add $25 for .40 S&W models.

NIB	Exc.	V.G.	Good	Fair	Poor
750	600	475	300	200	100

PRO CARRY
Pro Carry II

Introduced in 1998 this .45 ACP or .40 S&W model features a full-size aluminum frame and 4" slide and bull barrel. Other features are match grade trigger, beveled magazine well, full-length guide rod, low-profile combat sights, and 7-round magazine. Finish is matte black oxide. Weight is approximately 28 oz. In 2005 this model was offered in 9mm.

Pro TLE/RL II

Introduced in 2005 this model features a 45 ACP with 4" barrel with night sights. Slide and frame are steel with a steel finish. Accessory rail on frame. Magazine capacity is 7 rounds. Weight is about 36 oz.

NIB	Exc.	V.G.	Good	Fair	Poor
1150	950	700	495	300	150

Stainless Pro TLE/RL II

As above but with stainless steel frame and slide. Introduced in 2005.

NIB	Exc.	V.G.	Good	Fair	Poor
1250	925	750	525	350	175

SUPER CARRY SERIES
Super Carry Pro

1911-style semi-automatic pistol chambered in .45 ACP. Features include 8-round magazine; ambidextrous thumb safety; carry melt profiling; full length guide rod; aluminum frame with stainless slide; satin silver finish; super carry serrations; 4" barrel; micarta laminated grips; tritium night sights.

NIB	Exc.	V.G.	Good	Fair	Poor
1300	1125	950	500	300	200

Super Carry Custom HD

The .45 Carry Pro pistols feature a stainless steel slide and frame, match-grade barrel and bushing, ambidextrous thumb safety, beaver-tail tang, and directional serrations on the slide, mainspring housing and front strap. Other features include night sights, an 8-round magazine, rounded heel and "melt" treatment for easy carrying. Weight: 38 ounces, 5" barrel and Kim-Pro finish. Super Carry Pro has 4" barrel, Ultra has 3" and 6-round magazine.

NIB	Exc.	V.G.	Good	Fair	Poor
850	675	550	395	200	100

Pro Carry II Night Sights

As above but fitted with night sights.

NIB	Exc.	V.G.	Good	Fair	Poor
750	675	600	425	250	150

Pro Carry Stainless

Same as Pro Carry but with stainless steel slide. **NOTE:** Add $50 for .38 Super

Introduced in 2011.

magazine release. Weight is 17 ounces, barrel length 2.7". Width is 1.2" and overall length 5.5". Finish is Kim Pro or bright stainless. Introduced in 2011.

NIB	Exc.	V.G.	Good	Fair	Poor
1400	1200	1000	750	300	200

Super Carry Ultra Plus

Combines the full-size, round-heel frame of the Carry Pro with the short slide and 3" barrel of the Carry Ultra. Lightweight alloy frame reduces weight to 25 ounces with 8-round magazine. Introduced in 2011.

NIB	Exc.	V.G.	Good	Fair	Poor
650	535	450	400	300	200

ULTRA CARRY II SERIES

Ultra Carry

This model is chambered for the .45 ACP or .40 S&W cartridge. It is fitted with a 3" barrel with McCormick low profile sights. Grips are black synthetic. Magazine capacity is 7 rounds. Weight is about 25 oz. Black oxide finish. Introduced in 1999. **NOTE:** Add $100 for night sights.

NIB	Exc.	V.G.	Good	Fair	Poor
1350	1150	965	725	300	200

Solo Carry STS

A micro compact pistol designed for concealed carry, this is a single-action, striker-fired 9mm with stainless steel slide, alloy frame, 6-round magazine, ambidextrous thumb safety and

NIB	Exc.	V.G.	Good	Fair	Poor
765	600	475	350	200	100

NOTE: Add $100 for night sights.

Ultra Carry II

NIB	Exc.	V.G.	Good	Fair	Poor
800	625	500	375	225	125

Ultra Carry Stainless

Same as above but with stainless steel slide. **NOTE:** Add $25 for .40 S&W model. Add $100 for night sights.

NIB	Exc.	V.G.	Good	Fair	Poor
850	650	525	395	245	135

Ultra Carry Stainless II

NIB	Exc.	V.G.	Good	Fair	Poor
875	675	550	425	260	150

CUSTOM SHOP PISTOLS

Centennial Edition 1911

Highly artistic 1911-style semi-automatic pistol chambered in .45 ACP. Features include color case-hardened steel frame; extended thumb safety; charcoal-blue finished steel slide; 5" match grade barrel; special serial number; solid smooth ivory grips; nitre blue pins; adjustable sights; presentation case. Edition limited to 250 units. Finished by Doug Turnbull Restoration.

NIB	Exc.	V.G.	Good	Fair	Poor
4000	3600	3200	—	—	—

Royal Carry

This is a limited edition of 600 pistols. Chambered for .45 ACP and fitted with a 4" barrel with night sights. Hand checkered rosewood grips. Steel slide and aluminum frame. High polish blue finish. Magazine capacity is 7 rounds. Weight is approximately 28 oz. Introduced in 1998.

NIB	Exc.	V.G.	Good	Fair	Poor
1000	800	650	475	300	150

Elite Carry

Introduced in 1998 this custom shop pistol is limited to 1,200 pistols. Chambered for .45 ACP with a 4" barrel with night sights. Frame is aluminum with black oxide finish. Slide is steel with stainless steel finish. Ambidextrous extended thumb safety, checkered front strap, match trigger, and hand checkered rosewood grips. Magazine capacity is 7 rounds. Weight is about 28 oz.

NIB	Exc.	V.G.	Good	Fair	Poor
1000	800	650	475	300	150

Gold Guardian

This limited edition custom shop pistol is limited to 300 pistols. Chambered for .45 ACP and fitted with a 5" barrel with fixed night sights. Stainless steel slide and frame. Ambidextrous extended thumb safety, match grade barrel, extended magazine well, match trigger, and special markings and serial number. Magazine capacity is 8 rounds and weight is about 38 oz. Introduced in 1998.

NIB	Exc.	V.G.	Good	Fair	Poor
1500	1200	950	575	400	150

Combat Carry

This 4" barrel pistol is chambered for the .45 ACP or .40 S&W cartridge. Many custom features. Special markings. Stainless steel slide and blued frame. Night sights standard. Weight is approximately 28 oz. Introduced in 1999.

NIB	Exc.	V.G.	Good	Fair	Poor
1050	850	675	500	325	165

Gold Combat

This full-size pistol is chambered for the .45 ACP cartridge. Many custom features. Night sights standard. Special markings. Weight is about 38 oz. Blued slide and frame. Introduced in 1999.

NIB	Exc.	V.G.	Good	Fair	Poor
1680	1250	925	700	350	175

Gold Combat II

NIB	Exc.	V.G.	Good	Fair	Poor
1730	1300	925	750	425	200

Gold Combat Stainless

Same as the model above but with stainless steel slide.

NIB	Exc.	V.G.	Good	Fair	Poor
1725	1300	925	750	425	200

Gold Combat Stainless II

NIB	Exc.	V.G.	Good	Fair	Poor
1680	1250	925	700	350	175

Super Match

This is Kimber's most accurate .45 ACP pistol. Fitted with a 5" barrel and many special features. Adjustable sights. Weight is about 38 oz. Stainless steel slide and frame with two-tone finish. Introduced in 1999.

NIB	Exc.	V.G.	Good	Fair	Poor
1925	1500	900	600	350	175

Super Match II

NIB	Exc.	V.G.	Good	Fair	Poor
1985	1550	900	600	350	175

LTP II

Designed for limited pistol competition. Fitted with external extractor, flat top serrated slide with adjustable sights, and extended and beveled magazine well. Fitted with a 5" barrel with tungsten guide rod. Ten-round magazine. Front strap has 20 lpi checkering. Weight is about 38 oz.

NIB	Exc.	V.G.	Good	Fair	Poor
2100	1575	925	625	375	200

Raptor II

Introduced in 2005 this .45 ACP model features a 5" barrel with night sights. Blued finished. This model also has scale serrations on front strap and slide along with scaled zebra wood grips. Magazine capacity is 8 rounds. Weight is about 38 oz.

NIB	Exc.	V.G.	Good	Fair	Poor
1215	925	750	525	350	175

Pro Raptor II

Similar to the Raptor II except for a 4" barrel. Weight is about 35 oz. Introduced in 2005.

NIB	Exc.	V.G.	Good	Fair	Poor
1100	825	700	500	300	125

Grand Raptor II

This is a .45 ACP pistol with 5" match grade stainless steel barrel with adjustable night sights, black aluminum trigger, and rosewood grips. The slide serrations are lizard scale. Stainless steel frame. The slide is matte black and engraved with the Custom Shop logo.

NIB	Exc.	V.G.	Good	Fair	Poor
1500	1200	950	575	400	150

Ultra Raptor II

This .45 ACP model features a 3" ramped match grade bushingless bull barrel. Fixed night sights. Ambidextrous thumb safety. Lizard scale slide serrations. Introduced in 2005.

NIB	Exc.	V.G.	Good	Fair	Poor
1250	925	750	525	350	175

Ultra RCP II

Introduced in 2003 this pistol features a 3" barrel, aluminum frame, sight rail, and a 26 oz. weight. Chambered for the .45 ACP cartridge. Magazine capacity is 7 rounds. No longer in production.

NIB	Exc.	V.G.	Good	Fair	Poor
1300	975	795	550	370	195

Gold Combat RL II

Similar to the above model but with premium trigger, KimPro finish, and rosewood grips. Magazine capacity is 8 rounds. Weight is about 38 oz. Introduced in 2003.

NIB	Exc.	V.G.	Good	Fair	Poor
1775	1325	1100	700	425	245

Target Match

A limited edition of 1,000 pistols chambered for the .45 ACP cartridge. Matte black frame with adjustable sights. Match grade barrel and chamber. Solid aluminum trigger. Checkered front strap and underside of trigger guard. Special serial numbers: KTM0001-KTM1000. Introduced in 2005.

NIB	Exc.	V.G.	Good	Fair	Poor
1400	1050	875	650	395	175

Super America

Billed as Kimber's ultimate top-of-the-line custom 1911. Polished/matte blue finish, scroll engraving, mammoth ivory grips, presentation case with matching sheath knife. Introduced 2007.

NIB	Exc.	V.G.	Good	Fair	Poor
3000	2250	1700	1000	600	225

CDP SERIES (Custom Defense Package)

Ultra CDP

This custom shop model features a 3" barrel, night sights, hand checkered rosewood grips, numerous custom features. Finish is stainless steel slide and matte black frame. Chambered for .45 ACP cartridge. Magazine capacity is 6 rounds. Weight is about 25 oz. Introduced in 2000.

NIB	Exc.	V.G.	Good	Fair	Poor
1100	825	700	500	300	125

Ultra CDP II

Compact 1911-style semi-automatic pistol chambered in .45 ACP. Features include 7-round magazine; ambidextrous thumb safety; carry melt profiling; full length guide rod; aluminum frame with stainless slide; satin silver finish; checkered frontstrap; 3" barrel; rosewood double diamond Crimson Trace laser grips; tritium 3-dot night sights.

NIB	Exc.	V.G.	Good	Fair	Poor
1550	1350	850	525	350	175

Compact CDP

This model, introduced in 2000, features a 4" bull barrel, night sights, hand checkered rosewood grips, and other custom features. Stainless steel slide and matte black frame. Chambered for .45 ACP cartridge. Magazine capacity is 6 rounds. Weight is about 28 oz.

NIB	Exc.	V.G.	Good	Fair	Poor
1200	950	775	575	350	150

Compact CDP II

NIB	Exc.	V.G.	Good	Fair	Poor
1250	995	795	595	350	150

Pro CDP

This model is similar to the Compact CDP but with a full length grip. Magazine capacity is 7 rounds and weight is about 28 oz. Introduced in 2000.

NIB	Exc.	V.G.	Good	Fair	Poor
1100	825	700	500	300	125

Pro CDP II

NIB	Exc.	V.G.	Good	Fair	Poor
1175	900	775	550	350	150

Custom CDP

This .45 ACP full-size pistol is fitted with a 5" match grade barrel and stainless steel slide with front and rear beveled serrations. Matte black steel frame with checkered rosewood grips. Night sights standard. Introduced in 2001.

NIB	Exc.	V.G.	Good	Fair	Poor
1200	950	775	575	350	150

Custom CDP II

NIB	Exc.	V.G.	Good	Fair	Poor
1250	1000	800	600	375	165

ECLIPSE II SERIES

Eclipse Custom II

Chambered for the .45 ACP cartridge and fitted with a 5" barrel with match-grade bushing. Fixed night sights. Magazine capacity is 8 rounds. Weight is about 38 oz. Introduced in 2002. In 2005 this model was offered in 10mm. **NOTE:** Add $110 for 10mm model.

NIB	Exc.	V.G.	Good	Fair	Poor
1175	900	775	550	350	150

Eclipse Target II

Similar to the Eclipse Custom II with the addition of adjustable night sights. Introduced in 2002.

NIB	Exc.	V.G.	Good	Fair	Poor
1200	950	775	575	350	150

Eclipse Ultra II

This .45 ACP pistol with a 3" barrel has a slide machined from a stainless steel forging. Frontstrap checkering. Fixed night sights. Magazine capacity is 7 rounds. Weight is about 34 oz. Introduced in 2002.

NIB	Exc.	V.G.	Good	Fair	Poor
1100	825	700	500	300	125

Eclipse Pro II

This model is similar to the Eclipse Ultra II but features a full-length grip frame and a 4" barrel. Fixed night sights. Introduced in 2002.

NIB	Exc.	V.G.	Good	Fair	Poor
1100	825	700	500	300	125

Eclipse Pro Target II

Similar to the Eclipse Pro but fitted with adjustable night sights. Introduced in 2002.

NIB	Exc.	V.G.	Good	Fair	Poor
1190	950	725	525	325	150

TACTICAL SERIES

This series of pistols was introduced in 2003. Each pistol has 30 lpi checkering on the front strap and under the trigger guard, Meprolight three dot night sights, an extended and beveled magazine well, magazines with extended bumper pads, laminated grips, and match grade barrel and chamber.

Tactical Custom II

Chambered for the .45 ACP cartridge and fitted with a 5" barrel. Magazine capacity is 7 rounds. Weight is about 31 oz.

NIB	Exc.	V.G.	Good	Fair	Poor
1250	1000	800	600	375	165

Tactical Pro II

This model is fitted with a 4" barrel. Weight is about 28 oz.

NIB	Exc.	V.G.	Good	Fair	Poor
1250	1000	800	600	375	165

Tactical Ultra II

This model is fitted with a 3" barrel. Weight is about 25 oz.

NIB	Exc.	V.G.	Good	Fair	Poor
1250	1000	800	600	375	165

COVERT SERIES

Custom Covert II

1911-style semi-automatic carry gun chambered in .45 ACP. Aluminum frame, steel slide. Frame finished in Desert Tan; slide finished in matte black. Five-inch barrel with 3-dot sights. Introduced in 2007.

NIB	Exc.	V.G.	Good	Fair	Poor
1500	1200	950	575	400	150

Pro Covert II

Similar to Custom Covert II but with a 4" barrel. Introduced in 2007.

NIB	Exc.	V.G.	Good	Fair	Poor
1500	1200	950	575	400	150

Ultra Covert II

Similar to Pro Covert II but with a 3" barrel. Introduced 2007.

NIB	Exc.	V.G.	Good	Fair	Poor
1300	975	795	550	370	195

AEGIS SERIES
Pro Aegis II

1911-style semi-automatic carry gun chambered in 9mm Parabellum. Aluminum frame, steel slide. Frame finished in matte aluminum; slide finished in matte black. Four-inch bull barrel with 3-dot sights. Introduced in 2007.

NIB	Exc.	V.G.	Good	Fair	Poor
1000	800	650	475	300	150

Custom Aegis II

Full-size 1911-style semi-automatic carry gun chambered in 9mm Parabellum. Aluminum frame, steel slide. Frame finished in matte aluminum; slide finished in matte black. Five-inch bull barrel with 3-dot sights. Introduced in 2007.

NIB	Exc.	V.G.	Good	Fair	Poor
1100	825	700	500	300	125

Ultra Aegis II

Similar to Pro Aegis II but with 4" barrel. Introduced in 2007.

NIB	Exc.	V.G.	Good	Fair	Poor
1100	825	700	500	300	125

RIMFIRE SERIES
Rimfire Custom

Introduced in 2003 this .22 caliber pistol features a 5" barrel with fixed sights and 10-round magazine. Matte black or silver anodized finish. Weight is about 23 oz.

NIB	Exc.	V.G.	Good	Fair	Poor
750	525	365	225	150	100

Rimfire Target

As above but fitted with adjustable sights. In 2004 this model was also available in .17 Mach 2 caliber.

NIB	Exc.	V.G.	Good	Fair	Poor
800	575	400	275	200	125

Rimfire Super

This model was introduced in 2004 and features a serrated flat top slide with flutes in the upper corners, an ambidextrous thumb safety, an aluminum trigger, and two-tone finish. Weight is about 23 oz.

NIB	Exc.	V.G.	Good	Fair	Poor
1100	825	700	500	300	125

.22 LR Conversion Kit

Introduced in 1998 this Kimber kit features a complete upper assembly: slide, barrel, guide rod, shock buffer, and 10-round magazine. Finish is satin silver or satin blue. Will fit all Kimber 1911 .45 ACP models. In 2005 this kit was also offered for the .17 Mach 2 cartridge conversion.

NIB	Exc.	V.G.	Good	Fair	Poor
300	250	200	125	75	25

KING PIN
Unknown

Derringer

A .22 caliber spur trigger brass constructed single-shot pistol with a 2.5" barrel and walnut grips. Believed to have been made during the 1880s.

NIB	Exc.	V.G.	Good	Fair	Poor
—	—	675	200	100	50

KIRRIKALE, ENDUSTRISI
Ankara, Turkey

Kirrikale Pistol

A 7.65 or 9mm short caliber semi-automatic pistol with a 3.5" barrel and 6-shot magazine. Blued with plastic grips. The slide marked "MKE" ; and "Kirrikale Tufek Fb Cal.—." Imported by Firearms Center in Victoria, Texas, and also by Mandall Shooting Supplies. This was an unauthorized copy of the Walther PP that was imported into the U.S. briefly.

NIB	Exc.	V.G.	Good	Fair	Poor
450	350	275	225	150	100

KLEINGUENTHER/KDF, INC.
Kleinguenther Distinctive Firearms
Seguin, Texas

Condor

A 12 gauge boxlock over/under shotgun with 28" barrels with ventilated ribs, single-selective trigger and automatic ejectors. Blued with a walnut stock. Manufactured in Italy.

NIB	Exc.	V.G.	Good	Fair	Poor
—	700	600	525	375	275

Brescia

A 12 gauge boxlock double-barrel shotgun with 28" barrels, double triggers and extractors. Blued with a walnut stock. Manufactured in Italy.

NIB	Exc.	V.G.	Good	Fair	Poor
—	400	325	300	200	125

K-14 Insta Fire Rifle

A bolt-action sporting rifle manufactured in a variety of calibers with 24" or 26" barrels furnished without sights. Blued with a Monte Carlo-style walnut stock.

NIB	Exc.	V.G.	Good	Fair	Poor
—	1750	1350	1100	500	250

K-15

Similar to the above, with a 60-degree bolt angle and an accurized barrel guaranteed to fire a .5" group at 100 yards. Manufactured with a variety of optional features.

NIB	Exc.	V.G.	Good	Fair	Poor
—	1750	1350	1100	500	250

K-15 Pro-Hunter

As above, matte blued or electroless nickel-plated with a fiberglass stock.

NIB	Exc.	V.G.	Good	Fair	Poor
—	1750	1350	1100	500	250

K-15 Swat Rifle

A 7.62x54mm caliber bolt-action rifle with a 24" or 26" barrel furnished without sights, 4-shot magazine and Parkerized finish. Walnut stock.

NIB	Exc.	V.G.	Good	Fair	Poor
—	1800	1400	1150	700	350

K-15 Dangerous Game

As above, in .411 KDF caliber.

NIB	Exc.	V.G.	Good	Fair	Poor
—	2500	2000	1300	1000	700

Weight is about 7.7 lbs. **NOTE:** Add $50 for camo finish, $70 for stainless steel.

NIB	Exc.	V.G.	Good	Fair	Poor
325	250	200	175	150	100

T-Bolt Magnum

Available in .50 caliber with choice of blue or stainless steel 22" or 26" barrel. Adjustable rear sight. Composite stock with rubber recoil pad. Stock also available in camo. Adjustable trigger. Weight is about 8 lbs. **NOTE:** Add $50 for camo finish, $70 for stainless steel.

NIB	Exc.	V.G.	Good	Fair	Poor
400	325	275	225	150	100

LK-93 Wolverine

Available in .50 or .54 caliber with a choice of 22" blued or stainless steel barrel. Adjustable rear sight. Composite skeleton or thumbhole stock. Stock also available in black or camo. Adjustable trigger. Weight is about 6.5 lbs. **NOTE:** Add $50 for camo finish, $70 for stainless steel, $40 for thumbhole stock.

NIB	Exc.	V.G.	Good	Fair	Poor
265	200	150	100	75	25

LK-93 Wolverine Youth

Same as model above but with shorter length of pull. Offered in black stock only.

NIB	Exc.	V.G.	Good	Fair	Poor
275	225	175	125	100	75

American Knight

Available in .50 caliber with 22" blued barrel. Adjustable rear sight. Black composite stock. Non-adjustable trigger. Weight is approximately 6.3 lbs.

NIB	Exc.	V.G.	Good	Fair	Poor
200	150	100	75	50	25

MK-85 Hunter

This model is offered in .50 or .54 caliber with blued finish and walnut stock.

NIB	Exc.	V.G.	Good	Fair	Poor
550	450	375	325	250	200

MK-85 Predator

This is a stainless steel version of the Hunter model. Offered with composite stock or various camo finishes. **NOTE:** Add $50 for camo finish.

NIB	Exc.	V.G.	Good	Fair	Poor
650	525	450	300	250	200

MK-85 Stalker

This model is offered in .50 or .54 caliber with a variety of stock options. Standard stock is composite. Blued finish. **NOTE:** Add $50 for camo finish.

NIB	Exc.	V.G.	Good	Fair	Poor
565	450	375	325	250	200

MK-85 Knight Hawk

This model is offered in .50 or .54 caliber with black composite stock and stainless steel.

NIB	Exc.	V.G.	Good	Fair	Poor
750	600	500	400	300	200

MK-86 Shotgun

Available in 12 gauge with 24" extra full choked barrel. Black composite stock with blued finish.

NIB	Exc.	V.G.	Good	Fair	Poor
600	475	375	250	200	150

HK-94 Hawkeye Pistol

This is a .50 caliber pistol fitted with a 12" barrel and an overall length of 20" and a weight of 52 oz. Offered in stainless steel or blued finish. First offered in 1993 and discontinued in 1998. **NOTE:** Add $70 for stainless steel.

NIB	Exc.	V.G.	Good	Fair	Poor
400	300	250	200	150	100

Rolling Block Rifle

Rolling-block blackpowder rifle similar in design to the old Remington rolling block design. 209 primer ignition, .50 caliber barrel rifled for sabots. Finishes include blued/composite, stainless/camo, and all-camo. Introduced in 2007. Values shown are for stainless.

NIB	Exc.	V.G.	Good	Fair	Poor
375	300	200	125	100	50

Long Range Hunter

.45-, .50- or .52-caliber bolt-action muzzleloader with 27" fluted stainless barrel. Said to shoot 4" 3-shot groups at 200 yards. Laminated stock. Introduced in 2007.

NIB	Exc.	V.G.	Good	Fair	Poor
525	400	300	200	100	50

KNIGHT'S MANUFACTURING CO.
Vero Beach, Florida

STONER SR-15 RIFLES
SR-15 Match

Chambered for .223 Win. and fitted with a target contour 20" free floating barrel. Two-stage match trigger. Flat top receiver. No sights. Weight is approximately 7.9 lbs.

NIB	Exc.	V.G.	Good	Fair	Poor
1850	1400	1050	750	500	200

SR-15 M-5 Rifle

This .223 is fitted with a 20" standard weight barrel with two-stage target trigger. Handguard employs RAS accessory system. Fitted with flip-up low profile rear sight. Weight is about 7.6 lbs.

NIB	Exc.	V.G.	Good	Fair	Poor
1700	1250	950	700	400	200

SR-15 E3 URX Carbine

Similar to SR-15 M5 but with 16" barrel, telescoping buttstock and vertical fore-end grip. Introduced 2006.

NIB	Exc.	V.G.	Good	Fair	Poor
2100	1700	1250	950	500	200

SR-15 M-4 Carbine

This model also includes the RAS system and has a flip-up rear sight. Two-stage target trigger and 16" lightweight barrel. Weight is about 6.8 lbs.

NIB	Exc.	V.G.	Good	Fair	Poor
1700	1250	950	700	400	200

STONER SR-25 RIFLES

SR-25 Match

This rifle is chambered for the .308 caliber and fitted with a 24" target contour free floating barrel. Special rifling and twist rate. No sights. Weight is about 10.75 lbs.

NIB	Exc.	V.G.	Good	Fair	Poor
3495	2600	1850	950	600	400

SR-25 Lightweight Match

This .308 rifle is fitted with a 20" free floating barrel. No sights. Weight is about 9.5 lbs.

NIB	Exc.	V.G.	Good	Fair	Poor
2995	2250	1500	900	550	350

SR-25 Stoner Carbine

Fitted with a 16" free floating barrel and special short non-slip handguard. Weight is about 7.75 lbs.

NIB	Exc.	V.G.	Good	Fair	Poor
2995	2250	1500	900	—	—

SR-25 Competition Match

This rifle is chambered for either .308 or .260 cartridge and has a 26" match barrel. Fitted with a special forearm which rotates in 15 degree increments. Trigger is adjustable two-stage with extended trigger guard. Special bolt stop and charging handle. Adjustable buttstock. This model may be fitted with several extra costs options that will affect price.

NIB	Exc.	V.G.	Good	Fair	Poor
6000	4750	3000	1750	1000	600

SR-25 Mk11 Mod 0 Match Rifle

Introduced in 2004 this rifle features a heavy 20" free floating target grade barrel.

NIB	Exc.	V.G.	Good	Fair	Poor
5295	3900	2500	1650	100	475

SR-50 Rifle

This is a semi-automatic rifle chambered for the .50 BMG cartridge. Magazine feed. Weight is approximately 31 lbs.

NIB	Exc.	V.G.	Good	Fair	Poor
7000	5500	4000	3000	2000	750

KOHOUT & SPOLECNOST
Kdyne, Czechoslovakia

Mars

A 6.35 or 7.65mm caliber semi-automatic pistol, the larger caliber having a grip safety. Blued with plastic grips impressed with the word "Mars." The slide marked "Mars 7.65 (or 6.35) Kohout & Spol. Kdyne." Manufactured between 1928 and 1945.

NIB	Exc.	V.G.	Good	Fair	Poor
—	350	250	200	150	100

Niva, PZK

Similar to the above in 6.35mm caliber.

NIB	Exc.	V.G.	Good	Fair	Poor
—	350	250	200	150	100

KOLB, HENRY M.
Philadelphia, Pennsylvania

The revolvers listed were manufactured by Henry Kolb and Charles Foehl until 1912 when R.F. Sedgely replaced Foehl. Manufacture continued until approximately 1938.

Baby Hammerless

A .22 caliber folding-trigger double-action revolver with an enclosed hammer and 5-shot cylinder.

NIB	Exc.	V.G.	Good	Fair	Poor
—	300	200	150	100	50

New Baby Hammerless

Similar to the above, with a hinged barrel to facilitate loading.

NIB	Exc.	V.G.	Good	Fair	Poor
—	300	200	150	100	50

KOLIBRI/FREDERICH PFANNL
Rehberg, Austria

2.7mm

A 2.7mm semi-automatic pistol with a 7-round magazine. The F.P. trademark is on the grips as well as the Kolibri name at the bottom of the grips. A single cartridge may be worth as much as $75!

Courtesy James Rankin

NIB	Exc.	V.G.	Good	Fair	Poor
—	2500	1550	850	600	400

3mm

A 3mm semi-automatic pistol with a 6-round magazine. The 3mm version is the rarer of the two Kolibri pistols. The F.P. trademark is on the grips.

Courtesy James Rankin

NIB	Exc.	V.G.	Good	Fair	Poor
—	2800	2000	1500	1000	600

KOMMER, THEODOR WAFFENFABRIK
Zella Mehlis, Germany

Model 1

A 6.35mm semi-automatic pistol with an 8-shot magazine. Blued with plastic grips. Kommer name is both on the slide and the frame with T.K. trademark on the grips. Manufactured during the 1920s.

Courtesy James Rankin

NIB	Exc.	V.G.	Good	Fair	Poor
—	300	250	200	150	90

Model 2

A 6.35mm semi-automatic pistol with a 6-round magazine similar to the Model 1906 Browning. Barrel length is 2". Weight is about 13 oz. The Kommer name is on the slide. The late TH.K. trademark is on the grips. Manufactured in the 1930s.

Courtesy James Rankin

NIB	Exc.	V.G.	Good	Fair	Poor
—	300	250	200	150	90

Model 3

A 6.35mm semi-automatic pistol with a 9-round magazine. The Kommer name is on the slide and the TH.K. trademark is on the grips. Same as the Model 2 with extended grips straps for longer magazine.

Courtesy James Rankin

NIB	Exc.	V.G.	Good	Fair	Poor
—	300	250	200	150	90

Model 4

A 7.65mm caliber semi-automatic pistol with a 7-shot magazine and without a grip safety. Similar to the FN Model 1901. Barrel length is 3". Weight is about 20 oz. The slide marked "Waffenfabrik Kommer Zella Mehlis Kal. 7.65.". Manufactured between 1936 and 1940.

Courtesy James Rankin

NIB	Exc.	V.G.	Good	Fair	Poor
—	375	325	275	175	100

KONGSBERG
Norway

Thumbhole Sporter

Introduced in 1993, this bolt-action rifle is chambered for the .22-250 and .308 Win. cartridges. It is fitted with a 23" heavy barrel. The stock is American walnut with stippled thumbhole grip and wide fore-end. Cheekpiece is adjustable for height. Weight is about 8.5 lbs. Available in both right- and left-hand configurations. **NOTE:** Add 10 percent for left-hand model.

NIB	Exc.	V.G.	Good	Fair	Poor
1575	1250	900	550	350	200

Classic Rifle

This model was also introduced in 1993 and is chambered for a wide variety of calibers from .22-250 to .338 Win. Magnum. Fitted with a 23" barrel for standard calibers and a 26" barrel for magnum calibers. European walnut stock with straight comb. Hand checkered. Open sights. Weight is about 7.5 lbs. depending on caliber. Offered in both left- and right-hand configurations. **NOTE:** Add 10 percent for left-hand models and 10 percent for magnum calibers.

NIB	Exc.	V.G.	Good	Fair	Poor
995	800	650	375	225	125

KORRIPHILA
Germany

HSP

A 7.65mm Luger, .38 Special, 9mm Police, 9mm Luger, 9mm Steyr, 10mm ACP, and the .45 ACP caliber double-action semi-automatic pistol with a 4" barrel made of stainless steel.

NIB	Exc.	V.G.	Good	Fair	Poor
7500	6000	5000	2500	1250	550

HSP—Single-Action Only

NIB	Exc.	V.G.	Good	Fair	Poor
7500	6000	5000	2500	1250	550

Odin's Eye

Essentially the same model as above in the same calibers with choice of barrel lengths of 4" or 5". Frame and slide are made of Damascus steel.

NIB	Exc.	V.G.	Good	Fair	Poor
14000	10000	7500	4000	1500	500

KORTH
Germany

Korth started business in Ratzegurg, Germany, in 1954.

Semi-Automatic Pistol

A 9mm caliber double-action semi-automatic pistol with a 4" barrel, adjustable sights and 13-shot magazine. Other calibers are offered such as .40 S&W, .357 SIG, and 9x21. Optional 5" barrel is also offered. Weight is about 44 oz. Matte or polished blue with walnut grips. Introduced in 1985.

NIB	Exc.	V.G.	Good	Fair	Poor
7000	5000	3750	2750	1300	650

Combat Revolver

A .22 LR, .22 Magnum, .357 Magnum, and 9mm caliber revolver with a 3", 4", 5.25", or 6" barrel and 6-shot cylinder. The barrels and cylinders are interchangeable, matte or polished blue with walnut grips.

NIB	Exc.	V.G.	Good	Fair	Poor
5000	3900	3000	1750	1150	700

Match Revolver

Built in the same calibers as the Combat revolver with a choice of 5.25" or 6" barrel. Adjustable rear sight with adjustable sight notch widths. Machined trigger shoe. Grips are adjustable match grips with oiled walnut and matte finish.

NIB	Exc.	V.G.	Good	Fair	Poor
6250	5000	4000	2250	1500	1000

KRAUSER, ALFRED
Zella Mehlis, Germany

Helfricht or Helkra

A 6.35mm semi-automatic pistol with a 2" barrel. Produced in four models, the fourth with an enclosed barrel. Blued with composition grips. Manufactured from 1921 to 1929.

NIB	Exc.	V.G.	Good	Fair	Poor
—	475	400	350	250	150

KRICO
Stuttgart, West Germany

Sporting Rifle

A .22 Hornet or .222 caliber bolt-action rifle with 22", 24", or 26" barrels, single or double set trigger, adjustable sights and a 4-shot magazine. Blued with a walnut stock. Manufactured between 1956 and 1962.

NIB	Exc.	V.G.	Good	Fair	Poor
—	650	550	475	375	275

Sporting Carbine

As above, with a 20" barrel and full length stock.

NIB	Exc.	V.G.	Good	Fair	Poor
—	675	575	500	400	300

Varmint Special Rifle

The Sporting Rifle with a heavier barrel.

NIB	Exc.	V.G.	Good	Fair	Poor
—	650	550	475	375	275

Model 300

A .22 caliber bolt-action rifle with a 23.5" barrel, 5-shot magazine and grooved receiver. Blued with a walnut stock. Imported prior to 1989.

NIB	Exc.	V.G.	Good	Fair	Poor
—	700	600	550	400	300

Model 302 and 304

Variations of the above. Discontinued in 1986.

NIB	Exc.	V.G.	Good	Fair	Poor
—	700	600	550	400	300

Model 311 Smallbore

A .22 caliber bolt-action rifle with a 22" barrel, double set triggers, adjustable sights and a 5- or 10-shot magazine. Blued with walnut stock. Not imported after 1988.

NIB	Exc.	V.G.	Good	Fair	Poor
—	325	275	225	150	100

Model 320

As above, with a 19.5" barrel and full length stock. Discontinued in 1988.

NIB	Exc.	V.G.	Good	Fair	Poor
—	700	600	550	400	300

Model 340

A .22 caliber bolt-action rifle with a 21" heavy barrel furnished without sights, adjustable trigger and 5-shot magazine. Blued with a walnut stock. Not imported after 1988.

NIB	Exc.	V.G.	Good	Fair	Poor
—	750	625	575	425	325

Model 340 Mini-Sniper

As above, but matte finished, barrel fitted with a muzzlebrake and stock with a raised cheekpiece as well as ventilated hand guard.

NIB	Exc.	V.G.	Good	Fair	Poor
—	1000	850	750	500	400

Model 340 Kricotronic

The Model 340 fitted with an electronic trigger. Not imported after 1988.

NIB	Exc.	V.G.	Good	Fair	Poor
—	1450	1000	850	600	500

Model 360S Biathlon Rifle

Introduced in 1991 this model features a .22 Long Rifle straight pull bolt-action with 5-round magazine and fitted with a 21.25" barrel. Walnut stock with high comb and adjustable buttplate. Fully adjustable match peep sight. Fitted with 17 oz. match trigger. Weight is approximately 9.25 lbs.

NIB	Exc.	V.G.	Good	Fair	Poor
1950	1350	850	500	300	150

Model 360S2 Biathlon Rifle

Same as above but fitted with a black epoxy finished walnut stock with pistol grip. Weight is 9 lbs.

NIB	Exc.	V.G.	Good	Fair	Poor
1500	1250	800	400	200	100

Model 400 Match

Chambered for the .22 LR or the .22 Hornet this bolt-action rifle is fitted with a heavy match 23" barrel and a 5-round magazine. The match-style stock is of European walnut. Fitted with a double set of match triggers. Weight is about 8.8 lbs.

NIB	Exc.	V.G.	Good	Fair	Poor
900	775	650	500	300	150

Model 400 Sporter

A .22 Hornet caliber bolt-action rifle with a 23.5" barrel, open sights and 5-shot magazine. Blued with a walnut stock. Not imported after 1988.

NIB	Exc.	V.G.	Good	Fair	Poor
—	750	625	550	425	325

Model 420

As above, with a 19.5" barrel, double set triggers, and a full-length stock. Discontinued in 1988.

NIB	Exc.	V.G.	Good	Fair	Poor
—	900	750	675	500	400

Model 440

Similar to the Model 340. Not imported after 1988.

NIB	Exc.	V.G.	Good	Fair	Poor
—	950	800	700	500	375

Model 500 Kricotronic Match Rifle

Chambered for the .22 LR this bolt-action rifle is fitted with a 23.6" barrel with tapered bore. Walnut stock with match-type adjustable buttplate. Electronic ignition system gives fastest lock time. Weight is approximately 9.4 lbs.

NIB	Exc.	V.G.	Good	Fair	Poor
3900	3000	2400	1650	1000	400

Model 600 Sporter

A .17 Remington to .308 Winchester caliber bolt-action rifle with a 23.5" barrel, open sights and 3-shot magazine. Blued with a walnut stock. Not imported after 1988.

NIB	Exc.	V.G.	Good	Fair	Poor
—	1150	950	875	700	575

Model 600 Sniper Rifle

This bolt-action rifle is chambered for the .222, .223, .22-250, .243, and 308. It is fitted with a 25.6" heavy barrel with flack hider. The stock is walnut with adjustable rubber buttplate. Magazine holds 4 rounds. Weight is about 9.2 lbs.

NIB	Exc.	V.G.	Good	Fair	Poor
2900	2100	1500	1100	600	300

Model 600 Match Rifle

Chambered for the same calibers as the 600 Sniper with the addition of the 5.6x50 Mag. Fitted with a 23.6" barrel. The match stock is vented in forearm for cooling. Wood is walnut with cheekpiece. Weight is approximately 8.8 lbs.

NIB	Exc.	V.G.	Good	Fair	Poor
1500	1100	750	600	300	150

Model 620

As above, with a 20.5" barrel, double set triggers, and full-length stock.

NIB	Exc.	V.G.	Good	Fair	Poor
1500	1100	750	600	300	150

Model 640 Varmint Rifle

Similar to the above, in .22-250, .222 or .223 caliber with a 23.5" heavy barrel. Not imported after 1988.

NIB	Exc.	V.G.	Good	Fair	Poor
—	1250	1025	925	775	625

Model 640 Sniper Rifle

As above, but matte finished. Discontinued in 1988.

NIB	Exc.	V.G.	Good	Fair	Poor
1500	1100	750	600	300	150

Model 640 Deluxe Sniper Rifle

As above, in .223 or .308 caliber with a 23" barrel, stippled stock, and adjustable trigger. Not imported after 1988.

NIB	Exc.	V.G.	Good	Fair	Poor
—	1700	1250	1000	750	650

Model 700 Sporter

A .270 or .30-06 caliber bolt-action rifle with a 23.5" barrel, open sights, single set trigger, and 3-shot magazine. Blued with a walnut stock. Discontinued in 1988.

NIB	Exc.	V.G.	Good	Fair	Poor
—	1050	850	750	600	500

Model 720

As above, with a 20.5" barrel, double set triggers, and full-length stock. Discontinued in 1988.

NIB	Exc.	V.G.	Good	Fair	Poor
—	1200	900	750	600	500

Model 720 Limited Edition

As above, in .270 caliber only with gold-plated furniture and gold highlighted engraving. Not imported after 1988.

NIB	Exc.	V.G.	Good	Fair	Poor
—	2500	2000	1750	1400	900

KRIDER, J. H.
Philadelphia, Pennsylvania

Pocket Pistol

A .41 caliber percussion pocket pistol with a 3" barrel, German silver furniture and walnut stock. The barrel marked "Krider Phila." Manufactured during the 1850s and 1860s.

NIB	Exc.	V.G.	Good	Fair	Poor
—	—	1750	700	300	150

Militia Rifle

A .58 caliber percussion rifle with a 39" barrel and full length stock secured by two barrel bands. The barrel is browned, the lock marked "Krider." Case hardened and furniture of brass. Several hundred were manufactured in 1861.

Courtesy Milwaukee Public Museum, Milwaukee, Wisconsin

NIB	Exc.	V.G.	Good	Fair	Poor
—	—	4550	2000	750	225

KRIEGHOFF, HEINRICH, GUN CO.
Ulm, Germany

Krieghoff-manufactured Lugers are listed in the Luger section.

DRILLINGS AND COMBINATION GUNS

Plus Model

A three-barrel combination rifle/shotgun produced in a variety of gauges and calibers with 25" barrels, double triggers, and automatic ejectors. Blued with a walnut stock. Introduced in 1988.

NIB	Exc.	V.G.	Good	Fair	Poor
6600	5250	4100	3500	2000	750

Trumpf Model

A combination rifle/shotgun produced in a variety of calibers and gauges with 25" barrels and double triggers. Blued with a walnut stock.

NIB	Exc.	V.G.	Good	Fair	Poor
11000	7700	5100	3500	2000	750

Trumpf Dural

As above, lightweight boxlock with a Duraluminum frame. **NOTE:** For single trigger add $1,850. For free-floating barrel add $450.

NIB	Exc.	V.G.	Good	Fair	Poor
11000	7700	5100	3500	2000	750

Neptun

A combination over/under rifle/shotgun with sidelocks produced in a variety of gauges and calibers. Engraved, blued with a walnut stock.

NIB	Exc.	V.G.	Good	Fair	Poor
15000	12000	10500	5000	2500	1500

Neptun Dural

As above, lightweight boxlock with a Duraluminum frame.

NIB	Exc.	V.G.	Good	Fair	Poor
15000	12000	10500	5000	2500	1500

Neptun Primus

The Neptun with relief engraving and detachable sidelocks.

NIB	Exc.	V.G.	Good	Fair	Poor
20000	17000	14000	7500	3500	2000

Neptun Primus Dural

As above, lightweight sidelock with a Duraluminum frame.

NIB	Exc.	V.G.	Good	Fair	Poor
20000	18000	14000	7500	3500	2000

DOUBLE RIFLES

There are many optional engraving patterns available for these double rifles that may affect price. Consult an expert prior to a sale.

Teck Over/Under

A boxlock over/under rifle manufactured in a variety of calibers with 25" barrels, double triggers, extractors, and express sights. Blued with a walnut stock. **NOTE:** For .458 Win. Magnum add $1,500.

NIB	Exc.	V.G.	Good	Fair	Poor
9000	8250	6600	5000	2250	1500

Ulm Model

As above, with sidelocks.

NIB	Exc.	V.G.	Good	Fair	Poor
15000	12000	10500	7500	3000	2000

Ulm Primus

As above, with detachable sidelocks.

NIB	Exc.	V.G.	Good	Fair	Poor
23500	19500	16500	11500	7000	3000

Ultra

This boxlock over/under rifle is offered with several different options such as same caliber rifle barrels or different caliber rifle barrels. Built on a 20 gauge frame with game scene engraving. Weights are depending on calibers and combinations of calibers but are between 6.5 lbs. and 8 lbs.

NIB	Exc.	V.G.	Good	Fair	Poor
7500	6100	4400	3000	1500	800

Classic

This is a side-by-side rifle with side plates. Offered in 7x65R to 9.3x74R calibers with an optional interchangeable 20 gauge shotgun barrel. Single trigger. Choice of standard stock with cheekpiece or classic Bavaria style. Weight is approximately 7.25 to 8 lbs. depending on calibers.

NIB	Exc.	V.G.	Good	Fair	Poor
8800	6900	5000	3500	2000	800

Classic Big Five

Similar to the Classic but chambered for .375 H&H, .375 NE, .458 Win. Magnum, .416 Rigby, .470 NE, and .500 NE 3". Double trigger with hinged front trigger. Weighs approximately 9.25 to 10 lbs. depending on caliber. Interchangeable barrel are optional.

NIB	Exc.	V.G.	Good	Fair	Poor
10900	82500	5100	3500	2000	750

SHOTGUNS

Model 32 Standard

A 12, 20, 28 or .410 bore boxlock over/under shotgun with 26.5" to 32" barrels, single-selective trigger and automatic ejectors. Blued with a walnut stock. Discontinued in 1980. **NOTE:** 28 gauge or .410 two barrel set add 50 percent. Four-barrel Skeet set add 100 percent.

NIB	Exc.	V.G.	Good	Fair	Poor
—	3000	2500	2000	1100	750

San Remo Grade

NIB	Exc.	V.G.	Good	Fair	Poor
—	5000	3750	1900	1400	1000

Monte Carlo Grade

NIB	Exc.	V.G.	Good	Fair	Poor
—	6250	4850	2750	1650	1250

Crown Grade

Courtesy Bonhams & Butterfields

NIB	Exc.	V.G.	Good	Fair	Poor
—	8700	6500	4300	2200	1500

Super Crown Grade

NIB	Exc.	V.G.	Good	Fair	Poor
18000	14700	10500	6850	3750	2000

Single Barrel Trap Gun

The Model 32 with a single 32" to 34" barrel.

NIB	Exc.	V.G.	Good	Fair	Poor
—	3950	3250	1700	1075	600

Teck Over/Under

Similar to the Teck double rifle but offered in 12 and 16 gauge.

NIB	Exc.	V.G.	Good	Fair	Poor
12000	10000	7500	4550	3000	1750

Teck Dural

Same as above but with lightweight aluminum frame.

NIB	Exc.	V.G.	Good	Fair	Poor
12000	10000	7500	4550	3000	1750

Ulm

This sidelock over/under is offered in both 12 and 16 gauge.

NIB	Exc.	V.G.	Good	Fair	Poor
20000	16500	13000	8000	4500	3000

Ulm Dural

This is a lightweight version of the above model.

NIB	Exc.	V.G.	Good	Fair	Poor
20000	16500	13000	8000	4500	3000

Ulm Primus

This is a deluxe version of the Ulm series with sidelocks and extensive engraving.

NIB	Exc.	V.G.	Good	Fair	Poor
30000	22250	16500	12000	7000	3500

Ulm Primus Dural

This is a lightweight version of the above model.

NIB	Exc.	V.G.	Good	Fair	Poor
30000	22250	16500	12000	7000	3500

Ultra

This is a lightweight over/under gun offered in 12 or 20 gauge.

NIB	Exc.	V.G.	Good	Fair	Poor
—	6250	4850	2750	1650	1250

KS-5 Single Barrel Trap

This model is a boxlock 12 gauge only trap gun with 32" or 34" ventilated tapered rib barrel and case hardened frame with a satin gray finish. The barrel features an adjustable point of impact and is offered with screw-in choke tubes. Weight is approximately 8.6 lbs.

NIB	Exc.	V.G.	Good	Fair	Poor
8000	7500	5900	3650	1250	800

KS-5 Special

Same as above but furnished with adjustable rib and adjustable comb.

NIB	Exc.	V.G.	Good	Fair	Poor
8250	7750	6100	3900	1500	1000

K-80 Trap

This is a boxlock 12 gauge shotgun built to trap dimensions. This model is offered in many variations. Available in over/under trap with choice of 30" or 32" vent tapered step rib barrels. Also a single barrel is offered in 32" or 34" tapered step rib lengths. These single barrels are adjustable for point of impact. A top single barrel is available as well in 34" length. Trap combos are offered also. All barrels are offered with or without choke tubes. The checkered walnut stock is offered in Monte Carlo or straight trap dimensions. Trap guns weigh approximately 8.75 lbs. Prices listed are for Standard Grade. **NOTE:** Bavaria Grade add 70 percent. Danube Grade add 100 percent. Gold Target Grade add 200 percent.

Over/Under Trap

NIB	Exc.	V.G.	Good	Fair	Poor
12000	10500	7400	4850	2000	1000

Unsingle Trap

NIB	Exc.	V.G.	Good	Fair	Poor
12500	11000	8250	5400	2250	1250

Top Single Trap

NIB	Exc.	V.G.	Good	Fair	Poor
13250	11200	9500	6400	3300	1500

Trap Combos

NIB	Exc.	V.G.	Good	Fair	Poor
13000	10700	9600	7400	4300	1900

K-20 Sporting and Field

Compact frame variation of the K-80, chambered in 20 or 28 gauge, or .410 bore. Barrels are 30" or 32" with five choke tubes and tapered flat rib. Checkered walnut stock, auto ejectors and single selective trigger. Weight is approx. 7.25 lbs. Available with extra sets of barrels in other two gauges.

NIB	Exc.	V.G.	Good	Fair	Poor
9000	8000	7000	4000	2200	1000

K-80 Sporting Clays

The frame is the same as the trap model with the addition of a lightweight alloy model and is available in 12 gauge only. Barrel lengths for standard weight model are 28", 30", or 32" with tapered flat rib. The lightweight model is offered with 28" or 30" flat rib barrels. Select European walnut stock with hand checkering and supplied with a #3 Sporting stock with schnabel forearm. The standard weight model weighs about 8.25 lbs. while the lightweight model weighs 7.75 lbs. Prices listed are for the Standard Grade. **NOTE:** Bavaria Grade add 70 percent. Danube Grade add 100 percent. Gold Target Grade add 200 percent.

NIB	Exc.	V.G.	Good	Fair	Poor
9500	8000	7000	4000	2200	1000

K-80 Skeet

This model is offered in a number of variations. The standard weight skeet with 28" or 30" tapered or parallel ribs, lightweight skeet with 28" or 30" tapered or parallel ribs, International skeet with 28" parallel broadway rib, and the 4 barrel skeet set in 12, 20, and 28 gauge as well as .410 bore with 8mm rib. Stock is hand-checkered select European walnut with a choice of several skeet dimensions. Values listed are for Standard Grade. **NOTE:** Bavaria Grade add 70 percent. Danube Grade add 100 percent. Gold Target Grade add 200 percent. Optional Engravings available by special order on NIB or Exc. conditions guns: Parcours add $1500. Parcours Special add $2800. Super Scroll add $1100. Gold Super Scroll add $2900. Custom Bavaria $4700 over Bavaria Grade price.

Standard Weight Skeet

NIB	Exc.	V.G.	Good	Fair	Poor
7500	6250	4950	3300	2200	1000

Lightweight Skeet

NIB	Exc.	V.G.	Good	Fair	Poor
7500	6250	4950	3300	2200	1000

International Skeet

NIB	Exc.	V.G.	Good	Fair	Poor
7500	6250	4950	3300	2200	1000

4 Barrel Set

NIB	Exc.	V.G.	Good	Fair	Poor
17000	10000	7600	4400	3300	2200

SIDE-BY-SIDE DOUBLES

Essencia Boxlock

This high-grade model was introduced in 2003 and has a round-body receive with English-style scroll engraving and gold highlights. Offered in 12, 16, 20 and 28 gauges with 28" or 30" barrels and fixed IC/M chokes. Straight grip Turkish walnut checkered stock, single (non-selective) or double triggers and automatic ejectors. **NOTE:** Add $1000 for 28 gauge, $1000 for single trigger.

NIB	Exc.	V.G.	Good	Fair	Poor
22000	17500	15000	10000	3000	800

Essencia Sidelock

This model was also introduced in 2003 and is a back-action sidelock on three frame sizes designed for different gauges. Offered in 12, 16, 20 and 28 gauges. Barrel lengths are 18", 26.5" or 30" with fixed chokes or Briley choke tubes. Receiver is color case hardened with gold-inlayed engraving. Straight or pistol-grip Turkish walnut checkered stock, single (non-selective) or double triggers and automatic ejectors. **NOTE:** Add $1000 for 28 gauge, $1000 for single trigger, $1500 for Briley choke tubes.

NIB	Exc.	V.G.	Good	Fair	Poor
27000	22500	18000	12000	4000	800

KRNKA, KAREL
Vienna, Austria

Karel Krnka was a talented firearms inventor born in 1858. He began his career in firearms design as a member of the Austro-Hungarian army. He made many improvements to their service rifle design. After he left the military, he took the job of head engineer with the ill-fated and short-lived "Gatling Gun Company." This company ceased operations in 1890, and then Krnka went to work for the patent office and remained there for a few years. In 1898 he became foreman of the Roth Cartridge Company and worked with Roth on firearms designs until the death of Roth in 1909. After this he became associated with the Hertenberger Cartridge Company; and finally in 1922 he moved to Czechoslovakia, where he became a firearms designer for the firm of C.Z. He remained at this post until his death in 1926. He recorded his first firearm patent in 1888 for a mechanical repeater with a ring trigger. His best known innovations are the internal butt magazine that is loaded by means of a stripper clip and the rotating locked bolt with internal firing pin. These designs were never actually turned into a mass-marketed pistol but were major contributions in the development of a practical semi-automatic pistol design.

Model 1892

NIB	Exc.	V.G.	Good	Fair	Poor
—	—	8200	5500	2200	1050

KSN INDUSTRIES
Israel

Golan

A semi-automatic pistol, introduced in 1996, chambered for the 9mm or .40 S&W cartridge. Double-action trigger with ambidextrous controls. Barrel length is 3.9" and magazine capacity is 10 rounds in U.S. In rest of the world 15 rounds for 9mm and 11 rounds for the .40 S&W. Weight is 29 oz.

NIB	Exc.	V.G.	Good	Fair	Poor
650	525	400	325	200	100

Kareen MK II

This single-action semi-automatic pistol is chambered for the 9mm cartridge. The barrel length is 4.5". Ambidextrous safety and rubber grips. Steel slide and frame. Weight is about 34 oz.

NIB	Exc.	V.G.	Good	Fair	Poor
500	395	250	200	150	100

Kareen MK II—Compact

Same as above but fitted with a 3.9" barrel. Weight is about 32 oz.

NIB	Exc.	V.G.	Good	Fair	Poor
575	425	325	250	200	150

GAL

Same as the full size Kareen but chambered for the .45 ACP cartridge.

NIB	Exc.	V.G.	Good	Fair	Poor
575	425	325	250	200	150

KUFAHL, G. L.
Sommerda, Germany

Kufahl Needle-Fire Revolver

Designed and patented in Britain in 1852 by G.L. Kufahl, who tried unsuccessfully to interest a British company in producing it. He then went to the firm of Rheinmettal Dreyse, where a needle-fire gun was produced in 1838. This company manufactured his design. This revolver was chambered for a unique, totally consumed .30 caliber "cartridge." A lead projectile had the ignition percussion cap affixed to its base, with the propellant powder in the rear. The firing pin had to be long enough to penetrate the powder charge and hit the percussion cap. This does not sound efficient, but realize that these were the days before cartridges. This revolver has a 3.2" barrel and an unfluted cylinder that holds six shots. It is not bored all the way through but is loaded from the front. The finish is blued, with a modicum of simple engraving and checkered wood grips that protrude all the way over the trigger. The markings are "Fv.V. Dreyse Sommerda."

NIB	Exc.	V.G.	Good	Fair	Poor
—	—	2950	1600	650	400

KYNOCH GUN FACTORY
Birmingham, England

Established by George Kynoch in approximately 1886, this company ceased operation in 1890.

Early Double Trigger Revolver

A .45 caliber double trigger revolver with a 6" barrel, 6-shot cylinder and enclosed hammer. Blued with walnut grips. Manufactured in 1885.

NIB	Exc.	V.G.	Good	Fair	Poor
—	—	1600	950	575	350

Late Double Trigger Revolver

Similar to the above, but in .32, .38, or .45 caliber with the cocking trigger enclosed within the trigger guard. Approximately 600 of these revolvers were made between 1890 and 1896.

NIB	Exc.	V.G.	Good	Fair	Poor
—	—	2100	1575	900	575

L

LAGRESE
Paris, France

Lagrese Revolver

A large ornate revolver chambered for the .43 rimfire cartridge. It has a 6.25" barrel and a 6-shot fluted cylinder. This revolver has no top strap; and the frame, as well as the grip straps, are cast in one piece with the barrel screwed into the frame. It is loaded through a gate and has double-action lockwork. The outstanding feature about this well-made revolver is its extremely ornate appearance. There are more sweeps and curves than could be imagined and in general outline somewhat resmbles the leMat, though with a sisngle barrel. It is engraved and blued, with well-figured curved walnut grips. It is marked "Lagrese Bte a Paris" and was manufactured in the late 1860s.

NIB	Exc.	V.G.	Good	Fair	Poor
—	—	3500	2750	1300	875

LAHTI
Finland

See—Husqvarna

Lahti

This is a commercial version of the Finnish L-35 9mm pistol. These late pistols have the barrel and trigger guard design of the L-35 but the barrel extension of the Swedish M40. Produced in the late 1950s.

Courtesy J.B. Wood

NIB	Exc.	V.G.	Good	Fair	Poor
—	1250	1000	800	550	300

LAKELANDER
Gulfport, Mississippi

Model 389 Premium

This bolt action rifle is chambered for .270 Win., .308 Win., and .30-06 calibers. It is fitted with a 22" lightweight barrel. The stock is oil finished walnut with diamond checkering. Rosewood fore-end cap, black recoil pad, and Monte Carlo buttstock. Weight is approximately 7.6 lbs. Introduced in 1997.

NIB	Exc.	V.G.	Good	Fair	Poor
1750	1350	950	700	375	200

Model 389 Classic

Similar to the Premium grade rifle above but offered with traditional stock and checkering and less fancy walnut stock. Weight is approximately 7.3 lbs. Introduced in 1997.

NIB	Exc.	V.G.	Good	Fair	Poor
1725	1325	925	675	350	150

Model 389 Match-Maker

This bolt action is chambered for the .308 cartridge and is fitted with a 21.7" barrel. The stock is target style with adjustable chin support with benchrest-style buttpad. Weight is approximately 8.4 lbs. Introduced in 1997. **NOTE:** Add $50 for magnum calibers.

NIB	Exc.	V.G.	Good	Fair	Poor
2250	1850	1350	850	575	250

LAMB, H. C. & CO.
Jamestown, North Carolina

Muzzleloading Rifle

Chambered for .58 caliber and utilizes the percussion ignition system. It has a 33" barrel and a full-length oak stock held on by two barrel bands. There is a ramrod mounted under the barrel that is made of iron. All other trim is brass, and there is a bayonet lug at the muzzle. This rifle was made for the Confederacy and the workmanship was crude, as it was on most CSA weapons. The stock is marked "H.C.Lamb & Co., N.C." There were supposedly 10,000 rifles ordered, but actually there were approximately 250 manufactured between 1861 and 1863. The rarity of the guns of the Confederacy gives them a great deal of collector appeal.

Courtesy Milwaukee Public Museum, Milwaukee, Wisconsin

NIB	Exc.	V.G.	Good	Fair	Poor
—	—	35000	15000	2750	500

LAMES
Chiavari, Italy

Skeet or Trap Grade

An over/under shotgun chambered for 12 gauge with either 26" skeet-and-skeet barrels or 30" or 32" full-choked barrels. It has a competition-style wide vent rib and automatic ejectors. The trigger is single-selective, and the finish is blued. The trap gun has a Monte Carlo stock of checkered walnut. Both models feature recoil pads.

NIB	Exc.	V.G.	Good	Fair	Poor
—	700	575	4575	375	200

California Trap Grade

This over/under is similar to the standard trap model, with separated barrels. All other features are the same.

NIB	Exc.	V.G.	Good	Fair	Poor
—	775	650	575	475	225

Field Grade

Similar in design to the standard trap model, with 3" chambers and barrel lengths of 26", 28", or 30" and a field dimensioned stock. It features various choke combinations and was also available with the separated barrels of the California Trap for an additional 20 percent in cost.

NIB	Exc.	V.G.	Good	Fair	Poor
—	475	450	350	250	150

LANBER ARMAS S.A.
Vizcaya, Spain

Model 2072 Slug

Fixed choke double barrel slug gun with 3" chambers and 20" barrel with fiber-optic rifle sights. Weight is about 6 lbs. A hard-to-find gun.

NIB	Exc.	V.G.	Good	Fair	Poor
900	800	650	475	300	200

Model 844 ST

A 12-gauge over/under shotgun with 26" or 28" vent rib barrels. The chokes vary, and the gun features a single-selective trigger, extractors, and an engraved receiver with a blued finish and a walnut stock. This gun was manufactured until 1986.

NIB	Exc.	V.G.	Good	Fair	Poor
—	425	350	300	250	175

Model 844 MST

Similar to the Model 844 ST except that it is chambered for 3" Magnum and has 30" Full and Modified choked barrels.

NIB	Exc.	V.G.	Good	Fair	Poor
—	525	450	300	250	175

Model 844 EST

Similar to the others, but it features automatic ejectors.

NIB	Exc.	V.G.	Good	Fair	Poor
—	575	425	350	300	200

Model 844 EST CHR

Has automatic ejectors and double triggers. All other features are the same as the EST.

NIB	Exc.	V.G.	Good	Fair	Poor
—	550	400	325	275	175

Model 2004 LCH

An over/under chambered for 12 gauge and features 28" vent rib barrels with screw-in choke tubes. It has a single-selective trigger, automatic ejectors, and an engraved boxlock action that is matte finished, with a hand-checkered walnut stock. This model was also discontinued in 1986.

NIB	Exc.	V.G.	Good	Fair	Poor
—	775	650	550	475	375

Model 2008 LCH and Model 2009 LCH

The trap and skeet versions of the series. The basic differences are in the barrel lengths and the stock dimensions.

Model 2008 LCH

Model 2009 LCH

NIB	Exc.	V.G.	Good	Fair	Poor
—	900	750	650	575	475

Model 2067

This 20 gauge over/under with 3" chambers has 28" barrels, auto ejectors and an oil-finished walnut stock. Weight is about 6.6 lbs.

NIB	Exc.	V.G.	Good	Fair	Poor
775	650	550	450	375	200

Model 2077 Hunter Light

This is a 2.75" 12 gauge with 26" barrels and a lightweight alloy receiver. Weight is about 6.2 lbs.

NIB	Exc.	V.G.	Good	Fair	Poor
850	725	575	475	400	200

Model 2087 Hunter

This 12 gauge comes with 3" chambers, auto ejectors, oil-finished walnut stock and 28" or 30" barrel. Weight is about 7 lbs.

NIB	Exc.	V.G.	Good	Fair	Poor
775	650	550	450	375	200

Model 2097 Sporting

Sporting clays model in 12 gauge with 3" chambers and 28" or 30" barrels. Weight is about 7.7 lbs. Add $50 for Sporting LUX model.

NIB	Exc.	V.G.	Good	Fair	Poor
850	725	575	475	400	200

Model 2088 Rival I

Sporting clays model is a 2.75" 12 gauge with 28" barrels and case-hardened receiver. Weight is about 7.6 lbs.

NIB	Exc.	V.G.	Good	Fair	Poor
1600	1300	850	600	400	200

Model 2089 Rival II

This 2.75" 12 gauge sporting clays gun has 30" barrels, one fixed and the other threaded for choke tubes. Blued receiver. Weight is about 7.9 lbs.

NIB	Exc.	V.G.	Good	Fair	Poor
1600	1300	850	600	400	200

Model 2070 Becada

This 3" 12 gauge gun developed for woodcock hunting features one fixed choke barrel and one barrel threaded for chokes. Barrel length is 23". Weight is about 6 lbs.

NIB	Exc.	V.G.	Good	Fair	Poor
850	725	575	475	400	200

Model 2531 Victoria I

This 12 gauge semi-automatic has a 3" chamber and 28" barrel with an internal choke tube system. The stock is oil finished walnut and the receiver is blued. Weight is about 6.8 lbs.

NIB	Exc.	V.G.	Good	Fair	Poor
600	500	400	300	200	100

Model 2532 Victoria II

Similar to above and available with a 26" or 28" barrel.

NIB	Exc.	V.G.	Good	Fair	Poor
625	525	425	325	225	100

Model 2532 Victoria II EXT

Similar to above but with a 24.5" barrel and external choke tube system.

NIB	Exc.	V.G.	Good	Fair	Poor
625	525	425	325	225	100

Model 2534

This lighter version of the 2532 weighs about 6.4 lbs. with a 26" barrel.

NIB	Exc.	V.G.	Good	Fair	Poor
625	525	425	325	225	100

Model 2533 Victoria LUX

Semi-automatic 3" 12 gauge features a brushed silver finish, scrollwork and gold mallard on the receiver. The barrel is 26" or 28" and weight is about 6.8 lbs.

NIB	Exc.	V.G.	Good	Fair	Poor
650	550	450	350	250	100

Model 2533 Victoria LUX EXT

As above but with 24.5" barrel and external choke tube system.

NIB	Exc.	V.G.	Good	Fair	Poor
650	550	450	350	250	100

Model 2535 Victoria Slug

Dedicated slug gun has fiber-optic rifle sights atop a 24", fixed cylinder barrel.

NIB	Exc.	V.G.	Good	Fair	Poor
650	550	450	350	250	100

LANCASTER, CHARLES
London, England

4-Barreled Pistol

A unique pistol for several reasons. It is chambered for the .476 rimfire cartridge and has four 6.25" barrels. The bore has a slightly twisted oval pattern that imparts a spin to the bullet. The barrels are hinged at the bottom and break downward for loading. It is a double-action type lockwork with a long, difficult trigger pull. The pistol is well made; and the caliber, suitably heavy to insure stopping power. The primary goal was military; and it was successful, seeing action in the Sudan campaigns of 1882 and 1885. This powerful weapon was also popular with big game hunters as a backup sidearm. The finish is blued, with checkered walnut grips. It is marked "Charles Lancaster (Patent) 151 New Bond St. London." This model was introduced in 1881. There are smaller-caliber versions of this pistol with shorter barrels. They are not as well known as the large-caliber version, and the values would be similar as their rarity would be balanced by the desirability of the large bore models.

NIB	Exc.	V.G.	Good	Fair	Poor
—	—	8000	5750	2500	1500

2-Barreled Pistol

Similar to the 4 barreled version, with only two superposed barrels chambered for a variety of calibers from .320 to .577. It was also chambered for the 20 gauge and .410 bore shotshell. The advantage to the 2 barreled pistol is that it is lighter and better balanced. The 2 barrel is less common than the 4 barrel version.

Courtesy James Rankin

NIB	Exc.	V.G.	Good	Fair	Poor
—	—	6000	3750	1750	1000

4-Barreled Shotgun

This company also produced a shotgun in the 4 barrel configuration. It is chambered for 12 or 16 gauge and has 28" barrels. The gun is, as one would imagine, quite heavy and poorly balanced; and it was not a great success.

NIB	Exc.	V.G.	Good	Fair	Poor
—	—	6250	4000	2000	1000

Bolt-Action Rifle

A high-grade sporting rifle chambered for various different calibers. The barrel is 24" in length; and the finish is blued with a classic-styled, hand-checkered walnut stock. This rifle was discontinued in 1936.

NIB	Exc.	V.G.	Good	Fair	Poor
—	3500	1900	1250	800	600

LANG, J.
London, England

Percussion Pistol

Chambered for .60 caliber percussion. It is a single-barreled, muzzle-loading pistol with a 3.25" barrel. This is essentially a defensive weapon that was well made, with Damascus barrels and an ornate engraved hammer and frame.

NIB	Exc.	V.G.	Good	Fair	Poor
—	—	4510	3000	1100	600

Gas Seal Revolver

Chambered for the .42 caliber percussion and has a 4.75" barrel. The unfluted cylinder holds 6 shots and is spring-loaded to be forced into the barrel when cocked, in order to obtain the "Gas Seal" feature desired. This revolver was well made and finished. It is lightly engraved, with a case-colored cylinder and a blued barrel and frame. The grips are finely checkered walnut, and the markings are "J.Lang 22 Cockspur St. London." This type of firearm was the forerunner of later designs such as the Russian Nagant. This revolver was manufactured in the 1850s.

NIB	Exc.	V.G.	Good	Fair	Poor
—	—	3000	1500	1000	550

LANGENHAN, FRIEDRICH
Zella Mehlis, Germany

NOTE: F.L. Selbstlader is not a manufacturer but the German designation for the self-loader used on pistols made by Friedrich Langenhan.

Langenhan Army Model

A blowback-operated semi-automatic pistol chambered for the 7.65mm Auto Pistol cartridge. It has a 4" barrel and a detachable magazine that holds 8 rounds. Weight is about 24 oz. The pistol was made with a separate breechblock that is held into the slide by a screw. This feature doomed this pistol to eventual failure as when this screw became worn, it could loosen when firing and allow the breechblock to pivot upwards—and the slide would then be propelled rearward and into the face of the shooter. This pistol was produced with wood grips.

Courtesy James Rankin

NIB	Exc.	V.G.	Good	Fair	Poor
—	375	300	250	175	100

Langenhan Open Model

A semi-automatic pistol that is similar to the Army Model with some minor variations, and an open window in the frame. Checkered hard rubber grips with "FL" logo on each side.

Courtesy James Rankin

NIB	Exc.	V.G.	Good	Fair	Poor
—	400	325	275	200	100

Langenhan Closed Model

Similar to the Open Model with closed frame and other minor variations.

Courtesy James Rankin

NIB	Exc.	V.G.	Good	Fair	Poor
—	400	325	275	200	100

Model 2

A blowback-operated semi-automatic pistol chambered for the 6.35mm cartridge. It has a 3" barrel and an 8-round detachable magazine. Weight is about 18 oz. The pistol fires by means of a concealed hammer, and the breechblock is separate from the rest of the slide and is held in place by a heavy crossbolt. The finish is blued, and the grips are molded checkered black plastic with the monogram "F.L." at the top. The slide is marked "Langenhan 6.35." This model was manufactured between 1921 and 1936.

Courtesy James Rankin

NIB	Exc.	V.G.	Good	Fair	Poor
—	375	300	250	200	100

Model 3

Similar to the Model 2 except that it is somewhat smaller. The barrel is 2.25" in length, and the butt is only large enough to house a 5-round detachable magazine. Weight is about 17 oz. The markings are the same with the addition of "Model 111" on the slide. This model was also manufactured until 1936.

NIB	Exc.	V.G.	Good	Fair	Poor
—	325	275	250	200	150

LAR MFG. CO.
West Jordan, Utah

Grizzly Mark I

A .357 Magnum, .45 ACP, 10mm, or .45 Winchester Magnum semi-automatic pistol with a 5.4", 6.5", 8", or 10" barrel, Millett sights, ambidextrous safety and 7-shot magazine. Parkerized, blued, or hard-chrome plated with rubber grips. Available with cartridge conversion units, telescope mounts, or a compensator. Weight is approximately 48 oz. Introduced in 1984.

NIB	Exc.	V.G.	Good	Fair	Poor
1400	150	950	700	400	200

Grizzly Mark II

As above, with fixed sights and without the ambidextrous safety. Manufactured in 1986.

NIB	Exc.	V.G.	Good	Fair	Poor
—	1300	1050	775	475	300

Grizzly Mark IV

Similar to the Mark I but chambered for the .44 Magnum cartridge. Barrel length is 5.4" or 6.5". Choice of blue or Parkerized finish.

NIB	Exc.	V.G.	Good	Fair	Poor
1500	1100	775	500	400	200

Grizzly Mark V

Same as above model but chambered for .50 AE cartridge. Empty weight is 56 oz. Add $200 for nickel finish.

NIB	Exc.	V.G.	Good	Fair	Poor
1950	1350	1000	650	425	200

Grizzly State Pistol

This is a limited edition of 50 Grizzly pistols with serial numbers that match the order in which each state was admitted into the union. Each pistol features the state outline, the state seal, and the name of the state engraved in gold. Supplied with a cherry wood fitted case with glass top. Chambered for .45 Win. Mag cartridge.

NIB	Exc.	V.G.	Good	Fair	Poor
3000	—	—	—	—	—

Grizzly 50 Big Boar

A single-shot breech loading rifle chambered for the .50 caliber BMG cartridge. The barrel is 36" in length and the rifle weighs approximately 30 lbs. **NOTE:** Add $100 for Parkerized finish. Add $250 for nickel frame, and $350 for full nickel finish.

NIB	Exc.	V.G.	Good	Fair	Poor
2350	2000	1550	1100	550	300

LASALLE
France

Slide-Action Shotgun

Chambered for 12 or 20 gauge and is offered with a 26", 28", or 30" barrel with improved-cylinder, modified, or full chokes. The receiver is alloy, anodized blue and the vent rib barrel is blued. The stock is checkered walnut.

NIB	Exc.	V.G.	Good	Fair	Poor
—	275	225	200	150	100

Semi-Automatic Shotgun

A gas-operated semi-automatic shotgun chambered for 12 gauge only, with the same barrel length and choke combinations as are available on the slide-action model. The receiver is also alloy, and the stock is checkered walnut.

NIB	Exc.	V.G.	Good	Fair	Poor
—	325	250	200	175	100

LASERAIM ARMS
Little Rock, Arkansas

Series I

Offered in 10mm or .45 ACP this single-action semi-automatic pistol is fitted with a 6" barrel with compensator. Adjustable rear sight. Stainless steel frame and barrel with matte black Teflon finish. Introduced in 1993. Magazine capacity for 10mm is 8 rounds and 7 rounds for .45 ACP. Weight is about 46 oz.

NIB	Exc.	V.G.	Good	Fair	Poor
650	550	400	300	200	100

Series II

This is similar to the Series I except this model has no compensator. It is fitted with a 5" barrel and stainless steel finish. A compact version has a 3-3/8" barrel. Introduced in 1993. Weight is 43 oz. for 5" barrel and 37 oz. for compact version.

NIB	Exc.	V.G.	Good	Fair	Poor
625	525	375	275	175	100

Series III

This model is similar to the Series II except it is offered with 5" barrel only with a dual port compensator. Introduced in 1994. Weight is about 43 oz.

NIB	Exc.	V.G.	Good	Fair	Poor
650	550	400	300	200	100

LAURONA
Eibar, Spain

This company has manufactured quality shotguns in Spain since 1941, but there has not been a U.S. importer for many years. The last importer was Galaxy Imports of Victoria, Texas, which brought several models of over/under and side-by-side shotguns into the country from about 1967 to early 1990s. One of the unique features of the standard Laurona over/under series was a double trigger system with each trigger acting as a non-selective single trigger. One trigger fired the bottom barrel first, then the top barrel; the other trigger fired the top barrel first, then the bottom barrel. We thank Thomas Barker of Galaxy Imports for the information and specifications in these listings.

Model 67

The first over/under Laurona chambered for 12 gauge only with double triggers and 28" vent rib barrels with extractors. The boxlock action and barrels are blued, and the stock is checkered walnut in 20 lpi skip line checkering.

NIB	Exc.	V.G.	Good	Fair	Poor
—	400	250	150	75	50

Model 71

Similar to the Model 67 with minor cosmetic changes and improvements to facilitate ease of manufacturing. Receiver is bright chromed with roll engraving depicting dogs on the right side and birds on the left. This model was imported and sold by Sears & Roebuck in about 1973 and 1974. The earlier models had traditional solid center ribbed blued barrels, the later models having black chrome finished solid ribbed barrels.

NIB	Exc.	V.G.	Good	Fair	Poor
—	450	300	200	100	75

MODEL 82

Similar to the Model 71 with auto-ejectors. Chambered for 12 gauge only. All barrels separated without center rib with Black Chrome finish and hard chrome bores with long forcing cones in chambers. Firing pins changed to traditional round type. Many internal parts improved for reliability. Checkering changed from skip diamond to standard 20 lpi. In most respects the 82 Models are representative of present-day Laurona over/under shotguns and will share most internal parts. **NOTE:** The Super Models listed have nickel-finish receivers featuring delicate fine scroll engraving with black chrome relief. All barrels have a very durable rust-resistant black chrome finish.

Model 82 Game

Barrels are 28" with 2.75" or 3" chambers, long forcing cones, hard chrome bores, 5mm rib, and chokes. Finish on barrels is black chrome with nickel receiver with Louis XVI style engraving. Tulip fore-end, field-style stock with plastic buttplate. Weighs approximately 7 lbs.

NIB	Exc.	V.G.	Good	Fair	Poor
—	550	400	250	125	100

Model 82 Super Game

Similar to the Model 82 Game except with more elaborate and very delicate engraving

NIB	Exc.	V.G.	Good	Fair	Poor
—	600	500	300	125	100

Model 82 Trap Combi

Similar to the Model 82 Game except for 28" or 29" barrels. The rib is 8mm. The Trap stock is fitted with a rubber recoil pad. Weight is about 7.4 lbs.

NIB	Exc.	V.G.	Good	Fair	Poor
—	700	500	350	300	200

Model 82 Trap Competition

Similar to the Model 82 Trap Combi except for the 13mm aluminum rib with long white sight. Engraving consist of motifs on sides of receiver. Beavertail fluted fore-end and Monte Carlo Trap stock with black rubber special Trap recoil pad. Weight is approximately 8 lbs.

NIB	Exc.	V.G.	Good	Fair	Poor
—	700	500	300	250	200

Model 82 Super Trap (U only)

Similar to the Model 82 Trap Competition except for special trap Pachmayr recoil pad with imitation leather face. Engraving very delicate fine scroll. Weight is 7 lbs., 12 oz.

NIB	Exc.	V.G.	Good	Fair	Poor
—	650	500	350	300	250

Model 82 Super Skeet

Similar to the Model 82 Super Trap except fitted with 28" barrels choked sheet with field-style buttstock with plastic buttplate. Weight is approximately 7 lbs.

NIB	Exc.	V.G.	Good	Fair	Poor
—	650	500	300	250	200

Model 82 Pigeon Competition

Similar to the Model 82 Trap Competition except fitted with 28" barrels. Recoil pad is special competition-style Pachmayr with imitation leather face. Weight is about 7 lbs., 13 oz.

NIB	Exc.	V.G.	Good	Fair	Poor
—	650	500	350	300	250

Model 82 Super Pigeon

Similar to the Model 82 Super Trap except fitted with 28" barrels. Weight is approximately 7 lbs., 9 oz.

NIB	Exc.	V.G.	Good	Fair	Poor
—	675	575	450	300	250

MODEL 83/84/85

NOTE: The Super Game models listed were available with an extra set of 20 gauge multi-choke barrels in 26" or 28". Add $400 to Exc. value for these barrels. For models with cast-on stocks for left-hand shooters add $50 to Exc. value.

Model 84S Super Game

Similar to the Model 82 Super Game except for the new single-selective trigger which is designated by "S" in the model number. Chambered for the 12 gauge 3" magnum with 28" barrels with 8mm rib. Weight is approximately 7 lbs.

NIB	Exc.	V.G.	Good	Fair	Poor
—	500	400	350	200	100

Model 83MG Super Game

Similar to the Model 82 Super Game except this model was the advent of Laurona's new multi-choke. CAUTION! The Laurona multi-choke is not compatible with any other brand of screw-in chokes because of the black chrome plating on the metric threads. Do not attempt to interchange with other guns. Barrel for this model in 12 gauge are 28" in length and for the 20 gauge 26" or 28". Both are chambered for the 3" shell. Rib is 8mm. Weight is about 7 lbs.

NIB	Exc.	V.G.	Good	Fair	Poor
—	700	450	350	200	100

Model 85MS Super Game

Similar to the Model 83MG Super Game except for the single-selective trigger. Chambered for the 12 or 20 gauge 3" Magnum. Weight is about 7 lbs.

NIB	Exc.	V.G.	Good	Fair	Poor
—	750	650	450	250	200

Model 84S Super Trap

Single-selective trigger with 29" barrels. Chambered for 2.75" shells with long forcing cones. The aluminum rib is 13mm wide. Auto ejectors. Receiver is nickel plated with fine scroll engraving with black chrome relief. Beavertail forearm and choice of Monte Carlo or standard Trap stock. Weight is about 7 lbs., 12 oz.

NIB	Exc.	V.G.	Good	Fair	Poor
—	1000	750	550	350	250

Model 85MS Super Trap

Similar to the Model 82S Super Trap except multi-choke in bottom barrel with fixed choke on top barrel. Weight is about 7 lbs., 12 oz.

NIB	Exc.	V.G.	Good	Fair	Poor
—	1100	900	700	500	300

Model 85MS Super Pigeon

Similar to the Model 85MS Super Trap except with 28" barrels with fixed IM choke on top barrel and multi-choke on bottom barrel. Intended for live bird competition. Weight is about 7 lbs., 4 oz.

NIB	Exc.	V.G.	Good	Fair	Poor
—	1100	900	800	600	300

Model 85MS Special Sporting

Similar to the Model 85MS Super Pigeon except for field-style buttstock with plastic buttplate. Intended for upland game. Weight is approximately 7 lbs., 4 oz.

NIB	Exc.	V.G.	Good	Fair	Poor
—	1100	900	800	600	300

Model 84S Super Skeet

Similar to the Model 85MS Special Sporting except choked skeet and skeet. Weight is approximately 7 lbs.

NIB	Exc.	V.G.	Good	Fair	Poor
—	950	900	800	600	300

LAURONA OVER/UNDER MODELS SILHOUETTE 300

These guns are basically the same as the Super series above with these exceptions: They are readily identified by the white and black chrome stripped receiver with the model engraved on the side of the receiver. Barrels are multi-choked on both bores and have 11mm steel ribs. **NOTE:** Two types of chokes were used. Some guns came with knurl head-type as in the Super models and others were made with the flush invector style. A later option for ease of changing chokes is the knurl long choke, which is a flush-type with a knurl head added. Both later type chokes, the flush and the knurl long-type, can be used in the early multi-choke models with some extension showing.

Silhouette 300 Trap

This model has barrels 29" with 2.75" chambers and long forcing cones with hard chrome bores and 11mm rib. Beavertail forearm and straight comb trap stock fitted with a ventilated black rubber recoil pad are standard. Weight is approximately 8 lbs.

NIB	Exc.	V.G.	Good	Fair	Poor
—	1100	800	500	200	100

Silhouette 300 Sporting Clays

Similar to the Model 300 Trap except with 28" barrels. Some guns came with 3" chambers. The buttstock is field style with plastic buttplate or hard rubber sporting clays pad. Weight is about 8 lbs.

NIB	Exc.	V.G.	Good	Fair	Poor
—	950	700	600	200	100

Silhouette 300 Ultra Magnum

Similar to the Model 300 Sporting Clays except with 3.5" chamber in 12 gauge for waterfowl hunting. Weight is about 7 lbs., 8 oz.

NIB	Exc.	V.G.	Good	Fair	Poor
—	1000	800	500	275	150

LAURONA SIDE-BY-SIDE SHOTGUNS

Models with "X" after the model number were made after 1975 and finished with non-rusting black chrome on barrels and action with hard chrome bores. Guns were made in 12, 16, and 20 bore. Smaller gauges were made on special order. Side-by-side shotguns were discontinued by Laurona after 1978 to concentrate on the over/under market.

Model 11

Boxlock action with triple Greener-type round crossbolt. Independent firing pins bushed into the face of the action. Barrels of "Bellota" steel. Made in 12, 16, and 20 gauge.

NIB	Exc.	V.G.	Good	Fair	Poor
—	400	350	300	200	150

Model 13

Similar to the Model 11 except with Purdey-type bolting system. Extractor of double radius.

NIB	Exc.	V.G.	Good	Fair	Poor
—	400	350	300	200	150

Model 13X

Barrels and action finished in black chrome and hard chrome bores.

NIB	Exc.	V.G.	Good	Fair	Poor
—	500	400	300	250	200

Model 13E

Similar to the Model 13 except with automatic ejectors.

NIB	Exc.	V.G.	Good	Fair	Poor
—	500	400	300	250	200

Model 13XE

Similar to the Model 13E except black chrome finish and hard chrome bores.

NIB	Exc.	V.G.	Good	Fair	Poor
—	600	500	400	350	300

Model 15 Economic Pluma

Similar to the Model 13 except first model has hard chrome bores.

NIB	Exc.	V.G.	Good	Fair	Poor
—	450	400	300	250	200

Model 15X

Similar to the Model 15 except black chrome finish and hard chrome bores.

NIB	Exc.	V.G.	Good	Fair	Poor
—	500	400	300	250	200

Model 15E Economic Pluma

Similar to the Model 15 except with automatic ejectors.

NIB	Exc.	V.G.	Good	Fair	Poor
—	550	450	350	300	250

Model 15XE

Similar to the Model 15E except black chrome finish and hard chrome bores.

NIB	Exc.	V.G.	Good	Fair	Poor
—	600	500	400	350	300

Model 52 Pluma

Boxlock action with back of action scalloped and artistically engraved in fine English-style scroll. Churchill rib and double radius extractor. Hard chrome bores. Weight is about 6 lbs.

NIB	Exc.	V.G.	Good	Fair	Poor
—	750	650	500	400	350

Model 52E Pluma

Similar to the Model 52 except with automatic ejectors. Weight is approximately 6 lbs., 2 oz.

NIB	Exc.	V.G.	Good	Fair	Poor
—	850	750	600	500	450

LAURONA SIDE-BY-SIDE SIDELOCKS

Model 103

Blued sidelock with some light border engraving. Triple Purdey-type bolting system. Extractor of double radius. Barrels of special "Bellota" steel with hard chrome bores. Made in 12, 16, and 20 gauge.

NIB	Exc.	V.G.	Good	Fair	Poor
—	900	800	700	500	400

Model 103E

Similar to the Model 103 except with automatic ejectors.

NIB	Exc.	V.G.	Good	Fair	Poor
—	1000	800	700	600	500

Model 104X

Case-colored sidelocks with Purdey-type bolting system. Extractor with double radius. Fine double safety sidelocks. Gas relief vents. Articulated trigger. Hard chrome bores. Demi-block barrels of special "Bellota" steel. Black chrome barrels. Produced in 12, 16, and 20 gauge with smaller bores available on special order.

NIB	Exc.	V.G.	Good	Fair	Poor
—	1200	1000	800	700	600

Model 104XE

Same as Model 104X but with Holland automatic selective ejectors.

NIB	Exc.	V.G.	Good	Fair	Poor
—	1350	1100	900	800	700

Model 105X Feather

Same as the Model 104X but with concave rib. Weight in 12 gauge is approximately 6 lbs., 2 oz.

NIB	Exc.	V.G.	Good	Fair	Poor
—	1250	1000	800	700	600

Model 105XE Feather

Same as Model 105X but with Holland automatic selective ejectors.

NIB	Exc.	V.G.	Good	Fair	Poor
—	1400	1250	1000	800	750

Model 502 Feather

Fine sidelock with Purdey-type bolting system. Very fine double safety sidelocks, hand detachable. Gas relief vents. Holland automatic selective ejectors. Articulated trigger. Inside hard chromed demi-block barrels of special "Bellota" steel. Outside Black Chrome finish. Fine English-style scroll engraving. Marble gray or Laurona Imperial finish. Churchill or concave type rib. Weight: 12 gauge is approximately 6.25 lbs. Offered in 12, 16, and 20 gauge.

NIB	Exc.	V.G.	Good	Fair	Poor
—	2200	1800	1600	1500	1400

Model 801 Deluxe

Same as the Model 502 Feather but engraving is a true deluxe Renaissance style. Fully handmade with Imperial finish. First grade walnut stock and forearm.

NIB	Exc.	V.G.	Good	Fair	Poor
—	4400	4000	3750	2750	2250

Model 802 Eagle

Same as the Model 801 Deluxe except highly artistic base relief hand engraving of hunting scenes.

NIB	Exc.	V.G.	Good	Fair	Poor
—	5000	4500	4000	3500	3250

LAW ENFORCEMENT ORDNANCE CORP.
Ridgeway, Pennsylvania

Striker 12

A semi-automatic shotgun designed for self-defense. It is chambered for 12 gauge and has an 18.25" cylinder bored barrel. The unique feature about this gun is its 12-round drum magazine. The barrel is shrouded, and the stock folds. A fixed-stock model is also available. This gun was introduced primarily as a law enforcement tool, and the original models had 12" barrels and were legal for law enforcement agencies and Class 3 licensed individuals only. This shotgun is no longer imported into the U.S. This shotgun is now classified as a Class III weapon and subject to restrictions of the B.A.T.F.E. Be certain that the particular shotgun is transferable before purchase. If there are any questions contact B.A.T.F.E. before purchase. Striker 12 shotguns in excellent condition may sell for as much as $1500.

LAZZERONI ARMS COMPANY
Tucson, Arizona

Model 2000ST-F

This model, as with all Lazzeroni models, is chambered for the company's own proprietary calibers. The 6.17 (.243) Spitfire, 6.53 (.257) Scramjet, 6.71 (.264) Phantom, 7.21 (.284) Tomahawk, 7.82 (.308) Patriot, and the 8.59 (.338) Galaxy. Fitted with a 27" match grade barrel with fully adjustable trigger, and removable muzzlebrake. Conventional fiberglass stock.

NIB	Exc.	V.G.	Good	Fair	Poor
3700	3000	2200	1500	800	300

Model 2000ST-W

As above but fitted with a conventional black wood laminate stock. No longer offered.

NIB	Exc.	V.G.	Good	Fair	Poor
4800	3900	2700	1750	1000	350

Model 2000ST-FW

As above but fitted with a conventional fiberglass stock and an additional black wood laminate stock. No longer offered.

NIB	Exc.	V.G.	Good	Fair	Poor
5300	4250	3000	2000	1200	500

Model 2000ST-28

This model is a 28" barrel variation of the Model 2000 ST chambered for the 7.82 Warbird cartridge. Introduced in 1999.

NIB	Exc.	V.G.	Good	Fair	Poor
5300	4250	3000	2000	1200	500

Model 2000SLR

This model has a 28" extra-heavy fluted barrel with conventional fiberglass stock. Chambered for the 6.53 Scramjet, 7.21 Firehawk, and the 7.82 Warbird.

NIB	Exc.	V.G.	Good	Fair	Poor
3900	3100	2300	1600	900	400

Model 2000SP-F

This model is fitted with a 23" match grade barrel and Lazzeroni thumbhole fiberglass stock. Chambered for all Lazzeroni calibers.

NIB	Exc.	V.G.	Good	Fair	Poor
3700	3000	2200	1500	800	300

Model 2000SP-W

Same as above but with black wood laminate thumbhole stock. No longer offered.

NIB	Exc.	V.G.	Good	Fair	Poor
4800	3900	2700	1750	1000	350

Model 2000SP-FW

Same as above model but supplied with two stocks: a thumbhole fiberglass stock and a black wood laminate stock. No longer offered.

NIB	Exc.	V.G.	Good	Fair	Poor
5300	4250	3000	2000	1200	500

Model 2000SA

Designed as a lightweight mountain rifle. Chambered for .308, .284, or .338 propriety calibers. Barrel length is 24" and fluted except for .338 caliber. Offered in both right- and left-hand models. Stock has Monte Carlo cheekpiece. Weight is approximately 6.8 lbs.

NIB	Exc.	V.G.	Good	Fair	Poor
4000	3100	2300	1600	900	400

Model 2000DG

Offered in Saturn and Meteor calibers only and fitted with a 24" barrel this rifle weight about 10 lbs. Fibergrain stock finish, removable muzzlebrake, and threaded muzzle protector are standard.

NIB	Exc.	V.G.	Good	Fair	Poor
4400	3500	2700	1850	1050	450

Model 700ST

This rifle is built around a modified Remington 700 action and fitted with a 26" barrel. Chambered for all Lazzeroni long-action calibers except Saturn and Meteor. Weight is about 8 lbs. synthetic stock.

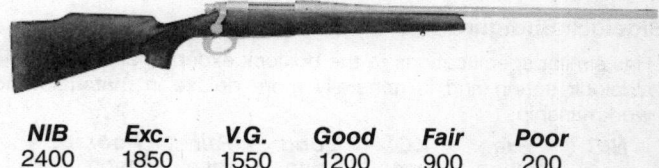

NIB	Exc.	V.G.	Good	Fair	Poor
2400	1850	1550	1200	900	200

Swarovski P.H. 3-12x50 Rifle

NIB	Exc.	V.G.	Good	Fair	Poor
1400	1150	925	600	400	150

Savage 16 LZ

Introduced in 2001 this model features a 24" stainless steel barrel, synthetic stock. It is chambered for the 7.82 Patriot and 7.21 Tomahawk cartridges. Weight is approximately 6.8 lbs. Base price is listed.

NIB	Exc.	V.G.	Good	Fair	Poor
900	775	500	375	200	100

Sako TRG-S

This model is fitted with a 26" stainless steel barrel and synthetic stock. It is chambered for the 7.82 Warbird and 7.21 Firebird cartridges. Weight is about 7.9 lbs. Base price is listed.

NIB	Exc.	V.G.	Good	Fair	Poor
1400	1150	925	600	400	150

Model 2005 Global Hunter

Features include a precision CNC-machined 17R stainless steel receiver; stainless steel, match-grade button-barrel; Jewel competition trigger; titanium firing pin; slim line graphite/composite stock; precision-machined aluminum-alloy floorplate/trigger guard assembly; Vais muzzle brake; and Limbsaver recoil pad. Base price is listed.

NIB	Exc.	V.G.	Good	Fair	Poor
6900	5900	4700	3250	1500	500

LE FORGERON
Liege, Belgium

Model 6020 Double Rifle

A boxlock-actioned side-by-side rifle that is chambered for the 9.3x74R cartridge. It has 25" barrels with double triggers and automatic ejectors. The finish is blued, and the pistol grip stock is checkered walnut.

NIB	Exc.	V.G.	Good	Fair	Poor
—	6100	4950	4400	3300	1250

Model 6040

Simply the Model 6020 with false sideplates. All other specifications are the same.

NIB	Exc.	V.G.	Good	Fair	Poor
—	6900	5750	4950	3850	1500

Model 6030

A double rifle that has a true sidelock action and is engraved. It has a deluxe French walnut stock.

NIB	Exc.	V.G.	Good	Fair	Poor
—	11000	8800	8000	6100	2000

Boxlock Shotgun

This is a side-by-side, double-barreled shotgun chambered for 20 or 28 gauge. The barrel lengths are optional, as are the choke combinations. This gun has a single-selective trigger and automatic ejectors. It is engraved and blued, with a deluxe French walnut stock. **NOTE:** False sideplates add 20 percent.

NIB	Exc.	V.G.	Good	Fair	Poor
—	5500	4400	3600	2500	1000

Sidelock Shotgun

Has similar specifications to the boxlock except that it has a true sidelock action and is generally more deluxe in materials and workmanship.

NIB	Exc.	V.G.	Good	Fair	Poor
—	13000	12000	9350	7250	2500

LE FRANCAIS
Francais D'Armes et Cycles de St. Etienne
St. Etienne, France

See—Manufrance

Gaulois

An 8mm palm pistol designed by Brun-Latrige and manufactured by Le Francais. Furnished with a 5-round magazine.

Courtesy James Rankin

NIB	Exc.	V.G.	Good	Fair	Poor
—	—	950	550	400	300

Le Francais Model 28 (Type Armee)

A unique pistol chambered for the 9mm Browning cartridge. It is a large pistol, with a 5" barrel that was hinged with a tip-up breech. This is a blowback-operated semi-automatic pistol that has no extractor. The empty cases are blown out of the breech by gas pressure. The one feature about this pistol that is desirable is that it is possible to tip the barrel breech forward like a shotgun and load cartridges singly, while holding the contents of the magazine in reserve. This weapon has fixed sights and a blued finish, with checkered walnut grips. It was manufactured in 1928.

Courtesy James Rankin

NIB	Exc.	V.G.	Good	Fair	Poor
—	1250	950	750	500	200

Police Model (Type Policeman)

A blowback-operated, double-action semi-automatic that is chambered for the .25 ACP cartridge. It has a 3.5" barrel and a 7-round magazine. It has the same hinged barrel feature of the Model 28 and is blued, with fixed sights and Ebonite grips. This model was manufactured 1913 to 1914.

Courtesy James Rankin

NIB	Exc.	V.G.	Good	Fair	Poor
—	800	650	450	300	150

Officer's Model (Pocket Model)

May also be referred to a "Staff Model". Also a blowback-operated semi-automatic chambered for the .25 ACP cartridge. It has a 2.5" barrel and a concealed hammer. It has fixed sights and the finish is blued. The grips are Ebonite. This model was manufactured between 1914 and 1938 in two variations: early and second type.

Courtesy James Rankin

Early variation Pocket

Courtesy James Rankin

Second variation Pocket

NIB	Exc.	V.G.	Good	Fair	Poor
—	300	250	200	150	100

Target Model (Type Champion)

Chambered for 6.35mm cartridge and fitted with a 6" barrel. Extended magazine base is for grip purchase, not additional cartridges.

Courtesy James Rankin

NIB	Exc.	V.G.	Good	Fair	Poor
—	900	700	550	400	275

LE MAT
Paris, France

LeMat

Has a somewhat unique background that makes it a bit controversial among collectors. It is a foreign-made firearm manufactured in Paris, France, as well as in Birmingham, England. It was designed and patented by an American, Jean Alexander Le Mat of New Orleans, Louisiana; and it was purchased for use by the Confederate States of America and used in the Civil War. This is a curious firearm as it is a huge weapon that has two barrels. The top 6.5" barrel is chambered for .42 caliber percussion and is supplied by a 9-shot unfluted cylinder that revolves on a 5", .63 caliber, smoothbore barrel that doubles as the cylinder axis pin. These two barrels are held together by a front and a rear ring. The rear sight is a notch in the nose of the hammer, and there is an attached ramrod on the side of the top barrel. The weapon is marked "Lemat and Girards Patent, London." The finish is blued, with checkered walnut grips. There were fewer than 3,000 manufactured, of which approximately one-half were purchased by the Confederate States of America. They were made between 1856 and 1865.

Courtesy Milwaukee Public Museum, Milwaukee, Wisconsin

NIB	Exc.	V.G.	Good	Fair	Poor
—	—	30000	25000	7500	1750

Baby LeMat

Similar in appearance (though a good deal smaller in size) to the standard model pistol. It is chambered for .32 caliber percussion and has a 4.25" top barrel and a .41 caliber smoothbore lower barrel. The cylinder is unfluted and holds 9 shots. The barrel is marked "Systeme Le Mat Bte s.g.d.g. Paris." It has British proofmarks and is blued, with checkered walnut grips. This is the scarcest model Le Mat, as there were only an estimated 100 manufactured and used by the Confederate States of America in the Civil War.

NIB	Exc.	V.G.	Good	Fair	Poor
—	—	28500	22000	1100	3300

LeMat Revolving Carbine

Chambered for the centerfire, rimfire cartridges, or percussion. Barrels are half round half octagon and 20" in length. Chambered for a variety of calibers but in percussion usually .42 caliber with a .62 caliber smoothbore lower barrel.

Courtesy Little John's Auction Service, Inc., Paul Goodwin photo

NIB	Exc.	V.G.	Good	Fair	Poor
—	—	31500	25000	11000	3000

LE PAGE SA.
Liege, Belgium

Pinfire Revolver

This company was in the business of revolver manufacture in the 1850s, producing a .40 caliber pinfire revolver that was similar to the Lefauchaux and other pinfires of the day. The barrel lengths vary, and the unfluted cylinder holds 6 shots. These pistols are double-action and are sometimes found with ornate, but somewhat crude engraving. The finish is blued, with wood grips. The quality of these weapons is fair. They were serviceable; but the ammunition created somewhat of a problem, as it is rather fragile and difficult to handle with the protruding primer pin to contend with.

NIB	Exc.	V.G.	Good	Fair	Poor
—	—	775	325	200	125

Semi-Automatic Pistol

A semi-automatic pistol with an open top slide, and exposed hammer. It is chambered for the 6.35mm, 7.65mm, 9mm Short, and 9mm Long cartridges. It has a large grip with finger grooves.

NIB	Exc.	V.G.	Good	Fair	Poor
—	875	675	525	300	200

Pocket Pistol

A semi-automatic pistol in caliber 6.35mm. Checkered hard rubber grips with crossed sword and pistol logo of Le Page on each side of the grip.

NIB	Exc.	V.G.	Good	Fair	Poor
—	325	275	225	175	75

LEBEAU COURALLY
Liege, Belgium

This company has been in business since 1865 and has made more guns for royalty than any other gun company in the world. The prices listed are for guns without engraving. There are other extra-cost options that will affect price. All guns are built to order, and there is virtually no upper end for the values to these infrequently-encountered guns. Values are certainly well in excess of $30,000 for any model in Very Good or better condition.

LEE FIREARMS CO.
Milwaukee, Wisconsin

Lee Single-Shot Carbine

A rare single-shot break-open carbine that pivots to the right side for loading. It is chambered for the .44 rimfire cartridge and has a 21.5" barrel with a hammer mounted in the center of the frame. The carbine has a walnut buttstock but no forearm and is marked "Lee's Firearms Co. Milwaukee, Wisc." There were approximately 450 manufactured between 1863 and 1865. There are few surviving examples, and one should be wary of fakes.

NIB	Exc.	V.G.	Good	Fair	Poor
—	—	6500	2200	900	400

Lee Sporting Rifle

Similar to the military carbine except that it has a longer octagonal barrel. The barrel length was varied, and there were more of these manufactured. The survival rate appears to have been better than for the carbine model.

NIB	Exc.	V.G.	Good	Fair	Poor
—	—	1750	700	300	150

LEECH & RIGDON
Greensboro, Georgia

Leech & Rigdon Revolver

This Confederate revolver was patterned after the 1851 Colt Navy. It is chambered for .36 caliber percussion and has a 6-shot unfluted cylinder. The 7.5" barrel is part-octagonal and has a loading lever beneath it. The frame is open-topped; and the finish is blued, with brass grip straps and walnut one-piece grips. The barrel is marked "Leech & Rigdon CSA." There were approximately 1,500 revolvers manufactured in 1863 and 1864. These were all contracted for by the Confederacy and are considered to be a prime acquisition for collectors. Beware of fakes!

NIB	Exc.	V.G.	Good	Fair	Poor
—	—	42000	27500	11000	2750

LEFAUCHAUX, CASIMER & EUGENE
Paris, France

Pinfire Revolver

The pinfire ignition system was invented by Casimir Lefauchaux in 1828 but was not widely used until the 1850s. It consists of a smooth rimless case that contains the powder charge and a percussion cap. A pin protrudes from the side of this case at the rear and when struck by the hammer is driven into the cap, thereby igniting the charge and firing the weapon. The pistols for this cartridge are slotted at the end of the cylinder to allow the pins to protrude and be struck by the downward blow of the hammer. This particular revolver is chambered for .43 caliber and has a 5.25" barrel. The cylinder holds 6 shots; and the finish is blued, with checkered walnut grips. This revolver was manufactured after 1865 and was selected for service by the French military.

NIB	Exc.	V.G.	Good	Fair	Poor
—	—	—	575	250	125

LEFEVER ARMS CO.
Syracuse, New York

Founded by Dan Lefever, who was a pioneer in the field of breech-loading firearms. This company was founded in 1884, with Lefever as the president. He was referred to as "Uncle Dan" within the firearms industry. He was responsible for many improvements in the double-barrel shotgun design. He developed the automatic hammerless system in the late 1880s. He also developed a compensating action that allowed simple adjustments to compensate for action wear. In 1901 he was forced out of the company and organized another company—the D.M. Lefever, Sons & Company—also in Syracuse. Dan Lefever died in 1906, and his new company went out of business. The original company was acquired by Ithaca in 1916. They continued to produce Lefever guns until 1948.

Sideplated Shotgun

A double-barrel, side-by-side shotgun chambered for 10, 12, 16, or 20 gauge. It was offered with 26", 28", 30", or 32" barrels with various choke combinations. The barrels are either Damascus or fluid steel. Damascus guns have become collectible and in better condition—very good to excellent—can bring nearly the same price as the fluid-steel guns. It features a fractional sidelock because the hammers were mounted in the frame and the sears and cocking indicators were mounted on the sideplates. After serial number 25,000, the entire locking mechanism was frame mounted and only the cocking indicators remained on the side plates. Double triggers are standard. The finish is blued, with a checkered walnut stock. There are a number of variations that differ in the amount of ornamentation and the quality of materials and workmanship utilized in their construction. Automatic ejectors are represented by the letter "E" after the respective grade designation. This shotgun was manufactured between 1885 and 1919. We strongly recommend that a qualified appraisal be secured if a transaction is contemplated. There was also an Optimus Grade and a Thousand Dollar Grade offered. These are extremely high-grade, heavily ornamented firearms inlaid with precious metals. They are extremely rare, and evaluating them on a general basis is impossible. **NOTE:** For all models listed: 20 gauge add 25 percent. Single-selective trigger add 10 percent.

H Grade

NIB	Exc.	V.G.	Good	Fair	Poor
—	1600	1250	950	550	350

HE Grade

NIB	Exc.	V.G.	Good	Fair	Poor
—	2400	1900	1550	900	650

G Grade

NIB	Exc.	V.G.	Good	Fair	Poor
—	1900	1500	1200	700	425

GE Grade

NIB	Exc.	V.G.	Good	Fair	Poor
—	2800	2150	1800	1000	650

F Grade

NIB	Exc.	V.G.	Good	Fair	Poor
—	2400	1900	1550	900	650

FE Grade

NIB	Exc.	V.G.	Good	Fair	Poor
—	3400	2650	2200	1300	800

E Grade

NIB	Exc.	V.G.	Good	Fair	Poor
—	3700	2950	2400	1400	900

EE Grade

Courtesy Rock Island Auction Company

NIB	Exc.	V.G.	Good	Fair	Poor
—	7500	6500	3100	1850	1150

D Grade

NIB	Exc.	V.G.	Good	Fair	Poor
—	4700	3650	3000	1800	1100

DS Grade

NIB	Exc.	V.G.	Good	Fair	Poor
—	1450	1150	900	500	300

DE Grade

Courtesy Rock Island Auction Company

NIB	Exc.	V.G.	Good	Fair	Poor
—	7250	5750	4600	2800	1750

DSE Grade

NIB	Exc.	V.G.	Good	Fair	Poor
—	1750	1400	1150	700	500

C Grade

NIB	Exc.	V.G.	Good	Fair	Poor
—	8500	5700	4200	2400	1500

CE Grade

NIB	Exc.	V.G.	Good	Fair	Poor
—	9500	6950	5650	3400	2100

B Grade

NIB	Exc.	V.G.	Good	Fair	Poor
—	10500	7700	5300	3200	2000

BE Grade

NIB	Exc.	V.G.	Good	Fair	Poor
—	15000	10000	6600	4000	2500

A Grade

NIB	Exc.	V.G.	Good	Fair	Poor
—	24000	18000	10100	6000	3700

AA Grade

NIB	Exc.	V.G.	Good	Fair	Poor
—	38000	22000	13200	8000	5000

LEFEVER, D. M. & SONS COMPANY
Syracuse, New York

In 1901, when Dan Lefever was forced out of Lefever Arms, the company he had founded in 1884, he organized another company to produce a line of high-grade, boxlock side-by-side doubles. He operated Lefever, D.M. & Sons until his death in 1906, at which time the firm closed its doors. During this five-year period, approximately 1,200 shotguns were made in several grades. This makes them quite rare and difficult to evaluate. It is important to get an appraisal from a trusted source before buying or selling. Prices shown are average values.

Lefever Double-Barrel Shotgun

A side-by-side, double-barrel shotgun chambered for 12, 16, or 20 gauge. It was offered with various-length barrels and choke combinations that were made to order. It features double triggers and automatic ejectors. A single-selective trigger was available as an option. The finish is blued, with a checkered walnut stock. The individual grades differ in the amount of ornamentation and the general quality of the materials and workmanship utilized in their construction. This model was discontinued in 1906. There are an "Optimus" and an "Uncle Dan" grade, which are top-of-the-line models, that features extremely high quality in materials and workmanship and a great deal of ornamentation. This firearm is extremely rare and seldom found in today's market. It is impossible to evaluate it on a general basis. **NOTE:** For all models listed: 20 gauge add 50 percent. Single-selective trigger add 25 percent.

O Excelsior Grade—Extractors

NIB	Exc.	V.G.	Good	Fair	Poor
—	2750	2200	1750	950	700

Excelsior Grade—Auto Ejectors

NIB	Exc.	V.G.	Good	Fair	Poor
—	3250	2700	2100	1250	900

F Grade, No. 9

NIB	Exc.	V.G.	Good	Fair	Poor
—	3700	2950	2350	1500	1100

E Grade, No. 8

NIB	Exc.	V.G.	Good	Fair	Poor
—	4750	4200	3200	2400	1700

D Grade, No. 7

NIB	Exc.	V.G.	Good	Fair	Poor
—	5800	5000	4000	2750	2000

C Grade, No. 6

NIB	Exc.	V.G.	Good	Fair	Poor
—	8000	7000	6000	3000	2500

B Grade, No. 5

NIB	Exc.	V.G.	Good	Fair	Poor
—	8700	8000	7000	3500	3000

AA Grade, No. 4

NIB	Exc.	V.G.	Good	Fair	Poor
—	11500	10500	9000	4200	2750

LEFEVER ARMS COMPANY, INC. (ITHACA)
Syracuse, New York

During 1916, the Ithaca Gun company purchased the gunmaking assets of the Syracuse, New York based, Lefever Arms Company. Between then and World War I, they continued to manufacture the same sideplate gun that had been made in Syracuse until about 1919 when they were discontinued. Prices for those guns are listed in the Sideplated Shotgun section. During 1921, Ithaca Gun Company, under the name the Lefever Arms Company, Inc., introduced a line of lower costs, boxlock guns. Eventually, six different models were produced. Ithaca's

Lefever guns were produced in 12, 16, and 20 gauges, and in .410 bore. Twenty gauge guns often command a price premium of 50 percent; a .410 bore gun may command up to a 200 percent premium.

Nitro Special

A side-by-side, double-barrel shotgun chambered for 12, 16, or 20 gauge, as well as .410. The barrels were offered in lengths of 26" to 32" with various choke combinations. It features a boxlock action with double triggers and extractors standard. The finish is blued, with a case-colored receiver and a checkered walnut stock. This model was manufactured between 1921 and 1948 and, incredible as it may seem, its price at introduction was $29. Add 100+ percent for .410. **NOTE:** Single-selective trigger add $100. Automatic ejectors add $200.

NIB	Exc.	V.G.	Good	Fair	Poor
—	600	400	250	200	100

Long Range Single-Barrel Trap and Field (Model 2)

Manufactured from 1927 to 1947, the Model 2 was a single-barrel gun with no rib. Like the Nitro Special, it had walnut stocks that were line cut checkered at the grip area of the buttstock and on the fore-end.

NIB	Exc.	V.G.	Good	Fair	Poor
—	500	300	200	150	100

Single-Barrel Trap Ventilated Rib (Model 3)

Manufactured from 1927 to 1942, the Model 3 was a single-barrel gun with the same ventilated rib that was used on the "Knick" trap gun. The walnut stocks had line cut checkering at the grip area of the buttstock and on the fore-end.

NIB	Exc.	V.G.	Good	Fair	Poor
—	1200	500	250	150	100

Double-Barrel Ventilated Rib Trap (Model 4)

Manufactured during 1929 but cataloged until 1939, the Model 4 was a double-barrel gun with a ventilated rib barrel. The walnut stocks had line cut checkering at the grip area of the buttstock and on the beavertail fore-end. Only about 200 units were produced.

NIB	Exc.	V.G.	Good	Fair	Poor
—	2000	1200	1000	700	300

A Grade (Model 5)

Manufactured from 1936 to 1939, the A Grade was a double-barreled gun. The walnut stocks had pointed checkering cut at the grip area of the buttstock and on the splinter fore-end. A line engraving outlined its nicely sculptured frame. **NOTE:** Single trigger add $200, automatic ejectors add $200, beavertail fore-end add $300.

NIB	Exc.	V.G.	Good	Fair	Poor
—	900	600	400	300	100

Skeet Special (Model 6)

Manufactured from 1936 to 1939, the A Grade was a double-barreled gun. The walnut stocks had pointed checkering cut at the grip area of the buttstock and on the beavertail fore-end. A beavertail fore-end, single trigger, automatic ejectors, a recoil pad, and ivory center and front sight were standard. The frame was sculptured and line engraved like the Model 5.

NIB	Exc.	V.G.	Good	Fair	Poor
—	1500	1200	1000	400	100

LEMAN, H. E.
Lancaster, Pennsylvania

Leman Militia Rifle

A .58 caliber percussion muzzleloader that has a 33" round barrel. The stock is full-length and is held on by two barrel bands. There is a ramrod mounted under the barrel. The trim is brass and the barrel is browned, with a case-colored lock. The lock is marked "H.E.Leman/Lancaster, Pa." There were approximately 500 manufactured between 1860 and 1864. They are believed to have been used by the Pennsylvania State Militia in the Civil War.

Courtesy Milwaukee Public Museum, Milwaukee, Wisconsin

NIB	Exc.	V.G.	Good	Fair	Poor
—	—	4750	2000	750	300

LEONARD, G.
Charlestown, Massachusetts

Pepperbox

A .31-caliber, four-barreled pepperbox with a concealed hammer. The barrels are 3.25" in length. There is a ring trigger used to cock the weapon, while a smaller trigger located outside the ring is used to fire the weapon. The barrels on this pistol do not revolve. There is a revolving striker inside the frame that turns to fire each chamber. The barrels must be removed for loading and capping purposes. The frame is iron and blued, with engraving. The rounded grips are walnut. The barrel is stamped "G. Leonard Jr. Charlestown". There were fewer than 200 manufactured in 1849 and 1850.

NIB	Exc.	V.G.	Good	Fair	Poor
—	—	1850	725	300	150

LES, INC.
Skokie, Illinois

Rogak P-18

A 9mm caliber double-action semi-automatic pistol with a 5.5" barrel and 18-shot magazine. Stainless steel. Discontinued.

NIB	Exc.	V.G.	Good	Fair	Poor
—	380	350	295	200	150

LEWIS MACHINE & TOOL COMPANY (LMT)
Milan, Illinois

This company was founded in 1980 and manufactures a wide range of military-type rifles. Originally, the firm made weapons for law enforcement and government agencies in the U.S., but now makes products for the civilian community and for foreign armed forces.

.308 Modular Weapon System (MWSE)

Gas piston operating system with monolithic rail system with one-piece upper receiver, free floated, cryogenically treated barrel which can quickly be changed to another size, two-stage trigger, 20-shot magazine.

NIB	Exc.	V.G.	Good	Fair	Poor
2500	2000	1550	1200	750	400

Defender Standard Model 16

Standard flattop upper receiver with 16" chrome-lined 1:7"-twist barrel, standard semi-automatic bolt carrier group, tactical charging handle, Generation 1 collapsible buttstock.

NIB	Exc.	V.G.	Good	Fair	Poor
1200	1000	750	500	350	200

CQB Series

Piston operated with CQB/MRP (Close Quarter Battle/Monolithic Rail Platform) upper receiver, 16" chrome lined 5.56 barrel with SOPMOD buttstock and standard trigger group. Also offered in 6.8 SPC. **NOTE:** Add $200 for 6.8 SPC.

NIB	Exc.	V.G.	Good	Fair	Poor
1900	1650	1250	750	450	250

LIDDLE & KAEDING
San Francisco, California

Pocket Revolver

Manufactured by Forehand and Wadsworth and stamped with the above name. This company was a dealer in California and had nothing whatever to do with the production of this revolver. It is chambered for the .32 rimfire cartridge and has a 3.25" octagonal barrel and a 5-shot fluted cylinder. The frame is iron and the finish is blued, with walnut grips. There were a few hundred manufactured between 1880 and 1886. The dealer's name is marked on the top strap.

NIB	Exc.	V.G.	Good	Fair	Poor
—	—	575	450	200	75

LIEGEOISE D ARMES
Liege, Belgium

Side-by-Side Boxlock Shotgun

This double-barreled gun is chambered for 12 and 20 gauge. The barrels are 28" or 30" in length, and the choke combinations are varied. It has a single trigger and automatic ejectors. The action is moderately engraved and the finish is blued, with a checkered walnut stock.

NIB	Exc.	V.G.	Good	Fair	Poor
—	900	700	500	400	200

Liegeoise Pistol

A semi-automatic pistol in 6.35mm caliber.

Courtesy James Rankin

NIB	Exc.	V.G.	Good	Fair	Poor
—	250	200	175	125	75

LIGNOSE
Suhl, Germany

In 1921, Bergmann Industriewerke was incorporated into Aktiengesellschaft Lignose, Berlin, with a manufacturing division in Suhl.

Liliput Model I

Manufactured in caliber 6.35mm during the 1920s.

NIB	Exc.	V.G.	Good	Fair	Poor
—	400	300	200	150	100

Lignose Model 2

The Pocket Model in 6.35mm caliber.

Courtesy James Rankin

NIB	Exc.	V.G.	Good	Fair	Poor
—	450	400	350	250	150

Lignose Model 3

The same as the Model 2 but with a 9-round magazine capacity.

NIB	Exc.	V.G.	Good	Fair	Poor
—	750	650	500	400	250

Einhand Model 2A

This unique design resembled the Swiss Chylewski. It allows the shooter to cock and fire this blowback-operated semi-automatic pistol with one hand (Einhand). It is chambered for the 6.35mm cartridge and has a 2" barrel. The magazine holds 6 shots, and the finish is blued, with molded horn grips marked "Lignose." The trigger guard on this pistol has a reverse curve that fits the finger, and it moves backward to cock the slide. The short-grip model without the Einhard feature was the Model 2; the long grip model without the Einhand was the Model 3. The first 9,000 to 10,000 examples (all four variations serial numbered in the same series) were marketed under the Bergmann name; only later Lignose. It was manufactured in the early 1920s by the Bergman Company, but the firm was merged with Lignose under whose name it was produced.

Courtesy James Rankin

NIB	Exc.	V.G.	Good	Fair	Poor
—	750	650	500	400	250

Einhand Model 3A

Similar to the Model 2A, with a longer grip that houses a 9-shot magazine. All other specifications are the same as the Model 2A.

Courtesy Orvel Reichert

NIB	Exc.	V.G.	Good	Fair	Poor
—	850	700	650	500	300

LILLIPUT
See—Menz

LINDE, A.
Memphis, Tennessee

Pocket Pistol

This company manufactured a small, concealable firearm patterned after the Henry Deringer Philadelphia-type pistol. It is chambered for .41 caliber percussion and has a 2.5" barrel, German silver mountings and a walnut stock. It was manufactured in the 1850s.

NIB	Exc.	V.G.	Good	Fair	Poor
—	—	2150	875	300	150

LINDSAY, JOHN P.
Union Knife Company
Naugatuck, Connecticut

The Union Knife Company manufactured the Lindsay 2-shot pistols for the inventor, John P. Lindsay. There are three separate and distinct models listed.

2 Shot Belt Pistol

An oddity. It is a single-barreled, .41 caliber percussion pistol with a double chamber that contains two powder charges and projectiles that are simultaneously fired by two separate hammers. The hammers are released by a single trigger that allows them to fall in the proper sequence. The 5.5" octagonal barrel is contoured into a radical stepped-down shape, and there is a spur trigger. The frame is brass and has scroll engraving. The barrel is blued and is marked "Lindsay's Young America." There were estimated to be fewer than 100 manufactured between 1860 and 1862.

NIB	Exc.	V.G.	Good	Fair	Poor
—	—	4400	1500	700	300

2 Shot Pocket Pistol

A smaller version of the Belt Pistol. It is chambered for the same caliber but has a 4" barrel. There were approximately 200 manufactured between 1860 and 1862.

Courtesy W. P. Hallstein III and son Chip

NIB	Exc.	V.G.	Good	Fair	Poor
—	—	3500	3000	1100	400

2 Shot Martial Pistol

A large version of the Lindsay design. It is chambered for .45 caliber smoothbore and has an 8.5" part-round, part-octagonal barrel. In other respects it is similar to the smaller models. The inventor tried to sell this pistol to the government but was unsuccessful. It was estimated that there were 100 manufactured between 1860 and 1862.

NIB	Exc.	V.G.	Good	Fair	Poor
—	—	—	5400	2200	700

LINS, A. F.
Philadelphia, Pennsylvania

Pocket Pistol

Chambered for .41 caliber percussion and a copy of the Henry Deringer pistol. It has a 3" barrel and a walnut stock and is marked "A. Fred. Lins. Philada." This pistol was manufactured between 1855 and 1860.

NIB	Exc.	V.G.	Good	Fair	Poor
—		2100	1075	350	200

Rifled Musket

A single-shot, muzzleloading, percussion rifle chambered for .58 caliber. It has a 39" barrel and a full-length walnut stock held on by three barrel bands. There is an iron ramrod mounted under the barrel. The mountings are iron, and there is a bayonet lug combined with the front sight. The lock is marked "A. Fred. Lins/ Philada." This is a rare weapon that was used by Union forces in the Civil War. There were approximately 200 manufactured in 1861 and 1862.

Courtesy Milwaukee Public Museum, Milwaukee, Wisconsin

NIB	Exc.	V.G.	Good	Fair	Poor
—	—	5500	2000	825	300

LITTLE SHARPS RIFLE MFG. CO.
Big Sandy, Montana

Little Sharps Rifle

This hand-built reproduction of the single-shot Sharps rifle is 20 percent smaller than the original. Chambered for a wide variety of calibers from .22 Long Rifle to .375 LSR. A number of extra cost options are available for this rifle. The price listed is for the basic model.

NIB	Exc.	V.G.	Good	Fair	Poor
3250	2750	2000	1500	900	500

LJUTIC INDUSTRIES
Yakima, Washington

Bi-Matic Semi-Automatic

A custom-built, gas-operated, semi-automatic shotgun that is known for its low level of felt recoil. It is chambered for 12 gauge and has 26" to 32" barrels choked for either skeet or trap. The stock specifications are to the customer's order. Add 15 percent for interchangeable chokes.

NIB	Exc.	V.G.	Good	Fair	Poor
2750	2100	1300	800	400	200

Dynatrap Single-Barrel

A single-shot trap gun chambered for 12 gauge. It has a 33" vent rib full-choke barrel and features a push-button opener and a manual extractor. The stock is made to trap specifications. There are many options that affect the value.

NIB	Exc.	V.G.	Good	Fair	Poor
2500	1500	1000	800	400	200

Model X-73 Single-Barrel

Similar features to the Dynatrap, with a high competition rib. Appraisal is recommended. Add 15 percent for interchangeable chokes.

NIB	Exc.	V.G.	Good	Fair	Poor
2750	2100	1300	800	400	200

Mono Gun Single-Barrel

Chambered for 12 gauge and has a 34" vent rib barrel. It is essentially a custom-order proposition that is available with a standard, as well as a release, trigger. There are many value-affecting options available. Add 15 percent for interchangeable chokes.

NIB	Exc.	V.G.	Good	Fair	Poor
6500	5700	4200	3000	1000	—

LTX Model

A deluxe version of the Mono Gun with a 33" medium-height vent rib and a high-grade walnut stock with fine hand checkering. Options raise values drastically.

NIB	Exc.	V.G.	Good	Fair	Poor
7500	6200	5000	3500	1500	—

Space Gun

A unique single-barrel gun chambered for 12 gauge, with trap choking. It has a stock and forearm that reminds one of a crutch in appearance but which allows the shooter to have in-line control with little felt recoil. The barrel, forearm, and stock are all on one line. There is a recoil pad and a high ventilated rib.

NIB	Exc.	V.G.	Good	Fair	Poor
3750	3000	2250	1500	900	200

Bi-Gun Over/Under

An over/under double chambered for 12 gauge. It has 30" or 32" vent ribbed barrels that are separated. The choking is to trap specifications, and the stock is deluxe hand-checkered walnut.

NIB	Exc.	V.G.	Good	Fair	Poor
7250	6000	4000	1000	600	200

Bi-Gun Combo

The over/under Bi-Gun supplied with a high ribbed single-barrel in addition to the separated over-and-under barrels.

NIB	Exc.	V.G.	Good	Fair	Poor
10000	7000	4000	2000	1000	200

LM-6 Super Deluxe

This is an over/under gun made to the customer's specifications. Available in 12 gauge with barrel lengths from 28" to 34". All other specifications are custom. **NOTE:** Extra single-barrel add $7,000.

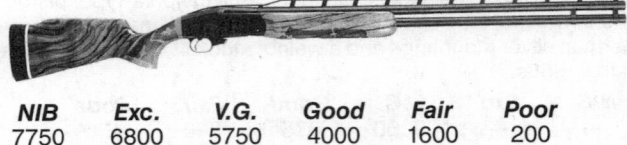

NIB	Exc.	V.G.	Good	Fair	Poor
7750	6800	5750	4000	1600	200

LLAMA
Manufactured by Gabilondo y Cia
Vitoria, Spain

This is the same firm that was founded in 1904 and produced several inexpensive revolvers and pistols prior to 1931. In 1931 the company began to produce a semi-automatic pistol based on the Colt Model 1911. They were of high quality and have been sold around the world. After the Spanish civil war the company moved its facilities to Vitoria, Spain, where it continued to build handguns under the Llama trade name. In the 1980s the firm introduced a new line of pistols that were more modern in design and function. The Llama pistol is still produced today. For Llama pistols built prior to 1936 the slide marking reads: "GABILONDO Y CIA ELOEIBAR (ESPANA) CAL 9MM/.380IN LLAMA." For pistols built after 1936 the slide marking reads: "LLAMA GABILONDO Y CIA ELOEIBAR (ESPANA) CAL 9MM .380." Current production Llama pistols will show a slide marking with either "LLAMA CAL..." or "GABILONDO Y CIA VITORIA (ESPANA)" and the Llama logo. "Llama" is now a trade name for handguns manufactured by Bersa of Argentina.

SEMI-AUTOMATICS

Model I-A

This is a 7.65mm blowback design introduced in 1933. Magazine capacity is 7 rounds. The barrel was 3.62", overall length 6.3", and weight about 19 oz.

NIB	Exc.	V.G.	Good	Fair	Poor
—	275	225	125	100	75

Model II

Chambered for the 9mm Short introduced in the same year. Identical to the Model I. Discontinued in 1936.

NIB	Exc.	V.G.	Good	Fair	Poor
—	265	200	150	125	100

Model III

An improved version of the Model II. Introduced in 1936 and discontinued in 1954.

NIB	Exc.	V.G.	Good	Fair	Poor
—	275	225	175	125	100

Model III-A

Similar to the Model III, chambered for the .380 ACP, but with the addition of the Colt-type grip safety. Introduced in 1955. Weight is about 23 oz.

NIB	Exc.	V.G.	Good	Fair	Poor
—	300	250	195	125	100

Model IV

Chambered for the 9mm Largo or .380 ACP. Is not fitted with a grip safety. Introduced in 1931, it is the first of the Llama designs.

NIB	Exc.	V.G.	Good	Fair	Poor
—	275	225	175	125	100

Model V

The same as the Model IV but was intended for export to the United States and is stamped "made in Spain" on the slide.

NIB	Exc.	V.G.	Good	Fair	Poor
—	275	225	175	125	100

Model VI

Chambered for the 9mm Short and without a grip safety.

NIB	Exc.	V.G.	Good	Fair	Poor
—	275	225	175	125	100

Model VII

Introduced in 1932 and manufactured until 1954. Chambered for the .38 Auto cartridge. It does not have a grip safety.

NIB	Exc.	V.G.	Good	Fair	Poor
—	400	300	225	150	100

Model VIII

This model was introduced in 1955 and is chambered for the .45 ACP, .38 Auto, or 9mm Largo. It is fitted with a grip safety. Barrel length is 5", overall length is 8.5", and weight is about 38 oz. Magazine capacity is 7 rounds. **NOTE:** Many of these pistols are marked ".38." It is unclear whether these pistols were intended for use with the .38 Super cartridge or with the milder .38 Automatic. We do not recommend full-house Super loadings in these pistols.

NIB	Exc.	V.G.	Good	Fair	Poor
—	400	300	225	150	100

Model IX

Chambered for the 7.65mm Para, 9mm Largo, or .45 ACP, this model has a locked breech with no grip safety. Built from 1936 to 1954.

NIB	Exc.	V.G.	Good	Fair	Poor
—	400	300	200	150	100

Model IX-A

This version of the Model IX is fitted with a grip safety. Current production models are chambered for the .45 ACP only. Weighs about 30 oz. with 5" barrel.

NIB	Exc.	V.G.	Good	Fair	Poor
—	400	300	200	150	100

Model IX-B

This version of the Model IX series is chambered in .45 ACP. It is fitted with an extended slide release, black plastic grips, and target-type hammer. Offered in blue or satin chrome finish.

NIB	Exc.	V.G.	Good	Fair	Poor
400	300	250	175	125	100

Model IX-C

This is the last large-frame version of the Model IX. It is chambered for the .45 ACP and is fitted with a 5.125" barrel. Blade front sight with adjustable rear sight. Magazine capacity is 10 rounds. Weight is approximately 41 oz.

NIB	Exc.	V.G.	Good	Fair	Poor
400	300	250	200	150	100

Model IX-D

This model is a compact frame version with a 4.25" barrel and chambered for the .45 ACP cartridge. Stocks are black rubber. Fixed front sight with adjustable rear. Introduced in 1995. Magazine capacity is 10 rounds. Weight is about 39 oz.

NIB	Exc.	V.G.	Good	Fair	Poor
450	350	250	200	150	100

Model X

First produced in 1935, this model is chambered for the 7.65mm cartridge. It has no grip safety.

NIB	Exc.	V.G.	Good	Fair	Poor
—	295	225	150	100	75

Model X-A

This version is similar to the Model X but with a grip safety. Produced from 1954 to the present.

NIB	Exc.	V.G.	Good	Fair	Poor
—	300	225	150	100	75

Model XI

Chambered for the 9mm Parabellum cartridge this model is different from previous models with a longer curved butt, ring hammer, and vertically grooved walnut grips. Magazine capacity is 9 rounds. Barrel length is 5". Discontinued in 1954.

NIB	Exc.	V.G.	Good	Fair	Poor
—	350	300	250	175	125

Model XI-B

Similar to the Model XI but with a spur hammer and shorter barrel.

NIB	Exc.	V.G.	Good	Fair	Poor
400	375	275	150	100	75

Model XII-B

This model is chambered for the .40 S&W cartridge. It has a compact frame.

NIB	Exc.	V.G.	Good	Fair	Poor
400	375	275	150	100	75

Model XV

Chambered for the .22 Long Rifle this model is marked "Especial." It is fitted with a grip safety and comes in several finishes and with different grip styles. The barrel length is 3.6", the overall length is 6.5", and the weight is about 17 oz.

NIB	Exc.	V.G.	Good	Fair	Poor
—	325	275	195	125	100

Model XVI

This is a deluxe version of the Model XV with engraving, ventilated rib, and adjustable sights.

NIB	Exc.	V.G.	Good	Fair	Poor
—	350	275	200	150	100

Model XVII "Especial"

This vest pocket-sized model is chambered for the .22 Short. It is small version of the Model XV with a finger-contoured grip.

NIB	Exc.	V.G.	Good	Fair	Poor
—	275	225	175	125	100

Model XVIII

Introduced in 1998 this model is chambered for the .25 ACP cartridge and offered with gold or chrome finish and stag grips.

NIB	Exc.	V.G.	Good	Fair	Poor
—	300	225	175	150	125

Model Omni

This pistol is chambered for the .45 ACP or 9mm cartridge and fitted with a 4.25" barrel. Blued finish. Adjustable rear sight. Magazine capacity is 7 rounds for the .45 ACP and 13 rounds for the 9mm. Weight is approximately 40 oz. Produced between 1984 and 1986.

Courtesy J.B. Wood

NIB	Exc.	V.G.	Good	Fair	Poor
475	350	250	150	125	100

Model Max-I

Introduced in 1995 this 1911 design single-action model features a choice of 9mm or .45 ACP chambers with a 4.25" barrel or a 5.125" barrel. Black rubber grips with blade front sight and adjustable rear sight. Weight is 34 oz. for compact model and 36 oz. for Government model. **NOTE:** For compact model add $25. For duo-tone model add $25.

NIB	Exc.	V.G.	Good	Fair	Poor
450	400	300	175	125	95

Micro-Max

This pistol is chambered for the .32 ACP or .380 cartridge. It operates on a straight blowback system with a single-action trigger. Black polymer grips. Barrel length is 3.6". Overall length is 6.5" and height is 4.37". Weight is approximately 23 oz. Introduced in 1999. **NOTE:** Add $20 for satin chrome finish.

NIB	Exc.	V.G.	Good	Fair	Poor
400	350	250	175	150	100

Model Mini-Max

This version is chambered for the 9mm, .40 S&W, or .45 ACP. Furnished with a 6-round magazine. Barrel length is 3.5". Checkered rubber grips. Introduced in 1996. Weight is about 35 oz. Choice of blue, duo-tone, satin chrome, or stainless steel. **NOTE:** Add $40 for satin chrome finish. Add $60 for stainless. Add $20 for duo-tone finish.

NIB	Exc.	V.G.	Good	Fair	Poor
400	375	275	150	100	75

Model 82

This is a large-frame double-action semi-automatic pistol. It features plastic grips, ambidextrous safety, 3-dot sights. The barrel length is 4.25" and overall length is 8". Weight is approximately 39 oz. Choice of blue or satin chrome finish.

NIB	Exc.	V.G.	Good	Fair	Poor
650	500	350	250	150	100

Model 87 Competition

Chambered for the 9mm cartridge and fitted with a integral muzzle compensator. Has a number of competition features such as beveled magazine well and oversize safety and magazine release. Magazine capacity is 14 rounds. Offered between 1989 and 1993.

NIB	Exc.	V.G.	Good	Fair	Poor
1200	925	650	525	300	150

Llama Compact Frame Semi-Automatic

A 9mm or the .45 ACP caliber semi-automatic pistol with a 4.25" barrel and either a 7- or 9-shot detachable magazine. Blued. Introduced in 1986.

NIB	Exc.	V.G.	Good	Fair	Poor
400	375	275	150	100	75

Mini-Max Sub Compact

This semi-automatic is chambered for the 9mm, .40 S&W, or .45 ACP cartridge. It is fitted with a 3.14" barrel with an overall length of 6.5" and a height of 4.5". Skeletonized combat-style hammer. Grips are black polymer. Weight is about 31 oz. Introduced in 1999. **NOTE:** Add $40 for satin chrome finish. Add $60 for stainless. Add $20 for duo-tone finish.

NIB	Exc.	V.G.	Good	Fair	Poor
400	375	275	150	100	75

Model Max-I with Compensator

Similar to the Max-I with the addition of a compensator. This model introduced in 1996. Weight is about 42 oz.

NIB	Exc.	V.G.	Good	Fair	Poor
350	300	225	150	100	75

Llama Small Frame Semi-Automatic

A .22, .32 ACP, and the .380 ACP caliber semi-automatic pistol with a 3-11/16" barrel and 7-shot detachable magazine. Either blued or satin chrome finished. **NOTE:** Add $75 for satin chrome finish.

NIB	Exc.	V.G.	Good	Fair	Poor
350	300	225	150	100	75

Llama Large Frame Semi-Automatic

A 9mm, .38 Super or .45 ACP caliber semi-automatic pistol with a 5.25" barrel and either a 7- or 9-shot detachable magazine, depending on the caliber. Blued or satin chrome. **NOTE:** Add $125 for satin chrome finish.

NIB	Exc.	V.G.	Good	Fair	Poor
450	400	300	175	125	100

Mugica

Eibar gun dealer Jose Mugica sold Llama pistols under his private trade name. They are marked "mugica-ebir-spain" on the slide. These pistols do not seem to have any additional value over and above their respective Llama models. For the sake of clarification the Mugica models are listed with their Llama counterparts:

Mugica Model 101	Llama Model X
Mugica Model 101-G	Llama Model X-A
Mugica Model 105	Llama Model III
Mugica Model 105-G	Llama Model III-A
Mugica Model 110	Llama Model VII
Mugica Model 110-G	Llama Model VIII
Mugica Model 120	Llama Model XI

Tauler

In an arrangement similar to Mugica, a gun dealer in Madrid sold Llama pistols under his own brand name. Most of these pistols were sold in the early 1930s to police and other government officials. The most common Llama models were Models I to VIII. Slide inscriptions were in English and had the name Tauler in them. No additional value is attached to this private trademark.

REVOLVERS

RUBY EXTRA MODELS

These revolvers were produced in the 1950s and were copies of Smith & Wessons. They were marked "RUBY EXTRA" on the left side of the frame. At the top of the grips was a Ruby medallion. The barrel address is stamped: gabilondo y cia elgoeibar espana. The Ruby Extra Models represent the company's attempts to produce and sell a low-cost revolver.

Model XII

This model is chambered for the .38 Long cartridge and is fitted with a 5" barrel and a squared butt.

NIB	Exc.	V.G.	Good	Fair	Poor
—	200	150	125	100	75

Model XIII

Chambered for the .38 Special, this revolver has a round butt with 4" or 6" ventilated rib barrel. The 6" barreled gun was fitted with adjustable sights and target grips.

NIB	Exc.	V.G.	Good	Fair	Poor
—	225	175	150	125	100

Model XIV

Offered in .22 LR or .32 caliber, this model was available in a wide choice of barrel lengths and sights.

NIB	Exc.	V.G.	Good	Fair	Poor
—	200	150	125	100	75

Model XXII Olimpico

This model was designed as a .38 Special target revolver. It features an adjustable anatomic grip, adjustable rear sight, ventilated rib barrel, and a web that joins the barrel to the ejector shroud.

NIB	Exc.	V.G.	Good	Fair	Poor
—	275	225	150	125	100

Model XXIX Olimpico

This is the Model XXI I chambered for the .22 LR.

NIB	Exc.	V.G.	Good	Fair	Poor
—	250	200	150	125	100

Model XXVI

Chambered for the .22 LR, it features traditional grips and shrouded ejector rod.

NIB	Exc.	V.G.	Good	Fair	Poor
—	175	150	125	100	75

Model XXVII

Similar to the model above but fitted with a 2" barrel and chambered for the .32 Long cartridge.

NIB	Exc.	V.G.	Good	Fair	Poor
—	175	150	125	100	75

Model XXVIII

This model is chambered for the .22 LR and is fitted with a 6" barrel. It has a ramp front sight and adjustable rear sight.

NIB	Exc.	V.G.	Good	Fair	Poor
—	200	175	150	100	75

Model XXXII Olimpico

This model is a .32 target revolver with an unusual cylinder and frame design.

NIB	Exc.	V.G.	Good	Fair	Poor
—	400	300	250	200	150

Llama Martial

A .22 or the .38 Special caliber double-action revolver with a 6-round swingout cylinder, a 4" or 6" barrel and adjustable sights. Blued, with checkered hardwood grips. Manufactured between 1969 and 1976. **NOTE:** Add $500 for engraved chrome, $600 for engraved blue, and $1,000 to $3,000 for gold model.

NIB	Exc.	V.G.	Good	Fair	Poor
—	275	225	200	150	125

Llama Comanche I

This .22 caliber revolver is fitted with a 6" barrel and has a 9 shot cylinder. Rubber grips with adjustable sights. Choice of blue or stainless steel. Weight is about 39 oz.

NIB	Exc.	V.G.	Good	Fair	Poor
240	175	125	100	75	50

Llama Comanche II

As above, in .38 Special caliber with 6 shot cylinder. Choice of 3" or 4" barrel. Rubber grips and adjustable sights. Blue or stainless steel. Weight is about 30 oz.

NIB	Exc.	V.G.	Good	Fair	Poor
225	175	125	100	75	50

Llama Comanche III

As above, in .357 Magnum with a 3", 4", 6", barrel and adjustable sights. Rubber grips. Blue or stainless steel. Weight is about 30 oz. for 3" or 4" barrel guns and 39 oz. for 6" gun. Introduced in 1975. **NOTE:** Add 20 percent for satin chrome finish.

NIB	Exc.	V.G.	Good	Fair	Poor
275	225	175	125	100	75

Llama Super Comanche

As above, in .357 or .44 Magnum with a 10" ventilated rib barrel and adjustable sights. Blued, with walnut grips. Weight is about 47 oz.

NIB	Exc.	V.G.	Good	Fair	Poor
325	250	200	150	100	75

LOEWE, LUDWIG & CO.
Berlin, Germany
See—Borchardt

During the 1870s and 1880s this firm manufactured a close copy of the Smith & Wesson Russian Model for the Russian government. They are marked "Ludwig Loewe Berlin" on the top of the barrel.

Loewe Smith & Wesson Russian Revolver

NIB	Exc.	V.G.	Good	Fair	Poor
—	—	1250	600	325	125

LOHNER, C.
Philadelphia, Pennsylvania

Pocket Pistol

A .44 caliber single-shot percussion pistol with a 5" barrel, German silver mounts and walnut grip. The barrel marked "C. Lohner." Manufactured during the 1850s.

NIB	Exc.	V.G.	Good	Fair	Poor
—	—	1600	675	250	125

LOMBARD, H. C. & CO.
Springfield, Massachusetts

Pocket Pistol

A .22 caliber single-shot spur trigger pistol with a 3.5" octagonal barrel. The frame is silver plated, barrel blued and grips are of walnut. Barrel marked "H.C. Lombard & Co. Springfield, Mass."

NIB	Exc.	V.G.	Good	Fair	Poor
—	—	500	225	150	100

LONDON ARMOURY COMPANY
London

This firm was established in 1856, by Robert Adams. In addition to marketing revolvers based upon Adams' designs, the London Armoury Company were major retailers of other arms, particularly Enfield Pattern 53 Percussion Rifles. During the 1870s, the London Armoury distributed Colt pistols. During its business life, the London Armoury Company was located at these addresses:

Henry Street	1857-1863
36 King William Street	1864-1868
54 King William Street	1868-1883
118 Queen Victoria Street	1884-1886
114 Queen Victoria Street	1887-1905
1 Lawrence Pounty Hill	1905-1910
31 Bury Street, St. James	1910-1939
10 Ryder Street, St. James	1940-1950

Although the firm continued in business after 1950, its operations were restricted to the trade of used arms.

LONE STAR RIFLE COMPANY
Conroe, Texas

This company builds custom blackpowder rifles. They are built on the rolling block design and are offered in two basic configurations. There are a wide number of options that will affect the price of these rifles.

Sporting Rifle

This is a basic configuration that features a straight grip stock with semi-crescent butt. Offered in a wide variety of calibers from .32-40 to .50-90. Barrel lengths, barrel configurations, wood, triggers, sights, engraving, finishes, hammers, and accessories will greatly affect the final price. Basic retail price: $2195.

Target Rifle

This is a basic configuration that features a straight grip stock with semi-crescent butt. Offered in a wide variety of calibers from .32-40 to .50-90. Barrel lengths, barrel configurations, wood, triggers, sights, engraving, finishes, hammers, and accessories will greatly affect the final price. Basic retail price: $2195.

LORCIN ENGINEERING CO., INC.
Mira Loma, California

This company was in business from 1989 to 1999.

Model L-25

A .25 caliber semi-automatic pistol with a 2.5" barrel and 7-shot magazine. Weight is 14.5 oz. Overall length is 4.8". Introduced in 1989.

NIB	Exc.	V.G.	Good	Fair	Poor
125	100	75	40	30	20

Model LT-25

Same as above but with aluminum alloy frame. Introduced in 1989.

NIB	Exc.	V.G.	Good	Fair	Poor
125	100	75	40	30	20

Model L-22

Chambered for the .22 LR cartridge with a 2.5" barrel. Magazine capacity is 9 rounds. Introduced in 1989. Weight is 16 oz.

NIB	Exc.	V.G.	Good	Fair	Poor
125	100	75	40	30	20

Model L-380

This semi-automatic pistol is chambered for the .380 ACP cartridge. Barrel length is 3.5" with a magazine capacity of 7 rounds. Introduced in 1992. Weight is about 23 oz.

NIB	Exc.	V.G.	Good	Fair	Poor
125	100	75	40	30	20

Model I-380 10th Anniversary

Same as above but frame and slide are plated in 24 karat gold. Limited edition model.

NIB	Exc.	V.G.	Good	Fair	Poor
125	100	75	40	30	20

Model L-32

Same as above but chambered for the .32 ACP cartridge. Introduced in 1992

NIB	Exc.	V.G.	Good	Fair	Poor
125	100	75	40	30	20

Model LH-380

This semi-automatic pistol is chambered for the .380 ACP cartridge. The barrel length is 4.5" and the magazine capacity is 10 rounds. Offered in black, satin or bright chrome finishes.

NIB	Exc.	V.G.	Good	Fair	Poor
150	125	100	75	60	50

Model L-9mm

Same as above but chambered for 9mm cartridge. Weight is 36 oz.

NIB	Exc.	V.G.	Good	Fair	Poor
150	125	100	75	60	50

Derringer

This over/under pistol is chambered for the .38 Special, .357 Magnum, and .45 ACP. Barrel length is 3.5". Overall length is 6.5".

NIB	Exc.	V.G.	Good	Fair	Poor
140	120	95	65	50	40

LOWELL ARMS CO.

See—Rollin White Arms Co.

LOWER, J. P.

See—Slotter & Co.

LUGERS
Various Manufacturers

Just before the turn of the 20th century, Georg Luger redesigned the Borchardt semi-automatic pistol so that its mainspring was housed in the rear of the grip. The resulting pistol was to prove extremely successful and his name has become synonymous with the pistol despite the fact his name never appeared on it.

These companies manufactured Luger pattern pistols at various times.

1. DWM - Deutsch Waffen und Munitions - Karlsruhe, Germany
2. The Royal Arsenal of Erfurt Germany
3. Simson & Company - Suhl, Germany
4. Mauser - Oberndorf, Germany
5. Vickers Ltd. - England
6. Waffenfabrik Bern - Bern, Switzerland
7. Heinrich Krieghoff - Suhl, Germany

DEUTSCH WAFFEN UND MUNITIONS

1899/1900 Swiss Test Model

4.75" barrel, 7.65mm caliber. The Swiss Cross in Sunburst is stamped over the chamber. The serial range runs to three digits. With fewer than 100 manufactured and only one known to exist, it is one of the rarest of the Lugers and the first true Luger that was produced. This model is far too rare to estimate an accurate value.

1900 Swiss Contract

4.75" barrel, 7.65mm caliber. The Swiss Cross in Sunburst is stamped over the chamber. The military serial number range is 2001-5000; the commercial range, 01-21250. There were approximately 2,000 commercial and 3,000 military models manufactured. **NOTE:** Wide trigger add 20 percent.

Courtesy Gale Morgan

Swiss Cross & Sunburst

NIB	Exc.	V.G.	Good	Fair	Poor
—	8000	6750	4000	1500	1000

1900 Commercial

4.75" barrel, 7.65mm caliber. The area above the chamber is blank. The serial range is 01-19000, and there were approximately 5,500 manufactured for commercial sale in Germany or other countries. Some have "Germany" stamped on the frame. These pistols were imported into the U.S., and some were even stamped after bluing.

Courtesy Gale Morgan

NIB	Exc.	V.G.	Good	Fair	Poor
—	8500	6000	3000	1000	650

1900 American Eagle

4.75" barrel, 7.65mm caliber. The American Eagle crest is stamped over the chamber. The serial range is between 2000-200000, and there were approximately 11,000-12,000 commercial models marked "Germany" and 1,000 military test models without the commercial import stamp. The serial numbers of this military lot have been estimated at between 6100-7100.

NIB	Exc.	V.G.	Good	Fair	Poor
—	6500	4500	1500	850	600

1900 Bulgarian Contract

An old model, 1900 Type, with no stock lug. It has a 4.75" barrel and is chambered for the 7.65mm cartridge. The Bulgarian crest is stamped over the chamber, and the safety is marked in Bulgarian letters. The serial range is 20000-21000, with 1,000 manufactured. This is a military test model and is quite rare as most were rebarreled to 9mm during the time they were used. Even with the 9mm versions, approximately 10 are known to exist. It was the only variation to feature a marked safety before 1904.

Courtesy Gale Morgan

NIB	Exc.	V.G.	Good	Fair	Poor
—	12500	8500	4000	2500	1800

1900 Carbine

11.75" barrel, 7.65mm caliber. The carbines have a gracefully contoured and finely checkered walnut forearm and detachable shoulder stock. The rear sight on this extremely rare variation is a five-position sliding model located on the rear link. The area above the chamber is blank. The serial range is three digits or under, and this may have been a prototype as less than 100 were produced. This model is far too rare to estimate an accurate value.

1902 Prototype

6" barrel, 7.65mm caliber. The serial numbers are in the 10000 range with a capital B, and the chamber is blank. The 6" barrel is of a heavy contour, and there were less than 10 manufactured. The rarity of this variation precludes estimating value.

1902 Commercial—"Fat Barrel"

Thick 4" barrel, 9mm caliber. The area above the chamber is blank. It is chambered for the 9mm cartridge, and the serial numbers fall within the 22300-22400 and the 22900-23500 range. There were approximately 600 manufactured, and the greater part of those noted were marked "Germany" for export purposes.

NIB	Exc.	V.G.	Good	Fair	Poor
—	12500	9500	6000	4000	1500

1902 American Eagle

As above, with an American Eagle stamped over the chamber. It is chambered for the 9mm cartridge, and the serial numbers fall within the 22100-22300 and the 22450-22900 range. This model was solely intended for export sales in the U.S.A., and all are marked "Germany" on the frame. There were approximately 700 manufactured.

NIB	Exc.	V.G.	Good	Fair	Poor
—	14000	9000	5500	3750	1300

1902 American Eagle Cartridge Counter

As above, with a "Powell Indicating Device" added to the left grip. A slotted magazine with a numbered window that allows visual access to the number of cartridges remaining. There were 50 Lugers altered in this way at the request of the U.S. Board of Ordnance, for U.S. Army evaluation. The serial numbers are 22401-22450. Be especially wary of fakes!

NIB	Exc.	V.G.	Good	Fair	Poor
—	40000	29000	16000	6000	3500

1902 Carbine

11.75" barrel, 7.65mm caliber. The sight has four positions and is silver-soldered to the barrel. A stock and forearm were sold with this weapon. The serial range was 21000-22100 and 23500-24900. There were approximately 2,500 manufactured for commercial sale in and out of Germany. Many were imported into the United States, but none here have been noted with the "Germany" export stamp. **NOTE:** Prices include matching stock.

Courtesy Gale Morgan

NIB	Exc.	V.G.	Good	Fair	Poor
—	22500	17000	10000	3500	2500

1902 Presentation Carbine

11.75" barrel, 7.65mm caliber. These carbines have the initials of the owner gold-inlaid above the chamber. They are furnished with a checkered walnut stock and forearm. Only four have been noted in the 9000C serial number range. They have the initials "GL" for Georg Luger on the back of the rear toggle. They are too rare to estimate value.

1902/06 Carbine (Transitional)

11.75" barrel, 7.65mm caliber. Assembled from Model 1902 parts with a new toggle assembly. They have the four-position sliding sight, silver-soldered to the barrel, and a checkered walnut stock and forearm. There were approximately 100 manufactured in the 23600 serial number range. **NOTE:** Prices include matching stock.

Paul Goodwin photo

NIB	Exc.	V.G.	Good	Fair	Poor
—	17000	14500	8000	5000	3000

1903 Commercial

4" barrel, 7.65mm caliber. The chamber area is blank. There were approximately 50 manufactured for export to France, serial numbered 25000-25050. The extractor on this model is marked "CHARGE".

NIB	Exc.	V.G.	Good	Fair	Poor
—	17000	13000	5000	3200	2500

1904 Navy

6" thick barrel, 9mm caliber. The chamber area is blank, and the extractor is marked "Geladen". The safety is marked "Gesichert". There were approximately 1,500 manufactured in the one- to four-digit serial range, for military issue to the German Navy. The toggle has a "lock" comparable to 1900 types. **NOTE:** It is advised that a professional appraisal be obtained before purchase.

NIB	Exc.	V.G.	Good	Fair	Poor
—	63000	42000	16000	6000	4500

1906 Navy Commercial

This is a new model, 1906 Type, with stock lug. It has a 6" barrel and is chambered for the 9mm cartridge. The chamber is blank, and the extractor is marked "Geladen." The safety is marked "Gesichert," and some have the "Germany" export stamp. The proper magazine has a wood bottom with concentric circles on the sides. There were approximately 2,500 manufactured in the 25050-65000 serial range. They were produced for commercial sales in and outside of Germany.

NIB	Exc.	V.G.	Good	Fair	Poor
—	8000	5800	2700	1500	1000

1906 Commercial

4" barrel, 9mm caliber. The extractor is marked "Geladen," and the area of the frame under the safety in its lower position is polished and not blued. The chamber is blank. There were approximately 4,000 manufactured for commercial sales. Some have the "Germany" export stamp. The serial range is 26500-68000.

Courtesy Orvel Reichert

NIB	Exc.	V.G.	Good	Fair	Poor
—	5000	4000	1600	800	600

1906 Commercial (Marked Safety)

As above, with the area of the frame under the safety in its lowest position is marked "Gesichert" and the barrel is 4.75" in length and chambered for the 7.65mm cartridge. There were approximately 750 manufactured, serial numbered 25050-26800.

NIB	Exc.	V.G.	Good	Fair	Poor
—	5500	4500	2000	800	600

1906 American Eagle

4" barrel, 9mm caliber. The chamber area has the American Eagle stamped upon it. The extractor is marked "Loaded" and the frame under the safety at its lowest point is polished and not blued. This model has no stock lug. There were approximately 3,000 manufactured for commercial sale in the U.S.A. in the serial range 25800-69000. They were supplied with a "Caliber 9mm Magnum".

NIB	Exc.	V.G.	Good	Fair	Poor
—	6500	4000	1200	700	500

1906 American Eagle (Marked Safety)

4.75" barrel, 7.65mm caliber. The frame under the safety at its lowest point is marked "Gesichert". There were approximately 750 manufactured in the 25100-26500 serial number range.

Courtesy Gale Morgan

NIB	Exc.	V.G.	Good	Fair	Poor
—	7000	5000	2000	1200	800

1906 American Eagle 4.75" Barrel

As above but with polished bright safety area. Approximately 8,000 manufactured in the 26500-69000 serial range.

NIB	Exc.	V.G.	Good	Fair	Poor
—	5000	3000	1100	700	450

1906 U.S. Army Test Luger .45 Caliber

5" barrel, .45 ACP caliber. Sent to the United States for testing in 1907. The chamber is blank; the extractor is marked "Loaded," and the frame is polished under the safety lever. The trigger on this model has an odd hook at the bottom. Only five of these pistols were manufactured. Buyer Caution: Perfect copies of this pistol are currently being produced.

1906 Swiss Commercial

4.75" barrel, 7.65mm caliber. The Swiss Cross in Sunburst appears over the chamber. The extractor is marked "Geladen,", and the frame under the safety is polished. There is no stock lug, and the proofmarks are commercial. There were approximately 1,000 manufactured in the 35000-55000 serial number range.

Courtesy Bonhams & Butterfields, San Francisco, California

NIB	Exc.	V.G.	Good	Fair	Poor
—	5800	4700	2500	1400	800

1906 Swiss Military

As the Swiss Commercial, except with military proofmarks.

NIB	Exc.	V.G.	Good	Fair	Poor
—	5500	3800	2200	900	700

1906 Swiss Police Cross in Shield

As above, with a shield replacing the sunburst on the chamber marking. There were 10,215 of both models combined. They are in the 5000-15215 serial number range.

Courtesy Gale Morgan

NIB	Exc.	V.G.	Good	Fair	Poor
—	5200	4200	2000	1000	700

1906 Dutch Contract

4" barrel, 9mm caliber. It has no stock lug, and the chamber is blank. The extractor is marked "Geleden" on both sides, and the safety is marked "RUST" with a curved upward pointing arrow.

This pistol was manufactured for military sales to the Netherlands, and a date will be found on the barrel of most examples encountered. The Dutch refinished their pistols on a regular basis and marked the date on the barrels. There were approximately 4,000 manufactured, serial numbered between 1 and 4000.

Courtesy Gale Morgan

NIB	Exc.	V.G.	Good	Fair	Poor
—	4500	3500	1500	800	600

1906 Royal Portuguese Navy

4" barrel, 9mm caliber, and has no stock lug. The Royal Portuguese Naval crest, an anchor under a crown, is stamped above the chamber. The extractor is marked "CARREGADA" on the left side. The frame under the safety is polished. There were approximately 1,000 manufactured with one- to four-digit serial numbers.

NIB	Exc.	V.G.	Good	Fair	Poor
—	11000	8000	6500	4000	2500

1906 Royal Portuguese Army (M2)

4.75" barrel, 7.65mm caliber. It has no stock lug. The chamber area has the Royal Portuguese crest of Mannuel II stamped upon it. The extractor is marked "CARREGADA." There were approximately 5,000 manufactured, with one- to four-digit serial numbers.

NIB	Exc.	V.G.	Good	Fair	Poor
—	4000	3200	1200	600	500

1906 Republic of Portugal Navy

4" barrel, 9mm caliber. It has no stock lug, and the extractor was marked "CARREGADA". This model was made after 1910, when Portugal had become a republic. The anchor on the chamber is under the letters "R.P." There were approximately 1,000 manufactured, with one- to four-digit serial numbers.

LUGERS • 653

NIB	Exc.	V.G.	Good	Fair	Poor
—	10500	8000	5500	2500	1500

1906 Brazilian Contract

4.75" barrel, 7.65mm caliber. It has no stock lug, and chamber area is blank. The extractor is marked "CARREGADA," and the frame under the safety is polished. There were approximately 5,000 manufactured for military sales to Brazil.

NIB	Exc.	V.G.	Good	Fair	Poor
—	3750	2900	1100	750	450

1906 Bulgarian Contract

4.75" barrel, 7.65mm caliber. It has no stock lug, and the extractor and safety are marked in cyrillic letters. The Bulgarian crest is stamped above the chamber. Nearly all of the examples located have the barrels replaced with 4" 9mm units. This was done after the later 1908 model was adopted. Some were refurbished during the Nazi era, and these pistols bear Waffenamts and usually mismatched parts. There were approximately 1,500 manufactured, with serial numbers of one- to four-digits.

NIB	Exc.	V.G.	Good	Fair	Poor
—	10000	7500	5000	3500	1500

1906 Russian Contract

4" barrel, 9mm caliber. It has no stock lug, and the extractor and safety are marked with cyrillic letters. Crossed Nagant rifles are stamped over the chamber. There were approximately 1,000 manufactured, with one- to four-digit serial numbers; but few survive. This is an extremely rare variation, and caution should be exercised if purchase is contemplated.

Courtesy Gale Morgan

NIB	Exc.	V.G.	Good	Fair	Poor
—	14500	12500	6500	4000	2500

1906 Navy 1st Issue

6" barrel, 9mm caliber. The safety and extractor are both marked in German, and the chamber area is blank. There is a stock lug, and the unique two-position sliding Navy sight is mounted on the rear toggle link. There were approximately 12,000 manufactured for the German Navy, with serial numbers of one- to five-digits. The wooden magazine bottom features concentric rings. **NOTE:** Many of these pistols had their safety changed so that they were "safe" in the lower position. Known as "1st issue altered". Value at approximately 20 percent less.

Courtesy Gale Morgan

NIB	Exc.	V.G.	Good	Fair	Poor
—	8500	6500	4000	1500	950

1906 Navy 2nd Issue

As above, but manufactured to be safe in the lower position. Approximately 11,000 2nd Issue Navies manufactured, with one- to five-digit serial numbers—some with an "a" or "b" suffix. They were produced for sale to the German Navy.

Courtesy Gale Morgan

NIB	Exc.	V.G.	Good	Fair	Poor
—	7000	4500	2500	1200	700

1908 Commercial

4" barrel, 9mm caliber. It has no stock lug, and the chamber area is blank. The extractor and the safety are both marked in German, and many examples are marked with the "Germany" export stamp. There were approximately 9,000 manufactured in the 39000-71500 serial number range.

NIB	Exc.	V.G.	Good	Fair	Poor
—	5000	3500	750	600	450

1908 Navy Commercial

6" barrel, 9mm caliber. It has a stock lug, no grip safety, and the characteristic two-position sliding sight mounted on the rear toggle link. The chamber area is blank, and the safety and extractor are both marked. The "Germany" export stamp appears on some examples. There were approximately 1,500 manufactured, in the 44000-50000 serial number range.

NIB	Exc.	V.G.	Good	Fair	Poor
—	6500	5000	2500	1750	1250

1908 Navy

As above, with the "Crown M" military proof. They may or may not have the concentric rings on the magazine bottom. There were approximately 40,000 manufactured, with one- to five-digit serial numbers with an "a" or "b" suffix. These Lugers are quite scarce as many were destroyed during and after WWI.

NIB	Exc.	V.G.	Good	Fair	Poor
—	7000	5000	2000	1100	800

1914 Navy

Similar to the above, but stamped with the dates from 1914-1918 above the chamber. Most noted are dated 1916-1918. There were approximately 30,000 manufactured, with one- to five-digit serial numbers with an "a" or "b" suffix. They are scarce as many were destroyed as a result of WWI. **WARNING:** Many counterfeit pistols reported.

NIB	Exc.	V.G.	Good	Fair	Poor
—	6700	4700	2500	950	700

1908 Military 1st Issue

4" barrel, 9mm caliber. It has no stock lug, and the extractor and safety are both marked in German. The chamber is blank. There were approximately 20,000 manufactured, with one- to five-digit serial numbers—some with an "a" suffix.

NIB	Exc.	V.G.	Good	Fair	Poor
—	2850	2000	1000	500	350

1908 Military Dated Chamber (1910-1913)

As above, with the date of manufacture stamped on the chamber.

NIB	Exc.	V.G.	Good	Fair	Poor
—	2500	1700	800	500	350

1913 Commercial

As above, with a grip safety. Approximately 1,000 manufactured, with serial numbers 71000-72000; but few have been noted, and it is considered to be quite rare.

NIB	Exc.	V.G.	Good	Fair	Poor
—	3200	2200	1300	850	600

1914 Military

As above, with a stock lug.

NIB	Exc.	V.G.	Good	Fair	Poor
—	2500	1700	600	500	350

1914 Artillery

8" barrel, 9mm caliber. It features a nine-position adjustable sight that has a base that is an integral part of the barrel. This model has a stock lug and was furnished with a military-style flat board stock and holster rig (see Accessories). The chamber is dated from 1914-1918, and the safety and extractor are both marked. This model was developed for artillery and machine gun crews; and many thousands were manufactured, with one- to five-digit serial numbers—some have letter suffixes. This model is quite desirable from a collector's standpoint and is rarer than its production figures would indicate. After the war many were destroyed as the allies deemed them more insidious than other models, for some reason. **NOTE:** For models stamped with 1914 date add 75 percent.

Courtesy Gale Morgan

NIB	Exc.	V.G.	Good	Fair	Poor
—	5000	3500	1700	1500	900

DWM Double Dated

4" barrel, 9mm cartridge. The date 1920 or 1921 is stamped over the original chamber date of 1910-1918, creating the double-date nomenclature. These are arsenal-reworked WWI military pistols and were then issued to the German military and/or police units within the provisions of the Treaty of Versailles. Many thousands of these Lugers were produced.

NIB	Exc.	V.G.	Good	Fair	Poor
—	1800	1000	550	400	300

1920 Police Rework

As above, except that the original manufacture date was removed before the rework date was stamped. There were many thousands of these produced. **NOTE:** It is not unusual to find with one or two "Police Matched" magazines.

NIB	Exc.	V.G.	Good	Fair	Poor
—	1800	1200	500	350	300

1920 Commercial

Similar to the above, with 3.5" to 6" barrels in 7.65mm or 9mm and marked "Germany" or "Made in Germany" for export. Others are unmarked and were produced for commercial sale inside Germany. Some of these pistols are military reworks with the markings and the proofmarks removed; others were newly manufactured. The extractors and safety are both marked, and the chamber is blank. The serial number range is one to five digits, and letter suffixes often appear. **NOTE:** Add 15 percent for 9mm.

NIB	Exc.	V.G.	Good	Fair	Poor
—	2000	1300	950	450	350

1920 Commercial Navy

6" barrel, 9mm caliber. Some have a stock lug; others have been noted without. The chamber area is generally blank, but some have been found with 1914-1918 dates stamped upon them. These were reworked by DWM from Military Navy Lugers after

WWI for commercial sales. They are marked "Germany" or "Made in Germany" and were sold by Stoeger Arms, among others. The extractor and safety are both marked, and the unique Navy sight is on the rear toggle link. No one knows exactly how many were produced, but they are quite scarce.

NIB	Exc.	V.G.	Good	Fair	Poor
—	7000	3500	2100	1100	850

1920 Commercial Artillery

8" barrel, 9mm caliber. Erfurt-manufactured pistols, as well as DWM-manufactured pistols, were reworked in this manner. The export markings "Germany" or "Made in Germany" are found on most examples. The number produced is not known, but examples are quite scarce.

NIB	Exc.	V.G.	Good	Fair	Poor
—	4500	3000	1100	700	450

1920 Long Barrel Commercial

10" to 24" barrels, 7.65mm or 9mm caliber. The extractor and safety are both marked, and an artillery model rear sight is used. This model was often built to a customer's specifications. They are rare, and the number manufactured is not known.

NIB	Exc.	V.G.	Good	Fair	Poor
—	5000	3450	1500	1000	800

1920 Carbine

11.75" barrel, 7.65mm caliber. The chamber is blank, and the extractor is marked either "Geleden" or "Loaded". The safety is not-marked. The carbine has a checkered walnut forearm and stock, and most have the "Germany" or "Made in Germany" export stamp. There were few of these carbines manufactured for commercial sales in and outside of Germany. **NOTE:** Prices include stock.

NIB	Exc.	V.G.	Good	Fair	Poor
—	14000	10500	5000	2500	1500

1920 Navy Carbine

Assembled from surplus Navy parts with the distinctive two position, sliding navy sight on the rear toggle link. Most are marked with the export stamp and have the naval military proofmarks still in evidence. The safety and extractor are marked, and rarely one is found chambered for the 9mm cartridge. Few were manufactured.

NIB	Exc.	V.G.	Good	Fair	Poor
—	19500	11000	5250	3000	1700

1920 Swiss Commercial

3.5"-6" barrels, 7.65mm or 9mm caliber. The Swiss Cross in Sunburst is stamped over the chamber, and the extractor is marked "Geladen". The frame under the safety is polished. There were a few thousand produced, with serial numbers in the one- to five-digit range, sometimes with a letter suffix.

NIB	Exc.	V.G.	Good	Fair	Poor
—	4000	1800	1200	800	600

1923 Stoeger Commercial

3.5" to 24" barrels, 7.65mm or 9mm caliber. There is a stock lug. The chamber area is either blank or has the American Eagle stamped on it. The export stamp and "A.F.Stoeger Inc. New York" is found on the right side of the receiver. The extractor and safety are marked in German or English. This was the model that Stoeger registered with the U.S. Patent office to secure the Luger name, and some examples will be so marked. There were less than 1,000 manufactured, with one- to five-digit serial numbers without a letter suffix. Individual appraisal must be secured on barrel lengths above 6". Be wary as fakes have been noted. The values given here are for the shorter barreled models. **NOTE:** For barrel lengths over 8" add 25 percent.

Courtesy Gale Morgan

NIB	Exc.	V.G.	Good	Fair	Poor
—	6000	4500	1800	1000	700

Abercrombie & Fitch Commercial 100

Swiss Lugers were made for commercial sale in the United States by "Abercrombie & Fitch Co. New York. Made in Switzerland." — in either one or two lines—is stamped on the top of the barrel. The barrel is 4.75" in length, and there were 49 chambered for 9mm and 51 chambered for the 7.65mm cartridge. This pistol has a grip safety and no stock lug. The Swiss Cross in Sunburst is stamped over the chamber. The extractor is marked, but the safety area is polished. The serial range is four digits—some with a letter suffix. This is a rare and desirable Luger. Be careful of fakes on models of this type and rarity.

NIB	Exc.	V.G.	Good	Fair	Poor
—	10000	8000	4500	3000	2000

1923 Commercial

7.5" barrel, 7.65mm caliber. It has a stock lug, and the chamber area is blank. The extractor and safety are both marked in German. These pistols were manufactured for commercial sales in and outside of Germany. There were approximately 18,000 produced, with serial numbers in the 73500-96000 range.

NIB	Exc.	V.G.	Good	Fair	Poor
—	2000	1400	800	600	450

1923 Commercial Safe & Loaded

As above, except that the extractor and safety are marked in English "Safe" & "Loaded." There were approximately 7,000 manufactured in the 73500-96000 serial number range.

Courtesy Gale Morgan

NIB	Exc.	V.G.	Good	Fair	Poor
—	3200	2200	1000	800	500

1923 Dutch Commercial & Military

4" barrel, 9mm caliber. It has a stock lug, and the chamber area is blank. The extractor is marked in German, and the safety is marked "RUST" with a downward pointing arrow. This model was sold commercially and to the military in the Netherlands. There were approximately 1,000 manufactured in the one- to three-digit serial range, with no letter suffix.

NIB	Exc.	V.G.	Good	Fair	Poor
—	4000	2800	1000	850	550

Royal Dutch Air Force

4" barrel, 9mm caliber. Marked with the Mauser Oberndorf proofmark and serial numbered in the 10000 to 14000 range. The safety marked "RUST."

NIB	Exc.	V.G.	Good	Fair	Poor
—	4500	2900	1000	800	550

VICKERS LTD.

NOTE: Vickers was not a manufacturer but an intermediary marketer.

1906 Vickers Dutch

4" barrel, 9mm caliber. There is no stock lug, and it uses a grip safety. The chamber is blank, and the extractor is marked "Geleden.". "Vickers Ltd." is stamped on the front toggle link. The safety is marked "RUST" with an upward pointing arrow. Examples have been found with an additional date as late as 1933 stamped on the barrel. These dates indicate arsenal refinishing and in no way detract from the value of this variation. Arsenal reworks are matte-finished, and the originals are a higher-polished rust blue. There were approximately 10,000 manufactured in the 1-10100 serial-number range.

NIB	Exc.	V.G.	Good	Fair	Poor
—	3800	3000	1800	1200	750

ERFURT ROYAL ARSENAL

1908 Erfurt

4" barrel, 9mm caliber. It has no stock lug; and the year of manufacture, from 1910-1913, is stamped above the chamber. The extractor and safety are both marked in German, and "ERFURT" under a crown is stamped on the front toggle link. There were many thousands produced as Germany was involved in WWI. They are found in the one- to five-digit serial range, sometimes with a letter suffix.

NIB	Exc.	V.G.	Good	Fair	Poor
—	2100	1350	600	400	350

1914 Erfurt Military

4" barrel, 9mm caliber. It has a stock lug and the date of manufacture over the chamber, 1914-1918. The extractor and safety are both marked in German, and the front link is marked "ERFURT" under a crown. The finish on this model is rough; and as the war progressed in 1917 and 1918, the finish got worse. There were many thousands produced with one- to five-digit serial numbers, some with letter suffixes.

NIB	Exc.	V.G.	Good	Fair	Poor
—	1300	950	600	400	350

1914 Erfurt Artillery

8" barrel, 9mm caliber. It has a stock lug and was issued with a flat board-type stock and other accessories which will be covered in the section of this book dealing with same. The sight is a nine-position adjustable model. The chamber is dated 1914 and the extractor and safety are both marked in German. "ERFURT" under a crown is stamped on the front toggle link. There were a great many manufactured with one- to five-digit serial numbers, some with a letter suffix. This model is similar to the DWM Artillery except that the finish is not as fine.

NIB	Exc.	V.G.	Good	Fair	Poor
—	3400	2200	1100	800	600

Double Date Erfurt

4" barrel, 9mm caliber. The area above the chamber has two dates: the original 1910-1918, and the date of rework, 1920 or 1921. The extractor and safety are both marked in German, and this model can be found with or without a stock lug. "ERFURT" under a crown is stamped on the front toggle link. Police or military unit markings are found on the front of the grip straps more often than not. There were thousands of these produced by DWM as well as Erfurt.

NIB	Exc.	V.G.	Good	Fair	Poor
—	1000	700	500	400	350

SIMSON & CO. SUHL, GERMANY

NOTE: Simson was the official rework firm for the German army. Thanks to Edward Tinker for his contributions to this section.

Simson & Co. Rework

4" barrels, 9mm caliber. The chamber is blank, but some examples are dated 1917 or 1918. The forward toggle link is stamped "SIMSON & CO. Suhl". The extractor and safety are marked in German. Most examples have stock lugs; some have been noted without them. The only difference between military models and commercial models is the proofmarks.

NIB	Exc.	V.G.	Good	Fair	Poor
—	2500	1650	900	600	500

Simson Grip Safety Rework

4" barrel, 9mm caliber and a grip safety was added. There is a stock lug. The chamber area is blank; the extractor is marked but the safety is not. There were only a few of these commercial reworks manufactured, and caution should be taken to avoid fakes.

NIB	Exc.	V.G.	Good	Fair	Poor
—	3700	2600	1500	850	550

Simson Dated Military

4" barrel, 9mm caliber. There is a stock lug, and the year of manufacture from 1925-1926 is stamped above the chamber (below serial number 700). The extractor and the safety are both marked in German. The checkered walnut grips of Simson-made Lugers are noticeably thicker than others. This is an extremely rare variation. Approximately 2,000 were manufactured with one- to three-digit serial numbers, and few seem to have survived.

NIB	Exc.	V.G.	Good	Fair	Poor
—	4000	2600	1800	900	650

Simson S Code

4" barrel, 9mm caliber. The forward toggle link is stamped with a Gothic S, possibly for "Simson". It has a stock lug, and the area above the chamber is blank. The extractor and the safety are both marked. The grips are also thicker. There were fewer than 12,000 manufactured with one- to five-digit serial numbers—some with the letter "a" suffix. This pistol is quite rare on today's market.

NIB	Exc.	V.G.	Good	Fair	Poor
—	5000	3250	1500	1000	750

EARLY NAZI ERA REWORKS MAUSER

Produced between 1930 and 1933, and normally marked with Waffenamt markings.

Deaths Head Rework

4" barrel, 9mm caliber. It has a stock lug; and a skull and crossbones are stamped, in addition to the date of manufacture, on the chamber area. This date was from 1914-1918. The extractor and safety are both marked. The Waffenamt proof is present. It is thought that this variation was produced for the 1930-1933 era "SS" division of the Nazi Party. Mixed serial numbers are encountered on this model and do not lower the value. This is a rare Luger on today's market.

NIB	Exc.	V.G.	Good	Fair	Poor
—	2900	1900	950	600	450

Kadetten Institute Rework

4" barrel, 9mm caliber. It has a stock lug, and the chamber area is stamped "K.I." above the date 1933. This stood for Cadets Institute, an early "SA" and "SS" officers' training school. The extractor and safety are both marked, and the Waffenamt is present. There were only a few hundred reworked, and the variation is quite scarce. Be wary of fakes.

NIB	Exc.	V.G.	Good	Fair	Poor
—	3700	2900	1100	800	600

Mauser Unmarked Rework

4" barrel, 9mm caliber. The entire weapon is void of identifying markings. There is extensive refurbishing, removal of all markings, rebarreling, etc. The stock lug is present, and the extractor and safety are marked. The Waffenamt proofmark is on the right side of the receiver. The number manufactured is not known.

NIB	Exc.	V.G.	Good	Fair	Poor
—	2100	1350	850	600	450

MAUSER MANUFACTURED LUGERS 1930-1942 DWM

Mauser Oberndorf

4" barrel, 9mm caliber. It has a stock lug, blank chamber area and a marked extractor and safety. This is an early example of Mauser Luger, and the front toggle link is still marked DWM as leftover parts were intermixed with new Mauser parts in the production of this pistol. This is one of the first Lugers to be finished with the "Salt" blue process. There were approximately 500 manufactured with one- to four-digit serial numbers with the letter "v" suffix. This is a rare variation.

NIB	Exc.	V.G.	Good	Fair	Poor
—	7000	6100	2000	1500	900

1934/06 Swiss Commercial Mauser

4.75" barrel, 7.65mm caliber. There is no stock lug, but it has a grip safety. The Swiss Cross in Sunburst is stamped above the chamber. The extractor and safety are marked in German. The front toggle link is marked with the Mauser banner. There were approximately 200 manufactured for commercial sale in Switzerland. This variation is very well finished, and the serial numbers are all four digits with a "v" suffix.

NIB	Exc.	V.G.	Good	Fair	Poor
—	8000	6000	4000	1800	1000

1935/06 Portuguese "GNR"

4.75" barrel, 7.65mm caliber. It has no stock lug but has a grip safety. The chamber is marked "GNR," representing the Republic National Guard. The extractor is marked "Carregada"; and the safety "Seguranca". The Mauser banner is stamped on the front toggle link. There were exactly 564 manufactured according to the original contract records that the Portuguese government made public. They all have four-digit serial numbers with a "v" suffix.

NIB	Exc.	V.G.	Good	Fair	Poor
—	4500	3300	1800	900	750

1934 Mauser Commercial

4" barrel, 7.65mm or 9mm caliber. It has a stock lug, and the chamber area is blank. The extractor and the safety are marked. The Mauser banner is stamped on the front toggle link. The finish on this pistol was very good, and the grips are either checkered walnut or black plastic on the later models. There were a few thousand manufactured for commercial sales in and outside of Germany.

NIB	Exc.	V.G.	Good	Fair	Poor
—	4000	3500	1650	1100	700

S/42 K Date

4" barrel, 9mm caliber. It has a stock lug, and the extractor and safety are marked. This was the first Luger that utilized codes to represent maker and date of manufacture. The front toggle link is marked S/42 in either Gothic or script; this was the code for Mauser. The chamber area is stamped with the letter "K," the code for 1934, the year of manufacture. Approximately 10,500 were manufactured with one- to five-digit serial numbers—some with letter suffixes.

NIB	Exc.	V.G.	Good	Fair	Poor
—	9500	7000	3000	1200	1000

S/42 G Date

As above, with the chamber stamped "G," the code for the year 1935. The Gothic lettering was eliminated, and there were many thousands of this model produced.

Courtesy Orvel Reichert

NIB	Exc.	V.G.	Good	Fair	Poor
	3500	2500	1200	650	450

Dated Chamber S/42

4" barrel, 9mm caliber. The chamber area is dated 1936-1940, and there is a stock lug. The extractor and safety are marked. In 1937 the rust blue process was eliminated entirely, and all subsequent pistols were salt blued. There were many thousands manufactured with one- to five-digit serial numbers—some with the letter suffix. **NOTE:** Rarest variation is early 1937 with rust blued and strawed parts, add 20 percent.

NIB	Exc.	V.G.	Good	Fair	Poor
—	2700	2100	1100	500	400

S/42 Commercial Contract

4" barrel, 9mm caliber. It has a stock lug, and the chamber area is dated. It has a marked extractor and safety. The unusual feature is that, although this was a commercial pistol, the front toggle link is stamped S/42, which was the military code for Mauser. There were only a few hundred manufactured, so perhaps the toggles were left over from previous military production runs. The serial number range is four digits with the letter "v".

NIB	Exc.	V.G.	Good	Fair	Poor
—	3500	2500	1200	750	450

Code 42 Dated Chamber

4" barrel, 9mm caliber. The new German code for Mauser, the number 42, is stamped on the front toggle link. There is a stock lug. The chamber area is dated 1939 or 1940. There were at least 50,000 manufactured with one- to five-digit serial numbers; some have letter suffixes.

NIB	Exc.	V.G.	Good	Fair	Poor
—	2500	1400	1000	600	350

41/42 Code

As above, except that the date of manufacture is represented by the final two digits (e.g. 41 for 1941). There were approximately 20,000 manufactured with the one- to five-digit serial number range.

NIB	Exc.	V.G.	Good	Fair	Poor
—	2500	1750	1200	800	500

byf Code

As above, with the "byf" code stamp on the toggle link. The year of manufacture, either 41 or 42, is stamped on the chamber. This model was also made with black plastic, as well as walnut grips. There were many thousands produced with the one- to five-digit serial numbers—some with a letter suffix.

NIB	Exc.	V.G.	Good	Fair	Poor
—	3000	1800	950	450	350

Persian Contract 4"

4" barrel, 9mm caliber. It has a stock lug, and the Persian crest is stamped over the chamber. All identifying markings on this variation—including extractor, safety and toggle—are marked in Farsi, the Persian alphabet. There were 1,000 manufactured. The serial numbers are also in Farsi.

NIB	Exc.	V.G.	Good	Fair	Poor
—	7000	5500	3500	2500	2000

Persian Contract Artillery

As above, with an 8" barrel and nine-position adjustable sight on the barrel. This model is supplied with a flat board stock. There were 1,000 manufactured and sold to Persia.

NIB	Exc.	V.G.	Good	Fair	Poor
—	8500	5500	3500	1750	1000

1934/06 Dated Commercial

4.75" barrel, 7.65mm caliber. It has a grip safety but no stock lug. The year of manufacture, from 1937-1942, is stamped above the chamber, and the Mauser banner is stamped on the front link. The extractor is marked, but the safety is not. There were

approximately 1,000 manufactured with one- to three-digit serial numbers—some with the letter suffix.

NIB	Exc.	V.G.	Good	Fair	Poor
—	4200	3100	1400	900	500

1934 Mauser Dutch Contract

4" barrel, 9mm caliber. The year of manufacture, 1936-1940, is stamped above the chamber. The extractor is marked "Geladen" and the safety is marked "RUST" with a downward pointing arrow. The Mauser banner is stamped on the front toggle link. This was a military contract sale, and approximately 1,000 were manufactured with four-digit serial numbers with a letter "v" suffix.

NIB	Exc.	V.G.	Good	Fair	Poor
—	4500	3650	2000	1100	850

1934 Mauser Swedish Contract

4.75" barrel, 9mm or 7.65mm caliber. The chamber is dated 1938 or 1939. The extractor and safety are both marked in German, and there is a stock lug. The front toggle link is stamped with the Mauser banner. There were only 275 dated 1938 and 25 dated 1939 in 9mm. There were only 30 chambered for 7.65mm dated 1939. The serial number range is four digits with the letter "v" suffix.

NIB	Exc.	V.G.	Good	Fair	Poor
—	5200	3800	2000	1500	700

1934 Mauser Swedish Commercial

4" barrel, 7.65mm caliber. 1940 is stamped over the chamber; "Kal. 7.65" is stamped on the left side of the barrel. The extractor and safety are both marked, and the Mauser banner is stamped on the front toggle link. There is a stock lug. This model is rare as there were only a few hundred manufactured with four digit serial numbers with the letter "w" suffix.

NIB	Exc.	V.G.	Good	Fair	Poor
—	4500	2950	1200	850	600

1934 Mauser German Contract

4" barrel, 9mm caliber. The chamber is dated 1939-1942, and the front toggle link is stamped with the Mauser banner. There is a stock lug, and the extractor and safety are both marked. The grips are either walnut or black plastic. There were several thousand manufactured with one- to five-digit serial numbers—some with letter suffixes. They were purchased for issue to police or paramilitary units.

NIB	Exc.	V.G.	Good	Fair	Poor
—	3500	3200	1500	800	550

Austrian Bundes Heer (Federal Army)

4" barrel, 9mm caliber. The chamber is blank, and there is a stock lug. The extractor and safety are marked in German, and the Austrian Federal Army Proof is stamped on the left side of the frame above the trigger guard. There were approximately 200 manufactured with four-digit serial numbers and no letter suffix.

NIB	Exc.	V.G.	Good	Fair	Poor
—	3400	2350	1200	700	500

Mauser 2 Digit Date

4" barrel, 9mm caliber. The last two digits of the year of manufacture—41 or 42—are stamped over the chamber. There is a stock lug, and the Mauser banner is on the front toggle link. The extractor and safety are both marked, and the proofmarks were commercial. Grips are either walnut or black plastic. There were approximately 2,000 manufactured for sale to Nazi political groups. They have one- to five-digit serial numbers; some have the letter suffix.

NIB	Exc.	V.G.	Good	Fair	Poor
—	3500	2600	1500	900	650

Ku Luger (Prefix or suffix)

A 4" barrel, 9mm Luger probably manufactured by Mauser for the German Luftwaffe in the early 1940s. The serial number (on the left side receiver area) has a "Ku" prefix or suffix. Total production is estimated at 5000 pieces.

Courtesy Gale Morgan

NIB	Exc.	V.G.	Good	Fair	Poor
—	3900	2400	1200	900	550

KRIEGHOFF MANUFACTURED LUGERS

1923 DWM/Krieghoff Commercial

4" barrel, 7.65mm or 9mm caliber. The chamber is dated 1921 or left blank. There is a stock lug. The front toggle is marked DWM, as they manufactured this Luger to be sold by Krieghoff. "Krieghoff Suhl" is stamped on the back above the lanyard loop. The second "F" in Krieghoff was defective, and all specimens have this distinctive die strike. The safety and extractor are marked in German. There were only a few hundred manufactured with four-digit serial numbers with the letter "i" suffix.

NIB	Exc.	V.G.	Good	Fair	Poor
—	5000	3500	1700	900	500

DWM/Krieghoff Commercial

As above, but marked "Heinrich Krieghoff Waffenfabrik Suhl" on the right side of the frame. Some examples have the "Germany" export stamp. There were several hundred manufactured with four-digit serial numbers with a letter suffix.

NIB	Exc.	V.G.	Good	Fair	Poor
—	4800	3650	2000	950	800

Krieghoff Commercial Inscribed Side Frame

4" or 6" barrel, 7.65mm or 9mm caliber. 1,000 were marked "Heinrich Krieghoff Waffenfabrik Suhl" on the left side of the frame, and 500 were devoid of this marking. All have the dagger and anchor trademark over "H.K. Krieghoff Suhl" on the front toggle link. The extractor and the safety are both marked. There is a stock lug, and the grips are of brown checkered plastic. There were approximately 1,500 manufactured with one- to four-digit serial numbers with a "P" prefix.

NIB	Exc.	V.G.	Good	Fair	Poor
—	8500	6400	3000	2000	1000

S Code Krieghoff

4" barrel, 9mm caliber. The Krieghoff trademark is stamped on the front toggle link, and the letter "S" is stamped over the chamber. There is a stock lug, and the extractor and safety are both marked. The grips are wood on early manufactured pistols and brown checkered plastic on later examples. There were approximately

4,500 manufactured for the Luftwaffe with one- to four-digit serial numbers.

NIB	Exc.	V.G.	Good	Fair	Poor
—	7750	5500	2000	950	750

Grip Safety Krieghoff

4" barrel, 9mm caliber. The chamber area is blank, and the front toggle link is stamped with the Krieghoff trademark. There is a stock lug and a grip safety. The extractor is marked "Geleden," and the safety is marked "FEUER" (fire) in the lower position. The grips are checkered brown plastic. This is a rare Luger, and the number produced is not known.

NIB	Exc.	V.G.	Good	Fair	Poor
—	8500	5900	3400	1700	900

36 Date Krieghoff

4" barrel, 9mm caliber. It has a stock lug and the Krieghoff trademark on the front toggle link. The safety and extractor are marked, and the grips are brown plastic. The two-digit year of manufacture, 36, is stamped over the chamber. There were approximately 700 produced in the 3800-4500 serial number range.

NIB	Exc.	V.G.	Good	Fair	Poor
—	8500	5250	2600	1200	950

4 Digit Dated Krieghoff

As above, with the date of production, 1936-1945, stamped above the chamber. There were approximately 9,000 manufactured within the 4500-14000 serial number range.

Courtesy Gale Morgan

NIB	Exc.	V.G.	Good	Fair	Poor
—	7500	6000	3000	1500	750

2nd Series Krieghoff Commercial

4" barrel, 9mm caliber. There is a stock lug, and the Krieghoff trademark is stamped on the front link. The chamber area is blank, and the extractor and safety are marked. There were approximately 500 manufactured for commercial sales inside Germany. The date of manufacture is estimated at 1939-1940, as this variation has the dark finish that results from bluing without polishing the surface, which was done during these years. The grips are coarsely checkered black plastic. The serial number range is one to three digits with a "P" prefix.

NIB	Exc.	V.G.	Good	Fair	Poor
—	6500	4200	2200	1300	800

Post-War Krieghoff

4" barrel, 9mm caliber. There is a stock lug, and the chamber area is blank. The extractor and safety are marked, and the serial numbers in the one- to three-digit range are unusually large—about 3/16ths of an inch. There were 300 of these post-war Lugers produced for the occupation forces. They were assembled from leftover parts, and only 150 have the Krieghoff trademark on the front toggle link—the second 150 have blank links.

NIB	Exc.	V.G.	Good	Fair	Poor
—	6000	3500	2000	750	650

Krieghoff Post-War Commercial

As above, in 7.65mm caliber and the extractor not marked. Approximately 200 manufactured with standard-sized two- or three-digit serial numbers. They were supposedly sold to the occupation forces in the PX stores.

NIB	Exc.	V.G.	Good	Fair	Poor
—	6500	3500	2200	700	550

LUGER ACCESSORIES
Detachable Carbine Stocks

Approximately 13" in length, with a sling swivel and horn buttplate.

NIB	Exc.	V.G.	Good	Fair	Poor
—	6500	4500	3000	1000	700

Artillery Stock with Holster

The artillery stock is of a flat board style approximately 13.75" in length. There is a holster and magazine pouches with straps attached. This is a desirable addition to the Artillery Luger.

NIB	Exc.	V.G.	Good	Fair	Poor
—	3500	2500	1000	800	600

Navy Stock without Holster

As above, but 12.75" in length with a metal disc inlaid on the left side.

NIB	Exc.	V.G.	Good	Fair	Poor
—	4500	3000	1500	800	400

Ideal Stock/Holster with Grips

A telescoping metal tube stock with an attached leather holster. It is used in conjunction with a metal-backed set of plain grips that correspond to the metal hooks on the stock and allow attachment. This Ideal Stock is U.S. patented and is so marked.

NIB	Exc.	V.G.	Good	Fair	Poor
—	3000	2000	1500	700	450

Drum Magazine 1st Issue

A 32-round, snail-like affair that is used with the Artillery Luger. It is also used with an adapter in the German 9mm sub-machine gun. The 1st Issue has a telescoping tube that is used to wind the spring. There is a dust cover that protects the interior from dirt.

NIB	Exc.	V.G.	Good	Fair	Poor
—	2500	2000	1500	550	300

Drum Magazine 2nd Issue

As above, with a folding spring winding lever.

NIB	Exc.	V.G.	Good	Fair	Poor
—	2000	1700	1000	550	300

Drum Magazine Loading Tool

This tool is slipped over the magazine and allows the spring to be compressed so that cartridges could be inserted.

NIB	Exc.	V.G.	Good	Fair	Poor
—	800	550	500	300	200

Drum Carrying Case

NIB	Exc.	V.G.	Good	Fair	Poor
—	500	350	125	100	50

LATE PRODUCTION MAUSER LUGERS MANUFACTURED DURING THE 1970S
P.08 Interarms

4" or 6" barrel, 7.65mm or 9mm caliber.

NIB	Exc.	V.G.	Good	Fair	Poor
1750	1000	550	400	350	300

Swiss Eagle Interarms

Swiss-style straight front grip strap and the American Eagle crest over the chamber. It is chambered for 7.65mm or 9mm and is offered with a 4" or 6" barrel.

NIB	Exc.	V.G.	Good	Fair	Poor
1800	950	650	350	325	300

Cartridge Counter

Chambered for 9mm cartridge and fitted with a slotted grip to show cartridge count in magazine.

NIB	Exc.	V.G.	Good	Fair	Poor
2100	1600	1100	750	500	350

Commemorative Bulgarian

The Bulgarian crest is stamped over the chamber. There were only 100 produced.

NIB	Exc.	V.G.	Good	Fair	Poor
2200	1600	1100	750	500	350

Commemorative Russian

Crossed Nagant rifles are stamped over the chamber. There were 100 produced.

NIB	Exc.	V.G.	Good	Fair	Poor
2200	1600	1100	750	500	350

Modern Production Carbine

This splendid reproduction was produced on a limited basis. The workmanship is excellent, and the carbine and stock are furnished in a case.

NIB	Exc.	V.G.	Good	Fair	Poor
6000	4500	4000	3200	2500	2000

JOHN MARTZ CUSTOM LUGERS
Martz Luger Carbine

16" barrel. Fewer than 100 were manufactured.

NIB	Exc.	V.G.	Good	Fair	Poor
—	8700	7000	4500	2500	1000

.45 ACP or .357 SIG

6" barrel, .45 ACP caliber. Assembled from two Luger pistols that were split and welded together. Fewer than 100 manufactured.

NIB	Exc.	V.G.	Good	Fair	Poor
—	5500	4000	3000		

Baby Luger 9mm & 7.65mm

A compact Luger pistol. Fewer than 300 were produced.

Courtesy Gale Morgan

NIB	Exc.	V.G.	Good	Fair	Poor
—	4000	2500	1500	—	—

Baby Luger .380 ACP

As above, in .380 caliber. Seven were manufactured.

Courtesy Gale Morgan

NIB	Exc.	V.G.	Good	Fair	Poor
—	7500	6000	4000	—	—

LUNA
Zella-Mehlis, Germany
Model 200 Free Pistol

A .22 caliber Martini action single-shot pistol with an 11" barrel, adjustable sights, and walnut grips. Manufactured prior to WWII.

NIB	Exc.	V.G.	Good	Fair	Poor
—	1850	1250	800	500	300

Model 300 Free Pistol

This model is a single-shot target pistol chambered for .22 Short cartridge. Fitted with an 11" barrel, set trigger, walnut stocks and forearm with adjustable palm rest. Built from about 1929 to 1939.

NIB	Exc.	V.G.	Good	Fair	Poor
—	1950	1250	800	500	300

Target Rifle

A .22 or .22 Hornet caliber Martini action single-shot rifle with a 20" barrel, adjustable sights, and walnut stock. Manufactured prior to WWII.

NIB	Exc.	V.G.	Good	Fair	Poor
—	1800	1350	850	500	250

LYMAN
Middletown, Connecticut
Lyman In-Line

Introduced in 1998 this in-line muzzleloader is offered in either .50 or .54 caliber. Fitted with a 22" barrel. Hardwood stock. Add $80 for stainless steel version.

NIB	Exc.	V.G.	Good	Fair	Poor
300	250	200	125	75	50

Deerstalker Rifle

Available in either .50 or .54 caliber percussion or flintlock. Fitted with a 24" barrel and hardwood stock. A stainless steel version is also offered for an additional $80.

NIB	Exc.	V.G.	Good	Fair	Poor
375	250	200	150	100	50

Deerstalker Carbine

Same as above but with 21" barrel. Offered in .50 caliber only.

NIB	Exc.	V.G.	Good	Fair	Poor
375	250	200	150	100	50

Great Plains Rifle

This rifle is offered in .50 or .54 caliber flint or percussion. Barrel length is 32". Hardwood stock. **NOTE:** Add $25 for flintlock version and $10 for left-hand rifles. Early models in Excellent condition are showing significant collector potential.

NIB	Exc.	V.G.	Good	Fair	Poor
525	400	300	175	125	100

Trade Rifle

This rifle is offered in either .50 or .54 caliber with 28" octagonal barrel and hardwood stock. Polished brass furniture. Add $25 for flintlock rifle.

NIB	Exc.	V.G.	Good	Fair	Poor
300	250	200	125	75	50

Plains Pistol

Available in .50 or .54 caliber percussion.

NIB	Exc.	V.G.	Good	Fair	Poor
375	250	200	125	75	50

M.O.A. CORP.
Dayton, Ohio

Maximum

A single-shot pistol manufactured in a variety of calibers from .22 rimfire to .454 Casull with an 8.5", 10", or 14" barrel, adjustable sights, stainless steel receiver blued barrel and walnut grip. Introduced in 1986. **NOTE:** Add 100 percent for stainless steel barrel.

NIB	Exc.	V.G.	Good	Fair	Poor
800	600	475	325	250	125

NOTE: Add 100 percent for stainless steel barrel.

Carbine

As above with an 18" barrel. Discontinued.

NIB	Exc.	V.G.	Good	Fair	Poor
1000	675	525	350	275	150

MAC
See—Ingram

MADSEN
Copenhagen, Denmark

Model 47

NIB	Exc.	V.G.	Good	Fair	Poor
—	700	525	400	275	125

MAGNUM RESEARCH, INC.
Minneapolis, Minnesota
See Also—Desert Eagle

BFR (Long Cylinder)

This is a single-action revolver with a long cylinder chambered for .22 Hornet, .30-30, .475/.480, .444, .45-70, .460 S&W, and .45 LC/.410 with 7.5" or 10" barrel and .444 Marlin with 10" barrel. Also chambered for .500 S&W Magnum. Fitted with adjustable sights and stainless steel finish. Weight is about 4 lbs. with 7.5" barrel. Introduced in 1998.

NIB	Exc.	V.G.	Good	Fair	Poor
900	775	500	350	200	100

BFR Little Max (Short Cylinder)

This single-action revolver has a standard cylinder chambered for the .454 Casull (6.5", 7.5", or 10" barrel), .45 Long Colt (6.5" or 7.5" barrel), .22 Hornet (7.5" barrel), or .50 A.E (7.5" barrel). Weight is about 3.5 lbs. with 7.5" barrel. Introduced in 1998. Discontinued.

NIB	Exc.	V.G.	Good	Fair	Poor
800	675	500	350	200	100

IMI SP-21

This is semi-automatic double-action pistol chambered for the 9mm, .40 S&W, or .45 ACP cartridge. Barrel length is 3.9". Magazine capacity is 10 rounds for all calibers. Polymer frame with steel slide and barrel. Weight is about 26 oz. Made in Israel by Israel Military Industries. Discontinued.

NIB	Exc.	V.G.	Good	Fair	Poor
550	400	300	200	150	100

MALIN, F. E.
London, England

Boxlock and sidelock shotguns made by Malin were imported into the United States for a number of years. As these arms were all essentially built to specific customer's requirements, values listed are rough estimates only.

Boxlock Basic Model

Features an Anson & Deeley action and high-grade walnut. All other specification were on a custom-order basis. This gun should definitely be individually appraised as values will fluctuate greatly with options.

NIB	Exc.	V.G.	Good	Fair	Poor
4800	4000	3500	2500	1850	1000

Sidelock Basic Model

Features a Holland & Holland-type detachable sidelock action, and all other features (as on the boxlock) were on a custom-order basis. This model should also be appraised individually.

NIB	Exc.	V.G.	Good	Fair	Poor
7000	6000	4750	3000	2500	1250

MALTBY, HENLEY AND CO.
New York, New York
Spencer Safety Hammerless Revolver

A .32 caliber double-action revolver with a 3" barrel and 5-shot cylinder. The frame and barrel made of brass and the cylinder of steel. The barrel marked "Spencer Safety Hammerless Pat. Jan. 24, 1888 & Oct. 29, 1889". Several thousand were manufactured during the 1890s.

Courtesy Mike Stuckslager

NIB	Exc.	V.G.	Good	Fair	Poor
—	—	325	225	125	75

MANHATTAN FIREARMS COMPANY
Norwich, Connecticut
Newark, New Jersey
Bar Hammer Pistol

A .31, .34, or .36 caliber single-shot percussion pistol with a 2" or 4" barrel. The hammer marked "Manhattan F.A. Mfg. Co. New York". Blued with walnut grips. Approximately 1,500 were made during the 1850s.

NIB	Exc.	V.G.	Good	Fair	Poor
—	—	1050	750	300	150

Shotgun Hammer Pistol

A .36 caliber bar hammer single-shot percussion pistol with a 5.5" half octagonal barrel marked as above. Blued with walnut grips. Approximately 500 were made.

NIB	Exc.	V.G.	Good	Fair	Poor
—	—	1050	750	300	150

Pepperbox

A .28 or .31 caliber double-action percussion pepperbox with 3", 4", or 5" barrels and 5- or 6-shot barrel groups. Blued, case hardened with walnut grips. Marked as above and also "Cast Steel". The major variations of this pistol are as follows:

Courtesy Milwaukee Public Museum, Milwaukee, Wisconsin

Three-shot with 3" Barrel
Manually rotated barrels.

NIB	Exc.	V.G.	Good	Fair	Poor
—	—	950	550	250	125

Five-shot with 3", 4", 5" Barrel
Automatically rotated barrels.

NIB	Exc.	V.G.	Good	Fair	Poor
—	—	1100	650	450	250

Six-shot with 3" or 4" Barrel
Automatic rotation.

NIB	Exc.	V.G.	Good	Fair	Poor
—	—	1100	650	450	250

Six-shot with 5" Barrel
Automatic rotation.

NIB	Exc.	V.G.	Good	Fair	Poor
—	—	1600	1200	550	350

Pocket Revolver

A .31 caliber percussion revolver with a 4", 5", or 6" barrel and either 5-shot or 6-shot cylinder. Blued, case hardened with walnut grips. The barrel marked, "Manhattan Firearms/Manufg. Co. New York" on the 5-shot model, serial numbers from 1 to approximately 1,000, and "Manhattan Firearms Mfg. Co. New York" on the 6-shot model. The frame marked "December 27, 1859".

Courtesy Milwaukee Public Museum, Milwaukee, Wisconsin

First Model—Five-Shot

NIB	Exc.	V.G.	Good	Fair	Poor
—	—	1200	600	450	150

Second Model—Six-Shot

NIB	Exc.	V.G.	Good	Fair	Poor
—	—	1200	600	450	150

London Pistol Company

As above, but marked "London Pistol Company". Approximately 200 manufactured between 1859 and 1861.

NIB	Exc.	V.G.	Good	Fair	Poor
—	—	1400	750	450	150

.36 Caliber Percussion Revolver

A .36 caliber percussion revolver with a 4", 5", or 6.5" octagonal barrel and 5- or 6-shot cylinder. Blued, case hardened with walnut grips. Approximately 78,000 were made between 1859 and 1868. There were five variations.

Courtesy Milwaukee Public Museum, Milwaukee, Wisconsin

Model I

A 5-shot cylinder marked "Manhattan Firearms Mfg. Co. New York". The serial numbers from 1 through 4200. **NOTE**: The 6" barreled version would be worth a 15 percent premium.

NIB	Exc.	V.G.	Good	Fair	Poor
—	—	1500	1050	550	150

Model II

As above with the 1859 patent date marked on the barrel. The serial range is 4200 to 14500.

NIB	Exc.	V.G.	Good	Fair	Poor
—	—	1650	1350	550	150

Model III

A 5-shot cylinder and marked, "Manhattan Firearms Co. Newark NJ", together with the 1859 patent date. The serial numbers are from 14500 to 45200.

NIB	Exc.	V.G.	Good	Fair	Poor
—	—	1575	1200	500	150

Model IV

As above, with a modified recoil shield and the patent date March 8, 1864, added to the barrel inscription. Serial numbers from 45200 to 69200.

NIB	Exc.	V.G.	Good	Fair	Poor
—	—	1600	1250	450	150

Model V

NIB	Exc.	V.G.	Good	Fair	Poor
—	—	1700	1350	550	200

.22 Caliber Pocket Revolver

A .22 caliber spur trigger revolver with a 3" barrel and 7-shot cylinder. Blued, silver plated with walnut or rosewood grips. Approximately 17,000 were made during the 1860s. A fairly close copy of the S&W No. 1.

Courtesy Milwaukee Public Museum, Milwaukee, Wisconsin

NIB	Exc.	V.G.	Good	Fair	Poor
—	—	550	300	250	100

Manhattan-American Standard Hero

A .34 caliber single-shot percussion pistol with a 2" or 3" round barrel that unscrews for loading. Blued, brass frame with walnut grips. Marked "A.S.T. Co./HERO". Made by the American Standard Tool Company, Manhattan's successor. Approximately 30,000 manufactured between 1868 and 1873.

Manhattan Manufactured

Marked, "HERO/M.F.A.Co." Approximately 5,000 were produced.

NIB	Exc.	V.G.	Good	Fair	Poor
—	—	625	550	250	100

American Standard Manufactured

Approximately 25,000 were produced.

NIB	Exc.	V.G.	Good	Fair	Poor
—	—	625	500	225	100

MANN, FRITZ
Suhl, Germany

6.35mm Pocket Pistol

A 6.35mm caliber semi-automatic pistol with a 1.65" barrel and 5-shot magazine. Blued with plastic grips having the name "Mann" cast in them. This pistol, which weighs only 9 oz., is one of the smallest semi-automatic pistols ever manufactured. Made between 1920 and 1922.

NIB	Exc.	V.G.	Good	Fair	Poor
—	395	295	200	150	100

7.65mm Pocket Pistol

A 7.65mm or 9mm short semi-automatic pistol with a 2.35" barrel and 5-shot magazine. Blued with plastic grips that have the name "Mann" cast in them. Manufactured between 1924 and 1929.

NIB	Exc.	V.G.	Good	Fair	Poor
—	375	275	200	150	100

MANNLICHER PISTOL
Steyr, Austria
See—Steyr

MANNLICHER SCHOENAUER
Steyr, Austria

For military models and their history, technical data, descriptions, and prices see the *Standard Catalog of Military Firearms* under "Austria-Hungary". For currently imported Mannlicher models, see Steyr.

Model 1903 Carbine

A 6.5x54mm caliber bolt-action rifle with a 17.7" barrel. Rotary magazine capacity is 5 rounds. Folding rear leaf sight, double set triggers, and full-length walnut stock. Discontinued prior to WWII.

NIB	Exc.	V.G.	Good	Fair	Poor
—	2200	1650	1300	1000	550

Model 1905 Carbine

As above but chambered for the 9x56mm cartridge. Discontinued prior to WWII.

NIB	Exc.	V.G.	Good	Fair	Poor
—	1850	1500	1000	750	550

Model 1908 Carbine

As above but chambered for the 7x57mm or 8x56mm cartridge. Discontinued prior to WWII.

NIB	Exc.	V.G.	Good	Fair	Poor
—	1950	1600	1000	750	550

Model 1910 Carbine

As above but chambered for the 9.5x57mm cartridge. Discontinued prior to WWII.

NIB	Exc.	V.G.	Good	Fair	Poor
—	1850	1500	1000	750	550

Model 1924 Carbine

As above but chambered for the .30-06 cartridge. Discontinued prior to WWII.

NIB	Exc.	V.G.	Good	Fair	Poor
—	2750	2250	1750	1000	550

High Velocity Rifle

As above, but in 7x64mm Brenneke, .30-06, 8x60Smm Magnum, 9.3x62mm, and the 10.75x68mm caliber with a 23.5" barrel and folding leaf sight. Half-length walnut stock. Discontinued prior to WWII. **NOTE:** Takedown Model add 75 percent.

NIB	Exc.	V.G.	Good	Fair	Poor
—	2750	2250	1750	1000	550

Model 1950

A .257 Roberts, .270 Winchester, and .30-06 caliber bolt-action rifle with a 24" barrel and 5-shot rotary magazine. Blued with a half length walnut stock. Manufactured between 1950 and 1952.

NIB	Exc.	V.G.	Good	Fair	Poor
2000	1600	1250	800	650	450

Model 1950 Carbine

As above, with a 20" barrel and a full-length stock.

NIB	Exc.	V.G.	Good	Fair	Poor
2200	1750	1250	800	650	450

Model 1950 6.5 Carbine

As above, in 6.5x54mm Mannlicher Schoenauer caliber with a 18.5" barrel and full-length stock.

NIB	Exc.	V.G.	Good	Fair	Poor
2300	1900	1400	1000	650	300

Model 1952

Similar to the above, with a turned back bolt handle. Manufactured between 1952 and 1956.

NIB	Exc.	V.G.	Good	Fair	Poor
2400	2100	1850	1300	650	300

Model 1952 Carbine

Similar to the Model 1950 carbine, but additionally in 7x57mm caliber. Manufactured between 1952 and 1956.

NIB	Exc.	V.G.	Good	Fair	Poor
2450	2100	1850	1300	650	300

Model 1952 6.5mm Carbine

As above, in 6.5x54mm Mannlicher Schoenauer caliber with an 18.5" barrel. Manufactured between 1952 and 1956.

NIB	Exc.	V.G.	Good	Fair	Poor
2400	2000	1500	850	650	300

Model 1956 Rifle

A .243 or .30-06 caliber bolt-action rifle with a 22" barrel and Monte Carlo-style stock. Manufactured between 1956 and 1960.

NIB	Exc.	V.G.	Good	Fair	Poor
2100	1900	1700	950	650	300

Model 1956 Carbine

As above, with a 20" barrel and full-length stock. Manufactured between 1956 and 1960.

NIB	Exc.	V.G.	Good	Fair	Poor
2100	1900	1700	950	650	300

Model 1961 MCA Rifle

As above, but modified for easier use with a telescopic sight.

NIB	Exc.	V.G.	Good	Fair	Poor
1750	1550	1250	1000	800	650

Model 1961 MCA Carbine

As above, with a 20" barrel and half-length stock.

NIB	Exc.	V.G.	Good	Fair	Poor
1950	1650	1250	1100	700	600

Model M72 LM Rifle

Fitted with a 23" fluted barrel, double set or single trigger and full-length stock. Manufactured between 1972 and 1980.

NIB	Exc.	V.G.	Good	Fair	Poor
—	1300	1050	700	550	450

MANUFRANCE
St. Etienne, France
See—Le Francais

Auto Stand

A .22 caliber semi-automatic pistol manufactured by Pyrenees and sold by Manufrance under the trade name Auto Stand.

NIB	Exc.	V.G.	Good	Fair	Poor
—	250	225	200	150	100

Buffalo Stand

A .22 caliber bolt-action pistol with a 12" barrel and adjustable sights. Blued with a walnut stock. Manufactured prior to 1914.

NIB	Exc.	V.G.	Good	Fair	Poor
—	250	225	200	150	100

Le Agent

An 8mm caliber double-action revolver with a 5" barrel. Blued with walnut grips.

NIB	Exc.	V.G.	Good	Fair	Poor
—	200	100	175	150	75

Le Colonial

As above, with an enclosed hammer.

NIB	Exc.	V.G.	Good	Fair	Poor
—	200	175	150	100	75

LeFrancais

A semi-automatic pistol chambered for the 7.65mm cartridge. Built on the blowback design. The 7.65mm pistols were first built in 1950 and production stopped in 1959. Very few of these pistols are in the U.S.

Courtesy J.B. Wood

NIB	Exc.	V.G.	Good	Fair	Poor
—	525	425	300	200	100

MANURHIN
Saint-Bonnet-le-Chateau, France

This company manufactured the Walther PP and PPK models under license and these are marked "Manufacture de Machines du Haut-Rhin" on the left front of the slide and "Lic Excl. Walther" on the left rear. These arms were imported into the U.S.A. in the early 1950s by Thalson Import Company of San Francisco, California, and later by Interarms. The latter are marked "Mark 11" and "Made in France". Manurhin is now owned by Chapuis Armes. **NOTE:** For all models, add 15 percent for police markings.

Model PP

Similar to the Walther Model PP, with a revised safety. Discontinued.

NIB	Exc.	V.G.	Good	Fair	Poor
—	400	350	300	225	150

Model PPK/S

Similar to the Walther Model PPK/S, with a revised safety. Discontinued.

NIB	Exc.	V.G.	Good	Fair	Poor
—	400	350	300	225	150

Model PP Sports

This is a target version of the PP chambered for the .22 caliber shell. Available in various barrel lengths. Discontinued.

NIB	Exc.	V.G.	Good	Fair	Poor
—	400	350	300	225	150

Model 73 Defense Revolver

A .38 Special or .357 Magnum caliber double-action swing-out cylinder revolver with a 2.5", 3", or 4" barrel having fixed sights. Blued with walnut grips.

NIB	Exc.	V.G.	Good	Fair	Poor
1150	1000	850	750	500	350

Model 73 Gendarmerie

As above, with a 5.5", 6", or 8" long barrel and adjustable sights.

NIB	Exc.	V.G.	Good	Fair	Poor
1250	1100	900	800	550	400

Model 73 Sport

Similar to the above, with a shortened lock time and target-style adjustable sights.

NIB	Exc.	V.G.	Good	Fair	Poor
1250	1100	900	800	550	400

Model 73 Convertible

As above, with interchangeable .22, .32, or .38 caliber barrels and cylinders.

NIB	Exc.	V.G.	Good	Fair	Poor
2250	1850	1600	1400	950	750

Model 73 Silhouette

Similar to the Model 73 Sport, but in .22 to .357 Magnum caliber with a 10" or 10.75" shrouded barrel and form fitting walnut grips.

NIB	Exc.	V.G.	Good	Fair	Poor
1200	1050	850	750	500	350

MARATHON PRODUCTS, INC.
Santa Barbara, California

.22 First Shot

A .22 caliber single-shot bolt-action rifle with a 16.5" barrel and overall length of 31". Blued with a walnut stock. Manufactured between 1985 and 1987.

NIB	Exc.	V.G.	Good	Fair	Poor
—	75	55	45	30	25

.22 Super Shot

As above, with a 24" barrel. Manufactured between 1985 and 1987.

NIB	Exc.	V.G.	Good	Fair	Poor
—	75	55	45	30	25

.22 Hot Shot Pistol

A .22 caliber bolt-action pistol with a 14.5" barrel. Blued with a walnut stock. Manufactured in 1986 and 1987.

NIB	Exc.	V.G.	Good	Fair	Poor
—	100	55	45	30	25

Centerfire Rifle

A bolt-action sporting rifle manufactured in a variety of calibers with a 24" barrel, open sights, adjustable trigger and 5-shot magazine. Blued with a walnut stock. Manufactured in 1985 and 1986.

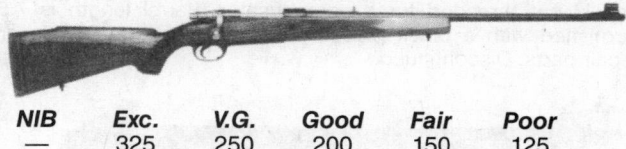

NIB	Exc.	V.G.	Good	Fair	Poor
—	325	250	200	150	125

MARBLE'S ARMS & MFG. CO.
Gladstone, Michigan
Marble's Game Getter Gun—NFA, curio or relic

Marble's suspended sales of the Game Getter in the United States after the Treasury Department ruled it was a "firearm" under the NFA, but continued sales abroad. Its retail price in 1934 was about $24 (12" or 15" barrels) to $26 (18" barrels). The Bureau of Internal Revenue removed the 18" barrel variation from the NFA in a Letter Ruling dated March 1, 1939. Today, the 12" and 15" barrel variations are controlled under the NFA in the "any other weapon" category. If the shoulder stock is removed from a 12", 15", or 18" barreled Game Getter, however, ATF has ruled it to be a NFA "firearm" subject to a $200 transfer tax.

Model 1908

Serial numbered from A to M; then 001 to 10000.

NIB	Exc.	V.G.	Good	Fair	Poor
—	1800	1200	750	550	425

The Model 1908 was available in two variations. Model 1908A has a flexible rear tang sight and the Model 1908B has a filler block. Some confusion about the serial numbering exists, because some Marble's factory representatives gave out incorrect information during the 1960s and 1970s. According to some letters from this period, on Marble's factory letterhead, serial numbers began with number 700 and ended with 9999. Original factory records, however, disclose that the Model 1908 was first shipped from the factory in 1909, serial numbered with letters A through M, before beginning numerically with serial number 001 through 10000, when production ended in May, 1914. Serial number 001 was shipped from the factory on March 3, 1909 and the last Model 1908 was shipped on May 22, 1918.

The markings on the Model 1908 are:

    Type I (serial 1 to about 4000)
    Type II (about serial 4000 to 9999)

LEFT SIDE:
MANUFACTURED BY THE
MARBLE SAFETY AXE CO.
GLADSTONE, MICH. U.S.A.
Marble Arms & Mfg. Co.

MANUFACTURED BY THE
MARBLE SAFETY AXE CO.
GLADSTONE, MICH. U.S.A.

SUCCESSOR

RIGHT SIDE:
Calibers 22 & 44
Patent Allowed

Calibers 22 & 44
Patent Allowed

Each of the markings on the right side is enclosed within an elongated circle.

OTHER CHARACTERISTICS: Separate flat buttplate attached with two screws up to approximately serial number 1200; afterwards, a flattened buttplate was integrally formed from the same round steel used to form the skeleton stock. Early stocks have drop adjustment with a knurled collar 3/8" diameter by 13/16" long; at approximately serial number 2500, the collar was changed to 1/2" by 5/8" long. The hammer spur is curved down up to approximately serial number 2,000, then the curve at hammer is up.

The Model 1908 was originally designed for .22 short, long or LR and .44 shot and ball ammunition, but the most satisfactory load was the long-cased .44-40 that held the shot in place with a disk and mouth crimp. The 1915 Marble's catalog stated the Model 1908 was available for use with the 2" .410 shotgun shell; chambering is slightly different from that of the .44-40, but is seldom encountered. Production of the Model 1908 was not resumed because of World War I.

Model 1921

NIB	Exc.	V.G.	Good	Fair	Poor
—	1800	1200	750	550	425

To meet the continuing demand for the extremely popular 1908, Marble's produced an entirely new gun in 1921. The grip, folding stock (made from cold-rolled sheet metal and nickel-plated), and other features were redesigned. The serial number range for the Model 1921 is 10001 (shipped in October 1921) to 20076. Most production of the Model 1921 apparently ended around the time of World War II; however, factory records disclose that Marble's was exporting 15" barrel Model 1921s into Canada in 1955, where their registration was not required at that time. Marble's also assembled approximately 200 Model 1921s from parts circa 1960-61, and sold them (without the holster) for $200 each.

The Model 1921 was originally designed for the 2" .410 shotgun shell, but Marble's changed the extractor marking on some guns to 2" or 2-1/2" to indicate factory rechambering for the 2.5" shell, which has been reported to have started in 1924. However, the change to a 2-1/2" chamber may not have been uniform, because both 2" and 2-1/2" marked guns have been observed in low (14000) and high (19000) serial number ranges. The lowest serial number with 2-1/2" marking observed so far is 14601. The range from approximately 14500 to 17000 have plastic rather than walnut grips, a single-bladed rear sight rather than multiple-blade and blued rather than case-hardened hammer. Outside this range, only 19288 has the 2" marking; and number 19692 is marked 2-1/2". No Model 1921 Game Getters are known to have been factory chambered for the 3" .410 shell.

The markings on the Model 1921 are:

LEFT SIDE:
Marble's
Game Getter Gun
Marble Arms & Mfg.Co.
Gladstone, Mich.U.S.A.

RIGHT SIDE: **UPPER BARREL 22 S.L. LR.&N.R.A
LOWER BARREL .44GG & .410 2"**

OTHER CHARACTERISTICS: Other barrel markings for the Model 1921 in .410 are **.410 2" and .410 2-1/2"**; the latter appears in the serial number range from approximately 15000 to 16600 and in the low 19000 range.

NOTE: Boxed guns (wooden box, Model 1908; cardboard box, Model 1921) with accessories, or 18" barrel variations, nonstandard calibers (.25-20, .32-20, .38-40, etc.) command premiums of 50 to 200 percent or more; an original holster is $75 to $150. Two (2) new-in-box Model 1908 with 15" and 18" barrels sold for $2,700 and $3,600, respectively, in 1994. An original wooden Model 1908 box alone may sell for $500 to $900. All 18" barrel variations are rare.

Marble's Game Getter Pistol and other special-order or experimental Game Getters—NFA, curio or relic

Contemporary articles and advertisements in Hunter-Trader-Trapper and some early Marble's catalogs, state that a small number of Model 1908 Game Getters were originally manufactured (with rifled barrels) for .25-20, .32-20, and .38-

40 cartridges. An illustrated advertisement in a 1910 issue of Hunter-Trapper-Trader states that 12", 15" and 18" barrel Game Getters were available for delivery in .25-20, .32-20 and .38-40 and that these firearms were designed as over/under rifles with rifled barrels. An article in the October 1913 issue of Outdoor Life states that Marble's was manufacturing a Game Getter pistol, with 10" barrels and that any barrel length could be ordered.

Original factory records have confirmed the manufacture of the foregoing Game Getters, and clarified their designs. All original guns are thus correctly classified as experimental or special-order guns, and all are extremely rare. Factory records disclose that about 20 each of the Model 1908 were manufactured with .22/25-20 and .22/.32-20 over/under rifled barrels, but the barrel lengths are not specified. No .22/.38-40 Model 1908 Game Getters are listed in the factory records, but that may not have precluded a later factory alteration to that configuration. It is important to note that any Model 1908 Game Getter with over/under rifled barrels less than 18" in length is currently subject to registration under the NFA as a short barreled rifle, with a $200 transfer tax. Under current law, if these firearms are not registered they are contraband and cannot be legally owned unless B.A.T.F.E. administratively removes them from the NFA as collector's items.

Factory records disclose that eight Model 1908 Game Getter pistols were manufactured and all were shipped to a Minneapolis hardware store. Two specimens have been located: serial number 3810, with a 8" .22/.44 smooth bore barrel, and serial number 3837, with a 10" .22/.44 smooth bore barrel. Inspection of serial numbers 3810 and 3837 (including removal of the grips) reveal they were never fitted with shoulder stocks, because the portion of the frame which would have accommodated the stock was never machined out to receive one. Under current law, an original Marble's Game Getter pistol is subject to registration under the NFA as an "Any Other Weapon" with a $5 transfer tax. According to very incomplete factory records, a relatively small number—about a dozen—Model 1921 Game Getters were manufactured with .22/.38-40 rifled barrels, but the barrel lengths are not specified. It is possible that other factory-original configurations exist, such as .22/.25-20 and others.

MARGOLIN
Tula, Soviet State Arsenal
Model MT Sports

This is a semi-automatic .22 caliber pistol with no barrel weights and is not threaded for a compensator. Barrel length is 7.5". Furnished with a black plastic case with spare magazine and repair parts. Discontinued.

Courtesy Orvel Reichert

NIB	Exc.	V.G.	Good	Fair	Poor
—	600	500	400	300	200

Model MTS-1

A .22 short semi-automatic pistol with a 5.9" barrel having an integral muzzle brake (7.4" overall), adjustable walnut grips and a 6-shot magazine. Normally, accompanied by a wooden case with cleaning accessories. Discontinued.

Courtesy Orvel Reichert

NIB	Exc.	V.G.	Good	Fair	Poor
—	1300	1025	800	450	350

Model MTS-2

As above, in .22 LR with a 5.9" barrel. Discontinued.

Courtesy Orvel Reichert

NIB	Exc.	V.G.	Good	Fair	Poor
—	1200	900	600	400	350

MARIETTE BREVETTE
Liege, Belgium

A number of European manufacturers produced percussion pepperbox pistols based upon a patent issued to Mariette during the 1840s and 1850s. These pistols have detachable barrels that are loaded at the breech, double-action ring triggers, and internally mounted hammers. They are normally blued and foliate engraved.

4" Barrel Pepperbox

NIB	Exc.	V.G.	Good	Fair	Poor
—	—	2250	900	400	—

6" Barrel Pepperbox

NIB	Exc.	V.G.	Good	Fair	Poor
—	—	2250	900	400	—

MARLIN FIREARMS CO.
Madison, North Carolina

Marlin, along with its subsidiaries Harrington & Richardson/NEF, is now owned by the Freedom Group Family of Companies.

BALLARD RIFLES

Established by John Mahlon Marlin in 1863. Marlin manufactured pistols until 1875 when he began production of Ballard rifles. In 1881 he made his first lever-action repeating rifle for which his company became famous.

BALL & WILLIAMS BALLARDS
First Model

This model was the first Ballard produced. It was introduced in 1861 and was offered with a 24" or 28" octagonal barrel. The frame is case colored, and the barrel is blued. The walnut stock is varnished. The major identifying feature of this model is the inside extractor. This was the only Ballard that had this feature before Marlin began to manufacture the rifle in 1875. The barrel is stamped "Ball & Williams/Worchester, Mass." and "Ballards Patent/Nov. 5, 1861". There were approximately 100 manufactured and serial numbered from 1-100.

NIB	Exc.	V.G.	Good	Fair	Poor
—	—	3000	2500	900	400

Military Rifle

There is not enough known about these rifles and probably never will be. They were chambered most frequently for the .44 and .54 rimfire cartridges and feature the outside tangs and extractors. They were offered with a 30" round barrel and full-length forearm. There are three barrel bands and sling swivels. The government ordered only 35 of these for use in the Civil War; and if one was to be definitely authenticated as a genuine martial specimen, it would be quite valuable. Many of these rifles were marked "Kentucky" on top of the receiver because the militia of that state armed its men with the Ballard rifles and carbines. This marking was a sales aid used by the company and does not indicate militia ownership. The number manufactured is not known. Barrel markings are as on the First Model.

NIB	Exc.	V.G.	Good	Fair	Poor
—	—	5000	2850	1250	300

Civil War Military Carbine

This model has a 22" part-round, part-octagonal barrel and is chambered for the .44 rimfire cartridge. It has the outside tang and extractor. The stock and forearm are walnut with a barrel band sling swivel. The buttstock bears an oval cartouche surrounding the inspector's marks, "MM." These letters also appear stamped on major metal parts. There were 1,509 ordered by the government for use in the Civil War. The barrel was marked the same as the rifle.

NIB	Exc.	V.G.	Good	Fair	Poor
—	—	5500	3750	1500	500

Sporting Rifle

This model is chambered for the .32, .38, and .44 rimfire cartridges. The octagonal barrel is 24", 26", or 28" in length and is blued. The frame is case colored. The stock and forearm are varnished walnut, and there is a knob that protrudes in front of the frame to operate the outside manual extractor. There is a crescent buttplate standard. There were approximately 6,500 manufactured, and barrel markings are the same as on the First Model.

NIB	Exc.	V.G.	Good	Fair	Poor
—	—	2000	1550	500	200

Sporting Carbine

This model is similar in appearance to the Sporting Rifle with a 22" part-round, part-octagonal barrel. It is chambered for the .44 and .54 caliber cartridge, and the sling swivel is found on a barrel band in the front. The knob on the bottom activates the outside extractor. There have been some encountered with "Kentucky" stamped on the top, but this does not affect the value. The markings are the same as on the previous models. There are no production figures available, but some estimate approximately 2,000 were manufactured.

NIB	Exc.	V.G.	Good	Fair	Poor
—	—	2200	1750	600	250

Dual Ignition System

This system allows the use of the rimfire cartridge or percussion method by simply turning the striker on the hammer from one position to the other. This model features a percussion nipple mounted on the breechblock, and the hammer is marked "Patented Jan. 5, 1864". The patent was held by Merwin and Bray. This swivel system is usually found on the sporting models and would increase the value of the weapon by 20 percent.

MERRIMACK ARMS CO. AND BROWN MANUFACTURING CO. (BALLARDS)

The values for the Ballard rifles manufactured by these two firms are the same, and the specifications are similar. The identifying difference is in the markings, "Merrimack Arms & Mfg. Co./ Newburyport Mass." or "Brown Mfg. Co. Newburyport, Mass." Merrimack produced approximately 3,000 of these rifles between 1867 and 1869 serial numbered in the 18000-20000 range. Brown produced approximately 1,800 between 1869 and 1873 in the 20000-22000 serial number range.

Sporting Rifle

This model was produced in .22 (rare), .32, .38, .44, .46, and .52 caliber rimfire or percussion, as most encountered featured the dual ignition system and had the nipple in the breechblock. They have either a round or octagonal barrel in 24", 26", or 28" lengths. The appearance and finish is similar to the Ball & Williams rifles; and the major difference is the inside tang. The extractor was still outside mounted and manually activated. Exact production breakdown is unknown. There is no premium for the dual ignition system on these later guns.

NIB	Exc.	V.G.	Good	Fair	Poor
—	—	1700	1250	450	200

Sporting Carbine

This model is quite similar in appearance to the Sporting Rifle, with a 22" part-round, part-octagonal barrel.

NIB	Exc.	V.G.	Good	Fair	Poor
—	—	1800	1350	550	300

Military Rifle

The Military Rifle is similar to the sporting version except that it has a 30" round barrel and full-length forearm with three barrel bands. It is chambered for the .44 and .52 caliber rimfire or percussion with the dual ignition system.

NIB	Exc.	V.G.	Good	Fair	Poor
—	—	2000	1500	650	300

Shotgun

This model is similar to the Sporting Rifle in appearance but is chambered for 24 gauge, with a 30" round barrel. There is a groove milled in the top of the frame to use as a sight. The buttplate is shotgun-style instead of the usual crescent shape.

NIB	Exc.	V.G.	Good	Fair	Poor
—	—	1200	800	350	200

MARLIN-BALLARD RIFLES

Commencing in 1875 the Ballard single-shot rifle was made by John Marlin for Schoverling and Daly. In 1881 the business was incorporated and became the Marlin Firearms Co. All the Ballards made from then until 1891, when they were discontinued, were produced under this banner. The only real difference in the rifles manufactured during these periods was in the markings. The earlier rifles are stamped "J.M. Marlin New Haven. Conn. U.S.A./ Ballards Patent. Nov. 5, 1861"; and the post-1881 models are stamped "Marlin Firearms Co. New Haven Ct. U.S.A./Patented Feb. 9, 1875/Ballards Patent Nov. 5, 1861".

Ballard Hunters Rifle

This model resembles the earlier Brown Manufacturing Company rifles, and it utilizes many leftover parts acquired by Marlin. It is chambered for the .32, .38, and .44 rimfire and centerfire and features John Marlin's unique reversible firing pin that allows the same gun to use both rimfire and centerfire ammunition simply by rotating the firing pin in the breechblock. This model still had the external ejector and bears the J.M. Marlin markings. There were approximately 500 manufactured in the 1 to 500 serial range. They were produced in 1875 and 1876.

NIB	Exc.	V.G.	Good	Fair	Poor
—	—	3700	2750	950	400

Ballard No. 1 Hunters Rifle

This model bears the early J.M. Marlin marking only, as it was manufactured from 1876 until 1880 and was discontinued before the incorporation. It has a 26", 28", and 30" barrel and is chambered for the .44 rimfire or centerfire cartridge. It has the reversible firing pin and also the new internal extractor. Production figures are not available, but the serial number range is between 500 and 4000.

NIB	Exc.	V.G.	Good	Fair	Poor
—	—	4500	3000	1000	400

Ballard No. 1-1/2 Hunters Rifle

This model is similar to the No. 1 except that it is chambered for the .45-70, .40-63, and the .40-65 cartridges and does not have the reversible firing pin. The barrel length is 30" and 32". It was manufactured between 1879 and 1883. This model is found with both early and later markings.

NIB	Exc.	V.G.	Good	Fair	Poor
—	—	5200	3750	1500	500

Ballard No. 1-3/4 "Far West" Hunters Rifle

This model was made by J. M. Marlin only and is similar to the 1-1/2, the difference being the addition of double-set triggers and a ring on the opening lever. It was manufactured in 1880 and 1881.

NIB	Exc.	V.G.	Good	Fair	Poor
—	—	6300	4750	2000	600

Ballard No. 2 Sporting Rifle

This model is chambered for the .32, .38 rimfire or centerfire cartridges, and the .44 centerfire. It has the reversible firing pin and was offered in 26", 28", and 30" barrel lengths. This model features "Rocky Mountain" sights and was manufactured between 1876 and 1891. It is found with both early and late markings.

NIB	Exc.	V.G.	Good	Fair	Poor
—	—	3200	2000	650	200

Ballard No. 3 Gallery Rifle

This model is similar to the No. 2 rifle but is chambered for the .22 rimfire cartridge and has a manually operated external extractor. The sights are the same and a 24" barrel was offered in addition to the 26", 28", and 30". This rifle was manufactured between 1876 and 1891.

NIB	Exc.	V.G.	Good	Fair	Poor
—	—	3200	2000	650	200

Ballard No. 3F Gallery Rifle

This is a deluxe version of the No. 3. It has a pistol-grip stock, a nickel-plated Schutzen-style buttplate, and an opening lever like a repeating rifle. It features a 26" octagonal barrel and an oil-finished stock. It was manufactured in the late 1880s and is quite scarce in today's market.

No. 3 F Fine Gallery Rifle.

NIB	Exc.	V.G.	Good	Fair	Poor
—	—	6500	4250	1750	500

Ballard No. 4 Perfection Rifle

This model is chambered for a number of centerfire calibers from .32-40 to .50-70. The barrel lengths are from 26" to 30", and the sights are of the "Rocky Mountain" type. This model was manufactured between 1876 and 1891.

NIB	Exc.	V.G.	Good	Fair	Poor
—	—	6500	4250	1750	500

Ballard No. 3-1/2 Target Rifle

This model is similar to the No. 4 Perfection Rifle except that it has a checkered stock with a shotgun-style buttplate, a 30" barrel, and a tang peep sight with globe front sight. It was chambered for the .40-65 cartridge and was manufactured from 1880-1882.

NIB	Exc.	V.G.	Good	Fair	Poor
—	—	6500	4250	1750	500

Ballard No. 4-1/2 Mid Range Rifle

This model is also a variation of the No. 4 Perfection model. It has a higher-grade checkered stock with a shotgun buttplate. It has a 30" part-round, part-octagonal barrel and is chambered for the .38-40, .40-65, and the .45-70 cartridges. It features a Vernier tang peep sight and a globe front sight. It was manufactured between 1878 and 1882.

NIB	Exc.	V.G.	Good	Fair	Poor
—	—	6750	4500	2000	500

Ballard No. 4-1/2 A-1 Mid Range Target Rifle

This is a deluxe version of the No. 4-1/2" rifle. It features scroll engraving on the frame with "Ballard A-1" on the left and "Mid-Range" on the right. It is chambered for the .38-50 and the .40-65 cartridge and has a high-grade checkered stock with a horn fore-end tip. The sights are the highest-grade Vernier tang sight and a spirit lever front sight. The shotgun or rifle-style butt was optional. This model was manufactured between 1878 and 1880.

NIB	Exc.	V.G.	Good	Fair	Poor
—	—	9000	7250	3500	750

Ballard No. 5 Pacific Rifle

This model has a 30" or 32" medium to heavyweight barrel, with a ramrod mounted underneath. It is chambered for many different calibers from .38-50 to .50-70. This model features "Rocky Mountain" sights, a crescent butt, double-set triggers, and a ring-style opening lever. It was manufactured between 1876 and 1891.

NIB	Exc.	V.G.	Good	Fair	Poor
—	—	5500	4750	2000	500

Ballard No. 5-1/2 Montana Rifle

This model is similar to the Pacific Rifle, with an extra heavyweight barrel, and is chambered for the .45 Sharps cartridge only. It features a checkered steel shotgun-style buttplate. It was manufactured from 1882-1884 and has the late markings only.

NIB	Exc.	V.G.	Good	Fair	Poor
—	—	15000	10000	5500	1250

Ballard No. 6 Schuetzen Off Hand Rifle

This model has a 30" or 32" octagonal barrel and is chambered for the .40-65, .44-75, and the .38-50 cartridges. The stock is of select walnut in the high-combed Schuetzen style. The buttplate is nickel-plated, and the receiver is not engraved. The sights are Vernier tang type on the rear and a spirit lever front. The triggers are double set, and the opening lever has a ring and a spur. This model is marked J.M. Marlin only and was manufactured between 1876 and 1880.

NIB	Exc.	V.G.	Good	Fair	Poor
—	—	—	6500	2500	500

Ballard No. 6 Schuetzen Rifle

This model is similar to the Off Hand model but was produced by the later Marlin Firearms Company and was so marked. It is a more deluxe version with checkered stock, horn fore-end tip, and a fully engraved receiver. This model was chambered for the .32-40 and the .38-55 cartridges and was manufactured between 1881 and 1891.

NIB	Exc.	V.G.	Good	Fair	Poor
—	—	13000	8500	4500	1250

Ballard No. 6-1/2 Off Hand Mid Range Rifle

This model is chambered for the .40-54 Everlasting cartridge only. It has a 28" or 30" part-round, part-octagonal barrel, a Schuetzen-style stock, and a plain non-engraved receiver. It was manufactured between 1880 and 1882.

NIB	Exc.	V.G.	Good	Fair	Poor
—	20000	9500	5500	2500	500

Ballard No. 6-1/2 Rigby Off Hand Mid Range Rifle

This model is chambered for the .38-50 and the .40-65 cartridges. It features the Rigby ribbed-style barrel in 26" and 28" lengths, with Vernier rear and globe front sights and a high grade, checkered walnut, Schuetzen-style stock with horn fore-end tip, and pistol-grip cap. The buttplate is nickel-plated, and the opening lever is of the ring type with a single trigger and extensively engraved receiver. This model was manufactured from 1880 to 1882.

No. 6½ Off-Hand Rifle.

NIB	Exc.	V.G.	Good	Fair	Poor
—	—	14500	9000	5500	1250

Ballard No. 6-1/2 Off Hand Rifle

This model is chambered for the .32-40 and .38-55 cartridges and features barrel lengths of 28" and 30". It has a checkered, high-grade walnut, Schuetzen-style stock with nickel-plated buttplate. The fore-end tip and pistol-grip cap are of horn, and the receiver is engraved. This model has a single trigger, full-ring opening lever, Vernier tang rear sight, and spirit lever front sight. The 6-1/2 Off Hand was made by the Marlin Firearms Company between 1883 and 1891 and is found with the later markings only.

NIB	Exc.	V.G.	Good	Fair	Poor
—	—	14000	9000	5500	1250

Ballard No. 7 "Creedmore A-1" Long Range Rifle

This model is commonly chambered for the .44-100 or the .45-100 cartridges. It has a 34" part-round, part-octagonal barrel and a high grade checkered pistol-grip stock, with a horn fore-end tip and shotgun-style butt. The sights are a special 1,300-yard Vernier tang rear and a spirit level front. There is another sight base on the heel of the stock for mounting the rear sight for ultra long-range shooting. The opening lever is similar to a repeating rifle, and a single trigger is featured. The receiver is engraved and marked "Ballard A-1" on the left and "Long Range" on the right. This model was manufactured between 1876 and 1886 and is found with both early and late markings.

Courtesy Milwaukee Public Museum, Milwaukee, Wisconsin

NIB	Exc.	V.G.	Good	Fair	Poor
—	—	15000	9700	5500	1250

Ballard No. 7 Long Range Rifle

This model is similar to the "Creedmore A-1" but is slightly less deluxe. The engraving is less elaborate, and the lettering on the receiver is absent. This model was manufactured between 1883 and 1890 and is found with the later markings only.

No. 7 Long Range Rifle.

Courtesy Marlin Firearms Co.

NIB	Exc.	V.G.	Good	Fair	Poor
—	—	13500	8000	4500	850

Ballard No. 7A-1 Long Range Rifle

This model is a higher grade version of the "Creedmore A-I," with fancier walnut and a checkered straight stock. Better sights and deluxe engraving are also featured. This model was manufactured between 1879 and 1883 and is found with both markings.

No. 7 A-I Long Range Rifle.

Courtesy Marlin Firearms Co.

NIB	Exc.	V.G.	Good	Fair	Poor
—	—	16000	1000	5500	1250

Ballard No. 7A-1 Extra Grade Long Range Rifle

This is the highest grade version of the No. 7 rifles. It features a 34" "Rigby" -type ribbed, round barrel. This was usually a special-order rifle with most features to customer specifications. The model was manufactured in limited numbers between 1879 and 1883. It is found with both markings.

Courtesy Marlin Firearms Co.

NIB	Exc.	V.G.	Good	Fair	Poor
—	—	19500	11500	6500	1500

Ballard No. 8 Union Hill Rifle

This model has a 28" and 30" part-round, part-octagonal barrel and is chambered for the .32-40 and the .38-55 cartridges. It has a checkered pistol-grip stock with nickel-plated buttplate; and the opening lever is fully enclosed ring, as on the repeaters. There is a double-set trigger and a tang peep with globe front sight. The receiver is not engraved. This model was manufactured between 1884 and 1890 and is found only with the late markings. This was one of the most popular rifles in the Ballard line.

Courtesy Milwaukee Public Museum, Milwaukee, Wisconsin

NIB	Exc.	V.G.	Good	Fair	Poor
—	—	7000	4250	1750	500

Ballard No. 9 Union Hill Rifle

This model is similar to the No. 8 except that it features a single trigger and better sights. It was manufactured between 1884 and 1891 and has the later markings only.

Courtesy Bonhams & Butterfields, San Francisco, California

NIB	Exc.	V.G.	Good	Fair	Poor
—	—	7000	4250	1750	500

Ballard No. 10 Schuetzen Junior Rifle

This model is simply a heavier barreled version of the No. 9. The barrel is 32" long, and the checkered pistol-grip stock is of the off-hand style. The rear sight is a Vernier Mid Range model, and the front sight is a spirit-level type. This was a popular model that was manufactured between 1885 and 1891. It is found with the later markings only.

NIB	Exc.	V.G.	Good	Fair	Poor
—	—	7000	4750	2000	650

MARLIN HANDGUNS

1st Model Derringer

This was the first handgun produced by Marlin. The barrel is 2-1/16" long and pivots to the side for loading. There is a plunger under the frame that is depressed to free the barrel. This device is a Ballard patent. This pistol is chambered for the .22 rimfire cartridge, and there is no extractor. The frame is brass and usually nickel-plated. It has two grooves milled beneath the blued barrel. The grips are of rosewood. The barrel is stamped "J.M. Marlin, New Haven, Ct." There were approximately 2,000 manufactured between 1863 and 1867. They are quite scarce on today's market.

NIB	Exc.	V.G.	Good	Fair	Poor
—	—	1350	750	300	100

O.K. Model Derringer

The O.K. Model is chambered for .22, .30 and .32 rimfire cartridges. The barrel is 2-1/8" or 3-1/8" on the .32. There is no extractor and it functions as the 1st Model. The frame is plated brass with flat sides, and the barrel is found either blued or nickel-plated. The grips are rosewood. The markings are the same as on the 1st Model but are located on the right side of the barrel. The top of the barrel is marked "O.K." There were approximately 5,000 manufactured between 1863 and 1870.

NIB	Exc.	V.G.	Good	Fair	Poor
—	—	1350	750	300	100

Victor Model Derringer

This model is similar in appearance to the "O.K." Model but is larger in size and is chambered for the .38-caliber rimfire cartridge. The barrel is 2-11/16" long; and there was, for the first time, an extractor. The finish and function were unchanged. The right side of the barrel is stamped "J.M. Marlin/New Haven, Ct./Pat. April 5.1870". "Victor" is stamped on the top of the barrel. There were approximately 4,000 manufactured between 1870 and 1881.

NIB	Exc.	V.G.	Good	Fair	Poor
—	—	1600	1250	500	150

Nevermiss Model Derringer

This model was made in three different sizes chambered for the .22, .32, and .41 rimfire cartridges. The barrel is 2.5" long and swings sideways for loading. The frame is plated brass, and the barrels are either blued or nickel-plated. The grips are rosewood. The frame is grooved under the barrels as on the 1st model. There is an extractor on this model. The barrel markings are the same as on the "Victor", with the top of the barrel marked "Nevermiss". There were approximately 5,000 manufactured between 1870 and 1881.

.22 Caliber Model

NIB	Exc.	V.G.	Good	Fair	Poor
—	—	1500	1150	500	100

.32 Caliber Model

NIB	Exc.	V.G.	Good	Fair	Poor
—	—	1200	750	350	100

.41 Caliber Model

Courtesy Marlin Firearms Co.

NIB	Exc.	V.G.	Good	Fair	Poor
—	—	3750	2500	1000	400

Stonewall Model Derringer

This model is identical to the .41-caliber "Nevermiss", but the top of the barrel is marked "Stonewall". It is rarely encountered.

Courtesy Marlin Firearms Co.

NIB	Exc.	V.G.	Good	Fair	Poor
—	—	6000	4250	2000	750

O.K. Pocket Revolver

This is a solid-frame, spur-trigger, single-action revolver chambered for the .22 rimfire short. The round barrel is 2.25", and the 7-shot cylinder is unfluted. The frame is nickel-plated brass with a blue or nickel-plated barrel, and the bird's-head grips are rosewood. The cylinder pin is removable and is used to knock the empty cases out of the cylinder. The top of the barrel is marked "O.K." and "J.M. Marlin. New Haven, Conn. U.S.A." There were approximately 1,500 manufactured between 1870 and 1875.

Courtesy Marlin Firearms Co.

NIB	Exc.	V.G.	Good	Fair	Poor
—	—	700	500	200	75

Little Joker Revolver

This model is similar in appearance to the "O.K." model; some are reported to have engraving and ivory or pearl grips. There were approximately 500 manufactured between 1871 and 1873.

Courtesy Marlin Firearms Co.

NIB	Exc.	V.G.	Good	Fair	Poor
—	—	500	500	350	125

J.M. MARLIN STANDARD POCKET REVOLVERS

In 1872 Marlin began production of its Smith & Wesson look-alike. The Manhattan Firearms Company had developed a copy of the Model 1 S&W .22 cartridge revolver. In 1868 the company ceased business and the revolvers were produced by the American Standard Tool Company until their dissolution in 1873. In 1872 Marlin had entered into an agreement with this company to manufacture these revolvers, which were no longer protected by the Rollin White patent after 1869. The Marlin revolvers are similar to those made by American Standard. The only real difference being that Marlin grips are of the bird's-head round configuration. A contoured grip frame and a patented pawl spring mechanism is utilized on the Marlin revolvers.

Marlin XXX Standard 1872 Pocket Revolver

This is the first in the series of four Standard model revolvers. It is chambered for the .30 caliber rimfire. The earlier model has an octagonal 3-1/8" barrel; and the later, a round 3" barrel. There are round and octagonal barrel variations (with unfluted cylinder) and round barrel variations (with short and long fluted cylinders). All of the barrels are ribbed and tip up for loading. They have plated brass frames, and the barrels are nickel-plated. The bird's-head grips are of rosewood or hard rubber, bearing the monogram "M.F.A. Co." inside a star. There is a spur trigger. The markings "J.M. Marlin-New Haven Ct." appear on the earlier octagonal barreled models. "U.S.A. Pat. July 1. 1873" was added to the later round barreled models. All barrels are marked "XXX Standard 1872". There were approximately 5,000 of all types manufactured between 1872 and 1887.

Octagon Barrel—Early Variation

NIB	Exc.	V.G.	Good	Fair	Poor
—	—	900	500	300	75

Round Barrel—Non-Fluted Cylinder

NIB	Exc.	V.G.	Good	Fair	Poor
—	—	800	400	275	75

Round Barrel—Short Fluted Cylinder

NIB	Exc.	V.G.	Good	Fair	Poor
—	—	750	350	200	75

Round Barrel—Long Fluted Cylinder

NIB	Exc.	V.G.	Good	Fair	Poor
—	—	750	450	150	75

Marlin XX Standard 1873 Pocket Revolver

This model is similar in appearance to the XXX 1872 model except that it is chambered for the .22 long rimfire and is marked "XX Standard 1873". There are three basic variations: the early octagonal barrel model with non-fluted cylinder, the round barrel model with non-fluted cylinder and the round barrel with fluted cylinder. Function and features are the same as described for the "XXX Standard 1872" model. There were approximately 5,000 manufactured between 1873 and 1887.

Early Octagon Barrel Model

Courtesy Marlin Firearms Co.

NIB	Exc.	V.G.	Good	Fair	Poor
—	—	900	600	200	100

Round Barrel—Fluted Cylinder

Courtesy Marlin Firearms Co.

NIB	Exc.	V.G.	Good	Fair	Poor
—	—	750	500	200	75

Round Barrel—Non-Fluted Cylinder

Courtesy Marlin Firearms Co.

NIB	Exc.	V.G.	Good	Fair	Poor
—	—	875	650	400	100

Marlin No. 32 Standard 1875 Pocket Revolver

This model is also similar in appearance to the "XXX Standard 1872" model except that it is chambered for the .32 rimfire cartridge. The 3" barrel is round with a rib. The 5-shot cylinder is fluted and is in two different lengths to accommodate either the .32 Short or Long cartridge. The finish, function and most markings are the same as on previous models with the exception of the barrel top marking "No. 32 Standard 1875". There were approximately 8,000 manufactured between 1875 and 1887.

Courtesy Marlin Firearms Co.

NIB	Exc.	V.G.	Good	Fair	Poor
—	—	675	450	200	75

Marlin 38 Standard 1878 Pocket Revolver

This model is different than its predecessors in that it features a steel frame and flat bottom butt, with hard rubber monogram grips. There was still a spur trigger and the 3.25" ribbed round barrel still tipped up for loading. This model is chambered for the .38 centerfire cartridge. The finish is full nickel plate and the top of the barrel is marked "38 Standard 1878". There were approximately 9,000 manufactured between 1878 and 1887.

Courtesy Marlin Firearms Co.

Carbine 20" Barrel and Saddle Ring on Left Side of Receiver

Courtesy Marlin Firearms Co.

NIB	Exc.	V.G.	Good	Fair	Poor
—	—	2250	1250	500	250

Musket

30" barrel with full-length stock, 68 made in .44-40.

NIB	Exc.	V.G.	Good	Fair	Poor
—	—	6500	3000	1250	650

Model 1891 Lever-Action Rifle

This was Marlin's first rifle designed to fire the .22 rimfire and the first repeating rifle to accept the .22 Short, Long, and LR cartridges interchangeably. It was also chambered for the .32 rimfire and centerfire. The 24" octagonal barrel is standard, with a buckhorn rear and blade front sight. The finish is blued with a case colored hammer, lever and buttplate. The stock is plain walnut. The first variation is marked "Marlin Fire-Arms Co. New Haven, Ct. U.S.A./Pat'd Nov.19.1878.April 2.1889. Aug.12 1890" on the barrel, with the solid-topped frame marked "Marlin Safety". The second variation was marked the same with "March 1,1892" added. There were approximately 18,650 manufactured between 1891 and 1897.

1st Variation

.22 rimfire only, side loading, appr. 5,000 made.

NIB	Exc.	V.G.	Good	Fair	Poor
—	—	2500	1000	550	300

2nd Variation

.22 and .32 rimfire, .32 centerire, tube loading, Model 1891 on later model tangs (3rd variation). **NOTE:** Add 20 percent for .22 rifle with "1891" stamped on tang. Deduct 50 percent for .32 caliber.

NIB	Exc.	V.G.	Good	Fair	Poor
—	—	1500	500	300	150

Model 1892 Lever-Action Rifle

This is basically an improved version of the Model 1891 and is similar to the second variation of the 1891. The only notable exceptions were the tang marking "Model 1892" and "Model 92" on later models. The .22 rimfire was scarce in the Model 1892. There were approximately 45,000 manufactured between 1895 and 1916. There were many options and these special-order guns must be individually appraised to ascertain value and authenticity.

.22 Rimfire

NOTE: Antique (pre-1898) add 20 percent.

NIB	Exc.	V.G.	Good	Fair	Poor
—	—	1350	400	250	150

.32 Rimfire and Centerfire

NIB	Exc.	V.G.	Good	Fair	Poor
—	—	950	350	150	100

Model 1893 Lever-Action Rifle

This model was the first rifle Marlin designed for the then new smokeless powder cartridges. It is chambered for the .25-36, .30-30, .32 Special, .32-40, and the .38-55. It was offered standard with either a round or octagonal barrel, in lengths of 24" to 32". Buckhorn rear and blade front sights were also standard. The receiver, lever, hammer, and buttplate are case colored, and the rest is blued. The stock is varnished walnut.

As with all of these early Marlins, many options were offered and when encountered, will drastically alter the value of the particular rifle. For this reason we supply the values for the basic model and urge securing competent appraisal on non-standard specimens. The barrel on earlier guns is marked "Marlin FireArms Co. New Haven, Ct.U.S.A./ Patented Oct.11. 1887.April 2.1889. Aug.1.1893". In 1919 the markings were changed to "The Marlin Firearms Corporation/ New Haven, Conn.U.S.A.Patented". The rifles manufactured after 1904 are marked "Special Smokeless Steel" on the left side of the barrel. The upper tang is marked "Model 1893" on early guns; and "Model 93" on later specimens. There were approximately 900,000 manufactured between 1893 and 1935. Factory records are incomplete on the Model 1893.

Antique Production (Pre-1898)

Courtesy Bonhams & Butterfields, San Francisco, California

NIB	Exc.	V.G.	Good	Fair	Poor
—	3000	2000	650	450	275

Modern Production 1899-1935

NOTE: Add 100 percent premium for musket. Deduct 50 percent for B model with blued receiver.

NIB	Exc.	V.G.	Good	Fair	Poor
—	2000	1100	550	350	225

Model 1894 Lever-Action Rifle

This model is similar to the Model 1893, but with a shorter action. It is chambered for the .25-20, .32-20, .38-40, and the .44-40. 24" to 32" round or octagonal barrels with full-length magazine tubes are standard, as are buckhorn rear and blade front sights. The finish is case colored receiver, lever, hammer, and buttplate, with the rest blued. The walnut stock is varnished. The first versions were marked "Marlin Fire-Arms Co., New Haven, Ct.U.S.A./Patented Oct.11, 1887. April 2,1889". The top of the frame is marked "Marlin Safety", and the model designation is not stamped on the tang. These early rifles were chambered for .38-40 and .44-40 only. The later rifles added the patent date

"Aug. 1, 1893"; and "Model 1894" was stamped on the tang. On the latest versions this was shortened to "Model 94". There were approximately 250,000 manufactured between 1894 and 1935. This model was also produced with a great many options. Individual appraisal should be secured when confronted with these features.

Antique Production (Pre-1898)

NIB	Exc.	V.G.	Good	Fair	Poor
—	1850	1150	650	450	275

Modern Production (1899-1935)

NOTE: Add 100 percent premium for musket. Add 25 percent premium for saddle ring carbine. Add 30 percent premium for "Baby" carbine.

NIB	Exc.	V.G.	Good	Fair	Poor
—	1600	850	550	350	225

Model 1895 Lever-Action Rifle

This is a large rifle designed to fire the larger hunting cartridges. It is chambered for the .33 W.C.F., .38-56, .40-65, .40-70, .40-83, .45-70, and the .45-90. It came standard with round or octagonal barrels from 26" to 32" in length. A bull-length magazine tube was also standard, as were buckhorn rear and blade front sights. The finish is case colored receiver, lever, and hammer; the rest is blued with a varnished walnut stock. The barrel markings are the same as the Model 1894, and the top tang is marked "Model 1895". After 1896 "Special Smokeless Steel" was stamped on the barrel. There were also many options available for this model and they have a big effect on the value. There were approximately 18,000 manufactured between 1895 and 1917.

Antique Production (Pre-1898)

NIB	Exc.	V.G.	Good	Fair	Poor
—	3750	2850	2000	1250	600

Modern Production (1899-1917)

NIB	Exc.	V.G.	Good	Fair	Poor
—	2400	1500	875	650	500

Model 1897 Lever-Action Rifle

This model is an improved version of the Model 1892. It was chambered for the .22 rimfire only and came standard with a 24", 26", or 28" round, octagonal, or part-round, part-octagonal barrel. The standard sights are buckhorn rear and blade front and all were manufactured as takedown rifles. They have case colored receiver, lever, and hammer. The rest is blued and the walnut stock is varnished. There were approximately 125,000 manufactured between 1897 and 1917. In 1922 production was begun with the designation changed to "Model 39" which is produced to this day. There were also options offered with this rifle that have great effect on the value; take this into consideration and seek qualified appraisal.

Standard Production Rifle

NOTE: For first year production antique add 40 percent.

NIB	Exc.	V.G.	Good	Fair	Poor
—	2200	1500	1100	650	200

Deluxe Rifle

Checkering and fancy pistol-grip stock.

NIB	Exc.	V.G.	Good	Fair	Poor
—	3000	2000	1500	850	300

MODERN PRODUCTION MARLIN RIFLES

Model 18

This slide-action model is chambered for the .22 rimfire cartridges. It was offered standard with a 20" round or octagonal barrel, open sights, and a straight walnut stock. It has an exposed hammer and blued finish with blued steel buttplate. There is a half-length tubular magazine, and the stock features a quick takedown screw on the top tang which was marked "Model 18". This rifle was manufactured between 1906 and 1909.

Courtesy Marlin Firearms Co.

NIB	Exc.	V.G.	Good	Fair	Poor
—	650	495	200	150	80

Model 20

The Model 20 slide-action was chambered for the .22 rimfire cartridges and was offered standard with a 24" octagonal barrel and open sight, with an exposed hammer. This rifle was only made as a "Takedown" receiver model and is blued with a straight walnut stock. It was manufactured between 1907 and 1922.

NIB	Exc.	V.G.	Good	Fair	Poor
—	600	450	200	125	75

Model 25

This slide-action model was chambered for the .22 Short only and was not a commercial success. The 23" round or octagonal barrel is standard, as are open sights. It is called a takedown model, but only the stock is removable—the receiver does not separate. It has an exposed hammer, tubular magazine, and straight walnut stock. The finish is blued. This rifle was manufactured in 1909 and 1910.

Model 25 rifle.

Courtesy Marlin Firearms Co.

NIB	Exc.	V.G.	Good	Fair	Poor
—	850	625	475	300	175

Model 27

This is a centerfire slide-action rifle chambered for the .25-20 and .32-20 cartridges. Also chambered for the .25 caliber rimfire cartridge. It features a 24" octagonal barrel with two-thirds-length magazine tube that holds 7 shots. It has open sights, a blued finish and straight walnut stock with crescent buttplate. It was manufactured in from 1910 to 1916. **NOTE:** Deduct 20 percent for rifles chambered for the .25 rimfire.

NIB	Exc.	V.G.	Good	Fair	Poor
1100	950	700	475	275	100

Model 27S

The Model 27S is similar to the Model 27 but with a sliding button on the right side of the receiver that permitted the gun to be opened while a cartridge was in the chamber. It was offered with a round (1913) or octagonal 24" barrel. The .25 rimfire cartridge was added in 1913 to those already available. This model was introduced in 1910 and was manufactured until 1932. **NOTE:** Deduct 20 percent for rifles chambered for the .25 rimfire.

NIB	Exc.	V.G.	Good	Fair	Poor
1100	950	700	475	275	100

Model 29

This slide action model is identical to the Model 20 with a 23" round barrel and smooth walnut fore-end instead of a grooved one as found on the Model 20. It was manufactured between 1913 and 1916. **NOTE:** Deduct 20 percent for rifles chambered for the .25 rimfire.

Courtesy Marlin Firearms Co.

NIB	Exc.	V.G.	Good	Fair	Poor
—	600	450	300	225	75

Model 32

This model was the first of the hammerless slide-action rifles. It is chambered for the .22 rimfire and has a 24" octagonal barrel and half-length magazine tube. The Model 32 is a takedown rifle with adjustable sights and features "Ballard" rifling. It is blued, with a pistol-grip walnut stock. The advent of WWI and the need for Marlin to produce military arms cut short the production of this model. It was manufactured in 1914 and 1915 only.

Courtesy Marlin Firearms Co.

NIB	Exc.	V.G.	Good	Fair	Poor
1000	850	650	300	150	100

Model 37

This slide-action model is the same as the Model 29 with a 24" round barrel and full-length magazine tube. It was manufactured between 1913 and 1916.

Courtesy Marlin Firearms Co.

NIB	Exc.	V.G.	Good	Fair	Poor
—	500	350	200	125	75

Model 38

This was the hammerless model slide-action introduced after the end of WWI to replace the Model 32. It is similar in appearance but features a Rocky Mountain adjustable rear and an ivory bead front sight instead of the distinctive round Swebilius sight on the Model 32. The Model 38 was manufactured between 1920 and 1930.

NIB	Exc.	V.G.	Good	Fair	Poor
—	500	400	300	175	115

Model 40

This slide-action model is identical to the Model 27S centerfire rifle except that the barrel is marked "Marlin-Rockwell". The top tang is stamped "Marlin/Mod. 40". This is a rare model and not many marked in this manner have been noted.

NIB	Exc.	V.G.	Good	Fair	Poor
1000	850	575	375	225	150

Model 47

This model is similar to the Model 20, with a 23" round barrel and an improved magazine tube. The Model 47 has a case colored receiver and a checkered buttstock. This model was not offered for sale nor was it listed in Marlin's catalog but was offered free of charge to anyone purchasing four shares of Marlin stock for $100. One other fact about this model is that it was the first Marlin to be case colored with the new cyanide method; this created a tiger-striped pattern that is peculiar to the Model 47 Rifle.

NIB	Exc.	V.G.	Good	Fair	Poor
—	750	600	400	250	160

Model 1936, Rifle or Carbine

This lever-action model is a direct descendant of the Model 1893. It is chambered for the .30-30 and the .32 Special cartridge. The stock is streamlined with a pistol grip added and a 20" round barrel. A barrel band and improved sights are utilized. It has a 7-shot tube magazine and a semi-beavertail forearm. The receiver, lever and hammer are case colored; the rest is blued. This model was manufactured between 1936 and 1948. It was designated the Model 36 in 1937.

1st Variation (early 1936)

This variation has a slight "fish-belly" forearm, long tang, case colored receiver, lever and hammer, with no serial number prefix. These are rare.

NIB	Exc.	V.G.	Good	Fair	Poor
—	1200	850	400	175	125

2nd Variation (late 1936-1947)

This variation has thicker forearm, short tang, and "B" serial number prefix.

NIB	Exc.	V.G.	Good	Fair	Poor
—	1000	650	300	150	100

Model 36 Rifle or Carbine (1937-1948)

First and Second variations of this lever-action both have case colored receiver and "C" serial number prefix. Second variation tapped for receiver sight.

NIB	Exc.	V.G.	Good	Fair	Poor
—	800	600	400	195	125

1st & 2nd Variations

NIB	Exc.	V.G.	Good	Fair	Poor
—	800	600	400	195	125

3rd Variation—Blued Receiver

NIB	Exc.	V.G.	Good	Fair	Poor
—	600	400	300	175	100

Model 36 Sporting Carbine

This model is similar to the 1936 Carbine, with a 20" barrel. It features a two-thirds-length magazine tube and holds 6 shots instead of 7. The front sight is a ramp sight with hood.

NIB	Exc.	V.G.	Good	Fair	Poor
—	800	600	400	195	125

Model 36A-DL Rifle

This lever-action model is similar to the Model 36A, with a deluxe checkered stock. It features sight swivels and is furnished with a leather sling.

NIB	Exc.	V.G.	Good	Fair	Poor
—	800	650	400	225	150

MODEL 336

Information on the Model 336 were provided by Doug Murray, author and publisher of *The 336* (1983). **NOTE:** Beginning in the 1980s, Marlin used the "S" suffix on its model numbers (e.g., 336CS, 1895S, etc.), to designate models with the new crossbolt safety. This suffix has now been dropped in most cases, even though the safety remains.

Model 336 Carbine (R.C. Regular Carbine)

This model was introduced in 1948 and was an improved version of the Model 36. It features a new-type round bolt, chrome-plated with improved extractor and redesigned cartridge carrier that improved feeding. It is chambered for the .30-30 and the .32 Special cartridges and has a 20" tapered round barrel with Ballard-type rifling. The finish is blued, with the receiver top matted to reduce reflections. The pistol-grip stock and semi-beavertail fore-end are of American walnut. It features Rocky Mountain-style rear and bead front sights. The hammer is lowered to facilitate scope mounting.

NIB	Exc.	V.G.	Good	Fair	Poor
—	475	325	175	125	100

Model 336C

The same as the Model 336 Carbine. In 1951 the catalog model designation was changed. In 1952 the .35 Remington cartridge was added to the line. In 1963 the .32 Special was discontinued.

NIB	Exc.	V.G.	Good	Fair	Poor
—	475	325	175	125	100

Model 336A

This model is similar to the 336C, with a 24" barrel and steel fore-end tip instead of a barrel band. The magazine tube is two-thirds-length and holds 6 shots. This model was introduced in 1948 and built until 1962. It was reintroduced in 1973 and discontinued in 1980. In 1950 the .35 Rem. was introduced and in 1960 the .32 Special was discontinued.

NIB	Exc.	V.G.	Good	Fair	Poor
—	475	325	175	125	100

Model 336ADL

This model differs from the Model 336A by having a deluxe wood checkered stock and fore-end, quick detachable swivels, better grade finish and a sling.

NIB	Exc.	V.G.	Good	Fair	Poor
—	650	500	300	150	125

Model 336SC (Sporting Carbine)

This is basically a 336A with fore-end tip and two-thirds magazine but has a 20" barrel instead of the 24" found on the 336A.

NIB	Exc.	V.G.	Good	Fair	Poor
—	400	300	200	150	100

Model 336SD (Sporting Deluxe Carbine)

This is the 336 SC in a deluxe checkered stock version, with quick detachable swivels and supplied with a sling. **NOTE:** This is a scarce model as only 4,392 were built.

NIB	Exc.	V.G.	Good	Fair	Poor
—	1000	750	400	200	125

Model 336 MicroGroove Zipper

This model was advertised as a fast-handling, lever-action carbine chambered for the .219 Zipper cartridges flat trajectory, varmint-type round. It has a 20" heavy barrel, which was the feature that doomed it to failure as this was too short to coax the maximum performance and accuracy from the cartridge. The "MicroGroove" rifling that was used did not yield long barrel life; and the model survived from 1955 through 1959, when it was discontinued. It is externally similar to the 336 SC. **NOTE:** The first few thousand Zippers were made in standard weight barrels, not heavy weight. These are scarce and found in the "M" prefix code number. Add 100 percent.

NIB	Exc.	V.G.	Good	Fair	Poor
—	1600	950	550	300	150

Model 336T (Texan)

This is a straight-stock version of the 336C, chambered for the .30-30 cartridge, with an 20" barrel. Also produced in .35 Rem. from 1953 to 1964, and .44 Magnum from 1965 to 1967. It was manufactured from 1953-1983.

NIB	Exc.	V.G.	Good	Fair	Poor
—	650	475	395	250	175

Model 336DT

A deluxe-stock version of the "Texan", with the map of Texas and a longhorn carved on the butt. It was manufactured between 1962 and 1964. Calibers are .30-30 and .35 Rem.

NIB	Exc.	V.G.	Good	Fair	Poor
—	700	550	425	275	175

Model 336 "Marauder"

This is simply a 336T with a 16.25" barrel and a slimmer fore-end. It is chambered for either the .30-30 or .35 Remington cartridges, has a gold trigger and is drilled and tapped for both scope mounts and receiver sights. It was manufactured in 1963 and 1964.

NIB	Exc.	V.G.	Good	Fair	Poor
—	750	675	550	300	150

Model 336 .44 Magnum

This is the 336 "Marauder" with a 20" MicroGroove barrel chambered for the .44 Magnum cartridge. It holds 10 shots and was introduced in 1963. Not very successful, reportedly because of feeding difficulties.

NIB	Exc.	V.G.	Good	Fair	Poor
—	600	450	295	150	100

Model 336 "Centennial"

In 1970 a 100th year medallion was embedded into the buttstock of the 336 Carbines, the 336 Texan, and the 444 Rifle.

NIB	Exc.	V.G.	Good	Fair	Poor
—	625	500	375	250	150

1970 100th Year Commemorative Matched Pair

This is a deluxe octagonal barreled .30-30 with an engraved receiver and deluxe wood with an inlaid medallion, accompanied by a matching Model 339 .22 rimfire rifle. They are numbered the same and are furnished in a deluxe luggage case. There were 1,000 sets manufactured in 1970. These are commemoratives and as such it should be noted that collectors usually will only show interest if they are new and unfired in the original packaging. All accessories and brochures should be included for them to be worth top dollar. Once a commemorative has been used, it has no more value than as a shooter.

NIB	Exc.	V.G.	Good	Fair	Poor
1800	1400	900	600	400	300

Model 336 "Zane Grey Century"

This model was introduced in 1972, the 100th anniversary of the birth of Zane Grey, the famous Western author. This model has a 22" octagonal barrel chambered for the .30-30. The stock is high grade walnut and features a brass buttplate and pistol-grip cap. A Zane Grey medallion is inlaid into the receiver. There were 10,000 manufactured in 1972. This is a commemorative rifle and must be new in the box to generate the top collector appeal.

NIB	Exc.	V.G.	Good	Fair	Poor
600	425	275	200	150	100

Model 336 Octagon

This model was introduced to utilize the octagonal barrel making equipment that was on hand from the manufacture of the commemoratives. It is essentially a 336T with a 22" tapered octagonal barrel chambered for .30-30 only. It features a full-length magazine tube, slim fore-end with steel cap, and a classic-style hard rubber buttplate. The walnut stock is straight and the lever is square. The finish, including the trigger, is blued. This model was made in 1973 only.

NIB	Exc.	V.G.	Good	Fair	Poor
725	600	500	325	175	150

Model 336ER (Extra Range)

This model was introduced in 1983 and was advertised as being chambered for the .307 Winchester and the .356 Winchester cartridges. The .307 was never produced. The .356 Winchester was supposed to add new capabilities to this classic rifle, but it never caught on with the shooting public and was discontinued in 1986 after only 2,441 Model ERs were manufactured. It has a 20" barrel and 5-shot tube magazine.

NIB	Exc.	V.G.	Good	Fair	Poor
—	825	550	300	250	150

Model 336C

This is the current carbine model of this line. It has a hammer-block safety and is chambered for the .30-30, .35 Remington, and until 1988 the .375 Winchester. The barrel is 20" and the magazine tube holds 6 shots. The pistol-grip stock and semi-beavertail forearm are American walnut. This model has been manufactured since 1984. The 1983 model was known as the 336C and had no hammer-block safety. Weight is approximately 7 lbs.

NIB	Exc.	V.G.	Good	Fair	Poor
475	350	225	200	175	150

Model 336SS

Similar to the Model 336C but in .30-30 only and with stainless steel barrel and receiver.

NIB	Exc.	V.G.	Good	Fair	Poor
525	400	250	200	150	100

Model 336LTS

This is the latest version of the old "Marauder" carbine. It was dubbed the LTS or "Lightweight" model instead of the Marauder as it was feared that the latter designation would be inappropriate in today's society. The model features a 16.5" barrel with full-length tube magazine that holds 5 shots. The walnut stock has a straight grip and there is a barrel band on the forearm. The butt has a rubber rifle pad. This model was introduced in 1988. Discontinued.

NIB	Exc.	V.G.	Good	Fair	Poor
675	450	300	250	200	150

Model 336 Cowboy

This model is similar to the Model 336 CS. It is available in both .30-30 and .38-55 calibers. It is fitted with 24" tapered octagon barrel. Rear sight is Marble buckhorn. Tubular magazine holds 6 rounds. Straight grip walnut stock has a hard rubber buttplate. Weight is about 7.5 lbs. First introduced in 1999.

NIB	Exc.	V.G.	Good	Fair	Poor
875	650	525	325	175	150

Model 336M

Introduced in 2000, this model is chambered for the .30-30 cartridge. It features a stainless steel receiver and barrel; all other parts are nickel plated. Barrel length is 20". Magazine capacity is 6 rounds. Checkered walnut stock has a Mar-Shield finish. Rubber buttpad. Weight is about 7 lbs. Marlin's first stainless steel rifle.

NIB	Exc.	V.G.	Good	Fair	Poor
675	550	425	275	175	125

Model 336CC

Chambered for the .30-30 cartridge and fitted with a 20" barrel this model features a Mossy Oak Break-Up camo finish. Adjustable rear sight. Weight is about 7 lbs. Introduced in 2001.

NIB	Exc.	V.G.	Good	Fair	Poor
500	390	325	250	200	100

Model 336W

Similar to Model 336C but in .30-30 only and with gold-plated trigger and hardwood stock. Also available with factory-mounted 3x9 scope. **NOTE:** Add 10 percent for scope package.

NIB	Exc.	V.G.	Good	Fair	Poor
450	395	325	250	200	100

Model 336Y "Spike Horn"

Chambered for the .30-30 cartridge and fitted with a 16.5" barrel, this rifle features a checkered walnut stock with pistol grip. Magazine capacity is 5 rounds. Adjustable rear sight. Weight is about 6.5 lbs. Introduced in 2003.

NIB	Exc.	V.G.	Good	Fair	Poor
575	425	300	200	150	100

Model 336XLR

Lever-action chambered in 30/30 or .35 Remington, with 5-shot tubular magazine, 24" stainless steel barrel, along with stainless steel receiver, trigger, trigger guard plate, magazine tube, loading gate and lever. Full pistol grip, swivel studs and Ballard-type rifling precision fluted bolt. Features solid top receiver with side-ejection, adjustable folding semi-buckhorn rear sight, ramp front sight, tapped for scope mount. Designed for Hornady LEVERevolution cartridges. Introduced 2006.

NIB	Exc.	V.G.	Good	Fair	Poor
625	500	375	250	175	100

Model 336BL

Lever action rifle chambered for .30-30. Features include 6-shot full length tubular magazine; 18" blued barrel with Micro-Groove rifling (12 grooves); big-loop finger lever; side ejection; blued steel receiver; hammer block safety; brown laminated hardwood pistol-grip stock with fluted comb; cut checkering; deluxe recoil pad; blued swivel studs.

NIB	Exc.	V.G.	Good	Fair	Poor
525	400	250	200	150	100

Model 30AS

This model is similar to the 336 CS, but the stock is made of walnut-finished hardwood instead of genuine American walnut. It is chambered for .30-30 only.

NIB	Exc.	V.G.	Good	Fair	Poor
395	285	200	175	125	100

Model 375

This model was introduced in 1980. It has a 20" MicroGroove barrel and is chambered for the .375 Winchester cartridge. Its appearance is much the same as the Model 336, with walnut pistol stock and steel fore-end tip. This model was discontinued in 1983 after 16,315 were manufactured.

NIB	Exc.	V.G.	Good	Fair	Poor
625	500	375	250	175	100

Model 444

This model was introduced in 1965. It is chambered for the .444 Marlin. The rifle is essentially a Model 336 action modified to accept the larger cartridge. It has a 24" round barrel that was cut back to 22" in 1971. It holds 5 shots total and when introduced, featured a straight-gripped Monte Carlo stock and semi-beavertail fore-end with barrel band. Another band holds the two-thirds-length magazine tube in place. In 1971 the stock was changed to a pistol grip without the Monte Carlo comb.

NIB	Exc.	V.G.	Good	Fair	Poor
—	600	450	300	175	125

Model 444S

This model was introduced in 1972 and is essentially the later 444 with a steel fore-end tip instead of the barrel bands.

NIB	Exc.	V.G.	Good	Fair	Poor
—	500	350	175	150	125

Model 444SS

In 1984 the company added a crossbolt hammer-block safety to the 444 S and re-designated it the 444 SS. This Model is currently in production as the Model 444, the "S" suffix having been dropped.

NIB	Exc.	V.G.	Good	Fair	Poor
550	395	300	225	150	125

Model 444P Outfitter

Introduced in 1999 this model is chambered for the .444 Marlin cartridge. It is fitted with a 18.5" ported barrel. Tubular magazine capacity is 5 rounds. Walnut stock with straight grip and ventilated recoil pad standard. Weight is approximately 6.75 lbs. Discontinued 2002.

NIB	Exc.	V.G.	Good	Fair	Poor
725	600	425	335	275	200

Model 444XLR

Similar to Model 1895XLR but chambered in .444 Marlin. Introduced 2006.

NIB	Exc.	V.G.	Good	Fair	Poor
625	500	375	250	175	100

Model 1894

The production of the Model 336 in .44 Magnum was a frustrating experience as the action was simply too long for a short pistol case. In 1969 Marlin reintroduced the Model 1894 chambered for the .44 Magnum cartridge. The barrel is 20" and the full-length magazine tube holds 10 rounds. It features an adjustable rear and a ramp-type front sight. The finish is blued, with a matted receiver top. The walnut stock has a straight grip; and the fore-end, a barrel band. From 1969 to 1971 there was a brass saddle ring.

NIB	Exc.	V.G.	Good	Fair	Poor
525	375	300	200	150	100

Model 1894 Octagon Barrel

This is basically the same as the Model 1894, with a 20" octagonal barrel and a steel fore-end tip instead of the barrel band. There were 2,957 manufactured in 1973 only.

NIB	Exc.	V.G.	Good	Fair	Poor
—	650	525	350	225	100

Model 1894 Sporter

This variation has a 20" round barrel, half-length magazine tube that holds 6 shots and a hard rubber classic-style buttplate. Only 1,398 were manufactured in 1973.

NIB	Exc.	V.G.	Good	Fair	Poor
625	475	325	250	175	125

Model 1894P

This model was introduced in 2000 and is chambered for the .44 Magnum or .44 Special cartridges. Barrel length is 16.25". Magazine capacity is 8 rounds. Adjustable rear sight. Blued finish with bead blasted receiver top. Drilled and tapped for scope mount. Weight is about 5.75 lbs.

NIB	Exc.	V.G.	Good	Fair	Poor
600	450	375	300	150	100

Model 1894CS

This model is chambered for the .38 Special and .357 Magnum cartridges. It features an 18.5" round barrel, with full-length magazine tube and two barrel bands. It holds 9 shots and has a walnut straight-grip stock. This model was manufactured between 1969 and 1984. In 1984 a hammer-block crossbolt safety was added and the model number was changed to 1894 CS. All other specifications remained the same. The Model is now known, again, as the Model 1894C.

NIB	Exc.	V.G.	Good	Fair	Poor
—	525	375	275	125	100

Model 1894M

This model is similar to the other 1894 rifles except that it is chambered for the .22 Magnum cartridge and features an outside loading tube magazine that holds 11 shots. The barrel is 20" long and there is a steel fore-end tip instead of a barrel band. This model was manufactured between 1983 and 1988 and was only produced with the crossbolt safety.

NIB	Exc.	V.G.	Good	Fair	Poor
—	550	450	325	275	150

Model 1894S

This model was introduced in 1984. It is chambered for the .41 Magnum and the .44 Special/.44 Magnum cartridges. In 1988 the .45 Colt chambering was offered. This model has a 20" barrel and a straight-grip stock. The fore-end has a steel cap. This model is currently produced as the Model 1894 and features the hammer-block safety.

NIB	Exc.	V.G.	Good	Fair	Poor
550	450	375	275	175	125

Model 1894CL (Classic)

This model was introduced in 1988 and is the same basic rifle chambered for the old .25-20 and .32-20 cartridges. The rifle is also chambered for the .218 Bee cartridge. The barrel is 22" and the half-length magazine tube holds 6 shots. The walnut stock has no white spacers and has a black buttplate. Discontinued in 1993. **NOTE:** Collector interest has been growing in this model since it was discontinued in 1993.

NIB	Exc.	V.G.	Good	Fair	Poor
750	550	450	300	250	150

Model 1894CL (Classic) New

Reintroduced in 2005 this model is chambered for the .32-20 cartridge and fitted with a 22" barrel with open sights. Tubular magazine capacity is 6 rounds. Checkered straight grip walnut stock. Weight is about 6 lbs. Discontinued.

NIB	Exc.	V.G.	Good	Fair	Poor
700	600	475	395	300	125

Model 1894 Century Limited

An anniversary edition of the Marlin Model 1894 is limited to 2,500 rifles chambered in .44-40 caliber. Frame engraved and case colored. It is fitted with a 24" octagon barrel with 10-round magazine tube. The stock is semi-fancy walnut with straight grip and cut checkering with brass crescent buttplate.

NIB	Exc.	V.G.	Good	Fair	Poor
950	700	425	300	200	100

Model 1894 Century Limited Employee Edition

Same as above but limited to 100 rifles. The gun has a finer grade wood and the Marlin man on the horse logo is inlaid in gold on the right side of the receiver.

NIB	Exc.	V.G.	Good	Fair	Poor
1500	825	700	425	300	200

Model 1894 Cowboy

Introduced in 1996 this lever-action rifle features a 24" tapered octagon barrel with a 10-round tubular magazine. It is chambered for the .45 Long Colt, a popular cartridge for "Cowboy Action Shooting". Straight-grip checkered stock with blued steel forearm cap. Weight is approximately 7.5 lbs.

NIB	Exc.	V.G.	Good	Fair	Poor
750	600	450	300	225	150

Model 1894 Cowboy 32

As above but chambered for the .32 H&R Magnum cartridge. Introduced in 2004.

NIB	Exc.	V.G.	Good	Fair	Poor
750	600	450	300	225	150

Model 1894 Cowboy II

Introduced in 1997 and is the same as the Model 1894 Cowboy but is chambered for several cartridges. Available in .44-40, .357 Magnum .38 Special, and .44 Magnum/.44 Special.

NIB	Exc.	V.G.	Good	Fair	Poor
650	525	300	225	150	100

Model 1894CP

This model is chambered for the .375 Magnum cartridge and fitted with a 16.25" ported barrel. Tubular magazine holds 8 rounds. Checkered American black walnut stock. Adjustable semi-buckhorn rear sight. Receiver drilled and tapped for scope mount. Weight is about 5.75 lbs. Introduced in 2001.

NIB	Exc.	V.G.	Good	Fair	Poor
626	575	450	300	225	100

Model 1894SS

This lever-action rifle is chambered for the .44 Magnum and .44 Special cartridges. Fitted with a 20" barrel with 10-round magazine. Stainless steel barrel and receiver. Checkered walnut stock with straight grip. Rubber buttpad. Weight is about 6 lbs. Introduced in 2002.

NIB	Exc.	V.G.	Good	Fair	Poor
650	500	400	300	200	100

Model 1894PG

Introduced in 2003, this lever-action model is chambered for the .44 Rem. Magnum cartridge and fitted with a 20" barrel. Checkered walnut stock with pistol grip. Magazine capacity is 10 rounds. Adjustable rear sight. Blued finish. Weight is about 6.5 lbs.

NIB	Exc.	V.G.	Good	Fair	Poor
575	450	300	225	150	100

Model 1894FG

This lever-action model is chambered for the .41 Rem. Magnum cartridge and fitted with a 20" barrel. Checkered walnut stock with pistol grip. Magazine capacity is 10 rounds. Weight is about 6.5 lbs. Introduced in 2003.

NIB	Exc.	V.G.	Good	Fair	Poor
600	450	300	225	150	100

Model 1894 Cowboy

Fitted with a 20" barrel and chambered for the .38 Special cartridge, this rifle is designed for Cowboy Action Shooting. Special hand-tuned parts. Magazine capacity is 10 rounds. Walnut stock with straight grip. Case colored receiver, bolt, trigger plate and lever. Weight is about 6 lbs. Introduced in 2002. In 2003 this model was offered chambered for the .45 Colt cartridge.

NIB	Exc.	V.G.	Good	Fair	Poor
825	750	600	500	300	150

Marlin 1894 Deluxe

Lever action rifle chambered in .44 Magnum/.44 Special. Features include 10-shot tubular magazine; squared finger lever; side ejection; richly polished deep blued metal surfaces; solid top receiver; hammer block safety; #1 grade fancy American black walnut straight-grip stock and fore-end; cut checkering; rubber rifle butt pad; Mar-Shield finish; blued steel fore-end cap: swivel studs; deep-cut Ballard-type rifling (6 grooves).

NIB	Exc.	V.G.	Good	Fair	Poor
600	500	400	325	250	150

Marlin 1894CSS

Lever action rifle chambered in .357 Magnum/.38 Special. Features include 9-shot tubular magazine; stainless steel receiver, barrel, lever, trigger and hammer; squared finger lever; side ejection; solid top receiver; hammer block safety; American black walnut straight-grip stock and fore-end; cut checkering; rubber rifle butt pad; Mar-Shield finish.

NIB	Exc.	V.G.	Good	Fair	Poor
725	600	450	350	300	200

Marlin 1894 CSBL

Chambered in .357/.38 Special with 7-round capacity. Barrel is 16.25", stock gray/black laminated. Other features include Marlin's Big Loop lever, stainless steel barrel, receiver, trigger guard plate and loading gate. Ghost-ring sighting system with mounting rail for optical sights. Introduced in 2011.

NIB	Exc.	V.G.	Good	Fair	Poor
800	725	600	500	400	300

Model 1895 and 1895SS

The Model 1895 was reintroduced on the Model 336 action that had been modified to handle the .45-70 cartridge. This was done to capitalize on the nostalgia wave that descended on the country in the early 1970s. This model features a 22" round barrel with a two-thirds-length magazine tube that holds 4 shots. The walnut stock had a straight grip until the Model 1895 S was released in 1980, when a pistol-grip stock was used. In 1983 the Model 1895 SS with the crossbolt hammer-block safety was added; it is currently produced in this configuration. **NOTE:** For early "B" prefix guns below serial number 12000 add 25 percent.

NIB	Exc.	V.G.	Good	Fair	Poor
600	500	325	200	150	100

Model 1895M

Similar to the Model 1895 but chambered in .450 Marlin.

NIB	Exc.	V.G.	Good	Fair	Poor
600	500	325	200	150	100

Model 1895 Century Limited

Chambered for the .45-70 cartridge this model features a 4-shot tubular magazine, 24" half round/half octagon barrel, semi-fancy walnut stock with pistol grip. The receiver is French grayed and engraved with the Marlin man on one side and two bears on the other. Weight is about 7.5 lbs. Discontinued. 299 produced.

NIB	Exc.	V.G.	Good	Fair	Poor
1200	1050	700	500	300	150

Model 1895 Century Limited Employee Edition

Similar to the above model but limited to 100 rifles. The company logo is inlaid in gold on the right side and the left side has two cow elk and a bull elk.

NIB	Exc.	V.G.	Good	Fair	Poor
2750	2400	1800	1000	—	—

Model 1895G Guide Gun

This model is chambered for the .45-70 Government cartridge. It has a 18.5" ported barrel. Straight grip walnut stock with cut checkering and ventilated recoil pad. Adjustable rear sight. Weight is about 6.75 lbs. Introduced in 1998.

NIB	Exc.	V.G.	Good	Fair	Poor
650	550	450	350	250	150

Model 1895GS Guide Gun

Introduced in 2001, this .45-70 rifle is fitted with a 18.5" ported barrel with 4-round magazine. Stainless steel receiver and barrel. American black walnut stock with cut checkering and ventilated recoil pad. Adjustable rear semi-buckhorn sight. Weight is about 7 lbs. Early models had ported barrel, now discontinued.

NIB	Exc.	V.G.	Good	Fair	Poor
6	75	550	450	350	100

Model 1895 Cowboy

This rifle is chambered for the .45-70 cartridge and fitted with a 26" tapered octagon barrel. Tubular magazine has a 9-round capacity. Adjustable semi-buckhorn rear sight. American black stock with cut checkering. Hard rubber butt. Weight is about 8 lbs. Introduced in 2001.

NIB	Exc.	V.G.	Good	Fair	Poor
650	550	450	350	200	100

Model 1895XLR

Lever-action chambered in .45-70 Government or .450 Marlin with a 4-shot tubular magazine, 24" stainless steel barrel, along with stainless steel receiver, trigger, trigger guard plate, magazine tube, loading gate, and lever. Full pistol grip, swivel studs, and Ballard-type rifling precision fluted bolt. Features solid top receiver with side-ejection, adjustable folding semi-buckhorn rear sight, ramp front sight, tapped for scope mount. Designed for Hornady LEVERevolution cartridges. Introduced 2006.

NIB	Exc.	V.G.	Good	Fair	Poor
700	600	525	400	300	150

Model 1895MXLR

Similar to Model 1895XLR but chambered in .450 Marlin. Introduced 2006.

NIB	Exc.	V.G.	Good	Fair	Poor
700	600	525	400	300	150

Model 1895 SBLR

Similar to Model 1895GS Guide Gun but with stainless steel barrel (18.5"), receiver, large loop lever and magazine tube. Black/gray laminated buttstock and fore-end, XS ghost ring rear sight, hooded ramp front sight, receiver/barrel-mounted top rail for mounting accessory optics. Chambered in .45-70 Government. Overall length 42.5". Weight: 7.5 lbs.

NIB	Exc.	V.G.	Good	Fair	Poor
875	700	600	525	400	150

Model 1895GBL

Lever action rifle chambered in .45-70 Government. Features include 6-shot, full-length tubular magazine; 18.5" barrel with deep-cut Ballard-type rifling (6 grooves); big-loop finger lever; side ejection; solid-top receiver; deeply blued metal surfaces; hammer block safety; pistol-grip two tone brown laminate stock with cut checkering; ventilated recoil pad; Mar-Shield finish, swivel studs. Introduced 2010.

NIB	Exc.	V.G.	Good	Fair	Poor
550	500	425	350	250	150

Model 308MXLR

Similar to the Model 1895MXLR but chambered in the proprietary .308 Marlin Express cartridge.

NIB	Exc.	V.G.	Good	Fair	Poor
700	600	525	400	300	150

Model 308MX

Similar to the Model 308MXLR but with blued receiver and barrel.

NIB	Exc.	V.G.	Good	Fair	Poor
550	450	350	250	150	100

Model 338MXLR

Lever-action rifle chambered for .338 Marlin Express. 24" stainless steel barrel, stainless steel receiver, lever and magazine tube. Black/gray laminated checkered stock and fore-end. Hooded ramp front sight and adjustable semi-buckhorn rear; drilled and tapped for scope mounts. Receiver-mounted crossbolt safety. Overall length 42.5". Weight: 7.5 lbs.

NIB	Exc.	V.G.	Good	Fair	Poor
700	600	525	400	300	150

Model 338MX

Similar to Model 338MXLR but with blued metal and walnut stock and fore-end.

NIB	Exc.	V.G.	Good	Fair	Poor
550	450	350	250	150	100

Model 1897 Century Limited

Introduced in 1997 this model is chambered for the .22 caliber cartridge and commemorates the 100th anniversary of the Model 1897. It is fitted with a 24" half round/half octagon barrel with adjustable Marble rear sight and Marble front sight with brass bead. Blued receiver is engraved and gold inlaid with semi-fancy walnut stock and hard rubber buttplate. Weight is about 6.5 lbs.

NIB	Exc.	V.G.	Good	Fair	Poor
900	700	575	475	300	200

Model 1897 Century Limited Employee Edition

Similar to the model above but with additional gold engraving on the lever. Limited to 100 rifles.

NIB	Exc.	V.G.	Good	Fair	Poor
1300	1150	900	700	400	250

Model 1897 Cowboy

This .22 caliber lever-action rifle is fitted with a 24" tapered octagon barrel with adjustable Marble buckhorn sight and Marble front sight with brass bead. Full-length tubular magazine holds 26 Shorts, 21 Longs, and 19 LR cartridges. Walnut straight grip stock with hard rubber buttplate. Weight is 7.5 lbs. Introduced in 1999.

NIB	Exc.	V.G.	Good	Fair	Poor
700	550	450	350	200	100

Model 1897 Annie Oakley

Introduced in 1998 this .22 caliber model features an 18.5" tapered octagon barrel, adjustable Marble rear sight and Marble front sight. The blued receiver is roll engraved with gold signature. Stock is straight grip with blued end cap and hard rubber buttplate. Weight is approximately 5.5 lbs.

NIB	Exc.	V.G.	Good	Fair	Poor
700	600	400	300	200	125

Model 1897 Texan

Chambered for the .22 caliber cartridge and fitted with a 20" octagon barrel, this rifle has a walnut stock with straight grip. Magazine capacity is 14 to 21 cartridges depending on type. Weight is about 6 lbs. Introduced in 2002.

NIB	Exc.	V.G.	Good	Fair	Poor
700	600	400	300	200	125

Glenfield Lever-Action Rifles

The Glenfield line of rifles was designed to be sold in large outlet chain stores and were simply cheaper versions that were to be sold for less money. The rifles functioned fine, but birch was used instead of walnut and pressed checkering instead of handcut. These rifles were manufactured under the Glenfield name between 1964 and 1983. There are five models of Lever-Action Glenfields: the 30, 30A, 30AS, 30GT and 36G. They are chambered for the .30-30 cartridge, and the basic differences are slight and in most cases, merely cosmetic. They are good,

serviceable rifles but have little or no collector interest or investment potential.

NIB	Exc.	V.G.	Good	Fair	Poor
295	250	200	150	125	100

Model 30AW

This lever-action rifle is chambered for the .30-30 cartridge. It has a 20" barrel and 6-round magazine tube. The stock is walnut finished birch with pistol-grip cap and hard rubber buttplate. Introduced in 1998.

NIB	Exc.	V.G.	Good	Fair	Poor
300	250	200	150	125	100

MODEL 39

This model originally evolved from the Model 1891 invented by L.L. Hepburn. The 1891 rifle became the 1892 and eventually developed into the takedown Model 1897. The latter two were produced until 1915, when they were discontinued in favor of machine gun production for WWI. In 1922, when the company was sold to John Moran and became the Marlin Firearms Corp., the .22 rimfire lever-action was reintroduced as the Model 39. It has been in production in one form or another ever since.

Model 39

As it was introduced in 1922, the Model 39 was chambered for the .22 rimfire, had a 24" octagonal barrel and a takedown receiver. It has a full-length magazine tube which holds 25 Shorts, 20 Longs, or 18 LR cartridges. Most Model 39s had a spring-loaded button outer magazine tube release. Very early variations had the Model '97 type knurled latch release. As the Model 39As were being phased in around 1939 many have the more modern removable inner magazine tube. It has a solid top frame and side ejection, a Rocky Mountain rear and ivory bead front sight. The receiver, lever and hammer are case colored; the barrel is blued. The pistol-grip stock and steel-capped forearm are varnished walnut. This model was manufactured in this form between 1922 and 1938 with a number of options that could affect value and would warrant individual appraisal. Model 39s with a "star" stamped on the tang were considered high grade guns by the factory inspector and will command a premium in better condition examples. **NOTE:** Model 39s made prior to 1932 that have either no prefix or the prefix S on the serial number should not be used with high-speed ammunition. The prefix HS indicates the improved bolt that is safe for this ammunition.

Standard Rifle

NIB	Exc.	V.G.	Good	Fair	Poor
—	4000	3000	2000	1000	750

Deluxe Rifle

Factory checkering, fancy wood and "star" stamp on tang.

NIB	Exc.	V.G.	Good	Fair	Poor
—	4500	3500	2200	1000	750

Model 39A

This is an improved version of the Model 39. It has a heavier, tapered round barrel, semi-beavertail forearm and a redesigned pistol-grip stock. The rubber buttplate was replaced by one of a synthetic fiber; otherwise, specifications were similar to the Model 39. This model was manufactured from 1939 to 1960. Several variations are listed.

Pre-war Variations (1939-1941)

Case colored receiver, no serial number prefix (1939) or "B" prefix (1940-1941).

NIB	Exc.	V.G.	Good	Fair	Poor
—	2000	1200	800	500	400

Post-war Variations (1945-1953)

Serial number prefixes up to letter "K." Ballard-type deep rifling. **NOTE:** Add 20 percent premium of C prefix 1st post-war variation with figured wood.

NIB	Exc.	V.G.	Good	Fair	Poor
—	700	575	425	250	200

Post-war Variations (1954-1956)

Serial number prefixes L, M, N, with MicroGroove barrel.

NIB	Exc.	V.G.	Good	Fair	Poor
—	600	495	395	225	125

"Golden 39A's" (1954-1963)

Gold trigger, MicroGroove rifling. Serial number prefixes L through W.

NIB	Exc.	V.G.	Good	Fair	Poor
—	550	450	325	195	125

Model 39A Mountie

This is basically a carbine version of the Model 39A. It features a 20" tapered round barrel, straight-grip walnut stock and slimmed-down forearm. It was manufactured between 1953 and 1960.

1st Variation

K prefix and 24" barrel, fat forearm. **NOTE:** Add 20 percent for slim forearm.

NIB	Exc.	V.G.	Good	Fair	Poor
—	600	450	300	200	100

Standard

NIB	Exc.	V.G.	Good	Fair	Poor
—	450	325	175	125	100

Model 39A 1960 Presentation Model

Released in 1960, this was Marlin's 90th Anniversary model. It is similar to the 39A but has a chrome-plated barrel and receiver with a high grade, checkered walnut stock and fore-end. There is a squirrel carved on the right side of the buttstock. There were 500 produced in 1960. This is a commemorative and as such will be desirable to collectors only if NIB with all boxes and papers with which it was originally sold.

NIB	Exc.	V.G.	Good	Fair	Poor
1200	900	500	300	175	125

Model 39M Mountie 1960 Presentation Model

This is the carbine version of the 90th Anniversary model. This is the same as the 39A with a 20" barrel and straight-grip stock. There were 500 of this model manufactured in 1960.

NIB	Exc.	V.G.	Good	Fair	Poor
1200	900	500	300	175	125

Model 39ADL

This model is the same as the 90th Anniversary issue except that it is blued instead of chrome-plated. There were 3,306 manufactured between 1960 and 1963.

NIB	Exc.	V.G.	Good	Fair	Poor
1000	850	500	300	175	125

Model Golden 39A

This model is similar to the 39A, with a gold-plated trigger and sling swivels. It was manufactured between 1960 and 1983.

NIB	Exc.	V.G.	Good	Fair	Poor
—	650	550	400	250	125

Model 39 Carbine

This is a slimmer, lighter version of the Model 39A. It features a slimmer fore-end and thinner barrel. There were 12,140 manufactured between 1963 and 1967.

NIB	Exc.	V.G.	Good	Fair	Poor
—	550	400	250	175	100

Model 39 Century Limited

The introduction of this model marked the 100th Anniversary of the Marlin Company. This model features a 20" octagonal barrel with semi-buckhorn rear and brass blade front sight. The stock is fancy walnut, with a straight grip, a brass fore-end tip and buttplate. There is a medallion inlaid into the right side of the receiver and a brass plate on the stock. There were 34,197 manufactured in 1970. As a commemorative this model needs to be as it came from the factory to command collector interest.

NIB	Exc.	V.G.	Good	Fair	Poor
950	550	300	150	125	100

Model 39A Article II

This model commemorated the National Rifle Association's 100th Anniversary in 1971. It has a 24" octagonal barrel, high grade walnut pistol-grip stock, brass fore-end tip and buttplate. The right side of the receiver has the NRA's Second Amendment "Right to Keep and Bear Arms" medallion inlaid. Manufactured in 1971.

NIB	Exc.	V.G.	Good	Fair	Poor
750	450	300	150	125	100

Model 39M Article II

This model is the same as the Model 39A Article II except that it is a carbine version with a 20" octagonal barrel and a straight-grip stock. There were 3,824 manufactured in 1971. As commemoratives NIB condition is essential to collector interest.

NIB	Exc.	V.G.	Good	Fair	Poor
775	475	325	175	150	100

Model 39A Octagon

This model was produced because the company had the machinery and some leftover barrels from the two commemorative models produced in 1970 and 1971. This was a regular production run that was meant to be used and was not a special issue. It has a 24", tapered octagonal barrel and is chambered for the .22 rimfire cartridges. It has a pistol-grip walnut stock, with steel fore-end tip. There were 2,551 manufactured in 1972 and 1973. This was not a commercially successful model and it was discontinued for that reason.

NIB	Exc.	V.G.	Good	Fair	Poor
800	600	400	250	200	175

Model 39M Octagon

This is the 20", octagonal barreled carbine version with a straight-grip stock. There were 2,140 manufactured in 1973.

NIB	Exc.	V.G.	Good	Fair	Poor
750	600	400	250	200	175

Model 39D

This is essentially the Model 39M carbine, 20" barrel version with a pistol-grip stock. It was manufactured in 1971 and reintroduced in 1973. The 1971 version has white line spacers and pistol-grip caps. The 1973 version has neither of these features.

NIB	Exc.	V.G.	Good	Fair	Poor
—	625	475	325	195	125

Golden 39A

This is the current production model of this extremely popular .22 rifle. It features the hammer-block crossbolt safety and sling swivel studs. It is similar in appearance to its predecessors. Takedown style.

NIB	Exc.	V.G.	Good	Fair	Poor
650	550	425	325	225	200

Model 39TDS

Similar to the Model 39AS, with a 20" carbine barrel and straight-grip stock. It replaced the Model 39M and was introduced in 1988. Superseded by the current Golden 39A, which is a takedown design.

NIB	Exc.	V.G.	Good	Fair	Poor
600	475	300	200	150	100

Model 39AWL

This is a limited edition of 2,000 rifles distributed solely through Wal-Mart. Fitted with a 24.5" octagon barrel, select checkered walnut stock, gold filled engraving, and stamped "Wildlife For Tomorrow".

NIB	Exc.	V.G.	Good	Fair	Poor
750	600	400	300	200	125

Model 56 Levermatic

This is a streamlined version of the lever-action. It features a short lever throw and a one-piece walnut stock. The 22" barrel is round and is chambered for the .22 rimfire cartridges. There is a 7-shot detachable magazine, open sights and a gold-plated trigger. The receiver on this model was made of aluminum after 1956. There were 31,523 manufactured between 1955 and 1964.

NIB	Exc.	V.G.	Good	Fair	Poor
—	325	225	150	75	50

Model 56 "Clipper King" Levermatic

This is the same as the Model 56 except that it is specially packaged and comes with a 4X .22 scope. The name "Clipper King" is stamped on the barrel and the buttplate is red hard rubber. There were only 152 of these manufactured in 1959.

NIB	Exc.	V.G.	Good	Fair	Poor
—	350	250	175	100	75

Model 57 Levermatic

This model is similar to the Model 56, with a tube magazine and Monte Carlo stock. In 1960 Marlin went back to a steel receiver on this model. There were 34,628 manufactured from 1959 to 1965.

NIB	Exc.	V.G.	Good	Fair	Poor
—	325	225	150	75	50

Model 57M Levermatic

This is the Model 57 chambered for the .22 Magnum cartridge. There were 66,889 manufactured between 1959 and 1969.

NIB	Exc.	V.G.	Good	Fair	Poor
—	450	350	250	175	100

Model 62 Levermatic

This model is similar in appearance to the Model 57 except that it is chambered for the centerfire .256 Magnum cartridge and has a 4-shot magazine. In 1966 the .30 carbine cartridge was added. This model has a 23" "MicroGroove" barrel with open sights and a walnut one-piece stock. The first 4,000 Model 62s were shipped without serial numbers in violation of federal law. The company recalled the rifles for numbering; and, to this day, the owner of a centerfire Model 62 can return the rifle for numbering. There were 15,714 manufactured between 1963 and 1969. Add 15 percent for .256. **NOTE:** From 1969 to 1972, the first digit of the serial number indicates the year of manufacture. In 1973, the system was changed by having the first two digits subtracted from 100 to find the year of production. For example: 2717793=100-27=1973.

NIB	Exc.	V.G.	Good	Fair	Poor
—	600	475	375	225	100

MISCELLANEOUS RIMFIRE RIFLES

The Marlin Firearms Company produced a great many bolt-action rifles, both single-shot and repeaters, starting in 1930 and continuing today. These rifles were low-priced and designed primarily as utility rifles. They also manufactured many autoloaders of the same type during these years. The Glenfield name will also be found on these models, as many were produced to be marketed by the large chain outlets. These rifles have limited value as collectibles at the present time, but no one can deny that they're durable, accurate, good-natured little rifles.

Model 70P "Papoose"

Semi-automatic takedown carbine chambered for the .22 rimfire family of cartridges. It has a 16.25" barrel and a 7-shot detachable magazine. It is supplied with 4X scope and bright red case that will float if dropped overboard. The stock is walnut-finished birch, with a pistol grip and rubber buttplate. It was introduced in 1986.

Single Shot		Repeater	
Model 65	1935-37	Model 80	1935-59
Model 65E	1935-37	Model 80E	1935-39
Model 100	1935-59	Model 81	1939
Model 100S	1937-38	Model 81E	1939
Model 101	1941-77	Model 81DL	1939
Model 101 DL	1941-45	Model 80B	1940
Model 100 SB	1941	Model 80BE	1940
Model 101	1959	Model 81B	1940
Model 122	1962-65	Model 81BE	1940
		Model 80 CSB	1941
		Model 80DL	1941-64
		Model 80C	1941-71
		Model 980	1966-71
		Model 780	1971-88
		Model 781	1971-88
		Model 782	1971-88
		Model 783	1971-88
		Model 880	1988-Pres.
		Model 881	1988-Pres.
		Model 882	1988-Pres.
		Model 883	1988-Pres.

AUTOLOADERS

Model 50	1931-34	Model 98	1950-61
Model 50E	1931-34	Model 99	1959-61
Model A-1	1935-46	Model 99C	1962-78
Model A-1 E	1935-46	Model 99G	1960-65
Model A-1C	1940-46	Model DL	1960-65
Model A-1 DL	1940-46	Model 60	1960-Pres.
Model 88-C	1947-56	Model 49	1968-71
Model 88-DL	1953-56	Model 49DL	1971-78
Model 89-C	1950-61	Model 990	1979-87
Model 89-DL	1950-61	Model 995	1979-Pres.

NIB	Exc.	V.G.	Good	Fair	Poor
275	200	150	100	75	50

Model 70PSS

Same as Model 70P above but furnished with a 10-round magazine and finished in stainless steel with synthetic stock. Automatic last shot bolt hold-open.

NIB	Exc.	V.G.	Good	Fair	Poor
245	175	125	100	85	60

Model 70HC

This is the Model 70 .22 rimfire semi-automatic that has been produced since 1983 with a high-capacity, 25-round "Banana" magazine.

NIB	Exc.	V.G.	Good	Fair	Poor
200	160	140	110	85	75

Model 9 Camp Carbine

This model has a 16.5" barrel and is chambered for the 9mm Parabellum pistol cartridge. It has a 12- or 20-shot detachable magazine, walnut-finished hardwood pistol-grip stock and a sandblasted matte-blued finish. There are open sights and the receiver is drilled and tapped for scope mounting. This model was introduced in 1985.

NIB	Exc.	V.G.	Good	Fair	Poor
625	500	395	250	175	125

The year of manufacture of Marlin modern production rifles made between 1946 and 1968 can be determined by the letter prefix on the serial number.

The prefixes are as follows:

1946–C	1951–H	1956–N	1961–U	1966–AB
1947–D	1952–J	1957–P	1962–V	1967–AC
1948–E	1953–K	1958–R	1963–W	1968–AD
1949–F	1954–L	1959–S	1964–Y, Z	
1950–G	1955–M	1960–T	1965–AA	

Model 9N

Similar to the Model 9mm Carbine but furnished with nickel-plated metal parts.

NIB	Exc.	V.G.	Good	Fair	Poor
650	525	425	275	195	125

Model 45 Camp Carbine

This is the same as the 9mm version but is chambered for the .45

ACP cartridge and has a 7-shot detachable magazine. This is a very hot collectible.

NIB	Exc.	V.G.	Good	Fair	Poor
675	600	425	300	225	175

Model 922M

First offered in 1993 this model is a semi-automatic .22 Win. Magnum Rimfire rifle. It features a 7-shot clip, 20.5" MicroGrove barrel. The receiver is sandblasted and drilled and tapped for scope mounting. Monte Carlo black walnut stock with rubber rifle buff pad. Adjustable rear sight and ramp front sight with hood. Rifle weighs 6.5 lbs.

NIB	Exc.	V.G.	Good	Fair	Poor
550	450	375	225	150	125

Model 995

Semi-automatic .22 LR only rifle features a 7-shot clip, 18" MicroGroove barrel. Receiver is grooved for scope mount and receiver has a serrated non-glare top. Adjustable sights. Monte Carlo American black walnut stock with checkered pistol grip and forearm. White buttplate spacer is standard. Rifle weighs 5 lbs. Introduced in 1979.

NIB	Exc.	V.G.	Good	Fair	Poor
175	110	80	70	60	40

Model 995SS

Same as above but with stainless steel finish and black fiberglass stock. Introduced in 1995.

NIB	Exc.	V.G.	Good	Fair	Poor
195	125	100	85	60	50

Model 990L

This semi-automatic .22 LR Marlin features a tubular 14-round magazine with 22" MicroGrove barrel. The trigger is gold plated. The receiver is grooved for a scope mount while the stock is a two-tone brown birch Monte Carlo. Rubber rifle buttpad is standard. Rifle weighs 5.75 lbs.

NIB	Exc.	V.G.	Good	Fair	Poor
150	120	100	80	65	50

Model 7000

This model was first offered in 1997 and is a semi-automatic .22 caliber rifle with 18" heavy barrel. Magazine holds 10 rounds. Black synthetic stock with Monte Carlo comb and molded checkering. Receiver grooved for scope mount. No sights included. Weight about 6 lbs.

NIB	Exc.	V.G.	Good	Fair	Poor
200	150	125	100	75	50

Model 7000T

This target rifle is fitted with an 18" barrel with recessed muzzle. No sights. The stock is laminated red, white and blue with pistol grip. Serrated rubber buttplate is adjustable for length of pull, height and angle. Weight is about 7.5 lbs. Introduced in 1999.

NIB	Exc.	V.G.	Good	Fair	Poor
425	375	325	275	150	100

Model 795

Similar to the Model 7000 above but with an 18" standard weight barrel. Weight is about 5 lbs. Also available with 4X scope. **NOTE:** Add $5 for scope.

NIB	Exc.	V.G.	Good	Fair	Poor
150	115	—	—	—	—

Model 795SS

As above but with stainless steel action and barrel with black fiberglass stock. Weight is about 4.5 lbs. Introduced in 2002.

NIB	Exc.	V.G.	Good	Fair	Poor
200	150	125	100	75	50

Model 60

This semi-automatic 14-shot .22 caliber LR features a 22" MicroGroove barrel with adjustable rear sight. Receiver is grooved for scope mount and stock is birch with Monte Carlo comb. Rifle weighs 5.5 lbs. Introduced in 1960.

NIB	Exc.	V.G.	Good	Fair	Poor
175	125	90	60	50	40

Model 60SS

Introduced in 1993 this model is similar to the Model 60 except that it features a stainless barrel, bolt, and magazine tube. All other metal parts are nickel plated. The stock is a two-tone black and gray laminated birch Monte Carlo.

NIB	Exc.	V.G.	Good	Fair	Poor
275	225	150	125	75	50

Model 60SN

Similar to Model 60SS but with black synthetic stock with molded checkering and swivel studs. Blued metal. Introduced in 2007. Available with factory-mounted 3x9 scope. **NOTE:** Add 10 percent for scope package.

NIB	Exc.	V.G.	Good	Fair	Poor
200	150	125	100	75	50

Model 60S-CF

Similar to Model 60SN but with carbon fiber-dipped black synthetic stock, giving it a – quote – "racy, high tech look". Woo-hoo!

NIB	Exc.	V.G.	Good	Fair	Poor
250	225	175	125	100	75

Model 60SB

Introduced in 1998 this model features a stainless steel 22" barrel, bolt and magazine tube. The stock is birch with Monte Carlo and hard rubber buttplate.

NIB	Exc.	V.G.	Good	Fair	Poor
175	125	90	60	50	40

Model 60SSK

Similar to the Model 60SB with the addition of a black synthetic Monte Carlo stock with checkering.

NIB	Exc.	V.G.	Good	Fair	Poor
195	195	150	125	100	75

Model 60C

Similar to the Model 60 but with Realtree camo finish. Introduced in 2000.

NIB	Exc.	V.G.	Good	Fair	Poor
195	195	150	125	100	75

Model 60DL

Introduced in 2004 this model features a Monte Carlo hardwood stock with Walnutone walnut pattern finish with full pistol grip. Weight is about 5.5 lbs.

NIB	Exc.	V.G.	Good	Fair	Poor
175	125	90	60	50	40

Model 60DLX

Semi-automatic rifle chambered for .22 LR. Features include 14-shot tubular magazine; side ejection; manual and automatic last-shot bolt hold-opens; receiver top with serrated, non-glare finish; cross-bolt safety; steel charging handle; Monte Carlo American walnut-finished hardwood; full pistol grip; tough Mar-Shield finish; 19" barrel with Micro-Groove rifling. Limited availability.

NIB	Exc.	V.G.	Good	Fair	Poor
225	175	125	100	75	50

Model 2000

This is a bolt-action single-shot target rifle chambered for the .22 LR. The barrel is a 22" long MicroGroove design with match chamber and recessed muzzle. The rear sight is a fully adjustable target peep sight with a hooded front sight supplied with 10 aperture inserts. The stock is a Marlin blue fiberglass/Kevlar material with adjustable buttplate. There is an aluminum forearm rail with forearm stop and quick detachable swivel. Rifle weighs 8 lbs. Discontinued.

NIB	Exc.	V.G.	Good	Fair	Poor
425	325	250	200	150	125

Model 2000A

This is a 1996 version of the Model 2000 introduced in 1994 that features an adjustable comb and an ambidextrous pistol grip. A Marlin logo is molded into the side of the buttstock. Weighs approximately 8.5 lbs. Discontinued.

NIB	Exc.	V.G.	Good	Fair	Poor
425	350	250	200	150	125

Model 2000L

Introduced in 1996 this version of the Model 2000 features a black/gray laminated stock. It is fitted with a heavy 22" barrel with a match chamber. Fitted with a two-stage target trigger and a rubber buttplate that is adjustable for length of pull, height and angle. Weight is about 8 lbs. Discontinued.

NIB	Exc.	V.G.	Good	Fair	Poor
450	400	300	250	175	125

Model 880

This is a bolt-action clip-fed rifle chambered for the .22 LR caliber. The clip is a 7-shot magazine. The MicroGroove barrel is 22" and has adjustable folding rear sight and ramp front sight with hood. Rifle weighs 5.5 lbs. and was introduced in 1988. Discontinued in 2004.

NIB	Exc.	V.G.	Good	Fair	Poor
160	135	110	90	75	50

Model 880SS

Introduced in 1994 this .22 caliber rifle features a synthetic stock and a stainless steel receiver and barrel. The barrel is 22" long and a 7-shot magazine is standard. Discontinued in 2004.

NIB	Exc.	V.G.	Good	Fair	Poor
250	175	150	125	75	60

Model 880SQ

Similar to the Model 880 but fitted with a 22" heavy barrel and no sights. Introduced in 1996. Weight is approximately 7 lbs. Discontinued in 2004.

NIB	Exc.	V.G.	Good	Fair	Poor
285	225	200	150	100	75

Model 881

Bolt-action .22 caliber rifle has a tubular magazine that holds 25 Shorts, 19 longs, and 17 LR. A 22" MicroGroove barrel has adjustable folding rear sight and ramp front sight with hood. Stock is black walnut with Monte Carlo and a rubber rifle buttpad with sling swivels. Rifle weighs 6 lbs. First offered in 1988. Discontinued in 2004.

NIB	Exc.	V.G.	Good	Fair	Poor
175	150	125	100	80	60

Model 882SS

This bolt-action magazine rifle is chambered for the .22 Magnum cartridge. It has a stainless steel barrel and action with black synthetic stock. It has Marlin "Fire Sights" installed. Introduced in 1998. Discontinued in 2004.

NIB	Exc.	V.G.	Good	Fair	Poor
225	175	150	100	75	50

Model 25N

A Marlin promotional model. Bolt-action rifle chambered for the .22 LR only. Seven-shot clip magazine with a 22" MicroGroove barrel. Receiver grooved for scope mount. Walnut finished birch stock. Gun weighs 5.5 lbs.

NIB	Exc.	V.G.	Good	Fair	Poor
125	90	80	70	50	40

Model 25NC

Similar to the model above but with Mossy Oak Break-Up camo finish. Introduced in 2000.

NIB	Exc.	V.G.	Good	Fair	Poor
125	100	80	70	50	40

Model 25MN

Same as above but chambered for the .22 Win. Magnum Rimfire cartridge. Gun weighs 6 lbs.

NIB	Exc.	V.G.	Good	Fair	Poor
175	150	125	100	80	60

Model 25MNC

Similar to the above model but with Mossy Oak Break-Up camo finish. Weight is about 6 lbs. Introduced in 2001.

NIB	Exc.	V.G.	Good	Fair	Poor
195	160	125	100	80	60

Model 17V

Introduced in 2002 this bolt-action rifle is chambered for the .17 Hornady Magnum Rimfire cartridge. Fitted with a 22" heavy barrel. Hardwood stock. No sights. Magazine capacity is 7-round detachable magazine. Weight is about 6 lbs.

NIB	Exc.	V.G.	Good	Fair	Poor
225	200	150	115	90	50

Model 17VS

As above but with stainless steel heavy barrel and action and laminated stock. Weight is about 7 lbs. Discontinued.

NIB	Exc.	V.G.	Good	Fair	Poor
285	225	200	150	100	75

Model 15YN "Little Buckaroo"

A Marlin promotional model referred to as the "Little Buckaroo". A bolt-action .22 caliber single-shot rifle for the beginner. Features a MicroGroove 16.25" barrel adjustable rear sight and receiver grooved for scope mount. Birch stock. Rifle weighs 4.25 lbs.

NIB	Exc.	V.G.	Good	Fair	Poor
125	100	75	60	50	40

Model 15N

This bolt-action rifle is chambered for .22 S, L and LR. It is fitted with an adjustable rear sight. It has a full size birch stock interchangeable with the Model 15YN. Weight is about 4.25 lbs. Introduced in 1998.

NIB	Exc.	V.G.	Good	Fair	Poor
185	145	100	75	60	40

Model 15YS (Youth)

This is single-shot bolt-action rifle with a shorter-than-standard length of pull. Barrel length is 16.25". Hardwood stock. Weight is about 4.25 lbs. Introduced in 2002.

NIB	Exc.	V.G.	Good	Fair	Poor
175	140	110	65	50	35

Model 81TS

This is a bolt-action rifle chambered for the .22 Short, Long, and LR cartridges. It is fitted with a 22" barrel and has a tubular magazine. It comes with a black Monte Carlo synthetic stock and adjustable rear sight. Weight is about 6 lbs. Introduced in 1998. Discontinued in 2004.

NIB	Exc.	V.G.	Good	Fair	Poor
175	140	110	65	50	35

Model 882

Bolt-action rifle chambered for .22 Win. Magnum Rimfire cartridge. A 7-shot clip is standard. A MicroGroove 22" barrel with adjustable rear sight and ramp front sight with hood. Receiver grooved for scope mount. Black walnut stock with Monte Carlo and rubber rifle butt. Rifle weighs 6 lbs. Introduced in 1988. Discontinued in 2004.

NIB	Exc.	V.G.	Good	Fair	Poor
285	225	200	150	100	75

Model 882L

Same as above but furnished with a two-tone brown hardwood

Monte Carlo stock. Rifle weighs 6.25 lbs. Discontinued in 2004.

NIB	Exc.	V.G.	Good	Fair	Poor
275	215	190	145	90	60

Model 882SS

Same as above but furnished in stainless steel. With black fiberglass stock. Introduced in 1995. Discontinued in 2004.

NIB	Exc.	V.G.	Good	Fair	Poor
285	225	200	150	100	75

Model 882SSV

This variation of the Model 882, introduced in 1997, is all in stainless steel and chambered for the .22 WMR cartridge. It is fitted with a nickel plated 7-round magazine and 22" barrel. The stock is black synthetic with molded checkering. Receiver is grooved for scope mount. 1" brushed aluminum scope ring mounts included. Weighs about 7 lbs. Discontinued in 2004.

NIB	Exc.	V.G.	Good	Fair	Poor
285	225	200	150	100	75

Model 83TS

Chambered for the .22 Win. Magnum cartridge and fitted with a 22" barrel with 12-round tubular magazine. Adjustable rear sight. Bolt-action with synthetic stock. Weight is about 6 lbs. Introduced in 2001. Discontinued in 2004.

NIB	Exc.	V.G.	Good	Fair	Poor
250	200	165	145	100	75

Model 883

Bolt-action rifle chambered for .22 Win. Magnum cartridge with 12-shot tubular magazine. Furnished with a 22" MicroGroove barrel and adjustable rear sight, ramp front sight with hood. Checkered American black walnut stock with Monte Carlo. Rifle weighs 6 lbs. Introduced in 1988. Discontinued in 2004.

NIB	Exc.	V.G.	Good	Fair	Poor
285	225	200	150	100	75

Model 883N

Same as above but furnished with stainless steel barrel, receiver, front breech bolt, and striker. All other metal parts, except for sights, are nickel plated. Discontinued in 2004.

NIB	Exc.	V.G.	Good	Fair	Poor
285	225	200	150	100	75

Model 883SS

Introduced in 1993 this model is similar to the Model 883 but with all metal parts in stainless steel or nickel and the stock is a two-tone brown birch Monte Carlo that is not checkered. Discontinued in 2004.

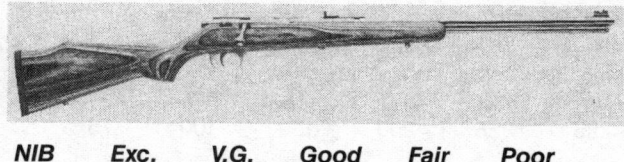

NIB	Exc.	V.G.	Good	Fair	Poor
275	215	190	145	90	60

Model 717M2

Introduced in 2005 this semi-automatic model is chambered for the .17 Mach 2 cartridge. Laminated hardwood stock with Monte Carlo comb. Fitted with an 18" barrel with iron sights. Magazine capacity is 7 rounds. Weight is about 5 lbs.

NIB	Exc.	V.G.	Good	Fair	Poor
300	250	200	175	150	125

MODEL 900 SERIES

This bolt action rimfire series was introduced into the Marlin line in 2004 and features a T-900 fire control system. This is a trigger and safety system that features a wide serrated trigger and improved trigger pull. The safety activation is also improved. The 900 series also features drilled and tapped receivers on all models.

Model 983T

Chambered for the .22 WMR cartridge and fitted with a 22" barrel. Monte Carlo black fiberglass stock with checkering. Adjustable sights. Tubular 12-round magazine. Weight is about 6 lbs.

NIB	Exc.	V.G.	Good	Fair	Poor
285	225	200	150	100	75

Model 983S

As above but with laminated two-tone stock.

NIB	Exc.	V.G.	Good	Fair	Poor
285	225	200	150	100	75

Model 983

This .22 WMR model features a Monte Carlo stock of American

black walnut with full pistol grip and checkering.

NIB	Exc.	V.G.	Good	Fair	Poor
285	225	200	150	100	75

Model 917

Bolt-action rifle chambered in .17 Hornady Magnum Rimfire; 7-shot clip magazine; fiberglass-filled synthetic stock with full pistol grip; swivel studs and molded-in checkering. Adjustable open rear sight, ramp front. 22" barrel. Introduced 2006.

NIB	Exc.	V.G.	Good	Fair	Poor
285	225	200	150	100	75

Model 917V

This model is chambered for the .17 HMR cartridge and fitted with a 22" heavy barrel. Hardwood Monte Carlo stock with full pistol grip. No sights. Detachable magazine with 7-round capacity. Weight is about 6 lbs.

NIB	Exc.	V.G.	Good	Fair	Poor
285	225	200	150	100	75

Model 917VR

Similar to Model 917 but with fiberglass-filled synthetic stock. Introduced 2006.

NIB	Exc.	V.G.	Good	Fair	Poor
285	225	200	150	100	75

Model 917VS

As above but with gray/black laminated hardwood stock. No sights. Magazine is nickel plated. Weight is about 7 lbs. Scope bases included.

NIB	Exc.	V.G.	Good	Fair	Poor
285	225	200	150	100	75

Model 917VS-CF

Similar to Model 917VS but with carbon fiber-patterned stock.

NIB	Exc.	V.G.	Good	Fair	Poor
285	225	200	150	100	75

Model 917VSF

Chambered for the .17 HMR cartridge and fitted with a 22" heavy stainless steel fluted barrel with no sights. Nickel magazine capacity is 7 rounds. Laminated gray stock with Monte Carlo comb. Weight is about 6.75 lbs. Introduced in 2005.

NIB	Exc.	V.G.	Good	Fair	Poor
300	250	200	175	150	125

Model 917VT

Similar to above but with laminated brown thumbhole stock. Introduced 2008.

NIB	Exc.	V.G.	Good	Fair	Poor
350	300	250	175	145	110

Model 917VST

Similar to above but with laminated gray/black thumbhole stock. Introduced 2008.

NIB	Exc.	V.G.	Good	Fair	Poor
400	350	295	245	125	100

Model 917M2

This model is chambered for the .17 Mach 2 cartridge and fitted with a 22" heavy barrel. Monte Carlo hardwood stock with full pistol grip. No sights but scope bases included. Magazine capacity is 7 rounds. Weight is about 5.5 lbs.

NIB	Exc.	V.G.	Good	Fair	Poor
300	250	200	175	150	125

Model 917M2S

As above but with Monte Carlo gray/black laminated stock with full pistol grip. Stainless steel barrel and receiver. Nickel plated magazine.

NIB	Exc.	V.G.	Good	Fair	Poor
325	275	225	200	175	125

Model 982S

This model is chambered for the .22 WMR cartridge and fitted with a 22" stainless steel barrel with adjustable sights. Black fiberglass stock with Monte Carlo and full pistol grip. Detachable 7-round nickel magazine. Weight is about 6 lbs.

NIB	Exc.	V.G.	Good	Fair	Poor
285	225	200	150	100	75

Model 982L

As above but for a gray/black laminated stock. Weight is about 6.25 lbs.

NIB	Exc.	V.G.	Good	Fair	Poor
300	250	200	175	150	125

Model 982

Similar to 982S but with American black walnut checkered stock with Monte Carlo and full pistol grip. Adjustable sights. Weight is about 6 lbs.

NIB	Exc.	V.G.	Good	Fair	Poor
285	225	200	150	100	75

Model 982VS

As above but with black fiberglass Monte Carlo stock. Heavy 22" stainless steel barrel. Nickel plated 7-round magazine. No sights. Weight is about 7 lbs.

NIB	Exc.	V.G.	Good	Fair	Poor
325	275	225	200	175	125

Model 982VS-CF

As above but with synthetic stock with dipped carbon-fiber textured finish.

NIB	Exc.	V.G.	Good	Fair	Poor
325	275	225	200	175	125

Model 925M

As above but with hardwood stock and full pistol grip. Fitted with 22" standard weight barrel. Adjustable sights. Weight is about 6 lbs.

NIB	Exc.	V.G.	Good	Fair	Poor
250	200	165	145	100	75

Model 925RM

Similar to Model 925M but with black fiberglass-filled synthetic stock.

NIB	Exc.	V.G.	Good	Fair	Poor
250	200	165	145	100	75

Model 925MC

As above but with Monte Carlo stock with Mossy Oak Break-up camo stock. Weight is about 6 lbs.

NIB	Exc.	V.G.	Good	Fair	Poor
285	225	200	150	100	75

Model 980V

This model is chambered for the .22 LR cartridge and fitted with a 22" heavy barrel. Black fiberglass stock with Monte Carlo and full pistol grip. No sights. Magazine capacity is 7 rounds. Weight is about 7 lbs.

NIB	Exc.	V.G.	Good	Fair	Poor
285	225	200	150	100	75

Model 980S

As above but with standard weight 22" barrel and 7-round nickel plated magazine and stainless steel barrel and receiver. Adjustable sights. Weight is about 6 lbs.

NIB	Exc.	V.G.	Good	Fair	Poor
285	225	200	150	100	75

Model 980S-CF

As above but with carbon fiber stock. Introduced in 2007.

NIB	Exc.	V.G.	Good	Fair	Poor
285	225	200	150	100	75

Model 981T

This model is chambered to handle interchangeably the .22 Short, Long, or LR cartridges in a tubular magazine. Black Monte Carlo fiberglass stock with full pistol grip. Adjustable sights. Fitted with a standard weight 22" barrel. Weight is about 6 lbs.

NIB	Exc.	V.G.	Good	Fair	Poor
285	225	200	150	100	75

Model 981TS

Bolt action rifle chambered in .22 S/L/LR. Features include tubular magazine (holds 25 Short, 19 Long or 17 Long Rifle) cartridges; thumb safety; red cocking indicator; black fiberglass-filled synthetic stock with full pistol grip; molded-in checkering and swivel studs; 22" stainless steel barrel with Micro-Groove rifling (16 grooves). Adjustable semi-buckhorn folding rear sight, ramp front with high visibility, orange front sight post; cutaway Wide-Scan hood. Receiver grooved for scope mount; drilled and tapped for scope bases.

NIB	Exc.	V.G.	Good	Fair	Poor
300	250	225	150	100	75

Model 925

This model is chambered for the .22 LR cartridge and fitted with a 22" standard weight barrel with adjustable sights. Monte Carlo hardwood stock with full pistol grip. Seven-round magazine. Weight is about 5.5 lbs.

NIB	Exc.	V.G.	Good	Fair	Poor
225	175	150	125	95	75

Model 925R

As above but with factory-mounted 3x9 scope.

NIB	Exc.	V.G.	Good	Fair	Poor
250	200	165	145	100	75

Model 925C

As above but with Monte Carlo hardwood stock with Mossy Oak Break-up camo pattern. Adjustable sights.

NIB	Exc.	V.G.	Good	Fair	Poor
250	200	165	145	100	75

Model 915Y Compact

Single-shot .22 rimfire rifle with 16.25" barrel, hardwood stock with impressed checkering and iron sights.

NIB	Exc.	V.G.	Good	Fair	Poor
200	150	125	100	75	50

Model 915YS Compact

Similar to above but with stainless steel receiver and barrel, no checkering and fiber optic sights.

NIB	Exc.	V.G.	Good	Fair	Poor
225	175	150	125	95	75

Model 322

This model is chambered for the .222 cartridge and has a 24" medium-weight barrel with MicroGroove rifling. It has a checkered walnut pistol-grip stock. The magazine holds 4 shots, and the adjustable trigger and sights are Sako products. The Sako receiver is fitted for Sako scope mounting bases. Non-Sako receivers were apparently also used. The MicroGroove rifling in the barrel was not successful for this caliber, and accuracy fell off after as few as 500 shots—so this model was dropped and replaced. The serial numbers were Sako and there were 5,859 manufactured between 1954 and 1959.

NIB	Exc.	V.G.	Good	Fair	Poor
—	950	600	500	325	200

Model 422

This model is the successor to the Model 322. It is simply the same rifle fitted with a 24", featherweight, stainless steel barrel and named the "Varmint King". The stock features a Monte Carlo stock with a cheekpiece. There were only 354 manufactured between 1956 and 1958.

NIB	Exc.	V.G.	Good	Fair	Poor
—	—	—	—	—	—

Model 455

This model is built on the Fabrique Nationale Belgian Mauser action. It is chambered for the .308 and the .30-06 cartridges. It has a stainless steel barrel made by Marlin and has a 5-shot magazine. It has a Bishop checkered walnut stock with detachable sling swivels and a leather sling. The rear sight is a Lyman 48, and the front is a ramp type with a detachable hood. The receiver is drilled and tapped for scope mounts. The trigger is an adjustable Sako unit. There were 1,079 manufactured in .3006 and only 59 in .308 between 1955 and 1959.

NIB	Exc.	V.G.	Good	Fair	Poor
—	700	595	425	300	200

Model MR-7

Introduced in 1996, this was an American-made bolt-action centerfire rifle of a totally new design. Chambered for the .25-06 (first offered in 1997), .243, .270 Win. .280, .308, or .30-06 cartridges it is fitted with a 22" barrel. It has an American black walnut stock and a 4-shot detachable box magazine. Offered with or without sights. Weight is approximately 7.5 lbs. Discontinued 1999.

NIB	Exc.	V.G.	Good	Fair	Poor
450	350	300	250	175	150

Model MR-7B

Similar to the MR-7 but fitted with a 4-round blind magazine and birch stock. Offered in .30-06 or .270 with or without sights. Introduced in 1998. Discontinued.

NIB	Exc.	V.G.	Good	Fair	Poor
375	300	250	175	150	100

Model XL7

Introduced in 2008, this is a centerfire bolt-action rifle with adjustable Pro-Fire trigger system. 4+1 capacity . Chambered in .25-06, .270 and .30-06 with a crowned, precision-rifled 22" barrel that is joined to the receiver with a pressure nut. Black synthetic stock with raised cheekpiece and Soft-Tech recoil pad. No sights; drilled and tapped for mounts. **NOTE:** Add $50 for factory scope package.

NIB	Exc.	V.G.	Good	Fair	Poor
325	275	225	200	175	125

Model XL7C

Similar to above but with Realtree APG HD camo finish.

NIB	Exc.	V.G.	Good	Fair	Poor
350	300	250	175	145	110

Model XS7 Short-Action

Similar to Model XL7 but chambered in 7mm-08, .243 Winchester and .308 Winchester. **NOTE:** Add $50 for factory scope package.

NIB	Exc.	V.G.	Good	Fair	Poor
325	275	225	200	175	125

Model XS7Y Youth Rifle

Similar to above but with smaller dimensions.

NIB	Exc.	V.G.	Good	Fair	Poor
325	275	225	200	175	125

Model XS7C Camo

Similar to above but with Realtree APG HD camo stock.

NIB	Exc.	V.G.	Good	Fair	Poor
350	300	250	175	145	110

Model XS7S

Bolt action rifle; similar to Model XS7 but with stainless steel barrel, receiver and trigger group. Short action.

NIB	Exc.	V.G.	Good	Fair	Poor
375	325	275	175	150	100

Model XL7

Entry-level bolt action rifle chambered in .25-06 Rem., .270 Win., .30-06 Spr. Features include 4+1 magazine capacity; pillar bedded 22" barrel; Pro-Fire adjustable trigger system; 2-position safety; red cocking indicator; swivel studs; matte blue/black finish; black synthetic stock with molded in checkering and Soft-Tech recoil pad. No sights.

NIB	Exc.	V.G.	Good	Fair	Poor
325	285	235	200	150	75

MARLIN PUMP SHOTGUNS

Model 1898

This model was made in 12 gauge, with an exposed hammer. It has a takedown receiver and walnut pistol-grip stock and fore-end. There is a 5-shot tube magazine, and the barrel lengths are from 26" and 32". They were manufactured between 1898 and 1905.

Grade A

This variation has a 38", 30", or 32" barrel, is Full choke, and is the plainest grade.

Courtesy Marlin Firearms Co.

NIB	Exc.	V.G.	Good	Fair	Poor
—	475	425	325	125	75

Grade A Brush or Riot

This is the same shotgun with a 26" cylinder-bore barrel.

NIB	Exc.	V.G.	Good	Fair	Poor
—	425	375	250	150	100

Grade B

This is the same as the Grade A with a special smokeless steel barrel and a checkered stock.

NIB	Exc.	V.G.	Good	Fair	Poor
—	675	550	350	150	100

Grade C

This is a more deluxe version with engraving and fancier wood.

NIB	Exc.	V.G.	Good	Fair	Poor
—	1150	850	550	275	125

Grade D

This variation has a Damascus barrel and the greatest amount of engraving.

NIB	Exc.	V.G.	Good	Fair	Poor
—	2100	1400	900	450	250

Model 16

This model is exactly the same as the Model 1898 except that it is chambered for 16 gauge only. The four grades are the same also. They were manufactured between 1903 and 1910.

Grade A

NIB	Exc.	V.G.	Good	Fair	Poor
—	500	450	400	250	150

Grade B

NIB	Exc.	V.G.	Good	Fair	Poor
—	650	550	400	200	100

Grade C

NIB	Exc.	V.G.	Good	Fair	Poor
—	1100	850	500	300	150

Grade D

NIB	Exc.	V.G.	Good	Fair	Poor
—	2000	1400	950	425	250

Model 17

This model is an exposed-hammer gun with a solid frame and a straight-grip stock. It is chambered for 12 gauge, with a 30" or

32" barrel. The Model 17 was manufactured between 1906 and 1908.

NIB	Exc.	V.G.	Good	Fair	Poor
—	525	450	275	150	75

Model 17 Brush Gun

This variation is similar to the standard Model 17, with a 26" cylinder-bore barrel.

NIB	Exc.	V.G.	Good	Fair	Poor
—	550	475	325	200	100

Model 17 Riot Gun

This variation has a 20" cylinder-bore barrel.

NIB	Exc.	V.G.	Good	Fair	Poor
—	600	525	325	150	125

Model 19

This is a takedown gun, chambered for 12 gauge. It is basically an improved and lightened version of the Model 1898. It is available in the same four grades. It was manufactured in 1906 and 1907.

Grade A

NIB	Exc.	V.G.	Good	Fair	Poor
—	500	450	250	150	100

Grade B

NIB	Exc.	V.G.	Good	Fair	Poor
—	600	550	500	350	225

Grade C

NIB	Exc.	V.G.	Good	Fair	Poor
—	750	675	5550	425	300

Grade D

Courtesy Marlin Firearms Co.

NIB	Exc.	V.G.	Good	Fair	Poor
—	1850	1500	1050	400	200

Model 21 "Trap"

This model is basically the same as the Model 19 with a straight-grip stock. The 1907 catalog listed it as a Trap model. This model was manufactured in 1907 and 1908. The four grades are similar to the previous models.

Grade A

NIB	Exc.	V.G.	Good	Fair	Poor
—	450	450	300	200	100

Grade B

NIB	Exc.	V.G.	Good	Fair	Poor
—	600	550	350	200	100

Grade C

NIB	Exc.	V.G.	Good	Fair	Poor
—	750	675	500	350	200

Grade D

NIB	Exc.	V.G.	Good	Fair	Poor
—	1600	1300	1050	700	550

Model 24

This model is actually an improved version of the Model 21. It has a pistol-grip stock and exposed hammer. It features an automatic recoil lock on the slide and a matte rib barrel. Otherwise, it is quite similar to its predecessor. It was manufactured between 1908 and 1917.

Grade A

Courtesy Marlin Firearms Co.

NIB	Exc.	V.G.	Good	Fair	Poor
—	475	400	350	150	100

Grade B

NIB	Exc.	V.G.	Good	Fair	Poor
—	600	550	450	350	225

Grade C

NIB	Exc.	V.G.	Good	Fair	Poor
—	750	675	550	425	300

Grade D

NIB	Exc.	V.G.	Good	Fair	Poor
—	1600	1300	900	600	400

Marlin "Trap Gun"

This model is unique in that it has no numerical designation and is simply known as the "Trap Gun". It is a takedown gun with interchangeable barrels from 16" to 32". It has a straight-grip buttstock and is quite similar in appearance to the Model 24. It was manufactured between 1909 and 1912.

NIB	Exc.	V.G.	Good	Fair	Poor
—	1000	700	525	350	200

Model 26

This model is similar to the Model 24 Grade A, with a solid frame. It has 30" or 32" barrels.

NIB	Exc.	V.G.	Good	Fair	Poor
—	525	450	325	125	100

Model 26 Brush Gun

This model has a 26" cylinder-bored barrel.

NIB	Exc.	V.G.	Good	Fair	Poor
—	550	475	325	200	100

Model 26 Riot Gun

This variation has a 20" cylinder-bored barrel.

NIB	Exc.	V.G.	Good	Fair	Poor
—	600	525	325	150	125

Model 28 Hammerless

This model was the first of the Marlin hammerless shotguns. It is a takedown 12 gauge, with barrels from 26" to 32" in length. The stock has a pistol grip, and it comes in four grades like its predecessors. The Model 28 was manufactured between 1913 and 1922.

Grade A

NIB	Exc.	V.G.	Good	Fair	Poor
—	400	335	200	100	70

Grade B

NIB	Exc.	V.G.	Good	Fair	Poor
—	600	550	350	350	225

Grade C

NIB	Exc.	V.G.	Good	Fair	Poor
—	750	625	550	425	300

Grade D

Courtesy Marlin Firearms Co.

NIB	Exc.	V.G.	Good	Fair	Poor
—	1700	1200	800	600	300

Model 28TS Trap Gun

This variation is the same as the Model 28 with a 30" Full choke barrel with matte rib and a high-comb straight grip stock. It was manufactured in 1915.

NIB	Exc.	V.G.	Good	Fair	Poor
—	725	600	525	425	300

Model 28T Trap Gun

This variation is the deluxe model, similar to the Model 28TS, with engraving, high-grade walnut and hand checkering. It was manufactured in 1915.

NIB	Exc.	V.G.	Good	Fair	Poor
—	750	625	550	425	300

Model 30

This model is an improved version of the Model 16, 16 gauge shotgun. Its features are similar, with the addition of the improved takedown system and the automatic recoil lock on the slide. This model was manufactured between 1910 and 1914.

Grade A

NIB	Exc.	V.G.	Good	Fair	Poor
—	550	475	350	200	100

Grade B

NIB	Exc.	V.G.	Good	Fair	Poor
—	600	550	450	200	100

Grade C

NIB	Exc.	V.G.	Good	Fair	Poor
—	750	675	550	250	150

Grade D

NIB	Exc.	V.G.	Good	Fair	Poor
—	1400	1200	1000	700	550

Model 30 Field Grade

This model is similar to the Model 30 Grade B, with a 25" modified-choke barrel and a straight-grip stock. It was manufactured in 1913 and 1914.

NIB	Exc.	V.G.	Good	Fair	Poor
—	450	375	250	150	100

Model 31

This model is a smaller version of the Model 28 hammerless takedown shotgun, chambered for 16 and 20 gauge. It was produced with barrel lengths of 26" and 28" and was available in the usual four grades, with various different chokes. This model was manufactured between 1915 and 1922.

Grade A

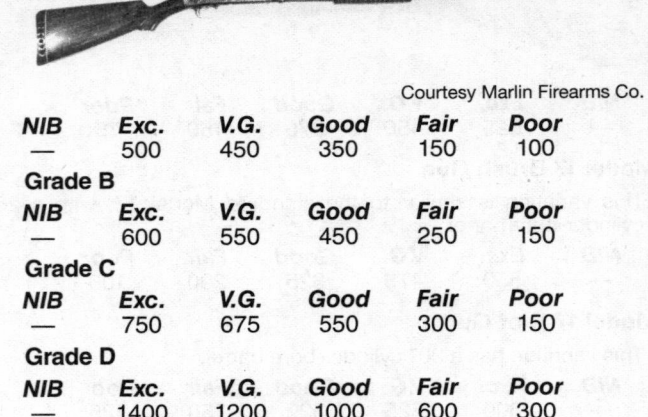

Courtesy Marlin Firearms Co.

NIB	Exc.	V.G.	Good	Fair	Poor
—	500	450	350	150	100

Grade B

NIB	Exc.	V.G.	Good	Fair	Poor
—	600	550	450	250	150

Grade C

NIB	Exc.	V.G.	Good	Fair	Poor
—	750	675	550	300	150

Grade D

NIB	Exc.	V.G.	Good	Fair	Poor
—	1400	1200	1000	600	300

Model 42/42A

This model was originally listed as the Model 42; but in the second year of production, the designation was changed to /42A for no more apparent reason than standardization of models. This model is similar to the Model 24 except that the barrel markings are different. It is still an exposed hammer takedown gun chambered for 12 gauge. It was manufactured between 1922 and 1933.

NIB	Exc.	V.G.	Good	Fair	Poor
—	375	325	200	150	100

Model 43A

This hammerless model was quite similar to the Model 28, with different markings and less attention to finishing detail. It was manufactured between 1923 and 1930.

NIB	Exc.	V.G.	Good	Fair	Poor
—	400	350	250	150	75

Model 43T

This model is the same as the Model 43A takedown hammerless with a 30" or 32" matte rib barrel. The straight-grip stock is of high grade walnut, with a non-gloss oil finish and fitted recoil paid. This model was manufactured between 1922 and 1930.

NIB	Exc.	V.G.	Good	Fair	Poor
—	500	450	350	200	100

Model 43TS

This is a custom-order version of the Model 43T, the same in all respects except that the stock could be ordered to any specifications the shooter desired. It was manufactured between 1922 and 1930.

NIB	Exc.	V.G.	Good	Fair	Poor
—	700	625	550	250	150

Model 44A

This model is similar to the Model 31 and was advertised as its successor. It is a hammerless takedown chambered for the 20 gauge. It features an improved bolt opening device located in the trigger guard area instead of at the top of the receiver and has a shorter 4-shot magazine tube. The model was manufactured from 1922 until 1933.

Courtesy Marlin Firearms Co.

NIB	Exc.	V.G.	Good	Fair	Poor
—	475	400	275	150	100

Model 44S

This model is similar to the Model 44A, with a higher grade walnut stock that featured hand-cut checkering.

NIB	Exc.	V.G.	Good	Fair	Poor
—	500	425	300	200	100

Model 49

This model is a 12-gauge, exposed-hammer takedown that combines features of the Model 42 and the Model 24. It is basically a lower-priced model that was never listed in the Marlin catalog. This model was part of Frank Kenna's money-raising program—anyone who purchased four shares of stock for $25 per share was given one, free of charge. This model was manufactured between 1925 and 1928.

NIB	Exc.	V.G.	Good	Fair	Poor
—	700	625	550	250	150

Model 53

This model is a hammerless, takedown, 12 gauge that was not in production for long. It is theorized that the Model 53 was produced to use up old parts on hand when the Model 43 was introduced. It was manufactured in 1929 and 1980.

Courtesy Marlin Firearms Co.

NIB	Exc.	V.G.	Good	Fair	Poor
—	450	400	275	175	125

Model 63

This was the last of the slide-action shotguns produced by Marlin until the Model 120 in 1971. It is a hammerless, takedown 12 gauge and replaced the Model 43A in the Marlin catalog. This model had improvements over the earlier guns, but its introduction during the Depression did little to bolster sales. This model was also offered free of charge to anyone purchasing four shares of Marlin stock at $25 per share. It was manufactured between 1931 and 1933.

NIB	Exc.	V.G.	Good	Fair	Poor
—	500	450	350	200	100

Model 63T

This is the trap-grade version of the Model 63. It has a better grade hand-checkered stock, with a fitted recoil pad and oil finish. It was manufactured between 1931 and 1933.

NIB	Exc.	V.G.	Good	Fair	Poor
—	600	525	450	200	125

Model 63TS

This variation is the same as the Model 63T except that the stock dimensions were custom-made to the customer's specifications. It was manufactured between 1931 and 1933.

NIB	Exc.	V.G.	Good	Fair	Poor
—	700	625	550	250	150

Premier Mark I

This model was made by Manufrance and called the LaSalle. Marlin was able to purchase them without the barrels at a good enough price for them to barrel and market them under their own name. This model is 12 gauge only, with an alloy receiver and seven interchangeable barrels in 26"-30" lengths and various chokes. The plain stock is French walnut. The biggest problem with this gun is that the light weight (six pounds) produced severe recoil and it was less than enjoyable to shoot. This model was in production from 1959 through 1963, with approximately 13,700 sold.

NIB	Exc.	V.G.	Good	Fair	Poor
—	325	225	175	150	100

Premier Mark II

This model is similar to the Mark I, with light engraving and a checkered stock.

NIB	Exc.	V.G.	Good	Fair	Poor
—	325	225	175	150	100

Premier Mark IV

This model is similar to the Mark II, with more engraving on the receiver. **NOTE:** Add 10 percent for vent rib.

NIB	Exc.	V.G.	Good	Fair	Poor
—	325	225	175	150	100

Model 120

This model was styled to resemble the Winchester Model 12 and was advertised as an all steel and walnut shotgun. It was offered with interchangeable barrels from 26" to 40" and various chokes were available. The checkered stock is of walnut, with a fitted recoil pad. The tube magazine holds 5 shots, 4 in 3". There was a Trap Model available (1973-1975), as well as a slug gun (1974-1984). This model was manufactured between 1971 and 1985. A really nice gun, if a bit heavy. **NOTE:** Add 10 percent for 36" "Long Tom" barrel.

NIB	Exc.	V.G.	Good	Fair	Poor
—	350	300	250	150	125

Model 778 (Glenfield)

This model is similar to the Model 120, with a walnut finished hardwood stock instead of walnut, and the Glenfield name stamped on it. It was manufactured between 1979 and 1984.

NIB	Exc.	V.G.	Good	Fair	Poor
—	275	225	175	125	100

MARLIN OVER/UNDER & TOP-BREAK SHOTGUNS

Model 60 Single-Barrel Shotgun

This is a break-open, exposed-hammer, top lever-opening 12 gauge with either 30" or 32" full-choke barrel. It has a pistol grip stock. There were approximately 60 manufactured in 1923.

NIB	Exc.	V.G.	Good	Fair	Poor
—	400	350	250	150	75

Model 90 Over/Under Shotgun

This gun was produced in response to a request from Sears Roebuck that Marlin should manufacture an over/under shotgun for Sears to market in their stores. The guns produced for Sears have the prefix 103 in their serial numbers and were marked "Ranger" before WWII and "J.C. Higgins" after the war. Prior to 1945 they were not marked Marlin; after that date Sears requested that the company stamp their name on the guns. They were also produced as the Marlin Model 90 during the same period and were chambered for 12, 16 and 20 gauge, as well as .410 bore. The 16 and 20 gauge guns were first offered in 1937 with 26" or 28" barrels. In 1939 the .410 bore was first offered with 26" barrel and 3" chambers. The barrels are either 26", 28", or 30" with various chokes. The action is a boxlock with extractors. Guns made prior to 1950 were solid between the barrels; after that date there was a space between the barrels. They can be found with double or single triggers and a checkered walnut stock. A ventilated rib was also offered as an option beginning in 1949. Be aware that this model was also available as a combination gun in .22 LR/.410, .22 Hornet/.410 and .218 Bee/.410. There were approximately 34,000 Model 90s manufactured between 1937 and 1963. **NOTE:** Single trigger add 33 percent. Add 25 percent for 20 gauge guns and 300 percent for .410 bores. Add a 300 percent premium for combination guns. There are other rare gauge and barrel combinations that may affect value.

Marlin Model 90 Combination Gun

Courtesy Marlin Firearms Co.

Marlin Model 90 .410 bore

NIB	Exc.	V.G.	Good	Fair	Poor
—	550	425	350	275	200

MARLIN LEVER-ACTION SHOTGUNS

Model .410 Lever-Action Shotgun (Original)

This was a unique venture for the Marlin Company—a lever-action shotgun based on the Model 1893 action with a longer loading port, modified tube magazine that held 5 shots and a smoothbore barrel chambered for the .410 shot shell. The finish of this gun is blued, with a walnut pistol grip stock and grooved beavertail fore-end. It has a hard rubber rifle-type buttplate. The model was available with either a 22" or 26" full-choke barrel. This gun was also part of the stock purchase plan and was given free of charge to anyone purchasing four shares at $25 per share. It was also cataloged for sale and was manufactured between 1929 and 1932.

Courtesy Mike Stuckslager

NIB	Exc.	V.G.	Good	Fair	Poor
—	1600	1000	650	500	200

Model .410 Deluxe (Original)

This variation was never cataloged and is essentially the same as the standard version with a hand-checkered stock. The fore-end does not have the grooves found on the standard model. Be wary of fakes!

NIB	Exc.	V.G.	Good	Fair	Poor
—	2200	1200	800	400	200

Model .410 (New)

A lever-action shotgun chambered for the 2.5" .410 shot shell. Checkered walnut stock, fluorescent front sight. Based on the Model 336 action. Discontinued.

NIB	Exc.	V.G.	Good	Fair	Poor
700	625	550	450	300	—

Model 410XLR 410 XLR

New in 2009, this is the latest Marlin .410 shotgun. It's built on the M1895 chassis and is chambered for 2.5" .410 shot shells. Receiver and barrel are stainless and the stock is laminated wood.

NIB	Exc.	V.G.	Good	Fair	Poor
750	675	575	450	300	—

MARLIN BOLT-ACTION SHOTGUNS

Model 50DL

This bolt-action 12 gauge shotgun is available with a 28" modified barrel, black synthetic stock. Ventilated recoil pad is standard. Brass bead front sight. Weight is approximately 7.5 lbs.

NIB	Exc.	V.G.	Good	Fair	Poor
300	275	225	150	125	100

Model 55

This model is chambered for 12, 16 and 20 gauge, with Full or adjustable choke and barrels of 26" or 28". It is a bolt-action with 2-shot box magazine. The pistol grip stock is plain. This model was manufactured between 1950 and 1965.

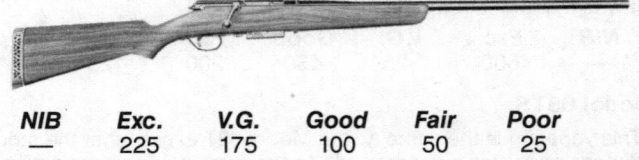

NIB	Exc.	V.G.	Good	Fair	Poor
—	225	175	100	50	25

Model 55 Swamp Gun

This is simply the Model 55 with a 3" Magnum, 20" barrel and an adjustable choke. It was manufactured between 1963 and 1965.

NIB	Exc.	V.G.	Good	Fair	Poor
—	300	250	175	75	50

Model 55 Goose Gun

This is the Model 55 with a 3" chambered, 36" Full choke 12 gauge barrel and a recoil pad and sling. It was introduced in 1962.

NIB	Exc.	V.G.	Good	Fair	Poor
375	250	175	150	75	50

Model 55S Slug Gun

This is the Model 55 with a 24" cylinder-bore barrel and rifle sights. It was manufactured between 1974 and 1983.

NIB	Exc.	V.G.	Good	Fair	Poor
—	250	200	150	100	50

Model 5510 Goose Gun

This model is chambered for the 3.5" 10 gauge. It has a 34" Full choke barrel and a recoil pad and sling. It was manufactured between 1976 and 1985.

NIB	Exc.	V.G.	Good	Fair	Poor
—	400	300	250	175	100

Model 55GDL

This bolt-action shotgun is fitted with a 36" full choke barrel and reinforced black synthetic stock. Magazine holds two rounds. Ventilated recoil pad is standard. First introduced in 1997. Weight is about 8 lbs. Discontinued.

NIB	Exc.	V.G.	Good	Fair	Poor
350	325	275	200	150	100

Model 512 Slugmaster

Introduced in 1994 this bolt-action shotgun features a rifled 21" barrel. It is equipped with a two-shot detachable magazine and a ventilated recoil pad. A special scope is also provided. Weight is approximately 8 lbs. Discontinued.

NIB	Exc.	V.G.	Good	Fair	Poor
350	325	275	200	150	100

Model 512DL Slugmaster

Introduced in 1997 this bolt-action model features a black synthetic stock with a fully rifled 21" barrel chambered for the 12 gauge shell. A two-round magazine is standard. Adjustable rear sight with ramp front sight. In 1998 this model was furnished with "Fire Sights". Receiver drilled and tapped for scope mount. Weight is about 8 lbs. Discontinued.

NIB	Exc.	V.G.	Good	Fair	Poor
395	250	200	150	125	100

Model 512P

Introduced in 1999 this model is similar to the Model 512 DL with the addition of a 21" fully rifled and ported barrel. Fire sights are standard. Weight is about 8 lbs. Discontinued.

NIB	Exc.	V.G.	Good	Fair	Poor
395	250	200	150	125	100

Model 25MG

This bolt-action .22 Win. Magnum shot shell only gun is fitted with a 22" smoothbore barrel. It has a 7-round magazine. Hardwood stock. Weight is about 6 lbs. First introduced in 1999.

NIB	Exc.	V.G.	Good	Fair	Poor
225	175	145	125	100	75

MODERN L.C. SMITH SHOTGUNS

The modern line of L.C. Smith shotguns is made in Europe and imported into the USA under the Marlin name.

Model LC410-DB

A side-by-side .410 bore, with fleur-de-lis checkered walnut stock, single selective trigger, selective automatic ejectors, three choke tubes (IC, M, F) and 26" chrome-lined barrels with solid rib and bead front sight. Its case-colored receiver has gold game bird embossed on the side and bottom.

NIB	Exc.	V.G.	Good	Fair	Poor
1600	1175	900	700	500	300

Model LC28-DB

Similar to above but in 28 gauge.

NIB	Exc.	V.G.	Good	Fair	Poor
1750	1275	900	700	500	300

Model LC12-DB

This 12 gauge double barrel features 3" chambers, a single trigger, selective automatic ejectors, three choke tubes (IC, M, F), 28" barrels with a solid rib and a bead front sight. Its walnut stock is checkered and has a fluted comb, a beavertail forearm and a recoil pad. Case-coloring on receiver and side plates.

NIB	Exc.	V.G.	Good	Fair	Poor
1100	950	800	575	400	250

Model LC20-DB

Similar to above but in 20 gauge.

NIB	Exc.	V.G.	Good	Fair	Poor
1100	950	800	575	400	250

Model LC12-OU

This over/under features 3" chambers, a single selective trigger, selective automatic ejectors, automatic safety, three choke tubes (IC, M, F), 28" barrels with ventilated rib and bead front sight. It has a checkered walnut stock with a fluted comb and recoil pad and features case-coloring on its receiver and sideplates.

NIB	Exc.	V.G.	Good	Fair	Poor
950	825	600	450	300	200

Model LC20-OU

Similar to above but in 20 gauge.

NIB	Exc.	V.G.	Good	Fair	Poor
950	825	600	450	300	200

MARLIN MODERN MUZZLELOADERS

Model MLS-50/54

These Marlin in-line muzzleloaders were introduced in 1997. They are stainless steel and available in either .50 or .54 caliber. The barrel is 22" long. Adjustable Marble rear sight, ramp front sight with brass bead. Drilled and tapped for scope mount. Black synthetic stock with molded in checkering. Weight is about 7 lbs. Discontinued and not particularly easy to take down for cleaning.

NIB	Exc.	V.G.	Good	Fair	Poor
300	225	200	150	75	50

MAROCCHI ARMI
Brescia, Italy

Model 2000

A 12 gauge Magnum single-shot shotgun with a 28" barrel, exposed hammer and automatic ejector. Blued with a walnut stock.

NIB	Exc.	V.G.	Good	Fair	Poor
—	100	80	65	50	35

Field Master I

A 12 gauge over/under shotgun with 26" or 28" ventilated rib barrels fitted for choke tubes, single trigger and automatic ejectors. Blued, French case hardened with a walnut stock.

NIB	Exc.	V.G.	Good	Fair	Poor
—	500	395	300	200	150

Field Master II

As above, with a single-selective trigger.

NIB	Exc.	V.G.	Good	Fair	Poor
—	525	450	350	225	175

CONQUISTA SERIES

Grade I is the standard grade with a special polished steel finish and machined engraved. The stock and forearm are select walnut and hand checkered 20 lpi. Grade II has roll engraved game scenes. The stock is select figured walnut. Grade III is hand engraved by a master engraver featuring game scenes. Finely figured walnut stock.

Sporting Clays Model

Offered in 12 gauge with 28", 30" or 32" ventilated rib barrels. Screw in chokes are standard. Adjustable trigger. Weight is approximately 8 lbs.

Grade I

NIB	Exc.	V.G.	Good	Fair	Poor
1950	1700	1175	850	600	300

Grade II

NIB	Exc.	V.G.	Good	Fair	Poor
2350	1900	1475	950	700	350

Grade III

NIB	Exc.	V.G.	Good	Fair	Poor
3350	2850	1825	1150	800	400

Sporting Light—Grade I

Same as above but slightly smaller dimensions. Available in 28" or 30" barrel length. Weight is about 7.5 lbs.

NIB	Exc.	V.G.	Good	Fair	Poor
2050	1700	1175	850	600	300

Sporting Clays Left-Hand Model—Grade I

Same as Sporting Clays Model but designed for the left-handed shooter.

NIB	Exc.	V.G.	Good	Fair	Poor
2150	1700	1175	850	600	300

Lady Sport Model

Offered in 12 gauge only with choice of 28" or 30" vent rib barrels. Slightly smaller dimensions for women. Weight 7.75 lbs.

Grade I

NIB	Exc.	V.G.	Good	Fair	Poor
2150	1700	1175	850	600	300

Spectrum Grade—Colored Frame

NIB	Exc.	V.G.	Good	Fair	Poor
2100	1750	1200	850	600	300

Lady Sport Left-Handed

Same as above but for left-handed shooters.

Grade I

NIB	Exc.	V.G.	Good	Fair	Poor
2100	1750	1200	850	600	300

Spectrum Grade

NIB	Exc.	V.G.	Good	Fair	Poor
2175	1800	1225	850	600	300

Trap Model

Built for the competition shooter this model features a choice of 30" or 32" vent rib barrels. Trap dimension stock. Weight approximately 8.25 lbs.

Grade I

NIB	Exc.	V.G.	Good	Fair	Poor
2025	1750	1200	850	600	300

Grade II

NIB	Exc.	V.G.	Good	Fair	Poor
2400	1950	1500	1000	750	350

Grade III

NIB	Exc.	V.G.	Good	Fair	Poor
3400	2700	18900	1500	800	400

Skeet Model

This model is designed for the competition shooter. Only a 28" vent rib barrel is offered as standard. Skeet dimension stock. Skeet chokes. Weight is approximately 7.75 lbs.

Grade I

NIB	Exc.	V.G.	Good	Fair	Poor
2025	1750	1200	850	600	300

Grade II

NIB	Exc.	V.G.	Good	Fair	Poor
2425	1950	1525	1000	750	350

Grade III

NIB	Exc.	V.G.	Good	Fair	Poor
3400	2700	1900	1500	800	400

Classic Doubles Model 92

Offered in 12 gauge only with 30" vent rib barrels. Adjustable trigger. Walnut stock with 18 lpi checkering. Weight is approximately 8.12 lbs.

NIB	Exc.	V.G.	Good	Fair	Poor
1650	1350	875	600	500	250

Model 99—Grade I

This over/under gun features a silver-grayed receiver, boxlock action with single-selective trigger, pistol-grip stock and schnabel forearm. Sporting models are offered with 28", 30" or 32" barrels. Trap models are offered with 30" or 32" barrels, and skeet models with 28" or 30" barrels. All barrels are supplied with five extended choke tubes.

NIB	Exc.	V.G.	Good	Fair	Poor
3125	2350	1800	750	700	300

Model 99—Grade III

This model has all of the above features in addition to five flush-mounted choke tubes and silver game scene engraved receiver.

NIB	Exc.	V.G.	Good	Fair	Poor
5200	3400	2200	950	800	300

MARS

See—Gabbet-Fairfax or Bergmann

MARSTON, S.W.

New York, New York

Double-Action Pepperbox

A .31 caliber double-action percussion pepperbox with a 5" barrel group and ring trigger. Blued with walnut grips. Manufactured between 1850 and 1855.

NIB	Exc.	V.G.	Good	Fair	Poor
—	—	2000	1125	600	250

2-Barrel Pistol

A .31 or .36 revolving barrel 2-shot pistol with a ring trigger. The barrel marked "J.Cohn & S.W.Marston-New York". Blued, brass frame with walnut grips. Manufactured during the 1850s.

NIB	Exc.	V.G.	Good	Fair	Poor
—	—	2700	1250	450	200

MARSTON, W. W. & CO.

New York, New York

W.W. Marston & Company manufactured a variety of firearms some of which are marked only with the trade names: Union Arms Company, Phoenix Armory, Western Arms Company, Washington Arms Company, Sprague and Marston and Marston and Knox.

Double-Action Single-Shot Pistol

A .31 or .36 caliber bar hammer percussion pistol with a 2.5" or 5" half octagonal barrel. Blued with walnut grips. Manufactured during the 1850s.

NIB	Exc.	V.G.	Good	Fair	Poor
—	—	650	325	150	100

Pocket Revolver

A .31 caliber percussion revolver with a 3.25" to 7.5" barrel and 6-shot cylinder. Blued with walnut grips. Approximately 13,000 were manufactured between 1857 and 1862.

NIB	Exc.	V.G.	Good	Fair	Poor
—	—	1250	550	200	125

Navy Revolver

A .36 caliber percussion revolver with a 7.5" or 8.5" octagonal barrel and 6-shot cylinder. Blued with walnut grips. Manufactured between 1857 and 1862.

NIB	Exc.	V.G.	Good	Fair	Poor
—	—	3100	1400	600	200

Single-Action Pistol

A .31 or .36 caliber percussion pistol with a 4" or 6" barrel. Blued with walnut grips. Manufactured during the 1860s.

NIB	Exc.	V.G.	Good	Fair	Poor
—	—	675	580	250	100

Breech-Loading Pistol

A .36 caliber breech loading percussion pistol with a 4" to 8.5" half octagonal barrel and either a brass or iron frame. Blued, case hardened with walnut grips. Approximately 1,000 were manufactured in the 1850s.

Courtesy Milwaukee Public Museum, Milwaukee, Wisconsin

Brass Frame

NIB	Exc.	V.G.	Good	Fair	Poor
—	—	4400	3600	1650	500

Iron Frame

NIB	Exc.	V.G.	Good	Fair	Poor
—	—	3900	3000	1100	300

Double-Action Pepperbox

A .31 caliber double-action 6-shot percussion pepperbox with 4" or 5" barrel groups and a bar hammer. Blued, case hardened with walnut grips. Manufactured during the 1850s.

Courtesy Milwaukee Public Museum, Milwaukee, Wisconsin

NIB	Exc.	V.G.	Good	Fair	Poor
—	—	3200	2500	1150	300

3-Barrel Derringer

A .22 caliber 3-barreled spur-trigger pocket pistol with a sliding knife blade mounted on the left side of the 3" barrel group. Blued, silver-plated with walnut grips. The barrel marked "Wm. W. Marston/New York City". Approximately 1,500 were manufactured between 1858 and 1864.

Knife Blade Model

Courtesy Milwaukee Public Museum, Milwaukee, Wisconsin

NIB	Exc.	V.G.	Good	Fair	Poor
—	—	5575	4100	1650	400

Without Knife

Courtesy Milwaukee Public Museum, Milwaukee, Wisconsin

NIB	Exc.	V.G.	Good	Fair	Poor
—	—	2550	2000	775	200

3-Barrel Derringer .32 Caliber

Similar to the above, but in .32 caliber with either 3" or 4" barrels and not fitted with a knife blade. Approximately 3,000 were manufactured between 1864 and 1872.

Courtesy Milwaukee Public Museum, Milwaukee, Wisconsin

NIB	Exc.	V.G.	Good	Fair	Poor
—	—	3750	3000	825	200

MASQUELIER, S. A.
Liege, Belgium

Carpathe

A .243, .270, .7x57mm, 7x65Rmm or .30-06 caliber single-shot rifle with a 24" barrel, adjustable trigger and adjustable sights. Blued, with an engraved receiver and walnut stock. Imported until 1986.

NIB	Exc.	V.G.	Good	Fair	Poor
—	3750	2950	1950	1250	750

Express

A .270, .30-06, 8x57JRSmm or 9.3x74Rmm caliber over/under double-barrel rifle with 24" barrels, single-selective trigger and automatic ejectors. Blued, engraved with a walnut stock. Not imported after 1986.

NIB	Exc.	V.G.	Good	Fair	Poor
—	3800	2950	1950	1250	750

Ardennes

As above, but made on custom order only. Discontinued in 1986.

NIB	Exc.	V.G.	Good	Fair	Poor
—	8000	6000	3750	2500	1000

Boxlock Side-by-Side Shotgun

A 12 gauge boxlock double-barrel shotgun manufactured in a variety of barrel lengths with a single-selective trigger and automatic ejectors. Blued with a walnut stock. Imported prior to 1987.

NIB	Exc.	V.G.	Good	Fair	Poor
—	4750	3500	2500	1500	850

Sidelock Side-by-Side Shotgun

Similar to the above, but with detachable sidelocks and finely engraved. Imported prior to 1987.

NIB	Exc.	V.G.	Good	Fair	Poor
—	14500	11750	7000	5000	1750

MASSACHUSETTS ARMS CO.
Chicopee Falls, Massachusetts

Wesson & Leavitt Dragoon

A .40 caliber percussion revolver with a 7" round barrel, 6-shot cylinder and side-mounted hammer. Blued, case hardened with walnut grips. Approximately 800 were manufactured in 1850 and 1851.

Early Model with 6" Barrel

Approximately 30 made.

NIB	Exc.	V.G.	Good	Fair	Poor
—	—	8500	6600	275	750

Fully Marked 7" Barrel Standard Model

NIB	Exc.	V.G.	Good	Fair	Poor
—	—	8000	6050	2200	650

Wesson & Leavitt Belt Revolver

A .31 caliber percussion revolver with a 3" to 7" round barrel and 6-shot cylinder. Similar in appearance to the above. Approximately 1,000 were manufactured in 1850 and 1851.

Courtesy Milwaukee Public Museum, Milwaukee, Wisconsin

NIB	Exc.	V.G.	Good	Fair	Poor
—	—	3000	1900	775	250

Maynard Primed Belt Revolver

Similar to the above, with a Maynard tape primer. Approximately 1,000 were manufactured between 1851 and 1857.

Courtesy Milwaukee Public Museum, Milwaukee, Wisconsin

NIB	Exc.	V.G.	Good	Fair	Poor
—	—	3700	2750	880	250

Maynard Primed Pocket Revolver

Similar to the above, but in .28 or .30 caliber with 2.5" to 3.5" octagonal or round barrels. Approximately 3,000 were made between 1851 and 1860.

Courtesy Milwaukee Public Museum, Milwaukee, Wisconsin

NIB	Exc.	V.G.	Good	Fair	Poor
—	—	1950	1400	625	200

Adams Patent Navy Revolver

As above, in .36 caliber with a 6" octagonal barrel. Approximately 600 of the 1,000 made were purchased by the U.S. government. **NOTE:** Those bearing inspection marks will bring approximately a 20 percent premium over the values listed.

Courtesy Milwaukee Public Museum, Milwaukee, Wisconsin

NIB	Exc.	V.G.	Good	Fair	Poor
—	—	3750	2500	825	300

Single-Shot Pocket Pistol

A .31 caliber single-shot percussion pistol with a 2.5" to 3.5" half octagonal barrel and a Maynard tape primer. The barrel marked "Mass. Arms Co/Chicopee Falls" and the primer door "Maynard's Patent Sept. 22, 1845". Blued, case hardened with walnut grips. Manufactured in the 1850s.

NIB	Exc.	V.G.	Good	Fair	Poor
—	—	4000	2750	925	300

MAYNARD CARBINE

This is a single-shot breechloader chambered for .35 or .50 caliber percussion. The barrel is round and 20" in length. The trigger guard is the lever that pivots the barrel in break-open fashion when it is lowered. The finish is blued, with a case colored frame. The buttstock is walnut and there is no fore-end. This carbine was designed by the same Maynard who invented the tape primer system. There are two models—a 1st and a 2nd. They were made for both sporting use and as a U.S. Martial carbine. The 2nd Model was used considerably during the Civil War.

1st Model

This model is marked "Maynard Patentee/May 27, 1851/June 17, 1856". It has an iron patchbox and a curved buttplate. It has a Maynard tape primer system and a tang sight. Later production was fitted with a sling swivel. There are approximately 400 of these carbines that are U.S. marked, but the total manufactured in the late 1850s is unknown.

Courtesy Milwaukee Public Museum, Milwaukee, Wisconsin

U.S. Martially Marked

NIB	Exc.	V.G.	Good	Fair	Poor
—	—	6500	4050	2000	700

Commercial Model

NIB	Exc.	V.G.	Good	Fair	Poor
—	—	4000	3000	1250	400

2nd Model

This model is chambered for .50 caliber only and does not have the tape primer system or the tang sight. There is no patchbox, and the buttplate is not as curved as on the 1st Model. It is marked "Manufactured By/Mass. Arms Co./Chicopee Falls". There were approximately 20,000 manufactured between 1860 and 1865. This model was used by Union forces during the Civil War.

Courtesy Milwaukee Public Museum, Milwaukee, Wisconsin

NIB	Exc.	V.G.	Good	Fair	Poor
—	—	2500	2050	700	500

Maynard Patent Sporting Rifle

Sporting rifles bearing the designations Model 1865, 1873 and 1882 were manufactured in a wide variety of calibers, gauges, stock styles, finishes and options.

Courtesy Milwaukee Public Museum, Milwaukee, Wisconsin

NIB	Exc.	V.G.	Good	Fair	Poor
—	—	2500	1650	660	200

MATEBA ARMS
Italy

AutoRevolver

Introduced in 2000, this revolver is chambered for the .357 Magnum or .44 Magnum with 4", 6" or 8" barrel. The gun features a single-action trigger that has a reciprocating cylinder that fires from the bottom chamber rather than the top. The firing of the gun cocks the hammer and cycles the action for the next round. Available with or without compensator. Offered in blue or nickel finish. Extra barrels available. Distributed in USA by American Western Arms (AWA). **NOTE:** Guns without compensator deduct $80. For nickel finish add $50. For extra barrel add $140.

NIB	Exc.	V.G.	Good	Fair	Poor
1600	1100	900	600	400	200

AutoRevolver Carbine

Similar in principle to handgun but with 16" or 18" barrel and walnut buttstock, pistol grip and fore-end.

NIB	Exc.	V.G.	Good	Fair	Poor
1800	1300	1000	700	500	300

MATRA MANURHIN DEFENSE
Mulhouse, France
See—Manurhin

MAUNZ MFG., INC.
Maumee, Ohio

Manufacturer (1970s-1980s) of high-end law enforcement and competition rifles based primarily on the M14 military rifle.

Model 77 Service Match Rifle

Semi-automatic rifle chambered in .308 Winchester and other chamberings on custom order. 22" barrel standard; medium and heavy barrels also available. Charcoal gray parkerized finish. Custom rifles had heavyweight Kevlar or graphite/fiberglass stocks covered in black gelcoat. Red/white/blue stocks were also produced. 300 produced.

NIB	Exc.	V.G.	Good	Fair	Poor
—	2500	2250	2000	1850	1500

Model 87 Maunz Match Rifle

Semi-automatic rifle chambered in .308 Winchester and 6.30 Maunz; Limited .338 and .45 Maunz chamberings on custom order. Sold only to Master competitors and American Shooters Union members.

NIB	Exc.	V.G.	Good	Fair	Poor
—	2500	2200	2000	1500	1200

Model 57 M1A

Semi-automatic rifle chambered in .30-06, .276 and .308 Winchester, also .45 Maunz (rare). M1 Garand receiver with M14 parts and National Match barrels. Custom-built glass-bedded stock. Approximately 200 made.

NIB	Exc.	V.G.	Good	Fair	Poor
—	1500	1250	1000	800	600

Model 67 Match Grade for Practice

Semi-automatic rifle chambered in .308 Winchester, 6.30 Maunz and .45 Maunz. Camp Perry stamped. Not allowed for Service Rifle competition. Combination of M1 Garand and M14 parts. Approximately 250 made.

NIB	Exc.	V.G.	Good	Fair	Poor
—	2000	1800	1500	1200	1500

MAUSER WERKE

Established in 1869 by Peter and Wilhelm Mauser, this company came under the effective control of Ludwig Loewe and Company of Berlin in 1887. In 1896 the latter company was reorganized under the name Deutsches Waffen und Munition or as it is better known, DWM. **NOTE:** For historical information, technical details, photos and prices see the *Standard Catalog of Military Firearms*.

EARLY MODEL 98 SPORTING RIFLES

A wide variety of commercial Model 98 Sporting Rifles were made, most of which had 23.5" ribbed barrels, open sights, 5-shot magazines, single or double set triggers and either full or semi-pistol grip stocks. **NOTE:** The values listed here are representative.

Type A—Short Action

NIB	Exc.	V.G.	Good	Fair	Poor
—	6000	5200	3300	1850	700

Type A—Medium Action

NIB	Exc.	V.G.	Good	Fair	Poor
—	5000	4000	3000	1600	700

Type A—Long Action

NIB	Exc.	V.G.	Good	Fair	Poor
—	6000	5200	3300	1850	700

Type B

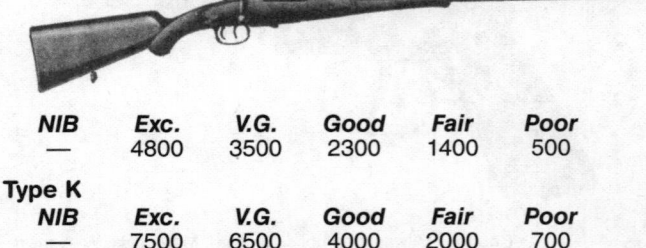

NIB	Exc.	V.G.	Good	Fair	Poor
—	4800	3500	2300	1400	500

Type K

NIB	Exc.	V.G.	Good	Fair	Poor
—	7500	6500	4000	2000	700

Type M					
NIB	**Exc.**	**V.G.**	**Good**	**Fair**	**Poor**
—	4500	3900	3300	1850	700
Type S					
NIB	**Exc.**	**V.G.**	**Good**	**Fair**	**Poor**
—	4500	3900	3300	1850	700

MODEL 1896 BROOMHANDLE MAUSER PISTOL

Manufactured from 1896 to 1939, the Model 1896 Pistol was produced in a wide variety of styles as listed. It is recommended that those considering the purchase of any of the models listed should consult Breathed & Schroeders's *System Mauser* (Chicago 1967) as it provides detailed descriptions and photographs of the various models. **NOTE:** Prices listed are for the pistol only. A correct, matching stock/holster will add approximately 40 percent to value of each category. Non-matching stock/holster will add $350 and $600 to prices.

"BUYER BEWARE" ALERT by Gale Morgan: I have personally seen English Crest, the U.S. Great Seal, unheard-of European dealers, aristocratic Coats-of-Arms and Middle East Medallions beautifully photo-etched into the magazine wells and rear panels of some really common wartime commercials with price tags that have been elevated to $2,500 plus. They are quite eye-catching and if they are sold as customized/modified Mausers, the seller can price the piece at whatever the market will bear. However, if sold as a factory original—BUYER BEWARE.

Large Ring Cutaway

Courtesy Gale Morgan

Six-Shot Step-Barrel Cone Hammer

A 7.63mm semi-automatic pistol with a 5.5" barrel, fixed rear sight and checkered walnut grips. Marked "Ruecklauf Pistole System Mauser, Oberndorf am/Neckar 1896". Very few were manufactured. Too rare to price.

Twenty-Shot Step-Barrel Cone Hammer

As above, with a 20-shot extended magazine and tangent rear sight. Engraved "system mauser" on top of chamber. Too rare to price.

System Mauser 10-Shot Cone Hammer

As above, with either fixed or tangent rear sight. Step barrel (pictured) is very rare as is tapered barrel. Magazine capacity 10 rounds.

Courtesy Joe Schroeder

NIB	**Exc.**	**V.G.**	**Good**	**Fair**	**Poor**
—	25000	17000	12000	8000	7000

Six-Shot Standard Cone Hammer

Similar to the above but with no step in the barrel, 6-shot magazine and marked "Waffenfabrik Mauser, Oberndorf A/N" over the chamber. May have fixed, or rarely, tangent rear sight.

Courtesy Joe Schroeder

NIB	**Exc.**	**V.G.**	**Good**	**Fair**	**Poor**
—	12000	9000	6750	4500	3000

Twenty-Shot Cone Hammer

As above, with an extended magazine holding 20 cartridges. May have panels or flat sides.

Courtesy Joe Schroeder

NIB	**Exc.**	**V.G.**	**Good**	**Fair**	**Poor**
—	40000	35000	20000	10000	7000

Standard Cone Hammer

As above, with a 10-shot magazine and 23-groove grips.

Courtesy Rock Island Auction Company

NIB	**Exc.**	**V.G.**	**Good**	**Fair**	**Poor**
—	7500	5000	2000	1400	800

Fixed Sight Cone Hammer

Similar to the standard Cone Hammer except that a fixed, integral sight is machined into the barrel extension.

Courtesy Joe Schroeder

NIB	Exc.	V.G.	Good	Fair	Poor
—	7000	5500	3500	2000	1000

Turkish Contract Cone Hammer

As above, but sight marked in Farsi and bearing the crest of Sultan Abdul-Hamid II on the frame. Approximately 1,000 were made.

Courtesy Gale Morgan

Courtesy Joe Schroeder

NIB	Exc.	V.G.	Good	Fair	Poor
—	15000	12000	8500	5000	2000

Early Transitional Large Ring Hammer

This variation has the same characteristics of the "Standard Cone Hammer" except the hammer has a larger, open ring.

Courtesy Wallis & Wallis, Lewes, Sussex, England

NIB	Exc.	V.G.	Good	Fair	Poor
—	5500	4000	2500	1150	800

Model 1899 Flat Side—Italian Contract

Similar to the above, with a 5.5" barrel, adjustable rear sight and the frame sides milled flat. Left flat of chamber marked with "DV" proof. Approximately 5,000 were manufactured in 1899.

Courtesy Joe Schroeder

NIB	Exc.	V.G.	Good	Fair	Poor
—	5000	4000	2000	1200	900

Early Flat Side

Similar to the above, except with "pinned" rear sight and without the Italian markings.

NIB	Exc.	V.G.	Good	Fair	Poor
—	5000	3500	2800	1000	750

Late Flat Side

Similar to the above, with an integral pin mounted adjustable rear sight and often marked with dealer's names such as "Von Lengerke & Detmold, New York".

NIB	Exc.	V.G.	Good	Fair	Poor
—	4000	3200	2000	1000	750

Flat Side Bolo

Similar to the above, but with a 3.9" barrel, fixed sights and checkered walnut grips. Very rare.

NIB	Exc.	V.G.	Good	Fair	Poor
—	7500	6000	4000	3000	2000

Early Large Ring Hammer Bolo

As above, with a milled frame, adjustable rear sight and grooved wood or hard rubber grips cast with a floral pattern. 10-shot magazine.

NIB	Exc.	V.G.	Good	Fair	Poor
—	4700	3700	2000	1500	1000

Shallow-Milled Panel Model

Full size. Similar to the above, with a 5.5" barrel and either 23-groove walnut or checkered hard rubber grips. Shallow frame panels.

NIB	Exc.	V.G.	Good	Fair	Poor
—	3800	2700	1000	750	500

Deep-Milled Panel Model

As above, with deeper milled panels on the sides of the receiver.

NIB	Exc.	V.G.	Good	Fair	Poor
—	4500	3000	2000	1000	750

Late Large Ring Hammer Bolo

Similar to the Early Large Ring Hammer Bolo, but with the late style adjustable rear sight.

Courtesy Joe Schroeder

NIB	Exc.	V.G.	Good	Fair	Poor
—	4000	3000	2000	1000	750

Six-Shot Large Ring Bolo

Similar to the above Large Ring Bolo but with six-shot magazine. This model may be equipped with either fixed or tangent sights.

Courtesy James Rankin

NIB	Exc.	V.G.	Good	Fair	Poor
—	8900	6500	5000	3000	1800

Early Small Ring Hammer Model, Transitional

The Model 96 with an early long extractor, a hammer with a small-diameter hole and a 5.5" barrel. The grips have 34 grooves.

Courtesy Joe Schroeder

NIB	Exc.	V.G.	Good	Fair	Poor
—	3200	2000	1500	1000	500

Early Small Ring Hammer Bolo Model

As above, with a 3.9" barrel and wood or hard rubber grips cast with a floral pattern. Serial numbers in the 40,000 range.

NIB	Exc.	V.G.	Good	Fair	Poor
—	4500	3000	2000	1500	600

Six-Shot Small Ring Hammer Model

As above, with 27-groove walnut grips.

NIB	Exc.	V.G.	Good	Fair	Poor
—	8000	6500	3000	1800	1000

Standard Pre-war Commercial

A Model 96 with a 5.5" barrel, late-style adjustable rear sight and either 34-groove walnut grips or checkered hard rubber grips. Often found with dealers markings such as "Von Lengerke & Detmold".

Courtesy Joe Schroeder

NIB	Exc.	V.G.	Good	Fair	Poor
—	3000	2500	1200	650	300

9mm Export Model

As above, in 9mm Mauser with 34-groove walnut grips.

NIB	Exc.	V.G.	Good	Fair	Poor
—	3250	2250	1500	1000	700

Mauser Banner Model

Standard pre-war features except chamber stamped with the Mauser Banner trademark and 32-groove walnut grips. Approximately 10,000 were manufactured.

Courtesy Joe Schroeder

NIB	Exc.	V.G.	Good	Fair	Poor
—	4000	3200	2300	1100	600

Persian Contract

Persian rampant lion on left rear panel. Prospective purchasers should secure a qualified appraisal prior to acquisition. Serial numbers in the 154000 range.

NIB	Exc.	V.G.	Good	Fair	Poor
—	4700	4000	2700	1400	1000

Standard Wartime Commercial

Identical to the pre-war Commercial Model 96, except that it has 30 groove walnut grips and the rear of the hammer is stamped "NS" for new safety. Many also bear German or Austrian military acceptance proofs.

Courtesy Gale Morgan

NIB	Exc.	V.G.	Good	Fair	Poor
—	2500	1750	1000	500	350

9mm Parabellum Military Contract

As above, in 9mm Parabellum caliber with 24 groove grips, stamped with a large "9" filled with red paint.

9mm "Full Rig" shown.

Courtesy Gale Morgan

NIB	Exc.	V.G.	Good	Fair	Poor
—	3200	2000	1000	700	450

1920 Rework

A Model 96 modified to a barrel length of 3.9" and in 7.63mm Mauser or 9mm Parabellum caliber. Often encountered with police markings.

Courtesy Bonhams & Butterfields, San Francisco, California

NIB	Exc.	V.G.	Good	Fair	Poor
—	1500	1000	500	400	350

Luger Barreled 1920 Rework

Similar to the above, but fitted with a Luger 4" barrel, 23 groove walnut grips and 9mm caliber.

Front Sight of Luger Barreled 1920 Rework

Courtesy Gale Morgan

NIB	Exc.	V.G.	Good	Fair	Poor
—	2000	1200	700	500	450

Early Post-war Bolo Model

A Model 96 in 7.63mm caliber with a 3.9" barrel, adjustable rear sight and 22-groove walnut grips.

NIB	Exc.	V.G.	Good	Fair	Poor
—	3000	2100	1000	400	200

Late Post-war Bolo Model

As above, with the Mauser Banner trademark stamped on the left rear panel.

Courtesy Gale Morgan

Courtesy James Rankin

NIB	Exc.	V.G.	Good	Fair	Poor
—	2700	2000	1000	400	200

French Gendarme Model

A standard Model 96 fitted with a 3.9" barrel and checkered hard rubber grips. Although reputed to have been made under a French contract, no record of that has been found to date.

Courtesy James Rankin

NIB	Exc.	V.G.	Good	Fair	Poor
—	4000	2500	1000	600	350

Early Model 1930

A 7.63mm caliber Model 96 with a 5.2" stepped barrel, grooved side rails, 12-groove walnut grips and late-style safety.

NIB	Exc.	V.G.	Good	Fair	Poor
—	3000	2000	1700	800	500

Late Model 1930

Similar to the above, except for solid receiver rails.

NIB	Exc.	V.G.	Good	Fair	Poor
—	3500	2200	1700	800	400

Model 1930 Removable Magazine

Similar to the above, but with a detachable magazine. Prospective purchasers should secure a qualified appraisal prior to acquisition. Too rare to price.

CARBINE MODELS

Cone Hammer Flat Side Carbine

A 7.63mm caliber carbine with an 11.75" barrel, early adjustable sight, flat frame and detachable buttstock. The barrel has a full length "rib". Prospective purchasers should secure a qualified appraisal prior to acquisition. Too rare to price. **NOTE:** Watch for fakes.

Large Ring Hammer Transitional Carbine

Similar to the above with milled frame panels. Prospective purchasers should secure a qualified appraisal prior to acquisition.

NIB	Exc.	V.G.	Good	Fair	Poor
—	25000	18000	11000	5000	3000

Large Ring Hammer Flatside Carbine

Similar to the above, with a 14.5" barrel. Prospective purchasers should secure a qualified appraisal prior to acquisition.

NIB	Exc.	V.G.	Good	Fair	Poor
—	23000	17000	10000	5000	3000

Small Ring Hammer Carbine

Similar to the above, with the hammer having a smaller diameter hole at its tip. Prospective purchasers should secure a qualified appraisal prior to acquisition. Some late carbines were chambered for the 9mm export.

Courtesy Gale Morgan

Small Ring Hammer Carbine with serial numbers 1035 and 1045, the highest known manufactured by Mauser

NIB	Exc.	V.G.	Good	Fair	Poor
—	21000	18000	15000	6000	4000

CHINESE COPIES

Chinese Marked, Handmade Copies

Crude copies of the Model 96 and unsafe to fire.

NIB	Exc.	V.G.	Good	Fair	Poor
—	500	400	350	250	175

Taku-Naval Dockyard Model

Approximately 6,000 copies of the Model 96 were made at the Taku-Naval Dockyard in several variations, both flat and paneled sides.

NIB	Exc.	V.G.	Good	Fair	Poor
—	3500	1500	1000	600	400

Shansei Arsenal Model

Approximately 8,000 Model 96 pistols were manufactured in .45 ACP caliber. Copies of the Model 96 were made by Unceta (Astra) and Zulaica y Cia (Royal) and marketed by the firm of Beistegui Hermanos. These copies are covered in their own sections of this text. **NOTE:** Within the past several years, a large quantity of Model 96 pistols exported to or made in China have been imported into the United States. It has been reported that some newly made copies of the Shansei .45 were recently exported from China. Proceed with caution.

Shansei Panel Marking

Courtesy Gale Morgan

NIB	Exc.	V.G.	Good	Fair	Poor
—	5000	3500	2250	1500	1300

MAUSER POCKET PISTOLS

Model 1910

A 6.35mm (.25 ACP) caliber pistol with a 3" barrel, 9-shot magazine and either a checkered walnut or (scarce) hard rubber wraparound grip. Early examples (below serial 60,000 or so) have a pivoting takedown latch above the trigger guard and are identified as "Sidelatch" models by collectors. Later production Models 1910s are often identified as the Model 1910/14. Manufactured from 1910 to 1934.

Sidelatch Model

NIB	Exc.	V.G.	Good	Fair	Poor
—	1200	900	600	300	300

Later Production (Model 1910/14)

NIB	Exc.	V.G.	Good	Fair	Poor
—	550	300	200	150	100

Model 1914

A larger version of the Model 1910, chambered for 7.65mm Browning (.32 ACP) with a 3.5" or (rarely) 4.5" barrel. Very early examples up to serial 2500 or so had a contoured hump on the slide and are called "Humpbacks" by collectors; these bring a considerable premium. Model 1914s with police or military markings bring a small premium. Manufactured between 1914 and 1934.

Model 1914 "Humpback"

NIB	Exc.	V.G.	Good	Fair	Poor
—	4000	3000	1750	800	400

Model 1914 (later)

NIB	Exc.	V.G.	Good	Fair	Poor
—	475	300	200	150	100

Model 1912/14

While Mauser's pocket pistols were very successful on the commercial market, Mauser was also trying to develop a larger caliber pistol for military use. The most successful of these was the Model 1912/14, though only about 200 were ever made. A few of these did reach the commercial market and it's likely the pistol would have continued in production had WWI not broken out. Higher serial numbered guns were slotted for a Model 1896-style holster stock and a few of these also had tangent sights. **NOTE:** Add 50 percent for shoulder stock.

NIB	Exc.	V.G.	Good	Fair	Poor
—	31000	20000	11000	8000	4000

Model WTP I

This was Mauser's first post-WWI new design and first vest pocket pistol, with a 2.5" barrel and 6-shot magazine capacity. Grips were plastic wraparound, with one, two or three grip screws depending on production period. Production ended in the late 1930s, when the WTP II was introduced.

NIB	Exc.	V.G.	Good	Fair	Poor
—	600	300	250	175	125

Model WTP II

The WTP II was a much more compact design that its predecessor, with a 2" barrel and separate grip panels instead of Mauser's usual wraparound grip. Production was limited by the outbreak of WWII, so the WTP II is much scarcer than the WTP I. Under French occupation at least several hundred WTP IIs were assembled and sold; these can be identified by their very low electric penciled serial numbers and lack of German proofing and bring a slight premium over the pre-war German manufactured pistols.

Courtesy Gale Morgan

NIB	Exc.	V.G.	Good	Fair	Poor
—	650	450	325	250	175

Model 1934

In response to competition from Walther and others, in 1934 Mauser spruced up its aging 1910/14 and 1914 pistols with a new high-polish finish and form-fitting swept back grips. Nickel finish was also offered, but is very rare (50 percent premium, but beware of re-nickeled blued guns). The 7.65mm pistols became popular with both the military and police, but those so marked can bring a considerable premium.

Courtesy Orvel Reichert

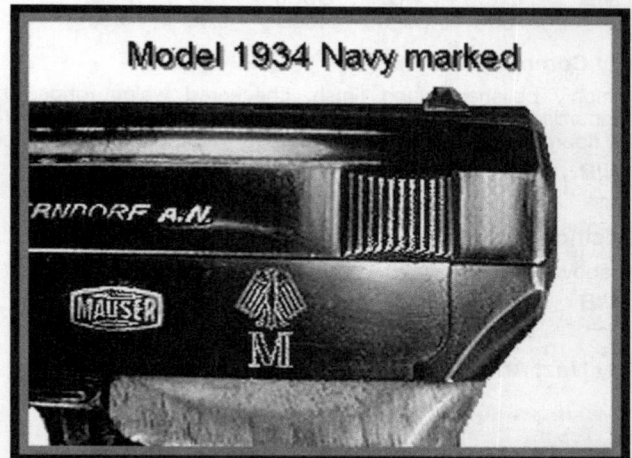

Model 1934 Navy marked

Courtesy Gale Morgan

6.35mm

NIB	Exc.	V.G.	Good	Fair	Poor
—	525	325	250	200	125

7.65mm Commercial

NIB	Exc.	V.G.	Good	Fair	Poor
—	450	325	250	200	125

7.65mm Eagle L proofed

NIB	Exc.	V.G.	Good	Fair	Poor
—	675	450	300	250	150

7.56mm Large Eagle over M (Navy)

NIB	Exc.	V.G.	Good	Fair	Poor
—	1200	750	450	300	200

MODEL HSc

The HSc was a totally new design, chambered for 7.65mm Browning and featuring double-action lockwork and a partially concealed external hammer. Introduced just as WWII broke out, the HSc was produced through the war for both commercial sale and military use. Serials started at 700,000 and the first 1500 or so had the grip screws located near the bottom of the grip and bring a large premium. Finish deteriorated as the war progressed and some HSc pistols were even produced under French occupation after the war ended. **NOTE:** Add 20 percent for Waffenamt markings and 50 percent for Navy marked front straps.

Courtesy Orvel Reichert

Low Grip Screw Model

As above, with screws that attach the grip located near the bottom of the grip. Highly-polished blue, checkered walnut grips and the early address without the lines and has the Eagle N proof. Some have been observed with Nazi Kreigsmarine markings. Approximately 2,000 were manufactured.

NIB	Exc.	V.G.	Good	Fair	Poor
—	7000	5000	1800	750	650

Early Commercial Model

A highly polished blued finish, checkered walnut grips, the standard Mauser address on the slide and the Eagle N proofmark. The floorplate of the magazine stamped with the Mauser Banner.

NIB	Exc.	V.G.	Good	Fair	Poor
—	650	500	350	175	125

Transition Model

As above, but not as highly finished.

NIB	Exc.	V.G.	Good	Fair	Poor
—	525	400	300	150	100

Early Nazi Army Model

Courtesy Orvel Reichert

NIB	Exc.	V.G.	Good	Fair	Poor
—	650	550	400	200	125

Late Nazi Army Model

NIB	Exc.	V.G.	Good	Fair	Poor
—	450	375	250	150	100

Early Nazi Navy Model

NIB	Exc.	V.G.	Good	Fair	Poor
—	1000	800	550	400	300

Wartime Nazi Navy Model

NIB	Exc.	V.G.	Good	Fair	Poor
—	800	600	500	400	200

Early Nazi Police Model

NIB	Exc.	V.G.	Good	Fair	Poor
—	600	500	425	250	175

Wartime Nazi Police Model

NIB	Exc.	V.G.	Good	Fair	Poor
—	500	400	350	250	175

Wartime Commercial Model

As above, without acceptance markings on the trigger guard.

NIB	Exc.	V.G.	Good	Fair	Poor
—	425	350	300	200	125

French Manufactured Model

Blued or Parkerized with walnut or plastic grips and the trigger guard marked on the left side with the monogram "MR".

NIB	Exc.	V.G.	Good	Fair	Poor
—	375	275	225	150	100

Model HSc Post-war Production

In the late 1960s Mauser resumed production of the HSc in both 7.65mm and 9mm Browning short (.380). Five thousand post-war HSc pistols were specially marked with an American eagle and bring a slight premium over standard marked pistols. In the 1980s Mauser licensed HSc production to Gamba in Italy, which produced an enlarged frame version of the HSc with a double-column magazine. In both German and Italian production, .380s bring about a 20 percent premium over .32s.

Mauser Production (.32)

NIB	Exc.	V.G.	Good	Fair	Poor
—	525	450	300	175	125

Gamba Production

In recent years Mauser has licensed several firms other than Gamba to produce pistols bearing the Mauser trademark, such as a Browning Hi Power knockoff made in Hungary. In 1999 Mauser was bought by SIG-Sauer and a new large caliber Mauser pistol was announced.

NIB	Exc.	V.G.	Good	Fair	Poor
—	600	475	325	200	100

MAUSER RIFLES—RECENT PRODUCTION

In February 1999 SIGARMS announced the acquisition of the Mauser line of small arms. With the acquisition, SIG assumes the rights to the Mauser name and will integrate the Mauser product line into SIGARMS' line of small arms.

Model 2000

A .270, .308 or the .30-06 caliber bolt-action rifle with a 24" barrel, open sights and a 5-shot magazine. Blued, with a checkered walnut stock. Manufactured between 1969 and 1971 by Heym.

NIB	Exc.	V.G.	Good	Fair	Poor
—	600	450	300	200	150

Model 3000

As above, with a 22" barrel, no sights and Monte Carlo-style stock. Manufactured from 1971 to 1974 by Heym.

NIB	Exc.	V.G.	Good	Fair	Poor
—	600	450	300	200	150

Model 3000 Magnum

As above, in 7mm Rem. Magnum, .300 Win. Magnum and the .375 H&H Magnum caliber with a 26" barrel and a 3-shot integral magazine. Blued, with a checkered walnut stock. Produced by Heym.

NIB	Exc.	V.G.	Good	Fair	Poor
—	675	525	375	250	200

Model 4000

Similar to the Model 3000, but in .222 or .223 caliber with folding open sights. Produced by Heym.

NIB	Exc.	V.G.	Good	Fair	Poor
—	550	400	250	200	150

Model 225

A .243 to. 300 Weatherby Magnum caliber bolt-action rifle with a 24" or 26" barrel, no sights, adjustable trigger or 3- or 5-shot magazine. Blued with a walnut stock.

NIB	Exc.	V.G.	Good	Fair	Poor
1400	1250	1000	750	600	500

Model ES340

A .22 caliber single-shot bolt-action rifle with a 25.5" barrel, open sights and walnut stock. Manufactured before WWII.

NIB	Exc.	V.G.	Good	Fair	Poor
—	300	250	225	175	125

Model DSM34

Similar to the above, with a 25" barrel and full-length walnut stock. Manufactured prior to WWII.

NIB	Exc.	V.G.	Good	Fair	Poor
—	325	275	250	200	150

Model MS420B

Similar to the above, with a 25" barrel and 5-shot magazine. Manufactured before WWII.

NIB	Exc.	V.G.	Good	Fair	Poor
—	375	325	300	275	200

Model ES350

A .22 caliber single-shot bolt-action rifle with a 27.5" barrel and checkered pistol grip walnut stock. Manufactured before WWII.

NIB	Exc.	V.G.	Good	Fair	Poor
—	450	400	375	350	275

Model M410

Similar to the above, with a 23.5" barrel and 5-shot magazine. Manufactured before WWII.

NIB	Exc.	V.G.	Good	Fair	Poor
—	375	325	300	275	200

Model M420

As above, with a 25.5" barrel.

NIB	Exc.	V.G.	Good	Fair	Poor
375	325	300	275	200	

Model EN310

A .22 caliber single-shot bolt-action rifle with a 19.75" barrel, open sights and plain walnut stock. Manufactured before WWII.

NIB	Exc.	V.G.	Good	Fair	Poor
—	250	225	200	150	100

Model EL320

As above, with a 23.5" barrel and checkered walnut stock.

NIB	Exc.	V.G.	Good	Fair	Poor
—	275	250	225	175	125

Model KKW

A .22 caliber single-shot bolt-action rifle with a 26" barrel, ladder rear sight and full-length walnut stock. Manufactured prior to WWII.

NIB	Exc.	V.G.	Good	Fair	Poor
—	400	350	300	225	150

Model MS350B

A .22 caliber bolt-action rifle with a 26.75" barrel, adjustable rear sight and 5-shot magazine. Blued with a walnut stock.

NIB	Exc.	V.G.	Good	Fair	Poor
—	475	400	350	275	200

Model ES340B

Similar to the above, but in single-shot form.

NIB	Exc.	V.G.	Good	Fair	Poor
—	375	300	250	175	100

Model MM41OBN

A .22 caliber bolt-action rifle with a 23.5" barrel, adjustable sights and 5-shot magazine. Blued with a walnut stock.

NIB	Exc.	V.G.	Good	Fair	Poor
—	400	350	300	200	125

Model MS420B

As above, with a 26.75" barrel and target-style stock.

NIB	Exc.	V.G.	Good	Fair	Poor
—	400	350	300	200	125

Model 107

This is a bolt-action rifle chambered for the .22 LR. Barrel length is 21.6" and box magazine has a 5-shot capacity. The beechwood checkered Monte Carlo stock is full size with pistol grip, plastic buttplate. The rear sight is adjustable. Metal finish is blue. Weighs about 5 lbs.

NIB	Exc.	V.G.	Good	Fair	Poor
265	225	180	150	125	100

Model 201 Standard

This model features a 21" medium heavy free-floating barrel. The receiver accepts all rail mounts and is also drilled and tapped for scope mount. Magazine capacity is 5-shot. Chambered for .22 LR or .22 WMR cartridge. The beechwood stock is hand checkered with plastic buttplate. The Monte Carlo stock is fitted with cheekpiece. Weighs about 6.5 lbs.

NIB	Exc.	V.G.	Good	Fair	Poor
600	500	350	200	150	100

Model 66 Standard

This is a centerfire bolt-action rifle fitted with a European Walnut hand-checkered oil finish stock. Stock is half stock design. Rosewood fore-ends and pistol grip caps are standard. Fitted with rubber recoil pad and 1" quick disconnect sling swivels. Barrels are interchangeable on this model. Barrels with standard calibers is 24" and approximate weight is 7.5 lbs. Standard calibers are: .243 Win., .270, .308, .30-06, 5.6x57, 6.5x57, 7.64 and 9.3x62.

NIB	Exc.	V.G.	Good	Fair	Poor
1700	1450	1100	700	550	350

Model 66 Magnum

Same as above but chambered for 7mm Rem. Magnum, .300 and .338 Win. Magnum, 6.5x68, 8x86S, 9.3x64. Fitted with a 26" barrel and weighs about 7.9 lbs.

NIB	Exc.	V.G.	Good	Fair	Poor
1800	1550	1200	800	600	400

Model 66 Safari

Same as above but chambered for .375 H&H and .458 Win. Magnum. Fitted with a 26" barrel and weighs about 9.3 lbs.

NIB	Exc.	V.G.	Good	Fair	Poor
2600	2000	1250	850	650	400

Model 66 Stuzen

Same as the Standard Model 66 but fitted with a full stock. Barrel length is 21" and calibers are same as Standard. Weighs about 7.5 lbs.

NIB	Exc.	V.G.	Good	Fair	Poor
2500	2100	1500	800	600	400

IDF Mauser Rifle Model 66SP

This is a bolt-action rifle chambered for the .308 Win. cartridge. Adjustable trigger for pull and travel. Barrel length is 27". Specially designed stock has broad fore-end and a thumbhole pistol grip. Cheekpiece is adjustable as is the recoil pad. Supplied with case. This rifle is military issue. Fewer than 100 imported into the U.S. by Springfield Armory.

NIB	Exc.	V.G.	Good	Fair	Poor
2250	1575	1100	850	650	400

Model 77

Fitted with a 24" barrel this bolt-action rifle is chambered for the .243, .270, 6.5x57, 7x64, .308, and .30-06 calibers. Detachable box magazine. Set trigger. Walnut stock with cheekpiece and hand checkering. Weight is about 7.25 lbs.

NIB	Exc.	V.G.	Good	Fair	Poor
1250	950	800	650	450	200

Model 77 Ultra

This model is fitted with a 20" barrel and chambered for the 6.5x57, 7x64, and .30-06 calibers. Weight is about 7.5 lbs.

NIB	Exc.	V.G.	Good	Fair	Poor
1250	950	800	650	450	200

Model 77 Mannlicher

Similar to the Ultra Model but with a full-length Mannlicher stock. Set trigger. Weight is about 7.5 lbs.

NIB	Exc.	V.G.	Good	Fair	Poor
1250	950	800	650	450	200

Model 77 Big Game

Chambered for the .375 H&H Magnum cartridge and fitted with a 26" barrel. Weight is about 8.5 lbs.

NIB	Exc.	V.G.	Good	Fair	Poor
1100	900	750	600	500	200

Model 86-SR

Introduced in 1993 this bolt-action .308 is sometimes referred to as the Specialty Rifle. Fitted with a laminated wood and special match thumbhole stock or fiberglass stock with adjustable cheekpiece. Stock has rail in forearm and an adjustable recoil pad. Magazine capacity is 9 rounds. Finish is a non-glare blue. The barrel length with muzzlebrake is 28.8". Many special features are found on this rifle from adjustable trigger weight to silent safety. Mauser offers many options on this rifle, as well, that will affect the price. Weight is approximately 11 lbs.

NIB	Exc.	V.G.	Good	Fair	Poor
9500	7500	5000	3500	1800	1000

Model 93 SR

Introduced in 1996 this is a tactical semi-automatic rifle chambered for the .300 Win. Magnum or the .338 Lapua cartridge. Barrel length is 25.5" with an overall length of 48.4". Barrel is fitted with a muzzlebrake. Magazine capacity is 6 rounds for .300 and 5 rounds for .338 caliber. Weight is approximately 13 lbs.

NIB	Exc.	V.G.	Good	Fair	Poor
10000	9000	7500	5000	3500	1500

Model 96

This bolt-action rifle is chambered for the .25-06, .270 Win., 7x64, .308, or .30-06 cartridge. It is fitted with a 22" barrel (24" Magnum calibers) and has a 5-round top loading magazine. Receiver is drilled and tapped. Checkered walnut stock. No sights. Approximately weight is 6.25 lbs.

NIB	Exc.	V.G.	Good	Fair	Poor
700	600	500	300	125	100

Model 98 (SIG ARMS)

Built in Germany this bolt-action rifle features a select walnut stock with oil finish. Express rear sight and single stage trigger. Chambered for the .416 Rigby, .450 Dakota, .458 Lott, and .500 Jeffery. Weight is approximately 8.8 lbs. **NOTE:** Add $1,000 for .500 Jeffery.

NIB	Exc.	V.G.	Good	Fair	Poor
1000	900	700	500	350	150

Model 99 Standard

This model is a bolt-action centerfire sporting rifle. It is offered with two stock designs: a classic with straight oil finish stock or high luster with cheekpiece and schnabel fore-end and Monte Carlo with rosewood fore-end tip and pistol grip cap. Chambered for standard calibers: .243, .25-06, .270, .308, .30-06, 5.6x57, 6.5x57, 7x57, 7x64. Barrel length is 24". Weight about 8 lbs.

NIB	Exc.	V.G.	Good	Fair	Poor
900	700	600	500	400	300

Model 99 Magnum

Same as above but chambered for magnum calibers: 7mm Rem. Magnum, .257 Wby., .270 Wby., .300 Wby., .300 and .338 Win. Magnum, 8x68S, and 9.3x64. Fitted with 26" barrel. Weighs about 8 lbs.

NIB	Exc.	V.G.	Good	Fair	Poor
950	750	650	550	400	300

CURRENT MAUSER PRODUCTION PISTOLS

Model 80 SA

This single-action semi-automatic pistol is based on the Browning Hi-Power design. Chambered for the 9mm Parabellum cartridge it has a barrel length of 4.66" and a magazine capacity of 14 rounds. Weighs approximately 35 oz.

NIB	Exc.	V.G.	Good	Fair	Poor
550	475	295	175	125	100

Model Compact DA

Same as above but double-action trigger and shorter barrel: 4.13". Weighs approximately 33 oz.

NIB	Exc.	V.G.	Good	Fair	Poor
340	320	250	175	125	100

Model 90 DA

Similar to the Model 80 but with a double-action trigger.

NIB	Exc.	V.G.	Good	Fair	Poor
550	475	295	175	125	100

Model M2 (Imported by SIG ARMS)

Introduced in 2000 this pistol is chambered for the .45 ACP, .40 S&W, or .357 SIG cartridges. It has an aluminum alloy frame and steel slide. The action is an enclosed hammerless striker-fired design. Barrel length is 3.5". Fixed sights. Weight is about 29 oz. Magazine capacity for .45 ACP is 8 rounds, for .40 S&W and .357 SIG capacity is 10 rounds.

NIB	Exc.	V.G.	Good	Fair	Poor
475	400	300	200	150	100

MAVERICK ARMS, INC.
Subsidiary of O. F. Mossberg & Sons, Inc.
Eagle Pass, Texas

Model 88

A 12 gauge Magnum slide-action shotgun with 28" or 30" barrels, anodized receiver and composition stock. Introduced in 1989.

NIB	Exc.	V.G.	Good	Fair	Poor
250	150	125	100	75	50

Model 88 Slug Pump Shotgun

A 12 gauge Magnum pump-action shotgun with an interchangeable Cylinder-bore barrel. Black synthetic stock and forearm, blued metal finish, 6-shot magazine. **NOTE:** Add $20 for rifled 24" barrel with adjustable rifle sights.

NIB	Exc.	V.G.	Good	Fair	Poor
295	200	100	75	60	50

Model 88 Six-Shot Security Model

A 12 gauge Magnum pump-action shotgun with a 6-shot magazine and an interchangeable 18.5" Cylinder-bore fixed choke barrel. A rugged black synthetic stock and forearm, blued metal finish and brass front sight bead are also included. **NOTE:** Add 5 percent for Eight-Shot Security Model with 20" Cylinder-bore fixed choke barrel. Add 10 percent for heat shield.

NIB	Exc.	V.G.	Good	Fair	Poor
295	200	100	75	60	50

MAYNARD/PERRY
Keen, Walker & Co.
Danville, Virginia

Brass Framed Carbine

Overall length 40"; barrel length 22.5"; caliber .54. Browned, blued barrel, brass frame and walnut stock. Manufactured in 1861 and 1862. Fewer than 300 produced.

NIB	Exc.	V.G.	Good	Fair	Poor
—	—	33000	14000	800	1500

M.B. ASSOCIATES-GYROJET
San Ramon, California

Established in 1960 by R. Maynard and Art Biehl, M.B. Associates produced the Gyrojet pistols and carbines from 1962 to 1970. Basically a hand held rocket launcher, shooting a 12mm or 13mm spin stablized rocket cartridge, composed of four-part solid rocket fuel. The nose of the round was forced rearward onto a stationary firing pin, igniting the fuel, expelling the round and recocking for the next shot. These were not very accurate and led to MBA's demise. Ammunition typically sells for $35 per round or more. By Dave Rachwal.

Mark I Model A Commemorative

13mm pistol, cased with a Goddard commemorative medal and 10 dummy rounds, black anodized finish, with walnut grips.

NIB	Exc.	V.G.	Good	Fair	Poor
—	2195	1500	1200	900	500

Mark I Model B Commemorative

13mm pistol, cased with the commemorative Goddard medal and 10 dummy rounds, black with walnut grips or antique nickel with pearlite grips.

NIB	Exc.	V.G.	Good	Fair	Poor
—	1895	1695	1000	600	300

Mark I Model B

13mm pistol, cardboard box, black anodized with walnut grips usually. This model was produced in many variations and finishes.

NIB	Exc.	V.G.	Good	Fair	Poor
—	995	800	650	400	200

Mark II Model C

12mm pistol, black anodized with walnut grips. This was manufactured for the 12mm round to conform with the 1968 gun control act, because 13mm is 51 caliber and 12mm is 49 caliber.

NIB	Exc.	V.G.	Good	Fair	Poor
—	995	800	650	400	200

Mark I Model A Carbine

13mm, black anodized finish with walnut stock and carrying handle.

NIB	Exc.	V.G.	Good	Fair	Poor
—	2495	2195	1700	1000	600

Mark I Model B Carbine

13mm, antique nickel finish with walnut stock. This was the sporter carbine and had a flared muzzle and sleek lines.

NIB	Exc.	V.G.	Good	Fair	Poor
—	1495	800	900	400	200

McMILLAN & CO. INC., G.
(Later: Harris/McMillan Gunworks, Harris Gunworks)
Phoenix, Arizona

Competition Model

A custom order bolt-action rifle in .308, 7mm-08 and the .300 Winchester Magnum caliber with the barrel length, stock type, and dimensions to the customer's specifications. Introduced in 1988.

NIB	Exc.	V.G.	Good	Fair	Poor
1700	1500	1150	800	600	300

Model 86 Sniper's Rifle

A custom order rifle in .308 Winchester or the .300 Winchester Magnum calibers with a synthetic stock and a choice of scope systems. Introduced in 1988.

NIB	Exc.	V.G.	Good	Fair	Poor
3250	2700	1900	1100	600	300

Model 86 System

As above, with the Ultra scope, mounting system, bipod and fitted case. Introduced in 1988.

NIB	Exc.	V.G.	Good	Fair	Poor
3700	3250	2300	1800	850	550

Model 87 Long Range Sniper's Rifle

A large stainless steel, single-shot bolt-action rifle in .50 BMG caliber featuring a 29" barrel with an integral muzzlebrake. Camouflaged synthetic stock. Weight 21 lbs. Accurate to 1,500 meters. Introduced in 1988.

NIB	Exc.	V.G.	Good	Fair	Poor
6000	5200	4000	2750	1000	500

Model 87 System

As above, with a bipod and a 20X Ultra scope, mounting system, and a fitted case. Introduced in 1988.

NIB	Exc.	V.G.	Good	Fair	Poor
6500	5700	4400	3150	1200	600

Signature Model

A bolt-action sporting rifle manufactured in a variety of calibers up to .375 Holland & Holland with a 22" or 24" stainless barrel, composition stock and either 3- or 4-shot magazine. Introduced in 1988.

NIB	Exc.	V.G.	Good	Fair	Poor
2200	1750	1250	800	600	300

Signature Stainless

Same as model above but barrel and action made of stainless steel. Fiberglass stock. Left- or right-hand model. The .416 Rigby is also offered in this configuration. Introduced in 1990.

NIB	Exc.	V.G.	Good	Fair	Poor
2500	2050	1650	1000	750	400

Signature Alaskan

This model, introduced in 1989, is offered in .270 .280 Rem., .30-06, 7mm Rem. Magnum, .300 Win. Magnum, .300 Wby. Magnum, .358 Win. Magnum, .340 Wby. Magnum, .375 H&H. Match grade barrel from 22" to 26" in length. Single leaf rear sight and barrel band front sight.

NIB	Exc.	V.G.	Good	Fair	Poor
3000	2700	2000	1500	950	500

Signature Titanium Mountain

Offered in calibers from .270 Win. to 7mm Rem. Magnum. Match grade barrel is produced from titanium. Stock is graphite. Weight is about 6.5 lbs.

NIB	Exc.	V.G.	Good	Fair	Poor
3500	3000	2500	1800	950	500

Signature Varminter

Available in calibers such as .223, .22-250, .220 Swift, .243, 6mm Rem., .25-06, 7mm-08, .308. Barrel lengths from 22" to 26". Heavy barrel configuration with hand bedded fiberglass stock. Field bipod is standard. Introduced in 1989.

NIB	Exc.	V.G.	Good	Fair	Poor
2500	2000	1500	900	600	400

Talon Safari

Bolt-action rifle offered in various calibers from .300 Win. Magnum to .458 Win. Magnum. Stainless steel barrel is 24". Four-round magazine. Fiberglass stock. Introduced in 1989. Weight is approximately 10 lbs.

NIB	Exc.	V.G.	Good	Fair	Poor
3750	3250	2200	6500	950	500

Talon Sporter

Offered in calibers from .25-06 to .416 Rem. Magnum. 24" barrel with no sights. Built on a pre-1964 Winchester Model 70 action. Choice of walnut or fiberglass stock. Weight is about 7.5 lbs.

NIB	Exc.	V.G.	Good	Fair	Poor
2500	2000	1750	1250	600	250

Model 300 Phoenix Long Range Rifle

Introduced in 1992 and chambered for the .300 Phoenix cartridge. Fitted with a 28" barrel with no sights. Fiberglass stock. Weight is approximately 12.5 lbs.

NIB	Exc.	V.G.	Good	Fair	Poor
3000	2500	2050	1450	600	350

Model 40 Sniper

This bolt-action rifle chambered for the .308 cartridge was introduced in 1990. Fitted with a 24" match grade heavy weight barrel. No sights. Weight is about 9 lbs.

NIB	Exc.	V.G.	Good	Fair	Poor
2500	2000	1500	1150	500	300

Model 92 Bullpup

This is a single-shot rifle chambered for the .50 caliber BMG. Fitted with a 26" barrel and no sights. Fiberglass bullpup stock. First introduced in 1995.

NIB	Exc.	V.G.	Good	Fair	Poor
4500	3750	2800	2200	1000	500

Model 93 SN

This is a bolt-action rifle chambered for the .50 BMG and fitted with a 29" barrel with muzzlebrake. Magazine holds 10 rounds. No sights. Weight is approximately 21.5 lbs. Folding fiberglass stock. Introduced in 1995.

NIB	Exc.	V.G.	Good	Fair	Poor
4750	4250	3500	2450	1450	750

McMillan LRHR

Long Range Hunting Rifle, designed for precision shooting. Custom made, benchrest tolerances in a long or short action. Chambered in .243 Winchester, .308 Winchester, 7mm Remington, .300 Winchester and .338 Lapua Magnum. Action is pillar bedded. Barrel lengths: 24", 26" or 27", depending on caliber. McMillan A-3 fiberglass stock is standard

NIB	Exc.	V.G.	Good	Fair	Poor
4750	4000	3000	2500	—	—

MEAD & ADRIANCE
St. Louis, Missouri

This company retailed a variety of single-shot percussion pistols most of which were manufactured by Ethan Allen of Grafton, Massachusetts. In general, the value for pistols marked "Mead & Adriance" are listed.

Single-Shot Pistols

NIB	Exc.	V.G.	Good	Fair	Poor
—	—	2500	1650	550	250

MENDENHALL, JONES & GARDNER
Greensboro, North Carolina

Muzzleloading Rifle

A .58 caliber percussion rifle with a 33" barrel and full-length walnut stock secured by two barrel bands. Finished in the white with the lock marked "M.J.&G.,N.C."

NIB	Exc.	V.G.	Good	Fair	Poor
—	—	39000	33000	14000	5000

MENZ, AUGUST
Suhl, Germany

Established prior to WWI to manufacture Beholla pistols, this company was purchased by Lignose in 1937.

Menta

Identical to the Beholla, which is listed separately.

NIB	Exc.	V.G.	Good	Fair	Poor
—	350	250	200	150	100

Liliput

A 4.25mm caliber semi-automatic pistol with a 2" barrel and 6-shot magazine. Overall length 3.5", weight 10 oz. The slide marked "Liliput Kal. 4.25". Also manufactured in 6.35mm caliber. These pistols have an overall length of 4". Blued with composition grips.

NIB	Exc.	V.G.	Good	Fair	Poor
—	800	600	450	300	200

Menz Model II

As above in 7.65mm caliber.

NIB	Exc.	V.G.	Good	Fair	Poor
—	400	300	250	200	125

Menz VP Model

Similar to the Model 2, but in 6.35mm caliber with a 2.35" barrel, 6-shot magazine and fitted with a cocking indicator.

NIB	Exc.	V.G.	Good	Fair	Poor
—	400	300	250	200	125

Model III

A total redesign. It has a closed-top slide and the quality is much better than the previous Menz pistols. It has a fixed barrel and is similar to the Model 1910 Browning with an exposed hammer. This model was produced until 1937.

NIB	Exc.	V.G.	Good	Fair	Poor
—	450	350	300	250	150

MERCURY
Liege, Belgium

Model 622 VP

A .22 caliber semi-automatic rifle with a 20" barrel, open sights and 7-shot magazine. Blued with a walnut stock. Manufactured by Robar & Son.

NIB	Exc.	V.G.	Good	Fair	Poor
—	325	275	250	200	125

MERCURY
Eibar, Spain

Double-Barreled Shotgun

A 10, 12 or 20 gauge Magnum boxlock double-barrel shotgun with 28" or 32" barrels, double triggers and extractors. Blued with a walnut stock. **NOTE:** Add 75 percent for 10 gauge.

NIB	Exc.	V.G.	Good	Fair	Poor
—	325	250	225	175	125

MERIDEN FIREARMS CO.
Meriden, Connecticut

Pocket Pistol

A .32 or .38 caliber double-action revolver manufactured in a variety of barrel lengths and with either an exposed or enclosed hammer. Nickel-plated with rubber grips. The barrel marked "Meriden Firearms Co. Meriden, Conn. USA." Manufactured between 1895 and 1915.

NIB	Exc.	V.G.	Good	Fair	Poor
—	—	375	200	75	50

Double-Barrel Shotguns

From 1905-1918 Meriden Fire Arms Co., successor to A.J. Aubrey, made 12, 16 and 20 gauge sidelock double-barrel shotguns. These were better quality hammer and hammerless side-by-sides fitted with twist, laminated, Damascus and steel barrels in grades A to G. Some of these guns were beautifully engraved by the same artisans who worked for Parker Bros. and other Connecticut gunmakers. Prices in 1910 ranged from $40 to $250 but they represented great value for the money as they were superior to the popular Crescent guns which they closely resembled. Current values depend on model, grade, gauge and condition. It is difficult to find examples in excellent condition as these were sold by Sears to customers who put them to hard use. In good condition their current values range from $250 for plain Janes to $3,500 or more for the top grades, of which few specimens are known.

Single-Barrel Shotguns and Rifles

Meriden Fire Arms Co. also made many single-barrel shotguns and rifles whose current values are determined by growing collector interest and condition.

MERKEL, GEBRUDER
Suhl, Germany

The Merkel brothers began manufacturing rifles and shotguns in Suhl, Germany in 1898. The company is best known for its over/under and side-by-side shotguns, but has also produced double-barreled express rifles, drillings with various rifle/shotgun combinations, falling block single-shot rifles and bolt-action rifles. Many experts consider Merkels to be equal in quality to some of the better Italian and English guns. Because of the company's long and complex history, including the years during which it operated behind the Iron Curtain, there are many un-catalogued models that may be encountered. Merkel firearms are imported by Merkel USA, a subsidiary of Steyr Arms in Trussville, Alabama.

SIDE-BY-SIDE SHOTGUNS

Model 8

This model has a self-cocking Deeley boxlock action with cocking indicators. The locking mechanism is a Greener cross-bolt with double-barrel locking lug. Triggers are single-selective or double. The safety is automatic and tang mounted. This model has an extractor. Offered in 12 and 16 gauge with 28" solid rib barrels or 20 gauge with 26.75" barrels. Available with straight or pistol grip oil-finished walnut stock. Receiver is case colored with light scroll engraving. The 12 and 16 gauge guns weigh about 6.8 lbs. while the 20 gauge weighs approximately 6 lbs.

NIB	Exc.	V.G.	Good	Fair	Poor
1500	1150	900	600	500	400

Model 117/117E

Offered in 12 and 16 gauge with various barrel lengths, this model featured a boxlock action with double triggers and extractors. Ejectors were available under the "E" designation. The boxlock action body was scrupled at the rear with fine line scroll engraving.

NIB	Exc.	V.G.	Good	Fair	Poor
—	6000	4350	1950	1000	500

Model 118/118E

Also offered in 12 and 16 gauge this model is similar to above model with slightly more engraving and better wood. This model also has some engraving coverage on the breech end of the barrels.

NIB	Exc.	V.G.	Good	Fair	Poor
—	7100	4900	2800	1200	650

Model 124/125

Similar to the above models but supplied with extractors for the Model 124 and ejectors for the Model 125. Both models have more engraving coverage with game scenes. Finer checkering and fancy wood is seen on this model.

Model 124

NIB	Exc.	V.G.	Good	Fair	Poor
—	5400	4350	2500	1500	700

Model 125

NIB	Exc.	V.G.	Good	Fair	Poor
—	6000	4600	3500	2000	1000

Model 130

This was one of Merkel's highest grade side-by-side shotguns. It featured a sidelock action, extra fancy wood, fine line checkering and full coverage game scene engraving.

NIB	Exc.	V.G.	Good	Fair	Poor
—	25500	17500	10000	3200	300

Model 126

Similar to the Model 130 but fitted with removable sidelocks.

NIB	Exc.	V.G.	Good	Fair	Poor
—	18500	15500	82700	4500	300

Model 170

This model was offered in 12 gauge only with automatic ejectors. The boxlock action was engraved with fine full coverage scroll.

NIB	Exc.	V.G.	Good	Fair	Poor
—	6000	4900	3900	2500	300

Model 127

This model was Merkel's finest side-by-side shotgun. The sidelock action featured full coverage fine line scroll engraving of the best quality.

NIB	Exc.	V.G.	Good	Fair	Poor
—	25000	19500	14500	6000	300

Model 47E

Same as above but fitted with ejectors. Offered in 12, 16 or 20 gauge. Supplied with fitted luggage case.

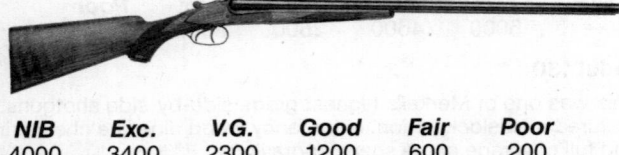

NIB	Exc.	V.G.	Good	Fair	Poor
4000	3400	2300	1200	600	200

Model 147

Same as Model 8 but with silver grayed receiver with fine engraved hunting scenes, engraved border and screws. This model has been discontinued.

NIB	Exc.	V.G.	Good	Fair	Poor
3700	3250	2300	1100	600	200

Model 147E

Same as above but fitted with ejectors. Offered in 12, 16, 20 or 28 gauge. Supplied with fitted luggage case.

NIB	Exc.	V.G.	Good	Fair	Poor
4750	3850	2700	1500	1000	300

Model 147EL

Similar to the Model 147E but with fancy walnut stock. Supplied with fitted luggage case.

NIB	Exc.	V.G.	Good	Fair	Poor
6000	4950	3400	2200	1000	3000

Model 122

This model features the same specifications as the above models but has false sideplates. This model is fitted with ejectors and the receiver is silver grayed with fine engraved hunting scenes on false sideplates, engraved border and screws.

NIB	Exc.	V.G.	Good	Fair	Poor
4000	3500	3000	1900	950	300

Model 47SL

Same as above but with scroll engraving in place of hunting scenes.

NIB	Exc.	V.G.	Good	Fair	Poor
8200	6100	4400	3000	1750	300

Model 147SL

This model features true Holland and Holland-style sidelocks with cocking indicators. Gauge and barrel lengths are as above. Stock is fancy walnut. However, 20 gauge gun weighs 6.4 lbs., 28 gauge gun weighs about 6.1 lbs.

NIB	Exc.	V.G.	Good	Fair	Poor
10000	7000	5500	3850	2250	300

Model 147SSL

Similar to the Model 147SL but fitted with removable side plates. Fancy walnut stock. Supplied with fitted luggage case.

NIB	Exc.	V.G.	Good	Fair	Poor
8800	6500	5200	3000	2500	300

Models 247S/347S

These models are the same as the Model 147S with the exception of the types of engraving.

Model 247S

Large scroll engraving.

NIB	Exc.	V.G.	Good	Fair	Poor
7700	5800	4400	2500	2000	300

Model 347S

Medium scroll engraving.

NIB	Exc.	V.G.	Good	Fair	Poor
7100	6100	4950	3850	2250	300

Model 447SL

Small scroll engraving. **NOTE:** For wood upgrade add $1,200. For custom stock dimensions add $ 1,400. For left-hand stocks add $900.

NIB	Exc.	V.G.	Good	Fair	Poor
9900	7300	6000	4400	2700	300

Model 280

This is a boxlock gun chambered for the 28 gauge shell and fitted with 28" barrels choked Improved Cylinder and Modified. Double triggers with ejectors. Straight-grip walnut stock. Scroll engraving with case colored receiver. Weight is about 5.2 lbs.

NIB	Exc.	V.G.	Good	Fair	Poor
4000	3600	2650	1900	950	300

Model 280EL

This model features an Anson & Deely boxlock action with engraved hunting scenes on a silver-grayed action. Double triggers. Fancy walnut with straight grip stock. Offered in 28 gauge with 28" barrels. Fitted luggage case standard. Weight is about 5.2 lbs. First imported in 2000.

NIB	Exc.	V.G.	Good	Fair	Poor
6500	5500	3850	2500	1500	300

Model 280SL

Similar to the Model 280EL, but with English-style scroll engraving on H&H style sidelocks with choice of pistol-grip or straight-grip fancy walnut stock. Fitted luggage case standard. First imported in 2000.

NIB	Exc.	V.G.	Good	Fair	Poor
8250	7700	5500	3600	1700	300

Model 360

This boxlock model is the same as the Model 280 but chambered for the .410 bore. Straight grip walnut stock. Scroll engraving on case colored receiver. Barrel is 28" choke Modified and Full. Weight is about 5.2 lbs.

NIB	Exc.	V.G.	Good	Fair	Poor
4200	3600	2650	1400	800	300

Model 360EL

This model is the same as the Model 280EL but chambered for the .410 shell and fitted with 28" barrels. Fancy walnut and fitted case. Weight is about 5.5 lbs. First imported in 2000.

NIB	Exc.	V.G.	Good	Fair	Poor
7000	5700	4100	2750	1300	300

Model 360SL

Same as the Model 360EL but with English-style scroll engraving on H&H style sidelocks and choice of pistol grip or straight grip stock. First imported in 2000.

NIB	Exc.	V.G.	Good	Fair	Poor
10500	8100	5900	3750	1600	300

Model 280/360 Two Barrel Set

This set consists of a 28 gauge 28" barrel and a .410 bore 28" barrel with scroll engraving and oil finish walnut stock. Double triggers and straight grip stock.

NIB	Exc.	V.G.	Good	Fair	Poor
6500	6000	5000	3750	1600	500

Model 280/360EL Two Barrel Set

This set consists of a 28 gauge 28" barrel and a .410 bore 28" barrel with engraved hunting scenes and fancy walnut stock. Double triggers and straight-grip stock. First imported in 2000.

NIB	Exc.	V.G.	Good	Fair	Poor
9500	8000	6000	3750	1600	500

Model 280/360SL Two Barrel Set

Same as above but with English-style scroll engraving and choice of pistol-grip or straight-grip stock. First imported in 2000.

NIB	Exc.	V.G.	Good	Fair	Poor
15500	11500	8000	5500	3500	500

Model 1620

This is a boxlock side-by-side gun chambered for the 16 gauge shell. Fitted with 28" barrels with double triggers. Barrel chokes Improved Cylinder and Modified. Ejectors. Straight-grip walnut stock with oil finish. Case colored receiver finish. Light scroll engraving. Fitted luggage case. Weight is about 6.1 lbs. **NOTE:** For two-barrel set add $2,300. Second set is 20 gauge with 28" barrels.

NIB	Exc.	V.G.	Good	Fair	Poor
4200	3600	2500	1800	1000	300

Model 1620E

Similar to Model 1620 but with fine engraved hunting scenes on silver-grayed receiver.

NIB	Exc.	V.G.	Good	Fair	Poor
5000	4000	3000	2000	1000	300

Model 1620EL

As above but with high-grade walnut straight-grip stock and deeply engraved hunting scenes. **NOTE:** For two-barrel set add $2,900. Second set is 20 gauge with 28" barrels.

NIB	Exc.	V.G.	Good	Fair	Poor
6000	5000	3850	2200	1100	300

Model 1620SL

Similar to the 1620 models above but with grayed sidelocks with deeply engraved hunting scenes. High-grade walnut stock with oil finish. Weight is 6.6 lbs. **NOTE:** For two-barrel set add $3,800. Second set is 20 gauge with 28" barrels.

NIB	Exc.	V.G.	Good	Fair	Poor
11000	8400	6100	3750	1800	500

Model 1622

Introduced in 2006, this 16 gauge boxlock side-by-side features full sideplates, case hardened receiver with cocking indicators, ejectors, single selective or double triggers and pistol grip or English style stock. Fixed IC and Mod. chokes. **NOTE:** Add 50 percent for 2-barrel set (second set is 28" 20 gauge).

NIB	Exc.	V.G.	Good	Fair	Poor
4000	3200	2550	1700	1400	300

Model 1622E

Similar to 1622 but with fine engraved hunting scenes on silver-grayed receiver.

NIB	Exc.	V.G.	Good	Fair	Poor
7500	5700	4100	2750	1300	300

Model 1622EL

Similar to Model 1622E but with luxury grade wood. **NOTE:** Add 30 percent for 2-barrel set (second set is 28" 20 gauge).

NIB	Exc.	V.G.	Good	Fair	Poor
8800	6500	5200	3000	2500	300

OVER/UNDER SHOTGUNS

Model 102E

This was Merkel's standard over/under boxlock model. Offered in 12 gauge with 28" barrels or 16 gauge with 26" barrels. Both are fitted with double triggers, semi-pistol grip and ejectors.

NIB	Exc.	V.G.	Good	Fair	Poor
—	1800	1450	1100	650	400

Model 103E

Similar to the standard but with more English scroll engraving coverage and better wood. This model was offered in 12, 16 and 20 gauge.

NIB	Exc.	V.G.	Good	Fair	Poor
—	2450	1650	1350	950	600

Model 204E

This model is essentially a Model 203E with finer engraving. This model was discontinued prior to 1939.

NIB	Exc.	V.G.	Good	Fair	Poor
—	6600	4900	3300	2200	1750

Model 301E

This is a boxlock model with scalloped action chambered for the 12, 16, 20, 24, 28 and 32 gauge. The engraving is an English scroll and the trigger guard is horn. Double triggers and pistol grip are standard. This model was produced prior to 1939.

NIB	Exc.	V.G.	Good	Fair	Poor
—	4900	4000	2500	2000	1850

Model 302E

Similar to the Model 301E but fitted with sideplates. The full-coverage engraving features game scenes. This model produced prior to WWII.

NIB	Exc.	V.G.	Good	Fair	Poor
—	13250	11000	8250	4400	2000

Model 303 Luxus

This over/under Merkel is custom built to the customer's specifications. Each gun is unique and should be appraised by a knowledgeable individual who is familiar with quality European shotguns.

NIB	Exc.	V.G.	Good	Fair	Poor
22000	18500	15000	—	—	—

Model 304E

This pre-war model was the highest grade in Merkel's over/under shotgun line. A sidelock gun with full coverage scroll engraving of the highest quality. Fine line checkering and extra fancy wood make this gun difficult to appraise due to its rarity.

Model 400E

A higher grade over/under fitted with Kersten crossbolt, finer engraving and fancy wood. Merkel offered this grade in 12, 16, 20, 24, 28 and 32 gauge with choice of barrel lengths. This model was produced prior to 1939.

NIB	Exc.	V.G.	Good	Fair	Poor
—	1950	1450	1000	600	400

Model 401E

Similar to the model above but with full coverage game scene engraving.

NIB	Exc.	V.G.	Good	Fair	Poor
—	2750	2000	1350	800	600

Model 200E

The action on this model is a self-cocking Blitz where the hammers are attached to the trigger plates. The locking mechanism is a Kersten double crossbolt lock with release. Trigger may be either single-selective or double. The manual safety is mounted on the tang. Fitted with coil spring ejectors. Offered in 12 and 16 gauge with 28" solid rib barrels or 20 gauge with 26.75" barrels. The oil-finished stock is offered with straight or pistol grip. The receiver is case colored with engraved border and screws. The 12 gauge weighs 7 lbs., the 16 gauge 6.8 lbs., and the 20 gauge 6.4 lbs.

NIB	Exc.	V.G.	Good	Fair	Poor
2900	2200	1650	1000	800	500

Model 201E

Same as Model 200E but with silver grayed receiver with fine engraved hunting scenes, engraved border and screws.

NIB	Exc.	V.G.	Good	Fair	Poor
3700	3100	2500	1650	1000	750

Model 202E

This model has the same basic specifications as the Model 201E but is fitted with false side plates with cocking indicators.

NIB	Exc.	V.G.	Good	Fair	Poor
8200	5500	3850	2500	1500	1000

Model 200ES

This model features a Blitz action with cocking indicators and Kersten double cross bolt lock with release. The trigger is single-selective with tang-mounted manual safety. Coil spring ejectors are standard. Offered in 12 gauge only with 26.75" or 28" ventilated rib barrel. The walnut stock has skeet dimensions with pistol grip. Receiver is silver grayed with 112 coverage scroll engraving, engraved borders and screws. Weighs approximately 7.3 lbs.

NIB	Exc.	V.G.	Good	Fair	Poor
4400	3600	2750	2200	1500	1000

Model 200ET

Same as Model 200ES, but in a trap configuration. The ventilated rib barrel length offered is 30".

NIB	Exc.	V.G.	Good	Fair	Poor
4700	3850	3000	2250	1750	1000

Model 200SC (Sporting Clays)

Introduced in 1995 this model is offered in 12 gauge only with 3" chambers and 30" barrels with ventilated rib. It is fitted with a single-selective trigger adjustable for length of pull. It has a special walnut oil finished stock with 26 lpi checkering. Pistol grip and Pachmayr Sporting Clays recoil pad is standard. Weight is approximately 7.6 lbs. **NOTE:** With Briley choke tubes add $500.

NIB	Exc.	V.G.	Good	Fair	Poor
7200	6000	3300	1500	900	450

Model 201ES

Same as Model 200SC but with full coverage scroll engraving.

NIB	Exc.	V.G.	Good	Fair	Poor
4950	4050	3300	2500	2000	1000

Model 201ET

Same as Model 210ES but fitted with a 30" barrel and trap stock dimensions.

NIB	Exc.	V.G.	Good	Fair	Poor
4950	4100	3300	2750	2000	1000

Model 203E

This model has true Holland & Holland-style sidelocks with cocking indicators. These sideplates are removable with cranked screw. The gauge selection and barrel are the same as those listed above. The silver grayed receiver has English-style large scroll engraving. This model has been discontinued.

NIB	Exc.	V.G.	Good	Fair	Poor
13500	10400	8250	5000	2500	1000

Model 303E

Same as Model 203E but with detachable sidelock plates with integral retracting hook. The Model 303E also has medium scroll work engraving and Holland & Holland-type ejectors.

NIB	Exc.	V.G.	Good	Fair	Poor
18700	16500	13400	7500	5000	2500

Model 303EL

This model features H&H-style sidelocks that are quick detachable without tools. Receiver is engraved with hunting scenes. Offered in 12, 20 and 28 gauge. Double triggers and fancy walnut stock with pistol or straight grip. Weight for 12 gauge is about 7 lbs, for the 20 gauge about 6.4 lbs. and for the 28 gauge about 6.4 lbs. Fitted luggage case standard.

NIB	Exc.	V.G.	Good	Fair	Poor
26000	18700	13000	7500	5000	2500

Model 2000EL

This model features a Kersten crossbolt lock, scroll engraving on a silver grayed receiver and a modified Anson & Deely boxlock action. This gun is offered in 12, 20 or 28 gauge with ejectors, single-selective or double triggers, fancy wood, and choice of pistol or straight grip stock. Weight is about 7 lbs. for 12 gauge, 6.4 lbs. for 20 gauge and 6.4 lbs. for 28 gauge.

NIB	Exc.	V.G.	Good	Fair	Poor
7200	5100	3600	2200	1500	750

Model 2000EL Sporter

Similar to the above model but fitted with 30" barrels on the 12 gauge and 28" barrels on the 20 and 28 gauge.

NIB	Exc.	V.G.	Good	Fair	Poor
7200	5200	3600	2200	1500	750

Model 2000CL

Introduced in 2005 this model is chambered for the 12, 20 or 28 gauge with 28" barrels choked improved cylinder and modified. Scroll engraved receiver with case colors. Single selective trigger with auto ejectors. High grade wood with semi-pistol grip and straight grip.

NIB	Exc.	V.G.	Good	Fair	Poor
7700	5800	3750	2200	1500	750

Model 2000CL Sporter

As above but with 30" barrel for the 12 gauge with vent rib and 28" barrels with solid rib for the 20 and 28 gauge guns. Pistol grip stock. Introduced in 2005. **NOTE:** Deduct $500 for 20 and 28 gauge models.

NIB	Exc.	V.G.	Good	Fair	Poor
8100	6100	3750	2200	1500	750

Model 2001EL

Similar to the Model 2000 but with finely engraved hunting scenes. This model is offered in 28 gauge as well as 12 and 20 gauge.

NIB	Exc.	V.G.	Good	Fair	Poor
9000	7500	4950	2900	2000	1000

Model 2001EL Sporter

Same as above but with 30" barrels for 12 gauge, 28" barrels for 20 and 28 gauge.

NIB	Exc.	V.G.	Good	Fair	Poor
11000	7300	5300	3600	2000	1000

Model 2002EL

This model features finely engraved hunting scenes with arabesque style. Offered in 12, 20 and 28 gauges.

NIB	Exc.	V.G.	Good	Fair	Poor
11000	8800	6000	4400	2200	1200

Model 2016EL

This is a 16 gauge gun with 28" barrels and single non-selective trigger and ejectors. Fixed chokes. Checkered walnut stock with semi-pistol grip. Scroll engraving on the case colored receiver. Weight is about 6.6 lbs.

NIB	Exc.	V.G.	Good	Fair	Poor
8750	7000	5000	3000	1500	750

Model 2016EL Two Barrel Set

As above but with extra set of 20 gauge 28" barrels with fixed chokes.

NIB	Exc.	V.G.	Good	Fair	Poor
12000	10500	8000	5000	3000	1000

Model 2116EL

This 16 gauge model is similar to the above but with game scene engraving on the case colored receiver.

NIB	Exc.	V.G.	Good	Fair	Poor
9100	7700	5500	3200	2000	1000

Model 2116EL Two Barrel Set

As above with extra set of 20 gauge 28" barrels with fixed chokes.

NIB	Exc.	V.G.	Good	Fair	Poor
13000	9300	6950	4400	2900	2000

PRE-WAR SINGLE-SHOT AND BOLT-ACTION RIFLES

Merkel built special single-shot rifles and bolt-action rifles. These guns were produced prior to WWII and are seldom seen in the United States. The buyer should exercise caution and seek expert assistance prior to a sale.

Model 180

This is a top-lever single rifle with double under lugs built on a boxlock action. The stock is 3/4 with pistol grip. Commonly referred to as a stalking rifle. Offered in a variety of European calibers. A rare Merkel.

NIB	Exc.	V.G.	Good	Fair	Poor
—	3300	2400	1650	1000	500

Model 183

This top lever model features a Holland & Holland-type sidelock action with the sidelock on the left side and the removable sideplate on the right side. Fitted with a straight-grip stock and full-length forearm with sling swivels, fine line checkering and fancy wood. A rare rifle.

NIB	Exc.	V.G.	Good	Fair	Poor
—	8300	5500	3850	2000	1200

Model 190

This is Merkel's version of a Sporting rifle built on a Mauser action. Offered in a variety of European calibers. These were special order rifles and will be seen in a variety of configurations.

NIB	Exc.	V.G.	Good	Fair	Poor
6000	5000	3500	2000	1100	650

DOUBLE RIFLES, COMBINATION GUNS, DRILLINGS

Model 410E

Merkel's base boxlock model with ejectors. Produced prior to WWII.

NIB	Exc.	V.G.	Good	Fair	Poor
—	2500	1950	1350	750	500

Model 411E

Similar to the above but with the addition of a small coverage of scroll engraving.

NIB	Exc.	V.G.	Good	Fair	Poor
—	2750	2200	1650	1100	600

Model 300

A boxlock hammerless four barrel shotgun/rifle combination. The shotgun barrels were 12, 16 or 20 gauge, while the top rifle barrel was .22 rimfire with the bottom rifle barrel .30-30 or .25-35. Probably any combination of rifle and shotgun could be used as this was a special order gun. Very rare.

Model 311E

This combination gun has additional English scroll engraving.

NIB	Exc.	V.G.	Good	Fair	Poor
—	8600	7200	5500	2250	1250

Model 312E

This model is fitted with sideplates and game scene engraving.

NIB	Exc.	V.G.	Good	Fair	Poor
—	10400	9000	7500	4000	2000

Model 313E

This model has sidelocks with fine, full coverage scroll engraving. An expert appraisal is recommended due to this model's rarity and unique features.

NIB	Exc.	V.G.	Good	Fair	Poor
18000	13000	11750	8800	4400	2000

Model 314E

This sidelock model is also rare and unique. An expert appraisal is recommended prior to a sale. Extra barrels will frequently be seen with this model.

Model 128E

This side-by-side double rifle is a droplock design with scroll and game scene engraving. The wood is Circassian walnut with fine line checkering. Offered in a variety of European calibers.

Model 132E

Similar to the Model 128E but with full coverage scroll engraving and fancy wood.

Model 140-1

This model features a Greener cross bolt, scroll engraving with case hardened receiver. Extractors and double triggers with pistol grip stock are standard. Offered in a wide variety of European and American calibers.

NIB	Exc.	V.G.	Good	Fair	Poor
6500	5200	4100	2900	2000	1000

Model 140-1.1

Same as above model but with finely engraved hunting scenes.

NIB	Exc.	V.G.	Good	Fair	Poor
7400	6100	4400	2900	2000	1000

Model 140-2

This double rifle has an Anson & Deely boxlock action. Double triggers. Barrel length is 23.6". Chambered for .375 H&H, .416 Rigby and the .470 NE. Pistol grip stock with cheekpiece on oil finish walnut. Weight is about 10.7 lbs. depending on caliber.

NIB	Exc.	V.G.	Good	Fair	Poor
11500	8250	6000	3750	2200	1500

Model 140-2.1

This model is similar to the one above but is engraved with African game scenes.

NIB	Exc.	V.G.	Good	Fair	Poor
13400	9300	6600	3750	2200	1500

Model 150-1

This model features an arabesque engraving on a silver grayed receiver. Extractors, double triggers and pistol grip are standard.

NIB	Exc.	V.G.	Good	Fair	Poor
8250	6600	5100	3000	2000	900

Model 150-1.1

Same as above model but with finely engraved hunting scenes.

NIB	Exc.	V.G.	Good	Fair	Poor
9500	7700	6000	3500	2500	1000

Model 160S Luxus Double Rifle

This double rifle is part of the Luxus series and features the highest quality sidelock action, wood, and fittings. It is offered in .222 Rem., 5.6x5OR Magnum, .243, 6.5x57R, 7x57, 7x65, .3006, .30R Blaser, 8x57IRS, 8x57RS, .308 Win., and 9.3x74R. Weighs approximately 8 lbs. An expert appraisal should be sought prior to a sale due to the unique nature of this model.

NIB	Exc.	V.G.	Good	Fair	Poor
15000	12500	8500	5750	4300	1200

Model 160S-2.1

Same as above but with finely engraved hunting scenes. Chambered for the .470 Nitro Express. Weight is about 11 lbs.

NIB	Exc.	V.G.	Good	Fair	Poor
28500	20750	16500	12000	7500	1500

Model 211E Rifle/Shotgun Combination

This over/under model features a gray metal boxlock action with hunting scenes. The top barrel is available in 12, 16 or 20 gauge and the bottom barrel is offered in .22 Hornet, 5.6R Magnum, 5.6R, .222 Rem., .243 Win., 6.5x55, 6.5x57R, 7x57R, 7x65R, .30-06, 8x57IRS, 9.3x74R and .375 H&H Magnum. The barrel has a solid rib and the trigger is single-selective. The select walnut stock is hand checkered. Weight is about 7 lbs.

NIB	Exc.	V.G.	Good	Fair	Poor
6600	4950	3850	2250	1500	700

Model 210E Rifle/Shotgun Combination

Same as above model but features a scroll engraved case hardened receiver. This model has been discontinued.

NIB	Exc.	V.G.	Good	Fair	Poor
6900	5500	4400	2750	1200	700

Model 211E Rifle/Shotgun Combination

Similar to the above model but with finely engraved hunting scenes.

NIB	Exc.	V.G.	Good	Fair	Poor
8300	6600	4900	3000	1500	750

Model 213E Rifle/Shotgun Combination

This combination gun features sidelocks with English style large scroll engraving on a silver grayed receiver. Also is fitted with double triggers and pistol grip with cheekpiece.

NIB	Exc.	V.G.	Good	Fair	Poor
13000	10000	8200	5500	1900	900

Model 313E Rifle/Shotgun Combination

Same as above model but with finer scroll engraving and fancy wood.

NIB	Exc.	V.G.	Good	Fair	Poor
19000	15000	8250	6500	2000	1000

Model 220E Over/Under Double Rifle

This is a boxlock design with a Kersten double cross bolt, scroll engraved case hardened receiver, Blitz action, double triggers and pistol-grip stock with cheekpiece.

NIB	Exc.	V.G.	Good	Fair	Poor
10000	6600	4950	3800	1700	825

Model 221E Over/Under Double Rifle

Similar to the model above but with game scene engraving on a silver grayed receiver.

NIB	Exc.	V.G.	Good	Fair	Poor
12500	9350	6300	4500	2300	900

Model 223E Over/Under Double Rifle

This model is fitted with sidelocks and features English-style arabesque engraving in large scrolls on silver grayed receiver.

NIB	Exc.	V.G.	Good	Fair	Poor
16000	14000	11000	8000	4200	1000

Model 240-1

This is a boxlock double rifle and shotgun chambered for the 7x65R, .30R Blaser, 6.5x57R, 8x57IRS, 9.3x74R, .30-06 and the .308 Win. Shotgun barrels are 20 gauge. Fitted with 23.6" barrels and double triggers. Ejectors. Scroll engraving. Walnut stock with pistol grip and cheekpiece. Weight is about 10 lbs.

NIB	Exc.	V.G.	Good	Fair	Poor
8000	6300	5000	4000	3000	1300

Model 240-1.1

As above but with hunting scene engraving on grayed receiver.

NIB	Exc.	V.G.	Good	Fair	Poor
9100	7100	6000	5000	4000	1500

Model 323E Over/Under Double Rifle

Similar to the above model but with finer engraving.

NIB	Exc.	V.G.	Good	Fair	Poor
25000	19000	13500	9500	3200	1500

Model 95K Drilling

This model is a three-barrel shotgun/rifle combination. The top two barrels are chambered for 12, 16 or 20 gauge and the bottom barrel is available in rifle calibers from .22 Hornet to .375 H&H Magnum. The action is a boxlock design with scroll engraving on borders and screws. The stock is select grade walnut with raised comb, pistol grip with cap, cheekpiece and plastic butt-plate. Weighs about 7.7 lbs. This model has been discontinued

NIB	Exc.	V.G.	Good	Fair	Poor
9400	7400	4700	3000	2000	1000

Model 96K

Similar to the above model but with scroll engraving on a case hardened frame.

NIB	Exc.	V.G.	Good	Fair	Poor
9800	7800	5000	3700	2200	1000

Model 96K—Engraved

Same as above but with finely engraved hunting scenes with arabesque engraving on a silver grayed receiver.

NIB	Exc.	V.G.	Good	Fair	Poor
11000	8500	5500	4000	2700	1100

K-SERIES STALKING RIFLES

Model K-1 Jagd

Introduced in 2003 this single-shot break-open rifle is chambered for the .243, 270, 7x57R, .308 Win., .30-06, 7mm Rem. Magnum, .300 Win. Magnum and the 9.3x74R cartridge. Fitted with a 23.6" barrel. Hunting scene engraving. Weight is about 5.4 lbs.

NIB	Exc.	V.G.	Good	Fair	Poor
4200	2750	1900	1600	1100	600

POST-WAR BOLT-ACTION RIFLES

KR-1 Premium

A short-stroke bolt-action rifle chambered for .243, .308 or .30-06 and 7mm Rem. Magnum and .300 Win. Magnum calibers. Barrel length for standard calibers is 20" or 22" and for magnum calibers 22" or 24". Checkered walnut stock with hog-back comb. Magazine capacity is 3 rounds. Single set trigger. Interchangeable barrels. Arabesque engraving on bolt housing and trigger plate. Select walnut stock with Bavarian cheekpiece. Weight is about 6.4 lbs. depending on caliber and barrel length. Introduced in 2005. **NOTE:** Add $200 for magnum calibers.

NIB	Exc.	V.G.	Good	Fair	Poor
3550	2900	2200	1650	900	450

KR-1 Weimar

As above but with rounded bolt housing with hand chiselled engraving with game scenes. Trigger and lock bolt head are gold titanium nitride plated. Select walnut stock with rosewood forearm tip and Bavarian double fold cheekpiece. Introduced in 2005. **NOTE:** Add $200 for magnum calibers.

NIB	Exc.	V.G.	Good	Fair	Poor
11000	8800	7100	5500	3000	600

MERRILL
Fullerton, California

Sportsman

A single-shot pistol manufactured in a variety of calibers with either a 9" or 12" octagonal barrel having a wide ventilated rib, adjustable sights and integral telescope mounts. Blued with walnut grips. **NOTE:** Interchangeable barrels add $100. Wrist support add $25.

NIB	Exc.	V.G.	Good	Fair	Poor
—	700	575	325	175	125

MERRILL, JAMES H.
Baltimore, Maryland

Merrill Rifle

A single-shot breechloading rifle that is chambered for .54 caliber and utilizes the percussion ignition system. The breech opens for loading by lifting and pulling back on a lever. The barrel is 33" in length and there is a full-length walnut stock held on by two barrel bands. The mountings and patch box are brass; and the lock is case colored, with a browned barrel. The lock is marked "J.H. Merrill Balto./Pat. July 1858". There are military acceptance marks on the stock. There were approximately 775 of these rifles manufactured and purchased by the government for use during the Civil War. They were made in 1864 and 1865.

Courtesy Milwaukee Public Museum, Milwaukee, Wisconsin

NIB	Exc.	V.G.	Good	Fair	Poor
—	—	7800	6350	2750	750

Merrill Carbine

Similar in appearance to the rifle except that the barrel length is 22" and the stock is only half-length with one barrel band. There are some variations that are quite subtle in appearance but which have a considerable effect on values. We recommend that an independent appraisal be secured. The values given are for the standard 1st and 2nd Types. There were approximately 15,000 total manufactured and most were used in the Civil War.

1st Type

No eagle stamped on the lock, and the breech lever is flat.

Courtesy Milwaukee Public Museum, Milwaukee, Wisconsin

NIB	Exc.	V.G.	Good	Fair	Poor
—	—	3750	2750	1500	500

2nd Type

An eagle stamped on the lock and the stock has no patch box. The breech lever has a round tip.

Courtesy Milwaukee Public Museum, Milwaukee, Wisconsin

NIB	Exc.	V.G.	Good	Fair	Poor
—	—	4250	3000	1750	600

MERRILL, LATROBE & THOMAS
S. Remington—Maker
Ilion, New York

Carbine

A .58 caliber breech loading percussion carbine with an overall length of 38" and barrel length of 21". The lock marked "S. Remington/Ilion, N.Y." and the barrel "Merrill, Latrobe & Thomas/Baltimore, Md./Patent Applied For". Approximately 170 were made in 1855.

NIB	Exc.	V.G.	Good	Fair	Poor
—	—	45000	35000	12500	700

MERRIMACK ARMS
See—Brown Manufacturing Co.

MERWIN & BRAY
Worcester, Massachusetts

This company marketed a number of firearms produced by various manufacturers under its own name.

Merwin & Bray Pocket Pistol

A .32 caliber spur trigger single-shot pistol with a 3.5" barrel. Blued, silver-plated with walnut grips. The barrel marked "Merwin & Bray New York".

NIB	Exc.	V.G.	Good	Fair	Poor
—	—	—	300	150	75

MERWIN HULBERT & CO.
New York, New York

Merwin Hulbert & Co., New York City. Founder Joseph Merwin had previously been involved in Merwin & Bray. Merwin Hulbert & Co. or its principals were also involved in Phoenix Rifle Company, Evans Rifle Company, American Cartridge Company and Hopkins & Allen of Norwich, CT. Most Merwin Hulbert revolvers will be marked with the Hopkins & Allen name, in addition to Merwin Hulbert. They were made for a fairly brief period, with most production apparently taking place during the 1870s & early 1880s. There has been some confusion over a classification system for MH revolvers. The system adopted here is based on the distinctions listed in Art Phelps' book, The Story of Merwin Hulbert & Co. Firearms. We believe this is the first time the Phelps system has been adapted to a list format.

LARGE-FRAME MERWIN HULBERT SIXGUNS

There has been a marked increase in interest in Merwin Hulbert & Co. over the past decade, with many coming to recognize them as one of the pre-eminent makers of large-frame revolvers used in the American West. Total production of large-frame revolvers has been estimated at a few thousand by some sources. However, the frequency with which they are encountered suggests possibly greater production.

MH used a unique system of opening, loading & unloading their revolvers which was supposed to allow selective ejection of spent shells, leaving remaining cartridges in place. A latch on the bottom of the frame is pushed toward the rear of the gun and the barrel and cylinder are rotated to the right (clockwise, as viewed from the rear of the revolver) 90 degrees. The barrel and cylinder are then pulled forward, far enough to allow empty brass to fall free. This system required exceptional quality machining and some modern authorities are on record as considering the Merwin Hulbert to have the finest workmanship of all revolvers of the era.

All are .44 caliber 6-shot large-frame revolvers. Beyond that, to fully identify a large-frame Merwin Hulbert, you must specify the following:

1. **MODEL DESIGNATION** — First Model has an open top and scoop flutes, round barrel, and two small screws above the trigger guard. Second Model is similar to the first, except with only one screw above the trigger guard. Third Model has a top-strap with standard flutes and a round barrel. Fourth Model is similar to the third, except that it has a ribbed barrel. The open-top 1st and 2nd Models seem to be more sought after. The 4th Model is rare, and will bring a premium from a serious Merwin collector.

2. **FRONTIER ARMY or POCKET ARMY** — Frontier Army models have a square butt, and were made in 1st through 4th models. Pocket Army models have a bird's-head butt with a pointed extension with lanyard hole, and are found in 2nd or 3rd Model configuration. Generally, the Frontier Army will bring more than the Pocket Army.

3. **SINGLE-ACTION or DOUBLE-ACTION** — The topstrap models, 3rd and 4th, were manufactured in both single-action and double-action. The single-action models tend to bring more.

4. **BARREL LENGTH** — Standard barrel length on the Frontier Army 1st, 2nd, & 3rd Models is 7", with a 5-1/2" barrel common on the 4th Model. Standard barrel length on the Pocket Army was a more "pocket-sized" 3-1/2". However, somewhat ironically, bird's-head butt models marked "Pocket Army" were also produced with full length 7" barrels. Generally, these longer barrels will bring a bit more than the shorter ones.

5. **CALIBER** — Most common is .44-40 (designated "Winchester Calibre 1873"). Merwins were also chambered for .44 Merwin Hulbert (somewhat similar to the S&W .44 American cartridge), and .44 Russian. The less common calibers may bring a small premium from serious Merwin collectors.

6. **FOREIGN COPIES** — The Merwin Hulbert design was relatively widely copied during the period of use, particularly in Spain. It seems that much of this production may have gone to Mexico, and some found their way to the U.S. Although these Spanish copies may bear markings such as "System Merwin Hulbert" or other usage of the words "Merwin Hulbert," they generally will not be found with the Hopkins & Allen marking. Spanish firms making Merwin copies included Orbea Hermanos and Anitua y Charola. These Spanish copies may bring half or less of what an original Merwin will bring, and it can sometimes take a fairly experienced eye to tell the difference.

7. **ENGRAVING** — Special order engraving was available, and it was usually executed in a distinctive and colorful "punch dot" style, which has come to be associated with Merwins (although it is occasionally encountered on other makes of firearms). For a long time, this style was somewhat dismissed as a bit crude and lacking in artistry. However, a new appreciation of Merwin engraving has emerged, and factory engraved pieces will bring a significant premium. Often, a panel scene depicts an animal, object, or landmark. These panel scenes have an almost "folk art" quality to them, and will enhance the value further. Engraved Merwins are sometimes encountered with the engraving filled with colored enamel, quite rare, and, if original, this will bring a further premium.

8. **FINISH** — The vast majority were nickel plated. Original blued guns will bring a premium.

Courtesy Supica's Old Town Station

Top: Open Top Pocket Army. Bottom: Topstrap Double-Action Pocket Army

First Model Frontier Army, .44 Open Top

Two screws, square butt, 7" barrel.

NIB	Exc.	V.G.	Good	Fair	Poor
—	—	5500	3000	1500	500

Second Model Frontier Army, .44 Open Top

One screw, square butt, 7" barrel.

NIB	Exc.	V.G.	Good	Fair	Poor
—	—	4500	2750	1000	500

Second Model Pocket Army, .44 Open Top

Bird's-head butt. 3.5" barrel standard, 7" will bring a premium.

NIB	Exc.	V.G.	Good	Fair	Poor
—	—	3500	2000	700	400

Third Model Frontier Army, Single-Action, .44 Topstrap

Square butt, 7" barrel.

NIB	Exc.	V.G.	Good	Fair	Poor
—	—	3750	2250	800	450

Third Model Frontier Army, Double-Action, .44 Topstrap

Square butt, 7" barrel.

NIB	Exc.	V.G.	Good	Fair	Poor
—	—	3250	1750	700	400

Third Model Pocket Army, Single-Action, .44 Topstrap

Bird's-head butt. 3.5" barrel standard, 7" will bring a premium.

NIB	Exc.	V.G.	Good	Fair	Poor
—	—	3250	1750	700	400

Third Model Pocket Army, Double-Action, .44 Topstrap

Bird's-head butt. 3.5" barrel standard, 7" will bring a premium.

NIB	Exc.	V.G.	Good	Fair	Poor
—	—	3000	1600	650	400

Fourth Model Frontier Army, Single-Action, .44 Topstrap

Ribbed barrel, scarce. 5.5" barrel seems to be most common, also offered in 7" and 3.5".

NIB	Exc.	V.G.	Good	Fair	Poor
—	—	5000	2750	800	550

Fourth Model Frontier Army, Double-Action, .44 Topstrap

Ribbed barrel. Barrel lengths as above.

NIB	Exc.	V.G.	Good	Fair	Poor
—	—	4750	2500	750	550

SMALL-FRAME MERWIN HULBERT POCKET REVOLVERS

The .32 & .38 centerfire revolvers were manufactured with the unique Merwin Hulbert twist-open system, like the large frame revolvers. They were often advertised as chambered for the .32 MH & Co. or .38 MH & Co. cartridges, but it appears as if these cartridges may have been essentially the same as the .32 S&W and .38 S&W rounds. Of course, the Merwin Hulbert revolvers were manufactured for the original lower pressure black-powder loadings of these cartridges. Saw-handled grip frames were standard, although some were manufactured with the distinctive Pocket Army type pointed "skullcrusher" bird's-head grip frames and these will generally bring a premium. Most common barrel length for most models is 3.5", with 5.5" barrels somewhat scarcer in most models and 2.75" barrels quite scarce and worth a premium. A number of police departments purchased small frame Merwin Hulbert revolvers in the late 19th century. Department marked guns will bring a premium.

Terminology alert—note that the .44 caliber "Pocket Army" model is a large-frame and is listed in the section above.

The .22 Merwin Hulbert revolver is the only one not to use the MH twist-open system. It is, instead, a tip-up revolver closely resembling the S&W Model One.

Courtesy Supica's Old Town Station

Top: Single-Action Pocket Revolver. Bottom: Double-Action Pocket Revolver

First Pocket Model Single-Action

Spur-trigger, cylinder pin exposed at front of frame, round loading aperture in recoil shield (no loading gate), five-shot .38, scarce.

NIB	Exc.	V.G.	Good	Fair	Poor
—	—	1250	800	300	175

Second Pocket Model Single-Action

Spur-trigger, cylinder pin exposed, sliding loading gate, five-shot .38.

NIB	Exc.	V.G.	Good	Fair	Poor
—	—	1000	650	285	150

Third Pocket Model Single-Action Spur-Trigger

Enclosed cylinder pin, sliding loading gate, five-shot .38.

NIB	Exc.	V.G.	Good	Fair	Poor
—	—	950	600	225	125

Third Pocket Model Single-Action w/Trigger Guard

Five-shot .38.

NIB	Exc.	V.G.	Good	Fair	Poor
—	—	1000	675	285	150

Double-Action Pocket Model, Small Frame

.32 caliber five shot. Patent marked folding hammer spur will bring a small premium.

NIB	Exc.	V.G.	Good	Fair	Poor
—	—	800	550	185	125

Double-Action Pocket Model, Medium Frame

Usually .38 five shot. Scarce .32 seven shot will bring a 25 percent to 50 percent premium. Patent marked folding hammer spur will bring a small premium.

NIB	Exc.	V.G.	Good	Fair	Poor
—	—	900	900	225	150

Tip-Up .22 Spur-Trigger

.22 rimfire, a S&W patent infringement, looks similar to S&W Model. One Third Issue. Scarce. "Made by Merwin Hulbert & Co. for Smith & Wesson" marking will bring a small premium.

NIB	Exc.	V.G.	Good	Fair	Poor
—	—	1000	650	275	175

MERWIN HULBERT RIFLES

Very similar in design to Hopkins & Allen single-shot breech loaders. Advertised in .22 and .32 rimfire, as well as .32 WCF, .38 WCF, and .44 WCF. May have been offered in .32-40 and .38-55 chamberings. A 20 gauge shotgun barrel was offered separately for these rifles. Features included set trigger, rebounding hammer, pistol grip stock and takedown. Seldom encountered, the Merwin Hulbert name on these should bring a premium over standard Hopkins & Allen single-shot rifles. A small frame "Merwin Hulbert & Co's. Junior" rifle was also offered, chambered for .22 rimfire.

METROPOLITAN ARMS CO.
New York, New York

Established in February 1864, this company manufactured copies of the Colt Model 1851 and 1861 Navy Revolvers, as well as copies of the Colt Model 1862 Police Revolver. Two of the firm's principle officers were Samuel and William Syms (formerly of Blunt & Syms) and it is believed that they were responsible for production. Curiously, although, most Metropolitan pistols were produced during the 1864 to 1866 period. The company itself was not dissolved until 1920.

1851 Navy Revolver

A .36 caliber percussion revolver with a 7.5" octagonal barrel and 6-shot cylinder. Blued, case hardened with walnut grips. The barrel marked "Metropolitan Arms Co. New York". Approximately 6,000 of these revolvers were made during the 1860s. Those bearing H.E. Dimick markings are worth considerably more than the standard marked examples.

Standard Navy Model

NIB	Exc.	V.G.	Good	Fair	Poor
—	—	—	4100	1400	500

H.E. Dimick Navy Model

NIB	Exc.	V.G.	Good	Fair	Poor
—	—	—	8000	3000	850

1861 Navy Revolver

A .36 caliber percussion revolver with a 7.5" round barrel and 6-shot cylinder. The loading lever of the rack-and-pinion type. Blued, case hardened with walnut grips. The barrel marked "Metropolitan Arms Co. New York". Approximately 50 were made in 1864 and 1865.

NIB	Exc.	V.G.	Good	Fair	Poor
—	—	—	8000	3300	950

Police Revolver

A .36 caliber percussion revolver with either 4.5", 5.5" or 6.5" round barrels and a fluted 5-shot cylinder. Blued, case hardened with walnut grips. The barrel normally marked "Metropolitan Arms Co. New York", although examples have been noted without any markings. Approximately 2,750 were made between 1864 and 1866.

NIB	Exc.	V.G.	Good	Fair	Poor
—	—	2400	1650	650	250

MIIDA
Marubeni America Corp.
Japan

Model 612

A 12 gauge boxlock over/under shotgun with 26" or 28" ventilated rib barrels, single-selective trigger and automatic ejectors. Blued with a walnut stock. Imported between 1972 and 1974.

NIB	Exc.	V.G.	Good	Fair	Poor
—	900	750	600	400	250

Model 612 Skeet

As above, with 27" Skeet choked barrels and some engraving. Imported between 1972 and 1974.

NIB	Exc.	V.G.	Good	Fair	Poor
—	900	750	600	400	250

Model 2100 Skeet

Similar to the Model 612 but with more engraving coverage.

NIB	Exc.	V.G.	Good	Fair	Poor
—	950	800	650	450	300

Model 2200 Trap or Skeet

As above, with either 30" trap or 27" skeet bored barrels and more finely engraved. Imported between 1972 and 1974.

NIB	Exc.	V.G.	Good	Fair	Poor
—	1100	850	700	450	300

Model 2300 Trap or Skeet

A more finely finished Model 2200. Imported from 1972 until 1974.

NIB	Exc.	V.G.	Good	Fair	Poor
—	1200	900	750	500	300

Model GRT Trap or GRS Skeet

A 12 gauge boxlock shotgun fitted with false sideplates, 27" skeet or 29" Full choked barrels, single-selective trigger and automatic ejector. Imported between 1972 and 1974.

NIB	Exc.	V.G.	Good	Fair	Poor
—	2250	1850	1250	800	500

MILLER ARMS
Sturgis, South Dakota

NOTE: There are a large number of extra costs options available for these rifles.

Standard Rifle

This is single shot falling block rifle. Fitted with a 26" round barrel chambered for centerfire cartridges up to .375 caliber. Stock is checkered XXX walnut with pistol grip. Quarter rib scope base. Weight depends on caliber.

NIB	Exc.	V.G.	Good	Fair	Poor
4500	3500	2000	1300	700	350

Low Boy

This model features a 24" half round/half octagon barrel. All other features as above.

NIB	Exc.	V.G.	Good	Fair	Poor
5000	4000	2250	1300	700	350

Model F

This model is similar to the standard rifle with the addition of a 26" octagon barrel with tang sight and globe front sight. All calibers to .45-110.

NIB	Exc.	V.G.	Good	Fair	Poor
6000	4750	3000	2200	1300	500

MILTECH
Los Altos, California

This company rebuilds and refinishes selected military firearms. All firearms are thoroughly inspected for safety and are considered safe to shoot. All firearms have their original receivers and markings. These rifles are not stamped with the Miltech name but do have a unique Miltech pine crate serial numbered to the gun as standard. The company will verify that it did the rebuild if asked. All guns come with manual, sling and other selected accessories depending on model.

German Mauser Model 98k

NIB	Exc.	V.G.	Good	Fair	Poor
1495	1150	900	750	550	300

M1 Garand

NOTE: For International Harvester and Winchester add $225.

NIB	Exc.	V.G.	Good	Fair	Poor
1595	1200	850	700	500	300

M1D Garand

NIB	Exc.	V.G.	Good	Fair	Poor
2950	2500	1900	1350	700	400

M1 Carbine

NOTE: For Rockola and Winchester add $200-300.

NIB	Exc.	V.G.	Good	Fair	Poor
1295	1050	800	575	375	200

Model 1941 Johnson

NIB	Exc.	V.G.	Good	Fair	Poor
5000	4000	3000	2000	1000	500

Model 1903 Springfield

NIB	Exc.	V.G.	Good	Fair	Poor
1495	1150	900	750	550	300

Model 1903A3 Springfield

NIB	Exc.	V.G.	Good	Fair	Poor
1495	1150	900	750	550	300

Model 1903 Mark I Springfield

NIB	Exc.	V.G.	Good	Fair	Poor
1550	1225	975	800	575	325

Model 1917 U.S. Enfield

NIB	Exc.	V.G.	Good	Fair	Poor
1495	1150	900	750	550	300

MINNEAPOLIS F. A. CO.
Minneapolis, Minnesota

Palm Pistol

A .32 caliber radial cylinder pistol with a 1.75" barrel manufactured by the Ames Manufacturing Company (see the Ames entry). Nickel-plated with hard rubber grips. The sideplates marked "Minneapolis Firearms Co." and "The Protector". Several thousand were sold during the 1890s.

NIB	Exc.	V.G.	Good	Fair	Poor
—	—	2250	1850	950	300

MIROKU, B. C.
Miroku, Japan

Firearms produced by this manufacturer have been imported and marketed by a variety of companies such as Charles Daly, Browning, Winchester and SKB.

MITCHELL ARMS, INC.
Santa Ana, California

An importer and distributor of foreign-made firearms, this company is no longer in business. However, some Mitchell models were available under Brolin Arms through 1998. Brolin Arms was no longer in business as of 1999. This company also imported Yugoslavian-manufactured semi-automatic AK-47 rifles in 7.62x39mm, as well as 7.62x54mm.

RIFLES

Galil

A .22 or .22 Magnum caliber copy of the Galil rifle. Introduced in 1987.

NIB	Exc.	V.G.	Good	Fair	Poor
500	400	300	150	125	100

MAS

A .22 or .22 Magnum caliber copy of the French MAS Bullpup Service Rifle. Introduced in 1987.

NIB	Exc.	V.G.	Good	Fair	Poor
400	325	200	150	125	100

AK-22

A .22 or .22 Magnum caliber copy of the AK-47 rifle. Introduced in 1985.

NIB	Exc.	V.G.	Good	Fair	Poor
400	300	250	125	100	75

M-16

A .22 rimfire copy of the Colt AR-15. Introduced in 1987.

NIB	Exc.	V.G.	Good	Fair	Poor
325	250	150	125	100	75

PPSH-30/50

A .22 or .22 Magnum caliber copy of the PPSH Submachine gun.

NIB	Exc.	V.G.	Good	Fair	Poor
375	325	225	150	75	60

HANDGUNS

Trophy II

A semi-automatic pistol chambered for the .22 LR cartridge. Offered in either 7.25" fluted or 5.5" bull barrel. Barrels are interchangeable. Trigger is adjustable for weight and pull. Walnut grips with thumb rest are standard.

NIB	Exc.	V.G.	Good	Fair	Poor
400	325	275	200	150	100

Citation II

Similar to the Trophy II but with a matte satin finish.

NIB	Exc.	V.G.	Good	Fair	Poor
375	300	250	200	150	100

Sharpshooter II

This is a stainless steel target pistol with 5.5" bull barrel to which barrel weights can be added. Fully adjustable rear sight and checkered walnut grips are standard.

NIB	Exc.	V.G.	Good	Fair	Poor
325	275	225	200	150	100

Olympic I.S.U.

This competition pistol features a 6.75" barrel with integral stabilizer. Rear sight is adjustable as is the trigger. Barrel weights are adjustable as well as removable.

NIB	Exc.	V.G.	Good	Fair	Poor
525	475	400	300	200	100

Victor II

This .22 caliber pistol is built from stainless steel and has interchangeable barrels in 4.5" or 5.5" lengths. Barrels have full length ventilated ribs, checkered walnut grips with thumb rest. Gold plated trigger is adjustable.

NIB	Exc.	V.G.	Good	Fair	Poor
450	375	325	250	175	125

Victor II with Weaver Rib

NIB	Exc.	V.G.	Good	Fair	Poor
525	450	375	275	175	125

High Standard Collectors' Association Special Editions

Limited run of Mitchell's version of the High Standard pistol with special roll marking on the slide "High Standard / Collectors Association / Special Edition" and a special serial number series with a HSCA prefix. Manufactured by Pastucek Industries, Fort Worth, Texas.

Trophy II

5.5" barrel. See standard Mitchell guns for rest of description.

NIB	Exc.	V.G.	Good	Fair	Poor
420	325	—	—	—	—

Victor II

4.5" barrel. See standard Mitchell guns for rest of description.

NIB	Exc.	V.G.	Good	Fair	Poor
450	325	—	—	—	—

Citation II

7.25" barrel. See standard Mitchell guns for rest of description.

NIB	Exc.	V.G.	Good	Fair	Poor
400	300	—	—	—	—

Three Gun Set

Includes Trophy II, Olympic ISU and Victor II. Eleven sets manufactured.

NIB	Exc.	V.G.	Good	Fair	Poor
1400	1100	—	—	—	—

Six Gun Set

Includes 5.5" Trophy II, 6.75" Olympic II, 4.5" Victor II, Sharpshooter II, Citation II and 4.5" Sport King II. Nineteen sets manufactured.

NIB	Exc.	V.G.	Good	Fair	Poor
2450	1975	—	—	—	—

Skorpion

A .32 caliber semi-automatic pistol with a 4.75" barrel and either 20- or 30-shot magazine. Blued with plastic grips. Imported from Yugoslavia in 1987 and 1988 only.

NIB	Exc.	V.G.	Good	Fair	Poor
—	600	500	425	350	175

Spectre

A 9mm caliber semi-automatic pistol with an 8" shrouded barrel and either 30- or 50-shot magazine. Blued with plastic grips. Also produced with an 18" barrel and folding buttstock. Imported from Yugoslavia in 1987 and 1988.

NIB	Exc.	V.G.	Good	Fair	Poor
—	600	500	425	350	175

MITCHELL'S MAUSERS
Fountain Valley, California

Black Arrow

This is a .50 caliber bolt-action rifle with 5-round box magazine. Fitted with a recoil compensator. Iron sights. Bipod.

NIB	Exc.	V.G.	Good	Fair	Poor
6000	5000	4000	2700	1600	500

Centurion

This is a double-action revolver with either a 4" or 6" barrel. Chambered for the .357 Magnum cartridge. Blued or stainless steel.

NIB	Exc.	V.G.	Good	Fair	Poor
695	550	400	300	200	100

Valkyrie

This revolver is chambered for the .44 Magnum cartridge and has a choice of 4" or 6" barrel. Blued or stainless steel.

NIB	Exc.	V.G.	Good	Fair	Poor
895	700	500	400	300	200

Gold Series '03

Chambered for the 9mm, .40 S&W or .45 ACP cartridge. Built on the Model 1911 Government Model. Blued or stainless steel.

NIB	Exc.	V.G.	Good	Fair	Poor
795	600	450	325	250	150

Escalade

This is a slide-action shotgun chambered for the 12 gauge shell. Fitted with a choice of 18.5" barrel, 28" vent rib barrel or 22" barrel with Turkey choke. Turkish walnut stock. Blued.

NIB	Exc.	V.G.	Good	Fair	Poor
395	300	250	200	150	100

Sabre

This is a semi-automatic 12 gauge shotgun with choice of 22" vent rib barrel or 28" vent rib barrel. Blued.

NIB	Exc.	V.G.	Good	Fair	Poor
495	400	350	300	250	150

Mauser M98 North American

This bolt-action rifle is fitted with a Mauser 98 action and offered in most standard hunting calibers. **NOTE:** For magnum calibers add $2,000.

NIB	Exc.	V.G.	Good	Fair	Poor
7000	6000	4500	2275	1500	400

Mauser M98 Varmint

As above but chambered for .22-250 or .220 Swift.

NIB	Exc.	V.G.	Good	Fair	Poor
6000	5000	3500	1775	1000	300

Mauser M98 African/Alaskan

Chambered for heavy calibers up to .500 Jeffery.

NIB	Exc.	V.G.	Good	Fair	Poor
8000	7500	6500	2500	1500	500

MK ARMS, INC.
Irvine, California

Model 760

A 9mm caliber semi-automatic carbine with a 16" shrouded barrel, fixed sights, and 14-, 24- or 36-shot magazine. Parkerized with a folding stock. Introduced in 1983.

NIB	Exc.	V.G.	Good	Fair	Poor
950	700	575	400	250	125

MKE
Ankara, Turkey

Kirrikale

A 7.65 or 9mm short semi-automatic pistol with a 4" barrel and 7-shot magazine. It is an unauthorized copy of the Walther PP. Blued with plastic grips.

NIB	Exc.	V.G.	Good	Fair	Poor
450	375	275	225	150	100

MODESTO SANTOS CIA.
Eibar, Spain

Action, Corrientes, and M.S.

A 6.35mm or 7.65mm caliber semi-automatic pistol of low quality marked on the slide "Pistolet Automatique Model 1920". Blued with composition grips having the monogram "M.S." cast in them. Manufactured between 1920 and 1935.

NIB	Exc.	V.G.	Good	Fair	Poor
—	275	175	125	75	50

Action

A 6.35mm or 7.65mm semi-automatic pistol marked on the slide "Pistolet Automatique Modele 1920". Often found bearing the trade name "Corrientes" as well as the maker's trademark "MS".

NIB	Exc.	V.G.	Good	Fair	Poor
—	275	175	115	80	60

MONTENEGRAN-GASSER
See—Gasser, Leopold

MOORE'S PATENT FIREARMS CO.
Brooklyn, New York

In 1866 this company became known as the National Arms Company.

No. 1 Derringer

A .41 caliber spur trigger all metal pistol with a 2.5" barrel. Blued or silver-plated. Approximately 10,000 were manufactured between 1860 and 1865. This model was also marketed as the No. 1 Derringer by the Colt Company after they purchased the National Arms Company in 1870.

Courtesy Milwaukee Public Museum, Milwaukee, Wisconsin

1st Variation Marked "Patent Applied For"

NIB	Exc.	V.G.	Good	Fair	Poor
—	—	3200	2500	1100	400

2nd Variation Marked "D. Moore Patented Feb. 19 1861"

NIB	Exc.	V.G.	Good	Fair	Poor
—	—	2200	1500	700	250

Standard Model Marked "Moore's Pat F.A. Co."

NIB	Exc.	V.G.	Good	Fair	Poor
—	—	1200	850	350	150

National Arms Co. Production

Courtesy Milwaukee Public Museum, Milwaukee, Wisconsin

NIB	Exc.	V.G.	Good	Fair	Poor
—	—	1250	875	385	150

Iron Model

NIB	Exc.	V.G.	Good	Fair	Poor
—	—	1300	1100	550	250

Pocket Revolver

A .32 teat fire caliber spur trigger revolver with a round 3.25" barrel and 6-shot cylinder. Blued or silver plated with walnut grips. Approximately 30,000 were manufactured between 1864 and 1870.

NIB	Exc.	V.G.	Good	Fair	Poor
—	—	800	550	275	100

Belt Revolver

A .32 rimfire caliber revolver with a 4", 5" or 6" octagonal barrel and 7-shot cylinder. The barrel and cylinder blued, the brass frame sometimes silver-plated with walnut grips. The barrel marked "D. Moore Patent Sept. 18, 1860". Several thousand were manufactured between 1861 and 1863.

Courtesy Milwaukee Public Museum, Milwaukee, Wisconsin

Courtesy Rudolph R. Massenzi

Belt Revolver and holster belonging to Capt. Henry Kellogg, Illinois 33rd during American Civil War.

NIB	Exc.	V.G.	Good	Fair	Poor
—	—	1450	950	350	150

MORGAN & CLAPP
New Haven, Connecticut

Single-Shot Pocket Pistol

A .22 or .23 caliber spur trigger single-shot pistol with a 3.5" octagonal barrel. Blued, silver-plated frame with walnut grips. The barrel marked "Morgan & Clapp New Haven". Active 1864 to 1867.

NIB	Exc.	V.G.	Good	Fair	Poor
—	—	1150	650	250	100

MORINI
Italy

C-80 Standard

A .22 caliber single-shot pistol with a free floating 10" barrel, match sights, adjustable frame and adjustable grips. Discontinued in 1989.

NIB	Exc.	V.G.	Good	Fair	Poor
—	1100	800	675	550	250

CM-80 Super Competition

As above, with a trigger adjustable from 5 to 120 grams pressure, Plexiglass front sight and a polished finish. Discontinued in 1989.

NIB	Exc.	V.G.	Good	Fair	Poor
—	1200	900	750	650	300

Model 84E Free Pistol

Introduced in 1995 this competition pistol features an 11.4" barrel chambered for the .22 LR. It is a single-shot. Adjustable sights with adjustable electronic trigger. Weight is about 44 oz.

NIB	Exc.	V.G.	Good	Fair	Poor
1650	1150	900	700	500	200

MORRONE
Hope Valley, Rhode Island

See—Rhode Island Arms Company

MORSE
Greenville, South Carolina
State Armory

Morse Carbine

Overall length 40"; barrel length 2"; caliber .50 (other calibers are known to have been made on an experimental basis). The round barrel is blued, the frame is of brass and the stock is of either walnut or beechwood. Approximately 1,000 were manufactured during the Civil War.

Courtesy Milwaukee Public Museum, Milwaukee, Wisconsin

Courtesy Milwaukee Public Museum, Milwaukee, Wisconsin

NIB	Exc.	V.G.	Good	Fair	Poor
—	—	27000	23000	7500	1500

MOSSBERG, O. F. & SONS, INC.
North Haven, Connecticut

Founded by Oscar F. Mossberg in 1892 at Fitchburg, Massachusetts, this company for a time was located at Chicopee Falls, Massachusetts and since 1962 has been in North Haven, Connecticut. It is the oldest family-owned firearms manufacturer in America.

HANDGUNS

Brownie

A .22 caliber four-barreled pocket pistol with a revolving firing pin. This pistol resembles a semi-automatic. Manufactured from 1906 to approximately 1940. Premium for in box with papers.

NIB	Exc.	V.G.	Good	Fair	Poor
750	450	325	300	225	150

RIFLES

Model K

A .22 caliber slide-action rifle with a 22" barrel, tubular magazine, internal hammer and takedown system. Blued with a walnut stock. Discontinued in 1931.

NIB	Exc.	V.G.	Good	Fair	Poor
—	350	250	150	75	50

Model M

As above, with a 24" octagonal barrel. Manufactured from 1928 and 1931.

NIB	Exc.	V.G.	Good	Fair	Poor
—	350	250	150	75	50

Model L

A .22 caliber Martini-style single-shot takedown rifle with a 24" barrel. Manufactured from 1927 to 1932.

NIB	Exc.	V.G.	Good	Fair	Poor
—	600	475	350	175	100

Beginning in 1930, the Mossberg company manufactured a variety of utilitarian single-shot and repeating bolt-action rifles. Later they introduced a similar line of semi-automatic rifles. As these arms were intended for extensive use and were low-priced, the values for them may be categorized as listed.

Bolt-Action Rifles

Model10	Model 25	Model 340M
Model 14	Model 25A	Model 341
Model 140B	Model 26B	Model 342K
Model 140K	Model 26C	Model 346B
Model 142A	Model 30	Model 346K
Model 142K	Model 320B	Model 352K
Model 144	Model 320K	
Model 144LS	Model 321K	
Model 146B	Model 340B	
Model 20	Model 340K	

Model 140B

NIB	Exc.	V.G.	Good	Fair	Poor
400	300	200	100	75	50

Semi-Automatic Rifles

Model 50	Model 152K
Model 51	Model 350K
Model 51M	Model 351C
Model 151K	Model 351K
Model 151M	Model 432
Model 152	

Model 51M

NIB	Exc.	V.G.	Good	Fair	Poor
350	300	200	150	100	50

RECENT PRODUCTION RIFLES

Targo Smoothbore Series

In the early 1940s, Mossberg produced a series of bolt-action .22 rimfire rifles with smoothbore barrels. These rifles were mainly designed for a clay target game called Targo, in which shooters used .22 LR shot ammunition. The game never achieved much popularity. A rifled barrel section several inches long could be attached to the muzzle, which allowed the use of standard ammunition. Some models came with a smoothbore attachment that extended the length of the barrel. Other accessories included a clay target launcher that attached to the barrel, a case designed for the rifle and a supply of the small clay targets. There were several model variations: a single shot (Model 26T), two repeater models with 7-round magazines (42T and 42TR) and a fourth version with an extended 15-round clip (B42T). Most of these rifles were produced from 1940-1942 and again in the late '40s after WWII. Two models were introduced briefly in the early 1960s, the Model 320TR single shot and 340TR repeater. **NOTE:** Add 50 percent for original case and all original accessories. Add 20 percent for Model 26T or B42T, the rarest models of this series.

NIB	Exc.	V.G.	Good	Fair	Poor
500	425	350	250	200	100

Model 400 Palomino

A .22 caliber lever-action rifle with a 22" barrel, open sights and tubular magazine. Also made with an 18.5" barrel. Blued with a walnut stock. Manufactured from 1959 to 1964.

NIB	Exc.	V.G.	Good	Fair	Poor
350	300	200	150	100	50

Model 702 Plinkster

Introduced in 2004 this 22 caliber semi-automatic rifle is fitted with a 18" barrel with adjustable sights. Detachable 10-round magazine. Blued finish and choice of black synthetic, hardwood, synthetic thumb-hole, solid pink, pink camo or Mossy Oak New Break-up camo finish stock. Weight is about 4 lbs. Also available as scope package (add 10 percent) and with tiger maple or carbon fiber stock and chromed barrel and receiver. By 2008, a variety of color and stock options, including a modern synthetic version of Mossberg's old flip-down fore-end and thumb-hole stocks had been added to the line and these will bring more or less than the values listed, according to local demand.

NIB	Exc.	V.G.	Good	Fair	Poor
175	145	110	75	50	25

Model 702 International Plinkster

This model features a 21" chrome barrel with iron sights. Black synthetic stock. Weight is about 4.5 lbs. **NOTE:** Add $75 for muzzle brake.

NIB	Exc.	V.G.	Good	Fair	Poor
195	160	125	90	65	40

Model 817 Varmint

Introduced in 2008, this offering by Mossberg International features a 21" free-floating blued or brushed chrome barrel, hardwood or black synthetic stock, factory Weaver mounts, detachable box magazine and .17 HMR chambering.

NIB	Exc.	V.G.	Good	Fair	Poor
175	150	125	100	75	50

Tactical .22

An AR-styled rimfire auto-loading rifle with an 18", free-floating barrel. Matte blue finish. Matte black synthetic stock with fixed or adjustable length of pull. Magazine capacity, 10 or 25 rounds. Quad fore-end for unlimited mounting opportunities of optical or light systems. Peep rear and front post sight are standard.

NIB	Exc.	V.G.	Good	Fair	Poor
235	200	160	120	100	80

Model 100 ATR (All-Terrain Rifle)

Introduced in 2005, this bolt action rifle is chambered for the .270 or .30-06 calibers. Fitted with a 22" barrel with no sights. Choice of black synthetic, synthetic walnut or camo stock. Matte blue or all-weather finish. Weight is about 7 lbs. .243, 308. Also available as 3X9 scope package. **NOTE:** Add 10 percent for scope, $40 for all-weather finish.

NIB	Exc.	V.G.	Good	Fair	Poor
360	300	250	200	150	100

Model 100 ATR Night Train

Similar to above but with black synthetic stock, factory-mounted 4x16 scope, bipod and .308 Winchester chambering. Introduced 2008.

NIB	Exc.	V.G.	Good	Fair	Poor
375	325	275	225	165	125

Model 100 ATR Super Bantam

Similar to Model 100 ATR but chambered only in .243 and .308. No sights. Synthetic black stock adjustable for length of pull. Introduced in 2007.

NIB	Exc.	V.G.	Good	Fair	Poor
360	300	250	200	150	100

Model 800

A bolt-action rifle manufactured in a variety of calibers with a 22" barrel and folding leaf rear sight. Blued with a walnut stock. Introduced in 1967.

NIB	Exc.	V.G.	Good	Fair	Poor
400	325	200	150	100	75

Model 800D

As above, with a comb stock, rosewood fore-end tip and pistol grip cap. Manufactured from 1970 to 1973.

NIB	Exc.	V.G.	Good	Fair	Poor
400	300	250	200	150	100

Model 800V

As above, with a 24" heavy barrel not fitted with sights. Introduced in 1968.

NIB	Exc.	V.G.	Good	Fair	Poor
400	300	225	150	100	75

Model 800M

As above, with a Mannlicher-style stock.

NIB	Exc.	V.G.	Good	Fair	Poor
500	375	250	200	150	100

Model 800SM

As above, with a 4X scope.

NIB	Exc.	V.G.	Good	Fair	Poor
550	425	275	225	150	100

Model 801 Half-Pint Plinkster

Entry-level .22 LR single-shot rifle with removable magazine plug to allow insertion of 10-round magazine. 16" barrel, hardwood stock, adjustable open sights. Overall weight 4 lbs. Introduced 2008.

NIB	Exc.	V.G.	Good	Fair	Poor
150	125	100	75	50	25

Model 802 Plinkster

Bolt-action rifle chambered in .22 LR with 18" steel barrel and black synthetic stock with schnabel. Also available with 4X scope package (add 10 percent). Introduced 2006.

NIB	Exc.	V.G.	Good	Fair	Poor
150	125	100	75	50	25

Model 817 Plinkster

Similar to Model 802 Plinkster bolt-action but chambered in .17 HMR. Introduced in 2007.

NIB	Exc.	V.G.	Good	Fair	Poor
175	150	125	100	75	50

Model 810

A .270 to .338 Winchester Magnum caliber bolt-action rifle with a 22" or 24" barrel fitted with a folding rear sight. Blued with a Monte Carlo-style stock. Introduced in 1970.

NIB	Exc.	V.G.	Good	Fair	Poor
—	275	250	200	150	100

Model 472C

A .30-30 or .35 Remington caliber lever-action rifle with a 20" barrel, open sights and tubular magazine. Blued with a walnut stock. Introduced in 1972.

NIB	Exc.	V.G.	Good	Fair	Poor
—	250	195	150	100	75

Model 472P

As above, with a pistol grip stock and not fitted with a saddle ring.

NIB	Exc.	V.G.	Good	Fair	Poor
—	250	195	150	100	75

Model 472 One in Five Thousand

As above, with an etched receiver, brass buttplate, saddle ring and barrel band. A total of 5,000 were made in 1974.

NIB	Exc.	V.G.	Good	Fair	Poor
—	400	350	300	200	150

Model 479 PCA

Similar to the Model 472C in .30-30 caliber with a 20" barrel. Blued with a walnut stock.

NIB	Exc.	V.G.	Good	Fair	Poor
—	250	195	150	100	75

Model 479 RR (Roy Rogers)

As above, with a gold-plated trigger, barrel band as well as "Roy Rogers" signature. A total of 5,000 were made in 1983.

NIB	Exc.	V.G.	Good	Fair	Poor
—	325	250	200	150	100

Model 464 Lever-Action Centerfire

Side-loading, top-ejecting lever rifle with button-rifled 20" barrel, blued finish and hardwood stock. Straight or pistol-grip stock. Tang-mounted thumb safety. Chambered in .30-30.

NIB	Exc.	V.G.	Good	Fair	Poor
—	400	350	300	200	150

Model 464 Lever-Action Rimfire

A rimfire version of the above with 18" barrel.

NIB	Exc.	V.G.	Good	Fair	Poor
—	375	300	250	200	150

SSi-One Sporter

Introduced in 2000 this is a single-shot rifle chambered for the .223, .243, 270 Win., .308 and .30-06 cartridges. Fitted with a 24" barrel without sights. Matte blue finish. Checkered walnut stock. Weight is about 8 lbs. Interchangeable barrels including 12 gauge.

NIB	Exc.	V.G.	Good	Fair	Poor
475	375	300	225	175	125

SSi-One Varmint

Similar to the single-shot model above, but fitted with a 24" bull barrel chambered for the .22-250 cartridge. Walnut stock. Weight is about 10 lbs. Introduced in 2000. Interchangeable barrels.

NIB	Exc.	V.G.	Good	Fair	Poor
475	375	300	225	175	125

SSi-One Slug

This single-shot model is similar to the other SSi-One guns but is fitted with a 24" fully rifled 12 gauge barrel. Walnut stock. Weight is about 8 lbs. Interchangeable barrels. Introduced in 2000.

NIB	Exc.	V.G.	Good	Fair	Poor
475	375	300	225	175	125

SSi-One Turkey

Same as above but with 24" smoothbore barrel. Will handle 3.5" magnum 12 gauge shells. Weight is about 7.5 lbs. Introduced in 2001.

NIB	Exc.	V.G.	Good	Fair	Poor
475	375	300	225	175	125

Model 1500

A .223 to .338 Winchester Magnum bolt-action rifle with a 22" or 24" barrel, 5- or 6-shot magazine and various sights. Blued with a hardwood or walnut stock. Manufactured by Howa in Japan and also known as the Smith & Wesson Model 1500. Offered in 1986 and 1987.

Mountaineer Grade I

NIB	Exc.	V.G.	Good	Fair	Poor
—	350	250	225	150	125

Mountaineer Grade II

NIB	Exc.	V.G.	Good	Fair	Poor
—	325	275	250	175	125

Varmint

24" heavy barrel.

NIB	Exc.	V.G.	Good	Fair	Poor
—	350	300	275	200	150

Model 1550

As above, but in .243, .270 or .30-06 caliber. Offered in 1986 and 1987.

NIB	Exc.	V.G.	Good	Fair	Poor
—	325	275	250	175	125

Model 1700 LS

Similar to the above and in the same calibers with a 22" barrel not fitted for sights, machine jeweled bolt and knurled bolt handle. Blued with a walnut stock and schnabel fore-end. Offered in 1986 and 1987.

NIB	Exc.	V.G.	Good	Fair	Poor
—	400	350	275	200	150

Mossberg 4X4

Bolt-action centerfire rifle chambered in .25-06, .270, .30-06, 7mm Rem Magnum, .300 Win Magnum, .338 Win Magnum. Barrel length 22" (iron sight) or 24" (sightless). Detachable box magazine, two-position safety. Walnut, laminated or black synthetic stock with lightening cutouts in butt and fore-end. Scope package also available. Introduced in 2007.

NIB	Exc.	V.G.	Good	Fair	Poor
475	375	300	225	175	125

Mossberg 4X4 Classic Stock Synthetic

Similar to above but with black synthetic stock and Marinecote metal surfaces.

NIB	Exc.	V.G.	Good	Fair	Poor
—	450	350	275	200	125

Mossberg 4X4 Scoped Combo

Similar to above but with matte blue finish and 3x9 scope. Various stock compositions, including laminate.

NIB	Exc.	V.G.	Good	Fair	Poor
—	450	350	275	200	125

Mossberg 4X4 Classic Walnut Stock

Similar to above but with checkered walnut stock.

NIB	Exc.	V.G.	Good	Fair	Poor
—	500	450	350	225	150

SHOTGUNS

Mossberg manufactured a variety of shotguns that were sold at low to moderate prices. The values for these arms are approximately all the same.

Miscellaneous Bolt-Action Shotguns

Model 73	Model 195D
Model 173	Model 195K
Model 173Y	Model 385K
Model 183D	Model 385T
Model 183K	Model 390K
Model 183T	Model 390T
Model 185D	Model 395K
Model 185K	Model 395S
Model 190D	Model 395T
Model 190K	

Model 190D

NIB	Exc.	V.G.	Good	Fair	Poor
—	150	125	90	65	35

Model 695

Introduced in 1969 this bolt-action shotgun is chambered for the 12 gauge shell. Barrel length is 22" with either a rifled bore or plain bore. Finish is matte blue. In 1997 this model was offered with a 22" plain ported barrel with rifled bore. Magazine capacity is 3 rounds. Weight is about 7.5 lbs.

NIB	Exc.	V.G.	Good	Fair	Poor
275	225	175	150	125	100

Model 695 Camo

Introduced in 2000 this model is the same as the standard Model 695 with the addition of Woodlands camo finish.

NIB	Exc.	V.G.	Good	Fair	Poor
375	325	275	250	195	150

Model 200K

A 12 gauge slide-action shotgun with a 28" barrel and Mossberg select choke. Blued with a composition slide handle and walnut stock. Manufactured from 1955 to 1959.

NIB	Exc.	V.G.	Good	Fair	Poor
—	150	125	100	75	50

MODEL 500 SERIES

A 12, 20 or .410 bore slide-action shotgun manufactured in a variety of barrel lengths and styles as listed.

Model 500 Regal

NIB	Exc.	V.G.	Good	Fair	Poor
—	250	200	150	100	75

Model 500 Field Grade

NIB	Exc.	V.G.	Good	Fair	Poor
285	250	200	150	100	75

Model 500 Steel Shot

Chrome bore.

NIB	Exc.	V.G.	Good	Fair	Poor
—	300	250	200	125	100

Model 500 Slugster

Crown grade, iron sights.

NIB	Exc.	V.G.	Good	Fair	Poor
—	275	250	200	150	100

Model 500 Camper

18.5" barrel, camo case.

NIB	Exc.	V.G.	Good	Fair	Poor
—	295	275	225	175	100

Model 500 Hi-Rib Trap

NIB	Exc.	V.G.	Good	Fair	Poor
—	275	250	200	150	100

Model 500 Super Grade

NIB	Exc.	V.G.	Good	Fair	Poor
—	300	275	225	175	100

Model 500 Pigeon Grade

NIB	Exc.	V.G.	Good	Fair	Poor
—	375	300	250	200	125

Model 500 Pigeon Grade Trap

NIB	Exc.	V.G.	Good	Fair	Poor
—	450	375	300	250	175

Model 500 Persuader

Riot gun, 18.5" barrel in 12 gauge. 20" barrel in 20 gauge (added 2008).

NIB	Exc.	V.G.	Good	Fair	Poor
300	275	225	175	100	75

Model 500 Mariner

Marinecote finish.

NIB	Exc.	V.G.	Good	Fair	Poor
400	325	225	200	150	125

Model 500 Cruiser

Pistol grip only.

NIB	Exc.	V.G.	Good	Fair	Poor
375	300	250	200	125	100

Model 500 Muzzleloader Combo

NIB	Exc.	V.G.	Good	Fair	Poor
350	325	275	225	200	150

Model 500 Bantam

Introduced in 1996 this model is slightly smaller overall than the full-size guns. Chambered for the 20 gauge shell it is fitted with a 22" shotgun barrel or 24" rifled vent rib barrel. Walnut stock. Weight is about 6.9 lbs.

NIB	Exc.	V.G.	Good	Fair	Poor
275	225	200	150	125	100

Model 500 Super Bantam Field

Introduced in 2005 this model features a 20 gauge 3" chamber with 22" ventilated rib barrel with choke tubes. Blued finish. Synthetic stock with adjustabe length of pull. Weight is about 5.25 lbs.

NIB	Exc.	V.G.	Good	Fair	Poor
315	275	175	125	100	75

Model 500 Super Bantam Turkey

This 20 gauge 3" model has a 22" vent rib ported barrel with extra full choke. Synthetic camo stock. Adjustable stock for length of pull. Weight is about 5.25 lbs. Introduced in 2005.

NIB	Exc.	V.G.	Good	Fair	Poor
375	325	250	175	150	100

Model 500 Super Bantam Slug

This 20 gauge model features a full rifled 24" ported barrel with adjustable sights. Synthetic stock with blue or camo finish. Weight is about 5.25 lbs. Introduced in 2005. In 2008, a version with an integrated scope base was added to this series.

NIB	Exc.	V.G.	Good	Fair	Poor
375	325	250	175	150	100

Model 500 Super Bantam Combo

This model introduced in 2005, features a 22" vent rib barrel with choke tubes and a 24" fully rifled ported barrel. Camo finish with adjustable length of pull synthetic stock. Weight is about 5.25 lbs.

NIB	Exc.	V.G.	Good	Fair	Poor
400	325	275	200	150	125

Model 500 Bullpup

A 12 gauge slide-action Bullpup shotgun with an 18.5" or 20" shrouded barrel. Matte black finish with a composition stock. Introduced in 1986. Discontinued. Values shown are for 6-shot version. **NOTE:** Add 215 percent for 8-shot.

NIB	Exc.	V.G.	Good	Fair	Poor
600	500	375	250	150	100

Model 500 Slug Gun Viking Grade

Introduced in 1996 this model is a 12 gauge gun with 24" rifled barrel with iron sights and green synthetic stock. **NOTE:** In 1997 Mossberg introduced ported barrels on some of its slug models. These ported barrels will be seen on rifled barrels only.

NIB	Exc.	V.G.	Good	Fair	Poor
300	275	225	175	100	75

Model 500 Grand Slam Turkey

This 12 or 20 gauge 3" gun was introduced in 2004. Offered with a 20" vent rib barrel with adjustable fiber optic sights and ported Extra Full choke tube. Available in Realtree Hardwood or Mossy Oak Break-Up camo pattern. Weight is about 7 lbs. for the 12 gauge gun and about 6.75 lbs. for the 20 gauge.

NIB	Exc.	V.G.	Good	Fair	Poor
375	325	250	175	150	100

Model 500 Flyway Series

Introduced in 2005 this model is a 12 gauge 3.5" gun with 28" vent rib barrel with fiber optic front sight. Choke tubes. Advantage camo synthetic stock. Weight is about 7.5 lbs.

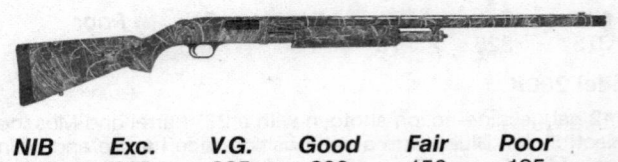

NIB	Exc.	V.G.	Good	Fair	Poor
400	325	225	200	150	125

Model 500 Combo

The 500 series has a total of nine combination sets available to choose from. They are a combination of shotgun barrels and rifled barrels for different hunting applications. They are offered in both 12 and 20 gauge sets of the same gauge only.

NIB	Exc.	V.G.	Good	Fair	Poor
400	325	275	225	175	125

Model 500 USA

Introduced in 1997 this model is similar to the military model. It has a Parkerized finish with heavy-duty sling swivels. Fitted with a plain 20" barrel choked Cylinder. Stock is black synthetic. Magazine capacity is 6 rounds. Weight is about 7.2 lbs.

NIB	Exc.	V.G.	Good	Fair	Poor
250	200	175	150	125	100

Model 500 HS (Home Security)

This shotgun is chambered for the .410 shell and fitted with an 18.5" barrel. Five-round magazine capacity. Synthetic stock and blue finish. **NOTE:** In 1999 Mossberg offered a .50 muzzleloader 24" fully rifled barrel that will fit directly onto any six-shot Model 500.

NIB	Exc.	V.G.	Good	Fair	Poor
350	325	275	225	200	150

Porting on most 500 series and 835 series vent rib and slug barrels

Model 500 Rolling Thunder

This home defense/tactical model is a 3" 12 gauge featuring a pistol grip, 23" barrel with heat shield and recoil-reducing stabilizer and six-round capacity.

NIB	Exc.	V.G.	Good	Fair	Poor
400	325	275	225	175	125

Model 500 Tactical Cruiser "Door Buster"

Similar to above but with serrated muzzle. A TALO exclusive.

NIB	Exc.	V.G.	Good	Fair	Poor
525	425	325	225	175	125

Model 500 Tactical

The Model 500 Tactical 8-shot pump has a 20" barrel and ghost ring sights. Black synthetic pistol-grip stock can be adjusted to provide a 10.75" to a 14-5/8" length of pull. Weight: 6.25 lbs. Capacity: 7+1. Matte blue finish.

NIB	Exc.	V.G.	Good	Fair	Poor
480	440	400	370	320	280

Model 500 JIC (Just In Case)

This survival model is a 3" 12 gauge featuring a pistol grip, 18.5" barrel and a weatherproof pack tube. Three different models available with different finishes and accessory packages. **NOTE:** Add 15 percent for nickel finish. Add 10 percent for JIC II with black finish in black nylon case.

NIB	Exc.	V.G.	Good	Fair	Poor
375	325	250	175	150	100

Model 505 Youth

Offered in 20 gauge or .410 bore this model is fitted with a 20" vent rib barrel with choke tubes for the 20 gauge and fixed modified choke for the .410 bore. Wood stock with recoil pad. Blued finish. Weight is about 5.25 lbs.

NIB	Exc.	V.G.	Good	Fair	Poor
315	275	175	125	100	75

Model 510 Mini Shotgun

Compact pump-action shotgun based on Model 500 action, chambered in 3" 20 gauge and .410 bore. Features include an 18.5" vent rib barrel with interchangeable (20 gauge) or fixed (.410 bore) choke, black synthetic stock, inserts to adjust length of pull from 10.5" to 11.5" and 4-shot capacity. Weight 5 lbs.

NIB	Exc.	V.G.	Good	Fair	Poor
315	275	175	125	100	75

MODEL 535 SERIES

Model 535 ATS (All Terrain Shotgun) Field

Introduced in 2005 this 12 gauge 3.5" model features a 28" vent rib barrel with choke tubes. Blued finish with checkered wood stock with pistol grip. Weight is about 6.75 lbs.

NIB	Exc.	V.G.	Good	Fair	Poor
375	325	250	175	150	100

Model 535 ATS Turkey

As above but with 22" vent rib barrel with extra full choke and fiber optic front sight. Synthetic stock with matte blue or camo finish. Weight is about 6.5 lbs. Introduced in 2005. **NOTE:** Add $55 for camo finish.

NIB	Exc.	V.G.	Good	Fair	Poor
375	325	250	175	150	100

Model 535 ATS Waterfowl

This model is fitted with 28" vent rib barrel with choke tubes and fiber optic front sight. Synthetic stock with matte blue or camo finish. Weight is about 6.75 lbs. Introduced in 2005. **NOTE:** Add $55 for camo finish.

NIB	Exc.	V.G.	Good	Fair	Poor
375	325	250	175	150	100

Model 535 ATS Slugster

Fitted with a fully rifled 24" vent rib barrel with adjustable sights. Choice of matte blue or camo finish and synthetic stock. Weight is about 7 lbs.

NIB	Exc.	V.G.	Good	Fair	Poor
375	325	250	175	150	100

Model 535 ATS Combos

This set is offered in several different configurations: Field/Deer, 28" and 24"; Turkey/Deer, 22" and 24"; Turkey/Slug/Waterfowl,

22" and 28". Weights are from 6.5 to 7 lbs. depending on barrel length. Introduced in 2005. **NOTE:** Add $55 for camo finish.

NIB	Exc.	V.G.	Good	Fair	Poor
475	400	350	225	150	175

MODEL 590 SERIES

Model 590 Special Purpose

Fitted with a 20" shrouded barrel, bayonet lug, Parkerized or blued finish. Speed feed stock and ghost ring sights. Introduced in 1987. Weight is about 7.25 lbs.

NIB	Exc.	V.G.	Good	Fair	Poor
325	275	200	175	125	100

Model 590 Mariner

Marinecote finish.

NIB	Exc.	V.G.	Good	Fair	Poor
425	350	275	225	150	100

Model 590DA

This 12 gauge model, introduced in 2000, features a 6-round tubular magazine and an 18.5" barrel. Choice of plain bead sight or ghost ring sights. Choke is fixed Modified. Weight is about 7 lbs. A 14" barreled model is also offered but NFA rules apply. **NOTE:** Add $50 for ghost ring sights.

NIB	Exc.	V.G.	Good	Fair	Poor
500	400	300	200	150	100

Model 590 Bullpup

The Model 500 with a 20" barrel and 9-shot magazine. Introduced in 1989. Discontinued.

NIB	Exc.	V.G.	Good	Fair	Poor
600	500	400	250	200	125

Model 590A1 Blackwater

The 590A1 Blackwater pump is a 12 gauge with 3" chamber, a 20" long heavy-walled barrel, measures 41" overall and has ghost ring/AR-style sights. Length of pull is 13-7/8". Features a synthetic Speedfeed stock and Parkerized finish. Thumb safety is atop the receiver. Capacity is 8+1 rounds, weight is 7.25 lbs. Blackwater logo etched on receiver.

NIB	Exc.	V.G.	Good	Fair	Poor
585	500	425	350	300	150

Model 590 Tri Rail

The Tri-Rail Model 590 pump gun is chambered for 3" 12 gauge loads and features a protective heat shield on its 20" barrel. Overall length is 40-7/8". Has synthetic Speedfeed stock and bead front sight. Features a Tri-Rail fore-end with removable side rails and an integral bottom rail. Extended magazine gives the gun an 8+1 capacity. Matte blue finish. Length of pull is 13.8". Weight: 7.25 lbs.

NIB	Exc.	V.G.	Good	Fair	Poor
540	490	440	390	300	150

Model 590 A1

The Model 590A1 features an adjustable aluminum stock and ghost ring sights. Heavy-walled barrel is 20" long. Length of pull can be adjusted between 10.5" and 14.25". Weight: 7.5 lbs. Capacity: 8+1. Parkerized finish.

NIB	Exc.	V.G.	Good	Fair	Poor
480	420	325	250	200	125

MODEL 835 SERIES

Model 835 Ulti-Mag

A 12 gauge Magnum slide-action shotgun with a choice of 24" or 28" ventilated rib barrel fitted for choke tubes, 6-shot magazine and either composition camo or walnut stock. Barrel is ported. Introduced in 1988. In 1998 this model was offered with Shadow Grass camo pattern on both stock and barrel. In 1999 this model was offered with Woodland camo. Weight is 7.3 to 7.7 lbs. In 2000 this model was offered with Realtree Hardwoods camo finish.

NIB	Exc.	V.G.	Good	Fair	Poor
425	350	275	225	150	100

Model 835 Ulti-Mag Viking Grade

Introduced in 1996 this model features a 12 gauge 3.5" magnum chambered with green synthetic stock and Modified choke tube. Furnished with 28" vent rib barrel.

NIB	Exc.	V.G.	Good	Fair	Poor
300	250	200	175	125	100

Model 835 Ulti-Mag Crown Grade

The Crown Grade features checkered walnut stock with fluted comb. It is chambered for the 12 gauge with 3.5" chamber. Offered in 24" or 28" vent rib barrels with blued or camo finish. Weight is about 7.3 to 7.7 lbs.

NIB	Exc.	V.G.	Good	Fair	Poor
375	300	225	200	150	100

Model 835 Ulti-Mag Crown Grade Combo Model

Same as above but offered with both a 28" vent rib barrel and a 24" rifled barrel with iron sights.

NIB	Exc.	V.G.	Good	Fair	Poor
425	325	250	225	175	150

Model 835 Ulti-Mag Grand Slam Turkey

Introduced in 2004 this 12 gauge 3.5" model features a 20" vent rib overbored barrel with Extra Full ported choke tube. Magazine capacity is 6 rounds for 2.75" shells, 5 rounds for 3" and 4 rounds for 3.5" shells. Adjustable fiber optic sights. Available in Realtree Hardwoods camo or Mossy Oak Break-Up. Weight is about 7.25 lbs.

NIB	Exc.	V.G.	Good	Fair	Poor
400	325	275	225	175	125

Model 835 Ulti-Mag Thumbhole Turkey

New in 2006, this dedicated pump-action 12 gauge turkey gun features a thumbhole stock and overbored barrel. Chambered for 3.5" shells. X-Factor ported choke tube. Barrel is 20" and has adjustable fiber-optic front and rear sights. Weight is about 7.75 lbs. Available in Mossy Oak New Break-Up camo or Realtree Hardwoods Green camo.

NIB	Exc.	V.G.	Good	Fair	Poor
475	400	325	250	200	125

Model 835 Ulti-Mag Tactical Turkey

Same as above but with extended pistol grip stock that is adjustable for length of pull from 10.75" to 14.5".

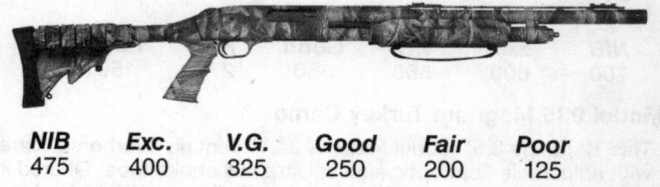

NIB	Exc.	V.G.	Good	Fair	Poor
475	400	325	250	200	125

Model 835 Wild Turkey Federation

As above, with a Wild Turkey Federation medallion inlaid in the stock. Introduced in 1989.

NIB	Exc.	V.G.	Good	Fair	Poor
475	400	325	250	200	125

Model 835 American Field

This 12 gauge model has a checkered walnut stock, 28" ventilated rib barrel with Modified choke tube. Weight is about 7.7 lbs.

NIB	Exc.	V.G.	Good	Fair	Poor
300	275	225	200	150	100

MODEL 935 MAGNUM SERIES

The 935 Magnum series of guns was introduced in 2004.

Model 935 Magnum Waterfowl Camo

This 12 gauge 3.5" semi-automatic shotgun is available with either a 26" or 28" vent rib overbored barrel with fiber optic bead and choke tubes. Offered with choice of Mossy Oak Break-Up or Advantage Max-4 camo pattern. Magazine capacity is 5 rounds of 3" and 4 rounds of 3.5". Weight is about 7.75 lbs.

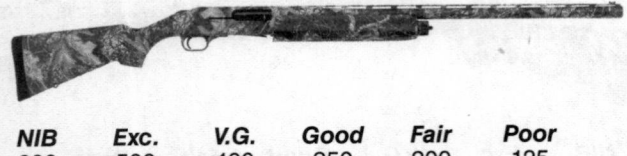

NIB	Exc.	V.G.	Good	Fair	Poor
600	500	400	250	200	125

Model 935 Magnum Slugster

Similar to above but with 24" fully rifled barrel, rifle sights, Realtree AP camo overall.

NIB	Exc.	V.G.	Good	Fair	Poor
600	500	400	250	200	125

Model 935 Magnum Turkey/Deer Comb

Similar to above but with interchangeable 24" Turkey barrel, Mossy Oak New Break-up camo overall.

NIB	Exc.	V.G.	Good	Fair	Poor
700	600	500	350	275	150

Model 935 Magnum Turkey Camo

This 12 gauge 3.5" model features a 24" vent rib overbored barrel with adjustable fiber optic sights. Ultra Full choke tube. Offered in Mossy Oak Break-Up or Hardwoods HD-Green. Weight is about 7.75 lbs.

NIB	Exc.	V.G.	Good	Fair	Poor
600	500	400	250	200	125

Model 935 Magnum Turkey Pistol Grip

Similar to above but with full pistol grip stock.

NIB	Exc.	V.G.	Good	Fair	Poor
625	525	425	275	225	150

Model 935 Magnum Waterfowl Synthetic

This 12 gauge 3.5" gun features a choice of 26" or 28" vent rib overbored barrel with choke tubes. Fiber optic bead. Matte black finish with black synthetic stock. Weight is about 7.75 lbs.

NIB	Exc.	V.G.	Good	Fair	Poor
550	450	350	250	150	125

Model 935 Magnum Turkey Synthetic

As above but with 24" vent rib overbored barrel with Ultra Full choke tube. Weight is about 7.75 lbs.

NIB	Exc.	V.G.	Good	Fair	Poor
550	450	350	250	150	125

Model 935 Magnum Waterfowl/Turkey Combo

Similar to above but with 24" Turkey and 28" Waterfowl barrels, Mossy Oak New Break-up finish overall.

NIB	Exc.	V.G.	Good	Fair	Poor
800	650	500	400	250	150

Model 935 Grand Slam Turkey

This 12 gauge 3.5" model features a a 22" vent rib overbored barrel with Extra Full ported choke tube. Adjustable fiber optic sights. Offered in Realtree Hardwoods green or Mossy Oak Break-Up camo pattern. Camo sling included. Weight is about 7.5 lbs.

NIB	Exc.	V.G.	Good	Fair	Poor
650	550	450	275	225	150

MODEL 930 SERIES

This is a 12 gauge 3" chamber semi-automatic shotgun series introduced in 2005.

Model 930 Field

This 12 gauge 3" gun is fitted with either 26" or 28" vent rib barrels with choke tubes. The barrel is ported. Checkered walnut stock with recoil pad. Magazine capacity is 5 rounds. Blued finish. Weight is about 7.75 lbs.

NIB	Exc.	V.G.	Good	Fair	Poor
525	425	325	225	175	125

Model 930 Turkey

Fitted with a synthetic stock and 24" vent rib ported barrel. Chokes are extra full extended tubes. Offered with matte blue finish or camo finish. Weight is about 7.5 lbs. **NOTE:** Add $100 for camo finish.

NIB	Exc.	V.G.	Good	Fair	Poor
500	400	300	200	150	100

Model 930 Turkey Pistol Grip

Similar to above but with full pistol grip stock, matte black or Mossy Oak Obsession camo finish overall.

NIB	Exc.	V.G.	Good	Fair	Poor
650	550	450	275	225	150

Model 930 Waterfowl

This model is fitted with a 28" vent rib ported barrel with choke tubes. Choice of matte blue or camo finish. Weight is about 7.75 lbs. **NOTE:** Add $100 for camo finish.

NIB	Exc.	V.G.	Good	Fair	Poor
500	400	300	200	150	100

Model 930 Slugster

This model features a 24" vent rib ported barrel with choice of plain or Monte Carlo synthetic stock. Matte blue or camo finish. Weight is about 7.5 lbs. **NOTE:** Add $100 for camo finish.

NIB	Exc.	V.G.	Good	Fair	Poor
525	425	325	225	175	125

Model 930 Tactical

This 3" 12 gauge has an 18.5" barrel and cylinder bore. Synthetic stock with matte black finish. **NOTE:** Add $75 for ventilated heat shield.

NIB	Exc.	V.G.	Good	Fair	Poor
500	400	300	200	150	100

Model 930 Road Blocker

Similar to above but with muzzle brake.

NIB	Exc.	V.G.	Good	Fair	Poor
525	425	325	225	175	125

Model 930 SPX

Billed as a "home security" model, the 3" 12 gauge SPX has a 7-round magazine tube, 18.5" barrel, picatinny rail, ghost ring rear sight and fiber-optic front sight. **NOTE:** Deduct 10 percent for white dot sights.

NIB	Exc.	V.G.	Good	Fair	Poor
500	400	300	225	150	125

Model 930 Home Security/Field Combo

Combo unit with 18.5" Cylinder bore barrel and 28" ported Field barrel; black synthetic stock and matte black finish.

NIB	Exc.	V.G.	Good	Fair	Poor
600	500	400	300	200	150

MODEL 3000 SERIES

Model 3000

A 12 or 20 gauge slide-action shotgun manufactured in a variety of barrel lengths and styles. Blued with a walnut stock. Also known as the Smith & Wesson Model 3000.

NIB	Exc.	V.G.	Good	Fair	Poor
—	325	250	175	125	75

Model 3000 Waterfowl

As above, but matte finished, fitted with sling swivels and accompanied by a camouflage sling. Produced in 1986.

NIB	Exc.	V.G.	Good	Fair	Poor
—	350	275	200	150	100

Model 3000 Law Enforcement

As above, with an 18.5" or 20" cylinder-bore barrel. Manufactured in 1986 and 1987.

NIB	Exc.	V.G.	Good	Fair	Poor
—	375	275	200	150	100

MODEL 1000 SERIES

Model 1000

A 12 or 20 gauge semi-automatic shotgun manufactured in a variety of barrel lengths and styles. The receiver of an aluminum alloy and blued. Also known as the Smith & Wesson Model 1000. Offered in 1986 and 1987.

NIB	Exc.	V.G.	Good	Fair	Poor
—	300	250	200	150	100

Model 1000 Slug

As above, with a 22" barrel fitted with rifle sights. Offered in 1986 and 1987.

NIB	Exc.	V.G.	Good	Fair	Poor
—	325	250	200	125	100

Model 1000 Super Series

As above, with a steel receiver and a self-regulating gas system that allows the use of either standard or Magnum shells.

NIB	Exc.	V.G.	Good	Fair	Poor
—	375	300	250	150	100

Model 1000 Super Waterfowl

Matte finish.

NIB	Exc.	V.G.	Good	Fair	Poor
—	375	300	250	150	100

Model 1000 Super Slug
Rifle sights.

NIB	Exc.	V.G.	Good	Fair	Poor
—	375	300	250	150	100

Model 1000 Super Trap
30" high rib barrel.

NIB	Exc.	V.G.	Good	Fair	Poor
—	395	325	275	175	125

Model 1000 Super Skeet
25" barrel.

NIB	Exc.	V.G.	Good	Fair	Poor
—	395	325	275	175	125

MODEL 9200 SERIES
This model has a variety of configurations. It is a 12 gauge semi-automatic with a choice of walnut stock or camo synthetic stock. Barrel lengths are from 22" to 28". Weights range from 7 to 7.7 lbs.

Model 9200 Viking Grade

NIB	Exc.	V.G.	Good	Fair	Poor
350	300	275	200	100	75

Model 9200 USST Crown Grade

NIB	Exc.	V.G.	Good	Fair	Poor
400	350	300	200	100	75

Model 9200 Combos

NIB	Exc.	V.G.	Good	Fair	Poor
475	425	350	250	150	100

Model 9200 Special Hunter
28" vent rib barrel with synthetic stock.

NIB	Exc.	V.G.	Good	Fair	Poor
475	425	350	250	150	100

Model 9200 Deer Combo

NIB	Exc.	V.G.	Good	Fair	Poor
475	425	350	250	150	100

Model 9200 Turkey Camo

NIB	Exc.	V.G.	Good	Fair	Poor
475	425	350	250	150	100

Model 9200 Crown Grade Bantam

NIB	Exc.	V.G.	Good	Fair	Poor
395	350	300	250	125	75

Model 9200 Jungle Gun
This is a 12 gauge auto-loader fitted with a plain 18.5" barrel with bead sight. Barrel choked Cylinder. Chambers are 2.75". Magazine capacity is 5 rounds. Parkerized finish. Synthetic stock.

NIB	Exc.	V.G.	Good	Fair	Poor
525	450	325	200	150	125

Model SA-20
This synthetic-stocked, matte black 20 gauge autoloader is chambered for 3" shells. It has a 26" or 28" vent-rib barrel and comes with five choke tubes. Weight is about 6 lbs. The Bantam model has a 1" shorter length of pull and 24" barrel. Weighs about 5.6 lbs. Introduced in 2008.

NIB	Exc.	V.G.	Good	Fair	Poor
400	350	300	200	100	75

Model SA-20 Tactical
Mossberg's SA-20 Tactical Autoloader is in 20 gauge only. Easy-Load elevator facilitates fast, one-handed reloading. Top-mounted Picatinny-style rail accommodates optical sights, while the magazine tube rail allows mounting lights, lasers and other accessories. Ghost ring rear and fiber optic front sights. Gas-

operated action. Capacity: 4+1. Cylinder-bore barrel is 20" long. Available with conventional black synthetic or synthetic pistol grip stock. Weight is approximately 6 lbs.

NIB	Exc.	V.G.	Good	Fair	Poor
480	440	400	370	320	280

Model 5500 MKI I

A 12 gauge semi-automatic shotgun supplied with either a 26" barrel for 2.75" shells or a 28" barrel for 3" shells. Blued with a walnut stock. Introduced in 1989.

NIB	Exc.	V.G.	Good	Fair	Poor
300	235	200	175	150	125

RESERVE SERIES

Introduced in 2005 and 2008 these are over/under side-by-side guns in 12, 20, 28 gauge and .410 bore. Made in Turkey.

Silver Reserve Field Over/Under

Offered in 12 gauge with 28" vent rib barrels, 20 gauge with 26" or 28" vent rib barrels, 28 gauge with 26" vent rib barrels, .410 with 26" vent rib barrels. All gauges have choke tubes except for the .410 with fixed chokes. Steel silvered receiver with scroll engraving and game scenes in gold. Checkered walnut stock with recoil pad. Single trigger. Weight is from 6 lbs. to 7.7 lbs. depending on gauge. **NOTE:** Add 20 percent for 28 gauge and .410 bore.

NIB	Exc.	V.G.	Good	Fair	Poor
600	500	300	200	150	100

Silver Reserve Sporting Over/Under

As above but in 12 gauge only with 28" vent 10mm rib barrels with choke tubes and ported barrels. Weight is about 7.7 lbs.

NIB	Exc.	V.G.	Good	Fair	Poor
700	600	425	300	225	125

Silver Reserve Side-by-Side

New in 2008, the side-by-side version of the Silver Reserve comes in 12 gauge with 26" or 28" barrels, 20 and 28 gauge with 26" barrels. The stock and fore-end is select black walnut with satin finish. The receiver is satin-finished silver with scroll engraving and barrels are blued. Bores are chrome-plated. All models come with five choke tubes. Weight is 6.4 to 6.5 lbs. for 20 and 28 gauges; 7.2 lbs. for 12 gauge.

NIB	Exc.	V.G.	Good	Fair	Poor
850	750	600	450	250	150

Onyx Reserve Sporting Side-by-Side

Similar to Silver Reserve Sporting but with blued receiver.

NIB	Exc.	V.G.	Good	Fair	Poor
800	700	575	400	225	150

MOUNTAIN ARMS
Ozark, Missouri

Wildcat

Similar to Rau Arms Wildcat (q.v.) and Garcia Bronco but with plastic stock inserts. A takedown model was offered as well. Estimated 6,243 produced 1971-1978. The first several thousand bore the Rau Arms label.

NIB	Exc.	V.G.	Good	Fair	Poor
225	175	125	100	65	35

MOUNTAIN RIFLES, INC.
Palmer, Alaska

Mountaineer

This bolt-action rifle, introduced in 1997, is built on a Remington action with Model 70 style bolt release. A factory muzzlebrake is installed with open sights. A Timney trigger is standard. Stock is fiberglass. Finish is Parkerized. This model is chambered for many different calibers, from .223 Rem. to .416 Rem., including Dakota and Weatherby cartridges. Weight starts at about 6 lbs. and is dependent on caliber. There are several options that will affect price. A left-hand model is offered as an option.

NIB	Exc.	V.G.	Good	Fair	Poor
2195	1750	1400	1100	750	300

Super Mountaineer

Similar to the Mountaineer model but the bolt is fluted and hollow. Barrel is match grade stainless steel with muzzlebrake. Kevlar/Graphite stock. Wide variety of calibers. Weight starts at about 4.25 lbs. depending on caliber.

NIB	Exc.	V.G.	Good	Fair	Poor
2895	2350	1900	1500	1000	400

Pro Mountaineer

This model is built on a Winchester Model 70 action. Premium match grade barrel with muzzlebrake. Model 70 trigger. Stainless steel matte finish. Kevlar/Graphite stock. Wide variety of calibers. Weight starts at about 6 lbs.

NIB	Exc.	V.G.	Good	Fair	Poor
2895	2350	2350	1900	1500	400

Pro Safari

This model is built on an MRI action with controlled feed. Premium match grade barrel. Timney trigger. Matte blue finish. Exhibition grade walnut stock with custom bottom metal. Weight starts at about 7 lbs. depending on caliber. Caliber from .223 to .458 Lott.

NIB	Exc.	V.G.	Good	Fair	Poor
4495	3500	2300	1750	1200	500

Ultra Mountaineer

Built on an MRI action with premium match grade barrel and muzzlebrake. Timney trigger. Parkerized finish. Kevlar/Graphite stock. Calibers from .223 to .505 Gibbs. Weight begins at 5 lbs. depending on caliber. **NOTE:** Add $500 for Rigby-length calibers.

NIB	Exc.	V.G.	Good	Fair	Poor
2995	2500	2200	1900	1500	400

NIB	Exc.	V.G.	Good	Fair	Poor
—	—	50000	33000	14000	1500

MUGICA, JOSE
Eibar, Spain
See—Llama

A trade name found on Llama pistols that were manufactured by Gabilondo.

MURFEESBORO ARMORY
Murfeesboro, Tennessee

Established in 1861 by William Ledbetter. Made copies of U.S. Model 1841 Rifle complete with patchbox and double strapped nose cap. Barrel bands pinned to stock. Between 270 and 390 made from October of 1861 through March of 1862. Overall length 48.75"; barrel length 33"; .54 caliber. Unmarked except for serial number on various parts including the barrel.

NIB	Exc.	V.G.	Good	Fair	Poor
—	—	27500	16500	6600	2000

MURPHY & O'CONNEL
New York, New York

Pocket Pistol

A .41 caliber single-shot percussion pocket pistol with a 3" barrel, German silver mounts and a walnut stock. Manufactured during the 1850s.

NIB	Exc.	V.G.	Good	Fair	Poor
—	—	3500	2950	1100	450

MURRAY, J. P.
Columbus, Georgia

Percussion Rifle

A .58 caliber percussion rifle with a 33" barrel, full stock and brass mounts. Also made with a 23.5" to 24" barrel as a carbine. The lock marked "J.P. Murray/Columbus Ga." Several hundred were manufactured between 1862 and 1864.

Courtesy Milwaukee Public Museum, Milwaukee, Wisconsin

MUSGRAVE
Republic of South Africa
RSA NR I Single-Shot Target Rifle

A .308 caliber single-shot bolt-action rifle with a 26" barrel, match sights, adjustable trigger and target-style stock. Made of walnut. Manufactured between 1971 and 1976.

NIB	Exc.	V.G.	Good	Fair	Poor
—	550	425	300	225	125

Valiant NR6

A .243, .270, .308, .30-06 and 7mm Remington Magnum caliber bolt-action sporting rifle with a 24" barrel, open sights and English-style stock. Imported from 1971 to 1976.

NIB	Exc.	V.G.	Good	Fair	Poor
—	450	350	275	175	125

Premier NR5

As above, with a 26" barrel and pistol grip Monte Carlo-style stock. Discontinued in 1976.

NIB	Exc.	V.G.	Good	Fair	Poor
—	550	450	325	225	150

MUSKETEER RIFLES
Firearms International/Garcia
Washington, D.C.

Sporter

A .243 to .300 Winchester Magnum caliber bolt-action rifle with a 24" barrel without sights and Monte Carlo-style stock. Imported between 1963 and 1972. **NOTE:** Add 20 percent for magnum chamberings.

NIB	Exc.	V.G.	Good	Fair	Poor
—	500	375	275	195	120

Deluxe Sporter

As above, with an adjustable trigger and more finely figured walnut stock.

NIB	Exc.	V.G.	Good	Fair	Poor
—	550	400	300	200	125

Carbine

The Sporter with a 20" barrel.

NIB	Exc.	V.G.	Good	Fair	Poor
—	500	375	275	195	120

N

NATIONAL ARMS CO.
Brooklyn, New York
See—Moore's Patent Firearms Co.

The successor to the Moore's Patent Firearms Company in 1865. Purchased by the Colt Company in 1870.

Large Frame Teat-Fire Revolver

A .45 teat fire caliber revolver with a 7.5" barrel and 6-shot cylinder. Blued or silver-plated with walnut grips. The barrel marked "National Arms Co. Brooklyn". The exact number of these revolvers made is unknown, but it is estimated to be fewer than 30.

NIB	Exc.	V.G.	Good	Fair	Poor
—	—	24500	19000	6050	850

No. 2 Derringer

A .41 caliber spur trigger pocket pistol with a 2.5" barrel. Blued or silver-plated with walnut grips. Later manufactured by the Colt Company as their No. 2 Derringer.

Courtesy Rock Island Auction Company

NIB	Exc.	V.G.	Good	Fair	Poor
—	—	1750	1300	550	150

NAVY ARMS COMPANY
Martinsburg, West Virginia

Not a manufacturer but an importer. Founded in 1957 by Val Forgett to enhance the shooting of blackpowder firearms without destroying the originals. The first replica was the Colt 1851 Navy. Thus, the name of the new company, "Navy Arms". In the early 1980s Navy Arms began importing surplus firearms from European countries. Navy Arms continues to offer both blackpowder replicas and foreign imports. For a short period of time the company imported double-barrel shotguns. This was discontinued in 1990. Most if not all of the guns listed below are also to be found under the manufacturers' names as well as those of other importers.

SHOTGUNS

Model 83

A 12 or 20 gauge Magnum over/under shotgun manufactured in a variety of barrel lengths and styles with double triggers and extractors. Blued, engraved, with a walnut stock. Introduced in 1985.

NIB	Exc.	V.G.	Good	Fair	Poor
500	400	275	200	175	100

Model 93

As above, with automatic ejectors.

NIB	Exc.	V.G.	Good	Fair	Poor
575	475	300	250	200	100

Model 95

As above, with a single trigger and screw-in choke tubes.

NIB	Exc.	V.G.	Good	Fair	Poor
600	500	350	250	200	100

Model 96 Sportsman

As above, in 12 gauge only with a gold-plated receiver.

NIB	Exc.	V.G.	Good	Fair	Poor
600	500	350	250	200	100

Model 100

A 12, 20, 28 or .410 bore over/under boxlock shotgun with 26" ventilated rib barrels, single trigger and extractors. Blued, chrome-plated, with a walnut stock. Introduced in 1989. Add 20 percent for .410.

NIB	Exc.	V.G.	Good	Fair	Poor
450	350	200	150	100	75

Model 100 Side-by-Side

A 12 or 20 gauge Magnum boxlock double-barrel shotgun with 27.5" barrels, double triggers and extractors. Blued with a walnut stock. Imported between 1985 and 1987.

NIB	Exc.	V.G.	Good	Fair	Poor
—	475	350	250	200	100

Model 150

As above, with automatic ejectors.

NIB	Exc.	V.G.	Good	Fair	Poor
—	495	375	300	225	125

Model 105

A 12, 20 or .410 bore folding single barrel shotgun with a 26" or 28" barrel, chrome-plated engraved receiver, blued barrel and hardwood stock. Introduced in 1985.

NIB	Exc.	V.G.	Good	Fair	Poor
125	80	75	65	50	35

Model 105 Deluxe

As above, with vent rib barrel and a checkered walnut stock.

NIB	Exc.	V.G.	Good	Fair	Poor
150	100	85	75	60	45

REPLICA LONG GUNS

Harpers Ferry Flint Rifle

This model is a copy of the 1803 rifle in the original .54 caliber. It features a rust blued 35" barrel. Weight is 8.5 lbs.

NIB	Exc.	V.G.	Good	Fair	Poor
600	475	350	300	200	100

Harpers Ferry "Journey of Discovery" Rifle

Similar to the Harpers Ferry Flint Rifle above but with oil finished walnut stock, brass fittings brass patchbox engraved "Lewis and Clark's Journey of Discovery';1803 to 1806". Introduced in 2003.

NIB	Exc.	V.G.	Good	Fair	Poor
775	600	475	275	175	100

Brown Bess Musket

This replica is a copy of the second model used between 1760 and 1776. Bright finish on metal and one-piece walnut stock with polished brass locks. Barrel is 42" and weight is 9.5 lbs.

NIB	Exc.	V.G.	Good	Fair	Poor
800	625	500	300	200	100

Brown Bess Carbine

Same as above but fitted with a 30" barrel. Weighs 7.75 lbs.

NIB	Exc.	V.G.	Good	Fair	Poor
800	625	500	300	200	100

1777 Charleville Musket

Copy of French flintlock in .69 caliber. Fittings are steel with brass front sight and brass flashpan. Barrel length is 44.625" and weight is about 8.75 lbs

NIB	Exc.	V.G.	Good	Fair	Poor
900	700	550	400	300	150

1777 Standard Charleville Musket

Same as above with polished steel barrel and select walnut stock.

NIB	Exc.	V.G.	Good	Fair	Poor
900	700	550	400	300	150

1816 M.T. Wickham Musket

Furnished in .69 caliber with steel ramrod with button head. Brass flashpan and walnut stock are standard.

NIB	Exc.	V.G.	Good	Fair	Poor
600	550	450	350	250	200

1808 Springfield Musket

This model is a U.S. copy of the 1763 Charleville musket with 1808 Springfield markings. Barrel length is 44" and weight is 8.75 lbs.

NIB	Exc.	V.G.	Good	Fair	Poor
950	800	600	400	200	100

Pennsylvania Long Rifle

This model is offered in either percussion or flintlock ignition and is offered in a choice of .32 caliber or .45 caliber. It has an octagonal

40.5" rust blued barrel, polished lock, double set triggers, and brass furniture on a walnut stock. Weighs 7.5 lbs.

Percussion

NIB	Exc.	V.G.	Good	Fair	Poor
450	375	250	200	150	100

Flintlock

NIB	Exc.	V.G.	Good	Fair	Poor
475	400	275	225	150	100

Kentucky Rifle

Offered in either percussion or flintlock ignition it has a blue steel barrel, case colored lockplate, and a polished brass patch box inletted into a walnut stock. The barrel length is 35" and the rifle is available in .45 oz. 50 caliber. Weight is 6 lbs. 14 oz.

Percussion

NIB	Exc.	V.G.	Good	Fair	Poor
475	325	200	150	100	75

Flintlock

NIB	Exc.	V.G.	Good	Fair	Poor
495	335	225	150	100	75

Mortimer Flintlock Rifle

Offered in .54 caliber with rust blued barrel, walnut stock with cheekpiece and checkered straight grip. It also has a external safety and sling swivels. Barrel length is 36" and weight is 9 lbs. Optional shotgun barrel. Made by Pedersoli. Optional shotgun barrel add $240.

NIB	Exc.	V.G.	Good	Fair	Poor
900	750	600	500	450	150

Tryon Creedmoor Rifle

This .45 caliber model features a heavy blued 33" octagonal barrel, hooded front sight, adjustable tang sight, double set triggers, sling swivels, and a walnut stock. Weighs about 9.5 lbs.

NIB	Exc.	V.G.	Good	Fair	Poor
800	600	525	450	400	150

Standard Tryon Rifle

Same as above but without target sights.

NIB	Exc.	V.G.	Good	Fair	Poor
700	500	350	300	250	200

Deluxe Tryon Rifle

Same as above but with polished and engraved lock and patch box.

NIB	Exc.	V.G.	Good	Fair	Poor
750	525	375	325	250	200

Parker-Hale Whitworth Rifle

This is a replica of a British sniper rifle, .451 caliber, used by the Confederates during the Civil War. Round barrel is 36" and features a globe front sight and ladder rear sight. The walnut stock is hand checkered. Weighs 9 lbs. 10 oz. Limited edition telescope add $150.

NIB	Exc.	V.G.	Good	Fair	Poor
850	675	600	450	300	150

Parker-Hale Volunteer Rifle

A .451 caliber rifle with hand checkered walnut stock. Fitted with 32" barrel with globe front sight and ladder rear sight. Weighs 9.5 lbs.

NIB	Exc.	V.G.	Good	Fair	Poor
825	650	550	400	300	150

Parker-Hale 3 Band Volunteer Rifle

Same basic specifications as Whitworth rifle but furnished with Alexander Henry rifling.

NIB	Exc.	V.G.	Good	Fair	Poor
750	650	600	400	250	50

Rigby Target Rifle

The 1880s replica is chambered for the .451 caliber. It is fitted with adjustable front sight and vernier tang sight. The lock, breech plug, trigger guard, buttplate, and escutcheons are case colored. Barrel length is 32" and weight is 7 lbs. 12 oz.

NIB	Exc.	V.G.	Good	Fair	Poor
700	500	450	300	200	100

1861 Springfield Rifle

This .58 caliber replica is fitted with an 1855-style hammer. Barrel length is 40" and weight is 10 lbs. 4 oz.

NIB	Exc.	V.G.	Good	Fair	Poor
550	425	350	300	200	100

Model 1873 Springfield Officer's Trapdoor

This model features a single set trigger, case colored breechblock, deluxe walnut stock, adjustable rear peep sight with Beech front sight. Chambered for the .45-70 cartridge and fitted with a 26" round barrel. Weight is about 8 lbs. Introduced in 2003.

NIB	Exc.	V.G.	Good	Fair	Poor
900	750	495	350	300	200

1862 C.S. Richmond Rifle

This Confederate rifle is .58 caliber and is a faithful reproduction of those produced at the Richmond Armory. Barrel length is 40". Weighs 10 lbs. 4 oz.

NIB	Exc.	V.G.	Good	Fair	Poor
550	425	350	300	200	100

J.P. Murray Carbine

This Confederate cavalry .58 caliber carbine has a case colored lock and brass furniture on a walnut stock. Barrel length is 23.5" and weight is 8 lbs. 5 oz.

NIB	Exc.	V.G.	Good	Fair	Poor
495	325	250	200	150	100

1863 Springfield Rifle

An exact replica of the famous Springfield Musket. Barrel is 40" with 3 barrel bands. All metal parts are finished bright. Weighs 9.5 lbs.

NIB	Exc.	V.G.	Good	Fair	Poor
550	425	350	300	200	100

1841 Mississippi Rifle

Also known as the "Yager" rifle; offered in either .54 or .58 caliber. Barrel length is 33" and weighs 9.5 lbs.

NIB	Exc.	V.G.	Good	Fair	Poor
450	325	250	200	150	100

Zouave Rifle

This Civil War replica is a .58 caliber with polished brass hardware and blued 33" barrel. Weighs 9 lbs.

NIB	Exc.	V.G.	Good	Fair	Poor
450	325	250	200	150	100

Parker-Hale 1861 Musketoon

Made by Gibbs Rifle Company using 130-year-old gauges for reference. This .577 caliber replica features a 24" barrel with folding ladder military sight. The stock is walnut and the lock is case colored. All furniture is polished brass. Weighs 7.5 lbs.

NIB	Exc.	V.G.	Good	Fair	Poor
400	325	250	200	150	100

Navy Arms Musketoon

Same as above but manufactured in Italy.

NIB	Exc.	V.G.	Good	Fair	Poor
400	325	250	200	150	100

Parker-Hale 1858 Two Band Musket

This .577 caliber model is based on the 1858 Enfield naval pattern. Fitted with a military sight graduated to 1,100 yards. Case colored lock and walnut stock with brass fittings. Barrel length is 33" and weighs 8.5 lbs.

NIB	Exc.	V.G.	Good	Fair	Poor
550	425	350	300	200	100

Navy Arms 1858 Two Band Musket

Same as above but built in Italy.

NIB	Exc.	V.G.	Good	Fair	Poor
450	325	250	200	150	100

Parker-Hale Three Band Musket

This replica is based on the design produced between 1853 and 1863. The rear sight is based on an 1853 model graduated to 900 yards. Is fitted with a case colored lock and walnut stock with brass furniture. Barrel is 39" and weighs 9 lbs.

NIB	Exc.	V.G.	Good	Fair	Poor
600	475	400	300	200	100

Navy Arms Three Band Musket

Same as above but produced in Italy.

NIB	Exc.	V.G.	Good	Fair	Poor
475	350	300	250	200	100

Navy Arms Revolving Carbine

Fitted with a 20" barrel and chambered for the .357 Magnum, .44-40, or .45 Colt cartridge. This model has a revolving 6-shot cylinder. Straight-grip stock with brass buttplate and trigger guard. The action is based on the Remington Model 1874 revolver. Introduced in 1968 and discontinued in 1984.

NIB	Exc.	V.G.	Good	Fair	Poor
600	500	400	300	200	100

1859 Sharps Infantry Rifle

This is a .54 caliber copy of the three band Sharps. Barrel length is 30". Case hardened receiver and patch box. Blued barrel and walnut stock. Weight is about 8.5 lbs.

NIB	Exc.	V.G.	Good	Fair	Poor
1150	800	600	400	300	150

1859 Berdan Sharps Rifle

Similar to the 1859 Sharps above but with double set triggers.

NIB	Exc.	V.G.	Good	Fair	Poor
1200	850	650	450	325	150

1873 Sharps No. 2 Creedmore

Chambered for the .45-70 cartridge and fitted with a 30" round barrel. Polished nickel receiver. Target-grade rear tang sight and front globe sight with inserts. Checkered walnut stock with pistol grip. Weight is about 10 lbs. Introduced in 2002.

NIB	Exc.	V.G.	Good	Fair	Poor
1425	1000	750	550	375	200

Sharps #2 Silhouette Rifle

This model is identical to the standard No. 2 above but with a full octagon barrel. Weight is about 10.5 lbs. Introduced in 2003.

NIB	Exc.	V.G.	Good	Fair	Poor
1325	1000	750	550	375	200

Sharps #2 Sporting Rifle

Same as the No. 2 standard rifle but with case colored receiver. Introduced in 2003.

NIB	Exc.	V.G.	Good	Fair	Poor
1425	1000	750	550	375	200

1873 Sharps Quigley

This model is chambered for the .45-70 cartridge and fitted with a heavy 34" octagon barrel. Case hardened receiver with military patchbox. Open sights. Weight is about 13 lbs. Introduced in 2002.

NIB	Exc.	V.G.	Good	Fair	Poor
1490	1100	850	625	395	225

1874 Sharps Infantry Rifle

This model is fitted with a 30" round barrel and chambered for the .45-70 cartridge. Blued barrel with case hardened receiver. Walnut stock with 3 barrel bands. Weight is about 8.5 lbs.

NIB	Exc.	V.G.	Good	Fair	Poor
1150	800	600	400	300	150

1874 Sharps Sniper Rifle

Same as 1874 Infantry rifle but with double set triggers.

NIB	Exc.	V.G.	Good	Fair	Poor
1200	850	650	450	325	150

Sharps Cavalry Carbine

A breech-loading .54 caliber carbine with 22" blued barrel. Military-style sights, walnut stocks, and saddle bar with ring are standard. Weighs 7 lbs. 12 oz.

NIB	Exc.	V.G.	Good	Fair	Poor
1050	800	600	400	300	150

Sharps Cavalry Carbine Cartridge Model

Same as above but chambered for the .45-70 Government cartridge.

NIB	Exc.	V.G.	Good	Fair	Poor
1150	800	600	400	300	150

1874 Sharps Plains Rifle

This model features a case colored receiver, blued barrel, and checkered walnut stock. Offered in .44-70 or .54 caliber percussion. Barrel length is 28.5". Weight is 8 lbs. 10 oz.

NIB	Exc.	V.G.	Good	Fair	Poor
1150	800	600	400	300	150

1874 Sharps Sporting Rifle

Similar to the above model but features a full pistol grip, 32" medium weight octagonal barrel, double set triggers, and case colored frame. Weight is about 10.75 lbs.

NIB	Exc.	V.G.	Good	Fair	Poor
1325	1000	750	550	375	200

1874 Sharps Buffalo Rifle

Chambered for the .45-70 or .45-90 and fitted with a 28" heavy octagon barrel. Buttstock is checkered. Weight is approximately 12 lbs.

NIB	Exc.	V.G.	Good	Fair	Poor
1325	1000	750	550	375	200

1874 Sharps No. 3 Long Range Rifle

Built by Pedersoli this rifle is fitted with a 34" medium weight octagon barrel, globe target front sight and match grade rear tang sight. Double set trigger. Case hardened frame. Walnut stock. Weight is about 11 lbs.

NIB	Exc.	V.G.	Good	Fair	Poor
1800	1325	950	725	400	300

1873 Winchester Rifle

This replica features a case colored receiver, blued octagon 24" barrel, and walnut stocks. Offered in either .44-40 or .45 Long Colt. Weighs about 8 lbs. 4 oz.

NIB	Exc.	V.G.	Good	Fair	Poor
900	725	600	500	400	200

1873 Winchester Carbine

Same specifications as rifle above but fitted with a 19" round barrel, blued receiver, and saddle ring. Weighs 7 lbs. 4 oz.

NIB	Exc.	V.G.	Good	Fair	Poor
900	725	600	500	400	200

1873 Winchester Sporting Rifle

This model features a 24.25" octagonal barrel, case colored receiver, and checkered pistol grip. Offered in .44-40 or. 45 Long Colt. Weighs about 8 lbs. 14 oz.

NIB	Exc.	V.G.	Good	Fair	Poor
950	750	650	525	400	200

1873 Sporting Long Range Rifle

Similar to the Sporting Rifle above but chambered for the .44-40 cartridge and fitted with a 30" octagon barrel. Long-range rear tang sight. Weight is about 7.5 lbs. Introduced in 2002.

NIB	Exc.	V.G.	Good	Fair	Poor
1075	850	750	625	500	250

1873 Border Model

Introduced in 2000 this model features a 20" blued octagon barrel with buckhorn rear sight. Magazine capacity is 10 rounds. Checkered pistol-grip stock is walnut with oil finish. Chambered for the .357 Magnum, .44-40, or .45 Colt cartridge.

NIB	Exc.	V.G.	Good	Fair	Poor
975	800	700	550	450	225

1866 "Yellowboy" Rifle

This model features a brass receiver, 24" octagon barrel, and walnut stocks. Weighs 8.5 lbs.

NIB	Exc.	V.G.	Good	Fair	Poor
850	675	525	450	300	150

1866 "Yellowboy" Carbine

Same as above but fitted with a 19" round barrel and saddle ring. Weighs 7 lbs. 4 oz.

NIB	Exc.	V.G.	Good	Fair	Poor
850	675	525	450	300	150

1866 "Yellowboy" Short Rifle

Introduced in 2000 this model features a 20" barrel with buckhorn rear sight. Walnut stock with oil finish. Receiver is yellow brass.

Chambered for the .38 Special, .44-40, or .45 Colt cartridge. Magazine capacity is 10 rounds.

NIB	Exc.	V.G.	Good	Fair	Poor
850	675	525	450	300	150

Iron Frame Henry

This is a replica of the famous and rare .44-40 Iron Frame Henry that features a case colored frame. Barrel length is 24" and rifle weighs 9 lbs.

NIB	Exc.	V.G.	Good	Fair	Poor
925	750	650	500	400	200

Blued Iron Frame Henry

Same as above but furnished with a highly polished blued receiver.

NIB	Exc.	V.G.	Good	Fair	Poor
925	750	650	500	400	200

Military Henry

Based on the brass frame military version of the Henry rifle this model is furnished with sling swivels mounted on the left side. The buttplate is fitted with a trap door. Caliber is .44-40 and barrel length is 24". Weighs 9 lbs. 4 oz.

NIB	Exc.	V.G.	Good	Fair	Poor
900	725	625	500	400	200

Henry Carbine

This is the brass frame carbine version and features a 22" barrel. Chambered for the .44-40 cartridge. Weighs 8 lbs. 12 oz.

NIB	Exc.	V.G.	Good	Fair	Poor
875	700	600	500	400	200

Henry Trapper

This replica is not based on an actual Henry. Fitted with a unique 16.5" barrel, this brass frame model weighs 7 lbs. 7 oz. Chambered for the .44-40 cartridge.

NIB	Exc.	V.G.	Good	Fair	Poor
875	700	600	500	400	200

1892 Rifle

This lever-action rifle is chambered for the .357 Magnum, .44-40, .45 Colt, or .32-20 cartridge. Octagon barrel is 24.25". Walnut stock, crescent butt and blued or case colored receiver. Weight is about 6.25 lbs.

NIB	Exc.	V.G.	Good	Fair	Poor
525	425	350	300	250	200

1892 Short Rifle

Same as above but with 20" octagon barrel. Weight is about 6.25 lbs.

NIB	Exc.	V.G.	Good	Fair	Poor
525	425	350	300	250	200

1892 Carbine

Similar to the short rifle but fitted with a 20" round barrel and saddle ring on left side of receiver. Weight is about 5.75 lbs.

NIB	Exc.	V.G.	Good	Fair	Poor
450	350	300	250	200	150

1892 Brass Frame Carbine

Same as above but with polished brass receiver.

NIB	Exc.	V.G.	Good	Fair	Poor
450	350	300	250	200	150

1892 Brass Frame Rifle

This model is the same as the carbine but with polished brass receiver.

NIB	Exc.	V.G.	Good	Fair	Poor
525	425	350	300	250	200

No. 2 Creedmoor Target Rifle

This is a reproduction of the Remington No. 2 Creedmoor. It features a case colored receiver, tapered 30" octagonal barrel, hooded front sight, Creedmoor tang sight, and walnut stock with checkered pistol grip. Furnished in .45-70 Government. Weighs 9 lbs.

NIB	Exc.	V.G.	Good	Fair	Poor
900	725	625	500	400	200

Rolling Block Buffalo Rifle

This rifle is a replica of the Remington Buffalo rifle. It is fitted with a 26" or 30" octagonal or half octagonal barrel, case colored receiver, blade front sight, notch rear sight, brass trigger guard, with walnut stocks. Tang is drilled and tapped for tang sight.

NIB	Exc.	V.G.	Good	Fair	Poor
750	600	475	300	200	100

Half Octagon Barrel Model

NIB	Exc.	V.G.	Good	Fair	Poor
750	600	475	300	200	100

"John Bodine" Rolling Block Rifle

Chambered for the .45-70 cartridge and fitted with a 30" octagon barrel. Double set triggers. Match-grade rear tang sight. Weight is about 12 lbs. Introduced in 2002.

NIB	Exc.	V.G.	Good	Fair	Poor
1550	1150	800	575	350	200

1885 High Wall

Chambered for the .45-70 cartridge this rifle is fitted with a 30" medium heavy octagon barrel. Case colored receiver, target sights and walnut stocks. Also available with 28" round barrel. Reduce price by $100 for Buckhorn sights and $60 for 28" barrel.

NIB	Exc.	V.G.	Good	Fair	Poor
900	725	600	500	400	200

1873 Springfield Infantry Rifle

A copy of the Trapdoor Springfield. Chambered for .45-70 and fitted with a 32.5" barrel. Walnut stock and case hardened breechlock. Weight is approximately 8.25 lbs.

NIB	Exc.	V.G.	Good	Fair	Poor
975	800	600	500	400	200

1873 Springfield Cavalry Carbine

Same as above but with 22" barrel. Weight is about 7 lbs.

NIB	Exc.	V.G.	Good	Fair	Poor
875	700	600	500	400	200

Ithaca/Navy Hawken Rifle

Offered in either .50 or .54 caliber percussion. Features a 31.5" rust blued octagon barrel. The percussion lockplate is case colored, while the rest of the hardware is blued with the exception of the nose cap and escutcheons. Weighs about 9 lbs. 13 oz.

NIB	Exc.	V.G.	Good	Fair	Poor
350	300	250	200	150	100

Hawken Rifle

This model features a case colored lock, 28" blued octagon barrel, adjustable sights, double set triggers, and hooked breech. The polished brass furniture and patch box are mounted on a walnut stock. Weighs about 8.5 lbs.

NIB	Exc.	V.G.	Good	Fair	Poor
300	200	175	125	95	60

Hawken Hunter Rifle

Offered in .50, .54, or .58 caliber, this model features blued hardware, adjustable sights, case colored lock, and hooked breech. The walnut stock is hand checkered with a cheekpiece. Rubber recoil pad is standard. Barrel length is 28".

NIB	Exc.	V.G.	Good	Fair	Poor
295	190	150	100	75	60

Hawken Hunter Carbine

Same as above but fitted with a 22.5" barrel. Weighs about 6 lbs. 12 oz.

NIB	Exc.	V.G.	Good	Fair	Poor
295	190	150	100	75	60

Kodiak MKIV Double Rifle

Built in Europe by Pedersoli, this model is chambered for the .45-70 cartridge and features a walnut stock with cheekpiece and hand checkering. Barrel length is 24" with adjustable sights. Engraved sideplates are polished bright. Sling swivels standard. Weighs 10.2 lbs.

NIB	Exc.	V.G.	Good	Fair	Poor
4500	3350	2500	1500	600	400

Mortimer Flintlock or Percussion Shotgun

Replica of 12 gauge English Mortimer. This model features a waterproof pan, roller frizzen (flintlock only); external safety. All parts are case colored. Barrel is 36" long. Weighs 7 lbs.

NIB	Exc.	V.G.	Good	Fair	Poor
975	800	600	500	400	200

Fowler Shotgun

This 12 gauge model is a side-by-side with straight gripstock. The gun features a hooked breech and 28" blued barrels. The sideplates are engraved and case colored. Double triggers and checkered walnut stock are standard. Weighs 7.25 lbs.

NIB	Exc.	V.G.	Good	Fair	Poor
550	395	300	250	200	100

Navy Arms Steel Shot Magnum

Same as above but in 10 gauge. Weighs 7 lbs. 9 oz.

NIB	Exc.	V.G.	Good	Fair	Poor
575	400	295	125	100	75

T&T Shotgun

This turkey and trap model has a straight grip stock and 28" barrel choked Full and Full. Locks are case colored and engraved. Walnut stock is checkered. Weighs 7.5 lbs.

NIB	Exc.	V.G.	Good	Fair	Poor
550	395	300	250	200	100

Japanese Tanegashima Matchlock

This model is a .50 caliber with 41" barrels. Weighs 8.5 lbs.

NIB	Exc.	V.G.	Good	Fair	Poor
1150	800	600	400	300	150

HANDGUNS

Le Page Pistol

This .44 caliber percussion pistol has a 10.25" tapered octagon barrel, adjustable single set trigger. The lock, trigger guard, and buttcap are engraved. The walnut stocks are hand checkered. Weighs 36 oz.

NIB	Exc.	V.G.	Good	Fair	Poor
450	375	300	250	200	100

Single Cased Set

NIB	Exc.	V.G.	Good	Fair	Poor
580	530	475	400	300	150

Double Cased Set

NIB	Exc.	V.G.	Good	Fair	Poor
995	875	750	600	400	200

Flintlock

Same as above but with flintlock ignition. Weighs 41 oz.

NIB	Exc.	V.G.	Good	Fair	Poor
470	425	350	250	150	100

Smoothbore Flintlock Pistol

Same as above but with a smooth bore.

NIB	Exc.	V.G.	Good	Fair	Poor
470	425	350	250	150	100

Smoothbore Flintlock Pistol Single Cased Set

NIB	Exc.	V.G.	Good	Fair	Poor
800	700	600	400	300	150

Smoothbore Flintlock Pistol Double Cased Set

NIB	Exc.	V.G.	Good	Fair	Poor
1395	1275	1050	600	400	200

Kentucky Pistol

A percussion replica of a pistol developed in the 1840s. It has a 10.125" blued barrel, case colored lock, brass furniture and trigger guard with walnut stock. Weighs 32 oz.

NIB	Exc.	V.G.	Good	Fair	Poor
295	225	200	125	85	60

Single Cased Set

NIB	Exc.	V.G.	Good	Fair	Poor
350	275	225	175	125	75

Double Cased Set

NIB	Exc.	V.G.	Good	Fair	Poor
550	450	350	250	150	100

Flintlock Pistol

Same as above but with flintlock ignition.

NIB	Exc.	V.G.	Good	Fair	Poor
225	175	150	100	75	60

Flintlock Pistol Single Cased Set

NIB	Exc.	V.G.	Good	Fair	Poor
350	275	225	175	125	75

Flintlock Pistol Double Cased Set

NIB	Exc.	V.G.	Good	Fair	Poor
550	450	350	275	175	100

Harpers Ferry Pistol

This pistol has a .58 caliber rifled 10" barrel. Case hardened lock and walnut stock. Weight is approximately 39 oz.

NIB	Exc.	V.G.	Good	Fair	Poor
300	250	200	150	100	75

Pistol Single Cased Set

NIB	Exc.	V.G.	Good	Fair	Poor
350	275	225	175	125	100

LE MAT PISTOLS

18th Georgia Le Mat Pistol

This 9-shot .44 caliber percussion revolver has a 7.625" blued barrel and engraved cylinder. An engraved banner on the left side of the frame reads "DEO VINDICE". Hammer and trigger are case colored. Stocks are checkered walnut. Comes with Le Mat mould and velvet draped French fitted case. Weighs 55 oz.

NIB	Exc.	V.G.	Good	Fair	Poor
795	625	500	400	300	150

Beauregard Le Mat Pistol

This is a replica of the Cavalry model. Comes cased.

NIB	Exc.	V.G.	Good	Fair	Poor
1000	800	650	550	350	200

Navy Le Mat

This model features a knurled pin barrel release and spur barrel selector.

NIB	Exc.	V.G.	Good	Fair	Poor
795	625	500	400	300	150

Army Le Mat

This model features a knurled pin barrel release and cross pin barrel selector.

NIB	Exc.	V.G.	Good	Fair	Poor
795	625	500	400	300	150

Cavalry Le Mat

This model features a lanyard ring, spur trigger, lever type barrel release, and cross pin barrel selector.

NIB	Exc.	V.G.	Good	Fair	Poor
795	625	500	400	300	150

Starr Double-Action Model 1858 Army

This model is a double-action revolver chambered for .44 caliber. Fitted with a 6" barrel. Blued finish. Weight is about 48 oz.

NIB	Exc.	V.G.	Good	Fair	Poor
350	250	200	150	100	75

Starr Single-Action Model 1863 Army

This model is fitted with an 8" barrel and is chambered for .44 caliber. Blued finish and walnut stock. Weight is about 48 oz.

NIB	Exc.	V.G.	Good	Fair	Poor
350	250	200	150	100	75

1862 New Model Police

This replica is based on the Colt .36 caliber pocket pistol of the same name. It features a half fluted and re-dated cylinder, case colored frame and loading gate, and a polished brass trigger guard and backstrap. Barrel length is 5.5" and pistol weigh 26 oz.

NIB	Exc.	V.G.	Good	Fair	Poor
300	250	175	150	100	75

1862 New Model Book-Style Cased Set

NIB	Exc.	V.G.	Good	Fair	Poor
350	250	200	150	100	75

Paterson Revolver

This replica is the five-shot .36 caliber. The cylinder is scroll engraved with a stagecoach scene. The hidden trigger drops down when the hammer is cocked. Barrel is 9" and the pistol weighs 43 oz.

NIB	Exc.	V.G.	Good	Fair	Poor
475	425	350	250	150	100

Engraved Paterson Revolver

This model features hand engraving with silver inlays.

NIB	Exc.	V.G.	Good	Fair	Poor
575	475	350	250	200	100

1851 Navy

This Colt replica is offered in either .36 or .44 caliber. A naval battle scene is engraved in the cylinder. The octagon barrel length is

7.5". The trigger guard and backstrap are polished brass. The walnut grips are hand rubbed. Weighs 32 oz. Optional shoulder stock add $100.

NIB	Exc.	V.G.	Good	Fair	Poor
350	250	200	150	100	75

Single Cased Set

NIB	Exc.	V.G.	Good	Fair	Poor
375	275	225	150	100	75

Double Cased Set

NIB	Exc.	V.G.	Good	Fair	Poor
550	450	375	275	200	100

1851 Navy Conversion

This is a replica of the Colt 1851 Navy cartridge conversion. Offered in 38 Special or .38 Long Colt with choice of 5.5" or 7.5" barrels. Weight is about 40 oz.

NIB	Exc.	V.G.	Good	Fair	Poor
475	425	350	250	150	100

Augusta 1851 Navy Pistol

Available with either 5" or 7.5" barrel. Engraved with "A" coverage.

NIB	Exc.	V.G.	Good	Fair	Poor
350	250	200	150	100	75

Model 1851 Navy Frontiersman

Introduced in 2003 this revolver features a 5" .36 caliber barrel. The receiver, loading lever and hammer are case colored while the barrel and cylinder are charcoal blued. Fitted with a German silver backstrap and walnut grips.

NIB	Exc.	V.G.	Good	Fair	Poor
350	250	200	150	100	75

Reb Model 1860 Pistol

This is a replica of the Confederate Griswold and Gunnison revolver. It features a blued round 7.5" barrel, brass frame, trigger guard and backstrap. Offered in .36 or .44 caliber. Weighs 44 oz.

NIB	Exc.	V.G.	Good	Fair	Poor
165	150	125	90	75	35

Reb 1860 Sheriff's Model

Same as above but fitted with a 5" barrel. Weighs 40 oz.

NIB	Exc.	V.G.	Good	Fair	Poor
165	150	125	90	75	35

1847 Walker Dragoon

This is a replica of the rare Colt .44 caliber revolver. The barrel and cylinder are blued while the frame and loading lever are case colored. Barrel length is 9" and pistol weighs 75 oz.

NIB	Exc.	V.G.	Good	Fair	Poor
400	325	275	250	200	100

Single Cased Set

NIB	Exc.	V.G.	Good	Fair	Poor
450	375	325	250	200	100

Single Deluxe Cased Set

NIB	Exc.	V.G.	Good	Fair	Poor
525	425	350	300	200	100

1860 Army Pistol

This .44 caliber model features a case colored frame and loading lever with blued barrel, cylinder, and backstrap. The trigger guard is brass. The cylinder is engraved with a battle scene. Barrel is 8" and pistol weighs 41 oz.

NIB	Exc.	V.G.	Good	Fair	Poor
350	250	200	150	100	75

Single Cased Set

NIB	Exc.	V.G.	Good	Fair	Poor
375	275	225	150	100	75

Double Cased Set

NIB	Exc.	V.G.	Good	Fair	Poor
550	450	375	275	200	100

1860 Army Conversion

Chambered for the .38 Special or .38 Long Colt this model is fitted with either a 5.5" or 7.5" barrel. Blued finish. Walnut grips. Weight is about 40 oz.

NIB	Exc.	V.G.	Good	Fair	Poor
475	425	350	250	150	100

1858 New Model Remington-Style Pistol

This replica has a solid frame, as did the original. The frame and 8" barrel are blued, while the trigger guard is brass. Walnut grips are standard. Weighs 40 oz.

NIB	Exc.	V.G.	Good	Fair	Poor
350	250	200	150	100	75

Single Cased Set

NIB	Exc.	V.G.	Good	Fair	Poor
375	275	225	150	100	75

Double Cased Set

NIB	Exc.	V.G.	Good	Fair	Poor
550	450	375	275	200	100

Stainless Steel 1858 New Model Army

Same as above but in stainless steel. Weighs 40 oz.

NIB	Exc.	V.G.	Good	Fair	Poor
375	275	225	150	100	75

Single Cased Set

NIB	Exc.	V.G.	Good	Fair	Poor
375	275	225	150	100	75

Double Cased Set

NIB	Exc.	V.G.	Good	Fair	Poor
550	450	375	275	200	10

Brass Framed 1858 New Model Army

This version features a highly polished brass frame. Barrel length is 7.75".

NIB	Exc.	V.G.	Good	Fair	Poor
165	150	125	90	75	35

Single Cased Set

NIB	Exc.	V.G.	Good	Fair	Poor
250	200	150	100	75	60

Double Cased Set

NIB	Exc.	V.G.	Good	Fair	Poor
395	325	300	250	200	100

1858 Target Model

Same as above but features a patridge front sight and an adjustable rear sight. Barrel length is 8".

NIB	Exc.	V.G.	Good	Fair	Poor
300	225	175	125	75	50

Deluxe 1858 New Model Army

This replica is built to the exact dimensions as the original. The barrel is 8" with adjustable front sight. The trigger guard is silver plated. The action is tuned for competition. Weighs 46 oz.

NIB	Exc.	V.G.	Good	Fair	Poor
400	325	250	200	150	100

Spiller and Burr Pistol

This is a .36 caliber pistol with 7" blued octagon barrel. The frame is brass with walnut grips. Weighs 40 oz.

NIB	Exc.	V.G.	Good	Fair	Poor
350	250	200	150	100	75

Single Cased Set

NIB	Exc.	V.G.	Good	Fair	Poor
375	275	225	150	100	75

Double Cased Set

NIB	Exc.	V.G.	Good	Fair	Poor
550	450	375	275	200	100

Rogers and Spencer

This model features a 7.5" barrel with blued frame and barrel. Offered in .44 caliber. Walnut grips. Weighs 48 oz.

NIB	Exc.	V.G.	Good	Fair	Poor
375	275	225	150	100	75

"London Gray" Rogers and Spencer Pistol

Same as above but with a burnished satin chrome finish.

NIB	Exc.	V.G.	Good	Fair	Poor
375	275	225	150	100	75

Rogers and Spencer Target Model

Same as standard model but fitted with adjustable target sights.

NIB	Exc.	V.G.	Good	Fair	Poor
375	275	225	150	100	75

1861 Navy Conversion

Replica of the cartridge conversion of the 1861 Navy. Chambered for .38 Special or .38 Long Colt. Fitted with either a 5.5" or 7.5" barrel. Weight is about 40 oz.

NIB	Exc.	V.G.	Good	Fair	Poor
475	425	350	250	150	100

1872 Colt Open Top

This model features a 5.5" or 7.5" barrel with case hardened frame, blued barrel and cylinder, and silver-plated brass trigger guard and backstrap. Walnut grips. Chambered for .38 caliber cartridge. Weight is about 40 oz.

NIB	Exc.	V.G.	Good	Fair	Poor
500	375	225	175	150	125

1873 Colt-Style Single-Action Army

This replica features a case colored frame and hammer with blued round barrel in 3", 4.75", 5.5", or 7.5" lengths. Trigger guard and cylinder are blued. Offered in .44-40, .45 Long Colt, .357 Magnum, and .32-20.

NIB	Exc.	V.G.	Good	Fair	Poor
500	375	225	175	150	125

Model 1873 SAA Stainless Gunfighter

Introduced in 2003 this model is the same as the standard 1873, but features all stainless steel construction. Offered in .45 Colt and .357 Magnum caliber with choice of 4.75", 5.5", or 7.5" barrel. Weight is about 45 oz. depending on barrel length.

NIB	Exc.	V.G.	Good	Fair	Poor
525	400	250	195	150	125

Economy Model 1873 S.A.A.

Same as above but with brass trigger guard and backstrap.

NIB	Exc.	V.G.	Good	Fair	Poor
325	250	200	150	125	100

Nickel 1873 S.A.A.

NIB	Exc.	V.G.	Good	Fair	Poor
525	400	250	195	150	125

1873 U.S. Cavalry Model

This .45 Long Colt model features U.S. arsenal stampings, case colored frame, and walnut grips. Barrel length is 7.5" and pistol weighs 45 oz.

NIB	Exc.	V.G.	Good	Fair	Poor
500	375	225	175	150	125

1873 Pinched Frame Model

This is a replica of the "pinched" frame 1873 with "U" shape rear sight notch. Chambered for .45 Colt with 7.5" barrel.

NIB	Exc.	V.G.	Good	Fair	Poor
500	375	225	175	150	125

1873 Flat Top Target

This model features a windage adjustable rear sight on a flat top frame and a spring loaded front sight. Barrel length is 7.5". Offered in .45 Colt. Weight is about 40 oz. Introduced in 1998.

NIB	Exc.	V.G.	Good	Fair	Poor
500	375	225	175	150	125

Deputy Single-Action Army

Similar to the Model 1873 but with a bird's-head grip. Barrel lengths are 3", 3.5", 4", and 4.75". Chambered for .44-40 and .45 Colt.

NIB	Exc.	V.G.	Good	Fair	Poor
400	325	250	200	150	100

Shootist Model S.A.A.

This model is a reproduction of the Colt 1873. Parts are interchangeable with the originals. Blued barrel, cylinder, trigger guard, and backstrap. Case hardened frame and hammer. Walnut grips. Offered in 4.75", 5.5", and 7.5" barrel lengths. Chambered for .357 Magnum, .44-40, or .45 Colt.

NIB	Exc.	V.G.	Good	Fair	Poor
500	375	225	175	150	125

Scout Small Frame Revolver

This model is identical to the Colt 1873 SAA but with smaller dimensions. Offered in .38 Special with choice of 4.75" or 5.5" barrel. Weight is about 30 oz. Introduced in 2003.

NIB	Exc.	V.G.	Good	Fair	Poor
400	325	250	200	150	100

Deluxe 1873 Colt Revolver

This model is chambered for the .32-20 cartridge and features bright charcoal blue with case colored frame and hammer. Walnut grips. Fitted with a 5.5" barrel. Limited production. Weight is about 41 oz.

NIB	Exc.	V.G.	Good	Fair	Poor
500	375	225	175	150	125

Bisley Model

This model features the famous Bisley grip. Barrel length is 4.75", 5.5", and 7.5". Chambered for .44-40 or .45 Colt.

NIB	Exc.	V.G.	Good	Fair	Poor
500	375	225	175	150	125

Bisley Flat Top Target

Similar to the Bisley but with 7.5" barrel with flat top frame with adjustable front sight and windage adjustable rear sight. Chambered for .44-40 or .45 Colt. Weight is about 40 oz.

NIB	Exc.	V.G.	Good	Fair	Poor
525	400	250	195	150	125

1875 Remington-Style Revolver

The frame is case colored while all other parts are blued except for brass trigger guard. Available in .44-40 or .45 Long Colt. Furnished with walnut grips. Barrel length is 7.5". Weighs 41 oz.

NIB	Exc.	V.G.	Good	Fair	Poor
500	375	225	175	150	125

1890 Remington-Style Revolver

This is a modified version of the 1875 model that is also offered in .44-40 or .45 Long Colt. The web under the barrel has been eliminated. It has blued 5.5" steel barrel and frame. Lanyard loop is on bottom of walnut grips. Weighs 39 oz.

NIB	Exc.	V.G.	Good	Fair	Poor
500	375	225	175	150	125

TOP-BREAK REVOLVERS

Model 1875 Schofield—Wells Fargo 5" barrel

NIB	Exc.	V.G.	Good	Fair	Poor
750	650	525	450	350	125

Model 1875 Schofield—Cavalry 7" barrel

A reproduction of the S&W Model 3 top-break revolver in either .44-40 or .45 Long Colt. The Cavalry model has a 7" barrel while the Wells Fargo model has a 5" barrel. Weight is about 39 oz.

NIB	Exc.	V.G.	Good	Fair	Poor
750	650	525	450	350	125

Model 1875 Schofield—Deluxe

This model has a charcoal blue finish with gold inlays and "A" style hand engraving. Available in either the Cavalry or Wells Fargo model. Special order only.

NIB	Exc.	V.G.	Good	Fair	Poor
1000	800	675	550	425	200

Model 1875 Schofield—B Engraved

Available in Cavalry or Wells Fargo Model. This grade is "B" style engraved with 35 percent coverage. Special order only.

NIB	Exc.	V.G.	Good	Fair	Poor
1100	900	775	650	525	250

Model 1875 Schofield—C Engraved

This model is available in Cavalry or Wells Fargo with "C" style engraving with 50 percent coverage. Special order only.

NIB	Exc.	V.G.	Good	Fair	Poor
1150	950	800	675	55	275

Model 1875 Schofield Founder's Model

Introduced in 2003 to honor Val Forgett, Sr. and Aldo Uberti. This revolver features a charcoal blued barrel and cylinder with color case hardened receiver, backstrap, trigger guard and trigger. Grip are white ivory polymer. Limited production with special serial number prefix of "VF".

NIB	Exc.	V.G.	Good	Fair	Poor
750	650	525	450	350	125

Model 1875 Schofield—Hideout

This is a short-barrel variation of the Schofield. It is fitted with a 3.5" barrel and chambered for the .44-40 or .45 Colt cartridge. Weight is about 38 oz.

NIB	Exc.	V.G.	Good	Fair	Poor
750	650	525	450	350	125

New Model Russian

Built around the single-action Smith & Wesson Model 3, this revolver is chambered for the .44 Russian cartridge. It is fitted with a 6.5" barrel. Case colored spur trigger guard, latch and hammer. Blued frame, barrel and cylinder. Walnut grips. Weight is about 40 oz. Introduced in 1999.

NIB	Exc.	V.G.	Good	Fair	Poor
750	650	525	450	350	125

MILITARY SURPLUS ARMS

SKS Type 56 w/Scope Rail

This semi-automatic gas operated rifle is chambered for the 7.62x39 cartridge. It has a 10-round clip. This model is fitted with a scope rail on the left side of the receiver. Barrel length is 20.5". Weight is 8 lbs.

NIB	Exc.	V.G.	Good	Fair	Poor
400	325	250	200	150	100

Standard SKS Type 56

Same as above without the scope rail.

NIB	Exc.	V.G.	Good	Fair	Poor
400	325	250	200	150	100

Standard SKS Type 56 With Scope and Bipod

As above but fitted with a 2.75 power Type 89 scope and RPK style folding bipod.

NIB	Exc.	V.G.	Good	Fair	Poor
400	325	250	200	150	100

SKS "Cowboy's Companion" Carbine

Barrel length on this version is 16.5". Weighs 7 lbs. 8 oz.

NIB	Exc.	V.G.	Good	Fair	Poor
400	325	250	200	150	100

Military Version

This is the military version of the "Cowboy's Companion" fitted with a short cruciform folding bayonet.

NIB	Exc.	V.G.	Good	Fair	Poor
400	325	250	200	150	100

SKS "Hunter" Carbine

This model has a checkered composite Monte Carlo stock with full length pull. Comes with 5-round magazine.

NIB	Exc.	V.G.	Good	Fair	Poor
400	325	250	200	150	100

TT-Olympia Pistol

This is a reproduction of the Walther target pistol. Chambered for .22 LR. Barrel length is 4.625" and pistol weighs 27 oz.

NIB	Exc.	V.G.	Good	Fair	Poor
275	200	150	125	100	50

TU-90 Pistol

This model is based on the Tokagypt pistol. It features a wraparound grip with thumb rest. Barrel length is 4.5" and pistol weighs 30 oz.

NIB	Exc.	V.G.	Good	Fair	Poor
250	190	115	75	50	40

TU-KKW Training Rifle

Based on the 98 Mauser and chambered for the .22 LR cartridge. It is fitted with military sights, bayonet lug, cleaning rod and take down disc. Comes with detachable 5-round box magazine. Barrel length is 26" and weighs 8 lbs.

NIB	Exc.	V.G.	Good	Fair	Poor
325	275	200	150	100	60

TU-KKW Sniper Trainer

Same as above but fitted with a 2.75 power Type 89 scope and quick detachable mounting system.

NIB	Exc.	V.G.	Good	Fair	Poor
375	325	275	200	150	100

TU-33/40 Carbine

This model is based on the WWII Mauser G 33/40 mountain carbine. Chambered for the .22 LR or 7.62x39 cartridge. Barrel length is 20.75" and weighs 7.5 lbs.

NIB	Exc.	V.G.	Good	Fair	Poor
325	275	200	150	100	—

JW-15 Rifle

This model is a bolt-action design based on the BRNO Model 5 action. Chambered for the .22 LR it features adjustable sights, sling swivels, an detachable 5-round magazine. The top of the receiver is dovetailed for easy scope mounting. Barrel is 24" long and rifle weighs 5 lbs. 12 oz.

NIB	Exc.	V.G.	Good	Fair	Poor
100	80	70	60	50	35

Martini Target Rifle

A .444 or .45-70 caliber single-shot Martini-action rifle with a 26" or 30" octagonal barrel, tang sight, and walnut stock. Offered between 1972 and 1984.

NIB	Exc.	V.G.	Good	Fair	Poor
—	625	500	400	300	150

Parker-Hale Sniper Rifle

See—Parker-Hale.

RPKS-74

A 5.56mm or 7.62x39mm caliber semi-automatic rifle with a 19" barrel patterned after the Russian AK series rifles.

NIB	Exc.	V.G.	Good	Fair	Poor
550	450	375	275	200	10

No. 5 Enfield Jungle Carbine

This replica is chambered for .303 British cartridge and fitted with cupped buttplate and flashider. Barrel length is 20.5". Magazine capacity is 10 rounds. Weight is approximately 7 lbs.

NIB	Exc.	V.G.	Good	Fair	Poor
375	325	275	200	150	100

No. 6 Enfield Jungle Carbine

This reproduction is chambered for .303 British with 20.5" barrel with flashider. Weight is about 7 lbs. Ten-round magazine.

NIB	Exc.	V.G.	Good	Fair	Poor
375	325	275	200	150	100

Ishapore 2A No. 1 MK III Rifle

This is a refinished rifle with 25" barrel and chambered for .308 Win. cartridge. Magazine capacity is 12 rounds. Weight is about 9.3 lbs.

2A Tanker Carbine

This is a replica with a short 20" barrel. Chambered for .308 Win. Magazine capacity is 12 rounds. Weight is approximately 8.7 lbs.

NIB	Exc.	V.G.	Good	Fair	Poor
375	325	275	200	150	100

MK III Tanker Carbine

Similar to the above model but chambered for the .303 British cartridge. Magazine capacity is 10 rounds.

NIB	Exc.	V.G.	Good	Fair	Poor
375	325	275	200	150	100

Lithgow No. 1 MK III Rifle

These rifles are in unissued condition. Barrel length is 25". Chambered for .303 British cartridge. Magazine capacity is 10 rounds. Weight is about 9 lbs.

NIB	Exc.	V.G.	Good	Fair	Poor
400	325	250	200	150	100

No. 1 MK III Enfield Rifle

These rifles are standard MK III S.M.L.E. rifles that have been refinished. Barrel length is 25.25". Magazine capacity is 10 rounds of .303 British. Weight is about 9 lbs.

NIB	Exc.	V.G.	Good	Fair	Poor
375	325	275	200	150	100

No. 4 Tanker Carbine

This is a cut-down version of the No. 4 MK I Enfield. Barrel length is 20.5". Chambered for .303 with magazine capacity of 10 rounds. Weight is approximately 8.2 lbs.

NIB	Exc.	V.G.	Good	Fair	Poor
350	250	200	150	100	75

No. 4 MK I Enfield Rifle

This is a reconditioned rifle. Barrel length is 25". Magazine capacity is 10 rounds of .303 British. Weight is about 8.6 lbs.

NIB	Exc.	V.G.	Good	Fair	Poor
350	250	200	150	100	75

Savage No. 4 MK I Rifle

Chambered for .303 British cartridge with 25" barrel. Stocks are unissued. Magazine capacity is 10 rounds. Weight is approximately 8.7 lbs.

NIB	Exc.	V.G.	Good	Fair	Poor
375	325	275	200	150	100

Luger

A .22 caliber semi-automatic pistol with a 4", 6", or 8" barrel, fixed sights, and 10-shot magazine. Blued with walnut grips. Manufactured in the U.S.A. in 1986 and 1987.

NIB	Exc.	V.G.	Good	Fair	Poor
—	325	275	225	175	125

Grand Prix Silhouette Pistol

A .30-30, .44 Magnum, 7mm Special, and .45-70 caliber single-shot pistol with a 13.75" barrel, adjustable sights, and an aluminum, heat-disbursing rib. Matte-blued, walnut grips and forearm. Manufactured in 1985.

NIB	Exc.	V.G.	Good	Fair	Poor
—	450	375	295	225	150

NEAL, W.
Bangor, Maine

Under Hammer Pistol

A .31 caliber under hammer percussion pistol with 5" to 8" barrels, iron frame and walnut grip. The barrel marked "Wm. Neal/Bangor, Me."

NIB	Exc.	V.G.	Good	Fair	Poor
—	—	1350	1000	450	150

NEPPERHAN FIREARMS CO.
Yonkers, New York
Pocket Revolver

A .31 caliber percussion revolver with 3.5" to 6" barrels and a 5-shot cylinder. Blued, case hardened with walnut grips. The barrel marked "Nepperhan/Fire Arms Co" and on some additionally "Yonkers New York." The latter are worth a slight premium over the values listed. Approximately 5,000 were made during the 1860s.

NIB	Exc.	V.G.	Good	Fair	Poor
—	—	1400	1000	385	200

NESIKA BAY PRECISION, INC.
Sturgis, South Dakota
Hunting Rifles

Offered in a number of different calibers with several stock options to choose from. All rifles are fitted with adjustable trigger.

NIB	Exc.	V.G.	Good	Fair	Poor
4000	2900	2300	1500	750	400

Varmint Rifles

Offered in a variety of calibers and barrel lengths and weights. Single shot or repeater.

NIB	Exc.	V.G.	Good	Fair	Poor
3500	2900	2300	1500	750	400

Urban Tactical Rifle

Chambered for the .308 cartridge and fitted with a 20" fluted barrel. Detachable box magazine. Weight is about 10 lbs. Add 5-10 percent for Heavy Tactical version. **NOTE:** For .300 win. Mag add $100.

NIB	Exc.	V.G.	Good	Fair	Poor
5800	4800	3500	2700	800	500

NEW ENGLAND FIREARMS CO.
Gardner, Massachusetts

New England Firearms Company is owned by Marlin.

Model R22

.22 Magnum or .32 H&R Magnum double-action revolver with a 2.5", 4", or 6" barrel and either a 6- or 9-shot cylinder. Blued or nickel-plated with walnut grips. Introduced in 1988.

NIB	Exc.	V.G.	Good	Fair	Poor
150	100	80	70	60	40

Excell

Introduced in 2005 this model is chambered for the 12 gauge 3" shell and fitted with a 28" vent rib barrel with choke tubes. Checkered black synthetic stock. Magazine capacity is 5 rounds. Weight is about 7 lbs.

The NRA's National Firearms Museum

By Philip Schreier, NRA Museum Senior Curator
Photos by Michael Ives & Philip Schreier

When Mr. D. Barclay won a Nimschke-engraved Remington rolling block rifle at the 1874 National Matches, little did he know that his trophy gun would be the first in a long line of firearms that, nearly 140 years later, would number 6,000 and be the heart of one of the world's finest museums dedicated to firearms. It was with that first rifle that the new National Rifle Association of America began its collection. In 1935, the collection, supplemented by gifts from industry and manufacturers that submitted firearms for test and evaluation for the pages of *American Rifleman* magazine, opened its doors as a full-fledged museum to the general public in the hallways of the Barr Building, in Washington, D.C., just blocks from the White House. In 1994, NRA Headquarters moved from its venerable 1600 Rhode Island Avenue address to more spacious accommodations in Fairfax, Virginia, just 20 miles away. On May 28, 1998, a new and improved National Firearms Museum (NFM) opened at the NRA HQ.

Today's NFM is truly world class. It consists of 15 galleries comprised of 85 exhibit cases in a 15,000 square foot facility detailing and examining the nearly 700-year history of firearms with a special emphasis on firearms, freedom, and the American experience. Each gallery is evocative of a period of time in American history, from the stockade fort at Jamestown to the gun factories of New England. Numerous life-sized dioramas bring to life a nineteenth-century riflemaker's shop, a trench on the Western Front, and a shelled-out town square in Normandy. More than 3,000 firearms tell the stories of how they were used to provide security and sustenance to the early colonists, how they were used to secure our freedom and independence and have been used ever since to maintain and preserve those liberties. They also tell the stories of exploration, manufacturing, competition, hunting, and recreational shooting sports.

The museum is truly a dynamic and evolving institution. Since our first grand opening, in 1998, the William B. Ruger Gallery has been host to numerous temporary exhibits, including the personal collections of Bill Ruger and Dr. Ugo Beretta. We've also highlighted exhibits from veterans of World War II, Thompson submachine guns, and, most recently, Hollywood Guns, a collection of actual movie-used firearms from some of your favorite actors and most beloved films. In 2010, following a unprecedented gift from Robert E. & Margie Petersen, another gallery was opened that highlights the finest collection of sporting arms and Gatling guns on public display anywhere in the world. Most recently, the National Park Service graciously entrusted the NFM with custody of nearly 100 priceless artifacts from Sagamore Hill National Historic Site, the home of NRA Life Member Theodore Roosevelt. Our exhibit "Theodore Roosevelt—Trappings of an Icon: the Oval Office of the Summer White House" opened in the Fall of 2012 as an exhibit gallery that had been designed in 1993 to replicate the twenty-sixth President's private library at his Oyster Bay, Long Island, home. And there's more ahead! In the Spring of 2013, the NFM and Bass Pro Shops will open the NRA Sporting Arms Museum in Springfield, Missouri, and make available to the general public mroe than 1,000 firearms and treasures from the NFM collection in a brand new museum environment at the Bass Pro flagship facility.

The museum continues to grow, and our outreach programs continue to keep up with advancing technology as we venture into a museum without walls via the realm of the internet. A very interactive www.nramuseum.com site allows visitors access to the museum's collection via thousands of high-resolution photos of every firearm currently on exhibit. Links on our website will take the visitor to the NFM YouTube site that now has had more than three million views, as well as our own Facebook page that features fast-breaking news from the museum about our future exhibits, tours, television appearances, and museum store specials.

Drop on by and visit us, whether you arrive via the interstate or the Internet, we offer free admission. Museum hours in Fairfax, Virginia are 9:30 a.m. to 5 p.m. daily, seven days a week (closed on some major holidays).

The Mayflower Wheelock—Perhaps the crown jewel of the NFM collection, this European wheelock was found in the home of Mayflower Pilgrim John Alden during a restoration of his home in the early 20th century. Alden was a signer of the Mayflower Compact, our first document of freedom, as well as the first man to set foot ashore after the landing at Plymouth Rock.

This Joseph Manton fowler was made for Fredrick Augustus, the Duke of York and second eldest son of King George III of Great Britain.

This English fowler was made for King James II and abandoned with the Royal baggage train in Ireland, in 1688.

This highly embellished flintlock long rifle was made by John Palm (1782-1865) in Womelsdorf, Berks County, Pennsylvania. The swivel barrel allowed the shooter to get off two shots quickly.

The Nock Volley Gun—This seven barreled .46-caliber shoulder cannon was purchased by the British Ordinance Board for use in the arms lockers of the Royal Navy during the days of fighting sails. This particular Nock was used by the actor Richard Widmark in John Wayne's film The Alamo (1960). Gift of the Robert E. Petersen Estate.

be LeMat was also known as the "Grape Shot" revolver by ...ue of the 20-gauge central shotgun barrel and nine-shot ...caliber revolver chambers. Imported from Europe, it was ...vorite arm of Confederate General J.E.B. Stuart. Gift of ...Robert E. Petersen Estate.

This highly engraved and embellished Browning M-1900 .32 auto was the personal property of President Theodore Roosevelt. After President William McKinley's assassination in 1901, Roosevelt carried a pistol for personal protection for the rest of his life. Gift of Cornelius V.S. Roosevelt.

This is one of the many Winchester Model 1886 rifles owned by Theodore Roosevelt. He was said to have purchased this rifle with his winnings from a tennis match. It was returned to Winchester for refinishing and refitting no less than five times by Roosevelt. On Loan from Sagamore Hill National Historic Site, NPS.

This Kornbrath engraved double rifle in .450-500 was imported by Frederick Adolph in 1910 and presented to President Roosevelt following his successful year-long safari in Africa. The chamber of each barrel bears the engraved seal of the United States.

The Gatling Gun exhibit in the NFM's new Robert E. Petersen Gallery represents the largest collection of Gatling guns on public display in the world and include one of only three known original crated Gatlings. Gift of the Robert E. Petersen Estate.

This 8-gauge double-barreled Colt's shotgun is the only one ever made by Colt's and it was a presentation model for President Grover Cleveland. Gift of the Robert E. Petersen Estate.

The 1907 pistol trials concluded with the selection of the John Browning-designed .45 ACP pistol that is world renowned today as the Colt 1911. The NFM's exhibit on the centennial of the 1911 featured the Grant Hammond Savage 1907 in .45 ACP, the Colt/Browning 1907, and the 1902 Luger. Gift of Bailey & Taz Brower.

Boss and Co. has, since 1812, been considered Great Britain's most venerable gun maker. Producing only "Best Guns" has kept Boss & Co. head and shoulders above their competition for the past 200 years. Gift of the Robert E. Petersen Estate.

Boss & Co.

This remarkable Howdah pistol by Alexander Henry is chambered in .577 and cased with ivory and gold accoutrements. Exquisitely engraved and inlayed in gold and blued, it is the finest Howdah pistol known to the museum staff. Gift of the Robert E. Petersen Estate.

Thompson Model of 1921—This nearly mint example of a Thompson Model of 1921 was manufactured by Colt's in Hartford, Connecticut. Originally made with a 20-round magazines, eventually 30-round stick magazines and 50- and 100-round drum magazines were manufactured for use on the gun "that made the '20s roar." Gift of Tracie Hill.

This Japanese Garand was one of eight known to have been made shortly before V-J Day in August of 1945. Gift of General Julian Hatcher.

At top, the Colt .38 was used by New Jersey shooting phenomenon A.P. Lane to capture five Olympic Gold and one Olympic Bronze medals in the 1912 and 1920 Summer games. At left is a Model 102 High Standard, intended for rapid fire competition and bearing the stamp "1960 Olympics, Rome."

This single-shot .22 is called the Camp Perry Model and is named after the site of the NRA Annual Matches held annually in Ohio since 1907. Gift of General Julian Hatcher.

John Wayne's Model 1892 Winchester was branded with "BATJAC" on the stock, the name of his production company. This particular rifle was used by the Duke in Hondo (1953) McClintock! (1963) and Big Jake (1971) Loaned by Chris Hearn.

General Dwight David Eisenhower favored this Winchester Model 21 in 20-gauge above all his shotguns. A gift from Coca Cola CEO Robert Woodruff, the trigger guard has the General's initials, as well as five gold stars signifying his rank. Gift of General John S.D. Eisenhower.

"Go ahead, make my day." From the pen of writer and director John Milius to the script of Dirty Harry (1971) and the spoken lines of actor Clint Eastwood, those five simple words helped propel the modest Smith & Wesson Model 29 .44 Magnum to international stardom. This is one of the three actual Model 29s used in both Dirty Harry and Magnum Force (1973). On loan from John Milius, a gift to him from Clint Eastwood & Warner Brothers.

Right: This stunning Holland & Holland Royal 28-gauge. Is known as The Empire Gun and was executed by A. M. Brown of H&H. Highlighted scenes of Greco-Roman mythology are rendered in three types of gold and numerous other precious metals. Gift of the Robert E. Petersen Estate.

The Parker Invincibles—These three shotguns represent the penultimate in artisanship and craftsmanship ever exhibited in an American-made shotgun. Thought to be the finest example of the gun maker's art ever executed in the United States, it is estimated that their combined value is five million dollars. Parker brothers manufactured just three Invincible grade guns in the late 1920s. Gift of the Robert E. Petersen Estate.

NIB	Exc.	V.G.	Good	Fair	Poor
450	375	295	225	150	100

Excell Waterfowl

As above but with Real Tree Advantage Wetlands camo finish. Introduced in 2005.

NIB	Exc.	V.G.	Good	Fair	Poor
475	400	325	250	175	125

Excell Turkey

This model is fitted with a 22" barrel with choke tubes and fiber optic front sight. Real Tree Advantage Hardwoods camo finish. Weight is 7 lbs. Introduced in 2005.

NIB	Exc.	V.G.	Good	Fair	Poor
475	400	325	250	175	125

Excell Combo

This model has a black synthetic stock and two barrels: 28" vent rib with choke tubes, and 24" rifled barrel. Weight is about 7 lbs. depending on barrel length. Introduced in 2005.

NIB	Exc.	V.G.	Good	Fair	Poor
500	425	345	260	185	135

Pardner

A 12, 16, 20 or .410 bore single-shot shotgun with a 24", 26", or 28" barrel. Blued with a walnut stock. Introduced in 1987.

NIB	Exc.	V.G.	Good	Fair	Poor
150	100	80	70	60	40

Pardner Youth

Similar to the above model but offered only in 20 and 28 gauge as well as .410. Fitted with a 26" barrel. Weight is between 5 and 6 lbs.

NIB	Exc.	V.G.	Good	Fair	Poor
150	100	80	70	60	40

Special Purpose

This is a similar model but it is offered only in 10 gauge. It is available in several different configurations: A 10 gauge model with hardwood stock with 28" barrel, a camo model with 28" barrel, a camo model with 32" barrel choked Modified, and a black matte finish model with 24" barrel with screw-in turkey Full choke. Weight is about 9.5 lbs.

NIB	Exc.	V.G.	Good	Fair	Poor
250	175	125	100	75	50

Pardner Pump Turkey

This model is chambered for the 12 gauge 3" shell and fitted with 22" barrel with turkey choke tube. Magazine capacity is 5 rounds. Weight is about 7.5 lbs. Introduced in 2005.

NIB	Exc.	V.G.	Good	Fair	Poor
275	225	175	125	100	75

Pardner Pump Walnut Shotgun

12- or 20-gauge pump-action shotgun with American walnut furniture, 28- or 26-inch vent rib barrel, 3-inch chamber and screw-in choke tube. Weight 7-1/2 lbs.

NIB	Exc.	V.G.	Good	Fair	Poor
—	275	225	175	125	100

Pardner Pump Synthetic Shotgun

Similar to above but with black synthetic buttstock and forend.

NIB	Exc.	V.G.	Good	Fair	Poor
—	225	175	150	100	75

Pardner Pump Field Shotgun

Similar to above but with Realtree APG HD camo finish.

NIB	Exc.	V.G.	Good	Fair	Poor
—	275	225	175	125	100

Pardner Pump Compact Field Shotgun

Similar to above but with 1-1/4-inch shorter length of pull and 21 inch barrel.

NIB	Exc.	V.G.	Good	Fair	Poor
—	225	175	150	100	75

Pardner Pump Compact Walnut Shotgun

Similar to Pardner Pump Walnut model but with 1-1/4 inch shorter length of pull and 21 inch barrel. Weight 6-1/4 lbs.

NIB	Exc.	V.G.	Good	Fair	Poor
—	225	175	150	100	75

Pardner Pump Compact Synthetic Shotgun

Similar to above but with black synthetic buttstock and forend.

NIB	Exc.	V.G.	Good	Fair	Poor
—	225	175	150	100	75

Pardner Pump Combo

Introduced in 2005 this model features two 12 gauge 3" barrels. One 28" with vent rib and choke tubes, and the other 22" rifled slug barrel. Walnut stock. Weight is about 7.5 lbs. depending on barrel length.

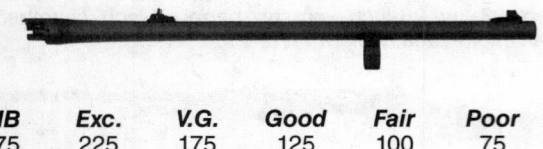

NIB	Exc.	V.G.	Good	Fair	Poor
275	225	175	125	100	75

Pardner Pump Protector

Similar to Pardner Pump but with matte black finish throughout and synthetic buttstock and forend. Also available with carbon fiber dipped stock.

NIB	Exc.	V.G.	Good	Fair	Poor
—	225	175	150	100	75

Survivor

Based on a single-shot break-action design this rifle or shotgun is fitted with a synthetic stock with integral storage compartments. Offered in .410/.45 Colt, 12 and 20 gauge, .223 Rem., and .357 Mag. Barrel length is 22". Weight is about 6 lbs.

NIB	Exc.	V.G.	Good	Fair	Poor
200	175	150	125	100	75

Handi-Rifle (aka Handi-Gun)

.22 Hornet, .223, .243, .270, .280, .30-30, .44 Magnum, or .45-70 caliber version of the above with a 22" barrel fitted with open sights. Blued, with a walnut stock. Introduced in 1989. In 2003 this model was offered in stainless steel. In 2004 the .22-250, .25-06, and .204 calibers were added. In 2005 the .500 S&W was added.

NIB	Exc.	V.G.	Good	Fair	Poor
275	200	150	125	100	75

Tracker

This single-shot break-open shotgun is offered in both 12 and 20 gauge with rifled barrel or cylinder bore barrel. Both are 24" in length. Equipped with adjustable rifle sights. Weight is about 6 lbs.

NIB	Exc.	V.G.	Good	Fair	Poor
150	125	100	75	60	50

Super Light Rifle

This single-shot rifle is chambered for the .22 Hornet or .223 Rem. It is fitted with a 20" light weight barrel. Choice of scope mount and no sights or adjustable rear sight and ramp front sight. Black polymer stock with semi-beavertail fore-end. Weight is about 5.5 lbs.

NIB	Exc.	V.G.	Good	Fair	Poor
175	125	100	75	60	50

Huntsman

This is a blackpowder gun with break-open action hardwood pistol-grip stock. Fitted with a 24" barrel. Chambered for .50 or .45 caliber slug. Recoil pad. Weight is about 6.5 lbs. Introduced in 2002. In 2003 this model was offered in stainless steel.

NIB	Exc.	V.G.	Good	Fair	Poor
175	125	100	75	60	50

Tracker II

Combination two-barrel set of blackpowder barrel and 12 gauge slug barrel. Case colored frame. Hardwood stock.

NIB	Exc.	V.G.	Good	Fair	Poor
275	225	175	125	100	—

Handi-Rifle Combo

Combination two-barrel set of .50 blackpowder barrel and .243 Win. barrel. Hardwood stock. No iron sights.

NIB	Exc.	V.G.	Good	Fair	Poor
275	225	175	125	100	—

Sportster

This is a single shot .22 caliber short/LR or .22 WMR rifle with a 20" barrel. No iron sights. Black polymer Monte Carlo stock with matte black metal finish. Scope mount rail. Weight is about 5.5 lbs.

NIB	Exc.	V.G.	Good	Fair	Poor
175	125	100	75	60	50

Sportster Youth

As above but with standard stock. Weight is about 5.25 lbs.

NIB	Exc.	V.G.	Good	Fair	Poor
175	125	100	75	60	50

Sportster .17 HMR

This single-shot model is chambered for the .17 HMR cartridge and fitted with a 22" heavy varmint barrel. No iron sights. Black polymer Monte Carlo stock with matte black metal finish. Weight is about 7 lbs.

NIB	Exc.	V.G.	Good	Fair	Poor
175	125	100	75	60	50

Sportster .17 M2

As above but chambered for the .17 Mach2 cartridge. Introduced in 2005.

NIB	Exc.	V.G.	Good	Fair	Poor
175	125	100	75	60	50

Sportster SL

This is a semi-automatic rifle chambered for the .22 LR cartridge. Fitted with a 19" barrel. Walnut finished hardwood stock with Monte Carlo and pistol grip. Adjustable sights. Ten-round magazine. Weight is about 5.5 lbs. Introduced in 2004.

NIB	Exc.	V.G.	Good	Fair	Poor
150	125	100	75	60	50

Sportster Versa-Pack

This is a two-barrel set with a 22" .410 barrel and the other a 20" .22 caliber barrel. Hardwood stock with straight grip. Iron sights. Weight about 5.5 lbs.

NIB	Exc.	V.G.	Good	Fair	Poor
250	175	125	100	75	50

Sidekick Muzzleloader

Introduced in 2004 this model features a break-open action with side lever release chambered for the .50 caliber ball. Barrel length is 24" or 26". American hardwood stock with pistol grip and recoil pad. Black matte finish or stainless steel. Adjustable fiber optic sights. Weight is about 6.5 lbs. **NOTE:** Add $70 for stainless steel.

NIB	Exc.	V.G.	Good	Fair	Poor
200	165	125	100	75	50

NEWBURY ARMS CO.
Catskill, New York
Albany, New York

Pocket Pistol

A .25 caliber spur trigger pocket pistol with a 4" octagonal barrel. Blued, silver-plated with walnut grips.

NIB	Exc.	V.G.	Good	Fair	Poor
—	—	2400	2050	875	200

Pocket Revolver

A .26 caliber double-action percussion revolver with a 5" barrel and C-shaped exposed trigger. Blued with an iron or brass frame and walnut grips. The barrel marked "Newbury Arms Co. Albany." Produced in limited numbers between 1855 and 1860.

NIB	Exc.	V.G.	Good	Fair	Poor
—	—	7800	6900	3000	750

NEWCOMB, H. G.
Natchez, Mississippi

Pocket Pistol

A .41 caliber percussion pocket pistol with a 2.5" barrel, German silver mounts and a walnut stock. Manufactured in the 1850s.

NIB	Exc.	V.G.	Good	Fair	Poor
—	—	2400	1850	700	250

NEWTON ARMS CO.
Buffalo, New York

Also known as the Buffalo Newton Rifle Company and the Charles Newton Rifle Company. In operation from 1913 to 1932. **NOTE:** Any of the rifles listed chambered for a Newton caliber will bring a premium over standard calibers of about 25 percent.

Newton-Mauser Rifle

A .256 Newton caliber bolt-action rifle with a 24" barrel and double set triggers. Blued with a walnut stock. Manufactured circa 1914.

NIB	Exc.	V.G.	Good	Fair	Poor
—	—	1300	850	500	300

Standard Rifle First Type

A .22, .256, .280, .30, .33, and .35 Newton as well as .30-06 caliber bolt-action rifle with a 24" barrel, open or aperture sights and double set triggers. Blued with a walnut stock. Manufactured between 1916 and 1918.

Courtesy Amoskeag Auction Company, Inc.

NIB	Exc.	V.G.	Good	Fair	Poor
—	2500	2150	1500	900	400

Standard Rifle Second Model

A .256, .30, or .35 Newton as well as .30-06 caliber bolt-action rifle as above, but with an Enfield-style bolt handle. Manufactured after 1918.

NIB	Exc.	V.G.	Good	Fair	Poor
—	2500	2150	1500	900	400

Buffalo Newton Rifle

As above, but marked "Buffalo Newton Rifle Company."

NIB	Exc.	V.G.	Good	Fair	Poor
—	2000	1650	1000	600	300

NICHOLS & CHILDS
Conway, Massachusetts

Percussion Belt Revolver

A .34 caliber percussion revolver with a 6" round barrel and 6-shot cylinder. Blued or browned with walnut grips. It is estimated that fewer than 25 were made in 1838.

NIB	Exc.	V.G.	Good	Fair	Poor
—	—	1450	1175	4900	1250

Revolving Percussion Rifle

A .36 or .40 caliber percussion rifle with a 22", 26", or 30" barrel and a 5-, 6-, 7- or 9-shot cylinder. Blued or browned with a walnut stock with a patch box. It is believed that approximately 150 were made between 1838 and 1840.

NIB	Exc.	V.G.	Good	Fair	Poor
—	—	25000	16500	6600	2000

NIGHTHAWK CUSTOM
Berryville, Arkansas

Custom Talon/Talon II

1911-style semi-auto with 5" (Talon) or 4.25" (Talon II) barrel and fixed or adjustable sights. Several other barrel lengths/finishes available.

NIB	Exc.	V.G.	Good	Fair	Poor
2400	1950	1550	1200	700	300

Custom Predator

1911-style semi-auto with 5" barrel or 4.25" and fixed or adjustable sights. Several other barrel lengths/finishes available.

NIB	Exc.	V.G.	Good	Fair	Poor
2800	2350	1850	1400	750	300

GRP

Global Response Pistol. 1911-style semi-auto with 5" or 4.25" barrel and fixed or adjustable sights. Several other barrel lengths/finishes available.

NIB	Exc.	V.G.	Good	Fair	Poor
2400	1950	1550	1200	700	300

NOBLE
Haydenville, Massachusetts

In business between 1946 and 1971, this company manufactured a variety of plain, utilitarian firearms. In general, these arms are all worth approximately the same, that is, less than $200 in excellent condition. Noble firearms represent an attractive opportunity for the beginning collector as most can be had very inexpensively.

RIFLES

Model 10

A .22 caliber bolt-action single rifle with a 24" barrel. Pistol grip stock with no checkering. Open sights. Produced in the late 1950s.

NIB	Exc.	V.G.	Good	Fair	Poor
—	75	60	50	40	30

Model 20

A .22 caliber bolt-action rifle fitted with a 22" barrel. Open sights. Produced from the late 1950s to the early 1960s.

NIB	Exc.	V.G.	Good	Fair	Poor
—	75	60	50	40	30

Model 33

This is a .22 caliber slide-action rifle fitted with a 24" barrel and tubular magazine and Tenite stock. Produced from the late 1940s to the early 1950s.

NIB	Exc.	V.G.	Good	Fair	Poor
—	80	70	60	50	40

Model 33A

Same as above but fitted with a wood stock.

NIB	Exc.	V.G.	Good	Fair	Poor
—	75	60	50	40	30

Model 222

This is a single-shot bolt-action rifle chambered for the .22 caliber cartridge. Plain pistol-grip stock.

NIB	Exc.	V.G.	Good	Fair	Poor
—	85	75	60	50	40

Model 235

A rather dopey but kinda cute .22 caliber slide-action rifle with a 24" barrel and tubular magazine. Plain pistol-grip stock and groved slide handle.

NIB	Exc.	V.G.	Good	Fair	Poor
—	200	125	75	60	50

Model 275

A .22 caliber lever-action rifle with tubular magazine. Fitted with a 24" barrel. The plain stock has a semi-pistol grip.

NIB	Exc.	V.G.	Good	Fair	Poor
—	175	100	80	60	50

SHOTGUNS

Model 40

This is a hammerless slide-action shotgun chambered for the 12 gauge shell. It is fitted with a tubular magazine and 28" barrel with multi choke. Plain pistol stock with grooved slide handle.

NIB	Exc.	V.G.	Good	Fair	Poor
—	125	100	85	70	50

Model 50

Same as above but without the multi choke.

NIB	Exc.	V.G.	Good	Fair	Poor
—	115	90	80	65	50

Model 60

A hammerless slide-action shotgun in 12 or 16 gauge with tubular magazine and fitted with a 28" barrel with adjustable choke. Plain pistol grip stock with grooved slide handle.

NIB	Exc.	V.G.	Good	Fair	Poor
—	175	150	125	100	75

Model 65

Same as above but without adjustable choke.

NIB	Exc.	V.G.	Good	Fair	Poor
—	150	125	100	75	60

Model 66CLP

Offered in 12 or 16 gauge this slide-action shotgun is fitted with a 28" plain barrel and a keyed lock fire control system.

NIB	Exc.	V.G.	Good	Fair	Poor
—	160	140	110	85	70

Model 66RCLP

Similar to above but fitted with a 28" vent rib barrel and checkered pistol-grip stock. Adjustable choke is standard.

NIB	Exc.	V.G.	Good	Fair	Poor
—	200	175	150	125	100

Model 66RLP

Same as above but without adjustable choke.

NIB	Exc.	V.G.	Good	Fair	Poor
—	175	150	125	100	75

Model 66XL

Similar to the above models but with plain barrel, and checkering only on the slide handle.

NIB	Exc.	V.G.	Good	Fair	Poor
—	150	125	100	75	60

Model 70CLP

Similar to the Model 66 series but offered in .410 bore with 26" barrel and adjustable choke. Both the buttstock and slide handle are checkered.

NIB	Exc.	V.G.	Good	Fair	Poor
—	175	150	125	100	75

Model 70RCLP

This variation is fitted with a 26" ventilated rib barrel.

NIB	Exc.	V.G.	Good	Fair	Poor
—	200	175	150	125	100

Model 70RLP

This model has a vent rib barrel and no adjustable choke.

NIB	Exc.	V.G.	Good	Fair	Poor
—	175	150	125	100	75

Model 70XL

This version has no adjustable choke but is fitted with a 26" vent rib barrel. Stock is checked.

NIB	Exc.	V.G.	Good	Fair	Poor
—	125	100	80	70	60

Model 602RCLP

This is a hammerless slide-action shotgun chambered for the 20 gauge shell. It is fitted with a 28" vent barrel and adjustable choke. Checkered pistol grip stock with slide handle.

NIB	Exc.	V.G.	Good	Fair	Poor
—	225	200	175	125	100

Model 602CLP

Same as above but with plain barrel.

NIB	Exc.	V.G.	Good	Fair	Poor
—	175	150	125	100	75

Model 602RLP

Same as Model RCLP except without the addition of an adjustable choke device.

NIB	Exc.	V.G.	Good	Fair	Poor
—	200	175	150	125	100

Model 602XL

Same as above but with only the slide handle checkered.

NIB	Exc.	V.G.	Good	Fair	Poor
—	150	125	100	75	60

Model 662

This 20 gauge slide-action shotgun has a plain aluminum barrel with checkered pistol grip and slide handle. The receiver is made from aluminum. Produced in the late 1960s.

NIB	Exc.	V.G.	Good	Fair	Poor
—	200	175	150	125	100

Model 80

This model is a semi-automatic inertia-operated shotgun chambered for the .410 shell. It is fitted with a 26" barrel, plain pistol stock with slotted forearm. Produced in the early to mid 1960s.

NIB	Exc.	V.G.	Good	Fair	Poor
—	250	200	150	125	100

Model 166L

This is a 12 gauge slide-action shotgun with a key lock system. It is fitted with a 24" barrel bored for rifled slug. Lyman peep rear sight with post front sight. Checkered pistol and slide handle.

NIB	Exc.	V.G.	Good	Fair	Poor
—	250	200	150	125	100

Model 420

This shotgun is a box lock design side-by-side with double triggers and offered in 12, 16, 20 gauge, as well as .410 bore. Barrel lengths are 28" for all gauges except .410 where it is 26". Lightly engraved frame. Checkered walnut stock and splinter forearm.

NIB	Exc.	V.G.	Good	Fair	Poor
—	300	250	200	150	100

Model 450E

This model is similar to the Model 420 with the addition of automatic ejectors and not offered in .410 bore. Checkered pistol grip stock with beavertail forearm. Produced in the late 1960s.

NIB	Exc.	V.G.	Good	Fair	Poor
—	350	275	225	175	125

NORINCO
Peoples Republic of China
China North Industries Corp.

Norinco is a state-owned conglomerate in China that exported firearms to the United States from 1988 to 1995. Importation of Norinco firearms was banned in conjunction with the 1994 Crime Bill and various trade sanctions against China, with the exception of several shotguns that were marketed between 1999 and 2002.

ATD .22

A .22 caliber semi-automatic rifle with a 19.4" barrel and 11-shot magazine located in the butt. Blued with a hardwood stock. Importation began in 1987.

NIB	Exc.	V.G.	Good	Fair	Poor
200	150	125	100	75	50

EM-321

A .22 caliber slide-action rifle with a 19.5" barrel and 10-shot tubular magazine. Blued with a hardwood stock. Introduced in 1989.

NIB	Exc.	V.G.	Good	Fair	Poor
150	100	85	75	65	50

Model HL-12-203 Shotgun

A 12 gauge boxlock over/under shotgun with 30" ventilated rib barrels fitted for choke tubes, single trigger and automatic ejectors. Blued with a hardwood stock. Introduced in 1989.

NIB	Exc.	V.G.	Good	Fair	Poor
400	325	275	225	175	125

Model HL-12-102 Shotgun

A 12 gauge slide-action shotgun with a 28" barrel and 3-shot magazine. Blued with a hardwood stock. Introduced in 1989.

NIB	Exc.	V.G.	Good	Fair	Poor
275	225	200	175	125	100

Model 97 Hammer Pump

Similar in appearance to the Winchester Model 1897 shotgun. Fitted with a 20" barrel with cylinder choke. Hardwood stock.

NIB	Exc.	V.G.	Good	Fair	Poor
375	275	200	150	100	75

Type 54-1 Tokarev

A 7.62x25mm caliber semi-automatic pistol with a 4.6" barrel, fixed sights, and 8-shot magazine. Blued with plastic grips. Imported in 1989.

NIB	Exc.	V.G.	Good	Fair	Poor
—	300	250	200	100	80

1911 A1

Steel-framed clone of the 1911 .45 A1 semi-auto. Very popular with competition shooters as a platform for custom guns. No longer imported.

NIB	Exc.	V.G.	Good	Fair	Poor
—	400	350	200	100	80

Model 213 Pistol

A copy of the Browning P-35 semi-automatic pistol. Sold in 1988 only.

NIB	Exc.	V.G.	Good	Fair	Poor
—	250	200	150	100	75

Type 59 Makarov

A .380 or 9mm Makarov caliber double-action semi-automatic pistol with a 3.5" barrel and 8-shot magazine. Blued with plastic grips.

NIB	Exc.	V.G.	Good	Fair	Poor
—	275	250	225	175	125

SKS Rifle

A 7.62x39mm caliber semi-automatic rifle with a 20.5" barrel, folding bayonet and either a 10-shot fixed magazine or 30-shot detachable magazine. Blued with a hardwood stock. Importation began in 1988.

NIB	Exc.	V.G.	Good	Fair	Poor
—	400	300	225	150	100

Type 84S AK

Similar to the AKS service rifle, in 5.56mm caliber with a 16" barrel and 30-shot magazine.

NIB	Exc.	V.G.	Good	Fair	Poor
900	800	700	550	350	200

Type 84S-1

As above, with an underfolding metal stock.

NIB	Exc.	V.G.	Good	Fair	Poor
1050	900	750	575	375	225

Type 84S-3

As above, with a composition stock.

NIB	Exc.	V.G.	Good	Fair	Poor
1000	850	700	600	400	225

NORTH AMERICAN ARMS
Provo, Utah

Mini-Revolver

A .22 or .22 Magnum caliber spur trigger revolver with a 1" or 2.5" barrel and 5-shot cylinder. Stainless steel with plastic or laminated rosewood grips. Introduced in 1975 and made in the styles listed.

Standard Rimfire Version

NIB	Exc.	V.G.	Good	Fair	Poor
225	175	150	—	125	100

2 Cylinder Magnum Convertible Version

NIB	Exc.	V.G.	Good	Fair	Poor
275	200	175	—	145	125

Viper Belt Buckle Version

NIB	Exc.	V.G.	Good	Fair	Poor
225	175	150	—	125	100

Magnum Version

NIB	Exc.	V.G.	Good	Fair	Poor
250	200	175	—	150	100

Standard 3 Gun Set

NIB	Exc.	V.G.	Good	Fair	Poor
725	575	400	—	300	225

Deluxe 3 Gun Set

NIB	Exc.	V.G.	Good	Fair	Poor
800	650	475	—	375	275

Cased .22 Magnum

NIB	Exc.	V.G.	Good	Fair	Poor
350	250	200	—	150	125

Companion

This is a .22 caliber cap-and-ball mini revolver. It has a 1.125" barrel. Overall length is 4.6" and weight is about 5 oz.

NIB	Exc.	V.G.	Good	Fair	Poor
200	165	150	125	100	75

Super Companion

Same as above but with longer cylinder. It has a 1.62" barrel and weighs about 7 oz.

NIB	Exc.	V.G.	Good	Fair	Poor
200	165	150	125	100	75

Black Widow

This is a five-shot fixed-sight revolver with oversize black rubber grips with a 2" or 4" barrel. Chambered for .22 LR or .22 Win. Mag. Stainless steel. Weight is approximately 8.8 oz. **NOTE:** Add $20 for adjustable sights.

NIB	Exc.	V.G.	Good	Fair	Poor
280	225	175	125	100	75

Mini-Master

This model is similar to the Black Widow with a 2" or 4" barrel. This model also gives a choice of either .22 LR or .22 Win. Mag. Stainless steel. Weight is approximately 10.7 oz. **NOTE:** Add $20 for adjustable sights.

NIB	Exc.	V.G.	Good	Fair	Poor
280	225	175	125	100	75

"The Earl" Single-Action Revolver

Single-action mini-revolver patterned after 1858-style Remington percussion revolver. Chambered in .22 Magnum with .22 Long Rifle accessory cylinder. Features include a 4" octagonal barrel, spur trigger, five-shot cylinder, faux loading lever that serves as cylinder pin release, wood grips, fixed notch rear sight and barleycorn front sight. Overall length 7-3/4". Weight: 6.8 oz.

.22 Magnum only

NIB	Exc.	V.G.	Good	Fair	Poor
290	225	175	125	100	75

.22 convertible

NIB	Exc.	V.G.	Good	Fair	Poor
325	275	200	150	125	100

Single-Action Revolver

A polished stainless steel single-action revolver chambered for the .45 Winchester Magnum and the .450 Magnum Express cartridge. It has a 7.5" barrel and a 5-shot cylinder. There is a transfer bar safety, and the grips are walnut. This model was discontinued in 1988. Available with two cylinders. **NOTE:** Add $200 for extra cylinder.

NIB	Exc.	V.G.	Good	Fair	Poor
—	1200	950	700	400	250

Guardian

This is a semi-automatic double-action-only pocket pistol chambered in .32 ACP, .32 NAA or .25 NAA. Magazine capacity is 6 rounds and the barrel length is 2.2". Overall length of the pistol is 4.4" and weight empty is 13.5 oz. Introduced in 1998. Add 25 percent for Crimson Trace laser grips.

NIB	Exc.	V.G.	Good	Fair	Poor
400	300	225	175	150	125

Guardian .380

Similar to the above model but chambered for the .380 cartridge. Barrel length is 2.5". Magazine capacity is 6 rounds. Weight is about 19 oz. Add $25 percent for Crimson Trace lasergrips.

NIB	Exc.	V.G.	Good	Fair	Poor
450	350	250	195	175	150

NORTH AMERICAN ARMS CORP.
Toronto, Canada

Brigadier

A .45 ACP caliber semi-automatic pistol with a 5" barrel, 8-shot magazine and alloy frame. Weight 4.5 lbs. Produced in limited quantity between 1948 and 1951. Rarely if ever seen; value should be in excess of $5000 in Excellent or better condition.

NORTH AMERICAN SAFARI EXPRESS
Liege, Belgium
SEE—Francotte

A trade name used by Francotte on their double rifles imported and distributed by Armes De Chasse of Chads Ford, Pennsylvania.

NORTH & COUCH
New York, New York

Animal Trap Gun

A .28 or. 30 caliber percussion pepperbox with either a 1.75" or 2.12" barrel group and a hammer made with or without a spur. Marked "North & Couch, Middletown, Conn." or "North & Couch New York." Manufactured during the 1860s.

Disk Hammer Model

NIB	Exc.	V.G.	Good	Fair	Poor
—	—	2200	1850	700	300

Spur Hammer Model

NIB	Exc.	V.G.	Good	Fair	Poor
—	—	3000	2750	900	350

NORTON ARMAMENT CORPORATION
Mt. Clemens, Michigan
SEE—Budischowsky

This firm manufactured Budischowsky Model TP-70 semi-automatic pistols prior to 1979. After that date, these arms were made by the American Arms and Ammunition Company. Values below are for early Michigan production. Deduct 15 percent for later Florida and Utah production.

NIB	Exc.	V.G.	Good	Fair	Poor
—	500	375	250	125	100

NOSLER CUSTOM
Bend, Oregon

Nosler Custom Model 48 Sporter

Bolt-action centerfire rifle chambered in various calibers, 24" barrel, round top receiver, onyx gray composite stock. Introduced 2007. Price shown includes scope. Limited edition series has high grade walnut stock, double square bridge action with integral scope bases. Only 500 made. **NOTE:** Add 50 percent for limited edition model.

NIB	Exc.	V.G.	Good	Fair	Poor
2495	2000	1600	900	500	300

NORWICH PISTOL CO.
Norwich, Connecticut

Established in 1875 by the New York retailer Maltby, Curtis & Company, this firm manufactured a wide variety of inexpensive spur trigger revolvers that were sold under these trade names: America, Bulldozer, Challenge, Chieftain, Crescent, Defiance, Hartford Arms, Maltby Henley, Metropolitan Police, Nonpariel, Norwich Arms, Parole, Patriot, Pinafore, Prairie King, Protector, Spy, True Blue, U.M.C. Winfield Arms. The company ceased operations in 1881. The value for any of its arms listed is approximate.

NIB	Exc.	V.G.	Good	Fair	Poor
—	—	300	200	75	50

NOWLIN MANUFACTURING COMPANY
Claremore, Oklahoma

Match Classic

This 1911 pistol has a wide range of features. It can be chambered in 9mm, .38 Super, 9x23, .40 S&W, and .45 ACP. It has a 5" barrel, adjustable trigger, checkered main spring housing, hardwood grips, front and rear cocking serrations. The price listed is for the basic pistols. Options will greatly affect price.

NIB	Exc.	V.G.	Good	Fair	Poor
1600	1250	800	600	400	250

Compact Carry

This pistol is similar to the Match Classic with the exception of a 4" barrel on a full-size frame. Again options will greatly affect price.

NIB	Exc.	V.G.	Good	Fair	Poor
1495	1100	700	500	300	200

Match Master

These hand-built pistols offered a choice of S.T.I., Caspian Hi-Cap, or Nowlin STD Gov't frames. Available in 9mm, 9x23, .38 Super, .40 S&W, and .45 ACP. Many special features are included in standard pistol and many extra cost options are available.

NIB	Exc.	V.G.	Good	Fair	Poor
2400	1750	1200	800	600	300

O.D.I.
Midland Park, New Jersey

Viking

A .45 caliber double-action semi-automatic pistol with a 5" barrel and 7-shot magazine. Stainless steel with teak grips. Manufactured in 1981 and 1982.

NIB	Exc.	V.G.	Good	Fair	Poor
700	625	375	300	200	100

Viking Combat

As above, with a 4.25" barrel.

NIB	Exc.	V.G.	Good	Fair	Poor
700	625	375	300	200	100

O.K.
Unknown

See—Marlin

O'CONNELL, DAVID
New York, New York

Pocket Pistol

A .41 caliber percussion pocket pistol with a 2.5" barrel, German silver mounts, and walnut stock. Manufactured during the 1850s.

NIB	Exc.	V.G.	Good	Fair	Poor
—	—	3650	3000	1025	300

O'DELL, STEPHEN
Natchez, Mississippi

Pocket Pistol

A .34 to .44 caliber percussion pocket pistol with a 2" to 4" barrel, German silver mounts and walnut stock. Manufactured during the 1850s.

NIB	Exc.	V.G.	Good	Fair	Poor
—	—	6750	6000	2500	950

OBREGON
Mexico City, Mexico

This is a .45 caliber semi-automatic pistol with a 5" barrel. Similar to the Colt M1911A1 but with a combination side and safety latch on the left side of the frame. The breech is locked by rotating the barrel, instead of the Browning swinging link. This unusual locking system results in a tubular front end appearance to the pistol. Originally designed for the Mexican military it was not adopted as such and only about 1,000 pistols were produced and sold commercially. The pistol is 8.5" overall and weighs about 40 oz. The magazine holds seven cartridges. This is a rare pistol; an independent appraisal is suggested prior to sale.

NIB	Exc.	V.G.	Good	Fair	Poor
—	3750	2300	1850	1550	800

OHIO ORDNANCE INC.
Chardon, Ohio

Model 1918A3 Self-Loading Rifle

This rifle is a semi-automatic version of the famed Browning Automatic Rifle. It is chambered for the .30-06 cartridge and has a 20-round magazine. It was introduced in this configuration in 1996. **NOTE:** Add $200 for .308 or 8mm caliber guns. Subtract 10 percent for bakelite stock.

NIB	Exc.	V.G.	Good	Fair	Poor
3800	3300	2500	1850	1500	750

Colt Browning Water Cooled Gun

Introduced in 2001, this is a semi-automatic version of the famous Browning Model 1928 belt-fed machine gun. This model features a .30-06 or 7.65 Argentine caliber belt-fed gun with tripod, wooden ammo box, water hose, water can, and one 250 cloth belt. **NOTE:** Add $200 for .308 or 8mm caliber guns.

NIB	Exc.	V.G.	Good	Fair	Poor
3700	3300	2500	1850	1500	750

1919A4

Semi-automatic version of the air-cooled, belt-fed .30-caliber 1919 machine gun. Chambered for .308/7.62 NATO.

NIB	Exc.	V.G.	Good	Fair	Poor
3250	2800	2000	1250	1100	500

OJANGUREN Y VIDOSA
Eibar, Spain

This typical Eibar company produced mediocre firearms from the early 1920s and was forced out of business during the Spanish Civil War.

Apache (Model 1920)

A typical Eibar Browning copy that is chambered for the 6.35mm cartridge. It is of the typical low quality associated with most Spanish arms of this era. The slide is marked "Pistole Browning Automatica Cal. 6.35 Apache". The finish is blued, and the plastic grips have a head with a beret and the word "Apache" molded into them.

NIB	Exc.	V.G.	Good	Fair	Poor
—	250	175	125	75	50

As above but chambered for the 7.65mm cartridge.

Courtesy James Rankin

NIB	Exc.	V.G.	Good	Fair	Poor
—	275	225	190	100	75

Ojanguren

The trade name this company used to cover the line of revolvers they produced in the 1930s. They produced two in .32 caliber and two chambered for the .38 Special cartridge. They are similar in appearance and have barrel lengths of either 3" or 6". The finishes are blued, and they have plastic grips. One of the .38 caliber models the "Legitimo Tanque" is a reasonably well-made gun that was popular with the Spanish target shooters. These guns have little collector value, little practical value and are all priced alike.

NIB	Exc.	V.G.	Good	Fair	Poor
—	175	125	100	75	50

Tanque

A blowback-operated semi-automatic chambered for the 6.35mm cartridge. It has a 1.5" barrel and is actually an original design, which was rarely found on Eibar guns of this period. It has an oddly shaped slide, and the barrel is retained by means of a screw in the front of the frame. It has a 6-shot magazine, and the slide is marked "6.35 Tanque Patent". The plastic grips have a tank molded into them and the word "Tanque", as well as the letters "O&V".

NIB	Exc.	V.G.	Good	Fair	Poor
—	175	125	100	75	50

OLD WEST GUN CO.
Houston, Texas

See—Cimarron Arms

An importer of reproduction firearms primarily manufactured by Aldo Uberti of Italy. In 1987 this company purchased the inventory of Allen Firearms and subsequently changed their name to Cimarron Arms.

OLYMPIC ARMS, INC.
Olympia, Washington

PISTOLS

Black Widow

A .45 caliber semi-automatic pistol with a 3.9" barrel and 6-shot magazine. Nickel-plated with ivory Micarta grips with a spider engraved on them.

NIB	Exc.	V.G.	Good	Fair	Poor
700	575	450	350	300	200

Enforcer

A .45 caliber semi-automatic pistol with a 3.8" barrel and 6-shot magazine. Parkerized, anodized or nickel-plated with rubber grips. Weight is approximately 36 oz.

NIB	Exc.	V.G.	Good	Fair	Poor
650	500	400	350	300	200

Match Master

As above, with a 5" barrel and 7-shot magazine. Weight is about 40 oz.

NIB	Exc.	V.G.	Good	Fair	Poor
650	500	400	350	300	200

Match Master 6"

Same as above but with 6" barrel and slide. Weight is approximately 44 oz.

NIB	Exc.	V.G.	Good	Fair	Poor
675	550	400	350	300	200

Cohort

Fitted with a 4" bull barrel with a full size frame. Magazine capacity is 7 rounds. Weight is about 38 oz.

NIB	Exc.	V.G.	Good	Fair	Poor
675	550	400	350	300	200

Safari G.I.

This model is built on a Match Master frame with 5" barrel with fixed sights. Finish is flat black Parkerized. Checkered walnut grips.

NIB	Exc.	V.G.	Good	Fair	Poor
600	450	400	350	300	200

Schuetzen Pistol Works Big Deuce

This model is made in Olympic Arms specialty shop called Schuetzen Pistol Works. Marked "Schuetzen Pistol Works" on the slide and "Safari Arms" on the frame. Introduced in 1995. This semi-automatic pistol is chambered for the .45 ACP cartridge and fitted with a 6" barrel, smooth walnut grips, and a number of other custom features. Magazine capacity is 7 rounds. Weight is approximately 40 oz. Black slide with stainless steel frame.

NIB	Exc.	V.G.	Good	Fair	Poor
950	800	700	500	275	150

Schuetzen Pistol Works Crest

Similar to the above model with the same markings. This version features a .45 ACP pistol with 4.5", 5", or 5.5" barrel. Checkered walnut grips. Offered in both right- and left-hand configurations. Stainless steel finish. Introduced in 1993. Weight is about 39 oz. depending on barrel length. **NOTE:** Left-hand model will bring a small premium.

NIB	Exc.	V.G.	Good	Fair	Poor
800	650	500	400	275	150

Schuetzen Pistol Works Griffon

Similar to the above specialty models. This version is fitted with a 5" barrel and smooth walnut grips. Magazine capacity is 10 rounds. Stainless steel finish. Numerous custom features. Introduced in 1995.

NIB	Exc.	V.G.	Good	Fair	Poor
1300	1150	975	650	400	200

Schuetzen Pistol Works Carrier

Special built model along the lines of the Detonics Score Master with adjustable sights.

NIB	Exc.	V.G.	Good	Fair	Poor
700	600	500	400	250	150

Black-Tac

Semi-automatic .45 ACP pistol treated with "black-tac" process – advantages of hard chrome without its drawbacks such as embrittlement.

NIB	Exc.	V.G.	Good	Fair	Poor
800	650	500	400	275	150

Constable

Semi-automatic pistol chambered for .45 ACP with 4" barrel, 5.75" sight radius, 7+1 capacity, 35 oz. Introduced 2006.

NIB	Exc.	V.G.	Good	Fair	Poor
950	800	700	500	275	150

Custom Street Deuce

Semi-automatic chambered for .45 ACP with 5.2" bull barrel, 7" sight radius, 7+1 capacity, 38 oz. Many options. Introduced 2006.

NIB	Exc.	V.G.	Good	Fair	Poor
1300	1150	975	650	400	200

Custom Journeyman

Semi-automatic chambered for .45 ACP with 4" bull barrel, 6" sight radius, 6+1 capacity, 35 oz. Many options. Introduced 2006.

NIB	Exc.	V.G.	Good	Fair	Poor
1100	800	675	500	300	150

Trail Boss

Semi-automatic pistol in the Westerner line chambered for .45 ACP, with 6" barrel, 8" sight radius, 7+1 capacity, 43 oz. Introduced 2006.

NIB	Exc.	V.G.	Good	Fair	Poor
950	800	700	500	275	150

Westerner

Semi-automatic pistol chambered for .45 ACP with 5" barrel, 7" sight radius, 7+1 capacity, 39 oz. Introduced 2006.

NIB	Exc.	V.G.	Good	Fair	Poor
950	800	700	500	275	150

Model OA-93-PT

Similar to OA-93-CAR but with F8R handguard with vertical grip, post-ban muzzle brake, and detachable stock.

NIB	Exc.	V.G.	Good	Fair	Poor
1100	800	675	500	300	150

Wolverine

Polymer-frame, vent-rib replica of the old "ray gun" .22 Whitney Wolverine semi-automatic pistol. Cool, baby!

NIB	Exc.	V.G.	Good	Fair	Poor
300	265	250	200	150	100

RIFLES

SGW Ultra Match (PCR-1)

A match grade copy of the AR-15 with a 20" or 24" barrel and not fitted with a carrying handle. Weight is about 10 lbs.

NIB	Exc.	V.G.	Good	Fair	Poor
1250	1000	800	500	400	200

Model PCR-2

Similar to the above model but fitted with a 16" match grade barrel, post front and E2 rear sight. Weight is approximately 8.2 lbs.

NIB	Exc.	V.G.	Good	Fair	Poor
1300	1050	850	550	450	225

Model PCR-3

Same as above model but with forged T-12 upper receiver.

NIB	Exc.	V.G.	Good	Fair	Poor
1300	1050	850	550	450	225

Model PCR-4

This version is fitted with a 20" steel barrel with post front sight and A-1 style rear sight. Weight is approximately 8.5 lbs.

NIB	Exc.	V.G.	Good	Fair	Poor
900	725	575	450	350	150

Model PCR-5

Similar to the above but fitted with a 16" barrel. Weight is about 7 lbs.

NIB	Exc.	V.G.	Good	Fair	Poor
900	725	575	450	350	150

Model PCR-6

This AR-15 style rifle is chambered for the 7.62x39 Russian caliber. It is fitted with a 16" barrel with a post front sight and a A-1 style rear sight. Weight is about 7 lbs.

NIB	Exc.	V.G.	Good	Fair	Poor
900	725	575	450	350	150

Model PCR-7 "Eliminator"

This model is a shortened version of the PCR-4. It is fitted with a 16" barrel, A2 handguard, A2 stock, and an A2 pistol grip. Weight is about 7.6 lbs.

NIB	Exc.	V.G.	Good	Fair	Poor
900	725	575	450	350	150

Model PCR-Service Match

This .223 caliber rifle has a 20" stainless steel match barrel. It is fitted with a post front sight and a E-2 style rear sight. Weight is about 8.7 lbs.

NIB	Exc.	V.G.	Good	Fair	Poor
1100	800	675	500	300	150

Ultra CSR Tactical Rifle

This is a bolt-action rifle chambered for the .308 Winchester cartridge. Barrel length is 26". Magazine capacity is 5 rounds. Tactical-style stock is black synthetic with aluminum bedding block. Comes complete with scope rings and Harris bipod in a hardcase. Weight is approximately 9.4 lbs.

NIB	Exc.	V.G.	Good	Fair	Poor
1100	800	675	500	300	150

Model CAR-97

Chambered for the .223 cartridge or optional 9mm, .40 S&W, or .45 ACP pistol cartridges. Fitted with a 16" barrel and non-collapsible CAR-style stock. Overall length is 34". Weight is about 7 lbs. **NOTE:** Add $50 for pistol cartridge conversion.

NIB	Exc.	V.G.	Good	Fair	Poor
900	725	575	450	350	150

Model OA-96

This model has a 6" barrel with pistol grip only, no buttstock. The 30-round magazine is pinned and cannot be detached. Break-open-action allows loading with stripper clips. Overall length is 15.75". Weight is about 4.2 lbs. BATFE approved.

NIB	Exc.	V.G.	Good	Fair	Poor
1100	800	675	500	300	150

Model OA-98

Similar to the OA-93 but with lightening holes on the grip, mount, magazine. Fitted with a 6" barrel with no vertical grip. Weight is about 3 lbs. No buttstock.

NIB	Exc.	V.G.	Good	Fair	Poor
1100	800	675	500	300	150

UM-1P

Gas-operated .223 semi-automatic target rifle based on AR-15 chassis. Features include 24" stainless steel bull barrel, anodized finish, pistol grip with bottom swell, Picatinny rail, Harris bipod, and competition trigger.

NIB	Exc.	V.G.	Good	Fair	Poor
900	725	575	450	350	150

UM-1

Similar to UM-1P but with 20" stainless steel bull barrel, standard pistol grip, no bipod.

NIB	Exc.	V.G.	Good	Fair	Poor
900	725	575	450	350	150

SM-1P

Tricked-out AR-15 in .223 with 20" stainless steel barrel, free-floating sleeve handguard, carry handle upper or Picatinny rail flattop, pneumatic recoil buffer, Bob Jones interchangeable sight system, competition trigger and Maxhard receivers.

NIB	Exc.	V.G.	Good	Fair	Poor
1300	1050	850	550	450	225

SM-1

Similar to SM-1P but with standard receivers, trigger and sights. No pneumatic recoil buffer.

NIB	Exc.	V.G.	Good	Fair	Poor
1000	700	575	450	300	150

ML-1

Similar to SM-1 but with 16" barrel with flash hider, 6-position collapsible buttstock and free-floating aluminum tube handguard.

NIB	Exc.	V.G.	Good	Fair	Poor
1000	700	575	450	300	150

ML-2

Similar to ML-1 but with flat-top upper receiver with Picatinny rails, standard buttstock and bull barrel.

NIB	Exc.	V.G.	Good	Fair	Poor
1000	700	575	450	300	150

Model K8

Similar to ML-2 but with 20" barrel and extended aluminum tube handguard.

NIB	Exc.	V.G.	Good	Fair	Poor
1000	700	575	450	300	150

Model K8-MAG

Similar to K8 but with 24" bull barrel and chambered in .223 WSM, .243 WSM or .25 WSM.

NIB	Exc.	V.G.	Good	Fair	Poor
1000	700	575	450	300	150

K3B

Features include 16" chrome-moly barrel with flash-hidefully adjustable rear sight, 6-position collapsible buttstock and carbine-length handguard.

NIB	Exc.	V.G.	Good	Fair	Poor
900	725	575	450	350	150

K3B-M4

Similar to K3B but with M4S fiberite handguard with heatshield and 32.25" overall length.

NIB	Exc.	V.G.	Good	Fair	Poor
900	725	575	450	350	150

K3B-CAR

Similar to K3B but with 30.5" overall length.

NIB	Exc.	V.G.	Good	Fair	Poor
900	725	575	450	350	150

K3B-FAR

Similar to K3B but with Featherweight barrel and weight of 5.84 lbs.

NIB	Exc.	V.G.	Good	Fair	Poor
900	725	575	450	350	150

K4B

Similar to K3B but with 20" barrel and rifle-length fiberite handguard.

NIB	Exc.	V.G.	Good	Fair	Poor
900	725	575	450	350	150

K4B-A4

Similar to K4B but with ventilated FIRSH rifle-length handguard.

NIB	Exc.	V.G.	Good	Fair	Poor
950	775	600	475	375	175

LTF

Features include 16" chrome-mol barrel, free-floating FIRSH handguard with Picatinny rails, ACE FX skeleton stock, ERGO pistol grip and multiple-aperture flipup sight system.

NIB	Exc.	V.G.	Good	Fair	Poor
1100	800	675	500	350	150

LT-M4

Similar to LTF but with 16" stainless steel barrel.

NIB	Exc.	V.G.	Good	Fair	Poor
1100	800	675	500	350	150

K16

Similar to K8 but with 16" bull chrome-moly barrel.

NIB	Exc.	V.G.	Good	Fair	Poor
800	625	475	400	300	125

GI-16

Basic AR-15-inspired semi-automatic rifle chambered in .223. 16" chrome-moly barrel with flash-hider, 6-position collapsible buttstock, carbine-length handguard and rear sight adjustable for windage only.

NIB	Exc.	V.G.	Good	Fair	Poor
900	725	575	450	350	150

Plinker Plus

Similar to GI-16 but with standard buttstock.

NIB	Exc.	V.G.	Good	Fair	Poor
800	625	475	400	250	100

Plinker Plus 20

Similar to Plinker Plus but with 20" barrel and rifle-length handguard.

NIB	Exc.	V.G.	Good	Fair	Poor
850	675	525	425	300	125

K7 Eliminator

Similar to K4B but with 16" barrel with extended handguard and sight radius of 20" barreled models.

NIB	Exc.	V.G.	Good	Fair	Poor
900	725	575	450	350	150

K30

Similar to GI-16 but chambered in .30 Carbine. Includes mag well insert to accept military-spec magazines.

NIB	Exc.	V.G.	Good	Fair	Poor
900	725	575	450	350	150

K9/K10/K40/K45

Similar to K30 but chambered, respectively, for 9mm Parabellum, 10mm, .40 S&W and .45ACP. Models use converted surplus military magazines.

NIB	Exc.	V.G.	Good	Fair	Poor
900	725	575	450	350	150

K9-GL/K40-GL

Similar to K9 and K40 but accept standard Glock pistol magazines.

NIB	Exc.	V.G.	Good	Fair	Poor
900	725	575	450	350	150

Model OA-93-CAR

Features include OA-93 FT recoil-reducing upper, 16" chrome-moly barrel with Phantom flash hider, and side-folding buttstock.

NIB	Exc.	V.G.	Good	Fair	Poor
1000	700	575	450	300	150

Model OA-93-PT

Similar to OA-93-CAR but with F8R handguard with vertical grip, post-ban muzzle brake, and detachable stock.

NIB	Exc.	V.G.	Good	Fair	Poor
1000	700	575	450	300	150

Olympic Arms Gamestalker

Sporting AR-style rifle chambered in .223, .243 and .25 WSSM and .300 OSSM. Features include forged aluminum upper and lower; flat top receiver with Picatinny rail; gas block front sight; 22" stainless steel fluted barrel; free-floating slotted tube handguard; camo finish overall; ACE FX skeleton stock. Price: $1,359.

OMEGA
Springfield Armory
Geneseo, Illinois

Omega Pistol

A high-grade target-type pistol that is patterned after the Colt Model 1911 pistol, with marked improvements. It is chambered for the .38 Super, 10mm, and the .45 ACP cartridges. The barrel is either 5" or 6" in length and has polygonal rifling. The barrels are furnished either ported or plain and feature a lockup system that eliminates the barrel link and bushing associated with the normal Browning design. This pistol has a dual extractor system, adjustable sights, and Pachmayr grips. It was introduced in 1987.

NIB	Exc.	V.G.	Good	Fair	Poor
900	725	575	450	350	150

Over/Under Shotgun

A 12, 20, 28 or .410 bore boxlock over/under shotgun with 26" or 28" ventilated rib barrels, single trigger and extractors. Blued with a walnut stock.

NIB	Exc.	V.G.	Good	Fair	Poor
—	450	300	200	150	125

Side-by-Side Shotgun

A 20, 28 or .410 bore boxlock double-barrel shotgun with 26" barrels, double triggers and extractors. Blued with a hardwood stock.

NIB	Exc.	V.G.	Good	Fair	Poor
—	350	250	150	100	75

Single Barreled Shotgun

A 12, 20 or .410 bore single barrel shotgun manufactured in a variety of barrel lengths and fitted with an extractor. Blued with a hardwood stock.

NIB	Exc.	V.G.	Good	Fair	Poor
—	125	85	65	50	35

OMEGA FIREARMS CO.
Flower Mound, Texas

Bolt-Action Rifle

A .25-06 to .358 Norma Magnum bolt-action rifle with a 22" or 24" barrel, octagonal bolt, adjustable trigger and rotary magazine. Blued with a two-piece walnut or laminated stock. Discontinued circa 1975.

NIB	Exc.	V.G.	Good	Fair	Poor
—	800	650	550	424	200

OPUS SPORTING ARMS, INC.
Long Beach, California

Opus One

A .243, .270, or .30-06 caliber bolt-action rifle with a 24" barrel, well figured walnut stock and an ebony pistol grip cap as well as fore-end tip. Built on a Model 70 Winchester action. Manufactured in 1987 and 1988.

NIB	Exc.	V.G.	Good	Fair	Poor
—	2250	1600	1150	700	350

Opus Two

As above, in 7mm Remington Magnum and .300 Winchester Magnum.

NIB	Exc.	V.G.	Good	Fair	Poor
—	2500	1750	1250	750	350

Opus Three

As above, in .375 Holland & Holland and .458 Winchester Magnum.

NIB	Exc.	V.G.	Good	Fair	Poor
—	3000	2000	1500	900	500

ORBEA & CIA
Eibar, Spain

Pocket Pistol

A 6.35mm semi-automatic pistol with a 2.5" barrel. Blued with plastic grips. The slide marked "Orbea y Cia Eibar Espana Pistola Automatica Cal. 6.35". Manufactured from approximately 1918 to 1936.

NIB	Exc.	V.G.	Good	Fair	Poor
—	250	175	125	75	50

ORTGIES, HEINRICH & CO.
Erfurt, Germany

Ortgies Pistol

A 6.35mm or 7.65mm semi-automatic pistol with a 2.75" or 3.25" barrel. Blued with walnut grips. The slide marked "Ortgies & Co. Erfurt". After 1921, these pistols were manufactured by Deutsche Werke. **NOTE:** Deduct $100 for 6.35mm.

NIB	Exc.	V.G.	Good	Fair	Poor
—	550	300	175	125	85

ORVIS
Sunderland, Vermont

An importer and retailer of sporting goods including foreign manufactured firearms. Orvis sells some of these side-by-side and over/under guns under its own name. Most are made by Beretta, Arrieta or other Italian manufacturers. Values approximate those of similar models made by the gunmakers.

OSBORN, S.
Canton, Connecticut

Under Hammer Pistol

A .34 caliber under hammer percussion pistol with a 7" half octagonal barrel, brass mounts and a walnut grip. The barrel marked "S. Osborn/Canton, Conn."

NIB	Exc.	V.G.	Good	Fair	Poor
—	—	800	550	250	125

OSGOOD GUN WORKS
Norwich, Connecticut

Duplex Revolver

A .22 caliber spur trigger revolver with two super-imposed barrels, the upper most of .22 caliber and the lower a .32 caliber. The cylinder with eight .22 chambers. The hammer fitted with a movable firing pin so that the pistol can be used either as a revolver or as a single shot with a .32 caliber barrel. Blued or nickel-plated with hard rubber grips. The barrel marked "Osgood Gun Works-Norwich Conn." and "Duplex". An unknown quantity were manufactured during the 1880s.

Courtesy Milwaukee Public Museum, Milwaukee, Wisconsin

NIB	Exc.	V.G.	Good	Fair	Poor
—	—	1600	875	350	100

OVERTON, JOHN
Nashville, Tennessee

Formerly armorer at Harpers Ferry Armory. He delivered 81 rifles copying the U.S. Model 1841 but with a saber bayonet lug on the right side of the barrel. Unmarked externally but are serial numbered internally. Overall length ca. 48.75"; barrel length 33"; .54 caliber.

NIB	Exc.	V.G.	Good	Fair	Poor
—	—	18500	14000	5500	2000

OWA
Osterreiche Werke Anstalt
Vienna, Austria

OWA Pocket Pistol

A 6.35mm semi-automatic pistol with a 2" barrel. "OWA" logo cast in the grips. Blued with plastic grips. Manufactured between 1920 and 1925.

Courtesy Orvel Reichert

NIB	Exc.	V.G.	Good	Fair	Poor
—	400	325	200	150	1000

P.38
THE GERMAN WWII SERVICE PISTOL

NOTE: For history, technical data, descriptions, photos, and prices, see *The Standard Catalog of Military Firearms.*

WALTHER COMMERCIAL

The Commercial version of the P.38 is identified by commercial proofmarks of a crown over N or an eagle over N. Production started at around serial number 1000 and went through serial number 26659. This was the first of the commercial pistols and was a high-quality, well made gun with a complete inscription on the left slide. A few of these early pistols were equipped with checkered wooden grips. The quality decreased as the war progressed. There are many variations of these commercial models and values can range up to more than $30,000. It is suggested that these pistols be appraised and evaluated by an expert. For post-war Walther P.38 pistols see the Walther section.

A few of the Walther Commercial Model variations are listed.

MOD HP

H Prefix w/rectangular firing pin

NIB	Exc.	V.G.	Good	Fair	Poor
—	3200	2000	950	750	450

Early w/High Gloss Blue

NIB	Exc.	V.G.	Good	Fair	Poor
—	3000	1750	750	600	400

.30 caliber, extremely rare

NIB	Exc.	V.G.	Good	Fair	Poor
—	28000	—	—	—	—

Early w/High Gloss Blue & Alloy Frame

NIB	Exc.	V.G.	Good	Fair	Poor
—	10000	6500	3500	2000	1000

Croatian Contract

100 built, 6 known

NIB	Exc.	V.G.	Good	Fair	Poor
—	10000				

Late w/Military Blue Finish

NOTE: Add $500 for "Eagle/359" on right side.

NIB	Exc.	V.G.	Good	Fair	Poor
—	2000	1400	750	550	350

MOD P38—Late with Military Blue

1800 produced.

NIB	Exc.	V.G.	Good	Fair	Poor
—	2700	1750	750	600	400

"ac45" Zero Series

1200 made.

NIB	Exc.	V.G.	Good	Fair	Poor
—	2800	1750	750	600	400

WALTHER MILITARY
ZERO SERIES

First Issue

NIB	Exc.	V.G.	Good	Fair	Poor
—	9500	8000	6000	3500	1500

Second Issue

NIB	Exc.	V.G.	Good	Fair	Poor
—	8000	6750	5250	2000	1000

Third Issue

NIB	Exc.	V.G.	Good	Fair	Poor
—	3500	2200	1250	800	500

480 CODE

NIB	Exc.	V.G.	Good	Fair	Poor
—	7000	5000	3250	1750	1000

"AC" CODES

This variation follows the 480 code.

"ac" (no date)

NIB	Exc.	V.G.	Good	Fair	Poor
—	9000	7500	5000	3000	2000

"AC40"

Added

NIB	Exc.	V.G.	Good	Fair	Poor
—	3800	2500	1750	1000	600

Standard

NIB	Exc.	V.G.	Good	Fair	Poor
—	3000	2000	1200	700	500

"AC41"

1st Variation

NIB	Exc.	V.G.	Good	Fair	Poor
—	2200	1100	700	500	350

2nd Variation

NIB	Exc.	V.G.	Good	Fair	Poor
—	2000	1000	700	450	300

3rd Variation

NIB	Exc.	V.G.	Good	Fair	Poor
—	1500	800	600	400	300

"AC42"

1st Variation

NOTE: Add $800 for "byf" Mauser code

NIB	Exc.	V.G.	Good	Fair	Poor
—	1300	550	400	350	275

2nd Variation

NIB	Exc.	V.G.	Good	Fair	Poor
—	1100	500	400	300	250

"AC43"

1st Variation

NIB	Exc.	V.G.	Good	Fair	Poor
—	900	450	300	250	200

2nd Variation

NIB	Exc.	V.G.	Good	Fair	Poor
—	900	450	300	250	200

Single Line Slide

NIB	Exc.	V.G.	Good	Fair	Poor
—	1200	550	450	350	250

"AC44"

NOTE: Add $300 for FN frame (Eagle/140).

NIB	Exc.	V.G.	Good	Fair	Poor
—	800	450	300	250	200

"AC45"

NOTE: Add $200 for pistols with Czech barrels; barrel code "fnh".

1st Variation

NIB	Exc.	V.G.	Good	Fair	Poor
—	800	450	300	250	200

2nd Variation

NIB	Exc.	V.G.	Good	Fair	Poor
—	950	500	325	300	250

3rd Variation

NIB	Exc.	V.G.	Good	Fair	Poor
—	750	400	300	250	200

MAUSER MILITARY

"byf42"

NIB	Exc.	V.G.	Good	Fair	Poor
—	2200	1200	700	500	300

"byf43"

NIB	Exc.	V.G.	Good	Fair	Poor
—	950	550	300	250	200

"byf44"

NOTE: Add $100 for dual tone finish that is a combination of blue and gray components.

NIB	Exc.	V.G.	Good	Fair	Poor
—	950	550	300	250	200

AC43/44—FN slide

NIB	Exc.	V.G.	Good	Fair	Poor
—	2200	1200	725	550	400

"SVW45"

German Proofed

NIB	Exc.	V.G.	Good	Fair	Poor
—	2900	2000	1300	550	400

French Proofed

NIB	Exc.	V.G.	Good	Fair	Poor
—	650	400	300	250	200

"svw46"— French Proofed

NIB	Exc.	V.G.	Good	Fair	Poor
—	800	500	400	350	300

MAUSER "POLICE" P.38

"byf/43"

NIB	Exc.	V.G.	Good	Fair	Poor
—	2500	1700	1200	800	500

"byf/44"

NIB	Exc.	V.G.	Good	Fair	Poor
—	2500	1700	1200	800	500

"ac/43"

NIB	Exc.	V.G.	Good	Fair	Poor
—	5000	3500	2000	1250	800

"ac/44"

NIB	Exc.	V.G.	Good	Fair	Poor
—	5000	3500	2000	1250	800

"svw/45"

NIB	Exc.	V.G.	Good	Fair	Poor
—	6000	4500	2500	1600	1000

SPREEWERKE MILITARY

"cyq"

Eagle /211 on frame

2 known.

NIB	Exc.	V.G.	Good	Fair	Poor
—	5000	—	—	—	—

1st Variation

NIB	Exc.	V.G.	Good	Fair	Poor
—	1400	1000	750	600	500

Standard Variation

NOTE: If "A" or "B" prefix add $250.

NIB	Exc.	V.G.	Good	Fair	Poor
—	800	400	275	250	200

Zero Series

NOTE: Add $250 for AC43 or AC44 marked "FN" slide.

NIB	Exc.	V.G.	Good	Fair	Poor
—	1250	550	400	350	275

POST-WAR PISTOLS

Standard Slides

NIB	Exc.	V.G.	Good	Fair	Poor
—	400	250	200	175	150

Single Line Code (Rare)

NIB	Exc.	V.G.	Good	Fair	Poor
—	1000	550	350	250	200

Manurhin

NIB	Exc.	V.G.	Good	Fair	Poor
—	400	300	200	175	150

P.A.F.
Pretoria Small Arms Factory
Pretoria, South Africa

P.A.F. Junior

A .22 or .25 caliber semi-automatic pistol with a 2" barrel and 6-shot magazine. Blued with plastic grips. Slide marked "Junior Verwaardig in Suid Afrika Made in South Africa." Manufactured during the 1950s.

NIB	Exc.	V.G.	Good	Fair	Poor
—	350	250	125	100	70

PAGE-LEWIS ARMS CO.
Chicopee Falls, Massachusetts

Model A Target

A .22 caliber single-shot lever-action rifle with a 20" barrel and open sights. Blued with a walnut stock. Manufactured from 1920 to 1926.

NIB	Exc.	V.G.	Good	Fair	Poor
—	300	225	175	125	100

Model B Sharpshooter

As above, with a 24" barrel and longer fore-end.

NIB	Exc.	V.G.	Good	Fair	Poor
—	300	225	175	125	100

Model C Olympic

As above, with a 24" barrel and improved sights.

NIB	Exc.	V.G.	Good	Fair	Poor
—	375	275	200	150	100

Challenge Model 49

Single shot .22 LR boy's rifle, manufactured c. 1925-1930. Stamped on top of barrel "Page Lewis Arms Co., Chicopee Falls, Mass USA/22 LR" Model 49. 22" long barrel, fixed front and rear sights.

NIB	Exc.	V.G.	Good	Fair	Poor
—	150	100	75	50	35

PALMER
Windsor, Vermont
E. G. Lamson & Co.

Palmer Bolt-Action Carbine

A .50 caliber single-shot bolt-action carbine with a 20" round barrel, walnut half stock and full sidelock. Blued and case hardened. The receiver marked "Wm. Palmer / Patent / Dec.22, 1863" and the lock "G.Lamson & Co./ Windsor, Vt." Approximately 1,000 were made in 1865.

NIB	Exc.	V.G.	Good	Fair	Poor
—	3000	2250	1500	700	250

PARA USA (PARA-ORDNANCE)
Pineville, North Carolina

Previously known as Para-Ordnance of Scarborough, Ontario, Canada. In 2009 the company relocated to Pineville, North Carolina.

Para 1911 100th Anniversary

Classic 1911 styling to commemorate the centennial of the design. Caliber .45 ACP, military-style thumb and grip safeties, solid muzzle bushing and hammer, and three-dot sights. Weight 39 ounces, 5" barrel, Covert Black finish. Smooth cocobolo grips. Comes with one 7- and one 8-round magazine.

NIB	Exc.	V.G.	Good	Fair	Poor
925	775	665	500	350	200

Model P14.45

Similar in appearance to the Colt Government model this .45 ACP semi-automatic pistol features a 5" barrel, flared ejection port, combat style hammer beveled magazine well and a 13-round magazine capacity. Overall length is 8.5" and weight is 40 oz. for steel and stainless steel version and 31 oz. for alloy frame model. Finish is black except for stainless steel model. **NOTE:** Add $50 for steel frame, $45 for stainless steel, and $30 for duo-tone.

NIB	Exc.	V.G.	Good	Fair	Poor
700	550	500	400	300	200

Model P14.45 Limited

Similar to the above model but with extra features such as full length recoil guide, beavertail grip safety, adjustable rear sight, competition hammer, lowered ejection port, front and rear slide serrations, and trigger overtravel stop. Match grade barrel. Choice of black carbon steel or stainless steel finish. Weight is about 40 oz.

NIB	Exc.	V.G.	Good	Fair	Poor
1200	900	725	575	400	200

Model P14.45 LDA/P14.45 LDA Stainless

This model is essentially the same as the P14.45 but with a double-action trigger. Offered in black carbon steel only. Weight is about 40 oz. First introduced in 1999. **NOTE:** Add $50 for stainless steel.

NIB	Exc.	V.G.	Good	Fair	Poor
800	600	400	350	225	150

Model P16.40

This is essentially the same as the Model 14.45 except that it is chambered for the .40 S&W cartridge. The magazine capacity is 15 rounds. **NOTE:** Add $50 for steel frame, $45 for stainless steel, and $30 for duo-tone.

NIB	Exc.	V.G.	Good	Fair	Poor
800	600	400	350	225	150

Model P16.40 Limited

Similar to the above model but with extra features such as full length recoil guide, beavertail grip safety, adjustable rear sight, competition hammer, lowered ejection port, front and rear slide serrations, and trigger overtravel stop. Match grade barrel. Black carbon steel finish.

NIB	Exc.	V.G.	Good	Fair	Poor
1200	900	725	575	400	200

Model P16.40 LDA

This model is a double-action version of the P16.40 in black carbon steel only. First offered in 1999.

NIB	Exc.	V.G.	Good	Fair	Poor
800	600	400	350	225	150

Model P13.45

Introduced in 1994 this .45 ACP model features a 4.25" barrel with a 13-round magazine. The grip is .25" longer than the 12.45 model. Offered in light alloy, carbon, or stainless steel. Overall length is 7.75" and the height is 5.25". Weight is about 36 oz. in steel version and 28 oz. in alloy version. **NOTE:** Add $50 for steel frame, $45 for stainless steel, and $30 for duo-tone.

NIB	Exc.	V.G.	Good	Fair	Poor
600	450	350	300	200	100

Model P13.45/P12.45 Limited

Similar to the above model but with extra features such as full length recoil guide, beavertail grip safety, adjustable rear sight, competition hammer, lowered ejection port, front and rear slide serrations, and trigger overtravel stop. Match grade barrel. Black carbon steel finish.

P13.45

P12.45

NIB	Exc.	V.G.	Good	Fair	Poor
800	600	400	350	225	150

Model P12.45 LDA/P12.45 LDA

This model is fitted with a 3.5" barrel and has a magazine capacity of 12 rounds. It features a double-action trigger. Finish is black. Weight is about 34 oz. Introduced in 2000. **NOTE:** Add $50 for stainless steel.

NIB	Exc.	V.G.	Good	Fair	Poor
750	600	450	300	200	100

Model P12.45/P12.40

Similar to the Model P14 but in a smaller package. Introduced in 1993. Has all the same features as the Model P14 but has a magazine capacity of 11 rounds. Also available in alloy, steel, or stainless steel this model weighs 24 oz. in alloy model and 33 oz. in steel models. The P12.40 is the same model but chambered for .40 S&W cartridge. **NOTE:** Add $50 for steel frame, $45 for stainless steel, and $30 for duo-tone.

NIB	Exc.	V.G.	Good	Fair	Poor
800	600	400	350	225	150

Model P10.45/P10.40/P10.9

Introduced in 1996 this model at the time was the smallest semi-automatic .45 ACP in production. Overall length is 6.5" with height of 4.5". Magazine capacity is 10 rounds. Barrel length is 3.5". Offered in stainless steel, duo-tone, or black alloy finish. Also offered chambered for .40 S&W cartridge and the 9mm cartridge. Weight is about 31 oz. for stainless and 24 oz. for alloy model. **NOTE:** Add $50 for steel frame, $45 for stainless steel, and $30 for duo-tone.

NIB	Exc.	V.G.	Good	Fair	Poor
600	450	350	300	00	100

Model P10.45 Limited

Similar to the above model but with extra features such as full length recoil guide, beavertail grip safety, adjustable rear sight, competition hammer, lowered ejection port, front and rear slide serrations, and trigger overtravel stop. Match grade barrel. Black carbon steel finish.

NIB	Exc.	V.G.	Good	Fair	Poor
650	500	400	300	200	100

Model P18.9

This pistol is chambered for the 9mm cartridge and is fitted with a 5" barrel. Finish is stainless steel. Rear sight is adjustable; dovetail front sight. Magazine capacity is 18 rounds (10 rounds for US and Canada). Weight is approximately 40 oz.

NIB	Exc.	V.G.	Good	Fair	Poor
775	625	500	350	200	125

Model P18.9 LDA

This is a double-action version of the P18-9. Offered in black carbon steel only. Introduced in 1999.

NIB	Exc.	V.G.	Good	Fair	Poor
775	625	500	350	200	125

Model C7.45 LDA (Para Companion)

This .45 ACP pistol is fitted with a 3.5" barrel. Stainless steel slide and frame. Low profile fixed sights. Magazine is 7 rounds. Weight is about 32 oz.

NIB	Exc.	V.G.	Good	Fair	Poor
700	550	400	300	200	100

Model C6.45 LDA (Para Carry)

Similar to the model above but with 3" barrel and 6-round magazine. Weight is about 30 oz.

NIB	Exc.	V.G.	Good	Fair	Poor
750	575	550	375	200	100

Model Stealth Carry

This model, introduced in 2005, is chambered for the .45 ACP cartridge and fitted with a 3" barrel with Novak adjustable sights. LDA trigger. Black slide and frame with black polymer grips. Magazine capacity is 6 rounds. Weight is about 30 oz.

NIB	Exc.	V.G.	Good	Fair	Poor
775	575	400	300	200	100

Model Tac-Four

This .45 ACP model features the LDA trigger system. It is fitted with a 4.25" barrel and has a stainless steel slide and frame. Early models shipped with two pre-ban 13-round magazines. Later models will ship with two 10-round magazines. Weight is about 36 oz. Introduced in 2003.

NIB	Exc.	V.G.	Good	Fair	Poor
850	675	550	425	300	150

Model Para CCW

Introduced in 2003 this .45 ACP model features a 4.25" barrel with stainless steel receiver and frame. Magazine capacity is 7 rounds. Fitted with the LDA trigger system. Weight is about 34 oz.

NIB	Exc.	V.G.	Good	Fair	Poor
900	800	650	500	350	125

Model Tac-Four LE

Same as above but shipped with two 13-round magazines to certified law enforcement only, back in the ban days.

NIB	Exc.	V.G.	Good	Fair	Poor
900	800	650	500	350	125

PARA PXT SERIES PISTOLS

In 2004 the company introduced a new extractor called the Power Extractor (PXT). The company also added a number of new finishes and features for its PXT line. All Para pistols have integral ramp barrels that are of match grade quality. All pistols have full-length guide rod, match trigger, flared ejection port, extended slide lock safety, beavertail grip safety, cocobolo stocks with gold medallion and high-visibility, low-mount, dovetail, three-dot sights.

Para introduced five finishes:

1. Sterling—All stainless steel, black slide with polished sides.
2. Stealth—Black slide, black frame with black fire controls.
3. Black Watch—Black slide, green frame with green fire controls on hi-cap models, and black controls on single-stack models.
4. Regal—Black slide, black frame with stainless steel fire controls.
5. Spec Ops—Green slide, green frame with black fire controls.

SINGLE-ACTION, SINGLE STACK MODELS

Model LTC

This .45 ACP pistol has a 4.25" ramped match barrel with steel receiver and Regal finish. Fixed 3-dot sights. Cocobolo wood grips with gold medallion. Magazine capacity is 7 rounds. Weight is about 37 oz.

NIB	Exc.	V.G.	Good	Fair	Poor
900	800	650	500	350	125

Model Para Companion Carry Option

This model is similar to the CCW above but it is fitted with a 3.5" barrel. Weight is about 32 oz. Introduced in 2003.

NIB	Exc.	V.G.	Good	Fair	Poor
775	575	400	300	200	100

Model LTC Alloy

As above but with alloy frame. Weight is about 28 oz.

NIB	Exc.	V.G.	Good	Fair	Poor
775	575	400	300	200	100

Model LTC Stainless

Same as the Model LTC but with stainless steel frame and slide. Weight is about 35 oz. Introduced in 2005.

NIB	Exc.	V.G.	Good	Fair	Poor
800	625	500	400	150	125

Hawg 9

Chambered for the 9mm cartridge and fitted with a 3" ramped barrel. Alloy receiver and steel slide. Fixed 3-dot sights. Black polymer stocks with black slide, black frame and stainless steel fire controls. Weight is about 24 oz. 12-shot magazine. Introduced in 2005.

NIB	Exc.	V.G.	Good	Fair	Poor
800	625	500	400	150	125

Hawg 7

Caliber .45 ACP, single-action trigger, stainless steel slide, alloy frame with Griptor grooves, extended thumb and grip safeties, fiber optic front and 2-dot rear sights, 7-round magazine. Weight 32 ounces, 3.5" barrel with Covert Black finish. Introduced in 2011.

NIB	Exc.	V.G.	Good	Fair	Poor
800	675	550	400	300	200

Model OPS

This .45 ACP pistol is fitted with a 3.5" barrel. It has a stainless steel frame and slide. Low mount fixed sights. Cocobolo grips. Magazine capacity is 7 rounds. Weight is about 32 oz. Introduced in 2005.

NIB	Exc.	V.G.	Good	Fair	Poor
850	675	550	425	300	150

Model 1911

This .45 ACP model has a 5" barrel with steel receiver and Regal finish. Magazine capacity is 7 rounds. Weight is about 39 oz.

NIB	Exc.	V.G.	Good	Fair	Poor
775	575	400	300	200	100

1911 SSP

7+1 capacity .45 ACP 1911-style semi-automatic with 5" barrel. 39 oz. Competition triggers and hammers. Fixed sights. Cocobolo grip panels.

NIB	Exc.	V.G.	Good	Fair	Poor
925	800	675	500	400	175

GI Expert LTC

Caliber .45 ACP, single-action trigger, Commander-length stainless slide on alloy frame, extended grip safety, competition trigger, fiber optic front and 2-dot rear sights. Weight 28 ounces, 4.25" barrel with Covert Black finish. Magazine capacity 8-rounds.

NIB	Exc.	V.G.	Good	Fair	Poor
750	635	500	400	300	200

1911 Wild Bunch

Designed for SASS Traditional and Modern "Wild Bunch" shooting matches. Class 1911 features. Caliber .45 ACP, traditional thumb and grip safeties, hammer, solid trigger, recoil system, 7-round magazine, plain sights and barrel without integral ramp. Weight 39 oz., 5" barrel with Covert Black finish. Introduced in 2011.

NIB	Exc.	V.G.	Good	Fair	Poor
685	585	475	400	300	200

HIGH-CAPACITY, SINGLE ACTION MODELS
Warthog

Introduced in 2004 this .45 ACP pistol is fitted with a 3" barrel. The receiver is alloy. Black slide and frame with stainless steel fire controls. Overall length is 6.5". Height is 4.5". Magazine capacity is 10 rounds. Weight is about 24 oz. In 2005 this model was also chambered for the 9mm cartridge.

NIB	Exc.	V.G.	Good	Fair	Poor
925	800	675	500	400	175

Stainless Warthog

Stainless .45 ACP with 10+1 capacity. Barrel 3", 31 oz. Fixed, 3-dot sights and plastic grips. Introduced 2006.

NIB	Exc.	V.G.	Good	Fair	Poor
875	675	575	400	300	150

Stealth Warthog

Chambered for the .45 ACP cartridge and fitted with a 3" ramped barrel. Black alloy slide with black frame and black fire controls. Tritium night sights. Extended slide lock, beavertail grip and firing pin. Weight is about 24 oz. Introduced in 2004.

NIB	Exc.	V.G.	Good	Fair	Poor
850	675	550	425	300	150

Slim Hawg

A .45 ACP pistol with 6+1 capacity. Single-stack, single-action 1911. Barrel 3", 30 oz. Stainless construction, checkered wood grips. Fixed, 3-dot sights. Introduced 2006.

NIB	Exc.	V.G.	Good	Fair	Poor
850	675	550	425	300	150

Lite Hawg 9

Double-stack, 12+1 single-action 9mm in non-reflective black finish. Barrel 3", 31.5 oz and capacity. Fixed, 3-dot sights. Introduced 2006.

NIB	Exc.	V.G.	Good	Fair	Poor
850	675	550	425	300	150

P12.45

This .45 ACP model is fitted with a 3.5" barrel and has a stainless steel receiver with stainless finish. Magazine capacity is 10 (12) rounds. Weight is about 34 oz.

NIB	Exc.	V.G.	Good	Fair	Poor
800	625	500	400	150	125

P13.45

This .45 ACP pistol has a 4.25" barrel with stainless steel receiver and Spec Ops finish. Magazine capacity is 10 (13) rounds. Weight is about 36 oz.

NIB	Exc.	V.G.	Good	Fair	Poor
750	575	550	375	200	100

Midnight Blue P14-45

Double-stack, 14+1 single-action 45 ACP in non-reflective black. 5" barrel, fixed, 3-dot sights and black plastic grips. Introduced 2006.

NIB	Exc.	V.G.	Good	Fair	Poor
750	575	550	375	200	100

Hi-Cap LTC

Introduced in 2005 this model is chambered for the .45 ACP cartridge and fitted with a 4.25" barrel with low mount fixed sights. Green frame, green slide with black fire controls. Black polymer grips. Magazine capacity is 14 rounds. Weight is about 37 oz.

NIB	Exc.	V.G.	Good	Fair	Poor
850	675	550	425	300	150

Stealth P14.45

This .45 ACP model is fitted with a 5" barrel and has a steel receiver with Stealth finish. Magazine capacity is 10 (14) rounds. Weight is about 40 oz.

NIB	Exc.	V.G.	Good	Fair	Poor
850	675	550	425	300	150

P14.45

As above but with stainless steel receiver and finish.

NIB	Exc.	V.G.	Good	Fair	Poor
925	800	675	500	400	175

14.45 Tactical

Based upon the classic Para-Ordnance 14.45 high-capacity 1911 design in .45 ACP. Stainless steel slide and frame with 14-round, double-stack magazine. Custom features include Ed Brown National Match barrel, bushing, slide stop and checkered mainspring housing; Dawson Precision mag well; ambidextrous thumb safeties; extended grip tang and accessory rail. Sights are adjustable rear and fiber optic front. Covert Black finish. Weight is 42 ounces, barrel length 5". PXT Tactical model is same except for single-stack frame, 8-round magazine, 4.25" barrel and weight of 36 oz.

NIB	Exc.	V.G.	Good	Fair	Poor
1350	1150	875	650	350	200

P18.45

This model is chambered for the 9mm Parabellum cartridge and fitted with a 5" barrel. The receiver is stainless steel with stainless steel finish. Magazine is 10 (18) rounds. Weight is about 40 oz.

NIB	Exc.	V.G.	Good	Fair	Poor
850	675	525	375	200	125

HIGH-CAPACITY, SINGLE ACTION LIMITED MODELS

S12.45 Limited

This .45 ACP pistol has a 3.5" barrel with stainless steel receiver and Sterling finish. Magazine capacity is 10 (12) rounds. Weight is about 34 oz. Introduced in 2005.

NIB	Exc.	V.G.	Good	Fair	Poor
925	800	675	500	400	175

S13.45 Limited

A .45 ACP pistol with 4.25" barrel. Stainless steel receiver and Sterling finish. Spurless hammer. Magazine capacity is 10 (13) rounds. Weight is about 36 oz.

NIB	Exc.	V.G.	Good	Fair	Poor
925	800	675	500	400	175

Stealth S14.45 Limited

This .45 ACP pistol is fitted with a 5" barrel and has a steel receiver with Stealth finish. Magazine capacity is 10 (14) rounds. Weight is about 40 oz.

NIB	Exc.	V.G.	Good	Fair	Poor
925	800	675	500	400	175

S14.45 Limited

As above but with stainless steel receiver and Sterling finish.

NIB	Exc.	V.G.	Good	Fair	Poor
1000	795	600	450	275	225

Long Slide Limited

Lengthened barrel and slide for competition or hunting. Caliber .435 ACP. Weight is 41 oz., barrel length is 6". Front and rear slide serrations, ambidextrous thumb safeties, extended grip safety, adjustable rear and fiber optic front sight, 14-round magazine and stainless finish. Introduced in 2011.

NIB	Exc.	V.G.	Good	Fair	Poor
1200	1025	825	650	450	300

Stealth S16.40 Limited

This pistol is chambered for the .40 S&W cartridge and fitted with a 5" barrel. Receiver is steel with Stealth finish. Magazine capacity is 10 (16) rounds. Weight is about 40 oz.

NIB	Exc.	V.G.	Good	Fair	Poor
1100	950	750	500	400	175

S16.40 Limited

As above but with stainless steel receiver and Sterling finish.

NIB	Exc.	V.G.	Good	Fair	Poor
925	800	675	500	400	175

18.9 Limited

Chambered for the 9mm Parabellum, features include stainless steel slide and frame with dual grasping grooves, 18-round magazine, adjustable rear and fiber optic front sight, ambidextrous thumb safeties, extended grip tang and competition trigger. Weight is 40 oz., barrel length is 5", finish is bright stainless.

NIB	Exc.	V.G.	Good	Fair	Poor
1100	875	750	575	350	200

Todd Jarrett .40 USPSA P-16

A limited edition 16+1 (or 10+1) .40 S&W custom competition pistol with adjustable rear sight and fiber optic front sight. 5" barrel, 40 oz., covert non-reflective black or sterling.

NIB	Exc.	V.G.	Good	Fair	Poor
1500	1250	900	675	450	200

Todd Jarrett .45 USPSA

Limited edition 8+1 .45 ACP caliber custom competition pistol with adjustable rear sight and fiber optic front sight. 5" barrel, 39 oz.; covert non-reflective black or stainless finish.

NIB	Exc.	V.G.	Good	Fair	Poor
1500	1250	900	675	450	200

LDA, DOUBLE-ACTION, SINGLE STACK CARRY OPTION

Companion II

Caliber .45 ACP, Light Double Action (LDA) trigger, Commander-length stainless slide on full-size stainless frame, extended grip safety, fiber optic front sight and 8-round magazine. Weight 35 oz., 4.25" barrel with Covert Black finish. Introduced in 2011.

NIB	Exc.	V.G.	Good	Fair	Poor
775	650	550	400	300	200

Carry Model

This .45 ACP model has a 3" barrel and stainless steel receiver with stainless finish. Magazine capacity is 6 rounds. Weight is about 30 oz.

NIB	Exc.	V.G.	Good	Fair	Poor
925	800	675	500	400	175

Stealth Carry

Similar to the model above but with Stealth finish and Novak adjustable sights.

NIB	Exc.	V.G.	Good	Fair	Poor
925	800	675	500	400	175

CCO (Companion Carry Option)

This .45 ACP model is fitted with a 3.5" barrel. The receiver is stainless steel with a stainless finish. Magazine capacity is 7 rounds. Weight is about 32 oz.

NIB	Exc.	V.G.	Good	Fair	Poor
850	700	575	400	300	125

CCW

Similar to the model above but fitted with a 4.45" barrel. Weight is about 34 oz.

NIB	Exc.	V.G.	Good	Fair	Poor
850	700	575	400	300	125

DOUBLE-ACTION-ONLY, SINGLE STACK MODELS

Black Watch Companion

This .45 ACP pistol is fitted with a 3.5" barrel. Receiver is stainless steel with black watch finish. Magazine capacity is 7 rounds. Weight is about 32 oz.

NIB	Exc.	V.G.	Good	Fair	Poor
850	675	525	375	200	125

TAC-S

Chambered for the .45 ACP cartridge with a 4.45" barrel. Steel receiver and Spec Ops finish. Magazine capacity is 7 rounds. Weight is about 35 oz.

NIB	Exc.	V.G.	Good	Fair	Poor
750	575	550	375	200	100

Black Watch SSP

This .45 ACP pistol has a 5" barrel with steel receiver and Black Watch finish. Fixed 3-dot sights. Match trigger. Cocobolo wood grip with gold medallion. Magazine capacity is 7 rounds. Weight is about 39 oz.

NIB	Exc.	V.G.	Good	Fair	Poor
750	575	550	375	200	100

SSP

Similar to the model above but with stainless steel receiver and stainless finish.

NIB	Exc.	V.G.	Good	Fair	Poor
800	625	500	400	150	125

LDA, DOUBLE-ACTION, SINGLE STACK LIMITED MODELS

Stealth Limited

This .45 ACP pistol has a 5" barrel with adjustable sights. Receiver is steel with Stealth finish. Magazine capacity is 7 rounds. Weight is about 40 oz.

NIB	Exc.	V.G.	Good	Fair	Poor
850	700	575	400	300	125

Limited

This .45 ACP model has a 5" barrel and stainless steel receiver with Sterling finish. Magazine capacity is 7 rounds. Weight is about 40 oz. Adjustable sights.

NIB	Exc.	V.G.	Good	Fair	Poor
925	800	675	500	400	175

LDA, DOUBLE-ACTION, HIGH CAPACITY CARRY OPTION SERIES

Carry 12

This is a 45 ACP pistol with a 3.5" barrel fitted with night sights. Receiver is stainless steel with a stainless finish. Magazine capacity is 10 (12) rounds. Weight is about 34 oz.

NIB	Exc.	V.G.	Good	Fair	Poor
850	700	575	400	300	125

Tac-Four

This .45 ACP model is fitted with a 4.35" barrel. Stainless steel receiver with Spec Ops finish. Magazine capacity is 10 (13) rounds. Sight are 3-dot. Weight is about 36 oz.

NIB	Exc.	V.G.	Good	Fair	Poor
850	700	575	400	300	125

Tac-Five

Light double-action 9mm with 18+1 capacity. 5" barrel, 37.5 oz., stainless finish, adjustable rear sight, plastic grips.

NIB	Exc.	V.G.	Good	Fair	Poor
850	700	575	400	300	125

LDA, DOUBLE-ACTION, HIGH CAPACITY MODELS

Stealth Hi-Cap .45

This .45 ACP pistol has a 5" barrel with steel receiver and Stealth finish. Spurless hammer. sights are 3-dot. Magazine capacity is 10 (14) rounds. Weight is about 40 oz.

NIB	Exc.	V.G.	Good	Fair	Poor
800	625	500	400	150	125

Hi-Cap .45

Similar to the model above but with stainless steel receiver and stainless finish.

NIB	Exc.	V.G.	Good	Fair	Poor
800	625	500	400	150	125

Colonel

This .45 ACP pistol is fitted with a 4.25" barrel with low mount fixed sights. The slide and frame are green with black fire controls.

Black polymer grips. Magazine capacity is 14 rounds. Weight is about 37 oz. Introduced in 2005.

NIB	Exc.	V.G.	Good	Fair	Poor
800	625	500	400	150	125

Hi-Cap .40

This model is chambered for the .40 S&W cartridge and fitted with a 5" barrel with 3-dot sights. Stainless steel receiver with stainless finish. Magazine capacity is 10 (16) rounds. Weight is about 40 oz.

NIB	Exc.	V.G.	Good	Fair	Poor
800	625	500	400	150	125

Stealth Hi-Cap 9

This 9mm pistol is fitted with a 5" barrel with 3-dot sights and steel receiver with Stealth finish. Magazine capacity is 10 (18) rounds. Weight is about 40 oz.

NIB	Exc.	V.G.	Good	Fair	Poor
800	625	500	400	150	125

Hi-Cap 9

Similar to the model above but for stainless steel receiver and stainless finish.

NIB	Exc.	V.G.	Good	Fair	Poor
850	700	575	400	300	125

Covert Black Nite-Tac

Introduced in 2005 this .45 ACP pistol is fitted with a 5" barrel with covert black finish. Low mount fixed sights. Magazine capacity is 14 rounds. Weight is about 40 oz.

NIB	Exc.	V.G.	Good	Fair	Poor
850	700	575	400	300	125

Nite-Tac

As above but with stainless steel frame and slide. Introduced in 2005.

NIB	Exc.	V.G.	Good	Fair	Poor
800	625	500	400	150	125

Nite-Tac .40

A .40 S&W 16+1 capacity double-action duty pistol with fixed sights. 5" barrel, 40 oz., stainless finish.

NIB	Exc.	V.G.	Good	Fair	Poor
800	625	500	400	150	125

Nite-Tac 9

A 9mm 18+1 double-action duty pistol with fixed sights. 5" barrel, 40 oz., stainless finish.

NIB	Exc.	V.G.	Good	Fair	Poor
800	625	500	400	150	125

LDA, DOUBLE-ACTION, HIGH-CAPACITY LIMITED

Hi-Cap Limited .40

This .40 S&W pistol has a 5" barrel with 3-dot sights and a stainless steel receiver with Sterling finish. Magazine capacity is 16 rounds. Weight is about 40 oz.

NIB	Exc.	V.G.	Good	Fair	Poor
1000	875	725	575	400	200

Stealth Hi-Cap Limited 9

This model is chambered for the 9mm cartridge and fitted with a 5" barrel with 3-dot sights. The receiver is steel with Stealth finish. Magazine capacity is 18 rounds. Weight is about 40 oz.

NIB	Exc.	V.G.	Good	Fair	Poor
1000	875	725	575	400	200

Hi-Cap Limited 9

As above but with stainless steel receiver and Sterling finish.

NIB	Exc.	V.G.	Good	Fair	Poor
1200	975	825	650	450	225

Stealth Hi-Cap Ltd .45

This .45 ACP pistol has a 5" barrel with 3-dot sights and spurless hammer. Receiver is steel with Stealth finish. Magazine capacity is 10 (14) rounds. Weight is about 40 oz.

NIB	Exc.	V.G.	Good	Fair	Poor
1000	875	725	575	400	200

Hi-Cap Limited .45

This model is similar to the one above but with stainless steel receiver and Sterling finish.

NIB	Exc.	V.G.	Good	Fair	Poor
1100	975	825	650	450	225

TTR RIFLE SERIES

Para's Tactical Target Rifle is based on the AR platform with 16.5" barrel, 30-round magazine. Chambered in .223 Rem./5.56x45 NATO. Flat Top upper receiver, full-length Picatinny rail, short or long-rail forearm, adjustable buttstock. Delayed impingement gas system, front and rear flip-up sights. Accepts all M16 and AR-15 magazines. Manufactured 2009 - 2011.

NIB	Exc.	V.G.	Good	Fair	Poor
1950	1700	1450	1100	900	400

PARDINI
Italy

Standard Target Pistol

A .22 caliber semi-automatic pistol with a 4.7" barrel, adjustable rear sight and adjustable trigger. Blued with two sizes of walnut grips, one suitable for use by ladies. Introduced in 1986.

NIB	Exc.	V.G.	Good	Fair	Poor
1450	1200	975	800	600	350

Rapidfire Pistol

Similar to the above, in .22 short with an alloy bolt, 4.6" barrel and enclosed grip. Weight is about 43 oz. Introduced in 1995.

NIB	Exc.	V.G.	Good	Fair	Poor
1450	1200	975	800	600	350

Centerfire Pistol

Similar to the standard model, but in .32 Smith & Wesson caliber. Introduced in 1986.

NIB	Exc.	V.G.	Good	Fair	Poor
1450	1200	975	800	600	350

Free Pistol

A .22 caliber single-shot pistol with a 9.8" barrel, adjustable sights and adjustable grip. Furnished with barrel weights. Weight is about 35 oz. Introduced in 1995.

NIB	Exc.	V.G.	Good	Fair	Poor
1550	1300	1050	900	700	450

PARKER
Springfield, Massachusetts

4-Shot Pistol

A .33 caliber percussion pistol with a 4" half-octagonal barrel and a 4-shot sliding chamber. Marked "Albert Parker/Patent Secured/Springfield, Mass." Original finish unknown with walnut grips. Prospective purchasers are advised to secure a qualified appraisal prior to acquisition.

NIB	Exc.	V.G.	Good	Fair	Poor
—	—	1500	13500	6000	2000

PARKER BROS.
Meriden, Connecticut

Perhaps the best known of all American shotgun manufacturers. Established by Charles Parker shortly after the Civil War, this company has produced a wide variety of shotguns in a number of different styles over the years. In the early 1930s the company was purchased by Remington Arms Company.

Parker shotguns are among the most collectible of American-made shotguns. Both the beginning and the veteran collector should be aware that originality and condition are absolutely critical in establishing such high values for these shotguns. There are numerous upgraded and refinished guns that are represented as original. Beware that such misrepresentations exist because refinished and upgraded Parker guns should sell for as much as 50 to 75 percent below the price of an original gun. Extreme caution should be exercised and we would recommend that an expert be consulted. Even the most advanced collectors may benefit from such consultations. Also, the prices indicated for guns in excellent condition may fluctuate drastically, especially in high grade or small bore guns, due to their extreme rarity.

In addition, uncommon extras such as single triggers, ventilated ribs, beavertail forearms, straight-grip stocks, and skeleton steel buttplates may add substantial value to an individual gun. Extra sets of factory barrels that were installed at the time of delivery will add an average of a 30 percent premium. This premium will increase with grade and gauge; the higher the grade and smaller the gauge the higher the premium.

Letters of authenticity are available. These letters are a must in order for any Parker gun to attain maximum value. Contact: the Executive Secretary Parker Gun Collectors Association, P.O. Box 126502, Harrisburg, PA 17112. The letter is $40 for members of the PCGA and $100 for non-members.

VH

A 12, 16, 20, 28 or .410 bore boxlock double-barrel shotgun manufactured in a variety of barrel lengths with double triggers and extractors. Blued, case hardened receiver with a walnut stock. Only 2,297 guns had single triggers, only 3,983 guns had straight grip stocks. Approximately 78,659 were made: 10 gauge—20, 12 gauge—51,901, 16 gauge—14,446, 20 gauge—10,406, 28 gauge—1,417, .410 bore—469. Also made with automatic ejectors and known as the Model VHE. The E suffix was used on all models to denote automatic ejectors. **NOTE:** VHE add 40 percent, 20 gauge add 60 percent, 28 gauge add 500 percent, .410 add 500 percent.

Courtesy Bonhams & Butterfields

NIB	Exc.	V.G.	Good	Fair	Poor
—	5000	4000	2950	2000	1000

PH

Similar to the above, but with a small amount of scroll engraving. slightly better grade of walnut. Approximately 1,339 were made: 10 gauge—798, 12 gauge—839, 16 gauge—208, 20 gauge—204, 28 gauge—only 5, .410 bore—only 4. **NOTE:** PHE (ejectors) add 40 percent. For 20 gauge add 60 percent. For the extremely rare 28 and .410 models, prices can command a 1000 percent premium.

Courtesy Bonhams & Butterfields

NIB	Exc.	V.G.	Good	Fair	Poor
—	5500	4250	3350	2100	1000

GH

Similar to the above, with a modest amount of scroll and game scene engraving and the barrels marked "Parker Special Steel". Only about 430 G grades were built with straight grip stocks. Approximately 4,291 were made: 8 gauge—11, 10 gauge—63, 12 gauge—2,501, 16 gauge—607, 20 gauge—990, 28 gauge—91, .410 bore—28. **NOTE:** GHE (ejectors) add 35 percent, 16 gauge add 15 percent, 20 gauge add 50 percent, 28 gauge add 300 percent, .410 add 500 percent.

NIB	Exc.	V.G.	Good	Fair	Poor
—	7000	5500	4000	3000	1000

DH

As above, but more finely finished. Engraving coverage more profuse. Most modern D grade guns were fitted with Titanic barrels. Only about 280 were built with Parker single triggers, and only about 280 were built with ventilated ribs. Approximately 9,346 were made: 8 gauge—10, 10 gauge—45, 12 gauge—6,330, 16 gauge—1,178, 20 gauge—1,536, 28 gauge—187, .410 bore—60. **NOTE:** DHE (ejectors) add 35 percent, 16 gauge add 15 percent, 20 gauge add 50 percent, 28 gauge add 300 percent, .410 add 500 percent.

Courtesy Bonhams & Butterfields

NIB	Exc.	V.G.	Good	Fair	Poor
—	8500	7000	5000	3500	1000

CH

As above, with more scroll and game scene engraving coverage. Marked with Acme steel barrels. Only about 93 C grades had straight-grip stocks. Approximately 697 were made: 8 gauge— only 2, 10 gauge— only 9, 12 gauge—410, 16 gauge—105, 20 gauge—149, 28 gauge—only 16, .410 bore—only 6. **NOTE:** CHE (ejectors) add 35 percent, 16 gauge add 10 percent, 20 gauge add 40 percent, 28 gauge add 400 percent, .410 add 700 percent.

NIB	Exc.	V.G.	Good	Fair	Poor
—	20000	17000	13000	10000	2500

AH

As above, but highly engraved with finely figured walnut stocks. Most had Acme steel barrels. About 42 A grade guns were built with straight grip stocks. Approximately 167 were made: 10 gauge—only 1, 12 gauge—92, 16 gauge—23, 20 gauge—44, 28 gauge—only 6, .410 bore— only 1. **NOTE:** AHE (ejectors) add 30 percent, 16 gauge add 25 percent, 20 gauge add 75 percent, 28 gauge add 450 percent, .410 add 600 percent.

Courtesy Bonhams & Butterfields

NIB	Exc.	V.G.	Good	Fair	Poor
—	16000	14000	9000	6500	1500

BH

As above, but offered in a variety of different styles of engraved decoration. Only about 66 guns had straight-grip stocks, 29 had beavertail fore-ends, 20 were built with vent ribs, and 57 had single triggers. Approximately 512 were made: 10 gauge—only 2, 12 gauge—317, 16 gauge—71, 20 gauge—109, 28 gauge—13. **NOTE:** Prospective purchasers are advised to secure a qualified appraisal prior to acquisition. BHE (ejectors) add 35 percent, 16 gauge add 15 percent, 20 gauge add 50 percent, 28 gauge add 450 percent.

NIB	Exc.	V.G.	Good	Fair	Poor
—	35000	30000	20000	15000	2500

AAH

As above, with either Whitworth or Peerless barrels and not made in .410 bore. The engraving is more extensive and of the first quality. Only one AA grade has a ventilated rib, ten were built with single trigger and 95 had straight grip stocks. Approximately 238 were made: 10 gauge—only 2, 12 gauge—185, 16 gauge—19, 20 gauge—27, 28 gauge—only 5. **NOTE:** Due to the rarity of this grade prospective purchasers are advised to secure a qualified appraisal prior to acquisition. AAHE (ejectors) add 30 percent, 16 gauge add 35 percent, 20 gauge add 75 percent, 28 gauge add 250 percent.

NIB	Exc.	V.G.	Good	Fair	Poor
—	100000	80000	65000	35000	5000

Single-Barrel Trap

A 12 gauge single-shot shotgun with a 30", 32", or 34" barrel, automatic ejector and walnut stock. Produced in a variety of grades as listed. Prospective purchasers are advised to secure a qualified appraisal prior to acquisition.

NIB	Exc.	V.G.	Good	Fair	Poor
—	55000	45000	37500	20000	3000

A-1 Special

As above, but made strictly on special order and not manufactured in .410 bore. Two A-1 Specials were built with ventilated rib, 7 had single triggers, 3 had beavertail fore-ends, and 24 were built with straight-grip stocks. Approximately 79 were made: 12 gauge—55, 16 gauge—only 6, 20 gauge—11, and 28 gauge—only 7. **NOTE:** 16 gauge add 35 percent, 20 gauge add 75 percent, 28 gauge add 400 percent.

S.C. Grade

NIB	Exc.	V.G.	Good	Fair	Poor
—	8500	6500	4000	2000	1000

S.B. Grade

NIB	Exc.	V.G.	Good	Fair	Poor
—	10000	7500	5500	2400	1600

S.A. Grade

NIB	Exc.	V.G.	Good	Fair	Poor
—	14000	13000	10000	5000	2000

S.A.A. Grade

NIB	Exc.	V.G.	Good	Fair	Poor
—	25000	20000	15000	10000	5000

S.A-1 Special Grade

NIB	Exc.	V.G.	Good	Fair	Poor
—	30000	25000	18000	12000	5000

Under Lifter Hammer Gun

A side hammer double-barrel shotgun manufactured in a variety of gauges with the barrel release located in front of the triggerguards. Damascus barrels, case hardened locks, blued furniture with walnut stocks. Manufactured during the 1870s and later.

NIB	Exc.	V.G.	Good	Fair	Poor
—	6000	3200	1500	800	600

Trojan

A 12, 16, or 20 gauge boxlock double-barrel shotgun manufactured in a variety of barrel lengths with double triggers and extractors. Only 27 Trojans were built with single triggers. Blued, case hardened receiver with a walnut stock. Approximately 33,000 were made: 12 gauge—21,977, 16 gauge—6,573, 20 gauge—5450. **NOTE:** 20 gauge add 40 percent. 16 gauge add 20 percent.

NIB	Exc.	V.G.	Good	Fair	Poor
—	3800	3000	2000	1000	600

PARKER FIELD & SONS
London, England

Gas Seal Revolver

A .42 caliber percussion revolver with a 6" barrel and 6-shot cylinder. Blued, case hardened with walnut grips. Manufactured during the 1860s.

NIB	Exc.	V.G.	Good	Fair	Poor
—	—	2500	1950	900	450

PARKER-HALE LTD.
Birmingham, England

S&W Victory Conversion

A .22 caliber double-action revolver with a 4" barrel and 6-shot cylinder. Blued with walnut grips. An alteration of the Smith & Wesson Victor model.

NIB	Exc.	V.G.	Good	Fair	Poor
—	295	200	150	100	75

Model 1200

A .22-250 to .300 Winchester Magnum bolt-action rifle with a 24" barrel and open sights. Blued, with walnut stock.

NIB	Exc.	V.G.	Good	Fair	Poor
700	550	450	400	350	250

Model 1100 Lightweight

As above, with a 22" barrel and 4-shot magazine. Introduced in 1985.

NIB	Exc.	V.G.	Good	Fair	Poor
600	475	400	300	250	200

Model 81 Classic

A .22-250 to 7mm Remington Magnum bolt-action rifle with a 24" barrel and open sights. Blued with a walnut stock. Introduced in 1985.

NIB	Exc.	V.G.	Good	Fair	Poor
875	750	600	500	400	350

Model 81 African

As above, but in .375 Holland & Holland caliber. Introduced in 1986.

NIB	Exc.	V.G.	Good	Fair	Poor
1750	1200	1100	700	500	350

Model 84 Target

Similar to the Model 81, but in .308 caliber with adjustable rear sights and an adjustable cheekpiece.

NIB	Exc.	V.G.	Good	Fair	Poor
1300	1000	800	600	450	250

Model 85 Sniper

As above, with a scope and bipod.

NIB	Exc.	V.G.	Good	Fair	Poor
3250	2500	975	—	—	—

Model 640E Shotgun

A 12, 16, or 20 gauge boxlock double-barrel shotgun manufactured in a variety of barrel lengths with double triggers and extractors. Blued, French case hardened with a walnut stock. Introduced in 1986.

NIB	Exc.	V.G.	Good	Fair	Poor
575	450	400	300	250	200

Model 640A

As above, with a pistol grip, beavertail fore-end, and single trigger. Introduced in 1986.

NIB	Exc.	V.G.	Good	Fair	Poor
675	550	500	400	300	200

Model 645E

As above, but more finely finished and engraved.

NIB	Exc.	V.G.	Good	Fair	Poor
700	550	500	400	300	200

Model 670E

A sidelock double-barrel shotgun made on special order. Introduced in 1986.

NIB	Exc.	V.G.	Good	Fair	Poor
3000	2500	1850	1200	750	400

Model 680E—XXV

As above, with case hardened lockplates and 25" barrels.

NIB	Exc.	V.G.	Good	Fair	Poor
3000	2500	1850	1200	750	400

BLACKPOWDER REPRODUCTIONS

1853 Enfield Rifle Musket

This is a three band version in .577 caliber. Barrel length is 39". Rear sight graduated to 900 yards. Weight about 9 lbs.

NIB	Exc.	V.G.	Good	Fair	Poor
600	475	375	250	175	75

1858 Enfield Naval Pattern Rifle

This is the Naval version with two bands in .577 caliber. Barrel length is 33". Walnut stock with brass furniture. Rear sight adjustable to 1100 yards. Weight is approximately 8.5 lbs.

NIB	Exc.	V.G.	Good	Fair	Poor
550	425	325	200	125	50

1861 Enfield Artillery Carbine Musketoon

This is the Artillery version in .577 caliber with 24" barrel. Walnut stock with brass furniture. Rear sight adjustable to 600 yards. Weight is about 7.5 lbs.

NIB	Exc.	V.G.	Good	Fair	Poor
550	425	325	200	125	50

Whitworth Military Target Rifle

This model is in .451 caliber. Barrel length is 36". Weight is about 9.9 lbs.

NIB	Exc.	V.G.	Good	Fair	Poor
875	700	550	400	200	100

Whitworth Sniping Rifle

Same as above but with brass scope and mounts.

NIB	Exc.	V.G.	Good	Fair	Poor
1400	1050	800	550	300	150

Volunteer Percussion Target Rifle

This rifle is in .451 caliber and fitted with a 33" barrel. It is the two banded design with walnut stock and brass furniture. Adjustable rear sight. Weight is approximately 9.5 lbs.

NIB	Exc.	V.G.	Good	Fair	Poor
850	650	550	400	200	100

PARKER REPRODUCTIONS
Japan

This company had exact reproductions of Parker D, DHE, B and A-1 Special shotguns made in Japan. They are of the finest quality and workmanship. The styles of engraving and features of these shotguns correspond exactly to the original Parker Arms. The following following values are a starting point.

DHE Grade

This side-by-side shotgun is offered in 12, 20, and 28 gauge. Barrel lengths are 26" or 28" with sold matte rib. Stocks are select walnut with choice of pistol or straight grip. Choice splinter or beavertail forearms are offered. Single or double triggers are available as well. The receiver is case colored and scroll engraved with game scenes to match the original Parker DHE grade. Weight of 12 gauge is 6.75 lbs., 20 gauge is 6.5 lbs., and 28 gauge weighs 5.3 lbs. **NOTE:** For 28 gauge add 40 percent, 20 gauge add 30 percent.

12 Gauge

NIB	Exc.	V.G.	Good	Fair	Poor
4000	3000	2400	1800	1200	400

16/20 Combination

Introduced in 1993 and limited to 500 sets. Offered with 28" barrels only this set features a 16 gauge barrel on a 20 gauge frame. Weighs 6.25 lbs.

NIB	Exc.	V.G.	Good	Fair	Poor
11000	8900	7500	3500	200050	650

28 Gauge

NIB	Exc.	V.G.	Good	Fair	Poor
6000	4250	3000	2000	1400	400

28 Gauge/.410 Bore Combination

NOTE: Add $990 for an additional barrel and $170 for beavertail forearm. For the D Grade, three-barrel sets are offered in 16/20/20 combinations for an additional $2300.

NIB	Exc.	V.G.	Good	Fair	Poor
15000	12000	9000	7500	3000	1000

DHE Grade Steel-Shot Special

Offered in 12 gauge only with 28" barrels. Fitted with 3" chambers and special chrome lined barrels. Weighs 7 lbs.

NIB	Exc.	V.G.	Good	Fair	Poor
6000	5000	3950	2200	1200	400

BHE Grade Limited Edition

This model features engraving similar to the original Parker BHE Grade. Fancy walnut stocks with fine line checkering was standard. It was offered in 12, 20, and 28 gauge. A 28 gauge/.410 bore combination was also offered. Only 100 shotguns in this grade were produced in 1989.

NIB	Exc.	V.G.	Good	Fair	Poor
8500	6500	5000	2250	900	450

2-Barrel Set

NIB	Exc.	V.G.	Good	Fair	Poor
15000	11500	9500	4000	2000	750

A-1 Special

Introduced in 1988, this grade featured fine scroll engraving and presentation French walnut with custom checkering pattern. The stock was hand carved with fleur-de-lis and features 32 lpi checkering. The grip cap was rosewood and gold or gold initial plate on straight grip guns. Gold wire was used on the breech end on the barrels. Serial numbers were in gold relief as were the word "SAFE" and "L" and "R" on models with selective single trigger. Barrel flats and frame water table were jeweled. This grade was offered in 12, 20, and 28 gauge with a few early guns sold with 28 gauge/.410 bore combinations. Furnished with English-style oak-and-leather case with canvas and leather cover, engraved snap caps, and engraved oil bottle.

12 or 20 Gauge

NIB	Exc.	V.G.	Good	Fair	Poor
13000	11500	9000	6500	5000	700

28 Gauge

NIB	Exc.	V.G.	Good	Fair	Poor
16000	14000	9500	7000	3500	600

A-1 Special Custom Engraved

This model is a custom A-1 Special hand-engraved to each individual customer's specifications. Only a limited number of these shotguns were built. Initial price in 1989 was $10,500. The sky's the limit on a gun of this sort.

PEABODY
Providence, Rhode Island
Providence Tool Company

For historical information, photos, and data on Peabody military rifles see the Standard Catalog of Military Firearms.

Peabody Rifle and Carbine

A .43 Spanish, .443, .45 Peabody, .45-70, .50 or .50-70 caliber single-shot rifle with a 33" or 20" (carbine) barrel and either a full-length or half stock. The receiver marked "Peabody's Patent July 22, 1862 / Manf'd by Providence Tool Co. Prov. R.I." Blued, with a walnut stock. Produced in large quantities during the 1860s and 1870s.

Courtesy Milwaukee Public Museum, Milwaukee, Wisconsin

NIB	Exc.	V.G.	Good	Fair	Poor
—	—	1950	900	300	100

Sporting Rifle

As above, in a sporting configuration with either 26" or 28" barrels. The frame marked, "Peabody's Patent, July 22, 1862 / Manf'd by Providence Tool Co., Prov. R.I." Blued, case hardened with a walnut stock. Manufactured from approximately 1866 to 1875.

NIB	Exc.	V.G.	Good	Fair	Poor
—	—	5500	3000	1100	400

PEABODY-MARTINI SPORTING RIFLES

For historical information, photos, and data on Peabody-Martini military rifles see the *Standard Catalog of Military Firearms*.

Creedmoor

A .40-90 or .44-100 caliber Martini-action single-shot rifle with a 32" round/octagonal barrel, butt-mounted vernier rear sight, combination wind gauge and spirit level front sight. The receiver marked, "Peabody & Martini Patents" and the barrel "Manufactured by the Providence Tool Co. Providence R.I. U.S.A." Blued, case hardened with a walnut stock.

Courtesy Milwaukee Public Museum, Milwaukee, Wisconsin

NIB	Exc.	V.G.	Good	Fair	Poor
—	—	8250	3850	1650	550

Creedmoor Mid-Range

Similar to the above, but in .40-70 or .40-90 caliber with a 28" round/octagonal barrel, vernier tang sight and wind gauge front sight. Blued, case hardened with a walnut stock.

NIB	Exc.	V.G.	Good	Fair	Poor
—	—	6600	3700	1400	400

What Cheer

The Creedmoor without a pistol grip.

NIB	Exc.	V.G.	Good	Fair	Poor
—	—	6600	3600	1350	400

What Cheer Mid-Range

The Mid-Range Creedmoor without a pistol grip.

NIB	Exc.	V.G.	Good	Fair	Poor
—	—	5500	3100	1100	300

Kill Deer

A .45-70 caliber single-shot Martini-action rifle with 28" or 30" round/octagonal barrels, adjustable tang rear sight and globe front sights. Blued, case hardened with a walnut stock.

NIB	Exc.	V.G.	Good	Fair	Poor
—	—	8250	4700	1650	500

PEAVY, A. J.
South Montville, Maine

Knife-Pistol

A .22 caliber single-shot knife pistol constructed of steel and brass with a folding trigger. The sideplates marked "A.J. Peavy Pat. Sept. 5, '65 & Mar. 27, '66." Produced between 1866 and 1870.

NIB	Exc.	V.G.	Good	Fair	Poor
—	—	6000	4700	1900	500

PECARE & SMITH
New York, New York

Pepperbox

A .28 caliber 4-shot or 1-shot percussion pepperbox with a folding trigger and 4" barrel group. The barrel group enclosed within an iron casing. Blued, silver-plated frame with walnut grips. The barrel casing marked "Pecare & Smith". Manufactured during the 1840s and early 1850s.

NIB	Exc.	V.G.	Good	Fair	Poor
—	—	4800	3000	1300	350

Ten-Shot Pepperbox (rare)

NIB	Exc.	V.G.	Good	Fair	Poor
—	—	9500	6600	2750	600

PEDERSEN, JOHN D.
Denver, Colorado & Jackson, Wyoming

Pedersen Rifle

NIB	Exc.	V.G.	Good	Fair	Poor
—	15000	7500	5000	2500	500

Pedersen Carbine

NIB	Exc.	V.G.	Good	Fair	Poor
—	17500	8500	6000	3000	—600

PEDERSEN CUSTOM GUNS
North Haven, Connecticut

A division of the O.F. Mossberg Company operated between 1973 and 1975.

Model 4000 Shotgun

The Mossberg Model 500 slide-action shotgun in 12, 20 or .410 bore with 26", 28", or 30" ventilated rib barrels. Blued, engraved with a walnut stock. Manufactured in 1975.

NIB	Exc.	V.G.	Good	Fair	Poor
—	400	350	250	200	100

Model 4000 Trap

Chambered for 12 gauge only with 30" Full choke barrel. Monte Carlo stock with factory recoil pad.

NIB	Exc.	V.G.	Good	Fair	Poor
—	500	400	300	200	100

Model 4500

As above, but with a reduced amount of engraving.

NIB	Exc.	V.G.	Good	Fair	Poor
—	425	325	225	175	100

Model 4500 Trap

Same as the Model 4000 Trap but with less engraving.

NIB	Exc.	V.G.	Good	Fair	Poor
—	400	350	250	200	100

Model 1500

A 12 gauge Magnum over/under shotgun with 26", 28", or 30" ventilated rib barrels, single-selective trigger and automatic ejectors. Blued with a walnut stock. Weight is about 7.5 lbs. depending on barrel length. Manufactured between 1973 and 1975.

NIB	Exc.	V.G.	Good	Fair	Poor
—	900	775	550	300	200

Model 1500 Skeet

Similar to the above model but fitted with a skeet-style stock, 27" barrels and skeet chokes.

NIB	Exc.	V.G.	Good	Fair	Poor
—	950	825	600	350	200

Model 1500 Trap

This model is fitted with a Monte Carlo-style stock a choice of 30" or 32" barrels.

NIB	Exc.	V.G.	Good	Fair	Poor
—	950	825	600	350	200

Model 1000

As above, but manufactured in two grades of decoration. Manufactured between 1973 and 1975.

Grade I

NIB	Exc.	V.G.	Good	Fair	Poor
—	1750	1250	800	500	200

Grade II

NIB	Exc.	V.G.	Good	Fair	Poor
—	1500	1000	750	400	200

Model 1000 Magnum

This model is chambered for the 12 gauge 3" shell and fitted with 30" barrels.

Grade I

NIB	Exc.	V.G.	Good	Fair	Poor
—	1600	1200	800	500	200

Grade II

NIB	Exc.	V.G.	Good	Fair	Poor
—	1400	1100	750	400	200

Model 1000 Skeet

Offered in 12 gauge only with 26" or 28" barrels. Skeet-style stock and skeet chokes.

Grade I

NIB	Exc.	V.G.	Good	Fair	Poor
—	1750	1250	800	400	200

Grade II

NIB	Exc.	V.G.	Good	Fair	Poor
—	1500	1000	750	400	200

Model 1000 Trap

This model is chambered for 12 gauge and fitted with 30" or 32" barrels. Trap-style Monte Carlo stock.

Grade I

NIB	Exc.	V.G.	Good	Fair	Poor
—	1600	1200	800	500	200

Grade II

NIB	Exc.	V.G.	Good	Fair	Poor
—	1400	1100	750	400	200

Model 2000

A 12 or 20 gauge boxlock double-barrel shotgun with 26", 28", or 30" barrels, single-selective trigger and automatic ejectors. Produced in two grades of decoration. Manufactured in 1973 and 1974.

Grade I

NIB	Exc.	V.G.	Good	Fair	Poor
—	2000	1500	1000	600	200

Grade II

NIB	Exc.	V.G.	Good	Fair	Poor
—	1750	1250	800	400	200

Model 2500

A 12 or 20 gauge boxlock double-barrel shotgun with 26" or 28" barrels, double triggers and automatic ejectors. Blued with a walnut stock.

NIB	Exc.	V.G.	Good	Fair	Poor
—	400	300	250	150	200

Model 3000

A Mossberg Model 810 bolt-action rifle manufactured in .270 to .338 Winchester Magnum caliber with a 22" or 24" barrel with open sights. Produced in three grades.

Grade III—Plain

NIB	Exc.	V.G.	Good	Fair	Poor
—	450	400	350	150	200

Grade II

NIB	Exc.	V.G.	Good	Fair	Poor
—	525	425	350	150	200

Grade I

NIB	Exc.	V.G.	Good	Fair	Poor
—	800	650	500	200	200

Model 4700

The Mossberg Model 472 lever-action in .30-30 or .35 Remington caliber with a 24" barrel and 5-shot tubular magazine. Blued with a walnut stock.

NIB	Exc.	V.G.	Good	Fair	Poor
—	450	375	275	175	100

PEDERSOLI, DAVIDE
Brescia, Italy

Davide Pedersoli & Co. was founded in 1957 by the late Davide Pedersoli. In the nearly half-century since, Pedersoli has established itself as a manufacturer of extremely high-quality replica and modern firearms. Pedersoli products are frequently marked with the importer's or retailer's name (e.g., Dixie Gun Works or Cabela's) rather than the Pedersoli brand, usually at widely varying discounts. Many muzzleloading rifles and pistols are available in kit form at reduced prices. **NOTE:** Rapidly-fluctuating currency markets can result in values for newly-imported Pedersoli guns being 10-15 percent higher than the values listed below.

HANDGUNS

Mang In Graz Pistol

Recreation of single-shot percussion pistol made c. 1850 by Martin Mang. .38 or .44 caliber. **NOTE:** Add 10 percent for target model, 20 percent for deluxe.

NIB	Exc.	V.G.	Good	Fair	Poor
1100	750	500	400	300	150

Kuchenreuter Pistol

Recreation of single-shot percussion pistol made c. 1854 by Bartholomaus Kuchenreuter of Steinweg, Germany. .38 or .44 caliber. **NOTE:** Add 20 percent for deluxe.

NIB	Exc.	V.G.	Good	Fair	Poor
1350	900	600	500	400	200

Mortimer Pistol

Recreation of single-shot pistol first made c. 1810 by H. W Mortimer & Son of London. .44 caliber, smooth or rifled barrel. Percussion and flint versions available. **NOTE:** Add 10 percent for Match model, 20 percent for deluxe.

NIB	Exc.	V.G.	Good	Fair	Poor
895	755	525	375	250	100

LePage Dueller

Recreation of single-shot duelling pistol made by Henry LePage c. 1840. Percussion and flint versions available. .31, .36 or .44 caliber. **NOTE:** Add 20 percent for deluxe.

NIB	Exc.	V.G.	Good	Fair	Poor
895	755	525	375	250	100

Charles Moore Duelling Pistol

Recreation of single-shot duelling pistol made by Charles Moore of London c. 1800. Percussion and flint versions available. .36 or .44 caliber. **NOTE:** Add 10 percent for target model.

NIB	Exc.	V.G.	Good	Fair	Poor
600	450	300	200	100	50

Carleton Underhammer Pistol

Recreation of saw-handled underhammer percussion pistol c. 1850. .36 caliber.

NIB	Exc.	V.G.	Good	Fair	Poor
750	600	450	300	150	75

Remington Pattern Target Revolver

Replica of Remington "1858-style" .44-caliber percussion revolver.

NIB	Exc.	V.G.	Good	Fair	Poor
450	350	250	100	75	50

Rogers & Spencer Target Percussion Target Revolver

Replica of the .44-caliber Rogers and Spencer revolver that didn't quite make it in time for the Civil War.

NIB	Exc.	V.G.	Good	Fair	Poor
425	325	250	100	75	50

Kentucky Pistol

Recreation of single-shot pistol of American colonial era. Flint and percussion versions available. .45, .50 and .54 caliber. **NOTE:** Add 50 percent for "Silver Star" models.

NIB	Exc.	V.G.	Good	Fair	Poor
300	250	225	150	100	50

Bounty Pistol

Similar to Kentucky Pistol standard version but with 16" barrel. .45 or .50 caliber only.

NIB	Exc.	V.G.	Good	Fair	Poor
300	250	225	150	100	50

Navy Moll Pistol

Similar to Kentucky pistol but with brass trim. Flint and percussion versions available. .45 caliber.

NIB	Exc.	V.G.	Good	Fair	Poor
425	325	250	100	75	50

Harper's Ferry Pistol

Recreation of .58-caliber flintlock pistol procured for the U. S. Navy in 1806.

NIB	Exc.	V.G.	Good	Fair	Poor
425	325	250	100	75	50

Queen Anne Pistol

Recreation of English 17th-century cannon-barrel flintlock pistol. .50-caliber smoothbore barrel. Steel or brass construction.

NIB	Exc.	V.G.	Good	Fair	Poor
375	295	225	75	50	25

An IX Pistol

Recreation of .69-caliber Napoleonic flintlock cavalry pistol of 1803. Brass trim.

NIB	Exc.	V.G.	Good	Fair	Poor
500	400	300	200	100	50

An XIII Pistol

Simplified 1806 version of the An IX pistol.

NIB	Exc.	V.G.	Good	Fair	Poor
500	400	300	200	100	50

Remington Rider Derringer

Recreation of Remington Rider single-shot .177 percussion parlor pistol. Available in the white or with casehardened, gold-toned or engraved/silvered finish. Pricing for basic model.

NIB	Exc.	V.G.	Good	Fair	Poor
175	150	100	75	50	25

Derringer Liegi

Recreation of c. 1850 screw-barrel percussion pocket pistol with folding trigger and bag grip. .44 caliber. **NOTE:** Add 10 percent for engraved model.

NIB	Exc.	V.G.	Good	Fair	Poor
175	150	100	75	50	25

Zimmer Pistol

Recreation of c. 1850 single-shot percussion parlor pistol. .177 caliber; fluted grip with butt cap. Discontinued.

NIB	Exc.	V.G.	Good	Fair	Poor
500	400	300	200	100	50

Saloon Pistol

Recreation of c. 1850 single-shot percussion parlor pistol. .36 or .177 caliber. Discontinued.

NIB	Exc.	V.G.	Good	Fair	Poor
500	400	300	200	100	50

RIFLES

Swivel-Breech Rifle

Muzzleloading over/under rotating percussion rifle in .45, .50, or .54 caliber. Browned barrel, walnut stock. Discontinued.

NIB	Exc.	V.G.	Good	Fair	Poor
700	625	500	350	175	100

Bristlen A. Morges Target Rifle

Recreation of 1850-vintage percussion target rifle made by Marc Bristlen of Morges, Switzerland. Schuetzen-style buttplate, double triggers, false muzzle. Shoots .35- or .45-caliber elongated conical. **NOTE:** Add 20 percent for deluxe model.

NIB	Exc.	V.G.	Good	Fair	Poor
1350	900	600	500	400	200

Waadtlander Target Rifle

Similar to Bristel A. Morges target rifle but rifled for .45-caliber round ball. **NOTE:** Add 20 percent for deluxe version.

NIB	Exc.	V.G.	Good	Fair	Poor
1350	900	600	500	400	200

Swiss Rifle

Similar to Waadtlander Target Rifle but in flintlock with 29.5" barrel.

NIB	Exc.	V.G.	Good	Fair	Poor
1350	900	600	500	400	200

Wurttemberg Mauser

Replica of 1857 Mauser military percussion rifle made from 1857 to 1856. Shoots .54 Minié ball. Designed for 100m target shooting.

NIB	Exc.	V.G.	Good	Fair	Poor
1000	850	700	575	400	125

Gibbs Rifle

Recreation of the 1865-vintage long-range percussion rifle made by George Gibbs of London. Shoots elongated .40- or .45-caliber conicals.

NIB	Exc.	V.G.	Good	Fair	Poor
1350	900	600	500	400	200

Tryon Rifle

Recreation of noteworthy American percussion plains rifle c. 1850. .45-, .50-, or .54-caliber. **NOTE:** Add 10 percent for Creedmore model; 20 percent for deluxe target model.

NIB	Exc.	V.G.	Good	Fair	Poor
750	600	450	300	150	75

Mortimer Rifle

Recreation of arms made c. 1850 by H. W Mortimer & Son of London. Percussion and flint versions available. Various configurations including Whitworth, Vetterli, and 12-gauge fowler.

NIB	Exc.	V.G.	Good	Fair	Poor
1050	875	600	500	400	175

Indian Trade Musket

Recreation of 18th-century flintlock smoothbore fusil as typified by colonial and early 19th-century trading companies.

NIB	Exc.	V.G.	Good	Fair	Poor
825	750	650	500	400	175

Frontier Rifle

Recreation of typical American hunting rifle c. 1800 - 1840. .32-, .36-, .45-, .50- and .54-caliber versions available in flintlock and percussion. Various barrel lengths.

NIB	Exc.	V.G.	Good	Fair	Poor
750	600	450	300	150	75

Kentucky Rifle

Recreation of Pennsylvania-style rifle c. 1800. .32-, .45- and .50-caliber percussion or flintlock. **NOTE:** Add 35 percent for "Silver Star" model.

NIB	Exc.	V.G.	Good	Fair	Poor
750	600	450	300	150	75

Alamo Rifle

Recreation of long rifle used in Mexican War of the 1840s. Double triggers; .32-, .45- or .50-caliber.

NIB	Exc.	V.G.	Good	Fair	Poor
825	750	650	500	400	175

Cub

Scaled-down Pennsylvania-type rifle in .36, .45 or .50 caliber. Percussion or flint. **NOTE:** Add 25 percent for flint.

NIB	Exc.	V.G.	Good	Fair	Poor
550	425	350	250	200	100

Country Hunter

Exceedingly simple half-stock .50-caliber percussion or flintlock rifle.

NIB	Exc.	V.G.	Good	Fair	Poor
500	425	350	250	200	100

Jager Rifle

Massive, decidedly Germanic .54-caliber percussion or flintlock rifle based on Teutonic hunting arms c. 1750-1850.

NIB	Exc.	V.G.	Good	Fair	Poor
950	875	700	550	375	200

Leger 1763 Charleville Musket

Recreation of Revolution-era .69-caliber smoothbore flintlock musket.

NIB	Exc.	V.G.	Good	Fair	Poor
1050	875	600	500	400	175

Revolutionnaire 1777 Musket

Similar to Charleville musket but in detail patterned after muskets used in French Revolution.

NIB	Exc.	V.G.	Good	Fair	Poor
1050	875	600	500	400	175

Corrige An IX

Similar to Revolutionnaire 1777 musket but differing in details of frizzen, etc.

NIB	Exc.	V.G.	Good	Fair	Poor
1050	875	600	500	400	175

An IX Dragoon Musket

Similar to Corrige An IX musket but with 40.5" cavalry-length barrel.

NIB	Exc.	V.G.	Good	Fair	Poor
1050	875	600	500	400	175

Austrian 1798 Flintlock Musket

Similar to 1777 musket but with Austrian modifications in barrel bands, bayonet mount, etc.

NIB	Exc.	V.G.	Good	Fair	Poor
1050	875	600	500	400	175

Prussian 1809 Flintlock Musket

Similar to French 1777 musket but in .75 caliber with "Potsdam" markings.

NIB	Exc.	V.G.	Good	Fair	Poor
1050	875	600	500	400	175

Brown Bess Flintlock Musket

Recreation of legendary .75-caliber smoothbore musket as used by British troops before, during and after the American Revolutionary War.

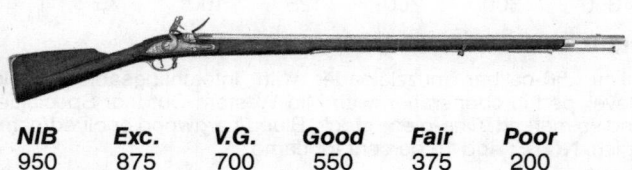

NIB	Exc.	V.G.	Good	Fair	Poor
950	875	700	550	375	200

Springfield 1795 Musket

Recreation of America's first indigenous military arm. .69-caliber smoothbore.

NIB	Exc.	V.G.	Good	Fair	Poor
950	875	700	550	375	200

Harper's Ferry 1816 Musket

Recreation of U.S. martial .69-caliber smoothbore flintlock musket.

NIB	Exc.	V.G.	Good	Fair	Poor
950	875	700	550	375	200

Rocky Mountain Hawken

Faithful recreation of legendary plains rifle. .54 caliber.

NIB	Exc.	V.G.	Good	Fair	Poor
850	695	550	400	250	125

Springfield 1861 Rifle

Recreation of .58-caliber percussion rifle as used in American Civil War.

NIB	Exc.	V.G.	Good	Fair	Poor
950	875	700	550	375	200

Kodiak Combination Gun

Percussion side-by-side rifle/shotgun combination gun with 12-gauge smoothbore barrel and .50-, .54- and .58-caliber rifled barrel.

NIB	Exc.	V.G.	Good	Fair	Poor
1100	850	600	425	300	200

Kodiak Double Rifle

Side-by-side double percussion rifle in .50, .54, .58 and .72 caliber. Sights regulated to 75 yards.

NIB	Exc.	V.G.	Good	Fair	Poor
1200	950	700	475	325	200

Rolling Block Rifle

Replica of famous Remington rolling block single-shot rifle 1867 – c. 1890. Various centerfire chamberings and configurations including Baby carbine. Prices shown are for standard version in .45-70.

NIB	Exc.	V.G.	Good	Fair	Poor
950	875	700	550	375	200

1859 Sharps Cavalry Carbine

Replica of Sharps percussion carbine with 22" barrel, patchbox and elvator sight; .54 caliber. Also available as Infantry Rifle with 30" barrel.

NIB	Exc.	V.G.	Good	Fair	Poor
895	825	775	675	475	200

1862 Robinson Confederate Sharps

Similar to 1859 Sharps carbine but with different barrel band, receiver details, and rear sight.

NIB	Exc.	V.G.	Good	Fair	Poor
800	675	575	400	300	125

Sharps 1863 Sporting Rifle

Replica of Sharps sporting rifle with 32" barrel, set trigger and sculpted fore-end; .45 or .54 caliber. .45 version rifled for elongated conicals.

NIB	Exc.	V.G.	Good	Fair	Poor
850	725	625	450	350	150

1874 Sharps

High-quality replica of first Sharps chambered for metallic cartridges. Chamberings include .45-70, .45-90, .45-110, .45-120, .50-70 and .50-90. Several variations available including Sporting Standard Sporting, Cavalry Rifle, Cavalry Carbine, Sporting Deluxe, Sporting Extra Deluxe, Silhouette Standard, Silhouette Deluxe, Boss, Business Rifle, Buffalo, Billy Dixon, Long Range, Quigley, Creedmore #2 and Competition Standard. Prices given are for Standard Sporting model.

NIB	Exc.	V.G.	Good	Fair	Poor
1100	850	600	425	300	200

1873 Trapdoor Springfield

Replica of famous single-shot cartridge rifle chambered in .45-70. Several variations available including Standard Rifle, Standard Carbine, Officer's Model and Long Range Model. Prices given are for Standard Rifle. **NOTE:** Add 30 percent for deluxe models.

NIB	Exc.	V.G.	Good	Fair	Poor
1100	850	600	425	300	200

Kodiak Mark IV Express Rifle

Side-by-side double rifle chambered for .45-70 cartridge.

NIB	Exc.	V.G.	Good	Fair	Poor
4500	3750	3000	2000	900	300

Pedersoli Lightning Rifle

Updated replica of Model 1883 Colt Lightning Magazine Rifle. Pump action with magazine disconnector. Chambered for .44-40 and .45 Colt.

NIB	Exc.	V.G.	Good	Fair	Poor
1100	850	600	425	300	200

SHOTGUNS

Double Percussion Shotgun

Side-by-side muzzleloading shotgun in 10, 12 and 20 gauge. Interchangeable chokes. Camo models available. Prices given are for basic version in 12 gauge.

NIB	Exc.	V.G.	Good	Fair	Poor
650	550	475	300	175	125

Coach Shotgun

Side-by-side 12-gauge percussion shotgun with 20" barrels. Discontinued.

NIB	Exc.	V.G.	Good	Fair	Poor
600	525	450	275	150	125

Mortimer Shotgun

Recreation of 12-gauge fowlers made c. 1830 to 1850 by H. W Mortimer & Son of London. Percussion and flint versions available.

NIB	Exc.	V.G.	Good	Fair	Poor
1100	850	600	425	300	200

MODERN MUZZLELOADERS

Denali

In-line .50-caliber muzzleloader with lever-operated break-open action. Walnut/blue or camo/blue finish. **NOTE:** Add 15 percent for camo.

NIB	Exc.	V.G.	Good	Fair	Poor
380	350	275	200	100	50

Brutus 94

Inline .50-caliber muzzleloader. Blued/composite, blued/synthetic or stainless/blued/walnut finish. **NOTE:** Add 15 percent for camo.

NIB	Exc.	V.G.	Good	Fair	Poor
350	300	200	125	100	75

Brutus Ovation

Inline .50-caliber muzzleloader with interchangeable barrels. Developed in cooperation with Mid-Western Outdoor Specialties and so marked. One-piece stock. Blued/hardwood or blued/camo finish. **NOTE:** Add 15 percent for camo.

NIB	Exc.	V.G.	Good	Fair	Poor
350	300	200	125	100	75

Rolling Block Percussion Rifle

.50-caliber muzzleloading version of Remington rolling block rifle. Blued/hardwoods or blued/camo finish.

NIB	Exc.	V.G.	Good	Fair	Poor
350	300	200	125	100	75

PERAZZI
Brescia, Italy

This company was founded in 1957. During the 1970s Ithaca and Winchester imported and sold Perazzi shotguns. Perazzi has now taken over its own importation and distribution in the United States with the creation of Perazzi USA, Inc. Many shooters consider the Perazzi to be the finest currently produced shotgun in the world. Perazzi has an extensive variety of models to choose from. In addition, each model may be available in different grades. These grades are based on the type of finish, engraving, and wood quality. The vast majority of Perazzi shotguns that are sold in this country are Standard Grade guns. According to Perazzi USA, these Standard Grade guns account for approximately 98 percent of North American sales. Therefore, it is unlikely that the shooter or collector will encounter high-grade Perazzi guns. It should be pointed out that in some models no Extra Grade or Extra Gold Grade shotguns have ever been sold in the United States.For the benefit of the reader an approximate description of each grade follows. It is a general description because the Perazzi customer may order practically any combination of finishes or engraving patterns he or she desires. Use this list as a general guide. It is suggested that anyone wanting to know more about Perazzi guns buy a copy of Karl Lippard's book, Perazzi Shotguns. He can be reached at P.O. Box 60719, Colorado Springs, CO.

OUT-OF-PRODUCTION SHOTGUNS

NOTE: Very high premiums on early SCO and higher grades.

COMP 1-SB TRAP (Standard Grade)

This model is a single barrel trap gun in 12 gauge only with 32" or 34" vent rib barrel.

NIB	Exc.	V.G.	Good	Fair	Poor
—	2500	1750	1000	750	500

COMP 1-TRAP (Standard Grade)

This is an over/under version of the above model.

NIB	Exc.	V.G.	Good	Fair	Poor
—	4800	4000	3000	2250	500

Light Game Model (Standard Grade)

Offered in 12 gauge with a 27.5" vent rib barrel. Trigger group is not detachable. Produced between 1972 and 1974.

NIB	Exc.	V.G.	Good	Fair	Poor
—	6250	4750	3000	1400	500

MT-6 Model (Standard Grade)

This model was offered in 12 gauge with a tapered vent rib. The trigger group was not removable. Discontinued in 1983.

NIB	Exc.	V.G.	Good	Fair	Poor
—	3800	3000	2000	1000	400

MX3

This model was discontinued in 1988 and was available in 12 gauge only for single barrel trap, over/under trap, combination trap, skeet, and sporting configurations. **NOTE:** Add 50 percent for Combination Trap Guns.

Standard Grade

NIB	Exc.	V.G.	Good	Fair	Poor
—	3500	3000	2250	1750	400

SC3 Grade

NIB	Exc.	V.G.	Good	Fair	Poor
—	5000	4000	3000	2200	500

SCO Grade

NIB	Exc.	V.G.	Good	Fair	Poor
—	6500	5500	4000	2500	500

Gold Grade

NIB	Exc.	V.G.	Good	Fair	Poor
10000	8500	5900	2700	—	700

Grand American Special

This model was introduced in 1988 and features a high ramped rib similar to the MX3 model. The fore-end was grooved. Discontinued in 1991. It was offered in single barrel trap, combination trap, and over/under trap configurations.

Standard Grade

NIB	Exc.	V.G.	Good	Fair	Poor
—	5250	4250	3500	2000	700

SC3 Grade

NIB	Exc.	V.G.	Good	Fair	Poor
—	6500	5250	4500	3000	700

SCO Grade

NIB	Exc.	V.G.	Good	Fair	Poor
—	8000	6500	5500	3750	700

Gold Grade

NIB	Exc.	V.G.	Good	Fair	Poor
—	10000	7500	6000	4000	700

SCO Grade w/Sideplates

NIB	Exc.	V.G.	Good	Fair	Poor
—	13500	10000	7500	6000	700

Gold Grade w/Sideplates

NIB	Exc.	V.G.	Good	Fair	Poor
—	15000	12000	8500	6500	700

SHO Model

This over/under sidelock model is available in 12 gauge only in both Type 1 and Type 2 configurations. Type 1 does not have rebounding firing pins and is worth approximately 50 percent less than Type 2 models that are fitted with rebounding firing pins. There are no parts available in this country or at the factory for Type 1 guns. An expert appraisal is recommended for this model due to its unique features.

The SHO model features a silver finish with fine scroll engraving with game scenes to customer's specifications. Select walnut stock built to customer's dimensions with fine line checkering. A custom built shotgun. Special order only. The sky's the limit.

DHO Model

This is a side-by-side shotgun offered in 12 gauge only. It has full sidelocks and a silver receiver finish with scroll and game scene engraving of the same quality as the SHO Model. Fancy walnut stock with fine line checkering. An expert appraisal is recommended for this model due to its unique features. Special order only. The sky's the limit.

DHO Extra Gold

Available in any gauge and barrel length combination. Only the finest presentation walnut and checkering. A totally custom built shotgun. Special order only. The sky's the limit.

RECENT PRODUCTION SHOTGUNS

MX9

Introduced in 1993 this model features removable inserts on rib to adjust point of impact and a walnut stock with adjustable comb. Offered in 12 gauge with 32" or 34" barrel with screw-in chokes in trap configuration and single barrels in Trap/Combo models. A competition version is also offered with unique vent rib inserts to correct for point of impact. The trigger group is removable. Available in several different grades of ornamentation.

Standard Grade

NIB	Exc.	V.G.	Good	Fair	Poor
—	6500	5000	3500	1800	700

SC3 Grade

NIB	Exc.	V.G.	Good	Fair	Poor
—	11500	6000	5000	3000	700

SCO Grade

MX9 Trap Combo Model

NIB	Exc.	V.G.	Good	Fair	Poor
—	18000	8000	7000	3500	7000

Standard Grade Trap Combo

NIB	Exc.	V.G.	Good	Fair	Poor
—	9500	6500	5000	3500	900

MX10

This model was introduced in 1993. Its Single Barrel Trap models feature a different method of rib height and pattern adjustment. This model also has an adjustable stock. Available in 12 gauge with 32" or 34" barrels. Trap/Combo models are offered in 12 gauge with 29.5" or 31.5" over/under barrels with 32" or 34" single barrel. Chokes are fixed. Competition models are offered in 12- and 20 gauge with choice of 29.5" or 31.5" barrel for 12 gauge and 29.5" barrel for 20 gauge. The ventilated rib height is adjustable as is the comb position on the stock. Trigger is removable.

Standard Grade

NIB	Exc.	V.G.	Good	Fair	Poor
—	8250	7000	6000	4300	700

SC3 Grade

NIB	Exc.	V.G.	Good	Fair	Poor
—	10000	8500	7000	5200	700

SCO Grade

MX 10 Competition model

NIB	Exc.	V.G.	Good	Fair	Poor
—	13500	11000	8500	6750	700

Standard Grade Combo Model

NIB	Exc.	V.G.	Good	Fair	Poor
—	15000	13000	10500	5000	700

TM I Special Standard Grade

This basic single barrel Perazzi Trap model is offered in 12 gauge with 32" or 34" barrel. Trigger is adjustable.

NIB	Exc.	V.G.	Good	Fair	Poor
—	4000	2000	1250	850	700

TMX Special

Similar to TM I Special with select walnut.

Standard Grade

NIB	Exc.	V.G.	Good	Fair	Poor
—	5000	4200	2700	1900	700

SCO Grade

NIB	Exc.	V.G.	Good	Fair	Poor
—	8000	6000	5000	2100	700

MX8 Special

This model features a low contour vent rib, adjustable trigger, and grooved fore-end. **NOTE:** Some SCO engraving patterns on early models have sold in the $30,000 to $45,000 price range. depending on the engraver. Get an expert appraisal. Beware of counterfeits.

Standard Grade

NIB	Exc.	V.G.	Good	Fair	Poor
—	5500	4000	3000	2000	700

SC3 Grade

NIB	Exc.	V.G.	Good	Fair	Poor
—	7500	5500	3800	2500	700

SCO Grade

MX 8 Special Trap Combo

NIB	Exc.	V.G.	Good	Fair	Poor
—	13000	10500	8000	5000	700

Standard Grade Trap Combo

NIB	Exc.	V.G.	Good	Fair	Poor
—	7500	5000	3500	2000	700

MX8/20

This model was first introduced in 1993. It features a removable trigger group. Available in 20 gauge only with choice of 27.5", 28.375", 29.5" flat ventilated rib barrels. Choice of fixed or screw-in chokes on sporting model. Stock is custom made to customer's dimensions with beavertail fore-end.

Standard Grade

NIB	Exc.	V.G.	Good	Fair	Poor
10000	8500	6500	4800	2000	—

SC3 Grade

NIB	Exc.	V.G.	Good	Fair	Poor
16000	14500	12000	7500	3000	—

SCO Grade

NIB	Exc.	V.G.	Good	Fair	Poor
30000	24000	17500	12000	5000	—

MX8/20-8/20C

Introduced in 1993 and offered in 20 gauge with 26" or 27.625" vent rib barrels. The trigger group on this model is removable. The stock is a high-grade walnut custom made to customers' specifications. The fore-end is round. The MX8/20 is supplied with fixed chokes while the MX8/20C has 5 screw-in choke tubes. **NOTE:** Add $400 for MX8/20C values.

Standard Grade

NIB	Exc.	V.G.	Good	Fair	Poor
10500	9000	7000	5000	2250	—

SC3 Grade

NIB	Exc.	V.G.	Good	Fair	Poor
16500	13500	10000	8000	4000	—

SCO Grade

NIB	Exc.	V.G.	Good	Fair	Poor
32000	25000	20000	14000	7000	—

MX7 Standard Grade

Introduced in 1993. This an over/under trap model that is offered in 12 gauge with 29.5" or 31.5" over/under barrels with either 32" or 34" single barrel. This model has a non-renewable trigger group feathering fixed coil spring trigger mechanism. The trigger is selective and works in conjunction with the safety catch. The vent rib is ramped on the Combo Trap model. The walnut is custom made to the customer's dimensions.

NIB	Exc.	V.G.	Good	Fair	Poor
—	4500	3200	2500	1750	700

MX7C Standard Grade

Introduced in 1993 this model is offered in 12 gauge with a non-renewable trigger group. It has a coil spring mechanism, fully selective in conjunction with the safety. Offered in 27.5", 29.5", or 31.5" flat vent rib barrels. Screw-in chokes are standard. Walnut stock is custom made to customer's dimensions. The fore-end is beavertail.

NIB	Exc.	V.G.	Good	Fair	Poor
—	5500	4000	3000	2000	700

DB81 Special

This model, offered in 12 gauge only and features a high ramped ventilated rib. Trigger is adjustable with internal selector. Barrel length are 29.5" or 31.5". **NOTE:** Add $1,000 for two fore-ends and two triggers for Trap/Combo models.

Standard Grade

NIB	Exc.	V.G.	Good	Fair	Poor
—	8700	6500	5200	2500	700

SC3 Grade

NIB	Exc.	V.G.	Good	Fair	Poor
—	11000	8000	7000	3500	700

SCO Grade

NIB	Exc.	V.G.	Good	Fair	Poor
—	17500	12500	10000	6500	700

COMPETITION MODELS

Competition versions are over/under shotguns in trap, skeet, pigeon, and sporting models. Stock dimensions are based on the particular model chosen. Trap models feature trap stock dimensions and forearm designed for that purpose. The other models also have their own particular specifications. However, prices are based on a common style referred to by Perazzi as Competition. Thus, all models within this group are priced the same regardless of specific type.

Mirage Special Standard Grade

This model features an adjustable trigger and is available in 12 gauge with choice of 27.5", 28.375", 29.5", or 31.5" ventilated rib barrels.

NIB	Exc.	V.G.	Good	Fair	Poor
—	5500	3750	2500	1100	700

Mirage Special Sporting Standard Grade

Similar to the Mirage Special listed above, but with external trigger selection and screw-in chokes. Offered in 12 gauge only with choice of 27.5", 28.375", or 29.5" vent rib barrels.

NIB	Exc.	V.G.	Good	Fair	Poor
—	4500	3250	2500	1100	700

Mirage Special Sporting Classic Standard Grade

This model features the same basic specifications as the Mirage Special Sporting with the addition of a scroll border on the receiver and triggerguard. The wood is of slightly higher quality. Offered in 12 gauge only with 27.5", 28.375", or 29.5" vent rib barrels.

NIB	Exc.	V.G.	Good	Fair	Poor
—	4500	3250	2500	1100	700

Mirage MX8 Standard Grade

NIB	Exc.	V.G.	Good	Fair	Poor
—	5800	4250	3000	1500	700

SCO Model

This model is similar to the MX8 but offered only in 12 gauge with barrel lengths from 27.5" to 31.5". The trigger is adjustable instead of removable.

NIB	Exc.	V.G.	Good	Fair	Poor
—	10500	6000	4500	3000	700

Mirage Special 4-Gauge Set

Similar to the Mirage Special in appearance and specifications but fitted with four barrel sets with 27.62" barrels in 12, 20, 28 gauge, and .410 bore. **NOTE:** For 28.37" barrels add $2,000 and for 29.5" barrels add $3,000.

Standard Grade

NIB	Exc.	V.G.	Good	Fair	Poor
—	—	10000	7000	4500	700

SC3 Grade

NIB	Exc.	V.G.	Good	Fair	Poor
—	21000	15000	10000	7500	700

SCO Grade

NIB	Exc.	V.G.	Good	Fair	Poor
—	28000	19000	12500	8500	700

MX12/12C

Offered in 12 gauge only with 26.75" or 27.5" vent rib barrels. The single-selective trigger is nonrefillable. The walnut stock is fitted with a schnabel fore-end and the receiver has a light-scroll engraved border. The MX12 is supplied with fixed chokes while the MX12C is fitted with 5 screw-in choke tubes. **NOTE:** Add $400 to MX12 prices to get MX12C values.

Standard Grade

NIB	Exc.	V.G.	Good	Fair	Poor
11000	9000	6800	4500	2000	1000

SC3 Grade

NIB	Exc.	V.G.	Good	Fair	Poor
18000	15000	12000	9000	5000	1200

SCO Grade

NIB	Exc.	V.G.	Good	Fair	Poor
30000	26000	20000	15000	10000	3000

MX20/20C

This model is offered in 20 gauge. It features a nonremovable trigger group. The frame is smaller than 12 gauge. Offered with 26" or 27.5" vent rib barrels. The MX20 has fixed chokes while the MX20C is supplied with 5 screw-in choke tubes. **NOTE:** Add $400 to MX20 prices to get MX20C values.

Standard Grade

NIB	Exc.	V.G.	Good	Fair	Poor
11500	9000	6800	4500	2000	1000

SC3 Grade

NIB	Exc.	V.G.	Good	Fair	Poor
18500	15000	12000	9000	5000	1200

SCO Grade

NIB	Exc.	V.G.	Good	Fair	Poor
32000	25000	20000	13500	7000	3000

MX28 and MX410

Introduced in 1993 these two models feature a non-removable trigger group and a special small frame for each. The MX28, .28 gauge, weighs about 5.5 lbs. while the MX410, .410 bore, weighs slightly less. Both are supplied with fixed chokes, flat ribs, custom made stocks, and round fore-ends. Each model is offered with a choice of 26" or 27.5" barrels. Both the MX28 and MX410 are priced the same.

Standard Grade

NIB	Exc.	V.G.	Good	Fair	Poor
21000	16000	12000	9000	6000	1000

SCO Grade

NIB	Exc.	V.G.	Good	Fair	Poor
42000	36000	29000	20000	10000	3000

PERRY & GODDARD
Renwick Arms Co.
New York, New York

Derringer

A .44 caliber single-shot spur trigger pistol with a 2" octagonal barrel. Blued or silver-plated with walnut or gutta-percha grips. The barrel may be swiveled so that either end can serve as the chamber and is marked "Double Header/ E.S. Renwick". Produced in limited quantities during the 1860s.

NIB	Exc.	V.G.	Good	Fair	Poor
—	—	21000	9400	1500	500

PERRY PATENT FIREARMS CO.
Newark, New Jersey

Perry Single-Shot Pistol

A .52 caliber breech-loading percussion pistol with a 6" round barrel. Blued with walnut grips. The barrel marked "Perry Patent Firearms Co./Newark, N.J." Approximately 200 were made between 1854 and 1856 in two styles.

1st Type

Long, contoured trigger guard, opening lever.

NIB	Exc.	V.G.	Good	Fair	Poor
—	—	4950	1900	500	200

2nd Type

S curved shorter trigger guard and an automatic primer feed that protrudes from the butt.

NIB	Exc.	V.G.	Good	Fair	Poor
—	—	4700	1650	500	200

Perry Carbine

A .54 caliber breech-loading percussion carbine with a 20.75" barrel and half-length walnut stock secured by one barrel band. Blued with a case hardened lock. Approximately 200 were made.

Courtesy Milwaukee Public Museum, Milwaukee, Wisconsin

NIB	Exc.	V.G.	Good	Fair	Poor
—	27500	13000	8250	3600	1000

PERUGINI & VISINI
Brescia, Italy

Arms by this maker were imported by W.L. Moore of Westlake Village, California.

Liberty Model

A side-by-side 12, 20, 28 gauge and .410 bore shotgun with 28" barrels. Anson & Deeley action with a double Purdy lock. Blued overall with checkered walnut stock.

NIB	Exc.	V.G.	Good	Fair	Poor
7500	6000	4500	2500	1250	750

Classic Model

A 12 or 20 gauge double-barrel shotgun with a Holland & Holland-style sidelock and a double Purdy lock. The barrels are 28" in length. Single trigger and automatic ejectors. The sidelocks and mounts and engraved and blued. Well figured and checkered walnut stock.

NIB	Exc.	V.G.	Good	Fair	Poor
15000	11500	9500	4000	2000	1000

Bolt-Action Rifle

A Mauser-type bolt-action rifle available in a variety of chamberings, with 24" or 26" barrels. Sights not furnished. Well figured checkered walnut stock.

NIB	Exc.	V.G.	Good	Fair	Poor
6500	4250	3000	1500	900	500

Deluxe Bolt-Action Rifle

As above with first quality walnut stocks and a case.

NIB	Exc.	V.G.	Good	Fair	Poor
7500	5000	3500	1500	1000	600

Eagle Single-Shot

An Anson & Deeley single-shot rifle fitted with either 24" or 26" barrels, open sights, automatic ejector and adjustable trigger. Stock of checkered walnut.

NIB	Exc.	V.G.	Good	Fair	Poor
7500	4250	4000	1500	1000	600

Boxlock Express Rifle

An Anson & Deeley action double-barrel rifle chambered for .444 Marlin or 9.3x74R cartridges. The barrel length is 24" and is fitted with express sights. Double triggers and automatic ejectors. Receiver case hardened and the barrels as well as mounts blued.

Checkered walnut stock.

NIB	Exc.	V.G.	Good	Fair	Poor
7000	5500	3750	2000	1500	500

Magnum Over/Under

An Anson & Deeley action over/under rifle available .375 Holland & Holland and .458 Winchester Magnum. The barrels are 24" in length and fitted with express sights. Double triggers and automatic ejectors. Receiver and barrels blued, the stock of checkered walnut.

NIB	Exc.	V.G.	Good	Fair	Poor
7000	5500	3750	2000	1500	500

Super Express Rifle

A Holland & Holland-style sidelock double-barrel rifle. Having 24" barrels fitted with express sights. Available in a variety of chamberings. The receiver and sidelocks are either case hardened or finished in the bright and fully engraved. Checkered walnut stock.

NIB	Exc.	V.G.	Good	Fair	Poor
20000	17500	13000	10000	6500	1000

Victoria Side-by-Side Rifle

Similar to the Boxlock Express Rifle but chambered for .30-06, 7x65R, or 9.3x74R cartridges. Either 24" or 26" barrels were available. Double triggers and automatic ejectors. Blued with minimal engraving. Stock of checkered walnut.

NIB	Exc.	V.G.	Good	Fair	Poor
6500	5250	4000	3000	1500	750

Selous Side-by-Side Rifle

First quality double-barrel express rifle with 24" or 26" barrels. Fully detachable Holland & Holland-style sidelocks, double triggers and automatic ejectors. Fully engraved with well figured checkered walnut stocks.

NIB	Exc.	V.G.	Good	Fair	Poor
22500	17500	12500	6000	3000	1500

PETTINGILL C. S.
New Haven, Connecticut
Rogers, Spencer & Co.
Willowvale, New York

Pocket Revolver

A hammerless, double-action .31 caliber percussion revolver having a 4" octagonal barrel. The frame of brass or iron. Blued barrel, the grips of oil finished walnut. The First and Second Models are marked "Pettingill's Patent 1856" as well as "T.K. Austin". The Third Model is marked "Pettengill Patent 1856", and "Raymond and Robitaille Patented 1858". Approximately 400 were manufactured in the late 1850s and early 1860s.

1st Model

Brass frame.

NIB	Exc.	V.G.	Good	Fair	Poor
—	—	2750	2000	1100	400

2nd Model

Iron frame.

NIB	Exc.	V.G.	Good	Fair	Poor
—	—	1650	1000	660	200

3rd Model

Iron frame and improved action.

NIB	Exc.	V.G.	Good	Fair	Poor
—	—	1400	800	450	200

Navy Revolver

As above but in .34 caliber with a 4.5" barrel and a 6-shot cylinder. The frame of iron, blued overall, and the grips of walnut. This model is marked "Pettengill's Patent 1856" and "Raymond & Robitaille Patented 1858". Approximately 900 were manufactured in the late 1850s and early 1860s.

Courtesy Milwaukee Public Museum, Milwaukee, Wisconsin

NIB	Exc.	V.G.	Good	Fair	Poor
—	—	3500	1900	775	250

Army Model Revolver

As above but of .44 caliber and fitted with a 7.5" barrel. The frame of iron that is case hardened, the octagonal barrel blued, the grips of oil finished walnut. Early production models are marked as the Navy models, while later production examples are marked "Petingill's Patent 1856, pat'd July 22, 1856 and July 27, 1858". It is believed that 3,400 were made in the 1860s. **NOTE:** Some examples will be found with government inspector's marks and are worth approximately 25 percent more.

Courtesy Milwaukee Public Museum, Milwaukee, Wisconsin

NIB	Exc.	V.G.	Good	Fair	Poor
—	—	4950	2250	1650	500

PFANNL, FRANCOIS
Krems, Austria

Erika

A 4.25mm semi-automatic pistol with a hinged barrel assembly. The barrel either 1.5" or 2.25" in length. The grips are marked "Erika". Approximately 3,500 made between 1912 and 1926.

NIB	Exc.	V.G.	Good	Fair	Poor
—	3000	2500	1750	900	500

PGM PRECISION
France

Model PGM

This is a highly sophisticated semi-automatic rifle designed and built on a modular component system. Barrel change is fast and available calibers are .308 Win., .300 Savage, 7mm-08, .243, and .22-250. Match grade barrel length is 23.4". Fully adjustable trigger and buttstock with adjustable bipod. Five-round magazine is standard. Weight is approximately 13 lbs.

NIB	Exc.	V.G.	Good	Fair	Poor
13500	9000	7000	3500	1750	1000

PHILLIPS & RODGERS INC.
Huntsville, Texas

Medusa Model 47

Introduced in 1996 this unique multi-caliber revolver is designed to chamber, fire, and extract almost any cartridge using 9mm, .357, or .38 cartridges—a total of about 25 different calibers. The barrel lengths are 2.5", 3", 4", 5", or 6". Rubber grips and interchangeable front sights. Finish is matte blue. Rarely if ever encountered. Discontinued.

NIB	Exc.	V.G.	Good	Fair	Poor
1100	850	550	450	275	150

Ruger 50 Conversion

This conversion, executed on a new revolver, converts a .44 Magnum Ruger into a .50 Action Express. Stainless steel or blue with 5-shot cylinder. Barrel length is 6.5".

NIB	Exc.	V.G.	Good	Fair	Poor
1000	800	550	450	275	150

PHOENIX
Lowell, Massachusetts

Pocket Pistol

A rare .25 ACP semi-automatic pistol with a 2.25" barrel and 6-round magazine. Receiver and slide are blued, the grips are of hard rubber. Manufactured during the 1920s.

NIB	Exc.	V.G.	Good	Fair	Poor
—	950	700	350	200	100

PHOENIX ARMS
Ontario, California

HP22

A pocket-size semi-automatic pistol chambered for the .22 LR cartridge. Barrel length is 3". Magazine capacity is 11 rounds. Offered in bright chrome or polished blue finish with black checkered grips. Top of gun is fitted with vent rib. Overall length is 4.1" and weight is about 20 oz.

NIB	Exc.	V.G.	Good	Fair	Poor
175	125	90	65	40	25

HP25

This model is the same as above but chambered for the .25 ACP cartridge. Magazine capacity is 10 rounds.

NIB	Exc.	V.G.	Good	Fair	Poor
175	125	90	65	40	25

HP22/HP25 Target

A conversion kit to convert the HP22/HP25 into a target pistol. Kit includes extended vent rib barrel and a convertible 10-round magazine. Finish is either blue or nickel.

NIB	Exc.	V.G.	Good	Fair	Poor
100	75	60	40	30	25

Raven

A small pocket-size semi-automatic pistol chambered for the .25 ACP cartridge. Magazine capacity is 6 rounds. Barrel length is 2.4" with fixed sights. Offered in 3 finishes: bright chrome, satin nickel, or polished blue. Grips are either ivory, pink pearl, or black. Overall length is 4.8" and weight is approximately 15 oz.

NIB	Exc.	V.G.	Good	Fair	Poor
175	125	90	65	40	25

PHOENIX ARMS CO.
Liege, Belgium

See—Robar and de Kirkhave

PICKERT, FRIEDRICH
Arminius Waffenfabrik
Zella-Mehlis, Germany

This firm produced revolvers bearing the trade name "Arminius". The revolvers manufactured by Pickert are of the double-action type, with or without exposed hammers. Some models are fitted with ejectors, while others have removable cylinders. Calibers and barrel lengths vary. After WWII, the trade name was acquired by Hermann Wiehauch.

Arminius 7.65mm

A five-shot concealed hammer revolver in 7.65mm caliber. The Arminius head is on the grips.

Courtesy James Rankin

NIB	Exc.	V.G.	Good	Fair	Poor
—	350	225	175	125	90

Arminius Single-Shot Target Pistol

A single-shot target pistol chambered for the 22 caliber cartridge. Some of these were built under the name PICKERT. The Arminius name is seen on the frame.

Courtesy James Rankin

NIB	Exc.	V.G.	Good	Fair	Poor
—	900	700	600	400	300

Pickert Revolver

Similar to the Arminius revolver but with a half-round, half-octagon barrel. Chambered for the 7.54mm cartridge.

Courtesy James Rankin

NIB	Exc.	V.G.	Good	Fair	Poor
—	275	225	175	150	100

PIEPER, HENRI & NICOLAS
Liege, Belgium

Originally founded by Henri Pieper in 1859, the company was reorganized in 1898 when his son, Nicolas, assumed control. The firm is perhaps best known for a series of semi-automatic pistols that are listed below, but Pieper also manufactured a bewildering variety of drillings, combination guns, cape guns, rook rifles, salon rifles and even volley guns. These guns must be evaluated on their own merits, and their value is strictly a function of what the market will bear.

Pieper Model 1907

A 6.35 or 7.65mm semi-automatic pistol featuring a hinged barrel assembly 2.5" in length. Receiver and barrel are blued, the grips are of hard rubber with the firm's trademark cast in them. The Model 1907 variation does not have a hinged barrel assembly. The Model 1908 is also known as the "Basculant", and the Model 1918 as the "Demontant".

Courtesy Orvel Reichert

NIB	Exc.	V.G.	Good	Fair	Poor
—	250	150	125	100	75

Model 1908/Basculant

This is a tipping barrel pistol chambered for the 6.35mm Auto cartridge. Similar in appearance to the Model 1907 this model had several improvements. The front end of the barrel was retained by a pivot bolt and the recoil spring rod had a hook that engaged the lug on the slide.

Courtesy Orvel Reichert

NIB	Exc.	V.G.	Good	Fair	Poor
—	275	175	150	125	100

Pieper Bayard Revolver

In competition with the Nagant gas seal revolver, Henri Pieper developed a superior design. Revolvers of this type have 5" barrels and are chambered for 8mm cartridges. The first model of this revolver had an automatic ejection system, while the second version utilized a swing-out cylinder. Standard finish is blued, with checkered hard rubber grips.

NIB	Exc.	V.G.	Good	Fair	Poor
—	1000	750	500	250	100

Legia

This model was patterned after that of the Browning, and is chambered for the 6.35mm cartridge. The standard magazine holds 6 cartridges but a 10-round magazine was also available.

NIB	Exc.	V.G.	Good	Fair	Poor
—	250	150	125	100	75

Bayard

A 6.35, 7.65 or 9mm short semi-automatic pistol with a 2.5" barrel. Standard magazine capacity 6 rounds. The slide is stamped "Anciens Etablissement Pieper Liege, Belgium".

NIB	Exc.	V.G.	Good	Fair	Poor
—	250	150	125	100	75

PILSEN, ZBROVKA
Pilsen, Czechoslovakia

Pocket Pistol

Essentially a Model 1910 Browning semi-automatic pistol without a grip safety, this pistol was of 7.65mm caliber and had a 3.5" barrel with a 6-round magazine. The slide is marked "Akciova Spolecnost drive Skodovny zavody Zbrovka Plzen". Standard finish is blued, the grips of hard rubber. Manufactured during the 1920s.

NIB	Exc.	V.G.	Good	Fair	Poor
—	300	200	150	125	100

PIOTTI
Brescia, Italy

This Italian gun making firm is located in Gardone Val Trompia in the province of Brescia. Its shotguns are hand crafted and limited to a few each year. Each gun is made to individual specifications. Many consider them one of the best double shotguns made in the world today. Actions are either Anson & Deeley boxlock or Holland & Holland sidelock. Several features are offered on these shotguns at no additional cost: type of stock and forearm, barrel length and chokes, rib, action shape and finish.

Other features are considered extra cost options and will affect the value of the gun. There are: single triggers, detachable sidelocks, automatic safety, recoil pads, upgraded wood,

engraving, and multi-gauge sets. With the exception of a few grades Piotti guns are available in 10, 12, 16, 20, and 28 gauge, as well as .410 bore. Depending on gauge barrel lengths are from 25" to 32".

Model Piuma (BSEE)

This model is the firm's standard boxlock offering. Available in 12 gauge to .410 bore it features ejectors and a scalloped frame. Fine scroll and rosette engraving is standard. **NOTE:** Around serial number 9000, or 1989, Piotti began building the Model BSEE to the same standards as the King Model. Therefore, guns below serial number 9000 deduct about 40 percent from prices listed.

NIB	Exc.	V.G.	Good	Fair	Poor
14250	10500	7500	6000	4000	700

Westlake Model

This was Piotti's second quality model. It features a case colored receiver with gold line work. Offered in 12, 16, and 20 gauge. Discontinued in 1989.

NIB	Exc.	V.G.	Good	Fair	Poor
13000	10500	8000	6000	3500	700

Over/Under Gun

This model features King 2 engraving which has a light border scroll with 10 percent coverage. Custom engraving patterns available at extra charge.

NIB	Exc.	V.G.	Good	Fair	Poor
44750	33500	25000	17500	10000	1000

Model King No. I

This model features a sidelock with fine line scroll engraving with full coverage. A gold crown is inlaid on the top lever prior to 1989. H&H or Purdey-style engraving. Select walnut with hand checkering is standard. Chambered from 10 gauge to .410 bore.

NIB	Exc.	V.G.	Good	Fair	Poor
33000	25000	18000	12500	8000	2700

Monte Carlo Model

This model was a less expensive version of the King Model. It had H&H or Purdey-style engraving. It was discontinued in 1989 and was upgraded and became part of the King Model. This occurred around serial number 9000.

NIB	Exc.	V.G.	Good	Fair	Poor
14000	10000	7000	6000	3500	700

Model King Extra

This model is similar to the King No. 1 but with the addition of a number of engraving styles from English to game scenes with gold inlays. Because of the wide variety of engraving patterns offered on this model it is advisable to secure a qualified appraisal before purchase.

Model Lunik

This model is fitted with Holland & Holland sidelocks. Engraving is Renaissance-style relief cut scroll engraving. A gold crown is inlaid on the top lever. Offered in gauges from 10 to .410 bore.

NIB	Exc.	V.G.	Good	Fair	Poor
33000	25000	18000	12000	7000	1700

Model Monaco

This sidelock model features all of the best that Piotti has to offer and extra attention is paid to hand work and fitting. Only the finest European hardwoods are used. Available in 10 gauge to 410 bore. Offered with three different types of engraving designated No. 1, No. 2, and No. 4.

No. 1 or No. 2

NIB	Exc.	V.G.	Good	Fair	Poor
42000	35000	28000	19500	12000	2000

No. 3

NIB	Exc.	V.G.	Good	Fair	Poor
46000	40000	32000	22000	13000	2000

No. 4

NIB	Exc.	V.G.	Good	Fair	Poor
56000	45000	36000	28000	—	—

PLAINFIELD MACHINE CO.
Dunelien, New Jersey

Super Enforcer

A cut-down version of the U.S. M1 Carbine with a 12" barrel and pistol grip. The finish is blued and stocks are walnut.

NIB	Exc.	V.G.	Good	Fair	Poor
—	600	475	375	225	100

M1 Carbine

A commercial reproduction of the U.S. M1 Carbine. The finish is blued. Walnut stock.

NIB	Exc.	V.G.	Good	Fair	Poor
—	400	350	225	150	100

M1 Paratrooper Carbine

As above with a telescoping wire buttstock and walnut fore-end.

NIB	Exc.	V.G.	Good	Fair	Poor
—	475	375	275	200	125

PLAINFIELD ORDNANCE CO.
Middlesex, New Jersey

Model 71

A stainless steel .22 caliber semi-automatic pistol with a 10-shot magazine and 1" barrel. Also available in .25 ACP and conversion kits were available.

Conversion Kit

NIB	Exc.	V.G.	Good	Fair	Poor
—	50	40	30	25	20

.22 or .25 Caliber Pistol

NIB	Exc.	V.G.	Good	Fair	Poor
—	175	125	100	75	50

Model 72

As above except with an alloy frame.

NIB	Exc.	V.G.	Good	Fair	Poor
—	175	125	100	75	50

PLANT'S MANUFACTURING CO.
New Haven, Connecticut

Army Model Revolver

A large single-action revolver chambered for a .42 caliber cup-primed cartridge that loads from the front of the cylinder. Barrel length 6" and of octagonal form with a rib. The frame is made of either brass or iron. Finish is blued, with walnut or rosewood grips. Interchangeable percussion cylinders also were made for these revolvers. If present, the values would be increased approximately 30 percent. This revolver was marketed by Merwin & Bray. There were approximately 1,500 of the 1st and 2nd Models manufactured and 10,000 of the 3rd Model in the 1860s.

1st Model Brass Frame

Marked "Plant's Mfg. Co. New Haven, Ct." on the barrel, "M & B" on the side of the frame, and "Patented July 12, 1859" on the cylinder. Approximately 100 manufactured.

NIB	Exc.	V.G.	Good	Fair	Poor
—	—	2750	1025	700	150

1st Model Iron Frame

As above with an iron frame. Approximately 500 made.

NIB	Exc.	V.G.	Good	Fair	Poor
—	—	2750	1025	700	300

2nd Model Rounded Brass Frame

This model is distinguished by the markings "Merwin & Bray, New York" on the frame and the patent date "July 21, 1863". Approximately 300 made.

NIB	Exc.	V.G.	Good	Fair	Poor
—	—	3600	1400	700	300

2nd Model Iron Frame

As above with an iron frame.

NIB	Exc.	V.G.	Good	Fair	Poor
—	—	2500	825	500	300

3rd Model

As above with a flat brass frame.

Courtesy Milwaukee Public Museum, Milwaukee, Wisconsin

NIB	Exc.	V.G.	Good	Fair	Poor
—	—	1900	1300	450	150

Pocket Revolver

Similar to the Army model described above except chambered for .30 caliber cartridges. Barrel length 3.5", five-shot cylinder. The frame normally silver plated, barrel and cylinder blued and the grips of rosewood or walnut. This model is encountered with a variety of retailer's markings: Eagle Arms Co., New York, "Reynolds, Plant & Hotchkiss, New Haven, Ct.", and "Merwin & Bray Firearms Co., N.Y." Approximately 20,000 were made.

Courtesy Milwaukee Public Museum, Milwaukee, Wisconsin

NIB	Exc.	V.G.	Good	Fair	Poor
—	—	1100	600	250	100

POINTER
Hopkins & Allen
Norwich, Connecticut

Single-Shot Derringer

An unmarked Hopkins & Allen single-shot pistol stamped "Pointer" on the barrel. Barrel length 2.75", caliber .22, frame of nickel-plated brass. The barrel swings sideways for loading. Bird's-head walnut grips. It is believed that about 2,500 were made between 1870 and 1890.

NIB	Exc.	V.G.	Good	Fair	Poor
—	—	450	375	250	100

POLY-TECHNOLOGIES, INC./POLY-TECH
China

SKS

A semi-automatic rifle chambered for the 7.62x39mm cartridge with a 20.5" barrel and 10-shot fixed magazine. Based on the Soviet Siminov carbine. Finish is blued, and the stock and hand guard are made of a Chinese hardwood.

NIB	Exc.	V.G.	Good	Fair	Poor
425	375	200	150	100	50

AKS-762

A semi-automatic version of the Chinese-type 56 Assault rifle chambered for the 7.62x39mm cartridge with a 16.5" barrel. Furnished with a 20-round magazine and a Chinese bayonet. The finish is blued, and the stock is hardwood. **NOTE:** For folding stock model add $250. Add 15 percent for milled receiver.

NIB	Exc.	V.G.	Good	Fair	Poor
950	800	675	500	350	200

AK-47/S

Chambered for the 7.62x39 cartridge. **NOTE:** For folding stock model add $350. With a Soviet-style bayonet add $15.

NIB	Exc.	V.G.	Good	Fair	Poor
1350	1150	850	750	600	400

M-14/S

A reproduction of the U.S. M14 rifle chambered for the 7.62mm cartridge with a 22" barrel and 20-round magazine. Finish is blued and the stock is of hardwood.

NIB	Exc.	V.G.	Good	Fair	Poor
1000	875	675	500	350	200

POND, LUCIUS, W.
Worchester, Massachusetts

Pocket Revolver

A single-action, spur trigger .32 caliber revolver with octagonal barrels of 4", 5", or 6" length. The barrel top strap and cylinder pivot upwards for loading. Made with either brass or iron frames. A screwdriver is fitted in the butt. As these revolvers were an infringement of Rollin White's patent, they were discontinued. Some revolvers are to be found with the inscription "Manuf'd. for Smith & Wesson Pat'd. April 5, 1855". These examples are worth approximately 20 percent more than the values listed.

Courtesy Milwaukee Public Museum, Milwaukee, Wisconsin

Courtesy Milwaukee Public Museum, Milwaukee, Wisconsin

Brass Framed Revolver

NIB	Exc.	V.G.	Good	Fair	Poor
—	—	1100	875	350	100

Iron Framed Revolver

NIB	Exc.	V.G.	Good	Fair	Poor
—	—	1000	775	300	75

Separate Chamber Revolver

To avoid the Rollin White patent, this revolver is chambered for .22 or .32 caliber rimfire cartridges that fit into separate steel chamber inserts that can be removed from the front of the cylinder for loading. The .22 caliber version has a 3.5" octagonal barrel with a 7-round unfluted cylinder; the .32 caliber version has a 4", 5", or 6" octagonal barrel and 6-shot unfluted cylinder. Frames are of silver-plated brass and the barrels and cylinders are blued. Grips of walnut. Standard markings include "L.W. Pond, Worcester, Mass." and patent dates. Approximately 2,000 manufactured in .22 caliber and 5,000 in .32 caliber between 1863 and 1870.

.22 Caliber Version

NIB	Exc.	V.G.	Good	Fair	Poor
—	—	1750	1400	550	150

.32 Caliber Version

NIB	Exc.	V.G.	Good	Fair	Poor
—	—	1750	1400	550	150

PORTER, P. W.
New York, New York

Turret Revolver

An extremely rare 9-shot vertical cylinder .41 caliber percussion revolver with a 5.25" round barrel. The trigger guard is also a lever that turns the cylinder and cocks the hammer. An automatic primer system is also fitted to this revolver. Manufactured during the 1850s in an unknown quantity.

NIB	Exc.	V.G.	Good	Fair	Poor
—	—	23500	19500	8800	100

Turret Rifle

A 9-shot vertical cylinder .44 caliber rifle with either a 26" or 28" octagonal barrel. The only markings are "Address P.W. Porter/New York". Four variations of this rifle are known and the 22" barreled carbine would command a 25 percent premium. Approximately 1,250 were manufactured during the 1850s.

1st Model with Canister Magazine

Fitted with a 30-shot round canister magazine over the turret, this model was made in Tennessee and is extremely rare. Most often the canisters are not encountered and values reflect this. Approximately 25 were made.

NIB	Exc.	V.G.	Good	Fair	Poor
—	—	37500	30000	13500	2000

2nd Model (New York)

NIB	Exc.	V.G.	Good	Fair	Poor
—	—	15000	12000	5125	1000

3rd Model (New York)

This model has a screw-off cover over the magazine.

NIB	Exc.	V.G.	Good	Fair	Poor
—	—	13000	1050	5200	1000

4th Model (New York)

As above but without an automatic primer magazine and the nipples are exposed.

NIB	Exc.	V.G.	Good	Fair	Poor
—	—	10500	8800	4150	750

PRAHA ZBROJOVKA
Prague, Czechoslovakia

Established in 1918 by A. Novotny, this company ceased operations in 1926.

VZ2L

A 7.65mm semi-automatic pistol patterned after the Model 1910 Browning, but without a grip safety. Barrel length 3.5", magazine capacity 6 rounds, grips of wood. The slide is marked "Zbrojowka Praga Praha".

NIB	Exc.	V.G.	Good	Fair	Poor
—	400	250	200	150	100

Praga 1921

A 6.35mm semi-automatic pistol with a slide of stamped steel cut with a finger groove at the front. Folding trigger. The barrel 2" in length. The slide is marked "Zbrojowka Praga Praha Patent Cal 6.35". The grips of molded plastic, with the name "Praga" cast in them. A dangerous feature of this pistol is that it is striker-fired with no hammer and is intended to be carried fully loaded and cocked in the pocket with absolutely no safety of any kind. I do not recommend this. The folding trigger does not spring out until the slide is drawn back slightly by using the finger groove in the front of it.

NIB	Exc.	V.G.	Good	Fair	Poor
—	375	225	200	150	100

PRAIRIE GUN WORKS
Winnipeg, Manitoba, Canada

M-15

This is a lightweight mountain rifle chambered for .22-250, 6mm-284, .25-284, 6.5-284, 7mm-08, .308 Win., and most short calibers. Built on a Remington 700 action with 20" lightweight barrel. Stock is Kevlar and comes in either green, black or gray. Barrel length is usually 20". Weight is approximately 4.75 lbs.

NIB	Exc.	V.G.	Good	Fair	Poor
2600	2200	1750	1200	800	500

M-18

Similar to the above model but chambered for long action calibers and fitted with barrel lengths from 22" to 24". Weight is approximately 5.25 lbs.

NIB	Exc.	V.G.	Good	Fair	Poor
2600	2200	1750	1200	800	500

PRANDELLI & GASPARINI
Brescia, Italy

Boxlock Side-by-Side Shotgun

A good quality double-barrel 12 or 20 gauge shotgun with 26" or 28" barrels. Single-selective trigger, automatic ejectors and an Anson & Deeley action. Blued, stock of select walnut.

NIB	Exc.	V.G.	Good	Fair	Poor
—	2500	1750	1100	700	450

Sidelock Side-by-Side Shotgun

Similar to the above, but with full sidelocks.

NIB	Exc.	V.G.	Good	Fair	Poor
—	3500	2650	1500	900	500

Boxlock Over/Under Shotgun

An over/under double-barrel 12 or 20 gauge shotgun with 26" or 28" barrels, single triggers and automatic ejectors. Blued, with select walnut stock.

NIB	Exc.	V.G.	Good	Fair	Poor
—	2750	1850	1200	900	350

Sidelock Over/Under Shotgun

As above with full sidelocks.

NIB	Exc.	V.G.	Good	Fair	Poor
—	3000	2500	1800	950	450

PRATT, GEORGE
Middletown, Connecticut

Trap Gun

A doubled-barreled, stationary burglar alarm or animal trap gun that is chambered for .38 caliber centerfire. The barrel is 4" in length, and all of the components are made of cast iron with a galvanized finish. Barrels and action are mounted on a round base, which can turn 360 degrees. The patent date "Dec. 18, 1883" is marked on the gun. Many were manufactured between 1880 and the early 1890s.

NIB	Exc.	V.G.	Good	Fair	Poor
—	—	1800	1200	500	150

PRATT, H.
Roxbury, Massachusetts

Under Hammer Pistol

A .31 caliber percussion single-shot pistol with an 8.5" octagonal barrel. The frame marked "H. Pratt's/ Patent". Manufactured during the 1850s.

NIB	Exc.	V.G.	Good	Fair	Poor
—	—	1700	1350	650	200

PRECISION SMALL ARMS
Beverly Hills, California

PSA-25

This is a semi-automatic pistol chambered for the .25 ACP. The barrel length is 2.13". Magazine capacity is 6 rounds. The frame and slide is steel alloy. Weight is 9.5 oz. Overall length is 4.11". Grips are black polymer. Standard finish is black oxide. Modeled after the Browning Baby. **NOTE:** For brushed chrome finish add $50 and for stainless steel add $75.

NIB	Exc.	V.G.	Good	Fair	Poor
525	400	300	225	150	75

Featherweight Model

Same as above, but with aluminum frame and chrome slide with gold-plated trigger.

NIB	Exc.	V.G.	Good	Fair	Poor
1000	850	700	475	250	100

Diplomat Model

Black oxide with gold highlights and ivory grips.

NIB	Exc.	V.G.	Good	Fair	Poor
1900	1550	1100	800	500	100

Montreaux Model

Gold plated with ivory grips.

NIB	Exc.	V.G.	Good	Fair	Poor
2550	2000	1500	1050	800	100

Renaissance Model

Same as above but with hand engraved steel frame and slide. Antique stain chrome finish.

NIB	Exc.	V.G.	Good	Fair	Poor
3950	3200	2500	2000	1200	100

Imperiale

Inlaid gold filigree over blue with scrimshawed ivory grips.

NIB	Exc.	V.G.	Good	Fair	Poor
6500	5800	5000	4000	2100	100

PREMIER
Italy and Spain

A trade name used by various retailers on shotguns manufactured in Italy and Spain that were imported during the late 1950s and early 1960s.

Regent Side-by-Side Shotgun

A double-barrel shotgun with 26" to 30" barrels available in all standard gauges. Receiver blued, stock of walnut. Normally found with a pistol grip and beavertail fore-end.

NIB	Exc.	V.G.	Good	Fair	Poor
—	450	250	200	150	100

Regent Magnum

As above but chambered for the 3.5" 10 gauge Magnum cartridge. Barrels 32" in length and choked Full and Full.

NIB	Exc.	V.G.	Good	Fair	Poor
—	500	300	250	200	150

Brush King

Identical to the Regent Model except that it is fitted with 22" Modified and Improved Cylinder barrels and a straight-grip English-style stock.

NIB	Exc.	V.G.	Good	Fair	Poor
—	500	375	250	200	150

Ambassador Model

A more ornate version of the Regent Model.

NIB	Exc.	V.G.	Good	Fair	Poor
—	600	450	300	250	175

Presentation Custom Grade

A custom-order shotgun with game scenes as well as gold and silver inlays.

NIB	Exc.	V.G.	Good	Fair	Poor
—	2500	1750	1250	850	400

PRESCOTT, E. A.
Worcester, Massachusetts

Percussion Pocket Revolver

A .31 caliber percussion spur trigger revolver with either 4" or 4.25" octagonal barrel and a 6-shot cylinder. The frame of brass, and the grips of walnut. It is believed that approximately 100 were manufactured during 1860 and 1861.

NIB	Exc.	V.G.	Good	Fair	Poor
—	—	3700	2500	1125	200

Pocket Revolver

A .22 or .32 spur trigger revolver with a barrel of either 3" or 4" length. The .22 caliber version has a 7-shot cylinder and the .32 caliber version a 6-shot cylinder. The standard markings are "E.A. Prescott Worcester Mass. Pat. Oct. 2, 1860". Approximately 1,000 were manufactured between 1862 and 1867.

NIB	Exc.	V.G.	Good	Fair	Poor
—	—	1050	825	350	100

Navy Revolver

A single-action revolver fitted with a conventional trigger, chambered for .38 rimfire cartridges with a 7.25" octagonal barrel. The unfluted cylinder holds 6 shots. The frame is of either silver-plated brass or blued iron; and the barrel and the cylinder are blued, with walnut grips. The barrel marked "E.A. Prescott, Worcester, Mass. Pat. Oct. 2, 1860". It is believed that several hundred were manufactured between 1861 and 1863. The iron frame model will bring a small premium.

Courtesy Milwaukee Public Museum, Milwaukee, Wisconsin

NIB	Exc.	V.G.	Good	Fair	Poor
—	—	1850	1400	550	200

Army Revolver

Similar in appearance to the Navy model but with a larger frame. Chambered for .44 caliber rimfire cartridge. Fitted with a 9" octagon barrel with extractor rod and loading gate on right side of frame. Very rare.

NIB	Exc.	V.G.	Good	Fair	Poor
—	—	24500	19500	8800	600

Belt Revolver

Although similar in appearance to early Smith & Wesson revolvers, the Prescott has a solid frame. Available in either .22 or .32 caliber, the .22 caliber model has a 3" barrel and the .32 caliber a 5.75" barrel. Markings are identical found on the Pocket Revolver. Approximately 300 were manufactured between 1861 and 1863.

NIB	Exc.	V.G.	Good	Fair	Poor
—	—	1150	825	325	100

PRETORIA
Pretoria, South Africa

See—P.A.F.

PRINZ
Germany

Grade 1 Bolt-Action Rifle

A high quality bolt-action rifle chambered for the .243, .30-06, .308, 7mm Remington Magnum or the .300 Winchester Magnum cartridges. Barrel length 24", double-set triggers available. Finish is blued, stock is of oil-finished select walnut. Introduced in 1989.

NIB	Exc.	V.G.	Good	Fair	Poor
1200	950	700	450	325	150

Grade 2 Bolt-Action Rifle

As above with a rosewood fore-end tip and pistol grip cap.

NIB	Exc.	V.G.	Good	Fair	Poor
1300	1075	750	475	350	175

Tip Up Rifle

A high quality single-shot rifle available in a variety of American cartridges. Barrel length 24" and not furnished with sights. Finish blued, stock of select walnut.

NIB	Exc.	V.G.	Good	Fair	Poor
3000	2250	1700	1135	850	300

Model 85 "Princess"

A combination 12 gauge shotgun and rifle with 24" or 26" barrels, double triggers and automatic ejectors. Finish blued, stock of select walnut.

NIB	Exc.	V.G.	Good	Fair	Poor
3500	2850	2100	1650	1000	300

PROFESSIONAL ORDNANCE, INC.
Ontario, California

This company was purchased by Bushmaster.

Carbon-15 Pistol—Type 97

Introduced in 1996 this semi-automatic pistol is built on a carbon fiber upper and lower receiver. Chambered for the 5.56 cartridge it has a 7.25" fluted stainless steel barrel. Ghost ring sights are standard. Magazine is AR-15 compatible. Quick detach compensator. Furnished with a 10-round magazine. Weight is approximately 46 oz. **NOTE:** This pistol has several options that will affect value.

NIB	Exc.	V.G.	Good	Fair	Poor
925	700	550	425	300	150

Carbon-15 Rifle—Type 97

Similar to the above model but fitted with a 16" barrel, quick detachable buttstock, quick detach compensator, Weaver type mounting base. Overall length is 35". Weight is about 3.9 lbs.

NIB	Exc.	V.G.	Good	Fair	Poor
950	725	600	500	350	150

Carbon-15 Rifle—Type 97S

Introduced in 2000 this rifle incorporated several new features. Its foregrip is double walled and insulated with a sheet of ultra-lightweight amumina silica ceramic fiber. The recoil buffer has been increased in size by 30 percent for less recoil. A new ambidextrous safety has been added, and a new multi carry silent sling with Hogue grip is standard. Weight is approximately 4.3 lbs.

NIB	Exc.	V.G.	Good	Fair	Poor
1285	950	700	550	375	150

Carbon-15 Pistol—Type 21

Introduced in 1999 this model features a light profile stainless steel 7.25" barrel. Ghost ring sights are standard. Optional recoil compensator. A 30-round magazine is standard until supplies are exhausted. Weight is about 40 oz.

NIB	Exc.	V.G.	Good	Fair	Poor
925	700	550	425	300	150

Carbon-15 Rifle—Type 21

This model is fitted with a 16" light profile stainless steel barrel. Quick detachable stock, weaver mounting base. Introduced in 1999. Weight is approximately 3.9 lbs.

NIB	Exc.	V.G.	Good	Fair	Poor
1150	900	650	500	325	125

PROTECTION
Unknown
Protection Pocket Revolver

A .28 caliber percussion spur-trigger revolver with a 3.25" octagonal barrel and 6-shot cylinder roll engraved with a police arrest scene. The frame of brass and grips of walnut. The cylinder is marked "Protection". Approximately 1,000 were manufactured during the late 1850s and early 1860s.

1st Model
Roll engraved cylinder.

NIB	Exc.	V.G.	Good	Fair	Poor
—	—	1500	1150	450	100

2nd Model
Plain cylinder above serial no. 650.

NIB	Exc.	V.G.	Good	Fair	Poor
—	—	1300	950	350	100

PTK INTERNATIONAL, INC.
Atlanta, Georgia
See—Poly-Technologies, Inc.

PULASKI ARMORY
Pulaski, Tennessee

Founded in 1861, this firm produced rifles for the State of Tennessee. Overall length 48.5" to 49.5"; round barrels 32.5" to 33.25"; caliber .54. Resemble U.S. Model 1841 Rifles except without patchbox. Had single screw sporting locks with diamond-shaped ferrules. Usually marked on barrel "PULASKI T. C.S.A. 61". Production estimated to be about 300.

NIB	Exc.	V.G.	Good	Fair	Poor
—	—	16500	10000	5000	1500

PUMA
Model 92 Rifle

This model is a copy of the Winchester lever-action rifle. It is fitted with a 24" octagon barrel and chambered for the .44 Magnum, .357 Magnum, .454 Casull or .45 Colt cartridge. Offered in a variety of finishes such as stainless steel, blued, blued and brass, and blued and case colored. Fitted with a cresent butt and hardwood stock. **NOTE:** Add $50 for stainless steel.

NIB	Exc.	V.G.	Good	Fair	Poor
550	425	350	275	200	100

Model 92 Carbine

This model is also available with a 20" round barrel chambered as above and also in .454 Casull and .480 Ruger. Fitted with a shotgun butt. **NOTE:** Add $50 for stainless steel.

NIB	Exc.	V.G.	Good	Fair	Poor
550	425	350	275	200	100

Model 92 Trapper

Introduced in 2004 this model features a 16" barrel with large-loop lever and saddle ring. Available in all of the calibers noted above.

NIB	Exc.	V.G.	Good	Fair	Poor
550	425	350	275	200	100

PPS22

New in 2009, this is a .22 LR version of the Soviet PPSh sub-machine gun. Comes with one 50-round drum magazine.

NIB	Exc.	V.G.	Good	Fair	Poor
575	475	350	275	200	100

PURDEY, J. & SONS LTD.
London, England

Perhaps the finest manufacturer of shotguns, double-barrel and bolt-action rifles in the world. Virtually all their products are made on special order and it is impossible to establish general values for their products. Prospective purchasers are advised to seek qualified guidance prior to the acquisition of any arms made by this maker. The prices listed are for standard guns with no extras. Below are approximate base prices for new custom shotguns and rifles, based on the exchange rate between the English pound and the U.S. dollar as of August, 2012. Prices do not include VAT, which is approximately 20 percent. These guns are made to order to the buyer's specifications and can be made in any gauge or caliber.

CURRENT PRODUCTION

Hammerless Ejector Side-by-Side Game Gun

Available in 12, 16, 20, 28, and .410 bore. Engraved sidelocks.

NIB	Exc.	V.G.	Good	Fair	Poor
88000	—	—	—	—	—

Hammerless Ejector Over/Under Gun

This gun is offered in 12, 16, 20, 28, and .410 bore with sidelocks.

NIB	Exc.	V.G.	Good	Fair	Poor
100,000	—	—	—	—	—

Double-Barreled Rifle

A custom made side-by-side double rifle with sidelocks. **NOTE:** Up to .375 bore size: $140,000; .375 to .500 bore size: $154,000; .500 bore size and up: $170,000.

OLDER MANUFACTURED SHOTGUNS AND RIFLES

Best Quality Game Gun

NOTE: Add 50 percent for 20 gauge, 80 to 100 percent for 28 gauge or .410 bore.

NIB	Exc.	V.G.	Good	Fair	Poor
40000	35000	27500	20000	8000	—

Best Quality Heavy Duck Gun

NIB	Exc.	V.G.	Good	Fair	Poor
24000	20000	12500	7500	5000	—

Best Quality Over/Under

NOTE: Add 50 percent for 20 gauge, 100 percent for 28 gauge.

NIB	Exc.	V.G.	Good	Fair	Poor
50000	42000	32000	25000	9000	—

Double Rifle

.300 H&H

NIB	Exc.	V.G.	Good	Fair	Poor
—	55000	47500	40000	25000	—

.375 H&H

NIB	Exc.	V.G.	Good	Fair	Poor
—	70000	60000	50000	35000	—

.470 N.E.

NIB	Exc.	V.G.	Good	Fair	Poor
—	90000	75000	65000	45000	—

.600 N.E.

NIB	Exc.	V.G.	Good	Fair	Poor
—	100000	85000	70000	55000	—

PYRENEES
Hendaye, France

Founded in 1923, this company has produced a variety of models. The most popular of which was the "Unique" series. Prior to 1939, a variety of trade names were marked on their products such as these: Superior, Capitan, Cesar, Chantecler, Chimere Renoir, Colonial, Prima, Rapid Maxima, Reina, Demon, Demon-marine, Ebac, Elite, Gallia, Ixor, Le Majestic, St. Hubert, Selecta, Sympathique, Touriste, Le Sanspariel, Le Tout Acier, Mars, Perfect, Triomphe Francais, Unis & Vindex. Following 1939 this company's products are simply stamped "Unique". **NOTE:** During World War II production at this company was taken over by the Nazis. Consequently, the various models listed above will be found with German inspection marks. These arms are worth approximately 25 percent more than the values listed.

Model 10 Unique

A 6.35mm semi-automatic pistol similar to the Model 1906 Browning. The slide is marked "Le Veritable Pistolet Francais Unique". Introduced in 1923.

NIB	Exc.	V.G.	Good	Fair	Poor
—	295	195	165	100	75

Model 11

As above with a grip safety and loaded chamber indicator.

NIB	Exc.	V.G.	Good	Fair	Poor
—	325	225	195	150	100

Model 12

As above but without the loaded chamber indicator.

NIB	Exc.	V.G.	Good	Fair	Poor
—	295	195	165	100	75

Model 13

As above with a 7-shot magazine.

NIB	Exc.	V.G.	Good	Fair	Poor
—	295	195	165	100	75

Model 14

As above with a 9-shot magazine.

NIB	Exc.	V.G.	Good	Fair	Poor
—	295	195	165	100	75

Model 15

As above but in 7.65mm caliber. Introduced in 1923.

NIB	Exc.	V.G.	Good	Fair	Poor
—	295	195	165	100	75

Model 16

As above with a 7-shot magazine.

NIB	Exc.	V.G.	Good	Fair	Poor
—	295	195	165	100	75

Model 15

As above but in 7.65mm caliber. Introduced in 1923.

NIB	Exc.	V.G.	Good	Fair	Poor
—	295	195	165	100	75

Model 16

As above with a 7-shot magazine.

Courtesy Orvel Reichert

NIB	Exc.	V.G.	Good	Fair	Poor
—	295	195	165	100	75

Model 17

As above with a 9-shot magazine.

Courtesy Orvel Reichert

NIB	Exc.	V.G.	Good	Fair	Poor
—	325	225	195	150	100

Model 18

A 7.65mm caliber semi-automatic pistol patterned after the Model 1920 Browning but without a grip safety.

NIB	Exc.	V.G.	Good	Fair	Poor
—	295	195	165	100	75

Model 19

As above with a 7-shot magazine.

NIB	Exc.	V.G.	Good	Fair	Poor
—	295	195	165	100	75

Model 20

As above but with a 9-shot magazine.

NIB	Exc.	V.G.	Good	Fair	Poor
—	325	225	195	150	100

Model 21

As above except chambered for the 9mm short cartridge.

NIB	Exc.	V.G.	Good	Fair	Poor
—	325	225	195	150	100

POST-WAR UNIQUE

Model BCF66

A 9mm short semi-automatic pistol with a 3.5" barrel, open top slide and external hammer. The slide marked "Armes Unique Hendaye BP France". Blued finish blued, plastic grips.

QUACKENBUSH
Herkimer, New York

Quackenbush Safety Cartridge Rifle

A single-shot, takedown boy's rifle chambered for .22 rimfire cartridges in either .22 Short or .22 Long. Barrel length 18". Weight was about 4.5 lbs. All metal parts nickel-plated. The breech swings to the side for loading. Stock of walnut. Manufactured between 1886 and about 1920. Approximately 50,000 were produced. Quackenbush also made nickel-plated nutcrackers. Who'd'a thought?

NIB	Exc.	V.G.	Good	Fair	Poor
—	—	800	650	300	150

Junior Safety Rifle

Same as above but with skeleton stock. Built between 1893 and 1920. About 7,000 guns were manufactured. Weight was about 4 lbs.

NIB	Exc.	V.G.	Good	Fair	Poor
—	—	950	600	200	100

Bicycle Rifle

Chambered for the .22 cartridge, this rifle was fitted with a 12" barrel. Skeleton wire pistol grip.

NIB	Exc.	V.G.	Good	Fair	Poor
—	—	1300	750	350	150

QUINABAUG MFG. CO.
Southridge, Massachusetts

Under Hammer Pistol

A .31 caliber percussion under hammer pistol with barrels from 3" to 8" in length. Frame of blued iron, the grips of walnut or maple. The top of the frame is marked "Quinabaug Rifle M'g Co. Southbridge, Mass." The barrels are normally marked "E. Hutchings & Co. Agents". Manufactured during the 1850s.

NIB	Exc.	V.G.	Good	Fair	Poor
—	—	1900	1400	600	200

R

R. G. INDUSTRIES
Miami, Florida
Rohm Gmbh
Sontheim/Brenz, Germany

An importer of inexpensive handguns of dubious quality that ceased operations in 1986. Just about as crummy as it gets.

RG-25

A .25 caliber semi-automatic pistol available with either a blued or chrome-plated finish.

NIB	Exc.	V.G.	Good	Fair	Poor
—	75	65	50	25	—

RG-16

A double-barrel .22 caliber chrome-plated derringer.

NIB	Exc.	V.G.	Good	Fair	Poor
—	75	65	50	20	—

RG-17

As above except chambered for. 38 Special cartridge.

NIB	Exc.	V.G.	Good	Fair	Poor
—	75	70	60	25	—

RG-14

A .22 caliber double-action revolver with a 4" barrel and 6-shot cylinder. Blued finish, plastic grips.

NIB	Exc.	V.G.	Good	Fair	Poor
—	75	70	60	25	—

RG-30

A .22 LR or Magnum double-action revolver. Blued finish, plastic grips.

NIB	Exc.	V.G.	Good	Fair	Poor
—	75	65	50	25	—

RG-40

A .38 Special double-action revolver with swing-out cylinder. Blued finish, plastic grips.

NIB	Exc.	V.G.	Good	Fair	Poor
—	75	70	60	25	—

RG-57

A .357 or .44 Magnum double-action revolver with 6-shot cylinder. Blued finish, checkered wood grips.

NIB	Exc.	V.G.	Good	Fair	Poor
—	75	70	60	25	—

RG-63

A .22 caliber double-action revolver resembling a Colt Model 1873.

NIB	Exc.	V.G.	Good	Fair	Poor
—	75	70	60	25	—

RG-66

A .22 or .22 Magnum single-action revolver patterned after the Colt Model 1873.

NIB	Exc.	V.G.	Good	Fair	Poor
—	90	70	50	25	—

RG-66T

As above with adjustable sights.

NIB	Exc.	V.G.	Good	Fair	Poor
—	90	70	50	25	—

RG-74

A .22 caliber double-action revolver with swing-out cylinder.

NIB	Exc.	V.G.	Good	Fair	Poor
—	75	65	55	25	—

RG-88

A .357 Magnum double-action revolver with swing-out cylinder.

NIB	Exc.	V.G.	Good	Fair	Poor
—	75	65	55	25	—

R.E.
Valencia, Spain

The initials "R.E." stand for "Republica Espana". This copy of the Spanish Army Model 1921, also known as the Astra 400, was produced between 1936 and 1939 during the Spanish Civil War by the Republican forces. This variation can be identified by the "RE" monogram on the butt and the absence of any manufacturer's stampings.

NIB	Exc.	V.G.	Good	Fair	Poor
—	475	325	250	175	100

RADOM
Radom, Poland

For history, technical data, descriptions, photos and prices see the *Standard Catalog of Military Firearms*.

VIS-35 Reissue

This is an exact copy of the original VIS-35 pistol. Limited to 100 pistols with fewer than that number imported into the U.S. The importer, "Dalvar of USA" is stamped on the barrel. **NOTE:** Subtract 50 percent for "non-eagle" version.

NIB	Exc.	V.G.	Good	Fair	Poor
2300	2000	1500	1100	600	300

RANDALL FIREARMS CO.
Sun Valley, California

Randall matched set, serial-number RFOO010C. Made for the TV series "Magnum PI". (Photo by Steve Comus)

NOTE: Randall prototypes can be identified by a "T" prefix. Add 50 percent to the price for this variety. For serial numbers under 2000 add $100 to $150.

NOTE: At present (2009) the Randall market seems to be holding steady, possibly as a result of the profusion of high-end 1911s on the general market.

Randall Documentation & Collectors Club: Research letters on original Randall Letterhead are available at a cost of $30 each postpaid (Randal pistols only). Readers and collectors interested in joining the Randall Firearms/Pistol Collectors Association can contact the Randall Historian, Rick Kennerknecht at:

P.O. Box 1180, Mills, Wyoming 82644-1180
Web: www.Randall45.com
E-mail: Historian@Randal45.com
Phone: 877-464-0180
U.S. Fax: 419-464-0180; Euro-Fax: 44-(0870) 131-2598

Model A111

Caliber is .45 Auto, barrel length 5", round-slide top, right-hand with fixed sights. Total production: 3,431. **NOTE:** For original box add a premium of $100 for Exc. through Good prices.

Randall matched set, serial-number RFOO010C. Made for the TV series "Magnum PI." (Photo by Steve Comus)

NIB	Exc.	V.G.	Good	Fair	Poor
1050	950	650	400	350	200

Model A121

Caliber is .45 Auto, barrel length 5", flat-slide top, right-hand with fixed sights. Total production: 1,067. **NOTE:** For original box add a premium of $100 for Exc. through Good prices.

NIB	Exc.	V.G.	Good	Fair	Poor
1150	1000	800	425	375	200

Model A131

Caliber is .45 Auto, barrel length 5", flat-slide top, right-hand with Millet sights. Total production: 2,083. **NOTE:** For original box add a premium of $100 for Exc. through Good prices.

Randall A131/SO in .451 Detonics Magnum with Randall memorabilia. (Photo by Larry Gray)

NIB	Exc.	V.G.	Good	Fair	Poor
1300	1050	875	550	400	200

Model A112

Caliber is 9mm, barrel length 5", round-slide top, right-hand with fixed sights. Total production: 301. **NOTE:** For original box add a premium of $100 for Exc. through Good prices.

NIB	Exc.	V.G.	Good	Fair	Poor
1350	950	900	575	425	200

Model A122

Caliber 9mm. barrel length 5", flat-slide top, right-hand with fixed sights. Total production: 18. **NOTE:** For original box add a premium of $100 for Exc. through Good prices.

NIB	Exc.	V.G.	Good	Fair	Poor
1900	1600	1350	800	540	300

Model A211

Caliber .45 Auto, barrel length 4.25", round-slide top, right-hand with fixed sights. Total production: 922. **NOTE:** For original box add a premium of $100 for Exc. through Good prices.

NIB	Exc.	V.G.	Good	Fair	Poor
1150	1000	800	425	375	200

Model A231

Caliber .45 Auto, barrel length 4.25", flat-slide top, right-hand with Millet sights. Total production: 574. **NOTE:** For original box add a premium of $100 for Exc. through Good prices.

NIB	Exc.	V.G.	Good	Fair	Poor
1350	950	900	575	425	200

Model A212

Caliber 9mm, barrel length 4.25", round-slide top, right-hand with fixed sights. Total production: 76. **NOTE:** For original box add a premium of $100 for Exc. through Good prices.

NIB	Exc.	V.G.	Good	Fair	Poor
1450	1050	925	650	500	300

Model A232

Caliber 9mm. barrel length 4.25", flat-slide top, right-hand with Millet sights. Total production: 5. **NOTE:** For original box add a premium of $100 for Exc. through Good prices.

NIB	Exc.	V.G.	Good	Fair	Poor
2400	1900	1565	—	—	—

Model A311

Caliber .45 Auto, barrel length 4.25", round-slide top, right-hand with fixed sights. Total production: 361. **NOTE:** For original box add a premium of $100 for Exc. through Good prices.

A311B black oxide LeMay special order by Soldier of Fortune magazine for field testing in El Salvador. (Photo by Steve Comus)

NIB	Exc.	V.G.	Good	Fair	Poor
1700	1375	1150	900	700	300

Model A331 Curtis LeMay

Caliber .45 Auto, barrel length 4.25", flat-slide top, right-hand with Millet sights. Total production: 293.

NIB	Exc.	V.G.	Good	Fair	Poor
1800	1475	1250	950	735	300

Model A312

Caliber 9mm. barrel length 4.25", round-slide top, right-hand with fixed sights. Total production: 2. **NOTE:** For original box add a premium of $100 for Exc. through Good prices.

NIB	Exc.	V.G.	Good	Fair	Poor
3750	3300	2575	—	—	—

Model A332

Caliber 9mm. barrel length 4.25", flat-slide top, right-hand with Millet sights. Total production: 9. **NOTE:** For original box add a premium of $100 for Exc. through Good prices.

NIB	Exc.	V.G.	Good	Fair	Poor
2250	1775	1450	1000	750	300

Model B111

Caliber .45 Auto, barrel length 5", round-slide top, left-hand with fixed sights. Total production: 297. **NOTE:** For original box add a premium of $100 for Exc. through Good prices.

NIB	Exc.	V.G.	Good	Fair	Poor
1900	1550	1200	975	700	300

Model B121

Caliber .45 Auto, barrel length 5", flat-slide top, left-hand with fixed sights. Total production: 110. **NOTE:** For original box add a premium of $100 for Exc. through Good prices.

NIB	Exc.	V.G.	Good	Fair	Poor
2250	1775	1450	1000	750	300

Model B122

Caliber 9mm. barrel length 5", flat-slide top, left-hand with fixed sights. Total production: 2.

NIB	Exc.	V.G.	Good	Fair	Poor
4000	3500	2675	—	—	—

Model B123

Caliber .38 Super, barrel length 5", flat-slide top, left-hand with fixed sights. Total production: 2.

NIB	Exc.	V.G.	Good	Fair	Poor
4000	3500	2675	—	—	—

Model B131

Caliber .45 Auto, barrel length 5", flat-slide top, left-hand with Millet sights. Total production: 225. **NOTE:** For original box add a premium of $100 for Exc. through Good prices.

B131/SO left-hand service model with custom Chuck Stapel knife. (Photo by Steve Comus)

NIB	Exc.	V.G.	Good	Fair	Poor
2075	1700	1400	875	700	300

Model B311

Caliber .45 Auto, barrel length 4.25", round-slide top, left-hand with fixed sights. Total production: 52. **NOTE:** For original box add a premium of $100 for Exc. through Good prices.

NIB	Exc.	V.G.	Good	Fair	Poor
2250	1775	1450	1000	750	300

Model B312

Caliber 9mm. barrel length 4.25", round-slide top, left-hand with fixed sights. Total production: 9. **NOTE:** For original box add a premium of $100 for Exc. through Good prices.

Randall B312 left-hand 9mm LeMay, one of the most sought-after of the B-series guns. Only nine were manufactured. (Photo by Steve Comus)

Randall B312 with factory 45 ACP conversion unit. Only one of these factory units were made. (Photo by Steve Comus)

NIB	Exc.	V.G.	Good	Fair	Poor
3750	3300	2575	—	—	—

Model B331

Caliber .45 Auto, barrel length 4.25", flat-slide top, left-hand with Millet sights. Total production: 45. **NOTE:** For original box add a premium of $100 for Exc. through Good prices.

NIB	Exc.	V.G.	Good	Fair	Poor
2500	2050	1675	1100	600	300

Model C311

Caliber .45 Auto, barrel length 4.25", round-slide top, right-hand with fixed sights. Total production: 1.

NIB	Exc.	V.G.	Good	Fair	Poor
4250	—	—	—	—	—

Model C332

Caliber 9mm. barrel length 4.25", flat-slide top, right-hand with Millet sights. Total production: 4.

NIB	Exc.	V.G.	Good	Fair	Poor
1900	1550	1200	975	700	300

Model B321 SET

Randall B321 of the B321 set, serial-number REK1. (Photo by Steve Comus)

NIB	Exc.	V.G.	Good	Fair	Poor
24500	—	—	—	—	—

Model A111/111 Matched Set

Serial numbers: RFOOOOOC, RFOO001C, RFOO010-C, RFOO024C.

NIB	Exc.	V.G.	Good	Fair	Poor
9200	—	—	—	—	—

Austrian Randall

Total production: 5. **NOTE:** Prototypes with "T" serial numbers add 50 percent. For serial numbers under 2000 add $200 to $300. With factory box add $100 for A111, A121 and A131. Add $200 for all other right-hand models and $300 for all left-hand models.

Close-up view of Austrian proof marks. (Photos by Christopher Todd)

NIB	Exc.	V.G.	Good	Fair	Poor
32500	—	—	—	—	—

RANDALL MAGAZINES

.45 LeMay—Right-Hand

NIB	Exc.	V.G.	Good	Fair	Poor
100	90	80	80	—	—

.45 LeMay—Dogleg Right-Hand

NIB	Exc.	V.G.	Good	Fair	Poor
80	70	70	70	—	—

.45 LeMay—Left-Hand

NIB	Exc.	V.G.	Good	Fair	Poor
150	130	125	125	—	—

.45 LeMay—Dogleg Left-Hand

NIB	Exc.	V.G.	Good	Fair	Poor
140	130	120	120	—	—

.45 Service—Right-Hand

NIB	Exc.	V.G.	Good	Fair	Poor
60	45	40	40	—	—

.45 Service—Left-Hand

NIB	Exc.	V.G.	Good	Fair	Poor
125	115	100	100	—	—

9mm Service—Right-Hand

NIB	Exc.	V.G.	Good	Fair	Poor
125	115	100	100	—	—

9mm Service—Left-Hand

NIB	Exc.	V.G.	Good	Fair	Poor
200	175	150	150	—	—

RANGER ARMS, INC.
Gainesville, Texas

.22 Rifle

A bolt-action rifle produced in .22 LR with a checkered walnut Monte Carlo stock. Manufactured in the early 1970s.

NIB	Exc.	V.G.	Good	Fair	Poor
—	200	150	100	75	50

Statesman

A bolt-action rifle produced in various centerfire calibers with a 22" barrel, no sights and a checkered walnut stock. Standard finish blued. Manufactured in the early 1970s.

NIB	Exc.	V.G.	Good	Fair	Poor
—	900	750	600	350	200

Statesman Magnum

As above, but chambered for magnum calibers and with a 24" barrel.

NIB	Exc.	V.G.	Good	Fair	Poor
—	950	800	650	375	200

Senator

As above with a better finish.

NIB	Exc.	V.G.	Good	Fair	Poor
—	1000	850	700	525	250

Senator Magnum

As above chambered for magnum cartridges.

NIB	Exc.	V.G.	Good	Fair	Poor
—	1150	900	750	575	250

Governor

As above with better walnut and finer lined checkering.

NIB	Exc.	V.G.	Good	Fair	Poor
—	1300	1050	800	600	300

Governor Magnum

As above chambered for magnum cartridges.

NIB	Exc.	V.G.	Good	Fair	Poor
—	1540	1200	950	750	300

RAPTOR ARMS CO.
Shelton, Connecticut

Raptor Bolt-Action Rifle

An economy-class bolt rifle introduced in 1997 and chambered for the .270, .30-06, .243, .25-06 and .308 calibers. Fitted with a 22" barrel and black synthetic checkered stock. An upgrade model was available with wooden stock. Adjustable trigger. Weight is about 7.5 lbs.

NIB	Exc.	V.G.	Good	Fair	Poor
275	225	175	125	100	75

Peregrine Bolt-Action Rifle

Similar to above but with checkered hardwood stock. Special order.

NIB	Exc.	V.G.	Good	Fair	Poor
275	225	175	125	100	75

RAST & GASSER
See—Gasser

RAU ARMS CORP.
El Dorado, Kansas

Wildcat

Single-shot pivoting-barrel .22 rimfire rifle with skeletonized stock with walnut or mahogany inset. Fore-end acts as extractor. Similar in overall look to FIE/Garcia Bronco but in .22 only. Mfg. 1969-1970 with 2500-3000 produced. Later produced by Mountain Arms. See that listing.

Model 500

Blued with walnut stock insert.

NIB	Exc.	V.G.	Good	Fair	Poor
300	200	150	100	75	45

Model 600 Deluxe

Chrome finish with mahogany stock insert.

NIB	Exc.	V.G.	Good	Fair	Poor
325	225	175	125	95	50

RAVELL
Barcelona, Spain

Maxim Double Rifle

A Holland & Holland-styled sidelock double-barrel rifle available in either .375 Holland & Holland or 9.3x74R with 23" barrels having express sights. Double triggers and automatic ejectors. The sidelocks and mounts engraved, stock of well figured walnut normally fitted with a recoil pad.

NIB	Exc.	V.G.	Good	Fair	Poor
4500	3500	2750	1850	1250	850

RAVEN ARMS
Industry, California

P-25

A .25 caliber semi-automatic pistol with a 2.75" barrel and 6-round magazine. Available with a blued, chrome or nickel-plated finish and walnut grips. Manufacture ceased in 1984.

NIB	Exc.	V.G.	Good	Fair	Poor
—	100	75	50	35	25

MP-25

As above with a die-cast frame and imitation ivory grips.

NIB	Exc.	V.G.	Good	Fair	Poor
110	80	55	45	35	25

READ & WATSON
Danville, Virginia

During 1862 and 1863, Read & Watson produced approximately 900 altered Hall rifles for the State of Virginia. These arms were made from Hall rifles issued to the state prior to the Civil War. The original breech loading mechanisms were removed and a brass breech piece or receiver was secured in their place. New buttstocks were fitted and the original Hall furniture was reused. Carbines have an overall length of 42-1/8"; barrel length of 26" and are of .52 caliber. Position and style of serial numbers varies.

NIB	Exc.	V.G.	Good	Fair	Poor
—	—	18500	15500	7100	1000

RECORD-MATCH ANSCHUTZ
Zelia-Mehlis, Germany

Model 210 Free Pistol

A single-shot .22 caliber target pistol using a Martini falling block action. Barrel length 11", set trigger and adjustable sights. Blued finish with checkered walnut grips and fore-end. Manufactured during the 1930s.

NIB	Exc.	V.G.	Good	Fair	Poor
—	1500	1200	1000	825	400

Model 210A

As above with a lightweight alloy frame.

NIB	Exc.	V.G.	Good	Fair	Poor
—	1425	1125	975	775	350

Model 200 Free Pistol

As above without a set trigger.

NIB	Exc.	V.G.	Good	Fair	Poor
—	1125	1050	875	550	300

REEDER, GARY CUSTOM GUNS
Flagstaff, Arizona

This company offers complete guns as listed below. It also offers custom options built on customer guns as well. An extensive number of custom options is available on any of these models. Prices listed below reflect the standard for that particular model. Retail prices only are listed below due to lack of active secondary market for these limited edition guns. Reeder is a custom manufacturer, or re-stylist, working primarily with Ruger frames. Only a representative sampling of his works is presented here and the values are estimates only. Since many of Reeder's guns are made to custom specs, their value is largely a matter of finding the right buyer.

Arizona Ranger Classic

Built on a Ruger Vaquero this model is chambered for the .45 Long Colt cartridge and fitted with a choice of a 4.5", 5.5", or 7.5" barrel. Blue or stainless steel finish. Special engraving with Stag grips.

NIB	Exc.	V.G.	Good	Fair	Poor
1400	1225	975	—	—	—

Badlands Classic

Built on a Ruger Vaquero and chambered for the .45 Long Colt cartridge with an extra .45 ACP cylinder. Fitted with a 4.5" barrel. Special engraving. Pearl grips.

NIB	Exc.	V.G.	Good	Fair	Poor
1400	1225	975	—	—	—

Black Widow

Chambered for the .44 Magnum cartridge and fitted with a 4.625" barrel with black Chromex finish. Round butt with black Cape Buffalo grips. Engraved with Black Widow on each side of the cylinder. Built on a Ruger Super Blackhawk.

NIB	Exc.	V.G.	Good	Fair	Poor
1300	1075	850	—	—	—

Black Widow II

Similar to the Black Widow but chambered for the .45 Long Colt cartridge. Barrel length is 4.5".

NIB	Exc.	V.G.	Good	Fair	Poor
1350	1125	900	—	—	—

Cowboy Classic

Built on a Ruger Vaquero and chambered for the .45 Long Colt with a 6.75" barrel. Stainless steel or black Chromix finish. Ivory polymer or pearlite grips. Special engraving.

NIB	Exc.	V.G.	Good	Fair	Poor
1350	1125	900	—	—	—

Cowtown Classic

Built on a Ruger Vaquero and chambered for the .45 Long Colt with 7.5" barrel. Special engraving. Walnut grips.

NIB	Exc.	V.G.	Good	Fair	Poor
1350	1125	900	—	—	—

Gamblers Classic

Built on a Ruger Vaquero and chambered for the .45 Long Colt with a 2.5" barrel. Stainless steel or black Chromix finish. Choice of black or white pearl grips. No ejector rod. Special engraving.

NIB	Exc.	V.G.	Good	Fair	Poor
1350	1125	900	—	—	—

Lone Star Classic

Built on a Ruger Vaquero and chambered for the .45 Long Colt cartridge with 7.5" barrel. Stainless steel finish. Special engraving and walnut grips with five notches.

NIB	Exc.	V.G.	Good	Fair	Poor
1350	1125	900	—	—	—

Long Rider Classic

Built on a Ruger Vaquero and chambered for the .45 Long Colt cartridge with 4.5", 5.5" or 7.5" barrel. Special engraving with black Chromix finish. Gunfighter grip with simulated pearl or ivory.

NIB	Exc.	V.G.	Good	Fair	Poor
1350	1125	900	—	—	—

Texas Ranger Classic

Built on a Ruger Vaquero frame and chambered for the .45 Long Colt cartridge with 4.5", 5.5" or 7.5" barrel. Stainless steel finish. Special engraving. Simulated pearl gunfighter grips.

NIB	Exc.	V.G.	Good	Fair	Poor
1350	1125	900	—	—	—

Trail Rider Classic

Built on a Ruger Vaquero frame and chambered for the .45 Long Colt cartridge with 7.5" barrel. Black Chromix finish. Special engraving. Simulated pearl grips.

NIB	Exc.	V.G.	Good	Fair	Poor
1350	1125	900	—	—	—

Tombstone Classic

Built on a Ruger Vaquero frame and chambered for the .45 Long Colt cartridge with 3.5" barrel. Black Chromix finish. Special engraving. Simulated pearl or ivory bird's-head grips.

NIB	Exc.	V.G.	Good	Fair	Poor
1350	1125	900	—	—	—

Doc Holliday Classic

Built on a Ruger Vaquero frame and chambered for the .45 Long Colt cartridge with 3.5" barrel. Stainless steel or black Chromix finish. Special engraving. Simulated pearl gambler grips.

NIB	Exc.	V.G.	Good	Fair	Poor
1350	1125	900	—	—	—

Night Rider

Built on a Ruger Vaquero frame and chambered for the .44-40 cartridge with 7.5" barrel. Black Chromix finish. Special engraving. Stag grips.

NIB	Exc.	V.G.	Good	Fair	Poor
1350	1125	900	—	—	—

Ultimate Vaquero

Built on a Ruger Vaquero frame and chambered for the .45 Long Colt cartridge with 4" barrel. Stainless steel or black Chromix finish. Special engraving. Simulated pearl gambler grips.

NIB	Exc.	V.G.	Good	Fair	Poor
1350	1125	900	—	—	—

Ultimate Bisley

Built on a Ruger Vaquero frame and chambered for the .45 Long Colt or .44 Magnum cartridge with 4.5", 5.5", 6.5" or 7.5" barrel. Black Chromix finish. Special engraving. Simulated pearl or ivory Bisley grips.

NIB	Exc.	V.G.	Good	Fair	Poor
1350	1125	900	—	—	—

Long Colt Hunter

Built on a Ruger Blackhawk frame and chambered for the .45 Long Colt cartridge with 5.5" or 7.5" barrel. Stainless steel finish. Adjustable rear sight with gold bead front sight. Special engraving. Ebony grips.

NIB	Exc.	V.G.	Good	Fair	Poor
1350	1125	900	—	—	—

Long Colt Hunter II

Built on a Ruger Redhawk frame and chambered for the .45 Long Colt or .44 Magnum cartridge with 5" barrel. Stainless steel finish. Special engraving. Wooden gunfighter grips.

NIB	Exc.	V.G.	Good	Fair	Poor
1350	1125	900	—	—	—

African Hunter

Built on a Ruger Bisley or Super Blackhawk frame and chambered for the .475 or .500 Linebaugh cartridge with 6" barrel. Available with or without muzzlebrake. Adjustable rear sight and interchangeable front sights. Stainless steel or black Chromix finish. Special engraving. Ebony grips.

NIB	Exc.	V.G.	Good	Fair	Poor
1350	1125	900	—	—	—

Ultimate 41

Built on a Ruger Blackhawk frame and chambered for the .41 Magnum or .41 GNR cartridge with 4.5", 5.5" or 7.5" barrel. Unfluted cylinder. Stainless steel finish. Adjustable rear sights. Special engraving. Ebony grips.

NIB	Exc.	V.G.	Good	Fair	Poor
1500	1295	950	—	—	—

Coyote Classic

Built on a Ruger frame and chambered for the .22 Hornet, .22 K Hornet, .218 Bee, .218 Mashburn Bee, .17 Ackley Bee, .17 Ackley Hornet, .256 Winchester and .25-20 with 8" barrel. Adjustable rear sight and drilled and tapped for scope mount. Black Chromix or stainless steel finish. Special engraving. Laminated cherry grips.

NIB	Exc.	V.G.	Good	Fair	Poor
1350	1125	900	—	—	—

Classic Hunter

Built on a Ruger Vaquero frame and chambered for the .475 Linebaugh cartridge with heavy 6" barrel. Black Chromix finish. Special engraving. Laminated ironwood, cherry or walnut gunfighter grips.

NIB	Exc.	V.G.	Good	Fair	Poor
1500	1295	950	—	—	—

Alaskan Grizzly

Built on a Ruger Vaquero frame and chambered for the .475 or .500 Linebaugh cartridge with customer's choice of barrel. Black Chromix or stainless steel finish. Special engraving. Horn or black laminated gunfighter grips.

NIB	Exc.	V.G.	Good	Fair	Poor
1350	1125	900	—	—	—

Ultimate Back Up 2

Built on a Ruger Blackhawk or Super Blackhawk frame and chambered for the .475 or .500 Linebaugh cartridge with 3.5" ported barrel. Stainless steel finish. Special engraving. Laminated wood or Buffalo horn grips.

NIB	Exc.	V.G.	Good	Fair	Poor
1500	1295	950	—		

Montana Hunter

Built on a Ruger Blackhawk or Super Blackhawk frame and chambered for the .45 Long Colt or .44 Magnum cartridge with customer's choice of barrel. Stainless steel finish. Special engraving. Laminated gunfighter grips.

NIB	Exc.	V.G.	Good	Fair	Poor
1350	1125	900	—	—	—

Alaskan Survivalist

Built on a Ruger Redhawk frame and chambered for the .45 Long Colt or .44 Magnum cartridge with 3" barrel. Adjustable rear sight. Stainless steel finish. Special engraving. Ebony round butt grips.

NIB	Exc.	V.G.	Good	Fair	Poor
1350	1125	900	—	—	—

American Hunter

Built on a Winchester Model 94 big bore frame and chambered for the .444 Marlin cartridge. Black Chromix finish. Ghost ring rear sight. Special engraving. Checkering walnut stock.

NIB	Exc.	V.G.	Good	Fair	Poor
1350	1125	900	—	—	—

Alaskan Classic

Built on a Marlin Model 1895 frame and chambered for the .45-70 cartridge. Barrel length is 16.5". Black Chromix finish. Ghost ring rear sight. Special engraving. Checkering walnut stock.

NIB	Exc.	V.G.	Good	Fair	Poor
1500	1295	950	—	—	—

Buffalo Hunter

Built on a Marlin Model 1895 frame and chambered for the .475 GNR cartridge. Barrel length is 18". Full length magazine tube. Black Chromix finish. Peep rear sight. Special engraving. Checkering walnut stock.

NIB	Exc.	V.G.	Good	Fair	Poor
1500	1295	950	—	—	—

Kodiak Hunter

Built on a Contender frame and chambered for the .50 Action Express or .454 Casull cartridge. Barrel length is 10". Black Chromix finish. Adjustable rear sight with barrel band front sight. Special engraving. Walnut grips.

NIB	Exc.	V.G.	Good	Fair	Poor
1350	1125	900	—	—	—

Ultimate Encore

Built on a Thompson/Center frame and chambered for a variety of big bore cartridges. Fitted with a 15" barrel with muzzle-brake. Black Chromix finish. Ghost ring rear sight. Special engraving.

NIB	Exc.	V.G.	Good	Fair	Poor
1350	1125	900	—	—	—

Ultimate 44

Built on the customer's Ruger Hunter this model features an extra long five-shot cylinder, Bisley hammer and trigger, special grip frame with laminated cherry grips, Magna-Ported barrel, sling swivels and action job. Game scene engraving.

NIB	Exc.	V.G.	Good	Fair	Poor
1500	1295	950	—	—	—

Southern Comfort

Built on the customer's Blackhawk or Super Blackhawk Ruger this revolver features a five-shot cylinder chambered for the .454 Casull cartridge, tear drop hammer, special set back trigger, special grip frame and light engraving. Barrel length to the customer's choice.

NIB	Exc.	V.G.	Good	Fair	Poor
1500	1295	950	—	—	—

Professional Hunter

This model features a number of special features from an extended frame to a five-shot cylinder. Choice of calibers from .224 GNR to .500 Maximum. Fitted with a 8" barrel with heavy taper. Limited production.

NIB	Exc.	V.G.	Good	Fair	Poor
2750	2295	1650	—	—	—

Ultimate 480

This model is built on the customer's Ruger Blackhawk or Super Blackhawk and is chambered for the .480 cartridge. Cylinder has five rounds, heavy barrel to customer's length, special grip. Blued or stainless steel.

NIB	Exc.	V.G.	Good	Fair	Poor
1400	1195	875	—	—	—

Ultimate 500

This model is chambered for the .500 S&W cartridge. Fitted with a heavy five-shot cylinder and barrel length of customer's choice. Black or ivory Micarta grips. Engraved games scenes and other special features.

NIB	Exc.	V.G.	Good	Fair	Poor
2750	2295	1650	—	—	—

Classic 45

This model is chambered for the .45 Colt, .45 ACP or .45 Schofield cartridge without full moon clips. It is fitted with a six-shot unfluted cylinder. Special set back trigger, Bisley hammer, Super Blackhawk or Blackhawk stainless steel frame and other special features.

NIB	Exc.	V.G.	Good	Fair	Poor
1350	1125	900	—	—	—

Big 5 Classic

This single-shot rifle is built on the customer's Ruger No. 1 rifle. Chambered for the .500 Jeffery cartridge. Fitted with a heavy barrel to customer's length and muzzlebrake. Tuned action. Buttstock weight added. Game scene engraved.

NIB	Exc.	V.G.	Good	Fair	Poor
2200	1725	1150	—	—	—

The BMF

This model features a 4" barrel chambered for the .500 Maximum cartridge and Magna-Ported. Bisley grip. Satin stainless steel finish with black Micarta grips. Game scene engraved.

NIB	Exc.	V.G.	Good	Fair	Poor
2750	2295	1650	—	—	—

Double Duce

This Ruger Single Six revolver is fitted with an eight-shot cylinder and 8" barrel for the .22 WMR cartridge. Longer grip frame with red cherry grips. Game scene engraved.

NIB	Exc.	V.G.	Good	Fair	Poor
1350	1125	900	—	—	—

Ultimate Black Widow

This model, built on the customer's Blackhawk, Bisley or Super Blackhawk Ruger. Chambered for the .475 or .500 Linebaugh. Heavy duty five-shot cylinder. Barrel length to customer's choice. Bisley grip with black Micarta grips. Black Chromix finish.

NIB	Exc.	V.G.	Good	Fair	Poor
1350	1125	900	—	—	—

REFORM
August Schuler
Suhl, Germany

Reform Pistol

A 6.35 or .25 ACP four barreled double-action pistol constructed so that the barrel unit rises upward when the trigger is pulled. It superficially resembles a semi-automatic pistol. Blued with hard rubber grips. Manufactured between 1906 and about 1913.

NIB	Exc.	V.G.	Good	Fair	Poor
—	1750	1200	950	600	375

REID, JAMES
New York, New York

Model 1 Revolver

A spur trigger .22 caliber revolver with a 3.5" octagonal barrel and 7-shot unfluted cylinder. Blued with walnut grips. The barrel marked "J. Reid, New York". Approximately 500 were manufactured between 1862 and 1865.

NIB	Exc.	V.G.	Good	Fair	Poor
—	—	1175	950	375	100

Model 2 Revolver

As above but in .32 caliber, the barrel marked "Address W.P. Irving, 20 Cliff Street. N.Y." or "James P. Fitch. N.Y." Approximately 1,300 were manufactured between 1862 and 1865.

NIB	Exc.	V.G.	Good	Fair	Poor
—	—	1175	950	385	100

Model 3 Revolver

Similar to the above, but with the grip angle sharpened. Chambered for the .32 rimfire cartridge with a 4.75" barrel. The cylinder chambers are threaded so that percussion nipples can be inserted. The barrel is marked "J. Reid N.Y. City". Approximately 300 were made between 1862 and 1865.

NIB	Exc.	V.G.	Good	Fair	Poor
—	—	1550	1375	550	200

Model 4 Revolver

As above with barrel lengths varying from 3.75" to 8". Approximately 1,600 were manufactured between 1862 and 1865.

NIB	Exc.	V.G.	Good	Fair	Poor
—	—	1550	1375	550	200

"My Friend" Knuckle Duster

A 7-shot .22 caliber revolver constructed entirely of metal and without a barrel. The frame of silver-plated brass or blued iron and marked "My Friend Patd. Dec. 26, 1865". The grip is formed with a finger hole so that the pistol can be used as a set of brass knuckles.

Courtesy W.P. Hallstein III and son Chip

Brass Frame

NIB	Exc.	V.G.	Good	Fair	Poor
—	1550	1200	800	500	200

Iron Frame

NIB	Exc.	V.G.	Good	Fair	Poor
—	2800	2250	800	500	250

.32 Caliber Knuckle Duster

As above but .32 caliber. Approximately 3,400 were manufactured between 1869 and 1884.

Brass Frame

NIB	Exc.	V.G.	Good	Fair	Poor
—	1800	1500	800	600	200

Iron Frame

NIB	Exc.	V.G.	Good	Fair	Poor
—	2800	2250	1300	800	250

.41 Caliber Knuckle Duster

As above but .41 caliber and marked "J. Reid's Derringer". Approximately 300 were manufactured between 1875 and 1878.

NIB	Exc.	V.G.	Good	Fair	Poor
—	18500	15000	9000	6500	1500

Model No. 1 Knuckle Duster

As above with a 3" barrel. Approximately 350 were made between 1875 and 1880.

Courtesy W.P. Hallstein III and son Chip

NIB	Exc.	V.G.	Good	Fair	Poor
—	3350	2750	1300	850	250

Model No. 2 Knuckle Duster

As above with a 1.75" barrel. Approximately 150 were made between 1875 and 1880.

NIB	Exc.	V.G.	Good	Fair	Poor
—	3950	3000	1700	1250	500

Model No. 3 Derringer

A .41 caliber revolver with a 3" octagonal barrel and 5-shot fluted cylinder. The frame silver-plated and the barrel as well as cylinder blued. Approximately 75 were made between 1880 and 1884.

NIB	Exc.	V.G.	Good	Fair	Poor
—	2900	2500	1200	950	350

Model No. 4 Derringer

As above but with a brass frame and walnut grips and marked "Reid's Extra". Approximately 200 were made during 1883 and 1884.

NIB	Exc.	V.G.	Good	Fair	Poor
—	1800	1500	1000	700	250

New Model Knuckle Duster

Similar to the Model 2 with a 2" barrel and 5-shot cylinder. The barrel marked "Reid's New Model .32 My Friend". Approximately 150 were made in 1884.

NIB	Exc.	V.G.	Good	Fair	Poor
—	1800	1500	1050	650	250

REISING ARMS CO.
Hartford, Connecticut

Standard Model

A .22 caliber semi-automatic pistol with a hinged 6.5" barrel and 10-round magazine. Standard finish is blued, however, nickel-plated versions are known. The slide marked with the company's name and patent dates. Bakelite grips impressed with a bear's head and the motto "Reising, It's A Bear". Manufactured in both New York City and Hartford during the 1920s. **CAUTION:** High-velocity ammunition should not be used in these pistols.

Courtesy John J. Stimson, Jr.

New York Manufacture

NIB	Exc.	V.G.	Good	Fair	Poor
—	900	750	500	300	100

Hartford Manufacture

NIB	Exc.	V.G.	Good	Fair	Poor
—	450	350	275	175	100

REMINGTON ARMS COMPANY, INC.
Madison, North Carolina

Founded in 1816 by Eliphalet Remington, this company has the distinction of being the oldest firearms manufacturing firm in the United States. Since 1856 it has been known by four different names: between 1856 and 1888, E. Remington & Sons; 1888-1910, Remington Arms Company; 1910-1925, Remington Arms U.M.C. Company (Union Metallic Cartridge Company); and 1925 to the present, Remington Arms Company.

1st Model Remington-Beals Revolver

A .31 caliber 5-shot percussion revolver with a 3" octagonal barrel. The cylinder turning mechanism is mounted on the left outside frame. Blued, case hardened, silver-plated, brass trigger guard and gutta-percha grips. The barrel marked, "F. Beal's Patent, June 24, '56 & May 26, '57" and the frame, "Remington's Ilion, N.Y." Approximately 5,000 were manufactured in 1857 and 1858.

Courtesy Milwaukee Public Museum, Milwaukee, Wisconsin

NIB	Exc.	V.G.	Good	Fair	Poor
—	4500	3000	2500	500	300

2nd Model Remington-Beals Revolver

A spur trigger .31 caliber 5-shot percussion revolver with a 3" octagonal barrel. Blued, case hardened with a squared gutta-percha grip. The barrel marked, "Beals Patent 1856 & 57, Manufactured by Remingtons Ilion, N.Y." Approximately 1,000 were manufactured between 1858 and 1860.

NIB	Exc.	V.G.	Good	Fair	Poor
—	6000	5000	4500	2500	1000

3rd Model Remington-Beals Revolver

A .31 caliber 5-shot percussion revolver with a 4" octagonal barrel. A loading lever mounted beneath the barrel. Blued, case hardened with gutta-percha grips. The barrel marked, "Beals Pat. 1856, 57, 58" and also "Manufactured by Remingtons, Ilion, N.Y." Approximately 1,500 were manufactured in 1859 and 1860.

Courtesy Milwaukee Public Museum, Milwaukee, Wisconsin

NIB	Exc.	V.G.	Good	Fair	Poor
—	4500	4000	3350	1150	500

Remington-Rider Revolver

A double-action .31 caliber percussion revolver with a 3" barrel and 5-shot cylinder. Most of these revolvers were blued but a few were nickel-plated, case hardened with gutta-percha grips. This model is also encountered altered to .32 rimfire. The barrel marked, "Manufactured by Remingtons, Ilion, N.Y., Riders Pt. Aug. 17, 1858, May 3, 1859". Approximately 20,000 were manufactured between 1860 and 1873. **NOTE:** The cartridge variation is worth approximately 20 percent less than the original percussion version.

NIB	Exc.	V.G.	Good	Fair	Poor
—	2500	1400	1100	675	300

Remington-Beals Army Revolver

A .44 caliber percussion revolver with an 8" barrel and 6-shot cylinder. Blued, case hardened with walnut grips. The barrel marked "Beals Patent Sept. 14, 1858 Manufactured by Remington's Ilion, New York". Approximately 2,500 were manufactured between 1860 and 1862. **NOTE:** A martially marked example is extremely rare and would be worth approximately 35 percent additional.

NIB	Exc.	V.G.	Good	Fair	Poor
—	6500	4750	2500	1500	500

Remington-Beals Navy Revolver

Similar in appearance to Remington-Beals Army Revolver, but in .36 caliber with a 7.5" octagonal barrel. The first examples of this model were fitted with a loading lever that would not allow the cylinder pin to be completely removed. These examples are worth approximately 80 percent more than the standard model. Approximately 1,000 of these revolvers were purchased by the United States government and martially marked examples are worth approximately 40 percent more than the values listed below. Manufactured from 1860 to 1862 with a total production of approximately 15,000.

Courtesy Wallis & Wallis, Lewes, Sussex, England

NIB	Exc.	V.G.	Good	Fair	Poor
—	6500	4750	2500	1500	500

1861 Army Revolver

A .44 caliber percussion revolver with an 8" octagonal barrel and 6-shot cylinder. The loading lever is cut with a slot so that the cylinder pin can be drawn forward without the lever being lowered. Blued, case hardened with walnut grips. The barrel marked "Patented Dec. 17, 1861 Manufactured by Remington's, Ilion, N.Y." Some examples were converted to .46 caliber rimfire cartridge and would be worth approximately 25 percent more than the original, martially marked, standard percussion model. Approximately 12,000 were manufactured in 1862. This model is also known as the "Old Army Model".

Paul Goodwin photo

NIB	Exc.	V.G.	Good	Fair	Poor
—	7000	4750	2000	1000	500

1861 Navy Revolver

As above, but .36 caliber with a 7.25" octagonal barrel. Blued, case hardened with walnut grips. This model is also found altered to .38 metallic cartridge. Cartridge examples are worth approximately 35 percent less than the percussion versions. Approximately 8,000 were manufactured in 1862. **NOTE:** Add 25 percent for martial.

Paul Goodwin photo

NIB	Exc.	V.G.	Good	Fair	Poor
—	6000	5000	2500	1500	500

New Model Army Revolver

A .44 caliber 6-shot percussion revolver with an 8" octagonal barrel. Blued, case hardened with walnut grips. The barrel marked "Patented Sept. 14, 1858 E. Remington & Sons, Ilion, New York, U.S.A. New Model". Approximately 132,000 were made between 1863 and 1873.

Standard Model—Military Version

NIB	Exc.	V.G.	Good	Fair	Poor
—	7000	5750	3750	1800	400

Civilian Model—No Government Inspector's Markings

NIB	Exc.	V.G.	Good	Fair	Poor
—	6000	5000	3000	1000	400

.44 or .46 Cartridge Conversion

Courtesy Milwaukee Public Museum, Milwaukee, Wisconsin

NIB	Exc.	V.G.	Good	Fair	Poor
—	4800	3000	1400	875	400

New Model Navy Revolver

As above, but .36 caliber with a 7.23" octagonal barrel. Approximately 22,000 were made between 1863 and 1875.

Courtesy Milwaukee Public Museum, Milwaukee, Wisconsin

Military Version

NIB	Exc.	V.G.	Good	Fair	Poor
—	6200	5000	3200	1500	400

Civilian Version

NIB	Exc.	V.G.	Good	Fair	Poor
—	5200	4000	2400	1000	400

.38 Cartridge Conversion—1873 to 1888

NIB	Exc.	V.G.	Good	Fair	Poor
—	4200	2400	1000	450	300

New Model Single-Action Belt Revolver

As above, but with a 6.5" barrel. Blued or nickel-plated, case hardened with walnut grips. This model is sometimes encountered altered to .38 cartridge. Cartridge examples are worth approximately 25 percent less than the values listed below. Approximately 3,000 were made between 1863 and 1873. **NOTE:** Blued models will command a premium.

Paul Goodwin photo

NIB	Exc.	V.G.	Good	Fair	Poor
—	4800	3000	1500	1000	500

Remington-Rider Double-Action Belt Revolver

A double-action .36 caliber percussion revolver with a 6.5" octagonal barrel marked, "Manufactured by Remington's, Ilion, N.Y. Rider's Pt. Aug. 17, 1858, May 3, 1859". Blued or nickel-plated, case hardened with walnut grips. This model is also found converted to cartridge and such examples would be worth approximately 20 percent less than the values listed below. Several hundred of this model were made with fluted cylinders and are worth a premium of about 25 percent. Approximately 5,000 were made between 1863 and 1873.

Courtesy Milwaukee Public Museum, Milwaukee, Wisconsin

NIB	Exc.	V.G.	Good	Fair	Poor
—	4500	2750	1500	900	400

New Model Police Revolver

A .36 caliber percussion revolver with octagonal barrels ranging from 3.5" to 6.5" and with a 5-shot cylinder. Blued or nickel-plated, case hardened with walnut grips. This model is also found converted to cartridge and such examples would be worth approximately 20 percent less than the values listed below. Approximately 18,000 were manufactured between 1863 and 1873. **NOTE:** Blued models will command a premium.

Paul Goodwin photo

NIB	Exc.	V.G.	Good	Fair	Poor
—	4200	3000	2000	800	300

New Model Pocket Revolver

A .31 caliber spur trigger percussion revolver with octagonal barrels ranging from 3" to 4.5" in length and a 5-shot cylinder. Blued or nickel-plated, case hardened, walnut grips. The barrel marked, "Patented Sept. 14, 1858, March 17, 1863 E. Remington & Sons, Ilion, New York U.S.A. New Model.". Approximately 25,000 were manufactured between 1863 and 1873. **NOTE:** Add 15 percent for blued models.

1st Version

Brass frame and trigger.

NIB	Exc.	V.G.	Good	Fair	Poor
—	4200	3200	1800	1300	300

2nd Version

Iron frame, brass trigger.

NIB	Exc.	V.G.	Good	Fair	Poor
—	—	2750	1400	900	300

3rd Version

Iron frame, iron trigger.

NIB	Exc.	V.G.	Good	Fair	Poor
—	—	2400	1200	800	300

.32 Cartridge Conversion

NIB	Exc.	V.G.	Good	Fair	Poor
—	—	2200	1000	600	300

Remington-Rider Derringer

A small, silver-plated brass single-shot .17 caliber percussion pistol with a 3" round barrel. The barrel marked, "Rider's Pt. Sept. 13, 1859". Approximately 1,000 were manufactured between 1860 and 1863. Beware of fakes.

NIB	Exc.	V.G.	Good	Fair	Poor
—	—	6900	3300	975	300

Zig-Zag Derringer

A 6-shot .22 caliber revolving barrel pocket pistol with barrels 3.25" in length. The barrels are cut with zigzag grooves, which are part of the revolving mechanism. The trigger is formed as a ring that when moved forward and rearward turns the barrels and cocks the internal hammer. The barrel group marked "Elliot's Patent Aug. 17, 1858 May 29, 1860" as well as "Manufactured by Remington's Ilion, N.Y." Approximately 1,000 were manufactured in 1861 and 1862.

Paul Goodwin photo

NIB	Exc.	V.G.	Good	Fair	Poor
—	5000	3600	1650	650	300

Remington-Elliot Derringer

A 5-shot .22 or 4-shot .32 caliber pepperbox pistol with a revolving firing pin. Blued or nickel-plated with hard rubber grips. The barrel group marked "Manufactured by E. Remington & Sons, Ilion, N.Y. Elliot's Patents May 19, 1860 - Oct.1, 1861". Approximately 25,000 were manufactured between 1863 and 1888.

5-shot .22 caliber

NIB	Exc.	V.G.	Good	Fair	Poor
—	5000	3600	1500	750	200

4-shot .32 caliber

Courtesy W.P. Hallstein III and son Chip

NIB	Exc.	V.G.	Good	Fair	Poor
—	5000	3600	1500	750	200

Vest Pocket Pistol

A .22 caliber single-shot pistol with a 3.25" barrel. Blued or nickel-plated with walnut grips. The barrel marked "Remington's Ilion, N.Y. Patent Oct. 1, 1861". Early examples have been noted without any barrel markings. Approximately 25,000 were manufactured from 1865 to 1888. **NOTE:** Add a 35 percent premium for blued models.

Paul Goodwin photo

NIB	Exc.	V.G.	Good	Fair	Poor
—	3000	2000	1000	400	200

Large-Bore Vest Pocket Pistol

As above, but in .30, .32 or .41 caliber with barrel lengths of either 3.5" or 4". Blued or nickel-plated with walnut or rosewood grips. The barrel markings as above except for the addition of the patent date, November 15, 1864. The smaller caliber versions are worth approximately 20 percent more than the .41 caliber. Approximately 10,000 were made from 1865 to 1888. **NOTE:** Add a 35 percent premium for blued models.

NIB	Exc.	V.G.	Good	Fair	Poor
—	3300	2200	1200	350	150

Remington-Elliot Single-Shot Derringer

A .41 caliber single-shot pistol with a 2.5" round barrel. Blued or nickel-plated with walnut, ivory or pearl grips. The barrel marked "Remingtons, Ilion, N.Y. Elliot Pat. Aug. 27, 1867". Approximately 10,000 were manufactured between 1867 and 1888. **NOTE:** Add a 35 percent premium for blued models. For all variations of the Remington Over/Under Derringer below, examine closely for broken or cracked barrel hinge and subtract from value accordingly.

NIB	Exc.	V.G.	Good	Fair	Poor
—	3500	2500	1200	400	125

REMINGTON OVER/UNDER DERRINGERS

A double-barrel .41 caliber pocket pistol with 3" round barrels that pivot upward for loading. There is a lock bar to release the barrels on the right side of the frame. The firing pin raises and lowers automatically to fire each respective barrel. It has a spur trigger and bird's-head grip. The finish is either blued or nickel-plated; and it is featured with walnut, rosewood or checkered hard rubber grips. Examples with factory pearl or ivory grips would be worth a small premium. Approximately 150,000 were manufactured between 1866 and 1935.

Courtesy William F. Krause

Early Type I

Manufactured without an extractor, this type is marked "E. Remington & Sons, Ilion, N.Y." on one side and "Elliot's Patent Dec. 12, 1865" on the other side of the barrel rib. Only a few hundred were manufactured in 1866. **NOTE:** Add a 25 percent premium for blued models.

NIB	Exc.	V.G.	Good	Fair	Poor
—	5000	4500	3000	2000	1000

Type I Mid-Production

As above, but fitted with an extractor. Manufactured in the late 1860s. **NOTE:** Add a 25 percent premium for blued models.

NIB	Exc.	V.G.	Good	Fair	Poor
—	3500	2750	1100	550	250

Type I Late Production

Fitted with an automatic extractor and marked on the top of the barrel rib. Manufactured from the late 1860s to 1888. **NOTE:** Add a 25 percent premium for blued models.

NIB	Exc.	V.G.	Good	Fair	Poor
—	4500	3400	2200	1000	200

Type II

Marked "Remington Arms Co., Ilion, N.Y." on the barrel rib. Manufactured between 1888 and 1911. **NOTE:** Add a 25 percent premium for blued models.

NIB	Exc.	V.G.	Good	Fair	Poor
—	2500	1900	1200	600	200

Type III

Marked "Remington Arms - U.M.C. Co., Ilion, N.Y." on the barrel rib. Manufactured between 1912 and 1935. **NOTE:** For Type III models, blue or nickel prices are the same.

NIB	Exc.	V.G.	Good	Fair	Poor
—	1750	1000	875	450	200

Remington-Rider Magazine Pistol

A 5-shot .32 caliber magazine pistol with a spur trigger and 3" octagonal barrel. The magazine is located beneath the barrel and can be loaded from the front. Blued, nickel-plated or case hardened with walnut, pearl or ivory grips. The barrel marked "E. Remington & Sons, Ilion, N.Y. Riders Pat. Aug. 15, 1871". Approximately 10,000 were manufactured between 1871 and 1888. **NOTE:** For blued finish add a 50 percent premium.

NIB	Exc.	V.G.	Good	Fair	Poor
—	3000	1950	825	350	150

Model 1865 Navy Rolling Block Pistol

A spur trigger single-shot rolling block .50 caliber rimfire cartridge pistol with an 8.5" round barrel. Blued, case hardened with walnut grips and fore-end. The barrel marked "Remingtons, Ilion N.Y. U.S.A. Pat. May 3d Nov. 15th, 1864 April 17th, 1866". **NOTE:** Examples bearing military inspection marks are worth approximately 25 percent more than the values listed below. Examples are also to be found altered to centerfire cartridge and these are worth approximately 10 percent less than the values listed below. Approximately 6,500 were manufactured between 1866 and 1870.

NIB	Exc.	V.G.	Good	Fair	Poor
—	6000	4500	3000	1000	400

Model 1867 Navy Rolling Block Pistol

A .50 caliber single-shot rolling block pistol with a 7" round barrel. Blued, case hardened with walnut grips and fore-end. The majority of these pistols were purchased by the United **NOTE:** States government and civilian examples without inspection marks are worth approximately 30 percent more than the values listed.

NIB	Exc.	V.G.	Good	Fair	Poor
—	6000	4500	3000	1000	400

Model 1871 Army Rolling Block Pistol

A .50 caliber rolling block single-shot pistol with an 8" round barrel. Blued, case hardened with walnut grips and fore-end. The distinguishing feature of this model is that it has a rearward extension at the top of the grip and a squared butt. Approximately 6,000 were made between 1872 and 1888. **NOTE:** Engraved ivory-stocked versions, as pictured below, will bring considerable premiums.

NIB	Exc.	V.G.	Good	Fair	Poor
—	3500	2350	1800	875	400

Remington-Smoot No. 1 Revolver

A .30 caliber spur trigger revolver with a 2.75" octagonal barrel and 5-shot fluted cylinder. Blued or nickel-plated with walnut or hard rubber grips. The barrel rib is marked, "E. Remington & Sons, Ilion, N.Y. Pat. W. S. Smoot Oct. 21, 1873". Examples dating from the beginning of production are found with a revolving recoil shield. Such examples would command approximately a 300 percent premium over the values listed. **NOTE:** For blued finish add a 50 percent premium.

NIB	Exc.	V.G.	Good	Fair	Poor
—	2000	1650	1100	675	250

Remington-Smoot No. 2 Revolver

As above, except in .32 caliber; approximately 20,000 were made between 1878 and 1888. **NOTE:** For blued finish add a 50 percent premium.

NIB	Exc.	V.G.	Good	Fair	Poor
—	1800	875	600	275	100

Remington-Smoot No. 3 Revolver

Two variations of this spur trigger .38 caliber revolver exist. One with a rounded grip and no barrel rib, the other with a squared back, squared butt grip with a barrel rib. Centerfire versions are also known and they are worth approximately 10 percent more than the values listed below. Blued or nickel-plated with hard rubber grips. Approximately 25,000 were made between 1878 and 1888. **NOTE:** For blued finish add a 50 percent premium.

Paul Goodwin photo

NIB	Exc.	V.G.	Good	Fair	Poor
—	1700	650	550	325	100

New No. 4 Revolver

A .38 or .41 caliber spur trigger revolver with a 2.5" barrel and no ejector rod. Blued or nickel-plated with hard rubber grips. The barrel marked "E. Remington & Sons, Ilion, N.Y." Approximately 10,000 were manufactured between 1877 and 1888. **NOTE:** For blued finish add a 50 percent premium.

Paul Goodwin photo

NIB	Exc.	V.G.	Good	Fair	Poor
—	1700	775	475	225	100

Remington Iroquois Revolver

A .22 caliber spur trigger revolver with a 2.25" barrel and 7-shot cylinder. Blued or nickel-plated with hard rubber grips. The barrel marked "Remington, Ilion, N.Y." and "Iroquois". Some examples of this model will be found without the Remington markings. Approximately 10,000 were manufactured between 1878 and 1888. **NOTE:** For blued finish add a 50 percent premium.

NIB	Exc.	V.G.	Good	Fair	Poor
—	2000	1100	825	385	150

Model 1875 Single-Action Army

A .44 Remington or .44-40 or .45 caliber single-action revolver with a 7.5" barrel. Blued or nickel-plated, case hardened with walnut grips. Some examples are to be found fitted with a lanyard ring at the butt. The barrel marked "E. Remington & Sons Ilion, N.Y. U.S.A." Approximately 25,000 were manufactured between 1875 and 1889. **NOTE:** Blued version add 40 percent.

Courtesy Milwaukee Public Museum, Milwaukee, Wisconsin

NIB	Exc.	V.G.	Good	Fair	Poor
—	14000	10000	6000	3000	1000

Model 1890 Single-Action Army

A .44-40 caliber single-action revolver with a 5.5" or 7.5" barrel and 6-shot cylinder. Blued or nickel-plated with hard rubber grips bearing the monogram "RA" at the top. The barrel marked "Remington Arms Co., Ilion, N.Y." Approximately 2,000 were made between 1891 and 1894. Beware of fakes. **NOTE:** Blued version add 40 percent.

Paul Goodwin photo

NIB	Exc.	V.G.	Good	Fair	Poor
—	15000	10000	6000	3000	1000

Model 1891 Target Rolling Block Pistol

A .22, .25 Stevens or .32 S&W caliber single-shot rolling block pistol with a 10" half octagonal barrel fitted with target sights. Blued, case hardened with walnut grips and fore-end. The barrel marked "Remington Arms Co. Ilion, N.Y." and the frame "Remingtons Ilion N.Y. U.S.A. Pat. May 3 Nov. 15, 1864 April 17, 1866 P S". This is an extremely rare pistol, with slightly more than 100 manufactured between 1892 and 1898. Prospective purchasers are advised to secure a qualified appraisal prior to acquisition.

Paul Goodwin photo

NIB	Exc.	V.G.	Good	Fair	Poor
—	4000	3700	2750	1200	500

Model 1901 Target Rolling Block

As above, with the exception that the bridge block thumb piece has been moved out of the line of sight and the rear sight is mounted on the frame instead of the barrel. Approximately 735 were made between 1901 and 1909.

Paul Goodwin photo

NIB	Exc.	V.G.	Good	Fair	Poor
—	4000	3650	2750	1200	500

Mark III Signal Pistol

A 10 gauge spur trigger flare pistol with a 9" round barrel. The frame of brass and the barrel of iron finished matte black with walnut grips. The barrel marked "The Remington Arms - Union Metallic Cartridge Co., Inc. Mark III, Remington Bridgeport Works Bridgeport, Connecticut U.S.A." Approximately 25,000 were manufactured between 1915 and 1918.

Paul Goodwin photo

NIB	Exc.	V.G.	Good	Fair	Poor
—	—	725	375	110	55

Model 51

A .32 or .380 caliber semi-automatic pistol with a 3.5" barrel and magazines capable of holding either 7 or 8 cartridges depending on the caliber. Blued with hard rubber grips having the legend "Remington UMC" in a circle at the top. The slide marked "The Remington Arms - Union Metallic Cartridge Co., Inc. Remington Ilion Wks. Ilion, N.Y. U.S.A. Pedersen's Patents Pending". Later versions carried a 1920 and a 1921 patent date. The early examples have nine grooves on the slide; later models have 15 grooves with the frame marked "Remington Trademark". **NOTE:** Early variations are worth approximately 10 percent more than the values listed below and .32 caliber examples are worth approximately 25 percent additional. Approximately 65,000 were manufactured between 1918 and 1934.

Courtesy Orvel Reichert

NIB	Exc.	V.G.	Good	Fair	Poor
—	750	575	350	125	75

Model 53

Built in 1917 in .45 ACP for the U.S. government test. Similar to the Model 51 except for size and an external hammer. Tested by the US Army and Navy. Overall length is 8.25", weight is about 35 oz., and magazine capacity is 7 rounds. Too rare to price.

Courtesy James Rankin

1911R1 SERIES

Model 1911R1

Combines traditional 1911 features with modern touches. Caliber .45 ACP, carbon steel slide and frame, traditionally styled trigger, hammer, recoil system, walnut grips, 7-round magazine, thumb and grip safeties. Dovetailed front and rear sights with white dots, lowered and flared ejection port. Weight 38.5 oz., 5" barrel and Satin Black Oxide or stainless finish. Model 1911 Enhanced model has match-grade barrel and bushing, front cocking serrations, extended thumb safety and beavertail tang, textured grips, adjustable rear and fiber optic front sights and lightweight trigger and hammer. Introduced 2010. **NOTE:** Add 30 percent for Enhanced model.

NIB	Exc.	V.G.	Good	Fair	Poor
600	525	435	350	200	150

Model 1911R1 Centennial

Same features as 1911R1 but with special Centennial engravings on the slide, a Centennial serial number range, dovetailed brass-bead front and black serrated rear sight. Custom grips with Remington medallions.

Model 1911R1 Centennial Limited Edition

NIB	Exc.	V.G.	Good	Fair	Poor
1100	925	800	600	—	—

Same features as above with uniquely engraved slide with gold banner, custom charcoal blued finish, 24-karat gold front sight, smooth exhibition grade walnut grips. Each Limited Edition model is hand assembled and comes in a custom wood presentation case. Introduced in 2011 with production scheduled for only 300 units.

NIB	Exc.	V.G.	Good	Fair	Poor
2000	1900	1800	—	—	—

RIFLES

Model 1841 "Mississippi Rifle"

A .54 caliber percussion rifle with a 33" barrel and full stock secured by two barrel bands. The lock (marked Remington's Herkimer N.Y.) is case hardened, the barrel browned and the furniture of brass. The stock is fitted with a brass patch box on the right side. Approximately 20,000 were made between 1846 and 1855.

Paul Goodwin photo

NIB	Exc.	V.G.	Good	Fair	Poor
—	—	2000	1750	750	400

Model 1861 U.S. Rifle Musket

A .58 caliber percussion rifle with a 40" barrel and full length stock secured by three barrel bands. The lock marked "Remington's Ilion, N.Y." Finished in the white with a walnut stock. Approximately 40,000 were made between 1864 and 1866.

Paul Goodwin photo

NIB	Exc.	V.G.	Good	Fair	Poor
—	4500	3000	1250	500	200

Model 1863 Zouave Rifle

A .58 caliber percussion rifle with a 33" barrel and full length stock secured by two barrel bands. The lock case hardened and marked "Remington's Ilion N.Y.". The barrel blued and the furniture of brass. Approximately 12,500 were manufactured between 1862 and 1865.

Paul Goodwin photo

NIB	Exc.	V.G.	Good	Fair	Poor
—	6000	4000	2250	1500	500

Breech-Loading Carbine

A .46 or .50 rimfire single-shot rolling block carbine with a 20" barrel. Blued, case hardened with a walnut stock. The tang marked "Remington's Ilion, N.Y. Pat. Dec. 23, 1863 May 3 & Nov. 16, 1864". The .50 caliber version is worth approximately 15 percent more than the .46 caliber. Approximately 15,000 .50-caliber variations were made, most of which were sold to France. Approximately 5,000 carbines were made in .46 caliber. Manufactured from 1864 to 1866.

NIB	Exc.	V.G.	Good	Fair	Poor
—	—	3750	1500	500	200

Revolving Rifle

A .36 or. 44 caliber revolving rifle with either 24" or 28" octagonal barrels with a 6-shot cylinder. The trigger guard formed with a scrolled finger extension at the rear. Blued, case hardened with a walnut stock. These rifles are also encountered converted to cartridge and would be worth approximately 20 percent less than the percussion values listed below. The barrel marked "Patented Sept. 14, 1858 E. Remington & Sons, Ilion, New York, U.S.A. New Model". The .44 caliber model will bring a premium of about 15 percent and is rare. Approximately 1,000 were manufactured between 1866 and 1879.

Courtesy Buffalo Bill Historical Center, Cody, Wyoming

Courtesy Milwaukee Public Museum, Milwaukee, Wisconsin

NIB	Exc.	V.G.	Good	Fair	Poor
—	20000	11500	8000	5500	900

Remington-Beals Rifle

A .32 or .38 caliber sliding barrel single-shot rifle with octagonal barrels of 24", 26" or 28" length. The barrel can be moved forward by lowering the trigger guard/lever. This model is to be found with either frames made of brass or iron, the latter being worth approximately 20 percent more than the values listed below. Walnut stock. The barrel marked "Beals Patent June 28, 1864 Jan. 30, 1866 E. Remington & Sons, Ilion, New York.".Approximately 800 were manufactured between 1866 and 1888. A few examples are known to have been factory engraved. Prospective purchasers are advised to secure a qualified appraisal prior to acquisition.

Courtesy Milwaukee Public Museum, Milwaukee, Wisconsin

NIB	Exc.	V.G.	Good	Fair	Poor
—	2500	1500	950	400	150

U.S. Navy Rolling Block Carbine

NIB	Exc.	V.G.	Good	Fair	Poor
—	4000	3250	2750	1000	350

Model 1867 Navy Cadet Rifle

NIB	Exc.	V.G.	Good	Fair	Poor
—	3500	2750	1400	700	350

Rolling Block Military Rifles

NIB	Exc.	V.G.	Good	Fair	Poor
—	—	900	750	400	100

NO. 1 ROLLING BLOCK SPORTING RIFLE
Standard No. 1 Sporting Rifle

A single-shot rolling block rifle produced in a variety of calibers from .40-50 to .50-70 centerfire as well as .32, .44 and .46 rimfire. Standard barrel lengths were either 28" or 30" and of octagonal form.

Courtesy Milwaukee Public Museum, Milwaukee, Wisconsin

NIB	Exc.	V.G.	Good	Fair	Poor
—	4000	3500	2500	1500	500

Long-Range Creedmoor Rifle

A .44-90, .44-100 or .44-105 caliber rolling block rifle with a 34" half-octagonal barrel, long-range vernier tang sights and globe front sights. Blued, case hardened with a walnut stock and a checkered pistol grip. This rifle was available with a number of optional features and a qualified appraisal should be secured if those features are in doubt. Produced from 1873 to 1890.

Courtesy Bonhams & Butterfields, San Francisco, California

NIB	Exc.	V.G.	Good	Fair	Poor
—	10000	8500	5750	2500	500

Mid-Range Target Rifle

As above, except chambered for .40-70, .44-77, .45-70 or .50-70 caliber with 28" or 30" half-octagonal barrels. Produced from 1875 to 1890.

NIB	Exc.	V.G.	Good	Fair	Poor
—	—	6000	2750	1750	300

Short-Range Rifle

As above, chambered for cartridges between .38 and .44 caliber with 26" or 30" round or octagonal barrels. Open rear sight with beach front sight. The walnut stock is checkered. Produced from 1875 to 1890.

NIB	Exc.	V.G.	Good	Fair	Poor
—	—	5000	2750	1675	250

Black Hills Rifle

As above, in .45-60 caliber with a 28" round barrel fitted with open sights and a plain straight grip stock. Produced from 1877 to 1882.

NIB	Exc.	V.G.	Good	Fair	Poor
—	—	5000	2750	1675	250

Shotgun

As above, in 16 gauge with either a 30" or 32" Damascus or fluid steel barrels. Produced from 1870 to 1892.

NIB	Exc.	V.G.	Good	Fair	Poor
—	2800	1650	1200	750	150

Baby Carbine

As above, with a 20" thin round barrel chambered for the .44-40 cartridge and fitted with a saddle ring on the left side of the frame. Blued, case hardened with a walnut stock and a carbine buttplate. Manufactured from 1892 to 1902.

NIB	Exc.	V.G.	Good	Fair	Poor
—	8000	4250	2250	900	200

Model 1-1/2 Sporting Rifle

A lightweight variation of the above using a 1.25" wide, No. 1 rolling block action. Chambered for rimfire cartridges from .22 to the .38 Extra Long, as well as centerfire cartridges from .32-20 to the .44-40. Medium weight octagonal barrels from 24" to 28" in length, with open rear and a blade-type front sight. Blued, case hardened with a walnut stock. There were several thousand manufactured between 1888 and 1897.

Paul Goodwin photo

NIB	Exc.	V.G.	Good	Fair	Poor
—	2800	2000	950	400	100

Model 2 Sporting Rifle

As above, using a No. 2 action and chambered for various cartridges from .22 to .38 caliber with 24" or 26" octagonal barrels. Blued, case hardened with a walnut stock. This model was produced with a number of optional features that affect its value. Prospective purchasers are advised to secure a qualified appraisal prior to acquisition. Manufactured from 1873 to 1910.

Paul Goodwin photo

NIB	Exc.	V.G.	Good	Fair	Poor
—	2400	1500	600	250	100

No. 4 Rolling Block Rifle

Built on the lightweight No. 4 action, this rifle was available in .22, .25 Stevens or .32 caliber, with either a 22.5" or 24" octagonal

barrel. Blued, case hardened with a walnut stock. A takedown version was also made and these are worth approximately 10 percent more than the values listed. Approximately 50,000 were made between 1890 and 1933.

NIB	Exc.	V.G.	Good	Fair	Poor
—	900	700	400	200	75

Model No. 4 S Military Rifle

At the request of the United States Boy Scouts in 1913, the Remington Company designed a military style rifle having a 28" barrel and full length fore-end secured by one barrel band. A short upper hand guard was also fitted and a bayonet stud is to be found at the muzzle. In 1915 the designation of this model was changed from "Boy Scout" to "Military Model". Approximately 15,000 were made between 1913 and 1923.

Paul Goodwin photo

NIB	Exc.	V.G.	Good	Fair	Poor
—	—	2250	950	400	275

No. 5 Rolling Block Rifle

Built on the No. 5 action, this rifle was designed for smokeless cartridges and was made in a variety of barrel lengths, calibers and in a carbine version. Blued, case hardened with a walnut stock.

NIB	Exc.	V.G.	Good	Fair	Poor
—	—	2250	800	350	100

No. 5 Sporting or Target Rifle

Chambered for the .30-30, .303 British, 7mm, .30 U.S., .32-40, .32 U.S. and the .38-55 cartridges. This rifle was offered with 28" or 30" round barrels and features a plain, straight-grip stock with a half-length fore-end. It has open rear sights and was available with double-set triggers that would add approximately 10 percent to the value. It was manufactured between 1898 and 1905.

NIB	Exc.	V.G.	Good	Fair	Poor
—	—	5750	2250	850	300

Model 1897

A 7x57mm and .30 U.S. caliber full stock rolling block rifle. The Model 1902 is of identical form except that it was fitted with an automatic ejector. Manufactured from 1897 to 1902.

Paul Goodwin photo

NIB	Exc.	V.G.	Good	Fair	Poor
—	2800	1250	550	250	100

Carbine

As above, fitted with a 20" round barrel and a half-length fore-end secured by one barrel band.

NIB	Exc.	V.G.	Good	Fair	Poor
—	—	1750	750	350	100

No. 6 Rolling Block Rifle

A lightweight, small rifle designed expressly to be used by young boys. It is chambered for the .22 rimfire cartridge, as well as the

.32 Short or Long. It was also produced with a smoothbore barrel to be used with shot cartridges. The round barrel is 20" in length. It has a takedown action with a barrel held on by a knurled knob underneath the frame. It is a lightweight rolling block, with a thin operating knob on the breech. The finish is blued overall. Early models featured a case-colored frame and these versions would be worth approximately 10 percent additional. It has a straight-grip walnut stock with a small forearm. Over 250,000 manufactured between 1902 and 1903.

Paul Goodwin photo

NIB	Exc.	V.G.	Good	Fair	Poor
—	750	475	300	100	75

No. 7 Rolling Block Rifle

Readily identifiable by its accentuated checked pistol grip, this model was available in .22 or .25-10 Stevens caliber with 24", 26" or 28" half octagonal barrels. Fitted with a tang mounted aperture rear sight. Blued, case hardened with a walnut stock. Approximately 1,000 were made between 1903 and 1911.

NIB	Exc.	V.G.	Good	Fair	Poor
—	6500	5000	3000	2000	500

REMINGTON-HEPBURN RIFLES

Remington-Hepburn No. 3 Rifle

A lever activated falling block single-shot rifle designed by Lewis Hepburn available in a variety of calibers from .22 Winchester centerfire to .50-90 Sharps with octagonal or round barrels of 26", 28" or 30" length. Blued, case hardened with a walnut stock. This model was available with a variety of optional features that affect the value considerably. Prospective purchasers are advised to secure a qualified appraisal prior to acquisition. Approximately 10,000 were made between 1883 and 1907.

NIB	Exc.	V.G.	Good	Fair	Poor
—	—	4000	2000	1200	300

Remington-Hepburn No. 3 Match Rifle

As above, but fitted with a high comb buttstock and a nickel-plated Schuetzen buttplate. Manufactured in various calibers from .25-20 Stevens to .40-65 with 30" half octagonal barrels. This model was made in two versions: "A Quality" with a plain stock, tang mounted rear sight and a Beach front sight and; "B Quality" with a checkered walnut stock having a cheek rest, checkered fore-end, vernier rear sight and a combination wind gauge and spirit level front sight. Double set triggers were also available and these would add approximately 10 percent to the values listed below. Approximately 1,000 were made between 1883 and 1907.

A Quality

Paul Goodwin photo

NIB	Exc.	V.G.	Good	Fair	Poor
—	—	7500	4750	1800	350

B Quality

Paul Goodwin photo

NIB	Exc.	V.G.	Good	Fair	Poor
—	—	8250	5000	1900	500

Remington-Hepburn No. 3 Long-Range Creedmoor Rifle

As above, in .44 caliber with a 32" or 34" half-octagonal barrel, long-range vernier rear sight, combination wind gauge and spirit level front sight, deluxe checkered walnut stock and a rubber shotgun buttplate. Produced with a number of optional features that affect the value. Prospective purchasers are advised to secure a qualified appraisal prior to acquisition. Manufactured from 1880 to 1907.

Paul Goodwin photo

NIB	Exc.	V.G.	Good	Fair	Poor
—	—	7500	4750	1800	350

Remington-Hepburn No. 3 Mid-Range Creedmoor Rifle

As above, but chambered for the .40-65 cartridge and fitted with a 28" barrel.

NIB	Exc.	V.G.	Good	Fair	Poor
—	—	5000	2250	950	350

Remington-Hepburn No. 3 Long-Range Military Rifle

This is a rare variation that is chambered for the .44-20 Remington cartridge. It has a round 34" barrel and a full-length forearm held on by two barrel bands. The finish is blued, case-colored and the stock is walnut. There are two basic versions. The plain grade has an uncheckered, straight-grip stock with military-type sights. There is also a fancy grade that features a high-grade, checkered, pistol-grip stock with a full-length, checkered fore-end, vernier tang sight and wind gauge and spirit lever front sight. There were a few manufactured in the 1880s.

Paul Goodwin photo

Plain Grade

NIB	Exc.	V.G.	Good	Fair	Poor
—	6000	4500	2500	1200	400

Fancy Grade

NIB	Exc.	V.G.	Good	Fair	Poor
—	9000	7500	3750	1500	600

Remington-Hepburn No. 3 Schuetzen Match Rifle

As above, with the exception that instead of the side lever, the action is raised or lowered by means of the lever on the trigger guard. Chambered for various popular cartridges and offered with a 30" or 32" part-octagonal, heavy barrel. It features a vernier tang sight with a hooded front sight. It was standard with double-set triggers and a palm rest. The finish is blued and case-colored, with a high-grade checkered walnut stock and fore-end. It has an ornate, Swiss-type Schuetzen buttplate and is also known as the "Walker-Hepburn Rifle". There were two versions available. One, a standard breechloader with the Remington Walker-marked barrel; the other, a muzzleloading variation that was fitted with a removable false muzzle. This version was supplied with a brass bullet starter and other accessories. Prospective purchasers are advised to secure a qualified appraisal prior to acquisition.

Breechloading Version

NIB	Exc.	V.G.	Good	Fair	Poor
—	—	27500	12500	3500	900

Muzzleloading Version

NIB	Exc.	V.G.	Good	Fair	Poor
—	—	42500	17500	5000	1500

Remington-Hepburn No. 3 High-Power Rifle

The Model No. 3 was also made available in a variety of smokeless cartridges: .30-30, .30-40, .32 Special, .32-40 and .38-55. Standard barrel lengths were 26", 28" or 30". Produced from 1900 to 1907.

NIB	Exc.	V.G.	Good	Fair	Poor
—	4000	2500	1750	650	250

REMINGTON-KEENE MAGAZINE RIFLE

A bolt-action rifle chambered for the .40, .43 and .45-70 centerfire cartridges with 22", 24.5", 29.25" or 32.5" barrels. It is readily identifiable by the exposed hammer at the end of the bolt. Blued, case hardened hammer and furniture, with a walnut stock. The receiver marked "E. Remington & Sons, Ilion, N.Y." together with the patent dates 1874, 1876 and 1877. The magazine on this rifle was located beneath the barrel and the receiver is fitted with a cut-off so that the rifle could be used as a single-shot. Approximately 5,000 rifles were made between 1880 and 1888 in the variations listed.

Sporting Rifle

24.5" barrel.

Paul Goodwin photos

Remington-Keene Repeating Sporting Rifle Fancy Grade

NIB	Exc.	V.G.	Good	Fair	Poor
—	3450	2000	750	350	150

Army Rifle

Barrel length 32.5" with a full-length stock secured by two barrel bands.

NIB	Exc.	V.G.	Good	Fair	Poor
—	—	3500	950	450	

Navy Rifle

As above, with a 29.25" barrel.

NIB	Exc.	V.G.	Good	Fair	Poor
—	—	4500	1750	450	

Carbine

As above, with a 22" barrel and a half-length fore-end secured by one barrel band.

NIB	Exc.	V.G.	Good	Fair	Poor
—	—	5750	3250	1250	350

Frontier Model (aka Indiana Scout Carbine)

As above, with a 24" barrel and half-length fore-end secured by one barrel band. Those purchased by the United States Department of the Interior for arming the Indian Police are marked "U.S.I.D." on the receiver.

NIB	Exc.	V.G.	Good	Fair	Poor
—	—		5250	2500	850

REMINGTON-LEE RIFLES

Remington-Lee Magazine Rifle

Designed by James Paris Lee, rifles of this type were originally manufactured by the Sharps Rifle Company in 1880. The Remington Company began production of this model in 1881 after the Sharps Company ceased operations. Approximately 100,000 Lee magazine rifles were made between 1880 and 1907. Their variations are listed.

Remington-Lee Model 1879 Sharps Mfg.

Barrel length 28" with a full-length stock secured by two barrel bands. The barrel marked "Sharps Rifle Co. Bridgeport, Conn." and "Old Reliable" in a rectangular cartouche. Approximately 300 were made prior to 1881.

NIB	Exc.	V.G.	Good	Fair	Poor
—	—	4750	3000	2000	600

Remington-Lee Model 1879 U.S. Navy Model

NIB	Exc.	V.G.	Good	Fair	Poor
—	—	2250	1600	750	250

Remington-Lee Model 1879 Sporting Rifle

Barrel length 28" or 30", .45-70 or .45-90 caliber, checkered pistol-grip stock with a sporting-style fore-end. Markings on the receiver as above. Approximately 450 made.

NIB	Exc.	V.G.	Good	Fair	Poor
—	—	2500	1750	700	250

Remington-Lee Model 1879 Military Rifle

Identical to the Navy model, except chambered for the .43 Spanish cartridge. A limited number were also produced in .45-70 caliber. The Spanish versions are worth approximately 25 percent less than the values listed below. Approximately 1,000 were made. The majority of these rifles were made for export.

NIB	Exc.	V.G.	Good	Fair	Poor
—	—	1250	750	500	150

Remington-Lee Model 1882 Army Contract

NIB	Exc.	V.G.	Good	Fair	Poor
—	—	2000	1250	750	300

Remington-Lee Model 1885 Navy Contract

NIB	Exc.	V.G.	Good	Fair	Poor
—	—	2400	1750	750	300

Remington-Lee Model 1882 & 1885 Military Rifles

Barrel length 32", full-length stock secured by two barrel bands, chambered for .42 Russian, .43 Spanish, .45 Gardner or .45-70 cartridges. The values for those rifles not in .45-70 caliber would be approximately 25 percent less than those listed. Approximately 10,000 Model 1882 rifles were made and 60,000 Model 1885 rifles. The two models can be differentiated by the fact that the cocking piece on the bolt of the Model 1885 is larger. The majority of these rifles were made for foreign contracts and commercial sales.

NIB	Exc.	V.G.	Good	Fair	Poor
—	—	1795	950	400	150

Remington-Lee Model 1882 & 1885 Sporting Rifle

As above, chambered for .45-70 and .45-90 caliber with 26" or 30" octagonal barrels and walnut sporting stocks. Approximately 200 were made.

NIB	Exc.	V.G.	Good	Fair	Poor
—	—	2400	1750	750	200

Remington-Lee Model 1882 & 1885 Carbine

As above, with a 24" barrel and a half-length fore-end secured by one barrel band. Prospective purchasers are advised to secure a qualified appraisal prior to acquisition.

NIB	Exc.	V.G.	Good	Fair	Poor
—	—	2400	1750	750	200

Remington-Lee Model 1899

Designed for use with smokeless and rimless cartridges, this model is marked on the receiver "Remington Arms Co. Ilion, N.Y. Patented Aug. 26th 1884 Sept. 9th 1884 March 17th 1885 Jan 18th 1887". Produced from 1889 to 1907 in the variations listed.

Military Rifle

NIB	Exc.	V.G.	Good	Fair	Poor
—	—	1250	500	200	100

Military Carbine

NIB	Exc.	V.G.	Good	Fair	Poor
—	—	1750	700	300	100

Remington-Lee Sporting Rifle

As above, with a 24", 26" or 28" round or octagonal barrel and a half-length sporting stock with a checkered pistol grip. Approximately 7,000 were manufactured.

NIB	Exc.	V.G.	Good	Fair	Poor
—	—	1250	500	200	100

Remington Lebel Bolt-Action Rifle

NIB	Exc.	V.G.	Good	Fair	Poor
—	—	750	450	150	100

Remington Mosin-Nagant Bolt-Action Rifle

NIB	Exc.	V.G.	Good	Fair	Poor
—	—	600	300	100	75

U.S. Model 1917 Magazine Rifle

NIB	Exc.	V.G.	Good	Fair	Poor
—	—	1250	600	150	100

Remington-Whitmore Model 1874

A sidelock double-barrel shotgun, combination shotgun/rifle or double-barrel rifle with 28" or 30" fluid steel barrels. Also available with Damascus barrels. The barrels released by pushing forward the top lever. Blued, case hardened with a straight or semi-pistol grip walnut stock. The barrels marked "A. E. Whitmore's Patent Aug. 8, 1871, April 16, 1872". The rib between the barrels is marked "E. Remington & Sons, Ilion, N.Y." Several thousand were manufactured between 1874 and 1882.

Shotgun

NIB	Exc.	V.G.	Good	Fair	Poor
—	—	1750	850	450	100

Combination Gun (Rare)

NIB	Exc.	V.G.	Good	Fair	Poor
—	—	4250	3200	1500	300

Double Rifle

Very rare.

NIB	Exc.	V.G.	Good	Fair	Poor
—	—	9000	4250	1500	500

Model 1882 Shotgun

A sidelock double-barrel 10 or 12 gauge shotgun with 28" or 30" fluid steel or Damascus barrels. Blued, case hardened with a checkered pistol grip stock and hard rubber buttplate. The barrels are marked "E. Remington & Sons, Ilion, N.Y." and the lock is marked "Remington Arms Co." This model has a conventional top lever that moves to the side. Offered with optional engraving and such models should be individually appraised. Approximately 7,500 were manufactured between 1882 and 1889.

NIB	Exc.	V.G.	Good	Fair	Poor
—	—	1250	750	300	100

Model 1883 through 1889 Shotgun

A sidelock 10, 12 or 16 gauge double-barrel shotgun with fluid steel or Damascus barrels 28" to 32" in length. The models 1883, 1885, 1887 and 1889 are all somewhat alike, varying only in the form of their hammers and internal mechanisms. Blued, case hardened, checkered pistol-grip stock with a grip cap. Available in a variety of styles including highly engraved models that should be individually appraised. Approximately 30,000 were made between 1883 and 1909.

NIB	Exc.	V.G.	Good	Fair	Poor
—	—	1800	1100	800	200

Model 1893 (No. 9)

Single-barrel hammer gun in 10, 12, 16, 20, 24 and 28 gauge. Barrel lengths from 28" to 34". Case colored frame with hard rubber buttplate.

Courtesy William F. Krause

NIB	Exc.	V.G.	Good	Fair	Poor
—	—	—	600	250	100

Hammerless Shotgun Model 1894

A boxlock 10, 12 or 16 gauge double shotgun with fluid steel or Damascus barrels 26" to 32" in length. Blued, case hardened with a pistol-grip stock. Available in a variety of styles and it is advised that highly engraved examples should be individually appraised. **NOTE:** Fluid steel barrels add 25 percent premium.

NIB	Exc.	V.G.	Good	Fair	Poor
—	1750	1250	750	300	100

Model 1900 Shotgun

As above, in 12 and 16 gauge only. The same cautions apply to highly engraved examples.

NIB	Exc.	V.G.	Good	Fair	Poor
—	1500	1000	600	250	100

Model 8 Rifle

A .25, .30, .32 or .35 Remington semi-automatic rifle featuring a 22" barrel with open sights. The barrel is covered by a full-length tube that encloses the recoil spring. Blued with walnut stock. Approximately 60,000 were made between 1906 and 1936 in the styles listed. **NOTE:** Add 35 percent for .25 Remington. Some collectors will pay and demand, prices substantially in excess of those listed below for Grades C, D and E

Standard Grade

Courtesy Remington Arms

NIB	Exc.	V.G.	Good	Fair	Poor
1200	900	700	550	250	125

Model 8A

Checkered stock.

NIB	Exc.	V.G.	Good	Fair	Poor
1400	1000	800	600	300	150

Model 8C

NIB	Exc.	V.G.	Good	Fair	Poor
3000	2500	1500	900	500	300

8D Peerless

Light engraving.

NIB	Exc.	V.G.	Good	Fair	Poor
6000	5000	3500	1750	800	400

8E Expert

NIB	Exc.	V.G.	Good	Fair	Poor
7500	6000	4000	2250	1100	450

8F Premier

Heavily engraved.

Paul Goodwin photo

NIB	Exc.	V.G.	Good	Fair	Poor
10000	8500	7500	3750	1600	700

Model 81 Woodsmaster

An improved variation of the Model 8, chambered for the same calibers (but not the .25 apparently) as well as the .300 Savage cartridge. Produced from 1936 to 1950 in the styles listed. **NOTE:** Add 300 percent for police model with detachable 15-round magazine.

Standard Grade

NIB	Exc.	V.G.	Good	Fair	Poor
1100	900	750	500	250	125

Model 81A

NIB	Exc.	V.G.	Good	Fair	Poor
1200	1000	850	500	250	125

81D Peerless

Engraved.

NIB	Exc.	V.G.	Good	Fair	Poor
7500	6000	4000	2250	1100	450

81F Premier

Heavily engraved.

NIB	Exc.	V.G.	Good	Fair	Poor
10000	8500	7500	3750	1600	700

Model 12 or 12A

A .22 caliber slide-action rifle with a 22" round or octagonal barrel having open sights. Blued with a walnut stock. Manufactured from 1909 to 1936 in the styles listed.

Model 12A

NIB	Exc.	V.G.	Good	Fair	Poor
1000	800	600	300	225	150

Model 12B

.22 Short, Gallery Model.

NIB	Exc.	V.G.	Good	Fair	Poor
1500	1100	900	700	400	150

Model 12C

24" octagon barrel.

NIB	Exc.	V.G.	Good	Fair	Poor
1200	1000	750	500	300	175

12C N.R.A. Target

Limited production.

NIB	Exc.	V.G.	Good	Fair	Poor
1500	1300	1100	825	500	300

Model 12CS

.22 Remington Special.

NIB	Exc.	V.G.	Good	Fair	Poor
1300	1000	900	700	400	175

12D Peerless

Light engraving.

NIB	Exc.	V.G.	Good	Fair	Poor
6000	5000	3750	1800	1000	500

12E Expert

NIB	Exc.	V.G.	Good	Fair	Poor
8000	7500	4000	2250	1200	800

12F Premier

Heavily engraved.

Paul Goodwin photo

NIB	Exc.	V.G.	Good	Fair	Poor
10000	9000	5250	3150	1500	800

Model 121 and/or 121A

A .22 caliber slide-action rifle with a 24" round barrel. Blued with a walnut stock. Manufactured from 1936 to 1954 in the styles listed.

Standard Grade

NIB	Exc.	V.G.	Good	Fair	Poor
750	600	500	300	175	100

121D Peerless

Engraved.

NIB	Exc.	V.G.	Good	Fair	Poor
6500	5000	3750	1800	1000	500

121F Premier

Heavily engraved.

NIB	Exc.	V.G.	Good	Fair	Poor
9000	7500	5250	3150	1500	800

Model 121S

.22 WRF.

NIB	Exc.	V.G.	Good	Fair	Poor
1100	850	700	400	350	250

121SB—Smoothbore

There are four different variations of this smoothbore rifle. Seek expert advice before a sale.

NIB	Exc.	V.G.	Good	Fair	Poor
1200	1000	800	650	400	300

Model 14 or 14A

A .25, .30, .32 or .35 Remington caliber slide-action rifle with a 22" round barrel and open sights. Blued, plain walnut stock. Manufactured from 1912 to 1936. **NOTE:** Add 85 percent for .25 Remington.

NIB	Exc.	V.G.	Good	Fair	Poor
—	900	750	500	300	200

Model 14R

As above, with an 18.5" barrel.

NIB	Exc.	V.G.	Good	Fair	Poor
—	1500	800	500	300	200

Model 14-1/2

As above, except chambered for the .38-40 or .44-40 cartridge with a 22.5" barrel. A carbine with an 18.5" barrel known as the Model 14-1/2R, would be worth approximately 10 percent more than the values listed. Manufactured from 1912 to 1922.

NIB	Exc.	V.G.	Good	Fair	Poor
—	2000	1250	700	350	250

Model 16

A .22 caliber (Remington Automatic, not interchangeable with anything else) semi-automatic rifle with a 22" barrel and open sights. Blued with a walnut stock. Later production examples were known as the Model 16A. Manufactured from 1914 to 1928.

Courtesy Remington Arms

NIB	Exc.	V.G.	Good	Fair	Poor
1000	900	600	250	125	75

Model 141

A .30, .32 or .35 Remington caliber slide-action rifle with a 24" barrel having open sights. Blued with a plain walnut stock. Later production versions of this rifle were known as the Model 141A. Manufactured from 1936 to 1950.

Courtesy Remington Arms

NIB	Exc.	V.G.	Good	Fair	Poor
1500	1250	800	500	250	175

Model 25

A .25-20 or .32-20 caliber slide-action rifle with a 24" barrel having open sights. Blued with a walnut stock. Later production examples were known as the Model 25A and a carbine version with an 18" barrel as the Model 25R. Manufactured from 1923 to 1936. **NOTE:** For rifles with 18" barrels add 100 percent.

Model 25

NIB	Exc.	V.G.	Good	Fair	Poor
—	1000	750	400	250	200

Model 24

Designed by John M. Browning, this semi-automatic rifle is of .22 caliber with a 19" barrel and open sights. Blued with a walnut pistol grip stock. Later production versions were known as the Model 24A. Produced from 1922 to 1935.

NIB	Exc.	V.G.	Good	Fair	Poor
1200	1000	600	400	200	100

Model 241 Speedmaster

A .22 caliber takedown semi-automatic rifle with a 24" barrel and open sights. Blued with a walnut stock. Later production versions were known as the Model 241A. Approximately 56,000 were made between 1935 and 1949 in the styles listed.

Model 241

NIB	Exc.	V.G.	Good	Fair	Poor
750	550	400	250	200	150

Model 241D Peerless

Engraved.

NIB	Exc.	V.G.	Good	Fair	Poor
6500	5000	3750	1800	1000	500

Model 241E Expert

NIB	Exc.	V.G.	Good	Fair	Poor
8000	7500	4000	2250	1200	800

Model 241F Premier

Heavily engraved.

NIB	Exc.	V.G.	Good	Fair	Poor
10000	9000	5250	3150	1500	800

Model 550A

A .22 Short, Long or LR caliber semi-automatic rifle with a 24" barrel and open sights. Blued with a walnut pistol-grip stock. Approximately 220,000 were made between 1941 and 1971.

NIB	Exc.	V.G.	Good	Fair	Poor
—	350	275	150	100	75

Model 550P

As above, with an aperture rear sight.

NIB	Exc.	V.G.	Good	Fair	Poor
—	375	300	175	125	100

Model 550-2G

As above, except fitted with a shell deflector and a screw eye for securing it to a shooting gallery counter.

NIB	Exc.	V.G.	Good	Fair	Poor
500	400	375	225	135	75

Model 30A "Express"

A sporting rifle using the U.S. Model 1917 Enfield bolt-action chambered for various Remington cartridges as well as the 7x57mm and .30-06 cartridges. Barrel length 22". Checkered walnut stock. A carbine model fitted with a 20" barrel was known as the Model 30R. Manufactured from 1921 to 1940.

NIB	Exc.	V.G.	Good	Fair	Poor
—	950	700	475	175	100

Model 30S

As above, chambered for the .257 Roberts, 7x57 and the .30-06 cartridges. 24" barrel with a Lyman receiver sight. Select checkered walnut stock. Manufactured from 1930 to 1940.

NIB	Exc.	V.G.	Good	Fair	Poor
—	1300	975	495	250	150

Model 41A "Targetmaster"

This is a bolt-action rimfire rifle chambered for the .22 caliber Short, Long and LR. It is fitted with a 27" barrel with an open rear sight and bead front sight. The pistol-grip stock is plain. It was produced from 1936 to 1940.

NIB	Exc.	V.G.	Good	Fair	Poor
—	300	200	150	100	50

Model 41AS

Same as above but chambered for the .22 Remington Special or .22 WRF cartridge.

NIB	Exc.	V.G.	Good	Fair	Poor
—	275	175	125	100	75

Model 41P

Same as Model 41A with the addition of a rear peep sight and hooded front sight.

NIB	Exc.	V.G.	Good	Fair	Poor
—	325	225	175	125	50

Model 41SB

Same as Model 41A except for use with .22 shot cartridge. Barrel is smoothbore.

NIB	Exc.	V.G.	Good	Fair	Poor
—	350	275	195	150	75

Miscellaneous Remington Bolt Action Rimfires, 1930-1970

From 1930 to 1970 the Remington Company produced a variety of single-shot and repeating .22 caliber rifles. The values for these are much the same, consequently, they are listed for reference only.

Model 33	Model 510 X
Model 33 NRA	Model 511 A
Model 34	Model 511 P
Model 34 NRA	Model 511 X
Model 341 A	Model 512 A
Model 341 P	Model 512 P
Model 341 SB	Model 512 X
Model 510	Model 514
Model 510 P	Model 514 P
Model 510 SB	Model 514 BC

Model 510

Courtesy Remington Arms

Model 510 Carbine

Courtesy Remington Arms

NIB	Exc.	V.G.	Good	Fair	Poor
300	250	200	125	75	50

Model 37

A .22 caliber bolt-action magazine target rifle with a heavy 28" barrel featuring target-sights and telescope bases. Blued with a walnut target style stock. Manufactured from 1937 to 1940.

Courtesy Remington Arms

NIB	Exc.	V.G.	Good	Fair	Poor
1200	1000	600	400	300	250

Model 37-1940

As above, with an improved lock, trigger pull and redesigned stock. Manufactured from 1940 to 1954.

Courtesy Remington Arms

NIB	Exc.	V.G.	Good	Fair	Poor
1300	1100	750	500	300	200

Model 504

Introduced in 2004 this .22 caliber bolt action rifle is fitted with a 20" barrel with no sights. American walnut stock with checkering and pistol grip. Satin blue metal finish. Six round flush mounted detachable magazine. Receiver is drilled and tapped for scope mounts. Weight is about 6 lbs. Discontinued 2006.

NIB	Exc.	V.G.	Good	Fair	Poor
650	550	400	300	200	100

Model 504 Custom

Introduced in 2005 this model features a fancy walnut stock.

NIB	Exc.	V.G.	Good	Fair	Poor
1000	850	625	400	225	125

Model 504-T LS HB

Introduced in 2005 this model features a 20" heavy barrel with blued finish. Chambered for the .22 LR or the .17 HMR cartridge. Brown laminate stock with Monte Carlo comb. Weight is about 8.5 lbs.

NIB	Exc.	V.G.	Good	Fair	Poor
800	675	475	275	250	150

Model 541 S Custom

A .22 caliber bolt-action magazine rifle with a 24" barrel. Blued with a scroll engraved receiver and checkered walnut stock having a rosewood pistol grip cap and fore-end tip. Manufactured from 1972 to 1984.

NIB	Exc.	V.G.	Good	Fair	Poor
700	600	500	375	200	125

Model 541T

As above, drilled and tapped for telescopic sights. Introduced in 1986.

NIB	Exc.	V.G.	Good	Fair	Poor
375	275	200	175	125	75

Model 541T Heavy Barrel

This model is the same as the standard 541-T with the exception of a 24" heavy barrel. First introduced in 1993.

NIB	Exc.	V.G.	Good	Fair	Poor
450	350	300	250	200	125

Model 547

High-quality magazine-fed .17 or .22 rimfire sporter with walnut stock, crowned muzzle, tuned rigger and other goodies. Suspiciously similar to the defunct Model 504. A dealer exclusive for 2007.

NIB	Exc.	V.G.	Good	Fair	Poor
1000	775	600	400	275	200

Model 511 Scoremaster

A .22 caliber bolt-action magazine sporting rifle with a 22" barrel. Blued with a walnut stock. Six- round magazine.

NIB	Exc.	V.G.	Good	Fair	Poor
375	325	250	175	125	75

Model 512

Bolt-action .22 rimfire repeater identical to 511 except with tubular magazine located beneath the barrel. Capacity is 15 LR, 17 Long and 22 Short cartridges. Manufactured from 1940 to 1962. All 500 series models (510, 511, 512, 513 and 521) feature a red cocking indicator at the rear of the bolt.

NIB	Exc.	V.G.	Good	Fair	Poor
400	350	275	200	150	100

Model 513 TR Matchmaster

A .22 caliber bolt-action magazine target rifle with a heavy 27" barrel and Redfield aperture rear sight. Blued with a target-style walnut stock. Manufactured from 1940 to 1969.

NIB	Exc.	V.G.	Good	Fair	Poor
500	400	300	200	150	100

Model 513 S

As above, with Marble sights and a checkered walnut sporting-style stock. Manufactured from 1941 to 1956.

NIB	Exc.	V.G.	Good	Fair	Poor
—	750	625	475	375	225

Model 514

A bolt-action single-shot .22 rimfire rifle manufactured from 1948 to 1971. A total of 770,932 were made with standard barrels and sights. Another 5,617 were made with Routledge Bore barrels, which were meant for use only with .22 LR Shot loads and came with a shotgun-style bead front sight. These rifles have a 24" smoothbore barrel with a bore diameter of .22" that opens up to .40 for the last 12". The Routledge Bore Model 514 was never in the Remington catalog and was available only on special order. The design originated with Michigan trap shooter and gunsmith Fred Routledge in 1938. **NOTE:** Add $100 for Routledge barrel.

NIB	Exc.	V.G.	Good	Fair	Poor
300	250	200	125	75	50

Model 521 TL Jr.

A .22 caliber bolt-action magazine target rifle with a heavy 25" barrel and Lyman sights. Blued with a target-style walnut stock. Manufactured from 1947 to 1969.

NIB	Exc.	V.G.	Good	Fair	Poor
400	350	250	175	125	75

Model 760

A slide-action sporting rifle chambered for various popular centerfire cartridges from the .222 up to the .35 Remington cartridge, with a 22" round barrel and open sights. It features a detachable box magazine. Blued with a checkered, walnut, pistol-grip stock. Manufactured between 1952 and 1982. Examples of this rifle chambered for the .222, .223, .244 and the .257 Roberts are worth a premium of 100 to 200 percent over other calibers. This model was produced in the styles listed.

Standard Model

NIB	Exc.	V.G.	Good	Fair	Poor
—	500	395	275	195	150

Carbine

18.5" barrel.

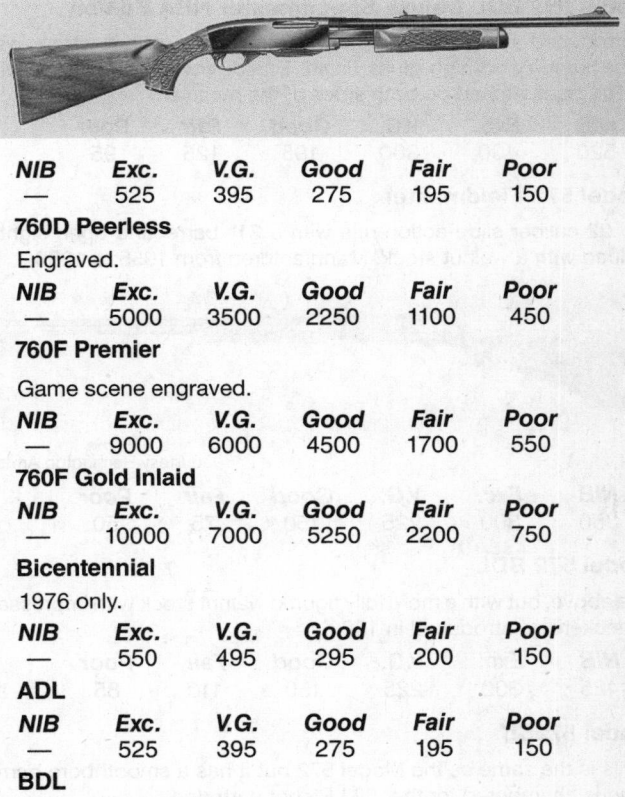

NIB	Exc.	V.G.	Good	Fair	Poor
—	525	395	275	195	150

760D Peerless

Engraved.

NIB	Exc.	V.G.	Good	Fair	Poor
—	5000	3500	2250	1100	450

760F Premier

Game scene engraved.

NIB	Exc.	V.G.	Good	Fair	Poor
—	9000	6000	4500	1700	550

760F Gold Inlaid

NIB	Exc.	V.G.	Good	Fair	Poor
—	10000	7000	5250	2200	750

Bicentennial

1976 only.

NIB	Exc.	V.G.	Good	Fair	Poor
—	550	495	295	200	150

ADL

NIB	Exc.	V.G.	Good	Fair	Poor
—	525	395	275	195	150

BDL

Basketweave checkering.

NIB	Exc.	V.G.	Good	Fair	Poor
—	525	395	275	195	150

Model 552A Speedmaster

A .22 caliber semi-automatic rifle with a 23" barrel and open sights. Blued with a pistol grip walnut stock. Manufactured from 1959 to 1988.

NIB	Exc.	V.G.	Good	Fair	Poor
300	250	225	150	75	50

Model 552 BDL

As above, with a more fully figured stock and impressed checkering. Introduced in 1966.

Courtesy Remington Arms

NIB	Exc.	V.G.	Good	Fair	Poor
425	300	225	150	100	75

Model 552 BDL Deluxe Speedmaster NRA Edition

Introduced in 2005 this model features a walnut stock with checkering and high gloss finish. Blued receiver and barrel with NRA logos etched on both sides of the receiver.

NIB	Exc.	V.G.	Good	Fair	Poor
520	400	300	195	125	95

Model 572 Fieldmaster

A .22 caliber slide-action rifle with a 21" barrel and open sights. Blued with a walnut stock. Manufactured from 1955 to 1988.

Courtesy Remington Arms

NIB	Exc.	V.G.	Good	Fair	Poor
350	300	225	150	75	50

Model 572 BDL

As above, but with a more fully figured walnut stock with impressed checkering. Introduced in 1966.

NIB	Exc.	V.G.	Good	Fair	Poor
425	300	225	150	110	85

Model 572SB

This is the same as the Model 572 but it has a smoothbore barrel and is chambered for the .22 LR shot cartridge.

NIB	Exc.	V.G.	Good	Fair	Poor
325	275	200	125	75	60

Model 572 BDL Smoothbore

Similar to Model 572 but with unrifled barrel for use with shot cartridges. Introduced as a special production item in 2007.

NIB	Exc.	V.G.	Good	Fair	Poor
425	300	225	150	110	85

Model 580

A .22 caliber single-shot bolt-action rifle with a 24" barrel, open sights and a Monte Carlo-style stock. Blued. Manufactured from 1968 to 1978.

Courtesy Remington Arms

NIB	Exc.	V.G.	Good	Fair	Poor
—	250	200	150	75	50

Model 580 BR

Same as above but with 1" shorter buttstock.

NIB	Exc.	V.G.	Good	Fair	Poor
250	200	150	175	75	50

Model 580 SB

This is the same as the Model 580 except with a smoothbore barrel for .22 LR shot cartridges.

NIB	Exc.	V.G.	Good	Fair	Poor
300	250	175	125	75	50

Model 581

A .22 caliber bolt-action magazine rifle, blued with a 24" barrel and walnut stock. Manufactured from 1967 to 1983.

NIB	Exc.	V.G.	Good	Fair	Poor
300	250	175	125	75	50

Model 581 Left-Hand

Same as above but built for a left-handed shooter.

NIB	Exc.	V.G.	Good	Fair	Poor
295	250	175	125	75	50

Model 581-S

As above, fitted with a 5-round detachable magazine. Introduced in 1986.

NIB	Exc.	V.G.	Good	Fair	Poor
300	250	175	125	75	50

Model 582

As above, fitted with a tubular magazine in place of the detachable box magazine. Manufactured from 1967 to 1983.

Courtesy Remington Arms

NIB	Exc.	V.G.	Good	Fair	Poor
300	250	175	125	75	50

Model 591

A 5mm rimfire Magnum bolt-action rifle with a 24" barrel and Monte Carlo-style stock. Approximately 20,000 were made between 1970 and 1973.

NIB	Exc.	V.G.	Good	Fair	Poor
450	300	225	175	125	75

Model 592

As above, with a tubular magazine. Approximately 7,000 were made.

NIB	Exc.	V.G.	Good	Fair	Poor
450	300	225	175	125	75

Model 740

A semi-automatic rifle with a 22" barrel and detachable box magazine. Chambered in .244 Rem., .280 Rem., .308 or .30-06. Blued with a plain walnut stock. Also available with an 18.5" barrel that would be worth approximately 10 percent more than the values listed below. 30 percent premium for .244 Remington. Manufactured from 1955 to 1960.

NIB	Exc.	V.G.	Good	Fair	Poor
—	300	225	200	150	100

ADL

As above, with a checkered walnut stock with a pistol grip.

NIB	Exc.	V.G.	Good	Fair	Poor
—	350	250	225	150	100

BDL

As above, with a more finely figured walnut stock.

NIB	Exc.	V.G.	Good	Fair	Poor
—	400	275	250	150	100

Model 742

A 6mm Remington, .243, .280, .30-06 or .308 caliber semi-automatic rifle with a 22" barrel and 4-shot magazine. Also available with an 18" barrel in calibers .308 and .30-06 that are worth approximately 10 percent more than the values listed below. Blued with a checkered walnut stock. Manufactured from 1960 to 1980.

Courtesy Remington Arms

NIB	Exc.	V.G.	Good	Fair	Poor
—	350	275	250	150	100

BDL Standard Grade

As above, with a Monte Carlo-style stock and basketweave checkering.

NIB	Exc.	V.G.	Good	Fair	Poor
—	375	275	225	175	125

742D Peerless

Engraved.

NIB	Exc.	V.G.	Good	Fair	Poor
—	5000	3500	2250	1100	450

742F Premier (Game Scene)

NIB	Exc.	V.G.	Good	Fair	Poor
—	9000	6000	4500	1700	550

742F Premier (Gold Inlaid)

NIB	Exc.	V.G.	Good	Fair	Poor
—	10000	7000	5250	2200	750

Bicentennial

Mfg. 1976 only.

NIB	Exc.	V.G.	Good	Fair	Poor
—	550	495	295	200	150

Model 76 Sportsman

A .30-06 slide-action rifle with a 22" barrel and 4-shot magazine. Blued with walnut stock. Manufactured from 1985 to 1987.

NIB	Exc.	V.G.	Good	Fair	Poor
—	325	225	175	125	75

Model 7600

A variation of the above, chambered for a variety of cartridges from 6mm Remington to .35 Whelen with a 22" barrel and a detachable magazine. Also available with an 18.5" barrel. Blued with a checkered walnut stock. In 1996 fine line engraving on the receiver was offered as standard.

Model 7600 with engraving

Close-up of engraving on Model 7600

Courtesy Remington Arms

Standard Grade

NIB	Exc.	V.G.	Good	Fair	Poor
615	450	325	225	150	100

7600D Peerless

Engraved.

NIB	Exc.	V.G.	Good	Fair	Poor
—	5000	3500	2250	1100	450

7600F Premier

Game scene engraved.

NIB	Exc.	V.G.	Good	Fair	Poor
—	9000	6000	4500	1700	550

Premier

Gold inlaid.

NIB	Exc.	V.G.	Good	Fair	Poor
—	10000	7000	5250	2200	750

Synthetic

Same as the standard grade Model 7600 with black synthetic stock. A .30-06 carbine version is also available. Introduced in 1998.

NIB	Exc.	V.G.	Good	Fair	Poor
510	375	275	200	150	100

Special Purpose

The same configuration as the standard Model 7600 but equipped with a special finish on both the wood and metal that is non-reflective. First offered in 1993.

NIB	Exc.	V.G.	Good	Fair	Poor
600	475	350	225	150	100

7600P Patrol

Introduced in 2002 this rifle is chambered for the .308 cartridge. It is fitted with a 16.5" barrel. Synthetic stock with matte black finish. Parkerized finish on metal. Wilson Combat rear ghost-ring sights with AO front sight. Weight is about 7 lbs.

NIB	Exc.	V.G.	Good	Fair	Poor
600	475	350	225	150	100

Buckmasters ADF (American Deer Foundation)

Introduced in 1997 and built only for that year this model is chambered for the .30-06 cartridge and is a limited edition item. Fitted with a 22" barrel and special fine line engraved receiver.

Close-up detail on engraving for Model 7600

NIB	Exc.	V.G.	Good	Fair	Poor
600	475	350	225	150	100

Model 7600 Custom Grade

This Custom Shop model is available in three levels of engraving, gold inlay, wood grade and finish, metal work finish, recoil pad/buttplate and dimensions. Each gun should be individually appraised prior to a sale.

D Grade

NIB	Exc.	V.G.	Good	Fair	Poor
—	5000	3500	2250	1100	450

F Grade

NIB	Exc.	V.G.	Good	Fair	Poor
—	9000	6000	4500	1700	550

F Grade with Gold Inlay

NIB	Exc.	V.G.	Good	Fair	Poor
—	10000	7000	5250	2200	750

Model Six

A centerfire slide-action rifle with a 22" barrel and a 4-shot detachable magazine. Blued with a walnut stock. Manufactured from 1981 to 1987.

NIB	Exc.	V.G.	Good	Fair	Poor
—	450	350	275	200	125

Model 7615 Tactical Pump Carbine

Pump-action rifle based on Model 7600 action and chambered in .223 Remington with 16.5" barrel. Folding synthetic stock. Introduced in 2007.

NIB	Exc.	V.G.	Good	Fair	Poor
600	475	350	225	150	100

Model 7615 Special Purpose Synthetic

Similar to Model 7615 Tactical but with fixed stock and picatinny rail. A dealer exclusive for 2007.

NIB	Exc.	V.G.	Good	Fair	Poor
625	500	375	250	175	125

Model 7615 Camo Hunter

Similar to Model 7615 Tactical but with fixed buttstock and entirely camo-finished except for action parts and trigger guard assembly. Introduced in 2007.

NIB	Exc.	V.G.	Good	Fair	Poor
650	525	400	265	195	150

Model 7615 Ranch Carbine

Similar to Model 7615 Tactical but with fixed buttstock, walnut buttstock and fore-end and 18.5" barrel. No iron sights but drilled and tapped for scope mounts. Introduced in 2007.

NIB	Exc.	V.G.	Good	Fair	Poor
625	500	375	250	175	125

Model 74 Sportsman

A .30-06 caliber semi-automatic rifle with a 22" barrel and a 4-shot detachable magazine. Blued with a walnut stock. Manufactured from 1985 to 1987.

NIB	Exc.	V.G.	Good	Fair	Poor
—	350	250	175	125	75

Model Four

As above, with a select Monte Carlo-style stock. Manufactured from 1982 to 1987.

NIB	Exc.	V.G.	Good	Fair	Poor
—	500	400	350	275	175

Model 7400

This is a semi-automatic rifle with a 22" barrel. It is chambered for the .243, .270, .280, .30-06, .308 and the .35 Whelen. Blued with a checkered walnut stock. Average weight is about 7.5 lbs. Introduced in 1982. In 1996 this model was offered with fine line engraving on the receiver as standard.

Model 7400 with engraving

Close-up of engraving for Model 7400

Courtesy Remington Arms

NIB	Exc.	V.G.	Good	Fair	Poor
600	475	350	250	200	100

Synthetic

Similar to the Model 7400 with black non-reflective synthetic stock. A .30-06 carbine is also offered. Introduced in 1998.

NIB	Exc.	V.G.	Good	Fair	Poor
550	400	300	200	150	100

Weathermaster

Introduced in 2003 this semi-automatic model features a weather-resistant black synthetic stock and matte nickel-plated receiver, barrel and magazine. Barrel length is 22" with iron sights. Chambered for the .30-06 or .270 Win. cartridges. Weight is about 7.5 lbs.

NIB	Exc.	V.G.	Good	Fair	Poor
650	525	400	300	200	100

Carbine

Same as above but with 18.5" barrel and chambered for the .30-06 cartridge.

NIB	Exc.	V.G.	Good	Fair	Poor
550	400	300	200	150	100

Special Purpose

The same configuration as the standard Model 7400 but equipped with a special finish on both the wood and metal that is non-eflective. First offered in 1993.

NIB	Exc.	V.G.	Good	Fair	Poor
450	350	300	250	200	100

Buckmasters ADF (American Deer Foundation)

Introduced in 1997 and built only in that year, this model is limited. Chambered for the .30-06 cartridge and fitted with a 22" barrel. Special fine line engraving and polished blue finish. American walnut stock with Monte Carlo and cut checkering. Weight is 7.5 lbs.

Close-up detail on engraving for Model 7400 Buckmasters ADF

NIB	Exc.	V.G.	Good	Fair	Poor
600	500	400	300	200	100

Model 7400 Custom Grade

This Custom Shop model is available in three levels of engraving, gold inlay, wood grade and finish, metal work finish, recoil pad/buttplate, and dimensions. Each gun should be individually appraised prior to a sale.

F Grade

NIB	Exc.	V.G.	Good	Fair	Poor
—	9000	6000	4500	1700	550

F Grade with Gold Inlay

NIB	Exc.	V.G.	Good	Fair	Poor
—	10000	7000	5250	2200	750

Model 750 Woodsmaster

Wood-stocked version of Model 7400 semi-automatic. Rifle version has 22" barrel; carbine has 18.5" barrel. Introduced 2006.

NIB	Exc.	V.G.	Good	Fair	Poor
650	550	400	275	175	100

Model 750 Synthetic

Similar to Model 750 Woodsmaster but with black synthetic stock and fore-end. Introduced in 2007.

NIB	Exc.	V.G.	Good	Fair	Poor
625	550	400	300	225	125

Model R-15 VTR Predator Rifle

AR-style rifle chambered for .223 Remington or .204 Ruger. Supplied with one 5-shot magazine but accepts AR-style higher-cap magazines. 22" fluted barrel; fixed stock. Finish: Advantage MAX-12 HD overall.

NIB	Exc.	V.G.	Good	Fair	Poor
1100	900	695	500	250	125

Model R-15 VTR Predator Carbine

Similar to above but with 18" barrel.

NIB	Exc.	V.G.	Good	Fair	Poor
1100	900	695	500	250	125

Model R-15CS VTR Predator Carbine

Similar to above but with collapsible buttstock.

NIB	Exc.	V.G.	Good	Fair	Poor
1145	950	750	550	275	150

Model R-15 Hunter

Similar to R-15 but in .30 Remington AR or .450 Bushmaster, 22" barrel, Realtree AP HD camo.

NIB	Exc.	V.G.	Good	Fair	Poor
1200	975	750	550	275	150

Model R-15 VTR Byron South Edition

.223, 18" barrel, Advantage MAX-1 HD camo.

NIB	Exc.	V.G.	Good	Fair	Poor
1200	975	750	550	275	150

Model R-15 VTR SS Varmint

As above but with 24" stainless steel barrel.

NIB	Exc.	V.G.	Good	Fair	Poor
1200	975	750	550	275	150

Model R-15 VTR Thumbhole

Similar to R-15 Hunter but with thumbhole stock.

NIB	Exc.	V.G.	Good	Fair	Poor
1300	1075	850	595	295	150

Model R-25 Modular Repeating Rifle

Enhanced AR-style semi-automatic rifle chambered in .243, 7mm-08 and .308 Winchester. Features include 20" chrome-moly barrel, single-stage trigger, four-round magazine, aluminum alloy upper and lower Mossy Oak Treestand camo finish overall. Overall length 38.25", weight: 7.75 lbs.

NIB	Exc.	V.G.	Good	Fair	Poor
1375	1100	850	650	275	150

REMINGTON'S "NYLON SERIES" .22 RIFLES

Model 10 Nylon

Bolt-action single shot. Approximately 10,700 (approx. 2000 smoothbore and only 200 of those with 24" barrel) produced from 1962-1964. Mohawk brown nylon stock with white accents, chrome spoon style bolt handle, safety engages upon cocking, .22 short, long and long rifle. This model is available in both rifled and smoothbore versions (smoothbore barrels are marked "smoothbore" and in barrel lengths of 19.5" and 24". **NOTE:** Add 100 percent+ for the 24" versions. Add 100 percent+ for NIB.

Courtesy Remington Arms

10 (model)

NIB	Exc.	V.G.	Good	Fair	Poor
—	700	600	500	300	200

10 (SB)

NIB	Exc.	V.G.	Good	Fair	Poor
—	1000	800	700	500	450

Model 11 Nylon

Bolt-action repeater, 6- or 10-round metal box magazine. Approximately 22,500 produced from 1962-1964. Mohawk brown nylon stock with white accents, chrome spoon style bolt handle, manual right side safety. .22 short, long or long rifle. Barrel lengths of 19.5" and 24". **NOTE:** Add 100 percent for the 24" version.

NIB	Exc.	V.G.	Good	Fair	Poor
—	475	375	300	275	175

Model 12 Nylon

Bolt-action repeater, 14 round external tubular magazine under the barrel. Approximately 27,600 produced from 1962-1964. Mohawk brown nylon stock with white accents, chrome spoon style bolt handle, manual right side safety. .22 short, long or long rifle. Barrel lengths of 19.5" and 24". **NOTE:** Add 100 percent for 24" version.

NIB	Exc.	V.G.	Good	Fair	Poor
—	475	375	300	275	175

Model 66 Nylon

Semi-automatic, 19.5" barrel, 14 round tubular magazine, fed through the buttplate. In excess of 1,000,000 produced from 1959-1987. Seven different variations of style and color were sold. Non-serialized prior to the 1968 gun control act of 1968. An "A" prefix was added to the serialization in 1977.

66 (MB) "Mohawk" Brown

Blued metal parts, dark chocolate brown stock with white accents, .22 LR ONLY. 1959-1987. Approx. 678,000.

66 (SG) "Seneca" Green

Blued metal parts, dark olive green stock (often confused with MB in artificial light) with white accents, .22 LR ONLY, 1959-1962. Approx. 45,000.

66 (AB) "Apache" Black

Bright chrome plated metal parts, black stock with white accents, .22 LR ONLY. 1962-1983. Approx. 220,000.

66 (BD) "Black Diamond"

Blued metal parts, black stock with black diamonds in the fore-end. The remainder of accents are white, .22 LR ONLY, 1978-1987. Approx. 56,000.

66 (GS) "Gallery Special"

Blued metal parts, dark brown stock with white accents. Barrel marked .22 SHORT. Distinguished by shell deflector over ejection port and a loop on the fore-end for the counter chain. 1961-1981. Approx. 6500.

66 (AN) "150th Anniversary Rifle"

Blued metal parts, dark brown stock with white accents, .22 LR ONLY. Distinguished by 150th Anniversary stamping on the left side of the receiver cover. 1966 ONLY. Approx. 4000.

66 (BI) "Bicentennial Rifle"

Blued metal parts, dark brown stock with white accents, .22 LR ONLY. Distinguished by the eagle and 1776/1976 stamping on the left side of the receiver cover. 1976 ONLY. Approx. 10,000.

66 (MB)

NIB	Exc.	V.G.	Good	Fair	Poor
400	350	300	150	125	100

66 (SG)

NIB	Exc.	V.G.	Good	Fair	Poor
600	550	450	325	275	175

66 (AB)

NIB	Exc.	V.G.	Good	Fair	Poor
600	500	425	350	250	125

66 (BD)

NIB	Exc.	V.G.	Good	Fair	Poor
450	425	375	300	250	150

66 (GS)

NIB	Exc.	V.G.	Good	Fair	Poor
1300	1200	950	700	450	300

66 (AN)

NIB	Exc.	V.G.	Good	Fair	Poor
750	700	600	450	300	250

66 (BI)

NIB	Exc.	V.G.	Good	Fair	Poor
700	600	500	325	275	200

Model 76 Nylon

Lever-action repeater. The only lever-action Remington ever produced. 19.5" barrel, 14 round tubular magazine, fed through the buttplate. Produced from 1962-1964 in three different variations.

76 (MB) "Trailrider"

Blued metal parts, dark brown stocks with white accents. Approximately 25,300 produced.

NIB	Exc.	V.G.	Good	Fair	Poor
—	1700	600	500	375	250

76 (AB) "Trailrider"

Bright chrome metal parts, black stock with white accents. Approximately 1600 produced.

NIB	Exc.	V.G.	Good	Fair	Poor
—	2000	800	700	500	400

76 (not cataloged)

Blued metal parts, black stock with white accents. Production numbers do not exist.

NIB	Exc.	V.G.	Good	Fair	Poor
—	1800	675	600	400	300

Model 77 Nylon

Known as the 77 (MB): Semi-automatic, 19.5" barrel, 5 round plastic box magazine. Blued metal parts, dark brown stock with white accents. .22 LR ONLY. 1970-1971. Approx. 15,300 produced. This model was replaced by the Model 10C in 1972. **NOTE:** Add 100 percent for NIB.

NIB	Exc.	V.G.	Good	Fair	Poor
—	500	375	300	200	150

Model 10C Nylon

Known as the 10C. An identical copy of the 77 (MB), except that the box magazine capacity was increased to 10 rounds. 1972-1978. Approx. 128,000 produced. **NOTE:** Add 50 percent for NIB.

NIB	Exc.	V.G.	Good	Fair	Poor
—	325	275	225	175	100

Model 77 Apache Nylon

Known as the "APACHE 77". Semi-automatic, 19.5" barrel, 10 round plastic box magazine. Metal parts coated with a black "teflon-like" finish, bright green stock with swirls of orange, brown and black (highly variable), not to be confused with the 66 (SG). This rifle was contracted as an "exclusive" run, marketed by K-Mart. The number manufactured is hazy, but estimates run from 54,000 to over 100,000. Produced from 1987-1989. **NOTE:** Add 100 percent for NIB.

NIB	Exc.	V.G.	Good	Fair	Poor
—	350	250	200	140	120

Model 522 Viper

Introduced in 1993 the Model 522 Viper is a new Remington .22 rimfire caliber semi-automatic design. The black stock is made from synthetic resin, while the receiver is made from a synthetic as well. It features a 20" barrel and a 10-shot detachable clip. The rifle weighs 4.6 lbs.

NIB	Exc.	V.G.	Good	Fair	Poor
160	120	100	80	60	40

MODEL 597 SERIES

Model 597

Introduced in 1997 this automatic .22 LR rimfire rifle features a carbon steel barrel with alloy receiver. All metal has a non-reflective matte black finish. Stock is dark gray synthetic. Barrel length is 20" and weight is approximately 5.5 lbs.

NIB	Exc.	V.G.	Good	Fair	Poor
225	150	100	70	50	25

Sporter

Introduced in 1998 this version of the Model 597 has a blued finish with a hardwood stock with beavertail-style forearm. Magazine capacity is 10 rounds.

NIB	Exc.	V.G.	Good	Fair	Poor
225	150	100	70	50	25

Stainless Sporter

Same as the Model 597SS but fitted with a hardwood stock. Introduced in 2000.

NIB	Exc.	V.G.	Good	Fair	Poor
275	200	150	100	75	25

LSS

This version of the Model 597 is similar to the above but with the addition of a laminated stock and stainless steel finish.

NIB	Exc.	V.G.	Good	Fair	Poor
300	225	175	125	100	50

SS

This version is also chambered for the .22 LR and has a stainless steel barrel on an alloy receiver. The stock is gray synthetic with beavertail style forearm. Magazine capacity is 10 rounds. Weight is about 5.5 lbs. Introduced in 1998.

NIB	Exc.	V.G.	Good	Fair	Poor
240	175	125	100	75	25

HB

Introduced in 2001 this model features a 20" carbon steel heavy barrel chambered for the .22 LR cartridge. Fitted with a brown laminated stock. No sights. Weight is about 6 lbs.

NIB	Exc.	V.G.	Good	Fair	Poor
275	225	165	125	75	25

HB Magnum

Same as model above but chambered for the .22 Winchester Magnum cartridge. Introduced in 2001.

NIB	Exc.	V.G.	Good	Fair	Poor
425	325	200	165	125	50

Magnum

This model features a 20" carbon steel barrel, alloy receiver and black synthetic stock. It is chambered for the .22 Win. Magnum cartridge. Weight is approximately 6 lbs.

NIB	Exc.	V.G.	Good	Fair	Poor
350	250	200	150	100	50

Magnum LS

Chambered for the .22 Magnum. The receiver and barrel are blued with a gray laminated hardwood stock with beavertail-style forearm. Magazine capacity is 10 rounds. Introduced in 1998. In 2003 this model was also offered chambered for the .17 HMR cartridge.

NIB	Exc.	V.G.	Good	Fair	Poor
375	275	195	145	100	50

Custom Target

This model is available on special order from the Custom Shop. It is chambered for the .22 LR cartridge and has a 20" stainless steel heavy target barrel without sights. The stock is a green, laminated-wood target style with pistol grip. Trigger is custom tuned. Weight is approximately 7.5 lbs. Introduced in 1998.

NIB	Exc.	V.G.	Good	Fair	Poor
600	475	400	275	200	150

Custom Target Magnum

Similar to the model above but chambered for the .22 Win. Magnum. Weight is approximately 8 lbs. Introduced in 1998. This is special order item only.

NIB	Exc.	V.G.	Good	Fair	Poor
750	600	500	375	250	175

LSS

Similar to Model 597 but with laminated stock, stainless barrel and 3-9X scope. Dealer exclusive for 2007.

NIB	Exc.	V.G.	Good	Fair	Poor
275	200	150	100	75	25

Synthetic Scope Combo

"Package rifle" similar to Model 597 but with 3-9X scope included. Introduced in 2007.

NIB	Exc.	V.G.	Good	Fair	Poor
300	225	175	125	100	50

TVP (Target/Varmint/Plinker)

Ultra-funky .22 LR autoloader built on the Model 597 chassis. Features include bolt-guidance system with twin, tool-steel guide rails; laminated, skeletonized wood stock; non-glare matte finish; 10-shot metal detachable magazine; and last-shot hold-open bolt for added safety. Scope rail. Introduced in 2008.

NIB	Exc.	V.G.	Good	Fair	Poor
530	465	395	275	175	125

Yellow Jacket

Similar to above but with yellow and black laminated stock.

NIB	Exc.	V.G.	Good	Fair	Poor
500	395	225	150	100	75

Blaze Camo

A Model 597 with synthetic stock molded in screamin' blaze orange and black.

NIB	Exc.	V.G.	Good	Fair	Poor
275	225	165	125	75	25

Pink Camo

Similar to above but with a pink – yes, pink – and black camo-pattern stock.

NIB	Exc.	V.G.	Good	Fair	Poor
275	225	165	125	75	25

FLX

Similar to Model 597 Blaze/Pink camo but with FLX Digital Camo stock.

NIB	Exc.	V.G.	Good	Fair	Poor
275	225	165	125	75	25

AAC

Same features as other 597 models except has 16.5" barrel that will accept AAC flash hider, muzzle break or suppressor. Staggered-stack magazine holds 10 rounds. Weight is 5.5 pounds.

NIB	Exc.	V.G.	Good	Fair	Poor
195	165	140	115	100	75

VTR - Quad Rail

Semi-automatic rifle chambered in .22 LR, styled to resemble AR. Features include matte blued finished and black synthetic stock; 16" barrel; Pardus A2-style collapsible pistol-grip stock; quad-rail free-floated tube; 10-round magazine.

NIB	Exc.	V.G.	Good	Fair	Poor
400	360	325	275	210	150

VTR A-2 Fixed Stock

Similar to Remington 597 VTR - Quad Rail but with fixed A2-style stock and standard handguard with quad rail.

NIB	Exc.	V.G.	Good	Fair	Poor
400	360	325	275	210	150

VTR Collapsible Stock

Similar to 597 VTR A-2 Fixed Stock but with Pardus A2-style collapsible pistol-grip stock.

NIB	Exc.	V.G.	Good	Fair	Poor
400	360	325	275	210	150

VTR A-TACS Camo

Semi-automatic rifle chambered in .22 LR, styled to resemble AR. Features include ATACS camo finish overall; 16" barrel; Pardus

A2-style collapsible pistol-grip stock; round handguard without rails; receiver-mounted optics rail; 10-round magazine.

NIB	Exc.	V.G.	Good	Fair	Poor
525	465	425	350	275	185

Model Five

.22 rimfire bolt-action sporter. Calibers: .22 LR or .22 WMR or .17 HMR; five-shot detachable magazine. Barrel: 22" blued with iron sights; receiver blued for scope mounts. Stock: laminated walnut with QD swivels. **NOTE:** Add 10 percent for .22 WMR. Introduced 2006.

NIB	Exc.	V.G.	Good	Fair	Poor
300	250	175	125	75	25

MODEL 40X SERIES

Target Rifle

A .22 caliber rimfire single-shot bolt-action rifle with a heavy 28" barrel fitted with Redfield Olympic sights or telescopic sight bases. Blued with a walnut target style stock having a hard rubber butt-plate. Manufactured from 1955 to 1964.

Courtesy Remington Arms

NIB	Exc.	V.G.	Good	Fair	Poor
875	750	550	425	350	300

Sporter

As above, with a 24" barrel, 5-shot magazine and a walnut sporting style stock. Fewer than 700 were made between 1969 and 1980.

Courtesy Remington Arms

NIB	Exc.	V.G.	Good	Fair	Poor
3500	2500	1700	1200	500	275

Centerfire Target

Chambered for .222, .222 Magnum, .308 or .30-06 centerfire cartridges. Manufactured from 1961 to 1964.

NIB	Exc.	V.G.	Good	Fair	Poor
—	700	500	400	300	200

40XB Rangemaster Centerfire

This model is built in the Custom Shop and features stainless steel barrel, receiver, and bolt. The receiver is drilled and tapped and fitted with a 27.25" heavy target barrel. The trigger is fully adjustable. There is a choice of walnut stock or synthetic stock. Starting in 1998 this model was offered with a special laminated thumbhole stock. Offered in calibers from .222 to .300 Win. Magnum. This rifle is built to order. Made since 1964.

Model 40XB with laminated thumbhole stock

NIB	Exc.	V.G.	Good	Fair	Poor
2100	1800	1325	1000	600	250

40XB BR

This is a bench rest Custom Shop version of the above model. This rifle has a 22" stainless heavy barrel chambered for the .22 BR Remington. Adjustable trigger. Built to order.

NIB	Exc.	V.G.	Good	Fair	Poor
1200	1000	850	600	450	200

40XB Tactical Rifle

First offered in 2003 this bolt-action rifle features a Teflon coated stainless steel 27.25" barrel chambered for the .308 Win. cartridge. Fitted with a H.S. Precision tactical stock with vertical pistol grip. Remington 40-X trigger.

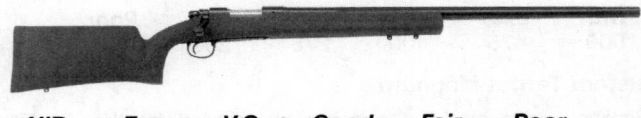

NIB	Exc.	V.G.	Good	Fair	Poor
2400	2100	1600	1200	700	350

40XS Tactical

Bolt-action rifle chambered in .308 Winchester or .338 Lapua Magnum. Features include 416 stainless steel Model 40-X 24" 1:12 barreled action; black polymer coating; McMillan A3 series stock with adjustable length of pull and adjustable comb; adjustable trigger and all-steel trigger guard; Harris bipod with quick adjust swivel lock Leupold Mark IV 3.5-10x40mm long range M1 scope with Mil Dot reticle; Badger Ordnance all-steel Picatinny scope rail and rings. **NOTE:** Deduct 50 percent if without Leupold scope, Harris Bipod, Badger Ordnance Picatinny rail.

NIB	Exc.	V.G.	Good	Fair	Poor
4000	3600	3000	2000	—	—

40XR KS Sporter

This Custom Shop version is also chambered for the .22 LR and is fitted with a 24" barrel. Fully adjustable trigger.

NIB	Exc.	V.G.	Good	Fair	Poor
1300	1000	850	600	450	350

Model XR-100 Rangemaster

Introduced in 2005 this model features a 26" barrel chambered for the .204 Ruger, .223 or .22-250 calibers. Black laminate stock with thumbhole and vented forearm. Adjustable trigger. Blued finish. Weight is about 9.12 lbs.

NIB	Exc.	V.G.	Good	Fair	Poor
880	675	500	395	275	150

Model XC KS

This is a Custom Shop position rifle with 24" stainless steel heavy barrel chambered for .223 Rem. and .308 Win. cartridges. Kevlar stock with palm rail. Weight is approximately 11 lbs.

NIB	Exc.	V.G.	Good	Fair	Poor
2650	2225	1850	1400	800	400

Model 673 Guide Rifle

Introduced in 2003 this bolt-action rifle features a 22" vent rib barrel chambered for the 6.5 mm Rem. Magnum, .308, .300 RUM or .350 Rem. Magnum cartridge. Adjustable rear sight. The stock is dark and light tan laminate with checkering. Magazine capacity is three rounds. Weight is about 7.5 lbs. Discontinued 2006. Slight premium for .300 RUM.

NIB	Exc.	V.G.	Good	Fair	Poor
650	525	400	300	200	150

Model 720A

A .257 Roberts, .270 or .30-06 bolt-action sporting rifle with a 22" barrel and a 5-shot integral magazine. Blued with a checkered walnut stock. Approximately 2,500 were manufactured in 1941. **NOTE:** Deduct 40 percent if .30-06 caliber.

Courtesy Remington Arms

NIB	Exc.	V.G.	Good	Fair	Poor
3000	2400	1875	1300	700	400

Model 721

A .264 Magnum, .270, .280 or .30-06 bolt-action rifle with a 24" barrel and a 4-shot magazine. Blued with a plain walnut stock. Manufactured from 1948 to 1962. ADL model has checkered stock. BDL has high grade stock.

Courtesy Remington Arms

Standard Version

NIB	Exc.	V.G.	Good	Fair	Poor
500	450	350	200	150	100

ADL

NIB	Exc.	V.G.	Good	Fair	Poor
550	475	375	250	200	125

BDL

NIB	Exc.	V.G.	Good	Fair	Poor
600	500	400	300	250	150

Model 721A Magnum

.300 H&H or .264 Win.

NIB	Exc.	V.G.	Good	Fair	Poor
650	550	400	350	275	150

Model 722

A short-action variation of the Model 721 chambered for .222 Rem., .222 Rem. Magnum, .243 Win., .244 Rem., .257 Roberts, .300 Savage, .308 Winchester. The BDL models featured high-grade, select walnut stocks; ADL had checkered stocks. Made from 1948 to 1962. **NOTE:** Add 25 percent for BDL, 10 percent for ADL. Add 25 percent for .222 Rem. Magnum, .243, .257 or .308 chamberings.

NIB	Exc.	V.G.	Good	Fair	Poor
550	450	350	200	150	100

Model 725 ADL

A short-lived but well-made model offered in .222 Rem., .243 Win., .244 Rem., .270 Win., .280 Rem., and .30-06 Springfield. Four-round magazine capacity (5 in .222). Adjustable open rear sight, hooded ramp front. Checkered walnut stock with Monte Carlo comb, sling swivels. Barrel length: 22" (24" .222). Weight: Approx. 7 lbs. Made from 1958 to 1961.

Courtesy Remington Arms

NIB	Exc.	V.G.	Good	Fair	Poor
—	800	525	275	225	150

Model 725 Kodiak

A .375 Holland & Holland Magnum or .458 Winchester Magnum, bolt-action sporting rifle with a 26" barrel, muzzlebrake, open sights and 3-shot magazine. Blued with a checkered walnut stock. Manufactured in 1961. Very limited production.

NIB	Exc.	V.G.	Good	Fair	Poor
5000	4000	3000	2000	1000	300

Model 78 Sportsman

A centerfire bolt-action sporting rifle with a 22" barrel and 4-shot magazine. Blued with a walnut stock. Introduced in 1985. Calibers: .223, .243, .270, .308, .30-06.

NIB	Exc.	V.G.	Good	Fair	Poor
335	275	225	200	150	100

Model 600

A centerfire bolt-action sporting rifle with an 18.5" ventilated rib barrel and a checkered walnut stock. Manufactured from 1964 to 1967. Calibers: .222 Rem., .223 Rem., 6mm Rem., .243, .308, .35 Rem. **NOTE:** Add 100 percent for .223 Rem.

Courtesy Remington Arms

NIB	Exc.	V.G.	Good	Fair	Poor
—	550	450	350	225	150

Model 600 Mohawk

As above, but with a plain barrel and chambered only for the .222 Remington, .243 Winchester or .308 Winchester cartridges. Manufactured from 1971 to 1979.

NIB	Exc.	V.G.	Good	Fair	Poor
—	450	375	225	175	125

Model 600 Magnum

As above, chambered for the 6.5mm Remington Magnum and .350 Remington Magnum cartridges. Stock of laminated walnut and beechwood. Manufactured from 1965 to 1967.

NIB	Exc.	V.G.	Good	Fair	Poor
—	1000	750	600	450	200

Model 660

An improved version of the Model 600. Manufactured from 1968 to 1971.

NIB	Exc.	V.G.	Good	Fair	Poor
—	550	425	350	250	200

Model 660 Magnum

As above, but chambered for either the 6.5mm Remington Magnum or .350 Remington Magnum cartridges and fitted with a laminated stock.

NIB	Exc.	V.G.	Good	Fair	Poor
—	1000	750	600	450	200

MODEL 700 SERIES

Model 700 ADL

A centerfire bolt-action sporting rifle with either a 20", 22" or 24" barrel; open sights and a 4-shot magazine. Blued with a checkered Monte Carlo-style walnut stock. Introduced in 1962. This model was available in most popular calibers from .222 Rem. to .300 Win. Magnum.

NIB	Exc.	V.G.	Good	Fair	Poor
425	325	250	200	150	100

Model 700 ADL Synthetic

This model features a black matte metal finish with 22" barrel or 24" on Magnums. The synthetic stock is black with checkering, recoil pad and sling swivel studs. Receiver is drilled and tapped for scope. Offered in .243, .270, .30-06 and 7mm Rem. Magnum. In 1998 this model was available in .223 Rem. and .300 Win. Magnum.

Courtesy Remington Arms

NIB	Exc.	V.G.	Good	Fair	Poor
350	300	250	200	150	100

Model 700 ADL Synthetic Youth

Introduced in 1998 this model has a shortened synthetic stock with a 13" lop. Offered in .243 and .308 calibers.

NIB	Exc.	V.G.	Good	Fair	Poor
400	300	250	200	150	100

Model 700 BDL

Same as above, with a hinged floorplate, cut checkering, black fore-end tip and pistol grip cap. Offered in a wide variety of calibers from the .17 Rem. to the .338 Rem. Ultra Magnum. Weights are between 7.25 lbs. to 7.62 lbs. depending on caliber and barrel length.

Courtesy Remington Arms

NIB	Exc.	V.G.	Good	Fair	Poor
715	525	400	275	225	150

Model 700 BDL LH (Left-Hand)

This model is also offered in selected calibers for left-hand shooters. They are: .270 Win., 7mm Rem. Magnum, .30-06 and .300 Rem. Ultra Magnum.

NIB	Exc.	V.G.	Good	Fair	Poor
800	700	500	325	250	150

Model 700 BDL (DM)

Same as above but introduced in 1995 with detachable magazine.

NIB	Exc.	V.G.	Good	Fair	Poor
715	525	400	300	225	150

Model 700 BDL LSS

This is a Model 700, introduced in 1996, with a synthetic stock and stainless steel bolt, floor plate, trigger guard and sling swivels. The action and barrel are stainless steel as well. In 1997 the .260 Rem. cartridge was also available.

Courtesy Remington Arms

NIB	Exc.	V.G.	Good	Fair	Poor
600	475	400	350	300	200

Model 700 BDL SS DM—Magnum Rifle

Introduced in 1996 this Model 700 version is fitted with a factory installed muzzlebrake on its Magnum calibers: 7mm Rem. Magnum, .300 Win. Magnum, .300 Wthby. Magnum, .338 Win. Magnum and the .338 Rem. Ultra Magnum. Weight is approximately 7.5 lbs. In 1997 the 7mm STW cartridge was added to this model.

Courtesy Remington Arms

NIB	Exc.	V.G.	Good	Fair	Poor
675	500	400	300	200	150

Model 700 BDL SS Short Action

Fitted with stainless steel 24" and chambered for the 7mm Rem. Ultra Magnum and the .300 Rem. Ultra Magnum Black synthetic stock. No sights. Weight is about 7.325 lbs. Introduced in 2003.

NIB	Exc.	V.G.	Good	Fair	Poor
775	625	500	395	300	175

Model 700 BDL SS Camo Special Edition (RMEF)

This is a special edition rifle for the Rocky Mountain Elk Foundation. Fitted with a 24" barrel and chambered for the .300 Rem. Ultra Magnum cartridge. Camo stock with stainless steel receiver and barrel. Weight is about 7.5 lbs. Introduced in 2001. In 2002 the 7mm Rem. Ultra Magnum chambering was added for one year only. In 2003 the .300 Rem. Ultra Magnum was offered.

NIB	Exc.	V.G.	Good	Fair	Poor
835	650	500	395	300	175

Model 700 50th Anniversary Edition

Introduced in 2012, this is a recreation of the original M700 BDL of 1962. The satin finished walnut stock has a cheek piece, cut fleur-de-lis checkering, white-line spacers, black fore-end and grip caps and black recoil pad. Laser engraving on the floorplate commemorates the 50th anniversary. Barrel length is 24" and chambering is for the 7mm Remington Magnum, the cartridge that was introduced with the Model 700 BDL.

NIB	Exc.	V.G.	Good	Fair	Poor
1250	1000	850	—	—	—

Model 700 EtronX

Introduced in 2000 this rifle features a new technology that electronically discharges the round resulting in nearly instant ignition. LED located on top of the grip that shows safe or fire and chamber status. There is also a low battery indicator and malfunction indicators as well. The rifle is fitted with a 26" stainless steel fluted barrel. The stock is fiberglass and graphite reinforced with Kevlar. Chambers are .220 Swift, .22-250 Rem. and .243 Win. cartridges. Average weight is about 8.88 lbs. The gun was a flopperoo but is now considered an almost-prime collectible. Discontinued 2004.

NIB	Exc.	V.G.	Good	Fair	Poor
1450	1300	1150	700	500	300

Model 700 Sendero

This Model 700 configuration is chambered for the .25-06, .270, 7mm Rem. Magnum, .300 Win. Magnum. It is fitted with a synthetic stock and a 26" heavy barrel.

NIB	Exc.	V.G.	Good	Fair	Poor
600	475	400	300	200	150

Model 700 Sendero SF

Introduced in 1996 this model features a stainless steel fluted barrel. It has a synthetic stock with full length bedding. It weighs about 8.5 lbs. Chambered for same calibers as the standard Sendero above except for the .270. In 1997 the 7mm STW cartridge was made available for this model. In 2003 the 7mm Rem. Ultra Magnum and the .300 Rem. Ultra Magnum were added calibers.

Courtesy Remington Arms

NIB	Exc.	V.G.	Good	Fair	Poor
900	800	600	450	350	200

Model 700 Sendero SF-II

Similar to Sendero SF but with HS Precision synthetic stock. Chambered in .264 WM, 7mm RM, 7mm RUM, .300 WM and .300 RUM. Introduced 2006.

NIB	Exc.	V.G.	Good	Fair	Poor
1150	985	835	700	500	300

Model 700 Sendero Composite

Introduced in 1999, this model features a composite barrel of graphite fiber with a stainless steel liner. Stock is synthetic. Calibers available are .25-06, 7mm STW and .300 Win. Magnum. Barrel length is 26". Weight is just under 8 lbs.

NIB	Exc.	V.G.	Good	Fair	Poor
1400	1250	975	700	475	300

Model 700 Mountain Rifle

As above, with a tapered 22" lightweight barrel, blued with checkered walnut stock. Introduced in 1986.

NIB	Exc.	V.G.	Good	Fair	Poor
425	325	250	200	150	100

Model 700KS Mountain Rifle

As above, with a lightweight Kevlar stock. Introduced in 1986.

NIB	Exc.	V.G.	Good	Fair	Poor
750	700	600	500	400	300

Model 700 Mountain Rifle (DM)

Same as standard Mountain Rifle but introduced in 1995 with detachable magazine. In 1998 this model was available in .260 Rem. caliber.

Courtesy Remington Arms

NIB	Exc.	V.G.	Good	Fair	Poor
780	575	425	300	250	175

Model 700 Safari Grade

As the Model 700BDL chambered for 8mm Remington Magnum, .375 Holland & Holland, 8mm Rem. Magnum, .416 Remington Magnum or .458 Winchester Magnum cartridges. 24" barrel and 3-shot magazine. Blued with a finely figured walnut checkered stock. The Model KS Safari Grade was fitted with a Kevlar stock and would be worth approximately 20 percent more than the values listed. Introduced in 1962.

NIB	Exc.	V.G.	Good	Fair	Poor
1500	1300	1000	700	400	300

Model 700 RS

As above, chambered for the .270 Winchester, .280 Remington or .30-06 cartridges, 22" barrel and 4-shot magazine. Blued with a DuPont Rynite stock. Manufactured during 1987 and 1988.

NIB	Exc.	V.G.	Good	Fair	Poor
—	550	425	350	250	150

Model 700 FS

As above, with a Kevlar stock.

NIB	Exc.	V.G.	Good	Fair	Poor
—	550	475	400	300	200

Model 700 BDL European

Available for the first time in 1993, this model features an oil finish stock with Monte Carlo comb and raised cheekpiece. The checkering is fine line. In addition the rifle has a hinged floorplate, sling swivel studs, hooded ramp front sight and adjustable rear sight. Offered in these calibers: .243, .207, .280, 7mm-08, 7mm Magnum, .30-06 and .308.

NIB	Exc.	V.G.	Good	Fair	Poor
675	400	350	300	250	200

Model 700 BDL Stainless Synthetic

Offered in 1993 this model features a stainless steel receiver, barrel and bolt. Synthetic stock has straight comb, raised cheekpiece and hinged floor plate. Metal is finished in a black matte non-reflective finish. Available in 14 calibers from .223 to .338 Win. Magnum. All barrel lengths regardless of caliber are 24".

NIB	Exc.	V.G.	Good	Fair	Poor
750	600	500	300	200	150

Model 700 BDL Stainless Synthetic (DM)

Same as above but introduced in 1995 with detachable magazine.

Courtesy Remington Arms

NIB	Exc.	V.G.	Good	Fair	Poor
800	650	525	350	200	150

Model 700 CDL

This model was introduced in 2004 and features a classic-style checkered walnut stock with black fore-end tip and grip cap. Hinged floor plate. Chambered for the .243, .270, 7mm-08, 7mm Rem. Magnum, 7mm Rem. Ultra Magnum, .30-06, .300 Win. Magnum and .300 Rem. Ultra Magnum. Standard calibers are fitted with a 24" barrel while magnum calibers have a 26" barrel. Weight is about 7.5 lbs. depending on caliber.

NIB	Exc.	V.G.	Good	Fair	Poor
740	550	400	295	200	125

Model 700 CDL SF (2009)

Similar to above but chambered in .257 Roberts.

NIB	Exc.	V.G.	Good	Fair	Poor
740	550	400	295	200	125

Model 700 CDL Boone and Crockett

Similar to Model 700 CDL but with B&C laser-engraved barrel. A dealer exclusive for 2007.

NIB	Exc.	V.G.	Good	Fair	Poor
750	560	400	295	200	125

Model 700 CDL SF Ltd.

Similar to Model 700 CDL but with engraved floorplate and stainless, fluted barrel. Chambered in .30-06 and .17 Remington Fireball. 2006 "Centennial" model commemorates the centennial of the .30-06 cartridge and was introduced in 2006 for one year only. Reintroduced in .260 Remington in 2008. .280 Remington added 2010.

NIB	Exc.	V.G.	Good	Fair	Poor
1100	900	675	450	275	150

Model 700 Mountain Rifle Stainless Synthetic

This model is the same as the Mountain Rifle but with stainless steel receiver, bolt and barrel. Offered in .25-06 Rem., .270, .280 and .30-06. All calibers are supplied with a 22" barrel. In 1998 this model was available in .260 Rem. caliber.

NIB	Exc.	V.G.	Good	Fair	Poor
830	600	450	300	225	150

Model 700 LSS Mountain Rifle

This model, introduced in 1999, is fitted with a two-tone laminated stock with black fore-end tip and cheekpiece. Stainless steel barrel and action. Offered in .260 Remington, 7mm-08 Rem., .270 Win., and .30-06. Barrel length is 22". Weight is approximately 6.5 lbs.

NIB	Exc.	V.G.	Good	Fair	Poor
830	625	450	300	200	100

Model 700 Titanium

Introduced in 2001 this model features a titanium receiver drilled and tapped for scope mounts. Fitted with a 22" stainless steel barrel chambered for both long and short calibers. Synthetic stock. Weight is approximately 5.25 lbs. In 2002 the .308 Win. chambering was added.

NIB	Exc.	V.G.	Good	Fair	Poor
1270	950	700	500	300	175

Model 700 Varmint Special Synthetic

The stock on this model is reinforced with DuPont Kevlar, fiberglass and graphite. Rifle is offered with a heavy barrel and all metal has a fine matte black finish. The barrel rest on a machined aircraft-grade aluminum bedding stock. The receiver is drilled and tapped for scope mounts. Offered in .22-250, .223 and .308 calibers. In 1993 the .220 Swift was added to the line. This model was later dropped from the product line. In 2000 it was reintroduced in all calibers above but the .220 Swift.

NIB	Exc.	V.G.	Good	Fair	Poor
600	475	400	350	300	200

Model 700 VS SF (Varmint Synthetic Stainless Fluted)

Introduced in 1994 this model features a stainless steel barrel, receiver and action. It is fitted with a 26" heavy varmint barrel that has a spherical concave crown contour. Six flutes reduce barrel weight and help cooling. A synthetic stock made from fiberglass reinforced with graphite is standard. The stock is dark gray. Offered in .223, .220 Swift, .22-250 and .308 calibers. The .243 Win. cartridge was added to this model in 1997. The rifle weighs about 8-3/8 lbs. In 1998 the barrel was fluted and ported.

NIB	Exc.	V.G.	Good	Fair	Poor
800	650	500	400	300	150

Model 700 Varmint Special Wood

Same as above but furnished with walnut stock and offered in these calibers: .222, .22-250, .223, 6mm, .243, 7mm-08 and .308.

NIB	Exc.	V.G.	Good	Fair	Poor
825	675	525	400	300	150

Model 700 Varmint Laminated Stock (VLS)

Same as above but furnished with special laminated stock. Introduced in 1995. The 7mm-08 Rem. cartridge was added to this model in 1997. In 1998 a beavertail fore-end was added to this model, as well as the .260 Rem. and the 6mm Rem. calibers.

Model 700 VLS with beavertail forearm   Courtesy Remington Arms

NIB	Exc.	V.G.	Good	Fair	Poor
750	575	425	300	250	150

Model 700 VS Composite (Varmint Synthetic Composite)

This model is fitted with a graphite fiber composite barrel and chambered for the .223 Rem., .22-250 or .308 cartridges. Stock is synthetic. Barrel lengths are 26". Weight is 7.9 lbs. Introduced in 1999.

NIB	Exc.	V.G.	Good	Fair	Poor
1675	1250	950	600	425	300

Model 700 LV SF (Light Varmint)

This model, introduced in 2004, features a black synthetic stock with 22" stainless steel fluted barrel. Chambered for the .17 Rem, .221 Rem Fireball, .223 and .22-250. Weight is about 6.75 lbs.

NIB	Exc.	V.G.	Good	Fair	Poor
950	700	475	300	225	125

Model 700 VS SF II

Introduced in 2005 this model features a varmint synthetic stock with stainless steel action and stainless fluted barrel chambered for the .204 Ruger, .220 Swift, 223 and .22-250. Barrel length is 26". Weight is about 8.5 lbs.

NIB	Exc.	V.G.	Good	Fair	Poor
1025	775	600	475	250	125

Model 700 VSF

Chambered for the .17 Remington Fireball, .204 Ruger, .220 Swift, .223 or .22-250 this model is fitted with a 26" blued fluted heavy barrel and tan synthetic stock. Weight is about 8.5 lbs. Introduced in 2005.

NIB	Exc.	V.G.	Good	Fair	Poor
930	700	475	300	225	125

Model 700 LSS LH (Laminated Stock SS Left-Hand)

Introduced in 1998 this model features a stainless steel barreled action with satin finish. Stock is similar to the BDL style with Monte Carlo comb and cheekpiece with hinged floor plate. Barrel is 24" with no sights. Offered in .270, .30-06, 7mm Rem. Magnum and .300 Win. Magnum.

NIB	Exc.	V.G.	Good	Fair	Poor
700	550	400	300	250	150

Model 700 SPS

This model introduced in 2005, features an improved synthetic stock, RS recoil pad and hinged floorplate. Chambered for short, standard and long action calibers. Supplied with sling swivels studs. Matte blue finish. Weight is about 7.5 lbs. depending on caliber and barrel length.

NIB	Exc.	V.G.	Good	Fair	Poor
575	450	300	200	150	100

Model 700 SPS Synthetic Left hand

Similar to Model 700 SPS but configured for left-handed shooters.

NIB	Exc.	V.G.	Good	Fair	Poor
575	450	300	200	150	100

Model 700 SPS Varmint

Varmint version of Model 700 SPS with 26" heavy-contour barrel and synthetic stock with weight-reducing cuts in the fore-end. Available in a variety of chamberings from .17 Remington Fireball to .308 Winchester. Introduced in 2007.

NIB	Exc.	V.G.	Good	Fair	Poor
575	450	300	200	150	100

Model 700 SPS Dangerous Game

Similar to 700 SPS but chambered in .375 H&H Magnum. A TALO exclusive.

NIB	Exc.	V.G.	Good	Fair	Poor
675	550	400	275	200	150

Model 700 SPS Stainless

As above but with matte stainless steel barrel and action. No Ultra magnum calibers offered in this configuration. Introduced in 2005.

NIB	Exc.	V.G.	Good	Fair	Poor
610	475	350	225	150	100

Model 700 SPS DM

This model is the same as the Model SPS but with detachable magazine. Matte blue finish. Introduced in 2005.

NIB	Exc.	V.G.	Good	Fair	Poor
575	450	300	200	150	100

Model 700 SPS Youth

Offered in both long and short action calibers this model features barrel lengths of 20" and 22" depending on caliber. Weight is about 7 lbs. Introduced in 2005.

NIB	Exc.	V.G.	Good	Fair	Poor
525	425	275	175	125	100

Model 700 SPS Tactical

Similar to Model 700 Police but with 20" barrel and in .223 and .308. Laser-engraved tactical barrel. A dealer exclusive for 2007.

NIB	Exc.	V.G.	Good	Fair	Poor
800	675	500	375	250	175

Model 700 SPS Tactical AAC

A Special Purpose Synthetic version of the Model 700 with a 20" heavy-contour, hammer-forged barrel with threaded muzzle. Chambered in .308 Winchester. Hogue Overmolded Ghillie Green pillar-bedded stock with semi-beavertail forearm, Super-Cell recoil pad. Remington X-Mark Pro externally adjustable trigger. Black oxide finish. Weight: 7.5 pounds.

NIB	Exc.	V.G.	Good	Fair	Poor
650	550	475	400	300	200

Model 700 VTR A-TACS Camo with Scope

Bolt action rifle chambered in .223 and .308 Win. Features include ATACS camo finish overall; triangular contour 22" barrel has an integral muzzle brake; black overmold grips; 1:9 (.223 caliber) or 1:12 (.308) twist; factory-mounted scope.

NIB	Exc.	V.G.	Good	Fair	Poor
875	750	625	550	380	225

Model 700 XCR

Introduced in 2005 this model features a stainless steel action and barrel with synthetic stock, rubber grip and forearm panels. Hinged floorplate. RS recoil pad. Chambered for the .270 Win., .280 Rem., 7mm Ultra Magnum, .30-06, .300 WSM and the .300 Win. Magnum cartridges. Barrel lengths are 24" and 26" depending on caliber. Weight is around 7.5 lbs. depending on caliber. **NOTE:** Add $25 for magnum calibers.

NIB	Exc.	V.G.	Good	Fair	Poor
865	650	500	375	295	125

Model 700 XCR (Rocky Mountain Elk Foundation)

As above but with camo stock, engraved floorplate and 7mm Rem. Magnum caliber. Introduced in 2005.

NIB	Exc.	V.G.	Good	Fair	Poor
865	650	500	375	295	125

Remington 700 XCR II

Bolt-action rifle chambered in .25-06 Remington, .270 Win, .280 Remington, 7mm Remington Magnum, 7mm Remington Ultra Magnum, .300 WSM, .300 Win Magnum, .300 Remington Ultra Magnum, .338 Win. Magnum, .338 Remington Ultra Magnum, .375 H&H, .375 Remington Ultra Magnum, .30-06 Springfield. Features include black TriNyte corrosion control system coating; coated stainless steel barrel and receiver; olive drab green Hogue overmolded synthetic stock; SuperCell recoil pad; X-Mark Pro Trigger System; 24" or 26" barrel, depending on chambering.

NIB	Exc.	V.G.	Good	Fair	Poor
825	735	600	500	350	200

Remington 700 XCR II - BoneCollector Edition

Similar to Remington 700 XCR II but with Realtree AP HD camo stock.

NIB	Exc.	V.G.	Good	Fair	Poor
900	785	675	550	380	225

Model 700 Classic

This limited edition model was furnished with a straight comb, satin finished walnut stock, sling swivel studs and hinged magazine floorplate. The series began in 1981 and each year Remington offered the Model 700 Classic in a special chambering, concluding the series in 2005. **NOTE:** Add 25 percent for .250 Savage, .257 Roberts, 6.5x55 or 7x57.

A list of chamberings by year.

1981 — 7MM Mauser	1994 — 6.5X55
1982 — .257 Roberts	1995 — .300 Win. Mag.
1983 — .300 H&H Mag.	1996 — .375 H&H Mag.
1984 — .250-3000	1997 — .280 Rem.
1985 — .350 Rem. Mag.	1998 — 8mm Rem. Mag.
1986 — .264 Win. Mag.	1999 — .17 Remington
1987 — .338 Win. Mag.	2000 — .223 Remington
1988 — .35 Whelen	2001 — 7mm-08
1989 — .300 Wthby. Mag.	2002 — .221 Rem.Fireball
1990 — .25-06 Rem.	2003 — .300 Savage
1991 — 7mm Wthby. Mag.	2004 — 8mm Mauser
1992 — .220 Swift	2005 — .308 Winchester
1993 — .222 Rem.	

NIB	Exc.	V.G.	Good	Fair	Poor
900	700	600	500	350	250

MODEL 700 CUSTOM

A special order rifle available in either American, English or California walnut. Stock can be fitted to customer's own dimensions. Engraving is available as is a large selection of calibers. Model 700 Custom rifles should be priced individually and an appraisal should be obtained.

"C" Grade

Introduced in 2003 this Custom Shop bolt-action rifle is fitted with fancy walnut with Monte Carlo stock and rosewood fore-end tip and grip cap. Offered in all standard calibers. Barrel length is 24" for all calibers except Ultra Magnums, which are 26".

NIB	Exc.	V.G.	Good	Fair	Poor
2700	2200	1700	1200	600	250

AWR (Alaskan Wilderness Rifle)

This model is built in the Custom Shop and features a blind magazine and stainless steel components on a black matte synthetic stock. Fitted with a 24" barrel, all metal parts are finished in a black satin. Offered in .300 Weatherby Magnum, 7mm Rem. Magnum, .300 Win. Magnum, .338, and .375 calibers. In 1998 the 7mm STW was added as an additional caliber to this model. Weighs about 6.75 lbs. Built to order.

NIB	Exc.	V.G.	Good	Fair	Poor
1400	1100	850	700	350	200

APR (African Plains Rifle)

This Custom Shop model features a hinged floorplate, a 26" barrel and blue metal finish. The stock is a laminated Monte Carlo style with cheekpiece and is fitted with black rubber recoil pad. Offered in same calibers as Model 700 AWR. Weighs about 7-3/4 lbs.

NIB	Exc.	V.G.	Good	Fair	Poor
2400	2000	1500	1000	500	250

ABG (African Big Game)

This Custom Shop rifle is fitted with a laminated stock, matte finished receiver and barrel and 3-round detachable magazine. Chambered for the .375 Rem. Ultra Magnum, .375 H&H, .416 Rem. Magnum and .458 Win. Magnum. Introduced in 2001. Many extra cost options are offered for Custom Shop firearms.

NIB	Exc.	V.G.	Good	Fair	Poor
2750	2350	1800	1250	750	350

Model 700 Safari KS Stainless

A new addition to the Remington line in 1993, the Safari KS Stainless has a special reinforced Kevlar stock in a non-reflective gray finish. Checkering is 18 lpi. Offered in these calibers: .375 H&H Magnum, .416 Rem. Magnum and the .458 Win. Magnum.

NIB	Exc.	V.G.	Good	Fair	Poor
925	800	650	450	300	200

Model 700 Police

Chambered for the .223 cartridge and fitted with a 26" heavy barrel (1-9" twist), black synthetic stock and Parkerized finish.

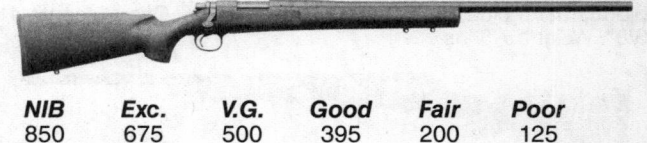

NIB	Exc.	V.G.	Good	Fair	Poor
850	675	500	395	200	125

Model 700 Police DM

Same as above but chambered for .308 Win. (1-12" twist) or .300 Win. Magnum (1-10" twist). Detachable magazine standard. **NOTE:** Add $20 for .300 Win. Magnum model.

NIB	Exc.	V.G.	Good	Fair	Poor
850	675	500	395	200	125

Model 700 Police Lightweight Tactical

This model is chambered for the .308 Win. cartridge and fitted with a 20" fluted barrel (1-12" twist). Stock is slim composite Kevlar with dual front swivel studs. Parkerized finish. Detachable magazine. Weight is approximately 7.5 lbs. Introduced in 1998.

NIB	Exc.	V.G.	Good	Fair	Poor
700	550	400	300	200	125

Model 700 XCR Tactical Long Range Rifle

Chambered in .223 Rem., .300 Lapua and .338 WM; 26" crowned stainless varmint contour barrel; olive drab Bell & Carlson synthetic stock. Coated overall with TriNyte Corrosion Control finish. Introduced in 2007. **NOTE:** Add 50 percent for .338 Lapua.

NIB	Exc.	V.G.	Good	Fair	Poor
925	800	675	500	300	150

Model 700 XCR Compact Tactical

Similar to above but with Black TriNyte PVD coating OD green stock; hinged floorplate magazine; dual front swivel studs and rear stud; free-floating 20-inch barrel with LTR-style fluting; 40-X externally adjustable trigger; tactical-style 1 in 9" (223 caliber) or 1 in 12" twist (308 caliber). Chambered in .223 and .308.

NIB	Exc.	V.G.	Good	Fair	Poor
1400	1150	875	650	475	200

Model 700 Target Tactical Rifle

Bolt-action rifle chambered in .308 Winchester. Features include a 26" triangular counterbored barrel with 1: 11-1/2 rifling, textured green Bell & Carlson varmint/tactical stock with adjustable comb and length of pull, adjustable trigger, satin black oxide finish on exposed metal surfaces, hinged floorplate, SuperCell recoil pad, matte blue on exposed metal surfaces. Overall length 45.75". Weight: 11.75 lbs.

NIB	Exc.	V.G.	Good	Fair	Poor
1800	1550	1175	850	675	300

Model 700 VTR Varmint-Tactical Rifle

Bolt-action rifle chambered in .17 Remington Fireball, .204 Ruger, .22-250, .223 Remington, .243 Winchester and .308 Winchester. Features include a 22" triangular counterbored barrel, olive drab overmolded or Digital Tiger TSP Desert Camo stock with vented semi-beavertail fore-end, tactical-style dual swivel mounts for bipod, matte blue on exposed metal surfaces. Overall length 41-5/8". Weight: 7.5 lbs.

NIB	Exc.	V.G.	Good	Fair	Poor
750	625	500	375	200	125

Model 700 VTR Desert Recon

Similar to above but with Digital Desert Camo stock and chambered for .223 and .308 Winchester only.

NIB	Exc.	V.G.	Good	Fair	Poor
750	625	500	375	200	125

Model 700 XHR Extreme Hunting Rifle

Bolt-action rifle chambered in .243 Winchester, .25-06, .270 Winchester, 7mm-08, 7mm Remington Magnum, .300 Winchester Magnum, 7mm Remington Ultra Magnum, .30-06 and .300 Remington Ultra Magnum. Features include a 24", 25" or 26" triangular magnum-contour counterbored barrel, adjustable trigger, synthetic stock finished in Realtree AG HD camo, satin black oxide finish on exposed metal surfaces, hinged floorplate, SuperCell recoil pad. Overall length 41-5/8" to 46.5". Weight: 7.25 lbs. to 7-5/8 lbs.

NIB	Exc.	V.G.	Good	Fair	Poor
850	675	500	395	200	125

Model 700 SPS Buckmasters Edition

Similar to Model 700 SPS but with engraved floorplate and camo stock. Also available in Youth model chambered in .243 only. Introduced in 2007.

NIB	Exc.	V.G.	Good	Fair	Poor
500	450	400	350	300	150

Model 700 Alaskan Ti

Lightweight (6.25 lbs.) version of Model 700 with titanium receiver, 24" fluted stainless barrel and Bell & Carlson synthetic stock. Chambered in a variety of long, short and super-short cartridges. Introduced in 2007.

NIB	Exc.	V.G.	Good	Fair	Poor
1600	1350	1050	775	500	200

Model 700 LSS 50th Anniversary of the .280 Remington

Similar to Model 700 LSS but in .280 Remington. A dealer exclusive for 2007.

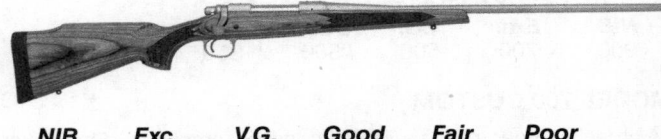

NIB	Exc.	V.G.	Good	Fair	Poor
800	675	500	375	250	175

Model 700 VL SS Thumbhole

Similar to Model 700 VS Composite but with brown laminated thumbhole stock and stainless steel barrel. Introduced in 2007.

NIB	Exc.	V.G.	Good	Fair	Poor
900	750	500	300	200	125

Model 700 Tactical Weapons System

This set is designed for law enforcement use and features a Model 700 Police chambered for the .308 Win. cartridge, a 24" barrel (1-12" twist), and detachable magazine. Also furnished with a Leupold VARI X III scope with rings and base and a Harris 1A2 bipod, sling, lens covers and case.

NIB	Exc.	V.G.	Good	Fair	Poor
2500	2000	1650	1150	800	500

Model 710

Introduced in 2001 this rifle is chambered for the .270 Win. or .30-06 cartridge. Fitted with a 22" barrel and dark gray synthetic stock. Detachable box magazine. Supplied with pre-mounted Bushnell Sharpshooter 3-9x scope. Barrel finish is ordnance gray steel with a matte finish. Weight is about 7.12 lbs. In 2004 the 7mm Rem. Magnum and .300 Win Magnum chamberings were added. In 2005 the receiver was extruded solid steel. Calibers: .243, 7mm RM, .300 WM.

NIB	Exc.	V.G.	Good	Fair	Poor
375	285	225	195	150	100

Model 710 Youth

Similar to Model 710 but with 20" barrel and 39.5" overall length. Chambered in .243 Win. Introduced 2006.

NIB	Exc.	V.G.	Good	Fair	Poor
375	285	225	195	150	100

Model 788

A centerfire bolt-action sporting rifle with either a 22" or 24" barrel and a plain walnut stock. An 18" barrel carbine was also manufactured and is worth approximately 10 percent more than the values listed below. Manufactured from 1967 to 1983. **NOTE:** Add a 30 percent premium for .44 Magnum, 25 percent for .30-30, and 20 percent premium for 7mm-08 caliber. Add 40 percent premium for left-hand models in 6mm and .308.

NIB	Exc.	V.G.	Good	Fair	Poor
—	500	425	375	300	250

Model Seven

A centerfire bolt-action sporting rifle with an 18.5" barrel and 4- or 5-shot magazine. Blued with a checkered walnut stock. Chambered for .17 Rem., .222 Rem., .223 Rem., .243 Rem., 6mm Rem., .260 Rem., 7mm-08 Rem. and .308 Win. Introduced into the Remington product line in 1982.

NIB	Exc.	V.G.	Good	Fair	Poor
600	475	325	275	200	100

Model Seven FS

As above with a Kevlar stock. Introduced in 1987.

NIB	Exc.	V.G.	Good	Fair	Poor
600	525	450	375	275	150

Model Seven Synthetic

Updated Synthetic short-action series in .223 Remington, .243 Winchester, .260 Remington, 7mm-08 Remington and .308 Winchester. 20" satin blue carbon steel barrel and matte black stock. Externally adjustable X-Mark Pro trigger is standard. No sights furnished. Weight: 6.5 pounds. Compact version has 18" barrel, chambered in .243 or 7mm-08 only.

NIB	Exc.	V.G.	Good	Fair	Poor
585	500	425	365	300	200

Model Seven SS (Stainless Synthetic)

Introduced in 1994 this model features a stainless steel barrel, receiver and bolt with a matte finish. It is fitted with a 20" barrel and a hinged floorplate. The synthetic stock is textured black.

Available in .243, 7mm-08 and .308. In 1997 the .260 Rem. cartridge was also offered. Weight approximately 6.25 lbs.

NIB	Exc.	V.G.	Good	Fair	Poor
625	450	350	300	200	150

Model Seven LSS

This model has a stainless steel barrel and action but is fitted with a satin finished laminated stock. Chambered for .22-250, .243, and 7mm-08 Rem. Weight is about 6.5 lbs. Introduced in 2000.

NIB	Exc.	V.G.	Good	Fair	Poor
625	500	375	300	200	100

Model Seven LS

This model offers a laminated stock but with a carbon steel blued barrel. Offered in five calibers: .22-250, .243, .260 Rem., 8mm-08 Rem. and .308 Win. Weight is about 6.5 lbs. Introduced in 2000.

NIB	Exc.	V.G.	Good	Fair	Poor
625	500	375	300	200	100

Model Seven MS

First introduced in 1993 and available through the Remington Custom Shop. This rifle features a 20" barrel with Mannlicher stock made from select grain wood and laminated for strength. Available in most short-action calibers including .222 Rem., .223 Rem., .22-250, .243 Win., 6mm Rem., .250 Savage, .257 Roberts, .260 Rem., 7mm-08, .308 Win., .35 Rem., .350 Rem. Magnum. **NOTE:** Add 20 percent for .250 Savage, .257 Roberts, .35 Rem.

NIB	Exc.	V.G.	Good	Fair	Poor
2000	1800	1500	500	350	250

Model Seven AWR

The Alaskan Wilderness Model has a black synthetic stock, stainless steel action, and a 22" barrel with a black matte Teflon finish. Weight: 6-1/8 lbs. Detachable 3-shot magazine. It was available from the Remington Custom Shop from 2002 - 2008 and chambered only in 6.8 Rem. SPC, 7mm Rem. SAUM or .300 Rem. SAUM. It was replaced by the Model Seven AWR II in 2008. This model came with a 20" or 22" stainless steel barrel, Bell & Carlson olive green fiberglass stock and hinged floorplate. Chamberings include .260 Rem., .270 WSM, 7mm-08, 7mm Rem. SAUM, .308 Win., .300 WSM, .300 Rem. SAUM and .350 Rem. Magnum. **NOTE:** Add 10 percent for AWR II

NIB	Exc.	V.G.	Good	Fair	Poor
2400	1800	1500	500	350	250

Model Seven Youth

First offered in 1993 this variation is a youth version of the standard Model 7. The buttstock is 1" shorter than standard. Available in

6mm, .243, and 7mm-08. In 1998 this model was available in .260 Rem. caliber.

NIB	Exc.	V.G.	Good	Fair	Poor
600	495	350	225	175	100

Model Seven CDL

Similar to Model Seven but with satin walnut, satin blue finish, sightless barrel and Limbsaver recoil pad. Introduced 2006.

NIB	Exc.	V.G.	Good	Fair	Poor
775	625	550	400	275	150

Model Seven XCR Camo

Similar to Model Seven LSS but with camo stock, fluted barrel and weather-resistant coating. Chambered in .243, 7mm-08, .308, .270 WSM and .300 WSM. Introduced in 2007.

NIB	Exc.	V.G.	Good	Fair	Poor
775	650	500	395	275	175

Model Seven 25th Anniversary Version

Similar to Model Seven but in 7mm-08 only with 25th anniversary medallion inset at the pistol grip cap area, high-sheen blued finish on the receiver, bolt and 22" standard-contour barrel, X-Mark Pro Trigger and SuperCell recoil pad. Introduced 2008.

NIB	Exc.	V.G.	Good	Fair	Poor
950	700	550	350	250	150

Model Seven Predator

Similar to Model Seven but with full coverage in Mossy Oak Brush camo; fluted, magnum contour 22" barrel, synthetic stock as on Model Seven XCR; X-Mark Pro Trigger. Chambered in .17 Remington Fireball, .204, .223, .22-250 and .243.

NIB	Exc.	V.G.	Good	Fair	Poor
800	650	500	395	275	175

Model 770

Package rifle similar to Model 710 but with redesigned bolt assembly and magazine catch. Chambered in .243, .270, 7mm-08, .308, .30-06 and .300 WM. Also available in Youth model chambered in .243 only. Introduced in 2007. In 2008 a version with stainless steel barrel and receiver and full camo finish was introduced. A 3-9X Bushnell scope is included. **NOTE:** Add $75 for camo finish.

NIB	Exc.	V.G.	Good	Fair	Poor
400	300	225	175	100	50

Model 770 Youth

Similar to Model 770 but with shorter stock and barrel.

NIB	Exc.	V.G.	Good	Fair	Poor
375	275	200	165	90	50

Model 715 Sportsman

Similar to Model 770. A dealer exclusive for 2007.

NIB	Exc.	V.G.	Good	Fair	Poor
375	275	200	165	90	50

Model 798

Long-action sporting rifle built on reworked 98 Mauser action. Calibers: .243, .308, .30-06, .270, .300 WM, .375 H&H, .458 WM. Barrel: 22" or 24" blued sightless. Stock: Brown laminated with recoil pad. Claw extractor, 2-position safety, hinged floorplate. Add 10 percent for Magnum chamberings; add 30 percent for .375 and .458. Introduced 2006.

NIB	Exc.	V.G.	Good	Fair	Poor
575	400	300	200	125	100

Model 798 Stainless Laminate

Similar to Model 798 but with laminated stock and stainless barrel. Chambered in .243, .25-06, .270, .30-06, 7mm Magnum, .300 WM and .375 H&H Magnum. Introduced in 2007. **NOTE:** Add 25 percent for .375.

NIB	Exc.	V.G.	Good	Fair	Poor
650	475	350	250	175	125

Model 798 SPS

Similar to Model 798 but with blued barrel and black synthetic stock. Introduced 2008.

NIB	Exc.	V.G.	Good	Fair	Poor
575	400	300	200	125	100

Model 798 Safari

Similar to Model 798 but chambered in .375 H&H or .458 Winchester Magnum. Introduced 2008.

NIB	Exc.	V.G.	Good	Fair	Poor
850	700	575	400	325	250

Model 799

Similar to Model 798 but short-action without recoil pad. Calibers: .22 Hornet, .222 Remington, .22-250, .223, 762X39. Introduced 2006.

NIB	Exc.	V.G.	Good	Fair	Poor
525	400	300	200	125	100

Model 1816 Commemorative Flint Lock Rifle

Introduced in 1995. It features a 39", .50 caliber octagonal barrel. Stock is hand finished extra fancy curly maple. Built for one year only. Special order only.

Courtesy Remington Arms

NIB	Exc.	V.G.	Good	Fair	Poor
1825	1200	850	700	500	300

Remington No. 1 Rolling Block Mid-Range

This classic rifle was reintroduced into the Remington line in 1997 and features a 30" half octagon, half-round barrel chambered for the .45-70 Government cartridge. Designed for use with black powder and lead cast bullets. The receiver is case colored. All barrel, receiver and metalwork markings match the original rifle. Rear tang-mounted vernier sight and front globe sight with interchangeable inserts. A single set trigger is standard. Steel buttplate. Weight is approximately 9.75 lbs.

NIB	Exc.	V.G.	Good	Fair	Poor
2200	1900	1500	1200	700	400

Remington Mid-Range Sporter Rolling Block

Introduced in 1998 this model features a 30" round barrel with pistol grip sporter stock. Adjustable rear sight. Chambered for .30-30, .444 Marlin and .45-70 Government. A number of extra cost options are available for this model including barrels, sights, fancy wood, etc. Prices listed below are for standard model.

NIB	Exc.	V.G.	Good	Fair	Poor
1800	1600	1350	900	600	350

Model SPR18 Single Shot Rifle

A break-action rifle with silvertone receiver and fluted barrel. Calibers: .223, .243, .270, .30-06, .308. Weight: 6.75 lbs. Imported; introduced 2005.

NIB	Exc.	V.G.	Good	Fair	Poor
260	225	175	150	100	75

Model SPR22 Double Rifle

Top-lever operated break-action SXS double rifle in .30-06 and .45-70. Double triggers, tang safety. Barrels can be regulated via jackscrew. Imported; introduced 2005.

NIB	Exc.	V.G.	Good	Fair	Poor
1000	850	700	600	450	300

Model SPR94 Combo Gun

Over/under rifle shotgun. Combinations: .410/.22 rimfire, .410/.17HMR, .41o/.22WMR, 12-gauge/.223, 12 gauge/.30-06, 12 gauge/.308. Double triggers, tang safety. Imported; introduced 2005.

NIB	Exc.	V.G.	Good	Fair	Poor
850	700	600	450	300	200

Model 412

Compact single-shot chambered for .22 LR. 19.5" blued barrel, hardwood stock. Introduced 2006.

NIB	Exc.	V.G.	Good	Fair	Poor
165	125	100	75	50	25

MODERN MUZZLELOADERS

Model 700 ML

This model was introduced in 1996. It is an in-line design and the first built on a modern action. It is chambered for the .50 or .54 caliber bullet. It is fitted with a synthetic stock and rubber recoil pad. The barrel length is 24" and the approximate weight is 7.75 lbs. A camo stock option was added to this model in 1997. Discontinued 2006.

Remington Model 700 ML Camo   Courtesy Remington Arms

NIB	Exc.	V.G.	Good	Fair	Poor
350	250	200	150	100	75

Model 700 ML Custom

Introduced in 1997 this new model is similar to the above model but features a satin metal finish and gray laminated thumbhole stock with roll-over cheekpiece. Discontinued.

NIB	Exc.	V.G.	Good	Fair	Poor
550	425	350	275	200	100

Model 700 MLS

Same as above but with stainless steel barrel and action. Discontinued.

Courtesy Remington Arms

Remington Model 700 MLS Camo

NIB	Exc.	V.G.	Good	Fair	Poor
400	300	250	200	150	100

Model 700 MLS Custom

Similar to the above model but with a satin stainless steel finish and a two-toned gray laminated thumbhole stock with roll-over cheekpiece. Introduced in 1997. Discontinued.

NIB	Exc.	V.G.	Good	Fair	Poor
600	475	375	325	225	125

Model 700 ML Youth

This model is similar to the Model ML with a shortened stock with 13" lop with a rubber recoil pad. Discontinued.

NIB	Exc.	V.G.	Good	Fair	Poor
370	300	250	200	150	100

Genesis Muzzleloaders

Fixed-breech hammer-fired muzzleloaders manufactured in a variety of configurations. Imported. Manufactured from 2006 to 2008.

NIB	Exc.	V.G.	Good	Fair	Poor
200	180	160	135	110	85

SHOTGUNS

Model 11

A 12, 16 or 20 gauge semi-automatic shotgun with barrels ranging in length from 26" to 32". Designed by John M. Browning and produced under license from Fabrique Nationale. Blued with a checkered walnut stock. Approximately 300,000 were made from 1911 to 1948. **NOTE:** Solid rib or vent rib add 30 percent to listed values.

NIB	Exc.	V.G.	Good	Fair	Poor
—	550	400	300	200	100

11B Special

Engraved.

NIB	Exc.	V.G.	Good	Fair	Poor
—	900	750	600	300	200

11D Tournament

NIB	Exc.	V.G.	Good	Fair	Poor
—	1000	895	675	500	300

11E Expert

Engraved.

NIB	Exc.	V.G.	Good	Fair	Poor
—	4500	3250	2700	1500	300

11F Premier

Heavily engraved.

NIB	Exc.	V.G.	Good	Fair	Poor
—	9000	7000	5000	3500	500

11R

20" barrel riot gun.

NIB	Exc.	V.G.	Good	Fair	Poor
—	475	350	250	175	100

Model 10A

A 12, 16 or 20 gauge slide-action shotgun with barrels ranging from 26" to 32". Takedown, blued with a plain walnut stock. Manufactured from 1907 to 1929.

Courtesy Remington Arms

NIB	Exc.	V.G.	Good	Fair	Poor
—	375	300	250	200	100

Model 17

A 20 gauge slide-action shotgun with barrels ranging in length from 26" to 32". Takedown, blued with a plain walnut stock. Approximately 48,000 were made from 1917 to 1933. **NOTE:** Vent rib add 25 percent.

Courtesy Remington Arms

NIB	Exc.	V.G.	Good	Fair	Poor
—	395	300	250	175	100

Model 29

As above, chambered for 12 gauge cartridges. Approximately 24,000 manufactured from 1929 to 1933. **NOTE:** For guns with 32" barrels add 40 percent. Vent rib add 25 percent.

NIB	Exc.	V.G.	Good	Fair	Poor
—	450	350	300	200	175

Model 31

A 12, 16 or 20 gauge slide-action shotgun with barrels ranging in length from 26" to 32" and a magazine capacity of either 2 or 4 rounds. Takedown, blued with a walnut stock. Approximately 160,000 were made from 1931 to 1949. **NOTE:** For guns with 32" barrel add 50 percent. For early models with checkered stocks add 40 percent. Solid rib or vent rib add 25 percent. For early banded barrels add 25 percent.

NIB	Exc.	V.G.	Good	Fair	Poor
—	450	325	275	200	125

MODEL 870 SERIES

Model 870 Wingmaster

A 12, 16, or 20 gauge slide-action shotgun with 26", 28", or 30" barrels and a 5-shot tubular magazine. Blued with a plain walnut stock. Manufactured from 1950 to 1963. **NOTE:** Vent rib add 10 percent.

NIB	Exc.	V.G.	Good	Fair	Poor
—	350	225	200	150	100

Model 870 Field Wingmaster

As above, with a checkered walnut stock and screw-in choke tubes. Introduced in 1964. In 1980 the 16 gauge was dropped as an offering but was later reinstated (see below).

NIB	Exc.	V.G.	Good	Fair	Poor
550	450	300	225	150	100

Model 870 Field Wingmaster 16 Gauge

In 2002 the 16 gauge was reintroduced into the Wingmaster line. Offered with 26" or 28" vent rib barrel with choke tubes. Walnut stock with blued finish. Weight is about 7 lbs. Offered in 16 gauge in other configurations listed.

NIB	Exc.	V.G.	Good	Fair	Poor
600	475	375	250	200	100

Model 870 Wingmaster Jr.

Introduced in 2005 this model features a 20 gauge gun with 18.75" vent rib barrel with choke tubes. Checkered walnut stock with recoil pad. Blued finish. Weight is about 6 lbs.

NIB	Exc.	V.G.	Good	Fair	Poor
550	450	300	225	150	100

Model 870 Field Wingmaster Small Bores

Introduced in 1999 this model is now offered in both 28 gauge and .410 bore. Checkered walnut stock. High polish blue finish. Both guns are fitted with 25" barrels. The 28 gauge has Rem chokes while the .410 comes with fixed Modified chokes. Weight is approximately 6 lbs. Price listed is for the .410 bore. **NOTE:** Add $50 for 28 gauge gun.

NIB	Exc.	V.G.	Good	Fair	Poor
600	475	395	300	275	200

Model 870 Magnum

As above, chambered for 12 or 20 gauge 3" Magnum shells. Introduced in 1964. Choke tubes introduced in 1987.

NIB	Exc.	V.G.	Good	Fair	Poor
575	425	300	225	150	100

Model 870 Express

As above, for 3", 12 gauge shells with a 28" ventilated rib and one choke tube. Parkerized with a matte finished stock. Introduced in 1987.

NIB	Exc.	V.G.	Good	Fair	Poor
330	250	200	150	100	75

Model 870 Express Synthetic

NIB	Exc.	V.G.	Good	Fair	Poor
330	250	200	150	100	75

Model 870 Express Synthetic Youth

NIB	Exc.	V.G.	Good	Fair	Poor
300	250	200	150	100	75

Model 870 Express Jr. NWTF Edition

This 20 gauge model is fitted with a 18.75" vent rib barrel with choke tubes. Synthetic stock has a camo finish. Metal is matte black. Weight is about 6 lbs. Introduced in 2005.

NIB	Exc.	V.G.	Good	Fair	Poor
320	250	200	150	100	75

Model 870 Express Super Magnum

Introduced in 1998, this 870 is similar to the 870 Express but is chambered for 3.5" 12 gauge. Offered in walnut stock with blued 28" barrel, matte black synthetic with 26" or 28" barrel or various camo finishes. Also available as a combo with extra 20" rifled deer barrel. **NOTE:** Add $100 for camo. Add 20 percent for combo with deer barrel. Introduced in 1998.

NIB	Exc.	V.G.	Good	Fair	Poor
425	330	225	175	125	100

Model 870 Express Super Magnum Fall Flight

Chambered for the 12 gauge with either 2.75", 3", or 3.5" shells. Fitted with 30" vent rib barrel with choke tubes. Skyline Fall Flight camo finish. Weight is about 7.75 lbs. Introduced in 2005.

NIB	Exc.	V.G.	Good	Fair	Poor
475	375	275	225	175	150

Remington 870 Express Synthetic Super Mag Turkey-Waterfowl Camo

Pump action shotgun chambered in 12 gauge, 2.75" to 3.5". Features include full Mossy Oak Bottomland camo coverage; 26" barrel with HiViz fiber-optics sights; Wingmaster HD Waterfowl and Turkey Extra Full RemChokes; SuperCell recoil pad; drilled and tapped receiver.

NIB	Exc.	V.G.	Good	Fair	Poor
515	440	375	315	200	150

Remington 870 Super Mag Turkey-Predator Camo with Scope

Pump action shotgun chambered in 12 gauge, 2.75" to 3.5". Features include 20" barrel; TruGlo red/green selectable illuminated sight mounted on pre-installed Weaver-style rail; black padded sling; Wingmaster HD Turkey/Predator RemChoke; full Mossy Oak Obsession camo coverage; ShurShot pistol grip stock with black overmolded grip panels; TruGlo 30mm Red/Green Dot Scope pre-mounted.

NIB	Exc.	V.G.	Good	Fair	Poor
575	500	425	350	200	150

MODEL 870 SERIES

Model 870TA Trap

As above, with a competition ventilated rib and checkered stock. Produced in 12 gauge only. Discontinued in 1986.

NIB	Exc.	V.G.	Good	Fair	Poor
500	400	300	200	150	100

Model 870TB Trap

As above, with a 28" or 30" Full choke, ventilated rib barrel and a trap-style walnut stock. Manufactured from 1950 to 1981.

NIB	Exc.	V.G.	Good	Fair	Poor
—	450	325	275	200	125

Model 870TC Trap

As above, with a finely figured walnut stock and screw-in choke tubes.

NIB	Exc.	V.G.	Good	Fair	Poor
575	475	400	350	250	150

Model 870 Express Deer Gun

This model is fitted with a 20" fully rifled barrel, iron sights, and Monte Carlo stock. Also offered with a 20" IC rifle sighted barrel. Available in 12 gauge only.

NIB	Exc.	V.G.	Good	Fair	Poor
370	275	200	150	125	100

Model 870 Express Deer/Turkey Combo

This 3" 12 gauge has a 21" barrel threaded for Remchokes for turkey hunting and a 23" rifled slug barrel with cantilever scope mount for deer hunting. Receiver and barrel are matte black; synthetic stock is Mossy Oak Break-Up camo.

NIB	Exc.	V.G.	Good	Fair	Poor
625	500	425	350	250	150

Model 870 Express Left-Hand

Left-hand version of the Express model fitted with a 28" vent rib barrel and checkered hardwood stock. Black matte finish.

NIB	Exc.	V.G.	Good	Fair	Poor
360	275	200	150	100	75

Remington 870 Express Synthetic Turkey Camo

Pump action shotgun chambered for 2.75" and 3" 12 gauge. Features include 21" vent-rib bead-sighted barrel; standard Express finish on barrel and receiver; Turkey Extra Full RemChoke; synthetic stock with integrated sling swivel attachment.

NIB	Exc.	V.G.	Good	Fair	Poor
445	385	325	275	200	150

Model 870 Express Super Magnum Turkey

This 12 gauge gun will handle 2.75", 3" or 3.5" shells. Fitted with a 23" vent rib barrel, black synthetic stock and matte black metal finish. Weight is about 7.25 lbs. Introduced in 1999.

NIB	Exc.	V.G.	Good	Fair	Poor
390	290	200	150	100	75

Model 870 Express Synthetic Deer

This model is fitted with a 20" fully rifled barrel with adjustable rifle sights. Black synthetic stock with Monte Carlo comb and matte black finish. Weight is about 7 lbs. Introduced in 1999.

NIB	Exc.	V.G.	Good	Fair	Poor
370	275	200	150	100	75

Model 870 Express Compact Deer

20 gauge; similar to Model 870 Express Synthetic Deer but with smaller dimensions.

NIB	Exc.	V.G.	Good	Fair	Poor
425	300	200	150	100	75

Model 870 Express Compact Pink Camo

20 gauge; similar to Model 870 Express but with pink camo synthetic stock.

NIB	Exc.	V.G.	Good	Fair	Poor
370	275	200	150	100	75

Model 870 Express Compact Synthetic

Similar to above but with matte black synthetic stock.

NIB	Exc.	V.G.	Good	Fair	Poor
370	275	200	150	100	75

Model 870 Express Compact Camo

Similar to above but with camo buttstock and forend.

NIB	Exc.	V.G.	Good	Fair	Poor
395	295	215	150	100	75

Model 870 Express Compact Jr.

Similar to above but with shorter barrel and LOP.

NIB	Exc.	V.G.	Good	Fair	Poor
370	275	200	150	100	75

Model 870 Express Combos

Offered in both 12 and 20 gauge with a 26" vent rib modified barrel and a 20" fully rifled deer barrel.

NIB	Exc.	V.G.	Good	Fair	Poor
500	395	250	200	150	100

Model 870 Express Youth Gun

Available in 20 gauge only, this shotgun is built for children. It has a 13" length of pull, a 21" vent rib barrel, and is sold with a Modified Rem. choke tube.

NIB	Exc.	V.G.	Good	Fair	Poor
330	250	200	150	125	100

Model 870 Express Turkey

Furnished in 12 gauge with 21" vent rib barrel with extra-full Remington choke Turkey tube.

NIB	Exc.	V.G.	Good	Fair	Poor
345	250	175	150	125	100

Model 870 Express Camo Turkey

Similar to the Express Turkey but with complete coverage of camo stock. Metal is matte black.

NIB	Exc.	V.G.	Good	Fair	Poor
400	300	225	150	100	75

Model 870 20 Gauge Express Youth Camo Turkey

Similar to the Model 870 Express Camo but in 20 gauge with shortened stock (13" lop).

NIB	Exc.	V.G.	Good	Fair	Poor
400	300	225	150	100	75

Model 870 Express Small Game

Offered in 20 gauge or .410, this model has a nonreflective metal and wood finish. The .410 bore is furnished with a 25" vent rib Full choke barrel, while the 20 gauge is available with a 26" or 28" vent rib barrel with Modified Rem. choke tube.

NIB	Exc.	V.G.	Good	Fair	Poor
225	200	175	150	125	100

Model 870 Express HD (Home Defense)

Introduced in 1995 this model features an 18" 12 gauge barrel with cylinder barrel with front bead sight. Weight approx. 7.25 lb.

Courtesy Remington Arms

NIB	Exc.	V.G.	Good	Fair	Poor
345	250	175	150	125	100

Model 870 Classic Trap

Introduced in 2000 this model features special fine line engraving with gold inlays. Stock is select walnut with Monte Carlo comb, 30" barrel with a contoured vent rib. Ventilated recoil pad with white-line spacers. Choke tubes. Weight is about 8 lbs.

NIB	Exc.	V.G.	Good	Fair	Poor
675	550	450	300	200	—

Model 870 Special Field

This Remington pump-action shotgun is available in either 12 or 20 gauge and features an English-style straight grip stock, 21" vent rib barrel and slim shortened slide handle. In 12 gauge the gun weighs 7 lbs. and in 20 gauge it weighs 6.25 lbs. Comes with a set of Remington choke tubes.

NIB	Exc.	V.G.	Good	Fair	Poor
650	550	375	250	150	100

Model 870 Rifled Deer Gun

This new 20 gauge model was introduced in 1994 and features a fully rifled 20" barrel. It has a new scope rail design that is more rigid. The finish is blue and the Monte Carlo stock is walnut. Is equipped with recoil pad and checkering.

Close-up of engraving detail on Model 870 Deer Gun

NIB	Exc.	V.G.	Good	Fair	Poor
450	400	350	300	200	100

Model 870 Brushmaster Deer Gun

This 12 gauge slide-action shotgun is fitted with a 20" Remington choke plain barrel and Monte Carlo stock. Available for either left-hand or right-hand shooters.

NIB	Exc.	V.G.	Good	Fair	Poor
350	300	250	200	150	100

Model 870 Express Youth Turkey Camo

Similar to the model above but chambered for the 20 gauge shell and finished with Realtree Camo. Weight is about 6 lbs.

NIB	Exc.	V.G.	Good	Fair	Poor
400	300	225	150	125	100

Model 870 Youth Deer Gun

Chambered for the 20 gauge shell and fitted with a 21" full choked barrel. Realtree Camo finish. Magazine capacity is 4 rounds. Weight is about 6 lbs.

NIB	Exc.	V.G.	Good	Fair	Poor
350	300	250	200	150	100

Model 870 Security

Offered in 12 gauge only this personal protection shotgun has an 18.5" Cylinder-choked plain barrel with front bead sight.

NIB	Exc.	V.G.	Good	Fair	Poor
350	300	250	200	150	100

Model 870 SPS-Camo

Offered in 12 gauge only and a choice of 26" or 28" vent rib barrel with Rem. choke tubes. The wood and metal are finished in a brown camo color. Introduced in 2001.

NIB	Exc.	V.G.	Good	Fair	Poor
600	425	325	225	175	125

Model 870 SPS Super Magnum Camo

This model is chambered for 12 gauge shells with chambers that will handle both 3" magnum and 3.5" magnum shells as well as all 2.75" shells. Barrel is 23" with ventilated rib and Rem. chokes. Finish is Mossy Oak camo. Weight is about 7.25 lbs. Introduced in 1999.

NIB	Exc.	V.G.	Good	Fair	Poor
600	425	325	225	175	125

Model 870 SPS-BG Camo

Available for the first time in 1993 this model features a 12 gauge 20" plain barrel with IC and Turkey Super Full Rem. choke tubes. The wood and metal are finished in a brown camo color.

NIB	Exc.	V.G.	Good	Fair	Poor
400	300	225	175	125	100

Model 870 SPS Fully Rifled Deer Gun

This 20 gauge model features an 18.5" fully rifled heavy barrel with no sights. Receiver has a cantilever scope mount. Black synthetic stock. Black matte finish. Weight is about 8 lbs. Magazine capacity is 4 rounds. Introduced in 2004.

NIB	Exc.	V.G.	Good	Fair	Poor
500	375	250	175	125	100

Model 870 SPS Super Slug Deer Gun

This model features a 23" fully rifled modified contour barrel which is equipped with a barrel mounted cantilever scope mount. Stock is black synthetic. Weight is approximately 8 lbs. Introduced in 1999.

NIB	Exc.	V.G.	Good	Fair	Poor
600	425	325	250	175	100

Model 870 SPS-T

This 12 gauge model comes standard with a 21" vent rib barrel, Rem. choke tubes in IC and Turkey Super Full, black synthetic stock, and black matte finish.

NIB	Exc.	V.G.	Good	Fair	Poor
575	475	400	350	250	150

Model 870 SPS-T Camo

Same as above with the exception of a 21" vent rib barrel with IC and Turkey Super Full Rem. choke tubes. Both wood and metal are finished in a green camo color.

NIB	Exc.	V.G.	Good	Fair	Poor
600	425	325	250	175	100

Model 870 SPS-T Youth Turkey Camo

This shotgun is finished in Mossy Oak Break-Up and chambered for the 12 gauge shell. Fitted with a 20" Super Full choke. Weight is about 7.125 lbs. Introduced in 2001.

NIB	Exc.	V.G.	Good	Fair	Poor
565	450	325	250	175	125

Model 870 SPS-T Super Magnum Camo

This 12 gauge model will handle 2.75", 3" and 3.5" shells. Fitted with a 23" barrel with Rem chokes. Finish is Mossy Oak camo. Weight is about 7.25 lbs. Introduced in 1999.

NIB	Exc.	V.G.	Good	Fair	Poor
615	425	325	250	175	125

Model 870 SPS-T Camo NWTF 25th Anniversary

This model, fitted with a 21" barrel has special fiber optic sighting system. NWTF logo on left side of receiver. Introduced in 1998.

NIB	Exc.	V.G.	Good	Fair	Poor
600	450	325	250	175	125

Model 870 SPS-T Super Mag

Similar to Model 870 SP-T Thumbhole but with pistol-grip stock and vent-rib barrel.

NIB	Exc.	V.G.	Good	Fair	Poor
630	450	350	275	200	150

Model 870 SPS-T/20

This 20-gauge turkey gun features a 3" chamber, 23" vent rib barrel, R3 recoil pad and full coverage in Mossy Oak New Break-Up camo. Drilled and tapped for scope mount.

NIB	Exc.	V.G.	Good	Fair	Poor
550	450	325	250	195	150

Model 870 SPS-T Camo

Chambered for the 20 gauge 3" shell and fitted with a 20" barrel with full choke. Stock is Mossy Oak camo. Fiber optic front sight. Weight is about 6 lbs. Introduced in 2003.

NIB	Exc.	V.G.	Good	Fair	Poor
600	450	325	250	175	125

Model 870 SP-T Super Magnum Thumbhole

This 12 gauge 3.5" gun is fitted with a 23" barrel with choke tubes. Mossy Oak Obsession finish. Open sights with fiber-optic front sight. Weight is about 8 lbs. Introduced in 2005.

NIB	Exc.	V.G.	Good	Fair	Poor
650	500	350	250	175	125

Model 870 Dale Earnhardt Limited Edition

This is a 12 gauge with a 28" vent rib barrel with choke tubes. Checkered walnut stock. The receiver is engraved with Earnhardt's likeness and gold signature. High polish blue finish. Weight is about 8 lbs. Introduced in 2005.

NIB	Exc.	V.G.	Good	Fair	Poor
650	500	350	250	175	125

Model 870 Marine Magnum

This 12 gauge shotgun has a nickel finish on the inside and outside of the receiver and barrel. Synthetic stock is checkered. The 18" barrel is bored cylinder and is fitted with a 7-round magazine. Sling swivel studs are standard.

NIB	Exc.	V.G.	Good	Fair	Poor
560	325	275	225	175	125

Model 870 SPS

Offered in 12 gauge only with synthetic stock and black matte finish. The barrel is either 26" or 28" with ventilated rib and Rem. choke tubes.

NIB	Exc.	V.G.	Good	Fair	Poor
325	275	225	175	125	100

Model 870 SPS-Deer

Available with a 20" rifle with plain barrel, this 12 gauge shotgun has a black synthetic stock and black matte finish. First introduced in 1993.

NIB	Exc.	V.G.	Good	Fair	Poor
550	450	325	250	195	150

Model 870 Police

This model comes in a wide variety (21) of 12 gauge configurations. Fitted with barrel from 14" (Class III), 18" or 20". Most with Parkerized finish, although some variations have blued finish. Wood stock, folding stock, Speedfeed stock or synthetic stock. Rifle or bead sights and some configurations with ghost ring and tritium night sights. Some variations have 7- or 8-round magazine extensions depending on barrel length.

NIB	Exc.	V.G.	Good	Fair	Poor
650	525	400	300	225	125

Model 870 Tac-2 SpecOps Stock

Tactical 3" 12 gauge is available with a Knoxx pistol-grip or folding stock. Barrel is 18" with fixed Cylinder choke. Magazine capacity is 6 shells. Weight is 7 lbs.

NIB	Exc.	V.G.	Good	Fair	Poor
615	425	325	250	175	125

Model 870 Tac-3 Speedfeed IV

Tactical 3" 12 gauge with pistol-grip stock and 20" barrel. Extended 7-round magazine. Weight is 7.5 lbs.

NIB	Exc.	V.G.	Good	Fair	Poor
600	450	325	250	175	125

Model 870 Tac-3 Folder

As above but with Knoxx Spec-Ops folding stock. Weight is 7 lbs.

NIB	Exc.	V.G.	Good	Fair	Poor
600	450	325	250	175	125

Remington 870 Express Tactical A-TACS Camo

Pump action shotgun chambered for 2.75" and 3" 12 gauge. Features include full A-TACS digitized camo; 18.5" barrel; extended ported Tactical RemChoke; SpeedFeed IV pistol-grip stock with SuperCell recoil pad; fully adjustable XS Ghost Ring Sight rail with removable white bead front sight; 7-round capacity with factory-installed 2-shot extension; drilled and tapped receiver; sling swivel stud.

NIB	Exc.	V.G.	Good	Fair	Poor
600	525	450	375	275	185

Model 870 Custom Grade

This Custom Shop model is available in three levels of engraving, gold inlay, wood grade and finish, metal work finish, recoil pad/buttplate and dimensions.

D Grade

NIB	Exc.	V.G.	Good	Fair	Poor
3000	200	1100	—	—	—

F Grade

NIB	Exc.	V.G.	Good	Fair	Poor
6000	4000	2250	—	—	—

F Grade with Gold Inlay

NIB	Exc.	V.G.	Good	Fair	Poor
10000	7500	5000	—	—	—

Model 870 SP-T Thumbhole

Introduced in 2005, this 3.5" 12 gauge is designed specifically for turkey hunting with full coverage in Mossy Oak Obsession camo and thumbhole stock. The 23" barrel features fiber-optic adjustable rifle sights and is drilled and tapped for scope mounting. Includes R3 recoil pad, sling, swivels and turkey super full choke tube.

NIB	Exc.	V.G.	Good	Fair	Poor
615	425	325	250	175	125

Model 870 Special Purpose Thumbhole

Laminated stock 12 gauge slug gun with 3" chamber and 23" fully rifled cantilever barrel.

NIB	Exc.	V.G.	Good	Fair	Poor
525	475	350	275	200	150

Model 870 XCS Marine Magnum

New in 2007, this weather-resistant 870 is a 3" 12 gauge with full black TriNyte coverage, 18" fixed Cylinder barrel and 7 round capacity. Weight is 7.5 lbs.

NIB	Exc.	V.G.	Good	Fair	Poor
675	495	400	300	200	125

Model 870 SPS MAX Gobbler

This dedicated turkey gun is a 3.5" 12 gauge featuring a length-adjustable Knoxx SpecOps stock, 23" barrel, fiber-optic rifle sights, Super Full turkey choke tube and full coverage in Realtree APG camo. Drilled and tapped for Weaver style mount. Weight is 8 lbs.

NIB	Exc.	V.G.	Good	Fair	Poor
650	550	425	350	225	150

Model 870 20 Gauge Lightweight Magnum

Fixed-choke, high-gloss 3" version of the Model 870 Wingmaster, with impressed checkering. Introduced mid-1980s. Also chambers 2.75" shells. Discontinued.

NIB	Exc.	V.G.	Good	Fair	Poor
550	450	325	250	195	150

Model 870 Wingmaster 100th Anniversary

This Commemorative Edition 12 gauge celebrating 100 years of Remington pump shotguns (dating from the introduction of the Model 10 in 1908) was introduced in 2008 and offered only for one year. Gold-inlaid logos on both sides of receiver and "B" Grade American Walnut stock with high-gloss finish. Includes three choke tubes.

NIB	Exc.	V.G.	Good	Fair	Poor
875	600	475	350	200	125

Model 870 with Claro Walnut

This 2008 upgrade to the 870 Wingmaster features a semi-fancy claro walnut stock and fore-end. It is available in 3" 12- and 20-gauge with 28" and 26" barrels, respectively. Three choke tubes included.

NIB	Exc.	V.G.	Good	Fair	Poor
875	600	475	350	200	125

Model 870 Express Magnum ShurShot Cantilever

This 3" 12 gauge has a 23", fully rifled barrel with cantilever scope mount. Matte black finish. Weight is about 7.75 lbs.

NIB	Exc.	V.G.	Good	Fair	Poor
550	450	325	250	195	150

Model 870 SPS ShurShot Synthetic Super Slug

Pump-action shotgun based on 870 platform. Chambers 12 gauge 2.75" and 3" shells interchangeably. Extra-heavy (1" dia.) 25.5" fully rifled barrel pinned to receiver. SuperCell recoil pad. Drilled and tapped for scope mounts with Weaver rail included. Matte black metal surfaces, Mossy Oak Treestand ShurShot buttstock and fore-end. Overall length 47". Weigh: 7-7/8 lbs.

NIB	Exc.	V.G.	Good	Fair	Poor
550	450	325	250	195	150

Model 870 Express Super Magnum Waterfowl

Introduced in 2008, this dedicated waterfowl gun is completely finished in Mossy Oak Duck Blind camo. The 3.5" 12 gauge has a 28" barrel, HiViz single bead sight and weighs about 7.5 lbs. Includes one choke tube.

NIB	Exc.	V.G.	Good	Fair	Poor
350	300	250	200	150	100

Model 870 Express Magnum ShurShot Turkey

This turkey-dedicated model has a matte black finish with a ShurShot pistol grip/thumbhole stock and fore-end finished in Mossy Oak Obsession camo. The 3" 12 gauge has a 21" barrel. Includes a Turkey Extra Full choke tube. Weight is about 7.5 lbs.

NIB	Exc.	V.G.	Good	Fair	Poor
500	400	325	250	175	100

Model 870 SPS ShurShot Turkey

New in 2008, this 12 gauge 870 is chambered for shells up to 3.5". It features Remington's ShurShot pistol grip/thumbhole stock and is fully covered in Realtree's APG HD camo. It has a 23" non-vent-rib barrel outfitted with fiber-optic rifle-type sights and includes an extended Turkey Rem Choke. Weight is about 7.5 lbs.

NIB	Exc.	V.G.	Good	Fair	Poor
625	495	400	300	200	125

Model 870 Express Tactical

Similar to Model 870 but in 12 gauge only (2.75" and 3" interchangeably) with 18.5" barrel, Tactical RemChoke extended/ported choke tube, black synthetic buttstock and fore-end, extended magazine tube, gray powdercoat finish overall. 38.5" overall length. Weight: 7.5 lbs.

NIB	Exc.	V.G.	Good	Fair	Poor
575	465	325	250	195	150

Model 870 Express Tactical with Ghost Ring Sights

Similar to Model 870 Express Tactical but with top-mounted accessories rail and XS ghost ring rear sight.

NIB	Exc.	V.G.	Good	Fair	Poor
625	495	400	300	200	125

Model 870 Tactical Desert Recon

This tactical version 870 features Digital Tiger desert camo on the synthetic stock and fore-end and an olive-drab powder-coated barrel and receiver. It is available with an 18" (six-round mag. capacity) or 20" (seven-round mag. capacity) barrel. Speedfeed I (shell holding) or Speedfeed IV (pistol grip) stock. Add 10 percent for Speedfeed IV stock.

NIB	Exc.	V.G.	Good	Fair	Poor
625	495	400	300	200	125

Model 887 Nitro Mag Pump Shotgun

Pump-action shotgun based on the Model 870. Chambers 3.5", 3" and 2.75" 12-gauge shells interchangeably. Black matte ArmorLokt rustproof coating throughout. SuperCell recoil pad. 28" barrel with solid rib and Hi-Viz front sight with interchangeable light tubes. Black synthetic stock with contoured grip panels.

NIB	Exc.	V.G.	Good	Fair	Poor
445	385	325	275	200	150

Model 887 Nitro Mag Waterfowl

Similar to above but with Advantage Max-4 camo overall.

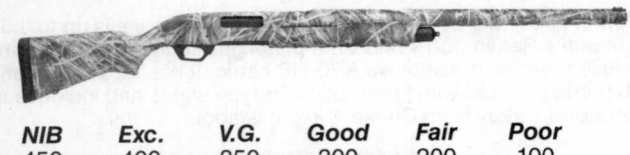

NIB	Exc.	V.G.	Good	Fair	Poor
450	400	350	300	200	100

Remington 887 Bone Collector Edition

Pump action shotgun chambered in 12 gauge, 2.75" to 3.5". Features include ArmorLokt rustproof coating; synthetic stock and fore-end; 26" barrel; full camo finish; integral swivel studs; SuperCell recoil pad; solid rib and HiViz front sight. Bone Collector logo.

NIB	Exc.	V.G.	Good	Fair	Poor
560	475	400	335	250	150

Remington 887 Nitro Mag Camo Combo

Pump action shotgun chambered in 12 gauge, 2.75" to 3.5". Features include 22" turkey barrel with HiViz fiber-optic rifle sights and 28" waterfowl with a HiViz sight; extended Waterfowl and Super Full Turkey RemChokes are included; SuperCell recoil pad; synthetic stock and fore-end with specially contoured grip panels; full camo coverage.

NIB	Exc.	V.G.	Good	Fair	Poor
625	535	460	385	325	200

Remington 887 Nitro Mag Tactical

Pump action shotgun chambered in 12 gauge, 2.75" to 3.5". Features include 18.5" barrel with ported, extended tactical RemChoke; 2-shot magazine extension; barrel clamp with integral Picatinny rails; ArmorLokt coating; synthetic stock and fore-end with specially contour grip panels.

NIB	Exc.	V.G.	Good	Fair	Poor
450	400	350	275	200	150

Model 48 Sportsman

A 12, 16 or 20 gauge semi-automatic shotgun with 26", 28" or 32" barrels and a 3-shot tubular magazine. Blued with a checkered walnut stock. Approximately 275,000 were made from 1949 to 1959. **NOTE:** Vent rib add 20 percent.

NIB	Exc.	V.G.	Good	Fair	Poor
—	325	300	250	175	100

Model 11-48

As above, with the addition of 28 gauge and .410 bore. Approximately 425,000 were made from 1949 to 1968. 225 percent premium for 28 ga.

NIB	Exc.	V.G.	Good	Fair	Poor
—	300	250	200	150	75

Model 58 Sportsman

A 12, 16 or 20 gauge semi-automatic shotgun with 26", 28" or 30" barrels and a 3-shot tubular magazine. The receiver is scroll engraved and blued. Checkered walnut stock. Approximately 270,000 were made from 1956 to 1963.

NIB	Exc.	V.G.	Good	Fair	Poor
—	300	250	200	150	75

Model 878 Automaster

As above, in 12 gauge only. Approximately 60,000 were made from 1959 to 1962.

NIB	Exc.	V.G.	Good	Fair	Poor
—	350	250	175	125	75

MODEL 1100 SERIES

A 12, 16, 20 or 28 gauge or .410 bore semi-automatic shotgun with barrels ranging in length from 26" to 30". Fitted with choke tubes after 1987. Blued with a checkered walnut stock. Manufactured beginning in 1963. **NOTE:** The smaller bore versions are worth approximately 20 percent more than the values listed.

NIB	Exc.	V.G.	Good	Fair	Poor
550	450	350	200	150	100

Model 1100 Classic Field

Introduced in 2003 this shotgun is chambered for the 16 gauge shell and fitted with a choice of 26" or 28" vent rib barrel with Remington choke tubes. Checkered walnut stock with pistol grip. High polish blue finish. Magazine capacity is four rounds. Weight is about 7 to 7.25 lbs. depending on barrel length.

NIB	Exc.	V.G.	Good	Fair	Poor
800	600	450	300	200	100

Model 1100 Small Game

Available in 20, 28 gauge or .410 bore fitted with 25" vent rib barrels. The 28 gauge and .410 have fixed chokes while the 20 gauge has Rem. choke tubes.

NIB	Exc.	V.G.	Good	Fair	Poor
500	450	400	350	250	150

Model 1100 Youth Gun

Offered in 20 gauge only with a 21" vent rib 2.75" barrel. The stock has a special 13" length of pull. Gun is supplied with a set of Rem. choke tubes.

NIB	Exc.	V.G.	Good	Fair	Poor
600	400	350	300	200	150

Model 1100 Youth Synthetic

Fitted with a 21" vent rib barrel this 20 gauge gun has a 1" shorter length of pull than standard. Matte black finish. Black synthetic stock. Weight is approximately 6.5 lbs. Introduced in 1999.

NIB	Exc.	V.G.	Good	Fair	Poor
575	400	300	225	150	100

Model 1100 Youth Synthetic Camo

Same as model above but with Realtree camo finish and chambered for 20 gauge 3" magnum shells. Weight is about 6.75 lbs. Introduced in 1999.

NIB	Exc.	V.G.	Good	Fair	Poor
695	475	325	225	175	100

Model 1100 Tournament Skeet

Offered in 20, 28 gauge, and .410 bore. The 28 gauge and .410 come with 25" Skeet choked vent rib barrels while the 20 gauge is supplied with a 26" Skeet choked vent rib barrel.

Courtesy Remington Arms

NIB	Exc.	V.G.	Good	Fair	Poor
800	650	500	400	250	150

Model 1100 Tournament Skeet, 12 Gauge

Introduced in 2003 this model is fitted with a 26" light contour vent rib barrel. Stock is semi-fancy walnut. Receiver is rolled-marked "tournament skeet". Supplied with extended choke tubes and gold-plated trigger. Weight is about 7.75 lbs.

NIB	Exc.	V.G.	Good	Fair	Poor
650	500	400	300	200	100

Model 1100 Classic Trap

This model features a 30" low-profile vent rib barrel. The stock is semi-fancy walnut with Monte Carlo comb and ventilated recoil pad. Receiver has fine line engraving with gold inlays and the trigger is gold. Weight is about 8.25 lbs.

NIB	Exc.	V.G.	Good	Fair	Poor
850	725	600	475	350	200

Model 1100 Sporting 12

Introduced in 2000 this 12 gauge model features a 28" low profile vent rib barrel. Stock is walnut with cut checkering and Sporting Clays-style recoil pad. Gold trigger and fine line engraving on the receiver. Weight is about 8 lbs.

NIB	Exc.	V.G.	Good	Fair	Poor
725	650	475	400	300	150

Model 1100 Sporting 20

This model has a high grade walnut stock with glass finish and recoil pad. It is fitted with a 28" barrel with target sights. Interchangeable chokes. Introduced in 1998.

NIB	Exc.	V.G.	Good	Fair	Poor
700	625	425	400	300	150

Model 1100 Sporting 28

Introduced in 1996 this version is chambered for the 28 gauge shell. It is fitted with interchangeable chokes and a 25" vent rib barrel. The stock is walnut with Tournament grade checkering and recoil pad.

Courtesy Remington Arms

NIB	Exc.	V.G.	Good	Fair	Poor
825	700	575	475	350	200

Model 1100 Competition Master

Introduced in 2003 this model features a 12 gauge gun chambered for the 2.75" shell. Fitted with a 22" vent rib barrel with Remington chokes and fiber optic front sight. Has a gray synthetic stock with matte black finish on receiver and barrel. Magazine extension has eight-round capacity. Receiver mounted ammo carrier for seven extra shells. Weight is about 8 lbs. Designed for practical shooting competition.

NIB	Exc.	V.G.	Good	Fair	Poor
725	600	425	400	300	150

Model 1100 Competition

Introduced in 2005 this model is chambered for the 12 gauge shells with 2.75" chamber. Fitted with a 30" target style barrel with 10mm vent rib. Extended choke tubes. Receiver is nickel plated. Stock is semi-fancy American walnut with checkering and high gloss finish. Adjustable comb offered as option. Weight is about 8 lbs. **NOTE:** Add $175 for adjustable comb model.

NIB	Exc.	V.G.	Good	Fair	Poor
950	775	650	525	350	175

Model 1100 LT-20

This 20 gauge model features a choice of 26" or 28" vent rib barrels with Rem choke tubes. It has a blue finish and walnut Monte Carlo stock. Recoil pad and cut checkering are standard. Weight is 6.75 to 7 lbs. depending on barrel length.

NIB	Exc.	V.G.	Good	Fair	Poor
600	450	400	300	200	150

Model 1100 LT-20 "Limited"

20 gauge lightweight Mode I 1100 Field gun with stock 1" shorter than standard and 23" barrel for youthful, beginner shooters of smaller stature.

NIB	Exc.	V.G.	Good	Fair	Poor
675	525	475	375	275	200

Model 1100 1 OF 3000

In September 1980, Remington announced the Model 1100 Limited Edition "One of Three Thousand". This was a high grade gun with positive cut checkered fancy American walnut wood with a fitted rosewood grip cap and thin brown butt pad. It is 14K gold trimmed and etched with a hunting scenes on the receiver. All metal parts including the receiver, barrel, bolt and magazine cap have a high-luster finish. Available only in 1980.

NIB	Exc.	V.G.	Good	Fair	Poor
2000	1600	1000	800	400	250

Model 1100 Special Field

In 12 gauge, 20 gauge or .410 bore, a shorter variation of the standard 1100. Barrel length was originally 21" (1983-1993) and was changed to 23" from (1994 to 1999) when the model was discontinued. Checkered walnut stock with straight grip. Ventilated rib on all models. **NOTE:** Add 20 percent for .410.

NIB	Exc.	V.G.	Good	Fair	Poor
600	500	400	350	300	150

Model 1100 TBMC Trap Gun

12 gauge with 30", vent rib barrel in full or modified trap chokes. This gun featured a figured and checkered stock and fore-end and had a rubber recoil pad. A Monte Carlo style stock was optional. A left-hand version of this gun was also available Due to a shortage of American walnut, in mid-year Remington began fitting some Model 1100 and Model 870 Field Grade shotguns with lightweight mahogany stocks and fore-ends.

NIB	Exc.	V.G.	Good	Fair	Poor
725	650	475	400	300	150

Model 1100 LT-20 Deer Gun

Same as above but fitted with a 21" barrel with adjustable sights and an improved cylinder choke. Satin finish with American walnut stock. Weight is approximately 6.5 lbs.

NIB	Exc.	V.G.	Good	Fair	Poor
525	450	400	300	200	150

Model 1100 LT-20 Synthetic

Same as above but fitted with a synthetic stock with recoil pad.

NIB	Exc.	V.G.	Good	Fair	Poor
550	375	325	275	200	150

Model 1100 LT-20 Magnum

This 20 gauge Model 1100 is chambered for the 3" 20 gauge shell. It is fitted with a 28" vent rib barrel with interchangeable chokes. Checkered walnut stock. Weight is about 7 lbs.

NIB	Exc.	V.G.	Good	Fair	Poor
575	395	400	300	200	150

Model 1100 LT-20 Synthetic Camo NWTF 25th Anniversary

This model is fitted with a 21" barrel with special fiber optic sighting system. NWTF logo on left side of receiver. Introduced in 1998.

NIB	Exc.	V.G.	Good	Fair	Poor
650	525	450	300	250	125

Model 1100 Synthetic

Introduced in 1995 this model is furnished with a black synthetic stock with black matte metal finish. Available in both 12 and 20 gauge. Weight is about 6.75 to 7 lbs. depending on barrel length. In 2003 this model was offered chambered for the 16 gauge shell.

Courtesy Remington Arms

NIB	Exc.	V.G.	Good	Fair	Poor
550	450	350	250	200	100

Model 1100 Synthetic Deer Gun

Same as above but fitted with a 21" fully rifled barrel with cantilever rail for scope mounting. Furnished with 2.75" chamber. Stock is black synthetic with checkering and Monte Carlo-style cheekpiece. Recoil pad is standard.

NIB	Exc.	V.G.	Good	Fair	Poor
525	450	400	300	200	150

Model 1100 Competition Synthetic

The 1100 Competition Synthetic is super-tuned for competitive shooters. Overbored 30" barrel with lengthened forcing cones. Optimized for 2.75" target loads and light field loads. Receiver and all internal parts have nickel-Teflon finish. Synthetic stock has SuperCell recoil pad. Twelve-gauge only; weight: 8.25 lbs.

NIB	Exc.	V.G.	Good	Fair	Poor
900	800	675	525	400	250

Model 1100 Custom Grade

This Custom Shop model is available in three levels of engraving, gold inlay, wood grade and finish, metal work finish, recoil pad/buttplate and dimensions. Each gun should be individually appraised prior to a sale.

D Grade

NIB	Exc.	V.G.	Good	Fair	Poor
3000	200	1100	—	—	—

F Grade

NIB	Exc.	V.G.	Good	Fair	Poor
6000	4000	2250	—	—	—

F Grade with Gold Inlay

NIB	Exc.	V.G.	Good	Fair	Poor
10000	7500	5000	—	—	—

Model 1100 G3

Introduced in 2006, this updated 1100 features a Realwood high gloss semi-fancy stock and forend. Available in 12 and 20 gauges with 26" or 28" barrel and chambered for 3" shells. Includes five Pro Bore chokes for 12 gauge and five Rem chokes for 20 gauge, R3 recoil pad and high-grade travel case. A left-handed version was added to this line in 2008.

NIB	Exc.	V.G.	Good	Fair	Poor
825	600	450	300	225	150

Model 1100 Tactical Speedfeed IV

All-black 2.75" 12 gauge has an 18" barrel with fixed Improved Cylinder choke and Speedfeed IV stock. Extended 6-round magazine. Weight is 7.5 lbs.

NIB	Exc.	V.G.	Good	Fair	Poor
825	600	450	300	225	150

Model 1100 Tactical Standard Stock

Tactical 2.75" 12 gauge has 22" barrel threaded for Remchokes. Extended 8-round magazine.

NIB	Exc.	V.G.	Good	Fair	Poor
825	600	450	300	225	150

Model 1100 Premier Sporting

Introduced in 2008 as a dedicated sporting clays gun, the Premier Sporting comes in 12, 20 and 28 gauge and .410 bore with 2.75" chamber (3" in .410). Polished nickel receiver with fine-line embellishments and gold accents. Stock and fore-end are semi-fancy American walnut with high-gloss finish. A full line of Briley choke tubes and Premier Sporting hard case are included. Weights are about 8 lbs. in 12 gauge; 7 lbs. in 20 gauge; and 6.5 lbs. in 28 gauge and .410. **NOTE:** Add 5 percent for 28 and .410.

NIB	Exc.	V.G.	Good	Fair	Poor
1150	1000	850	675	475	300

MODEL 11-87 SERIES
Model 11-87 Premier

A 3", 12 gauge semi-automatic shotgun with 26" to 32" ventilated rib barrels having screw-in choke tubes. Blued with a checkered walnut stock. Weight is approximately 7.75 lbs. Introduced in 1987. In 1999 this model was offered in a left-hand version.

Model 11-87 Premier left-hand model

NIB	Exc.	V.G.	Good	Fair	Poor
700	600	450	300	200	150

Model 11-87 Premier 20 Gauge

Introduced in 1999 this model is built on a small frame receiver. It will chamber both 2.75" and 3" shells. Available in both 26" and 28" vent rib barrels with twin beads. Barrels are built for Rem. chokes. Stock is walnut with gloss finish. Weight is about 7 lbs.

NIB	Exc.	V.G.	Good	Fair	Poor
675	575	425	300	225	125

Model 11-87 Dale Earnhardt Tribute

Introduced in 2003 to honor Dale Earnhardt this 12 gauge gun is fitted with a 28" vent rib barrel and walnut stock with checkering. Engraved on the receiver is a likeness of Earnhardt, his signature, and scroll work. Inlayed in gold. Serial numbers start with "DE3." Weight is about 7.75 lbs.

NIB	Exc.	V.G.	Good	Fair	Poor
675	575	425	300	225	125

Model 11-87 Upland Special

This model is offered in 12 or 20 gauge with 23" barrel with twin bead sights. Chambered for 3" shells. Stock is walnut with straight grip. Choke tubes standard. Weight is about 7.25 for 12 gauge and 6.5 lbs. for 20 gauge. Introduced in 2000.

NIB	Exc.	V.G.	Good	Fair	Poor
725	600	450	300	225	125

Model 11-87 Premier Cantilever Scope Mount Deer Gun

This semi-automatic model has a Monte Carlo stock and the option of a barrel-mounted scope (not included). Optional with a fully rifled barrel 21" long with a 1-in-35" twist. Also available in a 21" nonrifled barrel with Rifled and IC Rem. choke tubes. Available in 12 gauge only. Sling swivel studs and camo are standard.

NIB	Exc.	V.G.	Good	Fair	Poor
800	675	400	300	200	150

Model 11-87 Premier Trap

Available in either right- or left-hand models. Is available with either a straight or Monte Carlo comb, 2.75" chamber, 30" vent rib overbored barrel and special Rem. Trap choke tubes. This model is set up to handle 12 gauge target loads only.

NIB	Exc.	V.G.	Good	Fair	Poor
525	475	425	300	200	150

Model 11-87 Premier SC (Sporting Clays)

This model features a special target stock with a 3.16" length of pull longer than standard and 1/4" higher at the heel. The butt pad is radiused at the heel and rounded at the toe. The receiver top, barrel, and rib have a fine matte finish on the blueing. The vent rib is a medium wide 8mm with stainless steel mid bead and a Bradley-style front bead sight. Gun is supplied new with these Rem. choke tubes: Skeet, Improved Skeet, Improved Cylinder, Modified, and Full. Supplied from the factory with a two-barrel custom fitted hard case.

Courtesy Remington Arms

Model 11-87 Sporting Clays with new engraving

NIB	Exc.	V.G.	Good	Fair	Poor
750	600	450	350	200	150

Model 11-87 SC NP (Sporting Clays Nickel-Plated)

Same as above but with nickel-plated receiver.

NIB	Exc.	V.G.	Good	Fair	Poor
800	650	500	400	300	200

Model 11-87 SPS-BG Camo

This 12 gauge model is fitted with a rifle sighted 21" barrel with a brown camo finish on the stock and metal parts. Introduced in 1993.

NIB	Exc.	V.G.	Good	Fair	Poor
525	475	425	300	200	150

Model 11-87 SPS-T Camo

Same as above but supplied with a 21" vent rib barrel with IC and Turkey Super Full Rem. choke tubes. Camo finish is green. Introduced in 1993.

NIB	Exc.	V.G.	Good	Fair	Poor
550	450	350	250	200	150

Model 11-87 SPS

This 12 gauge model is furnished with a 26" or 28" vent rib barrel with IC, Mod., and Full Rem. choke tubes. The stock is a black synthetic material and the metal is finished in a black matte. In 1997 a camo version of this model was introduced.

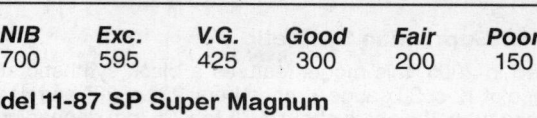

NIB	Exc.	V.G.	Good	Fair	Poor
700	595	425	300	200	150

Model 11-87 SP Super Magnum

Introduced in 2000 this model is chambered for the 12 gauge 3.5" Magnum shell. Fitted with a 26" or 28" vent rib barrel. Walnut stock with flat finish. Recoil pad. Matte black finish. Weight is about 8.25 lbs.

Remington Model 11-87 SPS Camo

NIB	Exc.	V.G.	Good	Fair	Poor
500	400	300	250	200	150

Model 11-87 SPS-Deer

The same as above but fitted with a 21" rifled, sighted barrel. First introduced in 1993.

NIB	Exc.	V.G.	Good	Fair	Poor
675	500	350	300	125	100

Model 11-87 SPS Super Magnum

Same as above but with a black synthetic stock. Introduced in 2000. Weight is about 8.25 lbs.

NIB	Exc.	V.G.	Good	Fair	Poor
525	475	425	300	200	150

Model 11-87 Waterfowl

This 12 gauge gun is fitted with a 28" vent rib barrel with choke tubes and Hi-Viz sights. Camo pattern is Mossy Oak Shadowgrass. Weight is about 8.25 lbs. Introduced in 2004.

NIB	Exc.	V.G.	Good	Fair	Poor
675	500	350	300	125	100

Model 11-87 SPS-T Super Magnum (NWTF Edition)

Introduced in 2005 this model features a 12 gauge 3.5" chamber with 23" barrel with choke tubes and iron sights. Mossy Oak Obsession camo stock with Monte Carlo comb. Weight is about 8 lbs.

NIB	Exc.	V.G.	Good	Fair	Poor
925	700	600	500	350	175

Model 11-87 SPS-T

Same as above but fitted with a 21" vent rib barrel with IC and Turkey Super Full Rem. choke tubes. In 1997 a camo version of this model was introduced.

NIB	Exc.	V.G.	Good	Fair	Poor
950	775	650	525	350	175

Model 11-87 Police

Offered chambered for 12 gauge shells, this model features a synthetic stock, 18" barrel with bead, rifle, or ghost ring sights, and 7-shot magazine extension. **NOTE:** Add $20 for rifle sights and $60 for ghost ring sights.

Remington Model 11-87 SPS-T Camo

NIB	Exc.	V.G.	Good	Fair	Poor
525	475	425	300	200	150

Model 11-87 SPS-T Camo NWTF 25th Anniversary

This model has a 21" barrel with special fiber optic sighting system. NWTF logo on left side of receiver. Introduced in 1998.

NIB	Exc.	V.G.	Good	Fair	Poor
675	500	350	300	125	100

Model 11-87 Custom Grade

This Custom Shop model is available in three levels of engraving, gold inlay, wood grade and finish, metal work finish, recoil pad/buttplate, and dimensions.

D Grade

NIB	Exc.	V.G.	Good	Fair	Poor
3000	200	1100	—	—	—

F Grade

NIB	Exc.	V.G.	Good	Fair	Poor
6000	4000	2250	—	—	—

F Grade with Gold Inlay

NIB	Exc.	V.G.	Good	Fair	Poor
10000	7500	5000	—	—	—

Model 11-87 Sportsman Synthetic

Introduced in 2005, this model features a black synthetic stock with choice of 12 or 20 gauge 3" chambers; 26" or 28" barrels with Mod. choke tube. Weight is about 7.75 to 8.25 lbs. depending on gauge and barrel length.

NIB	Exc.	V.G.	Good	Fair	Poor
675	500	350	300	125	100

Model 11-87 Sportsman Super Magnum

In 2008, Remington added this 3.5" version of the 11-87 Sportsman. It has a 28" barrel and weighs 8.25 lbs.

NIB	Exc.	V.G.	Good	Fair	Poor
750	625	550	400	300	200

Model 11-87 Sportsman Rifled

This is a 12 gauge 3" gun with 21" rifled barrel with cantilever scope mount. Black synthetic stock with black metal finish. Weight is about 8.5 lbs. Introduced in 2005.

NIB	Exc.	V.G.	Good	Fair	Poor
675	500	350	300	125	100

Model 11-87 Sportsman Youth

This is a 20 gauge 3" gun with 21" vent rib barrel with choke tubes. Black synthetic stock, length of pull is 13". Weight is about 6.5 lbs. Introduced in 2005.

NIB	Exc.	V.G.	Good	Fair	Poor
600	450	400	300	200	150

Model 11-87 Sportsman Compact Synthetic

Similar to Model 1-87 black synthetic but with reduced overall dimensions.

NIB	Exc.	V.G.	Good	Fair	Poor
700	595	500	350	225	150

Model 11-87 Sportsman Youth Camo

Same as above but with full coverage in Mossy Oak Break-Up camo.

NIB	Exc.	V.G.	Good	Fair	Poor
750	625	550	400	300	175

Model 11-87 Sportsman NRA Edition

This 12 gauge, 3" model is fitted with a 28" vent rib barrel with choke tubes. Synthetic stock with Mossy Oak New Break-Up camo. NRA logo on the left side of the matte black receiver. Introduced in 2005.

NIB	Exc.	V.G.	Good	Fair	Poor
675	500	350	300	125	100

Model 11-87 SP Thumbhole

Laminated, thumbhole-stock 12 gauge slug gun with 3" chamber and 21" fully rifled cantilever barrel.

NIB	Exc.	V.G.	Good	Fair	Poor
700	595	500	350	225	150

Model 11-87 SPS-T Super Magnum

Similar to Model 11-87 SP Thumbhole but with pistol-grip stock and vent rib barrel.

NIB	Exc.	V.G.	Good	Fair	Poor
750	625	550	400	300	200

Model 11-87 SP-T Thumbhole

This 12 gauge with 3.5" chamber is made specifically for turkey hunting. Camouflaged in Mossy Oak Obsession with an R3 recoil pad and thumbhole stock. The 23" barrel has fiber-optic adjustable rifle sights and is drilled and tapped for scope mounting. Includes a turkey super full choke tube and sling/swivels. Introduced 2006.

NIB	Exc.	V.G.	Good	Fair	Poor
750	625	550	400	300	200

Model 11-87 Sportsman Camo

New in 2007, the camo version of the Sportsman comes in 12 and 20 gauge with 26" or 28" barrel. Finished in Mossy Oak Break-Up camo.

NIB	Exc.	V.G.	Good	Fair	Poor
750	625	550	400	300	200

Model 11-87 Sportsman Camo Rifled

Camo 12 gauge slug gun with 21" barrel and cantilever scope mount.

NIB	Exc.	V.G.	Good	Fair	Poor
750	625	550	400	300	200

Model 11-87 Sportsman Camo Youth

Youth model in 20 gauge with shorter length of pull was introduced in 2007. Weight is about 6.5 lbs.

NIB	Exc.	V.G.	Good	Fair	Poor
700	595	500	350	225	150

Model 11-87 Sportsman Field

Semi-automatic shotgun chambered in 12 and 20 gauge, 2.75" and 3". Features include 26- (20) or 28" (12) barrel; vent rib; RemChokes (one supplied); sati-finished walnut stock and fore-end with fleur-de-lis pattern; dual sights; nickel-plated bolt and trigger: Suggested retail price: Starting at $845.

NIB	Exc.	V.G.	Good	Fair	Poor
680	575	435	350	225	150

Model 11-87 Sportsman Super Mag Synthetic

Semi-automatic shotgun chambered in 12 gauge, 3.5". Features include black matte synthetic stock and fore-end; rubber overmolded grip panels on the stock and fore-end; black padded sling; HiViz sights featuring interchangeable light pipe; 28" vent-rib barrel; SuperCell recoil pad; RemChoke. Price: $859.

NIB	Exc.	V.G.	Good	Fair	Poor
730	650	550	425	250	175

Model 11-87 Sportsman Super Mag Shurshot Turkey

Similar to 11-87 Sportsman Super Mag Synthetic but with ambidextrous ShurShot pistol-grip stock; full Realtree APG HD coverage; 23" barrel with fully adjustable TruGlo rifle sights. Wingmaster HD Turkey Choke included. Price: $972.

NIB	Exc.	V.G.	Good	Fair	Poor
875	750	625	500	300	175

Model 11-87 SPS Super Magnum Waterfowl

This 3.5" 12 gauge is finished in Mossy Oak Duck Blind camo. It has a 30" barrel and includes three chokes. Weight is 8.25 lbs.

NIB	Exc.	V.G.	Good	Fair	Poor
950	775	650	525	350	175

Model 11-87 Sportsman Super Mag ShurShot Turkey

New in 2008, this specialized turkey shotgun with ShurShot stock is a 3.5" chamber 12 gauge with a 23" non-vent-rib barrel. It comes with fiber-optic rifle-type sights, and a synthetic stock and fore-end. The gun is fully covered in Realtree APG HD camo. Weight is about 7.6 lbs.

NIB	Exc.	V.G.	Good	Fair	Poor
800	695	550	450	300	175

Model 11-87 Sportsman Super Magnum Waterfowl

With full coverage in Mossy Oak Duck Blind camo and shell-holding Speedfeed stock and three choke tubes.

NIB	Exc.	V.G.	Good	Fair	Poor
850	725	595	475	325	195

Model 11-87 Sportsman ShurShot Cantilever

This dedicated slug gun in 3" 12-gauge features a 23", fully rifled barrel with cantilever scope mount. It is matte black with synthetic stock and fore-end finished in Realtree Hardwoods HD camo. Weight is about 8 lbs.

NIB	Exc.	V.G.	Good	Fair	Poor
850	725	595	475	325	195

Model 11-96 Euro Lightweight

Introduced in 1996 this model is based on the Model 11-87 action. Two vent rib barrel lengths are offered: 26" and 28" supplied with three Rem chokes. Fine line engraving on the receiver and checkered Claro walnut stocks are standard. Blued finish. Weight is approximately 7 lbs. Made for one year only.

NIB	Exc.	V.G.	Good	Fair	Poor
1000	875	625	500	325	200

Model SP-10

A 3.5", 10 gauge semi-automatic shotgun with 26" or 30" ventilated rib barrels having screw-in choke tubes. Matte blued with a checkered walnut stock.

NIB	Exc.	V.G.	Good	Fair	Poor
1500	1275	950	775	600	300

Model SP-10 Magnum Camo

A new model introduced in 1993, this 10 gauge semi-automatic is designed for the turkey or deer hunter. Available with either 26" or 30" vent rib barrel or a 22" deer barrel. An additional barrel option is a 23" vent rib barrel with a camo finish. All barrels are fitted with Remington choke tubes.

NIB	Exc.	V.G.	Good	Fair	Poor
1550	1325	1000	825	625	325

Model SP-10 Magnum Camo NWTF 25th Anniversary

This model has a special fiber optic sighting system. The "NWTF" logo is on the left side of the receiver. Barrel length is 23". Introduced in 1998.

NIB	Exc.	V.G.	Good	Fair	Poor
1550	1325	1000	825	625	325

Model SP-10 Synthetic

This model features a black synthetic stock with 26" barrel chambered for 10 gauge shells. Matte black metal finish. Choke tubes standard. Introduced in 2000. Weight is about 10 lbs.

NIB	Exc.	V.G.	Good	Fair	Poor
1300	1150	900	775	575	300

Model SP-10 RC/VT

This 10 gauge gun was introduced in 2005 and is fitted with a 26" vent rib barrel with choke tubes. Mossy Oak Obsession finish. Weight is about 10.75 lbs.

NIB	Exc.	V.G.	Good	Fair	Poor
1300	1150	900	775	575	300

Model SP-10 Custom Grade

This Custom Shop model is available in three levels of engraving, gold inlay, wood grade and finish, metal work finish, recoil pad/

buttplate and dimensions. Limited production or activity on the used gun market. Price estimates for NIB models start at $2000 to $3000 and vary depending on the quality of custom features.

Model SP-10 Magnum Waterfowl

New in 2007, this waterfowl-specific model is a synthetic-stock 3.5" 10 gauge with Mossy Oak Duck Blind camo finish and 26" barrel. Includes three Briley ported choke tubes. Weight is about 10.9 lbs.

NIB	Exc.	V.G.	Good	Fair	Poor
1550	1325	1000	825	625	325

Model SP-10 Magnum Thumbhole Camo

Special turkey model features a synthetic thumbhole stock and complete Mossy Oak Obsession camo finish. Barrel is 23". Briley ported turkey choke included. Weight is 10.9 lbs.

NIB	Exc.	V.G.	Good	Fair	Poor
1650	1500	1200	900	675	350

Model 105CTi

New in 2006, this ultralight gas-operated 12 gauge autoloader features advanced recoil reduction and bottom feed and ejection. Available with 26" or 28" barrel. Satin finish walnut stock. Chambered for 3" shells. Includes three Pro Bore chokes. Weighs about 7 lbs. Discontinued in 2009.

NIB	Exc.	V.G.	Good	Fair	Poor
1175	950	800	600	475	275

Versa Max

The Versa Max gas-operated semi-automatic, shoots everything from 2.75" target loads to 3.5" magnums. Synthetic stock in black and camo finishes is fully adjustable for length-of-pull, drop-of-comb and cast. Twelve-gauge only; 26" and 28" barrels; 7.7 lbs. Introduced in 2011.

NIB	Exc.	V.G.	Good	Fair	Poor
1200	1100	1000	850	600	300

Model 32

A 12 gauge over/under shotgun with 26", 28" or 30" separated barrels and a single-selective trigger. Approximately 15,000 were made from 1932 to 1942. **NOTE:** Solid or vent rib add 10 percent.

Standard Grade

NIB	Exc.	V.G.	Good	Fair	Poor
—	2500	2250	1600	1250	1000

Skeet

NIB	Exc.	V.G.	Good	Fair	Poor
—	2750	2250	1950	1500	1250

TC

NIB	Exc.	V.G.	Good	Fair	Poor
—	2750	2500	2250	1750	1450

TC 32D Grade

NIB	Exc.	V.G.	Good	Fair	Poor
3000	200	1100	—	—	—

TC 32F Grade

NIB	Exc.	V.G.	Good	Fair	Poor
6000	4000	2250	—	—	—

TC 32E Expert

NIB	Exc.	V.G.	Good	Fair	Poor
10000	7500	5000	—	—	—

Model 3200

A 12 gauge over/under shotgun with 26", 28" or 30" separated ventilated rib barrels, single-selective trigger and automatic ejector. Blued with a checkered walnut stock. Manufactured from 1972 to 1984.

Field Grade

NIB	Exc.	V.G.	Good	Fair	Poor
—	800	725	600	450	300

Magnum

3" chambers.

NIB	Exc.	V.G.	Good	Fair	Poor
—	1000	850	750	550	300

Skeet

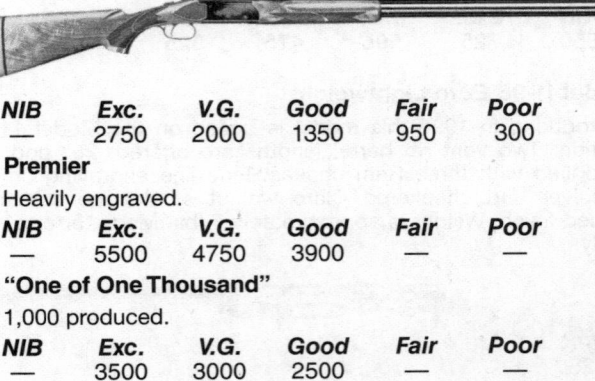

NIB	Exc.	V.G.	Good	Fair	Poor
—	1200	995	800	600	300

4-Gauge Set

NIB	Exc.	V.G.	Good	Fair	Poor
—	5500	4750	3500	2450	1500

Trap

NIB	Exc.	V.G.	Good	Fair	Poor
—	1200	995	800	600	300

Special Trap

Deluxe wood.

NIB	Exc.	V.G.	Good	Fair	Poor
—	1350	1150	750	700	300

Competition Trap

Engraved.

NIB	Exc.	V.G.	Good	Fair	Poor
—	2750	2000	1350	950	300

Premier

Heavily engraved.

NIB	Exc.	V.G.	Good	Fair	Poor
—	5500	4750	3900	—	—

"One of One Thousand"

1,000 produced.

NIB	Exc.	V.G.	Good	Fair	Poor
—	3500	3000	2500	—	—

Model 300 Ideal

This 12 gauge over/under shotgun, was introduced in 2000 and is offered with a choice of 26", 28" or 30" barrels. Single-selective trigger and automatic ejectors. Metal finish is blue. Stock is walnut with semi-gloss finish. Solid black recoil pad. Weight is about 7.62 lbs. for 28" barrels. Dropped from production in 2001.

NIB	Exc.	V.G.	Good	Fair	Poor
1650	1400	1150	700	575	300

Model 90-T Single-Barrel Trap

Offered in 12 gauge only, this single-barrel Trap shotgun is fitted with either a 32" or 34" overbored Full choke barrel.

NIB	Exc.	V.G.	Good	Fair	Poor
3600	2500	1450	1100	600	300

Model 90-T Single-Barrel Trap (High Rib)

The same shotgun as described above with the exception of an adjustable high rib for shooters who prefer a more open target picture and higher head position.

NIB	Exc.	V.G.	Good	Fair	Poor
3600	2500	1450	1100	600	300

Model 332

A reintroduction, in 2002, of the famous Remington Model 32 this model features a mechanical set trigger, automatic ejectors with a choice of vent rib barrel lengths in 26", 28" and 30". Checkered walnut stock. Black oxide metal finish. Chambered for the 12 gauge with 3" chambers. Weight is about 7.75 lbs. depending on barrel length.

NIB	Exc.	V.G.	Good	Fair	Poor
1250	900	750	600	400	250

Remington Peerless

Introduced in 1993, this new Remington over/under shotgun was offered in 12 gauge only. Available in 26", 28" and 30" vent rib barrel lengths and fitted with Remington choke tubes (IC, M, F). The sideplates are removable and the stock is American walnut. Production stopped in 1998.

NIB	Exc.	V.G.	Good	Fair	Poor
1250	900	750	600	400	250

Model 396 Sporting

Introduced in 1996 this over/under shotgun is designed for sporting clays shooting. It is offered in 12 gauge only with 30" barrels. Chokes are interchangeable Rem. choke system. Fancy American stock with satin finish. Scroll engraving on the receiver and blue finish. Weight is about 8 lbs.

Courtesy Remington Arms

NIB	Exc.	V.G.	Good	Fair	Poor
2150	1700	1150	875	500	300

Model 396 Skeet

Same but with a choice of 28" or 30" barrels.

Courtesy Remington Arms

NIB	Exc.	V.G.	Good	Fair	Poor
2150	1700	1150	875	500	300

Model 396 Custom Grade

This Custom Shop model is available in three levels of engraving, gold inlay, wood grade and finish, metal work finish, recoil pad/buttplate, and dimensions. Each gun should be individually appraised prior to a sale. Limited production or activity on the used gun market. Price estimates for NIB models start at $2000 to $3000 and vary depending on the quality of custom features.

PREMIER SERIES OVER/UNDERS

Introduced in 2006, the Italian-made over/unders in the Premier Series feature premium figured walnut stocks, Schnabel fore-ends, ProBore chokes, 3" chambers (2.75" in 28 gauge) and include a hardside case.

STS Competition

This 12 gauge with 28", 30" or 32" overbored barrels has an engraved, nickel-plated receiver and high-gloss finished stock. Weight is about 7.8 lbs. **NOTE:** Add 15 percent for adjustable-stock model.

NIB	Exc.	V.G.	Good	Fair	Poor
1500	1300	950	700	550	300

Field Grade

Available in 12, 20 and 28 gauges with satin finish and nickel receiver. Available with 26" or 28" barrels. Includes three flush chokes. Weight is about 6.5 lbs. for 20 and 28 gauges and 7.5 lbs. for 12 gauge.

NIB	Exc.	V.G.	Good	Fair	Poor
1400	1200	900	650	500	300

Upland Grade

As above but with oil finish stock and case colored receiver with gold game bird scene.

NIB	Exc.	V.G.	Good	Fair	Poor
1450	1250	900	675	525	300

RGS

This special Conservation Gun of the Year in 2007 for the Ruffed Grouse Society is a 20 gauge with 26" barrels, satin oil finished stock and satin black oxide receiver. Includes five choke tubes. Weight is 6.5 lbs.

NIB	Exc.	V.G.	Good	Fair	Poor
1650	1400	1150	700	575	300

Remington Parker AAHE Double

Built to order, this side-by-side double is exact in every respect to the original Parker Brothers shotguns made from the 1860s to 1937 and again until 1942 after Remington purchased the company. In 2006, Remington partnered with Connecticut Shotgun Mfg. Co., to build the high-grade AAHE model. It is offered in 28 gauge only with many options including stock dimensions and engraving patterns. Prices start at $49,000.

BOLT-ACTION HANDGUNS

Model XP-100

A .221 Remington Fireball or .223 Remington caliber bolt-action single-shot pistol available with or without a 14.5" ventilated rib barrel and adjustable sights. Blued with a nylon stock. Introduced in 1963. Discontinued.

NIB	Exc.	V.G.	Good	Fair	Poor
800	600	375	300	225	175

Model XP-100 Silhouette

As above, chambered for either the 7mm Remington or .35 Remington cartridges and fitted with a 15" barrel drilled and tapped for a telescope. Discontinued.

NIB	Exc.	V.G.	Good	Fair	Poor
725	525	325	250	200	125

Model XP-100 Custom

A custom-made version of the above with a 15" barrel and either a nylon or walnut stock. Available in .223 Remington, .250 Savage, 6mm Benchrest, 7mm Benchrest, 7mm-08, or .35 Remington calibers. Introduced in 1986. Discontinued.

NIB	Exc.	V.G.	Good	Fair	Poor
950	800	650	550	425	300

Model XP-100 Hunter

This model features a laminated wood stock, 14.5" drilled and tapped barrel, and no sights. It is offered in these calibers: .223 Rem., 7mm BR Rem., 7mm-08 Rem., and .35 Rem. Discontinued.

NIB	Exc.	V.G.	Good	Fair	Poor
800	675	375	300	250	175

Model XP-100R Repeater

Introduced in 1998, this model is chambered for the .22-250, .223, .260 and .35 Rem. cartridges. It is fitted with a 14.5" barrel that is drilled and tapped for sights. The receiver is drilled and tapped for scope mounts. Fiberglass stock. Weight is approximately 4.5 lbs. Manufactured 1998. Discontinued.

NIB	Exc.	V.G.	Good	Fair	Poor
950	800	500	450	225	200

SPARTAN GUNWORKS BY REMINGTON

This line of imported firearms was introduced into the Remington line in 2004 and discontinued in 2009.

Model SPR 210

This is a side-by-side gun with single-selective trigger and auto ejectors. The box lock receiver is nickel and is fitted with 26" or 28" barrels with choke tubes in 12 and 20 gauge, and fixed chokes in 28 and .410 bore. This model is also offered with 20" barrel with choke tubes and blued receiver. Checkered walnut stock with recoil pad. Weight is about 6.75 lbs. depending on gauge and barrel length. **NOTE:** Add $30 for 28 and .410 bore models.

NIB	Exc.	V.G.	Good	Fair	Poor
475	400	350	225	175	100

Model SPR 220

This is a double trigger model with 20" barrels with choke tubes. Extractors. Nickel or blued receiver. Walnut stock with recoil pad. Weight is about 6.25 lbs.

NIB	Exc.	V.G.	Good	Fair	Poor
425	375	300	200	150	100

Model SPR 310

This model is an over/under gun chambered for the 12, 20, 28 and .410 bore. Choice of 26" or 28" vent rib barrels with choke tubes or 26" barrels for the 28 and .410. Single selective trigger and auto ejectors. Checkered walnut stock with recoil pad. Weight is about 7.5 lbs.

NIB	Exc.	V.G.	Good	Fair	Poor
475	400	350	225	175	125

Model SPR 310S

This model is chambered for the 12 and 20 gauge 3" shell and is fitted with 29.5" (12 gauge) or 28.5" (20 gauge) ported barrels with choke tubes. Checked walnut stock with recoil pad. Weight is about 7.5 lbs.

NIB	Exc.	V.G.	Good	Fair	Poor
700	600	475	350	275	200

Model SPR 100/Sporting

This is a single shot gun chambered for the 12, 20 , or .410 bore and fitted with 29.5" (12 gauge), 28.5" (20 gauge), or 26" (.410) barrel. Single trigger with ejectors or extractors. A youth model is also offered with 24" barrel chambered for the .410 bore. Checkered walnut stock with recoil pad. Weight is about 6.25 lbs. **NOTE:** Add $40 for Sporting models.

NIB	Exc.	V.G.	Good	Fair	Poor
250	175	125	100	75	50

Model SPR 18

This is a single shot rifle chambered for the .223, .243, .270 or .30-06 calibers. Nickel receiver. Fitted with a 23.5" barrel with iron sights. Checkered walnut stock with recoil pad. Weight is about 6.75 lbs.

NIB	Exc.	V.G.	Good	Fair	Poor
275	200	150	125	95	75

Model SPR 22

This model is a side-by-side double rifle chambered for the .30-06 or .45-70 calibers and fitted with 23.5" barrels. Blued receiver and checkered walnut stock with recoil pad. Weight is about 7.5 lbs.

NIB	Exc.	V.G.	Good	Fair	Poor
1000	825	700	575	400	250

Model SPR 94

This model features an under/under rifle/shotgun combination. Chambered for the .410/17HMR, .410/.22WMR, 12/.223, 12/.30-06 or 12/.308. Fitted with a 24" barrel with iron sights. Checkered walnut stock with recoil pad. Blued receiver. Weight is about 8 lbs. depending on combination. **NOTE:** Add 30 percent for centerfire models.

NIB	Exc.	V.G.	Good	Fair	Poor
375	300	225	150	100	75

REMINGTON CUSTOM SHOP

The Remington Custom Shop builds a number of specialty rifles and shotguns as well as specific custom guns for its customers. Remington will build a wide number of special features from special wood type, finish, and styling options to engraving. These special order features add considerably to the cost of a gun and will affect its price. The Custom Shop can be reached at 1-800-243-9700 for current prices and availability.

REMINGTON 180TH ANNIVERSARY LIMITED EDITION RIFLES AND SHOTGUNS

Remington manufactured 180 each of these firearms to commemorate the founding of the company in 1816: Model 700, Model 7600, Model 7400, Model 870, and Model 11-87. These firearms featured fine line hand engraving with gold embellishments. The rifles were chambered for the .30-06 cartridge with 22" barrels and the shotguns were chambered for the 12 gauge shell with 26" vent rib barrels with Rem chokes. All guns had blue finishes with high gloss semi-fancy walnut stocks. If sold in a five-gun set each should have matching serial numbers. The suggested retail price for the five-gun set was $6,925 in 1996.

Individual guns carried these suggested retail prices:
Model 700 180th Anniversary Commemorative—$1,372
Model 7400 180th Anniversary Commemorative—$1,372

Model 7600 180th Anniversary Commemorative—$1,332
Model 870 180th Anniversary Commemorative—$1,305
Model 11-87 180th Anniversary Commemorative—$1,465

MODEL 870 SERIES

Model 870 Wingmaster NRA Edition

This is a 12 gauge 3" gun with a 28" vent rib barrel with choke tubes. Walnut stock with checkering. Blued receiver with NRA logos on both sides. Introduced in 2005.

NIB	Exc.	V.G.	Good	Fair	Poor
550	450	300	225	150	100

RENETTE, GASTINNE
Paris, France

SHOTGUNS

Model 105

An Anson & Deeley action 12 or 20 gauge double-barrel shotgun available in a variety of barrel lengths, with double triggers and automatic ejectors. Blued, case hardened with a checkered walnut stock.

NIB	Exc.	V.G.	Good	Fair	Poor
—	4000	3200	2500	1700	300

Model 98

As above, except more finely finished.

NIB	Exc.	V.G.	Good	Fair	Poor
—	5200	4500	3500	2800	300

Model 202

A 12 or 20 gauge sidelock double-barrel shotgun made only on custom order. French case hardened and blued with a checkered walnut stock.

NIB	Exc.	V.G.	Good	Fair	Poor
—	9000	7000	5000	3450	300

Model 353

A custom manufactured double-barrel shotgun with detachable sidelocks. Highly finished.

NIB	Exc.	V.G.	Good	Fair	Poor
—	35000	30000	1700	8000	500

RIFLES

Type G Rifle

A .30-06, 9.3x74R, or .375 Holland & Holland double-barrel rifle with 24" barrels, express sights, double triggers and automatic ejectors. Engraved, blued with a checkered walnut stock.

NIB	Exc.	V.G.	Good	Fair	Poor
—	5500	3700	3000	2000	650

Type R Deluxe

As above, engraved with hunting scenes and with a more finely figured walnut stock.

NIB	Exc.	V.G.	Good	Fair	Poor
—	7000	5000	3400	2900	750

Type PT President

As above, inlaid in gold with extremely well figured walnut stock.

NIB	Exc.	V.G.	Good	Fair	Poor
—	8000	6400	4000	3500	950

Mauser Bolt-Action

A custom-made bolt-action rifle built on a Mauser action. Choice of calibers and stock styles. Base price listed.

NIB	Exc.	V.G.	Good	Fair	Poor
—	11000	9000	6500	3000	750

Deluxe Mauser Bolt-Action

Same as above but with fancy wood and other options.

NIB	Exc.	V.G.	Good	Fair	Poor
—	20000	14000	9000	6500	1250

RENWICK ARMS CO.
See—Perry & Goddard

REPUBLIC ARMS, INC.
Chino, California

This company was in business from 1997 to 2001. The Republic Patriot pistol may still be available from Cobra Enterpises.

RAP 440

This pistol is chambered for the .40 S&W or 9mm cartridges. It is double-action/single-action operation. Fitted with a 3.75" barrel, it has a magazine capacity of 7 rounds. Grips are two-piece black plastic. Weight is approximately 32 oz. Sights are three dot with fixed ramp front and windage adjustable rear. Introduced in 1998. Imported by TSF of Fairfax, Virginia.

NIB	Exc.	V.G.	Good	Fair	Poor
550	450	300	200	150	100

Republic Patriot

This is a double-action-only .45 ACP caliber pistol with a 3" barrel and fixed sights. Black polymer frame with checkered grips and stainless steel slide. Magazine capacity is 6 rounds. Weight is about 20 oz. Introduced in 1997.

NIB	Exc.	V.G.	Good	Fair	Poor
325	250	200	150	100	75

RETOLAZA HERMANOS
Eibar, Spain

Brompetier

A folding trigger 6.35mm or 7.65mm caliber double-action revolver with a 2.5" barrel and a safety mounted on the left side of the frame. Manufactured until 1915.

NIB	Exc.	V.G.	Good	Fair	Poor
—	250	125	85	70	45

Gallus or Titan

A 6.35mm semi-automatic pistol normally marked "Gallus" or "Titan". Blued with plastic grips.

NIB	Exc.	V.G.	Good	Fair	Poor
—	275	150	100	75	50

Liberty, Military, Retolaza, or Paramount

A 6.35mm or 7.65mm semi-automatic pistol with a 3" barrel and 8-shot magazine. The slide marked with any of the trade names listed above.

NIB	Exc.	V.G.	Good	Fair	Poor
—	275	150	100	75	50

Puppy

A folding trigger .22 caliber double-action revolver with a 5-shot cylinder. The trade name "Puppy" stamped on the barrel.

NIB	Exc.	V.G.	Good	Fair	Poor
—	175	125	75	50	25

Stosel

A 6.35mm semi-automatic pistol marked on the slide "Automatic Pistol Stosel No. 1 Patent". Blued with plastic grips.

NIB	Exc.	V.G.	Good	Fair	Poor
—	275	150	100	75	50

Titanic

A 6.35mm semi-automatic pistol with a 2.5" barrel, the slide marked "1913 Model Automatic Pistol Titanic Eibar". Blued with plastic grips.

NIB	Exc.	V.G.	Good	Fair	Poor
—	275	150	100	75	50

REUNIES
Liege, Belgium

Dictator

A 6.35mm semi-automatic pistol with a 1.5" barrel, 5-shot magazine and the name "Dictator" together with the company's details stamped on the slide. This pistol features a bolt of tubular form, the front end of which is hollow and encloses the barrel breech. Manufactured from 1909 to approximately 1925.

NIB	Exc.	V.G.	Good	Fair	Poor
—	275	150	100	75	50

Texas Ranger or Cowboy Ranger

Patterned after the Colt Model 1873 revolver. This pistol is of .38 Special caliber and has a 5.5" barrel. The barrel is marked with the company's details and either the legend "Cowboy Ranger" or "Texas Ranger". Manufactured from 1922 to 1931.

NIB	Exc.	V.G.	Good	Fair	Poor
—	350	200	100	75	50

REUTH, F.
Hartford, Connecticut

Animal Trap Gun

A cast iron .28 to .50 caliber percussion trap gun with either single or double-barrels 3.5" or 5" in length. This firearm fires a barbed arrow and is triggered by a cord attached to an animal trap or bait. The barrels marked "F. Reuth's Patent, May 12, 1857". Several hundred were made between 1858 and 1862. **NOTE:** The single-barrel model is more common than the double-barrel and is worth approximately 20 percent less.

NIB	Exc.	V.G.	Good	Fair	Poor
—	—	2000	1650	550	150

REXIO DE ARMAS (COMANCHE)
Argentina

RS 22

A 9-shot revolver chambered for the .22 LR cartridge. Choice of blued or stainless steel frame. Fixed or adjustable sights. Barrel lengths are 4" or 6". Fitted with rubber grips. **NOTE:** Add $30 for stainless steel.

NIB	Exc.	V.G.	Good	Fair	Poor
235	175	150	125	75	50

RS 22M

Same as above but chambered for the .22 Win. Magnum cartridge. **NOTE:** Add $30 for stainless steel.

NIB	Exc.	V.G.	Good	Fair	Poor
235	175	150	125	75	50

RJ 22

This revolver is chambered for the .22 LR cartridge and fitted with a 3", 4" or 6" barrel. Checkered walnut grips or synthetic grips. Adjustable rear sight. Blued finish.

NIB	Exc.	V.G.	Good	Fair	Poor
175	125	95	75	50	25

RJ 38

Same as above but chambered for .38 Special cartridge.

NIB	Exc.	V.G.	Good	Fair	Poor
175	125	95	75	50	25

RS 357

Same as above but chambered for the .357 Magnum cartridge and offered with 3", 4" or 6" barrels. **NOTE:** Add $30 for stainless steel.

NIB	Exc.	V.G.	Good	Fair	Poor
235	175	125	95	75	50

Outfitter Single-Shot

This is a break down single pistol chambered for the .45 Colt/.410 .22 LR or .22 Win. Magnum. Blued 10" barrel with synthetic grip. Weight is about 43 oz.

NIB	Exc.	V.G.	Good	Fair	Poor
200	150	—	—	—	—

Outfitter Single-Shot Compact

Same as above but with 6" barrel in .22 Win. Magnum or .45 Colt/.410.

NIB	Exc.	V.G.	Good	Fair	Poor
200	150	125	95	75	50

RHEINMETALL
Sommerda, Germany

Dreyse 6.35mm Model 1907

A 6.35mm semi-automatic pistol with a 2" barrel, manual safety and 6-shot magazine. Weight is about 14 oz. The slide marked "Dreyse". Blued with hard rubber grips having the trademark "RFM" molded in them. The patent for this design was issued in 1909 to Louis Schmeisser.

Courtesy James Rankin

NIB	Exc.	V.G.	Good	Fair	Poor
—	400	250	200	150	100

Dreyse 7.65mm Model 1907

As above, but chambered for the 7.65mm cartridge, with a 3.6" barrel and a 7-shot magazine. Weight is about 25 oz. Blued with horn grips.

Courtesy Orvel Reichert

NIB	Exc.	V.G.	Good	Fair	Poor
—	300	200	150	125	75

Dreyse 9mm

As above, but chambered for the 9mm cartridge with a 5" barrel and an 8-shot magazine. Weight is about 37 oz. The slide marked "Rheinische Mettallwaaren Und Maschinenfabrik, Sommerda". Blued with hard rubber grips. Manufactured prior to 1916 and in small numbers.

Courtesy James Rankin

NIB	Exc.	V.G.	Good	Fair	Poor
—	4500	3750	2500	1500	750

Rheinmetall 32

A 7.65mm semi-automatic pistol with a 3.65" barrel and an 8-shot magazine. The slide marked "Rheinmetall ABT. Sommerda". Blued with walnut grips. Overall length is 6.5" and weight is about 23.5 oz. Production of this pistol began in 1920.

Courtesy James Rankin

NIB	Exc.	V.G.	Good	Fair	Poor
—	350	225	175	125	90

Rheinmetall 9mm

This is a 9mm version of the Rheinmetall and was built in 1935 to compete with the 9mm Parabellum German military pistols of that time. It was unsuccessful.

Courtesy James Rankin

NIB	Exc.	V.G.	Good	Fair	Poor
—Too Rare To Price	—	—	—	—	—

Dreyse Light Rifle or Carbine

Model 1907 in caliber 7.65 Browning. Fitted with a fixed stock and 6-round magazine.

Courtesy James Rankin

NIB	Exc.	V.G.	Good	Fair	Poor
—	1850	1400	1150	700	300

RHODE ISLAND ARMS CO.
Hope Valley, Rhode Island

Morrone

A 12 or 20 gauge over/under boxlock shotgun with 26" or 28" barrels, single trigger and automatic ejectors. Blued with either a straight or pistol grip walnut checkered stock. 450 were made in 12 gauge and 50 in 20 gauge. Manufactured from 1949 to 1953.

NIB	Exc.	V.G.	Good	Fair	Poor
—	1700	1200	850	600	350

RICHLAND ARMS CO.
Blissfield, Michigan

This company, which ceased operation in 1986, imported a variety of Spanish-made shotguns.

Model 41 Ultra Over/Under

A 20, 28, or .410 bore double-barrel shotgun with 26" or 28" ventilated rib barrels, single nonselective trigger and automatic ejectors. French case hardened receiver and checkered walnut stock.

NIB	Exc.	V.G.	Good	Fair	Poor
—	300	250	200	150	100

Model 747 Over/Under

As above, in 20 gauge only with a single-selective trigger.

NIB	Exc.	V.G.	Good	Fair	Poor
—	425	350	300	250	175

Model 757 Over/Under

A Greener-style boxlock 12 gauge double-barrel shotgun with 26" or 28" ventilated rib barrels, double triggers and automatic ejectors. Finished as Model 747.

NIB	Exc.	V.G.	Good	Fair	Poor
—	300	250	200	175	125

Model 787 Over/Under

As above, fitted with screw-in choke tubes.

NIB	Exc.	V.G.	Good	Fair	Poor
—	450	375	325	275	200

Model 808 Over/Under

A 12 gauge double-barrel shotgun with 26", 28" or 30" ventilated rib barrels, single trigger and automatic ejectors. Blued with checkered walnut stock. Manufactured in Italy from 1963 to 1968.

NIB	Exc.	V.G.	Good	Fair	Poor
—	425	350	300	250	175

Model 80 LS

A 12, 20 or .410 bore single-barrel shotgun with 26" or 28" barrels. Blued with checkered walnut stock.

NIB	Exc.	V.G.	Good	Fair	Poor
—	175	125	100	80	60

Model 200

An Anson & Deeley-style 12, 16, 20, 28 or .410 bore double-barrel shotgun with 22", 26" or 28" barrels, double triggers, and automatic ejectors. Blued with a checkered walnut stock.

NIB	Exc.	V.G.	Good	Fair	Poor
—	350	300	250	200	125

Model 202

As above, with an extra set of interchangeable barrels. Imported from 1963 to 1985.

NIB	Exc.	V.G.	Good	Fair	Poor
—	325	275	225	175	100

Model 711 Magnum

As above, chambered for 3" shells and fitted with 30" or 32" barrels.

NIB	Exc.	V.G.	Good	Fair	Poor
—	350	300	250	200	150

Model 707 Deluxe

As above, more finely finished and fitted with well figured walnut stocks.

NIB	Exc.	V.G.	Good	Fair	Poor
—	350	300	250	200	150

RICHMOND ARMORY
Richmond, Virginia

Carbine

This weapon was manufactured for use by the Confederate States of America and is extremely collectible. This muzzle-loading carbine is chambered for .58 caliber percussion and has a 25" round barrel and a full-length stock that is held on by two barrel bands. It was manufactured from parts that were captured at the Harper's Ferry Armory in 1861. The locks are marked "Richmond, VA" and dated from 1861 to 1865. There are sling swivels in front of the trigger guard and on the front barrel band; a third swivel is on the underside of the buttstock. The quantity manufactured is not known. They were made between 1861 and 1865.

Courtesy Milwaukee Public Museum, Milwaukee, Wisconsin

NIB	Exc.	V.G.	Good	Fair	Poor
—	—	28500	22000	8250	1000

Musketoon

This weapon is similar to the carbine except that the barrel is 30" in length and the front sight is also the bayonet lug. There is no sling swivel on the buttstock. This weapon was also manufactured between 1861 and 1865.

NIB	Exc.	V.G.	Good	Fair	Poor
—	—	24000	19000	7700	1000

Rifled Musket

This model is also similar to the Carbine, with a 40" barrel and a full-length stock held on by three barrel bands. The front sling swivel is on the middle barrel band instead of on the front band. The Rifled Musket was also manufactured between 1861 and 1865.

Courtesy Milwaukee Public Museum, Milwaukee, Wisconsin

NIB	Exc.	V.G.	Good	Fair	Poor
—	—	30000	22000	8250	1000

RIEDL RIFLE CO.
Westminster, California

Single-Shot Rifle

This company produced custom order dropping block single-shot rifles in a variety of calibers and barrel lengths. Rifles were normally fitted only with telescopic or target sight bases. Blued with a checkered walnut stock. Premium for African or magnum chamberings.

NIB	Exc.	V.G.	Good	Fair	Poor
—	1750	1500	1250	750	400

RIFLESMITH INC.
Sheridan, Montana
See—Axtell Rifle Co.

RIGBY, JOHN & CO., LTD.
London, England

This company was established in the 18th century in the U.K. and has produced a wide variety of firearms over the years. It traces its roots back to 1735 in Dublin where the company was known for its percussion dueling pistols. A branch was opened in London in 1865 where some of the world's finest double rifles were made for more than 130 years, many of them made to order. In 1997 a group of investors moved the company to Paso Robles, California where production continues on a limited number of Rigby models. Current prices start at $32,000 for double rifles and $40,000 for shotguns.

RIFLES

Magazine Rifle

Utilizing a Mauser action, this rifle is available in a number of calibers, barrel lengths and with either a 3- or 5-shot magazine. Checkered walnut stock.

Courtesy Faintich Auction Service, Paul Goodwin photo

NIB	Exc.	V.G.	Good	Fair	Poor
—	12500	10000	7000	4000	1000

African Express Magazine Rifle

Utilizing a square bridge Mauser action, this rifle is chambered for .375 Holland & Holland, .404 Gibbs, .416 Rigby, .458 Winchester Magnum and .505 Gibbs cartridges. Barrel lengths vary from 20" to 24" and a 4-shot magazine is standard.

NIB	Exc.	V.G.	Good	Fair	Poor
—	25000	20000	15000	10000	2000

Single-Shot Rifle

Utilizing a Farquharson falling block action, this rifle is chambered for a variety of cartridges and has a 24" barrel. The receiver finely engraved and blued. Stock of well figured walnut.

NIB	Exc.	V.G.	Good	Fair	Poor
—	8000	7000	5500	2500	600

Second Quality Boxlock Double Rifle

A double-barrel rifle chambered for cartridges from .275 Magnum to .577 Nitro Express with a 24" to 28" barrel fitted with express sights. Double triggers and automatic ejectors. Blued with light engraving and a checkered walnut stock.

NIB	Exc.	V.G.	Good	Fair	Poor
—	20000	17000	11000	5500	900

Best Quality Boxlock Double Rifle

As above, but more finely engraved and with better quality walnut stocks.

NIB	Exc.	V.G.	Good	Fair	Poor
—	30000	22500	15000	7500	1000

Best Quality Sidelock Double Rifle

As above, but fitted with full sidelocks, with best bouquet engraving and finely figured walnut stocks.

NIB	Exc.	V.G.	Good	Fair	Poor
—	50000	42500	33000	15000	1500

SHOTGUNS

Sidelock Double

Offered in all gauges with choice of barrel lengths, chokes, stock dimensions, grip and fore-end styles. Double triggers and automatic ejectors. Prices shown are for Sandringham Grade. Regal Grade has higher grade wood and engraving. Made in London prior to 1998. **NOTE:** Add 20 percent for Regal Grade, 30 percent for 20 gauge, 40 percent for 28 or .410.

NIB	Exc.	V.G.	Good	Fair	Poor
9000	7500	6000	4500	3000	1000

Boxlock Double

Same features and options as above except boxlock action. Prices shown are for Chatsworth Grade. Sackville Grade has higher grade wood and engraving. Made in London prior to 1998. **NOTE:** Add 30 percent for Sackville Grade, 20 percent for 20 gauge, 30 percent for 28 or .410.

NIB	Exc.	V.G.	Good	Fair	Poor
4500	3700	2800	2000	1500	500

RIGDON, ANSLEY & CO.
Augusta, Georgia
1851 Colt Navy Type

A .36 caliber percussion revolver with a 7.5" barrel and 6-shot cylinder. Blued with walnut grips. Initial production examples marked "Augusta, GA. C.S.A." and later models "C.S.A." Approximately 1,000 were manufactured in 1864 and 1865.

Courtesy Milwaukee Public Museum, Milwaukee, Wisconsin

Early Production Model

NIB	Exc.	V.G.	Good	Fair	Poor
—	—	70000	61000	27500	2000

Standard Production Model

NIB	Exc.	V.G.	Good	Fair	Poor
—	—	63500	4950	1925	1500

RIPOMANTI, GUY
St. Etienne, France
Side-by-Side Shotgun

A high-grade shotgun offered on a strictly made-to-order basis. There is a boxlock model that begins at $8,500 and a sidelock that is priced from $22,500. These prices rise depending on the options and embellishments desired. These guns are rarely seen on the used-gun market.

Side-by-Side Double Rifles

Extremely high-grade and basically made to order. They are rarely encountered on today's market. They have been imported since 1988. They range in price from $11,000 up.

Over/Under Double Rifle

A boxlock action over/under chambered for the 9.3x74R cartridge. The barrels are 23.5" in length and have express sights. There are double triggers and automatic ejectors. This model is highly engraved and features a high-grade, hand-checkered walnut stock.

NIB	Exc.	V.G.	Good	Fair	Poor
12500	9750	7750	5000	4000	900

RIVERSIDE ARMS CO.
Chicopee Falls, Massachusetts

See—Stevens, J. Arms Co.

Double-Barrel Shotguns

Brand name used by J. Stevens Arms Co. on many good quality double-barrel shotguns. Value depends on model, gauge and condition. From $100 to $1,600. See also Stevens.

Courtesy William Hammond

RIZZINI, BATTISTA
Bresica, Italy

NOTE: There are a number of extra cost options for Rizzini guns that can greatly affect price. Extra barrels and upgraded wood are such options.

SHOTGUNS
Aurum Light

This over/under model features a choice of 24.5" to 27.5". Vent rib barrel. Figured oil finish walnut stock with hand checkering and pistol grip. Game scene engraved receiver. Auto ejectors and single-selective trigger. Weight is about 6 lbs.

Courtesy William Larkin Moore & Co.

NIB	Exc.	V.G.	Good	Fair	Poor
2250	1650	1250	975	700	500

Artemis Classic

This model features engraved sideplates with game scenes. Offered in 12, 16, 20, 28 gauge as well as .410 bore. Barrel lengths from 24" to 27.5". Auto ejectors and single-selective trigger. Figured walnut stock with hand checkering and pistol grip. Weight is about 6 lbs.

Courtesy William Larkin Moore & Co.

NIB	Exc.	V.G.	Good	Fair	Poor
3200	2700	2300	1900	1000	500

Artemis Deluxe

Similar to the standard Artemis with the addition of gold inlaid game scenes and fancy walnut stock. Cased.

NIB	Exc.	V.G.	Good	Fair	Poor
5000	4200	3500	2500	1250	600

Artemis EL

This model features sideplates with hand engraved English scroll and game scenes. Extra fancy walnut stock. Cased.

NIB	Exc.	V.G.	Good	Fair	Poor
18000	13500	10000	8000	6000	900

Upland EL

NIB	Exc.	V.G.	Good	Fair	Poor
4000	3500	3000	2500	1250	600

S780 Emel

This boxlock model is offered in 12, 16, 20, 28 or .410. Barrel lengths from 24" to 27.5". Hand engraved receiver with game scenes. Auto ejectors and single-selective trigger. Fancy walnut stock with hand checkering. Leather case. Weight for 12 gauge is about 6.8 lbs. and the smaller gauges about 6 lbs.

NIB	Exc.	V.G.	Good	Fair	Poor
13500	11000	8750	7000	4250	900

S782 Emel Field Classic

This model is similar to the S792 but with the addition of hand engraved gold inlaid game scenes.

NIB	Exc.	V.G.	Good	Fair	Poor
15000	13000	10000	8750	5700	900

S790 Emel Field

This model is similar to the S780 with the exception of the engraving pattern. This model has a thistle-leaf style pattern.

NIB	Exc.	V.G.	Good	Fair	Poor
10500	8000	6500	5000	4250	900

S792 Emel Field

This model features sideplates engraved with English scroll and game scenes. Extra select walnut stock. Available in 12, 16, 20, 28 and .410 with barrel lengths from 24" to 27.5".

NIB	Exc.	V.G.	Good	Fair	Poor
11000	9750	8000	6750	5000	900

Premier Sporting

This model is offered in 12 or 20 gauge with choice of barrel lengths from 27.5" to 31.5". Blued boxlock action with auto ejectors and single-selective trigger. Select walnut stock with hand checkering and oil finish. Pistol grip stock and beavertail fore-end. Weight is about 7.5 lbs.

NIB	Exc.	V.G.	Good	Fair	Poor
3000	2750	2100	1600	900	500

Sporting EL

NIB	Exc.	V.G.	Good	Fair	Poor
3750	2800	2200	1750	975	600

S790 EL Sporting

This model is offered in 12 gauge only and choice of barrel from 27.5" to 31.5". Boxlock action with chrome plate. Auto ejectors and single-selective trigger. Pistol grip stock with fancy walnut. Weight is about 7.5 lbs.

NIB	Exc.	V.G.	Good	Fair	Poor
7500	6250	5000	3750	2900	800

EXPRESS RIFLES

Express 90 L

This over/under rifle is chambered for the 7x65R, 8x57JRS, 9.3x74R, .30-06, .308 Win., and .444 Marlin. Barrel length is 16". Boxlock action with case colored receiver. Auto ejectors and single trigger. Pistol-grip walnut stock with Bavarian cheekpiece. Hand checkered and oil finish stock. Weight is about 8 lbs.

NIB	Exc.	V.G.	Good	Fair	Poor
4750	4250	3500	2500	1750	800

Express 92 EL

Same calibers as above model but with sideplates engraved with English scroll and game scenes. Extra select walnut stock with pistol grip and round cheekpiece.

NIB	Exc.	V.G.	Good	Fair	Poor
11000	9500	8000	5500	2500	900

RIZZINI, FRATELLI
Brescia, Italy

Early guns were manufactured with Antonio Zoli. As a result, these were off-the-shelf guns of lower prices. These early guns were imported by Abercombie and Fitch of New York. Some of these guns will be stamped with the A&F address on the barrel. These side-by-side guns have a boxlock action. NOTE: At the present time this Italian gun company builds about 24 shotguns a year. Each gun is highly individualized for the customer. The company produces only two models. These are listed to give the reader some idea of the value of one of these models. None of these models includes the cost of engraving and multi barrel set and multi gauge sets are extra. Rizzini models with serial numbers above #1709 have their own patented action and the prices listed reflect that action. Guns listed have a H&H style action and should deduct approximately 30 percent from the prices listed.

Lusso Grade

12 gauge

NIB	Exc.	V.G.	Good	Fair	Poor
3200	2850	2200	1600	900	400

20 gauge

NIB	Exc.	V.G.	Good	Fair	Poor
3700	3250	2800	2200	1500	550

28 gauge and .410 bore

NIB	Exc.	V.G.	Good	Fair	Poor
4000	3600	3000	2500	1700	600

Extra Lusso Grade—Scalloped receiver

12 gauge

NIB	Exc.	V.G.	Good	Fair	Poor
4800	4150	3250	2700	1500	700

20 gauge

NIB	Exc.	V.G.	Good	Fair	Poor
5450	4600	3500	2900	1650	700

28 gauge

NIB	Exc.	V.G.	Good	Fair	Poor
5850	4900	3750	3250	1900	700

.410 bore

NIB	Exc.	V.G.	Good	Fair	Poor
6250	5250	3900	3500	2350	750

Model R-1

Available in 12 to .410 bore with choice of barrels from 25" to 30". Choice of single or double trigger, pistol or straight grip, rib, barrel length and chokes are standard items on this model. This model features a Holland & Holland sidelock action.

12, 16, or 20 gauge

NIB	Exc.	V.G.	Good	Fair	Poor
85000	72000	57500	40000	—	—

28 gauge or .410 bore

NIB	Exc.	V.G.	Good	Fair	Poor
90000	76000	62000	45000	—	—

Model R-2

This model has a boxlock action and a removable inspection plate on the bottom of the frame. The stock and forearm is fitted with Turkish Circassian walnut. Offered in 12 gauge to .410 bore.

NIB	Exc.	V.G.	Good	Fair	Poor
17000	14000	1000	7500	5000	700

NOTE: Engraving extras for above models will add $8,700 for English scroll pattern and $22,000 for Fracassi style engraving. Other types of engraving are offered. Extra set of barrels in same gauge add 15 percent.

ROBAR AND de KIRKHAVE
Liege, Belgium

Model 1909-1910

A 6.35mm or 7.65mm caliber semi-automatic pistol with a 3" barrel. The barrel is located under the recoil spring housing. The slide is marked "Pistolet Automatique Jieffeco Depose Brevete SGDG". Blued with plastic grips. Manufactured from 1910 to 1914. Copy of Browning Model 1900.

Courtesy James Rankin

NIB	Exc.	V.G.	Good	Fair	Poor
—	500	400	300	200	100

Model 1911

A semi-automatic pistol in caliber 6.35mm. Same as the Model 1909-1910. Slide serrations have been added at the muzzle.

Courtesy James Rankin

NIB	Exc.	V.G.	Good	Fair	Poor
—	500	400	300	200	100

Model 1912

A semi-automatic pistol in caliber 7.65mm. Similar to the Model 1909-1910. Slide serrations have been added at the muzzle.

Courtesy James Rankin

NIB	Exc.	V.G.	Good	Fair	Poor
—	500	400	300	200	100

Melior Model 1907

A semi-automatic pistol in calibers 6.35mm and 7.65mm. Barrel is located under the recoil spring housing.

Courtesy James Rankin

NIB	Exc.	V.G.	Good	Fair	Poor
—	500	400	300	200	100

Melior Model 1913-1914

A semi-automatic pistol in caliber 6.35mm and 7.65mm. Same as the Model 1907 but with slide serrations at the muzzle.

NIB	Exc.	V.G.	Good	Fair	Poor
—	500	400	300	200	100

Melior Pocket Model

A semi-automatic pistol in 6.35mm caliber. It is nearly identical to the Jieffeco's made by the same company, Robar. It was manufactured in the 1920s and imported into the U.S. by Phoenix Arms Company, Mass. The Phoenix name appears on the pistol. The model resembles the FN Browning Model 1910.

Courtesy James Rankin

NIB	Exc.	V.G.	Good	Fair	Poor
—	350	250	175	125	75

Melior Vest Pocket Model

A semi-automatic pistol in caliber 6.35mm with open-top slide. Blue finish with black checkered rubber grips with Robar logo "ROC" on each grip.

Courtesy James Rankin

NIB	Exc.	V.G.	Good	Fair	Poor
—	300	250	200	150	100

Melior Model .22 Long Rifle

A semi-automatic pistol chambered for the .22 LR cartridge. Very similar in appearance to the Pocket Model, but with no squeeze grip safety.

Courtesy James Rankin

NIB	Exc.	V.G.	Good	Fair	Poor
—	500	400	300	200	100

Melior Model .22 Target

A semi-automatic in .22 LR caliber. Barrel is detachable so that various lengths may be used. A knurled nut at the front of the slide allows for barrel changes.

Courtesy James Rankin

NIB	Exc.	V.G.	Good	Fair	Poor
—	500	400	300	200	100

New Model Jieffeco (7.65mm)

In the 1920s Robar and de Kirkhave introduced a New Model Jieffeco, similar to the FN Browning Model 1910. As this time the right to import the Jieffeco into the U.S. was arranged with Davis Warner Arms Corp., New York, whose company name was used on the pistol. The model is a semi-automatic pistol in caliber 7.65mm. On the slide is "Pistolet Automatique Jieffeco Repose".

Courtesy James Rankin

NIB	Exc.	V.G.	Good	Fair	Poor
—	350	250	175	125	75

New Model Jieffeco (6.35mm)

In the 1920s Robar and de Kirkhave introduced a New Model Jieffeco, similar to the FN Browning Model 1910. As this time the right to import the Jieffeco into the U.S. was arranged with Davis Warner Arms Corp., New York, whose company name was used on the pistol. The model is a semi-automatic pistol in caliber 7.65mm. On the slide is "Pistolet Automatique Jieffeco Made in Liege, Belgium. Davis Warmer Arms Corporation, New York".

Courtesy James Rankin

NIB	Exc.	V.G.	Good	Fair	Poor
—	350	250	175	125	75

Mercury

As above, in .22 caliber and imported by Tradewinds of Tacoma, Washington. The slide marked "Mercury Made in Belgium". Blue or nickel-plated. Manufactured from 1946 to 1958.

NIB	Exc.	V.G.	Good	Fair	Poor
—	200	150	125	100	75

ROBAR COMPANIES
Phoenix, Arizona

This company has been building precision rifles, shotguns, and pistol since 1983.

Robar Patriot Tactical Shotgun

Built on a Remington Model 870 this model features an 18" barrel, express sights, seamless extended magazine tube, sidesaddle shell carrier, Wolff springs, etc. as well as Roguard/NP3 finish.

NIB	Exc.	V.G.	Good	Fair	Poor
765	600	500	400	300	100

Robar Spec Ops Tactical Shotgun

Similar to the model above but fitted with tactical ghost ring night sights, tactical safety and tactical sling.

NIB	Exc.	V.G.	Good	Fair	Poor
990	800	700	600	400	100

Robar Elite Tactical Shotgun

This model features a number of special options such as Robar choke with forcing cone, modified bolt, Pachmayr pad, etc.

NIB	Exc.	V.G.	Good	Fair	Poor
1700	1350	1000	875	600	300

Robar MK I Tactical Rifle

This model is built on a Remington Model 700 action with a 24" heavy factory barrel. Chambered for the .308 or .223 cartridge. Fitted with a gray Choate Ultimate sniper stock, Robar bipod and adjustable trigger. Roguard/MP3 finish.

NIB	Exc.	V.G.	Good	Fair	Poor
3400	2900	2250	1600	900	300

Robar MK II Tactical Rifle

As above but chambered for the .308 cartridge only. Special trigger job and special hand finish of internal parts and chamber.

NIB	Exc.	V.G.	Good	Fair	Poor
3400	2900	2250	1600	900	300

Robar SR60 Precision Rifle

This model is a fully accurized Remington Mdeol 700 action with bench rest quality barrel and chamber. Custom stock with hand bedding and pillars. Choice of .308 with 20" or 24" barrel and .223 with 24" barrel.

NIB	Exc.	V.G.	Good	Fair	Poor
3900	3500	2900	2200	1400	500

ROBBINS & LAWRENCE
Windsor, Vermont

Pepperbox

A .28 or .31 caliber percussion 5 barrel pistol with the barrel groups measuring 3.5" or 4.5" in length. Ring trigger, blued iron frame with simple scroll engraving and browned barrels, which are marked "Robbins & Lawrence Co. Windsor, VT. Patent. 1849". The barrel groups for this pistol were made in two types: fluted in both calibers, and ribbed in .31 caliber only. Approximately 7,000 were made between 1851 and 1854.

NIB	Exc.	V.G.	Good	Fair	Poor
—	—	2700	2200	650	200

ROBERTSON
Philadelphia, Pennsylvania

Pocket Pistol

A .41 caliber single-shot percussion derringer with barrels ranging in length from 3" to 4.5". The barrel marked "Robertson, Phila."

NIB	Exc.	V.G.	Good	Fair	Poor
—	—	2000	1650	500	200

ROBINSON ARMAMENT CO.
Salt Lake City, Utah

Super VEPR

This semi-automatic rifle is made in Russia and is chambered for the .308, .223 or 7.62x39mm cartridge. Uses an RPK-type receiver. Chrome lined 21.65" barrel. Walnut thumbhole stock. Black oxide finish. Weight is about 8.5 lbs.

NIB	Exc.	V.G.	Good	Fair	Poor
1200	800	675	500	400	200

M-96 Expeditonary Rifle

Chambered for the .223 or 7.62x39mm cartridge. Can use either AK or AR magazines. With quick-change barrel. Adjustable gas operating system. Can interchange calibers without tools. Built in the U.S.A.

NIB	Exc.	V.G.	Good	Fair	Poor
1750	1400	1100	800	575	300

M-96 Carbine

As above but with shorter barrel.

NIB	Exc.	V.G.	Good	Fair	Poor
1750	1400	1100	800	575	300

M-96 Top Fed

This model has the same specifications as the rifle but with the magazine fitted to the top of the receiver.

NIB	Exc.	V.G.	Good	Fair	Poor
1900	1550	1175	900	625	350

ROBINSON, ORVIL
See—Adirondack Arms Company

ROBINSON, S.C.
Richmond, Virginia

From December of 1862 through March 1 of 1863, S.C. Robinson produced copies of the Sharps carbine. These arms had an overall length of 38.5", with .52 caliber barrels 21.5" long. The lockplates were marked "S.C. ROBINSON/ARMS MANUFACTORY/RICHMOND VA/1862" along with the serial number. The barrels were marked forward of the rear sight "S.C. ROBINSON/ARMS MANUFACTORY", as well as "RICHMOND VA/1862" to the rear of the sight. Total number made estimated to be slightly more than 1,900.

In March of 1863, the Robinson factory was taken over by the Confederate States Government. Carbines produced after that date are only stamped with the serial number on their lockplates and "RICHMOND VA" on their barrels. Total number made in excess of 3,400.

Robinson Sharps

NIB	Exc.	V.G.	Good	Fair	Poor
—	—	37000	30000	9300	1500

Confederate Sharps

NIB	Exc.	V.G.	Good	Fair	Poor
—	—	32000	27500	8250	1500

ROCK ISLAND ARMORY
(TRADE NAME OF ARMSCOR)
Pahrump, Nevada

Importer of various centerfire semi-automatic pistols manufactured in the Philippines and based on 1911 and CZ designs. All of these pistols typically retail for under $500 new, with used values ranging from 50-75 percent of that, depending on condition.

ROCK RIVER ARMS, INC.
Colona, Illinois

PISTOLS

Elite Commando

Built on a National Match frame with 4" National Match slide with double serrations and lowered ejection port (5" barrel optional). Front strap is 30 lpi. Night sights standard. Aluminum trigger and many more customs features. Checkered cocobolo grips. Guaranteed 2.5" groups at 50 yards. Chambered for the .45 ACP cartridge.

NIB	Exc.	V.G.	Good	Fair	Poor
1725	1300	950	775	500	300

Standard Match

Many of the same features as the above model without the night sights. Also chambered for the .45 ACP cartridge.

NIB	Exc.	V.G.	Good	Fair	Poor
1025	750	600	450	300	200

National Match Hardball

Similar features as above models but with adjustable rear Bomar sight with dovetail front sight. Chambered for .45 ACP cartridge.

NIB	Exc.	V.G.	Good	Fair	Poor
1500	1100	825	675	500	300

Bullseye Wadcutter

This model features Rock River slide scope mount. Guaranteed to shoot 1.5" groups at 50 yards. Chambered for .45 ACP.

NIB	Exc.	V.G.	Good	Fair	Poor
1650	1250	925	750	525	325

Basic Limited Match

Similar to the Bullseye Wadcutter but with Bomar adjustable rear sight and dovetail front sights. Chambered for the .45 ACP.

NIB	Exc.	V.G.	Good	Fair	Poor
1700	1300	950	750	525	325

Limited Match

This match pistol comes standard with many custom features. Guaranteed to shoot 1.5" groups at 50 yards. Chambered for the .45 ACP.

NIB	Exc.	V.G.	Good	Fair	Poor
2050	1550	1150	800	575	350

Hi-Cap Basic Limited

This model gives the customer the choice of STI, SVI, Para-Ordnance, or Entreprise frames. Many special features. Chambered for the .45 ACP. **NOTE:** Add $200 for Para-Ordnance or Entreprise frames.

NIB	Exc.	V.G.	Good	Fair	Poor
1895	1500	1200	800	575	300

Ultimate Match Achiever

This is an IPSC-style pistol with scope and three port muzzle compensator with many special features. Chambered for the .38 Super cartridge.

NIB	Exc.	V.G.	Good	Fair	Poor
2250	1750	1150	800	575	350

Match Master Steel

This is a Bianchi-style pistol with scope and three port muzzle-brake. Chambered fo the .38 Super Cartridge.

NIB	Exc.	V.G.	Good	Fair	Poor
2350	1850	1200	850	600	375

Basic Carry

Introduced in 2005 this .45 ACP model features a 5" match barrel. Checkered front strap, lowered and flared ejection port, Novak rear sight, dehorned for carry and rosewood grips. Many other special features.

NIB	Exc.	V.G.	Good	Fair	Poor
1525	1150	825	675	500	300

Pro Carry

Similar to Basic Carry but with 4.25", 5" or 6" barrel and choice of Heinie or Novak tritium sights and polished finish; guaranteed to shoot 2.5" group at 50 yards with select ammunition. Other options available.

NIB	Exc.	V.G.	Good	Fair	Poor
1795	1400	1100	675	500	250

Tactical Pistol

This .45 ACP pistol is fitted with a 5" slide with front serrations and match grade barrel. Heine or Novak rear sight, checkered front strap, tactical mag catch and safety. Dehorned for carry. Rosewood grips. Introduced in 2005. **NOTE:** Add $200 for Black "T" finish.

NIB	Exc.	V.G.	Good	Fair	Poor
1925	1450	1200	800	575	300

Limited Police Competition 9mm

This 9mm model features a 5" slide with double serrations. Three position rear sight with dovetail front sight. Checkered front strap. Deluxe blued finish. Deluxe grips. Many other special features. Introduced in 2005. **NOTE:** Add $200 for Black "T" finish.

NIB	Exc.	V.G.	Good	Fair	Poor
2310	1750	1150	800	575	350

Unlimited Police Competition 9mm

Similar to the above but with additional special features such as a 6" slide. Introduced in 2005. **NOTE:** Add $200 for Black "T" finish.

NIB	Exc.	V.G.	Good	Fair	Poor
2310	1750	1150	800	575	350

RIFLES

CAR A2

These are AR-15-style rifles chambered for the .223 cartridge. Fitted with a 16" barrel with CAR handguards. Two stage trigger. Choice of A2 or non-collapsible buttstock. Choice of black or green furniture. Weight is about 7 lbs. **NOTE:** Add $25 for non-collapsible buttstock.

NIB	Exc.	V.G.	Good	Fair	Poor
925	750	600	500	375	200

CAR A2M

Same as above but with mid-length handguard. **NOTE:** Add $25 for non-collapsible buttstock.

NIB	Exc.	V.G.	Good	Fair	Poor
925	750	600	500	375	200

CAR A4

Similar to the models above but with flattop receiver and CAR handguard. **NOTE:** Add $25 for non-collapsible buttstock.

NIB	Exc.	V.G.	Good	Fair	Poor
925	750	600	500	375	200

CAR A4M

Flattop receiver with mid-length handguard. **NOTE:** Add $25 for non-collapsible buttstock.

NIB	Exc.	V.G.	Good	Fair	Poor
925	750	600	500	375	200

Standard A2

The AR-15-style rifle is fitted with a 20" barrel and chambered for the .223 cartridge. Two stage trigger. Fixed stock and full-length hand guard. Weight is about 8.2 lbs.

NIB	Exc.	V.G.	Good	Fair	Poor
925	750	600	500	375	200

National Match A2

This model features a .22 Wylde chamber with a 20" Wilson air-gauged match stainless steel barrel. A2 receiver. Two stage trigger. Free float high tempeture thermo mold handguard. Match sights. Weight is about 9.7 lbs.

NIB	Exc.	V.G.	Good	Fair	Poor
1265	950	800	650	500	300

Standard A4 Flattop

Same as Standard A2 but with flattop receiver.

NIB	Exc.	V.G.	Good	Fair	Poor
925	750	600	500	375	200

Varmint Rifle

This flattop model is fitted with a 24" stainless steel barrel without sights. Chambered for the .223 cartridge. Fixed stock. Two-stage trigger. Weight is about 9.5 lbs.

NIB	Exc.	V.G.	Good	Fair	Poor
1050	875	600	475	375	200

Varmint EOP (Elevated Optical Platform)

Chambered for the .223 with a Wylde chamber and fitted with a Wilson air-gauged bull stainless steel barrel. Choice of 16", 18", 20" and 24" barrel lengths. Free float aluminum handguard. National Match two stage trigger. Weight is about 8.2 lbs with 16" barrel and 10 lbs with 24" barrel. **NOTE:** Add $10 for each barrel length over 16".

NIB	Exc.	V.G.	Good	Fair	Poor
1050	875	600	475	375	200

Advanced Hunter

Chambered for 5.56/.223 Remington. Carbine-style adjustable stock, 18" cryogenically treated stainless steel barrel with tactical muzzle brake. Half-quad free-floating mid-length hand guard, winter designed trigger guard, two-stage trigger. Numerous options. Introduced in 2011.

NIB	Exc.	V.G.	Good	Fair	Poor
1100	1000	850	700	400	250

NM A2-DCM Legal

Fitted with a 20" stainless steel barrel with National Match sleeve and specially selected upper and lower to ensure tight fit. Special high temp handguards. Two-stage trigger. National Match sights. Weight is about 9 lbs.

NIB	Exc.	V.G.	Good	Fair	Poor
1200	1000	825	600	450	200

Government Model

Chambered for the .223 cartridge and fitted with a 16" Wilson chrome barrel with A2 flash hider. National Match two stage trigger. A4 upper receiver. Flip-up rear sight. EOTech M951 light system. Surefire M73 Quad Rail handguard, and 6 position tactical CAR stock. Weight is about 8.2 lbs.

NIB	Exc.	V.G.	Good	Fair	Poor
2310	1750	1150	800	575	350

Tactical CAR A4

This .223 caliber rifle has a 16" Wilson chrome barrel with A2 flash hider. A4 upper receiver with detachable carry handle. Two stage National Match trigger. R-4 handguard. Six position tactical CAR stock. Weight is about 7.5 lbs.

NIB	Exc.	V.G.	Good	Fair	Poor
950	800	650	500	350	200

Elite CAR A4

As above but with mid-length handguard. Weight is about 7.7 lbs.

NIB	Exc.	V.G.	Good	Fair	Poor
950	800	650	500	350	200

Tactical CAR UTE (Universal Tactical Entry) 2

This .223 caliber rifle has a 16" Wilson chrome barrel with A2 flash hider. It has a R-2 handguard. The upper receiver is a UTE2 with standard A4 rail height. Two stage trigger and 6 position CAR tactical stock. Weight is about 7.5 lbs.

NIB	Exc.	V.G.	Good	Fair	Poor
950	800	650	500	350	200

Elite CAR UTE 2

As above but with mid-length handguard. Weight is about 7.7 lbs.

NIB	Exc.	V.G.	Good	Fair	Poor
950	800	650	500	350	200

Entry Tactical

This .223 model features a 16" Wilson chrome barrel with a R-4 profile. A4 upper receiver with detachable carry handle. National Match two stage trigger. Six position tactical CAR stock. R-4 handguard. Weight is about 7.5 lbs.

NIB	Exc.	V.G.	Good	Fair	Poor
950	800	650	500	350	200

TASC Rifle

This rifle features a 16" Wilson chrome barrel with A2 flash hider. A2 upper receiver with windage and elevation rear sight. R-4 handguard. A2 buttstock. Weight is about 7.5 lbs.

NIB	Exc.	V.G.	Good	Fair	Poor
925	750	600	500	375	200

ROGERS & SPENCER
Utica, New York

Army Revolver

A .44 caliber 6-shot percussion revolver with a 7.5" octagonal barrel. The barrel marked "Rogers & Spencer/Utica, N.Y." Blued, case hardened hammer with walnut grips bearing the inspector's mark "RPB". Approximately 5,800 were made between 1863 and 1865.

Courtesy Milwaukee Public Museum, Milwaukee, Wisconsin

NIB	Exc.	V.G.	Good	Fair	Poor
—	—	3500	2500	1000	550

ROGUE RIFLE COMPANY
Prospect, Oregon

See—Chipmunk Rifles

ROGUE RIVER RIFLEWORKS
Paso Robles, California

Boxlock Double Rifle

These rifles are custom fitted and available in any barrel length or caliber from .22 Hornet to .577 NE. Anson & Deeley boxlocks. Choice of finish, fore-end, engraving, wood and various other options. Each rifle should be appraised individually before a sale. Prices listed are for basic rifle with no extras.

NIB	Exc.	V.G.	Good	Fair	Poor
17500	15000	12000	9500	5000	900

Sidelock Double Rifle

These rifles are custom fitted and available in any barrel length or caliber from .22 Hornet to .577 NE. Holland & Holland pattern sidelocks. Choice of finish, fore-end, engraving, wood and various other options. Each rifle should be appraised individually before a sale. Prices listed are for basic rifle with no extras.

NIB	Exc.	V.G.	Good	Fair	Poor
50000	42500	30000	17000	7500	900

ROHM GMBH
Sonthein/Brenz, Germany

This firm produced a variety of revolvers marked with various trade names that were imported into the United States prior to 1968. Essentially, they are of three types: 1) solid-frame, gateloading models; 2) solid-frame, swingout-cylinder revolvers; and 3) solid-frame, swingout-cylinder revolvers. They are of low quality and little collector interest. Junk, with virtually no value.

ROHRBAUGH
Bayport, New York

R9/R9S

Introduced in 2004 this is a very small 9mm pistol. Offered with or without sights. Magazine capacity is 6 rounds. Barrel length is 2.9". Height is 3.7", length is 5.2", slide width is .812" and weight is about 12.8 oz. Values shown are for basic model.

Courtesy John J. Stimson, Jr.

NIB	Exc.	V.G.	Good	Fair	Poor
1200	950	775	600	400	200

380/380S

NIB	Exc.	V.G.	Good	Fair	Poor
—	950	775	600	400	200

ROMERWERKE
Suhl, Germany

Romer

A .22 caliber semi-automatic pistol with a 2.5" or 6.5" barrel and 7-shot magazine. The barrels are interchangeable and marked "Kal. .22 Long Rifle", the slide marked "Romerwerke Suhl". Blued, with plastic grips. Manufactured between 1924 and 1926.

NIB	Exc.	V.G.	Good	Fair	Poor
—	625	500	450	325	225

RONGE, J. B.
Liege, Belgium

Bulldog

A .32, .380 or .45 caliber double-action revolver with a 3" barrel. Unmarked except for the monogram "RF" on the grips. Various trade names have been noted on these revolvers and are believed to have been applied by retailers. Manufactured from 1880 to 1910.

NIB	Exc.	V.G.	Good	Fair	Poor
—	250	150	100	75	50

ROSS RIFLE CO.
Quebec, Canada

Designed in 1896 by Sir Charles Ross, this straight pull rifle was manufactured in a variety of styles. Due to problems with the bolt design, it never proved popular and was discontinued in 1915.

Mark 1

Barrel length 28", .303 caliber with a "Harris Controlled Platform Magazine" that can be depressed by an external lever to facilitate loading.

Courtesy Buffalo Bill Historical Center, Cody, Wyoming

NIB	Exc.	V.G.	Good	Fair	Poor
—	700	550	400	175	100

Mark 1 Carbine

As above, with a 22" barrel.

NIB	Exc.	V.G.	Good	Fair	Poor
—	650	500	350	150	75

Mark 2

As above, with a modified rear sight.

NIB	Exc.	V.G.	Good	Fair	Poor
—	650	500	350	150	75

Mark 3

Introduced in 1910 with improved lockwork and stripper clip guides.

Courtesy Buffalo Bill Historical Center, Cody, Wyoming

NIB	Exc.	V.G.	Good	Fair	Poor
—	1200	875	675	375	175

Mark 3B

As above, with a magazine cut-off.

NIB	Exc.	V.G.	Good	Fair	Poor
—	650	500	350	150	75

Sporting Rifle

A .280 Ross or .303 caliber straight pull sporting rifle with a 24" barrel and open sights. Blued with a checkered walnut stock.

Courtesy Buffalo Bill Historical Center, Cody, Wyoming

NIB	Exc.	V.G.	Good	Fair	Poor
—	950	650	400	150	125

ROSSI, AMADEO
São Leopoldo, Brazil

Rossi handguns are manufactured under license by Taurus.

SHOTGUNS

Overland Shotgun

An exposed hammer sidelock 12, 20 or .410 bore double-barrel shotgun with 26" or 28" barrels and double triggers. Manual extractors. Blued with a walnut stock. Discontinued in 1988.

NIB	Exc.	V.G.	Good	Fair	Poor
250	225	200	150	100	75

Squire Shotgun

A 12, 20 or .410 bore double-barrel shotgun with 20", 26" or 28" barrels, double triggers and manual ejectors. Blued with a walnut stock.

NIB	Exc.	V.G.	Good	Fair	Poor
350	300	250	200	150	100

Field Grade Shotgun

This is a single-shot, tip-open gun with oil-finish hardwood stock, low profile hammer and pistol grip. No checkering. Offered in 12 and 20 gauge, as well as .410 bore. Barrel length is 28". Weight is about 5.25 lbs. for 12 and 20 gauge and 4 lbs. for the .410 bore.

NIB	Exc.	V.G.	Good	Fair	Poor
115	75	50	25	—	10

Youth Model Shotgun

Same as above but with shorter length of pull and 22" barrel. Offered in 20 gauge and .410 bore only. Weight for 20 gauge is about 5 lbs. and 3.75 lbs. for the .410 bore.

NIB	Exc.	V.G.	Good	Fair	Poor
115	75	50	25	—	10

Matched Pair Combo Guns

This model matches a single-barrel shotgun with a .22 LR barrel. Offered in 12/.22, 20/.22 and .410/.22. Adjustable sights on the rifle barrel. Blued finish.

NIB	Exc.	V.G.	Good	Fair	Poor
165	125	100	65	50	25

Stainless Matched Pair Combo Guns

Similar to above but with stainless barrel/receiver. Introduced 2008.

NIB	Exc.	V.G.	Good	Fair	Poor
200	165	125	100	75	50

Trifecta

Similar to Matched Pair with a black synthetic stock and blued barrel; includes easily interchangeable .243 Winchester or .44 Magnum, .22 Long Rifle and 20-gauge barrels.

NIB	Exc.	V.G.	Good	Fair	Poor
300	250	200	150	100	75

Turkey Gun

Introduced in 2008. A specialized version of Rossi's 12 gauge single-shot shotgun. Features a 3.5" chamber, fiber optic sights, drilled and tapped barrel, included scope mount base and a removable Briley Extended Turkey Choke.

NIB	Exc.	V.G.	Good	Fair	Poor
200	165	125	100	75	50

Rossi Circuit Judge

Revolving shotgun chambered in .410 (2.5" or 3") .45 Colt. Based on Taurus Judge handgun. Features include 18.5" barrel; fiber optic front sight; 5-round cylinder; hardwood Monte Carlo stock.

NIB	Exc.	V.G.	Good	Fair	Poor
600	—	—	—	—	—

RIFLES

Model 62

A copy of the Winchester Model 62 rifle with either 16.5" or 23" round or octagonal barrels. Blued or stainless steel with a walnut stock. Imported from 1988 to 1998.

NIB	Exc.	V.G.	Good	Fair	Poor
200	165	125	100	75	50

Model 59

As above, in .22 Magnum caliber.

NIB	Exc.	V.G.	Good	Fair	Poor
250	200	150	110	85	60

Model 92

A copy of the Winchester Model 1892, chambered for .357 Magnum, .44 Magnum, .45 Colt or .44-40 with either a 16" or 20" barrel. Blued with a walnut stock. The engraved version of this model is worth approximately 20 percent more than the values listed. **NOTE:** Add $75 for stainless steel version introduced in 1997.

NIB	Exc.	V.G.	Good	Fair	Poor
475	350	295	225	175	100

Model 92 Rifle

Introduced in 1997 this model is fitted with a 24" half octagon barrel and brass blade front sight. Magazine capacity is 13 rounds of .45 Colt. Weight is about 6.8 lbs.

NIB	Exc.	V.G.	Good	Fair	Poor
500	375	325	250	200	125

Rossi Rio Grande

Variation of the Model 92 chambered for the .45-70 plus the .410-bore shotshell. Side ejection and hammer extension allow a scope to be mounted easily. Scope-mounting rail is atop the receiver. Barrel is 20" with adjustable rear open sight, bead front. Hardwood stock with recoil pad. Cross bolt safety.

NIB	Exc.	V.G.	Good	Fair	Poor
500	400	350	275	200	100

Model 92 Large Loop

This model has a 16" barrel and is chambered for the .44 Magnum or .45 Colt cartridge. Weight is about 5.5 lbs. Finish is blue. Introduced in 1997.

NIB	Exc.	V.G.	Good	Fair	Poor
475	350	295	225	175	100

Model 65

Similar to the Model 92, but chambered for either the .44 Special or .44 Magnum cartridge. Barrel length 20". Blued with a walnut stock. Introduced in 1989.

NIB	Exc.	V.G.	Good	Fair	Poor
500	375	325	250	200	125

Single-Shot Rifle

Offered in a variety of configurations and chambered for the .22 LR, .22 Magnum, .357 Magnum, .44 Magnum, .45 Colt, .223 Rem. and .243 calibers. Fitted with 23" barrel with wood stock and choice of matte blue or stainless steel finish. Weight varies from 4.75 lbs. to 6.25 lbs. depending on caliber. **NOTE:** For stainless steel add $30, for .357 and .44 add $10. For .223 or .243 add $30.

NIB	Exc.	V.G.	Good	Fair	Poor
225	175	125	100	75	50

Single Shot Rifle—Heavy Barrel

Chambered for the .223, .243 and .22-250. This rifle is fitted with a 23" heavy barrel with plain wood stock. Matte blue finish. Weight is about 7 lbs. introduced in 2005.

NIB	Exc.	V.G.	Good	Fair	Poor
230	175	125	100	75	50

Muzzleloading Rifle

This rifle has a .50 caliber bore and is fitted with a 23" barrel. Hardwood stock with recoil pad. Weight is about 6.3 lbs. Introduced in 2003. Blue or stainless steel. **NOTE:** For matte stainless steel finish add $35.

NIB	Exc.	V.G.	Good	Fair	Poor
165	130	100	75	50	25

Muzzleloader Matched Pair

This is a .50 caliber muzzleloader with an extra 20 gauge or .243 or .270 barrel. All matched pairs come with blued finish. Price listed is for 20 gauge barrel. **NOTE:** For .243 add $40 and for .270 add $150.

NIB	Exc.	V.G.	Good	Fair	Poor
250	200	150	100	75	50

Rossi Blued Synthetic Matched Pair

Single-shot combo outfit consisting of interchangeable rifle and shotgun barrels. Synthetic stock, blued barrel and receiver. Combinations include 12 or 20 gauge/.22LR, .22 WMR, .17 HMR, .223, .243, .270, .308, .30-06 and .410/.22 LR or .410/.17 HMR. Youth and full-size versions available.

NIB	Exc.	V.G.	Good	Fair	Poor
250	200	150	100	75	50

Rossi Stainless Synthetic Matched Pair

Single-shot combo outfit consisting of interchangeable rifle and shotgun barrels. Synthetic stock, stainless barrel and receiver. Combinations include 12 or 20 ga./.22LR, .22 WMR, .17 HMR, .223, .243, .270, .308, .30-06 and .410/.22 LR or .410/.17 HMR. Youth and full-size versions available.

NIB	Exc.	V.G.	Good	Fair	Poor
275	225	165	115	90	50

Rossi Wizard

Single shot rifle chambered in 23 different rimfire/centerfire/shotshell/muzzleloading configurations. Featured include drop-barrel action; quick, toolless barrel interchangeability; fiber optic front sight; adjustable rear sight with barrel-mounted optics rail; hardwood or camo Monte Carlo stock.

NIB	Exc.	V.G.	Good	Fair	Poor
225	200	175	150	110	80

Rossi Ranch Hand

Based upon Rossi's R92 lever-action rifle. Calibers: .38/.357, .44 Magnum or .45 Colt. Barrel length is 12", overall length 24", weight 4.9 pounds (empty). Large loop lever, 6-round tubular magazine, shortened hardwood buttstock. Open buckhorn rear sight, bead front. Blue or case-hardened carbon steel receiver with saddle ring.

NIB	Exc.	V.G.	Good	Fair	Poor
450	400	325	250	200	100

HANDGUNS

Model 51

A .22 caliber double-action revolver with a 6" barrel, adjustable sights and a 6-shot cylinder. Blued with walnut grips. Imported prior to 1986.

NIB	Exc.	V.G.	Good	Fair	Poor
—	150	100	75	50	40

Model 511 Sportsman

As above, with a 4" barrel and made of stainless steel with walnut grips. Introduced in 1986.

NIB	Exc.	V.G.	Good	Fair	Poor
225	200	150	125	100	75

Model 461

This is a 6-round revolver chambered for the .357 Magnum cartridge. Fitted with a 2" barrel. Rubber grips and blued finish. Weight is about 26 oz.

NIB	Exc.	V.G.	Good	Fair	Poor
300	225	195	150	125	75

Model 462

Same as above but with stainless steel finish.

NIB	Exc.	V.G.	Good	Fair	Poor
350	275	225	165	140	90

Model 68S

This new version was introduced in 1993 and features a shrouded ejector rod and fixed sights. Chambered for the .38 Special cartridge, it is offered with either 2" or 3" barrel. Grips wood or rubber. Finish is blue or nickel. Weighs about 23 oz.

NIB	Exc.	V.G.	Good	Fair	Poor
175	150	125	100	75	60

Model 69

As above, in .32 Smith & Wesson caliber with a 3" barrel and 6-shot cylinder. Imported prior to 1986.

NIB	Exc.	V.G.	Good	Fair	Poor
—	125	100	75	50	40

Model 70

As above, in .22 caliber with a 3" barrel and 6-shot cylinder. Imported prior to 1986.

NIB	Exc.	V.G.	Good	Fair	Poor
—	125	100	75	50	40

Model 84

A stainless steel, .38 Special caliber double-action revolver with ribbed 3" or 4" barrel. Blued with walnut grips. Imported in 1985 and 1986.

NIB	Exc.	V.G.	Good	Fair	Poor
—	175	150	125	100	75

Model 851

As above, with either a 3" or 4" ventilated rib barrel and adjustable sights.

NIB	Exc.	V.G.	Good	Fair	Poor
200	175	150	125	100	75

Model 68

A .38 Special double-action revolver with a 2" or 3" barrel and 5-shot cylinder. Blued or nickel-plated with walnut grips.

NIB	Exc.	V.G.	Good	Fair	Poor
225	175	150	125	100	75

Model 31

A .38 Special caliber double-action revolver with a 4" barrel and 5-shot cylinder. Blued or nickel-plated with walnut grips. Imported prior to 1986.

NIB	Exc.	V.G.	Good	Fair	Poor
225	175	150	125	100	75

Model 677

This model was first introduced in 1997 and is chambered for the .357 Magnum cartridge. It has a matte blue finish with 2" barrel and black rubber grips. Weight is about 26 oz.

NIB	Exc.	V.G.	Good	Fair	Poor
300	250	200	150	125	100

Model 88S

Introduced in 1993 this improved model has the same features of the Model 68 with the addition of a stainless finish. It is chambered for the .38 Special cartridge and is fitted with either a 2" or 3" barrel. Available with either wood or rubber grips. Cylinder holds 5 cartridges. Weighs approximately 22 oz.

NIB	Exc.	V.G.	Good	Fair	Poor
325	275	225	165	140	100

Model 351

This revolver is chambered for the .38 Special +P cartridge. Fitted with a 2" barrel and rubber grips. 5 round cylinder. Blued finish. Weight is about 24 oz.

NIB	Exc.	V.G.	Good	Fair	Poor
300	250	200	150	125	100

Model 352

Same as above but with stainless steel finish.

NIB	Exc.	V.G.	Good	Fair	Poor
325	275	225	165	140	100

Model 951

A .38 Special caliber double-action revolver with a 3" or 4" ventilated rib barrel and 6-shot cylinder. Blued with walnut grips. Introduced in 1985.

NIB	Exc.	V.G.	Good	Fair	Poor
300	250	200	150	125	100

Model 971

As above, in .357 Magnum caliber with a solid ribbed 4" barrel and enclosed ejector rod. Adjustable sights. Blued with walnut grips. Introduced in 1988.

NIB	Exc.	V.G.	Good	Fair	Poor
300	250	200	150	125	100

Model 971 Comp

Introduced in 1993. Similar to the Model 971 with the addition of a compensator on a 3.25" barrel. Overall length is 9" and weight is 32 oz. Chambered for .357 Magnum cartridge.

NIB	Exc.	V.G.	Good	Fair	Poor
335	265	200	150	125	100

Model 971 Comp Stainless

As above, but constructed of stainless steel with checkered black rubber grips. Introduced in 1989.

NIB	Exc.	V.G.	Good	Fair	Poor
350	275	225	150	125	100

Model 972

Revolver; 6-shot polished stainless double-action .357 Magnum. Adjustable rear sight and red insert on front sight. 6" barrel, rubber grip, 35 oz. Uses Taurus security system. Introduced 2006.

NIB	Exc.	V.G.	Good	Fair	Poor
375	295	250	150	125	100

Model 877

Introduced in 1996 this 6-shot revolver is chambered for the .357 Magnum cartridge. It is fitted with a 2" heavy barrel. Stainless steel with black rubber grips. Weight is about 26 oz.

NIB	Exc.	V.G.	Good	Fair	Poor
350	275	225	150	125	100

Model 89

As above, in .32 Smith & Wesson caliber with a 3" barrel.

NIB	Exc.	V.G.	Good	Fair	Poor
325	275	225	165	140	100

Model 971 VRC (vented rib compensator)

Introduced in 1996 this variation features a choice of a 6", 4" or 2.5" vent rib barrel with integral compensator. Stainless steel with black rubber grips. Weight is from 30 oz. to 39 oz. depending on barrel length.

NIB	Exc.	V.G.	Good	Fair	Poor
375	295	250	150	125	100

Model 988 Cyclops

Introduced in 1997 this model is chambered for the .357 Magnum cartridge and is fitted with four recessed compensator ports on each side of the muzzle. Offered in 8" or 6" barrel lengths this six-shot double-action revolver weighs about 44 ozs. for the 6" model and 51 ozs. for the 8" model. Stainless steel finish.

Cyclops with scope mounted

NIB	Exc.	V.G.	Good	Fair	Poor
525	475	350	275	200	150

Model 720

This double-action revolver is chambered for the .44 Special and features a five-round cylinder and 3" barrel. Overall length is 8" and weight is about 27.5 oz. Finish is stainless steel.

NIB	Exc.	V.G.	Good	Fair	Poor
525	475	350	275	200	150

ROTH-SAUER
See—Sauer, J. P. & Son

ROTTWEIL
Rottweil, West Germany

Model 650

A 12 gauge over/under shotgun with 28" ventilated rib barrels, screw-in choke tubes, single-selective trigger and automatic ejectors. The receiver is engraved and case hardened. Checkered stock of well figured walnut. Imported prior to 1987.

NIB	Exc.	V.G.	Good	Fair	Poor
—	900	700	550	425	150

Model 72

A 12 gauge over/under shotgun with 28" ventilated rib barrels, screw-in choke tubes, single-selective trigger and automatic ejectors. Blued with a well figured checkered walnut stock. Imported prior to 1988.

NIB	Exc.	V.G.	Good	Fair	Poor
—	2200	1550	975	650	350

Model 72 American Skeet

As above, with a 26.75" ventilated rib barrel, single-selective trigger and automatic ejectors. The receiver is also engraved. Imported prior to 1988.

NIB	Exc.	V.G.	Good	Fair	Poor
—	2200	1550	975	650	350

Model 72 Adjustable American Trap

As above, with a 34" ventilated rib barrel, adjustable to point of impact. Imported prior to 1987.

NIB	Exc.	V.G.	Good	Fair	Poor
—	2200	1550	975	650	350

Model 72 American Trap

As above, without the barrel being adjustable to the point of impact.

NIB	Exc.	V.G.	Good	Fair	Poor
—	2100	1450	875	550	300

Model 72 International Skeet

As above, with 26.75" ventilated rib barrels choked Skeet. Imported prior to 1988.

NIB	Exc.	V.G.	Good	Fair	Poor
—	2100	1450	875	550	300

Model 72 International Trap

As above, with 30" high ventilated rib barrels that are choked Improved Modified and Full. Imported prior to 1988.

NIB	Exc.	V.G.	Good	Fair	Poor
—	2100	1450	875	550	300

ROYAL AMERICAN SHOTGUNS
Woodland Hills, California

Model 100

A 12 or 20 gauge over/under shotgun with 26", 28" or 30" ventilated rib barrels, double triggers and extractors. Blued with a walnut stock. Imported from 1985 to 1987.

NIB	Exc.	V.G.	Good	Fair	Poor
—	550	375	250	175	150

Model 100AE

As above, with a single trigger and automatic ejectors.

NIB	Exc.	V.G.	Good	Fair	Poor
—	650	475	275	200	175

Model 600

A 12, 20, 28 or .410 bore double-barrel shotgun with 25", 26", 28" or 30" ventilated rib barrels, double triggers and extractors. Blued with a walnut stock. Imported from 1985 to 1987.

NIB	Exc.	V.G.	Good	Fair	Poor
—	600	425	300	200	175

Model 800

A 28 or .410 bore detachable sidelock double-barrel shotgun with 24", 26" or 28" barrels, double triggers and automatic ejectors. Blued, French case hardened with an English-style walnut stock. Imported from 1985 to 1987.

NIB	Exc.	V.G.	Good	Fair	Poor
—	1550	1200	900	675	400

RUBY ARMS COMPANY
Guernica, Spain

Ruby

A 6.35mm or 7.35mm caliber semi-automatic pistol with a 3.5" barrel and 6-shot magazine. The slide marked "Ruby". Blued with plastic grips.

NIB	Exc.	V.G.	Good	Fair	Poor
—	275	175	125	75	50

RUGER
See—Sturm, Ruger Co.

RUPERTUS, JACOB
Philadelphia, Pennsylvania

Navy Revolver

This model is equally as rare as the Army model. It is chambered for .36 caliber percussion. Otherwise it is quite similar in appearance to the Army model. There were approximately 12 manufactured in 1859. Both of these revolvers were manufactured for test purposes and were not well-received by the military, so further production was not accomplished.

NIB	Exc.	V.G.	Good	Fair	Poor
—	—	15000	11750	5500	1250

Pocket Model Revolver

This is a smaller version of the Army and Navy model, chambered for .25 caliber percussion. It has no loading lever and has a 3-1/8" octagonal barrel. There were approximately 12 manufactured in 1859.

NIB	Exc.	V.G.	Good	Fair	Poor
—	—	11000	8250	3600	950

NIB	Exc.	V.G.	Good	Fair	Poor
—	2100	1450	875	550	300

Double-Barrel Pocket Pistol

A .22 caliber double-barrel pistol with 3" round barrels and a spur trigger. The hammer fitted with a sliding firing pin. Blued with walnut grips.

NIB	Exc.	V.G.	Good	Fair	Poor
—	—	2400	1900	850	200

Army Revolver

This is an extremely rare revolver chambered for .44 caliber percussion. It has a 7.25" octagon barrel with an integral loading lever that pivots to the side instead of downward. The hammer is mounted on the side and there is a pellet priming device located on the backstrap. There is only one nipple on the breech that lines up with the top of the cylinder. The cylinder is unfluted and holds 6-shots. The finish is blued, with walnut grips; and the frame is marked "Patented April 19, 1859". There were less than 12 manufactured in 1859. It would behoove one to secure a qualified independent appraisal if a transaction were contemplated.

Courtesy Greg Martin Auctions

NIB	Exc.	V.G.	Good	Fair	Poor
—	—	28500	12000	5500	1500

Single-Shot Pocket Pistol

A .22, .32, .38 or .41 rimfire single-shot pistol with half-octagonal barrels, ranging in length from 3" to 5". The barrel marked "Rupertus Pat'd. Pistol Mfg. Co. Philadelphia". Blued with walnut grips. Approximately 3,000 were made from 1870 to 1885. **NOTE:** The .41 caliber variety is worth approximately 200 percent more than the values listed.

NIB	Exc.	V.G.	Good	Fair	Poor
—	—	900	650	225	75

Spur Trigger Revolver

A .22 caliber revolver with a 2.75" barrel and unfluted 7-shot cylinder. The top strap is marked "Empire Pat., Nov. 21, 71". Blued or nickel-plated with walnut grips. Also made in .32 and .32 rimfire with 5-shot semi-fluted cylinder. A larger model in .41 rimfire with 5-shot semi-fluted cylinder was made with top strap marked "Empire 41". Made during the 1870s and 1880s. **NOTE:** Add 20 percent for .41 caliber.

NIB	Exc.	V.G.	Good	Fair	Poor
—	—	450	250	175	100

RWS
Dynamit Nobel
Nurenberg, Germany

Model 820 S

A .22 caliber target rifle with 24" heavy barrel and adjustable aperture sights. The trigger is fully adjustable. Three-position adjustable match stock with stippled pistol grip and fore-end. Discontinued in 1986.

NIB	Exc.	V.G.	Good	Fair	Poor
1650	1275	975	625	450	250

Model 820 SF

As above with a heavier barrel. Discontinued in 1986.

NIB	Exc.	V.G.	Good	Fair	Poor
1700	1350	1000	550	400	250

Model 820 K

Offhand "Running Boar" model of the above with a lighter barrel. Furnished without sights. Discontinued in 1986.

NIB	Exc.	V.G.	Good	Fair	Poor
1700	1350	1000	550	400	250

S

S.A.E.
Miami, Florida

S.A.E. was an importer of Spanish shotguns, some of very fine quality. The most notable of these is the S.A.E. line of Sarasqueta shotguns from Eibar, Spain. Not all S.A.E. shotguns are marked with the maker's name.

Model 210S

A 12, 20 or .410 bore double-barrel shotgun with 26" or 28" barrels, double triggers and manual extractors. Blued, French case hardened with a checkered walnut stock. Imported in 1988.

NIB	Exc.	V.G.	Good	Fair	Poor
—	475	395	300	225	150

Model 340X

A Holland & Holland-style sidelock 10 or 20 gauge double-barrel shotgun with 26" barrels, double triggers and automatic ejectors. Blued, case hardened with a checkered English style walnut stock. Imported in 1988.

NIB	Exc.	V.G.	Good	Fair	Poor
—	850	675	500	400	200

Model 209E

As above, with the exception that it was also chambered for .410 bore cartridges, and was more finely engraved. Imported in 1988.

NIB	Exc.	V.G.	Good	Fair	Poor
—	1100	850	700	550	250

Model 70

A 12 or 20 gauge over/under shotgun with 26" ventilated rib barrels screw-in choke tubes, single trigger and automatic ejectors. The modestly engraved receiver is either blued or French case hardened. Stock of finely figured walnut. Imported in 1988.

NIB	Exc.	V.G.	Good	Fair	Poor
—	500	375	250	200	100

Model 66C

A 12 gauge over/under shotgun with 26" or 30" ventilated rib barrels choked for skeet or trap, single trigger and automatic ejectors. The boxlock action fitted with false sideplates, which are engraved and gold inlaid. Blued with a checkered Monte Carlo-style stock and a beavertail forearm. Imported in 1988.

NIB	Exc.	V.G.	Good	Fair	Poor
—	1100	850	700	575	300

S.E.A.M.
Eibar, Spain

This retailer sold a number of pistols produced by the firm of Urizar prior to 1935.

Praga

A 7.65 caliber semi-automatic pistol marked "Praga Cal 7.65" on the slide. Blued with plastic grips impressed with the trademark S.E.A.M.

NIB	Exc.	V.G.	Good	Fair	Poor
—	275	175	125	90	65

S.E.A.M.

A 6.35mm semi-automatic pistol with a 2" barrel. The slide marked "Fabrica de Armas SEAM". Blued with black plastic grips, having the trademark "SEAM" cast into them.

NIB	Exc.	V.G.	Good	Fair	Poor
—	250	175	125	90	65

Silesia

As above, but of 7.65mm caliber with a 3" barrel and having the word "Silesia" stamped on the slide.

NIB	Exc.	V.G.	Good	Fair	Poor
—	250	175	125	90	65

S.W.D., INC.
Atlanta, Georgia

Cobray M-11

A 9mm semi-automatic pistol with a 32-round magazine. Parkerized finish.

NIB	Exc.	V.G.	Good	Fair	Poor
—	550	495	400	275	100

M-11 Carbine

As above, with a 16.25" barrel enclosed in a shroud and fitted with a telescoping wire stock.

NIB	Exc.	V.G.	Good	Fair	Poor
—	800	650	550	275	100

Terminator

A 12 or 20 gauge single-shot shotgun with an 18" cylinder bored barrel. Parkerized finish. Said to be exceptionally rare but attracts little interest.

NIB	Exc.	V.G.	Good	Fair	Poor
—	150	80	70	60	50

SABATTI
See—European American Armory Corp.

SACKET, D. D.
Westfield, Massachusetts

Under Hammer Pistol

A .34 or .36 single-shot percussion pistol with a half octagonal 3" or 4" barrel marked "D. D. Sacket/Westfield/Cast Steel". Manufactured during the 1850s.

NIB	Exc.	V.G.	Good	Fair	Poor
—	—	1550	1200	550	165

SAFARI ARMS
Phoenix, Arizona

In operation from 1978 to 1987, this company was purchased by Olympic Arms of Olympia, Washington, in 1987 and the models listed are currently produced by that company under different trade names.

Enforcer

A .45 caliber semi-automatic pistol with a 3.9" barrel and 5-shot magazine. Patterned after the Colt Model 1911. Blued, Armaloy, electroless nickel-plate or Parkerized finish with checkered walnut or neoprene grips.

NIB	Exc.	V.G.	Good	Fair	Poor
700	600	500	400	350	150

Match Master
As above, with a 5" barrel.

NIB	Exc.	V.G.	Good	Fair	Poor
700	600	500	400	350	150

Black Widow
As above, with ivory Micarta grips etched with a black widow.

NIB	Exc.	V.G.	Good	Fair	Poor
700	600	500	400	350	150

Model 81
As above, without the grip etching. Also offered in .38 caliber.

NIB	Exc.	V.G.	Good	Fair	Poor
800	700	600	500	400	200

Model 81L
As above, with a 6" barrel.

NIB	Exc.	V.G.	Good	Fair	Poor
850	750	650	550	450	200

Ultimate Unlimited
A bolt-action single-shot pistol with a 15" barrel chambered for variety of cartridges. Blued with a laminated stock.

NIB	Exc.	V.G.	Good	Fair	Poor
850	750	650	550	450	200

Survivor I Conversion Unit
A conversion unit lifted to the Model 1911 frame that alters that pistol to a bolt-action carbine. Barrel length 16.25", caliber .223, folding stock.

NIB	Exc.	V.G.	Good	Fair	Poor
300	275	250	200	150	100

Counter Sniper Rifle
A .308 caliber bolt-action target rifle with a heavy 26" barrel and 20-round detachable magazine. Matte blued with a colored composite stock.

NIB	Exc.	V.G.	Good	Fair	Poor
1200	1050	850	650	450	200

SAIGA
Izhevsk, Russia

A series of AK type rifles and shotguns manufactured in Russia by Izhmash.

RIFLES

Model IZ-114, AZ-132
This Kalashnikov-type semi-automatic rifle is chambered in .223 Rem. (IZ-114) or 7.62x39mm (IZ-132). Black synthetic or wood stock and forearm, 16" or 20.5" barrel. Imported by several companies including EAA, U.S. Sporting Goods and others.

NIB	Exc.	V.G.	Good	Fair	Poor
325	300	275	225	200	150

Model AZ-139
Same as above except in .308 Win. and 22" barrel.

NIB	Exc.	V.G.	Good	Fair	Poor
500	425	350	300	250	150

Model 100
Hunting style semi-automatic rifle with synthetic stock in .223, 7.62x39, .308 or .30-06. Magazine capacity 3 or 10 rounds.

NIB	Exc.	V.G.	Good	Fair	Poor
685	600	500	350	250	150

SHOTGUNS
Model 109
Semi-automatic shotgun based on AK-47 design in 12 or 20 gauge or .410 bore. Black synthetic stock and forearm, 5- or 10-shot magazine. **NOTE:** Add $75 for .410 bore.

NIB	Exc.	V.G.	Good	Fair	Poor
550	475	425	300	250	150

SAKO
Riihimaki, Finland

NOTE: Arms produced by this company prior to 1972 are worth approximately 25 percent more than arms of the same type produced thereafter. Prices for fair and poor condition reflect the worth of the action. In 2000 Beretta Holding Co. purchased Sako and distributes the product line through Beretta U.S.A.

Standard Sporter
A bolt-action magazine rifle produced in a wide variety of calibers with varying barrel lengths, etc. Blued with checkered walnut stocks.

NIB	Exc.	V.G.	Good	Fair	Poor
—	750	650	450	400	300

Deluxe Model

As above, with an engraved floorplate and checkered Monte Carlo-style stock featuring a rosewood pistol grip cap and fore-end tip.

NIB	Exc.	V.G.	Good	Fair	Poor
—	900	750	600	450	400

Finnbear

As above, with a long action available in a variety of large bore calibers. Fitted with a 20" or 23.5" barrel. Blued with a checkered stock. For .458 Winchester Magnum (only 20 produced), values double. **NOTE:** Add 15 percent for other magnum chamberings or Deluxe version. Add 20 percent for Mannlicher Carbine version.

NIB	Exc.	V.G.	Good	Fair	Poor
—	1000	850	650	400	300

Forester

As above, with a shorter action suitable for use with intermediate cartridges. **NOTE:** Add 20 percent for Mannlicher Carbine version.

NIB	Exc.	V.G.	Good	Fair	Poor
—	1000	850	650	400	300

Vixen

As above, with a short action. **NOTE:** Add 20 percent for Mannlicher Carbine version.

NIB	Exc.	V.G.	Good	Fair	Poor
—	1000	850	650	400	300

FN Action

Manufactured from 1950 to 1957, this model utilized a Fabrique Nationale manufactured receiver and was chambered for .270 Winchester and .30-06 cartridges. Otherwise, as above.

NIB	Exc.	V.G.	Good	Fair	Poor
—	800	600	475	400	300

FN Magnum Action

As above, with a long action for .300 and .375 Holland & Holland.

NIB	Exc.	V.G.	Good	Fair	Poor
—	900	700	550	400	300

Anniversary Model

A 7mm Remington Magnum bolt-action rifle with a 24" barrel. Blued, checkered walnut stock. A total of 1,000 were manufactured. As with any commemorative firearm, this model should be NIB to realize its full resale potential.

NIB	Exc.	V.G.	Good	Fair	Poor
2500	850	750	450	400	300

Finnwolf

A 4-shot lever-action rifle produced in .243 and .308 calibers. Blued, checkered walnut stock. Manufactured from 1962 to 1974.

NIB	Exc.	V.G.	Good	Fair	Poor
—	1400	1200	750	450	300

Finnfire

This bolt-action rifle is chambered for the .22 LR cartridge. It is fitted with a 22" barrel with choice of iron sights or no sights and a European walnut stock. A 5-shot detachable magazine is standard. Weight is about 5.25 lbs.

Courtesy Stoeger

NIB	Exc.	V.G.	Good	Fair	Poor
1150	950	700	575	400	300

Finnfire Heavy Barrel

Same as above but fitted with a heavy barrel.

Courtesy Stoeger

NIB	Exc.	V.G.	Good	Fair	Poor
1150	950	700	575	400	300

Finnfire Hunter

Introduced in 2000 this bolt-action model is chambered for the .22 LR cartridge. It is fitted with a 22" barrel and a Sako 75 style select walnut stock. Weight is about 5.75 lbs.

NIB	Exc.	V.G.	Good	Fair	Poor
1150	950	700	575	400	300

Finnfire Sporter

This model is chambered for the .22 LR cartridge and is built on the P94S action. It has a walnut stock with adjustable cheekpiece and buttplate spacer system that allows for length of pull and buttplate angle adjustment. Trigger is adjustable. Introduced in 1999.

NIB	Exc.	V.G.	Good	Fair	Poor
1150	950	700	575	400	300

Sako Quad Combo

Introduced in 2005 this bolt-action rifle features four interchangeable barrels in four different rimfire calibers. Black synthetic stock. Detachable 5-round magazine. Included barrels are: .22 Long Rifle, .22 WMR, .17 HMR, and .17 Mach 2. All 22" in length. Blued finish. Weight is about 5.75 lbs. **NOTE:** NIB price for rifles with only one barrel is $948. Extra barrels are $260 each.

NIB	Exc.	V.G.	Good	Fair	Poor
1450	1300	1075	800	500	300

Hunter

This model is offered in three action lengths: short, medium and long. In the short action the calibers available are .17 Rem., .222, .223 in 21.25" barrel. In medium action the calibers are: .22-250, .243, .308, and 7mm-08 in 21.75" barrel. The long action calibers are: .25-06, .270 Win., .280 Rem., .30-06 for 22" barrel length. In 24" barrel the long action calibers are: 7mm Rem. Magnum, .300 Win. and .300 Wby. Magnum, .338 and .375 Win. Magnum and .416 Rem. Magnum. In 1996 the .270 Wthby Magnum, 7mm Wthby Magnum and the .340 Wthby was added to the long action calibers. Available in left-handed version for all but short action calibers. Adjustable trigger is standard. Checkered European walnut stock. Weight for short action is 6.25 lbs., for medium action 6.5 lbs., and long action calibers 7.75 to 8.25 depending on caliber.

Medium Action

NIB	Exc.	V.G.	Good	Fair	Poor
1200	1050	875	600	500	300

Short Action

NOTE: Add 10 percent to Medium Action prices for .222 Rem. and .223 Rem. For .17 Rem. add 20 percent to Medium Action prices.

Long Action

NOTE: For long action calibers in .300 and .338 Win. Magnum add 10 percent. For .375 H&H Magnum add 20 percent. For .416 Rem. Magnum add 25 percent.

NIB	Exc.	V.G.	Good	Fair	Poor
1400	1175	1000	750	600	300

Carbine

As above, with an 18.5" barrel. Produced with either a medium or long-length action.

NIB	Exc.	V.G.	Good	Fair	Poor
1200	1050	875	600	500	300

Long Range Hunting Rifle

Similar to the long action Hunter but fitted with a 26" fluted barrel. Chambered for the .25-06, .270 Win., 7mm Rem. Mag., and .300 Win. Mag. Introduced in 1996. **NOTE:** Add 10 percent to medium action prices for .222 Rem. and .223 Rem. For .17 Rem. add 20 percent to medium action and prices.

NIB	Exc.	V.G.	Good	Fair	Poor
1500	1300	1050	875	650	300

Laminated Model

This model features a laminated checkered hardwood stock made up of 36 layers. Solid recoil pad is standard as are quick detachable sling swivels. Available in both medium and long action calibers. Medium action calibers are: .22-250, .243, .308 and 7mm-08 with 21.75" barrel; weight of 6.5 lbs. Long action calibers are: .25-06, .270, .280, .30-06 with 22" barrel; weight is 7.75 lbs. Offered with 24" barrels are: 7mm Rem. Magnum, .300, .338 Win. Magnum and .375 H&H; weight is 7.75 lbs.

Medium Action

NOTE: Add 10 percent to prices for .222 Rem. and .223 Rem. For .17 Rem. add 20 percent.

NIB	Exc.	V.G.	Good	Fair	Poor
1200	1050	875	600	500	300

Long Action

NOTE: For long action calibers in .300 and .338 Win. Magnum add 10 percent. For .375 H&H Magnum add 20 percent. For .416 Rem. Magnum add 25 percent.

NIB	Exc.	V.G.	Good	Fair	Poor
1400	1175	1000	750	600	300

FiberClass

This model features a black plain fiberglass stock. Offered in long action calibers only. The .25-06, .270, .280, and .30-06 are fitted with 22" barrels and weigh 7.25 lbs. The 7mm Rem. Mag., .300 Win. Mag., .338 Win. Mag., and .375 H&H are fitted with 24" barrel and weigh 7.25 lbs. The .416 Rem. Mag. has a 24" barrel and weighs 8 lbs. **NOTE:** For long action calibers in .300 and .338 Win. Mag. add 10 percent. For .375 H&H Mag. add 20 percent. For .416 Rem. Mag. add 25 percent.

NIB	Exc.	V.G.	Good	Fair	Poor
1050	800	600	500	400	400

FiberClass Carbine

As above, with a fiberglass stock.

NIB	Exc.	V.G.	Good	Fair	Poor
1050	800	600	500	400	400

Carbine

This model features a Mannlicher-style stock with a two-piece forearm. It has a checkered walnut stock with oil finish. It is offered in both medium and short actions, all with 18.5" barrels. In medium action the .243 and .308 are available and weigh 6 lbs. The long action calibers are: .270, and .30-06, weighing 7.25 lbs.; and the .338 Win. Mag. and .375 H&H, weighing 7.75 lbs. **NOTE:** For long action calibers in .338 Win. Mag. add 10 percent. For .375 H&H Mag. add 20 percent.

Medium Action

NIB	Exc.	V.G.	Good	Fair	Poor
1200	1050	875	600	500	300

Long Action

NOTE: For long action calibers in .338 Win. Magnum add 10 percent. For .375 H&H Magnum add 20 percent.

NIB	Exc.	V.G.	Good	Fair	Poor
1200	1050	875	600	500	300

Varmint-Heavy Barrel

The checkered walnut stock on this model features an extra wide beavertail forearm with oil finish. Offered in both short and medium action, all are fitted with a 23" heavy barrel weighing 8.5 lbs. Short action calibers are .17 Rem., .222, and .223. Medium action calibers are: .22-250, .243, .308, and 7mm-08.

Short Action

NOTE: Add 10 percent for .222 and .223 Rem. Add 20 percent for .17 Rem. to above prices.

NIB	Exc.	V.G.	Good	Fair	Poor
1200	1050	875	600	500	300

Medium Action

NIB	Exc.	V.G.	Good	Fair	Poor
1200	1050	875	600	500	300

PPC Bench Rest/Varmint

Similar to the Varmint but single-shot. Fitted with 23.75" barrel and weighs 8.75 lbs. Available in short action special calibers .22 PPC and 6mm PPC.

NIB	Exc.	V.G.	Good	Fair	Poor
1350	1150	975	650	500	300

Classic Grade

Hand-checkered select walnut stock with matte lacquer finish is featured on this grade. Offered in medium and long action. Long action rifles are offered in left-hand model. The medium action caliber is .243 Win. with a 21.75" barrel and weight of 6 lbs. The long action calibers are: .270, .30-06, and 7mm Rem. Mag. with 24" barrels. Long action calibers weigh about 7.5 lbs.

NIB	Exc.	V.G.	Good	Fair	Poor
1200	1050	875	600	500	300

Deluxe Grade

This grade features a high grade European walnut stock with hand cut basket weave checkering. The forend tip and grip are fitted with rosewood. English-style recoil pad is standard. Long action models are offered in left-hand configuration. As with the Hunter model short, medium, and long action are available in the same calibers, barrel lengths and weights as the Hunter.

Medium Action

NIB	Exc.	V.G.	Good	Fair	Poor
1400	1175	1000	750	600	300

Short Action

NOTE: Add 10 percent to above prices for .222 and .223 Rem. Add 20 percent for .17 Rem.

Long Action

NOTE: For long action calibers in .300 and .338 Win. Magnum add 10 percent. For .375 H&H Magnum add 20 percent. For .416 Rem. Magnum add 25 percent. For left-hand models add $100.

NIB	Exc.	V.G.	Good	Fair	Poor
1400	1175	1000	750	600	300

Super Grade/Super Deluxe

Similar to Deluxe Grade but offered with fancy walnut stock with oak-leaf carving. Floor plate and trigger guard are engraved. Pistol grip cap has inlaid silver plate. Offered in same actions and calibers as Hunter and Deluxe Grades.

Medium Action

NIB	Exc.	V.G.	Good	Fair	Poor
2500	1750	1200	750	625	300

Short Action

NOTE: Add 10 percent to above prices for .222 and .223 Rem.

Long Action

NOTE: For long action calibers in .300 and .338 Win. Magnum add 10 percent. For .375 H&H Magnum add 20 percent. For .416 Rem. Magnum add 25 percent.

NIB	Exc.	V.G.	Good	Fair	Poor
2500	1750	1200	750	625	300

Safari Grade

As above, chambered for .300 Winchester Magnum, .338 Winchester Magnum, or .375 Holland & Holland cartridges.

NIB	Exc.	V.G.	Good	Fair	Poor
3250	2500	1900	1100	800	400

MODEL 75 SERIES

This model was introduced in March 1997. It is based on a new design by Sako. Each of the five different action sizes is manufactured for a specific range of calibers. Its action, barrel, and stocks are all redesigned components. It is offered in a variety of configurations and calibers. Sako actions are offered separately in carbon steel, in white, and stainless steel.

Sako 75 action

Model 75 Hunter

This model is available in five different action sizes for calibers from .17 Rem. to .416 Rem. Magnum. Weight varies from 6.37 lbs. to 9 lbs. and barrel lengths from 22" to 24.37". Choice of checkered walnut stock or black synthetic stock. All Hunter models are sold without sights as standard, but open sights are an option. Magazine is detachable except for .300 Rem. Ultra Magnum and the .416 Rem. Magnum. Single set trigger is an option. In 2003 a left-hand model was offered in .270 Win and .30-06. In 2004 the .270 WSM and .300 WSM calibers were added. **NOTE:** Add $30 for long action calibers from .270 to .416.

Sako Model 75 left-hand rifle

NIB	Exc.	V.G.	Good	Fair	Poor
1425	1050	700	500	400	300

Model 75 Stainless Synthetic

Same as above but available with synthetic stock and stainless steel barrel and action. Offered in calibers from .22-250 to .375 H&H. **NOTE:** Add $30 for long action calibers.

NIB	Exc.	V.G.	Good	Fair	Poor
1500	1100	750	600	400	300

Model 75 Deluxe

This model features all of the elements of the Hunter model with the addition of special checkering on select walnut stock with special black finish. All models have a hinged floor plate. In 2004 the .270 WSM and .300 WSM calibers were added. Weight is about 7.75 lbs. **NOTE:** Add $100 for long action calibers.

NIB	Exc.	V.G.	Good	Fair	Poor
1600	1050	800	700	500	400

Model 75 Big Game Deluxe

This model is similar to the M75 Deluxe except that it is chambered for the .416 Rem. Magnum cartridge and fitted with iron sights.

NIB	Exc.	V.G.	Good	Fair	Poor
1600	1050	800	700	500	400

Model 75 Varmint

This model is chambered for the .17 Rem., .222 Rem., .223 and .22-250, all with 24" heavy barrels. In 1999 Sako added the .22 PPC and 6mm PPC calibers. Other calibers are .260 Remington, .308 and .204 Ruger. It weighs about 8.4 lbs. Walnut stock.

NIB	Exc.	V.G.	Good	Fair	Poor
1250	950	750	600	450	400

Model 75 Varmint Set Trigger

As above but with a single set trigger. Introduced in 2005.

NIB	Exc.	V.G.	Good	Fair	Poor
1550	1100	875	700	500	400

Model 75 Varmint Stainless

Introduced in 1999 this model is similar to the Varmint 75 but with stainless steel barrel. Magazine is detachable but can be loaded through the ejection port. Trigger is adjustable. Offered in all of the calibers as the standard Model 75 Varmint. Weights vary from about 8 lbs. to 8.6 lbs. The stock is laminated.

NIB	Exc.	V.G.	Good	Fair	Poor
1200	1050	875	600	500	300

Model 75 Varmint Stainless Set Trigger

As above but with stainless steel barrel and receiver and laminated stock. Weight is about 9 lbs. Introduced in 2005.

NIB	Exc.	V.G.	Good	Fair	Poor
1400	1175	1000	750	600	300

Model 75 Finnlight

Introduced in 2001 this bolt-action rifle features short, medium, and long action calibers with stainless steel barrel lengths from 20.25" to 22.5" depending on caliber. Barrels are fluted. Synthetic stock. Weight is about 6.5 lbs. depending on caliber. In 2003 this model was offered in .300 WSM caliber.

NIB	Exc.	V.G.	Good	Fair	Poor
1300	1075	900	650	500	300

Model 75 Grey Wolf

This bolt action rifle is chambered for a wide variety of calibers from .223 to 7mm WSM. Stainless steel barrel is either 22.5" or 24.3" depending on caliber without sights. The gray stock is laminated and checkered. Rubber recoil pad. Detachable magazine. Weight is about 7.75 lbs. depending on caliber. Introduced in 2005.

NIB	Exc.	V.G.	Good	Fair	Poor
1400	1175	1000	750	600	300

Model 75 Custom Deluxe

Introduced in 2003 this model features an oil-finished premium-grade walnut stock with special fine-line checkering pattern. Factory recoil pad. Chambered for the .270 Win or .30-06 cartridges.

NIB	Exc.	V.G.	Good	Fair	Poor
3250	2500	1900	1100	800	400

Model 75 Custom Single Shot

Introduced in 2004 this single-shot model is chambered for the .308 cartridge and fitted with a 23.625" heavy fluted stainless steel barrel with no sights. Checkered laminated stock with beavertail forearm. Weight is about 9 lbs.

NIB	Exc.	V.G.	Good	Fair	Poor
3250	2500	1900	1100	550	400

Model 75 Super Deluxe

This is a special order rifle. Advise obtaining an expert opinion before a sale. Prices listed are for the base rifle.

NIB	Exc.	V.G.	Good	Fair	Poor
2500	2100	1600	1275	600	400

Model 78

A .22 or .22 Hornet bolt-action rifle with a 22" barrel. Blued with a checkered walnut stock. Discontinued in 1986.

NIB	Exc.	V.G.	Good	Fair	Poor
—	850	675	500	375	250

Model 2700 Finnsport

A .270 to .300 Winchester Magnum bolt-action rifle with a 22" barrel. Blued, checkered walnut stock. Discontinued in 1985.

NIB	Exc.	V.G.	Good	Fair	Poor
—	900	750	600	475	200

Safari 80th Anniversary Model

This is a limited edition rifle. Built on the Sako 75 magnum long action and chambered for the .375 H&H cartridge. Match grade heavy barrel. Select grade walnut stock with straight comb and ebony fore-end tip. Quarter rib. Equipped with Swarovski PV-1 1.25x24 scope. Engraved floor plate. Supplied with hand-made leather case with cleaning accessories. Limited to 80 rifles worldwide. Serial numbers 200101 to 200180.

NIB	Exc.	V.G.	Good	Fair	Poor
15950	12500	8500	—	—	—

Sako 85 Hunter

Bolt-action centerfire rifle chambered in short and long calibers ranging from .223 Remington to .375 H&H Magnum. Controlled round feeding, checkered walnut stock, satin blued sightless 22-7/16", 22-7/8" or 24-3/8" barrel. Introduced in 2007. **NOTE:** Thirty percent premium for .375.

NIB	Exc.	V.G.	Good	Fair	Poor
1100	900	775	600	475	300

Sako 85 Stainless Synthetic

Similar to Sako 85 Hunter but with stainless steel receiver and barrel. Introduced 2007.

NIB	Exc.	V.G.	Good	Fair	Poor
1200	1000	875	650	525	350

Sako 85 Finnlight

Similar to Sako 85 Stainless Synthetic but with recoil pad and ultra-lightweight synthetic stock. Chambered in long and short cartridges ranging from .243 to .300 Win Magnum. Introduced 2007.

NIB	Exc.	V.G.	Good	Fair	Poor
1550	1100	875	700	500	400

Sako 85 Varmint

Similar to Sako 85 Hunter but with recoil pad and 7.5-oz. set trigger. Chambered in .204 Ruger, .243, .22-250 or .308. Introduced 2007.

NIB	Exc.	V.G.	Good	Fair	Poor
1300	1075	900	650	500	300

Sako 85 Laminated SS Varmint

Similar to Sako 85 Varmint but with laminated stock and stainless steel barrel. Introduced 2007.

NIB	Exc.	V.G.	Good	Fair	Poor
1400	1175	1000	750	600	300

Sako A7 American Bolt-Action Rifle

Bolt-action rifle chambered in .22-250, .243 Win., .25-06, .260 Rem., .270 Win., .270 WSM, .300 WSM, .30-06, .300 WM, .308 Win., .338 Federal, .7mm Rem. Magnum, 7mm-08. Features include blued or stainless barrel (22-7/16" standard, 24-3/8" magnum) and receiver, black composite stock with sling swivels and recoil pad, two-position safety, adjustable trigger, detachable 3+1 box magazine. Weight 6 lbs., 3 oz. to 6 lbs., 13 oz.

NIB	Exc.	V.G.	Good	Fair	Poor
850	725	575	400	300	200

Sako A-7 Tecomate

Chambered in the .270 WSM (23" barrel) or .300 WSM (24.25") barrel. Magazine capacity 4 rounds. Features a new Bell & Carlson Medalist composite stock. Integral aluminum bedding system, CNC produced from aircraft quality 6061-T6 aluminum. Flat bottom receiver. Stainless action. Introduced in 2011.

NIB	Exc.	V.G.	Good	Fair	Poor
1200	1025	850	600	300	100

Sako Classic Deluxe

High grade version of Model 85 with oil-finished walnut stock with palm swell and cheekpiece, pronounced pistol grip, rosewood pistol and fore-end tip. Barrel band for sling swivel. Free-floating barrel. All metal parts are highly polished and blued. Medium or long action depending upon caliber. Adjustable trigger. Open sights are available. Five cartridges are available to include .270 Winchester, 7x64, .30-06, .370 Sako Magnum and .375 H&H. Introduced in 2011.

NIB	Exc.	V.G.	Good	Fair	Poor
3450	3100	2600	2000	1600	500

Sako 85 Bavarian

Available in full length or carbine style (shown). Offered in most standard calibers plus 6.5x55 Swedish. Comes with set trigger and adjustable express sights. Stock is oil finished high-grade checkered walnut with rosewood grip and fore-end caps. Carbine has full-length Mannlicher-style stock with Bavarian-style comb and cheekpiece. **NOTE:** Add 15 percent for Carbine model.

NIB	Exc.	V.G.	Good	Fair	Poor
1950	1750	1400	1000	750	250

Sako 85 Kodiak

Weatherproof design has stainless steel barrel and action, gray laminated stock reinforced with two crossbolts. Free-floating bull barrel in 21", 22.5" or 24.3" lengths. Offered in calibers from .22-250 to .375 H&H.

NIB	Exc.	V.G.	Good	Fair	Poor
1750	1525	1200	800	450	200

Sako Black Bear Series

Model 85 variation available in short and medium actions only. Short action is chambered in .308 Win. or .338 Federal; medium action in .30-06, 8x57 JS, 9.3x62 and 9.3x66 (.370) Sako. Controlled feeding, detachable magazine, single-stage adjustable trigger. Black injection molded stock with Soft Touch areas around pistol grip and fore-end. Open sights are available, scope can be mounted to integral Sako mounting system on receiver. Bull barrel, free-floating and hammer forged. Brown Bear model has similar features but with brown laminated hardwood stock and is chambered in .338 Win. Magnum or .375 H&H. Introduced in 2011.

NIB	Exc.	V.G.	Good	Fair	Poor
1600	1350	1100	950	600	300

TRG-S

This model features a unique cold-forged receiver. The stock is a special reinforced polyurethane Monte Carlo without checkering. The recoil pad has spacer for adjustable length of pull. The trigger is adjustable and the detachable magazine holds 5 rounds. Offered in a variety of calibers from .243 to .375 H&H. Non-Magnum calibers are fitted with a 22" barrel and weigh 7.75 lbs. and magnum calibers are fitted with a 24" barrel and also weigh 7.75 lbs. In 1996 the .270 Wthby Magnum, 7mm Wthby Magnum, .340 Wthby Magnum, as well as the 6.5x55S were added.

NIB	Exc.	V.G.	Good	Fair	Poor
1000	850	675	500	350	250

TRG-21

The receiver is similar to the TRG-S but the polyurethane stock features a unique design. Chambered for the .308 cartridge. The trigger is adjustable for length and two-stage pull and also for horizontal or vertical pitch. This model also has several options that would affect the price; muzzlebrake, one-piece scope mount, bipod, quick detachable sling swivels, and military nylon sling. The rifle is offered in .308 Win. only. It is fitted with a 25.75" barrel and weighs 10.5 lbs.

NIB	Exc.	V.G.	Good	Fair	Poor
3500	2750	1850	—	—	—

TRG-22

This model is similar to the TRG-21 but meets the exact specifications to comply with the Finish military requirements. Chambered for the .308 cartridge. Introduced in 2000. Offered in both green and black finish. Weight is about 10.25 lbs. **NOTE:** Add $2,250 for folding stock version.

NIB	Exc.	V.G.	Good	Fair	Poor
3589	2650	1750	—	—	—

TRG-41

Exactly the same as the TRG-21 except chambered for the .338 Lapua Magnum cartridge.

NIB	Exc.	V.G.	Good	Fair	Poor
4350	3500	2500	—	—	—

TRG-42

This model is similar to the TRG-41 but meets the exact specifications to comply with the Finish military requirements. Chambered for the .338 Lapua or .300 Win. Magnum cartridge. Introduced in 2000. Weight is about 11.25 lbs.

NIB	Exc.	V.G.	Good	Fair	Poor
4000	3000	2000	—	—	—

SAM, INC.
Special Service Arms Mfg., Inc.
Reston, Virginia

Model 88 Crossfire

A semi-automatic combination 12 gauge/.308 caliber shotgun/rifle, with a 7-shot shotgun magazine and 20-shot rifle magazine. Barrel length 20", matte black finish with a composition stock. This weapon can be fired in either mode by means of a selector switch mounted on the receiver.

NIB	Exc.	V.G.	Good	Fair	Poor
1900	1500	1175	800	550	300

SAMCO GLOBAL ARMS, INC.
Miami, Florida

This firm imports a variety of military surplus firearms that under current law are marked with the importer's name.

SARASQUETA, FELIX
Eibar, Spain

Merke

A 12 gauge over/under double-barrel shotgun with 22" or 27" ribbed and separated barrels, nonselective trigger and manual extractors. Blued, checkered walnut stock. Imported in 1986 only.

NIB	Exc.	V.G.	Good	Fair	Poor
—	500	375	200	150	100

SARASQUETA, J. J.
Eibar, Spain

Model 107E

A 12, 16 or 20 gauge boxlock double-barrel shotgun with a variety of barrel lengths, double triggers and automatic ejectors. Blued with a checkered walnut stock. Discontinued in 1984.

NIB	Exc.	V.G.	Good	Fair	Poor
—	425	300	275	225	100

Model 119E

As above, with a more finely figured walnut stock.

NIB	Exc.	V.G.	Good	Fair	Poor
—	525	400	375	325	150

Model 130E

As above, but engraved.

NIB	Exc.	V.G.	Good	Fair	Poor
—	950	700	600	450	250

Model 131E

As above, with considerably more engraving.

NIB	Exc.	V.G.	Good	Fair	Poor
—	1350	900	800	650	350

Model 1882 E LUXE

As above, with a single-selective trigger and gold inlays. A silver inlaid version is sold for approximately 10 percent less.

NIB	Exc.	V.G.	Good	Fair	Poor
—	1750	1250	900	650	350

SARASQUETA, VICTOR
Eibar, Spain

Model 3

A 12, 16 or 20 gauge boxlock or sidelock double-barrel shotgun available in a variety of barrel lengths, with double triggers and automatic ejectors. Blued with a checkered straight stock. The sidelock version is worth approximately 20 percent more than the values listed. The basic Model 3 was offered in a variety of grades featuring different amounts of engraving and better quality wood. These shotguns are listed under the model designations of 4 to 12E.

NIB	Exc.	V.G.	Good	Fair	Poor
—	650	500	450	350	300

Model 4

NIB	Exc.	V.G.	Good	Fair	Poor
—	1200	1000	875	600	300

Model 4E (Auto-ejectors)

NIB	Exc.	V.G.	Good	Fair	Poor
—	1600	1400	1100	800	400

Model 203

NIB	Exc.	V.G.	Good	Fair	Poor
—	700	600	525	425	325

Model 203E

NIB	Exc.	V.G.	Good	Fair	Poor
—	900	750	625	475	375

Model 6E

NIB	Exc.	V.G.	Good	Fair	Poor
—	1400	1250	875	525	425

Model 7E

NIB	Exc.	V.G.	Good	Fair	Poor
—	1500	1350	1000	750	475

Model 10E

NIB	Exc.	V.G.	Good	Fair	Poor
—	2600	2100	1650	950	750

Model 11E

NIB	Exc.	V.G.	Good	Fair	Poor
—	3000	2600	2000	1150	850

Model 12E

NIB	Exc.	V.G.	Good	Fair	Poor
—	3200	2850	2200	1300	1000

SARDIUS
Israel

SD-9

A 9mm double-action semi-automatic pistol with a 3" barrel and 6-shot magazine. Matte black finish with composition grips. Imported since 1988.

NIB	Exc.	V.G.	Good	Fair	Poor
425	300	250	200	150	100

SARSILMAZ
Mercan/Istanbul, Turkey

Professional

CZ-75-style compensated semi-automatic in white chrome finish chambered for 9mm. Single-action with adjustable trigger, laser engraving. 16 or 18 round capacity. 42.3 oz.; 5.1" barrel. MSRP: $437.

K2

CZ-75-style double-action semi-automatic in white chrome or blued. Chambered for 9mm. 16 or 18 round capacity. 35.3 oz.; 4.6" barrel. Plastic grips.

NIB	Exc.	V.G.	Good	Fair	Poor
—	300	225	175	125	50

Kama Sport

CZ-75-style semi-automatic 9mm in white chrome or blued. Double-action with 3.9" compensated barrel, laser engraving. 15+1 or 17+1 capacity. 35.4 oz. Plastic grips.

NIB	Exc.	V.G.	Good	Fair	Poor
—	325	250	195	135	50

Kama

CZ-75-style semi-automatic 9mm in white chrome or blued. Double-action with 4.3" compensated barrel, laser engraving. 15+1 or 17+1 capacity. 35.4 oz.; 7.7". Plastic grips.

NIB	Exc.	V.G.	Good	Fair	Poor
—	300	225	175	125	50

Kilinc 2000 Mega

CZ-75-style semi-automatic 9mm in white chrome or blued. Double-action with 4.7" barrel. 16 or 18 capacity. 35 oz. Plastic grips. Fixed sights.

NIB	Exc.	V.G.	Good	Fair	Poor
—	300	225	175	125	50

Kilinc 2000 Light

CZ-75-style semi-automatic 9mm in white chrome, blued or camo. Double-action with 4.7" barrel, laser engraving. 15+1 or 17+1 capacity. 35.4 oz. Plastic grips.

NIB	Exc.	V.G.	Good	Fair	Poor
—	300	225	175	125	50

Hancer 2000/2000 Light

CZ-75-style semi-automatic 9mm in white chrome or blued. Double-action with 3.9" barrel, laser engraving. 13+1 capacity. 33.5 oz. (25.4 oz. Light model). Plastic grips.

NIB	Exc.	V.G.	Good	Fair	Poor
—	300	225	175	125	50

Bernardelli

CZ-75-style double-action semi-automatic in 9mm. Black/white or blued finish. The 15+1 model has a 4.7" barrel, 27 oz., Plastic grips. The 13+1 model has a 3.9" barrel; 26.7 oz. Plastic grips, fixed sights.

NIB	Exc.	V.G.	Good	Fair	Poor
—	300	225	175	125	50

SAUER & SON, J. P.
Suhl and Eckernfoerde, Germany

This is the oldest firearms manufacturing firm in Germany. It was founded in 1751 in Suhl. During this period the company produced high quality handguns and long guns. In 1938 it introduced a new double-action semi-automatic pistol, the Sauer 38H. This pistol had the first decocking lever ever used on a mass produced pistol. In 1951 the company relocated to Eckernfoerde where it continued to produced high quality forearms. **NOTE:** The Model 90 Supreme and Model 202 are currently imported by SIGARMS Inc.

Bolt-Action Rifle

A Mauser action sporting rifle chambered for a variety of cartridges with either a 22" or 24" barrel featuring a raised rib. Double set triggers, express sights, blued with a checkered walnut stock. Manufactured prior to WWII.

NIB	Exc.	V.G.	Good	Fair	Poor
—	1250	900	6500	400	300

Model 200

A bolt-action rifle chambered for a variety of cartridges with short or medium length actions, 24" barrels, set trigger, 4-round magazine. Blued, checkered walnut stock. Discontinued 1987. Extra barrels add $235.

NIB	Exc.	V.G.	Good	Fair	Poor
1350	1050	700	500	425	350

Model 200 Lightweight

As above, with an alloy receiver. Discontinued in 1987.

NIB	Exc.	V.G.	Good	Fair	Poor
—	1100	900	550	325	250

Model 200 Lux

As above, with a finely figured walnut stock, rosewood pistol grip cap and fore-end tip, gold-plated trigger and a machine jewelled bolt. Imported prior to 1988.

NIB	Exc.	V.G.	Good	Fair	Poor
—	1200	950	700	475	400

Model 200 Carbon Fiber

The Model 200 fitted with a carbon composition stock. Imported in 1987 and 1988.

NIB	Exc.	V.G.	Good	Fair	Poor
—	1300	1100	800	500	400

Model 202 Supreme

This is a bolt-action rifle with a barrel change feature. It is fitted with an adjustable two-stage trigger, quick-change fluted barrel, black rubber recoil pad and removable box magazine. The stock is select American claro walnut with high gloss finish and rosewood fore-end and grip cap. Buttstock has a Monte Carlo comb and cheekpiece. It is offered in .243, .270, .308, and .30-06. Barrel length for these calibers is 23.6". Weight for these calibers is about 7.7 lbs. In the Supreme Magnum series it is available in 7mm magnum, .300 Win. Magnum and .375 H&H Magnum. Barrel for these magnum calibers is 26". Weight for these caliber is 8.4 lbs.

NIB	Exc.	V.G.	Good	Fair	Poor
2700	2000	1350	1000	750	400

Model 202 Takedown

This model is a true takedown. Introduced in 2003 this rifle is chambered for the .300 Win. Magnum and the .375 H&H; other calibers will be offered in the future. Fancy Turkish walnut stock with Monte Carlo and rosewood fore-end tip. Base price listed.

NIB	Exc.	V.G.	Good	Fair	Poor
5700	4400	2900	2000	1200	400

Model S202 Wolverine

Similar to the Model 202 Supreme above but with 25.6" barrel, beavertail fore-end and adjustable cheekpiece. Chambered in various varmint calibers.

NIB	Exc.	V.G.	Good	Fair	Poor
—	2300	1950	1500	1050	400

Model S202 Highland

Similar to the Model 202 Supreme above but with 20" barrel, schnabel fore-end and easily-detachable buttstock. Chambered in .308 Winchester and various European cartridges.

NIB	Exc.	V.G.	Good	Fair	Poor
—	2500	1950	1500	1050	400

Model S202 Forest

A carbine-style version of the Model 202 Highland above intended specifically for drive hunts. Has standard fore-end and 25.6" barrel and is chambered in various varmint calibers.

NIB	Exc.	V.G.	Good	Fair	Poor
—	2500	1950	1500	1050	400

Model S202 Hardwood

Similar to the Model 202 Highland above but, oddly enough, with a synthetic stock with orange inserts. Chambered in .308 Winchester and various European cartridges.

NIB	Exc.	V.G.	Good	Fair	Poor
—	2300	1950	1500	1050	400

Model S202 Match

Target version of the Model 202 with 26.8" match barrel, wide fore-end. Chambered in .300 Winchester Magnum and 6.5x55 Swedish.

NIB	Exc.	V.G.	Good	Fair	Poor
—	2500	1950	1500	1050	400

Model S202 Outback

Similar to the Model 202 Hardwood above but with lightweight construction and plain black synthetic stock

NIB	Exc.	V.G.	Good	Fair	Poor
—	2500	1950	1500	1050	400

Model S202 Team Sauer

Classically-styled sporter version of Model 202 with heavy medium or magnum-weight barrel and walnut Monte Carlo stock. Chambered in various European and American long-action cartridges from 6.5x55 Swedish up to .300 Winchester Magnum.

NIB	Exc.	V.G.	Good	Fair	Poor
—	1950	1600	1250	800	400

Model 90

A bolt-action rifle produced in a number of calibers in all action lengths with 23" or 26" barrels, with a detachable magazine. Blued with a checkered walnut stock.

NIB	Exc.	V.G.	Good	Fair	Poor
—	1300	1100	675	500	300

Model 90 Stutzen

As above, with a full-length Mannlicher-style stock. Imported prior to 1990.

NIB	Exc.	V.G.	Good	Fair	Poor
—	1350	1150	725	550	350

Model 90 Safari

The Model 90 made for use with the .458 Winchester Magnum cartridge and fitted with a 24" barrel. Imported from 1986 to 1988. **NOTE:** The Model 90 Series of bolt-action rifles was available in a deluxe version that differed with the grade of workmanship and materials utilized. This deluxe series would be worth approximately 60 percent additional.

NIB	Exc.	V.G.	Good	Fair	Poor
—	2300	2000	1250	900	400

Model 90 Supreme

Similar to the above, with a gold-plated trigger, machine jewelled bolt and finely figured checkered walnut stock. Introduced in 1987.

NIB	Exc.	V.G.	Good	Fair	Poor
—	2500	2200	1425	1000	400

SSG-3000

NIB	Exc.	V.G.	Good	Fair	Poor
3300	2650	1950	1500	11000	500

SG 550 Sniper

NIB	Exc.	V.G.	Good	Fair	Poor
5500	4750	3875	2700	2000	500

SHOTGUN/RIFLE COMBINATIONS

Luftwaffe M30 Survival Drilling

A double-barrel 12 gauge by 9.3x74R combination shotgun/rifle with 28" barrels. Blued with a checkered walnut stock and marked with Nazi inspection. Stampings on the stock and barrel breech. Normally, furnished with an aluminum case. **NOTE:** Add 50 percent to prices for case.

NIB	Exc.	V.G.	Good	Fair	Poor
20000	15000	9500	6000	3250	1500

Model 3000 Drilling

This model was chambered for a variety of gauges and calibers and is built upon a boxlock action with a Greener crossbolt. The action is lightly engraved. Blued, checkered walnut stock.

NIB	Exc.	V.G.	Good	Fair	Poor
5500	3700	2750	2000	1500	1250

Model 54 Combo

A combination rifle/shotgun chambered for a variety of gauges and calibers with an action as above. Discontinued in 1986.

NIB	Exc.	V.G.	Good	Fair	Poor
—	3000	2250	1750	1400	1200

SHOTGUNS

Model 60

A 12, 16 or 20 gauge double-barrel boxlock shotgun produced in a variety of barrel lengths with double triggers and manual extractors. Blued with checkered walnut stock. Produced prior to WWII.

NIB	Exc.	V.G.	Good	Fair	Poor
—	1300	950	725	550	400

Royal Model

A 12 or 20 gauge boxlock double-barrel shotgun with 26", 28", or 30" barrels, single-selective triggers with automatic ejectors. The frame is scalloped, blued with a checkered walnut stock. Manufactured from 1955 to 1977.

NIB	Exc.	V.G.	Good	Fair	Poor
—	1500	1250	1000	750	500

Grade I Artemis

A 12 gauge sidelock double-barrel shotgun with 28" barrels, single-selective trigger and automatic ejector. Engraved, blued with checkered walnut stock. Manufactured from 1966 to 1977.

NIB	Exc.	V.G.	Good	Fair	Poor
—	5000	4250	3500	2500	2000

Grade II Artemis

As above, but more finely finished.

NIB	Exc.	V.G.	Good	Fair	Poor
—	6500	5750	4750	3500	3000

Model 66

A 12 gauge sidelock double-barrel shotgun with a 26", 28", or 30" barrel, single-selective trigger and automatic ejectors. Blued, checkered walnut stock. This model was produced in three different grades that have different degrees of engraving. Produced from 1966 to 1975.

Grade I

NIB	Exc.	V.G.	Good	Fair	Poor
—	2000	1800	1500	1150	800

Grade II

NIB	Exc.	V.G.	Good	Fair	Poor
—	3000	2800	2500	2150	1800

Grade III

NIB	Exc.	V.G.	Good	Fair	Poor
—	3750	3500	2850	2500	2000

PISTOLS

Written and compiled by our very good friend Jim Cate.

Bär Pistol

Invented by Burkard Behr and made by Sauer. This was Sauer's first modern small pistol. It has stacked barrels (over/under configuration) that allow the shooter to fire two shots, rotate the barrel and then fire two more shots before loading. It was first patented in Germany in 1897 and in the USA in 1899. It shoots the 7mm Bär cartridge only. (DO NOT ATTEMPT TO FIRE THE .25 ACP/6.35mm CARTRIDGE IN THIS PISTOL.) It was made from 1897 to 1911 or 1912. Some pistols have Bakelite grips; some have diamond-pattern checkered wood grips. A case extractor rod screws into the bottom of the frame. No trigger guard. **NOTE:** Add $150 for original box and instructions.

NIB	Exc.	V.G.	Good	Fair	Poor
—	1250	800	450	275	–

Roth-Sauer Model

The very first automatic pistol produced by J.P. Sauer & Son and designed by Karl Krinka for George Roth. It is available only in 7.65 Roth-Sauer caliber. It is a locked breech design, beautifully finished and extremely well made. Later this design was modified and became the Roth-Steyr military pistol which was adopted by Austria in 1907. A difficult-to-find pistol.

NIB	Exc.	V.G.	Good	Fair	Poor
—	2500	1800	900	500	300

Sauer Model 1913

First Series, which incorporates an extra safety button on the left side of the frame near the trigger and the rear sight is simply a milled recess in the cocking knob itself. The serial number range runs from 1 to approximately 4750 and this first series is found only in 7.65mm caliber. All were for commercial sales as far as can be determined. Some were tested by various militaries, no doubt.

A. European variation—all slide legends are in the German language.
B. English Export variation—slide legends are marked, J.P. Sauer & Son, Suhl - Prussia, "Sauer's Patent" Pat'd May 20 1912.

Both were sold in thick paper cartons or boxes with the color being a reddish purple with gold colored letters, etc. Examples of the very early European variation are found with the English language brochure or manual as well as an extra magazine, cleaning brush and grease container. These were shipped to England or the U.S. prior to Sauer producing the English Export variation. **NOTE:** Original box with accessories and manual: Add $500 if complete and in very good to excellent condition.

A. European variation:

NIB	Exc.	V.G.	Good	Fair	Poor
—	1500	900	650	400	250

B. English Export variation

NIB	Exc.	V.G.	Good	Fair	Poor
—	1800	1200	800	500	300

SECOND SERIES

Extra safety button eliminated, rear sight acts as cocking knob retainer.

Commercial variation

Normal European/German slide markings are normally found; however it has been called to my attention that there are English Export pistols in this SECOND SERIES which have the English markings on the slide which are similar to those found on the FIRST SERIES of the Model 1913. This is applicable to both the 7.65mm and 6.35mm model 1919 pistols. These are exceptional scarce pistols and should command at least a 50 percent premium, perhaps more due to their rarity. This commercial variation had factory manuals printed in English, Spanish and German which came with the cardboard boxed pistols. **NOTE:** With the original Sauer box accessories and manual: Add $300 if in very good to excellent condition.

Caliber 7.65mm variation

NIB	Exc.	V.G.	Good	Fair	Poor
—	450	375	300	250	100

Caliber 7.65 variation with all words in English (i.e Son, Prussia, etc.)

NIB	Exc.	V.G.	Good	Fair	Poor
—	800	575	450	300	200

Police variations

These will be of the standard German Commercial configuration but nearly always having the Zusatzsicherung (additional safety) added to the pistol. This safety is found between the regular safety lever and the top of the left grip. Police used both calibers, 7.65mm and 6.35mm but the 7.65 was predominant. After the early part of the 1930s the 6.35 was not available to police departments. Thus the 6.35mm police marked Sauer is rather scarce in relation to the 7.65mm caliber. A few in 7.65mm are dated 1920 on the left side of the frame and were used by auxiliary policemen in Bavaria. Normal police property markings are on the front or rear gripstraps. Most were originally issued with at least two magazines and a police accepted holster. The mags were usually numbered and the holsters are found with and without pistol numbers. **NOTE:** Add 10 percent for one correctly numbered magazine, or 20 percent if found with both correctly numbered magazines. Add 30 percent if found with correct holster and magazines.

Caliber 6.35mm police marked without Zusatzsicherung

NIB	Exc.	V.G.	Good	Fair	Poor
—	500	350	275	200	75

Caliber 6.35mm police marked with Zusatzsicherung

NIB	Exc.	V.G.	Good	Fair	Poor
—	550	375	275	200	75

Caliber 7.65mm police marked without Zusatzsicherung

NIB	Exc.	V.G.	Good	Fair	Poor
—	575	325	275	175	125

Caliber 7.65mm police marked with Zusatzsicherung

NIB	Exc.	V.G.	Good	Fair	Poor
—	500	350	275	175	125

R.F.V. (Reich Finanz Verwaltung)

This Sauer variation is rarely found in any condition. The R.F.V. markings and property number could be 1 to 4 digits. This variation is found in both calibers and were used by the Reich's Customs and Finance department personnel.

Caliber 6.35mm R.F.V. marked pistols

NIB	Exc.	V.G.	Good	Fair	Poor
—	1000	750	500	350	250

Caliber 7.65mm R.F.V. marked pistols

NIB	Exc.	V.G.	Good	Fair	Poor
—	750	600	400	300	200

Imperial Military variations

These were normal German commercial variations of the time period having either the Imperial Eagle acceptance marking applied on the front of the trigger guard and having the small Imperial Army inspector's acceptance marking (crown over a scriptic letter) on the right side of the frame close to the Nitro proof; or having just the Imperial Army inspector's marking alone. Usually these pistols are found in the 40000 to 85000 range. However, the quantity actually Imperial Military accepted is quite low even though thousands were privately purchased by the officer corps. There are examples in 6.35mm which are Imperial Military accepted but these are very scarce. **NOTE:** Add 30 percent for 6.35mm.

Caliber 7.65mm Imperial Military accepted pistols

NIB	Exc.	V.G.	Good	Fair	Poor
—	700	500	350	275	150

SECOND SERIES

Paramilitary marked Sauer pistols of the 1925-35 period

A very few of the Model 1913 pistols will have been marked by paramilitary groups or organizations of this period. Usually this marking is no more than a series of numbers above another series of numbers, such as 23 over 12. These are found usually on the left side of the frame next to the left grip. Most of these numbers are indicative of property numbers assigned to a particular pistols belonging to a particular SA Group, Stahlhelm, or a rightwing organization such as the Red Front (early communist). Any pistol of this type should be examined by an expert to determine if it is an original example.

NIB	Exc.	V.G.	Good	Fair	Poor
—	450	375	275	200	100

Norwegian police usage, post World War II

After the war was over many surplus German weapons were put back into use by the government of Norway. The Germans had occupied this country and large numbers of weapons remained when the fighting ended. This included a large number of surplus Sauer pistols being utilized by the police (POLITI) forces. Most of the Sauers that were used by the Politi which have been imported into the U.S. have been the Model 1913; however there were a number of the Model 1930 pistols which reached our country as well. All examples, regardless of the model, have the word POLITI stamped on the slide as well as a rampant lion on a shield under a crown marking. Following this is the property number and this number is also stamped into the left side of the frame. Most saw much usage during the post-war period. All are in 7.65mm caliber.

NIB	Exc.	V.G.	Good	Fair	Poor
—	350	300	200	150	100

Model 1913/19 in 6.35mm

This particular pistol must be divided into three (3) sub-variations. This variation appears to be in a serial number range of its own. The first sub-variation appears to run from 1 to 40000. It is highly doubtful if this quantity was manufactured. The second sub-variation incorporates a Zusatzsicherung or Additional Safety which can be seen between the normal safety lever and the top of the left grip. It locked the trigger bar when in use. This second range appears to run from approximately serial number 40000 to 51000 which probably was continuous in the number produced. Lastly, the third sub-variation examples were manufactured during or after 1926. The trigger guard has a different shape; the slide has a greater area of vertical milled finger grooves; the added Additional safety (Zusatzsicherung) now acts as the hold open device as well. These are found up to approximately 57000. Then a few examples of the first sub-variation are found from 57000 up to about 62500. This was, no doubt, usage of remaining parts. **NOTE:** Any commercial pistol could be special ordered with a factory nickel finish, special grip material (pearl, wood, etc.) as well as different types of engraving. It would be in your best interest to have these pistols examined by an expert.

Caliber 6.35mm first sub-variation
NIB	Exc.	V.G.	Good	Fair	Poor
—	450	375	250	150	75

Caliber 6.35mm second sub-variation
NIB	Exc.	V.G.	Good	Fair	Poor
—	475	375	250	150	75

Caliber 6.35mm third sub-variation
NIB	Exc.	V.G.	Good	Fair	Poor
—	650	500	500	200	100

Caliber 6.35mm English export variation
NIB	Exc.	V.G.	Good	Fair	Poor
—	1000	700	500	300	200

1926 Export Model

This variation's name comes from actual Sauer factory records found in the Suhl Archive. It is an interim pistol produced during the 1926 to early 1929 period. It is found only in the 7.65mm caliber. This was an advancement of the normal 1913 design which included changes in (1) the safety lever's design that became a slide hold open device as well, (2) shape of the frame was altered in that the trigger guard became more streamlined and the rear of the frame was shortened, and serrations were added to the slide as well as the cocking knob. These are found in the 162000 to 169000 range in relatively small clusters. Two to four thousand are presumed to have been manufactured. A scarce Sauer pistol! To date, none have been seen in nickel.

NIB	Exc.	V.G.	Good	Fair	Poor
—	825	700	500	300	150

W.T.M.-Westentaschen Model—Vest Pocket Model

Several variations of vest pocket pistols were manufactured. The first was called a Model 1920 by the Sauer firm. We usually refer to it as the Model 1924. This pistol, as well as all other W.T.M. examples, were designed to carry in your pocket. They are quite small in size and are found only in the 6.35mm or .25 ACP caliber. Later on in 1928 an updated version became available and was referred to a the Model 1928. These differed in internal parts design, slide configuration and the bottom of the grip was marked, "Cal.6.35.28." The last version appeared in 1933 and still utilized the same grips but the trigger and some other small parts differed. All three were available in blue or nickel finish, as well as engraving and fancy grip material. A very few of the Model 1933 had stainless steel (NIROSTA marked) barrels.

Model 1920

Serrations on the front and rear of the slide.

NIB	Exc.	V.G.	Good	Fair	Poor
—	550	450	300	200	75

Model 1928

"Cal. 6.35.28" on the black Bakelite grips.

NIB	Exc.	V.G.	Good	Fair	Poor
—	500	450	300	185	75

Model 1933

Different type of trigger and found in the 253000 to early 254000 serial number range. **NOTE:** Add $200 for factory nickel, $250 for factory engraving, $250 for exotic grip material, $500 for factory paper box with cleaning brush, extra magazine and brochure, $750 in original factory imitation leather covered metal presentation case with accessories, $500 for NIROSTA marked stainless barrel.

NIB	Exc.	V.G.	Good	Fair	Poor
—	700	575	400	275	150

MODEL 1930 VARIATIONS

Dutch models

These different types of Dutch pistols will have JOH MUNTS - AMSTERDAM on the left side of the slide. The grips are usually a mottled gray color. Sauer manufactured different pistols for the Dutch police, Navy, Army, Department of Finance, S.M.N. (Steam Ships Netherlands) and possibly other agencies. **NOTE:** Accessories: cleaning rod, brush, aluminum oil bottle and manuals, add accordingly.

Dutch Police

First variation manufactured w/o adjustable front sight and w/o lanyard loop.

NIB	Exc.	V.G.	Good	Fair	Poor
—	650	450	350	250	125

Amsterdam Police

Manufactured without adjustable sight but having a lanyard loop.

NIB	Exc.	V.G.	Good	Fair	Poor
—	700	500	350	250	125

Navy

Made without adjustable sight and having the Anchor & Crown marked on the rear gripstrap.

NIB	Exc.	V.G.	Good	Fair	Poor
—	1000	750	400	250	125

S.M.N.

Found with and without adjustable front sights, no lanyard loop, S.M.N. marked horizontally near bottom of rear gripstrap.

NIB	Exc.	V.G.	Good	Fair	Poor
—	1000	700	375	225	100

Department of Finance

Found with and without adjustable front sight, no lanyard loop, DF over date-1933-on rear grip strap.

NIB	Exc.	V.G.	Good	Fair	Poor
—	850	700	385	250	150

1930 Commercial Model

These pistols were for sale in Germany and other countries through normal commercial outlets. A very few are factory nickeled, engraved or both; some are with the NIROSTA marked barrels and a very few were made in Duralumin or Dural. The standard caliber was 7.65mm hut a very limited number were made in .22 LR (.22 Long). Standard grip material is black Bakelite. Most of the regular pistols were purchased by military officers, some went to paramilitary groups, such as the SA. **NOTE:** For any variation listed add $100 for nickel finish; $500 for engraving; $600 for both nickel and engraving; with nickel, engraving, and with a fancy grip material (pearl or ebony, etc.) $750.

Standard Commercial

NIB	Exc.	V.G.	Good	Fair	Poor
—	600	450	300	200	125

Standard Commercial with NIROSTA marked barrel, 7.65mm

NIB	Exc.	V.G.	Good	Fair	Poor
—	900	600	350	275	150

Standard Commercial in .22 LR (.22 Long)

NIB	Exc.	V.G.	Good	Fair	Poor
—	2500	1800	1200	500	300

Duralumin (rural) Variation, 7.65mm

NIB	Exc.	V.G.	Good	Fair	Poor
—	3500	2750	2000	1200	450

BEHORDEN MODEL

The Behorden (Authority) Model is different from the Model 1930 in that it has a trigger safety and a loaded indicator provided.

Behorden Commercial

These are normally found with a high polished blued finish. It was available with a nickel finish, engraving, or both, as well as fancy grip material and a NIROSTA marked barrel. The regular caliber is 7.65mm, but a very few are know in .22 LR that are probably prototype pistols. **NOTE:** Add $100 for nickel finish, $250 for engraving, $350 for both, $500 with nickel, engraving, and a fancy grip material; $500 for NIROSTA marked stainless barrel. Add 300 percent for .22 caliber.

NIB	Exc.	V.G.	Good	Fair	Poor
—	675	550	400	350	200

Late Behorden Commercial

These are actually Model 1930 pistols found in the 220000 to 223000 serial number range which do not have the trigger safety and/or the indicator pin.

NIB	Exc.	V.G.	Good	Fair	Poor
—	600	450	300	200	125

Duralumin Model (Dural)

The frame and slide are made of the Duralumin material. These are rare pistols! **NOTE:** Add $250 for the stainless barrel.

Blue Anodized Variation

Found with and w/o NIROSTA marked barrels.

NIB	Exc.	V.G.	Good	Fair	Poor
—	4000	3500	2500	1500	850

Nonanodized Variation

Found with and w/o NIROSTA marked barrels.

NIB	Exc.	V.G.	Good	Fair	Poor
—	4000	3500	2500	1500	850

Presentation Examples of Anodized and Nonanodized Variations

Please consult an expert for pricing.

Police Models

Examples will be found with police acceptance on the left side of the trigger guard and in a few cases on the front or rear grip straps. Black Bakelite grips are standard.

Sunburst K Police Acceptance

Non-adjustable front sight (a round blade).

NIB	Exc.	V.G.	Good	Fair	Poor
—	600	500	350	275	200

Sunburst K Police Acceptance

Adjustable front sight.

NIB	Exc.	V.G.	Good	Fair	Poor
—	750	625	450	300	225

Diamond in Sunburst Police Acceptance

All known are with the adjustable front sight.

NIB	Exc.	V.G.	Good	Fair	Poor
—	1250	900	550	300	225

Grip Strap Marked Variations

(Having abbreviations of a city and the property number of the pistol on the grip strap.) Very few of these are known. Examples are S.Mg. 52, Sch. 78, etc.

NIB	Exc.	V.G.	Good	Fair	Poor
—	750	550	375	250	150

MODEL 36/37

These very few pistols are all prototype Sauer pistols which preceded the Model 38. They are in the 210,000 range. Please consult an expert to determine value! EXTREMELY RARE.

MODEL 38 AND 38-H (H MODEL) VARIATIONS
Model 38

This pistol started at 260000. It is Crown N Nitro proofed, has a cocking/decocking lever, and a loaded indicator pin, and is double-action. It has a high polish blue; is in 7.65m/m (the standard production pistol); is found without the thumbsafety on the slide; with a pinned mag release. VERY RARE.

(Having abbreviations of a city and the property number of the pistol on the grip strap.) Very few of these are known. Examples are S.Mg. 52, Sch. 78, etc.

One Line Slide Legend Variation (pinned magazine release button - no screw)

Crown N proofs. Approximately 250 produced. Extremely rare!

NIB	Exc.	V.G.	Good	Fair	Poor
—	3800	3000	2000	600	300

Two Line Slide Legend Variation (pinned magazine release button - no screw)

C/N proofs, blued, with pinned magazine release (about 850 produced) VERY RARE. **NOTE:** Add $250 for factory nickel; $350 for factory chrome; $1000 for engraving; $500 for NIROSTA marked barrel.

NIB	Exc.	V.G.	Good	Fair	Poor
—	2600	2000	1500	500	275

Two Line Slide Legend Variation (magazine release button)

C/N proofs, blued, magazine release button retained by a screw. RARE. **NOTE:** Add $250 for factory nickel; $350 for factory chrome; $1000 for engraving; $500 for NIROSTA marked barrel.

NIB	Exc.	V.G.	Good	Fair	Poor
—	2500	1500	900	500	275

SA der NSDAP Gruppe Thuringen Marked Variation

Blued, C/N proofs, with magazine release button held by a screw. VERY RARE.

NIB	Exc.	V.G.	Good	Fair	Poor
—	5000	4000	2500	650	275

Model 38 pistols converted to H Models by Sauer factory

Currently there are fewer than 30 known examples in collections. The thumbsafety levers were added. Unique milling on the left side of the slide determines these pistols in the 262xxx, 263xxx and 264xxx ranges. This includes SA der NSDAP Gruppe Thringen marked pistols.

NIB	Exc.	V.G.	Good	Fair	Poor
—	1800	1200	850	450	—

Model 38-H or H Model

This model has a thumbsafety on the slide, Crown N Nitro proof, high polish blued finish, a cocking/decocking lever, double-action and is found in 7.65m/m caliber as the standard production pistol. This model is found only with the two line slide legend or logo. Type 1, variation 2.

Standard Commercial Variation

NOTE: Add $100 for factory nickel (factory chromed has not been identified); $1000 for factory engraving; $250 for exotic grip material; $500 for NIROSTA marked stainless barrel.

NIB	Exc.	V.G.	Good	Fair	Poor
—	1200	900	600	300	175

SA der NSDAP Gruppe Thuringia Variation

Same as Standard. above except having SA markings on slide, with blued finish, VERY RARE. **NOTE:** Add $700 for SA marked Akah holster in excellent condition.

NIB	Exc.	V.G.	Good	Fair	Poor
—	4000	3000	2500	900	400

L.M. Model

(Leicht Model-lightweight model); frame and slide made of DURAL (Duralumin), in the 264800 range, with thumb safety, and regular black Bakelite grips. EXTREMELY RARE.

NIB	Exc.	V.G.	Good	Fair	Poor
—	6500	5000	3000	1500	850

Flash Light Model

Only four known examples of this variation. Battery flash light attached by four screws to the pistol. Carried by the SS night patrol at the Reich's chancellory in Berlin. No specific markings, but known serial numbers are 266814, 266842, 266845.

NIB	Exc.	V.G.	Good	Fair	Poor
—Too Rare To Price		—	—	—	—

Police Accepted Variation

Found with Police Eagle C acceptance on left trigger guard and having Crown N proofs. RARE.

NIB	Exc.	V.G.	Good	Fair	Poor
—	3000	2500	1850	500	175

TYPE TWO MODEL 38-H (H MODEL)

There are no Model 38 pistols in the Type Two description, only the H Model with thumbsafety. These begin at serial number 269100 and have the Eagle N Nitro proofs, with a blued high polish finish and black Bakelite grips. The normal caliber is 7.65mm.

A. H Model

Standard Commercial

NOTE: Add $1500 for boxed examples complete with factory manual, clean ring rod, all accessories, extra magazine, etc. $250 for factory nickel, $350 for factory chrome, $1000 for factory engraving.

NIB	Exc.	V.G.	Good	Fair	Poor
—	1000	850	600	300	200

.22 Caliber Variation

Slide and magazines are marked CAL. .22 LANG. (Some with steel frame and slides; some with Dural frames and slides.) Found in 269900 range. Very Rare.

NIB	Exc.	V.G.	Good	Fair	Poor
—	6000	4500	3000	1000	600

Jager Model

A special order pistol in .22 caliber which is similar in appearance to Walther's 1936 Jagerschafts pistol. Very rare.

NIB	Exc.	V.G.	Good	Fair	Poor
—	6250	5000	3000	1000	400

Police Eagle C and Eagle F Acceptance Variations

These are the first Eagle N (post January 1940) police accepted pistols are found in the 270000 to 276000 ranges. **NOTE:** Add 50 percent for E/F.

NIB	Exc.	V.G.	Good	Fair	Poor
—	1250	800	600	325	200

German Military Variation

This is the first official military accepted range of 2,000 pistols. It is in a range found between 271000 to 273000. Two Eagle 37 military acceptance marks are found on the trigger guard.

NIB	Exc.	V.G.	Good	Fair	Poor
—	2850	1500	1200	700	300

Second Military Variation

These pistols are found with the high polish finish but have only one Eagle 37 acceptance marks. The letter H is found on all small parts.

NIB	Exc.	V.G.	Good	Fair	Poor
—	1650	1450	800	400	200

Police Eagle C Acceptance

This variation includes the remainder of the high polish blued police accepted pistols. **NOTE:** Add $50 for matching magazine, $200 for both matching mags and correct police holster; $300 for both matching mags and correct matching numbered, police accepted and dated holster.

NIB	Exc.	V.G.	Good	Fair	Poor
—	950	600	450	275	175

TYPE THREE 38-H MODEL (H MODEL)

This terminology is used because of the change of the exterior finish of the Sauer pistols. Due to the urgency of the war, the order was received to not polish the exterior surfaces of the pistols as had been done previously. There was also a change in the formulation of the grip's material. Later in this range there will be found stamped parts, zinc triggers and magazine bottoms, etc. used to increase the pistol's production. Type Three has a full slide legend.

A. H Model

Military Accepted

One Eagle 37 Waffenamt mark.

NIB	Exc.	V.G.	Good	Fair	Poor
—	850	650	400	275	150

Commercial

Only Eagle N Nitro proof marks. **NOTE:** See Type Two Commercial, prices apply here also.

NIB	Exc.	V.G.	Good	Fair	Poor
—	725	500	400	250	150

Police Accepted with the Police Eagle C Acceptance

NOTE: See Type Two Police, prices apply here also.

NIB	Exc.	V.G.	Good	Fair	Poor
—	850	650	350	250	150

TYPE FOUR 38-H MODEL (H MODEL)

This is a continuation of the pistol as described in Type Three except the J.P. Sauer & Sohn, Suhl legend is dropped from the slide and only CAL. 7.65 is found on the left side. The word PATENT may or may not appear on the right side. Many are found with a zinc trigger.

A. H Model

Military Accepted

NIB	Exc.	V.G.	Good	Fair	Poor
—	850	650	400	275	150

Commercial

Having only the Eagle N Nitro proofs. **NOTE:** See Type Two Commercial info, prices apply here also.

NIB	Exc.	V.G.	Good	Fair	Poor
—	750	600	400	250	150

Police Accepted with the Police Eagle C Acceptance

NOTE: See Type Two Price info, prices apply here also.

NIB	Exc.	V.G.	Good	Fair	Poor
—	850	650	450	300	150

Eigentum NSDAP SA Gruppe Alpenland Slide Marked Pistols

These unique pistols are found in the 456000 and 457000 serial number ranges. They have thumb safety levers on the slides.

NIB	Exc.	V.G.	Good	Fair	Poor
—	4000	3000	2000	600	400

NSDAP SA Gruppe Alpenland Slide Marked Pistols

These unique pistols are found in the 465000 serial number range. They have thumbsafety levers on the slide.

NIB	Exc.	V.G.	Good	Fair	Poor
—	4000	3000	2000	600	400

Himmler Presentation Pistols

These desirable pistols have a high polish finish with DEM SCHARFSCHUTZEN - H. HIMMLER on the left side of the slide (with no other markings), and J.P. SAUER & SON over CAL. 7.65 on the right side (opposite of normal). These pistols came in imitation leather cover metal cases with cloth interiors having a cleaning brush, extra magazine and cartridges. Very rare pistols! Extremely rare if cased! Only 12 are known presently.

NIB	Exc.	V.G.	Good	Fair	Poor
—	25000	18500	12500	5000	1500

Model 38

To speed up production even more, the thumbsafety (Handsicherung-Hammer safety) was eliminated. The side continues to be marked only with CAL. 7,65. The frame's serial number changes from the right side to the left side at 472000 with overlaps up to 489000.

Military Accepted

One Eagle 37 Waffenamt mark.

NIB	Exc.	V.G.	Good	Fair	Poor
—	700	500	400	250	175

Commercial

Only the Eagle N Nitro proofs. **NOTE:** See Type Two Commercial info, prices apply here also.

NIB	Exc.	V.G.	Good	Fair	Poor
—	600	475	350	250	175

Police Accepted with the Police Eagle C Acceptance

NIB	Exc.	V.G.	Good	Fair	Poor
—	700	500	400	300	200

Police Accepted with the Police Eagle F Acceptance

NOTE: See Type Two Police info, prices apply here also.

NIB	Exc.	V.G.	Good	Fair	Poor
—	750	600	500	250	175

There are two different basic variations of the Type Five Sauer pistols. Either may or may not have a thumbsafety lever on the slide. The main criteria is whether the frame is factory numbered as per normal and follows the chronological sequence of those pistols in the preceding model. After the frames were used which were already numbered and finished upon the arrival of the U.S. Army, the last variation came about. Neither variation has any Nitro proof marks. **NOTE:** There are some pistols which have post-war Russian Crown N Nitro proofs. The Russians assembled or refurbished a very few pistols after the U.S. Army left this section after the war. Several have been found with newly made barrels in 7.65mm with a C/N proof. A hard to find Sauer!

NIB	Exc.	V.G.	Good	Fair	Poor
—	1800	750	450	250	175

TYPE FIVE MODEL 38 & H MODEL PISTOLS

First Variation

Factory numbered sequential frames starting on or near serial number 506800. Slides and breech blocks may or may not match.

NIB	Exc.	V.G.	Good	Fair	Poor
—	550	450	300	225	100

Second Variation

Started with serial number 1; made from mostly rejected parts, generally have notched trigger guards, may or may not be blued, no Nitro proofs, slides may or may not have factory legends, etc. Approximately 300 assembled. Definitely rare Sauer pistols.

NIB	Exc.	V.G.	Good	Fair	Poor
—	900	650	450	300	150

SAVAGE ARMS CORPORATION
Utica, New York
Westfield, Massachusetts

Model 1895

A .303 Savage caliber lever-action rifle with a 26" or 30" barrel and 5-shot rotary magazine. Identifiable by the hole in the breechbolt. The barrel marked "Savage Repeating Arms Co. Utica, N.Y. U.S.A. Pat. Feb. 7, 1893, July 25, 1893. CAL. .303". Blued with a walnut stock. Approximately 8,000 were manufactured between 1895 and 1899. **NOTE:** For carbine version add 100 percent.

Courtesy Rock Island Auction Company

NIB	Exc.	V.G.	Good	Fair	Poor
—	6000	5000	3750	2000	900

Model 1899-A 22" Barrel Short Rifle

Chambered for .303, .30-30, .25-35, .32-40, .38-55. Serial number range from 10000 to 220000. Produced from 1899 to 1922. Same cocking indicator as the 1899-A rifle. **NOTE:** Add 50 percent for .25-35, .32-40, and .38-55 calibers.

NIB	Exc.	V.G.	Good	Fair	Poor
—	1600	100	600	300	100

Model 1899-A 26" Round Barrel Rifle

A .25-35, .30-30, .303 Savage, .32-40 or .38-55, .300 Savage caliber lever-action rifle with 26" barrel marked "Savage Arms Company, Utica, N.Y. Pat. Feb. 7, 1893, July 25.'93, Oct.3.'99 .CAL.30." Manufactured between 1899 and 1926/27. Blued with a walnut stock. Serial number range 10000 to 300000. Block cocking indicator on bolt to s/n 90000 then changed to pin indicator on tang. **NOTE:** Add 50 percent for .25-35, .32-40, and .38-55 calibers.

Courtesy Rock Island Auction Company

NIB	Exc.	V.G.	Good	Fair	Poor
—	1500	1000	600	250	100

Model 1899-B 26" Octagon Barrel Rifle

In calibers .303, .30-30, .25-35, .32-40, .38-55. Manufactured between 1899 and 1915. Serial number range 10000 to 175000. Same cocking indicator as 1899-A rifle. **NOTE:** Add 50 percent for .25-35, .32-40, and .38-55 calibers.

Courtesy Rock Island Auction Company

NIB	Exc.	V.G.	Good	Fair	Poor
—	1900	1300	800	350	150

Model 1899-C 26" Half Octagon Barrel Rifle

In calibers .303, .30-30, .25-35, .32-40, .38-55. Manufactured between 1899 and 1915. Serial number range 10000 to 175000. Same cocking indicator as 1899-A rifle. **NOTE:** Add 50 percent for .25-35, .32-40, and .38-55 calibers.

Courtesy Rock Island Auction Company

NIB	Exc.	V.G.	Good	Fair	Poor
—	2300	1700	1100	400	150

Model 1899-D Military Musket

Chambered for .303 Savage only with 28" barrel. Fitted with full military stocks. Produced from 1899 to 1915. Several hundred produced for Canadian Home Guard during WWI. These will have rack number on buttplate.

NIB	Exc.	V.G.	Good	Fair	Poor
5800	4700	3200	1100	700	300

Model 1899-F Saddle Ring Carbine

Fitted with 20" barrel only in calibers .303, .30-30, .25-35, .32-40, .38-55. Built from 1899 to 1919 in serial number range 19000 to 200000. Same cocking indicator as 1899-A rifle. Earliest style with barrel band is rarest variation. **NOTE:** Add 100 percent for .25-35, .32-40, and .38-55 calibers. Add 200 percent for barrel band carbine.

Courtesy Rock Island Auction Company

NIB	Exc.	V.G.	Good	Fair	Poor
—	1800	1100	600	300	100

Model 1899-CD Deluxe Rifle

In calibers .303, .30-30, .25-35, .32-40, .38-55. Serial number range 50000 to 175000. Built from 1905 to 1917. Same cocking indicator as the 1899-A rifle. The standard Deluxe 1899 rifle with 26" round, octagon, or half octagon barrel with pistol grip stock and checkering. Takedown barrel or short 22" barrel. **NOTE:** Add 30 percent for .25-35, .32-40, and .38-55 calibers.

Courtesy Rock Island Auction Company

NIB	Exc.	V.G.	Good	Fair	Poor
—	3000	2200	1600	600	250

Model 1899-H Featherweight Rifle

Chambered for .303, .30-30, .25-35, and .22 HP Savage in 20" barrel. Serial number range 50000 to 220000. Built from 1905 to 1919. The revolutionary .22 HP cartridge was introduced in this model in 1912. Most 1899-Hs are found with takedown barrels. **NOTE:** Add 50 percent for .25-35, add 25 percent for .22HP.

Paul Goodwin photo

NIB	Exc.	V.G.	Good	Fair	Poor
—	1900	1400	700	300	100

Model 1899 .250-3000 Savage Rifle

This deluxe Model 1899 was developed to introduce the Charles Newton designed .250-3000 Savage cartridge. Fitted with a 22" featherweight takedown barrel, pistol grip, checkered perch belly stock, unique checkered trigger. Built from 1914 to 1921 in the 146500 to 237500 serial number range.

NIB	Exc.	V.G.	Good	Fair	Poor
—	1800	1500	800	350	100

Model 99-B 26"/24" Standard Weight Takedown

Chambered for .303, .30-30, and .300 Savage. Serial number range 200000 to 344000. Produced from 1920 to 1934. In 1926 a new 24" barrel with ramp front sight was introduced.

NIB	Exc.	V.G.	Good	Fair	Poor
—	1200	900	500	300	100

Model 99-C 22" Standard Weight Short Rifle

Chambered for .303, .30-30, and .300 Savage. Serial number range 238000 to 290000. Built from 1922 to 1926. This model looks like a shortened 26" rifle but with a heavily crowned muzzle.

NIB	Exc.	V.G.	Good	Fair	Poor
—	1100	800	500	200	100

Model 99-D 22" Standard Weight Takedown Rifle

Chambered for .303, .30-30, and .300 Savage. Serial number range 238000 to 290000. Built from 1922 to 1926. Same heavily crowned muzzle as 99-C.

NIB	Exc.	V.G.	Good	Fair	Poor
—	1200	900	500	200	100

Model 99-E Lightweight Rifle

Chambered for .22 HP, .30-30, .303, .250-3000, and .300 Savage. Manufactured between 1922 and 1934. Serial number range 238000 to 344000. In 1926 new ramp front sight introduced. **NOTE:** Add 25 percent for .22 Hi Power and .250-3000 calibers.

Courtesy Rock Island Auction Company

NIB	Exc.	V.G.	Good	Fair	Poor
—	1450	950	600	300	100

Model 99-F Lightweight Takedown Rifle

As above, but in lightweight takedown barrels in 20", 22", and 24". Chambered for .22 HP, .30-30, .303, .250-3000, and .300 Savage. These barrels were tapered lightweight barrels. Manufactured between 1920 and 1940. Serial number range 200000 to 398000. In 1926 new ramp front sight introduced. Early versions look similar to Model 1899-H featherweight. In 1938 checkered stocks offered this option is rare. **NOTE:** Add 50 percent for .22 HP, and .250-3000. Add 75 percent for 1938 checkered stocks.

NIB	Exc.	V.G.	Good	Fair	Poor
—	1700	1200	700	300	100

Model 99-G Deluxe Takedown Pistol Grip Rifle

Calibers and barrel lengths as above, with a pistol grip checkered stock. Manufactured between 1922 and 1941. Serial number range 238000 to 407000. No takedown Model 99s made after 1941. **NOTE:** Add 50 percent for .22 Hi Power and 25 percent for .250-3000.

Courtesy Rock Island Auction Company

NIB	Exc.	V.G.	Good	Fair	Poor
—	1950	1400	800	300	100

Model 99-H Carbine/Barrel Band Carbine

Fitted with 20" or 22" barrels and chambered for .30-30, .303, .250-3000, and .300 Savage. serial number range 220000 to 400000. Built between 1923 and 1940. Distinctive plain stocks with no flat pads on side of buttstock. Curved carbine style butt-plate. In 1931 barrel band added to fore-end, then commonly called the "barrel band carbine." In 1935 flat pads added to buttstock sides. Also front ramp sight added. **NOTE:** Add 50 percent for 1935 barrel band carbine. Add 25 percent for .250-3000, and .300 Savage.

Courtesy Rock Island Auction Company

NIB	Exc.	V.G.	Good	Fair	Poor
—	1200	800	500	200	100

Combination Cased Set .300 Savage/.410 Barrel

Fitted with 22" or 24" barrels with .410 barrels and .300 Savage in Model 99-F, 99-G, or 99-K configuration. In black fitted case. Serial number range 240000 to 350000. built from 1922 to 1934. Be aware that the barrel address on the .410 barrel matches that on the rifle barrel and that the .410 barrel takes up correctly on the receiver, and that the case fits the .410 barrel and receiver.

Courtesy Amoskeag Auction Company

NIB	Exc.	V.G.	Good	Fair	Poor
—	4000	2500	1500	800	300

Model 99-A 24" Featherweight Rifle

Fitted with a 24" barrel with new 1926 ramp front sight. Chambered for .303, .30-30, or .300 Savage. Serial number range 290000 to 370000. Built from 1926 to 1937. Buttplate is older 1899 crescent style.

NIB	Exc.	V.G.	Good	Fair	Poor
—	900	700	5500	250	75

Model 99-K Deluxe Engraved Rifle

The premier Savage Model 99 with an engraved receiver. Fitted with a checkered pistol grip stock of select American walnut and a takedown frame. Hand honed and hand fitted. Chambered for .22 HP, .30-30, .303, .250-3000 and .300 Savage. Fitted with 22" or 24" barrels. Serial number range 285000 to 398000. Manufactured between 1926 and 1940. **NOTE:** Add 30 percent for .22 caliber Hi Power. Some of these models found with cased set with .410 barrel. Add $700 for V.G. case and barrels.

Courtesy Rock Island Auction Company

NIB	Exc.	V.G.	Good	Fair	Poor
3500	3000	2500	1400	600	200

Model 99-R Heavy Stocked Rifle

This model features a heavy pistol grip checkered stock with rounded forend tip. Fitted with a 22" or 24" barrel and chambered for .250-3000, .303, .300 Savage, .308, .243, and .358 calibers. Serial number range 340000 to 1060000. Manufactured between 1932 and 1960. **NOTE:** Add 50 percent for .358 and 100 percent for rare uncataloged .30-30. Approximately 10 made for A.F. Stoeger of N.Y.C. for N.Y. State Police in 1935 in serial number range 348600. Most of these are found with Redfield No. 102 side peep sight and 1/4" rack number stamped in stock below pistol grip.

Courtesy Rock Island Auction Company

NIB	Exc.	V.G.	Good	Fair	Poor
—	1300	800	550	200	100

Model 99-RS Special Sights

As above, with a Lyman aperture rear tang sight. In 1940 this was changed to a Redfield micrometer tang sight. This was the first model fitted with Savage quick release sling swivels. No .30-30 calibers made in this model. Manufactured between 1932 and 1942. **NOTE:** Add 50 percent for .358.

Courtesy Rock Island Auction Company

NIB	Exc.	V.G.	Good	Fair	Poor
—	1500	1000	600	350	200

Model 99-EG Standard Weight Rifle

Produced with plain uncheckered pistol grip stock until 1940. Available in .22 Hi Power, .250 Savage, .30-30, .303 Savage, .300 Savage, .308, .243, and .358. Serial number range 350000 to 1060000. Manufactured between 1935 and 1960. **NOTE:** For pre-1940 uncheckered stocks add 20 percent. Add 100 percent for rifles chambered for .22 Hi Power and .358.

Courtesy Rock Island Auction Company

NIB	Exc.	V.G.	Good	Fair	Poor
—	900	650	400	200	75

Model 99-T Deluxe Featherweight Rifle

This is the classic short barrel deluxe Model 99 with semi-beavertail fore-end and distinct long checkering pattern. Fitted with 20" or 22" barrels and chambered for .250-3000, .30-30, .303, .22 HP or .300 Savage. Serial number range 350000 to 400000. Manufactured between 1935 and 1940. **NOTE:** Add 100 percent for .22 Hi Power caliber, 20 percent for .250-3000.

Courtesy Rock Island Auction Company

NIB	Exc.	V.G.	Good	Fair	Poor
2000	1750	1200	800	450	200

Model 99-F Featherweight Rifle

The first Savage made with the model designation visible on the outside. Located at the rear on the right side of the barrel. A true featherweight with slender 22" barrel, lightweight stocks with butt end hollowed out. Chambered for .250-3000, .300 Savage, .308, .243, .284 and .358 calibers. Serial number range 755000 to present. Built from 1955 to 1973. **NOTE:** Add 75 percent for .284 and .358 calibers, add 50 percent for .250 Savage.

NIB	Exc.	V.G.	Good	Fair	Poor
1200	1000	800	500	250	75

Model 99-DL Deluxe Monte Carlo Rifle

A deluxe version of the Model 99EG. Available in .243, .250 Savage, .300 Savage, .284, .358 and .308 calibers with a Monte Carlo-style stock. Serial number range 1000000 to present. Manufactured between 1960 and 1973. **NOTE:** Add 75 percent for .358 and .284 calibers.

NIB	Exc.	V.G.	Good	Fair	Poor
900	800	550	350	200	100

Model 99-E Economy Rifle

The ugly duckling of the Savage line. The Model 99-E lacked many of the standard features such as left side cartridge counter, tang sight holes, walnut stocks and capped pistol grip. Fitted with 20", 22" or 24" barrels and chambered for .250-3000, .300 Savage, .243 and .308 calibers. Serial number range 1000000 to present. Built from 1960 to 1984. **NOTE:** The Model 99-E was the last original rotary magazine Model 99 when production discontinued in 1984.

NIB	Exc.	V.G.	Good	Fair	Poor
850	750	575	375	150	50

Model 99-C Clip Magazine Rifle

The recent production model in .22-250, .243, .284 Winchester, 7mm-08 or .308 caliber with a 22" barrel and open sights. Blued with a walnut stock. This model features a clip magazine and is the first modification in the Model 99 in 66 years. Introduced in 1965. Dropped from production and reintroduced in 1995 in .243 and .308 calibers. Approximate weight is 7.75 lbs. **NOTE:** Add 50 percent for .22-250, .284 and 7mm-08.

NIB	Exc.	V.G.	Good	Fair	Poor
850	550	400	250	150	50

Model 99-DE Citation Grade Rifle

A premier Savage with an engraved receiver with nickel-like finish and impressed checkering on select walnut stocks. Marked 99-M. Offered in .243, .284 and .308 calibers with 22" barrel only. Serial number range 1140000 to present. Manufactured between 1965 and 1970. **NOTE:** Add 30 percent for .284 caliber.

NIB	Exc.	V.G.	Good	Fair	Poor
1750	1600	1200	700	400	200

Model 99-PE Presentation Grade Rifle

This model is a presentation grade Model 99 with an engraved receiver as well as a hand-checkered finely figured walnut stock. Mountain lion on right side of receiver and elk on left side. Chambered for .243, .284 and .308 caliber with 22" barrel. Serial number range 1140000 to present. Manufactured between 1965 and 1970. **NOTE:** Add 30 percent for .284 caliber.

NIB	Exc.	V.G.	Good	Fair	Poor
2500	2000	1500	800	500	300

Model 1895 Anniversary Edition

A .308 caliber reproduction of the Model 1895 with a 24" octagonal barrel, engraved receiver and walnut stock with a schnabel fore-end. Brass crescent buttplate, brass medallion inlaid in stock. There were 9,999 manufactured in 1970.

NIB	Exc.	V.G.	Good	Fair	Poor
950	775	600	450	300	200

Model 99-A Saddle Gun

A variation of the original Model 99A with a 20" or 22" barrel. Chambered for the .243, .250 Savage, .300 Savage, .308, and .375. Serial number range in new "A" series on left side. Manufactured between 1971 and 1982. **NOTE:** Add 25 percent for .375 caliber.

NIB	Exc.	V.G.	Good	Fair	Poor
1200	800	500	400	300	200

Model 99-.358 and 99-.375 Brush Guns

Similar to the Model 99-A straight grip saddle gun, but in .358 and .375 Win. (1980) calibers. Has plain grooved fore-end, rubber recoil pad. Serial number range in the "A" series on left side. Built from 1977 to 1980. **NOTE:** Add 25 percent for .358 Win. caliber.

NIB	Exc.	V.G.	Good	Fair	Poor
1200	800	500	400	300	200

Model 99-CD Deluxe Clip Model

The North American classic rifle with distinct stocks of checkered walnut with long grooved fore-end, deep shaped pistol grip, and Monte Carlo stock with cheekpiece. Fitted with 22" barrel and chambered for .250-3000, .308, or .243. Serial number range in new "A" series on left side. Built from 1975 to 1980.

NIB	Exc.	V.G.	Good	Fair	Poor
1100	850	600	400	300	200

Model 99-CE (Centennial Edition)

Introduced in 1995 this limited edition rifle is chambered for the .300 Savage cartridge. Limited to 1,000 rifles with serial numbers from AS0001 to AS1000. Engraved receiver with gold inlays. Select American walnut stock with Monte Carlo comb.

Courtesy Savage Arms

NIB	Exc.	V.G.	Good	Fair	Poor
1600	1300	900	750	500	250

Model 1903

A .22 caliber slide-action rifle with a 24" octagon barrel having open sights. Blued with a walnut stock. Manufactured between 1903 and 1922. Late model rifles have updated slide handle and pistol-grip stock in same style as Model 1914.

Courtesy Rock Island Auction Company

NIB	Exc.	V.G.	Good	Fair	Poor
600	500	400	250	150	100

Model 1903 Gallery Model

Same general specifications as Model 1903 except for a mechanical counter attached to record shots fired.

NIB	Exc.	V.G.	Good	Fair	Poor
700	600	500	350	150	100

Model 1903 Factory Engraved Models

NOTE: These models are seldom seen. Secure a qualified appraisal prior to a sale. Add premiums as shown.

Grade EF

Grade "B" checkering, fancy English walnut stock, Savage 22B front sights, and 21B rear sight. **NOTE:** Add 50 percent.

Expert Grade

Fancy American walnut stock, Grade "A" engraving, Grade "B" checkering, and standard sights. **NOTE:** Add 150 percent.

Grade GH

Plain American walnut stock, Grade "A" checkering, 22B front sight, and 21B rear sight. **NOTE:** Add 50 percent.

Gold Medal Grade

Plain American walnut stock, animal ornamentation on receiver, Grade "A" checkering, and standard sights. **NOTE:** Add 60 percent.

Model 1909

As above, with a 20" barrel. Manufactured between 1909 and 1915.

NIB	Exc.	V.G.	Good	Fair	Poor
700	600	500	350	150	100

Model 1911

Produced from 1911 to 1915 in .22 short only. Bolt-action repeater. American walnut stock. Shotgun steel buttplate, bead front sight with adjustable open rear sight. Tubular magazine is loaded through buttstock and has capacity of 20 rounds. Weight is approximately 4 lbs.

NIB	Exc.	V.G.	Good	Fair	Poor
—	475	425	225	125	100

Model 1912

A .22 caliber semi-automatic rifle with a 20" barrel, open sights and in takedown form. Magazine capacity is 7 rounds. Blued with a walnut stock. Manufactured between 1912 and 1916. Weight is about 4.5 lbs.

NIB	Exc.	V.G.	Good	Fair	Poor
650	550	450	300	125	90

Model 6

Similar to the above, with a 24" barrel and tubular magazine. The walnut stock checkered prior to 1938 and plain after 1965.

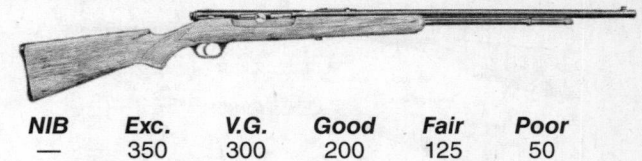

NIB	Exc.	V.G.	Good	Fair	Poor
—	350	300	200	125	50

Model 7

As above, with a detachable magazine. Manufactured between 1938 and 1954.

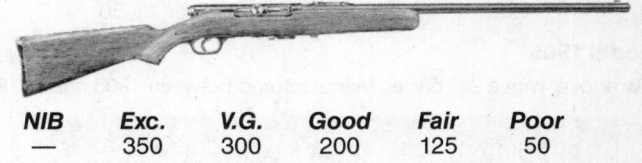

NIB	Exc.	V.G.	Good	Fair	Poor
—	350	300	200	125	50

Model 1914

As above, with a 24" octagonal barrel. Manufactured between 1914 and 1926.

NIB	Exc.	V.G.	Good	Fair	Poor
—	350	300	200	125	50

Model 25

A .22 caliber slide-action rifle with a 24" octagonal barrel, open sights and tubular magazine. Blued with a plain walnut stock. Manufactured between 1925 and 1929.

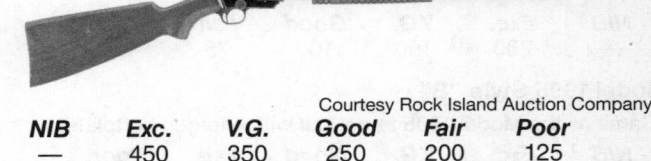

Courtesy Rock Island Auction Company

NIB	Exc.	V.G.	Good	Fair	Poor
—	450	350	250	200	125

Model 29

Similar to above but with a 22" octagonal barrel, later changed to round on post-war rifles, and a checkered walnut stock, later changed to plain on post-war rifles. Manufactured between 1929 and 1967.

NIB	Exc.	V.G.	Good	Fair	Poor
—	450	325	200	150	100

Model 170

A .30-30 or .35 Remington caliber slide-action rifle with a 22" barrel and 3-shot tubular magazine. Blued with a walnut stock. Manufactured between 1970 and 1981.

NIB	Exc.	V.G.	Good	Fair	Poor
—	550	400	250	175	100

Model 1904

A .22 caliber single-shot bolt-action rifle with an 18" barrel and walnut stock. Manufactured between 1904 and 1931. After 1915 this model became known as the Model 04.

NIB	Exc.	V.G.	Good	Fair	Poor
—	200	150	100	75	50

Model 1905

As above, with a 24" barrel. Manufactured between 1905 and 1919.

NIB	Exc.	V.G.	Good	Fair	Poor
—	200	150	100	75	50

Model 1905 Style "B"

Same as the Model 1905 target but with shotgun buttplate.

NIB	Exc.	V.G.	Good	Fair	Poor
—	375	300	200	150	50

Model 1905 Special Target Rifle

This model is the same as the Model 1905 Target Rifle except for hand checkered fancy American walnut stock.

NIB	Exc.	V.G.	Good	Fair	Poor
—	450	325	250	150	100

Model 19 NRA

A .22 caliber bolt-action rifle with a 25" barrel, detachable magazine and full-length military-style stock. Approximately 50,000 were manufactured total between 1919 and 1937.

NIB	Exc.	V.G.	Good	Fair	Poor
—	395	250	175	100	75

Model 19L

As above, with a Lyman receiver sight. Manufactured between 1933 and 1942.

NIB	Exc.	V.G.	Good	Fair	Poor
—	425	275	225	200	150

Model 19M

As above, with a 28" barrel fitted with telescope sight bases. Manufactured between 1933 and 1942.

NIB	Exc.	V.G.	Good	Fair	Poor
—	395	250	175	100	75

Model 19H

The Model 19 chambered for .22 Hornet. Manufactured between 1933 and 1942.

NIB	Exc.	V.G.	Good	Fair	Poor
—	600	475	350	300	200

Model 3

A .22 caliber single-shot bolt-action rifle with a 24" barrel, open sights and walnut stock. Manufactured between 1933 and 1952.

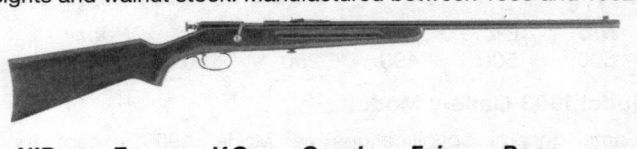

NIB	Exc.	V.G.	Good	Fair	Poor
—	200	150	100	75	50

Model 4

Similar to the above, with a 24" barrel and 5-shot magazine. Produced from 1932 to 1964.

NIB	Exc.	V.G.	Good	Fair	Poor
—	200	150	100	75	50

Model 4M

As above, in .22 Magnum. Produced from 1960 to 1964.

NIB	Exc.	V.G.	Good	Fair	Poor
—	225	175	110	75	50

Model 5

The Model 4 with a tubular magazine. Manufactured between 1933 and 1964.

NIB	Exc.	V.G.	Good	Fair	Poor
—	200	150	100	75	50

Model 1920

A .250-3000 or .300 Savage caliber bolt-action rifle with a 22" or 24" barrel, open sights and 5-shot magazine. Blued, with a walnut stock and schnabel fore-end. Manufactured between 1920 and 1929. An improved version of this rifle was introduced in 1926 that was heavier and had a Lyman #54 peep sight.

NIB	Exc.	V.G.	Good	Fair	Poor
—	1000	600	465	300	200

Model 1922

This model is a variation of the Model 19 NRA with a sporting-style stock and schnabel fore-end. Fitted with a 23" round barrel it was chambered for the .22 caliber cartridge. This model superceded the Model 23 and looks like a Model 23 sporter. Introduced in 1922 and discontinued in 1923. Very rare.

NIB	Exc.	V.G.	Good	Fair	Poor
—	750	600	475	300	200

Model 23A

This bolt-action .22 LR rifle was introduced in 1923 and features a 5-round detachable box magazine and 23" barrel with open sights. The large loading port on the left side of the receiver permitted easy single-shot loading. The stock was plain with pistol grip and a schnabel fore-end. A varnish wood finish was applied to this model. Production stopped in 1933.

NIB	Exc.	V.G.	Good	Fair	Poor
—	350	275	150	125	100

Model 23AA

This was an improved version of the Model 23A introduced in 1933. It features better speed lock, redesigned stock with oil finish. The receiver was tapped for No. 15 Savage extension peep sight. The rifle weighs approximately 6 lbs. Production ceased in 1942.

NIB	Exc.	V.G.	Good	Fair	Poor
—	395	295	200	150	125

Model 23B

Similar to the Model 23A except chambered for the .25-20 cartridge. Barrel length was 25" and forearm was a full 1.5" wide beavertail. Receiver was tapped for peep sight and magazine capacity was 4 rounds. Production on the Model 23B was from 1923 to 1940.

NIB	Exc.	V.G.	Good	Fair	Poor
—	375	325	250	200	100

Model 23C

The same configuration as the Model 23B with the exception of the caliber .32-20. Manufactured from 1923 to 1946.

NIB	Exc.	V.G.	Good	Fair	Poor
—	375	325	250	200	100

Model 23D

The same configuration as the Model 23B but chambered for the .22 Hornet cartridge. Manufactured from 1932 to 1948.

NIB	Exc.	V.G.	Good	Fair	Poor
—	375	325	250	200	100

Model 40 (Old Model)

Similar to the above but in .250-3000, .300 Savage, .30-30, and .30-06 caliber. Manufactured between 1928 and 1940.

NIB	Exc.	V.G.	Good	Fair	Poor
—	425	350	295	250	175

Model 45 Super

Similar to old Model 40, with a Lyman receiver sight and checkered walnut stock. Manufactured between 1928 and 1940.

NIB	Exc.	V.G.	Good	Fair	Poor
—	400	350	300	200	150

Model 35

A .22 caliber bolt-action rifle with a 22" barrel, open sights and 5-shot magazine. Blued with a Monte Carlo-style hardwood stock.

NIB	Exc.	V.G.	Good	Fair	Poor
—	175	150	125	75	50

Model 46

As above with a tubular magazine. Manufactured between 1969 and 1973.

NIB	Exc.	V.G.	Good	Fair	Poor
—	175	150	125	75	50

Model 340

A .22 Hornet, .222 Remington, .223, or .30-30 caliber bolt-action rifle with a 22" or 24" barrel, open sights and 4- or 5-shot magazine. Blued, with a plain walnut stock. Manufactured between 1950 and 1985.

NIB	Exc.	V.G.	Good	Fair	Poor
—	375	325	250	200	100

Model 342

As above, but in .22 Hornet caliber. Manufactured between 1950 and 1955.

NIB	Exc.	V.G.	Good	Fair	Poor
—	375	325	250	200	100

MODEL 110 SERIES

Model 110 Sporter

A bolt-action rifle manufactured in a variety of calibers with a 22" barrel, open sights and 4-shot magazine. Blued with a walnut stock. Manufactured between 1958 and 1963.

NIB	Exc.	V.G.	Good	Fair	Poor
400	325	250	175	125	100

Model 110-M

Similar to the above, in 7mm Magnum to .338 Winchester Magnum. Manufactured between 1963 and 1969.

NIB	Exc.	V.G.	Good	Fair	Poor
400	325	275	200	150	125

Model 110-D

Similar to the Model 110 in .22-250 to .338 Winchester Magnum caliber with a detachable magazine. Manufactured between 1966 and 1988.

NIB	Exc.	V.G.	Good	Fair	Poor
400	300	250	200	150	100

Model 110-P Premier Grade

As above, with a finely figured walnut stock, rosewood fore-end tip and pistol grip cap. Manufactured between 1964 and 1970.

NIB	Exc.	V.G.	Good	Fair	Poor
650	575	450	325	250	200

Model 110-PE

As above, with an engraved receiver, magazine floorplate and trigger guard. Manufactured between 1968 and 1970.

NIB	Exc.	V.G.	Good	Fair	Poor
900	800	700	500	400	300

Model 110-F

DuPont Rynite stock and sights. Discontinued.

NIB	Exc.	V.G.	Good	Fair	Poor
450	400	350	300	250	200

Model 110-FX

As above without sights. Discontinued.

NIB	Exc.	V.G.	Good	Fair	Poor
400	350	300	250	200	150

Model 110-FP

Composite stock and 24" heavy barrel. In 2003 the Savage AccuTrigger was added to this model. Discontinued.

NIB	Exc.	V.G.	Good	Fair	Poor
600	450	325	225	150	150

Model 110-G

Checkered hardwood stock and sights. Discontinued.

NIB	Exc.	V.G.	Good	Fair	Poor
425	325	275	225	175	125

Model 110-GX

As above without sights. Discontinued.

NIB	Exc.	V.G.	Good	Fair	Poor
400	300	250	200	150	100

Model 110-CY

A compact version of the Model 110 series. Shorter length of pull on walnut stock and 22" barrel. Overall length is 42-1/2". Weight is about 6-1/2 lbs. Chambered in .223, .243, .270, .300 Savage, and .308 calibers. Discontinued.

NIB	Exc.	V.G.	Good	Fair	Poor
400	300	250	200	150	100

Model 110-FP Tactical

Offered in calibers from .223 Rem. to .300 Win. Mag this bolt-action rifle has a 24" heavy barrel with recessed muzzle. The synthetic stock is black as are all other surfaces. Available in both right- and left-hand versions. Weight is approximately 8.5 lbs. Discontinued.

NIB	Exc.	V.G.	Good	Fair	Poor
600	450	325	225	150	150

Model 110-FP Duty

Introduced in 2002 this model is chambered for the .308 cartridge and features a 24" free-floating barrel with open sights. Black synthetic stock. Third swivel stud for bipod. Matte blue finish. Magazine capacity is 4 rounds. Weight is about 8.5 lbs. Discontinued.

NIB	Exc.	V.G.	Good	Fair	Poor
600	450	300	250	200	100

Model 110-FP-LE1

Similar to the Model 110FP-Duty (.308) but with a 20" barrel. No sights. Weight is about 8.25 lbs. Introduced in 2002. Discontinued.

NIB	Exc.	V.G.	Good	Fair	Poor
500	375	275	225	175	100

Model 110-FP-LE2

Same as the model above but fitted with a 26" barrel. Weight is about 8.75 lbs. Introduced in 2002. Discontinued.

NIB	Exc.	V.G.	Good	Fair	Poor
500	375	275	225	175	100

Model 110-Fiftieth Anniversary

Short-action rifle commemorating the 50th anniversary of the Model 10. Chambered in .300 Savage with 22-inch barrel. 1000 numbered rifles, high-luster blued barrel and action, unique checkering pattern on select walnut stock, high-grade hinged floorplate, Scroll pattern on receiver, 24-karat gold plated double barrel bands, 24-karat gold plated AccuTrigger, embossed recoil pad.

NIB	Exc.	V.G.	Good	Fair	Poor
1000	750	600	475	300	200

Savage Axis Series

Comes in long or short action, offered in eight cartridge choices from .223 Remington to .30-06 Springfield. Stainless action, natural color. Detachable box magazine. Right-hand action only. Synthetic stock with camo or black matte finish. Drilled and tapped for scope mounts. Also available with 3-9x40 mounted scope. Previously called "The Edge". **NOTE:** Add 15 percent for camo stock, 20 percent for scope.

NIB	Exc.	V.G.	Good	Fair	Poor
300	265	225	200	150	100

110 BA Law Enforcement Rifle

Bolt action rifle chambered .300 Win. Mag. And .338 Lapua Mag. Features include aluminum stock that features Savage's innovative three-dimensional bedding system; interchangeable buttstocks and pistol grips; three-sided accessory rail; 5-round detachable magazine; high-efficiency muzzle-brake; Magpul PRS adjustable stock; 26-inch carbon steel barrel.

NIB	Exc.	V.G.	Good	Fair	Poor
1900	1650	1400	1100	700	300

MODEL 111 SERIES

Model 111 Classic Hunter Series

All models under this series are fitted with a classic American designed straight comb stock with pistol grip. Chambered in 13 different calibers from .223 Rem. to the .338 Win. Mag. Weights vary with caliber and stock type but range from 6-3/8 to 7 lbs. Models are fitted with a detachable or internal magazine. All Hunter series rifles are drilled and tapped for scope mounts.

Model 111G

Top loading with walnut stock with recoil pad. chambered for the .25-06, .270, .30-06, 7mm Rem. Mag., or the .300 Win. Mag. Fitted with 22" or 24" barrel depending on caliber with iron sights. Weight is about 7 lbs.

NIB	Exc.	V.G.	Good	Fair	Poor
495	375	275	200	150	100

Model 111GCNS

This is a long action model as above with 22" or 24" barrel depending on caliber with no sights. Introduced in 2005.

NIB	Exc.	V.G.	Good	Fair	Poor
515	400	325	250	175	100

Model 111GC

Detachable magazine with walnut stock and recoil pad. Discontinued.

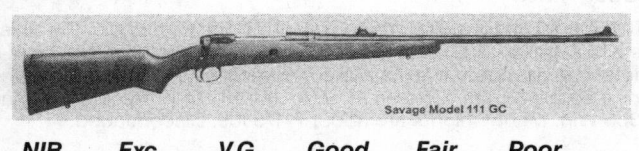

Savage Model 111 GC

NIB	Exc.	V.G.	Good	Fair	Poor
450	350	300	250	200	150

Model 111GL

Same as the Model 111G model but with left hand action.

NIB	Exc.	V.G.	Good	Fair	Poor
485	350	250	200	150	100

Model 111F

Top loading with graphite stock. Chambered for the .25-06, .270, .30-06, 7mm Rem. Mag., .300 Win. Mag., and the .338 Win. Mag. cartridges. Fitted with either a 22" or 24" barrel depending on caliber with iron sights. Black synthetic stock. Weight is about 6.75 lbs. depending on caliber.

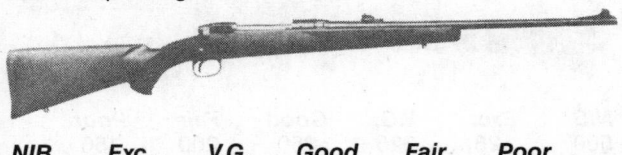

NIB	Exc.	V.G.	Good	Fair	Poor
485	350	250	200	150	100

Model 111FL

As above but with left hand action.

NIB	Exc.	V.G.	Good	Fair	Poor
485	350	250	200	150	100

Model 111FC

Detachable magazine with graphite stock. Discontinued.

NIB	Exc.	V.G.	Good	Fair	Poor
450	350	300	250	200	150

Model 111FCNS

Introduced in 2005 this model is chambered for the .25-06, .270, .30-06, 7mm Rem. Mag., .300 Win. Mag., and the .338 Win. Mag calibers. Fitted with 22" or 24" barrel with no sights. Black synthetic stock. Weight is about 6.75 lbs. depending on caliber.

NIB	Exc.	V.G.	Good	Fair	Poor
505	375	275	—	—	—

Model 111FXP3

Top loading with graphite stock and 3x9 scope, rings, and bases, and sling.

NIB	Exc.	V.G.	Good	Fair	Poor
515	400	350	300	200	150

Model 111FCXP3

Same as above but detachable magazine.

NIB	Exc.	V.G.	Good	Fair	Poor
515	400	350	300	200	150

Model 111FAK

Blued steel barrel, composite stock, muzzlebrake. Discontinued.

NIB	Exc.	V.G.	Good	Fair	Poor
450	350	300	250	200	150

MODEL 112 SERIES

Model 112BT / 112BT-S (Long Action)

Introduced for the first time in 1994 this model is a competition grade rifle. Chambered for the .223 Rem. and the .308 Win. it features a 26" heavy stainless steel barrel fitted to an alloy steel receiver. In 1995 the .300 Win. Magnum was added to the line referred to as the Model 112BT-S. The barrel finish is black. The stock is laminated with ambidextrous palm swell and adjustable cheek rest. Weight is about 11 lbs.

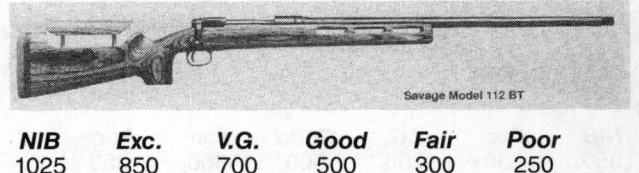

Savage Model 112 BT

NIB	Exc.	V.G.	Good	Fair	Poor
1025	850	700	500	300	250

Model 112 Series Varmint Rifles

This series of varmint rifles features 26" barrels. Offered with either composite or laminated wood stocks all Model 112s are top loading and all are drilled and tapped for scope mounting.

Available in .223, .22-250, and .220 Swift the BV configuration weighs about 10-1/2 lbs. while the FV configuration weighs about 9 lbs.

Model 112BVSS (Long Action)

This model has a laminated wood stock with high comb and ambidextrous palm swell. It is fitted with a stainless steel barrel, bolt and trigger guard. In 1996 the .300 Win. Mag., 7mm Rem. Mag., .308 Win., .30-06, and .25-06 was added to this model.

NIB	Exc.	V.G.	Good	Fair	Poor
720	550	400	275	200	150

Model 112BVSS-S

Same as above but single-shot.

NIB	Exc.	V.G.	Good	Fair	Poor
600	450	325	225	150	150

Model 112FVSS

This version also is fitted with a stainless steel barrel and a composite stock This version was fitted with a stainless steel "fluted" barrel in 1995. Several new calibers were added as well: 300 Win. Mag., 7mm Rem. Mag., .25-06 Rem. In 2003 the Savage AccuTrigger was added to this model.

NIB	Exc.	V.G.	Good	Fair	Poor
475	400	350	300	200	150

Model 112FVSS-S

This is a single-shot version of the above model.

NIB	Exc.	V.G.	Good	Fair	Poor
475	400	350	300	200	150

Model 112FV

This is similar to the model above but with a blued barrel.

NIB	Exc.	V.G.	Good	Fair	Poor
375	300	250	200	150	100

Model 112BT—Competition Grade

This model was introduced in 1996. It is a competition rifle. It features a 26" blackened stainless steel barrel and custom target style laminated stock with adjustable cheek rest. Chambered for .223 or .308 cartridges. Weight is approximately 11 lbs. The barrel is pillar bedded.

NIB	Exc.	V.G.	Good	Fair	Poor
950	850	700	500	300	250

MODEL 114 SERIES

Model 114C—Classic

This model, introduced in 2000, features a select grade oil finished walnut stock with cut checkering. No sights. Chambered for .270

and .30-06 with 22" barrel, and 7mm Mag. and .300 Win. Mag with 24" barrel.

NIB	Exc.	V.G.	Good	Fair	Poor
615	450	325	225	—	—

Model 114CE—Classic European

Introduced in 1996 this rifle is chambered for the .270 Win., .30-06, 7mm Rem. Mag., and .300 Win. Mag. Barrel lengths are 22" or 24" depending on caliber. It has an oil-finished stock with skip line checkering and cheekpiece. The fore-end tip is a schnabel type. Rubber recoil pad and pistol grip cap are standard. High luster blue finish. Approximate weight is 7.12 lbs. Discontinued.

Courtesy Savage Arms

NIB	Exc.	V.G.	Good	Fair	Poor
550	475	400	350	300	150

Model 114CU

This model has a select grade walnut oil finished stock. The finish is a high polish blue and the bolt has a laser etched Savage logo. A detachable magazine is standard. The receiver is drilled and tapped for a scope mount. Offered in .270, .30-06, 7mm Rem. Mag., and .300 Win. Mag. Weights are about 7-1/8 lbs. Discontinued.

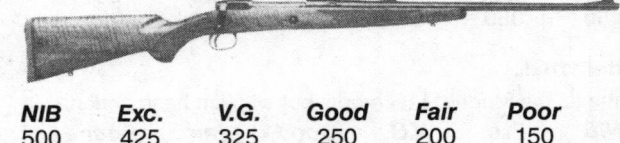

NIB	Exc.	V.G.	Good	Fair	Poor
500	425	325	250	200	150

Model 114U—Ultra

Introduced in 1999 this model features a high gloss walnut stock with custom checkering. Blued finish is high luster with a laser-etched Savage logo on the bolt body. Chambered for the .270 Win., .30-06, 7mm-08 Rem., and .300 Win. Mag cartridges. Barrel length is 22" and 24" depending on caliber. Weight is about 7 lbs.

NIB	Exc.	V.G.	Good	Fair	Poor
500	425	325	250	200	150

MODEL 116 SERIES

This series of rifles feature graphite stocks and stainless steel barreled actions. An adjustable muzzlebrake is also included. All rifles in the 116 series are drilled and tapped for scope mounts.

Model 116FCSAK (Long Action)

Features a detachable box magazine. The 22" barrel is fluted. Offered in .270, .30-06, 7mm Rem. Mag., .300 Win. Mag., and .338 Win. Mag. Weighs about 6-1/2 lbs.

NIB	Exc.	V.G.	Good	Fair	Poor
660	500	375	250	175	175

Model 116FSAK (Long Action)

Same as model above but with on-off choice for muzzlebrake given to shooter. AccuTrigger added in 2004.

NIB	Exc.	V.G.	Good	Fair	Poor
600	450	325	225	175	175

Model 116BSS

Introduced in 2001 this model features a laminated stock. It is chambered for the .270 Win., .30-06, 7mm Rem. Mag., .300 Win. Mag., and the .300 Rem. Ultra Mag. cartridges. Fitted with either a 24" or 26" stainless steel barrel depending on caliber. No sights. Weight is about 7.5 lbs. depending on caliber. Discontinued.

NIB	Exc.	V.G.	Good	Fair	Poor
625	500	365	225	175	175

Model 116FSS (Long Action)

This is the standard configuration for the 116 series. This model features a top-loading action with 22" or 24" barrel depending on caliber. There is no muzzlebrake fitted to this model. Weight is approximately 6-3/4 lbs. Offered in 7 calibers from .223 to .338 Win. Mag. AccuTrigger added in 2004.

NIB	Exc.	V.G.	Good	Fair	Poor
550	475	375	300	200	150

Model 116FCS

Same as above but with stainless steel removable box magazine.

NIB	Exc.	V.G.	Good	Fair	Poor
550	475	375	300	200	150

Model 116FSK—Kodiak (Long Action)

This model features a top loading action with a 22" barrel with muzzlebrake. Weight is approximately 7.25 lbs.

NIB	Exc.	V.G.	Good	Fair	Poor
575	495	385	300	200	150

Model 116SE—Safari Express

Introduced in 1994 this rifle features select grade walnut stock with ebony tip and deluxe checkering. Barrel and action are stainless steel with adjustable muzzlebrake. Offered in .300 Win. Mag., .338 Win. Mag., and .458 calibers. In 1995 the .425 Express cartridge was added. In 2000 this model had a stainless steel action and barrel. Weight is approximately 8-1/2 lbs. Discontinued.

NIB	Exc.	V.G.	Good	Fair	Poor
1100	950	775	600	475	300

Model 116US

Introduced in 1995 this model features a stainless steel action and barrel with a high gloss American walnut stock with ebony tip and custom checkering. Offered in .270 Win., .30-06, 7mm Rem. Mag., and .300 Win. Mag. Barrel is 22" on the two smaller calibers and 24" on the magnum calibers. Discontinued.

NIB	Exc.	V.G.	Good	Fair	Poor
600	500	400	300	250	200

MODEL 12 SERIES VARMINT

Introduced in 1998 this series features a short action heavy barrel line of rifles designed for long-range shooting.

Model 12BVSS

This model features a 26" fluted stainless steel barrel with recessed crown and a brown laminated stock with beavertail fore-end. Chambered for .223, .22-250, and .308. Magazine capacity is 4 rounds. Weight is approximately 9.5 lbs. Introduced in 1998. In 2003 the Savage AccuTrigger was added to this model.

NIB	Exc.	V.G.	Good	Fair	Poor
720	550	400	275	200	100

Model 12BVSS-S

Same as above but in a single-shot version chambered for .223 and .22-250. Weight is 9 lbs. In 2003 the Savage AccuTrigger was added to this model.

NIB	Exc.	V.G.	Good	Fair	Poor
720	550	400	275	200	150

Model 12BVSS-SXP

Introduced in 2003 this single-shot model is chambered for the .223 Rem. or .22-250 Rem. cartridge. Fitted with a 26" stainless steel fluted barrel. Savage AccuTrigger. Stock is a target-style heavy prone laminate. Weight is about 12 lbs.

NIB	Exc.	V.G.	Good	Fair	Poor
675	525	400	275	200	150

Model 12BTCSS

Similar to Model 12BVSS but with laminated thumbhole Monte Carlo stock with short action and detachable box magazine.

NIB	Exc.	V.G.	Good	Fair	Poor
725	550	400	275	200	100

Model 12FVSS

This model has a 26" stainless steel fluted barrel and a synthetic stock. Offered in .223, .22-250, and .308 calibers. Weight is about 9 lbs. Introduced in 1998. A left-hand version is also offered. In 2003 the Savage AccuTrigger was added to this model.

NIB	Exc.	V.G.	Good	Fair	Poor
600	500	375	250	200	100

Model 12FVSS-S

Same as above but in a single-shot configuration chambered for .223 or .22-250. Weight is about 9 lbs. In 2003 the Savage AccuTrigger was added to this model. Discontinued.

NIB	Exc.	V.G.	Good	Fair	Poor
550	450	325	225	175	100

Model 12FV (Short Action)

This model is similar to the other 12 Series rifles but with blued actions and 26" barrels that are nonfluted. Synthetic stock. Chambered for .223 or .22-250. Weight is about 9 lbs. Introduced in 1998. In 2003 the Savage AccuTrigger was added to this model.

NIB	Exc.	V.G.	Good	Fair	Poor
575	495	385	300	200	150

Model 12FLV

As above but with left hand action. Introduced in 2005.

NIB	Exc.	V.G.	Good	Fair	Poor
575	495	385	300	200	150

Model 12VSS—Varminter (Short Action)

Introduced in 2000 this model features a Choate adjustable black synthetic stock. A heavy fluted stainless steel barrel. Box magazine holds 4 rounds. Chambered for .223 or .22-250 cartridges. Weight is approximately 15 lbs. In 2003 the Savage AccuTrigger was added to this model.

NIB	Exc.	V.G.	Good	Fair	Poor
700	525	375	275	200	100

Model 12 Varminter Low Profile

Introduced in 2004 this model is chambered for the .223 Rem. or .22-250 cartridge and fitted with a 26" heavy fluted stainless steel barrel with no sights. Low-profile laminated stock with extra wide beavertail forearm. Adjustable trigger. Available as a repeater or single shot. Weight is about 10 lbs.

NIB	Exc.	V.G.	Good	Fair	Poor
600	500	375	250	200	100

Model 12 LRPV Long Range Precision Varminter

Similar to Model 12 FVSS but with 30" stainless bull barrel and various accurizing refinements. Chambered in .204 Ruger, .223 Remington and .22-250. Introduced in 2007. Available in single shot and 4+1 repeating versions.

NIB	Exc.	V.G.	Good	Fair	Poor
850	700	575	425	300	150

Model 12 Varminter Low Profile

Available in single shot and 4+1 repeating versions. Chambered in .22 Hornet, .204, .223, .22-250 and .243. Laminated stock, fluted 26-inch barrel. Left hand version available.

NIB	Exc.	V.G.	Good	Fair	Poor
950	800	650	500	350	175

12 FCV Varmint Rifle

The new model 12 FCV varmint rifle includes the AccuStock with beavertail fore-end, AccuTrigger, detachable box magazine and a heavy fluted barrel.

NIB	Exc.	V.G.	Good	Fair	Poor
675	600	525	450	300	150

Model 12 F-Class Target Rifle

International-class target rifle chambered in .6.5x284 Norma. Ventilated fore-end, laminated "under-hold" target stock, oversize bolt knob, AccuTrigger, 30" stainless barrel. Also available in Model 12F/TR version with conventional buttstock and elevated cheekpiece. Introduced in 2007.

NIB	Exc.	V.G.	Good	Fair	Poor
1200	1000	750	600	475	200

Model 12 Long Range Precision

Target series rifle with target style AccuTrigger, HS Precision fiberglass matte black stock. Fluted barrel 26" long. Detachable magazine with 4-round capacity. Weight is 11 pounds, overall length 46.25". Chambered for .243 winchester, .260 Remington or 6.5 Creedmoor.

NIB	Exc.	V.G.	Good	Fair	Poor
925	825	700	550	400	250

Model 12 Palma

Target rifle designed for Palma Trophy Match competition in .308 Win. caliber. Single shot with 30" stainless steel heavy barrel, laminated adjustable stock and Savage AccuTrigger.

NIB	Exc.	V.G.	Good	Fair	Poor
1800	1525	1250	900	500	250

MODEL 40 VARMINT HUNTER

Model 40 Varmint Hunter

This model, introduced in 2004, is chambered for the .22 Hornet or .223 Rem. cartridge. Fitted with a 24" heavy barrel with no sights. Laminated stock with wide beavertail forearm. Blued. Single shot. Weight is about 7.75 lbs. **NOTE:** Add $30 for .223 Rem. model.

NIB	Exc.	V.G.	Good	Fair	Poor
400	300	250	200	150	100

MODEL 10 SERIES

Model 10FP—Tactical (Short Action)

This is a short action model chambered for the .223 or .308 calibers. Fitted with a 24" barrel. Black synthetic stock. Drilled and tapped for scope mount. Weight is approximately 8 lbs. Introduced in 1998. In 2003 the Savage AccuTrigger was added to this model. Premium for Choate or McMillan stock.

NIB	Exc.	V.G.	Good	Fair	Poor
545	450	325	225	150	100

Model 10FLP

Same as above but in left-hand. In 2003 the Savage AccuTrigger was added to this model.

NIB	Exc.	V.G.	Good	Fair	Poor
550	450	325	225	150	100

Model 10FM—Sierra

This model features a 20" barrel chambered for .223, .243, or .308 calibers. In 2002 the .300 WSM caliber was added. Black synthetic stock. Magazine capacity is 4 rounds. Weight is approximately 6 lbs. Introduced in 1998. Discontinued.

NIB	Exc.	V.G.	Good	Fair	Poor
500	400	300	150	125	100

Model 10FCM—Sierra

Introduced in 2005 this model features a 20" light barrel with detachable magazine. Chambered for the .243, 7mm-08 Rem., .308, .270, and .300 WSM calibers. Black synthetic stock. Weight is about 6.25 lbs.

NIB	Exc.	V.G.	Good	Fair	Poor
550	450	325	225	150	100

Model 10FCM—Scout Rifle

Chambered for the 7mm-08 Rem. or .308 Win. cartridge this model is fitted with a 20" barrel, removable ghost ring rear sight, one-piece scope mount, and other special features. Weight is about 6.2 lbs. Introduced in 1999. Discontinued in 2005 but reintroduced in 2007.

NIB	Exc.	V.G.	Good	Fair	Poor
545	450	325	225	150	100

Model 10GY Youth

This model is similar to the Model 10FM but features a shortened hardwood stock. It is fitted with a 22" barrel and has open sights. It is chambered for .223, .243, or .308 calibers. Weight is about 6.25 lbs. Introduced in 1998.

NIB	Exc.	V.G.	Good	Fair	Poor
450	325	225	165	125	100

Model 10 Predator Hunter

Similar to Model 110FCM but with overall camo finish, 22" medium-contour barrel, and AccuTrigger. Chambered in .204 Ruger, .22-250 and .223. Introduced in 2007. **NOTE:** The Savage Predator line of rifles now includes a version with the new AccuStock Savage launched in 2009. This version has the AccuStock, AccuTrigger, detachable box magazine and a medium-contour fluted barrel. The stock is finished in Realtree Advantage Max 1 and the metal is matte black. MSRP is $864.

NIB	Exc.	V.G.	Good	Fair	Poor
600	475	350	275	200	100

Model 10XP Predator

Package rifle with factory-mounted scope, entirely covered in camo finish. 22-inch barrel, chambered in .204, .223 and .22-250. Introduced in 2008.

NIB	Exc.	V.G.	Good	Fair	Poor
650	500	395	300	225	125

Model 10XP Predator Hunter Bolt-Action Rifle Package

Bolt-action rifle similar to Model 10 but chambered in .223, .204, .22-250 or .243 Win. Includes 4-12x40 scope, 22" barrel, Accu-Trigger, choice of Realtree Snow or Mossy Oak Brush camo overall.

NIB	Exc.	V.G.	Good	Fair	Poor
725	575	425	325	250	150

LAW ENFORCEMENT SERIES

Model 10FP-LE1

Chambered for the .308 Win. cartridge and fitted with a 20" heavy barrel with no sights. Black synthetic stock. AccuTrigger. Weight is about 8.25 lbs. Introduced in 2003.

NIB	Exc.	V.G.	Good	Fair	Poor
550	450	325	225	150	100

Model 10FP-LE1A

As above but chambered for the .223 Rem. cartridge as well as the .308. Black synthetic Choate adjustable stock with accessory rail. Weight is about 10.75 lbs. Introduced in 2003.

NIB	Exc.	V.G.	Good	Fair	Poor
650	500	395	300	225	125

Model 10FP-LE2B

This bolt-action model is chambered for the .308 Win. cartridge and fitted with a McMillan fiberglass tactical stock. Barrel is 26" with no sights. AccuTrigger. Matte blue finish. Weight is about 10 lbs. Introduced in 2003.

NIB	Exc.	V.G.	Good	Fair	Poor
800	675	525	400	300	175

Model 10FP-LE2

Introduced in 2003 this model features a 26" barrel chambered for the .308 Win. cartridge and fitted with a black synthetic stock. AccuTrigger. Weight is about 8.75 lbs.

NIB	Exc.	V.G.	Good	Fair	Poor
650	500	395	300	225	125

Model 10FP-LE2A

This model is chambered for the .223 or .308 cartridge and fitted with a 26" heavy barrel with no sights. Black synthetic Choate adjustable stock with accessory rail. Weight is about 11.25 lbs. Introduced in 2003.

NIB	Exc.	V.G.	Good	Fair	Poor
725	575	425	325	250	150

Model 10FPXP-LEA

This item is a package of both rifle and scope with accessories. Features a Model 10FP with 26" barrel and black synthetic stock, Leupold 3.5-10x40 black matte scope with Mil Dot, scope covers and one-piece base. Harris bipod and heavy duty aluminum case. Rifle weighs about 10.5 lbs. Introduced in 2003.

NIB	Exc.	V.G.	Good	Fair	Poor
1950	1450	1100	700	450	300

Model 10FPXP-LE

As above but with Choate adjustable stock with accessory rail. Rifle weighs about 11.25 lbs. Introduced in 2003.

NIB	Exc.	V.G.	Good	Fair	Poor
1805	1350	1000	600	350	200

Model 10FCP-HS Precision

Similar to Model 110FP-LE1 but with one-piece HS Precision synthetic target stock and detachable box magazine. Introduced in 2007.

NIB	Exc.	V.G.	Good	Fair	Poor
650	500	395	300	225	125

Model 10FCP Choate

Similar to Model 10FP-LE1 but with Choate synthetic stock. Introduced in 2007.

NIB	Exc.	V.G.	Good	Fair	Poor
675	535	395	300	225	125

Model 10FCP McMillan

Similar to Model 10FP-LE1 but with synthetic McMillan precision stock. Introduced in 2007.

NIB	Exc.	V.G.	Good	Fair	Poor
1100	900	725	575	400	200

Model 10FPXP-HS Precision

Similar to Model 10FPXP-LEA but with HS Precision Tactical Stock. Introduced 2006.

NIB	Exc.	V.G.	Good	Fair	Poor
1725	1500	1250	800	600	300

Model 10FP-HS

Similar to Model 10FP-LE1 but with HS Precision Tactical stock. Introduced 2006.

NIB	Exc.	V.G.	Good	Fair	Poor
950	800	625	475	300	200

Model 10 Precision Carbine

Similar to Model 10 but with 20" medium contour barrel, synthetic camo Accu-Stock. Chambered in .223/.308.

NIB	Exc.	V.G.	Good	Fair	Poor
800	675	525	400	300	175

Model 10FLCP

Similar to Model 10 FCP but in left-hand configuration, with standard stock or Accu-Stock.

NIB	Exc.	V.G.	Good	Fair	Poor
800	675	525	400	300	175

Model 10 BAS Law Enforcement Bolt-Action Rifle

Bolt-action repeater based on Model 10 action but with 24" fluted heavy barrel with muzzle brake, M4-style collapsible buttstock, pistolgrip with palm swell, all-aluminum Accustock, picatinny rail for mounting optics. Chambered in .308 Winchester.

NIB	Exc.	V.G.	Good	Fair	Poor
1600	1350	1000	750	500	300

Model 10 BAT-S

Similar to above but with multi-adjustable buttstock.

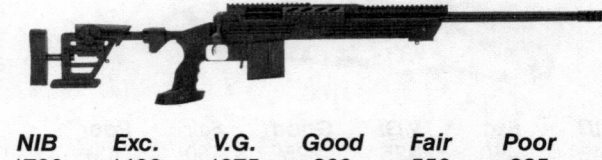

NIB	Exc.	V.G.	Good	Fair	Poor
1700	1400	1075	800	550	325

MODEL 10 SERIES MUZZLELOADER
Model 10ML-II

This model is fitted with a .50 caliber 24" barrel with adjustable sights. Synthetic stock. Blued finish. Weight is about 7.75 lbs.

NIB	Exc.	V.G.	Good	Fair	Poor
530	375	300	200	150	100

Model 10MLSS-II

As above in stainless steel.

NIB	Exc.	V.G.	Good	Fair	Poor
590	375	325	200	150	100

Model 10ML-II Camo

This model, introduced in 2002, has a camo stock finish with blued barrel and action.

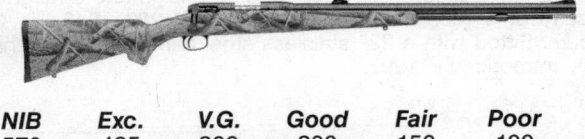

NIB	Exc.	V.G.	Good	Fair	Poor
570	425	300	200	150	100

Model 10MLSS-II Camo

This model has a camo stock finish with stainless steel barrel and action. Introduced in 2002.

NIB	Exc.	V.G.	Good	Fair	Poor
625	475	350	200	150	100

Model 10MLBSS-II

This model features a brown laminate stock with stainless steel action and barrel. Weight is 8.75 lbs. Introduced in 2002.

NIB	Exc.	V.G.	Good	Fair	Poor
665	500	375	200	150	100

Model 10ML-IIXP

Introduced in 2002 this model has a blued action and barrel with a synthetic stock. Fitted with a 3-9x40mm scope. Weight is 9.25 lbs.

NIB	Exc.	V.G.	Good	Fair	Poor
570	425	300	200	150	100

Model 10MLSS-IIXP

Same as above but with stainless steel barrel and action.

NIB	Exc.	V.G.	Good	Fair	Poor
625	475	350	200	150	100

MODEL 11 SERIES
Model 11F

This model features a short action chambered for the .223, .22-250, .243, or .308 calibers. Barrel lengths are 22" with open sights. Black synthetic stock. Weight is approximately 6.75 lbs. Introduced in 1998.

NIB	Exc.	V.G.	Good	Fair	Poor
485	350	250	175	125	100

Model 11FCNS

Introduced in 2005 this model is chambered for the .22-250, .243, 7mm-08, .308, .270 WSM, .7mm WSN, and the .300 WSM cartridges. Barrel length is 22" or 24" depending on caliber without sights. Detachable box magazine. Black synthetic stock. Weight is about 6.5 lbs. depending on caliber.

NIB	Exc.	V.G.	Good	Fair	Poor
500	375	250	175	125	100

Model 11 Lightweight Hunter

Chambered for five standard cartridges plus 6.5 Creedmoor. Lightweight at 5-1/2 pounds with a satin-finished American walnut wood stock. AccuTrigger, detachable box magazine, matte blue barrel and action with spiral fluted bolt. Barrel length is 20-inches.

NIB	Exc.	V.G.	Good	Fair	Poor
750	650	500	400	250	150

Model 11G

Chambered for .223, .243, .22-250, or .308 calibers and fitted with a 22" barrel. Wood stock has fancy checkering pattern, black recoil pad, and a gold medallion. Fitted with open sights. Weight is about 6.75 lbs. Introduced in 1998.

NIB	Exc.	V.G.	Good	Fair	Poor
500	375	250	175	125	100

Model 11BTH

Laminated, thumbhole-stock version of the Model 11 chambered in .204, .223, .22-250 and .22 Hornet. 22-inch blued barrel.

NIB	Exc.	V.G.	Good	Fair	Poor
625	475	350	200	150	100

Model 11GCNS

This model, introduced in 2005, is chambered for the .22-250, .243, 7mm-08, .308, .270 WSM, 7mm WSM, and the .300 WSM cartridges. Fitted with a 22" or 24" barrel depending on caliber without sights. Checkered walnut stock. Detachable box magazine. Weight is about 6.75 lbs. depending on caliber.

NIB	Exc.	V.G.	Good	Fair	Poor
525	400	300	200	150	100

Model 11FYCAK

Short-action youth model chambered in .243, 7mm-08, and .308. Barrel: 22-inch blued with muzzlebrake, no sights. Stock: Black composite. Weight 6.5 lbs.; 41.5-inch overall length. Introduced 2006.

NIB	Exc.	V.G.	Good	Fair	Poor
515	400	300	200	125	100

Model 111FYCAK

Similar to Model 11FYCAK but long-action chambered for .25-06, .270 and .30-06. Introduced 2006.

NIB	Exc.	V.G.	Good	Fair	Poor
515	400	300	200	125	100

Model 11BTH

Laminated, thumbhole-stock version of the Model 11 chambered in .204, .223, .22-250 and .22 Hornet. 22-inch blued barrel.

NIB	Exc.	V.G.	Good	Fair	Poor
625	475	350	200	150	100

Model 111FHNS

Similar to Model 111FCNS but with hinged floorplate. Introduced 2006.

NIB	Exc.	V.G.	Good	Fair	Poor
515	400	300	200	125	100

Model 11FCXP3

Similar to Model 111FCXP3 but in short-action. Introduced 2006.

NIB	Exc.	V.G.	Good	Fair	Poor
515	400	300	200	125	100

Model 11FYCXP3

Similar to Model 11FCXP3 but in youth version chambered in .243 Win.

NIB	Exc.	V.G.	Good	Fair	Poor
450	325	250	175	150	100

MODEL 14 SERIES

Model 14 Classic

Short-action chambered for .22-250, .243, .270 WSM, 7mm-08, .300 WSM and .308. Barrel: 22-inch or 24-inch polished blue without sights. Stock: Select lacquered walnut with contrasting forend. Introduced 2006. Also available in American Classic version with optional left hand action.

NIB	Exc.	V.G.	Good	Fair	Poor
600	500	400	300	200	100

Model 14 Left Hand

Similar to above but in left hand and chambered in .250 Savage and .300 Savage only. Suggested retail price: $779.

Model 114 Classic

Similar to Model 14 Classic but long-action chambered for .270, 7mm RM and .300 WM. Introduced 2006. Also available in American Classic version with optional left hand action.

NIB	Exc.	V.G.	Good	Fair	Poor
625	475	350	200	150	100

Model 14 Euro Classic

Similar to Model 14 Classic but with iron sights. Introduced 2006.

NIB	Exc.	V.G.	Good	Fair	Poor
625	475	350	200	150	100

Model 114 Euro Classic

Similar to Model 114 Classic but with iron sights. Introduced 2006.

NIB	Exc.	V.G.	Good	Fair	Poor
625	475	350	200	150	100

Model 14 / 114 American Classic Stainless

Traditional design has an oil-finished American walnut stock featuring wrap-around checkering, a back fore-end tip and no Monte-Carlo. Available in short and long-action versions. Short action is chambered for .243 or .308 Win., long action in .270 Winchester, .30-06 and 7mm Rem. Magnum, all with a 22-inch barrel. Introduced in 2011.

NIB	Exc.	V.G.	Good	Fair	Poor
825	750	650	500	350	150

MODEL 16 SERIES

Model 16FSS

This is a short action with a top-loading design and a magazine capacity of 4 rounds. Chambered for the .223, .243, or .308 calibers. Fitted with a 22" stainless steel barrel. Black synthetic stock. Introduced in 1998.

NIB	Exc.	V.G.	Good	Fair	Poor
550	425	325	250	200	100

Model 16FLSS

Same as above but with left-hand action.

NIB	Exc.	V.G.	Good	Fair	Poor
550	425	325	250	200	100

Model 16FCSAK

Introduced in 2005 this model is chambered for the .243, 7mm-08 Rem., .308, .270 WSM, 7mm WSM, and the .300 WSM cartridges. Fitted with a 22" or 24" barrel depending on caliber. Detachable box magazine. Black synthetic stock. Weights are between 7.75 and 7.25 lbs. depending on caliber.

NIB	Exc.	V.G.	Good	Fair	Poor
660	500	400	300	200	100

Model 16FCSS

This model is chambered for the .22-250, .243, 7mm-08 Rem., .308, .270 WSM, 7mm WSM, and the .300 WSM cartridges. Fitted with a 22" or 24" depending on caliber. Detachable box magazine. Black synthetic stock. Weight is about 6.5 lbs. depending on caliber. Introduced in 2005.

NIB	Exc.	V.G.	Good	Fair	Poor
570	425	375	250	175	125

Model 16BSS

Introduced in 2002 this model features a shot action chambered for the 7mm RSUM, .300 RSUM, and the .300 WSM cartridges. Fitted with a 24" stainless steel barrel drilled and tapped for scope mounts. Laminated stock with cut checkering. Weight is about 7.75 lbs. Discontinued.

NIB	Exc.	V.G.	Good	Fair	Poor
640	475	400	300	200	100

Model 16FHSAK

Similar to Model 116FHSAK but short-action only. Introduced 2006.

NIB	Exc.	V.G.	Good	Fair	Poor
600	475	350	200	150	100

Model 16FHSS

Similar to Model 16FSS but with hinged floorplate. Introduced 2006.

NIB	Exc.	V.G.	Good	Fair	Poor
600	475	350	200	150	100

Long Range Precision Varminter

Single-shot bolt action chambered in .204 Ruger, .223 or .22-250. Features include AccuTrigger and oversized bolt handle. Composite stock, sightless stainless steel fluted barrel. Weight: 11.25 lbs. Introduced 2006. about 6.5 lbs. depending on caliber. Introduced in 2005.

NIB	Exc.	V.G.	Good	Fair	Poor
900	750	600	450	300	200

Model 112 Varmint, Low Profile

Long-action bolt rifle chambered for .25-06 (4) and .300 WM (3). Stock: Brown laminated with recoil pad. Barrel: 26-inch sightless stainless steel bull. Weight: 11.25 lbs.

NIB	Exc.	V.G.	Good	Fair	Poor
600	475	350	200	150	100

Model 25 Lightweight Varminter

Short-action rifle chambered in .204 and .223. Medium-contour fluted barrel with recessed target crown, free-floating sleved barrel, dual pillar bedding, three locking lugs, 60-degree bolt lift, AccuTrigger adjustable from 2.5 to 3.25 lbs., detachable box magazine. Weight 8.25 lbs.

NIB	Exc.	V.G.	Good	Fair	Poor
575	450	325	250	150	100

Model 25 Lightweight Varminter Thumbhole

Similar to above but with thumbhole stock.

NIB	Exc.	V.G.	Good	Fair	Poor
650	525	400	325	275	125

Model 25 Classic Sporter

Short-action rifle chambered in .204 and .223. Free-floating sleeved barrel, Dual pillar bedding, three locking lugs, 60-degree bolt lift, AccuTrigger adjustable from 2.5 to 3.25 lbs., Detachable box magazine. Satin lacquer American walnut stock with contrasting forend tip and wraparound checkering.

NIB	Exc.	V.G.	Good	Fair	Poor
600	475	350	200	150	100

Model 25 Walking Varminter

Chambered for .204 Ruger, .22 Hornet, .222 Remington, .223 Remington and 5.7x28mm. Features a 22-inch barrel sleeved for rigidity. Triple pillar bedding and Weaver scope bases. Has a three-lug bolt with a 60-degree throw to allow mounting of a large diameter. AccuTrigger is standard, center feed detachable magazine and synthetic stock.

NIB	Exc.	V.G.	Good	Fair	Poor
475	425	350	250	200	150

Savage Edge Bolt Action Rifle

Entry-level bolt-action repeating rifle chambered in .223, .22-250, .243 Win., 7mm-08, .308 Win., .25-06, .270 Win., and .30-06. Features include 22-inch matte black barrel, synthetic black stock, 4-round capacity; detachable box magazine, drilled and tapped for scope mounts. Also available in camo finish (Edge Camo); XP variation (with 3x9 scope); and Camo XP (with camo finish and scope). In 2011 the name of this model was changed to the Axis. **NOTE:** Add 15 percent for camo stock, 20 percent for scope.

NIB	Exc.	V.G.	Good	Fair	Poor
300	265	225	200	150	100

RIMFIRE RIFLES

NOTE: As of 2006, virtually all Savage rimfire rifles (with the exception of the 30G and semi-autos) were equipped with an AccuTrigger as a standard feature.

Model 60

A .22 caliber semi-automatic rifle with a 20" barrel, open sights, and tubular magazine. Blued with a Monte Carlo-style walnut stock. Manufactured between 1969 and 1972.

NIB	Exc.	V.G.	Good	Fair	Poor
—	100	80	70	50	35

Model 64G

Introduced in 1996 this semi-automatic .22 long rifle has a 20.25" barrel and 10-shot detachable magazine. The finish is blue and the stock has a Monte Carlo with checkered pistol grip. Bead front sight with adjustable open rear sight is standard. Weight is about 5.5 lbs.

NIB	Exc.	V.G.	Good	Fair	Poor
160	125	90	60	50	40

Model 64GXP

As above but with unmounted 4x15mm scope.

NIB	Exc.	V.G.	Good	Fair	Poor
170	125	100	80	60	50

Model 64BTV

Similar to Model 64 but with laminated thumbhole stock.

NIB	Exc.	V.G.	Good	Fair	Poor
170	125	100	80	60	50

Model 64F

Introduced in 1997 this model features a black synthetic stock with blue finish. Chambered for .22 LR and fitted with a 20.25" barrel. Weight is approximately 5.5 lbs.

NIB	Exc.	V.G.	Good	Fair	Poor
140	120	90	65	50	25

Model 64FSS

Similar to the model above but with stainless steel action and barrel. Introduced in 2002.

NIB	Exc.	V.G.	Good	Fair	Poor
200	150	110	75	50	25

Model 64FV

Introduced in 1998 this model features a heavy 21" target barrel with no sights. A black synthetic stock is standard. Chambered for the .22 LR cartridge. Weight is about 6 lbs. Discontinued.

NIB	Exc.	V.G.	Good	Fair	Poor
150	125	90	65	50	25

Model 64FVXP

Similar to Model 64FV but with scope package. Introduced 2006.

NIB	Exc.	V.G.	Good	Fair	Poor
190	150	110	75	50	25

Model 64FVSS

Similar to the Model FV but with stainless steel action and barrel. Introduced in 2002. Discontinued.

NIB	Exc.	V.G.	Good	Fair	Poor
225	175	125	100	75	50

Model 64FXP

This is a package model that offers a .22 LR gun with 20.25" barrel with detachable 10-round magazine. It comes with a 4x15mm scope as well as open sights. Introduced in 1998. Weight is about 5.25 lbs.

NIB	Exc.	V.G.	Good	Fair	Poor
150	125	90	65	50	25

Model 88

As above, with a hardwood stock. Manufactured between 1969 and 1972.

NIB	Exc.	V.G.	Good	Fair	Poor
—	100	80	70	50	35

Model 90 Carbine

As above, with a 16.5" barrel and carbine-style stock. The forend is secured to the barrel by a barrel band. Discontinued.

NIB	Exc.	V.G.	Good	Fair	Poor
—	100	80	70	50	35

Model 93G

Introduced in 1996 this model is a bolt-action repeating rifle chambered for the .22 WMR cartridge. It is fitted with a 20.75" barrel with 5-shot magazine. It has a walnut-stained hardwood stock with cut checkering. Open sights standard. Weight is about 5.75 lbs. In 2001 this model was offered in a left-hand version (Model 93GL). AccuTrigger introduced 2006.

NIB	Exc.	V.G.	Good	Fair	Poor
195	150	100	75	60	50

Model 93FS

This .22 WMR model features a stainless steel finish with a 20.75" barrel and black synthetic stock. Five-round magazine. Front bead sight and sporting rear sight. Introduced in 1997. Weight is about 5.5 lbs. Discontinued.

NIB	Exc.	V.G.	Good	Fair	Poor
195	150	100	75	60	50

Model 93 Classic

Similar to Model 93G but with sporter-weight barrel and oil-finished premium walnut stock. AccuTrigger. Introduced in 2007.

NIB	Exc.	V.G.	Good	Fair	Poor
475	375	325	200	150	100

Model 93 Classic Thumbhole

Similar to above but with thumbhole stock.

NIB	Exc.	V.G.	Good	Fair	Poor
515	400	300	200	125	100

Model 93XP

.22 WMR package gun with 22-inch barrel and factory-mounted 3x9 scope. Finished overall with Mossy Oak Brush stock.

NIB	Exc.	V.G.	Good	Fair	Poor
400	325	250	150	100	75

Model 93FVSS

This model features a 21" heavy barrel chambered for the .22 WMR cartridge, recessed target muzzle and stainless steel barreled action. Equipped with black synthetic stock. Magazine capacity is 5 rounds. Weight is about 6 lbs. Introduced in 1998.

NIB	Exc.	V.G.	Good	Fair	Poor
275	200	150	100	70	50

Model 93BTVS

Similar to Model 93FVSS but with laminated thumbhole stock. Introduced in 2007.

NIB	Exc.	V.G.	Good	Fair	Poor
400	325	250	150	100	75

Model 93F

Similar to the above model but with blued finish and a synthetic stock with open sights. Weight is approximately 5 lbs. Introduced in 1998.

NIB	Exc.	V.G.	Good	Fair	Poor
185	125	95	65	50	25

Model 93R17-F

This bolt-action rifle is chambered for the .17 HMR cartridge and fitted with a 20.75" barrel with no sights. Black synthetic stock. Magazine capacity is 5 rounds. Blued finish. Weight is about 5 lbs. Introduced in 2003.

NIB	Exc.	V.G.	Good	Fair	Poor
225	175	125	100	75	50

Model 93R17-BVSS

Similar to the above model but with 21" stainless steel barrel with no sights and laminated hardwood stock. Weight is about 6 lbs. Introduced in 2003.

NIB	Exc.	V.G.	Good	Fair	Poor
325	250	190	125	75	50

Model 93R17-FSS

This .17 HMR caliber rifle has a 20.75" stainless steel barrel with no sights and black synthetic stock. Weight is about 5 lbs. Introduced in 2003.

NIB	Exc.	V.G.	Good	Fair	Poor
250	180	130	100	75	50

Model 93R17-Camo

As above but with Realtree Hardwoods camo stock. Weight is about 5 lbs. Introduced in 2003.

NIB	Exc.	V.G.	Good	Fair	Poor
250	180	130	100	75	50

Model 93R17-FVSS

As above but with 21" stainless steel heavy barrel. Weight is about 6 lbs. Introduced in 2003.

NIB	Exc.	V.G.	Good	Fair	Poor
275	210	150	125	75	50

Model 93R17-GV

This .17 HMR model has a walnut finished hardwood checkered stock and 21" heavy barrel with no sights. Blued finish. Weight is about 6 lbs. Introduced in 2003. A left-hand model is also available.

NIB	Exc.	V.G.	Good	Fair	Poor
230	175	125	100	75	50

Model 93R17-GVXP

Similar to Model 93R17-GV but with scope package. Introduced 2006.

NIB	Exc.	V.G.	Good	Fair	Poor
250	180	130	100	75	50

Model 93R17-FXP

Similar to Model 93R17-F but with scope package. Introduced 2006.

NIB	Exc.	V.G.	Good	Fair	Poor
250	180	130	100	75	50

Model 93FVSS-XP

Similar to Model 93FVSS but with scope package. Introduced 2006.

NIB	Exc.	V.G.	Good	Fair	Poor
300	225	150	125	75	50

Model 93FSS

Similar to discontinued Model 93FS but with no sights and AccuTrigger. Introduced 2006.

NIB	Exc.	V.G.	Good	Fair	Poor
275	210	150	125	75	50

Model 93FV

Similar to Model 93F but with AccuTrigger. Introduced 2006.

NIB	Exc.	V.G.	Good	Fair	Poor
250	180	130	100	75	50

Model 93R17-BTVS

Similar to Model 93R17-BVSS but with laminated thumbhole stock. Introduced 2006.

NIB	Exc.	V.G.	Good	Fair	Poor
350	295	245	195	150	100

Model 93R17BLTVS

Similar to above but in left hand. Suggested retail price: $441.

Model 93R17-BV

Similar to Model 93R17-GV but with brown laminated stock with wide beavertail forend. Introduced 2006.

NIB	Exc.	V.G.	Good	Fair	Poor
350	295	245	195	150	100

Model 93R17 Classic

Similar to Model 93R17 but with sporter-weight barrel and oil-finished premium walnut stock. AccuTrigger. Introduced in 2007.

NIB	Exc.	V.G.	Good	Fair	Poor
450	345	295	200	135	100

Model Mark II BRJ

Similar to Mark II, Model 93 but features spiral fluting pattern on a heavy barrel, blued finish and Royal Jacaranda wood laminate stock. In .22 LR, .22 WMR or .17 HMR.

NIB	Exc.	V.G.	Good	Fair	Poor
400	350	300	250	200	100

Model Mark II TRR-SR

Similar to Mark II, Model 93 but features heavy barrel, matte finish and a tactical-style wood stock.

NIB	Exc.	V.G.	Good	Fair	Poor
475	425	350	300	250	150

Model CUB-G (Mini-Youth)

Introduced in 2003 this single-shot bolt-action rifle is chambered for the .22 caliber cartridge. Barrel length is 16" and the walnut-stained hardwood stock is proportionally scaled down. Weight is about 3.3 lbs. In 2005 this model was offered in .17 HM2.

NIB	Exc.	V.G.	Good	Fair	Poor
155	125	100	75	50	25

Model CUB-T

Similar to Model CUB-G but with laminated thumbhole stock. Introduced in 2007.

NIB	Exc.	V.G.	Good	Fair	Poor
235	195	145	100	75	50

Model 30G "Stevens Favorite"

Based on the Stevens Favorite model, this lever-action single-shot .22 caliber rifle is fitted with a 21" half octagonal barrel. Walnut stock with schnabel forend. Blued finish. Weight is about 4.25 lbs. Introduced in 1999. Additional calibers added are .22 WMR and .22 Hornet. **NOTE:** Add $35 for .22WMR and $60 for .22 Hornet.

NIB	Exc.	V.G.	Good	Fair	Poor
325	275	225	150	100	50

Model 30G "Favorite" Takedown

Introduced in 2004 this model has a takedown feature. Offered in .17 HMR and .22 LR. The .17 HMR is fitted with a 21" full octagon barrel with sights and scope base included. The .22 LR model is fitted with a 21" half octagon barrel with sights. **NOTE:** Add $65 for .17 HMR model.

NIB	Exc.	V.G.	Good	Fair	Poor
325	275	225	150	100	50

MARK I & II SERIES

Introduced in 1996 this series of .22 caliber rifles feature both single-shot and repeating models. They are available in both right- and left-hand models.

Mark I-G

This is a bolt-action single-shot rifle chambered for the .22 Short, Long, or Long Rifle cartridges. It is fitted with a 20.75" barrel and has a cut checkered walnut finished stock. Bead front sight and open adjustable rear sight. Offered in both right- and left-hand models. Weight is about 5.5 lbs.

NIB	Exc.	V.G.	Good	Fair	Poor
150	100	80	70	60	50

Model Mark I-FVT

Similar to Model Mark I-G but with synthetic stock, rear peep sight and hooded front sight. Introduced 2006.

NIB	Exc.	V.G.	Good	Fair	Poor
200	150	100	80	70	60	—

Mark I-GY (Youth Model)

Same as above but fitted with a 19" barrel and shorter buttstock. Weight is about 5 lbs.

MARK I GY

NIB	Exc.	V.G.	Good	Fair	Poor
150	100	80	70	60	50

Mark I-GSB Smoothbore

This version of the Mark I is a smoothbore model made for .22 caliber shot cartridges. Barrel length is 20.75" and weight is about 5.5 lbs.

NIB	Exc.	V.G.	Good	Fair	Poor
150	100	80	70	60	50

Mark II-G

This model is a bolt-action repeater with 10-shot magazine. It is chambered for the .22 LR cartridge. Checkered walnut finished stock. Open sights. Barrel length is 20.75". Offered in both right- and left-hand versions. Weight is approximately 5.5 lbs.

NIB	Exc.	V.G.	Good	Fair	Poor
170	125	90	70	60	50

Mark II-GY (Youth Model)

Same as above but with 19" barrel and shorter stock.

NIB	Exc.	V.G.	Good	Fair	Poor
170	125	90	70	60	50

Mark II-GXP

Same as the Mark II-G model but includes an unmounted 4x15mm scope. Discontinued.

NIB	Exc.	V.G.	Good	Fair	Poor
130	100	80	70	60	50

Mark II-FSS

This is a stainless steel .22 caliber rifle with 20.75" barrel and 10-round magazine. Receiver is dovetailed for scope mounting. Stock is black synthetic. Weight is about 5 lbs.

NIB	Exc.	V.G.	Good	Fair	Poor
210	150	110	75	65	45

Mark II-LV

This .22 caliber is fitted with a 21" heavy barrel. It has a laminated hardwood stock with cut checkering. Blue finish and 10-round magazine. Weight is approximately 6.5 lbs. Introduced in 1997. Discontinued.

NIB	Exc.	V.G.	Good	Fair	Poor
200	150	110	75	65	45

Mark II-F

This model has the standard Mark II barreled action with a black synthetic stock. Detachable 10-round magazine is standard. Weight is about 5 lbs. Introduced in 1998. .17 Hornady Mach 2 added in 2006.

NIB	Exc.	V.G.	Good	Fair	Poor
150	110	80	70	65	45

Mark II-FXP

Similar to the Mark II-F but with a 4x15mm scope. Weight is approximately 5.25 lbs. First offered in 1998.

NIB	Exc.	V.G.	Good	Fair	Poor
155	110	80	70	65	45

Model Mark II Camo

Similar to Model Mark II-F but with forest camo synthetic stock. Introduced 2006.

NIB	Exc.	V.G.	Good	Fair	Poor
200	165	135	100	75	50

Mark II-FV

Introduced in 1998 this model features a 21" heavy barrel with blue alloy steel receiver. Stock is black synthetic. Magazine capacity is 5-round detachable magazine. Weight is about 6 lbs. .17 Hornady Mach 2 added in 2006.

NIB	Exc.	V.G.	Good	Fair	Poor
215	150	110	80	60	45

Model Mark II-FVXP

Similar to Model Mark II-FV but with scope package. Introduced 2006.

NIB	Exc.	V.G.	Good	Fair	Poor
250	195	150	125	75	50

Model Mark II-FVT

Similar to Model Mark II-FV but with rear peep sight and hooded front sight. Introduced 2006.

NIB	Exc.	V.G.	Good	Fair	Poor
315	250	195	145	100	75

Model Mark II-BV

This model features a 21-inch stainless steel bull barrel without sights and a brown laminate stock. Chambered in .22 LR. Introduced 2006.

NIB	Exc.	V.G.	Good	Fair	Poor
300	225	175	150	100	75

Model Mark II BTV

Similar to above but with laminated thumbhole vent stock, Accu-Trigger, blued receiver and bull barrel.

NIB	Exc.	V.G.	Good	Fair	Poor
375	325	250	150	125	100

Mark II BVTS

Similar to above but with stainless barrel/receiver; available in right- or left-hand (BTVLS) configuration. Suggested retail price: $393 (standard); $441 (left hand).

NIB	Exc.	V.G.	Good	Fair	Poor
395	350	265	165	140	125

Model Mark II Classic

Similar to Mark II-FV but with sporter-weight barrel and oil-finished premium walnut stock. AccuTrigger. Introduced in 2007. Add $50 for thumbhole stock.

NIB	Exc.	V.G.	Good	Fair	Poor
395	350	295	225	150	100

Model 900 Series

First offered in 1996 this series consists of .22 caliber rimfire target rifles in various configurations. All are available in both right- or left-hand versions.

Model 900B—Biathlon

This rifle features a hardwood stock with 5-round magazine, carrying and shooting rails, butt hook, and hand stop. The barrel length is 21" and comes with a snow cover. Receiver sight are peep variety and the front sight has 7 aperture inserts as standard. Weight is about 8.25 lbs.

NIB	Exc.	V.G.	Good	Fair	Poor
475	400	350	300	2175	125

Model 900 TR—Target

This model has a one-piece hardwood stock with shooting rail and hand stop. Rear sight is adjustable peep and front sight has 7 aperture inserts. Barrel length is 25". Five-shot magazine is standard. Weight is about 8 lbs.

NIB	Exc.	V.G.	Good	Fair	Poor
400	325	275	225	150	100

Model 900S—Silhouette

This version features a 21" heavy barrel with recessed target style crown. Fitted with a one-piece silhouette-style stock with high comb and satin walnut finish. Receiver is drilled and tapped for scope mount. Weight is about 8 lbs.

NIB	Exc.	V.G.	Good	Fair	Poor
400	325	275	225	150	100

Model 24

An external hammer combination rifle/shotgun with 24" barrels. Blued with a walnut stock. Manufactured from 1950 to 1965 in a variety of styles. The standard chambering was .22 by .410. Add 20 percent for centerfire chamberings.

NIB	Exc.	V.G.	Good	Fair	Poor
—	450	375	275	150	100

Model 24S

20 gauge.

Model 24MS

.22 Rimfire Magnum.

NIB	Exc.	V.G.	Good	Fair	Poor
—	475	395	325	175	125

Model 24DL

Satin chrome with checkered stock.

NIB	Exc.	V.G.	Good	Fair	Poor
—	450	375	325	175	125

Model 24 Field—Lightweight Version

NIB	Exc.	V.G.	Good	Fair	Poor
—	450	375	275	150	100

Model 24C

Nickel finish.

NIB	Exc.	V.G.	Good	Fair	Poor
—	450	375	275	150	100

Model 24VS

.357 Magnum or .357 Maximum/20 gauge, nickel finish.

NIB	Exc.	V.G.	Good	Fair	Poor
—	675	575	400	250	175

Model 24F

DuPont Rynite stock.

NIB	Exc.	V.G.	Good	Fair	Poor
500	400	325	250	150	100

Model 2400

A combination 12 gauge by .222 or .308 caliber over/under rifle/shotgun with 23.5" barrels and a Monte Carlo-style stock. Made by Valmet and imported between 1975 and 1980.

NIB	Exc.	V.G.	Good	Fair	Poor
—	700	575	450	350	275

SAVAGE SHOTGUNS

Model 411 Upland Sporter

SEE—Stevens.

Model 420

A 12, 16, or 20 gauge boxlock over/under shotgun with 26", 28", or 30" barrels, double triggers and extractors. Manufactured between 1937 and 1943.

Courtesy Nick Niles, Paul Goodwin photo

NIB	Exc.	V.G.	Good	Fair	Poor
—	500	400	300	200	150

Model 420 with Single Trigger

NIB	Exc.	V.G.	Good	Fair	Poor
—	500	400	300	200	150

Model 430

As above, with a checkered walnut stock and solid barrel rib. Produced from 1937 to 1943.

NIB	Exc.	V.G.	Good	Fair	Poor
—	550	450	350	200	150

Model 430 with Single Trigger

NIB	Exc.	V.G.	Good	Fair	Poor
—	600	450	300	200	150

Model 320

This is a side-by-side model.

NIB	Exc.	V.G.	Good	Fair	Poor
—	800	650	500	400	300

Model 412

.410 bore adapter.

NIB	Exc.	V.G.	Good	Fair	Poor
—	80	60	50	40	30

Model 412F

.410 bore adapter.

NIB	Exc.	V.G.	Good	Fair	Poor
—	50	45	40	35	25

Model 220

A 12, 16, 20 or .410 bore boxlock single barrel shotgun with 26" to 32" barrels. Blued with a walnut stock. Manufactured between 1938 and 1965.

NIB	Exc.	V.G.	Good	Fair	Poor
—	100	80	70	50	35

Model 210F

Introduced in 1996 this bolt-action shotgun has a 24" rifled barrel for slugs. It is chambered for the 3" 12 gauge shell. No sights. Magazine holds 2 rounds. Weight is about 7.5 lbs.

NIB	Exc.	V.G.	Good	Fair	Poor
575	500	425	350	200	125

Model 210F Slug Warrior Camo

As above but with camo stock.

NIB	Exc.	V.G.	Good	Fair	Poor
595	525	450	375	225	150

Model 210FT

Introduced in 1997 this is a 12 gauge bolt-action shotgun with a camouflage finish. Chambered for 3" shells and fitted with a 24" barrel. 2-round magazine. Approximate weight is 7.5 lbs. Drilled and tapped for scope mounting.

NIB	Exc.	V.G.	Good	Fair	Poor
575	500	425	350	200	125

Model 720

A 12 or 16 gauge semi-automatic shotgun with 26" to 32" barrels. Blued with a walnut stock. Manufactured between 1930 and 1949.

NIB	Exc.	V.G.	Good	Fair	Poor
—	450	375	275	225	100

Model 726 Upland Sporter

As above, with a 2-shot magazine. Manufactured between 1931 and 1949.

NIB	Exc.	V.G.	Good	Fair	Poor
—	450	375	275	225	100

Model 740C Skeet

The Model 726 with a 24.5" barrel featuring a Cutts compensator and skeet-style stock. Manufactured between 1936 and 1949.

NIB	Exc.	V.G.	Good	Fair	Poor
—	450	375	275	225	100

Model 745

The Model 720 in 12 gauge with an alloy receiver and 28" barrel. Manufactured between 1940 and 1949.

NIB	Exc.	V.G.	Good	Fair	Poor
—	450	375	275	225	100

Model 755

A 12 or 16 gauge semi-automatic shotgun with 26" to 30" barrels. Blued with a walnut stock. Also available with Savage Super Choke. Manufactured between 1949 and 1958.

NIB	Exc.	V.G.	Good	Fair	Poor
—	295	225	175	125	75

Model 775

As above, with an alloy receiver. Manufactured between 1950 and 1966.

NIB	Exc.	V.G.	Good	Fair	Poor
—	295	225	175	125	75

Model 750

A 12 gauge semi-automatic shotgun with a 26" or 28" barrel. The Model 750SC fitted with the Savage Super Choke and the Model 750AC with a Poly Choke. Blued with a walnut stock. Manufactured between 1960 and 1967.

NIB	Exc.	V.G.	Good	Fair	Poor
—	295	225	175	125	75

Model FA-1

This is Savage Fox semi-automatic shotgun imported from Japan in 1981 and 1982. Marked KTG. Offered in 12 gauge only with 28" or 30" vent rib barrels. Walnut stock with cut checkering. Magazine capacity is 4 rounds. Weight is about 7.5 lbs.

NIB	Exc.	V.G.	Good	Fair	Poor
—	350	300	250	200	150

Model FP-1

Similar to the above model but with 3" chambers and a 5-round magazine capacity.

NIB	Exc.	V.G.	Good	Fair	Poor
—	350	300	250	200	150

Model 21

This is a slide-action shotgun built between 1920 and 1928. Chambered for 12 gauge with 26", 28", 30", or 32" barrel. Walnut pistol grip stock and slide handle. Takedown. Almost identical to the famous Winchester Model 12. Offered in a number of different configurations including standard grade, Trap grade, Tournament grade, and Riot Model. About 13,000 were built.

NIB	Exc.	V.G.	Good	Fair	Poor
—	450	375	275	225	100

Model 28

This slide-action shotgun is an improved version of the Model 21. It was manufactured from 1928 to 1934. There are several variations of this gun including the Model 28-A, a standard grade; the Model 28-B, a standard grade with raised matted rib; a Model 28-C, a Riot gun; a Model 28-D, a Trap grade; and in 1931 a Model 28-3, an improved version with checkering and roll marked game scenes on the receiver.

NIB	Exc.	V.G.	Good	Fair	Poor
—	450	375	275	225	100

Model 30

A 12, 16, 20 or .410 bore slide-action shotgun with 26" to 30" ventilated rib barrels. Blued with a walnut stock. Manufactured between 1958 and 1978.

NIB	Exc.	V.G.	Good	Fair	Poor
—	300	195	150	100	75

Model 242

A .410 bore boxlock double-barrel over/under shotgun with 26" barrels, single trigger, extractors and exposed hammer. Manufactured between 1977 and 1981.

Courtesy Nick Niles, Paul Goodwin photo

NIB	Exc.	V.G.	Good	Fair	Poor
—	550	475	350	225	125

Model 550

A 12 or 20 gauge boxlock side-by-side double-barrel shotgun with 26", 28", or 30" barrels, single triggers and automatic ejectors. Blued with a hardwood stock. Manufactured between 1971 and 1973. Barrels were built by Valmet.

Courtesy Nick Niles, Paul Goodwin photo

NIB	Exc.	V.G.	Good	Fair	Poor
—	500	400	300	200	150

Model 440

An Italian made 12 or 20 gauge boxlock over/under shotgun with 26", 28", or 30" ventilated rib barrels, single-selective trigger and extractors. Blued with a walnut stock. Manufactured between 1968 and 1972.

NIB	Exc.	V.G.	Good	Fair	Poor
—	600	500	400	300	200

Model 440A

Courtesy Nick Niles, Paul Goodwin photo

NIB	Exc.	V.G.	Good	Fair	Poor
—	600	500	400	300	200

Model 440B-T

NIB	Exc.	V.G.	Good	Fair	Poor
—	800	650	500	350	250

Model 444 Deluxe

As above, with a more finely figured stock and automatic ejectors. Imported between 1969 and 1972.

NIB	Exc.	V.G.	Good	Fair	Poor
—	550	475	400	300	225

Model 444

NIB	Exc.	V.G.	Good	Fair	Poor
—	600	500	400	300	200

Model 444B

NIB	Exc.	V.G.	Good	Fair	Poor
—	700	550	400	300	250

Model 440T

A 12 gauge Model 440 with 30" barrels and a trap-style stock. Imported between 1969 and 1972.

NIB	Exc.	V.G.	Good	Fair	Poor
—	600	500	400	300	200

Model 330

A Valmet manufactured 12 or 20 gauge over/under shotgun with 26", 28", or 30" barrels, single-selective trigger and extractors. Blued with a walnut stock. Imported between 1970 and 1978.

Courtesy Nick Niles, Paul Goodwin photo

NIB	Exc.	V.G.	Good	Fair	Poor
—	800	650	500	350	250

Model 333

As above, with a ventilated rib and automatic ejectors. Imported between 1973 and 1980.

NIB	Exc.	V.G.	Good	Fair	Poor
—	700	550	400	300	200

Model 333T

As above, with a 30" barrel and trap-style stock. Imported between 1972 and 1980.

NIB	Exc.	V.G.	Good	Fair	Poor
—	800	650	500	350	250

Model 312 Field Over/Under

NIB	Exc.	V.G.	Good	Fair	Poor
—	800	600	450	300	200

Model 312 Trap

NIB	Exc.	V.G.	Good	Fair	Poor
—	700	600	550	350	200

Model 312 Sporting Clay

NIB	Exc.	V.G.	Good	Fair	Poor
—	800	600	450	300	200

Model 320 Field

NIB	Exc.	V.G.	Good	Fair	Poor
—	800	600	450	300	200

(SAVAGE) FOX B MODELS

The Fox Model B was introduced about 1939 by Savage for the hunter who wanted better fit and finish than offered by the Stevens brand Model 530. It was made in many variations until 1988.

Fox Model B—Utica, NY

NIB	Exc.	V.G.	Good	Fair	Poor
1000	800	600	450	400	350

Fox Model B—Chicopee Falls, Mass. (later Westfield, Mass.)

Courtesy Nick Niles, Paul Goodwin photo

NIB	Exc.	V.G.	Good	Fair	Poor
800	750	500	400	350	300

Fox Model B—Single Trigger

NIB	Exc.	V.G.	Good	Fair	Poor
900	800	600	500	400	300

Fox Model BDL

NIB	Exc.	V.G.	Good	Fair	Poor
1000	800	700	600	400	350

Fox Model BDE

Courtesy Nick Niles, Paul Goodwin photo

NIB	Exc.	V.G.	Good	Fair	Poor
1000	800	700	600	400	350

Fox Model BST

NIB	Exc.	V.G.	Good	Fair	Poor
800	700	600	500	400	300

Fox Model BSE

Courtesy Nick Niles, Paul Goodwin photo

NIB	Exc.	V.G.	Good	Fair	Poor
1000	750	650	550	450	350

Fox Model BE

NIB	Exc.	V.G.	Good	Fair	Poor
1000	800	600	450	400	350

Milano

This Italian-made over/under is available in 12, 20 and 28 gauges and .410-bore on frames scaled to match, all with 28" barrels and 3" chambers. Single selective trigger. Three choke tubes (fixed IC and Mod. on .410-bore). Automatic ejectors.

NIB	Exc.	V.G.	Good	Fair	Poor
1000	825	675	475	300	150

PISTOLS

Elbert Searle was granted a patent on an automatic pistol which utilized the bullet's torque to twist the barrel into a locking position with the slide. The patent also featured a double-row staggered magazine which increased the capacity over ordinary pistols. The patent was sold to Savage and the first Savage automatic pistol, the Model 1907 was produced. **NOTE:** Savage automatic pistols with the original cardboard box will bring between $50 and $100 premium. If the instruction pamphlet, cleaning brush, or other advertising material is present the price will escalate.

Model 1907

A .32 or .380 semi-automatic pistol with a 3.75" or 4.25" barrel depending upon caliber and a 9- or 10-shot magazine. Blued with hard rubber rectangular grips. This model is often incorrectly termed the Model 1905 or Model 1910. **NOTE:** The .380 caliber model is worth approximately 30 percent more than the values listed.

NIB	Exc.	V.G.	Good	Fair	Poor
—	525	350	250	150	100

Model 1907 Portugese Contract

Similar to the commercial guns but with a lanyard ring same as the French contract model. Original Portugese pistols will have the Portugese Crest on the grips. Only about 1,150 of these pistols were produced. Very rare. Proceed with caution.

NIB	Exc.	V.G.	Good	Fair	Poor
—	1700	1250	950	600	300

Model 1915

Similar to the Model 1907, except fitted with a grip safety and with an internal hammer. Approximately 6,500 pistols were produced in .32 caliber and 3,900 in the .380 caliber. Manufactured between 1915 and 1917. The rarest of the regular-production Savage automatic pistols.

Courtesy Orvel Reichert

.32 Caliber

NIB	Exc.	V.G.	Good	Fair	Poor
—	650	550	400	300	200

.380 Caliber

NIB	Exc.	V.G.	Good	Fair	Poor
—	1000	750	600	450	300

Model 1917

As above, with an external hammer and without the grip safety. The form of the grip frame widened in a kind of trapezoidal shape. Manufactured between 1917 and 1928. **NOTE:** Add $100 for .380.

NIB	Exc.	V.G.	Good	Fair	Poor
—	8000	7000	4000	2500	1000

Model 1907 Test Pistol

Manufactured in 1907 in .45 ACP this pistol was tested in the U.S. Army trials. About 290 pistols were produced for these trials. Double-stack magazine held 8 rounds.

NIB	Exc.	V.G.	Good	Fair	Poor
—	13500	11000	9500	6000	4000

Model 1910 Test Pistol

This was a modified Model 1907 with a heavier slide that was not concave like the Model 1907. There was a total of nine Model 1910s built. Too Rare To Price

NIB	Exc.	V.G.	Good	Fair	Poor

Model 1911 Test Pistol

This example was completely modified with a longer and thinner grip. Checkered wood grips were attached by friction instead of screws, the slide release was modified, a full grip safety was added, and a heavier serrated hammer (cocking lever) was added. Four of these pistols were built. Serial #1 has never been located. Too rare to price.

Model 101

.22 caliber single-shot pistol resembling a revolver with a 5.5" barrel. Blued with hardwood grips. This pistol was made in Chicopee Falls or Westfield, Mass. Manufactured between 1960 and 1968.

NIB	Exc.	V.G.	Good	Fair	Poor
—	225	175	125	100	75

500 HANDGUN SERIES

Introduced in 1998 this line of short action handguns features a left-hand bolt and a right-hand ejection. All are fitted with an internal box magazine, composite stock and 14" barrel.

Model 501F—Sport Striker

This handgun is fitted with a left-hand bolt and 10" free floating barrel. Detachable clip holds 10 rounds of .22 LR cartridges. Drilled and tapped for scope mount. Weight is about 4 lbs. Introduced in 2000.

Model 1917 with watch fob for salesmen samples

NIB	Exc.	V.G.	Good	Fair	Poor
—	395	275	225	175	100

Model 6.35mm

A small number of .25 caliber Savage pistols were manufactured between 1915 and 1919. Perhaps less than 25 were built. There are two major variations of this pistol. First, is the wide or 10-serrations grip, and second the 27-serrations grip variation. This change occured around 1917. Magazine capacity was 6 to 7 rounds. Very rare.

NIB	Exc.	V.G.	Good	Fair	Poor
350	295	250	175	150	100

Model 501FXP

Introduced in 2002 this model is similar to the one above but fitted with a 1.25-4x28mm scope with soft case.

NIB	Exc.	V.G.	Good	Fair	Poor
375	325	265	195	165	110

Model 502F—Sport Striker

Same as 501F but chambered for .22 WMR cartridge. Magazine capacity is 5 rounds. Introduced in 2000.

NIB	Exc.	V.G.	Good	Fair	Poor
375	325	265	195	165	110

Model 503F—Sport Striker

Same as the Model 502F-Sport Striker but chambered for the .17 HMR cartridge. Blued finish. Weight is about 4 lbs. Introduced in 2003.

NIB	Exc.	V.G.	Good	Fair	Poor
375	325	265	195	165	110

Model 503FSS—Sport Striker

As above but with stainless steel action and barrel.

NIB	Exc.	V.G.	Good	Fair	Poor
395	350	290	210	180	125

Model 510F Striker

Blued barrel action and chambered for .22-250, .243, or .308 calibers. Weight is approximately 5 lbs.

NIB	Exc.	V.G.	Good	Fair	Poor
475	400	350	295	175	150

Model 516FSS

Similar to the model above but with stainless steel barreled action.

NIB	Exc.	V.G.	Good	Fair	Poor
495	425	365	310	195	150

Model 516FSAK

Features a stainless steel barreled action with adjustable muzzlebrake.

NIB	Exc.	V.G.	Good	Fair	Poor
525	450	395	345	225	165

Model 516FSAK Camo

As above but with Realtree Hardwood camo stock. Chambered for the .300 WSM cartridge. Weight is about 5.5 lbs. Introduced in 2002.

NIB	Exc.	V.G.	Good	Fair	Poor
600	525	450	300	235	75

Model 516BSS

Fitted with a laminated thumbhole stock, left-hand bolt for right-hand ejection, 14" barrel. This model is chambered for the .223, .243, 7mm-08 Rem., .260 Rem., and .308 Win. calibers. Magazine capacity is 2 rounds. Weight is about 5 lbs. Introduced in 1999.

NIB	Exc.	V.G.	Good	Fair	Poor
600	525	450	300	235	75

Model 516BSAK

Similar to the model above but chambered for the .223 or .22-250 cartridges. The 14" barrel is fitted with an adjustable muzzlebrake. Introduced in 1999.

NIB	Exc.	V.G.	Good	Fair	Poor
600	525	450	300	235	75

SAVAGE & NORTH
Middletown, Connecticut

Figure 8 Revolver

A .36 caliber percussion revolver with a 7" octagonal barrel and 6-shot cylinder. The barrel marked "E. Savage, Middletown. CT./H.S. North. Patented June 17, 1856." The four models of this revolver are: (1) With a rounded brass frame, and the mouths of the chamber fitting into the end of the barrel breech; (2) with a rounded iron frame and a modified loading lever that is marked "H.S. North, Patented April 6, 1858"; (3) with a flat-sided brass frame having a round recoil shield; (4) with an iron frame. Approximately 400 of these revolvers were manufactured between 1856 and 1859.

First Model

NIB	Exc.	V.G.	Good	Fair	Poor
—	—	16500	7250	1500	500

Second Model

NIB	Exc.	V.G.	Good	Fair	Poor
—	—	9900	3850	850	400

Third Model

NIB	Exc.	V.G.	Good	Fair	Poor
—	—	9900	3850	850	400

Fourth Model

NIB	Exc.	V.G.	Good	Fair	Poor
—	—	11000	4400	1000	450

SAVAGE REVOLVING FIREARMS CO.
Middletown, Connecticut

Navy Revolver

A .36 caliber double-action percussion revolver with a 7" octagonal barrel and 6-shot cylinder. The frame marked "Savage R.F.A. Co./H.S. North Patented June 17, 1856/Jan. 18, 1859, May 15, 1860." Approximately 20,000 were manufactured between 1861 and 1865, of which about 12,000 were purchased by the U.S. Government.

NIB	Exc.	V.G.	Good	Fair	Poor
—	—	4250	1750	700	500

SCATTERGUN TECHNOLOGIES
Formerly—Nashville, Tennessee
Berryville, Arkansas

NOTE: In 1999 Scattergun Technologies was purchased by Wilson Combat and became a division of Wilson Combat.

TR-870

This model is based on the Remington Model 870 slide-action shotgun. It is offered in a wide variety of configurations with different features. The standard model is fitted with an 18" barrel and chambered for the 12 gauge shell. The stock is composite with recoil pad. Tactical fore-end has flashlight built in. Ghost Ring rear sight. Front sight has tritium insert. Six-round shell carrier on left side of receiver. Introduced in 1991. Weight for standard model is approximately 9 lbs. Prices listed are for the standard model.

NIB	Exc.	V.G.	Good	Fair	Poor
1000	800	650	550	300	200

Wilson Combat Current Production Models

NOTE: Add $100 to all models with Armor-Tuff finish

Standard Model

Based on the Remington 12 gauge 3" 870 Magnum this model is fitted with an 18" barrel with cylinder bore. Adjustable Ghost Ring rear sight with tritium front sight. Seven-round extended magazine. Side saddle shell carrier. Synthetic stock. Tactical sling is standard. Parkerized finish. Fitted with a SURE-FIRE tactical light.

NIB	Exc.	V.G.	Good	Fair	Poor
1150	850	625	500	400	300

Border Patrol Model

Similar to the standard model but without the tactical light. A 14" barrel is offered on this model but all NFA rules apply to the purchase of a short barrel shotgun.

NIB	Exc.	V.G.	Good	Fair	Poor
875	650	475	300	200	150

Professional Model

This model features all of the standard model components but it is fitted with a 14" barrel. Magazine capacity is 6 rounds. All NFA rules apply to purchase of short barrel shotgun.

NIB	Exc.	V.G.	Good	Fair	Poor
1175	875	650	500	400	300

Entry Model

This model has all the features of the standard model but is fitted with a 12.5" barrel. Magazine capacity is 5 rounds. All NFA rules apply to the purchase of a short barrel shotgun.

NIB	Exc.	V.G.	Good	Fair	Poor
950	700	600	500	400	300

K-9 Model

This model is built on a Remington 12 gauge 3" 11-87 Magnum semi-automatic. Fitted with Ghost Ring rear sights and tritium front sight. Extended magazine holds 7 rounds. Barrel is 18". Synthetic stock with side saddle shell carrier. Parkerized finish.

NIB	Exc.	V.G.	Good	Fair	Poor
1075	800	700	600	500	350

SWAT Model

Similar to the K-9 model but fitted with a tactical light and 14" barrel. All NFA rules apply to the purchase of a short barrel shotgun.

NIB	Exc.	V.G.	Good	Fair	Poor
1350	1000	800	650	550	400

SCHALK, G. S.
Pottsville, Pennsylvania

Rifle Musket

A .58 caliber percussion rifle with a 40" round barrel and full length stock secured by three barrel bands. The barrel marked "G. Schalk Poftsville 1861." Finished in white with a walnut stock. Approximately 100 were manufactured.

Courtesy Milwaukee Public Museum, Milwaukee, Wisconsin

NIB	Exc.	V.G.	Good	Fair	Poor
—	—	6900	3300	750	500

SCHALL & CO.
New Haven, Connecticut

Manufactured the Fiala repeating pistol for Fiala. Later, after Fiala's bankruptcy, Schall provided parts, repair service, and produced repeating pistols with the Schall name. Marketed by Schall between about 1930 and 1935.

Repeating Pistol

A .22 caliber pistol with 10-shot magazine. Tapered 6.5" barrel with fixed sights and blued finish. Rear sight is much simpler than those on the Fiala. Grips are wood with ribs running lengthwise. Typically marked "schall & co./new haven, conn usa" but guns exist with no markings. Note that the original Fiala pistols had 7.5" barrels, but not so the Schalls (a fact revealed to us by our friend Jack in Florida).

Courtesy Dr. Jon Miller

NIB	Exc.	V.G.	Good	Fair	Poor
—	500	425	325	190	170

SCHMIDT, HERBERT
Ostheim, West Germany

Model 11, Liberty 11, and Eig Model E-8

A .22 caliber double-action revolver with a 2.5" barrel and 6-shot cylinder. Blued with plastic grips.

NIB	Exc.	V.G.	Good	Fair	Poor
—	125	80	60	40	25

Model 11 Target

As above, with a 5.5" barrel and adjustable sights.

NIB	Exc.	V.G.	Good	Fair	Poor
—	150	120	75	45	30

Frontier Model or Texas Scout

.22 caliber revolver with a 5" barrel and 6-shot cylinder. Blued with plastic grips.

NIB	Exc.	V.G.	Good	Fair	Poor
—	125	80	60	40	25

SCHMIDT & COMPANY, E.
Houston, Texas

Pocket Pistol

A .45 caliber percussion single-shot pistol with a 2.5" barrel, German silver mounts and walnut stock. The barrel marked "E. Schmidt & Co. Houston." Manufactured between 1866 and 1870.

NIB	Exc.	V.G.	Good	Fair	Poor
—	—	9000	4400	1000	350

SCHNEIDER & CO.
Memphis, Tennessee

Pocket Pistol

A .41 caliber single-shot percussion pocket pistol with a 3.5" octagonal barrel, iron or German silver mounts and a walnut stock. The lock marked "Schneider & Co./Memphis, Tenn." Manufactured 1859 and 1860.

NIB	Exc.	V.G.	Good	Fair	Poor
—	—	4500	1850	650	300

SCHNEIDER & GLASSICK
Memphis, Tennessee

Pocket Pistols

A .41 caliber percussion pocket pistol with a 2.5" barrel, German silver mounts and walnut stock. The barrel marked "Schneider & Glassick, Memphis, Tenn." Manufactured 1860 to 1862.

NIB	Exc.	V.G.	Good	Fair	Poor
—	—	7000	5250	2500	800

SCHOUBOE
See—Dansk Rekylriffel Syndikat

SCHUERMAN ARMS, LTD.
Scottsdale, Arizona

Model SA40

Introduced in 2004 this bolt-action rifle is chambered for a wide variety of calibers from short action to long magnum. Offered in both right-hand and left-hand models. Barrel lengths from 20" to 26" in stainless steel. No sights. Stock is laminated fiberglass sporter style. Retail prices atart at $5440. **NOTE:** There are a number of extra costs options that may be ordered with this model. These options will affect price.

SCHULER, AUGUST
Suhl, Germany

Reform

A 6.35mm caliber four-barreled pocket pistol with 2.5" barrels. The barrel unit rises as the trigger is pulled. Blued with walnut or hard rubber grips. Manufactured between 1907 and 1914.

NIB	Exc.	V.G.	Good	Fair	Poor
—	850	750	650	450	300

SCHULTZ & LARSEN
Ofterup, Denmark

Model 47 Match Rifle

A .22 caliber single-shot bolt-action rifle with a 28" barrel, adjustable sights and adjustable trigger. Blued with an ISU-style stock.

NIB	Exc.	V.G.	Good	Fair	Poor
—	800	650	550	400	250

Model 61 Match Rifle

As above, but fitted with a palm rest.

NIB	Exc.	V.G.	Good	Fair	Poor
—	1000	850	750	600	300

Model 62 Match Rifle

Similar to the above, but manufactured for centerfire cartridges.

NIB	Exc.	V.G.	Good	Fair	Poor
—	1250	900	750	650	350

Model 54 Free Rifle

Similar to the above, with a 27" barrel and ISU stock.

NIB	Exc.	V.G.	Good	Fair	Poor
—	950	800	700	550	300

Model 68 DL

A .22-250 to .458 Winchester Magnum bolt-action rifle with a 24" barrel, adjustable trigger and well figured walnut stock.

NIB	Exc.	V.G.	Good	Fair	Poor
—	850	700	600	450	200

SCHWARZLOSE, ANDREAS
Berlin, Germany

Military Model 1898 (Standart)

A semi-automatic pistol with a 6.5" barrel, rotary locked bolt, 7-shot magazine and adjustable rear sight. Chambered for the 7.63x25mm Borchardt cartridge. Weight is about 28 oz. Blued with walnut grips. The pistol was neither a commercial or military success, and fewer than 500 were made. (CAUTION: Although the 7.63x25mm Mauser cartridge will chamber, it's too powerful for this firearm.)

NIB	Exc.	V.G.	Good	Fair	Poor
—	24000	20000	12000	5500	3000

SEARS, ROEBUCK & CO. BRAND
Chicago, Illinois

Double-Barrel Shotguns

Between 1892 and 1988 the world's largest mail order house carried a huge inventory of sporting doubleguns including any foreign and domestic brands whose makers did not object to Sears' famous price discounts. To increase sales volume, however, Sears also created its own brands which they supported with innovative design, extravagant advertising claims, unbeatable pricing and excellent quality control. These doubles, like many other firearms products handled by Sears, were listed in its very detailed semiannual catalog from about 1892, when the company first offered doubleguns, until about 1988 when social and political pressures made the company stop handling firearms. Sears marketing people gave birth to and successfully exploited many house and private brands which we no longer associate with Sears at all. In fact, many of these brands clearly rollmarked on guns are now unfamiliar to many collectors. Frequently seen and important in the market segment which many might describe as affordable doubles are some of the most often seen Sears trade names or brands. Listed in chronological order: T. Barker, S.R. & Co., Triumph, Thomas Barker, Sam Holt, Chicago

Long Range Wonder, American Bar Lock, Meriden Fire Arms Co., Norwich, A. J. Arbrey Gun Co., New England, Gladiator, Berkshire, Ranger, Eastern Arms Co., J.C. Higgins, Sears, and Ted Williams. These guns were of good quality but sold at bargain prices which gave them tremendous appeal. They were made for Sears to Sears' specifications by a number of American firms and a few foreign ones as well, all of which produced excellent shotguns under their own names. Among the best-known American companies were J. Stevens, Savage Arms, A.H. Fox, High Standard, N.R. Davis, Crescent Firearms, Ithaca, A. Fyrberg, Colton Mfg. Co., Marlin, Hunter Gun Co., Baker Gun Co., and probably a few others. Among the foreign makers were AYA, H. Pieper, Janssen, SKB, Rossi, CBC, and A. Zoli.Sears customers were not aware of this but they did trust Sears name and bought many millions of these shotguns over the nearly 100 years that Sears was in the business. Today these guns are becoming recognized as interesting and valuable collectibles in their own special niche. Their values range from $100 to $3,500 or more depending on make, model, decoration, if any, and relative rarity.

SEAVER, E.R.
New York, New York

Pocket Pistol

A .41 caliber percussion pocket pistol with a 2.5" barrel, German silver mounts and a walnut stock.

NIB	Exc.	V.G.	Good	Fair	Poor
—	—	2300	1825	975	400

SECURITY INDUSTRIES
Little Ferry, New Jersey

Model PSS

A .38 Special double-action revolver with a 2" barrel, fixed sights and 5-shot cylinder. Stainless steel with walnut grips. Manufactured between 1973 and 1978.

NIB	Exc.	V.G.	Good	Fair	Poor
—	250	150	125	100	75

Model PM357

As above, with a 2.5" barrel and in .357 Magnum caliber. Manufactured between 1975 and 1978.

NIB	Exc.	V.G.	Good	Fair	Poor
—	300	200	175	150	100

Model PPM357

As above, with a 2" barrel and a hammer without a finger spur. Manufactured between 1975 and 1978.

NIB	Exc.	V.G.	Good	Fair	Poor
—	300	200	175	150	100

SEDCO INDUSTRIES, INC.
Lake Elsinore, California

This company was in business from 1988 to 1990.

Model SP22

A .22 caliber semi-automatic pistol with a 2.5" barrel. Blackened or nickel-plated with plastic grips. Introduced in 1989.

NIB	Exc.	V.G.	Good	Fair	Poor
125	90	65	50	35	25

SEDGELY, R. F., INC.
Philadelphia, Pennsylvania

R.F. Sedgely produced specialized bolt-action rifles using the Model 1903 Springfield action. As these arms were for the most part custom order pieces, it is impossible to provide standardized values. It should be noted that his prime engraver was Rudolph J. Kornbrath.Sedgely also made a .22 caliber hammerless pistol. SEE— KOLB.

SEECAMP, L. W. CO., INC.
Milford, Connecticut

LWS .25 ACP Model

A .25 caliber semi-automatic pistol with a 2" barrel, fixed sights and 7-shot magazine. Stainless steel with plastic grips. Approximately 5,000 were manufactured between 1982 and 1985.

NIB	Exc.	V.G.	Good	Fair	Poor
500	400	300	200	150	100

LWS .32 ACP Model

A .32 caliber double-action semi-automatic pistol with a 2" barrel and 6-shot magazine. Matte or polished stainless steel with plastic grips.

NIB	Exc.	V.G.	Good	Fair	Poor
525	450	400	350	200	150

Matched Pair

A matched set of the above, with identical serial numbers. A total of 200 sets were made prior to 1968.

NIB	Exc.	V.G.	Good	Fair	Poor
—	900	800	700	500	350

LWS .380 Model

Same as the .32 caliber but chambered for the .380 cartridge. Essentially the same weight and dimensions as the .32 caliber pistol. Introduced in 1999.

NIB	Exc.	V.G.	Good	Fair	Poor
900	650	500	400	300	100

SEMMERLING
Waco, Texas

See—American Derringer Corporation

SERBU FIREARMS
Tampa, Florida

BFG-50 Rifle

This is .50 caliber single-shot bolt-action rifle fitted with a 29.5" barrel. Also offered with 36" barrel. Parkerized finish. Weight is about 22 lbs.

NIB	Exc.	V.G.	Good	Fair	Poor
2195	1600	1275	1000	700	350

BFG-50 Carbine

As above but fitted with a 22" barrel. Weight is about 17 lbs.

NIB	Exc.	V.G.	Good	Fair	Poor
2195	1600	1275	1000	700	350

BFG-50A

This model is a gas operated semi-automatic takedown rifle with a 25" barrel. Parkerized finish. Magazine capacity is 10 rounds. Weight is about 25 lbs.

NIB	Exc.	V.G.	Good	Fair	Poor
6700	5200	400	2750	1700	500

SHARPS ARMS CO., C.
Big Timber, Montana

This company was founded in 1975 in Richland, Washington, and moved to Big Timber, Montana, in 1980. It also produced custom-built rifles included the Model 1877 Sharps and others to individual customer specifications. The models listed are standard production models without extras.

Model 1874 Sharps Hartford Sporting Rifle

Chambered for a number of popular blackpowder calibers and fitted with either a 26", 28", or 30" tapered octagon barrel, double set triggers. American walnut stock with Hartford semi cresent steel butt. Silver nose cap. Case colored receiver with blued barrel. Optional sights. Weight depending on barrel length is about 10 lbs.

NIB	Exc.	V.G.	Good	Fair	Poor
2300	1775	1350	1200	800	500

Model 1874 Bridgeport Sporting Rifle

As above but with Bridgeport checkered steel butt. Schnabel-style forend.

NIB	Exc.	V.G.	Good	Fair	Poor
2300	1775	1350	1200	1000	500

Model 1875 Carbine—Hunters Rifle

Offered in a variety of calibers from .38-55 to .50-70. Fitted with a choice of tapered round military-style barrels of lengths from 22", 24", or 26". Full buckhorn and silver blade sights. Semi-cresent military-style butt with slender forend. Case colored receiver and blued barrel. Double set triggers.

NIB	Exc.	V.G.	Good	Fair	Poor
2300	1775	1350	1200	1000	500

Model 1874 Boss Gun

This model features engraved receiver, XXX fancy walnut, 34" #1 heavy tapered octagon barrel, long range tang sight, buckhorn rear sight, globe with post front sight, and Hartford nose cap. Calibers offered from .38-55 to .50-100. Weight is about 13.5 lbs. with 34" #1 barrel. **NOTE:** For Grade II add $750, for Grade III add $1,500.

NIB	Exc.	V.G.	Good	Fair	Poor
4395	3250	2250	1500	1000	500

Model 1875 Target & Sporting Rifle

Offered in a variety of calibers this rifle is fitted with a 30" heavy tapered round barrel. American walnut stock with pistol grip. Case colored receiver with blued barrel. Single trigger. Price listed is without sights.

NIB	Exc.	V.G.	Good	Fair	Poor
1500	1300	1075	900	775	400

Model 1875 Classic Rifle

This model features a receiver with octagon top and with tapered octagon barrel lengths from 26" to 30". American walnut stock with straight grip and crescent butt. Single trigger. German steel nose cap. Case colored receiver with blued barrel. Weight is about 9.5 lbs. with 30" barrel. Priced without sights.

NIB	Exc.	V.G.	Good	Fair	Poor
1500	1300	1075	900	775	400

Model 1885 High Wall Sporting Rifle

Offered with choice of .26", 28", or 30" tapered octagon barrel. Calibers are from .22 to .45-120. Single trigger. American walnut stock with straight grip and oil finish. Checkered steel butt plate. Schnabel forend. Priced without sights. Weight is about 9.25 lbs. with 30" barrel.

NIB	Exc.	V.G.	Good	Fair	Poor
2200	1750	1450	1195	750	400

Model 1885 High Wall Classic Rifle

As above but with crescent butt. Stock with cheek rest and silver inlay in forend.

NIB	Exc.	V.G.	Good	Fair	Poor
2200	1750	1450	1195	750	400

SHARPS RIFLE MANUFACTURING COMPANY
Hartford, Connecticut

The first Sharps rifles to be manufactured were made by A.S. Nippes of Mill Creek, Pennsylvania. Later they were made by Robbins & Lawrence of Windsor, Vermont. It was not until 1855 that Sharps established his own factory in Hartford, Connecticut. After his death in 1874, the company was reorganized as the Sharps Rifle Company and remained in Hartford until 1876 when it moved to Bridgeport, Connecticut. It effectively ceased operations in 1880. The following descriptions are just a brief guide and are by no means exhaustive.

Model 1849

A breechloading .44 caliber percussion rifle with a 30" barrel having a wooden cleaning rod mounted beneath it. The breech is activated by the trigger guard lever, and there is an automatic disk-type capping device on the right side of the receiver. The finish is blued and case colored. The stock is walnut with a brass patch box, buttplate, and forend cap. It is marked "Sharps Patent 1848." There were approximately 200 manufactured in 1849 and 1850 by the A.S. Nippes Company.

NIB	Exc.	V.G.	Good	Fair	Poor
—	—	23000	18000	7500	1500

Model 1850

As above, with a Maynard priming mechanism mounted on the breech. Marked "Sharps Patent 1848" on the breech and the barrel "Manufactured by A.S. Nippes Mill Creek, Pa." The priming device marked "Maynard Patent 1845." There were approximately 200 manufactured in 1850. This model is also known as the 2nd Model Sharps.

NIB	Exc.	V.G.	Good	Fair	Poor
—	—	21000	15000	6000	1200

Model 1851 Carbine

A single-shot breechloading percussion rifle in .36, .44, or .52 caliber with a 21.75" barrel and Maynard tape priming device.

Blued and case hardened with a walnut stock and forearm held on by a single barrel band. The buttplate and barrel band are brass, and the military versions feature a brass patch box. The tang marked "C. Sharps Patent 1848," the barrel "Robbins & Lawrence," and the priming device "Edward Maynard Patentee 1845." Approximately 1,800 carbines and 180 rifles were manufactured by Robbins & Lawrence in Windsor, Vermont, in 1851. **NOTE:** Those bearing U.S. inspection marks are worth approximately 75 percent more than the values listed.

Courtesy Milwaukee Public Museum, Milwaukee, Wisconsin

NIB	Exc.	V.G.	Good	Fair	Poor
—	—	12000	9500	4250	1000

Model 1852

Similar to the above, but with Sharps' Patent Pellet Primer. The barrel marked "Sharps Rifle Manufg. Co. Hartford, Conn." Blued, case hardened, brass furniture and a walnut stock. Manufactured in carbine, rifle, sporting rifle and shotgun form. Approximately 4,600 carbines and 600 rifles were made between 1853 and 1855.

Military Carbine

Courtesy Bonhams & Butterfields

NIB	Exc.	V.G.	Good	Fair	Poor
—	—	9000	6750	3000	750

Military Rifle

NIB	Exc.	V.G.	Good	Fair	Poor
—	—	12500	9750	4000	1000

Sporting Rifle

NIB	Exc.	V.G.	Good	Fair	Poor
—	—	6500	4250	1750	500

Shotgun

NIB	Exc.	V.G.	Good	Fair	Poor
—	—	4700	3250	1250	500

Model 1853

As above, but without the spring retainer for the lever hinge being mounted in the forestock. Approximately 10,500 carbines and 3,000 rifles were made between 1854 and 1858.

Military Carbine

Courtesy Milwaukee Public Museum, Milwaukee, Wisconsin

NIB	Exc.	V.G.	Good	Fair	Poor
—	—	8500	6250	2750	750

Military Rifle

NIB	Exc.	V.G.	Good	Fair	Poor
—	—	12000	9500	4000	1000

Sporting Rifle

Courtesy Bonhams & Butterfields

NIB	Exc.	V.G.	Good	Fair	Poor
—	—	4500	2750	1250	450

Shotgun

Courtesy Bonhams & Butterfields

NIB	Exc.	V.G.	Good	Fair	Poor
—	—	4300	2500	1000	450

Model 1855

As above, in .52 caliber and fitted with a Maynard tape primer that is marked "Edward Maynard Patentee 1845." Approximately 700 were made between 1855 and 1856.

NIB	Exc.	V.G.	Good	Fair	Poor
—	—	14500	10500	4250	1000

Model 1855 U.S. Navy Rifle

As above, with a 28" barrel, full-length stock and bearing U.S. Navy inspection marks. Approximately 260 were made in 1855.

Courtesy Milwaukee Public Museum, Milwaukee, Wisconsin

NIB	Exc.	V.G.	Good	Fair	Poor
—	—	13000	10500	4000	1000

Model 1855 British Carbine

The Model 1855 with British inspection marks. Approximately 6,800 were made between 1855 and 1857.

Courtesy Milwaukee Public Museum, Milwaukee, Wisconsin

NIB	Exc.	V.G.	Good	Fair	Poor
—	—	8750	6250	3000	850

SHARPS STRAIGHT BREECH MODELS

Model 1859 Carbine

Similar to the above models, but with the breech opening cut on an almost vertical angle.

22" Barrel, Brass Mountings

Courtesy Milwaukee Public Museum, Milwaukee, Wisconsin

NIB	Exc.	V.G.	Good	Fair	Poor
—	—	7700	6250	2500	500

Iron Mountings

Courtesy Milwaukee Public Museum, Milwaukee, Wisconsin

NIB	Exc.	V.G.	Good	Fair	Poor
—	—		3250	1500	500

Model 1863 Carbine

Courtesy Mike Stuckslager

NIB	Exc.	V.G.	Good	Fair	Poor
—	—	5000	3250	1500	500

Model 1863 Rifle

Without bayonet lug.

NIB	Exc.	V.G.	Good	Fair	Poor
—	—	4500	3750	1500	500

Model 1865 Rifle

Without bayonet lug.

NIB	Exc.	V.G.	Good	Fair	Poor
—	—	4200	3250	1000	500

Model 1865 Carbine

NIB	Exc.	V.G.	Good	Fair	Poor
—	—	4500	3750	1750	500

Model 1859 Rifle

30" Barrel

NIB	Exc.	V.G.	Good	Fair	Poor
—	—	5500	4250	2000	800

36" Barrel

NIB	Exc.	V.G.	Good	Fair	Poor
—	—	5500	4250	2000	800

Sporting Rifle

As above, with octagonal barrels, set triggers and finely figured walnut stocks. The Model 1853 Sporting rifle was built as a special order. About 32 were produced. The Model 1863 Sporting Rifle was also built on special order. About 16 were produced. No two of this model are alike. All reside in museums or collections.

Coffee-Mill Model

Some Sharps' carbines were fitted with coffee-mill style grinding devices set into their buttstocks. **CAUTION:** These arms are exceptionally rare and extreme caution should be exercised prior to purchase. Fakes exist.

Courtesy Milwaukee Public Museum, Milwaukee, Wisconsin

NIB	Exc.	V.G.	Good	Fair	Poor
—	—	65000	42500	15000	5000

Metallic Cartridge Conversions

In 1867 approximately 32,000 Model 1859, 1863 and 1865 Sharps were altered to .52-70 rimfire and centerfire caliber.

Courtesy Mike Stuckslager

NIB	Exc.	V.G.	Good	Fair	Poor
—	—	5500	4250	2000	600

Model 1869

A .40-50 to .50-70 caliber model produced in a military form with 26", 28", or 30" barrels; as a carbine with 21" or 24" barrels and in a sporting version with various barrel lengths and a fore-end stock fitted with a pewter tip. Approximately 650 were made.

Carbine

.50-70, saddle ring on frame.

NIB	Exc.	V.G.	Good	Fair	Poor
—	—	5500	4250	1750	500

Military Rifle

.50-70, 30" barrel with three barrel bands.

NIB	Exc.	V.G.	Good	Fair	Poor
—	—	6500	5250	2000	800

Sporting Rifle

26" barrel, .44-77 and .50-70.

NIB	Exc.	V.G.	Good	Fair	Poor
—	—	8000	6500	3000	950

Model 1870 Springfield Altered

Chambered for .50-70 caliber and fitted with a 35.5" barrel with two barrel bands, walnut stock, case hardened lock and breechlock. Buttplate stamped "US." Also built for Army trials with 22" barrel converted to centerfire.

First Type

Most common, straight breech.

Courtesy Bonhams & Butterfields

NIB	Exc.	V.G.	Good	Fair	Poor
—	—	5000	3750	1750	500

Second Type

Model 1874 action, serial #1 to 300.

NIB	Exc.	V.G.	Good	Fair	Poor
—	—	8000	6000	2750	750

Carbine

22" barrel converted to centerfire.

NIB	Exc.	V.G.	Good	Fair	Poor
—	—	10500	8250	5000	1250

Model 1874

This model was manufactured in a variety of calibers, barrel lengths, and stock styles. The barrel markings are of three forms: initially, "Sharps Rifle Manufg. Co. Hartford, Conn." ; then, "Sharps Rifle Co. Hartford, Conn." ; and finally "Sharps Rifle Co. Bridgeport, Conn." As of 1876 "Old Reliable" was stamped on the barrels. This marking is usually found on Bridgeport-marked rifles only. The major styles of this model are listed.

Military Carbine

.50-70, 21" barrel (460 made).

NIB	Exc.	V.G.	Good	Fair	Poor
—	—	7950	5500	2750	750

Military Rifle

In .45-70 and .50-70 centerfire caliber with a 30" barrel and full-length fore-end secured by three barrel bands. Approximately 1,800 made.

Courtesy Dennis Callender

NIB	Exc.	V.G.	Good	Fair	Poor
—	—	7500	5000	2250	750

Hunter's Rifle

In .40, .44, .45-70, and .50-70 caliber with 26", 28", or 30" round barrels having open sights. Approximately 600 were manufactured.

NIB	Exc.	V.G.	Good	Fair	Poor
—	—	8000	6250	2750	800

Business Rifle

In .40-70 and .45-75 Sharps caliber with a 26", 28", or 30" round barrel, adjustable sights and double-set triggers. Approximately 1,600 manufactured.

Courtesy Mike Stuckslager

NIB	Exc.	V.G.	Good	Fair	Poor
—	—	7750	6000	3250	1000

Sporting Rifle

Offered in a variety of calibers, barrel lengths, barrel weights, barrel styles and stock styles. Approximately 6,000 were manufactured.

Courtesy Milwaukee Public Museum, Milwaukee, Wisconsin

NIB	Exc.	V.G.	Good	Fair	Poor
—	—	15000	8500	4000	1500

Creedmoor Rifle

With a checkered pistol grip stock, vernier sights, combination wind gauge and spirit level front sight, set trigger and shotgun style butt. Approximately 150 were made.

NIB	Exc.	V.G.	Good	Fair	Poor
—	—	24000	17500	8500	2000

Mid-Range Rifle

Similar to the above, with a crescent buttplate. Approximately 180 were made.

Courtesy Bonhams & Butterfields

NIB	Exc.	V.G.	Good	Fair	Poor
—	—	22500	15000	6500	1500

Long-Range Rifle

As above with a 34" octagonal barrel. Approximately 425 were manufactured.

NIB	Exc.	V.G.	Good	Fair	Poor
—	—	23000	16500	6000	1500

Schuetzen Rifle

Similar to the above, with a checkered pistol grip stock and fore-end, a large Schuetzen style buttplate, double-set triggers and a vernier tang sight. Approximately 70 were manufactured.

Courtesy Bonhams & Butterfields

NIB	Exc.	V.G.	Good	Fair	Poor
—	—	22500	15000	6500	2000

Model 1877

Similar to the Model 1874, and in .45-70 caliber with a 34" or 36" barrel which is marked "Sharps Rifle Co. Bridgeport, Conn. Old Reliable." Approximately 100 were manufactured in 1877 and 1878.

NIB	Exc.	V.G.	Good	Fair	Poor
—	—	30000	10000	5000	2000

Model 1878 Sharps-Borchardt

An internal hammer breechloading rifle manufactured from 1878 to approximately 1880. The frame marked "Borchardt Patent Sharps Rifle Co. Bridgeport Conn. U.S.A." **NOTE:** Be advised that the actions on Borchardt Sporting Rifles are worth a minimum of $750. Military actions are not as difficult to locate as Sporting actions. For the sake of continuity rifles in poor condition, but with usable actions, are priced at the minimum of $750.

Carbine

Approximately 385 were made in .45-70 caliber with a 24" barrel. The fore-end is secured by one barrel band.

Courtesy Milwaukee Public Museum, Milwaukee, Wisconsin

NIB	Exc.	V.G.	Good	Fair	Poor
—	—	4700	3750	1500	750

Military Rifle

Approximately 12,000 were made in .45-70 caliber with 32.25" barrels and full stocks secured by two barrel bands.

NIB	Exc.	V.G.	Good	Fair	Poor
—	—	3000	1250	900	750

Sporting Rifle

Approximately 1,600 were made in .45-70 caliber with 30" round or octagonal barrels.

NIB	Exc.	V.G.	Good	Fair	Poor
—	—	6000	2500	800	750

Hunter's Rifle

Approximately 60 were made in .40 caliber with 26" barrels and plain walnut stocks.

NIB	Exc.	V.G.	Good	Fair	Poor
—	—	4500	1750	1000	750

Business Rifle

Approximately 90 were made with 28" barrels in .40 caliber.

NIB	Exc.	V.G.	Good	Fair	Poor
—	—	4500	2000	1000	750

Officer's Rifle

Approximately 50 were made in .45-70 caliber with 32" barrels and checkered walnut stocks.

NIB	Exc.	V.G.	Good	Fair	Poor
—	—	7500	3750	1500	750

Express Rifle

Approximately 30 were made in .45-70 caliber with 26" barrels, set triggers and checkered walnut stocks.

NIB	Exc.	V.G.	Good	Fair	Poor
—	—	12500	6000	2000	800

Short-Range Rifle

Approximately 155 were made in .40 caliber with 26" barrels, vernier rear sights, wind gauge front sight and a checkered walnut stock.

NIB	Exc.	V.G.	Good	Fair	Poor
—	—	7500	3750	1000	800

Mid-Range Rifle

Similar to the above, with a 30" barrel. Approximately 250 were manufactured.

NIB	Exc.	V.G.	Good	Fair	Poor
—	10000	7000	4000	2000	900

Long-Range Rifle

Similar to the above, with different sights. Approximately 230 were manufactured.

NIB	Exc.	V.G.	Good	Fair	Poor
—	—	16000	6500	2500	900

C. Sharps & Company and Sharps & Hankins Company Breechloading, Single-Shot Pistol

A .31, .34, or .36 caliber breechloading percussion pistol with 5" or 6.5" round barrels. Blued, case hardened with walnut stock.

NIB	Exc.	V.G.	Good	Fair	Poor
—	—	7000	5000	2000	600

Pistol-Grip Rifle

A .31 or .38 caliber breechloading percussion rifle resembling the above. Manufactured in a variety of barrel lengths. Blued, case hardened with a walnut stock having German silver mounts.

NIB	Exc.	V.G.	Good	Fair	Poor
—	—	6800	4750	2500	750

Percussion Revolver

A .25 caliber percussion revolver with a 3" octagonal barrel and 6-shot cylinder. Blued with walnut grips. The barrel marked "C. Sharps & Co., Phila. Pa." Approximately 2,000 were manufactured between 1857 and 1858.

NIB	Exc.	V.G.	Good	Fair	Poor
—	—	4250	3000	1250	500

4-Shot Pepperbox Pistols

Between 1859 and 1874, these companies manufactured 4 barrel cartridge pocket pistols in a variety of calibers, barrel lengths and finishes. The barrels slide forward for loading. The major models are listed.

Courtesy Buffalo Bill Historical Center, Cody, Wyoming

Model 1

Manufactured by C. Sharps & Co. and in .22 rimfire caliber.

NIB	Exc.	V.G.	Good	Fair	Poor
—	—	800	600	250	100

Model 2

As above, in .30 rimfire caliber.

NIB	Exc.	V.G.	Good	Fair	Poor
—	—	800	600	250	100

Model 3

Manufactured by Sharps & Hankins and marked "Address Sharps & Hankins Philadelphia Penn." on the frame. Caliber .32 short rimfire.

NIB	Exc.	V.G.	Good	Fair	Poor
—	—	950	750	300	150

Model 4

Similar to the above, in .32 Long rimfire and with a rounded bird's-head grip.

Courtesy John J. Stimson, Jr.

NIB	Exc.	V.G.	Good	Fair	Poor
—	—	950	750	300	150

Model 1861 Navy Rifle

A .52 Sharps & Hankins caliber breechloading single-shot rifle with a 32.75" barrel and full stock secured by three barrel bands. Blued, case hardened with a walnut stock. Approximately 700 were made in 1861 and 1862.

Courtesy Milwaukee Public Museum, Milwaukee, Wisconsin

NIB	Exc.	V.G.	Good	Fair	Poor
—	—	5000	300	2000	700

Model 1862 Navy Carbine

A .24 caliber breechloading carbine with a 24" leather covered barrel. Case hardened with a walnut stock. The frame marked "Sharps & Hankins Philada." Approximately 8,000 were manufactured between 1861 and 1862.

Courtesy Milwaukee Public Museum, Milwaukee, Wisconsin

NIB	Exc.	V.G.	Good	Fair	Poor
—	—	5000	3500	2000	700

Short Cavalry Carbine

Similar to the above, with a 19" blued barrel. Approximately 500 were manufactured.

NIB	Exc.	V.G.	Good	Fair	Poor
—	—	5000	3500	2000	700

Army Model

Similar to the above, with a 24" barrel that does not have a leather covering. Approximately 500 were purchased by the Army.

NIB	Exc.	V.G.	Good	Fair	Poor
—	—	4750	3000	1750	700

SHATTUCK, C. S.
Hatfield, Massachusetts

Double-Barrel Shotguns

In addition to single-barrel shotguns, Shattuck made about 1,000 hammerless doubles.

Courtesy Nick Niles

NIB	Exc.	V.G.	Good	Fair	Poor
—	1000	500	400	300	200

Boom

A .22 caliber spur trigger revolver with a 2" octagonal barrel and 6-shot cylinder. Nickel-plated with rosewood or walnut grips. The barrel marked "Boom" and "Pat. Nov. 4. 1879." Manufactured during the 1880s.

NIB	Exc.	V.G.	Good	Fair	Poor
—	—	400	150	100	75

Pocket Revolver

A .32 caliber spur trigger revolver with a 3.5" octagonal barrel and 5-shot cylinder. Nickel-plated with hard rubber grips. The barrel marked "C. S. Shattuck Hatfield, Mass. Pat. Nov. 4, 1879." Manufactured during the 1880s.

NIB	Exc.	V.G.	Good	Fair	Poor
—	—	500	200	150	100

SHAW & LEDOYT
Stafford, Connecticut

Under Hammer Pistol

A .31 caliber under hammer percussion pistol with a 2.5" to 3.5" half-octagonal barrel. Blued with a brass mounted walnut grip. The frame marked "Shaw & LeDoyt/Stafford. Conn." Manufactured during the 1850s.

NIB	Exc.	V.G.	Good	Fair	Poor
—	—	1750	1300	550	150

SHAWK & McLANAHAN
St. Louis, Missouri

Navy Revolver

A .36 caliber percussion revolver with an 8" round barrel and 6-shot cylinder. Blued with a brass frame and walnut grips. Marked "Shawk & McLanahan, St. Louis, Carondelet, Mo." Produced in limited quantities prior to 1860.

Courtesy Little John's Auction Service, Inc., Paul Goodwin photo

NIB	Exc.	V.G.	Good	Fair	Poor
—	—	15000	12000	5500	2000

SHERIDAN PRODUCTS, INC.
Racine, Wisconsin

Knockabout/Model D

A .22 caliber single-shot pistol with a 5" barrel having fixed sights. Blued with plastic grips. Manufactured between 1953 and 1960.

NIB	Exc.	V.G.	Good	Fair	Poor
—	350	225	175	100	50

SHILEN RIFLES, INC.
Ennis, Texas

Model DGA Bench Rest Rifle

A centerfire single-shot bolt-action rifle with a 26" barrel and either fiberglass or walnut stock.

NIB	Exc.	V.G.	Good	Fair	Poor
—	1750	1400	1100	850	500

Model DGA Sporter

A .17 Remington to .308 Winchester caliber bolt-action sporting rifle with a 24" barrel furnished without sights. Blued with a walnut stock.

NIB	Exc.	V.G.	Good	Fair	Poor
—	1750	1400	1100	850	500

Model DGA Varminter

As above, in varmint calibers with a 25" barrel.

NIB	Exc.	V.G.	Good	Fair	Poor
—	1750	1400	1100	850	500

Model DGA Silhouette Rifle

As above, in .308 Winchester only.

NIB	Exc.	V.G.	Good	Fair	Poor
—	1750	1400	1100	850	500

SHILOH RIFLE MFG. CO., INC.
Big Timber, Montana

Established in Farmingdale, New York, in 1976, this company moved to Big Timber, Montana, in 1983 with the name Shiloh Products. It changed its name to Shiloh Rifle Manufacturing Co. in that same year. In 1985 the company began marketing its products factory direct. In 1991 Robert, Phyllis, and Kirk Bryan purchased the company. Those interested in the Sharps reproduction rifles manufactured by this company are advised to contact them in Big Timber. **NOTE:** The company will build a rifle to customers' specifications. It is therefore possible that many of these rifles have special-order features that are not reflected in the base model price. Since Shiloh is in effect a custom (or at least semi-custom) manufacturer, the rifles listed here are representative but not inclusive.

Model 1863 Military Rifle

A .54 caliber percussion rifle with a 30" barrel, single- or double-set triggers and full-length walnut stock secured by three barrel bands.

NIB	Exc.	V.G.	Good	Fair	Poor
1900	1650	1100	900	700	500

Model 1863 Sporting Rifle

As above, with a 30" octagonal barrel, sporting sights and a half-length stock.

NIB	Exc.	V.G.	Good	Fair	Poor
1800	1550	1050	850	600	450

Model 1863 Military Carbine

The Model 1863 with a 22" round barrel and carbine stock secured by one barrel band.

NIB	Exc.	V.G.	Good	Fair	Poor
1900	1650	1100	900	700	500

Model 1862 Confederate Robinson

As above, with a 21.5" barrel, brass buttplate and barrel band.

NIB	Exc.	V.G.	Good	Fair	Poor
1900	1650	1100	900	700	500

Model 1874 Creedmore Target Rifle

This model is furnished with a 32" 1/2 round, 1/2 octagon barrel. Extra-fancy wood stock with pistol grip, no cheek rest, and shotgun butt. Single trigger. No sights.

NIB	Exc.	V.G.	Good	Fair	Poor
2700	2250	1700	1300	800	500

Model 1874 Buffalo Rifle (Quigley)

Offered in .45-70 or .45-110 with 34" heavy octagon barrel. Mid-range tang sight with globe front sight. Semi buckhorn rear sight. Double-set triggers. Military buttstock with patch box. No cheek rest and straight-grip stock.

NIB	Exc.	V.G.	Good	Fair	Poor
3300	2750	2100	1700	1200	500

Model 1874 Long Range Express Rifle

Manufactured in a variety of calibers with a 34" octagonal barrel, double-set triggers, vernier rear sight and globe front sight.

NIB	Exc.	V.G.	Good	Fair	Poor
2200	1750	1450	1195	750	400

Model 1874 Montana Roughrider Rifle

As above, with either octagonal or half-octagonal barrels ranging in lengths from 24" to 34".

NIB	Exc.	V.G.	Good	Fair	Poor
2200	1750	1450	1195	750	400

Saddle Rifle

As above, with a 26" barrel and shotgun butt.

NIB	Exc.	V.G.	Good	Fair	Poor
2200	1750	1450	1195	750	400

No. 1 Sporter Deluxe Rifle

Similar to the above, with a 30" octagonal barrel.

NIB	Exc.	V.G.	Good	Fair	Poor
2200	1750	1450	1195	750	400

No. 3 Standard Sporter

As above, with a military-style stock.

NIB	Exc.	V.G.	Good	Fair	Poor
2200	1750	1450	1195	750	400

The Business Rifle

As above, with a heavy 28" barrel.

NIB	Exc.	V.G.	Good	Fair	Poor
2200	1750	1450	1195	750	400

Model 1874 Military Rifle

The Model 1874 with a 30" round barrel, military sights and full-length stocks secured by three barrel bands.

NIB	Exc.	V.G.	Good	Fair	Poor
2200	1750	1450	1195	750	400

Model 1874 Carbine

Similar to the above, with a 24" round barrel.

NIB	Exc.	V.G.	Good	Fair	Poor
2000	1550	1150	750	500	300

The Jaeger

The Model 1874 with a 26" half-octagonal barrel, open sights and pistol-grip stock with a shotgun butt.

NIB	Exc.	V.G.	Good	Fair	Poor
2200	1750	1450	1195	750	400

Hartford Model

A reproduction of the Sharps Hartford Model.

NIB	Exc.	V.G.	Good	Fair	Poor
2200	1750	1450	1195	750	400

Model 1874 Military Carbine

Similar to the Military Rifle, but with a 22" round barrel.

NIB	Exc.	V.G.	Good	Fair	Poor
2200	1750	1450	1195	750	400

SIG
Neuhausen, Switzerland

P 210

A 7.65mm or 9mm semi-automatic pistol with a 4.75" barrel and 8-shot magazine. Blued with plastic grips. In 1996 the 9mm version was the only one imported. Weight is about 32 oz. **NOTE:** For 1996 a .22 caliber conversion unit serialized to the gun was available. Add $600 for this option.

NIB	Exc.	V.G.	Good	Fair	Poor
2300	1500	1300	1100	800	500

P 210-1

As above, with an adjustable rear sight, polished finish and walnut grips. Imported prior to 1987.

NIB	Exc.	V.G.	Good	Fair	Poor
2500	2200	1500	1150	800	400

P 210-2

NIB	Exc.	V.G.	Good	Fair	Poor
2000	1750	1350	1000	750	300

P 210-5

As above, with an extended length barrel, adjustable rear sight and walnut grips.

NIB	Exc.	V.G.	Good	Fair	Poor
2250	1850	1650	1000	800	400

P 210-6

As above, with a 4.75" barrel.

NIB	Exc.	V.G.	Good	Fair	Poor
2750	2250	1500	1150	800	400

SIG-HAMMERLI
Lenzburg, Switzerland

Model P240 Target Pistol

A .32 Smith & Wesson Long Wadcutter or .38 Midrange caliber semi-automatic pistol with a 5.9" barrel, adjustable rear sight, adjustable trigger and 5-shot magazine. Blued, with adjustable walnut grips. Imported prior 1987.

Courtesy John J. Stimson, Jr.

NIB	Exc.	V.G.	Good	Fair	Poor
—	1300	1150	950	750	600

.22 Conversion Unit

A barrel, slide, and magazine used to convert the above to .22 caliber.

NIB	Exc.	V.G.	Good	Fair	Poor
—	500	450	400	300	200

Model P208S

This is a semi-automatic target pistol chambered for the .22 LR cartridge. The barrel length is 5.9" long with adjustable sights. Sight radius is 8.2". Trigger has adjustable pull weight, travel, slack weight, and creep. Grips are stippled walnut with adjustable palm shelf. Weight is approximately 37 oz. empty.

NIB	Exc.	V.G.	Good	Fair	Poor
1900	1600	1300	1100	750	500

Model P280

This model is a semi-automatic pistol chambered for the .22 LR cartridge or the .32 S&W Long Wadcutter. Single-action-only. Barrel length is 4.6" with a sight radius of 8.7". Adjustable sights. Trigger is adjustable for pull weight, take-up, let-off, and creep. Stippled walnut grip with adjustable palm shelf. Weight is 35 oz. for the .22 caliber and 42 oz. for the .32 caliber. Magazine capacity is six .22 caliber rounds and five .32 caliber rounds.

NIB	Exc.	V.G.	Good	Fair	Poor
1200	10000	800	650	500	300

Model P160/162

This .22 LR single-shot pistol is designed for international free pistol competition. Barrel length is 11.3" with a sight radius of 14.6". Trigger is fully adjustable as are the sights. Stippled walnut grips with adjustable palm shelf and rake angle. The Model 160 has a mechanical trigger while the Model 162 is fitted with an electric trigger.

NIB	Exc.	V.G.	Good	Fair	Poor
2300	2000	1700	1250	800	400

Trailside PL 22

Introduced in 1999 this semi-automatic pistol is chambered for the .22 LR cartridge. Barrel length is 4.5" or 6" with fixed sights. Synthetic grips. Two-tone finish. Magazine capacity is 10 rounds. Weight is about 28 oz. with 4.5" barrel and 30 oz. with 6" barrel. **NOTE:** Add $90 for 6" barrel.

NIB	Exc.	V.G.	Good	Fair	Poor
575	500	375	295	200	100

Trailside PL 22 Target

Similar to the PL 22 with the addition of adjustable sights and walnut grips. Introduced in 1999. **NOTE:** Add $25 for 6" barrel.

NIB	Exc.	V.G.	Good	Fair	Poor
595	525	400	325	225	125

Trailside Competition

Introduced in 2004 this .22 caliber model features a 6" barrel with adjustable sights and adjustable competition grip, counterweights, and two-tone finish. Magazine capacity is 10 rounds. Weight is about 36 oz.

NIB	Exc.	V.G.	Good	Fair	Poor
800	675	500	425	300	150

SIGARMS/SIG-SAUER
Eckernforde, West Germany

NOTE: SIGARMS currently offers an almost innumerable variety of semi-auto pistols. The main models are listed here. Values for similar models (i.e., those with similar model numbers) are generally comparable to the values given here with a 5-10 percent premium for scarce or desirable options.

PISTOLS

CLASSIC SERIES

P210

This model was reintroduced into the U.S. in 2001 and is based on the Swiss military version first built in 1949. It is designed primarily as a target pistol and is furnished in four different variations. All variations are chambered for the 9mm cartridge. **NOTE:** Older P210 models imported before 1968 without importer stamps and pistols built during the late 1940s and early 1950s may bring a premium to the collector. Be aware that extra barrels, conversion kits, and other special order features will add additional value. For pistols with factory installed night sights add $90. Add $45 for pistols with K-Kote finish. Add $35 for nickel slides.

P210-8-9

This variation has adjustable target sights, select wood grips, lateral magazine catch, blued sandblasted finish, and adjustable trigger stop. Heavy frame. Barrel length is 4.8". Weight is about 37 oz.

NIB	Exc.	V.G.	Good	Fair	Poor
4275	3500	2750	2000	1000	500

P210-6-9

This variation has adjustable target sights, wood grips, target grade trigger, and blued sandblasted finish. Barrel length is 4.8". Weight is about 32 oz.

NIB	Exc.	V.G.	Good	Fair	Poor
2695	2000	1750	1400	800	500

P210-5-9

This variation has extended 5.85" barrel with compensator, ribbed front frame grip, wood grip plates, adjustable target sights, and target trigger. Weight is about 34 oz.

NIB	Exc.	V.G.	Good	Fair	Poor
4000	3500	3000	2400	1000	500

P210-2-9

This variation is similar to the Swiss Army service pistol and has wood grip plates and standard fixed sights. Barrel length is 4.8". Weight is about 32 oz. **NOTE:** A .22 LR conversion is available for the P210-2/5/6 series but not the P210-8. Retail price is $1,400.00.

NIB	Exc.	V.G.	Good	Fair	Poor
2200	1900	1600	1250	700	300

P210-9-6S

This 9mm pistol is fitted with a heavy frame, target sights, wood grips, and U.S.-style magazine release. Introduced in 2004.

NIB	Exc.	V.G.	Good	Fair	Poor
3300	2950	2500	2000	1450	500

P210 Legend

An updated variation of the P210. Features include a side-mounted magazine release, improved and extended beavertail, black Nitron finish and a choice of fixed or adjustable sights. Available only in 9mm. Introduced in 2011. **NOTE:** Add $200 for adjustable sights.

NIB	Exc.	V.G.	Good	Fair	Poor
1950	1750	1500	1000	700	450

P220

This is a high-quality, double-action semi-automatic pistol chambered for .38 Super, .45 ACP, and 9mm Parabellum. It has a 4.41" barrel and fixed sights and features the de-cocking lever that was found originally on the Sauer Model 38H. There are two versions of this pistol—one with a bottom magazine release (commonly referred to as the European model) and the other with the release on the side (commonly referred to as the American model) as on the Model 1911 Colt. The frame is a lightweight alloy that is matte-finished and is available in either blue, nickel, or K-Kote finish with black plastic grips. The .45 ACP magazine capacity is 7 rounds and the pistol weighs 25.7 oz.; the .38 Super magazine capacity is 9 rounds and the pistol weighs 26.5 oz.; the 9mm magazine holds 9 rounds and the overall weight is 26.5 oz. This model was manufactured from 1976 and is still in production. The 9mm and .38 Super versions are no longer in production. The prices listed are for guns with a standard blue finish. **NOTE:** For the K-Kote finish add $40, for nickel slide add $40. Stainless steel add $100. In 2004 a blued version with tactical rail was offered.

NIB	Exc.	V.G.	Good	Fair	Poor
825	600	400	300	200	150

P220 .22

As above, chambered for the .22 LR cartridge.

NIB	Exc.	V.G.	Good	Fair	Poor
500	400	300	200	150	100

P220 ST

As above, chambered for the .45 ACP cartridge and features a stainless steel frame and slide with tactical rail. Also includes a SIGARMS tactical knife and aliminum carrying case. Weight is about 39 oz.

NIB	Exc.	V.G.	Good	Fair	Poor
875	700	550	425	300	150

P220 Sport

Introduced in 1999, this .45 ACP pistol is similar to the P220 with the addition of 5.5" barrel with stainless steel compensator. The frame and slide are stainless steel. Magazine capacity is 7 rounds. Weight is about 44 oz.

NIB	Exc.	V.G.	Good	Fair	Poor
1400	1250	1000	775	500	300

P220R SAO

An 8+1 or 10+1 capacity single-action semi-auto chambered for .45 ACP. Polymer grip and Nitron finish, 4.4" barrel, 30.4 oz., 5-lb. trigger. Picatinny rail. Introduced 2006.

NIB	Exc.	V.G.	Good	Fair	Poor
750	600	475	350	200	150

P220R DAK

Semi-auto with 8+1 or 10+1 capacity chambered for .45 ACP. Polymer grip and Nitron finish, 4.4" barrel, 30.4 oz., 7.5-lb. trigger. Picatinny rail. Introduced 2006.

NIB	Exc.	V.G.	Good	Fair	Poor
875	700	600	475	350	200

P220 SAS

An 8+1 capacity double-action semi-auto chambered for .45 ACP. Fixed sights, wood grips, 4.4" barrel, 30.4 oz., 6.5-lb. trigger. Introduced 2006.

NIB	Exc.	V.G.	Good	Fair	Poor
1000	875	725	600	400	200

P220 Carry SAS

An 8+1 capacity double-action semi-auto chambered for .45 ACP. Fixed sights, wood grips, 3.9" barrel, 30.4 oz., 6.5-lb. trigger. Introduced 2006.

NIB	Exc.	V.G.	Good	Fair	Poor
900	795	700	550	400	200

P220 Carry

An 8+1 or 10+1 capacity single/double-action semi-auto chambered for .45 ACP. Fixed sights, polymer grips, 3.9" barrel, 30.4 oz. Introduced 2006.

NIB	Exc.	V.G.	Good	Fair	Poor
875	725	600	450	350	200

P220R Equinox

An 8+1 or 10+1 capacity single/double-action semi-auto chambered for .45 ACP. Fixed sights, wood grips, 4.4" barrel, 30.4 oz. Introduced 2006.

NIB	Exc.	V.G.	Good	Fair	Poor
1200	1050	750	600	450	300

P220R Carry Equinox

An 8+1 or 10+1 capacity single/double-action semi-auto chambered for .45 ACP. Fixed sights, wood grips, 3.9" barrel, 30.4 oz. Introduced 2006.

NIB	Exc.	V.G.	Good	Fair	Poor
875	700	575	450	350	200

P220 Langdon Edition

This .45 ACP pistol, introduced in 2004, features a 4.4" barrel, Nill wood grips, fiber optic sight, competition rear sight, front serrations, short trigger and other special features. Two-tone finish. Magazine capacity is 8 rounds. Weight is about 41 oz. 500 manufactured.

NIB	Exc.	V.G.	Good	Fair	Poor
1300	1050	800	600	450	250

P220 Combat

Similar to P220 but with sand-colored alloy slide and steel frame. Threaded barrel for suppressor. Capacity 8+1 or 10+1. Designed for SOCOM sidearm trials. Introduced in 2007.

NIB	Exc.	V.G.	Good	Fair	Poor
1100	950	750	600	400	200

P220 Match

Similar to P220 but with 5-inch barrel and adjustable sights. Introduced 2007.

NIB	Exc.	V.G.	Good	Fair	Poor
950	800	675	500	300	150

P220 Super Match

Super-accurized version of P220 Match with single-action-only trigger, beavertail safety and custom wood grips. Limited edition.

NIB	Exc.	V.G.	Good	Fair	Poor
1200	975	850	600	400	200

P220 Compact

Similar to P220 but with 3.9-inch barrel and 6+1 capacity. Single-action-only or single-/double-action. Various finishes, grip and sight options.

NIB	Exc.	V.G.	Good	Fair	Poor
950	800	675	500	375	200

P220 Elite

Similar to P220 but with SIG's new Short Reset Trigger or SRT. Beavertail safety, front cocking serrations, front strap checkering, SIGLITE\xa8 Night Sights and custom wood grips. Introduced in 2008. Also available in single action-only model.

NIB	Exc.	V.G.	Good	Fair	Poor
950	800	675	500	375	200

P220 Elite Stainless

Similar to above but in stainless. Introduced 2008.

NIB	Exc.	V.G.	Good	Fair	Poor
1250	1100	875	650	450	200

P220 Carry Elite Stainless

Compact version of above with 3.9-inch barrel; chambered in .45 ACP with 8-round capacity. Introduced 2008.

NIB	Exc.	V.G.	Good	Fair	Poor
1250	1100	875	650	450	200

P220 Platinum Elite

Fine-tuned, enhanced version of P220 Elite with front cocking serrations, front strap checkering, SIGLITE Adjustable Combat Night Sights and custom aluminum grips.

NIB	Exc.	V.G.	Good	Fair	Poor
1000	825	700	550	400	200

P224

Sub-compact variation of the P220/229 series with double-stack magazine, steel slide, alloy frame, black wood grips and Siglite night sights. In 9mm, .357 Sig or .40 S&W. Available with DA/SA or DAK trigger. Introduced in 2012

NIB	Exc.	V.G.	Good	Fair	Poor
1000	875	675	500	400	250

P225

This is similar to the Model P220 except that it is chambered for 9mm cartridge. It is a more compact pistol, with a 3.86" barrel. It has an 8-shot detachable magazine and adjustable sights. The finish is matte blue, K-Kote, or electroless nickel plate with black plastic grips.The overall length is 7.1" with an overall height of 5.2". The pistol weighs 26.1 oz. No longer in production. **NOTE:** For K-Kote finish add $70. For nickel slide add $70.

NIB	Exc.	V.G.	Good	Fair	Poor
625	575	500	400	200	150

P225 Limited

This 9mm 3.9" model features a Novak low-carry rear sight, three magazines, SIG-Sauer range bag. Introduced in 2004. Weight is about 26 oz.

NIB	Exc.	V.G.	Good	Fair	Poor
800	625	500	395	275	150

P226

This model is a full size, high-capacity pistol with a 4.41" barrel chambered for the 9mm or .40 S&W cartridge. In 1996 this model was also available chambered for the .357 SIG cartridge. It is available with a 15- or 20-round detachable magazine and high-contrast sights. It is either blued, electroless nickel plated, or has a polymer finish known as K-Kote. Overall length is 7.7" and overall height is 5.5". The pistol weighs 26.5 oz. This model was introduced in 1983. Add $50 for K-Kote finish and $50 for nickel slide. In 2003 this pistol was available with an integral rail system on the frame. In 2004 this pistol was offered with optional Crimson Trace laser grips. **NOTE:** Add $125 for Crimson Trace laser grips.

NIB	Exc.	V.G.	Good	Fair	Poor
825	600	550	450	300	200

P226BR .22

Similar to above but in .22 LR. **NOTE:** Add $125 for Crimson Trace laser grips.

NIB	Exc.	V.G.	Good	Fair	Poor
550	475	350	250	175	100

P226 Navy Seal

This special limited edition 9mm pistol is fitted with a 4.4" barrel and special serial numbers from "nsw0001" and above. Black finish.

NIB	Exc.	V.G.	Good	Fair	Poor
1400	900	750	550	400	300

P226 ST

Similar to P226 but with stainless steel frame and slide. Offered in 9mm, .40 S&W, and .357 SIG. Barrel length is 4.4". Magazine capacity is 10 rounds. Weight is about 39 oz. Introduced in 2002.

NIB	Exc.	V.G.	Good	Fair	Poor
1000	850	700	575	400	200

P226 Sport Stock

Introduced in 2002 this 9mm pistol features a heavy match barrel and adjustable rear sight. Hand tuned. Specifications are the same as the P226 ST. Available by special order only.

NIB	Exc.	V.G.	Good	Fair	Poor
1600	1450	1200	950	700	300

P226 Sport

Introduced in 2001 this model is similar to the other SIG Sport models and is chambered for the 9mm Luger cartridge. Stainless steel slide and frame with adjustable target sights and competition barrel weight.

NIB	Exc.	V.G.	Good	Fair	Poor
1350	1175	1000	850	700	300

JP226 Jubilee Pistol

This variation is a special limited edition of the P226. Each gun carries a special serial number prefixed JP. The grips are hand carved select European walnut. The slide and frame are covered with solid gold wire inlays, while the trigger, hammer, decocking lever, slide catch lever, and magazine catch are all gold plated. Each pistol comes in a custom fitted hard case of full leather. This pistol is no longer imported into the U.S. Fewer than 250 were imported between 1991 and 1992.

NIB	Exc.	V.G.	Good	Fair	Poor
1795	1500	1200	900	700	400

P226 ST

This .40 caliber model, introduced in 2004, features a reverse two-tone finish, 3-dot sights, and Hogue rubber grips. Weight is about 31 oz. Magazine capacity is 10 rounds.

NIB	Exc.	V.G.	Good	Fair	Poor
900	775	600	450	300	200

P226R DAK

Introduced in 2005 this model features double action only DAK trigger system with double strike capability. Chambered for the 9mm, .357 SIG, or .40 S&W cartridge with a 4.4" barrel. Fixed sights. Magazine capacity is 10, 12, or 15 rounds depending on caliber. Weight is about 32 oz. for 9mm and 34 oz. for .357 SIG or .40 S&W models.

NIB	Exc.	V.G.	Good	Fair	Poor
900	775	600	450	300	200

P226 X-Five

This single action model is chambered for the 9mm or .40 S&W cartridge and fitted with a 5" barrel. Adjustable rear sight and adjustable trigger pull. Slide has front cocking serrations. Checkered wood Null grips. Magazine capacity is 19 rounds for the 9mm and 14 rounds for the .40 S&W. Stainless steel finish. Weight is about 47 oz.

NIB	Exc.	V.G.	Good	Fair	Poor
1700	1525	1275	900	550	300

P226 Tactical

This 9mm pistol has a 4.98" extended threaded barrel. Fixed sights. Alloy frame. Magazine capacity is 15 rounds. Weight is about 32 oz. Black finish. Ellett Brothers exclusive. Introduced in 2005.

NIB	Exc.	V.G.	Good	Fair	Poor
900	795	600	450	300	150

P226 SAS

Double-action semi-auto with 12+1 capacity chambered for .40 S&W. Fixed sights, wood grips, 4.4" barrel, 34 oz., 6.5-lb. trigger. Introduced 2006.

NIB	Exc.	V.G.	Good	Fair	Poor
875	750	600	475	300	150

P226R Equinox

An 10+1 or 12+1 capacity single/double-action semi-auto chambered for .40 S&W. Fixed sights, wood grips, 4.4" barrel, 34 oz. Introduced 2006.

NIB	Exc.	V.G.	Good	Fair	Poor
1175	1025	875	700	550	350

P226 SCT

An all black, Nitron finished P226 featuring front cocking serrations, a SIGLITE rear night sight, a TRUGLO tritium fiber optic front sight and comes with four newly designed 20-round magazines for the 9mm version or four 15-round magazines for the .40S&W version.

NIB	Exc.	V.G.	Good	Fair	Poor
950	825	700	575	400	200

P226 Elite

Introduced 2008. Similar to P226 but with redesigned short-reset trigger and improved ergonomics. Chambered in 9mm, .40 S&W and .357 SIG. Model P226 Enhanced Elite has same features as P226 Elite with the addition of ergonomic one-piece reduced-reach polymer grips.

NIB	Exc.	V.G.	Good	Fair	Poor
1050	900	825	675	450	250

P226 Elite Stainless

Similar to above but in stainless steel.

NIB	Exc.	V.G.	Good	Fair	Poor
1100	1000	900	750	475	275

P226 Platinum Elite

Fine-tuned, enhanced version of P226 Elite with front cocking serrations, front strap checkering, SIGLITE Adjustable Combat Night Sights and custom aluminum grips.

NIB	Exc.	V.G.	Good	Fair	Poor
1250	1175	950	775	500	300

Mosquito

This model is essentially a P226 reduced to 90 percent of its original size. Double action/single action trigger and fitted with a 3.98" barrel chambered for the .22 Long Rifle cartridge. Polymer frame with Picatinny rail. Fixed sights. Magazine capacity is 10 rounds. Weight is about 24.5 oz. Black finish. Introduced in 2005.

NIB	Exc.	V.G.	Good	Fair	Poor
325	300	250	200	150	100

P228

This model is a compact version of the P226 fitted with a 3.86" barrel and chambered for the 9mm cartridge. Like the P 226 it is available in blue, K-Kote, or nickel finish with black grips. Overall length is 7.1" and overall height is 5.4". Pistol weighs 26.1 oz. No longer in production. **NOTE:** For K-Kote finish add $50 and for nickel slide add $50.

NIB	Exc.	V.G.	Good	Fair	Poor
725	600	475	350	200	150

P228 Limited (New Model)

Reintroduced in 2004 in a limited edition, this 9mm pistol features a Hi-Viz fiber optic front sight and 2-dot rear sight. One 15-round pre-ban magazine magazine included. Weight is about 26 oz.

NIB	Exc.	V.G.	Good	Fair	Poor
800	675	550	400	250	150

P229

This model is similar to the P228 except that it is chambered for the .40 S&W cartridge and has a blackened stainless steel slide and lightweight aluminum alloy frame. The slide is slightly larger to accommodate the more powerful cartridge. In 1996 the 9mm chamber was also offered in this model. Its overall length is 7.1" and overall height is 5.4". Introduced in 1992. The pistol weighs 27.54 oz. and has a magazine capacity of 12 rounds. In 1994 the company introduced a new caliber for this model; the .357 SIG developed by Federal. Magazine capacity is 12 rounds.

NIB	Exc.	V.G.	Good	Fair	Poor
800	675	550	400	250	150

P229 Nickel

Same as the standard P229 but with full nickel finish over a stainless steel slide and alloy frame. Weight is about 27.5 oz. Introduced in 1998.

NIB	Exc.	V.G.	Good	Fair	Poor
850	525	600	450	275	175

P229 Stainless

Introduced in 2005, has all the same features as the standard P229 except for the stainless steel slide and frame. Weight is about 41 oz. Magazine capacity is 12 rounds.

NIB	Exc.	V.G.	Good	Fair	Poor
900	775	600	475	300	150

P229 Sport

Chambered for the .357 SIG cartridge this model is fitted with a 4.8" barrel with a muzzle compensator. Adjustable target sights. Both frame and slide are stainless steel. Magazine capacity is 10 rounds. Weight is approximately 41 oz. Introduced in 1998.

NIB	Exc.	V.G.	Good	Fair	Poor
1500	1350	1175	950	600	400

P229 Limited

This .40 S&W pistol features a 3.9" barrel with fixed sights. Stainless steel slide with Nitron finish. Scroll engraving on top of slide, high polished 24 kt gold accents on trigger, hammer, magazine catch, and grip screws. Hardwood grips.

NIB	Exc.	V.G.	Good	Fair	Poor
950	825	675	500	350	200

P229 Combo

This pistol is chambered for the .40 S&W cartridge and fitted with a 3.9" barrel. Fixed sights. Black Nitron finish. A spare barrel chambered for the .357 SIG is included. Magazine capacity is 10 rounds. Weight is about 30 oz. Introduced in 2004.

NIB	Exc.	V.G.	Good	Fair	Poor
900	775	625	450	300	175

P229 Elite

The P229 Elite features an ergonomic beavertail grip, front cocking serrations, front strap checkering, SIGLITE Night Sights, custom wood grips and the new Short Reset Trigger or SRT. Available in 9mm and .40 S&W. Model P229 Enhanced Elite has same features as P229 Elite with the addition of ergonomic one-piece reduced-reach polymer grips.

NIB	Exc.	V.G.	Good	Fair	Poor
1100	900	825	675	450	250

P229 Platinum Elite

Fine-tuned, enhanced version of P229 Elite with front cocking serrations, front strap checkering, SIGLITE Adjustable Combat Night Sights and custom aluminum grips.

NIB	Exc.	V.G.	Good	Fair	Poor
1100	900	800	695	475	300

1911 C3

1911-style 6+1 autoloader in .45 ACP. 4-2/4-inch barrel, alloy frame. Introduced in 2008.

NIB	Exc.	V.G.	Good	Fair	Poor
900	775	600	475	300	150

1911 Platinum Elite

1911-style 8+1 autoloader in .45 ACP. 5-inch barrel, Nitron frame, aluminum grips. Introduced in 2008.

NIB	Exc.	V.G.	Good	Fair	Poor
1100	950	800	675	500	300

1911 Platinum Elite Carry

Compact version of the above with 4.5-inch barrel. Introduced in 2008.

NIB	Exc.	V.G.	Good	Fair	Poor
1250	1025	875	750	575	350

1911-22

Same dimensions as standard 1911 pistol. Caliber .22 LR, alloy frame and slide, 10-round magazine, blowback operated, extended thumb safety, extended beavertail grip safety, magazine disconnect safety, skeletonized hammer and trigger. Weight: 18 ounces, Nitron finish.

NIB	Exc.	V.G.	Good	Fair	Poor
340	285	235	200	165	100

1911 Scorpion

Caliber .45 ACP, stainless steel slide and frame, 8-round magazine, extended thumb safety, extended beavertail grip safety, skeletonized hammer and flat trigger, checkered front strap and mainspring housing, Low-Mount night sights and accessory rail. Frame and slide has Cerkote desert tan finish, grips are Hogue G10 Magwell with Piranha texture.

NIB	Exc.	V.G.	Good	Fair	Poor
975	850	700	500	300	150

Model GSR

This .45 ACP pistol was introduced in 2004. Fitted with a 5" barrel. Single-action only. It is offered with white stainless steel frame and slide or blued frame and slide. Also offered with black Nitron finish. Tac rail standard. Hand fitted. Magazine capacity is 8 rounds. Weight is about 39 oz.

NIB	Exc.	V.G.	Good	Fair	Poor
775	650	500	375	250	150

REVOLUTION SERIES

Revolution

All-stainless frames and slides in four configurations. Novak Night Sights, Rose- or Diamond Wood custom grips. Stainless or Nitron finish. 8+1 capacity, 45 ACP, single-action, 5" barrel, 40.3 oz. Introduced 2006.

NIB	Exc.	V.G.	Good	Fair	Poor
900	775	600	475	300	150

Revolution Custom STX

Single-action .45 ACP stainless semi-auto with 8+1 capacity. Adjustable combat night sights and custom wood grip panels, 5" barrel, 40.6 oz. Introduced 2006.

NIB	Exc.	V.G.	Good	Fair	Poor
1100	950	800	675	500	300

Revolution TTT

Stainless semi-auto with 8+1 capacity. Single-action .45 ACP. Adjustable combat night sights and custom wood grip panels, 5" barrel, 40.3 oz. Introduced 2006.

NIB	Exc.	V.G.	Good	Fair	Poor
1000	850	675	575	425	300

Revolution XO

Single-action .45 ACP stainless semi-auto with 8+1 capacity. Polymer grip panels. 8.65" LOA, 5" barrel, 40.3 oz. Introduced 2006.

NIB	Exc.	V.G.	Good	Fair	Poor
900	775	600	475	300	150

Revolution Target

Single-action .45 ACP stainless semi-auto with 8+1 capacity. Adjustable target night sights. Custom wood grip panels, 5" barrel, 40.3 oz. Stainless or Nitron finish. Introduced 2006.

NIB	Exc.	V.G.	Good	Fair	Poor
950	825	650	495	325	150

Revolution Carry

Single-action .45 ACP stainless semi-auto with 8+1 capacity. Fixed sights. Custom wood grip panels, 4" barrel, 35.4 oz. Stainless or Nitron finish. Introduced 2006.

NIB	Exc.	V.G.	Good	Fair	Poor
900	775	600	475	300	150

Revolution Compact

Stainless semi-auto single-action .45 ACP with 6+1 capacity. Fixed sights. Custom wood grip panels, 4" barrel, 30.3 oz. Stainless or Nitron finish. Introduced 2006.

NIB	Exc.	V.G.	Good	Fair	Poor
950	825	650	495	325	150

Revolution Compact SAS

Dehorned version of Revolution Compact.

NIB	Exc.	V.G.	Good	Fair	Poor
950	825	650	495	325	150

Revolution Compact C3

Similar to Revolution Compact but with black anodized alloy frame and stainless or Nitron-finished slide.

NIB	Exc.	V.G.	Good	Fair	Poor
950	825	650	495	325	150

Revolution Custom Compact RCS

Stainless semi-auto single-action .45 ACP with 6+1 capacity. Fixed sights. Custom wood grip panels, 4" barrel, 30.3 oz. Stainless or Nitron finish. Introduced 2006.

NIB	Exc.	V.G.	Good	Fair	Poor
950	825	650	495	325	150

P229R DAK

Introduced in 2005 this model features double action only DAK trigger system with double strike capability. Chambered for the 9mm, .357 SIG, or .40 S&W cartridge with a 4.4" barrel. Fixed sights. Magazine capacity is 10, 12, or 15 rounds depending on caliber. Weight is about 32 oz. for 9mm and 34 oz. for .357 SIG or .40 S&W models.

NIB	Exc.	V.G.	Good	Fair	Poor
850	525	600	450	275	175

P229 SCT

All black, Nitron finished P229 featuring front cocking serrations, a SIGLITE rear night sight, a TRUGLO tritium fiber optic front sight and comes with four newly designed 17-round magazines for the 9mm version or four 14-round magazines for the .40S&W version.

NIB	Exc.	V.G.	Good	Fair	Poor
1100	950	800	675	500	300

P238

A compact .380 single-action with 1911-style controls, but no grip safety. Offered in many grip and finish variations. Ambidextrous safety available. **NOTE:** Add $100 for rosewood grips or Hogue rubber grips, $50 for ambidextrous safety.

NIB	Exc.	V.G.	Good	Fair	Poor
635	550	450	400	300	200

P938

A slightly larger version of the P238 and chambered in 9mm. Other features are similar to the P238. Available with several grip and finish options.

NIB	Exc.	V.G.	Good	Fair	Poor
700	620	515	450	350	225

P239

Introduced in 1996 this pistol is chambered for the 9mm, .40 S&W, or .357 SIG cartridge. It is double/single-action or double-action-only. The barrel is 3.6" long and the overall length is 6.6". Weight is 25 oz. It is fitted with a single column magazine with 7 rounds for the .357 SIG and 8 rounds for the 9mm. **NOTE:** All of the above SIG pistols from the P220 to the P239 are available with "SIGLITE" night sights. Add $80 for these optional sights.

NIB	Exc.	V.G.	Good	Fair	Poor
725	600	475	350	200	150

P239 Limited

This .40 S&W model features a rainbow titanium slide. Trigger, hammer, grip screws, and control levers also rainbow titanuim. Magazine capacity is 7 rounds. Weight is about 27 oz. Introduced in 2004.

NIB	Exc.	V.G.	Good	Fair	Poor
725	600	475	350	200	150

P230

This is a semi-automatic, compact, pocket-type pistol chambered for .22 LR, .32 ACP, .380 ACP, and 9mm Ultra. It has a 3.62" barrel and either a 10-, 8-, or 7-round magazine, depending on the caliber chambered. The pistol weighs between 16.2 oz. and 20.8 oz. The finish is blued or stainless, with black plastic grips; and it was manufactured from 1976. In 1996 a two-tone finish was offered. No longer in production. **NOTE:** For stainless steel finish add $85 and for stainless steel slide add $35.

NIB	Exc.	V.G.	Good	Fair	Poor
450	375	300	250	200	150

P232

An improved model of the P230. Incorporates numerous changes to improve function and reliability. Basic features, operation, and dimensions remain the same as the P230.

NIB	Exc.	V.G.	Good	Fair	Poor
450	375	300	250	200	150

P232 (1998 Model)

In 1998 this model has as standard features night sights and Hogue grips with an all stainless steel finish. Chambered for .380 ACP, the pistol has a 7-round magazine capacity. Weight is about 21 oz.

NIB	Exc.	V.G.	Good	Fair	Poor
500	375	300	250	200	150

P232 Limited

This .380 pistol features a black finish, night sights, and satin nickel accents. Hogue rubber grips with finger grooves. Magazine capacity is 7 rounds. Weight is about 28 oz. Introduced in 2004.

NIB	Exc.	V.G.	Good	Fair	Poor
575	450	375	250	200	100

P245 Compact

Introduced in 1999 this model is chambered for the .45 ACP cartridge. It is fitted with a 3.9" barrel. Magazine capacity is 6 rounds. Overall length is 7.3". Weight is about 28 oz. Available finishes are blue and K-Kote. SIGLITE night sights are also available.

NIB	Exc.	V.G.	Good	Fair	Poor
775	650	500	375	250	150

P245 Custom Shop

Introduced in 2004 this .45 ACP pistol is limited to 75 guns. It features a Teflon-impregnated nickel slide, frame, trigger, hammer, etc. Hand-tuned action. Target crowned barrel. Novak low-carry sights, limited edition markings. Weight is about 27 oz.

NIB	Exc.	V.G.	Good	Fair	Poor
2100	1700	1450	1000	600	350

P250 Compact

Introduced in 2008. A 9mm semiauto pistol of so-called "modular design" that enables the shooter to quickly remove the functional mechanism and place it into the polymer grip of his choice. This allows an immediate change in caliber and size; (subcompact, compact and full). And after any change the pistol delivers both outstanding accuracy and reliable functionality. Its modularity not only provides incredible ease of maintenance, but also provides a solution for accommodating different hand sizes— there are 6 different ergonomic combinations for each size, accomplished by changes in grip circumference and trigger style. Matte or duotone finish.

NIB	Exc.	V.G.	Good	Fair	Poor
650	525	450	375	300	150

P290

New micro-compact pistol for concealed carry. Caliber 9mm Parabellum, is double-action only with stainless steel slide, polymer frame, 6-round magazine, three-dot sights and removable grip panels. Weight is 20.5 ounces, barrel length 2.9-inches. Finish is Nitron or two-tone stainless. Available with detachable laser sight. **NOTE:** Add $70 for laser sight.

NIB	Exc.	V.G.	Good	Fair	Poor
650	550	465	400	325	150

SIG PRO SERIES

SP2340

Introduced in 1998 this model is chambered for the .357 SIG or .40 S&W cartridge. It is built on a polymer frame with accessory rails on the dust cover. Barrel length is 3.9". Standard finish is blue. Weight is about 28 oz. Comes with two sets of interchangeable grips and two 10-round magazines. Available in single-action/double-action or double-action-only.

NIB	Exc.	V.G.	Good	Fair	Poor
650	525	450	375	300	150

SP2009

Similar to the SP2340 but chambered for the 9mm cartridge. Weight is about 25 oz. Magazine capacity is 10 rounds.

NIB	Exc.	V.G.	Good	Fair	Poor
500	425	350	225	175	100

SP2022

Chambered for the 9mm, .357 SIG, or .40 S&W cartridges and fitted with a 3.85" barrel with fixed sights. Polymer frame. Black finish. Weight is about 27 to 30 oz. depending on caliber. Magazine capacity is 10 or 12 rounds depending on caliber.

NIB	Exc.	V.G.	Good	Fair	Poor
575	450	325	250	200	150

SHOTGUNS

Model SA3 Hunter

Introduced in 1997 this over/under shotgun is chambered for the 20 gauge shell and fitted with 26" or 28" barrels. It has single-selective trigger and automatic ejectors. The stock is figured walnut with pistol grip. The receiver is polished steel with engraved game scenes. Weight is approximately 6.8 lbs.

NIB	Exc.	V.G.	Good	Fair	Poor
1200	1050	750	600	400	300

Model SA3 Sporting

This 12 gauge over/under gun was introduced in 1998 and features a 28" or 29.5" barrel with wide 11mm rib and front and mid-target sights. Both barrels and action are blued. Walnut stock with pistol grip and recoil pad. Weight is about 7.3 lbs.

NIB	Exc.	V.G.	Good	Fair	Poor
1675	1250	1000	700	500	400

Model SA5 Sporting

Introduced in 1998 this 12 gauge is fitted with a choice of 28" or 29.5" barrels. Single-selective trigger and automatic ejectors are standard. Barrels are fitted with a 10mm rib. Receiver is polished steel with engraved clay target on each side. Weight is about 7.6 lbs.

NIB	Exc.	V.G.	Good	Fair	Poor
2500	2000	1500	1100	750	500

AURORA SERIES

These shotguns were first imported and introduced into the SIG product line in 2000. They are made in Italy by B. Rizzini. All the guns in this series are over/under guns.

Aurora TR Field Shotguns

All of the TR field guns are offered in 12, 20, and 28 gauge as well as .410 bore. All have single triggers and ejectors. Barrel lengths are 26" or 28". Weights vary from 7 lbs. for the 12 gauge to 6 lbs. for the .410. Select walnut stock with oil finish. Cut checkering of 20 lpi. Choke tubes on the 12 and 20 gauge models and fixed chokes on the 28 and .410 models.

TR 20U

This model features a boxlock action with case hardened frame. No engraving. Straight-grip stock.

NIB	Exc.	V.G.	Good	Fair	Poor
2000	1750	1475	1200	900	400

TR 20

This model features a boxlock action with nickel finish and no engraving. Pistol grip.

NIB	Exc.	V.G.	Good	Fair	Poor
1850	1500	1325	1000	750	300

TR 30

This model features a case hardened action with side plates. No engraving. Pistol grip.

NIB	Exc.	V.G.	Good	Fair	Poor
2225	1850	1550	1375	1000	400

TR 40 Silver

This model features a silver action with side plates with gold inlaid game scenes. Pistol grip.

Aurora TR 40 Silver

NIB	Exc.	V.G.	Good	Fair	Poor
2575	2100	1550	1200	950	450

TR 40 Gold

This features a case hardened action with side plates and gold inlaid game scenes. Pistol grip.

NIB	Exc.	V.G.	Good	Fair	Poor
2675	2000	1450	1100	800	500

New Englander

Introduced in 2000 jointly by SIG and L.L. Bean this over/under gun is chambered in 12 and 20 gauge with choice of 26" or 28" barrels. Single-selective trigger, auto ejectors, choke tubes all standard. L.L. Bean logo inlaid in gold on receiver. Select turkish walnut stock with oil finish. Prince of Wales-style pistol grip and rubber recoil pad.

NIB	Exc.	V.G.	Good	Fair	Poor
1995	1500	1200	900	700	350

TT 25 Competition

This model is offered in both 12 and 20 gauge with a choice of 28" to 32" barrels for the 12 gauge and 28" or 30" barrels for the 20 gauge. Choke tubes. Single-selective auto ejectors are standard. Wide competition vent rib. Pistol grip on select walnut stock with 20 lpi checkering. Weight for 12 gauge is about 7.25 lbs. while the 20 gauge weighs about 6.75 lbs.

NIB	Exc.	V.G.	Good	Fair	Poor
1995	1500	1200	900	700	350

TT45

Similar to the TT25 but with the addition of a case hardened receiver and side plates with engraving and gold inlay game scenes.

NIB	Exc.	V.G.	Good	Fair	Poor
3275	2795	2200	1775	1300	450

RIFLES

SIG AMT

This is a semi-automatic rifle chambered for .308 cartridge. Fitted with a 19" barrel and wooden buttstock and forearm. Folding bipod standard. Box magazine capacity is 5, 10, or 20 rounds. Weight is about 10 lbs. Built from 1960 to 1974.

Courtesy Rock Island Auction Company

NIB	Exc.	V.G.	Good	Fair	Poor
4500	3800	3100	2500	1500	1000

SIG PE-57

Similar to the above but chambered for the 7.5x55 Swiss cartridge.

NIB	Exc.	V.G.	Good	Fair	Poor
4500	3800	3000	2500	1500	1000

SIG 550

This semi-automatic rifle is chambered for .223 cartridge and fitted with a 18" barrel.

NIB	Exc.	V.G.	Good	Fair	Poor
9000	7000	5500	3000	1800	1000

SIG 551

Same as above but fitted with a 16" barrel.

NIB	Exc.	V.G.	Good	Fair	Poor
10500	9500	7500	4000	2000	1000

SSG 2000

This is a high-grade, bolt-action, sniping-type rifle chambered for .223, 7.5mm Swiss, .300 Weatherby Magnum, and .308 Winchester. It has a 24" barrel and was furnished without sights. It has a 4-round box magazine. The finish is matte blue with a thumbhole-style stippled walnut stock with an adjustable cheekpiece. This model was discontinued in 1986.

NIB	Exc.	V.G.	Good	Fair	Poor
8000	6000	3500	2700	1500	—

SSG 3000

Chambered for the .308 Win. cartridge this model is fitted with a 23.4" barrel and ambidextrous McMillian Tactical stock. Magazine capacity is 5 rounds. Overall length is 46.5", and approximate weight is 12 lbs. This model comes in three different packages.

Level I

Base model with no bipod or scope, but with carrying case.

NIB	Exc.	V.G.	Good	Fair	Poor
2550	2000	1600	1350	950	600

Level II

At this level a Leupold Vari-X III 3.5-10x40mm Deplex scope and Harris bipod with carrying case.

NIB	Exc.	V.G.	Good	Fair	Poor
3500	2750	2300	1700	1200	600

Level III

Rifle is supplied with a Leupold Mark 4 M1-10x40mm Mil-Dot Scope with Harris bipod and carrying case.

NIB	Exc.	V.G.	Good	Fair	Poor
4500	3500	2700	2400	1500	700

Conversion Kit—.22 LR

In 2001 a .22 caliber conversion was offered for the SSG 3000 rifle. The kit includes a heavy contured barrel, bolt, and 5-round magazine.

NIB	Exc.	V.G.	Good	Fair	Poor
750	—	—	—	—	—

Model SHR 970

Introduced in 1998 this bolt-action rifle is chambered for the .25-06 Rem., .270, .280 Rem., .30-06, or .308 cartridges. It has a 22" barrel and the receiver is drilled and tapped for scope mounts. Detachable box magazine. Stock is black synthetic or walnut. Barrels are interchangeable. Weight is about 7.2 lbs. **NOTE:** Add $30 for walnut stock.

NIB	Exc.	V.G.	Good	Fair	Poor
725	650	575	400	300	200

Model SHR 970 Magnum

Same as above but chambered for 7mm Rem. Mag or .300 Win. Mag. Barrel length is 24". Weight is about 7.4 lbs. **NOTE:** Add $30 for walnut stock.

NIB	Exc.	V.G.	Good	Fair	Poor
775	725	625	450	350	250

Model SHR 970 Tactical

This model was introduced in 2000 and features a McMillan stock, non-reflective metal coating, heavy fluted contoured barrel, integral muzzlebrake. The rifle is chambered for .308 Win. or .300 Win. Mag cartridges. Receiver is drilled and tapped for scope mount and the stock has a fitted rubber recoil pad.

NIB	Exc.	V.G.	Good	Fair	Poor
1400	1200	1000	775	600	400

Model 202 Standard

This bolt-action rifle features a choice of synthetic or Turkish walnut stock. Bolt is jeweled. Detachable 3-round box magazine. Offered in standard calibers from .22-250 to .30-06 and magnum calibers from 7mm Rem. Mag. to .375 H&H Mag. Barrel length is 24" for standard calibers and 26" for magnum calibers. Weight is about 7.5 lbs. depending on caliber.

NIB	Exc.	V.G.	Good	Fair	Poor
1650	1200	975	750	600	400

Model 202 Lightweight

This model features a black synthetic stock fluted barrel chambered for the .22-250, .243, .25-06, .270, or .30-05 calibers. Barrel length is 24". Magazine capacity is 3 rounds. Alloy receiver and quick change barrel system are standard. Weight is about 6.5 lbs. Introduced in 2001.

NIB	Exc.	V.G.	Good	Fair	Poor
1600	1150	925	700	550	350

Model 202 Varmint

This model is chambered for the .22-250, .243, or .25-06 cartridge. Fitted with a 26" fluted bull barrel. Stock is Turkish walnut with adjustable cheekpiece. Three-round detachable box magazine. Quick change barrel system. Weight is approximately 9.5 lbs.

NIB	Exc.	V.G.	Good	Fair	Poor
1600	1150	925	700	550	350

Model 202 Supreme

This bolt-action model is chambered for .243, .25-06, 6.5x55 Swedish, .270 Win., .308 Win., or .30-06. It is fitted with a 24" barrel with choice of synthetic or walnut stock. Magazine capacity is 3 rounds. Weight is approximately 7.7 lbs. No sights. **NOTE:** Add $50 for walnut stock.

NIB	Exc.	V.G.	Good	Fair	Poor
1800	1650	1400	1100	800	400

Model 202 Supreme Magnum

As above but chambered for 7mm Rem. Mag, .300 Win. Mag, .300 Wby Mag., or .375 H&H Mag. Magazine capacity is 3 rounds. Choice of synthetic or walnut stock. Weight is about 8.4 lbs. **NOTE:** Add $50 for walnut stock.

NIB	Exc.	V.G.	Good	Fair	Poor
1875	1725	1475	1150	850	450

SIG 556

Generally similar to the SIG 556 but made in the USA. Chambered in 5.56 NATO. Collapsible stock, 16" mil-spec barrel, picatinny rail and all the trendy tactical goodies. Introduced 2006.

NIB	Exc.	V.G.	Good	Fair	Poor
1200	1000	850	750	500	400

SIG 556 SWAT

The SIG556 SWAT features a 16-inch military grade cold hammer forged barrel, chambered in 5.56mm NATO, with a twist rate of 1 in 7". High performance flash suppressor, vented tactical quad rail forearm machined from aircraft grade aluminum alloy and hard coat anodized for durability, quad rail with four picatinny rails, picatinny equipped receiver. The rifle comes standard with the flip-up combat front and rear sight system. The trigger housing is machined from an aircraft grade aluminum alloy forging with a hard-coat anodized finish designed to survive extreme conditions. The rifle comes equipped with a smooth two-stage trigger, ambidextrous safety and is designed to accept standard AR magazines.

NIB	Exc.	V.G.	Good	Fair	Poor
1500	1300	1100	950	875	600

SIG 556 HOLO

Similar to above but with holographic sight and without quad rail and other features.

NIB	Exc.	V.G.	Good	Fair	Poor
1550	1350	1100	900	800	400

SIG 556 DMR

A sniper version of the SIG 556 SWAT with bipod and other accurizing features.

NIB	Exc.	V.G.	Good	Fair	Poor
1650	1500	1350	1000	850	500

SIG-Sauer SIG516 Gas Piston Rifle

AR-style rifle chambered in 5.56 NATO. Features include 14.5", 16", 18" or 20" chrome-lined barrel; free-floating, aluminum quad rail fore-end with four M1913 Picatinny rails; threaded muzzle with a standard (0.5x28TPI) pattern; aluminum upper and lower receiver is machined; black anodized finish; 30-round magazine; flattop upper; various configurations available.

NIB	Exc.	V.G.	Good	Fair	Poor
1100	950	800	650	500	300

SIG-Sauer SIG716 Tactical Patrol Rifle

AR-10 type rifle chambered in 7.62 NATO/.308 Winchester. Features include gas-piston operation with 3 round-position (4-position optional) gas valve; 16", 18" or 20" chrome-lined barrel with threaded muzzle and nitride finish; free-floating aluminum quad rail fore-end with four M1913 Picatinny rails; telescoping buttstock; lower receiver is machined from a 7075-T6 Aircraft grade aluminum forging; upper receiver, machined from 7075-T6 aircraft grade aluminum with integral M1913 Picatinny rail.

NIB	Exc.	V.G.	Good	Fair	Poor
1900	1750	1500	1250	900	450

Sauer SSG 3000

Imported by SIGARMS. A 5-round bolt action sniper rifle chambered in .308 Winchester. The heavy-contoured, hammer forged barrel is fitted with a flash suppressor/muzzle brake to provide greater accuracy with reduced muzzle signature. Both the barrel and the receiver feature a black oxide finish to eliminate glare. The short, smooth 60 degree bolt throw allows for rapid operation and, like the safety release, the bolt action is quiet. A massive six-lug lockup system is used to give the SSG 3000 greater strength and accuracy. Pistol grip and fully adjustable stock to give the shooter a custom fit. The trigger is adjustable for trigger position, trigger take up, let-off point, and trigger pull weight. The receiver on the SSG 3000 features a dovetail that will accept a wide range of sighting systems, including a factory available M1913 rail.

NIB	Exc.	V.G.	Good	Fair	Poor
4000	3550	2700	2000	1200	600

SIG 50

Bolt-action tactical rifle chambered for the .50 BMG cartridge. Designed for ultra long-range tactical applications. Match-grade trigger that is set for 3-1/2 pounds. Stock has adjustable cheekpiece, pistol grip and length of pull. Barrel is 29-inch heavy fluted with muzzle brake. Full length machined rails allow the mounting of accessories. Fluted bolt, heavy duty steel bipod, Duracoat coating. Weight is 23.5 pounds. Introduced in 2011.

NIB	Exc.	V.G.	Good	Fair	Poor
8300	7400	6350	—	—	—

SILMA
Italy

STANDARD MODELS

Model 70 EJ

This over/under gun is chambered for the 12 or 20 gauge shell with 28" vent rib barrels with choke tubes. Single-selective trigger and auto ejectors. Checkered walnut stock. Weight for 12 gauge is about 7.6 lbs. and for the 20 gauge about 6.9 lbs. Silver engraved receiver.

12 Gauge

NIB	Exc.	V.G.	Good	Fair	Poor
950	800	675	495	300	200

20 Gauge

NIB	Exc.	V.G.	Good	Fair	Poor
875	725	600	400	265	150

DELUXE MODELS

Model 70 EJ

This model is chambered for the 12, 20, 28, or .410 shell and fitted with 28" vent rib barrels. Checkered select walnut stock with deluxe engraved receiver. Weights are 7.6 lbs. for 12 gauge and 6.9 lbs. for smaller gauges.

12 Gauge

NIB	Exc.	V.G.	Good	Fair	Poor
1050	750	600	475	350	200

20 Gauge

NIB	Exc.	V.G.	Good	Fair	Poor
950	700	550	425	300	175

28 and .410 Gauge

NIB	Exc.	V.G.	Good	Fair	Poor
1075	800	650	525	400	250

Superlight

This model is offered in 12 or 20 gauge with 28" barrels with choke tubes. Checkered select walnut stock. Receiver is made from alloy steel. Weight for 12 gauge is about 6.7 lbs. and about 6.3 lbs. for the 20 gauge.

NIB	Exc.	V.G.	Good	Fair	Poor
1100	825	675	550	425	275

Clays Model

This model is designed for sporting clays and is chambered for the 12 gauge 3" shell. Fitted with a 28" barrel with choke tubes and wide ventilated rib. Checkered select walnut stock.

NIB	Exc.	V.G.	Good	Fair	Poor
1300	975	775	625	500	400

SIMPLEX
Unknown

Simplex

A German design based on the Bergmann-Mars pistol. An 8mm caliber semi-automatic pistol with a 2.6" barrel and a front mounted 5-round magazine. Blued with hard rubber grips having the trade name "Simplex" cast in them. Manufactured from approximately 1901 to around 1906. Early samples may have come from Germany and later pistols are thought to have been produced in Belgium.

NIB	Exc.	V.G.	Good	Fair	Poor
—	1650	1050	550	400	200

SIMPSON, R. J.
New York, New York

Pocket Pistol

A .41 caliber single-shot percussion pocket pistol with a 2.5" barrel, German silver mounts and walnut stock. Manufactured during the 1850s and 1860s.

NIB	Exc.	V.G.	Good	Fair	Poor
—	—	2400	1750	700	300

SIMSON & COMPANY
Suhl, Germany

See—Luger

NOTE: The models listed and pictured are taken from a mid-1930s Simson catalog. Because the company was Jewish-owned the Nazis took control in the mid-1930s changing the name to "Berlin Suhler Waffen." Prices are estimates.

SHOTGUNS

Model 235

Side-by-side shotgun chambered for 12 or 16 gauge with Anson & Deely action. Scalloped frame with scroll engraving. Walnut stock with pistol grip. Double triggers.

Courtesy Jim Cate

NIB	Exc.	V.G.	Good	Fair	Poor
—	900	700	550	400	350

Model 73

Similar to the above model but with more scroll engraving coverage.

Courtesy Jim Cate

NIB	Exc.	V.G.	Good	Fair	Poor
—	950	750	600	400	350

Model 74

This model features deep cut game scene engraving. Select walnut stock with fine-line checkering.

Courtesy Jim Cate

NIB	Exc.	V.G.	Good	Fair	Poor
—	1100	800	600	450	350

Model 74E

Same as above but with automatic ejectors.

Courtesy Jim Cate

NIB	Exc.	V.G.	Good	Fair	Poor
—	1200	850	650	450	350

Model 76

This side-by-side model is fitted with game scene engraved side plates and offered in 12 or 16 gauge.

Courtesy Jim Cate

NIB	Exc.	V.G.	Good	Fair	Poor
—	1400	1100	800	550	400

Model 76E

As above but with automatic ejectors.

Courtesy Jim Cate

NIB	Exc.	V.G.	Good	Fair	Poor
—	1500	1200	850	550	400

PISTOLS

Model 1922

A 6.35mm semi-automatic pistol with a 2" barrel and 6-shot magazine. The slide marked "Selbstlade Pistole Simson DRP" and "Waffenfabrik Simson & Co Suhl." Blued, with black plastic grips.

NIB	Exc.	V.G.	Good	Fair	Poor
—	600	475	400	300	100

Model 1927

Similar to the above, with a slimmer frame stamped with the trademark of three overlapping triangles having the letter "S" enclosed.

NIB	Exc.	V.G.	Good	Fair	Poor
—	600	475	400	300	100

SIRKIS INDUSTRIES, LTD.
Ramat-Gan, Israel

SD9

A 9mm double-action semi-automatic pistol with a 3" barrel, fixed sights and 7-shot magazine. Blued with plastic grips. Also known as the Sardius.

NIB	Exc.	V.G.	Good	Fair	Poor
—	325	275	225	175	100

Model 35 Match Rifle

A .22 caliber single-shot bolt-action rifle with a 26" free floating barrel, adjustable rear sight and adjustable trigger. Blued with a walnut stock.

NIB	Exc.	V.G.	Good	Fair	Poor
—	600	550	500	400	200

Model 36 Sniper's Rifle

A 7.62x54mm caliber semi-automatic rifle with a 22" barrel. Matte blued with a composition stock.

NIB	Exc.	V.G.	Good	Fair	Poor
—	675	600	550	450	200

SKB ARMS COMPANY
Tokyo, Japan

SIDE-BY-SIDE GUNS

Model 100

A boxlock 12 or 20 gauge double-barrel shotgun with 25" to 30" barrels, single-selective trigger and automatic ejectors. Blued with a walnut stock. Imported prior to 1981. Discontinued.

NIB	Exc.	V.G.	Good	Fair	Poor
1200	1000	900	800	550	400

Model 150

As above, with some engraving, a beavertail forearm and a figured walnut stock. Imported from 1972 to 1974.

NIB	Exc.	V.G.	Good	Fair	Poor
1250	1000	900	800	550	400

Model 200

As above, with a French case hardened and scalloped receiver. Discontinued.

NIB	Exc.	V.G.	Good	Fair	Poor
1300	1150	900	675	500	400

Model 200E

As above, with an English-style stock. Imported prior to 1989.

NIB	Exc.	V.G.	Good	Fair	Poor
1350	1200	850	650	450	350

Model 280

Same as the Model 200 but fitted with a straight grip stock. Discontinued.

NIB	Exc.	V.G.	Good	Fair	Poor
1400	1200	850	650	450	350

Model 300

As above, with more engraving and a figured walnut stock. Discontinued.

NIB	Exc.	V.G.	Good	Fair	Poor
1450	1250	900	700	475	350

Model 385

Similar to the Model 300 but chambered for the 12, 20 or 28 gauge shell. Scroll engraved frame with semi-fancy walnut. Pistol-grip or straight-grip stock. Limited quantities imported. Weight is approximately 7 lbs. depending on barrel length and gauge. Discontinued.

NIB	Exc.	V.G.	Good	Fair	Poor
1800	1600	1475	1100	700	400

Model 385 2 Barrel Set

Same as above but with a 20 and 28 gauge set of barrels in either 26" or 28". Discontinued.

NIB	Exc.	V.G.	Good	Fair	Poor
2600	2500	2250	1300	900	500

Model 385 Sporting Clays

This model is chambered for 12, 20, or 28 gauge and fitted with a 28" barrel. Pistol-grip stock. Weight is about 7 lbs. depending on gauge. Discontinued. **NOTE:** For extra set of 20 or 28 gauge barrels add $900.

NIB	Exc.	V.G.	Good	Fair	Poor
1850	1750	1475	1100	700	400

Model 400E

As above, with engraved false sideplates and an English-style stock. Imported prior to 1990.

NIB	Exc.	V.G.	Good	Fair	Poor
1750	1600	1400	900	700	400

Model 480E

As above, with a French case hardened receiver and more finely figured walnut stocks. Discontinued.

NIB	Exc.	V.G.	Good	Fair	Poor
1800	1650	1475	1100	700	400

Model 485

This model features an engraved sideplate boxlock action chambered for 12, 20, or 28 gauge with 26" or 28" barrels. Choke tubes. Weight is approximately 7.7 lbs. Discontinued.

NIB	Exc.	V.G.	Good	Fair	Poor
2750	2100	1500	900	650	300

Model 485 2 Barrel Set

Same as above but with an extra set of barrels in 20/28 gauge combinations with 26" barrels. Choice of pistol-grip or straight-grip stock. Discontinued.

NIB	Exc.	V.G.	Good	Fair	Poor
3900	3000	1850	1500	1200	500

OVER/UNDER GUNS

MODEL 85TSS SERIES

This series, introduced in 2004, features a low-profile boxlock action fitted with an inertia trigger (12 and 20 gauge), mechanical on 28 and .410 bore. Single-selective trigger with manual safety. Silver nitride finish. Barrels have automatic ejectors, ventilated rib and choke tubes. Pigeon porting is optional. Stocks are American walnut with matte finish and fitted with Pachmayr recoil pad. Adjustable comb stock is optional.

Model 85TSS Sporting Clays

Chambered for the 12, 20, 28 gauge, and .410 bore, this model features a choice of 28", 30", or 32" barrels on the 12 gauge guns and 28" or 30" barrels on the small bore guns. Choke tubes. Choice of fixed or adjustable comb. Choice of multiple barrel sets. Weight on 12 gauge guns is about 8.5 lbs. depending on barrel length and 7.5 lbs. on the smaller bore guns. **NOTE:** Add $175 for adjustable comb, $1,200 for two-barrel sets and $2,800 for three-barrel 20, 28 and .410 set.

NIB	Exc.	V.G.	Good	Fair	Poor
1875	1600	1425	1075	800	450

Model 85TSS Trap

This 12 gauge 3" trap model is fitted with a choice of 30" or 32" backbored barrels with adjustable 12mm rib. Choice of fixed or adjustable comb with or without Monte Carlo. Weight is about 8.75 lbs. **NOTE:** Add $175 for adjustable comb.

NIB	Exc.	V.G.	Good	Fair	Poor
1875	1600	1425	1075	800	450

Model 85TSS Trap Unsingle

This model is a single barrel trap gun with choice of 32" or 34" adjustable rib barrel with choice of standard comb or Monte Carlo with or without adjustable comb. Weight is about 9 lbs. **NOTE:** Add $175 for adjustable comb.

NIB	Exc.	V.G.	Good	Fair	Poor
2100	1900	1625	1250	1000	500

Model 85TSS Trap Unsingle Combo

This model features a 32" or 34" single barrel and 30" or 32" over/under barrels. Barrel rib is adjustable. Choice of Monte Carlo or standard stock with or without adjustable comb. **NOTE:** Add $175 for adjustable comb.

NIB	Exc.	V.G.	Good	Fair	Poor
3175	2500	2250	1875	1300	600

Model 85TSS Skeet

This model is offered in 12, 20, and 28 gauge as well as .410 bore. The 12 gauge model is offered with a choice of 28", 30" or 32" backbored barrels with 9.5mm rib. Small gauges are offered with a choice of 28" or 30" backbored barrels with 8.5mm rib. Weight for 12 gauge gun is about 8.35 lbs. and 7.5 lbs. for smaller gauges. Choice of fixed or adjustable comb. **NOTE:** Add $175 for adjustable comb. Add $2,800 for three-barrel set.

NIB	Exc.	V.G.	Good	Fair	Poor
2100	1900	1625	1250	1000	500

Model 500

A 12, 20, 28 gauge or .410 bore over/under shotgun with 26", 28" or 30" ventilated rib barrels. Blued with a walnut stock. Imported from 1966 to 1979.

NIB	Exc.	V.G.	Good	Fair	Poor
850	700	575	400	325	200

Model 505 Field

The 505 Series is also produced in sporting clays, trap and skeet configurations, which are valued at approximately 10 percent additional.

NIB	Exc.	V.G.	Good	Fair	Poor
1270	950	700	500	350	250

Model 505 3-Gauge Skeet Set

As above, with 3 sets of barrels.

NIB	Exc.	V.G.	Good	Fair	Poor
2500	1800	1400	975	650	650

Model 585

Similar to the Model 505 but offered in 12, 20, and 28 gauge and .410 bore as well. Barrel lengths are 26" or 28". Weight is about 7.25 lbs. for small bores and 8 lbs. for 12 gauge guns.

NIB	Exc.	V.G.	Good	Fair	Poor
1550	1200	950	650	400	300

Model 585 Gold Package

Has all of the features of the 585 series with the addition of a gold-plated trigger, gold-plated game scenes, and schnabel fore-end. Choice of blued or silver receiver.

NIB	Exc.	V.G.	Good	Fair	Poor
1600	1250	975	675	425	300

Model 585 Skeet

Offered in 12, 20, or 28 gauge as well as .410 bore with 28" barrels. Skeet stock and beavertail forearm. Black recoil pad. Weight in 12 gauge about 8 lbs.

NIB	Exc.	V.G.	Good	Fair	Poor
1600	1250	975	675	425	300

Model 585—3 Barrel Skeet Set

Fitted with 20, 28 gauge and .410 bore barrels. Skeet choked.

NIB	Exc.	V.G.	Good	Fair	Poor
2500	2250	1875	1300	600	400

Model 585—3 Barrel Skeet Set Gold Package

Same as above but with engraving and choice of silver or blued receiver.

NIB	Exc.	V.G.	Good	Fair	Poor
2600	2350	1875	675	600	400

Model 585 Youth/Ladies

This model is similar to the 585 but with a shortened length of pull to 13.5". Weight of 20 gauge model is approximately 6.6 lbs. Weight of 12 gauge is about 7.5 lbs.

NIB	Exc.	V.G.	Good	Fair	Poor
1525	1300	975	700	350	200

Model 585 Youth Gold Package

Same as above but with gold trigger, gold-plated game scenes, and schnabel forend. Choice of silver or blued receiver.

NIB	Exc.	V.G.	Good	Fair	Poor
1625	1375	1025	750	400	200

Model 585 Upland

Similar to the 585 series except for straight-grip stock. Offered in 12, 20, and 28 gauge all with 26" barrels. Weight for 12 gauge is about 7.75 lbs. and for 20 and 28 gauge about 6.75 lbs.

NIB	Exc.	V.G.	Good	Fair	Poor
1525	1300	975	700	350	200

Model 585 Upland Gold Package

This model has the additional gold package features of gold trigger, gold game scenes, and schnabel fore-end. Choice of silver or blued receiver.

NIB	Exc.	V.G.	Good	Fair	Poor
1600	1375	1025	750	350	225

Model 600

Similar to Model 585, with a silver-plated receiver.

NIB	Exc.	V.G.	Good	Fair	Poor
1000	875	650	500	350	200

Model 600 Magnum

As above, chambered for 3", 12 gauge cartridges. Imported from 1969 to 1972.

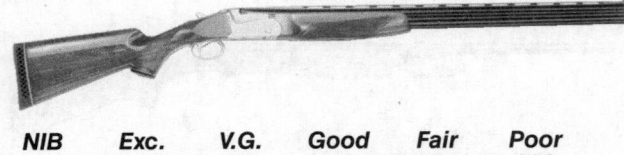

NIB	Exc.	V.G.	Good	Fair	Poor
—	900	675	525	375	200

Model 600 Trap Gun

As above, with 30" or 32" barrels trap choked, with a high comb walnut stock.

NIB	Exc.	V.G.	Good	Fair	Poor
1000	875	650	500	350	200

Model 600 Skeet Gun

As above, chambered for 12, 20, 28 or .410 bore cartridges with 26" or 28" barrels that are skeet choked.

NIB	Exc.	V.G.	Good	Fair	Poor
1000	875	650	500	350	200

Model 600 Skeet Combo Set

As above, with an extra set of three interchangeable barrels. Furnished with a carrying case.

NIB	Exc.	V.G.	Good	Fair	Poor
2900	2550	2100	1650	1200	600

Model 605

Similar to Model 600, with an engraved and French case hardened receiver. **NOTE:** The 605 Series is also available in trap or skeet configurations. The values are similar.

NIB	Exc.	V.G.	Good	Fair	Poor
1250	950	700	500	400	400

Model 605 3-Gauge Skeet Set

As above, with three extra sets of barrels.

NIB	Exc.	V.G.	Good	Fair	Poor
2900	2550	2100	1650	1200	600

Model 680E

Similar to the Model 600, with an engraved receiver and English-style stock. Imported from 1973 to 1976.

NIB	Exc.	V.G.	Good	Fair	Poor
1400	1100	850	600	500	250

Model 685

This over/under shotgun is offered in 12, 20, and 28 gauge as well as .410 bore. Barrel lengths are 26" or 28" with choke tubes. The engraved receiver has a silver finish with gold inlays. The walnut stock is semi-fancy.

NIB	Exc.	V.G.	Good	Fair	Poor
1400	1100	850	600	500	250

Model 700 Trap Gun

Similar to the Model 600 Trap, with a wider rib, additional engraving and a figured walnut stock. Imported from 1969 to 1975.

NIB	Exc.	V.G.	Good	Fair	Poor
1600	1250	975	675	425	300

Model 700 Skeet Gun

As above, with skeet chokes.

NIB	Exc.	V.G.	Good	Fair	Poor
1700	1350	1050	775	500	350

Model 785

Offered in 12, 20, and 28 gauge as well as .410 bore this over/under features 26" or 28" barrels with choke tubes, single trigger, ejectors, and checkered walnut stock. The silver receiver is scroll engraved. Weight is about 8 lbs. for 12 gauge and 7.25 lbs. for small bores.

NIB	Exc.	V.G.	Good	Fair	Poor
1800	1500	900	750	500	300

Model 785—2 Barrel Set

These two barrel sets are in combination 12/20, 20/28, and 28/.410 bore with 26" and 28" barrels.

NIB	Exc.	V.G.	Good	Fair	Poor
2900	2650	2200	1775	1200	600

Model 785 Sporting Clays

Chambered for 12, 20, and 28 gauge with barrels lengths from 28" to 32" in 12 gauge and 28" in 20 and 28 gauge. Recoil pad standard. **NOTE:** For Sporting Clays set add $900.

NIB	Exc.	V.G.	Good	Fair	Poor
2250	1750	1150	1400	900	500

Model 785 Skeet

Offered in 12, 20, 28, and .410 bore with 28" barrels. Recoil pad standard.

NIB	Exc.	V.G.	Good	Fair	Poor
2250	1750	1150	1400	900	500

Model 785 3-Gauge Skeet Set

This model furnished with 12, 20, and 28 gauge barrel all 28" in length. Weight is about 7.3 lbs. regardless of gauge.

NIB	Exc.	V.G.	Good	Fair	Poor
4400	3250	2500	1700	1200	600

Model 785 Trap

Offered in 12 gauge with or without Monte Carlo stock. Barrel length either 30" or 32". Ventilated recoil pad standard.

NIB	Exc.	V.G.	Good	Fair	Poor
2250	1750	1150	1400	900	500

Model 785 Trap Combo

Features a 30" or 32" over/under barrels with a single 32" or 34" barrel. Choice of standard stock or Monte Carlo.

NIB	Exc.	V.G.	Good	Fair	Poor
3050	2250	1250	100	700	375

Model 800 Trap Gun

As above, but with trap chokes and more engraving. Imported from 1969 to 1975.

NIB	Exc.	V.G.	Good	Fair	Poor
2000	1000	850	650	550	250

Model 800 Skeet Gun

As above, in 12 or 20 gauge with 26" or 28" skeet choked barrels. Imported from 1969 to 1975.

NIB	Exc.	V.G.	Good	Fair	Poor
2000	1000	850	650	550	250

Model 880 Crown Grade

A false sidelock 12, 20, 28 or .410 bore boxlock double-barrel shotgun with a single-selective trigger and automatic ejectors. The engraved sideplates and receiver are French case hardened, and the figured walnut stock is checkered. Imported prior to 1981.

NIB	Exc.	V.G.	Good	Fair	Poor
1900	1700	1350	1100	900	450

Model 885

A false sidelock 12, 20, 28 or .410 bore boxlock shotgun. Similar to the Model 800.

NIB	Exc.	V.G.	Good	Fair	Poor
1600	1250	1050	900	700	300

Model 5600

This over/under gun is offered in 12 gauge only in either trap or skeet configurations.

NIB	Exc.	V.G.	Good	Fair	Poor
875	775	650	500	400	200

Model 5700

Similar to the above but with light scroll engraving on the receiver and figured walnut stock.

NIB	Exc.	V.G.	Good	Fair	Poor
900	800	675	525	425	200

Model 5800

Similar to the Model 5600 but with more engraving coverage on the receiver and fancy walnut stock.

NIB	Exc.	V.G.	Good	Fair	Poor
950	800	700	550	450	175

Model 7300

A 12 or 20 gauge slide-action shotgun. Blued with a walnut stock. Imported prior to 1981.

NIB	Exc.	V.G.	Good	Fair	Poor
—	300	250	200	150	100

Model 7900

As above, but skeet choked.

NIB	Exc.	V.G.	Good	Fair	Poor
400	300	250	200	150	100

Model 300

A 12 or 20 gauge semi-automatic shotgun with 26", 28", or 30" barrels. Blued with a walnut stock. Imported from 1968 to 1972. **NOTE:** Ventilated rib barrel add 20 percent.

NIB	Exc.	V.G.	Good	Fair	Poor
—	450	395	350	300	200

Model 1300

A redesigned version of the Model 300 with a ventilated rib barrel and screw-in choke tubes. Imported since 1988.

NIB	Exc.	V.G.	Good	Fair	Poor
450	400	350	300	200	150

Model XL 900 MR

A 12 gauge, semi-automatic shotgun with 26" to 30" ventilated-rib barrels, and etched alloy receiver and checkered walnut stock. Imported prior to 1981.

NIB	Exc.	V.G.	Good	Fair	Poor
—	475	425	375	325	200

Model 1900

As above, but also chambered for 20 gauge shells and available with 22", 26", or 28" ventilated rib barrels and screw-in choke tubes. Blued with a walnut stock.

NIB	Exc.	V.G.	Good	Fair	Poor
500	425	375	300	250	175

Model 3000

Similar to the above, with a modified receiver design. Imported prior to 1990.

NIB	Exc.	V.G.	Good	Fair	Poor
—	475	400	350	250	150

SLOTTER & CO.
Philadelphia, Pennsylvania

Pocket Pistol

A .41 caliber percussion pocket pistol with a 2.5" to 3.5" barrel, German silver mounts and walnut stock. Marked "Slotter & Co. Phila." Manufactured during 1860s.

NIB	Exc.	V.G.	Good	Fair	Poor
—	—	3000	2200	950	250

SMITH AMERICAN ARMS COMPANY
Springfield, Massachusetts

Smith Carbine

A .50 caliber breechloading percussion carbine with a 21.75" round barrel having an octagonal breech. Blued, case hardened with a walnut stock. The barrel marked "Address/Poultney & Trimble/ Baltimore, USA" and the frame "Smith's Patent/June 23, 1857" as well as "American Arms Co./Chicopee Falls." Approximately 30,000 were manufactured, most of which were purchased by the United States government. The sales agents were Poultney & Trimble of Baltimore, Maryland.

NIB	Exc.	V.G.	Good	Fair	Poor
—	—	2750	1200	500	200

SMITH, L. C.
Syracuse, New York
Hunter Arms Company
Fulton, New York

One of the finest American-made double-barrel shotguns and very collectible in today's market. It was manufactured between 1880 and 1888 in Syracuse, New York; and between 1890 and 1945 in Fulton, New York, by the Hunter Arms Company. In 1945 Marlin Firearms Company acquired Hunter Arms, and the L.C. Smith was made until 1951. In 1968 the L.C. Smith was resurrected for five years, and production ceased in 1973. Marlin brought the L.C. Smith brand to market with models imported from Italy from 2004 to 2010. The values given are approximate for standard production models; and we strongly feel that competent, individual appraisals should be secured, especially on the rarer and higher grade models, if a transaction is contemplated.

The values given are for fluid steel, hammerless guns only. Damascus-barreled guns have become collectible if they are in very good or better condition, and values are approximately the same as for the fluid steel models. Damascus guns in less than good condition are worth considerable less.

Early Hammerless Shotguns

The models listed were manufactured between 1890 and 1913. They are chambered for 10, 12, 16, and 20 gauge and were produced with various barrel lengths and choke combinations. They feature full sidelock actions. The difference in the models and their values is based on the degree of ornamentation and the quality of materials and workmanship utilized in their construction. The general values furnished are for 10, 12 or 16 gauge guns only.

NOTE: 20 gauge add 50 percent. A premium for 25 percent for 10 gauge and 16 gauge guns should be added. Single-selective trigger add $250. Automatic ejectors add 30 percent.

00 Grade
60,000 manufactured.

NIB	Exc.	V.G.	Good	Fair	Poor
—	2050	1800	1300	650	400

0 Grade
30,000 manufactured.

NIB	Exc.	V.G.	Good	Fair	Poor
—	2150	1900	1400	700	450

No. 1 Grade
10,000 manufactured.

NIB	Exc.	V.G.	Good	Fair	Poor
—	3150	2600	1950	800	550

No. 2 Grade
13,000 manufactured.

NIB	Exc.	V.G.	Good	Fair	Poor
—	3500	2900	1625	900	700

No. 3 Grade
4,000 manufactured.

NIB	Exc.	V.G.	Good	Fair	Poor
—	4250	3400	2275	1000	750

Pigeon Grade
1,200 manufactured.

NIB	Exc.	V.G.	Good	Fair	Poor
—	6500	5200	4000	1800	1000

No. 4 Grade
500 manufactured.

NIB	Exc.	V.G.	Good	Fair	Poor
—	8800	7300	5800	3000	2000

A-1 Grade
700 manufactured, all damascus, No 20 gauge.

NIB	Exc.	V.G.	Good	Fair	Poor
—	6500	4250	2750	1750	1000

No. 5 Grade
500 manufactured.

NIB	Exc.	V.G.	Good	Fair	Poor
—	9750	8100	5800	3250	2000

Monogram Grade
100 manufactured.

NIB	Exc.	V.G.	Good	Fair	Poor
—	13000	9750	6900	3750	2500

A-2 Grade
200 manufactured.

NIB	Exc.	V.G.	Good	Fair	Poor
—	17500	11500	8550	4500	3750

A-3 Grade
20 manufactured. This is too rare to generalize a value.

Later Production Hammerless Shotguns

These were manufactured at Fulton, New York, between 1914 and 1951. They are side-by-side double-barrel shotguns chambered for 12, 16, and 20 gauge, as well as the .410. They are offered with various barrel lengths and choke combinations. They feature a full sidelock action and are available with double or single triggers, extractors, and automatic ejectors. The finishes are blued and case colored, with checkered walnut stocks that are of either straight, semi-pistolgrip, or pistolgrip configurations. The various models differ as to the degree of ornamentation and the quality of materials and workmanship utilized in their construction. These are highly collectible American shotguns. Because these guns were manufactured as late as 1951, mint original specimens and even unfired new in the box guns will be offered for sale occasionally. These guns are worth considerably more than excellent condition guns and more than ever an individual, expert authentication and appraisal is recommended if a transaction is anticipated.

NOTE: The values supplied are for 12 gauge models only. For 16 gauge add 25 percent premium. For 20 gauge add 50 percent premium. For .410 bore add 200 percent premium (field grade), 300 percent to 400 percent for higher grades. Single-selective triggers add $250 premium. For automatic ejectors add 30 percent premium.

Courtesy Milwaukee Public Museum, Milwaukee, Wisconsin

Field Grade

NIB	Exc.	V.G.	Good	Fair	Poor
—	1800	1500	1125	700	350

Specialty Grade

Courtesy William Hammond

NIB	Exc.	V.G.	Good	Fair	Poor
—	3400	3150	2150	1200	400

Skeet Special Grade

Courtesy William Hammond

NIB	Exc.	V.G.	Good	Fair	Poor
—	3400	3150	2225	1300	500

Premier Skeet Grade

NIB	Exc.	V.G.	Good	Fair	Poor
—	3700	3150	2250	1350	500

Eagle Grade

NIB	Exc.	V.G.	Good	Fair	Poor
—	5350	4350	3150	1700	500

Crown Grade

With this grade, automatic ejectors became standard equipment. The .410 is extremely rare in this model and nonexistent in higher grades; there were only six manufactured, and they cannot be generally evaluated.

NIB	Exc.	V.G.	Good	Fair	Poor
—	7000	5350	4400	2950	500

Ideal Grade

With this grade, automatic ejectors became standard equipment. The .410 is extremely rare in this model and nonexistent in higher grades; there were only six manufactured, and they cannot be generally evaluated.

NIB	Exc.	V.G.	Good	Fair	Poor
—	2350	1950	1700	900	500

Trap Grade

With this grade, automatic ejectors became standard equipment. The .410 is extremely rare in this model and nonexistent in higher grades; there were only six manufactured, and they cannot be generally evaluated.

NIB	Exc.	V.G.	Good	Fair	Poor
—	2800	2350	1900	1100	500

Monogram Grade

There were two higher grades offered: the Premier Grade and the Deluxe Grade. They are extremely rare, and there have not been enough transactions to generally evaluate them. This version is offered standard with automatic ejectors and a single-selective trigger.

NIB	Exc.	V.G.	Good	Fair	Poor
—	15000	12000	8750	600	500

HUNTER ARMS BOXLOCKS

These shotguns are inexpensive, high quality boxlocks built with quality equal to the Field Grade L.C. Smith. The receiver, forend iron, trigger guard and triggers are all machined from forgings. Durability of these guns has proven to be excellent.

Fulton Model

A utility side-by-side boxlock shotgun chambered for 12, 16, 20 gauge and .410 bore. It was offered with various barrel length and choke combinations. It has double triggers and extractors with a non-selective single trigger option. Values given are for 12 gauge only. **NOTE:** For 20 gauge add 50 percent premium. For .410 bore add 250 percent premium. For 16 gauge add 25 percent. For single trigger add $150.

NIB	Exc.	V.G.	Good	Fair	Poor
—	1150	925	600	425	150

Fulton Special

A slightly higher grade version of the Fulton Model featuring modest engraving and pointed checkering. **NOTE:** For 20 gauge add 50 percent premium. For 16 gauge add 25 percent. For single trigger add $200.

Courtesy William Hammond

NIB	Exc.	V.G.	Good	Fair	Poor
—	1400	1050	750	500	200

Hunter Special

Similar to the Fulton Model but features the L.C. Smith rotary locking bolt. **NOTE:** For 20 gauge add 75 percent premium. For .410 bore add 300 percent premium. for 16 gauge add 25 percent.

Courtesy William Hammond

NIB	Exc.	V.G.	Good	Fair	Poor
—	1100	950	750	500	200

Single Barrel Trap Guns

High quality, break-open, single-shot trap guns chambered for 12 gauge only. They feature 32" or 34" vent rib barrels that are full-choked. They have boxlock actions and are standard with automatic ejectors. The finish is blued and case colored, and they have a checkered walnut stock with a recoil pad. The various models differ in the amount of ornamentation and the quality of the materials and workmanship utilized in their construction. There was a total of approximately 2,650 manufactured between 1917 and 1951. Although these firearms are actually rarer and just as high in quality as their side-by-side counterparts, they are simply not as collectible as the side-by-side variations.

NOTE: There were only two Premier Grade and three Deluxe Grade trap guns manufactured. This rarity makes it unrealistic to give an estimate of values. Beware of fakes.

Olympic Grade

NIB	Exc.	V.G.	Good	Fair	Poor
—	2050	1775	1300	900	500

Specialty Grade

NIB	Exc.	V.G.	Good	Fair	Poor
—	2600	1950	1400	1000	800

Crown Grade

NIB	Exc.	V.G.	Good	Fair	Poor
—	4250	3700	2800	1850	500

Monogram Grade

NIB	Exc.	V.G.	Good	Fair	Poor
—	7650	6500	4350	2800	500

1968 Model

A side-by-side double-barrel shotgun chambered for 12 gauge with a 28" vent rib barrel, choked Full and Modified. It features a sidelock action with double triggers and extractors. The finish is blued and case colored, with a checkered walnut stock. This shotgun was offered by Marlin between 1968 and 1973. These are less desirable than earlier models because of manufacturing expedients used. Investment cast receiver rather than machined forgings were used. Cyanide case-hardening replaced bone charcoal hardening and aluminum vent ribs were used. A thin brown polymer layer was used to create the fit between the lock plates and buttstock which is a departure from traditional fitting.

NIB	Exc.	V.G.	Good	Fair	Poor
1750	1475	1100	850	450	300

1968 Deluxe Model

Similar to the 1968 model but features a Simmons floating rib and a beavertail-type forearm. It was manufactured by Marlin between 1971 and 1973.

NIB	Exc.	V.G.	Good	Fair	Poor
2200	1800	1350	1100	700	400

L.C. SMITH NEW MODEL (MARLIN)

Model LC12-DB

Introduced in 2005 this Italian-made side-by-side gun is chambered for the 12 gauge 3" shell. Single trigger, selective ejectors, and 3 choke tubes. Barrel length is 28". Checkered walnut stock with pistol grip. Beavertail forearm. Recoil pad. Weight is about 6.25 lbs.

NIB	Exc.	V.G.	Good	Fair	Poor
1500	1250	950	800	675	300

Model LC20-DB

As above but chambered for the 20 gauge 3" shell and fitted with a 26" barrel. Weight is about 6 lbs. Introduced in 2005.

NIB	Exc.	V.G.	Good	Fair	Poor
1500	1250	950	800	675	300

Model LC12-OU

This is a 12 gauge 3" over/under gun with 28" vent rib barrels. Checkered walnut stock with pistol grip. Choke tubes. Weight is about 7.25 lbs. Introduced in 2005.

NIB	Exc.	V.G.	Good	Fair	Poor
1000	875	725	600	400	300

Model LC20-OU

As above but in 20 gauge with 3" chamber. Barrel length is 26". Weight is about 6.75 lbs. Introduced in 2005.

NIB	Exc.	V.G.	Good	Fair	Poor
1000	875	725	600	400	300

Model LC28/LC410-DB

The 28 gauge and .410 bore models were introduced in 2007. Both have 2.75" chambers and 26" barrels. Selective automatic ejectors. Case-colored receiver with gold game bird. Three choke tubes. Weight is about 6.5 lbs.

NIB	Exc.	V.G.	Good	Fair	Poor
1100	975	825	675	450	350

SMITH, OTIS
Rockfall, Connecticut

This company manufactured a line of single-action, spur-trigger revolvers that are chambered for .22, .32, .38, and .41 rimfire cartridges. The pistols have varying barrel lengths. The cylinder access pin is retained by a button on the left side of the frame. The cylinder usually holds five shots. The finishes are either blued or nickel-plated, with bird's-head grips. The quality was considered to be mediocre.

Model 1883 Shell-Ejector

A single-action, break-open, self ejecting revolver with a ribbed 3.5" barrel chambered for .32 centerfire. It has a 5-shot fluted cylinder and a spur trigger. It was quite well made. The finish is nickel-plated, with black plastic grips.

NIB	Exc.	V.G.	Good	Fair	Poor
—	—	500	275	100	75

Model 1892

A double-action, concealed-hammer revolver chambered for the .38 centerfire cartridge. It has a 4" barrel and, for the first time, a conventional trigger and trigger guard. It is gateloaded and has a solid frame. It is nickel-plated with black plastic grips and also appeared under the Maltby, Henley & Company banner marked "Spencer Safety Hammerless" or "Parker Safety Hammerless." The Otis Smith Company ceased operations in 1898.

NIB	Exc.	V.G.	Good	Fair	Poor
—	—	500	275	100	75

SMITH & WESSON
Springfield, Massachusetts

SMITH & WESSON ANTIQUE HANDGUNS

NOTE: A surprising number of pistols are still found in their original boxes, even for older models. This can add 100 percent to the value of the pistol.

Model 1, 1st Issue Revolver

This was the first metallic-cartridge arm produced by Smith & Wesson. It is a small revolver that weighs approximately 10 oz. and is chambered for the .22 Short rimfire cartridge. The octagonal barrel is 3.25" long. It holds 7 cartridges. The barrel and nonfluted cylinder pivot upward upon release of the under the frame. This model has a square butt with rosewood grips. The oval brass frame is silver-plated. The barrel and cylinder are blued. The barrel is stamped with the company name and address; the patent dates also appear. The sides of the frame are rounded on the 1st issue. Other characteristics which distinguish the more valuable 1st issue from later issues include a perfectly round side plate and a hinged hammer spur. Smith & Wesson manufactured approximately 11,000 of these revolvers between 1857 and 1860. Since this was the first of its kind, it is not difficult to understand the need for the number of variations within this model designation. Many small improvements were made on the way to the next model. These variations are as follows:

1st Type

Serial range 1 to low 200s, revolving recoil shield, bayonet type catch on frame. **NOTE:** Rarity makes valuation speculative.

NIB	Exc.	V.G.	Good	Fair	Poor
—	—	15000	10000	8000	1000

2nd Type

Serial range low 200s to 1130, improved recoil plate.

NIB	Exc.	V.G.	Good	Fair	Poor
—	—	10000	6000	2500	500

3rd Type

Serial range 1130 to low 3000s, bayonet catch dropped for spring-loaded side catch.

Courtesy Jim Supica, Old Town Station

Typical configuration for 3rd-6th type, Model 1 1st Issue

NIB	Exc.	V.G.	Good	Fair	Poor
—	7500	5500	4000	2500	500

4th Type

Serial range low 3000s to low 4200s, recoil shield made much smaller.

NIB	Exc.	V.G.	Good	Fair	Poor
—	3000	2250	1800	1250	300

5th Type

Serial range low 4200s to low 5500s, has 5-groove rifling instead of 3.

NIB	Exc.	V.G.	Good	Fair	Poor
—	3000	2250	1800	1250	300

6th Type

Serial range low 5500s to end of production 11670. A cylinder ratchet replaced the revolving recoil shield.

NIB	Exc.	V.G.	Good	Fair	Poor
—	2000	1600	1400	1000	250

Model 1, 2nd Issue

Similar in appearance to the 1st Issue this 2nd Issue variation has several notable differences that make identification rather simple. The sides of the frame on the 2nd Issue are flat not rounded as on the 1st Issue. The sideplate is irregular in shape—not round like on the 1st Issue. The barrel was 3-3/16" in length. The barrel is stamped "Smith & Wesson" while the cylinder is marked with the three patent dates: April 3, 1858, July 5 1859, and December 18, 1860. There have been 2nd Issue noted with full silver or nickel-plating. Smith & Wesson manufactured approximately 115,000 of these revolvers between 1860 and 1868. The serial numbers started around 1100 where the 1st Issue left off and continued to 126400. There were approximately 4,400 revolvers marked "2D Quality" on the barrels. These revolvers were slightly defective and were sold at a lesser price. They will bring an approximate 100 percent premium on today's market.

Courtesy Mike Stuckslager

NIB	Exc.	V.G.	Good	Fair	Poor
—	900	750	600	250	100

Model 1, 3rd Issue

This is a redesigned version of its forerunners. Another .22 Short rimfire, 7-shot revolver, this model has a fluted cylinder and round barrel with a raised rib. This variation was manufactured totally from wrought iron. The three patent dates are stamped on top of the ribbed barrel as is "Smith & Wesson." It features bird's-head type grips of rosewood and is either fully blued nickel-plated, or two-toned with the frame nickel and the barrel and cylinder blued. There are two barrel lengths offered: 3.25" and 2-11/16". The shorter barrel was introduced in 1872. Serial numbering began with #1 and continued to 131163. They were manufactured between 1868 and 1882. The Model 1 3rd Issue was the last of the tip-up style produced by Smith & Wesson.

Courtesy Mike Stuckslager

Shorter Barreled Version
Rare.

NIB	Exc.	V.G.	Good	Fair	Poor
—	1500	1350	800	400	100

Longer Barreled Version

NIB	Exc.	V.G.	Good	Fair	Poor
—	750	500	275	200	100

Model 1-1/2 1st Issue (1-1/2 Old Model)

This model was the first of the .32-caliber Rimfire Short revolvers that S&W produced. It is a larger version of the Model 1 but is physically similar in appearance. The Model 1-1/2 was offered with a 3.5" octagonal barrel and has a 5-shot nonfluted cylinder and a square butt with rosewood grips. In 1866 a 4" barrel version was produced for a short time. It is estimated that about 200 were sold. The finish is blued or nickel-plated. The serial numbering on this model ran from serial number 1 to 26300; and, interestingly to note, S&W had most of the parts for this revolver manufactured on contract by King & Smith of Middletown, Connecticut. Smith & Wesson merely assembled and finished

them. They were produced between 1865 and 1868. **NOTE:** Add a 50 percent premium for the 4" barrel variation.

Courtesy Mike Stuckslager

NIB	Exc.	V.G.	Good	Fair	Poor
—	795	650	400	200	100

Model 1-1/2 2nd Issue (1-1/2 New Model)

The factory referred to this model as the New Model 1-1/2 and it is an improved version of the 1st Issue. It is somewhat similar in appearance with a few notable exceptions. The barrel is 2.5" or 3.5" in length, round with a raised rib. The grip is of the bird's-head configuration, and the 5-shot cylinder is fluted and chambered for the .32 Long rimfire cartridge. The cylinder stop is located in the top frame instead of the bottom. The finish and grip material are the same as the 1st Issue. There were approximately 100,700 manufactured between 1868 and 1875.

Courtesy Mike Stuckslager

3.5" Barrel

Courtesy Mike Stuckslager

NIB	Exc.	V.G.	Good	Fair	Poor
900	800	650	375	175	100

2.5" Barrel
Rare. Watch for fakes.

NIB	Exc.	V.G.	Good	Fair	Poor
2500	1500	1100	600	350	100

Model 1-1/2 Transitional Model

Approximately 650 of these were produced by fitting 1st Issue cylinders and barrels to 2nd Issue frames. They also have 1st Model octagon barrels with 2nd Model bird's-head grips. These revolvers fall into the serial number range 27200-28800.

NIB	Exc.	V.G.	Good	Fair	Poor
—	—	3000	1500	800	300

Model 2 Army or Old Model

Similar in appearance to the Model 1 2nd Issue, this revolver was extremely successful from a commercial standpoint. It was released just in time for the commencement of hostilities in the Civil War. Smith & Wesson had, in this revolver, the only weapon able to fire self-contained cartridges and be easily carried as a backup by soldiers going off to war. This resulted in a backlog of more than three years before the company finally stopped taking orders. This model is chambered for .32 Long rimfire cartridge and has a 6-shot nonfluted cylinder and 4", 5", or 6" barrel lengths. It has a square butt with rosewood grips and is either blued or nickel-plated. There were approximately 77,155 manufactured between 1861 and 1874. Rare.

Courtesy Chester Krause

5" or 6" Barrel
Standard barrel.

NIB	Exc.	V.G.	Good	Fair	Poor
—	2450	1500	950	450	300

4" Barrel
Rare, use caution. **NOTE:** A slight premium for early two-pin model. For rare 8" model add 800 percent.

NIB	Exc.	V.G.	Good	Fair	Poor
—	—	6000	3650	1500	500

.32 Single-Action (so-called "1-1/2 Frame" Centerfire)

This model represented the first .32 S&W centerfire caliber top-break revolver that automatically ejected the spent cartridges upon opening. It is similar in appearance to the Model 1-1/2 2nd Issue. This model has a 5-shot fluted cylinder and a bird's-head grip of wood or checkered hard rubber and was offered with barrel lengths of 3", 3.5", 6", 8", and 10". The 8" and 10" barrel are rare and were not offered until 1887. This model pivots downward on opening and features a rebounding hammer that made the weapon much safer to fully load. There were approximately 97,599 manufactured between 1878 and 1892.

Courtesy W.P. Hallstein III and son Chip

Early Model w/o Strain Screw—Under #6500

Courtesy Mike Stuckslager

NIB	Exc.	V.G.	Good	Fair	Poor
—	1200	600	300	175	75

Later Model with Strain Screw

Courtesy Mike Stuckslager

NIB	Exc.	V.G.	Good	Fair	Poor
—	1000	450	300	150	75

8" or 10" Barrel
Very rare; use caution.

NIB	Exc.	V.G.	Good	Fair	Poor
—	—	4500	2500	800	400

.38 Single-Action 1st Model (Baby Russian)

This model is sometimes called the "Baby Russian." It is a top break, automatic-ejecting revolver chambered for the .38 S&W centerfire cartridge. Offered with either a 3.25" or 4" round barrel with a raised rib, has a 5-shot fluted cylinder, and finished in blue or nickel plating. A 5" barrel was added as an option a short time later. The butt is rounded, with wood or checkered hard rubber grips inlaid with the S&W medallion. It has a spur trigger. Approximately 25,548 were manufactured in 1876 and 1877, of which 16,046 were nickel and 6,502 were blued.

Courtesy Mike Stuckslager

NIB	Exc.	V.G.	Good	Fair	Poor
—	2000	1200	900	350	150

.38 Single-Action 2nd Model

With the exception of an improved and shortened extractor assembly and the availability of additional barrel lengths of 3.25",

4", 5", 6", 8", and 10" with the 8" and 10" barrel lengths being the most rare, this model is quite similar in appearance to the 1st Model. There were approximately 108,225 manufactured between 1877 and 1891.

Courtesy Mike Stuckslager

8" and 10" Barrel

Very rare, use caution.

NIB	Exc.	V.G.	Good	Fair	Poor
—	—	4000	2250	950	500

3.25", 4", 5", and 6" Barrel Lengths

Small premium for 5" or 6" lengths.

NIB	Exc.	V.G.	Good	Fair	Poor
—	700	350	225	175	75

.38 Single-Action 3rd Model

This model differs from the first two models because it is fitted with a trigger guard. It is chambered for the .38 S&W centerfire cartridge, has a 5-shot fluted cylinder, and is a top break design with automatic ejection upon opening. The barrel lengths are 3.25", 4", and 6". The finish is blued or nickel-plated. The butt is rounded, with checkered hard rubber grips featuring S&W medallions. There were approximately 26,850 manufactured between 1891 and 1911.

Courtesy Mike Stuckslager

NIB	Exc.	V.G.	Good	Fair	Poor
—	2000	1300	1000	600	200

.38 Single-Action Mexican Model

This extremely rare model is quite similar in appearance to the 3rd Model Single-Action. The notable differences are the flat hammer sides with no outward flaring of the spur. The spur trigger assembly was not made integrally with the frame but is a separate part added to it. One must exercise extreme caution as S&W offered a kit that would convert the trigger guard assembly of the Third Model to the spur trigger of the Mexican Model. This, coupled with the fact that both models fall within the same serial range, can present a real identification problem. Another feature of the Mexican Model is the absence of a half cock. The exact number of Mexican Models manufactured between 1891 and 1911 is unknown but it is estimated that the number is small.

NIB	Exc.	V.G.	Good	Fair	Poor
—	3950	3650	1500	950	400

.32 Double-Action 1st Model

This is one of the rarest of all S&W revolvers. There were only 30 manufactured. It also has a straight-sided sideplate that weakened the revolver frame. Perhaps this was the reason that so few were made. This model was the first break-open, double-action, automatic-ejecting .32 that S&W produced. It features a 3" round barrel with raised rib, a 5-shot fluted cylinder, and round butt with plain, uncheckered, black hard rubber grips. The finish is blued or nickel-plated. All 30 of these revolvers were manufactured in 1880. **NOTE:** Rarity makes valuation speculative.

NIB	Exc.	V.G.	Good	Fair	Poor
—	—	12000	7500	4000	1000

.32 Double-Action 2nd Model

This revolver is chambered for the .32 S&W cartridge and has a 3" round barrel with a raised rib. The 5-shot cylinder is fluted, and the finish is blued or nickel-plated. It is a top break design with a round butt. The grips are either checkered or floral-embossed hard rubber with the S&W monogram. This model has an oval sideplate, eliminating the weakness of the 1st Model. There were approximately 22,142 manufactured between 1880 and 1882.

Courtesy Mike Stuckslager

NIB	Exc.	V.G.	Good	Fair	Poor
—	700	350	225	175	75

.32 Double-Action 3rd Model

This model incorporates internal improvements that are not evident in appearance. The most notable identifiable difference between this model and its predecessors is in the surface of the cylinder. The flutes are longer; there is only one set of stops instead of two; and the free groove is no longer present. There were approximately 21,232 manufactured in 1882 and 1883.

Courtesy Mike Stuckslager

NIB	Exc.	V.G.	Good	Fair	Poor
—	625	350	225	175	75

.32 Double-Action 4th Model

This model is quite similar in appearance to the 3rd Model except that the trigger guard is oval in shape instead of the squared back of the previous models. There were also internal improvements. There were approximately 239,600 manufactured between 1883 and 1909. **NOTE:** Add a 50 percent premium for revolvers built before 1898.

Courtesy Mike Stuckslager

NIB	Exc.	V.G.	Good	Fair	Poor
—	575	300	200	125	65

.32 Double-Action 5th Model

The only difference between this model and its predecessors is that this model has the front sight machined as an integral part of the barrel rib. On the other models, the sight was pinned in place. There were approximately 44,641 manufactured between 1909 and 1919.

Courtesy Mike Stuckslager

NIB	Exc.	V.G.	Good	Fair	Poor
—	500	375	250	125	100

SAFETY HAMMERLESS

This model was a departure from what was commonly being produced at this time. Some attribute the Safety Hammerless design to D.B. Wesson's hearing that a child had been injured by cocking and firing one of the company's pistols. This story has never been proven. Nevertheless, the concealed hammer and grip safety make this an ideal pocket pistol for those needing concealability in a handgun. This is a small revolver chambered for .32 S&W and .38 S&W cartridges. It has a 5-shot fluted cylinder and is offered with a 2", 3", and 3.5" round barrel with a raised rib. The butt is rounded and has checkered hard rubber grips with the S&W logo. The finish is blue or nickel plated. The revolver is a top break, automatic-ejecting design; and the 1st Model has the latch for opening located in the rear center of the top strap instead of at the sides. The latch is checkered for a positive grip. This model is commonly referred to as the "Lemon Squeezer" because the grip safety must be squeezed as it is fired.

Courtesy Mike Stuckslager

.32 Safety Hammerless (aka .32 New Departure or .32 Lemon Squeezer) 1st Model

Push button latch serial number 1- 91417, built 1888-1902. **NOTE:** Add a 50 percent premium for revolvers built before 1898.

NIB	Exc.	V.G.	Good	Fair	Poor
—	475	275	165	100	50

.32 Safety Hammerless 2nd Model

T-bar latch, pinned front sight, serial number 91418-169999, built 1902 to 1909.

Courtesy Mike Stuckslager

NIB	Exc.	V.G.	Good	Fair	Poor
—	450	275	165	100	50

.32 Safety Hammerless 3rd Model

T-bar latch, integral forged front sight, serial number 170000-242981, built 1909 to 1937. **NOTE:** For 2" barrel, Bicycle Model add 200 percent.

NIB	Exc.	V.G.	Good	Fair	Poor
—	450	325	265	150	50

.38 Double-Action 1st Model

This model is similar in appearance to the .32 1st Model, having a straight cut side-plate, but is chambered for the .38 S&W cartridge. The grips are checkered, and there were 4,000 manufactured in 1880.

NIB	Exc.	V.G.	Good	Fair	Poor
—	1200	650	400	250	75

.38 Double-Action 2nd Model

This is similar in appearance to the .32 2nd Model but is chambered for the .38 S&W cartridge. There were approximately 115,000 manufactured between 1880 and 1884.

Courtesy Mike Stuckslager

NIB	Exc.	V.G.	Good	Fair	Poor
—	550	375	225	200	100

.38 Double-Action 3rd Model

Essentially the same in appearance as the .32 Model but chambered for the .38 S&W cartridge, it is also offered with a 3.25", 4", 5", 6", 8", and 10" barrel. There were numerous internal changes in this model similar to the .32 Double-Action 3rd Model. There were approximately 203,700 manufactured between 1884 and 1895.

8" and 10" Barrel

Rare, use caution.

Courtesy Mike Stuckslager

NIB	Exc.	V.G.	Good	Fair	Poor
—	—	2500	1500	800	200

Standard Barrel

NIB	Exc.	V.G.	Good	Fair	Poor
—	550	450	325	200	75

.38 Double-Action 4th Model

This is the .38 S&W version of the 4th Model and is identical in outward appearance to the 3rd Model. The relocation of the sear was the main design change in this model. There were approximately 216,300 manufactured between 1895 and 1909. **NOTE:** Add a 20 percent premium for revolvers built before 1898.

NIB	Exc.	V.G.	Good	Fair	Poor
—	495	230	225	150	75

.38 Double-Action 5th Model

This model is the same as the .32 except that it is chambered for the .38 S&W cartridge. There were approximately 15,000 manufactured between 1909 and 1911.

Courtesy Mike Stuckslager

NIB	Exc.	V.G.	Good	Fair	Poor
—	525	385	225	150	75

.38 Double-Action Perfected

A unique top-break with both a barrel latch similar to the other top-breaks and a thumbpiece similar to the hand ejectors; also the only top-break where the trigger guard is integral to the frame rather than a separate piece. Produced from 1909 to 1911 in their own serial number range. About 59,400 were built.

NIB	Exc.	V.G.	Good	Fair	Poor
—	600	525	295	165	85

.38 Safety Hammerless 1st Model

Z-bar latch, serial number range 1 to 5250, made 1887 only. **NOTE:** Also offered with a 6" barrel. RARE! Add 50 percent.

NIB	Exc.	V.G.	Good	Fair	Poor
—	900	600	425	250	100

.38 Safety Hammerless 2nd Model

Push button latch protrudes above frame, serial number 5251-42483, built 1887-1890.

Courtesy Mike Stuckslager

NIB	Exc.	V.G.	Good	Fair	Poor
—	500	350	250	175	100

.38 Safety Hammerless 3rd Model

Push button latch flush with frame, serial number 42484-116002, 1890-1898.

NIB	Exc.	V.G.	Good	Fair	Poor
—	475	355	225	165	100

.38 Safety Hammerless Army Test Revolver

There were approximately 100 sold to U.S. government in 1890. They have 3rd Model features but are in the 2nd Model serial number range, 41333-41470. Fitted with 6" barrels and marked "US." CAUTION: Be wary of fakes. **NOTE:** Rarity makes valuation speculative.

NIB	Exc.	V.G.	Good	Fair	Poor
—	—	10,000	7500	4000	—

.38 Safety Hammerless 4th Model

This model was produced in .38 S&W only, and the only difference in the 4th Model and the 3rd Model is the adoption of the standard T-bar type of barrel latch as found on most of the top break revolvers. ".38 S&W Cartridge" was also added to the left side of the barrel. There were approximately 104,000 manufactured between 1898 and 1907; serial number range 116003 to 220000.

Courtesy Mike Stuckslager

NIB	Exc.	V.G.	Good	Fair	Poor
—	450	335	275	110	50

.38 Safety Hammerless 5th Model

This is the last of the "Lemon Squeezers," and the only appreciable difference between this model and the 4th Model is that the front sight blade on the 5th Model is an integral part of the barrel and not a separate blade pinned onto the barrel. There were approximately 41,500 manufactured between 1907 and 1940;

serial number range 220001 to 261493. **NOTE:** 2" barrel version add 50 percent.

Courtesy Mike Stuckslager

NIB	Exc.	V.G.	Good	Fair	Poor
—	500	395	275	110	50

Model 3 American 1st Model

This model represented a number of firsts for the Smith & Wesson Company. It was the first of the top break, automatic ejection revolvers. It was also the first Smith & Wesson in a large caliber (it is chambered for the .44 S&W American cartridge as well as the .44 Henry rimfire on rare occasions). It was also known as the 1st Model American. This large revolver is offered with an 8" round barrel with a raised rib as standard. Barrel lengths of 6" and 7" were also available. It has a 6-shot fluted cylinder and a square butt with walnut grips. It is blued or nickel-plated. It is interesting to note that this model appeared three years before Colt's Single-Action Army and perhaps, more than any other model, was associated with the historic American West. There were only 8,000 manufactured between 1870 and 1872.

Standard Production Model

NOTE: Add 25 percent for "oil hole" variation found on approximately the first 1,500 guns. Add 50 percent for unusual barrel lengths other than standard 8". Original "Nashville Police" marked guns worth a substantial premium.

NIB	Exc.	V.G.	Good	Fair	Poor
—	—	7000	3500	1500	500

Transition Model

Serial number range 6466-6744. Shorter cylinder (1.423"), improved barrel catch.

NIB	Exc.	V.G.	Good	Fair	Poor
—	—	6000	3000	1500	500

U.S. Army Order

Serial number range 125-2199. One thousand (1,000) produced with "U.S." stamped on top of barrel; "OWA," on left grip.

NIB	Exc.	V.G.	Good	Fair	Poor
—	—	17500	7500	3000	500

.44 Rimfire Henry Model

Only 200 produced throughout serial range. **NOTE:** Rarity makes valuation speculative.

NIB	Exc.	V.G.	Good	Fair	Poor
—	—	12000	6000	3000	500

Model 3 American 2nd Model

An improved version of the 1st Model. The most notable difference is the larger diameter trigger pivot pin and the frame protrusions above the trigger to accommodate it. The front sight blade on this model is made of steel instead of nickel silver. Several internal improvements were also incorporated into this model. This model is commonly known as the American 2nd Model. The 8" barrel length was standard on this model. There were approximately 20,735 manufactured, including 3,014 chambered for .44 rimfire Henry, between 1872 and 1874. **NOTE:** There have been 5.5", 6", 6.5", and 7" barrels noted; but they are extremely scarce and would bring a 40 percent premium over the standard 8" model. Use caution when purchasing these short barrel revolvers.

.44 Henry Rimfire

NIB	Exc.	V.G.	Good	Fair	Poor
—	—	6500	3250	1500	500

Standard 8" Model, .44 American Centerfire

NIB	Exc.	V.G.	Good	Fair	Poor
—	6750	5000	3000	1250	500

Model 3 Russian 1st Model

This model is quite similar in appearance to the American 1st and 2nd Model revolvers. S&W made several internal changes to this model to satisfy the Russian government. The markings on this revolver are distinct; and the caliber for which it is chambered, .44 S&W Russian, is different. There are approximately 20,000 Russian-Contract revolvers. The serial number range is 1-20000. They are marked in Russian Cyrillic letters. The Russian double-headed eagle is stamped on the rear portion of the barrel with inspector's marks underneath it. All of the contract guns have 8" barrels and lanyard swivels on the butt. These are rarely encountered, as most were shipped to Russia. The commercial run of this model numbered approximately 4,655. The barrels are stamped in English and include the words "Russian Model." Some are found with 6" and 7" barrels, as well as the standard 8". There were also 500 revolvers that were rejected from the Russian contract series and sold on the commercial market. Some of these are marked in English; some, Cyrillic. Some have the Cyrillic markings ground off and the English restamped. This model was manufactured from 1871 to 1874.

Russian Contract Model, Cyrillic Barrel Address

NIB	Exc.	V.G.	Good	Fair	Poor
—	—	7000	3500	2000	500

Commercial Model

NIB	Exc.	V.G.	Good	Fair	Poor
—	—	5000	2750	1250	500

Rejected Russian Contract Model

NIB	Exc.	V.G.	Good	Fair	Poor
—	—	5000	2750	1250	500

Model 3 Russian 2nd Model

This revolver was known as the "Old Model Russian." This is a complicated model to understand as there are many variations within the model designation. The serial numbering is quite complex as well, and values vary greatly due to relatively minor model differences. Before purchasing this model, it would be advisable to secure competent appraisal as well as to read reference materials solely devoted to this firearm. This model is chambered for the .44 S&W Russian, as well as the .44 Henry rimfire cartridge. It has a 7" barrel and a round butt featuring a projection on the frame that fits into the thumb web. The grips are walnut, and the finish is blue or nickel-plated. The trigger guard has a reverse curved spur on the bottom. There were approximately 85,200 manufactured between 1873 and 1878.

Courtesy Jim Supica, Old Town Station

Commercial Model

6,200 made, .44 S&W Russian, English markings.

NIB	Exc.	V.G.	Good	Fair	Poor
—	—	3250	1500	850	400

.44 Rimfire Henry Model

500 made.

NIB	Exc.	V.G.	Good	Fair	Poor
—	—	4750	2250	1000	500

Russian Contract Model

70,000 made; rare, as most were shipped to Russia. Cyrillic markings; lanyard swivel on butt.

NIB	Exc.	V.G.	Good	Fair	Poor
—	—	3500	1750	950	500

1st Model Turkish Contract

.44 rimfire Henry, special rimfire frames, serial-numbered in own serial number range 1-1000.

NIB	Exc.	V.G.	Good	Fair	Poor
—	—	6000	3750	1750	500

2nd Model Turkish Contract

Made from altered centerfire frames from the regular commercial serial number range. 1,000 made. Use caution with this model.

NIB	Exc.	V.G.	Good	Fair	Poor
—	—	4500	2250	1000	500

Japanese Govt. Contract

Five thousand made between the 1-9000 serial number range. The Japanese naval insignia, an anchor over two wavy lines, found on the butt. The barrel is Japanese proofed, and the words "Jan.19, 75 REISSUE July 25, 1871" are stamped on the barrel, as well.

NIB	Exc.	V.G.	Good	Fair	Poor
—	—	3500	1700	950	500

Model 3 Russian 3rd Model

This revolver is also known as the "New Model Russian." The factory referred to this model as the Model of 1874 or the Cavalry Model. It is chambered for the .44 S&W Russian and the .44 Henry rimfire cartridge. The barrel is 6.5", and the round butt is the same humped-back affair as the 2nd Model. The grips are walnut; and the finish, blue or nickel-plated. The most notable differences in appearance between this model and the 2nd Model are the shorter extractor housing under the barrel and the integral front sight blade instead of the pinned-on one found on the previous models. This is another model that bears careful research before attempting to evaluate. Minor variances can greatly affect values. Secure detailed reference materials and qualified appraisal. There were approximately 60,638 manufactured between 1874 and 1878.

Commercial Model

.44 S&W Russian, marked "Russian Model" in English, 13,500 made.

NIB	Exc.	V.G.	Good	Fair	Poor
—	—	9000	5000	2500	500

.44 Henry Rimfire Model

NIB	Exc.	V.G.	Good	Fair	Poor
—	—	4500	2700	900	500

Turkish Model

Five thousand made from altered centerfire frames. Made to fire .44 Henry rimfire. "W" inspector's mark on butt. Fakes have been noted; be aware.

NIB	Exc.	V.G.	Good	Fair	Poor
—	—	4500	2700	900	500

Japanese Contract Model

One thousand made; has the Japanese naval insignia, an anchor over two wavy lines, stamped on the butt.

NIB	Exc.	V.G.	Good	Fair	Poor
—	—	3100	1950	850	500

Russian Contract Model

Barrel markings are in Russian Cyrillic. Approximately 41,100 were produced.

NIB	Exc.	V.G.	Good	Fair	Poor
—	—	3100	1950	850	500

Model 3 Russian 3rd Model (Loewe & Tula Copies)

The German firm of Ludwig Loewe produced a copy of this model that is nearly identical to the S&W. This German revolver was made under Russian contract, as well as for commercial sales. The contract model has different Cyrillic markings than the S&W and the letters "HK" as inspector's marks. The commercial model has the markings in English. The Russian arsenal at Tula also produced a copy of this revolver with a different Cyrillic dated stamping on the barrel.

Courtesy Mike Stuckslager

Loewe

NIB	Exc.	V.G.	Good	Fair	Poor
—	—	2900	1750	700	400

Tula

NIB	Exc.	V.G.	Good	Fair	Poor
—	—	3350	2000	800	400

Model 3 Schofield 1st Model

"US" Contract

3,000 issued.

NIB	Exc.	V.G.	Good	Fair	Poor
—	12500	7500	4250	2250	500

Civilian Model

No "US" markings, 35 made, Very Rare. **NOTE:** Use caution. UNABLE TO PRICE. At least double the military model values. Expert appraisal needed.

Model 3 Schofield 2nd Model

No "US" markings, 35 made, Very Rare.

"US" Contract

4,000 issued.

NIB	Exc.	V.G.	Good	Fair	Poor
—	10500	6500	4000	2250	500

Civilian Model

646 made.

NIB	Exc.	V.G.	Good	Fair	Poor
—	12000	7000	4000	2000	500

Model 3 Schofield—Surplus Models

After the government dropped the Schofield as an issue cavalry sidearm, the remaining U.S. inventory of these revolvers was sold off as military surplus. Many were sold to National Guard units; and the remainder were sold either to Bannerman's or to Schuyler, Hartley & Graham, two large gun dealers who then resold the guns to supply the growing need for guns on the Western frontier. Schuyler, Hartley & Graham sold a number of guns to the Wells Fargo Express Co. These weapons were nickel-plated and had the barrels shortened to 5", as were many others sold during this period. Beware of fakes when contemplating purchase of the Wells Fargo revolvers.

Wells Fargo & Co. Model

NIB	Exc.	V.G.	Good	Fair	Poor
—	—	8000	4000	2000	500

Surplus Cut Barrel—Not Wells Fargo

NIB	Exc.	V.G.	Good	Fair	Poor
—	—	3500	2000	1200	500

New Model No. 3 Single-Action

Always interested in perfecting the Model 3 revolver D.B. Wesson redesigned and improved the old Model 3 in the hopes of attracting more sales. The Russian contracts were almost filled so the company decided to devote the effort necessary to improve on this design. In 1877 this project was undertaken. The extractor housing was shortened; the cylinder retention system was improved; and the shape of the grip was changed to a more streamlined and attractive configuration. This New Model has a 3.5", 4", 5", 6", 6.5", 7", 7.5", or 8" barrel length with a 6-shot fluted cylinder. The 6.5" barrel and .44 S&W Russian chambering is the most often encountered variation of this model, but the factory considered the 3-1/2" and 8" barrels as standard and these were kept in stock as well. The New Model No. 3 was also chambered for .32 S&W, .32-44 S&W, .320 S&W Rev. Rifle, .38 S&W, .38-40, .38-44 S&W, .41 S&W, .44 Henry rimfire, .44 S&W American, .44-40, .45 S&W Schofield, .450 Rev., .45 Webley, .455 MkI and .455 MkII. They are either blued or nickel-plated and have checkered hard rubber grips with the S&W logo molded into them, or walnut grips. There are many sub-variations within this model designation, and the potential collector should secure detailed reference material that deals with this model. There were approximately 35,796 of these revolvers manufactured between 1878 and 1912. Nearly 40 percent were exported to fill contracts with Japan, Australia, Argentina, England, Spain, and Cuba. There were some sent to Asia, as well. The proofmarks of these countries will establish their provenance but will not add appreciably to standard values.

Standard Model

6.5" barrel, .44 S&W Russian.

Courtesy Mike Stuckslager

NIB	Exc.	V.G.	Good	Fair	Poor
—	5000	3700	2000	1000	500

Japanese Naval Contract

This was the largest foreign purchaser of this model. There were more than 1,500 produced with the anchor insignia stamped on the frame.

Courtesy Mike Stuckslager

NIB	Exc.	V.G.	Good	Fair	Poor
—	—	3700	2000	1000	500

Japanese Artillery Contract

This variation is numbered in the 25000 serial range. They are blued, with a 7" barrel and a lanyard swivel on the butt. Japanese characters are stamped on the extractor housing.

NIB	Exc.	V.G.	Good	Fair	Poor
—	—	5000	2500	1250	500

Maryland Militia Model

This variation is nickel-plated, has a 6.5" barrel, and is chambered for the .44 S&W Russian cartridge. The butt is stamped "U.S.," and the inspector's marks "HN" and "DAL" under the date 1878 appear on the revolver. There were 280 manufactured between serial-numbers 7126 and 7405. **NOTE:** Rarity makes valuation speculative.

NIB	Exc.	V.G.	Good	Fair	Poor
—	—	10000	6000	3000	500

Argentine Model

This was essentially not a factory contract but a sale through Schuyler, Hartley and Graham. They are stamped "Ejercito/ Argentino" in front of the trigger guard. The order amounted to some 2,000 revolvers between the serial numbers 50 and 3400.

NIB	Exc.	V.G.	Good	Fair	Poor
—	—	7000	3500	1750	500

Australian Contract

This variation is nickel-plated, is chambered for the .44 S&W Russian cartridge, and is marked with the Australian Colonial Police Broad Arrow on the buff. There were 250 manufactured with 7" barrels and detachable shoulder stocks. The stock has the Broad Arrow stamped on the lower tang. There were also 30 manufactured with 6.5" barrels without the stocks. They all are numbered in the 12000-13000 serial range.

Courtesy Mike Stuckslager

Revolver with Stock and Holsters

NOTE: Deduct 40 percent for no stock.

NIB	Exc.	V.G.	Good	Fair	Poor
—	—	8000	4750	2750	500

Turkish Model

This is essentially the New Model No. 3 chambered for the .44 rimfire Henry cartridge. It is stamped with the letters "P," "U" and "AFC" on various parts of the revolver. The barrels are all 6.5"; the finish, blued with walnut grips. Lanyard swivels are found on the butt. There were 5,461 manufactured and serial numbered in their own range, starting at 1 through 5461 between 1879 and 1883.

NIB	Exc.	V.G.	Good	Fair	Poor
—	—	7000	3500	1750	500

New Model No. 3 Target Single-Action

This revolver is similar in appearance to the standard New Model No. 3, but was the company's first production target model. It has a 6.5" round barrel with a raised rib and 6-shot fluted cylinder and is finished in blue or nickel-plated. The grips are either walnut or checkered hard rubber with the S&W logo molded into them. This model is chambered in either .32 S&W or .38 S&W. The company referred to these models as either the .32-44 Target or the .38-44 Target depending on the caliber. The designation of .44 referred to the frame size, i.e. a .32 caliber built on a .44 caliber frame. This model was offered with a detachable shoulder stock as an option. These stocks are extremely scarce on today's market. There were approximately 4,333 manufactured between 1887 and 1910. **NOTE:** Shoulder stock add 50 percent.

Courtesy Mike Stuckslager

NIB	Exc.	V.G.	Good	Fair	Poor
—	—	3100	1350	850	400

New Model No. 3 Frontier Single-Action

This is another model similar in appearance to the standard New Model No. 3. It has a 4", 5", or 6.5" barrel and is chambered for the .44-40 Winchester Centerfire cartridge. Because the original New Model No. 3 cylinder was 1-7/16" in length this would not accommodate the longer .44-40 cartridge. The cylinder on the No. 3 Frontier was changed to 1-9/16" in length. Later the company converted 786 revolvers to .44 S&W Russian and sold them to Japan. This model is either blued or nickel-plated and has checkered grips of walnut or hard rubber. They are serial numbered in their own range from 1 through 2072 and were manufactured from 1885 until 1908. This model was designed to compete with the Colt Single-Action Army but was not successful.

Courtesy Mike Stuckslager

.44-40—Commercial Model

NIB	Exc.	V.G.	Good	Fair	Poor
—	—	5000	2500	1250	500

Japanese Purchase Converted to .44 S&W Russian

NIB	Exc.	V.G.	Good	Fair	Poor
—	—	4000	2000	1000	500

New Model No. 3—.38 Winchester

This variation was the last of the New Model No. 3s to be introduced. It was offered in .38-40 Winchester as a separate model from 1900 until 1907. The finish is blue or nickel-plate, and the grips are checkered hard rubber or walnut. Barrel lengths of 4" or 6.5" were offered. This model was not at all popular, as only 74 were manufactured in their own serial range 1 through 74. Today's collectors are extremely interested in this extremely rare model. **NOTE:** Rarity makes valuation speculative.

Courtesy Mike Stuckslager

NIB	Exc.	V.G.	Good	Fair	Poor
—	—	14000	8000	4000	500

.44 Double-Action 1st Model

This model is a top break revolver that automatically ejects the spent cartridge cases upon opening. The barrel latch is located at the top and rear of the cylinder; the pivot, in front and at the bottom. This model was also known as "The D.A. Frontier" or "The New Model Navy." The revolver is chambered for the .44 S&W Russian and was built on a modified Model 3 frame. It is also found on rare occasions chambered for the .38-40 and the .44-40 Winchester. The barrel lengths are 4", 5", 6", and 6.5", round with a raised rib. A 3-1/2" barrel was produced on this model by special request. Collectors should be aware that the barrel for this model and the New Model No. 3 were interchangeable and the factory did in fact use barrels from either model. The serial number on the rear of the barrel should match the number on the butt, cylinder and barrel latch. The cylinder holds 6 shots and is fluted. It has double sets of stop notches and long free grooves between the stops. It is serial numbered in its own range, beginning at 1. There were approximately 54,000 manufactured between 1881 and 1913.

Courtesy Bonhams & Butterfields, San Francisco, California

Standard .44 S&W Russian

NIB	Exc.	V.G.	Good	Fair	Poor
—	—	2000	1300	700	400

Model .44 Double-Action Wesson Favorite

The Favorite is basically a lightened version of the 1st Model D.A. .44. The barrel is thinner and is offered in 5" length only. There are lightening cuts in the frame between the trigger guard and the cylinder; the cylinder diameter was smaller, and there is a groove milled along the barrel rib. The Favorite is chambered for the .44 S&W Russian cartridge and has a 6-shot fluted cylinder with the same double-cylinder stop notches and free grooves as the 1st Model Double-Action .44. The company name and address, as well as the patent dates, are stamped into the edge of the cylinder instead of on the barrel rib. It is serial-numbered in the same range, between 9000 and 10100. The revolver was most often nickel-plated but was also offered blued. The grips are walnut or checkered hard rubber with the S&W logo molded in. There were approximately 1,000 manufactured in 1882 and 1883. Use caution when purchasing a blued model. **NOTE:** Rarity makes valuation speculative. Blued finish add 25 percent.

NIB	Exc.	V.G.	Good	Fair	Poor
—	—	9000	5000	2500	500

Model .44 Double-Action Frontier

Chambered for the .44-40 cartridge. This is a separate model from the .44 Double-Action 1st Model. It has a longer 19/16" cylinder like the later .44 double-action 1st Model's. Produced from 1886 to 1916 with their own serial number range. Approximately 15,340 built.

NIB	Exc.	V.G.	Good	Fair	Poor
—	—	1850	1200	750	400

Model .38 Winchester Double-Action

Similar to the .44 Double-Action 1st Model except for the chamber. Fitted with long cylinder. Approximately 276 produced in their own serial number range from 1900 to 1910.

NIB	Exc.	V.G.	Good	Fair	Poor
—	—	5500	3000	1250	500

1st Model Single-Shot

This unusual pistol combines the frame of the .38 Single-Action 3rd Model with a single-shot barrel. This model is a top break and functions exactly as the revolver models do. The barrel length is 6", 8", or 10"; and the pistol is chambered for .22 LR, .32 S&W, and .38 S&W. The finish is blue or nickel plated, with a square butt. The grips are checkered hard rubber extension types for a proper target hold. This pistol is considered quite rare on today's market, as only 1,251 were manufactured between 1893 and 1905.

.22 L.R.
NIB	Exc.	V.G.	Good	Fair	Poor
—	2000	1500	1000	600	400

.32 S&W
NIB	Exc.	V.G.	Good	Fair	Poor
—	2200	1750	1275	700	500

.38 S&W
NIB	Exc.	V.G.	Good	Fair	Poor
—	2500	1900	1400	750	50

2nd Model Single-Shot

The 2nd Model single-shot has a frame with the recoil shield removed, is chambered for the .22 LR only, and is offered with the 10" barrel. The finish is blue or nickel plated, and the grips are checkered hard rubber extension types. There were approximately 4,617 manufactured between 1905 and 1909.

Courtesy Mike Stuckslager

NIB	Exc.	V.G.	Good	Fair	Poor
—	1500	1100	650	350	175

3rd Model Single-Shot

The basic difference between this model and the 2nd Model is that this pistol could be fired double-action as well as single-action, and the frame came from the double-action perfected model. There were 6,949 manufactured between 1909 and 1923.

Courtesy Mike Stuckslager

NIB	Exc.	V.G.	Good	Fair	Poor
—	2000	1400	1200	600	300

SMITH & WESSON • 1033

Straight Line Single-Shot

This is a unique pistol that very much resembles a semi-automatic. The barrel is 10" in length and pivots to the left for loading. It is chambered for .22 LR cartridge and is finished in blue, with walnut grips inlaid with the S&W medallions. The hammer is straight-line in function and does not pivot. There were 1,870 manufactured between 1925 and 1936.

Courtesy Bonhams & Butterfields, San Francisco, California

NIB	Exc.	V.G.	Good	Fair	Poor
—	2500	1750	900	700	400

.32 Hand Ejector Model of 1896 or .32 Hand Ejector 1st Model

This model was the first time S&W made a revolver with a swing-out cylinder. Interestingly, there is no cylinder latch; but the action opens by pulling forward on the exposed portion of the cylinder pin. This frees the spring tension and allows the cylinder to swing free. Another novel feature of this model is the cylinder stop location, which is located in the top of the frame over the cylinder. This model is chambered for the .32 S&W Long cartridge, has a 6-shot fluted cylinder, and is offered with 3.25", 4.25", and 6" long barrels. It is available with either a round or square butt, has checkered hard rubber grips, and is blued or nickel-plated. Factory installed target sights were available by special order. The company name, address, and patent dates are stamped on the cylinder instead of on the barrel. There were approximately 19,712 manufactured between 1896 and 1903.

Courtesy Mike Stuckslager

NIB	Exc.	V.G.	Good	Fair	Poor
900	650	425	350	200	150

Hand Ejector Model of 1903

This model is quite different from its predecessor. The cylinder locks front and back; the cylinder stop is located in the bottom of the frame, and the familiar sliding cylinder latch is found on the left side of the frame. The barrel lengths are 3.25", 4.25", and 6". The 6-shot cylinder is fluted, and the revolver is chambered for .32 S&W Long. It is offered either blued or nickel-plated, and the round butt grips are checkered hard rubber. There were approximately 19,425 manufactured in 1903 and 1904; serial number range 1 to 19425.

Courtesy Mike Stuckslager

NIB	Exc.	V.G.	Good	Fair	Poor
—	550	350	200	150	100

.32 Hand Ejector Model of 1903 1st Change

This model differs from the model of 1903 internally, and the serial number range 19426 to 51126 is really the only way to differentiate the two. There were approximately 31,700 manufactured between 1904 and 1906.

NIB	Exc.	V.G.	Good	Fair	Poor
—	1400	1200	950	650	300

.32 Hand Ejector Model of 1903 2nd Change

Produced from 1906 to 1909 in serial number range 51127 to 95500. A total of 44,373 manufactured.

.32 Hand Ejector Model of 1903 3rd Change

Produced from 1909 to 1910 in serial number range 95501 to 96125. A total of 624 manufactured.

.32 Hand Ejector Model of 1903 4th Change

Produced in 1910 in serial number range 96126 to 102500. A total of 6,374 manufactured.

.32 Hand Ejector Model of 1903 5th Change

Produced from 1910 to 1917 in serial number range 102500 to 263000. A total of 160,500 manufactured.

.32 Hand Ejector Third Model

Produced from 1911 to 1942 in serial number range 263001 to 536684. A total of 273,683 were manufactured.

NIB	Exc.	V.G.	Good	Fair	Poor
—	650	500	375	250	150

K-32 Hand Ejector First Model

This is one of the rarest pre-war K-frame revolvers. Chambered for the .32 S&W Long cartridge, less than 100 were made between 1936 and 1941. After WWII this model was part of the K-22/K-32/K-38 Masterpiece series of 6-inch barreled, target-sighted revolvers. Due to the rarity of this model, an expert appraisal is essential.

NIB	Exc.	V.G.	Good	Fair	Poor
—	18000	13500	9000	3500	800

.22 Ladysmith 1st Model

This model was designed primarily as a defensive weapon for women. Its small size and caliber made it ideal for that purpose. The 1st Model Ladysmith is chambered for .22 Long cartridge and has a 7-shot fluted cylinder and 3" and 3.5" barrel lengths. This little revolver weighed 9-5/8 ounces. It is either blued or nickel-plated and has a round butt with checkered hard rubber grips.

The 1st Model has a checkered cylinder-latch button on the left side of the frame. There were approximately 4,575 manufactured between 1902 and 1906.

NIB	Exc.	V.G.	Good	Fair	Poor
—	2300	1550	1050	650	450

.22 Ladysmith 2nd Model

This is essentially quite similar in appearance to the 1st Model, the difference being in the pull-forward cylinder latch located under the barrel, replacing the button on the left side of the frame. The new method allowed lockup front and back for greater action strength. The 2.25" barrel length was dropped; caliber and finishes are the same. There were approximately 9,374 manufactured between 1906 and 1910; serial number range 4576 to 13950. **NOTE:** Use caution. UNABLE TO PRICE. At least double the military model values. Expert appraisal needed.

Courtesy Mike Stuckslager

NIB	Exc.	V.G.	Good	Fair	Poor
—	2000	1250	1000	600	400

.22 Ladysmith 3rd Model

This model is quite different in appearance to the 2nd Model, as it features a square butt and smooth walnut grips with inlaid S&W medallions. The barrel lengths remained the same, with the addition of a 2.25" and 6" variation. The under barrel cylinder lockup was not changed, nor were the caliber and finishes. There were approximately 12,200 manufactured between 1910 and 1921; serial number range 13951 to 26154. **NOTE:** Add a 50 percent premium for 2.25" and 6" barrel lengths.

Courtesy W.P. Hallstein III and son Chip

NIB	Exc.	V.G.	Good	Fair	Poor
—	1750	1200	950	600	400

K-22 Outdoorsman/Masterpiece

Pre-war version of the K-22 K-frame, 6" barreled revolver chambered for the .22 Short, Long and Long Rifle. Walnut grips, adjustable rear sight, ribbed barrel. Manufactured from 1931 to 1940. In 1940 the name was changed to K-22 Masterpiece and an improved adjustable rear sight was added. The S&W short action was another improvement. Only about 1,000 K-22 Masterpieces were manufactured in 1940. **NOTE:** Add 100 percent premium for 1940 manufacture in 682,420 - 696,952 serial number range.

NIB	Exc.	V.G.	Good	Fair	Poor
2500	2000	1600	1000	500	300

.38 Hand Ejector Military & Police 1st Model or Model of 1899

This was an early swing-out cylinder revolver, and it has no front lockup for the action. The release is on the left side of the frame. This model is chambered for .38 S&W Special cartridge and the .32 Winchester centerfire cartridge (.32-20), has a 6-shot fluted cylinder, and was offered with a 4", 5", 6", 6.5", or 8" barrel in .38 caliber and 4", 5", and 6-1/2" in .32-20 caliber. The finish is blued or nickel-plated; the grips, checkered walnut or hard rubber. There were approximately 20,975 manufactured between 1899 and 1902 in .38 caliber; serial number range 1 to 20975. In the .32-20 caliber 5,311 were sold between 1899 and 1902; serial number range 1 to 5311.

Courtesy Mike Stuckslager

Commercial Model

NIB	Exc.	V.G.	Good	Fair	Poor
—	1500	1200	800	450	350

U.S. Navy Model

One thousand produced in 1900, .38 S&W, 6" barrel, blued with checkered walnut grips, "U.S.N." stamped on butt, serial number range 5000 to 6000.

NIB	Exc.	V.G.	Good	Fair	Poor
—	3000	2500	1200	500	300

U.S. Army Model

One thousand produced in 1901, same as Navy Model except that it is marked "U.S.Army/Model 1899" on butt, "K.S.M." and "J.T.T." on grips, serial number range 13001 to 14000.

NIB	Exc.	V.G.	Good	Fair	Poor
—	3000	2500	1200	500	300

.38 Hand Ejector M&P 2nd Model or Model of 1902

The 2nd Model is similar in appearance to the 1st Model. The major difference is the addition of the front lockup under the barrel, and the ejector rod was increased in diameter. Barrel lengths for the .38 S&W were 4", 5", 6" or 6.5" while the .32-20 was available in 4", 5" or 6.5" barrel lengths. Both calibers were offered in round butt only configuration. There were approximately 12,827 manufactured in .38 S&W in 1902 and 1903; serial number range 20976 to 33803. In the .32-20 caliber 4,499 were produced; serial number range 5312 to 9811. **NOTE:** Add 250 percent for U.S. Navy Model.

NIB	Exc.	V.G.	Good	Fair	Poor
—	1200	900	500	250	100

.38 Hand Ejector M&P 2nd Model, 1st Change

Built between 1903 and 1905 this variation represents the change to the square butt, which made for better shooting control and standardized frame shape. Both the .38 S&W and the .32-20 were available in 4", 5", or 6-1/2" barrel lengths. The company manufactured 28,645 .38 calibers; serial number range 33804 to 62449 and produced 8,313 .32-20s; serial number 9812 to 18125.

NIB	Exc.	V.G.	Good	Fair	Poor
—	1100	800	400	250	100

.38 Hand Ejector Model of 1905

This model was a continuation of the .38 M&P Hand Ejector series. Built from 1905 to 1906 it was available in 4", 5", 6", and 6-1/2" barrels for both the .38 and .32-20 calibers. Finished in either blue or nickel with round or square butt the .38 caliber model serial number range was from 62450 to 73250 or about 10,800 produced. The .32-20 caliber serial number range spans 18126 to 22426 or 4,300 produced. **NOTE:** Prices for the following four variations will be the same as those noted above.

NIB	Exc.	V.G.	Good	Fair	Poor
—	1200	950	650	400	150

.38 Hand Ejector Model of 1905, 1st Change

Produced from 1906 to 1908 this model is similar to the original model of 1905 with regard to barrel lengths, finish and butt styles. The 1st change in .38 caliber was produced in serial number range 73251 to 120000 with 46,749 sold. In .32-20 caliber the serial-number range was 22427 to 33500 with 11,073 sold.

.38 Hand Ejector Model of 1905, 2nd Change

Produced from 1908 to 1909 only internal changes were made to this model. The best approach to differentiate this model is by serial number. The .38 caliber serial number range was from 120001 to 146899 with 26,898 produced. In the .32-20 caliber the serial number range is between 33501 and 45200 with 11,699 produced.

.38 Hand Ejector Model of 1905, 3rd Change

Produced from 1909 to 1915 the 3rd Change variation was available in only 4" or 6" barrel lengths for both the .38 and .32-20 models. The .38 caliber serial number range was between 146900 to 241703 with 94,803 sold.

Courtesy Mike Stuckslager

.38 Hand Ejector Model of 1905, 4th Change

This last variation was also the longest production run. Produced from 1915 to 1942 the .38 caliber model was available in 2", 4", 5", or 6", barrel lengths while the .32-20 caliber was offered in 4", 5", or 6" barrel lengths. The .38 caliber serial number range was from 241704 to 1000000. The .32-20 caliber model was produced from 1915 to 1940 in serial number range from 65701 to 144684.

Courtesy Mike Stuckslager

.22-32 Hand Ejector

This is a very interesting model from the collector's point of view. Phillip B. Bekeart, a San Francisco firearms dealer requested that S&W manufacture a .22 caliber target-grade revolver on the heavier .32 frame. He believed in his idea so passionately that he immediately ordered 1,000 of the guns for himself. This initial order is found within the serial number range 1 to 3000 and are known to collectors as the authentic Bekearts. The remainder of the extensive production run are simply .22-32 Hand Ejectors. This model is chambered for .22 LR cartridge and has a 6-shot fluted cylinder with 6" barrel. The finish is blue, with square butt and checkered extension-type walnut grips. There were only 292 revolvers of his initial order delivered to Mr. Bekeart, but the first 1,000 pistols are considered to be True Bekearts. The production number of each respective pistol is stamped into the base of the extended wooden grips. S&W went on to manufacture several hundred thousand of these revolvers between 1911 and 1953.

Courtesy Mike Stuckslager

"The True Bekeart"

Serial number range 138226 to 139275 in the .32 Hand Ejector series, production number stamped on butt. Professional appraisal should be secured.

NIB	Exc.	V.G.	Good	Fair	Poor
—	1500	1400	900	700	250

Standard Model

NIB	Exc.	V.G.	Good	Fair	Poor
—	600	400	250	200	125

.44 Hand Ejector 1st Model

This model is also known by collectors as the ".44 Triple Lock" or "The New Century." The Triple Lock nickname came from a separate locking device located on the extractor rod shroud that is used in addition to the usual two locks. This model is chambered for the .44 S&W Special cartridge or the .44 S&W Russian. On a limited basis it is also chambered in .44-40, .45 Colt, and .38-40. The fluted cylinder holds 6 shots, and the barrel was offered in standard lengths of 5" or 6.5". A limited quantity of 4" barrel was produced. The finish is blued or nickel-plated; and the grips are checkered walnut, with the gold S&W medallion on later models. There were approximately 15,375 manufactured between 1908 and 1915.

Courtesy Mike Stuckslager

.44 S&W Special

NIB	Exc.	V.G.	Good	Fair	Poor
—	3250	1800	1175	600	500

Other Calibers (Rare)

NIB	Exc.	V.G.	Good	Fair	Poor
—	4000	2000	1300	750	500

.44 Hand Ejector 2nd Model

This model is quite similar in appearance to the 1st Model. The major difference is the elimination of the third or triple lock device and the heavy ejector rod shroud. Other changes are internal and not readily apparent. This model is also standard in .44 S&W Special chambering but was offered rarely in .38-40, .44-40, and .45 Colt. Specimens have been noted with adjustable sights in 6-1/2" barrel lengths. Standard barrel lengths were 4", 5", and 6-1/2". There were approximately 17,510 manufactured between 1915 and 1937 in serial number range 15376 to 60000.

.44 S&W Special

NIB	Exc.	V.G.	Good	Fair	Poor
—	2300	1800	1250	500	200

.38-40, .44-40 or .45 Colt

NIB	Exc.	V.G.	Good	Fair	Poor
—	3700	3000	2400	1000	500

.44 Hand Ejector 3rd Model or Model of 1926

This model is similar in appearance to the 2nd Model but brought back the heavy ejector rod shroud of the 1st Model without the triple lock device. Barrel lengths were 4", 5", and 6-1/2". The .44 Hand Ejector Model was manufactured between 1926 and 1949.

Courtesy Mike Stuckslager

.44 S&W Special

NIB	Exc.	V.G.	Good	Fair	Poor
—	3000	2400	2000	1000	500

.44-40 or .45 Colt

NIB	Exc.	V.G.	Good	Fair	Poor
—	4500	3500	3000	2000	500

.44 Hand Ejector 4th Model (Target Model)

The 4th Model featured a ribbed barrel, micrometer adjustable sight, and short throw hammer. Never a popular seller this model had only 5,050 pistol produced between 1950 and 1966.

NIB	Exc.	V.G.	Good	Fair	Poor
—	3000	2400	2000	1000	500

.45 Hand Ejector U.S. Service Model of 1917

WWI was on the horizon, and it seemed certain that the United States would become involved. The S&W people began to work with the Springfield Armory to develop a hand ejector model that would fire the .45-caliber Government cartridge. This was accomplished in 1916 by the use of half-moon clips. The new revolver is quite similar to the .44 Hand Ejector in appearance. It has a 5.5" barrel, blued finish with smooth walnut grips, and a lanyard ring on the butt. The designation "U.S.Army Model 1917" is stamped on the butt. After the war broke out, the government was not satisfied with S&W's production and actually took control of the company for the duration of the war. This was the first time that the company was not controlled by a Wesson. The factory records indicate that there were 163,476 Model 1917s manufactured between 1917 and 1919, the WWI years. After the war, the sale of these revolvers continued on a commercial and contract basis until 1949, when this model was finally dropped from the S&W product line.

Military Model

NIB	Exc.	V.G.	Good	Fair	Poor
—	1500	1200	1000	400	200

Brazilian Contract

25,000 produced for the Brazilian government in 1938. The Brazilian crest is stamped on the sideplate.

NIB	Exc.	V.G.	Good	Fair	Poor
—	1100	800	500	250	125

Commercial Model

High gloss blue and checkered walnut grips.

Courtesy Mike Stuckslager

NIB	Exc.	V.G.	Good	Fair	Poor
—	2000	1500	1000	475	300

.455 Mark II Hand Ejector 1st Model

This model was designed the same as the .44 Hand Ejector 1st Model with no caliber stamping on the barrel. It has a barrel length of 6.4". Of the 5,000 revolvers produced and sold only 100 were commercial guns, the rest were military. Produced between 1914 and 1915. The commercial model is worth a premium.

NIB	Exc.	V.G.	Good	Fair	Poor
—	1400	1150	700	400	200

.455 Mark II Hand Ejector 2nd Model

Similar to the first model without an extractor shroud. Barrel length was also 6.5". Serial number range was 5000 to 74755. Manufactured from 1915 to 1917.

NIB	Exc.	V.G.	Good	Fair	Poor
—	1300	1050	600	350	175

S&W .35 Automatic Pistol

Production of the .35 Automatic was S&W's first attempt at an auto-loading pistol. As was always the case, the company strived for maximum safety and dependability. This model has a 3.5" barrel and a 7-shot detachable magazine and is chambered in .35 S&W Automatic, a one-time-only cartridge that eventually proved to be the major downfall of this pistol from a commercial standpoint. There were two separate safety devices—a revolving cam on the backstrap and a grip safety on the front strap that had to be fully depressed simultaneously while squeezing the trigger. The finish is blue or nickel-plated; and the grips are walnut, with the S&W inlaid medallions. The magazine release slides from side to side and is checkered, expensive to manufacture, and destined to be modified. There were approximately 8,350 manufactured.

NIB	Exc.	V.G.	Good	Fair	Poor
—	750	450	300	200	150

S&W .32 Automatic Pistol

In 1921 it became apparent to the powers that controlled S&W that the .35-caliber automatic was never going to be a commercial success. Harold Wesson, the new president, began to redesign the pistol to accept the .32 ACP, a commercially accepted cartridge, and to streamline the appearance to be more competitive with the other pistols on the market, notably Colt's. This new pistol used as many parts from the older model as possible for economy's sake. The pivoting barrel was discontinued, as was the cam-type safety in the rear grip strap. A magazine disconnector and a reduced-strength recoil spring to ease cocking were employed. The barrel length was kept at 3.5", and the 7-shot magazine was retained. The finish is blued only, and the grips are smooth walnut. There were only 957 of these manufactured between 1924 and 1936. They are eagerly sought by collectors.

Courtesy James Rankin

NIB	Exc.	V.G.	Good	Fair	Poor
—	2500	1750	1100	700	500

SMITH & WESSON MODERN HANDGUNS

NOTE: A surprising number of pistols are still found in their original boxes even for older models. This can add 100 percent to the value of the pistol.

With the development of the Hand Ejector Models and the swingout cylinders, Smith & Wesson opened the door to a number of new advancements in the revolver field. This new system allowed for a solid frame, making the weapon much stronger than the old top break design. The company also developed different basic frame sizes and gave them letter designations. The I frame, which later developed into the slightly larger J frame, was used for the .22-32 and the small, concealable .38 revolvers. The medium K frame was used for .38 duty- and target-type weapons. The N frame was the heavy-duty frame used for the larger .357 and .44 and .45 caliber revolvers. The hand ejector went through many evolutionary changes over the years. Beginning in 1959, all S&W models were given numerical designations — Model 10, Model 14, etc. Models are cataloged here by their numerical designations, brief description are given, and current values offered. It is important to note that the S&W revolver that we see marketed by the company today has undergone many changes in reaching its present configuration. The early models featured five screws in their construction, not counting the grip screw. There were four screws fastening the sideplate and another through the front of the trigger guard that retained the cylinder stop plunger. The first change involved the elimination of the top sideplate screw, and the five-screw Smith & Wesson became the four-screw. Later the frame was changed to eliminate the cylinder stop plunger screw, and the three-screw was created. Some models were offered with a flat cylinder latch that was serrated instead of the familiar checkering. In 1978, the method of attaching the barrel to the frame was changed; and the familiar pin was eliminated. At the same time, the recessed cylinder commonly found on magnum models was also eliminated. All of these factors have a definite affect on the value and collectibility of a particular S&W handgun.

NOTE: The pre-model number designations are listed in parentheses after the model number.

Courtesy Smith & Wesson

Model 10 (.38 Military & Police)

This model has been in production in one configuration or another since 1899. It was always the mainstay of the S&W line and was originally known as the .38 Military and Police Model. The Model 10 is built on the K, or medium frame, and was always meant as a duty gun. It was offered with a 2", 3", 4", 5", or 6" barrel. Currently only the 4" and 6" are available. A round or square butt is offered. It is chambered for the .38 Special and is offered in blue or nickel-plate, with checkered walnut grips. The model designation is stamped on the yoke on all S&W revolvers. This model, with many other modern S&W pistols, underwent several engineering changes. These changes may affect the value of the pistol and an expert should be consulted. The dates of these changes are as follows:

10-NONE-1957	10-1-1959	10-2-1961
10-3-1961	10-4-1962	10-5-1962
10-6-1962		

NIB	Exc.	V.G.	Good	Fair	Poor
500	300	200	150	125	90

Victory Model

Manufactured during WWII, this is a Model 10 with a sandblasted and parkerized finish, a lanyard swivel, and smooth walnut grips. The serial number has a V prefix. This model was available in only 2" and 4" barrel lengths. The Victory Model was discontinued on April 27, 1945, with serial number VS811119. **NOTE:** Top strap marked Navy will bring a 75 percent premium. Navy variation with both top strap and side plate marked will bring a 100 percent premium. Navy variation marked "N.Y.M.I." will bring a 125 percent premium. Revolvers marked "U.S.G.C." or "U.S.M.C." will bring a premium of unknown amount. Exercise caution.

NIB	Exc.	V.G.	Good	Fair	Poor
—	600	395	250	100	75

Model 11 (.38/200 British)

First produced in 1947 S&W received many contracts for this service pistol. Nicknamed the .38/200 British Service Revolver, the company sold many of these models throughout the 1950s and 1960s. There are several rare variations of this model that will greatly affect its value. Consult an expert if special markings and barrel lengths are encountered.

NIB	Exc.	V.G.	Good	Fair	Poor
—	500	375	225	100	75

Model 12 (.38 Military & Police Airweight)

The Model 12 was introduced in 1952, starting serial number C223999, and is merely a Model 10 with a lightweight alloy frame and cylinder. In 1954 the alloy cylinder was replaced with one of steel that added an additional 4 ounces in weight. Discontinued in 1986. **NOTE:** Aluminum cylinder model add 40 percent.

NIB	Exc.	V.G.	Good	Fair	Poor
—	700	500	250	125	100

USAF M-13 (Aircrewman)

This model was manufactured in the early 1950s for the U.S. Air Force on the Model 12 K-frame. The revolvers were chambered in .38 Special and have an alloy frame and cylinder. They were to be carried by pilots and other flight-crew members for emergency use. The Air Force ultimately rejected the model because of problems encountered with the alloy cylinder and most were destroyed. Because of this, the Aircrewman is one of the rarest modern-day Smith & Wesson revolvers. Serial numbers are in the C247000 to C406000 range and it is not known how many still exist. The genuine model is seldom seen for sale. Numerous fakes have been documented, so it is strongly suggested that a knowledgeable S&W expert be consulted for an appraisal. A few "Baby" Aircrewman 5-shot revolvers were made on the S&W J-frame and it is believed that fewer than 15 of these guns still exist. Because of the rarity of these two models and the few actual transactions that have occurred in recent years, it is not possible to list meaningful values.

Model 13 (.357 Military & Police)

This is simply the Model 10 M&P chambered for the .357 Magnum and fitted with a heavy barrel. It was introduced in 1974.

NIB	Exc.	V.G.	Good	Fair	Poor
525	425	350	275	175	125

Model 14 (K-38 Masterpiece)

This model is also known as the "K-38." In 1957 "Model 14" was stamped on the yoke. This model is offered in a 6" barrel with adjustable sights. In 1961 a single-action version with faster lock time was offered. This would be worth a small premium. This model was discontinued in 1981. **NOTE:** Single-action model add 25 percent.

NIB	Exc.	V.G.	Good	Fair	Poor
675	600	450	200	175	125

Model 15 (K-38 Combat Masterpiece)

Also known as the "Combat Masterpiece" this model was produced at the request of law enforcement officers who wanted the "K-38" fitted with a 4" barrel. The model went into production in 1950 and was discontinued in 1987.

NIB	Exc.	V.G.	Good	Fair	Poor
600	475	350	200	175	125

Model 16 (K-32 Masterpiece)

Also known as the "K-32" until 1957, this model is identical in appearance to the Model 14 except that it is chambered for .32 S&W. The Model 16 did not enjoy the commercial popularity of the Model 14 and was dropped from the line in 1973. Only 3,630 K-32s/Model 16s were sold between 1947 and 1973. Reintroduced in 1990 in .32 Magnum and discontinued in 1993. **NOTE:** Add 25 percent for 1946 - 1957 production (no Model 16 marking).

Courtesy Mike Stuckslager

NIB	Exc.	V.G.	Good	Fair	Poor
2750	2200	1800	1200	400	200

Model 16 (.32 Magnum)

Reintroduced in 1990 in .32 Magnum and discontinued in 1993.

NIB	Exc.	V.G.	Good	Fair	Poor
1250	800	450	200	150	100

K-32 Combat Masterpiece

S&W produced a limited number of 4" barreled K-32 revolvers. They were never given a number designation, as they were discontinued before 1957 when the numbering system began.

NIB	Exc.	V.G.	Good	Fair	Poor
2600	2000	1500	900	350	300

Model 17 (K-22)

This is the numerical designation that S&W placed on the "K-22" in 1957. This target model .22 rimfire revolver has always been popular since its introduction in 1946. It is offered in 4", 6", and 8-3/8" barrel lengths, with all target options. The 8-3/8" barrel was dropped from the product line in 1993. The finish is blued, and it has checkered walnut grips.

Courtesy Mike Stuckslager

NIB	Exc.	V.G.	Good	Fair	Poor
650	475	300	175	125	100

Model 17 Plus

Introduced in 1996 this new version of the old Model 17 has a 10-round cylinder for its .22 LR cartridges. It features a 6" full lug barrel with Patridge front sight and adjustable rear sight. The hammer is semi-target style and the trigger is a smooth combat style. Finish is matte black and the grips are Hogue black rubber. Drilled and tapped for scope mounts. Weight is about 42 oz. Discontinued.

NIB	Exc.	V.G.	Good	Fair	Poor
650	475	300	175	125	100

Model 617 Plus

Identical to the Model 17 but furnished with stainless steel frame and cylinder.

NIB	Exc.	V.G.	Good	Fair	Poor
575	400	250	200	150	100

Model 647

Introduced in 2003 this revolver is chambered for the .17 HMR cartridge. Fitted with a 8.375" barrel with full lug. Six-round cylinder capacity. Stainless steel finish. Adjustable rear sight. Hogue rubber grips. Fitted with a target trigger and hammer. Drilled and tapped for scope. Weight is about 52.5 oz. Discontinued.

NIB	Exc.	V.G.	Good	Fair	Poor
775	525	375	225	175	100

Model 648

Identical to the Model 617 but chambered for the .22 Magnum rimfire cartridge.

NIB	Exc.	V.G.	Good	Fair	Poor
675	500	375	225	175	100

Model 648 (New Model)

Introduced in 2003 this medium frame revolver is chambered for the .22 WMR cartridge and fitted with a 6" full lug barrel. Pinned Patridge front sight and adjustable rear sight. New extractor

system. Drilled and tapped for scope mount. Stainless steel finish. Weight is 45 oz.

NIB	Exc.	V.G.	Good	Fair	Poor
700	525	395	250	200	125

Note On "K Frame" Target Models:
1. The factory eliminated the upper corner screw from the side plate in 1955. The 5-screw became a 4-screw. This change occurred around serial number K260000.

2. Model number designations were stamped on the yoke in 1957.

Model 18 (K-22 Combat Masterpiece)

This is the model designation for the 4"-barrel "Combat Masterpiece" chambered for the .22 rimfire.

NIB	Exc.	V.G.	Good	Fair	Poor
—	675	475	300	200	125

Model 19 (.357 Combat Magnum)

Introduced in 1954 at the urging of Bill Jordan, a competition shooter with the U.S. Border Patrol who went on to become a respected gun writer, this model is one of Smith and Wesson's most popular pistols. It was built on the "K-Frame" and was the first medium frame revolver chambered for the powerful .357 Magnum cartridge. Since its inception the Model 19 has been one of S&W's most popular revolvers. It was the first revolver to be introduced as a three-screw model. Originally it was offered with a 4" heavy barrel with extractor shroud; the 6" became available in 1963. The finish is blued or nickel plated, and the grips are checkered walnut. The Goncalo Alves target stocks first appeared in 1959. In 1968 a 2.5" round butt version was introduced. The Model 19 has been the basis for two commemoratives—the Texas Ranger/with Bowie Knife and the Oregon State Police/with Belt Buckle. This model is no longer in production.

Combat Magnum (Pre-Model 19, 1954-1958)

NOTE: Add 50 percent for nickel finish.

NIB	Exc.	V.G.	Good	Fair	Poor
1600	1300	1000	650	350	200

Model 19, 19-1

NOTE: Add 40 percent for nickel finish.

NIB	Exc.	V.G.	Good	Fair	Poor
1200	950	750	500	300	200

Model 19-2, 19-3

NIB	Exc.	V.G.	Good	Fair	Poor
650	550	450	375	300	200

Oregon State Police Cased with Buckle

NIB	Exc.	V.G.	Good	Fair	Poor
900	—	—	—	—	—

Texas Ranger Cased with Knife

NIB	Exc.	V.G.	Good	Fair	Poor
700	—	—	—	—	—

Model 20 (.38/.44 Heavy Duty)

Known as the ".38/.44 Heavy Duty" before the change to numerical designations this model was brought out in 1930 in response to requests from law enforcement personnel for a more powerful sidearm. This model, along with the .38-44 S&W Special cartridge, was an attempt to solve the problem. The revolver was manufactured with a standard 5" long barrel but has been noted rarely as short as 3.5" and as long as 8-3/8". It was built on the large N-frame and is blued or nickel-plated, with checkered walnut grips. Eventually the popularity of the .357 Magnum made the Model 20 superfluous, and it was discontinued in 1966. Post-war production for this model was about 20,000 revolvers. **NOTE:** Pre-war add 50 percent.

Courtesy Mike Stuckslager

NIB	Exc.	V.G.	Good	Fair	Poor
1250	1000	850	600	450	200

Model 21 (1950 Military)

This model was known as the "1950 Military" and the "4th Model .44 Hand Ejector" before the Model 21 designation was applied in 1957. The Model 21 was chambered for the .44 Special cartridge and equipped with fixed sights. The Model 21 was built on the N frame and is quite rare, as only 1,200 were manufactured in 16 years of production. It was discontinued in 1966.

NIB	Exc.	V.G.	Good	Fair	Poor
2800	2500	1800	950	650	500

Model 21 Thunder Ranch

This limited edition variation is a 4" barreled .44 Special with a gold-plated logo of the legendary Arizona shooting school on the frame.

NIB	Exc.	V.G.	Good	Fair	Poor
800	650	500	400	300	200

Model 696

Introduced in 1997 this model features a 3" underlug barrel. chambered for the .44 Special and fitted on an L-frame, capacity is 5 rounds. Grips are Hogue black rubber. Finish is stainless steel. Weight is approximately 48 oz.

NIB	Exc.	V.G.	Good	Fair	Poor
850	725	600	450	300	—

Model 22 (1950 .45 Military)

This model was known as the "1950 .45 Military" before 1957. It was actually introduced in 1951 and is similar in appearance to the Model 21 except that it is chambered for the .45 Auto Rim or .45 ACP cartridge. Half-moon clips are used with the latter. There were 3,976 manufactured between 1951 and 1966. Beginning serial number for this model was S85,000.

NIB	Exc.	V.G.	Good	Fair	Poor
1850	1550	1350	950	650	500

Model 23 (.38-44 Outdoorsman)

The .38-44 Outdoorsman was the model name of this N-frame revolver before the 1957 designation change. This is simply the Model 20 with adjustable sights. It was introduced in 1931 as a heavy-duty sporting handgun with hunters in mind. S&W produced 4,761 of these pre-war revolvers. It features a 6.5" barrel and blued finish and was the first S&W to have the new checkered walnut "Magna" grips. After 1949 this revolver was thoroughly modernized and had the later ribbed barrel. There were a total of 8,365 manufactured before the model was discontinued in 1966. 6,039 were of the modernized configuration. **NOTE:** Add 50 percent for pre-war production.

Courtesy Mike Stuckslager

NIB	Exc.	V.G.	Good	Fair	Poor
1700	1500	1200	600	250	200

Model 22 – Thunder Ranch .45 ACP

Limited edition six-shot single/double-action chambered for .45 ACP. Blued with 4" tapered barrel, 37.5 oz. Cocobolo grips engraved with Thunder Ranch insignia. Fixed sights. Serial numbers begin with TRR0000.

NIB	Exc.	V.G.	Good	Fair	Poor
—	850	675	500	250	200

Model 24 (.44 Target Model of 1950)

This model was introduced as the .44 Target Model of 1950. It is simply the N-frame Model 21 with adjustable target sights.

This revolver was quite popular with the long-range handgunning devotees and their leader, Elmer Keith. The introduction of the .44 Magnum in 1956 began the death knell of the Model 24, and it was finally discontinued in 1966. S&W produced a total of 5,050 Model 24s. It was reintroduced in 1983 and 1984—and then was dropped again. **NOTE:** Add 25 percent for 4" barrel, 40 percent for 5". Deduct 60 percent for 1983-84 model.

NIB	Exc.	V.G.	Good	Fair	Poor
2500	2000	1600	1000	650	500

Model 25 (.45 Target Model of 1950)

Prior to the model designation change in 1957 this model was also known as the .45 Target Model of 1955, this was an improved version of the 1950 Target .45. The Model 25 features a heavier barrel 4", 6.5", or 8" in length with blued or nickel-plated finish. All target options were offered. The Model 25 is chambered for the .45 ACP or .45 Auto-rim cartridges. This model was later chambered for .45 Colt as the Model 25-5. **NOTE:** Add 100 percent premium for .45 Colt.

NIB	Exc.	V.G.	Good	Fair	Poor
1750	1550	1350	950	650	500

Model 25-3 125th Anniversary with Case

NIB	Exc.	V.G.	Good	Fair	Poor
1300	—	—	—	—	—

Model 25-2

This is the discontinued modern version of the Model 25 chambered in .45 ACP. The 6.5" barrel is shortened to 6" and is available in a presentation case.

NIB	Exc.	V.G.	Good	Fair	Poor
900	775	650	400	300	150

Model 25 Mountain Gun

Introduced in 2004 this .45 Colt N-frame round butt model features a 4" tapered barrel with black blade front sight and adjustable rear sight. Cocobolo wood grips. Blued finish. Weight is about 40 oz.

NIB	Exc.	V.G.	Good	Fair	Poor
750	625	500	425	300	150

Model 625-2

This is the stainless steel version of the Model 25-2. It is fitted with a 5" barrel and has Pachmayr SK/GR gripper stocks as standard. Designed for pin shooting. Weight is about 45 oz.

NIB	Exc.	V.G.	Good	Fair	Poor
750	625	500	425	300	150

Model 625 IDPA

As above but fitted with a 4" barrel, adjustable rear sight, patridge front sight, and Hogue grips. Introduced in 2002. Weight is about 43 oz.

NIB	Exc.	V.G.	Good	Fair	Poor
1000	850	700	575	400	200

Model 625 JM (Jerry Miculek)

Introduced in 2005 this model is chambered for the .45 ACP cartridge and fitted with a 4" full lug barrel with adjustable rear sight and Patridge front sight. Capacity is 6 rounds. Wood grips. Weight is about 43 oz.

NIB	Exc.	V.G.	Good	Fair	Poor
750	625	500	425	300	150

Model 625 Mountain Gun

Offered for the first time in 1996 this model is chambered for the .45 Colt cartridge. It is fitted with a 4" tapered barrel with ramp front sight and adjustable rear sight. The frame is drilled and tapped for a scope mount. In 2000 this model was offered in .45 Colt caliber. **NOTE:** The Model 625 Mountain Gun is a limited production revolver limited to between 2,500 and 3,000 guns. When those units are sold the model is no longer in production until re-issued by S&W.

NIB	Exc.	V.G.	Good	Fair	Poor
650	500	400	300	200	125

Model 610

Introduced in 1998 this revolver is chambered for the 10mm cartridge. It is fitted with a 6.5" full-lug barrel and an unfluted cylinder. Hogue grips are standard. Adjustable rear sight. Interchangeable front sight. Weight is approximately 52 oz.

NIB	Exc.	V.G.	Good	Fair	Poor
750	625	500	425	300	150

Model 26 (1950 .45 Target)

This is the numerical designation of the 1950 .45 Target Model. This large N-frame revolver is basically the same as the Model 25 but has a lighter, thinner barrel. This caused its unpopularity among competitive shooters who wanted a heavier revolver. This brought about the Model 25 and the demise of the Model 26 in 1961 after only 2,768 were manufactured. The Model 26 also has two additional variations and are marked 26-1 and 26-2.

NIB	Exc.	V.G.	Good	Fair	Poor
3500	2500	1800	1000	500	200

Factory Registered .357 Magnum

In the early 1930s, a gun writer named Phillip B. Sharpe became interested in the development of high performance loads to be used in the then-popular .38-44 S&W revolvers. He repeatedly urged the company to produce a revolver especially made to handle these high pressure loads. In 1934 S&W asked Winchester to produce a new cartridge that would create the ballistics that Sharpe was seeking. This new cartridge was made longer than the standard .38 Special case so that it could not inadvertently be fired in an older gun. The company never felt that this would be a commercially popular venture and from the onset visualized the ".357 Magnum" as a strictly deluxe hand-built item. They were to be individually numbered, in addition to the serial number, and registered to the new owner. The new Magnum was to be the most expensive revolver in the line. The gun went on the market in 1935, and the first one was presented to FBI Director J. Edgar Hoover. The gun was to become a tremendous success. S&W could only produce 120 per month, and this did not come close to filling orders. In 1938 the practice of numbering and registering each revolver was discontinued after 5,500 were produced. The ".357 Magnum," as it was designated, continued as one of the company's most popular items.

The Factory Registered Model was built on the N-frame. It could be custom ordered with any barrel length from 3.5" up to 8-3/8". The finish is blue, and the grips are checkered walnut. This model was virtually hand-built and test targeted. A certificate of registration was furnished with each revolver. The registration number was stamped on the yoke of the revolver with the prefix "Reg." This practice ceased in 1938 after 5,500 were produced.

NOTE: For top dollar, all accessories and registration letter must be present.

Courtesy Mike Stuckslager

NIB	Exc.	V.G.	Good	Fair	Poor
13500	10000	8500	5000	2000	500

Pre-war .357 Magnum

This is the same as the Factory Registered Model without the certificate and the individual numbering. Approximately 1,150 were manufactured between 1938 and 1941. Production ceased for WWII weapons production.

NIB	Exc.	V.G.	Good	Fair	Poor
6000	5000	4000	3000	600	300

Model 27 (.357 Magnum)

In 1948 after the end of WWII, production of this revolver commenced. The new rebound slide operated hammer block and short throw hammer were utilized, and the barrel lengths offered were 3.5", 5", 6", 6-1/2", and 8-3/8". In 1957 the model designation was changed to Model 27; and in 1975 the target trigger, hammer and Goncalo Alves target grips were made standard. This revolver is still available from S&W and has been in production longer than any other N-frame pistol. Some additional variations may be of interest to the collector. Around serial number S171584 the three-screw side plate model was first produced. In 1960 the model designation -1 was added to the model to indicate the change to a left-hand thread to the extractor rod. In 1962 the cylinder stop was changed, which disposed of the need for a plunger spring hole in front of the trigger guard. This change was indicated by a -2 behind the model number. **NOTE:** Add $1,000 premium for pre-1957 production.

NIB	Exc.	V.G.	Good	Fair	Poor
725	525	300	250	200	150

Model 627

This is special edition stainless steel version of the Model 27 and is offered with a 5-1/2" barrel. Manufactured in 1989 only. Approximately 4,500 produced.

NIB	Exc.	V.G.	Good	Fair	Poor
650	450	350	300	200	150

Model 627 Pro Series

Introduced in 2008. This is an eight-shot .357 revolver with stainless steel frame, adjustable sights, 4-inch barrel and various accurizing refinements.

NIB	Exc.	V.G.	Good	Fair	Poor
—	900	675	495	300	150

Model 28 (Highway Patrolman)

The Model 27 revolver was extremely popular among law enforcement officers, and many police agencies were interested in purchasing such a weapon—except for the cost. In 1954 S&W produced a new model called, at the time, the "Highway Patrolman." This model had all the desirable performance features of the deluxe Model 27 but lacked the cosmetic features that drove up the price. The finish is a matte blue; the rib is sandblasted instead of checkered or serrated, and the grips are the standard checkered walnut. Barrel lengths are 4" and 6.5". On late models the 6.5" barrel was reduced to 6", as on all S&Ws. The model designation was changed to Model 28 in 1957. S&W discontinued the Model 28 in 1986.

NIB	Exc.	V.G.	Good	Fair	Poor
—	625	475	325	250	100

Model 29 (.44 Magnum)

In the early 1950s, handgun writers, under the leadership of Elmer Keith, were in the habit of loading the .44 Special cartridge to high performance levels and firing them in the existing .44 Hand Ejectors. They urged S&W to produce a revolver strong enough to consistently fire these heavy loads. In 1954 Remington, at the request of S&W produced the .44 Magnum cartridge. As was the case with the .357 Magnum, the cases were longer so that they would not fit in the chambers of the older guns. The first .44 Magnum became available for sale in early 1956. The first 500 were made with the 6.5" barrel; the 4" became available later that year. In 1957 the model designation was changed to 29, and the 8-3/8" barrel was introduced. The Model 29 is available in blue or nickel-plate. It came standard with all target options and was offered in a fitted wood case. The Model 29 is considered by many knowledgeable people to be the finest revolver S&W has ever produced. The older Model 29 revolvers are in a different collector category than most modern S&W revolvers. The early four-screw models can be worth a 50 percent premium in excellent condition. These early models were produced from 1956 to 1958 and approximately 6,500 were sold. One must regard these revolvers on a separate basis and have them individually appraised for proper valuation. In 1993 the 4" barrel was dropped from production. This model is no longer in production.

NIB	Exc.	V.G.	Good	Fair	Poor
1500	1000	550	350	200	150

Early 5-Inch Barrel Model 29

This is the rarest of the Model 29s. A total of 500 were manufactured in 1958. Collectors are cautioned to exercise care before purchasing one of these rare Model 29 variations.

NIB	Exc.	V.G.	Good	Fair	Poor
4000	3200	2500	1500	500	300

Model 629

This revolver is simply a stainless steel version of the Model 29 chambered for the .44 Magnum. In 2002 this model was offered with HiViz sights.

NIB	Exc.	V.G.	Good	Fair	Poor
700	550	400	300	200	125

Model 629 Classic

This model has additional features that the standard Model 629 does not have such as: Chamfered cylinder, full lug barrel, interchangeable front sights, Hogue combat grips, and a drilled and tapped frame to accept scope mounts.

NIB	Exc.	V.G.	Good	Fair	Poor
700	550	400	300	200	125

Model 629 Classic DX

Has all of the features of the Model 629 Classic, introduced in 1991, plus two sets of grips and five interchangeable front sights. Available in 6.5" or 8-3/8" barrel. A 5" barrel option was offered in 1992 but dropped in 1993.

NIB	Exc.	V.G.	Good	Fair	Poor
750	600	500	400	300	200

Model 629 Mountain Gun

This limited edition 6-shot revolver, introduced in 1993, features a 4" barrel chambered for the .44 Magnum. Built on the large N frame this pistol is made from stainless steel and is drilled and tapped for scope mounts. It is equipped with a Hogue round butt rubber monogrip. Standard sights are a pinned black ramp front sight and an adjustable black rear blade. Weight is approximately 40 oz. Model was re-introduced in 1999.

NIB	Exc.	V.G.	Good	Fair	Poor
675	450	400	350	300	150

Model 629 Backpacker

This 1994 variation of the Model 629 is built on the N-frame with round butt. Cylinders are fluted and chamfered. Barrel length is 3" with adjustable rear sight. The finish is stainless steel and Hogue rubber grips are standard. Weight is approximately 40 oz.

NIB	Exc.	V.G.	Good	Fair	Poor
750	600	500	400	300	200

Model 629 Classic Powerport

Introduced in 1996 this model offers a integral compensator with a 6.5" full lug barrel. The Patridge front sight is pinned and the rear sight is fully adjustable. The frame is drilled and tapped for scope mounts. Synthetic Hogue combat-style grips are standard. Weight is approximately 52 oz.

NIB	Exc.	V.G.	Good	Fair	Poor
700	550	400	300	200	125

Fiftieth Anniversary Model 29

A commemorative edition of the classic .44 Magnum. Carbon steel with polished blue finish. Double-action 6-shot. LOA 12", 6.5" barrel, 48.5 oz. Cocobolo wood grips with 24kt gold anniversary logo.

NIB	Exc.	V.G.	Good	Fair	Poor
1500	1000	550	350	200	150

NIGHT GUARD SERIES REVOLVERS
Model 310 Night Guard

Large-frame snubnose revolver chambered in 10mm/.40 S&W (interchangeable). Six-shot cylinder, 2.75" barrel, fixed tritium sights, synthetic grips. Scandium frame, stainless steel cylinder, matte black finish throughout. Weight 28 oz.

NIB	Exc.	V.G.	Good	Fair	Poor
900	775	600	475	300	150

Model 357 Night Guard

Don't let the model name fool you. Large-frame snubnose revolver chambered in .41 Magnum. Six-shot cylinder, 2.75" barrel, fixed tritium sights, synthetic grips. Scandium frame, stainless steel cylinder, matte black finish throughout. Weight 29.7 oz.

NIB	Exc.	V.G.	Good	Fair	Poor
900	775	600	475	300	150

Model 325 Night Guard

A 2-1/2" snubbie chambered for .45 ACP. Tritium sights, scandium alloy frame, matte black finish overll. Neoprene grips. Introduced 2008.

NIB	Exc.	V.G.	Good	Fair	Poor
900	775	600	475	300	150

Model 327 Night Guard

Large-frame snubnose revolver chambered in .357 Magnum/.38 Special +P (interchangeable). Six-shot cylinder, 2.5" barrel, fixed tritium sights, synthetic grips. Scandium frame, stainless steel cylinder, matte black finish throughout. Weight 27.6 oz.

NIB	Exc.	V.G.	Good	Fair	Poor
900	775	600	475	300	150

Model 329 Night Guard

Large-frame snubnose revolver chambered in .44 Magnum/.44 Special (interchangeable). Six-shot cylinder, 2.5" barrel, fixed tritium sights, synthetic grips. Scandium frame, stainless steel cylinder, matte black finish throughout. Weight 29.3 oz.

NIB	Exc.	V.G.	Good	Fair	Poor
900	775	600	475	300	150

Model 386 Night Guard

Medium-frame snubnose revolver chambered in .357 Magnum/.38 Special +P (interchangeable). Seven-shot cylinder, 2.5" barrel, fixed tritium sights, synthetic grips. Scandium frame, stainless steel cylinder, matte black finish throughout. Weight 24.5 oz.

NIB	Exc.	V.G.	Good	Fair	Poor
850	725	550	425	300	150

Model 396 Night Guard

Medium-frame snubnose revolver chambered in .44 Special. Five-shot cylinder, 2.5" barrel, fixed tritium sights, synthetic grips. Scandium frame, stainless steel cylinder, matte black finish throughout. Weight 24.2 oz.

NIB	Exc.	V.G.	Good	Fair	Poor
850	725	550	425	300	150

Model 315 Night Guard

Medium-frame snubnose revolver chambered in .38 Special +P. Six-shot cylinder, 2.5" barrel, fixed tritium sights, synthetic grips. Scandium frame, stainless steel cylinder, matte black finish throughout. Weight 24.0 oz.

NIB	Exc.	V.G.	Good	Fair	Poor
850	725	550	425	300	150

Model 30 (The .32 Hand Ejector)

This model was built on the small I frame and based on the .32 Hand Ejector Model of 1903. This older model was dropped from production in 1942. It was re-introduced in 1949 in a more modern version but still referred to as the .32 Hand Ejector. In 1957 the model designation was changed to Model 30. In 1960 this frame size was dropped, and the J frame, which had been in use since 1950, became standard for the Model 30. S&W stamped -1 behind the model number to designate this important change in frame size. The Model 30 is chambered for the .32 S&W long cartridge. It has a 6-shot cylinder and 2", 3", 4", and 6" barrel lengths. It has fixed sights and is either blued or nickel-plated. The butt is round, with checkered walnut grips. It was discontinued in 1976.

Courtesy W.P. Hallstein III and son Chip

NIB	Exc.	V.G.	Good	Fair	Poor
—	425	300	200	150	100

Model 31 (.32 Regulation Police)

This model is the same as the Model 30 with a square butt. It was known as the .32 Regulation Police before 1957. Discontinued.

NIB	Exc.	V.G.	Good	Fair	Poor
—	425	300	200	150	100

Model 31 (.32 Regulation Police Target)

The Target model of the Regulation Police is rare. Only 196 of these special variations were produced in 1957. All specifications are the same as the Model 31 except for the addition of adjustable sights.

NIB	Exc.	V.G.	Good	Fair	Poor
—	1500	925	750	525	300

Model 32 (.38/.32 Terrier)

This model, known as the Terrier prior to 1957, was introduced in 1936. It is essentially a .38 Regulation Police chambered for .38 S&W and with a 2" barrel and round butt. Like the Model 30 and 31 this revolver was originally built on the I-frame, which was changed to the J frame in 1960. The -1 behind the model number signifies this change. It is offered in blue or nickel-plate and has a 5-shot cylinder, fixed sights, and checkered walnut grips. This model was discontinued in 1974. **NOTE:** A limited production version with alloy frame and steel cylinder was produced as the Model 032. Add 30 percent for this model.

NIB	Exc.	V.G.	Good	Fair	Poor
—	425	300	200	150	100

Model 33 (.38 Regulation Police)

This model is simply the .38 Regulation Police with a square butt and 4" barrel chambered for the .38 S&W. The factory referred to this model as the .38-.32 revolver. It, too, was built on the small I frame and later changed to the J frame in 1960. The Model 33 was discontinued in 1974.

Courtesy Mike Stuckslager

NIB	Exc.	V.G.	Good	Fair	Poor
—	425	300	200	150	100

Model 34 (.22/.32 Kit Gun)

Introduced in 1936 as the .22-32 Kit Gun, it has a 2" or 4" barrel, either round or square butt, and adjustable sights. This model

underwent several modifications before it reached its present form. S&W modernized this revolver in 1953 with the addition of a coil mainspring and micro-click sights. The Model 34 is built on this improved version. The revolver is a .32 Hand Ejector chambered for the .22 rimfire. It is built on the I frame until 1960 when the changeover to the improved J frame occurred. The -1 behind the model number indicates this variation. The Model 34 is offered blued or nickel-plate.

Courtesy Mike Stuckslager

NIB	Exc.	V.G.	Good	Fair	Poor
550	425	300	250	175	100

Model 35 (.22/.32 Target)

This is a square-butt, 6"-barreled version of the .22/32 Hand Ejector. It was known prior to 1957 as the .22/32 Target. It underwent the same changes as the Model 34 but was discontinued in 1973.

Courtesy Mike Stuckslager

NIB	Exc.	V.G.	Good	Fair	Poor
1000	800	600	400	275	100

AIRLITE SERIES (titanium cylinder—aluminum alloy frame)
Model 317 AirLite

This 8-round revolver was introduced in 1997 and is chambered for the .22 LR cartridge. It is fitted with a 2" barrel, serrated ramp front sight, fixed rear sight, and Dymondwood boot grips. It is produced from carbon and stainless steel and also aluminum alloy on a J frame. Its weight is about 9.9 oz.

NIB	Exc.	V.G.	Good	Fair	Poor
550	400	375	295	175	100

Model 317 AirLite Kit Gun

This version of the Model 317 was introduced in 1998 and is fitted with a 3" barrel with adjustable rear sight. Choice of Dymondwood grips or Uncle Mike's Combat grips. Weight is about 12 oz. In 2001 this model was offered with HiViz green dot front sight.

NIB	Exc.	V.G.	Good	Fair	Poor
700	550	425	300	200	150

Model 317 AirLite Ladysmith

This model features a 2" barrel and Dymondwood grips. Display case is standard. Weight is about 10 oz.

NIB	Exc.	V.G.	Good	Fair	Poor
700	550	425	300	200	150

Model 325PD

Introduced in 2004 this 6-round large frame revolver is chambered for the .45 ACP cartridge. Fitted with a 2.75" barrel. Wooden grips and HiViz sights. Black oxide finish. Weight is about 21.5 oz.

NIB	Exc.	V.G.	Good	Fair	Poor
900	775	600	450	300	150

Model 331 AirLite

This model is chambered for the .32 H&R Magnum cartridge on a J frame. Barrel length is 1-7/8". Exposed hammer offers single or double-action. The frame is aluminum, as is the barrel shroud and yoke. The cylinder is titanium. The barrel has a stainless steel liner. Matte finish. Because the revolver is made from aluminum and titanium it has a two-tone appearance because of the two different materials. Choice of wood or rubber boot grips. Capacity is 6 rounds. Weight is about 12 oz. with rubber grip and 11.2 oz. with wood grip. Introduced in 1999.

NIB	Exc.	V.G.	Good	Fair	Poor
700	550	425	300	200	150

Model 332 AirLite

This model is similar to the Model 331 above but with a concealed hammer, double-action configuration. Weight is 12 oz. with rubber grips and 11.3 oz. with wood grips.

NIB	Exc.	V.G.	Good	Fair	Poor
700	550	425	300	200	150

Model 337 AirLite

This model has an aluminum frame, exposed hammer, titanium cylinder. Front sight is black and pinned. Smooth trigger. Cylinder capacity is five rounds. Chambered for .38 Special +P ammo. Barrel length is 1-7/8". Wood or rubber grips. Weight with wood grips is about 11.2 oz., with rubber grips about 12 oz. Introduced in 1999.

NIB	Exc.	V.G.	Good	Fair	Poor
600	450	325	250	175	100

Model 337 Kit Gun

Similar to the Model 337 but fitted with a 3" barrel. Adjustable rear sight. Weight is about 13.5 oz. In 2001 this model was offered with HiViz green dot front sight.

NIB	Exc.	V.G.	Good	Fair	Poor
650	475	325	250	175	100

Model 337 PD

Similar to the Model 337 but with a matte black finish over the aluminum frame and Hogue Bantam grips. Weight is 10.7 oz. Introduced in 2000.

NIB	Exc.	V.G.	Good	Fair	Poor
600	450	325	250	175	100

Model 340

Introduced in 2001 this hammerless model features a Scandium alloy frame and is fitted with a 1.875" barrel. Chambered for the .357 Magnum cartridge with a 5-round cylinder. Matte stainless gray finish. Pinned black front sight. Hogue Bantam grips standard. Weight is about 12 oz.

NIB	Exc.	V.G.	Good	Fair	Poor
700	550	425	300	200	150

Model 340 PD

Same as the Model 340 but with a gray/black finish. Also introduced in 2001.

NIB	Exc.	V.G.	Good	Fair	Poor
750	500	375	275	200	150

Model 342 AirLite

This is similar to the above model but with double-action-only concealed hammer. Weight is 11.3 oz. with wood grips and 12 oz. with rubber grips. Introduced in 1999.

NIB	Exc.	V.G.	Good	Fair	Poor
700	550	425	300	200	150

Model 342 PD

Similar to the Model 337 but with matte black finish over the aluminum frame and Hogue Bantam grips. Weight is about 10.8 oz. Introduced in 2000.

NIB	Exc.	V.G.	Good	Fair	Poor
700	550	425	300	200	150

Model 351PD

This 7-shot revolver is chambered for the .22 Magnum cartridge and fitted with a 1.875" barrel. Black oxide finish. Rubber grips. HiViz sights. Weight is about 10.6 oz.

NIB	Exc.	V.G.	Good	Fair	Poor
625	475	350	225	175	75

Model 360

This J frame model features a Scandium alloy frame with exposed hammer and 5-shot cylinder. Fixed sights on a 1.875" barrel. Matte stainless grey finish. Weight is about 12 oz. Introduced in 2001.

NIB	Exc.	V.G.	Good	Fair	Poor
700	550	425	300	200	150

Model 360 Kit Gun

This version of the M360 is fitted with a 3.125" barrel with HiViz green dot front sight and adjustable rear sight. Weight is about 14.5 oz. Introduced in 2001.

NIB	Exc.	V.G.	Good	Fair	Poor
700	550	425	300	200	150

Model 386

Introduced in 2001 this L frame model features a 6-shot cylinder chambered for the .357 Magnum cartridge. Fitted with a 3.125" barrel with HiViz green dot front sight and adjustable rear sight. Scandium alloy frame with matte stainless gray finish. Weight is about 18.5 oz. Hogue Batam grips.

NIB	Exc.	V.G.	Good	Fair	Poor
800	675	500	400	300	200

Model 386 PD

Same as above but with gray/black finish and 2.5" barrel with red ramp front sight and adjustable rear sight. Weight is about 17.5 oz.

NIB	Exc.	V.G.	Good	Fair	Poor
800	675	500	400	300	200

Model 386 Sc/S

Single-/double-action L-frame revolver in .38/.357 Magnum. 7-shot cylinder, 2.5" barrel, Patridge front sight, adjustable rear, scandium/alloy frame, matte black finish, rubber grips. Introduced 2007.

NIB	Exc.	V.G.	Good	Fair	Poor
750	600	475	350	250	175

Model 386 XL Hunter

Single/double action L-frame revolver chambered in .357 Magnum. Features include 6-inch full-lug barrel, 7-round cylinder, Hi-Viz fiber optic front sight, adjustable rear sight, candium frame, stainless steel cylinder, black matte finish, synthetic grips.

NIB	Exc.	V.G.	Good	Fair	Poor
750	625	550	465	350	150

Model 396 Mountain Lite

This L frame revolver is chambered for the .44 Special cartridge. It is fitted with a five round titanium cylinder and aluminum alloy frame. Barrel length is 3" and has a green HiViz front sight and an adjustable rear sight. Introduced in 2000. Weight is approximately 19 oz.

NIB	Exc.	V.G.	Good	Fair	Poor
750	600	475	350	250	175

Model 242

This medium frame revolver is chambered for the .38 Special +P cartridge. Semi-concealed hammer and 2.5" barrel. Pinned black ramp front sight. Black rubber boot grips. Seven-round cylinder. Matte alloy and titanium finish. Weight is about 19 oz. Introduced in 1999. This model is no longer in production.

NIB	Exc.	V.G.	Good	Fair	Poor
550	450	300	225	175	75

Model 296

Also a medium frame revolver chambered for the .44 Special cartridge. Fitted with a 2.5" barrel. Concealed hammer. Cylinder capacity is 5 rounds. Weight is about 19 oz. Introduced in 1999.

NIB	Exc.	V.G.	Good	Fair	Poor
700	550	425	300	200	150

Model 586

Six or seven shot double action revolver (L frame) chambered for the .357 Magnum cartridge. It will also chamber and fire .38 Special cartridges. The 686 has been available with 2-1/2-; 3-; 4-; 5- 6- and 8-3/8-inch barrel lengths. Blued frame and cylinder, adjustable sights, walnut Magna or rubber grips.

NIB	Exc.	V.G.	Good	Fair	Poor
550	425	300	200	150	100

Model 686

Six or seven shot double action revolver (L frame) chambered for the .357 Magnum cartridge. It will also chamber and fire .38 Special cartridges. The 686 has been available with 2-1/2-; 3-; 4-; 5- 6- and 8-3/8-inch barrel lengths. Stainless steel frame and cylinder, adjustable sights, walnut Magna or rubber grips. Introduced in 1980.The Performance Center also made a limited number of 686s in .38 Super for competitive shooters. Add 50% for Super.

NIB	Exc.	V.G.	Good	Fair	Poor
700	550	425	300	200	150

Model 329PD

Chambered for the .44 Magnum cartridge and fitted with a 4" barrel, this large frame revolver has a Scandium frame with matte black finish. Orange dot front sight and adjustable rear sight. Cylinder capacity is six rounds. Wood or rubber grips. Weight is approximately 26.5 oz. Introduced in 2003.

NIB	Exc.	V.G.	Good	Fair	Poor
800	675	500	400	300	200

Model 610 (2007 Reintroduction)

This N frame model is chambered for the 10mm cartridge and fitted with a variety of barrel lengths. Adjustable rear sight. Six-round non-fluted cylinder. Hogue rubber combat grips. Stainless steel finish. Weight is about 50 oz. for 4-inch model. Reintroduced in 2007.

NIB	Exc.	V.G.	Good	Fair	Poor
750	600	475	350	250	175

Model 36 (.38 Chief's Special)

This model, known as the Chief's Special, was introduced in 1950. It was built on the J frame and is chambered for the .38 Special cartridge. It holds 5 shots, has a 2" or 3" barrel, and was initially offered in a round butt. In 1952 a square-butt version was released. It is finished in blue or nickel-plate and has checkered walnut grips. A 3" heavy barrel was first produced in 1967 and became standard in 1975. The 2" barrel was dropped from production in 1993.

NIB	Exc.	V.G.	Good	Fair	Poor
575	375	275	200	150	100

Model 36LS (.38 Ladysmith)

This model is similar to the Model 36 with the exception that it is only offered with a 2" barrel, comes with rosewood grips and a soft carrying case. Weighs 20 oz.

NIB	Exc.	V.G.	Good	Fair	Poor
625	450	300	200	150	100

Model 36 (Chief's Special Target)

Since 1955 a limited number of Chief's Specials with adjustable sights have been manufactured. They have been offered with 2" or 3" barrels, round or square butts, and either blue or nickel-plated. Between 1957 and 1965, these target models were stamped Model 36 on the yoke. The revolvers manufactured between 1965 and the model discontinuance in 1975 were marked Model 50. This is a very collectible revolver. A total of 2,313 of these special target models were sold in various model designations. Some are more rare than others.

Courtesy W.P. Hallstein III and son Chip

NIB	Exc.	V.G.	Good	Fair	Poor
—	775	575	300	200	125

Model 37

Introduced in 1952 as the Chief's Special Airweight, this revolver initially had an alloy frame and cylinder. In 1954, following many complaints regarding damaged revolvers, the cylinders were made of steel. Barrel lengths, finishes, and grip options on the Airweight are the same as on the standard Chief Special. In 1957 the Model 37 designation was adopted. These early alloy frame and cylinder revolvers were designed to shoot only standard velocity .38 Special cartridges. The use of high velocity ammunition was not recommended by the factory. **NOTE:** All 1998 and later production models were rated for +P ammunition.

NIB	Exc.	V.G.	Good	Fair	Poor
575	375	275	200	150	100

Model 637

Same as the model above but with aluminum frame and stainless steel finish. **NOTE:** Current production models are now rated for +P ammunition.

NIB	Exc.	V.G.	Good	Fair	Poor
575	375	275	200	150	100

Model 637 Carry Combo

As above but supplied with Kydex carry holster. Introduced in 2004.

NIB	Exc.	V.G.	Good	Fair	Poor
575	375	275	200	150	100

Model 637 Power Port Pro Series

Aluminum J-frame 5-shot revolver with stainless steel cylinder chambered for .38 Special (5 shots). 2-1/8-inch ported black stainless barrel. Introduced 2008. Dealer sets pricing.

NIB	Exc.	V.G.	Good	Fair	Poor
575	375	275	200	150	100

Model 637CT

Same as Model 6377 but with Crimson Trace lasergrips.

NIB	Exc.	V.G.	Good	Fair	Poor
650	575	375	275	200	100

Model 38 (Airweight Bodyguard)

This model was introduced in 1955 as the Airweight Bodyguard. This was a departure from S&W's usual procedure in that the alloy-framed version came first. The Model 38 is chambered for .38 Special and is available with a 2" barrel standard. Although a 3" barrel was offered, it is rarely encountered. The frame of the Bodyguard is extended to conceal and shroud the hammer but at the same time allow the hammer to be cocked by the thumb. This makes this model an ideal pocket revolver, as it can be drawn without catching on clothing. It is available either blue or nickel-plated, with checkered walnut grips. **NOTE:** All 1998 and later production models were rated for +P ammunition.

NIB	Exc.	V.G.	Good	Fair	Poor
525	350	225	175	125	100

Model 638

Same as the model above but with aluminum frame and stainless steel finish. **NOTE:** Current production models are now rated for +P ammunition.

NIB	Exc.	V.G.	Good	Fair	Poor
475	375	300	225	175	125

Model 49 (Bodyguard)

This model was introduced in 1959 and is identical in configuration to the Model 38 except that the frame is made of steel.

NIB	Exc.	V.G.	Good	Fair	Poor
—	575	450	300	250	200

Model 649 (Bodyguard Stainless)

This stainless steel version of the Model 49 was introduced in 1985. It is also available in .357 Magnum. As of 1998 this model was also offered in a .38 Special-only version.

NIB	Exc.	V.G.	Good	Fair	Poor
500	350	225	200	175	125

Model 40 (aka Model 42) Centennial

This model was introduced in 1952 as Smith & Wesson's 100th anniversary and appropriately called the "Centennial Model." It is of the Safety Hammerless design. This model was built on the J frame and features a fully concealed hammer and a grip safety. The Model 40 is chambered for the .38 Special cartridge. It is offered with a 2" barrel in either blue or nickel plate. The grips are checkered walnut. The Centennial was discontinued in 1974.

Courtesy Mike Stuckslager

NIB	Exc.	V.G.	Good	Fair	Poor
625	550	375	225	150	100

Model 42—Airweight Centennial

This model is identical in configuration to the Model 40 except that it was furnished with an aluminum alloy frame. It was also discontinued in 1974. Editors **NOTE:** The first 37 Model 42s were manufactured with aluminum alloy cylinders. They weigh 11-1/4 ounces compared to 13 ounces for the standard model. The balance of Model 42 production was with steel cylinders. Add 300 percent for this extremely rare variation.

NIB	Exc.	V.G.	Good	Fair	Poor
450	400	325	200	150	100

Model 640 Centennial

A stainless steel version of the Model 40 furnished with a 2" or 3" barrel. Both the frame and cylinder are stainless steel. The 3" barrel was no longer offered as of 1993. As of 1998 this model was also offered in a .38 Special-only version.

NIB	Exc.	V.G.	Good	Fair	Poor
500	375	250	200	150	100

Model 640 Centennial .357 Magnum

Introduced in 1995 this version of the Model 640 is chambered for the .357 cartridge and fitted with a 2-1/8" barrel. The gun is stainless steel with a fixed notch rear sight and pinned black ramp front sight. It is 6-3/4" in length and weighs 25 oz.

NIB	Exc.	V.G.	Good	Fair	Poor
525	400	250	200	150	100

Model 642 Centennial Airweight

Identical to the Model 640 with the exception of a stainless steel cylinder and aluminum alloy frame. Furnished with a 2" or 2.5" barrel. Discontinued in 1992. Replaced by the Model 442 which was introduced in 1993. This model was reintroduced in 1996. **NOTE:** Current production models are now rated for +P ammunition.

NIB	Exc.	V.G.	Good	Fair	Poor
450	300	250	200	150	100

Model 642CT (Crimson Trace)

As above but fitted with Crimson Trace laser grips. Weight is about 15 oz. Introduced in 2004.

NIB	Exc.	V.G.	Good	Fair	Poor
650	575	375	275	200	100

Model 642LS Ladysmith

Similar to Model 642 but fitted with smooth combat wood grips and a softside carry case. **NOTE:** Current production models are now rated for +P ammunition.

NIB	Exc.	V.G.	Good	Fair	Poor
575	450	325	275	175	100

Model 642 PowerPort Pro Series

Similar to Model 642 buit with gray aluminum frame and black stainless ported barrel. Dealer sets pricing. Introduced 2008.

NIB	Exc.	V.G.	Good	Fair	Poor
575	450	325	275	175	100

Model 631

This revolver is chambered for the .32 Magnum cartridge and is fitted with a 2" (fixed sights) or 4" (adjustable sights) barrel. Stainless steel finish. Weight with 23" barrel is 22 oz. Produced in 1990.

NIB	Exc.	V.G.	Good	Fair	Poor
650	575	375	275	200	100

Model 631 Lady Smith

Similar to the above model but with rosewood grips and laser etched. Fitted with 2" barrel.

NIB	Exc.	V.G.	Good	Fair	Poor
650	575	375	275	200	100

Model 632 Centennial

This model is similar to the other Centennial models but is chambered for the .32 H&R Magnum cartridge. It comes standard with a 2" barrel, stainless steel cylinder and aluminum alloy frame. Dropped from the product line in 1993.

NIB	Exc.	V.G.	Good	Fair	Poor
650	575	375	275	200	100

Smith & Wesson Model 632 PowerPort Pro Series

J-frame revolver chambered in .327 Federal Magnum. Six-shot cylinder, 3" full-lug ported barrel with full-length extractor. Pinned, serrated front sight, adjustable rear. Synthetic grips. Stainless steel frame and cylinder.

NIB	Exc.	V.G.	Good	Fair	Poor
775	650	495	350	250	175

Smith & Wesson Models 637 CT/638 CT/642 CT

Similar to Models 637, 638 and 642 but with Crimson Trace Laser Grips. Suggested retail price $920.

Model 042 Centennial Airweight

This model was produced in 1992 but is not catalogued. It is chambered for .38 Special and fitted with a 2" barrel. The frame is alloy. Marked "MOD 042." No grip safety. Blued finish. Weight is about 16 oz. Supposedly a reworked Model 642 "blemish gun" distributed through a national wholesaler.

NIB	Exc.	V.G.	Good	Fair	Poor
650	575	375	275	200	100

Model 442 Centennial Lightweight

This 5-shot revolver is chambered for the .38 Special and is equipped with a 2" barrel, aluminum alloy frame, and carbon steel cylinder. It has a fully concealed hammer and weighs 15.8 oz. The front ramp sight is serrated and the rear sight is a fixed square notch. Rubber combat grips from Michael's of Oregon are standard. Finish is either blue/black or satin nickel. Introduced in 1993. **NOTE:** Current production models are now rated for +P ammunition.

NIB	Exc.	V.G.	Good	Fair	Poor
400	300	250	200	150	100

Model 442/642/640/632 Pro Series Revolvers

Double action only J-frame with concealed hammers chambered in .38 Special +P (442 & 642), .357 Magnum (640) or .327 Federal (632). Features include 5-round cylinder, matte stainless steel frame, fixed sights or dovetail night sights (632, 640), synthetic grips, cylinder cut for moon clips (442, 642, 640). Suggested retail price $640 (standard) to $916 (night sights).

Model 438

J-frame double-action-only revolver chambered in .38 Special +P. Five-shot cylinder, 1.87" barrel, fixed front and rear sights, synthetic grips. Aluminum alloy frame, stainless steel cylinder. Matte black finish throughout.

NIB	Exc.	V.G.	Good	Fair	Poor
575	450	325	275	175	100

Model 940

Styled like the other Centennial models, this model is chambered for the 9mm Parabellum cartridge. It has a stainless steel cylinder and frame and is furnished with a 2" or 3" barrel. The 3" barrel version was dropped from production in 1993.

NIB	Exc.	V.G.	Good	Fair	Poor
700	550	425	300	200	150

Model 43 (.22/.32 Kit Gun Airweight)

This model was built on the J frame, is chambered for .22 rimfire, has a 3.5" barrel, and is offered in a round or square butt, with checkered walnut grips. It has adjustable sights and is either blued or nickel-plated. The frame is made of aluminum alloy. Except for this, it is identical to the Model 34 or .22/.32 Kit Gun. This model has a rare 2" barrel configuration as well as a .22 WRM model. The Model 43 was introduced in 1954 and was discontinued in 1974.

Courtesy Mike Stuckslager

NIB	Exc.	V.G.	Good	Fair	Poor
650	575	375	275	200	100

Model 51 (.22/.32 Kit Gun Magnum)

This model is simply the Model 34 chambered for the .22 Winchester Magnum rimfire. It was first introduced in 1960 beginning with serial number 52637. Available in both round and square butt with the round butt variation having a total production of only 600. The Model 51 was discontinued in 1974.

NIB	Exc.	V.G.	Good	Fair	Poor
—	675	400	250	200	125

Model 651

This stainless steel version of the Model 51 .22 Magnum Kit Gun was manufactured between 1983 and 1987.

NIB	Exc.	V.G.	Good	Fair	Poor
—	675	400	250	200	125

Model 73

Produced in about 1973 this revolver was built on a special "C" size frame. Cylinder holds 6 rounds and is chambered for the .38 Special cartridge. Fitted with a 2" barrel. A total of 5,000 were built. All but 20 were destroyed. An extremely rare S&W revolver. Marked, "MOD 73" on yoke.

Courtesy Jim Supica, Old Town Station

NIB	Exc.	V.G.	Good	Fair	Poor
8500	—	—	—	—	—

Model 45 (Post Office)

This model is a special purpose K-frame Military & Police Model chambered for the .22 rimfire. It was designed as a training revolver for police departments and the U.S. Postal Service. This model was manufactured in limited quantities between 1948 and 1957. In 1963 production abruptly began and ended again. There were 500 of these revolvers released on a commercial basis, but they are rarely encountered.

NIB	Exc.	V.G.	Good	Fair	Poor
1250	800	650	450	300	100

Model 48 (K-22 Masterpiece Magnum)

Introduced in 1959 and is identical to the Model 17 or K-22 except that it is chambered for the .22 WRM cartridge. Offered in 4", 6", and 8-3/8" barrel lengths, it has a blued finish. Discontinued in 1986.

NIB	Exc.	V.G.	Good	Fair	Poor
700	500	275	225	150	100

Model 53 (Magnum Jet)

Introduced in 1961 and chambered for the .22 Jet, a Remington cartridge. The barrel lengths were 4", 6", and 8-3/8" and the finish is blued. Sights were adjustable and the revolver was furnished with cylinder inserts that would allow .22 rimfire cartridges to be fired. The frame had two firing pins. Approximately 15,000 were produced before it was discontinued in 1974. Price includes guns with individual chambered inserts. **NOTE:** Add $150 for auxiliary .22 LR cylinder.

NIB	Exc.	V.G.	Good	Fair	Poor
1500	750	450	350	250	200

Model 57

This revolver was introduced in 1964 and is chambered for the .41 Magnum cartridge. It is built on the N frame. Offered in 4", 6", and 8-3/8" barrel lengths, it has a blued frame and adjustable sights. Model designations are: 57-1 1982; 57-2 1988; 57-3 1990; 57-4 1993.

NIB	Exc.	V.G.	Good	Fair	Poor
600	400	275	225	200	150

Model 657

This is a stainless steel version of the Model 57 and was introduced in 1980. Still in production. In 2001 this model was reintroduced again with a 7.5" barrel with pinned front sight and adjustable rear sight. Hogue rubber combat grips. Weight is about 52 oz.

NIB	Exc.	V.G.	Good	Fair	Poor
670	525	425	295	200	150

Model 56 (KXT-38 USAF)

Introduced in 1962 this is a 2" heavy barrel built on the K frame. It is chambered for the .38 Special. There were approximately 15,000 of these revolvers built when it was discontinued in 1964. It was marked "US" on the backstrap. A total of 15,205 produced but most destroyed.

NIB	Exc.	V.G.	Good	Fair	Poor
4500	1750	1250	750	500	250

Model 58

This model is chambered for the .41 Magnum and is fitted with fixed sights. Offered in blued or nickel finish and with 4" barrel. Checkered walnut grips are standard. Introduced in 1964.

NIB	Exc.	V.G.	Good	Fair	Poor
1100	650	450	300	225	125

Model 547

Introduced in 1980 and chambered for the 9mm cartridge and offered with either 3" or 4" barrel. Finish is blued. Discontinued.

NIB	Exc.	V.G.	Good	Fair	Poor
650	475	375	275	200	125

Model 460 XVR

Introduced in 2005 this model is chambered for the .460 S&W magnum, which has the highest muzzle velocity of any production handgun. Fitted with a 8-3/8" barrel with interchangeable compensators. Frame size is extra large. Capacity is 5 rounds. Adjustable sights with Hi-Viz front sight. Finger groove grips. Satin stainless finish. Weight is about 72.5 oz. **NOTE:** Add $135 for 4" barrel model.

NIB	Exc.	V.G.	Good	Fair	Poor
1000	875	750	600	400	300

Model 460V

X-frame double-action trigger and 5" barrel in .460 S&W Magnum caliber. Also accepts .454 Casull and .45 Colt. Sorbothane recoil-reducing grip, interchangeable muzzle compensator. 5-shot, stainless with satin finish. 62.5 oz. Introduced 2006.

NIB	Exc.	V.G.	Good	Fair	Poor
1000	875	750	600	400	300

Model 500

Introduced in 2003 this revolver is chambered for the .500 S&W Magnum cartridge. Fitted with a 8.375" barrel with compensator and built on the X frame. Cylinder holds five rounds. Stainless steel frame and barrel. Interchangeable front blade sight and adjustable rear sight. K-frame size Hogue grips. Weight is about 72.5 oz. In 2004 this model was offered with a 4" barrel with compensator. Weight is about 56 oz. 6.5-inch model introduced 2008. **NOTE:** Add $135 for 4" barrel model.

S&W Model 500 with 4" barrel

NIB	Exc.	V.G.	Good	Fair	Poor
1000	875	750	600	400	300

Model 60

Introduced in 1965 this model is similar to the Model 36 but in stainless steel. Offered in 2" barrel with fixed sights, walnut grips, and smooth trigger. Some 2" Model 60s were produced with adjustable sights add 50 percent. The 3" barrel version comes with a full underlug, adjustable sights, serrated trigger, and rubber grips. The 2" version weighs about 20 oz. while the 3" version weighs approximately 25 oz. In 1996 this model was offered chambered for the .357 Magnum cartridge. This new version is fitted with a 2-1/8" barrel. The 2-1/8" barrel weighs about 23 oz. This model was also offered in a .38 Special-only version.

2" Barrel

NIB	Exc.	V.G.	Good	Fair	Poor
450	350	300	200	125	100

3" Barrel

NIB	Exc.	V.G.	Good	Fair	Poor
475	375	350	250	150	100

5" Barrel

Introduced in 2005.

NIB	Exc.	V.G.	Good	Fair	Poor
550	475	375	295	200	125

Model 60LS (LadySmith)

Chambered for the .38 Special with 2" barrel and stainless steel frame and cylinder. This slightly smaller version of the Model 60 is made for small hands. A new version offered in 1996 is chambered for the .357 Magnum cartridge.

NIB	Exc.	V.G.	Good	Fair	Poor
450	350	300	200	125	100

Model 60 with Hi-Viz Sight

Similar to Model 60 but with light-gathering Hi-Viz red dot front sight and adjustable rear sight. Introduced 2007.

NIB	Exc.	V.G.	Good	Fair	Poor
525	400	300	225	175	100

Model 60 Pro Series

Similar to Model 60 but in .38/.357 with night front sights, "high-hold" enforcing walnut grips, 3-inch battel and matte stainless finish. Introduced 2008.

NIB	Exc.	V.G.	Good	Fair	Poor
650	475	375	275	200	125

Model 63

This model, introduced in 1977, is simply the Model 34 made of stainless steel.

NIB	Exc.	V.G.	Good	Fair	Poor
500	375	250	225	200	150

Model 64 (Military & Police Stainless)

This model is the stainless steel version of the Model 10 M&P. It was introduced in 1970. The Model 64-1 variation was introduced in 1972 and is the heavy barrel version.

NIB	Exc.	V.G.	Good	Fair	Poor
500	325	275	225	175	125

Model 65 (.357 Military & Police Heavy Barrel Stainless)

This is the stainless steel version of the Model 13 M&P .357 Magnum. It was introduced in 1974.

NIB	Exc.	V.G.	Good	Fair	Poor
425	300	275	225	175	125

Model 66 (.357 Combat Magnum Stainless)

Released in 1970, this is the stainless steel version of the Model 19 or Combat Magnum. It is chambered for the .357 Magnum, has adjustable sights, a square butt with checkered walnut grips, and was initially offered with a 4" barrel. In 1974 a 2.5" barrel, round butt version was made available. It was available in a 6" barrel, as well as all target options until discontinued in 1993.

NIB	Exc.	V.G.	Good	Fair	Poor
575	400	250	200	150	125

Model 67 (.38 Combat Masterpiece Stainless)

Introduced in 1972 this is a stainless steel version of the Model 15 with a 4" barrel. It is chambered for the .38 Special cartridge. Model designation changes are as follows: {None} 1972 to 1977; {-1} 1977 to 1988; {-2} 1988 to 1993; {-3} 1993 to present.

NIB	Exc.	V.G.	Good	Fair	Poor
500	300	250	200	150	100

Model 650

Introduced in 1983 this stainless steel model is built on a J frame with a 3" heavy barrel chambered for the .22 WRM. It has a round butt and fixed sights. Discontinued in 1988.

NIB	Exc.	V.G.	Good	Fair	Poor
600	450	250	175	125	100

Model 651

This J-frame model was introduced in 1983 and chambered for the .22 WRM and fitted with a 4" barrel. Stainless steel finish and adjustable sights. Designation changes are: {None} 1983 to 1988; {-1} 1988 to 1990; {-2} 1988 to 1990.

NIB	Exc.	V.G.	Good	Fair	Poor
575	400	250	200	150	100

Model 686 Powerport

Introduced in 1995 this version of the Model 686 features a 6" full lug barrel with integral compensator. The frame is drilled and tapped for scope mounts. Hogue grips are furnished as standard.

NIB	Exc.	V.G.	Good	Fair	Poor
650	550	450	400	300	200

Model 686 Plus Mountain Gun

This model is fitted with a 4" tapered barrel and chambered for the .357 Magnum cartridge. It has adjustable rear sights. Hogue rubber grips are standard. Stainless steel finish. Weight is about 44 oz.

NIB	Exc.	V.G.	Good	Fair	Poor
650	475	450	400	300	200

Model 686 Magnum Plus

Offered for the first time in 1996 this model features a 7-shot cylinder. It is available with 2.5", 4", or 6" barrel lengths. It is fitted with a red ramp front sight and a fully adjustable rear sight. The frame is drilled and tapped for scope mounts. Hogue synthetic grips are standard. The stainless steel is satin finished. Weight is between 35 oz. and 45 oz. depending on barrel length.

NIB	Exc.	V.G.	Good	Fair	Poor
625	500	450	400	300	200

Model 686—5" Barrel

This .357 Magnum stainless steel model is fitted with a 5" barrel with HiViz front sight and adjustable rear sight. Cylinder holds 7 rounds. Cocobolo wood grips. Weight is about 41 oz. Introduced in 2004.

NIB	Exc.	V.G.	Good	Fair	Poor
575	475	395	300	200	100

Model 686 Plus

Single-/double-action L-frame revolver in .38/.357 Magnum. 7-shot cylinder, 3" barrel, Patridge front sight, adjustable rear, stainless finish, rubber grips. Introduced 2007.

NIB	Exc.	V.G.	Good	Fair	Poor
600	550	450	400	300	200

Model 686 Plus Pro Series

Single/double-action L-frame revolver chambered in .357 Magnum. Features include 5-inch barrel with tapered underlug, 7-round cylinder, satin stainless steel frame and cylinder, synthetic grips, interchangeable and adjustable sights. Suggested retail price $1,059.

Model 619

This model is chambered for the .357 Magnum cartridge and fitted with a 4" two-piece semi-lug barrel with fixed sights. Stainless steel frame and barrel. Capacity is 7 rounds. Medium frame. Weight is about 37.5 oz. Rubber grips. Introduced in 2005.

NIB	Exc.	V.G.	Good	Fair	Poor
575	475	395	300	200	100

Model 620

Similar to the model above but with a 4" barrel with adjustable rear sight and red ramp front sight. Weight is about 37.9 oz. Introduced in 2005.

NIB	Exc.	V.G.	Good	Fair	Poor
600	550	450	400	300	200

Model 3 Schofield

A reintroduction of the famous Schofield revolver. This is a single-action top-break model chambered for the .45 S&W cartridge. Barrel length is 7". Frame and barrel are blue while hammer and trigger are case hardened. Sights are a fixed rear notch and half moon post front. Walnut grips. Weight is 40 oz. Reintroduced in 2000. In 2002 this model was offered in a 7" nickel version as well as a 5" blue and 5" nickel configuration.

NIB	Exc.	V.G.	Good	Fair	Poor
1750	1400	1050	800	500	300

HERITAGE SERIES REVOLVERS

These revolvers are built by the S&W Performance Center and produced for Lew Horton Distributing Co. Each model is similar in appearance to the original but has modern internal features. These handguns are produced in limited runs of from 100 units to 350 units.

Model 1917

Chambered for the .45 ACP cartridge and fitted with a 5.5" heavy tapered barrel. High-profile front blade sight with fixed rear sight. Checkered service grips with lanyard ring. Offered in blue, case-colored, or military finish. Shipped in a S&W collectible box. **NOTE:** Add $60 for case color finish.

NIB	Exc.	V.G.	Good	Fair	Poor
900	775	600	450	300	150

Model 15

This revolver is chambered for the .38 S&W Special. Fitted with a 4" barrel. Grips are S&W checkered target. Adjustable rear sight. Offered in nickel or color case hardened.

NIB	Exc.	V.G.	Good	Fair	Poor
800	675	550	400	250	125

Model 15 McGivern

Similar to the above model but fitted with 5" barrel and checkered diamond grips. Engraved sideplate of McGivern's speed record. Blue finish.

NIB	Exc.	V.G.	Good	Fair	Poor
900	775	600	450	300	150

Model 17

Chambered for the .22 caliber cartridge and fitted with a 6" barrel with patridge front sight and adjustable rear sight. Four screw sideplate. Diamond checkered S&W walnut grips. Blue or case colored finish. **NOTE:** Add $30 for case colored finish.

NIB	Exc.	V.G.	Good	Fair	Poor
800	675	550	400	250	125

Model 24

This model is chambered for the .44 Special cartridge and fitted with a 6.5" tapered barrel. McGivern gold-bead front sight with adjustable rear sight. Four-screw sideplate, chamfered charge holes, checkered diamond grips. **NOTE:** Add $60 for case colored finish.

NIB	Exc.	V.G.	Good	Fair	Poor
900	775	600	450	300	150

Model 25

Similar to the Model 24 but chambered for the .45 Colt cartridge. Blue or case colored finish. **NOTE:** Add $30 for case colored finish.

NIB	Exc.	V.G.	Good	Fair	Poor
900	775	600	450	300	150

Model 29

Similar to the Model 24 and Model 25 but chambered for the .44 Magnum cartridge. Oversized wood grips. Blue or nickel finish. Was to be produced in 2002 only. Serial numbers to begin with "DBW2005."

NIB	Exc.	V.G.	Good	Fair	Poor
900	775	600	450	300	150

CLASSIC SERIES

Model 14 Classic

Recreation of the vintage Model 14 revolver chambered in .38 Special +P. Six-shot cylinder, 6" barrel with pinned Patridge front sight and micro-adjustable rear. Carbon steel frame and cylinder with blued finish. Weight 34.5 oz.

NIB	Exc.	V.G.	Good	Fair	Poor
800	675	525	400	275	150

Model 14 Classic (nickel)

Same as above but with nickel finish. Discontinued.

NIB	Exc.	V.G.	Good	Fair	Poor
900	775	600	500	375	200

Model 15 Classic

Identical to Model 14 Classic, except with 4" barrel.

NIB	Exc.	V.G.	Good	Fair	Poor
800	675	525	400	275	150

Model 17 Masterpiece Classic

Recreation of the K-22 Masterpiece in .22 LR with blue finish, 6" barrel, adjustable rear sight and wood grips.

NIB	Exc.	V.G.	Good	Fair	Poor
850	725	550	400	275	150

Model 36 Classic

Replica of vintage Model 36 Chief's Special in .38 Special. Five-shot cylinder. Carbon steel frame, 1-7/8" or 3" barrel, fixed sights. Blued, case colored, or nickel finish with Altamont wood grips. Introduced 2007.

NIB	Exc.	V.G.	Good	Fair	Poor
500	400	250	150	100	

Model 21 Classic

Replica of vintage Model 21 N-frame revolver in .44 Special. Six-shot cylinder. Carbon steel frame, 4" barrel, fixed sights. Blued, case colored, or nickel finish with Altamont wood grips. Introduced 2007.

NIB	Exc.	V.G.	Good	Fair	Poor
900	750	525	400	275	150

Model 22 Classic

Replica of vintage Model 22 N-frame revolver in .45 ACP. Six-shot cylinder. Carbon steel frame, 4" barrel, fixed sights. Blued, case colored, or nickel finish with Altamont wood grips. Introduced 2007.

NIB	Exc.	V.G.	Good	Fair	Poor
900	750	525	400	275	150

Model 22 of 1917 Classic

Similar to Model 22 Classic but without ejector rod shroud and with lanyard ring on butt. Replica of U.S. Army WWI-era revolver. Introduced 2007.

NIB	Exc.	V.G.	Good	Fair	Poor
900	700	525	400	275	150

Model 24 Classic

In .44 Special with 6.5" barrel, wood grips with square butt and adjustable rear sight.

NIB	Exc.	V.G.	Good	Fair	Poor
850	725	550	400	275	150

Model 25 Classic

Identical to Model 24 Classic, except chambered for .45 Colt.

NIB	Exc.	V.G.	Good	Fair	Poor
850	725	550	400	275	150

Model 27 Classic

Reintroduction of vintage Model 27. Available in blue or bright nickel finish. 6.5" barrel, walnut grips. Introduced 2008. **NOTE:** Add 25 percent for 75th Anniversary Model.

NIB	Exc.	V.G.	Good	Fair	Poor
900	700	525	400	275	150

Model 29 Classic

Replica of original (1956) Model 29 N-frame revolver in .44 Magnum. Six-shot cylinder. Carbon steel frame, 6.5" barrel, fixed sights. Blued or nickel finish with or without engraving. Altamont wood grips. Introduced 2007.

NIB	Exc.	V.G.	Good	Fair	Poor
900	775	600	500	375	200

Model 10 Classic

Single/double action K frame revolver chambered in .38 Special. Features include bright blue steel frame and cylinder, checkered wood grips, 4" barrel, adjustable patridge-style sights.

NIB	Exc.	V.G.	Good	Fair	Poor
600	500	450	375	275	150

Model 40/42 Centennial Classic

This recreation of the 5-shot J-frame model, is designed for double-action only operation with a fully concealed hammer and grip safety. The Model 40 has a steel frame and weighs 19 oz. Model 42 has an alloy frame and weighs 13 oz.

NIB	Exc.	V.G.	Good	Fair	Poor
650	550	450	375	300	200

Model 48 Classic

Single/double action K frame revolver chambered in .22 Magnum Rimfire (.22 WMR). Features include bright blue steel frame and cylinder, checkered wood grips, 4" or 6" barrel, adjustable patridge-style sights.

NIB	Exc.	V.G.	Good	Fair	Poor
750	625	500	400	275	150

MILITARY & POLICE (M&P) SERIES
M&P340

Double-action-only revolver built on Centennial (hammerless J) frame. .357 Magnum/.38 Special; five-shot cylinder; 1.87" barrel with fixed night sights. Matte black finish on scandium/alloy frame. Introduced 2007.

NIB	Exc.	V.G.	Good	Fair	Poor
700	575	400	250	150	100

M&P340CT

Similar to above but with Crimson Trace lasergrips. Introduced 2007.

NIB	Exc.	V.G.	Good	Fair	Poor
825	700	600	500	350	175

M&P360

Double-action-only revolver built on Chief's Special (hammered J) frame. .357 Magnum/.38 Special; five-shot cylinder; 1.87" barrel with fixed night sights. Matte black finish on scandium/alloy frame. Introduced 2007.

NIB	Exc.	V.G.	Good	Fair	Poor
700	575	400	250	150	100

M&PR8

Double-action-only revolver built on large (N) frame. .357 Magnum/.38 Special; eight-shot cylinder; 5" barrel with adjustable Patridge sights with interchangeable inserts. Matte black finish on scandium/alloy frame. Introduced 2007.

NIB	Exc.	V.G.	Good	Fair	Poor
1100	850	600	500	375	200

Governor

Built on the Smith & Wesson L frame, this six-shot revolver can fire .410 shotshells, .45 Colt and .45 ACP (with moon clips) ammunition. Scandium alloy frame, stainless steel cylinder, Tritium night sight, internal security lock and Hogue synthetic grips. Barrel length is 2.75-inches, weight 29.6 ounces, overall length 8.5-inches with matte black finish. Available with Crimson Trace Laser grips. Introduced in 2011. **NOTE:** Add $200 for Crimson Trace Laser grips.

NIB	Exc.	V.G.	Good	Fair	Poor
650	525	425	365	250	150

SEMI-AUTOMATIC PISTOLS

NOTE: For pistols with Smith and Wesson factory-installed night sights add $100 to NIB and Exc. prices. For S&W factory engraving add $1,000 for Class C (1/3 coverage), $1,250 for Class B (2/3 coverage), $1,500 for Class A (full coverage).

Model 39

This was the first double-action semi-automatic pistol produced in the United States. It was introduced in 1957. It had an alloy frame and was chambered for the 9mm Parabellum or .30 Luger. The barrel was 4" and the finish was either blued or nickel with checkered walnut grips. The rear sight was adjustable. Magazine capacity is 8 rounds. Discontinued in 1982. The .30 Luger model is very rare and was mostly sold in Europe. **NOTE:** Add 150 percent for .30 Luger.

NIB	Exc.	V.G.	Good	Fair	Poor
600	450	250	200	150	100

Model 39 Steel Frame

A total of 927 steel frame Model 39s were produced. A rare pistol; use caution.

NIB	Exc.	V.G.	Good	Fair	Poor
1750	1200	700	550	400	250

Model 59

Introduced in 1971 this pistol is similar to the Model 39 but with a wide grip to hold a double column magazine of 14 rounds. Furnished with black checkered plastic grips. Discontinued in 1982.

NIB	Exc.	V.G.	Good	Fair	Poor
575	500	350	200	150	100

Model 439

Introduced in 1979 this is an improved version of the Model 39. Furnished with adjustable rear sight. Discontinued in 1988.

NIB	Exc.	V.G.	Good	Fair	Poor
600	450	350	325	250	100

Model 639

This is a stainless steel version of the Model 439. Introduced in 1984 and discontinued in 1988.

NIB	Exc.	V.G.	Good	Fair	Poor
600	450	350	325	250	100

Model 459

This improved-sight version of the 15-shot Model 59 9mm pistol was introduced in 1979 and discontinued in 1987.

NIB	Exc.	V.G.	Good	Fair	Poor
600	450	350	325	250	100

Model 659

This stainless steel version of the Model 459 9mm pistol features an ambidextrous safety and all other options of the Model 459. Introduced in 1982 and discontinued in 1988.

NIB	Exc.	V.G.	Good	Fair	Poor
550	425	350	300	250	150

Model 539

This is yet another version of the Model 439 9mm pistol. It incorporates all the features of the Model 439 with a steel frame instead of aluminum alloy. This model was introduced in 1980 and discontinued in 1983.

NIB	Exc.	V.G.	Good	Fair	Poor
525	400	350	300	250	200

Model 559

This variation of the Model 459 9mm pistol has a steel frame instead of aluminum alloy. It is identical in all other respects.

NIB	Exc.	V.G.	Good	Fair	Poor
475	400	350	300	250	200

Model 469

The Model 469 was brought out in answer to the need for a more concealable high-capacity pistol. It is essentially a "Mini" version of the Model 459. It is chambered for the 9mm Parabellum and has a 12-round detachable magazine with a finger-grip extension and a shortened frame. The barrel is 3.5" long; the hammer is bobbed and does not protrude; the safety is ambidextrous. The finish is matte blue, with black plastic grips. The Model 469 was introduced in 1983 and discontinued in 1988.

NIB	Exc.	V.G.	Good	Fair	Poor
450	375	325	275	200	150

Model 669

This is a stainless steel version of the Model 469 9mm pistol. All of the features of the 469 are incorporated. The Model 669 was manufactured from 1986 to 1988.

NIB	Exc.	V.G.	Good	Fair	Poor
475	425	350	300	250	200

Model 645

The Model 645 is a large-framed, stainless steel double-action pistol chambered for the .45 ACP cartridge. It has a 5" barrel, adjustable sights, and a detachable 8-shot magazine. It is offered with fixed or adjustable sights and an ambidextrous safety. The grips are molded black nylon. S&W manufactured this pistol between 1985 and 1988.

NIB	Exc.	V.G.	Good	Fair	Poor
600	450	375	325	250	150

Model 745—IPSC

This model is similar in outward appearance to the Model 645 but is quite a different pistol. The Model 745 is a single-action semi-automatic chambered for the .45 ACP cartridge. The frame is made of stainless steel, and the slide of blued carbon steel. The barrel is 5", and the detachable magazine holds eight rounds. The sights are fully adjustable target types. The grips are checkered walnut. Introduced in 1986 and discontinued in 1990.

NIB	Exc.	V.G.	Good	Fair	Poor
775	600	500	400	350	250

TARGET PISTOLS

Model 41

NOTE: For full set of steel and aluminum barrel weights add up to $500 depending on condition. For .22 Short conversion kit add $750 depending on condition. For military marked pistols add 400 percent.

Model 41 barrel types

Courtesy John J. Stimson, Jr.

NIB	Exc.	V.G.	Good	Fair	Poor
1100	850	600	500	325	150

Model 41 (New Model)

This model was restyled in 1994 featuring recontoured hardwood stocks, a Millet adjustable rear sight, and a drilled and tapped barrel for scope mounting.

NIB	Exc.	V.G.	Good	Fair	Poor
775	600	500	400	350	250

Model 41-1

This model was introduced in 1960 and is chambered for the .22 Short rimfire only. It was developed for the International Rapid Fire competition. In appearance it is quite similar to the Model 41 except that the slide is made of aluminum alloy, as well as the frame, in order to lighten it to function with the .22 Short cartridge. This model was not a commercial success like the Model 41, so it was discontinued after fewer than 1,000 were manufactured.

NIB	Exc.	V.G.	Good	Fair	Poor
1200	900	725	500	375	225

Model 41 Fiftieth Anniversary Edition

Similar to original Model 41 but machine-engraved with Class A+ coverage, gold plated borders, and glass-topped presentation case. Introduced 2008. Serial Number Range: FYA0001 - FYA0500.

NIB	Exc.	V.G.	Good	Fair	Poor
1600	1400	1200	900	600	400

Model 46

This was a lower-cost version of the Model 41. It was developed for the Air Force in 1959. Its appearance was essentially the same as the Model 41 with a 7" barrel. Later a 5" barrel was introduced, and finally in 1964 a heavy 5.5" barrel was produced. This economy target pistol never had the popularity that the more expensive Model 41 had, and it was discontinued in 1968 after approximately 4,000 pistols were manufactured.

Courtesy Mike Stuckslager

NIB	Exc.	V.G.	Good	Fair	Poor
1100	900	800	650	400	200

Model 61 Escort

In 1970 the Model 61 was introduced as the only true pocket automatic that S&W produced. It was chambered for the .22

LR cartridge with a 2-1/2" barrel and 5-round magazine. It was offered in either blued or nickel finish with black checkered plastic grips. It was dropped from the product line in 1974.

NIB	Exc.	V.G.	Good	Fair	Poor
300	225	200	150	100	75

Model 52A

Introduced in 1961 in the .38 AMU caliber for the Army marksmanship training. Army rejected the pistol and the 87 units built were released to the public. The letter "A" is stamped behind the model designation. A rare find; only 87 were produced. Use caution.

NIB	Exc.	V.G.	Good	Fair	Poor
3000	2500	2000	1500	750	500

Model 52 (.38 Master)

Introduced in 1961 as a target pistol chambered for the .38 Special mid-range wad cutter cartridge. It is similar in appearance to the Model 39 but is single-action-only by virtue of a set screw. Fitted with a 5" barrel and a 5-round magazine. It has a blued finish with checkered walnut grips. About 3,500 of these pistols were produced in this configuration until discontinued in 1963.

NIB	Exc.	V.G.	Good	Fair	Poor
975	750	550	450	300	200

Model 52-1

In 1963 this variation featured a true single-action design and were produced until 1971.

NIB	Exc.	V.G.	Good	Fair	Poor
850	725	450	350	300	200

Model 52-2

Introduced in 1971 with a coil spring-style extractor. Model was discontinued in 1993.

NIB	Exc.	V.G.	Good	Fair	Poor
750	600	475	400	300	200

Model 2214 (The Sportsman)

This semi-automatic pistol is chambered for the .22 LR and designed for casual use. It is fitted with a 3" barrel and has a magazine capacity of 8 rounds. The slide is blued carbon steel and the frame is alloy. Introduced in 1990, discontinued 1997.

NIB	Exc.	V.G.	Good	Fair	Poor
250	200	150	125	100	50

Model 2206

This .22 LR pistol is offered with either a 4-1/2" or 6" barrel. Magazine capacity is 12 rounds. Adjustable rear sight. Stainless steel frame and slide.

NIB	Exc.	V.G.	Good	Fair	Poor
300	250	175	125	100	50

Model 2206 TGT (Target)

Introduced in 1995 this version of the Model 2206 features a selected 6" barrel, bead blasted sighting plane and polished flat side surfaces. A Patridge front sight and Millet adjustable rear sight are standard. In addition the model has a serrated trigger with adjustable trigger stop and a 10-round magazine.

NIB	Exc.	V.G.	Good	Fair	Poor
350	300	250	200	150	100

Model 422 Field

Introduced in 1987 this .22 LR pistol has a 4-1/2" barrel or 6" barrel with an alloy frame and steel slide. The magazine capacity is 10 rounds. This model has fixed sights and black plastic grips. Finish is matte blue.

NIB	Exc.	V.G.	Good	Fair	Poor
350	275	225	125	100	50

Model 422 Target

Same as the Field model but fitted with adjustable sights and checkered walnut grips.

NIB	Exc.	V.G.	Good	Fair	Poor
350	275	225	125	100	50

Model 622 Field

This is a stainless steel version of the Model 422 Field.

NIB	Exc.	V.G.	Good	Fair	Poor
400	300	225	150	125	75

Model 622 Target

This is the stainless steel version of the Model 422 Target.

NIB	Exc.	V.G.	Good	Fair	Poor
400	300	225	150	125	75

Model 622VR

Redesigned in 1996 this .22 caliber model features a 6" ventilated rib barrel. It is fitted with a matte black trigger and a new trigger guard. The front sight is a serrated ramp style with an adjustable rear sight. Weight is approximately 23 oz. Grips are black polymer.

NIB	Exc.	V.G.	Good	Fair	Poor
375	275	200	150	100	75

Model 22A Sport

Introduced in 1997 this model features a choice of 4", 5.5", or 7" barrel. It is chambered for the .22 LR cartridge. Magazine capacity is 10 rounds. Rear sight is adjustable. Grips are either two-piece polymer or two-piece Soft Touch. Frame and slide are aluminum alloy and stainless steel. Finish is blue. Weight is approximately 28 oz. for 4" model and 32 oz. for 5.5" model. Weight of 7" model is about 33 oz. Prices quoted are for 4" model. In 2001 this model was furnished with a Hi-Viz green dot front sight. In 2008 a full-camo version was introduced (add $40).

NIB	Exc.	V.G.	Good	Fair	Poor
290	200	150	100	75	50

Model 22S Sport

This model, also introduced in 1997, is similar to the above model but with 5.5" and 7" barrel on stainless steel frames. Weight is about 41 oz. and 42 oz. respectively. In 2001 this model was furnished with a Hi-Viz green dot front sight.

NIB	Exc.	V.G.	Good	Fair	Poor
300	225	175	150	100	50

Model 22A Target

This .22 caliber target pistol has a 10-round magazine, adjustable rear sight, and target grips with thumb rest. The barrel is 5.5" bull barrel. Finish is blue. Weight is about 39 oz. Introduced in 1997.

NIB	Exc.	V.G.	Good	Fair	Poor
290	200	150	100	75	45

Model 22S Target

Same as above but with stainless steel frame and slide. Weight is approximately 48 oz.

NIB	Exc.	V.G.	Good	Fair	Poor
300	225	175	150	100	50

Model 22A Camo

Introduced in 2004 this .22 LR model features a Mossy Oak Break-Up finish. Weight is about 39 oz.

NIB	Exc.	V.G.	Good	Fair	Poor
325	250	175	150	100	50

Model 3904

In 1989 S&W redesigned the entire line of 9mm semi-automatic handguns. The 3904 is chambered for the 9mm Parabellum and has an 8-shot detachable magazine and 4" barrel with a fixed bushing. The frame is alloy, and the trigger guard is squared for two-hand hold. The magazine well is beveled, and the grips are one-piece wrap-around made of delrin. The three-dot sighting system is employed. This model has been discontinued.

NIB	Exc.	V.G.	Good	Fair	Poor
450	400	325	300	275	225

Model 3906

This is the stainless steel version of the Model 3904. The features are the same. It was introduced in 1989. This model has been discontinued.

NIB	Exc.	V.G.	Good	Fair	Poor
450	400	325	300	275	225

Model 3914

Offered as a slightly smaller alternative to the Model 3904, this 9mm pistol has a 3-1/2" barrel, 8-round magazine, and blued carbon steel slide and alloy frame.

NIB	Exc.	V.G.	Good	Fair	Poor
525	450	400	350	300	250

Model 3913

This version is similar to the Model 3914 but features a stainless steel slide and alloy frame.

NIB	Exc.	V.G.	Good	Fair	Poor
525	450	400	350	300	250

Model 3914LS

This is a redesigned Model 3914 that has a more modern appearance. The LS refers to LadySmith and is chambered for the 9mm cartridge. All other features are the same as the Model 3914 including the blued carbon slide and alloy frame.

NIB	Exc.	V.G.	Good	Fair	Poor
525	450	400	350	300	200

Model 3913LS

This model is identical to the Model 3914LS with the exception of the stainless steel slide.

NIB	Exc.	V.G.	Good	Fair	Poor
525	450	400	350	300	200

Model 3954

Similar to the Model 3914 but offered in double-action-only. Discontinued in 1993.

NIB	Exc.	V.G.	Good	Fair	Poor
525	450	400	350	300	200

Model 915

Introduced in 1993 this model is chambered for the 9mm cartridge and features a 4" barrel, matte blue finish, fixed rear sight, and wraparound rubber grips. Overall length is 7.5" and weight is about 28 oz.

NIB	Exc.	V.G.	Good	Fair	Poor
400	350	250	200	150	100

Model 5904

This is a full high capacity, 15-shot version of the Model 3904. It was introduced in 1989 and features a slide mounted decocking lever and 4" barrel. This version has a blued carbon steel slide and alloy frame. This model is no longer in production.

NIB	Exc.	V.G.	Good	Fair	Poor
525	450	375	325	275	200

Model 5903

The same caliber and features as the Model 5904 and Model 5906, but furnished with a stainless steel slide and alloy frame.

NIB	Exc.	V.G.	Good	Fair	Poor
525	450	400	350	300	250

Model 5906

This is a stainless steel version of the Model 5904. Both the slide and frame are stainless steel.

NIB	Exc.	V.G.	Good	Fair	Poor
525	450	375	275	200	—

Model 5906 Special Edition

A double-action semi-automatic pistol chambered for the 9mm with a 15-round magazine. The frame and slide have a special machine finish while the grips are one-piece wrap-around Xenoy. The front sight is a white dot post and the rear sight is a Novak L-Mount Carry with two white dots. This model has a manual safety/decocking lever and firing pin safety. Introduced in 1993.

NIB	Exc.	V.G.	Good	Fair	Poor
575	450	350	300	250	150

Model 5926

S&W offers a 9mm pistol similar to the 5906 but with a frame mounted decocking lever. Both the slide and frame are stainless steel. Discontinued in 1993.

NIB	Exc.	V.G.	Good	Fair	Poor
525	450	375	300	250	150

Model 5946

This 9mm pistol offers the same features as the Model 5926, but in a double-action-only mode. The hammer configuration on this model is semi-bobbed instead of serrated.

NIB	Exc.	V.G.	Good	Fair	Poor
525	450	400	350	300	250

Model 5967

This is a 9mm model with a M5906 frame and a 3914 slide. It has a stainless steel frame and blued slide. Novak Lo-Mount fixed sights. Introduced in 1990 and sold through Lew Horton.

NIB	Exc.	V.G.	Good	Fair	Poor
600	475	400	350	300	250

Model 6904

This is the concealable, shortened version of the Model 5904. It has a 12-shot magazine, fixed sights, bobbed hammer, and a 3.5" barrel.

NIB	Exc.	V.G.	Good	Fair	Poor
525	450	400	350	300	250

Model 6906

This version has a stainless steel slide and alloy frame but otherwise is similar to the Model 6904.

NIB	Exc.	V.G.	Good	Fair	Poor
525	450	400	350	300	200

Model 6946

This is a double-action version of the Model 6906.

NIB	Exc.	V.G.	Good	Fair	Poor
525	450	400	350	300	200

Model 4003

This pistol is chambered for the .40 S&W cartridge and is fitted with a 4" barrel, 11-round magazine, serrated hammer with a stainless steel slide and alloy frame.

NIB	Exc.	V.G.	Good	Fair	Poor
575	500	400	350	300	200

Model 4004

Identical to the Model 4003 except for a blue carbon steel slide and alloy frame. Discontinued in 1993.

NIB	Exc.	V.G.	Good	Fair	Poor
575	500	400	350	300	200

Model 4006

This model is identical to the Model 4003 except that both the slide and frame are made from stainless steel. This adds 8 oz. to the weight of the pistol.

NIB	Exc.	V.G.	Good	Fair	Poor
575	500	400	350	300	200

Model 4026

Similar to the Model 4006 this version has a frame-mounted decocking lever.

NIB	Exc.	V.G.	Good	Fair	Poor
575	500	400	350	300	200

Model 4046

Similar to the Model 4006 but with a double-action-only configuration.

NIB	Exc.	V.G.	Good	Fair	Poor
575	500	400	350	300	250

Model 4013

A compact version of the 4000 series, this .40 caliber model features a 3-1/2" barrel, eight-round magazine, and stainless steel slide and alloy frame.

NIB	Exc.	V.G.	Good	Fair	Poor
575	500	400	350	300	200

Model 4014

Identical to the Model 4013 except for a blued carbon steel slide and alloy frame.

NIB	Exc.	V.G.	Good	Fair	Poor
575	500	400	350	300	200

Model 4053

Identical to the Model 4013, stainless steel slide and alloy frame, except offered in a double-action-only configuration.

NIB	Exc.	V.G.	Good	Fair	Poor
575	500	400	350	300	200

Model 4054

This model is the same as the Model 4053 except for a blued carbon steel slide and alloy frame. Dropped from S&W product line in 1992.

NIB	Exc.	V.G.	Good	Fair	Poor
575	500	400	300	250	200

Model 411

This model was introduced in 1993 as a no frills model and features an alloy frame, 4" barrel, matte blue finish, fixed sights, and wrap-around rubber grips. Chambered for .40 S&W cartridge with 11-round magazine capacity. Overall length is 7.5" and weight is approximately 29 oz.

NIB	Exc.	V.G.	Good	Fair	Poor
400	350	300	250	200	150

Model 1006

This is a full-size 10mm pistol with a 5" barrel, nine-round magazine, and choice of fixed or adjustable sights. Both the slide and frame are stainless steel.

NIB	Exc.	V.G.	Good	Fair	Poor
675	550	400	350	300	200

Model 4056 TSW

This is a double-action-only pistol chambered for the .40 S&W cartridge. Fitted with a 3.5" barrel with white dot sights. Curved backstrap. Stainless steel and alloy frame. Stainless steel finish. Magazine capacity is nine rounds. Introduced in 1997. Weight is approximately 36 oz.

NIB	Exc.	V.G.	Good	Fair	Poor
700	575	400	325	250	150

Model 1066

This is a slightly smaller version of the Model 1006 and is furnished with a 4-1/4" barrel. Discontinued in 1993.

NIB	Exc.	V.G.	Good	Fair	Poor
675	550	400	350	300	200

Model 1076

Identical to the Model 1066 with the exception of the frame mounted decocking lever.

NIB	Exc.	V.G.	Good	Fair	Poor
675	550	400	350	300	200

Model 1086

Similar to the Model 1066 but offered in double-action-only. This model was discontinued in 1993.

NIB	Exc.	V.G.	Good	Fair	Poor
650	525	375	300	250	200

Model 1026

Similar to the Model 1006 with a 5" barrel this model has a frame mounted decocking lever.

NIB	Exc.	V.G.	Good	Fair	Poor
675	550	400	350	300	200

Model 4506

This is the newly designed double-action .45 ACP pistol. It is all stainless steel and has a 5" barrel, 8-shot detachable magazine, and wrap-around black Delrin grips. This model is no longer in production.

NIB	Exc.	V.G.	Good	Fair	Poor
550	475	400	350	300	250

Model 4505

This version is identical to the Model 4506 with the exception of a blued slide and frame.

NIB	Exc.	V.G.	Good	Fair	Poor
550	475	400	350	300	250

Model 4516

Offered in a .45 caliber this 4500 series is a compact version of the full size .45 caliber S&W autos. Furnished with a 3-3/4" barrel and a 7-round magazine this model has a stainless slide and frame. Discontinued in 1991. This model was reintroduced in 1994.

NIB	Exc.	V.G.	Good	Fair	Poor
550	475	425	375	300	250

Model 4536

A compact version and similar to the Model 4616 this pistol is offered with a decock lever on the frame.

NIB	Exc.	V.G.	Good	Fair	Poor
550	475	400	350	300	250

Model 4546

A full size version of the Model 4506 but offered in double-action-only.

NIB	Exc.	V.G.	Good	Fair	Poor
550	475	400	350	300	250

Model 4040PD

When introduced in 2003 this was the first Scandium frame S&W pistol. Chambered for the .40 S&W cartridge and fitted with a 3.5' barrel. White dot front sight with Novak Lo Mount rear sight. Matte black finish. Magazine capacity is seven rounds. Soft rubber grips. Weight is about 25.6 oz.

NIB	Exc.	V.G.	Good	Fair	Poor
700	575	400	325	250	150

Model SW1911

Introduced in 2003 this is a full size pistol chambered for the .45 ACP and 9mm Parabelluum cartridges. Fitted with a 5" barrel with white dot front sight and Novak Lo-Mount rear sight. Stainless steel frame and slide. Checkered black rubber grips. Magazine capacity is 8 rounds (9 in 9mm). Weight is about 39 oz. In 2005 this model was also offered with wood grips and black oxide finish.

NIB	Exc.	V.G.	Good	Fair	Poor
965	750	600	500	375	200

Model SW1911 Adjustable

As above but fitted with adjustable sights. Introduced in 2004.

NIB	Exc.	V.G.	Good	Fair	Poor
850	700	600	500	375	200

Model SW1911Sc

This .45 ACP model is fitted with a Commander size slide and Scandium frame. Fixed sights. Checkered wood grips. Black oxide finish. Weight is about 28 oz. Introduced in 2004.

NIB	Exc.	V.G.	Good	Fair	Poor
900	750	650	550	400	250

Model 1911 PD

This .45 ACP model is offered with either a 4.25" barrel or 5" barrel with Novak low mount sights. Wood grips. The frame is alloy with black finish. Magazine capacity is 8 rounds. Weight is about 28 oz. for 4.25" model and 29.5 oz. for the 5" model.

NIB	Exc.	V.G.	Good	Fair	Poor
850	700	600	500	375	200

Model SW1911 E Series

Full-size 1911-style pistol. Caliber .45 ACP, stainless steel frame and slide with "fish scale" scalloped slide serrations front and rear. Other features include checkered front strap and mainspring housing, oversized extractor, enlarged ejection port, titanium firing pin and laminated textured wood grips. Available with Crimson Trace Laser grips. Introduced in 2011. **NOTE:** Add 20 percent for Crimson Trace Laser grips. Add 30 percent for integral accessory rail.

NIB	Exc.	V.G.	Good	Fair	Poor
800	685	575	450	300	150

Model SW1911 DK (Doug Koenig)

Introduced in 2005 this .45 ACP model is fitted with a 5" stainless steel barrel. Adjustable rear sight with black blade front sight. Frame is stainless steel with black carbon steel slide. Wood grips. Magazine capacity is 8 rounds. Weight is about 41 oz.

NIB	Exc.	V.G.	Good	Fair	Poor
850	700	600	500	375	200

Model SW1911 Pro Series

Similar to Model SW1911 but with Novak fiber optic sights, skeletonized trigger and various tactical/performance enhancements. Introduced 2008.

NIB	Exc.	V.G.	Good	Fair	Poor
950	800	700	600	475	250

Smith & Wesson Model 1911 Sub-Compact Pro Series

Chopped 1911-style semi-auto pistol chambered for .45 ACP. 7+1 capacity, 3" barrel. Wood grips, scandium frame with stainless steel slide, matte black finish throughout. Overall length 6.9". Weight 26.5 oz.

NIB	Exc.	V.G.	Good	Fair	Poor
1100	950	700	600	475	250

TSW SERIES (Tactical Smith & Wesson)

This series is an upgrade of the older Smith & Wesson pistol series, many of which have been discontinued. These pistols come with either a traditional double-action trigger or a double-action-only trigger. All TSW pistols have an equipment rail for mounting lights or lasers. All are marked "TACTICAL S&W" on the slide.

3913/3953 TSW

Chambered for 9mm cartridge and fitted with a 3.5" barrel. White dot front sight and Novak Lo-Mount rear sight. Aluminum alloy frame. Magazine capacity is 7 rounds. Weight is about 25 oz. Stainless steel finish. The 3913 is traditional double-action while the 3953 is double-action-only.

NIB	Exc.	V.G.	Good	Fair	Poor
650	525	475	400	325	125

4013/4053 TSW

This pistol is chambered for the .40 S&W cartridge and fitted with a 3.5" barrel. White dot front sight and Novak Lo-Mount rear sight. Aluminum alloy frame and stainless steel slide. Magazine capacity is 9 rounds. Weight is about 27 oz. The 4013 is traditional double-action while the 4053 is double-action-only.

NIB	Exc.	V.G.	Good	Fair	Poor
650	525	475	400	325	125

4513/4553 TSW

This model is chambered for the .45 ACP cartridge and fitted with a 3.75" barrel. White dot front sight and Novak Lo-Mount rear sight. Aluminum alloy frame with stainless steel slide. Magazine capacity is 7 rounds. Weight is about 29 oz. The 4513 is traditional double-action while the 4553 is double-action-only. **NOTE:** The double-action-only model 4553 is $50 less.

NIB	Exc.	V.G.	Good	Fair	Poor
650	525	475	400	325	125

5903/5906/5943/5946 TSW

These pistols are chambered for the 9mm cartridge and fitted with a 4" barrel. Fixed sights standard (5903, 5906, 5943, 5946) adjustable sights (5906) optional as well as night sights (5906). Offered in traditional double-action (5903, 5906) as well as double-action-only (5943, 5946). Magazine capacity is 10 rounds and weight is about 38 oz. Stainless steel finish. **NOTE:** Add $100 for night sights, add $50 for adjustable sights.

NIB	Exc.	V.G.	Good	Fair	Poor
650	525	475	400	325	125

4003/4006/4043/4046 TSW

This model comes in the same configurations as the 5903 group except these pistols are chambered for the .40 S&W cartridge. Magazine capacity is 10 rounds. Weight is about 28 oz. **NOTE:** Add $100 for night sights, add $50 for adjustable sights.

NIB	Exc.	V.G.	Good	Fair	Poor
650	525	475	400	325	125

4563/4566/4583/4586 TSW

Similar to the above model but chambered for the .45 ACP cartridge and fitted with a 4.25" barrel. Same configurations as above. Weight is about 31 oz. **NOTE:** Add $100 for night sights, add $50 for adjustable sights.

NIB	Exc.	V.G.	Good	Fair	Poor
650	525	475	400	325	125

CHIEF'S SPECIAL SERIES

CS9

Chambered for 9mm cartridge and fitted with a 3" barrel, this model has a stainless steel slide and aluminum alloy frame. Also available in blued finish. Hogue wraparound grips are standard. Fixed sights. Magazine capacity is 7 rounds. Weight is approximately 21 oz.

NIB	Exc.	V.G.	Good	Fair	Poor
550	395	315	250	200	125

CS45

Similar to the model above but chambered for the .45 ACP cartridge. Barrel length is 3.25". Magazine capacity is six rounds. Weight is about 24 oz.

NIB	Exc.	V.G.	Good	Fair	Poor
575	400	315	250	200	125

CS40

This Chief's Special model is chambered for the .40 S&W cartridge. Barrel length is 3.25". Magazine capacity is seven rounds. Weight is about 24 oz.

NIB	Exc.	V.G.	Good	Fair	Poor
550	395	315	250	200	125

CS40 Two-Tone

Same as above but with alloy frame and black slide. Limited edition. Introduced in 2000.

NIB	Exc.	V.G.	Good	Fair	Poor
575	400	315	250	200	125

SIGMA SERIES

SW40F

This new pistol was introduced in 1994 and was a departure from the traditional S&W pistol. The pistol features a stainless steel barrel, carbon steel slide, and polymer frame. Offered in .40 S&W and 9mm calibers with 15-round and 17-round capacities.

NIB	Exc.	V.G.	Good	Fair	Poor
450	400	350	300	250	200

SW9C

Same as above but with barrel and slide 1/2" shorter than full size Sigma. Offered in both .40 S&W and 9mm.

NIB	Exc.	V.G.	Good	Fair	Poor
450	400	350	300	250	200

SW9M

Introduced in 1996 this pistol is chambered for the 9mm cartridge. It is fitted with a 3.25" barrel and has a magazine capacity of seven rounds. The frame is polymer and the slide carbon steel. Height is 4.5" and overall length is 6.25". Weight is 18 oz.

NIB	Exc.	V.G.	Good	Fair	Poor
450	400	350	300	250	200

SW9V

Chambered for the 9mm cartridge this model is fitted with a 4" barrel and 10-round magazine. It has a traditional double action.

White dot sights are standard. Grips are integral to the frame. Stainless steel slide. Satin stainless finish with choice of gray or black frame. Weight is about 25 oz. Introduced in 1997.

NIB	Exc.	V.G.	Good	Fair	Poor
450	400	350	300	250	200

SW9P

Same as the Model SW9V with the addition of a ported barrel. Introduced in 2001.

NIB	Exc.	V.G.	Good	Fair	Poor
450	400	350	300	250	200

SW9G

Same as the standard SW9 but with a black Melonite stainless steel slide and NATO green polymer frame. Introduced in 2001.

NIB	Exc.	V.G.	Good	Fair	Poor
450	400	350	300	250	200

SW40V

Same as above but chambered for .40 S&W cartridge. Weight is 25 oz. Introduced in 1997.

NIB	Exc.	V.G.	Good	Fair	Poor
450	400	350	300	250	200

SW40P

Same as the Model SW40V but with the addition of a ported barrel. Introduced in 2001.

NIB	Exc.	V.G.	Good	Fair	Poor
450	400	350	300	250	200

SW40G

Same as the standard SW40 pistol but with a black Melonite stainless steel slide and NATO green polymer frame. Introduced in 2001.

NIB	Exc.	V.G.	Good	Fair	Poor
450	400	350	300	250	200

SW380

Introduced in 1995 this model is chambered for the .380 ACP cartridge. Barrel length is 3" with overall length 5.8". Empty weight is 14 oz. with a magazine capacity of 6 rounds.

NIB	Exc.	V.G.	Good	Fair	Poor
325	275	200	150	100	75

ENHANCED SIGMA SERIES

Introduced in 1999 this series features a shorter trigger pull, slide stop guard, redesigned extractor and ejector. The ejection port is also lower. These pistols are also fitted with an accessory groove. Checkering pattern is more aggressive.

SW9E

Chambered for the 9mm cartridge this model has a 4" barrel with Tritium sights. Stainless steel slide with black Melonite finish. Magazine capacity is 10 rounds. Weight is about 25 oz.

NIB	Exc.	V.G.	Good	Fair	Poor
375	300	225	175	150	75

SW40E

Similar to the above model but chambered for the .40 S&W cartridge. Weight is about 24 oz.

NIB	Exc.	V.G.	Good	Fair	Poor
375	300	225	175	150	75

SW9VE

This model is chambered for the 9mm cartridge and fitted with a 4" barrel. Fixed sights and stainless steel slide. Weight is about 25 oz.

NIB	Exc.	V.G.	Good	Fair	Poor
375	300	225	175	150	75

SW40VE

Similar to the model above but chambered for the .40 S&W cartridge. Weight is about 24 oz.

NIB	Exc.	V.G.	Good	Fair	Poor
375	300	225	175	150	75

SW99

This model features a polymer frame designed and manufactured in Germany by Walther. The slide and barrel are manufactured by S&W in the U.S. Chambered for either the 9mm or .40 S&W cartridge this model is fitted with a 4" barrel on the 9mm model and a 4.125" barrel on the .40 S&W model. Adjustable rear sights. Decocking slide-mounted lever. Barrel and slide are stainless steel with black Melonite finish. Trigger is traditional double-action. Magazine capacity is 10 rounds. Weight is about 25 oz. Introduced in 1999.

NIB	Exc.	V.G.	Good	Fair	Poor
400	350	300	225	150	75

SW99 Compact

Introduced in 2003 this model is similar to the full size SW99 but with a 3.5" barrel and shorter grip frame. Chambered for both the 9mm or .40 S&W cartridge. Stainless steel barrel and slide with polymer frame. Magazine capacity is 10 rounds for 9mm and eight rounds for the .40 S&W. Weight is about 23 oz.

NIB	Exc.	V.G.	Good	Fair	Poor
400	350	300	225	150	75

SW99 .45 ACP

Same as the SW99 but chambered for the .45 ACP cartridge. Magazine is nine rounds. Weight is about 26 oz. Introduced in 2003.

NIB	Exc.	V.G.	Good	Fair	Poor
500	400	325	250	150	100

SW990L Compact

Introduced in 2005 this model is chambered for the 9mm or .40 S&W cartridge. Barrel length is 3.5". Adjustable rear sight with dot front sight. Polymer frame with stainless steel slide with Melonite finish. Plastic grips. Magazine capacity is 10 rounds for the 9mm and 8 rounds for the .40 S&W model. Weight is about 23 oz.

NIB	Exc.	V.G.	Good	Fair	Poor
475	400	300	225	150	100

SW990L Full Size

Similar to the above model but chambered for the 9mm, .40 S&W and .45 ACP cartridges. Barrel lengths are 4" for the 9mm; 4.125" for the .40 S and 4.25" for the .45 ACP. Magazine capacity is 16 rounds for the 9mm and 12 rounds for the .40 S&W model. Weight is about 25 oz. Introduced in 2005. **NOTE:** Add $40 for .45 ACP model.

NIB	Exc.	V.G.	Good	Fair	Poor
500	400	325	250	150	100

410

This model was first introduced in 1996. It features an alloy frame with carbon steel slide. It is chambered for the .40 S&W cartridge. Barrel length is 4". The magazine capacity is 10 rounds and the overall length is 7.5". Weight is approximately 29 oz.

NIB	Exc.	V.G.	Good	Fair	Poor
450	400	325	250	150	100

410 Two-Tone

Same as the Model 410 but with alloy finish frame and black slide. Limited edition.

NIB	Exc.	V.G.	Good	Fair	Poor
475	400	325	250	150	100

410S

Introduced in 2003 this is a stainless steel version of the Model 410. Weight is about 28 oz.

NIB	Exc.	V.G.	Good	Fair	Poor
475	400	300	250	150	100

457

Introduced in 1996 this .45 ACP model features a 3.75" barrel with rounded trigger guard and double-action. It is fitted with a single side decocker. Magazine capacity is seven rounds. Overall length is 7.25" and weight is about 29 oz. The frame is alloy and the slide a carbon steel. Finish is matte black.

NIB	Exc.	V.G.	Good	Fair	Poor
500	400	325	250	150	100

457S

Same as above but in stainless steel. Weight is about 29 oz. Introduced in 2003.

NIB	Exc.	V.G.	Good	Fair	Poor
500	400	325	250	150	100

908

Introduced in 1996 this is an economy compact pistol. It is chambered for the 9mm cartridge and is fitted with a 3.5" barrel. The action is traditional double-action. Fixed rear sight. Magazine capacity is eight rounds. Overall length is 6-7/8" and weight is about 26 oz.

NIB	Exc.	V.G.	Good	Fair	Poor
450	400	325	225	150	100

908S

Same as the Model 908 but in stainless steel. Weight is about 24 oz. Introduced in 2003.

NIB	Exc.	V.G.	Good	Fair	Poor
475	425	350	250	150	100

908S Carry Combo

Introduced in 2004 this model is the same as above with the addition of a Kydex carry holster.

NIB	Exc.	V.G.	Good	Fair	Poor
500	400	325	250	150	100

909

Introduced in 1995 this pistol is chambered for the 9mm cartridge. It has a blue carbon steel slide, aluminum alloy frame, and is double-action. It has a single column magazine and curved backstrap.

NIB	Exc.	V.G.	Good	Fair	Poor
405	350	250	150	100	75

910

Also introduced in 1995. Same as above model but with double-column magazine and straight backstrap.

NIB	Exc.	V.G.	Good	Fair	Poor
400	300	200	150	100	75

910S

Introduced in 2003 this is a stainless steel version of the Model 910. Weight is about 28 oz.

NIB	Exc.	V.G.	Good	Fair	Poor
400	325	250	150	100	75

MILITARY & POLICE (M&P) SERIES

Model M&P9m

Full-size Military and Police semi-auto chambered in 9mm. Capacity 17+1, 4.25" barrel, 6.5 lb. trigger, 24.25 oz. Picatinny rail and polymer frame. Optional tritium low-light sights. Introduced 2006.

NIB	Exc.	V.G.	Good	Fair	Poor
500	425	300	225	150	75

Model M&P9-JG

Similar to above but with interchangeable palmswell grip panels, including two pink ones. Dealer sets pricing. Introduced 2008.

NIB	Exc.	V.G.	Good	Fair	Poor
475	425	300	225	150	75

Model M&P9 Pro Series

Similar to M&P9 and M&P40 but with green fiber optic sights and interchangeable palmswell grip panels. Black Melonite finish. Introduced 2008.

NIB	Exc.	V.G.	Good	Fair	Poor
600	475	350	250	150	75

Model M&P9L

Similar to M&P9 but with 5-inch barrel. Introduced 2008.

NIB	Exc.	V.G.	Good	Fair	Poor
575	425	300	225	150	75

M&P 40

Full-size semi-automatic chambered in .40 S this is the first of the new Military and Police series. Capacity 15+1, 4.25" barrel, .5 lb. trigger, 24.25 oz. Polymer frame and Picatinny rail. Optional tritium low-light sights. Introduced 2006.

NIB	Exc.	V.G.	Good	Fair	Poor
475	425	300	225	150	75

M&P .357 SIG

Full-size Military and Police semi-auto chambered in .357 Magnum. Capacity 15+1, 4.25" barrel, 6.5 lb. trigger, 24.25 oz. Polymer frame and Picatinny rail. Optional tritium low-light sights. Introduced 2006.

NIB	Exc.	V.G.	Good	Fair	Poor
575	425	300	225	150	75

M&P45

Semi-auto; similar to M&P40 but in .45 ACP. Black or Dark Earth Brown finish. Introduced 2007.

NIB	Exc.	V.G.	Good	Fair	Poor
575	425	300	225	150	75

M&P45 with Thumb Safety

Similar to above but with ambidextrous thumb safety. Introduced 2008.

NIB	Exc.	V.G.	Good	Fair	Poor
585	435	310	235	160	75

M&P9c

Semi-automatic; compact model; similar to M&P9 but with 3.5" barrel, short grip frame and 10+1 or 12+1 capacity. Black Melonite finish. Introduced 2007.

NIB	Exc.	V.G.	Good	Fair	Poor
475	425	300	225	150	75

M&P40c

Semi-automatic; compact model; similar to M&P9c but in .40 S&W. Black Melonite finish. Introduced 2007.

NIB	Exc.	V.G.	Good	Fair	Poor
475	425	300	225	150	75

M&P357c

Semi-auto; compact model; similar to M&P40c but in .357 SIG. Black Melonite finish. Introduced 2007.

NIB	Exc.	V.G.	Good	Fair	Poor
575	425	300	225	150	75

SW9VE Allied Forces

Similar to SW9VE but with black Melonite slide. Adopted by Afghanistan internal security and border forces. Introduced 2007. Add 75 percent for "Disaster Ready Kit" (case and emergency supplies).

NIB	Exc.	V.G.	Good	Fair	Poor
575	425	300	225	150	75

SW40VE Allied Forces

Similar to SW9VE Allied Forces but in .40 S&W. Introduced 2007. Add 75 percent for "Disaster Ready Kit" (case and emergency supplies).

NIB	Exc.	V.G.	Good	Fair	Poor
575	425	300	225	150	75

S&W M&P VTAC

Caliber 9mm Parabellum/.40 S&W. Magazine capacity: 19 (9mm), 17 (.40). Stainless steel slide, polymer frame, with Flat Dark Earth finish. Striker fired, double-action-only, ambidextrous slide release and reversible magazine catch. Weight is 24 ounces, 4.25-inch barrel with VTAC Warrior night sights.

NIB	Exc.	V.G.	Good	Fair	Poor
665	550	475	400	300	150

M&P22

Rimfire version of the M&P pistol. Striker-fired with aluminum alloy slide and polymer frame. Magazine capacity, 10 or 12 rounds. Ambidextrous thumb safety and slide release, and reversible magazine catch. Weight is 24 ounces, barrel length is 4.1-inches. Introduced in 2011.

NIB	Exc.	V.G.	Good	Fair	Poor
375	325	275	225	150	100

SMITH & WESSON COMMEMORATIVES (REFERENCE ONLY)

Smith & Wesson has, over the years, built many special edition handguns. These guns have been to commemorate some important national or regional event or group. The company has also built a large number of special edition handguns for certain distributors such as Lew Horton which is listed. There are well over 200 special production guns not reflected in this pricing guide. Not even Smith & Wesson has all of the information on these guns and with many the number is so small that a market price would not be possible to establish. Listed are a number of Smith & Wesson Commemoratives that we do have information on. Due to the difficulty in determining value only the original retail price is listed. Remember to receive full value for these guns they must be NIB, unfired with unturned cylinders.

Model 14 Texas Ranger Comm.

Introduced in 1973. Supplied with 4" barrel and cased. Edition limited to 10,000. 8,000 of these had knives. Serial numbers TR 1 to TR 10000. Original Retail Introductory Price: $250.00

Model 25-3 S&W 125th Anniversary Comm.

Introduced in 1977. Limited edition of 10,000. Serial numbers SW0000 to SW10000. Deluxe models marked 25-4. Original Retail Introductory Price: $350.00

Model 26-4 Georgia State Police Comm.

Introduced in 1988/1989 and supplied with a 5" barrel. Total production of 802 guns. Known Serial numbers BBY00354 to BBY0434. Original Retail Introductory Price: $405.00

Model 27 .357 50th Anniversary Comm.

Introduced in 1985 and supplied with a 5" barrel and cased. Limited edition to 2,500 guns. Serial numbers REG0001 to REG2500. Original Retail Introductory Price: N/A

Model 29-3 Elmer Keith Comm.

Introduced in 1986 and supplied with a 4" barrel. Gun etched in gold. Limited edition of 2,500 guns. Serial numbers EMK0000 to EMK0100 for Deluxe models and EMK 010 to EMK2500 for standard model. Original Retail Introductory Price: $850.00

Model 544 Texas Wagon Train 150 Anniversary Comm.

Introduced in 1986 and limited to 7801 guns. Serial numbers TWT0000 to TWT7800. Original Issue Introductory Price: N/A

Model 586 Mass. State Police Comm.

Introduced in 1986 and fitted with a 6" barrel. Limited to 631 guns. Serial numbers with ABT-AUC prefix.Original Retail Introductory Price: N/A

Model 629-1 Alaska 1988 Iditarod Comm.

Introduced in 1987 and limited to 545 guns. Serial numbers from AKI0001 to AKI0545.Original Retail Introductory Price: N/A

Model 745 IPSC Comm.

Introduced in 1986 and limited to 5362 guns. Serial numbers DVC0000 to DVC5362.Original Retail Introductory Price: N/A

Model 4516-1 U.S. Marshall Comm.

Introduced in 1990 and limited to 500 guns. Serial numbers USM0000 to USM0499.Original Retail Introductory Price: $599.95

Model SW1911 PD Gunsite Commemorative

Honors Lt. Col. Jeff Cooper's Gunsite Training Academy. Scandium alloy, single-action .45 ACP with 4.25" barrel and 8+1 capacity. Fixed sights. 28 oz. Introduced 2006.

NIB	Exc.	V.G.	Good	Fair	Poor
950	700	600	500	350	175

Model SW1911 – Rolling Thunder Commemorative

Limited edition commemorates American POW-MIAs. Rolling Thunder and POW-MIA logos in imitation bonded ivory grips. Chambered for .45 ACP. Blued, 8+1 capacity, 5" barrel, 38.5 oz. Introduced 2006.

NIB	Exc.	V.G.	Good	Fair	Poor
950	700	600	500	350	175

SMITH & WESSON PERFORMANCE CENTER HANDGUNS (REFERENCE ONLY)

The role of Smith & Wesson's Performance Center has changed since it was established in 1990. What was once a specialized tune-up and competition one-off production department has now become a separate facility in providing specialized and limited handguns to the public often with distributors participation. This change came about around 1991, when the Performance Center initiated its own limited edition designs. These editions are generally limited to between 300 and 600 pistols for each model. The Performance Center, in fact, has its own distinct product line. Performance Center pistols are made in its own shop using its own designers. One of these distributors that has played a major role in offering these special guns to the public is the Lew Horton Distribution Company. The Center still continues to offer action jobs and accurate work but no longer executes one-of-a-kind customizing. The Performance Center has built about eight to twelve different models in the last two years. Plans call for more of these unique handguns to be built in the future. Pistols that are available from a certain distributor or the Performance Center will be noted in the description of each pistol.

Limited Edition Pistols and Revolvers of 1990

One of the first limited special series of Performance Center handguns was this offering, which consisted of custom engraved S&W handguns limited to 15 units on any current (1990) production pistol or revolver. This Limited Edition featured: 24 karat gold and sterling inlays, special bright mirror finish, decorated in light scroll pattern, specially assigned serial number beginning with the prefix "PEC," tuned action, solid walnut presentation case inlaid with blue or burgundy leather insert, embossed with gold with performance center logo. Interior of case is custom fitted with a matching colored velvet. Each handgun is hand numbered and has a signed certificate of authenticity. Because of the unique nature of the Limited Edition offering it is strongly recommended to secure a professional appraisal.

.40 S&W Tactical

A limited edition semi-automatic handgun offered exclusively by Lew Horton through the Performance Center. This special pistol is fitted with a 5" match-grade barrel, hand fit spherical barrel bushing, custom tuned action, special trigger job, oversized frame and slide rails, wrap-around straight backstrap grip. Replaceable front and Novak rear sights. Special serial numbers. Offered in 1992 and limited to 200 units.

Suggested Retail Introductory Price: $1,500

.40 S&W Compensated

Similar to the .40 S&W Tactical but furnished with a 4.625" barrel and single chamber compensator. This is also a Lew Horton/Performance pistol. A production of 250 units. Offered in 1992.

Suggested Retail Introductory Price: $1,700

.40 S&W Performance Action Pistol

Offered in limited quantities in 1990, this Performance Center .40 S&W semi-automatic pistol was used by the Smith & Wesson shooting team. The frame and barrel are stainless steel with blued carbon steel slide, two port compensator, two fitted and numbered 13-round magazines, 5.25" match grade barrel extended frame beavertail, square combat trigger guard, oversize magazine release button, spherical barrel bushing, wrap-around straight backstrap grip, extended magazine funnel, and BoMar adjustable rear sight. The action is tuned for accuracy and precision.

Suggested Retail Introductory Price: N/A

Model 681 Quadport

A Lew Horton revolver limited to 300 guns with special serial numbers. This 7-shot revolver has a 3" barrel underlug quadport barrel. The action is tuned, cylinders are chamfered and the trigger has an overtravel stop. Sights are fixed combat type. Suggested Retail Introductory Price: $675

Model 686 Competitor

Introduced by Lew Horton and the Performance Center for 1993 this limited edition revolver features a match grade barrel and unique under barrel weight system. The action has been custom tuned and the receiver is drilled and tapped for scope mounts. Charge holes are chambered, ejector rod housing is enclosed, and the grip is an extended competition type. Special serial numbers. Suggested Retail Introductory Price: $1,100

Model 686 Hunter

Similar to the Model 686 Competitor. This is also a limited edition Lew Horton revolver chambered for the .357 Magnum and features the under barrel weight system, internal scope mount, and custom tuned action. Special serial numbers. Suggest Retail Introductory Price: $1,154

Model 686 Carry Comp 4"

Offered in limited quantities by Lew Horton and the Performance Center in 1992 this new design features the unique single chamber integral barrel compensator. Front is windage adjustable and the action is custom tuned. Chambered for the .357 Magnum cartridge. Special serial numbers. Suggested Retail Introductory price: $1,000

Model 686 Carry Comp 3"

The 1993 Lew Horton limited edition version of the Model 686 Carry Comp 4" model with a 3" barrel. The same features apply to both models. Suggested Retail Introductory Price: $1,000

Model 686 Plus

This Lew Horton model features a 7-round cylinder with chamfered charge holes for use with full moon clips for both .38 Special and .357 Magnum cartridges. Fitted with a tapered 6" barrel with countersunk muzzle. Gold bead front sight and adjustable rear sight. Altamont wood grips are standard. Stainless steel finish. Weight is approximately 44 oz. Suggested Retail Introductory Price: $930

Model 686 - .38 Super

Introduced in 2003 this six-round revolver is chambered for the .38 Super cartridge and fitted with a 4" barrel with tapered lug. Interchangeable red ramp front sight and adjustable rear sight. Stainless steel with glass bead finish. Cocobolo grips. Weight is about 37 oz. Distributed by Bangers. Suggested Retail Introductory Price: N/A

Model 629 Hunter

Introduced in 1992 by Lew Horton and the Performance Center this limited edition revolver features a new design that utilizes a 6" under barrel weight system, special integral barrel compensator. The action has been custom tuned and the receiver has an integral scope mount. Chambered for the .44 Magnum. Special finger groove grips are standard. Special serial numbers. Suggested Retail Introductory Price: $1,234

Model 629 Hunter II

Another Lew Horton/Performance Center limited edition revolver that features 2x Nikon scope with steel see-through rings. The barrel is Mag-Na-Ported and incorporates the Performance Center's under barrel weight arrangement. The action is custom tuned and the revolver is supplied with a ballistic nylon range carry bag. Special serial numbers. Suggested Retail Introductory Price: $1,234

Model 629 Comped Hunter

Offered through RSR this model features a 6" barrel with 4-port detachable compensator. The cylinder is unfluted. Sights are adjustable, fitted with Altamount wood grips. Tuned action. Stainless steel. Weight is approximately 59 oz. Suggested Retail Introductory Price: $1,100

Model 629 12" Hunter/7.5" Hunter

Introduced in 2000 this Lou Horton revolver is fitted with a 12" barrel with Patridge front sight and Wilson silhouette adjustable rear sight. Hogue Combat grips. Finish is glassbead stainless steel. Comes with a Waller 21" gun rug. Weight is about 65 oz. A 7.5-inch version was introduced in 2008. Suggested Retail Introductory Price: $1,025

Model 629 Magnum Hunter Trail Boss

Exclusive to RSR this limited edition model is chambered for the .44 Magnum cartridge and is fitted with a 3" barrel. Stainless steel finish. Suggested Retail Introductory Price: $733

Model 629 Compensated Hunter

Chambered for the .44 Magnum cartridge and fitted with a 7.5" barrel with compensator. Barrel also has removable stainless steel scope mount. Open sights fitted with adjustable orange ramp front and adjustable rear sight. Rosewood grips. Six-round cylinder. Weight is 52 oz. Talo exclusive. Introduced in 2001. Suggested Retail Introductory Price: $1190

Model 629 Stealth Hunter

Fitted with a 7.5" ported barrel and chambered for the .44 magnum cartridge. Six-round cylinder. The finish is black-T and NATO green. Red ramp Millett front sight and adjustable rear sight. Hogue rubber combat grips standard. Furnished with lockable aluminum case. Weight is about 56 oz. Introduced in 2001. Camfour Distributor exclusive. Suggested Retail Introductory Price: $1,025

Model 629 Extreme

Chambered for the .44 Magnum cartridge and fitted with a 12" barrel with sling swivel. Bomar sights. Rubber grips. Suggested Retail Introductory Price: $1,025

Model 629 Carry Comp

Introduced in 1992 by Lew Horton and the Performance Center this limited edition revolver is chambered for the .44 Magnum cartridge. It features an integral ported 3" barrel, fluted cylinder, radiused charge holes, dovetail front and fixed groove rear sight. Fitted with a rubber combat grip. The action is custom by the Performance Center. Special serial numbers. Suggested Retail Introductory Price: $1,000

Model 629 Carry Comp II

A limited edition 1993 offering by Lew Horton and the Performance

Center similar to the 1992 Model 629 Carry Comp with the exception that this 1993 model has a special unfluted cylinder and fully adjustable rear sight. Special serial numbers. Suggested Retail Introductory Price: $1,000

Model 629 Comped Hunter

Chambered for the .44 Magnum cartridge and built with a 7.5" barrel with a tapered full length lug and compensator. Front sight is drift adjustable orange ramp. Adjustable rear sight. Stainless steel with glass bead finish. Removable scope mount. Rosewood grips. Weight is about 52 oz. Introduced in 2003. Suggested Retail Introductory Price: $1,100

Model 610

Introduced in 1998 by Lew Horton this model features a 3" full lug barrel chambered for the 10mm cartridge. Nonfluted cylinder, red ramp front sight and white outline rear sight. Rosewood grips. Limited to 300 revolvers. Suggested Retail Introductory Price: $740

Model 640 Carry Comp

Introduced in 1991 by Lew Horton and the Performance Center this revolver is chambered for the .38 S&W Special, but with a strengthened action to handle +P loads. Fitted with a heavy 2.625" barrel with unique integral barrel compensator. The front sight is replaceable and adjustable for windage. The rear sight is a fixed groove. Custom trigger job and custom tuned action are also part of the package. Special serial numbers. Suggested Retail Introductory Price: $750

Model 640 .357 Quadport

Introduced in 1996. Similar to the model above but chambered for the .357 Magnum cartridge and quadported. Limited to 190 revolvers. Special serial numbers. Suggested Retail Introductory Price: $675

Model 460 Airweight

Chambered for the .38 Special cartridge, this model is fitted with a 2" Mag-Na-Ported barrel and a five-shot cylinder. Fixed sights. Eagle Secret Service grips. Weight is about 16 oz. Limited to 450 revolvers. Introduced in 1994. Suggested Retail Introductory Price: $580

Model 625 Light Hunter

This is a large frame revolver chambered for the .45 Colt. It is fitted with a 6" Mag-Na-Ported barrel with integral Weaver-style base. It has a stainless steel finish and black Hogue rubber grips. Drift adjustable Millet front and fully adjustable rear sight. Offered in limited quantities. Introduced in 1997 by RSR. Suggested Retail Introductory Price: $580

Model 625

Introduced in 1998 this model is chambered for the .45 ACP or .45 Colt cartridge. Fitted with a 3" full lug barrel, fluted cylinder, and rosewood grips. Limited to 150 revolvers in each chambering. Suggested Retail Introductory Price: $755

Model 625 V-Comp

Chambered for the .44 Magnum cartridge this model is fitted with a 4" barrel and removable three-port compensator. Front sight is a red ramp with black adjustable rear sight. Hogue wood combat grips. Furnished with aluminum case. Weight is about 43 oz. Finish is stainless steel. Distributed by RSR. Introduced in 1999. Suggested Retail Introductory Price: $1,000

Model 625—5.25"

Introduced in 2001 this model features a special Jerry Miculek Hogue laminated combat grip. Chambered for the .45 ACP cartridge and fitted with a 5.25" barrel. Stainless steel finish. Interchangeable gold bead front sight and adjustable rear sight. Weight is about 42 oz. Camfour exclusive. Suggested Retail Introductory Price: N/A

Model 627—8 Shot

Chambered for the .357 Magnum cartridge this revolver has an 8-round capacity. Drilled and tapped with adjustable sights on a 5" tapered and contoured barrel. Tuned action. Hogue wood grips. Satin stainless steel finish. Weight is approximately 44 oz. A Lew Horton exclusive. Introduced in 1997. Suggested Retail Introductory Price: $1,160

Model 627 Defensive—8 Shot

Chambered for the .357 Magnum this model is fitted with an eight-round unfluted cylinder recessed for full moon clips. Barrel length is 2-5/8". Adjustable rear sight and drift adjustable front sight. Wooden eagle boot grips. Weight is about 38 oz. Introduced in 1999. Furnished with aluminum case. Suggested Retail Introductory Price: $1,025

Model 651

This is a limited edition revolver by RSR chambered for the .22 WMR cartridge. Fitted with a 2" barrel and boot grips. Stainless steel finish. Suggested Retail Introductory Price: $492

"Shorty-Forty" .40 S&W

Introduced in 1992 and available exclusively from Lew Horton, this limited edition Performance Center pistol features a light alloy frame, oversize slide rails, and spherical barrel bushing. A match grade barrel is joined to a custom tuned action. Special serial numbers. Suggested Retail Introductory Price: $950

Model 647 Varminter

Introduced in 2003 this model is chambered for the .17 HMR cartridge and fitted with a 12" fluted barrel with a removable black Patridge front sight. Adjustable rear sight. Integral scope mount on barrel. Six-round cylinder. Stainless steel finish. Weight is about 54 oz. Suggested Retail Introductory Price: $1,100

Model 500 Magnum Hunter

Introduced in 2003 this revolver is chambered for the .500 S&W cartridge and fitted with a 10.5" barrel with compensator. Sling swivel studs and sling are standard. Orange dovetail ramp front sight and adjustable rear sight. Stainless steel with glass bead finish. Hogue rubber grips. Weight is approximately 82 oz. Suggested Retail Introductory Price: $1390

Model 460XVR

Built for serious handgun hunters. Chambered for the .460 S&W Magnum. Stainless steel cylinder, frame and barrel, 5-round capacity, adjustable rear and removable Partridge front sight.

Other features include sling swivels, dual accessory rails and synthetic grips. Weight is a hefty 79.2 ounces, 12-inch fluted barrel with compensator. Re-introduced in 2011 by the Performance Center. Suggested Retail Introductory Price: $1,619.

"Shorty Forty" Mark III

Offered in 1995 this Lew Horton exclusive features low-mount adjustable sights, hand-fitted titanium barrel bushing, checkered front strap. The action as been hand honed and the pistol is sold with two magazines; one 11 rounds and the other nine rounds. Suggested Retail Introductory Price: $1,000

Shorty .45

Introduced by Lew Horton in 1996 this .45 ACP pistol has a hand-fitted titanium barrel bushing, oversize frame and slide rails, match grade barrel, checkered front strap, hand honed double-action, and special serial numbers. Suggested Retail Introductory Price: $1,095

Shorty Nine

This Lew Horton exclusive is limited to 100 units. It features a hand-fitted titanium barrel bushing, oversize slide rails, action job, low mount adjustable sights, checkered front strap, match grade barrel, and two tone finish. Furnished with two 12-round magazines. Suggested Retail Introductory Price: $1,000

9 Recon

This is an RSR exclusive and introduced in 1999. Chambered for the 9mm cartridge this model is fitted with a 3.5" barrel. Rear sight is Novak Lo-Mount. Hogue wraparound rubber grips. The slide is black carbon steel with an alloy frame. Magazine capacity is 12 rounds. Weight is about 27 oz. Suggested Retail Introductory Price: $1,178

Performance Center .45 Limited

This Lew Horton model is a full-size single-action pistol. Handfitted titanium barrel bushing, fitted slide lock, match grade barrel, adjustable sights, oversize magazine well, tuned action, and checkered front strap. Suggested Retail Introductory Price: $1,400

45 Recon

Another RSR pistol chambered for the .45 ACP cartridge, this model is an enhanced version of the "Shorty 45." The 4.25" barrel is ported with Novak Lo-Mount sights. Hogue wraparound rubber grips. Stainless steel slide and barrel with aluminum frame. Weight is about 28 oz. Magazine capacity is 7 rounds. Matte black finish. Furnished with aluminum case. Suggested Retail Introductory Price: $1,221

Shorty .356 TSW

This new cartridge is also available in another Lew Horton/ Performance Center limited edition pistol with a 4" barrel. It features a steel frame and hand-fitted slide, with spherical barrel bushing. The double-action is custom tuned by the Performance Center. Magazine holds 12 rounds. Similar in appearance to the "Shorty-Forty." Offered in 1993. Special serial numbers. Suggested Retail Introductory Price: $1,000

Model .356 TSW "Limited" Series

This is a Lew Horton gun. This model is chambered for the new .356 TSW caliber (TSW stands for Team Smith & Wesson). This is a new caliber, actually a 9mm x 21.5mm cartridge, with ballistics of around 1,235 fps with a 147-grain bullet. Designed as a low-end .357 competition pistol. Built for the competitive shooter (IPSC) it features a 15-round magazine and distinctive profile and markings. The single-action trigger is adjustable for reach while the slide, frame, and barrel are custom fitted. The gun comes with a spherical barrel bushing and adjustable BoMar sights. The frame grip is checked 20 line to the inch, the magazine well is extended as is the magazine release. The magazine is fitted with a pad. Suggested Retail Introductory Price: $1,350

Model 5906 Performance Center

Introduced in 1998 this 9mm pistol features front slide serrations, ambidextrous decocker, titanium coated barrel bushing, match grade barrel, and Novak Lo-Mount sights. Sold with one 15-round magazine and one 10-round magazine. Stainless steel finish. Suggested Retail Introductory Price: $1,200

Model 845 of 1998

This .45 ACP caliber model has a 5" match grade barrel with hand lapped rails on frame and slide. Patridge front sight and adjustable Bomar rear sight. Single-action trigger is tuned and the slide has front serrations. Magazine capacity is 8 rounds. Stainless steel finish. Limited to 150 pistols. Suggested Retail Introductory Price: $1,500

Model 945 Black Model

This Performance Center Model features a 3.25" barrel with black stainless steel slide. Frame is aluminum. Novak Lo-Mount sights. Hogue checkered wood laminate grips. Furnished with two 6-round magazines and a locking aluminum gun case. Weight is about 24 oz. Exclusive with RSR. Suggested Retail Introductory Price: $1,550

Model .45 CQB Combat

Introduced in 1998 this Lew Horton model features a 4" match grade barrel. Novak Lo-Mount sights. Double-action trigger with ambidextrous decocker. Available in both a matte black and stainless steel finish. Matte black model has alloy frame and weighs about 30 oz. Stainless steel version has stainless frame and weighs about 38 oz. Suggested Retail Introductory Price: $1,200

Model 945-40

This PC model is fitted with a 3.75" barrel chambered for the .40 S&W cartridge. Novak Lo-Mount sights and Hogue checkered wood laminate grips are standard. Furnished with two 7-round magazines and a locking aluminum case. Clear glassbead finish. Exclusive with Sports South. Suggested Retail Introductory Price: $1,275

Model 945

This is a single-action-only pistol chambered for the .45 ACP cartridge. Fitted with a 5" match grade barrel and Bomar adjustable rear sight. Grips are checkered black/silver wood laminate with matte stainless steel slide and frame. Magazine capacity is 8 rounds. Empty weight is approximately 44 oz. Introduced in 1998. Suggested Retail Introductory Price: $1,600

Model 945 Micro

Similar to the Model 945 Black Model but with stainless steel finish. Exclusive with Camfour Distributor. Suggested Retail Introductory Price: $1,300

Model SW945

This .45 ACP pistol is fitted with a 5" barrel with Wilson Combat adjustable rear sight. Scalloped slide serrations both front and rear. Checkered wood grips. Many special features. Weight is about 40.5 oz. Suggested Retail Introductory Price: $2,085

Model SW1911

Chambered for the .45 ACP cartridge and fitted with a 5" barrel with adjustable rear sight. Checkered wood grips. Many special features. Scalloped slide serrations front and rear. Black Melonite finish. Magazine capacity is 8 rounds. Weight is about 41 oz. Also offered in a stainless steel version for $160 less. Suggested Retail Price: $2,270

Model SW1911 DK

This model is chambered for the .38 Super cartridge and fitted with a 5" barrel with adjustable rear sight. Smooth wood grips with DK logo. Stainless steel finish with scalloped serrations at rear of slide. Many special features. Magazine capacity is 10 rounds. Weight is about 41.5 oz. Introduced in 2005. Suggested Retail Price: $2,320

SW1911 Tactical Rail

One of Tactical Rail Series for SWAT Teams and tactical applications. Picatinny rail and fixed sights. Blued or stainless, single-action .45 ACP with 5" barrel and 8+1 capacity. 39 oz. Introduced 2006. MSRP: $1,057.

Model 66 .357 Magnum F-Comp

A Performance Center revolver designed as a carry gun. Furnished with a 3" ported barrel and full underlug. The thumbpiece has been cut down to accommodate all speed loaders and the charge holes are countersunk. The K-frame action has been custom tuned and the rear sight is a fully adjustable black blade while the front sight features a Tritium dot night sight. Furnished with a round butt combat-style rubber grip. This revolver has a stainless steel finish. Weight is about 35 oz. This is a Lew Horton special limited edition, 300 units. **NOTE:** In 2003 this revolver was produced for all S&W stocking dealers. Suggested Retail Introductory Price: $800

Model 66

An RSR exclusive this model is chambered for the .357 Magnum cartridge and fitted with a 3" barrel. Red ramp front sight. Stainless steel finish. Limited edition. Suggested Retail Introductory Price: $490

Model 681 Quad Port

Chambered for the .357 Magnum cartridge and fitted with a 3" barrel with Quad porting. Fixed rear sight. Seven-round cylinder with moon clips. Two sets of grips are standard: Hogue Bantam and checkered wood laminate. Stainless steel finish. Weight is about 35 oz. Camfour exclusive. A 4" barrel version is also available. Suggested Retail Introductory Price: $850

Model 25

This PC model is a reintroduction of the original Model 25. Chambered for the .45 Colt cartridge and fitted with a tapered 6" barrel with pinned gold bead patridge front sight. Four screw frame. Furnished with locking aluminum case. Weight is about 42 oz. Sports South exclusive.

NIB	Exc.	V.G.	Good	Fair	Poor
900	750	650	550	375	—

Model 657

This Lew Horton/Performance Center revolver is fitted with a 3" full lug barrel chambered for the .41 Magnum cartridge. Fluted cylinder with red ramp front sight and white outline rear. Rosewood grips. Limited to 150 revolvers in 1998. Suggested Retail Introductory Price: $720

Model 657 Classic

Offered in limited quantities of 350 units this Lew Horton/Performance Center revolver features an unfluted cylinder and 6.5" barrel on a drilled and tapped N frame. Chambered for the .41 Magnum cartridge this handgun is fitted with adjustable rear sight. Special serial numbers. Suggested Retail Introductory Price: $550

Model 657 Defensive

Introduced in 1999 by Lou Horton, this .41 Magnum revolver is fitted with a 2-5/8" barrel with drift adjustable Millet front sight and fully adjustable rear sight. Stainless steel finish with 6-shot nonfluted cylinder. Hogue combat grips. Weight is about 40 oz. Furnished with aluminum case. Suggested Retail Introductory Price: $1,025

Model 657 Hunter

Introduced in 1995 this is an RSR Wholesale Guns exclusive. Fitted with an integral weaver base, Mag-Na-Ported 6" barrel with Millet red ramp front sight and adjustable rear sight. This model has a stainless steel finish, special serial numbers, chamfered charge holes, and adjustable trigger stop. Limited to 500 guns. Suggested Retail Introductory Price: $1,000

Model 19 .357 Magnum K-Comp

This is the same gun as the F-Comp but furnished with a black matte finish and is sold through stocking dealers on a unlimited basis. Suggested Retail Introductory Price: $800

Model 60 Carry Comp

Introduced in the summer of 1993 this J-frame revolver is fitted with a 3" full underlug barrel with integral compensator. The charge holes are radiused for quick loading and the action is tuned by the Performance Center. The pistol is rated for +P ammunition. The grips are fancy wood contoured for speed loaders. This Lew Horton revolver is limited to 300 guns and has special serial numbers. Suggested Retail Introductory Price: $795

Paxton Quigley Model 640

This is a Performance Center offering restricted to 300 revolvers. Built around the Model 640 this limited edition handgun has a 2" compensated barrel, windage adjustable front sight, specially tuned action, and a tapestry soft gun case. Each gun has a distinct serial number range. Suggested Retail Introductory Price: $720

Model 640 Centennial Powerport

Introduced in 1996 this model is a Lew Horton exclusive. It is fitted with a 2-1/8" barrel with integral compensator. The front sight is a black blade with Tritium insert and the rear is a fixed notch. The cylinder holds five .357 or .38 rounds. Stainless steel with Pachmayr decelerator compact grips. Overall length is 6.75" and weight is about 25 oz. Limited to 300 units. Suggested Retail Introductory Price: $675

Model 327 Carry

Introduced in 2004 this 8-shot model is chambered for the .357 Magnum cartridge. Barrel length is 2" with dovetail .260 orange ramp. Scandium alloy frame with stainless steel barrel, titanium cylinder and shroud. Black oxide finish except for gray cylinder. Cocobolo wood grips. Weight is about 21 oz. Suggested Retail Price: $1,226

Model 940 Centennial .356

Offered exclusively from Lew Horton this J-frame revolver is chambered for the new .356 cartridge and has a 2" compensated barrel. It will also fire the 9mm cartridge. This gun features a tuned action, radius hammer and trigger and special serial numbers. Suggested Retail Introductory Price: $760

Model 13 .357

This is a Lew Horton exclusive that features a 3" barrel with 4 Mag-Na-Ports, a bobbed hammer for double-action-only, chambered charge holes, beveled cylinder, contoured grip and thumb latch for speed loader clearance, overtravel trigger stop, and FBI grips. Limited to 300 guns. Suggested Retail Introductory Price: $730

Model 845 Single-Action

Offered by Lew Horton this pistol is chambered for the .45 ACP and is designed for the competitive shooter. Adjustable reach trigger precision fitted slide, frame and barrel are some of the special features. The barrel bushing is spherical and the front sight is dovetailed. The magazine well is extended as is the magazine release and safety. Both front and rear sight are adjustable. Suggested Retail Introductory Price: $1,470

Model 952

Chambered for the 9mm cartridge, this semi-automatic pistol has 5" barrel. Stainless steel frame and slide. Adjustable rear sight. Checkered wood grips. Magazine capacity is nine rounds. Weight is about 41 oz. Suggested Retail Introductory Price: $2,030

Model 1911

This .45 ACP PC model features a 5" barrel, micro-click adjustable black rear sight and dovetail black front sight. Checkered wine laminate grips. Stainless steel frame and slide with black oxide finish. Magazine capacity is 8 rounds. Weight is about 41 oz. Introduced in 2004. Suggested Retail Price: $2,270

SMITH & WESSON LONG ARMS

.320 Revolving Rifle Model

This model is rare and unique—a prize to a S&W collector. The Revolving Rifle is chambered for the .320 S&W Revolving Rifle cartridge, has a 6-shot fluted cylinder and is offered with a 16", 18", and 20" barrel. Only 76 of the rifles are nickel-plated, and the remainder of the production is blued. The butt is rounded, with red hard rubber checkered grips and a forearm of the same material. There is a detachable shoulder stock with a black hard rubber buttplate featuring the S&W logo. The rifle was furnished in a leather carrying case with accessories. As fine a firearm as this was, it was a commercial failure for S and they finally came to the realization that the public did not want a revolving rifle. They manufactured only 977 of them between 1879 and 1887. **NOTE:** Values are for complete unit. Deduct 40 percent without stock. Add 10 percent for 16" or 20" barrels.

NIB	Exc.	V.G.	Good	Fair	Poor
—	8000	5500	3500	2000	1500

Model A Rifle

A bolt-action with 23.75" barrel, chambered for .22-250, .243, .270, .308, .30-06, 7mm Magnum, and .300 Winchester Magnum. It has a folding rear sight and a checkered Monte Carlo stock with contrasting rosewood fore-end tip and pistol grip cap. It was manufactured for S&W by Husqvarna of Sweden. From 1969 to 1972.

NIB	Exc.	V.G.	Good	Fair	Poor
400	325	275	200	150	100

Model B

As above, with a schnabel fore-end and 20.75" barrel.

NIB	Exc.	V.G.	Good	Fair	Poor
425	350	295	200	150	100

Model C

As above, with a cheekpiece.

NIB	Exc.	V.G.	Good	Fair	Poor
425	350	295	225	175	125

Model D

As above, with a Mannlicher-style stock.

NIB	Exc.	V.G.	Good	Fair	Poor
700	600	400	350	250	150

Model 1500 Series

A bolt-action series of hunting rifles made for Smith & Wesson by Howa of Japan in 1983 and 1984. Calibers included .222 Rem., .223 Rem., .22-250 Rem., .243 Win., .25-06 Rem., .270 Win., 7mm Rem. Mag., .308 Win., .30-06 and .300 Win. Mag.. Offered in several variations with blue or stainless receiver, plain or checkered wood stock (Deluxe model). Barrel lengths are 22-inches except 24-inches for magnum calibers. A heavy barrel varmint version was available. The Model 1700 Classic Hunter was similar, except for a removable magazine and schnabel fore-end. **NOTE:** Add 10 percent for Deluxe or Varmint model, 15 percent for Model 1700.

NIB	Exc.	V.G.	Good	Fair	Poor
450	400	350	300	250	150

I-Bolt Rifle

This bolt-action hunting rifle was made in the U.S.A. by Smith & Wesson from 2008 to 2009 in .25-06, .270 Win., .30-06, 7mm Rem. Mag. and .300 Win. Mag.. Offered with wood, synthetic or camo stock, and blue or stainless finish. Integral Picatinny rail. **NOTE:** Add 10 percent for camo stock.

NIB	Exc.	V.G.	Good	Fair	Poor
475	425	365	300	250	150

M&P15 Military and Police Tactical Rifle

Gas-operated semi-auto built along lines of AR-15. Caliber: 5.56mm NATO. Magazine capacity: 30. Barrel: 16-inch 1:9. Stock: Six-position telescoping composite. Weight: 6.74 lbs. unloaded. Sights: Adjustable front and rear. Variants: M&P15A & M&P15T (no carry handle; folding battle sight). Introduced 2006.

NIB	Exc.	V.G.	Good	Fair	Poor
1200	950	800	675	450	200

M&P 15 PC

Generally similar to the M&P rifle but with accurized tubular floated barrel, 2-stage match trigger, 20" matte stainless barrel. No sights. Introduced 2007.

NIB	Exc.	V.G.	Good	Fair	Poor
1750	1300	950	800	550	250

M&P 15 Sport

A more economical addition to the M&P rifle line. Chambered for the 5.56 NATO with a black anodized upper and lower receiver of 7075 T6 aluminum. Polymer hand guard, 16-inch 4140 steel barrel. Adjustable sights, single-stage trigger, chrome-lined gas key and bolt carrier. Flash suppressor compensator. Introduced in 2011.

NIB	Exc.	V.G.	Good	Fair	Poor
665	550	475	400	300	150

M&P 15PC Camo

AR-style semi-auto rifle chambered for .223 Remington/5.56 NATO. A2 configuration, 10-round magazine. No sights but integral front and rear optics rails. Two-stage trigger, aluminum lower, stainless 20" barrel with 1:8 twist. Finished in Realtree Advantage Max-1 camo. Overall length 38.5", weight 8.2 lbs.

NIB	Exc.	V.G.	Good	Fair	Poor
1500	1075	875	750	500	275

M&P 15VTAC Viking Tactics

AR-style semi-auto rifle chambered in .223 Remington/5.56 NATO. Six-position CAR stock. 16" barrel. Surefire flash-hider and G2 light with VTAC light mount; VTAC/JP handguard; JP single-stage match trigger and speed hammer; three adjustable picatinny rails; VTAC padded two-point adjustable sling. Overall length 35" extended, 32" collapsed; weight 6.5 lbs. 30-round magazine.

NIB	Exc.	V.G.	Good	Fair	Poor
1750	1300	950	800	550	250

M&P 15 Piston Rifle

Similar to AR-derived M&P15 but with gas piston. Chambered in 5.56 NATO. Features include adjustable gas port, optional Troy quad mount handguard, chromed bore/gas key/bolt carrier/chamber, 6-position telescoping or MagPul MOE stock, flattop or folding MBUS sights, aluminum receiver, alloy upper and lower, black anodized finish, 30-round magazine, 16-inch barrel with birdcage. Suggested retail price $1531 (standard handguard), $1692 (Troy quad mount handguard).

M&P 15-22

.22 LR rimfire verson of AR-derived M&P tactical autoloader. Features include blowback action, 15.5- or 16-inch barrel, 6-position telescoping or fixed stock, quad mount Picatinny rails, plain barrel or compensator, alloy upper and lower, matte black finish, 10- or 25-round magazine. Price: $589.

Model 916

A series of slide-action shotguns made in the U.S.A. by Smith & Wesson from 1972 to 1981. Made in 12, 16 and 20 gauge in various barrel lengths with fixed chokes. Ventilated rib or plain barrel. Offered in both solid-frame and takedown versions. **NOTE:** Add 10 percent for ventilated rib, 10 percent for takedown model.

NIB	Exc.	V.G.	Good	Fair	Poor
200	180	150	120	100	75

Model 3000

Slide-action shotgun made in Japan by Howa for Smith & Wesson and imported from 1982 to about 1989. In 12 or 20 gauge with a 3-inch chamber, checkered wood stock and fore-end, and fixed chokes or choke tubes. Standard barrel lengths of 26, 28 or 30-inches. Also offered in 18 or 20-inches in police model, and 22-inches in a slug gun with rifle sights. **NOTE:** Add 10 percent for choke tubes.

NIB	Exc.	V.G.	Good	Fair	Poor
350	320	280	225	180	100

Model 1000

A series of gas-operated semi-auto shotguns patterned after the Remington Model 1100. Offered in 12 or 20 gauge with barrel length from 22 to 30-inches and with fixed chokes or interchangeable tubes. Checkered walnut stock and fore-end, engraved aluminum receiver. Available in several variations including waterfowl, trap and skeet models. **NOTE:** Add 25 percent for waterfowl model, 50 percent for trap gun.

NIB	Exc.	V.G.	Good	Fair	Poor
400	350	285	220	150	100

Model 1012/1020

This series of gas-operated semi-autos were imported by S&W from 2007 to 2009. Available in 12 gauge (1012) or 20 gauge (1020) with barrel lengths from 24 to 30-inches, and five choke tubes. Stock is adjustable for length and drop. Satin finished walnut or black synthetic stock, or total camo coverage. **NOTE:** Add 20 percent for camo coverage, 30 percent for 3.5-inch 12 ga. model.

NIB	Exc.	V.G.	Good	Fair	Poor
500	425	385	325	250	200

Elite Gold & Silver Series

Elite Gold model is a side-by-side in 20 gauge only with quality double-gun features. Grade III checkered walnut stock with English-style straight grip or pistol grip, and a choice of single or double triggers. Automatic ejectors, color case hardened frame, fixed chokes of IC/M or M/F with barrel lengths of 26 or 28-inches. Weight is approx. 6.5 lbs. Elite Silver is over/under in 12 gauge only with features similar to Elite Gold except the over/under has five choke tubes, single trigger and recoil pad. Weight is approx. 7.5 lbs. Both of these models were imported from Turkey from 2007 to 2010.

NIB	Exc.	V.G.	Good	Fair	Poor
1800	1500	1100	800	500	250

SNAKE CHARMER
Sporting Arms Manufacturing, Inc.
Little Field, Texas

Snake Charmer

A .410 bore single-shot shotgun with an 18.5" barrel. Stainless steel with a composition stock.

NIB	Exc.	V.G.	Good	Fair	Poor
200	125	100	75	50	25

SNEIDER, CHARLES E.
Baltimore, Maryland

Two-Cylinder Revolver

A .22 caliber spur trigger revolver with a 2.75" octagonal barrel and twin seven-shot cylinders that can be pivoted. The barrel marked "E. Sneider Pat. March 1862." Produced in limited quantities during the 1860s.

NIB	Exc.	V.G.	Good	Fair	Poor
—	—	14000	11000	5500	1250

SODIA, FRANZ
Ferlach, Austria

A wide variety of double-barrel shotguns, drillings, and combination shotgun/rifles are made by this maker.

SOKOLOVSKY CORP. SPORT ARMS
Sunnyvale, California

.45 Automaster

A .45 caliber stainless steel semi-automatic pistol with a 6" barrel fitted with Millet adjustable sights and six-shot magazine. Approximately 50 of these pistols have been made since 1984.

NIB	Exc.	V.G.	Good	Fair	Poor
4850	3800	2750	2000	1500	500

SPALDING & FISHER
Worcester, Massachusetts

Double Barreled Pistol

A .36 caliber percussion double-barrel pocket pistol with 5.5" barrels, blued iron frame and walnut grips. The top of the barrels marked "Spalding & Fisher." Produced during the 1850s.

NIB	Exc.	V.G.	Good	Fair	Poor
—	—	1350	925	400	100

SPANG & WALLACE
Philadelphia, Pennsylvania

Pocket Pistol

A .36 caliber percussion pocket pistol with a 2.5" to 6" barrel, German silver furniture and checkered walnut stock. The barrel marked "Spang & Wallace/Phila." Manufactured during late 1840s and early 1850s.

Courtesy Bonhams & Butterfields

NIB	Exc.	V.G.	Good	Fair	Poor
—	—	2850	1500	750	200

SPENCER
Boston, Massachusetts

Spencer Carbine

This was one of the most popular firearms used by Union forces during the Civil War. It is chambered for a metallic rimfire cartridge known as the "No. 56." It is actually a .52 caliber and was made with a copper case. The barrel is 22" in length. The finish is blued, with a carbine-length walnut stock held on by one barrel band. There is a sling swivel at the butt. There were approximately 50,000 manufactured between 1863 and 1865.

Courtesy Bonhams & Butterfields, San Francisco, California

NIB	Exc.	V.G.	Good	Fair	Poor
—	—	7500	5000	2500	500

Military Rifle—Navy Model

This model is similar to the carbine, with a 30" round barrel and a full-length walnut stock held on by three barrel bands. It features an iron fore-end tip and sling swivels. The Civil War production consisted of two models. A Navy model was manufactured between 1862 and 1864 (there were approximately 1,000 of these so marked).

NIB	Exc.	V.G.	Good	Fair	Poor
—	—	10000	7500	5000	1000

Military Rifle—Army Model

There were approximately 11,450 produced for the Army during the Civil War. They are similar to the Navy model except that the front sight doubles as a bayonet lug. They were manufactured in 1863 and 1864.

Courtesy Milwaukee Public Museum, Milwaukee, Wisconsin

NIB	Exc.	V.G.	Good	Fair	Poor
—	—	8000	6000	2500	600

Springfield Armory Post-war Alteration

After the conclusion of the Civil War, approximately 11,000 carbines were refurbished and rechambered for .50 caliber rimfire. The barrels were sleeved, and a device known as the "Stabler cut-off" was added to convert the arm to single-shot function. Often they were refinished and restocked. The inspector's marks "ESA" will be found in an oval cartouche on the left side of the stock. These alterations took place in 1867 and 1868.

NIB	Exc.	V.G.	Good	Fair	Poor
—	—	5250	3950	1700	500

Model 1865 Contract

This model was manufactured by the Burnside Rifle Company in 1865. They are similar to the Civil War-type carbine and are marked "By Burnside Rifle Co./Model 1865." There were approximately 34,000 manufactured. Old records show that 30,500 were purchased by the United States government, and 19,000 of these had the Stabler cut-off device.

Courtesy Wallis & Wallis, Lewes, Sussex, England

NIB	Exc.	V.G.	Good	Fair	Poor
—	—	5300	3250	1250	500

SPENCER ARMS CO.
Windsor, Connecticut

Slide-Action Shotgun

From 1882 to 1889 they manufactured the first successful slide action repeating shotgun. Designed by Christopher M. Spencer who also designed the Civil War era Spencer military carbines. The shotgun came in both solid and takedown models in both 12 and 10 gauge. In 1890 Francis Bannerman & Sons of New York bought the patents and machinery and moved the operation to Brooklyn, New York. They produced what is known as the Spencer Bannerman models from 1890 to 1907. The later Bannerman models are worth 50 percent less than the Spencer models. **NOTE:** The takedown model is worth 20 percent premium and 10 gauge models are worth a 10 percent premium.

NIB	Exc.	V.G.	Good	Fair	Poor
—	—	1000	600	200	125

SPENCER REVOLVER
Maltby, Henley & Company
New York, New York

Safety Hammerless Revolver

A .32 caliber hammerless double-action revolver with a 3". barrel. The frame and barrel made of brass, the cylinder of steel and the grips are of walnut. The barrel is marked "Spencer Safety Hammerless Pat. Jan. 24, 1888 & Oct. 29, 1889." Manufactured by the Norwich Pistol Company circa 1890.

NIB	Exc.	V.G.	Good	Fair	Poor
—	—	500	225	150	100

SPHINX
Sphinx Engineering SA
Porrentru, Switzerland
Imported by Sile Distributors Inc.

AT-380

This semi-automatic pistol is a small .380 caliber in double-action-only. The magazine capacity is 11 rounds. It is offered in stainless steel, blued, or two-tone finish. The barrel is 3.27" and overall length is 6.03". Sights are fixed and grips are black checkered plastic. Weight is 25 oz.

NIB	Exc.	V.G.	Good	Fair	Poor
600	550	400	300	200	100

AT-2000 series pistols

This is a series number applied to several different variations of the same basic design. Based on the CZ 75 pistol the AT-2000 is a semi-automatic pistol offered in 9mm and .40 S&W. Barrel lengths are different depending on variation, but the AT-2000 can be converted from double-action to double only in just a matter of minutes.

AT-2000S/SDA

This model is chambered for the 9mm or .40 S&W cartridge. The barrel length is 4.53" and overall length is 8.12". Magazine capacity is 15 rounds for 9mm and 13 rounds for .40 S&W. Available in double-action (S) or double-action-only (SDA). Offered with two-tone or all blued finish. Weighs 35 oz.

NIB	Exc.	V.G.	Good	Fair	Poor
1500	1150	875	675	600	300

AT-2000P/PDA

This is a slightly smaller of the AT-2000S. Magazine capacity is 13 rounds for 9mm and 11 rounds for .40 S&W. The features are the same except that the barrel length is 3.66", overall length 7.25", and weight is 31 oz.

NIB	Exc.	V.G.	Good	Fair	Poor
1500	1150	875	675	600	300

AT-2000PS

This version, sometimes referred to as the Police Special, features the shorter barrel of the AT-2000P model on the larger AT-2000S frame. Barrel length is 3.66" and magazine capacity is 15 rounds for 9mm and 13 rounds for the .40 S&W.

NIB	Exc.	V.G.	Good	Fair	Poor
1500	1150	875	675	600	300

AT-2000H/HDA

This is the smallest version of the AT-2000 series. Magazine capacity is 10 rounds for 9mm and 8 rounds for .40 S&W. The barrel length is 3.34" and overall length is 6.78". Weight is 26 oz.

NIB	Exc.	V.G.	Good	Fair	Poor
1500	1150	875	675	600	300

AT-2000C

This is the competitor model. It features a competition slide, dual port compensator, match barrel, and Sphinx scope mount. Offered in double-action/single-action. Available in 9mm, 9x21, and .40 S&W.

NIB	Exc.	V.G.	Good	Fair	Poor
2200	1600	1200	800	600	400

AT-2000CS

Same as above model but fitted with BoMar adjustable sights.

NIB	Exc.	V.G.	Good	Fair	Poor
2250	1650	1250	850	650	425

AT-2000GM

The Grand Master model. Features are similar to the AT-2000C but offered in single-action-only.

NIB	Exc.	V.G.	Good	Fair	Poor
3000	2550	2100	1750	1250	500

AT-2000GMS

Same as above but fitted with BoMar adjustable sights.

NIB	Exc.	V.G.	Good	Fair	Poor
3050	2600	2150	1800	1300	525

3000

16+1 autoloader chambered in 9mm or .45 ACP. Stainless steel frame and slide, manual safety, saingle/double/decocking action, weight 40.56 oz. Also available in compact version.

NIB	Exc.	V.G.	Good	Fair	Poor
2000	1650	1150	500	300	200

SPIES, A. W.
New York, New York

Pocket Pistol

A .41 caliber percussion pocket pistol with a 2.5" barrel, German silver furniture and a checkered walnut stock. Produced during the 1850s.

NIB	Exc.	V.G.	Good	Fair	Poor
—	—	1950	1775	900	300

SPILLER & BURR
Atlanta, Georgia

Navy Revolver

A .36 caliber percussion revolver with a 6" or 6.5" octagonal barrel and 6-shot cylinder. The barrel and cylinder blued, the frame of brass with walnut grips. Some pistols are marked "Spiller & Burr" while others are simply marked "C.S." Approximately 1,450 were made between 1862 and 1865. .

Courtesy Milwaukee Public Museum, Milwaukee, Wisconsin

NIB	Exc.	V.G.	Good	Fair	Poor
—	—	45000	22500	15500	1500

SPITFIRE
JSL (Hereford) Ltd.
Hereford, England

This semi-automatic pistol is a design based on the CZ 75. This is a hand-built pistol designed by John Slough and built from a solid block of steel. The stainless steel frame and slide are cut with spark erosion and diamond grinding. Barrels are built and bored in the same factory. This is primarily a competition pistol. Manufactured 1992-1994.

Standard Model (G1)

Chambered for the 9x21, 9mm Parabellum, or .40 S&W cartridges this pistol uses the locked breech concept. The trigger system is single and double-action and it is fitted with an ambidextrous safety. The barrel is 3.7" and the overall length is 7.1". Magazine capacity of the 9mm is 15 rounds. Sights are fixed. Empty weight is 35 oz. Finish is stainless steel. Comes supplied with presentation box, two magazines, and allen key.Discontinued.

NIB	Exc.	V.G.	Good	Fair	Poor
1300	900	700	500	300	200

Master Model

This is similar to the Standard Model but without sights. It is fitted with a stainless steel bridge mount to take an Aimpoint sight. Also has a dual port compensator. Supplied with presentation box and two magazines. Discontinued.

NIB	Exc.	V.G.	Good	Fair	Poor
2100	1750	1250	800	400	200

Squadron Model

This model has a Standard Model frame, adjustable rear sight slide, adjustable rear sight slide with compensator, Master Model slide and barrel with stainless steel bridge mount and Aimpoint sight, four magazines, screwdriver, allen key, oil bottle, spare springs, cleaning kit, and fitted leather case. Discontinued.

NIB	Exc.	V.G.	Good	Fair	Poor
6000	4800	2100	900	450	200

Sterling Model (G2)

This model is chambered for the 9x21, 9mm Parabellum, or .40 S&W cartridges. Its features are the same as the Standard Model with the exception that it has adjustable sights. Discontinued.

NIB	Exc.	V.G.	Good	Fair	Poor
1400	1000	800	600	300	200

Super Sterling (G7)

Also chambered for the 9x21, 9mm Parabellum, and .40 S&W this model features a single port compensator, 4.3" barrel, and overall length of 8.25". Weight is approximately 36 oz. Discontinued.

NIB	Exc.	V.G.	Good	Fair	Poor
1600	1200	900	700	350	200

Competition Model (G3)

Chambered for 9x21, 9mm Parabellum, or .40 S&W cartridge this model features a tapered slide rib, adjustable rear sight, dual pod compensator, match hammer, adjustable trigger stop with presentation box. Barrel is 5.27" with compensator and weight is 40 oz. Discontinued.

NIB	Exc.	V.G.	Good	Fair	Poor
1800	1400	1000	800	400	200

Battle of Britain Commemorative

This is a limited edition of 1,056 Spitfires in 9mm Parabellum. Each one represents one of the Spitfire aircraft. The stainless steel slide has the inscription "Battle of Britain-50th Anniversary," the grips are checkered walnut, log book of history of that particular aircraft, and a wooden presentation box with engraved plaque. Discontinued.

NIB	Exc.	V.G.	Good	Fair	Poor
1950	1400	1000	800	400	200

Westlake Britarms

This is a .22 LR Match pistol. Barrel length is 5.77", sight base is 8.42", magazine capacity is 5 rounds. Weight is approximately 47 oz. Trigger is adjustable for length, front and rear trigger stops, adjustable palm rest on contoured wood grips, take-down barrel design with removable weight. Limited importation.

NIB	Exc.	V.G.	Good	Fair	Poor
1850	1400	1000	800	400	200

SPRINGFIELD ARMORY INC.
Geneseo, Illinois

RIFLES

M1 Garand Rifle

A .270 (discontinued), .308 or .30-06 caliber semi-automatic rifle with a 24" barrel and 8-shot magazine. Patterned directly after the U.S. M1 Rifle.

Courtesy Milwaukee Public Museum, Milwaukee, Wisconsin

NIB	Exc.	V.G.	Good	Fair	Poor
—	1000	825	550	400	300

Iwo Jima M1 Garand

Similar to standard M1 Model but shipped in reproduction WWII-era crate with signed decorative lithograph. Introduced 2006.

NIB	Exc.	V.G.	Good	Fair	Poor
1600	1300	1000	800	400	200

M1A Basic Rifle

Chambered for .308 Win. and fitted with a painted black fiberglass stock. Barrel length is 22" without flash suppressor. Front sights are military square post and rear military aperture (battle sights). Magazine capacity is 5, 10, or 20 box. Rifle weighs 9 lbs.

NIB	Exc.	V.G.	Good	Fair	Poor
1250	1000	850	650	400	250

D-Day M1 Garand Limited Edition

Introduced in 2005 this model is chambered for the .30-06 cartridge and fitted with a 24" barrel. Military style sights. Two-stage military trigger. Limited to 1,944 rifles, each with a military-style wooden crate. Each side of the buttstock has stamped memorials to D-Day.

NIB	Exc.	V.G.	Good	Fair	Poor
1600	1200	925	675	425	250

M1A Standard Rifle

This model is chambered for the .308 Win. or .243 cartridge. Also fitted with a 22" barrel but with adjustable rear sight. Fitted with a walnut stock with fiberglass hand guard, it comes equipped with a 20-round box magazine. Weighs 9 lbs.

NIB	Exc.	V.G.	Good	Fair	Poor
1500	1100	850	650	400	250

M1A-A1 Bush Rifle

Chambered for .308 or .243 cartridge with choice of walnut stock, black fiberglass, or folding stock (no longer produced). Fitted with 18.25" barrel. Rifle weighs 8.75 lbs. **NOTE:** Add $250 for folding stock.

NIB	Exc.	V.G.	Good	Fair	Poor
1400	1100	850	650	400	250

M1A Scout Squad Rifle

This .308 model is fitted with an 18" barrel and a choice of fiberglass or walnut stock. Military sights. Supplied with 10-round magazine. Weight with fiberglass stock is about 9 lbs., with walnut stock about 9.3 pounds.

NIB	Exc.	V.G.	Good	Fair	Poor
1800	1100	750	550	300	175

M1A National Match

Chambered for .308 as standard or choice of .243 cartridge. Fitted with a medium weight National Match 22" glass bedded barrel and walnut stock. Special rear sight adjustable to half minute of angle clicks. Weighs 10.06 lbs.

NIB	Exc.	V.G.	Good	Fair	Poor
2050	1400	1000	700	500	250

M1A Super Match

This is Springfield's best match grade rifle. Chambered for .308 as standard and also .243 cartridge. Fitted with special oversize heavy walnut stock, heavy Douglas match glass bedded barrel, and special rear lugged receiver. Special rear adjustable sight. Weighs 10.125 lbs. **NOTE:** For walnut stock and Douglas barrel add $165. For black McMillan stock and Douglas stainless steel barrel add $600. For Marine Corp. camo stock and Douglas stainless steel barrel add $600. For adjustable walnut stock and Douglas barrel add $535. For adjustable walnut stock and Krieger barrel add $900.

NIB	Exc.	V.G.	Good	Fair	Poor
2500	1850	1350	900	600	300

M1A Model 25 Carlos Hathcock

Introduced in 2001 this model features a match trigger, stainless steel heavy match barrel, McMillan synthetic stock with adjustable cheek pad, Harris Bi-pod, and other special featirtes. Chambered for the .308 cartridge. Weight is about 12.75 lbs. A special logo bears his signature.

NIB	Exc.	V.G.	Good	Fair	Poor
4650	3450	2500	1750	800	400

M21 Law Enforcement/Tactical Rifle

Similar to the Super Match with the addition of a special stock with rubber recoil pad and height adjustable cheekpiece. Available as a special order only. Weighs 11.875 lbs.

NIB	Exc.	V.G.	Good	Fair	Poor
3000	2600	2000	1500	650	350

M1A SOCOM 16

This M1A1 rifle features a 16.25" barrel with muzzlebrake. Black fiberglass stock with steel buttplate. Forward scout-style scope mount. Front sight post has tritium insert. Weight is about 9 lbs. Introduced in 2004.

NIB	Exc.	V.G.	Good	Fair	Poor
1575	1250	875	650	400	250

M1A SOCOM II

Introduced in 2005 this model features a full length top rail and short bottom rail for accessories. Weight is about 11 lbs.

NIB	Exc.	V.G.	Good	Fair	Poor
1700	1450	950	700	450	300

M1A SOCOM Urban Rifle

Similar to the SOCOM but with black and white camo stock. Introduced in 2005.

NIB	Exc.	V.G.	Good	Fair	Poor
1725	1475	950	700	450	300

IDF Mauser Rifle Model 66SP

This is a bolt-action rifle chambered for the .308 Win. cartridge. Adjustable trigger for pull and travel. Barrel length is 27". Specially designed stock has broad fore-end and a thumb hole pistol grip. Cheekpiece is adjustable as is the recoil pad. Supplied with case. This rifle is military issue. Fewer than 100 imported into the U.S.

NIB	Exc.	V.G.	Good	Fair	Poor
2200	1750	950	700	450	300

SAR-48

This is the pre-ban version of the SAR-4800.

NIB	Exc.	V.G.	Good	Fair	Poor
1400	1200	850	600	500	250

SAR-4800

This is a semi-automatic gas operated rifle, similar in appearance to the FN-FAL/LAR rifle, chambered for the .308 Win. cartridge. It is fitted with a 21" barrel and has a fully adjustable rear sight. Weight is approximately 9.5 lbs. No longer imported.

NIB	Exc.	V.G.	Good	Fair	Poor
1600	1200	800	600	400	250

SAR-8

This semi-automatic rifle is similar in appearance to the HK-91. It is chambered for the .308 Win. and is of the recoil operated delayed roller-lock design. Barrel length is 18" and the rear sight is fully adjustable. Weight is about 8.7 lbs. No longer imported.

NIB	Exc.	V.G.	Good	Fair	Poor
950	750	600	400	300	200

SAR-8 Tactical

Similar to the above model but fitted with a heavy barrel. Introduced in 1996. No longer imported. Fewer than 100 imported into U.S.

NIB	Exc.	V.G.	Good	Fair	Poor
1450	1100	750	600	400	300

M6 Scout

A .22, .22 Magnum, or .22 Hornet and .410 bore over-and-under combination shotgun rifle with an 18" barrel. Black anodized finish with a synthetic stock. Discontinued. The US-made version commands a premium over the Czech-made. Add 30 percent for Hornet. Values shown are for US-made version.

NIB	Exc.	V.G.	Good	Fair	Poor
600	450	295	200	100	50

M6 Scout—Stainless Steel

Same as above but in stainless steel. First introduced in 1996. Discontinued.

NIB	Exc.	V.G.	Good	Fair	Poor
625	475	325	225	150	75

M6 Scout Pistol

As above but with 10" barrel and no folding stock. Parkerized or stainless steel finish. Weight is about 28 oz. Introduced in 2002. Discontinued. **NOTE:** Add $30 for stainless steel.

NIB	Exc.	V.G.	Good	Fair	Poor
575	425	295	200	100	50

PISTOLS

Model 1911-A1

A 9mm, .38 Super or .45 caliber copy of the Colt Model 1911-A1 semi-automatic pistol. Blued or Parkerized. Introduced in 1985.

NIB	Exc.	V.G.	Good	Fair	Poor
625	425	375	350	300	250

Model 1911-A1 Service Model

Introduced in 2003 this .45 ACP pistol has a 5" barrel with Bo-Mar adjustable three-dot rear sight. This model also has a number of special features such as extended mag well, titanium firing pin, and beavertail grip safety. Stainless steel magazine capacity is seven rounds. Black stainless steel finish. Weight is about 35 oz.

NIB	Exc.	V.G.	Good	Fair	Poor
925	750	600	500	400	200

Model 1911-A1 Service Mil-Spec

Chambered for the .45 ACP cartridge and fitted with a 5" barrel. Fixed sights. Matte stainless steel finish. Black plastic grips. Weight is about 36 oz. Introduced in 2003.

NIB	Exc.	V.G.	Good	Fair	Poor
610	475	375	350	300	250

Model 1911-A1 Service Model Lightweight

This .45 ACP pistol has a 5" barrel with lightweight alloy frame and bi-tone finish. Novak Lo-Mount sights. A large number of special features. Checkered cocobolo grips. Magazine capacity is seven rounds. Weight is about 30 oz. Introduced in 2003.

NIB	Exc.	V.G.	Good	Fair	Poor
875	700	600	500	400	200

Model 1911-A1 Stainless

Similar to the standard Model 1911 but chambered for the .45 ACP cartridge and offered in stainless steel. Equipped with three-dot sights, beveled magazine well, and checkered walnut grips. Weighs about 39.2 oz. **NOTE:** For Bomar sights add $50.

NIB	Exc.	V.G.	Good	Fair	Poor
900	750	625	400	350	200

Model 1911-A1 Factory Comp

Chambered for the .45 ACP or the .38 Super this pistol is fitted with a three chamber compensator. The rear sight is adjustable, an extended thumb safety and Videcki speed trigger are standard features. Also checkered walnut grips, beveled magazine well and Commander hammer are standard. Weighs 40 oz. **NOTE:** Factory Comp pistols chambered for .38 Super may bring a small premium.

NIB	Exc.	V.G.	Good	Fair	Poor
1050	925	750	600	500	300

Model 1911-A1 Factory Comp High Capacity

Same as above but with 13-round magazine.

NIB	Exc.	V.G.	Good	Fair	Poor
1050	925	750	600	500	300

Model 1911-A2 S.A.S.S.

This is a single-shot pistol built on the Model 1911 frame. Available in two barrel lengths; 10.75" and 14.9". Offered in .22 LR, .223, 7mm-08, 7mmBR, .357 Magnum, .308 and .44 Magnum calibers. This conversion kit is available for those wishing to use it on their own Model 1911 pistol frames.

NIB	Exc.	V.G.	Good	Fair	Poor
500	400	325	275	200	100

Model 1911-A1 Defender

Chambered for the .45 ACP cartridge this pistol is fitted with a tapered cone dual port compensator. It also is fitted with reversed recoil plug, full length recoil spring guide, fully adjustable rear sight, serrated front strap, rubberized grips, and Commander-style hammer. Eight-round magazine capacity. The finish is bi-tone. Weighs 40.16 oz.

NIB	Exc.	V.G.	Good	Fair	Poor
875	700	600	500	400	200

Model 1911-A1 Loaded Defender Lightweight

As above but with loaded features: precision fit frames, slides and barrels, flat serrated mainspring housing, lowered and flared ejection port, Delta lightweight hammer, loaded chamber indicator, titanium firing pin, carry bevel treatment, ambidextrous thumb safety, high hand beavertail grip safety, dovetail front sight, Novak or adjustable rear sight, and adjustable speed trigger.

NIB	Exc.	V.G.	Good	Fair	Poor
950	775	675	550	450	250

Model 1911-A1 Compact

Available in blue or bi-tone this .45 ACP is fitted with a 4.5" barrel and compact compensator. It is equipped with Commander-style hammer and three-dot sights. Walnut grips are standard. Comes with 7-round magazine. Weighs 37.2 oz. **NOTE:** For stainless steel add $40.

NIB	Exc.	V.G.	Good	Fair	Poor
900	750	625	400	350	200

Lightweight Compact Comp

Fitted with a 4-1/2" barrel and single port compensator. Magazine hold 8 rounds of .45 ACP. Frame is alloy and weight is 30 oz.

NIB	Exc.	V.G.	Good	Fair	Poor
900	750	625	400	350	200

Model 1911-A1 Compact Mil-Spec

This model is the same as the standard blued steel Compact model but with a Parkerized finish.

NIB	Exc.	V.G.	Good	Fair	Poor
850	700	575	350	300	200

Model 1911-A1 Long Slide

This model features a 6" barrel, 3-dot fixed sights, checkered wooden grips, and an 8-round magazine capacity. Finish is stainless steel. Weight is about 38 oz. Introduced in 1997.

NIB	Exc.	V.G.	Good	Fair	Poor
950	775	675	550	450	250

Model 1911-A1 Loaded Long Slide

As above but with loaded features: precision fit frames, slides and barrels, flat serrated mainspring housing, lowered and flared ejection port, Delta lightweight hammer, loaded chamber indicator, titanium firing pin, carry bevel treatment, ambidextrous thumb safety, high hand beavertail grip safety, dovetail front sight, Novak or adjustable rear sight, and adjustable speed trigger.

NIB	Exc.	V.G.	Good	Fair	Poor
1100	950	775	600	475	350

Model 1911-A1 Champion

This .45 ACP pistol has a shortened slide, barrel, and reduced size frame. The Champion is fitted with 4" barrel, 8-round magazine,

Commander hammer, checkered walnut grips, and special 3-dot sights. Weighs 33.4 oz.

NIB	Exc.	V.G.	Good	Fair	Poor
795	650	500	400	295	150

Model 1911-A1 Champion Mil-Spec

Same as above but with a Parkerized finish.

NIB	Exc.	V.G.	Good	Fair	Poor
700	600	400	350	225	125

Model 1911-A1 Stainless Champion

Same as above but offered in stainless steel. Weighs about 33.4 oz.

NIB	Exc.	V.G.	Good	Fair	Poor
850	700	575	350	300	200

Model 1911-A1 Loaded Champion Stainless

As above but with loaded features: precision fit frames, slides and barrels, flat serrated mainspring housing, lowered and flared ejection port, Delta lightweight hammer, loaded chamber indicator, titanium firing pin, carry bevel treatment, ambidextrous thumb safety, high hand beavertail grip safety, dovetail front sight, Novak or adjustable rear sight, and adjustable speed trigger.

NIB	Exc.	V.G.	Good	Fair	Poor
1000	875	700	575	500	300

Champion Compact

Includes same features as Champion but with a shortened grip frame length and a 7-round magazine. Weighs 32 oz.

NIB	Exc.	V.G.	Good	Fair	Poor
850	700	575	350	300	200

Model 1911 Loaded Champion Lightweight

This model has a lightweight aluminum frame with Novak night sights. Checkered rubber grips. Finish is OD green and Black Armory Kote. Weight is about 28 oz. Introduced in 2004.

NIB	Exc.	V.G.	Good	Fair	Poor
850	700	575	350	300	200

Ultra Compact 1911-A1

This model features a 3-1/2" barrel with a 7-1/8" overall length. It has a stainless steel frame, beveled mag well, speed trigger, match grade barrel, and walnut grips. Weighs 31 oz.

NIB	Exc.	V.G.	Good	Fair	Poor
850	700	575	350	300	200

Ultra Compact Lightweight MD-1

Same as above but in .380 caliber with alloy frame. Weighs 24 oz.

NIB	Exc.	V.G.	Good	Fair	Poor
700	600	400	350	225	125

Ultra Compact 1911-A1 Mil-Spec

Same as the Ultra Compact Model but with a Parkerized or blued finish.

NIB	Exc.	V.G.	Good	Fair	Poor
750	650	450	350	225	125

V10 Ultra Compact 1911-A1

Same as the Ultra Compact 1911-A1 but fitted with a compensator built into the barrel and slide.

NIB	Exc.	V.G.	Good	Fair	Poor
900	750	625	400	350	200

V10 Ultra Compact 1911-A1 Mil-Spec

Same as above but with Parkerized finish.

NIB	Exc.	V.G.	Good	Fair	Poor
850	700	575	350	300	200

Model 1911-A1 High Capacity

This model is chambered in .45 ACP (10-round magazine) or 9mm caliber (16-round magazine). Standard features include Commander hammer, walnut grips, and beveled magazine well. Blued finish. Weighs 42 oz. In 1997 this model was offered in stainless steel and Parkerized finish. **NOTE:** For stainless steel add $40, for Parkerized finish deduct $25.

NIB	Exc.	V.G.	Good	Fair	Poor
650	525	400	300	200	100

Compact High Capacity

Same as above but with an 11-round magazine.

NIB	Exc.	V.G.	Good	Fair	Poor
650	525	400	300	200	150

Ultra Compact High Capacity

This .45 ACP model is offered in three different 3.5" barrel variations: stainless steel, Parkerized, and ported. Standard magazine capacity is 10 rounds. Weight is about 31 oz. **NOTE:** Add $60 for stainless steel and $100 for ported models.

NIB	Exc.	V.G.	Good	Fair	Poor
700	600	400	350	225	125

1104 • SPRINGFIELD ARMORY INC.

Micro Compact—Parkerized

Chambered for the .45 ACP cartridge and fitted with a 3" bull barrel. Aluminum frame with steel slide. Novak night sights. Cocobolo grips. Offered with Parkerized finish. Weight is about 24 oz. Magazine capacity is six rounds. Introduced in 2002.

NIB	Exc.	V.G.	Good	Fair	Poor
850	700	575	350	300	200

Micro Compact—Stainless

As above but with stainless steel frame and slide and Novak tritium night sights. Weight is about 24 oz. Introduced in 2003.

NIB	Exc.	V.G.	Good	Fair	Poor
900	750	625	400	350	200

Micro Compact—O.D. Green

As above but with Armory Kote green finish. Pearce grips. Introduced in 2003.

NIB	Exc.	V.G.	Good	Fair	Poor
900	750	625	400	350	200

Micro Compact—Black Stainless

As above but with black stainless steel finish and Slimline cocobolo grips. Weight is about 32 oz. Introduced in 2003.

NIB	Exc.	V.G.	Good	Fair	Poor
900	750	625	400	350	200

Micro Compact Lightweight

This model is similar to the other Micro models but is fitted with an aluminum frame and Novak night sights. Cocobolo wood grips. Bi-Tone finish. Equipped with XML Mini Light. Introduced in 2004. Weight is about 24 oz.

NIB	Exc.	V.G.	Good	Fair	Poor
900	750	625	400	350	200

Loaded Micro Compact Lightweight

As above but with loaded features: precision fit frames, slides and barrels, flat serrated mainspring housing, lowered and flared ejection port, Delta lightweight hammer, loaded chamber indicator, titanium firing pin, carry bevel treatment, ambidextrous thumb safety, high hand beavertail grip safety, dovetail front sight, Novak or adjustable rear sight, and adjustable speed trigger. Introduced in 2005.

NIB	Exc.	V.G.	Good	Fair	Poor
1000	975	775	600	475	300

Model 1911-A1 Mil-Spec Operator

Chambered for the .45 ACP and fitted with a 5" barrel. This model features a Picatinny rail system on the frame. Fixed sights. Magazine capacity is 7 rounds. Parkerized finish.

NIB	Exc.	V.G.	Good	Fair	Poor
900	750	625	400	350	200

Model 1911-A1 Loaded Operator

Introduced in 2002 this model features a integral Picatinny rail on the frame. Chambered for the .45 ACP cartridge and fitted with a 5" barrel. Novak night sights. Parkerized finish. Magazine capacity is 7 rounds.

NIB	Exc.	V.G.	Good	Fair	Poor
1150	950	700	500	375	250

Combat Commander

A copy of the Colt Model 1911-A1 Combat Commander chambered for .45 ACP only. Introduced in 1988.

NIB	Exc.	V.G.	Good	Fair	Poor
600	500	400	350	225	125

Trophy Match

This model has special features such as fully adjustable target sights, match grade 5" barrel, and special wide trigger. Weight is approximately 36 oz. Available in blue, stainless steel, or bi-tone finish. In 1997 this model was offered chambered for the 9mm cartridge. Values would be the same for both .45 ACP and the 9mm models. **NOTE:** For stainless steel add $40.

NIB	Exc.	V.G.	Good	Fair	Poor
1000	975	775	600	475	300

Loaded Leatham Trophy Match

Introduced in 2005 this .40 S&W pistol is fitted with a 5" barrel with fully adjustable target sights. Black Polymer grips. Dawson magazine well, tuned trigger, match barrel and bushing, checkered front strap and other special features. Black finish. Weight is about 39 oz.

NIB	Exc.	V.G.	Good	Fair	Poor
1200	1075	900	700	575	300

1911 GI SERIES

Full Size

Chambered for the .45 ACP cartridge and fitted with a 5" barrel. Old style fixed sights. Standard checkered brown plastic grips. Lanyard loop on mainspring housing. Stainless steel frame and slide. Magazine capacity is 7 rounds. Weight is about 36 oz. Introduced in 2004. This model is also offered with Parkerized finish or OD green finish. Also offered in stainless steel. **NOTE:** Deduct $45 for Parkerized or OD finish. Add $30 for stainless steel.

NIB	Exc.	V.G.	Good	Fair	Poor
560	450	375	325	250	125

Full Size High-Capacity

As above but with 10-round magazine. Weight is about 38 oz. Introduced in 2005.

NIB	Exc.	V.G.	Good	Fair	Poor
600	500	425	375	295	175

Champion

This model is a scaled-down version of the full-size model above. Fitted with a 4" fully supported barrel and low-profile military sights. This model also has double diamond walnut grips. Black finish. Weight is about 34 oz. Introduced in 2004. Also offered with Parkerized finish.

NIB	Exc.	V.G.	Good	Fair	Poor
600	500	425	375	295	175

Champion Lightweight

Introduced in 2005 this .45 ACP model is fitted with a 4" barrel with fully supported ramp. Low profile military sights. Checkered walnut grips. Weight is about 28 oz.

NIB	Exc.	V.G.	Good	Fair	Poor
600	500	425	375	295	175

Micro-Compact

As above but fitted with a 3" fully supported and ramped barrel. Magazine capacity is 6 rounds. Weight is about 32 oz. Introduced in 2004.

NIB	Exc.	V.G.	Good	Fair	Poor
600	500	425	375	295	175

P9 SERIES

This is a double-action 9mm, .45 ACP, or .40 S&W pistol based on the Czech CZ 75 design. It incorporates several design features including: stainless steel trigger, sear safety mechanism, extended sear safety lever, redesigned back strap, lengthened beavertail grip area, and a new high strength slide stop. This model discontinued in 1993.

Model P9 Standard

This is the standard pistol fitted with a 4.7" barrel, low profile target sights, and a ribbed slide. The 9mm has a 16-round magazine, the .45 ACP has a 10-round magazine, and the .40 S&W holds 12 rounds. Offered in either blue or stainless finish. Weighs about 35 oz.

NIB	Exc.	V.G.	Good	Fair	Poor
600	500	425	375	295	175

Model P9 Factory Comp.

This is a competition pistol fitted with triple port compensator, extended magazine release, adjustable rear sight, slim competition wood grips, and bi-tone finish. Weighs 34 oz. Dropped from the Springfield product line in 1993.

NIB	Exc.	V.G.	Good	Fair	Poor
700	600	400	350	225	125

Model P9 Ultra (IPSC Approved)

This competition pistol features a longer slide and barrel, 5". Special target sights, rubberized competition grips. Pistol is engraved with IPSC logo. Available in bi-tone finish only. Weighs 34.5 oz. Dropped from production in 1993.

NIB	Exc.	V.G.	Good	Fair	Poor
775	575	425	350	250	200

Super Tuned Champion

Introduced in 1997 this model features a 4" barrel chambered for the .45 ACP cartridge, Novak fixed Lo-Mount sights. Tuned and polished extractor and ejector. Polished feed ramp and barrel throat. Magazine capacity is 7 rounds. Choice of blued or Parkerized finish. Weight is approximately 36 oz.

NIB	Exc.	V.G.	Good	Fair	Poor
850	700	575	350	300	200

Super Tuned V10

Similar to the model above but with 3.5" barrel. Finish is bi-tone or stainless steel. Weight is about 33 oz. Introduced in 1997. Add $100 for stainless steel.

NIB	Exc.	V.G.	Good	Fair	Poor
1000	895	700	600	400	250

Super Tuned Standard

This model features a 5" barrel with stainless steel finish. Weight is about 39 oz. Has all other super tune features. Introduced in 1997.

NIB	Exc.	V.G.	Good	Fair	Poor
1000	895	700	600	400	250

Armory Range Officer

A 1911 pistol ready to compete out of the box. Caliber: .45 ACP. Five-inch barrel with blue finish, forged steel slide and frame, 7-round magazine. Other features include adjustable rear sight, match grade barrel and bushing, checkered mainspring housing, lightweight Delta hammer, extended thumb safety and beavertail grip tang. Weight is 40 ounces.

NIB	Exc.	V.G.	Good	Fair	Poor
800	675	550	450	350	200

Tactical Response Pistol (TRP)

This .45 ACP pistol is fitted with a 5" barrel and choice of stainless steel or black Armory Kote finish. Fully checkered front strap and mainspring housing. Novak Lo-Mount sights. Magazine capacity 8 rounds. Weight is about 37 oz.

NIB	Exc.	V.G.	Good	Fair	Poor
1360	1150	850	600	400	250

TRP Champion

Same as above but with a 3.9" barrel and black Armory Kote finish. Weight is about 33 oz.

NIB	Exc.	V.G.	Good	Fair	Poor
1175	950	800	600	400	200

TRP Pro

This model is fitted with a 5" barrel and many special features including Novak Lo-Mount tritium sights. Magazine capacity is 7 rounds. Meets specifications for FBI SWAT team. Weight is 36 oz.

NIB	Exc.	V.G.	Good	Fair	Poor
2000	1750	1200	900	675	300

TRP Operator

This model has all the features of the TRP series with the addition of an integral light rail on the frame. Fitted with a 5" barrel. Adjustable night sights. Introduced in 2002. **NOTE:** Add $60 for night sights. Add $100 for OD green frame and slide.

NIB	Exc.	V.G.	Good	Fair	Poor
1350	1025	800	600	400	250

Lightweight Operator

Blued, semi-auto .45 ACP with 5" bull barrel. Fixed sights, 5-6-lb. trigger pull, Cocobolo grips, 31 oz. Picatinny rail. Introduced 2006.

NIB	Exc.	V.G.	Good	Fair	Poor
850	700	575	350	300	200

Lightweight Champion Operator

Similar to above but with 4" bull barrel. Introduced 2006.

NIB	Exc.	V.G.	Good	Fair	Poor
850	700	575	350	300	200

Enhanced Micro Pistol (EMP)

Tiny little 1911-style semi-automatic chambered in 9mm Parabellum or .40 S&W. Short-action single-action design, 7-shot capacity, 3" bull barrel, fixed sights, stainless frame that is 1/8" shorter than the company\qs Compact models. Premium for night sights and other refinements.

NIB	Exc.	V.G.	Good	Fair	Poor
1175	950	800	600	400	200

XD SERIES

These pistols are fitted with a polymer frame, grip safety, chamber indicator and raised firing pin indicator. Offered in black finish as well as O.D. green.

XD 4"

Chambered for the 9mm, .40 S&W, .357 SIG, or .45 GAP cartridges. Barrel length is 4". Magazine capacity for 9mm is 15 rounds; for .40 S&W 12 rounds, for the .357 SIG 12 rounds, and for the .45 GAP 9 rounds. Weight is about 23 oz. **NOTE:** Add $60 for night sights. Add $100 for OD green frame and slide.

NIB	Exc.	V.G.	Good	Fair	Poor
550	450	350	250	175	125

XD 4" Bi-Tone

Offered in 9mm or .40 S&W this 4" pistol has a black polymer frame and stainless steel slide. Magazine capacity is 10 rounds. Weight is about 26 oz. Introduced in 2003.

NIB	Exc.	V.G.	Good	Fair	Poor
585	495	375	275	200	150

XD V-10 Ported 4"

Similar to XD but with 4" ported barrel chambered for the 9mm, .40 S&W or .357 SIG. Black finish. Weight is about 26 oz.

NIB	Exc.	V.G.	Good	Fair	Poor
550	450	350	250	175	125

XD 5" Tactical

This model is fitted with a 5" barrel and chambered for the 9mm, .40 S&W or .357 SIG cartridges. Magazine capacity is 10 rounds. Weight is about 26 oz. Offered in black or O.D. green finish. In 2005 the .45 GAP cartridge was also offered for this model. Magazine capacity for 9mm is 15 rounds; for .40 S&W 12 rounds, for the .357 SIG 12 rounds, and for the .45 GAP 9 rounds. Weight is about 31 oz.

NIB	Exc.	V.G.	Good	Fair	Poor
600	450	350	250	200	150

XD 5" Tactical Pro

Introduced in 2003 this model features a Robar NP3 finish, fiber optic front sight and fixed rear sight. The frame is built with an oversized beavertail frame extension of a higher grip. Chambered for the 9mm, .357 SIG., 40 S&W, or the .45 GAP cartridge. Magazine capacity for 9mm is 15 rounds; for .40 S&W 12 rounds, for the .357 SIG 12 rounds, and for the .45 GAP 9 rounds. Weight is about 31 oz.

NIB	Exc.	V.G.	Good	Fair	Poor
875	750	600	500	375	250

XD 5" Bi-Tone Tactical

Introduced in 2005 this model is chambered for the .45 GAP cartridge and fitted with a 5" barrel. Black polymer frame and stainless steel slide. Magazine capacity is 9 rounds. Weight is about 31 oz.

NIB	Exc.	V.G.	Good	Fair	Poor
600	500	400	300	200	125

XD Sub-Compact

Introduced in 2003 this polymer pistol is chambered for the 9mm or .40 S&W cartridge and fitted with a 3" barrel. Fitted with light rail on the dust cover. Grip safety and safe action trigger. Magazine capacity is 10 rounds. Weight is about 20 oz. Fixed sights. **NOTE:** For night sights add $60. Add $70 for XML Mini light.

NIB	Exc.	V.G.	Good	Fair	Poor
550	450	350	250	175	125

XD 45 ACP

Polymer semi-auto in black, green or bi-tone holds 13+1 .45 ACP. Imported from Croatia. Fixed sights. Service model: 4" barrel, 30 oz. Tactical model: 5" barrel, 32 oz. Picatinny rail. Introduced 2006.

NIB	Exc.	V.G.	Good	Fair	Poor
585	495	375	275	200	150

LEATHAM LEGEND SERIES

This series was introduced in 2003 and will be identified with a unique series markings, serial number, and certificate of authenticity. Two sets of grips will come with each pistol: one cocobolo with lazer engraved signature of Rob Leatham and the other a black micarta double diamond slimline grips. A custom aluminum case is standard for this series.

TGO 1

This is a full custom pistol from the Springfield Custom Shop with Nowlin Match Grade throated barrel and bushing, Robar bi-tone finish, Bomar low-mount adjustable sights, and a number of other custom features. Chambered for the .45 ACP cartridge. Weight is about 38 oz. Four magazines are standard.

NIB	Exc.	V.G.	Good	Fair	Poor
2400	1875	1500	—	—	—

TGO 2

Similar to the TGO 1, but hand-built by the Springfield Armory.

NIB	Exc.	V.G.	Good	Fair	Poor
1900	1500	1200	—	—	—

TGO 3

This model is an enhanced high-end production model with a lightweight aluminum slide. Bi-tone finish. Weight is about 30 oz.

NIB	Exc.	V.G.	Good	Fair	Poor
1295	1025	800	—	—	—

XD(M)

Enhanced variation of XD series with interchangeable backstraps, improved magazine release and disassembly design. Offered in 9mm, .40 S&W or .45 ACP with 4.5-inch barrel. Three-dot sights with night sights available. Black or two-tone polymer frame Ultra Safety Assurance trigger, striker fired, grip safety, ambidextrous magazine releases, accessory rail, loaded chamber and cocked striker indicators. Weight is approx. 27 ounces with empty magazine. Also available in competition model (9mm only) with 5.25-inch barrel with lightening cut on top of slide

NIB	Exc.	V.G.	Good	Fair	Poor
650	525	400	300	200	100

XDM-3.8

Sub-compact model chambered in 9mm Parabellum (19+1) and .40 S&W (16+1). Features include 3.8-inch steel full-ramp barrel; dovetail front and rear 3-dot sights (tritium and fiber-optics sights available); polymer frame; stainless steel slide with slip-resistant slide serrations; loaded chamber indicator; grip safety. Black, bi-tone or stainless steel finish. Overall length 7 inches, weight 27.5 oz. (9mm).

NIB	Exc.	V.G.	Good	Fair	Poor
650	525	400	300	200	100

SPRINGFIELD CUSTOM SHOP

This specialty shop was formed to build custom pistols to the customer's own specifications. When these one-of-a-kind pistols are encountered it is advisable for the shooter or collector to get an independent appraisal. The Springfield Custom also offers standard custom and Racegun packages that are readily available and in stock. These pistols are commercially available.

Custom Carry

Chambered for the following cartridges: .45 ACP, 9mm Parabellum, .38 Super, 10mm, .40 S&W, 9mm x 21. Pistol is fitted with fixed 3-dot sights, speed trigger, Match barrel and bushing, extended thumb safety, beveled magazine well, Commander hammer, polished feed ramp and throated barrel, tuned extractor, lowered and flared ejection port, fitted slide to frame, full length spring guide rod, and walnut grips. Supplied with two magazines and plastic carrying case.

NIB	Exc.	V.G.	Good	Fair	Poor
1600	1450	1075	800	500	300

Basic Competition Model

Chambered for the .45 ACP this model features a variety of special options for the competition shooter. Special BoMar sights, match trigger, custom slide to frame fit, polished feed-ramp and throated barrel are just some of the features of this pistol.

NIB	Exc.	V.G.	Good	Fair	Poor
1800	1600	1275	1050	650	400

N.R.A. PPC

Designed to comply with NRA rules for PPC competition this pistol is chambered for the .45 ACP cartridge with a match grade barrel and chamber. It has a polished feedramp, throated barrel, recoil buffer system, walnut grips, and fully adjustable sights. It is sold with a custom carrying case.

NIB	Exc.	V.G.	Good	Fair	Poor
1600	1450	1075	800	500	300

Trophy Master Expert Limited Class

Chambered for .45 ACP Adjustable BoMar rear sight, match barrel, polished ramp and throated barrel, extended ambidextrous thumb safety, beveled and polished magazine well, full length recoil spring guide, match trigger, Commander hammer, lowered and flared ejection port, tuned extractor, fitted slide to frame, extended slide release, flat mainspring housing, Pachmayr wraparound grips, two magazines with slam pads and plastic carrying case.

NIB	Exc.	V.G.	Good	Fair	Poor
2100	1750	1300	950	600	400

Expert Pistol

Similar to the above model but progressive triple port compensator.

NIB	Exc.	V.G.	Good	Fair	Poor
2200	1850	1400	1000	650	400

Bureau Model 1911-A1

Introduced in 1998 this model features a 5" match barrel, a speed trigger, lowered and flared ejection port, beavertail grip safety, Lo-Mount Novak night sights, front strap checkering, Black T finish and special serial numbers with FBI prefix. Bureau Model markings on slide.

NIB	Exc.	V.G.	Good	Fair	Poor
2100	1750	1300	950	600	400

Springfield Formula "Squirtgun"

Chambered for .45 ACP, .38 Super, 9mmx19, 9mmx21, and 9mmx23. Fitted with a high capacity 20-round frame, customer specifications sights, hard chrome frame and slide, triple chambered tapered cone compensator, full recoil spring guide and reverse plug, shock butt, lowered and flared ejection port, fitted trigger, Commander hammer, polished feed ramp and throated barrel, flat checkered mainspring housing, extended ambidextrous thumb safety, tuned extractor, checkered front strap, bottom of trigger guard checkered, rear of slide serrated, cocking sensations on front of slide, built in beveled magazine well, and checkered wood grips.

NIB	Exc.	V.G.	Good	Fair	Poor
3500	2950	2500	2000	1400	700

Bullseye Wadcutter

Chambered for .45 ACP, .38 Super, 10mm, and .40 S&W. Slide is fitted with BoMar rib. Standard features include full length recoil spring guide rod, speed trigger, Commander hammer, lowered and flared ejection port, tuned extractor, fitted slide to frame, beveled magazine well, checkered front strap, checkered main spring housing, removable grip cope mount, match barrel and bushing, polished feed ramp and throated barrel, walnut grips, and two magazines with slam pads.

NIB	Exc.	V.G.	Good	Fair	Poor
1800	1600	1275	1050	650	400

Trophy Master Distinguished Pistol

This model is chambered for the following cartridges: .45 ACP, .38 Super, 10mm, .40 S&W, 9mmx21. Special BoMar adjustable rear sight with hidden rear leaf, triple port compensator on match barrel, full length recoil spring guide rod and recoil spring retainer, shock butt, lowered and flared ejection port, fitted speed trigger, Commander hammer, polished feed ramp and throated barrel, flat checkered magazine well and mainspring housing matched to beveled magazine well, extended ambidextrous thumb safety, tuned extractor, checkered front strap, flattened and checkered trigger guard, serrated slide top and compensator, cocking sensations on front of slide, checkered walnut grips, two magazines with slam pads, and carrying case.

NIB	Exc.	V.G.	Good	Fair	Poor
2450	1900	1350	1000	650	500

Distinguished Limited Class

Similar to the above model but built to comply with USPSA "Limited Class" competition rules. This model has no compensator.

NIB	Exc.	V.G.	Good	Fair	Poor
2695	2000	1500	1000	650	500

CMC Formula "Squirtgun"

Chambered for .45 ACP, .38 Super, 9mmx19, 9mmx21, 9mmx23. This pistol has a 20-round magazine and a modular frame. All other features the same as the Trophy Master.

NIB	Exc.	V.G.	Good	Fair	Poor
2750	2000	1200	800	400	200

National Match Model

As above, with a National Match barrel and bushing, adjustable sights and checkered walnut grips. Introduced in 1988.

NIB	Exc.	V.G.	Good	Fair	Poor
1535	1150	850	600	400	300

Competition Grade

As above, hand-tuned, Match Grade trigger, low-profile combat sights, an ambidextrous safety, and a Commander-type hammer. Furnished with Pachmayr grips. Introduced in 1988.

NIB	Exc.	V.G.	Good	Fair	Poor
1600	1200	900	650	400	350

A Model Master Grade Competition Pistol

Similar to the Custom Carry Gun, with a National Match barrel and bushing. Introduced in 1988.

NIB	Exc.	V.G.	Good	Fair	Poor
1700	1500	1250	850	400	350

Model B-1 Master Grade Competition Pistol

Specially designed for USPSA/IPSC competition. Introduced in 1988.

NIB	Exc.	V.G.	Good	Fair	Poor
2000	1750	1250	850	400	350

High Capacity Full-House Race Gun

Built with all available race gun options. Offered in .45 ACP, 9x25 Dillon, .38 Super, and custom calibers on request.

NIB	Exc.	V.G.	Good	Fair	Poor
3085	2300	1700	1200	700	400

Night Light Standard

Introduced in 1996 as a limited edition from Springfield distributor Lew Horton this full size Model 1911A1 pistol is chambered for the .45 ACP. It has a lightweight frame and slide with Millett night sights with Hogue rubber wraparound grips. Fitted with extended beavertail safety. Weight 29 oz.

NIB	Exc.	V.G.	Good	Fair	Poor
620	500	400	300	200	100

Night Light Compact

This model was also introduced by Lew Horton in 1996 and is similar to the above model but fitted with a 4.25" barrel and lightweight frame and slide. Weight is 27 oz.

NIB	Exc.	V.G.	Good	Fair	Poor
620	500	400	300	200	100

Night Compact

Same as above but with a steel frame and slide.

NIB	Exc.	V.G.	Good	Fair	Poor
620	500	400	300	200	100

Omega

A .38 Super, 10mm Norma, or .45 caliber semi-automatic pistol with a 5" or 6" polygon rifled barrel, ported or unported, adjustable sights and Pachmayr grips. Patterned somewhat after the Colt Model 1911. Introduced in 1987. **NOTE:** Caliber Conversion Units add $400.

NIB	Exc.	V.G.	Good	Fair	Poor
650	500	350	250	200	125

XD Custom Pro

This pistol is built in the Custom Shop and is available in service and tactical sizes. Tactical calibers offered are: 9mm, .40 S&W, and .45 GAP. In Tactical sizes the following calibers are offered: 9mm, .40 S&W, .357 SIG, and .45 GAP. Among some of the special features are: high hand frame relief, overtravel stop, low-mount Bomar sights. Extended magazine release. National Match barrel and special finish.

NIB	Exc.	V.G.	Good	Fair	Poor
1500	1100	825	675	500	300

XD Carry Pro

This model is offered in subcombact, service and tactical sizes. In subcompact size the following calibers are offered: 9mm and .40 S&W. Many special features as listed above.

NIB	Exc.	V.G.	Good	Fair	Poor
750	550	400	300	200	100

SPRINGFIELD ARMS COMPANY
Springfield, Massachusetts

Belt Model

A .31 caliber percussion revolver with 4", 5", or 6" round barrels, centrally mounted hammer, and an etched 6-shot cylinder. Made with or without a loading lever. Early production versions of this revolver are marked "Jaquith's Patent 1838" on the frame and later production were marked "Springfield Arms" on the top strap. Approximately 150 were made.

NIB	Exc.	V.G.	Good	Fair	Poor
—	—	2600	1925	875	200

Warner Model

As above, but is marked "Warner's Patent Jan. 1851." Approximately 150 of these were made.

NIB	Exc.	V.G.	Good	Fair	Poor
—	—	3200	2750	1325	250

Double Trigger Model

As above, with two triggers, one of which locks the cylinder. Approximately 100 were made in 1851.

NIB	Exc.	V.G.	Good	Fair	Poor
—	—	2750	2200	875	200

Pocket Model Revolver

A .28 caliber percussion revolver with 2.5" round barrel, centrally mounted hammer, no loading lever and etched 6-shot cylinder. Marked "Warner's Patent Jan. 1851" and "Springfield Arms Company." Blued, case hardened with walnut grips. Early production examples of this revolver do not have a groove on the cylinder and have a rounded frame. Approximately 525 were made in 1851.

Courtesy Milwaukee Public Museum, Milwaukee, Wisconsin

NIB	Exc.	V.G.	Good	Fair	Poor
—	—	1750	1250	585	150

Ring Trigger Model

As above, but fitted with a ring trigger that revolved the cylinder. Approximately 150 were made in 1851.

Courtesy Milwaukee Public Museum, Milwaukee, Wisconsin

NIB	Exc.	V.G.	Good	Fair	Poor
—	—	1725	1275	550	200

Double Trigger Model

As above, with two triggers set within a conventional trigger guard. The forward trigger revolves the cylinder. Approximately 350 were made in 1851.

Courtesy Milwaukee Public Museum, Milwaukee, Wisconsin

NIB	Exc.	V.G.	Good	Fair	Poor
—	—	1625	1275	550	200

Late Model Revolver

As above, except that the cylinder is automatically turned when the hammer is cocked. The top strap marked "Warner's Patent/James Warner, Springfield, Mass." Approximately 500 were made in 1851.

NIB	Exc.	V.G.	Good	Fair	Poor
—	—	1300	875	325	100

Dragoon

A .40 caliber percussion revolver with either a 6" or 7.5" round barrel, some fitted with loading levers, others without. The top strap marked "Springfield Arms Company." Blued with walnut grips. Approximately 110 revolvers were manufactured in 1851.

NIB	Exc.	V.G.	Good	Fair	Poor
—	—	10000	8800	3850	950

Navy Model

A .36 caliber percussion revolver with a 6" round barrel, centrally mounted hammer, and 6-shot etched cylinder. The top strap marked "Springfield Arms Company." Blued, case hardened with walnut grips. This model was manufactured in two variations, one with a single trigger and the other with a double trigger, the forward one of which locks the cylinder. Both variations had loading levers. Approximately 250 of these pistols were made in 1851.

NIB	Exc.	V.G.	Good	Fair	Poor
—	—	6000	4250	1650	500

Double-Barrel Shotguns

The Springfield Arms Co. was bought by Stevens who used the Springfield brand name on many good quality single and double-barrel shotguns. Values range from $100 to $1,600 depending on model, gauge, and condition. See also Stevens.

SQUIBBMAN

SEE—Squires Bingham Mfg. Co., Inc.

SQUIRES BINGHAM MFG. CO., INC.

Rizal, Philippine Islands

Firearms produced by this company are marketed under the trademark Squibbman.

Model 100D

A .38 Special caliber double-action swingout cylinder revolver with a 3", 4", or 6" ventilated rib barrel, adjustable sights, matte black finish and walnut grips.

NIB	Exc.	V.G.	Good	Fair	Poor
—	175	100	80	60	40

Model 100DC

As above, without the ventilated rib.

NIB	Exc.	V.G.	Good	Fair	Poor
—	200	100	80	60	40

Model 100

As above, with a tapered barrel and uncheckered walnut grips.

NIB	Exc.	V.G.	Good	Fair	Poor
—	200	100	80	60	40

Thunder Chief

As above, but in .22 or .22 Magnum caliber with a heavier ventilated rib barrel, shrouded ejector, and ebony grips.

NIB	Exc.	V.G.	Good	Fair	Poor
—	225	125	100	80	60

SSK INDUSTRIES

Bloomingdale, Ohio

SSK-Contender

A custom-made pistol available in 74 different calibers from .178 Bee to .588 JDJ and built on a Thompson/Center action.

NIB	Exc.	V.G.	Good	Fair	Poor
1250	1050	875	600	550	300

SSK-XP100

A custom-made pistol utilizing a Remington XP100 action. Available in a variety of calibers and sight configurations.

NIB	Exc.	V.G.	Good	Fair	Poor
1400	1225	900	625	575	400

.50 Caliber XP100

As above, with an integral muzzlebrake and reinforced composition stock.

NIB	Exc.	V.G.	Good	Fair	Poor
1750	1500	1250	1000	750	450

STAFFORD, T. J.

New Haven, Connecticut

Pocket Pistol

A .22 caliber single-shot spur trigger pistol with a 3.5" octagonal barrel marked "T.J. Stafford New Haven Ct.," silver-plated brass frame and walnut or rosewood grips.

Courtesy W.P. Hallstein III and son Chip

NIB	Exc.	V.G.	Good	Fair	Poor
—	—	775	600	250	100

Large Frame Model

As above, but in .38 rimfire caliber with a 6" barrel.

NIB	Exc.	V.G.	Good	Fair	Poor
—	—	1050	850	400	200

STAG ARMS
New Britain, Connecticut

NOTE: All Stag rifles are available in left hand configuration. The prices are approximately $25-$40 higher than the right handed models listed here.

Stag-15 Model 1 Pre-Ban

Basic M-4 Carbine pattern. Cal. 5.56mm/.223. 16-inch M-4 barrel with flash hider and bayonet lug. A2 upper receiver with adjustable rear sight. Six-position collapsible buttstock.

NIB	Exc.	V.G.	Good	Fair	Poor
950	800	675	500	350	200

Stag-15 Model 2 Pre-Ban

As above but with a flat top upper receiver. Includes MI ERS flip type rear sight assembly.

NIB	Exc.	V.G.	Good	Fair	Poor
950	800	675	500	350	200

Stag-15 Model 2 T

As above but with a A.R.M.S. sight system and Samson MRFS-C four sided hand guard.

NIB	Exc.	V.G.	Good	Fair	Poor
1050	900	775	600	400	250

Stag-15 Model 3 Pre-Ban

M-4 type carbine featuring a flat top receiver and gas block with picatinny rails. Six position collapsible buttstock.

NIB	Exc.	V.G.	Good	Fair	Poor
950	800	675	500	350	200

Stag-15 Model 4 Pre-Ban

An A-2 type rifle featuring a 20-inch barrel. Flash hider and bayonet lug.

NIB	Exc.	V.G.	Good	Fair	Poor
950	800	675	500	350	200

Stag 6.8 Model 5 Pre-Ban

Cal. 6.8 SPC. 16-inch barrel. Flat top receiver with picatinny rail. Six position collapsible buttstock. 25-round magazine.

NIB	Exc.	V.G.	Good	Fair	Poor
1050	900	775	600	400	250

Stag-15 Model 6 Pre-Ban Super Varminter

24-inch heavy barrel. No flash hider. Flat top receiver with picatinny rail. Two stage trigger. Free float round hand guard. A2 type fixed stock.

NIB	Exc.	V.G.	Good	Fair	Poor
1050	900	775	600	400	250

STALCAP, ALEXANDER T.F.M.
Nashville, Tennessee

First in business during the 1850s, Stalcap received a contract in 1862, to modify sporting arms for military use. Overall length 50-7/8" to 51-3/4"; octagonal barrels 35-1/4" - 36" turned round at muzzle for socket bayonets; .54 caliber. Rifles assembled with sporting locks, new stocks and brass furniture. At least 102 rifles were delivered in 1862. These arms are unmarked.

NIB	Exc.	V.G.	Good	Fair	Poor
—	—	6500	4250	2000	1000

STANDARD ARMS CO.
Wilmington, Delaware
Model G

Chambered for .25 Remington, .30 Remington, and .35 Remington, with a 22" barrel, and open sights. Integral box magazine and closable gas port that allowed the rifle to be used as a slide action. Blued with a walnut stock. Produced in limited quantities, circa 1910. A notorious jamamatic. Bronze alloy buttplate and forend.

NIB	Exc.	V.G.	Good	Fair	Poor
—	750	600	450	250	150

Model M

Manually-operated pump-only version of Model G.

NIB	Exc.	V.G.	Good	Fair	Poor
—	900	725	550	300	150

STAR, BONIFACIO ECHEVERRIA
Eibar, Spain

SEE—Echeverria

STARR, EBAN T.
New York, New York

Single-Shot Derringer

A .41 caliber single-shot pistol with a pivoted 2.75" round barrel. The hammer mounted on the right side of the frame and the trigger formed in the shape of a button located at the front of the frame. The frame marked "Starr's Pat's May 10, 1864." The brass frame silver-plated, the barrel blued or silver-plated with checkered walnut grips. Manufactured from 1864 to 1869.

Courtesy Milwaukee Public Museum, Milwaukee, Wisconsin

NIB	Exc.	V.G.	Good	Fair	Poor
—	—	2300	1850	825	200

Four Barreled Pepperbox

A .32 caliber 4 barreled pocket pistol with 2.75" to 3.25" barrels. The frame marked "Starr's Pat's May 10, 1864." Brass frames, silver-plated. The barrel is blued with plain walnut grips. This pistol was produced in six variations.

Courtesy Milwaukee Public Museum, Milwaukee, Wisconsin

First Model

Fluted breech and a barrel release mounted on the right side of the frame.

NIB	Exc.	V.G.	Good	Fair	Poor
—	—	3900	2750	875	200

Second Model

Flat breech.

NIB	Exc.	V.G.	Good	Fair	Poor
—	—	2500	1925	650	200

Third Model

Rounded breech with a visible firing-pin retaining spring.

NIB	Exc.	V.G.	Good	Fair	Poor
—	—	2350	1650	550	150

Fourth Model

Rounded breech without visible springs.

NIB	Exc.	V.G.	Good	Fair	Poor
—	—	2100	1650	550	150

Fifth Model

A larger, more angular grip.

NIB	Exc.	V.G.	Good	Fair	Poor
—	—	1950	1400	450	150

Sixth Model

The frame length of this variation is of increased size.

NIB	Exc.	V.G.	Good	Fair	Poor
—	—	2100	1650	550	150

STARR ARMS COMPANY
New York, New York

1858 Navy Revolver

A .36 caliber double-action percussion revolver with a 6" barrel and 6-shot cylinder. Blued, case hardened with walnut grips. The frame marked "Starr Arms Co. New York." Approximately 3,000 were made between 1858 and 1860.

Courtesy Milwaukee Public Museum, Milwaukee, Wisconsin

Standard Model

NIB	Exc.	V.G.	Good	Fair	Poor
—	—	4100	3250	1100	350

Martially Marked (JT)

NIB	Exc.	V.G.	Good	Fair	Poor
—	—	5100	4250	1750	700

1858 Army Revolver

A .44 caliber double-action percussion revolver with a 6" barrel and 6-shot cylinder. Blued, case hardened with walnut grips. The frame marked "Starr Arms Co. New York." Approximately 23,000 were manufactured.

NIB	Exc.	V.G.	Good	Fair	Poor
—	6200	4300	2500	1100	300

1863 Army Revolver

Similar to the above, but single-action and with an 8" round barrel. Approximately 32,000 were manufactured between 1863 and 1865.

Courtesy Milwaukee Public Museum, Milwaukee, Wisconsin

NIB	Exc.	V.G.	Good	Fair	Poor
—	6750	4700	3250	1500	350

Percussion Carbine

A .54 caliber breechloading percussion carbine with a 21" round barrel secured by one barrel band. Blued, case hardened with a walnut stock. The lock marked "Starr Arms Co./Yonkers, N.Y."

Courtesy Milwaukee Public Museum, Milwaukee, Wisconsin

NIB	Exc.	V.G.	Good	Fair	Poor
—	—	3500	2750	1250	400

Cartridge Carbine

Similar to the above, but in .52 rimfire caliber. Approximately 5,000 were manufactured.

Courtesy Milwaukee Public Museum, Milwaukee, Wisconsin

NIB	Exc.	V.G.	Good	Fair	Poor
—	—	3750	2500	1000	350

STEEL CITY ARMS, INC.
Pittsburgh, Pennsylvania

Double Deuce

A .22 caliber stainless steel double-action semi-automatic pistol with a 2.5" barrel, 7-shot magazine and plain rosewood grips. Introduced in 1984.

Courtesy J.B. Wood

NIB	Exc.	V.G.	Good	Fair	Poor
—	300	250	200	150	100

STENDA WAFFENFABRIK
Suhl, Germany

Pocket Pistol

A 7.65mm semi-automatic pistol similar to the "Beholla," the "Leonhardt," and the "Menta." Stenda took over the production of the Beholla pistol design at the close of WWI. The only major difference in the Stenda design was the elimination of the Beholla's worst feature, the pin that went through the slide and retained the barrel. It was replaced by a sliding catch that anchored it in place and unlocked the slide so that the barrel could be removed without the need of a vise and drift pin. The Stenda pistol can be identified by the fact that there are no holes through the slide and there is a catch on the frame above the trigger. The finish blued, with plastic grips; and the slide is marked "Waffenfabrik Stendawerke Suhl." Approximately 25,000 manufactured before production ceased in 1926.

NIB	Exc.	V.G.	Good	Fair	Poor
—	450	275	225	165	100

STERLING ARMAMENT LTD.
London, England

Parapistol MK 7 C4

A 9mm semi-automatic pistol with a 4" barrel, and detachable magazines of 10-round capacity. Black wrinkled paint finish with plastic grips.

NIB	Exc.	V.G.	Good	Fair	Poor
600	475	400	300	200	100

Parapistol MK 7 C8

As above, with a 7.8" barrel.

NIB	Exc.	V.G.	Good	Fair	Poor
625	500	400	300	200	100

Sterling MK 6

A semi-automatic copy of the Sterling submachine gun with a 16.1" barrel, folding metal stock and side mounted magazine. Finished as above.

NIB	Exc.	V.G.	Good	Fair	Poor
1500	950	750	500	300	200

Sterling AR 180

A copy of the Armalite Model AR18, 5.56mm rifle. Finished with either black wrinkled paint or, more rarely, blued.

NIB	Exc.	V.G.	Good	Fair	Poor
1100	750	600	500	350	200

STERLING ARMS CORPORATION
Gasport, New York

Model 283 Target 300

This pistol is similar in appearance to Hi-Standard semi-automatic pistols. Chambered for the .22 LR cartridge it was offered with 4", 4-1/2", or 8" barrels. Rear sight is adjustable and magazine holds 10 rounds. Grips are black plastic. Weight is approximately 36 oz.

NIB	Exc.	V.G.	Good	Fair	Poor
300	250	175	100	75	60

Model 284 Target 300L

Similar to the above model except for 4-1/2" or 6" tapered barrel with barrel band.

Courtesy John J. Stimson, Jr.

NIB	Exc.	V.G.	Good	Fair	Poor
325	275	175	100	75	60

Model 285 Husky

Similar to the Model 283 with the exception of fixed sights. Offered with 4-1/2" barrel only.

NIB	Exc.	V.G.	Good	Fair	Poor
300	250	175	100	75	60

Model 286 Trapper

Similar to the Model 284 except for fixed sights.

NIB	Exc.	V.G.	Good	Fair	Poor
300	250	175	100	75	60

Model 287 PPL .380

This is a pocket-size semi-automatic pistol chambered for the .380 ACP cartridge. Fitted with a 1" barrel it has a 5-1/4" length overall. Magazine holds 6 rounds. Weight is approximately 22 oz.

NIB	Exc.	V.G.	Good	Fair	Poor
225	175	125	75	50	25

Model PPL .22

This is a small pocket pistol similar to the Model 287 but chambered for the .22 LR cartridge. Barrel is 1" long. Pistol weighs about 24 oz.

NIB	Exc.	V.G.	Good	Fair	Poor
275	225	150	75	60	50

Model 300

Similar to the Model 287 but chambered for the .25 ACP cartridge. It has a 2-1/4" barrel with a 6-round magazine. Length is 5" overall and the weight is about 14 oz.

NIB	Exc.	V.G.	Good	Fair	Poor
250	225	150	75	50	40

Model 300S

This is the stainless steel version of the Model 300.

NIB	Exc.	V.G.	Good	Fair	Poor
265	235	165	75	50	40

Model 302

Identical to the Model 300 except that it is chambered for the .22 LR cartridge.

NIB	Exc.	V.G.	Good	Fair	Poor
250	225	150	75	50	40

Model 302S

Same as above but in stainless steel.

NIB	Exc.	V.G.	Good	Fair	Poor
265	235	165	75	60	50

Model 400

This is a double-action semi-automatic pistol chambered for the .380 ACP cartridge with a 3-1/2" barrel. Magazine holds 7 rounds. Pistol is 6-1/2" overall and the weight is approximately 24 oz.

NIB	Exc.	V.G.	Good	Fair	Poor
300	275	200	125	100	75

Model 400S

This is the stainless steel version of the Model 400.

NIB	Exc.	V.G.	Good	Fair	Poor
325	300	2255	125	100	75

Model 402

Similar to the Model 400 except chambered for the .22 LR cartridge.

NIB	Exc.	V.G.	Good	Fair	Poor
250	225	150	75	60	40

Model X-Caliber

A single-shot .22 LR, .22 WMR, .357 Magnum, or .44 Magnum pistol with interchangeable barrels from 8" and 10". Adjustable rear sight. Finger groove grips. Deduct 50 percent for rimfire.

NIB	Exc.	V.G.	Good	Fair	Poor
450	400	300	225	150	100

STEVENS ARMS CO., J.
Chicopee Falls, Massachusetts

In 1864 this firm began doing business as J. Stevens & Company. In 1888 it was incorporated as the J. Stevens Arms & Tool Company. it operated as such until 1920, when it was taken over by Savage Arms Company. It has operated as an independent division in this organization since. This company produced a great many firearms—most that were of an affordable nature. They are widely collected, and one interested in the, should take advantage of the literature available on the subject.

Vest Pocket Pistol

This is a single-shot pocket pistol chambered for the .22 and the .30 rimfire cartridges. The .22 caliber version is rarely encountered and would be worth approximately 25 percent more than the values illustrated. It has a 2.75" part-octagonal barrel that pivots upward for loading. It has an external hammer and a spur-type trigger. The frame is nickel-plated or blued, with a blued barrel. The odd shaped flared grips are made of rosewood. The first models were marked "Vest Pocket Pistol" only. Later models have the barrels marked "J. Stevens & Co. Chicopee Falls, Mass." There were approximately 1,000 manufactured between 1864 and 1876.

Courtesy Milwaukee Public Museum, Milwaukee, Wisconsin

NIB	Exc.	V.G.	Good	Fair	Poor
—	5000	3450	2300	1300	1000

Pocket Pistol

This is a more conventional-appearing, single-shot pocket pistol chambered for either the .22 or the .30 rimfire cartridges. It has a 3.5" part-octagonal barrel that pivots upward for loading. It features a plated brass frame with either a blued or nickel-plated barrel and rosewood, two-piece grips. The barrel is marked "J. Stevens & Co. Chicopee Falls, Mass." There were approximately 15,000 manufactured between 1864 and 1886.

Courtesy Milwaukee Public Museum, Milwaukee, Wisconsin

NIB	Exc.	V.G.	Good	Fair	Poor
—	700	500	250	125	100

Gem Pocket Pistol

This is a single-shot, derringer-type pocket pistol chambered for either the .22 or .30 rimfire cartridges. It has a 3" part-octagonal barrel that pivots to the side for loading. It has a nickel-plated brass frame with either a blued or plated barrel. It has bird's-head grips made of walnut or rosewood. The barrel is marked "Gem." The Stevens name or address does not appear on this firearm. There were approximately 4,000 manufactured between 1872 and 1890.

NIB	Exc.	V.G.	Good	Fair	Poor
—	1100	900	600	425	300

.22 or .41 Caliber Derringer

This is a single-shot pocket pistol chambered for the .22 or .41 caliber rimfire cartridge. It has a 4" part-octagonal barrel that pivots upward for loading. It has a spur trigger and an external hammer. The frame is plated brass with a blued barrel. It has walnut bird's-head grips. This firearm is completely unmarked except for a serial number. There were approximately 100 manufactured in 1875.

.22 Caliber

NIB	Exc.	V.G.	Good	Fair	Poor
—	6500	6000	5000	3000	1500

.41 Caliber

NIB	Exc.	V.G.	Good	Fair	Poor
—	6200	5600	4000	2500	1400

No. 41 Pistol

This is a single-shot pocket pistol chambered for the .22 and .30 Short cartridges. It has a 3.5" part-octagonal barrel that pivots upward for loading. It features an external hammer and a spur-type trigger. It has an iron frame with the firing pin mounted in the recoil shield. It is either blued or nickel-plated, with square-butt walnut grips. There were approximately 90,000 manufactured between 1896 and 1916.

Courtesy Rock Island Auction Company

NIB	Exc.	V.G.	Good	Fair	Poor
—	500	425	300	250	135

Single-Shot Pistol

This is a single-shot pistol chambered for the .22 or .30 rimfire cartridges. It has a 3.5" part-octagonal barrel that pivots upward for loading. It is quite similar in appearance to the original pocket pistol. It has a plated brass frame and either a blued or nickel-plated barrel with walnut, square-butt grips. The barrel is marked "J. Stevens A&T Co." There were approximately 10,000 manufactured between 1886 and 1896.

NIB	Exc.	V.G.	Good	Fair	Poor
—	550	400	300	200	150

Stevens Tip Up Rifles

This series of rifles was produced by Stevens beginning in the 1870s through 1895. There are a number of variations, but they are all quite similar in appearance. They feature a distinctive sloped frame made of iron and nickel-plated. Most frames are similar in size, but there is a slightly lighter frame used on the "Ladies Model" rifles. These Tip Up rifles are chambered for various calibers from the .22 rimfire to the .44 centerfire cartridges. They are offered with barrel lengths of 24", 26", 28", or 30". The actions are nickel-plated, as well as the trigger guards and the buttplates. The barrels are blued, and the two-piece stocks are of walnut. They are offered with various buttplates and sights. A shotgun version is also offered. There are a number of variations that differ only slightly, and the model numbers are not marked on the rifles. We suggest securing a qualified appraisal if in doubt. The major variations and their values are as follows:

Courtesy Milwaukee Public Museum, Milwaukee, Wisconsin

Ladies Model—.22 or .25 Rimfire Only, 24" or 26" Barrel

NIB	Exc.	V.G.	Good	Fair	Poor
—	3750	3200	2400	1500	700

Tip Up Rifle—Without Fore-end

NIB	Exc.	V.G.	Good	Fair	Poor
—	750	650	500	250	200

Tip Up Rifle—With Fore-end, Swiss-Type Buttplate

NIB	Exc.	V.G.	Good	Fair	Poor
—	1250	1000	600	400	250

Tip Up Shotgun—All Gauges, 30" or 32" Barrel

NIB	Exc.	V.G.	Good	Fair	Poor
—	600	500	300	150	100

Ideal Single-Shot Rifle

This excellent rifle was manufactured by Stevens between 1896 and 1933. It is a single-shot, falling-block type action that is activated by a trigger guard-action lever. It was produced in many popular calibers from .22 rimfire up to .30-40. It was also manufactured in a number of special Stevens calibers. It was offered with various length barrels in many different grades, from plain Spartan starter rifles up to some extremely high-grade Schuetzen-type target rifles with all available options. In 1901 Harry Pope of Hartford, Connecticut, went to work for Stevens and brought his highly respected barrel to the Stevens Company. He remained an employee for only two years, and the firearms produced during this period have the name "Stevens-Pope" stamped on the top of the barrel in addition to the other factory markings. Rifles marked in this manner and authenticated would be worth an approximate 50 percent premium if they are in very good to excellent condition. Due to numerous variations and options offered, we strongly recommend securing a qualified appraisal, especially on the higher-grade Ideal series rifles, before a purchase.

No. 44

This version is chambered for various calibers and is offered with a 24" or 26" barrel. It has an open rear sight with a Rocky Mountain-type front sight. The finish is blued and case colored, with a walnut stock. There were approximately 100,000 manufactured between 1896 and 1933.

NIB	Exc.	V.G.	Good	Fair	Poor
—	1300	1080	700	400	225

No. 44-1/2

This rifle is similar in appearance to the No. 44 but features an improved action. It has barrel lengths up to 34" and will be found with the Stevens-Pope barrel. It was manufactured between 1903 and 1916.

Courtesy J.B. Barnes

NIB	Exc.	V.G.	Good	Fair	Poor
—	2175	1950	1500	1000	725

No. 044-1/2

This version is also known as the English Model rifle and is similar to the No. 44-1/2 except that it has a shotgun butt and a tapered barrel. There were a number of options offered that would affect the value. It was manufactured between 1903 and 1916.

Courtesy Mike Stuckslager

NIB	Exc.	V.G.	Good	Fair	Poor
—	2175	1950	1500	1000	725

No. 45

This version is also known as the Range Rifle, It is chambered for various calibers from the .22 rimfire to the .44-40. Its identifying features are the Beach sights with an additional vernier tang sight and a Swiss-type buttstock. It is offered with a 26" or 28" part-octagonal barrel. It was manufactured between 1896 and 1916. Values listed are for the standard version. **NOTE:** Deduct 25 percent for .44 action.

NIB	Exc.	V.G.	Good	Fair	Poor
—	2375	2150	1600	1100	825

No. 46

Same as the No. 45 but with a fancy wood stock. Manufactured from 1896 to 1902. Built in No. 44 action-only.

NIB	Exc.	V.G.	Good	Fair	Poor
—	2700	2375	1900	1500	1100

No. 47

This version is similar to the No. 45, with a pistol grip buttstock. **NOTE:** Deduct 25 percent for .44 action.

NIB	Exc.	V.G.	Good	Fair	Poor
—	5400	4750	3600	3000	1200

No. 48

Same as the No. 47 but with a fancy wood checkered stock. Manufactured from 1896 to 1902. Built in a No. 44 action-only. This is a very rare model.

NIB	Exc.	V.G.	Good	Fair	Poor
—	6000	5100	4200	3000	2000

No. 49

This model is also known as the "Walnut Hill Rifle." It is a high grade target rifle chambered for many calibers between the .22 rimfire and the .44-40. It is offered with a 28" or 30" part-octagonal barrel that is medium- or heavy-weight. It was furnished with a globe front sight and a vernier tang sight. It is blued with a case-colored frame and has a high-grade, checkered, varnished walnut stock that has a high comb and features a pistol grip, cheekpiece, Swiss-type buttplate, and a loop-type trigger guard lever that resembles that of a lever-action rifle. The receiver is engraved, and there were a number of options available that would increase the value when present. We recommend an appraisal when in doubt. This rifle was manufactured between 1896 and 1916.

Courtesy J.B. Barnes

NIB	Exc.	V.G.	Good	Fair	Poor
—	8000	7500	4500	3000	2000

Model 50

This version is identical to the Model 49 but was offered with a higher-grade walnut stock. This is a very rare model.

Courtesy J.B. Barnes

NIB	Exc.	V.G.	Good	Fair	Poor
—	9200	8600	5200	3500	2400

Model 51

This version is known as the "Schuetzen Rifle" and is quite similar to the No. 49 except that it features double-set triggers, a higher-grade walnut stock, a wooden insert in the trigger guard action lever, and a heavy, Schuetzen-type buttplate. There were many options available on this model, and we recommend securing an appraisal when in doubt. It was manufactured between 1896 and 1916.

Courtesy J.B. Barnes

NIB	Exc.	V.G.	Good	Fair	Poor
—	15000	13000	8250	5000	2500

No. 52

This version is also known as the "Schuetzen Junior". It is similar to the No. 51 except that it features more engraving and a higher-grade walnut stock. It was manufactured between 1897 and 1916.

Courtesy J.B. Barnes

NIB	Exc.	V.G.	Good	Fair	Poor
—	15000	13000	8250	5000	2500

No. 53

This model is the same as the No. 51 except for the addition of a fancy wood stock and palm rest. Produced from 1896 to 1902 and offered only with a No. 44 action. This is a rare rifle.

NIB	Exc.	V.G.	Good	Fair	Poor
—	13000	10000	8000	5000	2500

No. 54

This is similar to the No. 52 except that it has double-set triggers and a palm rest, as well as a heavy, Swiss-style buttplate. It is offered with a 30" or 32" part-octagonal heavy barrel. This was Stevens' top-of-the-line rifle. It was offered with many options, and an appraisal should be secured if in doubt. It was manufactured between 1897 and 1916. **NOTE:** The prices are based on a No. 44-1/2 action. A No. 44 action will bring 20 percent less than the prices listed above.

NIB	Exc.	V.G.	Good	Fair	Poor
—	19500	17500	12500	9000	5500

No. 55

This version is one of the Stevens' Ideal Ladies Models. It is chambered for the smaller rimfire calibers between .22 Short and .32 Long rimfire. It features a 24" or 26" part-octagonal barrel with a vernier tang sight. The finish is blued and case-colored, with a checkered pistol grip walnut stock that features a Swiss-type buttplate. This is a lighter weight rifle that was manufactured between 1897 and 1916.

NIB	Exc.	V.G.	Good	Fair	Poor
—	7000	5500	3750	2200	1100

No. 56

This Ladies' Model rifle is similar to the No. 55 except that it is chambered for centerfire cartridges and has a higher-grade walnut stock. It was made on the improved No. 44-1/2 action. It was manufactured between 1906 and 1916.

Courtesy J.B. Barnes

NIB	Exc.	V.G.	Good	Fair	Poor
—	7500	6000	4250	2400	1200

No. 404

This version is chambered for the .22 rimfire cartridge only. It features a 28" round barrel with a globe front sight and a Lyman No. 42 receiver sight. The finish is blued and case-colored. It has a walnut straight-grip stock with a semi-beavertail fore-end. It features a shotgun-type buttplate. It was manufactured between 1910 and 1916.

NIB	Exc.	V.G.	Good	Fair	Poor
—	1300	1075	875	750	600

No. 414

This version is also known as the Armory Model and is chambered for the .22 LR cartridge only. It was built on a No. 44 action and features a 26" round barrel. It has a Rocky Mountain front sight with a Lyman receiver sight at the rear. The finish is blued and case-colored, with a straight-grip walnut stock and fore-end held on by a single barrel band. It was manufactured between 1912 and 1932.

Courtesy Mike Stuckslager

NIB	Exc.	V.G.	Good	Fair	Poor
—	1000	750	550	300	275

No. 417 Walnut Hill Model

This is a heavy single-shot, lever action target rifle chambered for the .22 LR, .22 Short, or .22 Hornet cartridges. Weight is approximately 10.5 lbs. Produced from 1932 to 1940.

NIB	Exc.	V.G.	Good	Fair	Poor
—	1625	1300	850	600	400

No. 417 1/2 Walnut Hill Model

This model is a sporting version of the Model 417. Weight is about 8.5 lbs. Manufactured from 1932 to 1940.

NIB	Exc.	V.G.	Good	Fair	Poor
—	1725	1400	950	700	450

No. 418 Walnut Hill Jr.

This is a light single-shot lever action target rifle chambered for .22 LR or .22 Short. Weight is about 6.5 lbs. Manufactured from 1932 to 1940.

NIB	Exc.	V.G.	Good	Fair	Poor
—	975	800	550	300	200

No. 418 1/2 Walnut Hill Jr.

Similar to the Model 418 but chambered for .25 rimfire or .22 WRF cartridges. It is also fitted with sporting sights. Manufactured from 1932 to 1940.

NIB	Exc.	V.G.	Good	Fair	Poor
—	975	800	550	300	200

BOY'S RIFLES

The Stevens Company produced an extensive line of smaller, single-shot rifles chambered for small calibers and intended primarily for use by young shooters. These firearms have become quite collectible and are considered a field of specialty by many modern collectors. **NOTE:** There are many variations that were available with a number of options that would affect their value. We supply information and values for the major variations but would recommend securing a qualified appraisal if in doubt.

"FAVORITE" RIFLES

This series of rifles is chambered for the .22, .25, and .32 rimfire. It has a 22" part-octagonal barrel and is blued, with a case-colored frame. It has a takedown-type action with an interchangeable barrel feature. It was available with optional sights, as well as buttplates. There were approximately 1,000,000 manufactured between 1893 and 1939. The variations are listed.

Courtesy Mike Stuckslager

1st Model Favorite

This version is chambered for the .22 or .25 rimfire cartridge. It has a removable sideplate on the right side of the receiver not found on any other variation. There were approximately 1,000 manufactured between 1893 and 1894.

NIB	Exc.	V.G.	Good	Fair	Poor
—	1300	875	700	500	350

No. 17

This is the standard, plain version with open sights.

NIB	Exc.	V.G.	Good	Fair	Poor
—	600	435	325	175	125

No. 20

This version is chambered for the .22 or .32 rimfire shot cartridges and has a smoothbore barrel and no rear sight.

NIB	Exc.	V.G.	Good	Fair	Poor
—	650	475	350	175	125

No. 21

This version is known as the Bicycle rifle and features a 20" barrel with open sights standard. It was furnished with a canvas carrying case that would be worth approximately a 30 percent premium. It was manufactured between 1898 and 1903.

NIB	Exc.	V.G.	Good	Fair	Poor
—	800	625	375	170	110

No. 21 Ladies Model

This version bears the same model number as the Bicycle rifle but has a 24" barrel and a high grade, checkered walnut stock with a Swiss buttplate. It features a vernier tang sight. It was manufactured between 1910 and 1916.

NIB	Exc.	V.G.	Good	Fair	Poor
—	7000	5500	3750	2200	1100

No. 16

This version is known as the "Crack Shot." It is chambered for .22 or .32 rimfire cartridges with a 20" round barrel. It has a rolling-block-type action with a thumb lever on the side. It is a utility-type rifle with open sights, a blued and case-colored finish, and a plain two-piece walnut stock with a rubber buttplate. The barrel is marked "Crack Shot" along with the standard Stevens' barrel address markings. It was manufactured between 1900 and 1913.

NIB	Exc.	V.G.	Good	Fair	Poor
—	600	500	350	225	100

No. 16-1/2

This version is similar to the No. 16 except that it is chambered for the .32 rimfire shot cartridge with a smoothbore barrel. It was manufactured between 1900 and 1913.

NIB	Exc.	V.G.	Good	Fair	Poor
—	625	525	375	250	125

No. 23—Sure Shot

This version is chambered for the .22 rimfire cartridge. It has a 20" round barrel that pivots to the right for loading. There is a barrel release on the frame. This version is blued and case-colored, with a plain walnut buttstock and no fore-end. It was manufactured between 1894 and 1897.

NIB	Exc.	V.G.	Good	Fair	Poor
—	2700	2375	1500	1000	600

No. 15

This version is also known as the "Maynard Junior." It is chambered for the .22 rimfire cartridge and has an 18" part-octagonal barrel. The action is similar to the Civil War Maynard rifle with a trigger guard-activating lever. The finish is all blued, with a bored-type buttstock and no forearm. The barrel is marked "Stevens Maynard, J. R." in addition to the standard Stevens' barrel address. It was manufactured between 1902 and 1912.

Courtesy Mike Stuckslager

NIB	Exc.	V.G.	Good	Fair	Poor
—	600	500	350	225	100

No. 15-1/2

This is a smoothbore version of the No. 15.

NIB	Exc.	V.G.	Good	Fair	Poor
—	625	525	375	250	125

No. 14

This version is also known as the "Little Scout." It is a utility, takedown rifle that is blued, with a one-piece bored-type stock. It features a rolling-block-type action and was manufactured between 1906 and 1910.

NIB	Exc.	V.G.	Good	Fair	Poor
—	550	425	300	225	100

No. 14-1/2

This version is similar to the No. 14 except that it has a two-piece stock. It is also marked "Little Scout." It was manufactured between 1911 and 1941.

NIB	Exc.	V.G.	Good	Fair	Poor
—	500	375	200	150	100

No. 65

This version is known as the "Little Krag". It is a single-shot bolt-action rifle chambered for the .22 rimfire cartridge. It has a one-piece stock and a 20" round barrel that was marked "Little Krag". This version is quite scarce. It was manufactured between 1903 and 1910.

NIB	Exc.	V.G.	Good	Fair	Poor
—	600	500	350	200	100

No. 12

This version is also known as the "Marksman". It is chambered for the .22, .25, and the .32 rimfire cartridges. It has a 22" barrel that pivots upward for loading. It is activated by an S-shaped trigger guard lever. It was manufactured between 1911 and 1930.

Courtesy Mike Stuckslager

NIB	Exc.	V.G.	Good	Fair	Poor
—	550	425	300	225	100

No. 26

This version is also known as the "Crack Shot". It has a rolling block-type action and is chambered for .22 or the .32 rimfire cartridges. It is offered with an 18" or 20" round barrel. It is blued and has a two-piece stock. It was manufactured between 1912 and 1939.

Courtesy Mike Stuckslager

NIB	Exc.	V.G.	Good	Fair	Poor
—	550	425	300	225	100

No. 26-1/2

This is the smoothbore version of the No. 26.

NIB	Exc.	V.G.	Good	Fair	Poor
—	550	500	350	250	100

No. 11—Junior

This is a single-shot, rolling block rifle chambered for the .22 rimfire cartridge. It has a 20" barrel, is blued, and has a bore-type stock without a buttplate. This was the last model offered in the Boy's Rifle series. It was manufactured between 1924 and 1931.

NIB	Exc.	V.G.	Good	Fair	Poor
—	550	425	300	225	100

Model 71

This was a reintroduced version of the "Stevens Favorite." It is chambered for the .22 LR cartridge and has a 22" octagonal barrel. The finish is blued and case-colored, with a plain walnut stock that has an inlaid medallion and a crescent buttplate. There were 10,000 manufactured in 1971.

NIB	Exc.	V.G.	Good	Fair	Poor
400	300	175	125	100	75

Model 72

This is a reintroduced version of the "Crack Shot" that features a single-shot, falling block action. It is chambered for the .22 rimfire cartridge and has a 22" octagon barrel with open sights. It is blued and case-colored, with a straight walnut stock. It was introduced in 1972.

NIB	Exc.	V.G.	Good	Fair	Poor
400	300	175	125	100	75

Model 70

This is a slide-action rifle chambered for the .22 rimfire cartridge. It is also known as the "Visible Loading Rifle." It features a 20" round barrel with a 3/4-length, tubular magazine. The finish is blued and case-colored, and it has a walnut stock. It features open sights but was available with other options. It was offered as the No. 70-1/2, 71, 71-1/2, 72, and 72-1/2. These different model numbers denote various sight combinations. Otherwise, they are identical. They were manufactured between 1907 and 1932.

NIB	Exc.	V.G.	Good	Fair	Poor
—	450	350	225	100	75

No. 80

This is a slide-action repeating rifle chambered for the .22 rimfire cartridge. It has a 24" round barrel with a tubular magazine. It features open sights and is blued, with a walnut stock. It was manufactured between 1906 and 1910.

NIB	Exc.	V.G.	Good	Fair	Poor
—	500	350	225	175	100

High Power Rifle

This is a series of lever-action hunting rifles chambered for the .25, .300, .32, and the .35 Remington centerfire cartridges. It features a 22" round barrel with a tubular magazine. The finish is blued, with a walnut stock. It is available in four variations: the No. 425, No. 430, No. 435, and No. 440. These designations denote increased ornamentation and high quality materials and workmanship used in construction. There were approximately 26,000 manufactured between 1910 and 1917.

No. 425

NIB	Exc.	V.G.	Good	Fair	Poor
—	1150	900	600	300	200

No. 430

NIB	Exc.	V.G.	Good	Fair	Poor
—	1300	1000	650	400	300

No. 435

NIB	Exc.	V.G.	Good	Fair	Poor
—	1750	1400	1000	600	400

No. 440

NIB	Exc.	V.G.	Good	Fair	Poor
—	3350	3000	2400	1600	850

SPORTING PISTOLS

Beginning in 1869 the Stevens Company produced a series of single-shot, break-open target and sporting pistols that pivot upward for loading. They are chambered for the .22 and the .25 rimfire cartridges, as well as various centerfire cartridges from the .32 Short Colt to the .44 Russian. These pistols were made with various barrel lengths and have either a spur trigger or conventional trigger with a guard. They are all single-actions with exposed hammers. The finishes are nickel-plated frames with blued barrels and walnut grips. These variations and their values are listed.

Six-inch Pocket Rifle

This version is chambered for the .22 rimfire cartridge and has a 6" part-octagonal barrel with open sights. The barrel is marked "J. Stevens & Co. Chicopee Falls, Mass." There were approximately 1,000 manufactured between 1869 and 1886.

NIB	Exc.	V.G.	Good	Fair	Poor
—	750	500	400	350	200

No. 36

This version is known as the Stevens-Lord pistol. It is chambered for various rimfire and centerfire calibers up to .44 Russian. It is offered with a 10" or 12" part-octagonal barrel and features a firing pin in the frame with a bushing. It has a conventional trigger with a spurred trigger guard. It features the standard Stevens barrel address. It was named after Frank Lord, a target shooter well-known at this time. There were approximately 3,500 manufactured from 1880 to 1911.

Courtesy J.B. Barnes

NIB	Exc.	V.G.	Good	Fair	Poor
—	1750	1400	1000	650	400

First Issue Stevens-Conlin

This version is chambered for the .22 or .32 rimfire cartridges. It has a 10" or 12" part-octagonal barrel. It features a plated brass frame with a blued barrel and checkered walnut grips with a weighted buttcap. This version has a spur trigger either with or without a trigger guard. It was named after James Conlin, the owner of a shooting gallery located in New York City. There were approximately 500 manufactured between 1880 and 1884.

Courtesy J.B. Barnes

NIB	Exc.	V.G.	Good	Fair	Poor
—	2700	2300	1700	900	500

Second Issue Stevens-Conlin No. 38

This version is similar to the First Issue, with a conventional trigger and spurred trigger guard, as well as a fully adjustable rear sight. There were approximately 6,000 manufactured between 1884 and 1903.

NIB	Exc.	V.G.	Good	Fair	Poor
—	1850	1625	1200	800	450

No. 37

This version is also known as the Stevens-Gould and was named after a 19th century firearms writer. It resembles the No. 38 without the spur on the trigger guard. There were approximately 1,000 manufactured between 1889 and 1903.

Courtesy J.B. Barnes

NIB	Exc.	V.G.	Good	Fair	Poor
—	2600	2200	1300	850	450

No. 35

This version is chambered for the .22 rimfire, the .22 Stevens-Pope, and the .25 Stevens cartridges. It is offered with a 6", 8", 10", or 12.25" part-octagonal barrel. The firing pin has no bushing. It features an iron frame that is either blued or plated with a blued barrel. It has plain walnut grips with a weighted buttcap. It featured open sights. There were approximately 43,000 manufactured between 1923 and 1942. **NOTE:** Longer barrels worth a premium.

NIB	Exc.	V.G.	Good	Fair	Poor
—	450	325	275	175	100

No. 35 Target

This version is similar to the No. 35 but has a better quality trigger guard and sights. There were approximately 35,000 manufactured between 1907 and 1916.

NIB	Exc.	V.G.	Good	Fair	Poor
—	500	400	325	200	100

STEVENS NO. 35 OFF-HAND SHOT GUN NFA, CURIO OR RELIC

Stevens No. 35 Auto-Shot

The Stevens No. 35 is a .410 bore pistol manufactured by the J. Stevens Arms Co., Chicopee Falls, Massachusetts. It was available with an 8" or 12.25" smoothbore barrel, for 2.5" shells only, in two variations: the Off-Hand Shot Gun (1923 to 1929) and the Auto-Shot (1929 to 1934). Total production is unknown because the .410 and .22 rimfire variations of the No. 35 share the same serial number range. Researcher Ken Cope estimates total Auto-Shot production

was approximately 2,000, and Off-Hand production at 20,000 to 25,000. Production was halted after the government ruled the .410 Stevens to be a "firearm" in the "any other weapon" category under the NFA in 1934, when its retail price was about $12. The Stevens does not possess the same collector appeal as other .410 smoothbore pistols, because (1) its relatively light weight makes it an uncomfortable shooter, and (2) the gun is not well made. **NOTE:** 8" barrel commands a 25 to 50 percent premium.

Off-Hand Shot Gun

Serial range from 1 to 43357.

Courtesy John J. Stimson, Jr.

NIB	Exc.	V.G.	Good	Fair	Poor
—	400	250	200	100	75

Auto-Shot

NIB	Exc.	V.G.	Good	Fair	Poor
—	450	300	200	125	100

No. 43

This version is also called the Diamond and was produced in two distinct variations called the First Issue and the Second Issue. The First Issue has a brass frame; and the Second Issue, an iron frame and no firing pin bushing. Otherwise they are quite similar and would be valued the same. They are chambered for the .22 rimfire cartridge and are offered with either a 6" or 10" part-octagonal barrel. The frames are either nickel-plated or blued with blued barrels and square-butt walnut grips. There were approximately 95,000 manufactured between 1886 and 1916. **NOTE:** Add a 25 percent premium for 10" barrels.

Paul Goodwin photo

NIB	Exc.	V.G.	Good	Fair	Poor
—	600	400	250	150	75

No. 10 Target Pistol

This version was a departure from its predecessors. It very much resembles a semi-automatic pistol but is, in reality, a single-shot. It is chambered for the .22 rimfire cartridge and has an 8" round barrel that pivots upward for loading. It has a steel frame and is blued, with checkered rubber grips. Instead of the usual exposed hammer, this version has a knurled cocking piece that extends through the rear of the frame. There were approximately 7,000 manufactured between 1919 and 1933.

Courtesy John J. Stimson, Jr.

NIB	Exc.	V.G.	Good	Fair	Poor
—	400	300	200	150	100

POCKET RIFLES

This series of pistols is similar to the target and sporting pistols except that these were produced with detachable shoulder stocks that bear the same serial number as the pistol with which they were sold. They are sometimes referred to as Bicycle rifles. The collector interest in these weapons is quite high; but it would behoove one to be familiar with the provisions of the Gun Control Act of 1968 when dealing in or collecting this variation—as when the stock is attached, they can fall into the category of a short-barreled rifle. Some are considered to be curios and relics, and others have been totally declassified; but some models may still be restricted. We strongly recommend securing a qualified, individual appraisal on these highly collectible firearms if a transaction is contemplated. **NOTE:** The values supplied include the matching shoulder stock. If the stock number does not match the pistol, the values would be approximately 25 percent less; and with no stock at all, 50 percent should be deducted.

Old Model Pocket Rifle

This version is chambered for the .22 rimfire cartridge and has an 8" or 10" part-octagonal barrel. It has a spur trigger and an external hammer on which the firing pin is mounted. The extractor is spring-loaded. It has a plated brass frame, blued barrel, and either walnut or rosewood grips. The shoulder stock is either nickel-plated or black. The barrel is marked "J. Stevens & Co. Chicopee Falls, Mass." There were approximately 4,000 manufactured between 1869 and 1886.

NIB	Exc.	V.G.	Good	Fair	Poor
—	900	700	550	325	200

Reliable Pocket Rifle

This version is chambered for the .22 rimfire cartridge and in appearance is quite similar to the Old Model. The basic difference is that the extractor operates as a part of the pivoting barrel mechanism instead of being spring-loaded. The barrel is marked "J. Stevens A&T Co." There were approximately 4,000 manufactured between 1886 and 1896.

NIB	Exc.	V.G.	Good	Fair	Poor
—	800	625	500	400	300

No. 42 Reliable Pocket Rifle

This version is similar to the first issue Reliable except that it has an iron frame with the firing pin mounted in it without a bushing. The shoulder stock is shaped differently. There were approximately 8,000 manufactured between 1896 and 1916.

NIB	Exc.	V.G.	Good	Fair	Poor
—	700	575	475	350	250

First Issue New Model Pocket Rifle

This version is the first of the medium-frame models with a frame width of 1". All of its predecessors have a 5/8" wide frame. This model is chambered for the .22 and .32 rimfire cartridges and is offered with barrel lengths of 10", 12", 15", or 18" that are part-octagonal in configuration. The external hammer has the firing pin mounted on it. It has a plated brass frame, blued barrel, and either walnut or rosewood grips. The shoulder stock is nickel-plated and fitted differently than the small-frame models in that there is a dovetail in the butt and the top leg is secured by a knurled screw. The barrel is marked "J. Stevens & Co. Chicopee Falls, Mass." There were approximately 8,000 manufactured between 1872 and 1875.

Courtesy Mike Stuckslager

NIB	Exc.	V.G.	Good	Fair	Poor
—	1100	1000	650	500	400

Second Issue New Model Pocket Rifle

This version is similar to the First Issue except that the firing pin is mounted in the frame with a bushing. There were approximately 15,000 manufactured between 1875 and 1896.

Paul Goodwin photo

NIB	Exc.	V.G.	Good	Fair	Poor
—	975	850	600	500	350

Vernier Model

This version is similar to the Second Issue except that it features a vernier tang sight located on the back strap. There were approximately 1,500 manufactured between 1884 and 1896.

Courtesy Rock Island Auction Company

NIB	Exc.	V.G.	Good	Fair	Poor
—	1200	900	650	525	300

No. 40

This version is similar to its medium-frame predecessors except that it has a longer grip frame and a conventional trigger with trigger guard. There were approximately 15,000 manufactured between 1896 and 1916.

Courtesy Rock Island Auction Company

NIB	Exc.	V.G.	Good	Fair	Poor
—	975	850	650	400	300

No. 40-1/2

This version is similar to the No. 40, with a vernier tang sight mounted on the back strap. There were approximately 2,500 manufactured between 1896 and 1915.

NIB	Exc.	V.G.	Good	Fair	Poor
—	1100	975	700	550	400

No. 34 (Hunter's Pet)

This is the first of the heavy-frame pocket rifles that featured a 1.25" wide frame. This version is also known as the "Hunter's Pet." It is chambered for many popular cartridges from the .22 rimfire to the .44-40 centerfire. It is offered with a part-octagonal 18", 20", 22", or 24" barrel. It has a nickel-plated iron frame and blued barrel. The detachable stock is nickel-plated, and the grips are walnut. There were few produced with a brass frame; and if located, these would be worth twice the value indicated. The firing pin is mounted in the frame with the bushing, and it features a spur trigger. There were approximately 4,000 manufactured between 1872 and 1900.

NIB	Exc.	V.G.	Good	Fair	Poor
—	1250	1050	700	450	350

No. 34-1/2

This version is similar to the No. 34 except that it features a vernier tang sight mounted on the back strap. There were approximately 1,200 manufactured between 1884 and 1900.

NIB	Exc.	V.G.	Good	Fair	Poor
—	1425	1250	900	650	450

STEVENS BOLT-ACTION UTILITY RIFLES

The Stevens Company produced a number of inexpensive, utilitarian, bolt-action rifles. These were both single-shot and repeaters. They have been popular over the years as starter rifles for young shooters. Their values are quite similar, and they are listed for reference purposes only.

Model 053—Single-Shot   Model 056—5-Shot Magazine
Model 066—Tube Magazine   Model 083—Single-Shot
Model 084—5-Shot Magazine   Model 086—Tube Magazine
Model 15—Single-Shot   Model 15Y—Single-Shot
Model 419—Single-Shot   Model 48—Single-Shot
Model 49—Single-Shot   Model 50—Single-Shot
Model 51—Single-Shot   Model 52—Single-Shot
Model 53—Single-Shot   Model 56—5-Shot Magazine
Model 66—Tube Magazine

NIB	Exc.	V.G.	Good	Fair	Poor
—	—	200	100	70	50

Model 416

This is a target rifle chambered for the .22 LR cartridge. It has a 24" heavy barrel with aperture sights. It features a 5-round detachable magazine and is blued, with a target-type walnut stock.

NIB	Exc.	V.G.	Good	Fair	Poor
—	450	350	200	150	100

Model 322

This is a bolt-action sporting rifle chambered for the .22 Hornet cartridge. It has a 20" barrel with open sights and a detachable box magazine. The finish is blued, with a plain walnut stock.

NIB	Exc.	V.G.	Good	Fair	Poor
—	175	125	100	75	50

Model 322-S

This version features an aperture rear sight.

NIB	Exc.	V.G.	Good	Fair	Poor
—	225	125	100	75	50

Model 89

This is a single-shot, Martini-type, falling-block rifle chambered for the .22 LR cartridge. It has an 18.5" barrel and a trigger guard loop-lever activator. The finish is blued, with a straight walnut stock. It was introduced in 1976 and is no longer manufactured.

NIB	Exc.	V.G.	Good	Fair	Poor
—	125	80	70	60	40

Model 87M

Designed to look like the M1 Garand this rifle was chambered for the .22 rimfire cartridge.

Courtesy Richard M. Kumor, Sr.

NIB	Exc.	V.G.	Good	Fair	Poor
—	600	500	375	225	150

Model 987

This is a blowback-operated semi-automatic rifle chambered for the .22 LR cartridge. It has a 20" barrel with a 15-round tubular magazine. The finish is blued, with a hardwood stock.

NIB	Exc.	V.G.	Good	Fair	Poor
—	150	100	75	50	25

STEVENS ECONOMY LINE (SAVAGE, 2006)

Stevens Model 200

Long- or short-action bolt rifle chambered in .223, .22-250, .243, 7MM-08, .308, .25-06, .270, .30-06, 7mm RM, or .300 WM. Gray checkered synthetic stock and 22-inch (short-action) or 24-inch (long-action) blued sightless barrel. Introduced 2006.

NIB	Exc.	V.G.	Good	Fair	Poor
325	275	225	175	125	100

Model 200XP Long or Short Action Package Rifle

Similar to above but with 4x12 scope.

NIB	Exc.	V.G.	Good	Fair	Poor
375	300	250	200	150	125

Model 200XP Camo

Similar to above but with camo stock.

NIB	Exc.	V.G.	Good	Fair	Poor
400	325	275	225	175	150

Stevens Cadet Mini-Youth

Similar to Savage Cub .22 rimfire. Introduced 2006.

NIB	Exc.	V.G.	Good	Fair	Poor
200	150	125	100	75	50

Stevens Model 315 Youth

Similar to Cadet Mini-Youth but with sightless barrel. Introduced 2006.

NIB	Exc.	V.G.	Good	Fair	Poor
200	150	125	100	75	50

Stevens Model 310

Five-shot bolt-action repeater chambered for .17 HMR. Detachable box magazine, synthetic stock, blued 20.75-inch sightless barrel. Introduced 2006.

NIB	Exc.	V.G.	Good	Fair	Poor
200	150	125	100	75	50

Stevens Model 310 Heavy Barrel

Similar to Stevens Model 310 but with 21-inch bull barrel. Introduced 2006.

NIB	Exc.	V.G.	Good	Fair	Poor
225	175	150	115	75	50

Stevens Model 300

Clip-fed bolt-action repeater chambered for .22 rimfire. Gray synthetic stock and 20.75-inch blued barrel. Also available with scope package (add 10 percent). Introduced 2006.

NIB	Exc.	V.G.	Good	Fair	Poor
200	150	125	100	75	50

Stevens Model 305

Similar to Model 310 but chambered in .22 WMR. Introduced 2006.

NIB	Exc.	V.G.	Good	Fair	Poor
225	175	150	115	75	50

MISCELLANEOUS STEVENS SINGLE-SHOT SHOTGUNS

This company manufactured a number of single barrel break-open, single-shot shotguns. They were produced chambered for various gauges with various-length barrels and chokes. They are quite similar in appearance and were designed as inexpensive utility-grade weapons. There is little or no collector interest in them at this time and their values are similar. They are listed for reference purposes only.

Model 89	Model 97	Model 108	Model 170
Model 90	Model 100	Model 110	Model 180
Model 93	Model 102	Model 120	Model 944
Model 94	Model 104	Model 125	Model 958
Model 94A	Model 105	Model 140	Model 970
Model 94C	Model 106	Model 160	
Model 95	Model 107	Model 165	

Model 107

Model 94C

NIB	Exc.	V.G.	Good	Fair	Poor
—	150	100	75	50	25

Model 182

This is a single-shot, break-open shotgun chambered for 12 gauge. It is offered with a 30" or 32" trap choked barrels and features a hammerless action with an automatic ejector and a lightly engraved receiver. The finish is blued, with a checkered trap-grade stock.

NIB	Exc.	V.G.	Good	Fair	Poor
—	175	125	100	75	50

Model 185

This version features a half-octagonal barrel with an automatic ejector and a checkered walnut stock. **NOTE:** Damascus barrel deduct 25 percent.

NIB	Exc.	V.G.	Good	Fair	Poor
—	175	125	100	75	50

Model 190

This is a 12-gauge hammerless gun with an automatic ejector. It is lightly engraved with a half-octagonal barrel. **NOTE:** Damascus barrel deduct 25 percent.

NIB	Exc.	V.G.	Good	Fair	Poor
—	175	125	100	75	50

Model 195

This is another deluxe version that features engraving, a half-octagonal barrel, and a high-grade, checkered walnut stock. **NOTE:** Damascus barrel deduct 25 percent.

NIB	Exc.	V.G.	Good	Fair	Poor
—	350	250	200	150	100

Model 240

This over/under model features a boxlock frame with exposed hammers.

NIB	Exc.	V.G.	Good	Fair	Poor
—	400	300	250	200	150

Model .22/.410

Over/under .22/.410 combo gun with Tenite stock. Manufactured 1939-1950.

NIB	Exc.	V.G.	Good	Fair	Poor
—	350	300	250	175	100

STEVENS DOUBLE-BARREL SHOTGUNS

STEVENS BRAND

The firm of J. Stevens and its successors produced a number of utility-grade, side-by-side double-barrel shotguns between 1877 and 1988. They are chambered for 10, 12, 16, or 20 gauge as well as the .410 bore. Stevens shotguns in 10 gauge and .410 bore will normally bring a premium as do guns with single triggers and ejectors. They have various length barrels and choke combinations. They feature double triggers and extractors except where noted. A complete list of Stevens brand models including the three in-house brands: Riverside, Springfield, and Super Value, are listed.

Model 1877—Hammer Boxlock

NIB	Exc.	V.G.	Good	Fair	Poor
—	575	450	350	250	200

Model 250—Hammer Sidelock

NIB	Exc.	V.G.	Good	Fair	Poor
—	575	450	350	250	200

Model 225—Hammer Boxlock

Courtesy Nick Niles, Paul Goodwin photo

NIB	Exc.	V.G.	Good	Fair	Poor
—	575	450	350	250	200

Model 260—Hammer Sidelock

NIB	Exc.	V.G.	Good	Fair	Poor
—	575	450	350	250	200

Model 270—Hammer Sidelock

NIB	Exc.	V.G.	Good	Fair	Poor
—	575	450	350	250	200

Model 280—Hammer Sidelock

NIB	Exc.	V.G.	Good	Fair	Poor
—	575	450	350	250	200

Model 325—Hammerless Boxlock

NIB	Exc.	V.G.	Good	Fair	Poor
—	450	400	350	250	200

Model 350—Hammerless Boxlock

NIB	Exc.	V.G.	Good	Fair	Poor
—	450	400	350	250	200

Model 360—Hammerless Boxlock

NIB	Exc.	V.G.	Good	Fair	Poor
—	450	400	350	250	200

Model 370—Hammerless Boxlock

NIB	Exc.	V.G.	Good	Fair	Poor
—	450	400	350	250	200

Model 380—Hammerless Boxlock

NIB	Exc.	V.G.	Good	Fair	Poor
—	575	450	350	250	200

Model 235—Hammer Boxlock

NIB	Exc.	V.G.	Good	Fair	Poor
—	450	400	350	250	200

Model 335 (Early)—Hammerless Boxlock

Courtesy Nick Niles, Paul Goodwin photo

NIB	Exc.	V.G.	Good	Fair	Poor
—	450	400	350	250	200

Model 335 (Late)—Hammerless Boxlock

NIB	Exc.	V.G.	Good	Fair	Poor
—	450	400	350	250	200

Model 255—Hammer Sidelock

NIB	Exc.	V.G.	Good	Fair	Poor
—	450	400	350	250	200

Model 265—Hammer Sidelock

Courtesy Nick Niles, Paul Goodwin photo

NIB	Exc.	V.G.	Good	Fair	Poor
—	450	400	350	250	200

Model 355—Hammerless Boxlock

NIB	Exc.	V.G.	Good	Fair	Poor
—	800	575	450	350	250

Model 365—Hammerless Boxlock

Courtesy Nick Niles, Paul Goodwin photo

NIB	Exc.	V.G.	Good	Fair	Poor
—	925	625	500	400	300

Model 375 (London Proofs)—Hammerless Boxlock

NIB	Exc.	V.G.	Good	Fair	Poor
—	1500	950	700	450	350

Model 375 (U.S.)—Hammerless Boxlock

NIB	Exc.	V.G.	Good	Fair	Poor
—	1100	700	575	400	300

Model 385 (London Proofs)—Hammerless Boxlock

NIB	Exc.	V.G.	Good	Fair	Poor
—	1650	1050	700	450	350

Model 385 (U.S.)—Hammerless Boxlock

NIB	Exc.	V.G.	Good	Fair	Poor
—	1200	850	575	450	300

Model 345—Hammerless Boxlock

Courtesy Nick Niles, Paul Goodwin photo

NIB	Exc.	V.G.	Good	Fair	Poor
—	575	450	350	250	200

Model 330—Hammerless Boxlock

Stevens Model 330 early fork-type cocking lever

Stevens Model 330 late spade-type cocking lever

NIB	Exc.	V.G.	Good	Fair	Poor
—	450	400	350	250	200

Model 515—Hammerless Boxlock

NIB	Exc.	V.G.	Good	Fair	Poor
—	625	525	450	350	300

Model 515—Single Trigger Hammerless Boxlock

NIB	Exc.	V.G.	Good	Fair	Poor
—	750	575	450	350	300

Model 500—Skeet Hammerless Boxlock

Courtesy Nick Niles, Paul Goodwin photo

NIB	Exc.	V.G.	Good	Fair	Poor
—	1250	925	800	700	400

Model 530—Hammerless Boxlock

NIB	Exc.	V.G.	Good	Fair	Poor
—	450	400	350	250	200

Model 530M—Tenite Hammerless Boxlock

NIB	Exc.	V.G.	Good	Fair	Poor
—	450	400	350	250	200

Model 530M—Tenite Single Trigger Hammerless Boxlock

NIB	Exc.	V.G.	Good	Fair	Poor
—	750	575	450	350	300

Model 530A—Hammerless Boxlock

Courtesy Nick Niles, Paul Goodwin photo

NIB	Exc.	V.G.	Good	Fair	Poor
—	450	400	350	250	200

Model 530A—Single Trigger Hammerless Boxlock

NIB	Exc.	V.G.	Good	Fair	Poor
—	525	450	350	300	250

Model 311—Tenite Hammerless Boxlock

NIB	Exc.	V.G.	Good	Fair	Poor
—	450	400	350	250	200

Model 331—Single Trigger Hammerless Boxlock

NIB	Exc.	V.G.	Good	Fair	Poor
—	525	400	300	250	200

Model 311—Tenite Single Trigger Hammerless Boxlock

NIB	Exc.	V.G.	Good	Fair	Poor
—	575	500	450	350	300

Model 311A—Hammerless Boxlock

NIB	Exc.	V.G.	Good	Fair	Poor
—	525	450	350	250	200

Model 311C—Hammerless Boxlock

Courtesy Nick Niles, Paul Goodwin photo

NIB	Exc.	V.G.	Good	Fair	Poor
—	400	350	250	200	150

Model 311D—Hammerless Boxlock

Courtesy Nick Niles, Paul Goodwin photo

NIB	Exc.	V.G.	Good	Fair	Poor
—	450	400	350	250	200

Model 311E—Hammerless Boxlock

NIB	Exc.	V.G.	Good	Fair	Poor
—	600	450	400	300	250

Model 311F—Hammerless Boxlock

NIB	Exc.	V.G.	Good	Fair	Poor
—	450	400	350	250	200

Model 311H—Hammerless Boxlock

NIB	Exc.	V.G.	Good	Fair	Poor
—	450	400	350	250	200

Model 311H—Vent Rib Hammerless Boxlock

Courtesy Nick Niles, Paul Goodwin photo

NIB	Exc.	V.G.	Good	Fair	Poor
—	500	450	350	300	250

Model 311J/R—Hammerless Boxlock

Courtesy Nick Niles, Paul Goodwin photo

NIB	Exc.	V.G.	Good	Fair	Poor
—	400	350	250	200	150

Model 311J/R—Solid Rib Hammerless Boxlock

NIB	Exc.	V.G.	Good	Fair	Poor
—	400	350	250	200	150

Model 311H—Waterfowler Hammerless Boxlock

NIB	Exc.	V.G.	Good	Fair	Poor
—	700	575	450	350	250

Model 240—.410 Over/Under Hammer Tenite

RIVERSIDE BRAND
Model 215—Hammer Boxlock

Courtesy Nick Niles, Paul Goodwin photo

NIB	Exc.	V.G.	Good	Fair	Poor
—	750	525	400	250	200

Model 315 (Early)—Hammerless Boxlock

NIB	Exc.	V.G.	Good	Fair	Poor
—	575	450	350	250	200

Model 315 (Late)—Hammerless Boxlock

NIB	Exc.	V.G.	Good	Fair	Poor
—	575	450	350	250	200

SUPER VALUE BRAND
Model 511—Hammerless Boxlock

NIB	Exc.	V.G.	Good	Fair	Poor
—	525	400	300	200	150

Model 511—Sunken Rib Hammerless Boxlock

NIB	Exc.	V.G.	Good	Fair	Poor
—	575	450	350	200	150

SPRINGFIELD BRAND
Model 215—Hammer Boxlock

NIB	Exc.	V.G.	Good	Fair	Poor
—	575	450	350	250	150

Model 311—Hammerless Boxlock

Courtesy Nick Niles, Paul Goodwin photo

NIB	Exc.	V.G.	Good	Fair	Poor
—	575	450	350	250	150

Model 315—Hammerless Boxlock

Courtesy Nick Niles, Paul Goodwin photo

NIB	Exc.	V.G.	Good	Fair	Poor
—	575	450	350	250	200

Model 3150—Hammerless Boxlock

NIB	Exc.	V.G.	Good	Fair	Poor
—	700	575	400	250	200

Model 3151—Hammerless Boxlock

NIB	Exc.	V.G.	Good	Fair	Poor
—	850	700	450	350	250

Model 3151—Single Trigger Hammerless Boxlock

NIB	Exc.	V.G.	Good	Fair	Poor
—	950	800	575	450	300

Model 311—Single Trigger Hammerless Boxlock

NIB	Exc.	V.G.	Good	Fair	Poor
—	800	700	575	450	300

Model 5151—Hammerless Boxlock

Courtesy Nick Niles, Paul Goodwin photo

NIB	Exc.	V.G.	Good	Fair	Poor
—	575	450	350	250	200

Model 5151—Single Trigger Hammerless Boxlock

NIB	Exc.	V.G.	Good	Fair	Poor
—	700	525	400	300	200

Model 311—New Style Hammerless Boxlock

Courtesy Nick Niles, Paul Goodwin photo

NIB	Exc.	V.G.	Good	Fair	Poor
—	575	450	350	250	150

Model 311—New Style Tenite Hammerless Boxlock

NIB	Exc.	V.G.	Good	Fair	Poor
—	575	450	350	250	150

Model 511—Sunken Rib Hammerless Boxlock

NIB	Exc.	V.G.	Good	Fair	Poor
—	575	450	350	250	150

Model 511—Hammerless Boxlock

NIB	Exc.	V.G.	Good	Fair	Poor
—	525	400	300	200	150

Model 511A—Hammerless Boxlock

NIB	Exc.	V.G.	Good	Fair	Poor
—	525	400	300	200	150

STEVENS/SAVAGE SHOTGUNS

Model 411 Upland Sporter

Introduced in 2003 this side-by-side shotgun is chambered for the 12 or 20 gauge, as well as the .410 bore. The 12 gauge is fitted with 28" barrels, while the 28 and .410 have 26" barrels. Single trigger with ejectors. False sideplates are laser engraved. European walnut stock with pistol grip and splinter forend. Weight is about 6.75 to 6.5 lbs. depending on gauge. **NOTE:** Add 50 percent for 20 and .410 models.

NIB	Exc.	V.G.	Good	Fair	Poor
550	425	350	300	200	125

STEVENS DATE CODES

Collectors will find a date code stamped on every double-barrel shotgun in the Stevens brands produced between March 1949 and December 1968. Usually, it is behind the hinge pin or ahead of the trigger guard on the bottom of the frame. It will appear as a small circle containing a number and letter. The letters correspond to the years shown in the following table. Significance of the numbers is not known.

DATE CODES			
A-1949	B-1950	C-1951	D-1952
E-1953	F-1954	G-1955	H-1956
I-1957	J-1958	K-1959	L-1960
M-1961	N-1962	P-1963	R-1964
S-1965	T-1966	U-1967	V-1968
W-1969	X-1970		

STEVENS BOLT-ACTION SHOTGUNS

The Stevens Company produced a number of bolt-action shotguns that are either single-shot or repeaters. They are chambered for the 20 gauge or .410 and blued with walnut stocks. The values for these utility-grade shotguns are similar.

Model 237—Single-Shot
Model 258—Clip Fed
Model 37—Single-Shot
Model 38—Clip Fed
Model 39—Tube Magazine
Model 58—Clip Fed
Model 59—Tube Magazine

Model 58

Model 59

NIB	Exc.	V.G.	Good	Fair	Poor
—	125	100	75	50	35

STEVENS SLIDE-ACTION UTILITY-GRADE SHOTGUNS

The J. Stevens Arms Company also produced a series of utility-grade slide-action shotguns. They are chambered for various gauges with various barrel lengths and chokes. The finishes are blued with walnut stocks. The values are similar and are listed for reference purposes.

Model 67
Model 67-VR
Model 77
Model 77-AC
Model 77-M
Model 77-SC
Model 520
Model 522
Model 620
Model 621
Model 820

NIB	Exc.	V.G.	Good	Fair	Poor
—	225	150	125	100	75

Model 620 U.S. Marked Trench Gun

NOTE: Add $150 for bayonet.

Courtesy Richard M. Kumor Sr.

NIB	Exc.	V.G.	Good	Fair	Poor
—	3000	2500	1650	1200	750

Model 124

This is a manually-operated bolt-action shotgun chambered for 12 gauge. It has a 28" barrel with various chokes, is blued, and has a brown plastic Tenite stock. Ann odd duck: it looks like a semi-auto and is often mistaken for such.

NIB	Exc.	V.G.	Good	Fair	Poor
—	225	175	75	65	50

Model 67

This is a slide-action shotgun chambered for 12 and 20 gauge, as well as .410. It has 3" chambers. It is offered with various length barrels and choke tubes with a 5-shot tube magazine. It features a steel receiver and is blued, with a walnut stock. It was discontinued in 1989.

NIB	Exc.	V.G.	Good	Fair	Poor
—	250	175	150	100	75

Model 675

This is a slide-action shotgun chambered for 12 gauge with a 24" vent rib barrel with iron sights. The finish is blued, with a hardwood stock and recoil pad. It was manufactured in 1987 and 1988.

NIB	Exc.	V.G.	Good	Fair	Poor
—	275	240	200	150	100

Model 69-RXL

This is a matte-finished riot version of the Model 67 series slide-action shotgun. It has an 18.25" cylinder-bore barrel and is furnished with a recoil pad. It was discontinued in 1989.

NIB	Exc.	V.G.	Good	Fair	Poor
—	250	175	150	100	75

Stevens Model 350 Pump Shotgun

Pump-action shotgun chambered for 2.75- and 3-inch 12-ga. Features include all-steel barrel and receiver; bottom-load and -eject design; black synthetic stock; 5+1 capacity. Price: $267 (Field Model w/ 28-inch barrel, screw-in choke); $241 (Security Model w/ 18-inch barrel, fixed choke); $307 (Combo Model with Field and Security barrels); $254 (Security Model with 18.25-inch barrel w/ ghost ring rear sight).

STEYR
Steyr, Austria

STEYR & MANNLICHER PISTOLS

By Joseph Schroeder: Not all Mannlicher pistols were made by Steyr, and many of the pistols made by Steyr were not designed by Mannlicher. However, since by far the greatest number of Mannlicher's pistols were made by Steyr we believe it will be appropriate to include all of Ferdinand Ritter von Mannlicher's pistols along with other Steyr designs under this heading.

Schoenberger

Considered by many to be the first "commercial" semi-automatic pistol even though apparently at the most only about two dozen were made in 1892. The Steyr-made 8mm Schoenberger was based on patents granted to Laumann in 1890-91 and had a magazine in front of the trigger guard. Too rare to price.

Mannlicher Model 1894

Mannlicher's first "successful" self-loading pistol, the Model 1894 had a blow-forward action and double-action lockwork. Earliest examples were made in Austria, probably by Steyr, in 7.6mm but the greatest number were made by SIG in 1896-97 for Swiss army tests. These 100 pistols had a shorter barrel and smaller frame and were in 6.5mm. Prices are for Swiss examples. **NOTE:** Add 20 percent for 7.6mm pistols.

Courtesy Rock Island Auction Company

NIB	Exc.	V.G.	Good	Fair	Poor
—	13200	9900	6600	5500	3000

Mannlicher Model 1896/03

This is one of the most confusing of Mannlicher's pistols. Earliest examples, which have a fixed magazine and ribbed barrel, may have been made by Steyr and are very rare. Later versions, with a removable box magazine, have been called "Model 1896/03" and "Model 1901," and were made as both a pistol and pistol-carbine, possibly in Switzerland. Chambered for the 7.65mm Mannlicher cartridge, which is really a 7.65mm Borchardt. Prices listed are for the standard later model pistol or pistol-carbine (12" barrel, tangent sight); double prices for early pistol or late model pistol with detachable holster stock.

Courtesy Joseph Schroeder

NIB	Exc.	V.G.	Good	Fair	Poor
—	8250	5500	3850	2750	1500

Mannlicher Model 1899

Earliest version of Mannlicher's final semi-automatic pistol design, only about 250 were made by Dreyse in Soemmerda, Germany. Chambered for a tapered case 7.63mm Mannlicher cartridge. Distinguished by the large safety lever on the left side, takedown screw under the barrel, and the Dreyse markings.

Courtesy Joseph Schroeder

NIB	Exc.	V.G.	Good	Fair	Poor
—	9400	7150	4950	3850	2000

Mannlicher Model 1901

Marked "WAFFENFABRIK Steyr" on the left side and "SYSTEM MANNLICHER" on the right, the Model 1901 is distinguished by its checkered grips, rear sight located on the rear of the barrel, 8-round fixed magazine, and serial numbers to a little over 1000.

Courtesy Joseph Schroeder

NIB	Exc.	V.G.	Good	Fair	Poor
—	3300	2450	1750	900	700

Mannlicher Model 1905

Improved version of the Model 1901, with longer grip holding 10 rounds, grooved wooden grips, rear sight on rear of breechblock, and "MODEL 1905" added to right side. Later production moved all markings to the left side so Argentine crest could be placed on right side. **NOTE:** Prices listed are for an original commercial Model 1905, NOT a reblued Argentine contract with the crest ground off. Subtract 60 percent for reworked examples.

Courtesy Joseph Schroeder

NIB	Exc.	V.G.	Good	Fair	Poor
—	2425	1875	1350	800	400

Argentine Contract

NIB	Exc.	V.G.	Good	Fair	Poor
—	2750	2250	1650	900	500

Roth Steyr Model 1907

Based on the patents granted to Karel Krnka and Georg Roth, the 8mm Model 1907 had a rotating barrel locking system and was the first self-loading pistol adopted by the Austro-Hungarian Army. **NOTE:** Add 20 percent for early Steyr examples without a large pin visible on right side of frame, or for those made in Budapest instead of Steyr. Slight premium for correct stripper clips.

Courtesy Joseph Schroeder

NIB	Exc.	V.G.	Good	Fair	Poor
—	1250	750	600	350	250

Steyr Model 1908 Pocket Pistol

Based on the Belgian patents of Nicholas Pieper, these .25 and .32 caliber pocket pistols featured tipping barrels were built by Steyr under license from Pieper in Liege. Production was suspended during WWI but may have resumed after the war ended. Prices are for either caliber.

NIB	Exc.	V.G.	Good	Fair	Poor
—	385	275	165	100	75

Steyr Hahn Model 1911 Commercially Marked

NOTE: For military versions of this model see the *Standard Catalog of Military Firearms*.

NIB	Exc.	V.G.	Good	Fair	Poor
—	2200	1650	1220	875	450

Steyr Model SP

Steyr's first post WWII pistol, the Model SP was a beautifully made .32 ACP which, being double-action-only and more expensive than most of its contemporaries, was not competitive and was discontinued in the early 1960s after fewer than 1,000 were made. Slide marked "STEYR-DAIMLER-PUCH A.G. MOD.SP KAL. 7.65mm."

Courtesy Joseph Schroeder

NIB	Exc.	V.G.	Good	Fair	Poor
—	950	825	550	385	200

Steyr Model GB

The GB was introduced in the mid-1970s as a 9mm Parabellum military pistol, large in size but with an 18-round magazine capacity. Other features included polygon rifling and a gas trap around the barrel to delay breech opening. Initially produced as the Rogak P-18 by L.E.S. of Morton Grove, Illinois, but discontinued due in part to quality control problems after just over 2,000 were made. Later production by Steyr as the GB was to much higher standards, but the GB never achieved much popularity and was discontinued in 1988.

Rogak P-18

NIB	Exc.	V.G.	Good	Fair	Poor
—	425	350	250	175	125

Steyr GB

NIB	Exc.	V.G.	Good	Fair	Poor
—	800	675	525	400	200

RIFLES

THE FOLLOWING STEYR/MANNLICHER GUNS WERE IMPORTED BY GSI INC. TRUSSVILLE, ALABAMA

NOTE: For earlier models, see Mannlicher Schoenauer.

SPORTER SERIES

This series includes rifles that are lightweight and have a reduced overall length. All Sporter models have an interchangeable 5-round rotary magazine. The stock is oil-finished walnut in either the Mannlicher full stock design or the half stock version. In both stock configurations an oval European cheekpiece is standard. These rifles are offered in four different action lengths: SL (super light), L (light), M (medium), or S (magnum). They are also available with either single trigger or double set triggers.

Model M72 L/M

A .243, .270, 7x57mm, 7x64mm, .308 or .30-06 caliber bolt-action rifle with a 23" fluted barrel, and single or double set triggers. Blued, checkered walnut stock. Manufactured from 1972 to 1980.

NIB	Exc.	V.G.	Good	Fair	Poor
—	1325	1025	750	550	450

Model SL

This model features the super light action and is offered with 20" barrel in full stock version or 23-1/6" barrel in half stock version. A rubber buttpad is standard. This model does not have a forend tip on its half stock variation. Offered in the following calibers: .222 Rem., .222 Rem. Mag., .223, and 5.6x50 Mag. Weighs approximately 6.2 lbs. with full stock and 6.3 lbs. with half stock.

NIB	Exc.	V.G.	Good	Fair	Poor
2000	1650	1000	750	500	300

Model SL Carbine

As above, with a 20" fluted barrel and Mannlicher-style stock.

NIB	Exc.	V.G.	Good	Fair	Poor
1950	1750	1050	800	550	350

Varmint Model

This model features a heavy 26" barrel chambered for the .222 Rem., .223, 5.6x57, .243 Win., .308 Win., and .22-250. The forend of the stock is ventilated. The grip is enlarged and textured. Choice of single or double set triggers. Recoil pad is standard. Weighs about 8 lbs.

NIB	Exc.	V.G.	Good	Fair	Poor
1950	1750	1050	800	550	350

Model L

This rifle has the light action and is offered in the same stock configuration and barrel lengths as the Model SL. The calibers are: 5.6x57, .243 Win., .308, .22-250, and 6mm Rem. Weighs about 6.3 lbs. with full stock and 6.4 lbs. with half stock.

NIB	Exc.	V.G.	Good	Fair	Poor
1850	1650	1000	750	500	300

Luxus Series

This luxury model offers a choice of full or half stock variations in select walnut with fine line checkering. The pistol grip is steeply angled. The Luxus rifles are fitted with a swept back European cheekpiece. A single set trigger is standard. The box magazine holds 3 rounds. Optional engraving and stock carving may be encountered on these modes that will dramatically affect price. The Luxus rifles are available with light, medium, or magnum length actions.

Luxus Model L

Same dimensions and barrel lengths as the Sporter version. The calibers are: 5.6x57, .243 Win., .308, .22-250, and 6mm Rem.

NIB	Exc.	V.G.	Good	Fair	Poor
2400	2000	1100	800	600	350

Luxus Model M

Same dimensions and barrel lengths as the Sporter Model M. Available in these calibers: 6.5x57, .270 Win., 7x64, .30-06, 9.3x 626.5x55, 7.5 Swiss, 7x57, and 8x57JS.

NIB	Exc.	V.G.	Good	Fair	Poor
2400	2000	1100	800	600	350

Luxus Model S

Same as the Sporter Model S. Offered in the following calibers: 6.5x68, 7mm Rem. Mag., .300 Win. Mag., and 8x68S.

NIB	Exc.	V.G.	Good	Fair	Poor
2400	2000	1100	800	600	350

Model M

This model features the medium action and has the same barrel and stock configurations as the other two models listed above with the exception that it has no buttpad and it does have a forend tip on its half stock variation. Available in these calibers: 6.5x57, .270 Win., 7x64, .30-06, 9.3x62, 6.5x55, 7.5 Swiss, 7x57, and

8x57JS. Weighs approximately 6.8 lbs. with full stock and 7 lbs. with half stock.

NIB	Exc.	V.G.	Good	Fair	Poor
2500	2100	1200	900	600	300

Professional Model M

This model is fitted with a medium weight action and features a black synthetic checkered stock. Comes fitted with a ventilated rubber recoil pad. Offered with 20" or 23.6" barrel it is available with single or double set trigger. Available in these calibers: 6.5x57, .270 Win., 7x64, .30-06, 9.3x62, 6.5x55, 7.5 Swiss, 7x57, and 8x57JS. Weighs approximately 7.25 lbs.

NIB	Exc.	V.G.	Good	Fair	Poor
1500	1200	950	700	600	300

Model S/T

Similar to the model above but in a heavy barreled version. Offered in these calibers: 9.3x64, .375 H&H, and .458 Win. Mag. An optional buttstock magazine is available. Weighs about 9 lbs.

NIB	Exc.	V.G.	Good	Fair	Poor
2100	1900	1400	1100	800	500

Tropical Rifle

As above, with a 26" heavy barrel chambered for .375 Holland & Holland and .458 Winchester Magnum. Not imported after 1985.

NIB	Exc.	V.G.	Good	Fair	Poor
—	2000	1750	1100	650	450

Model MIII Professional

Introduced in 1995 this is an economy version of the Model M Professional. It is fitted with a 23.5" barrel, black synthetic stock, and choice of single or double set triggers. Offered in .25-06, .270 Win., .30-06, and 7x64 calibers. Weight is approximately 7 lb. 5 oz. **NOTE:** With checkered walnut stock add $100.

NIB	Exc.	V.G.	Good	Fair	Poor
1000	800	600	400	300	200

Steyr SBS (Safe Bolt System)

This series was introduced in 1997 and features a newly designed bolt. It is offered in two distinct models the SBS Forester and the SBS ProHunter.

SBS ProHunter

This model has a 23.6" barrel with 4-round magazine and single adjustable trigger. Offered in .243 Win., .25-06, .270 Win., 7mm-08, .308 Win., .30-06, 7mm Rem. Mag., .300 Win. Mag., and several European calibers. Weight is approximately 7.5 lbs. This model is furnished with a black synthetic stock with recoil pad

and buttspacers. Introduced in 1999. **NOTE:** Add $150-$300 for custom metric calibers. Add approximately $30 for 7mm Mag and .300 Win. Mag calibers.

NIB	Exc.	V.G.	Good	Fair	Poor
750	650	575	400	300	150

SBS ProHunter Stainless Steel

Same as the ProHunter model but with stainless steel action and barrel. Introduced in 2000. **NOTE:** Add $150-$300 for custom metric calibers. Add approximately $30 for 7mm mag and .300 Win. Mag calibers.

NIB	Exc.	V.G.	Good	Fair	Poor
900	750	675	500	400	250

SBS ProHunter Camo

Same as standard ProHunter but with camo synthetic stock. **NOTE:** Add $150-$300 for custom metric calibers. Add approximately $30 for 7mm mag and .300 Win. Mag calibers.

NIB	Exc.	V.G.	Good	Fair	Poor
1000	850	700	575	400	200

SBS ProHunter Camo Stainless Steel

Same as above but with stainless steel action and barrel. **NOTE:** Add $150-$300 for custom metric calibers. Add approximately $30 for 7mm mag and .300 Win. Mag calibers.

NIB	Exc.	V.G.	Good	Fair	Poor
1050	900	750	600	475	250

SBS ProHunter Mountain Rifle

Chambered for .243, .25-06, .270, and 7mm-08 calibers, this model is fitted with a 20" barrel with no sights. Receiver engraved "Mountain Rifle." Synthetic stock with recoil pad standard. Weight is 7.25 lbs. Introduced in 1999.

NIB	Exc.	V.G.	Good	Fair	Poor
1000	850	700	575	400	200

SBS ProHunter Mountain Stainless Steel

Same as the ProHunter Mountain but with stainless steel action and barrel. Introduced in 2000.

NIB	Exc.	V.G.	Good	Fair	Poor
1050	900	750	600	425	200

SBS ProHunter Mountain Camo

Same as the ProHunter but with camo synthetic stock. Introduced in 2000.

NIB	Exc.	V.G.	Good	Fair	Poor
1150	1000	850	700	475	250

SBS ProHunter Mountain Camo Stainless Steel

Same as above but with stainless steel action and barrel. Introduced in 2000.

NIB	Exc.	V.G.	Good	Fair	Poor
1150	1000	850	700	475	250

SBS ProHunter (Youth/Ladies)

This model is fitted with a walnut stock with buttspacers (to create a shorter length of pull) and extra thick recoil pad. Chambered for .243, 7mm-08, and .308. Weight is about 7.25 lbs. Introduced in 1999.

NIB	Exc.	V.G.	Good	Fair	Poor
1000	850	700	575	400	200

SBS ProHunter Compact

Same as above but with black synthetic stock. Also offered with stainless steel action and barrel. **NOTE:** Add $80 for stainless steel model.

NIB	Exc.	V.G.	Good	Fair	Poor
1000	850	700	575	400	200

SBS ProHunter 376 Steyr

This model is chambered for the .376 Steyr cartridge. Fitted with a 20" barrel with iron sights. Synthetic stock with special thick pad. Weight is about 8 lbs. Introduced in 1999.

NIB	Exc.	V.G.	Good	Fair	Poor
1200	950	800	675	400	200

SBS Forester

Same as Pro Hunter model but furnished with a walnut stock with recoil pad. **NOTE:** Add $150-$300 for custom metric calibers. Add $30 for 7mm Rem. Mag and .300 Win. Mag.

NIB	Exc.	V.G.	Good	Fair	Poor
850	725	625	500	400	200

SBS Classic American

This model features a 23.6" barrel with a single adjustable trigger and stain finish walnut stock with recoil pad. Offered in calibers from .243 to .300 Win. Mag. Weight is about 7.2 lbs. Introduced in 2000. **NOTE:** Add $150-$300 for custom metric calibers. Add approximately $30 for 7mm Mag and .300 Win. Mag calibers.

NIB	Exc.	V.G.	Good	Fair	Poor
1500	1100	850	650	500	300

SBS Classic Mannlicher

Offered in the same calibers as above except for 7mm Rem. Mag and .300 Win. Mag. and fitted with a 25.6" barrel. The walnut stock is the full Mannlicher style with recoil pad. Fitted with open sights. Weight is about 7.2 lbs. Introduced in 2000.

NIB	Exc.	V.G.	Good	Fair	Poor
2300	2000	1600	1000	675	400

SBS Forester Mountain Rifle

Walnut stock with 20" barrel and no sights. Chambered for a variety of calibers including .243, .25-06, .270, 7mm-08, .308, .30-06 and 6.5x55. Receiver engraved "Mountain Rifle." Introduced in 1999.

NIB	Exc.	V.G.	Good	Fair	Poor
850	725	625	500	400	200

Mannlicher SBS European—Half Stock

Fitted with a 23.6" barrel with iron sights and chambered for a wide variety of American and European calibers from .243 to 9.3x62. European style figured walnut stock. Adjustable trigger. Recoil pad. Weight is about 7.5 lbs.

NIB	Exc.	V.G.	Good	Fair	Poor
2795	2200	1750	1200	700	400

Mannlicher SBS European—Half Stock Carbine

Same as model above but with 20" barrel.

NIB	Exc.	V.G.	Good	Fair	Poor
2795	2200	1750	1200	700	400

Mannlicher SBS European—Full Stock

Same as above but with full European stock covering a 20" barrel.

NIB	Exc.	V.G.	Good	Fair	Poor
2895	2300	1800	1250	750	450

Mannlicher SBS Magnum European—Half Stock

This model is chambered for the 7mm Rem. Mag., .300 Win. Mag., and the 6.5x68 and 8x68S calibers. Fitted with a 25.6" barrel with iron sights. Walnut stock. Weight is about 7.75 lbs.

NIB	Exc.	V.G.	Good	Fair	Poor
2895	2300	1800	1250	750	450

Steyr Scout—Jeff Cooper Package

Developed by Col. Jeff Cooper this model is chambered for the .308 Win. cartridge. It is fitted with a 19" fluted barrel. Stock is gray synthetic with removable buttspacers and folding bi-pod. Magazine capacity is 5 rounds with optional 10-round magazines available. Weight is approximately 7 lbs. with scope. Weight is 6.3 lbs. with no scope. Adjustable single trigger. Factory-installed Leupold M8 2.5x28mm scope. Introduced in 1998.

STEYR SCOUT

NIB	Exc.	V.G.	Good	Fair	Poor
2600	2000	1600	1100	650	400

Steyr Scout Package

Similar to the Jeff Cooper Package but without the Jeff Cooper logo. Stock is black synthetic. Also offered in .223 Rem., .243 Win., 7mm-08 as well as .308 and .375 Steyr calibers.

NIB	Exc.	V.G.	Good	Fair	Poor
2100	1800	1550	1000	700	400

Steyr Scout

Same as above but rifle only.

NIB	Exc.	V.G.	Good	Fair	Poor
2100	1800	1550	1000	700	400

Steyr Scout Tactical

This model has a 19.25" fluted barrel and is chambered for the .223 or .308 Win. cartridge. Integral bipod. Emergency Ghost Ring sights. **NOTE:** Add $100 for stainless steel model.

NIB	Exc.	V.G.	Good	Fair	Poor
2050	1500	1000	800	750	425

PRECISION/TACTICAL RIFLES

Model SSG-PI

This model features a black synthetic stock originally designed as a military sniper rifle. Fitted with a cocking indicator, single or double set trigger, 5-round rotary magazine, or 10-round magazine. Receiver is milled to NATO specifications for Steyr ring mounts. Barrel length is 26". Rifle weighs about 9 lbs. Offered in .308 Win. **NOTE:** This model was originally called the SSG 69.

NIB	Exc.	V.G.	Good	Fair	Poor
1700	1300	1000	800	600	400

SSG-PII Police Rifle

This version of the SSG has a heavier 26" barrel and a larger knob-style bolt handle. Weighs about 10 lbs. 11 oz.

NIB	Exc.	V.G.	Good	Fair	Poor
1700	1300	1000	800	600	400

SSK-PIIK Police Kurz

Similar to the above model but with a 20" heavy barrel. Weight is about 10 lbs.

NIB	Exc.	V.G.	Good	Fair	Poor
1700	1300	1000	800	600	400

SSG-PII & PIIK McMillan

Fitted with a McMillan A-3 stock with adjustable cheekpiece and removable buttspacers. Special forearm rail.

NIB	Exc.	V.G.	Good	Fair	Poor
2300	1750	1350	950	750	500

SSG-PIV

Again similar to the above PIIK but with a 16.75" heavy barrel with a removable flash hider. Barrel is threaded. Weight is about 9 lbs. 11 oz.

NIB	Exc.	V.G.	Good	Fair	Poor
2500	2000	1500	1000	750	500

Match

NIB	Exc.	V.G.	Good	Fair	Poor
3000	2500	2000	1500	800	500

Match UIT

Designed as an international target rifle this model features special shaped pistol grip, an adjustable trigger for length of pull and pressure. Enlarged bolt handle and nonglare barrel. Chambered for .308 Win. cartridge.

NIB	Exc.	V.G.	Good	Fair	Poor
3900	3500	3000	2000	1500	1000

JAGD Match

Introduced in 1995 this model features a choice of 23.5" or 20" barrel with sights. The stock is laminated. A full stock version is offered on 20" barrel models and a half stock is offered on the 23.5" barrel models. Available in a variety of configurations with calibers from .222 Rem. to .458 Win. Mag.

NIB	Exc.	V.G.	Good	Fair	Poor
1750	1250	900	500	350	200

SBS TACTICAL SERIES

SBS Tactical

Fitted with a black synthetic stock and 20" barrel with no sights. This model is chambered for the .308 cartridge. Removable buttspacers. Black bolt body. Receiver engraved "SBS Tactical." Introduced in 1999. Weight is about 7.25 lbs. **NOTE:** Add $100 for stainless steel model (introduced 2000).

NIB	Exc.	V.G.	Good	Fair	Poor
1150	950	700	550	300	200

SBS Tactical Heavy Barrel

This model also has a black synthetic stock but is fitted with a 26" heavy barrel and no sights. Black bolt body. Receiver engraved "SBS Tactical HB." Weight is about 8 lbs. Introduced in 1999. Also offered with 20" barrel called "HBC." Both barrel lengths chambered for .308 cartridge.

NIB	Exc.	V.G.	Good	Fair	Poor
1250	1050	800	650	300	200

SBS Tactical Heavy Barrel Carbine

This model features a 20" heavy barrel, no sights, matte blue finish. Chambered for .308 caliber. Introduced in 2000.

NIB	Exc.	V.G.	Good	Fair	Poor
1150	950	700	550	300	200

SBS Tactical McMillan

This model is fitted with a 26" barrel chambered for the .308 cartridge and has a McMillan A-3 stock. Oversize bolt handle. Weight is about 9.8 lbs. Introduced in 1999.

NIB	Exc.	V.G.	Good	Fair	Poor
1600	1250	950	750	60	400

SBS CISM Rifle

This model is chambered for the .308 cartridge and fitted with a 19.7" heavy barrel. The stock is laminated wood with black lacquer finish. The stock has a forearm rail with handstop, adjustable

buttplate, and cheekpiece. The trigger is adjustable. Weight is approximately 10.25 lbs. Introduced in 1999.

NIB	Exc.	V.G.	Good	Fair	Poor
3295	2500	1950	1600	1200	700

SBS Tactical Elite Heavy Barrel

This model, introduced in 2000, features a 26" heavy barrel, no sights, matte blue finish, Zytel stock with adjustable cheekpiece and adjustable buttplate. Full length Picatinny mounting rail. Magazine capacity is 5 or 10 rounds. Chambered for .308 cartridge. **NOTE:** Add $100 for stainless steel model. Add $1,000 for ZF optics.

NIB	Exc.	V.G.	Good	Fair	Poor
2400	1750	1400	1000	700	400

SBS Tactical Elite Heavy Barrel Carbine

Same as the Tactical Elite Heavy Barrel model but fitted with a 20" heavy barrel. Introduced in 2000.

NIB	Exc.	V.G.	Good	Fair	Poor
2400	1750	—	—	—	—

Steyr AUG

A 5.56mm semi-automatic, Bullpup rifle with a 20" barrel incorporating a Swarovski 1.5x telescopic sight. Green carbon composite stock. Weight is about 8.5 lbs. Recommend independent, local appraisals.

NIB	Exc.	V.G.	Good	Fair	Poor
3700	3100	2500	1600	1300	650

Steyr AUG—Police Model

Same as above but with black stock and 16" barrel.

NIB	Exc.	V.G.	Good	Fair	Poor
3700	3100	2500	1600	1300	650

Steyr AUG Special Receiver

Receiver only. Special flattop with Stanag mounting.

NIB	Exc.	V.G.	Good	Fair	Poor
3700	3100	2500	1600	1300	650

Steyr USR

This model is the post-ban version of the AUG. Fitted with a Swarovski 1.5x scope and gray synthetic stock.

NIB	Exc.	V.G.	Good	Fair	Poor
3700	3100	2500	1600	1300	650

Steyr Zephyr

This model is a .22 caliber rimfire bolt-action carbine. It has a 5-round detachable magazine, dovetailed receiver for scope rings. It is fitted with a full stock. Made from 1953 to 1968.

NIB	Exc.	V.G.	Good	Fair	Poor
—	1800	1475	1150	800	400

PISTOLS

Model SPP

Introduced in 1993 this is a 9mm semi-automatic pistol. It is made from synthetic materials and operates on a delayed blowback, rotating barrel system. The magazine capacity is either 15 or 30 rounds. The barrel is 5.9" in length overall length is 12.75" and weight is about 42 oz. Due to its appearance and design this pistol was banned for importation into the United States shortly after its introduction. Because of this circumstance the price of this pistol may fluctuate widely.

NIB	Exc.	V.G.	Good	Fair	Poor
1000	900	750	600	500	400

Model M

Chambered for the .40 S&W, 9mm, or .357 SIG cartridge this semi-automatic pistol has a polymer frame and 3 user selectable safety systems. Loaded chambered indicator. Triangle/Trapezoid sights. Limited access lock with key. Weight is about 28 oz. Magazine capacity is 10 rounds. Introduced in 1999.

STEYR HAHN
SEE—Steyr

STEYR MANNLICHER
SEE—Steyr

STI INTERNATIONAL
Georgetown, Texas

LS9 & LS40

Single stack pistol chambered for the 9mm or .40 S&W cartridge. Fitted with a 3.4" barrel and short grip. Heine Low Mount sights. Rosewood grips. Matte blue finish. Magazine capacity is 7 rounds for 9mm and 6 rounds for .40 S&W. Weight is about 28 oz.

NIB	Exc.	V.G.	Good	Fair	Poor
850	675	550	400	300	200

BLS9 & BLS40

Same as above but with full length grip. Magazine capacity is 9 rounds for 9mm and 8 rounds for .40 S&W.

NIB	Exc.	V.G.	Good	Fair	Poor
825	650	525	375	275	200

Ranger

Chambered for the .45 ACP cartridge and fitted with a 3.9" barrel with short grip. Fixed STI sights. Blued frame with stainless steel slide. Weight is about 29 oz.

NIB	Exc.	V.G.	Good	Fair	Poor
950	775	600	500	400	200

Ranger II

Chambered for the .45 ACP cartridge and fitted with a 4.15" ramped bull barrel. Slide is flat top with rear serrations and chamfered fore end. Ambidextrous safety and high rise grip safety. Adjustable rear sight. Hard chrome upper with blued lower frame. Weight is about 39 oz.

NIB	Exc.	V.G.	Good	Fair	Poor
925	800	675	525	400	200

Trojan

Chambered for the .45 ACP, .40 Super, .40 S&W, and 9mm cartridge. Fitted with a 5" barrel. Rosewood grips. Matte blue finish. Eight-round magazine capacity. Weight is about 36 oz. **NOTE:** For .40 Super with .45 ACP conversion add $275. For Trojan with 6" slide add $250.

NIB	Exc.	V.G.	Good	Fair	Poor
1150	925	750	600	500	300

Tactical 4.15

Chambered for the 9mm, .40 S&W, or the 45 ACP cartridge. Fully supported ramped 4.15" bull barrel. Frame has tactical rail. Slide has rear serrations. Fixed rear sight. Aluminum magazine well. Black polycoat finish. Weight is about 34.5 oz.

NIB	Exc.	V.G.	Good	Fair	Poor
1750	1475	1150	900	650	350

Tactical

As above but with 5" barrel. Flat blue finish. Weight is about 39 oz.

NIB	Exc.	V.G.	Good	Fair	Poor
1750	1475	1150	900	650	350

Trubor

Chambered for the 9mm major, 9x23, or .38 Super cartridges. Steel frame. Fully supported and ramped one piece with bull barrel with integral compensator. Slide has front and rear serrations. Sights are C-More or OK Red Dot reflix. Blued finish. Weight is about 42.5 oz. with scope.

NIB	Exc.	V.G.	Good	Fair	Poor
2500	2100	1600	1200	900	500

Lawman

This .45 ACP pistol has a 5" ramped barrel with match grade bushing. Aluminum trigger. Series 70 grip safety. Novak 3 dot sights. Checkered walnut grips. Polymer finish with brown slide over tan frame. Weight is about 36 oz.

NIB	Exc.	V.G.	Good	Fair	Poor
1200	975	825	675	500	250

Xcaliber Single Stack

Chambered for the .450 SMC cartridge and fitted with a 6" slide. Adjustable rear sight. Weight is about 38 oz. Blue finish. Single stack magazine. Discontinued.

NIB	Exc.	V.G.	Good	Fair	Poor
1475	1275	1050	775	500	350

Xcaliber Double Stack

Same as the Xcaliber Single Stack except that this model has a double stack magazine. Discontinued.

NIB	Exc.	V.G.	Good	Fair	Poor
1800	1600	1175	900	600	400

Executive

Chambered for the .40 S&W cartridge. Fitted with a 5" ramped bull barrel. Adjustable rear sight. Gray synthetic grip and hard chrome slide. Weight is about 39 oz. Double stack magazine.

NIB	Exc.	V.G.	Good	Fair	Poor
2350	2000	1650	1100	725	400

VIP

Chambered for the .45 ACP cartridge and fitted with a 3.9" ramped bull barrel. Stainless steel flat top slide. Fixed rear sight. Ten-round magazine capacity. Weight is about 25 oz.

NIB	Exc.	V.G.	Good	Fair	Poor
1400	1100	800	650	400	250

Edge

Chambered for the 9mm, 10mm, .40 S&W, and .45 ACP cartridge with 5" ramped bull barrel. Dual stack magazine. Bomar style sights. Blue finish. Weight is about 39 oz.

NIB	Exc.	V.G.	Good	Fair	Poor
1800	1400	1000	700	500	300

Eagle

Chambered for customer's choice of caliber and fitted with 5" ramped bull barrel. Fixed sights. Blued frame and stainless steel slide. Weight is about 30 oz.

NIB	Exc.	V.G.	Good	Fair	Poor
1700	1200	900	600	400	250

Duty One

Chambered for the 9mm, .40 S&W, or .45 ACP cartridges. Five-inch bull barrel is fully supported and ramped. Steel frame with single stack magazine with front strap checkering and tactical rail. Grips are rosewood. Slide has front and rear serrations. Adjustable sights. Finish is flat blue. Weight is about 38 oz.

NIB	Exc.	V.G.	Good	Fair	Poor
1100	900	750	500	400	250

Duty CT

1911-style steel frame single-stack with integral tactical rail and rosewood grips. 5" slide/barrel, fixed 2-dot tritium rear sight. 36.6 oz. Also available in 4.15" commander size. Blued.

NIB	Exc.	V.G.	Good	Fair	Poor
1100	900	750	500	400	250

Competitor

Chambered for the .38 Super cartridge and fitted with a 5.5" ramped bull barrel with compensator. Fitted with a C-More scope. Stainless steel slide. Weight is about 44 oz. with scope and mount. Discontinued.

NIB	Exc.	V.G.	Good	Fair	Poor
2350	2000	1650	1100	725	400

Grandmaster

Custom built to customer's specifications in 9mm major, 9x23, and .38 Super.

NIB	Exc.	V.G.	Good	Fair	Poor
2800	2500	2000	1500	850	500

Rangemaster

Fitted with a 5" fully supported and ramped bull barrel and chambered for the 9mm or .45 ACP cartridge, this pistol has a full length dust cover, checkered front strap and mainspring housing and square trigger guard. Front and rear slide serrations. Adjustable sights. Rose grips. Polished blue finish. Weight is about 38 oz.

NIB	Exc.	V.G.	Good	Fair	Poor
1500	1350	1100	800	500	250

Rangemaster II

Single-stack blued variation of Rangemaster. Chambered for 9mm, .40 S&W, .45 ACP. 5" slide/barrel, 37 oz. Introduced 2006.

NIB	Exc.	V.G.	Good	Fair	Poor
1300	1125	900	600	400	200

Targetmaster

As above but with 6" barrel.

NIB	Exc.	V.G.	Good	Fair	Poor
1650	1250	900	650	400	250

Stinger

Chambered for the 9mm or .38 Super cartridge. Fitted with a 3.9" barrel with compensator. Sights are OKO or C-More on STI mount. Blued finish. Weight is about 38 oz.

NIB	Exc.	V.G.	Good	Fair	Poor
2775	2275	1850	1450	900	500

Hawk 4.3

This pistol is modeled on the 1911 design and is equipped with a 4.3" barrel with steel slide. The frame of the pistol is made from polymer and features and increased magazine capacity while retaining the 1911 grip thickness. Chambered for .38 Super, .45 ACP, .40 S&W, 10mm, and 9x25 calibers. Built primarily for competition shooting. Discontinued.

NIB	Exc.	V.G.	Good	Fair	Poor
1700	1200	900	600	400	250

Night Hawk 4.3

Chambered for .45 ACP only with 4.3" bull barrel and a host of special features such a narrow tactical safety, front and rear slide serrations, and extended dust cover. Tritium sights optional. Blued finish. Weight is 33 oz. Discontinued.

NIB	Exc.	V.G.	Good	Fair	Poor
1925	1600	1300	1050	750	400

Falcon 3.9

Similar to the above model but fitted with a 3.9" barrel. Weight is approximately 30 oz. with steel frame and 25 oz. with aluminum frame. Discontinued.

NIB	Exc.	V.G.	Good	Fair	Poor
1925	1600	1300	1050	750	400

Sparrow 5.0

Chambered for the .22 LR cartridge only and fitted with a 5" bull barrel with fixed sights. Weight is approximately 30 oz. Discontinued.

NIB	Exc.	V.G.	Good	Fair	Poor
925	800	675	525	400	200

Edge 5.1

Chambered for .40 S&W only with 5" bull barrel and many special features. BoMar front and rear sights. Weight is 39 oz.

NIB	Exc.	V.G.	Good	Fair	Poor
1800	1400	1000	700	500	300

Eagle 5.1

Similar to the Model 2011 Hawk but furnished with a 5" barrel. Comes standard with BoMar adjustable sights.

NIB	Exc.	V.G.	Good	Fair	Poor
1925	1600	1300	1050	750	400

Eagle 5.5

Similar to above model but furnished with a 5-1/2" barrel with compensator.

NIB	Exc.	V.G.	Good	Fair	Poor
2395	1950	1600	1200	850	500

Eagle 6.0

Chambered for 9mm, .38 Super, .40 S&W, or .45 ACP cartridges. Fitted with a 6" bull barrel. Many special features. BoMar front and rear sights. Blued finish. Weight is about 42 oz.

NIB	Exc.	V.G.	Good	Fair	Poor
1925	1600	1300	1050	750	400

Hunter 6.0

Chambered for the 10mm cartridge only and fitted with a 6" bull barrel. Heavy extended frame. Many special features. Leupold 2x scope. Blued finish. Weight with scope 51 oz.

NIB	Exc.	V.G.	Good	Fair	Poor
2350	1900	1600	1200	850	500

Special Edition

Chambered for the 9mm, .40 S&W or .45 ACP cartridge and fitted with a fully supported and ramped 5" bull barrel. Hi-Rise grip. Sights are Dawson fiber optic with adjustable rear. Slide has Saber Tooth serrations and custom engraving. Finish is 24 karat gold on all steel parts except barrel. Weight is about 38 oz.

NIB	Exc.	V.G.	Good	Fair	Poor
2900	2500	1975	1600	1200	500

I.P.S.C. 30th Anniversary

Similar to the Special Edition but with hard chrome upper with color inlays and blued lower.

NIB	Exc.	V.G.	Good	Fair	Poor
2775	2400	1700	1400	950	450

TruSight

Semi-auto pistol chambered for 9mm, .40 S&W, .45 ACP; double-stack magazine. Steel frame, 4.15" slide/barrel. Dawson fiber optic front sight, adjustable rear sight. 36.1 oz. Blued with multiple options. IPSC, USPSA approved. Introduced 2006.

NIB	Exc.	V.G.	Good	Fair	Poor
1800	1575	1200	900	600	350

Legacy

Chambered for .45 ACP single-stack. 5" slide/barrel, LOA 8.5", 38 oz. with adjustable rear sight. Cocobola smooth grips. IDPA, USPSA approved. Introduced 2006.

NIB	Exc.	V.G.	Good	Fair	Poor
1500	1300	1050	750	600	300

GP6

Polymer-framed single/double action pistol with ambidextrous safeties and fized three-dot sight system. Chambered in 9mm Parabellum.

NIB	Exc.	V.G.	Good	Fair	Poor
650	500	375	250	175	75

Sentinel Premier

Top-of-the-line ISPC and IDPA competition 1911 with Dawson Precision/STI "Perfect Impact" style white outline tritium adjustable sights and the STI Tritium competition front; forged steel, government length, standard-width frame; and many other refinements. The Sentinel Premier comes standard with case, owner's manual, and one Wilson Combat \xa8 Elite Tactical magazine.

NIB	Exc.	V.G.	Good	Fair	Poor
1700	1500	1300	1000	800	450

Limited Edition 20th Anniversary

1911-style semi-auto pistol chambered in 9x19, .38 Super, .40 S&W, and .45 ACP to commemorate 20th anniversary. Features include ambidextrous thumb safeties and knuckle relief high-rise beavertail grip safety; gold TiN (or Titanium Nitride) coating; full length steel bar stock slide with custom serrations specific to this model; 5-inch fully ramped and supported bull barrel; STI adjustable rear sight and a Dawson fiber optic front sight. STI will only build 200 of these pistols and the serial numbers reflect this (1 of 200, 2 of 200, etc.)

NIB	Exc.	V.G.	Good	Fair	Poor
3200	2900	2600	—	—	—

Duty One

1911-style semi-auto pistol chambered in .45 ACP. Features include government size frame with integral tactical rail and 30 lpi checkered front strap; milled tactical rail on the dust cover of the frame; ambidextrous thumb safeties; high rise beavertail grip safety; lowered and flared ejection port; fixed rear sight; front and rear cocking serrations; 5-inch fully supported STI International ramped bull barrel.

NIB	Exc.	V.G.	Good	Fair	Poor
1300	1100	850	700	300	200

Apeiro

1911-style semi-auto pistol chambered in 9x19, .40 S&W, and .45 ACP. Features include Schuemann "Island" barrel; patented modular steel frame with polymer grip; high capacity double-stack magazine; stainless steel ambidextrous thumb safeties and knuckle relief high-rise beavertail grip safety; unique sabertooth rear cocking serrations; 5-inch fully ramped, fully supported "island" bull barrel, with the sight milled in to allow faster recovery to point of aim; custom engraving on the polished sides of the (blued) stainless steel slide; stainless steel magwell; STI adjustable rear sight and Dawson fiber optic front sight; blued frame.

NIB	Exc.	V.G.	Good	Fair	Poor
2200	1850	1500	1200	800	400

Eclipse

Compact 1911-style semi-auto pistol chambered in 9x19, .40 S&W, and .45 ACP. Features include slide with rear cocking serrations, over-sized ejection port; 2-dot tritium night sights recessed into the slide; high-capacity polymer grip; single sided blued thumb safety;bobbed, high-rise, blued, knuckle relief beavertail grip safety; 3-inch barrel. Also comes with alloy frame as Escort model.

NIB	Exc.	V.G.	Good	Fair	Poor
1625	1400	1185	900	600	300

Texican Single Action Revolver

SAA-styled revolver chambered in .38 Special and .45 Colt. Features include 4.75- or 6.5-inch (.45) or 5.25-inch barrel (.38). Features include competition sights, springs, triggers and hammers; color case hardening and blued finish standard.

NIB	Exc.	V.G.	Good	Fair	Poor
1100	935	775	600	300	200

FPI 2260 Rifle

Chambered for the .22 Long Rifle cartridge. Aluminum receiver with adjustable trigger and quick magazine release. Integral scope mount.

NIB	Exc.	V.G.	Good	Fair	Poor
1000	850	675	500	300	150

Sporting Competition Rifle

AR-style semi-auto rifle chambered in 5.56 NATO. Features include 16-inch 410 stainless 1:8 barrel; mid-length gas system; Nordic Tactical Compensator and JP Trigger group; custom STI Valkyrie hand guard and gas block; flat-top design with Picatinny rail; anodized finish with black Teflon coating. Also available in Tactical configuration.

NIB	Exc.	V.G.	Good	Fair	Poor
1175	1000	825	650	350	250

STOCK, FRANZ
Berlin, Germany

Stock

A .22, 6.35mm or 7.65mm semi-automatic pistol with an open topped slide. The frame marked "Franz Stock Berlin." Blued with black composition grips impressed with the name "Stock" at the top. Manufactured from 1918 to the early 1930s.

Courtesy J.B. Wood

NIB	Exc.	V.G.	Good	Fair	Poor
—	525	400	300	250	150

STOCKING & CO.
Worcester, Massachusetts

Pepperbox

A .28 or .316 barreled percussion pepperbox revolver with barrel lengths from 4" to 6". The hammer is fitted with a long cocking piece at the rear and the trigger guard may or may not be made with a spur at the rear. Blued with walnut grips. The barrel group marked "Stocking & Co., Worcester." Manufactured between 1846 and 1854.

NIB	Exc.	V.G.	Good	Fair	Poor
—	—	1950	1650	600	200

Single-Shot Pistol

A .36 caliber single-shot percussion pistol of the same pattern as the pepperbox with a 4" half octagonal barrel. Marked as above. Manufactured from 1849 to 1852.

NIB	Exc.	V.G.	Good	Fair	Poor
—	—	1200	850	350	100

STOEGER, A. F./STOEGER INDUSTRIES

The first guns shown, the pistols, were imported many years ago to South Hackensack, New Jersey, but all the rest have been imported by Stoeger Industries in: Accokeek, Maryland

HANDGUNS

.22 Luger

A .22 caliber simplified copy of the German Model P.08 semi-automatic pistol with a 4.5" or 5.5" barrel and an aluminum frame. The word "Luger" is roll engraved on the right side of the frame. Blued with checkered brown plastic grips. Made by Erma.

NIB	Exc.	V.G.	Good	Fair	Poor
—	350	275	200	150	100

Target Luger

As above, with adjustable target sights. Made by Erma.

NIB	Exc.	V.G.	Good	Fair	Poor
—	375	295	225	175	125

Luger Carbine

As above, with an 11" barrel, walnut fore-end and checkered walnut grips. Furnished with a red velvet lined black leatherette case. Manufactured during the 1970s. Made by Erma.

NIB	Exc.	V.G.	Good	Fair	Poor
—	1100	775	500	350	150

American Eagle Luger

This is identical to the German design. It is chambered for the 9mm with a 7-round magazine and fitted with a 4" barrel. Checkered walnut grips. Stainless steel. Weight is about 32 oz.

NIB	Exc.	V.G.	Good	Fair	Poor
1100	975	650	450	300	100

American Eagle Navy Model

Same as above but with a 6" barrel.

NIB	Exc.	V.G.	Good	Fair	Poor
1200	1075	700	450	300	100

Cougar

Double-action semi-automatic offered in 9mm. .40 S&W or .45 ACP. Manufactured in Turkey and based on the Beretta model of the same name. Traditional DA/SA design with ambidextrous safety/decocking lever, white dot sights and Picatinny rail (.45 only). Also made in compact variation.

NIB	Exc.	V.G.	Good	Fair	Poor
425	375	325	275	200	150

Pro Series 95

Target pistol in .22 LR with 5.5" or 7.25" barrel, adjustable trigger and sights. Imported by Stoeger in 1995 and 1996. **NOTE:** Add $75 for bull barrel.

NIB	Exc.	V.G.	Good	Fair	Poor
450	400	350	300	250	150

SHOTGUNS

Model 2000

This is a semi-automatic shotgun chambered for the 12 gauge shell. Fitted with 26", 28", or 30" vent rib barrel. Single trigger with screw-in chokes. Weight is about 7 lbs. Introduced in 2001.

NIB	Exc.	V.G.	Good	Fair	Poor
500	400	300	200	150	75

Model 2000 Deluxe

Same as above but with high grade walnut stock and etched receiver with gold trigger.

NIB	Exc.	V.G.	Good	Fair	Poor
625	500	400	300	250	125

Model 2000 Camo

As above but with Advantage Timber HD camo stock.

NIB	Exc.	V.G.	Good	Fair	Poor
500	400	300	200	150	75

Model 2000 Slug

This model is chambered for the 12 gauge shell with 3" chamber. Barrel length is 24". The gun is fitted with a black synthetic stock. Smooth bore barrel. Adjustable rifle-type sights. Optional field-style barrels in 24", 26", or 28". Weight is approximately 6.7 lbs. Introduced in 2003.

NIB	Exc.	V.G.	Good	Fair	Poor
450	350	250	175	125	50

Model 2000 Synthetic

As above but choice of 24", 26", or 28" vent rib barrel and black synthetic stock. Weight is about 6.8 lbs. Introduced in 2003.

NIB	Exc.	V.G.	Good	Fair	Poor
500	400	300	200	150	75

Model 3500

This 12-gauge auto-loader comes with either a 24-, 26- or 28-inch barrel fitted with a ventilated, stepped rib and fiber-optic front sight. Inertia operation. Weight is 7.5 lbs. The alloy receiver is drilled and tapped and includes a Weaver-style scope base. All M3500s come supplied with five choke tubes (Extra-full turkey, Full, Modified, Improved Cylinder and Cylinder). A shim kit provides drop and cast adjustment. A threaded steel recoil reducer (included) can be installed in the buttstock to help manage felt recoil from heavy Magnum loads. Available in three different finishes: matte black synthetic, Realtree APG or Realtree Max-4. **NOTE:** Add 20 percent for total camo coverage.

NIB	Exc.	V.G.	Good	Fair	Poor
535	450	385	325	250	200

Coach Gun

This is a side-by-side gun chambered for the 12 or 20 gauge shell as well as the .410 shell. Fitted with 20" barrels with double triggers. Improved Cylinder and Modified fixed chokes. Weight is about 7 lbs. **NOTE:** Add $50 for nickel finish.

NIB	Exc.	V.G.	Good	Fair	Poor
400	275	225	175	125	75

Silverado Coach Gun

Offered in 12 and 20 gauge as well as .410 bore with straight- or pistol-grip stock and matte nickel finish. Straight-stock version is offered in 12 and 20 gauge only. Weight is about 6.5 lbs.

NIB	Exc.	V.G.	Good	Fair	Poor
450	320	250	175	125	75

Coach Gun Supreme

This model is similar to the above but offered with blue, stainless, or nickel receiver. Introduced in 2004. **NOTE:** Add $10 for stainless and $30 for nickel.

NIB	Exc.	V.G.	Good	Fair	Poor
450	320	250	175	125	75

Uplander

This side-by-side shotgun is chambered for the 12, 16, 20, 28, and .410 bores. with choice of 26" or 28" barrels. Fixed chokes. Double triggers. Weight is about 7.25 lbs.

NIB	Exc.	V.G.	Good	Fair	Poor
375	275	175	125	100	75

Uplander Special

As above but with straight grip and oil finish stock. Offered in 12, 20, or 28 gauge. Weight is about 7.3 lbs.

NIB	Exc.	V.G.	Good	Fair	Poor
395	300	200	150	100	75

Uplander Supreme

Same as above but with select wood and screw-in chokes.

NIB	Exc.	V.G.	Good	Fair	Poor
425	350	250	175	125	100

Uplander English

This variation is fitted with a straight-grip stock and chambered for the 20 gauge or .410 bore. Fitted with 24" barrels. Weight is about 7 lbs. Also available with a short stock.

NIB	Exc.	V.G.	Good	Fair	Poor
395	300	200	150	100	75

Uplander Youth

Offered in 20 gauge or .410 bore this model features a 13" LOP with 22" barrels choked Improved Modified and Modified. Weight is about 6.75 lbs.

NIB	Exc.	V.G.	Good	Fair	Poor
375	275	175	125	100	75

Condor

This over/under shotgun is chambered 12, 16 and 20 gauges and .410 bore. Available with 26" and 28" barrels in all gauges and 26" barrel in .410 bore. Single trigger. Blued finish. The 16-gauge is chambered for 2.75" shells. All others have 3" chambers. Weights run from 6 lbs. to 7.4 lbs. depending on bore.

NIB	Exc.	V.G.	Good	Fair	Poor
375	275	175	125	100	75

Condor Special

Similar to the standard Condor model but with matte stainless receiver and rubbed oil finish stock. Introduced in 2003.

NIB	Exc.	V.G.	Good	Fair	Poor
475	375	295	200	125	100

Condor Combo

This model, introduced in 2004, features a two-barrel set of 12 and 20 gauge. Barrel length on the 12 gauge is 28" and 26" on the 20 gauge. Choke tubes. Offered in 3 grades: Field, Special, and Supreme. Introduced in 2004.

Field

NIB	Exc.	V.G.	Good	Fair	Poor
500	400	300	200	100	75

Special

NIB	Exc.	V.G.	Good	Fair	Poor
650	500	400	275	175	125

Supreme

NIB	Exc.	V.G.	Good	Fair	Poor
775	650	500	300	200	150

Condor Supreme Deluxe

Similar to the above model but with cut checkering and high polish blue. Offered in 12 and 20 gauge with 26" or 28" barrels as well as 24" barrels for the 20 gauge. Automatic ejectors.

NIB	Exc.	V.G.	Good	Fair	Poor
500	400	300	200	100	75

Condor Competition

These 3" 12 and 20 gauge over/unders feature 30" barrels, AA Grade wood and adjustable combs. Three choke tubes. Weight is about 7.3 lbs. in 20 gauge and 7.8 lbs. in 12 gauge.

NIB	Exc.	V.G.	Good	Fair	Poor
650	500	400	275	175	125

Condor Competition Combo

As above with 12 gauge and 20 gauge barrels.

NIB	Exc.	V.G.	Good	Fair	Poor
775	650	500	300	200	150

Condor Outback

New in 2007, the Outback comes in 12 and 20 gauge chambered for 3" shells. The finish is either A Grade satin walnut stock with blued barrels and receiver or matte black walnut stock with polished barrels and receiver. Barrels are 20" with rifle sights. Includes two choke tubes. Add $40 for black/nickel finish.

NIB	Exc.	V.G.	Good	Fair	Poor
375	275	175	125	100	75

Single Barrel Classic Youth

Available in 20 gauge or .410 bore with a 13" length of pull and 22" vent rib barrel. Straight-grip stock. Weight is about 5 lbs.

NIB	Exc.	V.G.	Good	Fair	Poor
125	100	75	50	25	10

Single Barrel Classic

As above but with standard length of pull and available in 12, 20 or .410 bore. Barrel length on 12 gauge is 26" or 28"; on 20 gauge length is 26". On .410 bore barrel length is 24". Open pistol grip. Weight is about 5.5 lbs.

NIB	Exc.	V.G.	Good	Fair	Poor
125	100	75	50	25	10

Single Barrel Special

As above but with stainless steel frame. Offered in 12, 20, or .410 bore. Weight is about 5.5 lbs.

NIB	Exc.	V.G.	Good	Fair	Poor
125	100	75	50	25	10

P-350

This pump-action 12 gauge shotgun was introduced in 2005. All versions are chambered for 3.5" shells. Available with 24", 26" or 28" barrel in matte black synthetic or Advantage Timber camo finish; available with 26" or 28" barrel in Max-4 camo finish. Comes with 5 choke tubes. Weight is about 6.8 lbs. Also available is a Defense model with 18.5" barrel and fixed cylinder bore. Add 15 percent for camo models.

NIB	Exc.	V.G.	Good	Fair	Poor
275	225	175	125	100	50

P-350 Camo

This pump-action 12 gauge is chambered for 3.5" shells. It has a 24", 26" or 28" barrel and a matte black, Max-4, Timber or APG finish. There are also some pistol-grip stock offerings with 24" barrels. Includes five choke tubes. Weight is about 6.8 lbs. Add $20 for pistol-grip stock. Add $75 for camo finish.

NIB	Exc.	V.G.	Good	Fair	Poor
350	275	225	150	125	75

P-350 Defense

Same as above in a matte black finish with 18.5", fixed cylinder choke barrel. Add $20 for pistol-grip stock.

NIB	Exc.	V.G.	Good	Fair	Poor
300	225	175	125	100	50

STREET SWEEPER
Atlanta, Georgia

Street Sweeper

A 12 gauge semi-automatic double-action shotgun with an 18" barrel and 12-shot rotary, drum magazine. Matte black finish. Introduced in 1989. **NOTE:** This firearm is now on the restricted list as a Class III weapon and is subject to NFA rules. This model requires registration with the BATFE to avoid federal penalties. Make sure that the shotgun is transferable prior to sale.

NIB	Exc.	V.G.	Good	Fair	Poor
2195	—	—	—	—	—

STURDIVANT, LEWIS G.
Talladega, Alabama

Received contract from the state of Alabama for 2,000 "Mississippi" or "Enfield" rifles. Two hundred and eighty were received on this contract. These arms resemble U.S. Model 1841 Rifles without patchboxes. Overall length 48.5"; barrel length 33"; .577 caliber. Unmarked.

STURM, RUGER & CO.
Southport, Connecticut

SEMI-AUTOMATIC RIMFIRE PISTOLS

Standard Model "Red Eagle Grips"

This is a blowback semi-automatic with a fixed, exposed, 4.75" barrel. The receiver is tubular, with a round bolt. There is a 9-shot detachable magazine, and the sights are fixed. The finish is blued, and the black hard rubber grips on this first model feature a red Ruger eagle or hawk medallion on the left side. There were approximately 25,600 manufactured before Alexander Sturm's death in 1951, but this model may be seen as high as the 35000 serial number range. Because variations of this model exist an expert opinion should be sought before a final price is established. **NOTE:** Factory verified plated pistols will bring between $2,500 and $5,000 depending on condition. For pistols in factory original wood "cod box" shipping carton add $2,000.

NIB	Exc.	V.G.	Good	Fair	Poor
750	550	450	325	250	150

Standard Model

This model is identical to the Red Eagle except that after Sturm's death the grip medallions were changed from red to black and have remained so ever since. This pistol was produced from 1952-1982 in 4-3/4" and 6" barrels. There are a great many variations of this pistol, but a book dealing with this pistol alone should be consulted as the differences in variations are subtle and valuation of these variations is definitely a matter for individual appraisal.

NIB	Exc.	V.G.	Good	Fair	Poor
400	350	275	125	100	85

Standard Model—Marked "Hecho en Mexico"

These pistols were assembled and sold in Mexico. Approximately 200 were built with 4.75" barrels and about 50 were produced with 6" barrels. Only a few of these pistols have been accounted for and for this reason an expert should be consulted.

NIB	Exc.	V.G.	Good	Fair	Poor
1600	1500	1200	850	600	400

Mark I Target Model

The success of the Ruger Standard Model led quite naturally to a demand for a more accurate target model. In 1951 a pistol that utilized the same frame and receiver with a 6-7/8", target-type barrel and adjustable sights was introduced. Early target models number 15000 to 16999 and 25000 to 25300 have Red Eagle grips. In 1952 a 5-1/4" tapered barrel model was introduced, but was soon discontinued. In 1963 the popular 5-1/2" bull barrel model was introduced. These models enjoyed well deserved success and were manufactured from 1951-1982.

Red Eagle 6-7/8" barrel

NIB	Exc.	V.G.	Good	Fair	Poor
725	675	500	250	200	150

Black or Silver Eagle 6-7/8" barrel

NOTE: For original hinged box add 35 percent. With factory supplied muzzlebrake add $75-100. For other Mark I Target models under serial number 72500 in original hinged box add 50 percent.

NIB	Exc.	V.G.	Good	Fair	Poor
450	400	300	175	150	125

5-1/4" Tapered Barrel Model

NOTE: Add 50 percent if in original 5-1/4" marked hinged box.

NIB	Exc.	V.G.	Good	Fair	Poor
800	700	600	400	250	125

5-1/2" Bull Barrel Model

NIB	Exc.	V.G.	Good	Fair	Poor
425	375	275	150	125	95

Rollmarked with U.S. on Top of Frame

These pistols will have either 1/16" or 1/8" high serial numbers. **NOTE:** Add 25 percent to price if pistol has 1/8" high serial numbers.

NIB	Exc.	V.G.	Good	Fair	Poor
800	700	500	300	200	150

Stainless Steel 1 of 5,000

This model is a special commemorative version of the first standard with the "Red Eagle" grips. It is made of stainless steel and is rollmarked with Bill Ruger's signature on it. The pistol is encased in a wood "salt cod" case.

NIB	Exc.	V.G.	Good	Fair	Poor
395	350	300	225	175	125

MARK II .22 CALIBER PISTOL SPECIFICATIONS

Supplied in .22 LR with various barrel weights and lengths. Magazine capacity is 10 rounds. Trigger is grooved with curved finger surface. High speed hammer provides fast lock time. Grips are sharply checkered and made of black gloss delrin material. Stainless steel models have a brushed satin finish. Today, each

model except the MK-10 and KMK-10, comes from the factory with a lockable plastic case and Ruger lock. **NOTE:** Beginning n 2004 all Ruger adjustable sight .22 pistols were drilled and tapped for an included Weaver-type scope base adapter.

STANDARD MODEL MARK II

This is a generally improved version of the first Ruger pistol. There is a hold-open device, and the magazine holds 10 rounds. This model was introduced in 1982.

Model MK4

Blued finish with 4.75" barrel. Checkered composition grips. Weight about 35 oz.

NIB	Exc.	V.G.	Good	Fair	Poor
350	250	150	125	100	75

Model MK450

Introduced in 1999 to commemorate the 50th anniversary of the first Ruger rimfire pistol. Fitted with a 4.75" barrel with fixed sights. Chambered for the .22 LR cartridge. The pistols grips have a red Ruger medallion and Ruger crest on the barrel. Furnished in a red case. Weight is about 35 oz. Production limited to one year.

NIB	Exc.	V.G.	Good	Fair	Poor
385	350	250	175	125	75

Model MK6

Same as above but with 6" barrel. Weight 37 oz.

NIB	Exc.	V.G.	Good	Fair	Poor
350	275	225	125	100	75

Model KMK4

This model is the same as the Mark II Standard except that it is made of stainless steel.

NIB	Exc.	V.G.	Good	Fair	Poor
375	300	200	150	125	100

Model KMK6

Same as above but with 6" barrel. Weight is about 37 oz. **NOTE:** In 1997, Ruger produced 650 of the Model MK6 with special features for the "Friends of the NRA" auction of the same year. These guns have high polish blueing, faux ivory grips panels, a gold inlaid National Rifle Association inscription and a gold inlaid number of "1 of 650" to "650 of 650". The NIB price for these pistols is $550.

NIB	Exc.	V.G.	Good	Fair	Poor
375	300	200	150	125	100

Target Model

This model incorporates the same improvements as the Mark II Standard but is offered with 5.5" bull, 6-7/8" tapered and 10" heavy barrel. A 5-1/4" tapered barrel was added in 1990 but discontinued in 1994. Blued finish. This model has adjustable target sights and was introduced in 1982. **NOTE:** In 1989, approximately 2,000 5-1/2" bull barrel Mark II pistols with blue barreled receivers and stainless steel grip frames were produced by Ruger on order from a Ruger distributor. They exist in the 215-25xxx to 215-43xxx serial number range. The NIB price for these pistols is $375.

NIB	Exc.	V.G.	Good	Fair	Poor
315	275	200	150	125	100

Stainless Steel Target Model

This model is the same as the blued version but is made of stainless steel.

NIB	Exc.	V.G.	Good	Fair	Poor
350	285	250	200	175	125

Government Model

This model is similar to the blue Mark II Target, with a 6-7/8" bull barrel. It is the civilian version of a training pistol that the military is purchasing from Ruger. The only difference is that this model does not have the U.S. markings.

NIB	Exc.	V.G.	Good	Fair	Poor
450	325	225	200	150	100

Stainless Steel Government Model

Stainless steel version of the Government Model. **NOTE:** Same with U.S. markings. These are found in the serial number range of 210-00001 to 210-18600. Only a couple dozen are in civilian hands. The NIB price for these pistols is $1,000.00.

NIB	Exc.	V.G.	Good	Fair	Poor
475	350	250	225	175	125

Competition Model KMK678GC

The Competition model features a stainless steel frame with checkered laminated hardwood thumb rest grips, heavy 6-7/8" bull barrel factory drilled and tapped for scope mount, Partridge type front sight undercut to prevent glare and an adjustable rear sight. Pistol weighs 45 oz. **NOTE:** In 1997 Ruger produced 204 of these pistols in blue instead of stainless steel for one of their distributors. They are very scarce. The NIB for these pistols is $350. In 1995 Ruger produced a similar blued pistol (1,000 total, 500 each with or without scope rings) with 5-1/2" slab side barrels. These are not marked "Competition Target Model" like the previously described variation. The NIB price for these pistols was $350 and with rings $375.

NIB	Exc.	V.G.	Good	Fair	Poor
400	325	275	200	125	100

Bull Barrel Model MK4B

Introduced in 1996 this bull barrel variation has a blued finish with a 4" barrel. Grips are checkered composition. Weight is about 38 oz.

NIB	Exc.	V.G.	Good	Fair	Poor
400	325	275	200	125	100

RUGER 22/45 MODEL

This .22 LR caliber pistol has the same grip angle and magazine latch as the Model 1911 .45 ACP. The semi-automatic action is stainless steel and the grip frame is made from Zytel, a fiberglass reinforced lightweight composite material. Front sight is Patridge-type. This model is available in several different configurations. A 4" tapered barrel and standard model sights, a 5.25" tapered barrel with target sights, or a 5.5" bull barrel with target sights. The 5.25" barrel was discontinued in 1994.

KP4

This model features a 4.75" standard weight barrel with fixed sights. Pistol weighs 28 oz.

NIB	Exc.	V.G.	Good	Fair	Poor
300	275	250	200	125	75

KP514

Furnished with a target tapered barrel 5.25" in length. Comes with adjustable sights. Pistol weighs 38 oz. Model now discontinued.

NIB	Exc.	V.G.	Good	Fair	Poor
300	200	175	150	100	75

KP512

This model is equipped with a 5.5" bull barrel with adjustable sights. Weighs 42 oz. **NOTE:** In 1995 Ruger produced 500 22/45s with stainless steel 6-7/8" Government type barreled receivers for one of their distributors. They appear around the 220-59xxx serial number range. The NIB price for these pistols is $350.00. In 1997 another Ruger distributor succeeded in contracting Ruger to make a similar 22/45 only in blue and with 6-7/8" slab side bull barrels. Approximately 1,000 were produced with serial numbers extending to the 220-87xxx serial number range. The NIB price is $300.00.

NIB	Exc.	V.G.	Good	Fair	Poor
300	200	175	150	100	75

P4

A limited number, about 1,000, of this variation were produced in 1995 with a 4" bull barrel on a P frame. It was introduced into the product line as a production pistol in 1997. Weight is approximately 31 oz.

NIB	Exc.	V.G.	Good	Fair	Poor
350	200	150	100	75	50

22/45 Threaded Barrel

Variation of Model 22/45 with muzzle threaded to accept various accessories. Muzzle is capped to protect threads, receiver and barrel drilled and tapped to accept accessory rails. Weight is 32 ounces; 4.5-inch barrel with blue finish.

NIB	Exc.	V.G.	Good	Fair	Poor
375	325	285	200	135	100

P512

This variation of the stainless steel version has a blued receiver with P-style frame.

NIB	Exc.	V.G.	Good	Fair	Poor
350	250	150	100	75	60

MARK III .22 CALIBER PISTOL SPECIFICATIONS

The Mark III series was introduced in 2004. This series features a newly designed magazine release button located on the left side of the frame. Mark III pistols also have a visible loaded chamber indicator, an internal lock, magazine disconnect, re-contontured sights and ejection port.

Standard Pistol

Introduced in 2005 this .22 caliber pistol is fitted with a 4.75" or 6" barrel. Fixed rear sight. Blued finish. Magazine capacity is 10 rounds. Black checkered grips. Weight is about 35 oz. depending on barrel length.

NIB	Exc.	V.G.	Good	Fair	Poor
300	250	185	150	100	75

Hunter

This .22 caliber pistol is fitted with a 6.88" target crowned fluted stainless steel barrel. Adjustable rear sight with Hi-Viz front sight. Checkered Cocobolo grips. Drilled and tapped for scope mount. Supplied with green case, scope base adapter, and 6 interchangeable LitePipes for front sight. Weight is about 41 oz. Introduced in 2005. Add 50 percent for Crimson Trace lasergrips (limited edition for 2008).

NIB	Exc.	V.G.	Good	Fair	Poor
350	275	225	175	125	75

Competition

This .22 caliber model features a 6.88" flat sided heavy barrel with adjustable rear sight and Patridge front sight. Stainless steel finish. Checkered wood grips. Weight is about 45 oz. Introduced in 2005.

NIB	Exc.	V.G.	Good	Fair	Poor
425	315	245	200	150	75

Mark III 22/45 Standard Pistol

This .22 caliber pistol has a grip frame similar to the Colt 1911 pistol. The 4" bull barrel is flat sided. Blued steel frame. Fixed sights. Magazine capacity is 10 rounds. Grips are checkered black polymer. Weight is about 29 oz.

NIB	Exc.	V.G.	Good	Fair	Poor
300	225	175	125	100	75

Mark III 22/45 Stainless

Similar to above but with stainless barrel and receiver.

NIB	Exc.	V.G.	Good	Fair	Poor
425	375	325	250	175	125

Mark III 512 Pistol

This .22 LR pistol has a 5.5" bull barrel and adjustable rear sight. Steel frame is blued. Checkered black synthetic grips. Weaver-style scope base adapter included. Magazine capacity is 10 rounds. Weight is about 41 oz.

Ruger® Mark III Pistol
MKIII512

NIB	Exc.	V.G.	Good	Fair	Poor
350	300	225	175	125	100

Mark III 22/45 Hunter

Similar to 22/45 .22 pistol but with Mark III-style improvements. 6-7/8" or 4-1/2" fluted barrel, HiViz front sight with six interchangeable inserts. Blued or stainless finish. Pricing is for stainless model. Introduced in 2007.

NIB	Exc.	V.G.	Good	Fair	Poor
465	395	300	225	150	100

Mark III 22/45RP Pistol

Semiauto pistol chambered in .22 LR. Features include polymer frame with grip panels that recreate feel of 1911; 1911-style controls including magazine button, manual safety, and bolt stop locations as the classic 1911 pistol; slim polymer grip frame with serrated front strap and checkered back strap; blued alloy steel 5.5-inch bull barrel with a fixed front sight and micro-adjustable rear sight; adjustable sights, drilled/tapped for Weaver mounts. MSRP: $380.

Charger

Introduced in 2008. A 10-inch-barrel pistol version of the 10/22 .22 LR rifle. Black matte finish, black laminated stock (other colors available), bipod, and Weaver-style mounts. Includes one 10-round magazine.

NIB	Exc.	V.G.	Good	Fair	Poor
375	300	225	175	125	100

OLD MODEL SINGLE-ACTION REVOLVERS (PRE-TRANSFER BAR)

Single Six Revolver

This is a .22 rimfire, 6-shot, single-action revolver. It was first offered with a 5-1/2" barrel length and a fixed sight. In 1959 additional barrel lengths were offered for this model in 4-5/8", 6-1/2", and 9-1/2". It is based in appearance on the Colt Single-Action Army, but internally it is a new design that features coil springs instead of the old-style, flat leaf springs. It also features a floating firing pin and is generally a stronger action than what was previously available. The early model had a flat loading gate and was made this way from 1953-1957, when the contoured gate became standard. Early models had checkered hard rubber grips changed to smooth varnished walnut by 1962. Black eagle grip medallions were used from the beginning of production to 1971 when a silver eagle grip medallion replaced it. No "Red Eagle" single-sixes were ever produced. This model was manufactured from 1953-1972.

Flat Gate Model

60,000 produced.

NOTE 1: Be aware that revolvers serial numbered under 2000 will bring a premium of 25 percent to 125 percent depending on condition, low serial number, and color of cylinder frame—bright reddish purple the most desirable.

NOTE 2: Values cited below are for unconverted examples and for converted examples with original parts present.

Courtesy John C. Dougan

NIB	Exc.	V.G.	Good	Fair	Poor
900	700	500	450	225	150

Contoured Gate Model

Introduced 1957. There were 258 5.5" barrel factory engraved pistols in this model. Add a 25 percent premium for 3-screw models. **NOTE:** Be aware that 4-5/8" and 9.5" barrel lengths will bring a premium. Add $3,500 to $6,000 for factory engraved and cased models.

NIB	Exc.	V.G.	Good	Fair	Poor
700	600	500	350	200	125

Single Six Convertible

This model is similar to the Single Six but is furnished with an extra .22 rimfire Magnum cylinder. **NOTE:** Barrel lengths in 4-5/8" and 9.5" will bring a premium.

NIB	Exc.	V.G.	Good	Fair	Poor
650	550	450	375	225	150

Single Six .22 Magnum Model

This model is similar to the Single Six except that it is chambered for the .22 rimfire Magnum and the frame was so marked. It was offered in the 6.5" barrel length only and was manufactured for three years. An extra long rifle cylinder was added later in production. The serial numbers are in the 300000-340000 range.

NIB	Exc.	V.G.	Good	Fair	Poor
600	500	400	350	200	125

Lightweight Single Six

This model is similar to the Single Six, with an aluminum alloy frame and 4-5/8" barrel. This variation was produced between 1956 and 1958 and was in the 200000-212000 serial number range.

Approximately the first 6,500 were produced with alloy cylinders with steel chamber inserts. **NOTE:** Stamped after the serial number or on the bottom of the frame. Varieties of "S" marked lightweights exist. Individual evaluation and appraisal is recommended. These are factory seconds and are verifiable. **NOTE:** For original Lightweight Single-Six boxes add 25 percent to 40 percent.

Courtesy Know Your Ruger Single-Action Revolvers 1953-63
Blacksmith Corp.

Courtesy Know Your Ruger Single-Action Revolvers 1953-63
Blacksmith Corp.

Silver Anodized Frame with Aluminum Cylinder Model with Martin Hardcoat Finish

NIB	Exc.	V.G.	Good	Fair	Poor
850	775	550	400	225	195

Black Anodized Aluminum Frame and Cylinder Model

NIB	Exc.	V.G.	Good	Fair	Poor
950	850	600	500	300	250

Black Anodized Frame with Blue Steel Cylinder Model

NIB	Exc.	V.G.	Good	Fair	Poor
650	550	450	350	225	195

Silver Anodized with Blue Steel Cylinder Model

Only a few hundred pistols in this variation were produced by the factory with an "S" suffix.

NIB	Exc.	V.G.	Good	Fair	Poor
1200	1100	850	600	400	200

Super Single Six

Introduced in 1964, this is the Single Six with adjustable sights. Prices listed are for pistols with 5.5" and 6.5" barrels. **NOTE:** The listed models are factory verifiable.

Courtesy Know Your Ruger Single-Actions: The Second Decade.
Blacksmith Corp.

NIB	Exc.	V.G.	Good	Fair	Poor
600	500	400	350	200	125

4-5/8" Barrel

200 built.

NIB	Exc.	V.G.	Good	Fair	Poor
1200	1100	900	750	400	200

Nickel-Plated Model

Approximately 100 built.

NIB	Exc.	V.G.	Good	Fair	Poor
2350	1900	1600	1200	600	300

Bearcat (Old Model)

This is a scaled-down version of the single-action. It is chambered for .22 rimfire and has a 4" barrel and an unfluted, roll engraved cylinder. The frame is alloy, and it has a brass colored anodized alloy trigger guard. The finish is blue and the grips are plastic impregnated wood until 1963, thereafter, walnut with eagle medallions were used. This model was manufactured from 1958-1970.

Courtesy Know Your Ruger Single-Actions: The Second Decade.
Blacksmith Corp.

Serial Number under 30000

NIB	Exc.	V.G.	Good	Fair	Poor
575	500	350	225	150	125

Alphabet Model

NIB	Exc.	V.G.	Good	Fair	Poor
575	500	400	295	275	225

Black Anodized Trigger Guard Model

109 built.

NIB	Exc.	V.G.	Good	Fair	Poor
800	700	600	500	400	—

Serial Number over 30000 or with 90-prefix

NIB	Exc.	V.G.	Good	Fair	Poor
450	350	300	265	225	175

Super Bearcat (Old Model)

This model is similar to the with a steel frame and, on later models, a blued steel trigger guard and grip frame. The early examples still used brass. This model was manufactured from 1971 to 1974.

Courtesy W.P. Hallstein III and son Chip

NIB	Exc.	V.G.	Good	Fair	Poor
575	500	395	275	225	175

Flattop—.357 Magnum

The success of the Single Six led to the production of a larger version chambered for the .357 Magnum cartridge. This model is a single-action, with a 6-shot fluted cylinder and a flat top strap with adjustable "Micro sight." The barrel length is 4-5/8", 6.5", and 10". The finish is blue with checkered hard rubber grips on the early examples and smooth walnut on later ones. There were approximately 42,600 manufactured between 1955 and 1962.

Courtesy Know Your Ruger Single-Action Revolvers 1953-63.
Blacksmith Corp.

4-5/8" Barrel

NIB	Exc.	V.G.	Good	Fair	Poor
1200	1000	600	350	250	200

6-1/2" Barrel

NIB	Exc.	V.G.	Good	Fair	Poor
1000	850	600	450	350	250

10" Barrel

NIB	Exc.	V.G.	Good	Fair	Poor
2800	2500	1000	850	750	600

Blackhawk Flattop .44 Magnum

In 1956 the .44 Magnum was introduced, and Ruger jumped on the bandwagon. This is similar in appearance to the .357 but has a slightly heavier frame and a larger cylinder. It was available in a 6.5", 7.5", and 10" barrel. It was manufactured from 1956-1963. There were approximately 29,700 manufactured.

Courtesy Know Your Ruger Single-Action Revolvers 1953-63.
Blacksmith Corp.

6-1/2" Barrel

NIB	Exc.	V.G.	Good	Fair	Poor
1250	800	600	450	350	250

7-1/2" Barrel

NIB	Exc.	V.G.	Good	Fair	Poor
1325	950	700	600	450	300

10" Barrel

NIB	Exc.	V.G.	Good	Fair	Poor
3000	2000	1200	800	700	400

Blackhawk

This model is similar to the "Flattop," but the rear sight is protected by two raised protrusions—one on each side. It was available chambered for the .30 Carbine, .357 Magnum, .41 Magnum, or the .45 Colt cartridge. Barrel lengths are 4-5/8" or 6.5" in .357 Magnum and .41 Magnum. .45 Colt version has 4-5/8" and 7.5" barrel lengths. The .30 Carbine is furnished with a 7.5" barrel only. The finish is blue, and the grips are walnut with Ruger medallions. This model was produced from 1962 to 1972. Note that the "Old Style" Blackhawk (i.e., pre-transfer bar) is a popular platform for custom revolvers, so prices may exceed those shown depending on circumstances. **NOTE:** Add 20 percent for .41 Mag. and 50 percent for .45 Colt and 35 percent for .30 Carbine. Original verified factory brass grip frame will add at least $800 to above prices. It was available chambered for the .357 Magnum or .41 Magnum (4-5/8" or 6-1/2" barrel), or .45 Colt (4-5/8" or 7-1/2" barrel). The .41 Magnum with factory installed brass frame will bring $1000 to $2500 depending on condition.

Courtesy Know Your Ruger Single-Action Revolvers 1953-63.
Blacksmith Corp.

NIB	Exc.	V.G.	Good	Fair	Poor
700	500	350	200	150	125

Blackhawk Convertible

This model is the same as the Blackhawk with an extra cylinder to change or convert calibers. The .357 Magnum has a 9mm cylinder, and the .45 Colt has a .45 ACP cylinder. **NOTE:** The 4-5/8" barrel will bring a slight premium. Nonprefix serial numbered .357/9mm Blackhawks will bring a premium.

.357/9mm

NIB	Exc.	V.G.	Good	Fair	Poor
650	550	450	300	200	150

.45 L.C./.45 ACP

NIB	Exc.	V.G.	Good	Fair	Poor
1000	800	500	250	175	125

Super Blackhawk Old Model

The formidable recoil of the .44 Magnum cartridge was difficult to handle in a revolver with a small grip such as found on the Blackhawk, so it was decided to produce a larger-framed revolver with increased size in the grip. The rear of the trigger guard was squared off, and the cylinder was left unfluted to increase mass. This model was offered with a 7.5" barrel; 600 6.5" barrel Super Blackhawks were produced by factory error. This model is blued and has smooth walnut grips with medallions. The first of these revolvers were offered in a fitted wood case and are rare today. The Super Blackhawk was made from 1959-1972. **NOTE:** For pistols with verified factory installed brass grip frame each example should be appraised. For pistols with brass grip frames add $250 to the prices listed.

NIB	Exc.	V.G.	Good	Fair	Poor
800	600	400	300	200	150

Early Model in Wood Presentation Case

Courtesy Know Your Ruger Single-Action Revolvers 1953-63. Blacksmith Corp.

Super Blackhawk in scarce mahogany case, serial numbers 1-8500

NIB	Exc.	V.G.	Good	Fair	Poor
1200	1000	750	475	400	300

In Fitted White Cardboard Case

NIB	Exc.	V.G.	Good	Fair	Poor
1800	1600	1000	950	875	675

Long Grip Frame in Wood Case

300 guns built.

NIB	Exc.	V.G.	Good	Fair	Poor
2000	1800	1150	1050	800	675

Factory Verified 6-1/2" Barrel

Approximately 600 guns built in the 23000-25000 serial number range.

NIB	Exc.	V.G.	Good	Fair	Poor
1500	1300	950	700	450	375

Hawkeye Single-Shot

The shooting public wanted a small-caliber, high-velocity handgun. The Smith & Wesson Model 53, chambered for the .22 Jet, appeared in 1961; and the cartridge created extraction problems for a revolver. Ruger solved the problem with the introduction of the Hawkeye—a single-shot that looked like a six shooter. In place of the cylinder was a breech block that cammed to the side for loading. This pistol was excellent from an engineering and performance standpoint but was not a commercial success. The Hawkeye is chambered for the .256 Magnum, a bottleneck cartridge, and has an 8.5" barrel and adjustable sights. The finish is blued with walnut, medallion grips. The barrel is tapped at the factory for a 1" scope base. This pistol is quite rare as only 3,300 were produced in 1963 and 1964.

Courtesy John C. Dougan

NIB	Exc.	V.G.	Good	Fair	Poor
2500	1900	1400	850	600	500

EDITOR'S COMMENT: All of the above single-action Ruger pistols fitted with factory optional grips will bring a premium regardless of model. This premium applies to pistols manufactured from 1954 to 1962 only. For the optional grips the premium is: Ivory $800, Stag $400.

NEW MODEL SERIES

The Ruger firm in 1973 completely modified their single-action lockwork to accommodate a hammer block or transfer bar. This hammer block or transfer bar prevented accidental discharge should a revolver be dropped. In doing so, the company circumvented a great deal of potential legal problems and made collectibles out of the previous models.

Super Single Six Convertible (New Model)

This model is similar in appearance to the old model but has the new hammer block safety system. The frame has two pins instead of three screws, and opening the loading gate frees the cylinder stop for loading. Barrel lengths are 4-5/8", 5.5", 6.5", and 9.5". The sights are adjustable; the finish is blued. The grips are walnut with a medallion, and an interchangeable .22 Magnum cylinder is supplied. This model was introduced in 1973 and is currently in production.

NIB	Exc.	V.G.	Good	Fair	Poor
450	350	250	200	175	125

Stainless Steel Single Six Convertible

The same as the standard blued model but made from stainless steel. Offered with a 4-5/8", 6-1/2", and 9-1/2" barrel. **NOTE:** Pre-warning pistols (1973-1976) with 4-5/8" or 9-1/2" barrel will bring an additional 40 percent premium. Pistols with 4-5/8" barrels with "made in the 200th year of American Liberty" rollmark on the barrel will bring at least 100 percent premium to the NIB prices.

NIB	Exc.	V.G.	Good	Fair	Poor
475	400	300	250	225	175

New Model Single Six (.22 LR only) "Star" Model

This model was produced in blue and stainless for one year only in 4-5/8", 5-1/2", 6-1/2", and 9-1/2" barrel lengths. Very low production on this model.

Blue Variation 5.5" or 6.5" Barrel

NIB	Exc.	V.G.	Good	Fair	Poor
450	400	350	300	275	200

9.5" Barrel—Rare

NIB	Exc.	V.G.	Good	Fair	Poor
550	500	450	400	350	250

4.62" Barrel—Very Rare

NIB	Exc.	V.G.	Good	Fair	Poor
800	750	450	400	350	250

Stainless Variation 5.5" or 6.5" Barrel

NIB	Exc.	V.G.	Good	Fair	Poor
450	350	275	225	175	150

9.5" Barrel

NIB	Exc.	V.G.	Good	Fair	Poor
600	500	400	300	225	175

4.62" Barrel—Rare

NIB	Exc.	V.G.	Good	Fair	Poor
650	550	500	400	300	200

Fixed Sight New Model Single Six

First made as drift adjustable rear sight (500 each in 4-5/8", 5-1/2", and 6-1/2" blue) and now a catalogued item as a pinched frame style fixed rear sight. Barrel lengths are offered in 5-1/2" and 6-1/2" lengths. Finish is blued or glossy stainless steel. Rear sight is fixed. Weights are between 32 and 38 oz. depending on barrel length and cylinder.

Blued Finish

NIB	Exc.	V.G.	Good	Fair	Poor
325	295	250	165	125	100

Stainless Steel

NIB	Exc.	V.G.	Good	Fair	Poor
395	300	250	200	150	125

Colorado Centennial Single Six

This model had a stainless steel grip frame, and the balance is blued. It has walnut grips with medallion insert. The barrel is 6-1/2", and the revolver is furnished with a walnut case with a centennial medal insert. There were 15,000 manufactured in 1975.

NIB	Exc.	V.G.	Good	Fair	Poor
500	400	300	200	125	100

Model "SSM" Single Six

This is the Single Six chambered for the .32 H&R Magnum cartridge. The first 800 pistols were marked with "SSM" on the cylinder frame and will bring a slight premium. Sold from 1984 to 1997. Adjustable sights.

NIB	Exc.	V.G.	Good	Fair	Poor
700	525	375	225	150	125

New Model Single Six Fixed Sight

Introduced in 2000 this revolver is chambered for the .32 H&R Magnum cartridge and fitted with a 4.625" barrel. Offered in blue or stainless steel. Short (1/4" shorter) simulated ivory grips. Vaquero-style frame with fixed sights. **NOTE:** Values shown are for stainless. Deduct 25 percent for blued.

NIB	Exc.	V.G.	Good	Fair	Poor
525	400	300	225	175	125

New Model Single Six 50th Anniversary Model

Introduced in 2003 this model features a 4.625" barrel with blued finish. Top of barrel is rollmarked "50 years of single six 1953-2003". Comes standard with both .22 LR and .22 WMR cylinders. Cocobolo grips with red Ruger medallion. Packaged in a red plastic case with special "50 Year" label. Offered only in 2003.

NIB	Exc.	V.G.	Good	Fair	Poor
425	350	300	225	175	125

New Model Super Single Six

Chambered for the .22 LR and a separate cylinder for the .22 WMR cartridge. Barrel lengths are 4.625", 5.5", 6.5", and 9.5". Rosewood grips and adjustable or fixed sights. Blued finish except for optional stainless steel on 5.5" or 6.5" revolvers. Weight is about 35 oz. depending on barrel length. **NOTE:** For stainless steel models add $80.

NIB	Exc.	V.G.	Good	Fair	Poor
375	325	275	225	175	125

New Model Super Single Six, .17 HMR

As above but with 6.5" barrel and chambered for the .17 HMR cartridge. Weight is about 35 oz. Introduced in 2003.

NIB	Exc.	V.G.	Good	Fair	Poor
400	350	275	225	175	125

New Model Single Six Hunter Convertible

This model is chambered for the .17 HMR/.17 Mach 2. Fitted with a 7.5" barrel with adjustable rear sight. Stainless steel finish with black laminate grips. The integral barrel rib machined for scope rings. Weight is about 45 oz. Introduced in 2005.

NIB	Exc.	V.G.	Good	Fair	Poor
675	500	500	300	250	175

Single-Ten

A 10-shot version of the Single-Six with a 5.5-inch barrel and walnut Gunfighter grips. Other features include a satin stainless finish and Williams adjustable fiber optic sights. Introduced in late 2011.

NIB	Exc.	V.G.	Good	Fair	Poor
525	450	385	300	220	150

Buckeye Special

This model was built in 1989 and 1990. It is chambered for the .38-40 or 10mm and .32-20 or .32 H&R cartridges.

NIB	Exc.	V.G.	Good	Fair	Poor
750	600	400	275	200	125

New Model Blackhawk

This model is similar in appearance to the old model Blackhawk, offered in the same calibers and barrel lengths. It has the transfer bar safety device. It was introduced in 1973 and is no longerin production.

NIB	Exc.	V.G.	Good	Fair	Poor
550	425	300	200	150	125

50th Anniversary New Model Blackhawk NVB34-50

Introduced in 2005 this model features a smaller, original size XR-3 grip and smaller main frame with checkered hard rubber grips. Adjustable rear sight. Special commemorative gold roll mark on top of barrel. Chambered for the .357 Mag and fitted with a 4.625" barrel. Weight is about 45 oz. All Blackhawk revolvers now feature this new/old smaller main frame.

NIB	Exc.	V.G.	Good	Fair	Poor
575	425	300	200	150	125

New Model Blackhawk

Similar to above but without the fancy trimmings. Chambered in .327, .357, .44 Special, and .45 L.C. Weight is about 45 oz.

NIB	Exc.	V.G.	Good	Fair	Poor
575	425	300	200	150	125

Stainless Steel Blackhawk (New Model)

This is simply the New Model Blackhawk made from stainless steel. To date it has been offered in .357, .44, and .45 L.C. calibers.

NIB	Exc.	V.G.	Good	Fair	Poor
400	325	275	225	175	150

Blackhawk Convertible (New Model)

This model is the same as the Blackhawk with interchangeable conversion cylinders—.357 Magnum/9mm and .45 Colt/.45 ACP. Prices listed are for blued model.

NIB	Exc.	V.G.	Good	Fair	Poor
465	350	250	175	150	125

.45 ACP & .45 Long Colt Convertible (1998)

NIB	Exc.	V.G.	Good	Fair	Poor
550	450	350	275	225	150

Stainless Model .357/9mm

300 guns built.

NIB	Exc.	V.G.	Good	Fair	Poor
925	700	600	500	375	250

Fiftieth Anniversary .44 Magnum Flattop New Model Blackhawk

Six-shot, single-action .44 Magnum (also accepts .44 Special) with 6.5" barrel and adjustable rear sight, 47 oz. Recreation of original .44 Falt-Top Blackhawk. Blued with checkered rubber grips. Gold, color-filled rollmark on top of barrel. Introduced 2006.

NIB	Exc.	V.G.	Good	Fair	Poor
525	400	300	225	175	150

Model SRM Blackhawk .357 Maximum

This is the New Model Blackhawk with a 7.5" or 10.5" barrel. It was chambered for the .357 Maximum and was intended for silhouette shooting. This model experienced problems with gas erosion in the forcing cone and under the top strap and was removed from production in 1984 after approximately 9200 were manufactured.

NIB	Exc.	V.G.	Good	Fair	Poor
—	675	575	400	275	250

Super Blackhawk (New Model)

This model is similar in appearance to the Old Model but has the transfer bar safety device. It was manufactured from 1973 to the present and commenced at serial number 81-00001.

NIB	Exc.	V.G.	Good	Fair	Poor
425	350	275	225	175	125

Super Blackhawk Stainless Steel

This model is the same as the blued version but is made of stainless steel. In 1998 this model was offered in 4-5/8" or 7-1/2" barrels with hunter grip frame and laminated grip panels. **NOTE:** Add $50 to prices for hunter grip frame and laminated grip panels.

NIB	Exc.	V.G.	Good	Fair	Poor
450	400	300	250	200	150

Super Blackhawk Hunter

Introduced in 2002 this .44 or .41 Magnum model features a 7.5" barrel with integral full-length solid rib for scope mounts. Stainless steel. Adjustable rear sight. Scope rings included. Weight is about 52 oz.

NIB	Exc.	V.G.	Good	Fair	Poor
675	575	485	400	300	175

50th Anniversary Matched Set .357 and .44 Magnum

Matched pair of Ruger New Blackhawks, one in .44 and the other in .357, commemorating 50th anniversary of Ruger Blackhawk revolver. Gold-filled rollmarked 6-1/2" and 4-5/8" barrels, respectively. Includes presentation case. Production limited. Introduced 2007.

NIB	Exc.	V.G.	Good	Fair	Poor
1350	1150	900	775	600	400

Bisley Model

This model has the modified features found on the famous old Colt Bisley Target model—the flat top frame, fixed or adjustable sights, and the longer grip frame that has become the Bisley trademark. The Bisley is available chambered for .22 LR, .32 H&R Magnum, .357 Magnum, .41 Magnum, .44 Magnum, and .45 Long Colt. The barrel lengths are 6.5" and 7.5"; cylinders are either fluted or unfluted and roll engraved. The finish is a satin blue, and the grips are smooth Goncalo Alves with medallions. The Bisley was introduced in 1986. **NOTE:** Approximately 750 stainless grip frame .22 caliber Bisleys were made. These will demand a premium. Add $100 for stainless and $125 for convertible stainlesss.

.22 LR and .32 H&R Magnum

NOTE: Add $100 for .32 Magnum Bisley.

NIB	Exc.	V.G.	Good	Fair	Poor
425	375	225	200	150	125

.357 Magnum, .41 Magnum, .44 Magnum, and .45 Long Colt

NIB	Exc.	V.G.	Good	Fair	Poor
450	365	275	250	200	175

Shootists Bisley

Produced in 1994 for the Shootist organization in memory of Tom Ruger. Chambered for the .22 cartridge these revolvers were limited to 52 total produced. They were stainless steel and were fitted with 4-5/8" barrels. The barrels were marked, "IN MEMORY OF OUR FRIEND TOM RUGER THE SHOOTIST 1994". Some of these revolvers, but not all, have the name of the owner engraved on the backstrap. **Value Speculative.**

Courtesy Jim Taylor

Old Army Percussion Revolver

This model is a .45 caliber percussion revolver with a 5" or 7-1/2" barrel. It has a 6-shot cylinder, with a blued finish and walnut grips. Beginning in 1994 this model was offered with fixed sights. Weight is about 46 oz. Add 20 percent for 5.5-inch model. All models now discontinued. **NOTE:** For pistols with original factory installed brass grip frame add $150 to prices listed.

NIB	Exc.	V.G.	Good	Fair	Poor
575	475	375	250	175	150

Old Army Stainless Steel

This model is the same as the blued version except that it is made of stainless steel. Add 200 percent for stainless 200th Year model.

NIB	Exc.	V.G.	Good	Fair	Poor
650	525	400	275	225	150

Ruger Vaquero

This single-action pistol was introduced in 1993 and was voted handgun of the year by the shooting industry. It is a fixed sight version of the New Model Blackhawk. It is available in stainless steel or blued with case-colored frame. Offered in three different barrel lengths: 4.62", 5.5", and 7.5". Chambered for the .45 Long Colt. In 1994 the .44-40 and .44 Magnum calibers were added to the Vaquero line. Capacity is 6 rounds. Weighs between 39 and 41 oz. depending on barrel length. Discontinued; superseded by New Vaquero. **NOTE:** Vaqueros with 4-5/8" barrel chambered for .44 Magnum in both blue and stainless are uncatalogued, add 25 percent.

NIB	Exc.	V.G.	Good	Fair	Poor
500	425	325	200	150	100

Ruger Bisley Vaquero

Introduced in 1997 this model features a 5.5" barrel chambered for .44 Magnum or .45 Long Colt. Grips are smooth rosewood. Finish is blued with case colored frame. Blade front sight and notch rear. Weight is about 40 oz. Discontinued.

NIB	Exc.	V.G.	Good	Fair	Poor
500	425	325	200	150	100

Ruger Vaquero Bird's-head

Introduced in 2001 this model features a bird's-head grip. Chambered for the .45 Long Colt cartridge and fitted with a 5.5" barrel. Offered in stainless steel and blued finish. Weight is about 40 oz. Discontinued. **NOTE:** In 2002 this model was offered with 3.75" barrel and black Micarta grips. In 2003 this model was offered chambered for the .357 Magnum cartridge. Simulated ivory grips are also offered.

NIB	Exc.	V.G.	Good	Fair	Poor
650	550	400	300	175	125

"Cowboy Pair"

Matched pair of engraved and consecutively serial-numbered New Vaquero revolvers in .45 Colt. Includes lined wood collector case. Production limited to 500 sets. Introduced 2007.

NIB	Exc.	V.G.	Good	Fair	Poor
3500	3000	2500	1350	1000	600

Ruger New Vaquero ("Small Frame")

Introduced in 2005 this model features a slimmer pre-1962 XR-3 style grip frame with color case finish. The cylinder frame is mid-size. The cylinder is beveled. The ejector rod head is crescent shaped. Chambered for the .357 Mag or .45 Colt. Barrel lengths are 4.625", 5.5", and 7.5" (not in .357). Choice of case colored finish or stainless steel. Black checkered grips. Weight is about 37 oz depending on barrel length.

NIB	Exc.	V.G.	Good	Fair	Poor
575	475	400	300	200	100

Ruger New Model Bisley Vaquero

Similar to New Vaquero but with Bisley-style hammer and grip frame. Chambered in .357 and .45 Colt. Features include a 5.5" barrel, simulated ivory grips, fixed sights, six-shot cylinder. Overall length 11.12". Weight: 45 oz. Add 15 percent for stainless steel finish.

NIB	Exc.	V.G.	Good	Fair	Poor
565	425	325	225	165	150

New Ruger Bearcat (Super Bearcat)

This old favorite was reintroduced in 1994. This new version is furnished with a .22 LR cylinder and a .22 WMR cylinder. Barrel length is 4" with fixed sights. Grips are walnut. Offered with blued finish. **NOTE:** There was a factory recall on the magnum cylinders. Bearcats with both cylinders are very rare.

Blue

NIB	Exc.	V.G.	Good	Fair	Poor
425	325	250	175	125	100

Stainless Steel

NIB	Exc.	V.G.	Good	Fair	Poor
450	350	275	200	150	125

Convertible (Recalled)

NIB	Exc.	V.G.	Good	Fair	Poor
1100	1000	900	650	400	200

New Model Super Bearcat

Reintroduced in 2002 this .22 caliber model features a stainless steel or blued finish, 4" barrel with fixed sights and rosewood grips. Weight is about 24 oz. **NOTE:** Add $50 for stainless steel version.

NIB	Exc.	V.G.	Good	Fair	Poor
425	325	250	175	125	100

Fiftieth Anniversary New Bearcat

Gussied-up version of the New Bearcat (.22 LR only) commemorating the 50th anniversary of the original Bearcat.

Blued finish with gold-filled anniversary script, gold-colored trigger guard and special box with anniversary booklet. Manufactured in 2008 only.

NIB	Exc.	V.G.	Good	Fair	Poor
700	600	500	—	—	—

DOUBLE-ACTION REVOLVERS

Security Six

This revolver, also known as the Model 117, is chambered for the .357 Magnum cartridge and has a 2.75", 4", or 6" barrel. It features adjustable sights, with blue or stainless finish and a square butt, with checkered walnut grips. It was manufactured between 1970 and 1985. Early guns with fixed sights and square butt were also marked "Security-Six". The model was later termed "Service-Six" and was so marked. The prices listed are only for the adjustable sight and square butt "Security-Six" models. **NOTE:** Fixed sight guns marked Security-Six and round butt Security-Sixes with adjustable sights are worth a premium.

NIB	Exc.	V.G.	Good	Fair	Poor
450	400	350	295	200	150

Speed Six

This model is known as the Model 207, chambered for .357 Magnum; Model 208, chambered for .38 Special; and Model 209, chambered for 9mm. It has a 2.75" or 4" barrel, fixed sights, and a round butt with checkered walnut grips and was blued. There are some with factory bobbed hammers. This model was introduced in 1973. Discontinued. Add 200 percent for military (lanyard ring) and .38 S&W (not .38 Special) marked models.

NIB	Exc.	V.G.	Good	Fair	Poor
400	350	300	250	200	150

Models 737, 738, 739

These are the designations for the stainless steel versions of the Speed-Six. They are the same revolver except for the material used in the manufacture. **NOTE:** Add $150 for 739.

NIB	Exc.	V.G.	Good	Fair	Poor
500	425	350	300	225	125

GP-100

This model is chambered for the .327 Federal or .357 Magnum/.38 Special. It is available with fixed or adjustable sights in barrel lengths of 3", 4", or 6" barrel and has a frame designed for constant use of heavy magnum loads. The rear sight has a white outline, and the front sight features interchangeable colored inserts. The finish is blued, and the grips are a new design made of rubber with smooth Goncalo Alves inserts. This model was introduced in 1986. Discontinued.

NIB	Exc.	V.G.	Good	Fair	Poor
425	375	200	150	125	100

GP-100 Stainless

This model is the same as the GP-100 except that the material used is stainless steel.

NIB	Exc.	V.G.	Good	Fair	Poor
450	385	225	150	150	100

SP-101

This model is similar in appearance to the GP-100 but has a smaller frame and is chambered for the .22 LR (6-shot), .38 Special (5-shot), .357 Magnum (5-shot), and 9mm (5-shot). The grips are all black synthetic, and the sights are adjustable for windage. Barrel lengths are 2" or 3", and construction is of stainless steel. This model was introduced in 1989. 6" barrel is available for .22 caliber. .327 Federal Magnum chambering added 2008. Add $100 for Crimson Trace lasergrips (limited edition for 2008).

NIB	Exc.	V.G.	Good	Fair	Poor
525	425	300	200	150	125

SP-101 Spurless-Hammer

This model was introduced in 1993 and features an SP-101 without an exposed hammer spur. Available in two calibers: .38 Special and .357 Magnum with 2-1/4" barrel. This double-action revolver has fixed sights, holds 5 rounds and weighs about 26 oz.

NIB	Exc.	V.G.	Good	Fair	Poor
515	375	300	250	200	150

Redhawk

This model is a large-frame, double-action revolver which was chambered for the .357 and .41 Magnums until 1992, and currently for the .44 Magnum and .45 Colt cartridges. The barrel lengths are 5-1/2" and 7-1/2". The finish is blued, and the grips are smooth walnut. The Redhawk was introduced in 1979. **NOTE:** Add 100 percent for .357 and 50 percent for .41.

NIB	Exc.	V.G.	Good	Fair	Poor
550	475	350	250	200	150

Redhawk Stainless Steel

The same as the blued version except constructed of stainless steel. It was chambered for .357 Magnum until 1985, the .41 Magnum until 1992, and currently for the .44 Magnum. In 1998 this model was offered chambered for .45 Long Colt cartridge in barrel lengths of 4", 5.5" and 7.5". **NOTE:** Add 100 percent for .357 and 50 percent for .41.

NIB	Exc.	V.G.	Good	Fair	Poor
700	600	500	375	250	150

Redhawk 4-Inch .45 Colt (2008)

Similar to original stainless Redhawk but in .45 Colt only and with a 4" barrel. Hogue molded grips.

NIB	Exc.	V.G.	Good	Fair	Poor
800	700	600	450	300	200

Super Redhawk

This is a more massive version of the Redhawk. It weighs 53 oz. and is offered with a 7.5" or 9.5" barrel. It is made of stainless steel with either brushed or dull grey finish, and the barrel rib is milled to accept the Ruger scope-ring system. The grips are the combination rubber and Goncalo Alves-type found on the GP-100. This revolver was introduced in 1987. In 1999 this model was offered chambered for the .454 Casull cartridge with 7.5" or 9.5" barrel. In 2001 this model was offered in .480 Ruger caliber in 7.5" or 9.5" barrel. Also available in .44 Magnum. **NOTE:** Add $200 for .454 Casull or .480 Ruger caliber. Revolvers chambered for the .454 Casull also accept .45 Long Colt cartridges.

NIB	Exc.	V.G.	Good	Fair	Poor
740	550	400	275	200	150

Super Redhawk Alaskan

This revolver is chambered for the .454 Casull and the .45 Colt interchangeable or the .480 Ruger cartridge. Barrel length is 2.5" with adjustable rear sight. Cylinder capacity is 6 rounds. Stainless steel finish. Hogue Tamer rubber grips. Weight is about 42 oz. Introduced in 2005. .44 Magnum chambering added 2007.

NIB	Exc.	V.G.	Good	Fair	Poor
850	700	500	375	250	200

Police Service-Six

This model is also known as the Model 107, chambered for .357 Magnum; the Model 108, chambered for the .38 Special; and the 109, chambered for the 9mm. The barrel is 2.75" or 4". A few 6" barrel Service-Sixes were also produced and these are worth a premium. It has fixed sights and a square butt, with checkered walnut grips. The finish is blued. The 9mm was discontinued in 1984; the other two calibers, in 1988. **NOTE:** Add 60 percent for 9mm.

NIB	Exc.	V.G.	Good	Fair	Poor
425	350	300	200	150	100

Model 707 and 708

This is the designation for the stainless versions of the Police Service-Six. It was not produced in 9mm, and only the 4" barrel was offered. This model was discontinued in 1988.

NIB	Exc.	V.G.	Good	Fair	Poor
450	375	300	200	150	100

Ruger LCR Lightweight Compact Revolver

Polymer-framer compact revolver chambered in .22 LR, .38 Special and .357 Magnum. Features include a five-shot stainless steel cylinder finished in Advanced Target Gray, 1.875" stainless steel barrel, fixed sights, Hogue or Crimson Trace grips, matte black frame. Overall length 6.5". Weight: 13 oz. **NOTE:** Add $75 for .357 Magnum chambering, add $200 for Crimson Trace Lasergrips.

NIB	Exc.	V.G.	Good	Fair	Poor
450	400	325	200	150	100

SEMI-AUTOMATIC CENTERFIRE HANDGUNS

P-85

This model represents Ruger's entry into the wonder-nine market. The P-85 is a double-action, high-capacity (15-shot detachable magazine) semi-automatic, with an alloy frame and steel slide. It has a 4.5" barrel, ambidextrous safety, and three-dot sighting system. It has a matte black finish and black synthetic grips. The latest option for this model is a decocking device to replace the standard safety. There is also an optional molded locking case and extra magazine with loading tool available. It is more reasonably priced than many of its competitors. This pistol was introduced in 1987 and was sold at large premium for some time due to limited supply and great demand. As of this writing, Ruger is producing this pistol in a new plant in Prescott, Arizona; and the premium situation no longer exists. This model is also produced in a 9x21 cartridge for non-NATO countries. In 1991 the internal mechanism was changed slightly with the result that a name change occurred "P85 Mark II".

NIB	Exc.	V.G.	Good	Fair	Poor
435	360	300	275	200	150

KP85

This model is the same as the matte black version except that the receiver assembly is made of stainless steel.

NIB	Exc.	V.G.	Good	Fair	Poor
475	375	325	295	200	150

KP89X

Introduced in 1993 this pistol features a stainless steel convertible safety model which comes with both 9mm and .30 Luger barrels. The barrels are interchangeable without the use of tools. Magazine capacity is 15 rounds. Less than 6,000 produced.

NIB	Exc.	V.G.	Good	Fair	Poor
500	400	345	245	200	150

P89

Introduced in 1991 this semi-automatic pistol is chambered for the 9mm cartridge. It has a blued finish and a 15-round magazine. The safety is a manual ambidextrous lever type. The barrel is 4.5" and the empty weight is approximately 36 oz.

NIB	Exc.	V.G.	Good	Fair	Poor
350	300	200	150	100	80

KP89

This model is the same configuration as the P89 but furnished with a stainless steel finish. Introduced in 1991.

NIB	Exc.	V.G.	Good	Fair	Poor
400	300	250	200	150	100

P89DC

This model features a blued finish and is chambered for the 9mm Parabellum cartridge but is fitted with a decock-only lever (no manual safety). After decocking the gun can be fired by a double-action pull of the trigger.

NIB	Exc.	V.G.	Good	Fair	Poor
425	375	350	250	200	150

KP89DC

This is the stainless steel version of the P89DC with decock only.

NIB	Exc.	V.G.	Good	Fair	Poor
425	375	350	250	200	150

KP89DAO

Chambered for the 9mm cartridge this model is the stainless steel double-action-only version of the above model.

NIB	Exc.	V.G.	Good	Fair	Poor
425	375	350	250	200	150

KP90

Chambered for the .45 ACP cartridge, this model is in stainless steel and holds 7 rounds in the magazine. It is fitted with a manual safety. Introduced in 1991.

NIB	Exc.	V.G.	Good	Fair	Poor
475	375	275	200	150	100

KP90DC

This stainless steel version of the KP90 has a decock-only system. Chambered for the .45 ACP cartridge.

NIB	Exc.	V.G.	Good	Fair	Poor
475	375	275	200	150	100

P90

Same as above model but with blued finish. Introduced in 1998.

NIB	Exc.	V.G.	Good	Fair	Poor
450	350	275	200	150	100

KP91DC

This model features a stainless steel finish and is chambered for the .40 S&W cartridge. Magazine capacity is 11 rounds. It has a decock-only system. Introduced in 1992. Discontinued.

NIB	Exc.	V.G.	Good	Fair	Poor
475	375	325	295	200	150

KP91DAO

Chambered for the .40 S&W with stainless steel finish it features a double-action-only system. Discontinued.

NIB	Exc.	V.G.	Good	Fair	Poor
475	375	325	295	200	150

P93D

This is a blued version with ambidextrous decocker and 3.9" barrel. Introduced in 1998.

NIB	Exc.	V.G.	Good	Fair	Poor
400	300	250	200	150	100

KP93DC

Introduced in 1993 this pistol is a new addition to the P series as a compact model. Stainless steel and chambered for the 9mm cartridge it has a magazine capacity of 15 rounds. Available in decock-only configuration. Barrel length is 3.9" and the weight is about 24 oz. empty.

NIB	Exc.	V.G.	Good	Fair	Poor
500	400	300	250	150	100

KP93DAO

The double-action-only version of the KP93 compact series.

NIB	Exc.	V.G.	Good	Fair	Poor
490	400	300	250	150	100

KP94

Introduced in 1994 this model is smaller than the full-size P series pistols and the compact P93 pistols. Offered in 9mm or .40 S&W calibers this pistol has an aluminum alloy frame and stainless steel slide. Barrel length is 4-1/4" and magazine capacity for the 9mm is 15 rounds and for the .40 11 rounds. Weight is approximately 33 oz. It is offered in double-action-only as well as traditional double-action. A decock-only model is available also.

NIB	Exc.	V.G.	Good	Fair	Poor
415	350	300	250	200	150

KP94DC

This is similar to the model above but in decock only.

NIB	Exc.	V.G.	Good	Fair	Poor
415	350	300	250	200	150

P94

This is a blued version of the KP94. Introduced in 1998.

NIB	Exc.	V.G.	Good	Fair	Poor
400	300	250	200	150	100

KP94DAO

Same as the KP94 model but in double-action-only.

NIB	Exc.	V.G.	Good	Fair	Poor
400	350	300	250	200	150

KP944

Chambered for the .40 S&W cartridge this model has a stainless steel tapered slide, an 11-round magazine, and a manual safety. Models made after September 1994 have a 10-round magazine.

NIB	Exc.	V.G.	Good	Fair	Poor
415	350	300	250	200	150

KP944DC

Same as a model above but fitted with a decock-only system.

NIB	Exc.	V.G.	Good	Fair	Poor
415	350	300	250	200	150

KP944DAO

Same as model above but with a double-action-only model of fire.

NIB	Exc.	V.G.	Good	Fair	Poor
415	350	300	250	200	150

P95

Introduced in 1996 this 9mm pistol features a 3.9" barrel, polymer frame and stainless steel slide. Decocker only. Fixed 3-dot sights are standard. Overall length is 7.3". Empty weight is about 29 oz. In 2001 this model was offered with a manual safety and blued finish.

NIB	Exc.	V.G.	Good	Fair	Poor
450	350	300	225	150	100

KP95DC

This model is the same as the matte black version of the P95, only this is in stainless steel. It has a decock only safety.

NIB	Exc.	V.G.	Good	Fair	Poor
450	350	300	225	150	100

P95DAO

Same as above but in double-action-only.

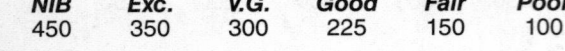

NIB	Exc.	V.G.	Good	Fair	Poor
450	350	300	225	150	100

KP95DAO

Same as the model above but in double-action-only. In 2001 this model was offered with a manual safety and blued finish.

NIB	Exc.	V.G.	Good	Fair	Poor
450	350	300	225	150	100

KP97D

Introduced in 1999 this decock-only model is chambered for the .45 ACP cartridge. It has a stainless steel slide. Magazine capacity is 7 rounds. Fixed sights. Weight is about 27 oz.

NIB	Exc.	V.G.	Good	Fair	Poor
450	350	300	225	150	100

KP97DAO

Same specifications as the model above but in double-action-only. Introduced in 1999.

NIB	Exc.	V.G.	Good	Fair	Poor
450	350	300	225	150	100

KP345

Introduced in 2004 this .45 ACP model features a 4.2" stainless steel barrel and stainless steel slide. Fixed sights. Internal lock, loaded chamber indicator, magazine disconnect, and a new cam block design to reduce recoil. Black polymer checkered grips. Magazine capacity is 8 rounds. Weight is about 29 oz. Available with ambidextrous safety or decocker.

NIB	Exc.	V.G.	Good	Fair	Poor
550	425	300	250	175	125

KP345PR

Similar to the model above but fitted with a Picatinny-style rail under the forward portion of the frame. Introduced in 2004.

NIB	Exc.	V.G.	Good	Fair	Poor
550	425	300	250	175	125

SR9 / SR40

Introduced in 2008. Ruger's first striker-fired semi-auto pistol. Chambered in 9mm Parabellum or .40 S&W. Double-action only with 4.14-inch barrel, 17+1 capacity. Available in three finish configurations: stainless steel slide with matte black frame; blackened stainless slide with matte black frame; and blackened stainless slide with matte black frame. **NOTE:** Ruger recalled all early-production SR9 pistols with a "330" serial number prefix because of a potential safety issue. SR40 has a 15-round magazine.

NIB	Exc.	V.G.	Good	Fair	Poor
450	350	300	225	150	100

SR9c Compact Pistol

Compact double-action only semiauto pistol chambered in 9mm Parabellum. Features include 1911-style ambidextrous manual safety; internal trigger bar interlock and striker blocker; trigger safety; magazine disconnector; loaded chamber indicator; two magazines, one 10-round and the other 17-round; 3.5-inch barrel; 3-dot sights; accessory rail; brushed stainless or blackened alloy finish. Weight 23.40 oz. MSRP: $525.

LCP (Lightweight Compact Pistol)

Introduced in 2008. Ruger's first true pocket pistol. Chambered in .380 (6+1 capacity) with a 2.75-inch barrel. Double action only. Glass-filled nylon frame with steel barrel. Black matte finish.

NIB	Exc.	V.G.	Good	Fair	Poor
350	300	250	200	150	100

LCP Crimson Trace

Similar to above but with CT laser grips.

NIB	Exc.	V.G.	Good	Fair	Poor
590	475	375	250	200	150

LC9

Subcompact 9mm pistol designed for concealed carry. Magazine capacity is seven rounds, barrel length is 3.12-inches and weight: 17.1 ounces. Steel slide, glass-filled nylon receiver, double-action-only trigger, hammer-fired operation. Three-dot sights, loaded-chamber indicator, manual safety, magazine disconnect and slide stop. **NOTE:** Add $100 for Crimson Trace LG-431 laser sight.

NIB	Exc.	V.G.	Good	Fair	Poor
385	335	285	200	150	100

SR1911

After years of rumors, there is a Ruger 1911 pistol. Caliber .45 ACP, stainless steel slide and frame, 8-round magazine, extended thumb safety, grip tang and magazine release, Novak Lo-Mount 3-dot sights, checkered mainspring housing and hardwood grips. Standard 1911 dimensions and controls. Introduced in 2011.

NIB	Exc.	V.G.	Good	Fair	Poor
685	600	500	375	225	150

SEMI-AUTOMATIC RIFLES

10/22 Standard Carbine With Walnut Stock

This model has an 18.5" barrel and is chambered for the .22 LR. It has a 10-shot, detachable rotary magazine and a folding rear sight. The stock is smooth walnut, with a barrel band and carbine-style buttplate. This rifle enjoys a fine reputation for accuracy and dependability and is considered an excellent value. It was introduced in 1964. **NOTE:** Birch stock deduct $20.

NIB	Exc.	V.G.	Good	Fair	Poor
275	225	125	100	75	50

10/22 Standard Carbine Stainless Steel

Same as above but with stainless steel barrel and receiver.

NIB	Exc.	V.G.	Good	Fair	Poor
300	250	150	125	100	75

10/22 Magnum

Introduced in 1999, this model is chambered for the .22 Magnum cartridge. Barrel length is 18.5". Folding rear sight and gold bead front sight. Hardwood stock. Weight is about 5.5 lbs. Discontinued.

NIB	Exc.	V.G.	Good	Fair	Poor
635	500	300	200	150	100

10/22 Sporter (Finger Groove Old Model)

This model is similar to the Standard Carbine except that it has a Monte Carlo stock, finger-groove forend, and no barrel band. It was manufactured between 1966 and 1971. **NOTE:** Factory hand checkering add 300 percent.

NIB	Exc.	V.G.	Good	Fair	Poor
—	500	400	300	175	125

10/22 Deluxe Sporter

The same as the Sporter with a checkered stock and better buttplate. Introduced in 1971.

NIB	Exc.	V.G.	Good	Fair	Poor
325	250	150	125	100	75

10/22 International Carbine

This model is similar to the Standard Carbine, with a full-length, Mannlicher-style stock. It was manufactured between 1966 and 1971 and is fairly rare on today's market. **NOTE:** Factory hand checkering add 50 percent.

NIB	Exc.	V.G.	Good	Fair	Poor
—	1100	625	450	300	250

10/22 International Carbine (New Model)

This 1994 model is a reintroduction of the older version. It is offered in either a blued or stainless steel finish. Barrel length is 18-1/2". Magazine capacity is 10 rounds. The hardwood stock had no checkering when this model was first introduced. Shortly after introduced the factory began checkering these stocks. Weight is about 5.2 lbs. Discontinued.

NIB	Exc.	V.G.	Good	Fair	Poor
465	300	225	—	—	—

Model 10/22T

Introduced in 1996 this model is a target version of the 10/22 line. It has a laminated American hardwood stock with blued heavy barrel with hammer-forged spiral finish. Rifle comes standard without sights. Barrel length is 20". Weight is approximately 7.25 lbs.

NIB	Exc.	V.G.	Good	Fair	Poor
450	350	275	200	150	100

Model 10/22TNZ

This target model features a 20" stainless steel barrel and receiver with laminated thumbhole stock. No sights. Weight is about 7 lbs. Introduced in 2001.

NIB	Exc.	V.G.	Good	Fair	Poor
500	375	275	200	150	100

Model 10/22 Canadian Centennial

In 1966 and 1967 approximately 4,500 10/22 Sporters were built for the Canadian Centennial. The first 2,000 were sold with a Remington Model 742 in .308 caliber with matching serial numbers. The Ruger Sporter may be checkered or uncheckered. The two-gun set was either boxed separately or together.

Two Gun Set

NIB	Exc.	V.G.	Good	Fair	Poor
700	—	—	—	—	—

10/22 Only

NIB	Exc.	V.G.	Good	Fair	Poor
450	—	—	—	—	—

10/22 Laminated Stock Carbine

Produced in varying quantities since 1986 these models are becoming quite collectible. The stocks range in color from dark green to gray and various shades of brown. Because there are so many different variations each should be individually appraised. Prices listed are for blued carbine models. **NOTE:** In stainless steel add approximately $40 to NIB price.

NIB	Exc.	V.G.	Good	Fair	Poor
250	200	175	150	125	100

10/22 Laminated Stock Sporter Model

This model has a tree bark laminated stock.

NIB	Exc.	V.G.	Good	Fair	Poor
325	275	225	175	150	100

10/22 Laminated Stock International

This stainless steel model was an exclusive Wal-Mart product. A few of these models in blue were also produced.

Blue

NIB	Exc.	V.G.	Good	Fair	Poor
400	325	250	200	150	100

Stainless Steel

NIB	Exc.	V.G.	Good	Fair	Poor
350	275	225	175	125	100

10/22 All Weather

This model is fitted with a stainless steel barrel and action and synthetic stock. Introduced in 1997. In 2001 this model was offered with blued finish. **NOTE:** Deduct $40 for blued model.

NIB	Exc.	V.G.	Good	Fair	Poor
300	225	175	125	100	70

Model 10/22 Carbine 40th Anniversary

This model is blued with hardwood stock. It is equipped with a 40th anniversary clear magazine with red rotor and original scope base adapter. A nickel-silver medallion is inlaid on the right side of the buttstock.

NIB	Exc.	V.G.	Good	Fair	Poor
280	225	175	125	100	75

Ruger 10/22 Compact Rifle 10/22 CRR

Similar to 10/22 standard rifle but with 16.25-inch blued barrel, shorter hardwood stock, fiber optic sights and 34.5-inch overall length. Introduced 2006.

NIB	Exc.	V.G.	Good	Fair	Poor
275	225	175	125	100	75

K10/22T Ruger 10/22 Target Stainless

Similar to 10/22 Target but with stainless steel barrel and laminated stock.

NIB	Exc.	V.G.	Good	Fair	Poor
495	425	350	275	200	150

10/22-T

Similar to 100/22 Target Stainless but with blued steel barrel and blued receiver. Introduced in 2007.

NIB	Exc.	V.G.	Good	Fair	Poor
450	350	275	200	150	100

10/22RPFCARH (Lipsey's Distributor's Special)

Similar to 10/22 but covered throughout with RealTree Hardwoods HD camo finish. Introduced 2008.

NIB	Exc.	V.G.	Good	Fair	Poor
275	225	175	125	100	75

K10/22-USST "Barracuda" (Distributor Exclusive)

Wow! A funkalicious 10/22 with red/white/blue laminated thumbhole stock and other goodies. Introduced 2008. Pricing not available. (**NOTE:** Compare styling to that of Remington Model 592 Yellow Jacket.)

10/22VLEH Target Tactical Rifle

Semi-auto rimfire rifle chambered in .22 LR. Features include precision-rifled, cold hammer-forged, spiral-finished 16-1/8-inch crowned match barrel; Hogue® OverMolded® stock; 10/22T target trigger; precision-adjustable bipod for steady shooting from the bench; 10-round rotary magazine. Weight: 6-7/8 lbs.

NIB	Exc.	V.G.	Good	Fair	Poor
485	400	350	300	225	150

Model 10/17

Introduced in 2004 this model is chambered for the .17 HMR cartridge. Fitted with a 20" barrel. Magazine capacity is 9 rounds. Weight is about 6.5 lbs. Discontinued.

NIB	Exc.	V.G.	Good	Fair	Poor
600	475	300	200	150	100

SR-22 Rifle

AR-style semi-auto rifle chambered in .22 LR, based on 0/22 action. Features include all-aluminum chassis replicating the AR-platform dimensions between the sighting plane, buttstock height, and grip; Picatinny rail optic mount includes a six-position, telescoping M4-style buttstock (on a Mil-Spec diameter tube); Hogue Monogrip pistol grip; buttstocks and grips interchangeable with any AR-style compatible option; round, mid-length hand-guard mounted on a standard-thread AR-style barrel nut; precision-rifled, cold hammer forged 16-1/8-inch alloy steel barrel capped with an SR-556/Mini-14 flash suppressor.

NIB	Exc.	V.G.	Good	Fair	Poor
535	460	385	325	250	150

Model 44 Carbine

This model is a short, 18.5" barreled, gas-operated carbine chambered for the .44 Magnum cartridge. It has a 4-shot, nondetachable magazine, a folding rear sight, and a plain walnut stock. This is a handy deer hunting carbine manufactured between 1961 and 1985.

NIB	Exc.	V.G.	Good	Fair	Poor
550	450	350	300	200	150

Deerstalker Model

The same as the Model 44 Carbine with "Deerstalker" stamped on it. This model was manufactured in 1961 and 1962 only.

NIB	Exc.	V.G.	Good	Fair	Poor
950	800	600	400	300	200

Model 44 RS

This is the Model 44 with sling swivels and an aperture sight. **NOTE:** "Liberty"-marked 44RS carbines are extremely rare and will bring a premium.

NIB	Exc.	V.G.	Good	Fair	Poor
—	600	550	350	200	150

Model 44 Sporter (Finger Groove Old Model)

This version has a Monte Carlo stock, finger groove fore-end, and no barrel band. It was manufactured until 1971. **NOTE:** Factory hand checkered models will bring at least a 75 percent premium.

NIB	Exc.	V.G.	Good	Fair	Poor
—	750	600	400	250	200

Model 44 International Carbine

This version features a full-length, Mannlicher-style stock. It was discontinued in 1971 and is quite collectible. **NOTE:** Factory hand checkered models will bring at least a 50 percent premium.

NIB	Exc.	V.G.	Good	Fair	Poor
—	800	600	425	350	275

Model 44 25th Anniversary Model

This version is lightly engraved, has a medallion in the stock and was only made in 1985, the last year of production.

NIB	Exc.	V.G.	Good	Fair	Poor
550	400	350	300	250	200

Model 99/44 Deerfield Carbine

A new and improved version, introduced in 2000, of the original Model 44 Carbine. Fitted with a 18.5" barrel this gas operated rifle has a hardwood stock and 4-round magazine capacity. Adjustable rear sight. Blued finish. Weight is about 6.2 lbs. This rifle will not cycle .44 Special ammo. Discontinued.

NIB	Exc.	V.G.	Good	Fair	Poor
700	525	400	275	200	150

Mini-14

This is a paramilitary-style carbine chambered for the .223 Remington and on a limited basis for the .222 cartridge. It has an 18.5" barrel and is gas-operated. The detachable magazines originally offered held 5, 10 or 20 rounds. The high-capacity magazines are now discontinued, and prices of them are what the market will bear. The Mini-14 has a military-style stock and aperture sight. It was introduced in 1975. 20-round magazine added 2009.

NIB	Exc.	V.G.	Good	Fair	Poor
600	500	400	275	200	150

Mini-14 Stainless Steel

The same as the Mini-14 except constructed of stainless steel.

NIB	Exc.	V.G.	Good	Fair	Poor
650	550	450	300	200	150

Mini-14 Target Rifle

Acccurized version of the Mini-14 but with matte stainless barrel and reciver, black laminated thumbhole stock, adjustable harmonic dampener. No sights. Also available with non-thumbhole synthetic stock. Introduced in 2007.

NIB	Exc.	V.G.	Good	Fair	Poor
1025	900	775	600	400	250

Mini-14 Ranch Rifle

This model is similar to the standard Mini-14, with a folding rear sight and the receiver milled to accept the Ruger scope-ring system. The rings are supplied with the rifle. 6.8 Remington chambering also available. **NOTE:** Models chambered in .222 caliber will bring a premium.

NIB	Exc.	V.G.	Good	Fair	Poor
625	500	450	350	250	175

Mini-14 Stainless All-Weather Ranch Rifle

Introduced in 1999 this model has all the features of the stainless steel Ranch Rifle with the addition of a black polymer stock. Weight is about 6.5 lbs.

NIB	Exc.	V.G.	Good	Fair	Poor
810	600	450	300	200	150

NRA Mini-14

Ruger NRA Mini-14 Rifle with two 20-round magazines, gold-tone medallion in grip cap, and special serial number sequence (NRA8XXXXX). Produced in 2008 only. Also available with 5-round magazines.

NIB	Exc.	V.G.	Good	Fair	Poor
1000	700	575	—	—	—

Mini-14 ATI Stock

Tactical version of Mini-14 but with six-position collapsible stock or folding stock, grooved pistol grip, multiple picatinny optics/accessories rails. Suggested retail price: $872.

NIB	Exc.	V.G.	Good	Fair	Poor
675	550	425	300	200	150

Mini-14 Tactical Rifle

Similar to Mini-14 but with 16-12" barrel with flash hider, black synthetic stock, adjustable sights.

NIB	Exc.	V.G.	Good	Fair	Poor
700	525	400	275	200	150

SR-556

AR-style semi-auto rifle chambered in 5.56 NATO. Feature include two-stage piston; quad rail hand-guard; Troy Industries sights; black synthetic fixed or telescoping buttstock; 16.12-inch 1:9 steel barrel with birdcage; 10- or 30-round detachable box magazine; black matte finish overall.

NIB	Exc.	V.G.	Good	Fair	Poor
1750	1400	1250	900	600	250

Mini-30

This model was brought out by Ruger in 1987 and is similar in appearance to the standard Mini-14 and is supplied with Ruger scope rings. Chambered in 7.63x39. 6.8mm chambering added 2007.

NIB	Exc.	V.G.	Good	Fair	Poor
550	450	300	250	200	150

Mini-30 Stainless with Synthetic Stock

NIB	Exc.	V.G.	Good	Fair	Poor
700	550	450	300	200	150

GB Model

This model has a factory-installed folding stock, flash suppressor, and bayonet lug. It was designed and sold by Ruger to law enforcement agencies. A number have come on the civilian market through surplus sales and police trade-ins. With the assault rifle hysteria, prices of this model have fluctuated wildly in some areas. Now that Ruger has discontinued the folding stock and the high-capacity magazines, this could become even less predictable. Note that this is a semi-automatic and totally different than the full-auto version of this weapon available only through Class 3 dealers.

NIB	Exc.	V.G.	Good	Fair	Poor
—	1350	1100	650	400	300

Ruger PC4/PC9 Carbine

This is a semi-automatic carbine chambered for the 9mm (PC9) or .40 S&W (PC4) cartridges. It is fitted with a 16.25" barrel and black synthetic stock. Post front sight with adjustable rear sight. A receiver is also offered. Detachable magazine has 10-round capacity. Weight is approximately 6.4 lbs. Introduced in 1998. Discontinued. **NOTE:** Add $30 for receiver sight.

NIB	Exc.	V.G.	Good	Fair	Poor
625	450	325	225	150	100

SINGLE-SHOT RIFLES

Ruger No. 1 Light Sporter (1-A)

This model features open sights, barrel band on lightweight barrel, and Alexander Henry-style forearm. Offered with a 22" barrel in four calibers. Rifle weighs 7.25 lbs. .300 Ruger Compact Magnum added 2009.

NIB	Exc.	V.G.	Good	Fair	Poor
965	725	550	375	250	200

Ruger Number 1 Light Standard (1-AB)

Similar to Light Sporter 1-A but with 22-inch sightless blued barrel. Chambered in .204 Ruger only; introduced 2006. MSRP: $1000.

Ruger No. 1 Standard (1-B)

This model is furnished with no sights, medium barrel, semi-beavertail forearm, and quarter rib with 1" Ruger scope rings. 6.5 Creedmore added 2010. Weighs 8 lbs.

NIB	Exc.	V.G.	Good	Fair	Poor
965	725	550	375	250	200

Ruger No. 1 Standard Stainless (1-B-BBZ)

Introduced in 2000 this model features a laminated wood stock. It is chambered for the .243 Win., .25-06, 7mm Mag., 7mm STW, .30-06, .300 Win. Mag. Fitted with a 26" barrel. Weight is approximately 8 lbs.

NIB	Exc.	V.G.	Good	Fair	Poor
995	750	550	375	250	200

Ruger No. 1 Tropical (1-H)

Fitted with open sights this model has a barrel band on a heavy barrel with Alexander Henry-style forearm. Rifle weighs 9 lbs. **NOTE:** In 2001 this model was also offered with stainless steel finish and black laminated stock in .375 H&H. In 2003 the .458 Lott and .405 Win. cartridges were added to this model. In 2008 the ..450/.400 Nitro Express was added. .416 Ruger added 2009. A few 24" heavy barrel 1-H rifles were chambered for the .45-70 Government cartridge up to 1976. These bring a substantial premium and should be appraised individually. The recently catalogued .404 Jeffery has been discontinued. Only a few of these rifles were produced. Add 100 percent for .404 Jeffery caliber.

NIB	Exc.	V.G.	Good	Fair	Poor
965	725	550	375	250	200

Ruger No. 1 International (1-RSI)

This No. 1 rifle features a lightweight barrel with full length forearm, open sights. Rifle weighs 7.25 lbs.

NIB	Exc.	V.G.	Good	Fair	Poor
995	750	550	375	250	200

Ruger No. 1 Medium Sporter (1-S)

The Medium Sporter is equipped with open sights, a barrel band on a medium weight barrel, and Alexander Henry-style forearm. Rifle weighs 8 lbs. In 2001 this model was also offered in stainless steel and black laminated stock in .45-70 caliber. .300 H&H, .338 Ruger Compact Magnum, .375 Ruger, .460 S&W Magnum, .480Ruger/.475 Linebaugh added 2009.

NIB	Exc.	V.G.	Good	Fair	Poor
965	725	550	375	250	200

Ruger No. 1 Special Varminter (1-V)

This model is furnished with no sights, a heavy barrel, target scope blocks with 1" Ruger scope rings, and semi-beavertail forearm. Rifle weighs about 9 lbs.

NIB	Exc.	V.G.	Good	Fair	Poor
965	725	550	375	250	200

Ruger No. 1 Stainless Varminter (1-V-BBZ)

Introduced in 2000 this model features a laminated wood stock and stainless steel finish. Chambered for .22-250 and fitted with a 24" barrel. Weight is approximately 9 lbs.

NIB	Exc.	V.G.	Good	Fair	Poor
995	750	550	375	250	200

Number 3 Carbine

This model is a less elaborate, inexpensive version of the Number 1. The action is the same except that the lever is less ornate in appearance and lacks the locking bar. The uncheckered stock is of a military carbine style with a barrel band. It is similar in appearance to the Model 44 and the 10/22. This serviceable rifle was chambered for the .45-70 when it was released in 1972. Later chamberings added the .22 Hornet, .30-40 Krag, .223, .44 Magnum, and the .375 Winchester. The barrel is 22" long, and there is a folding rear sight. This model was discontinued in 1987. Add premium for "neato" calibers.

NIB	Exc.	V.G.	Good	Fair	Poor
—	625	500	300	200	125

BOLT-ACTION RIFLES

Ruger introduced the Model 77R in 1968. It filled the need for a good quality, reasonably priced, bolt-action hunting rifle. It has been a commercial success. There are certain variations of this rifle that collectors actively seek. One should avail oneself of the specialized literature on this model and secure individual appraisals on the rare variations as the differences are slight and beyond the scope of this book.

Model 77-R/RS

This model was introduced in 1968. It is offered with a 22", 24", or 26" barrel. The Model 77 is chambered for most calibers from .22-250 through .458 Win. Mag. The action is of a modified Mauser-type, finished in blue with a checkered walnut stock and red rubber buttplate. The rifle is available milled for Ruger scope rings or in the round-top style that allows the mounting of any popular scope ring system. This model is designated 77R when supplied with rings only; and 77RS, when supplied with rings and sights. This model was replaced by the Model 77 MK II.

NIB	Exc.	V.G.	Good	Fair	Poor
500	400	350	300	250	200

Model 77-RS

NOTE: Add $400 for 6.5 Rem., .284, .350 Rem.

NIB	Exc.	V.G.	Good	Fair	Poor
550	450	400	300	250	200

Model 77 Flat Bolt

This is an example of the slight variations that make this model collectible. This is essentially the same rifle with the knob on the bolt handle flattened. They were only produced in the configuration until 1972. Watch for fakes, and read specialized material. Calibers such as the 6.5 Rem. Mag., .284, and .350 Rem. Mag. will bring a premium especially in the RS model. Nonprefixed rifles exists in calibers and configurations other than those advertised by Ruger. These should be individually appraised. **NOTE:** Add $400 for 6.5 Rem., .284, .350 Rem.

NIB	Exc.	V.G.	Good	Fair	Poor
—	650	500	400	350	275

Model 77 RL & RLS

This variation is similar to the standard model except that it features an ultralight 20" barrel and black forearm tip. This model was also available in an 18.5" carbine version with sights designated the RLS. This model was also in an 18.5" carbine version with sights designated the RLS. They were chambered for the .22-250, .243, .257, .270, .250-3000, .308, and .30-06. Weight is only 6 lbs.

NIB	Exc.	V.G.	Good	Fair	Poor
550	450	375	325	275	225

Model 77V Varmint

This variation is similar to the standard Model 77 except that it has a 24" heavy barrel that is drilled and tapped for target-scope bases and has a wider beavertail forearm. It is chambered for the .22-250, .243, 6mm, .25-06, .280, and .308. This model was also chambered for the .220 Swift in a 26" heavyweight barrel.

NIB	Exc.	V.G.	Good	Fair	Poor
500	400	350	300	250	200

Model 77 RSI

This version of the Model 77 has a full-length, Mannlicher-style stock and was chambered for the .22-250, .250-3000, .243, .270, 7mm-08, .308 and the .30-06.

NIB	Exc.	V.G.	Good	Fair	Poor
700	600	500	300	275	200

Model 77 RS African

This is a heavier-barreled version, with a steel trigger guard and floorplate. Earlier versions were stocked with fine-quality Circassian walnut. This rifle is chambered for the .458 Winchester Magnum. **NOTE:** Fewer than 50 rifles chambered for the .416 Taylor cartridge were produced up to 1976. Selling prices range from $3,000 to $5,000 and should be individually appraised. Add $100 for early models with Circassian walnut stocks.

NIB	Exc.	V.G.	Good	Fair	Poor
700	550	400	350	300	250

Model 77/17

Introduced in 2003, this rifle is chambered for the .17 HMR cartridge and fitted with a 22" barrel with no sights. Walnut stock with blued finish. Magazine capacity is nine rounds. Weight is about 6 lbs.

NIB	Exc.	V.G.	Good	Fair	Poor
610	475	350	250	175	125

Model 77/17 Synthetic

As above but with black synthetic stock and blued finish.

NIB	Exc.	V.G.	Good	Fair	Poor
625	475	350	250	175	125

Model 77/17 Varmint

As above but with black laminate stock and 24" stainless steel heavy barrel with no sights. Weight is about 7 lbs.

NIB	Exc.	V.G.	Good	Fair	Poor
685	500	375	265	195	145

Model 77/17RM2

Introduced in 2005 this model is chambered for the .17 Mach 2 caliber and fitted with a 20" barrel with no sights. Walnut stock with checkering. Blued finish. Weight is about 6.5 lbs.

NIB	Exc.	V.G.	Good	Fair	Poor
625	475	350	250	175	125

Model 77/17RM2 Stainless Steel

As above but with stainless steel finish and black laminate stock. Weight is about 7.25 lbs. Introduced in 2005.

NIB	Exc.	V.G.	Good	Fair	Poor
745	625	500	400	275	150

Model 77/22

This is a high quality, .22 rimfire (LR and WMR) rifle designed for the serious shooter. This model has a 20" barrel and a 10-shot, detachable rotary magazine. It is made of steel and stocked with checkered walnut. It is available with sights, scope rings, or both as an extra-cost ($20) option. This model was introduced in 1984. Early guns without the 77/22 rollmark on the receiver will bring a premium.

NIB	Exc.	V.G.	Good	Fair	Poor
625	450	350	250	175	125

Model 77/22 Synthetic Stock

This version is quite similar to the standard 77/22, with a black-matte-finished synthetic stock.

NIB	Exc.	V.G.	Good	Fair	Poor
625	450	350	250	200	150

Model 77/22 Stainless Steel/Synthetic Stock

This model is the same as the blued version except that it is made of stainless steel.

NIB	Exc.	V.G.	Good	Fair	Poor
610	475	375	275	225	150

Model 77/22 Varmint

Introduced in 1993 this model features a stainless steel finish, laminated wood stock, heavy 20" varmint barrel with no sights. Scope rings are included as standard. Chambered for the .22 LR or Win. Mag. Rimfire.

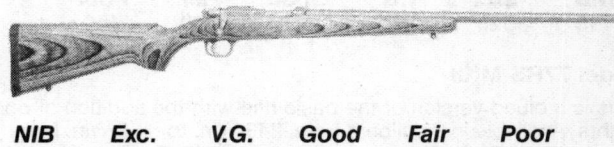

NIB	Exc.	V.G.	Good	Fair	Poor
650	525	425	300	250	150

Model 77/22M

This model is simply the 77/22 chambered for the .22 Magnum cartridge. The finish is blue, and the magazine capacity is 9 rounds.

NIB	Exc.	V.G.	Good	Fair	Poor
610	450	350	250	175	125

Model 77/22 Stainless Steel

This is the same as the blued 77/22M constructed of stainless steel.

NIB	Exc.	V.G.	Good	Fair	Poor
600	475	375	275	225	150

Model 77/22—.22 Hornet

Introduced in 1994 this version of the 77/22 series is chambered for the .22 Hornet cartridge. This model is furnished with or without sights. The barrel is 20" and it has a 6-round detachable rotary magazine. The stock is checkered walnut with sling swivels. Weight is approximately 6 lbs. This model is offered with (77/22RSH) or without (77/22RH) sights.

NIB	Exc.	V.G.	Good	Fair	Poor
650	500	375	275	225	150

Model K77/22VHZ

Introduced in 1995 this .22 Hornet variation features a stainless steel heavyweight barrel and laminated American hardwood stock. Offered without sights.

NIB	Exc.	V.G.	Good	Fair	Poor
685	525	425	300	250	150

Model 77R MKII

Introduced in 1992 this model is the basic Model 77 rifle. Features blued metal parts and no sights. Available in 15 different calibers from .223 to .338 Win. Mag. in barrel lengths from 22" to 24" depending on caliber. Comes from factory with scope bases and rings. Rifle weighs approximately 7 lbs.

NIB	Exc.	V.G.	Good	Fair	Poor
715	525	375	250	200	150

Model 77RP MKII

This model was also introduced in 1992 and differs from the Model 77R with the addition of stainless steel barrel and receiver and synthetic stock. Available in 10 calibers. In 1998 the .25-06 caliber was added to this model.

NIB	Exc.	V.G.	Good	Fair	Poor
715	525	375	250	200	150

Model 77RS MKII

This is a blued version of the basic rifle with the addition of open sights. Available in 9 calibers from .243 Win. to .458 Win. Mag.

NIB	Exc.	V.G.	Good	Fair	Poor
760	600	450	350	250	175

Model 77RSP MKII

The stainless version of the basic rifle with the addition of a synthetic stock and open sights. Available in 6 calibers: .243, .270, 7MM Rem. Mag., .30-06, .330 Win. Mag., .338 Win. Mag. Introduced in 1993.

NIB	Exc.	V.G.	Good	Fair	Poor
500	400	350	300	250	175

Model 77RSI MKII

Also introduced in 1993 this model features a blued barrel and full-length walnut stock. Offered in four calibers, all with 18" barrel. The calibers are: .243, .270, .30-06, and .308.

NIB	Exc.	V.G.	Good	Fair	Poor
820	600	450	350	250	175

Model 77RL MKII

This model features a short action in six calibers from .223 to .308, all with 20" barrel. Rifle weighs about 6 lbs. Introduced in 1992.

NIB	Exc.	V.G.	Good	Fair	Poor
770	575	425	300	200	150

Model 77LR MKII

This model is a left-handed rifle furnished in long action calibers: .270, 7mm Rem. Mag., .30-06, .300 Win. Mag. Introduced in 1992.

NIB	Exc.	V.G.	Good	Fair	Poor
770	575	425	300	200	150

Model 77RLP MKII

Introduced in 1999 this model is similar to the RL model above, but with an all-weather synthetic stock. Weight is about 6.5 lbs.

NIB	Exc.	V.G.	Good	Fair	Poor
715	525	400	275	200	150

Model 77VT MKII

This rifle was introduced in 1993 and is a target rifle. Furnished with no sights, heavy laminated wood stock with beavertail fore-end, and adjustable trigger. Barrel, bolt, and action are stainless steel. Weighs approximately 9.75 lbs. Furnished in eight calibers from .223 to .308.

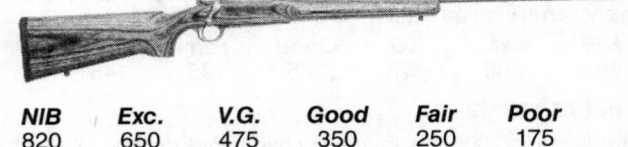

NIB	Exc.	V.G.	Good	Fair	Poor
820	650	475	350	250	175

Model 77RBZ MKII

This model features a stainless steel barrel and action fitted with laminated hardwood stock. No sights. Weight is approximately 7.25 lbs. Offered in a wide variety of calibers from .223 to .338 Win. Mag. Introduced in 1997.

NIB	Exc.	V.G.	Good	Fair	Poor
600	500	400	300	225	175

Model 77RSBZ MKII

Same as above but fitted with open sights. Introduced in 1997.

NIB	Exc.	V.G.	Good	Fair	Poor
800	650	475	350	250	125

Model 77CR MKII Compact Rifle

Introduced in 2001 this rifle features a 16.5" barrel with four-round magazine. Chambered for the .223 Rem., .243 Win., .260 Rem., and .308 Win. cartridges. Blued model is fitted with walnut stock and stainless steel model is fitted with black laminated stock. Weight is about 5.75 lbs. **NOTE:** Add $50 for stainless steel model (M77CRBBZ).

Top to bottom: M77 MK II Magnum, M77 MK II Standard, M77 MK II Compact

NIB	Exc.	V.G.	Good	Fair	Poor
715	525	400	275	200	150

Model 77 Express MKII

Introduced in 1992 the Ruger Express Mark II rifle features a select Circassian walnut straight comb checkered stock. The checkering is 22 lpi and the buttstock is fitted with a rubber recoil pad. The pistol grip is fitted with a metal grip cap. The barrel length is 22" and features a blade front sight, V-notch rear express sights, and the receiver is machined for scope mounts, which are included. Available in these calibers: .270, .30-06, 7mm Rem. Mag., .300 Win. Mag., .338 Win. Mag. Rifle weighs about 7.5 lbs.

NIB	Exc.	V.G.	Good	Fair	Poor
1200	850	650	550	400	200

Model 77 Magnum MKII

Similar in all respects to the Model 77 Express MKII except offered in these calibers: .375 H&H, .416 Rigby and .458 Lott. The .375 and weighs about 9.25 lbs. while the .416 and .458 Lott weigh about 10.25 lbs.

NIB	Exc.	V.G.	Good	Fair	Poor
1975	1500	1100	750	525	350

M77 MkII Frontier Rifle

Bolt-action rifle based on M77 MkII chassis but configured for "scout"-style scope mount system. Chambered in .243, .308, 7mm-08, .300 WSM, .325 WSM. 338 Federal. Gray laminated stock, 16.5-inch blued or stainless barrel (add 15 percent for stainless). Introduced 2005; stainless model introduced 2006 (add 10 percent). .338 Federal and .358 Winchester added 2008. Black laminated version discontinued 2008.

NIB	Exc.	V.G.	Good	Fair	Poor
600	500	400	300	225	175

Gunsite -Scout

Based on the Ruger M77 rifle design with a 16.5-inch barrel and forward mounted Picatinny rail for intermediate eye relief scopes. Chambered in .308 Win. with a 10-round detachable magazine, integral scope mounts with rings and a flash suppressor. Adjustable ghost-ring rear sight and ramp front. Black/gray laminated stock with checkering and a soft rubber recoil pad with spacers.

NIB	Exc.	V.G.	Good	Fair	Poor
850	750	600	450	300	200

Model 77/44RS

This bolt-action is chambered for the .44 Magnum cartridge. It features an 18.5" barrel with open sights. The stock is American walnut with rubber buttpad and checkering on forearm and pistol grip. Detachable rotary magazine has 4-round capacity. Weight is approximately 6 lbs. Introduced in mid-1997.

NIB	Exc.	V.G.	Good	Fair	Poor
575	465	375	250	175	125

Model 77/44RSP

Introduced in 1999 this model has a matte stainless steel barrel and action and a black synthetic stock. Chambered for .44 Magnum cartridge. Weight is about 6 lbs.

NIB	Exc.	V.G.	Good	Fair	Poor
575	465	375	250	175	125

Model 77/17RM

Similar in appearance to the .22 caliber Model 77 series this rifle is chambered for the .17 HMR and .17 Mach 2 cartridges. Fitted with a 22" barrel and walnut stock. Magazine capacity is nine rounds. Weight is about 6.25 lbs. Introduced in 2002.

NIB	Exc.	V.G.	Good	Fair	Poor
565	475	375	250	175	125

HAWKEYE SERIES

With a few exceptions, the Hawkeye Series, introduced in 2007, has replaced Ruger's M77 Mark II line. In 2010, the Hawkeye series began being offered in left-hand versions.

HM77R Hawkeye

Slimmed-down version of the M77. American walnut stock, blued barrel, Mauser-style controlled feed extractor, soft red rubber recoil pad, stainless steel bolt, new LC6 trigger, engraved solid steel floorplate. Chambered in .2506, 7mm-08, 7mm Magnum, .308, .30-06, .300 Win Mag, .338 Win Mag. Left-hand and laminate-stock versions available. Introduced in 2007. In 2008 a left-hand version (HM77LR) was introduced at no extra charge.

NIB	Exc.	V.G.	Good	Fair	Poor
650	550	400	225	175	125

M77 Hawkeye Ultra-Light

Similar to Hawkeye but with lightweight 20" blued barrel; chambered in .223, .243 Winchester, .257 Roberts, .270 Winchester, .308 Winchester and .30-06.

NIB	Exc.	V.G.	Good	Fair	Poor
700	600	450	300	225	175

M77 Hawkeye All-Weather Ultra-Light

Similar to above but with black synthetic stock and matte stainless barrel and receiver; chambered in .204, .223, .243 Winchester, .270 Winchester and .30-06.

NIB	Exc.	V.G.	Good	Fair	Poor
600	500	400	300	225	175

M77 Hawkeye Compact

Similar to M77 Hawkeye Ultra-Light but with 16.5" barrel and smaller overall dimensions; chambered in .223, .243 Winchester, .260 Remington, 7mm-08, .308 Winchester, 6.8 SPC, and 7.62x39.

NIB	Exc.	V.G.	Good	Fair	Poor
700	600	500	400	300	175

M77 Hawkeye Laminate Compact

Similar to above but with black laminate stock and matte stainless barrel and receiver.

NIB	Exc.	V.G.	Good	Fair	Poor
650	525	425	300	250	150

HK77RFP Hawkeye All-Weather

All-weather version of the HM77R Hawkeye but with synthetic stock and stainless barrel. Same chamberings as HM77R but with .338 Federal and .358 Winchester as well. Introduced in 2007. Left hand version introduced in 2008.

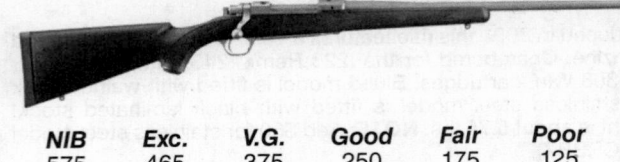

NIB	Exc.	V.G.	Good	Fair	Poor
575	465	375	250	175	125

HKM77PRCM Hawkeye Compact Magnum

Similar to Hawkeye but with 1/2-inch shorter synthetic stock and stainless steel barrel and receiver. Chambered for .416 Ruger, .375 Ruger, .300 Ruger Compact Magnum, .338 Ruger Compact Magnum. Introduced 2008.

NIB	Exc.	V.G.	Good	Fair	Poor
775	675	550	450	325	195

HKM77RCM Hawkeye Compact Magnum

Similar to above but with blued barrel and walnut stock. Introduced 2008.

NIB	Exc.	V.G.	Good	Fair	Poor
800	700	575	475	350	200

HM77RSPHAB Hawkeye Alaskan

Similar to HK77RFP but with iron sights, Diamond black finish, stainless or matte blued barrel/receiver and Hogue stock. Chambered in .375 Ruger or .416 Ruger. Introduced in 2007. Left hand model introduced 2008.

NIB	Exc.	V.G.	Good	Fair	Poor
850	725	600	475	300	200

HM77RSPHAB Hawkeye African

Similar to HK77RFP but with checkered walnut stock and express-style sights. Chambered in .375 Ruger, .223 Rem., 9.3x62, .300 Win. Mag. and .338 Win. Mag. Chambered in .375 Ruger. Introduced in 2007. A left-hand version was introduced in 2008.

NIB	Exc.	V.G.	Good	Fair	Poor
900	775	650	525	350	225

M77 Hawkeye Tactical

Similar to M77 Hawkeye but with 20" matte blue heavy barrel, overmolded Hogue synthetic stock; chambered in .223, .243 Winchester and .308 Winchester.

NIB	Exc.	V.G.	Good	Fair	Poor
875	750	625	500	300	200

M77 Hawkeye Predator

Similar to M77 Hawkeye but with 24" matte stainless barrel. Green-toned Green Mountain laminate stock; chambered in .204, .223 and .22-250.

NIB	Exc.	V.G.	Good	Fair	Poor
775	675	550	450	325	195

M77 Hawkeye International

Similar to Hawkeye but with 18.5" barrel and full-length Mannlicher-style stock; chambered in .243, .270 and .308 Winchester and .30-06.

NIB	Exc.	V.G.	Good	Fair	Poor
825	725	600	475	350	225

American Rifle

Budget-price bolt-action in .243, .270 Win., .308 or .30-06, with 4-shot rotary magazine, black composite stock and matte black finish. Other features include tang safety, adjustable trigger and free-floating hammer-forged barrel. Introduced in 2012.

NIB	Exc.	V.G.	Good	Fair	Poor
400	350	300	250	—	—

Model 77/50RS

This model is an in-line percussion rifle chambered for .50 caliber. It is fitted with a 22" barrel with open sights. Stock is birch with rubber buttplate and no checkering. Blued finish. Weight is approximately 6.5 lbs. Introduced in mid-1997. Discontinued.

NIB	Exc.	V.G.	Good	Fair	Poor
425	325	225	175	125	100

Model 77/50RSO

Similar to the model above but with a straight-grip checkered walnut stock with curved buttplate. Introduced in 1998.

NIB	Exc.	V.G.	Good	Fair	Poor
475	350	250	200	125	100

Model 77/50RSBBZ

This model was introduced in 1998 and features all of the specifications of the Model 77/50RS with the addition of a black/gray laminated stock and a stainless steel finish.

NIB	Exc.	V.G.	Good	Fair	Poor
500	375	275	225	125	100

Model 77/50RSP

This model is fitted with a stainless steel barrel and action and fitted with a black synthetic stock with pistol grip. Weight is about 6.5 lbs. Introduced in 1999.

NIB	Exc.	V.G.	Good	Fair	Poor
575	400	300	200	125	100

LEVER-ACTION RIFLES

Model 96/17

Introduced in 2003 this model is chambered for the .17 HMR cartridge and fitted with an 18.5" barrel. Magazine capacity is nine rounds. Hardwood stock and open sights. Weight is about 5.25 lbs.

NIB	Exc.	V.G.	Good	Fair	Poor
425	300	225	175	150	100

Model 96/22

Introduced into the Ruger line in 1996 this lever action rifle is chambered for the .22 LR. The stock is American hardwood and the barrel length is 18.5". Magazine capacity is 10 rounds. Open sights are standard. Weight is approximately 5.25 lbs. Apparently discontinued.

NIB	Exc.	V.G.	Good	Fair	Poor
325	275	200	175	150	100

Model 96/22M

Same as above but chambered for the .22 WMR cartridge. Magazine capacity is nine rounds.

NIB	Exc.	V.G.	Good	Fair	Poor
350	300	225	175	150	100

Model 96/44

Same as the .22 caliber except chambered for the .44 Magnum cartridge. Magazine capacity is four rounds and the weight is about 5-7/8 lbs. Discontinued.

NIB	Exc.	V.G.	Good	Fair	Poor
550	450	325	250	200	125

SHOTGUNS

Red Label Over/Under Early Production

Ruger introduced the Red Label in 20 gauge in 1977; the 12 gauge followed five years later. This high quality shotgun is offered with 3" chambers in 26" or 28" barrel lengths. Various chokes are available. They are boxlocks with automatic ejectors. The stock is of checkered walnut. The finish is blue on the earlier guns.

NIB	Exc.	V.G.	Good	Fair	Poor
1400	1150	900	500	300	250

Red Label Over/Under Late Production

The new 12 and 20 gauge Red Label shotgun has a stainless steel receiver and blued barrels. They are offered with screw-in choke tubes. Otherwise they are similar to the earlier models. In 1994 Ruger added the 28 gauge with 26" or 28" barrels to the Red Label line.

NIB	Exc.	V.G.	Good	Fair	Poor
1250	850	650	400	300	250

Red Label Over/Under Sporting Clays

Offered in 20 gauge this model was introduced in 1994 with 3" chambers and 30" barrels. Walnut stock has checkering and pistol grip. Weight is about 7 lbs. **NOTE:** Factory engraved Red Label shotguns are catalogued, as of 1996, as available with three different engraving coverages. A total of 375 were produced. Prices for these engraved guns are:

Grade 1—EXC.—$2200
Grade 2 (1/3 coverage)—EXC.—$2400
Grade 3 (2/3 coverage)—EXC.—$2750

Courtesy compliments of Bill Ruger, John C. Dougan

NIB	Exc.	V.G.	Good	Fair	Poor
1400	1200	900	600	325	225

Red Label All-Weather Over/Under

Offered in 12 gauge only with 26", 28", or 30" barrels this model is fitted with a black synthetic stock with pistol grip. Weight is about 7.5 lbs. Introduced in 1999.

NIB	Exc.	V.G.	Good	Fair	Poor
1200	875	650	400	300	250

Engraved Red Label Over/Under

This model features a scroll engraved receiver with a gold inlaid game bird appropriate to gauge. The 12 gauge: pheasant; 20 gauge: grouse; and 28 gauge: woodcock. Walnut stock. Other specifications same as standard Red Label shotguns. Introduced in 2000. Premium for 28 ga.

NIB	Exc.	V.G.	Good	Fair	Poor
1650	1300	1050	750	500	300

Engraved Red Label All-Weather Over/Under

Introduced in 2000 this model features a scroll engraved receiver with gold inlaid duck. Offered in 12 gauge only with 26", 28", or 30" barrel.

NIB	Exc.	V.G.	Good	Fair	Poor
1675	1325	1075	750	500	300

Ruger Woodside Over/Under

Introduced in 1995 this new model features a Circassian walnut stock with either pistol grip or straight grip. Available in 12 or 20 gauge with barrel lengths of 26", 28", or 30". Screw-in chokes are standard. **NOTE:** The Woodside shotgun was also available in three different engraving patterns. Discontinued 2002.

NIB	Exc.	V.G.	Good	Fair	Poor
1500	1300	950	650	300	250

Ruger Trap Model

Introduced in 2000 this model is a 12 gauge single-barrel trap gun with a 34" barrel choked Full and Modified. It is fitted with a mechanical trigger and auto ejector. The stock is select walnut with adjustable cheekpiece and buttplate. Receiver is engraved. Weight is approximately 9 lbs.

NIB	Exc.	V.G.	Good	Fair	Poor
3000	2500	1750	1200	900	500

Ruger Gold Label Side-by-Side

Introduced in 2002 this model is chambered for the 12 gauge 3" shell. Offered with 28" barrels with choke tubes. Choice of pistol or straight grip checkered walnut stock. Ejectors and single trigger. Weight is about 6.33 lbs. Discontinued 2008.

NIB	Exc.	V.G.	Good	Fair	Poor
3000	2450	1975	1300	700	450

SUNDANCE INDUSTRIES, INC.
North Hollywood, California

This company was in business from 1989 to 2002.

Model D-22M

A .22 or .22 Magnum caliber double-barrel over/under pocket pistol with 2.5" barrels and an aluminum alloy frame. Blackened finish or chrome-plated with either simulated pearl or black grips. Introduced in 1989.

NIB	Exc.	V.G.	Good	Fair	Poor
—	225	175	125	100	75

Model BOA

Introduced in 1991 this semi-automatic pistol is chambered for the .25 ACP cartridge. Fitted with a 2.5" barrel with fixed sights. Grip safety. Choice of black or chrome finish. Magazine capacity is 7 rounds. Weight is about 16 oz.

NIB	Exc.	V.G.	Good	Fair	Poor
125	100	80	70	50	25

Model A-25

Similar to the BOA but without grip safety.

NIB	Exc.	V.G.	Good	Fair	Poor
125	100	80	70	50	25

Model Laser 25

Similar to the Model BOA with grip safety but equipped with a laser sight. Laser activated by squeezing grip safety. Weight with laser 18 oz. Introduced in 1995.

NIB	Exc.	V.G.	Good	Fair	Poor
220	175	125	100	75	50

Sundance Point Blank

This is an over/under derringer chambered for the .22 LR cartridge. It is fitted with a 3" barrel and double-action trigger. Enclosed hammer. Matte black finish. Weight is about 8 oz. Introduced in 1994.

NIB	Exc.	V.G.	Good	Fair	Poor
95	80	70	50	25	10

SUPER SIX LTD.
Fort Atkinson, Wisconsin

Bison Bull

Massive single-action .45-70 revolver with blued carbon steel (Bison Bull) or engraved molybdenum bronze (Golden Bison Bull) frame. Adjustable sights, 10.5" barrel, 17.5" overall length, weight 6 lbs. Introduced 2006. Value shown is for blued version. Add 350 percent for engraved version.

NIB	Exc.	V.G.	Good	Fair	Poor
1200	1050	900	775	600	500

SUTHERLAND, S.
Richmond, Virginia

Pocket Pistol

A .41 caliber percussion single-shot pistol with round barrels of 2.5" to 4" in length, German silver mounts and a walnut stock. The lock normally marked "S. Sutherland" or "S. Sutherland/Richmond". Manufactured during the 1850s.

NIB	Exc.	V.G.	Good	Fair	Poor
—	—	2950	2200	800	300

SYMS, J. G.
New York, New York

Pocket Pistol

A .41 caliber single-shot percussion pistol with 1.5" to 3.5" barrels, German silver mounts and a walnut stock. The lock normally marked "Syms/New York". Manufactured during the 1850s.

NIB	Exc.	V.G.	Good	Fair	Poor
—	—	2600	2150	825	300

T

TACONIC FIREARMS LTD.
Cambridge, New York

M98 Ultimate Hunter

This bolt-action rifle is based on the M98 Mauser action. It is available in calibers from .22-250 to .358 Win. Stainless steel and barrel length is 22". Titanium grip cap. Stock is XXX English walnut with cheekpiece and oil finish. Ebony fore-end tip. Scope bases are integral to the receiver. The prices listed are for the standard rifle. There are an extensive list of options which will greatly affect price. For example an optional quarter rib will add $1000 to the base price of the gun. Value speculative.

NIB	Exc.	V.G.	Good	Fair	Poor
6000 — 10000					

TALLASSEE
Tallassee, Alabama

Carbine

A .58 caliber single-shot percussion carbine with a 25" round barrel and full-length stock secured by two barrel bands. Fitted with sling swivels. Barrel and lock finished in the bright, brass furniture and walnut stock. The lock marked "C.S./Tallassee/ Ala." Approximately 500 of these carbines were manufactured in 1864. Very Rare.

Courtesy Milwaukee Public Museum, Milwaukee, Wisconsin

NIB	Exc.	V.G.	Good	Fair	Poor
—	—	100000	70000	40000	10000

TANFOGLIO
Valtrompia, Italy

The products of this company, which was established in the late 1940s, have been imported into the United States by various companies including Eig Corporation, F.I.E. of Hialeah, Florida, and Excam.

Sata

A .22 or 6.35mm caliber semi-automatic pistol with a 3" barrel. The slide marked "Pistola SATA Made in Italy" and the grips "SATA". Blued with black plastic grips.

NIB	Exc.	V.G.	Good	Fair	Poor
—	250	175	125	90	75

Titan

A 6.35mm caliber semi-automatic pistol with a 2.5" barrel and external hammer. The slide marked "Titan 6.35" and on U.S. imported examples, "EIG". Blued with plastic grips.

NIB	Exc.	V.G.	Good	Fair	Poor
—	250	175	125	90	75

Super Titan

Similar in design to above but with larger frame and in .380 ACP. Walnut grips.

NIB	Exc.	V.G.	Good	Fair	Poor
—	265	195	150	125	95

TA 90 or TZ-75

A 9mm caliber semi-automatic pistol with a 4.75" barrel and 15-shot magazine. Blued or chrome-plated with walnut or rubber grips. Those imported by Excam were known as the Model TA 90, while those imported by F.I.E. are known as the Model TZ-75.

NIB	Exc.	V.G.	Good	Fair	Poor
450	400	350	300	250	200

TA 90B

As above, with a 3.5" barrel, 12-shot magazine and Neoprene grips. Introduced in 1986.

NIB	Exc.	V.G.	Good	Fair	Poor
450	400	350	300	250	200

TA 90 SS

As above, with a ported 5" barrel, adjustable sights and two-tone finish. Introduced in 1989.

NIB	Exc.	V.G.	Good	Fair	Poor
650	600	500	450	400	300

TA 41 AE

As above, in .41 Action Express caliber. Introduced in 1989.

NIB	Exc.	V.G.	Good	Fair	Poor
500	450	400	350	300	250

TA 41 SS

As above, with a ported 5" barrel, adjustable sights and two-tone finish. Introduced in 1989.

NIB	Exc.	V.G.	Good	Fair	Poor
650	600	500	450	400	300

TA 76

A .22 caliber single-action revolver with a 4.75" barrel and 6-shot cylinder. Blued or chrome-plated with a brass back strap and trigger guard. Walnut grips.

NIB	Exc.	V.G.	Good	Fair	Poor
100	90	80	65	50	25

TA 76M Combo

As above, with a 6" or 9" barrel and an interchangeable .22 Magnum caliber cylinder.

NIB	Exc.	V.G.	Good	Fair	Poor
110	100	90	75	60	35

TA 38SB

A .38 Special caliber over/under double-barrel pocket pistol with 3" barrels and a hammer block safety. Blued with checkered nylon grips. Discontinued in 1985.

NIB	Exc.	V.G.	Good	Fair	Poor
—	100	90	80	60	40

TANNER, ANDRE
Switzerland

Model 300 Free Rifle

A 7.5mm Swiss or .308 caliber single-shot rifle with varying length barrels having adjustable target sights, adjustable trigger, and a walnut stock fitted with a palm rest and adjustable cheekpiece. Blued.

NIB	Exc.	V.G.	Good	Fair	Poor
4750	3750	3000	2500	1500	750

Model 300S

As above, with a 10-shot magazine and not fitted with a palm rest. Discontinued in 1988.

NIB	Exc.	V.G.	Good	Fair	Poor
4500	3500	2750	2250	1250	750

Model 50F

As above, in .22 caliber with a thumb hole stock. Discontinued in 1988.

NIB	Exc.	V.G.	Good	Fair	Poor
3750	3000	2500	1750	900	500

TARPLEY, J. & F. AND E. T. GARRETT & CO.
Greensboro, North Carolina

Carbine

A .52 caliber breechloading single-shot percussion carbine with a 22" round barrel and a plain walnut buttstock. Blued with a case hardened frame. The tang marked "J H Tarpley's./Pat Feb 14./1863". Over 400 of these carbines were manufactured.

NIB	Exc.	V.G.	Good	Fair	Poor
—	—	80000	65000	30000	10000

TAURUS INTERNATIONAL MFG. CO.
Porto Alegre, Brazil

PISTOLS

PT-92C

This 9mm model is a large capacity semi-automatic pistol with a 4.25" barrel. Drift adjustable 3-dot combat rear sight. Magazine holds 13 rounds in a double column. Choice of blued, stain nickel, or stainless steel finish. Brazilian hardwood grips are standard. Weighs 31 oz.

NIB	Exc.	V.G.	Good	Fair	Poor
450	325	275	220	160	100

PT-92

A slightly larger and heavier version of the PT-92C. This model has a 5" barrel with drift adjustable 3-dot combat rear sight. Magazine capacity is 15 rounds. This model is 1" longer overall than the above model and weighs 34 oz. Also available in blued, nickel, and stainless steel. **NOTE:** Add $20 for stainless steel and $50 for blue with gold finish, $60 for stainless steel with gold accents. A blued or stainless steel .22 LR conversion kit will add $250.

NIB	Exc.	V.G.	Good	Fair	Poor
400	300	225	150	100	75

PT-99

Similar in appearance and specifications to the PT-92, this version has the additional feature of fully adjustable 3-dot rear sight. **NOTE:** Add $20 for stainless steel finish.

NIB	Exc.	V.G.	Good	Fair	Poor
425	325	250	150	100	75

PT-92AF

A 9mm caliber double-action semi-automatic pistol with a 4.92" barrel, exposed hammer, and 15-shot magazine. Blued or nickel-plated with plain walnut grips.

NIB	Exc.	V.G.	Good	Fair	Poor
400	350	300	250	200	150

PT-100

This model is similar to the other full-size Taurus semi-automatics except that it is chambered for the .40 S&W cartridge. Supplied with a 5" barrel, with drift adjustable rear sight, it has a magazine capacity of 11 rounds. Also available in blued, nickel, or stainless steel. Weighs 34 oz. **NOTE:** For Special Edition, blued steel with gold fixtures and rosewood grips add $50. For blued steel with gold fixtures and pearl grips add $110.

NIB	Exc.	V.G.	Good	Fair	Poor
500	400	300	200	150	100

PT-101

Same as the model above but furnished with fully adjustable rear 3-dot combat sight.

NIB	Exc.	V.G.	Good	Fair	Poor
450	350	300	250	150	100

Deluxe Shooter's Pak

Offered by Taurus as a special package it consists of the pistol, with extra magazine, in a fitted custom hard case. Available for these models: PT-92, PT-99, PT-100, and PT-101. **NOTE:** Add approximately 10 percent to the prices of these models for this special feature.

PT-138

Introduced in 1998 this polymer frame pistol is chambered for the .380 cartridge. It is fitted with a 4" barrel in either blue or stainless steel. Weight is about 16 oz. Magazine capacity is 10 rounds.

Blue

NIB	Exc.	V.G.	Good	Fair	Poor
350	250	200	175	125	100

Stainless Steel

NIB	Exc.	V.G.	Good	Fair	Poor
375	275	225	175	125	100

PT-908

A semi-automatic double-action pistol chambered for the 9mm Parabellum cartridge. It is fitted with a 3.8" barrel, with drift adjustable rear 3-dot combat sight. Magazine capacity is 8 rounds in a single column. Available in blued, satin nickel, or stainless steel. Stocks are black rubber. Pistol weighs 30 oz. Introduced in 1993.

NIB	Exc.	V.G.	Good	Fair	Poor
375	325	275	225	150	100

PT-911

This model was introduced in 1997 and is chambered for the 9mm cartridge. It is fitted with a 4" barrel and has a magazine capacity of 10 rounds. Choice of blue or stainless steel. Weight is about 28 oz. Black rubber grips are standard. **NOTE:** Add $20 for stainless steel.

NIB	Exc.	V.G.	Good	Fair	Poor
450	350	275	225	175	125

PT-111

Chambered for the 9mm cartridge and fitted with a 3.25" barrel. Magazine is 10 rounds. Weight is about 19 oz. **NOTE:** For matte stainless steel finish add $15. For night sights add $80.

NIB	Exc.	V.G.	Good	Fair	Poor
375	300	250	175	125	100

PT-140

Chambered for the .40 S&W cartridge and fitted with a 3.25" barrel. Magazine capacity is 10 rounds. Weight is about 19 oz. **NOTE:** For matte stainless steel finish add $15. For night sights add $80.

NIB	Exc.	V.G.	Good	Fair	Poor
350	300	265	180	125	100

PT-140 Millennium

Chambered for the .40 S&W cartridge and fitted with a 3.25" barrel, this model features a polymer frame and either a blue or stainless steel slide. Fixed sights. Magazine capacity is 10 rounds. Weight is about 19 oz. **NOTE:** For night sights add $75.

Blue

NIB	Exc.	V.G.	Good	Fair	Poor
345	315	225	150	100	75

Stainless Steel

NIB	Exc.	V.G.	Good	Fair	Poor
375	325	250	175	100	75

PT-145 Millennium

Similar to the PT-140 but chambered for the .45 ACP cartridge. Barrel length is 3.27". Weight is about 23 oz. Magazine capacity is 10 rounds. Weight is about 19 oz. **NOTE:** For night sights add $75.

Blue

NIB	Exc.	V.G.	Good	Fair	Poor
345	315	225	150	100	75

Stainless Steel

NIB	Exc.	V.G.	Good	Fair	Poor
375	325	250	175	100	75

Millennium Pro

Introduced in 2003 this pistol is a third generation series in the Millennium line. It features a captured dual spring and guide assembly, a re-engineered magazine release, and an internal firing pin lock. A larger 3-dot sighting system, positive slide serrations, internal magazine base extension, and an enlarged external safety with positive click are other improvements.

NIB	Exc.	V.G.	Good	Fair	Poor
365	300	200	150	100	75

Model 609TI-PRO

Similar to Millennium Pro but with titanium slide. Chambered in 9mm Parabellum. Features include 13+1 capacity, 3.25" barrel, checkered polymer grips, Heinie Straight-8 sights. Overall length 6.125". Weight: 19.7 oz.

NIB	Exc.	V.G.	Good	Fair	Poor
500	450	325	225	175	125

PT-400/400SS

Chambered for the .400 CorBon cartridge and fitted with a 4.25" ported barrel with fixed sights. Magazine capacity is 8 rounds. Offered in blue or stainless steel. Rubber grips. Weight is about 30 oz.

Blue

NIB	Exc.	V.G.	Good	Fair	Poor
375	300	200	150	100	75

Stainless Steel

NIB	Exc.	V.G.	Good	Fair	Poor
420	325	225	150	100	75

PT-132

Chambered for the .32 ACP cartridge and fitted with a 3.25" barrel. Magazine capacity is 10 rounds. Weight is about 20 oz. **NOTE:** For matte stainless steel finish add $15.

NIB	Exc.	V.G.	Good	Fair	Poor
325	275	200	150	100	75

PT-58

This model was introduced in 1988. Chambered for the .380 ACP cartridge it is fitted with a 4" barrel with drift adjustable rear sight. It is a conventional double-action design. Available in blued, satin nickel, or stainless steel. It is fitted with Brazilian hardwood grips. Pistol weighs 30 oz.

NIB	Exc.	V.G.	Good	Fair	Poor
300	250	200	150	100	75

PT-145

Chambered for the .45 ACP cartridge and fitted with a 3.25" barrel. Magazine capacity is 10 rounds. Weight is about 23 oz. **NOTE:** For matte stainless steel finish add $15. For night sights add $80.

NIB	Exc.	V.G.	Good	Fair	Poor
325	275	250	200	150	100

PT-45

Introduced in 1994 this semi-automatic double-action pistol is chambered for the .45 ACP cartridge. The barrel is 3.75" in length and the magazine capacity is 8 rounds. Offered in blued or stainless steel with grips of Brazilian hardwood. Fixed sights are standard. Overall length is 7.1" and weight is approximately 30 oz.

Blue

NIB	Exc.	V.G.	Good	Fair	Poor
350	275	200	150	100	75

Stainless Steel

NIB	Exc.	V.G.	Good	Fair	Poor
400	325	250	200	150	100

PT-745B/SS

Chambered for the .45 ACP cartridge and fitted with a 3.25" barrel. Fixed sights. Polymer grips. Blue or stainless steel. Magazine capacity is 6 rounds. Weight is about 21 oz. Introduced in 2004. **NOTE:** Add $15 for stainless steel.

NIB	Exc.	V.G.	Good	Fair	Poor
375	315	275	225	125	175

PT-640B/SS

Similar to the above model but chambered for the .40 S&W cartridge. Magazine capacity is 10 rounds. Weight is about 24 oz.

Introduced in in 2004. **NOTE:** Add $15 for stainless steel.

NIB	Exc.	V.G.	Good	Fair	Poor
375	315	275	225	125	175

PT-24/7-45B

This .45 ACP pistol is fitted with a 4.25" barrel with fixed sights. Ribbed grips. Blued receiver. Magazine capacity is 12 rounds. Weight is about 27 oz. Introduced in 2004. **NOTE:** Add $15 for stainless steel slide.

NIB	Exc.	V.G.	Good	Fair	Poor
400	300	285	225	150	100

24/7 G2

Double/single action semi-automatic pistol chambered in 9mm Parabellum (15+1), .40 S&W (13+1), and .45 ACP (10+1). Features include blued or stainless finish; "Strike Two" capability; new trigger safety; low-profile adjustable rear sights for windage and elevation; ambidextrous magazine release; 4.2" barrel; Picatinny rail; polymer frame; polymer grip with metallic inserts and three interchangeable backstraps. Also offered in compact model with shorter grip frame and 3.5" barrel.

NIB	Exc.	V.G.	Good	Fair	Poor
425	350	300	250	175	125

24/7-PRO Standard

4" barrel; stainless, duotone or blued finish.

NIB	Exc.	V.G.	Good	Fair	Poor
400	300	285	225	150	100

24/7-PRO Compact

3.2" barrel; stainless, titanium or blued finish.

NIB	Exc.	V.G.	Good	Fair	Poor
400	300	285	225	150	100

24/7-PRO Long Slide

5.2" barrel; matte stainless, blued or stainless finish.

NIB	Exc.	V.G.	Good	Fair	Poor
400	300	285	225	150	100

PT-24/7-9B

As above but chambered for the 9mm cartridge. Magazine capacity is 17 rounds. Weight is about 27 oz. Introduced in 2005. **NOTE:** Add $15 for stainless steel slide.

NIB	Exc.	V.G.	Good	Fair	Poor
400	300	285	225	150	100

PT-24/7-40B

As above but chambered for the .40 S&W cartridge. Magazine capacity is 15 rounds. Weight is about 27 oz. Introduced in 2005. **NOTE:** Add $15 for stainless steel slide.

NIB	Exc.	V.G.	Good	Fair	Poor
400	300	285	225	150	100

PT-24/7LS-9SS-17

Full-size stainless semi-automatic chambered for 9mm. Long grip, long slide. Capacity 17+1. Single/double action. 5" barrel, 27.2 oz. Fixed, 2-dot rear sight. Also in short grip 10+1 capacity. Introduced 2006. Price is for stainless.

NIB	Exc.	V.G.	Good	Fair	Poor
425	345	295	245	175	125

PT-24/79SSC-17

Compact stainless semi-automatic chambered for 9mm, short grip, short slide. Capacity 15+1. Single/double action. 5" barrel, 27.2 oz. Fixed, 2-dot rear sight. Also in short grip 10+1 capacity. Introduced 2006. Price is for stainless.

NIB	Exc.	V.G.	Good	Fair	Poor
400	300	285	225	150	100

PT-24/7PLS-9SSPTi-17

Full-size semi-automatic chambered for 9mm. Capacity 17+1 or 10+1. Single/double action. Titanium slide, 4" barrel, 27.2 oz. Introduced 2006.

NIB	Exc.	V.G.	Good	Fair	Poor
400	300	285	225	150	100

24/7 OSS

Introduced in 2007. Available in .45 ACP, .40 S&W and 9mm Parabellum. 12+1 capacity (.45), single-/double-action. Ambidextrous decock and safety, match grade barrel, polymer frame with steel upper. Claimed to exceed all requirements set by United States Special Operations Command and developed to compete is SOCOM pistol trials. **NOTE:** Add 5 percent for stainless.

NIB	Exc.	V.G.	Good	Fair	Poor
425	345	295	245	175	125

PT-24/7PLS-9SSCTi-17

Compact semi-automatic chambered for 9mm. Capacity 17+1. Single/double action. Titanium slide, 3.3" barrel, 25.4 oz. Introduced 2006.

NIB	Exc.	V.G.	Good	Fair	Poor
425	345	295	245	175	125

24/7PLS

Similar to above but with 5" barrel. Chambered in 9mm Parabellum, .38 Super, and .40 S&W.

NIB	Exc.	V.G.	Good	Fair	Poor
425	345	295	245	175	125

2045 Large Frame Pistol

Similar to Taurus Model 24/7 but chambered in .45 ACP only. Features include polymer frame, blued or matte stainless steel slide, 4.2" barrel, ambidextrous "memory pads" to promote safe finger position during loading, ambi three-position safety/decocker. Picatinny rail system, fixed sights. Overall length 7.34". Weight: 31.5 oz.

NIB	Exc.	V.G.	Good	Fair	Poor
450	375	325	250	175	125

809-B 9mm

Introduced in 2008. Basically a Model 24/7 OSS but with an exposed hammer. 17+1 capacity, black Tenifer finish.

NIB	Exc.	V.G.	Good	Fair	Poor
550	425	350	275	200	150

800 Series Compact

Compact double/single action semi-automatic pistol chambered in 9mm (12+1), .357 SIG (10+1) and .40 cal (10+1). Features include 3.5" barrel; external hammer; loaded chamber indicator; polymer frame; blued or stainless slide.

NIB	Exc.	V.G.	Good	Fair	Poor
485	410	350	275	200	150

PT191140B

1911-style .40 caliber semi-automatic. Blued steel. 5" barrel, 8+1 capacity, 32 oz. Fixed Heinie two-dot straight-eight sight. Blue or stainless. Introduced 2006. **NOTE:** Add 10 percent for stainless.

NIB	Exc.	V.G.	Good	Fair	Poor
675	550	425	300	200	125

PT1911

Blued or stainless 1911-style single action in .45 ACP. 8+1 capacity. LOA 8.5", 32 oz., 5" barrel, fixed Heinie two-dot straight-eight sight. Numerous options. Introduced 2006. **NOTE:** Add 10 percent for alloy frame and picatinny rail versions (added 2007). Add 10 percent for stainless.

NIB	Exc.	V.G.	Good	Fair	Poor
675	550	425	300	200	125

Model 1911B-9

Similar to above but chambered in 9mm Parabellum (9+1).

NIB	Exc.	V.G.	Good	Fair	Poor
675	550	425	300	200	125

Model 1911B-38

Similar to above but chambered in .38 Super.

NIB	Exc.	V.G.	Good	Fair	Poor
675	550	425	300	200	125

Model 1911HC

Similar to Taurus Model 1911 but with 12+1 capacity; .45 ACP only.

NIB	Exc.	V.G.	Good	Fair	Poor
725	600	475	375	250	150

PT-745GB

Blued semi-automatic in .45 GAP with 7+1 capacity. 3.25" barrel, fixed sights, 22 oz., polymer grip plates. Introduced 2006.

NIB	Exc.	V.G.	Good	Fair	Poor
375	300	225	175	125	100

PT745B/SS-LS

Blued or stainless semi-automatic in .45 ACP. 4.25" barrel, 23.3 oz. 7+1 capacity, polymer grip plates. Introduced 2006.

NIB	Exc.	V.G.	Good	Fair	Poor
375	300	225	175	125	100

PT917B20

9mm blued or stainless semi-automatic with 20+1 capacity. Fixed sights, 4" barrel, 31.8 oz. Introduced 2006.

NIB	Exc.	V.G.	Good	Fair	Poor
375	300	225	175	125	100

PT609Ti-13

This 9mm semi-automatic has a titanium finish plus 13+1 capacity, 3.25" barrel. Fixed sights, 19.2 oz. Introduced 2006.

NIB	Exc.	V.G.	Good	Fair	Poor
500	425	300	225	150	100

PT138BP12 Millennium Pro

Blued or stainless SA/DA semi-automatic in .380 ACP with 12+1 capacity. Fixed sights, 3.25" barrel, 18.7 oz. Introduced 2006. Also available in .32 ACP and .40 S&W.

NIB	Exc.	V.G.	Good	Fair	Poor
400	300	285	225	150	100

PT-38B/SS

Chambered for the .38 Super cartridge and fitted with a 4.25" barrel with fixed sights. Grips are checkered rubber. Blued or stainless steel. Magazine capacity is 10 rounds. Weight is about 30 oz. Introduced in 2004. **NOTE:** Add $15 for stainless steel.

NIB	Exc.	V.G.	Good	Fair	Poor
425	345	295	245	175	125

PT-38SSSPRL

Introduced in 2005 this model is chambered for the .38 Super cartridge and fitted with a 4.25" barrel. Magazine capacity is 10 rounds. Finish is stainless steel and gold. Weight is about 30 oz. **NOTE:** Deduct $60 for stainless steel only.

NIB	Exc.	V.G.	Good	Fair	Poor
475	400	300	225	150	100

738 TCP Compact Pistol

Lightweight DAO semi-automatic pistol chambered for .380 ACP. Features include a 3.35" barrel; polymer frame; blued (738B), stainless (738SS) or titanium (738Ti) slide; concealed hammer; low-profile fixed sight; ambi safety; loaded chamber indicator. Capacity 6+1 (standard magazine) or 8+1 (extended magazine). Overall length 5.195". Weight: 9 oz. (titanium slide) to 10.2 oz.

NIB	Exc.	V.G.	Good	Fair	Poor
300	275	250	225	150	100

709 "Slim"

Semi-automatic pistol chambered in 9mm Parabellum. Features include a streamlined profile, 3.25" barrel, 7+1 capacity, fixed sights, checkered polymer grips, choice of blued (709B) or stainless (709SS) slide. Single/double action. Overall length 6.25". Weight: 10 oz.

NIB	Exc.	V.G.	Good	Fair	Poor
400	300	285	225	150	100

638 Pro Compact

Caliber .380 ACP, steel slide, polymer frame, 15-round magazine. Barrel length is 3.2". Single-action trigger has integral safety. Other features include ambidextrous thumb safety, accessory rail, adjustable rear sight and loaded chamber and cocked striker indicators. Taurus Security System. Weight is 28 ounces. Blue or matte stainless finish.

NIB	Exc.	V.G.	Good	Fair	Poor
410	350	300	250	200	150

DT Hybrid

Caliber: 9mm Parabellum/.40 S&W, steel slide, polymer/steel frame, 3.2" barrel. Magazine capacity is 13 rounds, 11 for .40.

Single-action trigger has Strike Two capability. Integral trigger safety, manual safety and Taurus Security System. Ambidextrous magazine release, adjustable rear sight and loaded-chamber indicator. Weight is 24 ounces. Finish is blue or matte stainless.

NIB	Exc.	V.G.	Good	Fair	Poor
465	400	350	285	200	150

917

Lightweight, compact semi-automatic chambered in 9mm Parabellum. Matte blue or stainless finish, 17+1 or 20+1 capacity. Introduced 2007.

NIB	Exc.	V.G.	Good	Fair	Poor
400	300	285	225	150	100

PT-945C

Introduced in 1995 this .45 ACP double-action pistol features a 4" barrel with an 8-round magazine. The grips are black rubber. The sights are drift adjustable 3-dot combat style. Approximate weight is 30 oz. Offered in blue or stainless steel with or without ported barrel.

Blue

NOTE: Add $45 for blued finish with gold accents and ported barrel. Add $35 for ported barrel and blue finish. Add $40 for ported barrel.

NIB	Exc.	V.G.	Good	Fair	Poor
450	350	250	200	150	100

Stainless Steel

NOTE: Add $40 for ported barrel with stainless steel finish or Stainless steel finish with gold accents.

NIB	Exc.	V.G.	Good	Fair	Poor
475	400	300	250	150	100

PT-945S

Same as the model above but chambered for the .45 Super cartridge. Introduced in 1998.

Blue

NIB	Exc.	V.G.	Good	Fair	Poor
450	350	250	200	150	100

Stainless Steel

NIB	Exc.	V.G.	Good	Fair	Poor
475	375	275	225	150	100

PT-940

Similar to the PT-945 except chambered for the .40 S&W cartridge. Fitted with a 4" barrel. Magazine capacity is 10 rounds. Choice of blue or stainless steel. Black rubber grips. Weight is approximately 28 oz. Introduced in 1997. **NOTE:** Add $20 for stainless steel.

NIB	Exc.	V.G.	Good	Fair	Poor
425	315	265	200	125	75

PT-938

This model is chambered for the .380 ACP cartridge and fitted with a 3" barrel. Black rubber grips and choice of blue or stainless steel. Weight is about 27 oz. Introduced in 1997.

NIB	Exc.	V.G.	Good	Fair	Poor
365	300	245	175	80	50

922 Sport

Introduced in 2003 this semi-automatic .22 caliber pistol features a lightweight polymer frame. Single- or double-action trigger. Barrel length is 6". Magazine capacity is 10 rounds. Adjustable sights. Weight is about 25 oz. **NOTE:** For matte stainless steel finish add $15.

NIB	Exc.	V.G.	Good	Fair	Poor
310	250	175	150	100	75

PT-22

This is a semi-automatic double-action-only pistol that features a 2.75" barrel with fixed sights and a manual safety. It is chambered for the .22 LR cartridge and has a magazine capacity of 8 rounds. The stocks are Brazilian hardwood and the finish is available in either blue, blue with gold trim, nickel, or two-tone. Pistol weighs 12.3 oz. **NOTE:** For Special Edition, blued steel with gold fixtures and rosewood grips, add $50. For blued steel with gold fixtures and pearl grips add $110.

NIB	Exc.	V.G.	Good	Fair	Poor
250	175	250	75	60	50

PT-922

This .22 caliber pistol has a 6" barrel with fiber optic adjustable sights. Polymer grips. Ten-round magazine. Blued finish. Weight is about 29 oz. Introduced in 2004.

NIB	Exc.	V.G.	Good	Fair	Poor
365	300	245	175	80	50

PT-25

Similar in appearance to the PT-22, this model is chambered for the .25 ACP cartridge and has a magazine capacity of 9 rounds. This model is also fitted with a 2.75" barrel. Offered in blue, blue with gold trim, two-tone finish, or nickel. **NOTE:** For Special Edition, blued steel with gold fixtures and rosewood grips, add $50. For blued steel with gold fixtures and pearl grips add $110.

NIB	Exc.	V.G.	Good	Fair	Poor
250	175	125	75	60	50

22PLY/25PLY Small Polymer Frame Pistols

Similar to Taurus Models PT-22 and PT-25 but with lightweight polymer frame. Features include .22 LR (22PLY, 9+1) or .25 ACP (25PLY, 8+1) chambering, 2.33" tip-up barrel, matte black finish, extended magazine with finger lip, manual safety. Overall length 4.8". Weight 10.8 oz.

NIB	Exc.	V.G.	Good	Fair	Poor
225	200	175	—	—	—

REVOLVERS

Model 17MB2/MSS2

This 8-shot revolver is chambered for the .17 HMR cartridge and fitted with a 1.75" barrel with fixed sights. Blued or stainless steel. Hard rubber grips. Weight is about 22 oz. Introduced in 2004. **NOTE:** Add $45 for stainless steel.

NIB	Exc.	V.G.	Good	Fair	Poor
360	280	225	175	150	100

Model 73

A .32 Smith & Wesson Long double-action swing-out cylinder revolver, with a 3" barrel and 6-shot cylinder. Blued or nickel plated with walnut grips.

NIB	Exc.	V.G.	Good	Fair	Poor
250	195	150	125	100	75

Model 80

A full-size 6-round .38 Special with 3" or 4" heavy tapered barrel. Supplied with fixed sights and offered with blued or stainless steel (offered new in 1993) finish. Brazilian hardwood grips are standard. Weighs 30 oz. **NOTE:** Add $45 for stainless steel

NIB	Exc.	V.G.	Good	Fair	Poor
285	195	135	110	85	700

Model 82

Nearly identical to the Model 80, the Model 82 has a 3" or 4" heavy, solid rib barrel in place of the heavy tapered barrel. Pistol weighs 34 oz. **NOTE:** Add $40 for stainless steel.

NIB	Exc.	V.G.	Good	Fair	Poor
285	195	135	110	85	70

Model 82B4

Chambered for the .38 Special +P cartridge and fitted with a 4" heavy solid rib barrel. Cylinder holds 6 rounds. Rubber grips. Fixed sights. Blue finish. Weight is about 37 oz.

NIB	Exc.	V.G.	Good	Fair	Poor
295	250	200	125	100	75

Model 82SS4

Same as above but with stainless steel finish. Weight is about 37 oz.

NIB	Exc.	V.G.	Good	Fair	Poor
315	265	185	125	100	75

Model 827B4

Chambered for the .38 Special +P cartridge and fitted with a 4" heavy barrel with solid rib. Cylinder is 7 shots. Rubber grips. Blued finish. Weight is about 37 oz. Fixed sights.

NIB	Exc.	V.G.	Good	Fair	Poor
300	250	200	150	100	75

Model 827SS4

Same as above but with stainless steel finish. Weight is about 35 oz.

NIB	Exc.	V.G.	Good	Fair	Poor
350	300	250	175	125	75

Model 83

Similar to the Model 82 except for a fully adjustable rear sight and Patridge-type front sight. Offered with 4" barrel only with blued or stainless steel (new for 1993) finish. Pistol weighs 34 oz.

NIB	Exc.	V.G.	Good	Fair	Poor
300	250	200	150	100	75

Model 86

Similar to the Model 83 with the exception of a 6" barrel, target hammer, adjustable trigger, and blue-only finish. Weighs 34 oz.

NIB	Exc.	V.G.	Good	Fair	Poor
325	275	225	175	125	75

Model 85

A double-action revolver chambered for the .38 Special. This model is available in either a 2" or 3" heavy, solid rib barrel fitted with ejector shroud. Sights are fixed. Blued finish and stainless steel (new for 1993) are offered with Brazilian hardwood grips. Pistol weighs 21 oz. with 2" barrel. Beginning in 1996 this model was furnished with Uncle Mike's Boot Grips. **NOTE:** For Special Edition, blued steel with gold fixtures and rosewood grips, add $50. For blued steel with gold fixtures and pearl grips add $110.

NIB	Exc.	V.G.	Good	Fair	Poor
300	225	175	125	100	75

Model 85 Stainless

As above, in stainless steel. Beginning in 1996 this model was furnished with Uncle Mike's Boot Grips.

NIB	Exc.	V.G.	Good	Fair	Poor
350	275	225	200	150	100

Model 85CH

Same as above but offered in 2" or 3" barrel with shrouded hammer. Double-action-only. **NOTE:** Add $50 for stainless steel and $25 for ported barrel on 2" models.

NIB	Exc.	V.G.	Good	Fair	Poor
300	225	175	125	100	75

Model 85 UL

This double-action revolver is built on a small aluminum frame and is chambered for the .38 Special cartridge. It is fitted with a 2" barrel. Choice of blue or stainless steel finish. Weight is approximately 17 oz. Introduced in 1997. **NOTE:** For Special Edition, blued steel with gold fixtures and rosewood grips add $50. For blued steel with gold fixtures and pearl grips add $110. Add $30.00 for stainless steel.

NIB	Exc.	V.G.	Good	Fair	Poor
325	250	195	150	125	100

Model 85 Hy-Lite Magnesium

Similar to Model 85 but weighs only 13.8 oz. Gray alloy frame and Hy-Lite sights. Introduced 2007.

NIB	Exc.	V.G.	Good	Fair	Poor
375	300	250	200	175	125

Model 85 Ultra-Lite Gray

Similar to Model 85 but with lightweight magnesium frame. Fixed or fiber-optic front sight. Introduced 2007.

NIB	Exc.	V.G.	Good	Fair	Poor
375	300	250	200	175	125

Model 85 Ultra-Lite Titanium

NIB	Exc.	V.G.	Good	Fair	Poor
475	400	275	200	175	125

Model 850

Chambered for the .38 Special cartridge. Fitted with a 2" barrel with fixed sights. Hammerless with 5-round cylinder. Rubber grips. Weight is about 23 oz. Choice of blue or stainless steel. **NOTE:** Add $50 for stainless steel.

NIB	Exc.	V.G.	Good	Fair	Poor
375	300	250	200	175	125

Model 850 Ultra-Lite Blue

Similar to Model 850 but with lightweight alloy frame. Introduced 2007.

NIB	Exc.	V.G.	Good	Fair	Poor
375	300	250	200	175	125

Model 850 Ultra-Lite Stainless Steel

Similar to Model 850 Ultra-Lite Blue but with stainless finish. Introduced 2007.

NIB	Exc.	V.G.	Good	Fair	Poor
375	300	250	200	175	125

Model 605

Similar to Model 650 but with ultra-lightweight frame. Blue or stainless finish. Weight 23 oz. Introduced 2007.

NIB	Exc.	V.G.	Good	Fair	Poor
375	300	250	200	175	125

Taurus Polymer Protector

Single/double action revolver chambered in .38 Special +P. Features include 5-round cylinder; polymer frame; faux wood rubber-feel grips; fixed sights; shrouded hammer with cocking spur; blued finish; 2.5" barrel. Weight 18.2 oz.

NIB	Exc.	V.G.	Good	Fair	Poor
380	320	275	230	200	150

Model 650

Same as Model 850 but chambered for the .357 Magnum cartridge. **NOTE:** Add $50 for stainless steel.

NIB	Exc.	V.G.	Good	Fair	Poor
375	300	250	200	175	125

Taurus 405 Revolver

Chambered for .40 S&W with steel cylinder, alloy frame, 5-round capacity, 2" barrel. Taurus Security System and Ribber grips.

Weight is 29 oz. Blue or matte stainless finish. Available in .44 Special as Model 445 with weight of 22 oz. **NOTE:** Add 15 percent for stainless finish.

NIB	Exc.	V.G.	Good	Fair	Poor
385	325	275	235	200	150

Model 851 and 651 Revolvers

Small-frame SA/DA revolvers similar to Taurus Model 85 but with Centennial-style concealed-hammer frame. Chambered in .38 Special +P (Model 851) or .357 Magnum (Model 651). Features include five-shot cylinder; 2" barrel; fixed sights; blue, matte blue, titanium or stainless finish; Taurus security lock. Overall length 6.5". Weight: 15.5 oz. (titanium) to 25 oz. (blued and stainless).

NIB	Exc.	V.G.	Good	Fair	Poor
400	300	285	225	150	100

Model 94

This double-action revolver is chambered for the .22 LR cartridge. The swing-out cylinder holds 9 rounds. It is available with a heavy, solid rib, 3" or 4" barrel. In 1996 a 5" barrel option was added to this model in both blue and stainless steel. Ramp front sight with fully adjustable rear sight. Offered in blued or stainless steel with Brazilian hardwood grips. Pistol weighs 25 oz. with 4" barrel.

Blue

NIB	Exc.	V.G.	Good	Fair	Poor
350	275	225	200	150	100

Stainless Steel

NIB	Exc.	V.G.	Good	Fair	Poor
375	300	250	225	175	125

Model 94 UL

Introduced in 1997 this model is built on a small aluminum frame with 2" barrel and chambered for the .22 LR cartridge. Choice of blue or stainless steel. Weight is approximately 14 oz.

NIB	Exc.	V.G.	Good	Fair	Poor
400	300	285	225	150	100

Model 941

Similar in appearance to the Model 94 this version is chambered for the .22 WMR. Available with a choice of 3" or 4" heavy, solid rib barrel. In 1996 a 5" barrel option was added to this model. This model holds 8 rounds. Ramp front sight with fully adjustable rear sight. Available in blued or stainless steel with Brazilian hardwood grips. Pistol weighs 27.5 oz.

Blue

NIB	Exc.	V.G.	Good	Fair	Poor
350	250	175	125	100	75

Stainless Steel

NIB	Exc.	V.G.	Good	Fair	Poor
375	275	200	150	100	75

Model 941 UL

Same as the standard Model 941 but with an aluminum frame and 2" barrel. Weight is about 18 oz. Introduced in 1997.

NIB	Exc.	V.G.	Good	Fair	Poor
400	300	285	225	150	100

Model 96

A full-size .22 LR revolver with 6" heavy, solid rib barrel. Fully adjustable rear sight with target hammer and adjustable target trigger. Cylinder holds 6 rounds. Available in blued only with Brazilian hardwood grips. Pistol weighs 34 oz.

NIB	Exc.	V.G.	Good	Fair	Poor
300	250	200	150	125	100

Model 741

This double-action revolver is chambered for the .32 H&R Magnum cartridge. It features a 3" or 4" heavy, solid rib barrel with fully adjustable rear sight. Swing-out cylinder holds 6 rounds. Available in either blued or stainless steel (stainless steel model introduced in 1993) with Brazilian hardwood grips. Pistol weighs 30 oz. **NOTE:** Add $40 for stainless steel.

NIB	Exc.	V.G.	Good	Fair	Poor
200	175	150	125	100	75

Model 761

Similar to the Model 741 this version has a 6" barrel, target hammer, adjustable target trigger, and is available in blued only. Weighs 34 oz.

NIB	Exc.	V.G.	Good	Fair	Poor
350	250	175	125	100	75

Model 65

This double-action revolver is chambered for the .357 Magnum cartridge. It is offered with 2.5" or 4" heavy, solid rib barrel with ejector shroud. Fitted with fixed sights and Brazilian hardwood grips it is available in blued or stainless steel. The 2.5" barrel is a new addition to the Model 65 for 1993. Pistol weighs 34 oz. with 4" barrel. **NOTE:** Add $40 for stainless steel.

NIB	Exc.	V.G.	Good	Fair	Poor
325	225	150	125	100	75

Model 605

Introduced in 1995 this revolver is chambered for the .357 Magnum cartridge. It is fitted with a 2.25" or 3" heavy barrel and is offered in blue or stainless steel. Weighs 25 oz.

Blue

NIB	Exc.	V.G.	Good	Fair	Poor
325	225	150	125	100	75

Stainless Steel

NIB	Exc.	V.G.	Good	Fair	Poor
375	275	200	150	100	75

Model 605 Custom (B2C)

Same as above but offered with a 2.25" compensated barrel.

Blue

NIB	Exc.	V.G.	Good	Fair	Poor
400	300	285	225	150	100

Stainless Steel

NIB	Exc.	V.G.	Good	Fair	Poor
450	350	300	250	150	100

Model 605CHB2/SS2

Chambered for the .357 Magnum cartridge and fitted with a 2.25" solid rib barrel and 5-shot cylinder. This model is also offered with a concealed hammer. Weight is about 24 oz.

Blue

NIB	Exc.	V.G.	Good	Fair	Poor
350	250	175	125	100	75

Stainless Steel

NIB	Exc.	V.G.	Good	Fair	Poor
375	275	200	150	100	75

Model 605CHB2C/SS2C

Same as above but with concealed hammer and ported barrels.

Blue

NIB	Exc.	V.G.	Good	Fair	Poor
350	250	175	125	100	75

Stainless Steel

NIB	Exc.	V.G.	Good	Fair	Poor
375	275	200	150	100	75

Model 66

Similar to the Model 65 but offered with a choice of 2.5", 4", or 6" barrel with fully adjustable rear sight. Offered with either blued or stainless steel. Weighs 35 oz. with 4" barrel. The 2.5" barrel was introduced in 1993.

NIB	Exc.	V.G.	Good	Fair	Poor
225	200	175	150	125	100

Model 66CP

This model is similar to the Model 66 but features a compensated heavy, solid rib 4" or 6" ejector shroud barrel. Introduced in 1993. Pistol weighs 35 oz.

NIB	Exc.	V.G.	Good	Fair	Poor
250	225	200	150	125	100

Model 66B4/SS4

Chambered for the .357 Magnum cartridge with 4" solid rib barrel and 7-shot cylinder. Adjustable sights. Rubber grips. Weight is about 38 oz.

Blue

NIB	Exc.	V.G.	Good	Fair	Poor
350	275	225	150	125	100

Stainless Steel

NIB	Exc.	V.G.	Good	Fair	Poor
400	325	275	225	150	100

Model 607

Introduced in 1995 this .357 Magnum model features a choice of 4" or 6.5" integral compensated barrel in either blue or stainless steel. The 6.5" barrel is fitted with a vent rib.

Blue

NIB	Exc.	V.G.	Good	Fair	Poor
325	275	225	200	150	100

Stainless Steel

NIB	Exc.	V.G.	Good	Fair	Poor
400	350	300	200	150	100

Model 606

Introduced in 1997 this 6-round model is chambered for the .357 Magnum cartridge. Fitted with a 2" solid rib barrel with ramp front sight and notched rear sight. Available in double-action, single or double-action-only. Offered in blue or stainless steel. Rubber grips are standard. Weight is approximately 29 oz. A number of variations are offered on this model. **NOTE:** For stainless steel models add $50.

NIB	Exc.	V.G.	Good	Fair	Poor
375	275	200	150	100	75

Model 608

Introduced in 1996 this revolver is chambered for the .357 Magnum cartridge. The cylinder is bored for 8 rounds. Offered in 4" and 6.5" barrel lengths with integral compensator. The front sight is serrated ramp with red insert and the rear is adjustable. Offered in both blued and stainless steel versions. Weight is approximately 51.5 oz. with 6.5" barrel.

Blue

NIB	Exc.	V.G.	Good	Fair	Poor
425	325	250	200	150	100

Stainless Steel

NIB	Exc.	V.G.	Good	Fair	Poor
450	350	300	200	150	100

Model 689

This model is chambered for the .357 Magnum cartridge and features a heavy, vent rib barrel in either 4" or 6" lengths. Fully adjustable rear sight is standard. Offered in blued or stainless steel. Pistol weighs 37 oz. In 1998 this model was fitted with a 7-round cylinder.

NIB	Exc.	V.G.	Good	Fair	Poor
375	275	200	150	100	75

Model 617

Chambered for the .357 Magnum cartridge with 7-round cylinder. It is fitted with a 2" barrel. Choice of blue or stainless steel finish. Some variations offered a ported barrel. Introduced in 1998.

Blue

NIB	Exc.	V.G.	Good	Fair	Poor
400	325	275	225	175	125

Stainless Steel

NIB	Exc.	V.G.	Good	Fair	Poor
400	325	275	225	175	125

Ported Barrel

NIB	Exc.	V.G.	Good	Fair	Poor
425	325	250	200	150	100

Model 617 CHB2/SS2

Chambered for the .357 Magnum cartridge this model features a concealed hammer, 2" solid rib barrel, and fixed sights.

Blue

NIB	Exc.	V.G.	Good	Fair	Poor
350	275	225	175	125	100

Stainless Steel

NIB	Exc.	V.G.	Good	Fair	Poor
425	325	250	200	150	100

Model 627 Tracker

This model is chambered for the .357 Magnum cartridge and has a 7-round cylinder. The 4" barrel is ported with a heavy underlug. Adjustable rear sight. Matte stainless steel finish. Introduced in 2000.

NIB	Exc.	V.G.	Good	Fair	Poor
450	325	275	225	175	125

Model 669

This model is chambered for the .357 Magnum cartridge and features a 4" or 6" heavy, solid rib barrel with full shroud. It has fully adjustable rear sight and is available with blued or stainless steel finish. Brazilian hardwood grips are standard. Pistol weighs 37 oz. with 4" barrel. **NOTE:** Add $60 for stainless steel.

NIB	Exc.	V.G.	Good	Fair	Poor
375	275	200	150	100	75

Model 669CP

This variation of the Model 669 was introduced in 1993 and features a 4" or 6" compensated barrel. Fully adjustable rear sights are standard and it is offered with either blue or stainless steel finish. Weighs 37 oz. In 1998 this model was fitted with a 7-round cylinder. **NOTE:** Add $60 for stainless steel.

NIB	Exc.	V.G.	Good	Fair	Poor
425	325	250	200	150	100

Model 415

Chambered for .41 Magnum cartridge and fitted with a 2.5" ported barrel. Fixed sights. Rubber grips. Matte stainless steel finish. Weight is about 30 oz.

NIB	Exc.	V.G.	Good	Fair	Poor
450	350	300	200	150	100

Model 431

Chambered for the .44 Special cartridge this double-action revolver is furnished with a 3" or 4" heavy, solid rib barrel with ejector shroud. Cylinder capacity is 5 rounds. Fixed sights are standard. Choice of blued or stainless steel finish. Pistol weighs 35 oz. **NOTE:** Add $60 for stainless steel.

NIB	Exc.	V.G.	Good	Fair	Poor
450	350	300	200	150	100

Model 817 (Ultra-Lite)

Chambered for the .357 Magnum cartridge and fitted with a 7-shot cylinder and 2" solid rib barrel, this model features an alloy frame. Stainless steel or blued finish. Some models are ported. Weight is about 21 oz. **NOTE:** Add $20 for ported barrels.

Blue

NIB	Exc.	V.G.	Good	Fair	Poor
350	275	225	175	125	100

Stainless Steel

NIB	Exc.	V.G.	Good	Fair	Poor
390	325	275	225	175	100

Model 441

Similar to the Model 431 but furnished with an additional choice of a 6" barrel as well as a 3" or 4". Comes standard with fully adjustable rear sight. Cylinder capacity is 5 rounds. Blued or stainless steel finish. Pistol weighs 40.25 oz. with 6" barrel. **NOTE:** Add $60 for stainless steel.

NIB	Exc.	V.G.	Good	Fair	Poor
395	300	240	150	125	100

Model 444 Multi

This model features a 4" barrel with adjustable sights chambered for the .44 Magnum cartridge. Cylinder holds 6 rounds. Frame is alloy with titanium cylinder. Grips have cushion inset. Weight is about 28 oz. Introduced in 2004.

NIB	Exc.	V.G.	Good	Fair	Poor
575	475	375	300	275	200

Model 905I-B1/SS1

Introduced in 2003 this revolver is chambered for the 9mm pistol cartridge. Barrel length is 2". Cylinder capacity is 5 rounds. Weight is about 21 oz. Blue or stainless steel finish. **NOTE:** For matte stainless steel finish add $45.

NIB	Exc.	V.G.	Good	Fair	Poor
385	325	250	175	100	75

Model 951SH2

Chambered for the 9mm cartridge and fitted with a 2" barrel with adjustable sights. Cylinder holds 5 rounds. Titanium frame and finish. Rubber grips. Weight is about 16 oz.

NIB	Exc.	V.G.	Good	Fair	Poor
475	350	265	200	150	100

Model 907SH2

This 9mm revolver has a 7-shot cylinder, 2" barrel with fixed sights and rubber grips. Titanium frame and finish. Weight is about 17 oz. Introduced in 2004.

NIB	Exc.	V.G.	Good	Fair	Poor
475	350	265	200	150	100

Model 907B2/SS2

Chambered for the 9mm cartridge and fitted with a 2" barrel with fixed sights. Rubber grips. Ultra light alloy frame in blue or stainless steel. Weight is about 18.5 oz. Introduced in 2004. **NOTE:** Add $45 for stainless steel.

NIB	Exc.	V.G.	Good	Fair	Poor
390	300	250	200	150	100

RAGING BULL SERIES

Model 218 Raging Bee

Introduced in 2002 this model is chambered for the .218 Bee cartridge and fitted with a 10" vent rib barrel with adjustable sights. Cylinder holds 8 rounds. Matte stainless steel finish.

NIB	Exc.	V.G.	Good	Fair	Poor
900	775	600	475	350	200

Model 22H Raging Hornet

This model is chambered for the .22 Hornet cartridge and has a 10" barrel with base mount and adjustable sights. Matte stainless steel finish. Cylinder holds 8 rounds. Rubber grips.

NIB	Exc.	V.G.	Good	Fair	Poor
750	675	550	400	300	200

Model 30C Raging Thirty

Chambered for the .30 Carbine cartridge and fitted with a 10" vent rib barrel with adjustable sights. Cylinder holds 8 rounds. Supplied with full moon clips. Matte stainless steel finish. Introduced in 2002.

NIB	Exc.	V.G.	Good	Fair	Poor
750	675	550	400	300	200

Model 416 Raging Bull

This model has a 6.5" vent rib ported barrel with adjustable sights. Chambered for the .41 Magnum cartridge. Matte stainless steel finish. Introduced in 2002. Cylinder holds 6 rounds.

NIB	Exc.	V.G.	Good	Fair	Poor
625	500	400	300	225	100

Model 454 Raging Bull

This model is chambered for the .454 Casull. It is built on a large frame with a 5-round capacity. Barrel lengths are 5", 6.5" or 8.375". Barrels are fitted with a ventilated rib and integral compensator. Sights are adjustable. Finish is blue or stainless steel. Black rubber or walnut grips. Weight is 53 oz. with 6.5" barrel. **NOTE:** Add $60 for stainless steel model. Introduced in 1997.

Blue

NIB	Exc.	V.G.	Good	Fair	Poor
700	650	575	450	325	175

Stainless Steel

NIB	Exc.	V.G.	Good	Fair	Poor
750	675	550	400	300	200

Black Stainless Steel

NIB	Exc.	V.G.	Good	Fair	Poor
750	675	550	400	300	200

Model 500 Magnum Raging Bull

Introduced in 2004 this revolver is chambered for the .500 Magnum cartridge. Ventilated barrel length is 10" with adjustable sights. Cushion inset grips. Stainless steel finish. Weight is about 72 oz.

NIB	Exc.	V.G.	Good	Fair	Poor
900	775	600	475	350	200

Model 500MSS2 Raging Bull

Stainless .500 S&W Magnum with 5-shot capacity, 2.25" barrel, soft rubber grips. 68 oz. Adjustable rear sight, single/double action. Introduced 2006.

NIB	Exc.	V.G.	Good	Fair	Poor
900	775	600	475	350	200

Model 44/444

Introduced in 1994 this heavy frame revolver is chambered for the .44 Magnum cartridge. Offered with choice of three barrel lengths: 4" with solid rib, 6.5" with vent rib, and 8-3/8" with vent rib. All Model 44s have a built in compensator. The front sight is a serrated ramp with adjustable rear sight. Offered in either blued or stainless finish. Weight of 6.5" barrel gun is 53 oz.

Blue

NIB	Exc.	V.G.	Good	Fair	Poor
—	425	300	200	150	100

Stainless Steel

NIB	Exc.	V.G.	Good	Fair	Poor
600	475	375	250	200	125

TRACKER SERIES

Model 17

Introduced in 2002 this model features a 6.5" or 12" vent rib barrel chambered for the .17 HMR cartridge. Adjustable sights. Matte stainless steel finish. Cylinder holds 7 rounds. Weight is about 41 oz. for 6.5" model and 50 oz. for the 12" model.

NIB	Exc.	V.G.	Good	Fair	Poor
375	300	225	175	125	100

Model 970

This model is chambered for the .22 LR cartridge and fitted with a 6.5" vent rib heavy barrel with adjustable sights. Matte stainless steel finish. Rubber grips. Cylinder holds 7 rounds. Introduced in 2002.

NIB	Exc.	V.G.	Good	Fair	Poor
300	200	165	125	100	75

Model 971

Same as the Model 970 but chambered for the .22 Magnum cartridge. Introduced in 2002.

NIB	Exc.	V.G.	Good	Fair	Poor
300	200	165	125	100	75

Tracker .22/.22 Mag.

Same as Model 971 except it is chambered for .22 LR with an interchangeable .22 WMR cylinder. Both cylinders hold 9 rounds.

Weight: 38 to 44 oz. with 4.5" or 6" barrel. Blue or matte stainless finish. **NOTE:** Add 10 percent for stainless.

NIB	Exc.	V.G.	Good	Fair	Poor
465	400	350	285	200	150

Model 425 Tracker

Chambered for the .41 Magnum cartridge this model features a 4" heavy underlug ported barrel. Adjustable rear sight. Cylinder is chambered for 5 rounds. Matte stainless steel finish. Introduced in 2000.

NIB	Exc.	V.G.	Good	Fair	Poor
425	325	250	200	150	100

Model 44 Tracker

This .44 Magnum revolver has a 4" barrel with adjustable sights and Ribber (ribbed) grips. Five-shot cylinder. Stainless steel finish. Weight is about 34 oz. Introduced in 2004.

NIB	Exc.	V.G.	Good	Fair	Poor
425	325	250	200	150	100

Tracker .45

Similar to other Tracker models but chambered in .45 ACP (via full-moon clips) with 5-shot cylinder. Four-inch barrel with Picatinny rail. Stainless steel frame and cylinder. Introduced 2007.

NIB	Exc.	V.G.	Good	Fair	Poor
450	350	275	225	175	125

Model 445

This small frame revolver is chambered for the .44 Special cartridge. It is fitted with a 2" barrel with ramp front sight and notched rear sight. Cylinder holds 5 rounds. Black rubber grips. Offered in blue or stainless steel. Weight is about 28 oz. Factory barrel porting, add $20, is optional. Introduced in 1997. **NOTE:** Add $50 for stainless steel.

NIB	Exc.	V.G.	Good	Fair	Poor
425	325	250	200	150	100

Model 450

Chambered for the .45 Long Colt cartridge this model features a 2" heavy solid rib barrel with 5-shot cylinder and fixed sights. Ported barrel. Rubber grips. Stainless steel finish. Weight is about 28 oz. **NOTE:** Add $30 for Ultra Lite model.

NIB	Exc.	V.G.	Good	Fair	Poor
450	350	275	225	175	125

Model 455

This model, introduced in 2002, is chambered for the .45 ACP cartridge. Offered with a choice of 2", 4", or 6.5" barrel. Barrels of 4" and 6.5" have adjustable sights. Matte stainless steel finish. Rubber grips. Supplied with full moon clips.

NIB	Exc.	V.G.	Good	Fair	Poor
450	350	275	225	175	125

Model 460

Chambered for the .45 Long Colt cartridge and fitted with either a 4" or 6.5" vent rib barrel with adjustable sights. Matte stainless steel finish. Introduced in 2002.

NIB	Exc.	V.G.	Good	Fair	Poor
450	350	275	225	175	125

Model 45

Chambered for the .45 Long Colt and fitted with a choice of 6.5" or 8-3/8" heavy vent rib barrels. Cylinder holds 6 rounds. Rubber grips, ported barrels, and adjustable sights are standard. Weight with 6.5" barrel is about 53 oz.

Blue

NIB	Exc.	V.G.	Good	Fair	Poor
450	350	275	225	175	125

Stainless Steel

NIB	Exc.	V.G.	Good	Fair	Poor
—	375	300	225	200	125

Model 627

This model is chambered for the .357 Magnum cartridge and fitted with a 4" ported or 6.5" vent rib ported barrel with adjustable sights. Rubber grips. Matte stainless steel finish. Introduced in 2002. **NOTE:** Add $200 for titanium model.

NIB	Exc.	V.G.	Good	Fair	Poor
425	350	275	225	150	100

Tracker 10mm 10TSS4

Matte stainless 10mm with 4" barrel and fixed sights. Five-shot, 34.8 oz, rubber grip. Introduced 2006.

NIB	Exc.	V.G.	Good	Fair	Poor
500	400	295	250	175	125

Tracker 10SS8

10mm 6-shot matte stainless with either 6.5" (54.5 oz.) or 8.375" (59.5 oz.) barrel. Fixed sights and rubber grips. Introduced 2006.

NIB	Exc.	V.G.	Good	Fair	Poor
500	400	295	250	175	125

Tracker 4510TKR

Shoots 2.5" .410 bore shells or .45 Colt. Holds 5 shots. Stainless or blued, 2.25" or 6.5" barrel, rubber grip. Single/double action, 32 oz., 9.1" LOA. Introduced 2006.

NIB	Exc.	V.G.	Good	Fair	Poor
500	400	295	250	175	125

Tracker Model 590 5mm Remington Magnum Rimfire

Nine-shot double-action stainless steel revolver chambered in 5mm Remington Magnum Rimfire. Introduced 2008. Discontinued 2011.

NIB	Exc.	V.G.	Good	Fair	Poor
400	350	300	225	200	150

JUDGE SERIES

Judge

Stainless steel- or lightweight alloy-frame version of Tracker Model 4410. Chambered in 3" .410/.45 Colt (4510TKR-3MAG) or 2.5" .410/.45 Colt (4510TKR-3UL) with 3" (3" Magnum) or 2.5" barrel (2.5"). Introduced 2007.

NIB	Exc.	V.G.	Good	Fair	Poor
525	425	300	265	195	150

Model 4510TKR-SSR

Similar to Judge but with ported barrel and tactical rail.

NIB	Exc.	V.G.	Good	Fair	Poor
600	525	425	300	265	175

Judge Public Defender Polymer

Single/double action revolver chambered in .45 Colt/.410 (2-1/2). Features include 5-round cylinder; polymer frame; Ribber rubber-feel grips; fiber-optic front sight; adjustable rear sight; blued or stainless cylinder; shrouded hammer with cocking spur; blued finish; 2.5" barrel. Weight 27 oz.

NIB	Exc.	V.G.	Good	Fair	Poor
550	450	375	300	250	150

Judge Public Defender Ultra-Lite

Single/double action revolver chambered in .45 Colt/.410 (2-1/2). Features include 5-round cylinder; lightweight aluminum frame; Ribber rubber-feel grips; fiber-optic front sight; adjustable rear sight; blued or stainless cylinder; shrouded hammer with cocking spur; blued finish; 2.5" barrel. Weight 20.7 oz.

NIB	Exc.	V.G.	Good	Fair	Poor
600	500	425	325	250	150

Raging Judge Magnum

Single/double action revolver chambered for .454 Casull, .45 Colt, 2.5" and 3" .410. Features include 3- or 6" barrel; fixed sights with fiber-optic front; blued or stainless steel finish; vent rib for scope mounting (6" only); cushioned Raging Bull grips.

NIB	Exc.	V.G.	Good	Fair	Poor
825	700	550	400	350	200

Raging Judge Magnum Ultra-Lite

Single/double action revolver chambered for .454 Casull, .45 Colt, 2.5" and 3" .410. Features include 3" or 6" barrel; aluminum alloy frame; fixed sights with fiber-optic front; blued or stainless steel finish; cushioned Raging Bull grips. Weight: 41.4 oz. (3" barrel).

NIB	Exc.	V.G.	Good	Fair	Poor
875	725	575	425	350	200

SILHOUETTE SERIES

Model 17-12

Chambered for the .17 HMR cartridge and fitted with a 12" vent rib silhouette barrel. Adjustable sights. Cylinder holds 7 rounds. Matte stainless steel finish. Introduced in 2002.

NIB	Exc.	V.G.	Good	Fair	Poor
700	600	475	350	200	150

Model 66

Chambered for the .357 Magnum cartridge and fitted with a 12" barrel with adjustable sights. Choice of blue or stainless steel finish. Rubber grips. Introduced in 2002. **NOTE:** Add $60 for stainless steel.

NIB	Exc.	V.G.	Good	Fair	Poor
525	425	300	265	195	150

Model 980

This model is chambered for the .22 LR cartridge. Fitted with a 12" target barrel with adjustable sights. Cylinder holds 7 rounds. Matted stainless steel finish. Rubber grips. Introduced in 2002.

NIB	Exc.	V.G.	Good	Fair	Poor
375	350	300	250	200	150

Model 981

This model is the same as the Model 980 but chambered for the .22 Magnum cartridge.

NIB	Exc.	V.G.	Good	Fair	Poor
375	350	300	250	200	150

Model 217

This model is chambered for the .218 Bee cartridge and fitted with a 12" vent rib barrel with adjustable sights. Cylinder holds 7 rounds. Matte stainless steel finish. Introduced in 2002.

NIB	Exc.	V.G.	Good	Fair	Poor
900	775	600	475	350	200

TITANIUM SERIES

Introduced in 1999 this series of revolvers features titanium barrels with stainless steel bore liners, titanium frames and cylinders. Hammers, triggers, latches, ejector rod and other small parts are made from case hardened chrome moly steel. All Taurus Titanium revolvers have factory porting and are rated for +P ammunition. Rubber grips are standard. Three different finishes are offered: Bright Spectrum blue, Matte Spectrum blue, and Matte Spectrum gold.

Model 85Ti

Chambered for .38 Special and fitted with a 2" barrel with 5-shot cylinder. Fixed sights.

NIB	Exc.	V.G.	Good	Fair	Poor
525	425	300	200	150	100

Model 731Ti

Chambered for the .32 H&R Magnum and fitted with a 2" barrel with 6-shot cylinder. Fixed sights.

NIB	Exc.	V.G.	Good	Fair	Poor
525	425	300	200	150	100

Model 617Ti

Chambered for .357 Magnum and fitted with a 2" barrel and 7-shot cylinder. Fixed sights. Weight is about 20 oz.

NIB	Exc.	V.G.	Good	Fair	Poor
600	525	425	300	265	175

Model 627Ti

This model features a 7-round cylinder chambered for the .357 Magnum cartridge. Fitted with a ported 4" barrel with adjustable sights. Gray finish. Weight is about 28 oz. depending on barrel length.

NIB	Exc.	V.G.	Good	Fair	Poor
700	600	475	350	200	150

Model 415Ti

Chambered for the .41 Magnum and fitted with a 2.5" barrel with 5-shot cylinder. Fixed sights. Weight is about 21 oz.

NIB	Exc.	V.G.	Good	Fair	Poor
600	475	350	250	150	125

Model 425Ti

This model is chambered for the .41 Magnum cartridge and has a 5-round cylinder. The barrel is ported and 4" with adjustable rear sight. Gray finish. Introduced in 2000.

NIB	Exc.	V.G.	Good	Fair	Poor
600	475	350	250	150	125

Model 450Ti

Chambered for the .45 Long Colt and fitted with a 2" barrel with 5-shot cylinder. Fixed sights. Weight is about 19 oz.

NIB	Exc.	V.G.	Good	Fair	Poor
600	475	350	250	150	125

Model 445Ti

Chambered for the .44 Special and fitted with a 2" barrel with 5-shot cylinder. Fixed sights. Weight is about 20 oz.

NIB	Exc.	V.G.	Good	Fair	Poor
600	475	350	250	150	125

Model UL/Ti

Chambered for the .38 Special this model has a Titanium cylinder and alloy frame. Fitted with a 2" unported barrel. Cylinder is 5 shot. Fixed sights.

NIB	Exc.	V.G.	Good	Fair	Poor
525	425	300	200	150	100

GAUCHO SERIES

S/A-45, B/S/SM

Chambered for the .45 Colt cartridge and fitted with a 5.5" barrel with fixed sights. Checkered wood grips. Blued or stainless steel finish. Weight is about 37 oz. Introduced in 2004. Discontinued. **NOTE:** Add $15 for stainless steel.

NIB	Exc.	V.G.	Good	Fair	Poor
400	325	275	225	175	125

S/A-45, S/S/CH

Chambered for the .45 Colt cartridge and fitted with a 5.5" barrel with fixed sights. Choice of Sundance stainless steel finish or case hardened blued finish. Weight is about 37 oz. Introduced in 2004.

NIB	Exc.	V.G.	Good	Fair	Poor
400	325	275	225	175	125

S/A-357-B, S/SM, S/S, CHSA

Single action 6-shot chambered for .357/.38 caliber. Barrel lengths 4.75" (36.2 oz.), 5.5" (36.7 oz.), 7.5" (37.7 oz.). Fixed sights. Blued, matte stainless, polished stainless or blued/case hardened receiver. Introduced 2006. **NOTE:** Add $15 for stainless steel.

NIB	Exc.	V.G.	Good	Fair	Poor
400	325	275	225	175	125

S/A-44-40-B, S/SM, S/S, CHSA

Single action 6-shot chambered for .44-40 caliber. Barrel lengths 4.75" (36.2 oz.), 5.5" (36.7 oz.), 7.5" (37.7 oz.). Fixed sights. Blued, matte stainless, polished stainless or blued/case hardened receiver. Introduced 2006.

NIB	Exc.	V.G.	Good	Fair	Poor
450	375	300	225	175	125

S/A-45-B12, S/SM12, S/S12, CHSA12

Single action Buntline-style 6-shot revolver chambered for .45 Colt. Barrel length 12" (41.5 oz.). Fixed sights. Blued, matte stainless, polished stainless or blued/case hardened receiver. Introduced 2006. Discontinued. **NOTE:** Add $15 for stainless steel.

NIB	Exc.	V.G.	Good	Fair	Poor
450	375	300	250	195	100

RIFLES

Model 62

Introduced in 2000 this is a replica of the Winchester Model 62 .22 caliber rifle. Fitted with a 23" barrel and adjustable rear sight. Magazine capacity is 13 rounds. Weight is about 5 lbs. Hardwood stock. **NOTE:** In 2003 this model was offered in both .22 WMR and .17 HMR calibers. Add 15 percent for stainless.

NIB	Exc.	V.G.	Good	Fair	Poor
350	300	225	175	125	75

Model 62 Carbine

Same as above but with a 16.5" barrel. Magazine capacity is 12 rounds. Weight is about 4.5 lbs. Introduced in 2000. **NOTE:** In 2003 this model was offered in .22 WMR and .17 HMR calibers. Add 10 percent for stainless.

NIB	Exc.	V.G.	Good	Fair	Poor
350	300	225	175	125	75

Model 62 Upstart

This model is similar to the Model 62 above but with a shorter buttstock. Introduced in 2002.

NIB	Exc.	V.G.	Good	Fair	Poor
350	300	225	175	125	75

Model 72

Same as the Model 62 but chambered for the .22 Magnum cartridge. **NOTE:** Add $15 for stainless steel.

NIB	Exc.	V.G.	Good	Fair	Poor
350	300	225	175	125	75

Model 72 Carbine

Same as the Model 62 Carbine but chambered for the .22 Magnum cartridge. **NOTE:** Add $15 for stainless steel.

NIB	Exc.	V.G.	Good	Fair	Poor
350	300	225	175	125	75

Model 63

Copy of the Winchester Model 63 in takedown. Chambered for the .22 LR cartridge and fitted with a 23" round barrel with adjustable rear sight. Offered in blue or stainless steel. Introduced in 2002. In 2003 this model was reportedly also offered chambered for the .17 HMR and .22 WMR. Discontinued.

NIB	Exc.	V.G.	Good	Fair	Poor
300	245	200	150	100	75

Model 62LAR Lever Rifle

Lever-action rifle chambered in .22 LR. 23" blued barrel, walnut-finish hardwood stock. Introduced 2006.

NIB	Exc.	V.G.	Good	Fair	Poor
300	250	200	150	125	100

Model 62LAR-SS

Similar to Model 62LAR but in stainless steel. Introduced 2006.

NIB	Exc.	V.G.	Good	Fair	Poor
350	300	225	175	150	125

Thunderbolt

This slide-action rifle is a knockoff of the Colt Lightning rifle and is chambered for the .45 Colt cartridge as well as the .38/.357 Magnum. Fitted with a 26" barrel with adjustable sights. Blued or stainless steel finish. Stocks are hardwood. Weight is about 8.125 lbs. Introduced in 2004. **NOTE:** Add $50 for stainless steel or bright "Sundance" stainless finish.

NIB	Exc.	V.G.	Good	Fair	Poor
550	450	325	250	175	150

CT9G2

Semi-automatic carbine with hybrid aluminum/polymer construction. Reinforced steel frame. Lower receiver made with high-strength polymer reinforced with steel. Upper receiver has a flat top Picatinny rail. Two-position safety lever. Adjustable rear sight, fixed front. Ambidextrous slide catch. Available in 9mm, .40 S&W, .45 ACP. Taurus Security System installed. Introduced in 2011.

NIB	Exc.	V.G.	Good	Fair	Poor
700	600	500	—	—	—

TAYLOR'S & CO., INC.
Winchester, Virginia

HANDGUNS

Napoleon Le Page Pistol (Model 551)

A percussion French-style duelling pistol. Chambered for .45 caliber and fitted with a 10" octagon barrel. Walnut stock silver plated buttcap and trigger guard. Double set triggers. Made by Uberti.

NIB	Exc.	V.G.	Good	Fair	Poor
450	375	300	250	200	100

Kentucky Pistol (Model 550)

Chambered for the .45 caliber ball and fitted with a 10" barrel. Bird's-head grip with brass ramrod thimbles and case hardened sidelock. Made by Uberti.

NIB	Exc.	V.G.	Good	Fair	Poor
295	225	200	125	85	60

Colt Model 1847 Walker (Model 500A)

Fitted with a 9" round barrel and chambered for .44 caliber. This model has a 6-round engraved cylinder. Steel frame and backstrap and brass trigger guard. One-piece walnut grips. Made by Uberti.

NIB	Exc.	V.G.	Good	Fair	Poor
400	325	275	250	200	100

Colt Model 1851 Navy

Offered with either brass or steel frame with brass backstrap and trigger guard. Chambered for .36 caliber and fitted with a 7.5" barrel. Cylinder holds 6 rounds. One-piece walnut grip. Brass frame model made by Armi San Marco. Steel frame model made by F.lli Pietta.

Brass Frame (Model 210)

NIB	Exc.	V.G.	Good	Fair	Poor
295	225	200	125	85	60

Steel Frame (Model 245)

NIB	Exc.	V.G.	Good	Fair	Poor
350	250	200	150	100	75

Remington Model 1858

This is a .44 caliber either a brass frame or steel frame and brass trigger guard model with 8" octagon barrel. Cylinder holds 6 rounds. Two-piece walnut grips. Brass frame made by F.lli Pietta. Steel frame made by Armi San Marco.

Brass Frame (Model 410)

NIB	Exc.	V.G.	Good	Fair	Poor
295	225	200	125	85	60

Steel Frame (Model 430)

NIB	Exc.	V.G.	Good	Fair	Poor
350	250	200	150	100	75

Colt Model 1848 Baby Dragoon (Models 470, 471, 472)

Chambered for the .31 caliber and fitted with a 5-round cylinder. Barrel length is 4". Choice of blued or white steel frame. Brass backstrap and trigger guard. One-piece walnut grip. Made by Uberti.

NIB	Exc.	V.G.	Good	Fair	Poor
350	250	200	150	100	75

Starr Model 1858 (Model 510, 511)

This model is offered in either double-action or single-action. Chambered for the .44 caliber and fitted with a 6" round barrel. Made by F.lli Pietta.

NIB	Exc.	V.G.	Good	Fair	Poor
350	250	200	150	100	75

Colt Model 1860 Army

This model features an 8" round barrel except for the Sheriff's model which is 5.5". Choice of brass or steel frame with brass backstrap and trigger guard. Chambered for .44 caliber. One-piece walnut grip. Brass frame model made by Armi San Marco and steel frame by Uberti. **NOTE:** A half-fluted cylinder model is also offered.

Brass Frame (Model 300)

NIB	Exc.	V.G.	Good	Fair	Poor
295	225	200	125	85	60

Steel Frame (Model 310, 312, 315)

NIB	Exc.	V.G.	Good	Fair	Poor
350	250	200	150	100	75

Colt Dragoon (Models 485A, 490A, 495A)

Offered in 1st, 2nd, and 3rd models each is fitted with a 7.5" barrel and chambered for .44 caliber. Steel frame and brass backstrap and trigger guard. The 2nd and 3rd models have a square cylinder stop. The loading lever is inverted on the 3rd model. All have one-piece walnut grip. Made by Uberti. **NOTE:** Add $15 for 3rd model.

NIB	Exc.	V.G.	Good	Fair	Poor
350	250	200	150	100	75

Colt Model 1861 Navy (Model 210)

This model is chambered for the .36 caliber and fitted with a 7.5" round barrel. Cylinder is 6 rounds. Brass frame and backstrap and trigger guard. One-piece walnut grip. Made by Uberti.

NIB	Exc.	V.G.	Good	Fair	Poor
295	225	200	125	85	60

Colt Model 1862 Police (Model 315B)

Fitted with a 6.5" round barrel and chambered for .36 caliber. Case hardened frame with brass backstrap and trigger guard. Made by Uberti.

NIB	Exc.	V.G.	Good	Fair	Poor
350	250	200	150	100	75

Colt Model 1862 Pocket (Model 315C)

Similar to the above model but fitted with a 6.5" octagonal barrel. Made by Uberti.

NIB	Exc.	V.G.	Good	Fair	Poor
350	250	200	150	100	75

Remington Model 1863 Pocket (Model 435)

This revolver is chambered for the .31 caliber ball and fitted with a 3.5" barrel. Cylinder is 5 rounds. Frame, backstrap and trigger guard are brass. Walnut grip. Made by Armi San Marco.

NIB	Exc.	V.G.	Good	Fair	Poor
295	225	200	125	85	60

Colt Model 1873 Cattleman (Models 700, 701, 702)

This famous replica is made in several different configurations. Offered in barrel lengths of 4.75", 5.5", and 7.5". Calibers are: .45 Colt, .44-40, .44 Special, .38-40, .357 Magnum, and .45 ACP. Frame is case hardened with steel backstrap. One-piece walnut grip. Made by Uberti. **NOTE:** Add $80 for dual cylinder and $80 for nickel finish.

NIB	Exc.	V.G.	Good	Fair	Poor
500	375	225	175	150	125

Colt Model 1873 Bird's-head (Models 703A, 703B, 703C)

Same as above but offered with bird's-head grip.

NIB	Exc.	V.G.	Good	Fair	Poor
500	375	225	175	150	125

Colt Model 1873 "Outfitter"

Chambered for the .45 Colt or .357 Magnum cartridge and fitted with a 4.75", 5.5", or 7.5" barrel. Stainless steel finish and walnut grips.

NIB	Exc.	V.G.	Good	Fair	Poor
500	375	225	175	150	125

HARTFORD ARMORY MODELS

Introduced to the Taylor product line in 2004, this company produces revolvers made entirely in the U.S. Each gun comes with a lifetime warranty. All Hartford Armory revolvers come in a numbered wooden case with brass snap caps and brass plaque.

Remington Model 1875

This model is offered in these calibers: .38/.357, .44-40, .44 Special/Magnum, or .45 Colt. Barrel lengths are 5.75" or 7.5". Walnut grips. Armory dark blue finish.

NIB	Exc.	V.G.	Good	Fair	Poor
900	800	700	600	450	300

Remington Model 1890

This model is offered in .38/.357, .44-40, .44 Special/Magnum, or .45 Colt. Choice of 5.5" or 7.5" barrel. Armory dark blue finish. Walnut grips.

NIB	Exc.	V.G.	Good	Fair	Poor
900	800	700	600	450	300

RIFLES

Kentucky Rifle

Offered in either flintlock or percussion this rifle is .40 caliber and fitted with a 3.5" barrel. One-piece stock with brass fixtures.

Flintlock (Model 183)

NIB	Exc.	V.G.	Good	Fair	Poor
495	335	225	150	100	75

Percussion (Model 182)

NIB	Exc.	V.G.	Good	Fair	Poor
475	325	200	150	100	75

Model 1842 U.S. Percussion Musket (Model 125)

This model is offered as a smoothbore or rifled musket with 42" .69 caliber barrel. Finish is in the white. One-piece walnut stock.

Smoothbore

NIB	Exc.	V.G.	Good	Fair	Poor
450	325	250	200	150	100

Rifled with Rear Sight (Model 126)

NIB	Exc.	V.G.	Good	Fair	Poor
450	325	250	200	150	100

Model 1855 U.S. Percussion Musket (Model 116)

This model has a .58 caliber 40" barrel with rear sight. One-piece walnut stock. White satin finish.

NIB	Exc.	V.G.	Good	Fair	Poor
500	375	225	175	150	125

Model 1853 3-Band Enfield Musket (Model 120)

This rifled musket has a 39" .58 caliber barrel. Blued finish. One-piece walnut stock. Brass buttplate, nosecap, and trigger guard.

NIB	Exc.	V.G.	Good	Fair	Poor
475	350	300	250	200	100

Model 1858 2-Band Enfield Musket (Model 121)

Similar to the above model but fitted with a .58 caliber 33" barrel.

NIB	Exc.	V.G.	Good	Fair	Poor
475	350	300	250	200	100

Model 1861 Springfield Musket (Model 110)

This model has a 40" .58 caliber barrel with one-piece walnut stock. White satin finish.

NIB	Exc.	V.G.	Good	Fair	Poor
550	425	350	300	200	100

Model 1862 C.S. Richmond Musket (Model 115)

This rifle is fitted with a 40" .58 caliber barrel with three barrel bands. Brass buttplate and nosecap. White satin finish. One-piece walnut stock.

NIB	Exc.	V.G.	Good	Fair	Poor
550	425	350	300	200	100

Model 1863 Remington Zouave (Model 140)

Fitted with a 33" barrel chambered for the .58 caliber ball. One-piece walnut stock with blued finish, brass buttplate, nosecap, trigger guard, patchbox, and barrel bands.

NIB	Exc.	V.G.	Good	Fair	Poor
450	325	250	200	150	100

Henry Rifle

This lever-action rifle is chambered for the .44-40 or .45 Colt cartridge. Fitted with a 24.25" octagon barrel. Walnut stock. Open sights.

Brass Frame (Model 198)

NIB	Exc.	V.G.	Good	Fair	Poor
875	700	600	500	400	200

Iron Frame (Model 199)

NIB	Exc.	V.G.	Good	Fair	Poor
925	750	650	500	400	200

Winchester Model 1866 (Model 201)

This model is chambered for the .44-40 or .45 Colt cartridge. Fitted with a 24.25" octagon barrel. Brass frame. Open sights. Made by Uberti.

NIB	Exc.	V.G.	Good	Fair	Poor
830	650	575	400	300	175

Winchester Model 1866 Yellowboy Carbine (Model 202)

Same as above but with 19" round barrel and the additional .38 Special caliber. Made by Uberti.

NIB	Exc.	V.G.	Good	Fair	Poor
850	675	525	450	300	150

Winchester Model 1873 (Model 200)

This lever action model is chambered for the .44-40 or .45 Colt cartridge and fitted with a 24.25" octagon barrel. Made by Uberti.

NIB	Exc.	V.G.	Good	Fair	Poor
900	725	600	500	400	200

Winchester Model 1873 Carbine (Model 200B)

Chambered for the .45 Long Colt cartridge and fitted with a 19" barrel. Magazine capacity is 10 rounds. Walnut stock and case colored frame.

NIB	Exc.	V.G.	Good	Fair	Poor
900	725	600	500	400	200

Winchester Model 1873 Sporting Rifle (Model 200C)

Chambered for the .45 Long Colt cartridge and fitted with a 30" octagon barrel. Checkered walnut stock with pistol grip. Case colored frame and blued barrel.

NIB	Exc.	V.G.	Good	Fair	Poor
900	725	600	500	400	200

Winchester Model 1885 High Wall (Model 203)

Offered with 30" or 32" barrels chambered for the .45-70 cartridge. Walnut stock.

NIB	Exc.	V.G.	Good	Fair	Poor
900	725	600	500	400	200

Winchester Model 1885 Low Wall Sporting Rifle (Model 204)

This single-shot rifle is chambered for the .22 LR, .32-20, or .38-40 cartridge. Checkered walnut stock.

NIB	Exc.	V.G.	Good	Fair	Poor
900	725	600	500	400	200

Winchester Model 92

Introduced in 2004 this lever-action rifle is chambered for the .32-20, .32 H&R Magnum, .357 Magnum, .38 Special, .38-40, .44-40, .44 S&W, or the .45 Colt. Barrel length is 20" or 24" octagon. Takedown feature. Hardwood stock with blued barrel finish and case colored frame.

NIB	Exc.	V.G.	Good	Fair	Poor
725	625	450	300	250	200

Sharps Model 1859 Infantry (Model 151)

This rifle is fitted with a 30" round barrel and is chambered for the .54 caliber cartridge. One-piece walnut with 3 barrel bands. Adjustable rear sight.

NIB	Exc.	V.G.	Good	Fair	Poor
1150	800	600	400	300	150

Sharps Model 1859 Berdan Military (Model 152)

This .54 caliber rifle is fitted with a 30" round barrel. One-piece walnut stock with 3 barrel bands. Adjustable rear sight. This model is fitted with double set triggers.

NIB	Exc.	V.G.	Good	Fair	Poor
1150	800	600	400	300	150

Sharps Model 1859 Cavalry (Model 153)

This model has a 22" round barrel with adjustable rear sight. Chambered for .54 caliber. Walnut stock is fitted with patch box.

NIB	Exc.	V.G.	Good	Fair	Poor
1150	800	600	400	300	150

Sharps Model 1863 Cavalry (Model 154)

Similar to the Model 1859 Cavalry but without the patch box.

NIB	Exc.	V.G.	Good	Fair	Poor
1150	800	600	400	300	150

Sharps Model 1863 Sporting Rifle (Model 131)

This .54 caliber model is offered with either 30" or 32" octagon barrel with single or double set triggers. Walnut stock. **NOTE:** Add $20 for double set trigger.

NIB	Exc.	V.G.	Good	Fair	Poor
1150	800	600	400	300	150

Sharps Model 1874 Sporting Rifle (Model 138)

This model is offered with a variety of features. Available in .45-70 with choice of 30" or 32" octagon barrel with a choice of single trigger or double set triggers. It is also available with Hartford-style pewter fore-end tip. In this configuration it is available in .45-70, .40-65, .45-90, or .45-120 calibers. Checkered stock with patch is optional. **NOTE:** Add $125 for Hartford-style fore-end tip. Add $250 for checkered stock with patch box.

NIB	Exc.	V.G.	Good	Fair	Poor
895	700	545	400	315	175

Sharps Model 1874 Deluxe Sporting Rifle (Model 155)

This .45-70 caliber model features a hand checkered walnut stock with oil finish. Receiver is in the white with standard scroll engraving. **NOTE:** For Deluxe Model 1874 with gold inlay add $800.

NIB	Exc.	V.G.	Good	Fair	Poor
1800	1350	1050	775	595	200

Sharps Model 1874 Infantry Rifle (Model 157)

This .45-70 caliber model features a 30" round barrel with 3 barrel bands. One-piece walnut stock. Adjustable rear sight. Single trigger. Patch box in stock.

NIB	Exc.	V.G.	Good	Fair	Poor
1325	1000	750	550	375	200

1210 • TAYLOR, L.B.

Sharps Model 1874 Berdan Rifle (Model 158)

Similar to the above model but with a double set trigger.

NIB	Exc.	V.G.	Good	Fair	Poor
1325	1000	750	550	375	200

Sharps Model 1874 Cavalry (Model 159)

This .45-70 caliber model is fitted with a 22" round barrel. Adjustable rear sight.

NIB	Exc.	V.G.	Good	Fair	Poor
1150	800	600	400	300	150

Spencer Model 1865 Carbine (Model 160)

This lever-action model is chambered in a choice of calibers: .56-50, .44 Russian, or .45 Schofield. Fitted with a 20" round barrel. Walnut stock. Case hardened receiver and blued barrel. Made by Armi Sport.

NIB	Exc.	V.G.	Good	Fair	Poor
1200	1050	875	750	500	400

Spencer Model 1865 Rifle

As above but with 30" barrel with three barrel bands. Chambered for the .56-50 cartridge.

NIB	Exc.	V.G.	Good	Fair	Poor
1200	1050	875	750	500	400

TAYLOR, L.B.
Chicopee, Massachusetts

Pocket Pistol

A .32 caliber spur trigger single-shot pocket pistol with a 3.5" octagonal barrel marked "L. B. Taylor & Co. Chicopee Mass." Silver-plated brass frame, blued barrel and walnut grips. Manufactured during the late 1860s and early 1870s.

NIB	Exc.	V.G.	Good	Fair	Poor
—	—	1150	875	385	100

TERRIER ONE

Terrier One

A .32 caliber double-action swing-out cylinder revolver with a 2.25" barrel and 5-shot cylinder. Nickel-plated with checkered walnut grips. Manufactured from 1984 to 1987.

NIB	Exc.	V.G.	Good	Fair	Poor
—	100	75	50	30	25

TERRY, J. C.
New York City, New York

Pocket Pistol

A .22 caliber spur trigger single-shot pocket pistol with a 3.75" round barrel. The back strap marked "J.C. Terry/Patent Pending". Silver-plated brass frame, blued barrel and rosewood or walnut grips. Manufactured in the late 1860s.

NIB	Exc.	V.G.	Good	Fair	Poor
—	—	1300	950	475	100

TEXAS CONTRACT RIFLES

Three contractors produced rifles for the State of Texas during 1862 and 1863. One of these patterns has a sporting back-action lock, Enfield barrel bands, an overall length of 47-3/8", heavy 32" long barrel of .58 caliber. Total deliveries by all contractors amounted to 1,464 rifles. Quality of these arms was decidedly inferior and often complained about.

TEXAS GUNFIGHTERS
Ponte Zanano, Italy

Shootist Single-Action

A .45 Long Colt caliber single-action revolver with a 4.75" barrel. Nickel-plated with one-piece walnut grips. This model is made by Aldo Uberti. Introduced in 1988.

NIB	Exc.	V.G.	Good	Fair	Poor
400	350	250	200	150	75

1-of-100 Edition

As above, with one-piece mother-of-pearl grips fitted in a case with an additional set of walnut grips. 100 were made in 1988.

NIB	Exc.	V.G.	Good	Fair	Poor
450	375	295	225	175	100

TEXAS LONGHORN ARMS, INC.
Richmond, Texas

Jezebel

A .22 or .22 Magnum single-shot pistol with a 6" barrel. Stainless steel with a walnut stock and fore-end. Introduced in 1987.

NIB	Exc.	V.G.	Good	Fair	Poor
750	675	600	550	500	350

Texas Border Special

A .44 Special or .45 Colt caliber single-action revolver with a 3.5" barrel and Pope-style rifling. Blued, case hardened with one-piece walnut grips.

NIB	Exc.	V.G.	Good	Fair	Poor
1500	1250	1000	800	600	300

Mason Commemorative

As above, in .45 Colt with a 4.75" barrel and the Mason's insignia. Gold inlaid. Introduced in 1987.

NIB	Exc.	V.G.	Good	Fair	Poor
1500	1250	1000	800	600	300

South Texas Army

As above, but with a 4.75" barrel also chambered for the .357 Magnum cartridge and fitted with conventional one-piece walnut grips.

NIB	Exc.	V.G.	Good	Fair	Poor
1500	1250	1000	800	600	300

West Texas Target

As above, with a 7.5" barrel, flat top frame and in .32-20 caliber in addition to the calibers noted above.

NIB	Exc.	V.G.	Good	Fair	Poor
1500	1250	1000	800	600	300

Grover's Improved Number Five

Similar to the above, in .44 Magnum with a 5.5" barrel. Serial Numbered K1 to K1200. Introduced in 1988.

NIB	Exc.	V.G.	Good	Fair	Poor
2300	1350	800	—	—	—

Texas Sesquicentennial Commemorative

As above, engraved in the style of Louis D. Nimschke with one-piece ivory grips and a fitted case.

NIB	Exc.	V.G.	Good	Fair	Poor
2500	2000	1500	900	750	400

THAMES ARMS CO.
Norwich, Connecticut

A .22, .32, or .38 caliber double-action top break revolver with varying length barrels normally marked "Automatic Revolver", which refers to the cartridge ejector. Nickel-plated with walnut grips.

NIB	Exc.	V.G.	Good	Fair	Poor
—	500	200	100	75	50

THIEME & EDELER
Eibar, Spain

Pocket Pistol

A 7.65mm caliber semi-automatic pistol with a 3" barrel marked "T E". Blued with black plastic grips. Manufactured prior to 1936.

NIB	Exc.	V.G.	Good	Fair	Poor
—	250	150	100	75	50

THOMPSON
See—Auto Ordnance Corp.

THOMPSON/CENTER ARMS
Springfield, Massachusetts

Thompson/Center Arms Co. was founded in Rochester, New York in 1965 by K.W. Thompson and Warren Center. The company's first gun was a break-open, single-shot pistol, known as the Contender. More than 400,000 were produced between 1967 and 2000, when the original model was discontinued. In 2007 Thompson/Center became a division of Smith & Wesson and production was moved to Springfield, Massachusetts.

CONTENDER

The standard version was offered with a 10" octagon barrel and later with a 10" Bull barrel, 10" vent rib barrel, 14" Super models, 14" Super with vent rib, 16" Super models, and 16" Super models with vent rib. A stainless steel finish was available on all models except the 10" octagon barrel. The action on these handguns is a single-shot, break open design. Unless otherwise stated the barrels are blued. The Competitor grip is walnut with rubber insert mounted on back of grip. A finger groove grip is also available made from walnut with finger notching and thumb rest. Fore-end is American black walnut in various length and designs depending on barrel size. Stainless steel models have rubber grips with finger grooves. Standard sights are standard Patridge rear with ramp front. An adjustable rear sight was offered as an option. Barrels with vent ribs were furnished with fixed rear sight and bead front sight. **NOTE:** Early frames with no engraving, called flatsides, and those with eagle engraving bring between $2,000 and $2,500 on the collector market.

NOTE: Barrel interchangeability is acceptable for blued barrels and frames with stainless steel barrels and frames. **DO NOT**

interchange Alloy II barrels and frames with either blued or stainless steel components.

10" Octagon Barrel Model

This was the first Contender design and was offered in .22 LR only. It was supplied with adjustable rear sight and mounting holes for scope. Grips are Competitor or rubber. Weighs about 44 oz.

NIB	Exc.	V.G.	Good	Fair	Poor
375	300	250	200	150	100

10" Bull Barrel Model

Comes standard with adjustable rear sight, mounting holes for scope mounts, and Competitor grips for blued models and rubber grips on stainless models. Available in blued or stainless steel. Offered in these calibers as complete pistols: .22 LR, .22 LR Match, .22 Win. Magnum (blued only), .22 Hornet, .223, 7mm T.C.U. (blued only), .30-30, .32-20 (blued only), .357 Magnum, .357 Rem. Max (blued only), .44 Magnum, .45 Colt, .410 bore. In 1994 Thompson/Center introduced the .300 Whisper cartridge to its Contender product line. Weighs approximately 50 oz.

NIB	Exc.	V.G.	Good	Fair	Poor
375	300	250	200	150	100

10" Vent Rib Model

This features a raised vent rib and is chambered for the .45 Long Colt/.410 bore. The rear sight is fixed and the front sight is a bead. A detachable choke screws into the muzzle for use with the .410 shell. Furnished with Competitor grips or rubber grips.

NIB	Exc.	V.G.	Good	Fair	Poor
370	320	270	220	150	100

Super 14" Model

This model features a 14" bull barrel. Furnished with adjustable rear sight and ramp front sight. Drilled and tapped for scope mounts. Competitor or rubber grips are offered. Available in blued or stainless steel finish. Furnished in these calibers in a complete pistol only: .22 LR, .22 LR Match, .17 Rem. (blued only), .22 Hornet, .222 Rem. (blued only), .223 Rem., 7mm T.C.U. (blued only), 7-30 Waters, .30-30, .357 Rem. Max (blued only), .35 Rem., .375 Win. (blued only), .44 Magnum (blued only). Weighs approximately 56 oz.

NIB	Exc.	V.G.	Good	Fair	Poor
400	360	300	250	200	150

Super 14" Vent Rib Model

Similar to the 10" vent rib model chambered for the .45 Long Colt/.410 bore but furnished with a 14" vent rib barrel.

NIB	Exc.	V.G.	Good	Fair	Poor
475	385	325	275	215	150

Super 16" Model

Fitted with a 16.25" tapered barrel, two position adjustable rear sight. Drilled and tapped for scope mount. Furnished with Competitor grips or rubber grips and choice of blued or stainless steel finish. Available in these calibers as complete pistols only: .22 LR, .22 Hornet, .223 Rem., 7-30 Waters, .30-30, .35 Rem., .45-70 Government. Weighs approximately 56 oz.

NIB	Exc.	V.G.	Good	Fair	Poor
370	320	275	215	150	100

Super 16" Vent Rib Model

Chambered for .45 Long Colt/.410 bore this model was offered for the first time in 1993. All other features are the same as the other Contender .45/.410 bore pistols.

NIB	Exc.	V.G.	Good	Fair	Poor
390	350	300	250	175	125

Contender Hunter Model

This model is designed for handgun hunting and is offered in two barrel lengths: 12" and 14". The barrels are fitted with a compensator and a 2.5 power scope. There are no iron sights fitted. A nylon carrying sling and soft leather carrying case are standard. Offered in these calibers: 7-30 Waters, .30-30 Win., .35 Rem., .45-70 Government, .44 Magnum, .223 Rem., and .375 Win. Fitted with Competitor grips and offered in blued or stainless steel finish. Weighs approximately 64 oz.

NIB	Exc.	V.G.	Good	Fair	Poor
575	500	400	300	200	100

G2 CONTENDER SERIES

Introduced in 2003, this is a second generation Contender that features a slightly different look, a simplified internal design that allows re-cocking the hammer without having to break open the action, and differently shaped grips that give more clearance between the grip and the finger guard. These G2 firearms will accept previously manufactured Contender barrels and fore-ends but not grips.

G2 Contender

Offered with both 12" and 14" barrels. Chambered for .22 Hornet, .357 Magnum, .44 Magnum, .45 Colt/.410 in 12" barrels. In 14" barrel chambered for the .17 HMR, .22 LR, .22 Hornet, .223 Rem., 7-30 Waters, .30-30, .44 Magnum, .45 Colt/.410 and the .45-70. Adjustable sights and drilled and tapped for scope mounts. Walnut grips. Weight for 12" barreled guns is about 3.5 lbs., for 14" barreled guns about 3.75 lbs. In 2004 the .204 Ruger and .375 JDJ calibers were added.

NIB	Exc.	V.G.	Good	Fair	Poor
560	450	375	300	250	175

G2 Contender Rifle

This rifle is fitted with a 23" barrel with no sights and is chambered for the .17 HMR, .22 LR, .223 Rem., .30-30, and the .45-70. Walnut stock with blued finish. Weight is about 5.4 lbs. In 2004 the .375 JDJ and .204 Ruger calibers were added.

NIB	Exc.	V.G.	Good	Fair	Poor
600	500	400	325	275	200

G2 Contender Shotgun

Chambered for the .410 bore shell and fitted with a 24" ventilated rib barrel. Walnut stock. Weight is about 5.4 lbs. Introduced in 2004.

NIB	Exc.	V.G.	Good	Fair	Poor
600	500	400	325	275	200

CONTENDER CARBINE MODEL

This model is built from the same design as the Contender Model. It features completely interchangeable barrels chambered for 12 different cartridges from .22 LR to .35 Rem. A .410 bore shotgun barrel is also offered. The standard model has a 21" barrel stocked with walnut. For stainless steel models a composite stock in fitted walnut is also available. All are drilled and tapped for scope mounts. Available in blued or stainless steel.

Standard 21" Carbine

This model is fitted with a 21" plain barrel and walnut stocks. Offered in these calibers as a complete gun only: .22 LR, .22 LR Match (blued only), .17 Rem. (blued only), .22 Hornet, .223 Rem., 7-30 Waters, .30-30, .35 Rem. (blued only), .375 Win. (blued only). Weighs 5 lbs. 3 oz.

NIB	Exc.	V.G.	Good	Fair	Poor
500	400	350	300	250	200

21" Carbine .410 Bore

Same as above but fitted with a vent rib barrel and screw-in choke.

NIB	Exc.	V.G.	Good	Fair	Poor
475	375	300	250	200	100

16" Youth Model Carbine

A special walnut buttstock with 12" length of pull and 16.25" barrel. Short buttstock can be replaced with standard buttstock. Blued or stainless steel finish. Complete guns are offered in the same calibers as the 21" Carbine with the exception of the .375 Win. and the addition of the .45 Long Colt/.410 bore with vent rib barrel.

NIB	Exc.	V.G.	Good	Fair	Poor
475	375	300	250	200	100

ENCORE SERIES

Encore Pistol

Introduced in 1996 this single-shot pistol will feature barrels chambered for the .30-06, .308 Win., 7mm-08 Rem., .223 Rem., .22-250 Rem., .44 Magnum, and 7mmBR. Offered with 10.625", 15", or 24" barrels this new handgun is designed for use with higher pressure cartridges. Barrels will not interchange with the Contender. Weight with 10.625" barrel is 56 oz., with 15" barrel about 4 lbs. and with 24" barrel about 6.75 lbs. **NOTE:** Add $60 for stainless steel frame and barrels.

NIB	Exc.	V.G.	Good	Fair	Poor
550	450	375	300	250	175

HotShot Youth Rifle

Single-shot dropping-barrel rifle chambered in .22 LR. Features include a crowned 19" steel barrel, exposed hammer, synthetic fore-end and buttstock, peep sight (receiver drilled and tapped for optics), three stock pattern options (black, Realtree AP and pink AP). Overall weight 3 lbs., 11.5" length of pull.

NIB	Exc.	V.G.	Good	Fair	Poor
195	165	125	100	75	50

Encore Rifle

Similar to the Encore pistol but with longer barrels and walnut stock and forearm. A wide variety of calibers are offered from .22-250 to .300 Win. Magnum, in barrels lengths from 24" to 26". Heavy barrels are offered in 7mm Rem Magnum, .300 Win. Magnum and .22-250. These are offered with no sights. Weight is about 6 lbs. 12 oz. for 7mm-08 with 24" barrel. Introduced in 1997. In 1998 the .260 Rem., .280 Rem., and .45-70 Government cartridges were added. In 1999 stainless steel frame and barrels were offered as well as blued. In 2003 the .375 H&H Magnum with a 26" barrel without sights was offered. In 2004 the .280 Rem.,

.204 Ruger, and the .405 Win. were added. **NOTE:** Add about $60 for stainless steel frame and barrels.

NIB	Exc.	V.G.	Good	Fair	Poor
650	550	425	300	225	175

Encore Katahdin Carbine

This model is fitted with a heavy 18" barrel with integral muzzle-brake. Offered in .444 Marlin, .450 Marlin, and .45-70 Government calibers. Blued finish with composite stock and adjustable fiber optic sights. Weight is about 6.75 lbs. Introduced in 2002.

NIB	Exc.	V.G.	Good	Fair	Poor
650	550	425	300	225	175

Encore Katahdin Turkey Gun

This is a 12 gauge 3" chamber gun with 20" barrel and screw-in Turkey chokes. Open sights. Realtree Hardwoods HD camo composite stock. Weight is about 6 lbs. Introduced in 2005.

NIB	Exc.	V.G.	Good	Fair	Poor
750	575	450	325	225	200

Encore Shotgun 20 Gauge

Introduced in 1998 this model is fitted with a 26" 20 gauge vent rib barrel with walnut stock and fore-end. Choke tubes are standard.

NIB	Exc.	V.G.	Good	Fair	Poor
650	550	425	300	225	175

Encore Camo Shotgun 12 Gauge

This model features a 24" smoothbore barrel with screw-in turkey choke, camo stock and metal pattern. Blued frame with composite stock. Introduced in 2002.

NIB	Exc.	V.G.	Good	Fair	Poor
750	575	450	325	225	200

Encore Shotgun 12 Gauge

This model features a 3" 26" ventilated rib barrel with bead front sight. Blued with walnut stock. Weight is about 6.6 lbs. Introduced in 2004.

NIB	Exc.	V.G.	Good	Fair	Poor
750	575	450	325	225	200

Encore Rifled Shotgun 20 Gauge

Introduced in 2000 this model features a 26" rifled shotgun barrel chambered for the 20 gauge shell. Adjustable rear sight. Walnut stock and blued finish.

NIB	Exc.	V.G.	Good	Fair	Poor
650	550	425	300	225	175

Encore Rifled Shotgun 12 Gauge

Introduced in 2002 this model is fitted with a 24" rifled barrel with adjustable fiber optic sights. Blued with walnut stock.

NIB	Exc.	V.G.	Good	Fair	Poor
650	550	425	300	225	175

Encore Turkey Gun

Introduced in 2005 this model is chambered for the 20 gauge shell with 3" chamber, 26" barrel with open sights and screw-in Turkey chokes. Realtree Hardwoods HD camo composite stock.

NIB	Exc.	V.G.	Good	Fair	Poor
650	550	425	300	225	175

PRO HUNTER SERIES

Pro Hunter

Similar to Encore rifle but with plain or fluted barrel and various finish and stock options. Barrels interchange with standard Encore barrels. Muzzleloading and pistol versions available. Introduced 2007.

NIB	Exc.	V.G.	Good	Fair	Poor
650	500	400	275	200	100

Pro Hunter Predator Rifle

Contender-style break-action single shot rifle chambered in .204 Ruger, .223 Remington, .22-250 and .308 Winchester. Features include 28" deep-fluted interchangeable barrel, composite buttstock and fore-end with non-slip inserts in cheekpiece, pistol grip and fore-end. Max 1 camo finish overall. Overall length: 42.5". Weight: 7.75 lbs.

NIB	Exc.	V.G.	Good	Fair	Poor
750	650	500	400	300	250

Pro Hunter Turkey Gun

Contender-style break-action single shot shotgun chambered in 12 - or 20 gauge and 3" shells. Features include 24" barrel with interchangeable choke tubes (Extra Full supplied), composite buttstock and fore-end with non-slip inserts in cheekpiece, pistol grip and fore-end. Adjustable fiber optic sights, Sims recoil pad, AP camo finish overall. Overall length: 40.5". Weight: 6.5 lbs.

NIB	Exc.	V.G.	Good	Fair	Poor
750	650	525	400	250	150

ICON SERIES

Icon

Bolt-action centerfire rifle chambered in .22-250, .243, .308 and .30 Thompson-Center. Barrel length 22" (iron sight) or 24" (sightless). Detachable box magazine, Introduced in 2007.

NIB	Exc.	V.G.	Good	Fair	Poor
900	800	675	525	300	200

Icon Classic Long Action Rifle

Similar to Icon but with long-action design and chambered for .270, .30-06, .300 Winchester Magnum and 7mm Remington Magnum.

NIB	Exc.	V.G.	Good	Fair	Poor
1000	850	700	600	400	200

Icon Weathershield Medium Action Rifle

Similar to Icon but with stainless steel barrel and receiver and black synthetic or Realtree AP Camo stock.

NIB	Exc.	V.G.	Good	Fair	Poor
1000	850	700	600	400	200

VENTURE SERIES

Venture Medium Action Rifle

Bolt action rifle chambered in .204, .22-250, .223, .243, 7mm-08, .308 and 30TC. Features include a 24" crowned medium weight barrel, classic styled composite stock with inlaid traction grip panels, adjustable 3.5 to 5 pound trigger along with a drilled and tapped receiver (bases included). 3+1 detachable nylon box magazine. Overall length: 7 lbs. Length: 43.5".

NIB	Exc.	V.G.	Good	Fair	Poor
500	400	325	250	175	100

Venture Predator PDX Rifle

Bolt action rifle chambered in .204, .22-250, .223, .243, .308. Similar to Venture Medium action but with heavy, deep-fluted 22" barrel and Max-1 camo finish overall. Overall length: 8 lbs. Length: 41.5".

NIB	Exc.	V.G.	Good	Fair	Poor
600	500	425	350	275	200

Venture Weather Shield

Advanced Weather Shield finish for durability. Classic styled composite stock with Hogue Overmolded Grip panels. Classic styled composite stock. T/C large bolt design for smooth operation. 60 degree bolt lift. Receiver drilled and tapped with bases included. Magazine capacity, 3+1. Available in short and long-action models for most standard, magnum and WSM cartridges.

NIB	Exc.	V.G.	Good	Fair	Poor
525	450	380	325	225	150

Dimension

Bolt-action rifle available in 10 calibers from .204 Ruger to .300 Win. Magnum. Barrel lengths are 22" or 24". Synthetic stock has competition cheekpiece. Other features are an aluminum receiver, free-floated barrel and choice of right or left-hand action. Introduced in 2012.

NIB	Exc.	V.G.	Good	Fair	Poor
600	525	450	400	350	200

OTHER RIFLES

Model R55

This semi-automatic rifle is chambered for the .17 Mach 2 cartridge and fitted with a 20" match grade barrel with adjustable sights. Black composite or laminated hardwood stock. Receiver is blued or stainless steel. Magazine capacity is 5 rounds. Weight is about 5.5 lbs. Introduced in 2005. **NOTE:** Add $65 for black composite stock.

NIB	Exc.	V.G.	Good	Fair	Poor
550	450	375	300	250	175

TCR 87 Hunter Model

This single-shot top lever rifle is chambered for cartridges from .22 LR to .308 Win. Fitted with a 23" barrel. The finish is blue with walnut stock. Discontinued as a regular production rifle in 1993.

NIB	Exc.	V.G.	Good	Fair	Poor
650	550	425	300	225	175

T/C 22 LR Classic

Introduced in 2000 this model is a semi-automatic rifle chambered for the .22 LR cartridge. It is fitted with a 22" match grade barrel. Walnut stock with Monte Carlo comb. Adjustable rear sight. Magazine capacity is 8 rounds. Weight is about 5.5 lbs.

NIB	Exc.	V.G.	Good	Fair	Poor
450	350	275	225	175	100

.22 Classic Benchmark

An updated version of the Classic with an 18" heavy barrel and no sights. Wood laminated target stock. Magazine capacity is 10 rounds. Weight is about 6.8 lbs. Introduced in 2003.

NIB	Exc.	V.G.	Good	Fair	Poor
475	375	300	250	200	100

Silver Lynx

This .22 caliber semi-automatic rifle, introduced in 2004, is fitted with a .20 stainless steel barrel. Black composite stock with Monte Carlo comb. Magazine capacity is 5 rounds. Weight is about 5.5 lbs.

NIB	Exc.	V.G.	Good	Fair	Poor
400	300	225	150	100	75

BLACKPOWDER FIREARMS

System 1

Introduced in 1997 this concept features a complete muzzleloading system with interchangeable barrels. Offered with .32, .50, .54, .58 caliber and 12 gauge shotgun barrels with walnut stock and blued finish. Or stainless steel with synthetic stock. Barrel lengths are 26". Approximate weight is 7.5 lbs. Sights are adjustable. **NOTE:** Add $30 for synthetic stock and stainless steel.

NIB	Exc.	V.G.	Good	Fair	Poor
350	300	225	175	125	75

Thunder Hawk

Introduced in 1993, this rifle features a .50 caliber caplock in-line ignition with 21" round barrel. Rear sight is adjustable with ramp front sight. The stock is a plain American black walnut with rubber recoil pad. Trigger is adjustable. In 1994 this model was available in stainless steel. Weighs 6.75 lbs.

NIB	Exc.	V.G.	Good	Fair	Poor
225	200	175	150	100	75

Thunder Hawk Shadow

Introduced in 1996, this model features an in-line ignition in .50 or .54 caliber with a 24" round barrel. It comes standard with a black checkered composite stock. Weight is approximately 7 lbs. In 1997 this model was offered with camouflage stock and blued finish.

NIB	Exc.	V.G.	Good	Fair	Poor
300	250	200	150	100	75

Grey Hawk

This stainless steel composite stock rifle is a .50 caliber cap-lock with 24" round barrel. It utilizes a hooked breech system. The lock is a heavy-duty coil spring with floral engraving pattern. Adjustable rear sight and bead front sight are standard. Weighs about 7 lbs.

NIB	Exc.	V.G.	Good	Fair	Poor
225	200	175	150	100	75

Hawken Caplock Rifle

Available in .45, .50, and .54 caliber this rifle has a 28" octagonal barrel and hooked breech system. Triggers are fully adjustable and can function as double set or single stage. Adjustable sights with bead front sight are standard. Trim is solid brass and stock is select American walnut with cheekpiece. Weighs about 8.5 lbs.

NIB	Exc.	V.G.	Good	Fair	Poor
300	250	200	150	100	75

Hawken Flintlock Rifle

Offered in .50 caliber with 28" octagonal barrel. All other features are the same as above.

NIB	Exc.	V.G.	Good	Fair	Poor
310	260	200	150	100	75

Hawken Custom/Elite

Introduced in 1994 this model is a .50 caliber traditional cap-lock rifle with double set triggers, crescent butt, and select American walnut stock with no patch box. The finish is a high luster blue.

NIB	Exc.	V.G.	Good	Fair	Poor
400	350	275	175	100	75

Omega 45/Omega 50

This muzzleloader is chambered for .45 or .50 and fitted with a 28" round barrel. Adjustable sights. Composite or laminated stock. Weight is about 7 lbs. Introduced in 2002. **NOTE:** For stainless steel add $50. Add $60 for Realtree camo stock.

NIB	Exc.	V.G.	Good	Fair	Poor
535	425	325	250	150	75

Omega Pivoting Breech Rifle

Introduced in 2004 this rifle has a 28" stainless steel fluted barrel bored for the .50 caliber slug. Laminated wood thumbhole stock. Fiber optic sights. Weight is about 7 lbs.

NIB	Exc.	V.G.	Good	Fair	Poor
400	350	275	175	100	75

Renegade Caplock Rifle

Offered in .50 or .54 caliber with 26" octagonal barrel. Adjustable triggers that can function as double set or single stage. Adjustable sights with blued trim. Walnut stock. Offered in either right hand or left hand models. Weighs about 8 lbs.

NIB	Exc.	V.G.	Good	Fair	Poor
460	350	250	150	100	75

Renegade Flintlock

Available in .50 caliber only and right hand only. Other features are the same as Caplock model.

NIB	Exc.	V.G.	Good	Fair	Poor
460	350	250	150	100	755

Big Boar Rifle

This hooked breech model features the .58 caliber with 26" octagonal barrel. Single trigger and adjustable sights are standard. Trim is blued steel. American walnut stock with rubber pad. Weighs about 7.75 lbs.

NIB	Exc.	V.G.	Good	Fair	Poor
550	400	300	250	200	100

High Plains Sporter

This is a .50 caliber caplock with a 24" round barrel. The lock is case-colored. Choice of adjustable open sights or tang sight. Trim is blued. The stock is walnut with rubber recoil pad, pistol grip, and sling swivel studs. Weighs about 7 lbs.

NIB	Exc.	V.G.	Good	Fair	Poor
275	250	200	150	100	75

Tree Hawk

Available in either .50 caliber caplock or 12 gauge caplock. The .50 caliber carbine has a 21" barrel and is offered in camo colors. The 12 gauge shotgun is fitted with a 27" barrel and also comes in camo colors. Weight is about 6.75 lbs.

Rifle

NIB	Exc.	V.G.	Good	Fair	Poor
275	250	200	150	100	75

Shotgun

NIB	Exc.	V.G.	Good	Fair	Poor
275	250	200	150	100	75

White Mountain Carbine

Available in either .45, .50, or .54 caliber caplock or .50 flintlock. Fitted with a 20-1/2" octagon barrel. The lock is case-colored and trim is blued. Stock is walnut with rubber recoil pad. Weighs about 6.5 lbs. Discontinued.

NIB	Exc.	V.G.	Good	Fair	Poor
400	350	275	175	100	75

Black Mountain Magnum

Introduced in 1999 this model features a 26" round barrel with choice of walnut or composite stock. Chambered for .50 or .54 caliber or 12 gauge with 27" round barrel. All models are caplock. Blued finish. Discontinued.

NIB	Exc.	V.G.	Good	Fair	Poor
400	350	275	175	100	75

Pennsylvania Hunter

Offered in .50 caliber caplock or flintlock and fitted with either a 31.5" octagon/round barrel or a 21.5" octagon/round barrel. Fully adjustable sights, walnut stock, and blued trim are standard. Rifle weighs about 7.5 lbs. while the carbine weighs about 6.5 lbs. Discontinued.

Rifle

NIB	Exc.	V.G.	Good	Fair	Poor
400	325	250	200	150	100

Carbine

NIB	Exc.	V.G.	Good	Fair	Poor
400	325	250	200	150	100

Pennsylvania Match Rifle

Similar to the Pennsylvania Hunter Rifle except equipped with a tang peep sight and a globe front sight. Discontinued.

NIB	Exc.	V.G.	Good	Fair	Poor
—	450	375	300	250	175

New Englander Rifle

Offered in either .50 or .54 caliber caplock with walnut stock and 26" round barrel. Adjustable sights. Weighs about 7 lbs. 15 oz. A 12" barrel is optional. Discontinued. **NOTE:** Add $150 for interchangeable shotgun barrel.

NIB	Exc.	V.G.	Good	Fair	Poor
350	275	200	150	100	75

New Englander Shotgun

Same as above, but fitted with a 27" 12 gauge barrel with screw in full choke. Weighs about 6 lbs. 8 oz. Discontinued.

NIB	Exc.	V.G.	Good	Fair	Poor
350	275	200	150	100	75

New Englander Composite

Offered with composite stock. The .50 or .54 caliber rifle has a 24" barrel and the 12 gauge shotgun has a 27" barrel. Discontinued.

Rifle

NIB	Exc.	V.G.	Good	Fair	Poor
350	275	200	150	100	75

Shotgun

NIB	Exc.	V.G.	Good	Fair	Poor
350	275	200	150	100	75

Scout Carbine

This is a muzzleloading carbine of .50 or .54 caliber with an in-line ignition system. Offered with either walnut stock or composite stock (first offered in 1993) it is fitted with a 21" round barrel. Adjustable rear sight and fixed blade front sight. Brass barrel band and trigger guard on walnut stock and blued barrel band and trigger guard on composite stock model. Weighs about 7 lbs. 4 oz. Discontinued.

Walnut Stock

NIB	Exc.	V.G.	Good	Fair	Poor
325	275	200	150	100	75

Composite Stock

NIB	Exc.	V.G.	Good	Fair	Poor
250	225	175	150	100	75

Scout Rifle

Similar to the Scout Carbine but fitted with a 24" stepped half-round, half-octagonal barrel. Weight is approximately 8 lbs. Discontinued.

Walnut Stock

NIB	Exc.	V.G.	Good	Fair	Poor
425	350	275	225	150	100

Composite Stock

NIB	Exc.	V.G.	Good	Fair	Poor
400	325	250	200	150	100

Scout Pistol

The same design as the Scout carbine this single-action pistol is available in .45, .50, or .54 caliber. Fitted with a 12" barrel, adjustable rear sight, and blued finish with brass trigger guard. Black walnut grips. Weighs 4 lbs. 6 oz. Discontinued.

NIB	Exc.	V.G.	Good	Fair	Poor
250	225	200	175	100	75

Fire Hawk Deluxe

Introduced in 1996 this is an in-line muzzleloader. Offered in either .50 or .54 caliber with blued or stainless steel. Semi-fancy checkered walnut stock has a cheekpiece. The round barrel is 24" long. Adjustable rear leaf sight with ramp style front bead. Weight is about 7 lbs.

NIB	Exc.	V.G.	Good	Fair	Poor
400	325	250	200	125	100

Fire Hawk

Similar to the Deluxe Fire Hawk but with standard American walnut stock or composition stock.

NIB	Exc.	V.G.	Good	Fair	Poor
300	250	200	150	100	75

Thumbhole Stock

NIB	Exc.	V.G.	Good	Fair	Poor
325	275	225	175	100	75

Camo Stock

NIB	Exc.	V.G.	Good	Fair	Poor
325	275	225	175	100	75

Bantam

NIB	Exc.	V.G.	Good	Fair	Poor
275	225	175	125	100	75

.32 & .58 caliber models

NIB	Exc.	V.G.	Good	Fair	Poor
300	250	200	150	100	75

Fire Storm

Offered as a percussion or flintlock and fitted with a 26" barrel chambered for .50 caliber. Black composite stock. Adjustable fiber optics rear sight. Weight is about 7 lbs. Introduced in 2000.

NIB	Exc.	V.G.	Good	Fair	Poor
375	300	225	150	100	75

Black Diamond

This is an in-line muzzleloading rifle with removable breech plug. Fitted with a 22.5" .50 caliber barrel. Stock is Rynite. Choice of blue or stainless steel. Introduced in 1998. Discontinued. **NOTE:** Add $50 for stainless steel.

NIB	Exc.	V.G.	Good	Fair	Poor
325	275	225	175	100	75

Black Diamond XR

This .45 caliber or .50 caliber muzzleloader is fitted with a 26" round barrel. Offered with blued finish, camo, or stainless steel.

Weight is about 6.75 lbs. Introduced in 2002. Discontinued.

NIB	Exc.	V.G.	Good	Fair	Poor
375	300	225	150	100	75

Triumph

Fifty-caliber toggle-breech inline muzzleloader with only four moving parts. Blued/synthetic, Weathershield/synthetic, or Weathershield/stainless finish. Introduced 2007.

NIB	Exc.	V.G.	Good	Fair	Poor
425	350	275	225	150	100

Impact Muzzleloading Rifle

50-caliber single shot rifle. Features include 209 primer ignition, sliding hood to expose removable breechplug, synthetic stock adjustable from 12.5" to 13.5", 26" blued 1:28 rifled barrel, adjustable fiber optic sights, aluminum ramrod, camo composite stock, QLA muzzle system. Weight 6.5 lbs. **NOTE:** Add $20 for camo stock.

NIB	Exc.	V.G.	Good	Fair	Poor
200	175	140	100	80	50

NorthWest Explorer Muzzleloading Rifle

50-caliber single shot rifle. Features include dropping block action, #11 percussion cap ignition, 28" blued or Weathershield 1:48 rifled barrel, adjustable fiber optic sights, aluminum ramrod, black or camo composite stock with recoil pad, QLA muzzle system. Weight 7 lbs. **NOTE:** Add $60 for Realtree Hardwoods camo stock.

NIB	Exc.	V.G.	Good	Fair	Poor
280	235	200	175	125	75

G2 Contender Muzzleloader

A 209x45 24" muzzleloader barrel. Will interchange with G2 Contender rifle barrels. Weight is about 5.5 lbs.

NIB	Exc.	V.G.	Good	Fair	Poor
600	500	400	325	275	200

G2 Contender Muzzeloader .50 caliber

In .50 caliber with 24" barrel. Weight is about 6.5 lbs. Introduced in 2005.

NIB	Exc.	V.G.	Good	Fair	Poor
600	500	400	325	275	200

Encore 209x50 Mag Rifle

This muzzleloading rifle is chambered for .50 caliber and fitted with a 26" barrel. Designed to handle magnum loads of up to 150 grains of FFG black powder. Blued or stainless steel finish. Introduced in 1998. **NOTE:** Add $75 for stainless steel. Add $140 for Realtree camo stock

NIB	Exc.	V.G.	Good	Fair	Poor
650	500	400	275	200	100

Encore 209x50 Mag Carbine

Similar to the above model but fitted with a 20" ported barrel. Realtree camo stock. Weight is about 6.75 lbs. Introduced in 2004.

NIB	Exc.	V.G.	Good	Fair	Poor
650	500	400	275	200	100

Encore 209x50 Pistol

This model features a 15" barrel chambered for .50 caliber. Walnut stock and blued finish. Approximate weight is 16 oz. Introduced in 2000.

NIB	Exc.	V.G.	Good	Fair	Poor
550	450	375	300	250	175

THUNDER FIVE
MIL Inc.
Piney Flats, Tennessee

Thunder-Five

Five shot, double-action revolver with 2" rifled barrel, matte finish, ambidextrous hammer block safety, Pachmayr grips, chambered in .45 Long Colt/.410 shotgun.

NIB	Exc.	V.G.	Good	Fair	Poor
575	425	345	250	200	150

TIKKA
Tikkakoski, Finland

RIFLES

Whitetail Hunter

This rifle features a hand checkered walnut stock with matte lacquer finish. These rifles are furnished without sights, but receiver is grooved. Magazine is detachable box type. Three action lengths are offered: short, medium, and long. In short action calibers the choices are: .17 Rem., .223, .22-250, .243, and .308 with 22.4" barrels and weight of 7 lbs. The medium action calibers are: .270 and .30-06 with 22.4" barrels and weight of 7.3 lbs. In long are the 7mm Rem. Magnum, .300 and .338 Win. Magnum with 24.4" barrel and weight of 7.5 lbs.

NIB	Exc.	V.G.	Good	Fair	Poor
725	600	500	400	200	150

Whitetail Hunter Deluxe

Similar to standard model above but furnished with cheekpiece, select walnut stock, rosewood pistol grip cap and fore-end tip. Metal surfaces are a highly polished blue. Same calibers as offered above.

NIB	Exc.	V.G.	Good	Fair	Poor
875	700	600	400	200	150

Whitetail/Battue Rifle

This rifle was originally designed for the French market. The barrel is 20.5" long and is fitted with a raised quarter rib. The walnut is checkered with rubber recoil pad standard. A black fiberglass stock is offered as an option. In the medium action the only caliber is .308. In a long action the calibers are: .270, .30-06, 7mm Rem. Magnum, .300 and .338 Win. Magnum. All models weigh about 7 lbs. In 2000 this was offered in a left-hand model. **NOTE:** Add $50 for stainless steel finish. Add $20 for magnum calibers. Add $60 for left hand model.

NIB	Exc.	V.G.	Good	Fair	Poor
650	500	400	275	200	100

Varmint/Continental Rifle

This model features a 23.5" heavy barrel without sights. The checkered walnut stock has a wide fore-end. Offered in .17 Rem., .223, .22-250, .243, and .308. Weighs approximately 8.5 lbs.

NIB	Exc.	V.G.	Good	Fair	Poor
725	600	500	400	200	150

Long Range Hunting

Same as above but in .25-06, .270, .7mm Magnum, and .300 Win. Magnum. Fitted with 26" heavy barrel.

NIB	Exc.	V.G.	Good	Fair	Poor
725	600	500	400	200	150

Sporter

Introduced in 1998 this model features a select walnut stock, adjustable cheekpiece, adjustable buttplate, adjustable trigger. Comes without open sights. Detachable 5-round magazine. Chambered for .223, .22-250, and .308 calibers.

NIB	Exc.	V.G.	Good	Fair	Poor
950	825	675	500	395	200

T3 Hunter

Introduced in 2003 this bolt-action rifle features a hand-forged barrel and adjustable trigger. Offered in standard and magnum calibers from .223 to .338 Win. Magnum. Walnut stock with recoil pad. Detachable magazine holds three rounds for all calibers except .223 (four). No sights. Barrel lengths are 22.5" and 24.25" for standard and magnum calibers respectively. Weight is about 6.75 lbs.

NIB	Exc.	V.G.	Good	Fair	Poor
750	625	500	400	200	150

T3 Lite

As above but fitted with a black synthetic stock with blued finish. Introduced in 2003.

NIB	Exc.	V.G.	Good	Fair	Poor
675	550	425	325	150	100

T3 Lite Stainless

As above but with stainless steel barrel and synthetic stock.

NIB	Exc.	V.G.	Good	Fair	Poor
725	600	500	400	200	150

T3 Big Boar

This bolt action rifle is chambered for the .308, .30-06, or .300 WSM cartridges. Fitted with a 19" barrel with no sights. Black synthetic stock with recoil pad. Blued finish. Magazine capacity is 3 rounds. Weight is about 6 lbs. Introduced in 2005.

NIB	Exc.	V.G.	Good	Fair	Poor
725	600	500	400	200	150

T3 Super Varmint

This bolt-action model is chambered for the .223 Rem., .22-250 Rem., or the .308 cartridge. Stainless steel receiver and barrel with Picatinny rail on receiver. Barrel length is 23.3". Black synthetic stock has adjustable comb. Adjustable trigger. Detachable magazine. Introduced in 2005.

NIB	Exc.	V.G.	Good	Fair	Poor
1575	1350	1100	750	575	300

T3 Varmint

Chambered for the .223, .22-250, and .308 cartridges. Fitted with a 23.3" barrel with no sights. Synthetic stock with blued finish. Adjustable trigger. Rubber recoil pad. **NOTE:** Add $70 for stainless steel version.

NIB	Exc.	V.G.	Good	Fair	Poor
850	725	575	400	295	150

T3 Tactical

Introduced in 2004 this rifle is chambered for the .223 or .308 cartridge. Fitted with a 20" barrel with muzzlebrake. Black synthetic varmint-style stock with adjustable cheekpiece. Detachable magazine capacity is 5 rounds. Picatinny rail on receiver top.

NIB	Exc.	V.G.	Good	Fair	Poor
1500	1350	1050	850	575	350

Tikka Target

This bolt-action rifle is chambered for the .223, .22-250, 7mm-08 Rem., .308 Win., and the 6.5x55 Swedish Mauser cartridge. Fitted with a 23.25" barrel and adjustable walnut target stock, the trigger is adjustable for weight. No sights. Weight is about 9 lbs.

NIB	Exc.	V.G.	Good	Fair	Poor
950	825	675	500	395	200

SHOTGUNS/DOUBLE RIFLES (FORMERLY VALMET)

Tikka, Valmet and Sako have been merged into one company, SAKO Ltd. These firearms are now manufactured in Italy under the brand name Tikka. Parts are interchangeable between the Valmet guns, made in Finland, and the Tikka guns, made in Italy.

412S Shotgun

This over/under shotgun is available in 12 gauge only with 26" or 28" barrels. The stock is checkered European walnut. Weighs about 7.25 lbs.

NIB	Exc.	V.G.	Good	Fair	Poor
950	800	650	500	300	200

412S Shotgun/Rifle

Same as above but with 12 gauge barrel and choice of .222 or .308 barrel. Barrel length is 24" and weighs 8 lbs.

NIB	Exc.	V.G.	Good	Fair	Poor
1000	850	700	500	300	200

412S Double Rifle

Same as above but fitted with a 24" over/under rifle barrel in 9.3x74R. Weighs about 8.5 lbs.

NIB	Exc.	V.G.	Good	Fair	Poor
1150	950	750	500	300	200

412S Sporting Clays

Introduced in 1993 this model is offered in 12 gauge with 28" barrels with choke tubes.

NIB	Exc.	V.G.	Good	Fair	Poor
1000	850	700	500	300	200

512S Field Grade

Introduced in 2000 this over/under gun is chambered for the 12 gauge 3" shell and fitted with either a 26" or 28" choke tube barrels. **NOTE:** For shotgun/rifle barrel sets add $650 per set.

NIB	Exc.	V.G.	Good	Fair	Poor
1125	850	750	500	300	200

512S Sporting Clays

This 12 gauge 3" model is fitted with a 30" barrel with choke tubes.

NIB	Exc.	V.G.	Good	Fair	Poor
1175	900	750	500	300	200

TIMBER WOLF

See—Action Arms Ltd.

TIPPING & LAWDEN

Birmingham, England

Thomas Revolver

A .320, .380, or .450 double-action revolver with a 4.5" barrel and 5-shot cylinder, utilizing a cartridge extraction system designed by J. Thomas of Birmingham in which the barrel and cylinder may be moved forward. Manufactured from 1870 to 1877.

NIB	Exc.	V.G.	Good	Fair	Poor
—	—	1400	950	400	175

TIPPMAN ARMS

Fort Wayne, Indiana

Model 1917

A .22 caliber semi-automatic one-half scale reproduction of the Browning Model 1917 water-cooled machine gun. Barrel length 10". A tripod was sold with this model. Manufactured in 1986 and 1987.

NIB	Exc.	V.G.	Good	Fair	Poor
5750	5250	—	—	—	—

Model 1919 A-4

A .22 caliber semi-automatic one-half scale reproduction of the Browning Model 1919 A-4 machine gun. Barrel length 11" and furnished with a tripod. Manufactured in 1986 and 1987.

NIB	Exc.	V.G.	Good	Fair	Poor
3000	2750	—	—	—	—

Model .50 HB

A .22 Magnum caliber semi-automatic one-half scale reproduction of the Browning .50 caliber machine gun. Barrel length 18.25", furnished with a tripod. Manufactured in 1986 and 1987.

NIB	Exc.	V.G.	Good	Fair	Poor
6000	5500	—	—	—	—

TISAS (TRABZON GUN INDUSTRY CORP.)

Trabzon, Turkey

Fatih 13

Beretta-style autopistol clone chambered in .32 ACP. Introduced 1994.

NIB	Exc.	V.G.	Good	Fair	Poor
300	225	150	125	75	50

Kanuni 16

Single-/double-action autopistol chambered in 9mm Parabellum with 15- or 17-shot capacity. Black, chrome or chrome/gold finish. Introduced 1999.

NIB	Exc.	V.G.	Good	Fair	Poor
325	225	150	125	75	50

Kanuni S

Lightweight version of Kanuni 16. Black, chrome or chrome/black finish. Introduced 2000.

NIB	Exc.	V.G.	Good	Fair	Poor
325	225	150	125	75	50

Zigana M16

Single-/double-action autopistol chambered in 9mm Parabellum with 15- or 17-shot capacity and 5" barrel. Introduced 2000.

NIB	*Exc.*	*V.G.*	*Good*	*Fair*	*Poor*
395	300	225	195	150	75

Zigana K

Compact version of Zigana M16 with 4" barrel. Introduced 2002.

NIB	*Exc.*	*V.G.*	*Good*	*Fair*	*Poor*
395	300	225	195	150	75

Zigana T

Longer (5.5") barrel version of Zigana M16. Introduced 2002.

NIB	*Exc.*	*V.G.*	*Good*	*Fair*	*Poor*
395	300	225	195	150	75

Zigana Sport

Compensated version of Zigana K with 4.5" barrel. Introduced 2005.

NIB	*Exc.*	*V.G.*	*Good*	*Fair*	*Poor*
395	300	225	195	150	75

Zigana C45

Similar to Zigana M16 but chambered in .45 ACP with 4.75" barrel. Introduced 2005.

NIB	*Exc.*	*V.G.*	*Good*	*Fair*	*Poor*
395	300	225	195	150	75

Zigana F

"Meltdown" version of Zigana M16 with radiused edges and improved ergonomics. Introduced 2007.

NIB	*Exc.*	*V.G.*	*Good*	*Fair*	*Poor*
395	300	225	195	150	75

TOBIN ARMS MANUFACTURING CO.
Norwich, Connecticut and Windsor, Ontario, Canada

The Tobin Arms Manufacturing Co. operated from about 1905 to 1925 making an exposed hammer double and two hammerless models in four grades. The "Simplex" was cleverly designed (based on a patent by C.M. Wollam) side plated double-barrel internal hammer shotgun which resembled the Hopkins and Allen guns of that time. Some may have been private branded. Most of the Tobin doubles were made in Norwich, Conn., and are so marked. After 1909 operations were transferred to Windsor, Ont., Canada, and some guns will be found with that address. Tobin guns are not often seen by collectors and are highly prized because of their relative rarity and because they were considered good guns by top dealers such as C.J. Godfrey Co. of New York City and Iver Johnson Sporting Goods of Boston. Values depend on condition and range from $200 in poor condition to $1000 and up for engraved versions in good to very good condition.

NOTE: Tobin also manufactured a .22 rimfire single-shot rifle apparently during the period 1910-1925. These are rather scarce and their value is estimated to be in the $500 - $700 range, depending on condition.

A rough timeline of the Tobin Arms Manufacturing Company follows:

1903: founded by Frank M. Tobin in Norwich, CT.

1904-1909: manufactured hammer and hammerless sidelock shotguns (12ga. and 16ga.) in Norwich, Connecticut, USA

1909: purchased by a group of Canadian Investors and moved to Woodstock, ON, CAN

1910-1923/25: manufactured shotguns and rifles (entire product list unknown)

1923/25: purchased by sporting goods distributor G.B.Crandall

1923/25-1951: G.B.Crandall continued production until 1951 (possibly under the name GB Crandall)

Thanks to Jack of Florida for furnishing us with this information!

TODD, GEORGE H.
Montgomery, Alabama

Rifled Musket

A .58 caliber single-shot percussion rifle with a 40" barrel and full length stock secured by three barrel bands. Barrel and lock finished in the bright, brass furniture and walnut stock. The lock marked "George H. Todd/ Montgomery, Ala." **Too rare to price.**

TOMISKA, ALOIS
Pilsen, Czechoslovakia

Little Tom

A 6.35mm or 7.65mm caliber semi-automatic pistol with a 2.5" barrel. The slide marked "Alois Tomiska Plzen Patent Little Tom" and the grips inlaid with a medallion bearing the monogram "AT". Blued with checkered walnut grips. Manufactured from 1908 to 1918. Subsequently produced by the Wiener Waffenfabrik.

NIB	Exc.	V.G.	Good	Fair	Poor
—	550	425	350	250	125

TORKELSON ARMS CO.
Harfield, Warren, and Worcester, Massachusetts

Double-Barrel Shotguns

Reinhard T. Torkelson's company made double-barrel, boxlock, side-by-side, hammerless shotguns in four models at several locations between 1885 and 1910. He worked with Iver Johnson at Fitchburg, Mass., and also built guns carrying the Lovell (Boston) name. His "New Worcester" marked guns are quite common. They were sold by Sears and other large and well known houses.

NIB	Exc.	V.G.	Good	Fair	Poor
—	600	300	200	150	100

TRADEWINDS
Tacoma, Washington

Model H-170

A 12 gauge semi-automatic shotgun with a 26" or 28" ventilated rib barrel and 5-shot tubular magazine. Blued, anodized alloy receiver and walnut stock.

NIB	Exc.	V.G.	Good	Fair	Poor
—	300	250	225	150	100

Model 260-A

A .22 caliber semi-automatic rifle with a 22.5" barrel, open sights and 5-shot magazine. Blued with a walnut stock.

NIB	Exc.	V.G.	Good	Fair	Poor
—	200	175	125	100	75

Model 311-A

A .22 caliber bolt-action rifle with a 22.5" barrel, open sights and a 5-shot magazine. Blued with a walnut stock.

NIB	Exc.	V.G.	Good	Fair	Poor
—	175	150	100	75	50

Model 5000 "Husky"

A centerfire bolt-action rifle with a 24" barrel, adjustable sights and 4-shot magazine. Blued with a walnut stock.

NIB	Exc.	V.G.	Good	Fair	Poor
—	350	300	275	200	100

TRADITIONS
Old Saybrook, Connecticut

OVER/UNDER SHOTGUNS

These shotguns are built by the Italian firm of Fausti Stefano and Emil Rizzini.

Hunter

Introduced in 2001 this model features a choice of 12 or 20 gauge chambers with 26" or 28" vent rib barrels with fixed chokes. Single-selective trigger. Extractors. Checkered walnut stock. Blued frame and barrels. Black rubber recoil pad. Weight is about 7.25 lbs. for 12 gauge and 6.75 lbs. for 20 gauge.

NIB	Exc.	V.G.	Good	Fair	Poor
650	525	400	300	225	150

Field I

This model is offered in 12, 20 and 28 gauge as well as .410 bore. Barrel lengths are 26". Fixed chokes. Single-selective trigger and extractors. Coin finish engraved receiver. Checkered walnut stock. Black rubber recoil pad. Weight is similar to the Hunter model with the .410 bore weighing about 6.5 lbs.

NIB	Exc.	V.G.	Good	Fair	Poor
575	450	375	275	200	125

Field II

Similar to the Field I but with the additional choice of a 16 gauge with 28" barrels. This model also features screw-in chokes and automatic ejectors.

NIB	Exc.	V.G.	Good	Fair	Poor
750	625	500	375	250	125

Field II Combo

This model features a 20 gauge and .410 bore two barrel set. Both barrels are 26" with fixed chokes. Checkered walnut stock. Weight is about 6 lbs. Introduced in 2004.

NIB	Exc.	V.G.	Good	Fair	Poor
1400	1200	950	800	500	300

Field III Gold

Similar to the other Field series of guns but offered in 12 gauge only with 26" or 28" barrels. Select oil finish walnut stock. Engraved receiver with gold pheasants and woodcock.

NIB	Exc.	V.G.	Good	Fair	Poor
1100	950	800	675	500	250

Upland II

Offered in both 12 and 20 gauge with 26" barrels in 12 gauge and 24" or 26" barrels in 20 gauge. Straight grip walnut stock. Engraved blued receiver. Schnabel fore-end. Choke tubes. Single-selective trigger and auto ejectors. Weight for 12 gauge gun is about 7.25 lbs. and for 20 gauge about 6.25 lbs.

NIB	Exc.	V.G.	Good	Fair	Poor
800	650	500	350	275	150

Upland III

Introduced in 2001 this model features a 12 gauge gun with 26" vent rib barrels. High grade checkered walnut stock with hand engraved receiver with gold. Schnabel fore-end. Single-selective trigger and auto ejectors standard. Screw-in chokes. Black rubber recoil pad. Weight is about 7.25 lbs.

NIB	Exc.	V.G.	Good	Fair	Poor
1400	1200	950	800	500	300

Sporting Clay II

This 12 gauge gas operated model has either 28" or 30" vent rib ported barrels. Screw-in extended choke tubes. Checkered walnut stock with blued receiver and barrels. Weight is about 8 lbs.

NIB	Exc.	V.G.	Good	Fair	Poor
900	775	650	475	300	150

Sporting Clay III

This model features a choice of 12 or 20 gauge with 28" or 30" vent rib barrels. High grade checkered walnut stock. Choke tubes. Weight is about 8.5 lbs. for 12 gauge and 8.25 lbs. for 20 gauge. **NOTE:** Add $200 for 20 gauge guns.

NIB	Exc.	V.G.	Good	Fair	Poor
1400	1200	950	800	500	300

Waterfowl II

Introduced in 2001 this 12 gauge model is fitted with 28" vent rib barrels and 3.5" chambers. Finish on stock and barrels is Advantage Wetlands camo. Blued engraved receiver. Recoil pad. Single-selective trigger with auto ejectors. Weight is about 7.25 lbs.

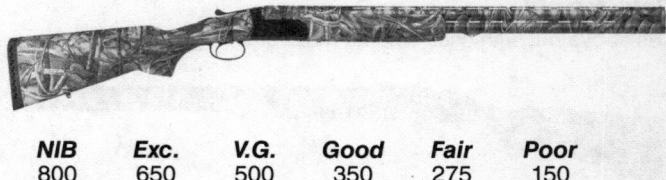

NIB	Exc.	V.G.	Good	Fair	Poor
800	650	500	350	275	150

Turkey II

Offered in 12 gauge with choice of 24" or 26" vent rib barrels with Mossy Oak Break-Up finish camo with blued receiver. X-Full choke. Single-selective trigger and auto ejectors. Weight is about 7 lbs.

NIB	Exc.	V.G.	Good	Fair	Poor
800	650	500	350	275	150

Mag Hunter II

This 12-gauge features 28" barrels with 3.5" chambers. Engraved blued receiver with walnut stock or blued receiver with Realtree Max-4 finish. Rubber recoil pad. Single selective trigger with auto ejectors. Screw-in chokes. Weight is about 7 lbs. Add 10 percent for camo model.

NIB	Exc.	V.G.	Good	Fair	Poor
900	765	650	500	350	175

Real 16

This 16 gauge gun is fitted with 26" vent rib barrels. Checkered walnut stock. Choke tubes. Single trigger with auto ejectors. Receiver is game scene engraved. Weight is about 6.75 lbs. Introduced in 2004.

NIB	Exc.	V.G.	Good	Fair	Poor
1100	950	800	675	500	250

Real 16 Gold

As above but with gold-filled birds on receiver.

NIB	Exc.	V.G.	Good	Fair	Poor
1400	1200	950	800	500	300

Gold Wing II Silver

Chambered for the 12 gauge 3" shell and fitted with 28" vent rib barrels with choke tubes. Single trigger and auto ejectors. Receiver is engraved with game scenes. High grade walnut stock with oil finish. Weight is about 7.5 lbs.

NIB	Exc.	V.G.	Good	Fair	Poor
1500	1300	1100	850	675	300

Gold Wing III

As above but with case colored receiver with gold inlays.

NIB	Exc.	V.G.	Good	Fair	Poor
2000	1750	1400	1050	800	400

Gold Wing III Silver

As above but with silver receiver with gold inlays.

NIB	Exc.	V.G.	Good	Fair	Poor
2100	1850	1500	1150	875	450

Gold Wing SL III

As above but with case colored side plates and gold inlays.

NIB	Exc.	V.G.	Good	Fair	Poor
2200	1950	1575	1225	950	450

Gold Wing SL III Silver

As above but with silver side plates and gold inlays.

NIB	Exc.	V.G.	Good	Fair	Poor
2300	2050	1675	1300	1000	500

SIDE-BY-SIDE SHOTGUNS

These side-by-side guns are imported from the Italian firm of Fausti Stanfano.

Elite I DT

This model is offered in 12, 20, and 28 gauge as well as .410 bore. All gauges are fitted with 26" barrels with fixed chokes. Double triggers and extractors. Walnut stock. Weight about 6 lbs. **NOTE:** Add $60 for 28 and .410 models.

NIB	Exc.	V.G.	Good	Fair	Poor
750	600	400	300	200	100

Elite I ST

Same as above but with single-selective trigger.

NIB	Exc.	V.G.	Good	Fair	Poor
900	750	550	425	300	150

Elite Hunter

Introduced in 2001 this model features either a 12 or 20 gauge gun with 26" barrels with screw-in chokes. Walnut stock with beavertail fore-end. Single non-selective trigger. Weight is about 6.5 lbs.

NIB	Exc.	V.G.	Good	Fair	Poor
950	800	600	475	350	200

Elite Field III ST

Introduced in 2001 this model is offered in either 28 or .410 bore with 26" barrels. High grade walnut stock with straight grip. Fixed chokes. Engraved receiver with gold. Weight is about 6.25 lbs.

NIB	Exc.	V.G.	Good	Fair	Poor
2000	1750	1400	1050	800	400

Uplander II Silver

Chambererd for the 12 gauge with 28" barrels or 20 gauge with 26" barrels. Choke tubes. Silver receiver with light scroll engraving. Checkered stock with high grade walnut. Straight grip. Single trigger and auto ejectors. Weight is about 6.75 lbs.

NIB	Exc.	V.G.	Good	Fair	Poor
2100	1850	1500	1150	875	450

Uplander III Silver

As above but with more extensive engraving with gold inlays.

NIB	Exc.	V.G.	Good	Fair	Poor
2700	2350	1950	1600	900	500

Uplander V Silver

As above but with sideplates, extensive engraving and gold inlays.

NIB	Exc.	V.G.	Good	Fair	Poor
3000	2650	2200	1800	1100	600

SEMI-AUTOMATIC SHOTGUNS

ALS Field

Introduced in 2001 this model is offered in both 12 and 20 gauge with 24", 26", or 28" vent rib barrel. Walnut stock with black pad. Blued receiver and barrels. Screw-in chokes. Weight is about 6.25 lbs.

NIB	Exc.	V.G.	Good	Fair	Poor
450	350	225	175	125	100

ALS Hunter

Same as above but with synthetic stock with 26" or 28" barrels.

NIB	Exc.	V.G.	Good	Fair	Poor
450	350	225	175	125	100

ALS Waterfowl

This 12 gauge model has Advantage Wetlands camo and is fitted with a 28" barrel with screw-in chokes. Weight is about 6.5 lbs.

NIB	Exc.	V.G.	Good	Fair	Poor
500	400	300	225	175	100

ALS Turkey

Same as above but with 21" barrel and Mossy Oak Break-up camo. Weight is about 6 lbs.

NIB	Exc.	V.G.	Good	Fair	Poor
500	400	300	225	175	100

TRANTER, WILLIAM
Birmingham, England

William Tranter produced a variety of revolvers on his own and a number of other makers produced revolvers based upon his designs. Consequently, "Tranter's Patent" is to be found on revolvers made by such firms as Deane, Adams and Deane, etc.

Model 1872

A .38 caliber double-action revolver with a 6" octagonal barrel and 6-shot cylinder. Blued with walnut grips.

Courtesy Wallis & Wallis, Lewes, Sussex, England

NIB	Exc.	V.G.	Good	Fair	Poor
—	—	2200	975	400	200

Model 1878

A .450 caliber double-action revolver with a 6" octagonal barrel. Blued with a walnut grip. Manufactured from 1878 to 1887.

NIB	Exc.	V.G.	Good	Fair	Poor
—	—	2750	1350	500	250

TRIPLETT & SCOTT/MERIDEN MANUFACTURING COMPANY
Meriden, Connecticut

Repeating Carbine

A .50 caliber carbine with either a 22" or 30" round barrel and a 7-shot magazine located in the butt. This model is loaded by turning the barrel until it comes in line with the magazine. Blued, case hardened with a walnut stock. Approximately 5,000 were made in 1864 and 1865. **NOTE:** Add 20 percent for even scarcer 22" barrel version.

Courtesy Milwaukee Public Museum, Milwaukee, Wisconsin

NIB	Exc.	V.G.	Good	Fair	Poor
—	—	3500	1500	500	200

TRISTAR SPORTING ARMS
N. Kansas City, Missouri

Tristar 300 series over/under guns are imported from Turkey. Tristar Nova series are imported from Italy. **NOTE:** In 2000 Tristar bought American Arms. American Arms no longer exists but some of its models will appear under the Tristar name. For American Arms firearms built prior to the sale see that section.

SILVER SERIES

This series of over/under guns is produced by the Spanish company Zabala.

Silver Sporting

Offered in 12 gauge with 28" or 30" barrels with single-selective trigger, auto ejectors, choke tubes, ported barrels with target rib, checkered walnut stock with pistol grip and recoil pad.

NIB	Exc.	V.G.	Good	Fair	Poor
800	675	525	400	200	125

Specialty Magnums

This is a 12 gauge magnum chambered for the 3.5" shell and fitted with a 28" barrel. Choke tubes. Checkered black walnut stock with pistol grip. **NOTE:** In 2003 a camo finish was offered for this model. Add $85 for camo.

NIB	Exc.	V.G.	Good	Fair	Poor
645	500	400	300	200	100

Silver Hunter

Offered in both 12 and 20 gauge with 26" or 28" vent rib barrels with single-selective trigger, choke tubes, engraved receiver with silver finish. Checkered walnut stock with pistol grip.

NIB	Exc.	V.G.	Good	Fair	Poor
625	500	400	300	200	100

Silver II

As above but also in 16 and 28 gauge as well as .410 bore. Fixed chokes for 16, 28, and .410 models.

NIB	Exc.	V.G.	Good	Fair	Poor
670	525	425	325	225	125

Silver Classic

This model is offered in both 12 and 20 gauge with 28" vent rib barrels and choke tubes. Frame is case colored and scroll engraved. Single-selective trigger and ejectors. Weight is about 6.75 lbs.

NIB	Exc.	V.G.	Good	Fair	Poor
800	650	500	400	300	175

BASQUE SERIES

This series of side-by-side shotguns was introduced in 2003. They are produced in Spain by Zabala.

Brittany Sporting

Offered in 12 and 20 gauge with 28" barrels with 3" chambers and choke tubes. The action is box lock with sideplates scroll engraved with case coloring. Semi-fancy checkered walnut stock with oil finish and pistol grip. Semi-beavertail fore-end. Single-selective trigger and ejectors. Weight is around 6.75 lbs.

NIB	Exc.	V.G.	Good	Fair	Poor
850	750	600	400	300	150

Brittany

This model features a boxlock action with case-colored frame with scroll engraving. Straight grip walnut stock with semi-beavertail fore-end. Offered in 12, 16, 20 and 28 gauge and .410 bore with 3" chambers and choke tubes. Weight is 6.2 - 7.4 lbs. depending on gauge.

NIB	Exc.	V.G.	Good	Fair	Poor
900	800	650	450	300	200

Brittany Classic

Enhanced Brittany model features fancy walnut wood and rounded pistol grip, cut checkering, engraved case colored frame and auto selective ejectors. Available in 12, 16, 20 and 28 gauges and .410 bore, all with 3" chambers and 27" barrels. Weight is about 6.7 lbs. in 12 gauge and slightly less in sub-gauges.

NIB	Exc.	V.G.	Good	Fair	Poor
1050	875	700	575	400	200

York

This side-by-side with blued engraved receiver and 3" chambers comes in 12 and 20 gauge with 26" or 28" barrels. Walnut, pistol grip stock and rubber recoil pad.

NIB	Exc.	V.G.	Good	Fair	Poor
625	500	400	300	200	100

Hunter Lite

Over/under with silver alloy engraved frame, 3" chambers, extractors, choke tubes and walnut pistol grip stock and forearm. 20-gauge with 26" barrels weighs 5.4 lbs.; 12 gauge with 28" barrels weighs 6 lbs.

NIB	Exc.	V.G.	Good	Fair	Poor
450	325	225	175	100	75

Hunter

Similar to Hunter Lite, but with blued steel frame.

NIB	Exc.	V.G.	Good	Fair	Poor
450	325	225	175	100	75

Field Hunter

Based on the Hunter, this model includes selective auto ejectors and five choke tubes.

NIB	Exc.	V.G.	Good	Fair	Poor
575	450	325	250	150	100

Gentry/Gentry Coach

This model is offered in 12, 16, 20 or 28 gauge and .410 bore in the Gentry and 12 and 20 gauge in the Gentry Coach. Barrel length are 28" for the Gentry (26" for 28 and .410) and 20" for the Gentry Coach. Boxlock action with engraved antique silver finish. Walnut stock with pistol grip. Choke tubes. Single-selective trigger. Weight is about 6.5 lbs. for Gentry and Gentry Coach depending on gauge.

NIB	Exc.	V.G.	Good	Fair	Poor
750	625	500	400	250	100

Derby Classic

This model features a sidelock frame and action that is engraved and case colored. Offered in 12 gauge with fixed chokes in modified and full. Fitted with 28" barrel. Double trigger and automatic ejectors. Weight is approximately 7.75 lbs.

NIB	Exc.	V.G.	Good	Fair	Poor
1200	1000	800	650	450	200

TSA SERIES

These gas-operated semi-automatics are available in 12 and 20 gauges with barrels from 24" to 26" depending on model.

TSA Field

Walnut fore-end and pistol grip stock, 3" chamber, 3 choke tubes and magazine-cut-off feature. Weight is around 5.7 lbs. in 20 gauge and 6.5 lbs. in 12 gauge, depending on barrel length. 20 gauge available in youth model.

NIB	Exc.	V.G.	Good	Fair	Poor
375	325	275	175	125	75

TSA Synthetic and Synthetic Mag

Same features as TSA Field Model but with non-glare black synthetic stock and fore-end. Also available with complete Realtree Max-4 coverage. Mag model has 3.5" chamber.

NIB	Exc.	V.G.	Good	Fair	Poor
375	325	275	175	125	75

300 SERIES

Tristar 300 series over/under guns were imported from Turkey.

Model 333

This over/under gun is available in 12 or 20 gauge with 26", 28", or 30" barrels in 12 gauge. Hand engraved frame. Fitted with 3" chambers and choke tubes. Single-selective triggers and auto ejectors. Fancy Turkish walnut stock. Weighs around 7.75 lbs. for 12 gauge and 7.5 lbs. for 20 gauge.

NIB	Exc.	V.G.	Good	Fair	Poor
650	600	425	325	225	150

Model 333SC

Similar to above model but with addition of 11mm sporting rib, recoil pad, forcing cones, and ported barrels. Extended choke tubes.

NIB	Exc.	V.G.	Good	Fair	Poor
700	650	475	375	250	175

Model 333SCL

Same features as Model 333SC but with special stock.

NIB	Exc.	V.G.	Good	Fair	Poor
700	650	475	375	250	175

Model 333L

This shotgun has the same features as the Model 333 but with a special stock designed for women. Length of pull is shorter with special Monte Carlo comb.

NIB	Exc.	V.G.	Good	Fair	Poor
650	600	425	325	225	150

Model 330

This over/under model has a standard Turkish walnut stock with etched engraved frame. Offered in 12 and 20 gauge. Single trigger with extractors and fixed chokes.

NIB	Exc.	V.G.	Good	Fair	Poor
450	325	225	175	100	75

Model 330D

This model is the same as the above but with the addition of selective auto ejectors.

NIB	Exc.	V.G.	Good	Fair	Poor
500	400	300	225	175	100

Model 300

This model features an underlug action lock with double triggers and extractors. Frame is etched. Offered in 12 gauge only with 26" or 28" barrels with fixed chokes.

NIB	Exc.	V.G.	Good	Fair	Poor
450	325	225	175	100	75

Model 311

This is a side-by-side gun in 12 or 20 gauge with 26" or 28" barrels with choke tubes. Standard Turkish walnut. Blued frame.

NIB	Exc.	V.G.	Good	Fair	Poor
500	400	300	225	175	100

Model 311R

Same as above but with 20" barrel choked Cylinder and Cylinder.

NIB	Exc.	V.G.	Good	Fair	Poor
500	400	300	225	175	100

EMILIO RIZZINI (Old Nova Series)

This gun line is no longer imported. Tristar Nova series were imported from Italy.

TR-L

Offered in 12 or 20 gauge with choice of 28" or 30" vent rib barrels. Choke tubes standard. Standard grade walnut with pistol grip. Action is silver finish boxlock with auto ejectors and single-selective trigger. Weight is approximately 7.5 lbs. Stock dimensions are made for a smaller shooter. Introduced in 1998.

NIB	Exc.	V.G.	Good	Fair	Poor
1000	850	700	575	400	200

TR-SC

Similar to the Nova L but offered in 12 gauge only with standard stock dimensions and semi-fancy walnut stock with pistol grip. Black sporting clays-style recoil pad. Weight is between 7.5 and 8 lbs. depending on barrel length. Introduced in 1998.

NIB	Exc.	V.G.	Good	Fair	Poor
1000	850	700	575	400	200

TR-I

Offered in 12 and 20 gauge with in 26" or 28" barrels with fixed chokes. Walnut stock with hand checkering and pistol grip. Beavertail fore-end. Boxlock action is blue with single-selective trigger and extractors. Weight is about 7.5 lbs. Introduced in 1998.

NIB	Exc.	V.G.	Good	Fair	Poor
650	600	425	325	225	150

TR-II (Nova II)

Same as above but fitted with automatic ejectors.

NIB	Exc.	V.G.	Good	Fair	Poor
700	650	475	375	250	175

TR-Mag

Similar to the Nova I but chambered for 10 and 12 gauge and 3.5" shell. Choice of 24" or 28" vent rib barrels with choke tubes. Non-reflective, non-glare blue finish. Introduced in 1998. **NOTE:** Add $175 for 12 gauge with ejectors and $350 for 10 gauge guns.

NIB	Exc.	V.G.	Good	Fair	Poor
750	650	475	375	250	175

TTR-Royal

This model is offered in 12, 20 or 28 gauge with 28" ported choke tube barrels, straight grip semi-fancy walnut stock, and auto ejectors. Silver receiver with gold engraving.

NIB	Exc.	V.G.	Good	Fair	Poor
1300	1250	1100	875	600	300

TR-Class SL

Top-of-the-line model with sculptured frame and engraved side plates. Offered in 12 gauge only.

NIB	Exc.	V.G.	Good	Fair	Poor
1775	1500	1250	1000	750	500

411 SERIES

These shotguns are made in Italy by R.F.M. Luciano Rota.

Model 411

This side-by-side double is imported from Italy and introduced in 1998. Chambered for 12, 20, and .410 bore with choice of 26" or 28" barrels with choke tubes or fixed chokes. Boxlock action with engraving and case coloring. Double triggers and extractors. Standard walnut stock with pistol grip and splinter forearm. Weight is between 6 and 6.5 lbs.

NIB	Exc.	V.G.	Good	Fair	Poor
850	675	500	375	250	150

Model 411R

Offered in 12 or 20 gauge with 20" barrel with fixed cylinder chokes. Extractors. Weight is about 6.5 lbs. for 12 gauge and 6 lbs. for 20 gauge.

NIB	Exc.	V.G.	Good	Fair	Poor
750	650	475	375	250	175

Model 411D

This model is similar to the Model 411 but with engraved case, colored finish on the receiver, auto ejectors, single trigger, and straight grip stock. Weight for 28 gauge is about 6.25 lbs. and for the 12 gauge about 7 lbs.

NIB	Exc.	V.G.	Good	Fair	Poor
1050	875	700	575	400	200

Model 411F

Same as the Model 411D but with silver engraved receiver.

NIB	Exc.	V.G.	Good	Fair	Poor
1600	1400	1050	800	600	400

PHANTOM SERIES

These shotguns are made in Turkey by Eqsilah and have been discontinued in favor of a new redesigned gun that is found under the Diana Series.

Phantom Field

This is a gas operated semi-automatic shotgun that is chambered for the 12 gauge and 2.75" or 3" shell. Fitted with 24", 26", or 28" barrel. Checkered walnut stock with pistol grip. Screw-in chokes. Five-round magazine. **NOTE:** For magnum models add $75.

NIB	Exc.	V.G.	Good	Fair	Poor
425	325	275	200	150	100

Phantom Synthetic

Same as above but with synthetic stock. **NOTE:** For magnum models add $75.

NIB	Exc.	V.G.	Good	Fair	Poor
395	300	225	195	150	75

Phantom HP

Same features as the phantom field except with synthetic stock, 19" barrel, and swivel studs.

NIB	Exc.	V.G.	Good	Fair	Poor
395	300	225	195	150	75

BREDA SERIES

These semi-automatic shotguns are made in Italy by Breda. This series of guns was first imported by Tristar in 2003.

Ermes

Chambered for the 12 gauge 3" shell and fitted with either a 26" or 28" vent rib barrel. Inertia operated recoil system. Checkered walnut stock with pistol grip. Choice of black, nickel, gold, or silver alloy receiver finish. Receiver is engraved with hunting scenes. Adjustable stock spacers. Weight is about 7.75 lbs.

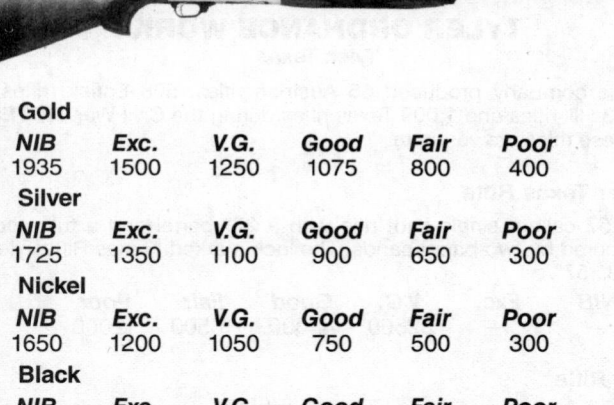

Gold

NIB	Exc.	V.G.	Good	Fair	Poor
1935	1500	1250	1075	800	400

Silver

NIB	Exc.	V.G.	Good	Fair	Poor
1725	1350	1100	900	650	300

Nickel

NIB	Exc.	V.G.	Good	Fair	Poor
1650	1200	1050	750	500	300

Black

NIB	Exc.	V.G.	Good	Fair	Poor
1260	975	750	600	500	250

Astra 20

This is a 20 gauge model with 26" vent rib barrel. Black receiver. Walnut with pistol grip and solid rubber recoil pad. Furnished with five choke tubes. Weight is about 6 lbs.

NIB	Exc.	V.G.	Good	Fair	Poor
1140	900	750	600	465	200

Mira Sporting

This semi-automatic shotgun is gas operated and chambered for the 12 gauge shell with 3" chamber. Fitted with a 30" vent rib barrel with 10mm wide rib. Checkered walnut stock with pistol grip. Weight is approximately 7 lbs.

NIB	Exc.	V.G.	Good	Fair	Poor
875	700	550	400	300	200

Mira Camo

As above but with 28" barrel and camo finish.

NIB	Exc.	V.G.	Good	Fair	Poor
875	700	550	400	300	200

CD DIANA SERIES

These shotguns are made in Turkey by Eqsilah. This line has replaced the Phantom Series and was first imported by Tristar in 2003.

CD Diana Field

This is a gas operated semi-automatic shotgun chambered for the 12 gauge 3" shell and fitted with a 26", 28", or 30" vent rib barrel. Checkered walnut stock with pistol grip. Choke tubes. Magazine cutoff. Weight is about 7 lbs. depending on barrel length.

NIB	Exc.	V.G.	Good	Fair	Poor
425	325	275	200	150	100

CD Diana Synthetic

As above but with black synthetic stock. Also offered with 3.5" chamber. Weight is about 6.75 lbs. **NOTE:** Add $90 for 3.5" Magnum model.

NIB	Exc.	V.G.	Good	Fair	Poor
400	300	250	200	150	100

CD Diana Slug

This 12 gauge gun is fitted with a 24" rifled slug barrel with open adjustable sights. Black synthetic stock. Weight is about 6.75 lbs.

NIB	Exc.	V.G.	Good	Fair	Poor
425	325	275	200	150	100

CD Diana Camo Mag

Similar to the models above but with camo stock and barrel and choice of 24" or 28" barrel with 3.5" chamber. Weight is about 6.75 lbs.

NIB	Exc.	V.G.	Good	Fair	Poor
575	450	350	225	175	100

Pee Wee

This is a single-shot bolt-action rifle chambered for .22 LR cartridges. Stock is walnut and it is about 1/2 the size of an adult rifle. Weight is about 2.75 lbs. Open sights. Finish is blue.

NIB	Exc.	V.G.	Good	Fair	Poor
200	150	100	75	50	25

TROCAOLA (TAC)
Eibar, Spain

Break-Top Revolvers

This maker produced a variety of .32, .38, and .44 caliber top break revolvers between approximately 1900 and 1936. These pistols can be identified by the monogram "TAC" stamped on the left side of the frame. **NOTE:** Add 50 percent premium for .44 models.

NIB	Exc.	V.G.	Good	Fair	Poor
—	275	175	125	100	75

TRYON, EDWARD K. & COMPANY
Philadelphia, Pennsylvania

Pocket Pistol

A .41 caliber single-shot percussion pocket pistol with a 2" or 4" barrel, German silver mounts and a walnut stock. The lock marked "Tryon/Philada". Manufactured during the 1860s and 1870s.

NIB	Exc.	V.G.	Good	Fair	Poor
—	—	2550	1900	750	200

TUCKER SHERARD & COMPANY
Lancaster, Texas

Dragoon

A .44 caliber percussion revolver with a 7.75" round barrel fitted with a loading lever and a 6-shot cylinder. The barrel marked "Clark, Sherard & Co., Lancaster, Texas" and the cylinder etched in two panels with crossed cannons and the legend "Texas Arms". Approximately 400 revolvers of this type were made between 1862 and 1867. Prospective purchasers are advised to secure a qualified appraisal prior to acquisition.

NIB	Exc.	V.G.	Good	Fair	Poor
—	—	60000	55000	22000	13000

TUFTS & COLLEY
New York, New York

Pocket Pistol

A .44 caliber single-shot percussion pocket pistol with a 3.5" barrel, German silver mounts and walnut stock. The lock marked "Tufts & Colley" and the barrel "Deringer/Pattn." Manufactured during the 1860s.

NIB	Exc.	V.G.	Good	Fair	Poor
—	—	2450	1900	825	200

TURBIAUX, JACQUES
Paris, France

See—Ames

TURNER, THOMAS
Redding, England

Pepperbox

A .476 double-action percussion pepperbox having 6 barrels. Blued, case hardened with walnut grips. The left side of the frame is engraved in an oval "Thomas Turner, Redding".

Courtesy Bonhams & Butterfields, San Francisco, California

NIB	Exc.	V.G.	Good	Fair	Poor
—	—	5500	1900	975	400

TYLER ORDNANCE WORKS
Tyler, Texas

This company produced 56 Austrian rifles, 508 Enfield rifles, 423 Hill rifles and 1,009 Texas rifles during the Civil War. **NOTE:** These rifles are very rare.

Tyler Texas Rifle

A .57 caliber single-shot rifle with a 27" barrel and a full stock secured by two barrel bands. The lock marked "Texas Rifle/Tyler/Cal. .57".

NIB	Exc.	V.G.	Good	Fair	Poor
—	—	62500	44000	16500	12000

Hill Rifle

A .54 caliber single-shot percussion rifle with a 27" barrel, full stock secured by two brass barrel bands and an iron trigger guard and buttplate. The lock marked "Hill Rifle/Tyler/Tex/ Cal. .54".

NIB	Exc.	V.G.	Good	Fair	Poor
—	—	58000	40000	15000	12000

U

U.S. ARMS CO.
Riverhead, New York
See—United Sporting Arms, Inc.

U.S. M1 CARBINE
Various Manufacturers

For history, technical data, descriptions, photos, and prices see the Standard Catalog of Military Firearms under United States, Rifles. The prices listed are for rifles in original, unaltered condition. **NOTE:** For rifles that have been refinished or restored deduct about 50 percent.

Inland
NIB	Exc.	V.G.	Good	Fair	Poor
2000	1800	1200	600	425	350

Underwood
NIB	Exc.	V.G.	Good	Fair	Poor
2000	1800	1250	550	400	275

S.G. Saginaw
NIB	Exc.	V.G.	Good	Fair	Poor
2000	1800	1400	700	450	375

IBM
NIB	Exc.	V.G.	Good	Fair	Poor
2200	1900	1500	1000	500	250

Quality Hardware
NIB	Exc.	V.G.	Good	Fair	Poor
2000	1700	1100	525	375	250

National Postal Meter
NIB	Exc.	V.G.	Good	Fair	Poor
2100	1800	1100	575	375	250

Standard Products
NIB	Exc.	V.G.	Good	Fair	Poor
2150	1900	1200	600	425	250

Rockola
NIB	Exc.	V.G.	Good	Fair	Poor
2400	2000	1400	750	475	350

SG Grand Rapids
NIB	Exc.	V.G.	Good	Fair	Poor
2400	2000	1400	600	425	350

Winchester
NIB	Exc.	V.G.	Good	Fair	Poor
2500	2200	1700	1100	600	375

Irwin Pedersen
NIB	Exc.	V.G.	Good	Fair	Poor
4200	3500	2500	1300	800	500

M1 Carbine Cutaway
NIB	Exc.	V.G.	Good	Fair	Poor
—	2500	1500	900	600	500

M1 Carbine Sniper with infra red conversion
NIB	Exc.	V.G.	Good	Fair	Poor
—	1450	1000	800	400	300

U.S. M1 A1 Paratrooper Model
NIB	Exc.	V.G.	Good	Fair	Poor
—	4500	3500	2500	1250	750

U.S. ORDNANCE
Reno, Nevada

The models listed are machined to military specifications and are semi-automatic only.

M-60

This is a 7.62mm belt-fed semi-automatic weapon modeled after the famous machine gun used in Vietnam. Fitted with a 22" barrel, the weight of the gun is about 24 lbs.

NIB	Exc.	V.G.	Good	Fair	Poor
10000	8900	7000	5500	4000	2500

M-60E3

A shorter, more lightweight version of the standard M-60 fitted with a 17" barrel. Weight reduced to about 18 lbs.

NIB	Exc.	V.G.	Good	Fair	Poor
8900	7000	5500	4000	3000	1750

Browning Model 1919

This belt-fed model is chambered for the 7.62mm/.30-06 cartridges. Fitted with a 23" barrel. Weight is about 30 lbs. Prices listed are for gun only. **NOTE:** For A6 stock, bipod, and carry handle add $125. For A4 tripod add $450.

Model 1919 with A4 tripod

Model 1919 A6

NIB	Exc.	V.G.	Good	Fair	Poor
2800	2400	1900	1500	1200	900

Vickers

This model is chambered for the .303 cartridge and is belt-fed. Weight is about 40 lbs. Prices listed are for gun only. **NOTE:** For tripod add $500.

NIB	Exc.	V.G.	Good	Fair	Poor
4800	4000	3000	2200	1700	900

U.S. REPEATING ARMS CO.

See—Winchester

UBERTI, ALDO/UBERTI USA

Ponte Zanano, Italy

This company manufactures high-grade reproductions of famous Western-style American firearms. Their products have been imported over the years by a number of different companies. They produce both blackpowder guns and the cartridge firearms that are included in this section. This Italian manufacturer builds high quality firearms of the American West. Featured are Colt, Winchester, and Remington. Each importer stamps its name on the firearm in addition to the Uberti address. In 2000 Beretta Holding Company purchased Uberti.

Paterson Revolver

This is an exact copy of the famous and rare Colt pistol. Offered in .36 caliber with engraved 5-shot cylinder, the barrel is 7.5" long and octagonal forward of the lug. The frame is casehardened steel as is the backstrap. Grips are one-piece walnut. Overall length is 11.5" and weight is about 2.5 lbs.

NIB	Exc.	V.G.	Good	Fair	Poor
400	300	200	125	100	75

Walker Colt Revolver

This is a faithful reproduction of the famous and highly sought-after Colts. Caliber is .44 and the round barrel is 9" in length. The frame is case hardened steel and the trigger guard is brass. The 6-shot cylinder is engraved with fighting dragoons scene. Grip is one-piece walnut. Overall length is 15.75" and weight is a hefty 70 oz.

NIB	Exc.	V.G.	Good	Fair	Poor
500	400	300	200	125	100

Colt Whitneyville Dragoon

This was the transition Walker. A reduced version of the Model 1847 Walker. Fitted with a 7.5" barrel and chambered for the .44 caliber.

NIB	Exc.	V.G.	Good	Fair	Poor
475	375	200	125	100	75

Colt 1st Model Dragoon Revolver

This was a shorter version of the Walker and evolved directly from that original design. This model is a 6-shot .44 caliber with a 7.5" barrel. The frame is color case hardened steel while the backstrap and trigger guard are brass. Grips are one-piece walnut. Overall length is 13.5" and weight is about 63 oz.

NIB	Exc.	V.G.	Good	Fair	Poor
400	300	250	125	100	75

Colt 2nd Model Dragoon Revolver

This differs from the 1st model in that the cylinder bolt slot is square instead of oval.

NIB	Exc.	V.G.	Good	Fair	Poor
400	300	250	125	100	75

Colt 3rd Model Dragoon Revolver

This model varies from the 2nd model as follows:
 a: Loading lever taper is inverted.
 b: Loading lever latch hook is different shape.
 c: Loading lever latch.
 d: Backstrap is steel and trigger guard is brass oval.
 e: Frame is cut for a shoulder stock.

NIB	Exc.	V.G.	Good	Fair	Poor
350	225	175	125	100	75

Colt Model 1849 Wells Fargo

This model has no loading lever. Chambered for .31 caliber cartridge. The barrel is octagonal. The frame is case colored and hardened steel while the backstrap and trigger guard are brass. Cylinder is engraved and holds 5 rounds. Grip is one-piece walnut. Overall length is 9.5" and weight is 34 oz.

NIB	Exc.	V.G.	Good	Fair	Poor
325	200	150	125	100	75

Pocket Revolver

Same as the Wells Fargo with the addition of a loading lever.

NIB	Exc.	V.G.	Good	Fair	Poor
325	200	150	125	100	75

Colt Model 1848 Baby Dragoon

Similar is appearance to the Model 1849 but with a 4" tapered octagonal barrel and a square back trigger guard. No loading lever. Weight is about 23 oz.

NIB	Exc.	V.G.	Good	Fair	Poor
325	200	150	125	100	75

Model 1851 Navy Colt

Chambered for .36 caliber with an engraved 6-shot cylinder. The tapered octagonal barrel is 7.5". The frame is case colored steel and the backstrap and oval trigger guard are brass. Grips are one-piece walnut. Overall length is 13" and weight is about 44 oz.

NIB	Exc.	V.G.	Good	Fair	Poor
400	300	250	125	100	75

Model 1861 Navy Colt

Sometimes referred to as the "New Navy" this model is similar in appearance to the Model 1851. Offered in two variations. The military version has a steel backstrap and trigger guard and is cut for a shoulder stock. The civilian version has a brass backstrap and trigger guard and is not cut for a shoulder stock.

Military Model

NIB	Exc.	V.G.	Good	Fair	Poor
400	300	250	125	100	75

Civilian Model

NIB	Exc.	V.G.	Good	Fair	Poor
400	300	250	125	100	75

Colt Model 1860 Army

Chambered for the .44 caliber ball and fitted with a round tapered 8" barrel, this revolver has a 6-shot engraved cylinder. Grips are one-piece walnut. Overall length is 13.75" and weight is approximately 42 oz.

Military

Steel backstrap and brass trigger guard and is cut for a shoulder stock.

NIB	Exc.	V.G.	Good	Fair	Poor
400	300	250	125	100	75

Fluted Cylinder Military

NIB	Exc.	V.G.	Good	Fair	Poor
400	300	250	125	100	75

Civilian

Brass backstrap and trigger guard and is not cut for a shoulder stock.

NIB	Exc.	V.G.	Good	Fair	Poor
400	300	250	125	100	75

Colt Model 1862 Police Revolvers

Chambered for .36 caliber and fitted with a round tapered barrel in 4.5", 5.5", or 6.5" barrel. The 5-shot cylinder is fluted, the frame color case hardened, and the backstrap and trigger guard are brass. Grips are one-piece walnut. Weight is about 25 oz.

NIB	Exc.	V.G.	Good	Fair	Poor
400	300	250	125	100	75

Colt Model 1862 Pocket Navy Revolver

Similar to the Model 1862 Police model but fitted with a 5-shot engraved nonfluted cylinder. Barrel lengths are 4.5", 5.5", and 6.5". Weight is about 27 oz.

NIB	Exc.	V.G.	Good	Fair	Poor
400	300	250	125	100	75

Colt Model 1868 Army Thuer Conversion

NIB	Exc.	V.G.	Good	Fair	Poor
450	325	225	175	150	100

Remington Model 1858 New Army .44 Caliber

Chambered for .44 caliber and fitted with a tapered octagonal 8" barrel. Cylinder holds 6-shots and the frame is blued steel. Trigger guard is brass. Grips are two-piece walnut. Overall length is 13.75" and weight is about 42 oz.

NIB	Exc.	V.G.	Good	Fair	Poor
300	200	150	125	100	75

Remington Model 1858 New Army .36 Caliber

Similar to above model but fitted with a 7-3/8" tapered octagonal barrel. Weight is approximately 40 oz.

NIB	Exc.	V.G.	Good	Fair	Poor
400	300	250	125	100	75

Remington Model 1858 New Army .44 Caliber Target

This version is fitted with a fully adjustable rear sight and ramp front sight.

NIB	Exc.	V.G.	Good	Fair	Poor
425	325	275	150	125	75

Remington Model 1858 New Army .44 Caliber Stainless Steel

All parts are stainless steel.

NIB	Exc.	V.G.	Good	Fair	Poor
425	325	275	150	125	75

Remington Model 1858 New Army .44 Cal. SS Target

Same as Target Model but all parts are stainless steel.

NIB	Exc.	V.G.	Good	Fair	Poor
450	325	250	200	125	75

Remington Model 1858 Target Revolving Carbine

Chambered for .44 caliber and fitted with an 18" octagon barrel. The frame is blued steel and the trigger guard is brass. Stock is select walnut. Overall length is 35" and weight is about 4.4 lbs.

NIB	Exc.	V.G.	Good	Fair	Poor
425	300	200	150	100	75

1875 Remington "Outlaw"

This is a replica of the original Remington cartridge pistol chambered for .357 Magnum, .44-40, .45 ACP, .45 ACP/.45 L.C. conversion, and .45 Colt. The frame is case colored steel and the trigger guard is brass. It is offered with a 7.5" round barrel and is either blued or nickel-plated, with two-piece walnut grips. Overall length is 13.75" and weight is about 44 oz.

NIB	Exc.	V.G.	Good	Fair	Poor
450	325	250	200	125	75

Remington Model 1875 Frontier

Introduced in 2005 this model features a 5.5" barrel chambered for the .45 Colt cartridge. Case colored frame with blued barrel, backstrap, and trigger guard. Two-piece walnut grips. Weight is about 40 oz.

NIB	Exc.	V.G.	Good	Fair	Poor
500	375	250	175	150	100

Remington Model 1890 Police

This is a 5.5"-barreled replica of the original Remington Pistol. It is chambered for .357 Magnum, .44-40, .45 ACP, .45 ACP/.45 L.C. conversion, and .45 Colt. The frame is case colored steel and the trigger guard is brass. It was available in either blued or nickel-plate. Grips are two-piece walnut and are fitted with a grip ring. Overall length is 11.75" and weight is about 41 oz.

NIB	Exc.	V.G.	Good	Fair	Poor
500	375	250	175	150	100

Model 1871 Rolling Block Pistol

This is a single-shot target pistol chambered for .22 LR, .22 Magnum, .22 Hornet, .222 Rem., 223 Rem., .45 Long Colt, or .357 Magnum. It has a 9.5" half-octagonal, half-round barrel and is blued, with a case colored receiver and walnut grip and forearm. The trigger guard is brass. Overall length is 14" and weight is about 44 oz.

NIB	Exc.	V.G.	Good	Fair	Poor
500	375	250	175	150	100

Model 1871 Rolling Block Carbine

This model is similar to the pistol, with a 22.5" half-octagonal, half-round barrel and a full-length walnut stock. trigger guard and buttplate are brass. Overall length is 35.5" and weight is approximately 4.8 lbs.

NIB	Exc.	V.G.	Good	Fair	Poor
650	525	400	275	200	125

Henry Rifle

This is a brass-framed reproduction of the famous Winchester/Henry Rifle. It is chambered for the .44-40 or .45 Colt cartridge, and this is basically the only departure from being a true and faithful copy. The octagonal barrel is 24.25" on the rifle model and 22.25" on the carbine model. There are also two Trapper models offered: an 18.5" barrel and a 16.5" version. This is a high-quality rifle and amazingly close to the original in configuration. There are three grades of engraving also available. Weights are: rifle 9.2 lbs., carbine 9 lbs., 18.5" trapper 7.9 lbs., 16.5" trapper 7.4 lbs. Finish can be steel, standard blued or charcoal blue. **NOTE:** Grade A add $350. Grade B add $450. Grade C add $600.

NIB	Exc.	V.G.	Good	Fair	Poor
900	700	550	450	350	200

Winchester Model 1866

This is a faithful replica of the Winchester 1866. It is chambered for .22 LR, .22 Magnum, .38 Special, and .44-40, and .45 Long Colt. The rifle version has a brass frame and a 24.25" tapered octagon barrel. The frame finish is brass, with a walnut stock. Weight is about 8 lbs.

NIB	Exc.	V.G.	Good	Fair	Poor
800	650	550	450	350	200

1866 Yellowboy Carbine

This model is similar to the standard rifle, but is offered with a 19" round tapered barrel.

NIB	Exc.	V.G.	Good	Fair	Poor
700	600	500	450	350	200

Winchester Model 1873 Carbine

This is a reproduction of the Winchester 1873 chambered for .357 Magnum, .45 Long Colt, and .44-40. It has a case colored steel receiver and a 19" round tapered barrel. The lever is also case colored. The stock and forearm are walnut. Overall length is 38.25" and weight is about 7.4 lbs.

NIB	Exc.	V.G.	Good	Fair	Poor
900	700	500	450	350	200

Winchester Model 1873 Rifle

This model is similar to the Carbine, with a 24.25" octagonal barrel. Overall length is 43.25" and weight is approximately 8.2 lbs. **NOTE:** Extra barrel lengths from 20" to 30" in .45 L.C. and .44-40 are also offered at extra cost.

NIB	Exc.	V.G.	Good	Fair	Poor
950	750	600	450	350	200

Winchester 1873 Short Sporting Rifle

As above but fitted with a 20" octagon barrel.

NIB	Exc.	V.G.	Good	Fair	Poor
950	800	600	450	350	200

Winchester 1873 Half-Octagon Rifle

Same as above but with 24.25" half octagon barrel. Stock has a checkered pistol grip.

NIB	Exc.	V.G.	Good	Fair	Poor
1000	800	600	450	350	200

Winchester 1873 Musket

Chambered for the .44-40 or .45 Long Colt cartridge and fitted

with a 30" barrel with full stock and three barrel bands. Magazine capacity is 14 rounds. Weight is about 9 lbs.

NIB	Exc.	V.G.	Good	Fair	Poor
1000	800	600	450	350	200

Model 1885 High Wall Single-Shot Carbine

Chambered for .38-55, .30-30, .44-40, .45 Colt, .40-65, or .45-70 with 28" barrel. Walnut stock.

NIB	Exc.	V.G.	Good	Fair	Poor
825	600	450	350	250	200

Model 1885 High Wall Single-Shot Rifle

Same as above but with 30" barrel.

NIB	Exc.	V.G.	Good	Fair	Poor
900	675	500	400	300	200

Model 1885 High Wall Single-Shot Rifle Pistol Grip

Fitted with a 30" or 32" barrel and checkered pistol-grip stock. Same calibers as above.

NIB	Exc.	V.G.	Good	Fair	Poor
1000	800	600	450	350	200

Winchester 1885 Low Wall Sporting Rifle

This version of the Low Wall Winchester is chambered for the .22 Hornet, .30-30, .44 Magnum or .45 Colt cartridges. Fitted with a 30" octagon barrel. Walnut stock with pistol grip. Weight is about 7.5 lbs. Introduced in 2004.

NIB	Exc.	V.G.	Good	Fair	Poor
950	800	600	450	350	200

Winchester 1885 Low Wall Schuetzen

As above but chambered for the .45 Colt cartridge and fitted with a palm rest and Swiss butt. Weight is about 7.75 lbs. Introduced in 2004.

NIB	Exc.	V.G.	Good	Fair	Poor
1200	950	800	600	450	350

Hawken Santa Fe

Based on the famous original rifle this reproduction is bored for .54 caliber and fitted with a 32" octagon barrel. A double set trigger and case hardened lock plate are standard. The stock ferrule and wedge plates are German silver. The stock is walnut with cheekpiece. Overall length is 50" and weight is about 9.5 lbs. Also available in kit form.

NIB	Exc.	V.G.	Good	Fair	Poor
350	300	250	200	150	100

Cattleman

This is a single-action revolver patterned closely after the Colt Single-Action Army. It is chambered in various popular calibers: .357 Magnum, .44-40, .44 Special, .45 ACP, .45 L.C./.45 ACP convertible, and .45 Colt. It is offered with barrel lengths of 4.75", 5.5", and 7.5". It is offered with either a modern or black powder-type frame and brass or steel backstraps. The finish is blued, with walnut grips. A Sheriff's Model with a 3" barrel and no ejector rod chambered for .44-40 and .45 Colt is also available and is valued the same. Weight is approximately 38 oz. for 5.5" barrel gun.

NIB	Exc.	V.G.	Good	Fair	Poor
400	275	225	150	100	75

Cattleman Flattop Target Model

This model is similar to the standard Cattleman, with an adjustable rear sight.

NIB	Exc.	V.G.	Good	Fair	Poor
435	350	275	225	175	125

Cattleman Gunfighter NM

Chambered for the .45 Colt cartridge and fitted with a 4.75", 5.5", or 7.5" barrel. Black checkered grip with matte blued finish. Weight is around 37 oz. Introduced in 2005.

NIB	Exc.	V.G.	Good	Fair	Poor
400	275	225	150	100	75

Cattleman Cody NM

As above but with nickel finish and ivory-style grips.

NIB	Exc.	V.G.	Good	Fair	Poor
500	375	250	175	150	100

Cattleman Frisco NM

As above but with charcoal blued barrel and case colored frame. Pearl grips.

NIB	Exc.	V.G.	Good	Fair	Poor
500	375	250	175	150	100

Cattleman El Patron CMS

Designed for Cowboy Mounted Shooter (CMS) competition. Caliber .357 Magnum or .45 Colt, steel cylinder, frame and barrel, 6 round capacity, single action trigger, low profile hammer, fixed sights and wood grips. Weight 36.8 ounces, 3.5" or 4" barrel with blue/case hardened or stainless finish. **NOTE:** Add 25 percent for stainless finish.

NIB	Exc.	V.G.	Good	Fair	Poor
525	425	350	300	225	150

Bisley

Chambered for the .32-20, .38 Special, .357 Magnum, .38-40, .44-40, and .44 Special and fitted with either 4.75", 5.5", or 7.5" barrel. Case hardened frame with two-piece walnut grips.

NIB	Exc.	V.G.	Good	Fair	Poor
435	350	275	225	175	125

Flattop

As above but with adjustable rear sight.

NIB	Exc.	V.G.	Good	Fair	Poor
435	350	275	225	175	125

Buntline Carbine

This version has the 18" barrel but is fitted with a permanently mounted shoulder stock with a brass buttplate and sling swivel. Chambered for .44-40, .45 Long Colt, .357 Magnum, and .44 Magnum. Offered with fixed or adjustable sights.

NIB	Exc.	V.G.	Good	Fair	Poor
450	400	350	300	250	200

Buckhorn Buntline

This version is chambered for the .44 Magnum. It has an 18" round barrel, and it is cut for attaching a shoulder stock. Steel backstrap and trigger guard. Overall length is 23" and weight is about 57 oz. **NOTE:** Detachable shoulder stock add 25 percent.

NIB	Exc.	V.G.	Good	Fair	Poor
400	325	300	250	200	100

Buckhorn Target

Same as above but fitted with an adjustable rear sight and ramp front sight. Has a flat upper frame.

NIB	Exc.	V.G.	Good	Fair	Poor
450	350	300	250	200	100

Phantom

Similar to the Buckhorn, but chambered for the .44 Magnum and the .357 Magnum. The barrel is a round 10.5" and the frame is blued with blued steel backstrap. One-piece walnut grips with anatomic profile. Adjustable sight. Weight is approximately 53 oz.

NIB	Exc.	V.G.	Good	Fair	Poor
400	275	225	150	100	75

New Thunderer Model

Designed and imported exclusively by Cimarron Arms for single-action shooting competition. Fitted with bird's-head grip with hard rubber, this model is chambered for the .357 Magnum, .44 Special, .44 WCF, and .45 Colt. Offered in barrel lengths of 3.5" and 4.75". Finish in nickel or blued with case colored frame.

4 3/4" WITH EJECTOR

3 1/2" WITH EJECTOR

NIB	Exc.	V.G.	Good	Fair	Poor
450	350	300	250	200	100

1873 Stallion

This is a scaled-down version, chambered for .22 LR/.22 Magnum. It is blued with a case colored frame and features one-piece walnut grips.

NIB	Exc.	V.G.	Good	Fair	Poor
350	295	250	200	150	100

Tornado

This five-shot revolver is chambered for the .454 Casull and fitted with a 4.75", 5.5" or 7.5" with ported barrel. Sandblasted nickel finish. Weight is about 47 oz.

NIB	Exc.	V.G.	Good	Fair	Poor
1000	900	750	600	500	400

No. 3 Schofield Revolver

Patterned after the original S&W revolver this model is chambered for the .44-40 or .45 Colt cartridge. It is fitted with a 7", 5", or 3.5" barrel. Weight with 7" barrel is approximately 40 oz.

NIB	Exc.	V.G.	Good	Fair	Poor
800	700	600	475	325	200

No. 3 New Model Russian

Chambered for the .44 Russian cartridge and fitted with a 6" or 7" barrel.

NIB	Exc.	V.G.	Good	Fair	Poor
900	800	700	575	400	300

Inspector Model

This is a double-action revolver built on the same general lines as the Colt Detective model. Cylinder holds six cartridges and is chambered for the .38 Special. Offered in these barrel lengths with fixed sights: 2", 2.125", 2.5", 3", 4", 6" and also offered in 4" and 6" barrel lengths with adjustable sights. Grips are walnut and finish is blued or chrome. With the 3" barrel the weight is about 24 oz.

NIB	Exc.	V.G.	Good	Fair	Poor
275	200	150	125	100	75

UHLINGER, WILLIAM P.
Philadelphia, Pennsylvania

Pocket Revolver

A .32 caliber spur trigger revolver with a 2.75" or 3" octagonal barrel and an unfluted 6-shot cylinder. Blued with rosewood or walnut grips. Manufactured during the late 1860s and early 1870s. Uhlinger-manufactured pistols will often be found with retailer's names on them, such as D.D. Cone, Washington, D.C.; J.P. Lower; and W.L. Grant.

Long Cylinder (1-3/16")

NIB	Exc.	V.G.	Good	Fair	Poor
—	—	800	600	250	100

Short Cylinder (1")

NIB	Exc.	V.G.	Good	Fair	Poor
—	—	650	425	175	75

.32 Rimfire Model (5", 6", or 7" Barrel)

NIB	Exc.	V.G.	Good	Fair	Poor
—	—	800	600	250	100

ULTIMATE
See—Camex-Blaser USA, Inc.

ULTRA LIGHT ARMS, INC./NEW ULTRA LIGHT ARMS
Granville, West Virginia

This maker manufactures a variety of bolt-action rifles fitted with Douglas barrels of varying lengths, custom triggers, and reinforced graphite stocks. The values for standard production models are listed.

Model 20 (Short Action)

Weight is 4.5 lbs. with 22" barrel. Composte stock with choice of colors or camo finish. Adjustable trigger. No sights. Offered in left- or right-hand.

NIB	Exc.	V.G.	Good	Fair	Poor
3100	2750	2500	1850	900	500

Model 20 RF Rimfire

Weight is about 4.5 lbs. with 22" barrel. Stock is synthetic with choice of colors or camo finish. No sights. Adjustable trigger. Available as a single-shot or repeater.

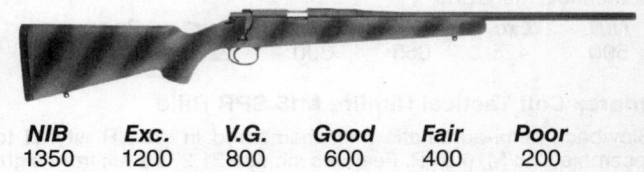

NIB	Exc.	V.G.	Good	Fair	Poor
1350	1200	800	600	400	200

Model 20 Hunter's Pistol

A bolt-action repeating pistol designed with the serious hunter in mind. It is offered in various popular calibers with a 14", high-quality Douglas heavy barrel. It has a 5-shot magazine and is matte blued, with a reinforced graphite Kevlar stock. It was introduced in 1987.

NIB	Exc.	V.G.	Good	Fair	Poor
1250	1000	800	625	500	300

Model 24 (Long Action)

Weight is approximately 5.25 lbs. with 22" barrel.

NIB	Exc.	V.G.	Good	Fair	Poor
3100	2750	2500	1850	900	500

Model 28 Magnum

Weight is about 5.75 lbs. with 24" barrel.

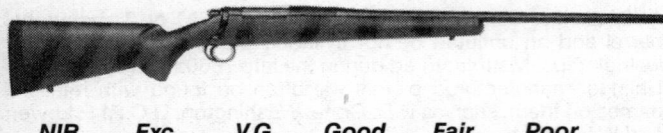

NIB	Exc.	V.G.	Good	Fair	Poor
3300	3050	2750	1950	900	500

Model 40 Magnum

Weight is about 7.5 lbs. with 26" barrel.

NIB	Exc.	V.G.	Good	Fair	Poor
3300	3050	2750	1950	900	500

Model 90

This is a muzzle-loading rifle built with either a .45 or .50 caliber barrel. Graphite stock. Williams sights. Barrel length is 28". Adjustable trigger. Weight is about 6 lbs.

NIB	Exc.	V.G.	Good	Fair	Poor
950	750	600	475	350	200

UMAREX USA
Fort Smith, Arkansas

Umarex Colt Tactical Rimfire M4 Ops Carbine

Blowback semi-automatic rifle chambered in .22 LR, styled to resemble Colt M16. Features include 16.2" barrel; front sight adjustable for elevation; adjustable rear sight; alloy lower; adjustable telestock; flattop receiver with removable carry handle; 10- or 30-round detachable magazine.

NIB	Exc.	V.G.	Good	Fair	Poor
500	425	365	300	225	150

Umarex Colt Tactical Rimfire M4 Carbine

Blowback semi-automatic rifle chambered in .22 LR, styled to resemble Colt M4. Features include 16.2" barrel; front sight adjustable for elevation; adjustable rear sight; alloy lower; adjustable telestock; flattop receiver with optics rail; 10- or 30-round detachable magazine.

NIB	Exc.	V.G.	Good	Fair	Poor
550	465	400	335	250	165

Umarex Colt Tactical Rimfire M16 Rifle

Blowback semi-automatic rifle chambered in .22 LR, styled to resemble Colt M16. Features include 21.2" barrel; front sight adjustable for elevation; adjustable rear sight; alloy lower; fixed stock; flattop receiver; removable carry handle; 10- or 30-round detachable magazine.

NIB	Exc.	V.G.	Good	Fair	Poor
500	425	365	300	225	150

Umarex Colt Tactical Rimfire M16 SPR Rifle

Blowback semi-automatic rifle chambered in .22 LR, styled to resemble Colt M16 SPR. Features include 21.2" barrel; front sight

adjustable for elevation; adjustable rear sight; alloy lower; fixed stock; flattop receiver with optics rail; removable carry handle; 10- or 30-round detachable magazine.

NIB	Exc.	V.G.	Good	Fair	Poor
575	485	425	360	275	185

Umarex H&K 416-22

Blowback semi-automatic rifle chambered in .22 LR, styled to resemble H&K 416. Features include metal upper and lower receivers; RIS - rail interface system; retractable stock; pistol grip with storage compartment; on-rail sights; rear sight adjustable for wind and elevation; 16.1" barrel; 10- or 20-round magazine. Also available in pistol version with 9" barrel.

NIB	Exc.	V.G.	Good	Fair	Poor
575	485	425	360	275	185

Umarex H&K MP5 A5

Blowback semi-automatic rifle chambered in .22 LR, styled to resemble H&K MP5. Features include metal receiver; compensator; bolt catch; NAVY pistol grip; on-rail sights; rear sight adjustable for wind and elevation; 16.1" barrel; 10- or 25-round magazine. Also available in pistol version with 9" barrel. Also available with SD-type fore-end.

NIB	Exc.	V.G.	Good	Fair	Poor
450	375	300	250	200	150

UNCETA
See—Astra-Unceta SA

UNION
Unknown

Pocket Pistol

.22 caliber spur trigger single-shot pistol with a 2.75" barrel marked "Union". Nickel-plated with walnut grips.

NIB	Exc.	V.G.	Good	Fair	Poor
—	—	650	400	100	75

UNION FIRE ARMS COMPANY
Toledo, Ohio

This company was incorporated in 1902 and used the names of Union Fire Arms, Union Arms Company, Illinois Arms Company (made for Sears) and Bee Be Arms Company. In 1917 the company was either bought up or absorbed by Ithaca Gun Company. **NOTE:** Union Fire Arms Company (or Union Firearms Company, as it is sometimes known) slide action shotguns are not commonly seen. Though not widely collected, they seem to attract considerable interest as oddities, much as the Spencer/Bannerman slide action shotguns do. The values given below are approximate; as always, true value lies in the eyes of the buyer, not the seller.

Double Barrel Shotguns

Union's predecessor, Colton Manufacturing Co. (1894-1902) made a double for Sears. It was cleverly designed with coil mainspring striker locks set into sideplates. The Union double in 12 and 16 gauge with steel or Damascus barrels derived from it, but was a traditional hammerless sidelock side-by-side well-made gun (1902-1913) and also sold by Sears. Values depend on grade and condition. Union also offered, about 1905, an unusual boxlock hammer gun, the Model 25 in 12 gauge only. It employs external hammers but they are mounted within the frame and the spurs protrude in front of the topsnap opener. These guns are hard to find and values range from $300 to $1,200 depending on condition. They are produced with steel, twist, or Damascus barrels but only in a plain grade.

Courtesy Nick Niles

NIB	Exc.	V.G.	Good	Fair	Poor
—	1300	525	4050	300	200

Model 24

Slide action, Model 25 Peerless that was a fancy version of the Model 24 and the Model 25A, which was a trap model, were manufactured from 1902 to 1913 in 12 or 16 gauge with 24", 26", 28", or 32" steel or Damascus barrels. This gun had a unique double trigger. The front trigger cocked and decocked an internal firing pin and the back trigger fired the gun. The gun is marked on the left side of the frame and the pump release is on the right side. This model had one serious drawback, in that the slide that extracted a spent shell extended back over the comb of the stock. This often hit the shooter's thumb knuckle and caused injury. In 1907 Union redesigned their slide by reducing its length and shielding it behind a steel plate that covered the rear half of the opening. These are the Model 24, 25, and 25A improved versions. Approximately 17,000 of all models combined were made.

NIB	Exc.	V.G.	Good	Fair	Poor
—	—	750	300	200	100

Model 50

Manufactured 1911 to 1913. This was basically a redesign of the Model 24. The main distinguishing feature of the Model 50 was that the frame sloped down to meet the comb of the stock and the double trigger system was replaced by a single trigger. It came in 12 or 16 gauge with a 26", 28", 30", or 32" Krupp steel barrel. Fewer than 3,000 were made.

NIB	Exc.	V.G.	Good	Fair	Poor
—	—	850	400	300	200

Model 22

This was essentially a no frills Model 23. It had the same barrel length and steel options, but it had a plain walnut stock and no engraving. There were fewer than 10,000 Model 22 and 23s made.

NIB	Exc.	V.G.	Good	Fair	Poor
—	—	300	100	75	50

Model 23

Hammerless double, manufactured between 1902 and 1913 with or without automatic ejectors. With some engraving, it came in both single and double trigger models; this was their top grade gun. Came in 12 and 16 gauge with 28", 30", or 32" steel, twist, or Damascus barrels.

NIB	Exc.	V.G.	Good	Fair	Poor
—	—	450	150	125	100

Diamond Grade

Single-shot, manufactured between 1905 and 1910. It had a unique octagonal breech in 12 gauge only with 30" steel, laminated, or Damascus barrel. This was their premium grade single-shot. Few of these were made.

NIB	Exc.	V.G.	Good	Fair	Poor
—	—	450	200	100	50

Model 18

Single-shot, manufactured 1906 to 1913 came in 12 or 16 gauge. 30", 32", 34", or 36" steel barrel. A plain single-shot. Very few made.

NIB	Exc.	V.G.	Good	Fair	Poor
—	—	200	75	50	25

Reifngraber

A .32 or .38 S&W caliber gas operated semi-automatic pistol, with a 3" barrel. Blued with walnut grips, approximately 100 of these pistols were manufactured.

NIB	Exc.	V.G.	Good	Fair	Poor
—	—	2250	1100	500	350

Automatic Revolver

.32 S&W caliber, similar to the Webley Fosbery semi-automatic revolver with a 3" barrel. Blued with either walnut or hard rubber grips. The cylinder has zigzag grooves.

NIB	Exc.	V.G.	Good	Fair	Poor
—	—	3250	1250	500	250

UNIQUE
Hendaye, France
See—Pyrenees

UNITED SPORTING ARMS, INC.
Tucson, Arizona

Blued Guns (Seville, etc.)

NIB	Exc.	V.G.	Good	Fair	Poor
N/A	500	450	350	—	—

Blue Silhouette (10.5" barrels)

NOTE: Add $100 for stainless, $250 for stainless long-frame models (calibers .357 Maximum/Super Magnum and .357 USA/Super Magnum).

NIB	Exc.	V.G.	Good	Fair	Poor
N/A	600	550	500	—	—

Silver Sevilles

NIB	Exc.	V.G.	Good	Fair	Poor
N/A	550	475	400	—	—

Stainless Steel Guns

NIB	Exc.	V.G.	Good	Fair	Poor
N/A	600	525	450	—	—

Tombstone Commemorative

NIB	Exc.	V.G.	Good	Fair	Poor
1000	750	625	525	—	—

Quik-Kit Stainless Steel

NOTE: For Quik-Kit guns with extra barrel and cylinder add $200 for each barrel and cylinder. Deduct 10 percent if United Sporting Arms, Hauppauge, N.Y. Deduct 20 percent if United Sporting Arms, Post Falls, ID. Add 20 percent if El Dorado Arms (either N.Y. or N.C.). Add 10 percent for 1.5" barrel Sheriff's Model. Add 20 percent for 10.5" barrel. Add 20 percent for bird's-head grip frame. Add 20 percent if brass grip frame.

NIB	Exc.	V.G.	Good	Fair	Poor
1500	1250	800	—	—	—

Quik-Kit Blued

NIB	Exc.	V.G.	Good	Fair	Poor
1200	1000	650	—	—	—

UNITED STATES ARMS
Otis A. Smith Company
Rockfall, Connecticut

Single-Action Revolver

A .44 rimfire and centerfire single-action revolver with a 7" barrel and integral ejector. The hammer nose is fitted with two firing pins so that rimfire or centerfire cartridges can be used interchangeably. The barrel marked "United States Arms Company - New York", the top strap "No. 44". Blued with either hard rubber or rosewood grips. Manufactured in limited quantities. Circa 1870 to 1875.

NIB	Exc.	V.G.	Good	Fair	Poor
—	—	4750	3250	1250	500

UNITED STATES FIRE ARMS MFG.
(Formerly United States Patent Firearms Mfg. Co.)
Hartford, Connecticut

This company began business in 1992. The company uses parts manufactured in the U.S. and fits, finishes, and assembles the gun in Hartford. Produces a wide variety of extremely high-quality replica arms. **NOTE:** This company offers a wide variety of special order options on its revolvers, from special bluing to grips to engraving. These special order options will affect price to a significant degree.

Single-Action Army Revolver

Offered in a wide variety of calibers including .22 rimfire, .32 WCF, .38 S&W, .357 Magnum, .38-40, .41 Colt, .44 Russian, .44-40, .45 Colt, and .45 ACP. Barrel lengths are 4.75", 5.5", and 7.5" with or without ejector. A modern cross pin frame is available for an additional $10. Prices listed are for standard grips and finish, Armory bone case finish, and Dome blue finish.

NIB	Exc.	V.G.	Good	Fair	Poor
975	900	800	675	525	300

Single-Action Army Revolver Pre-War

As above but with pre-war "P" frame.

NIB	Exc.	V.G.	Good	Fair	Poor
1395	1150	950	700	550	300

Shooting Master

A large-frame model in .357 Magnum with 7.5" barrel, U.S. hard rubber grips, blue finish and enlarged trigger guard. Adjustable rear sight, 6 round cylinder. Introduced in 2011. Also, available in .327 Federal with 8-shot cylinder (Sparrowhawk model).

NIB	Exc.	V.G.	Good	Fair	Poor
1300	1100	950	800	525	250

Flattop Target Model

This model is offered with the same calibers as the Single-Action Army above. Barrel lengths are 4.75", 5.5", and 7.5". Grips are two-piece hard rubber. Prices listed are given for standard finish. Introduced in 1997.

NIB	Exc.	V.G.	Good	Fair	Poor
1665	1450	1200	900	675	400

Rodeo

This single-action revolver is offered in .45 Colt, .44-40, .44 Special, .32-20, .38-40 and .38 Special calibers with a choice of 4.75" or 5.50" barrel. Satin blue finish with bone case hammer. "US" hard rubber grips are standard.

NIB	Exc.	V.G.	Good	Fair	Poor
625	550	450	350	250	175

Rodeo II

Similar to the Rodeo but with matte nickel finish and Burlwood grips.

NIB	Exc.	V.G.	Good	Fair	Poor
575	475	350	275	225	200

Buntline
This model features an all blued finish with 16" barrel. Chambered for the .45 Colt cartridge.

NIB	Exc.	V.G.	Good	Fair	Poor
2300	1750	1475	1100	700	450

Buntline Special
Fitted with a 16" barrel and chambered for the .45 Colt cartridge. Supplied with nickel stock. Limited edition. Cased.

NIB	Exc.	V.G.	Good	Fair	Poor
2895	2250	1750	1475	1100	700

China Camp Cowboy Action Gun
Chambered for .45 Colt cartridge but other calibers also available from .32 WCF to .44 WCF. Barrel lengths are 4.75", 5.5", and 7.5". Special action job. Two-piece hard rubber grips standard. Finish is silver steel.

NIB	Exc.	V.G.	Good	Fair	Poor
1395	1150	950	700	550	300

Henry Nettleton Revolver
This is an exact reproduction of the U.S. Government inspector model produced in the Springfield Armory. Offered in 7.5" and 5.5" models. Introduced in 1997. Discontinued.

NIB	Exc.	V.G.	Good	Fair	Poor
1575	1450	1200	900	600	350

.22 Plinker
Chambered for the .22 cartridge and fitted with a choice of barrel lengths of 4.75", 5.5", or 7.5". An extra .22 WMR cylinder is included.

NIB	Exc.	V.G.	Good	Fair	Poor
975	875	725	550	300	150

.22 Target
As above but with adjustable rear sight and replaceable front sight blade.

NIB	Exc.	V.G.	Good	Fair	Poor
1665	1450	1200	900	675	400

Gunslinger
Offered in .45 Colt, .44 Special, .44 WCF, .38 Special, .38 WCF, or .32 WCF and choice of 4.75", 5.5", or 7.5" barrel. Cross pin frame.

Hard rubber grips. Aged bluing finish. Black style frame optional. **NOTE:** Add $135 for black powder frame.

NIB	Exc.	V.G.	Good	Fair	Poor
1145	1025	800	625	500	250

Custer Battlefield Gun
Replica of 1873 revolver used during the height of Indian Wars, including Custer's Last Stand. Limited edition with cartouche of Ordnance Sub-inspector Orville W. Ainsworth; serial range 200-14,343. 7.5" barrel, six shot. Antique Patina aged blue. One-piece walnut stock.

NIB	Exc.	V.G.	Good	Fair	Poor
1625	1450	1200	900	675	400

Hunter
This revolver is chambered for the .17 HMR cartridge and fitted with a 7.5" barrel with adjustable rear sight and replaceable front sight blade. Finish is matte blue. Discontinued.

NIB	Exc.	V.G.	Good	Fair	Poor
975	875	725	550	300	150

Sheriff's Model
Chambered for a wide variety of calibers from the .45 Colt to the .32 WCF. Choice of 2.5", 3", 3.5", or 4" barrel. No ejector. **NOTE:** Add $250 for nickel finish.

NIB	Exc.	V.G.	Good	Fair	Poor
975	875	725	550	300	150

Omni-Potent Bird's-Head Model

Chambered for the .45 Colt, .45 ACP, .44 Special, .44 WCF, .38 Special, .38 WCF, or the .32 WCF cartridges. Offered with bird's-head grips and available with 3.5", 4", or 4.75" barrel lengths.

NIB	Exc.	V.G.	Good	Fair	Poor
1625	1450	1200	900	675	400

Omni-Potent Snubnose

As above but with 2", 3", or 4" barrel without ejector.

NIB	Exc.	V.G.	Good	Fair	Poor
1475	1300	1050	800	575	400

Omni-Potent Target

Choice of 4.75", 5.5", or 7.5" barrel with adjustable rear sight and replaceable front blade sight.

NIB	Exc.	V.G.	Good	Fair	Poor
1395	1150	950	700	550	300

Bisley Model

Based on the famous Bisley model this reproduction features barrel lengths of 4.75", 5.5", 7.5", and 10". The .45 Colt caliber is standard but .32 WCF, .38 S&W, .44 S&W, .41 Colt, .38 WCF, .44 WCF are optional. Introduced in 1997. **NOTE:** Add $60 for 10" models.

NIB	Exc.	V.G.	Good	Fair	Poor
1575	1450	1200	900	600	350

Target

As above but with adjustable rear sight and replaceable blade front sight.

NIB	Exc.	V.G.	Good	Fair	Poor
1625	1450	1200	900	675	400

Pony Express

This model features a 5.50" barrel with special finish and engraved frame and barrel. Ivory grips are etched with pony express rider. Custom gun.

NIB	Exc.	V.G.	Good	Fair	Poor
3895	3500	2950	2200	1500	700

Sears 1902 Colt

This model is a replica of the Sears 1902 Colt SAA. Fitted with a 5.50" barrel, pearl grips, and full coverage engraving with gold line work on the cylinder and barrel. Custom gun.

NIB	Exc.	V.G.	Good	Fair	Poor
8995	7500	6000	500	4000	1000

Model 1910

This model is a stylized version of the early Colt Model 1910 .45 ACP pistol.

NIB	Exc.	V.G.	Good	Fair	Poor
1895	1700	1550	1200	900	500

Model 1911 Army or Navy

This model is a faithful version of the early Colt Model 1911 military model.

NIB	Exc.	V.G.	Good	Fair	Poor
1875	1725	1500	1200	900	600

Ace .22 LR

Recreation of 1911-style Colt Ace. .22 LR with 10+1 capacity. Walnut grips. Introduced 2006.

NIB	Exc.	V.G.	Good	Fair	Poor
1995	1825	1600	1250	950	650

Super .38

1911-style semi-automatic. Blued finish; chambered for .38 Super Automatic with 9+1 capacity. Walnut grips. Introduced 2006.

NIB	Exc.	V.G.	Good	Fair	Poor
1875	1725	1500	1200	900	600

RIFLES

Cowboy Action Lightning

This is a copy of the Colt Lightning rifle chambered for the .44-40, .45 Colt, or the .38 WCF cartridge. Fitted with a 26" round barrel and walnut stock with crescent butt. Magazine capacity is 15 rounds. Introduced in the fall of 2003. Discontinued.

NIB	Exc.	V.G.	Good	Fair	Poor
1625	1450	1200	900	675	400

Cowboy Action Carbine

As above but with 20" round barrel. Magazine capacity is 12 rounds. Discontinued.

NIB	Exc.	V.G.	Good	Fair	Poor
1625	1450	1200	900	675	400

Lightning Magazine Rifle

This model is a premium version of the Cowboy Action Lightning and features a choice of 26" round, half round, or octagon barrel. Checkered American walnut forearm with non-checkered stock with oil finish. Many extra cost options are offered for this model. Discontinued. **NOTE:** Add $200 for half round barrel. Fancy wood, pistol grip, finish and engraving offered for this rifle.

NIB	Exc.	V.G.	Good	Fair	Poor
1625	1450	1200	900	675	400

Lightning Magazine Carbine

As above but with 20" round barrel. Discontinued.

NIB	Exc.	V.G.	Good	Fair	Poor
1625	1450	1200	900	675	400

Lightning Baby Carbine

This model is fitted with a 20" special round tapered barrel. Lightweight carbine forearm with border line. Discontinued.

NIB	Exc.	V.G.	Good	Fair	Poor
1995	1825	1600	1250	950	650

UNITED STATES HISTORICAL SOCIETY
Richmond, Virginia

The arms listed are manufactured by the Williamsburg Firearms Manufactory and the Virginia Firearms Manufactory. This company ceased business under this name in 1994 and resumed business under the name of America Remembers in Mechanicsville, Virginia.

UNITED STATES REVOLVER ASSOCIATION
See—Harrington & Richardson Arms Co.

UNITED STATES SMALL ARMS CO.
Chicago, Illinois
Huntsman Model Knife Pistol

Made from approximately 1918-1930. **Too Rare To Price.**

UNIVERSAL FIREARMS
Hialeah, Florida/Jacksonville, Arkansas

Universal merged with Iver-Johnson in 1985 and relocated to Arkansas in 1986. Universal operated out of Florida from the late 1950s to 1985.

Model 7312

A 12 gauge over/under shotgun with separated 30" ventilated rib barrels, single-selective trigger and automatic ejectors. The case hardened receiver engraved. Blued with a walnut stock. Imported from Italy.

NIB	Exc.	V.G.	Good	Fair	Poor
—	1250	900	450	300	175

Model 7412

As above, with extractors. Imported from Italy.

NIB	Exc.	V.G.	Good	Fair	Poor
—	1000	750	400	250	150

Model 7712

As above, with 26" or 28" barrels, nonselective single trigger and extractors. Imported from Italy.

NIB	Exc.	V.G.	Good	Fair	Poor
—	550	400	350	250	100

Model 7812

As above, with more detailed engraving and automatic ejectors. Imported from Italy.

NIB	Exc.	V.G.	Good	Fair	Poor
—	700	550	450	350	150

Model 7912

As above, with a gold wash frame and single-selective trigger. Imported from Italy.

NIB	Exc.	V.G.	Good	Fair	Poor
—	1350	1000	750	600	300

Model 7112

A 12 gauge double-barrel boxlock shotgun with 26" or 28" barrels, double triggers and extractors. Blued, case hardened with a walnut stock. Imported from Italy.

NIB	Exc.	V.G.	Good	Fair	Poor
—	450	300	250	200	100

Double Wing

A 10, 12, 20 or .410 bore boxlock double-barrel shotgun with 26", 28", or 30" barrels, double triggers and extractors. Blued with a walnut stock. Imported from Italy. Premium for .410 and 10 ga.

NIB	Exc.	V.G.	Good	Fair	Poor
—	450	300	250	200	100

Model 7212

A 12 gauge single-barrel trap shotgun with a 30" ventilated-rib ported barrel, and automatic ejector. Engraved, case hardened receiver and walnut stock. Imported from Italy.

NIB	Exc.	V.G.	Good	Fair	Poor
—	1200	850	650	450	300

Model 1000 Military Carbine

A copy of the U.S. M1 Carbine with an 18" barrel. Blued with a birchwood stock.

NIB	Exc.	V.G.	Good	Fair	Poor
—	400	250	200	100	75

Model 1003

As above, with a 16", 18", or 20" barrel.

NIB	Exc.	V.G.	Good	Fair	Poor
—	350	200	150	100	75

Model 1010

As above, but nickel-plated.

NIB	Exc.	V.G.	Good	Fair	Poor
—	375	225	175	125	100

Model 1015

As above, but gold-plated.

NIB	Exc.	V.G.	Good	Fair	Poor
—	400	250	200	150	125

Model 1005 Deluxe

As above, with a polished blue finish and Monte Carlo-style stock.

NIB	Exc.	V.G.	Good	Fair	Poor
—	375	225	150	100	75

Model 1006 Stainless

As the Model 1000, but in stainless steel.

NIB	Exc.	V.G.	Good	Fair	Poor
—	450	300	225	125	100

Model 1020 Teflon

As above, with a black or gray Dupont Teflon-S finish.

NIB	Exc.	V.G.	Good	Fair	Poor
—	375	225	175	125	100

Model 1256 Ferret

The Model 1000 in .256 Winchester Magnum caliber.

NIB	Exc.	V.G.	Good	Fair	Poor
—	350	200	175	125	100

Model 3000 Enforcer

A pistol version of the Model 1000 with an 11.25" barrel and 15- or 30-shot magazines. Prices are for blued models. **NOTE:** Nickel finish add 20 percent. Gold-plated add 40 percent. Stainless steel add 30 percent. Teflon-S add 20 percent.

NIB	Exc.	V.G.	Good	Fair	Poor
—	375	225	200	150	100

Model 5000 Paratrooper

The Model 1000, with a 16" or 18" barrel and folding stock. This model, in stainless steel, is known as the Model 5006.

NIB	Exc.	V.G.	Good	Fair	Poor
—	400	250	200	125	100

1981 Commemorative Carbine

A limited production version of the Model 1000 cased with accessories. Produced in 1981.

NIB	Exc.	V.G.	Good	Fair	Poor
500	350	250	200	100	75

Model 2200 Leatherneck

A .22 caliber version of the U.S. M1 Carbine with an 18" barrel and blowback action. Blued with a birchwood stock.

NIB	Exc.	V.G.	Good	Fair	Poor
—	300	175	150	100	75

URIZAR, TOMAS
Eibar, Spain

Celta, J. Cesar, Premier, Puma, and Union

A 6.35mm semi-automatic pistol with a 3" barrel. The slide marked with the trade names listed above. Blued with black plastic grips, cast with a wild man carrying a club.

NIB	Exc.	V.G.	Good	Fair	Poor
—	250	150	125	90	75

Dek-Du

A 5.5mm folding trigger double-action revolver with a 12-shot cylinder. Later versions were made in 6.35mm. Manufactured from 1905 to 1912.

NIB	Exc.	V.G.	Good	Fair	Poor
—	225	125	100	75	50

Express

A 6.35mm semi-automatic pistol with a 2" barrel. The slide marked "The Best Automatic Pistol Express". Blued with walnut grips. A 7.65mm variety exists with a 4" barrel.

NIB	Exc.	V.G.	Good	Fair	Poor
—	225	125	100	75	50

Imperial

A 6.35mm caliber semi-automatic pistol with a 2.5" barrel. This model was actually made by Aldazabal. Manufactured circa 1914.

NIB	Exc.	V.G.	Good	Fair	Poor
—	225	125	100	75	50

Le Secours or Phoenix

A 7.65mm semi-automatic pistol marked with either of the trade names listed above.

NIB	Exc.	V.G.	Good	Fair	Poor
—	225	125	100	75	50

Princeps

A 6.35mm or 7.65mm semi-automatic pistol marked on the slide "Made in Spain Princeps Patent".

NIB	Exc.	V.G.	Good	Fair	Poor
—	225	125	100	75	50

Venus

A 7.65mm semi-automatic pistol with the grips having the trade name "Venus" cast in them.

NIB	Exc.	V.G.	Good	Fair	Poor
—	225	125	100	75	50

USAS 12 DAEWOO PRECISION IND., LTD.
South Korea

USAS 12

A 12 gauge semi-automatic shotgun with a 18.25" cylinder-bored barrel, and either a 10-shot box magazine or 20-shot drum magazine. Parkerized, with a composition stock. This model is no longer imported. **WARNING:** As of May 1, 2001 this firearm must be registered with the BATFE and a transfer tax of $200 paid. This firearm is classified as a destructive device. Unregistered guns will be considered contraband after this date, and persons in possession will be in violation of federal law. Value speculative.

USELTON ARMS INC.
Goodlettsville, Tennessee

NOTE: Values shown are for basic models. The sky's the limit.

Compact Classic

This model is chambered for the .45 ACP cartridge and has a 5" barrel. Checkered rosewood grips. Low-profile sights. Black and gray finish. Magazine capacity is 7 rounds. Weight is about 32 oz.

NIB	Exc.	V.G.	Good	Fair	Poor
1995	1700	1500	1100	800	500

Ultra Compact Classic

1911-style semi-automatic .45 with fixed sights. 4.25" barrel, 34 oz. 3-4 lb. trigger pull, 7+1 capacity. Rosewood or imitation ivory grips. Introduced 2006.

NIB	Exc.	V.G.	Good	Fair	Poor
1995	1700	1500	1100	800	500

Compact Classic Companion

Chambered for the .357 Sig or .40 S&W cartridge and fitted with a 5" barrel. Low-profile sights. Black or polymer ivory grips. Stainless or gray finish. Magazine capacity is 7 rounds. Weight is about 32 oz.

NIB	Exc.	V.G.	Good	Fair	Poor
2250	1900	1700	1250	900	600

Carry Classic

Chambered for the .45 ACP cartridge and fitted with a 4.25" barrel with low-profile sights. Rosewood or polymer ivory grips, gray and black finish. Magazine capacity is 7 rounds. Weight is about 34 oz.

NIB	Exc.	V.G.	Good	Fair	Poor
1995	1700	1500	1100	800	500

Ultra Carry

This .45 ACP model features a Damascus slide and titanium frame. Fitted with a 3" barrel with low-profile sights. Magazine capacity is 7 rounds. Weight is about 27 oz. **NOTE:** This model is also offered in titanium and stainless for $2350 and stainless and black for $1850.

NIB	Exc.	V.G.	Good	Fair	Poor
3250	2900	2500	2000	1500	800

Tactical 1911

Chambered for the .45 ACP cartridge and fitted with as 5" barrel with Caspian adjustable sights. Rubber grips and moly coat finish. Magazine capacity is 8 rounds. Weight is about 40 oz.

NIB	Exc.	V.G.	Good	Fair	Poor
2200	1975	1600	1200	1000	500

Classic National Match

This .45 ACP pistol has a 5" barrel with Caspian adjustable sights. Black aluma grips and black finish. Magazine capacity is 8 rounds. Weight is about 40 oz. **NOTE**: Add $300 for compensator.

NIB	Exc.	V.G.	Good	Fair	Poor
2200	1975	1600	1200	1000	500

UZI ISRAELI MILITARY INDUSTRIES
See—Vector Arms, Inc.

Uzi Carbine Model A

Chambered for 9mm cartridge and fitted with a 16" barrel with 25-round magazine. Gray Parkerized finish. Built from 1980 to 1983.

NIB	Exc.	V.G.	Good	Fair	Poor
1600	1450	1200	800	600	450

Uzi Carbine Model B

A 9mm, .41 Action Express or .45 caliber semi-automatic carbine with a 16.1" barrel and 20-, 25-, or 32-shot box magazines. A 50-shot drum magazine is available in 9mm caliber. Black Parkerized finish, plastic grips and a folding stock. It is strongly suggested that a buyer or seller seek a qualified local appraisal. First produced in 1983. This model was no longer imported as of 1989.

NIB	Exc.	V.G.	Good	Fair	Poor
1500	1350	1100	750	550	400

Uzi Mini-Carbine

As above, in 9mm or .45 caliber with a 19.75" barrel. This model is no longer imported.

NIB	Exc.	V.G.	Good	Fair	Poor
2250	1600	1150	800	600	400

Uzi Pistol

As above in 9mm or .45 ACP, with a 4.5" barrel, pistol grip, no rear stock and a 20-shot magazine. This model is no longer imported.

NIB	Exc.	V.G.	Good	Fair	Poor
850	700	550	450	350	250

UZI EAGLE PISTOLS

As of 1999 these pistols were no longer imported into the U.S.

Full Size Model

Introduced in 1997 this is a double-action pistol chambered for the 9mm and .40 S&W cartridge. Barrel length is 4.4". Overall length is 8.1". Tritium night sights are standard.

NIB	Exc.	V.G.	Good	Fair	Poor
550	425	350	275	200	150

Short Slide Model

Introduced in 1997 this is a double-action pistol chambered for the 9mm, .40 S&W and .45 ACP cartridge. Barrel length is 3.7". Overall length is 7.5". Tritium night sights are standard.

NIB	Exc.	V.G.	Good	Fair	Poor
600	475	400	325	250	200

Compact Model

Introduced in 1997 this is a double-action pistol chambered for the 9mm, .40 S&W and .45 ACP cartridge. Barrel length is 3.5". Overall length is 7.2". Tritium night sights are standard. Magazine capacity is 8 rounds for the .45 ACP and 10 rounds for the other calibers. Double-action-only is an option for this model.

NIB	Exc.	V.G.	Good	Fair	Poor
600	475	400	325	250	200

Polymer Compact Model

Introduced in 1997 this is a double-action pistol chambered for the 9mm and .40 S&W cartridge. Barrel length is 3.5". Overall length is 7.2". Tritium night sights are standard.

NIB	Exc.	V.G.	Good	Fair	Poor
550	425	350	275	200	150

VALKYRIE ARMS, LTD.
Olympia, Washington

Valkyrie Arms filed for bankruptcy in early 2008.

Browning 1919 A4 .30 Caliber

This is a semi-automatic version of the famous Browning machine gun. It is chambered for the .30-06 or the .308 cartridge. It comes equipped with a tripod, pintle, T&E, belly linker and 200 links. An A6 configuration is available. Introduced in1996.

NIB	Exc.	V.G.	Good	Fair	Poor
2850	2000	1500	1100	750	600

U.S. M3-A1

A re-creation of the famous "grease gun" but in semi-automatic. Barrel length is 16.5". Supplied with three 30-round magazines. **NOTE:** For dummy suppressor add $50. For real suppressor add $300 plus transfer tax of $200. All NFA rules and state laws must be followed for suppressors.

NIB	Exc.	V.G.	Good	Fair	Poor
1500	1250	1000	750	500	300

DeLisle Carbine

A copy of the famous World War II commando carbine used by British forces. Chambered for .45 ACP. Integral suppressor. All NFA rules must be followed. Only 167 original WWII carbines were produced. **NOTE:** For dummy suppressor deduct $300.

NIB	Exc.	V.G.	Good	Fair	Poor
1575	1250	1000	750	500	300

VALMET, INC.
Jyvaskyla, Finland

M-62S

A semi-automatic copy of the Finnish M-62 service rifle in 7.62x39 caliber that is patterned after the Russian AK47. Fitted with a walnut or tubular steel stock. Manufactured after 1962.

NIB	Exc.	V.G.	Good	Fair	Poor
—	3000	2800	2300	900	750

M-71S

As above, in 5.56mm caliber and available with a composition stock.

NIB	Exc.	V.G.	Good	Fair	Poor
—	1350	1000	850	650	450

Model 76s

As above, in 5.56mm, 7.62x39mm, or 7.62x51mm with either a 16.75" or 20.5" barrel.

5.56mm

NIB	Exc.	V.G.	Good	Fair	Poor
—	1750	1500	1250	750	600

7.62x39mm

NIB	Exc.	V.G.	Good	Fair	Poor
—	3000	2750	2500	2000	1250

Model 78

As above, in 7.62x51mm, 7.62x39, or .223 with a 24.5" barrel, wood stock, and integral bipod.

NIB	Exc.	V.G.	Good	Fair	Poor
—	2150	1700	1300	850	600

Model 212 Lion

A 12 gauge over/under shotgun with 26", 28", or 30" barrels, single-selective trigger and extractors. Blued with a walnut stock. Manufactured from 1947 to 1968. Amazingly similar to the Savage Model 330 over/under. Values shown are for standard field grade.

NIB	Exc.	V.G.	Good	Fair	Poor
—	750	625	500	400	300

Model 412 Combination Gun

A 12 gauge .30-06 over/under combination gun built on the frame of the 12 gauge Lion shotgun. Discontinued.

NIB	Exc.	V.G.	Good	Fair	Poor
—	1900	1475	1200	1050	700

VALTRO
Italy

1998 A1

A Model 1911 clone chambered for .45 ACP and fitted with a match grade 5" barrel. Many special features include a checkered front strap, beavertail grip safety, deluxe wood grips, serrated slide front and back, beveled magazine well. Weight is approximately 40 oz. Introduced in 1998.

NIB	Exc.	V.G.	Good	Fair	Poor
2250	1950	1600	1275	800	500

Tactical 98 Shotgun

Chambered for 12 gauge and fitted with a 18.5" or 20" ported barrel. Choice of pistol grip or standard stock. Extended magazine with 5 or 7 rounds. Ghost ring sights.

NIB	Exc.	V.G.	Good	Fair	Poor
—	900	750	675	500	325

PM5

This is a slide-action shotgun chambered for the 12 gauge 3" shell. Barrel length is 20" choked Cylinder. Box-fed magazine. Value shown is for pre-ban model.

NIB	Exc.	V.G.	Good	Fair	Poor
—	—				

VARNER SPORTING ARMS, INC.
Marietta, Georgia

This company made several over/under shotguns and rifle/shotgun combination guns for the Savage Company. These are no longer being imported into this country. The rifles listed are all patterned after the Stevens Favorite model.

Hunter

.22 caliber single-shot rifle with a 21.5" half-octagonal, takedown barrel fitted with an aperture rear sight. Blued with well-figured walnut stocks. Introduced in 1988.

NIB	Exc.	V.G.	Good	Fair	Poor
375	300	250	200	150	100

Hunter Deluxe

As above, with a case hardened receiver and a more finely figured stock.

NIB	Exc.	V.G.	Good	Fair	Poor
500	400	350	250	175	125

Presentation Grade

As above, with a target hammer and trigger, and a hand checkered stock.

NIB	Exc.	V.G.	Good	Fair	Poor
575	475	425	350	250	200

No. 1 Grade
Engraved.

NIB	Exc.	V.G.	Good	Fair	Poor
650	550	500	450	350	200

No. 2 Grade

NIB	Exc.	V.G.	Good	Fair	Poor
775	650	600	500	400	200

No. 3 Grade

NIB	Exc.	V.G.	Good	Fair	Poor
1100	850	700	550	350	200

VECTOR ARMS, INC.
North Salt Lake, Utah

Mini Uzi

A smaller version of the full size Uzi chambered for the 9mm cartridge only. Fitted with 18" barrel.

Pre-Ban

NIB	Exc.	V.G.	Good	Fair	Poor
—	2000	1700	1400	1050	700

Post-Ban

NIB	Exc.	V.G.	Good	Fair	Poor
—	1500	1250	1050	700	500

Uzi

This is a semi-automatic, pre-ban Uzi carbine with 18" barrel chambered for the 9mm cartridge. Receiver built by Group Industries of Louisville, Kentucky, prior to May 1986. Receiver fixed parts manufacturing and receiver assembly by Vector Arms. Only 97 of these semi-automatic receivers were manufactured. **NOTE:** For .45 ACP or .22 caliber conversion kit, add $200.

Pre-Ban

NIB	Exc.	V.G.	Good	Fair	Poor
—	1500	1250	1050	700	500

Post-Ban

NIB	Exc.	V.G.	Good	Fair	Poor
—	1200	1050	800	675	500

VEKTOR
Pretoria, South Africa

This company made a variety of handguns and rifles for the U.S. market until 2001. It now only manufactures firearms for the south African military and law enforcement.

HANDGUNS

Model Z88

This is a semi-automatic pistol chambered for the 9mm cartridge. It has a 5" barrel and fixed sights. Weight is about 35 oz. Blue finish. Magazine capacity is 15 rounds or 10 in U.S. Clone of the Beretta 92.

NIB	Exc.	V.G.	Good	Fair	Poor
600	475	350	250	175	100

Model SP1 Service Pistol

This model is chambered for the 9mm cartridge and is fitted with a 4-5/8" barrel. Fixed sights. Weight is 35 oz. Blue finish. Magazine capacity is 15 rounds or 10 in U.S. **NOTE:** Add $30 for anodized or nickel finish.

NIB	Exc.	V.G.	Good	Fair	Poor
600	475	350	250	175	100

Model SP1 Sport

Similar to the SP1 this model features a 5" barrel with 3 chamber compensator. Blue finish. Weight is about 38 oz.

NIB	Exc.	V.G.	Good	Fair	Poor
725	575	450	350	275	175

Model SP1 Tuned Sport

This model also has a three-chamber compensator on a 5" barrel but it has an adjustable straight trigger and LPA 3-dot sighting system. Nickel finish. Weight is about 38 oz.

NIB	Exc.	V.G.	Good	Fair	Poor
1200	950	800	575	400	300

Model SP1 Target

This 9mm model is fitted with a 6" barrel with adjustable straight trigger. LPA 3 dot sighting system. Weight is about 40.5 oz. Two-tone finish.

NIB	Exc.	V.G.	Good	Fair	Poor
1200	950	800	575	400	300

Model SP1 Compact (General's Model)

A compact version of the 9mm pistol fitted with a 4" barrel. Fixed sights. Blue finish. Magazine capacity is 15 rounds or 10 for U.S. Weight is about 31.5 oz.

NIB	Exc.	V.G.	Good	Fair	Poor
650	525	400	300	200	75

Model SP2

A full size service pistol chambered for the .40 S&W cartridge. fitted with a 4-5/8" barrel. Fixed sights. Magazine capacity is 11 rounds or 10 for U.S. Blued finish. Weight is about 35 oz.

NIB	Exc.	V.G.	Good	Fair	Poor
650	525	400	300	200	75

Model SP2 Compact (General's Model)

A compact .40 S&W pistol with 4" barrel. Magazine capacity is 11 rounds or 10 for U.S. Weight is about 31.5 oz. Blue finish. Fixed sights.

NIB	Exc.	V.G.	Good	Fair	Poor
650	525	400	300	200	75

Model SP2 Competition

This model is chambered for the .40 S&W cartridge and fitted with a 5.88" barrel. It features enlarged safety levers and magazine catch. The frame has been thickened for scope mount. Beavertail grip and straight trigger. Weight is about 42 oz.

NIB	Exc.	V.G.	Good	Fair	Poor
1000	750	600	450	325	200

Model SP1 Ultra Sport

This model is designed for IPSC open-class competition. Barrel length is 6" with 3 chamber compensator. Chambered for 9mm cartridge. Optical scope mount with Weaver rails. Magazine capacity is 19 rounds or 10 for U.S. Weight is about 41.5 oz. Priced with Lynx scope.

NIB	Exc.	V.G.	Good	Fair	Poor
2150	1800	1575	1200	800	500

Model SP2 Ultra Sport

Same as model above but chambered for .40 S&W cartridge. Magazine capacity is 14 rounds or 10 for U.S.

NIB	Exc.	V.G.	Good	Fair	Poor
2150	1800	1575	1200	800	500

Model SP2 Conversion Kit

Made for the SP2 this is a 9mm conversion kit that consists of a 9mm barrel, recoil spring, and 9mm magazine.

NIB	Exc.	V.G.	Good	Fair	Poor
200	150	100	75	50	25

Model CP-1 Compact

Chambered for the 9mm cartridge and fitted with a 4" barrel this model has a polymer frame. Fixed sights. Weight is about 25 oz. Magazine capacity is 13 rounds standard, 12 rounds compact or 10 rounds for U.S. Offered with black or nickel slide. **NOTE:** This model was recalled in 2000 due to safety concerns.

NIB	Exc.	V.G.	Good	Fair	Poor
475	375	250	150	100	50

RIFLES

Vektor H5 Pump-Action Rifle

This pump-action rifle is chambered for the .233 cartridge. It is fitted with a thumbhole stock and a 22" barrel. Magazine capacity is 5 rounds.

NIB	Exc.	V.G.	Good	Fair	Poor
850	725	600	475	300	200

Vektor 98

Built on a Mauser action, this rifle is chambered for a variety of calibers from .243 to .375 H&H. Fitted with a one-piece walnut stock with hand checkering. Magazine capacity is 5 rounds. Open sights on magnum calibers only.

NIB	Exc.	V.G.	Good	Fair	Poor
1200	950	800	575	400	300

Vektor Lyttelton

This rifle features numerous special features and is fitted with a classic walnut stock with wraparound checkering. Fixed sights. Calibers offered are from .243 to .375 H&H.

NIB	Exc.	V.G.	Good	Fair	Poor
1595	1400	1100	800	575	300

VENUS WAFFENWERKE
Zella Mehlis, Germany
Venus

A 6.35mm, 7.65mm, or 9mm semi-automatic pistol with a 3.5" barrel. Slide is marked "Original Venus Patent" and the grips bear the monogram "OW". Designed by Oskar Will. Blued, plastic grips. Manufactured from 1912 to 1914.

NIB	Exc.	V.G.	Good	Fair	Poor
—	700	550	400	250	100

VERNEY-CARRON
St. Etienne, France
Concours

A 12 gauge over/under boxlock shotgun with 26" or 28" ventilated rib barrels, single-selective triggers, automatic ejectors and profuse engraving. Blued, French case hardened with checkered walnut stock. First imported in 1978.

NIB	Exc.	V.G.	Good	Fair	Poor
—	1450	900	700	600	300

Skeet Model

As above, with a 28" Skeet-choked barrel and a pistol-grip stock.

NIB	Exc.	V.G.	Good	Fair	Poor
—	1600	1050	700	600	300

Snake Charmer II

A .410 single-barrel break-action shotgun with stainless steel barrel and receiver and black ABS stock. Overall length 29".

NIB	Exc.	V.G.	Good	Fair	Poor
—	175	150	100	75	50

VERONA
Italy

HUNTING SHOTGUNS

Model SX401/S

This 12 or 20 gauge 3" semi-automatic model is offered with either a 26" or 28" vent rib barrel with choke tubes. Checkered Turkish walnut stock. Weight is about 6.75 lbs.

NIB	Exc.	V.G.	Good	Fair	Poor
800	600	475	350	150	100

Model SX405/S/L

As above but with black composite stock. Weight is about 6.5 lbs.

NIB	Exc.	V.G.	Good	Fair	Poor
700	600	550	300	100	75

Model SX405W/H/SW/SH

This 12 gauge 3" Magnum semi-automatic gun is offered with a choice of 26" or 28" vent rib barrel with wetland or hardwood camo pattern. Weight is about 6.5 lbs.

NIB	Exc.	V.G.	Good	Fair	Poor
800	600	475	350	150	100

LX501

This over/under shotgun is chambered for the 12, 20, 28, and .410 bore. Single-selective trigger. Ejectors. Blued steel receiver. Walnut stock with machine checkering. It is offered with 28" vent-rib barrels. Screw-in chokes for 12 and 20 gauges models. Fixed chokes for 28 and .410 bore. Chambers are 3" for all gauges except 28 gauge. Weight is between 6.25 lbs. and 6.75 lbs. depending on gauge. **NOTE:** For 28 gauge and .410 bore add $30.

NIB	Exc.	V.G.	Good	Fair	Poor
1000	875	600	400	300	225

LX692G

This model is also offered in 12, 20, 28, and .410 bore with 28" vent-rib barrels. Receiver is fitted with sideplates with gold inlaid hunting scenes on three sides. Matte finish walnut stock with schnabel forearm, hand-cut checkering. Weight is between 7.25 lbs. and 7.75 lbs. depending on gauge. **NOTE:** For 28 gauge add $40; for .410 bore add $25.

NIB	Exc.	V.G.	Good	Fair	Poor
1250	1100	875	725	500	300

LX692G-20/28

This model has the features as above, but features a 20 gauge gun with extra set of 28 gauge barrels. Choke tubes standard. Weight is about 7.5 lbs. with 20 gauge barrels.

NIB	Exc.	V.G.	Good	Fair	Poor
2000	1800	1500	1200	900	500

Model LX1001 Express Combo

This over/under gun features two sets of barrels; one for 20 gauge 2.75" and the other for either .223, .243, .270, .308, or .30-06. The 20 gauge barrels are 28" vent rib and the rifle barrels are 22". Checkered walnut stock with oil finish. Engraved receiver.

NIB	Exc.	V.G.	Good	Fair	Poor
2580	2300	1975	1600	900	600

LX702G

This model is offered in both 12 and 20 gauge with 28" barrel chambered for 3" shells. This model features a case colored receiver with side plates. The receiver is engraved on three sides with gold inlaid upland bird hunting scenes. Full-figured Turkish walnut with hand checkering and oil finish. Single-selective trigger, black recoil pad, ejectors and schnabel forearm. Weight for 12 gauge is about 7 lbs. For the 20 gauge about 6 lbs.

NIB	Exc.	V.G.	Good	Fair	Poor
1375	1200	950	700	500	350

SIDE-BY-SIDE SHOTGUNS

Model SS662GL

This side-by-side gun is offered in 20 or 28 gauge with 28" barrels choked Modified and Full. Double triggers. Engraved receiver. Checkered walnut stock with straight grip. Weight is about 6 lbs. Made by Bernardelli. **NOTE:** Add 20 percent for 28-gauge.

NIB	Exc.	V.G.	Good	Fair	Poor
2200	2000	1750	1400	1000	500

Model SS772GL

As above but with slightly more engraving. **NOTE:** Add 20 percent for 28-gauge.

NIB	Exc.	V.G.	Good	Fair	Poor
2450	2200	1850	1550	1175	550

SPORTING/COMPETITION SHOTGUNS

LX680

Chambered for 12 or 20 gauge shells with 2.75" chambers. Single-selective trigger, ejectors, lightly engraved steel receiver. Walnut stock with beavertail firearm and hand-cut checkering. Ventilated recoil pad standard. Fitted with 28" barrels with ventilated rib between barrels. Choke tubes. Weight is about 6.5 lbs. depending on gauge.

NIB	Exc.	V.G.	Good	Fair	Poor
1075	900	700	525	375	250

LX692GS

Similar to the above model but fitted with sideplates with gold inlaid hunting scenes.

NIB	Exc.	V.G.	Good	Fair	Poor
1425	1300	1050	750	500	350

LX680C S&T

This over/under model features a choice of 28" or 30" 11mm vent-rib barrels on a 12 gauge frame. Single-selective trigger, ejectors. Matte finish Turkish walnut stock with hand-cut checkering, beavertail forearm, wider comb. Lightly engraved steel receiver. Ventilated rib between barrels. Choke tubes. Weight is approximately 7.75 lbs. depending on barrel length. The 28" barrel model is designated as Skeet/Sporting and the 30" model is designated Trap.

NIB	Exc.	V.G.	Good	Fair	Poor
1175	1000	800	600	425	275

LX692GC S&T

Same as above but with sideplates with gold inlaid game scenes.

NIB	Exc.	V.G.	Good	Fair	Poor
1550	1400	1150	850	600	350

LX702GC S&T

This model features a case colored receiver and sideplates with gold inlaid birds. Offered in 12 gauge only with choice of 28" or 30" barrels. Weight is about 7.5 lbs.

NIB	Exc.	V.G.	Good	Fair	Poor
1625	1475	1175	800	600	350

Model SX801/L

This semi-automatic 12 gauge 2.75" shotgun is fitted with a choice of 28" or 30" vent-rib ported barrels with choke tubes and Hi-Viz sights. Walnut stock with choice of Monte Carlo comb or adjustable comb. Weight is about 6.75 lbs.

NIB	Exc.	V.G.	Good	Fair	Poor
865	700	575	400	275	200

Model SX801G/GL

As above but with higher grade walnut stock.

NIB	Exc.	V.G.	Good	Fair	Poor
1060	900	725	600	450	200

Model LX980CS

This 12 gauge 2.75" over/under gun is fitted with 30" ported barrels with extended choke tubes. Removable trigger assembly. Black receiver. Checkered select walnut stock. Weight is about 7.5 lbs.

NIB	Exc.	V.G.	Good	Fair	Poor
3525	3200	2500	2000	1550	600

Model LX980GCS/GCT

As above but with a choice of 30" or 32" ported barrels. Select walnut stock has adjustable comb. Weight is about 7.5 lbs.

NIB	Exc.	V.G.	Good	Fair	Poor
3775	3400	2800	2250	1700	650

VICKERS, LTD.
Crayford/Kent, England

Jubilee

A .22 caliber single-shot Martini-action rifle with a 28" barrel, adjustable sights and pistol grip walnut stock. Blued. Manufactured prior to WWII.

NIB	Exc.	V.G.	Good	Fair	Poor
—	1000	700	550	375	200

Empire

As above, with a 27" or 30" barrel and a straight stock.

NIB	Exc.	V.G.	Good	Fair	Poor
—	1000	700	550	375	200

VICTOR EJECTOR
See—Crescent F. A. Co.

VICTORY ARMS CO., LTD.
Northhampton, England

Model MC5
A 9mm, .38 Super, .41 Action Express, 10mm, or .45 caliber semi-automatic pistol with a 4.25", 5.75", or 7.5" barrel, 10-, 12-, or 17-shot magazine, decocking lever and Millett sights. Interchangeable barrels were available. Introduced in 1989.

NIB	Exc.	V.G.	Good	Fair	Poor
500	400	300	250	200	150

VIRGINIAN
See—Interarms

VOERE
Kufstein, Austria

In 1987 this company was purchased by Mauser-Werke. Voere actions are used in rifles made and sold by KDF, Inc. (Kleinguenther), of Seguin, Texas. Values for older-production rifles are listed.

Model 1007
Bolt-action rifle chambered for .22 LR cartridge and fitted with an 18" barrel. Open sights. Beech stock. Introduced in 1984. Discontinued in 1991.

NIB	Exc.	V.G.	Good	Fair	Poor
450	375	300	200	150	75

Model 1013
This bolt-action rifle is chambered for the .22 WMR cartridge and fitted with an 18" barrel. Magazine capacity is 8 rounds. Open sight with adjustable rear. Military-style stock is oil finished. Double set triggers.

NIB	Exc.	V.G.	Good	Fair	Poor
650	575	500	375	250	125

Model 2107
This .22 LR bolt-action rifle has a 19.5" barrel with Monte Carlo stock. Eight-round magazine. Weight is about 6 lbs.

NIB	Exc.	V.G.	Good	Fair	Poor
650	575	500	375	250	125

Model 2107 Deluxe
Bolt-action rifle chambered for .22 LR cartridge has checkered stock with raised cheekpiece. Discontinued in 1988.

NIB	Exc.	V.G.	Good	Fair	Poor
650	575	500	375	250	125

Model 2114S
This is a semi-automatic rifle chambered for .22 LR cartridge and fitted with a 18" barrel. Magazine capacity is 15 rounds. Open sight. Stock is beechwood. Single-stage trigger. No longer in production.

NIB	Exc.	V.G.	Good	Fair	Poor
450	375	300	200	150	75

Model 2115
Similar to the model above but with checkered stock. Weight is about 5.75 lbs. Discontinued in 1995.

NIB	Exc.	V.G.	Good	Fair	Poor
500	425	350	250	200	100

Model 2150
This is a bolt-action centerfire rifle chambered for calibers from .22-250 to .338 Win. Magnum. Fitted with 22" barrels (24" on magnums). Open sights with adjustable rear sight. Checkered walnut stock with oil finish. Built on M98 Mauser action. Weight is about 8 lbs. depending on caliber. Discontinued in 1995.

NIB	Exc.	V.G.	Good	Fair	Poor
—	1500	1200	850	550	300

Model 2155
Similar to the Model 2150 but with no sights and double set triggers. Discontinued in 1995.

NIB	Exc.	V.G.	Good	Fair	Poor
—	1650	1350	1000	700	225

Model 2165
Similar to the above model but with open sights, walnut stock with Bavarian cheekpiece and schnabel forearm. Rosewood grip cap. Discontinued.

NIB	Exc.	V.G.	Good	Fair	Poor
—	1650	1350	1000	700	225

Model 2185
This is a semi-automatic centerfire rifle chambered for 7x64, .308, and .30-06 cartridges. Fitted with a 20" barrel and open sights with adjustable rear sight. Checkered walnut stock. Available with full stock as well. NOTE: Add $100 for Mannlicher stock.

NIB	Exc.	V.G.	Good	Fair	Poor
—	1500	1200	950	850	400

Model 2185 Match

Same as the Model 2185 except for a 5-round magazine, hooded front sight, laminated stock with adjustable cheekpiece. Discontinued in 1994.

NIB	Exc.	V.G.	Good	Fair	Poor
4000	3400	2750	1150	650	400

Model Titan

This is a centerfire bolt-action rifle chambered in calibers from .243 to .375 H&H. Fitted with 24" or 26" barrels depending on caliber. No sights. Checkered Monte Carlo walnut stock with oil finish. Discontinued in 1988.

NIB	Exc.	V.G.	Good	Fair	Poor
—	1200	1000	775	500	350

Model Titan Menor

Bolt-action rifle chambered for .222 Rem, .223 Rem. Fitted with a 23.5" barrel and 3-round magazine. No sights. Checkered Monte Carlo walnut stock with rosewood grip cap. Introduced in 1986 and dropped in 1988.

NIB	Exc.	V.G.	Good	Fair	Poor
—	1000	800	600	400	250

Model VEC-91 Series

Bolt-action rifle that fires caseless 5.7mm ammo. Adjustable rear sight on a 20" barrel. Checkered walnut stock with cheekpiece. Electronic trigger. There was limited importation into the U.S. from 1991 to approximately 2008. It is seldom seen for sale on the used gun market, in part due to the expensive case-less ammunition.

NIB	Exc.	V.G.	Good	Fair	Poor
2000	1600	1450	1000	—	—

VOLCANIC ARMS COMPANY
New Haven, Connecticut
See—Winchester Repeating Arms Co.

VOLQUARTSEN CUSTOM
Carroll, Iowa

This company was started in 1973, and began specializing in Ruger 10/22 aftermarket conversions. In 1997 the company began producing its own receivers. **NOTE:** Volquartsen offers beaucoup options on a wide variety of rifles. The values shown below are for the more-or-less base models.

SEMI-AUTO RIFLES

These rifles are based on the Ruger 10/22 design. They are chambered for the .22 LR or .22 WMR cartridge.

Standard

Fitted with an 18.5" stainless steel barrel and either a Hogue rubber stock or brown laminated stock. No sights. Integral Weaver rail.

NIB	Exc.	V.G.	Good	Fair	Poor
1350	1200	950	700	550	300

Lightweight

This model has a 16.5" carbon-fiber barrel. Choice of rubber or laminated stock. Integral Weaver rail.

NIB	Exc.	V.G.	Good	Fair	Poor
1370	1220	975	725	550	300

Deluxe

This model has a 20" stainless steel fluted and compensated barrel. Choice of laminated or rubber stock.

NIB	Exc.	V.G.	Good	Fair	Poor
1360	1200	950	700	550	300

SIGNATURE SERIES

Fitted with a 20" stainless steel fluted and compensated barrel. Engraved receiver, trigger guard and rings. Comes with a Nikon 3.3x10 Titanium scope. Fancy walnut stock.

NIB	Exc.	V.G.	Good	Fair	Poor
3000	2650	2200	1600	1200	500

VG-1

This model has a 20" stainless steel fluted and compensated barrel. Fitted with a green McMillan fiberglass stock. Finish is black epoxy powder coating. Offered in .22 WMR only.

NIB	Exc.	V.G.	Good	Fair	Poor
1900	1700	1400	1150	900	500

VX-2500

This model features a 20" stainless steel fluted and compensated barrel. Fitted with a VX-2500 stock with aluminum forearm. Designed for benchrest shooting.

NIB	Exc.	V.G.	Good	Fair	Poor
2000	1750	1500	1200	900	500

VX-5000

Fitted with an 18" carbon-fiber lightweight barrel with compensator. Comes standard with VX-5000 stock with aluminum fore-end.

NIB	Exc.	V.G.	Good	Fair	Poor
2200	1950	1700	1400	1000	600

PISTOLS

These pistols are based on the Ruger MK II design.

Black Cheetah Pistol

Special order only.

Compact

Fitted with a 3.5" bull barrel and Hogue Monogrip. Adjustable rear sight and target front sight. Stainless steel finish. Weight is about 42 oz.

NIB	Exc.	V.G.	Good	Fair	Poor
1000	850	700	525	400	300

Deluxe

This model is fitted with a 5" to 10" special heavy barrel depending on the customer's requirements. Adjustable rear sight and target front sight. Target grips. Stainless steel finish.

NIB	Exc.	V.G.	Good	Fair	Poor
1250	1000	900	700	575	450

Masters

The Masters features a 6.5" barrel with aluminum alloy-finned underlug. The top rib has a front blade sight with an adjustable rear sight. Rib is cut to accommodate optics. Integral compensator. Weight is about 56 oz.

NIB	Exc.	V.G.	Good	Fair	Poor
1600	1350	1200	900	650	500

Olympic

The Olympic is designed for NRA or UIT competitive shooting. It has a 7.5" match barrel with a unique gas chamber for recoil-free shooting. Target front sight and adjustable rear sight. Weight is about 36 oz.

NIB	Exc.	V.G.	Good	Fair	Poor
1750	1450	1300	1000	650	500

Stingray

Fitted with a 7.5" match-grade barrel with radial flutes. Compensator standard. Supplied with either a Ultra Dot red dot optic or TL rear optic. Weight is about 56 oz.

NIB	Exc.	V.G.	Good	Fair	Poor
1600	1350	1200	900	650	500

Terminator

This model is fitted with a 7.5" match barrel with integral compensator. Choice of Weaver-style or 3/8" tip-off scope mounting system. **NOTE:** Add $150 for Ultra Dot optics.

NIB	Exc.	V.G.	Good	Fair	Poor
1600	1350	1200	900	650	500

Ultra-Lite Match

NIB	Exc.	V.G.	Good	Fair	Poor
1600	1350	1200	900	650	500

V-6

The V-6 has a 6" vent-rib triangular-shaped match barrel with full-length underlug. Adjustable rear sight and target front sight. Rubber target grips. Weight is about 36 oz.

NIB	Exc.	V.G.	Good	Fair	Poor
1350	1200	950	700	550	300

V-2000

Fitted with a 6" match barrel with alloy-finned underlug. Rubber target grips and adjustable rear sight with target front sight. Weight is about 37 oz.

NIB	Exc.	V.G.	Good	Fair	Poor
1350	1200	950	700	550	300

V-Magic II

This model has an 8" fluted match barrel with integral compensator. Rubber target grips and Ultra Dot red dot optic. No open sights. Weight is about 46 oz.

NIB	Exc.	V.G.	Good	Fair	Poor
1350	1200	950	700	550	300

VOLUNTEER ENTERPRISES
Knoxville, Tennessee
See—Commando Arms

VOUZELAUD
Paris, France

Model 315 E

A 12, 16, or 20 gauge boxlock shotgun with 20" barrels, double triggers, and straight-gripped stock. Blued, case hardened. Imported prior to 1988.

NIB	Exc.	V.G.	Good	Fair	Poor
—	7500	6000	4000	2000	900

Model 315 EL

As above, with more engraving and also available in .28 or .410 bore, which are worth approximately $1,000 more than the values listed.

NIB	Exc.	V.G.	Good	Fair	Poor
—	10000	8000	5000	2500	1100

Model 315 EGL

As above, with a French case hardened receiver. Discontinued in 1987.

NIB	Exc.	V.G.	Good	Fair	Poor
—	15000	12000	8500	4000	1500

Model 315 EGL-S

As above, with engraved hunting scenes. Discontinued in 1987.

NIB	Exc.	V.G.	Good	Fair	Poor
—	5500	4500	3500	2000	1000

WALCH, JOHN
New York, New York

Navy Revolver

A .36 caliber superimposed load percussion revolver with a 6" octagonal barrel and a 6-shot cylinder fitted with 12 nipples, two hammers, and two triggers. The barrel marked "Walch Firearms Co. NY." and "Patented Feb. 8, 1859." Blued with walnut grips.

NIB	Exc.	V.G.	Good	Fair	Poor
—	—	13000	9000	4000	950

Pocket Revolver

A spur trigger .31 caliber 10-shot percussion revolver with either a brass or iron frame and walnut grips. The iron frame version is worth approximately 50 percent more than the brass variety.

Courtesy Greg Martin Auctions

NIB	Exc.	V.G.	Good	Fair	Poor
—	—	5000	2750	1000	300

WALDMAN
Germany

Waldman

A 7.65mm semi-automatic pistol with a 3.5" barrel and 8-shot magazine. The slide marked "1913 Model Automatic Pistol" and some examples are marked "American Automatic Pistol." Blued with checkered walnut grips inlaid with a brass insert marked "Waldman."

NIB	Exc.	V.G.	Good	Fair	Poor
—	300	225	200	150	100

WALLIS & BIRCH
Philadelphia, Pennsylvania

Pocket Pistol

A .41 caliber single-shot percussion pocket pistol with a 2.5" or 3" barrel, German silver furniture and walnut stock. The barrel is marked "Wallis & Birch Phila." Produced during the 1850s.

NIB	Exc.	V.G.	Good	Fair	Poor
—	—	4050	2250	800	250

WALTHER, CARL
Zella Mehilis and Ulm/Donau, Germany

Model 1

A 6.35mm semi-automatic pistol barrel lengths of 2"-6". Blued with checkered hard rubber grips with the Walther logo on each grip. Introduced in 1908.

Courtesy James Rankin

NIB	Exc.	V.G.	Good	Fair	Poor
—	1000	700	400	200	200

Model 2

A 6.35mm semi-automatic pistol with a knurled bushing at the muzzle that retains the mainspring. There are two variations: one with a fixed rear sight, and one with a pop-up rear sight. Blued with checkered hard rubber grips with the Walther logo on each grip. Introduced in 1909.

Courtesy James Rankin

Fixed Sights

NIB	Exc.	V.G.	Good	Fair	Poor
—	800	600	300	200	150

Pop Up Sights

NIB	Exc.	V.G.	Good	Fair	Poor
—	1800	1000	600	400	300

Model 3

A 7.65mm semi-automatic pistol having a smooth barrel bushing. Blued with checkered hard rubber grips with the Walther logo on each. Introduced in 1910.

Courtesy James Rankin

Courtesy James Rankin

NIB	Exc.	V.G.	Good	Fair	Poor
3000	2000	1000	600	350	200

Model 4

A 7.65mm semi-automatic pistol larger than the preceding models. There were many variations of this model produced. Blued with checkered hard rubber grips with the Walther logo on each grip. Introduced 1910.

Courtesy James Rankin

NIB	Exc.	V.G.	Good	Fair	Poor
700	600	500	400	275	150

Model 5

A 6.35mm semi-automatic pistol that is almost identical to the Model 2. Fixed sights. Blued with checkered hard rubber grips with the Walther logo on each grip.

Courtesy James Rankin

NIB	Exc.	V.G.	Good	Fair	Poor
600	500	400	300	200	150

Model 6

A 9mm semi-automatic pistol. The largest of the Walther numbered pistols. Approximately 1,500 manufactured. Blued with checkered hard rubber grips with the Walther logo on each grip. Sometimes seen with plain checkered wood grips. Introduced 1915.

NIB	Exc.	V.G.	Good	Fair	Poor
8000	7000	5000	3000	1500	700

Model 7

A 6.35mm semi-automatic pistol in the same style as the Model 4. Blued with checkered hard rubber grips with the Walther logo on each side. Introduced in 1917.

Courtesy James Rankin

NIB	Exc.	V.G.	Good	Fair	Poor
800	700	500	300	200	150

Model 8

A 6.35mm semi-automatic pistol. Finish is either blue, silver, or gold. Most were unengraved, but three types of engraving coverage were available from the factory: slide only, slide and frame and complete coverage overall. The grips are checkered hard rubber with the WC logo on one grip, and 6.35mm on the opposite side. Ivory grips are seen with many of the engraved models. Introduced in 1920 and produced until 1944. **NOTE:** Add $500 for factory case.

Courtesy James Rankin

Blue, Silver or Gold Finish

NIB	Exc.	V.G.	Good	Fair	Poor
—	750	600	300	200	150

Engraved Slide

NIB	Exc.	V.G.	Good	Fair	Poor
—	1000	700	500	300	200

Engraved Slide and Frame

NIB	Exc.	V.G.	Good	Fair	Poor
—	2500	2000	1100	450	300

Engraved, Complete Coverage

NIB	Exc.	V.G.	Good	Fair	Poor
—	4000	3500	1400	500	300

Model 9

A 6.35mm semi-automatic pistol. Smaller than the Model 8, but built as the Model 1 with exposed barrel. Same finishes and engraving as the Model 8. Introduced 1921 and produced until 1944. All values the same as the Model 8.

Courtesy James Rankin

Sport Model 1926/ Walther Hammerless Target 22/ Walther Standard Sport/ Walther 1932 Olympia/ Sport Model Target/ Special Stoeger Model

All of these .22 LR caliber semi-automatic pistols are the same target pistol introduced by Walther in 1926. A well-made pistol with a barrel length of between 6"-16". It has one-piece checkered wrap-around wood grips. There was also a .22 Short version of the Olympia model produced for rapid fire Olympic shooting. There was also a torpedo-shape target weight available for shooters. **NOTE:** Add $200 for target weight. Add $500 for case.

Courtesy Orvel Reichert

NIB	Exc.	V.G.	Good	Fair	Poor
—	1000	850	550	350	250

Walther 1936 Olympia

This semi-automatic target pistol in .22 caliber resembled the earlier 1932 Olympia, but with many improvements. There were four standard models produced with many variations of each one. These variations included many barrel lengths, and both round and octagon barrels. There were duraluminum slides, frames and triggers. Various weight configurations to as many as four separate weights to one gun. One-piece wrap-around checkered wood grips in different configurations for the individual shooter. Produced until 1944. **NOTE:** Prices are for Standard Model. Add $100 for Pentathlon or Hunter, $200 for Rapid Fire. Add $250 for weights. The four models were:

1. **Funfklamph Pentathlon**
2. **Jagerschafts—Hunter**
3. **Sport or Standard Model**
4. **Schnellfeur—Rapid Fire**

Courtesy John J. Stimson, Jr.

Olympia without weights

NIB	Exc.	V.G.	Good	Fair	Poor
—	1500	1300	750	475	250

Model MP

A 9mm semi-automatic pistol that was the forerunner of the Model AP and P.38 series. Found in variations that resemble a large Model PP or the P.38. Blued finish with one-piece wrap-around checkered wood grips.

Courtesy James Rankin

NIB	Exc.	V.G.	Good	Fair	Poor
—	35000	30000	25000	20000	15000

Model AP

A 9mm semi-automatic pistol that was the forerunner of the Model P.38. A hammerless pistol in various barrel lengths. Sometimes with duraluminum frames, and some with stocks. Blued finish with one-piece wraparound checkered wood grips. **NOTE:** With stock add $4000.

NIB	Exc.	V.G.	Good	Fair	Poor
—	28000	25000	20000	15000	10000

Model PP

A semi-automatic pistol in .22, .25, .32 and .380 caliber. Introduced in 1928. It was the first successful commercial double-action pistol. It was manufactured in finishes of blue, silver, and gold, and with three different types of engraving. Grips were generally two-piece black or white plastic with the Walther banner on each grip. Grips in wood or ivory are seen, but usually on engraved guns. There are many variations of the Model PP and numerous NSDAP markings seen on the pre-1946 models that were produced during the Nazi regime. All reflect various prices.

.22 Caliber

NIB	Exc.	V.G.	Good	Fair	Poor
1200	800	600	350	250	150

.25 Caliber

NIB	Exc.	V.G.	Good	Fair	Poor
6500	5000	4500	2500	1500	600

.32 Caliber, High Polished Finish

Courtesy James Rankin

NIB	Exc.	V.G.	Good	Fair	Poor
1000	850	650	325	225	175

.32 Caliber, Milled Finish

NIB	Exc.	V.G.	Good	Fair	Poor
800	700	500	250	200	125

.380 Caliber

NIB	Exc.	V.G.	Good	Fair	Poor
2000	1600	1300	800	475	350

.32 Caliber, with Duraluminum Frame

NIB	Exc.	V.G.	Good	Fair	Poor
1000	900	700	550	400	200

.32 Caliber, with Bottom Magazine Release

NIB	Exc.	V.G.	Good	Fair	Poor
1500	1400	1000	600	400	200

.32 Caliber, with Verchromt Finish

NIB	Exc.	V.G.	Good	Fair	Poor
3000	2800	2500	1200	700	400

.32 Caliber, Allemagne Marked

NIB	Exc.	V.G.	Good	Fair	Poor
950	850	700	550	325	250

.32 Caliber, A. F. Stoeger Contract

NIB	Exc.	V.G.	Good	Fair	Poor
2700	2500	1750	1050	700	400

.32 Caliber, with Waffenampt Proofs, High Polished Finish

NIB	Exc.	V.G.	Good	Fair	Poor
1700	1500	1200	600	275	150

.32 Caliber, with Waffenampt Proofs, Milled Finish

NIB	Exc.	V.G.	Good	Fair	Poor
900	700	500	325	250	150

.32 Caliber, in Blue Finish and Full Coverage Engraving

NOTE: Add $500 for ivory grips. Add $700 for leather presentation cases. Add $1000 for .380 caliber.

NIB	Exc.	V.G.	Good	Fair	Poor
—	5000	4000	3000	1200	700

.32 Caliber, in Silver Finish and Full Coverage Engraving

NOTE: Add $500 for ivory grips. Add $700 for leather presentation cases. Add $1000 for .380 caliber.

NIB	Exc.	V.G.	Good	Fair	Poor
—	5500	4500	3000	1200	700

.32 Caliber, in Gold Finish and Full Coverage Engraving

NOTE: Add $500 for ivory grips. Add $700 for leather presentation cases. Add $1000 for .380 caliber.

NIB	Exc.	V.G.	Good	Fair	Poor
—	5800	5000	3500	1500	700

.32 Caliber, Police Eagle/C Proofed, High Polished Finish

NIB	Exc.	V.G.	Good	Fair	Poor
1600	1200	800	375	250	150

.32 Caliber, Police Eagle/C and Police Eagle/F Proofed, Milled Finish

NIB	Exc.	V.G.	Good	Fair	Poor
1000	900	600	375	275	150

.32 Caliber, NSKK Marked on the Slide

NOTE: Add $1,000 with proper NSKK DRGM AKAH holster.

NIB	Exc.	V.G.	Good	Fair	Poor
3500	3000	2700	850	550	300

.32 Caliber, NSDAP Gruppe Markings

NOTE: Add $1,000 with proper SA DRGM AKAH holster.

NIB	Exc.	V.G.	Good	Fair	Poor
2700	2500	2000	1000	500	300

.32 Caliber, PDM Marked with Bottom Magazine Release

NIB	Exc.	V.G.	Good	Fair	Poor
2400	2000	1500	1100	475	300

.32 Caliber, RJ Marked

NIB	Exc.	V.G.	Good	Fair	Poor
1400	900	700	475	400	150

.32 Caliber, RFV Marked, High Polished or Milled Finish

NIB	Exc.	V.G.	Good	Fair	Poor
1400	900	700	475	400	150

.32 Caliber, RBD Munster Marked

NIB	Exc.	V.G.	Good	Fair	Poor
2500	2200	1750	1200	650	400

.32 Caliber, RpLt Marked

NIB	Exc.	V.G.	Good	Fair	Poor
1650	1500	1200	700	375	200

.32 Caliber, Statens Vattenfallsverk Marked

NIB	Exc.	V.G.	Good	Fair	Poor
1650	1500	1200	700	375	200

.32 Caliber, AC Marked

NIB	Exc.	V.G.	Good	Fair	Poor
800	700	500	300	250	150

.32 Caliber, Duraluminum Frame

NIB	Exc.	V.G.	Good	Fair	Poor
1000	900	700	500	400	150

.380 Caliber, Bottom Magazine Release and Waffenampt Proofs

NIB	Exc.	V.G.	Good	Fair	Poor
2400	2000	1500	700	500	300

Model PPK

A semi-automatic pistol in .22, .25, .32 and .380 caliber. Introduced six months after the Model PP in 1929. A more compact version of the Model PP with one less round in the magazine and one-piece wraparound checkered plastic grips in brown, black, and white with the Walther banner on each side of the grips. The Model PPK will be found with the same types of finishes as the Model PP as well as the same styles of engraving. Grips in wood or ivory are seen with some of the engraved models. As with the Model PP there are many variations of the Model PPK and numerous NSDAP markings seen on the pre-1946 models that were produced during the Nazi regime. All reflect various prices.

Courtesy James Rankin

Courtesy Orvel Reichert

.22 Caliber

NIB	Exc.	V.G.	Good	Fair	Poor
1900	1700	1500	750	325	175

.25 Caliber

NIB	Exc.	V.G.	Good	Fair	Poor
8500	6000	4000	1850	1000	500

.32 Caliber, High Polished Finish

NIB	Exc.	V.G.	Good	Fair	Poor
1400	950	750	450	250	150

.32 Caliber, Milled Finish

NIB	Exc.	V.G.	Good	Fair	Poor
1300	900	700	400	250	150

.380 Caliber

Courtesy Orvel Reichert

NIB	Exc.	V.G.	Good	Fair	Poor
4250	3000	2500	1600	750	375

.32 Caliber, with Duraluminum Frame

NIB	Exc.	V.G.	Good	Fair	Poor
2000	1500	1300	600	400	200

.32 Caliber, Marked Mod. PP on Slide

NIB	Exc.	V.G.	Good	Fair	Poor
6000	5000	4000	2500	1500	1000

.32 Caliber, with Panagraphed Slide

NIB	Exc.	V.G.	Good	Fair	Poor
2000	1200	750	450	300	200

.32 Caliber, with Verchromt Finish

NIB	Exc.	V.G.	Good	Fair	Poor
3800	2800	2500	1200	700	350

.32 Caliber, in Blue Finish and Full Coverage Engraving

NOTE: Add $1,000 for ivory grips. Add $1,000 for leather presentation cases. Add $1,000 for .380 caliber.

NIB	Exc.	V.G.	Good	Fair	Poor
—	5000	3500	2500	1200	700

.32 Caliber, in Silver Finish and Full Coverage Engraving

NOTE: Add $1,000 for ivory grips. Add $1,000 for leather presentation cases. Add $1,000 for .380 caliber.

NIB	Exc.	V.G.	Good	Fair	Poor
—	6000	4000	3000	1500	700

.32 Caliber, in Gold Finish and Full Coverage Engraving

NOTE: Add $1,000 for ivory grips. Add $1,000 for leather presentation cases. Add $1,000 for .380 caliber.

NIB	Exc.	V.G.	Good	Fair	Poor
—	6500	5500	3500	1500	700

.32 Caliber, Czechoslovakian Contract

NIB	Exc.	V.G.	Good	Fair	Poor
2000	1850	1500	1000	550	300

.32 Caliber, Allemagne Marked

NIB	Exc.	V.G.	Good	Fair	Poor
1150	1000	800	600	400	250

.32 Caliber, with Waffenampt Proofs and a High Polished Finish

NIB	Exc.	V.G.	Good	Fair	Poor
2400	1900	1600	900	400	250

.32 Caliber, with Waffenampt Proofs and a Milled Finish

NIB	Exc.	V.G.	Good	Fair	Poor
1700	1500	1300	750	300	175

.32 Caliber, Police Eagle/C Proofed, High Polished Finish

NIB	Exc.	V.G.	Good	Fair	Poor
1500	1200	1000	500	300	175

.32 Caliber, Police Eagle/C Proofed. Milled Finish

NIB	Exc.	V.G.	Good	Fair	Poor
1100	900	700	375	275	175

.32 Caliber, Police Eagle/F Proofed, Duraluminum Frame, Milled Finish

NIB	Exc.	V.G.	Good	Fair	Poor
1600	1300	1000	550	350	225

.22 Caliber, Late War, Black Grips

NIB	Exc.	V.G.	Good	Fair	Poor
2400	1800	1500	600	450	300

.32 Caliber, Party Leader Grips, Brown

NIB	Exc.	V.G.	Good	Fair	Poor
8000	6000	5500	3000	2250	2000

.32 Caliber, Party Leader Grips, Black

NOTE: Add $1,500 with proper Party Leader DRGM AKAH holster.

NIB	Exc.	V.G.	Good	Fair	Poor
8000	6000	5500	3200	2550	2500

.32 Caliber, RZM Marked

NIB	Exc.	V.G.	Good	Fair	Poor
3000	2400	1700	800	400	300

.32 Caliber, PDM Marked with Duraluminum Frame and Bottom Magazine Release

NIB	Exc.	V.G.	Good	Fair	Poor
3500	3200	2800	1300	750	450

.32 Caliber, RFV Marked

NIB	Exc.	V.G.	Good	Fair	Poor
3000	2500	2000	1150	650	400

.32 Caliber, DRP Marked

NIB	Exc.	V.G.	Good	Fair	Poor
2800	2400	1800	1200	450	275

.32 Caliber, Statens Vattenfallsverk

NIB	Exc.	V.G.	Good	Fair	Poor
1700	1500	1200	700	450	300

WALTHER POST-WORLD WAR II

Manufactured by the firm of Manufacture de Machines du Haut Rhin at Mulhouse, France under license by Walther.

Model PP—Some with Duraluminum Frames

.22 Caliber

NIB	Exc.	V.G.	Good	Fair	Poor
850	750	600	400	275	175

.32 Caliber

NIB	Exc.	V.G.	Good	Fair	Poor
600	500	375	350	275	175

.380 Caliber

NIB	Exc.	V.G.	Good	Fair	Poor
850	750	600	400	275	175

Model PP—All Three Calibers Finished In Blue, Silver and Gold with Full Coverage Engraving

Blue

NIB	Exc.	V.G.	Good	Fair	Poor
—	1900	1500	900	600	300

Silver

NIB	Exc.	V.G.	Good	Fair	Poor
—	1900	1500	900	600	300

Gold

NIB	Exc.	V.G.	Good	Fair	Poor
—	1900	1500	900	600	300

Model PP Mark II

These Walthers were manufactured under license by Walther and produced by the Manurhin Company. They were sold exclusively by Interarms, Alexandria, Virginia. The Mark IIs were the same pistols as those above and have the same types of finish and engraving as well as the same value.

Model PP Manurhin

Manurhin Company manufactured with Manurhin logo and inscription. Usually "licensed by Walther" somewhere on the pistol. The same pistols as those above, bearing the same types of finish and engraving, and having the same values.

Model PP Sport, Manurhin

.22 caliber. This is the same gun as the Model PP with different barrel lengths running from 5-3/4" to 7-3/4". It is basically a target .22 with adjustable rear sights for elevation and windage. The front sight is also adjustable. There is a barrel bushing at the muzzle that attaches the front sight to the barrel. The grips are contoured checkered plastic and are either squared at the bottom of the grips or are in the shape of an inverted bird's-head.

NIB	Exc.	V.G.	Good	Fair	Poor
—	900	600	450	375	275

Model PP Sport C, Manurhin

.22 caliber. This is the same gun as the Model PP Sport but in single-action with a spur hammer. It has front and rear adjustable sights and squared target grips in checkered black, brown and plastic. Blued and silver finish.

NIB	Exc.	V.G.	Good	Fair	Poor
—	900	600	450	375	275

Model PP Sport, Walther

A .22 caliber Sport was manufactured by Manurhin, but sold by Walther with the Walther logo and inscription. This is the same gun as the Model PP Sport, Manurhin. Only sold for a period of two years.

NIB	Exc.	V.G.	Good	Fair	Poor
—	900	600	450	375	275

Model PP 50th Anniversary Commemorative Model

In .22 or .380 caliber. Blued with gold inlays and hand-carved grips with oak leaves and acorns. Walther banner carved into each side of the grips. Wood presentation case.

NIB	Exc.	V.G.	Good	Fair	Poor
—	1500	1000	750	500	300

Model PPK—Some with Duraluminum Frames

.22 Caliber

NIB	Exc.	V.G.	Good	Fair	Poor
—	750	600	400	275	175

.32 Caliber

NIB	Exc.	V.G.	Good	Fair	Poor
—	550	400	350	275	175

.380 Caliber

NIB	Exc.	V.G.	Good	Fair	Poor
—	750	600	400	275	175

Model PPK—All Three Calibers Finished In Blue, Silver and Gold With Full Coverage Engraving

Blue

NIB	Exc.	V.G.	Good	Fair	Poor
—	1900	1500	750	450	300

Silver

NIB	Exc.	V.G.	Good	Fair	Poor
—	1900	1500	750	450	300

Gold

NIB	Exc.	V.G.	Good	Fair	Poor
—	1900	1500	750	450	300

Model PPK Mark II

These Walthers were manufactured under license by Walther and produced by the Manurhin Company. They were sold exclusively by Interarms, Alexandria, Virginia. The Mark IIs were the same pistols as those above and have the same types of finish and engraving as well as the same value.

Model PPK Manurhin

Manurhin Company manufactured with Manurhin logo and inscription. Usually "Licensed by Walther" somewhere on the pistol. The same pistols as above, bearing the same types of finish and engraving, and having the same value.

Courtesy James Rankin

Model PPK 50th Anniversary Commemorative Model

In .22 or .380 caliber. Blued with gold inlays and hand-carved grips with oak leaves and acorns. Walther banner carved into each side of the grips. Wood presentation case.

NIB	Exc.	V.G.	Good	Fair	Poor
—	2100	1800	1250	1000	500

Model PPK American

In 1986 the Model PPK was licensed by the Walther Company to be manufactured in the United States. The finish is stainless steel. Caliber is .380.

NIB	Exc.	V.G.	Good	Fair	Poor
—	500	375	300	200	150

Model PPK/S

This Walther was manufactured in .22, .32 and .380 caliber for sale in the United States market after the introduction of the United States Gun Control Act of 1968. It is basically a Model PP with a cut-off muzzle and slide. It has two-piece black checkered plastic grips as seen on the Model PP. It was finished in blue, nickel, dull gold and verchromt.

NIB	Exc.	V.G.	Good	Fair	Poor
—	550	475	375	300	200

Model PPK/S American

Manufactured in the United States. The same as the German Model PPK/S. This pistol is finished in blue and stainless steel. Caliber is .380.

NIB	Exc.	V.G.	Good	Fair	Poor
—	500	375	300	200	150

Model TP

A Walther-manufactured semi-automatic pistol in .22 and .25 calibers patterned after the earlier Model 9. Finish is blue and silver black plastic checkered grips with Walther banner medallions in each grip.

NIB	Exc.	V.G.	Good	Fair	Poor
—	900	700	500	375	250

Model TPH

A Walther-manufactured semi-automatic pistol in .22 and .25 calibers. This is a double-action pistol with a duraluminum frame. Finished in blue or silver. Two-piece black checkered plastic grips. Full coverage engraving available. **NOTE:** Add $300 for the engraved model.

NIB	Exc.	V.G.	Good	Fair	Poor
—	650	500	450	350	250

Model TPH American

This semi-automatic is produced in both .22 and .25 calibers. It is licensed by Walther and manufactured in the United States. It is produced in stainless steel and has two-piece black plastic checkered grips. It is a double-action pistol.

NIB	Exc.	V.G.	Good	Fair	Poor
—	400	300	200	150	100

Model PP Super

This is a .380 and 9x18 caliber, double-action semi-automatic manufactured by Walther. It is similar in design to the Model PP, but with a P.38 type of mechanism. Finish is blue and the grips are wraparound black checkered plastic or a type of molded wood colored plastic.

Courtesy Orvel Reichert

NIB	Exc.	V.G.	Good	Fair	Poor
—	750	500	350	250	150

Model P.38

Following WWII, the P.38 was reintroduced in variety of calibers with a 5" barrel and alloy or steel frame.

.22 Caliber

NIB	Exc.	V.G.	Good	Fair	Poor
1200	850	650	500	350	200

Other Calibers

NIB	Exc.	V.G.	Good	Fair	Poor
750	600	500	400	300	200

Steel-Framed (Introduced 1987)

Factory-engraved versions of the P.38 pistol were blued, chrome, or silver or gold-plated. We suggest that a qualified appraisal be secured when contemplating purchase.

NIB	Exc.	V.G.	Good	Fair	Poor
1400	1250	1000	750	500	400

Model P.38K

As above, with a 2.8" barrel and front sight is mounted on the slide. Imported between 1974 and 1980.

NIB	Exc.	V.G.	Good	Fair	Poor
—	900	650	450	300	200

Model P.38 II

NIB	Exc.	V.G.	Good	Fair	Poor
—	800	550	350	250	200

Model P.38 IV

A redesigned version of the above, with a 4.5" barrel and 8-shot magazine. Fitted with a decocking lever and adjustable sights. Imported prior to 1983.

NIB	Exc.	V.G.	Good	Fair	Poor
—	900	650	450	300	200

CURRENTLY IMPORTED WALTHER HANDGUNS—WALTHER USA

In 1999 Carl Walther Gmbh of Germany and Smith & Wesson entered into a joint agreement to import and distribute Walther-branded firearms and accessories into the U.S. beginning August 1, 1999.

Model PP Limited Edition

This model was introduced in 2000 and is a limited edition of 100 pistols chambered in .380 ACP and 50 pistols chambered in .32 ACP. The finish is a high-polish blue with the slide marked "LAST EDITION 1929-1999." Supplied with a special case with certificate and video of history of Walther.

NIB	Exc.	V.G.	Good	Fair	Poor
1350	1100	900	700	500	300

Model PPK/E—Walther USA

Introduced in 2000 this pistol is chambered for the .380 or .32 ACP cartridges and later in that year the .22 LR. It has a double-action trigger. Produced in Hungary by Walther. Barrel length is 3.4". Magazine capacity is seven rounds for the .380 and eight rounds for the .32 ACP and .22 LR. Blued finish and plastic grips.

NIB	Exc.	V.G.	Good	Fair	Poor
400	325	250	195	125	75

Model PPK

Chambered for the .380 ACP or .32 ACP cartridge and fitted with a 3.35" barrel. Offered in blue or stainless steel. Black plastic grips. Fixed red-dot sights. Magazine capacity is six for the .380 ACP and seven for the .32 ACP. Weight is about 21 oz.

NIB	Exc.	V.G.	Good	Fair	Poor
550	425	300	250	175	75

Model PPK/S

Same as the PPK but with .25" longer grip. Magazine capacity is seven rounds for the .380 ACP and eight rounds for the .32 ACP. Weight is about 23 oz. Offered in blue, stainless steel and two-tone finish.

NIB	Exc.	V.G.	Good	Fair	Poor
550	425	300	250	175	75

Model PPS

Striker-fired compact DAO semi-auto pistol. Chambered in .40 S&W (6 rounds) or 9mm Parabellum (7 rounds). Features include polymer frame and grip, decocker button, loaded chamber indicator, 3.2-inch stainless steel barrel, integral Weaver-style accessory rail, black Tenifer finish overall.

NIB	Exc.	V.G.	Good	Fair	Poor
625	535	450	350	250	150

Seventy-fifth Anniversary PPK

Blued with wood grips, machine engraving and available in .380 ACP with 6+1 capacity. Special SN beginning with 0000PPK, shipped with glass-top display case. Single/double-action, 3.3" barrel, 20.8 oz. Windage-adjustable rear sight. Introduced 2006.

NIB	Exc.	V.G.	Good	Fair	Poor
800	700	600	400	—	—

Model P5

A 9mm semi-automatic pistol with a double-action firing mechanism. One of the first Walthers to have a decocker lever. Finish is a combination of black matte and high polish. It has black plastic checkered grips.

NIB	Exc.	V.G.	Good	Fair	Poor
1350	1000	750	500	300	200

Model P5, Compact

A shorter version of the standard Model P5.

NIB	Exc.	V.G.	Good	Fair	Poor
1450	1100	850	600	375	250

Model P5 One Hundred Year Commemorative

Blued with gold inlays and hand-carved grips with oak leaves and acorns. Walther banner carved into each side of the grips.

NIB	Exc.	V.G.	Good	Fair	Poor
2750	1950	1600	1000	750	400

Model P88

A 9mm semi-automatic in double-action with ambidextrous decocking lever. Fifteen-shot magazine and two-piece black checkered plastic grips. Combination of high polish and black matte finish.

NIB	Exc.	V.G.	Good	Fair	Poor
1700	1525	1275	975	700	400

Model P88 Compact

A shorter version of the standard Model P88.

NIB	Exc.	V.G.	Good	Fair	Poor
1600	1425	1135	850	600	400

Model P99

Introduced in 1997, this is a single- and double-action design with a 4" barrel and polymer frame. Chambered for 9mm or .40 S&W cartridge it has a magazine capacity of 10 rounds (16 rounds in 9mm and 12 rounds in .40 S&W for law enforcement). Front sight is interchangeable and rear sight is windage adjustable. Total length of pistol is 7" and weight is approximately 25 oz. Finish is blue tenifer.

NIB	Exc.	V.G.	Good	Fair	Poor
800	700	550	450	300	200

Model P99 Compact AS/QA

This model is chambered for the 9mm cartridge with a double action trigger and 9mm or .40 S&W cartridges. Quick action, striker fired. Barrel length is 3.5" with fixed sights. Magazine capacity is 10 rounds for 9mm and 8 rounds for .40 S&W models. Weight is about 19 oz.

NIB	Exc.	V.G.	Good	Fair	Poor
675	575	400	325	200	175

Model P990

A double-action-only version of the P99.

NIB	Exc.	V.G.	Good	Fair	Poor
675	550	400	325	200	175

Model P99 QPQ

Similar to the P99 but with silver tenifer finish.

NIB	Exc.	V.G.	Good	Fair	Poor
750	625	475	375	275	250

Model P990 QPQ

A double-action-only version of the P99 QPQ.

NIB	Exc.	V.G.	Good	Fair	Poor
750	625	475	375	275	250

Model P99 QA

Similar to the P99 pistol but with a constant short trigger pull. Trigger pull is approximately 6.5 lbs. Offered in both 9mm and .40 S&W calibers. Introduced in 2000.

NIB	Exc.	V.G.	Good	Fair	Poor
675	575	400	325	200	175

Model P99 Military

Similar to the P99 but with military finish.

NIB	Exc.	V.G.	Good	Fair	Poor
675	575	400	325	200	175

Model P99 La Chasse DU

This model features laser engraving on the blue tenifer slide.

NIB	Exc.	V.G.	Good	Fair	Poor
750	625	475	375	275	250

Model P99 La Chasse

.This model features hand engraving on a gray tenifer slide.

NIB	Exc.	V.G.	Good	Fair	Poor
1675	1350	1100	750	500	300

Model P99 Commemorative

This is a limited edition P99 that features a high polish blue slide with a special serial number and the marking" COMMEMORATIVE FOR THE YEAR 2000." Offered in both 9mm and .40 S&W calibers. Each handgun comes with a special certificate and video of the history of Walther.

NIB	Exc.	V.G.	Good	Fair	Poor
750	625	475	375	275	250

Walther PPQ

Caliber: 9mm Parabellum or .40 S&W. Steel slide, polymer frame with interchangeable backstraps. Magazine capacity, 15/12 (9mm) and 17/14 (.40). Other features include front slide serrations, Quick Defense Trigger with integral safety, ambidextrous slide and magazine release, adjustable rear sight and loaded-chamber indicator. Weight is 24.5 ounces, barrel length is 4.0-inches, finish matte black.

NIB	Exc.	V.G.	Good	Fair	Poor
625	525	450	380	325	200

Model P22 Standard

Introduced in 2002 this .22 caliber pistol is chambered for the LR cartridge. Barrel length is 3.4". Polymer frame with double-action trigger. Adjustable rear sight. Magazine capacity is 10 rounds. Weight is about 20 oz.

NOTE: In 2003 this model was offered with a military black slide and green frame or a silver slide with black frame. A carbon fiber-framed model is also available at about the same price as standard models. Barrels are interchangeable on both P22 pistols.

P22 with laser, laser optional

NIB	Exc.	V.G.	Good	Fair	Poor
400	325	250	200	150	75

Model P22 Target

Similar to the standard P22 model but with a 5" barrel with barrel weight. Weight is about 21 oz.

NIB	Exc.	V.G.	Good	Fair	Poor
425	350	275	225	175	75

Model FP

A .22 LR caliber, single-shot target pistol that fires electrically. It has micro-adjustable electric firing system along with micrometer sights and contoured wooden grips that are adjustable. The barrel is 11.7" and the finish is blued.

NIB	Exc.	V.G.	Good	Fair	Poor
—	2000	1600	1000	500	400

Model GSP

A semi-automatic target pistol in .22 LR and .32 calibers. This target pistol has a 4-1/2" barrel, 5-shot magazine and contoured wood target grips. Blued finish and sold with attache extra barrel, case and accessories.

Courtesy John J. Stimson, Jr.

NIB	Exc.	V.G.	Good	Fair	Poor
—	1600	1200	750	650	300

Model GSP-C

Almost the same pistol as the Model GSP, but in .32 caliber S&W wadcutter.

NIB	Exc.	V.G.	Good	Fair	Poor
—	1500	1100	750	650	300

Model OSP

A .22 Short semi-automatic target pistol that is similar to the Model GSP. This pistol is made for rapid fire target shooting. Blued finish with contoured wood grips.

Custom engraved OSP

NIB	Exc.	V.G.	Good	Fair	Poor
—	1800	1200	750	650	300

Free Pistol

A .22 caliber single-shot target pistol with an 11.7" barrel, micrometer sights, adjustable grips and an electronic trigger. Blued.

NIB	Exc.	V.G.	Good	Fair	Poor
1900	1600	1200	900	700	550

Model R99

This 6-shot revolver is chambered for the .357 Magnum cartridge. Barrel length is 3". Weight is about 28 oz. Offered in blue or stainless steel. Introduced in 1999. Said to be a close ringer for the S&W M19 but with different grips.

NIB	Exc.	V.G.	Good	Fair	Poor
1500	1300	1100	950	700	500

Model SP22-M1

.22 LR autoloader with aluminum frame and 4-inch barrel.

NIB	Exc.	V.G.	Good	Fair	Poor
400	325	350	150	100	75

Model SP22-M2

Similar to above but with a 6-inch barrel.

NIB	Exc.	V.G.	Good	Fair	Poor
400	325	250	150	100	75

Model SP22-M3

Similar to above but with match-grade barrel and adjustable trigger.

NIB	Exc.	V.G.	Good	Fair	Poor
475	400	325	200	150	100

Model SP22-M4

Similar to above but with wooden free-style grip assembly.

NIB	Exc.	V.G.	Good	Fair	Poor
750	675	550	400	250	150

RIFLES

Model B

A .30-06 caliber bolt-action rifle with a 22" barrel, 4-shot magazine and single or double set triggers. Double set triggers are worth approximately 20 percent more than the values listed. Blued with a walnut stock.

NIB	Exc.	V.G.	Good	Fair	Poor
—	775	700	450	250	175

Olympic Single-Shot

A .22 caliber bolt-action rifle with a 26" barrel, adjustable target sights and a walnut stock fitted with a palm rest and adjustable buttplate. Blued.

NIB	Exc.	V.G.	Good	Fair	Poor
—	1150	950	800	500	400

Model V

A .22 caliber single-shot bolt-action rifle with a 26" barrel and adjustable sights. Blued with a plain walnut stock. Manufactured before WWII.

NIB	Exc.	V.G.	Good	Fair	Poor
—	550	450	300	200	150

Model V Champion

As above, with a checkered walnut stock.

NIB	Exc.	V.G.	Good	Fair	Poor
—	600	500	350	250	200

Model KKM International Match

A .22 caliber single-shot bolt-action rifle with a 28" barrel and adjustable sights. Blued with a walnut stock fitted for a palm rest and with an adjustable buttplate. Manufactured after WWII.

NIB	Exc.	V.G.	Good	Fair	Poor
—	1550	1275	850	450	350

Model KKM-S

As above, with an adjustable cheekpiece.

NIB	Exc.	V.G.	Good	Fair	Poor
—	1625	1350	850	500	400

Model KKW

As above, with a military-style stock.

NIB	Exc.	V.G.	Good	Fair	Poor
—	1250	975	600	250	175

Model KKJ Sporter

A .22 caliber bolt action rifle with a 22.5" barrel and 5-shot magazine. Blued with a checkered walnut stock. This model was available with double set triggers and their presence would add approximately 20 percent to the values listed. Manufactured after WWII.

NIB	Exc.	V.G.	Good	Fair	Poor
—	900	800	550	350	300

Model KKJ-MA

As above, in .22 Magnum rimfire.

NIB	Exc.	V.G.	Good	Fair	Poor
—	850	750	550	350	300

Model KKJ-HO

As above, in .22 Hornet.

NIB	Exc.	V.G.	Good	Fair	Poor
—	950	850	650	450	350

Model SSV Varmint

A .22 caliber bolt-action single-shot rifle with a 25.5" barrel not fitted with sights and Monte Carlo-style stock. Blued. Manufactured after WWII.

NIB	Exc.	V.G.	Good	Fair	Poor
—	700	600	475	375	300

Model UIT BV Universal

As above, with adjustable target sights and a walnut stock fitted with a palm rest and adjustable buttplate.

NIB	Exc.	V.G.	Good	Fair	Poor
1750	1500	1250	900	650	500

Model UIT Match

As above, with a stippled pistol grip and fore-end. Also available with an electronic trigger that would add approximately $50 to the values listed.

NIB	Exc.	V.G.	Good	Fair	Poor
1350	1100	800	600	450	400

GX 1

As above, with an adjustable Free Rifle stock.

NIB	Exc.	V.G.	Good	Fair	Poor
2250	2000	1750	1250	850	700

Prone Model 400

Target rifle in .22 caliber with a prone position stock.

NIB	Exc.	V.G.	Good	Fair	Poor
800	700	600	450	350	300

Model KK/MS Silhouette

A .22 caliber bolt-action rifle with a 25.5" front-weighted barrel furnished without sights and a thumbhole stock with an adjustable buttplate. Introduced in 1984.

NIB	Exc.	V.G.	Good	Fair	Poor
1300	1100	850	700	550	400

Running Boar Model 500

As above, with a 23.5" barrel.

NIB	Exc.	V.G.	Good	Fair	Poor
1550	1350	950	750	600	450

Model WA-2000

A .300 Winchester Magnum or .308 caliber bolt-action sporting rifle produced on custom order. Imported prior to 1989.

NIB	Exc.	V.G.	Good	Fair	Poor
30000	25000	20000	—	—	—

Model G22

This is a .22 caliber rifle with a 20" barrel with adjustable sights. This model features a cocking indicator, integrated lock, slide safety, and multi function rail. Black or green finish. Weight is about 6 lbs. This model is also sold as a package.

NIB	Exc.	V.G.	Good	Fair	Poor
450	350	225	175	125	100

Package A1 with Walther rifle scope

NIB	Exc.	V.G.	Good	Fair	Poor
500	400	275	225	175	150

Package A2 with laser

NIB	Exc.	V.G.	Good	Fair	Poor
500	400	275	225	175	150

Package A3 with Walther rifle scope & laser

NIB	Exc.	V.G.	Good	Fair	Poor
500	400	275	225	175	150

Package A4 with Walther PS22 red-dot sight

NIB	Exc.	V.G.	Good	Fair	Poor
500	400	275	225	175	150

SHOTGUNS

Model SF

A 12 or 16 gauge boxlock double-barrel shotgun fitted with double triggers and extractors. Blued with a checkered walnut stock fitted with sling swivels.

NIB	Exc.	V.G.	Good	Fair	Poor
—	1150	900	750	600	450

Model SFD

As above, with the stock having a cheekpiece.

NIB	Exc.	V.G.	Good	Fair	Poor
—	1150	900	750	600	450

WALTHER MANURHIN
Mulhouse, France

The Manurhin-manufactured Walther pistols are listed in the Walther section under their respective model headings.

WARNANT, L. AND J.
Ognee, Belgium

Revolver

Modeled after pistols manufactured by Smith & Wesson, the Warnants produced a variety of revolvers in .32, .38, or .45 caliber, between 1870 and 1890.

NIB	Exc.	V.G.	Good	Fair	Poor
—	—	250	175	100	50

Semi-Automatic Pistol

A 6.35mm semi-automatic pistol with a 2.5" barrel and 5-shot magazine. The slide marked "L&J Warnant Bte 6.35mm." Blued with black plastic grips bearing the monogram "L&JW." Manufactured after 1908.

NIB	Exc.	V.G.	Good	Fair	Poor
—	350	200	150	100	75

1912 Model

A 7.65mm caliber semi-automatic pistol with a 3" barrel and 7-shot magazine. The slide marked "L&J Warnant Brevetes Pist Auto 7.65mm." Manufactured prior to 1915.

NIB	Exc.	V.G.	Good	Fair	Poor
—	350	200	150	100	75

WARNER ARMS CORPORATION
Brooklyn, New York and Norwich, Connecticut

Established in 1912, this firm marketed revolvers, rifles, semi-automatic pistols and shotguns made for them by other companies (including N.R. Davis & Sons, Ithaca Gun Company and so forth). In 1917, the company was purchased by N.R. Davis & Company. See also Davis-Warner. The arms marketed by Warner prior to 1917 are listed.

SHOTGUNS

Single Trigger Hammerless Utica Special Double-Barrel

In 12 gauge with 28", 30", or 32" barrels.

Double Trigger Hammerless Double-Barrel

In 12 or 16 gauge with 28", 30", or 32" barrels.

Grade X, SF, XT, SFT, XD and XDF Hammer Guns

In 12, 16 or 20 gauge with 28", 30", or 32" barrels.

Field Grade Hammer Gun

In 12 or 16 gauge with 28" or 30" barrels.

Boxlock Hammerless

In 12 or 16 gauge with 28", 30", or 32" barrels.

RIFLES

Number 522

A .22 caliber single-shot rifle with an 18" barrel.

Number 532

A .32 caliber single-shot rifle with an 18" barrel.

REVOLVERS

Double-Action

.32 and .38 caliber with 4" or 5" barrels.

Double-Action Hammerless

.32 and .38 caliber with 4" or 5" barrels.

SEMI-AUTOMATIC PISTOLS

"Faultless" : Warner-Schwarzlose Model C, .32 ACP

NIB	Exc.	V.G.	Good	Fair	Poor
—	—	500	300	200	100

WARNER, CHAS.
Windsor Locks, Connecticut

Pocket Revolver

A .31 caliber percussion revolver with a 3" round barrel and 6-shot unfluted cylinder. The cylinder marked "Charles Warner. Windsor Locks, Conn." Blued with walnut grips. Approximately 600 were made between 1857 and 1860.

NIB	Exc.	V.G.	Good	Fair	Poor
—	—	1625	1300	500	100

WARNER, JAMES
Springfield, Massachusetts

Revolving Carbines

A variety of revolving carbines were made by this maker, nearly all of which are of .40 caliber, with octagonal barrels measuring 20" to 24" in length. The most commonly encountered variations are listed.

Manually Revolved Grooved Cylinder

This model is fitted with two triggers, one of which is a release so that the cylinder can be manually turned. Not fitted with a loading lever. The top strap marked "James Warner/Springfield, Mass." Approximately 75 were made in 1849.

Courtesy Milwaukee Public Museum, Milwaukee, Wisconsin

NIB	Exc.	V.G.	Good	Fair	Poor
—	—	7500	4700	2200	500

Retractable Cylinder Model

This version has a cylinder that fits over the breech, and it must be retracted before it can be manually rotated. The cylinder release is a button located in front of the trigger. It is marked "James Warner/Springfield Mass" and with an eagle over the letters "U.S." The cylinder is etched, and there is no loading lever. It also has a walnut stock with patch box and no forearm. There were approximately 25 manufactured in 1849.

NIB	Exc.	V.G.	Good	Fair	Poor
—	—	9500	6900	3000	800

Automatic Revolving Cylinder

The cylinder is automatically turned when the hammer is cocked. This model is fitted with a loading lever and is marked "Warner's Patent/Jan. 1851" and "Springfield Arms Co." Approximately 200 were made during the 1850s.

Courtesy Milwaukee Public Museum, Milwaukee, Wisconsin

NIB	Exc.	V.G.	Good	Fair	Poor
—	—	7500	4700	1900	500

Belt Revolver

A .31 caliber double-action percussion revolver with a 4" or 5" round barrel and 6-shot etched cylinder. Blued with walnut grips. No markings appear on this model except for the serial number. Manufactured in 1851.

Courtesy Milwaukee Public Museum, Milwaukee, Wisconsin

NIB	Exc.	V.G.	Good	Fair	Poor
—	—	2100	1650	675	100

Pocket Revolver

A .28 caliber percussion revolver with a 3" octagonal barrel marked "James Warner, Springfield, Mass., USA" and a 6-shot cylinder. Blued with walnut grips. Approximately 500 were made.

NIB	Exc.	V.G.	Good	Fair	Poor
—	—	1050	725	275	100

Second Model

As above, with either a 3" or 4" barrel and marked "Warner's Patent 1857."

Courtesy Wallis & Wallis, Lewes, Sussex, England

NIB	Exc.	V.G.	Good	Fair	Poor
—	—	1100	750	325	100

Third Model

As above, but in .31 caliber.

NIB	Exc.	V.G.	Good	Fair	Poor
—	—	1000	650	300	100

Single-Shot Derringer

A .41 caliber rimfire single-shot pocket pistol with a 2.75" round barrel, brass frame and walnut grips. As this model is unmarked, it can only be identified by the large breechblock which lifts upward and to the left for loading.

NIB	Exc.	V.G.	Good	Fair	Poor
—	—	22500	19000	7250	1000

Pocket Revolver

A .30 caliber rimfire revolver with a 3" barrel marked "Warner's Patent 1857" and 5-shot cylinder. Blued or nickel-plated with walnut grips. Approximately 1,000 were made during the late 1860s.

NIB	Exc.	V.G.	Good	Fair	Poor
—	—	975	600	165	75

WEATHERBY
Paso Robles, California

This company was founded by Roy Weatherby in 1945 in South Gate, California. His original rifles were custom guns made to order on Mauser actions. In 1956 he contracted with both Sako and Schultz & Larsen to manufacture complete rifles, while he continued to make custom guns in California. In 1958, Weatherby introduced his Mark V action, which was designed to handle the high pressures of his proprietary cartridges. The Mark V action was made in the U.S. with the rifles assembled and finished in the Weatherby shop in South Gate. The Mark V featured a very modern stock design with a glossy finish, a high comb for scope use and contrasting grip and fore-end caps. Beginning in 1959, the rifles were made in what was then West Germany. In 1972 production was moved to Japan, where the rifles were made until 1995. Since that year, Weatherby rifles have all been made in the U.S. The barreled action for the Mark V is made by ATEK in Brainerd, Minnesota and the action for the Vanguard is made by Howa in Japan. Both the Mark V and the Vanguard are assembled in the Paso Robles, California Weatherby shop. For many years, Weatherby shotguns were made in Japan or Italy. Current models are made in Turkey.

Mark V

This is a deluxe, bolt-action repeating rifle chambered for various popular standard calibers, as well as the full line of Weatherby cartridges from .240 Weatherby Magnum to .300 Weatherby Magnum. It is furnished with either a 24" or 26" barrel without sights. It has either a 3- or 5-round magazine, depending on the caliber. It has a deluxe, high-polish blued finish with a select, skip-line checkered walnut stock with a rosewood forearm tip and pistol grip cap. This rifle is available with a left-hand action.

NIB	Exc.	V.G.	Good	Fair	Poor
1200	1050	800	600	500	250

Weatherby Mark V Deluxe

Stepped-up version of classic Mark V. Features include deluxe Claro walnut Monte Carlo stock with rosewood for-end, 26" or 28" high-polish blued sightless barrel. Chambered in .257, .270, 7mm, .300, .30-378, .340, .378, .416 and .460 Weatherby Magnum. Also available in short-action model in .22-250, .243 Win., .240 Weatherby, .25-06, .270 Win., 7mm-08, .280 Rem., .308 Win., .30-06. **NOTE:** Add 25 percent for .30-378 Weatherby Magnum.

NIB	Exc.	V.G.	Good	Fair	Poor
2000	1500	1300	1075	800	350

Mark V Sporter

Introduced in 1993 this model is identical to the Mark V Deluxe without the custom features. The metal is a low luster finish, the stock is Claro walnut with high gloss finish. A Monte Carlo comb with raised cheekpiece and black 1" recoil pad are standard features on this model. Available in Weatherby calibers from .257 through .340 plus .270 Win., .30-06, 7mm Rem. Mag., .300 Win Mag., .338 Win. Mag. Weighs 8 to 8.5 lbs. depending on caliber.

NIB	Exc.	V.G.	Good	Fair	Poor
1100	950	800	650	500	300

Mark V .375 Weatherby Magnum

This version was manufactured in Germany only and is chambered for the currently obsolete .375 Weatherby Magnum cartridge. This version has become very collectible.

NIB	Exc.	V.G.	Good	Fair	Poor
5000	3500	3000	2500	2000	1500

Mark V .378 Weatherby Magnum

This version is chambered for the .378 Weatherby Magnum cartridge. It is furnished with a 26" barrel only. **NOTE:** For German guns in this caliber add 50 percent.

NIB	Exc.	V.G.	Good	Fair	Poor
2000	1825	1550	1200	850	500

Mark V .416 Weatherby Magnum

This is an extremely powerful rifle suitable for hunting the biggest game. It was introduced in 1989.

NIB	Exc.	V.G.	Good	Fair	Poor
2000	1825	1550	1200	850	500

Mark V .460 Weatherby Magnum

This is said to be the most powerful commercial rifle available in the world, with the possible exception of some of the recently-reintroduced British nitro chamberings. It is available with a 24" or 26" heavy barrel with an integral, recoil-reducing muzzlebrake. It has a custom reinforced stock. **NOTE:** For German guns in this caliber add 100 percent.

NIB	Exc.	V.G.	Good	Fair	Poor
2500	2200	1850	1500	1000	600

Mark V Dangerous Game Rifle

This model was introduced in 2001 and features a synthetic stock with Monte Carlo and 24" or 26" barrel with barrel band and hooded front sight depending on caliber. Chambered for the .378 Weatherby Mag., .416 Weatherby Mag., and the .460 Weatherby Mag. Adjustable trigger. Weight is between 8.74 and 9.5 lbs. depending on caliber. In 2003 the .458 Lott was offered for this model.

NIB	Exc.	V.G.	Good	Fair	Poor
2500	2200	1850	1500	1000	600

Mark V Euromark

This model features a hand-checkered, oil-finished, Claro walnut stock with an ebony fore-end tip and pistol grip cap. It has a satin blued finish. It was introduced in 1986.

NIB	Exc.	V.G.	Good	Fair	Poor
1500	1300	1050	800	575	350

Mark V Fluted Stainless

Introduced late in 1996 this model features a fluted stainless steel barrel chambered for the .257 Weatherby Magnum to the .300 Weatherby Magnum calibers as well as the 7mm Rem. Mag. and the .300 Win. Mag. The stock is synthetic with raised comb and checkered stock. Weight varies depending on caliber.

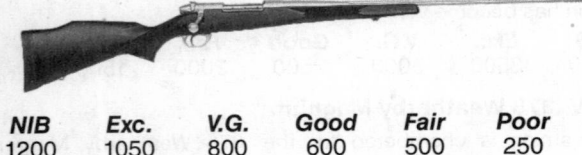

NIB	Exc.	V.G.	Good	Fair	Poor
1200	1050	800	600	500	250

Mark V Fluted Synthetic

This model is similar to the above model with a blued carbon steel action and barrel with synthetic stock. Introduced late in 1996.

NIB	Exc.	V.G.	Good	Fair	Poor
1000	850	650	450	400	200

Mark V SLS

This model features a stainless steel barreled action with laminated wood stock fitted with a 1" black recoil pad. Rifle is chambered for .257 through .340 Weatherby Magnum calibers as well as 7mm Rem. Mag., .300 and .338 Win. Mag., and the .375 H&H Mag. Weight is about 8.25 lbs. depending on caliber. Introduced in late 1996.

NIB	Exc.	V.G.	Good	Fair	Poor
1200	1050	800	600	500	250

Mark V Varmint

This version is chambered for the .22-250 and the .224 Weatherby cartridge. It is offered with a 24" or 26" heavy barrel. **NOTE:** For German built add 50 percent.

NIB	Exc.	V.G.	Good	Fair	Poor
975	800	750	550	450	400

Mark V Lazermark

This version had a laser-carved pattern on the stock and forearm in place of the usual checkering. It was introduced in 1985.

NIB	Exc.	V.G.	Good	Fair	Poor
2000	1750	1500	1100	600	300

Mark V Fibermark Composite

This version has a matte blue finish and is furnished with a synthetic black, wrinkle-finished stock. Chambered for calibers from .22-250 to .375 H&H with barrel lengths from 24" to 26" depending on caliber.

NIB	Exc.	V.G.	Good	Fair	Poor
1250	1000	800	550	400	250

Mark V Ultramark

This is a custom-finished version with a glass-bedded action and a special, high-polish blue. The action is hand-honed, and the walnut stock features basket weave checkering. It was introduced in 1989.

NIB	Exc.	V.G.	Good	Fair	Poor
2400	2000	1650	1200	800	500

Mark V Accumark

Introduced in 1995 this rifle features a Mark V Magnum action. The trigger is preset at the factory for 3.5 lbs. of pull. It is fully adjustable for sear engagement at let-off weight. The action metal is black oxide coated with a bead blast matte finish. The stainless steel barrel is 26" in length with a low luster brushed finish. Weight is approximately 8 lbs. and is offered in caliber from .257 to .340 Weatherby Magnum, 7mm Rem. Magnum, and .300 Win. Magnum. The company announced that this model would also be offered in the .30-.378 Weatherby caliber. In 1997 this model was offered chambered for the 7mm STW cartridge.

Mark V Accumark

NIB	Exc.	V.G.	Good	Fair	Poor
1400	1100	950	800	500	300

Mark V Accumark Left-Hand

This is a left-hand version of the Accumark. Introduced in 1999.

NIB	Exc.	V.G.	Good	Fair	Poor
1400	1100	950	800	500	300

35th Anniversary Commemorative Mark V

This specially embellished rifle commemorated the 35th anniversary of the company. There were 1,000 produced in 1980. As with all commemoratives, it must be NIB with all furnished materials to be worth top dollar.

NIB	Exc.	V.G.	Good	Fair	Poor
1600	1300	1050	750	500	350

1984 Olympic Commemorative Mark V

This is a specially embellished Mark V rifle that has gold-plated accents and an exhibition-grade walnut stock with a star inlay. There were 1,000 manufactured in 1984. This is a commemorative rifle and must be NIB to bring premium value.

NIB	Exc.	V.G.	Good	Fair	Poor
1600	1300	1050	750	500	350

Safari Grade Mark V

This is a custom-order version that is available chambered from the .300 Weatherby Magnum through the .460 Weatherby Magnum. It is available with a number of custom options and can be ordered with an 8- to 10-month delivery delay.

NIB	Exc.	V.G.	Good	Fair	Poor
4500	3500	2750	2000	1200	600

Crown Grade Mark V

This is Weatherby's best-grade rifle and is available on a custom-order basis only. It features an engraved receiver and barrel with an exhibition-grade, hand-checkered walnut stock. It is also furnished with an engraved scope mount.

NIB	Exc.	V.G.	Good	Fair	Poor
8000	7000	5500	4000	1500	500

Mark V Super Varmint Master (SVM)

Introduced in 2000 this model features a 26" stainless steel barrel. The stock is laminated with Monte Carlo comb. Fully adjustable trigger. Chambered for .220 Swift, .223 Rem., .22-250, .243 Win., 7mm-08, and .308 Win. Also offered in a single-shot configuration. Weight is about 8.5 lbs.

NIB	Exc.	V.G.	Good	Fair	Poor
1675	1400	1200	900	600	350

Mark V Special Varmint Rifle (SVR)

Introduced in 2003 this model features a 22" Krieger heavy barrel, a Monte Carlo composite stock, a black recoil pad and matte black finish. Adjustable trigger is standard. Available in .223 Rem. and .22-250. Weight is approximately 7.25 lbs.

NIB	Exc.	V.G.	Good	Fair	Poor
1100	1000	800	700	500	300

MARK V LIGHTWEIGHT RIFLES
Mark V Synthetic Lightweight

Chambered in calibers from .22-250 to .308 Win. fitted with a 24" barrel. Synthetic stock with Monte Carlo comb. Magazine capacity is 5 rounds. Weight is approximately 6.5 lbs. A carbine version is offered with 20" barrel in .243, 7mm-08, and .308. Weight is about 6 lbs.

NIB	Exc.	V.G.	Good	Fair	Poor
900	750	600	475	350	250

Mark V Stainless Lightweight

Similar to the model above but with stainless steel barrel and action. Weight is about 6.5 lbs. Carbine version also available.

NIB	Exc.	V.G.	Good	Fair	Poor
1100	950	800	650	525	300

Mark V Sporter Lightweight

Chambered for calibers ranging from .22-250 to .308 Win. and fitted with a 24" barrel. Stock is Claro walnut with Monte Carlo comb. Weight is approximately 6.75 lbs.

NIB	Exc.	V.G.	Good	Fair	Poor
1050	900	750	600	475	250

Mark V Accumark Lightweight

Chambered for calibers from .22-250 to .300 Wby. and fitted with a 24" barrel. Magazine capacity is 5 rounds. Special laminated synthetic stock. Weight is approximately 7 lbs. Introduced in 1998.

NIB	Exc.	V.G.	Good	Fair	Poor
1250	1000	900	800	650	400

Mark V Ultra Lightweight

Similar to the above model but with lightened components. Calibers begin with .243 and go to .300 Wby. Fitted with a 24" or 26" barrel depending on caliber. Weight is about 5.75 lbs. Introduced in 1998. In 2000 this model was offered in a left-hand version. In 2001 this model was available chambered for the .338-06 A-Square cartridge.

NIB	Exc.	V.G.	Good	Fair	Poor
1450	1200	950	700	450	300

Mark V Deluxe Lightweight

This model, in its lightweight configuration, is offered in calibers from .22-25- to .30-06. These calibers are fitted to a 24" barrel. Fitted with hand select walnut Monte Carlo stock with rosewood fore-end tip and pistol grip cap. Fine line checkering. Weight is about 6.75 lbs. Introduced in 1999.

NIB	Exc.	V.G.	Good	Fair	Poor
1650	1250	1000	800	600	400

Mark V SPM (Super Predator Master)

Introduced in 2001 this rifle features a 24" blackened stainless steel fluted barrel. Chambered for the .223 Rem., .22-250 Rem., .243 Win., 7mm-08 Rem., and the .308 Win. cartridges. Fully adjustable trigger. Synthetic stock. Weight is about 6.5 lbs. Right-hand only.

NIB	Exc.	V.G.	Good	Fair	Poor
1600	1300	1050	750	500	350

Mark V SBGM (Super Big Game Master)

This model features a 24" blackened stainless steel barrel Krieger fluted barrel (26" for magnum calibers). Fully adjustable trigger. Tan composite stock with raised comb Monte Carlo. Pachmayr Decelerator recoil pad. Offered in a wide variety of caliber from .240 Weatherby Mag. to .300 Weatherby Mag. Weight is about 5.75 lbs. and 6.75 lbs. for magnum rifles. Introduced in 2002. **NOTE:** Add $60 for magnum calibers.

NIB	Exc.	V.G.	Good	Fair	Poor
1650	1250	1000	800	600	400

THREAT RESPONSE RIFLE SERIES

These rifles are based on the Mark V action.

TRR

Chambered for the .223 or .308 Win. cartridge and fitted with a 22" heavy-contour black Krieger barrel. Black composite stock with raised comb Monte Carlo. Flat-bottom forearm. Fully adjustable trigger. Recoil pad. Introduced in 2002.

NIB	Exc.	V.G.	Good	Fair	Poor
1250	1000	900	800	650	400

TRR Magnum

As above but chambered for the .300 Win. Mag., .300 Wby. Mag., .30-378 Wby. Mag., or the .338-378 Wby. Mag. Barrel length is 26". **NOTE:** Add $150 for .30-378 and .338-378 calibers.

NIB	Exc.	V.G.	Good	Fair	Poor
1450	1200	950	700	450	300

TRR Magnum Custom

This model has all the features of the TRR Magnum with the addition of a fully adjustable stock. DO NOT use this model until the company performs a safety upgrade to the bolt. The rifle can accidentally discharge without the bolt being fully engaged. The affected rifles bear serial numbers from one of these series on the receiver: 00001 through 03810; V00001 through V80966; VX00001 through VX44065; VS00001 through VS23699; VL00001 through VL46984; W00001 through W0099; NV0001 through NV0099. For more information contact Weatherby at 800-227-2018. **NOTE:** Add $150 for .30-378 or .338-378 calibers.

NIB	Exc.	V.G.	Good	Fair	Poor
2500	2200	1900	1600	1250	500

VANGUARD

Vanguard (early production)

This was Weatherby's Japanese-manufactured economy rifle. It is chambered for various popular standard American cartridges from .22-50 to the .300 Winchester Magnum cartridge. It is a bolt-action repeater with a 24" barrel furnished without sights. It has either a 3-shot or 5-shot magazine; and the finish is polished blue, with a select, checkered walnut stock with a rosewood fore-end tip and pistol-grip cap. This model was discontinued in 1988.

NIB	Exc.	V.G.	Good	Fair	Poor
—	1100	925	750	600	350

Vanguard VGS

This satin-finish version was also discontinued in 1988.

NIB	Exc.	V.G.	Good	Fair	Poor
—	1000	825	650	500	300

Vanguard VGL

This is a lightweight carbine version that has a 20" barrel. It was discontinued in 1988.

NIB	Exc.	V.G.	Good	Fair	Poor
—	900	725	550	400	250

Fiberguard

This version has a matte-blued finish with a green fiberglass stock. It was discontinued in 1988.

NIB	Exc.	V.G.	Good	Fair	Poor
—	750	575	400	300	200

Vanguard Classic I

This version is chambered for various popular standard calibers and has a 24" barrel and either a 3- or 5-shot magazine. It has a satin blue finish and a select checkered, oil-finished walnut stock. It was introduced in 1989.

NIB	Exc.	V.G.	Good	Fair	Poor
700	600	500	400	300	200

Vanguard Classic II

This is a more deluxe version with a higher-grade walnut stock.

NIB	Exc.	V.G.	Good	Fair	Poor
725	625	525	425	325	225

Vanguard VGX Deluxe

This version has a high-gloss, Monte Carlo-type stock and a high-polished blued finish. It was introduced in 1989.

NIB	Exc.	V.G.	Good	Fair	Poor
800	700	600	500	400	300

Vanguard Weatherguard

This version has a wrinkle-finished, black synthetic stock. It was introduced in 1989. In 2003 this model was offered in stainless steel. **NOTE:** Add $120 for stainless steel.

NIB	Exc.	V.G.	Good	Fair	Poor
650	500	400	300	225	175

Vanguard Synthetic

This model features an upgraded composite stock with Monte Carlo comb, a ring/base scope mounting system, a 24" barrel, and calibers from .223 Rem. to .338 Win. Mag., including the .257 Weatherby. Weight is about 7.75 lbs. Introduced in 2004.

NIB	Exc.	V.G.	Good	Fair	Poor
400	350	300	250	175	100

Vanguard Stainless

Similar to Vanguard Synthetic but with stainless steel barrel and receiver.

NIB	Exc.	V.G.	Good	Fair	Poor
575	500	450	350	275	125

Vanguard Sporter

Similar to the model above but with a figured walnut stock, rosewood fore-end tip and fine line checkering. Chambered for calibers from .270 to .338 Win. Mag. Barrel length is 24". Weight is about 8 lbs. Introduced in 2004. Also available with detachable magazine.

NIB	Exc.	V.G.	Good	Fair	Poor
550	450	350	250	175	100

Vanguard Sporter SS

Similar to Vanguard Sporter but with stainless steel barrel and receiver.

NIB	Exc.	V.G.	Good	Fair	Poor
675	575	475	375	275	125

Vanguard Varmint Special

Chambered in .223, .22-250, or .308. 22-inch blued #3 contour heavy crowned barrel, adjustable trigger, synthetic tan composite stock with black spiderweb pattern. Introduced 2006.

NIB	Exc.	V.G.	Good	Fair	Poor
575	475	375	275	195	125

Vanguard Synthetic Package

Introduced in 2004 this model features a 24" barrel with adjustable trigger. Chambered for a variety of calibers from the .223 Rem. to the .338 Win. Mag. Supplied with a Bushnell Banner 3-9x40 scope, sling, and hard case. Weight is about 7.75 lbs.

NIB	Exc.	V.G.	Good	Fair	Poor
650	550	350	275	225	150

Vanguard Sub-MOA Matte or Stainless

Introduced in 2005 this model features a guarantee to shoot .99" at 100 yards. Calibers from .223 Rem. to .338 Win. Mag. Barrel length is 24" with Monte Carlo Fiberguard stock. Adjustable trigger. Weight is about 7.75 lbs. Also available in stainless steel. **NOTE:** Add $120 for stainless steel.

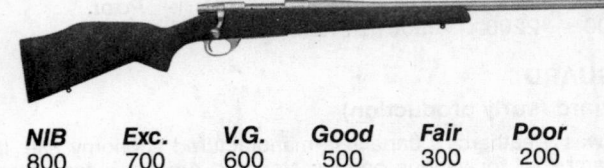

NIB	Exc.	V.G.	Good	Fair	Poor
800	700	600	500	300	200

Vanguard Sub-MOA Varmint

Similar to Vanguard Varmint Special but with ventilated beavertail fore-end. Chambered in .204, .223, .22-250, and .308. Introduced 2006.

NIB	Exc.	V.G.	Good	Fair	Poor
925	800	650	500	300	200

Vanguard Compact

This model, chambered for the ..223, 22-250, .243, or .308, is fitted with a 20" barrel and scaled-down hardwood stock with shorter length of pull. Also included is a full size composite stock. Weight is about 6.75 lbs. Introduced in 2005.

NIB	Exc.	V.G.	Good	Fair	Poor
550	450	350	250	175	100

Vanguard Youth Compact

Similar to above but with synthetic stock. Introduced 2008.

NIB	Exc.	V.G.	Good	Fair	Poor
550	450	350	250	175	100

Vanguard Deluxe

Similar to Vanguard but features 24-inch polished blued barrel, glossy select Monte Carlo walnut stock with rosewood fore-end, adjustable trigger. Chambered in .270, .30-06, .257 Weatherby Mag., and .300 Weatherby Mag. Introduced 2006.

NIB	Exc.	V.G.	Good	Fair	Poor
750	650	550	450	325	225

Vanguard Series II

Proven Mauser-style bolt, twin-locking lugs, 3-position safety. Available in 15 popular calibers from .223 Rem. to .338 Win. Mag., including .257 and .300 Weatherby Magnums. Adjustable match-quality two-stage trigger, 24-inch barrel on all models. Sub-MOA guaranteed. New stock design with Griptonite inserts, raised comb, right-hand side palm swell. Matte bead blast blue finish or stainless. **NOTE:** Add 35 percent for stainless finish.

NIB	Exc.	V.G.	Good	Fair	Poor
425	375	325	275	200	150

Weathermark

Introduced in 1993 this model features a checkered composite stock with matte blue metal finish. Available in Weatherby calibers from .257 through .340 and .270 Win., 7mm Rem. Mag., .30-06, .300 and .338 Win. Mag. Weighs 7.5 lbs.

NIB	Exc.	V.G.	Good	Fair	Poor
550	450	350	250	175	100

Weathermark Alaskan

Similar to the Weathermark with checkered composite stock the barreled action is electroless nickel with nonglare finish. Muzzlebrake is optional. Available in same calibers as Weathermark. Weighs 7.7 lbs.

NIB	Exc.	V.G.	Good	Fair	Poor
750	650	550	450	325	225

Mark XXII

This is a semi-automatic rifle chambered for the .22 LR cartridge. There are two versions—one with a detachable magazine and the other with a tubular magazine. It has a 24" barrel with adjustable sights and a select checkered walnut stock with a rosewood forearm tip and pistol-grip cap. This model was originally produced in Italy and was later manufactured in Japan. Introduced in 1965 and discontinued in 1989. **NOTE:** Premium for Italian guns.

Mark XXII Clip Model

Mark XXII Tube Model

NIB	Exc.	V.G.	Good	Fair	Poor
550	450	350	275	225	200

Mark XXII Bolt Action

Based on Anschutz design. Available in .22 Long Rifle or .17 HMR. Classic Mark V-style high-gloss walnut Monte Carlo stock with precision cut checkering, rosewood fore-end tip and grip cap. Target-grade barrel is 23-inches, weight 6.5 pounds. Fully adjustable single-stage trigger. Introduced in 2007. **NOTE:** Add 10 percent for .17 HMR.

NIB	Exc.	V.G.	Good	Fair	Poor
800	685	560	450	400	300

CUSTOM RIFLES

NOTE: Weatherby custom rifles are offered with many different options that will affect price. Consult an expert prior to a sale.

Vanguard Sage Country Custom

Introduced in 2008, this is similar to the Vanguard Synthetic but with injection-molded Desert Camo stock. Available in a variety of chamberings from .223 to .338 Winchester Magnum.

NIB	Exc.	V.G.	Good	Fair	Poor
600	500	400	300	225	175

Vanguard Back Country Custom

Introduced in 2008, this is a lightweight version of the Vanguard Synthetic with a fluted barrel, textured stock and overall weight of 6-3/4 lbs. Available in a variety of chamberings from .257 Weatherby Magnum to .300 Weatherby Magnum.

NIB	Exc.	V.G.	Good	Fair	Poor
950	850	725	625	425	200

Classic Custom

This model features an oil-finished French walnut stock with 20 lpi checkering, ebony fore-end tip, metal grip cap, and skeltonized steel buttplate. All metal work is matte blue. Calibers are all Weatherby from .257 Wby. Mag to .340 Wby. Mag.

NIB	Exc.	V.G.	Good	Fair	Poor
5100	4600	3500	2250	900	500

Safari Grade Custom

This model features an oil-finish French walnut stock with Monte Carlo comb with fleur-de-lis checkering. Ebony fore-end tip and pistol-grip cap. Damascened bolt and follower with checkered bolt handle. Quarter rib. Engraved floorplate "Safari Custom." Calibers from .257 Wby. Mag. to .460 Wby. Mag.

NIB	Exc.	V.G.	Good	Fair	Poor
5300	4800	3700	2450	1050	550

Crown Custom

This model features a hand-carved walnut stock with buttstock inlay, damascened bolt and follower with checkered bolt handle. Engraved barrel, receiver and trigger guard. Floorplate engraved with gold inlays.

NIB	Exc.	V.G.	Good	Fair	Poor
7500	6250	5000	3000	1500	750

Royal Custom

Introduced in 2002 this model features a Monte Carlo hand-checkered stock of fancy Claro walnut with high-gloss finish. Engraved receiver, bolt sleeve, and floorplate. Barrel length is 26". Available in a wide variety of calibers.

NIB	Exc.	V.G.	Good	Fair	Poor
5300	4800	3700	2450	1050	550

Outfitter Custom

This model features a Bell & Carlson synthetic stock with custom camo and Pachmayr pad. Lightweight stainless steel fluted barrel. Titanium nitride finish on all metalwork.

NIB	Exc.	V.G.	Good	Fair	Poor
2250	1700	1400	1100	700	400

Outfitter Krieger Custom

This model features a Bell & Carlson synthetic stock with custom camo and Pachmayr pad. Custom Krieger stainless steel fluted barrel. Titanium nitride finish on all metalwork.

NIB	Exc.	V.G.	Good	Fair	Poor
3500	3000	2500	2000	1300	600

SEMI-AUTO & PUMP SHOTGUNS

PA-08 PUMP-ACTION SERIES

Weatherby introduced this line of pump-action shotguns in 2008. All models come in 12 gauge with 3" chambers and have chrome-lined barrels. Knoxx stock models reduced recoil and are adjustable in length.

PA-08 Upland

This model has a walnut stock and fore-end with low-lustre finish and matte black metal work. Available with 28" or 26" barrel. Includes three choke tubes.

NIB	Exc.	V.G.	Good	Fair	Poor
325	275	225	175	125	75

PA-08 Knoxx Strutter X

Strutter models feature a synthetic stock and 24" vent rib barrel. Three choke tubes included. Add 15 percent for Apparition Excel camo pattern.

NIB	Exc.	V.G.	Good	Fair	Poor
425	375	325	250	175	100

PA-08 Knoxx HD

Home defense model features an 18" non-vent-rib barrel and cylinder choke.

NIB	Exc.	V.G.	Good	Fair	Poor
425	375	325	250	175	100

PA-08 Field/Slug Combo

Field and Slug-gun Combo pump features both a 28" field barrel for hunting birds and a 24" rifled slug barrel for deer. The field barrel is chrome lined and has a ventilated rib. Integral choke system features Briley thread pattern, and comes with improved cylinder, Modified and full-choked tubes. The 8-groove Slug barrel has a Weaver-compatible cantilevered scope mount base. Matte black finish. Weight: approx. 6.75 lbs. Introduced in 2011.

NIB	Exc.	V.G.	Good	Fair	Poor
430	380	340	300	270	220

PA-459 Turkey Camo

This pump gun features Mothwing Camo's Spring Mimicry pattern on stock and fore-end. The 12-gauge gun has a 19" barrel, a 13.5" length of pull and overall length of 40". Weight: approx. 6.5 lbs. Integral Picatinny rail allows mounting optical sights or other accessories. The rail has a clamp-style LPA ghost-ring rear sight adjustable for windage and elevation.

NIB	Exc.	V.G.	Good	Fair	Poor
450	390	360	320	290	250

Centurion

This is a gas-operated semi-automatic shotgun chambered for 12 gauge. It is offered with various barrel lengths and chokes. It has a checkered walnut stock. It was manufactured between 1972 and 1981.

NIB	Exc.	V.G.	Good	Fair	Poor
450	400	300	250	200	150

Centurion Deluxe

This version is slightly engraved and features a vent-ribbed barrel and higher-grade wood.

NIB	Exc.	V.G.	Good	Fair	Poor
500	400	325	275	225	175

Model 82

This is a gas-operated semi-automatic shotgun chambered for 12 gauge with 2.75" or 3" chambers. It has various barrel lengths with vent-ribs and screw-in choke tubes. It features an alloy receiver and a deluxe, checkered walnut stock. It is also available as the Buckmaster with a 22" open-choked barrel. This model was introduced in 1983.

NIB	Exc.	V.G.	Good	Fair	Poor
500	450	400	350	300	250

Model SAS Field

Introduced in 1999 this gas-operated semi-automatic model features a high-grade Claro walnut stock with black pistol-grip cap. Fine-line checkering. Chambered for 12 or 20 gauge and fitted with 26", 28", or 30" vent-rib barrels in 12 gauge and 26" or 28" vent-rib barrels in 20 gauge. The 12 gauge models weigh around 7.5 lbs. depending on barrel length, and the 20 gauge weighs around 7 lbs. depending on barrel length. Fitted with Briley choke tubes.

NIB	Exc.	V.G.	Good	Fair	Poor
700	550	450	325	250	200

Model SAS Camo

This model is offered with either Shadowgrass or Superflauge camo stocks. Available in 12 gauge only with 3" chambers. Shadowgrass model offered with 26" or 28" barrels; the Superflauge model with 24" or 26" barrels. Weight is about 7.5 lbs.

Shadow Grass

NIB	Exc.	V.G.	Good	Fair	Poor
750	600	500	375	300	225

Superflauge

NIB	Exc.	V.G.	Good	Fair	Poor
750	600	500	375	300	225

Model SAS Slug Gun

This model features a 22" rifled barrel chambered for the 3" 12 gauge shell. The barrel has a cantilever base for scope mounts. Walnut stock has a raised Monte Carlo comb. Sling swivel studs. Weight is about 7.25 lbs. Introduced in 2003.

NIB	Exc.	V.G.	Good	Fair	Poor
750	600	500	375	300	225

Model SAS Sporting Clays

This 12 gauge gun is fitted with a 28" or 30" vent-rib ported barrel. Walnut stock with pistol grip. Choke tubes standard. Weight is about 7.5 lbs. Introduced in 2002.

NIB	Exc.	V.G.	Good	Fair	Poor
800	650	550	425	350	250

Model SAS Synthetic

This model features a black synthetic stock chambered for 12 or 20 gauge barrels as above. Introduced in 2000.

NIB	Exc.	V.G.	Good	Fair	Poor
525	450	375	300	250	175

SA-08 Upland

This semi-automatic was new in 2008. It features a walnut stock with oil finish. Available in 12 and 20 gauge with 3" chambers and 28" or 26" barrels. Three choke tubes included.

NIB	Exc.	V.G.	Good	Fair	Poor
650	550	450	250	175	150

SA-08 Youth

As above but in 20 gauge with 26" barrel only and shorter 12.5" length of pull.

NIB	Exc.	V.G.	Good	Fair	Poor
550	425	300	250	175	150

SA-08 Entré Rios

The Entré Rios autoloader has a scaled-down frame for the 28 gauge. Features include a select, cut-checkered walnut stock and a high-gloss finish on barrel and receiver. Comes equipped with skeet, improved cylinder and modified choke tubes. Weight: 5.25 lbs. Available with 26" or 28" barrel.

NIB	Exc.	V.G.	Good	Fair	Poor
600	500	425	365	310	200

SA-459 TR

This gas-operated autoloader features a bolt with an oversized hourglass design that's easily located in the dark. It comes equipped with a new TR accessory rail for mounting tactical lights or laser sights. Also has a fully adjustable, LPA-style ghost ring sight. Pistol-grip buttstock has rubber-textured grip. Available in 12 or 20 gauge. Barrel length: 18.5". Weight: 7 lbs.

NIB	Exc.	V.G.	Good	Fair	Poor
625	550	400	325	250	150

OLDER MODEL PUMP SHOTGUNS

Patrician

This is a slide-action shotgun chambered for 12 gauge. It is offered with various barrel lengths and choke combinations. It has a vent-rib barrel, a blued finish and a checkered walnut stock. It was manufactured between 1972 and 1981.

NIB	Exc.	V.G.	Good	Fair	Poor
400	350	325	300	250	175

Patrician Deluxe

This is a slightly engraved version with fancier-grade walnut.

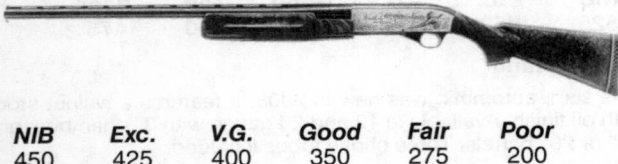

NIB	Exc.	V.G.	Good	Fair	Poor
450	425	400	350	275	200

Model 92

This is a slide-action shotgun chambered for 12 gauge with 2.75" or 3" chambers. It is offered with 26", 28" or 30" ventilated rib barrels with screw-in choke tubes. It features a short, twin-rail slide action and an engraved alloy receiver. The finish is blued, with a deluxe checkered walnut stock. A Buckmaster model with a 22" open-choke barrel and rifle sights is also available.

NIB	Exc.	V.G.	Good	Fair	Poor
350	300	250	200	175	125

SIDE-BY-SIDE GUNS

These shotguns are built in Spain.

Athena SBS

Introduced in 2002 this model features a case colored boxlock receiver with false sideplates with scroll engraving. Offered in 12 or 20 gauge with 26" or 28" barrels. Choke tubes. Turkish walnut stock with straight grip and recoil pad. Checkering is 22 lpi. Single trigger and ejectors. Weight is about 7 lbs.

NIB	Exc.	V.G.	Good	Fair	Poor
1550	1200	1000	750	500	400

Athena D'Italia

Introduced in 2005 this gun is chambered for the 12, 20, or 28 gauge and fitted with 28" barrels for the 12 gauge and 26" barrels for the 20 and 28 gauge guns. Receiver has silver sideplates with scroll engraving. Checkered walnut stock with straight grip. Weight is about 7 lbs. **NOTE:** Add $135 for 28 gauge.

NIB	Exc.	V.G.	Good	Fair	Poor
2840	2100	1600	1100	750	500

Athena D'Italia PG

Introduced in 2006, this model is offered in the same configurations as the D'Italia. It is identical in action and frame to the D'Italia but with a rounded pistol grip stock and single gold trigger. Laser-cut checkering at 20 lpi. Introduced 2006. Pricing is for 12 and 20 gauges. Add $200 for 28 ga.

NIB	Exc.	V.G.	Good	Fair	Poor
3200	2500	2000	1500	1050	500

Athena D'Italia Deluxe

Renaissance floral engraving with Bolino style game scene and AAA Fancy Turkish walnut with 24 lpi hand checkering adorn this straight grip stocked model. Available in 12, 20 and 28 gauges with 26" or 28" barrels with fixed IC and Mod. chokes. Single trigger. Introduced 2006.

NIB	Exc.	V.G.	Good	Fair	Poor
7000	6000	4750	3000	2200	600

Orion SBS

This model is a lower cost alternative to the Athena. Turkish walnut stock with pistol grips and 18 lpi checkering. Case colored boxlock receiver. Offered in 12, 20 and 28 gauge as well as .410 bore. Choke tubes except for .410. Choice of 26" or 28" barrels. Weight is about 7 lbs. Introduced in 2002.

NIB	Exc.	V.G.	Good	Fair	Poor
1750	1100	900	650	475	300

OVER/UNDER GUNS

Regency Field Grade

This is an over/under double-barrel shotgun chambered for 12 or 20 gauge. It has various length vent-ribbed barrels and a boxlock action with engraved false sideplates. It features a single-selective trigger and automatic ejectors. The finish is blued, with a checkered walnut stock. This model was imported from Italy between 1972 and 1980. It is also offered as a trap grade with the same value.

NIB	Exc.	V.G.	Good	Fair	Poor
1500	1200	1000	700	400	300

Olympian

This model is similar to the Regency, with less engraving. It was not imported after 1980. A skeet and a trap model, as well as a field-grade model, were available. The values were similar.

NIB	Exc.	V.G.	Good	Fair	Poor
1000	800	650	500	350	225

Orion Upland

This 12 or 20 gauge model features a Claro walnut stock with rounded pistol grip and slim forearm. Plain blued receiver. Choice of 26" or 28" vent-rib barrel with 3" chambers. Multi-choke system. Introduced in 1999.

NIB	Exc.	V.G.	Good	Fair	Poor
1200	1000	800	600	450	300

Orion Grade I

This is an over/under double-barrel shotgun chambered for 12 or 20 gauge with 3" chambers. It is offered with 26" or 28" vent-rib barrels with screw-in chokes. It has a single-selective trigger and automatic ejectors. The boxlock action features no engraving. The finish is blued, with a checkered walnut stock. It was introduced in 1989.

NIB	Exc.	V.G.	Good	Fair	Poor
1200	1000	800	650	450	300

Orion Grade II Skeet

This model is supplied with a Claro walnut checkered stock with full pistol grip with rosewood grip cap. The receiver is matte blue with scroll engraving. The barrel has a matte vent-rib with side vents and mid-point head with white bead front sight. Special ventilated recoil pad. Offered in 12 gauge and 20 gauge with 26" barrels. Fixed Skeet chokes are standard. The 12 gauge weighs 7.5 lbs. while the 20 gauge weighs 7.25 lbs.

NIB	Exc.	V.G.	Good	Fair	Poor
950	800	700	600	400	200

Orion Grade II Sporting Clays

Similar to the Classic model but with a full pistol grip with rosewood grip cap. The receiver is silver gray with scroll engraving. The Claro walnut stock is checkered with a high-gloss finish. Offered in 12 gauge with 28" to 30" vent-rib barrels. Supplied with five screw-in choke tubes.

NIB	Exc.	V.G.	Good	Fair	Poor
1300	1050	800	600	400	200

Orion Grade II Double Trap

This model features an integral multi-choke tube. The Monte Carlo stock has a rosewood pistol grip cap with diamond shaped inlay. The receiver is blue with scroll engraving. Available with 30" or 32" vent-rib barrels. Weighs 8 lbs.

NIB	Exc.	V.G.	Good	Fair	Poor
950	800	700	550	400	200

Orion Grade II Single Trap

Similar to the Double Trap but furnished with a single 32" barrel. Weighs 8 lbs.

NIB	Exc.	V.G.	Good	Fair	Poor
950	800	700	550	400	200

Orion Grade II

This version is lightly engraved and has a high-gloss finish. Otherwise, it is similar to the Grade I.

NIB	Exc.	V.G.	Good	Fair	Poor
1200	1050	925	800	600	250

Orion Grade II Classic Field

Introduced in 1993 this model features a rounded pistol grip and slim forearm design. The walnut stock is oil finished. The receiver is blued with game scene engraving. A solid recoil pad is standard. Available in 12 gauge, 20 gauge, and 28 gauge with vent-rib barrel lengths from 26" to 30" depending on gauge. Screw-in choke tubes standard. Weighs 6.5 lbs. to 8 lbs. depending on gauge.

NIB	Exc.	V.G.	Good	Fair	Poor
950	800	700	550	400	200

Orion Grade II Classic Sporting Clays

Introduced in 1993 this model has a rounded pistol grip with slender forearm with an oil-finished stock. The receiver is blued with scroll engraving. A stepped competition matte vent-rib with additional side vents is supplied. The recoil pad has a special radius heel. Offered in 12 gauge with 28" barrel. Furnished with five screw-in choke tubes. Weighs 7.5 lbs.

NIB	Exc.	V.G.	Good	Fair	Poor
1000	850	750	600	400	200

Orion Super Sporting Clays (SSC)

Introduced in 1999 this 12 gauge model features a walnut stock with sporter-style pistol grip and cast off. Barrel lengths are 28", 30" or 32" with 3" chambers and 12mm grooved rib. Barrels are also ported and backbored. Comes with five choke tubes. Weight is approximately 8 lbs.

NIB	Exc.	V.G.	Good	Fair	Poor
1750	1400	1150	925	750	350

Orion Grade III

This version has a game scene-engraved, coin-finished receiver and higher-grade walnut. It was introduced in 1989.

NIB	Exc.	V.G.	Good	Fair	Poor
1400	1100	850	650	500	300

Orion Grade III Classic Field

New for 1993, this model features a rounded pistol grip and slim forearm with oil finish, Claro walnut with fine line checkering. The receiver is silver gray with scroll engraving and gold game bird overlays. Available in 12 gauge with 28" vent-rib barrels and 20 gauge with 26" vent-rib barrels. Screw-in choke tubes standard.

NIB	Exc.	V.G.	Good	Fair	Poor
1600	1400	1000	750	500	300

Orion Grade III Classic English Field

This model features an English-style straight-grip stock with a choice of 12 gauge with 28" barrel or 20 gauge with 26" or 28" barrels. The receiver is engraved and the stock is oil-finished hand-checkered. Weight of 12 gauge gun is about 7 lbs. and 20 gauge is about 6.5 lbs. Introduced in 1996.

NIB	Exc.	V.G.	Good	Fair	Poor
1450	1200	925	800	600	250

Orion D'Italia

Engraved silver-finish metalwork and fineline, 20 lpi checkering. Turkish walnut stock with high-gloss finish. Available in 12 gauge with 28" barrel and 20 gauge with 26" barrel.

NIB	Exc.	V.G.	Good	Fair	Poor
1750	1500	1200	900	750	400

Athena Grade III Classic Field

Offered in 12 or 20 gauge this model features a hand select Claro walnut stock with oil finish. The pistol grip is rounded. The silver-gray sideplates feature a rose and scroll engraving pattern with gold overlaid hunting scenes. Available with 26" or 28" vent-rib barrels with multi-choke system. Weight is around 7.5 lbs. for 12 gauge and 7 lbs. for 20 gauge. Introduced in 1999. In 2001 a 28 gauge version was offered with 26" or 28" barrels.

NIB	Exc.	V.G.	Good	Fair	Poor
1700	1500	1250	900	600	350

Athena Grade IV

This is an over/under double-barrel shotgun chambered for 12, 20, and 28 gauge, as well as .410. It has 3" chambers. It is offered with various barrel lengths with vent-ribs and screw-in choke tubes. It has a boxlock action with Greener crossbolt, single-selective trigger, and automatic ejectors. It has engraved false sideplates and a satin nickel-plated action. The barrels are blued, with a select checkered walnut stock. This model was introduced in 1989.

NIB	Exc.	V.G.	Good	Fair	Poor
2100	1700	1500	1100	750	450

Athena Grade V Classic Field

Introduced in 1993 this model features a rounded pistol grip with slender forearm. The high-grade Claro walnut stock is oil finished with fine line checkering. The receiver has a side plate that is silver gray with rose and scroll engraving. The vent-rib barrels also have side vents. An Old English recoil pad is supplied. Offered in 12 gauge with 26", 28", or 30" barrels and 20 gauge with 26" and

28" barrels. Choke tubes are standard. Weatherby Athena Master skeet tube set, 12 gauge 28" skeet shotgun, plus two each 20, 28 and .410 gauge fitted, full-length Briley tubes with integral extractors. Packed in custom fitted aluminum case (not shown). **NOTE:** Add 50 percent for Master Skeet Set.

NIB	Exc.	V.G.	Good	Fair	Poor
2800	2400	1800	1400	900	500

Competition Model Athena

This is either a trap or skeet version with stock dimensions designed for either skeet or trap and competition-type ribs.

NIB	Exc.	V.G.	Good	Fair	Poor
1650	1400	1150	1000	750	600

HANDGUNS

Mark V – CFP (Compact Firing Platform)

Bolt-action handgun with 5+1 capacity. 16" barrel, adjustable trigger, composite stock. Available in .223, .22-250, .243 and 7mm-08. 5.25 lb. Introduced 2006.

NIB	Exc.	V.G.	Good	Fair	Poor
1300	1050	800	600	400	200

Mark V Accumark CFP

This model is similar to the Accumark rifle and features a synthetic stock of Kevlar and fiberglass. The stock has a matte black gel-coat finish. Offered in .223 Rem., .22-250, .243 Win., 7mm-08, and .308 Win. calibers. Fluted barrel length is 15". Weight is about 5 lbs. Introduced in 2000.

NIB	Exc.	V.G.	Good	Fair	Poor
1050	800	600	400	225	150

WEAVER ARMS
Escondido, California

Nighthawk Assault Pistol

A 9mm semi-automatic pistol with a 10" or 12" barrel, alloy receiver and ambidextrous safety. Blackened with plastic grips. Introduced in 1987.

NIB	Exc.	V.G.	Good	Fair	Poor
550	450	400	350	300	150

Nighthawk Carbine

As above, with a 16.1" barrel, retractable shoulder stock, 25-, 32-, 40-, or 50-shot magazine. Introduced in 1984.

NIB	Exc.	V.G.	Good	Fair	Poor
600	500	450	350	300	150

WEBLEY & SCOTT, LTD.
Birmingham, England

Established in 1860, this firm has produced a wide variety of firearms over the years and has been known as Webley & Scott, Ltd. since 1906. **NOTE:** For all Webley .455 revolvers deduct 35 percent if converted to .45 ACP/.45 Auto Rim.

Model 1872 Royal Irish Constabulary

A .450 double-action revolver with a 3.25" barrel, 5-shot cylinder and rotating ejector. This model was also offered with 2.5" and 3.5" barrels. Blued with checkered walnut grips.

NIB	Exc.	V.G.	Good	Fair	Poor
—	1000	750	475	250	150

Model 1880 Metropolitan Police

As above, with a 2.5" barrel and 6-shot cylinder.

NIB	Exc.	V.G.	Good	Fair	Poor
—	1000	750	475	250	150

Model 1878 Webley-Pryse

Chambered for the .455 and .476 Eley cartridge. **NOTE:** Add 200 percent premium for revolvers chambered for .577. Deduct 50 percent for revolvers chambered for cartridges below .442.

NIB	Exc.	V.G.	Good	Fair	Poor
—	2100	1500	950	550	300

New Model 1883 R.I.C.

Similar to the Model 1880, but in .455 caliber with a 4.5" barrel. Also made with a 2.5" barrel.

NIB	Exc.	V.G.	Good	Fair	Poor
—	900	750	425	250	100

Model 1884 R.I.C. Naval

As above, with a brass frame and oxidized finish. Barrel length 2.75" and of octagonal form.

NIB	Exc.	V.G.	Good	Fair	Poor
—	2250	1650	1225	600	500

British Bulldog

Similar to the new Model 1883 R.I.C. blued, checkered walnut grips. Those engraved on the back strap "W.R.A. Co." were sold through the Winchester Repeating Arms Company's New York sales agency and are worth a considerable premium over the values listed. Manufactured from 1878 to 1914. **NOTE:** Add a premium for U.S. dealer markings, see model description.

NIB	Exc.	V.G.	Good	Fair	Poor
—	900	550	325	200	150

Pug

Similar to the British Bulldog but somewhat smaller. Interesting in that it has a manual safety. Chambered in .450, .442, and possibly others as well.

NIB	Exc.	V.G.	Good	Fair	Poor
—	800	500	325	200	150

Model 1878 Army Express Revolver

A .455 caliber double-action revolver with a 6" barrel and integral ejector. Blued with one-piece walnut grips. **NOTE:** Add 100 percent premium for single-action version. Add 25 percent for .45 Long (.45 Colt) markings.

NIB	Exc.	V.G.	Good	Fair	Poor
—	2100	1500	850	500	350

Webley Kaufmann Model 1880

A top break, hinged-frame double-action revolver chambered for the .450 centerfire cartridge, with a 5.75" barrel and a curved bird's-head butt. Blued, with walnut grips.

NIB	Exc.	V.G.	Good	Fair	Poor
—	2300	1000	800	600	300

Webley-Green Model

A double-action, top break revolver chambered for the .455 cartridge, with a 6" ribbed barrel and a 6-shot cylinder. The cylinder flutes on this model are angular and not rounded in shape. Blued, with checkered walnut, squared butt grips with a lanyard ring on the butt. Introduced in 1882 and manufactured until 1896. Also known as the "WG" model.

NIB	Exc.	V.G.	Good	Fair	Poor
—	1900	1350	700	500	200

Mark I

A .442, .455, or .476 double-action top break revolver with a 4" barrel and 6-shot cylinder. Blued with checkered walnut grips. Manufactured from 1887 to 1894.

Courtesy Faintich Auction Services, Inc., Paul Goodwin photo

NIB	Exc.	V.G.	Good	Fair	Poor
—	950	550	375	250	150

Mark II

As above, with a larger hammer spur and improved barrel catch. Manufactured from 1894 to 1897.

NIB	Exc.	V.G.	Good	Fair	Poor
—	925	550	350	225	100

Mark III

As above, with internal improvements. Introduced in 1897.

NIB	Exc.	V.G.	Good	Fair	Poor
—	975	600	325	200	75

Mark IV

As above, with a .455 caliber 3", 4", 5", or 6" barrel. This model was also available in .22 caliber with 6" barrel, .32 caliber with 3" barrel, and .38 caliber with 3", 4", or 5" barrel.

Courtesy Faintich Auction Services, Inc., Paul Goodwin photo

NIB	Exc.	V.G.	Good	Fair	Poor
—	900	575	375	200	75

Mark IV Target

Chambered for the .22 caliber cartridge and fitted with a 6" barrel with target sights.

Courtesy Rock Island Auction Company

NIB	Exc.	V.G.	Good	Fair	Poor
—	1450	1000	800	500	300

Mark V

Similar to Mark IV, with a 4" or 6" barrel. Manufactured from 1913 to 1915.

Courtesy Faintich Auction Services, Inc., Paul Goodwin photo

NIB	Exc.	V.G.	Good	Fair	Poor
—	1000	695	395	250	150

Mark VI

Similar to Mark V in design but with a smaller frame, 4" or 6" barrel and modified grip. Chambered for .38/200 (.38 S&W).

NOTE: Pricing is for commercial version. Subtract 40 percent for WAR FINISH-marked examples.

Courtesy Faintich Auction Services, Inc., Paul Goodwin photo

NIB	Exc.	V.G.	Good	Fair	Poor
—	800	600	375	225	150

Mark VI .22 Rimfire

A standard-size Mark V chambered for the .22 rimfire cartridge used as a training pistol. Manufactured in 1918 and quite scarce.

Courtesy Faintich Auction Services, Inc., Paul Goodwin photo

NIB	Exc.	V.G.	Good	Fair	Poor
—	850	650	450	350	200

WEBLEY SEMI-AUTOMATIC PISTOLS

Webley-Fosbery Automatic Revolver

Recoil forces the top half of this unusual pistol back to cock the hammer, while a stud in the frame cams the cylinder around to bring a fresh chamber into position. Early examples under serial number 75 or so appear to be hand-made as no two seem to be identical; these bring a 100 percent premium over late-model pistols. Other low-number guns, under serial number 300 or so, also differ in appearance from the later production and bring a 25 percent premium. Early production was all in .455 Webley with a 6-round cylinder; a .38 ACP version with an 8-round cylinder was introduced about 1903 but is much scarcer than the .455.

Courtesy Joseph Schroeder

.455 Caliber

NIB	Exc.	V.G.	Good	Fair	Poor
—	9000	4500	3000	2000	1250

.38 Caliber

NIB	Exc.	V.G.	Good	Fair	Poor
—	10000	7250	4500	3000	2000

Model 1904

Made experimentally in both .38 ACP and .455 calibers, the highest serial numbered 1904 known is in the 30s and very few seem to have survived. A later Webley experimental, the Model 1906, made in .45 for the U.S. Army trial but apparently never submitted. Either model is too rare to price.

Model 1904

Courtesy Joseph Schroeder

Model 1905

Webley's first commercial semi-automatic pistol was this compact .32 caliber. The earliest Model 1905s have a diagonal flat machined on the slide and a hammer-mounted safety; these bring about a 50 percent premium. The Model 1905 was replaced by the Model 1908 after about perhaps 20,000 were made.

Courtesy Joseph Schroeder

NIB	Exc.	V.G.	Good	Fair	Poor
—	1200	1000	750	400	250

Model 1907

The 1907 is a .25 caliber pistol with an outside hammer and was one of Webley's most popular handguns; it remained in production until WWII and over 50,000 were made.

Courtesy Joseph Schroeder

NIB	Exc.	V.G.	Good	Fair	Poor
—	800	600	400	200	100

Model 1908

The Model 1908 is a slight redesign of the Model 1905. Webley's most popular self-loading pistol, it remained in production until WWII. Examples bearing a crown and the letters "MP" were made for the Metropolitan Police and bring a slight premium.

NIB	Exc.	V.G.	Good	Fair	Poor
—	650	550	350	175	125

Model 1909

The Model 1909 is a modified and enlarged version of the Model 1908, chambered for the 9mm Browning Long cartridge. It was never popular, and manufacture ended in 1914 with just under 1,700 made. Its most unusual feature was the slide release on top of the slide.

Courtesy Joseph Schroeder

NIB	Exc.	V.G.	Good	Fair	Poor
—	1475	850	500	300	200

Model 1910 .380

The Model 1910 .380 was simply a Model 1908 modified to accept the .380 cartridge. Never very popular, under 2,000 were sold.

NIB	Exc.	V.G.	Good	Fair	Poor
—	1500	875	525	—	—

Model 1910 .38 ACP

This was Webley's first locked-breech pistol, based closely on the experimental Model 1906 design and chambered for the .38 ACP cartridge. There are two models, both with internal hammers, but one with a grip safety and the later without. Total production for both was under 1,000, so both are rare.

Courtesy Joseph Schroeder

NIB	Exc.	V.G.	Good	Fair	Poor
—	2250	1500	900	500	350

Model 1911

The Model 1911 is a single-shot .22 caliber training version of the Model 1908, and developed specifically for the Metropolitan Police. It features a "blow open" action that ejects the fired cartridge but remains open for reloading, and the bottom of the frame is slotted for attaching a shoulder stock. **NOTE:** Stocks are quite rare, and will probably add more than 100 percent to the value of the pistol.

Courtesy Joseph Schroeder

NIB	Exc.	V.G.	Good	Fair	Poor
—	1750	1400	1100	800	300

Model 1912

A perceived need for a hammerless version of the Model 1907 .25 caliber led to the introduction of the Model 1912. It actually does have an internal hammer, but the recoil spring is two coils in the slide instead of the large V-spring under the right grip frame found in all other Webley semi-automatic pistols. Not as popular as the Model 1907, production totaled almost 15,000 vs. over 50,000 for the hammer model.

NIB	Exc.	V.G.	Good	Fair	Poor
—	1200	1000	750	400	200

Model 1913

The Model 1913 was the result of years of development in conjunction with the British government and was finally adopted in 1913 as the Model 1913 MK1N for Royal Navy issue. It has the same breech-locking system as the Model 1910, but has an external hammer and is chambered for the .455 Webley Self-Loading cartridge. About 1,000 Model 1913s were sold commercially and serial-numbered along with the smaller-caliber pistols. In 1915 a variation of the Model 1913 with butt slotted for a shoulder stock, an adjustable rear sight, and a hammer safety adopted for use by the Royal Horse Artillery. Shoulder stocks are very rare, and will double values listed for the RHA model. All militaries were numbered in their own series; about 10,000 made in both variations.

NIB	Exc.	V.G.	Good	Fair	Poor
—	1950	1200	800	500	300

Model 1913 (RHA model)

Courtesy Joseph Schroeder

NIB	Exc.	V.G.	Good	Fair	Poor
—	5000	4000	3000	1000	600

Model 1922

The Model 1922 was a redesign of the Model 1909 in hopes of military adoption. The grip safety was replaced by a manual safety mounted on the slide, the grip angle was changed, and a lanyard ring added to the butt. Unfortunately for Webley its only official use was by the Union Defense Force of South Africa (1,000 pistols). South African guns are marked with a large "U" with an arrow in it and bring a 20 percent premium.

NIB	Exc.	V.G.	Good	Fair	Poor
—	3000	2500	2000	1000	600

WEIHRAUCH, HANS HERMANN
Melrichstadt, West Germany

Model HW 60M

A .22 caliber single-shot bolt action rifle with a 26.75" barrel and adjustable sights. Blued with a walnut stock.

NIB	Exc.	V.G.	Good	Fair	Poor
800	650	550	400	350	250

Model HW 66

A .22 Hornet or .222 Remington bolt action rifle with a stainless steel 26" barrel and single- or double-set triggers. Blued with a walnut stock.

NIB	Exc.	V.G.	Good	Fair	Poor
700	550	500	350	300	200

Model HW-3

A double-action, solid-frame, swing-out cylinder revolver chambered for .22 LR or .32 Smith & Wesson long cartridges with a barrel length of 2.75", and a cylinder holding either seven or eight cartridges. Blued, with walnut grips. In America, this revolver was known as the Dickson Bulldog. In Europe it was known as the Gecado.

NIB	Exc.	V.G.	Good	Fair	Poor
—	100	75	50	35	25

Model HW-5

As above, with a 4" barrel. Sold in the United States under the trade name "Omega."

NIB	Exc.	V.G.	Good	Fair	Poor
—	100	75	50	35	25

Model HW-7

As above, in .22 caliber with a 6" barrel and 8-shot cylinder. Sold in the United States as the "Herter's Guide Model." Also available with target sights and thumbrest grips as the Model HW-7S.

NIB	Exc.	V.G.	Good	Fair	Poor
—	100	75	50	35	25

Model HW-9

These pistols all carry the Arminius trademark, a bearded head wearing a winged helmet. The model number will be found on the cylinder crane; the caliber, on the barrel; and the words "Made in Germany" on the frame.

NIB	Exc.	V.G.	Good	Fair	Poor
—	100	75	50	35	25

WEISBURGER, A.
Memphis, Tennessee

Pocket Pistol

A .41 caliber percussion single-shot pocket pistol with 2.5" barrel, German silver furniture and a walnut stock. Manufactured during the 1850s.

NIB	Exc.	V.G.	Good	Fair	Poor
—	6500	5100	3250	1800	

WESSON FIREARMS, DAN
Norwich, New York

Also See—Wesson Firearms Co., Inc., separate listing.

In 1996 the assets of the Wesson Firearms Co. was purchased by the New York International Corp. Full production of new models occurred in 1997. These firearms are laser marked on the barrel or frame with: "NYI" in an oval and below "DAN WESSON FIREARMS" on the next line "NORWICH, NEW YORK USA." In April, 2005 Dan Wesson Firearms was acquired by CZ-USA. Production continues at the Norwich, New York, facility.

NEW GENERATION SMALL-FRAME SERIES

NOTE: The "7" prefix denotes stainless steel frame and barrel. For models listed add between 4 percent and 9 percent depending on barrel length and for stainless steel.

Model 22/722

This is a 6-shot revolver chambered for .22 caliber cartridge. Interchangeable barrel lengths are 2.5", 4", 5.6", 8", and 10". Adjustable rear sight and interchangeable front sight. Hogue finger groove rubber grips. Weight is 36 oz. for 2.5" barrel and 58 oz. for 10" barrel.

NIB	Exc.	V.G.	Good	Fair	Poor
485	375	300	250	200	145

Model 22M/722M

Same as above but chambered for .22 Win. Mag. cartridge.

NIB	Exc.	V.G.	Good	Fair	Poor
525	400	300	225	175	145

Model 32/732

Same as above. Chambered for .32 H&R cartridge.

NIB	Exc.	V.G.	Good	Fair	Poor
550	425	325	250	195	165

Model 3220/73220

Same as above but chambered for the .32-20 cartridge.

NIB	Exc.	V.G.	Good	Fair	Poor
550	425	325	250	195	165

Model 15/715

Same as above but chambered for the .38 Special and .357 Magnum cartridges.

NIB	Exc.	V.G.	Good	Fair	Poor
525	400	300	225	175	145

Model 715 (Current Production)

Made from 100 percent stainless steel and chambered in .357 Magnum. Traditional double-action with dual cylinder lockup, six-round capacity, fully adjustable rear sight, transfer bar ignition and interchangeable barrel with ventilated rib. Includes barrel wrench kit. Weight 46 ounces, 6-inch barrel, bright stainless finish. Reintroduced in 2011.

NIB	Exc.	V.G.	Good	Fair	Poor
975	850	700	500	350	200

NEW GENERATION LARGE-FRAME SERIES

NOTE: The "7" prefix denotes stainless steel frame and barrel. For models listed add between 4 percent and 9 percent depending on barrel length and for stainless steel.

Model 41/741

This is a large-frame revolver with 6-shot cylinder. Interchangeable barrels in 4", 6", 8", and 10". Adjustable rear sight with interchangeable front sight. Hogue finger grip rubber grips standard. Weight is from 49 oz. for 4" barrel to 69 oz. for 10" barrels.

NIB	Exc.	V.G.	Good	Fair	Poor
575	475	350	225	175	125

Model 44/744

Same as above but chambered for .44 Magnum cartridge.

NIB	Exc.	V.G.	Good	Fair	Poor
575	475	350	225	175	125

Model 45/745

Same as above but chambered for .45 Colt cartridge.

NIB	Exc.	V.G.	Good	Fair	Poor
600	500	375	250	200	125

Model 360/7360

Same as above but chambered for .357 Magnum cartridge.

NIB	Exc.	V.G.	Good	Fair	Poor
575	475	350	225	175	125

Model 460/7460

Same as above but chambered for the .45 ACP, .45 Auto Rim, .45 Super, .45 Win. Mag, or .460 Rowland.

NIB	Exc.	V.G.	Good	Fair	Poor
750	625	500	400	300	200

NEW GENERATION SUPERMAG-FRAME SERIES

NOTE: The "7" prefix denotes stainless steel frame and barrel. For models listed add between 4 percent and 9 percent depending on barrel length and for stainless steel.

Model 40/740

This is a 6-shot revolver chambered for .the .357 Magnum, .357 Super Magnum/Maximum cartridges with interchangeable barrels in 4", 6", 8", or 10" lengths. Adjustable rear sight and interchangeable front sights. Hogue finger groove rubber grips standard. Weight range from 51 oz. for 4" barrel to 76 oz. for 10" barrel.

NIB	Exc.	V.G.	Good	Fair	Poor
1300	1125	850	675	400	250

Model 414/7414

Same as above but chambered for .414 Super Magnum cartridge.

NIB	Exc.	V.G.	Good	Fair	Poor
1300	1125	850	675	400	250

Model 445/7445

Same as above but chambered for .445 Super Mag. cartridge.

NIB	Exc.	V.G.	Good	Fair	Poor
1500	1325	1050	875	550	350

NEW GENERATION COMPENSATED SERIES

NOTE: The "7" prefix denotes stainless steel frame and barrel. For models listed add between 4 percent and 9 percent depending on barrel length and for stainless steel.

Model 15/715

This is a 6-shot revolver that is chambered for the .357 Magnum cartridge and offered with interchangeable barrels in 4", 6", or 10" lengths. Barrels have an integral compensator. Adjustable rear sight and interchangeable front sight. Hogue finger groove rubber grips.

NIB	Exc.	V.G.	Good	Fair	Poor
575	450	325	250	175	100

Model 41/741

Same as above but chambered for .41 Magnum cartridge.

NIB	Exc.	V.G.	Good	Fair	Poor
675	550	425	350	250	125

Model 44/744

Same as above but chambered for .44 Magnum cartridge.

NIB	Exc.	V.G.	Good	Fair	Poor
675	550	425	350	250	125

Model 45/745

Same as above but chambered for .45 Colt cartridge.

NIB	Exc.	V.G.	Good	Fair	Poor
675	550	425	350	250	125

Model 360/7360

Same as above but chambered for .357 Magnum on large frame.

NIB	Exc.	V.G.	Good	Fair	Poor
675	550	425	350	250	125

Model 445/7445 (Alaskan Guide)

Chambered for the .445 SuperMag cartridge. Fitted with a 4" heavy ported barrel. Special matte black coating over stainless steel. Introduced in 2002.

NIB	Exc.	V.G.	Good	Fair	Poor
1000	800	675	500	375	250

Model 460/7460

Same as above but chambered for the .45 ACP, .45 Auto Rim, .45 Super, .45 Win. Mag., or the .460 Rowland cartridgs.

NIB	Exc.	V.G.	Good	Fair	Poor
825	650	500	375	200	125

STANDARD SILHOUETTE SERIES

NOTE: All Standard Silhouette series revolvers are stainless steel.

Model 722 VH10

This is a 6-shot revolver chambered for the .22 caliber cartridge. Interchangeable barrel system. Choice of fluted or non-fluted cylinders. Patridge front sight and adjustable rear sight. Hogue finger groove rubber grips standard. Lightweight slotted 8" shroud.

NIB	Exc.	V.G.	Good	Fair	Poor
825	650	500	375	200	125

Model 7360 V8S

Same as above but chambered for the .357 Magnum cartridge.

NIB	Exc.	V.G.	Good	Fair	Poor
825	650	500	375	200	125

Model 741 V8S

Same as above but chambered for the .41 Magnum cartridge with 8" slotted shroud.

NIB	Exc.	V.G.	Good	Fair	Poor
825	650	500	375	200	125

Model 741 V10S

Same as above but with 10" slotted shroud.

NIB	Exc.	V.G.	Good	Fair	Poor
925	750	600	475	300	175

Model 744 V8S

Chambered for .44 Magnum cartridge and fitted with an 8" slotted shroud.

NIB	Exc.	V.G.	Good	Fair	Poor
825	650	500	375	200	125

Model 744 V10S

Same as above but fitted with a 10" slotted shroud.

NIB	Exc.	V.G.	Good	Fair	Poor
925	750	600	475	300	175

Model 740 V8S

Chambered for the .357 Super Mag. and fitted with an 8" slotted shroud.

NIB	Exc.	V.G.	Good	Fair	Poor
925	750	600	475	300	175

Model 7414 V8S

Chambered for the .414 Super Mag and fitted with an 8" slotted shroud.

NIB	Exc.	V.G.	Good	Fair	Poor
925	750	600	475	300	175

Model 7445 V8S

Chambered for the .445 Super Mag. and fitted with an 8" slotted shroud.

NIB	Exc.	V.G.	Good	Fair	Poor
925	750	600	475	300	175

Dan Wesson VH8

.445 SuperMag revolver designed for barrel interchangeability. Also fires standard .44-caliber rounds. Stainless, 6-shot; 8" barrel, 4.1 lb. Single/double action. Introduced 2006.

NIB	Exc.	V.G.	Good	Fair	Poor
1100	950	775	600	450	275

SUPER RAM SILHOUETTE SERIES

NOTE: All Super Ram Silhouette series revolvers are stainless steel.

Model 722 VH10 SRS1

This model is chambered for the .22 caliber cartridge and is fitted with a 10" slotted shroud barrel. Interchangeable barrel system. Adjustable Bomar rear sight. Bomar SRS-1 hood front sight. Fluted or non-fluted cylinders. Hogue finger groove rubber grips.

NIB	Exc.	V.G.	Good	Fair	Poor
925	750	600	475	300	175

Model 7360 V8S SRS1

Same as above but chambered for .357 Magnum cartridge. Fitted with an 8" slotted shroud.

NIB	Exc.	V.G.	Good	Fair	Poor
1100	950	775	600	450	275

Model 741 V8S SRS1

Same as above but chambered for .41 Magnum cartridge and fitted with an 8" slotted shroud.

NIB	Exc.	V.G.	Good	Fair	Poor
1100	950	775	600	450	275

Model 741 V10S SRS1

Same as above but fitted with a 10" slotted shroud.

NIB	Exc.	V.G.	Good	Fair	Poor
1100	950	775	600	450	275

Model 744 V8S SRS1

Same as above but chambered for the .44 Magnum cartridge and fitted with an 8" slotted shroud.

NIB	Exc.	V.G.	Good	Fair	Poor
1100	950	775	600	450	275

Model 744 V10S SRS1

Same as above but fitted with a 10" slotted shroud.

NIB	Exc.	V.G.	Good	Fair	Poor
1100	950	775	600	450	275

Model 740 V8S SRS1

Same as above but chambered for .357 Super Mag. and fitted with an 8" slotted shroud.

NIB	Exc.	V.G.	Good	Fair	Poor
1200	1050	875	700	550	300

Model 7414 V8S SRS1

Same as above but chambered for .414 Super Mag. and fitted with an 8" slotted shroud.

NIB	Exc.	V.G.	Good	Fair	Poor
1200	1050	875	700	550	300

Model 7445 V8S SS1

Same as above but chambered for .445 Super Mag. and fitted with an 8" slotted shroud.

NIB	Exc.	V.G.	Good	Fair	Poor
1200	1050	875	700	550	300

PISTOL PACK SERIES

This series consists of a Dan Wesson revolver of the customer's choice with adjustable rear sight and four barrel assemblies in the small-frame calibers (2.5", 4", 6", and 8"); the large frame and supermag frame have three barrel assemblies (4", 6", and 8"). Also included is a cleaning kit, wrench kit, extra exotic wood grips, instruction manual and fitted hard case. Choice of blue or stainless steel finish ("7" prefix).

Model 22/722

Chambered for .22 LR.

NIB	Exc.	V.G.	Good	Fair	Poor
1200	1050	875	700	550	300

Model 32/732

Chambered for .32 H&R Magnum.

NIB	Exc.	V.G.	Good	Fair	Poor
1200	1050	875	700	550	300

Model 3220/73220

Chambered for the .32-20.

NIB	Exc.	V.G.	Good	Fair	Poor
1200	1050	875	700	550	300

Model 15/715

Chambered for the .357 Magnum.

NIB	Exc.	V.G.	Good	Fair	Poor
1200	1050	875	700	550	300

Model 41/741

Chambered for the .41 Magnum.

NIB	Exc.	V.G.	Good	Fair	Poor
1450	1250	1050	850	650	350

Model 44/744

Chambered for the .44 Magnum.

NIB	Exc.	V.G.	Good	Fair	Poor
1450	1250	1050	850	650	350

Model 45/745

Chambered for the .45 Colt.

NIB	Exc.	V.G.	Good	Fair	Poor
1450	1250	1050	850	650	350

Model 460/7460

Chambered for the .45 ACP, .45 Auto Rim, .45 Super, .45 Win. Mag, .460 Rowland.

NIB	Exc.	V.G.	Good	Fair	Poor
1450	1250	1050	850	650	350

Model 40/740

Chambered for the .357 Maximum.

NIB	Exc.	V.G.	Good	Fair	Poor
1650	1300	1150	950	750	450

Model 414/7414

Chambered for the .414 Super Mag.

NIB	Exc.	V.G.	Good	Fair	Poor
1650	1300	1150	950	750	450

Model 445/7445

Chambered for the .445 Super Mag.

NIB	Exc.	V.G.	Good	Fair	Poor
1650	1300	—	—	—	—

HUNTER PACK SERIES

The Hunter Pack comes with a Dan Wesson revolver of the customer's choice with adjustable rear sight and two 8" barrel assemblies, one with open sights and one drilled and tapped with Burris or Weaver mount installed. Extra set of exotic wood grips, wrench kit, cleaning kit, and manual. Offered in blue or stainless steel ("7" prefix).

Model 22/722

Chambered for .22 LR.

NIB	Exc.	V.G.	Good	Fair	Poor
1200	950	—	—	—	—

Model 32/732

Chambered for .32 H&R Magnum.

NIB	Exc.	V.G.	Good	Fair	Poor
1200	950	—	—	—	—

Model 3220/73220

Chambered for .32-20.

NIB	Exc.	V.G.	Good	Fair	Poor
1200	1050	875	700	550	300

Model 15/715

Chambered for .357 Mag.

NIB	Exc.	V.G.	Good	Fair	Poor
1200	1050	875	700	550	300

Model 41/741

Chambered for the .41 Mag.

NIB	Exc.	V.G.	Good	Fair	Poor
1450	1250	1050	850	650	350

Model 44/744

Chambered for the .44 Mag.

NIB	Exc.	V.G.	Good	Fair	Poor
1450	1250	1050	850	650	350

Model 45/745

Chambered for the .45 Colt.

NIB	Exc.	V.G.	Good	Fair	Poor
1450	1250	1050	850	650	350

Model 460/7460

Chambered for the .45 ACP, .45 Auto Rim, .45 Super, .45 Win. Mag., .460 Rowland.

NIB	Exc.	V.G.	Good	Fair	Poor
1450	1250	1050	850	650	350

Model 40/740

Chambered for the .357 Maximum.

NIB	Exc.	V.G.	Good	Fair	Poor
1650	1300	1150	950	750	450

Model 414/7414

Chambered for the .414 Super Mag.

NIB	Exc.	V.G.	Good	Fair	Poor
1650	1300	1150	950	750	450

Model 445/7445

Chambered for the .445 Super Mag.

NIB	Exc.	V.G.	Good	Fair	Poor
1650	1300	1150	950	750	450

PISTOLS

Pointman Major

This is a semi-auto pistol chambered for the .45 ACP cartridge. Many special features including interchangeable front sight, Jarvis match barrel, adjustable rear sight, beveled magazine well, and others. Stainless steel slide and frame. Rosewood checkered grips. Slide serrations both front and rear. A high sighting rib with interchangeable sights. Introduced in 2000.

NIB	Exc.	V.G.	Good	Fair	Poor
1200	1050	800	625	500	300

Pointman Seven

Has many of the same features as the Pointman Major with blued slide and frame and no sighting rib.

NIB	Exc.	V.G.	Good	Fair	Poor
1100	950	700	525	400	300

Pointman Minor

Same as above except blued slide and frame and no match barrel.

NIB	Exc.	V.G.	Good	Fair	Poor
1100	950	700	525	400	300

Pointman Seven Stainless

Same as above with stainless steel frame and slide.

NIB	Exc.	V.G.	Good	Fair	Poor
1200	1050	800	625	500	300

Pointman Guardian

This model is fitted with a 4.25" barrel and match trigger group. Adjustable rear sight, plus many other special features. Blued frame and slide with sighting rib.

NIB	Exc.	V.G.	Good	Fair	Poor
1200	1050	800	625	500	300

Pointman Guardian Duce

Same as above but with blued steel slide and stainless steel frame.

NIB	Exc.	V.G.	Good	Fair	Poor
825	675	525	400	300	175

Pointman Major Australian

Introduced in 2002 this model features a fully adjustable Bomar-style target sight. Unique slide top configuration that features a rounded radius with lengthwise sight serrations. Slide has Southern Cross engraved on right side. Chambered for the .45 ACP cartridge only.

NIB	Exc.	V.G.	Good	Fair	Poor
1200	1050	800	625	500	300

Pointman Hi-Cap

This .45 ACP pistol is fitted with a 5" barrel and blued carbon alloy wide-body frame with a 10-round magazine. Fixed rear target sight. Extended thumb safety as well as other special features.

NIB	Exc.	V.G.	Good	Fair	Poor
1100	950	700	525	400	300

Pointman Dave Pruitt Signature Series

This pistol is fitted with a 5" match-grade barrel with a rounded top slide with bead blast matte finish. Chevron-style cocking serrations. Fixed rear sight with tactical/target ramp front sight. Many special features.

NIB	Exc.	V.G.	Good	Fair	Poor
1100	950	700	525	400	300

RZ-10

10mm single-action semi-auto with 8+1 capacity. 5" barrel, 2.4 lb. Fixed sights. Introduced 2006.

NIB	Exc.	V.G.	Good	Fair	Poor
1100	950	700	525	400	300

RZ-45 Heritage

Same as the discontinued RZ-10 except in .45 ACP. The RZ refers to "Razorback" which is based on the serrated Clark-style target rib machined onto the top of the slide. Introduced in 2010.

NIB	Exc.	V.G.	Good	Fair	Poor
1100	950	700	525	400	200

Guardian

Designed for concealed carry with Bobtail frame. Caliber is .45 ACP with steel slide, alloy frame, Novak Lo-Mount night sights, extended thumb and grip safeties, 8-round magazine and stippled Shadow grips. Weight 28.8 ounces, 4.3-inch barrel and black Duty finish.

NIB	Exc.	V.G.	Good	Fair	Poor
1300	1100	850	600	450	300

Valor

Full-size 1911-style .45 ACP with black ceramic coated or matte stainless finish. Slimline G10 grips, Heinie Ledge Straight-Eight Night Sights.

NIB	Exc.	V.G.	Good	Fair	Poor
1675	1350	1050	800	500	400

Pointman Nine

Full-size 1911-style in 9mm with 9+1 capacity. Front and rear slide serrations, adjustable rear sight, fiber optic front.

NIB	Exc.	V.G.	Good	Fair	Poor
1300	1100	850	600	450	300

PATRIOT SERIES

Patriot Marksman

Introduced in 2002 this .45 ACP pistol has a 5" match grade barrel. Fixed sights. Many special features such as a beveled mag well, lowered and flared ejection port. Checkered wood grips. Magazine capacity is 8 rounds. Weight is about 38 oz.

NIB	Exc.	V.G.	Good	Fair	Poor
795	650	525	400	300	175

Patriot Expert

As above but fitted with a Bomar target-style adjustable rear sight.

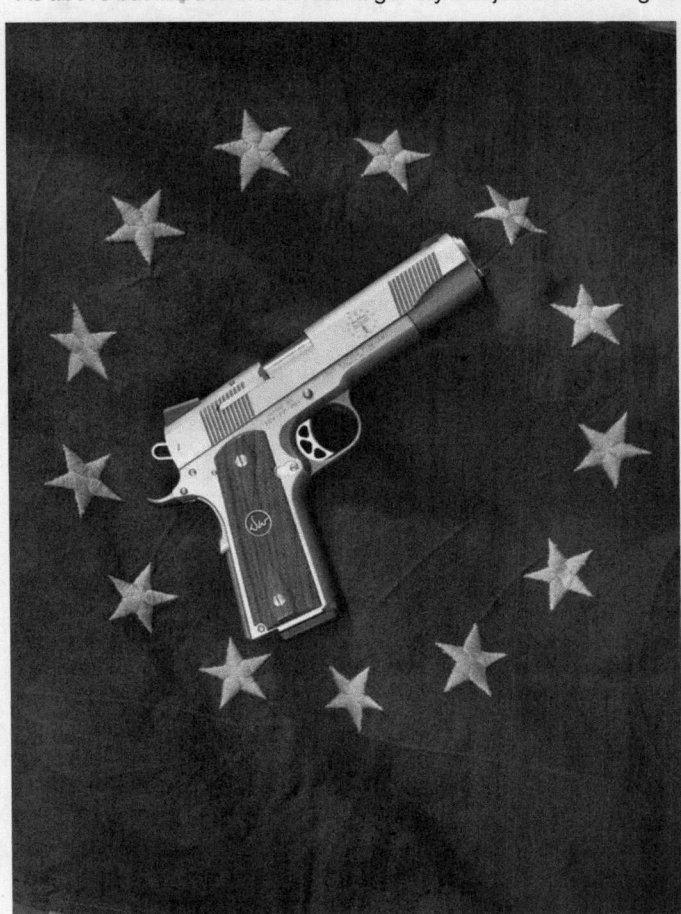

NIB	Exc.	V.G.	Good	Fair	Poor
900	750	625	500	400	225

RIFLES

Coyote Target

Chambered for the .22 LR or .22 Magnum cartridge and fitted with an 18.375" heavy bull barrel. Receiver is drilled and tapped for scope mount. Hardwood stock with high comb and flat-bottom fore-end. Magazine capacity is 6 or 10 rounds. **NOTE:** It is unknown whether the Dan Wesson Coyote rifles were ever actually produced; we suspect not. The values shown are based on 2002 suggested retail prices.

NIB	Exc.	V.G.	Good	Fair	Poor
275	—	—	—	—	—

Coyote Classic

This model is also chambered for the .22 LR or .22 Magnum cartridge. Fitted with a 22.75" barrel with open sights. Drilled and tapped for scope mount. Checkered hardwood stock. Magazine capacity is 6 or 10 rounds. Introduced in 2002.

NIB	Exc.	V.G.	Good	Fair	Poor
235	—	—	—	—	—

WESSON FIREARMS CO., INC.
Palmer, Massachusetts

The company was founded in 1968 by Daniel B. Wesson, the great-grandson of D.B. Wesson, co-founder of Smith & Wesson. This line of handguns is unique for its barrel/shroud interchangeability. Dan Wesson revolvers have established themselves as champion metallic silhouette competition guns. The company offers a comprehensive line of handguns for almost every use. The company will also custom build a handgun to customer specifications. Dan Wesson Arms was restructured on January 4, 1991, and identified as Wesson Firearms Company, Inc. Wesson handguns made after this date will be stamped with this new corporate name. In 1995 the company declared bankruptcy. (See WESSON FIREARMS, DAN)

Model 11

A .357 Magnum caliber double-action swing-out cylinder revolver with interchangeable 2.5", 4", or 6" barrels and a 6-shot cylinder. Blued with walnut grips. Manufactured in 1970 and 1971. **NOTE:** Extra barrels add 25 percent per barrel.

NIB	Exc.	V.G.	Good	Fair	Poor
300	275	150	125	100	75

Model 12

As above, with adjustable target sights.

NIB	Exc.	V.G.	Good	Fair	Poor
350	27	200	175	125	100

Model 14

As above, with a recessed barrel locking nut and furnished with a spanner wrench. Manufactured from 1971 to 1975.

NIB	Exc.	V.G.	Good	Fair	Poor
350	250	175	150	100	75

Model 15

As above, with adjustable target sights.

NIB	Exc.	V.G.	Good	Fair	Poor
375	275	200	175	125	100

Model 8

As above, in .38 Special caliber.

NIB	Exc.	V.G.	Good	Fair	Poor
325	225	150	125	100	75

Model 9

As the Model 15, with adjustable sights and in .38 Special caliber. Manufactured from 1971 to 1975.

NIB	Exc.	V.G.	Good	Fair	Poor
350	275	200	175	125	100

.22 CALIBER REVOLVERS

Model 22

This is a double-action target revolver chambered for the .22 LR cartridge. It is available in 2", 4", 6", and 8" barrel length with a choice of standard rib shroud, ventilated rib shroud, or ventilated heavy rib shroud. All variations feature an adjustable rear sight, red ramp interchangeable front sight and target grips. Offered in bright blue or stainless steel finish. For revolvers with standard barrel assembly weights are: 2"—36 oz., 4"—40 oz., 6"—44 oz., and 8"—49 oz.

Model 722

Same as above but with stainless steel finish.

Model 22M

Same as above but chambered for .22 Magnum with blued finish.

Model 722M

Same as above but chambered for .22 Magnum with stainless steel finish. **NOTE:** Add 10 percent to prices for stainless steel finish.

Standard Rib Shroud

NIB	Exc.	V.G.	Good	Fair	Poor
375	300	200	150	100	75

Ventilated Rib Shroud

NIB	Exc.	V.G.	Good	Fair	Poor
400	325	225	150	100	75

Ventilated Heavy Rib Shroud

NIB	Exc.	V.G.	Good	Fair	Poor
425	330	240	200	125	100

P22 Pistol Pac

This model is also a target revolver similar to the Model 22 and its variations. Chambered for the .22 LR or .22 Magnum, it is also offered with three types of barrel shrouds: standard, ventilated, or ventilated heavy. It is available in blued or stainless steel finish. The principal feature of the Pistol Pac is the three barrel assemblies in 2.5", 4", 6", and 8" with extra grips, four additional front sights, and a fitted carrying case. **NOTE:** Add 10 percent to prices for stainless steel finish.

Standard Rib Shroud

NIB	Exc.	V.G.	Good	Fair	Poor
750	550	400	350	300	150

Ventilated Rib Shroud

NIB	Exc.	V.G.	Good	Fair	Poor
800	600	500	450	350	150

Ventilated Heavy Rib Shroud

NIB	Exc.	V.G.	Good	Fair	Poor
800	600	500	450	350	150

HP22 Hunter Pac

This model is chambered for the .22 Magnum cartridge. The set includes a ventilated heavy 8" shroud, a ventilated 8" shroud only with Burris scope mounts and Burris scope in either 1.5x4X variable or fixed 2X, a barrel changing tool, and fitted carrying case. Finish is blued or stainless steel. **NOTE:** Hunter Pacs are a special order item and should be evaluated at the time of sale.

.32 CALIBER REVOLVERS

Model 32

This model is a target revolver chambered for the .32 H&R Magnum cartridge. It is offered in 2", 4", 6", or 8" barrel lengths with choice of rib shrouds. All variations are fitted with adjustable rear sight, red ramp interchangeable front sight, and target grips. Available in blued or stainless steel finish. Weights depend on barrel length and shroud type but are between 35 oz. and 53 oz.

Model 732

Same as above but with stainless steel finish.

Model 322

Same as above but chambered for .32-20 cartridge with blued finish.

Model 7322

Same as above but chambered for .32-20 cartridge with stainless steel finish. **NOTE:** Add 10 percent to prices for stainless steel finish.

Standard Rib Shroud

NIB	Exc.	V.G.	Good	Fair	Poor
475	325	200	150	100	75

Ventilated Rib Shroud

NIB	Exc.	V.G.	Good	Fair	Poor
500	350	225	150	100	75

Ventilated Heavy Rib Shroud

NIB	Exc.	V.G.	Good	Fair	Poor
525	375	250	150	100	75

P32 Pistol Pac

This set offers the same calibers, barrel shrouds, and finishes as the above models but in a set consisting of 2", 4", 6", and 8" barrels with extra grips, four additional sights, and fitted case. **NOTE:** Add 10 percent to prices for stainless steel finish.

Standard Rib Shroud

NIB	Exc.	V.G.	Good	Fair	Poor
1200	1000	650	500	400	300

Ventilated Rib Shroud

NIB	Exc.	V.G.	Good	Fair	Poor
1200	1000	650	500	400	300

Ventilated Heavy Rib Shroud

NIB	Exc.	V.G.	Good	Fair	Poor
1200	1000	650	500	400	300

329HP32 Hunter Pac

This model is chambered for the .32 H&R Magnum or .32-20 cartridge. The set includes a ventilated heavy 8" shroud, a ventilated 8" shroud only with Burris scope mounts and Burris scope in either 1.5x4X variable or fixed 2X, a barrel-changing tool, and fitted carrying case. Finish is blued or stainless steel.**NOTE:** Hunter Pacs are a special order item and should be evaluated at the time of sale.

.357 MAGNUM AND .38 CALIBER REVOLVERS

Model 14

This is a double-action service revolver chambered for the .357 Magnum cartridge. Available with 2", 4", or 6" barrel with service shroud. It has fixed sights, service grip, and is offered in blued or stainless steel finish.

Model 714

Same as above but with stainless steel finish.

Model 8

Same as above but chambered for .38 Special cartridge with blued finish.

Model 708

Same as above but chambered for .38 Special with stainless steel finish. **NOTE:** Add 10 percent to prices for stainless steel finish.

NIB	Exc.	V.G.	Good	Fair	Poor
400	350	250	125	100	75

P14/8 Pistol Pac

This set consists of a 2", 4", and 6" barrel with service shroud and fixed sights. It has an extra grip and fitted carrying case. The P14 is chambered for the .357 Mag. and the P8 is chambered for the .38 Special.

NIB	Exc.	V.G.	Good	Fair	Poor
800	700	600	500	400	300

Model 15

This model is designed as a double-action target revolver chambered for the .357 Magnum cartridge. It is available with 2", 4", 6", 8", and 10" barrel lengths with standard rib shroud. It features adjustable rear sight, red ramp interchangeable front sight, and target grips. Offered with blued finish. Weights according to barrel length are: 2"-32 oz., 4"-36 oz., 6"-40 oz., 8"-44 oz., 10"-50 oz.

Model 715

Same as above but with stainless steel finish.

Model 9

Same as above but chambered for .38 Special cartridge with blued finish.

Model 709

Same as above but with stainless steel finish. **NOTE:** Add 10 percent to prices for stainless steel finish.

Standard Rib Shroud

NIB	Exc.	V.G.	Good	Fair	Poor
800	700	600	500	400	300

Ventilated Rib Shroud

NIB	Exc.	V.G.	Good	Fair	Poor
800	700	600	500	400	300

Ventilated Heavy Rib Shroud

NIB	Exc.	V.G.	Good	Fair	Poor
800	700	600	500	400	300

330HP15 Hunter Pac

This model is chambered for the .357 Magnum cartridge. The set includes a ventilated heavy 8" shroud, a ventilated 8" shroud only with Burris scope mounts and Burris scope in either 1.5x4X variable or fixed 2X, a barrel changing tool, and fitted carrying case. Finish is blued or stainless steel. **NOTE:** Hunter Pacs are a special order item and should be evaluated at the time of sale.

331Model 40/Supermag

This model is a target revolver chambered for the .357 Maximum cartridge. It has an adjustable rear sight, red ramp interchangeable front sight, ventilated rib shroud, and target grip. Barrel lengths are 4", 6", 8", or 10". A ventilated slotted shroud is available in 8" only. For 1993 a compensated barrel assembly, "CBA," was added to the product line as a complete gun. Finish is blued. Weighs approximately 64 oz. with ventilated rib shroud barrel. Add 20 percent for Model 740 in stainless steel. **NOTE:** Add 10 percent to prices for stainless steel finish. For .357 Supermag with compensated barrel assembly add $30.

Ventilated Rib Shroud

NIB	Exc.	V.G.	Good	Fair	Poor
1100	950	750	600	450	300

Ventilated Slotted Shroud—8" barrel only

NIB	Exc.	V.G.	Good	Fair	Poor
1100	950	750	600	450	300

Ventilated Heavy Rib Shroud

NIB	Exc.	V.G.	Good	Fair	Poor
1100	950	750	600	450	300

332HP40 Hunter Pac

This model is chambered for the .357 Supermag cartridge. The set includes a ventilated heavy 8" shroud, a ventilated 8" shroud only with Burris scope mounts and Burris scope in either 1.5x4X variable or fixed 2X, a barrel changing tool, and fitted carrying case. Finish is blued or stainless steel. **NOTE:** Hunter Pacs are a special order item and should be evaluated at the time of sale.

Model 375

This model, also known as the .375 Supermag, is chambered for the .357 Maximum cartridge, based on the .375 Winchester cartridge. Offered in 6", 8", 10" barrels in ventilated, ventilated heavy, or ventilated slotted rib barrels. Sights are interchangeable and adjustable. Available in bright blue finish only. Weighs approximately 64 oz. with ventilated rib shroud barrel.

variable or fixed 2X, a barrel changing tool, and fitted carrying case. Finish is blued or stainless steel. **NOTE:** Hunter Pacs are a special order item and should be evaluated at the time of sale.

.41, .44 MAGNUM, AND .45 LONG COLT REVOLVERS

Model 44

This model is a target double-action revolver chambered for the .44 Magnum. It has 4", 6", 8", or 10" barrels with ventilated rib shrouds. Other features include: adjustable rear sight, red ramp interchangeable front sight, and target grips. Finish is bright blue. Weights with 4" barrel—40 oz., 6"—56 oz., 8"—64 oz., and 10"—69 oz.

Model 744

Same as above but with stainless steel finish.

301Model 41

Same as above but chambered for .41 Magnum with blued finish.

Ventilated Rib Shroud

NIB	Exc.	V.G.	Good	Fair	Poor
1100	950	750	600	450	300

Ventilated Heavy Rib Shroud

NIB	Exc.	V.G.	Good	Fair	Poor
1100	950	750	600	450	300

Ventilated Slotted Shroud—8" barrel only

NIB	Exc.	V.G.	Good	Fair	Poor
1100	950	750	600	450	300

P15/9 Pistol Pac

This model is a set with 2", 4", 6", and 8" barrels with standard rib shroud. Chambered for the .357 or .38 Special with standard rib shroud, four additional sights, and extra grip, and carrying case. The P15 is chambered for the .357 Mag. while the P9 is chambered for the .38 Special. **NOTE:** Add 10 percent to prices for stainless steel finish.

Standard Rib Shroud

NIB	Exc.	V.G.	Good	Fair	Poor
800	700	600	500	400	300

Ventilated Rib Shroud

NIB	Exc.	V.G.	Good	Fair	Poor
800	700	600	500	400	300

Ventilated Heavy Rib Shroud

NIB	Exc.	V.G.	Good	Fair	Poor
800	700	600	500	400	300

354HP375 Hunter Pac

This model is chambered for the .375 Supermag cartridge. The set includes a ventilated heavy 8" shroud, a ventilated 8" shroud only with Burris scope mounts and Burris scope in either 1.5x4X

302Model 741

Same as above but with stainless steel finish.

Model 45

Same as above but chambered for .45 Long Colt with bright blue finish.

Model 745

Same as above but with stainless steel finish. **NOTE:** Add 10 percent to prices for stainless steel finish.

Ventilated Rib Shroud

NIB	Exc.	V.G.	Good	Fair	Poor
1000	850	550	450	300	200

Ventilated Heavy Rib Shroud

NIB	Exc.	V.G.	Good	Fair	Poor
1000	850	550	450	300	200

P44/P41/P45 Pistol Pac

This set features a 6" and 8" barrel assembly with ventilated rib shroud, an extra grip, two additional front sights, and a fitted carrying case. Chambered for .41 Magnum, .44 Magnum, or .45 Long Colt. **NOTE:** Add 10 percent to prices for stainless steel finish.

Ventilated Rib Shroud

NIB	Exc.	V.G.	Good	Fair	Poor
1000	850	550	450	300	200

Ventilated Heavy Rib Shroud

NIB	Exc.	V.G.	Good	Fair	Poor
1000	850	550	450	300	200

357HP41/44 Hunter Pac

This model is chambered for either the .41 or .44 Magnum cartridge. The set includes a ventilated heavy 8" shroud, a ventilated 8" shroud only with Burris scope mounts and Burris scope in either 1.5x4X variable or fixed 2X, a barrel changing tool, and fitted carrying case. Finish is blued or stainless steel. **NOTE:** Hunter Pacs are a special order item and should be evaluated at the time of sale.

359Model 445

This double-action target revolver is chambered for the .445 Supermag cartridge. Barrel lengths offered are 8" with ventilated slotted rib shroud, 8" ventilated heavy slotted rib shroud, or 10" ventilated slotted rib shroud. Barrel lengths are also available in 4", 6", 8", and 10" with choice of ventilated rib or ventilated heavy rib shrouds. Introduced in 1993 is a compensated barrel assembly available as a complete gun. This is designated the "CBA." Fitted with adjustable rear sights, red ramp interchangeable front sight, and target grips. Finish is bright blue. Typical weight with 8" ventilated rib shroud barrel is about 62 oz.

Model 7445

Same as above but with stainless steel finish. **NOTE:** Add 10 percent to prices for stainless steel finish. For .44 Magnum and .445 Supermag with compensated barrel assembly add $30.

Ventilated Rib Shroud

NIB	Exc.	V.G.	Good	Fair	Poor
1100	950	750	600	450	300

Ventilated Heavy Rib Shroud

NIB	Exc.	V.G.	Good	Fair	Poor
1100	950	750	600	450	300

Model 7445 Alaskan Guide Special

This limited edition model (only 500 were produced) is chambered for the .445 Supermag cartridge. It features a 4" ventilated heavy compensated shroud barrel assembly, synthetic grips, and a matte black titanium nitride finish. Overall barrel length is 5.5" and the revolver weighs 56 oz.

NIB	Exc.	V.G.	Good	Fair	Poor
950	700	600	350	200	100

HP455 Hunter Pac

This model is chambered for the .445 Supermag cartridge. The set includes a ventilated heavy 8" shroud, a ventilated 8" shroud only with Burris scope mounts and Burris scope in either 1.5x4X variable or fixed 2X, a barrel changing tool, and fitted carrying case. Finish is blued or stainless steel. **NOTE:** Hunter Pacs are a special order item and should be evaluated at the time of sale.

FIXED BARREL HANDGUNS

Model 38P

This model is a 5-shot double-action revolver designed for the .38 Special cartridge. Barrel is 2.5" with fixed sights. Choice of wood or rubber grips. Finish is blued. Weighs 24.6 oz.

NIB	Exc.	V.G.	Good	Fair	Poor
350	225	150	125	100	75

Wesson Firearms Silhouette .22

This model is a 6-shot .22 LR single-action-only revolver with a 10" barrel. Fitted with compact-style grips, narrow notch rear sight with choice of ventilated or ventilated heavy rib shroud. Finish is blued or stainless steel. Weighs 55 oz. with ventilated rib shroud and 62 oz. with ventilated heavy rib shroud. **NOTE:** Add 10 percent to prices for stainless steel finish.

Ventilated Rib Shroud

NIB	Exc.	V.G.	Good	Fair	Poor
495	325	275	200	150	100

Ventilated Heavy Rib Shroud

NIB	Exc.	V.G.	Good	Fair	Poor
495	350	285	200	150	100

Model 738P

Same as above but with stainless steel finish.

NIB	Exc.	V.G.	Good	Fair	Poor
525	350	285	200	150	100

Model 45/745 Pin Gun

This model uses a .44 Magnum frame with 5" barrel with two-stage compensator. Choice of ventilated or ventilated heavy rib shroud configuration. Chambered for .45 ACP with or without half moon clips. Finish is blued or stainless steel. Weighs 54 oz. **NOTE:** Add 10 percent to prices for stainless steel finish.

Ventilated Rib Shroud

NIB	Exc.	V.G.	Good	Fair	Poor
1100	950	750	600	450	300

Ventilated Heavy Rib Shroud

NIB	Exc.	V.G.	Good	Fair	Poor
1100	950	750	600	450	300

Model 14/714 Fixed Barrel Service

Same features as the .357 Magnum Model 14 without the interchangeable barrels. Barrel length are either 2.5" or 4" with fixed sights. Offered in either blued or stainless steel. Weighs 30 oz. with 2.5" barrel and 34 oz. with 4" barrel. **NOTE:** Add 10 percent to prices for stainless steel finish.

NIB	Exc.	V.G.	Good	Fair	Poor
275	235	150	125	100	75

Model 15/715 Fixed Barrel Target

Same as the .357 Magnum Model 15 with target sights and grips. Fixed barrel lengths are either 3" or 5". Available in blued or stainless steel. Weighs 37 oz. with 3" barrel and 42 oz. with 5" barrel. **NOTE:** Add 10 percent to prices for stainless steel finish.

NIB	Exc.	V.G.	Good	Fair	Poor
300	250	160	125	100	75

WESSON, EDWIN
Hartford, Connecticut

Dragoon

A .45 caliber percussion revolver with a 7" round barrel and 6-shot unfluted cylinder. The barrel blued, the frame case hardened and the walnut grips fitted with a brass buttcap. Manufactured in 1848 and 1849.

NIB	Exc.	V.G.	Good	Fair	Poor
—	—	13500	9500	5000	1750

WESSON, FRANK
Worcester & Springfield, Massachusetts

Manual Extractor Model

A .22 caliber spur trigger single-shot pistol with a 4" octagonal barrel and thin brass frame. The barrel release is located in the front of the trigger. No markings. Approximately 200 were made in 1856 and 1857.

NIB	Exc.	V.G.	Good	Fair	Poor
—	—	1400	950	400	100

First Model Small Frame

As above, with a 3", 3.5", or 6" half-octagonal barrel. Blued with rosewood or walnut grips. The barrel marked "Frank Wesson Worcester Mass/Pat'd Oct. 25, 1859 & Nov. 11, 1862." Serial numbered from 1 to 2500.

NIB	Exc.	V.G.	Good	Fair	Poor
—	—	900	575	225	75

Second Type

As above, with a flat sighted frame and a circular sideplate.

NIB	Exc.	V.G.	Good	Fair	Poor
—	—	900	575	225	75

First Model Medium Frame

As above, in .30 or .32 rimfire with a 4" half-octagonal barrel and an iron frame. Approximately 1,000 were made between 1859 and 1862.

NIB	Exc.	V.G.	Good	Fair	Poor
—	—	950	600	225	75

Medium Frame Second Model

As above, with a longer spur trigger and a slightly wider frame at the barrel hinge. Manufactured from 1862 to 1870.

NIB	Exc.	V.G.	Good	Fair	Poor
—	—	950	600	225	75

Small Frame Pocket Rifle

A .22 caliber spur trigger single-shot pistol with a 6" half octagonal barrel and narrow brass frame. This model is adopted for use with a detachable skeleton shoulder stock. The barrel marked "Frank Wesson Worcester, Mass." Manufactured from 1865 to 1875 with approximately 5,000 made. **NOTE:** Matching shoulder stock add 100 percent. Prices are for pistols only.

NIB	Exc.	V.G.	Good	Fair	Poor
—	—	1500	925	350	100

Medium Frame Pocket Rifle

As above, in .22, .30, or .32 rimfire with a 10" or 12" half octagonal barrel. Approximately 1,000 were made from 1862 to 1870. **NOTE:** Matching shoulder stock add 100 percent. Prices are for pistols only.

NIB	Exc.	V.G.	Good	Fair	Poor
—	—	1000	650	200	75

Model 1870 Small Frame Pocket Rifle

As above, in .22 caliber with a 10", 12", 15", or 18" or 20" half octagonal barrel that rotates to the side for loading. This model was made with either a brass or iron frame. It has a half cocked notch on the hammer. **NOTE:** Matching shoulder stock add 100 percent. Prices are for pistol only.

NIB	Exc.	V.G.	Good	Fair	Poor
—	—	1000	650	200	75

1870 Medium Frame Pocket Rifle First Type

As above, but with a slightly larger frame chambered for .32 rimfire. Approximately 5,000 were made from 1870 to 1893. **NOTE:** Matching shoulder stock add 100 percent. Prices are for pistols only.

NIB	Exc.	V.G.	Good	Fair	Poor
—	—	1000	650	200	75

1870 Medium Frame Pocket Rifle Second Type

As above, with an iron frame and a push-button half cocked safety. **NOTE:** Matching shoulder stock add 100 percent. Prices are for pistols only

NIB	Exc.	V.G.	Good	Fair	Poor
—	—	900	475	175	75

1870 Medium Frame Pocket Rifle Third Type

As above, with three screws on the left side of the frame. **NOTE:** Matching shoulder stock add 100 percent. Prices are for pistols only.

NIB	Exc.	V.G.	Good	Fair	Poor
—	—	900	475	175	75

1870 Large Frame Pocket Rifle First Type

As above, in .32, .38, .42, or .44 rimfire with an octagonal barrel from 15" to 24" in length. The barrel marked "Frank Wesson Worcester, Mass Patented May 31, 1870." Fewer than 250 of these rifles were made between 1870 and 1880. **NOTE:** Matching shoulder stock add 100 percent. Prices are for pistols only.

NIB	Exc.	V.G.	Good	Fair	Poor
—	—	2750	1500	550	200

1870 Large Frame Pocket Rifle Second Type

As above, with a sliding extractor. **NOTE:** Matching shoulder stock add 100 percent. Prices are for pistols only.

NIB	Exc.	V.G.	Good	Fair	Poor
—	—	2750	1500	550	200

Small Frame Superposed Pistol

A .22 caliber spur trigger over/under pocket pistol with 2" or 2.5" octagonal barrels that revolve. Approximately 3,500 were made between 1868 and 1880. On occasion. this pistol is found with a sliding knife blade mounted on the side of the barrels. The presence of this feature would add approximately 25 percent to the values listed.

NIB	Exc.	V.G.	Good	Fair	Poor
—	—	3000	1750	850	250

Medium Frame Superposed Pistol

As above, in .32 rimfire with 2.5" or 3.5" barrels. As with the smaller version, this pistol is occasionally found with a sliding knife blade mounted on the barrels that would add 25 percent to the values listed. Manufactured from 1868 to 1880.

First Type Marked "Patent Applied For"

NIB	Exc.	V.G.	Good	Fair	Poor
—	—	2500	1250	400	100

Second Type Marked "Patent December 15, 1868"

NIB	Exc.	V.G.	Good	Fair	Poor
—	—	2450	1200	400	100

Third Type Full-Length Fluted Barrels

Courtesy W.P. Hallstein III and son Chip

NIB	Exc.	V.G.	Good	Fair	Poor
—	—	2750	1500	450	150

Large Frame Superposed Pistol

As above, in .41 rimfire with a 3" octagonal barrel fitted with a sliding knife blade. Approximately 2,000 were made from 1868 to 1880.

Courtesy W.P. Hallstein III and son Chip

NIB	Exc.	V.G.	Good	Fair	Poor
—	—	4200	2750	1250	400

No. 1 Long Range Rifle

A .44-100 or .45-100 caliber single-shot dropping block rifle with a 34" octagonal barrel. Blued with a checkered walnut stock. The barrel marked "F. Wesson Mfr. Worcester, Mass. Long Range Rifle Creedmoor." Manufactured in 1876.

NIB	Exc.	V.G.	Good	Fair	Poor
—	—	12500	4500	2000	500

No. 2 Mid-Range or Hunting Rifle

Similar to the above, with the firing pin located in a bolster on the right side of the receiver. The trigger guard has a rear finger loop. Standard barrel length 28", 32", and 34" and marked "F. Wesson Maker Worcester, Mass." The 32" and 34" barrels are occasionally marked "Long Range Rifle Creedmoor." Approximately 100 were made.

Courtesy Buffalo Bill Historical Center, Cody, Wyoming

NIB	Exc.	V.G.	Good	Fair	Poor
—	—	7250	3750	1750	500

No. 2 Sporting Rifle

A .38-100, .40-100, or .45-100 caliber single-shot dropping-barrel-action rifle with barrels ranging from 28" to 34" in length. Approximately 25 were made.

Courtesy Buffalo Bill Historical Center, Cody, Wyoming

NIB	Exc.	V.G.	Good	Fair	Poor
—	—	8250	3750	1750	500

Military Carbine

Fitted with a 24" barrel with sling swivels and chambered for the .44 caliber rimfire cartridge. Approximately 4,500 were manufactured. **NOTE:** Add 100 percent for martially marked examples.

NIB	Exc.	V.G.	Good	Fair	Poor
—	—	6000	2500	1100	500

WESSON & LEAVITT
Chicopee Falls, Massachusetts

Revolving Rifle

A .40 caliber percussion revolving rifle with a 16" to 24" round barrel and 6-shot cylinder. Blued with a walnut stock. Approximately 25 were made in 1849.

NIB	Exc.	V.G.	Good	Fair	Poor
—	—	13000	7500	3500	950

Dragoon

A .40 caliber percussion revolver with a 6.25" or 7" round barrel and 6-shot cylinder. These pistols are marked "Mass. Arms Co./ Chicopee Falls." Approximately 30 were made with the 6.25" barrel and 750 with the 7" barrel. Manufactured in 1850 and 1851.

Courtesy Milwaukee Public Museum, Milwaukee, Wisconsin

NIB	Exc.	V.G.	Good	Fair	Poor
—	—	9000	4750	2000	500

WESTERN ARMS
See—Bacon Arms Co.

WESTERN ARMS CORPORATION
See—Ithaca Gun Co.

WESTERN FIELD
Montgomery Ward

"Western Field" is the trade name used by Montgomery Ward & Company on arms that they retail. See Firearms Trade Names List at the end of this book.

WESTLEY RICHARDS & CO., LTD.
Birmingham, England

A wide variety of firearms have been produced by this company since its founding. Presently, it produces boxlock and sidelock double-barrel shotguns of both side-by-side and over/under form, bolt-action rifles and double-barrel rifles. Prospective purchasers are advised to secure individual appraisals prior to acquisition.

B Model SxS Boxlock, Pre-WWII

NOTE: Add 50 percent for 20 gauge, 80 percent for 28 gauge.

NIB	Exc.	V.G.	Good	Fair	Poor
5000	4250	3500	2800	—	—

Best Quality Sidelock, Current Model

Deluxe Sidelock

NIB	Exc.	V.G.	Good	Fair	Poor
30000	26500	22500	17500	—	—

Magazine Rifle

NIB	Exc.	V.G.	Good	Fair	Poor
12500	10000	8500	7250	—	—

Boxlock Double Rifle

NIB	Exc.	V.G.	Good	Fair	Poor
39000	33000	26500	22000	—	—

Best Quality Over/Under Shotgun, Current Model

NIB	Exc.	V.G.	Good	Fair	Poor
55000	47500	40000	32000	—	—

WHITE, ROLLIN
Lowell, Massachusetts

Pocket Pistol

A .32 or .38 rimfire spur trigger single-shot pistol with a 3" or 5" octagonal barrel. Brass or iron frames with walnut grips. The .38 caliber version with the 5" barrel was not produced in large quantities and therefore is worth approximately 25 percent more than the values listed. The barrels are marked "Rollin White Arms Co., Lowell, Mass."

NIB	Exc.	V.G.	Good	Fair	Poor
—	—	900	750	350	150

Pocket Revolver

A .22 caliber spur trigger revolver with a 3.25" octagonal barrel and 7-shot cylinder. The brass frame silver-plated, barrel blued and grips of walnut. This revolver was marked in a variety of ways including "Rollin White Arms Co., Lowell, Mass.," "Lowell Arms Co., Lowell, Mass.," or "Made for Smith & Wesson by Rollin White Arms Co., Lowell, Mass." Approximately 10,000 were made during the late 1860s.

NIB	Exc.	V.G.	Good	Fair	Poor
—	—	775	600	250	75

WHITNEY ARMS COMPANY
ELI WHITNEY, SR./P. & E.W. BLAKE/ELI WHITNEY, JR.

As the United States' first major commercial arms maker, Eli Whitney's New Haven plant, which began production in 1798 and continued under family control for the next 90 years, was one of the more important American arms manufactories of the 19th century. Its products, accordingly, are eminently collectible. Moreover, during its 90 years of operation, the Whitney clan produced a number of unusual arms, some exact copies of regulation U.S. martial longarms, others variations and derivatives of U.S. and foreign longarms, a variety of percussion revolvers, and finally a variety of single-shot and repeating breechloading rifles in an attempt to capture a portion of the burgeoning market in these cartridge arms during the post-Civil War period. Contrary to the prevailing myth, Eli Whitney, Sr., who also invented the cotton gin, did NOT perfect a system of interchangeability of parts in the arms industry. His contributions in this line were more as a propagandist for the concept that was brought to fruition by others, notably Simeon North and John Hall.

Eli Whitney, Sr. Armory Muskets, 1798-1824. 1798 U.S. Contract Muskets, Types I-IV

On 14 January 1798, Eli Whitney, Sr., having convinced the U.S. War Department that he could mass-produce interchangeable parts muskets, was awarded a contract for 10,000 muskets following the "Charlesville" (French M1766) pattern, then also being copied at the newly opened Springfield Armory and most of the U.S. musket contractors. Whitney's 1798 contract muskets measure between 58-7/8" and 57-3/4" in overall length, with the longer arms delivered earlier. The .69-caliber smoothbore barrels measure approximately 44", though most are shy of that length by anywhere from 1/16" to a maximum of 1-1/4". Lockplates are flat with a beveled edge and are marked "U.STATES" in a curve on the pointed tail and with a perched eagle with down folded wings over "NEW HAVEN" forward of the cock. Four differences in the material and manner of attachment of the pan distinguish the subtypes. The first deliver of 500 muskets in September of 1801 had an integral, faceted iron pan (Type I); the second delivery of 500 muskets in June of 1802 also had faceted iron pans, but were detachable (Type II). The 1,000 muskets delivered in September of 1802 and March of 1803 had faceted, detachable pans, but these were made of brass instead of iron (Type III). The final 8,000 muskets, delivered between 1803 and 1809, had detachable brass pans with a rounded bottom that Whitney copied from the French M1777 musket (Type IV) and a rounded cock, also copied from the French M1777 musket. Generally speaking, due to the limited production of Types I - III, they should command a higher price; prices are given for the more common Type IV 1798 contract musket. It should be noted however, that about 1804 Whitney delivered 112 Type IV muskets to Connecticut's "1st Company of Governor's Foot Guards." Although similar to the

Type IV musket, these 112 arms are distinguished by the absence of the "U.STATES" on the tail of the lock and the addition of the name "CONNECTICUT" to the left side plate. Such an arm should demand a considerable premium over the usual Type IV musket.

NIB	Exc.	V.G.	Good	Fair	Poor
—	—	7500	4500	2000	500

Whitney Connecticut, New York, and U.S. 1812 Contract Muskets

In 1808, Whitney received a contract from the state of New York for 2,000 muskets. In 1810, he received a second contract from the same source for an additional 2,000 muskets, all of which were eventually delivered by mid-1813. In the interim, in 1809, the state of Connecticut contracted with Whitney to deliver 700 muskets per year over the next three years. With the outbreak of the War of 1812, in July of 1812, a contract was let to Eli Whitney for 15,000 muskets (later extended by another 3,000 muskets), conforming to the pattern he had made for the state of New York, but with 42"-long barrels. All of these contract muskets shared most of the same features. Overall length was 58". The .69-caliber smoothbore barrel was nominally 42", though the two state contracts did not rigidly enforce that dimension. The lockplate of these muskets bore the inscription "NEW HAVEN" within a curving scroll forward of the cock. Like the Type III 1798 U.S. contract muskets, the lockplates incorporated a detachable round-bottomed brass pan and a round faced cock. The stock was distinguished by having a low, virtually nonexistent comb similar to that of the 1816 musket pattern. The New York state contract muskets are distinguished by having the state ownership mark "SNY" on the axis of the barrel near the breech. (It should be noted that the first 1,000 muskets delivered under the U.S. 1812 contract were also delivered to New York, but these have the mark across the breech at right angles to the axis of the barrel.) The Connecticut contract muskets are distinguishable by having the state-ownership mark "S.C." (for "state of Connecticut" on the barrel and the top of the comb of the stock. On Connecticut muskets in better condition, the Connecticut coat of arms (a shield with three clusters of grape vines) should also be visible struck into the wood on the left side of the musket opposite the lock. Verifiable Connecticut and New York contract muskets should bring a premium over the U.S. contract muskets.

NIB	Exc.	V.G.	Good	Fair	Poor
—	—	6000	3250	1500	500

Whitney (and P. & E.W. Blake) U.S. M1816/1822 Contract Muskets

The U.S. M1816/1822 muskets manufactured at Whitney's Armory were identical to those produced at the U.S. Armories at Springfield and Harpers Ferry. The overall length was 57-3/4". The 42"-long, .69-caliber smoothbore barrels were finished with a browning solution until 1831; after that date the metal was left in the polished "bright." The stock and the lock reflect Whitney's earlier attempts impart his design elements into the U.S. patterns. The stock had the low comb of his M1812 musket and the lock incorporated the rounded cock and round bottomed brass pan that he had championed from the French M1777 musket. The lock markings varied during the period that the arm was produced, though all were marked on the pointed tail with the vertical stamp: "NEW HAVEN" arced around the date (1825-1830), or in three vertical lines: "NEW / HAVEN / (date: 1831-1842)." Those made between 1825 and 1830 under the direct supervision of Whitney's nephews bore the two line mark "U.S. / P. & E.W. BLAKE" forward of the cock; those made from 1830 to 1837 bear the "U.S" over "E. WHITNEY" with a crossed arrow and olive branch between; after 1837 the crossed arrow and olive branch motif was eliminated in favor of the simple two lines. In addition to the Whitney Armory's federal contracts, Whitney executed at least one contract with the state of South Carolina in the mid-1830s for an estimated 800 to 2,000 muskets. Basically identical in configuration to the federal contract muskets, the South Carolina muskets were distinguished by the substitution of "S.C." for "U.S." over the "E. WHITNEY" stamp of the lockplate. They also bear the state ownership mark "So. CAROLINA" on the top of the barrel. Due to their relative rarity and Confederate usage (especially if altered to percussion by means of a brazed bolster), the South Carolina contract arms should bring a considerable premium.

NIB	Exc.	V.G.	Good	Fair	Poor
—	—	6500	3500	1500	500

Whitney Armory U.S. M1816/M1822 Muskets, Flintlock or Altered to Percussion and Adapted with "Sea Fencible" Heavy Buttplates

A number of the Whitney U.S. M1816/M1822 muskets were delivered to the Commonwealth of Massachusetts under the terms of the 1808 Militia Act. Many of these were subsequently altered to percussion at the Watertown Arsenal near Boston for the state after 1850. At some time in their career both some of the flintlock arms and those that had been altered to percussion were adapted to a heavy brass buttplate with a peculiar knob at its heel. In the process the buttstock was usually narrowed to conform to the width of the new buttplate. Because many of the muskets encountered with this buttplate bore the inspection mark of Samuel Fuller ("SF/V" within a lozenge), these arms were initially considered to have been made for the Massachusetts "Sea Fencible" organizations formed during and after the War of 1812. That appellation, however, has been dismissed, although the exact purpose of the new buttplate and the date of its application are not known. These butt-plates are usually (but not necessarily) found on Whitney contract muskets and invariably are marked with the Massachusetts state ownership mark "MS" on the barrel as well as rack numbers on the tang of the buttplate itself. Despite the unknown purpose of these arms, they command a considerable premium over standard flintlock or altered to percussion Whitney muskets.

NIB	Exc.	V.G.	Good	Fair	Poor
—	—	6500	3500	1250	400

Whitney Armory U.S. M1816/M1822 Muskets, Altered to Percussion

From 1850 through 1856, many of the contract muskets in store at the U.S. arsenals were altered from flintlock to percussion by means of the "Belgian" or "cone-in barrel" method. The system of alteration involved the removal of the flintlock battery from the lock, filing in the screw holes from those parts, substituting a percussion hammer for the cock, plugging the vent, removing the breech plug so as to "upset" the upper, right-hand side top of the barrel, drilling and threading the "upset" section for a cone, reinserting the breech plug, and screwing in a new percussion cone. The percussioned musket was effective but the barrel was considerably weakened by the process, and while some were rifled during the American Civil War, most saw service in that conflict as smoothbores. As a general rule, the muskets so altered generally command about one-third the price of the arm in original flintlock. Exceptions are those with state ownership marks (eg. "OHIO" in the stock), with regimental marks, or with the so-called "Sea Fencible" buttplate.

Whitney Armory Muskets, 1825-1842

Eli Whitney died in 1825. Although he had a son destined to take over the family business, Eli Whitney, Jr. was only 5 years old when his father passed away and could not assume legal possession until he turned 21 in 1842. In the interim, the company was administered by the senior Whitney's trustees, Henry Edwards and James Goodrich, while the plant itself was run by Whitney's nephews, Philo and Eli Whitney Blake. During their control of the factory, three contracts were fulfilled for the U.S. government, one awarded in August of 1822 for 15,000 muskets (delivered between 1826 and 1830), a second awarded in March of 1830 for 8,750 muskets (delivered between 1831 and 1836) and a final contract in January of 1840 for 3,000 muskets (delivered between 1840 and 1842). An additional 6,750 were delivered under annual allotments granted by the War Department between 1835 and 1839 over and above the contracts for distribution to the states under the 1808 Militia Act. Although the 1840 contract had originally called for U.S. M1840 muskets, in April of that year, the contract was altered so

that Whitney's plant could continue to deliver what it had delivered consistently from 1824, the U.S. M1816/1822 flintlock musket.

Eli Whitney, Jr. Armory Rifles and Rifle-Muskets, 1842-1865

Upon reaching the age of 21 in 1842, Eli Whitney, Jr. assumed command of his late father's gun making empire. Although he realized that the armory required updating to meet the improved tolerances adopted by the U.S. War Department, he also realized that a profit might be made in turning out arms of lesser standards for independent sale to the militia or the states. As a result, the younger Whitney's product line included not only several of the regulation U.S. longarms, but also a number of "good and serviceable" militia arms, including:

Whitney U.S. M1841 Contract Rifle (unaltered)

Between 1842 and 1855 Eli Whitney, Jr. received five contracts from the U.S. War Department to manufacture the newly adopted U.S. M1841 percussion rifle: 7,500 on October of 1842 (delivered between 1844 and 1847), 7,500 in March of 1848, subsequently extended to 10,000 in January of 1849 (delivered between 1849 and 1853) 5,000 (previously contracted for by Edward K. Tryon) in October of 1848 (delivered contiguous with the 1848 contract for 10,000), 5,000 in 1853 (delivered between 1853 and 1855), and 100 in 1855 (delivered that year). All except the final 1,100 delivered in 1855 conformed to the model made at Harpers Ferry, and of those 1,100, the only difference of 500 of them was the ramrod. This rifle was 49" in length, overall, having a 33" long browned barrel with .54 caliber rifled (7 groove) bore. The barrel bears the stamp of inspection at the breech, usually "U S /(inspectors' initials) / P," while the left flat (after mid-1848 for Whitney rifles) should also bear the stamping "STEEL" to indicate that the barrel had been rolled from "cast steel." Furniture is brass, the buttplate bearing the stamped letters, "U S." The lockplate is flat with a beveled edge and bears the horizontal two line inscription "E. WHITNEY" / "U S" forward of the hammer and the vertical, two line inscription "N. HAVEN" / (date) on the tail. (The date also appears on the breech plug tang). As originally made, the M1841 rifle was not adapted for a bayonet, though several modifications were made to the rifle between 1855 and 1862 to affect that adaptation.

NIB	Exc.	V.G.	Good	Fair	Poor
—	—	7500	4750	1750	500

Whitney U.S. M1841/1855 Contract Rifle, Adapted to Saber Bayonet and Long Range Sights

Before the final 600 rifles (of the 2,600 made in 1855) left the factory, the U.S. War Department contracted with Whitney to bring them up to the standards of the modified U.S. M1841 rifle then being produced or adapted at the Harpers Ferry Armory. The adaptation was two fold. First, a long range rear "ladder" style rear sight, having a 2-1/4" base was soldered to the top of the barrel; then a 1/2" long bayonet lug with 1" guide was brazed to the right side of the barrel, 2-1/2" from the muzzle. To permit disassembly, the old front band was removed and replaced with a shortened version. A new ramrod (also applied to 500 rifles without this adaptation), having an integral iron head cupped for the newly adopted "Minie ball" replaced the flat brass headed ramrod to complete the process; the rifle remained in .54 caliber with 7 grooves. Neither was the front sight modified. Bayonets were furnished by the Ames Manufacturing Company on a separate contract. Rifles so adapted at the Whitney Armory are among the rarer variants of the U.S. M1841 line and prices reflect that rarity.

NIB	Exc.	V.G.	Good	Fair	Poor
—	—	7500	4750	1750	650

Whitney U.S. M1841 Contract Rifles, Adapted to Saber Bayonets and Long Range Rear Sights (Colt 1862 Adaptation)

A large number of unaltered U.S. M1841 rifles remained on hand in U.S. Arsenals when the Civil War broke out, primarily those of Whitney's and Robbins & Lawrence's manufacture. To upgrade these rifles, revolver maker, Samuel Colt arranged to purchase 10,500 and adapt them to bayonets and long-range sights. The sight that he affixed consisted of the two leaf rear sight he had been using on his revolving rifles, with one leaf flopping forward and one flopping backward from the 100 yard block. The saber bayonet lug he attached consisted of a blued clamping ring with integral 1/2"-long lug attached that could fastened to the barrel so that the lug projected from the right side. These lugs were numbered both to the bayonet and the rifle's barrel, the number appearing on the lower surface of the barrel just behind the location of the clamping ring. Colt also bored the rifles up to .58 caliber, leaving some with 7 grooves but rerifling others with 3 wide grooves. An estimated half of the 10,200 rifles so modified by Colt were of Whitney's earlier production. Due to the Colt association, rifles so modified usually command slightly higher prices than other Civil War adaptations for saber or socket bayonets.

NIB	Exc.	V.G.	Good	Fair	Poor
—	—	7500	4750	1750	650

Whitney South Carolina Contract M1841 Rifle

To meet the perceived needs of South Carolina during the anti-slavery debates following the Mexican War Annexation, Whitney produced a variant of the U.S. M1841 rifle for that state, delivering only 274 in 1849. The marking of this rifle differed only in having the letters "S C" on the plate beneath the "E. WHITNEY" stamp. Because South Carolina had previously contracted for 1,000 variant M1841 rifles from William Glaze & Co. in 1853 which accepted a socket bayonet, Whitney provided the 274 1849 dated rifles with that provision also, although the lug was located under the barrel instead of atop it. Because the socket bayonet dominated the forward 3" of the barrel, the front sight was relocated to the top of the upper strap of the front band. Rifles from this contract are exceedingly rare.

NIB	Exc.	V.G.	Good	Fair	Poor
—	—	10000	6500	3250	950

Whitney "Good & Serviceable" M1841 Derivatives

From parts or entire rifles rejected for his federal contracts for U.S. M1841 rifles, between 1848 and 1860, Eli Whitney, Jr. assembled a number of rifles similar in overall characteristics to the federal contract rifles but differing both in quantity and in a number of minor details. At least four variations were produced between 1855 and 1862 and sold to various states or independent militia companies. Distinguishing characteristics of these four are:

Type I. M1841 rifle adapted to saber bayonet but not to long range sights. A 1/2" long saber bayonet lug (either with or without

the 1" guide) brazed to the right side of the barrel; long front band replaced with short double strapped band left over from 1855 contract. Some of this type (without 1" guide) are known with "OHIO" state ownership marks and are thought to be from among the 420 purchased by the state in 1861 from Schuyler, Hartley, & Graham. Examples are known with the lockplate dated 1855 and without any date or "US" stamp below "E. WHITNEY."

Type II. M1841 rifle adapted to saber bayonet and Sharps long range sight. These rifles also bear the 1/2" brazed saber bayonet lug (with the 1" guide) and the short front band, but they also have a Sharps M1853 "ladder" rear sight added in lieu of the standard notched iron block. Moreover, rifles in this configuration lack the brass patchbox lid and its underlying cavity for implements and greased patches.

Type III. M1841 rifle adapted to socket bayonet and Sharps long range sight. These late-production (1859-1860) derivatives of the M1841 rifle are adapted to the Sharps long-range sight used on the Type II. rifles but have a patch box. Unlike standard production, however, it is covered with an iron lid and hingle. The trigger guard strap is also iron. Lock plates delete both the date from the tail and the "US" under "E. WHITNEY." An iron stud is added below the barrel near the muzzle for a socket bayonet, necessitating the relocation of the brass blade front sight to the upper strap of the forward band. Probably fewer than 100 of this configuration were made, making it the most desirable of the derivative M1841 rifles.

Type IV. M1841 rifle unadapted using modified parts. Rifles of this configuration use the same markings as the type III rifles but delete entirely the patch box and its lid (like the type II rifles). The trigger guard strap is iron and the lock screws seem to be the same as Whitney used for his Whitney short Enfield derivative rifles. It is suspected that these rifles were purchased from New York dealers and sold to Georgia during the secession crisis of 1860-1861, thereby enhancing their collector's value, though in general Whitney M1841 derivative rifles are equal in pricing:

NIB	Exc.	V.G.	Good	Fair	Poor
—	—	6500	3250	1250	500

Whitney M1842 Rifled Musket Derivative

Using rejected U.S. M1842 barrels sold at auction by the Springfield Armory, Whitney assembled approximately 2,000 .69 caliber rifled muskets that he exchanged with the state of New Hampshire in 1858 for a number of old flintlock muskets owned by that state. These rifled muskets exhibit a number of anomalies from the U.S. M1842 musket, although overall length (57-3/4") and the barrel length (42") remain the same as that musket, the bores are rifles with 7 narrow grooves, and in addition to the dates and inspection marks placed at Springfield usually bear the state ownership mark "NEW HAMPSHIRE" on the top of the barrel. In finishing these rifled muskets, Whitney utilized a number of parts from other gun makers, including Sharps M1853 "ladder" style carbine rear sights, bands from the Robbins & Lawrence P1853 Enfield rifle-musket contract, and internal lock parts remaining from his M1841 rifles. Parts that are unique to these arms include the iron nosecap and the flat lockplate. The lockplates are unmarked, but the barrels usually show a letter/number code common to Whitney's production during this period. Despite a production of approximately 2,000 muskets, the survival rate for this type of arm is quite low.

NIB	Exc.	V.G.	Good	Fair	Poor
—	—	6500	3250	1250	400

Whitney P1853 "Long Enfield" Rifle-Musket Derivative

Having secured a number of bands and other furniture from the Robbins & Lawrence contract for P1853 Enfield rifle-muskets, about 1859 Whitney developed a derivative of that arm that combined those bands with a 40"-barrel .58 caliber, rifled with 7 grooves that basically resembled the configuration of the U.S. M1855 rifle-musket, a copy of which Whitney was also making. The 56"-long rifle-musket that resulted was sold to state militia companies and two states, Maryland purchasing 2,000 and Georgia contracting for 1,700 (of which 1,225 were delivered). Although several of the components of the furniture were from the Robbins & Lawrence contract, the nosecap was pewter (Enfield style), and the iron buttplate and brass trigger guard bow/iron strap were of a style peculiar to Whitney' Enfield series. The rear sight resembled the ladder pattern of the U.S. M1855 rifle musket. The unique flat, unbeveled lockplate simply bears the one line stamp, "E. WHITNEY" forward of the hammer.

NIB	Exc.	V.G.	Good	Fair	Poor
—	—	6500	3250	1250	600

Whitney P1853 "Short Enfield" Rifle Derivative

Total production of these rifles is estimated to have been between 800 and 1,000, with approximately half of the number going to southern states. Prices should not vary between the four types; however, confirmed Confederate usage will increase the value significantly. Type IV. Identical to Type III but with a new single leaf rear sight on a 1-1/4" long base.

NIB	Exc.	V.G.	Good	Fair	Poor
—	—	8500	4250	2000	600

Whitney M1855 Rifle Derivative

At the same time that Whitney advertised his Enfield derivative series of rifle-muskets and rifles, he also indicated the availability of a short rifle with saber bayonet. This rifle combined rejected barrels made at Harpers Ferry in 1858 for the U.S. M1855 rifles with rejected, unmilled Maynard tape primer lockplates that had been shaved of their top "hump," marked forward of the hammer with the single line stamp, "E. WHITNEY." The buttplate and the trigger guard also conform to that of the U.S. M1855 rifle, but the bands are brass, remaining from Whitney's M1841/1855 rifle contract. Early in production these rifles used round brass lock screw washers following the M1855 pattern; later production used the winged brass lock screw washers that Whitney inherited from the Robbins & Lawrence P1853 rifle-musket contract and which he used on his Enfield series derivatives. At least two patterns of saber bayonet were used on this rifle.

NIB	Exc.	V.G.	Good	Fair	Poor
—	—	7000	3500	1250	500

Whitney M1855 Rifle-Musket Derivative

In 1861, Whitney accepted a U.S. contract to produce 40,000 U.S. "M1855" rifle-muskets. What Whitney had in mind under this contract and what the War Department demanded were two different arms. Whitney's product was similar to the U.S. M1855 rifle-musket but differed in a number of respects. The 40" barrel was .58 caliber but was rifled with 7 rather than 3 grooves and was adapted to the English P1853 socket bayonet he had been using on his Enfield derivative rifle-muskets. The initial rear sight, while similar to the U.S. M1855 type, was slightly shorter, having a 2-5/16" base. (On later production, Whitney substituted a shorter, 1-1/4"-long base with a single, pierced leaf sight.) The nosecap, moreover, was made of pewter and followed the Enfield pattern rather than being malleable iron of the U.S. M1855 pattern. On later production, Whitney also substituted brass winged lock screw washers from his Enfield derivative series. The lockplates for these arms were drawn from complete Maynard locks made at the federal armories in 1858 and 1859 but later rejected for flaws. Upon these plates Whitney stamped "E. WHITNEY / N. HAVEN," as on his early Connecticut contract M1861 derivative rifle-muskets. Except for the letter/number code, the barrels are unmarked. Examples are known whose stocks bear indications of issue to the 8th Connecticut Infantry during the Civil War, suggesting Whitney may have sold the few made to Connecticut under his first state contract. Arms with these regimental marks should command a premium over unmarked arms.

NIB	Exc.	V.G.	Good	Fair	Poor
—	—	7000	3500	1250	500

Whitney M1861 Connecticut Contract Rifle-Musket Derivative

In 1861 and 1862, Eli Whitney, Jr. entered into two contracts with his home state of Connecticut for respectively 6,000 and 8,000 rifle-muskets generally conforming to the U.S. M1861 rifle musket. A number of exceptions to the U.S. model, however, were permitted. On the first contract, the 40" barrels were in .58 caliber but were made with 7 groove rifling instead of 3 groove; on the second contract, the arms were made with 3-groove rifling. Nosecaps for both contracts were of the U.S. M1855/1861 pattern but were cast in pewter instead of malleable iron. An exception was also permitted in the rear sights, which initially were the same 1-1/4" long base with pierced single leaf that Whitney had used on his Type IV short Enfield derivative rifles, though later the base was changed to conform to the pattern adopted for the U.S. M1861 rifle-musket but still retaining the single leaf. Lockplates were M1861-style, marked forward of the hammer "E. WHITNEY / N. HAVEN" on early production and with an eagle surmounting a panoply of flags and trophies over "WHITNEYVILLE" on later production. The barrels bore the typical Whitney letter/number code and were adapted to the Enfield pattern socket bayonets rather than the U.S. M1855 socket bayonets. Later production occasionally bears the inspection letters "G.W.Q."

NIB	Exc.	V.G.	Good	Fair	Poor
—	—	6000	2750	1150	400

Whitney "High Humpback" Lockplate M1861 Rifle-Musket Derivative

With the completion of his Connecticut contracts, Whitney combined the excess parts from its production with some of the unmilled and unshaved lockplates that he still had on hand from his M1855 Rifle Derivatives. The 56"-long rifle-muskets that resulted have 40" barrels in .58 caliber with 3-groove rifling and a rear sight that conforms to the U.S. M1861 pattern that Whitney began making in 1863. The flat, beveled unmilled lockplates bear the two line stamp "E. WHITNEY / N. HAVEN" that Whitney had used on his M1855 rifle-musket derivative and on the early M1861 Connecticut contract rifle-muskets, but showing considerable wear, to the extent that the second line is often incomplete or missing entirely. Photograph evidence indicates that the 21st Connecticut Infantry received some of these rifle-muskets. They are often mistaken as a southern purchase, which artificially raises the asking prices.

NIB	Exc.	V.G.	Good	Fair	Poor
—	—	7000	3250	1250	500

Whitney "Manton" M1861 Rifle-Musket Derivative

In order to dispose of some of his inferior arms from the second Connecticut state contract, Whitney assembled at least 1,300 bearing a fictitious Old English lock stamp "Manton" forward of the hammer and the date "1862" on its tail. In most respects this arm resembled the U.S. M1861 rifle musket, complete with 3-groove rifling in its .58-caliber, 40" barrel with typical Whitney letter/number code near the muzzle (and often also marked "G.W.Q. on its left flat). Nosecaps, in typical Whitney style, were case from pewter instead of being formed from malleable iron. The rear sight closely follows the M1861 pattern but lacks the step on its side walls since it utilized a simple pierced leaf instead of the compound double leaf of the M1861 rifle-musket. These arms were disposed of in the New York City market after the 1863 Draft Riot and issued to the New York National Guard.

NIB	Exc.	V.G.	Good	Fair	Poor
—	—	8250	4250	2000	600

Whitney "Direct Vent" M1861 Rifle-Musket Derivatives

In his continued efforts to dispose of surplus and rejected parts from his Connecticut and federal contracts, Whitney devised in 1863 a rifle-musket generally conforming to the M1861 rifle-musket except in two notable features. The bolster, instead of projecting considerably away from the barrel and having a clean-out screw was relatively short and flat faced. The process of making this bolster eliminated one production sequence, since it was not possible to drill the hole for the cone directly to the barrel. To accommodate the new cone position, the lockplates were made flat, without the bevel, and inletted flush with the stock. Lockplates bear the eagle surmounting the panoply of flags and trophies over "WHITNEYVILLE" stamp forward of the hammer, and are known with "1863" on the tail or without any date. The rear sight is the same as used on the "Manton" rifle-musket derivative. Arms with barrels than 40", 39", and 30" exist, all in .58 caliber with 3-groove rifling; however, the shortest of these may be post-war modifications for cadet use. Quantities made are not known, but surviving examples suggest limited production, probably to use faulty parts from the 1863 federal contract.

NIB	Exc.	V.G.	Good	Fair	Poor
—	—	7000	3250	1250	400

Whitney U.S. M1861 Contract Rifle-Musket

In October of 1863, Whitney secured a contract with the U.S. War Department to produce 15,000 U.S. M1861 rifle-muskets. The arms manufactured under this contract conform in all respects to the Springfield Model adopted in 1861. The 40" barrel is in .58 caliber and rifled with 3 grooves; its rear sight conforms to the two-leaf model with stepped side walls. Nosecap is M1861 style and made of malleable iron. Socket bayonets furnished with them conform to the U.S. M1855/M1861 pattern. Marks include "US" on buttplate and standard inspection marks on barrel and stock. Lockplate marked with eagle surmounting letters "US" forward of the hammer and "WHITNEYVILLE" on the forward projection of the plate; date, "1863" or "1864" stamped on tail of the plate.

NIB	Exc.	V.G.	Good	Fair	Poor
—	—	7000	3250	1250	400

Whitney U.S. Navy Contract Rifle

In July of 1861, Whitney entered a contact with the U.S. Navy to produce 10,000 rifles of the "Plymouth Pattern." So called after the U.S. Navy warship whereupon the first Harpers Ferry trial rifles had been developed, the new Navy rifle borrowed many of its characteristics from the French M1846 "carbine a tige." Overall length was 50" with a 34"-long barrel bearing a saber bayonet lug with guide extending nearly to the muzzle on its right side. The bore was .69 caliber, rifled with three broad lands and grooves. The rear sight copied the French M1846 and M1859 styles, i.e. it has an elevating ladder but no sidewalls. On early production the sights are serially numbered to the rifle's serial number (appearing on the breech plug tang). Barrels bear the standard U.S. inspection marks on the left quarter flat and the production date ("1863" or "1864") on the top of the barrel near the breech. Two lock markings have been encountered. The earlier production uses flat beveled plate marked with the date "1863" on its tail and an eagle surmounting a panoply of flags and trophies over the name "WHITNEYVILLE." In later (after serial no. 3,000) the lock's tail is marked "1864" and the stamping forward of the hammer matches that on the U.S. M1861 Whitney contract rifle-muskets, i.e. a small eagle over "U S" and "WHITNEYVILLE" in the forward projection of the plate. Inspector's initials (F.C.W.) appear on the barrel and in a cartouche on the stock.

NIB	Exc.	V.G.	Good	Fair	Poor
—	—	8250	4250	1750	600

The Whitney Arms Company, 1865-1888

With the close of the American Civil War, Eli Whitney, Jr. again turned his eyes to the manufacture of inexpensive arms from parts remaining on hand from his Civil War contracts. Extra barrels were turned into inexpensive muzzleloading shotguns, and a few breechloading designs were toyed with. Following Remington's example, Whitney soon realized that a substantial profit could be made in the production of single-shot martial arms for foreign governments. The result was a series of breechloading arms that copied many salient features of the Remington line, including a direct copy after the expiration of the Remington patent for the "rolling block" mechanism. Not until the late 1870s did Whitney

acquire the rights to several patents that led to the production of a lever-action repeating rifle. During the post-war period, revolver production, which had begun with evasions of Colt's patents in the decade prior to the Civil War, mushroomed with the production of small spur-trigger rimfire cartridge revolvers. Despite the variety of arms produced, by 1883 Whitney was considering the sale of his company. Business reverses over the next five years necessitated the sale of the firm to Winchester in 1888. Primarily interested securing in the patent rights for Whitney's lever-action series of rifles, Winchester closed the plant and moved its machinery to New Haven. After 90 years of production, the Whitneyville Armory ceased to exist.

Single Barreled Percussion Shotgun

This firearm was manufactured by Whitney out of surplus .58 caliber rifle barrels that were opened up and converted to smoothbore .60-caliber shotgun barrels. They are offered in lengths of 28" to 36" and are marked "Whitney Arms Co., Whitneyville, Conn. Homogeneous Wrought Steel." The finish is blued, with varnished walnut stocks that are crudely checkered. There were approximately 2,000 manufactured between 1866 and 1869. These guns are rarely encountered on today's market.

NIB	Exc.	V.G.	Good	Fair	Poor
—	—	1300	950	400	150

Double-Barreled Percussion Shotgun

The specifications for this version are similar to that of the single barrel except that there are two side-by-side barrels with double locks and hammers and double triggers. They are slightly more common than the single barreled version.

NIB	Exc.	V.G.	Good	Fair	Poor
—	—	1300	950	400	150

Swing-Breech Carbine

This is a single-shot breechloading carbine chambered for the .46-caliber rimfire cartridge. It has a 22" round barrel with a button-released breechblock that swings to the side for loading. The finish is blued, with a walnut stock. There were fewer than 50 manufactured in 1866.

NIB	Exc.	V.G.	Good	Fair	Poor
—	—	6000	3250	1750	600

Whitney-Cochran Carbine

This is a single-shot breechloading carbine chambered for the .44 rimfire cartridge. It has a 28" round barrel with a lever-activated breechblock that raises upward for loading. It was manufactured under license from J.W. Cochran. The finish is blued, with a walnut stock. There is a saddle ring on the left side of the frame. It is marked "Whitney Arms Co. - Whitneyville, Conn." This gun was produced for the 1867 Government Carbine Trials. There were fewer than 50 manufactured in 1866 and 1867.

Courtesy Milwaukee Public Museum, Milwaukee, Wisconsin

NIB	Exc.	V.G.	Good	Fair	Poor
—	—	7000	3500	1500	600

Excelsior

This is a single-shot rifle chambered for the .38, .44, or .50 rimfire cartridges. It is found with various-length octagonal or round barrels. The finish is blued, with a walnut stock and forearm held on by one barrel band. The breechblock pivots downward for loading. There is a center-mounted hammer. It is marked "Whitney Arms Co. Whitneyville Conn." The shorter barreled carbine versions have a saddle ring on the frame. There were approximately 200 manufactured between 1866 and 1870.

NIB	Exc.	V.G.	Good	Fair	Poor
—	—	6700	2750	1150	400

Whitney-Howard Lever Action ("Thunderbolt)

This is a single-shot breechloader that is chambered for the .44 rimfire cartridge. It has also been noted as a shotgun chambered for 20 gauge smoothbore with barrels from 30" to 40" in length. The rifle version has barrel lengths from 22" to 28". The breechblock is opened by means of a combination lever and trigger guard. There is also a carbine version with barrel lengths of 18.5" or 19". There were approximately 2,000 manufactured totally between 1866 and 1870.

Shotgun

Courtesy Buffalo Bill Historical Center, Cody, Wyoming

NIB	Exc.	V.G.	Good	Fair	Poor
—	—	1400	650	300	100

Rifle

Courtesy Milwaukee Public Museum, Milwaukee, Wisconsin

NIB	Exc.	V.G.	Good	Fair	Poor
—	—	1600	900	450	150

Carbine

Courtesy Milwaukee Public Museum, Milwaukee, Wisconsin

NIB	Exc.	V.G.	Good	Fair	Poor
—	—	2000	1250	500	200

Whitney Phoenix

There is little known about the origin of this model. It is built on a patent issued to Whitney in 1874. There are a number of variations that are all marked "Phoenix, Patent May 24, 74." The Whitney name is not marked on any of the versions. They are all single-shot breechloaders with a breechblock that lifts to the right side and upward for loading. The barrels are all blued, with either case colored or blued receivers and walnut stocks. There were approximately 25,000 total manufactured between 1867 and 1881. The models and values are listed.

Courtesy Milwaukee Public Museum, Milwaukee, Wisconsin

Gallery Rifle

This version is chambered for the .22 rimfire caliber and has a 24" half-octagonal barrel. Its production was quite limited.

NIB	Exc.	V.G.	Good	Fair	Poor
—	—	3250	1500	600	200

Shotgun

This is a smoothbore version chambered for 10, 12, 14, 16, or 22 gauge. It has smoothbore barrels between 26" and 32" in length. There were approximately 5,000 manufactured.

NIB	Exc.	V.G.	Good	Fair	Poor
—	—	1100	600	250	100

Military Rifle

This version is chambered for the .433, .45, or .50 caliber centerfire cartridges. It has a 35" round barrel with a full-length, two-piece walnut stock held on by three barrel bands. There were approximately 15,000 manufactured. Many were sent to Central or South America.

NIB	Exc.	V.G.	Good	Fair	Poor
—	—	5750	3000	1250	400

Schuetzen Rifle

This is a target-shooting version chambered for the .38, .40, or .44 centerfire cartridges. It has either a 30" or 32" octagonal barrel with a Schuetzen-type walnut stock and forearm that features hand checkering. It has a nickel-plated, Swiss-style buttplate and adjustable sights with a spirit level. This model has been noted with double-set triggers. There were few manufactured.

NIB	Exc.	V.G.	Good	Fair	Poor
—	—	6000	3250	1250	400

Civilian Carbine

Courtesy Milwaukee Public Museum, Milwaukee, Wisconsin

This version is chambered for the .44 caliber centerfire and has a 24" round barrel. The finish is blued, with a case colored frame and a walnut stock and forearm held on by one barrel band. It has military-type sights, buttplate, and a saddle ring mounted on the frame. There were approximately 500 manufactured.

NIB	Exc.	V.G.	Good	Fair	Poor
—	—	4800	2500	850	400

Military Carbine

Courtesy Milwaukee Public Museum, Milwaukee, Wisconsin

This version is chambered for the .433, .45, or .50 centerfire cartridges. It has a 20.5" round barrel and was manufactured for Central and South America. It is very rarely encountered on today's market.

NIB	Exc.	V.G.	Good	Fair	Poor
—	—	5000	2750	1000	400

Whitney-Laidley Model I Rolling Block

Whitney acquired manufacturing rights for this model from the inventors T. Laidley and C.A. Emery, who had received the patent in 1866. Whitney immediately started to modify the action to become competitive with the Remington Rolling Block. There were approximately 50,000 manufactured total between 1871 and 1881. There are a number of variations of this model.

Military Carbine

There were approximately 5,000 manufactured chambered for the .433, .45, or .50 centerfire cartridges. It has a 20.5" round barrel with military-type sights and a saddle ring on the receiver. The finish is blued, with a case colored frame and a walnut stock. Most of them were shipped to Central or South America.

NIB	Exc.	V.G.	Good	Fair	Poor
—	—	3500	1750	700	250

Civilian Carbine

This version is chambered for .44 rimfire or centerfire and .46 rimfire. It has either an 18.5" or 19.5" barrel. It is blued, with a case colored frame. The stock is walnut. A nickel-plated version is also available. There were approximately 1,000 of this version manufactured.

NIB	Exc.	V.G.	Good	Fair	Poor
—	—	2800	1750	700	250

Military Rifle

Courtesy Milwaukee Public Museum, Milwaukee, Wisconsin

This version is chambered the same as the Military Carbine but has either a 32.5" or 35" round barrel with a full-length two-piece stock held on by three barrel bands. The finish is blued, with a case colored receiver and a walnut stock. There were approximately 30,000 manufactured. Most were shipped to Central or South America.

NIB	Exc.	V.G.	Good	Fair	Poor
—	—	3950	2000	800	300

Gallery Rifle

This is a .22 caliber sporting-rifle version with a 24" octagonal barrel. The finish is similar to the Military Rifle. There were approximately 500 manufactured.

NIB	Exc.	V.G.	Good	Fair	Poor
—	—	3400	1750	700	250

Sporting Rifle

This version is chambered for .38, .40, .44, .45, or .50 centerfire, as well as .32, .38, or .44 rimfire. It features barrel lengths from 24" to 30" in either round or octagonal configurations. The finish is similar to the Military Rifle, and there were approximately 5,000 manufactured.

NIB	Exc.	V.G.	Good	Fair	Poor
—	—	3950	2000	750	300

Creedmoor No. 1 Rifle

This version is chambered for the .44 caliber cartridge and has a 32" or 34" barrel that is either round or octagonal in configuration. It has a blued finish with case colored frame and a hand checkered, select walnut stock and forearm. It features vernier adjustable sights with a spirit level. It is marked "Whitney Creedmoor." There were fewer than 100 manufactured.

NIB	Exc.	V.G.	Good	Fair	Poor
—	—	11500	6250	2750	850

Creedmoor No. 2 Rifle

This version is similar to the No. 1 Rifle except that it is chambered for the .40 caliber cartridge with either a 30" or 32" barrel.

NIB	Exc.	V.G.	Good	Fair	Poor
—	—	9500	4250	1750	500

Whitney-Remington Model 2 Rolling Block

When Remington's patent for the Rolling Block action expired, Whitney was quick to reproduce the action, labeling it his "New Improved System." It is essentially quite similar to Remington's Rolling Block and is easily recognized when compared with the Model 1 because it has only two parts — the hammer and the breechblock. The frame is also rounded. The tang on this model is marked "Whitney Arms Company, New Haven Ct USA." There were approximately 50,000 total manufactured between 1881 and 1888. There are a number of variations are listed.

Shotgun

This is a smoothbore version chambered for 12, 14, 16, or 20 gauge. It is offered with barrel lengths between 26" and 30". Twenty inch barrels have also been noted.

NIB	Exc.	V.G.	Good	Fair	Poor
—	—	1300	650	250	100

Military Carbine

This version is chambered for the .433 and .45 centerfire cartridges. It has a 20.5" barrel and is blued, with a case colored receiver and walnut stock. There were approximately 5,000 manufactured. Most were sent to South or Central America.

NIB	Exc.	V.G.	Good	Fair	Poor
—	—	3400	1750	700	300

Civilian Carbine

This version is chambered for the .44 rimfire or centerfire cartridge with an 18.5" round barrel. The finish is similar to the Military Carbine. There were approximately 2,000 manufactured.

NIB	Exc.	V.G.	Good	Fair	Poor
—	—	3100	1600	600	250

Military Rifle

Courtesy Buffalo Bill Historical Center, Cody, Wyoming

This version is chambered for the .433, .45, or .50 centerfire cartridge. It has a 32.5" or 35" barrel. It is finished similarly to the Military Carbine. There were approximately 39,000 manufactured.

NIB	Exc.	V.G.	Good	Fair	Poor
—	—	3950	2000	750	300

No. 1 Sporting Rifle

This version is chambered for various popular sporting cartridges and is offered with barrel lengths from 26" to 30", either round or octagonal in configuration. The finish is blued, with a case colored receiver and a varnished walnut stock. There were many options available that could radically affect the value, and a qualified appraisal would be advisable. There were approximately 3,000 manufactured.

NIB	Exc.	V.G.	Good	Fair	Poor
—	—	4850	2500	1000	400

No. 2 Sporting Rifle

This is a smaller version of the No. 1 Rifle, chambered for the .22 rimfire, .32, .38, and .44-40 centerfire cartridges. Again, a qualified appraisal would be helpful, as many options can affect the value.

NIB	Exc.	V.G.	Good	Fair	Poor
—	—	3400	1750	700	250

Whitney-Burgess-Morse Rifle

This is a lever action repeating rifle chambered for the .45-70 Government cartridge. There are three variations. All have a magazine tube mounted beneath the barrel with blued finishes and walnut stocks. The barrels are marked "G. W. Morse Patented

Oct. 28th 1856." The tang is marked "A. Burgess Patented Jan. 7th, 1873, Patented Oct 19th 1873." There were approximately 3,000 total manufactured between 1878 and 1882. The variations are listed.

Sporting Rifle

This version has a 28" octagonal or round barrel. The magazine tube holds 9 rounds. There are a number of options available that can increase the value drastically; and we recommend competent, individual appraisal. Value given is for a standard model.

NIB	Exc.	V.G.	Good	Fair	Poor
—	—	6500	3250	1250	400

Military Rifle

This version has a 33" round barrel with a full-length forearm held on by two barrel bands. It features military sights and has an 11-round tubular magazine. It has a bayonet lug and sling swivels. This variation is also found chambered for the .43 Spanish and .42 Russian cartridges. There were approximately 1,000 manufactured.

NIB	Exc.	V.G.	Good	Fair	Poor
—	—	8000	4250	2000	700

Carbine

This version has a 22" round barrel with a full-length forearm held on by one barrel band. It has a 7-round tubular magazine and a saddle ring attached to the frame. There were approximately 500 manufactured.

NIB	Exc.	V.G.	Good	Fair	Poor
—	—	9000	4750	2250	750

Whitney-Kennedy Rifle

This is a lever action repeating rifle that was manufactured in two sizes. It has a magazine tube mounted under the barrel and a blued finish with a case colored lever. The stock is walnut. The barrel is marked "Whitney Arms Co New Haven, Conn. U.S.A." Occasionally, the word "Kennedy" is marked after the Whitney name. There are two major variations. One features a standard-type action lever; and the other, the same "S"-shaped lever that is found on the Burgess model. This version would be worth approximately 10 percent additional. As with many of the rifles of this era, there were many options available that will affect the values. We strongly recommend securing a qualified appraisal for all but the standard models if a transaction is contemplated. There were approximately 15,000 manufactured between 1879 and 1886. The variations of the Whitney-Kennedy and their values are listed.

Courtesy Buffalo Bill Historical Center, Cody, Wyoming

Small Frame Sporting Rifle

This version is chambered for the .32-20, .38-40, and the .40-40 cartridges. It has a 24" barrel that is either round or octagonal in configuration. Examples will be noted with either a full-length or half-length tubular magazine.

NIB	Exc.	V.G.	Good	Fair	Poor
—	—	5000	2750	1200	500

Large Frame Sporting Rifle

This version is chambered for the .40-60, .45-60, .45-75, and the .50-90 cartridges. The .50-caliber version is uncommon and will bring a 20 percent premium. The barrel lengths offered are 26" or 28".

NIB	Exc.	V.G.	Good	Fair	Poor
—	—	6000	3000	1350	500

Military Rifle

This is a large-frame model, chambered for the .40-.60, .44-.40, and the .45-60 cartridges. It has a 32.25" round barrel and either an 11- or 16-round tubular magazine. It has a full-length walnut forend held on by two barrel bands and features a bayonet lug and sling swivels. There were approximately 1,000 manufactured. Most were shipped to Central or South America.

NIB	Exc.	V.G.	Good	Fair	Poor
—	—	6400	3750	1750	550

Military Carbine

Courtesy Buffalo Bill Historical Center, Cody, Wyoming

This is built on either the small-frame or large-frame action and is chambered for the .38-40, .44-40, .40-60, or .45-60 cartridges. It has either a 20" or 22" round barrel and a 9- or 12-round tubular magazine, depending on the caliber. It has a short forend held on by a single barrel band. There were approximately 1,000 manufactured. Most were sent to Central or South America.

NIB	Exc.	V.G.	Good	Fair	Poor
—	—	6400	3750	1750	550

Hooded Cylinder Pocket Revolver

This is an unusual revolver that is chambered for .28 caliber percussion. It has a manually rotated, 6-shot hooded cylinder that has etched decorations. The octagonal barrel is offered in lengths of 3" to 6". There is a button at the back of the frame that unlocks the cylinder so that it can be rotated. The finish is blued, with a brass frame and two-piece rounded walnut grips. It is marked "E. Whitney N. Haven Ct." There were approximately 200 manufactured between 1850 and 1853.

NIB	Exc.	V.G.	Good	Fair	Poor
—	—	5750	3250	1500	600

Two Trigger Pocket Revolver

This is a conventional-appearing pocket revolver with a manually rotated cylinder. There is a second trigger located in front of the conventional trigger guard that releases the cylinder so that it can be turned. It is chambered for .32 caliber percussion and has an octagonal barrel from 3" to 6" in length. It has a 5-shot unfluted cylinder that is etched and a brass frame. The remainder is blued, with squared walnut two-piece grips. An iron-frame version is also available, but only 50 were produced. It would bring approximately 60 percent additional. There were approximately 650 total manufactured between 1852 and 1854.

Courtesy Milwaukee Public Museum, Milwaukee, Wisconsin

NIB	Exc.	V.G.	Good	Fair	Poor
—	—	2750	2000	850	300

Whitney-Beals Patent Revolver

This was an unusual, ring-trigger pocket pistol that was made in three basic variations.

Courtesy Milwaukee Public Museum, Milwaukee, Wisconsin

First Model

This version is chambered for .31-caliber percussion and has barrels of octagonal configuration from 2" to 6" in length. It has a brass frame and a 6-shot cylinder. It is marked "F. Beals/New Haven, Ct." There were only 50 manufactured.

NIB	Exc.	V.G.	Good	Fair	Poor
—	—	5000	3500	1500	450

.31 Caliber Model

This version has an iron frame and a 7-shot cylinder. The octagonal barrels are from 2" to 6" in length. It is marked "Address E. Whitney/Whitneyville, Ct." There were approximately 2,300 manufactured.

NIB	Exc.	V.G.	Good	Fair	Poor
—	—	2500	1500	600	200

.28 Caliber Model

Except for the caliber, this model is similar to the .31 Caliber Model. There were approximately 850 manufactured.

NIB	Exc.	V.G.	Good	Fair	Poor
—	—	2750	1750	700	300

Whitney 1851 Navy

This is a faithful copy of the 1851 Colt Revolver. It is virtually identical. There is a possibility that surplus Colt parts were utilized in the construction of this revolver. There were approximately 400 manufactured in 1857 and 1858.

NIB	Exc.	V.G.	Good	Fair	Poor
—	—	9000	4250	1750	650

WHITNEY NAVY REVOLVER

This is a single-action revolver chambered for .36 caliber percussion. It has a standard octagonal barrel length of 7.5". It has an iron frame and a 6-shot unfluted cylinder that is roll engraved. The finish is blued, with a case colored loading lever and two-piece walnut grips. The barrel is marked either "E. Whitney/N. Haven" or "Eagle Co." There are a number of minor variations on this revolver, and we strongly urge competent appraisal if contemplating a transaction. There were 33,000 total manufactured between 1858 and 1862.

Courtesy Wallis & Wallis, Lewes, Sussex, England

First Model

Nearly the entire production of the First Model is marked "Eagle Co." The reason for this marking is unknown. There are four distinct variations of this model.

First Variation

This model has no integral loading-lever assembly and has a thin top strap. There were only 100 manufactured.

NIB	Exc.	V.G.	Good	Fair	Poor
—	—	5400	3750	1500	550

Second Variation

This version is similar to the First Variation, with an integral loading lever. There were approximately 200 manufactured.

NIB	Exc.	V.G.	Good	Fair	Poor
—	—	5000	3000	1200	400

Third Variation

This is similar to the Second, with a three-screw frame instead of four screws. The loading lever is also modified. There were approximately 500 manufactured.

NIB	Exc.	V.G.	Good	Fair	Poor
—	—	4800	2500	1000	300

Fourth Variation

This version has a rounded frame and a safety notch between the nipples on the rear of the cylinder. There have been examples noted marked "E. Whitney/N. Haven." There were approximately 700 manufactured.

NIB	Exc.	V.G.	Good	Fair	Poor
—	—	4800	2500	1000	300

Second Model

First Variation

This version features a more robust frame with a brass trigger guard. The barrel is marked "E. Whitney/N. Haven." The cylinder pin is secured by a wing nut, and there is an integral loading lever. There were approximately 1,200 manufactured.

NIB	Exc.	V.G.	Good	Fair	Poor
—	—	3750	2000	900	300

Second Variation

This version has six improved safety notches on the rear of the cylinder. There were approximately 10,000 manufactured.

NIB	Exc.	V.G.	Good	Fair	Poor
—	—	3200	1750	750	250

Third Variation

This version has an improved, Colt-type loading-lever latch. There were approximately 2,000 manufactured.

NIB	Exc.	V.G.	Good	Fair	Poor
—	—	3200	1750	750	250

Fourth Variation

This is similar to the Third except the cylinder is marked "Whitneyville." There were approximately 10,000 manufactured.

NIB	Exc.	V.G.	Good	Fair	Poor
—	—	3200	1750	750	250

Fifth Variation

This version has a larger trigger guard. There were approximately 4,000 manufactured.

NIB	Exc.	V.G.	Good	Fair	Poor
—	—	3200	1750	750	250

Sixth Variation

This version has the larger trigger guard and five-groove rifling instead of the usual seven-groove. There were approximately 2,500 manufactured.

NIB	Exc.	V.G.	Good	Fair	Poor
—	—	3200	1750	750	250

WHITNEY POCKET REVOLVER

This is a single-action revolver chambered for .31 caliber percussion. It has octagonal barrels between 3" and 6" in length. It has a 5-shot unfluted cylinder that is roll engraved and marked "Whitneyville." The frame is iron with a blued finish and a case colored integral loading lever. The grips are two-piece walnut. The development of this model, as far as models and variations go, is identical to that which we described in the Navy Model designation. The values are different, and we list them for reference. Again, we recommend securing qualified appraisal if a transaction is contemplated. There were approximately 32,500 manufactured from 1858 to 1862.

First Model
First Variation

NIB	Exc.	V.G.	Good	Fair	Poor
—	—	3750	2000	900	300

Second Variation

NIB	Exc.	V.G.	Good	Fair	Poor
—	—	2200	1250	500	200

Third Variation

NIB	Exc.	V.G.	Good	Fair	Poor
—	—	1900	1000	400	150

Fourth Variation

NIB	Exc.	V.G.	Good	Fair	Poor
—	—	1900	1000	400	150

Fifth Variation

NIB	Exc.	V.G.	Good	Fair	Poor
—	—	1900	1000	400	150

Second Model
First Variation

NIB	Exc.	V.G.	Good	Fair	Poor
—	—	1700	900	400	100

Second Variation

NIB	Exc.	V.G.	Good	Fair	Poor
—	—	1700	900	400	100

Third Variation

NIB	Exc.	V.G.	Good	Fair	Poor
—	—	1700	900	400	100

Fourth Variation

NIB	Exc.	V.G.	Good	Fair	Poor
—	—	1700	1000	425	125

New Model Pocket Revolver

This is a single-action, spur-triggered pocket revolver chambered for .28-caliber percussion. It has a 3.5" octagonal barrel and a 6-shot roll engraved cylinder. It features an iron frame with a blued finish and two-piece walnut grips. The barrel is marked "E. Whitney/N. Haven." There were approximately 2,000 manufactured between 1860 and 1867.

Courtesy Milwaukee Public Museum, Milwaukee, Wisconsin

NIB	Exc.	V.G.	Good	Fair	Poor
—	—	2000	1250	500	200

Rimfire Pocket Revolver

This is a spur-trigger, single-action, solid-frame pocket revolver that was produced in three frame sizes, depending on the caliber. It is chambered for the .22, .32, and .38 rimfire cartridges. The frame is brass, and it is found in a variety of finishes- nickel-plated or blued, or a combination thereof. The bird's-head grips are rosewood or hard rubber; ivory or pearl grips are sometimes encountered and will bring a slight premium in value. The barrels

are octagonal and from 1.5" to 5" in length. The barrels are marked "Whitneyville Armory Ct. USA." They have also been noted with the trade names "Monitor," "Defender," or "Eagle." They were commonly referred to as the Model No. 1, No. 1.5, Model 2, or Model 2.5. The values for all are quite similar. There were approximately 30,000 manufactured of all types between 1871 and 1879.

Courtesy Milwaukee Public Museum, Milwaukee, Wisconsin

NIB	Exc.	V.G.	Good	Fair	Poor
—	—	750	500	200	75

WHITNEY FIREARMS COMPANY
Hartford, Connecticut

Wolverine

A .22 caliber semi-automatic pistol with a 4.75" barrel. Blued or nickel-plated with plastic grips and an aluminum alloy frame. This pistol is readily distinguishable by its streamlined form. Approximately 13,000 examples were made with the blue finish and 900 with a nickel-plated finish. Some slides are marked "Wolverine Whitney Firearms Inc., New Haven, Conn USA." Others are marked "Whitney" only. The Wolverine-marked pistols are considered more rare. Pistol were produced in two locations: New Haven, Connecticut and Hartford, Connecticut. Manufactured from 1955 to 1962. Now being reproduced by Olympic Arms. Pricing is for original version.

Blue Finish

Blued pistols most often have brown or black grips.

NIB	Exc.	V.G.	Good	Fair	Poor
750	550	400	350	250	200

Nickel-Plated

Nickeled pistols most often have white plastic grips.

NIB	Exc.	V.G.	Good	Fair	Poor
2000	1800	1500	1250	800	500

WHITWORTH
See—Interarms

WICHITA ARMS, INC.
Wichita, Kansas

Classic Rifle

A single-shot bolt-action rifle produced in a variety of calibers with a 21" octagonal barrel. Offered with Canjar adjustable triggers. Blued with a checkered walnut stock.

NIB	Exc.	V.G.	Good	Fair	Poor
3000	2500	2250	1850	1250	1000

Varmint Rifle

As above, with a round barrel.

NIB	Exc.	V.G.	Good	Fair	Poor
2000	1750	1500	1250	1000	800

Silhouette Rifle

As above, with a 24" heavy barrel, gray composition stock and 2-oz. Canjar trigger.

NIB	Exc.	V.G.	Good	Fair	Poor
2200	1900	1700	1000	850	650

Wichita International Pistol

A single-shot pivoted barrel target pistol produced in a variety of calibers from .22 to .357 Magnum with a 10.5" or 14" barrel fitted with either adjustable sights or telescopic sight mounts. Stainless steel with walnut forestock and grips.

NIB	Exc.	V.G.	Good	Fair	Poor
800	650	400	350	300	200

Wichita Classic Pistol

A bolt action single-shot pistol chambered for a variety of calibers up to .308, with a left-hand action and 11.25" barrel. Blued with a walnut stock.

NIB	Exc.	V.G.	Good	Fair	Poor
3000	2500	2250	1850	1250	1000

Wichita Classic Engraved

As above, but embellished.

NIB	Exc.	V.G.	Good	Fair	Poor
5000	4250	3500	2500	2000	1500

Wichita Silhouette Pistol

As above, in 7mm HMSA or .308 with a 15" barrel. The walnut stock is made so that the pistol grip is located beneath the forward end of the bolt.

NIB	Exc.	V.G.	Good	Fair	Poor
1100	950	750	600	500	400

Wichita MK40

As above, with a 13" barrel, multi-range sights and either a composition or walnut stock. Standard finish is blued, however, this model was also made in stainless steel.

NIB	Exc.	V.G.	Good	Fair	Poor
1100	950	750	600	500	400

WICKLIFFE RIFLES
Triple S Development
Wickliffe, Ohio/Austinburg, Ohio

NOTE: The Wickliffe Rifle Company has been reorganized as a maker of custom single-shot rifles. Values below are for the original Wickliffe guns.

Model 76

A single-shot falling-block rifle produced in a variety of calibers from .22 Hornet to .45-70 with a 22" lightweight or 26" heavyweight barrel. Blued with a walnut stock. Introduced in 1976. Discontinued.

NIB	Exc.	V.G.	Good	Fair	Poor
—	1200	1000	750	550	300

Model 76 Deluxe

As above, with a nickel-silver pistol grip cap, machine jeweled breechblock and more finely figured walnut stock. Introduced in 1976.

NIB	Exc.	V.G.	Good	Fair	Poor
—	1450	1250	900	700	450

Traditionalist

The Model 76 in .30-06 or .45-70 caliber with a 24" barrel having open sights and a checkered walnut buttstock. Introduced in 1979.

NIB	Exc.	V.G.	Good	Fair	Poor
—	1200	1000	750	550	300

Stinger

Similar to the Model 76, but chambered for .22 Hornet or .223 Remington with a 22" barrel fitted with a Burris 6X power telescope. Blued with a checkered Monte Carlo-style stock. Introduced in 1979.

NIB	Exc.	V.G.	Good	Fair	Poor
—	1200	1000	750	550	300

Stinger Deluxe

As above, with a superior grade of finish and more finely figured walnut stock.

NIB	Exc.	V.G.	Good	Fair	Poor
—	1250	1050	800	575	300

WIENER WAFFENFABRIK
Vienna, Austria

Little Tom

A 6.35mm or 7.65mm double-action semi-automatic pistol with a 2.5" barrel. The slide marked "Wiener Waffenfabrik Patent Little Tom," and the caliber. Blued with either walnut or plastic grips inlaid with a medallion bearing the company's trademark. Approximately 10,000 were made from 1919 to 1925.

Little Tom—6.35mm

Courtesy J.B. Wood

NIB	Exc.	V.G.	Good	Fair	Poor
—	500	450	400	250	175

WILDEY FIREARMS CO., INC.
Cheshire, Connecticut
Newburg, New York
Warren, Connecticut

Wildey Auto Pistol

A gas-operated, rotary-bolt, double-action semi-automatic pistol chambered for the .357 Peterbuilt, the .45 Winchester Magnum, or the .475 Wildey Magnum cartridges. with 5", 6", 7", 8", or 10" ventilated rib barrels. The gas-operated action is adjustable and features a single-shot cutoff. The rotary bolt has three heavy locking lugs. Constructed of stainless steel with adjustable sights and wood grips. The values of this rarely encountered pistol are based on not only the condition, but the caliber—as well the serial-number range, with earlier-numbered guns being worth a good deal more than the later or current production models.

Cheshire, Connecticut, Address

Produced in .45 Winchester Magnum only and is serial numbered from No. 1 through 2489. **NOTE:** Serial numbers above 200 would be worth approximately $200 less respectively in each category of condition.

Serial No. 1 through 200

NIB	Exc.	V.G.	Good	Fair	Poor
2000	1500	1200	950	750	500

Survivor Model

This pistol is presently manufactured in Brookfield, Connecticut. **NOTE:** Add $100 for 12" barrel, $500 for 14" barrel, and $1,100 for 18" Silhouette model.

NIB	Exc.	V.G.	Good	Fair	Poor
1500	1000	750	550	450	300

Hunter Model

As above but with matte stainless steel finish.

NIB	Exc.	V.G.	Good	Fair	Poor
1775	1250	900	700	600	450

Pin Gun

Gas-operated auto-loading pistol in polished or matte stainless for competition shooting. With muzzle brake; variety of calibers and barrel lengths (7", 8", 10", 12", 14"). 4.09 lb. (8" barrel).

NIB	Exc.	V.G.	Good	Fair	Poor
2000	1500	1200	950	750	500

Wildey Carbine

This model features an 18" barrel with forearm in calibers from .44 Auto Mag to .475 Wildey Mag. Choice of polished or matte stainless steel. **NOTE:** Add $225 for matte stainless finish.

NIB	Exc.	V.G.	Good	Fair	Poor
2500	2000	1550	1000	750	500

Presentation Model

As above, but engraved and fitted with hand-checkered walnut grips.

NIB	Exc.	V.G.	Good	Fair	Poor
3000	2500	1950	1400	900	600

JAWS Viper

Jordanian Arms & Weapons System manufactured in Jordan. Semi-auto chambered for 9mm, .40 S&W, 45 ACP. Barrels: 4.4" and 5". 10-round magazine. Stainless finish with rubberized grip.

NIB	Exc.	V.G.	Good	Fair	Poor
—	725	500	375	250	150

WILKINSON ARMS CO.
Covina, California

Diane

A .25 caliber semi-automatic pistol with a 2.25" barrel and 6-shot magazine. Blued with plastic grips.

NIB	Exc.	V.G.	Good	Fair	Poor
—	400	325	200	150	100

Terry Carbine

A 9mm caliber semi-automatic carbine with a 16.25" barrel, adjustable sights, and 30-shot magazine. Matte blued with either a black composition or maple stock.

NIB	Exc.	V.G.	Good	Fair	Poor
—	675	450	325	200	125

WILLIAMSON
New York, New York

Derringer

A .41 caliber single-shot pocket pistol with a 2.5" sliding barrel. Blued, with a silver-plated furniture and a checkered walnut grip. Barrel marked "Williamson's Pat. Oct. 2, 1866 New York." This pistol was fitted with an auxiliary percussion cap chamber adaptor. Manufactured from 1866 to approximately 1870.

NIB	Exc.	V.G.	Good	Fair	Poor
—	—	—	1250	500	100

WILSON, J. P.
Ilion, New York

Percussion Alarm Gun

This unusual little device is chambered for .22 caliber percussion. It consists of approximately a 1" rectangular brass block with a chamber bored into it that accepts a blackpowder charge. There is no provision for a projectile. There is a spring retained arm on top, which works as a hammer. As the device is activated by a door or a window, the hammer snaps closed, striking a percussion cap that causes the charge to fire, thereby creating an alarm notifying that the perimeter has been breached. It is marked "J. P. Wilson/Patented Feb. 8, 1859/Ilion, NY."

NIB	Exc.	V.G.	Good	Fair	Poor
—	—	1200	850	350	100

WILSON COMBAT
Berryville, Arkansas

Wilson's began making custom 1911-style pistols using Colt slides and frames in 1977. This company produces a wide range of quality components for the 1911 pistol, such as slides, triggers, safeties, barrels, etc. The models listed are for complete factory-built-and-assembled guns. These factory-built pistols are sold with a lifetime warranty, even to subsequent buyers. The pistols listed are divided into two categories. Semi-custom pistols are off-the-shelf guns available through participating dealers. Custom pistols are special order guns. The models listed below are representative, not inclusive.

POLYMER FRAME PISTOLS

Tactical Carry (KZ-45)

Chambered for .45 ACP cartridge and fitted with a 5" stainless steel match barrel, this model has numerous special features such as night sights and front and rear slide serrations. Frame is stainless steel and reinforced polymer. Magazine capacity is 10 rounds. Finish is black polymer. Weight is approximately 31 oz. Introduced in 1999. Discontinued.

NIB	Exc.	V.G.	Good	Fair	Poor
1050	900	750	600	500	300

KZ 9mm

Polymer-frame 1911 chambered for 9mm. Full size is 16+1 capacity with 5" barrel at 33 oz. Compact size is 14+1 capacity with 4.1" barrel at 31 oz. Introduced 2006. Discontinued.

NIB	Exc.	V.G.	Good	Fair	Poor
1500	1350	1200	900	750	300

Spec-Ops 9

This model is an upgrade based on the discontinued KZ-9. Like the KZ-9, it has a polymer frame and 16-round magazine. Chambering is 9mm only. Barrel is 4.5" and weight unloaded is 29.6 oz.

NIB	Exc.	V.G.	Good	Fair	Poor
1950	1500	1200	900	450	200

ADP 9mm

11-round capacity, polymer frame. 19.5 oz. 6.3" overall length, 3.75" barrel. Introduced 2006.

NIB	Exc.	V.G.	Good	Fair	Poor
675	525	400	300	200	125

SEMI-CUSTOM PISTOLS

Model 1996A2

This pistol, introduced in 1996, was offered in a number of different configurations. These configurations affect price. The base pistol is chambered for the .45 ACP cartridge, has snag-free sights and blue finish. Barrel length is 5", magazine capacity is 8 rounds and weight is approximately 38 oz. There are numerous special features on the standard pistol. **NOTE:** Add $70 for tritium night sights, $125 for Wilson adjustable sights, $275 for nights sights, ambi safety, hard chrome frame, $325 for Wilson adjustable sights, ambi safety, hard chrome frame.

NIB	Exc.	V.G.	Good	Fair	Poor
1450	1150	1000	800	625	300

Protector

This model is fitted to a 5" slide with match barrel adjustable sights, and numerous other special features. Weight is about 38 oz. Black polymer finish on slide and frame. Introduced in 1996. **NOTE:** Add $100 for stainless steel.

NIB	Exc.	V.G.	Good	Fair	Poor
1795	1450	1150	900	650	400

Protector Compact

Same as above but fitted with a 4.25" match-grade barrel. Weight is about 34 oz. Introduced in 1996.

NIB	Exc.	V.G.	Good	Fair	Poor
1795	1450	1150	900	650	400

Sentinel Ultra Compact

This .45 ACP pistol is fitted with a 3.6" heavy tapered cone handfitted barrel, night sights, high-ride beavertail and numerous special features. Magazine capacity is 6 rounds. Weight is about 29 oz. Finish is a black polymer.

NIB	Exc.	V.G.	Good	Fair	Poor
2100	1675	1300	950	700	450

Tactical

This .45 ACP pistol is fitted with a 5" tapered cone handfitted barrel. Cocking serrations on front and rear of slide. High-ride beavertail safety and other special features. Night sights are standard. Cocobolo grips. Weight is about 38 oz. finish is black polymer. Magazine capacity is 8 rounds. Introduced in 1999.

NIB	Exc.	V.G.	Good	Fair	Poor
1825	1450	1100	900	700	400

Classic

This model has a 5" barrel, adjustable sights, hard chrome finish on frame, and other special features. Weight is about 38 oz. Introduced in 1996. **NOTE:** Add $100 for stainless steel.

NIB	Exc.	V.G.	Good	Fair	Poor
1895	1500	1200	900	700	400

Service Grade Target

Chambered for the .45 ACP cartridge, this model features a 5" stainless steel match handfitted barrel with full length guide rod. Front and rear cocking serrations. Magazine well is beveled and grips are cocobolo. Numerous other special features. Weight is about 38 oz. Finish is black polymer. Magazine capacity is 8 rounds.

NIB	Exc.	V.G.	Good	Fair	Poor
1825	1450	1150	850	650	350

Custom Carry Revolver

Built on a Smith & Wesson .357 Magnum Model 66, this model features a 2.5" barrel with adjustable night sights. Cylinder is chambered and grip is black nylon with smooth finish. Stainless steel finish. Weight is about 30 oz.

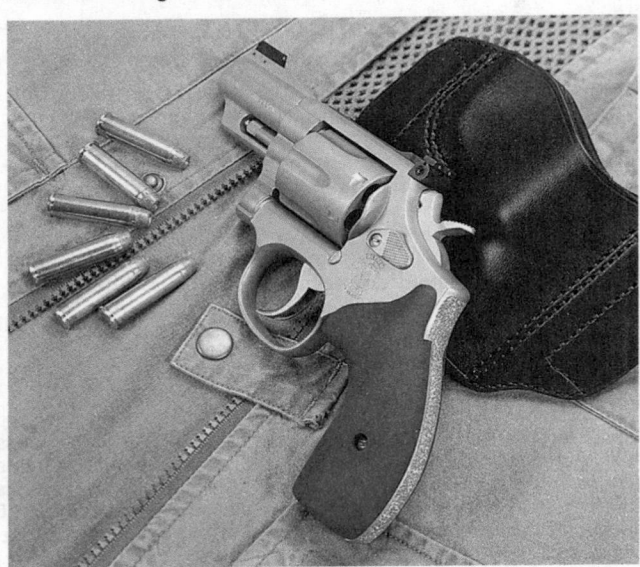

NIB	Exc.	V.G.	Good	Fair	Poor
1175	950	800	650	500	300

.22 Classic Rimfire Pistol

Chambered for the .22 caliber rimfire cartridge and fitted with a 5" barrel. Hard chrome frame and black anodized slide. Weight is less than standard .45 caliber pistol. Introduced in 1996.

NIB	Exc.	V.G.	Good	Fair	Poor
1125	975	800	625	500	250

CUSTOM-BUILT PISTOLS

Wilson Custom pistols bear the Wilson Combat or Wilson Custom label on the right side of the frame on the dust cover. Full custom guns are typically built on a Colt, Springfield Armory, Norinco, STI, Strayer Voight or Wilson Combat gun.

Combat Classic Super Grade (Tactical Super Grade)

Fitted with a 5" match-grade handfit stainless steel barrel. Adjustable sights, high ride beavertail safety, contoured magazine well and polymer slide with hard chrome frame. Weight is approximately 45 oz. In 9mm, .38 Super, .40 S&W, 10mm and .45 ACP.

NIB	Exc.	V.G.	Good	Fair	Poor
3595	2850	2300	1900	1500	600

Tactical Super Grade Compact

Similar to the above model but with a 4.1" match grade barrel. Magazine capacity is 7 rounds. Weight is about 40 oz. Introduced in 2003. Available in 9mm, .38 Super, .45 ACP.

NIB	Exc.	V.G.	Good	Fair	Poor
4475	3900	3200	2500	1850	650

Wilson X-TAC

Caliber .45 ACP, steel frame and slide, 8-round magazine, special XTAC-pattern slide serrations and texturing on front strap and mainspring housing, stainless match-grade barrel and bushing, extended thumb safety, beavertail tang, G10 grips and contoured mag well. Weight 38.1 ounces, 5-inch barrel with black Parkerized finish.

NIB	Exc.	V.G.	Good	Fair	Poor
2000	1700	1450	1150	750	300

CQB Light-Rail Lightweight

Calibers: 9mm Parabellum, .38 Super, .45 ACP. Compact size with 4-inch barrel, steel slide, alloy round butt frame. Weight is 27.34 ounces. Comes with two 8-round and one 7-round magazine, fiber optic front sight, integral accessory rail, G10 grips, extended thumb safety, beavertail tang, checkered front strap and mainspring housing. Several other sizes and variations available in CQB series.

NIB	Exc.	V.G.	Good	Fair	Poor
2300	1976	1650	1300	850	300

Ultralight Carry Series

A full-size 1911 with aluminum frame, steel slide. Chambered in 9mm Parabellum, .38 Super or .45 ACP. Stainless fluted 5-inch barrel. Comes with one 7- and two 8-round magazines. Other features include countersunk slide stop, integral accessory rail, contoured mag well, G10 grips, extended thumb safety, beavertail tang, checkered front strap and mainspring housing. Weight is 26.5 ounces. Several Armor-Tuff finish options including black, O.D., silver, tan or two-tone. Compact model has a 4-inch barrel (all calibers), Sentinel has 3.6-inch barrel (9mm only).

NIB	Exc.	V.G.	Good	Fair	Poor
2900	2400	2000	1600	1000	500

Stealth Defense System

Built with a 4.25" slide with match-grade stainless steel barrel. This model features night sights, checkered front strap and mainspring spring housing with numerous special features. Black polymer finish. Weight is approximately 34 oz. Offered in 9mm, .38 Super, .40 S&W, .45 ACP.

NIB	Exc.	V.G.	Good	Fair	Poor
2895	2250	1700	1300	900	400

Defensive Combat Pistol

This .45 ACP pistol is built with a 5" match-grade stainless steel barrel, night sights, and numerous special features. Finish is black polymer. Weight 38 oz.

NIB	Exc.	V.G.	Good	Fair	Poor
2395	1850	1250	1000	600	300

Classic Master Grade

This .45 ACP pistol is fitted with a 5" stainless steel handfitted match-grade barrel. Numerous special features such as ultralight hammer, ambidextrous safety, etc. Finish is stainless steel frame and black polymer slide. Weight is about 38 oz. and magazine capacity is 8 rounds.

NIB	Exc.	V.G.	Good	Fair	Poor
2895	2250	1700	1300	900	400

Tactical Elite

This is similar to other Wilson pistols with the addition of the special tactical heavy tapered cone barrel.

NIB	Exc.	V.G.	Good	Fair	Poor
2895	2250	1700	1300	900	400

Defensive Combat Pistol Deluxe

This model has a 5" match-grade stainless steel barrel and numerous special features. Fitted with adjustable sights. Weight is about 38 oz. Finish is black polymer.

NIB	Exc.	V.G.	Good	Fair	Poor
2595	2000	1350	1050	700	300

Professional Model Pistol

Introduced in 2004 this .45 ACP pistol features a 4.1" stainless steel match barrel, tactical combat sights with tritium inserts. Many custom features. Magazine capacity is 8 rounds. Offered in gray/black, green/black, or all-black finish. Weight is about 35 oz.

NIB	Exc.	V.G.	Good	Fair	Poor
1215	1650	1375	1100	750	450

Competition Pistols

Wilson Combat offers a custom-built pistol to the customer's specifications. An expert appraisal is recommended prior to sale.

TACTICAL RIFLES

UT-15 Urban Tactical

This semi-auto rifle is fitted with a 16.25" fluted barrel with tactical muzzlebrake. Flattop receiver. Aluminum handguard. Chambered for the .223 cartridge. Parkerized finish. Accepts all M-16/AR-15 magazines. Weight is about 6.5 lbs. **NOTE:** Add $100 for Armor-Tuff finish.

NIB	Exc.	V.G.	Good	Fair	Poor
1900	1700	1450	1100	900	500

Tactical Hunter LW 6.8

Chambered for the Remington 6.8 SPC with 15-round magazine. Stainless lightweight match-grade 16- or 18-inch barrel. Forged upper and lower receivers. Enhanced bolt and carrier with NP3 coating. Wilson Combat Quadrail, Accu-Tac flash hider. Armor Tuff polymer finish in black, gray or tan. Collapsible stock.

NIB	Exc.	V.G.	Good	Fair	Poor
2000	1700	1450	1150	750	300

TPR-15 Tactical Precision Rifle

This model is fitted with a match-grade 18" fluted barrel. Free-floating aluminum handguard. Chambered for .223 cartridge.

Weight is about 6.5 lbs. Parkerized finish. **NOTE:** Add $100 for Armor-Tuff finish.

NIB	Exc.	V.G.	Good	Fair	Poor
2500	2300	1950	1300	1100	600

M-4T Tactical Carbine

This model features a 16.25" M-4 style heavy barrel with muzzlebrake. Flattop receiver. Chambered for .223 cartridge. Parkerized finish. Weight is about 6.5 lbs. **NOTE:** Add $100 for Armor-Tuff finish.

NIB	Exc.	V.G.	Good	Fair	Poor
1900	1700	1450	1100	900	500

TL-15 Tactical Lightweight

Introduced in 2002, this flattop model features a match-grade 16.25" lightweight barrel with muzzlebrake. Aluminum handguard and fixed buttstock. Chambered for the .223 cartridge. Black Mil-Spec finish. **NOTE:** Add $100 for Armor-Tuff finish.

NIB	Exc.	V.G.	Good	Fair	Poor
1900	1700	1450	1100	900	500

Super Sniper

Fitted with a 20" stainless steel match grade barrel with a 1 in 8 twist. Flat top receiver. Offered in Parkerized or Armor-Tuff finish. **NOTE:** Add $100 for Armor-Tuff finish.

NIB	Exc.	V.G.	Good	Fair	Poor
2350	2100	1800	1500	1150	600

WINCHESTER REPEATING ARMS
New Haven, Connecticut

The prices given here are for the most part standard guns without optional features that were so often furnished by the factory. These optional or extra-cost features are too numerous to list and can affect the price of a shotgun or rifle to an enormous degree. In some cases these options are one of a kind. Collectors and those interested in Winchester firearms have the benefit of some of the original factory records. These records are now stored in the Cody Firearms Museum, Buffalo Bill Historical Center, P.O. Box 1000, Cody, Wyoming (307) 587-4771. For a $25 fee, the museum will provide factory letters containing the original specifications of certain Winchester models using the original factory records. CAUTION: Buyers should confirm by Cody letter any special-order feature on any Winchester within the Cody record range before paying a premium for a scarce feature.

Hunt Repeating Rifle

Walter Hunt described his repeating rifle as the Volition Repeater. Hunt was granted U.S. patent number 6663 in August 1849 for his repeating rifle that was to pave the way for future generations of Winchester repeating rifles. Hunt's rifle design was unique and innovative as was his patent number 5701 for a conical lead bullet that was to be fired in his rifle. This ingenious bullet had a hole in its base filled with powder and closed by a disc with an opening in the middle to expel the ignition from an independent priming source that used priming pellets made of fulminate of mercury. The rifle actually worked but only the patent model was built; it is now in the Cody Firearms Museum.

Jennings

Second in the evolutionary line of Winchester rifles is the Jennings. Made by Robbins & Lawrence of Windsor, Vermont, this rifle incorporated the original concept of the Hunt design with the additional improvements utilized by Lewis Jennings. The Jennings rifle is important not only as a link in the chain of repeating-rifle development but also because it introduced Benjamin Henry Tyler to the concept of the tubular magazine lever-action repeating rifle. The Jennings rifle was built in three separate and distinct models. While total production of the three types was contracted for 5,000 guns, it is probable that only about 1,000 were actually produced.

First Model

Courtesy Milwaukee Public Museum, Milwaukee, Wisconsin

The First Model Jennings was built in a .54 caliber, breech-loading, single-shot configuration with a ring trigger, oval trigger guard, and 26" barrel. A ramrod was fixed to the underside of the barrel as well. This variation was made from 1850 to 1851.

NIB	Exc.	V.G.	Good	Fair	Poor
—	—	35000	25000	7000	1500

Second Model

Courtesy Milwaukee Public Museum, Milwaukee, Wisconsin

The Second Model Jennings was produced adopting the improvements made by Horace Smith. This Second Model is a breech-loading repeating rifle with an under barrel magazine tube and a 26" barrel. The frame is sculpted, unlike the First Model. The ring trigger is still present, but the trigger guard was removed as part of the design change. The caliber remained a .54, and the rifle was fitted with a 25" barrel. The Second Model was produced in 1851 and 1852.

NIB	Exc.	V.G.	Good	Fair	Poor
—	—	30000	20000	5000	1200

Third Model

The Third Model represents an attempt by investors to use the remaining parts and close out production. The .54 caliber Third Model was a muzzleloading rifle with a ramrod mounted under the barrel and a 26-1/2" barrel. The frame was the same as that used on the First Model, but the trigger was more of the conventional type. The trigger guard had a bow in the middle giving this model a distinctive appearance. This variation was produced in 1852 and marks the end of the early conceptual period in repeating rifle development.

NIB	Exc.	V.G.	Good	Fair	Poor
—	—	23500	9500	4500	1500

Smith & Wesson Volcanic Firearms

An interesting connection in the evolution of the lever-action repeating firearm is found in the production of a small group of pistols and rifles built in Norwich, Connecticut, by Horace Smith and Daniel Wesson under the firm name of Smith & Wesson. The company built two types of Volcanic pistols. One was a large-frame model with an 8" barrel and chambered in .41 caliber. About 500 of these large frames were produced. The other pistol was a small-frame version with a 4" barrel chambered in .31 caliber. Slightly more of these small-frame pistols were built, about 700, than the large-frame version. In both variations the barrel, magazine, and frame were blued. Smith & Wesson also produced a lever-action repeating rifle. These rifles are exceedingly rare with fewer than 10 having been built. They were chambered for the .528 caliber and were fitted with 23" barrels. Because of the small number of rifles built, no value is offered.

Courtesy Buffalo Bill Historical Center, Cody, Wyoming

4" Pistol

NIB	Exc.	V.G.	Good	Fair	Poor
—	—		11000	4000	1000

8" Pistol

Courtesy Buffalo Bill Historical Center, Cody, Wyoming

NIB	Exc.	V.G.	Good	Fair	Poor
—	—	—	13000	6000	1500

Volcanic Firearms (Volcanic Repeating Arms Company)

With the incorporation of the Volcanic Repeating Arms Company, a new and important individual was introduced who would have an impact on the American arms industry for the next 100 years: Oliver F. Winchester. This new company introduced the Volcanic pistol using the improvements made by Horace Smith and Daniel Wesson. Volcanic firearms are marked on the barrel, "THE VOLCANIC REPEATING ARMS CO. PATENT NEW HAVEN, CONN. FEB. 14, 1854." The Volcanic was offered as a .38 caliber breechloading tubular magazine repeater with blued barrel and bronze frame. These pistols were available in three barrel lengths. **NOTE:** A few Volcanic pistols were produced with detachable shoulder stocks. These are considered quite rare. For original guns with this option, the prices listed should be increased by 25 percent.

Courtesy Milwaukee Public Museum, Milwaukee, Wisconsin

6" Barrel

NIB	Exc.	V.G.	Good	Fair	Poor
—	—	—	7000	3500	1500

8" Barrel

NIB	Exc.	V.G.	Good	Fair	Poor
—	—	—	7000	3500	1500

16" Barrel

Courtesy Buffalo Bill Historical Center, Cody, Wyoming

NIB	Exc.	V.G.	Good	Fair	Poor
—	—	—	14000	5500	2500

Volcanic Firearms (New Haven Arms Company)

In 1857 the New Haven Arms Company was formed to continue the production of the former Volcanic Repeating Arms Company. Volcanic firearms continued to be built but were now marked on the barrel, "NEW HAVEN, CONN. PATENT FEB. 14, 1854." The Volcanic pistols produced by the New Haven Arms Company were built in .30 caliber and used the same basic frame as the original Volcanic. These pistols were produced in 3-1/2" and 6" barrel lengths.

3-1/2" Barrel

NIB	Exc.	V.G.	Good	Fair	Poor
—	—	6500	5000	2500	1500

6" Barrel

NIB	Exc.	V.G.	Good	Fair	Poor
—	—	7500	5750	3000	1500

Lever Action Carbine

New Haven Arms introduced, for the first time, a Volcanic rifle that featured a full-length slotted magazine tube with a spring-activated thumbpiece follower that moved along the entire length of the magazine tube. These rifles were chambered for .38 caliber cartridge and were offered in three barrel lengths: 16", 20", and 24".

Courtesy Buffalo Bill Historical Center, Cody, Wyoming

16" Barrel

NIB	Exc.	V.G.	Good	Fair	Poor
—	40000	26000	16000	6000	2000

20" Barrel

NIB	Exc.	V.G.	Good	Fair	Poor
—	45000	23000	19000	8000	3000

24" Barrel

Courtesy Little John's Auction Service, Inc., Paul Goodwin photo

NIB	Exc.	V.G.	Good	Fair	Poor
—	55000	37000	22500	10000	3000

Henry Rifle

With the development of B. Tyler Henry's improvements in the metallic rimfire cartridge and his additional improvements in the Volcanic frame, the direct predecessor to the Winchester lever-action repeater was born. The new cartridge was the .44 caliber rimfire, and the Henry rifle featured a 24" octagon barrel with a tubular magazine holding 15 shells. The rifle had no forearm, but was furnished with a walnut buttstock with two styles of buttplates: an early rounded heel crescent shape seen on guns produced from 1860 to 1862 and the later sharper heel crescent butt found on guns built from 1863 to 1866. The early models, produced from 1860 to 1861, were fitted with an iron frame, and the later models, built from 1861 to 1866, were fitted with brass frames. About 14,000 Henry rifles were made during the entire production period; only about 300 were iron frame rifles.

Courtesy Bonhams & Butterfields, San Francisco, California

Iron Frame Rifle

Courtesy Bonhams & Butterfields, San Francisco, California

NIB	Exc.	V.G.	Good	Fair	Poor
—	—	85000	65000	30000	13000

Brass Frame Rifle

NIB	Exc.	V.G.	Good	Fair	Poor
—	—	53000	37500	17500	9000

Martially Inspected Henry Rifles

Beginning in 1863 the Federal Government ordered 1,730 Henry Rifles for use in the Civil War. Most of these government-inspected rifles fall into serial number range 3000 to 4000 while the balance are close to this serial-number range. They are marked "C.G.C." for Charles G. Chapman, the government inspector. These Henry rifles were used under actual combat conditions and for that reason it is doubtful that there are any rifles that would fall into the excellent condition category. Therefore no price is given. **NOTE:** There are many counterfeit examples of these rifles. It is strongly advised that an expert in this field be consulted prior to a sale.

NIB	Exc.	V.G.	Good	Fair	Poor
—	—	45000	34000	17500	12000

Winchester's Improvement Carbine

Overall length 43-1/2"; barrel length 24"; caliber .44 rimfire. Walnut stock with a brass buttplate; the receiver and magazine cover/fore-end of brass; the barrel and magazine tube blued. The magazine loading port is exposed by sliding the fore-end forward. This design was protected by O.F. Winchester's British Patent Number 3285 issued December 19, 1865. Unmarked except for internally located serial numbers. Approximately 700 manufactured in December of 1865 and early 1866, the majority of which were sold to Maximilian of Mexico. Prospective purchasers are strongly advised to secure an expert appraisal prior to acquisition.

NIB	Exc.	V.G.	Good	Fair	Poor
—	35000	27500	19500	13000	9000

Model 1866

In 1866 the New Haven Arms Company changed its name to the Winchester Repeating Arms Company. The first firearm to be built under the Winchester name was the Model 1866. This first Winchester was a much-improved version of the Henry. A new magazine tube developed by Nelson King, Winchester's plant superintendent, was a vast improvement over the slotted magazine tube used on the Henry and its predecessor. The old tube allowed dirt to enter through the slots and was weakened because of it. King's patent, assigned to Winchester, featured a solid tube that was much stronger and reliable. His patent also dealt with an improved loading system for the rifle. The rifle now featured a loading port on the right side of the receiver with a spring-loaded cover. The frame continued to be made from brass. The Model 1866 was chambered for the .44 caliber Flat Rimfire or the .44 caliber Pointed Rimfire. Both cartridges could be used interchangeably.

The barrel on the Model 1866 was marked with two different markings. The first, which is seen on early guns up to serial number 23000, reads "HENRY'S PATENT-OCT. 16, 1860 KING'S PATENT-MARCH 29, 1866." The second marking reads, "WINCHESTER'S-REPEATING-ARMS.NEW HAVEN, CT. KING'S-IMPROVEMENT-PATENTED MARCH 29, 1866 OCTOBER 16, 1860." There are three basic variations of the Model 1866:

1. Sporting Rifle round or octagon barrel. Approximately 28,000 were produced.
2. Carbine round barrel. Approximately 127,000 were produced.
3. Musket round barrel. Approximately 14,000 were produced.

The rifle and musket held 17 cartridges, and the carbine had a capacity of 13 cartridges. Unlike the Henry, Model 1866s were fitted with a walnut forearm. The Model 1866 was discontinued in 1898 with approximately 170,000 guns produced. The Model 1866 was sold in various special order configurations, such as barrels longer or shorter than standard, including engraved guns. The prices listed represent only standard-model 1866s. For guns with special-order features, an independent appraisal from an expert is highly recommended.

Courtesy Milwaukee Public Museum, Milwaukee, Wisconsin

First Model Rifle

This first style has both the Henry and King patent dates stamped on the barrel, a flat-loading port cover, and a two-screw upper tang. Perhaps the most distinctive feature of the First Model is the rapid drop at the top rear of the receiver near the hammer. This is often referred to as the "Henry Drop," a reference to the same receiver drop found on the Henry rifle. First Models will be seen up through the 15000 serial number range.

NIB	Exc.	V.G.	Good	Fair	Poor
—	45000	30000	19000	13000	4000

First Model Carbine

NIB	Exc.	V.G.	Good	Fair	Poor
—	40000	26000	17000	11000	3000

Second Model Rifle

The second style differs from the first most noticeably in its single screw upper tang and a flare at the front of the receiver to meet the forearm. The Second Model also has a more gradual drop at the rear of the receiver than the First Model. The Second Style Model 1866 appears through serial number 25000.

NIB	Exc.	V.G.	Good	Fair	Poor
—	25000	19000	10500	7500	4000

Second Model Carbine

NIB	Exc.	V.G.	Good	Fair	Poor
—	25000	16000	9500	6750	3500

Third Model Rifle

The third style's most noticeable characteristic is the more moderately curved receiver shape at the rear of the frame. The serial number is now stamped in block numerals behind the trigger, thus allowing the numbers to be seen for the first time without removing the stock. The barrel marking is stamped with the Winchester address. The Third Model is found between serial numbers 25000 and 149000. For the first time, a musket version was produced in this serial-number range.

NIB	Exc.	V.G.	Good	Fair	Poor
—	22000	15000	8000	5000	3000

Third Model Carbine

NIB	Exc.	V.G.	Good	Fair	Poor
—	25000	17000	9500	5500	3500

Third Model Musket

NIB	Exc.	V.G.	Good	Fair	Poor
—	12000	10000	8000	4500	2500

Fourth Model Rifle

The fourth style has an even less pronounced drop at the top rear of the frame, and the serial number is stamped in script on the lower tang under the lever. The Fourth Model is seen between serial number 149000 and 170100 with the late guns having an iron buttplate instead of brass.

NIB	Exc.	V.G.	Good	Fair	Poor
—	12000	10000	8500	4000	3000

1330 • WINCHESTER REPEATING ARMS

Fourth Model Carbine

NIB	Exc.	V.G.	Good	Fair	Poor
—	18000	13000	11000	3500	2500

Fourth Model Musket

NIB	Exc.	V.G.	Good	Fair	Poor
—	14500	11000	8000	3500	2500

Model 1866 Iron Frame Rifle Musket

Overall length 54-1/2"; barrel length 33-1/4"; caliber .45 centerfire. Walnut stock with case hardened furniture, barrel burnished bright, the receiver case hardened. The finger lever catch mounted within a large bolster at the rear of the lever. Unmarked except for serial numbers that appear externally on the receiver and often the buttplate tang. Approximately 25 made during the early autumn of 1866.26Value speculative.

Model 1866 Iron Frame Swiss Sharpshooters Rifle

As above, but in .41 Swiss caliber and fitted with a Scheutzen style stock supplied by the firm of Weber Ruesch in Zurich. Marked Weber Ruesch, Zurich on the barrel and serial numbered externally. Approximately 400 to 450 manufactured in 1866 and 1867.

Model 1867 Iron Frame Carbine

Overall length 39-1/4"; barrel length 20"; caliber .44 rimfire. Walnut stock with case hardened furniture; the barrel and magazine tube blued; the receiver case hardened. The finger lever catch mounted within the rear curl of the lever. Unmarked except for serial numbers that appear externally on the receiver and often the buttplate tang. Approximately 20 manufactured. Prospective purchasers are strongly advised to secure an expert appraisal prior to acquisition.

Model 1868 Iron Frame Rifle Musket

Overall length 49-1/2" (.455 cal.), 50-1/2" or 53" (.45 and .47 cal.); barrel length 29-1/2" (.455 cal.) and 30-1/4" or 33" (.45 and .47 cal.); calibers .45, .455, and .47 centerfire. Walnut stock with case hardened or burnished bright (.45 and .47 cal.) furniture; the barrel burnished bright; the receiver case hardened or burnished bright (.45 and .47 cal.). The finger lever catch mounted on the lower receiver tang. The rear of the finger lever machined with a long flat extension on its upper surface. Unmarked except for serial number. Approximately 30 examples made in .45 and .455 caliber and 250 in .47 caliber.

Model 1868 Iron Frame Carbine

Overall length 40"; barrel length 20"; caliber .44 centerfire. Walnut stock with case hardened furniture; barrel and magazine tube blued; the receiver case hardened. The finger lever catch as above. Unmarked except for serial numbers (receiver and buttplate tang). Approximately 25 manufactured.

Model 1873

This Winchester rifle was one of the most popular lever-actions the company ever produced. This is the "gun that won the West" and with good reason. It was chambered for the more powerful centerfire cartridge, the .44-40. Compared to the .44 Henry, this cartridge was twice as good. With the introduction of the single-action Colt pistol in 1878, chambered for the same cartridge, the individual had the convenience of a pistol for protection and the accuracy of the Winchester for food and protection. The .44-40 was the standard cartridge for the Model 1873. Three additional cartridges were offered but were not as popular as the .44. The .38-40 was first offered in 1879 and the .32-20 was introduced in 1882. In 1884 the Model 1873 was offered in .22 caliber rimfire with a few special order guns built in .22 extra long rimfire. Approximately 19,552 .22 caliber Model 1873s were produced.

Early model 1873s were fitted with an iron receiver until 1884, when a steel receiver was introduced. The Model 1873 was offered in three styles:

1. Sporting Rifle, 24" round, octagon, or half-octagon barrel. Equipped standard with a crescent iron buttplate, straight-grip stock and capped forearm.
2. Carbine, 20" round barrel. Furnished standard with a rounded iron buttplate, straight-grip stock, and carbine style fore-end fastened to the barrel with a single barrel band.
3. Musket, 30" round barrel. Standard musket is furnished with a nearly full-length forearm fastened to the barrel with three barrel bands. The buttstock has a rounded buttplate.

The upper tang was marked with the model designation and the serial number was stamped on the lower tang. Caliber stampings on the Model 1873 are found on the bottom of the frame and on the breech end of the barrel. Winchester discontinued the Model 1873 in 1919, after producing about 720,000 guns. The Winchester Model 1873 was offered with a large number of extra-cost options that greatly affect the value of the gun. For example, Winchester built two sets of special Model 1873s: the 1-of-100 and the 1-of-1000. Winchester sold only eight 1-of-100 Model 1873s, and 136 of the 1-of-1000 guns that were built. In 1991 a few of these special guns were sold at auction and brought prices exceeding $75,000. The prices listed here are for standard guns only. For Model 1873 with special features, it is best to secure an expert appraisal. Model 1873s with case colored receivers will bring a premium.

The Winchester Model 1873 was offered with a large number of extra-cost options that greatly affect the value of the gun. For example, Winchester built two sets of special Model 1873's: the 1-of-100 and the 1-of-1000. Winchester sold only eight 1-of-100 Model 1873s, and 136 of the 1-of-1000 guns that were built. In 1991 a few of those special guns were sold at auction and brought prices exceeding $75,000. The prices listed here are for standard guns only. For Model 1873 with special features, it is best to secure an expert appraisal. Model 1873s with case colored receivers will bring a premium.

Courtesy Bonhams & Butterfields, San Francisco, California

First Model Rifle

The primary difference between the various styles of the Model 1873 is found in the appearance and construction of the dust cover. The First Model has a dust cover held in place with grooved guides on either side. A checkered oval finger grip is found on top of the dust cover. The latch that holds the lever firmly in place is anchored into the lower tang with visible threads. On later First Models, these threads are not visible. First Models appear from serial number 1 to about 31000.

NIB	Exc.	V.G.	Good	Fair	Poor
—	18000	15000	6000	3000	1400

First Model Carbine

NIB	Exc.	V.G.	Good	Fair	Poor
—	22000	18000	7500	4000	2500

First Model Musket

NIB	Exc.	V.G.	Good	Fair	Poor
—	14000	12000	5000	2500	1000

Second Model Rifle

The dust cover on the Second Model operates on one central guide secured to the receiver with two screws. The checkered oval finger grip is still used, but on later Second Models this is changed to a serrated finger grip on the rear of the dust cover. Second Models are found in the 31000 to 90000 serial number range.

NIB	Exc.	V.G.	Good	Fair	Poor
—	10000	8000	4000	2000	1250

Second Model Carbine

NIB	Exc.	V.G.	Good	Fair	Poor
—	15000	13000	7000	3000	1000

Second Model Musket

NIB	Exc.	V.G.	Good	Fair	Poor
—	5000	4000	2000	1250	900

Third Model Rifle

The central guide rail is still present on the Third Model, but it is now integrally machined as part of the receiver. The serrated rear edges of the dust cover are still present on the Third Model.

NIB	Exc.	V.G.	Good	Fair	Poor
—	6000	4000	2000	1000	750

Third Model Carbine

NIB	Exc.	V.G.	Good	Fair	Poor
—	12500	8000	5000	2000	800

Third Model Musket

NIB	Exc.	V.G.	Good	Fair	Poor
—	7000	2700	1500	850	500

Model 1873 .22 Rimfire Rifle

Winchester's first .22 caliber rifle and the first .22 caliber repeating rifle made in America was introduced in 1884 and discontinued in 1904. Its drawback was the small caliber. The general preference during this period of time was for the larger-caliber rifles. Winchester sold a little more than 19,000 .22 caliber Model 1873s.

NIB	Exc.	V.G.	Good	Fair	Poor
—	8000	6500	3000	1700	750

Model 1876

Winchester's Model 1876, sometimes referred to as the Centennial Model, was the company's response to the public's demand for a repeater rifle capable of handling larger and more potent calibers. Many single-shot rifles were available at this time to shoot more powerful cartridges, and Winchester redesigned the earlier Model 1873 to answer this need. The principal changes made to the Model 1873 were a larger and stronger receiver to handle more powerful cartridges. Both the carbine and the musket had their forearms extended to cover the full length of the magazine tube. The carbine barrel was increased in length from 20" to 22", and the musket barrel length was increased from 30 to 32". The Model 1876 was the first Winchester to be offered with a pistol-grip stock on its special Sporting Rifle. The Model 1876 was available in these calibers: .45-77 W.C.F., .50-95 Express, .45-60 W.C.F., .40-60 W.C.F. The Model 1876 was offered in four different styles:

1. Sporting Rifle, 28" round, octagon, or half-octagon barrel. This rifle was fitted with a straight-grip stock with a crescent iron buttplate. A special sporting rifle was offered with a pistol-grip stock.
2. Express Rifle, 26" round, octagon, or half-octagon barrel. The same sporting rifle stock was used.
3. Carbine, 22" round barrel with full-length forearm secured by one barrel band and straight grip stock.
4. Musket, 32" round barrel with full-length forearm secured by one barrel band and straight grip stock. Stamped on the barrel is the Winchester address with King's patent date. The caliber marking is stamped on bottom of the receiver near the magazine tube and the breech end of the barrel. Winchester also furnished the Model 1876 in 1-of-100 and 1-of-1000 special guns. Only eight 1-of-100 1876s were built and 54 1-of-1000 76s were built. As with their Model 1873 counterparts, these rare guns often sell in the $75,000 range or more. Approximately 64,000 Model 1876s were built by Winchester between 1876 and 1897. As with other Winchesters, the prices given are for standard guns.

First Model Rifle

As with the Model 1873, the primary difference in model types lies in the dust cover. The First Model has no dust cover and is seen between serial number 1 and 3000.

NIB	Exc.	V.G.	Good	Fair	Poor
—	17500	12000	6000	2750	1000

First Model Carbine

NIB	Exc.	V.G.	Good	Fair	Poor
—	12000	9500	6500	2500	1000

First Model Musket

NIB	Exc.	V.G.	Good	Fair	Poor
—	20000	19000	10000	5000	1500

Second Model Rifle

The Second Model has a dust cover with guide rail attached to the receiver with two screws. On the early Second Model an oval finger guide is stamped on top of the dust cover while later models have a serrated finger guide along the rear edge of the dust cover. Second Models range from serial numbers 3000 to 30000.

NIB	Exc.	V.G.	Good	Fair	Poor
—	11000	7500	4000	2000	1000

Second Model Carbine

NIB	Exc.	V.G.	Good	Fair	Poor
—	11000	7500	4000	2000	1000

Second Model Musket

NIB	Exc.	V.G.	Good	Fair	Poor
—	20000	15000	8000	1750	1000

Second Model Northwest Mounted Police Carbine

The folding rear sight is graduated in meters instead of yards.

Courtesy Little John's Auction Service, Inc., Paul Goodwin photo

NIB	Exc.	V.G.	Good	Fair	Poor
—	15000	9000	4500	2000	1250

Third Model Rifle

The dust cover guide rail on Third Model 76s is integrally machined as part of the receiver with a serrated rear edge on the dust cover. Third Model will be seen from serial numbers 30000 to 64000.

NIB	Exc.	V.G.	Good	Fair	Poor
—	9000	5500	3250	1500	750

Third Model Carbine

NIB	Exc.	V.G.	Good	Fair	Poor
—	12500	8000	3000	2000	1250

Third Model Musket

NIB	Exc.	V.G.	Good	Fair	Poor
—	14000	10000	7500	4000	1000

Winchester Hotchkiss Bolt-Action Rifle

This model is also known as the Hotchkiss Magazine Gun or the Model 1883. This rifle was designed by Benjamin Hotchkiss in 1876, and Winchester acquired the manufacturing rights to the rifle in 1877. In 1879 the first guns were delivered for sale. The Hotchkiss rifle was a bolt-action firearm designed for military and sporting use. It was the first bolt-action rifle made by Winchester. The rifle was furnished in .45-70 Government, and although the 1884 Winchester catalog lists a .40-65 Hotchkiss as being available, no evidence exists that such a chamber was ever actually furnished. The Model 1883 was available in three different styles: 1.Sporting Rifle, 26" round, octagon, or half-octagon barrel fitted with a rifle-type stock that included a modified pistol grip or straight-grip stock. 2.Carbine, 24" round or 22-1/2" round barrel with military-style straight-grip stock. 3.Musket, 32" or 28" round barrel with almost full-length military-style straight-grip stock. Winchester produced the Model 1883 until 1899, having built about 85,000 guns.

Courtesy Bonhams & Butterfields, San Francisco, California

First Model Sporting Rifle

This model has the safety and a turn button magazine cut-off located above the trigger guard on the right side. The Sporting Rifle is furnished with a 26" round or octagon barrel while the carbine has a 24" round barrel with a saddle ring on the left side of the stock. The musket has a 32" round barrel with two barrel bands, a steel forearm tip, and bayonet attachment under the barrel. The serial number range for the First Model is between 1 and about 6419.

NIB	Exc.	V.G.	Good	Fair	Poor
—	2000	1650	1250	800	400

First Model Carbine

NIB	Exc.	V.G.	Good	Fair	Poor
—	5500	2500	1500	900	500

First Model Musket

NIB	Exc.	V.G.	Good	Fair	Poor
—	2000	1650	1250	800	400

Second Model Sporting Rifle

On this model the safety is located on the top left side of the receiver, and the magazine cutoff is located on the top right side of the receiver to the rear of the bolt handle. The sporting rifle remains unchanged from the First Model with the above exceptions. The carbine has a 22-1/2" round barrel with a nickeled forearm cap. The musket now has a 28" barrel. Serial number range for the Second Model runs from 6420 to 22521.

Courtesy Milwaukee Public Museum, Milwaukee, Wisconsin

Second Model Carbine

NIB	Exc.	V.G.	Good	Fair	Poor
—	1750	1400	900	600	300

Second Model Musket

NIB	Exc.	V.G.	Good	Fair	Poor
—	4500	2250	1000	750	500

Third Model Sporting Rifle

The Third Model is easily identified by the two-piece stock separated by the receiver. The specifications for the sporting rifle remain the same as before, while the carbine is now fitted with a 20" barrel with saddle ring and bar on the left side of the frame. The musket remains unchanged from the Second Model with the exception of the two-piece stock. Serial numbers of the Third Model range from 22552 to 84555.

NIB	Exc.	V.G.	Good	Fair	Poor
—	1650	1250	800	500	300

Third Model Carbine

NIB	Exc.	V.G.	Good	Fair	Poor
—	1650	1250	800	500	300

Third Model Musket

NIB	Exc.	V.G.	Good	Fair	Poor
—	1650	1250	800	500	300

Model 1885 (Single-Shot)

The Model 1885 marks an important development between Winchester and John M. Browning. The Single-shot rifle was the first of many Browning patents that Winchester would purchase and provided the company with the opportunity to diversify its firearms line. The Model 1885 was the first single-shot rifle built by Winchester. The company offered more calibers in this model than any other. A total of 45 centerfire calibers were offered from the .22 extra long to the 50-110 express, as well as 14 rimfire caliber from .22 B.B. cap to the .44 flat Henry. Numerous barrel lengths, shapes and weights were available as were stock configurations, sights, and finishes. These rifles were also available in solid frame and takedown styles. One could almost argue that each of the 139,725 Model 1885s built are unique. Many collectors of Winchester Single-Shot specialize in nothing else. For this reason it is difficult to provide pricing that will cover most of the Model 1885s that the collector will encounter. However the prices given here are for standard guns in standard configurations.

The Model 1885 was offered in two basic frame types:

A. The High Wall was the first frame type produced and is so called because the frame covers the breech and hammer except for the hammer spur.

B. The breech and hammer are visible on the Low Wall frame with its low sides. This frame type was first introduced around the 5000 serial number range.

Both the High Wall and the Low Wall were available in two type frame profiles; the Thickside and the Thinside. The Thickside frame has flat sides that do not widen out to meet the stock. The Thickside is more common on the low wall rifle and rare on the High Walls. The Thinside frame has shallow milled sides that widen out to meet the stock. Thinside frames are common on High Wall guns and rare on Low Wall rifles.

1. The standard High Wall rifle was available with octagon or round barrel with length determined by caliber. The buttstock and forearm were plain walnut with crescent buttplate and blued frame.

2. The standard Low Wall featured a round or octagon barrel with length determined by caliber and plain walnut stock and forearm with crescent buttplate.

3. The High Wall musket most often had a 26" round barrel chambered for the .22 caliber cartridge. Larger calibers were available as were different barrel lengths. The High Wall Musket featured an almost full length forearm fastened to the barrel with a single barrel band and rounded buttplate.

4. The Low Wall musket is most often referred to as the Winder Musket named after the distinguished marksman, Colonel C.B. Winder. This model features a Lyman receiver sight and was made in .22 caliber.

5. The High Wall Schuetzen rifle was designed for serious target shooting and was available with numerous extras including a 30" octagon barrel and medium weight without rear sight seat; fancy walnut checkered pistol grip Schuetzen-style buttplate; checkered forearm; double set triggers; spur finger lever, and adjustable palm rest.

6. The Low Wall carbine was available in 15", 16", 18", and 20" round barrels. The carbine featured a saddle ring on the left side of the frame and a rounded buttplate.

7. The Model 1885 was also available in a High Wall shotgun in 20 gauge with 26" round barrel and straight grip stock with shotgun style rubber buttplate. The Model 1885 was manufactured between 1885 and 1920 with a total production of about 140,000 guns.

CALIBER NOTE: As stated above it is difficult to provide pricing on specific rifles, especially calibers, because of the wide range of variables. However, the collector may find it useful to know that the most common rimfire calibers were the .22 Short, .22 WCF, and .22 Long, in that order, with the .22 Long Rifle a distant fourth. The most common centerfire chambers were the .32 WCF and the .32-40. Other popular centerfire calibers were the .38-55, .25-20, .44 WCF, .32 Long WCF, and the .45-70. There were a number of chamberings that are extremely rare (one of each built). It is strongly recommended that research is done prior to a sale.

Courtesy Bonhams & Butterfields, San Francisco, California

Standard High Wall Rifle

NIB	Exc.	V.G.	Good	Fair	Poor
—	5000	3500	2200	1500	950

Standard Low Wall Rifle

Courtesy Bonhams & Butterfields, San Francisco, California

NIB	Exc.	V.G.	Good	Fair	Poor
—	1800	1500	1400	1200	900

High Wall Musket

NIB	Exc.	V.G.	Good	Fair	Poor
—	1600	1300	1000	700	425

Low Wall Musket (Winder Musket)

Courtesy Buffalo Bill Historical Center, Cody, Wyoming

NIB	Exc.	V.G.	Good	Fair	Poor
—	1400	1200	800	500	300

High Wall Schuetzen Rifle

NIB	Exc.	V.G.	Good	Fair	Poor
—	10000	7000	3000	1850	1000

Low Wall Carbine

NIB	Exc.	V.G.	Good	Fair	Poor
—	7500	5000	3500	2750	1500

High Wall Shotgun

Courtesy Buffalo Bill Historical Center, Cody, Wyoming

NIB	Exc.	V.G.	Good	Fair	Poor
—	4500	3000	2250	1250	850

Model 1886

Based on a John Browning patent, the Model 1886 was one of the finest and strongest lever-actions ever utilized in a Winchester rifle. Winchester introduced the Model 1886 in order to take advantage of the more powerful centerfire cartridges of the time.

Model 1886 Rifles and carbines were furnished with black, walnut stocks, case hardened frames, and blued barrels and magazine tubes. In 1901 Winchester discontinued the use of case hardened frames on all its rifles and used blued frames instead. For this reason, case hardened Model 1886 rifles will bring a premium. Winchester provided a large selection of extra cost options on the Model 1886, and for rifles with these options, a separate evaluation should be made by a reliable source. The Model 1886 was produced from 1886 to 1935 with about 160,000 in production.

The rifle was available in 10 different chambers:

.45-70 U.S. Government	.50-110 Express
.45-90 W.C.F.	.40-70 W.C. F.
.40-82 W.C.F.	.38-70 W.C. F.
.40-65 W.C.F.	.50-100-450
.38-56 W.C.F.	.33 W.C. F.

The most popular caliber was the .45-70 Government. Prices of the Model 1886 are influenced by caliber, with the larger calibers bringing a premium. The 1886 was available in several different configurations.

1. Sporting Rifle, 26", round, octagon and half-octagon barrel, full or half magazine and straight-grip stock with plain forearm.

2. Fancy Sporting Rifle, 26" round or octagon barrel, half or full magazine and fancy checkered walnut pistol-grip with checkered forearm.

3. Takedown Rifle, 24" round barrel, full or half magazine with straight-grip stock fitted with shotgun rubber buttplate and plain forearm.

4. Extra Lightweight Takedown Rifle, 22" round barrel, full or half magazine with straight-grip stock fitted with shotgun rubber buttplate and plain forearm.

5. Extra Lightweight Rifle, 22" round barrel, full or half magazine with straight-grip stock fitted with a shotgun rubber buttplate and plain forearm.

6. Carbine, 22" round barrel, full or half magazine with straight-grip stock and plain forearm.
7. Musket, 30" round barrel, musket-style forearm with one barrel band. Military-style sights. About 350 Model 1886 Muskets were produced.

NOTE: For .50 Express add a premium of 20 percent. Case colored Model 1886s will bring a premium of 20 percent.

Sporting Rifle

Courtesy Bonhams & Butterfields, San Francisco, California

NIB	Exc.	V.G.	Good	Fair	Poor
—	15000	15000	7500	5000	2500

Fancy Sporting Rifle

NIB	Exc.	V.G.	Good	Fair	Poor
—	25000	14500	8000	6000	3000

Takedown Rifle—Standard

NIB	Exc.	V.G.	Good	Fair	Poor
—	12500	900	4200	2000	700

Extra Lightweight Takedown Rifle—.33 caliber

NIB	Exc.	V.G.	Good	Fair	Poor
—	9000	5000	2000	750	400

Extra Lightweight Takedown Rifle—Other Calibers

NIB	Exc.	V.G.	Good	Fair	Poor
—	8750	6000	1800	1250	500

Extra Lightweight Rifle—.33 caliber

NIB	Exc.	V.G.	Good	Fair	Poor
—	6000	4000	1800	1000	500

Extra Lightweight Rifle—Other Calibers

NIB	Exc.	V.G.	Good	Fair	Poor
—	7000	5500	3000	950	500

Carbine

Courtesy Bonhams & Butterfields, San Francisco, California

Model 1886 carbine barrels are 22". A few were Trappers with 20" barrels. Add 50 percent if Trapper.

NIB	Exc.	V.G.	Good	Fair	Poor
—	19000	11000	7500	4500	2000

Musket

NIB	Exc.	V.G.	Good	Fair	Poor
—	19000	15000	9000	3500	1500

Model 71

When Winchester dropped the Model 1886 from its line in 1935, the company replaced its large-bore lever-action rifle with the Model 71 chambered for the .348 caliber. The Model 71 is similar in appearance to the Model 1886 with some internal parts strengthened to handle the powerful .348 cartridge. The rifle was available in three basic configurations:

1. Standard Rifle, 24" round barrel, 3/4 magazine, plain walnut pistol-grip stock and semi-beavertail forearm.
2. Standard Rifle (Carbine), 20" round barrel, 3/4 magazine, plain walnut pistol-grip stock and semi-beavertail forearm.
3. Deluxe Rifle, 24" round barrel, 3/4 magazine, checkered walnut pistol-grip stock and checkered semi-beavertail forearm. The frames and barrels were blued on all models of this rifle.
4. Deluxe Rifle (Carbine), 20" round barrel, 3/4 magazine, checkered walnut pistol-grip stock and checkered semi-beavertail forearm. The frames and barrels were blued on all models of this rifle.

The Model 71 was produced from 1935 to 1957 with about 47,000 built. **NOTE:** For pre-war Model 71s add a premium of 20 percent. The pre-war Model 71 has a longer tang than its post-war equivalent. For a bolt peep sight add 10 percent.

Standard Rifle

NIB	Exc.	V.G.	Good	Fair	Poor
—	1500	1200	800	400	300

Standard Rifle (Carbine)

NIB	Exc.	V.G.	Good	Fair	Poor
—	3250	2000	1600	1200	650

Deluxe Rifle

NIB	Exc.	V.G.	Good	Fair	Poor
—	3500	3050	800	525	425

Deluxe Rifle (Carbine)

NIB	Exc.	V.G.	Good	Fair	Poor
—	4100	3500	2000	1250	700

Model 1892

The Model 1892 was an updated successor to the Model 1873 using a scaled down version of the Model 1886 action. The rifle was chambered for the popular smaller cartridges of the day, namely the .25-20, .32-20, .38-40, .44-40, and the rare .218 Bee. The rifle was available in several different configurations.

1. Sporting Rifle, solid frame or takedown (worth an extra premium of about 20 percent), 24" round, octagon, or half-octagon barrel with 1/2, 3/3 or full magazines. plain straight-grip walnut stock with capped forearm.
2. Fancy Sporting Rifle, solid frame or takedown (worth an extra premium of about 20 percent), 24" round, octagon, or half-octagon barrel with 1/2, 3/3 or full magazines. Checkered walnut pistol-grip walnut stock with checkered capped forearm.
3. Carbine, 20" round barrel, full or half magazine, plain walnut straight-grip stock with one barrel band forearm. Carbines were offered only with solid frames.
4. Trapper's Carbine, 18", 16", 15", or 14" round barrel with the same dimensions of standard carbine. Federal law prohibits the possession of rifles with barrel lengths shorter then 16". The Model 1892 Trapper's Carbine can be exempted from this law as a curio and relic with federal permit providing the trapper is an original trapper and left the factory with the short trapper barrel.
5. Musket, 30" round barrel with full magazine. Almost full length forearm held by two barrel bands. Buttstock is plain walnut with straight grip.

The Model 1892 was built between 1892 and 1932 with slightly more than 1 million sold. The Model 1892 carbine continued to be offered for sale until 1941. **NOTE:** Antique Winchester Model 1892s (pre-1898 manufacture) will bring a premium of 10 percent.

Sporting Rifle

Courtesy Bonhams & Butterfields, San Francisco, California

NIB	Exc.	V.G.	Good	Fair	Poor
—	5000	3500	1250	700	350

Fancy Sporting Rifle

Courtesy Bonhams & Butterfields, San Francisco, California

NIB	Exc.	V.G.	Good	Fair	Poor
—	12000	7500	4000	2500	1000

Carbine

Courtesy Bonhams & Butterfields, San Francisco, California

NIB	Exc.	V.G.	Good	Fair	Poor
—	3500	2500	1700	1200	600

Trapper's Carbine

NOTE: Add 20 percent for 15" barrel. Add 50 percent for carbines chambered for .25-20 cartridge.

Courtesy Bonhams & Butterfields, San Francisco, California

NIB	Exc.	V.G.	Good	Fair	Poor
—	12000	8500	4000	2500	1250

Musket

NIB	Exc.	V.G.	Good	Fair	Poor
—	—	9500	4500	2500	1500

Model 1894

Based on a John M. Browning patent, the Model 1894 was the most successful centerfire rifle Winchester ever produced. This model is still in production, and the values given here reflect those rifles produced before 1964, or around serial number 2550000. The Model 1894 was the first Winchester developed especially for the smokeless powder and was chambered for these cartridges: .32-40, .38-55, .25-35 Winchester, .30-30 Winchester, and the .32 Winchester Special. The rifle was available in several different configurations:

1. Sporting Rifle, 26" round, octagon or half-octagon barrel, in slid frame or takedown. Full, 2/3, or 1/2 magazines were available. Plain walnut straight or pistol-grip stock with crescent buttplate and plain capped forearm.
2. Fancy Sporting Rifle, 26" round, octagon or half-octagon barrel, in slid frame or takedown. Full, 2/3, or 1/2 magazines were available. Fancy walnut checkered straight or pistol-grip stock with crescent buttplate and checkered fancy capped forearm.
3. Extra Lightweight Rifle, 22" or 26" round barrel with half magazine. plain walnut straight-grip stock with shotgun buttplate and plain capped forearm.
4. Carbine, 20" round barrel, plain walnut straight-grip stock with carbine style buttplate. Forearm was plain walnut uncapped with one barrel band. Carbines were available with solid frame only. Carbines made prior to 1925 were fitted with a saddle ring on the left side of the receiver and worth a premium over carbines without a saddle ring.
5. Trappers Carbine, 18", 16", 15", or 14". Buttstock, forearm, and saddle ring specifications same as standard carbine. All Model 1894s were furnished with blued frames and barrels, although case hardened frames were available as an extra-cost option. Case colored Model 1894s are rare and worth a considerable premium, perhaps as much as 1,000 percent. Guns with extra-cost options should be evaluated by an expert to determine proper value. Between 1894 and 1963, approximately 2,550,000 Model 1984s were sold.

NOTE: Antique Winchester Model 1894s (pre-1898 manufacture) will bring a premium of 10 percent. First year production guns, October 1894 to December 1894, documented by the Cody Museum will command a 100 percent premium. Values are for guns with saddle rings. For carbines without saddle rings deduct 35 percent. Add 25 percent for carbines chambered for .25-35 or .38-55 cartridge.

First Model Sporting Rifle

Very early model that incorporates a screw entering the receiver over the loading port from the outside. Rare.

NIB	Exc.	V.G.	Good	Fair	Poor
—	7000	4000	2000	1250	500

Sporting Rifle

NOTE: Takedown versions are worth approximately 20 percent more.

Courtesy Bonhams & Butterfields, San Francisco, California

NIB	Exc.	V.G.	Good	Fair	Poor
—	4000	3000	1500	850	450

Fancy Sporting Rifle

NOTE: Takedown versions are worth approximately 20 percent more. Fancy Sporting Rifles were also engraved at the customer's request. Check factory where possible and proceed with caution. Factory engraved Model 1894s are extremely valuable.

Courtesy Bonhams & Butterfields, San Francisco, California

NIB	Exc.	V.G.	Good	Fair	Poor
—	12000	7500	3500	2000	900

Extra Lightweight Rifle

Courtesy Bonhams & Butterfields, San Francisco, California

NIB	Exc.	V.G.	Good	Fair	Poor
—	5000	3500	1500	1000	450

Carbine

NIB	Exc.	V.G.	Good	Fair	Poor
—	3000	2000	600	400	200

Trapper's Carbine

NOTE: Add 30 percent for carbines chambered for .25-35 or .38-55 calibers.

Courtesy Bonhams & Butterfields, San Francisco, California

NIB	Exc.	V.G.	Good	Fair	Poor
—	6500	4250	2500	1500	700

Model 53

This model was in fact a slightly more modern version of the Model 1892 offered in these calibers: .25-20, .32-20, and the .44-40. It was available in only one style: the Sporting Rifle, 22" round barrel, half magazine, straight- or pistol-grip plain walnut stock with shotgun butt. It was available in solid frame or takedown with blued frame and barrel. The Model 53 was produced from 1924 to 1932 with about 25,000 built. **NOTE:** Add 10 percent for takedown model. Add 40 percent for rifles chambered for .44-40 cartridge. A few of these rifles were fitted with stainless steel barrel in the early 1930s. If the black paint on these barrels is in good condition, they will bring a substantial premium.

NIB	Exc.	V.G.	Good	Fair	Poor
—	3000	2000	1000	500	300

Sporting Rifle

NIB	Exc.	V.G.	Good	Fair	Poor
—	3000	2000	1000	500	300

Model 55

This model was a continuation of the Model 1894 except in a simplified version. Available in the same calibers as the Model 1894, this rifle could be ordered only with a 24" round barrel, plain walnut straight-grip stock with plain fore-end and shotgun butt. Frame and barrel were blued with solid or takedown features. This model was produced between 1924 and 1932 with about 21,000 sold. Serial numbers for the Model 55 were numbered separately until about serial number 4500; then the guns were numbered in the Model 1894 sequence. **NOTE:** .25-35 caliber will bring about a 60 percent premium. Add 10 percent for models with solid frames.

NIB	Exc.	V.G.	Good	Fair	Poor
—	1500	1000	650	450	200

Standard Rifle

NIB	Exc.	V.G.	Good	Fair	Poor
—	1500	1000	650	450	200

Model 64

An improved version of the Model 55, this gun featured a larger magazine, pistol-grip stock, and forged front sight ramp. The trigger pull was also improved. Frame and barrel were blued. Chambered for the .25-35 Win., .30-30 Win., .32 Win. Special, and the .219 zipper added in 1938 (and discontinued in the Model 64 in 1941). Serial number of the Model 64 was concurrent with the Model 1894. Built between 1933 and 1957, approximately 67,000 were sold. This model was reintroduced in 1972 and discontinued in 1973. The values listed are for the early version only. **CALIBER NOTE:** As stated above it is difficult to provide pricing on specific rifles, especially calibers, because of the wide range of variables. However, the collector may find it useful to know that the most common rimfire calibers were the .22 Short,

.22 WCF, and .22 Long, in that order, with the .22 Long Rifle a distant fourth. The most common centerfire chambers were the .32 WCF and the .32-40. Other popular centerfire calibers were the .38-55, .25-20, .44 WCF, .32 Long WCF, and the .45-70. There were a number of chamberings that are extremely rare (one of each built). It is strongly recommended that research is done prior to a sale.

NIB	Exc.	V.G.	Good	Fair	Poor
—	1200	900	500	300	200

Standard Rifle

20" barrel. **NOTE:** For Deluxe model add 50 percent to prices. For Carbine model add 50 percent to above prices. For rifles chambered for the .219 Zipper and .25-35 cartridges add 100 percent. Add 10 percent for bolt peep sight. Model 64s in .219 Zipper left the factory with bolt peep sights as original equipment.

Courtesy Bonhams & Butterfields, San Francisco, California

NIB	Exc.	V.G.	Good	Fair	Poor
—	1200	900	500	300	200

Carbine

NIB	Exc.	V.G.	Good	Fair	Poor
—	1550	1000	650	500	250

Model 65

This model was a continuation of the Model 53 and was offered in three calibers: .25-20, .32-20, and .218 Bee. It had several improvements over the Model 53, namely the magazine capacity was increased to seven cartridges, forged ramp for front sight, and a lighter trigger pull. The Model 65 was available only in solid blued frame with blued barrel and pistol grip with plain walnut stock. Only about 5,700 of these rifles were built between 1933 and 1947. **NOTE:** Add 10 percent for bolt peep sight. Model 65s in .218 Bee left the factory with bolt peep sights as original equipment.

Model 65 in .218 Bee   Courtesy Rock Island Auction Company

NIB	Exc.	V.G.	Good	Fair	Poor
—	4000	3500	2000	1000	500

Standard Rifle

NIB	Exc.	V.G.	Good	Fair	Poor
—	4000	3500	2000	1000	500

NOTE: Add 10 percent for bolt peep sight. Model 65s in .218 Bee left the factory with bolt peep sights as original equipment.

Model 1895

The Model 1895 was the first nondetachable box magazine rifle offered by Winchester. Built on a John M. Browning patent, this rifle was introduced by Winchester to meet the demand for a rifle that could handle the new high-power, smokeless hunting cartridges of the period. The Model 1895 was available in these calibers: .30-40 Krag, .38-72 Winchester, .40-72 Winchester, .303 British, .35 Winchester, .405 Government, 7.62 Russian, .30-03, and .30-06. The rifle gained fame as a favorite hunting rifle of Theodore Roosevelt. Because of its box magazine, the Model 1895 has a distinctive look like no other Winchester lever-action rifle. The rifle was available in several different configurations:

1. Sporting Rifle, 28" or 24" (depending on caliber) round barrel, plain walnut straight-grip stock with plain fore-end. The first 5,000 rifles were manufactured with flat-sided receivers, and the balance of production were built with the receiver sides contoured. After serial-number 60000, a takedown version was available.
2. Fancy Sporting Rifle, 28" round barrel, fancy walnut checkered straight-grip stock and fancy walnut checkered forearm. Rifles with serial numbers below 5000 had flat sided frames.
3. Carbine, 22" round barrel, plain walnut straight-grip stock with military-style hand guard forend. Some carbines are furnished with saddle rings on left side of receiver.
4. Musket:

A. Standard Musket, 28" round, plain walnut straight-grip stock with musket style fore-end with two barrel bands.
B. U.S. Army N.R.A. Musket, 30" round barrel, Model 1901 Krag-Jorgensen rear sight. Stock similar to the standard musket. This musket could be used for "Any Military Arm" matches under the rules of the National Rifle Association.
C. N.R.A. Musket, Models 1903 and 1906, 24" round barrel with special buttplate. Also eligible for all matches under "Any Military Arm" sponsored by the NRA. This musket was fitted with the same stock as listed above.
D. U.S. Army Musket, 28" round barrel chambered for the .30-40 Krag. Came equipped with or without knife bayonet. These muskets were furnished to the U.S. Army for use during the Spanish-American War and are "US" marked on the receiver.
E. Russian Musket, similar to standard musket but fitted with clip guides in the top of the receiver and with bayonet. Approximately 294,000 Model 1895 Muskets were sold to the Imperial Russian Government between 1915 and 1916. The first 15,000 Russian Muskets had 8" knife bayonets, and the rest were fitted with 16" bayonets.

The Model 1895 was produced from 1895 to 1931 with about 426,000 sold. **NOTE:** Add a 10 percent premium for rifles built before 1898.

Sporting Rifle

NOTE: Flat-side rifles will bring a premium of 100 percent. Takedown rifles will add an additional 15 percent.

Courtesy Bonhams & Butterfields, San Francisco, California

Flat-side rifle

NIB	Exc.	V.G.	Good	Fair	Poor
—	5000	3000	1200	700	300

Fancy Sporting Rifles

NIB	Exc.	V.G.	Good	Fair	Poor
—	7000	5000	1500	1100	500

NOTE: Flat-side rifles will bring a premium of 100 percent. Takedown rifles will add an additional 15 percent.

Carbine

Courtesy Bonhams & Butterfields, San Francisco, California

NIB	Exc.	V.G.	Good	Fair	Poor
—	5500	3250	1550	900	300

Standard Musket

NIB	Exc.	V.G.	Good	Fair	Poor
—	3200	1800	1000	600	300

U.S. Army N.R.A. Musket

NIB	Exc.	V.G.	Good	Fair	Poor
—	4500	2000	1200	800	400

N.R.A. Musket, Model 1903 and 1906

NIB	Exc.	V.G.	Good	Fair	Poor
—	5500	2500	1200	800	400

U.S. Army Musket

NIB	Exc.	V.G.	Good	Fair	Poor
—	5000	3000	1500	850	450

Russian Musket

NIB	Exc.	V.G.	Good	Fair	Poor
—	4000	2500	1000	500	250

Breechloading Double-Barrel Shotgun

Winchester imported an English-made shotgun sold under the Winchester name between 1879 and 1884. The gun was available in 10 and 12 gauge with 30" or 32" Damascus barrels. It was sold in five separate grades referred to as "classes." The lowest grade was the "D" and the best grade was called the "Match Grade." These were marked on the sidelocks. The center rib was stamped "Winchester Repeating Arms Co., New Haven, Connecticut, U.S.A." Prices shown for "D" grade. Add 10 percent for "C" grade; 20 percent for "B" grade; and 30 percent for "A" grade. About 10,000 of these guns were imported by Winchester.

Class A, B, C, and D

NIB	Exc.	V.G.	Good	Fair	Poor
—	2500	2250	1250	850	500

Match Gun

NIB	Exc.	V.G.	Good	Fair	Poor
—	5000	4000	1800	850	500

Model 1887 Shotgun

Winchester enjoyed a great deal of success with its imported English shotgun, and the company decided to manufacture a shotgun of its own. In 1885 it purchased the patent for a lever-action shotgun designed by John M. Browning. By 1887 Winchester had delivered the first model 1887 in 12 gauge and shortly after offered the gun in 10 gauge. Both gauges were offered with 30" or 32" Full choked barrels, with the 30" standard on the 12 gauge and 32" standard on the 10 gauge. A Riot Gun was offered in 1898 both in 10, and 12 gauge with 20" barrels choked cylinder. Both variations of the Model 1887 were offered with plain walnut pistol-grip stocks with plain fore-end. The frame was case hardened and the barrel blued. Between 1887 and 1901 Winchester sold approximately 65,000 Model 1887 shotguns.

Standard Shotgun

Courtesy Milwaukee Public Museum, Milwaukee, Wisconsin

NIB	Exc.	V.G.	Good	Fair	Poor
—	2750	1500	850	500	300

Riot Shotgun

Courtesy Bonhams & Butterfields, San Francisco, California

NIB	Exc.	V.G.	Good	Fair	Poor
—	3000	2000	950	600	400

Model 1901 Shotgun

This model is a redesign of the Model 1887 shotgun and was offered in 10 gauge only with a 32" barrel choked Full, Modified, or Cylinder. The barrel was reinforced to withstand the new smokeless powder loads and the frame was blued instead of case hardened. The stock was of plain walnut with a modified pistol and plain forearm. The Model 1901 was built between 1901 and 1920 with about 65,000 guns sold.

NIB	Exc.	V.G.	Good	Fair	Poor
—	1500	1000	600	400	250

Model 1893

This was the first slide-action repeating shotgun built by Winchester. It featured an exposed hammer and side ejection. Based on a John M. Browning patent, this model was not altogether satisfactory. The action proved to be too weak to handle smokeless loads, even though the gun was designed for black powder. The gun was offered in 12 gauge with 30" or 32" barrels choked Full. Other chokes were available on special order and will command a premium. The stock was plain walnut with a modified pistol grip, grooved slide handle, and hard rubber buttplate. The receiver and barrel were blued. Winchester produced the Model 1893 between 1893 and 1897, selling about 31000 guns.

Courtesy Bonhams & Butterfields, San Francisco, California

NIB	Exc.	V.G.	Good	Fair	Poor
—	1000	700	600	325	250

Model 1897

The Model 1897 replaced the Model 1893, and while similar to the Model 1893, the new model had several improvements such as a stronger frame, chamber made longer to handle 2.75" shells, frame top was covered to force complete side ejection, the stock was made longer and with less drop. The Model 1897 was available in 12 or 16 gauge with the 12 gauge offered either in solid or takedown styles and the 16 gauge available in takedown only. The Model 1897 was available with barrel lengths of 20", 26", 28", 30" and 32" and in practically all choke options from full to cylinder. The shotgun could be ordered in several different configurations:

1. Standard Gun, 12 or 16 gauge, 30" barrel in 12 gauge and 28" barrel in 16 gauge, with plain walnut modified pistol-grip stock and grooved slide handle. Steel buttplate standard.

2. Trap Gun 12 or 16 gauge, 30" barrel in 12 gauge and 28" barrel in 16 gauge, fancy walnut stock with oil finish checkered pistol-grip or straight-grip stock with checkered slide handle. Marked "TRAP" on bottom of frame.

3. Pigeon Gun, 12 or 16 gauge, 28" barrel on both 12 and 16 gauge, straight- or pistol-grip stock same as Trap gun, receiver hand engraved.

4. Tournament Gun, 12 gauge only with 30" barrel, select walnut checkered straight-grip stock and checkered slide handle, top of receiver is matted to reduce glare.

5. Brush Gun, 12 or 16 gauge, 26" barrel, Cylinder choke, has a slightly shorter magazine tube than standard gun, plain walnut modified pistol-grip stock with grooved slide handle.

6. Brush Gun, Takedown, same as above with takedown feature and standard length magazine tube.

7. Riot Gun, 12 gauge, 20" barrel bored to shoot buckshot, plain walnut modified pistol-grip stock with grooved slide handle. Solid frame or takedown.

8. Trench Gun, same as Riot Gun but fitted with barrel hand guard and bayonet.

The Winchester Model 1897 was a great seller for Winchester. During its 60-year production span, 1,025,000 guns were sold.

NOTE: Add 100 percent for 16 gauge guns in excellent, very good and good condition.

Standard Gun

NIB	Exc.	V.G.	Good	Fair	Poor
—	1300	850	650	300	200

Trap Gun

NIB	Exc.	V.G.	Good	Fair	Poor
—	1500	1200	800	500	400

Pigeon Gun/High Grade

NIB	Exc.	V.G.	Good	Fair	Poor
—	8000	6000	5000	4000	500

Tournament Gun

NIB	Exc.	V.G.	Good	Fair	Poor
—	2000	1700	900	750	400

Brush Gun

NIB	Exc.	V.G.	Good	Fair	Poor
—	950	750	600	500	400

Riot Gun

Courtesy Bonhams & Butterfields, San Francisco, California

NIB	Exc.	V.G.	Good	Fair	Poor
—	1600	1050	750	450	300

Trench Gun

Courtesy Bonhams & Butterfields, San Francisco, California

NIB	Exc.	V.G.	Good	Fair	Poor
—	3500	2900	2250	1500	600

Winchester-Lee Straight Pull Rifle

U.S. Navy Musket

NIB	Exc.	V.G.	Good	Fair	Poor
—	2500	2000	1500	700	500

Commercial Musket

NIB	Exc.	V.G.	Good	Fair	Poor
—	2500	2000	1500	700	500

Sporting Rifle

Courtesy Amoskeag Auction Company

NIB	Exc.	V.G.	Good	Fair	Poor
—	2500	2000	1500	700	500

Model 1890

The Model 1890 was the first slide-action rifle ever produced by Winchester. Designed by John and Matthew Browning, this rifle was chambered for the .22 Short, Long, and Winchester Rimfire cartridges (the WRF cartridge was developed by Winchester specifically for the Model 1890) not on an interchangeable basis. In 1919 the .22 LR cartridge was offered as well. The rifle was a slide-action top ejecting rifle with an 18" under barrel magazine tube. All Model 1890s were furnished standard with plain walnut straight stocks with crescent buttplate and 12 groove slide handle. This rifle was one of the company's best selling small caliber firearms and was in worldwide use. The Model 1890 came in three separate and distinct variations that greatly affect its value:

1. First Model, solid frame, 24" octagon barrel, case hardened frame, and fixed rear sight. Approximately 15,552 of these First Model guns were produced, and their distinctive feature is concealed locking lugs and solid frame. Serial numbered on the lower tang only. Built from 1890 to 1892.
2. Second Model, takedown, 24" octagon barrel, case hard ened frame, and adjustable rear sight. Serial numbered from 15553 to 112970 (on lower tang only) these Second Model guns feature the same concealed locking lugs but with the added takedown feature. A Deluxe version was offered with fancy walnut checkered straight- or pistol-grip stock and grooved slide handle.
2A. Second Model (blued frame variation), same as above but with blued frame. Serial numbered from 112971 to 325250 (on lower tang until 232328, then also on bottom front end of receiver) these blued frame Second Models are much more numerous than the case hardened variety.

A Deluxe version was offered with fancy walnut checkered straight- or pistol-grip stock and grooved slide handle.
3. Third Model, takedown, 24" octagon barrel, blued frame, adjustable rear sight. Serial numbered from 325251 to as high as 853000 (numbered on both the lower tang and bottom front of receiver) the distinctive feature of the Third Model is the locking cut made on the front top of the receiver to allow the breech bolt to lock externally. A Deluxe version was offered with fancy walnut checkered stock, straight or pistol grip with grooved slide handle. Winchester offered many extra-cost options for this rifle that will greatly affect the value. Secure an expert appraisal before proceeding. The Model 1890 was produced from 1890 to 1932 with approximately 775,000 guns sold.

NOTE: For Third Models chambered for .22 LR add 25 percent premium.

First Model—Standard Grade

NIB	Exc.	V.G.	Good	Fair	Poor
—	9000	5000	2500	1250	750

Second Model—Case Hardened Frame Standard

Courtesy Bonhams & Butterfields, San Francisco, California

NIB	Exc.	V.G.	Good	Fair	Poor
—	6000	3500	2000	1000	500

First Model Deluxe

NIB	Exc.	V.G.	Good	Fair	Poor
—	10000	7000	3500	2000	1000

Second Model—Blued Frame Standard

NIB	Exc.	V.G.	Good	Fair	Poor
—	2500	1700	1500	750	250

Second Model Deluxe

NIB	Exc.	V.G.	Good	Fair	Poor
—	7500	5500	3000	1500	750

Third Model Standard

NIB	Exc.	V.G.	Good	Fair	Poor
—	2000	1400	900	450	250

Third Model Deluxe

NIB	Exc.	V.G.	Good	Fair	Poor
—	6500	4000	2000	1000	750

Model 1906

In 1906 Winchester decided to offer a lower-cost version of the Model 1890. The Model 1906 used the same receiver but was fitted with a 20" round barrel and plain gumwood straight-grip stock. When the Model 1906 was first introduced, it sold for two-thirds of the price of the Model 1890. For the first two years the gun was chambered for the .22 Short cartridge only. In 1908 the rifle was modified to shoot .22 Short, Long, and LR cartridges interchangeably. This modification ensured the Model 1906's success, and between 1906 and 1932 about 800,000 were sold. All Model 1906s were of the takedown variety. The Model 1906 is available in three important variations:

1. 22 Short Only, 20" round barrel, straight-grip gumwood stock and smooth slide handle. These were built from serial number 1 to around 113000.
2. Standard Model 1906, 20" round barrel, straight-grip gumwood stock with 12 groove slide handle. Serial

numbered from 113000 to 852000.

3. Model 1906 Expert, 20" round barrel, pistol-grip gumwood stock with fluted smooth slide handle. Expert was available from 1918 to 1924 and was offered in three different finishes regular blued finish, half nickel (receiver, guard, and bolt), and full nickel (receiver, guard, bolt, and barrel nickeled).

Model 1906 .22 Short Only

Courtesy Bonhams & Butterfields, San Francisco, California

NIB	Exc.	V.G.	Good	Fair	Poor
—	2500	1750	750	500	200

Standard Model 1906

Courtesy Bonhams & Butterfields, San Francisco, California

NIB	Exc.	V.G.	Good	Fair	Poor
2000	1500	750	400	400	200

Model 1906 Expert

Courtesy Bonhams & Butterfields, San Francisco, California

NIB	Exc.	V.G.	Good	Fair	Poor
—	2500	1850	950	500	300

NOTE: Prices are for half-nickel Experts. Add 10 percent for blued guns and 100 percent for full nickel.

Model 61

Winchester developed the Model 61 in an attempt to keep pace with its competitors' hammerless .22 rifles. The Model 61 featured a 24" round or octagonal barrel and could be ordered by the customer in a variety of configurations. Collector interest in this rifle is high because of the fairly large number of variations. The Model 61 is often considered a companion to the Winchester Model 12 and Model 42 shotguns. The following is a list of chamber and barrel variations found in this model:

1. 24" round barrel, .22 Short, Long, LR
2. 24" octagonal barrel, .22 Short only add 150 percent.
3. 24" octagonal barrel, .22 LR only add 150 percent.
4. 24" octagonal barrel, .22 W.R.F. only add 100 percent.
5. 24" round barrel, .22 LR Shot only add 200 percent.
5A. 24" round barrel, shot only Routledge bore add 200 percent.
6. 24" round barrel, .22 W.R.F. only add 125 percent.
7. 24" round barrel, .22 LR only add 50 percent.
8. 24" round barrel, .22 Winchester Magnum add 50 percent.
9. 24" round barrel, .22 Short only add 100 percent.

The Model 61 was fitted with a plain walnut pistol-grip stock with grooved slide handle. All Model 61s were of the take down variety. Pre-war models will have a short slide handle.

Manufactured between 1932 and 1963, approximately 342,000 guns were sold.

Pre-war

NOTE: Single caliber models will command a premium of 50 percent depending on caliber. Octagon barrel models will command a premium of 75 percent. .22 LR shot only models will bring a premium of 250 percent.

NIB	Exc.	V.G.	Good	Fair	Poor
3000	2200	1600	800	400	200

Post-war

Courtesy Bonhams & Butterfields, San Francisco, California

NIB	Exc.	V.G.	Good	Fair	Poor
2000	1400	1200	600	300	250

Magnum

NOTE: This variation (Model 61 Magnum) was produced from 1960 to 1963.

NIB	Exc.	V.G.	Good	Fair	Poor
2800	2400	1600	775	600	400

Model 62 and 62A

When the Model 1890 and Model 1906 were dropped from the Winchester product line in 1932, the company introduced the Model 62 to take their place. An updated version of the earlier slide-action .22 rifles, the Model 62 was fitted with a 23" round barrel and was capable of shooting .22 Short, Long and LR cartridges interchangeably. Winchester offered a Gallery version of the Model 62 that was chambered for .22 Short only. Some of these Gallery guns have "Winchester" stamped on the left side of the receiver. Winchester Model 62 Gallery rifles have a triangular loading port on the loading tube that the standard models did not have. A change in the breech bolt mechanism brought about a change in the name designation from Model 62 to Model 62A. This occurred around serial number 98000. The letter "A" now appears behind the serial number. This model stayed in production until 1958 and collectors will concede a premium for guns built prior to WWII with small slide handles. The stock was of plain walnut with straight grip and grooved slide handle. Both the receiver and barrel were blued. All Model 62 and 62As were takedown. Approximately 409,000 guns were sold.

Pre-war

NOTE: Barrels marked with Model 62 are worth more than barrels marked with Model 62A by approximately 15 percent. Gallery models will bring a premium of 300 percent.

NIB	Exc.	V.G.	Good	Fair	Poor
2200	1500	850	400	250	150

Post-war

Courtesy Bonhams & Butterfields, San Francisco, California

NIB	Exc.	V.G.	Good	Fair	Poor
1100	850	600	500	225	125

Model 62 Gallery

.22 Short only with triangular loading port & "winchester" stamped on side of receiver. **NOTE:** A Model 62 with "Winchester" stamped on the side of the receiver is more desirable than one without the stamping. Deduct 10 percent for Gallery rifles without this stamping.

NIB	Exc.	V.G.	Good	Fair	Poor
3200	2000	1000	650	400	200

Model 1903

The first semi-automatic rifle produced by Winchester was designed by T.C. Johnson. This rifle was offered in a takedown version only and was available in a 20" round barrel chambered for the .22 Winchester Automatic Rimfire. This ammunition is no longer produced and when found is very expensive. The tubular magazine is located in the buttstock and holds 10 cartridges. The rifle was available in two different configurations:

1. Standard Rifle, 20" round barrel, plain walnut straight-grip stock with plain fore-end. Steel crescent butt was standard.
2. Deluxe Rifle, 20" round barrel, fancy checkered walnut pistol-grip stock with checkered forearm. Manufactured from 1903 to 1932, about 126,000 were sold.

Standard

NIB	Exc.	V.G.	Good	Fair	Poor
—	850	550	325	200	100

Deluxe

NOTE: The first 5,000 guns were built without safeties, and the first 15,000 guns were furnished with bronze firing pins instead of steel. These early Model 1903s will bring a premium of 30 percent.

Courtesy Bonhams & Butterfields, San Francisco, California

NIB	Exc.	V.G.	Good	Fair	Poor
—	1800	1100	700	500	250

Model 63

The Model 63 took the place of the Model 1903 in 1933 in an attempt by Winchester to solve the problem of having to use a special .22 caliber cartridge in the gun to operate the blowback system. It is a very high quality semi-automatic rifle. Many collectors and shooters considered it the best rimfire semi-automatic rifle ever produced. The Model 63 was chambered for the .22 LR cartridge and was available in a 20" barrel for the first four years or until about serial number 9800. Thereafter, the model was offered with a 23" round barrel for the remainder of the production period. The gun was fitted with a plain walnut pistol-grip stock and forearm. The tubular magazine was located in the buttstock that came with a steel buttplate. The last 10,000 Model 63s were sold with a grooved receiver top to make the addition of a scope easier. Manufactured between 1933 and 1958, about 175,000 guns were sold. **NOTE:** Grooved top receivers command a premium of 20 percent.

20" Barrel

Courtesy Bonhams & Butterfields, San Francisco, California

NIB	Exc.	V.G.	Good	Fair	Poor
2750	1400	800	500	400	250

23" Barrel

Courtesy Bonhams & Butterfields, San Francisco, California

NIB	Exc.	V.G.	Good	Fair	Poor
2200	1600	900	600	400	200

Model 1905

The Model 1905 was a larger version of the Model 1903, developed by T.C. Johnson to handle the more powerful centerfire cartridges. It was chambered for the .32 Winchester Self-Loading and .35 Self-Loading cartridges, loading by means of a detachable box magazine. Available in takedown only, this model was offered in two different styles:

1. Sporting Rifle, 22" round barrel, plain walnut straight grip (changed to pistol grip in 1908) stock with plain fore-end.
2. Fancy Sporting Rifle, 22" round barrel, fancy walnut checkered pistol-grip stock with checkered fore-end. This model was the first Winchester semi-automatic rifle to fire centerfire cartridges. Produced from 1905 to 1920 with about 30,000 rifles sold.

Sporting

NIB	Exc.	V.G.	Good	Fair	Poor
—	700	550	350	175	125

Fancy Sporting

NIB	Exc.	V.G.	Good	Fair	Poor
—	900	750	500	200	150

Model 1907

The Model 1907 was an improved version of the Model 1905 and chambered for the new .351 Winchester Self-Loading cartridge. Outward appearance was the same as Model 1905 except for 20" round barrel. This rifle was available in three different styles:

1. Sporting Rifle, 20" round barrel, plain walnut pistol-grip stock with plain fore-end. Discontinued in 1937.
2. Fancy Sporting Rifle, 20" round barrel, fancy walnut checkered pistol-grip stock and checkered fore-end.
3. Police Rifle, 20" round barrel, plain walnut pistol-grip stock and beavertail fore-end. This version was fitted with a leather sling and with or without knife bayonet. First introduced in 1937. Winchester discontinued this model in 1957 after having sold about 59,000 guns.

NOTE: Post-WWII Model 1907s command a premium over the values shown below.

Sporting

NIB	Exc.	V.G.	Good	Fair	Poor
—	750	500	350	175	125

Fancy Sporting

NIB	Exc.	V.G.	Good	Fair	Poor
—	850	650	450	200	150

Police

NIB	Exc.	V.G.	Good	Fair	Poor
—	950	750	575	300	250

Model 1910

This model was similar to the Model 1907 but the action was made stronger to handle the new Winchester .401 Self-Loading cartridge. The specifications for this model are the same as the Model 1907. Built between 1907 and 1936, only about 21,000 of these guns were sold.

Sporting

Courtesy Bonhams & Butterfields, San Francisco, California

NIB	Exc.	V.G.	Good	Fair	Poor
—	900	750	550	400	200

Fancy Sporting

NIB	Exc.	V.G.	Good	Fair	Poor
—	1000	800	600	450	250

Model 55 (Rimfire Rifle)

Not to be confused with the lever-action model, this .22 caliber rifle was a semi-automatic (auto-ejecting, actually) single-shot with a 22" round barrel. Fitted with a plain walnut pistol-grip one-piece stock and fore-end. The safety goes on when each cartridge is inserted into the chamber. This model was not serial numbered and was produced from 1957 to 1961 with about 45,000 guns sold.

NIB	Exc.	V.G.	Good	Fair	Poor
—	400	350	225	150	75

Model 74

This was a semi-automatic chambered for either the .22 Short or the .22 LR. The rifle has a tubular magazine in the buttstock and a 24" round barrel. The bolt on this rifle was designed to be easily removed for cleaning or repair. The stock was plain walnut pistol-grip with semi-beavertail fore-end. A Gallery Special was offered that was chambered for the .22 Short and fitted with a steel shell deflector. This gallery model was also available with chrome trimmings at extra cost.

Sporting

Courtesy C.H. Wolfersberger

NIB	Exc.	V.G.	Good	Fair	Poor
—	400	300	225	150	100

Gallery Special—.22 Short Only

NOTE: For Gallery models with chrome trimmings, add a premium of 50 percent.

NIB	Exc.	V.G.	Good	Fair	Poor
—	800	600	325	225	150

Model 77

This rifle was built on the blow-back design for semi-automatic rifles and is chambered for the .22 LR. It features a 22" round barrel and either a detachable box magazine or under barrel tubular magazine. The rifle has a trigger guard made of nylon. It has a plain walnut pistol-grip stock with semi-beavertail fore-end and composition buttplate. Built between 1955 and 1963, Winchester sold about 217,000 of these rifles. **NOTE:** Models with tubular magazines will bring a premium of 10 percent to 20 percent.

NIB	Exc.	V.G.	Good	Fair	Poor
—	500	375	250	175	75

Model 100

This rifle is a gas operated semi-automatic and chambered for the .243, .308, and .284 caliber cartridges. The Model 100 was the first commercial Winchester self-loading, centerfire rifle made since the Winchester Model 1905, the Model 1907, and the Model 1910. These models were produced until 1936/37. Winchester did produce the M1 Carbine during WWII. It was available in a rifle version with a 22" round barrel and a carbine version with a 19" barrel. Both were furnished with a detachable box magazine. The stock was a one-piece design with pistol grip and was offered in either hand-cut checkering or pressed basket weave checkering. Rifles were introduced in 1960 and the carbine in 1967. The Model 100 was last produced in 1973 with about 263,000 guns sold.

Rifle

NOTE: Pre-1964 models 15 percent premium. Prices given are for .308 caliber; for .243 add 15 percent, for .284 add 20 percent.

NIB	Exc.	V.G.	Good	Fair	Poor
—	600	475	350	250	200

Carbine

Only about 53,000 carbines were made, about one for every five rifles. **NOTE:** Add 25 percent premium for .243, and 100 percent for .284.

NIB	Exc.	V.G.	Good	Fair	Poor
—	675	525	400	325	225

Model 88

The Model 88 was a modern short-stroke lever-action chambered for the .243, .308, 284 and .358 calibers. It was available in a rifle version with 22" round barrel and a carbine version with 19" round barrel. The carbine model was not chambered for the .358 cartridge. Both were furnished with a detachable box magazine. The stock was a one-piece design with pistol grip and was offered with hand-cut checkering or pressed basket weave checkering after 1964. The rifle was introduced in 1955 and the carbine was first offered in 1968. Both versions were discontinued in 1973 with about 283,000 sold.

Rifle

NOTE: Pre-1964 models add 25 percent premium. Prices are for .308 caliber; for .243 add 15 percent, .284 add 75 percent, and for 358 add 100 percent. This model was offered with no front or rear sights (Gopher Special) for a few years prior to 1962. Add 100 percent for this variant. Beware of fakes.

NIB	Exc.	V.G.	Good	Fair	Poor
—	900	750	500	300	250

Carbine

Only 28,000 carbines were built, about 1 for every 10 rifles. Rarely encountered. **NOTE:** Add 25 percent for .243, add 100 percent for .284 calibers. The carbine was not offered in .358 caliber.

NIB	Exc.	V.G.	Good	Fair	Poor
—	1300	1150	900	650	300

Model 99 or Thumb Trigger

This rifle was a modification of the Model 1902 without a traditional trigger. The rifle was fired by depressing the trigger with the thumb, which was part of the sear and extractor located behind the bolt. The rifle was chambered for the .22 Short and Long until 1914 when it was also chambered for the .22 Extra Long. All cartridges could be shot interchangeably. The stock was the same as the Model 1902, Gumwood stained walnut, without the trigger or trigger guard. This model was not serial numbered. Built between 1904 and 1923. Winchester sold about 76,000 rifles.

Courtesy Bonhams & Butterfields, San Francisco, California

NIB	Exc.	V.G.	Good	Fair	Poor
—	2400	2000	1000	700	500

Model 1900

This single-shot bolt-action .22 caliber rifle was based on a John M. Browning design. The rifle was furnished with an 18" round barrel and chambered for the .22 Short and Long interchangeably. The stock was a one-piece plain gumwood straight grip without a buttplate. The rifle was not serial numbered. It was produced from 1899 to 1902 with about 105,000 sold.

Courtesy Buffalo Bill Historical Center, Cody, Wyoming

NIB	Exc.	V.G.	Good	Fair	Poor
—	2000	1000	450	300	200

Model 1902

Also a single-shot, this model was of the same general design as the Model 1900 with several improvements: a special shaped metal trigger guard was added, a shorter trigger pull, a steel buttplate, a rear peep sight, and the barrel was made heavier at the muzzle. The rifle was chambered for the .22 Short and Long cartridges until 1914 when the .22 Extra Long was added. In 1927 the .22 Extra Long was dropped in favor of the more popular .22 LR. All of these cartridges were interchangeable. The stock was a one-piece plain gumwood with straight grip (the metal trigger guard added a pistol grip feel) and steel buttplate, which was changed to composition in 1907. This model was not serial numbered. About 640,000 Model 1902s were sold between 1902 and 1931 when it was discontinued.

NIB	Exc.	V.G.	Good	Fair	Poor
—	1000	750	400	225	125

Model 1904

This model was a slightly more expensive version of the Model 1902. It featured a 21" round barrel, a one-piece plain gumwood straight-grip stock (the metal trigger guard gave the rifle a pistol grip feel) with a small lip on the fore-end. Rifle was chambered for the .22 Short and Long until 1914 when the .22 Extra Long was added. The .22 LR cartridge was added in place of the Extra Long in 1927. This model was not serial numbered. Produced between 1904 and 1931, about 303,000 rifles were sold.

NIB	Exc.	V.G.	Good	Fair	Poor
—	900	675	350	200	100

Model D Military Rifle

Overall length 46-3/8"; barrel length 26"; caliber 7.62mm. Walnut stock with blued barrel, receiver, magazine housing and furniture.

Receiver ring over barrel breech stamped with serial number and Winchester proofmark. A total of 500 Model D Rifles were shipped to Russia for trial in March of 1917. **Value Speculative.**

Imperial Bolt-Action Magazine Rifle (Model 51)

Designed by T.C. Johnson, approximately 25 of these rifles were made during 1919 and 1920 in two different styles and three calibers. The takedown variation has an overall length of 42-1/4", barrel length 22" and was made in .27, .30-06 and .35 Newton calibers. The solid frame version is identical in form, dimensions and calibers. Sight configurations and markings vary. **Value Speculative.**

Model 43

Introduced in 1949, this rifle was chambered for the .218 Bee, .22 Hornet, .25-20 Winchester, and the .32-20 Winchester. The rifle was a bolt-action with detachable box magazine, fitted with a 24" round barrel and front sight ramp forged integrally with barrel. **This model was not drilled and tapped for scope blocks except for a few late rifles.** This model was available in two styles:

1. Standard Rifle, 24" round barrel, plain walnut pistol-grip stock and fore-end. One inch sling swivels are standard.
2. Special Rifle, 24" round barrel, select walnut checkered pistol-grip stock and checkered fore-end. Furnished with either open sporting rear sight or Lyman 57A micrometer receiver sight.

The Model 43 was produced from 1949 to 1957 with about 63,000 sold. **NOTE:** For rifles chambered for .25-20 and .32-20 add a 50 percent premium. For rifles with non-factory drilled and tapped scope holes deduct 40 percent.

Standard

NIB	Exc.	V.G.	Good	Fair	Poor
—	800	700	550	300	200

Special or Deluxe

NIB	Exc.	V.G.	Good	Fair	Poor
—	1500	1200	800	450	175

Model 47

This model was a single-shot bolt-action rifle chambered for the .22 Short, Long, and LR interchangeably. The rifle was furnished with a 25" round barrel, plain walnut pistol-grip stock and fore-end. The bolt, bolt handle, and trigger are chrome plated. This model has a special bolt with a post on the underside. This moves into the safety position when the bolt is closed. This model was not serial numbered. Produced between 1948 and 1954, Winchester sold about 43,000 guns. **NOTE:** Add 10 percent premium for Model 47 with factory peep sight.

Courtesy Buffalo Bill Historical Center, Cody, Wyoming

NIB	Exc.	V.G.	Good	Fair	Poor
—	450	350	250	200	150

Target Rifle

Fitted with a 28" round standard weight or heavyweight barrel, plain walnut modified pistol-grip stock with correct bolt.

NIB	Exc.	V.G.	Good	Fair	Poor
—	750	600	450	250	150

Model 52

One of the finest small-caliber bolt-action rifles ever built, the Model 52 was Winchester's answer to the increased demand for a military-style target rifle following WWI. The Model 52 was a well-made quality-built bolt-action rifle. The rifle was chambered for the .22 LR cartridge. Designed by T.C. Johnson, this rifle was built in several different configurations over its production life:

1. Model 52 with finger groove in fore-end and one barrel band. Produced from 1920 to 1929.
2. Model 52 Target Rifle, same as above but without finger groove in fore-end and has first speed lock. Made from 1929 to 1932.
3. Model 52A Target Rifle, same as above with addition of reinforced receiver and locking lug. Made from 1932 to 1935.
4. Model 52B Target Rifle, same as above with addition of adjustable sling swivel and single-shot adapter. Made from 1935 to 1947.
5. Model 52C Target Rifle, same as above with addition of an easily adjustable vibration-free trigger mechanism. Made from 1947 to 1961.
6. Model 52D Target Rifle, this is a single-shot rifle with free-floating barrel and new design stock with adjustable hand-stop channel.
7. Model 52 Bull Gun, same as target rifle but fitted with extra heavyweight barrel. Made from 1939 to 1960. The Bull Barrel measures 1.125" at the receiver juncture while the heavyweight measures 1". Both barrels measure .875" at the muzzle.
8. Model 52 International Match, a free-style stock with thumb hole and adjustable buttstock and fore-end introduced in 1969. International Prone model with no thumb hole or adjustable buttplate and fore-end was introduced in 1975. Both discontinued in 1980.
9. Model 52 Sporter, 24" round barrel, select walnut checkered pistol-grip stock with cheekpiece and fore-end with black plastic tip. Pistol grip was furnished with hard-rubber grip cap. The Model 52 Sporter was introduced in 1934 and discontinued in 1958. It went through the same improvements as the Target Rifle, thus the designation Model 52A Sporter, etc.

Standard

NIB	Exc.	V.G.	Good	Fair	Poor
—	1250	1000	750	250	300

Target

Courtesy Rock Island Auction Company

NIB	Exc.	V.G.	Good	Fair	Poor
—	1750	1500	1150	900	350

Target—Speed Lock

NIB	Exc.	V.G.	Good	Fair	Poor
—	1700	1400	1050	900	350

Model 52A Target Heavy Barrel—Rare

NIB	Exc.	V.G.	Good	Fair	Poor
—	1700	1400	1050	900	350

Model 52B Target Heavy & Standard Barrel

NIB	Exc.	V.G.	Good	Fair	Poor
—	1500	1300	950	700	300

Model 52B Target Bull Barrel

NIB	Exc.	V.G.	Good	Fair	Poor
—	1700	1400	1050	900	350

Model 52C Target

Courtesy Amoskeag Auction Company

NIB	Exc.	V.G.	Good	Fair	Poor
—	1700	1400	1050	800	500

Model 52D Target

Courtesy Amoskeag Auction Company

NIB	Exc.	V.G.	Good	Fair	Poor
—	1800	1500	1300	1050	500

Model 52B Bull Gun

NIB	Exc.	V.G.	Good	Fair	Poor
—	1800	1500	1300	1050	500

Model 52C Bull Gun

NIB	Exc.	V.G.	Good	Fair	Poor
—	1800	1500	1300	1050	500

International Match

Approximately 300 manufactured.

Free Style

NIB	Exc.	V.G.	Good	Fair	Poor
—	3550	2900	2050	1200	600

Prone

NIB	Exc.	V.G.	Good	Fair	Poor
—	1600	1350	1150	800	600

Model 52C Sporter

NIB	Exc.	V.G.	Good	Fair	Poor
5000	4100	3400	2300	1800	900

Model 52B Sporter

NIB	Exc.	V.G.	Good	Fair	Poor
4000	3600	2750	2000	1500	500

Model 52B Sporter

NIB	Exc.	V.G.	Good	Fair	Poor
4500	3900	3200	2400	1850	600

Model 54

The Model 54 was to centerfire cartridges what the Model 52 was to rimfire cartridges. The Model 54 was also a quality-made bolt-action rifle with a nondetachable box magazine and was chambered for a variety of calibers: .270, .30-06, .30-30, 7mm, 7.65, 9mm, .250-3000, .22 Hornet, .220 Swift, and .257 Roberts. This was Winchester's first bolt-action rifle built for heavy, high velocity ammunition. The rifle was available in several different styles:

1. Standard Rifle, 24" or 20" round barrel (except .220 Swift which was 26"), plain walnut checkered pistol-grip stock and fore-end.
2. Carbine, 20" round barrel, plain walnut pistol-grip stock with finger groove on each side of fore-end.
3. Sniper's Rifle, 26" round heavyweight barrel, plain walnut pistol-grip stock and fore-end.
4. N.R.A. Rifle, 24" round barrel, select walnut checkered pistol-grip stock and fore-end.
5. Super Grade Rifle, 24" round barrel, select walnut checkered pistol-grip stock with cheekpiece and checkered fore-end with black plastic tip. Pistol grip was capped with hard rubber cap. Super Grade was equipped with 1" detachable sling swivels.
6. Target Rifle, 24" round heavyweight barrel, plain walnut checkered pistol-grip stock and fore-end.
7. National Match Rifle, 24" round barrel, plain walnut special target stock and fore-end.

The Model 54 was introduced in 1925 and was discontinued in 1936 with about 50,000 guns sold. **NOTE:** The rare calibers are the 7mm, 7.65mm and the 9mm, which bring considerable premiums (in some cases as much as 250 percent) over standard calibers. Popular calibers such as .22 Hornet, .220 Swift, .30-30, and .257 Roberts will also bring a premium. Proceed with caution on Model 54s with rare caliber markings.

Standard

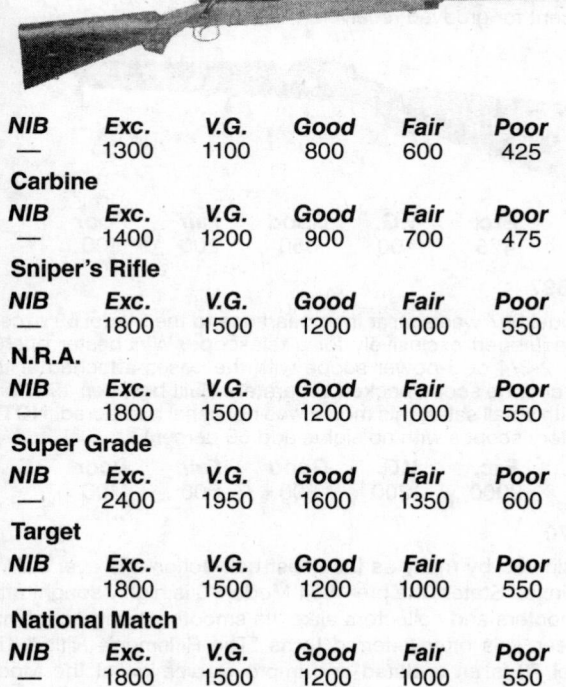

NIB	Exc.	V.G.	Good	Fair	Poor
—	1300	1100	800	600	425

Carbine

NIB	Exc.	V.G.	Good	Fair	Poor
—	1400	1200	900	700	475

Sniper's Rifle

NIB	Exc.	V.G.	Good	Fair	Poor
—	1800	1500	1200	1000	550

N.R.A.

NIB	Exc.	V.G.	Good	Fair	Poor
—	1800	1500	1200	1000	550

Super Grade

NIB	Exc.	V.G.	Good	Fair	Poor
—	2400	1950	1600	1350	600

Target

NIB	Exc.	V.G.	Good	Fair	Poor
—	1800	1500	1200	1000	550

National Match

NIB	Exc.	V.G.	Good	Fair	Poor
—	1800	1500	1200	1000	550

Model 56

This model was designed to be a medium-priced bolt-action rimfire rifle. It featured a detachable box magazine and was chambered for the .22 Short or .22 LR cartridges. The rifle was offered in two styles:

1. Sporting Rifle, 22" round barrel, plain walnut pistol-grip stock and fore-end.
2. Fancy Sporting Rifle, 22" round barrel, fancy walnut checkered pistol-grip stock and fore-end.

Both styles had a fore-end with a distinctive lip on the fore-end

tip. The rifle was introduced in 1926 and was discontinued in 1929 with about 8,500 rifles sold. **NOTE:** Add a 50 percent premium for rifles chambered for .22 Short only.

Sporting

NIB	Exc.	V.G.	Good	Fair	Poor
—	1500	1000	750	525	400

Fancy Sporting

Very rare, use caution.

NIB	Exc.	V.G.	Good	Fair	Poor
—	3000	2000	1500	900	750

Model 57

The Model 57 was close in appearance to the Model 56 with the addition of a heavier stock, target sights, and swivel bows attached to the stock. The rifle was chambered for the .22 Short or .22 LR and featured a 22" round barrel with detachable box magazine. The stock was plain walnut with pistol grip and plain fore-end. The rifle was introduced in 1927 and dropped from the Winchester line in 1936 having sold only about 19,000 guns. **NOTE:** Add 20 percent premium for web sling.

NIB	Exc.	V.G.	Good	Fair	Poor
—	950	700	450	325	250

Model 58

This model was an attempt by the company to market a low-priced .22 caliber rimfire rifle in place of its Models 1902 and 1904. This was a single-shot bolt-action, cocked by pulling the firing pin head to the rear. It had an 18" round barrel and was chambered for the .22 Short, Long, and LR interchangeably. The stock was a one-piece plain wood with straight grip. This model was not serial-numbered. The Model 58 was introduced in 1928 and discontinued in 1931. About 39,000 were sold.

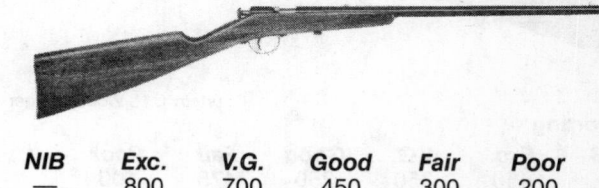

NIB	Exc.	V.G.	Good	Fair	Poor
—	800	700	450	300	200

Model 59

The Model 59 was essentially a Model 58 with the addition of a pistol-grip stock and a 23" round barrel. Introduced in 1930, it was dropped from the product line in the same year with a total sales of about 9,000 guns.

Courtesy Olin Corporation

NIB	Exc.	V.G.	Good	Fair	Poor
—	1000	800	550	400	200

Model 60 and 60A

This rifle used the same action as that of the Model 59. When the rifle was first introduced in 1931, it was furnished with a 23" round barrel which was changed to 27" in 1933. Several other mechanical improvements were included with this model; perhaps the most noticeable were the chrome-plated bolt, bolt handle, and trigger. The stock was plain wood with pistol grip. In 1933 the Model 60A was added, which was the same rifle but in a target configuration. The front sight was a square top military blade with a Lyman 55W receiver sight. The Model 60 was discontinued in 1934 with about 166,000 rifles sold. The Model 60A was dropped in 1939 with only about 6,100 rifles sold.

Courtesy Buffalo Bill Historical Center, Cody, Wyoming

Model 60

NIB	Exc.	V.G.	Good	Fair	Poor
—	375	250	200	150	100

Model 60A

NIB	Exc.	V.G.	Good	Fair	Poor
—	500	425	300	200	100

Model 67

Winchester again upgraded and improved the Model 60 with an expansion of the styles offered to the shooting public. The standard chamber for the rifle was .22 Short, Long, and LR interchangeably with the W.R.F. only added in 1935:

1. Sporting Rifle, 27" round barrel, stock similar to the Model 60.
2. Smoothbore Rifle, 27" barrel, chambered for the .22 long shot or .22 LR shot.
3. Junior Rifle, 20" round barrel and shorter stock.
4. Rifle with miniature target boring, 24" round barrel, chambered for .22 LR shot.

Model 67s were not serial numbered for domestic sales but were numbered for foreign sales. Introduced in 1934 the gun was dropped from the line in 1963 having sold about 384,000. Many of these models were fitted at the factory with telescopes and the bases were mounted on the rifle and the scope was packed separately.

Courtesy C.H. Wolfersberger

Sporting

NIB	Exc.	V.G.	Good	Fair	Poor
—	450	350	250	175	100

Smoothbore

Courtesy Buffalo Bill Historical Center, Cody, Wyoming

NIB	Exc.	V.G.	Good	Fair	Poor
—	800	600	400	250	200

Junior

NIB	Exc.	V.G.	Good	Fair	Poor
—	500	350	275	200	125

Miniature Target Rifle

This model is marked "for shot only" and has beads instead of standard iron rifle sights.

NIB	Exc.	V.G.	Good	Fair	Poor
—	1200	900	700	400	300

Model 677

This model looked the same as the Model 67 but was manufactured without iron sights and therefore will have no sight cuts in the barrel. The rifle was furnished with either 2-3/4 power scopes or 5 power scopes. This model was not serial numbered. Introduced in 1937 and discontinued in 1939. **NOTE:** Add 100 percent premium for rifles chambered for .22 WRF.

NIB	Exc.	V.G.	Good	Fair	Poor
—	2400	1800	1100	600	300

Model 68

Another takeoff on the Model 67, this model differed only in the sight equipment offered. Winchester fitted this rifle with a peep sight. First sold in 1934 the Model 68 was dropped in 1946 with sales of about 101,000. **NOTE:** Rifles with factory scopes and no sights add 50 percent. For rifles with factory scopes and no sights chambered for .22 WRF add 400 percent.

Courtesy C.H. Wolfersberger

With Scope

NIB	Exc.	V.G.	Good	Fair	Poor
—	900	775	450	300	200

Without Scope

NIB	Exc.	V.G.	Good	Fair	Poor
—	300	225	150	100	75

Model 69 and 69A

This model was designed by Winchester to answer the demand for a medium-priced hunting and target .22 rimfire bolt-action rifle. The rifle had a detachable box magazine, and many were offered with factory-installed telescopes in 2-3/4 and 5 power. The stock was plain walnut with pistol grip and plain fore-end. This model was not serial numbered. The 69A version was introduced in 1937 and featured an improved cocking mechanism. Introduced in 1935 as the Model 69, this gun was dropped in 1963 with sales of about 355,000 guns. **NOTE:** Add 25 percent for Target Model. Add 35 percent for grooved receiver.

NIB	Exc.	V.G.	Good	Fair	Poor
—	475	400	350	200	100

Model 697

The Model 697 was similar in appearance to the Model 69 except it was equipped exclusively for a telescope. Winchester offered either a 2-3/4 or 5-power scope with the bases attached at the factory and the scope packed separately. Built between 1937 and 1941 with small sales, this model was not serial numbered. **NOTE:** For factory scopes with no sights add 50 percent.

NIB	Exc.	V.G.	Good	Fair	Poor
—	2000	1200	800	600	400

Model 70

Considered by many as the finest bolt-action rifle ever built in the United States, the pre-1964 Model 70 is highly sought after by shooters and collectors alike. Its smooth, strong action has no peer. It is often referred to as "The Riflemen's Rifle." The Model 70 is an updated and improved version of the Model 54 and features a hinged floorplate, new speed locks, new safety design that does not interfere with telescope, manually releasable bolt stop, more attractive buttstock and fore-end, and forged steel trigger guard. Like many Winchesters, the Model 70 was available with several extra-cost options that should be evaluated by an expert. The values listed are given for pre-1964 Model 70s with serial numbers from 1 to 581471. This rifle was available in several different styles:

1. Standard Grade, 24" round barrel (except 26" round barrel for .220 Swift and .300 H&H Magnum—25" round barrel for .375 H&H Magnum after 1937), plain walnut checkered pistol stock and fore-end. Built from 1936 to 1963.

2. Standard Grade Carbine, 20" round barrel, chambered for .22 Hornet, .250-3000, .257 Roberts, .270, 7mm, and .30-06, same stock as Standard Grade. Built from 1936 to 1946.

3. Super Grade Rifle, same barrel and calibers as Standard Grade, select walnut checkered and capped pistol-grip stock with cheekpiece and checkered fore-end with plastic tip. Built from 1936 to 1960.

4. Featherweight, 22" round barrel chambered for .243, .264, .270, .308, .30-06, and .358. Fitted with aluminum trigger guard, aluminum buttplate, and aluminum floor plate. Later versions with plastic buttplate. Built from 1952 to 1963.

5. Featherweight Super Grade, same as above except not chambered for the .358 cartridge, but fitted with Super Grade stock. Built from 1952 to 1963.

6. National Match, same as Standard Grade but fitted with target type stock and telescope bases. Chambered for .30-06 only. Discontinued in 1960.

7. Target, 24" round medium-weight barrel with same stock as National Match in .243 and .30-06 calibers. Discontinued in 1963.

8. Varmint, 26" round heavy barrel, with heavier varmint stock, chambered for .243 and the rare .220 Swift. Built from 1956 to 1963.

9. Westerner, 26" round barrel with Standard Grade stock, chambered for .264 Winchester Magnum. Built from 1960 to 1963. Fitted with a solid rubber pad for early production guns and a vented pad for later guns.

10. Alaskan, 25" round barrel, with Standard Grade stock, chambered for .338 Winchester Magnum and .375 H&H Magnum. Built from 1960 to 1963. Fitted with a solid rubber pad marked Winchester for early production guns and a vented pad both marked Winchester for later guns.

11. Bull Gun, 28" round barrel, same stock as National Match, chambered for .30-06 and .300 H&H Magnum. Built from 1936 to 1963. The standard calibers offered for the Model 70 are these, in order of rarity: .300 Savage, .35 Rem., .458 Win Magnum, 7mm, .358 Win., .250-3000 Savage, .300 Win Magnum, .338 Win. Magnum, .375 H&H Magnum, .257 Roberts, .220 Swift, .22 Hornet, .264 Win. Magnum, .300 H&H Magnum, .308 Win., .243 Win., .270 W.C.F., .30-06.

Prices for the Model 70 are, in many cases, based on the caliber of the rifle; the more rare the caliber, the more premium the gun will command. Many pre-1964 Model 70s are still available in new condition in the original box with all papers. Add 25 to 50 percent if the box is serial numbered to the gun. Use caution prior to purchase of NIB guns due to fake boxes and papers.

PRICING NOTE: The asterisk (*) signifies the value of the rifle with respect to a usable action. Model 70 unaltered receivers bring $500 regardless of the condition of the barrel and stock. If the receiver is unusable then the rifle is worth the value of its usable parts, i.e. less than $500.

For Model 70s with "X" or "D" prefix add a collector premium of 10 percent. These letters indicate that there were two rifles mistakenly stamped with the same serial number.

Standard Rifle .30-06 Springfield (1937-1963)
Pre-War

NIB	Exc.	V.G.	Good	Fair	Poor
—	2200	1600	1100	500*	500*

Post-War

NIB	Exc.	V.G.	Good	Fair	Poor
—	1450	1200	800	500*	500*

.270 Win. (1937-1963)
Pre-War

NIB	Exc.	V.G.	Good	Fair	Poor
—	2200	1900	1000	500*	500*

Post-War

NIB	Exc.	V.G.	Good	Fair	Poor
—	1550	1400	900	500*	500*

.243. Win. (1955-1963)

NOTE: Post-WWII Model 1907s command a premium over the values shown below.

NIB	Exc.	V.G.	Good	Fair	Poor
—	2750	2200	1100	500*	500*

.300 H&H Magnum (1937-1963)
Pre-War

NIB	Exc.	V.G.	Good	Fair	Poor
—	3100	2500	1700	1000	500*

Post-War

NIB	Exc.	V.G.	Good	Fair	Poor
—	2650	2000	1400	850	500*

.264 Win. Magnum (1959-1963)

NIB	Exc.	V.G.	Good	Fair	Poor
—	2500	2000	1400	850	500*

.22 Hornet (1937-1958)
Pre-War

NIB	Exc.	V.G.	Good	Fair	Poor
—	3000	2400	2000	1000	500*

Post-War

NIB	Exc.	V.G.	Good	Fair	Poor
—	2750	2000	1500	750	500*

.220 Swift (1937-1963)
Pre-War

NIB	Exc.	V.G.	Good	Fair	Poor
—	3000	2400	1750	900	500*

Post-War

NIB	Exc.	V.G.	Good	Fair	Poor
—	2500	1750	1200	650	500*

.257 Roberts (1937-1959)
Pre-War

NIB	Exc.	V.G.	Good	Fair	Poor
—	3200	2500	1500	950	500*

Post-War

NIB	Exc.	V.G.	Good	Fair	Poor
—	2900	2100	1400	750	500*

.375 H&H Magnum (1937-1963)
Pre-War

NIB	Exc.	V.G.	Good	Fair	Poor
—	4300	3700	2200	1350	500*

Post-War

NIB	Exc.	V.G.	Good	Fair	Poor
—	3200	2500	1800	1000	500*

.338 Win. Magnum (1959-1963)

NIB	Exc.	V.G.	Good	Fair	Poor
—	3150	2550	1550	900	500*

.300 Win. Magnum (1962-1963)

NIB	Exc.	V.G.	Good	Fair	Poor
—	2650	2250	1200	750	500*

.250-3000 Savage (1937-1949)

NIB	Exc.	V.G.	Good	Fair	Poor
—	4750	3500	2500	1200	500*

7mm (1937-1949)

NIB	Exc.	V.G.	Good	Fair	Poor
—	5900	4800	2700	1700	700

Relative Caliber Rarity*
Model 70
1936 - 1963

Caliber categories (left to right): .300 Savage, .35 Rem, .458 Win Mag., 7MM, .358 Win., .250-3000 Savage, .300 Win. Mag., .338 Win. Mag., .375 H&H Mag., .257 Roberts, .220 Swift, .22 Hornet, .264 Win. Mag., .300 H&H Mag., .308 Win., .243 Win.

.35 Rem. (1944-1947)

NIB	Exc.	V.G.	Good	Fair	Poor
—	8900	6050	3700	2000	950

.300 Savage (1944-1950s?)

NIB	Exc.	V.G.	Good	Fair	Poor
—	9400	8300	3800	2000	950

.458 Win. Magnum African

Built in Supergrade only, 1956-1963.

NIB	Exc.	V.G.	Good	Fair	Poor
—	7400	5350	4200	2750	1350

Featherweight

NOTE: Add 100 percent for .358 Win. For .264 and .270 calibers add 25 percent.

NIB	Exc.	V.G.	Good	Fair	Poor
—	2200	1450	1075	700	450

Featherweight Super Grade

NIB	Exc.	V.G.	Good	Fair	Poor
—	5400	4300	3200	1650	1000

Standard Grade Carbine

NOTE: For Supergrade rifles add 100 percent.

NIB	Exc.	V.G.	Good	Fair	Poor
—	2900	2000	1400	950	650

National Match

NIB	Exc.	V.G.	Good	Fair	Poor
—	3400	2550	1850	950	600

Target

NIB	Exc.	V.G.	Good	Fair	Poor
—	2450	2100	1150	750	550

Varmint

NOTE: Add 40 percent premium for .220 Swift.

NIB	Exc.	V.G.	Good	Fair	Poor
—	2350	1950	950	600	375*

Bull Gun

NIB	Exc.	V.G.	Good	Fair	Poor
—	3900	3200	2450	850	600

Model 72

This model is a bolt-action rifle with tubular magazine. It is chambered for the .22 Short, Long and LR cartridges interchangeably.

Early rifles were available with 2.75 or 5 power telescopes, but the majority were furnished with either open sights or peep sights. This rifle was available in two different configurations:

1. Sporting Rifle, 25" round barrel, chambered for the .22 Short, Long, and LR cartridges, one-piece plain walnut pistol-grip stock and fore-end.
2. Gallery Special, 25" round barrel, chambered for .22 Short only, stock same as Sporting Rifle.

This model was not serial numbered. It was built between 1938 and 1959 with about 161,000 rifles sold. **NOTE:** Gallery Special will command a premium of 100 percent. For rifles with factory scopes and no sights add 200 percent depending on condition. Add 25 percent premium for peep sights. Add 20 percent for Model 72A with grooved receiver.

Courtesy C.H. Wolfersberger

NIB	Exc.	V.G.	Good	Fair	Poor
—	425	350	275	200	125

Model 75

Available in two styles:

1. Sporting Rifle, 24" round barrel, chambered for .22 LR, select walnut checkered pistol-grip stock and fore-end. This rifle was furnished with either open rear sights or a Lyman 57E receiver sight.
2. Target Rifle, 28" round barrel, chambered for .22 LR, plain walnut pistol-grip stock and fore-end. The Target Rifle was furnished with either a Winchester 8-power telescope or a variety of target sights.

This model was discontinued in 1958 with about 89,000 sold.

Sporter

NIB	Exc.	V.G.	Good	Fair	Poor
—	1500	1000	800	500	350

Target

NIB	Exc.	V.G.	Good	Fair	Poor
—	900	700	600	500	200

Model SXR Super X Rifle

Gas-operated semi-automatic patterned after Browning BAR ShortTrac and LongTrac. Calibers: .30-06 (4), .300WM (3), .270 WSM (3), .300 WSM (3). Barrel: 22" (.30-06), 24". Weight: 7.25 lbs. Stock: Two-piece checkered walnut. Introduced 2006.

NIB	Exc.	V.G.	Good	Fair	Poor
600	500	400	325	250	125

SHOTGUNS

Model 12

This model was designed by T.C. Johnson and was the first slide-action hammerless shotgun built by Winchester. The Model 12 enjoyed great success in its 68-year history, and over two million were sold. This was a high quality, well-made shotgun that is still in use in the hunting and shooting fields across the country. All Model 12s were of the takedown variety. The Model 12 was dropped from regular product line in 1963, but a special model was produced in the Custom Shop until 1979. In 1972 Winchester resurrected the Model 12 in its regular production line in 12 gauge only and ventilated rib. This reintroduced Model 12 was dropped in 1980. The prices listed are for guns made prior to 1964 or for guns with serial numbers below 1968307. This shotgun was offered in several different styles:

1. Standard Grade, 12, 16, 20, and 28 gauge, with plain, solid rib, or vent rib round barrels of standard lengths (26", 28", 30", 32"), plain walnut pistol-grip stock with grooved slide handle. Built from 1912 to 1963.
2. Featherweight, same as above with lightweight alloy trigger guard. Built between 1959 and 1962.
3. Riot Gun, in 12 gauge only with 20" round choked cylinder, stock same as Standard Grade. Built between 1918 and 1963.
4. Trench Gun, chambered for 12 gauge only with 20" round barrel with ventilated hand guard over barrel, fitted with bayonet lug. All metal surfaces are "Parkerized," and these shotguns should be U.S. marked as a military firearm. Introduced in 1918 and built for U.S. Armed Forces on special order.
5. Skeet Grade, chambered for 12, 16, 20, and 28 gauge with 26" round barrel with solid or ventilated rib, select walnut checkered pistol stock and special checkered extension slide handle (longer than standard). Built from 1933 to 1963.
6. Trap Grade, chambered for 12 gauge only with 30" round barrel with solid rib or ventilated rib, select walnut pistol or straight-grip stock, checkered extension slide handle. Built from 1914 to 1963.
7. Heavy Duck Gun, chambered in 12 gauge only with 30" or 32" round barrel with plain, solid, or ventilated rib, plain walnut pistol-grip stock fitted with Winchester solid red rubber recoil pad, plain grooved slide handle. Built from 1935 to 1963.
8. Pigeon Grade, chambered for 12, 16, 20, and 28 gauges with standard barrel lengths and choice of ribs. This was a special order shotgun and will be seen in many different variations, most of these guns were factory engraved. Built 1914 to 1963.

The Model 12 shotgun will be seen in many different combinations of gauges, barrel lengths, ribs and stocks, all of which determine value. The more rare a particular combination, the higher the price. The buyer is urged to be extremely cautious before purchasing the more rare combinations, such as a 28 gauge. The best advice is to seek assistance from an expert and get as many opinions as possible. The prices listed are for guns in standard configurations. **NOTE:** The following applies to all models. For 16 gauge add 10 percent. For 20 gauge add 50 percent. For 28 gauge add 600 percent. For guns with solid rib add 20 percent. For guns with Winchester Special ventilated rib add 30 percent. For guns with milled rib add 40 percent. Add 20 percent for 32" barrels on any Model 12 model. Add 30 percent premium for original box and papers.

Courtesy Bonhams & Butterfields, San Francisco, California

Standard Grade—12 gauge

NIB	Exc.	V.G.	Good	Fair	Poor
—	1000	800	600	500	200

Featherweight

NIB	Exc.	V.G.	Good	Fair	Poor
—	1300	900	700	575	200

Riot Gun

NIB	Exc.	V.G.	Good	Fair	Poor
—	1800	1300	900	700	250

Trench Gun

NIB	Exc.	V.G.	Good	Fair	Poor
—	3500	2800	1600	900	400

Skeet Grade

NIB	Exc.	V.G.	Good	Fair	Poor
—	1750	1500	900	600	350

Trap Grade

NIB	Exc.	V.G.	Good	Fair	Poor
—	1400	1000	800	550	400

Heavy Duck Gun

NOTE: For Heavy Duck Guns with solid ribs add 25 percent premium.

NIB	Exc.	V.G.	Good	Fair	Poor
—	1150	900	350	425	300

Pigeon Grade

NIB	Exc.	V.G.	Good	Fair	Poor
—	3750	2300	1600	750	500

Model 25

This model is similar in appearance to the Model 12 but does not have the takedown feature. All guns were solid frame. The Model 25 was furnished in 12 gauge with 26" or 28" plain round barrel, plain walnut pistol-grip stock with grooved slide handle. This was an attempt by Winchester to introduce a less expensive version of the Model 12. Introduced in 1949 it was dropped from the product line in 1954 having sold about 88,000 guns.

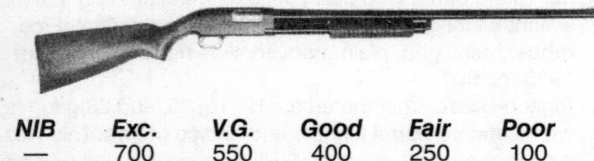

NIB	Exc.	V.G.	Good	Fair	Poor
—	700	550	400	250	100

Model 20

In order to utilize the expanded production facilities left over from WWI, Winchester introduced a series of three different models of single-shot shotguns; the Model 20 was the first of the three. This model has a visible hammer and a top lever frame. It was the first Winchester to have this type of breakdown action. It was chambered for the .410, 2.5" shell. The barrel is 26" round choked full, plain walnut pistol-grip stock with hard rubber buttplate. The fore-end has a small lip on the front end. The Model 20 was dropped from the product line in 1924 having sold about 24,000 guns.

Courtesy C.H. Wolfersberger

NIB	Exc.	V.G.	Good	Fair	Poor
—	750	500	350	200	150

Model 36

The Model 36 was the second of the single-shot shotguns to be introduced in 1920. This model features a bolt-action that is cocked by pulling the firing pin head to the rear. It is fitted with an

18" round barrel, chambered for the 9mm Long Shot, 9mm Short Shot and 9mm Ball interchangeably, plain gumwood straight-grip stock with special metal pistol grip trigger guard. Winchester referred to this model as the "Garden Gun" for use against birds and pests around the house and barn. This model was not serial numbered. It was dropped from the product line in 1927 having sold about 20,000 guns.

NIB	Exc.	V.G.	Good	Fair	Poor
—	1000	775	475	300	225

Model 41

This was the third of the low-priced single-shot shotguns to be announced in 1920. Like the Model 36, the Model 41 was a bolt-action arrangement but of much stronger construction and design. It features a 24" round barrel, chambered for the .410 2-1/2" shell, plain walnut pistol-grip stock and fore-end. Straight-grip stock was furnished at no extra charge. This model was not serial numbered. It was discontinued in 1934 having sold about 22,000 guns.

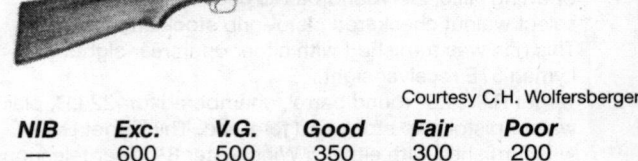

Courtesy C.H. Wolfersberger

NIB	Exc.	V.G.	Good	Fair	Poor
—	600	500	350	300	200

MODEL 21

The Model 21 was Winchester's finest effort with regard to quality, reliability, and strength. Developed in the late 1920s the introduction of this fine side-by-side shotgun was delayed by the company's financial troubles. When Winchester was purchased by the Olin family, the Model 21 was assured the attention it richly deserved due to John M. Olin's love for the gun. Despite the Model 21 being offered as a production gun it was, in fact, a hand-built custom-made shotgun. Almost each Model 21 built has a personality of its own because each shotgun is slightly different with regard to chokes, barrel lengths, stock dimensions, and embellishments. The gun was introduced in 1931. From 1931 to 1959 the Model 21 was considered a production line gun and about 30,000 were sold. In 1960, when the Custom Shop was opened, the Model 21 was built there using the same procedures. Sales during the Custom Shop era were about 1,000 guns. Winchester changed the name of some of the Model 21 styles but the production methods stayed the same. In 1981 Winchester sold its firearms division to U.S. Repeating Arms Company including the right to build the Model 21. Again the production procedures stayed the same as did many of the former employees. U.S. Repeating Arms expanded and changed some of the style designations for the Model 21. Production was discontinued in about 1991. No sales figures are available for this time period. Collectors and shooters will be given the price breakdown for all three eras of production separately.

NOTE: Fewer than 50 .410 Model 21s were built between 1931 and 1959 in all grades. The number of 28 gauge Model 21s built is unknown but the number is probably no greater than the .410 bore.

Model 21—1931 to 1959

The Model 21 was available in several different styles and configurations:

1. Standard Grade, chambered in 12, 16, and 20 gauge with barrel length from 26", 28", 30", and 32" with matted rib or ventilated rib, select walnut checkered pistol- or straight-grip stock with checkered beavertail fore-end. Built from 1931 to 1959.
2. Tournament Grade, same as above with special dimension stock. Marked "TOURNAMENT" on bottom of trigger plate. Built from 1933 to 1934. 3.Trap Grade, same as above with slightly better-grade wood and stock made to customers' dimensions. Marked "TRAP" on trigger plate. Built from 1932 to 1959.
4. Skeet Grade, same as above with the addition of the 28 gauge, stock furnished with checkered butt. Marked "SKEET" on trigger plate. Built from 1936 to 1959.
5. Duck Gun, chambered for 12 gauge 3" magnum shells, 30" or 32" barrels, Standard Grade stock except for shorter length of pull. Marked "DUCK" on trigger plate. Built from 1940 to 1952.
6. Magnum Gun, chambered for 3" 12 or 20 gauge, same stock as Duck Gun. Not marked on trigger plate. Built from 1953 to 1959.
7. Custom Built/Deluxe Grade, chambered for 12, 16, 20, 28, and .410, barrel lengths from 26" to 32", stock built to customers specifications using fancy walnut. Marked "CUSTOM BUILT" on top of rib or "DELUXE" on trigger plate. These grades are frequently but not always engraved. Built from 1933 to 1959.

NOTE: Some early Model 21s were furnished with double triggers, extractors, and splinter fore-ends. This combination reduces the price of the gun regardless of grade. Deduct about 25 percent. Add 30 percent for 20 gauge Magnum. Factory ventilated ribs command a premium of about $1,800 on 12 gauge guns and $2,500 on 20 and 16 gauge guns. Models 21s with factory furnished extra barrels will bring an additional premium of about $2,500. Refinished and restored Model 21s are in a somewhat unique category of American-made collectible shotguns. A gun that has been professionally refinished by a master craftsman will approximate 90 percent of the value of factory original guns.

Model 21 - 1931 to 1959

Standard Grade - 12 gauge

NIB	Exc.	V.G.	Good	Fair	Poor
—	6000	5000	3750	2400	2000

Standard Grade - 16 gauge

NIB	Exc.	V.G.	Good	Fair	Poor
—	8500	6700	5650	4700	4200

Standard Grade - 20 gauge

NIB	Exc.	V.G.	Good	Fair	Poor
—	9500	7500	6500	5100	4700

Model 21—1931 to 1959

Tournament Grade - 12 gauge

NIB	Exc.	V.G.	Good	Fair	Poor
—	6500	5200	4150	3500	3300

Model 21 - 1931 to 1959

Tournament Grade - 16 gauge

NIB	Exc.	V.G.	Good	Fair	Poor
—	8500	7200	6000	5000	4500

Tournament Grade - 20 gauge

NIB	Exc.	V.G.	Good	Fair	Poor
—	10000	8200	7200	6000	4800

Model 21—1931 to 1959

Trap Grade - 12 gauge

NIB	Exc.	V.G.	Good	Fair	Poor
—	6800	5300	4250	3800	3600

Model 21 - 1931 to 1959

Trap Grade - 16 gauge

NIB	Exc.	V.G.	Good	Fair	Poor
—	8500	7300	6100	5300	4900

Trap Grade - 20 gauge

NIB	Exc.	V.G.	Good	Fair	Poor
—	9000	7500	6550	5800	5300

Model 21—1931 to 1959

Skeet Grade - 12 gauge

NIB	Exc.	V.G.	Good	Fair	Poor
—	6500	5000	3950	3400	3200

Model 21 - 1931 to 1959

Skeet Grade - 16 gauge

NIB	Exc.	V.G.	Good	Fair	Poor
—	8200	7200	6000	4900	4400

Skeet Grade - 20 gauge

NIB	Exc.	V.G.	Good	Fair	Poor
—	9500	7800	6600	5000	4500

Model 21—1931 to 1959

Duck/Magnum Gun

NIB	Exc.	V.G.	Good	Fair	Poor
—	6500	5100	4450	4000	3800

Custom Built/Deluxe Grade

The prices paid for guns of this grade are determined by gauge, barrel and choke combinations, rib type, stock specifications and engraving. Expert appraisal is recommended. It is best to secure a factory letter from the Cody Firearms Museum. With respect to such a letter, it is important to note that these records are incomplete and may be inaccurate in a few cases. Records for Model 21s built during the 1930s may be missing. Special-order guns may have incomplete records. In such cases, a written appraisal from an authoritative collector or dealer may be helpful.

12 gauge

NIB	Exc.	V.G.	Good	Fair	Poor
—	8000	7000	5750	4500	4000

16 gauge

NIB	Exc.	V.G.	Good	Fair	Poor
—	9000	8000	6750	5500	4500

20 gauge

NIB	Exc.	V.G.	Good	Fair	Poor
—	10500	8500	7250	6000	5000

Custom Built .410 Bore

NIB	Exc.	V.G.	Good	Fair	Poor
—	50000	40000	31000	26000	22000

Custom Shop Model 21s—1960 to 1981

When Winchester moved the production of the Model 21 into the Custom Shop, the number of styles was greatly reduced. There were now three distinct styles:

1. Custom Grade, chambered in 12, 16, 20, 28 gauge and .410 bore in barrel lengths from 26" to 32". Matted rib, fancy walnut checkered pistol- or straight-grip stock with checkered fore-end. Guns with pistol grips furnished with steel grip cap. A small amount of scroll engraving was provided on the frame of this grade.
2. Pigeon Grade, same chambers and barrel lengths as above with the addition of choice of matted or ventilated rib, leather-covered recoil pad, style "A" carving on stock

and fore-end, and gold engraved pistol grip cap. The frame was engraved with the 21-6 engraving pattern.

3. Grand American Grade, same chambers and barrel lengths as Pigeon Grade with the addition of "B" carving on the stock and fore-end, 21-6 engraving with gold inlays, extra set of interchangeable barrels with extra fore-end. All of this was enclosed in a leather trunk case.

Editor's Comment: According to Ned Schwing's excellent book, *Winchester's Finest, The Model 21*, there were only eight 28 gauge and five .410-bore models made during the Custom Shop production era from 1960 to 1981. Any price estimates would be highly speculative.

Custom Grade—12 Gauge
NOTE: Add $4,000 for 16 gauge. Add $5,000 for 20 gauge.

NIB	Exc.	V.G.	Good	Fair	Poor
—	10000	8500	7300	6000	5200

Pigeon Grade—12 Gauge
NOTE: Add $6,000 for 16 gauge. Add $5,000 for 20 gauge.

NIB	Exc.	V.G.	Good	Fair	Poor
—	19000	16500	12500	10000	8000

Grand American—12 Gauge
NOTE: Add $15,000 for 16 gauge (extremely rare). Add $5,000 for 20 gauge.

NIB	Exc.	V.G.	Good	Fair	Poor
—	32000	25000	17500	14000	13000

ENGRAVED MODEL 21s

Winchester catalogued a number of special-order engraving patterns which ranged from a small amount of scroll (#1) to full-coverage game scene and scroll (#6). In addition, there were a few guns engraved on special order to the customer's request. Engraved guns are extremely rare, and the value added will vary with the rarity of the gauge and the date of manufacture. The following table represents the value added for various standard engraving patterns on 12 gauge guns for the "Custom Shop" (1960-1982) and "Pre-Custom Shop" (1932-1959) periods. However, it is advisable to seek the opinion of an authorative collector or dealer prior to a sale.

Engraving Pattern	Pre-Custom Shop	Custom Shop
#1	30 percent	20 percent
#2	40 percent	30 percent
#3	60 percent	45 percent
#4	70 percent	50 percent
#5	90 percent	70 percent
#6	100 percent	80 percent

Custom Shop Model 21s—1982 to 1993

When U.S. Repeating Arms Company took over the production of the Model 21, the Pigeon Grade was dropped from the line. The Grand American Grade was retained with all the features of its predecessor but with the addition of a small-bore set featuring a 28 gauge and .410 bore set of barrels. Two new grades were introduced in 1983: the Standard Custom Grade and the Special Custom Built. In addition to these grades, the factory would undertake to build for its customers whatever was desired. Due to the unique nature of these guns, it is advised that an expert appraisal be sought to establish a value. While the changeover from Winchester to U.S. Repeating Arms was a transfer of business assets and the craftsmen and personnel remained the same, collectors are reluctant to assign the same values to U.S. Repeating Arms Model 21s as those produced by Winchester. No official production figures are available for U.S.R.A. Model 21s, but the number is most likely small; perhaps around 200 guns.

Standard Custom Built
NIB	Exc.	V.G.	Good	Fair	Poor
9000	7000	6000	5000	4500	4000

Grand American
NIB	Exc.	V.G.	Good	Fair	Poor
19000	14000	10500	8500	6000	5000

Grand American Small Gauge Set—28 or .410 bore
NIB	Exc.	V.G.	Good	Fair	Poor
62500	46500	37500	27000	22000	20000

CURRENT MODEL 21 PRODUCTION

In 1995, Connecticut Shotgun Mfg. Co. purchased the assets of the Winchester Model 21 Custom Shop. Beginning in 2002, Winchester licensed CSMC to build Model 21s on a custom-order basis in a wide variety of grades and models, made to the buyer's specifications. For more information, see the listing for Connecticut Shotgun Mfg. Co. in this edition.

Model 24

The Model 24 was Winchester's attempt to develop a medium-priced double-barrel shotgun. Like the Model 21, it was a top lever breakdown model that was available in 12, 16, and 20 gauge in various barrel lengths from 26" to 30". Offered in a Standard model only with double triggers, raised matted rib, plain walnut pistol- or straight-grip stock with semi-beavertail fore-end, the Model 24 was introduced in 1939 and was discontinued in 1957 with about 116,000 guns sold. **NOTE:** Add 10 percent for 16 gauge. Add 25 percent for 20 gauge.

Top: Model 24 Standard; bottom: Model 24 Improved

NIB	Exc.	V.G.	Good	Fair	Poor
—	750	500	400	250	200

Model 37

This model was developed to keep pace with Winchester's competitors in the low-price single-barrel exposed-hammer shotgun market. The shotgun was available in 12, 16, 20, 28 gauge and .410 bore with barrel lengths from 26" to 30". The stock was plain walnut with pistol grip and semi-beavertail fore-end. This model was not serial numbered. Introduced in 1936 it stayed in the company line until 1963, having sold slightly over 1,000,000 guns. **NOTE:** Add 15 percent premium for so-called "red letter" (red-filled "W" on bottom of receiver).

Courtesy C.H. Wolfersberger

12 gauge
NIB	Exc.	V.G.	Good	Fair	Poor
—	400	350	300	250	100

16 gauge
NIB	Exc.	V.G.	Good	Fair	Poor
—	450	400	350	300	75

20 gauge
NIB	Exc.	V.G.	Good	Fair	Poor
—	600	525	500	425	100

28 gauge
NIB	Exc.	V.G.	Good	Fair	Poor
—	2000	1600	1150	850	450

.410 bore
NIB	Exc.	V.G.	Good	Fair	Poor
—	1000	850	500	300	100

NOTE: For 12 and 16 gauge guns add a 50 percent premium for 32" barrels. Use caution for 28 gauge guns. Many fakes are seen for sale.

Youth Model

26" Modified choke barrel, Win. red factory pad. 20 gauge only.

NIB	Exc.	V.G.	Good	Fair	Poor
—	600	550	450	350	125

Model 42

Commentary and values by Bud Bugni.

This was the first slide-action shotgun ever developed exclusively for the .410 bore. Invented by William Roemer, the Model 42 was in effect, at least in outward appearance, a miniature Model 12. This shotgun was a quality-built, fast-handling, racy looking shotgun that many refer to as "Everybody's Sweetheart". The Model 42 was the first American .410 bore chambered for the new 3" shell as well as the 2.5" shell. The Model 42 was offered in several different configurations throughout its production. These configurations will greatly influence value:

1. Standard Grade, 26" or 28" plain or solid rib barrel, plain walnut pistol-grip stock with grooved slide handle, fitted with composition buttplate. A straight grip was offered on the Standard Grade on a special order basis, but it is extremely rare. Built from 1933 to 1963.
2. Skeet Grade, 26" or 28" plain, solid rib, or ventilated rib barrel, select walnut checkered pistol or straight-grip stock with checkered extension slide handle. The Skeet Grade was offered in Full, Modified, Improved Cylinder, Cylinder as well as Skeet chokes. Built from 1933 to 1963.
3. Trap Grade, 26" or 28" plain or solid rib barrel, fancy walnut special checkered pistol or straight-grip stock with special checkered extension slide handle. The Trap Grade checkering pattern has one closed diamond on each side of the pistol grip or, in the case of the straight grip, the diamond is located on the underside of the grip. The extension slide handle has two uncut diamonds on each side. Most were stamped "TRAP" on the bottom of the receiver under the serial number. Built from 1934 to 1939.
4. Deluxe Grade, a continuation of the Trap Grade, available with ventilated rib in 1954. Some early models stamped "DELUXE" on bottom of receiver. This stamping is seldom seen and was probably discontinued around 1949. Built from 1940 to 1963.
5. Pigeon Grade, same as above Deluxe Grade but engraved with a pigeon on the lower magazine tube. Very few of this grade were built by Winchester, and the majority were done in the late 1940s. Authentic Pigeon Grade 42s appear to have been built between 1945 and 1949. Some estimate that less than 50 were produced. this is a rare Model 42. Seek an expert opinion before a sale.

As of late, I have heard horror stories from sincere, honest, decent folks who have purchased misrepresented guns from either unscrupulous sellers or sellers who simply do not know their products. In some cases there are no return privileges, or the buyer was unable to authenticate his purchase in a timely manner. This often has resulted in a heavy financial loss and that's a dish served cold. Contributors are listed in the Standard Catalog of Firearms. These knowledgeable and dedicated people are eager to assist readers, or refer them to sources who can.—Bud Bugni

NOTE: Engraved Model 42s will occasionally be seen. Collectors are urged to seek expert advice on these rare and expensive guns. The Model 42 was produced from 1933 to 1963. About 164,000 were sold. Factory service and repair for this model were discontinued in February of 1972.

Extra Barrels: Winchester offered extra interchangeable barrels for its Model 42s at the customer's request beginning in 1934. These extra sets of barrels are a rare option. Both barrels should have the same barrel markings and matching serial numbers before originality can be considered. Values are difficult to determine, but as a general rule add 60 percent to the price of a Model 42 if it has a factory-original extra barrel.

Editor's Comment: Contrary to traditional views, Winchester did install factory ventilated ribs on its Model 42. Former employees and factory drawings substantiate this fact. However, the subject of what is a factory rib and what is not has been covered in great detail in an excellent book on the Model 42. Seek expert advice before selling or purchasing any Model 42 with a ventilated rib. **NOTE:** For Pigeon Grade Model 42s with documentation on expert authentication add 100 percent. Must be individually appraised. Proceed with caution.

Cutts Compensator Guns: Approximately 66 original Cutts Compensator guns were produced in the factory, making this one of the rarest options on the Model 42. New information reveals Cutts Compensators were available as early as 1950, appearing in the retail price list dated Dec. 15, 1950. These original guns will have no choke markings and were only offered with a vent rib. Add 25 percent for original Cutts guns, deduct 50 percent for non-original Cutts guns.

Standard Grade

NOTE: For Standard Grade guns with solid ribs add 50 percent. For pre-war guns add 25 percent.

NIB	Exc.	V.G.	Good	Fair	Poor
3000	1950	1150	900	700	400

Skeet Grade—Solid Rib

NOTE: Add 25 percent guns chambered for 2.5" shells. For pre-war guns add 30 percent. For Skeet Grade guns with no rib deduct 25 percent.

NIB	Exc.	V.G.	Good	Fair	Poor
6500	5000	4250	3500	1950	1250

Skeet Grade—Ventilated Rib

NOTE: Add 25 percent of guns chambered for 2.5" shells.

NIB	Exc.	V.G.	Good	Fair	Poor
7500	6000	4750	3500	2200	1250

Trap Grade - Plain or Solid Rib

NIB	Exc.	V.G.	Good	Fair	Poor
—	12500	10500	9500	5500	3000

Deluxe Grade—Solid Rib

NIB	Exc.	V.G.	Good	Fair	Poor
12000	9500	8500	6000	3500	1250

Deluxe Grade—Ventilated Rib

NIB	Exc.	V.G.	Good	Fair	Poor
14000	12000	10950	7500	4800	2400

Model 1911

This was Winchester's first self-loading shotgun and was developed by T.C. Johnson in order to keep pace with the Remington Auto-Loading Shotgun Model 11, which was developed by John M. Browning with help from T.C. Johnson. Because of the delays involved in developing a brand new design, the Model 1911 was introduced on October 7, 1911. The shotgun was a recoil operated mechanism, had a tubular magazine and had the takedown feature. The shotgun was available in two styles:

1. Plain Model 1911, 26" or 28" barrel, 12 gauge, choked full, modified, or cylinder, plain birch laminated pistol-grip stock and fore-end with hard rubber buttplate.
2. Fancy Model 1911, same as above with fancy birch laminated stock.

Because of the hurry in getting the model ready for production, the shotgun demonstrated design weakness and never proved satisfactory. It was discontinued in 1925 with about 83,000 guns sold.

Plain

NIB	Exc.	V.G.	Good	Fair	Poor
—	650	375	300	250	200

Fancy

NIB	Exc.	V.G.	Good	Fair	Poor
—	800	500	400	300	250

Model 40

This model represents Winchester's second attempt to build a self-loading long recoil-operated repeating shotgun. This shotgun was a hammerless tubular magazine gun without the hump at the rear of the receiver. Available in 12 gauge only with barrel lengths from 28" to 30". The Standard Grade had plain walnut pistol-grip stock and fore-end. The Skeet Grade was fitted with select walnut checkered pistol-grip stock and checkered fore-end. The Model 40 suffered from the same design problems as the Model 11, and sales were small. Introduced in 1940 and discontinued in 1941, Winchester sold about 12,000 guns.

Standard Grade

NIB	Exc.	V.G.	Good	Fair	Poor
—	650	500	400	275	200

Skeet Grade

NIB	Exc.	V.G.	Good	Fair	Poor
—	950	600	500	300	250

Model 50

The Model 50 was the company's third attempt to produce a satisfactory self-loading repeating shotgun. Winchester went to the short recoil system, utilizing a floating chamber design. This model was available in several different styles:

1. Standard Grade, 12 or 20 gauge with plain or ventilated rib in lengths from 26" to 30", plain walnut checkered pistol-grip stock and fore-end.
2. Skeet Grade, 12 or 20 gauge with 26" ventilated rib barrel. Walnut checkered pistol-grip stock and fore-end.
3. Trap Grade, 12 gauge with 30" ventilated rib barrel, walnut checkered Monte Carlo stock and fore-end.
4. Pigeon Grade, 12 or 20 gauge with barrel lengths to customers' specifications. Fancy walnut checkered stock and fore-end. Made on special orders only.
5. Featherweight, a lighter version of all the above except Trap Grade.

This model begins with serial number 1000. This model was successful and was built between 1954 and 1961. Winchester sold about 200,000 guns. **NOTE:** Add 10 percent for 20 gauge. Add 20 percent for vent rib on standard grade guns.

Standard Grade

NIB	Exc.	V.G.	Good	Fair	Poor
—	550	400	300	200	150

Skeet Grade

NIB	Exc.	V.G.	Good	Fair	Poor
—	600	500	350	250	200

Trap Grade

NIB	Exc.	V.G.	Good	Fair	Poor
—	600	500	350	250	200

Pigeon Grade

NIB	Exc.	V.G.	Good	Fair	Poor
—	1800	1200	750	450	250

Featherweight

NIB	Exc.	V.G.	Good	Fair	Poor
—	600	500	350	250	200

The fourth and final pre-1964 Winchester self-loading shotgun, featured a steel and fiberglass barrel with aluminum alloy receiver. The gun was available in 12 gauge only with barrel lengths from 26" to 30" with a variety of chokes. In 1961 Winchester introduced the "Versalite" choke tube, which gave the shooter a choice of Full, Modified, or Improved Cylinder chokes in the same barrel. This model was available in two different styles:

1. Standard Grade, plain walnut checkered pistol-grip stock and fore-end.
2. Pigeon Grade, select walnut checkered pistol-grip and fore-end.

Winchester sold about 82,000 of these guns between 1960 and 1965. **NOTE:** This shotgun was also made in 10 gauge (very rare), 20 gauge and 14 gauge. If any of these very low production or prototype guns are encountered, use extreme caution and seek an expert appraisal. **NOTE:** Add 40 percent premium for barrels with three Versalite chokes and wrench. Add 20 percent premium for original box and papers.

Model 59

Standard Grade

Courtesy Bonhams & Butterfields, San Francisco, California

NIB	Exc.	V.G.	Good	Fair	Poor
—	650	550	450	350	250

Pigeon Grade

NIB	Exc.	V.G.	Good	Fair	Poor
—	2500	2000	1200	600	300

POST-1963 RIFLES

Model 121

This is a single-shot, bolt-action rifle chambered for the .22 rimfire cartridge. It has a 20.75" barrel with open sights. The finish is blued, with a plain walnut stock. It was manufactured between 1967 and 1973. A youth model with a shorter stock was designated the 121Y and is valued the same.

Courtesy Buffalo Bill Historical Center, Cody, Wyoming

NIB	Exc.	V.G.	Good	Fair	Poor
—	225	150	100	60	40

Model 131

This is a bolt-action repeater chambered for the .22 rimfire cartridge. It has a 20.75" barrel with open sights and a 7-round, detachable magazine. The finish is blued, with a plain walnut stock. It was manufactured between 1967 and 1973. A tubular magazine version was designated the Model 141 and is valued the same.

NIB	Exc.	V.G.	Good	Fair	Poor
—	250	175	100	60	40

Model 310

This is a single-shot, bolt-action rifle chambered for the .22 rimfire cartridge. It features a 22" barrel with open sights. The finish is blued, with a checkered walnut stock. It was manufactured between 1972 and 1975.

Courtesy Buffalo Bill Historical Center, Cody, Wyoming

NIB	Exc.	V.G.	Good	Fair	Poor
—	250	150	125	100	75

Model 320

This is a bolt-action repeating rifle that is similar in configuration to the Model 310 single-shot. It has a 5-round, detachable box magazine. It was manufactured between 1972 and 1974.

NIB	Exc.	V.G.	Good	Fair	Poor
—	400	300	250	175	125

Model 250

This is a lever-action repeating rifle with a hammerless action. It is chambered for the .22 rimfire cartridge and has a 20.5" barrel with open sights and a tubular magazine. The finish is blued, with a checkered pistol-grip stock. It was manufactured between 1963 and 1973.

NIB	Exc.	V.G.	Good	Fair	Poor
—	200	125	80	60	40

Model 250 Deluxe

This version is similar to the Model 250 and is furnished with select walnut and sling swivels. It was manufactured between 1965 and 1971.

NIB	Exc.	V.G.	Good	Fair	Poor
—	275	195	125	100	75

Model 255

This version is simply the Model 250 chambered for the .22 WMR cartridge. It was manufactured between 1964 and 1970.

NIB	Exc.	V.G.	Good	Fair	Poor
—	225	150	100	70	50

Model 255 Deluxe

This version was offered with select walnut and sling swivels. It was manufactured between 1965 and 1973.

NIB	Exc.	V.G.	Good	Fair	Poor
—	375	250	175	125	75

Model 490

This is a blowback-operated, semi-automatic rifle chambered for the .22 LR cartridge. It has a 22" barrel with open sights and a 5-round, detachable magazine. The finish is blued, with a checkered stock. It was manufactured between 1975 and 1980.

NIB	Exc.	V.G.	Good	Fair	Poor
—	350	225	165	100	75

Model 270

This is a slide-action rifle chambered for the .22 rimfire cartridge. It has a 20.5" barrel and a tubular magazine. The finish is blued, with a checkered walnut stock. It was manufactured between 1963 and 1973.

NIB	Exc.	V.G.	Good	Fair	Poor
—	350	225	165	100	75

Model 63 (1997)

Introduced in 1997 this is a re-creation of the famous Model 63 .22 caliber auto. Fitted with a 23" barrel and 10-round tubular magazine. The receiver top is grooved for scope mounting.

Grade I

NIB	Exc.	V.G.	Good	Fair	Poor
800	525	—	—	—	—

High Grade

Engraved receiver with gold accents and select walnut stock.

NIB	Exc.	V.G.	Good	Fair	Poor
1050	850	700	575	400	300

Wildcat

Bolt-action repeater styled after Mosin-Nagant military sporter. Caliber: .22 LR. Magazine: 5- and 10-round detachable. Stock: checkered walnut with schnabel. Barrel: 21-inch blued. Weight: 4.5 lbs. Imported. Introduced 2006. Sporter and Target/Varmint versions available. Add 5 percent for Target/Varmint.

NIB	Exc.	V.G.	Good	Fair	Poor
240	175	150	125	95	50

Model 94

This is the post-1964 lever-action carbine chambered for the .30-30, 7-30 Waters, and the .44 Magnum cartridges. It is offered with a 20" or 24" barrel and has a 6- or 7-round, tubular magazine depending on barrel length. The round barrel is offered with open sights. The forearm is held on by a single barrel band. The finish is blued, with a straight-grip walnut stock. In 1982 it was modified to angle ejection to simplify scope mounting. It was introduced as a continuation of the Model 94 line in 1964. In 2003 a top-tang safety was installed and the .480 Ruger caliber was added. The Model 94 series was discontinued in 2006. Premium for unusual chamberings such as 7-30 Waters, etc.

NIB	Exc.	V.G.	Good	Fair	Poor
800	600	425	300	200	100

Model 94 Traditional—CW

As above but with checkered walnut stock. Chambered for the .30-30, .44 Mag., and the .480 Ruger cartridge. **NOTE:** For .44 Mag. add $20. For the .480 Ruger add $70.

NIB	Exc.	V.G.	Good	Fair	Poor
850	575	450	325	225	125

Model 94 Ranger

Chambered for .30-30 cartridge and fitted with a 20" barrel. Weight is about 6.25 lbs. In 2003 a top-tang safety was installed.

NIB	Exc.	V.G.	Good	Fair	Poor
—	450	300	225	150	100

Model 94 Ranger Compact

Introduced in 1998 this model features a 16" barrel with 12.5" lop. Chambered for .30-30 or .357 Magnum. Furnished with black recoil pad. Post-style front sight with adjustable rear sight. Hardwood stock. Weight is approximately 5.87 lbs

NIB	Exc.	V.G.	Good	Fair	Poor
—	475	325	250	150	100

Model 94 Black Shadow

This model features a black synthetic stock with nonglare finish and black recoil pad. Offered in .30-30, .44 Magnum, or .444 Marlin. Fitted with a 20" barrel. Weight is about 6.5 lbs. Introduced in 1998.

NIB	Exc.	V.G.	Good	Fair	Poor
600	475	375	250	225	175

Model 94 Deluxe

Checkered stock.

NIB	Exc.	V.G.	Good	Fair	Poor
850	675	550	400	300	200

Model 94 Win-Tuff

Laminated stock.

NIB	Exc.	V.G.	Good	Fair	Poor
500	400	275	225	165	125

Model 94 XTR

Select, checkered walnut stock, discontinued 1988.

NIB	Exc.	V.G.	Good	Fair	Poor
—	700	450	350	250	175

Model 94 XTR Deluxe

Fancy checkering.

NIB	Exc.	V.G.	Good	Fair	Poor
—	725	475	375	275	200

Model 94 Trapper

16" barrel. Chambered for the .30-30, .357 Mag., .44 Mag, or .45 Colt cartridge. In 2003 a top-tang safety was installed.

NIB	Exc.	V.G.	Good	Fair	Poor
750	575	450	350	250	150

Model 94 Antique Carbine

Gold-plated saddle ring.

NIB	Exc.	V.G.	Good	Fair	Poor
—	800	600	475	350	200

Model 94 Wrangler

.32 Win. Special.

NIB	Exc.	V.G.	Good	Fair	Poor
—	900	725	525	400	250

Model 94 Wrangler II

Loop lever.

NIB	Exc.	V.G.	Good	Fair	Poor
700	525	425	300	150	—

Model 94 Legacy 20-inch

This Model 94 is fitted with a 20" barrel and chambered for the .30-30 Win. but it is fitted with a half pistol-grip stock. Both walnut buttstock and forearm are cut checkered. Weight is 6.5 lbs. In 2003 a top-tang safety was installed.

NIB	Exc.	V.G.	Good	Fair	Poor
900	750	600	475	300	200

Model 94 Legacy 24-inch

Introduced in 2005 this model features a 24" round barrel with full length magazine. Checkered walnut stock with semi-pistol grip. Chambered for the .30-30, .357 Mag., .44 Rem. Mag. or the .45 Colt cartridge. Drilled and tapped for scope mount. Blued finish. Weight is about 6.75 lbs.

NIB	Exc.	V.G.	Good	Fair	Poor
900	750	600	475	300	200

Model 94 Legacy 26-inch

Similar to the model above but offered in both round and octagon barrel and blue or case colored receiver. Marbles' tang sight. Chambered for the .30-30 or .38-55 calibers. Weight is about 7 lbs. Introduced in 2005. Premium for .38-55. **NOTE:** Add $55 for case colored receiver. Add $100 for octagon barrel.

NIB	Exc.	V.G.	Good	Fair	Poor
1100	875	750	575	400	300

Model 94 XTR Big Bore

This version is chambered for the .307, .356, or the .375 Win. cartridges. It features the angle-ejection and is blued with a walnut, Monte Carlo-type stock and recoil pad. The round barrel is 20" in length. It has a 6-round, tubular magazine. It was introduced in 1978. Deduct 12.5 percent for .375.

NIB	Exc.	V.G.	Good	Fair	Poor
1050	900	775	575	400	300

Model 94 Centennial Limited Editions

Introduced in 1994 these models celebrate the 100-year anniversary of the Winchester Model 1894. Offered in three grades, these models are of limited production. The Grade I is limited to 12,000 rifles while the High Grade is limited to 3,000 rifles. Only 94 of the Custom Limited model were produced. Each Limited model has different grades of select walnut and engraving coverage. All are chambered for the .30-30 Winchester cartridge.

Grade I

NIB	Exc.	V.G.	Good	Fair	Poor
1200	1000	900	700	575	400

High Grade

NIB	Exc.	V.G.	Good	Fair	Poor
1900	1300	1075	900	750	600

Custom High Grade

NIB	Exc.	V.G.	Good	Fair	Poor
4750	3900	2500	1000	750	450

Model 94 Heritage—Limited 1 of 1000

Introduced in 2002 and limited to 1,000 rifles. Fitted with half round/half octagon 26" barrel. Engraved with #3 pattern with gold plate. Fancy walnut stock. Chambered for the .38-55 cartridge.

NIB	Exc.	V.G.	Good	Fair	Poor
5000	4000	3000	1750	1200	600

Model 94 Heritage—Custom 1 of 100

Similar to the above model but with finer wood and engraved with #2 pattern with gold. Limited to 100 rifles. Introduced in 2002.

NIB	Exc.	V.G.	Good	Fair	Poor
7500	—	—	—	—	—

Model 94 Trails End

This model is chambered for the .357 Mag., .44 Mag., and .45 Colt. Offered with standard-size loop lever or Wrangler-style loop. Introduced in 1997. Add $500 to NIB for .25-35 Win.

NIB	Exc.	V.G.	Good	Fair	Poor
1375	1050	825	600	450	300

Model 94 Trails End Octagon

As above but with 20" octagon barrel and choice of blued or case colored receiver. Crescent butt. Weight is about 6.75 lbs. Introduced in 2004. **NOTE:** Add $60 for case colored receiver.

NIB	Exc.	V.G.	Good	Fair	Poor
1395	1100	850	600	450	300

Model 94 Trails End Hunter

Offered in .25-35 Win, .30-30 Win, or .38-55 Win and fitted with a 20" round or octagon barrel. Plain walnut stock. Blued finish on round barrel model and case colored finish on octagon model. Weight is about 6.5 lbs. Introduced in 2005. **NOTE:** Add $290 for octagon barrel model.

NIB	Exc.	V.G.	Good	Fair	Poor
1375	1050	825	600	450	300

Model 94 Timber Carbine

Introduced in 1999 this model is chambered for the .444 Marlin cartridge. Barrel is 17.75" long and ported. Hooded front sight. Magazine capacity is 5 rounds. Weight is about 6 lbs. Finish is blue. Walnut stock. In 2004 this rifle was chambered for the .450 Marlin cartridge.

NIB	Exc.	V.G.	Good	Fair	Poor
1000	850	700	600	400	300

Model 94 Timber Scout

This model, introduced in 2005, features an 18" barrel chambered for the .30-30 Win. or .44 Rem. Mag. cartridges with a quick detachable scope mount attached to the barrel for long eye relief. Plain walnut stock with pistol grip. Blued finish. Weight is about 6 lbs. Scope not included.

NIB	Exc.	V.G.	Good	Fair	Poor
900	750	600	475	300	200

Model 94 Pack Rifle

This lever-action model features an 18" barrel chambered for the .30-30 or .44 Magnum. It has a walnut stock with pistol grip and no checkering. Magazine is 3/4-style and has a 4-round capacity

for the .30-30, and five rounds for the .44 Mag. Open sights. Weight is about 6.25 lbs. Introduced in 2000.

NIB	Exc.	V.G.	Good	Fair	Poor
900	750	600	475	300	200

Winchester Model 1894 Custom Grade

Lever-action rifle chambered in .30-30. Features include 24" half-round, half octagon deeply blued barrel; buckhorn rear sight with Marbles gold bead front sight; Grade IV/V walnut stock and fore-end with a rich, high gloss finish; deep scroll engraving on both sides of the blued receiver. Commemorates the 200th anniversary of Oliver F. Winchester's birth. An early Winchester Repeating Arms crest graces the left side of the receiver, with the right side bearing the words, "Two Hundred Years, Oliver F. Winchester", and the dates, "1810 - 2010", in gold. The barrel is deeply polished, with the signature of Oliver F. Winchester in gold on the top of the bolt. Sold individually in limited quantities and in 500 sets with the High Grade.

NIB	Exc.	V.G.	Good	Fair	Poor
1800	1550	1300	—	—	—

Winchester Model 1894 High Grade

Lever-action rifle chambered in .30-30. Features include 24" half-round, half octagon deeply blued barrel; buckhorn rear sight with Marbles gold bead front sight; silver nitride receiver; Grade II/III high gloss walnut stock and fore-end with a rich, high gloss finish; delicate scroll work, with Oliver F. Winchester's signature in gold on top of the bolt. The left side of receiver bears an early Winchester Repeating Arms crest; on right side are the words, "Two Hundred Years, Oliver F. Winchester", and the dates, "1810 - 2010". Sold individually in limited quantities and in 500 sets with the Custom Grade.

NIB	Exc.	V.G.	Good	Fair	Poor
1300	1100	900	—	—	—

Model 71

A true reproduction of the original. Drilled and tapped for a receiver sight. Barrel is 24", polished blue and round. Oil finished American walnut stock for fore-end cap, no checkering. Marble gold bead front sight, buckhorn rear sight. Chambered for original caliber only, .348 WCF. Introduced in 2011.

NIB	Exc.	V.G.	Good	Fair	Poor
1300	1100	—	—	—	—

Model 94 Short Rifle

New for 2011, the latest incarnation of the famous Model 94 Carbine with 20" round barrel and straight grip walnut stock. Rifle-styled fore-end has black grip cap and full-length magazine. Receiver drilled and tapped for scope mounts with hammer extension included. Marble gold bead front sight, semi-buckhorn rear. Overall length 38" and weight is 6.75 lbs. Chambered in .30-30 Winchester only.

NIB	Exc.	V.G.	Good	Fair	Poor
1000	875	750	—	—	—

Model 94 Sporter

Reminiscent of the original Model 1894 Rifle, this new for 2011 model has a 24" half-round, half-octagon blued barrel and a satin oil-finished American walnut stock with steel crescent buttplate and double-line bordering checkering pattern. Blue receiver drilled and tapped for optical sights. Gold bead front sight, buckhorn sight at rear. Hammer extension included. Available in .30-30 or .38-55 Winchester.

NIB	Exc.	V.G.	Good	Fair	Poor
1175	1000	850	—	—	—

Model 1886 Short Rifle

Reintroduction of a version of the famed Model 1886 with Grade I American walnut stock. Blue steel fore-end cap and crescent buttplate. Barrel is 24" with full-length tubular magazine that holds six cartridges. Chambered in .45-70 Government. Elegant satin finish on all wood, no checkering. Deep blue receiver, barrel and lever. Top tang safety, adjustable rear buckhorn sight with fine gold Marble front sight.

NIB	Exc.	V.G.	Good	Fair	Poor
1125	975	825	—	—	—

Model 1892 Carbine

New version of the rifle made famous by actor John Wayne. Chambered for .357 Magnum, .44 Remington Magnum or .45 Colt. American walnut stock with straight grip. 21" round barrel, receiver and lever are deeply polished and blued. Full-length magazine. Front and rear iron sights.

NIB	Exc.	V.G.	Good	Fair	Poor
950	800	700	—	—	—

MODEL 9400 SERIES

Model 9410

Introduced in 2001 this model features a .410 shotgun in a lever-action configuration. Barrel length is 24" and is smoothbore with cylinder choke or Invector chokes. Chambered is 2.5". Magazine capacity is nine rounds. Tru-glo front sight. Weight is about 6.75 lbs. In 2003 a top-tang safety was installed.

NIB	Exc.	V.G.	Good	Fair	Poor
1450	1100	900	750	600	400

Model 9410 Semi-Fancy

As above but with semi-fancy walnut stock with checkering. Introduced in 2004.

NIB	Exc.	V.G.	Good	Fair	Poor
1600	1200	975	825	650	400

Model 9410 Packer

Introduced in 2002 this model features a 20" barrel with 3/4 magazine and pistol-grip stock. Weight is about 6.5 lbs.

NIB	Exc.	V.G.	Good	Fair	Poor
1000	850	700	600	400	300

Model 9410 Packer Compact

Introduced in 2003 this model features a reduced length of pull to 12-1/2". Fitted with Invector chokes. Weight is about 6.25 lbs.

NIB	Exc.	V.G.	Good	Fair	Poor
1000	850	700	600	400	300

Model 9410 Ranger

This version is the same as the standard or traditional Model 9410 but hardwood stock without checkering. Weight is about 6.75 lbs. Fitted with top-tang safety. Introduced in 2003.

NIB	Exc.	V.G.	Good	Fair	Poor
900	750	575	450	300	250

Model 9422

Introduced in 1972 this model is chambered for the .22 rimfire and .22 Magnum rimfire cartridges. It was fitted with a 20.5" barrel, front ramp sight with hood, and adjustable semi-buckhorn rear sight. Tubular magazine holds 21 Shorts, 17 Longs, and 15 LR cartridges. The Magnum version holds 11 cartridges. Weight is about 6.25 lbs. Two-piece American walnut stock with no checkering. Between 1972 and 1992 approximately 750,000 Model 9422s were produced.

NIB	Exc.	V.G.	Good	Fair	Poor
850	675	525	375	225	125

Model 9422 XTR

This is a deluxe lever-action rifle chambered for the .22 rimfire cartridge. It is a takedown rifle with a 20.5", round barrel and a tubular magazine. The finish is blued with a checkered, high-gloss, straight-grip walnut stock. It was introduced in 1978.

A .22 Magnum version is also available and would be worth approximately $100 additional.

NIB	Exc.	V.G.	Good	Fair	Poor
1000	850	700	600	400	300

Model 9422 XTR Classic

This version is similar to the standard Model 9422 XTR except that it features a 22.5" barrel and a satin-finished, plain, pistol-grip walnut stock. It was manufactured between 1985 and 1987.

NIB	Exc.	V.G.	Good	Fair	Poor
1100	925	750	650	450	325

Model 9422 WinTuff

This model features an uncheckered laminated wood stock that is brown in color. Chambered for both the .22 Rimfire and the .22 Winchester Magnum Rimfire. Weighs 6.25 lbs. Other features are the same as the standard Model 9422.

NIB	Exc.	V.G.	Good	Fair	Poor
850	675	525	375	225	125

Model 9422 WinCam

This model is chambered only for the .22 Winchester Magnum Rimfire. The laminated stock is a green color. Weighs 6.25 lbs.

NIB	Exc.	V.G.	Good	Fair	Poor
850	675	525	375	225	125

Model 9422 Trapper

Introduced in 1996 this model features a 16.5" barrel. It has an overall length of 33". Weight is 5.5 lbs.

NIB	Exc.	V.G.	Good	Fair	Poor
850	675	525	375	225	125

Model 9422 High Grade

This variation of the Model 9422 series features a specially engraved receiver and fancy wood stock. Barrel length is 20.5". Weight is about 6 lbs.

NIB	Exc.	V.G.	Good	Fair	Poor
1000	850	700	600	400	300

Model 9422 25th Anniversary Rifle

Introduced in 1997 this model features 20.5" barrel. Limited quantities.

Grade I

Engraved receiver.

NIB	Exc.	V.G.	Good	Fair	Poor
1000	850	700	600	400	300

High Grade

Engraved receiver with silver border.

NIB	Exc.	V.G.	Good	Fair	Poor
1450	1100	900	750	600	400

Model 9422 Legacy

This model has a semi-pistol-grip stock of checkered walnut. Will shoot .22 caliber LR, L, or S cartridges. Fitted with a 16" barrel. Weight is about 6 lbs. Introduced in 1998.

NIB	Exc.	V.G.	Good	Fair	Poor
850	675	525	375	225	125

Model 9422 Large Loop & Walnut

Introduced in 1998 this model features a walnut stock with large loop lever. Large loop offered on .22 LR, L, or S model. Standard lever on .22 WMR version. Fitted with 16" barrel. Weight is about 6 lbs.

NIB	Exc.	V.G.	Good	Fair	Poor
900	750	575	450	300	250

Model 9422 High Grade Series II

This model features a high-grade walnut stock with cut checkering. Receiver engraved with dogs and squirrels. Fitted with 16" barrel. Weight is about 6 lbs. Introduced in 1998.

NIB	Exc.	V.G.	Good	Fair	Poor
1450	1100	900	750	600	400

Model 9417 Traditional

Introduced in 2003 this model is chambered for the .17 HMR cartridge and fitted with a 20.5" barrel. Adjustable sights. Checkered walnut stock with straight grip. Weight is about 6 lbs.

NIB	Exc.	V.G.	Good	Fair	Poor
1200	975	850	675	400	300

Model 9417 Legacy

Similar to the model above but fitted with a 22.5" barrel and checkered walnut with pistol grip. Weight is about 6 lbs. Introduced in 2003.

NIB	Exc.	V.G.	Good	Fair	Poor
1200	975	850	675	400	300

MODEL 9422 TRIBUTE SERIES

As of 2005 the Model 9422 production will end. These final production Model 9422s will be limited to a total production of 9,422 rifles. Each rifle will have the Winchester Horse and Rider on one side and the Model 9422 tribute logo on the other side.

Traditional Tribute

This model features a 20.5" barrel with high grade checkered walnuty stock. Blued receiver with high-relief silver inlay on both sides of the receiver.

NIB	Exc.	V.G.	Good	Fair	Poor
1400	1200	975	825	650	300

Legacy Tribute

Similar to the model above but with semi-pistol grip and 22.5" barrel.

NIB	Exc.	V.G.	Good	Fair	Poor
1500	1300	1075	925	650	300

Custom Traditional Tribute

This model is fitted with a 20.5" barrel, high grade checkereed walnut stock. High-relief scroll engraved receiver with gold logos on both sides. Limited to 222 rifles.

NIB	Exc.	V.G.	Good	Fair	Poor
2600	2200	1650	1200	800	500

Special Edition Traditional Tribute

This model has a 20.5" barrel with checkered walnut straight grip stock and engraved blued receiver. Engraved logos on both sides of receiver.

NIB	Exc.	V.G.	Good	Fair	Poor
1200	975	850	675	400	300

Special Edition Legacy Tribute

This 22.5" barrel model has a checkered semi-pistol grip stock Blued receiver with engraved logos on both sides.

NIB	Exc.	V.G.	Good	Fair	Poor
1200	975	850	675	400	300

Model 64 (Post-'64)

This is a post-1964 version of the lever-action Model 64. It is chambered for the .30-30 cartridge and has a 24" round barrel with open sights and a 5-round, 2/3-length tubular magazine. The finish is blued with a plain walnut pistol-grip stock. It was manufactured between 1972 and 1974.

NIB	Exc.	V.G.	Good	Fair	Poor
—	800	650	550	375	250

Model 1885 Low Wall

Introduced in fall of 1999 this single-shot model is chambered for the .22 LR or .17 Mach II cartridge. It is fitted with a 24.5" half octagon barrel with leaf rear sight. Drilled and tapped for a tang sight. Crescent steel buttplate. Walnut stock. Weight is about 8 lbs. Limited to 2,400 rifles.

Grade I

NIB	Exc.	V.G.	Good	Fair	Poor
1050	900	750	600	500	300

High Grade

NIB	Exc.	V.G.	Good	Fair	Poor
1300	1050	875	750	600	400

Model 1885 High Wall Hunter

Single-shot; patterned after original Model 1885 designed by John Browning. Calibers: .223, .22-250, .270 WSM, 7mm WSM, .300 WSM, .325 WSM. Stock: Checkered walnut. Barrel: 28-inch blued, sightless octagon with Pachmayr pad. Weight: 8-1/2 lbs.

NIB	Exc.	V.G.	Good	Fair	Poor
1100	925	750	650	450	325

Model 1885 .30-06 Centennial High Wall Hunter

Similar to Model 1885 High Wall Hunter but with premium wood and gold inlay on receiver. Commemorates centennial of .30-06 cartridge. Introduced 2006.

NIB	Exc.	V.G.	Good	Fair	Poor
1300	1125	875	750	550	325

Model 1885 Low Wall Classic

This single-shot rifle is chambered for the .17 HMR cartridge and fitted with a 24" octagon barrel. Checkered walnut stock with straight grip and schnabel fore-end. Adjustable sights. Weight is about 8 lbs. Introduced in 2003. In 2005 the .17 Mach 2 caliber was offered in this model.

NIB	Exc.	V.G.	Good	Fair	Poor
1100	925	750	650	450	325

Model 1885 Low Wall 17 Mach 2

Similar to Model 1885 High Wall but with low-profile receiver, crescent buttplate, and 24-inch barrel. Chambered for 17 Mach 2 rimfire cartridge. Introduced 2006.

NIB	Exc.	V.G.	Good	Fair	Poor
1050	900	750	600	500	300

Model 1892

Introduced in mid-1997 this model is chambered for the .357 Magnum, .44-40 and .45 Colt cartridges. It features a straight grip, full magazine, and crescent buttplate.

Grade I

2,500 rifles with engraved receiver.

NIB	Exc.	V.G.	Good	Fair	Poor
900	800	700	550	450	325

High Grade

1,000 rifles with gold accents.

NIB	Exc.	V.G.	Good	Fair	Poor
1500	1300	1075	925	650	300

Model 1892 Short Rifle

This model is fitted with a 20" barrel and chambered for the .45 Colt, .357 Magnum, .44 Magnum and .44-40 cartridges. Walnut stock and blued barrel and receiver. Weight is about 6.25 lbs. Introduced in 1999.

NIB	Exc.	V.G.	Good	Fair	Poor
1200	975	850	675	400	300

Model 1892 Carbine

Similar to 1892 Short Rifle with satin-finished stock, full-length 10-shot magazine with barrel band. Introduced in 2011. Also available with large-loop lever.

NIB	Exc.	V.G.	Good	Fair	Poor
1000	850	700	500	350	200

John Wayne Model 1892 High Grade

Features silver-nickel receiver with engraved portrait of actor on the receiver. Banners on sides of receiver have silver-nickel engraving: "John Wayne-American 1907-2007" and "Courage, Strength, Grit". In .44-40 caliber with 18.5" barrel, large-loop lever, adjustable rear sight, blue hammer and trigger. Custom Grade has checkered stock, gold engraving, blue receiver. Limited editions with 4,000 High Grade and 1,000 Custom Grade. Manufactured 2007-2009. **NOTE:** Add $1000 for Custom Grade.

NIB	Exc.	V.G.	Good	Fair	Poor
W	1750	1650	1550	—	—

Model 1886

Introduced to the Winchester line in 1997 this was a non-cataloged item. This model features a 26" octagon barrel, semi-pistol grip, and crescent buttplate.

Grade I

2,500 rifles blued receiver.

NIB	Exc.	V.G.	Good	Fair	Poor
1050	900	750	600	500	300

High Grade

1,000 rifles with gold accents on receiver.

NIB	Exc.	V.G.	Good	Fair	Poor
1500	1300	1075	925	650	300

Model 1886 Take Down Classic

Introduced in 1999 this model is chambered for the .45-70 cartridge and features a 26" barrel with takedown feature. Walnut stock with pistol grip and crescent butt. Magazine capacity is 8 rounds. Weight is about 9.25 lbs.

NIB	Exc.	V.G.	Good	Fair	Poor
1300	1125	875	750	550	325

Model 1886 Extra Light

This model is similar to the Model 1886 Classic but fitted with a 22" round tapered barrel and half magazine. Chambered for the .45-70 cartridge. Shotgun butt. Weight is about 7.25 lbs. Limited edition. Introduced in 2000.

Grade I (3,500)

NIB	Exc.	V.G.	Good	Fair	Poor
1100	925	750	650	450	325

High Grade (1,000)

NIB	Exc.	V.G.	Good	Fair	Poor
1500	1300	1075	925	650	300

Model 1895 Limited Edition

Introduced in 1995 this reproduction of the famous Model 1895 is offered in .30-06 caliber with 24" barrel. Magazine capacity is 4 rounds. Weight is approximately 8 lbs. Available in two grades, each limited to 4,000 rifles. Reintroduced in 2010 in .30-40 Krag caliber.

Grade I

NIB	Exc.	V.G.	Good	Fair	Poor
1050	900	750	600	500	300

High Grade

NIB	Exc.	V.G.	Good	Fair	Poor
1500	1300	1075	925	650	300

Model 1895—Limited Edition for the year 2000

Same as above but chambered for the .405 Win. cartridge. Introduced in 2000.

Grade I

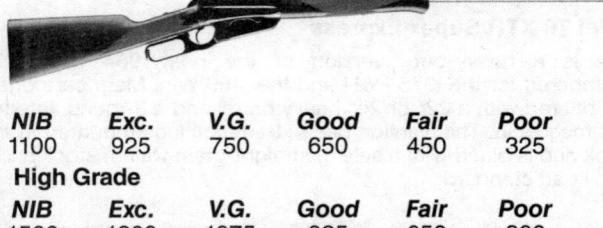

NIB	Exc.	V.G.	Good	Fair	Poor
1100	925	750	650	450	325

High Grade

NIB	Exc.	V.G.	Good	Fair	Poor
1500	1300	1075	925	650	300

Model 1895 Saddle Ring Carbine

Patterned after original Model 1895 carbine. Features include blued 22-inch barrel, ladder style rear sight; D&T for Lyman side mount; saddle ring on left side of receiver; rollmarked -inch.30 Gov't 06.-inch Chambered in .30-06 only; commemorates centennial of .30-06 cartridge. Introduced 2006.

NIB	Exc.	V.G.	Good	Fair	Poor
1200	975	850	675	400	300

Model 1895 Theodore Roosevelt Safari Centennial High Grade

Lever-action rifle patterned after original Winchester Model 1895. Chambered in .405 Winchester; commemorates Theodore Roosevelt's 1909 African Safari. 24" blued round barrel, 4-round box magazine, checkered walnut fore-end and buttstock with inlaid "TR" medallion, engraved and silvered receiver. Weight: 8 lbs.

NIB	Exc.	V.G.	Good	Fair	Poor
1600	1375	1075	925	650	300

Custom Grade

Similar to above but with jeweled hammer, fancier wood and engraving, gold-filled highlights and numerous accessories. Production limited to 1000 sets.

NIB	Exc.	V.G.	Good	Fair	Poor
3000	2500	1950	1575	1200	700

Model 52B Sporting Rifle

A 1993 limited-edition rifle (6,000 guns) that is a faithful reproduction of the famous Winchester Model 52 Sporter. Equipped with a 24" barrel, adjustable trigger, and "B" style cheekpiece. This model was reissued in 1997 and limited to 3,000 rifles.

NIB	Exc.	V.G.	Good	Fair	Poor
750	600	475	350	225	150

POST-1964 MODEL 70

These post-Model 70 rifles were fitted with redesigned actions and bolt with free-floating barrels and new style stocks with impressed checkering. In 1994, U.S. Repeating Arms reintroduced the pre-1964 Model 70 action on many of its Model 70 rifles. At the present time this new action does not affect values but may do so in the future depending on shooter reaction. In October of 2007, Winchester Repeating Arms announced that the pre-'64-style Model 70 would once again be produced – this time at the FN plant in Columbia, So. Carolina.

Model 70—Standard Grade

This is a bolt-action sporting rifle chambered for various popular calibers such as the .22-250, .222 Rem., .243 Win., .270 Win., .30-06, and .308 Win. It features a 22" barrel with open sights and a 5-round, integral box magazine. The finish is blued with a Monte Carlo-type stock furnished with sling swivels. It was manufactured between 1964 and 1971.

NIB	Exc.	V.G.	Good	Fair	Poor
—	600	475	325	175	110

Model 70 Varmint

Chambered for the .22-25, .222 Rem., and .243 Win. cartridges this rifle is fitted with a 24" heavyweight barrel with no sights. Magazine capacity is 5 rounds. Weight is about 9.75 lbs. Built from 1964 to 1971.

NIB	Exc.	V.G.	Good	Fair	Poor
—	600	450	300	150	100

Model 70 Westerner

This model is chambered for the .264 Win. Magnum and .300 Win. Magnum cartridges. Open sights, 24" barrel. Ventilated recoil pad. Weight is about 7.25 lbs. Built from 1964 to 1971.

NIB	Exc.	V.G.	Good	Fair	Poor
—	650	475	325	175	110

Model 70 African

Chambered for the .458 Win. Magnum cartridge this rifle is fitted with a 22" barrel with open sights. Magazine capacity is 3 rounds. Weight is about 8.5 lbs. Built from 1964 to 1971.

NIB	Exc.	V.G.	Good	Fair	Poor
—	925	750	485	275	175

NIB	Exc.	V.G.	Good	Fair	Poor
—	500	400	350	300	125

Model 70 Magnum

Chambered for the 7mm Rem. Mag., .300 Win. Mag., and .375 H&H cartridges. Barrel length is 24". Weight is about 7.75 lbs. Built from 1964 to 1971.

NIB	Exc.	V.G.	Good	Fair	Poor
—	750	585	375	225	175

Model 670

Economy-grade version of the Model 70. Hardwood stock, iron sights, non-hinged floorplate, 22" blued barrel. Manufactured from 1967 to 1973.

NIB	Exc.	V.G.	Good	Fair	Poor
—	450	400	300	250	100

Model 70 Deluxe

Built from 1964 to 1971, this rifle features a Monte Carlo stock with hand checkering and ebony fore-end tip. Offered in .243, .270, .30-06, .300 Win. Mag. Fitted with 22" barrel except magnums, which have 24" barrel. Weight is about 7.5 lbs.

NIB	Exc.	V.G.	Good	Fair	Poor
—	750	575	350	175	125

Model 70 XTR Featherweight

This gun was built after the takeover by the U.S.R.A. Company. It is a bolt-action sporting rifle chambered for various calibers from .22-250 up to the .30-06 cartridges. It has a 22" barrel that is furnished without sights and features either a short- or medium-length action. It has a 5-round, integral magazine. The finish is blued, with a checkered walnut stock. It was introduced in 1981.

Model 70 Mannlicher

This is a full-length, Mannlicher-type stocked version of the Model 70 bolt-action rifle that is chambered for the .243, .270, .308, and the .30-06 cartridges. It was introduced in 1969. It features a 19" barrel with open sights. The finish is blued. It was discontinued in 1972. Only 2,401 were produced. Excellent quality.

NIB	Exc.	V.G.	Good	Fair	Poor
—	975	825	625	425	310

NIB	Exc.	V.G.	Good	Fair	Poor
—	725	625	450	325	265

Model 70 Fiftieth Anniversary Model

This is a commemorative version of the post-1964 Model 70 bolt-action rifle. It is chambered for the .300 Win. Mag. and is offered with a 24" barrel. It is engraved and high-gloss blued with a deluxe, checkered walnut stock. There were 500 manufactured in 1987. In order to realize collector potential, it must be NIB with all supplied materials.

Model 70 Target Rifle

This version is chambered for the .308 or the .30-06 cartridges. It was offered with a 24" heavy barrel without sights. It is furnished with bases for a target scope. The finish is blued with a heavy walnut target stock with a palm rest. Weight is approximately 10.25 lbs.

NIB	Exc.	V.G.	Good	Fair	Poor
—	875	775	575	375	260

NIB	Exc.	V.G.	Good	Fair	Poor
1500	1400	1200	900	500	300

Model 70 XTR Super Express

This is a heavy-duty version of the post-1964 Model 70 chambered for the .375 H&H and the .458 Win. Mag. cartridges. It is offered with a 22" or 24" heavy barrel and a 3-round, integral box magazine. This version has extra recoil lugs mounted in the stock and is blued with a select, straight-grain walnut stock and a recoil pad standard.

Model 70 International Match Army

This version is chambered for the .308 cartridge and has a 24" heavy barrel furnished without sights. It has an adjustable trigger and is blued, with a target-type heavy stock that had an accessory rail and an adjustable butt.

NIB	Exc.	V.G.	Good	Fair	Poor
—	950	850	600	400	300

NIB	Exc.	V.G.	Good	Fair	Poor
1100	925	750	650	450	325

Model 70A

This is a utility version of the bolt-action post-1964 Model 70. It was furnished without a hinged floorplate. The finish is blued, with a walnut stock. It was manufactured between 1972 and 1978.

Model 70 XTR Varmint

This version is chambered for the .22-250, .223, and the .243 cartridges. It has a 24" heavy barrel and is furnished without sights. It has a 5-round magazine and is blued with a heavy walnut stock. It was introduced in 1972.

NIB	Exc.	V.G.	Good	Fair	Poor
650	550	400	250	200	100

Model 70 Winlight

This version is offered in various calibers between .270 and the .338 Win. Mag. It features a matte-blue finish and a fiberglass stock. It is offered with a 22" or a 24" barrel and a 3- or 4-round magazine. It was introduced in 1986.

NIB	Exc.	V.G.	Good	Fair	Poor
700	550	400	250	200	100

Ranger (Model 70)

This is a utility-grade, bolt-action rifle chambered for the .270 Win., .30-06, and the 7mm Rem. Mag. cartridges. It is offered with a 22" or a 24" barrel with open sights and has a 3- or 4-round box magazine. The finish is blued with a plain hardwood stock.

NIB	Exc.	V.G.	Good	Fair	Poor
450	300	275	225	150	100

Model 70 Featherweight

Bolt-action rifle chambered in .22-250, .243, 7mm-08, .308, .270 WSM, 7mm WSM, .300 WSM, .325 WSM, .25-06, .270, .30-06, 7mm Remington Magnum, .300 Winchester Magnum, .338 Winchester Magnum. 22" blued barrel (24" in magnum chamberings), satin-finished checkered Grade I walnut stock, controlled round feeding. Capacity 5 rounds (short action) or 3 rounds (long action). Weight: 6-1/2 to 7-1/4 lbs. Pachmayr Decelerator pad. No sights but drilled and tapped for scope mounts. Values shown are for long action. Deduct 15 percent for short action. **NOTE:** In 2003 a left-hand model was offered. Add $35. For stainless steel model add $60.

NIB	Exc.	V.G.	Good	Fair	Poor
850	650	450	375	225	125

Model 70 Featherweight Classic All-Terrain

Introduced in 1996, this model features a weather-resistant stainless steel barrel and action with fiberglass/graphite black synthetic stock. Offered in .270 Win., .30-06, 7mm Rem. Mag., .330 Win. Mag. Weight is about 7.25 lbs. Also offered with the BOSS system. **NOTE:** Add $100 for BOSS.

NIB	Exc.	V.G.	Good	Fair	Poor
950	650	450	325	225	125

Model 70 Featherweight Super Short

Introduced in 2003 this rifle features a shorter receiver to handle the .223 WSSM and .243 WSSM cartridges. Fitted with a 22" barrel and a checkered walnut stock with solid recoil pad. Weight is about 6 lbs.

NIB	Exc.	V.G.	Good	Fair	Poor
770	600	500	400	300	200

Model 70 Classic Laredo

First offered in 1996, this model features a heavy 26" barrel with pre-1964 action on a gray synthetic stock. Chambered for the 7mm Rem. Mag and the .300 Win. Mag. The forearm is a beavertail. Finish is matte blue. In 1997 this model was offered chambered for the 7mm STW cartridge. In 1998 this model was offered with fluted barrel. **NOTE:** Add $100 for BOSS. Add $125 for fluted barrel.

NIB	Exc.	V.G.	Good	Fair	Poor
750	650	550	500	400	300

Model 70 Classic Compact

Introduced in 1998, this model is a scaled-down version of the Featherweight. It has a length of pull of 12.5" and a 20" barrel. Chambered for .243, .308, and 7mm-08 calibers. Checkered walnut stock. Weight is about 6.5 lbs.

NIB	Exc.	V.G.	Good	Fair	Poor
750	650	550	500	400	300

Model 70 Classic Sporter LT

Introduced in 1999, this model is chambered for a wide variety of calibers from .25-06 to .338 Win. Mag. Fitted with a 24" or 26" barrel depending on caliber and no sights. Walnut stock with butt pad. Blued finish. Also offered in left-hand models from .270 to .338 Win. Mag. Weight is about 8 lbs. **NOTE:** Add $30 for left-hand models.

NIB	Exc.	V.G.	Good	Fair	Poor
750	650	550	500	400	300

Model 70 Classic Safari Express

This model is chambered for the .375 H&H Magnum, .416 Rem. Magnum and .458 Win. Magnum. Fitted with a 24" barrel and magazine capacity is 4 rounds. Walnut stock with open sights. Left-hand model offered in .375 H&H. Weight is about 8.5 lbs. Introduced in 1999. **NOTE:** Add $30 for .375 H&H left-hand model.

NIB	Exc.	V.G.	Good	Fair	Poor
1350	1100	900	650	500	300

Model 70 Super Grade

Another U.S.R.A. rifle that features a select walnut stock, claw-controlled round feed, a single reinforced cross bolt, 24" barrel shipped with bases and rings. The buttstock has a straight comb with classic cheekpiece and deep-cut checkering. Available in .270, .30-06, 7mm Rem. Magnum, .300 Win. Magnum, .338 Win. Magnum, .270 WSM, .300 WSM. Rifle weighs approximately 7.75 lbs.

NIB	Exc.	V.G.	Good	Fair	Poor
1500	1300	1075	925	650	300

Model 70 RMEF Super Grade

As above but with stainless steel action and barrel. Chambered for the .300 Win. Mag. cartridge. Fitted with a 26" barrel. Checkered walnut stock with solid recoil pad. Weight is about 8 lbs. Introduced in 2003. Special RMEF (Rock Mountain Elk Foundation) emblem on grip cap. Limited production.

NIB	Exc.	V.G.	Good	Fair	Poor
1600	1400	1175	975	650	300

Model 70 RMEF Super Grade III

This model is chambered for the .325 WSM or .300 WSM calibers and fitted with a 24" stainless steel barrel without sights. Super Grade walnut checkered stock with shadow line cheek piece. Weight is about 7.75 lbs. RMEF grip cap medallion. Introduced in 2005.

NIB	Exc.	V.G.	Good	Fair	Poor
1200	950	875	650	500	300

Model 70 Classic Super Grade III

Similar to the model above but chambered for a variety of short action calibers including WSM calibers. Fitted with a 24" barrel with no sights except for .300 Win. Magnum and .338 Win. Magnum which have 26" barrels. Weight is about 7.75 to 8 lbs. depending on caliber. Introduced in 2005.

NIB	Exc.	V.G.	Good	Fair	Poor
1400	1100	875	650	500	300

Model 70 Super Express

A U.S.R.A. version of the post-1964 XTR Super Express. Specifications are the same as the earlier model. Rifle weighs 8.5 lbs. Introduced in 1993.

NIB	Exc.	V.G.	Good	Fair	Poor
1500	1200	1075	975	650	300

Model 70 Heavy Varmint

Introduced by U.S.R.A. in 1993, this rifle features a fiberglass/graphite stock with heavy 26" stainless steel barrel. Offered in .223, .22-250, .243, and .308. In 1997, this model was offered chambered for the .222 Rem. cartridge. Rifle weighs about 10.75 lbs.

NIB	Exc.	V.G.	Good	Fair	Poor
750	575	500	425	375	200

Model 70 Heavy Varmint—Fluted Barrel

Introduced in 1997, this model is similar to the above Varmint with the addition of a fluted barrel. Calibers are also the same as the above model.

NIB	Exc.	V.G.	Good	Fair	Poor
825	625	500	475	350	250

Model 70 Stainless

All-metal parts are stainless steel, including the barrel, with synthetic stock. Available with 24" barrel and chambered for .270, .30-06, 7mm Rem. Mag., .300 Win. Mag., and .338 Win. Mag. Weighs about 7.5 lbs. Currently in production. In 2001 this model was offered chambered for the .300 Winchester Short Magnum (WSM) cartridge.

NIB	Exc.	V.G.	Good	Fair	Poor
850	650	450	375	225	125

Model 70 Classic Laminated Stainless

Introduced in 1998 this model features a laminated stock and stainless steel barrel and action. Offered in .270, .30-06, 7mm Rem. Mag., .300 Win. Mag., and .338 Win. Mag. Pre-1964 action. Bolt is jeweled and bolt handle is knurled. Barrel lengths are 24" and 26", depending on caliber. Weight is about 8 lbs. In 2001, this model was offered chambered for the .300 Winchester Short Magnum (WSM) cartridge.

NIB	Exc.	V.G.	Good	Fair	Poor
850	650	450	375	225	125

Model 70 Classic Camo Stainless

This model features a Sporter-style stock with 24" or 26" barrel and Mossy Oak Treestand camo on the stock. Chambered for .270 Win., .30-06, 7mm Rem. Mag., and .300 Win Mag. Magazine capacity is 5 rounds. Weight is about 7.5 lbs. Introduced in 1998.

NIB	Exc.	V.G.	Good	Fair	Poor
850	650	450	375	225	125

Model 70 SM

This rifle features a synthetic stock with black matte finish. Barrel length is 24". Available in 10 calibers from .223 Rem. to .375 H&H Mag. Depending on caliber, rifle weighs between 7 and 8 lbs.

NIB	Exc.	V.G.	Good	Fair	Poor
850	650	450	375	225	125

Model 70 DBM-S

Similar to Model 70 SM but fitted with detachable box magazine. The metal parts are blued and the stock is synthetic. Offered in eight calibers from .223 Rem. to .338 Win. Mag. Furnished with scope bases and rings are open sights. Rifle weighs about 7.25 lbs., depending on caliber. Introduced in 1993.

NIB	Exc.	V.G.	Good	Fair	Poor
650	550	450	375	225	125

Model 70 Varmint

Similar to the Model 70 Heavy Varmint but furnished with a traditional walnut stock and 26" medium-heavy barrel. Offered in .223 Rem., .22-250, .243, and .308. Weighs 9 lbs.

NIB	Exc.	V.G.	Good	Fair	Poor
700	600	450	325	225	150

Model 70 DBM

DBM stands for detachable box magazine. Fitted with a straight-comb walnut stock. Jeweled bolt with blued receiver. Shipped with scope bases and rings or open sights. Rifle offered in eight calibers from .223 Rem. to .300 Win. Mag. Rifle weighs about 7.35 lbs., depending on caliber. Introduced in 1993.

NIB	Exc.	V.G.	Good	Fair	Poor
700	600	450	325	225	150

Model 70 Sporter

U.S.R.A.'s basic Model 70 offering. Straight-comb walnut stock with checkering, jeweled bolt and blued receiver and barrel are standard. Available in 12 calibers from .223 Rem. to .338 Win. Mag. including .270 Weatherby Mag. and .300 Weatherby Mag. Barrel length is 24" and is available with either scope bases and rings or open sights. Rifle weighs about 7.5 lbs.

NIB	Exc.	V.G.	Good	Fair	Poor
700	600	450	325	225	150

Model 70 WinTuff

Similar to the Sporter except fitted with a laminated hardwood straight-comb stock with cheekpiece. Offered in 24" barrel lengths with a choice of 6 calibers from .270 Win. to .338 Win. Mag. Furnished with scope bases and rings. Rifle weighs about 7.65 lbs., depending on caliber.

NIB	Exc.	V.G.	Good	Fair	Poor
700	600	450	325	225	150

Model 70 Lightweight

Similar to the Model 70 Winlight. Offered with straight-comb checkered walnut stock with knurled bolt and blued receiver and barrel. The barrel is 22" without sights. Offered in 5 calibers: .223, .243, .270, .308, and .30-06. Rifle weighs about 7 lbs., depending on caliber.

NIB	Exc.	V.G.	Good	Fair	Poor
700	600	450	325	225	150

Model 70 Black Shadow

Chambered for the .270, .30-06, 7mm Rem. Mag., and .300 Win. Mag. and fitted with a 22" or 24" barrel, depending on caliber. Finish is matte black with composite stock. Push-feed action. Weight is 7.25 lbs. Introduced in 1998.

NIB	Exc.	V.G.	Good	Fair	Poor
550	450	375	325	225	150

Model 70 Ultimate Shadow

Introduced in 2003 this bolt-action model features a new black synthetic stock design with improved gripping surfaces and soft recoil pad. This model has a blued action and barrel. Chambered for the .300 WSM, .270 WSM, or the 7mm WSM cartridges. Fitted with a 24" barrel. Weight is about 6.75 lbs. Also offered with stainless action and barrel. **NOTE:** For stainless steel model add $45.

NIB	Exc.	V.G.	Good	Fair	Poor
800	700	425	350	275	125

Model 70 Ultimate Shadow Camo

As above but with Mossy Oak New Break-Up camo. Introduced in 2004.

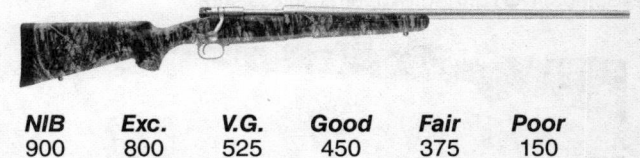

NIB	Exc.	V.G.	Good	Fair	Poor
900	800	525	450	375	150

Model 70 Super Shadow Super Short

Similar to the above model but chambered for the .223 WSM or .243 WSM cartridge. Fitted with a 22" barrel and blind magazine. Weight is about 6 lbs. Introduced in 2003.

NIB	Exc.	V.G.	Good	Fair	Poor
700	600	450	325	225	150

Model 70 Super Shadow

Similar to the Ultimate Shadow but fitted with a controlled round push feed bolt. Chambered for the .300 WSM, .270 WSM, or the 7mm WSM cartridge. Fitted with a 22" barrel, composite stock and blind magaziine. Weight is about 6.75 lbs. Introduced in 2003. New calibers: .243, .308, .270, .30-06, .300WM.

NIB	Exc.	V.G.	Good	Fair	Poor
700	600	450	325	225	150

Model 70 Stealth

This is a varmint model with 26" heavy barrel chambered for .223 Rem., .22-250, or .308 Win. It has a push-feed bolt-action. Black synthetic stock. Matte black finish. Weight is approximately 10.85 lbs. In 2004 the .223 WSSM, .243 WSSM and the .25 WSSM calibers were added.

NIB	Exc.	V.G.	Good	Fair	Poor
850	650	450	375	225	125

Model 70 Coyote

This model, introduced in 2000, has a push-feed bolt-action and is chambered for the .223 Rem, .22-250, and .243 Win. calibers. Fitted with a medium-heavy 24" stainless steel barrel with laminated stock and large fore-end. Weight is about 9 lbs. In 2002 the rifle was offered in .270 WSM, 7mm WSM, and .300 WSM. In 2005 the .325 WSM was added to this model. Discontinued 2006.

NIB	Exc.	V.G.	Good	Fair	Poor
750	650	450	375	225	125

Model 70 Coyote Lite

Introduced in 2005 this model features a lightweight composite stock with skeletonized aluminum block bedding. Recoil pad. Fluted 24" medium-heavy barrel with no sights. Offered in .223 Rem and all WSSM and WSM calibers. New calibers: .22-250, .243, .308. **NOTE:** Add $40 for stainless steel.

NIB	Exc.	V.G.	Good	Fair	Poor
850	650	450	375	225	125

Model 70 Ladies/Youth Ranger

A scaled-down version of the Ranger. Length of pull is 1" shorter than standard. Rifle weighs 6.5 lbs. Chambered in .243 and .308. In 1997 this model was offered chambered for the .223 Rem. and the 7mm-08 Rem. cartridges.

NIB	Exc.	V.G.	Good	Fair	Poor
450	300	275	225	150	100

Model 70 Shadow Elite Stainless

Bolt-action rifle. Calibers: .22-250, .243, .308, .270, .30-06, .300 WM, .338 WM, .375 H&H, .270 WSM, 7mm WSM, .300 WSM, .325 WSM. Barrel: Stainless steel, 24-inch or 26-inch (.300, .338 WM). Stock: Overmolded composite. Weight: 6-1/2 – 7-3/4 lbs. Magazine capacity: 3 or 5 (.22-250, .243, .308, .270, .30-06). Introduced 2006.

NIB	Exc.	V.G.	Good	Fair	Poor
800	700	425	350	275	125

Model 70 Shadow Elite Camo Stainless

Similar to Shadow Elite Stainless but with Mossy Oak New Break Up camo synthetic stock.

NIB	Exc.	V.G.	Good	Fair	Poor
850	750	475	350	275	125

Model 70 Pro Shadow Blued

Bolt-action rifle. Calibers: .22-250, .243, .308, .270, .30-06, 7mm RM, .300 WM, .270 WSM, 7mm WSM, .300 WSM, .325 WSM. Barrel: Blued steel, 22-inch (standard) or 24-inch (magnum). Stock: Overmolded composite. Weight: 6-1/2 – 7 lbs. Magazine capacity: 3 (magnum) or 5 (standard). Introduced 2006.

NIB	Exc.	V.G.	Good	Fair	Poor
650	550	375	250	175	125

Model 70 Pro Shadow Stainless

Similar to Pro Shadow blued but with stainless steel barrel and .338 WM and .375 H&H chamberings.

NIB	Exc.	V.G.	Good	Fair	Poor
700	600	450	325	225	150

Model 70 Laminated Coyote Outback Stainless

Similar to Model 70 Coyote Lite but with skeletonized laminated stock and stainless steel only. Calibers: .22-250, .243, .308, .270, .30-06, 7mm RM, .300 WM, .270 WSM, 7mm WSM, .300 WSM, .325 WSM. Weight: 7-3/4 lbs. Introduced 2006.

NIB	Exc.	V.G.	Good	Fair	Poor
750	650	450	375	225	125

Model 70 Laminated Coyote Gray or Brown Stainless

Similar to Model 70 Laminated Coyote Outback but with non-fluted barrel and choice of brown or gray laminated stock.

NIB	Exc.	V.G.	Good	Fair	Poor
700	600	450	325	225	150

POST-2007 MODEL 70

In 2006, Winchester closed its factory in New Haven, CT and discontinued production of the Model 70 and Model 94 rifles. Late in 2007, it was announced that production of the Model 70 would resume at the FN plant in Columbia, SC. FN (Fabrique Nationale of Belgium) is the parent company of Winchester. The following models are produced at the South Carolina plant.

Model 70 Featherweight Deluxe

Pre-64 action, three-position safety, jeweled bolt, knurled bolt handle, walnut stock with slight schnabel, cut checkering, Pachmayr Decelerator recoil pad., 22- or 24-inch barrel depending on caliber. Chambered for a variety of cartridges from .243 to .325 Winchester Short Magnum. Weight 6.5 to 7 lbs. Introduced in 2008.

NIB	Exc.	V.G.	Good	Fair	Poor
950	650	450	325	225	125

Model 70 Sporter Deluxe

Similar to above but with non-schnabel forend and cheekpiece.

NIB	Exc.	V.G.	Good	Fair	Poor
950	650	450	325	225	125

New Model 70 Super Grade Special Limited Edition

Very fancy version of the Model 70 featuring post-'64 action, ultra-premium walnut, gold-filled engraving, black forend cap, steel grip cap, and shadowline cheekpiece. Only 250 produced in 2008. Chambered in .300 Winchester Magnum only.

NIB	Exc.	V.G.	Good	Fair	Poor
2400	2000	1650	1300	900	500

Model 70 Extreme Weather SS

Post-'64 style action with 22-, 24- or 26-inch barrel depending on chambering. Three-position safety, fluted stainless barrel and Bell and Carlson composite stock. Chambered for a variety of cartridges from .243 to .325 Winchester Short Magnum.

NIB	Exc.	V.G.	Good	Fair	Poor
1000	750	550	425	275	175

Model 70 FW Compact

Featherweight Compact made for smaller-framed shooters. Light mountain type rifle weighing 6.5 pounds with 20-inch barrel. Pre-'64 Controlled Round Feed and three-position safety. M.O.A. adjustable trigger system. Jeweled bolt body with knurled bolt handle. Walnut stock with fancy checkering pattern. Chambered for .22-250 Remington, .243 Winchester, 7mm-08 Remington or .308 Winchester. Introduced in 2011.

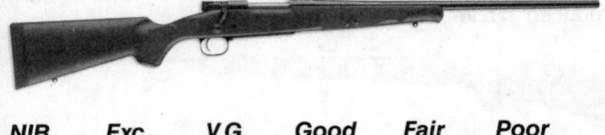

NIB	Exc.	V.G.	Good	Fair	Poor
765	650	550	450	350	200

Model 70 Safari Express

Designed for dangerous game, calibers include .375 H&H, .416 Rem. Mag. or .458 Win. Mag. Express sights, 24-inch barrel, satin finished and checkered walnut stock. Other features include reinforced crossbolts, dual recoil lugs and Pachmayr Decelerator recoil pad. Weight: 9- pounds.

NIB	Exc.	V.G.	Good	Fair	Poor
1200	1000	800	650	500	350

Model 70 75th Anniversary Super Grade

To commemorate the 75th anniversary of the rifle, Winchester introduced in 2012 this special edition in .30-06 caliber with a Grade IV/V Full Fancy walnut stock. One-piece bottom metal has engraving with scroll pattern of 75th Model 70 emblem. Other features include pre-64 style controlled-round feed with claw extractor and Pachmayr Decelerator recoil pad.

NIB	Exc.	V.G.	Good	Fair	Poor
1800	1700	1600	—	—	—

WINCHESTER CUSTOM GUN SHOP

NOTE: There were a number of special order options offered by the Custom shop that greatly affect price, such as special-order engraving, stock carving, wood, sights, etc. It is strongly suggested that an independent appraisal be secured prior to a sale.

Model 94 Custom Limited Edition New Generation

This lever-action rifle is stocked with fancy checkered walnut with pistol grip and long nose fore-end. Custom engraved with gold inlaid moose on right side and gold inlaid buck and doe on the left side. Fitted with tang safety. Barrel is 20" and chambered for the .30-30 cartridge. Introduced in 2003. Weight is about 6.25 lbs.

NIB	Exc.	V.G.	Good	Fair	Poor
3000	2500	2100	—	—	—

Model 70 Featherweight Ultra Grade

Limited to 1,000 rifles, this model is profusely engraved with game scene and gold line inlaid. Serial number inlaid in gold. Offered in .270 caliber with very fine-figured walnut stock with fine line checkering. Mahogany fitted case. Strongly suggest a qualified appraisal before sale.

NIB	Exc.	V.G.	Good	Fair	Poor
4000	3500	—	—	—	—

Model 70 Custom Featherweight

Introduced in 2003 this rifle is chambered for the .270, 7mm Win. Mag., or the .30-06. Fitted with a 22" barrel. Semi-fancy walnut stock with schnabel fore-end. Offered in blued or stainless steel finish in either right- or left-hand models. Weight is about 7.25 lbs.

NIB	Exc.	V.G.	Good	Fair	Poor
3500	—	—	—	—	—

Model 70 Custom Carbon

This rifle features a stainless steel action with Shilen barrel wrapped in graphite epoxy. Fitted with a black composite stock. Chambered for the .270 WSM, 7mm WSM, .300 WSM, .25-06 Rem., or the .338 Win. Mag. cartridge. Fitted with a 24" barrel on all calibers but the .338 (26"). Weight is about 6.5 lbs. on the WSM calibers and 7 lbs. of the others. Magazine capacity is three rounds. Introduced in 2003.

NIB	Exc.	V.G.	Good	Fair	Poor
3200	—	—	—	—	—

Model 70 Custom Sharpshooter

A U.S.R.A. Custom Shop gun. This model is fitted with a stainless steel Schneider barrel with hand-honed action and hand fitted. The stock is a custom McMillan A-2 glass bedded stock. Offered in .223 Rem., .22-250 Rem., .308 Win. and .300 Win. Mag. Comes from the factory with a hard case. Currently in production.

NIB	Exc.	V.G.	Good	Fair	Poor
2500	—	—	—	—	—

Model 70 Custom Classic Sharpshooter II

Same as above but introduced in 1996 with an H-S heavy target stock, a pre-1964 action stainless steel H-S barrel. Weight is about 11 lbs. Offered in .22-250, .308, .30-06, and .300 Win. Mag.

NIB	Exc.	V.G.	Good	Fair	Poor
2250	—	—	—	—	—

Model 70 Custom Sporting Sharpshooter

Essentially a take-off on the Custom Sharpshooter but configured for hunting. Fitted with a McMillan sporter-style gray stock and Schneider stainless steel barrel. Offered in .270 Win., .300 Win., and 7mm STW. Introduced in 1993.

NIB	Exc.	V.G.	Good	Fair	Poor
2000	—	—	—	—	—

Model 70 Custom Classic Sporting Sharpshooter II

Introduced in 1996 this is an updated version of the model above. It features a pre-1964 action with H-S special fiberglass stock and stainless steel barrel. Available in 7mm STW, .300 Win. Mag. Weight is about 8.5 lbs.

NIB	Exc.	V.G.	Good	Fair	Poor
2500	—	—	—	—	—

Model 70 Custom Grade

This custom built Model 70 is hand finished, polished, and fitted in the Custom Shop. Internal parts are hand honed while the barrel is lead lapped. The customer can order individual items to his or her own taste, including engraving, special stock dimensions and carvings, etc. Each Custom Grade Model 70 should be priced on an individual basis.

Model 70 Custom Express

Also built in the Custom Shop this model features figured walnut, hand-honed internal parts, bolt and follower are engine turned. A special 3-leaf rear sight is furnished also. Offered in .375 H&H Mag., .375 JRS, .416 Rem. Mag., .458 Win. Mag., and .470 Capstick.

NIB	Exc.	V.G.	Good	Fair	Poor
3000	—	—	—	—	—

Model 70 Custom African Express

Introduced in 1999 this model is chambered for the .340 Wby., .358 STA, .375 H&H, .416 Rem. Mag., and the .458 Win. Mag. Fitted with a 24" barrel and a magazine capacity of 4 rounds. Express sights. Weight is about 9.75 lbs. Ebony pistol grip cap, and select walnut stock.

NIB	Exc.	V.G.	Good	Fair	Poor
3850	—	—	—	—	—

Model 70 Custom Safari Express

This model has a figured walnut stock with the bolt and follower engine turned. Express sights. Chambered in .340 Wby., .358

STA, .375 H&H, .416 Rem. Mag., and .458 Win. Mag. Barrel length is 24". Weight is about 9.5 lbs. Introduced in 1999.

NIB	Exc.	V.G.	Good	Fair	Poor
2500	—	—	—	—	—

Model 70 Custom "Ultra Light" Mannlicher

This model features a full-length stock of figured walnut with smooth tapered barrel and blued action. Chambered for .260 Rem., .308 Win., and 7mm-08. Fitted with a 19" barrel with optional open sights. Weight is about 6.75 lbs. Introduced in 1999.

NIB	Exc.	V.G.	Good	Fair	Poor
2500	—	—	—	—	—

Model 70 Ultimate Classic

This model features a number of special options as standard. Included is a pre-1964 action, choice of round, round fluted, 1/2 octagon 1/2 round barrel, full tapered octagon barrel, blued or stainless steel barrel actions, fancy American walnut stock, special Custom Shop serial numbers and proof stamp, inletted swivel bases, red recoil pad, fine cut checkering, and a hard case. Offered in a wide variety of calibers from .25-06 to .338 Win. Mag. Weight is about 7.5 to 7.75 lbs. depending on caliber. Also available in stainless steel. **NOTE:** In 1997 this model was introduced in a left-hand version.

NIB	Exc.	V.G.	Good	Fair	Poor
2450	—	—	—	—	—

Model 70 Custom Short Action

This custom shop model is fitted with a 22" match-grade barrel Controlled feed. Chambered for short-action calibers from .243 to .358. Semi-fancy walnut stock. Hand-cut checkering. Supplied with hard case. Weight is about 7.5 lbs. Introduced in 2000. In 2003 this model was offered in a left-hand version.

NIB	Exc.	V.G.	Good	Fair	Poor
2700	—	—	—	—	—

Model 70 Custom Extreme Weather

This custom shop model is fitted with a round or fluted 24" match-grade barrel. Both barrel and action are stainless steel. McMillan fiberglass stock with cheekpiece. Chambered in calibers from .25-06 to .338 Win. Mag. Weight is about 7.5 lbs. Introduced in 2000. Lightweight Extreme Weather II model introduced 2006 (6-1/4 – 7 lbs.). MSRP: $2800.

NIB	Exc.	V.G.	Good	Fair	Poor
1950	—	—	—	—	—

Model 70 Custom Take Down

Introduced in 1998 this composite stock rifle has a special take down feature. Chambered for .375 H&H, .416 Rem. Mag., .300 Win Mag., 7mm STW. Magazine capacity is 3 rounds. Barrel length is 26". Weight is between 8.5 and 9 lbs. Offered in fluted barrel in .300 Win. Mag. and 7mm STW.

NIB	Exc.	V.G.	Good	Fair	Poor
3300	—	—	—	—	—

Model 70 Custom 100th Anniversary .30-06

Semi-fancy walnut Featherweight stock with single steel crossbolt, one-piece engraved floorplate, high-lustre blued and engraved 22-inch barrel. Commemorates centennial of .30-06 cartridge. Introduced 2006; only 100 manufactured.

NIB	Exc.	V.G.	Good	Fair	Poor
2700	—	—	—	—	—

Model 70 Custom Special "70 Years of the Model 70"

Calibers: .270, .30-06 Springfield, .300 WM. Barrel: 24-inch or 26-inch (.300 WM) blued sightless. Engraved floorplate and barrel. Stock: semi-fancy checkered walnut. Introduced 2006, only 70 manufactured per caliber.

NIB	Exc.	V.G.	Good	Fair	Poor
2800	—	—	—	—	—

Model 70 Custom Maple

Calibers: .284, .270, .308, .30-06. Barrel: 24-inch blued. Weight: 7-3/4 lbs. Stocked in fiddleback maple with pre-'64 pattern checkering. Quantities "very limited." Introduced 2006.

NIB	Exc.	V.G.	Good	Fair	Poor
4400	—	—	—	—	—

Model 70 Custom Continental Hunter

Calibers: .284, .270, .308, .30-06. Barrel: 22-inch blued or stainless Krieger. Stock: glossy claro walnut, round knob pistol grip, schnabel fore-end.

NIB	Exc.	V.G.	Good	Fair	Poor
5300	—	—	—	—	—

Model 70 Custom Stainless Laminate

Calibers: .270 WSM, 7mm WSM, .300 WSM, .325 WSM. Barrel: 24-inch stainless sporter. Stock: black/gray or brown Featherweight laminated with schnabel and Pachmayr pad.

NIB	Exc.	V.G.	Good	Fair	Poor
2300	—	—	—	—	—

Model 94 Custom Limited Edition

This is essentially a special order Model 94 with choice of engraving and stock carving. Chambered for the .44-40 and fitted with a 24" octagonal barrel. Fancy walnut stock. Limited to 75 rifles. Weight is about 7.75 lbs. Suggest an appraisal prior to a sale.

NIB	Exc.	V.G.	Good	Fair	Poor
2300	—	—	—	—	—

Model 9410 Custom

Introduced in 2005 this .410 shotgun is fitted with a 24" round barrel and full length magazine. Case colored receiver with semi-fancy checkered walnut stock. Weight is about 7 lbs.

NIB	Exc.	V.G.	Good	Fair	Poor
2300	—	—	—	—	—

POST-1964 SHOTGUNS

MODEL 12 "Y" SERIES

Model 12 Field Grade

This is a later version of the slide-action Model 12, chambered for 12 gauge only. It was offered with a 26", 28", or 30" vent rib barrel with various chokes. The finish is blued with a jeweled bolt and a hand-checkered, select walnut stock. This version is easily recognizable as it has the letter Y serial number prefix. It was manufactured between 1972 and 1976.

NIB	Exc.	V.G.	Good	Fair	Poor
—	950	800	650	485	300

Model 12 Super Pigeon Grade

This is a deluxe version that features extensive engraving and fancy checkering. It was offered with a turned action and select, fancy-grade walnut. It was a limited-production item produced between 1964 and 1972. It was briefly reintroduced in 1984 and discontinued again in 1985.

NIB	Exc.	V.G.	Good	Fair	Poor
—	3000	2400	1850	1400	950

Model 12 Skeet

This version is similar to the Field Grade but is offered with a 26", vent rib, skeet-bored barrel. The finish is blued, with a skeet-type stock and recoil pad. It was manufactured between 1972 and 1975.

NIB	Exc.	V.G.	Good	Fair	Poor
—	950	850	750	450	300

Model 12 Trap Grade

This version features a 30" vent rib barrel with a Full choke. It is blued with a trap-type, standard, or Monte Carlo stock with a recoil pad. It was manufactured between 1972 and 1980.

NIB	Exc.	V.G.	Good	Fair	Poor
—	935	830	725	425	215

Model 12 (Limited Edition)

Available in 20 gauge only. Furnished with a 26" vent rib barrel choked Improved Cylinder. The walnut stock is checkered with pistol grip. Introduced in 1993 and available in three different grades.

Grade I

4,000 guns.

NIB	Exc.	V.G.	Good	Fair	Poor
1000	800	650	450	200	100

Grade IV

1,000 guns, gold highlights.

NIB	Exc.	V.G.	Good	Fair	Poor
1400	1100	850	500	200	100

Model 42 (Limited Edition)

A reproduction of the famous Winchester Model 42 .410 bore slide-action shotgun. Furnished with a 26" ventilated rib barrel choked Full. The receiver is engraved with gold border. Introduced in 1993 and limited to 850 guns.

NIB	Exc.	V.G.	Good	Fair	Poor
1800	1400	1000	500	300	150

Model 1200

This is a slide-action shotgun chambered for 12, 16, or 20 gauge. It was offered with a 26", 28", or 30", vent rib barrel with various chokes. It has an alloy receiver and is blued, with a checkered walnut stock and recoil pad. It was manufactured between 1964 and 1981. This model was offered with the plastic Hydrocoil stock, and this would add approximately 35 percent to the values given.

NIB	Exc.	V.G.	Good	Fair	Poor
—	300	250	200	150	100

Ducks Unlimited Model

Available through Ducks Unlimited chapters. An independent appraisal is suggested.

MODEL 1300 SERIES

Discontinued in 2006.

Model 1300 XTR

Chambered for 12 and 20 gauge with 3" chambers. It is a takedown gun that is offered with various-length vent rib barrels with screw-in choke tubes. It has an alloy frame and is blued with a walnut stock. It was introduced in 1978.

NIB	Exc.	V.G.	Good	Fair	Poor
475	350	275	200	150	100

Model 1300 Waterfowl

This version is chambered for 12 gauge, 3" only. It has a 30" vent rib barrel with screw-in choke tubes. It is matte-blued, with a satin-finished walnut stock and a recoil pad. It was introduced in 1984. A laminated WinTuff stock was made available in 1988 and would add $10 to the value.

NIB	Exc.	V.G.	Good	Fair	Poor
400	300	250	200	150	100

Model 1300 New Shadow Grass

Introduced in 2004 this 12 gauge 3" gun is fitted with either a 26" or 28" vent rib barrel with choke tubes. Composite stock has New Shadow Grass camo pattern. Weight is about 7 lbs.

NIB	Exc.	V.G.	Good	Fair	Poor
470	370	250	200	150	100

Model 1300 WinCam Turkey Gun

This version is similar to the Model 1300 Turkey Gun, with a green, laminated hardwood stock. It was introduced in 1987. A WinTuff version is also available and would add $20 to the values given.

NIB	Exc.	V.G.	Good	Fair	Poor
475	350	275	200	150	100

Model 1300 Stainless Security

This version is chambered for 12 or 20 gauge and is constructed of stainless steel. It has an 18" cylinder-bore barrel and a 7- or 8-shot tubular magazine. It is available with a pistol-grip stock, which would add approximately 50 percent to the values given.

NIB	Exc.	V.G.	Good	Fair	Poor
475	350	275	200	150	100

Model 1300 Turkey

This slide-action model features a 22" vent rib barrel chambered for 3" 12 gauge shells. Supplied with choke tubes. Gun weighs 7.25 lbs.

NIB	Exc.	V.G.	Good	Fair	Poor
475	350	275	200	150	100

Model 1300 Realtree Turkey

Introduced in 1994, this model features a synthetic stock camouflaged with Realtree. The receiver and 22" barrel are matte finish.

NIB	Exc.	V.G.	Good	Fair	Poor
475	350	275	200	150	100

Model 1300 Mossy Oak Break-Up Turkey

Same as above but with Mossy Oak Break-Up camo stock and gun. Introduced in 2000.

NIB	Exc.	V.G.	Good	Fair	Poor
475	350	275	200	150	100

Model 1300 Black Shadow Turkey

This model was also introduced in 1994 and features a black composite stock with a nonglare finish on the barrel, receiver, bolt, and magazine. Barrel has vent rib and is 22" in length.

NIB	Exc.	V.G.	Good	Fair	Poor
475	350	275	200	150	100

Model 1300 National Wild Turkey Federation Series III

Engraved receiver, camo stock, open sights on a 22" plain barrel, and all metal and wood parts are nonglare. Comes with a quick detachable sling. Offered in 12 gauge only. Gun weighs 7.25 lbs.

NIB	Exc.	V.G.	Good	Fair	Poor
575	420	350	250	150	100

Model 1300 National Wild Turkey Federation Series IV

Introduced in 1993, this model is similar to the Series II with the addition of a 22" vent rib barrel. Stock is black laminated. Comes with quick detachable sling. Gun weight 7 lbs.

NIB	Exc.	V.G.	Good	Fair	Poor
600	520	350	250	150	100

Model 1300 NWTF Short Turkey

This 12 gauge gun is fitted with an 18" barrel with extended choke tubes. Fiber Optic sights. Mossy Oak camo stock. NWTF medallion on pistol grip cap. Weight is about 6.5 lbs. Introduced in 2005.

NIB	Exc.	V.G.	Good	Fair	Poor
475	350	275	200	150	100

Model 1300 Whitetails Unlimited Slug Hunter

This slide-action model features a full-length rifle barrel chambered for 3" 12 gauge shells. Barrel is choked Cylinder. Fitted with a checkered walnut stock with engraved receiver. Receiver is drilled and tapped for bases and rings, which are included. Comes equipped with camo sling. Weighs 7.25 lbs.

NIB	Exc.	V.G.	Good	Fair	Poor
475	350	275	200	150	100

Model 1300 Slug Hunter

Similar to the Whitetails Unlimited model, but without the engraved receiver.

NIB	Exc.	V.G.	Good	Fair	Poor
475	350	275	200	150	100

Model 1300 Buck and Tom

Introduced in 2002 for both deer and turkey. Camo stock. Fitted with a 22" barrel with choke tubes for both deer and turkey. Receiver drilled and tapped for scope mount. Weight is about 6.75 lbs.

NIB	Exc.	V.G.	Good	Fair	Poor
525	400	325	250	175	125

Model 1300 Universal Hunter

Introduced in 2002, this model features a camo stock with 26" vent rib barrel. Choke tubes. Weight is about 7 lbs.

NIB	Exc.	V.G.	Good	Fair	Poor
550	425	375	275	225	125

Model 1300 Black Shadow Deer

Introduced in 1994, this 12 gauge Model 1300 features a black composite stock with nonglare finish on the bolt, barrel, receiver, and magazine. Barrel is 22" with ramp front sight and adjustable rear sight. In 2000 this model was offered with a rifled barrel for shooting sabot slugs. **NOTE:** Add $25 for rifled barrel.

NIB	Exc.	V.G.	Good	Fair	Poor
475	350	275	200	150	100

Model 1300 Black Shadow Field

Same as above but fitted with a 26" or 28" vent rib barrel chambered for 3" Mag. shells. Weight is about 7 lbs.

NIB	Exc.	V.G.	Good	Fair	Poor
475	350	275	200	150	100

Model 1300 Sporting/Field

This 12 gauge gun has a 28" vent rib barrel with five choke tubes. Checkered walnut stock. Black recoil pad. Weight is about 7.5 lbs. Introduced in 2002.

NIB	Exc.	V.G.	Good	Fair	Poor
475	350	275	200	150	100

Model 1300 Sporting/Field Compact

As above but with 24" barrel and 1" shorter length of pull. Introduced in 2002.

NIB	Exc.	V.G.	Good	Fair	Poor
475	350	275	200	150	100

Model 1300 Walnut Field

This 12 gauge 3" gun is fitted with either 26" or 28" vent rib barrels with choke tubes. Checkered walnut stock with recoil pad. Weight is about 7.25 lbs. Introduced in 2004.

NIB	Exc.	V.G.	Good	Fair	Poor
475	350	275	200	150	100

Model 1300 Slug Hunter Sabot (Smoothbore)

Similar to the Slug Hunter but furnished with a smoothbore barrel with a special extended screw-in choke tube that is rifled.

NIB	Exc.	V.G.	Good	Fair	Poor
425	300	225	150	125	100

Model 1300 Upland Special

This 12 gauge slide-action shotgun is fitted with a 24" vent rib barrel and straight-grip walnut stock. Weight is about 7 lbs. Introduced in 1999. In 2000 this model was offered in 20 gauge with 24" vent rib barrel.

NIB	Exc.	V.G.	Good	Fair	Poor
600	500	400	300	200	100

Model 1300 Upland Special Field

This model, introduced in 2004, features a choice of 12 or 20 gauge 3" guns with 24" vent rib barrel with choke tube. Checkered walnut stock with straight grip. Weight is about 6.75 lbs.

NIB	Exc.	V.G.	Good	Fair	Poor
600	500	400	300	200	100

Model 1300 Ranger

This slide-action shotgun is a lower-cost version of the Model 1300. Furnished with a hardwood stock and available in 12 or 20 gauge with 26" or 28" vent rib barrel. WinChokes are included.

NIB	Exc.	V.G.	Good	Fair	Poor
300	225	190	165	125	100

Model 1300 Ranger Ladies/Youth-Compact

Available in 20 gauge only this model has a 1" shorter than standard length of pull and a 22" vent rib barrel. Choke tubes are included. Gun weighs 6.75 lbs.

NIB	Exc.	V.G.	Good	Fair	Poor
300	225	190	165	125	100

Model 1300 Ranger Deer Slug

Comes in two principal configurations: a 12 gauge 22" smooth barrel with Cylinder choke; and a 12 gauge 22" rifled barrel. Both are chambered for 3" shells and weigh 6.75 lbs.

NIB	Exc.	V.G.	Good	Fair	Poor
300	200	175	150	125	100

Model 1300 Ranger Deer Combo

The Model 1300 Ranger Deer Combos are available in three different configurations. One: 12 gauge 22" smooth barrel and 28" vent rib barrel with WinChokes. Two: 12 gauge 22" rifled barrel with 28" vent rib barrel with WinChokes. Three: 20 gauge 22" smooth barrel with 28" vent rib barrel with WinChokes.

12 Gauge Combo

NIB	Exc.	V.G.	Good	Fair	Poor
375	275	225	190	165	100

20 Gauge Combo

NIB	Exc.	V.G.	Good	Fair	Poor
375	275	225	190	165	100

Model 1300 Defender Combo

This personal defense slide-action shotgun features an 18" Cylinder choked barrel and a 28" vent rib barrel with modified WinChoke and an accessory pistol grip. A hardwood stock comes fitted to the gun.

NIB	Exc.	V.G.	Good	Fair	Poor
425	300	225	150	125	100

Model 1300 Defender 5-Shot

Same as above but furnished with a hardwood stock only and 18" barrel.

NIB	Exc.	V.G.	Good	Fair	Poor
425	300	225	150	125	100

Model 1300 Camp Defender

Introduced in 1999 this 12 gauge model features a 22" barrel and walnut stock. Magazine capacity is five rounds. Barrel fitted with rifle sights. Weight is about 7 lbs. Comes with Cylinder choke tube.

NIB	Exc.	V.G.	Good	Fair	Poor
425	300	225	150	125	100

Model 1300 Defender 8-Shot

Same as above but furnished with an 18" barrel with extended magazine tube.

NIB	Exc.	V.G.	Good	Fair	Poor
425	300	225	150	125	100

Model 1300 Defender Synthetic Stock

Same as above but fitted with a black synthetic full stock. Available in either 12 or 20 gauge.

NIB	Exc.	V.G.	Good	Fair	Poor
425	300	225	150	125	100

Model 1300 Defender Pistol Grip

Same as above but fitted with a black synthetic pistol grip and extended magazine tube.

NIB	Exc.	V.G.	Good	Fair	Poor
425	300	225	150	125	100

Model 1300 Lady Defender

Chambered for the 20 gauge shell, this model features an 18" barrel with 8-round capacity. Pistol-grip stock. Introduced in 1997.

NIB	Exc.	V.G.	Good	Fair	Poor
425	300	225	150	125	100

Model 1300 Stainless Marine

This 12 gauge slide-action shotgun comes with a black synthetic full stock with all metal parts chrome plated. Barrel is 18" and magazine tube holds 7 rounds. Gun weighs 6.75 lbs.

NIB	Exc.	V.G.	Good	Fair	Poor
600	500	400	300	200	100

Model 1300 Stainless Marine with Pistol Grip

Same as above with black synthetic pistol grip in place of full buttstock. Gun weighs 5.75 lbs.

NIB	Exc.	V.G.	Good	Fair	Poor
600	500	400	300	200	100

SPEED PUMP SERIES

This family of inertia-assisted slide-action shotguns was introduced in 2008 to take the place of the discontinued Model 1300. The 3" 12 gauge is available with a 26" or 28" barrel. Three choke tubes included. Weight is 7 to 7.25 lbs.

Speed Pump Walnut Field

High-gloss walnut with traditional checkering.

NIB	Exc.	V.G.	Good	Fair	Poor
375	325	275	200	150	100

Speed Pump Black Shadow Field

Synthetic stock and fore-end with matte black metal.

NIB	Exc.	V.G.	Good	Fair	Poor
375	325	275	200	150	100

Speed Pump Defender

This home-security 12 gauge has an 18", cylinder choke barrel and 5-round magazine tube. Weight is about 6.5 lbs.

NIB	Exc.	V.G.	Good	Fair	Poor
375	325	275	200	150	100

Model SXP Series

The Super X Pump is successor to Speed Pump series and features the same inertia-assisted action. Comes in 12 gauge only, with 3" chamber, 26" or 28" back-bored barrel with Invector choke tubes. Weight is approx. 6.8 lbs. Field grade model has Black Shadow composite stock. Waterfowl variation (shown) has full coverage Mossy Oak Duck Blind camo. Also available with 18", straight cylinder barrel as Defender model. Prices are for Black Shadow field model. **NOTE:** Add 20 percent for Waterfowl model, deduct 20 percent for Defender.

NIB	Exc.	V.G.	Good	Fair	Poor
400	360	325	275	225	150

Model 9410

A variation of the Model 94 lever-action rifle chambered for the .410-bore shotgun. Available in several versions. **SEE:** Model 9400 Series in the lever-action rifle section.

Model 1500 XTR

This is a gas-operated, semi-automatic shotgun chambered for 12 or 20 gauge, with a 28" vent rib barrel with screw-in chokes. The finish is blued, with a walnut stock. It was manufactured between 1978 and 1982.

NIB	Exc.	V.G.	Good	Fair	Poor
550	425	325	225	175	150

Super X Model 1

This is a self-compensating, gas-operated, semi-automatic shotgun chambered for 12 gauge. It was offered with a 26", 28", or 30" vent rib barrel with various chokes. It features all-steel construction and is blued, with a checkered walnut stock. It was manufactured between 1974 and 1981.

NIB	Exc.	V.G.	Good	Fair	Poor
—	800	675	525	400	250

Super X Model 1 Custom Competition

This is a custom-order trap or skeet gun that features the self compensating, gas-operated action. It is available in 12 gauge only from the Custom Shop. It is offered with a heavy degree of engraving on the receiver and a fancy, checkered walnut stock. Gold inlays are available and would add approximately 50 percent to the values given. This model was introduced in 1987.

NIB	Exc.	V.G.	Good	Fair	Poor
1450	1100	925	775	650	500

Super X2 3.5" Magnum

Introduced in 1999, this model is a gas-operated design chambered for 3.5" 12 gauge shells. Fitted with a black synthetic stock and choice of 24", 26" or 28" vent rib barrels. Invector chokes. Magazine capacity is five rounds. Weight is about 7.5 lbs. depending on barrel length. Matte black finish.

NIB	Exc.	V.G.	Good	Fair	Poor
950	875	700	525	450	300

Super X2 Turkey

Similar to the X2 Magnum but with 24" vent rib barrel with truglo sights. Extra-Full choke. Weight is about 7.25 lbs. Black synthetic stock. Introduced in 1999.

NIB	Exc.	V.G.	Good	Fair	Poor
950	875	700	525	450	300

Super X2 Turkey Mossy Oak Break-Up

Same as above but with Mossy Oak Break-Up camo on stock and gun. Introduced in 2000.

NIB	Exc.	V.G.	Good	Fair	Poor
1025	900	700	525	450	350

Super X2 NWTF Turkey

Introduced in 2005 this 3.5" 12 gauge gun is fitted with a 24" vent rib barrel with extra full extended choke tubes. Three dot TRUGLO sights. Mossy Oak camo stock. A brass NWTF medallion on the pistol grip cap. Weight is about 7.5 lbs.

NIB	Exc.	V.G.	Good	Fair	Poor
1235	950	1025	900	700	450

Super X2 Universal Hunter

Similar to the Super X2 Turkey but with a 26" barrel with Extra-Full choke tube. Weight is about 7.75 lbs. Introduced in 2002.

NIB	Exc.	V.G.	Good	Fair	Poor
1025	900	700	525	450	350

Super X2 Camo Waterfowl

Chambered for 12 gauge 3.5" shells and fitted with a 28" vent rib barrel, this model features a Mossy Oak camo finish. Weight is about 8 lbs. Introduced in 1999. In 2004 a New Shadow Grass camo pattern was added.

NIB	Exc.	V.G.	Good	Fair	Poor
1025	900	700	525	450	350

Super X2 Magnum Greenhead

Introduced in 2002, this model is chambered for the 12 gauge 3.5" shell and has a composite stock that is green in color. Fitted with 28" barrel. Weight is about 8 lbs.

NIB	Exc.	V.G.	Good	Fair	Poor
1025	900	700	525	450	350

Super X2 Magnum Field

This model is chambered for the 12 gauge 3" shell and is offered with either a walnut stock or black synthetic stock. Choice of 26" or 28" vent rib barrel with Invector chokes. Weight is about 7.25 lbs. Introduced in 1999.

NIB	Exc.	V.G.	Good	Fair	Poor
950	875	700	525	450	300

Super X2 Light Field

Checkered walnut stock with choice of 26" or 28" vent rib barrel with choke tubes are featured on this 12 gauge gun. Weight is about 6.5 lbs. Introduced in 2005.

Super X2 Cantilever Deer

This 12 gauge model has a 22" fully rifled barrel with fold-down rear sight and scope mount. Black composite stock. Weight is about 7.25 lbs. Introduced in 2002.

NIB	Exc.	V.G.	Good	Fair	Poor
950	875	700	525	450	300

Super X2 Practical

Introduced in 2002, this model is designed for competition shooting. Fitted with a 22" barrel with ghost ring sight and 8-round magazine. Black composite stock. Weight is about 8 lbs.

NIB	Exc.	V.G.	Good	Fair	Poor
1025	900	700	525	450	350

Super X2 Sporting Clays

Introduced in 2001, this model features a 12 gauge gun with choice of 28" or 30" barrels with high post rib. Barrels are back bore with Invector chokes. Adjustable comb. Weight is about 8 lbs.

NIB	Exc.	V.G.	Good	Fair	Poor
1200	950	750	575	500	350

Super X2 Sporting Clays Signature II

This 3" 12 gauge gun is fitted with a 30" barrel with choke tubes. The hardwood stock is painted black metallic. The receiver is a red anodized alloy. Weight is about 8.25 lbs. Introduced in 2005.

NIB	Exc.	V.G.	Good	Fair	Poor
1025	900	700	525	450	350

Super X2 Signature Red Sporting

This 12 gauge 3" shell model features a hardwood stock with red Dura-Touch coating. Fitted with a 30" vent rib barrel with five choke tubes. Weight is about 8 lbs. Introduced in 2003.

NIB	Exc.	V.G.	Good	Fair	Poor
950	875	700	525	450	300

SUPER X3 SERIES

Introduced in 2006, The Super X3 12 gauge features weight and recoil reducing features and a .742" back-bored barrel. It is available in a variety of configurations weighing under 7 lbs. in the 3" Field model and about 7.5 lbs. in composite, camo and 3.5" models. All models except Cantilever Deer included three choke tubes.

Super X3 Field

Walnut stock and 26" or 28" barrel.

NIB	Exc.	V.G.	Good	Fair	Poor
1200	950	750	575	500	350

Super X3 Composite

Matte black stock and fore-end. Available in 26" or 28" barrel and 3" or 3.5" chamber. **NOTE:** Add $100 for 3.5" model.

NIB	Exc.	V.G.	Good	Fair	Poor
1200	950	750	575	500	350

Super X3 Camo

Composite camo stock with 3.5" chamber. Available in various camo patterns with 26" and 28" barrel.

NIB	Exc.	V.G.	Good	Fair	Poor
1200	950	750	575	500	350

Super X3 Cantilever Deer

Slug gun with 22" barrel with cantilever scope mount and 3" chamber.

NIB	Exc.	V.G.	Good	Fair	Poor
950	875	700	525	450	300

Super X3 "Flanigun" Exhibition/Sporting

With a red receiver and fore-end cap, this is a duplicate of the gun used by exhibition shooter Patrick Flanigan but with a shorter magazine tube. It has a 3" chamber and 28" barrel.

NIB	Exc.	V.G.	Good	Fair	Poor
1200	950	750	575	500	350

Super X3 Classic Field

Introduced in 2008, the Classic Field is similar to the Super X3 Field but with traditional sharp checkering on pistol grip and fore-end. Barrel length is 26" or 28".

NIB	Exc.	V.G.	Good	Fair	Poor
950	875	700	525	450	300

Super X3 Turkey

New in 2008, this dedicated turkey model has a 3.5" chamber, 24" barrel, extra-full choke tube and complete coverage in Mossy Oak New Breakup camo. Price includes a TruGlo red-dot scope. Weight is 7.5 lbs.

NIB	Exc.	V.G.	Good	Fair	Poor
1200	950	750	575	500	350

Model 1400

This is a gas-operated, semi-automatic shotgun chambered for 12, 16 or 20 gauge. It was offered with a 26", 28" or 30" vent rib barrel with various chokes. The finish is blued, with a checkered walnut stock. It was manufactured between 1964 and 1981. The Hydrocoil plastic stock was available on this model and would add approximately 35 percent to the values given.

NIB	Exc.	V.G.	Good	Fair	Poor
450	350	300	250	200	125

New Model 1400

This is a gas-operated, semi-automatic shotgun chambered for 12 or 20 gauge. It is offered with a 22" or 28" vent rib barrel with screw-in chokes. The finish is blued, with a checkered walnut stock. It was introduced in 1989.

NIB	Exc.	V.G.	Good	Fair	Poor
450	350	300	250	200	125

Model 1400 Ranger

This is a utility-grade, gas-operated, semi-automatic shotgun chambered for 12 or 20 gauge. It is offered with a 28" vent rib barrel with screw-in chokes, as well as a 24" slug barrel with rifle sights. The finish is blued, with a checkered stock. A combination two-barrel set that includes the deer barrel would be worth approximately 20 percent additional. This model was introduced in 1983.

NIB	Exc.	V.G.	Good	Fair	Poor
400	300	250	200	150	100

Model 1400 Quail Unlimited

This 12 gauge semi-automatic shotgun model was introduced in 1993. It features compact engraved receiver with 26" vent rib barrel supplied with WinChoke tubes. Stock is checkered walnut. Gun weighs 7.25 lbs.

NIB	Exc.	V.G.	Good	Fair	Poor
400	300	250	200	150	100

Model 1400 Ranger Deer Combo

This model features a 12 gauge 22" smooth barrel and a 28" vent rib barrel with three WinChokes.

NIB	Exc.	V.G.	Good	Fair	Poor
400	300	250	200	150	100

Model 37A

Introduced in 1973. It is single-shot shotgun with exposed hammer. Offered in 12, 16, 20, and 28 gauge as well as .410 bore. All guns choked Full except youth model choked Modified. Walnut finish on hardwood stock. Pistol-grip cap with white spacer. Weight is about 6 lbs. About 395,000 were produced until 1980.

NIB	Exc.	V.G.	Good	Fair	Poor
—	350	250	225	175	115

Model 22

Introduced in 1975 this side-by-side shotgun was manufactured by Laurona in Spain to Winchester's specifications for the European market. It had an oil-finished stock with checkered pistol grip semi-beavertail forearm and hand engraved receiver. The finish was black chrome. The gun was fitted with double triggers, matted rib and offered in 12 gauge only with 28" barrels. It weighs 6-3/4 lbs. Rare.

NIB	Exc.	V.G.	Good	Fair	Poor
1250	950	700	550	400	200

Model 91

This over/under shotgun was built for Winchester by Laurona for its European markets. Offered in 12 gauge only with 28" barrels the barrels were fitted with a ventilated rib. The gun was offered with single or double triggers with hand-checkered walnut stock with oil finish and hand-engraved receiver. The finish was black chrome. Gun weighs 7-1/2 lbs. Rare.

NIB	Exc.	V.G.	Good	Fair	Poor
1100	800	600	500	400	200

Supreme Field

Introduced in 2000, this over/under gun is chambered for the 12 gauge 3" shell and fitted with 28" vent rib barrels with Invector chokes. Walnut stock with pistol grip and blued engraved receiver. Weight is about 7.5 lbs.

NIB	Exc.	V.G.	Good	Fair	Poor
1025	900	700	525	450	350

Supreme Sporting

Similar to the above model but fitted with a choice of 28" or 30" barrels chambered for 12 gauge 2.75" shells. Barrels are ported. Adjustable trigger. Polished silver receiver with blued barrels. Weight is about 7.5 lbs. Introduced in 2000.

NIB	Exc.	V.G.	Good	Fair	Poor
1200	950	750	575	500	350

Supreme Elegance

Introduced in 2003 this over/under model is chambered for the 12 gauge 3" shell. Choice of 26" or 28" vent rib barrels with three choke tubes. Grayed receiver with scroll and bird scenes. Weight is about 7 lbs. depending on barrel length.

NIB	Exc.	V.G.	Good	Fair	Poor
1400	1100	850	500	200	100

MODEL 23 SERIES

Model 23 XTR

This is a side-by-side, double-barrel shotgun chambered for 12 or 20 gauge. It is offered with 25.5", 26", 28" or 30" vent rib barrels with 3" chambers and various choke combinations. It is a boxlock gun that features a single trigger and automatic ejectors. It is scroll-engraved with a coin-finished receiver, blued barrels and a checkered, select walnut stock. It was introduced in 1978. This model is available in a number of configurations that differ in the amount of ornamentation and the quality of materials and workmanship utilized in their construction. These models and their values are listed. Discontinued.

NIB	Exc.	V.G.	Good	Fair	Poor
2000	1800	1400	1050	850	500

Pigeon Grade

With WinChokes.

NIB	Exc.	V.G.	Good	Fair	Poor
—	2300	1950	1600	1300	5000

Pigeon Grade Lightweight

Straight stock.

NIB	Exc.	V.G.	Good	Fair	Poor
—	2450	2100	1750	1400	500

Model 23 Golden Quail

This series was available in 28 gauge and .410, as well as 12 or 20 gauge. It features 25.5" barrels that are choked improved cylinder/modified. It features a straight-grip, English-style stock with a recoil pad. This series was discontinued in 1987. **NOTE:** Add 20 percent for 20 gauge, 50 percent for 28 gauge or .410 bore.

NIB	Exc.	V.G.	Good	Fair	Poor
3000	2700	2400	2000	1200	500

Model 23 Light Duck

This version is chambered for 20 gauge and was offered with a 28" Full and Full-choked barrel. There were 500 manufactured in 1985.

NIB	Exc.	V.G.	Good	Fair	Poor
3100	2900	2600	1800	800	500

Model 23 Heavy Duck

This version is chambered for 12 gauge with 30" Full and Full-choked barrels. There were 500 manufactured in 1984.

NIB	Exc.	V.G.	Good	Fair	Poor
3200	3000	2600	1800	800	500

Model 21

This is a high-quality, side-by-side, double-barrel shotgun that features a boxlock action and is chambered for 12, 16, 20, and 28 gauges, as well as .410. See previous Model 21 entry.

MODEL 101 SERIES

Model 101 Field Grade

This is an over/under, double-barrel shotgun chambered for 12, 20 and 28 gauge, as well as .410. It was offered with 26", 28" or 30" vent rib barrels with various choke combinations. Since 1983 screw-in chokes have been standard and models so furnished would be worth approximately $50 additional. This is a boxlock gun with a single-selective trigger and automatic ejectors. The receiver is engraved; the finish, blued with a checkered walnut stock. It was manufactured between 1963 and 1987. **NOTE:** 28 gauge add 40 percent; .410 add 50 percent.

NIB	Exc.	V.G.	Good	Fair	Poor
1500	1350	1200	1050	850	500

Waterfowl Model

This version of the Model 101 is chambered for 12 gauge with 3" chambers. It has 30" or 32" vent rib barrels and a matte finish.

NIB	Exc.	V.G.	Good	Fair	Poor
—	1900	1675	1400	800	400

Model 101 Magnum

This version is similar to the Field Grade, chambered for 12 or 20 gauge with 3" Magnum chambers. It was offered with 30" barrels with various chokes. The stock is furnished with a recoil pad. It was manufactured between 1966 and 1981.

Model 101 Skeet Grade

This version was offered with 26" skeet-bored barrels with a competition rib and a skeet-type walnut stock. It was manufactured between 1966 and 1984.

NIB	Exc.	V.G.	Good	Fair	Poor
—	1500	1250	1050	850	500

Model 101 Three-Gauge Skeet Set

This combination set was offered with three barrels, chambered for 20 and 28 gauge, as well as .410. It was furnished with a fitted case and manufactured between 1974 and 1984.

NIB	Exc.	V.G.	Good	Fair	Poor
—	3500	2600	1800	800	500

Model 101 Trap Grade

This version is chambered for 12 gauge only and was offered with 30" or 32" competition ribbed barrels, choked for trap shooting. It is furnished with a competition-type stock. It was manufactured between 1966 and 1984.

NIB	Exc.	V.G.	Good	Fair	Poor
—	1400	1100	925	700	500

Model 101 Pigeon Grade

This is a more deluxe-engraved version of the Model 101, chambered for 12, 20, or 28 gauge, as well as .410. It features a coin-finished receiver with a fancy checkered walnut stock. It was introduced in 1974.

NIB	Exc.	V.G.	Good	Fair	Poor
—	3000	2600	1800	1275	750

Model 101 Super Pigeon Grade

This is a deluxe version of the Model 101, chambered for 12 gauge. It is heavily engraved with several gold inlays. The receiver is blued, and it features a high-grade walnut stock with fleur-de-lis checkering. It was imported between 1985 and 1987.

NIB	Exc.	V.G.	Good	Fair	Poor
—	5500	4200	3500	2800	1000

Model 101 Diamond Grade

This is a competition model, chambered for all four gauges. It was offered in either a trap or skeet configuration with screw-in chokes, an engraved matte-finished receiver, and a select checkered walnut stock. The skeet model features recoil-reducing muzzle vents.

NIB	Exc.	V.G.	Good	Fair	Poor
—	2000	1625	1250	900	680

Model 101 Pigeon Grade Trap

This deluxe dedicated trap gun was introduced in 2008. It features a Grade III/IV walnut stock with a high-gloss finish and a raised comb. Barrels are 30" or 32" . Three choke tubes included. Weight is 7.5 to 7.75 lbs. Add 5 percent for adjustable comb stock.

NIB	Exc.	V.G.	Good	Fair	Poor
1750	1500	1300	975	600	400

Model 501 Grand European

This is an over/under, double-barrel shotgun chambered for 12 or 20 gauge. It was available in trap or skeet configurations and was offered with a 27", 30", or 32" vent rib barrel. It is heavily engraved and matte-finished, with a select checkered walnut stock. It was manufactured between 1981 and 1986.

NIB	Exc.	V.G.	Good	Fair	Poor
—	2700	2100	1700	1300	500

Model 501 Presentation Grade

This is a deluxe version chambered in 12 gauge only. It is ornately engraved and gold-inlaid. The stock is made out of presentation-grade walnut. It was furnished with a fitted case. It was manufactured between 1984 and 1987.

NIB	Exc.	V.G.	Good	Fair	Poor
—	3400	2750	2200	1600	500

Select Model 101 Field

This Belgian-made version of Winchesters popular Model 101 was introduced in 2007. It features Grade II/III walnut, 26" or 28" barrels and deep-relief engraving on the blued receiver that mimics the original 101. Classic white line spacer and vented recoil pad. Three choke tubes. Weight is about 7.2 lbs. Introduced in 2007.

NIB	Exc.	V.G.	Good	Fair	Poor
1600	1400	1150	900	650	400

Select Model 101 Sporting

Similar to Field model plus competition features such as a wider rib, adjustable trigger, white mid-bead and five extended Signature choke tubes. Ported barrels are 28", 30" or 32".

NIB	Exc.	V.G.	Good	Fair	Poor
1675	1475	1225	1050	775	450

Combination Gun

This is an over/under rifle/shotgun combination chambered for 12 gauge over .222, .223, .30-06, and the 9.3x74R cartridges. It features 25" barrels. The shotgun tube has a screw-in choke. It is engraved in the fashion of the Model 501 Grand European and features a select checkered walnut stock. It was manufactured between 1983 and 1985.

NIB	Exc.	V.G.	Good	Fair	Poor
—	3000	2500	1600	1200	700

Express Rifle

This is an over/under, double-barreled rifle chambered for the .257 Roberts, .270, 7.7x65R, .30-06, and the 9.3x74R cartridges. It features 23.5" barrels with a solid rib and express sights. It is engraved with game scenes and has a satin-finished receiver. The stock is checkered select walnut. It was manufactured in 1984 and 1985.

NIB	Exc.	V.G.	Good	Fair	Poor
—	3500	3000	2100	1700	900

Model 96 Xpert

This is a utility-grade, over/under, double-barrel shotgun that is mechanically similar to the Model 101. Chambered for 12 or 20 gauge and offered with various barrel lengths and choke combinations. It has a boxlock action with single-selective trigger and automatic ejectors. The plain receiver is blued, with a checkered walnut stock. Manufactured between 1976 and 1982. A competition-grade model for trap or skeet was also available and would be worth approximately the same amount.

NIB	Exc.	V.G.	Good	Fair	Poor
—	1025	900	700	525	350

Model 1001 Field

A new addition to the U.S.R.A. product line for 1993. This over/under shotgun was available in 12 gauge only, with a 28" ventilated rib barrel furnished with WinPlus choke tubes. A walnut checkered pistol stock is standard. The finish is blued with scroll engraving on the receiver. The receiver top has a matte finish. The gun weighs 7 lbs. subject to a 1995 recall.

NIB	Exc.	V.G.	Good	Fair	Poor
1000	850	700	500	350	200

Model 1001 Sporting Clays I & II

This model features different stock dimensions, a fuller pistol grip, a radiused recoil pad, and a wider vent rib fitted on a 28" barrel (Sporting Clays I model, the Sporting Clays II features a 30" barrel). Comes complete with choke tubes. The frame has a silver nitrate finish and special engraving featuring a flying clay target. Introduced in 1993. Gun weighs 7.75 lbs. Subject to a 1995 recall.

NIB	Exc.	V.G.	Good	Fair	Poor
1100	950	800	600	350	200

SELECT OVER/UNDER SERIES

This series of over/under shotguns was introduced into the Winchester line in 2004. The series features a low-profile receiver with unique engraving, lightweight barrels and contoured walnut stocks with distinctive checkering patterns.

Select Midnight

High-gloss bluing on receiver and barrels with gold accent game bird pattern on both sides and bottom of the receiver. Satin finished Grade II/III walnut. Oval checkering pattern. Choke tubes. Introduced 2006. Available in 26" and 28" barrels.

NIB	Exc.	V.G.	Good	Fair	Poor
1600	1400	1150	900	650	400

Select White Field

An engraved silver nitride receiver is featured on both versions of the White Field. The Traditional model has traditional checkering and the Extreme model features the Select Series' unique oval checkering pattern. Both versions have choke tubes and are available in 26" and 28" barrels. Introduced 2006.

NIB	Exc.	V.G.	Good	Fair	Poor
1300	1200	1100	900	650	400

Select Energy Sporting

Chambered for the 12 gauge 2.75" shell and offered with a choice of 28", 30", or 32" vent rib barrels with choke tubes and porting. Truglo front sight. Adjustable trigger shoe. Walnut stock with recoil pad. Weight is about 7.62 lbs. Adjustable comb available. **NOTE:** Add $150 for adjustable comb.

NIB	Exc.	V.G.	Good	Fair	Poor
1600	1400	1150	900	650	400

Select Energy Trap

This 12 gauge model is fitted with a choice of 30" or 32" back-bored ported barrels. Wide vent rib. Choke tubes. Walnut stock with Monte Carlo comb. Weight is about 7.8 lbs. Adjustable comb available. **NOTE:** Add $150 for adjustable comb.

NIB	Exc.	V.G.	Good	Fair	Poor
1600	1400	1150	900	650	400

Select Elegance (Supreme)

This 12 gauge gun features full coverage engraving with game scenes. Choice of 26" or 28" vent rib barrels with choke tubes. Walnut stock with unique checkering pattern. Weight is about 7 lbs.

NIB	Exc.	V.G.	Good	Fair	Poor
1800	1400	1150	900	650	400

Select Field

This 12 gauge 3" gun is fitted with a choice of 26" or 28" vent ribs barrels with choke tubes. Engraved receiver with oval checkering pattern. Weight is about 7 lbs.

NIB	Exc.	V.G.	Good	Fair	Poor
1400	1200	950	700	450	300

Select Traditional Elegance

Similar to the Extreme Elegance but with traditional checkering pattern.

NIB	Exc.	V.G.	Good	Fair	Poor
1400	1200	950	700	450	300

Select Deluxe Field

New in 2007, this Belgian-made 3" 12 gauge features an engraved steel receiver with silver nitride finish and Grade II walnut. Barrels are 26", 28" or 30". Three chokes included. Weight is about 7.25 lbs.

NIB	Exc.	V.G.	Good	Fair	Poor
1600	1400	1150	900	650	400

Select Platinum Field

This 3" 12 gauge was introduced in 2007. It is Belgian-made and comes with 28" or 30" barrels, Grade II/III walnut and deep relief engraving. Includes three Signature extended choke tubes and hard case.

NIB	Exc.	V.G.	Good	Fair	Poor
2050	1800	1575	1200	900	500

Select Platinum Sporting

Similar to the Platinum Field with 28", 30" or 32" ported barrels, wide rib, adjustable trigger shoe and five Signature extended choke tubes and hard case.

NIB	Exc.	V.G.	Good	Fair	Poor
2200	1950	1725	1375	1075	500

WINCHESTER COMMEMORATIVE RIFLES

Beginning in the early 1960s, Winchester produced a number of special Model 1894 rifles and carbines that commemorated certain historic events, places or individuals. In some cases they are slightly embellished and in others are quite ornate. If a Winchester commemorative rifle has been cocked leaving a line on the hammer or the lever, many collectors will show little or no interest in its acquisition. If they have been fired, they will realize little premium over a standard, Post-1964 Model 94. A number of commemorative's have been ordered by outside concerns and are technically not factory issues. Most have less collectibility than the factory-issued models. There are a number of concerns that specialize in marketing the total range of Winchester commemorative rifles. Listed are the factory-issue commemorative's with their current value, issue price and the number manufactured.

1964 Wyoming Diamond Jubilee—Carbine

NIB	Issue	Amt. Mfg.
1200	100	1,500

1966 Centennial—Rifle

NIB	Issue	Amt. Mfg.
700	125	102,309

1966 Centennial—Carbine

NIB	Issue	Amt. Mfg.
700	125	102,309

1966 Nebraska Centennial—Rifle

NIB	Issue	Amt. Mfg.
1200	100	2,500

1967 Canadian Centennial—Rifle

NIB	Issue	Amt. Mfg.
650	125	—

1967 Canadian Centennial—Carbine

NIB	Issue	Amt. Mfg.
650	125	90,301

1967 Alaskan Purchase Centennial—Carbine

NIB	Issue	Amt. Mfg.
1250	125	1,500

1968 Illinois Sesquicentennial—Carbine

NIB	Issue	Amt. Mfg.
600	110	37,648

1968 Buffalo Bill—Carbine

NIB	Issue	Amt. Mfg.
700	130	112,923

1968 Buffalo Bill—Rifle

NIB	Issue	Amt. Mfg.
700	130	—

1968 Buffalo Bill "1 or 300" —Rifle

NIB	Issue	Amt. Mfg.
3500	1000	300

1969 Theodore Roosevelt—Rifle

NIB	Issue	Amt. Mfg.
700	135	—

1969 Theodore Roosevelt—Carbine

NIB	Issue	Amt. Mfg.
700	135	52,386

1969 Golden Spike Carbine

NIB	Issue	Amt. Mfg.
700	120	69,996

1970 Cowboy Commemorative Carbine

NIB	Issue	Amt. Mfg.
750	125	27,549

1970 Cowboy Carbine "1 of 300"

NIB	Issue	Amt. Mfg.
3500	1000	300

1970 Northwest Territories (Canadian)

NIB	Issue	Amt. Mfg.
1000	150	2,500

1970 Northwest Territories Deluxe (Canadian)

NIB	Issue	Amt. Mfg.
1300	250	500

1970 Lone Star—Rifle

NIB	Issue	Amt. Mfg.
700	140	—

1970 Lone Star—Carbine

NIB	Issue	Amt. Mfg.
700	140	38,385

1971 NRA Centennial—Rifle

NIB	Issue	Amt. Mfg.
700	150	21,000

1971 NRA Centennial—Musket

NIB	Issue	Amt. Mfg.
700	150	23,400

1971 Yellow Boy

NIB	Issue	Amt. Mfg.
1300	250	4,900

1971 Royal Canadian Mounted Police (Canadian)

NIB	Issue	Amt. Mfg.
900	190	9,500

1971 Mounted Police (Canadian)

NIB	Issue	Amt. Mfg.
1000	190	5,100

1971 Mounted Police, Presentation

NIB	Issue	Amt. Mfg.
10000	—	10

1974 Texas Ranger—Carbine

NIB	Issue	Amt. Mfg.
800	135	4,850

1974 Texas Ranger Presentation Model

NIB	Issue	Amt. Mfg.
3500	1000	150

1974 Apache (Canadian)

NIB	Issue	Amt. Mfg.
900	150	8,600

1974 Commanche (Canadian)

NIB	Issue	Amt. Mfg.
900	230	11,500

1974 Klondike Gold Rush (Canadian)

NIB	Issue	Amt. Mfg.
900	240	10,200

1975 Klondike Gold Rush—Dawson City Issue (Canadian)

NIB	Issue	Amt. Mfg.
8500	—	25

1976 Sioux (Canadian)

NIB	Issue	Amt. Mfg.
900	280	10,000

1976 Little Bighorn (Canadian)

NIB	Issue	Amt. Mfg.
1000	300	11,000

1976 U.S. Bicentennial Carbine

NIB	Issue	Amt. Mfg.
800	325	19,999

1977 Wells Fargo

NIB	Issue	Amt. Mfg.
800	350	19,999

1977 Legendary Lawman

NIB	Issue	Amt. Mfg.
800	375	19,999

1977 Limited Edition I

NIB	Issue	Amt. Mfg.
1600	1500	1,500

1977 Cheyenne—.22 Cal. (Canadian)

NIB	Issue	Amt. Mfg.
1100	320	5,000

1977 Cheyenne—.44-40 Cal. (Canadian)

NIB	Issue	Amt. Mfg.
900	300	11,225

1977 Cherokee—.22 Cal. (Canadian)

NIB	Issue	Amt. Mfg.
1100	385	3,950

1977 Cherokee—.30-30 Cal. (Canadian)

NIB	Issue	Amt. Mfg.
900	385	9,000

1978 "One of One Thousand" (European)

NIB	Issue	Amt. Mfg.
8250	5000	250

1978 Antler Game Carbine

NIB	Issue	Amt. Mfg.
800	375	19,999

1979 Limited Edition II

NIB	Issue	Amt. Mfg.
1600	1500	1,500

1979 Legendary Frontiersman Rifle

NIB	Issue	Amt. Mfg.
800	425	19,999

1979 Matched Set of 1,000

NIB	Issue	Amt. Mfg.
2800	3000	1,000

1979 Bat Masterson (Canadian)

NIB	Issue	Amt. Mfg.
900	650	8,000

1980 Alberta Diamond Jubilee (Canadian)

NIB	Issue	Amt. Mfg.
1000	650	2,700

1980 Alberta Diamond Jubilee Deluxe (Canadian)

NIB	Issue	Amt. Mfg.
1800	1900	300

1980 Saskatchewan Diamond Jubilee (Canadian)

NIB	Issue	Amt. Mfg.
1000	695	2,700

1980 Saskatchewan Diamond Jubilee Deluxe (Canadian)

NIB	Issue	Amt. Mfg.
1800	1995	300

1980 Oliver Winchester

NIB	Issue	Amt. Mfg.
900	375	19,999

1981 U.S. Border Patrol

NIB	Issue	Amt. Mfg.
1000	1195	1,000

1981 U.S. Border Patrol—Member's Model

NIB	Issue	Amt. Mfg.
1000	695	800

1981 Calgary Stampede (Canadian)

NIB	Issue	Amt. Mfg.
1800	2200	1,000

1981 Canadian Pacific Centennial (Canadian)

NIB	Issue	Amt. Mfg.
900	800	2,000

1981 Canadian Pacific Centennial Presentation (Canadian)

NIB	Issue	Amt. Mfg.
1800	2200	300

1981 Canadian Pacific Employee's Model (Canadian)

NIB	Issue	Amt. Mfg.
900	800	2,000

1981 John Wayne (Canadian)

NIB	Issue	Amt. Mfg.
1600	600	1,000

1981 John Wayne

NIB	Issue	Amt. Mfg.
1600	600	49,000

1981 Duke

NIB	Issue	Amt. Mfg.
3750	2250	1,000

1981 John Wayne "1 of 300" Set

NIB	Issue	Amt. Mfg.
7500	10000	300

1982 Great Western Artist I

NIB	Issue	Amt. Mfg.
1550	2200	999

1982 Great Western Artist II

NIB	Issue	Amt. Mfg.
1500	2200	999

1982 Annie Oakley

NIB	Issue	Amt. Mfg.
1300	699	6,000

1983 Chief Crazy Horse

NIB	Issue	Amt. Mfg.
800	600	19,999

1983 American Bald Eagle

NIB	Issue	Amt. Mfg.
800	895	2,800

1983 American Bald Eagle—Deluxe

NIB	Issue	Amt. Mfg.
4000	2995	200

1983 Oklahoma Diamond Jubilee

NIB	Issue	Amt. Mfg.
1750	2250	1,001

1984 Winchester—Colt Commemorative Set

NIB	Issue	Amt. Mfg.
2750	3995	3,250

1985 Boy Scout 75th Anniversary .22 Cal.

NIB	Issue	Amt. Mfg.
1100	615	15,000

1985 Boy Scout 75th Anniversary—Eagle Scout

NIB	Issue	Amt. Mfg.
6000	2140	1,000

Texas Sesquicentennial Model—Rifle .38-55 Cal.

NIB	Issue	Amt. Mfg.
2750	2995	1,500

Texas Sesquicentennial Model—Carbine .38-55 Cal.

NIB	Issue	Amt. Mfg.
1000	695	15,000

Texas Sesquicentennial Model Set with Bowie Knife

NIB	Issue	Amt. Mfg.
6500	7995	150

1986 Model 94 Ducks Unlimited

NIB	Issue	Amt. Mfg.
900	—	2,800

1986 Statue of Liberty

NIB	Issue	Amt. Mfg.
9000	6500	100

1986 120th Anniversary Model—Carbine .44-40 Cal.

NIB	Issue	Amt. Mfg.
950	995	1,000

1986 European 1 of 1,000 Second Series (European)

NIB	Issue	Amt. Mfg.
1000	6000	150

1987 U.S. Constitution 200th Anniversary .44-40

NIB	Issue	Amt. Mfg.
15000	12000	17

1990 Wyoming Centennial—30-30

NIB	Issue	Amt. Mfg.
1600	895	500

1991 Winchester 125th Anniversary

NIB	Issue	Amt. Mfg.
6500	4995	61

1992 Arapaho—30-30

NIB	Issue	Amt. Mfg.
1600	895	500

1992 Ontario Conservation—30-30

NIB	Issue	Amt. Mfg.
1600	1195	400

1992 Kentucky Bicentennial—30-30

NIB	Issue	Amt. Mfg.
1600	995	500

1993 Nez Perce—30-30

NIB	Issue	Amt. Mfg.
1600	995	600

1995 Florida Sesquicentennial Carbine

NIB	Issue	Amt. Mfg.
1600	1195	360

1996 Wild Bill Hickok Carbine

NIB	Issue	Amt. Mfg.
1600	1195	350

2008 John Wayne 1892 .44-40

NIB	Issue	Amt. Mfg.
2000	2000	N/A

WINDSOR
Windsor, Vermont
Robbins & Lawrence
Hartford, Connecticut

Windsor Rifle-Musket

A .577 caliber single-shot percussion rifle with a 39" round barrel secured by three barrel bands. The lock marked "Windsor". Rifles of this pattern were contracted for by the British Government. The lock and barrel finished in the white, brass furniture and a walnut stock. Approximately 16,000 were made from 1855 to 1858.

NIB	Exc.	V.G.	Good	Fair	Poor
—	—	3750	3000	950	300

WINSLOW ARMS CO.
Camden, South Carolina

Bolt Action Rifle

A high-grade, semi-custom sporting rifle built upon a number of actions and offered in all popular calibers from .17 Remington to the .458 Winchester Magnum with a 24" barrel and a 3-shot magazine. The larger Magnum models have a 26" barrel and a 2-shot magazine. Two basic stocks are offered—the Conventional Bushmaster, which features a standard pistol grip and a beavertail forearm; and also the Plainsmaster, which has a full curled, hooked pistol grip and a wide, flat beavertail forearm. Both have Monte Carlo-style stocks with recoil pads and sling swivels. Offered in a choice of popular woods with rosewood fore-end tips and pistol gripcaps. Eight different grades of this rifle are available and the following lists the values applicable for each.

Commander Grade

Figured walnut stock. Rosewood forearm tip and grip cap. White line recoil pad. FN Supreme action.

NIB	Exc.	V.G.	Good	Fair	Poor
—	1450	1050	925	700	550

Regal Grade

All features of Commander Grade plus ivory and ebony inlay on stock, French-style checkering, jeweled bolt.

NIB	Exc.	V.G.	Good	Fair	Poor
—	2200	1800	1225	900	600

Regent Grade

As above with addition of hand-carved checkering.

NIB	Exc.	V.G.	Good	Fair	Poor
—	2375	1850	1250	900	600

Regimental Grade

As above but with addition of basket weave carving, two ivory stock inlays and large ivory and ebony inlay on both side of butt stock with animal silhouette.

NIB	Exc.	V.G.	Good	Fair	Poor
—	3000	2200	1500	1200	650

Crown Grade

As above but with more elaborate ivory inlays on stock.

NIB	Exc.	V.G.	Good	Fair	Poor
—	3700	2550	1800	1500	650

Royal Grade

As above but with addition even more elaborate stock carving and ivory and ebony inlay.

NIB	Exc.	V.G.	Good	Fair	Poor
—	4500	3250	2000	1600	650

Imperial Grade

As above but with addition of engraved barrel from receiver to 11" forward. Engraved receiver ring, bolt handle and trigger guard. Engraved scope mounts and rings.

NIB	Exc.	V.G.	Good	Fair	Poor
—	5000	3750	2500	2000	700

Emperor Grade

As above but with addition of gold raised relief animals engraved receiver and forward part of barrel with muzzle tip engraved engraved as well. Highest Winslow grade.

NIB	Exc.	V.G.	Good	Fair	Poor
—	6250	5000	4000	3000	700

WISEMAN, BILL & CO.
Bryan, Texas

Rifle

A custom order bolt-action rifle utilizing a Sako action, McMillan stainless steel barrel and laminated stock. The action components Teflon coated. It is made in four styles: the Hunter, Hunter Deluxe, Maverick, and the Varminter.

NIB	Exc.	V.G.	Good	Fair	Poor
—	2500	2150	1750	1500	600

Silhouette Pistol

A custom made single-shot pistol produced in a variety of calibers with a 14" fluted stainless steel barrel and laminated pistol-grip stock. Furnished without sights. Introduced in 1989.

NIB	Exc.	V.G.	Good	Fair	Poor
—	1750	1450	1100	800	600

WITNESS
See—European American Armory

WOLF SPORTING PISTOLS
Importer—Handgunner Gunshop
Topton, Pennsylvania

Wolf SV Target

Chambered for 9x19, 9x21, 9x23, .38 Super, .40 S&W or .45 ACP. Barrel is 4.5" long. Weight is 44 oz. Many special features. Built in Austria. Price listed is for basic pistol. A number of special order items are offered. Check with importer before a sale. First imported in 1998.

NIB	Exc.	V.G.	Good	Fair	Poor
2000	1600	1250	1000	750	600

Wolf SV Match

Chambered for 9x19, 9x21, 9x23, .38 Super, .40 S&W or .45 ACP. Barrel is 5.5" long. Weight is 44 oz. Many special features. Built in Austria. Price listed is for basic pistol. A number of special order items are offered. Check with importer before a sale. First imported in 1998.

NIB	Exc.	V.G.	Good	Fair	Poor
2000	1600	1250	1000	750	600

WOODWARD, JAMES & SONS
London, England

Prior to WWII, this company produced a variety of boxlock and sidelock shotguns that are regarded as some of the best made. Prospective purchasers should secure a qualified appraisal prior to acquisition.

WURFFLEIN, ANDREW & WILLIAM
Philadelphia, Pennsylvania

Pocket Pistol

A .41 caliber percussion single-shot pocket pistol with either a 2.5" or 3" barrel, German silver furniture and checkered walnut stock. The lock marked "A. Wurfflein / Phila." Manufactured during the 1850s and 1860s.

NIB	Exc.	V.G.	Good	Fair	Poor
—	—	2600	1750	700	200

Single-Shot Target Pistol

A .22 caliber single-shot pistol with half-octagonal barrels measuring from 8" to 16" in length. The barrel pivots downward for loading and is marked "W. Wurfflein Philad'a Pa. U.S.A. Patented June 24th, 1884". Blued with walnut grips. This model is also available with a detachable shoulder stock, which if present, would add approximately 35 percent to the values listed. Manufactured from 1884 to 1890.

NIB	Exc.	V.G.	Good	Fair	Poor
—	—	2600	1750	700	200

Single-Shot Rifle

A single-shot rifle produced in a variety of calibers with octagonal barrels of 24" to 28" length. This rifle was available with a wide variety of optional features.

NIB	Exc.	V.G.	Good	Fair	Poor
—	—	2400	1250	350	150

Mid-range Model

As above, with a 28" or 30" half-octagonal barrel.

NIB	Exc.	V.G.	Good	Fair	Poor
—	—	4250	3000	950	400

Model No. 25

The highest grade rifle manufactured by Wurfflein.

NIB	Exc.	V.G.	Good	Fair	Poor
—	—	4500	3500	1250	600

XL
HOPKINS & ALLEN
Norwich, Connecticut

Derringer

A .41 caliber spur trigger single-shot pistol with a 2.75" octagonal barrel and either iron or brass frame. Blued, nickel-plated with rosewood grips. The barrel marked "XL Derringer". Manufactured during the 1870s.

NIB	Exc.	V.G.	Good	Fair	Poor
—	1650	1295	950	500	150

Vest Pocket Derringer

As above, in .22 caliber with a 2.25" round barrel and normally full nickel-plated. The barrel marked "XL Vest Pocket". Manufactured from 1870s to 1890s.

NIB	Exc.	V.G.	Good	Fair	Poor
—	—	1350	750	325	125

XPERT
HOPKINS & ALLEN
Norwich, Connecticut

Xpert Derringer

A .22 or .30 caliber spur trigger single-shot pistol with round barrels, 2.25" to 6" in length and a nickel-plated finish with rosewood grips. The breechblock pivots to the left side for loading. The barrel marked "Xpert-Pat. Sep. 23. 1878". Manufactured during the 1870s.

NIB	Exc.	V.G.	Good	Fair	Poor
—	—	875	700	400	125

Xpert Pocket Rifle

Similar to the derringer with the same size frame but fitted with a 7.5" barrel and chambered for the .22 cartridge, as well as the .30 caliber rimfire. Supplied with wire stock. Values are for gun with stock. Produced from about 1870 to 1890s.

NIB	Exc.	V.G.	Good	Fair	Poor
—	—	1475	1150	500	150

Z

Z-B RIFLE CO.
Brno, Czechoslovakia

Model ZKW-465 Varmint Rifle

A Mauser bolt-action rifle chambered for the .22 Hornet cartridge. It has a 23" barrel with a three-leaf, folding rear sight. It is offered standard with double-set triggers. The finish is blued, with a select walnut checkered stock.

NIB	Exc.	V.G.	Good	Fair	Poor
—	1600	1150	975	800	500

ZANOTTI, FABIO
Brescia, Italy

Model 625

A 12 to .410 bore boxlock double-barrel shotgun with automatic ejectors and single-selective trigger. Blued with checkered walnut stock.

NIB	Exc.	V.G.	Good	Fair	Poor
6500	5200	4700	3500	2500	500

Model 626

As above, engraved with either scroll work or hunting scenes.

NIB	Exc.	V.G.	Good	Fair	Poor
7000	5700	5200	4000	2800	500

Giacinto

An external hammer boxlock shotgun produced in a variety of gauges with double triggers.

NIB	Exc.	V.G.	Good	Fair	Poor
6500	5200	4700	3500	2500	500

Maxim

Similar to the Model 625, but fitted with detachable sidelocks.

NIB	Exc.	V.G.	Good	Fair	Poor
7000	5700	5200	4000	2800	500

Edward

As above, but more intricately engraved.

NIB	Exc.	V.G.	Good	Fair	Poor
12000	9000	6500	4500	3000	1500

Cassiano I

As above, with exhibition grade engraving.

NIB	Exc.	V.G.	Good	Fair	Poor
13000	9000	7000	6000	4000	2000

Cassiano II

As above, with gold inlays.

NIB	Exc.	V.G.	Good	Fair	Poor
14500	12000	9500	7000	5000	2500

Cassiano Executive

A strictly custom-made shotgun produced to the client's specifications.

NIB	Exc.	V.G.	Good	Fair	Poor
45000	—	—	—	—	—

ZEHNER, E. WAFFENFABRIK
Suhl, Germany

Zehna

A 6.35mm semi-automatic pistol with a 2.5" barrel and 5-shot magazine. The slide marked "Zehna DRPA", and the caliber on later production models. Blued with a black plastic grips bearing the monogram "EZ". Approximately 20,000 were made from 1921 to 1927.

NIB	Exc.	V.G.	Good	Fair	Poor
—	395	300	250	175	100

ZEPHYR
Eibar, Spain
Importer—Stoegers

Woodlander II

A 12 or 20 gauge boxlock shotgun with varying barrel lengths, double triggers and extractors. Blued with a walnut stock.

NIB	Exc.	V.G.	Good	Fair	Poor
600	450	400	300	200	100

Uplander

A 12, 16, 20, 28 or .410 bore sidelock double-barrel shotgun with varying barrel lengths, double triggers, and automatic ejectors. Blued with a walnut stock.

NIB	Exc.	V.G.	Good	Fair	Poor
850	700	500	400	300	150

Upland King

As above, in 12 or 16 gauge with ventilated-rib barrels.

NIB	Exc.	V.G.	Good	Fair	Poor
1150	800	700	600	400	250

Vandalia

A 12 gauge single-barrel trap gun with a 32" full choked barrel. Blued with a walnut stock.

NIB	Exc.	V.G.	Good	Fair	Poor
750	600	550	450	300	150

Sterlingworth II

Identical to the Woodlander, but with sidelocks.

NIB	Exc.	V.G.	Good	Fair	Poor
850	700	550	450	300	150

Victor Special

A 12 gauge boxlock double-barrel shotgun with 25", 28", or 30" barrels, double triggers and extractors. Blued with a walnut stock.

NIB	Exc.	V.G.	Good	Fair	Poor
525	400	300	250	175	100

Thunderbird

A 10 gauge magnum boxlock double-barrel shotgun with 32" full choked barrels, double triggers, and automatic ejectors. Blued with a walnut stock.

NIB	Exc.	V.G.	Good	Fair	Poor
950	700	600	500	400	200

Honker

A 10 gauge magnum single-barrel shotgun with a 36" full choked and ventilated rib barrel. Blued with a walnut stock.

NIB	Exc.	V.G.	Good	Fair	Poor
600	450	400	300	200	100

ZM WEAPONS
Bernardton, Massachusetts

LR-300 Sport Rifle

This is a highly modified AR-15 chambered for the .223 cartridge. It is fitted with a 16.25" barrel and a true folding stock. A ghost ring rear sight and an adjustable post front sight with tritium insert is standard. Weight is approximately 7.2 pounds. Introduced in 1997.

NIB	Exc.	V.G.	Good	Fair	Poor
—	1600	1200	950	775	500

ZOLI USA, ANGELO
Brescia, Italy

Slide-Action Shotgun

A 12 gauge magnum slide-action shotgun produced with a variety of barrel lengths with detachable choke tubes. Blued with a walnut stock.

NIB	Exc.	V.G.	Good	Fair	Poor
400	300	250	200	150	100

Diano I

A 12, 20 or .410 bore single-shot folding barrel shotgun. Produced in a variety of barrel lengths. Blued with a walnut stock.

NIB	Exc.	V.G.	Good	Fair	Poor
175	100	90	80	60	40

Diano II

As above, but with a bottom lever instead of a top release lever.

NIB	Exc.	V.G.	Good	Fair	Poor
175	100	90	80	60	40

Apache

A 12 gauge magnum lever-action shotgun with a 20" barrel fitted with detachable choke tubes. Blued with a walnut stock.

NIB	Exc.	V.G.	Good	Fair	Poor
500	400	350	300	250	150

Quail Special

A .410 magnum bore double-barrel shotgun with 28" barrels and a single trigger. Blued with a walnut stock.

NIB	Exc.	V.G.	Good	Fair	Poor
325	200	150	125	100	75

Falcon II

As above with 26" or 28" barrels and double triggers.

NIB	Exc.	V.G.	Good	Fair	Poor
325	200	150	125	100	75

Pheasant

A 12 gauge magnum double-barrel shotgun with 28" barrels, single trigger, and automatic ejectors. Blued with a walnut stock.

NIB	Exc.	V.G.	Good	Fair	Poor
450	350	300	250	200	150

Classic

As above, with 26" to 30" barrels fitted with detachable choke tubes, single-selective trigger, and automatic ejectors. Blued with a walnut stock.

NIB	Exc.	V.G.	Good	Fair	Poor
850	700	600	500	300	200

Snipe

A .410 bore over/under shotgun with 26" or 28" barrels and a single trigger.

NIB	Exc.	V.G.	Good	Fair	Poor
400	300	200	175	150	100

Dove

Similar to the above.

NIB	Exc.	V.G.	Good	Fair	Poor
400	300	200	175	150	100

Texas

A 12, 20 or .410 bore over/under shotgun with 26" or 28" barrels, double triggers, and a bottom barrel release lever.

NIB	Exc.	V.G.	Good	Fair	Poor
350	250	200	150	100	75

Field Special

A 12 or 20 gauge magnum double-barrel shotgun produced in a variety of barrel lengths with a single trigger and extractors. Blued with a walnut stock.

NIB	Exc.	V.G.	Good	Fair	Poor
550	400	300	250	200	100

Pigeon Model

As above, but more finely finished.

NIB	Exc.	V.G.	Good	Fair	Poor
550	400	300	250	200	100

Standard Model

Similar to the above but in 12 and 20 gauge only.

NIB	Exc.	V.G.	Good	Fair	Poor
500	400	300	250	200	100

Special Model

As above, with detachable choke tubes and a single-selective trigger.

NIB	Exc.	V.G.	Good	Fair	Poor
600	450	300	250	200	100

Deluxe Model

As above, but engraved and with better quality walnut.

NIB	Exc.	V.G.	Good	Fair	Poor
800	600	500	400	300	150

Presentation Model

As above, with false sidelocks and finely figured walnut stock.

NIB	Exc.	V.G.	Good	Fair	Poor
950	700	600	450	350	200

St. George's Target

A 12 gauge over/under shotgun trap or skeet bore with various barrel lengths, single-selective trigger, and automatic ejectors. Blued with a walnut stock.

NIB	Exc.	V.G.	Good	Fair	Poor
1200	900	700	600	550	250

St. George Competition

A 12 gauge single-barrel gun with an extra set of over/under barrels.

NIB	Exc.	V.G.	Good	Fair	Poor
1950	1600	1200	950	500	300

Express Rifle

A .30-06, 7x65Rmm or 9.3x74Rmm over/under double-barrel rifle with single triggers and automatic ejectors. Blued with a walnut stock.

NIB	Exc.	V.G.	Good	Fair	Poor
4250	3500	2500	1750	1200	600

Express EM

As above, but more finely finished.

NIB	Exc.	V.G.	Good	Fair	Poor
5500	4000	3000	1500	1000	750

Savana E

As above, with double triggers.

NIB	Exc.	V.G.	Good	Fair	Poor
6500	5250	4500	3500	2750	1500

Savana Deluxe

As above, but engraved with hunting scenes.

NIB	Exc.	V.G.	Good	Fair	Poor
8000	7000	6000	4750	3500	2000

AZ 1900C

A .243, .270, 6.5x55mm, .308, or .30-06 bolt-action rifle with a 24" barrel having open sights. Blued with a walnut stock.

NIB	Exc.	V.G.	Good	Fair	Poor
850	700	500	400	300	150

AZ 1900M

Same as above but fitted with a Bell & Carlson composite stock.

NIB	Exc.	V.G.	Good	Fair	Poor
750	600	450	350	275	200

AZ 1900 Deluxe

As above, but more finely finished.

NIB	Exc.	V.G.	Good	Fair	Poor
1100	800	650	500	400	200

AZ 1900 Super Deluxe

As above, but engraved with a finely figured walnut stock.

NIB	Exc.	V.G.	Good	Fair	Poor
1500	1000	800	600	450	250

Patricia Model

As above, in .410 magnum bore with 28" ventilated rib barrels, various chokes, single-selective trigger, and automatic ejectors. Engraved, blued with finely figured walnut stock.

NIB	Exc.	V.G.	Good	Fair	Poor
1500	1100	950	750	650	400

Condor

A .30-06 or .308 and 12 gauge over/under combination shotgun rifle with double triggers, extractors and sling swivels. Blued with a walnut stock.

NIB	Exc.	V.G.	Good	Fair	Poor
1500	1050	850	700	500	300

Airone

As above, with false sidelocks.

NIB	Exc.	V.G.	Good	Fair	Poor
1650	1250	1000	800	600	300

Leopard Express

A .30-06, .308, 7x65Rmm, or .375 Holland & Holland over/under double-barrel rifle with 24" barrels having express sights, double triggers and extractors. Blued with a walnut stock.

NIB	Exc.	V.G.	Good	Fair	Poor
1750	1400	1000	800	600	300

ZOLI, ANTONIO
Brescia, Italy

Silver Hawk

A 12 or 20 gauge boxlock double-barrel shotgun produced in a variety of barrel lengths and chokes with a double trigger. Engraved, blued with walnut stock.

NIB	Exc.	V.G.	Good	Fair	Poor
—	1025	900	850	600	450

Ariete M2

A 12 gauge boxlock double-barrel shotgun with 26" or 28" barrels, non-selective single trigger and automatic ejectors. Engraved, blued with a walnut stock.

NIB	Exc.	V.G.	Good	Fair	Poor
—	1150	1000	850	700	350

Empire

As above, in 12 or 20 gauge with 27" or 28" barrels. Engraved, French case hardened, blued with a walnut stock.

NIB	Exc.	V.G.	Good	Fair	Poor
—	2300	1950	1400	1250	400

Volcano Record

A 12 gauge sidelock double-barrel shotgun with 28" barrels available in a variety of chokes, single-selective trigger and automatic ejectors. Engraved, French case hardened, blued with a walnut stock.

NIB	Exc.	V.G.	Good	Fair	Poor
—	7000	6000	5000	4000	500

Volcano Record ELM

This model is strictly a custom-ordered shotgun produced to the purchaser's specifications. Value speculative.

NIB	Exc.	V.G.	Good	Fair	Poor
—	16000	13500	10500	8500	500

Silver Snipe

A 12 or 20 gauge over/under shotgun produced with varying lengths, ventilated rib barrels, single trigger and extractors. Engraved, blued with a walnut stock.

NIB	Exc.	V.G.	Good	Fair	Poor
—	600	450	400	325	275

Golden Snipe

As above, but more finely finished and fitted with automatic ejectors.

NIB	Exc.	V.G.	Good	Fair	Poor
—	650	500	450	350	300

Delfino

As above, in 12 or 20 gauge magnum with 26" or 28" ventilated rib barrels, non-selective single trigger and automatic ejectors. Engraved, blued with walnut stock.

NIB	Exc.	V.G.	Good	Fair	Poor
—	575	425	325	275	250

Ritmo Hunting Gun

As above, in 12 gauge magnum with 26" or 28" separated ventilated rib barrels, single-selective trigger and automatic ejectors. Engraved, blued with a walnut stock.

NIB	Exc.	V.G.	Good	Fair	Poor
—	650	500	450	400	350

Condor Model

As above, in 12 gauge with 28" skeet bored barrels having a wide competition rib, single-selective trigger and automatic ejectors. Engraved, French case hardened, blued with a walnut stock.

NIB	Exc.	V.G.	Good	Fair	Poor
—	1100	800	650	500	400

Angel Model

As above, in a field grade version.

NIB	Exc.	V.G.	Good	Fair	Poor
—	1100	800	600	500	400

Ritmo Pigeon Grade IV

As above, with 28" separated ventilated rib barrels, single-selective trigger, automatic ejectors and extensively engraved. French case hardened, blued with a finely figured walnut stock.

NIB	Exc.	V.G.	Good	Fair	Poor
—	2250	1600	1200	800	600

Model 208 Target

As above, with 28" or 30" trap or skeet bored barrels fitted with a wide ventilated rib.

NIB	Exc.	V.G.	Good	Fair	Poor
—	1200	850	700	600	500

Model 308 Target

As above, but more finely finished.

NIB	Exc.	V.G.	Good	Fair	Poor
—	1500	1100	850	700	500

Combinato

A .222 or .243 and 12 or 20 gauge over/under combination rifle/shotgun with an engraved boxlock-action, double triggers, and a folding rear sight. French case hardened, blued with a walnut stock.

NIB	Exc.	V.G.	Good	Fair	Poor
—	2500	1700	1250	950	500

Safari Deluxe

As above, but with false sidelocks that are engraved with scrolls or hunting scenes.

NIB	Exc.	V.G.	Good	Fair	Poor
—	5000	4000	2850	1500	650

ZULAICA, M.
Eibar, Spain

Zulaica

A solid-frame .22 caliber revolver with a 6-shot cylinder that has zigzag grooves on its exterior surface. It is fired by an external hammer and the frame is hollow with a rod inside of it that connects to the breechblock. There is a serrated cocking piece connected to this rod that is found at the top rear of the frame. When fired, the cartridge case blows from the cylinder and activates the breechblock similar to a semi-automatic pistol.

NIB	Exc.	V.G.	Good	Fair	Poor
—	1000	800	600	350	250

ROYAL

The name Royal was applied to a number of pistols produced by this company, as listed.

Royal

A 6.35mm or 7.65mm semi-automatic pistol that is normally marked on the slide "Automatic Pistol 6.35 Royal" or "Automatic Pistol 7.65 Royal".

NIB	Exc.	V.G.	Good	Fair	Poor
—	300	175	100	75	50

As above, in 7.65mm caliber with a 5.5" barrel and 12-shot magazine.

NIB	Exc.	V.G.	Good	Fair	Poor
—	325	200	125	100	75

A rather poor copy of the Mauser Model C/96 semi-automatic pistol with fixed lockwork.

NIB	Exc.	V.G.	Good	Fair	Poor
—	900	700	500	300	150

Vincitor

A 6.35mm or 7.65mm caliber semi-automatic pistol patterned after the Model 1906 Browning. The slide marked "SA Royal Vincitor". Blued with plastic grips.

NIB	Exc.	V.G.	Good	Fair	Poor
—	300	175	100	75	50

FIREARMS TRADE NAMES

A.A. Co.: Inexpensive pocket revolvers of unknown manufacture.

Acme:
a) Trade name used by the W.H. Davenport Firearms Co. on shotguns.
b) Trade name used by the Hopkins and Allen Co. on revolvers produced for the Merwin, Hulbert and Co. and the Herman Boker Co. of New York.
c) Trade name used by the Maltby, Henley and Co. of New York on inexpensive pocket revolvers.

Acme Arms Company: Trade name used by the J. Stevens Arms and Tool Co. on pistols and shotguns produced for the Cornwall Hardware Co. of New York.

Aetna: Trade name used by the firm of Harrington and Richardson on inexpensive pocket revolvers.

Alamo Ranger: The name found on inexpensive Spanish revolvers.

Alaska: Trade name used by the Hood Firearms Co. on inexpensive pocket revolvers.

Alert: Trade name used by the Hood Firearms Co. on inexpensive pocket revolvers.

Alexander Gun Company: Trade name believed to have been used by E.K. Tryon of Philadelphia on imported shotguns.

Alexis: Trade name used by the Hood Firearms Co. on inexpensive pocket revolvers.

Allen 22: Trade name used by the Hopkins and Allen Co. on inexpensive pocket revolvers.

America: Trade name used by the Crescent Firearms Co. on inexpensive pocket revolvers.

American: Trade name used by the Ely and Wray on inexpensive pocket revolvers.

American Barlock Wonder: Trade name used by the H. & D. Folsom Arms Co. on shotguns made for the Sears, Roebuck Co. of Chicago.

American Boy: Trade name used on firearms retailed by the Townley Metal and Hardware Co. of Kansas City, Missouri.

American Bulldog: Trade name used by the Iver Johnson Arms and Cycle Works on inexpensive pocket revolvers.

American Bulldog Revolver: Trade name used by Harrington and Richardson Arms Co. on an inexpensive pocket revolver.

American Eagle: Trade name used by the Hopkins and Allen Co. on inexpensive pocket revolvers.

American Gun Company: Trade name used by H. & D. Folsom Arms Co. on pistols and shotguns that firm retailed.

American Gun Barrel Company: Trade name used by R. Avis of West Haven, Connecticut, between 1916 and 1920.

American Nitro: Trade name used by H. & D. Folsom Arms Co. on shotguns.

Americus: Trade name used by the Hopkins and Allen Co. on inexpensive pocket revolvers.

Angel: Trade name found on inexpensive pocket revolvers of unknown manufacture.

Arab, The: Trade name used by the Harrington and Richardson Arms Co. on shotguns.

Aristocrat:
a) Trade name used by the Hopkins and Allen Co. on inexpensive pocket revolvers.
b) Trade name used by the Supplee-Biddle Hardware Co. of Philadelphia on firearms they retailed.

Armory Gun Company: Trade name used by H. & D. Folsom Arms Co. on shotguns.

Aubrey Shotgun: Trade name found on shotguns made for the Sears, Roebuck and Co. of Chicago by Albert Aubrey of Meriden, Connecticut.

Audax: Trade name used by the Manufacture d'Armes Pyrenees on semiautomatic pistols.

Aurora: Trade name found on inexpensive Spanish semiautomatic pistols.

Autogarde: Trade name used by the Societe Francaise des Munitions on semiautomatic pistols.

Automatic:
a) Trade name used by the Forehand and Wadsworth Co. on inexpensive pocket revolvers.
b) Trade name used by the Harrington and Richardson Arms Co. on inexpensive pocket revolvers.
c) Trade name used by the Iver Johnson Arms and Cycle Works on inexpensive pocket revolvers.

Auto Stand: Trade name used by the Manufacture Francaise d'Armes et Cycles, St. Etiene on semiautomatic pistols.

Avenger: Trade name found on inexpensive pocket revolvers of unknown manufacture.

Baby Hammerless: Trade mark used successively by Henry Kolb and R.F. Sedgley on pocket revolvers they manufactured.

Baby Russian: Trade name used by the American Arms Co. on revolvers they manufactured.

Baker Gun Company: Trade name used by the H. & D. Folsom Arms Co. on shotguns they retailed.

Baker Gun and Forging Company: Trade name used by the H. & D. Folsom Arms Co. on shotguns they retailed.

Bang: Trade name found on inexpensive pocket revolvers of unknown manufacture.

Bang Up: Trade name used on inexpensive pocket revolvers retailed by the Graham and Haines Co. of New York.

Bartlett Field: Trade name used on shotguns retailed by Hibbard, Spencer, Bartlett and Co. of Chicago.

Batavia: Trade name used on shotguns produced by the Baker Gun Co.

Batavia Leader: Trade name used on shotguns produced by the Baker Gun Co.

Bay State: Trade name used by the Harrington and Richardson Arms Co. on both inexpensive pocket revolvers and shotguns.

Belknap: Trade name used by the Belknap Hardware Co. of Louisville, Kentucky, on shotguns made by the Crescent Fire Arms Co., which they retailed.

Bellmore Gun Company: Trade name used by the H. & D. Folsom Arms Co. on shotguns made for them by the Crescent Fire Arms Co.

Berkshire: Trade name used by the H. & D. Folsom Arms Co. on shotguns made for the Shapleigh Hardware Co. of St. Louis, Missouri.

Bicycle: Trade name used on firearms made by the Harrington and Richardson Arms Co.

Big All Right: Trade name used on shotguns manufactured by the Wright Arms Co.

Big Bonanza: Trade name found on inexpensive pocket revolvers of unknown manufacture.

Bismarck: Trade name found on inexpensive pocket revolvers of unknown manufacture.

Black Beauty: Trade name used by the Sears, Roebuck and Co. on imported shotguns retailed.

Black Diamond: Trade name found on Belgian made shotguns retailed by an unknown American wholesale house.

Black Diana: Trade name used by the Baker Gun Co. on shotguns.

Blackfield: Trade name used by the Hibbard, Spencer, Bartlett and Co. of Chicago on shotguns they retailed.

Blackhawk: Trade name found on inexpensive pocket revolvers of unknown manufacture.

Black Prince: Trade name used by the Hopkins and Allen Co. on inexpensive pocket revolvers.

Bliss: Trade name believed to have been used by the Norwich Arms Co.

Blood Hound: Trade name found on inexpensive pocket revolvers of unknown manufacture.

Bluefield: Trade name used by the W.H. Davenport Firearms Co. on shotguns.

Bluegrass: Trade name used by the Belknap Hardware Co. of Louisville, Kentucky, on shotguns they retailed.

Bluegrass Arms Company: Trade name of shotguns made by H. & D. Folsom Arms Co. for Belknap Hardware of Louisville, Kentucky.

Blue Jacket: Trade name used by the Hopkins and Allen Co. on inexpensive pocket revolvers they made for the Merwin, Hulbert and Co. of New York.

Blue Leader: Trade name found on inexpensive pocket revolvers of unknown manufacture.

Blue Whistler: Trade name used by the Hopkins and Allen Co. on inexpensive pocket revolvers they made for the Merwin, Hulbert and Co. of New York.

Bogardus Club Gun: Trade name found on Belgian made shotguns retailed by an unknown American wholesaler (possibly B. Kittredge and Co. of Cincinnati, Ohio).

Boltun: Trade name used by F. Arizmendi on semiautomatic pistols.

Bonanza: Trade name used by the Bacon Arms Co. on inexpensive pocket revolvers.

Boom: Trade name used by the Shattuck Arms Co. on inexpensive pocket revolvers.

Boone Gun Company: Trade name used by the Belknap Hardware Co. of Louisville, Kentucky, on firearms they retailed.

Boss:
a) Trade name used by E.H. and A.A. Buckland of Springfield, Massachusetts, on single-shot derringers designed by Holt & Marshall.
b) Trade name used on inexpensive pocket revolvers of unknown American manufacture.

Boys Choice: Trade name used by the Hood Firearms Co. on inexpensive pocket revolvers.

Bride Black Prince: Trade name used by H. & D. Folsom Arms Co. on shotguns.

Bridge Gun Company: Registered trade name of the Shapleigh Hardware Co., St. Louis, Missouri.

Bridgeport Arms Company: Trade name used by H. & D. Folsom Arms Co. on shotguns.

Bright Arms Company: Trade name used by H. & D. Folsom Arms Co.

British Bulldog: Trade name found on inexpensive pocket revolvers of unknown American and English manufacture.

Brownie:
a) Trade name used by the W.H. Davenport Firearms Co. on shotguns.
b) Trade name used by the O.F. Mossberg Firearms Co. on a four-shot pocket pistol.

Brutus: Trade name used by the Hood Firearms Co. on inexpensive pocket revolvers.

Buckeye: Trade name used by the Hopkins and Allen Co. on inexpensive pocket revolvers.

Buffalo: Trade name used by Gabilongo y Urresti on semiautomatic pistols.

Buffalo: Trade name found on bolt action rifles made in France.

Buffalo: Trade name used by the Western Arms Co. on an inexpensive pocket revolver.

Buffalo Bill: Trade name used by the Iver Johnson Arms and Cycle Works on an inexpensive pocket revolver.

Buffalo Stand: Trade name used by the Manufacture Francaise d'Armes et Cycles on target pistols.

Bull Dog: Trade name used by the Forehand and Wadsworth Co. on inexpensive pocket revolvers.

Bull Dozer:
a) Trade name used by the Norwich Pistol Co. on inexpensive pocket revolvers.
b) Trade name used by the Forehand and Wadsworth Co. on inexpensive pocket revolvers.
c) Trade name on Hammond Patent pistols made by the Connecticut Arms and Manufacturing Co.

Bull Frog: Trade name used by the Hopkins and Allen Co. on rifles.

Bulls Eye: Trade name used by the Norwich Falls Pistol Co. (O.A. Smith) on inexpensive pocket revolvers.

Burdick: Trade name used by the H. & D. Folsom Arms Co. on shotguns made for the Sears, Roebuck and Co. of Chicago.

Cadet: Trade name used by the Crescent Firearms Co. on rifles.

Canadian Belle: Trade name used by H. & D. Folsom Arms Co. on shotguns.

Cannon Breech: Trade name used by the Hopkins and Allen Co. on shotguns.

Captain: Trade name used by Manufacture d'Armes de Pyrenees on semiautomatic pistols.

Captain Jack: Trade name used by Hopkins & Allen on inexpensive pocket revolvers.

Carolina Arms Company: Trade name used by the H. & D. Folsom Arms Co. on shotguns produced for the Smith, Wadsworth Hardware Co. of Charlotte, North Carolina.

Caroline Arms: Trade name used by the H. & D. Folsom Arms Co.

Caruso: Trade name used by the Crescent Firearms Co. on shotguns made for the Hibbard, Spencer, Bartlett and Co. of Chicago.

Centennial 1876:
a) Trade name used by the Deringer Pistol Co. on inexpensive pocket revolvers.

b) Trade name used by the Hood Firearms Co. on inexpensive pocket revolvers.

Central Arms Company: Trade name used by the W. H. Davenport Firearms Co. on shotguns made for the Shapleigh Hardware Co. of St. Louis, Missouri.

Century Arms Company: Trade name used by the W. H. Davenport Firearms Co. on shotguns made for the Shapleigh Hardware Co. of St. Louis, Missouri.

Challenge:
a) Trade name found on inexpensive pocket revolvers of unknown manufacture.
b) Trade name used by the Sears, Roebuck and Co. of Chicago on shotguns made by Albert Aubrey of Meriden, Connecticut.

Challenge Ejector: Trade name used by the Sears, Roebuck and Co. of Chicago on shotguns made by Albert Aubrey of Meriden, Connecticut.

Champion:
a) Trade name used by H.C. Squires on shotguns.
b) Trade name used by J.P. Lovell on shotguns.
c) Trade name used by the Iver Johnson Arms and Cycle Works on shotguns and inexpensive pocket revolvers.
d) Trade name used by the Norwich Arms Co. on inexpensive pocket revolvers.

Chantecler: Trade name used by Manufacture d'Armes de Pyrenees on semiautomatic pistols.

Charles Richter Company: Trade name used by the H. & D. Folsom Arms Co. on firearms made for the New York Sporting Goods Co. of New York.

Chatham Arms Company: Trade name used by H. & D. Folsom Arms Co. used on shotguns.

Cherokee Arms Company: Trade name used by the H. & D. Folsom Arms Co. on shotguns made for C.M. McLung and Co. of Knoxville, Tennessee.

Chesapeake Gun Company: Trade name used by the H. & D. Folsom Arms Co. of New York.

Chicago: Trade name found on shotguns retailed by the Hibbard, Spencer, Bartlett and Co. of Chicago.

Chicago Ledger: Trade name used by the Chicago Firearms Co. on inexpensive pocket revolvers.

Chicago Long Range Wonder: Trade name used by the H. & D. Folsom Arms Co. on shotguns made for the Sears, Roebuck and Co. of Chicago.

Chichester: Trade name used by Hopkins & Allen on inexpensive pocket revolvers.

Chicopee Arms Company: Trade name used by the H. & D. Folsom Arms Co. of New York.

Chieftan: Trade name found on inexpensive pocket revolvers of unknown manufacture.

Christian Protector: Trade name found on inexpensive pocket revolvers of unknown manufacture.

Climax XL: Trade name used by Herman Boker and Co. of New York on revolvers, rifles and shotguns.

Club Gun: Trade name used by B. Kittredge and Co. of Cincinnati, Ohio, on shotguns they retailed.

Cock Robin: Trade name used by the Hood Firearms Co. on inexpensive pocket revolvers.

Colonial: Trade name used by Manufacture d'Armes de Pyrenees on semiautomatic pistols.

Colonial: Trade name used by H. & D. Folsom Co. on shotguns.

Columbian Automatic: Trade name used by Foehl & Weeks on inexpensive pocket revolvers.

Colton Arms Company: Trade name used by the Shapleigh Hardware Co. of St. Louis, Missouri, on imported shotguns they retailed.

Colton Firearms Company: Trade name used by the Sears, Roebuck and Co. of Chicago on shotguns they retailed.

Columbia:
a) Trade name found on inexpensive pocket revolvers of unknown manufacture.
b) Trade name used by H.C. Squires on shotguns.

Columbia Arms Company: Registered trade name of Henry Keidel, Baltimore, Maryland.

Columbian: Trade name found on inexpensive pocket revolvers of unknown manufacture.

Columbian Firearms Company:
a) Trade name used by the Maltby, Henly and Co. on inexpensive pocket revolvers.
b) Trade name used by the Crescent Firearms Co. on shotguns.

Combat: Trade name used by Randall Firearms Co. for its service model with a flat rib top and fixed sights.

Comet: Trade name used by the Prescott Pistol Co. on inexpensive pocket revolvers.

Commander: Trade name used by the Norwich Arms Co. on inexpensive pocket revolvers.

Commercial: Trade name used by the Norwich Falls Pistol Co. (O.A. Smith) on inexpensive pocket revolvers.

Compeer: Trade name used by the H. & D. Folsom Arms Co. on firearms made for the Van Camp Hardware and Iron Co. of Indianapolis, Indiana.

Competition: Trade name used by John Meunier of Milwaukee, Wisconsin, on rifles.

Conestoga Rifle Works: Trade name of Henry Leman, Philadelphia, Pennsylvania.

Connecticut Arms Company: Trade name used by H. & D. Folsom Arms Co. on shotguns.

Constable: Trade name used by Astra on semiautomatic pistols.

Constabulary: Trade name used by L. Ancion-Marx of Liege on revolvers.

Continental: Trade name used by the Great Western Gun Works of Pittsburgh, Pennsylvania, on firearms they retailed.

Continental Arms Company: Trade name used by the Marshall Wells Co. of Duluth, Minnesota, on firearms they retailed.

Cotton King: Trade name found on inexpensive pocket revolvers of unknown manufacture.

Cowboy: Trade name used by the Hibbard, Spencer, Bartlett and Co. of Chicago on imported, inexpensive pocket revolvers they retailed.

Cowboy Ranger: Trade name used by the Rohde Spencer Co. of Chicago on inexpensive pocket revolvers.

Crack Shot: Trade name used by the J. Stevens Arms and Tool Co. on rifles.

Cracker Jack: Trade name used by the J. Stevens Arms and Tool Co. on pistols.

Creedmoore:
a) Trade name used by the Hopkins and Allen

Co. on inexpensive pocket revolvers.
b) Trade name used by the Chicago Firearms Co. on inexpensive pocket revolvers.
c) Trade name used by William Wurflein on rifles.

Creedmoore Armory: Trade name used by A.D. McAusland of Omaha, Nebraska on rifles.

Creedmoore Arms Company: Trade name found on imported shotguns retailed by an unknown American wholesaler.

Crescent: Trade name used by the Crescent Arms Co. on inexpensive pocket revolvers.

Crescent International 1XL: Trade name used by Herman Boker and Co. of New York on shotguns.

Creve Coeur: Trade name used by the Isaac Walker Hardware Co. of Peoria, Illinois, on imported shotguns they retailed.

Crown: Trade name used by the Harrington and Richardson Arms Co. on inexpensive pocket revolvers.

Crown Jewel: Trade name used by the Norwich Arms Co. on inexpensive pocket revolvers.

Cruso: Trade name used by the H. & D. Folsom Arms Co. on shotguns made for Hibbard, Spencer, Bartlett and Co. of Chicago.

Cumberland Arms Company: Trade name used by the H. & D. Folsom Arms Co. on shotguns made for the Gray and Dudley Hardware Co. of Nashville, Tennessee.

Czar:
a) Trade name used by the Hopkins and Allen Co. on inexpensive pocket revolvers.
b) Trade name used by the Hood Firearms Co. on inexpensive pocket revolvers.

Daisy:
a) Trade name used by the Bacon Arms Co. on inexpensive pocket revolvers.
b) Registered proprietary trade name engraved on firearms made by the Winchester Repeating Arms Co. for the F. Lassetter and Co., Limited of Sydney, Australia.

Daniel Boone Gun Company: Trade name used by H. & D. Folsom Arms Co. on shotguns made for Belknap Hardware Co. of Louisville, Kentucky.

Daredevel: Trade name used by Lou J. Eppinger of Detroit, Michigan, on pistols.

Dash: Trade name found on inexpensive pocket revolvers of unknown manufacture.

Davis Guns: Trade names used successively by N.R. Davis, Davis Warner, and the Crescent-Davis Arms Co. on various firearms.

Dead Shot:
a) Trade name found on inexpensive pocket revolvers of unknown manufacture.
b) Trade name used by the Meriden Firearms Co. on rifles.

Deer Slayer: Trade name used by J. Henry and Son of Boulton, Pennsylvania on rifles.

Defender:
a) Trade name used by the Iver Johnson Arms and Cycle Works on inexpensive pocket revolvers.
b) Trade name used by the U.S. Small Arms Co. on knife pistols.

Defiance: Trade name used by the Norwich Arms Co. on inexpensive pocket revolvers.

Delphian Arms Company:
a) Trade name used by the Supplee-Biddle Hardware Co. of Philadelphia, Pennsylvania, on shotguns they retailed that were supplied by the H. & D. Folsom Co. of New York.
b) Trade name used by the H. & D. Folsom Arms Co. of New York on shotguns.

Delphian Manufacturing Company: Trade name used by the H. & D. Folsom Arms Co. of New York on shotguns.

Demon: Trade name used by Manufacture d'Armes de Pyrenees on semiautomatic pistols.

Demon Marine: As above.

Dexter: Trade name found on inexpensive pocket revolvers of unknown manufacture.

Diamond Arms Company: Trade name used by the Shapleigh Hardware Co. of St. Louis, Missouri, on imported shotguns they retailed.

Dictator: Trade name used by the Hopkins and Allen Co. on inexpensive pocket revolvers.

Dominion Pistol: Trade name found on inexpensive pocket revolvers of unknown manufacture.

Double Header: Trade name used by E.S. Renwick on Perry and Goddard Patent derringers.

Douglas Arms Company: Trade name used by the Hopkins and Allen Co. on shotguns.

Dreadnought: Trade name used by the Hopkins and Allen Co. on shotguns and inexpensive pocket revolvers.

Duchess: Trade name used by the Hopkins and Allen Co. on inexpensive pocket revolvers.

Duke: Trade name found on inexpensive pocket revolvers which may have been made by the Hopkins and Allen Co.

Dunlop Special: Trade name used by the Davis Warner Arms Co. on shotguns made for the Dunlop Hardware Co. of Macon, Georgia.

Duplex: Trade name used by the Osgood Gun Works of Norwich, Connecticut.

E.B.A.C.: Trade name used by Manufacture d'Armes de Pyrenees on semiautomatic pistols.

Eagle: Trade name used by the Iver Johnson Arms and Cycle Works on inexpensive pocket revolvers.

Eagle Arms Company: Trade name used by the Iver Johnson Arms and Cycle Works on inexpensive pocket revolvers.

Earlhood: Trade name used by E.L. Dickinson on inexpensive pocket revolvers.

Earnest Companion: Trade name found on inexpensive pocket revolvers of unknown manufacture.

Earthquake: Trade name used by E.L. Dickinson on inexpensive pocket revolvers.

Eastern Arms Company: Trade name used by the Sears, Roebuck and Co. of Chicago on both shotguns and inexpensive revolvers made by the Iver Johnson Arms and Cycle Works.

Eclipse:
a) Trade name found on single-shot derringers of unknown manufacture.
b) Trade name used by E.C. Meacham on imported shotguns.

Electric: Trade name found on inexpensive pocket revolvers of unknown manufacture.

Electric City Single Hammer: Trade name found on single-shot shotguns retailed by the Wyeth Hardware and Manufacturing Co. of St. Joseph, Missouri.

Elector: Trade name found on inexpensive pocket revolvers of unknown manufacture.

Elgin Arms Company: Trade name used by the H. & D. Folsom Arms Co. on shotguns made for the Strauss and Schram Co. of Chicago.

Elita: Trade name used by the W.H. Davenport Fire Arms Co. on shotguns.

Empire:
a) Trade name used by the Rupertus Patented Pistol Manufacturing Co. on inexpensive pocket revolvers.
b) Trade name used by the Crescent Firearms Co. on shotguns.

Empire Arms Company: Trade name used by the H. & D. Folsom Arms Co. on firearms made for the Sears, Roebuck and Co. of Chicago.

Enders Royal Shotgun: Trade name used by the Crescent Davis Firearms Co. on shotguns made for the Simmons Hardware Co. of St. Louis, Missouri.

Enders Special Service: Trade name used by the Crescent Davis Firearms Co. on shotguns made for the Simmons Hardware Co. of St. Louis, Missouri.

Enterprise: Trade name used by the Enterprise Gun Works on inexpensive pocket revolvers.

Essex Gun Works: Trade name used by the Crescent - Davis Firearms Co. on shotguns made for the Belknap Hardware Co. of Louisville, Kentucky.

Eureka: Trade name used by the Iver Johnson Arms and Cycle Works on inexpensive pocket revolvers.

Excel: Trade name used by both the H. & D. Folsom Arms Co. and the Iver Johnson Arms and Cycle Works on shotguns made for the Montgomery Ward and Co. of Chicago.

Excelsior:
a) Trade name found on inexpensive pocket revolvers of unknown manufacture.
b) Trade name used by the Iver Johnson Arms and Cycle Works on shotguns.

Expert:
a) Trade name found on single-shot derringers of unknown manufacture.
b) Trade name used by the W.J. Davenport Firearms Co. on shotguns made for the Witte Hardware Co. of St. Louis, Missouri.

Express: Trade name used by the Bacon Arms Co. on inexpensive pocket revolvers.

Express: Trade name used by Tomas de Urizar on a variety of semiautomatic pistols.

Farwell Arms Company: Trade name used by the Farwell, Ozmun, Kirk and Co. of St. Paul, Minnesota, on shotguns.

Fashion: Trade name found on inexpensive pocket revolvers of unknown manufacture.

Faultless: Trade name used by the H. & D. Folsom Arms Co. on shotguns made for the John M. Smythe Merchandise Co. of Chicago.

Faultless Goose Gun: Trade name used by the H. & D. Folsom Arms Co. on shotguns made for the John M. Smythe Merchandise Co. of Chicago.

Favorite:
a) Trade name used by the J. Stevens Arms and Tool Co. on rifles.
b) Trade name used by the Iver Johnson Arms and Cycle Works on inexpensive pocket revolvers.

Favorite Navy: Trade name used by the Iver Johnson Arms and Cycle Works on inexpensive pocket revolvers.

Featherlight: Trade name used by the Sears, Roebuck and Co. of Chicago on firearms they retailed.

Federal Arms Company: Trade name used by Meriden Firearms Co.

Folks Gun Works: Trade name of William and Samuel Folk of Bryan, Ohio on rifles and shotguns.

Frank Harrison Arms Company: Trade name used by the Sickles and Preston Co. of Davenport, Iowa, on firearms they retailed.

Freemont Arms Company: Trade name found on shotguns distributed by an unknown retailer.

Frontier: Trade name used by the Norwich Falls Pistol Co. (O.A. Smith) on inexpensive pocket revolvers made for the firm of Maltby, Curtis and Co. of New York.

Fulton: Trade name used by the Hunter Arms Co. on shotguns.

Fulton Arms Company: Trade name used by the W.H. Davenport Firearms Co. on shotguns.

Furor: Trade name used by Manufacture d'Armes de Pyrenees on semiautomatic pistols.

Gallia: Trade name used by Manufacture d'Armes de Pyrenees on semiautomatic pistols.

Game Getter: Registered trade mark of the Marble Arms and Manufacturing Co. on combination rifle-shotguns.

Gaulois: Trade name used by Manufacture d'Armes et Cycles on squeezer type pistols (see also Mitrailleuse).

Gem:
a) Trade name used by the J. Stevens Arms and Tool Co. on single-shot pocket pistols.
b) Trade name used by the Bacon Arms Co. on inexpensive pocket revolvers.

Gen Curtis E. LeMay: Trade name used for Randall Firearms Co. for its small compact pistol made from the General's own gun.

General: Trade name used by the Rupertus Patented Pistol Manufacturing Co. on inexpensive pocket revolvers.

General Butler: Trade name found on inexpensive pocket revolvers of unknown manufacture.

Gerrish: Trade name of G.W. Gerrish of Twin Falls, Idaho, used on shotguns.

Gibralter: Trade name of Albert Aubrey on shotguns made for the Sears, Roebuck and Co. of Chicago.

Gladiator: Trade name of Albert Aubrey on shotguns made for the Sears, Roebuck and Co. of Chicago.

Gold Field: Trade name found on inexpensive pocket revolvers of unknown manufacture.

Gold Hibbard: Trade name used by Hibbard, Spencer, Bartlett and Co. of Chicago on firearms they retailed.

Gold Medal Wonder: Trade name used by H. & D. Folsom Arms Co. on shotguns.

Governor: Trade name used by the Bacon Arms Co. on inexpensive pocket revolvers.

Guardian: Trade name used by the Bacon Arms Co. on inexpensive pocket revolvers.

Gut Buster: Trade name found on inexpensive pocket revolvers of unknown manufacture.

Gypsy: Trade name found on inexpensive pocket revolvers of unknown manufacture.

Half Breed: Trade name found on inexpensive pocket revolvers of unknown manufacture.

Hamilton Arms: Registered trade name of the Wiebusch and Hilger Co., New York.

Hammerless Auto Ejecting Revolver: Trade name of the Meriden Firearms Co. used on revolvers made for the Sears, Roebuck and Co. of New York.

Hanover Arms Co.: If no foreign proofmarks then trade name used by H. & D. Folsom Arms Co.

Hardpan: Trade name found on inexpensive American pocket revolver.

Hard Pan: Trade name used by Hood Arms Co. on inexpensive pocket revolvers.

Hart Arms Company: Trade name used by a Cleveland, Ohio, wholesaler (possibly the George Worthington Co.).

Hartford Arms Company: Trade name used by the H. & D. Folsom Arms on shotguns made for the Simmons Hardware Co. of St. Louis, Missouri.

Harvard: Trade name used by the H. & D. Folsom Arms Co. on shotguns made for the George Worthington Co. of Cleveland, Ohio.

Hercules: Trade name used by the Iver Johnson Arms and Cycle Works on shotguns made for the Montgomery Ward and Co. of Chicago.

Hermitage Arms Company: Trade name used by the H. & D. Folsom Arms Co. on shotguns made for the Gray and Dudley Hardware Co. of Nashville, Tennessee.

Hero:
a) Trade name used by the American Standard Tool Co. on percussion pistols.
b) Trade name used by the Manhattan Firearms Manufacturing Co. on percussion pistols.

Hexagon: Trade name used by the Sears, Roebuck and Co. of Chicago on shotguns they retailed.

Hinsdale: Trade name used by the Hopkins and Allen Co. on inexpensive pocket revolvers.

Hornet: Trade name used by the Prescott Pistol Co. on inexpensive pocket revolvers.

Howard Arms Company: Trade name used by the H. & D. Folsom Arms Co. on shotguns they distributed.

Hudson: Trade name used by the Hibbard, Spencer, Bartlett and Co. of Chicago on shotguns they retailed.

Hunter: Trade name used by the H. & D. Folsom Arms Co. on shotguns made for the Belknap Hardware Co. of Louisville, Kentucky.

Hunter, The: Trade name used by the Hunter Arms Co. on shotguns.

Hurricane: Trade name found on inexpensive pocket revolvers of unknown manufacture.

I.O.A.: Trade name used by the Brown, Camp Hardware Co. of Des Moines, Iowa on firearms they retailed.

I.X.L.:
a) Trade name used by B.J. Hart on percussion revolvers.
b) Trade name used by the W.H. Davenport Firearms Co. on shotguns made for the Witte Hardware Co. of St. Louis, Missouri.

Illinois Arms Company: Trade name used by the Rohde, Spencer Co. of Chicago on firearms they retailed.

Imperial: Trade name used by the Lee Arms Co. on inexpensive pocket revolvers.

Imperial Arms Company: Trade name used by the Hopkins and Allen Co. on inexpensive pocket revolvers.

Infallible: Trade name used by the Lancaster Arms Co. of Lancaster, Pennsylvania on shotguns they retailed.

Infallible Automatic Pistol: Trade name used by the Kirtland Brothers Co. of New York on inexpensive pistols they retailed.

International:
a) Trade name found on inexpensive pocket revolvers of unknown manufacture.

b) Trade name used by E.C. Meacham on shotguns.

Interstate Arms Company: Trade name used by the H. & D. Folsom Arms Co. on shotguns made for the Townley Metal and Hardware Co. of Kansas City, Missouri.

Invincible: Trade name used by the Iver Johnson Arms and Cycle Works on both shotguns and inexpensive pocket revolvers.

Ixor: Trade name used by Manufacture d'Armes de Pyrenees on semiautomatic pistols.

J.J. Weston: Trade name used by the H. & D. Folsom Arms Co. on shotguns.

J.S.T. & Company: Trade name used by the Iver Johnson Arms and Cycle Works on inexpensive pocket revolvers.

Jackson Arms Company: Trade name used by the H. & D. Folsom Arms Co. on shotguns made for C.M. McLung and Co. of Knoxville, Tennessee.

Jewel: Trade name used by the Hood Fire Arms Co. on inexpensive pocket revolvers.

John M. Smythe & Company: Trade name used by H. & D. Folsom Arms Co. for shotguns made for John M. Smythe Hardware Co. of Chicago.

John W. Price: Trade name used by the Belknap Hardware Co. of Louisville, Kentucky, on firearms they retailed.

Joker: Trade name used by the Marlin Firearms Co. on inexpensive pocket revolvers.

Joseph Arms Company (Norwich, Connecticut): Trade name used by H. & D. Folsom Arms Co.

Judge: Trade name found on inexpensive pocket revolvers of unknown manufacture.

Jupitor: Trade name used by Fabrique d'Armes de Grand Precision, Eibar, Spain, on semiautomatic pistols.

K.K.: Trade name used by the Hopkins and Allen Co. on shotguns made for the Shapleigh Hardware Co. of St. Louis, Missouri.

Keno: Trade name found on inexpensive pocket revolvers of unknown manufacture.

Kentucky: Trade name used by the Iver Johnson Arms and Cycle Works on inexpensive pocket revolvers.

Keystone Arms Company: Trade name used by the W.H. Davenport Firearms Co. on shotguns made for the E.K. Tryon Co. of Philadelphia, Pennsylvania.

Kill Buck: Trade name of the Enterprise Gun Works (James Bown), Pittsburgh, Pennsylvania.

Killdeer: Trade name used by the Sears, Roebuck and Co. of Chicago on firearms bearing their trade name Western Arms Co.

King Nitro: Trade name used by the W.H. Davenport Firearms Co. on shotguns made for the Shapleigh Hardware Co. of St. Louis, Missouri.

King Pin: Trade name found on inexpensive single-shot and revolving pocket pistols.

Kingsland Gun Company: Trade name used by the H. & D. Folsom Arms Co. on shotguns made for the Geller, Ward and Hasner Co. of St. Louis, Missouri.

Kirk Gun Company: Trade name used by Farwell, Ozmun, and Kirk Co. of St. Paul, Minnesota.

Knickerbocker: Trade name used by the Crescent-Davis Firearms Co. on shotguns.

Knickerbocker Club Gun: Trade name used by Charles Godfrey of New York on imported shotguns he retailed.

Knockabout: Trade name used by the Montgomery Ward and Co. of Chicago on shotguns they retailed.

Knox-All: Trade name used by the Iver Johnson Arms and Cycle Works on firearms they made for the H. & D. Folsom Arms Co. of New York.

L'Agent: Trade name used by Manufacture Francaises d'Armes et Cycles on revolvers.

Lakeside: Trade name used by the H. & D. Folsom Arms Co. on firearms they made for the Montgomery Ward and Co. of Chicago.

Le Colonial: Trade name used by Manufacture Francaises d'Armes et Cycles on revolvers.

Le Colonial: As above.

Le Francais: Trade name used by Manufacture Francaises d'Armes et Cycles on semiautomatic pistols.

Le Francais: As above on semiautomatic pistols.

Le Petit Forminable: Trade name used by Manufacture Francaises d'Armes et Cycles on revolvers.

Le Petit Forminable: As above on revolvers.

Le Protecteur: Trade name used by J.E. Turbiaux of Paris on squeezer pistols of the type later made by the Ames Sword Co.

Le Terrible: Trade name used by Manufacture Francaises d'Armes et Cycles on revolvers.

Leader:
a) Trade name used by the Shattuck Arms Co. on inexpensive pocket revolvers.
b) Trade name used by the Harrington and Richardson Arms Co. on inexpensive pocket revolvers.

Leader Gun Company: Trade name used by the H. & D. Folsom Arms Co. on shotguns they made for the Charles Williams Stores, Inc. of New York.

Lee's Hummer: Trade name used by the H. & D. Folsom Arms Co. on firearms they made for the Lee Hardware Co. of Salina, Kansas.

Lee's Special: Trade name used by the H. & D. Folsom Arms Co. on firearms they made for the Lee Hardware Co. of Salina, Kansas.

Liberty: Trade name used by the Norwich Falls Pistol Co. (O.A. Smith) on inexpensive pocket revolvers.

Liege Gun Company: Trade name used by the Hibbard, Spencer, Bartlett and Co. of Chicago on imported shotguns they retailed.

Lion: Trade name used by the Iver Johnson Arms and Cycle Works on inexpensive pocket revolvers.

Little Giant: Trade name used by the Bacon Arms Co. on inexpensive pocket revolvers.

Little John: Trade name used by the Hood Firearms Co. on inexpensive pocket revolvers.

Little Joker: Trade name found on inexpensive pocket revolvers of unknown manufacture.

Little Pal: Registered trade name for knife pistols made by L.E. Pulhemus.

Little Pet: Trade name used by the Sears, Roebuck and Co. of Chicago on inexpensive pocket revolvers they retailed.

London Revolver: Trade name found on inexpensive pocket revolvers of unknown manufacture.

Lone Star: Trade name found on inexpensive pocket revolvers of unknown manufacture.

Long Range Winner: Trade name used by the Sears, Roebuck and Co. of Chicago on shotguns they retailed.

Long Range Wonder: Trade name used by the Sears, Roebuck and Co. of Chicago on shotguns they retailed.

Long Tom: Trade name used by the Sears, Roebuck and Co. of Chicago on shotguns they retailed.

Looking Glass: Trade name used on semiautomatic pistols of unknown Spanish manufacture.

Marquis of Horne: Trade name used by Hood Arms Co. on inexpensive pocket revolvers.

Mars: Trade name used by Manufacture d'Armes de Pyrenees on semiautomatic pistols.

Marshwood: Trade name used by the H. & D. Folsom Arms Co. on shotguns they made for the Charles Williams Stores Inc. of New York.

Marvel: Trade name used by the J. Stevens Arms and Tool Co. on various firearms.

Massachusetts Arms Company: Trade name used by both the J. Stevens Arms and Tool Co. and the H. & D. Folsom Arms Co. on firearms made for the Blish, Mizet and Silliman Hardware Co. of Atchinson, Kansas.

Maximum: Trade name found on inexpensive pocket revolvers of unknown manufacture.

Metropolitan: Trade name used by the H. & D. Folsom Arms Co. on firearms they made for the Siegal-Cooper Co. of New York.

Metropolitan Police:
a) Trade name used by the Maltby, Curtiss and Co. on inexpensive pocket revolvers.
b) Trade name used by the Rohde-Spencer Co. of Chicago on inexpensive pocket revolvers.

Midget Hammerless: Trade name used by the Rohde-Spencer Co. of Chicago on inexpensive pocket revolvers.

Mikros: Trade name used by Manufacture d'Armes de Pyrenees on semiautomatic pistols.

Minnesota Arms Company: Trade name used by the H. & D. Folsom Arms Co. on shotguns they made for the Farwell, Ozmun, Kirk and Co. of St. Paul, Minnesota.

Missaubi Arms Company: Trade name used by the Hunter Arms Co., possibly for the Farwell, Ozmun, Kirk and Co. of St. Paul, Minnesota.

Mississippi Arms Company: Trade name used by the H. & D. Folsom Arms Co. on firearms made for the Shapleigh Hardware Co. of St. Louis, Missouri.

Mississippi Valley Arms Company: Trade name used by the H. & D. Folsom Arms Co. on firearms made for the Shapleigh Hardware Co. of St. Louis, Missouri.

Mitrailleuse: Alternate trade name of the Gaulois squeezer pistol.

Mohawk: Trade name used by the H. & D. Folsom Arms Co. on firearms made for the Blish, Mizet and Silliman Hardware Co. of Atchinson, Kansas.

Mohegan: Trade name used by the Hood Firearms Co. on inexpensive pocket revolvers.

Monarch:
a) Trade name used by the Hopkins and Allen Co. on inexpensive pocket revolvers.
b) Trade name used by the Osgood Gun Works on Duplex revolvers.

Monitor:
a) Trade name used by the Whitneyville Armory on inexpensive pocket revolvers.
b) Trade name used by the H. & D. Folsom Arms Co. on firearms made for the Paxton and Gallagher Co. of Omaha, Nebraska.

Montgomery Arms Company: Trade name used by the H. & D. Folsom Arms Co. on a variety of firearms.

Mountain Eagle: Trade name used by the Hopkins and Allen Co. on inexpensive pocket revolvers.

Mount Vernon Arms Company: Trade name used by the H. & D. Folsom Arms Co. on firearms made for the Carlin, Hullfish Co. of Alexandria, Virginia.

My Companion: Trade name found on inexpensive pocket revolvers of unknown manufacture.

My Friend: Trade name used by James Reid of New York.

N.R. Adams: Trade name used by the N.R. Davis and Co. on shotguns.

Napoleon: Trade name used by the Thomas J. Ryan Pistol Manufacturing Co. of Norwich, Connecticut, on inexpensive pocket revolvers.

National Arms Company: Trade name used by the H. & D. Folsom Arms Co. on firearms made both for the May Hardware Co. of Washington, D.C., and the Moskowitz and Herbach Co. of Philadelphia, Pennsylvania.

Nevermiss: Trade name used by the Marlin Firearms Co. on single-shot pocket pistols.

New Aubrey: Trade name used by Albert Aubrey of Meriden, Connecticut, on both revolvers and shotguns made for the Sears, Roebuck and Co. of Chicago.

New Britain Arms Company: Trade name used by H. & D. Folsom Arms Co.

New Defender: Trade name used by Harrington & Richardson on revolvers.

New Elgin Arms Company: Trade name used by H. & D. Folsom Arms Co.

New Empire: Trade name used by H. & D. Folsom Arms Co.

New England Arms Company: Trade name believed to have been used by Charles Godfrey on shotguns made for the Rohde-Spencer Co. of Chicago.

New Era Gun Works: Trade name used by the Baker Gun Co. on firearms made for an unknown retailer.

New Haven Arms Company: Trade name found on Belgian shotguns imported by either E.K. Tryon of Philadelphia or the Great Western Gun Works of Pittsburgh, Pennsylvania.

New Liberty: Trade name used by the Sears, Roebuck and Co. of Chicago on inexpensive pocket revolvers they retailed.

New Rival: Trade name used by the H. & D. Folsom Arms Co. on firearms made for the Van Camp Hardware and Iron Co. of Indianapolis, Indiana.

New Worcester: Trade name used by the Torkalson Manufacturing Co. of Worcester, Massachusetts.

New York Arms Company: Trade name used by the H. & D. Folsom Arms Co. on firearms made for the Garnet Carter Co. of Chattanooga, Tennessee.

New York Gun Company: Trade name used by the H. & D. Folsom Arms Co. on firearms made for the Garnet Carter Co. of Chattanooga, Tennessee.

New York Club: Trade name used by the H. & D. Folsom Arms Co. on rifles.

New York Machine Made: Trade name used by the H. & D. Folsom Arms Co.

New York Pistol Company: Trade name used by the Norwich Falls Pistol Co. (O.A. Smith) on inexpensive pocket revolvers.

Newport:
a) Trade name found on inexpensive pocket revolvers of unknown manufacture.
b) Trade name used by the H. & D. Folsom Arms Co. on shotguns made for Hibbard, Spencer, Bartlett and Co. of Chicago.

Nightingale: Trade name found on inexpensive pocket revolvers of unknown manufacture.

Nitro Bird: Trade name used by the Richards and Conover Hardware Co. of Kansas City, Missouri.

Nitro Hunter: Trade name used by the H. & D. Folsom Arms Co. on shotguns made for the Belknap Hardware Co. of Louisville, Kentucky.

Nitro King: Trade name used by the Sears, Roebuck and Co. of Chicago on shotguns of unknown manufacture.

Nitro Special: Trade name used by the J. Stevens Arms and Tool Co. on shotguns.

Northfield Knife Company: Trade name used by the Rome Revolver and Novelty Works of Rome, New York, on inexpensive pocket revolvers.

Norwich Arms Company:
a) Trade name used by the Hood Firearms Co. on inexpensive pocket revolvers.
b) Trade name found on shotguns retailed by the Marshall, Wells Co. of Duluth, Minnesota, and Winnipeg, Manitoba, Canada.

Norwich Falls Pistol Company: Trade name used by the O.A. Smith Co. on inexpensive pocket revolvers made for Maltby, Curtis and Co. of New York.

Norwich Lock Manufacturing Company: Trade name used by F.W. Hood Firearms Co. on inexpensive pocket revolvers.

Not-Nac Manufacturing Company: Trade name used by the H. & D. Folsom Arms Co. on firearms made for the Canton Hardware Co. of Canton, Ohio.

Novelty: Trade name used by D.F. Mossberg & Sons on Shattuck Unique pistols.

OK:
a) Trade name used by the Marlin Firearms Co. on single-shot pocket pistols.
b) Trade name used by Cowles and Son of Chicopee Falls, Massachusetts, on single-shot pocket pistols.
c) Trade name found on inexpensive pocket revolvers of unknown manufacture.

Old Hickory:
a) Trade name found on inexpensive pocket revolvers of unknown manufacture.
b) Trade name used by the Hibbard, Spencer, Bartlett and Co. of Chicago on shotguns they retailed.

Old Reliable: Trade name used by the Sharps Rifle Co.

Olympic:
a) Trade name used by the J. Stevens Arms and Tool Co. on rifles and pistols.
b) Trade name used by the Morley and Murphy Hardware Co. of Green Bay, Wisconsin, on firearms they retailed (possibly made by the J. Stevens Arms and Tool Co.).

Osprey: Trade name used by Lou J. Eppinger of Detroit, Michigan, on firearms he made.

Our Jake: Trade name used by E.L. and J. Dickinson of Springfield, Massachusetts, on inexpensive pocket revolvers.

Oxford Arms Company: Trade name used by the H. & D. Folsom Arms Co. on firearms made for the Belknap Hardware Co. of Louisville, Kentucky.

Pagoma: Trade name used by the H. & D. Folsom Arms Co. on firearms made for the Paxton and Gallagher Co. of Omaha, Nebraska.

Peoria Chief: Trade name found on inexpensive pocket revolvers.

Perfect: Trade name used by the Foehl and Weeks Firearms Manufacturing Co. of Philadelphia, Pennsylvania, on inexpensive pocket revolvers.

Perfect: Trade name used by Manufacture d'Armes de Pyrenees on semiautomatic pistols.

Perfection:
a) Trade name used by the H. & D. Folsom Arms Co. on firearms made for the H.G. Lipscomb and Co. of Nashville, Tennessee.
b) Trade name used by the John M. Smythe Merchandise Co. of Chicago on firearms they retailed.

Pet: Trade name found on inexpensive pocket revolvers of unknown manufacture.

Petrel: Trade name found on inexpensive pocket revolvers of unknown manufacture.

Phenix: Trade name used by J. Reid of New York on revolvers.

Phoenix:
a) Trade name used by J. Reid of New York on revolvers.
b) Trade name used by the Whitneyville Armory on percussion revolvers.

Piedmont: Trade name used by the H. & D. Folsom Arms Co. on firearms made for the Piedmont Hardware Co. of Danville, Pennsylvania.

Pinafore: Trade name used by the Norwich Falls Pistol Co. (O.A. Smith) on inexpensive pocket revolvers.

Pioneer: Trade name found on inexpensive pocket revolvers of unknown manufacture.

Pioneer Arms Company: Trade name used by the H. & D. Folsom Arms Co. on firearms made for the Kruse and Baklmann Hardware Co. of Cincinnati, Ohio.

Pittsfield: Trade name used by the Hibbard, Spencer, Bartlett and Co. of Chicago on firearms probably made by the H. & D. Folsom Arms Co.

Plug Ugly: Trade name found on inexpensive pocket revolvers of unknown manufacture.

Plymouth: Trade name used by Spear and Co. of Pittsburgh, Pennsylvania, on firearms they retailed.

Pocahontas: Trade name found on inexpensive pocket revolvers of unknown manufacture.

Pointer: Trade name found on single-shot pocket pistols of unknown manufacture.

Prairie Fire: Trade name found on inexpensive pocket revolvers of unknown manufacture.

Prairie King:
a) Trade name used by the Bacon Arms Co. on inexpensive pocket revolvers.
b) Trade name used by the H. & D. Folsom Arms Co. on inexpensive pocket revolvers.

Premier:
a) Trade name used by the Thomas E. Ryan Co. on inexpensive pocket revolvers.
b) Trade name used by the Harrington and Richardson Arms Co. on revolvers.
c) Trade name used by the Montgomery Ward and Co. of Chicago on firearms they retailed.
d) Registered trade name of Edward K. Tryon and Co. of Philadelphia, Pennsylvania.

Premium: Trade name used by the Iver Johnson Arms and Cycle Works on inexpensive pocket revolvers.

Princess: Trade name found on inexpensive pocket revolvers of unknown American manufacture.

Progress: Trade name used by Charles J. Godfrey of New York on shotguns.

Protection: Trade name used by the Whitneyville Armory on revolvers.

Protector:
a) Trade name found on inexpensive pocket revolvers of unknown manufacture.
b) Trade name used by the Chicago Firearms Co. on inexpensive pocket revolvers.

Protector Arms Company: Trade name used by the Rupertus Patented Pistol Manufacturing Co. on inexpensive pocket revolvers.

Providence: Trade name found on inexpensive pocket revolvers of unknown manufacture.

Puppy: Trade name found on inexpensive pocket revolvers made by several European makers.

Quail: Trade name used by the Crescent-Davis Arms Co. on shotguns.

Queen:
a) Trade name used by the Hood Firearms Co. on inexpensive pocket revolvers.
b) Trade name used by the Hyde and Shattuck Co. on inexpensive single-shot pocket pistols.

Queen City: Trade name used by the H. & D. Folsom Arms Co. on firearms made for the Elmira Arms Co. of Elmira, New York.

Raider: Randall Firearms Co. Commander size pistol named after Gen Randall's flight squadron; "Randall's Raiders".

Ranger:
a) Trade name found on inexpensive pocket revolvers of unknown manufacture.
b) Trade name used by the Eastern Arms Co. on various firearms made for the Sears, Roebuck and Co. of Chicago.
c) Trade name of the Sears, Roebuck and Co. of Chicago on a wide variety of firearms marketed by that firm.

Rapid-Maxim: Trade name used by Manufacture d'Armes de Pyrenees on semiautomatic pistols.

Reassurance: Trade name found on inexpensive pocket revolvers of unknown manufacture.

Red Chieftan: Trade name used by the Supplee Biddle Hardware Co. of Philadelphia Pennsylvania, on inexpensive pocket pistols they retailed.

Red Cloud: Trade name used by the Ryan Pistol Manufacturing Co. on inexpensive pocket revolvers.

Red Hot: Trade name found on inexpensive pocket revolvers of unknown manufacture.

Red Jacket:
a) Trade name used by the Lee Arms Co. on inexpensive pocket revolvers.
b) Trade name used by the Hopkins and Allen Co. on inexpensive pocket revolvers.

Reliable: Trade name found on inexpensive pocket revolvers of unknown manufacture.

Reliance: Trade name used by John Meunier of Milwaukee, Wisconsin, on rifles.

Rev-O-Noc: Trade name used by the H. & D. Folsom Arms Co. on firearms made for the Hibbard, Spencer, Bartlett and Co. of Chicago.

Rich-Con: Trade name used by the H. & D. Folsom Arms Co. for shotguns made for Richardson & Conover Hardware Co.

Richmond Arms Company: Trade name used by the H. & D. Folsom Arms Co. on firearms made for an unknown retailer.

Rickard Arms Company: Trade name used by the H. & D. Folsom Arms Co. on firearms made for the J.A. Rickard Co. of Schenectady, New York.

Rip Rap: Trade name used by the Bacon Arms Co. on inexpensive pocket revolvers.

Rival: Trade name used by the H. & D. Folsom Arms Co. on firearms made for the Van Camp Hardware and Iron Co. of Indianapolis, Indiana.

Riverside Arms Company: Trade name used by the J. Stevens Arms and Tool Co. on various types of firearms.

Robin Hood: Trade name used by the Hood Firearms Co. on inexpensive pocket revolvers.

Rocky Hill: Trade name found on inexpensive cast iron percussion pocket pistols made in Rocky Hill, Connecticut.

Rodgers Arms Company: Trade name used by the Hood Firearms Co. on firearms made for an unknown retailer.

Royal Gun Company: Trade name used by the Three Barrel Gun Co.

Royal Service: Trade name used by the Shapleigh Hardware Co. of St. Louis, Missouri, on firearms they retailed.

Rummel Arms Company: Trade name used by the H. & D. Folsom Arms Co. on firearms made for the A.J. Rummel Arms Co. of Toledo, Ohio.

Russel Arms Company: Registered trade name of the Wiebusch and Hilger Co. of New York.

Russian Model: Trade name used by the Forehand and Wadsworth Co. on inexpensive pocket revolvers.

S. Holt Arms Company: Trade name used by the Sears, Roebuck and Co. of Chicago on shotguns they retailed.

S.A.: Trade mark of the Societe d'Armes Francaises.

S.H. Harrington: If no foreign proofmarks then trade name used by H. & D. Folsom Arms Co.

Safe Guard: Trade name found on inexpensive pocket revolvers of unknown manufacture.

Safety Police: Trade name used by the Hopkins and Allen Co. on inexpensive pocket revolvers.

Scott: Trade name used by the Hopkins and Allen Co. on inexpensive pocket revolvers.

Secret Service Special: Trade name used by the Rohde-Spencer Co. of Chicago on inexpensive pocket revolvers.

Selecta: Trade name used by Manufacture d'Armes de Pyrenees on semiautomatic pistols.

Senator: Trade name found on inexpensive pocket revolvers of unknown manufacture.

Sentinal: Trade name found on inexpensive pocket revolvers of unknown manufacture.

Service Model C: The predecessor to the "Raider" pistol.

Sheffield, The: Trade name used by the A. Baldwin and Co., Limited of New Orleans, Louisiana, on shotguns they retailed.

Sickels-Arms Company: Trade name used by the Sickels and Preston Co. of Davenport, Iowa, on firearms they retailed.

Simson: Trade name used by the Iver Johnson Arms and Cycle Works on firearms made for the Iver Johnson Sporting Goods Co. of Boston, Massachusetts.

Sitting Bull: Trade name found on inexpensive pocket revolvers of unknown manufacture.

Skue's Special: Trade name used by Ira M. Skue of Hanover, Pennsylvania, on shotguns.

Smoker: Trade name used by the Iver Johnson Arms and Cycle Works on inexpensive pocket revolvers.

Southern Arms Company: Trade name used by the H. & D. Folsom Arms Co. on firearms made for an unknown retailer.

Southerner:
a) Trade name used by the Brown Manufacturing Co. and the Merrimac Arms Manufacturing Co. on single-shot pocket pistols.
b) Registered trade name of Asa Farr of New York on pistols.

Southron: Trade name found on inexpensive pocket pistols of unknown manufacture.

Special Service: Trade name used by the Shapleigh Hardware Co. of St. Louis, Missouri, on inexpensive pocket revolvers.

Spencer Gun Company: Trade name used by the H. & D. Folsom Arms Co.

Splendor: Trade name found on inexpensive pocket revolvers of unknown manufacture.

Sportsman, The: Trade name used by the H. & D. Folsom Arms Co. on firearms made for the W. Bingham Co. of Cleveland, Ohio.

Springfield Arms Company: Trade name used by the J. Stevens Arms and Tool Co.

Spy: Trade name found on inexpensive pocket revolvers of unknown manufacture.

Square Deal: Trade name used by the H. & D. Folsom Arms Co. on firearms made for the Stratton, Warren Hardware Co. of Memphis, Tennessee.

St. Louis Arms Company: Trade name used by the H. & D. Folsom Arms Co. on firearms made for the Shapleigh Hardware Co. of St. Louis, Missouri.

Standard: Trade name used by the Marlin Firearms Co. on revolvers.

Stanley Arms: Registered trade name of the Wiebusch and Hilger Co. of New York on firearms they retailed.

Stanley Double Gun: Trade name used by the H. & D. Folsom Arms Co. on shotguns they retailed.

Star:
a) Trade name found on inexpensive single-shot pocket pistols of unknown manufacture.
b) Trade name used by the Prescott Pistol Co. on inexpensive pocket revolvers.
c) Trade name used by Johnson & Bye on single-shot cartridge derringers.

State Arms Company: Trade name used by the H. & D. Folsom Arms Co. on firearms made for the J.H. Lau and Co. of New York.

Sterling:
a) Trade name used by E.L. and J. Dickinson of Springfield, Massachusetts, on single-shot pistols.
b) Trade name used by the H. & D. Folsom Arms Co. on shotguns they retailed.

Stinger: Registered proprietary trade name engraved on firearms made by the Winchester Repeating Arms Co. for the Perry Brothers Limited of Brisbane, Australia.

Stonewall:
a) Trade name used by the Marlin Firearms Co. on single-shot derringers.
b) Trade name used by T.F. Guion of Lycoming, Pennsylvania, on single-shot percussion pistols he retailed.

Striker: Trade name found on inexpensive pocket revolvers of unknown manufacture.

Sullivan Arms Company: Trade name used by the H. & D. Folsom Arms Co. on firearms made for the Sullivan Hardware Co. of Anderson, South Carolina.

Superior: Trade name of the Paxton and Gallagher Co. of Omaha, Nebraska, on revolvers and shotguns.

Super Range: Trade name of the Sears, Roebuck and Co. of Chicago on shotguns.

Sure Fire: Trade name found on inexpensive pocket revolvers of unknown manufacture.

Swamp Angel: Trade name used by the Forehand and Wadsworth Co. on inexpensive pocket revolvers.

Swift: Trade name used by the Iver Johnson Arms and Cycle Works on firearms made for the John P. Lovell & Sons, Boston, Massachusetts.

Syco: Trade name used by the Wyeth Hardware Co. of St. Joseph, Missouri, on firearms they retailed.

Sympathique: Trade name used by Manufacture d'Armes de Pyrenees on semiautomatic pistols.

T. Barker: Trade name used by the H. & D. Folsom Arms Co. of New York on shotguns they retailed.

Ten Star: Trade name used by the H. & D. Folsom Arms Co. on firearms made for the Geller, Ward and Hasner Co. of St. Louis, Missouri.

Terrier: Trade name used by the Rupertus Patented Pistol Manufacturing Co. on inexpensive pocket revolvers.

Terror: Trade name used by the Forehand and Wadsworth Co. on inexpensive pocket revolvers.

Texas Ranger: Trade name used by the Montgomery Ward and Co. of Chicago on inexpensive pocket revolvers they retailed.

Thames Arms Company: Trade name used by the Harrington and Richardson Arms Co. on firearms they made for an unknown wholesaler.

Tiger:
a) Trade name used by the Iver Johnson Arms and Cycle Works on inexpensive pocket revolvers.
b) Trade name used by the J.H. Hall and Co. of Nashville, Tennessee, on shotguns they retailed.

Tobin Simplex: Trade name used on shotguns of unknown manufacture that were retailed by the G.B. Crandall Co., Limited of Woodstock, Ontario, Canada.

Toledo Firearms Company:
a) Trade name used by the Hopkins and Allen Co. on inexpensive pocket revolvers.
b) Trade name used by E.L. and J. Dickinson on inexpensive pocket revolvers.

Toronto Belle: Trade name found on inexpensive pocket revolvers of unknown manufacture.

Touriste: Trade name used by Manufacture d'Armes de Pyrenees on semiautomatic pistols.

Tower's Police Safety: Trade name used by Hopkins & Allen on inexpensive pocket revolvers.

Townley's Pal and Townley's American Boy: Trade name used by H. & D. Folsom Arms Co. for shotguns made for Townley Metal and Hardware Co. of Kansas City, Missouri.

Tramps Terror: Trade name used by the Forehand and Wadsworth Co. on inexpensive pocket revolvers.

Traps Best: Trade name believed to have been used by the H. & D. Folsom Arms Co. on firearms made for the Watkins, Cottrell Co. of Richmond, Virginia.

Triumph: Trade name used by the H. & D. Folsom Arms Co. on shotguns.

Trojan: Trade name found on inexpensive pocket revolvers of unknown manufacture.

True Blue: Trade name found on inexpensive pocket revolvers of unknown manufacture.

Tryon Special: Trade name used by the Edward K. Tryon Co. of Philadelphia, Pennsylvania, on shotguns they retailed.

Tycoon: Trade name used by the Iver Johnson Arms and Cycle Works on inexpensive pocket revolvers.

U.S. Arms Company: Trade name used successively by the Alexander Waller and Co. (1877), the Barton and Co. (1878) and the H. & D. Folsom Arms Co. (1879 forward) on a variety of firearms.

U.S. Revolver: Trade name used by the Iver Johnson Arms and Cycle Works on inexpensive pocket revolvers.

U.S. Single Gun: Trade name used by the Iver Johnson Arms and Cycle Works on single barrel shotguns.

Uncle Sam: Trade name used by Johnson & Bye on percussion pocket pistols.

Union:
a) Trade name found on inexpensive single-shot pocket pistols of unknown manufacture.
b) Trade name used by the Hood Firearms Co. on inexpensive pocket revolvers.
c) Trade name used by the Prescott Pistol Co. on inexpensive pocket revolvers.

Union Arms Company: Trade name used by the H. & D. Folsom Arms Co. on firearms made for the Bostwick, Braun Co. of Toledo, Ohio.

Union Jack: Trade name found on inexpensive pocket revolvers of unknown manufacture.

Union N.Y.: Trade name used by the Whitneyville Armory on inexpensive pocket revolvers.

Unique: Trade name used by the C.S. Shattuck Arms Co. on revolvers and four barrel pocket pistols.

United States Arms Company: Trade name used by Norwich Falls Pistol Co. (O.A. Smith) on inexpensive pocket revolvers.

Universal: Trade name used by the Hopkins and Allen Co. on inexpensive pocket revolvers.

Utica Firearms Company: Trade name used by the Simmons Hardware Co. of St. Louis, Missouri, on firearms they retailed.

Valient: Trade name used by the Spear and Co. of Pittsburgh, Pennsylvania, on firearms they retailed.

Veiled Prophet: Trade name used by the T.E. Ryan Pistol Manufacturing Co. on inexpensive pocket revolvers.

Venus: Trade name used by the American Novelty Co. of Chicago on inexpensive pocket revolvers.

Veteran: Trade name found on inexpensive pocket revolvers of unknown manufacture.

Veto: Trade name found on inexpensive pocket revolvers of unknown manufacture.

Victor:
a) Trade name used by the Marlin Firearms Co. on single-shot pocket pistols.
b) Trade name used by the Harrington and Richardson Arms Co. on inexpensive pocket revolvers.
c) Trade name used by the H. & D. Folsom Arms Co. on inexpensive pocket pistols and revolvers.

Victor Arms Company: Trade name used by the H. & D. Folsom Arms Co. on firearms made for the Hibbard, Spencer, Bartlett and Co. of Chicago.

Victor Special: Trade name used by the H. & D. Folsom Arms Co. on firearms made for the Hibbard, Spencer, Bartlett and Co. of Chicago.

Victoria: Trade name used by the Hood Firearms Co. on inexpensive pocket revolvers.

Vindix: Trade name used by Manufacture d'Armes de Pyrenees on semiautomatic pistols.

Viper: Trade name used on inexpensive pocket revolvers of unknown American manufacture.

Virginia Arms Company: Trade name used by the H. & D. Folsom Arms Co. and later the Davis-Warner Arms Co. on firearms made for the Virginia-Carolina Co. of Richmond, Virginia.

Volunteer: Trade name used by the H. & D. Folsom Arms Co. on inexpensive pocket revolvers made for the Belknap Hardware Co. of Louisville, Kentucky.

Vulcan: Trade name used by the H. & D. Folsom Arms Co. on firearms made for the Edward K. Tryon Co. of Philadelphia, Pennsylvania.

Walnut Hill: Trade name used by the J. Stevens Arms and Tool Co. on rifles.

Warner Arms Corporation: Trade name used by the H. & D. Folsom Arms Co. on firearms made for the Kirtland Brothers, Inc. of New York.

Wasp: Trade name found on inexpensive pocket revolvers of unknown manufacture.

Wautauga: Trade name used by the Whitaker, Holtsinger Hardware Co. of Morristown, Tennessee on firearms they retailed.

Western: Trade name used by the H. & D. Folsom Arms Co. on firearms made for the Paxton and Gallagher Co. of Omaha, Nebraska.

Western Arms Company:
a) Trade name used by the Bacon Arms on various types of firearms.
b) Trade name used by W.W. Marston on revolvers.
c) Trade name used by Henry Kolb and later R.F. Sedgly of Philadelphia, Pennsylvania, on Baby Hammerless revolvers.
d) Trade name used by the Ithaca Gun Co. on shotguns believed to have been made for the Montgomery Ward and Co. of Chicago.

Western Field: Trade name used by Montgomery Ward and Co. of Chicago on shotguns of various makes that they retailed.

Western Field: Trade name used by Manufacture d'Armes de Pyrenees on revolvers.

Whippet: Trade name used by the H. & D. Folsom Arms Co. on firearms made for the Hibbard, Spencer, Bartlett and Co. of Chicago.

Whistler: Trade name used by the Hood Firearms Co. on inexpensive pocket revolvers.

White Powder Wonder: Trade name used by Albert Aubrey of Meriden, Connecticut on shotguns made for the Sears, Roebuck and Co. of Chicago.

Wildwood: Trade name used by the H. & D. Folsom Arms Co. for shotguns made for Sears, Roebuck & Co.

Wilkinson Arms Company: Trade name used by the H. & D. Folsom Arms Co. on firearms made for the Richmond Hardware Co. of Richmond, Virginia.

Wiltshire Arms Company: Trade name used by the H. & D. Folsom Arms Co. on firearms made for the Stauffer, Eshleman and Co. of New Orleans, Louisiana.

Winfield Arms Company: Trade name used by the H. & D. Folsom Arms Co. on various types of firearms.

Winner: Trade name found on inexpensive pocket revolvers of unknown manufacture.

Winoca Arms Company: Trade name used by the H. & D. Folsom Arms Co. on firearms made for the N. Jacobi Hardware Co. of Wilmington, North Carolina.

Witte's Expert: Trade name used by the Witte Hardware Co. of St. Louis, Missouri, on shotguns they retailed.

Witte's IXL: Trade name used by the Witte Hardware Co. of St. Louis, Missouri, on shotguns they retailed.

Wolverine Arms Company: Trade name used by the H. & D. Folsom Arms Co. on firearms made for the Fletcher Hardware Co. of Wilmington, North Carolina.

Woodmaster: Trade name found on Belgian shotguns imported by an unknown wholesaler.

Worlds Fair: Trade name used by the Hopkins and Allen Co. on shotguns.

Worthington Arms Company: Trade name used by the H. & D. Folsom Arms Co. on various types of firearms.

Wyco: Trade name used by the Wyeth Hardware and Manufacturing Co. of St. Joseph, Missouri, on firearms they retailed.

XL:
a) Trade name used by the Hopkins and Allen Co. on inexpensive pocket revolvers.
b) Trade name used by the Marlin Firearms Co. on single-shot pocket pistols.

Xpert:
a) Trade name used by the Hopkins and Allen Co. on inexpensive pocket revolvers.
b) Trade name used by the Iver Johnson Arms and Cycle Works on inexpensive single-shot pocket pistols.

XXX Standard: Trade name used by the Marlin Firearms Co. on revolvers.

You Bet: Trade name used on inexpensive pocket revolvers of unknown American manufacture.

Young America: Trade name used by J.P. Lindsay of New York on superimposed - load percussion pistols.

Young American: Trade name used by the Harrington and Richardson Arms Co. on revolvers.

FIREARMS MANUFACTURERS AND IMPORTERS

Accu-Tek
4510 Carter Ct.
Chino, CA 91710
909-627-2404
FAX: 909-627-7817
www.accu-tekfirearms.com

AcuSport Corporation
One Hunter Place
Bellefontaine, OH 43311
513-593-7010
FAX: 513-592-5625
www.acusport.com

American Derringer Corp.
127 N. Lacy Drive
Waco, TX 76715
254-799-9111
FAX: 254-799-7935
www.amderringer.com

American Frontier Firearms
40725 Brook Trails Way
Aguanga, CA 92536
909-763-0014
FAX: 909-763-0014

AR-7 Industries
998 N. Colony Rd.
Meriden, CT 06450
203-630-3536
FAX: 203-630-3637
www.ar-7.com

ArmaLite, Inc.
P.O. Box 299
Geneseo, IL 61254
309-944-6939
FAX: 309-944-6949
www.armalite.com

Armscorp USA Inc.
4424 John Avenue
Baltimore, MA 21227
410-247-6200
FAX: 410-247-6205

A-Square Co. Inc.
205 Fairfield Avenue
Jeffersonville, IN 47130
812-283-0577
FAX: 812-283-0375

Austin & Halleck
2150 South 950 East
Provo, UT 84606
877-543-3256
FAX: 801-374-9998
www.austinhalleck.com

Autauga Arms
Pratt Plaza Mall No. 13
Pratville, AL 36067
800-262-9563
FAX: 334-361-2961

Auto-Ordnance Corp.
P.O. Box 220
Blauvelt, NY 10913
845-735-4500
FAX: 845-735-4610
www.auto-ordnance.com

Axtell Rifle Company
Riflesmith, Inc.
353 Mill Creek Road
Sheridan, MT 59749
406-842-5814
www.riflesmith.com

Aya-Agiurre Y Aranzabal, S.A.L.
P.O. Box 45
Eibar (Guipuzcoa), Spain
+34 943 82 04 37
FAX: +34 943 20 01 33

B.C. Outdoors
P.O. Box 61497
Boulder City, NV 89005
702-294-3056
FAX: 702-294-0413

Ballard Rifle and Cartridge Co.
113 W. Yellowstone Ave.
Cody, WY 82414
307-587-4914
FAX: 307-527-6097
www.ballardrifles.com

Barrett Firearms Mfg.
P.O.Box 1077
Murfreesboro, TN 37133
615-896-2938
FAX: 615-896-7313

Benelli U.S.A.
17603 Indian Head Highway
Accokeek, MD 20607
301-283-6981
FAX: 301-283-6988
www.benelliusa.com

Beretta U.S.A. Corp.
17601 Beretta Drive
Accokeek, MD 20607
301-283-2191
FAX: 301-283-0435
www.berettausa.com

Bernardelli Vincenzo, S.P.A.
Via Grande, 10
Sede Legale Torbole Casaglia
Brescia, Italy
+39 30 8912851-2-3
FAX: +39 030 215 0963

Bond Arms
P.O. Box 1296
Grandbury, TX 76048
817-573-4445
FAX: 817-573-5636
www.bondarms.com

Briley Mfg. Company
1230 Lumpkin Road
Houston, TX 77043
800-331-5718
FAX: 713-932-1043

Brown, E. Arthur Co.
4353 State Highway 27 East
Alexandria, MN 56308
320-762-8847
FAX: 320-763-4310
www.eabco.com

Brown Precision Inc.
7786 Molinos Ave.
P.O. Box 270 W.
Los Molinos, CA 96055
530-384-2506
FAX: 530-384-1638
www.brownprecision.com

Brown, Ed Products
P.O. Box 492
Perry, MO 63462
573-565-3261
FAX: 573-565-2791
www.edbrown.com

Browning
One Browning Place
Morgan, UT 84050
801-876-2711
Parts & Service
800-322-4626
www.browning.com

Bushmaster Firearms
999 Roosevelt Trail
Windham, ME 04062
800-998-7928
FAX: 207-892-8068
www.bushmaster.com

Caspian Arms, Ltd.
14 N. Main St.
Hardwick, VT 05843
802-472-6454
FAX: 802-472-6709

Casull Arms Company, Inc.
P.O. Box 1629
Afton, WY 83110
307-886-0200
www.casullarms.com

Century International Arms
430 S. Congress Ave., Suite 1.
Delray Beach, FL 33445-4701
800-527-1252
FAX: 561-265-4520
www.centuryarms.com

Champlin Firearms
P.O. Box 3191/Woodring Airport
Enid, OK 73702
580-237-7388
FAX: 580-242-6922

Charter 2000, Inc.
273 Canal Street
Shelton, CT 06484
203-922-1652
FAX: 203-922-1469

Cimarron Arms
P.O. Box 906
105 Winding Oak Road
Fredericksburg, TX 78624
830-997-9090
FAX: 830-997-0802
www.cimarron-firearms.com

Cobra Enterprises
1960 S. Milestone Dr., Suite F
Salt Lake City, UT 84104
801-908-8300
FAX: 801-908-8301
www.cobrapistols.com

Colt Firearms
P.O. Box 1868
Hartford, CT 06144
800-962-COLT
FAX: 860-244-1449
www.colt.com

Colt Blackpowder Arms Co.
110 8th Street
Brooklyn, NY 11215
212-925-2159
FAX: 212-966-4986

Competitor Corporation Inc.
26 Knight Street, Unit 3
Jaffrey, NH 03452
603-532-9483
FAX: 603-532-8209
www.competitor-pistol.com

Connecticut Shotgun Manufacturing Co.
A. H. Fox Shotguns
35 Woodland Street
Box 1692
New Britain, CT 06051
860-225-6581
FAX: 860-832-8708

Connecticut Valley Arms, Inc. (CVA)
5988 Peachtree Corners East
Norcross, GA 30071
770-449-4687
FAX: 770-242-8546
www.cva.com

Cooper Arms
P.O. Box 114
Stevensville, MT 59870
406-777-0373
FAX: 406-777-5228

CZ-U.S.A.
P.O. Box 171073
Kansas City, KS 66117- 0073
913-321-1811
FAX: 913-321-2251
www.cz-usa.com

Dakota Arms, Inc.
130 Industry Rd.
Sturgis, SD 57785
605-347-4686
FAX: 605-347-4459
www.dakotaarms.com

Daly, Charles Inc.
P.O. Box 6625
Harrisburg, PA 17112
866-325-9486
FAX: 717-540-8567
www.charlesdaly.com

Dixie Gun Works
P.O. Box 130
Union City, TN 38281
731-885-0700
FAX: 731-885-0440

Downsizer Corp.
P.O. Box 710316
Santee, CA 92072
619-448-5510
www.downsizer.com

DSA, Inc.
P.O. Box 370
27 West 990 Industrial Ave.
Barrington, IL 600110
847-277-7258
FAX: 847-277-7259
www.dsarms.com

Dumoulin, Ernst
Rue Florent Boclinville 8-10
13-4041 Votten, Beligium
41 27 78 78 92

Eagle Imports
1750 Brielle Ave., Unit B1
Wanamassa, NJ 07712
908-493-0333

Ellett Bros.
P.O. Box 128
Chapin, SC 29036
803-345-3751
FAX: 803-345-1820

EMF Co., Inc.
1900 E. Warner Ave. Suite 1-D
Santa Ana, CA 92705
949-261-6611
FAX: 949-756-0133

Entreprise Arms Inc.
5321 Irwindale Ave.
Irwindale, CA 91706
626-962-8712
FAX: 626-962-4692
www.entreprise.com

Euro-Imports
412 Slayden St.
Yoakum, TX 77995
361-293-9353
FAX: 361-293-9353

European American Armory
P.O. Box 1299
Sharpes, FL 32959
321-639-4842
FAX: 321-639-7006
www.eacorp.com

F.N. Manufacturing, Inc.
P.O. Box 24257
Columbia, SC 29224
803-736-0522

Fieldsport
3313 W. South Airport Road
Traverse City, MI 49684
616-933-0767

Fiocchi Of America
5030 Fremont Road
Ozark, MO 65721
417-725-4118
FAX: 417-725-1039

Fletcher-Bidwell
305 E. Terhune Street
Viroqua, WI 54665
866-637-1860
FAX: 608-637-6922

Francotte, Aug.
Rue du 3 Juin, 109
4400 Herstal-Liege, Belgium
32-4-948-11-79

Freedom Arms
P.O. Box 150
Freedom, WY 83120
307-883-2468
FAX: 307-883-2005
www.freedomarms.com

Furr Arms
91 North 970 West
Orem, UT 84057
801-226-3877
FAX: 801-226-3877

Galaxy Imports
P.O. Box 3361
Victoria, TX 77903
361-573-4867
FAX: 361-576-9622

Gamba, Renato
Via Artigiana 93
25063 Gardone Val Trompia
  Brescia, Italy
+39 30 8911640
FAX: +39 30 8912180

Gamba, U.S.A.
P.O. Box 60452
Colorado Springs, CO 80960
719-578-1145
FAX: 719-444-0731

Glock, Inc.
6000 Highlands Parkway
Smyrna, GA 30082
770-432-1202
FAX: 770-433-8719
www.glock.com

Griffin & Howe, Inc.
33 Claremont Road
Bernardsville, NJ 07924
908-766-2287
FAX: 908-766-1068
www.griffinhowe.com

GSI, Inc. (Merkel)
7661 Commerce Lane
P.O. Box 129
Trussville, AL 35173
205-655-8299
FAX: 205-655-7078
www.gsifirearms.com

H-S Precision, Inc.
1301 Turbine Drive
Rapid City, SD 57703
605-341-3006
FAX: 605-342-8964
www.hsprecision.com

Hammerli USA
19296 Oak Grove Circle
Groveland, CA 95321
209-962-5311
FAX: 209-962-5931
www.hammerliusa.com

Hanus, Bill Birdguns
P.O. Box 533
Newport, OR 97365
541-265-7433
FAX: 541-265-7400

Harrington & Richardson (H&R 1871)
60 Industrial Rowe
Gardner, MA 01440
508-632-9393
FAX: 508-632-2300
www.hr1871.com

Heckler & Koch, Inc.
21480 Pacific Boulevard
Sterling, VA 20166
703-450-1900
FAX: 703-450-8160
smww.hecklerkoch-usa.com

Henry Repeating Arms Co
110 8th Street
Brooklyn, NY 11215
718-499-5600
FAX: 718-768-8056

Heritage Manufacturing, Inc.
4600 NW 135th St.
Opa Locka, FL 30054
305-685-5966
FAX: 305-687-6721

High Standard Mfg. Co.
5200 Mitchelldale, Suite E-17
Houston, TX 77092
713-462-4200
FAX: 713-681-5665
www.highstandard.com

Horton, Lew, Distributing Co., Inc.
15 Walkup Drive
Westboro, MA 01581
508-366-7400
FAX: 508-366-5332

Ithaca Classic Doubles
No. 5 Railroad Street
Victor, NY 14564
716-924-2710
FAX: 716-924-2737

Ithaca Gun/Ithaca Acq. Corp.
901 Route 34B
King Ferry, NY 13081
315-364-7171
FAX: 315-364-5134
www.ithacagun.com

KDF
2485 Highway 46 North
Seguin, TX 78155
830-379-8141
FAX: 830-379-5420

Kahr Arms
P.O. Box 220
Blauvelt, NY 10913
845-735-4500
FAX: 845-735-4610
www.kahr.com

Kel-Tec CNC, Inc.
1475 Cox Rd.
Cocoa, FL 32926
321-631-0068
FAX: 321-631-1169
www.kel-tec.com

Kimber
1 Lawton Street
Yonkers, NY 10705
800-880-2418
www.kimberamerica.com

Knight Rifles/Modern Muzzleloading, Inc.
21852 Hwy. J46
P.O. Box 130
Centerville, IA 52544
641-856-2626
www.knightrifles.com

Knight's Manufacturing Co.
701 Columbia Blvd.
Titusville, FL 32780
321-607-9900
FAX: 321-268-1498

Krieghoff International
P.O. Box 549
7528 Easton Rd.
Ottsville, PA 18942
610-847-5173
FAX: 610-847-8691
www.krieghoff.com

L.A.R. Manufacturing
4133 West Farm Road
West Jordan, UT 84088
801-280-3505
FAX: 801-280-1972

Laurona
P.O. Box 260
20600 Eibar (Guipuzcoa), Spain
34-43-700600
FAX: 34-43-700616

Lazzeroni Arms Co.
P.O. Box 26696
Tucson, AZ 85726
888-492-7247
FAX: 520-624-4250
www.lazzeroni.com

Legacy Sports International
206 South Union Street
Alexandria, VA 22314
703-548-4837

FAX: 549-7826
www.legacysports.com

Les Baer Custom Inc.
29601 34th Ave.
Hillsdale, IL 61257
309-658-2716
FAX: 309-658-2610
www.lesbaer.com

Ljutic Industries
732 N. 16th Ave. Suite 22
Yakima, WA 98902
509-248-0476
FAX: 509-576-8233
www.ljuticgun.com

Lone Star Rifle Company
11231 Rose Road
Conroe, TX 77303
936-856-3363
FAX: 936-856-3363

Lyman
475 Smith Street
Middletown, CT 06457
860-632-2020
FAX: 860-632-1699

Magnum Research, Inc.
7110 University Avenue N.E.
Minneapolis, MN 55432
763-574-1868
FAX: 763-574-0109
www.magnumresearch.com

Marlin Firearms
P.O. Box 248
North Haven, CT 06473
800-544-8892
www.marlinfirearms.com

Maverick Arms Inc.
7 Grasso Ave.
P.O. Box 497
North Haven, CT 06473
203-230-5300
FAX: 203-230-5420

McMillan (McBros Rifles)
1638 W. Knudsen No. 102
Phoenix, AZ 85027
623-582-3713
FAX: 623-582-3930
www.mcmfamily.com

M.O.A. Corp.
285 Government Valley Rd.
Sundance, WY 82729
307-283-3030
www.moaguns.com

Moore, William Larkin & Co.
8340 E. Raintree Dr., Suite B-7
Scottsdale, AZ 85260
480-951-8913
FAX: 480-951-3677

Mossberg, O. F., & Sons, Inc.
7 Grasso Avenue
North Haven, CT 06473
203-230-5300
FAX: 203-230-5420
www.mossberg.com

Navy Arms Co.
219 Lawn St.
Martinsburg, WV 25401
304-262-9870
FAX: 304-262-1658
www.navyarms.com

New England Arms Co.
Lawrence Lane
Box 278
Kittery Point, ME 03905
207-439-0593
FAX: 207-439-6726
www.newenglandarms.com

New England Custom Gun Service
438 Willow Brook Road
Plainfield, NH 03781
603-469-3450
FAX: 603-469-3471

New England Firearms
60 Industrial Rowe
Gardner, MA 01440
978-632-9393
FAX: 978-632-2300

North American Arms
2150 South 950 East
Provo, UT 84606
801-374-9990
FAX: 801-374-9998
www.naaminis.com

Northwest Arms
26884 Pearl Road
Parma, ID 83660
208-722-6771
FAX: 208-722-1062
www.northwest-arms.com

Nowlin Manufacturing Co.
20622 South 4092 Road
Claremore, OK 74019
918-342-0689
FAX: 918-342-0624
www.nowlinguns.com

Ohio Ordnance Works
P.O. Box 687
310 Park Drive
Chardon, Ohio 44024
440-285-3481
FAX: 286-8571

Olympic Arms, Inc.
624 Old Pacific Highway SE
Olympia, WA 98513
360-459-7940
FAX: 360-491-3447
www.olyarms.com

Para-Ordnance
980 Tapscott Rd.
Toronto, Ontario M1X 1C3
416-297-7855
FAX: 416-297-1289
www.paraord.com

Pedersoli Davide & Co.
Via Artigiani, 57-25063
Gardone Val Trompia, Brescia
Italy 25063

Perazzi U.S.A. Inc.
1010 West Tenth
Azusa, CA 91702
626-334-1234
FAX: 626-334-0344

Phoenix Arms
4231 Brickell St.
Ontario, CA 91761
909-937-6900
FAX: 909-937-0060

Prairie Gun Works
1-761 Marion Street
Winnipeg, Manitoba
Canada R2J OK6
204-231-2976
FAX: 204-231-8566

Reeder, Gary Custom Guns
2601 7th Avenue East
Flagstaff, AZ 86004
928-526-3313
FAX: 928-526-1287
www.reedercustomguns.com

Remington Arms Co., Inc.
P.O. Box 700
870 Remington Drive
Madison, NC 27025-0700
800-243-9700
FAX: 336-548-7801
www.remington.com

Rock River Arms Inc.
1042 Cleveland Rd.
Colona, IL 61241
866-980-7625
FAX: 309-792-5781
www.rockriverarms.com

Rogue Rifle Co.
1140 36th Street N, Suite B
Lewiston, ID 83501
208-743-4355
FAX: 208-743-4163
www.roguerifle.com

Rogue River Rifleworks
500 Linne Rd., Suite D
Paso Robles, CA 93446
805-227-4706
FAX: 805-227-4723

Savage Arms
100 Springdale Road
Westfield, MA 01085
413-568-7001
FAX: 413-568-8386
www.savagearms.com

Seecamp, L.W.C.
301 Brewster Rd.
Milford, CT 06460
203-877-3429

Shiloh Rifle Mfg. Co., Inc.
P.O. Box 279
201 Centennial Drive
Big Timber, MT 59011
406-932-4454
FAX: 406-932-5627
www.shilohrifle.com

SIGARMS, Inc.
18 Industrial Drive
Exeter, NH 03833
603-772-2302
FAX: 603-772-9082
www.sigarms.com

SKB Shotguns
4325 South 120th St.
Omaha, NE 68137
800-752-2767
FAX: 402-330-8029
www.skbshotguns.com

Smith & Wesson
2100 Roosevelt Road
Springfield, MA 01104
800-331-0852
FAX: 413-747-3317
www.smith-wesson.com

Springfield Armory, Inc.
420 West Main Street
Geneseo, IL 61254
309-944-5631
FAX: 309-944-3676
www.springfield-armory.com

SSK Industries
590 Woodvue Lane
Wintersville, OH 43953
740-264-0176
FAX: 740-264-2257
www.sskindustries.com

S.T.I. International, Inc.
114 Halmar Cove
Georgetown, TX 78628
800-959-8201
FAX: 512-819-0465
www.stiguns.com

Stoeger Industries
17603 Indian Head Highway
Accokeek, MD 20607
301-283-6300
FAX: 301-283-6986

Sturm Ruger & Co., Inc
Lacey Place
Southport, CT 06890
203-259-7843
FAX: 203-256-3367
www.ruger-firearms.com

Taconic Firearms Ltd.
P.O. Box 553
Perry Lane
Cambridge, NY 12816
518-677-2704
FAX: 518-677-5974

Taurus International
16175 NW 49th Av.
Miami, FL 33014
305-624-1115
FAX: 305-623-1126
www.taurususa.com

Thompson/Center Arms Co.
Farmington Road
P.O. Box 5002
Rochester, NH 03867
603-332-2394
FAX: 603-332-5133
www.tcarms.com

Traditions Performance Firearms
1375 Boston Post Road
P.O. Box 776
Old Saybrook, CT 06475
860-388-4656
FAX: 860-388-4657

Tristar Sporting Arms
P.O. Box 7496
18116 Linn St.
North Kansas City, MO 64116
816-421-1400
FAX: 816-421-4182
www.tristarsportingarms.com

Turnbull, Doug Restoration, Inc.
6680 Route 5 & 20
P.O. Box 471
Bloomfield, NY 14469
585-657-6338
FAX: 585-657-6338
www.turnbullrestoration.com

U.S. Repeating Arms/ Winchester
275 Winchester Ave.

New Haven, CT 06511
800-333-3288
www.winchester-guns.com

United States Fire Arms Manufacturing Co.
55 Van Dyke Av.
Hartford, CT 06106
877-277-6901
FAX: 860-724-6809
www.usfirearms.com

Valtro U.S.A.
24800 Mission Blvd.
Hayward, CA 94544
510-489-8477
FAX: 510-489-8477

Vector Arms, Inc.
270 W. 500 N.
North Salt Lake, UT 84054
801-295-1917
FAX: 801-295-9316
www.vectorarms.com

Volquartsen Custom
24276 240th Street
Carroll, IA 51401
712-792-4238
FAX: 712-792-2542
www.volquartsen.com

Weatherby, Inc.
3100 El Comino Real
Atascadero, CA 93422
805-466-1767
FAX: 805-466-2527
www.weatherby.com

Wesson, Dan Firearms
5169 Highway 12 South
Norwich, NY 13815
607-336-1174
FAX: 607-336-2730
www.danwessonfirearms.com

Westley Richards & Co. Ltd.
40 Grange Road, Bournbrook
Birmingham, England B29 5A
44 121 472 2953
FAX: 44 121 414 1138

Wichita Arms
923 E. Gilbert
Wichita, KS 67211
316-265-0061
FAX: 316-265-0760
www.wichitaarms.com

Wildey, Inc.
45 Angevine Rd.
Warren, CT 06754
860-355-9000
FAX: 860-354-7759
www.wildeyguns.com

Wilson Combat
2234 CR 719
P.O. Box 578
Berryville, AR 72616
870-545-3635
FAX: 870-545-3310
www.wilsoncombat.com

ZM Weapons
203 South Street
Bernardston, MA 01337
413-648-9501
FAX: 413-648-0219

Zoli, Antonio
Via Zanardelli, 39
I-25063 Gardone V.T. (BS) Italy

GUN COLLECTORS ASSOCIATIONS

Alabama Gun Collectors
P.O. Box 70965
Tuscalossa, AL 35407

Alaska Gun Collectors Association
5240 Litte Tree
Anchorage, AK 99507

American Society of Arms Collectors
P.O. Box 2567
Waxahachie, TX 75165

Arizona Arms Association
4837 Bryce Ave.
Glendale, AZ 85301

Ark-La-Tex Gun Collectors Association
919 Hamilton Road
Bossier City, LA 71111

Bay Colony Weapons Collectors, Inc.
Box 111
Hingham, MA 02043

Boardman Valley Collectors Guild
County Road 600
Manton, MI 49663

Browning Collectors Association
2749 Keith Dr.
Villa Ridge, MO 63089

California Arms and Collectors Assoc.
8290 Carburton St.
Long Beach, CA 90808

Colorado Gun Collectors
2553 South Quitman Street
Denver, CO 80219

Colt Collectors Association
25000 Highland Way
Los Gatos, CA 95030

Derringer Collectors Association
500 E. Old 66
Shamrock, TX 79079

Florida Gun Collectors Association
P.O. Box 43
Branford, FL 32008

Freedom Arms Collectors Association
P.O. Box 160302
Miami, FL 33116

High Standard Collectors Association
540 W 92nd Street
Indianapolis, In 46260

Houston Gun Collectors Association
P.O. Box 741429
Houston, TX 77274

Indianhead Firearms Association
Route 9, Box 186
Chippewa Falls, WI 54729

Indian Territory Gun Collectors Association
Box 4491
Tulsa, OK 74159

International Society of Mauser Arms Collectors
P.O. Box 277
Alpharetta, GA 30239

Iroquois Arms Collectors Association
P.O.Box 142
Ransomville, NY 14131

Jefferson State Arms Collectors
521 South Grape
Medford, OR 97501

Jersey Shore Antique Arms Collectors
P.O. Box 100
Bayville, NJ 08721

Kentuckiana Arms Collectors Association
P.O. Box 1776
Louisville, KY 40201

Kentucky Gun Collectors Association
P.O. Box 64
Owensboro, KY 42376

Lehigh Valley Military Collectors Association
P.O. Box 72
Whitehall, PA 18052

Long Island Antique Gun Collectors Association
35 Beach Street
Farmingdale, L.I., NY 11735

Marlin Firearms Collectors Association
44 Main Street
Champaign, IL 61820

Maryland Arms Collectors Association
P.O. Box 20388
Baltimore, MD
21284-0388

Memphis Antique Weapons Association
4672 Barfield Road
Memphis, TN 38117

Minnesota Weapons Collectors Association
P.O. Box 662
Hopkins, MN 55343

Missouri Valley Arms Collectors Association
P.O. Box 33033
Kansas City, MO 64114

Montana Arms Collectors Association
308 Riverview Drive
East Great Falls, MT 59404

National Automatic Pistol Collectors Association
Box 15738-TOGS
St. Louis, MO 63163

National Rifle Association
11250 Waples Mill Rd.
Fairfax, VA 22030

New Hampshire Arms Collectors, Inc.
P.O. Box 5
Cambridge, MA 02139

Northeastern Arms Collectors Association, Inc.
P.O. Box 185
Amityville, NY 11701

Ohio Gun Collectors Association
P.O. Box 9007
Maumee, OH 43537

Oregon Arms Collectors
P.O. Box 13000-A
Portland, OR 97213

Pelican Arms Collectors Association
P.O. Box 747
Clinton, LA 70722

Pennsylvania Antique Gun Collectors Association
28 Fulmer Avenue

Havertown, PA 19083

Pikes Peak Gun Collectors Guild
406 E. Uintah
Colorado Springs, CO 80903

Potomac Arms Collectors Association
P.O. Box 1812
Wheaton, MD 20915

Randall Collectors Club
228 Columbine Dr.
Casper WY 82609-3948

Remington Society of America
8267 Lone Feather
Las Vegas, NV 89123

Ruger Collectors Association, Inc.
P.O. Box 240
Greens Farms, CT 06436

Sako Collectors Association, Inc.
202 N. Locust
Whitewater, KS 67154

Santa Barbara Antique Arms Collectors Association
P.O. Box 6291
Santa Barbara, CA 93160-6291

San Bernardino Valley Arms Collectors
1970 Mesa Street
San Bernardino, CA 92405

Santa Fe Gun Collectors Association
1085 Nugget
Los Alamos, NM 87544

San Fernando Valley Arms Collectors Association
P.O. Box 65
North Hollywood, CA 91603

Shasta Arms Collectors Association
P.O. Box 3292
Redding, CA 96049

Smith & Wesson Collectors Association
2711 Miami St.
St. Louis, MO 63118

Tampa Bay Arms Collectors Association
2461 67th Avenue South
St. Petersburg, FL 33712

Texas Gun Collectors Association
P.O. Box 12067
El Paso, TX 79913

Washington Arms Collectors, Inc.
P.O. Box 7335
Tacoma, WA 98407

Weapons Collectors Society of Montana
3100 Bancroft
Missoula, MT 59801

Weatherby Collectors Association, Inc.
21569 448th Avenue
Oldham, SD 57051

Willamette Valley Arms Collectors Association, Inc.
P.O. Box 5191
Eugene, OR 97405

Winchester Arms Collectors Association
P.O. Box 6754
Great Falls, MT 59406.

Ye Connecticut Gun Guild
U.S. Route 7
Kent Road
Cornwall Bridge, CT 06754

Zumbro Valley Arms Collectors, Inc.
Box 6621
Rochester, MN 55901

BIBLIOGRAPHY

Bady, Donald *Colt Automatic Pistols.* Alhambra, California: Borden Publishing Company, 1973.

Baer, Larry L. *The Parker Gun.* Los Angeles, California: Beinfeld Publications, 1980.

Bailey, D. and Nie, D. *English Gunmakers.* London: Arms and Armour Press, 1978.

Ball, W.D., *Remington Firearms: The Golden Age of Collecting,* Iola, WI: Krause Publications, 1995.

Ball, W.D., *Mauser Military Rifles of the World.* Iola, WI: Krause Publications, 1996.

Belford, James & Dunlap, Jack *The Mauser Self-Loading Pistol.* Alhambra, California: Borden Publishing, 1969.

Bishop, Chris and Drury, Ian *Combat Guns.* Secaucus, New Jersey: Chartwell Books, 1987.

Blackmore, H. *Gunmakers of London.* York, Pennsylvania: Geo. Shumway, 1986.

Blackmore, H. *Guns and Rifles of the World.* New York, New York: Viking Press, 1965.

Blair, C. *Pistols of the World.* London: B.T. Batsford, Ltd., 1968.

Bogdanovic & Valencak *The Great Century of Guns.* New York, New York: Gallery Books, 1986.

Bowen, T.G. *James Reid and his Catskill Knuckledusters.* Lincoln, Rhode Island: Andrew Mowbray, Inc., 1989.

Breathed, J. and Schroeder, J. *System Mauser.* Glenview, Illinois: Handgun Press, 1967.

Brophy, Lt. Col. William S., USAR, Ret. *The Krag Rifle.* Los Angeles, California: Beinfeld Publications, 1980.

Brophy, Lt. Col. William S., USAR, Ret. *L.C. Smith Shotguns.* Los Angeles, California: Beinfeld Publications, 1977.

Brophy, W. *Marlin Firearms.* Harrisburg, Pennsylvania: Stackpole Books, 1989.

Browning, J. and Gentry, C. *John M. Browning; American Gunmaker.* Ogden, Utah: Browning, 1989.

Butler, David F. *The American Shotgun.* New York, New York: Winchester Press, 1973.

Buxton, Warren *The P 38 Pistol.* Dallas, Texas: Taylor Publishing Company, 1978.

Carr, J. *Savage Automatic Pistols.*

Chant, Christopher *The New Encyclopedia of Handguns.* New York, New York: Gallery Books.

Conley, F.F. *The American Single Barrel Trap Gun.* Carmel Valley, California: F.F. Conley, 1989.

Cope, K.L. *Stevens Pistols and Pocket Rifles.* Ottawa, Ontario: Museum Restoration Service.

Cormack, A.J.R. *Small Arms, a Concise History of Their Development.* Profile Publications, Ltd.

Cormack, A.J.R. *Small Arms in Profile, Volume I.* Garden City, New York: Doubleday & Company, Inc.,1973.

deHass, Frank *Bolt Action Rifles.* Northfield, Illinois: Digest Books, Inc., 1971.

deHass, Frank *Single-shot Rifles and Actions.* Northfield, Illinois: Digest Books, Inc., 1969.

Eastman, Matt, *Browning Sporting Arms of Distinction*; 1903-1992. Fitzgerald, Georgia, 1994.

Eberhart, L. D. & Wilson, R. L. *The Deringer in America: Volume Two - The Cartridge Era.* Lincoln, RI: Andrew Mowbray Inc., 1993.

Dance, T. *High Standard: A Collector's Guide to the Hamden & Hartford Target Pistols.* Lincoln, RI: Andrew Mowbray Inc., 1991

Dunlap, J. *Pepperbox Firearms.* Palo Alto, California: Pacific Books, 1964.

Ezell, Edward C. *Small Arms Today.* Harrisburg, Pennsylvania: Stackpole Books.

Frasca & Hill *The 45-70 Springfield.* Northridge, California: Springfield Publishing Company, 1980.

Fuller, C. *The Whitney Firearms.* Huntington, West Virginia: Standard Pub., Inc., 1946.

Gaier & Francotte, *FN 100 Years; The Story of a Great Liege Company, 1889-1989.* Brussels, Belgium, 1989.

Gander, Terry, editor, *Janes Infantry Weapons,* 23rd edition, Surry, England, 1997.

Goddard, W. H. D. *The Government Models.* The Development of the Colt Model of 1911. Lincoln, RI: Andrew Mowbray Inc., 1988.

Graham, R., Kopec, J., Moore, C. *A Study of the Colt Single Action Army Revolver.* Dallas, Texas: Taylor Publishing Co., 1978.

Greener, W. *The Gun and Its Development.* Secaucus, New Jersey: Chartwell Books, 1988.

Gun Digest 1967 through 1989 Editions. Northfield, Illinois: DBI Books.

Guns of the World Los Angeles, California: Petersen Publishing Company, 1972.

Hayward, J.F. *Art of the Gunmaker, Vol.* 1. London: Barrie & Rockliff, 1962; Vol. 2. London: Barrie & Rockliff, 1963.

Henshaw, Thomas, et. al., *The History of Winchester Firearms 1866-1992, 6th Ed.* Winchester Press, 1993.

Hiddleson, C. *Encyclopedia of Ruger Semi-Automatic Pistols: 1949-1992.* Iola, WI: Krause Publications, 1993.

Hinman, Bob *The Golden Age of Shotgunning,* New York, N.Y., Winchester Press, 1975.

Hoff, A. *Airguns and Other Pneumatic Arms.* London: Barrie & Jenkins, 1972.

Hoffschmidt, E.J. *Know Your. 45 Auto Pistols Models 1911 & AI.* Southport, Connecticut: Blacksmith Corporation, 1974.

Hoffschmidt, E.J. *Know Your Walther PP & PPK Pistols.* Southport, Connecticut: Blacksmith Corporation, 1975.

Hogg, Ian V. *German Pistols and Revolvers 1871-1945.* Harrisburg, Pennsylvania: Stackpole Books, 1971.

Hogg, Ian V. and Weeks, John *Military Small Arms of the 20th Century.* Fifth Edition. Northfield, Illinois: DBI Books, 1985.

Hogg, Ian V. and Weeks, John *Pistols of the World. Revised Edition.* Northfield, Illinois: DBI Books, 1982.

Honeycutt, Fred L., Jr. *Military Pistols of Japan.* Lake Park, Florida: Julin Books, 1982.

Houze, H. *The Winchester Model 52: Perfection in Design,* Iola, WI: Krause Publications, 1997.

Houze, H. *To The Dreams Of Youth: Winchester .22 Caliber Single-shot Rifle.* Iola, WI: Krause Publications, 1993.

Houze, H. *Winchester Repeating Arms Company Its History and Development 1865 to 1981.* Iola, WI: Krause Publications, 1994.

Houze, H. *Colt Rifles & Muskets: 1847-1870.* Iola, WI: Krause Publications, 1996.

Jamieson, G. Scott *Bullard Arms.* Erin, Ontario: Boston Mills Press, 1988.

Jinks, R.G. *History of Smith A. Wesson.* Beinfeld Pub., Inc., 1977.

Karr, C.L. and C.R. *Remington Handguns.* Harrisburg, Pennsylvania: Stackpole Co., 1956.

Kenyon, C. *Lugers at Random.* Glenview, Illinois: Handgun Press, 1990.

Kindig, J., Jr. *Thoughts on the Kentucky Rifle in its Golden Age.* New York, New York: Bonanza Books, 1964.

Laidacker, John S. *Collected Notes Concerning Developmental Cartridge Handguns In .22 Calibre As Produced in the United States and Abroad From 1855 to 1875.* Bloomsburg, PA: J.S. Laidacker, 1994.

Larson, Eric *Variations of the Smooth Bore H&R Handy-Gun.* Takoma Park, Maryland: 1993.

Leithe, Frederick E. *Japanese Handguns.* Alhambra, California: Borden Publishing Company, 1968.

Lenk, T. *The Flintlock, Its Origins and Development.* New York, New York: Bramhall House, 1965.

Lewis, Jack, editor, *Gun Digest Book of Assault Weapons,* 4th edition, Krause Publications, Iola, WI, 1996.

Lippard, K. *Fabbri Shotguns,* Colorado Springs, Colorado, VM Publications, 1998.

Lippard, K, *Perazzi Shotguns,* Colorado Springs, Colorado, VM Publications, 1996.

Lugs, J. *Firearms Past and Present.* London: Grenville, 1975.

Madis, George *The Winchester Model 12.* Brownsboro, Texas: Art & Reference House, 1982.

Madis, George *The Winchester Book.* Brownsboro, Texas: Art & Reference House, 1977.

Marcot, R. *Spencer Repeating Firearms.* Irvine, California: Northwood Heritage Press, 1990.

Markham, George *Japanese Infantry Weapons of World War Two.* New York, New York: Hippocrene Books, Inc., 1976.

McDowell, R. *Evolution of the Winchester.* Tacoma, Washington: Armory Pub., 1985.

McDowell, R. *A Study of Colt Conversions and Other Percussion Revolvers,* Iola, WI; Krause Publications, 1997.

McIntosh, Michael *A.H. Fox; The Finest Gun in the World.* Countrysport Press, 1992.

Moller, G. D. *American Military Shoulder Arms, Volume 1, Colonial and Revolutionary War Arms.* Niwot, CO: University Press of Colorado, 1993.

Murphy, J. M.D. *Confederate Carbines & Musketoons.* J. Murphy, M.D., n.p.: 1986.

Murray, Douglas P. *The 99: A History of the Savage Model 99 Rifle.* Murray, 1976.

Myatt, Major Frederick, M.D. *Pistols and Revolvers.* New York, New York: Crescent Books, 1980.

Nutter, W.E. *Manhattan Firearms.* Harrisburg, Pennsylvania: Stackpole Co., 1958.

Olson, Ludwig *Mauser Bolt Rifles.* Third Edition. Montezuma, Iowa: Brownell & Sons, 1976.

Parsons, J. E. *Henry Deringer's Pocket Pistol.* New York, New York: Wm. Morrow & Co., 1952.

Pender, Roy G. *III Mauser Pocket Pistols 1910-1946.* Houston, Texas: Collectors Press, 1971.

Peterson, H.L. *Arms and Armor in Colonial America.* New York, New York: Brandhall House, 1956.

Petty, Charles E. *High Standard Automatic Pistols 1932-1950.* Highland Park, NJ: The Gun Room Press, 1989.

Rankin, J. *Walther Models PP and PPK.* Coral Gables, Florida: Rankin, 1989.

Rankin, J. *Walther Volume III,* 1908-1980. Coral Gables, Florida: Rankin, 1981.

Reese, Michael *11 Luger Tips.* Union City, Tennessee: Pioneer Press, 1976.

Reilly, R. *United States Martial Flintlocks.* Lincoln, Rhode Island: Andrew Mowbray, Inc., 1986.

Reilly, R. *United States Military Small Arms 1816-1865.* Baton Rouge, Louisiana: Eagle Press, Inc., 1970.

Renneberg, R.C. *The Winchester Model 94: The First 100 Years.* Iola, WI: Krause Publications, 1992.

Riling, R. *The Powder Flask Book.* New York, New York: Bonanza Books, 1953.

Rosenberger, R.F.& Kaufmann, C. *The Long Rifles of Western Pennsylvania-Allegheny and Westmoreland Counties.* Pittsburgh, PA: University of Pittsburgh Press, 1993.

Rule, R. *The Rifleman's Rifle: Winchester's Model 70, 1936-1963.* Northridge, California: Alliance Books, 1982.

Ruth, L. *War Baby! Comes Home-The U.S. Caliber .30 Caliber Carbine Volume II.* Toronto, Ontario: Collector Grade Publications, Inc., 1993.

Ruth, L. *War Baby! The U.S. Caliber .30 Carbine.* Toronto, Ontario: Collector Grade Publications, Inc., 1992.

Schroeder, Joseph J. *Gun Collector's Digest, Volume II* Northfield, Illinois: Digest Books, Inc., 1977.

Schwing, N. *Winchester's Finest, The Model 21.* Iola, WI: Krause Pub., 1990.

Schwing, N. *The Winchester Model 42.* Iola, WI: Krause Pub., 1990.

Schwing, N. *Winchester Slide Action Rifles, Vol. Model 1890 and Model 1906.* Iola, WI: Krause Publications, 1992.

Schwing, N. *Winchester Slide Action Rifles, Vol. Model 61 and Model 62.* Iola, WI: Krause Publications, 1993.

Schwing, N. *The Browning Superposed: John Browning's Last Legacy.* Iola, WI: Krause Publications, 1996.

Sellers, F. *Sharps Firearms.* North Hollywood, California: Beinfeld Pub., Inc., 1978.

Sellers, F. *American Gunsmiths.* Highland Park, New Jersey: Gun Room Press, 1983.

Sellers, F. and Smith, S. *American Percussion Revolvers.* Ottawa, Ontario: Museum Restoration Service, 1971.

Serven, James E. *200 Years of American Firearms.* Chicago, Illinois: Follett Publishing Company, 1975.

Serven, J. *Collecting of Guns.*

Sharpe, P. *The Rifle in America.* Funk and Wagnalls Co., 1953.

Sheldon, Douglas G. *A Collector's Guide to Colt's. 38 Automatic Pistols.* Sheldon, 1987.

Smith, W. *The Book of Pistols and Revolvers.* Harrisburg, Pennsylvania: Stackpole Co., 1962.

Stadt, R.W. *Winchester Shotguns and Shotshells.* Tacoma, Washington: Armory Publications, 1984.

Stevens, R. *The Browning High Power Automatic Pistol.* Toronto, Canada: Collector Grade Publications, 1990.

Stoeger's Catalog & Handbook. 1939 Issue. Hackensack, New Jersey: Stoeger Arms Corporation.

Supica J. & Nahas R., *Standard Catalog of Smith & Wesson.* Iola, WI: Krause Publications, 1996.

Sutherland, R.Q. & Wilson, R. L. *The Book of Colt Firearms.* Kansas City, Missouri: R.Q. Sutherland, 1971.

Tivey, T. *The Colt Rifle, 1884-1902.* N.S.W. Australia: Couston & Hall, 1984.

Vorisek, Joseph T *Shotgun Markings: 1865 to 1940,* Canton, CT: Armsco Press 1990.

Wahl, Paul *Wahl's Big Gun Catalog II.* Cut And Shoot, Texas: Paul Wahl Corporation, 1988.

Walter, John *The German Rifle.* Ontario, Canada: Fortress Publishing, Inc., 1979.

Whitaker, Dean H. *The Winchester Model 70 1937-1964.* Dallas, Texas: Taylor Publishing Company, 1978.

Wilkerson, Don *The Post War Colt Single Action Army Revolver.* Dallas, Texas: Taylor Publishing Company, 1978.

Wilson, R.L. *Colt An American Legend.* New York, New York: Abbeville Press, 1985.

Wilson, R.L. *Colt Engraving.* Beinfeld Publishing, Inc., n.p., 1982.

Wilson, R.L. *Winchester Engraving.* Palm Springs, California: Beinfeld Books, 1989.

Wilson, R.L. *The Colt Heritage.* New York, New York: Simon & Schuster, 1979.

Wilson, R.L. *Winchester An American Legend.* New York, New York: 1991.

Winant, L. *Early Percussion Firearms.* New York, New York: Wm. Morrow & Co., 1959.

Winant, L. *Firearms Curiosa.* New York, New York: Greenburg Pub., 1955.

Workman, W.E. *The Ruger 10/22,* Iola, WI: Krause Publications, 1994.

Zhuk, A.B. *The Illustrated Encyclopedia of Handguns.* London, England, Greenhill Books, 1995.

MODEL INDEX

1428

GunDigest
THE WORLD'S FOREMOST GUN AUTHORITY

ENTER TO WIN
NEW PRIZES BEING ADDED ALL THE TIME!

FEDERAL PREMIUM AMMUNITION GOLD MEDAL

HIGH CALIBER
SWEEPSTAKES
www.GunDigest.com

ENTER ONLINE TO WIN! CHECK BACK OFTEN!